# 2005

## 109TH CONGRESS
## 1ST SESSION

### VOLUME LXI

**Congressional Quarterly Inc.**

1255 22nd Street, N.W.
Washington, D.C. 20037

**President & Editor-in-Chief**   Robert W. Merry
**Editor, Sr. V.P.**   David Rapp

**Executive Editors**
Susan Benkelman, Anne Q. Hoy, Mike Mills

**Managing Editors**
David Hawkings, Mark Stencel, Randy Wynn

**Senior Editors**
Adriel Bettelheim, Bob Benenson, John Cranford,
Mike Christensen, Caitlin Hendel, Chris Lehmann

**Department Editors**
John Bicknell, Jonathan Broder, Paul Hendrie,
Katherine Rizzo, Jodi Schneider

**Deputy Editors**
Maureen Conners, Pat Joy, Greg McDonald,
Frank Oliveri, Michael Remez, Kathleen Silvassy,
Joe Warminsky, Chris Wright

**Senior Writers**
Rebecca Adams, Jill Barshay, John Cochran,
Gregory L. Giroux, David Nather, Alan K. Ota,
Joseph J. Schatz, Shawn Zeller

**Reporters**
Kate Barrett, Laura Blinkhorn, Charlene Carter,
Jean Chemnick, Michael R. Crittenden,
Elizabeth B. Crowley, Steven T. Dennis,
John M. Donnelly, Susan Ferrechio, Jacob Freedman,
Libby George, Shweta Govindarajan, Liriel Higa,
Cheyenne Hopkins, Marie Horrigan,
Rachel Kapochunas, Victoria McGrane,
Kathleen Hunter, Martin Kady II, Keith Perine,
Anne Plummer, Daphne Retter, Catharine Richert,
Michael Sandler, Kate Schuler, Eleanor Stables,
Tim Starks, Seth Stern, Joelle Tessler,
Michael Teitelbaum, Jeff Tollefson, Rachel Van Dongen,
Alex Wayne, Kathryn A. Wolfe

# CQ
## 2005
## ALMANAC *Plus*

**Editor**
Jan Austin

**Production Editor**
Melinda W. Nahmias

**Design Director**
Jamie Baylis

**Art Directors**
Marilyn Gates-Davis, Jamey Fry

**Staff Photographer**
Scott J. Ferrell

**Graphics**
Lindsay Magum, Chris Wilson

**Copy Editors**
Neal Conway, Victoria Lemley, Charles Southwell

**News Research**
Nell Benton (Supervisor),
Jeff Austin, Rachel Bloom, Ryan Kelly,
Jody Kyle, Greg Vadala

**Indexer**
Susan Nedrow

**BUSINESS OPERATIONS**
**Publisher & Sr. V.P.**   Keith White

**Advertising Sales, V.P.**   Beth Bronder

**Circulation Sales**
**Vice President**   Jim Gale
**National Sales Manager**   Sean F. Doyle
**Senior Sales Representatives**   Joanna Matthews, David Stevens

**Chief Marketing Officer**   Greg Hamilton

**Chief Financial Officer**   Diane Atwell

**Chief Information Officer**   Larry Tunks

**Customer Relations**
**Customer Service Manager**   Lorri Porter
**Managing Deputy**   LaWanda D. Council

**Strategy & Development**
**Senior Director**   Neil Maslansky

**CQ Press**
**Publisher, Sr. V.P.**   John A. Jenkins

**Published by**
**CONGRESSIONAL QUARTERLY INC.**

**Chairman**   Paul C. Tash
**Vice Chairman**   Andrew P. Corty
**Founder**   Nelson Poynter
(1903-1978)

# Congressional Quarterly Inc.

CONGRESSIONAL QUARTERLY INC. is a publishing and information services company and the recognized national leader in political journalism. For more than a half-century, CQ has served clients in the fields of business, government, news and education with complete, timely and nonpartisan information on Congress, politics and national issues.

The flagship publication is the CQ Weekly, a news magazine on government, commerce and politics. It covers all the forces that shape public policy, from Capitol Hill to K Street to the White House.

CQ Today is a legislative news-daily providing a morning news report on Congress and the scheduled hearings and markups of congressional committees. It provides a comprehensive breaking news report of everything that just happened or is about to happen on Capitol Hill.

CQ also offers the most comprehensive, detailed and up-to-the-minute legislative tracking information on the World Wide Web. CQ.com provides immediate access to exclusive CQ coverage of bill action, votes, schedules and member profiles, with direct links to relevant texts of bills, committee reports, testimony and verbatim transcripts.

CQ Press, a division of Congressional Quarterly Inc., serves the academic and education markets with a variety of reference works and political science text books, both in print and online, plus reference books on the federal government, national elections and politics.

The CQ Press catalogue includes the signature CQ reference work, "Politics in America 2006," with original profiles of every member of the 109th Congress, written and edited by the CQ staff.

CQ Press also publishes a unique weekly publication — The CQ Researcher — with each weekly issue focused exclusively on a single topic of current interest. And CQ Press offers a line of print and Web-based directories, such as the Congressional Staff Directory.

The "Congressional Quarterly Almanac ®," published annually, provides a legislative history for each session of Congress. "Congress and the Nation," published every four years, provides a record of government for a presidential term.

### Copyright 2006, Congressional Quarterly Inc. (CQ)

Library of Congress Catalog Number 47-41081
ISBN: 0-87289-426-6   ISSN: 0095-6007

**CONGRESSIONAL QUARTERLY OFFERS A COMPLETE LINE OF PUBLICATIONS AND RESEARCH SERVICES.**

# The 2005 CQ Almanac

THIS BOOK MARKS THE 61ST EDITION of the CQ Almanac. Beginning with the first session of the 79th Congress in 1945, Congressional Quarterly has produced and published an annual account of the major legislative action in each session of Congress.

The 2005 edition covers the first session of the 109th Congress. It begins with an overview of the year, followed by 17 chapters filled with narrative accounts of major legislation.

Each chapter was written especially for the book, based on reporting and analysis done throughout the year by Congressional Quarterly's news staff. We added "Plus" to our title in 2001 to highlight the original nature of the material.

The 2005 Almanac provides a detailed look at all the major bills considered during the year — whether or not they became law. It examines how the bills changed as they moved from committee markup to floor votes and conference negotiations. The stories also identify the main provisions of the legislation and look at the roles played by individual members of Congress.

Republicans began the 109th invigorated by the November 2004 elections, which increased their majorities in both chambers. Their 55 seats in the Senate, in particular, enabled them to finish several major items that had been languishing: an energy overhaul sought by President Bush since 2001, a rewrite of bankruptcy law that had been stalled for eight years, bills to limit class action lawsuits and gunmakers' liability, and legislation to implement Bush's top trade priority, the Central American Free Trade Agreement.

Congress completed all of the fiscal 2006 appropriations bills without resorting to an omnibus package, while holding discretionary spending within the $843 billion limit proposed by Bush. But lawmakers also cleared more than $200 billion in supplemental funds during the year for the war in Iraq, hurricane response, veterans' health care and preparations for a possible flu pandemic. None of that money counted against either the fiscal 2005 or fiscal 2006 discretionary spending limits.

The year was also notable for the opportunity it gave Bush and the Republican majority in Congress to begin putting their stamp on the Supreme Court. John G. Roberts Jr. was confirmed as the 17th chief justice of the United States, following the death of William H. Rehnquist, who served for 20 years in that role. Conservative federal appellate judge Samuel A. Alito Jr. was nominated to fill another opening created when Sandra Day O'Connor, the first woman on the court, announced her retirement. His confirmation hearings were scheduled for 2006.

Congress nearly completed a budget reconciliation bill that promised the first reductions in entitlement spending since 1997 and affected programs ranging from Medicaid and Medicare to student loans, federal deposit insurance and welfare.

The second half of the session was heavily influenced by factors outside Congress' control: Hurricane Katrina, which devastated Gulf Coast states requiring tens of billions of dollars in aid; growing public unhappiness with the war in Iraq; rising gasoline prices; and revelations about secret government activities related to the war on terrorism. Added to that were the ethics problems of House Majority Leader Tom DeLay, R-Texas, who stepped down from his leadership post, at least temporarily, in September after being indicted in Texas on charges he violated state campaign finance laws.

The final weeks of the session were a mad scramble, as Congress raced to finish the two biggest spending bills and other major legislation, some of which was left for the second session.

In addition to stories on all these issues and more, the Almanac contains a series of data-filled reference appendixes:

● **Congress and its members.** In addition to an 11-page glossary of terms that arise in discussing Congress and legislation, and a list of members of the House and Senate in the first session of the 109th Congress, this year we have included a study of the characteristics of our elected representatives, from age and ethnicity to religious preferences and former occupations.

● **Vote studies.** CQ's popular annual analysis of voting patterns in Congress. Continued partisanship was the order of the day in 2005, with Democrats displaying almost the same level of party discipline as the Republicans, who have remained remarkably united since 1995. Other studies analyze the level of presidential support and member participation during the year, providing aggregate scores for each chamber along with individual ratings for each member.

● **Key votes.** An account of the votes chosen by CQ editors as most critical in determining the outcome of congressional action on major issues during the year.

● **Texts.** Bush's inaugural address, his Sept. 15 speech on Katrina from Jackson Square in New Orleans, and Roberts' opening statement at his confirmation hearing .

● **Public laws.** A detailed list of all the bills enacted into law during the year.

● **Roll call votes.** A complete set of roll call vote charts for both chambers, describing every vote and showing every member's position on each vote.

CQ produces the Almanac for public policy specialists, scholars, journalists, and all interested citizens and students of the U.S. legislative system.

We believe our 61st edition remains true to the mandate laid out by CQ founders Nelson and Henrietta Poynter: "Congressional Quarterly presents the facts in as complete, concise and unbiased form as we know how. The editorial comment on the acts and votes of Congress, we leave to our subscribers."

*Jan Austin*
*Editor, CQ Almanac*

**CQ** *"By providing a link between the local newspaper and Capitol Hill we hope Congressional Quarterly can help to make public opinion the only effective pressure group in the country. Since many citizens other than editors are also interested in Congress, we hope that they too will find Congressional Quarterly an aid to a better understanding of their government."*

Foreword, Congressional Quarterly, Vol. I, 1945
Henrietta Poynter, 1901-1968
Nelson Poynter, 1903-1978

# Summary Table of Contents

# TABLE OF CONTENTS

## CHAPTER 1 – INSIDE CONGRESS

## CHAPTER 2 – APPROPRIATIONS

## CHAPTER 3 – BANKING & FINANCIAL SERVICES

# CHAPTER 4 – BUDGET

# CHAPTER 5 – CONGRESSIONAL AFFAIRS

# CHAPTER 6 – DEFENSE

# CHAPTER 7 – EDUCATION

# CHAPTER 8 – ENERGY & ENVIRONMENT

# CHAPTER 9 – FOREIGN POLICY & INTELLIGENCE

# CHAPTER 10 – GOVERNMENT OPERATIONS

# CHAPTER 11 – HEALTH & SCIENCE

# CHAPTER 12 – HOMELAND SECURITY

# CHAPTER 13 – IMMIGRATION

# CHAPTER 14 – LEGAL AFFAIRS

# CHAPTER 15 – TAXES

# CHAPTER 16 – TECHNOLOGY & COMMUNICATIONS

# CHAPTER 17 – TRADE

# CHAPTER 18 – TRANSPORTATION & INFRASTRUCTURE

# APPENDIXES

**Chapter 1**

# INSIDE CONGRESS

# Supreme Court Nominees, Katrina, War Weariness Reshape Agenda

REPUBLICANS OPENED the 109th Congress brimming with confidence from their 2004 election victories, which gave President Bush a second term and expanded the party's majorities in both chambers. "We begin the new Congress with a sense of purpose and optimism. It's been a long time since Republicans have had this much power in Washington," David Dreier, R-Calif., chairman of the House Rules Committee, told his colleagues Jan. 4, the first day of the session.

The leadership promised an activist agenda focused on issues such as border security, curbs on civil-liability lawsuits, indefinitely extending the Bush tax cuts and simplifying the tax code. Republicans also anticipated one or more Supreme Court vacancies during the year, which would allow them to help shape the high court for years to come.

Democratic leaders, though in the minority, vowed to press for more funding for education and first-responders, expanded health care, a higher minimum wage, and the importation of cheaper prescription drugs from Canada.

The Republicans came out of the 2004 elections with 232 seats or 53 percent in the House, the largest number of seats won by GOP candidates since just after World War II. In the Senate, a four-seat gain gave Republicans a solid 55-seat majority that the leadership believed would allow them to overcome the nearly united Democrats, who had managed to to block several top Republican priorities in the last Congress. *(2004 Almanac, pp. 18-14, 18-17)*

During the first half of the session, the leadership delivered on its promise to clear a string of bills that had been hung up in Congress, including a six-year surface transportation bill, an energy overhaul sought by Bush since 2001 and a rewrite of bankruptcy law that had been stalled for eight years. Congress also cleared a bill to limit class action lawsuits and legislation to implement Bush's top trade priority, the Central American Free Trade Agreement (CAFTA).

But the new majorities were not enough to ensure the sweeping changes GOP leaders had hoped for. Democrats reacted by becoming more unified than ever, and the Republican leadership often found itself navigating between conservatives and the party's small moderate wing.

The second half of the session, beginning after the August recess and lasting into Christmas week, was dominated by factors outside the control of any party leaders. First and most dramatic were hurricanes Katrina and Rita and their costly aftermath. At the same time, lawmakers were feeling the public's growing disillusionment with the war in Iraq and the way it was being conducted, worries over the economy, their president's declining popularity and the mounting ethical problems of House Majority Leader Tom DeLay, R-Texas.

By the end of the session, the Republican caucus seemed to be unraveling, and Democrats looked forward to the 2006 elections when they hoped to unseat enough Republicans to get their turn again at running at least one chamber.

But Republican leaders also emerged with more victories to add to those of the first six months. They confirmed a new chief justice to the Supreme Court, won enactment of the first reduction in mandatory spending since 1997, cleared all 11 of the regular appropriations bills without having to resort to an omnibus package, provided $102.7 billion to support U.S. forces in Iraq and Afghanistan, and took innumerable steps to assist Gulf Coast states in recovering from the hurricanes.

## REPUBLICANS COME OUT FIGHTING

Emboldened by the party's increased hold on the Senate, Majority Leader Bill Frist, R-Tenn., used his opening speech on Jan. 4 to warn Democrats to "exercise self-restraint and do not filibuster judicial nominees" or expect him to follow through on threats to diminish the power of the minority. Democrats had used filibusters to halt action on 10 appellate court nominees in the 108th Congress. *(2004 Almanac, p. 12-15)*

On the other side of the Capitol, J. Dennis Hastert, R-Ill., was re-elected Speaker of the House over Nancy Pelosi of California, in her second term as House Democratic leader, 226-199. Hastert, who was catapulted to the position from chief deputy whip in 1999, was on track to become the longest-serving Republican Speaker. "The 109th Congress will be the Reform Congress," an ebullient Hastert told the House on Jan. 4. "In this Congress, big plans will stir men's blood." *(House vote 2, p. H-4)*

The House also adopted a leadership rules package for the 109th Congress on a 220-195 party-line vote. Democrats were particularly angered by a rules change that allowed ethics complaints to lapse without investigation unless a majority of the evenly divided Committee on Standards of Official Conduct agreed to proceed. *(House vote 6, p. H-4)*

Under pressure from their own members, Republican leaders had abandoned plans for an additional change that would have significantly curtailed the power of the ethics committee, and they agreed to reverse a November decision — aimed at protecting DeLay — that would have let GOP leaders keep party posts even if they were criminally indicted.

Democrats and congressional watchdog groups had vigorously criticized the proposed change, and individual Republicans had gotten an earful from the folks back home. "It's never a good idea to tie your shoelaces together right out of the gate," said J.D. Hayworth, R-Ariz., praising the leadership's responsiveness to the rank and file. *(DeLay, p. 5-3; ethics committee, p. 5-6)*

# Congressional Leaders: 109th Congress, 1st Session

## HOUSE

Speaker of the House — J. Dennis Hastert, R-Ill.

### REPUBLICANS
Majority Leader — Tom DeLay, Texas[1]
Majority Whip — Roy Blunt, Mo.
Conference Chairwoman — Deborah Pryce, Ohio
Conference Vice Chairman — Jack Kingston, Ga.
Conference Secretary — John T. Doolittle, Calif.
Policy Committee Chairman — John Shadegg, Ariz.
Chairman, National Republican Congressional Committee —
    Thomas M. Reynolds, N.Y.
Chief Deputy Majority Whip — Eric Cantor, Va.

### DEMOCRATS
Minority Leader — Nancy Pelosi, Calif.
Minority Whip — Steny H. Hoyer, Md.
Caucus Chairman — Robert Menendez, N.J.
Caucus Vice Chairman — James E. Clyburn, S.C.
Assistant to the Minority Leader — John M. Spratt Jr., S.C.
Chairman, Democratic Congressional Campaign Committee —
    Rahm Emanuel, Ill.
Senior Chief Deputy Minority Whip — John Lewis, Ga.

## SENATE

President Pro Tempore — Ted Stevens, R-Alaska

### REPUBLICANS
Majority Leader — Bill Frist, Tenn.
Majority Whip — Mitch McConnell, Ky.
Conference Chairman — Rick Santorum, Pa.
Conference Vice Chairwoman — Kay Bailey Hutchison, Texas
Policy Committee Chairman — Jon Kyl, Ariz.
Chairwoman, National Republican Senatorial Committee —
    Elizabeth Dole, N.C.
Chief Deputy Majority Whip — Robert F. Bennett, Utah

### DEMOCRATS
Minority Leader — Harry Reid, Nev.
Minority Whip — Richard J. Durbin, Ill.
Conference Secretary — Debbie Stabenow, Mich.
Policy Committee Chairman — Byron L. Dorgan, N.D.
Steering & Outreach Committee Chairwoman —
    Hillary Rodham Clinton, N.Y.
Chairman, Democratic Senatorial Campaign Committee —
    Charles E. Schumer, N.Y.
Chief Deputy Minority Whip — Barbara Boxer, Calif.

[1]DeLay was required by GOP Conference rules to temporarily vacate the position after his Sept. 28 indictment in Texas on campaign finance charges. Speaker J. Dennis Hastert, Ill., named Roy Blunt, Mo., to act as majority leader for the remainder of the session.

House leaders also made it clear they would punish party members who were not sufficiently loyal, starting with Christopher H. Smith, R-N.J., who was removed as chairman of the Veterans' Affairs Committee on the first day of the session, to be replaced by Steve Buyer, R-Ind. Smith had frequently clashed with GOP leaders in his bid to increase funding levels for veterans' programs. It was the first time since Republicans took power a decade before that they deposed a sitting chairman.

Smith was followed not long after by Joel Hefley, R-Colo., who was replaced as chairman of the ethics committee by Doc Hastings, R-Wash. The move was punishment for the panel's admonishments of DeLay for ethical lapses in 2004. In one other change, Jerry Lewis, R-Calif., took the helm in the Appropriations Committee, succeeding C.W. Bill Young, R-Fla., who stepped down due to GOP-imposed term limits.

On the Senate side, committees for the first time felt the impact of the GOP term limits for chairmen. Four senators — Alaska's Ted Stevens on Appropriations, Arizona's John McCain on Commerce, Science and Transportation, Utah's Orrin G. Hatch on Judiciary and Pennsylvania's Arlen Specter on Veterans' Affairs — had to move to other positions. The resulting musical chairs left a total of nine committees under new chairmen.

### CONFIRMING CABINET MEMBERS AND JUDGES
The Senate began the year by confirming all but one of Bush's nominees for high-level jobs in his second term. The exception was John R. Bolton, whose nomination as ambassador to the United Nations was blocked by Senate Democrats. Senators twice voted against invoking cloture, which would have allowed a vote on Bolton's nomination.

Bush later used his constitutional recess appointment powers to install Bolton at the U.N. during Congress' August recess. *(Bolton, p. 10-4)*

The newly confirmed Cabinet members included Alberto R. Gonzales, the first Hispanic to serve as attorney general; Condoleezza Rice, the national security adviser in Bush's first term, who took over the State Department; and Michael Chertoff, who became the second head of the Department of Homeland Security. *(Cabinet, p. 10-3)*

When it came to Bush's court nominees, however, the Senate seemed headed toward a showdown. Frist set a date for a test vote in May and appeared ready to follow through on his threat to employ an arcane parliamentary maneuver, dubbed the "nuclear option," to deny Democrats the ability to continue filibustering Bush's picks as they had done in the 108th Congress. But the confrontation some conservatives had hoped for was averted at the last minute, when a group of seven senators from each party took matters in their own hands. The group, which became known as the Gang of 14, struck a deal to let all but a few whom the Democrats considered the most objectionable judges win confirmation. When the test came May 24, the deal held and the Senate agreed to limit debate on the nomination of Priscilla R. Owen by a vote of 81-18. The deal remained in effect throughout the year. *(Gang of 14, p. 14-8)*

### LEGISLATIVE TO-DO LIST
Topping the Republicans' legislative agenda were bills that had languished in prior years, mainly in the Senate.

On Feb. 17, the House cleared a business-backed bill that limited plaintiffs' ability to pursue class action lawsuits in sympathetic state courts (PL 109-2). A centerpiece of the GOP "tort reform" agenda for

years, the legislation also was high on Bush's second-term wish list for Congress. Frist had pulled the bill in 2004 when he was unable to get the 60 votes needed to halt a Democratic filibuster. This time, the 55-vote majority enabled him to fend off Democratic amendments and send a clean bill to the House. *(Class action, p. 14-11)*

The enlarged Senate majority also enabled Frist to defeat an amendment that had prevented enactment of a bankruptcy overhaul prized by the credit card and financial services industries. Supporters had been trying to clear the legislation for eight years.

The law, enacted in April (PL 109-8), applied a means test to force more individuals filing for bankruptcy to repay their debts over several years, rather than having much of their debts discharged. The obstacle to enactment in recent years had been an amendment by Sen. Charles E. Schumer, D-N.Y., to prevent violent protesters, particularly anti-abortion protesters, from filing for bankruptcy protection to escape court-ordered fines. The amendment was anathema to conservatives and the Bush White House. This time, the amendment failed, 46-53, enabling the Senate to pass the bill and send it to the House, where it easily cleared. *(Bankruptcy, p. 3-3)*

The Senate had been the graveyard in 2004 for another top Republican priority: an energy policy overhaul that Bush had been seeking since 2001. The Senate easily cleared the bill in late July (PL 109-58), but this time the real turn-around came in the House. At White House insistence, DeLay backed off a demand that the bill protect manufacturers of the gasoline additive methyl tertiary butyl ether, or MTBE, from liability lawsuits over water contamination. The MTBE liability waiver had been the deal breaker in the Senate the previous year. *(Energy, p. 8-3)*

After a legislative struggle that spanned two years and two Congresses, lawmakers also cleared a $286.5 billion, six-year surface transportation bill in late July (PL 109-59). The legislation had been left stranded at the end of the 108th Congress, mainly because of a conflict with the White House over how much money to provide and the related regional issue of how much each state would get back from the excise taxes it contributed to the highway fund.

A change in the tax treatment of ethanol fuels in 2004 (PL 108-357) that channeled more money into the trust fund paved the way for the administration to increase its six-year total for transportation spending to $284 billion in early 2005. House and Senate conferees had tentatively settled on $299 billion in 2004. This time, they agreed on an amount $2.5 billion over Bush's number, close enough to win White House acceptance. The total was sufficient to guarantee all states enough of an increase in highway aid to get the bill to Bush's desk. *(Surface transportation, p. 18-3)*

In a major victory for Bush's free-trade policy, legislation to implement a free-trade agreement with five Central American countries and the Dominican Republic cleared in late July (PL 109-53). But the bitter battle and narrow House tally also underscored growing skepticism about the benefits of free trade. The largely unified Democratic opposition forced Republican leaders and the White House to make deals to win solid backing from their own party. *(CAFTA, p. 17-3)*

## BUDGET DISCIPLINE

Getting a budget resolution in place was another top priority for the leadership, which was determined to avoid a politically embarrassing repeat of 2004, when Republicans were unable to agree on a budget. *(2004 Almanac, p. 4-9)*

On April 28, both chambers signed off on a fiscal 2006 budget resolution (H Con Res 95) that mirrored the budget request Bush had sent to Congress on Feb. 7, the most stringent fiscal blueprint of his presidency. The budget resolution gave appropriators an $843 billion limit on discretionary spending, as Bush proposed. It also included instructions for writing two reconciliation bills later in the year — one to extend expiring portions of Bush's 2001 and 2003 tax cuts (PL 107-16, PL 108-27), and the other to make the first reductions in nearly a decade in politically sacrosanct entitlement programs such as Medicaid and crop subsidies. *(Bush's budget, p. 4-3; budget resolution, p. 4-9)*

The reconciliation instructions were a critical step because they protected tax and savings bills from filibusters in the Senate. That meant Republicans could prevail with a simple majority, rather than the 60 votes needed to cut off debate. The instructions included protection for another long-stymied GOP goal: opening portions of Alaska's Arctic National Wildlife Refuge (ANWR) to oil and gas drilling.

The leadership put off writing the actual reconciliation bills until the fall; the appropriations process was a more immediate priority. But before the appropriators could get started on the fiscal 2006 spending bills, they had to finish a fiscal 2005 supplemental spending bill requested by Bush to fund operations in Iraq and Afghanistan. The $82 billion measure, cleared May 10 (PL 109-13), brought total appropriations for Iraq and Afghanistan and related expenses since Sept. 11, 2001, to $350.6 billion, according to the Congressional Research Service. *(War supplemental, p. 2-52)*

Lewis and the other House appropriators kept their chamber on a tight schedule, passing all 11 regular fiscal 2006 appropriations bills before the July Fourth recess. Thad Cochran, R-Miss., who took over as Senate Appropriations chairman, proceeded at a slower pace, though the Senate amended and passed five of the bills before the August recess. Congress cleared two of the bills — for the Interior Department and EPA (PL 109-54) and the legislative branch (PL 109-55) before leaving.

## NO SILVER LINING

Republicans left Washington for the August recess with an ample list of bragging rights — and a full agenda for the fall.

When they returned, they would have nine annual appropriations bills left to complete, a package of mandatory spending cuts to write, a defense authorization bill, an extension of Bush's tax cuts and renewal of the 2001 anti-terrorism law known as the Patriot Act. On top of that would be the confirmation of a new Supreme Court justice. On July 1, Justice Sandra Day O'Connor, the first woman on the high court, announced her retirement. On July 19, Bush announced his choice of John G. Roberts Jr. to replace O'Connor. The Senate Judiciary Committee scheduled confirmation hearings to begin Sept. 6.

Yet for the GOP leadership there also were signs of trouble that would become increasingly pronounced in the second half of the session.

Republicans had made party unity a hallmark of their control of Congress, and they maintained that pattern in the House, actually increasing their party loyalty a bit over 2004, though not quite matching the record high they set in 1995. But in the Senate, Republicans fell off the pace in 2005, dropping well below the level of partisan cohesion they had reached in the highly partisan 2003 session.

Democrats, meanwhile, were taking a leaf from the GOP playbook and demanding strict adherence to party discipline. As a result, House Democrats were more unified in 2005 than at any time in the previous half-century. Senate Democrats were almost as united as they had been at their high point in 1989. Overall, congressional Republicans maintained a 90 percent unity rate on party unity votes, while Democrats were close behind at 88 percent. *(Party unity, p. B-8)*

As a result, Republicans could not automatically translate their larg-

# Highlights: 109th Congress, First Session

## CONGRESS DID

- Confirm John G. Roberts Jr. as the first new chief justice of the United States since 1986.
- Complete work on all 11 fiscal 2006 appropriations bills.
- Appropriate $102.7 billion for the military operations in Iraq and Afghanistan but dictated that 2006 be a year of "significant transition" to Iraqi sovereignty and required quarterly reports from President Bush on progress toward that goal.
- Appropriate $62.3 billion, provided about $19 billion in tax relief and altered federal policies on many fronts to assist Gulf Coast states in recovering from Hurricane Katrina, the most economically damaging storm in U.S. history.
- Revise the bankruptcy code to require more debt repayment.
- Overhaul federal energy policy, with an emphasis on enhanced production, four years after a similar plan was proposed by the president.
- Authorize $286.5 billion for federal highway, mass transit and road safety programs through 2009.
- Bar cruel, inhuman or degrading treatment of enemy detainees, but limited access to federal courts by prisoners at Guantánamo Bay, Cuba.
- Provide $3.8 billion for preparations against a potential flu pandemic and shield makers of flu vaccine from liability.
- Implement a free-trade agreement between the United States and five Central American countries and the Dominican Republic.
- Require uniform national standards for state-issued driver's licenses and tighten limits on people seeking asylum.
- Shield gun and ammunition manufacturers, distributors and dealers from civil liability when third parties misuse their products.
- Limit class action litigation by shifting more such cases to federal court.
- Speed the process for reconstituting the House after a catastrophic attack.

## CONGRESS DID NOT

- Complete work on a bill to reduce expected entitlement spending over the next five years by $38.8 billion.
- Take any action in response to the president's top second-term domestic initiative, an overhaul of the Social Security program to allow future beneficiaries to divert some of their payroll taxes to investment accounts.
- Extend 16 expiring provisions of a 2001 law, known as the Patriot Act, that had enhanced law enforcement powers to investigate suspected terrorists.
- Enact or extend any tax reductions, the first year since 2000 without a new tax cut.
- Open the Arctic National Wildlife Refuge in Alaska to energy exploration.
- Create a compensation pool for victims of asbestos exposure.
- Expand the federal role in embryonic stem cell research, although it did fund research on umbilical cord blood cells.
- Update federal policy toward immigrant workers and the treatment of businesses that violate immigration law.
- Confirm John R. Bolton as ambassador to the United Nations; Bush instead used his recess appointment power to install that envoy.
- Reauthorize programs run by the Homeland Security and State departments, the Coast Guard and the Army Corps of Engineers.
- Update the Head Start early childhood education program.
- Reauthorize the federal law regulating higher education policy.
- Revamp governance of the U.S. Postal Service.
- Advance a constitutional amendment to ban gay marriage.
- Reach bipartisan agreement to increase the federally guaranteed minimum wage above $5.15, which was set in 1997.
- Rewrite the Clean Air Act to enact the president's "Clear Skies" initiative to curb power plant emissions.

---

er majorities into victory, particularly in the Senate. With Democrats united in opposition, GOP leaders had to keep their caucus in tight lock step — a feat they could not always accomplish, especially toward the end of the year when the Republican caucus was badly fragmented.

Troubles of another kind were also brewing for Republicans: a steady accumulation of questions and doubts about DeLay's ethics problems and the party's efforts to sidestep them. In March, the media began to raise questions about the majority leader's connections with Washington lobbyist Jack Abramoff, who was already under investigation.

Democrats on the ethics committee had responded to the January rules changes, the deposing of Hefley and the subsequent firing of several committee staff, by refusing to approve operating rules for the committee itself. That effectively shut down the panel at a time of rising reports of ethics problems. On April 27, the House voted overwhelmingly to reverse all of the rules changes, though the committee remained largely moribund for the rest of the session.

### KATRINA AND IRAQ: AN AGENDA TRANSFORMED

Before lawmakers could return to Washington and start on their burgeoning fall agenda, Hurricane Katrina ripped through coastal areas of Louisiana, Mississippi and Alabama on Aug. 29, leaving staggering problems in its wake. The levees that protected New Orleans were breached and the rising water flooded 80 percent of the city. The federal government was caught flat-footed, and Americans watched round-the-clock coverage as tens of thousands of people sought help that did not come. The public seemed to know more about the deteriorating conditions than the federal government did. Disillusionment and anger grew over the government's slow response at all levels.

Lawmakers cut short their vacations and dashed back to Washington to a congressional agenda turned upside down by forces beyond their control. Everything lawmakers would do for the rest of the year would be colored in some way by Katrina and by Hurricane Rita, which hit the Gulf Coast Sept. 24, doing major damage to the nation's oil and natural gas infrastructure.

Republicans faced the added danger that public dismay over the federal response to the calamity would converge with the growing disillusionment over war in Iraq and anger at the climbing cost of gasoline to create a perfect storm for the party. For nearly two years, public opinion polls had shown growing dissatisfaction with the war and with the direction the country was headed. Bush's own approval rating fell from just above 50 percent in January to the low 40s in September.

With midterm elections coming in 2006, GOP lawmakers, whether moderate or conservative, began looking to their own political futures, and fissures in the party burst into the open. Republicans were left scrambling for direction and a unified message.

It did not help that DeLay had to step aside as majority leader Sept. 28, following his indictment by a Texas grand jury in a fundraising scandal. Majority Whip Roy Blunt, R-Mo., took over as acting majority

leader, but DeLay vowed to return to power after clearing his name of what he said were baseless charges.

The immediate task in early September, however, was obvious: Within 10 days of the disaster, two supplemental spending bills totaling $62.3 billion were enacted (PL 109-61, PL 109-62). In addition, lawmakers introduced dozens of bills aimed at cutting red tape and addressing myriad problems — from providing education for relocated students, to health care problems of poor people who no longer had addresses, to issues such as the need to relocate federal courts and provide temporary identification for those whose possessions were lost in the disaster. Many of the bills were enacted individually; dozens more were tucked into other bills that became law.

On Sept. 2, Frist announced that he had asked Susan Collins, R-Maine, chairwoman of the Senate Homeland Security and Governmental Affairs Committee, to hold oversight hearings on the responses of the federal government, the Federal Emergency Management Agency and the Department of Homeland Security. In the House, the leadership announced a select committee to investigate government actions before and after Katrina. Democrats boycotted the panels, arguing that an outside commission should be created. "The Republican Congress will not investigate this Republican administration," predicted House Minority Leader Pelosi.

## RESHAPING THE SUPREME COURT

Amid the preoccupation with Katrina, the Judiciary Committee prepared to open its hearing on Roberts' nomination to the Supreme Court. Then on Sept. 3, three days before the hearing was to begin, ailing Chief Justice William H. Rehnquist died after 20 years in the office. Bush quickly nominated Roberts to serve as the 17th chief justice. After a six-day delay, Roberts delivered a flawless performance at his confirmation hearing and was easily confirmed by the Senate on Sept. 29. He was sworn in later the same day. (Roberts, p. 14-3)

Roberts' smooth confirmation was a much-needed victory for Bush, but within days, the president undercut himself. On Oct. 3, he announced his selection of White House counsel Harriet Miers to take O'Connor's place on the high court. Miers, a Texas lawyer before she followed Bush to the White House in 2001, had little in her background to indicate where she stood on most issues. The nomination generated criticism and outrage from the political right, which was counting on Bush to pick a proven conservative with a clear record on issues such as abortion. On Oct. 27, with the nomination clearly unsustainable, Bush withdrew Miers' name. (Miers, p. 14-7)

It was the most emphatic rejection yet from a Republican-run Congress that had mostly deferred to Bush and his agenda throughout his presidency. The implosion of Miers' nomination also revealed disarray and divisions within the broader GOP coalition, with Bush looking more and more like a lame duck. Democrats mostly sat back and watched the show.

On Oct. 31, Bush moved to assuage his allies on the right by tapping conservative federal appellate judge Samuel A. Alito Jr. to replace O'Connor. Conservatives rejoiced; liberals promised to closely scrutinize Alito's lengthy legal record. The White House hoped to have Alito in place by the end of the year, but Judiciary Chairman Specter announced that the confirmation hearing would begin Jan. 9, 2006.

## WAR WEARINESS

In no area was the growing disconnect between Bush and congressional Republicans more evident than on the conduct of the war in Iraq.

On Nov. 15, the Senate voted 79-19 to adopt an amendment by Frist and John W. Warner, R-Va., chairman of the Armed Services Commit-

tee, requiring the president to send Congress quarterly unclassified reports on the course of the war and on progress toward drawing down U.S. forces. It also stated that 2006 should be a turning point in the war. The amendment to the defense authorization bill was offered as an alternative to a Democratic proposal that was nearly identical except for an additional provision requiring the Pentagon to set a schedule for a phased withdrawal from Iraq. The Democratic amendment was rejected. (Senate vote 323, p. S-63; defense authorization, p. 6-3)

Still, the Frist-Warner amendment was the most powerful statement of congressional oversight on Iraq policy since the 2003 invasion. "Congress got back in the game," said Jeremy Rosner, a Democratic pollster specializing in foreign affairs. House negotiators agreed to include most of the language in the conference report on the bill.

"Members are feeling the heat, and they want to weigh in more aggressively on what we're doing," said Pennsylvania's Curt Weldon, the second-ranking Republican on House Armed Services.

On Nov. 17, two days after the Senate vote, Rep. John P. Murtha of Pennsylvania, the ranking Democrat on the House Defense Appropriations Subcommittee and a decorated former Marine who had voted for the Iraq War, called for a withdrawal of troops over the next six months. "The military has done everything that has been asked of them. The U.S. cannot accomplish anything further in Iraq militarily," Murtha said. "It is time to bring them home."

Meanwhile, reports of abuse at military detention centers had prompted the Senate in early October, to add language to the fiscal 2006 Defense appropriations bill calling for a ban on "cruel, inhuman or degrading" treatment of detainees. Amendment author McCain, who had been held as a prisoner of war in North Vietnam, also succeeded in attaching the language to the defense authorization bill. Despite intense White House pressure, including a visit by Vice President Dick Cheney, McCain refused to back down.

With House leaders opposed to the amendment and the White House threatening to veto any legislation that contained it, Senate leaders held back the two defense bills. Then on Dec. 14, the House supported McCain's amendment in an overwhelming vote of 308-122. The next day, Bush reversed course and accepted the language in an Oval Office meeting with McCain and Warner. McCain agreed to add protections for U.S. interrogators who were performing "officially authorized" actions. (House vote 630, p. H-202)

Lawmakers also were growing dissatisfied with the level of administration secrecy about the war on terrorism. On Nov. 10, the Senate voted to demand a classified report on U.S.-run secret detention facilities overseas. The move came in response to a Washington Post report about a secret overseas system of CIA prisons for terrorists. In a non-binding ballot Dec. 16, the House voted to include the provision in the final defense authorization bill. However, it was dropped in conference as outside the jurisdiction of the Armed Services committees.

The New York Times on Dec. 16 ran a story revealing that the president in 2002 had authorized the National Security Agency to monitor overseas telephone calls by U.S. citizens without court permission. Angry reaction spilled into Senate debate on a bill to reauthorize expiring provisions of the Patriot Act that focused on enhanced surveillance powers. The House adopted the conference report on the reauthorization bill (HR 3199), but four Republicans joined nearly all Democrats in the Senate to reject cloture, blocking a vote on the conference report in that chamber. Frist switched his vote to "no" so he could move to reconsider the vote later.

With the provisions set to expire Dec. 31, Bush and Frist reversed an earlier refusal to consider a short-term bill and settled for a five-week

# 109th Congress, 1st Session: By the Numbers

The first session of the 109th Congress began, as the Constitution and federal law required, at noon Jan. 3, 2005. Under the terms of the adjournment resolution (H Con Res 326), the House adjourned sine die at 4:36 p.m. Dec. 22; the Senate adjourned sine die at 8:04 p.m. the same day. Following are some statistical comparisons of the two chambers over the past decade:

| | | 2005 | 2004 | 2003 | 2002 | 2001 | 2000 | 1999 | 1998 | 1997 | 1996 |
|---|---|---|---|---|---|---|---|---|---|---|---|
| **Days in Session** | Senate | 159 | 133 | 167 | 149 | 173 | 141 | 162 | 143 | 153 | 132 |
| | House | 140 | 110 | 133 | 123 | 142 | 135 | 137 | 119 | 132 | 122 |
| **Time in Session** (hours) | Senate | 1,222 | 1,032 | 1,454 | 1,043 | 1,236 | 1,018 | 1,184 | 1,095 | 1,093 | 1,037 |
| | House | 1,067 | 879 | 1,015 | 772 | 922 | 1,054 | 1,125 | 999 | 1,004 | 919 |
| **Average Length of Daily Session** (hours) | Senate | 7.7 | 7.8 | 8.7 | 7.0 | 7.1 | 7.2 | 7.3 | 7.7 | 7.1 | 7.9 |
| | House | 7.6 | 8.0 | 7.6 | 6.3 | 6.5 | 7.8 | 8.2 | 8.4 | 7.6 | 7.5 |
| **Public Laws Enacted**[1] | | 147 | 300 | 198 | 241 | 136 | 410 | 170 | 241 | 153 | 245 |
| **Bills and Resolutions Introduced** | Senate | 2,616 | 1,318 | 2,398 | 1,558 | 2,212 | 1,546 | 2,352 | 1,321 | 1,840 | 860 |
| | House | 5,703 | 2,338 | 4,616 | 2,711 | 4,318 | 2,701 | 4,241 | 2,254 | 3,728 | 1,899 |
| | **Total** | **8,319** | **3,656** | **7,014** | **4,269** | **6,530** | **4,247** | **6,593** | **3,575** | **5,568** | **2,759** |
| **Recorded Votes** | Senate | 366 | 216 | 459 | 253 | 380 | 298 | 374 | 314 | 298 | 306 |
| | House[2] | 671 | 544 | 677 | 484 | 512 | 603 | 611 | 547 | 640 | 455 |
| | **Total** | **1,037** | **760** | **1,136** | **737** | **892** | **901** | **985** | **861** | **938** | **761** |
| **Vetoes** | | 0 | 0 | 0 | 0 | 0 | 7[3] | 5 | 5 | 3[4] | 6 |

SOURCE: Congressional Record

[1] Bills signed into law during congressional session  [2] Includes quorum calls  [3] Includes pocket vetoes  [4] Does not include line-item vetoes

extension (PL 109-160). (*Anti-terrorism law, p. 12-3*)

"For a long time, the Republican majority has been willing to simply be foot soldiers for the president," Thomas E. Mann, a political scholar at the Brookings Institution in Washington, said near the end of the session. "Enough has happened that you're beginning to see them act in a more natural fashion, to reflect public opinion, to be a little more insistent on real congressional oversight."

## FINISHING THE APPROPRIATIONS BILLS

After a brief hiatus, lawmakers went back to work on the appropriations bills, clearing all but two of the remaining nine bills by the Thanksgiving break. The last two did not clear until Dec. 21. Appropriators had made the job slightly easier by a shifting about $6 billion from Defense to other programs; the Defense funds could be made up in the next supplemental. Still, when all the spending bills were finished, Congress had made the first reduction in non-Defense discretionary spending since the Reagan administration.

The tight spending limits made it particularly difficult to muster support for the Labor, Health and Human Services (HHS), and Education spending bill (PL 109-149). House leaders suffered an embarrassing defeat shortly before Thanksgiving, when 22 Republicans joined Democrats in rejecting the Labor-HHS conference report. Members were angry over the elimination of their individual earmarks and reduced spending for health care and education. The House accepted a slightly modified conference report Dec. 14, but there was so much opposition in the Senate that GOP leaders had to wait until the last moment when they could push the conference report through as part of the final flurry of business. (*Labor-HHS-Education, p. 2-37*)

The Defense spending bill (PL 109-48) was held up until mid-December by the fight over the McCain amendment. Also, GOP leaders held it as a must-pass vehicle to carry $3.8 billion in emergency appropriations to prepare for a possible flu pandemic, a year-end installment on hurricane relief, and a 1 percent across-the-board cut in virtually all fiscal 2006 discretionary spending, a top demand of the fiscal conservatives. The cut did not apply to veterans' programs or emergency war spending. (*Defense, p. 2-14*)

## SPENDING AND TAX CUTS ALIVE

The leadership had planned to handle the budget and tax reconciliation bills outlined in the budget resolution in the crowded end of the session. By that point, however, the Gulf Coast hurricanes, the war in Iraq and the president's growing unpopularity had changed the dynamic. Fiscal conservatives looked at a yawning federal deficit and demanded offsets for all hurricane spending. They honed in on earmarks — projects inserted into bills by individual members — scolding lawmakers for taking money home that was needed in the Gulf Coast.

On the other side, moderate Republicans such as Olympia J. Snowe of Maine fought against spending cuts in mandatory programs such as Medicaid, the federal-state health program for the poor, and food stamps. They cited the poor in New Orleans whose suffering had captured the nation's attention and reminded Americans of the continuing need to respond to poverty in their midst.

With Democrats almost unanimous in their opposition to the mandatory spending cuts, GOP leaders in both chambers had to walk a narrow path between their own conservative and moderate wings. The Senate passed a bill with a net $35 billion in savings over five years. Fis-

cal conservatives wanted deeper cuts, but influential moderates including Gordon H. Smith of Oregon refused to support more than $10 billion in reductions to Medicaid and held fast against other cuts to programs for the poor. Senate leaders did, however, have enough votes to keep ANWR provisions in the bill.

House leaders just barely got $49.9 billion in net savings through their chamber, but they had to drop ANWR along with some of their proposed cuts to Medicaid and food stamps. In conference, the cuts to Medicaid, which were at the heart of the negotiations, were whittled down to $4.8 billion, less than half what the House sought and a fraction of the $60 billion over 10 years that the White House requested in February.

The final bill was expected to cut mandatory spending by a net $38.8 billion over five years. While the total was far less than fiscal conservatives had hoped for, they could point to having helped force the first cut in entitlement spending since 1997. The biggest savings came from changes to federal student loan programs, Medicare and Medicaid. The bill also required higher premiums for the federal pension guarantee agency and counted on additional funds from auctioning portions of the electromagnetic spectrum. Those funds were used to offset some mandatory spending and to help pay for new expenditures that were included in the bill. *(Budget reconciliation, p. 4-13)*

Republicans put off plans to complete the second reconciliation bill aimed at extending Bush's tax cuts. The House passed a version of the bill focused on tax breaks for dividend and capital gains income, while the Senate concentrated on modifying the alternative minimum tax. In addition to the difficulty of finding time for a conference in the crowded end-of-year schedule, many members were uncomfortable voting for tax cuts in tandem with the cuts to entitlement programs. *(Tax reconciliation, p. 15-3)*

With the big package put on hold, lawmakers broke out $7.8 billion in additional tax incentives for the Gulf Coast and cleared it Dec. 16 (PL 109-135). At the insistence of House social conservatives, Senate tax writers agreed to limit the breaks that would flow to certain businesses such as casinos, racetracks and liquor stores.

## CHAOTIC END TO THE SESSION

As the session dragged into December, it became increasingly chaotic. House Democrats remained united on vote after vote, leaving the interim Republican leadership under Blunt to assemble separate majorities for each roll call, trading provisions in one bill for votes on another. The budget-reconciliation package, the Defense appropriations and authorization bills, the Labor-HHS-Education bill, and the Patriot Act reauthorization were all pulled at one point or another into a massive round of deal making.

An unexpected addition to the year-end mix was an immigration bill, introduced Dec. 6 by Judiciary Committee Chairman James F. Sensenbrenner Jr., R-Wis., and marked up by his committee two days later. The bill (HR 4437), which the House passed Dec. 16, focused on border security and criminal penalties for illegal immigrants and those who aided them. It was the subject of a raucous floor debate and highlighted deep divisions within the GOP. While House passage was a win for the Immigration Reform Caucus, a group of more than 90 House conservatives, many other Republicans argued that border control had to be paired with a plan to allow "guest worker" visas and give some illegal immigrants already in the country a pathway to legal immigration. *(Immigration, p. 13-3)*

The defense authorization and the Labor-HHS-Education measure, the largest of all the appropriations bills, cleared by voice vote four days before Christmas. The Defense spending bill cleared the same day.

Senate Democrats successfully challenged several provisions of the budget reconciliation bill on procedural grounds, causing the conference report to fall on a point of order. Only the vote of the vice president, which broke a 50-50 tie, allowed the Senate to send an amended version of the bill back to the House for final action in 2006. The bill was signed Feb. 8 (PL 109-171).

Indicative of the horse-trading and rapid change of fortunes in the last days of the session, provisions to open parts of ANWR to drilling were sacrificed to get other high-priority legislation through. The Senate-passed version of the budget reconciliation bill included ANWR. But House leaders concluded they could not get enough votes from moderate Republicans to get the conference report through their chamber as long as the provisions remained. *(ANWR, p. 8-18)*

Stevens, a tireless proponent of opening the wildlife refuge to drilling, agreed to move the provisions to the conference report on the fiscal 2006 Defense appropriations bill. That angered enough senators to halt work on the conference report, leaving the leadership with no choice but to drop the language. In a fitting coda to the year, a bitter Stevens told his Senate colleagues, "I'm going to go to every one of your states, and I'm going to tell them what you've done." ∎

**Chapter 2**

# APPROPRIATIONS

# Appropriations

# Fiscal 2006 Spending Bills Finished, Plus $200 Billion in Emergency Funds

Republican leaders succeeded in clearing all of the regular fiscal 2006 appropriations bills by year's end without resorting to an omnibus spending package. It was only the third time in a decade that Congress had managed to do so. In addition, the bills officially stayed within the $843 billion limit on discretionary spending set by President Bush and ratified by Congress in its fiscal 2006 budget resolution (H Con Res 95).

But Congress also cleared more than $200 billion in emergency supplemental spending during the year — much of it for fiscal 2005. Under the budget rules, none of that counted against the spending caps. The Bush administration continued its practice of funding the wars in Iraq and Afghanistan through supplemental appropriations rather than in the regular Defense budget. In addition, Congress was called on during the year to provide emergency funds for veterans' health care, preparations for a potential flu pandemic, and relief and recovery efforts following hurricanes Katrina and Rita, which devastated the Gulf Coast at the end of August.

## REGULAR BILLS A TIGHT SQUEEZE

Congress sent 11 regular fiscal 2006 spending bills to the White House before adjourning. The change from the longtime tradition of 13 bills was the result of reorganization plans carried out separately by the House and Senate Appropriations committees. One consequence of the reorganization was that, in several cases, companion House and Senate bills covered slightly different accounts, a problem that was only sorted out when the bills went to conference.

The new chairman of the House Appropriations Committee, Jerry Lewis, R-Calif., met his ambitious goal of getting all of the bills through the House by the July Fourth recess. Thad Cochran, R-Miss., who took over as Senate Appropriations chairman, did not set out to move that quickly, though the Senate passed five bills before the August recess. The job became much harder in the fall, when the Senate's top priorities became confirming a new Supreme Court justice and rushing hurricane relief to the Gulf Coast.

Both chairmen gave their subcommittees a little breathing space under the discretionary caps by cutting some money out of what Bush wanted for Defense — about $3 billion in the House and $7 billion in the Senate — and using it for domestic programs. The shift was a safe move since the money could be made up in supplemental appropriations.

All but two of the 11 bills were ready for Bush by Thanksgiving. The last two did not clear until Dec. 21. House members were so dissatisfied with the spending limits in the Labor, Health and Human Services (HHS), and Education bill — particularly the elimination of projects for their districts — that they shocked the leadership by rejecting the first conference report in mid-November. Arlen Specter, R-Pa., who chaired the Senate Labor-HHS-Education Appropriations Subcommittee, threatened at one point to vote against the compromise bill because he

felt it short-changed the National Institutes of Health and other programs. He later relented, but Senate GOP leaders had to wait until the last moment to push the conference report through as part of a final flurry of business before adjournment.

The must-pass Defense spending bill was also held up — at first by an Iraq-related controversy and later by the desire to use it to carry several last-minute items. The main obstacle was a dispute over language by Sen. John McCain, R-Ariz., to bar "cruel, inhuman or degrading" treatment of military detainees. From September on, the White House threatened to veto the bill if the provision remained. The administration finally backed down Dec. 15, a day after the House strongly supported the language. As part of end-of-session business, the Defense bill ended up carrying supplemental funds for the Gulf Coast and preparations for a avian flu pandemic, as well as a 1 percent across-the-board cut in discretionary spending in all the regular fiscal 2006 bills except for veterans' programs and emergency war funding.

Since only two of the bills had cleared when fiscal 2006 began Oct. 1, Congress also had to clear a series of three short-term "continuing resolutions" to tide the government over while lawmakers finished the rest of the bills. The three continuing resolutions were PL 109-77, signed Sept. 30; PL 109-105, signed Nov. 19; and PL 109-128, signed Dec. 18.

## SUPPLEMENTAL SPENDING

Congress also cleared several emergency supplemental appropriations during the year:

● **Defense.** An $82 billion fiscal 2005 supplemental bill enacted in May (PL 109-13) was devoted mainly to funding operations in Iraq and Afghanistan, though it also had funds for border security, homeland defense and aid to victims of a December 2004 tsunami. In December, Congress provided another $50 billion in supplemental spending for the Iraq and Afghanistan wars as part of the fiscal 2006 Defense bill (PL 109-148). The money was considered a "bridge" to keep funds flowing until Bush sent Congress a new supplemental request in early 2006.

● **Veterans.** Congress provided $1.5 billion in emergency supplemental spending to make up an unexpected shortfall in fiscal 2005 funding for veterans' health care programs. The money was enacted as part of the fiscal 2006 Interior-Environment spending bill (PL 109-54). Another $1.2 billion in emergency veterans' health care funding was enacted in November as part of the Military Construction-Veterans Affairs bill (PL 109-114).

● **Katrina.** A pair of fiscal 2005 emergency supplemental bills enacted in September (PL 109-61, PL 109-62) provided $62.3 billion for hurricane relief and cleanup efforts. In December, Congress included a $29 billion package of hurricane recovery money in the Defense bill, although $23.4 billion of it was reallocated from the earlier hurricane bills.

● **Flu pandemic.** The Defense bill also carried $3.8 billion in emergency supplemental fiscal 2006 money to stockpile vaccines and antiviral drugs and take other steps to prepare for a possible flu pandemic. ■

# Appropriations Mileposts
## 109th Congress — First Session

| Bill | House Action | Senate Action | House Final* | Senate Final* | President Signed | Story |
|---|---|---|---|---|---|---|
| **FY 2006 Agriculture** (HR 2744 — PL 109-97) | Passed 6/8/05 | Passed, amended 9/22/05 | 10/28/05 | 11/3/05 | 11/10/05 | 2-5 |
| **FY 2006 Commerce-Justice-Science** (HR 2862— PL 109-108) | Passed 6/16/05 | Passed, amended 9/15/05 | 11/9/05 | 11/16/05 | 11/22/05 | 2-9 |
| **FY 2006 Defense** (HR 2863 — PL 109-148) | Passed 6/20/05 | Passed, amended 10/7/05 | 12/19/05 | 12/21/05 | 12/30/05 | 2-14 |
| **FY 2006 District of Columbia** (Included in HR 3058 — PL 109-115) | Passed HR 3058 6/30/05 | Passed, amended, in HR 3058 10/20/05 | 11/18/05 | 11/21/05 | 11/30/05 | 2-20 |
| **FY 2006 Energy-Water Development** (HR 2419 — PL 109-103) | Passed 5/24/05 | Passed, amended 7/1/05 | 11/9/05 | 11/14/05 | 11/19/05 | 2-22 |
| **FY 2006 Foreign Operations** (HR 3057 — PL 109-102) | Passed 6/28/05 | Passed, amended 7/20/05 | 11/4/05 | 11/10/05 | 11/14/05 | 2-25 |
| **FY 2006 Homeland Security** (HR 2360 — PL 109-90) | Passed 5/17/05 | Passed, amended 7/14/05 | 10/6/05 | 10/07/05 | 10/18/05 | 2-28 |
| **FY 2006 Interior-Environment** (HR 2361 — PL 109-54) | Passed 5/19/05 | Passed, amended 6/29/05 | 7/28/05 | 7/29/05 | 8/2/05 | 2-33 |
| **FY 2006 Labor-HHS-Education** (HR 3010 — PL 109-149) | Passed 6/24/05 | Passed, amended 10/27/05 | 12/14/05 | 12/21/05 | 12/30/05 | 2-37 |
| **FY 2006 Legislative Branch** (HR 2985 — PL 109-55) | Passed 6/22/05 | Passed, amended 6/30/05 | 7/28/05 | 7/29/05 | 8/2/05 | 2-41 |
| **FY 2006 Military Construction-Veterans Affairs** (HR 2528 — PL 109-114) | Passed 6/30/05 | Passed, amended 9/22/05 | 11/18/05 | 11/18/05 | 11/30/05 | 2-43 |
| **FY 2006 Transportation-Treasury-Housing** (HR 3058 — PL 109-115) | Passed 6/30/05 | Passed, amended 10/20/05 | 11/18/05 | 11/21/05 | 11/30/05 | 2-47 |
| **FY 2005 War Supplemental** (HR 1268 — PL 109-13) | Passed 3/16/05 | Passed, amended 4/21/05 | 5/5/05 | 5/10/05 | 5/11/05 | 2-52 |
| **FY 2005 Veterans Supplemental** (HR 3130, included in HR 2361 — PL 109-54) | Passed 6/30/05 | —— | 7/28/05 | 7/29/05 | 8/2/05 | 2-57 |
| **FY 2005 Hurricane Supplementals** (HR 3645 — PL 109-61) | Passed 9/2/05 | Cleared 9/2/05 | —— | —— | 9/2/05 | 2-58 |
| (HR 3673 — PL 109-62) | Passed 9/8/05 | Cleared 9/8/05 | —— | —— | 9/8/05 | 2-58 |
| **FY 2006 Continuing Resolutions** (H J Res 68 — PL 109-77) | Passed 9/29/05 | Cleared 9/30/05 | —— | —— | 9/30/05 | |
| (H J Res 72 — PL 109-105) | Passed 11/17/05 | Cleared 11/18/05 | —— | —— | 11/19/05 | |
| (H J Res 75 — PL 109-128) | Passed 12/17/05 | Cleared 12/17/05 | —— | —— | 12/18/05 | |

*Adoption of conference report

# Congress Delays Food-Labeling Rule

CONGRESS CLEARED A $101 BILLION fiscal 2006 spending bill for Agriculture Department programs and the Food and Drug Administration (FDA). President Bush signed the measure into law Nov. 10 (HR 2744 — PL 109-97).

The measure funded crop subsidies and other farm programs; food and nutrition programs such as food stamps; rural conservation; food safety programs and foreign food aid.

Although the bill exceeded the previous year's funding by 13 percent, virtually all of the increase was due to the growth in mandatory programs such as food stamps and farm crop subsidies. Overall, entitlement programs accounted for more than 80 percent of the bill.

The $17 billion for discretionary programs — funding over which appropriators had direct control — was a less-than-inflation increase of about 1 percent over the fiscal 2005 spending law (PL 108-447). It was later offset by a 1 percent cut in discretionary spending enacted as part of the Defense appropriations bill (PL 109-148). *(2004 Almanac, p. 2-5)*

Congress used the fiscal 2006 bill to delay mandatory country-of-origin food labeling for two years. For the third year in a row, House and Senate conferees bowed to a White House veto threat and dropped a House provision that would have allowed individuals and wholesalers to import prescription drugs from Canada and other countries.

The House started in June by passing a $100.3 billion version of the bill that included $16.8 billion in discretionary funds. The Senate passed a larger, $100.7 billion measure in September that included $17.3 billion for discretionary programs. These included some conservation programs, agricultural and food safety, research, rural development, the supplemental nutrition program for women, infants and children (WIC), and international food aid. Bush requested $100.1 billion overall, including $16.7 billion in discretionary spending.

Although the money differences were not large, they were significant in a year of tight limits on discretionary spending. The two chambers also had to resolve policy issues, including the House provisions on drug importation and country-of-origin labeling and Senate language to bar states from hiring private companies to handle certain administrative parts of the food stamp program.

## HIGHLIGHTS

The fiscal 2006 Agriculture spending bill included the following components:

● **Agriculture programs.** $35.5 billion for a variety of agriculture programs, an increase of $8.4 billion, or 31 percent, over fiscal 2005. Most of the total, $25.7 billion, was for the Commodity Credit Corporation, which funded mandatory crop support programs authorized by the 2002 farm law (PL 107-171). The corporation got an increase of $9.2 billion over fiscal 2005 to replenish funds used the previous year; the amount needed each year is tied to crop and weather conditions. The bill also included $3.2 billion for the Federal Crop Insurance Corporation, another mandatory program, which got $936 million less than in the previous year.

● **Food and nutrition programs.** $58.9 billion — more than half the

**BILL:**
HR 2744 — PL 109-97

**LEGISLATIVE ACTION:**

**House** passed HR 2744 (H Rept 109-102), 408-18, on June 8.

**Senate** passed HR 2744, amended (S Rept 109-92), 97-2, on Sept. 22.

**House** adopted the conference report (H Rept 109-255), 318-63, on Oct. 28.

**Senate** cleared the bill, 81-18, on Nov. 3.

**President** signed Nov. 10.

funds in the bill — for food stamps and other domestic nutrition programs. That was an increase of 12 percent or $6.5 billion over fiscal 2005 levels. The total included:

▶ $40.7 billion for the food stamp program, an increase of 16 percent or $5.6 billion over fiscal 2005.

▶ $12.7 billion for school lunches and other child nutrition programs, a 7.5 percent increase.

▶ $5.3 billion in discretionary funds, virtually the same as the previous year, for WIC.

● **Conservation.** $1 billion for discretionary conservation programs managed by the Natural Resources Conservation Service. That was only about 1 percent more than provided in fiscal 2005, but it was 23 percent more than Bush requested.

The bill also reduced spending on some mandatory conservation programs from amounts authorized under the 2002 farm law. The Environmental Quality Incentives Program, an entitlement program providing assistance to livestock producers and farmers for water quality improvements, received $1 billion, compared with an authorization of $1.2 billion. The Wetlands Reserve Program, which offered landowners incentives to protect and restore wetlands, was limited to 150,000 acres in fiscal 2006 rather than 250,000.

● **Rural development.** $2.5 billion, about 5 percent more than under the fiscal 2005 law, for housing programs, community facilities, infrastructure and business development in low-income rural areas. Bush had requested about $70 million less.

● **Trade and global food aid.** $1.5 billion, about $37 million less than in fiscal 2005, to provide food aid abroad and promote U.S. agricultural exports. About $1.2 billion of the total went to the Food for Peace program (PL 480), which provided commodities to developing countries and emerging democracies.

● **Food safety.** $1.5 billion, $40 million more than fiscal 2005 funding but $10 million less than requested, for the agency responsible for regulating food, cosmetics, drugs and medical devices. In addition, the funding for farm programs included $838 million for the Food Safety and Inspection Service, a 3 percent increase over the previous year, and $820 million for the Animal and Plant Health Inspection Service (APHIS), a 1 percent increase.

● **Country-of-origin-labeling.** A delay until Sept. 2008 of an Agriculture Department rule requiring that retailers provide country-of-origin information on fruit, vegetables, meat and fish. Under prior law, the labeling would have become mandatory on Sept. 30, 2006.

## LEGISLATIVE ACTION
### HOUSE SUBCOMMITTEE ACTION

The House Agriculture Appropriations Subcommittee gave voice vote approval May 16 to a $100.3 billion draft bill that included $16.8 billion in discretionary spending — the amount House appropriators had allocated for the bill, and the same as fiscal 2005 spending.

Chairman Henry Bonilla, R-Texas, included a provision in the draft to block use of money in the bill to carry out country-of-origin labeling. The 2002 farm law had set Sept. 30, 2004, as the start date for mandatory labeling. Bonilla, who represented the interests of meat-

## WHERE THE MONEY GOES — FISCAL 2006 APPROPRIATIONS

# AGRICULTURE

## HR 2744 — PL 109-97

*(figures are in thousands of dollars of new budget authority)*

|  | Fiscal 2005 appropriations | Fiscal 2006 Bush request | House passed | Senate passed | Conference report |
|---|---|---|---|---|---|
| **GRAND TOTAL** | $89,439,376 | $100,132,911 | $100,321,593 | $100,722,949 | $100,981,758 |
| Discretionary spending | 16,832,417 | 16,739,462 | 16,829,760 | 17,348,000 | 17,031,085 |
| **MAIN COMPONENTS** |  |  |  |  |  |
| **Domestic food programs** | $52,488,361 | $58,956,717 | $58,700,579 | $58,711,717 | $58,949,950 |
| **Farm programs** | 27,041,494 | 35,081,521 | 35,195,960 | 35,451,185 | 35,469,627 |
| **Rural and community development programs** | 2,413,768 | 2,458,132 | 2,470,958 | 2,534,453 | 2,528,337 |
| **Foreign food assistance and loans** | 1,520,935 | 1,219,436 | 1,440,962 | 1,483,512 | 1,483,545 |
| **Food and Drug Administration** | 1,450,098 | 1,499,726 | 1,485,978 | 1,492,009 | 1,489,617 |
| **Conservation programs** | 991,901 | 814,393 | 939,770 | 963,987 | 1,004,207 |

TABLE: House and Senate Appropriations committees

packers and ranchers, had already delayed the labeling by two years for everything but fish as part of the fiscal 2004 Agriculture appropriations law (PL 108-199). Putting the language in this bill would keep the provision in law until a fiscal 2007 bill could be enacted, even if that bill were delayed past the start of the fiscal year.

Meatpackers and retailers argued that the labeling was too expensive and would drive up retail beef costs. Beef producers in the Plains states, on the other hand, supported earlier enforcement of the labeling rule because they viewed it as a marketing tool that could give them an edge over Canadian and Mexican competitors.

The subcommittee draft included:

▶ $1.5 billion for the FDA, $36 million more than the previous year and $14 million less than Bush requested.

▶ $837 million for the Food Safety Inspection Service, including $90 million for protection against bovine spongiform encephalopathy, or mad cow disease. The total was $20 million more than in fiscal 2005 and $127 million more than requested. The committee did not include a $139 million administration-proposed user fee for overtime costs in meat, poultry and egg inspections.

▶ $829 million for APHIS, a $16 million increase over fiscal 2005 but $32 million less than requested.

▶ $5.3 billion for WIC, $22 million more than fiscal 2005 spending but $253 million less than Bush requested. The appropriations were reduced after the Office of Management and Budget reported that estimates for participation and food costs had declined since Bush's budget request in February.

▶ $940 million for discretionary conservation programs, $52 million less than fiscal 2005 spending but $125 million more than requested.

▶ $2.5 billion for rural economic and community development, $48 million less than in fiscal 2005 but $120 million more than requested.

During the markup, the subcommittee:

▶ Adopted by voice vote a proposal by Jo Ann Emerson, R-Mo., to bar the FDA from using funds in the bill to enforce its ban on prescription drug imports. Similar language was added to the bill the previous year but removed in conference.

▶ Adopted by voice vote an amendment by Rosa DeLauro, D-Conn., to block the use of funds in the bill to produce prepackaged news stories that failed to disclose federal funding. The amendment was sparked by reports of administration efforts to distribute stories to television stations around the country that touted Bush's policies but did not disclose that the government produced the material.

### HOUSE COMMITTEE ACTION

The full House Appropriations Committee approved the bill (HR 2744 — H Rept 109-102) by voice vote May 25, with little change from the subcommittee version. "Every year is difficult, but this one was especially difficult," Bonilla said of the discretionary spending allocation.

During the markup, the committee:

▶ Rejected, 25-31, an amendment by Maurice D. Hinchey, D-N.Y., to authorize the FDA to require drugmakers to test the safety of medications after they were approved for sale. Hinchey cited high-profile cases of FDA-approved drugs — such as Merck & Co.'s recalled painkiller Vioxx — that were later discovered to have dangerous side effects. Bonilla and Appropriations Chairman Jerry Lewis, R-Calif., said the authorizers on the Energy and Commerce Committee were better suited to address the issue.

Harold Rogers, R-Ky., deferred to the Republican leadership but expressed frustration with the FDA's response to misuse of the painkiller OxyContin. "I would hope that the authorizing committee would take action," he said.

▶ Rejected, after heated debate, two amendments by Jesse L. Jackson Jr., D-Ill., to increase funding for the Food for Peace program and count the money as emergency spending. "It's time we put America first," argued Virgil H. Goode Jr., R-Va. "We can't keep being the sugar daddy for everyone around the world."

### HOUSE FLOOR ACTION

The House passed the $100.3 billion bill June 8 by an overwhelming vote of 408-18, after defeating an attempt to drop the language delaying mandatory country-of-origin labeling. *(House vote 238, p. H-76)*

Although the White House renewed its opposition to the drug importation proposal on the eve of the House vote, there was no attempt to remove the language on the floor. Amendment supporters

warned, however, that the administration would pressure lawmakers to kill the plan as they had the previous year. "In the dark of the night, mark my word, they will strip this out," said Rahm Emanuel, D-Ill.

The June 7 White House statement said the administration strongly opposed the amendment, but stopped short of threatening a veto. "Prohibiting the FDA from enforcing current laws designed to protect the health and safety of American consumers is not the best way to address the issue of drug affordability," the statement said.

During the floor debate, the House:

▶ Rejected, 187-240, an amendment by Denny Rehberg, R-Mont., that would have stripped out the delay in labeling. Roy Blunt, R-Mo., who was the majority whip, said the Agriculture Department needed the delay to ensure it could implement the regulation properly. "This is a marketing issue, not a food safety issue, and puts an unnecessary burden on processors if not handled in the right way," Blunt said. *(House vote 231, p. H-74)*

▶ Adopted, 218-210, an amendment by Hinchey to prevent the FDA from appointing scientists to advisory panels if they had conflicts of interest or financial stakes in the drugs and devices they would be evaluating. "There should be no question as to whether that committee's members are looking out for the public health," Hinchey said. The amendment's opponents said that because of the way research was financed, most top scientists in each field typically had industry ties. *(House vote 232, p. H-74)*

▶ Adopted, 269-158, an amendment by John E. Sweeney, R-N.Y., to bar use of funds in the bill to pay salaries or expenses of government inspectors who examined horses intended to be slaughtered for human consumption. *(House vote 233, p. H-74)*

▶ Adopted by voice vote an amendment by Bonilla to boost funds for Rural Cooperative Development grants by $40 million and increase the Watershed Rehabilitation account by $20 million, offset by cuts elsewhere in the bill. A similar Bonilla amendment added $40 million for the Environmental Quality Incentives program.

An attempt by Hinchey to revive his amendment authorizing additional tests of FDA-approved drugs was ruled out of order.

## SENATE COMMITTEE ACTION

The Senate Appropriations Committee approved a $100.7 billion version of the bill (HR 2477 — S Rept 109-92) by a vote of 28-0 on June 23. The Agriculture Appropriations Subcommittee had approved a draft of the bill by voice vote June 21.

The measure included $17.3 billion in discretionary spending, about $518 million more than was allocated to the bill in the House.

Highlighting increased spending for rural development, food safety and the FDA, ranking subcommittee Democrat Herb Kohl of Wisconsin said, "I think we've come up with something that we can all be satisfied with and proud of."

The bill recommended:

▶ $1.5 billion for the FDA, $7 million above the House bill.

▶ $837 million for the Food Safety and Inspection Service, about the same as the House bill.

▶ $964 million for discretionary conservation programs, $242 million more than in the House bill.

▶ $812 million for APHIS, $35 million less than in the House bill. Senate appropriators included Bush's proposal for $10.9 million in fees, which the House left out.

▶ $2.5 billion for rural economic and community development, $63 million more than in the House bill.

▶ $1.2 billion for the Food for Peace program, $42 million more than the House approved.

Issues such as country-of-origin food labeling, prescription drug importation, conflicts of interest on drug advisory panels and the slaughter of horses for human consumption did not come up.

## SENATE FLOOR ACTION

The Senate passed the $100.7 billion bill by a vote of 97-2 on Sept. 22, after adding language to restrict administration efforts to turn some jobs over to the private sector. *(Senate vote 241, p. S-47)*

During the floor debate, the Senate:

▶ Adopted by voice vote an amendment by Tom Harkin, D-Iowa, to bar states from contracting out to the private sector the job of processing applications for food stamps. The bill already contained a ban on privatizing certain administrative jobs related to rural development and farm loan programs. The latter provision was also in the House bill. The White House strongly opposed attempts to limit its "competitive sourcing" policies.

▶ Adopted, 72-26, an amendment by Ben Nelson, D-Neb., to block funding for a proposed Agriculture Department rule that would reopen U.S. markets to Japanese boneless beef, unless the president certified to Congress that Japan had granted open access for U.S. beef and beef products. Japan banned U.S. beef imports after the first U.S. mad cow case in Washington state in 2003 and had not lifted that ban. *(Senate vote 236, p. S-47)*

▶ Adopted by voice vote a proposal by Daniel K. Akaka, D-Hawaii, to make permanent a 2004 Agriculture Department ban on allowing "downer" cattle — animals no longer able to stand up — into the human food chain. Akaka also proposed to expand the law to include sheep, swine, horses and mules. The House bill had no similar ban.

▶ Adopted 69-28 a proposal by John Ensign, R-Nev., similar to the House provision, to ban the slaughter of horses for human consumption or sale overseas. *(Senate vote 237, p. S-47)*

▶ Adopted by voice vote a proposal by Richard J. Durbin, D-Ill., to restrict the FDA's ability to allow scientists with conflicts of interest to serve on the agency's advisory panels.

▶ Adopted, 55-39, a proposal by Tom Coburn, R-Okla., to specify that earmarks from the House and Senate reports on the bill would have to be included in the conference report to be considered approved by both chambers. *(Senate vote 238, p. S-47)*

David Vitter, R-La., filed a drug import amendment in the Senate but decided not to bring it up, saying he feared that he would lose too many votes because of the cost of administering drug safety requirements. The White House threatened to veto any bill that relaxed drug import curbs, citing safety considerations.

## CONFERENCE/FINAL ACTION

House and Senate negotiators reached agreement Oct. 26 on a $101 billion Agriculture bill with $17 billion in discretionary spending. The total was $660 million more than the original House-passed bill, $259 million more than the Senate-passed version and $849 million more than Bush requested. The House adopted the conference report (H Rept 109-255) with broad bipartisan support, 318-63, on Oct. 28. The Senate cleared the bill, 81-18, on Nov. 3. *(House vote 555, p. H-176; Senate vote 282, p. S-56)*

Conferees spent much of their time resolving differences on specific policy provisions. These included:

● **Country-of-origin labeling.** This was the most contentious issue in conference. The Senate originally ignored the question in its version of the bill, but Sens. Craig Thomas, R-Wyo., and Conrad Burns,

R-Mont., had vowed to strip the provision in conference. In the end, the House prevailed. In fact, the conferees went further and postponed the required labeling for two years until October 2008.

● **Drug imports.** As predicted, conferees dropped the House provision that would have blocked the FDA from enforcing a ban on prescription drug imports. Although the Senate version did not address the issue, there was strong support in the Senate for loosening drug import rules. The Senate Commerce, Science and Transportation Committee voted in July to allow Americans to order prescription drugs from an FDA-approved Canadian pharmacy.

● **Contracting jobs.** Harkin's amendment to bar states from contracting out to the private sector for the job of processing food stamp applications was also dropped.

● **FDA conflict of interest.** Conferees retained compromise Senate language on conflict of interest waivers that required FDA advisory commission members to provide advance notice of potential conflicts of interest.

● **Horse meat.** Negotiators rejected attempts by some Republicans to drop the provision banning the slaughter of horses for human consumption.

● **Japanese beef.** Conferees dropped the Senate ban on Japanese boneless beef imports and substituted less restrictive language instructing the administration to quickly resolve Japan's continuing ban on U.S. beef.

● **Discretionary spending.** An agreement to provide $17 billion for discretionary programs — $201 million more than House appropriators sought but $317 million less than in the Senate bill — facilitated a number of spending compromises. The final bill included:

▸ $1 billion for the Natural Resources Conservation Service, exceeding the House bill by $64 million and the Senate bill by $40 million.

▸ $2.5 billion for rural economic and community development, $57 million more than the House sought but about $6 million less than the Senate approved.

$1.5 billion for the FDA, $4 million above the House figure but $2 million less than the Senate wanted, including $30 million to research methods of preventing mad cow disease.

▸ $838 million for the Food Safety Inspection Service. The total was about the same as recommended by both chambers, but conferees agreed with the House and dropped Bush's proposal for $139 million in new user fees.

▸ $820 million for APHIS, $27 million less than in the House bill but $8 million more than the Senate proposed. Like the House, conferees left out Bush's proposal for $10.9 million in new fees. The funding included $17 million to conduct surveillance of mad cow disease and $28 million to control and manage avian influenza, or bird flu.

▸ $1.2 billion for Food for Peace, the same as in the Senate bill and $43 million more than the House wanted. ∎

# Justice Gets a Boost in C-J-S Bill

CONGRESS CLEARED a $61.8 billion fiscal 2006 spending bill for the departments of Commerce, Justice and State plus related agencies and science programs. Of the total, $57.9 billion was discretionary funding that Congress could allocate as it chose. That was a 3 percent increase over fiscal 2005 — roughly keeping pace with inflation — but 4 percent less than President Bush requested. Bush signed the bill into law Nov. 22 (HR 2862 — PL 109-108).

Lawmakers were more generous than the president with most agencies funded by the bill. The biggest apparent difference was over the Commerce Department, which got 31 percent less than Bush requested. However, the difference was the result of an administration assumption that Congress would agree to shift a number of community development programs to Commerce from the Department of Housing and Urban Development (HUD), which was funded under a separate bill. Leaving aside that proposal, which Congress rejected, the bill provided 13 percent more than requested for the Commerce Department and related agencies such as the National Oceanic and Atmospheric Administration (NOAA).

The Justice Department, which accounted for more than a third of the C-J-S bill, received 5 percent more than Bush requested. The State Department and international broadcasting agencies got 10 percent less than in fiscal 2005 — but 10.5 percent more if emergency supplemental spending in 2005 was not counted.

In addition to funding the three Cabinet departments, the bill provided money for two independent agencies newly added to the bill — NASA and the National Science Foundation (NSF) — as well as the Securities and Exchange Commission, the Small Business Administration (SBA), the Legal Services Corporation and the Federal Communications Commission.

The totals do not reflect a 1 percent across-the-board cut in most fiscal 2006 discretionary appropriations enacted as part of the Defense spending bill (PL 109-148).

The House started work on the bill in June, passing a $61.3 billion version that included $57.5 billion in discretionary funds. The Senate passed a $52.4 billion version, with $48.6 billion in discretionary funds, in September that did not cover the State Department. State was funded under the Senate's Foreign Operations spending bill (PL 109-102). The differences resulted from separate reorganizations of the House and Senate Appropriations panels earlier in the year. Appropriators from both chambers agreed that the final bill would reflect the House structure. *(Foreign operations, p. 2-25)*

In negotiating the final version, conferees stripped out several of the most controversial provisions, including a House amendment that would have limited the FBI's ability to access library and bookstore records under the 2001 anti-terrorism law known as the Patriot Act (PL 107-56). The amendment had drawn a White House veto threat.

Conferees also removed a proposal to give the Drug Enforcement Administration (DEA) the power to control the entry of new prescription painkillers into the market. The provision, championed by Rep. Frank R. Wolf, R-Va., was removed at the Senate's request.

**BOX SCORE 2006 FISCAL YEAR COMMERCE-JUSTICE-SCIENCE**

**BILL:** HR 2862 — PL 109-108

**LEGISLATIVE ACTION:**

**House** passed HR 2862 (H Rept 109-118), 418-7, on June 16.

**Senate** passed HR 2862, amended (S Rept 109-88), 91-4, Sept. 15.

**House** adopted the conference report (H Rept 109-272), 397-19, on Nov. 9.

**Senate** cleared the bill, 94-5, on Nov. 16.

**President** signed Nov. 22.

House conferees were successful in blocking a Senate attempt to include $4.3 billion in emergency spending for hurricane victims. House conferees opposed the funds, saying most of the money would go to programs administered by HUD, which did not come under the C-J-S bill.

## HIGHLIGHTS

The following are major components of the fiscal 2006 Commerce, Justice, State appropriations law:

● **Commerce Department.** $6.6 billion for the Commerce Department and related agencies, a cut of less than 1 percent from fiscal 2005, although inflation made it deeper in real terms. Bush requested $2.9 billion more, but his proposal included $3.7 billion for the HUD community development programs that he wanted to transfer to Commerce.

More than half the Commerce funding, $3.9 billion, was for NOAA, the agency responsible for monitoring the environment, managing fisheries and coastlines and running the National Weather Service. The total was virtually the same as in fiscal 2005 but about 10 percent more than Bush requested. The National Institute of Standards and Technology (NIST), which works with industry to develop and apply innovative technologies, got $762 million, a 9 percent increase over fiscal 2005 and 43 percent more than requested. Bush wanted to cut the program to $532 million.

● **Justice Department.** $21.7 billion, a 4 percent increase over fiscal 2005 and 5 percent more than requested. The total included $5.8 billion for the FBI — 10.5 percent more than in fiscal 2005 and 1 percent above the request. As in previous years, Congress rebuffed the administration's request for massive cuts to state and local law enforcement grants, juvenile justice and Community Oriented Policing Services (COPS) programs, but still provided less than the programs received the year before.

● **State Department.** $9 billion for the State Department and $652 million for the Broadcasting Board of Governors, which handles U.S. government-sponsored international broadcasting services. The combined total of $9.7 billion was a 10 percent cut from fiscal 2005 funding and about 3 percent less than Bush requested. Excluding $2 billion in emergency spending for 2005, however, State got 10.5 percent more than in the previous year.

● **NASA.** $16.5 billion for the space agency, a less-than-inflation 2 percent increase and virtually the same as Bush's request.

● **NSF.** $5.7 billion, 3 percent above fiscal 2005 funding and about equal to Bush's request.

## LEGISLATIVE ACTION
### HOUSE COMMITTEE ACTION

The House Appropriations Committee gave voice vote approval June 7 to a $61.3 billion C-J-S bill, $57.5 billion of which was discretionary spending (H Rept 109-118). The measure was drafted by the Subcommittee for Science, State, Justice, Commerce and Related Agencies, chaired by Wolf, which approved it by voice vote May 24.

The committee-approved bill included:

● **Commerce Department.** $5.8 billion for the department and related agencies, a cut of 14 percent from fiscal 2005 spending. More than

## WHERE THE MONEY GOES — FISCAL 2006 APPROPRIATIONS
# COMMERCE-JUSTICE-SCIENCE

### HR 2862 — PL 109-108

*(figures are in thousands of dollars of new budget authority)*

| | Fiscal 2005 appropriations | Fiscal 2006 Bush request | House passed | Senate* passed | Conference report |
|---|---|---|---|---|---|
| **GRAND TOTAL** | $62,939,025 | $64,158,909 | $61,293,285 | $63,209,272 | $61,797,098 |
| Discretionary spending | 56,241,882 | 60,351,223 | 57,452,424 | 58,229,511 | 57,854,000 |
| **MAIN COMPONENTS** | | | | | |
| **Justice Department** | $20,893,834 | $20,562,785 | $21,759,882 | $21,497,385 | $21,669,456 |
| FBI | 5,219,603 | 5,701,237 | 5,761,237 | 5,320,726 | 5,766,345 |
| **NASA** | 16,196,400 | 16,456,400 | 16,471,050 | 16,396,400 | 16,456,800 |
| **State Department and related agencies** | 10,780,207 | 9,935,252 | 9,581,629 | 9,790,278 | 9,685,574 |
| **Commerce Department and related agencies** | 6,654,204 | 9,554,079 | 5,752,734 | 7,396,811 | 6,617,140 |
| National Oceanic and Atmospheric Administration | 3,925,167 | 3,581,219 | 3,379,000 | 4,476,000 | 3,946,000 |
| **National Science Foundation** | 5,472,824 | 5,605,000 | 5,643,370 | 5,530,959 | 5,653,370 |

*Senate totals are recalculated to include the State Department, which was not covered in the original Senate-passed bill.

TABLE: House Appropriations Committee

half the proposed cuts were from NOAA, which was to get $3.4 billion, 13 percent less than the previous year and 6 percent less than requested. Appropriators also provided:

▸ $228 million for the Economic Development Administration (EDA), which granted aid and trade adjustment assistance to communities facing economic dislocation. That was 20 percent below fiscal 2005 funding. Bush wanted to eliminate the EDA and fold the programs into a new Strengthening America's Communities grant program for which he requested $3.7 billion. The committee did not fund that request.

▸ $549 million for NIST, 21.5 percent below 2005 funding but 3 percent more than Bush wanted.

● **Justice.** $21.7 billion, a 4 percent increase over fiscal 2005 spending, and $1.1 billion more than Bush requested. The biggest winner was the FBI, which was slated to get $5.8 billion, a 10 percent increase over fiscal 2005. The committee said in its report on the bill that it was "disappointed" by how slowly Justice had worked to develop civil rights safeguards related to the war on terrorism and by the unsuccessful implementation of the FBI's Virtual Case File system. Earlier in the year, FBI Director Robert S. Mueller III had told the panel that a long-delayed computer system was being scrapped after $170 million had been spent.

The bill also called for:

▸ $5 billion for the federal prison system, a 4 percent increase over fiscal 2005 funding and 5 percent more than requested.

▸ $800 million for the U.S. Marshals Service, a 5 percent increase over 2005 and 1 percent more than requested.

▸ $1 billion for state and local law enforcement grants, a 22 percent cut from fiscal 2005. Bush wanted to zero out the program.

▸ $520 million for COPS, a 13 percent cut from 2005; Bush wanted to end the program. The committee report said that "according to the Department of Justice, every $1 we invest in COPS grants contributes to a decline of 10 violent crimes and 27 property crimes per 100,000 residents."

▸ $334 million for juvenile justice programs, a 12 percent cut. Bush requested no funding.

● **State Department.** $9.7 billion for the department and the Broadcasting Board of Governors, a cut of $1.1 billion or 10 percent from fiscal 2005 funding including supplemental appropriations, and 3 percent less than Bush requested. The committee cut $130 million from Bush's request for the United Nations and other international organizations. Setting aside emergency supplemental funding, the committee proposal was a 10 percent increase over 2005.

● **NASA.** $16.5 billion, about $15 million more than Bush requested, but with a different set of priorities. The bill included $65 million for projects not in the president's request, for example, $40 million for science programs at NASA, while excluding $50 million that Bush sought for some space exploration programs, such as the space station.

Addressing the one source of debate during the markup, the panel adopted by voice vote an amendment by Anne M. Northup, R-Ky., to block use of funds in the bill to implement language in recent trade agreements with Australia, Morocco and Singapore that would make it more difficult to import prescription drugs from those countries. Appropriations Chairman Jerry Lewis, R-Calif., made it clear that House GOP leaders opposed the amendment language.

### HOUSE FLOOR ACTION

The House passed the bill, 418-7, on June 16 after three days of debate dominated by bipartisan efforts to find more aid for state and local law enforcement. *(House vote 268, p. H-86)*

In all, the House voted to redirect $125 million to Justice Department grant programs, with funding coming at the expense of the 2010 census, NOAA and U.S. contributions to the United Nations. Otherwise, the $61.3 billion spending bill was largely the same as the version approved by the Appropriations Committee. The new total for Justice was $21.8 billion; the total for Commerce was $5.8 billion; and State fell to $9.6 billion.

The only controversial change was language added by Vermont independent Bernard Sanders to bar the use of funds in the bill to search library circulation records, library patron lists, book sales records,

or book customer lists under the Foreign Intelligence Surveillance Act (PL 95-511). The power to conduct such searches was granted under the 2001 anti-terrorism law known as the Patriot Act (PL 107-56). The amendment was adopted, 238-187, with Sanders gaining the support of 38 Republicans despite a White House warning that Bush would likely veto the bill if it contained such language. Adoption of the amendment was seen at the time as a sign of bipartisan unease about portions of the sweeping anti-terrorism law. *(House vote 258, p. H-82; anti-terrorism law, p. 12-3)*

During three days of debate, the House also:

▸ Adopted, 260-168, a proposal by Brian Baird, D-Wash., to take $20 million from the 2010 census and divide it equally between efforts to curtail international trafficking of methamphetamine and grants to train local law enforcement and prosecutors. *(House vote 248, p. H-80)*

▸ Adopted, 231-195, an amendment by David Dreier, R-Calif., to shift $50 million to the State Criminal Alien Assistance Program from NOAA. *(House vote 250, p. H-80)*

▸ Adopted by voice vote several other amendments to shift funds to state and local law enforcement.

▸ Adopted, 242-182, an amendment by John Hostettler, R-Ind., to prohibit the enforcement of a recent federal district court ruling that ordered the removal of a display of the Ten Commandments from public property. *(House vote 257, p. H-82)*

▸ Adopted, 415-8, an amendment by Edward J. Markey, D-Mass., to prohibit actions barred by the U.N. Convention Against Torture. It aimed to block the United States from transferring prisoners to foreign governments that might torture them. *(House vote 261, p. H-82)*

▸ Rejected, 196-230, a proposal by David R. Obey of Wisconsin, ranking Democrat on the Appropriations Committee, to redirect $200 million from NASA to increase the grants for local law enforcement. House Majority Leader Tom DeLay, R-Texas, a vocal supporter of the space agency, objected that the amendment would force NASA to send astronauts "into the unknown on the cheap." DeLay had added the Johnson Space Center to his Houston-area district as part of a Texas redistricting plan that he helped engineer. *(House vote 244, p. H-78)*

▸ Rejected, 175-252, an amendment by Lee Terry, R-Neb., to make an across-the-board cut of 0.448 percent in the bill to pay for an extra $286 million for the Byrne grant program for state and local law enforcement. Terry and a group of bipartisan backers from mostly rural Midwestern districts said the increase was needed to help combat methamphetamine abuse, which he said was "overwhelming our communities." *(House vote 245, p. H-78)*

▸ Rejected, 210-216, an attempt by Jeff Flake, R-Ariz., to relax the trade embargo against Cuba to allow the shipment of gift parcels. The amendment encountered strong resistance from Florida's GOP delegation and DeLay, who said the goods would wind up in the hands of the Castro regime. The White House had warned that such an amendment might trigger a veto. *(House vote 254, p. H-80)*

▸ Rejected, 161-264, an amendment by Maurice D. Hinchey, D-N.Y., to block the Justice Department from prosecuting medical marijuana usage in states that had legalized it. Hinchey noted that the vote tally was the highest he had received in the three years he had offered the amendment. *(House vote 255, p. H-82)*

## SENATE COMMITTEE ACTION

The Senate Appropriations Committee approved a $52.4 billion version of the bill (HR 2862 — S Rept 109-88), along with two other appropriations measures, by a single 28-0 vote June 23. Discretionary spending accounted for $48.6 billion of the bill. The Commerce-Justice-Science Subcommittee, which approved the bill by voice vote June 21, allocated significantly more money to the Commerce Department than did House appropriators. The $8.9 billion difference between the House and Senate totals for the bill was due in part the Senate appropriators' decision to handle State Department funding in a separate spending measure.

The Senate committee's bill included:

● **Commerce.** $7.2 billion, $1.4 billion more than in the House-passed bill and $533 million more than the department got in fiscal 2005. Like the House, Senate appropriators ignored Bush's proposed transfer to the department of community development programs.

Much of the increase over the House bill went to NOAA. The Senate recommended $4.5 billion for the agency, $1.1 billion more than in the House bill. The committee report said the panel was "intensely disappointed" by Bush's request of $3.6 billion, 9 percent below fiscal 2005 spending. "I strongly believe, as many of you do, that NOAA's budget should move in the opposite direction," said Richard C. Shelby, R-Ala., chairman of the Commerce-Justice-Science Subcommittee.

The bill also included:

▸ $315 million for the EDA, compared with $228 million in the amended House bill. (An additional $210 million in emergency funding was added on the Senate floor.)

▸ $845 million for NIST, compared with $549 million in the House version.

● **Justice.** $21.2 billion, $557 million less than in the House bill but still $602 million more than Bush requested. (As passed by the Senate, the bill provided $21.5 billion for Justice.) The total included:

▸ $5.3 billion for the FBI, $440 million less than in the House bill and $380 million less than requested.

▸ $5.1 billion for the federal prison system, $146 million more than in the House bill and $360 million more than requested.

▸ $776 million for the U.S. Marshals Service, $24 million less than in the House bill and $14 million less than requested.

▸ $1.1 billion for state and local law enforcement grants, virtually the same as in the House bill. (The total was increased to $1.4 billion on the Senate floor.)

▸ $515 million for COPS, compared with $567 million in the amended House bill.

▸ $350 million for juvenile justice programs, compared to $334 million in the House bill.

● **NASA.** $16.4 billion, $75 million less than in the House version. The Senate bill included an extra $250 million to prepare a mission to service the Hubble Space Telescope, a priority of Barbara A. Mikulski of Maryland, ranking Democrat on the subcommittee. In its report, the committee expressed concern about NASA's ambitious agenda of manned and unmanned space flights, which it suggested "will likely be very difficult to sustain at the estimated levels" and which could cause NASA to "neglect areas that will only tangentially benefit from, or that do not fit within, the proposed vision."

## SENATE FLOOR ACTION

The Senate passed the bill, 91-4, on Sept. 15 after adding a total of $4.3 billion in emergency funds for aid and recovery in the aftermath of Hurricane Katrina, which devastated the Gulf Coast region Aug. 29. The extra funding, added in a series of floor amendments, did not count against discretionary spending caps set by the fiscal 2006 budget resolution (H Con Res 95). *(Senate vote 235, p. S-46)*

● **Katrina.** To provide assistance for hurricane recovery, the Senate:

▸ Adopted, 96-0, a proposal by Olympia J. Snowe, R-Maine, to sup-

ply $595 million in emergency disaster aid to Katrina victims through modified Small Business Administration programs for business owners, homeowners and renters. *(Senate vote 233, p. S-46)*

▶ Adopted by voice vote a proposal by Paul S. Sarbanes, D-Md., to make federal rent assistance available to Katrina evacuees. The bill appropriated $3.5 billion for the program. The government would cover all of the housing costs — including utilities, relocation and security deposits — for families until their income was restored.

▶ Adopted by voice vote an amendment by Max Baucus, D-Mont., to allow emergency spending totaling $210 million for economic development activity in areas affected by the hurricane.

● **Trade.** The Senate also:

▶ Adopted by voice vote an amendment by Debbie Stabenow, D-Mich., to bar use of funds in the bill to include language in any new trade agreements that would make it more difficult to import prescription drugs.

▶ Adopted, 99-0, an amendment by Charles E. Grassley, R-Iowa, to encourage trade negotiators not to weaken U.S. safeguards against unfair trade practices in trade agreements. The Senate rejected, 39-60, an alternative by Byron L. Dorgan, D-N.D., that would have prohibited the use of funds in the bill to negotiate a trade agreement that would weaken any U.S. law that provided safeguards from unfair foreign trade practices. *(Senate votes 231, 232, p. S-46)*

● **Justice Department.** The Senate:

▶ Agreed by voice vote to dedicate money to investigate the manufacture of fraudulent U.S. identity and travel documents, accelerate FBI background checks of backlogged visa applications, and postpone an increase in consumer phone bills intended to pay for a program that funds Internet connections in schools and libraries.

▶ Adopted by voice vote an amendment by Jim Talent, R-Mo., and Christopher J. Dodd, D-Conn., to create a "cold case" section in the Justice Department's civil rights division that would investigate pre-1970 civil rights violations that resulted in deaths, such as the 1955 murder of black teenager Emmett Till.

▶ Rejected a proposal by Joseph R. Biden Jr., D-Del., to add $1 billion in emergency funding for the COPS program. Biden failed, 41-56, to waive a budget point of order against the emergency designation. *(Senate vote 226, p. S-45)*

▶ Rejected an attempt by Stabenow to provide $5 billion for grants to state and local first responders for interoperable communications equipment. Stabenow failed, 40-58, to waive a budget point of order. *(Senate vote 227, p. S-45)*

▶ Voted, 68-29, to table (kill) an amendment by Tom Coburn, R-Okla., to eliminate funding for the Advanced Technology Program and increase funding for NOAA, COPS and state and local law enforcement assistance. *(Senate vote 230, p. S-46)*

▶ Rejected an attempt by Dorgan to establish a special Senate committee to investigate the awarding and carrying out of contracts in Afghanistan and Iraq. Dorgan failed, 44-54, to suspend the rule against legislating on an appropriations bill. An attempt by Hillary Rodham Clinton, D-N.Y., to establish an independent commission to examine the federal, state, and local response to Hurricane Katrina failed, 44-54, on a similar procedural vote. *(Senate votes 259, 229, pp. S-51, S-45)*

▶ Adopted by voice vote an amendment by Talent and Dianne Feinstein, D-Calif., to make it harder for illicit methamphetamine labs to obtain pseudoephedrine, an ingredient used in production of the drug. The amendment required that retailers put medicines containing pseudoephedrine behind counters and limit to 7.5 grams the amount of such medicines that consumers could buy per month.

## CONFERENCE/FINAL ACTION

House and Senate conferees reached agreement on a final bill Nov. 4, after stripping the most controversial provisions including the House amendment that would have limited the FBI's ability to access library and bookstore records. The House adopted the conference report (H Rept 109-272) by a vote of 397-19 on Nov. 9. The Senate cleared the bill, 94-5, on Nov. 16. *(House vote 581, p. H-184; Senate vote 329, p. S-64)*

Appropriators agreed to use House jurisdictional rules, which meant the final bill included State Department funding. The conferees resolved most major differences behind closed doors, including the wide gap in funding for NOAA.

● **Commerce.** As had been the case in previous years, NOAA got less than the Senate wanted but more than in the House bill. Conferees agreed to $3.9 billion compared with $3.4 billion in the House bill and $4.5 billion in the Senate version. That decision largely resolved the $1.6 billion gap between the two bills on the Commerce Department. Commerce and related agencies got $6.6 billion — $864 million more than in the House bill but $780 million less than the Senate recommended. Conferees provided:

▶ $762 million for NIST, closer to the Senate figure

▶ $284 million for the EDA, $56 above the House figure but $241 million less than the Senate wanted.

● **Justice.** Conferees largely agreed with the House in providing $1.1 billion more for the Justice Department than Bush requested. The total was $21.7 billion — $90 million less than the House recommended and about $172 million more than in the Senate bill. The $5.8 billion for the FBI was just $5 million above the House figure but $446 million more than in the Senate bill.

The DEA got $1.7 billion, but conferees dropped a proposal championed by Wolf that would have given the agency the power to control the entry of new prescription painkillers into the market. Wolf wanted to give the DEA more power to stop abuse of prescription painkillers such as OxyContin. Pharmaceutical manufacturers and some physicians objected, saying the provision could hurt patient care.

Conferees also dropped the Senate amendment that would have required stores to keep cold medicines containing pseudoephedrine behind the counter. House conferees objected that it was authorizing language and should not be included in an appropriations bill.

The final bill also included:

▶ $802 million for the U.S. marshals, close to the higher House number and nearly 6 percent above fiscal 2005 spending.

▶ $5 billion for the federal prison system, close to the lower House figure and a 4 percent increase over 2005.

▶ $1.1 billion for state and local law enforcement grants, $74 million more than the House wanted, $211 million less than in the Senate-passed bill and about 11 percent below 2005 funding.

▶ $478 million for the COPS program, less than either chamber recommended and 20 percent below the previous year's funding.

▶ $343 million for juvenile justice programs, splitting the difference between the two chambers and falling about 10 percent below 2005 funds.

● **State.** The two chambers were only about $209 million apart on funds for the State Department and Broadcast Board of Governors. Conferees split the difference, approving $9.7 billion.

● **NASA.** The $16.5 billion in the bill for the space agency was $14 million less than the House wanted but $60 million more than the Senate had approved. The conferees included an increase of $50 million above the budget request for the Hubble Space Telescope, for a total of $271 mil-

lion, to pay for a repair mission to keep the telescope operational.

● **SBA.** The House proposed $655 million for the SBA, 44 percent more than Bush requested. The Senate raised that to $1.2 billion, a 168 percent increase. In the end, Congress approved $456 million, just $3 million more than requested and $1 billion, or 70 percent, below fiscal 2005 spending excluding emergency supplemental funds.

● **Other decisions.** Conferees also:

▸ Accepted Senate language to bar the use of funds in the bill to include language in future trade agreements that would make it more difficult to import prescription drugs to the United States.

▸ Dropped House bill language to prohibit use of funds in violation of the U.N. Convention Against Torture. However, the conference report stated that no funds in the bill were to be used in contravention of the U.N. torture convention.

▸ Agreed with Senate language blocking "primary line" restrictions in the Universal Service Fund that subsidizes telephone and Internet service in rural states. Rural lawmakers said the restriction, which limited universal service subsidies to a single connection to a home or business, would make it far more expensive for small businesses to operate in their states. "It's of extreme importance to us," said Sen. Ted Stevens, R-Alaska.

▸ Dropped Senate provisions that would have added $4.3 billion in emergency spending for Hurricane Katrina victims. House appropriators opposed appropriating the funds in the C-J-S measure because most of the money would go to programs administered by HUD, which was funded under a separate bill.

Congress already had cleared a pair of emergency supplemental bills totaling $62.3 billion (PL 109-61, PL 109-62) to help the hurricane-ravaged states. Subsequently, Congress included a $29 billion package of hurricane relief in the Defense appropriation bill (PL 109-148) signed Dec. 30. About $23.4 billion of that was reallocated from funds granted to FEMA under the earlier bills. *(Hurricane supplementals, p. 2-58)* ■

# Last-Minute Disputes Slow Defense Bill

IN ONE OF ITS LAST ACTS of the session, the Senate cleared a $403.5 billion fiscal 2006 Defense spending bill after jettisoning unrelated provisions that would have opened Alaska's Arctic National Wildlife Refuge (ANWR) to oil and gas drilling.

In addition, it included $50 billion in emergency supplemental funds for the wars in Iraq and Afghanistan to tide over the Pentagon until President Bush submitted a new supplemental request, expected in February 2006. Bush signed the measure into law Dec. 30 (HR 2863 — PL 109-148)

Lawmakers also used the bill to carry $29 billion in emergency hurricane relief for Gulf Coast areas hit by hurricanes Katrina and Rita, $3.8 billion to protect against a potential flu epidemic and a 1 percent across-the-board cut in fiscal 2006 discretionary spending — other than for veterans and emergency war funding — which was expected to save $8.5 billion.

The total for Defense — $4.4 billion below the president's request, excluding supplemental war funding — promised to squeeze the military's modernization and procurement accounts during wartime, making the Pentagon even more reliant on supplemental spending than it had been.

C.W. Bill Young, R-Fla., chairman of the House Defense Appropriations Subcommittee, said the 1 percent cut would not affect veterans or combat funds for the wars in Iraq and Afghanistan, but that it would shave about $4 billion from regular Defense programs.

As part of the final bill, conferees provided $8.8 billion for what Young called a "fairly aggressive" shipbuilding program. That was a substantial increase over the $5.6 billion that the Bush administration requested for four ships — half the number of vessels covered in the fiscal 2005 law (PL 108-287). *(2004 Almanac, p. 2-12)*

Conferees agreed to meet Bush's request of $1.1 billion in research and $716 million for procurement of the Navy's next-generation DD(X) destroyer. But they trimmed funds for other modernization programs, including the Future Combat System, the Army's top modernization program, the Transformational Satellite Communications program and the Joint Strike Fighter, a next-generation multirole fighter aircraft for all services based on a common airframe.

Usually one of the first spending bills to clear Congress, the fiscal 2006 measure became the last — and arguably the most contentious — regular appropriations bill enacted.

The House got off to a quick start, easily passing its version of the bill June 20. But the measure slowed in the Senate, where lawmakers wanted to wait until the chamber finished its stalled defense authorization bill (HR 1815 — PL 109-163). Among the problems holding up that bill was a pending amendment by John McCain, R-Ariz., to ban abusive treatment of terror suspects in U.S. custody. *(Defense authorization, p. 6-3)*

After the new fiscal year started Oct. 1, the Pentagon warned lawmakers repeatedly that it would run out of money if they did not finish the appropriations bill soon. The Senate passed its version in early October, after agreeing overwhelmingly to attach McCain's detainee provision. A month later, the Senate added the provision to the

---

**BOX SCORE 2006** FISCAL YEAR

**DEFENSE**

**BILL:**
HR 2863 — PL 109-148

**LEGISLATIVE ACTION:**

**House** passed HR 2863 (H Rept 109-119), 398-19, on June 20.

**Senate** passed HR 2863, amended (S Rept 109-141), 97-0, on Oct. 7.

**House** adopted the conference report on HR 2863 (H Rept 109-359), 308-106, on Dec. 19.

**Senate** adopted S Con Res 74, 48-45, on Dec. 21, to strip ANWR language from HR 2863 once the bill was cleared.

**Senate** cleared HR 2863, 93-0, on Dec. 21.

**House** adopted S Con Res 74 by voice vote Dec. 22.

**President** signed Dec. 30.

---

authorization bill as well. The White House strongly opposed the McCain language, which left both bills in limbo. But after the House overwhelmingly endorsed the language in a non-binding vote in mid-December, Bush dropped his opposition.

As pressure increased to finish the bill, especially the $50 billion for troops in Iraq and Afghanistan, the measure turned into a magnet for other legislation. By the time House and Senate conferees met in a rare weekend session Dec. 18, the bill had been selected to carry the hurricane disaster aid and funds to prepare for a flu pandemic. At the insistence of House GOP leaders, it also provided an across-the-board spending cut, and the leadership decided to attach the ANWR drilling plan.

The House adopted the conference report, but the Senate would not accept it until the ANWR provisions were removed. Congress finally finished the bill four days before Christmas.

## HIGHLIGHTS

The fiscal 2006 Defense spending bill provided $97 billion for military personnel ($6.7 billion less than fiscal 2005 funding), $123.6 billion for operations and maintenance (a $2.6 billion increase), $76.5 billion for weapons procurement ($1.1 billion less) and $72.1 billion for research and development ($2.2 billion more). The following are some of the major features of the bill:

● **Prisoner abuse.** A prohibition on "cruel, inhuman or degrading treatment" of detainees in U.S. custody. Military interrogators were required to rely on standards set in an Army field manual that complied with the Geneva Conventions.

● **Iraq 'bridge fund'.** $50 billion in emergency funding for military operations in Iraq and Afghanistan, including $1 billion for additional equipment for the Army Air National Guard and the Army Reserve.

● **Higher troop levels.** Funding for 10,000 more personnel for the active-duty Army, for a new total of 512,400, and funding to increase the Marine Corps by 1,000, to 179,000.

● **Missile defense.** $7.8 billion for ballistic missile defense programs, $21 million more than requested, including funds for the initial deployment of a national missile defense system based in Alaska and California.

● **New destroyer.** $1.1 billion for research and development and $716 million, as requested, for procurement of the Navy's next-generation surface combat ship, the DD(X).

● **Raptor.** $3.8 billion, as requested, to procure 24 F-22A Raptors. The Air Force's controversial next generation premier fighter was intended to replace the F-15, and designed to have both air-to-air and air-to-ground fighter capabilities.

● **Joint Strike Fighter.** $4.7 billion for research and development of the next-generation multirole fighter, based on a common airframe and components for use by the Air Force, Navy and Marine Corps.

● **Future Combat System.** $3.2 billion for the Army's next generation of combat vehicles and weapons systems, part of Defense Secretary Donald H. Rumsfeld's plan to "transform" the Army into a lighter,

## WHERE THE MONEY GOES — FISCAL 2006 APPROPRIATIONS

# DEFENSE

## HR 2863 — PL 109-148

*(figures are in thousands of dollars of new budget authority)*

|  | Fiscal 2005 appropriations | Fiscal 2006 Bush request | House passed | Senate passed | Conference report* |
|---|---|---|---|---|---|
| **GRAND TOTAL** | $391,153,312 | $397,214,410 | $439,456,182 | $445,448,117 | $442,789,753 |
| **Total adjusted for scorekeeping\*\*** | 391,172,312 | 407,948,893 | 404,936,046 | 400,950,600 | 403,524,236 |
| Discretionary spending | 390,932,912 | 407,704,293 | 404,691,446 | 400,706,000 | 403,279,636 |
| **MAIN COMPONENTS** | | | | | |
| **Operation and maintenance** | 121,062,969 | 126,902,542 | 124,087,392 | 124,966,516 | 123,615,593 |
| **Military personnel** | 103,731,158 | 98,235,263 | 97,405,563 | 95,680,837 | 96,997,063 |
| **Procurement** | 77,679,803 | 76,635,410 | 76,806,886 | 75,817,187 | 76,539,415 |
| **Research, development, testing** | 69,932,182 | 69,356,040 | 71,656,892 | 70,407,582 | 72,132,238 |
| **Iraq, Afghanistan emergency funds** | — | — | 45,254,619 | 51,300,000 | 50,000,000 |

\*Totals do not include emergency funding for hurricane relief and pandemic flu preparation.
\*\*Does not include emergency supplemental funds.

TABLE: House Appropriations Committee

more mobile force.

● **Military pay raise.** Funding for an average 3.1 percent pay increase for military personnel in fiscal 2006.

● **Hurricane relief.** $29 billion in emergency supplemental spending, $11.9 billion more than requested, for disaster assistance to areas along the Gulf Coast affected by hurricanes Katrina and Rita. The bulk of this funding — $23.4 billion — was reallocated from amounts provided to the Federal Emergency Management Agency (FEMA) as part of two supplemental appropriations acts (PL 109-61, PL 109-62). The rest came from the across-the-board cut and other rescissions in the bill. The emergency funding included $11.5 billion for Community Development Block Grants, $2.9 billion for the Army Corps of Engineers, a net $4.4 billion for the Defense Department and $2.8 billion for emergency repairs to highways, roads and bridges.

● **Flu pandemic.** $3.8 billion, about half the amount requested, for various agencies to prepare for and respond to a possible influenza pandemic, such as an avian flu outbreak.

● **Across-the-board cut.** A 1 percent cut in most fiscal 2006 discretionary spending, for an estimated savings of $8.5 billion. The cuts did not apply to veterans' programs or to emergency funds for combat operations in Iraq and Afghanistan. The savings were used to offset part of the hurricane relief and flu preparation activities.

## LEGISLATIVE ACTION
### HOUSE COMMITTEE ACTION

The House Appropriations Committee approved a $404.9 billion Defense spending bill by voice vote June 7 (HR 2863 — H Rept 109-119) that also included $45.3 billion in emergency funds for operations in Iraq and Afghanistan. The Defense Appropriations Subcommittee approved a draft of the measure by voice vote May 24.

Because of a committee reorganization earlier in the year, the bill no longer covered several accounts — including the Defense Health Program, for which Bush requested $19.8 billion — which were moved to the military construction and Veterans Affair bill (PL 109-114).

Leaving aside the emergency funds for Iraq, the bill included $363.7 billion for regular Defense accounts, $3.3 billion less than Bush

requested. Discretionary spending accounted for $363.4 billion of the total, equal to the amount the committee had allocated for the bill.

House appropriators said they could bolster those funds with an additional $5 billion in spending that would be offset by rescissions and other savings, which would bring the total to $368.4 billion — slightly more than the president had sought.

The committee generally met or exceeded the administration's request for major weapons, with the exception of the new DD(X) destroyer. Appropriators also added $1.4 billion in unrequested funds for a new guided-missile destroyer for the Navy.

The measure included:

● **Raptor.** $3.8 billion to procure 24 F-22A fighter jets, equal to Bush's request. The administration wanted to end production of the plane after fiscal 2008.

● **Joint Strike Fighter.** $4.9 billion for research and development, as requested, but none of the $152 million requested for advance procurement.

● **C-130.** $321 million for four Marine Corps KC-130Js, down from $1.1 billion requested for 12 of the planes. Appropriators included $744 million for the Air Force to purchase nine C-130J transport planes that were not in Bush's budget. The Pentagon had said it wanted to cancel the program after fiscal 2006, but it had reversed that decision under congressional pressure in May.

● **Missile defense.** $7.6 billion for missile defense programs, $144 million less than Bush wanted and $1.2 billion below fiscal 2005 spending.

● **DD(X).** $670 million to continue development, compared with $1.1 billion requested. The committee also deleted $716 million that Bush requested for advance procurement, and rescinded $304 million in fiscal 2005 advance procurement funding. The committee cited cost increases and technical problems with the program. The recommendation was consistent with the House defense authorization bill.

● **DDG-51.** $1.4 billion in unrequested funds to procure one DDG-51 *Arleigh Burke*-class guided-missile destroyer, bringing the total provided for the ship in the bill to $1.6 billion. The administration did not request any funding to build new DDG ships, which were supposed to be replaced by the DD(X). The committee said the ship would be

needed because of delays in developing the DD(X).

● **Future Combat System.** $3 billion for research and development, a $449 million cut from the president's request. The committee said the reduction was due to development and contract delays, and instructed the Army to report by Dec. 1 with a detailed list and description of the systems included for each stage of development.

● **Military personnel.** $84.1 billion, $830 million less than requested. Appropriators said the funds would allow for a 3.1 percent pay raise.

● **Iraq funds.** $45.3 billion, about 80 percent of it earmarked to pay military personnel and keep operations and maintenance accounts from drying up. Inclusion of the funding reflected concerns that the Pentagon's share of an $82 billion supplemental spending bill (PL 109-13) enacted in May would run out before the fiscal 2006 Defense spending bill took effect. "We are being told the Army will once again be out of money by the end of August," said Young. The subcommittee chairman said the bridge fund would be available upon enactment.

During the markup, the committee:

▸ Rejected, 18-40, an amendment by ranking full committee Democrat David R. Obey of Wisconsin to offset part of the cost of the bridge fund by increasing taxes on the wealthy, which he said would generate $25.8 billion.

▸ Rejected by voice vote an Obey proposal to require the Budget Committee to draft an additional budget resolution if any proposed war appropriation would push the deficit beyond the $382.7 billion cap set in the fiscal 2006 budget resolution (H Con Res 95).

▸ Adopted by voice vote an amendment by Obey to condemn "coercive and abusive religious proselytizing" at the U.S. Air Force Academy in Colorado and require the Air Force to submit a plan to address the reported problem. Accounts of proselytizing by Evangelical Christians at the academy were the subject of an Air Force investigation.

### HOUSE FLOOR ACTION

The House passed the $408.9 billion Defense bill on a 398-19 vote June 20. *(House vote 287, p. H-90)*

During floor action, the House:

▸ Adopted by voice vote an amendment by Duncan Hunter, R-Calif., chairman of the Armed Services Committee, who led an attack on the Air Force Academy provision. Hunter substituted language to require the Air Force secretary to develop a plan to "maintain a positive climate of religious freedom and tolerance" at the academy. The House rejected, 198-210, an attempt by Obey to restore language similar to the committee amendment. *(House vote 283, p. H-90)*

The issue sparked a protracted debate, with Republicans arguing that Obey's provision could curtail Christian religious expression and that it implied guilt before the academy had a chance to finish ongoing internal reviews. "Like a moth to a flame," said John Hostettler, R-Ind., "Democrats can't help themselves when it comes to denigrating and demonizing Christians." That prompted an angry response from Democrats. "I'm just as much of a churchgoer as you are," the usually mild-mannered John P. Murtha, D-Pa., shouted at Hostettler. Republicans eventually agreed to strike Hostettler's comments from the record.

▸ Adopted by voice vote an amendment by Edward J. Markey, D-Mass., stating that none of the funds in the bill could be used to break laws or rules implementing the United Nations Convention Against Torture. The bill already contained language expressing Congress' reaffirmation that the torture of prisoners of war and detainees was illegal and did not reflect the policies of the U.S. government or the values of the people of the United States.

Minority Leader Nancy Pelosi, D-Calif., tried to add language to require the president to outline criteria for withdrawing U.S. troops from Iraq. Her amendment was ruled out of order on the grounds that it was an attempt to legislate on an appropriations bill. "If our troops are to return when we have succeeded, we need to know how success is defined," Pelosi said, calling the war in Iraq a "grotesque mistake."

### SENATE COMMITTEE ACTION

The Senate Appropriations Committee approved a $440.2 billion version of the bill (HR 2863 — S Rept 109-141) by a vote of 28-0 on Sept. 28. The total included $50 billion in supplemental funding for the wars in Iraq and Afghanistan. The Defense Appropriations Subcommittee approved a draft of the measure by voice vote Sept. 26.

The panel had broader reach than its House counterpart — including jurisdiction over the Defense Health Program — and a larger discretionary allocation: $400.7 billion vs. $363.4 billion for the House subcommittee.

The Senate bill included:

● **Raptor.** $3.8 billion for procurement of 24 F-22As, as requested and passed by the House, and $455 million for research and development, $25 million less than in the House bill.

● **Joint Strike Fighter.** $4.6 billion for research and development, $276 million less than in the House bill, and $152 million as requested for procurement.

● **C-130.** $516 million for seven Air Force C-130Js and $447 million for six Marine Corps KC-130Js, a different mix than in the House bill.

● **Missile defense.** $7.8 billion, $207 million above the House figure.

● **DD(X).** $1.1 billion for research and development, $371 million more than in the House bill, and $766 million for advance procurement, $50 million more than requested; the House had no procurement funds.

● **DDG-51.** $30 million, compared with $1.6 billion in the House bill.

● **New attack submarine.** $2.4 billion, the same as in the House bill, to procure the next *Virginia*-class attack submarine, and $194 million for research and development, slightly more than in the House bill.

● **Future Combat System.** $3.3 billion, $298 million more than in the House bill.

● **Iraq funds.** $50 billion for operations in Iraq and Afghanistan, $4.7 billion more than in the House bill. Senate appropriators included about $1.8 billion less for military personnel but $5.7 billion more for procurement.

● **Military personnel.** $95.7 billion for military personnel, $1.7 billion less than the House recommended for comparable accounts. Like the House bill, it provided for a 3.1 percent across-the-board pay raise for military personnel.

### SENATE FLOOR ACTION

The Senate passed an amended version of the bill Oct. 7 by a vote of 97-0, despite a White House veto threat because it fell $7 billion below the president's request for the Pentagon, not counting the supplemental war money. The appropriators had shifted most of the $7 billion to domestic spending bills. Given the importance of the Defense funding, few senators took the veto warning very seriously. Ted Stevens, R-Alaska, chairman of the Defense Appropriations Subcommittee, said the White House "indicated they're dissatisfied," but that he didn't think he had been handed a "real veto threat." *(Senate vote 254, p. S-50)*

In addition, senators voted overwhelmingly to add McCain's requirement that combat detainees be treated in accord with the Geneva Conventions, despite the fact that the White House had threatened to veto any bill that included the language, saying it would restrict the pres-

# Threat of Flu Leads to Emergency Funds

CONCERN ABOUT THE SPREAD of a new strain of flu virus led Congress to appropriate $3.8 billion in emergency fiscal 2006 funds for programs to prepare for and respond to a potential flu pandemic. The funds cleared as part of the Defense appropriations bill (PL 109-148), which President Bush signed Dec. 30. The provisions also gave liability protection to vaccine manufacturers. (*Defense, p. 2-14*)

Of the total, $3.3 billion went to the Department of Health and Human Services (HHS), with $350 million provided to help state and local governments and $267 million for international activities and surveillance.

The legislation barred lawsuits against drugmakers who supplied drugs or vaccines that were needed to cope with a disease that HHS has designated as a public health emergency. Instead, the department could create a compensation schedule for individuals who suffered serious injury or death because of the drug. Manufacturers could be sued in cases of public epidemics only on grounds of willful misconduct related to drugs or vaccines. The liability language was added to the conference report by Senate Majority Leader Bill Frist, R-Tenn.

The new virus — known as the H5N1 virus, or avian flu — had been found in birds in Asia and had shown that it could jump to humans, with sometimes deadly results. Public health officials said that if the virus were to adapt so that it could spread from one human to another, it could very well result in the next human pandemic.

The Senate took the lead Sept. 29, adopting by voice vote a proposal by Tom Harkin, D-Iowa, to add $3.9 billion in emergency flu funds to the Defense spending bill. Harkin took up the cause again when the Senate considered the Labor-HHS-Education bill. He won voice vote approval Oct. 27 to add $8 billion for preparation to combat avian flu. "The possibility of a deadly outbreak of avian flu is real, and time is of the essence," Harkin said. (*Labor-HHS, p. 2-37*)

Supporters said the amendment was necessary because the Bush administration had not released any plans to combat a possible flu pandemic.

Bush subsequently sent a proposal to Congress asking for $7.1 billion in emergency funding to prepare for a possible avian flu pandemic. The Nov. 1 request included $251 million to detect and contain flu outbreaks before they spread around the world; $2.8 billion to accelerate development of cell-culture technology; $800 million to develop new treatments and vaccines; $1.5 billion for HHS and the Pentagon to purchase influenza vaccines; $1 billion to stockpile antiviral medications for first-responders and high-risk populations; and $644 million to coordinate preparedness and response plans at the federal, state and local levels. The plan also included a government subsidy to help states buy antiviral medications.

Republican leaders considered several possibilities but settled on the Defense bill to carry the flu money. The $3.8 billion was $3.3 billion below Bush's request. The House Appropriations Committee said it would fund roughly the fiscal 2006 portion of the White House request.

---

ident's authority to protect the public against terrorism.

The Senate began floor action on the bill Sept. 29 and quickly amended it to include $5.2 billion in additional emergency supplemental funding. The added dollars were dedicated to buying new equipment for the National Guard and protecting against an outbreak of avian flu.

Stevens called on senators to pass the bill quickly. "It is imperative that we get this bill to the president so it can be signed and make the money available by the middle of November," he said. "Already we are starting to get amendments not germane to this bill, and I hope that will not go on," he added later.

● **Emergency funds.** The additional emergency funding was added in two amendments adopted by voice vote the first day. Tom Harkin, D-Iowa, added $3.9 billion to prepare for a potential outbreak of avian flu. Christopher S. Bond, R-Mo., co-chairman of the Senate National Guard Caucus, and Patrick J. Leahy, D-Vt., a caucus member, added $1.3 billion for new National Guard equipment. When the next big disaster, like Hurricane Katrina strikes, warned Leahy "our National Guard is not going to have a basic level of resources to do the job right."

● **Detainees.** The Senate adopted the McCain amendment on prison abuse, 90-9 on Oct. 5; all nine of the opponents were Republicans. (*Senate vote 249, p. S-49*)

The amendment banned "cruel, inhuman or degrading treatment" of detainees in U.S. custody, and required that military interrogators rely on standards set in an Army field manual that complied with the Geneva Conventions. McCain, a Navy pilot who was captured and tortured by the North Vietnamese for five years during the Vietnam War, insisted the language be added to both the spending and the author-

ization bills. The action was a response to revelations in 2004 of brutal methods used by military interrogators on detainees at Abu Ghraib in Iraq and Guantánamo Bay, Cuba. (*2004 Almanac, p. 6-5*)

Bush had distinguished between prisoners captured as uniformed military personnel fighting on behalf of a nation and detainees held as "unlawful enemy combatants." The administration said the latter category applied to non-uniformed foreign fighters who committed acts of terrorism — and that the Geneva Conventions do not apply to them. McCain said he did not oppose Bush's attempt to distinguish between regular soldiers and enemy combatants and to treat them differently, but he insisted that Congress should spell out the rules relied on for the treatment of all detainees.

The Senate reaffirmed its support for the McCain amendment Nov. 4, adding it to the defense authorization bill by voice vote. McCain said his opponents might try to the strip the language in conference, but he warned, "This issue is not going away."

● **Defense authorization.** Stevens succeeded Oct. 5 in rebuffing an effort by John W. Warner, R-Va., chairman of the Armed Services Committee, to attach the Senate's stalled fiscal 2006 defense authorization bill (S 1042) to the appropriations measure, along with two "manager's packages" containing a total of nearly 100 provisions. The Senate rejected, by a vote of 49-50, Warner's claim that the amendment was "germane" to the bill. (*Senate vote 247, p. S-49*)

Majority Leader Bill Frist, R-Tenn., had pulled the authorization bill from the floor in July when he was unable to limit debate on a long list of amendments. Stevens initially was supportive of the plan to attach it to the spending bill, but when it became clear that doing so would bog down the appropriations measure with dozens of secondary

amendments, Stevens objected.

The heated debate crossed party lines and pitted appropriators against authorizers. At one point Stevens warned Warner that their "friendship [was] very close to the brink."

● **Other amendments.** In other action on the bill, the Senate:

▸ Adopted by voice vote a proposal by Richard J. Durbin, D-Ill., to make up the difference in salaries of federal employees who were members of the National Guard or reserves and were called to serve in combat. Durbin had attached a similar provision to the fiscal 2005 Iraq supplemental (PL 109-13), but it was dropped in conference.

▸ Adopted by voice vote an amendment expressing the sense of the Senate that funding for additional soldiers and Marines should be requested and provided through annual appropriations, not supplemental bills. Jack Reed, D-R.I., had proposed transferring $3.9 billion from the $50 billion contingency war spending to the annual operations and maintenance and personnel budget of the Army and Marine Corps. Reed agreed to the sense of the Senate language instead.

▸ Voted, 65-32, to table (kill) an amendment by Tom Coburn, R-Okla., that would have blocked funding of a Defense Department Web-based travel system. Coburn said the program was not worth the high price tag because the military would not own the software. But Warner and Levin stepped in to defend the program, contending that it would ultimately save resources. *(Senate vote 253, p. S-50)*

▸ Adopted by voice vote a proposal by Mark Dayton, D-Minn., to appropriate an additional $100 million for family assistance programs and National Guard counterdrug activities.

▸ Defeated an attempt by Evan Bayh, D-Ind., to add $361 million to the bill to buy armored vehicles. Bayh failed, 56-43, to overcome a point of order that the amendment violated budget rules; 60 votes were required to prevail. *(Senate vote 248, p. S-49)*

▸ Rejected, 50-49, an attempt by John Kerry, D-Mass., to overcome a similar challenge to an amendment that would have provided $3.1 billion in emergency funding for the Low Income Home Energy Assistance Program. *(Senate vote 250, p. S-49)*

▸ Struck down, 48-51, an amendment by Debbie Stabenow, D-Mich., to establish a formula to allow funding for veterans' health care programs to keep pace with inflation and population growth. *(Senate vote 251, p. S-50)*

Democrat Mary L. Landrieu of Louisiana held up final action on the bill until Oct. 7, taking to the floor the night before to demand legislation that would allow federal disaster loans to hurricane-ravaged areas to be forgiven.

### CONFERENCE/FINAL ACTION

Conferees filed a report on the bill (H Rept 109-359) shortly before midnight on Dec. 18. The House adopted the conference report, 308-106, on Dec. 19. But the Senate became caught up in a bitter dispute that forced GOP leaders to drop the controversial section added in conference that would have opened a part of ANWR to drilling. The Senate then cleared the bill, 93-0, on Dec. 21. *(House vote 669, p. H-212; Senate vote 366, p. S-71)*

● **ANWR.** The Senate had passed the ANWR provisions, fervently backed by Stevens, as part of its budget reconciliation bill (S 1932), but House Republican leaders said they could not get that measure through their chamber with the ANWR language. Stevens added it to the Defense conference report instead, successfully bypassing opposition from House GOP moderates. *(ANWR, p. 8-18)*

In a bid to sweeten the deal, Stevens had earmarked part of the future profits from ANWR drilling for additional hurricane recovery on the Gulf Coast and for border security. None of that was enough in the Senate, however. On Dec. 21, senators rejected a motion to limit debate on the Defense conference report as long as it included the ANWR language. The vote was 56-44, four votes short of the number needed to invoke cloture. *(Senate vote 364, p. S-71)*

Stevens argued that ANWR was related to national security because drilling would reduce reliance on foreign oil supplies. Democrats insisted that including it violated Senate rules because it was not germane to the bill and the provisions had not been part of either the House- or Senate-passed versions of the spending measure. Ranking Appropriations Democrat Robert C. Byrd of West Virginia, a longtime friend of Stevens, said, "I love this man, but I love the Senate more!"

Because most House members had already departed for the holidays, Senate GOP leaders agreed to use an enrolling resolution to get rid of the ANWR package. The Senate adopted the resolution, 48-45, and then cleared the Defense spending bill in its last recorded vote of the year. The House adopted the enrolling resolution by voice vote Dec. 22. *(Senate vote 365, p. S-71)*

An angry and emotional Stevens accepted the decision but warned senators, "I'm going to go to every one of your states, and I'm going to tell them what you've done."

Before the 11th-hour fight over ANWR, completion of the conference report was stalled by disagreements over the McCain amendment and over plans by House GOP leaders to attach across-the-board cuts in discretionary spending. Leaders from both chambers also negotiated behind closed doors over adding aid for hurricane victims as well as funds to prepare for a flu pandemic at a time of growing concern about avian flu.

● **Detainees.** McCain's amendment presented a particular problem. Since September, the White House had threatened to veto any bill that included it. Vice President Dick Cheney came to Capitol Hill to argue that civilian personnel such as CIA interrogators should be exempt from prosecution for alleged abuse of prisoners, and that the new restrictions could inhibit intelligence operators from obtaining important information. House GOP leaders came out in opposition as well.

On Dec. 14, however, the House voted overwhelmingly for a motion by Murtha to instruct House conferees to include the McCain amendment in the conference report. The motion was adopted, 308-122, with support from 107 Republicans. Although it was non-binding, the vote sent a powerful signal to the White House that both chambers wanted a clear codification of the ban on detainee abuse. *(House vote 630, p. H-202)*

Faced with such opposition, as well as growing unease among U.S. allies overseas, Bush backed down Dec. 15 and accepted virtually all of McCain's language, clearing the way for its inclusion in the conference agreements on both the Defense appropriations bill and the separate defense authorization bill. The compromise added provisions to protect U.S. interrogators in lawsuits based on activities that were officially authorized and deemed lawful at the time they were conducted, and to allow the government to pay attorney fees in such a suit.

"We've sent a message to the world that the United States is not like the terrorists," McCain said at a Dec. 15 White House news conference.

● **Iraq funds.** Of the $50 billion for ongoing military operations agreed to by conferees, $8 billion was earmarked to buy equipment lost in combat, including Humvees, trucks, radios, electronic jammers, Tomahawk cruise missiles and ammunition. The package also included $1.4 billion for testing and fielding new equipment to thwart roadside bombs, and $1 billion in emergency funding for National Guard and Reserve equipment.

The $50 billion brought to approximately $362 billion the total that had been appropriated for military operations and other activities in Iraq and Afghanistan.

● **Detainee legal rights.** The conference agreement included an amendment prohibiting detainees held at Guantánamo Bay, Cuba, from suing for habeas corpus, though they gained a limited right to appeal their detention. The amendment, by Lindsey Graham, R-S.C., was originally added to the Defense authorization bill and was enacted as part of that measure as well.

● **Regular Defense funding.** Leaving aside the supplemental funds, conferees agreed to a fiscal 2006 spending total for the Pentagon of $403.5 billion — $4.4 billion less than requested. That was much closer to the $3.3 billion cut recommended by the House for comparable programs, including the Defense Health Program, than to the $7 billion reduction proposed by the Senate.

● **DD(X).** Conferees agreed to the $1.1 billion for research and $716 million for procurement requested by Bush. The Senate had agreed with Bush, but the House, citing past difficulties with the program, wanted to provide $670 million in research, with no funds for procurement and a $304 million rescission of fiscal 2005 funding. The Pentagon protested the House proposal, contending in an "appeal" paper to conferees that the low funding plan would render the program "unexecutable."

Since the agreement fully funded the DD(X), the conference report did not include the extra $1.4 billion added by the House to procure the DDG-51 *Arleigh Burke*-class guided-missile destroyer.

● **Future Combat System.** Conferees cut $240 million from the $3.4 billion requested, providing $3.2 billion. The House wanted to cut $449 million; the Senate proposed a $100 million cut.

● **Joint Strike Fighter.** They also cut $232 million from the Pentagon's $4.9 billion request, providing $4.7 billion. The House had agreed to the request; the Senate sought to cut $270 million.

● **Space programs.** Conferees said they funded most of the administration's request for major space programs. However, they cut $400 million from the $836 million requested for the Transformational Satellite Communications Program, saying the Pentagon had not acknowledged the risks associated with the program.

● **Raptor.** Like both chambers, conferees agreed to the Air Force's request for $3.8 billion to buy 24 F-22A aircraft, the most expensive jet fighter ever built.

The Bush administration had proposed ending the program after fiscal 2008, thereby saving $10 billion. The plane had been plagued by cost overruns, technical problems and questions over whether the Air Force should be directing its resources to expensive manned aircraft when newer technologies and strategies might be more effective and less costly. The conferees said consideration should be given to options for continuing procurement after 2009, and called on the Pentagon to report to Congress by March 30, 2006, on "alternatives for the continued acquisition" of the aircraft.

● **C-130.** The conferees recommend $690 million for eight Air Force C-130Js, and $384 million for five KC-130Js for the Marines in fiscal 2006, and a total of $138 million in advance procurement funding for those same quantities for fiscal 2007.

● **Bunker buster.** The bill did not include $4.5 million originally requested to research the feasibility of modifying a nuclear weapon to tunnel into the earth and destroy reinforced underground command posts and weapons arsenals. However, conferees provided $4 million for the Air Force to work on a conventional (non-nuclear) version of the so-called bunker buster, and $7 million for the Navy to study using submarine-launched intermediate range ballistic missiles to penetrate such targets.

Sen. Pete Domenici, R-N.M., announced Oct. 25 that the administration had dropped its request for a nuclear earth penetrator and would focus on a conventional weapon.

Critics had claimed for years that doing research on a nuclear earth penetrator would encourage other countries to follow suit and could spur a new arms race. A National Academy of Sciences report had found that earth-penetrating nuclear weapons, while effective at destroying military targets deep underground, would cause "massive casualties" above ground.

Another $4 million, requested as part of the Energy-Water appropriations bill, was also dropped. *(Energy-Water, p. 2-22)*

● **Pandemic flu.** Republican appropriators agreed to include $3.8 billion for use in preparing for a flu pandemic. Frist added a last-minute provision in conference that granted liability protection to vaccine manufacturers, a move that infuriated House Democrats. Frist's spokeswoman said the conferees and leadership were in agreement on the matter. *(Flu funding, p. 2-17)* ■

# $603 Million for D.C. Clears Easily

THE DISTRICT OF COLUMBIA government received $603 million in federal funds for fiscal 2006, a $47 million increase over the previous year and nearly $30 million more than President Bush requested for the nation's capital. The annual federal payment was mainly in place of taxes, which the federal government does not pay. The bill also approved a total operating budget of $8.7 billion for the District in fiscal 2006.

The funding was included in the Transportation-Treasury-Housing appropriations bill, which Bush signed into law Nov. 30 (HR 3058 — PL 109-115). The totals do not reflect a 1 percent across-the-board cut in most non-emergency discretionary appropriations enacted as part of the fiscal 2006 Defense spending bill (PL 109-148). *(Transportation-Treasury-Housing, p. 2-47)*

As part of a reorganization earlier in the year, the House Appropriations Committee had eliminated its District of Columbia Subcommittee and folded the spending into its Transportation-Treasury bill. Senate appropriators, by contrast, retained a separate D.C. subcommittee to the satisfaction of local leaders who, despite their desire to keep Congress out of the city's day-to-day affairs, still wanted a venue where federal-city issues could receive the undivided attention of lawmakers. Both chambers agreed to follow the House lead in conference.

The bill did little to change the operations of the city, which had begun to win praise from lawmakers for turning its once-troubled finances around. But it did continue some initiatives pushed by conservative Republicans.

One proposal, endorsed by the city's liberal Democratic House delegate, Eleanor Holmes Norton, established a $3 million pilot program to create "marriage development accounts" aimed at reducing the number of children raised out of wedlock.

## HIGHLIGHTS

The final bill included:

● **Education.** $40 million for school improvement, less than 1 percent more than in fiscal 2005. The total included $14 million in federal funds for vouchers that could be used to send children to private schools — a program favored by social conservatives but opposed by city leaders. Lawmakers complained that the city's public schools continued to perform poorly. In addition, the bill provided $33 million, a 3 percent increase, to allow District residents to pay in-state tuition rates at public universities nationwide.

● **D.C. courts.** $464 million for courts and court-related services, a 14 percent increase over fiscal 2005 funding.

● **Capital projects.** $10 million for capital projects — $7 million for the D.C. Water and Sewer Authority and $3 million for the Anacostia Waterfront Initiative. In addition, the bill provided $5 million for a new bioterrorism and forensics laboratory, on the condition that the District put up $1.5 million in matching funds.

● **Homeland security.** $13.5 million for emergency planning and security costs to the District, a 9 percent decrease.

---

**BOX SCORE 2006**
FISCAL YEAR

DISTRICT OF COLUMBIA

**BILL:**
HR 3058 — PL 109-115

**LEGISLATIVE ACTION:**

**House** passed HR 3058 (H Rept 109-153), 405-18, on June 30.

**Senate** passed HR 3058, amended, 93-1, on Oct. 20, after adding D.C. appropriations (S 1446 — S Rept 109-106) by voice vote Oct. 18.

**House** adopted the conference report on HR 3058 (H Rept 109-307), 392-31, on Nov. 18.

**Senate** cleared bill by voice vote Nov. 21.

**President** signed Nov. 30.

---

● **Marriage promotion.** $3 million for the new pilot program of marriage development accounts.

## LEGISLATIVE ACTION
### HOUSE ACTION

The House Appropriations Committee included $603.4 million for the District in its Transportation-Treasury-Housing bill (HR 3058 — H Rept 109-153), approved by voice vote June 21. The Transportation-Treasury-Housing Appropriations Subcommittee had approved the measure by voice vote June 15. The bill also approved the District's $8.7 billion budget.

The House passed the bill, 405-18, on June 30. Before signing off on the D.C funds, however, the House adopted a controversial amendment aimed at relaxing the city's gun control laws, which were among the most stringent in the nation. *(House vote 358, p. H-110)*

The amendment, adopted 259-161, would have barred the use of either city or federal funds to enforce language in a 1976 D.C. gun control law requiring that residents with registered firearms in the home keep them unloaded and disassembled or bound by a trigger lock. Handguns could not kept in the home unless they were purchased prior to the 1976 law. The law did allow registered gun owners to keep loaded firearms at their place of business for self-defense. *(House vote 349, p. H-108)*

"I believe the constitutional right to bear arms supersedes local authority," said Mark Souder, R-Ind., who offered the amendment. "This is about self-protection in your home." D.C. officials opposed the amendment.

### SENATE ACTION

The Senate Appropriations Committee approved a stand-alone D.C. spending bill (S 1446 — S Rept 109-106) by a vote of 28-0 on July 21. The bill provided for a federal payment to the District of $593 million, $10 million less than under the House bill, and approved the city's $8.7 billion budget.

Senate appropriators did not include the House gun ownership language. The bill contained a new provision to transfer 15 acres of federal land at RFK Stadium to the District of Columbia to be used for educational purposes.

Sam Brownback, R-Kan., chairman of the D.C. Appropriations Subcommittee, also included a first-of-its-kind, $3 million pilot project to encourage marriage in the District by providing a 3-to-1 match for married couples who saved money for several specific purposes, including buying a house or starting a small business. Brownback said the provision was put in the bill because almost 57 percent of babies in the District were born to single mothers. In a sign of the improved relations between Congress and the District, Brownback was able to win Norton's support for the initiative.

The Senate passed its Transportation-Treasury Housing bill by a vote of 93-1 on Oct. 20, after agreeing by voice vote to add the D.C. appropriations bill as an amendment. *(Senate vote 264, p. S-52)*

## CONFERENCE/FINAL ACTION

Although House and Senate conferees were not yet in accord on the larger Transportation-Treasury bill, they agreed Nov. 11 to a federal payment of $603 million to the District. Brownback had said he would back the House gun-ownership provision in conference, but the language did not appear in the final bill. Norton credited that to "quiet, behind-the-scenes work."

The House adopted the conference report (H Rept 109-307) by a vote of 392-31 on Nov. 18. The Senate cleared the bill by voice vote Nov. 21. *(House vote 605, p. H-192)*

Conferees included the Senate provision transferring 15 acres of federal land to the District to be used for educational purposes. They also continued a number of previous restrictions including:

▶ A ban on the use of federal or local funds for the District's needle exchange program. (The Senate would have allowed the use of local funds.)

▶ A prohibition on using federal funds to implement a District law that gave health insurance benefits to unmarried domestic partners of city employees, regardless of gender.

▶ A ban on using federal or local funds for a petition drive or civil action intended to obtain District voting representation in Congress. (The Senate bill would not have barred the use of local funds.)

▶ A ban on the use of federal or local funds for abortions, except to save the life of the woman or in cases of rape or incest. The bill also stated that any local legislation regarding the provision of contraceptive coverage by health insurance plans should include a "conscience clause" providing exceptions for religious beliefs and moral conviction.

▶ A prohibition on using federal or local funds to implement a 1998 D.C. initiative allowing medical use of marijuana.

▶ A $4,000 cap on attorney fees in special-education lawsuits against the city. ■

# Bill Cuts Back Yucca Mountain Funding

CONGRESS CLEARED a $30.5 billion Energy-Water spending bill for fiscal 2006 that provided far less than requested for the planned nuclear waste dump at Yucca Mountain in Nevada, but supplied more for the Army Corps of Engineers than either chamber had planned. The total was 2 percent above fiscal 2005 levels and almost 3 percent more than the White House requested. President Bush signed the bill into law Nov. 19 (HR 2419 – PL 109-103)

Most of the funding – $ 24.3 billion – was for Energy Department defense and nuclear activities, energy research and renewable energy and conservation programs. In addition to the corps' civil works projects, the bill also funded Interior Department water projects and the Nuclear Regulatory Commission. The totals are after scorekeeping; they do not reflect a 1 percent across-the-board cut in most discretionary spending enacted as part of the fiscal 2006 Defense spending bill (PL 109-148).

The House passed a $29.8 billion Energy-Water bill in late May, and the Senate passed a $31.2 billion version on July 1. Along with the spending differences, the two chambers had to resolve disputes over money management at the corps, strategies for nuclear waste disposal and spending on research for a new breed of nuclear weapon.

House leaders threatened to abandon negotiations in late October, accusing the Senate of backing out of a carefully written compromise for setting new restrictions on corps' contracting and spending. David L. Hobson, R-Ohio, chairman of the House Appropriations subcommittee on Energy and Water Development, said the corps' practice of transferring money among various projects had become routine and that Congress needed to clamp down to ensure the agency was properly managing its money and following congressional directives. Hobson's Senate counterpart, Pete V. Domenici, R-N.M., argued that the corps needed flexibility to efficiently manage projects.

The two eventually compromised, setting new limits on reprogramming and contracting, while not barring the disputed practices outright. Hobson said he hoped the compromise would serve to improve management of the corps. "If it doesn't, we'll be back next year," he said.

The bill provided $450 million for construction at Yucca Mountain, only about a third of what the Energy Department had said in the past that it needed each year to keep the project on track. Even the repository's most ardent supporters, however, accepted the reduced funding without much opposition because the facility was mired in delays, including a court battle over safety requirements.

A House-Senate dispute over whether to provide funds for research into a nuclear "bunker-buster" – a low-yield weapon known as the Robust Nuclear Earth Penetrator designed to destroy underground bunkers – was averted in the fall when the administration abandoned plans for a nuclear version of the weapon.

## HIGHLIGHTS

The following are major components of the final bill:
● **Energy Department.** $24.3 billion, virtually the same as requested and slightly less than fiscal 2005 funding for the Energy Department. More than two-thirds of the money – $16.4 billion – was devoted to

**BOX SCORE 2006** FISCAL YEAR

**ENERGY-WATER**

**BILL:**
HR 2419 — PL 109-103

**LEGISLATIVE ACTION:**

**House** passed HR 2419 (H Rept 109-86), 416-13, on May 24.

**Senate** passed HR 2419, amended (S Rept 109-84), 92-3, on July 1.

**House** adopted the conference report (H Rept 109-275), 399-17, on Nov. 9.

**Senate** cleared the bill, 84-4, on Nov. 14.

**President** signed Nov. 19.

defense activities associated with maintaining U.S. nuclear weapons and reducing the threat from weapons of mass destruction.

The bill also deferred $257 million in unspent appropriations until 2007 for an Energy Department clean-coal technology program, which was a White House priority.
● **Nuclear weapons.** $9.2 billion, more than 50 percent of the Energy Department's defense funding, for the National Nuclear Security Administration, a semiautonomous Energy Department agency that maintains and refurbishes the country's nuclear weapons and carries out non-proliferation activities. The amount was about 2 percent above 2005 spending but 2 percent less than requested.

The funding included $6.4 billion for weapons activities and $1.6 billion for defense nuclear non-proliferation programs to detect and counter the international spread of nuclear weapons.

Funding for defense-related environmental cleanup was reduced by 9 percent below 2005 to $6.2 billion. Bush requested $6 billion.
● **Nuclear waste disposal.** $450 million for Yucca Mountain, 21 percent less than fiscal 2005 spending and about 31 percent less than the White House requested. The bill also included new funding – $50 million, not derived from the industry-funded Nuclear Waste Fund – for the Energy Department to plan a facility for recycling nuclear waste, with construction to begin in fiscal 2010.
● **Energy science.** $3.6 billion, less than 1 percent above 2005 funding but about 5 percent more than Bush requested, for research in areas such as high energy physics, nuclear physics and basic energy sciences. Much of the funding was earmarked for specific institutions.
● **Energy supply and conservation.** $1.8 billion, including $1.2 billion for energy efficiency and renewable energy resources. The total was a less-than-inflation increase of 1 percent over 2005 and 5 percent over Bush's request.
● **Army Corps of Engineers.** $5.4 billion for waterway navigation and flood control projects. The total was nearly 7 percent more than fiscal 2005 funding, not counting emergency supplemental appropriations following Hurricane Katrina. Counting the Katrina funds, the corps got $57 million less than the previous year. The funding included hundreds of millions of dollars in earmarks for popular local projects such as river restoration and flood protection.

Bush requested $4.3 billion for the corps, a cut of $1.1 billion.
● **Interior Department.** $1.1 billion for water and dam projects in Western states carried out by the Bureau of Reclamation – 12 percent more than requested and nearly 5 percent above fiscal 2005 funding. Bush had requested a cut of $66 million from 2005.

## LEGISLATIVE ACTION
### HOUSE COMMITTEE ACTION

The House Appropriations Subcommittee on Energy and Water Development and Related Agencies approved the spending bill by voice vote May 12. The full Appropriations Committee approved it May 18 (H Rept 109-86), also by voice vote.

Hobson, who drafted the bill, met Bush's request for $29.7 billion

## WHERE THE MONEY GOES — FISCAL 2006 APPROPRIATIONS
# ENERGY-WATER

### HR 2419 — PL 109-103

| | Fiscal 2005 appropriations | Fiscal 2006 Bush request | House passed | Senate passed | Conference report |
|---|---|---|---|---|---|
| | *(figures are in thousands of dollars of new budget authority)* | | | | |
| **GRAND TOTAL** | $31,166,027* | $29,730,600 | $30,282,630 | $31,763,000 | $31,009,000 |
| **Total adjusted for scorekeeping** | 29,832,280 | 29,746,728 | 29,768,630 | 31,249,000 | 30,495,000 |
| **MAIN COMPONENTS** | | | | | |
| **Energy Department**\*\* | $24,419,197 | $24,213,307 | $24,317,857 | $25,077,259 | $24,289,863 |
| Nuclear weapons activity | 6,331,590 | 6,630,133 | 6,181,121 | 6,574,024 | 6,433,936 |
| Science | 3,599,871 | 3,462,718 | 3,666,055 | 3,702,718 | 3,632,718 |
| Defense nuclear non-proliferation | 1,493,033 | 1,637,239 | 1,500,959 | 1,729,066 | 1,631,151 |
| Nuclear waste disposal | 572,384 | 651,447 | 661,447 | 577,000 | 500,000 |
| **Army Corps of Engineers** | 5,439,948* | 4,332,000 | 4,746,021 | 5,298,000 | 5,383,000 |
| **Interior Department** | 1,017,546 | 951,055 | 1,011,486 | 1,081,055 | 1,065,000 |

\* Includes emergency supplemental spending.
\*\* Includes advance appropriations.

TABLE: House Appropriations Committee

in discretionary funds, but he proposed significant changes in two major programs: the Yucca Mountain repository and and the corps' civil projects.

● **Nuclear waste.** The bill included $651 million for the Yucca Mountain site, as requested. But because the administration had announced that the site would not open before 2012, Hobson added another $10 million for the department to provide interim storage for waste that was accumulating at nuclear facilities across the country. The report directed the department "to take action in fiscal year 2006 to begin accepting spent commercial fuel from the nuclear utilities and placing it in centralized interim storage at one or more [Energy Department] sites."

The measure also set aside $5.5 million for an integrated spent fuel recycling initiative. The report directed the department to select a spent-fuel reprocessing technology by the end of fiscal 2007 and to begin planning fuel reprocessing sites and facilities to handle part of the accumulating nuclear waste. The United States had not reprocessed radioactive fuel since 1977 because of proliferation worries.

● **Army Corps of Engineers.** Hobson included $4.7 billion for the corps — about 10 percent more than Bush requested — but moved to assert more control over the way the corps managed and spent its money.

Instead of the traditional approach — appropriating a lump sum and suggesting in the report accompanying the bill how the money should be allocated — House appropriators sought to make the allocations binding. In addition, the House bill proposed to limit the corps' ability to shift money between projects — a practice known as reprogramming. Under the bill, the corps could transfer no more than $2 million, or 10 percent of a project's total funding, whichever was less.

Hobson said the corps made as many as 20,000 reprogramming transactions a year for about 2,000 projects. The goal of the transfers was to enable the agency to spend 99 percent of its budget annually — a target directed by Congress in the past. The corps tried to reach that threshold by shuffling excess funds from one project to others in need of resources, and then repaying the donor projects later.

Hobson said that strategy put the donor projects at risk and created a messy financial paper trail. In addition, he said, the corps was using some of the reprogrammed funds to pay for projects the administra-

tion never requested and Congress never approved. "We can't allow that kind of thing to happen," Hobson said.

Critics, such as the nonpartisan group Taxpayers for Common Sense, said the proposed changes could be a way for lawmakers to protect their pet projects. "We are not trying to protect projects," Hobson responded. "We are trying to manage the corps."

The committee report also took issue with an administration proposal to cut several projects based on their low remaining benefit-to-cost ratio. The president's budget targeted 31 previously funded projects that were expected to deliver less than $3 in benefits to the nation in the future for every $1 of government investment. The committee report said the proposed ranking system would penalize projects that had already yielded the bulk of their anticipated benefits, and that it did not account for the broader effect of water projects on national economic development.

The bill included a total of $24.3 billion for the Energy Department, a very slight increase over Bush's request. Appropriators recommended $6.2 billion for nuclear weapons programs, nearly 7 percent less than Bush requested. The bill allowed no money for the administration's proposed study of the nuclear bunker buster.

### HOUSE FLOOR ACTION

The House passed the $29.8 billion bill May 24 by a 416-13 vote. *(House vote 211, p. H-68)*

John J. "Jimmy" Duncan Jr., R-Tenn., chairman of the Transportation and Infrastructure Subcommittee on Water Resources and Environment, succeeded in striking a provision in the committee bill that would have prevented the corps from letting contractors do more work on a project in a fiscal year than the amount appropriated by Congress. Duncan raised a point of order, saying the provision was legislating on an appropriations bill.

"Civil works projects are dynamic in nature," Duncan and Don Young, R-Alaska, chairman of the Transportation and Infrastructure Committee, wrote in a May 23 letter to top House appropriators. "The corps needs some flexibility to manage these projects and meet unexpected conditions."

Democrats used the floor debate to rail against high gas prices, cit-

ing prices as high as $2.53 per gallon at the pump. "All over the country people are crying out for relief at the pump," said Minority Leader Nancy Pelosi, D-Calif.

During the debate, the House:

▶ Rejected, 174-253, an amendment by Bart Stupak, D-Mich., that would have suspended oil deliveries to the Strategic Petroleum Reserve. *(House vote 209, p. H-68)*

▶ Rejected, 110-312, an amendment by Edward J. Markey, D-Mass., to reduce nuclear waste disposal funding by $15.5 million and spend it on energy efficiency and conservation. *(House vote 207, p. H-68)*

## SENATE COMMITTEE ACTION

The Senate Appropriations Committee approved a $31.2 billion version of the bill (S Rept 109-84) on June 16 by a vote of 28-0. Senate Energy-Water appropriators had more money to work with than their House counterparts, and they used much of it to boost funding for corps civilian water projects. The Energy-Water subcommittee had approved the measure by voice vote June 14.

The Senate bill included:

▶ $5.3 billion for the corps, 22 percent above Bush's request and $552 million more than in the House bill. "The Senate came through," said National Waterways Conference President Worth Hager. "It's amazing what you can do when you actually have some money to work with."

Senate appropriators rejected the White House proposal to base the distribution of funds on the project's remaining cost-benefit ratios. "I don't believe the formula is fair, and we've ignored it for the purposes of identifying projects to fund in this bill," Domenici said.

The measure gave the corps more flexibility to reprogram funds than the House version. Appropriators reiterated previous guidance that cumulative reprogramming should be no more than 25 percent of the budget for general investigations and studies, and 15 percent of the budget for construction. No limit was set on the amount that could be shifted in an individual transaction, and unlimited reprogramming authority would be granted for operations and maintenance.

"It is imperative to allow the corps ample flexibility to manage the program," the committee said in its report on the bill.

▶ $25.1 billion for the Energy Department, compared with $24.3 billion in the House bill. Both figures included advance appropriations. Domenici said retaining funding for science facilities that the president had proposed cutting was a major priority.

▶ $6.6 billion for nuclear weapons activities, $393 million more than the House approved. Domenici's state was home to the Sandia and Los Alamos national laboratories, and he regularly pushed for more money than in the House bill for nuclear weapons projects.

▶ $577 million for Yucca Mountain, the same as in fiscal 2005 and $84 million less in than in the House bill. The committee did not include funds for temporary waste storage. Minority Leader Harry Reid of Nevada, a staunch opponent of Yucca Mountain and ranking Democrat on the subcommittee, said, "A far more serious effort than the half-baked approach taken by the House is required to address the mounting failures of the Yucca Mountain program."

## SENATE FLOOR ACTION

The Senate passed the $31.2 billion bill, 92-3, on July 1. *(Senate vote 172, p. S-34)*

Prior to passage, senators rejected, 43-53, an attempt to strip all $4 million in funding for research on the nuclear bunker buster. Amendment sponsor Dianne Feinstein, D-Calif., said the Bush administration's plan for the weapon could trigger a nuclear arms race. *(Senate vote 171, p. S-34)*

"The time has come to send a clear message to the White House," Feinstein said. "We will not support funding for programs to develop new nuclear weapons." Republicans said the money was only for research. "This is not the testing of a weapon, this is not the design of a weapon, this is simply a feasibility study," said Jon Kyl, R-Ariz.

## CONFERENCE/FINAL ACTION

House and Senate conferees reached agreement Nov. 7 on a $30.5 billion Energy-Water bill. The House adopted the conference report (H Rept 109-275) by a vote of 399-17 on Nov. 9 . The Senate cleared the bill, 84-4, on Nov. 14. *(House vote 580, p. H-182; Senate vote 321, p. S-63)*

Conferees agreed to provide:

● **Nuclear waste disposal.** $450 million for Yucca Mountain — $100 million from the industry-funded Nuclear Waste Fund and $350 million for defense-related nuclear disposal. In addition, the bill provided $50 million to develop a spent fuel recycling plan. Additional research funds were provided under the department's integrated spent fuel recycling program. The conference report directed the Energy secretary to submit a detailed plan to the Appropriations committees by March 31, 2006, and to initiate a site selection competition by June 30, 2006. Site selection was to be completed and construction was to begin in 2010.

Republican leaders in both chambers insisted this did not mean that Congress was backing away from plans for a permanent waste dump at Yucca Mountain. "We have to keep it going, but we have to do some other things," Domenici said. "I think it's the beginning of a re-evaluation of a bigger policy that will include Yucca."

The agreement did not include the House provision that would have directed the department to begin consolidating the interim storage of nuclear waste starting in 2006

● **Army Corps of Engineers.** Conferees were more generous in the wake of Hurricane Katrina, which exposed weaknesses in the nation's flood-protection systems, many of which were built and maintained by the corps. They provided $5.4 billion for the corps, $85 million more than in the Senate bill and $637 million more than the House had recommended. The funding included hundreds of millions of dollars in earmarks for popular local projects such as river restoration and flood protection.

● **Nuclear weapons.** $9.2 billion for the National Nuclear Security Administration, roughly half way between the House and Senate amounts. Domenici announced Oct. 25 that conferees had dropped the $4 million for the nuclear bunker buster at the request of the Energy Department. The administration had argued that it was seeking funds for a study, not a weapon, but the plan had stirred vociferous objections from members who said it could be the start of a new round of nuclear weapons and could undercut non-proliferation efforts.

The total included $1.6 billion for nuclear non-proliferation programs (compared with $1.5 billion in the House bill and $1.7 billion in the Senate version), and $6.4 billion for nuclear weapons activities (compared with $6.2 billion in the House bill and $6.6 billion in the Senate measure). ■

# Foreign Aid Enjoys Singular Boost

IN A YEAR OF LITTLE OR NO growth in most non-Defense appropriations, foreign aid funding climbed by 13 percent, not counting supplemental funds. The fiscal 2006 Foreign Operations appropriations bill, cleared in November, provided $21 billion — an increase of about $2.4 billion over the previous year's regular appropriations, excluding supplemental spending for the wars in Iraq and Afghanistan. President Bush signed the bill into law Nov. 14 (HR 3057 — PL 109-102).

Bush had asked for about $1.9 billion more for foreign aid than Congress provided. The bill cut back on his request for the Millennium Challenge Account (MCA), the president's signature foreign aid initiative for the world's poorest countries, and it provided more than he sought for programs to combat HIV/AIDS, tuberculosis and malaria. Congress also provided only a fraction of the money requested for reconstruction in Iraq. The totals do not reflect a 1 percent across-the-board cut in most discretionary appropriations enacted as part of the fiscal 2006 Defense spending bill (PL 109-148).

Bush asked for $22.9 billion for foreign operations, an increase of almost 23 percent over fiscal 2005, at a time when much of the budget was flat; by contrast, he sought a 4.3 percent increase for Defense.

The foreign operations bill funded most U.S. foreign assistance — including bilateral economic aid provided by the U.S. Agency for International Development (USAID), military aid, contributions to multilateral aid institutions and export assistance.

The House passed a $20.3 billion foreign aid bill in June. The Senate bill, passed in July, called for $31.8 billion, but $9.7 billion of that was for the State Department and related agencies, which the House covered in a separate spending bill. The difference in handling the State Department was the result of separate reorganizations in the House and Senate Appropriations committees early in the year. Appropriators ultimately agreed to follow the outlines of the House foreign operations bill for fiscal 2006, then switch to the Senate jurisdictions for fiscal 2007. For fiscal 2006, State Department funding came under the Commerce-Justice-Science-appropriations bill (PL 109-108). *(C-J-S, p. 2-9)*

Other significant differences between the House and Senate foreign operations bills that had to be resolved in conference included funding for the MCA, HIV/AIDS programs and reconstruction in Iraq, and policy on funding international family planning organizations.

## HIGHLIGHTS

The following are major components of the final bill:
● **Bilateral economic aid.** $14.6 billion for direct, bilateral economic assistance, including the costs of operating USAID. The aid included $2.6 billion for the Economic Support Fund, of which $240 million went to Israel and $495 million was for Egypt. The total for bilateral aid was an increase of 11 percent over fiscal 2005 law, not counting supplemental spending, but it was $1.7 billion or 10.5 percent below Bush's request. *(2004 Almanac, p. 2-22)*
● **Millennium Challenge Account.** $1.8 billion for the MCA, $1.2 billion or 41 percent less than Bush requested. The reduction was responsible for most of the difference between Bush's bilateral aid budget and

the final bill. Appropriators maintained — as they had the previous two years — that the fledgling program could not absorb the sums requested. The MCA, which was created to promote modernization and economic change in the world's developing countries, required recipient countries to show that they were encouraging free economies, open government and human rights. Madagascar, Honduras, Nicaragua and Cape Verde had received the first four awards under the program.
● **Military aid.** $4.8 billion, about 4 percent less than fiscal 2005 funding not counting emergency spending. Israel, traditionally the lead recipient of U.S. aid, got $2.3 billion under the foreign military financing program, a 3.5 percent increase and equal to the president's request. Egypt received $1.3 billion, about a 1 percent increase, as requested.
● **HIV/AIDS.** $2.8 billion to combat global HIV/AIDS, tuberculosis and malaria, about 10 percent more than the $2.6 billion Bush requested under the foreign aid bill. (Bush requested an additional $596 million under other appropriations bills.)

## LEGISLATIVE ACTION
### HOUSE COMMITTEE ACTION

The House Foreign Operations Appropriations Subcommittee drafted a $20.3 billion foreign aid bill that was about $2.6 billion below Bush's budget. The appropriators scaled back Bush's request for the MCA and dropped his bid for Iraq reconstruction aid.

The subcommittee approved the bill by voice vote June 16, and the full Appropriations Committee approved it June 21 (HR 3057 — H Rept 109-152), also by voice vote. Although the bill was about 11 percent less than Bush requested, it was still 4 percent more than was appropriated for fiscal 2005. Subcommittee Chairman Jim Kolbe, R-Ariz., said he was constrained by the $20.3 billion discretionary spending cap the committee had placed on the bill, but he said there was a chance the cuts could be restored in conference with the Senate, which allocated about $2 billion more for foreign operations.

The House bill included:
▶ $1.75 billion for the MCA, nearly halving Bush's $3 billion request. Kolbe admitted he was taking a risk in angering the administration. "The White House has indicated to me this is their highest priority in our bill, and I do not believe that this level will be considered adequate," he said.
▶ None of the $459 million requested for Iraq reconstruction. Kolbe said ongoing reconstruction needs could be met from the approximately $3.5 billion remaining from the original $18.4 billion Iraq reconstruction package enacted in 2003. *(2003 Almanac, p. 2-27)*
▶ None of the $108 million requested for the Global Environmental Facility (GEF), an independent organization that provided aid for environmental programs in developing countries. Kolbe said the group had not established a "performance-based" system for giving out money. Nita M. Lowey of New York, the ranking subcommittee Democrat, objected. "The GEF is the largest single funder of projects to improve the global environment," she said. "Simply put, the GEF is a cost-effective way to undertake efforts to ensure global environmental sustainability."

## WHERE THE MONEY GOES — FISCAL 2006 APPROPRIATIONS

# FOREIGN OPERATIONS

## HR 3057 — PL 109-102

*(figures are in thousands of dollars of new budget authority)*

| | Fiscal 2005 appropriations | Fiscal 2006 Bush request | House passed | Senate passed | Conference report |
|---|---|---|---|---|---|
| **GRAND TOTAL** | $18,585,336* | $22,867,945 | $20,311,677 | $22,122,189** | $20,978,490 |
| Discretionary spending | 18,542,836 | 22,826,245 | 20,269,977 | 22,080,489 | 20,936,790 |
| **MAIN COMPONENTS** | | | | | |
| **Bilateral economic assistance** | $16,325,440 | $16,282,413 | $14,080,395 | $15,675,999 | $14,574,500 |
| U.S. Agency for International Development | 4,393,064 | 4,179,368 | 4,156,400 | 4,567,400 | 4,299,700 |
| Millennium Challenge Corporation | 1,488,000 | 3,000,000 | 1,750,000 | 1,800,000 | 1,770,000 |
| **U.S. military assistance** | 5,501,812 | 4,871,144 | 4,706,844 | 4,886,144 | 4,761,744 |
| **World Bank, other intl. financial institutions** | 1,219,199 | 1,335,330 | 1,227,830 | 1,269,396 | 1,290,138 |

\* Does not include supplemental spending

\*\* As passed by the Senate, the bill totaled $31.8 billion, including $9.7 billion for the State Department. For conference, however, the Senate followed the House lead and moved State Department funding to the separate Commerce-Justice-Science bill (HR 2862).

TABLE: House Appropriations Committee

▶ $150 million for economic assistance for the West Bank and Gaza. But the committee mandated that the money flow through USAID, with no funds going directly to the Palestinian Authority, reflecting concerns about official corruption.

▶ $2.7 billion for HIV/AIDS spending, $131 million more than requested. The total included $1.9 billion for Bush's State Department-run Global HIV/AIDS Initiative, about $50 million less than requested. The appropriators recommended $400 million from various accounts, twice what Bush requested, for the Global Fund to Fight AIDS, Tuberculosis and Malaria, an international organization created to fight disease in the developing world.

▶ $2.5 billion for Israel, as requested.

▶ $1.8 billion for Egypt, as requested. Some Democrats questioned the aid, saying Egypt had not embraced democracy and modernization. The United States had pledged billions of dollars a year to Egypt and Israel as part of the 1979 Israel-Egypt Peace Treaty. "Sooner or later we have to ask ourselves, is [Egypt] the same agent of change it was 20 years ago?" said David R. Obey of Wisconsin, the ranking Democrat on the committee. "With respect to democracy, I suspect it is stalling out."

The committee persuaded Minority Whip Steny H. Hoyer, D-Md., to withdraw a proposal to transfer $40 million from the $1.3 billion in the bill for military financing to economic aid. Instead the appropriators agreed by voice vote to an amendment by Obey to earmark $50 million of the $495 million in economic aid to Egypt for democracy and human rights and $50 million for education programs.

### HOUSE FLOOR ACTION

The House passed the $20.3 billion bill, 393-32, on June 28. *(House vote 335, p. H-104)*

During the floor debate, the House:

▶ Adopted, 313-114, an amendment to effectively prohibit the Export-Import Bank from loaning $5 billion to help the British-owned nuclear division of the Westinghouse Co. provide nuclear power technology to help China build four nuclear plants. The amendment was offered jointly by Bernard Sanders, I-Vt., one of the most liberal members of the House, and conservative Republican Dana Rohrabacher of California.

"It's absurd that U.S. taxpayers are subsidizing construction of nuclear power plants in China," Sanders said. *(House vote 332, p. H-104)*

▶ Adopted, 293-132, an amendment by Anthony Weiner, D-N.Y., to prohibit any financial aid for Saudi Arabia. Weiner asserted that Saudi Arabia exported terrorism and sent its extremists to Iraq to attack U.S. troops. The amendment was symbolic: The bill included just $25,000 for the Saudis. *(House vote 331, p. H-102)*

▶ Adopted, 294-132, an amendment by Nathan Deal, R-Ga., to bar the use of funds in the bill to aid any country that had an extradition treaty with the United States but refused to extradite certain accused criminals. Deal said his amendment was directed at Mexico. *(House vote 333, p. H-104)*

▶ Rejected, 87-326, an attempt by Joe Pitts, R-Pa., to cut $750 million from military aid for Egypt and shift it to USAID child survival and health accounts. *(House vote 326, p. H-102)*

▶ Rejected, 189-234, an amendment by Jim McGovern, D-Mass., to cut funding for the Andean Counterdrug Initiative by $100 million, to $635 million. *(House vote 329, p. H-102)*

### SENATE COMMITTEE ACTION

On June 30, the Senate Appropriations Committee approved a $31.8 billion version of the bill (HR 3057 — S Rept 109-96) that included funding for the State Department. The bill, which was approved 28-0, contained $22.1 billion for foreign aid programs, about $1.8 billion more than the House had passed.

The committee-approved bill included:

▶ $1.8 billion for the MCA, slightly more than in the House bill but $1.2 billion below Bush's request.

▶ $459 million, as requested, for Iraq reconstruction.

▶ $107.5 million, as requested, for the GEF.

▶ $9.7 billion for the State Department, $228 million less than requested by Bush and $1.2 billion less than fiscal 2005 funding.

▶ $2.9 billion to fight HIV/AIDS, malaria and tuberculosis, $176 million more than in the House bill and $307 million more than Bush requested. Senate appropriators included $2 billion for Bush's Global HIV/AIDS Initiative, and earmarked $500 million for the Geneva-

based Global Fund to Fight AIDS, Tuberculosis and Malaria.

Although several senators expressed concern over the $1.3 billion in military aid to Egypt, there was no change.

The bill sought to overturn the so-called Mexico City policy embraced by the Bush administration, which prohibited U.S. funding for any organization that provided or actively promoted abortion as a method of family planning, even if it did so with its own money. (Mexico City policy, 2001 Almanac, p. 2-28)

## SENATE FLOOR ACTION

The Senate passed the bill with little change by a vote of 98-1 on July 20. (Senate vote 197, p. S-39)

Two days before the vote, the White House issued a statement of administration policy saying that in addition to reversing the Mexico City policy, the bill would weaken the Kemp-Kasten amendment, a provision of law that extended the prohibition to any organization that "participates in the management" of a program of coercive abortion or forced sterilization. The statement warned that Bush would veto any bill that contained such provisions. The administration also said it would push Congress to increase funding for the MCA, saying it was "a critical part of the president's foreign assistance program."

During the debate, which stretched over four days, the Senate:

▶ Adopted, 86-12, an amendment by Saxby Chambliss, R-Ga., to withhold funding from any country that refused to extradite criminal suspects facing capital charges in the United States. The amendment was aimed at certain Latin American countries, including Nicaragua, Mexico and Costa Rica, that refused to extradite a suspect to the United States if the suspect might face the death penalty or even life in prison. (Senate vote 196, p. S-39)

▶ Adopted by voice vote an amendment by Sam Brownback, R-Kan., to specify that $50 million of economic aid to Egypt be devoted to education. The bill already set aside $35 million for promoting democracy.

▶ Adopted by voice vote an amendment by Patrick J. Leahy, D-Vt., to specify that U.S. family planning aid for the U.N. Population Fund (UNFPA) be limited to six specific uses. The bill already required that the organization keep the money in a separate account and spend none of it for abortions or programs in China. Like the House bill, the measure included $35 million for the UNFPA, but without the restrictions that had blocked delivery of the aid.

▶ Rejected, 37-62, an attempt by Tom Coburn, R-Okla, and Barbara Boxer, D-Calif., to block the use of federal funds for an Export-Import Bank loan to help the British-owned nuclear division of the Westinghouse Co. build nuclear power plants in China. (Senate vote 192, p. S-38)

## CONFERENCE/FINAL ACTION

House and Senate conferees agreed Nov. 1 on a final, $21 billion version of the bill that included $20.9 billion in discretionary spending. The House adopted the conference report (H Rept 109-265) by a vote of 358-39 on Nov. 4. The Senate cleared the bill, 91-0, on Nov. 10. (House vote 569, p. H-180; Senate vote 320, p. S-62)

Rep. Mike Pence of Indiana, chairman of the Republican Study Committee, a group of fiscal conservatives, praised the appropriations panel for managing to get a complicated bill to the floor "on time and on budget." He said the measure showed it was possible to "fund the nation's national and international priorities in a fiscally responsible way."

The final bill provided:

▶ $1.77 billion for the MCA, a compromise between the $1.75 billion in the House bill and the $1.8 billion passed in the Senate. The Bush administration pushed hard to expand the funding, arguing the program had brought greater accountability and transparency to programs benefiting the world's poorest nations.

▶ $2.8 billion to fight HIV/AIDS, malaria and tuberculosis — $125 million more than the House proposed, but $151 million below the Senate figure. The total included about $2 billion for Bush's HIV/AIDS Initiative, of which $200 million was for the Global Fund to Fight AIDS, Tuberculosis and Malaria. Another $250 million through USAID brought the total for the Geneva-based fund to $450 million.

▶ $1.6 billion for USAID's Child Survival and Health account, part of which went for HIV/AIDS programs. The total was 27 percent more than Bush requested; both chambers recommended an increase.

▶ $2.5 billion for Israel, including $240 million in economic assistance. Egypt received $1.8 billion, including $495 million in economic aid. The amounts were equal to the president's request for the two main recipients of U.S. bilateral aid. Conferees earmarked $50 million of the money for Egypt for education and $50 million to promote democracy.

▶ $931 million for Afghanistan, including the $430 million Bush requested for economic assistance; however, conferees retained a House provision withholding $225 million of the economic funds until the secretary of State certified that Afghan officials were cooperating with programs to eradicate opium-poppy cultivation and interdicting narcotics trafficking and $235 million in counternarcotics funding.

▶ $638 million for Pakistan — $300 million for economic assistance, $300 million for military aid, and $38 million for counternarcotics funding.

▶ $150 million for the West Bank and Gaza, as requested, but only for USAID projects, not direct assistance to the Palestinian authority.

▶ $61 million for reconstruction programs in Iraq, less than one-fourth of the $459 million requested by Bush and passed in the Senate.

▶ $80 million for the GEF, compared with zero funding in the House bill and the requested $107.5 million in the Senate version.

▶ $432 million for bilateral family planning programs, the same as in the House bill and $18 million less than the Senate approved. Conferees dropped the Senate's attempt to end the Mexico City policy and modify the Kemp-Kasten amendment. The final bill included $34 million for the UNFPA, subject to those restrictions, which had typically resulted in the money being withheld. On Sept. 17, the State Department announced that it was withholding the $34 million provided as part of the fiscal 2005 appropriations bill. Conferees also dropped the Senate amendment outlining acceptable uses for the UNFPA money. ■

# Border Security Gets Funding Boost

CONGRESS CLEARED a $31.9 billion fiscal 2006 Homeland Security spending bill Oct. 7 that boosted funding for border security while cutting back on grants to first-responders and targeting them more to areas at high risk of an attack. President Bush signed the bill into law Oct. 18 (HR 2360 — PL 109-90).

This was the third annual funding increase for the department, which opened its doors in early 2003. The bill provided $30.8 billion in discretionary appropriations, an increase of nearly 5 percent over the fiscal 2005 law (PL 108-334), not counting emergency funding and a one-time appropriation of $2.5 billion for Project Bioshield that year. It was 4 percent more than the $29.6 billion that Bush requested. The totals do not reflect a 1 percent across-the-board cut in most discretionary appropriations enacted as part of the fiscal 2006 Defense spending bill (PL 109-148). *(2004 Almanac, p. 2-26)*

Republican appropriators, who repeatedly stressed their intent to keep the bill "threat-based," devoted nearly two-thirds of the discretionary funding to border security-related functions. They also provided a significant increase for programs dealing with the danger of a biological, chemical and nuclear attack. Those increases came at the expense of funding for transportation security and for disaster preparedness and response.

The bill endorsed a reorganization of the Homeland Security Department, announced by Secretary Michael Chertoff in July, which included the creation of a new Directorate for Preparedness, leaving the Federal Emergency Management Agency (FEMA) to focus exclusively on disaster response and recovery. Democrats challenged the wisdom of separating disaster preparedness and response, but Republicans argued that FEMA would be better able to respond to disasters if that was its sole focus. Other changes initiated by Chertoff included establishing a new Office of Intelligence and Analysis, and moving the federal air marshals to the Transportation Security Agency (TSA).

Democrats objected that the funding allocations in the bill did not reflect lessons learned during the year, from the terrorist bombings of the London subway in July to the chaotic response by FEMA and others to Hurricane Katrina in late August. They wanted to add at least $1.7 billion to the bill, and they were particularly critical of cuts in the grant programs for police, firefighters and other first-responders, and to a decision to keep transit security funding stagnant at $150 million.

Judd Gregg, R-N.H., chairman of the Senate Appropriations Homeland Security Subcommittee, acknowledged FEMA's inadequacies in responding to Katrina but said the agency's problems could not be tied to a lack of money. "At this time putting more money in this bill, on top of the $60 billion in emergency funds already provided and the funds that will soon be coming in the next supplemental, is not the solution," he said after the conference committee completed its work on the bill.

Many Democrats disagreed. "We should be beefing up our support for all of our response partners rather than leaving them in a position of having to do more with less," said Sen. Joseph I. Lieberman, D-Conn.

The House passed its version of the bill in May, and the Senate fol-

**BOX SCORE 2006** FISCAL YEAR

HOMELAND SECURITY

**BILL:**
HR 2360 — PL 109-90

**LEGISLATIVE ACTION:**

**House** passed HR 2360 (H Rept 109-79), 424-1, on May 17.

**Senate** passed HR 2360, amended (S Rept 109-83), 96-1, on July 14.

**House** adopted the conference report on HR 2360 (H Rept 109-241), 347-70, on Oct. 6.

**Senate** cleared the bill by voice vote Oct. 7.

**President** signed Oct. 18.

lowed suit in July. Both versions totaled $31.9 billion, with $30.8 billion in discretionary funds and $1 billion for mandatory Coast Guard retirement benefits. Appropriators were not able to complete the bill until the fall, in part because they needed to revise the measure in light of Chertoff's plans to restructure the department.

## HIGHLIGHTS

The following are major components of the fiscal 2006 law:

● **Customs and Border Protection.** $6 billion, a 10 percent boost over fiscal 2005 appropriations and 7 percent more than Bush requested. An additional $1.1 billion in expected fees brought the total to $7.1 billion for the directorate charged with keeping terrorists from entering the country.

● **Immigration and Customs Enforcement.** $3.2 billion, a 22 percent increase over fiscal 2005 funding not counting funds for the federal air marshals, which were shifted to the TSA under Chertoff's reorganization. The appropriation was 7 percent above Bush's budget. The directorate, which was created to enforce immigration and customs laws inside U.S. borders, was also expected to receive $254 million in fees, bringing the total available funding to $3.4 billion.

● **TSA.** $3.9 billion, virtually the same as the fiscal 2005 appropriations, if the air marshals were included, but 68 percent more than Bush requested. Counting another $2 billion in anticipated fees, the TSA was expected to have a budget of $6.3 billion. Bush said his budget would give the TSA a similar amount, but that assumed an extra $1.7 billion from a proposed $3 increase in the airline passenger fee that Congress was unwilling to approve.

● **Coast Guard.** $7.8 billion, an increase of 6 percent over fiscal 2005, not counting supplemental spending, but about 2 percent less than requested. The total included $1 billion in mandatory funds for retiree pay. Congress provided $933 million for the Deepwater fleet modernization program, 29 percent above previous year funding but about 3 percent less than Bush wanted.

● **Domestic preparedness office.** $3.3 billion, 6 percent less than requested and 16 percent less than in fiscal 2005. The three major first-responder grant programs got a total of $1.7 billion, 28 percent less than in fiscal 2005. Congress also used the bill to reorient the way first-responder grants were distributed. As under prior law, each state was guaranteed at least 0.75 percent of the available funds. The Homeland Security secretary could allocate the rest based on the risk of a terrorist attack, and, to a lesser degree, of natural disaster — rather than on population, as in the past.

● **FEMA.** $2.6 billion for the agency's basic budget, about 15 percent less than the Bush administration requested and 11 percent less than FEMA received the previous year, not counting emergency spending and the one-time spending on biodefense.

● **Science and technology.** $1.5 billion for the agency that conducted most of the department's work on defenses against biological, chemical and nuclear weapons. That was a jump of nearly 35 percent over fiscal 2005 funding and 10 percent over Bush's request.

## WHERE THE MONEY GOES — FISCAL 2006 APPROPRIATIONS
# HOMELAND SECURITY SPENDING

### HR 2360 — PL 109-90

*(figures are in thousands of dollars of new budget authority)*

|  | Fiscal 2005 appropriations | Fiscal 2006 Bush request | House-passed | Senate-passed | Conference report |
|---|---|---|---|---|---|
| **GRAND TOTAL** | $100,210,103 | $30,568,748 | $31,860,080 | $33,360,080 | $31,860,080 |
| **Total adjusted for scorekeeping** | 33,065,236* | 30,568,748 | 31,860,080 | 31,860,080 | 31,860,080 |
| Discretionary spending** | 31,979,776 | 29,554,668 | 30,846,000 | 30,846,000 | 30,846,000 |
| **MAIN COMPONENTS** |  |  |  |  |  |
| **Customs and Border Protection**** | $5,408,631 | $5,574,751 | $5,784,751 | $6,012,570 | $5,952,554 |
| **Immigration and Customs Enforcement**** | 2,609,478 | 2,958,977 | 3,130,777 | 3,129,112 | 3,175,195 |
| **Transportation Security Administration**** | 3,923,275 | 2,330,652 | 3,961,774 | 3,744,181 | 3,925,065 |
| **Coast Guard***** | 7,373,280 | 7,961,632 | 7,458,232 | 7,779,628 | 7,796,857 |
| **Secret Service** | 1,175,008 | 1,203,782 | 1,232,680 | 1,192,337 | 1,212,009 |
| **Domestic preparedness** | 3,984,846 | 3,561,210 | 3,661,400 | 3,572,846 | 3,346,300 |
| **FEMA** | 5,458,372* | 3,090,995 | 2,969,865 | 2,757,947 | 2,632,865 |

\* Excludes $67,144,867,000 in emergency appropriations; includes $2,507,776,000 in advance appropriations for Project Bioshield.
\*\* Calculated after scorekeeping adjustments.
\*\*\* Does not include revenue from various fees and/or offsetting receipts appropriated by the bill, which allow higher spending.
\*\*\*\* Excludes emergency funds.

TABLE: House, Senate Appropriations committees

## LEGISLATIVE ACTION
### HOUSE COMMITTEE ACTION

The House Appropriations Committee approved a $31.9 billion version of the bill by voice vote May 10 (HR 2360 — H Rept 109-79). The measure was largely unchanged from a draft that the Homeland Security Subcommittee approved by voice vote May 4. Although the bill called for an overall increase in the department's budget, it came with a sharp rebuke and punitive cuts that subcommittee Chairman Harold Rogers, R-Ky., said should be a "wake-up call" to agencies that had not complied with committee directives or requests for information.

"At times, the department has made the mistake of assuming that appropriators are simply here to rubber-stamp their budgets," Rogers said. "That is a bad assumption." Altogether, Rogers cut about $485 million from Bush's request, and withheld another $310 million pending specific actions by the department, including progress on screening air cargo. The warning was aimed mainly at two of the department's biggest components — the Coast Guard and the TSA. The committee said in its report on the bill that 123 of 169 reports required from the department were overdue.

Democrats stood united with Republicans on steps designed to punish the department. "This agency is a mess, and it needs to be recognized on both ends of Pennsylvania Avenue," said David R. Obey of Wisconsin, the ranking Democrat on the full committee.

The committee-approved bill included:

● **Coast Guard.** $7.5 billion, about $500 million or 6 percent below Bush's request. Most of the cuts — $466 million — were aimed at the Coast Guard's multi-year, multibillion-dollar Deepwater program to replace its aging ships, aircraft and communications systems. Rogers said the Coast Guard had failed to upgrade its baseline plan for the program to reflect its post-Sept. 11 missions; funding in the bill was reduced to the pre-Sept. 11 level of $500 million. "Just as it is the mission of the Coast Guard to protect our nation's ports and waterways,

it is the mission of Congress to wisely appropriate taxpayer dollars," Rogers said.

● **Customs and Border Protection.** $5.8 billion, combined with $1.1 billion in anticipated fees, for a total of $6.9 billion — $210 million above Bush's request. That included an extra $150 million to pay for new 790 border patrol agents, in addition to the 210 new agents supported by Bush's budget and another 500 funded under the supplemental appropriations bill enacted in May (PL 109-13).

● **Immigration and Customs Enforcement.** $3.1 billion, after subtracting $487 million in offsetting fees. When an additional $229 million in expected fees was added, the total came to $3.4 billion. That was $172 million above the request and included funds to pay for 250 additional Immigration and Customs Enforcement employees and 1,920 new detention beds. In its report, the committee said it was "extremely concerned and disappointed by the persistent financial troubles" of the agency, which it said were a direct result of the Homeland Security Department's "total failure . . . to deal with major costs and financial management issues" inherited from the agencies that were merged to form Immigration and Customs Enforcement. The committee called for a number of improvements and directed the secretary to submit monthly reports on the agency's financial condition.

● **TSA.** $4 billion, plus about $2.4 billion in anticipated fees, which brought the projected total to $6.4 billion. That included the federal air marshal program, which Chertoff transferred from Immigration and Customs Enforcement. Bush requested $6.3 billion, but his total included $1.7 billion from an increase in passenger fees, which the committee rejected. Rogers said it was a "fee we simply cannot and will not agree to place on American travelers." Rogers said he was able to find other funds to make up for the lost dollars.

The TSA funding included $60 million for air cargo security, $20 million more than requested; $10 million of the increase was to hire 100 new air cargo inspectors. The report said the committee was "deeply disappointed" that TSA officials had not yet fully implemented a pro-

vision in the fiscal 2005 law requiring them to triple the screening of air cargo on passenger aircraft. Some of the TSA money in the bill was fenced off pending action on cargo security and other issues.

● **First-responders.** $3.7 billion — $100 million more than requested but $320 million less than fiscal 2005 funding — for the office that coordinated federal funding for state and local police, firefighters and other first-responders. Rogers said that until more than $6 billion in past funds were distributed, it made no sense to provide more. Committee Democrats disagreed, arguing that more funding still was necessary. It was one of the rare areas where they broke with the panel's majority.

The total in the bill included $750 million for formula-based state homeland security grants; $850 million for discretionary grants to high-threat, high-density urban areas; $400 million for law enforcement grants for terrorism prevention and $650 million for firefighter assistance. The committee proposed that the formula grants be distributed using the existing 0.75 percent minimum guarantee, but unlike in past years, the bill directed that remaining funds be distributed based on risk instead of population. The administration proposed guaranteeing all states 0.25 percent of the formula grants, with the rest based on risk and vulnerability.

Funding for other major accounts in the bill included $1.3 billion for the department's Science and Technology arm, and $1.2 billion for the Secret Service.

Democrats withdrew all but one of their amendments. Martin Olav Sabo, D-Minn., won voice vote adoption of an amendment to limit the number of TSA employees who could designate documents as "sensitive security information,"or "SSI." Sabo said the department had abused the designation to keep routine information secret. He said the Government Accountability Office found that TSA had no internal control procedures for SSI designation, and that potentially every TSA employee could stamp something 'SSI.' The conference committee subsequently replaced the provision with a requirement that the department report on specific improvements.

### HOUSE FLOOR ACTION

The House passed the bill, 424-1, on May 17. *(House vote 180, p. H-60)*

"Mr. Chairman, it is a simple equation," Rogers said of his cuts to Deepwater and other programs. "No information equals no funding."

But the attempts to fence off funding drew fire from Christopher Cox, R-Calif., then-chairman of the Homeland Security Committee. Moving to protect what he considered the authorizers' turf, Cox persuaded the Rules Committee to leave 35 different provisions of the bill open to challenge on the floor. Cox said many of them constituted legislating on an appropriations bill, a violation of House rules. Others sought changes to departmental structure or to the formula for distributing grants to first-responders.

Democrats who had backed the provisions penalizing the department said they might withdraw their support of the bill if they were dropped. A showdown was averted at the last minute after Cox reached a deal with Appropriations Chairman Jerry Lewis, R-Calif. Cox agreed not to raise points of order, and Rogers agreed to "follow the will of the authorizing committee" when the spending bill went to conference.

The House adopted several amendments to add funding for specific programs, all of which were offset by cuts elsewhere in the bill. During the debate, the House:

▶ Adopted 226-198, a proposal by Obey to add $100 million to help states comply with driver's license standards set by the immigration provisions of the fiscal 2005 supplemental spending law (PL 109-13). *(House vote 179, p. H-60; asylum, p. 13-3)*

▶ Adopted by voice vote an amendment by Sabo that added $50 million for firefighter grants, bringing the total in the bill to $650 million.

▶ Adopted, 225-198, an amendment by Robert Menendez, D-N.J., to add another $50 million to first-responder grants for chemical plant security. *(House vote 176, p. H-58)*

The White House issued a statement of administration policy the day of the vote that criticized cuts to the Coast Guard and other accounts. The administration said it made "every effort to comply with deadlines" for reports, but that "the committee's requirement of delivery of reports of complicated matters before receiving funding could inhibit the department's efforts to secure the homeland."

### SENATE COMMITTEE ACTION

The Senate Appropriations Committee approved its version of the bill (HR 2360 — S Rept 109-83) on a bipartisan 28-0 vote June 16. The Homeland Security Subcommittee had approved it by voice vote two days earlier. Like the House bill, the Senate measure contained $30.8 billion in discretionary funds, plus $1 billion in mandatory spending for Coast Guard retirement pay.

Gregg, who chaired the subcommittee and drafted the bill, made it clear his priority was to strengthen border security and defenses against catastrophic attacks, even if it meant less funding for state and local grants and transportation screening. "This bill attempts to refocus resources, and it does so very aggressively," Gregg said.

Senate appropriators did not go as far as the House in seeking to cut or withhold hundreds of millions of dollars in an effort to win management improvements and cooperation with Congress, but the bill still proposed to fence off some funding.

"This bill would focus our limited resources on future threats, not just yesterday's problems," agreed the full committee's ranking Democrat, Robert C. Byrd of West Virginia. "It's balanced, it's fair and it's based on the greatest risk."

The committee-approved bill included:

● **Customs and Border Protection.** $6 billion, combined with anticipated fees and a small rescission, for a total of $7.1 billion — $213 million more than in the House bill and 9 percent above fiscal 2005 funding. Like the House, appropriators included funds for 1,000 new border patrol agents, in addition to the 500 included in the supplemental.

● **Immigration and Customs Enforcement.** $3.8 billion, plus expected fees, for a total of $4 billion — just $24 million below the House bill. The committee said the bill would pay for 2,240 more detention beds and enhanced technology. Both chambers were interested in improving technology in the hope of reducing the number of agents needed.

● **TSA.** $3.7 billion, plus about $2.4 billion in anticipated fees, which brought the total (including funding for the federal air marshals) to $6.2 billion. That was $217 million below the House figure. Gregg said the airline industry's situation was too dire to impose new passenger fees. In addition, the Commerce Committee had ruled out the fee increase, which Gregg said sealed its fate.

The Senate bill included $50 million for air cargo security.

Gregg voiced "serious reservations" about the department's entry-exit program, called U.S. Visitor and Immigrant Status Indicator Technology (US-VISIT), which collected fingerprints and photographs of foreign visitors to authenticate their travel documents upon arrival in the United States. The bill included $340 million for the program, the same as in the previous year but 13 percent less than Bush requested. Of that amount, according to report language, $160 million could not be used until the department submitted a comprehensive plan that detailed its compliance with several management requirements.

- **First-responders.** $3.6 billion for the office coordinating state and local preparedness, about $90 million less than the House recommended. The committee allocated $1.5 billion for state and local assistance, without specifying how much was for formula-based state grants and how much was for urban area grants. It also provided $400 million for law enforcement terrorism prevention grants and $665 million for grants to firefighters.
- **Coast Guard.** $7.8 billion, plus a $100 million rescission of past funding, for a total of $7.9 billion — $321 million below the House bill. The committee proposed awarding $906 million for Deepwater, all but about $60 million of what Bush wanted and $406 million more than the House wanted.

## SENATE FLOOR ACTION

The Senate passed the $31.9 billion bill July 14 by a vote of 96-1. Despite proposals to shore up mass transit security in the aftermath of terrorist bombings of the London transit system a week earlier, the Senate left rail and transit security funding unchanged from the $100 million approved in committee — $50 million below fiscal 2005. *(Senate vote 189, p. S-37)*

In all, senators rejected more than $25 billion worth of proposals to boost funding not only for transit security but also for first-responders and border security. After a week of sometimes testy debate, the bill looked much as Gregg originally designed it.

- **First-responders.** The biggest change to the bill on the floor was the adoption of a new distribution formula for grants to police, firefighters and other responders. Lawmakers had repeatedly disagreed over how to distribute those funds — how much each state should get and how far lawmakers should go toward making all grants risk-based as the Sept. 11 commission and other experts had recommended.

During the floor debate, the Senate:

▶ Adopted, 71-26, an amendment by Susan Collins, R-Maine, and Lieberman to guarantee each state 0.55 percent of the grant pool, with a higher amount for more populous states on a sliding scale, up to 3 percent. The remaining funds would be distributed based on the risk of attack as estimated by the Homeland Security Department, under certain guidelines. *(Senate vote 175, p. S-35)*

Under existing law, each state got at least 0.75 percent from several grant pools, and the rest was distributed based on population.

▶ Rejected, 32-65, an amendment by Dianne Feinstein, D-Calif., and John Cornyn, R-Texas, similar to a House-passed bill (HR 1544) that would lower each state's guaranteed funds to 0.25 percent of the pool. The rest would be distributed based on risk. *(Senate vote 176, p. S-35)*

The debate pitted rural lawmakers against those from more urban states. Frank R. Lautenberg, D-N.J., said the target of the deadly July 7 London subway attacks was not Portsmouth, England, and "the odds are that it won't be Portsmouth, Maine." Collins stressed the accountability provisions in her amendment, saying they would "ensure that no longer will Homeland Security funds be spent to purchase air-conditioned garbage trucks in the state of New Jersey." Collins and others had used the anecdote repeatedly as an example of wasteful spending.

- **Rail security.** In a debate that turned testy at times, Charles E. Schumer of New York and others rejected an assertion by Chertoff that transit security was primarily a local responsibility and that the department's focus should be on greater threats.

The Senate:

▶ Rejected an attempt by Richard C. Shelby, R-Ala., to add $1.2 billion for transit security. Gregg, who also chaired the Budget Committee, challenged it because it would exceed the budget. The amendment

fell, 53-45, seven votes short of the 60 needed to overcome the procedural challenge. *(Senate vote 186, p. S-37)*

▶ Rejected, 46-52, an alternative by Gregg to provide an additional $100 million for transit security. The amendment was backed by GOP leaders, but it drew fire because it would have offset the cost with cuts to state and local aid accounts. *(Senate vote 185, p. S-37)*

Other failed amendments included proposals to add $368 million for border protection, $1.4 billion for rail and transit security and $70 million to track hazardous materials shipments.

For Gregg, the question was where best to spend the money. He said it was more difficult to defend rail and transit than aviation, where people could be easily funneled into specific locations for security checks. But supporters of higher spending said additional funding would help pay for surveillance cameras, bomb-sniffing dog teams and other needed security measures.

## CONFERENCE/FINAL ACTION

In addition to differences over issues such as the Deepwater program and first-responder grants, the Appropriations staffs had to give the bill a makeover to accommodate Chertoff's restructuring of the department. House and Senate conferees reached agreement Sept. 29. The House adopted the conference report (H Rept 109-241) by a vote of 347-70, on Oct. 6, and the Senate cleared the measure by voice vote Oct. 7. *(House vote 512, p. H-162)*

Democrats attempted to provide $1.7 billion more for disaster planning and mitigation, first-responders, and transit, port, chemical and border security. The amendment, which Republicans noted included no offsetting cuts, fell on an 8-10 vote. Democrats also failed to delay the plan to reorganize FEMA. Sabo tried to get the House to instruct its conferees to insist that the department retain its existing structure for disaster preparedness and response activities for fiscal 2006, but his motion was rejected, 196-227. *(House vote 497, p. H-156)*

The following are among the issues decided in conference.

- **Customs and Border Protection.** The $6 billion in the final bill was about 3 percent more than the House recommended and 1 percent less than in the Senate bill. It included an extra $241 million to fund an additional 1,500 border patrol agents. The bill included $139 million for the Container Security Initiative to screen cargo at foreign ports.

The agreement appropriated $456 million for automation modernization, and $400 million for air and marine interdiction operations to provide border and airspace security.

- **Immigration and Customs Enforcement.** The final bill had $3.2 billion, plus expected fees, for a total of $3.4 billion — about 2 percent more than the House recommended but 15 percent less than in the Senate bill.

It included $90 million for additional bed space for a total of 20,300 detention beds. It included $42 million to hire an additional 250 criminal investigators, $10 million for alternatives to detention and $9 million for an additional 100 immigration enforcement agents. The conference report directed the department to submit a plan by Dec. 1 for hiring the agents, and to report within 30 days of enactment on the total number of detention beds to be funded in fiscal 2006.

Conferees agreed to the Senate plan to provide $340 million for the US-VISIT program, $50 million less than in Bush's budget or in the House bill. They withheld $160 million until the Appropriations committees received and approved an expenditure plan.

- **TSA.** The final bill appropriated $3.9 billion, plus $2.4 billion in anticipated fees, for a total of $6.3 billion for the TSA.

More than 70 percent of TSA's funding — $4.6 billion — was devot-

ed to aviation security, a 7 percent increase over prior funding, virtually the same as in the House bill and 3.5 percent more than the Senate sought. The $2 billion in aviation security fees brought the net amount to $2.6 billion. The bulk of the money, $3.6 billion, was for screening operations.

The bill also:

▶ Renewed the cap of 45,000 full-time airport screeners. It provided $140 million for airports that decided to opt-out of federal screening, and shielded airports from legal liability for any error by transportation screeners, an attempt to lure airports into returning to private sector screening. That initiative had stalled because of airports' fear of lawsuits.

▶ Provided $57 million, 40 percent less than requested, for Secure Flight, the airline passenger-screening program that had worried privacy advocates in both parties. The bill banned purchasing information on citizens for the program from commercial data brokers.

▶ Provided $686 million for the federal air marshals, a 4 percent increase over fiscal 2005 funding,

▶ Provided $55 million for air cargo inspection, splitting the difference between the House and Senate. It included $10 million to hire 100 more inspectors. Another $30 million was provided through the Science and Technology directorate for three air cargo screening programs. The conference report directed the TSA to work with other agencies in the department to develop technologies that make it possible to screen 100 percent of the air cargo on passenger planes.

▶ Specified that if the department did not comply with a mandate in the fiscal 2005 spending law to at least triple the percentage of cargo on passenger aircraft that was inspected, it would have to provide biweekly reports beginning Oct. 1.

▶ Directed the TSA to use existing checked-baggage screeners and explosives-detection systems to screen cargo carried on passenger aircraft, and provide monthly reports on how much cargo was screened at each airport.

● **First-responders.** Under the restructuring, state and local first-responder assistance was coordinated by the Office of Domestic Pre-paredness, which became part of the new Preparedness Directorate. The office received $3.3 billion — less than Bush or either chamber had proposed.

The grant funding included $550 million for formula-based state homeland security grants; $765 million for grants to high-density, high-threat urban areas; $655 million for firefighter assistance grants; and $400 million for law enforcement terrorist prevention grants.

Conferees were unable to agree on a new distribution plan, so they agreed to use the existing formula guaranteeing each state at least 0.75 percent of the total funding for formula grants. However, they gave the secretary discretion to distribute the rest of the funding based on the risk of terrorism, and, to a lesser degree, of natural disaster.

The new formula applied only to fiscal 2006 funding, but members from high-risk areas hoped it would set a precedent. "It's irreversible," said House Homeland Security Chairman Peter T. King, R-N.Y. "It sets a pattern and provides a framework." But Sen. Schumer cautioned that "While New York will get a bigger piece of the pie, the overall pie is smaller."

The conferees directed the department to report by Feb. 10, 2006, on the status of all open grants made before fiscal 2003, why the funding had not been spent, and what actions could be taken to ensure grant funds were spent in a timely manner.

● **Coast Guard.** $933 million for Deepwater, less than the administration request of $966 million but more than either the $906 million recommended by the Senate or the $500 proposed in the House bill. Aides said the Coast Guard's well-regarded performance during Katrina search-and-rescue operations helped convince skeptics on Capitol Hill to increase the funding. Rogers also said the administration had come through with information his committee had requested. "The oversight of our subcommittee worked," he said. "We were unable to get that until we withheld money."

In conference, lawmakers adopted, by voice vote, an amendment by Obey that required the Bush administration to detail credit-card expenditures, contracting agreements and other Hurricane Katrina-related costs not previously required in its weekly reports to Congress. ■

# Interior Bill Is First to Cross Finish Line

CONGRESS CUT FUNDING for the Department of the Interior, the EPA and related agencies by 3 percent for fiscal 2006, providing $26.2 billion in a spending bill that was signed into law Aug. 2 (HR 2361 — PL 109-54). President Bush had proposed an even deeper cut to $25.7 billion, nearly 5 percent below fiscal 2005 spending.

The annual spending bill funded Interior Department land management activities, the National Park Service, the U.S. Forest Service, programs for American Indians, and arts and cultural programs. A reorganization of the House and Senate Appropriations committees early in the year added the EPA to the measure. Energy research programs, which formerly were part of the Interior bill, were moved to the separate Energy-Water appropriations measure.

The Interior bill was the first of the fiscal 2006 spending measures to clear, in part because there were few major differences between the $26.2 billion version the House passed in May and the $26.3 billion bill the Senate passed in June. Virtually all of the money was discretionary spending. Because the bill was moving quickly, appropriators also made it the vehicle for $1.5 billion in supplemental fiscal 2005 funds to cover a shortfall in veterans' health care funding. The need for the veterans' funding in the midst of a war made the bill a must-pass item before the August recess. (Veterans supplemental, p. 2-57)

The totals do not reflect a 1 percent across-the-board cut in most non-emergency discretionary appropriations enacted as part of the fiscal 2006 Defense spending bill (PL 109-148).

Fiscal constraints kept both chambers focused largely on the spending trade-offs, rather than on environmental policy, land-use restrictions and other issues that had stalled Interior bills in years past. The biggest policy dispute that arose in 2005 was over whether to allow the EPA to use data from pesticide tests on humans. The final bill required a new EPA rule that met strict criteria.

Negotiators alleviated some of the pressure to cut programs with a 0.48 percent across-the-board cut, which produced $126 million in headroom, more than the $100 million difference in discretionary spending levels between the House and Senate versions of the bill.

Still, the final bill cut money from an array of programs. Overall, the Interior Department received $9.9 billion, a very slight reduction from fiscal 2005 funding (PL 109-447). The chief losers, compared with fiscal 2005 funding, were the EPA and the Agriculture Department's Forest Service. Among the winners were National Park Service operations and the Indian Health Service, which was under the Department of Health and Human Services (HHS). (2004 Almanac, p. 2-30)

## HIGHLIGHTS

The Interior bill included the following major components:
- **EPA.** $7.7 billion, $294 million or nearly 4 percent less than the agency received in fiscal 2005. Much of the reduction came from a $191 million cut to the Clean Water State Revolving Fund, a source of funding for state and local water and sewage treatment projects. The fund got $900 million, down from $1.1 billion in fiscal 2005, though that still was $170 million more than Bush requested. Appropriators managed to provide $73 mil-

**BOX SCORE 2006** FISCAL YEAR

**INTERIOR-ENVIRONMENT**

**BILL:**
HR 2361 — PL 109-54

**LEGISLATIVE ACTION:**
**House** passed HR 2361 (H Rept 109-80), 329-89, on May 19.

**Senate** passed HR 2361, amended (S Rept 109-80), 94-0, on June 29.

**House** adopted the conference report on HR 2361 (H Rept 109-188), 410-10, on July 28.

**Senate** cleared the bill, 99-1, on July 29.

**President** signed Aug. 2.

lion for the Leaking Underground Storage Tank Program, a $3.6 million increase over fiscal 2005 and $1.3 billion for the superfund hazard waste cleanup program, a $13 million increase.
- **BLM.** $1.8 billion for the Bureau of Land Management (BLM), about 2 percent less than the agency got in fiscal 2005 and $21 million more than Bush requested. The total included $861 million to manage some 262 million acres of public land in Western states and $767 million for wildland fire management.
- **National Park Service.** $2.3 billion, 3 percent below fiscal 2005 spending and $40 million more than requested. Although total spending fell, appropriators included an increase of almost 4 percent for park service operations. The biggest cut was in the account for land acquisition and state assistance, which got $65 million, less than half the amount provided in fiscal 2005.
- **Fish and Wildlife Service.** $1.3 billion, virtually the same as fiscal 2005 spending and $7 million more than requested.
- **U.S. Forest Service.** $4.3 billion, 11 percent less than fiscal 2005 funding if prior-year emergency firefighting money is counted, and $198 million more than Bush requested. The total included $1.8 billion in firefighting funds for fiscal 2006.
- **Land acquisition.** $145 million for land acquisition covered under the Land and Water Conservation Fund, about 43 percent below fiscal 2005 spending but more than three times the amount in the House bill, which recommended $43 million. Of the total, the measure allocated $65 million to the National Park Service, $42.5 million to the Forest Service, $28 million to the Fish and Wildlife Service and $9 million to the BLM.
- **Indian programs.** $3.1 billion for the Indian Health Service, a 4 percent increase over fiscal 2005 and about $43 million more than requested. The bill also included $2.3 billion for the Interior Department's Bureau of Indian Affairs, $121 million above the request and just enough to offset the bill's half-percentage-point across-the-board cut.
- **Arts programs.** $126 million for the National Endowment for the Arts and $143 million for the National Endowment for the Humanities, increases of about 4 percent over fiscal 2005 spending. The Smithsonian Institution got a less-than-inflation increase to $624 million.

## LEGISLATIVE ACTION
### HOUSE COMMITTEE ACTION

The House Appropriations Committee gave voice vote approval May 10 to a $26.2 billion Interior-Environment bill (HR 2361 — H Rept 109-80), after a bipartisan lament that many popular programs would not be adequately funded. The panel's Interior-Environment Subcommittee approved the measure by voice vote May 4. Members of both parties were vocal in their praise for subcommittee Chairman Charles H. Taylor, R-N.C., for trying to balance competing interests within a tight discretionary spending allocation.

The total was 3 percent below the $27 billion allocated to comparable programs in fiscal 2005, but nearly 2 percent more than Bush requested.

The committee's toughest choices came in the environmental area,

## WHERE THE MONEY GOES — FISCAL 2006 APPROPRIATIONS

# INTERIOR-ENVIRONMENT

## HR 2361 — PL 109-54

*(figures are in thousands of dollars of new budget authority)*

| | Fiscal 2005 appropriations | Fiscal 2006 Bush request | House passed | Senate passed | Conference report |
|---|---|---|---|---|---|
| **GRAND TOTAL** | $27,017,724 | $25,724,328 | $26,159,125 | $26,256,625* | $26,201,541* |
| Discretionary spending** | 26,701,659 | 25,672,203 | 26,107,000 | 26,207,000 | 26,159,000 |
| **MAIN COMPONENTS** | | | | | |
| **Interior Department** | $9,955,228 | $9,792,069 | $9,799,693 | $9,867,741 | $9,926,107 |
| National Park Service | 2,365,683 | 2,249,275 | 2,228,963 | 2,315,332 | 2,289,900 |
| Bureau of Indian Affairs | 2,295,702 | 2,187,469 | 2,317,976 | 2,269,371 | 2,308,229 |
| Bureau of Land Management | 1,816,910 | 1,759,042 | 1,755,115 | 1,788,310 | 1,780,506 |
| U.S. Fish and Wildlife Service | 1,332,591 | 1,322,894 | 1,306,168 | 1,315,037 | 1,330,179 |
| **Environmental Protection Agency** | 8,026,485 | 7,520,600 | 7,708,027 | 7,881,989 | 7,732,354 |
| **U.S. Forest Service (Agriculture)** | 4,770,598 | 4,065,000 | 4,241,358 | 4,122,767 | 4,263,489 |
| **Indian Health Service (HHS)** | 2,985,066 | 3,047,966 | 3,103,072 | 3,067,966 | 3,090,783 |

\* Bill also includes $1.5 billion in fiscal 2005 supplemental funds for the Veterans Health Administration that is not reflected in grand total.
\*\* Calculated after scorekeeping adjustments.

TABLE: House, Senate Appropriations committees

which was new to the panel's jurisdiction in 2005. Appropriators made deep cuts in clean-water programs to sustain superfund cleanup of hazardous substances, environmental education activities and remediation of contaminated former industrial sites known as brownfields.

The committee-approved bill included:

● **EPA.** $7.7 billion, $187 million more than Bush requested but 4 percent below fiscal 2005 spending. The Clean Water State Revolving Fund was slated to get $850 million, more than Bush wanted but a 22 percent reduction from the previous year.

● **BLM.** $1.8 billion, virtually the same as the president's request, but $62 million below fiscal 2005 funding.

● **National Park Service.** $2.2 billion, $20 million less than requested and $137 million below fiscal 2005 spending. The committee proposed $1.8 billion for park operations, a $71 million increase.

● **Indian Health Service.** $3.1 billion, an increase of nearly $118 million over fiscal 2005 and $55 million above Bush's request. Within that total, the committee proposed to fund Indian school construction at $35 million below the fiscal 2005 level of $319 million and provide $50 million for construction of Indian health centers, a reduction of $38 million from 2005.

● **Forest Service.** $4.2 billion, $529 million below the previous year's spending, counting emergency funds, but $156 million more than Bush's request.

● **Land acquisition and construction.** $43 million, mostly to administer existing holdings. That was a drop of $212 million or 83 percent, from fiscal 2005. Taylor argued the federal government should be a better steward of the land it already had before adding new acreage.

### HOUSE FLOOR ACTION

After sorting through nearly two dozen amendments on topics ranging from wild horses to sewage, the House passed the $26.2 billion bill by a vote of 329-89 on May 19. *(House vote 199, p. H-64)*

Democratic appropriators praised Taylor for trying to fairly allocate scarce funds among dozens of popular programs. But they also used the opportunity to argue that the GOP-written fiscal 2006 budget resolution (H Con Res 95) was forcing choices they said should not have been necessary.

During the floor debate, the House:

▶ Adopted, 249-159, a proposal by Nick J. Rahall II, D-W.Va., and Edward Whitfield, R-Ky., to repeal a provision of the fiscal 2005 omnibus spending law (PL 108-447) that made it easier to sell wild horses from public lands. The lawmakers said there were inadequate safeguards to prevent the animals from being sold for slaughter. Horse meat is considered a delicacy in some countries. *(House vote 196, p. H-64)*

Western lawmakers blasted the proposal, warning that horse herds could double every five years, affecting ranchers and leaving many horses sick and housed in harsh conditions. But lawmakers wanted firmer assurances that these icons of the American frontier would not end up on dinner tables in Europe.

▶ Adopted by voice vote an amendment by Hilda L. Solis, D-Calif., and Timothy H. Bishop, D-N.Y., to prohibit the EPA from using funds in the bill to conduct, consult or rely on studies that intentionally exposed humans to pesticides.

▶ Adopted by a voice vote an amendment by Barbara Cubin, R-Wyo., to increase funding for the federal Payment in Lieu of Taxes program, which compensates local governments for the loss of potential tax revenue from land owned by the federal government. Cubin proposed to pay for the increase by reducing administrative funds for the Interior Department.

▶ Adopted by voice vote an amendment by Louise M. Slaughter, D-N.Y., to increase funding for the National Foundation on the Arts and the Humanities by $15 million, offset by cuts elsewhere in the bill.

▶ Rejected, 157-262, an attempt by John E. Peterson, R-Pa., to end a moratorium on drilling for natural gas in the Outer Continental Shelf to get a better inventory of what was available. Peterson said the soaring cost of natural gas was driving companies out of business or out of the country. *(House vote 192, p. H-64)*

But in a debate that pitted advocates of more robust exploration

against defenders of pristine coastline, Peterson faced skeptics of his claim that natural gas exploration, unlike oil exploration, could be done without putting the environment in jeopardy. C.W. Bill Young, R-Fla., insisted that an adequate inventory already existed and questioned how Peterson's proposal would result in lower natural gas prices.

▶ Rejected, 186-235, an amendment by David R. Obey of Wisconsin, the top Democrat on the Appropriations Committee, to shift $100 million to the Clean Water State Revolving Fund from other grants for states and tribal governments. An earlier attempt by Obey to add $500 million to the fund, paid for by raising taxes on those with annual incomes in excess of $1 million, was cut short by a parliamentary point of order. (House vote 194, p. H-64)

▶ Rejected, 76-344, a proposal by Lee Terry, R-Neb., to add $130 million to the $1.3 billion already in the bill for the superfund hazardous waste cleanup program. Terry proposed taking the funds from the $765 million that would be provided under the bill for EPA science and technology programs. (House vote 193, p. H-64)

A showdown over roadbuilding in Alaska's Tongass National Forest was averted when an amendment by Steve Chabot, R-Ohio, and Robert E. Andrews, D-N.J, to bar taxpayer-subsidized roads in the forest was ruled out of order.

## SENATE COMMITTEE ACTION

The Senate Appropriations Committee approved a $26.3 billion version of the bill (HR 2361 — S Rept 109-80) by a vote of 28-0 on June 9; the panel's subcommittee had approved the measure by voice vote two days earlier. Appropriators proposed to increase spending for water and conservation programs beyond the amounts passed by the House, setting up a possible conflict later in conference. The bill included:

● **EPA.** $7.9 billion, $173 million more than in the House bill. The Senate bill included $1.1 billion for the Clean Water State Revolving Loan Fund, the amount provided in fiscal 2005 and significantly more than the $850 million in the House bill. Norm Dicks of Washington, the ranking Democrat on the House Interior and Environment Appropriations Subcommittee, called the Senate action on the loan fund a "step in the right direction," adding: "Let's hope we can get close to the Senate number in conference."

● **BLM.** $1.8 billion, $33 million more than in the House bill.

● **National Park Service.** $2.3 billion, of which $1.7 billion was for park operations. The total for the park service was $86 million above the House figure.

● **Indian programs.** $2.7 billion, about $35 million less than in the House bill, for the Indian Health Service, and $2.3 billion, $49 million less than in the House bill, for the Bureau of Indian Affairs.

● **Forest Service.** $4.1 billion, $119 million below the House level.

● **Small engines.** Interior Appropriations Subcommittee Chairman Conrad Burns, R-Mont., sought to keep the bill free of earmarks and policy riders. The one exception revived a battle from late 2003. Christopher S. Bond, R-Mo., inserted a provision to delay final EPA regulations on emissions from small engines until the agency completed a study of the possible fire hazards of affixing such engines with catalytic converters. Bond raised the issue in 2003, trying to block new engine emission rules in California that he worried could send jobs, including some in Missouri, overseas.

But Dianne Feinstein, D-Calif., who had similarly stepped in in 2003, pushed Bond into a compromise that included a requirement that the study be completed within six months and that allowed tougher regulations even if domestic jobs would be affected.

The House bill did not address the issue.

## SENATE FLOOR ACTION

The Senate easily passed the $26.3 billion bill June 29 by a 94-0 vote. Before passage, senators agreed to attach $1.5 billion in emergency fiscal 2005 supplemental spending to fill a recently disclosed gap in funding for veterans' health care. (Senate vote 168, p. S-34)

Decrying the overall cut in funding, Burns said, "Simply keeping pace with pay costs and health benefits for park and forest rangers, Indian health care professionals, and other critical personnel requires a significant increase in funding over last year."

Although the bill remained relatively free of policy riders, the Senate adopted a pair of conflicting amendments regarding the EPA's consideration of pesticide tests on humans. The amendments came in response to draft EPA rules to let the agency consider data from tests conducted on humans in determining whether to grant government approval of pesticides. The draft rules did not include some recommendations made by the National Academy of Sciences in 2004 that would have imposed stricter guidelines on human testing.

During floor debate, the Senate:

▶ Adopted 57-40, an amendment by Burns, who supported EPA use of the test data, directing the agency administrator to review all third-party studies that involved human testing based on six principles outlined in the National Academy of Sciences report. The amendment required that within 180 days of the bill's enactment, the administrator issue a final rule on ethical standards for such studies. "We live in a chemically reactive world," Burns said. "The more we know about it, the more we know about our own environment and those steps we have to take in order to protect it." (Senate vote 161, p. S-32)

▶ Adopted 60-37, a proposal by Barbara Boxer, D-Calif., identical to the House amendment barring the EPA from using funds in the bill to accept, consider, conduct or rely on intentional human studies of the effects of pesticides. Boxer called Burns' amendment a "fig leaf, cover-yourself amendment," that would be worse than the status quo. Without her amendment, Boxer said, the EPA could rely on tests on pregnant women, fetuses and ill infants. (Senate vote 162, p. S-32)

▶ Adopted, 96-0, an amendment by Patty Murray, D-Wash., to provide $1.5 billion in emergency fiscal 2005 supplemental funds to the Department of Veterans Affairs for medical care provided by the Veterans Health Administration. (Senate vote 166, p. S-33)

▶ Rejected, 39-59, an attempt by John E. Sununu, R-N.H., to bar the use of federal funds to build roads used by logging companies in the Tongass National Forest. (Senate vote 164, p. S-33)

Sununu said the roads were primarily for the benefit of private timber companies. "I don't think it is too much to ask to simply require that those companies pay the expense of the roadbuilding themselves and not ask the taxpayers to provide that subsidy," he said. But opponents, led by Alaska's GOP Sens. Ted Stevens and Lisa Murkowski, questioned why Sununu was focusing on one national forest, saying that it would cost hundreds of jobs in the timber industry. "What we have today is an amendment that singles out the Tongass National Forest and no other national forest in the country," Murkowski said.

▶ Rejected, on a procedural vote, an attempt by Byron L. Dorgan, D-N.D., to offer an amendment that would allow travel to Cuba to visit immediate family members for funerals and other humanitarian purposes. The vote was 60-35; Dorgan needed a two-thirds majority to suspend the rule. (Senate vote 167, p. S-33)

## CONFERENCE/FINAL ACTION

With few major differences — and with Republicans eager to get the VA funding issue behind them after weeks of Democratic criticism that

the administration had ignored the shortfall — House and Senate conferees quickly completed the bill. The House adopted the conference report (H Rept 109-188), 410-10, on July 28, and the Senate followed suit, 99-1, on July 29. *(House vote 450, p. H-138; Senate vote 210, p. S-42)*

"I believe this bill addresses the most critical needs," said Taylor. Obey said the bill was "far from where it ought to be," but he and other Democrats said they could not vote against legislation carrying the money for veterans.

The following were among the issues settled in conference:

● **Pesticide testing.** In a decision that pleased critics of the draft EPA regulations, conferees prohibited the agency from accepting data collected from pesticide testing on humans until it adopted a new rule on such studies. The rule had to be issued within 180 days of the bill's enactment, and it could not allow the use of pregnant women, infants or children as subjects. It also had to be consistent with principles in the 2004 National Academy of Sciences study and the Nuremberg Code relating to human experimentation.

● **Outsourcing.** Despite White House objections, conferees agreed to include language limiting the amount that could be spent on competitive sourcing studies to $3.45 million for the Interior Department and $3 million for the Forest Service. The House and Senate bills both had similar language, which was aimed at restricting studies on contracting out government work to private companies.

● **Payment in Lieu of Taxes.** The measure provided $236 million for payments in lieu of taxes to local governments, a program of particular interest to members from Western states, where the federal government owns large amounts of land. The total was a compromise between the House and Senate amounts. It was 4 percent above previous-year spending and 18 percent more than Bush requested.

● **Abandoned mine funds.** Sen. Robert C. Byrd, D-W.Va., won on another issue by including a temporary extension of existing law on the Abandoned Mine Land Reclamation Fund for nine months.

"It is my hope that this nine-month extension will finally give Congress the time and the opportunity to put aside regional differences and reach an agreement to accomplish the top priority of this program - namely, reclaiming the hundreds of abandoned mine sites across the country," Byrd said in a release.

● **Small engines.** The final bill included the Senate language.

● **King memorial.** House and Senate negotiators wrangled publicly during a brief open conference meeting over $10 million in federal funding for a proposed Martin Luther King Jr. memorial in Washington, D.C. Thad Cochran, R-Miss., chairman of the Senate Appropriations Committee, and Byrd wanted the money, but Taylor said he objected to spending federal money to jump-start a private project. They ultimately agreed to provide the money contingent upon collection of an equal amount in private funds. ■

# Education, HHS Funds Hotly Contested

THE SENATE CLEARED THE LARGEST of the fiscal 2006 spending bills — for the departments of Labor, Health and Human Services (HHS) and Education — on Dec. 21 as one of the last acts of the first session. The bill's difficult path through Congress was largely the result of tight spending limits that left many lawmakers deeply dissatisfied about funding for education and health care, in particular. President Bush signed the measure into law Dec. 30 (HR 3010 — PL 109-149).

Sen. Arlen Specter, R-Pa., chairman of the Appropriations subcommittee that wrote the Senate version, was one of the leading critics of the final bill, saying it shortchanged health and school programs. Specter ultimately agreed to support the bill, noting that the programs would get even less money if Congress kept them operating through a long-term continuing resolution. "I'm going to be constrained to hold my nose and vote in favor of the bill," Specter said.

The bill provided $601.6 billion for the three departments and various independent agencies. That was $100.3 billion, or 20 percent, more than the fiscal 2005 version (PL 108-447), but the extra funding went entirely to mandatory programs. Funding to execute the new Medicare prescription drug benefit, scheduled to begin Jan. 1, 2006, was responsible for about half the mandatory funding increase. *(2004 Almanac, p. 2-33)*

Mandatory funds for Medicaid, Medicare and other entitlement programs accounted for $459.5 billion, more than 75 percent of the bill. Discretionary funds, those allocated by the appropriators, shrank slightly to $142.5 billion from $142.7 billion in fiscal 2005. Totals do not reflect a 1 percent across-the-board cut in most discretionary programs enacted under the fiscal 2006 Defense spending bill (PL 109-148).

The House passed a $601.6 billion version of the bill in June with $142.5 billion in discretionary spending. The Senate passed a $612.4 billion bill in October that officially included $141.5 billion in discretionary funds. However, Specter used several bookkeeping maneuvers to create more room for discretionary programs, including a $1.1 billion increase over fiscal 2005 for the National Institutes of Health (NIH). During the floor debate, senators also added nearly $8 billion in emergency spending to combat a feared avian flu pandemic.

House appropriators rejected most of the Senate's efforts to expand spending under the bill. Conferees said, among other things, that the tight spending caps forced them to scrap $1 billion worth of earmarks for members, a sticking point for many in the House. The House narrowly adopted the conference report on the bill Dec. 14, after stunning the GOP leadership in mid-November by rejecting an earlier version. The second conference report contained only a few adjustments, including an increase in funding for rural health care.

Although the changes were enough to win House adoption, a number of senators, including Specter, said they would vote against the conference report because it shortchanged NIH and other programs. Specter eventually relented, and the Senate cleared the bill by voice vote as part of an effort to complete its work and adjourn for the year.

**BOX SCORE 2006** FISCAL YEAR

LABOR-HHS-EDUCATION

**BILL:**
HR 3010 — PL 109-149

**LEGISLATIVE ACTION:**

**House** passed HR 3010 (H Rept 109-143), 250-151, on June 24.

**Senate** passed HR 3010, amended (S Rept 109-103), 94-3, Oct. 27.

**House** rejected the conference report on HR 3010 (H Rept 109-300), 209-224, on Nov. 17.

**House** adopted revised conference report (H Rept 109-337), 215-213, on Dec. 14.

**Senate** cleared the bill by voice vote Dec. 21.

**President** signed Dec. 30.

## HIGHLIGHTS

The fiscal 2006 Labor-HHS-Education law included $95.8 billion in advance fiscal 2007 appropriations, $400 million in advance fiscal 2008 appropriations and $13.4 billion from trust funds. Advance appropriations were routinely provided for the first quarter of the succeeding fiscal year for certain education and health programs. The following are the law's major funding components:

● **Education.** $63.5 billion, including $15 billion in advance funds for fiscal 2007. The total was $4.3 billion or 7 percent more than the fiscal 2005 appropriation and $4.6 billion more than Bush requested. The increase for education was due almost entirely to Congress' decision to provide $4.3 billion to pay off the accumulated shortfall in the Pell Grant program.

Education funding included:

▸ $14.6 billion for Title I grants to low-income school districts, about 2 percent less than in fiscal 2005. The funding was $1.8 billion less than Bush's request, mainly because Congress did not provide $1.2 billion requested for a high school intervention initiative, which had not been authorized.

▸ $10.7 billion for state special education grants, $100 million or 1 percent more than in fiscal 2005 but $408 million less than requested.

▸ $13.2 billion for Pell grants, 7 percent above the 2005 level but $22 million less than Bush sought. The bill kept the maximum Pell grant award at $4,050.

● **Health and Human Services.** $474.1 billion, including $67.1 billion in advance fiscal 2007 appropriations and $3.2 billion from trust funds. About 80 percent of the funding was for mandatory programs, including $219.7 billion for grants to states under Medicaid, the federal-state health program for the poor, and $177.7 billion for Medicare.

The total included $54 billion to fund the new Medicare prescription drug benefit. In addition, the bill appropriated more than $800 million in discretionary funds to pay the administrative costs of implementing the new benefit.

Total HHS discretionary spending was $63.4 billion, a less-than-1 percent increase over fiscal 2005. It included:

▸ $28.6 billion for NIH, $253 million or about 1 percent above 2005 funding and $107 million more than requested.

▸ $5.9 billion for the Centers for Disease Control and Prevention (CDC), an increase of $1.4 billion or 31 percent above 2005 funding and $1.8 billion more than requested.

▸ $6.9 billion for Head Start, the early childhood program for low-income children. The amount was virtually the same as fiscal 2005 funding and Bush's request. It included about $1.4 billion in advance fiscal 2007 funding.

● **Labor.** $14.8 billion for the Labor Department, $558 million or 4 percent less than fiscal 2005 funding and about $40 million more than Bush's request. The total included $11.1 billion in appropriations and $3.6 billion from trust funds.

# LABOR-HEALTH & HUMAN SERVICES-EDUCATION

## HR 3010 — PL 109-149

*(figures are in thousands of dollars of new budget authority)*

| | Fiscal 2005 appropriations | Fiscal 2006 Bush request | House passed | Senate Passed | Conference Report |
|---|---|---|---|---|---|
| **GRAND TOTAL** | $501,344,992 | $596,122,425 | $601,642,273 | $612,406,934 | $601,643,301 |
| **Total adjusted for scorekeeping** | 496,899,953 | 596,987,102 | 601,990,838 | 601,095,899 | 601,991,778 |
| Discretionary spending | 142,677,055 | 141,729,324 | 142,513,060 | 141,538,121 | 142,514,000 |
| **MAIN COMPONENTS** | | | | | |
| **Department of Health and Human Services** | $379,200,874 | $473,484,522 | $473,893,464 | $484,265,742 | $474,144,909 |
| Medicare | 119,825,800 | 177,822,200 | 177,742,200 | 177,822,200 | 177,742,200 |
| Medicaid grants to states | 182,296,309 | 219,738,244 | 219,738,244 | 219,738,244 | 219,738,244 |
| National Institutes of Health | 28,364,515 | 28,509,784 | 28,506,805 | 29,414,515 | 28,617,484 |
| Children and Families Services | 9,007,452 | 8,377,293 | 8,688,707 | 9,025,953 | 8,922,213 |
| **Department of Education** | 59,212,775 | 58,939,040 | 63,706,584 | 63,749,975 | 63,538,021 |
| Education for the Disadvantaged (Title I) | 14,843,974 | 16,431,473 | 14,728,735 | 14,532,785 | 14,627,435 |
| Student financial aid | 14,265,749 | 15,050,977 | 15,283,752 | 15,103,795 | 15,077,752 |
| Special education grants to states | 10,589,746 | 11,097,746 | 10,739,746 | 10,689,746 | 10,689,746 |
| **Department of Labor** | 15,321,804 | 14,724,465 | 14,801,322 | 14,957,122 | 14,764,129 |
| Training and employment services | 5,337,772 | 5,055,513 | 5,121,792 | 5,250,806 | 5,115,411 |

TABLE: House, Senate Appropriations committees

## LEGISLATIVE ACTION

### HOUSE COMMITTEE ACTION

The House Appropriations Committee approved a $601.6 billion version of the bill (HR 3010 — H Rept 109-143) by voice vote June 16. The Labor-HHS-Education Subcommittee, which drafted the bill, approved the measure by voice vote June 9. The bill included $142.5 billion in discretionary spending, $164 million less than in the fiscal 2005 law but $784 million more than Bush requested.

Subcommittee Chairman Ralph Regula, R-Ohio, told his panel that he wanted to provide more but was hampered by the need to accommodate $890 million in discretionary spending to administer the new Medicare prescription drug benefit, due to begin Jan. 1. For the previous two years, the costs had been paid from money mandated in the 2003 law (PL 108-173) that created the program, rather than through the appropriations process. *(2003 Almanac, p. 11-3)*

The bill included:

▶ $14.7 billion for Title I programs, $115 million less than in fiscal 2005 and $1.7 billion less than what Bush requested. The committee did not include $1.2 billion that was requested for a high school intervention initiative aimed at improving achievement and graduation rates. The committee expressed support for the president's goals, but noted that the program had not been authorized.

▶ $10.7 billion for state grants for educating disabled children, a $150 million increase over 2005; Bush sought a $508 million increase.

▶ $13.4 billion for Pell grants, $1 billion above 2005 funding and $184 million more than requested. The House proposed to increase individual grants to $4,100 from $4,050.

▶ $28.5 for NIH, a slight increase of $142 million over 2005 and about equal to what Bush requested.

▶ $5.9 billion for the CDC, $1.6 billion more than 2005 funding and $1.9 billion more than Bush requested.

▶ $2 billion for the Low Income Home Energy Assistance Program (LIHEAP), virtually the same as requested and about $175 million below fiscal 2005 funding.

During the Appropriations markup, the committee:

▶ Approved by voice vote an amendment by ranking Democrat David R. Obey of Wisconsin to provide $400 million in advance fiscal 2008 funding for the Corporation for Public Broadcasting (CPB). Appropriators typically provided two years of advance funding for the CPB, but Regula did not cover fiscal 2008 in the original bill, citing mounting federal budget deficits. Advocates for public radio and television launched a campaign to restore the proposed cut, charging that some House Republicans wanted to eliminate the CPB. Under the bill, fiscal 2006 CPB funding was reduced by 23 percent to $300 million.

▶ Rejected, 29-36, an amendment by Dave Weldon, R-Fla., to ban NIH funding to any entity that funded human cloning or any research that used cloned embryos. Weldon said his amendment was necessary because scientists were making rapid advances in cloning. Opponents said the provision would curtail embryonic stem cell research that could help find cures for diseases. Appropriations Chairman Jerry Lewis, R-Calif., said the issue should be handled by the responsible authorizing committee, not the appropriators.

▶ Rejected, 28-35, an amendment by James T. Walsh, R-N.Y., to eliminate a rescission of $125 million out of $175 million in federal funds provided (PL 107-38) to the New York state workers' compensation program that administered claims resulting from the Sept. 11, 2001, terrorist attacks. The administration said the state had spent only $50 million. Amendment backers said a recent study showed half the 12,000 rescue workers at the World Trade Center site needed further treatment.

### HOUSE FLOOR ACTION

The House passed the $601.6 billion bill by a vote of 250-151 on June 24, following two days of intense and often partisan debate that featured sparring over public television, pensions and immigration. The

bill was backed by 44 Democrats and opposed by 10 Republicans. *(House vote 321, p. H-100)*

During the debate, the House:

▸ Adopted, 284-140, a proposal by Obey to restore $100 million for the CPB, bringing the fiscal 2006 total to $400 million offset with cuts elsewhere in the bill. *(House vote 305, p. H-96)*

▸ Adopted, 219-185, an amendment by George Miller, D-Calif., to prevent the Pension Benefit Guaranty Corporation (PBGC) from spending any federal money to carry out its agreement with United Airlines to take over the airline's pension plan. Miller and others said the PBGC acted too quickly to take over the plan, forcing significant cuts to promised benefits for employees. Opponents argued the amendment would nullify two previous court decisions and potentially push the airline into liquidation. *(House vote 309, p. H-98)*

▸ Adopted, 224-178, a proposal by Chris Van Hollen, D-Md., to bar the use of funds in the bill to pay lenders a rate of return on student loans that was 6 percent higher than the return lenders received on regular student loans. *(House vote 316, p. H-100)*

▸ Adopted, 285-121, an amendment by Steve King, R-Iowa, to bar the use of funds in the bill to pay for drugs prescribed for the treatment of impotence. *(House vote 312, p. H-98)*

▸ Rejected, 187-218, an amendment by Maurice D. Hinchey, D-N.Y, to bar the use of funds by any federal agency to try to direct or control the content or distribution of public telecommunications programs and services. *(House vote 314, p. H-98)*

▸ Rejected, 192-210, an attempt by Hinchey to bar the use of funds in the bill to distribute personal information of Medicare and Medicaid beneficiaries to private companies for marketing purposes. The Bush administration opposed the amendment. *(House vote 319, p. H-100)*

▸ Rejected, 165-234, an amendment by Rosa DeLauro, D-Conn., to bar the use of funds in the bill to carry out a settlement agreement between the Labor Department and Wal-Mart that would give Wal-Mart 15 days' advance notice of any investigation or audit of possible child labor violations. *(House vote 318, p. H-100)*

▸ Rejected by voice vote an amendment by Tom Tancredo, R-Colo., to bar the use of funds in the bill to pay salaries of federal employees who reimbursed hospitals for providing medical care to illegal immigrants. Representatives from border states said the proposal would unfairly penalize their hospitals, which were required under federal law to accept emergency patients regardless of citizenship status.

## SENATE COMMITTEE ACTION

The Senate Appropriations Committee approved a $604.4 billion version of the bill (HR 3010 — S Rept 109-103) by a vote of 27-0 on July 14. The Labor-HHS-Education Subcommittee, which drafted the bill, squeezed in $1.1 billion in additional funds for NIH along with other spending increases before approving the measure by voice vote July 12.

Technically, the bill was close to the $141.3 billion discretionary spending cap set by the committee. But the accounting moves used by Specter to free up additional spending brought the actual discretionary total closer to $145.7 billion.

The biggest factor was language shifting $3.3 billion in mandatory Supplemental Security Income payments forward by a few days into fiscal 2007. Appropriators freed up another $105 million with language denying Medicaid and Medicare funding for drugs such as Viagra, Cialis and Levitra prescribed to treat impotence. The bill also included a rescission of $120 million in previously appropriated aid for New York.

The committee bill included:

▸ $29.4 billion for NIH, $908 million more than the House recom-

mended or Bush requested. Specter was a longtime supporter of increased funding for medical research, but the issue took on greater personal resonance after he announced in February that he was battling an advanced form of Hodgkin's disease, a cancer of the lymphatic system. "I look in the mirror, and I can't recognize who I am. I'm now engaging in a fierce battle," he said.

▸ $6.1 billion for the CDC, $118 million more than the House recommended.

▸ $14.5 billion for Title I grants, $196 million less than in the House bill and $1.9 billion less than requested. Like the House measure, the Senate bill did not include the $1.2 billion requested for high school intervention programs.

▸ $10.7 billion, $50 million less than in the House bill, for state grants to educate disabled students. Tom Harkin of Iowa, the ranking Democrat on Specter's subcommittee, said the government picked up 18.6 percent of the states' annual cost of educating children with disabilities in fiscal 2005, but that under the Senate bill the share would decline to 18 percent. "For the first time in 10 years, the federal government will slide backwards on its commitment to students with disabilities," Harkin said.

The Individuals with Disabilities Education Act (PL 108-446) authorized the federal government to pay up to 40 percent of a state's annual additional cost of educating children with disabilities.

"We would have liked to [have] done more," Specter said. "We stretched the dollars as far as we could."

▸ $15.1 billion for Pell grants, $206 million less than in the House bill. The committee proposed keeping the annual grant at $4,050.

▸ $2.2 billion for LIHEAP, including $300 million in emergency funds. The total was $176 million less than in the House bill.

## SENATE FLOOR ACTION

The Senate passed a $612.4 billion version of the bill Oct. 27 after adding nearly $8 billion to develop and produce a vaccine to combat avian flu. The vote was 94-3. The extra money was designated as emergency spending, which meant it did not count against the bill's discretionary spending cap. Without that designation and Specter's bookkeeping changes, total discretionary funding would have reached $153.7 billion. *(Senate vote 281, p. S-55)*

The $8 billion was added in an amendment by Harkin that was adopted by voice vote. "The possibility of a deadly outbreak of avian flu is real, and time is of the essence," Harkin said. The proposal included $3.3 billion for vaccine development, $3.1 billion to stockpile antiviral drugs such as Tamiflu, $600 million for state and local public health agencies, $750 million to manage a possible patient surge at hospitals in the event of a pandemic and $185 million for the CDC to handle any outbreak. The funds were to be distributed at the discretion of the president, after consultation with congressional leaders. The White House had not yet released a plan to prepare for a flu outbreak.

Much of the weeklong Senate debate on the bill focused on efforts to increase funding for politically popular education and health programs. Many of the amendments included no spending offsets and failed to get the 60 votes needed to waive budget points of order.

These included:

▸ A proposal by Jack Reed, D-R.I., to provide an additional $2.9 billion in emergency funds for LIHEAP, which fell on a 54-43 vote, six votes short. *(Senate vote 270, p. S-53)*

▸ A proposal by Robert C. Byrd, D-W.Va., to provide an additional $5 billion for Title I programs, which failed, 44-51. Byrd said the bill would provide $9.9 billion less than authorized under the 2001 edu-

cation law known as No Child Left Behind (PL 107-110), which required states to have all students proficient in math and reading by 2014 in exchange for federal funds. *(Senate vote 269, p. S-53)*

▶ A proposal by Hillary Rodham Clinton, D-N.Y., to add nearly $4 billion for state grants for disabled students. Clinton failed to overcome a point of order, 46-53. *(Senate vote 273, p. S-54)*

▶ An amendment by Budget Chairman Judd Gregg, R-N.H., to add $1.3 billion in LIHEAP funding, offset by a 0.9 percent across-the-board cut in all discretionary funds in the bill. Gregg's amendment was defeated, 46-53. *(Senate vote 271, p. S-53)*

### CONFERENCE/FINAL ACTION

House and Senate conferees reached agreement on a $601.6 Labor-HHS-Education bill Nov. 12, and appropriators expected to have it ready for the White House by the Thanksgiving recess. But the tight spending limits continued to raise hackles in both chambers, and on Nov. 17 the House dealt the GOP leadership a significant blow by rejecting the conference report (H Rept 109-300) by a vote of 209-224. Twenty-two Republicans crossed party lines to vote against the bill. No Democrats voted for the it. *(House vote 598, p. H-190)*

Leaders attributed the defeat to a variety of issues. Some lawmakers were upset about the lack of earmarks in the bill; others criticized cuts to rural health care programs and insufficient money for education. Ways and Means Chairman Bill Thomas, R-Calif., voted against the legislation because of a Senate provision that would have barred Medicare coverage of erectile dysfunction drugs. He said it could open the federal government to lawsuits from Medicare providers that had already set their formulas and begun marketing their plans. "Looking at those 22 members, there were 10 different issues," said acting Majority Leader Roy Blunt, R-Mo.

GOP appropriations leaders looked for relatively minor changes with the aim of winning over enough of those Republicans to get the conference report through. They boosted rural health funding by $90 million and deleted the provision that would have barred Medicare coverage of erectile dysfunction drugs, at an additional cost of $90 million. Conferees made up the $180 million by cutting $120 million from the $184 million in the bill for pandemic flu preparedness in the Public Health and Social Services Emergency Fund, and cutting $60 million from the funds provided for implementing the new Medicare prescription drug benefit.

House Republican leaders brought the revised conference report (H Rept 109-337) to the floor Dec. 14, but they still had to hold open the scheduled 15 minute vote for 31 minutes as some GOP moderates delayed voting. In the end, 12 Republicans voted against the bill, but 11 who opposed the first conference agreement supported the new version. The House adopted the conference report, 215-213. *(House vote 628, p. H-200)*

Senate leaders spent the last week of the session trying to round up enough votes to clear the measure. Although Specter warned at one point that he would vote against the conference report unless his vote was critical, he ultimately said he would be "a good soldier" and go along with the revised measure. The Senate finally cleared the bill by voice vote as part of its wrap up just four days before Christmas.

### CONFERENCE DECISIONS

At the insistence of House negotiators, conferees rejected the Senate's proposed funding shifts and the emergency funding to prepare for a possible flu pandemic. However, Congress provided $3.8 billion to combat a possible flu pandemic as part of the fiscal 2006 Defense appropriations bill (PL 109-148). *(Defense, p. 2-14)*

Conferees also insisted that about $1 billion worth of earmarks — discretionary funds set aside for specific programs — be excluded from the conference report to make more funding available for major education and health programs. According to the Congressional Research Service, the final bill included just eight earmarks, compared with 3,014 in the fiscal 2005 law.

In other decisions, the conferees:

▶ Leaned toward the lower House figure for NIH, providing $28.6 billion, $110 million more than in the House bill but $797 million less than the Senate wanted.

▶ Provided $5.9 billion for the CDC, slightly less than either chamber had wanted — $61 million less than the House and $179 million less than the Senate. Still, the CDC got $1.4 billion more than in the previous year and $1.8 billion more than Bush requested.

▶ Funded Title I grants at a total roughly halfway between the higher House and lower Senate numbers. The $14.6 billion for Title I programs included $12.8 billion for grants to local school districts, $100 million more than in 2005 but $503 million or 4 percent less than requested.

▶ Followed the Senate lead in providing $10.7 billion for state special education grants, $100 million above 2005 funding. The House wanted a $150 million increase.

▶ Agreed to $13.2 billion for Pell grants, as approved by the Senate but $206 million less than in the House bill. Conferees kept the annual grant at $4,050, as recommended by Bush and the Senate. They provided $4.3 billion, as approved by both chambers, to pay off the Pell Grant shortfall.

▶ Provided $1.3 billion for vocational education, $17 million below the 2005 level. Bush had requested no funding for vocational education programs.

▶ Provided $1.6 billion, close to the 2005 level, for the Job Corps, a Labor Department education and training program for at-risk youth. The bill also included $1.5 billion for dislocated worker assistance, equal to the 2005 level, and $950 million for youth training, $36 million less than in 2005.

▶ Agreed to $2.2 billion for LIHEAP, as recommended by the Senate. House appropriators rejected a Specter proposal to designate it as emergency spending not subject to discretionary budget caps, which would have freed up money for earmarks and other programs. A group of Senate GOP moderates from the Snow Belt won a last-minute promise from Majority Leader Bill Frist, R-Tenn., for a floor vote early in 2006 on additional funds for home heating subsidies.

▶ Provided $400 million for public broadcasting in fiscal 2006, plus $400 million in advance funding for each of fiscal years 2007 and 2008, as approved by both chambers. The bill also provided $30 million for digitalization and $35 million for satellite interconnection, close to the Senate recommendation. The House bill did not include those funds.

▶ Continued a provision added in the fiscal 2005 law to bar federal programs or state or local governments that received funds under the bill from discriminating against health care providers that did not provide abortion services or pay for them. The conference report also continued a provision, which began in the fiscal 1997 law, barring the use of funds in the bill for projects that involved the creation or destruction of human embryos.

▶ Dropped the House's United Airline pension provision, as well as the House amendment aimed at discouraging lenders from charging higher-than-normal rates of return on student loans. ∎

# Debate Centers on Visitor Center Costs

CONGRESS CLEARED A $3.8 BILLION fiscal 2006 Legislative Branch spending bill July 29 that included what lawmakers hoped would be the last installment of funds for the Capitol Visitor Center. President Bush signed the bill into law Aug. 2 (HR 2985 — PL 109-55).

The measure represented an increase of about 6 percent over the fiscal 2005 level for operations of the House and Senate, as well as congressional agencies such as the Library of Congress, the Government Accountability Office (GAO), the Government Printing Office (GPO) and the maintenance and security of the Capitol grounds.

Breaking with a longstanding practice, the bill removed a cap on congressional staff pay that had ensured that no congressional staff could make more than a member of Congress.

Much of the debate on the bill focused on the rising cost of the Capitol Visitor Center. The underground facility was originally budgeted at $265 million, but the GAO said the final cost would reach $522 million, plus an additional $37 million to cover "risks and uncertainties." Although the center was scheduled to be finished in September 2006, Bernard L. Ungar, the GAO director, said June 14 that a more realistic date was sometime between December 2006 and March 2007. Congress had provided no construction funds in fiscal 2005 but allowed $10 million to be transferred from the Capitol building account to cover anticipated funding gaps. The fiscal 2006 bill included $44 million.

The totals do not reflect a 1 percent across-the-board cut in most non-emergency discretionary appropriations enacted as part of the fiscal 2006 Defense spending bill (PL 109-148).

The two chambers easily passed versions of the bill in June. One of the main differences was the inclusion in the House version of so-called continuity of Congress provisions to establish a process under which states would hold special elections to fill vacancies in the House in the event of a catastrophe. House and Senate conferees agreed to retain the provisions and easily worked out other differences. Congress waited to adopt the conference report until another spending bill was ready for final action. Many members feared it would seem inappropriate to pay for their own operations before providing funds for other agencies and departments.

Once agreement was reached on the Interior-Environment bill (PL 109-54), the two measures moved in tandem to the White House.

## HIGHLIGHTS

The following are the main components of the bill:

● **House and Senate.** $1.1 billion for the House to cover staff salaries and operations, 2 percent more than fiscal 2005 spending and $8.5 million more than called for in the initial House bill. For the Senate, the bill provided $786 million, a 9 percent increase.

● **Architect of the Capitol.** $428 million for the Architect of the Capitol, 18 percent above fiscal 2005 spending, including the $44 million to complete the visitor center,

● **Capitol Police.** $249 million for the Capitol Police, a 3 percent increase above fiscal 2005. Congress eliminated funding for the mounted police unit, transferring the five horses to the U.S. Park Police.

● **Continuity of Congress.** House-passed language requiring states to

---

**BOX SCORE 2006**
FISCAL YEAR

LEGISLATIVE BRANCH

**BILL:**
HR 2985 — PL 109-55

**LEGISLATIVE ACTION:**

**House** passed HR 2985 (H Rept 109-139), 330-82, on June 22.

**Senate** passed HR 2985, amended (S Rept 109-89) by voice vote June 30.

**House** adopted the conference report (H Rept 109-189), 305-122, on July 28.

**Senate** cleared the bill, 96-4, on July 29.

**President** signed Aug. 2.

---

hold special elections within 49 days of the Speaker declaring that more than 100 vacancies exist in the House. The aim was to provide a mechanism for quickly reconstituting the House after a terrorist attack or other catastrophe. (*Continuity, p. 5-7*)

## LEGISLATIVE ACTION
### HOUSE COMMITTEE ACTION

The House Appropriations Committee approved a $2.9 billion version of the bill (HR 2985 — H Rept 109-139) by voice vote June 16. By custom, House and Senate appropriators deal only with funding for their own chambers and joint items, so the measure did not address Senate operations. The $3.6 billion fiscal 2005 legislative branch law (PL 108-447) included $2.8 billion for the House and joint operations. (*2004 Almanac, p. 2-37*)

The committee agreed by voice vote to an amendment, offered on behalf of Speaker J. Dennis Hastert, R-Ill., by Chairman Jerry Lewis, R-Calif., to provide for the replacement of House members in the case of a disaster that left a large number suddenly unable to serve. The House had passed the proposal as a stand-alone bill (HR 841) by a wide margin in March.

The committee-approved appropriations bill included:

▶ $1.1 billion for House staff and operations, including the costs of committees and leadership offices and members' official expenses.

▶ $317 million for the Architect of the Capitol, including $37 million for the visitor center — far less than the $72 million requested by the architect. Appropriators also called for a governing board for the center that would include members of the House and Senate leadership, along with the chairmen and ranking members of the Senate Rules and Administration and the House Administration committees.

▶ $240 million for the U.S. Capitol Police, about $2 million below fiscal 2005 spending and $50 million less than Chief Terrance W. Gainer had requested. The bill called for the mounted police program to be disbanded and its five horses transferred to the U.S. Park Police. It also called for an inspector general's office within the police department.

▶ $482 million for the GAO, an increase of 3 percent or $15 million.

### HOUSE FLOOR ACTION

The House passed the bill, 330-82, on June 22 after turning back virtually every attempt to modify it. The exception was an amendment to reduce spending for the GPO. (*House vote 303, p. H-96*)

During floor action, the House:

▶ Adopted by voice vote an amendment by Jeff Flake, R-Ariz., to cut GPO funds by $5 million.

▶ Rejected, by voice vote, an attempt by Patrick T. McHenry, R-N.C., to increase Capitol Police funding by $2 million.

▶ Rejected, 143-268, an amendment by Brian Baird, D-Wash., to strike the continuity of Congress provisions. (*House vote 299, p. H-94*)

▶ Rejected, 185-226, a bid by Jo Ann Davis, R-Va., to save the mounted police unit. (*House vote 300, p. H-94*)

▶ Rejected, 114-294, an amendment by Joel Hefley, R-Colo., to reduce spending in the bill by 1 percent. (*House vote 301, p. H-94*)

## WHERE THE MONEY GOES — FISCAL 2006 APPROPRIATIONS

# LEGISLATIVE BRANCH

## HR 2985 — PL 109-55

*(figures are in thousands of dollars of new budget authority)*

| | Fiscal 2005 appropriations | Fiscal 2006 Bush request | House** passed | Senate passed | Conference report |
|---|---|---|---|---|---|
| **GRAND TOTAL*** | $3,639,892 | $4,028,477 | $2,864,418 | $3,833,765 | $3,803,500 |
| **MAIN COMPONENTS** | | | | | |
| House of Representatives | $1,079,354 | $1,127,817 | $1,092,407 | $1,092,407 | $1,100,907 |
| Senate | 720,194 | 823,048 | N/A | 785,549 | 785,549 |
| Library of Congress | 545,362 | 590,795 | 542,950 | 579,562 | 560,566 |
| Government Accountability Office | 467,205 | 486,383 | 482,395 | 484,383 | 482,395 |
| Architect of the Capitol | 362,200 | 506,480 | 317,282 | 427,212 | 428,478 |
| Capitol Police | 241,469 | 290,139 | 239,695 | 264,600 | 249,456 |

\* All funding is discretionary.
\*\* By custom, the House bill does not include funds requested exclusively for the Senate; the Senate bill uses the House's numbers for funds requested by the House.

TABLE: House, Senate Appropriations committees

▶ Rejected, 180-232, a motion to recommit the bill to the committee. David R. Obey of Wisconsin, the ranking Democrat on the Appropriations Committee, offered the motion. He complained about the visitor center, which he said was out of control, and the continuity of Congress section, which he said was not germane to the bill. *(House vote 302, p. H-96)*

### SENATE COMMITTEE ACTION

The Appropriations Committee approved its version of the bill (S Rept 109-89) by voice vote June 23. With both chambers included, the total came to $3.8 billion. The Senate bill did not address the horse patrol or the continuity of Congress issue.

The Senate version included:

▶ $786 million for Senate operations and expenses.

▶ $427 million for the Architect of the Capitol, $110 million above the House level, including $44 million for the visitor center. The committee proposed an executive director position to help get the center in order.

▶ $265 million for the Capitol Police, only about half the 20 percent boost requested by Gainer. The amount was about $24 million above the House level, and the bill did not include the House-passed language to transfer the five-horse mounted patrol to the park police.

▶ $484 for the GAO, $2 million more than in the House version.

▶ $580 million for the Library of Congress, about $37 million more than in the House bill.

Wayne Allard, R-Colo., chairman of the Legislative Branch Appropriations Subcommittee initially included the continuity provision in deference to a House leadership request, but said he would defer to the full committee's wishes. The full committee gave voice vote approval

to an amendment by ranking Democrat Robert C. Byrd of West Virginia striking the language. "Continuity of Congress legislation is an issue of enormous consequence, and it's not something that should be decided by the House of Representatives alone," Byrd said.

### SENATE FLOOR ACTION

The Senate passed the bill by voice vote with little debate June 30.

### CONFERENCE/FINAL ACTION

House and Senate negotiators agreed to a final version of the bill July 26. The House adopted the conference report (H Rept 109-189), 305-122, on July 28. The Senate cleared the bill, 96-4, the next day. *(House vote 451, p. H-140; Senate vote 211, p. S-42)*

The House won on the continuity of Congress provisions, as well as on getting rid of the mounted patrols. Conferees also leaned toward the House position on police funding, providing $249 million, $10 million above the House figure. The Senate had hoped to boost the funding to $265 million. The conference report admonished the police for slow progress in making changes mandated by Congress. The bill established an inspector general to oversee audits and investigations within the department.

The Architect of the Capitol got $428 million under the bill, about $1 million more than in the Senate bill; the House had sought to cut the funding to $317 million.

The House prevailed on GAO funding, with $482 million, $2 million less than the Senate recommended. Conferees roughly split the difference on the Library of Congress, providing $561 million, $18 million above the House figure and $19 million less than the Senate wanted. ■

# Veterans' Health Care a Balancing Act

THE SENATE ON NOV. 18 cleared an $82.6 billion fiscal 2006 spending bill for military construction and the Department of Veterans Affairs (VA) that included $1.2 billion in emergency funding to help cover a shortfall in the VA's health care budget. President Bush signed the bill into law Nov. 30 (HR 2528 – PL 109-114).

The total was $3.8 billion or 5 percent more than comparable programs received in fiscal 2005, and $847 million or about 1 percent more than Bush requested. The discretionary portion – the funds that appropriators could allocate as they chose – was $44.1 billion or a little more than half the bill. That was $1.9 billion more than appropriators allocated in 2005, but Bush wanted $957 million more.

Mandatory spending – all of which was for veterans' programs – totaled $37.2 billion, a jump of $2.1 billion.

The totals do not reflect a 1 percent across-the-board cut in most discretionary programs – except those for veterans and emergency war costs – enacted in the fiscal 2006 Defense spending bill (PL 109-148).

The structure of the bill – combining military construction and funding for the VA – was new for fiscal 2006, the result of a reorganization earlier in the year by the House and Senate Appropriations committees. The initial House-passed bill included other defense accounts such as the $20 billion Defense Health Program and the Pentagon's housing allowance for military personnel. The Senate passed funding for those programs as part of its Defense appropriations bill. House and Senate negotiators ultimately agreed to follow the Senate structure for fiscal 2006. *(Defense, p. 2-14)*

The most difficult issue for Congress was balancing the political pressures to provide adequate care for the growing number of soldiers wounded in the Iraq and Afghanistan wars with the need to abide by deficit-driven budget constraints.

The House passed a $121.8 billion bill in May that included $85.2 billion in discretionary funds. When the bill was recalculated to cover only programs in the Senate bill, the total was $80.5 billion with $43.9 billion for discretionary programs.

The following month, the VA revealed a budget shortfall for veterans' health care that was eventually calculated at nearly $3 billion. VA officials blamed outdated forecasts that underestimated the rising costs of long-term care, and higher-than-anticipated numbers of returning Iraq and Afghanistan vets seeking health care. Democrats went on the attack, criticizing the administration for failing to acknowledge the shortfall earlier.

It was too late for the House to act, but Senate appropriators added $2 billion in emergency fiscal 2006 funds when they marked up their version of the bill in July. That brought the Senate bill, which passed in September, to $83 billion, with $46.4 billion in discretionary funds.

The emergency funds in the Senate bill and the inclusion of the additional Defense Department programs in the House measure were the chief differences between the chambers, and they were resolved relatively easily. Democrats who ultimately supported the bill still questioned whether the VA had adequately braced itself for the new generation of returning Iraq and Afghanistan veterans. Appropriators inserted bill

**BOX SCORE 2006** FISCAL YEAR

**MILITARY CONSTRUCTION-VA**

**BILL:** HR 2528 – PL 109-114

**LEGISLATIVE ACTION:**

**House** passed HR 2528 (H Rept 109-95), 425-1, on May 26.

**Senate** passed HR 2528, amended (S Rept 109-105), 98-0, Sept. 22.

**House** adopted the conference report (H Rept 109-305), 427-0, on Nov. 18.

**Senate** cleared the bill by voice vote Nov. 18.

**President** signed Nov. 30.

language requiring quarterly expense reports from the department.

In separate action, Congress attached $1.5 billion in emergency supplemental funds to the fiscal 2006 Interior-Environment bill (PL 109-54) to cover the portion of the VA health funding shortfall that fell in fiscal 2005. *(Veterans' supplemental, p. 2-57)*

## HIGHLIGHTS

● **Veterans Affairs.** About 85 percent of the bill was for the VA, which received $70.2 billion, including $33 billion in discretionary funding. That was a less-than-inflation increase of 2.5 percent over the previous year, although the funding for medical services got a bigger boost. The total for the VA included $1.2 billion in emergency VA health funds, though the president had to request that the money be designated as an emergency. He subsequently did so Jan. 28, 2006.

Funding for the department included:

▸ $29.1 billion for the Veterans Health Administration, comprised of $26.9 billion in direct appropriations and $2.2 billion in anticipated fees and other receipts. Veterans' medical services accounted for $22.5 billion of the spending, $1.7 billion or 8 percent more than was provided for fiscal 2005. The conference agreement specified that $2.2 billion be spent on mental health care. Both chambers rejected fee increases proposed by Bush, including a $250 annual enrollment fee for veterans with incomes above about $26,000, and an increase in co-payments for prescription drugs from $7 to $15 for the same veterans.

▸ $37.4 billion for the Veterans Benefits Administration, an increase of $2.1 billion or 6 percent over 2005 funding. Most of the money – $33.9 billion – was mandatory spending for veterans' compensation benefits and pensions.

● **Military construction.** The military construction portion of the bill appropriated $12.2 billion, $866 million or about 8 percent more than 2005 funding. The appropriations included:

▸ $6.2 billion for military construction – $5.1 billion for active-duty forces, and $1.1 billion for the National Guard and reserve forces. The combined total was $525 million less than 2005 funds.

▸ $4 billion for construction and maintenance of family housing, a decrease of about $55 million.

▸ $1.8 billion for Base Realignment and Closure (BRAC) accounts – $1.5 billion for the 2005 round and $255 million for environmental cleanup remaining from the 1990 round. *(BRAC, p. 6-8)*

## LEGISLATIVE ACTION
### HOUSE COMMITTEE ACTION

The House Appropriations Committee gave voice vote approval May 18 to $121.8 billion measure (HR 2528 – H Rept 109-95) that included $85.2 billion in discretionary funds, a 7 percent increase over funding for comparable programs in fiscal 2005.

The bill included:

▸ $68.1 billion for the VA, about 4 percent more than it got for fiscal 2005, including $31.5 billion in discretionary spending, a decrease

## WHERE THE MONEY GOES — FISCAL 2006 APPROPRIATIONS
# MILITARY CONSTRUCTION-VETERANS AFFAIRS
## HR 2528 — PL 109-114

(figures are in thousands of dollars of new budget authority)

| | Fiscal 2005 appropriations | Fiscal 2006 Bush request | House passed | Senate passed | Conference report |
|---|---|---|---|---|---|
| **GRAND TOTAL** | $78,799,417 | $81,726,037 | $80,531,818* | $82,984,618 | $82,573,514 |
| Discretionary spending** | 42,269,959 | 45,100,419 | 43,906,200 | 44,382,000 | 44,143,000 |
| **MAIN COMPONENTS** | | | | | |
| **Defense Department** | $11,300,304 | $12,116,611 | $12,262,392 | $12,116,611 | 12,166,611 |
| Military construction | 6,736,849 | 5,344,291 | 5,840,580 | 5,893,777 | 6,211,412 |
| Family housing | 4,074,603 | 4,242,169 | 4,201,661 | 4,133,683 | 4,019,048 |
| Base realignment and closure | 246,166 | 2,258,293 | 1,948,293 | 1,882,293 | 1,759,293 |
| **Veterans Affairs** | 67,338,832 | 69,454,300 | 68,112,300 | 70,710,881 | 70,249,277 |
| Veterans Benefits Administration | 35,261,848 | 36,780,131 | 36,780,131 | 36,780,131 | 37,360,027 |
| Veterans Health Administration | 29,688,875 | 30,180,684 | 28,820,684 | 31,332,943 | 29,115,252 |

* As originally passed by the House, the bill totaled $121.8 billion, including the Defense Health Program and the family housing allowance. For conference, however, the House followed the Senate's lead and moved those accounts to the separate Defense spending bill (HR 2863).
** Does not include emergency spending

TABLE: House, Senate Appropriations committees

of just over 2 percent. The committee did not include fee increases for medical care or prescription drugs for some veterans as requested by the administration.

▶ $28.8 billion for the Veterans Health Administration in the Department of Veterans Affairs. That included $21 billion for medical services, a 9 percent increase over 2005 spending not counting supplemental 2005 funds. But veterans' groups complained that after accounting for things like savings that were supposed to come from greater efficiency and fee collections that might not materialize, the increase would be closer to 3 percent. Even 9 percent, they said, would not be enough to keep pace with veterans' needs for medical services.

Joseph A. Violante, national legislative director for Disabled American Veterans, called the bill "a 10-month budget" and said it was "not enough to keep up with the current veterans in the system, let alone the new veterans coming back from Iraq and Afghanistan."

Chet Edwards of Texas, ranking Democrat on the subcommittee, complained about inadequate funding for veterans' health care, but noted that, "Despite these serious concerns … choices had to be made."

The report accompanying the bill stressed that the VA should prepare for the special needs of veterans returning from Iraq and Afghanistan, particularly those suffering post-traumatic stress disorder. The panel described mental health care as "one of the most pressing issues" facing the department and specified that $2.2 billion of the medical services money be set aside for speciality mental health care.

The committee also acknowledged the severity of the wounds that the new generation of veterans was dealing with. "Advances in battlefield medicine have resulted in dramatic increases over previous conflicts in the percentage of service personnel who survive their wounds," the report said. "The other side of this salutary change is an increase in certain medical cases, such as amputee and trauma cases."

▶ $20 billion for the Defense Health Program, $192 million more than Bush sought and $1.8 billion or 10 percent above fiscal 2005 fund-

ing. The program provided worldwide medical and dental services to active duty military personnel and their families.

▶ $5.8 billion for military construction for active-duty, National Guard and Reserve forces, $496 million or 9 percent more than requested and 4 percent more than fiscal 2005 funding.

▶ $4.2 billion for construction and maintenance of family housing, $127 million or 3 percent more than previous funding and $41 million less than requested.

▶ $13.3 billion for the basic housing allowance paid to troops who lived in commercial housing, the same as Bush's request and $1.2 billion or 10 percent more than was appropriated in fiscal 2005.

▶ $1.9 billion for base realignment and closure accounts, $1.6 billion of it for the 2005 round. The total was $310 million less than requested.

The only controversial amendment was offered by David R. Obey of Wisconsin, the committee's ranking Democrat. It would have increased funding for veterans' health care by $2.6 billion, mainly to provide medical services for an additional 10,000 veterans, offset by raising taxes for people making more than $1 million a year.

"There is very little sense of shared sacrifice in this country these days," said Obey, who proposed amendments highlighting the tax breaks to several spending bills.

"The Appropriations Committee does not have the power to manipulate the tax code," responded James T. Walsh, R-N.Y., chairman of the Military Quality of Life and Veterans' Affairs Subcommittee. The amendment was defeated, 27-34.

### HOUSE FLOOR ACTION

The House passed the $121.8 billion bill May 26 on a 425-1 vote after a debate that reflected the growing concern in Congress that not enough money was going to veterans' health care. (House vote 226, p. H-72)

"The bottom line is, we're at war," said Jim McGovern, D-Mass. "And there are more and more veterans coming back. And there is just not enough in this bill to take care of the needs." Republicans responded by pointing to consistent increases in veterans' health care funding since

fiscal 1999, when spending totaled $17.3 billion.

During the floor debate, the House:

▶ Narrowly defeated a proposal by Charlie Melancon, D-La., to add $53 million for veterans' programs, while cutting $169 million from the 2005 BRAC account. The vote was 213-214. *(House vote 224, p. H-72)*

▶ Rejected, 171-254, an amendment by Earl Blumenauer, D-Ore., to add $351 million to complete all environmental remediation at bases closed during the 1988 round, offset by an equal cut to the 2005 BRAC account. *(House vote 225, p. H-72)*

## SENATE COMMITTEE ACTION

The Senate Appropriations Committee voted 28-0 on July 21 to approve an $83 billion version of the bill (HR 2528 — S Rept 109-105), with $44.4 billion in discretionary spending, not including $2 billion in emergency fiscal 2006 funds for veterans' health care. The Military Construction-VA Subcommittee had added the $2 billion before approving the bill two days earlier. Bush requested the money July 14, although he did not ask that it be designated as emergency spending. About $300 million of the request was to replace fiscal 2005 VA funds the administration had thought would not be needed and could be carried over to fiscal 2006.

The committee-approved bill included:

▶ $70.7 billion overall for the Veterans Affairs Department, including $34.1 billion in discretionary funding. The total was $2.6 billion more than in the House version, which did not contain the extra veterans' health funding.

▶ $31.3 billion for the Veterans Health Administration within the VA account, $2.5 billion more than in the House bill. That included $23.3 billion for medical services, about $2.3 billion more than in the House bill.

▶ $5.9 billion for service-specific military construction, $53 million more than in the House bill, and $4.1 billion for family housing, $68 million below the House bill. The bill did not include funds for the basic housing allowance, which was covered in the Senate's Defense spending bill.

▶ $1.9 billion for BRAC, $66 million less than in the House bill.

In writing the bill, subcommittee Chairwoman Kay Bailey Hutchison, R-Texas, rejected White House fee proposals that she said would total nearly $1.2 billion, including a $250 enrollment fee for VA health care and increased prescription drug co-payments for some higher-income veterans. The subcommittee allocation for the bill was increased to make up for the absence of those revenues.

Hutchison won praise from Democrats for including a provision that would require quarterly expenditure reports from the VA in an effort to prevent future shortfalls.

The committee report said the Department of Defense should "submit and receive approval of a spending plan for BRAC 2005 before moving to obligate funds in this account." It also reiterated Congress' concern that the Pentagon integrate its decisions about base closings, the planned redeployment of overseas troops to home bases, and the need for housing facilities and base infrastructure to support the returning troops.

The committee also sought to short-circuit any closure or other changes in fiscal 2006 to 18 VA facilities that were under review, including a facility in Waco, Texas, Hutchison's home state.

## SENATE FLOOR ACTION

The Senate passed the bill with little debate Sept. 22. The vote was 98-0. *(Senate vote 243, p. S-47)*

During the brief floor debate, the Senate took only one roll call vote on an amendment, rejecting, 48-50, a proposal to shift funds from VA information technology to a veterans' counseling program. *(Senate vote 242, p. S-47)*

The Senate adopted several amendments by voice vote, including proposals by the following senators:

▶ Independent James M. Jeffords of Vermont, to provide training and protocols to enable medical clinicians to meet mental health care needs.

▶ Ken Salazar, D-Colo., to require the VA to report to Congress on any budget shortfall totaling 2 percent or more of the department's discretionary funding for the year.

▶ Tom Coburn, R-Okla., to require that earmarks or directives in either the House or Senate report be included in the conference report in order to be considered as having been approved by both chambers.

## CONFERENCE/FINAL ACTION

House and Senate conferees approved a final bill Nov. 17. The House adopted the conference report (H Rept 109-305) by a vote of 427-0 on Nov. 18, and the Senate cleared the bill by voice vote later the same day. *(House vote 604, p. H-194)*

Weeks earlier, House and Senate appropriators had resolved their jurisdictional disputes. The House agreed to put funding for several military-related accounts, including the Defense Health Program and the basic housing allowance, in the separate Defense appropriations bill, as the Senate preferred. Appropriators planned to alternate each year between the House and Senate structures for the bill.

Once those accounts were removed, the two bills were not that different: The House measure totaled $80.5 billion; the Senate bill was $81.1 billion, plus the $2 billion in emergency funds. Conferees agreed to $1.2 billion in emergency funds for veterans' health care, with the proviso that the president must declare it as emergency money before he could spend it. The designation allowed appropriators to remain below their cap on discretionary spending.

Lacking confidence that the administration could adequately track returning Iraq and Afghanistan veterans, appropriators included report language requiring quarterly updates on workloads and costs.

Several provisions of the conference report addressed the kinds of wounds being suffered by soldiers in Iraq and Afghanistan. The conferees called for the VA to create three "centers of excellence" for mental health/Post-Traumatic Stress Disorder (PTSD) care. They also required a comprehensive study of how to improve mental health research. Iraq veterans in particular were suffering from high rates of PTSD.

Democratic appropriators praised the increases for veterans' health care but questioned whether another shortfall was looming. Edwards said the VA continued to underestimate the number of veterans enrolling in the health care system.

Differing funding levels between the House and Senate for more than 100 military construction projects — many of them requested by lawmakers rather than the administration — also had to be settled before final passage.

A dispute between House and Senate appropriators over a $45 million family housing project at the Spangdahlem Air Base in Germany delayed final passage of the bill. House appropriators eventually won the funding for what they said was a needed upgrade to dangerously dilapidated housing, but only in return for a Senate-required report on the cost-effectiveness of the project.

Conferees also:

▶ Agreed, at the insistence of Sen. Dianne Feinstein, D-Calif., to allow

the Navy to keep $300 million from land sales to pay for environmental cleanup at closed bases, rather than putting the funds in a general Pentagon account.

▸ Prohibited the construction of new bases in the United States without a specific appropriation and barred the construction of new overseas bases without the prior notification of Congress.

▸ Barred the use of funds in the bill for military construction, land acquisition, or family housing projects at a military installation approved for closure in 2005. The Pentagon also was barred from transferring funds appropriated for such projects or land acquisitions to another account, or to use such funds for another purpose without congressional approval.

▸ Rescinded $29 million in previously appropriated funds for improvements to Karshi-Khanabad Air Base in Uzbekistan. The Uzbek government had asked U.S. forces to leave after the administration criticized the Uzbeks over human rights abuses.

▸ Required the Defense Department to give Congress prior notice of military exercises that involved more than $100,000 in construction costs.

▸ Dropped Senate language requiring that report language appear in the conference report to be considered adopted by both chambers. ■

# White House Prevails on Amtrak, Cuba

AFTER AVERTING A HALF-DOZEN White House veto threats, Congress in November cleared a $137.6 billion fiscal 2006 appropriations bill for the departments of Transportation, Treasury and Housing and Urban Development (HUD). The bill included $7.3 billion more than Bush requested and $4.1 billion more than comparable programs received the year before.

The final bill included $65.9 billion in discretionary funds, 4 percent more than Congress provided in fiscal 2005 and almost 9 percent more than the administration requested. President Bush signed the measure into law Nov. 30 (HR 3058 – PL 109-115).

The totals do not reflect a 1 percent across-the-board cut in most discretionary appropriations enacted as part of the fiscal 2006 Defense spending bill (PL 109-148).

Because of a reorganization in the House and Senate Appropriations committees early in the year, the measure for the first time covered not only the Transportation and Treasury departments, but also HUD, the federal judiciary and the District of Columbia.

It took a major push by appropriators to complete the complex bill before the Thanksgiving recess. The two chambers had significant differences over money – the House passed a $140 billion bill in June; the Senate passed a $142 billion version in July. They also were at odds over numerous specific accounts. The Senate, for example, wanted to appropriate $40.2 billion in highway funds, compared with $36.3 billion in the House version. The two bills attracted a number of controversial policy riders, and the White House identified six provisions that it said were likely to trigger a presidential veto.

"This is not a simple bill," said Christopher S. Bond, R-Mo., chairman of the Senate Transportation-Housing-Education Appropriations Subcommittee. "It is like a Rube Goldberg machine with many complex moving parts."

All the provisions that triggered veto warnings were ultimately dropped or modified to satisfy the White House.

Two of the highest-profile issues were Amtrak funding and a provision that would have made it easier to sell agricultural products to Cuba. The Bush administration had been pushing Congress for years to restructure the money-losing national passenger railroad or sell it off to states or private businesses. This time, the White House upped the ante by recommending no funding for Amtrak and promising a veto if the railroad got too much money without language overhauling operations. The final bill paired Amtrak funding with requirements that it separate its capital and operating budgets and take certain other steps.

Conferees struck the Cuba language from the final bill, although it had been adopted in both chambers.

They also dropped House provisions that would have restricted the administration's ability to bid out federal jobs to private companies and prevented the Federal Aviation Administration (FAA) from implementing an existing private contract for flight-servicing stations. They renewed existing language that banned coverage of abortions through federal employee health plans, except in cases of rape, incest or danger to the life of the woman. The Senate bill would have dropped the provision.

## HIGHLIGHTS

The following are major components of the fiscal 2006 Transportation-Treasury-HUD law:

● **Transportation Department.** $60.7 billion for the department, $2.4 billion or 4 percent more than requested and 2 percent above fiscal 2005 funding. The total included funding for the Federal Highway Administration, mass transit, the FAA and Amtrak.

● **Highways.** Authority to release a record $36 billion from the Highway Trust Fund to pay for construction and repairs on the Interstate Highway System and other roads. The total fulfilled mandates in the 2005 surface transportation law (PL 109-59). The measure also rescinded about $1.4 billion in previously appropriated spending, providing a net funding level of $34.7 billion for highways. The previous record was $34.4 billion, set in the fiscal 2005 spending law. Bush requested a net $34.7 billion. *(Fiscal 2005 law, 2004 Almanac, p. 2-43)*

● **Transit.** $8.6 billion for public mass transit programs, $809 million or 10 percent above Bush's request and a 12 percent increase over the previous year.

● **FAA.** A net total of $13.8 billion for programs administered by the FAA, $1.1 billion or nearly 9 percent more than Bush sought and about 2 percent above fiscal 2005 funding. The bill allowed the obligation of $3.6 billion from the Airport Trust Fund for federal airport improvement grants, $550 more than Bush requested and 2 percent above 2005 funding. It provided $8.2 billion for FAA operations, an increase of $473 million or 6 percent over 2005 and about equal to Bush's request.

● **Amtrak.** $1.3 billion in grants to Amtrak, nearly 9 percent more than in fiscal 2005. Bush's budget included $360 million to continue commuter rail operations in the event that Amtrak shut down, but no funds for the railroad itself.

● **Treasury.** $11.7 billion, 4 percent above fiscal 2005 spending and virtually the same as Bush's request. Most of Treasury's funding – $10.7 billion – was for the IRS.

● **HUD.** $34 billion, a 7 percent increase over 2005 spending and about 17 percent more than the $29.1 billion that Bush requested. A major reason for the difference with Bush was his request that Congress eliminate community and economic development programs under HUD, and consolidate them into a new grant program under the Commerce Department. Congress rejected that proposal and provided $4.2 billion for HUD's Community Development Fund.

● **Federal judiciary.** $5.8 billion for the federal courts, including the Supreme Court, federal district and appeals courts and the Court of International Trade. The total was $215 million or 4 percent less than Bush requested, but about 6 percent above 2005 funding. It included cost-of-living raises for federal judges.

● **District of Columbia.** $603 million for the federal payment to the district, an increase of about 9 percent over 2005 and $30 million or 5 percent over the request. *(D.C., p. 2-20)*

● **Office of Personnel Management.** $18.7 billion for the government's human resources agency, virtually all of it mandatory spending for federal employee retirement plans.

● **Executive Office of the President.** $735.5 million. For the fifth year,

## WHERE THE MONEY GOES — FISCAL 2006 APPROPRIATIONS

# TRANSPORTATION-TREASURY-HOUSING

## HR 3058 — PL 109-115

*(figures are in thousands of dollars of new budget authority)*

| | Fiscal 2005 appropriations | Fiscal 2006 Bush request | House passed | Senate passed* | Conference report |
|---|---|---|---|---|---|
| **GRAND TOTAL**** | $133,497,489 | $130,310,462 | $139,985,796 | $141,990,216 | $137,623,600 |
| Grand total after scorekeeping | 127,656,455 | 126,137,112 | $134,889,098 | 137,909,866 | 133,380,813 |
| Discretionary spending | 63,172,323 | 60,720,133 | 66,934,248 | 66,395,000 | 65,900,000 |
| **MAIN COMPONENTS** | | | | | |
| **Department of Transportation** | $59,722,623 | $58,296,854 | $63,468,595 | $64,244,175 | $60,676,546 |
| Federal Highway Administration | 34,422,400 | 34,700,000 | 36,287,100 | 40,194,259 | 36,032,344 |
| Federal Aviation Administration | 13,549,460 | 12,710,000 | 14,630,920 | 13,609,500 | 13,815,000 |
| Federal Transit Administration | 7,646,336 | 7,781,000 | 8,482,000 | 8,208,645 | 8,590,365 |
| Amtrak | 1,207,264 | 0*** | 1,176,248 | 1,450,000 | 1,315,000 |
| **Treasury Department** | 11,213,146 | 11,648,698 | 11,529,164 | 11,698,136 | 11,689,473 |
| **Department of Housing and Urban Development** | 31,915,207 | 29,147,486 | 33,670,898 | 34,758,734 | 33,974,171 |
| **The Judiciary** | 5,426,217 | 5,970,945 | 5,767,650 | 5,778,492 | 5,756,377 |
| **District of Columbia (federal payment)** | 555,521 | 573,397 | 603,397 | 593,000 | 603,000 |

* As originally passed by the Senate, the bill did not include District of Columbia funds.
** Total budgetary resources, including limitations on obligations and exempt obligations mainly from the Highway Trust Fund.
*** President Bush requested $360 million for rail service in the Northeast Corridor for use in the event Amtrak shut down.

TABLE: House Appropriations Committee

appropriators turned down Bush's request to consolidate White House funding into a single account.

## LEGISLATIVE ACTION

### HOUSE COMMITTEE ACTION

The House Appropriations Committee approved a $139.1 billion version of the bill (H Rept 109-153) by voice vote June 21. The Transportation-Treasury-Housing and Judiciary Appropriations Subcommittee — whose chairman, Joe Knollenberg, R-Mich., drafted the bill — approved the measure by voice vote June 15. The bill called for $6.5 billion or 5 percent more than fiscal 2005 funding and $9.7 billion more than Bush requested. The committee said that most of the increase was to provide spending levels for highway and transit programs that were required under the surface transportation law.

The bill included $66.9 billion in discretionary funding, $6.2 billion more than Bush sought. It also included $19 billion in mandatory spending and $48.2 billion in obligational authority, a special class of money derived primarily from the Highway Trust Fund.

● **Amtrak.** The most controversial feature of the bill was a proposal by Knollenberg to cut Amtrak funds by 54 percent. The bill included $550 million for the passenger railway, $657 million less than enacted the previous year, and it specified that none of the funds could be spent on routes that required subsidies of more than $30 per passenger. That would kill about 18 routes nationwide and allow federal dollars to be spent only on the Northeast and California corridors and some Midwestern spurs. Knollenberg said Amtrak could still seek money from states to keep the affected routes running, although states showed little interest in picking up the tab.

Then-Amtrak president David L. Gunn had said a $550 million appropriation would bankrupt the rail line and provide insufficient funds even to shut down operations because of the way union con-

tracts were structured.

● **CDBG.** In another rebuff to Bush, Knollenberg included $4.2 billion for the Community Development Fund, with $3.9 billion designated for the Community Development Block Grant (CDBG) program. Bush proposed to zero out the fund as part of his plan to consolidate community development programs under Commerce.

● **Other funding.** The bill also included:

▶ $36.3 billion for federal highway programs, compared to $34.7 billion requested by Bush. The amount was consistent with the House-passed surface transportation bill (HR 3).

▶ $8.5 billion for transit programs, $700 million above the request.

▶ $14.6 billion for the FAA, $1.9 billion more than the president requested. The total included $3.6 billion for airport improvement grants, $600 million more than Bush requested, and $8 million in unrequested funds to hire and train safety inspectors.

▶ $603.4 million for the District of Columbia.

In the full committee markup, appropriators:

▶ Rejected, 27-34, an amendment by John W. Olver, D-Mass., to boost Amtrak funding to $1.2 billion and add $250 million to the CDBG program. The amendment also would have added $180 million in IRS tax enforcement funds and provided $800 million for a voter-assistance program (PL 107-252) enacted in 2002 in response to problems that occurred at polling places during the 2000 presidential election. That law promised states $3.9 billion in grants to replace outdated voting machines and set up statewide voter databases. It also required states to offer safeguards to prevent the voting irregularities that occurred in 2000. So far, $3 billion had been appropriated for that purpose. *(2002 Almanac, p. 14-3)*

Olver proposed to offset the spending by rolling back a portion of the 2001 tax cut for the wealthiest individuals.

▶ Adopted by voice vote an amendment by Rosa DeLauro, D-Conn., to prohibit the use of government money to produce prepackaged news

stories that did not disclose their funding source. Similar language was included in the House Agriculture spending bill (HR 2744).

▶ Rejected by voice vote an amendment by Todd Tiahrt, R-Kan., to add the promotion of the aviation industry to the FAA's mandate.

▶ Adopted by voice vote an amendment by Minority Whip Steny H. Hoyer, D-Md., to ensure that federal civilian employees received annual pay raises equal to those of the Defense Department.

## HOUSE FLOOR ACTION

The House passed the bill by a vote of 405-18 on June 30, following two days of debate in which members more than doubled funding in the bill for Amtrak and rejected a series of amendments designed to ease restrictions on travel to Cuba. The total for the bill was calculated at $140 billion. *(House vote 358, p. H-110)*

The action allowed Appropriations Chairman Jerry Lewis, R-Calif., to achieve his goal of passing all 11 House spending bills by the July Fourth recess — the earliest the task had been completed since 1988.

The bill included $63.5 billion for the Transportation Department, $11.5 billion for the Treasury, $33.7 billion for HUD and $5.8 billion for the federal judiciary.

● **Amtrak.** While the floor debate was more civilized than the previous year's scorched-earth fight between appropriators and authorizers — which ended with 80 percent of the bill's funding deleted — the vote to stave off potentially fatal cuts to Amtrak's budget came as a major surprise. In recent years, the House had backed Bush administration proposals to slash the passenger railroad's funding to about $900 million — roughly half of Amtrak's request. The Senate then pressed for more funding and conferees split the difference, approving about $1.2 billion.

During the floor debate, the House:

▶ Adopted by voice vote a proposal to boost Amtrak funding to $1.2 billion, offset by taking bites out of several other accounts. The amendment was sponsored by Steven C. LaTourette, R-Ohio, chairman of the House Transportation and Infrastructure Railroads Subcommittee, and James L. Oberstar of Minnesota, the ranking Democrat on the full committee.

▶ Adopted, 269-152, an amendment by Corrine Brown, D-Fla., to strike the language that would have denied funding for several underused routes. *(House vote 336, p. H-104)*

● **Cuba.** Lawmakers bowed to a White House veto threat by rejecting several Cuba-related amendments. However, they did not try to remove language in the underlying bill aimed at blocking enforcement of a Feb. 25 administration rule that required agricultural shippers to receive payments prior to releasing shipments to Cuba. Like the amendments, that language had drawn a veto warning. The House:

▶ Defeated, 208-211, an amendment by Jim Davis, D-Fla., to repeal a 2004 Treasury Department regulation curtailing the number of visits Americans could pay to immediate family in Cuba. The regulation allowed such visits only once every three years for two weeks. Previously, Americans could visit Cuban relatives, including aunts, uncles and cousins, once a year without a time limit. In this test vote, 32 Republicans — mostly from agricultural states — voted "yea." Opponent Robert Menendez, D-N.J., argued that the amendment would send a message to Fidel Castro's regime that the United States was compromising on its stance against him. *(House vote 345, p. H-106)*

▶ Rejected, 187-233, an amendment by Barbara Lee, D-Calif., to nullify a 2004 regulation that curtailed educational travel to Cuba. *(House vote 346, p. H-106)*

▶ Rejected, 169-250, a proposal by Charles B. Rangel, D-N.Y., to end

the economic embargo on Cuba. *(House vote 348, p. H-108)*

Jeff Flake, R-Ariz., a strong advocate of easing sanctions on Cuba trade and travel, offered two Cuba-related amendments. One was ruled out of order on parliamentary grounds, and he withdrew the other. After the vote on Davis' amendment, Flake did not offer four other Cuba-related amendments.

● **Outsourcing.** Despite a veto warning, lawmakers supported two amendments aimed at limiting the administration's policy of seeking private bids for certain federal jobs. The House:

▶ Adopted, 222-203, an amendment by Chris Van Hollen, D-Md., to prohibit the administration from enforcing a 2003 Office of Management and Budget (OMB) rule allowing hundreds of thousands of federal jobs to be contracted out to private companies. Van Hollen argued that the rule gave unfair advantages to private companies over federal employees competing for the jobs, and did not do enough to ensure cost savings. Similar language added to the bill the previous two years had been removed or watered down in conference. *(House vote 357, p. H-110)*

▶ Adopted 238-177, an amendment by Bernard Sanders, I-Vt., to nullify an FAA contract with the Lockheed Martin Corp. that shut 38 of 61 flight service stations and privatized all but three of the rest. The stations provided general aviation pilots with weather, terrain, route and other flight information. The White House threatened to veto the bill over this provision, saying that canceling the contract would cost the FAA more than $300 million. *(House vote 347, p. H-106)*

● **Other amendments.** In action unrelated to the bill, the House:

▶ Adopted, 333-92, a provision aimed at blocking a Chinese energy company from acquiring a U.S.-owned oil and natural gas firm in a hostile takeover. The amendment barred the Treasury Department from using any funds to favorably recommend the sale of California-based Unocal Corp. to the China National Offshore Oil Corporation, a government-controlled company. *(House vote 353, p. H-108)*

▶ Adopted, 231-189, an amendment by Scott Garrett, R-N.J., to bar use of funds in the bill to enforce a June 23 Supreme Court ruling in *Kelo v. City of New London* that governments could use eminent domain to seize property for private development. *(House vote 350, p. H-108; eminent domain, p. 14-2)*

## SENATE COMMITTEE ACTION

The Senate Appropriations Committee approved a $141.4 billion version of the bill (HR 3058 — S Rept 109-109) by a vote of 28-0 on July 21. The measure, written by the panel's Transportation-Treasury-Judiciary-HUD Subcommittee, included $65.4 billion in discretionary spending.

Bond, the subcommittee chairman, said he hoped an Amtrak overhaul package could be enacted separately or combined with the appropriations bill. "If Amtrak is not reformed and money is put in [the spending bill], there will be a veto recommendation," he said.

The bill recommended $64.2 billion for the Transportation Department, $776 million more than in the House bill and $5.9 billion more that Bush requested.

Details included:

▶ $40.2 billion in highway spending, compared with $36.3 billion in the House version.

▶ $1.45 billion for Amtrak, compared to $1.2 billion in the House bill. The committee proposed some changes, including prohibiting the rail service from subsidizing food and beverage service or sleeper cars — activities that typically lost money — and allowing Amtrak to charge commuter rail systems for access to its Northwest Corridor. The bill also contained a provision to prevent Amtrak from lobbying members of

Congress on legislation "except to the extent that such efforts are consistent with the program and policies of the Amtrak board of directors." Gunn had not hesitated to publicly and privately advocate for more federal subsidies.

- ▶ $8.2 billion in transit spending, $273 million less than in the House bill.
- ▶ $13.6 billion for the FAA, $1 billion less than in the House version. Senate FAA funding included $3.5 billion for airport improvement grants vs. $3.6 billion in the House-passed bill.
- ▶ $34.8 billion for HUD, about $1 billion more than in the House version and $5.6 billion more than Bush requested.
- ▶ $4.3 billion for the Community Development Fund, compared with $4.2 billion in the House bill; it included $3.8 billion for CDBG formula grants.
- ▶ $11.7 billion for the Treasury Department vs. $11.6 billion in the House bill.
- ▶ $5.8 billion for the federal judiciary, equal to the House version.
- ▶ $593 million for the District, $10 million below the House bill.

## SENATE FLOOR ACTION

Ignoring six separate veto threats, the Senate passed what had become a $142 billion bill, 93-1, on Oct. 20. *(Senate vote 264, p. S-52)*

The cost of cleaning up after hurricanes Katrina and Rita, which had devastated the Gulf Coast a month earlier, dominated the sometimes-dramatic floor debate. An attempt to refocus previously appropriated money toward the needs of the storm-damaged region was angrily turned back.

- **Congressional pay raise.** In a nod to the growing expense of reconstruction efforts following the hurricanes, senators adopted, 92-6, an amendment by Jon Kyl, R-Ariz., to save about $2 million by forgoing an automatic cost-of-living adjustment (COLA) for members of Congress. House leaders of both parties said they favored the COLA, which was worth $3,100. *(Senate vote 256, p. S-51)*
- **Earmarks.** Conservative freshman Tom Coburn, R-Okla., exposed bitter divisions among Republicans over fiscal responsibility when he challenged several veteran senators' home-state projects, arguing that the cost of recovery from hurricanes Katrina and Rita required Congress to be more frugal. The Senate:
- ▶ Agreed, 86-13, to table (kill) a proposal to strip funding for projects such as a Nebraska art museum parking lot, an animal shelter in Rhode Island and a sculpture garden in Washington state. "I don't need a senator from Oklahoma telling me what's good for the state of Missouri," said Bond, the bill's floor manager. *(Senate vote 260, p. S-52)*
- ▶ Rejected, 15-82, a Coburn amendment to take money previously appropriated for Alaska bridge projects connecting Ketchikan with Gravina Island, and Anchorage with the Knik, and use the money for rebuilding the Interstate 10 bridge in New Orleans. Both Alaska bridges ended in sparsely populated areas, prompting critics to call them "bridges to nowhere." In a tirade on the Senate floor, Alaska Republican Ted Stevens threatened to resign if funds for the two bridges were cut. "This amendment is an offense to me," shouted Stevens, a 37-year veteran of the chamber. "It's not only an offense to me, it's a threat to every person in my state. This amendment is not going to pass. The Senate is warned." *(Senate vote 262, p. S-52)*
- ▶ Rejected, 33-61, a competing Stevens amendment to freeze all bridge money in the 2005 highway bill until New Orleans' I-10 bridge repairs were funded through non-emergency spending. *(Senate vote 263, p. S-52)*
- **Cuba.** Byron L. Dorgan, D-N.D., withdrew an amendment to lift the

prohibition on travel to Cuba, after John Ensign, R-Nev., offered a second-degree amendment that would have toughened abortion laws. In 2003 and 2004, the Senate version of the bill had included language to remove the Cuba travel ban. Though Dorgan withdrew the travel ban amendment, the underlying bill still contained language similar to that in the House bill to ease the sale of agricultural goods to the communist nation.

- **Minimum wage.** GOP leaders paired an effort by Edward M. Kennedy, D-Mass., to raise the minimum wage with a competing Republican plan, sending both to defeat. In both cases, the sponsors failed to overcome a budget point of order, a procedural step requiring 60 votes.

The Senate:

- ▶ Rejected, 47-51, Kennedy's proposal to increase the minimum hourly wage to $5.70 six months after the bill's enactment, and to $6.25 one year after enactment. The wage had remained at $5.15 since 1997. *(Senate vote 257, p. S-51)*
- ▶ Rejected, 42-57, the Republican amendment, offered by Michael B. Enzi of Wyoming, which was similar to Kennedy's but also included a number of tax breaks for small businesses. *(Senate vote 258, p. S-51)*
- **Other amendments.** In other action, the Senate:
- ▶ Rejected an attempt by Northeastern lawmakers to provide $3.1 billion more for the federal Low Income Home Energy Assistance Program (LIHEAP). Supporters failed, 53-46, to waive the Budget Act and allow the amendment — a step requiring 60 votes in the Senate. *(Senate vote 261, p. S-52)*
- ▶ Rejected, 44-54, an amendment by Dorgan to set up a task force, modeled on the Truman Commission during World War II, to probe contracting abuses stemming from the war in Iraq and the Gulf Coast reconstruction. Republicans were worried enough to have Vice President Dick Cheney in the chamber in case his vote was needed to break a tie. *(Senate vote 259, p. S-51)*
- ▶ Agreed by voice vote to a proposal by Susan Collins, R-Maine, to repeal a provision in the $51.8 billion Hurricane Katrina supplemental spending bill (PL 109-62) enacted in September that increased the amount federal employees could charge on government credit cards for "micropurchases" from $2,500 to $250,000. OMB already had ordered federal employees to ignore the controversial increase and stick to the old $2,500 cap. But Collins, who chaired the Homeland Security and Governmental Affairs Committee, wanted to put the change into law.
- ▶ Adopted by voice vote an amendment by Charles E. Grassley, R-Iowa, to stop funding the long-running independent counsel investigation of Henry G. Cisneros, HUD secretary under President Bill Clinton. Cisneros, who pleaded guilty in 1999 to a misdemeanor charge of lying to the FBI about payments he made to a woman with whom he was having an affair, had been under investigation since 1995. Clinton pardoned him in 2001, on his last day as president. Democrats had sought in the past to end the independent counsel investigation, calling it costly and unnecessary.

GOP leaders averted a floor fight over campaign finance with a last-minute decision to pull a provision that would have lifted all limits on the amounts that leadership political action committees (PACs) could give to political parties. The 2002 campaign finance law (PL 107-155) allowed leadership PACs to contribute $15,000 annually to a political party. The provision drew no attention until the spending bill was on the floor, where John McCain, R-Ariz., and Russ Feingold, D-Wis., two of the main authors of the 2002 law — raised strong objections. McCain threatened to hold up action on the entire bill unless the provision was removed. Bond had put the language in the bill, and he and Majority Leader Bill Frist, R-Tenn., agreed to drop it. *(2002 Almanac, p. 14-7)*

**CONFERENCE/FINAL**

House and Senate negotiators reached agreement on a $137.6 billion spending bill early in the morning of Nov 18. The House adopted the conference report (H Rept 109-307), 392-31, later in the day, and the Senate cleared the bill by voice vote Nov. 21. *(House vote 605, p. H-192)*

The following were among the issues settled in conference:

● **Cuba**. As expected, conferees dropped the provision in both bills that would have prevented the use of funds in the measure to implement the February regulation placing new restrictions on agricultural trade with Cuba. "The administration is simply flat, dead wrong on that one," Bond said. "The Treasury has imposed an impossible restriction on sales to Cuba."

● **Amtrak.** Congress appropriated $1.3 billion for Amtrak, halfway between the House and Senate bills. For the first time, it separated operations funding from capital funding. The bill provided $495 million for operating subsidy grants and $780 million to maintain and repair capital infrastructure. It required Amtrak to increase its operational efficiency, including changes in food and beverage service and first class service, and barred the railroad from offering discounts of more than 50 percent at peak hours. If the Transportation Department inspector general could not certify that Amtrak had shown "operational savings" by July 1, 2006, none of Amtrak's money could be used to subsidize food, beverage and sleeper car services.

● **Pay provisions.** The final bill included a 3.1 percent pay raise for federal civilian employees, equal to that for military personnel. Bush proposed a 2.3 percent increase for civilian personnel.

Conferees dropped the Senate provision that would have rejected the automatic COLA for lawmakers; as a result, they were set to get a 1.9 percent pay increase in 2006.

● **CDBG.** The conference agreement provided $4.2 billion for various community development activities financed through HUD's Community Development Fund, including $3.7 billion for CDBG formula grants.

● **Outsourcing.** Conferees dropped the House language that would have blocked changes to the rules for outsourcing government jobs, but they included modified Senate language to prevent the government from contracting out government jobs performed by more than 10 employees unless the change would save 10 percent or $10 million, whichever was less.

The House amendment that would have blocked the privatization of flight service stations also was dropped.

The conference agreement generally prevented federal agencies funded under the measure from contracting with expatriate companies that relocated overseas.

● **Eminent domain.** The final bill prohibited the use of funds for federal, state or local projects that used eminent domain to seize property primarily for private economic development.

● **Airport improvement grants.** The bill set an obligation limit of $3.6 billion, splitting the difference between the House and Senate bills, for Airport Trust Fund grants. The statement of managers directed that funding be provided to 124 specified "high priority" projects.

● **Earmarks.** Bowing to criticism of "pork-barrel" spending in light of mounting hurricane-relief costs and pressure to rein in the budget deficit, conferees redirected $454 million earmarked in the highway bill for the two bridges in Alaska, although the state still got the money to use at its discretion. ■

# War Supplemental Has Strings Attached

CONGRESS CLEARED AN $82 BILLION fiscal 2005 emergency supplemental spending bill in May, virtually all of it to pay for operations in Iraq and Afghanistan. While the total equaled President Bush's request, lawmakers altered the mix of funds, providing more for military operations and less for international assistance than the White House wanted. They also declined to give the Pentagon the near-full discretion it sought to determine how the funds would be allocated. Bush signed the measure into law May 11 (HR 1268 — PL 109-13).

The final bill also included a package of immigration-related provisions that tightened requirements for foreigners seeking asylum in the United States and established national standards for state driver's licenses. Though the changes were not part of Bush's request, they were a strong priority for House Republicans.

The supplemental brought the amount appropriated for operations in Iraq and Afghanistan and for enhanced security at U.S. military installations since Sept. 11, 2001, to $350.6 billion, according to the Congressional Research Service. Congress had already provided $25 billion in supplemental fiscal 2005 funds as part of the fiscal 2005 Defense appropriations bill (PL 108-287). Because the funding was classified as emergency spending, it did not count against limits on regular discretionary appropriations. *(2004 Almanac, p. 2-12)*

The Army was the big winner in the new bill, getting $17 billion for general operations and maintenance, $459 million for aircraft, $310 million for missiles and $2.6 billion for weapons and tracked combat vehicles. It also was in the most need of extra cash. To tide the Army over until the bill could be signed, the Pentagon shifted $1.1 billion of existing funds into Army coffers, saying the funding was "critically needed" to prevent exhausting operations and maintenance accounts.

Bush's $82 billion request, submitted Feb. 14, included $75 billion for the Department of Defense; $5.6 billion for foreign aid, peacekeeping and other foreign relations activities; $418 million for homeland security efforts; and $950 million for victims of the tsunami that caused widespread destruction in South Asia in December 2004.

While Congress was willing to meet the overall request, both chambers sought to change the way it would be allocated. The House passed an $81.4 billion version of the bill in March that favored military-related spending and attached provisions to make broad changes in immigration laws. The Senate passed an $81.2 billion bill in April that called for $2 billion less than the House for Defense spending but included more than the House for foreign policy activities and homeland security. The Senate bill also had far fewer immigration provisions.

The final bill provided about $900 million more than Bush requested for military operations in Iraq and Afghanistan through the end of fiscal 2005. It also provided about $766 million more than he sought for border security and other homeland security needs. Lawmakers made up the difference mainly by shaving about $500 million from the proposed funding for foreign policy activities and paying for another $1 billion by rescinding previously appropriated spending. The final bill also provided $907 million in tsunami relief.

**BOX SCORE 2005** FISCAL YEAR

**WAR SUPPLEMENTAL**

**BILL:**
HR 1268 — PL 109-13

**LEGISLATIVE ACTION:**

**House** passed HR 1268 (H Rept 109-16), 388-43, on March 16.

**Senate** passed HR 1268, amended (S Rept 109-52), 99-0, on April 21.

**House** adopted the conference report (H Rept 109-72), 368-58, on May 5.

**Senate** cleared the bill, 100-0, on May 10.

**President** signed May 11.

## HIGHLIGHTS

The following are the major components of the final bill:

- **Defense Department.** $75.9 billion, $909 million or about 1 percent more than Bush requested. Defense spending included:

  ▶ $37.1 billion for military operations in Iraq and Afghanistan, $975 million less than requested. The total included $5.7 billion to train and equip security forces in Iraq and $1.3 billion for security forces in Afghanistan.

  ▶ $17.4 billion, $1.2 billion more than requested, to replace equipment and munitions expended during the war in Iraq and other anti-terrorist operations. Much of the increase was for Army and Marine Corps force-protection measures, including additional trucks, truck and body armor, night-vision goggles, and electronic roadside-bomb jammers. The total included $611 million for add-on vehicle armor kits and $150 million for up-armored Army Humvees, both of which were needed to provide additional protection from anti-tank and anti-personnel mines.

  ▶ $17.4 billion for military personnel, $578 million more than requested, mainly to pay for increased death benefits.

  ▶ $5 billion, the full amount requested, for a multi-year initiative first announced in 2003 to restructure the Army and Marine forces into more flexible modular units that could be more easily deployed. The funding was spread through several accounts.

  ▶ $1.1 billion for military construction, $271 million less than requested, mainly for facilities in Iraq, Afghanistan and nations providing support for U.S. operations.

  ▶ Expanded benefits for survivors of service members who died in combat or combat-related activities. The law authorized $765 million to cover the higher cost of the benefits, some of which were retroactive.

- **Foreign affairs activities.** $5.1 billion, $464 million less than Bush requested, for foreign policy activities. However, a $1 billion rescission of previously appropriated but unused aid to Turkey brought the net total to $4.1 billion. The funds included $1.7 billion for continuing relief and reconstruction in Afghanistan; $680 million for international peacekeeping in the Darfur region of Sudan, as well as in Cote D'Ivoire, Haiti and Burundi, and $592 million for a new U.S. Embassy compound in Baghdad.

- **Homeland security.** $1.2 billion, $766 million more than requested, for what Congress described as "domestic appropriations for the war on terror." The total included $635 million for border security and $242 million for the Justice Department. But the category was also a bit of a grab bag. It included $112 million, as requested, for U.S. Coast Guard operations in support of operations in Iraq and Afghanistan, and $84 million for international nuclear nonproliferation.

- **Tsunami relief.** $907 million, $42 million less than requested, to aid victims of the December 2004 tsunami in South Asia.

- **Immigration.** Most of a House-passed measure that set tighter restrictions for state driver's licenses and for asylum, and waived state environmental laws to allow completion of a 14-mile U.S.-Mexico border fence near San Diego.

## LEGISLATIVE ACTION
### HOUSE COMMITTEE ACTION

The House Appropriations Committee approved an $81.3 billion version of the bill (HR 1268 — H Rept 109-16) by voice vote March 8, after agreeing to increase military death benefits and restore food aid for Sudan that had been requested by Bush but dropped from the draft written by committee Chairman Jerry Lewis, R-Calif.

The total was about $675 million below Bush's request, but several lawmakers on both sides of the aisle complained that it still included items that did not qualify as emergencies, such as funds for international peacekeeping, a U.S. embassy in Iraq and Army reorganization plans.

As approved by the committee, the bill included:
- **Defense.** $76.8 billion for the Pentagon, $1.9 billion more than requested. The bill recommended $18.2 billion — $2.1 billion more than Bush sought — for procurement, primarily for equipment to safeguard Army troops in Iraq.

The committee recommended full funding of the administration's request for $4.6 billion to reorganize the Army into more modular units. Although some members questioned whether this belonged in an emergency supplemental bill, the committee said the funds would be used for units that would deploy to Iraq or Afghanistan later in 2005 or in 2006.
- **Foreign affairs programs.** A total of $4.2 billion, about $1.6 billion less than requested, for foreign assistance, State Department activities, and peacekeeping programs in Sudan and elsewhere. The committee designated $3.2 billion of the total as emergency spending and $992 million as non-emergency funds, which it offset by rescinding $1 billion in previously appropriated but unused aid to Turkey. That brought net funding to $3.2 billion. The funds for Turkey, provided under the fiscal 2003 war supplemental (PL 108-11), had not been obligated because the Turkish parliament had never ratified an agreement not to deploy forces to the Kurdish region of northern Iraq.

Despite objections voiced during the markup, the panel approved $592 million, most of the $658 million requested, for a new U.S. Embassy in Baghdad. Critics questioned the need to fund the embassy in the supplemental rather than through the regular State Department appropriations bill. Republicans said money to begin construction of a highly secure compound was needed immediately.

In drafting the bill, Lewis dropped $400 million, the entire amount requested, for aid to U.S. allies that had provided troops in Iraq. He also cut $200 million from the request for international peacekeeping efforts, leaving just $10 million, and $570 million from reconstruction funds for Afghanistan. The committee generally welcomed Lewis' efforts to pare the foreign aid spending. Jim Kolbe, R-Ariz., chairman of the Foreign Operations Appropriations Subcommittee, said the reductions were intended to eliminate funds that ought to be considered during the regular appropriations process.

The bill included $200 million requested by Bush for economic development in the West Bank and Gaza Strip, but without a "national security waiver" that would allow Bush to send the funds directly to the Palestinian Authority, which many lawmakers viewed as corrupt.
- **Homeland security.** $358 million for domestic anti-terrorism programs, including $110 million for nonproliferation and $112 million for the Coast Guard..
- **Tsunami.** $656 million, $45 million less than requested.

During the markup, the committee:
▶ Adopted, 32-31, an amendment by Jesse L. Jackson Jr., D-Ill., to add $150 million in emergency food aid for the Darfur region of Sudan where government-sponsored mercenaries had waged a campaign of "ethnic cleansing" against the largely black Muslim population, leading to widespread death and displacement and increasing famine.
▶ Adopted, by voice vote, an amendment by David R. Obey of Wisconsin, ranking Democrat on the committee, to ensure that a Pentagon increase in death benefits would cover all personnel killed while on active duty. Bush's fiscal 2006 budget proposed increasing death benefits for soldiers killed in combat zones since the start of the war in Afghanistan in October 2001. Obey's proposal had bipartisan support, including nods from Lewis and John P. Murtha of Pennsylvania, ranking Democrat on the Defense Appropriations Subcommittee.
▶ Adopted by voice vote a proposal by Lewis to authorize the president's plan to increase benefits to families of those killed in Iraq and Afghanistan to $400,000 in subsidized life insurance and $100,000 in a death gratuity.
▶ Adopted by voice vote an amendment by Kolbe to require a White House report on progress made toward reform by the Palestinian Authority. Of the $200 million included in the bill for Palestinian assistance, $5 million would be used to fund an independent audit of the authority's financial system.
▶ Rejected, 25-39, a proposal by Obey to create a select committee to review contract awards for reconstruction work in Iraq and Afghanistan.

### HOUSE FLOOR ACTION

The House passed the bill, 388-43, on March 16, after adding another $100 million for disaster relief and refugee assistance. That brought the total to $81.4 billion, with a net total of $3.3 billion for foreign relations activities. *(House vote 77, p. H-26)*

During the floor debate, the committee:
▶ Adopted, 258-170, an amendment by Fred Upton, R-Mich., to bar use of funds in the bill for embassy construction. A majority from both parties, including 119 Republicans, voted for the amendment. The vote was part of a concerted effort by budget hawks to curb what they said was reckless spending in light of a growing budget deficit. Lewis indicated he would try to restore the money in conference. "The sooner we get [the embassy money], the better," he said, arguing that U.S. diplomatic personnel working in Baghdad needed a secure compound. *(House vote 73, p. H-24)*
▶ Added a set of immigration-related provisions by F. James Sensenbrenner Jr., R-Wis., chairman of the House Judiciary Committee. The language — from a bill (HR 418) the House had passed Feb. 10 — called for new uniform national driver's license standards, including a requirement that states verify that applicants were in the country legally. It also proposed tightening standards for asylum, expanding the definition of terrorist-related activities that would make an alien inadmissible or deportable, and requiring the Homeland Security secretary to waive environmental laws that could impede completion of a stretch of fence along the U.S.-Mexico border. The provisions were added to the bill as part of the rule governing floor debate (H Res 151 — H Rept 109-18), which was adopted by voice vote. *(Asylum restrictions, p. 13-3)*
▶ Adopted by voice vote the extra $100 million for disaster relief and refugee assistance for Sudan and other African countries. The amendment by Jackson was the only change to the bill's bottom line.
▶ Adopted by voice vote an amendment by James P. Moran, D-Va., urging the Pentagon to tell Congress its criteria for success in Iraq.
▶ Rejected, 191-236, an amendment by John F. Tierney, D-Mass., and Jim Leach, R-Iowa, to create a special committee to investigate the use of taxpayers' money in Iraq reconstruction. Amendment supporters questioned how the Defense Department had spent funds it had

already gotten, and noted that the Pentagon had failed to submit at least two reports on war costs required under previous laws. "Spending of this magnitude depends on strict accounting," said House Minority Leader Nancy Pelosi, D-Calif. *(House vote 72, p. H-24)*

▶ Rejected by voice vote a proposal by Tom Tancredo, R-Colo., to eliminate the $656 million for tsunami relief. "I'm not sure we need to provide extra taxpayer dollars," Tancredo said, citing large contributions by private donors.

### SENATE COMMITTEE ACTION

The Senate Appropriations Committee approved an $80.6 billion version of the bill (HR 1268 — S Rept 109-52) by a vote of 28-0 on April 6. The total was $1.5 billion less than Bush requested and $785 million less than the House-passed bill. The committee recommended about 3 percent less than the House for military activities and the same amount as the House for the U.S. Embassy in Baghdad.

Democrats used debate on the bill to criticize the Bush administration's prewar planning in Iraq and its reliance on emergency spending to fund its military operations, rather than using the regular appropriations process. Robert C. Byrd of West Virginia, ranking Democrat on the Appropriations Committee, said that by using supplemental bills, "the president avoids a debate about priorities and whether the war should be paid for."

The Senate committee-approved bill included:

● **Defense.** $74.4 billion for military activities, $2.4 billion less than the House proposed. Senate appropriators focused on priorities similar to the House's — such as replacing battle-damaged equipment and force-protection items — but with less cash. For instance, senators included less than half the money the House did to pay for devices intended to thwart roadside bombs.

Like the House, the committee approved Bush's request for $1.3 billion for Afghan security forces and $5.7 billion for Iraqi security forces.

Also like the House bill, the Senate measure proposed to increase life insurance coverage for troops killed in combat from $250,000 to $400,000 and increase the nation's "death gratuity" from $12,420 to $100,000. The boost would affect any service member killed on active duty after October 2001, when the war in Afghanistan began. Both bills would provide an additional $150,000 to survivors of troops killed in combat.

In addition to apportioning money, the committee used the bill as an opportunity to redirect Pentagon policy by prohibiting the use funds to enforce a "winner-take-all-strategy" for the Navy's next-generation destroyer program. Lawmakers with naval facilities in their home states wanted the Navy to divide work on the DD(X) destroyer between Bath Iron Works in Maine and Northrop Grumman Ship Systems in Mississippi, the home of Republican Thad Cochran, chairman of the Senate Appropriations Committee.

● **Foreign assistance.** $5.1 billion for foreign aid projects, including $592 million for construction of a U.S. Embassy in Iraq. A rescission of $1 billion in unused aid to Turkey reduced the net total to $4.1 billion. The funding included $1.3 billion in economic assistance for Afghanistan and $680 million for U.N. peacekeeping activities. In contrast, the House had included $739 million for the Afghanistan fund and $580 million for U.N. peacekeeping.

Senate appropriators also restored $200 million cut by the House to provide military assistance to allies deploying forces to Iraq and Afghanistan. However, the committee included just $40 million of the $200 million in economic aid that Bush had requested for the allies.

Cochran included in the bill a provision that would preserve $200 million in aid to the Palestinian Authority and give the president the national security waiver that the House omitted. Many senators regarded such waivers as a traditional courtesy to the president.

● **Tsunami relief.** $907 million, $260,000 less than in the House bill.

● **Immigration.** Senate appropriators did not include the House-passed provisions on national standards for driver's licenses, stiffer asylum requirements and completion of the U.S.-Mexico border fence.

● **Homeland security.** The Senate bill included $687 million for domestic anti-terrorism activities, about $329 million more than the House recommended, including $437 million for border security, $110 million for nonproliferation and $112 million for the Coast Guard.

During the markup, the committee:

▶ Agreed by voice vote to an amendment by Mitch McConnell, R-Ky., Sam Brownback, R-Kan., and Barbara A. Mikulski, D-Md., to give $50 million of the funds for the West Bank and Gaza to Israel for border control. The proposal was part of a larger "manager's amendment."

▶ Rejected, on a 13-15 party-line vote, an amendment by Byron L. Dorgan, D-N.D., to create a special congressional committee to investigate the billions of dollars spent on reconstruction in Iraq. Ted Stevens, R-Alaska, chairman of the Senate Defense Appropriations Subcommittee, said he opposed Dorgan's amendment because it would duplicate efforts by the Government Accountability Office, the investigative arm of Congress.

### SENATE FLOOR ACTION

The Senate passed the bill, 99-0, on April 21 after increasing the total to $81.2 billion. *(Senate vote 109, S-21)*

● **Immigration.** For almost a week, Senate action on the bill was sidetracked by a debate on immigration, but only one major amendment ultimately was attached to the bill. The Senate:

▶ Adopted, 94-6, language by Mikulski to exempt seasonal workers who worked in the United States in previous years from a cap on the number of so-called H-2B visas issued nationwide. Amendment supporters said the cap of 66,000 was reached early in the fiscal year, leaving an insufficient workforce for the summer tourism and seafood harvesting seasons. Hotels, restaurants, and the crab and lobster industries were among those who most relied on temporary immigrants. *(Senate vote 102, p. S-20)*

▶ Adopted by voice vote a refinement by Jon Kyl, R-Ariz., that would require the Department of Homeland Security to certify that visa recipients were returning workers.

▶ Rejected, 21-77, a cloture motion that would have ended debate on an amendment by Saxby Chambliss, R-Ga., to create a temporary guest worker program for farm laborers. Under his proposal, eligible workers could have worked in the United States for up to nine years, but they would be unable to obtain permanent resident status without returning home for at least a year and waiting in line with other applicants for green cards. A cloture motion requires 60 votes to prevail. *(Senate vote 97, p. S-20)*

▶ Rejected, 53-45, a cloture motion on a competing amendment by Larry E. Craig, R-Idaho, and Edward M. Kennedy, D-Mass., to create a two-step process for agricultural workers to apply for temporary and then permanent legal residency status. *(Senate vote 98, p. S-20)*

▶ Voted 100-0 to cut off debate on the underlying bill. The two guest worker amendments, and another by Dianne Feinstein, D-Calif., that would have expressed the sense of the Senate that immigration provisions should not be included in the final bill, were then all ruled non-germane and thrown out. *(Senate vote 103, p. S-20)*

● **Defense.** Senators increased funding for the Pentagon to $74.8 billion, still $2 billion less than in the House version. The Senate:

▶ Adopted by voice vote a Chambliss amendment to prohibit the Pentagon from using money in the bill to terminate the C-130J Hercules transport plane, made by Lockheed Martin Corp. in Marietta, Ga.

▶ Adopted, 58-38, an amendment by John W. Warner, R-Va., to require the Navy to maintain 12 aircraft carriers until certain conditions were met. Warner, chairman of the Armed Services Committee and a former Navy secretary with shipbuilding facilities in his home state, successfully argued that the Navy's plans to retire an aircraft carrier would limit the Pentagon's reach in the Pacific Ocean at a time when China was building up its military. He prevailed over Stevens, who argued that Congress should not interfere with the Navy's plans to modernize its force by shedding an older carrier. *(Senate vote 106, p. S-21)*

▶ Adopted, 61-39, an amendment to add $213 million for "up-armored" troop vehicles. Evan Bayh, D-Ind., initially pushed for $742 million, but Republicans opposed that amount. Bayh and Kennedy offered a second amendment, arguing successfully that $213 million was the amount the Defense Department said it needed to sustain maximum production of heavily armored Humvees through the end of fiscal 2005. *(Senate vote 108, p. S-21)*

▶ Adopted by voice vote an amendment by Craig to provide seriously injured troops with additional coverage under the military's life insurance plan, paying them $25,000 to $100,000. A modification offered by Mike DeWine, R-Ohio, and adopted by voice vote made the additional coverage retroactive for troops injured since October 2001.

▶ Adopted, 61-31, a Byrd amendment expressing the sense of the Senate that future funding requests for operations in Afghanistan and Iraq should be included in the president's annual budget, and that the president should submit an amended fiscal 2006 budget detailing war costs. *(Senate vote 96, p. S-20)*

● **Foreign affairs programs.** The Senate:

▶ Agreed, 54-45, to table (kill) an attempt by Tom Coburn, R-Okla., to reduce funding for the Baghdad Embassy to $106 million. *(Senate vote 104, p. S-21)*

▶ Agreed by voice vote to an amendment by Jon Corzine, D-N.J., to dedicate $90.5 million in funding for international peacekeeping specifically to help stop genocide in Sudan. Of the total, $50 million was for peacekeeping and $40.5 million for food aid for the Darfur region.

▶ Adopted by voice vote an amendment by Herb Kohl, D-Wis., to increase food aid to $470 million. The amendment found strong support on both sides of the aisle, including from Indiana Republican Richard G. Lugar, chairman of the Foreign Relations Committee.

● **Homeland security.** The Senate increased funding in the bill for homeland security to $1.2 billion, taking part of it from foreign affairs accounts. Senators:

▶ Adopted by voice vote a proposal by John Ensign, R-Nev., to shift $147 million from international peacekeeping activities to pay for hiring 1,050 border patrol agents and other personnel to manage immigration and customs.

▶ Adopted, 65-34, an amendment by Byrd to provide an extra $390 million to hire new border patrol agents, and pay for it by taking $400 million from State Department funds. *(Senate vote 105, p. S-21)*

● **Military benefits.** The Senate:

▶ Rejected, on 46-54 votes, two amendments offered by Patty Murray of Washington and cosponsored by more than a dozen other Democrats to add $2 billion to the bill to pay for veterans' health care. Murray failed to overcome points of order that the amendments violated

budget rules. Republicans argued that the money was not needed. *(Senate votes 89, 90, p. S-18)*

▶ Adopted by voice vote proposals by John Kerry, D-Mass., to lengthen the time family members could remain in military housing after a service member died and to expand the "death gratuity" benefit. The underlying Senate bill would have increased the death gratuity to $100,000 from $12,420, but the payment was restricted to those killed inside combat zones. Kerry proposed giving the gratuity to any service member killed while on active duty anywhere. Stevens tried to table the amendment on the grounds it would cost too much, but his motion was rejected, 25-75. *(Senate vote 92, p. S-19)*

▶ Adopted by voice vote an amendment by Richard J. Durbin, D-Ill., to make up the difference in salaries of federal employees who were members of the National Guard or reserves and were called to serve in combat. Durbin estimated that reservists lost an average of $368 per month when serving on active duty. An attempt by Stevens to table Durbin's amendment was rejected, 39-61. *(Senate vote 91, p. S-18)*

● **Other.** The Senate adopted, 98-0, an amendment by Byrd to require federal agencies to add disclaimers to video news releases they produced. The vote was a bipartisan rebuke of administration efforts to distribute prepackaged news stories to television stations around the country that touted Bush's policies but did not disclose that the government produced the material. *(Senate vote 95, p. S-19)*

### CONFERENCE/FINAL ACTION

House and Senate conferees began meeting in late April under intense pressure from the Pentagon, which said troops in Iraq would run out of money after the first week of May. They reached agreement on a conference report May 3. The House adopted the report (H Rept 109-72), 368-58, on May 5, after rejecting a motion by Obey to return it to the conference committee with instructions to adopt the higher Senate funding level for immigration and customs enforcement. Obey's motion was rejected, 201-225. The Senate cleared the measure, 100-0, on May 10. *(House votes 160, 161, p. H-52; Senate vote 117, p. S-23)*

While the overall funding levels were nearly identical in both versions of the bill, conferees had many details to spar over.

● **Defense.** Conferees provided $900 million more than Bush requested to equip Army troops in Iraq and Afghanistan — roughly splitting the $2 billion difference between the initial House and Senate figures.

Lawmakers on both sides of the aisle lobbied to included extra dollars for equipment that would protect soldiers, including $60 million for electronic jammers to thwart roadside bombs and $308 million for heavily armored Humvees. John P. Murtha of Pennsylvania, the veteran ranking Democrat on the House Defense Appropriations Subcommittee, said he and the panel's chairman, C.W. Bill Young of Florida, had toured many military facilities and learned of severe equipment shortages. When they asked whether more funding was needed for protective equipment and weapons, "the Army was very emphatic that they needed every cent, as soon as they could get it," he said.

Murtha and other lawmakers said that although the bill did not cover all of the Army's shortages, it went a long way toward correcting serious problems.

Conferees also:

▶ Included $5.7 billion for Iraq security forces and $1.3 billion for Afghanistan forces, as requested, but did not fully accept Bush's request to shift control over the funds from the State Department to the Pentagon. The final bill required that the State Department sign off on expenditures. It required that the Pentagon notify congressional com-

mittees five days in advance of any spending and provide them with quarterly reports.

▶ Kept Byrd's sense-of-the-Senate language calling for war costs to be included in the president's regular budget.

▶ Prohibited the Navy from retiring an aircraft carrier, terminating the C-130J cargo plane, or selecting a single naval yard to build the DD(X) destroyer.

▶ Barred the Pentagon and other federal agencies from distributing video news stories without identifying the source of information.

● **Military benefits.** Conferees provided $765 million to cover expanded benefits for survivors of service members who died in combat or combat-related activities. The bill increased the level of life insurance from $250,000 to $400,000 and increased death benefits to the service member's survivors from $12,240 to $100,000. The provisions were retroactive. The final bill also included a new insurance rider for traumatic injury protection of up to $100,000, and provided a one-year, rather than a six-month, extension of the basic housing allowance for dependents of those who died in Iraq and Afghanistan.

Conferees dropped a Senate provision that would have made up the difference between military and civilian pay of federal employees who were called to active duty as reservists.

● **Foreign affairs programs.** The final bill provided $5.1 billion for international activities — $43 million more than the Senate recommended and $866 million more than in the House bill. Like the House and Senate, conferees agreed to rescind $1 billion in unused aid to Turkey. That brought net funding for international activities to $4.1 billion, all of it emergency appropriations.

Conferees agreed to:

▶ $680 million out of the $780 million requested for international peacekeeping, mainly in Haiti and Africa (the House would have provided $580 million, the Senate $533 million), and $592 million of the $658 million sought to build a new embassy in Baghdad.

▶ $240 million for other countries' efforts in support of the U.S. war on terrorism — $30 million more than requested — but eliminated funding for a similar but separate account called "Global War on Terror Partners Fund." Bush had requested $200 million for the fund. The Senate would have provided $25.5 million; the House zeroed it out.

The conference agreement provided funding for a number of bilateral and international accounts, including:

▶ $200 million, as requested, for economic development in the West Bank and Gaza Strip. However, the conference report allocated the funds to specific programs, including $50 million dedicated to Israeli border control to ease the flow of goods and people between the two sides. The funding was subject to an existing prohibition on providing funds directly to the Palestinian Authority (PL 108-447), although that law allowed the president to waive the restriction if it was in the national security interest of the United States. In addition, the president was required to report to Congress on steps taken by the Palestinian Authority toward good governance, economic reform, and dismantling terrorist organizations.

▶ $1.1 billion in economic assistance for Afghanistan, instead of the $739 million proposed by the House or $1.3 billion requested by the president and supported by the Senate.

▶ $150 million in military support funds for Pakistan, as requested, for improved border security and to enhance interoperability with U.S. forces in the region.

▶ $200 million for Jordan, as requested, with half for economic assistance and half for military aid.

▶ About $400 million for humanitarian assistance in Africa, including about $238 million to aid in the Darfur region of Sudan. The funds came from a number of accounts, including economic aid, international humanitarian food assistance, disaster aid and international peacekeeping.

▶ $680 million for assessed contributions for international peacekeeping programs, most of which was for Sudan. The total was $100 million less than the president's request, but $100 million more than the House proposed and $147 million more than the Senate wanted. The funds were for U.S.-supported missions initiated after the fiscal 2005 budget was completed.

The bill also provided $240 million for voluntary contributions for international peacekeeping, including $200 million for coalition allies providing troops for operations in Iraq and Afghanistan.

● **Immigration.** The House provisions were kept largely intact. Senate conferees won a few concessions, but sponsors and opponents agreed that they made changes only on the margins.

The most significant changes to the original House provisions concerned asylum standards for those seeking U.S. residency to avoid persecution in their home countries. Conferees dropped language that would have allowed deportation of asylum applicants while their cases were pending in federal court. They also softened a provision on judicial review of asylum applicants' credibility. Human rights groups had expressed concern about language that would have allowed judges to consider applicants' demeanor, require corroborating evidence from the very governments that might be persecuting them, and require proof that a single motive explained the persecution.

Language added to the final bill allowed applicants to pick among five central reasons — race, religion, nationality, membership in a particular social group, or political opinion — to prove persecution, rather than requiring them to select a single reason. The final version also lifted the annual cap on the number of applicants granted conditional asylum who could qualify for longer-term status. Sensenbrenner said he supported the changes.

The final bill also:

▶ Softened a provision on easing environmental rules to allow completion of the stretch of fence along the U.S.-Mexico border. The bill authorized the Homeland Security secretary to waive environmental laws that interfered with expeditious completion of the project, but did not require him to do so as the House had recommended. The bill also allowed federal district court challenges to the constitutionality of such waivers — with appeals straight to the Supreme Court.

▶ Included the requirement for uniform national standards for driver's licenses that could be used for federal purposes, such as boarding airplanes, but also allowed states to issue a lower-tier document that would authorize driving for one year without proof of legal residency.

▶ Required states to share drivers' data among themselves and with the federal government. The House version would have gone further, giving states the option of sharing information more broadly through a compact that included Canada and Mexico.

▶ Preserved Mikulski's amendment lifting the cap on the number of H-2B visas for temporary seasonal workers.

● **Homeland security.** Conferees agreed to provide $1.2 billion, slightly less than the Senate wanted but more than three times what the House proposed, for the category of domestic appropriations for the war on terror. The total included $635 million for border security, appeasing senators who said there was an immediate need for more agents. Bush had not requested any funds for border security, and the House bill included none. ■

# Bill Fills Shortfall in Vets' Health Care

BEFORE DEPARTING for the August recess, Congress appropriated $1.5 billion in supplemental spending to make up an unexpected shortfall in fiscal 2005 funding for veterans' health care programs. The emergency money was attached to the fiscal 2006 Interior-Environment spending bill, which President Bush signed into law Aug 2 (HR 2361 — PL 109-54). *(Interior, p. 2-33)*

Six weeks earlier, Veterans Affairs Department officials had told stunned lawmakers that the VA faced shortages of $1 billion in fiscal 2005 and an unknown amount in fiscal 2006 because of faulty health care cost projections. Agency officials told the House Veterans' Affairs Committee June 23 their original spending requests for fiscal 2005 were based on a financial model that predated the 2003 invasion of Iraq. Spending growth had jumped from an expected 2.5 percent to 5 percent since then, and the number of patients had grown significantly because of the war. The officials said they had known about the mistake for two months.

House members were furious they had not been told about the shortfall before they passed their fiscal 2006 spending bill (HR 2528) for the Veterans Affairs Department and military construction in May. California Republican Jerry Lewis, chairman of the Appropriations Committee, said it "borders on stupidity" for the VA not to have come forward sooner.

Democrats, who had attempted earlier in the year to add billions in veterans' funding as part of an Iraq war supplemental (PL 109-13), crowed. "We hate to say, 'I told you so,' " Bob Filner of California said at a news conference with fellow Democrats, "but, 'I told you so.' "

Eager to act, the Senate voted, 96-0, on June 29 to attach $1.5 billion in fiscal 2005 funds for VA medical services to the Interior-Environment spending bill, figuring the funds could spill over into fiscal 2006 if needed. The measure passed later that day. *(Senate vote 166, p. S-33)*

House leaders took a different route, waiting for the administration to submit a request. On June 30, the White House asked Congress for a $975 million fiscal 2005 supplemental. The House passed a stand-alone bill (HR 3130) for that amount by a vote of 419-0 the same day. *(House vote 362, p. H-110)*

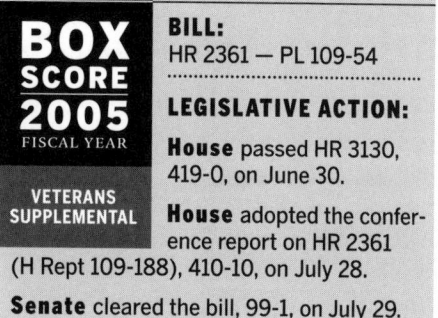

**BOX SCORE 2005** FISCAL YEAR

**VETERANS SUPPLEMENTAL**

**BILL:**
HR 2361 — PL 109-54
.......................................
**LEGISLATIVE ACTION:**
**House** passed HR 3130, 419-0, on June 30.

**House** adopted the conference report on HR 2361 (H Rept 109-188), 410-10, on July 28.

**Senate** cleared the bill, 99-1, on July 29.

**President** signed Aug. 2.

Senators dug in, saying they would accept nothing less than $1.5 billion, which they said would cover the immediate funding gap and give the VA a cushion for fiscal 2006 when the shortfall could amount to $2.7 billion. "I would want and hope the House could be with us on this issue," said Larry E. Craig, R-Idaho, the Senate Veterans' Affairs Committee chairman. "The Senate spoke in a very loud, bipartisan, unanimous way."

House Republicans, however, wanted to stick to the president's request. "They're making up numbers over in the Senate," said Steve Buyer, R-Ind., chairman of the House Veterans' Affairs Committee. "We're not going to make up numbers over here in the House."

The standoff delayed what lawmakers had hoped would be a quick solution, forcing them to go home for the July Fourth recess empty-handed.

After returning to Washington, senators reaffirmed their strong support for the $1.5 billion in emergency fiscal 2005 funding, voting 95-0 on July 12 to add the money to the fiscal 2006 Homeland Security spending bill (HR 2360) as well. *(Senate vote 174, p. S-35)*

On July 14, the White House acknowledged that more funding would be needed. It said the VA would need $2 billion more for health care in fiscal 2006 than Bush had assumed when he sent his budget to Capitol Hill in February. The revised request included $300 million to replace fiscal 2005 VA funds the administration had assumed would be available in fiscal 2006. The $300 million for fiscal 2005 was a surprise, but it helped convince the House to agree to the Senate's $1.5 billion figure.

Lawmakers' desire to get the veterans' funding approved before the August recess in turn helped make the Interior-Environment bill the first of the fiscal 2006 measures to clear. The House adopted the conference report (H Rept 109-188), 410-10, on July 28. The Senate cleared the bill, 99-1, on July 29. *(House vote 450, p. H-138; Senate vote 210, p. S-42)*

To make up the shortfall for fiscal 2006, Congress subsequently approved an extra $1.2 billion in emergency funds for VA health programs as part of the appropriations bill for military construction and Veterans Affairs. *(Military Construction-VA, p. 2-43)* ∎

# Congress Pays Katrina's High Price

HURRICANE KATRINA, which wreaked havoc on New Orleans and the Gulf Coast, was the costliest natural disaster the federal government had ever faced. Congress quickly cleared a pair of emergency supplemental appropriations bills totaling $62.3 billion to begin paying for relief and cleanup. At the end of December — after a furious lobbying effort by the Mississippi delegation — lawmakers came up with a $29 billion package to help the hurricane-ravaged states with urgent infrastructure needs. About $23.4 billion of that was money reallocated from the earlier emergency measures.

Katrina, which ripped through coastal areas of Louisiana, Mississippi and Alabama on Aug. 29, uprooted trees, smashed homes and businesses and left the entire region without power. The extent of the damage soared far beyond initial expectations when levees that protected New Orleans were breached and the rising water flooded 80 percent of the city. Tens of thousands of people crowded into the city's Convention Center and Superdome, where conditions quickly deteriorated.

As the extent of the disaster unfolded, the region's distress turned to growing anger over how long it took for federal and state agencies to reach survivors, many of whom were injured, displaced or without food and water for days. Most were poor and black, and their plight played out hour by hour on national television while the government seemed to do nothing.

On Sept. 2, Bush acknowledged that the relief efforts were "not acceptable," and the president and lawmakers raced to repair the public's faith in the government's willingness and ability to care for its citizens in times of crisis.

"Unacceptable here sadly means people are dying," said Rep. Elijah E. Cummings, D-Md., a member of the Congressional Black Caucus, which gathered as a group to express concern over the relief efforts. "We cannot allow it to be said by history that the difference between those who lived and those who died in the great storm and flood of 2005 was nothing more than poverty, age or skin color."

## $10.5 BILLION 'DOWN PAYMENT'

Congressional leaders cut short their summer recess and returned to Washington to clear a $10.5 billion emergency supplemental to meet immediate needs. The measure gave $10 billion to the Federal Emergency Management Agency (FEMA) and $500 million to the Defense Department. The House passed the bill and the Senate cleared it, both on voice votes, on Sept. 2. Bush, who had requested the funds, signed the bill into law a few hours later (HR 3645 — PL 109-61). During a tour of the region that day, he called it "a small down payment on the cost of this effort."

## $51.8 BILLION FOLLOW UP

On Sept. 8, Bush signed a $51.8 billion emergency spending bill — the largest non-war supplemental spending package in U.S. history (HR 3673 — PL 109-62). The House had passed the bill, 410-11, earlier

**BOX SCORE 2006** FISCAL YEAR

**HURRICANE SUPPLEMENTALS**

**BILLS:**
HR 3645 — PL 109-61;
HR 3673 — PL 109-62

**LEGISLATIVE ACTION:**

**House** passed HR 3645 by voice vote Sept. 2.

**Senate** cleared HR 3645 by voice vote Sept. 2.

**President** signed Sept. 2.

**House** passed HR 3673, 410-11, on Sept. 8.

**Senate** cleared HR 3673, 97-0, on Sept. 8.

**President** signed Sept. 8.

that day, and the Senate cleared it, 97-0. *(House vote 460, p. H-144; Senate vote 223, p. S-44)*

True cost projections could not be tallied with any precision because the last holdouts had yet to be evacuated from the ghost town of New Orleans; the Army Corps of Engineers was expected to take weeks to pump fetid water from the inundated city; and no attempt had been made to account for the thousands presumed dead. But the White House warned that "substantially more" would soon be needed to continue the recovery and begin reconstruction. Congressional leaders predicted that costs to the government would reach $150 billion to $200 billion.

The second supplemental provided $50 billion for FEMA, $1.4 billion for the Defense Department and $400 million for the Army Corps of Engineers. Although Congress included $15 million for an audit of the spending by the inspector general, the supplemental essentially was a government piggy bank with few restrictions.

About half the FEMA money was for human resources and relief, including $2,000 debit cards that were distributed to thousands of families, as well as costs associated with unemployment insurance, housing and medical needs, according to Joshua B. Bolten, director of the White House Office of Management and Budget. A quarter of the FEMA funds were to be disbursed to other federal agencies, including the Department of Health and Human Services, for providing medical care. The remainder was for operations and logistics, including restoration of public infrastructure.

Despite minor grumbling that the bills did not go through regular order, which would have allowed Congress to perform its oversight function, the time-sensitive nature of both requests ensured swift passage. At the time, some lawmakers estimated that the total federal costs for hurricane response could reach $200 billion.

While members were united in their intent to get aid to hurricane survivors as quickly as possible, they also clashed bitterly over who should be held responsible for the initially slow and chaotic response to the storm and over the trustworthiness of FEMA.

"I intend to find out why the federal response, particularly the response of FEMA, was so incompetent and insulting to the people of our states," Democrat Mary L. Landrieu, Louisiana's senior senator, said in her floor speech. "We know that FEMA was unaware that 20,000 Americans were stranded at the Convention Center without food, without water, without security, without clothes, without buses, without toilets and with no way out, and I had to stand there and listen to the news media say these people were lawless. We know that someone has to be accountable."

There was also partisan bickering in the House after Republicans blocked an attempt by David R. Obey of Wisconsin, the ranking Democrat on the Appropriations Committee, to offer an amendment to the supplemental that would have restored FEMA to the status of an independent agency reporting directly to the president and required the FEMA director to have relevant expertise.

"We have a responsibility to know that that money is going to be

spent in the most efficient, the most effective way to save lives, to rebuild communities," Obey said. "We cannot have that confidence under the existing management of this agency."

The House agreed, 221-193, to a procedural move by Lincoln Diaz-Balart, R-Fla., that blocked the FEMA amendment. Republicans argued that this was not the time to make wholesale changes and that amending the supplemental could delay the aid package. House Appropriations Chairman Jerry Lewis, R-Calif., said he understood Obey's frustration. "We are all frustrated at the moment. I can't tell you how many times I've woken up in the middle of the night wondering if there is anything more I can do," he said. *(House vote 458, p. H-142)*

FEMA spending slowed dramatically in the weeks that followed, however. Even Hurricane Rita, which hit southeastern Texas and southwestern Louisiana Sept. 24, did not put a great dent in FEMA's disaster relief funds.

On Oct. 7, Congress reallocated $750 million in previously appropriated FEMA funds to a community disaster loan program that provided loans to local governments for maintaining government services such as police and fire (PL 109-88). Landrieu and Sen. David Vitter, R-La., said their state needed the money before Congress started the weeklong Columbus Day recess to prevent more layoffs of government employees. At that time, more than $42 billion of the $62.3 billion Congress had appropriated had yet to be spent or allocated to hurricane relief efforts.

## $29 BILLION END-OF-YEAR PACKAGE

In October, the administration sent Congress a $17.1 billion reallocation request to redirect FEMA money to a variety of agencies, largely for repairing and replacing critical infrastructure such as highways, levees and military facilities.

But Senate Appropriations Chairman Thad Cochran, R-Miss., said it would not be enough. Along with Mississippi's influential Republican Gov. Haley Barbour, Cochran pressed for $35 billion and eventually persuaded House GOP leaders to agree to a $29 billion year-end package in late December. The package, which was enacted as part of the conference report on the fiscal 2006 Defense appropriations bill (PL 109-148), reallocated $23.4 billion in funds originally granted to FEMA. The additional funds were financed in part by an across-the-board spending cut in almost all fiscal 2006 discretionary programs except those for veterans and emergency war funding. The cut was enacted as part of the Defense bill. *(Defense appropriations, p. 2-14)*

The huge cost of the relief and reconstruction efforts had led fiscal conservatives — the 100-plus member Republican Study Committee in the House and a smaller band of senators — to call for funding offsets.

Republican leaders and the administration rejected many of the suggestions, such as delaying the Medicare prescription drug benefit. But the fiscal conservatives pushed GOP leaders to call for deeper-than-planned cuts in mandatory spending programs in the year-end budget-reconciliation bill. That bill totaled $38.8 billion in savings over five years (PL 109-171). *(Budget reconciliation, p. 4-13)* ■

**Chapter 3**

# BANKING &
# FINANCIAL SERVICES

# Banking & Financial Services

# Long-Awaited Bankruptcy Rewrite Focuses on Debt Repayment

AN EIGHT-YEAR DRIVE to rewrite bankruptcy law reached fruition April 20, when President Bush signed a far-reaching bankruptcy overhaul bill into law (S 256 — PL 109-8). Enactment was a victory, for the credit card and financial services industries, which had been pushing the legislation since 1997.

The centerpiece of the new law was the establishment of a means test aimed at forcing more consumers to file under Chapter 13 of the bankruptcy code, rather than Chapter 7. Under Chapter 7, individuals could have much of their debt discharged, or erased, while Chapter 13, by contrast, required debtors to enter into a court-ordered plan to repay their debts over several years.

The new law also bolstered the legal rights of creditors, required potential bankruptcy filers to receive credit counseling and increased the fees and paperwork requirements related to filing for bankruptcy.

Supporters argued the changes would help stem the rise in personal bankruptcy filings and prevent abuse of the system by wealthy filers who could repay their debts but used the bankruptcy system as a "financial planning tool." Opponents said the measure was a windfall for the credit card industry and faulted the bill for not addressing corporate bankruptcy in the wake of accounting scandals at Enron Corp. and WorldCom Inc. They also criticized the bill for putting the burden of proof on those attempting to file under Chapter 7 to show they were not abusing the law. They said the provisions would force filers to pay additional lawyers' fees and complete paperwork tied to the means test, potentially worsening their financial woes.

The legislation was first introduced in 1997. Supporters tried to win enactment through four Congresses, but each time the bill was derailed. The primary stumbling block was an amendment by Senate Democrat Charles E. Schumer of New York that was aimed at preventing violent protesters from escaping court-ordered judgments or fines by filing for bankruptcy protection.

Because it was originally aimed at anti-abortion protesters, the amendment was anathema to conservative Republicans, and it doomed the legislation in both the 107th and 108th Congresses. GOP leaders were so fed up with what they considered a "poison pill" that they decided not to bring the bankruptcy bill to the floor in 2004, rather than risk having the Schumer amendment adopted.

Supporters of the bill were able to overcome the Schumer amendment in 2005 because of the increased Republican majority in the Senate following the 2004 elections and the defection of a small group of Senate Democrats that waylaid any attempts to filibuster. Once the Senate had passed the bill, House GOP leaders steered the same measure through their chamber without amendment, avoiding the need for a House-Senate conference, a step that had stalled the legislation in previous years.

**BOX SCORE**

**BILL:** S 256 — PL 109-8

**LEGISLATIVE ACTION:**

**Senate** passed S 256, 74-25, on March 10.

**House** cleared the bill, 302-126, on April 14.

**President** signed April 20.

## HIGHLIGHTS

The following are some of the main provisions of the new law:

● **Means test.** The means test was created to determine whether an individual was eligible to file for protection under Chapter 7, or whether the case had to be converted to Chapter 13. Filers generally were not eligible for Chapter 7 if they earned more than their state's median income, and their income — after deducting allowable expenses — was sufficient to repay up to $6,000 over a five-year period. In general, filing under Chapter 7 without meeting this requirement was considered an abuse of the law, and it was up to the individual to show it was not. Under previous law, debtors could use Chapter 7 even if they could repay their debts.

● **Homestead exemption.** The law limited the home equity a debtor could protect during bankruptcy proceedings to $125,000 for a home purchased within 40 months of the bankruptcy filing.

● **Non-dischargeable debts.** Certain debts were made non-dischargeable, meaning they could not be erased. These included alimony and child support, certain money owed for luxury goods, qualified student loans, fines or penalties under federal election laws, and any debt incurred while paying a debt that was non-dischargeable — for example, a credit card charge that was used to pay state or local taxes.

● **Repeat filers.** If an individual filed for bankruptcy within one year of a previous filing, the bankruptcy court could terminate or restrict the automatic stay that would otherwise block creditors from trying to collect debts outside the bankruptcy process as soon as the case was filed. The individual had to show evidence that the new case was filed in good faith. The law also extended from six to eight years the allowable time between completion of a Chapter 7 case and a new Chapter 7 bankruptcy filing. Filers were required to wait four years for a Chapter 13 filing after a previous Chapter 7, 11, or 12 discharge of debts. A subsequent Chapter 13 filing could be made two years after a previous Chapter 13 filing.

● **Consumer education.** The law included a number of provisions aimed at increasing a debtor's knowledge about bankruptcy and money management. Consumers were required to get credit counseling before filing for bankruptcy, and their debts could only be canceled if they took a course to learn to better manage their finances.

● **Consumer protection.** Credit card companies were required to include a number of new sections in billing statements such as an example of the time it would take to repay the balance at a specified interest rate, warnings that paying only the minimum payment would increase the minimum amount of interest that had to be paid and a toll-free number for consumers to get information on how long it would take to repay a credit card balance if only the minimum was paid.

● **Business provisions.** Small-business debtors — those with less than $2 million in debts — were required to file a reorganization plan within 180 days of filing for bankruptcy, and to file periodic financial reports after that. The law also created a new chapter of the bankruptcy code to address transnational bankruptcy cases.

## BACKGROUND

The campaign to rewrite the bankruptcy code began in the late 1990s in response to a spike in consumer bankruptcy filings. The number of filings, which peaked at nearly 1.4 million in 1998, led a coalition of credit card companies, banks and retailers to argue the code needed tightening to prevent rampant abuse by borrowers who could afford to repay some of their debts but instead took advantage of permissive bankruptcy rules. Consumer advocates, on the other hand, blamed much of the rise in bankruptcies on aggressive marketing by credit card companies and opposed what they said were attempts to help the banks at the expense of low-wage workers. The battle continued through four Congresses.

● **105th Congress.** The House and Senate passed significantly different bankruptcy bills in 1998, with the House calling for a strict means test and the Senate proposing less stringent criteria to determine eligibility under Chapter 7. Negotiators managed to work out a compromise under which a person with an income above the median who could pay off at least 25 percent of their unsecured debt over five years would have been required to file under Chapter 13. The House adopted the conference report on the bill, but Senate Democrats balked, saying the means test was too stringent and that Senate consumer provisions had been dropped. An attempt to attach the legislation to an omnibus spending bill died after Republicans were unable to find a compromise acceptable to both President Bill Clinton and the credit industry. *(1997 Almanac, p. 2-81; 1998 Almanac, p. 5-15)*

● **106th Congress.** The House and Senate each passed versions of the bill — the House in 1999, the Senate in 2000 — and negotiators produced a conference report after scrapping a minimum wage increase and tax sweeteners that were in the Senate bill. But Clinton pocket-vetoed the measure, citing the deletion of Schumer's abortion protester language and the inclusion of a homestead exemption limit of $100,000 for homes bought within two years of the bankruptcy filing, which he decried as a loophole for the wealthy. *(1999 Almanac, p. 5-37; 2000 Almanac, p. 5-3)*

● **107th Congress.** Both chambers easily passed bankruptcy bills in 2001, but negotiations on a conference report stalled until July 2002, when Schumer and House abortion foe Henry J. Hyde, R-Ill., reached agreement on the abortion provision. The compromise would have barred individuals from using bankruptcy protection to escape fines and civil judgments if they had interfered with, intimidated, obstructed or injured those who provided "lawful goods or services," including abortions. The language specified the provision was not related to activities protected by the First Amendment. Although the deal was acceptable to Hyde, other anti-abortion activists in the House rejected it and blocked a vote on the conference report. *(2001 Almanac, p. 4-3; 2002 Almanac, p. 5-3)*

● **108th Congress.** The House easily passed the bill again in 2003, but Senate GOP leaders were unwilling to bring the measure to the floor unless they could find a way around the Schumer amendment. The House tried once more in 2004, inserting an amendment-free version of the bill into a Senate measure providing a short-term extension of farm bankruptcy provisions. But Senate Democrats refused to participate in talks on the legislation and it died at the end of the Congress. *(2003 Almanac, p. 13-8; 2004 Almanac, p. 12-14)*

## LEGISLATIVE ACTION
### SENATE COMMITTEE ACTION

The Senate Judiciary Committee approved S 256 by a vote of 12-5 on Feb. 17. The bill largely mirrored the legislation that had died in the previous Congress.

Democrats held many of their most contentious amendments for the floor, in part out of respect for the wishes of Chairman Arlen Specter, R-Pa., who had announced the previous day that he had an advanced form of Hodgkin's disease. Orrin G. Hatch, R-Utah, chaired the session in Specter's absence and said Specter wanted to move the bill out of the committee swiftly. However, a few of the panel's Democrats offered a preview of what was to come.

During the markup, the committee:

▸ Defeated, 7-9, a proposal by Richard J. Durbin, D-Ill., to give bankruptcy courts the power to go back four years and invalidate transactions that benefited top corporate executives. The idea was to ensure that shareholders, creditors and employees could recover money in such situations, but Hatch said the amendment was too broadly written.

▸ Rejected a half-dozen amendments by Russ Feingold, D-Wis., including a proposal to increase the exemption for home equity for elderly people. Feingold argued that the exemption in many states had not kept pace with inflation, leaving elderly people in danger of losing their homes. The amendment was rejected on a 7-9 vote.

In an effort to expedite the committee's work, Hatch agreed to accept without objection other amendments, including proposals by Edward M. Kennedy, D-Mass., to expand bankruptcy courts' authority to limit retention bonuses and severance pay of corporate insiders, and clarify what would qualify as reasonable medical expense for the means test to determine eligibility for Chapter 7 bankruptcy.

Kennedy reluctantly agreed to withdraw an amendment to create an exemption from the means test for people who faced financial ruin because of crises such as catastrophic medical bills that were beyond their control.

### SENATE FLOOR ACTION

The Senate passed the bill, 74-25, on March 10, after nearly two weeks of sometimes vitriolic debate. GOP leaders held their caucus together to defeat dozens of Democratic amendments aimed at exempting certain groups from the means test and placing new restrictions on the credit card industry. House leaders had signaled that any amendments would jeopardize the measure's chances in their chamber. *(Senate vote 44, p. S-11)*

● **Means test.** Critics of the legislation, led by Schumer and Kennedy, targeted the means test, which they said would saddle legitimate filers with extra lawyers' fees and more paperwork. They won only one exemption. During the debate, the Senate:

▸ Rejected 38-58, a proposal by Durbin to exempt members of the armed forces, as well as veterans who could prove their service led to their bankruptcy filing. The amendment also covered spouses, including spouses of service members who died in military service. Instead, the Senate adopted, 63-32, a GOP alternate to allow bankruptcy courts to consider a call to active duty as a "special circumstance" when deciding whether a person who did not meet the means test could still file under Chapter 7. *(Senate votes 13, 12, p. S-7)*

▸ Adopted, 99-0, a Durbin amendment to exempt disabled veterans whose debts occurred primarily while they were on active duty or performing homeland defense duties. *(Senate vote 40, p. S-11)*

▸ Rejected, 39-58, a Kennedy proposal to exempt debtors whose financial troubles were due to medical expenses. *(Senate vote 16, p. S-7)*

▶ Rejected, 37-60, a Jon Corzine, D-N.J., amendment to exempt debtors who went into debt paying medical costs for a family member, or took a lower-paying job to have time to care for a family member. *(Senate vote 18, p. S-7)*

▶ Rejected, 37-61, an amendment by Bill Nelson, D-Fla., to exempt victims of identity theft. *(Senate vote 21, p. S-8)*

● **Consumer protection.** The Senate rejected Democratic attempts to limit the interest that companies could charge on extended credit, require credit card companies to increase disclosure to consumers and discourage predatory lending. *(Senate votes 15, 20, 22, pp. S-7, S-8)*

● **Homestead exemption.** Democrats tried unsuccessfully to create special homestead exemptions for the elderly, those with high medical expenses and eligible members of the military. The provision for the elderly, by Feingold, was defeated, 40-59. It was vigorously opposed by Hatch, who said it would upset the "grand compromise" between the Senate and House on bringing the bill to the floor after eight years of unsuccessful attempts. "The Feingold amendment would bring the bill down," Hatch said. *(Senate vote 14, p. S-7)*

● **Schumer amendment.** The long-awaited vote on the Schumer amendment came March 8. In an impassioned floor speech, Schumer said the Senate should not "protect those who use violence," and warned, "A vote against this amendment is against the rule of law." But Republicans mustered enough votes to defeat it, 46-53. *(Senate vote 28, p. S-9)*

With that hard-won victory in hand, Republicans easily prevailed on a cloture motion later the same day. With the support of 14 Democrats, the Senate voted 69-31 to limit debate and block any effort to filibuster, clearing the way for passage. *(Senate vote 29, p. S-9)*

### HOUSE COMMITTEE ACTION

Chairman F. James Sensenbrenner Jr., R-Wis., urged the House Judiciary Committee to "vigorously oppose" all amendments to avoid the need for a conference. Committee Republicans followed his wishes, approving the Senate-passed bill without change March 16 by a mostly party-line vote of 22-13.

Democrats offered 15 amendments; all were rejected. Like their Senate counterparts, they tried to limit the bill and target predatory lending practices. They sought exemptions from the means test for victims of identity theft, disabled veterans and those with high medical expenses. Other amendments would have prevented creditors from seeking repayment for credit offered at an annual interest rate that exceeded 50 percent, as well as preventing "payday" lenders from offering loans to members of the military with an annual interest rate exceeding 36 percent.

### HOUSE FLOOR ACTION

The House passed the bill, 302-126, after about two hours of debate April 14, clearing it for the president. *(House vote 108, p. H-36)*

Many Democrats were outspoken in their opposition to the bill and to the strategy GOP leaders used in pushing it through. The leadership-controlled Rules Committee had approved a closed rule for floor debate that barred any amendments.

Democrats tried to recommit the bill to the Judiciary Committee with instructions to exempt members of the National Guard and reserve from the means test if their indebtedness occurred during or shortly after the time they were on active duty. The motion was rejected, 200-229. *(House vote 107, p. H-36)* ■

---

## [PROVISIONS]
# Chapter 7 Means Test at

*Following are the major provisions of the 2005 bankruptcy law (PL 109-8) that President Bush signed into law April 20.*

### CONSUMER BANKRUPTCY
#### MEANS TEST

The law creates a means test to determine whether a debtor is eligible to file for personal bankruptcy under Chapter 7 or whether the case will be converted to a Chapter 13 proceeding.

● **Means test and definition of "abuse."** Under the new law, individuals are not eligible for Chapter 7 relief if their "current monthly income" is at or above the median income in their state and, when multiplied by 60, is equal to or greater than 25 percent of their non-priority unsecured claims or $6,000. Secured claims are those involving collateral, such as a house. Priority claims are paid before other unsecured debts. If the individual exceeds this threshold, there is a "presumption of abuse," which will result in the case being dismissed or converted to Chapter 13. Under prior law, there was a presumption in favor of granting relief under Chapter 7.

● **Definition of "current monthly income."** The definition of "current monthly income" in the law is the debtor's average monthly income from all sources in the six months preceding a bankruptcy filing, including both taxable and non-taxable income. The figure also includes any amount paid on a regular basis by outside sources for the household expenses of a debtor or the debtor's dependents. Excluded

from the calculation are Social Security benefits, and payments to victims of war crimes, crimes against humanity or international or domestic terrorism. The six-month period used to calculate current monthly income ends on the last day of the calendar month immediately preceding the bankruptcy filing.

● **Allowable monthly expenses.** In calculating current monthly income, the filer may first deduct a number of expenses, including applicable monthly expenses as defined by the IRS. Eligible expenses include food and clothing, "reasonably necessary" expenses to protect the debtor and his family from certain types of violence and some expenditures for health insurance, disability insurance and health savings accounts. Bankruptcy filers in a Chapter 13 case are also allowed to deduct the administrative expenses stemming from the administration of a court-ordered repayment plan.

Separate provisions allow filers to deduct "reasonable and necessary" expenses for the care or support of any elderly, chronically ill or disabled household members, as well as up to $1,500 per dependent child for public or private elementary or secondary school education. The school expenses can be deducted only if they are documented and the debtor can show why they are necessary and are not already accounted for by the IRS standards.

● **Secured debts.** Filers may also deduct payments on secured debts from their current monthly income figure. For Chapter 13 filings, the debtor may deduct any additional payments necessary to maintain pos-

session of a house, vehicle or other property needed to support themselves or their dependents if it is collateral for secured debts.

● **Exceptions.** Filers that exceed the income threshold may still use Chapter 7 under special circumstances such as a serious medical condition or a call to active duty in the armed forces, but only if those circumstances justify additional expenses or reductions in monthly income. To be eligible, a filer must provide the bankruptcy court with a detailed explanation of the special circumstances and must testify under oath as to the accuracy of the claims.

● **Creditor rights.** The law for the first time allows "parties of interest," such as creditors, to seek to have a Chapter 7 bankruptcy filing dismissed or converted to Chapter 11. Under prior law, only the bankruptcy courts or a U.S. trustee could seek to have a case dismissed, and then only if the court found that the Chapter 7 filing was a "substantial abuse" of the bankruptcy system. Under the new law, the standard is reduced to "abuse."

● **Safe harbor provisions.** The law stipulates that if a debtor's current monthly income is less than the state median, only a judge, federal trustee or bankruptcy administrator — not a creditor — can seek to dismiss a Chapter 7 filing for abuse. No motion for dismissal based on a debtor's ability to pay may be filed by any party if the debtor's income is below the state median income threshold. Disabled veterans whose bankruptcy occurred primarily during a time when they were on active duty or performing a homeland defense activity are exempted from the means test.

● **Bad-faith provision.** If a filer falls below the means-test threshold, the court is required to consider whether the Chapter 7 filing was made in bad faith or the debtor's overall financial situation suggests some sort of abuse. Included among the factors the court can consider in this situation is whether a debtor refuses to sign a personal services contract — a legally binding agreement with a creditor to repay various debts.

● **Attorney sanctions.** A debtor's attorney is liable for civil penalties and administrative costs if a bankruptcy filing is found to be false or abusive. The attorney can be required to reimburse a bankruptcy trustee for trial costs if the bankruptcy court or a creditor makes such a request and the request is granted. Additionally, creditors or the court can make a motion to assess civil penalties against an attorney representing a bankruptcy filer.

The law stipulates that the attorney's signature on any petition, pleading or written motion makes the attorney responsible for performing a "reasonable investigation" into the debtor's circumstances and for determining that the filing is being made in good faith and does not constitute abuse under the means test. The attorney's signature is also regarded as a certification that the financial information required by the means test is accurate.

● **Creditor sanctions.** The court can award the debtor reasonable costs, including applicable attorney fees, if a creditor files a motion claiming abuse by the debtor and the motion is not granted. In such situations, the court can determine the party of interest — typically a creditor — or the lawyer that actually filed the motion, did so to coerce the debtor into waiving his or her rights or entering into a repayment plan.

● **Filing requirements.** Individuals and couples filing for bankruptcy must file a statement of current monthly income, including calculations showing whether or not they are eligible for Chapter 7 under the new means test and how each amount was arrived at.

● **Procedures following a bankruptcy filing.** Under the law, a bankruptcy trustee or administrator must review an individual debtor's bankruptcy filing and file a statement with the bankruptcy court within 10 days after meeting with the creditors, stating whether the debtor is eli-

gible for Chapter 7. The court must notify all of the debtor's creditors within five days after the trustee or administrator makes their determination. Within 30 days, the trustee or bankruptcy administrator must either file a motion to dismiss or convert the Chapter 7 filing to Chapter 13, or file a statement detailing why they are not doing so.

If a debtor does not qualify for Chapter 7 based on the means test, the clerk of the bankruptcy court must notify all of the debtor's creditors within 10 days after the beginning of the case that the "presumption of abuse" applies. This gives creditors the opportunity to file a motion to dismiss the bankruptcy filing or push the debtor into a Chapter 13 repayment plan.

● **Information from creditors.** The law allows creditors to provide virtually any information on a debtor to the bankruptcy courts, trustees or administrators.

● **Dismissal for crimes of violence and drug trafficking.** The court can dismiss a Chapter 7 filing if the debtor has been convicted of a crime of violence or drug trafficking and is already being sued by a victim of that crime. If dismissal is in the best interest of the victim, the court can dismiss the bankruptcy filing unless the debtor can prove that he or she is filing for Chapter 7 relief to make child support payments.

● **Chapter 13 disposable income.** In a Chapter 13 case, the court can — under certain circumstances — force a debtor to pay all his "disposable income" to unsecured creditors. Disposable income is calculated by taking into account all of the debtor's income and deducting all expenses for the support of the debtor and his dependents, child support payments, charitable contributions that do not exceed 15 percent of annual gross income and payments to operate a business. Debtors can deduct the cost of health insurance for themselves and their dependents if they document the cost and the court determines the cost is reasonable.

● **IRS expense standards.** The bankruptcy act expresses the sense of Congress that the secretary of the Treasury can adjust the IRS expense standards used as part of the means test if necessary. Additionally, the law requires the Executive Office for United States Trustees to submit a report to Congress within two years of enactment on the use of the IRS expense standards as part of the means test, including possible changes to the Bankruptcy Code.

● **Notice of alternatives.** Prior to the start of a bankruptcy case that primarily involves consumer debt, the clerk of the bankruptcy court must supply the debtor with a brief description of Chapters 7, 11, 12 and 13 of the bankruptcy code and the costs and benefits of each. The clerk must also provide information about services offered by credit counseling agencies, a statement warning the debtor the information he or she supplies can be examined by the attorney general, and a warning that concealing assets or making false statements under oath can be punishable by fine or imprisonment.

● **Mandatory credit counseling.** To be eligible for relief, a debtor must have received credit counseling during the six months before filing for bankruptcy. The counseling must be provided by an approved nonprofit agency, and must include either an individual or group briefing on opportunities for available credit counseling and assistance in performing a budget analysis. The briefing can occur over the telephone or Internet, and is not required if the bankruptcy trustees determine that adequate credit counseling is not available in the district where the debtor lives.

● **Exemptions from credit counseling.** A debtor can be temporarily exempted from the credit counseling requirement if he or she attempts to obtain counseling from an approved agency, but is unable to do so because of extraordinary circumstances approved by the court.

The requirement does not apply if the court determines a filer cannot complete the course because of mental incapacity, physical disability or active military duty in a combat zone.

● **Approved credit counseling agencies.** The law requires the trustees or bankruptcy administrators to determine whether approved credit counseling agencies are available in individual bankruptcy court districts, and allows them to disapprove of individual counseling agencies if necessary. The bankruptcy court clerk is required to keep a list of approved credit counseling agencies and make it available.

● **Liability of credit counseling agencies.** Credit counseling agencies cannot provide information about a debtor's decision to seek financial management training to a credit reporting agency. A debtor can recover court costs, attorneys' fees and actual damages if a credit counseling agency willfully or negligently fails to comply with the bankruptcy code.

● **Financial management instruction.** A bankruptcy court can only discharge remaining debts under Chapter 7 or 11 if the debtor completes a financial management training course. This requirement can be waived if the trustee or bankruptcy administrator determines the approved instructional courses in the district are not adequate or if the court determines the debtor cannot comply because of incapacity, disability or active military duty in a military combat zone.

● **Financial management pilot training program.** The law requires the Executive Office for United States Trustees to establish a pilot training program and materials to educate debtors about managing their finances. The program must be tested over an 18-month period in six of the bankruptcy court's districts beginning within nine months of enactment. The director must submit a report to Congress within three months after the test program is completed regarding the effectiveness and cost of the financial management program.

## CONSUMER PROTECTIONS

● **Creditor's refusal to negotiate.** The court may reduce an unsecured consumer claim by up to 20 percent if the debtor can show the creditor refused to negotiate a reasonable alternative repayment plan that was approved by an approved credit counseling agency on the debtor's behalf.

● **Mandatory disclosure for reaffirmation agreements.** The law requires any reaffirmation agreement that a debtor signs with a creditor to include certain disclosures and explanations. A reaffirmation agreement is an agreement for the repayment of a particular debt that would otherwise be discharged during the bankruptcy proceedings. Typically, the debts a debtor agrees to repay in such an agreement are secured by collateral that could be repossessed or foreclosed on in the absence of an agreement. The reaffirmation agreement must include a statement of the total amount of debt the debtor is agreeing to pay, the annual percentage rate for the agreement, any lien on goods or property under the agreement and a long statement clarifying the possible repercussions to the debtor of signing a reaffirmation agreement. The debtor's attorney must certify the debtor voluntarily agrees to the agreement and that it will not impose an undue hardship.

● **Enforcement.** The attorney general is required to appoint a U.S. attorney for each judicial district and an FBI agent for each field office to oversee the enforcement of laws pertaining to abusive reaffirmation agreements and "materially fraudulent" statements made in bankruptcy filings. The bankruptcy courts are directed to develop a procedure for referring bankruptcy cases to the U.S. attorney in cases where a fraudulent filing has been made.

● **Study on reaffirmation agreements.** The law instructs the comptroller general to report to Congress within 18 months of enactment on the overall treatment of consumers during the debt reaffirmation process. The report may include recommendations for legislation to address any abusive or coercive tactics used by creditors against consumers.

● **Child support payments.** To make child support payments a priority claim during bankruptcy proceedings, the law stipulates a debtor must pay all legally settled support payments before a court can approve a debt repayment plan, and makes child support obligations non-dischargeable. Additionally, trustees in bankruptcy cases are required to provide those receiving child support and appropriate state agencies the address of the debtor and information on their bankruptcy case.

● **Discharge of qualified educational loans.** The law allows for the discharge of debts for certain types of qualified educational loans if repayment would impose an undue hardship on the debtor or their dependents.

● **Bankruptcy filing preparers.** In an effort to protect consumers from unsavory bankruptcy filing services, the law creates a number of new rules for non-attorney bankruptcy petition preparers, including a requirement that they notify debtors they cannot practice law or give legal advice. The law also allows for the creation of guidelines setting the maximum fees bankruptcy filing services can charge, and it allows bankruptcy courts to fine non-attorney bankruptcy preparers for violating the provisions.

● **Protection of retirement savings.** An individual debtor is allowed to exempt from bankruptcy proceeding certain types of tax-exempt retirement funds that have not already been offered as collateral for the extension of credit. The law puts a $1 million cap on the exemption, with periodic adjustments for inflation. Debt owed to a pension, profit-sharing, stock bonus or other retirement plan is made non-dischargeable in the bankruptcy proceedings.

● **Protection of education savings.** Prior law is amended to protect educational individual retirement accounts in bankruptcy proceedings. The debtor's child, stepchild, grandchild or step-grandchild must be the beneficiary of the account, and the funds are only protected if they were placed in the account more than a year before the bankruptcy filing. Funds deposited between 720 days and 365 days before the filing are only protected up to $5,000.

● **Restrictions on debt relief agencies.** A number of provisions are aimed at reining in the behavior of debt relief agencies — organizations that provide bankruptcy assistance for a fee. These firms are prohibited from encouraging an "assisted person" — someone whose non-exempt assets are less than $150,000 — to make false or misleading statements in a bankruptcy filing. They also are prohibited from misrepresenting the services they provide or the benefits and risks of bankruptcy. The agencies may not encourage debtors to take on additional debt while filing for bankruptcy relief, or to incur additional debt to pay the agency fees for preparing a bankruptcy case.

When dealing with assisted persons, debt relief agencies must have a written contract signed by both parties, and provide certain written notifications about the requirements of filing for bankruptcy. Debt relief agencies that violate these restrictions are subject to civil penalties.

● **Child support study.** Within 270 days of enactment, the comptroller general must report to Congress on the cost and effectiveness of having bankruptcy trustees provide the Office of Child Support Enforcement in the Department of Health and Human Services with a debtor's information to determine any outstanding child support payments the debtor may have.

● **Sale of personal information.** The law prohibits bankruptcy trustees

from selling or leasing personally identifiable information about a debtor to unaffiliated third parties if the debtor has an existing privacy policy in place. The trustee may sell the information in certain circumstances, but only if specific conditions are met or if the court approves the sale following the appointment of a consumer privacy ombudsman.

Consumers have the right to protect the names of any children that are minors, as well as personal information that could be used for identity theft or could cause injury if made public.

## DISCOURAGING BANKRUPTCY ABUSE

● **Repeat filings.** The law allows the court to assume that a filing was made in bad faith if the debtor has filed more than one case in a one-year period, the previous filing was dismissed and there has been no material change in the individual's financial situation. The language places the onus on the debtor to present convincing evidence that the most recent filing is necessary. If a debtor is not successful in convincing the court, the automatic stay against creditor actions is lifted after 30 days.

● **Abusive filings.** If a bankruptcy filing is found to have been part of a scheme to delay, hinder or defraud creditors, creditors whose claims are secured by real property may be granted two-year relief from the automatic stay.

● **Retention of personal property.** Chapter 7 debtors can retain personal property used as collateral on a debt only if they enter into a reaffirmation agreement on the debt within 45 days after the first meeting of creditors, or if they redeem the property. If the debtor does not act within 45 days, the property is forfeited.

● **State exemptions.** The law extends from 180 days to 730 days the time a debtor must live in a particular state before he or she can claim that state's exemptions.

● **Homestead exemption.** The new law aims to limit the ability of debtors to use state homestead exemption laws to shield their assets. The law requires a debtor to be a resident of a state for at least two years before being eligible to claim that state's homestead exemption, making it more difficult to benefit from the laws in those states that have unlimited homestead exemptions. The amount of home equity that can be protected in a bankruptcy proceeding is also capped at $125,000 if the home was bought within 40 months of filing. The $125,000 limit is waived if it involves the primary residence of a family farmer.

The $125,000 limit applies, regardless of when a house was purchased, for any debtor who owes money because of a violation of federal or state securities law or who caused serious physical injury or death to another within the five years prior to the bankruptcy filing.

The home equity exemption is reduced if the debtor has attempted to hide assets from a creditor by investing them in the house within a 10-year period prior to filing for bankruptcy.

● **Luxury goods.** To make it more difficult to escape paying for luxury goods bought on credit, the law requires that a debtor pay any amount over $500 owed to a single creditor for such goods purchased within 90 days of a bankruptcy filing; the previous limit was $1,075 for goods bought within 60 days of the filing. The debtor also must repay all cash advances that total $750 or more and were made within 70 days; the previous limit was $1,075.

● **Eviction of debtors.** The new law lifts the automatic stay that previously prevented landlords from evicting tenants who filed for bankruptcy in certain situations. Landlords may now take back possession of their property if they have already obtained a judgment against a debtor/resident prior to the bankruptcy filing, or if the landlord offers evidence of specific debtor offenses including the illegal use of con-

trolled substances. The tenant can challenge the claims of the property owner; then it is up to the court to decide whether the eviction notice will be allowed.

● **Reducing frequency of bankruptcy relief.** The law prohibits a filer from entering Chapter 7 for a second time within eight years of the original discharge, increasing the limit from six years under prior law. Additionally, it denies a Chapter 13 discharge to any debtor who received a discharge under Chapter 7, 11 or 12 within the preceding four years, or under Chapter 13 within the two previous years.

● **Definition of "household goods."** The law uses a modified version of the Federal Trade Commission's definition of "household goods" to determine what pieces of a debtor's property can be subject to a lien. The definition excludes antiques, jewelry and electronic equipment worth more than $500, works of art not created by the debtor or their family, more than one personal computer, and various motor vehicles, boats and recreational vehicles.

● **Required filings and notices to creditors.** Debtors are required to file copies of their federal tax returns with the bankruptcy court, with evidence of employer payments received, anticipated income or expenditure increases and monthly net income projections. For Chapter 13 cases, the debtor must file a statement of income and expenditure for the preceding tax year. The debtor must also provide a driver's license, passport or other photo identification to the court.

The creditor in a Chapter 7 or Chapter 11 case may request the debtor's bankruptcy relief petition, tax schedules and statement of financial affairs. All mandatory documentation is available for parties of interest to copy or inspect upon request.

● **Automatic dismissal for failure to file information.** If a debtor in a Chapter 7 or Chapter 13 case fails to file all the information required by the bankruptcy law within 45 days of filing, the case is automatically dismissed. The court can extend the window by 45 days for justifiable reasons.

● **Chapter 13 confirmation hearing.** A Chapter 13 hearing must be held no sooner than 20 days and no later than 45 days after the first meeting of creditors.

● **Chapter 13 repayment plans.** Debtors must enter repayment plans of at least five years in length if their current monthly income, when combined with that of their spouse, exceeds a certain monetary limit. If the current monthly income figure falls below the threshold, the plan cannot be more than three years without court approval, and then the period cannot be longer than five years.

● **Termination of automatic stay.** If the court does not decide on a Chapter 7, 11 or 13 case within 60 days, a creditor can request a termination of the automatic stay. The stay will remain in place if the court decides on the overall case prior to the 60-day deadline, the parties agree to a deadline extension, or the debtor requests a specific extension for good cause as determined by the court.

● **Filing fees.** The act makes it more expensive to file for Chapter 7 relief, increasing the fee to $200 from $155 for an individual case. The fee for filing a Chapter 13 case is reduced to $150 from $155, while the Chapter 11 fee is increased to $1,000 from $800. The fee increases are earmarked for the salaries of additional bankruptcy judgeships created by the law. The court can waive the Chapter 7 filing fee and other fees if it determines the debtor is unable to pay the fees in installments.

● **Involuntary bankruptcy records.** The law allows the court to seal any records relating to an involuntary bankruptcy petition filed against a debtor if the court dismisses the petition because it was not justified. The court also can prohibit consumer credit agencies from using such involuntary bankruptcy petitions against a debtor, and debtors can file

a motion with the court to expunge any records relating to the involuntary bankruptcy petition.

## BUSINESS BANKRUPTCY

Business bankruptcies are governed by Chapter 11 of the Bankruptcy Code. Chapter 11 allows businesses to reorganize themselves, giving them an opportunity to restructure debt and escape from some leases and contracts. A business is usually allowed to continue operating while it is in Chapter 11 under the supervision of the bankruptcy court. Family farmers are protected under Chapter 12.

● **Applicable securities regulations.** In the case of a business filing for bankruptcy, the automatic stay does not prevent a self-regulatory securities organization or securities exchange from taking enforcement actions against a debtor or from delisting the debtor's securities.

● **Committee of creditors.** The law allows the bankruptcy court to increase the size of a committee of creditors during a Chapter 11 proceeding upon the request of a party of interest that is a small business. To include the small business on the committee, the court must find the claims held by the business are disproportionately large compared to its annual gross revenue. Additionally, the law requires creditor committees to give creditors who are not on the committee access to salient information.

● **Acceptance or rejection of a Chapter 11 plan.** A holder of a claim against a debtor in a Chapter 11 case can be asked to either reject or accept a reorganization plan if the request was made prior to the beginning of the case and in accordance with applicable non-bankruptcy laws.

● **Venue for certain Chapter 11 proceedings.** The law amends the federal judicial code to require that a proceeding to try to recover a non-consumer debt of less than $10,000 from a non-insider at the debtor company must take place in the district court for the district where the defendant resides. For consumer debts, a proceeding to recover less than $15,000 must convene in the defendant's district court.

● **Time limit for filing reorganization plan.** The law limits the time period available for a debtor to file a Chapter 11 reorganization plan to within 18 months after an order for relief in the case. Debtors must also obtain acceptance of the plan from creditors within 20 months after the order for relief.

● **Disinterested person.** The act eliminates a longstanding conflict-of-interest prohibition that prevented investment bankers that advised or consulted for a debtor prior to a bankruptcy filing from continuing to advise the debtor during the bankruptcy proceedings.

● **Small business debtors.** The law generally defines a small-business debtor as a business with less than $2 million in secured and unsecured debt when it files for bankruptcy protection. The act calls for the adoption of standardized disclosure statements and reorganization plans for small-business debtors, as well as uniform national reporting requirements aimed at providing sufficient information without excessive costs to the business.

Small-business debtors are required to file a reorganization plan within 180 days after filing for bankruptcy, and to file additional financial reports periodically at the direction of the court.

● **Small business debtor study.** The Small Business Administration is required by the law to report to Congress on the reasons small businesses file for bankruptcy and how federal bankruptcy law can be adjusted to help small businesses remain viable.

● **Collection of bankruptcy data.** The federal judicial code is amended to require the clerk of each district, or a clerk of the bankruptcy court, to compile bankruptcy statistics for debtors seeking relief under Chapters 7, 11 and 13. It is the sense of Congress that the public record data compiled in electronic form should be disseminated to the public after taking precautions to protect filers' privacy. The legislation also requires the Administrative Office of the U.S. Courts to report to Congress annually on the statistics.

● **Discharge of tax debts.** The law prevents certain taxes from being discharged in Chapter 7 or 13 cases, including taxes from a return within three years of the bankruptcy filing, taxes assessed within 240 days of filing, and taxes stemming from an unfiled return or false return.

● **Dismissal of bankruptcy filing for failure to file taxes.** The law amends previous statute to allow tax authorities to request a dismissal or conversion of a bankruptcy case if the debtor fails to file a tax return or obtain an extension after filing for bankruptcy. Debtors are given 90 days to file the tax return or request an extension, after which the court can decide to convert or dismiss the case based on the best interest of creditors and the debtor's estate.

● **Cross-border bankruptcies.** The legislation creates a new chapter of the bankruptcy code, Chapter 15, to deal with situations involving cross-border bankruptcies and to allow U.S. bankruptcy courts, debtors and trustees to interact with representatives from other countries. The act allows for bankruptcies involving a single debtor to occur at the same time in separate countries, and sets legal limits on the access foreign representatives and creditors have to both federal and state courts.

● **Financial contract and netting provisions.** The law includes provisions to help clarify how financial contracts between firms are to be treated when a financial institution becomes insolvent and to reflect the 2000 Commodity Futures Modernization Act (PL 106-554). It encourages the use of so-called netting arrangements to ensure that bankruptcy claims involving various types of financial contracts can be settled quickly. Under a netting arrangement, parties that have existing financial contracts with a bankrupt financial institution offset or "net" their various contractual obligations to settle their claims. Netting provisions have previously received support from the Federal Reserve and other regulators to reduce the chances the bankruptcy of a single firm could cause massive market complications.

● **Permanent Chapter 12 protection.** The law makes permanent Chapter 12 of the bankruptcy code, created in 1986 to provide bankruptcy relief for family farmers that have a regular income. Chapter 12 requires farmers to reorganize their debts pursuant to a repayment plan, but is generally thought to be less complex and expensive than other sections of the bankruptcy code.

● **Definition of a family farmer.** The law broadens the definition of a family farmer for bankruptcy purposes. Previously, to qualify for Chapter 12 protection a farmer could have no more than $1.5 million in debt, 80 percent of which came from farming. Under the new law, an eligible farmer can have up to $3.2 million in debt, at least 50 percent of it from farming, and the limit can be adjusted periodically for inflation. Instead of having to receive over 50 percent of their income from farming in the year before filing for bankruptcy, farmers must have gotten 50 percent of it from farming in one of the three years prior to filing.

● **Family fishermen.** The law extends Chapter 12 bankruptcy relief to include "family fishermen" with regular income. For the purpose of the statute, a family fisherman is any individual involved in a commercial fishing operation that has debt up to $1.5 million, at least 80 percent of which stems from the fishing operation. Additionally, at least 50 percent of the individual's income must come from fishing in the year prior to filing for bankruptcy to be eligible for Chapter 12 relief.

● **Health care business bankruptcies.** The act creates new procedures to

ensure the proper disposal of patient records in the event a health care company or other medical-related business files for bankruptcy. It directs a bankruptcy trustee to destroy patient records if they have not been picked up within 365 days after the trustee has published a notice in various newspapers and attempted to directly contact the patients by mail.

The trustee must also make an effort to move patients from a health care facility that is being closed to a similar facility in the vicinity of the original business that provides comparable services.

The bankruptcy court can appoint an ombudsman to monitor the quality of patient care within 30 days of a Chapter 7, 9 or 11 filing by a health care business. Chapter 9 applies to municipalities.

● **Debts stemming from intoxication.** Under existing law, debts resulting from death or personal injury caused by an individual who was intoxicated and operating a motor vehicle are non-dischargeable, meaning they have to be paid. The new law closes a loophole that allowed individuals operating aircraft or watercraft to escape from this provision. Now, anyone who is intoxicated and operating a motor vehicle, aircraft or watercraft is responsible for debts resulting from a death or personal injury caused by his operation of the vehicle. Both motor-powered and unpowered vehicles are included.

● **Single-asset real estate.** The act repeals a provision of bankruptcy law that set a $4 million ceiling on the debt that could be held by so-called single-asset real estate debtors — typically defined as any enterprise in which the principal asset of the business consists of real estate. The act makes these debtors subject to the small-business provisions, and excludes family farmers from the definition of single-asset real estate debtors.

● **New judgeships.** The act allows for the appointment of 28 temporary bankruptcy judges throughout the United States, and extends current temporary judgeships in Alabama, Delaware, Puerto Rico and Tennessee.

● **Consumer credit studies.** The Federal Reserve is directed to study whether credit card companies indiscriminately offer credit without making any effort to ensure the consumers will be able to repay their debt. In addition to allowing the Fed to pass regulations requiring additional disclosures to consumers, the law directs it to take steps to ensure that credit industry practices are responsible and helpful in preventing consumer debt and insolvency.

The act also directs the Fed to study and report to Congress on the type of information credit card companies provide to consumers, and on existing consumer protections from identity theft and other unauthorized uses of credit cards. The Fed is also required to report to Congress on the effect of credit card offers to dependent college students on the number of federal bankruptcy case.

● **New consumer disclosures.** The law takes a number of steps to ensure that consumers are better informed about open-ended credit plans, such as those offered by most credit card firms. Billing statements for such plans must include an example of the time it would take to pay the balance at a specified interest rate; a toll-free number consumers can call to receive an estimate of the time it would take to pay the balance if only the minimum was paid and warnings that paying only the minimum amount on a balance increases the minimum amount of interest that must be paid.

The consumer protection provisions also require additional disclosures regarding introductory interest rates on credit cards, Internet-based credit card offers and late payment deadlines and penalties. Creditors are barred from terminating an open-end account prior to its expiration date solely because a consumer pays off the balance consistently.

● **Asset-protection trusts.** The law allows a bankruptcy court to gain access to funds in certain types of "asset protection trusts" if the court can prove the funds were transferred during the previous 10 years in an effort to shield the money from creditors. Five states allow the creation of such trusts to protect assets in bankruptcy.

The law also permits a bankruptcy trustee to access funds transferred within two years of the bankruptcy filing if the transfer was made to defraud a creditor or for the benefit of a company insider.

● **Retiree benefits.** The law allows the court to reinstate retiree benefits that a company modified within six months of filing for bankruptcy if the company was insolvent when the changes were made.

● **Employee benefit plans.** The cap on wage and employee benefit claims eligible for priority treatment under the Bankruptcy Code is increased from $4,650 earned within 90 days of the bankruptcy filing to $10,000 earned within 180 days of the filing.

● **Securities laws violations.** Any debt incurred before, on or after a bankruptcy filing is made non-dischargeable if the debt was incurred through the violation of securities laws.

● **Effective date.** The bankruptcy law takes effect 180 days after the date of enactment, which was April 20. ∎

# Attempts to Rein In Mortgage Giants Stall

EFFORTS TO TIGHTEN THE regulation of mortgage finance giants Fannie Mae and Freddie Mac were unsuccessful for the third straight year, derailed by partisan disagreements over proposals to restrict the firms' investment portfolios and to set up an affordable housing fund. The House passed a version of the overhaul legislation (HR 1461) in October. A Senate committee approved a companion bill (S 190) in July, but that measure never reached the floor.

Lawmakers in both chambers had been pushing for stronger oversight of Fannie Mae and Freddie Mac for more than three years, as multibillion-dollar accounting scandals came to light, leading to the ouster of a number of executives. As recently as December 2004, Fannie Mae's chairman, Franklin D. Raines, was ousted, and the firm's chief financial officer, J. Timothy Howard, resigned after the Securities and Exchange Commission forced the company to restate its earnings by as much as $9 billion.

But aggressive lobbying by the two firms and the inability of lawmakers and the Bush administration to agree on a new regulatory framework stymied the efforts. *(2004 Almanac, p. 3-3)*

Both the House and Senate bills called for a new regulator for the two government-sponsored enterprises, along with the 12 Federal Home Loan Banks. Lawmakers agreed that the new regulator would be independent of existing agencies, exist outside of the appropriations process and have broader authority to oversee the firms than the existing regulator, the Office of Federal Housing Enterprise Oversight. The chambers differed, however, on how to regulate the firms' trillion-dollar investment portfolios and whether to require them to set aside a percentage of their profits to create an affordable housing fund.

The inclusion of affordable housing fund language in the House bill allowed supporters to win easy bipartisan approval in the Financial Services Committee in May. But objections from the conservative Republican Study Committee (RSC) delayed floor action and led sponsors to add language that would strictly limit the groups that would be eligible for grants from the fund.

The Senate Banking, Housing and Urban Affairs Committee approved its version of the bill in late July, but the party-line vote all but guaranteed there would be no further action before 2006. The Senate measure, championed by Banking Chairman Richard C. Shelby, R-Ala., included portfolio restrictions but not the affordable housing fund.

## LEGISLATIVE ACTION

### HOUSE COMMITTEE ACTION

The House Financial Services Committee approved its oversight bill (HR 1461 — H Rept 109-171, Part 1) by a vote of 65-5 on May 25, rejecting White House calls for changes.

Chairman Michael G. Oxley, R-Ohio, was at odds with the administration over how best to rein in the massive investment portfolios held by Fannie Mae and Freddie Mac, which combined totaled about $1.5 trillion.

The White House sent lawmakers a proposal May 19 urging them to insert language in the bill greatly limiting the types of assets the two firms could purchase for their portfolios, with the aim of reducing the portfolios' size.

Critics of the mortgage finance companies said their huge portfo-

**BOX SCORE**

**BILLS:** HR 1461, S 190

**LEGISLATIVE ACTION:**

**Senate** Banking, Housing and Urban Affairs Committee approved S 190, 11-9, on July 28.

**House** passed HR 1461 (H Rept 109-171), 331-90, on Oct. 26.

lios were not essential to their mission of increasing home ownership and instead served to enrich executives and shareholders. In a May 19 speech, Federal Reserve Chairman Alan Greenspan said the holdings of mortgage-backed securities concentrated interest rate risk at the two companies and posed a systemic risk to the economy.

Company supporters said the holdings provided liquidity to the mortgage market, allowing lenders to offer more loans at lower interest rates.

Oxley resisted pressure to add the administration provisions, choosing instead to retain language in the bill that would give the new regulator discretion to restrict the portfolios if that were found necessary for reasons of fiscal safety and soundness.

"There is nothing in the bill as written that would stop the new regulator . . . from pursuing exactly the same policies on portfolios that the administration is calling for," bill sponsor Richard H. Baker, R-La., said in a statement. Baker said the overall legislation should not be derailed "by minor disagreements over a portfolio issue that nobody was even talking about six months ago."

Barney Frank of Massachusetts, the lead Democrat on the panel, said the bill was not what "we would have written," but he and other committee Democrats voted to approve it.

The key to their support was a provision that Oxley included to beef up the affordable housing responsibilities of the two firms. Fannie Mae and Freddie Mac would be required to donate 5 percent of their after-tax profits to an affordable-housing fund to be used for community and economic development programs.

The committee rejected, 53-17, an attempt by Ed Royce, R-Calif., to strike the provision, which he called "an experiment in socialism." Baker, who rarely differed from Oxley on financial matters, said he was concerned that there was no cap on the size of the funds and not enough guidance on how the money would be disbursed. But Democrats, joined by a number of Republicans, praised the provision as appropriate to the firms' housing mission.

The committee adopted several other amendments, including one to require the companies to disclose charitable contributions to nonprofit organizations and another requiring them to review interest-rate disparities on mortgages offered to minority borrowers. The committee also adopted amendments authorizing studies into alternatives to Fannie Mae and Freddie Mac, affordable housing opportunities for long-term care facilities and loan guarantee fees charged to lenders.

### HOUSE FLOOR ACTION

Brushing off Democratic concerns and White House opposition, House Republicans passed the bill, 331-90, on Oct. 26. *(House vote 547, p. H-172)*

Opposition by conservatives to the affordable housing fund had delayed floor action for months. Despite bill language specifically aimed at preventing the fund from being used for partisan purposes, the RSC said liberal lobbying groups could use the money to defeat GOP candidates and interests. The RSC only relented when Oxley agreed to add language restricting the groups that could receive grants. Democrats fell just short of defeating Oxley's amend-

ment adding the language.

GOP supporters defended the provision, saying groups would have to decide whether housing or political activities were more important. "The question is what do you have to give up to do affordable housing," Baker said.

During the floor debate, the House:

▸ Adopted, 210-205, a managers' amendment by Oxley that included language specifying that groups would be deemed ineligible for affordable housing fund grants if they had been involved in any political activity in the previous year, including nonpartisan voter registration and get-out-the-vote programs. The amendment also reduced contributions to the fund to 3.5 percent of after-tax profits in the first two years, and required the program to end after five years. Thirteen Republicans crossed party lines to vote with the Democrats, while two Democrats joined with Republicans to back the amendment. *(House vote 541, p. H-170)*

Critics, including civil rights groups and faith-based charities, said the restrictions ran afoul of the First Amendment, as well as the 1993 "motor voter" law (PL 103-31) that required many nonprofits to get involved in registering voters. *(1993 Almanac, p. 199)*

▸ Rejected, 200-220, a motion by Frank to send the bill back to committee with instructions to add language clarifying that housing must be among a nonprofit organization's primary purposes and that recipients of money from the affordable housing fund could participate in any voter registration or get-out-the-vote-activity conducted in a nonpartisan basis. Frank noted that the RSC language would affect only nonprofit groups. For-profit companies still could receive funds, regardless of their political activities and donations. "Whatever happened to your belief in helping faith-based organizations?" Frank chided Republicans. *(House vote 546, p. H-172)*

▸ Rejected, 73-346, an amendment by Royce that would have authorized the new regulator to reduce the size of the portfolios if they did in fact pose a "systemic risk" to the economy. *(House vote 543, p. H-172)*

The White House issued a statement of administration policy the day of the vote stating its opposition to the bill because it would not restrict the mortgage giants' portfolios. The White House said the bill "fails to include key elements that are essential to protect the safety and soundness of the housing finance system and the broader financial system at large."

## SENATE COMMITTEE ACTION

The Senate Banking Committee approved its bill (S 190) by a 11-9 party-line vote July 28, with no Democrats voting in favor. The bill — which proposed restrictions on the firms' portfolios and avoided creation of an affordable housing fund — adhered more closely to the White House's wishes than did Oxley's bill.

In April 2004, Shelby had pushed similar legislation through his committee with the support of only one panel Democrat. That effectively killed the measure, which never was acted upon by the full Senate. Lawmakers on both sides of the aisle expressed optimism that this time the legislation would not face a similar fate. "I would hope over the August break we can work together and find some compromise," Christopher J. Dodd, D-Conn., said at the markup.

The major sticking point was a provision, opposed by the Democrats, that would give the new regulator authority to limit the types of assets the two companies could hold in their portfolios.

Charles E. Schumer, D-N.Y., said requiring the companies to have smaller portfolios would reduce the nation's overall commitment to housing. Schumer said the winners would be the private banks. Unlike Fannie Mae and Freddie Mac, which were chartered by Congress to further the nation's housing goals, he said, banks were not required to help provide affordable housing.

Some GOP panel members also expressed concern. Robert F. Bennett of Utah said he disagreed with claims the companies posed a systemic risk to the economy, but said he would vote in favor of Shelby's bill to get it through the committee. "We need to get to conference . . . and ultimately craft a bill we all can agree on," Bennett said.

Democrats also were unhappy that the bill did not include the affordable housing fund. A substitute amendment by ranking Democrat Paul S. Sarbanes of Maryland that included the affordable housing proposal was rejected, 9-11.

Following House passage, Shelby said he still considered the legislation a priority, but he did not give a timeline or any sense of how a consensus could be reached. ∎

# House, Senate Start on Pension Overhaul

THE HOUSE AND SENATE each passed bills aimed at forcing private companies to better fund their pension plans and shoring up the finances of the Pension Benefit Guaranty Corporation (PBGC), the federal agency that insured traditional pension plans. The job of reconciling the two bills was left to the second session.

A series of high-profile bankruptcy filings by companies in the airline, steel and auto parts industries had led to increased concern in Congress over the health of the private pension system and the impact on the PBGC. In May, for example, a bankruptcy court allowed United Airlines to terminate its four pension plans, which were underfunded by about $9.8 billion, causing the PBGC to assume about $6.6 billion in liabilities for the plans. On Nov. 15, the agency reported that its fiscal 2005 deficit was $22.8 billion. For law-

**BOX SCORE**

**BILLS:**
HR 2830, S 1783

**LEGISLATIVE ACTION:**

**Senate** passed S 1783, 97-2, on Nov. 16.

**House** passed HR 2830, 294-132, on Dec. 15.

makers, the PBGC's problems raised the specter of a taxpayer bailout of the agency.

Finding solutions was particularly difficult, however. To strengthen the PBGC, lawmakers agreed they needed to increase premiums. Many experts also believed it was necessary to ensure the health of private pension plans by tightening accounting rules and requiring greater disclosure. But such changes could backfire if companies concluded they would be better off walking away from their pensions and transferring their obligations to the PBGC.

Efforts on a broad overhaul of the pension system began in January, when Labor Secretary Elaine L. Chao outlined a Bush administration plan to simplify the pension contribution process and increase incentives for companies that adequately funded their pension plans. The proposal applied only to single-employer defined-benefit pension plans

— those that paid employees a set amount after retirement. It called for the annual premium rate, last changed in 1991, to rise to $30 per worker from $19; after that, it would be indexed to increases in workers' wages. Companies with credit ratings below investment grade or with underfunded plans would pay an additional risk-adjusted premium.

The plan would change the benchmark for measuring a company's pension liabilities, using a yield curve pegged to corporate bond rates instead of the interest rate on 30-year Treasury bonds. A temporary change enacted in 2004 (PL 108-218) used a corporate bond rate, but it was good only until the end of 2005. *(2004 Almanac, p. 8-3)*

Lawmakers used the White House proposal as a starting point but made some provisions less stringent. Business and labor groups pushed to have any changes that would increase their costs phased in. Business groups — among them the U.S. Chamber of Commerce, the ERISA Industry Committee and the American Benefits Council — cautioned against sweeping changes, arguing that the perceived crisis in pensions was actually limited to a handful of troubled companies. They called for generous phase-in periods for new rules to avoid encouraging more firms to default on their obligations.

The Senate passed a pension overhaul bill (S 1783) in November, based on legislation approved by the Health, Education, Labor and Pensions and Finance committees.

Two House committees — Education and the Workforce and Ways and Means — marked up a pension bill (HR 2830), but that measure stalled on its way to the floor because of objections from the United Auto Workers. With time in the first session running short, bill sponsors secured a last-minute endorsement from the powerful union, a step that won some Democratic support and enabled them to pass the bill in mid-December.

Both bills proposed to increase the PBGC premium to $30 per employee and require companies to fund 100 percent of the benefits they had pledged to employees, though the full-funding requirements would be phased in over different periods, depending on the health of companies.

The biggest differences included provisions in the Senate bill, but not the House version, to give special treatment to airlines and to use a company's credit rating as a factor in determining how well it had funded its pension plans. The White House opposed industry-specific language and said the president's advisers would recommend a veto if the legislation weakened existing funding requirements for pension plans.

One provision — the PBGC premium increases — was included in the budget reconciliation bill that the House cleared Feb. 1, 2006. Language in the reconciliation bill increased the annual premium per plan participant to $30. Companies that terminated their plans while under bankruptcy protections would have to pay additional premiums once they left bankruptcy. *(Budget reconciliation, p. 4-13)*

## LEGISLATIVE ACTION
### HOUSE COMMITTEE ACTION
● **Education and the Workforce.** On June 30, the House Education and the Workforce Committee approved a bill (HR 2830 — H Rept 109-232, Part 1) introduced by Chairman John A. Boehner, R-Ohio. The vote was 27-0, with all 27 Republicans voting in favor, and all 22 Democrats voting "present" to protest what they said was the quick pace of the legislation; the bill had been introduced earlier in the month.

The panel's Subcommittee on Employer-Employee Relations had approved a draft by voice vote June 22.

The bill included provisions to raise PBGC premiums to $30 per employee, change the benchmark for measuring pension liabilities to

be similar to that in Bush's plan and force companies to fully fund their plans over time.

The committee adopted a number of amendments during the two-day markup, including a substitute offered by Boehner that would give legal certainty to so-called cash-balance plans, and a five-year phase-in period for companies to increase funding of their plans to 100 percent. Existing law generally allowed 90 percent funding.

Other adopted amendments would expand the investment options available to pension fund investment managers and provide more flexibility for robustly funded plans to use credit balances. The panel rejected a number of amendments offered by Democrats, including one tying executives' retirement benefits to employees' pensions.

Democrats also expressed concern about a section of the bill that would allow employers to provide workers with access to investment advisers. Robert E. Andrews of New Jersey said he was worried about conflicts of interest that could result from investment advisers giving advice to employees while trying to sell financial products.

Boehner discounted Andrews' concern, saying the bill included safeguards to ensure that advice would be provided without conflicts. Also, he said, any conflicts of interest paled in comparison with the "greater risk to our nation as a whole if we don't get quality investment advice" into the hands of workers.

● **Ways and Means.** The House Ways and Means Committee approved its version of the bill (HR 2830 — H Rept 109-232, Part 2) on a mostly party-line 23-17 vote Nov. 9.

Republican leaders had considered a broader retirement package that included an overhaul of the Social Security system, as called for by Bush. But with little support for Social Security changes, Ways and Means Chairman Bill Thomas, R-Calif., settled for attaching some modest retirement provisions to the pension bill.

The panel gave voice vote approval to an amendment by Thomas that added a number of provisions dealing with defined contribution plans, such as 401(k)s. The provisions would make it easier to contribute to Individual Retirement Accounts (IRAs) and make permanent a tax credit for low-income people who contributed to qualified retirement plans.

The committee also gave voice vote approval to three amendments offered by Benjamin L. Cardin, D-Md., that included making IRAs more available to disabled individuals and allowing rollover of retirement plans by non-spouse beneficiaries.

### HOUSE FLOOR ACTION
The House passed HR 2830 by a vote of 294-132 on Dec. 15. The rule for floor debate (H Res 602 — H Rept 109-346) substituted a version that combined provisions from the two committees, with a modification that secured the support of the UAW. *(House vote 635, p. H-202)*

The measure won support from both sides of the aisle, with 70 Democrats voting for the bill despite an effort by their leaders to whip the caucus against it. The Democratic support was due in part to a change in the UAW position. Boehner and Thomas won the union's endorsement for the bill Dec. 13 after agreeing to modify certain provisions.

They agreed to a five-year phase-in of a provision that would prohibit plans that were less than 80 percent funded from increasing pension benefits, unless the benefits were immediately paid for by increased contributions. Another element of the agreement permitted plans that were at least 80 percent funded to use pension assets to pay plant shutdown benefits.

Opponents said the bill would do more harm than good. Calling it

an "assault" on the retirement security of American workers, George Miller, D-Calif., said it would cause more companies to freeze traditional plans or dump them on the PBGC.

Democrat David Scott of Georgia, who voted for the bill, said he hoped language helping the airline industry would be added during conference talks.

### SENATE COMMITTEE ACTION

● **Finance Committee.** The Senate Finance Committee gave voice vote approval July 26 to a bipartisan bill (S 1953 — S Rept 109-174) sponsored by Chairman Charles E. Grassley, R-Iowa, and ranking Democrat Max Baucus of Montana.

The Grassley-Baucus bill would require companies to fully fund their pension plans and use a bond curve to more accurately estimate their pension liabilities. It would increase the PBGC premium to $30 per worker and eliminate "smoothing," an accounting technique that critics said masked deterioration in plan assets.

Like the House bill, the measure would offer greater legal certainty to cash-balance, or hybrid, benefit plans. Left in legal limbo by a 2003 court decision, the plans combined aspects of pension and defined contribution plans. The bill would set age-discrimination standards and parameters for companies to convert a pension plan to a cash-balance system.

● **Health, Education, Labor and Pensions.** The Senate Health, Education, Labor and Pensions Committee (HELP) voted 18-2 on Sept. 8 to approve a bill offered jointly by Chairman Michael B. Enzi, R-Wyo., and the ranking Democrat, Edward M. Kennedy of Massachusetts.

Like the other bills, the legislation would establish new rules to calculate companies' pension liabilities, require companies to fully fund their pension plans, and increase PBGC premiums to $30 per worker.

But the bill also included a number of provisions considered more business-friendly than those in either the Senate Finance or House measures. Under the HELP bill, companies would have 10 years to make up for any underfunding of a plan, compared with five years in the House bill and seven years in the Senate Finance legislation.

The bill included airline-industry specific language that would allow certain "legacy carriers" to make up any funding requirements over 14-years as opposed to 10.

Other provisions would adjust the funding rules for multi-employer pension plans, and postpone certain payment and funding deadlines for companies with plans that were affected by Hurricane Katrina.

### SENATE FLOOR ACTION

The Senate passed a version of the bill negotiated by Grassley and Enzi (S 1783) by a vote of 97-2 on Nov. 16. The only two "no" votes came from Michigan Democrats Carl Levin and Debbie Stabenow, who expressed concern about the legislation's effect on manufacturing

jobs in their state. *(Senate vote 328, p. S-64)*

The Senate compromise was generally more lenient in the way it dealt with distressed firms than either the House proposal or the earlier Finance Committee bill.

The bill required companies to use a modified yield curve to determine their plan's funding status and to fund 100 percent of their pension obligations. Companies with underfunded plans would have seven years to reach 100 percent; they would be ineligible to offer additional pension benefits if their plans were less than 80 percent funded. The bill included the premium increase to $30 per year. Employers would be required to provide more detailed information to pensioners about the funding status of their plans.

During floor debate, the Senate adopted two amendments, both of which addressed pension issues in the airline industry.

The first, by Johnny Isakson, R-Ga., would give airlines 20 years to make up any underfunding in their pension plans. The companies would then have seven years to phase in the more stringent funding requirements included in the legislation. As originally written, airlines would have had 14 years before the new rules would take effect. It was adopted by voice vote.

The second, by Daniel K. Akaka, D-Hawaii, would lower to 60 the age at which pilots could receive maximum pension benefits allowed by the PBGC, resolving a discrepancy in federal law that required pilots to retire at age 60 but did not allow them to draw maximum benefits unless they retired at 65. It was adopted 58-41. *(Senate vote 327, p. S-64)*

### BUDGET RECONCILIATION

The 2005 budget reconciliation bill — which promised a net reduction of $38.8 billion from mandatory spending programs over five years — included provisions to increase PBGC premiums. The measure was signed into law Feb. 8 (S 1932 — PL 109-171).

The PBGC provisions:

▶ Increased the premiums paid by single-employer defined-benefit plans to $30 from $19 per participant, and increased premiums for multi-employer pension plans to $8 from $2.60 per worker. Future premium levels would be indexed to account for increases in average wages. The changes were effective starting in 2006.

▶ Established a new premium for companies that terminated their pension plans while in bankruptcy. Those companies would have to pay $3,750 over three years for each plan participant once they emerged from bankruptcy protection.

The House Education and the Workforce Committee had approved a $30 per participant premium. The Senate Health, Education, Labor and Pensions Committee approved a jump to $46.75 per participant in its budget-reconciliation markup held Oct. 18.

The provisions in the final bill were expected to bring in $3.6 billion over five years. ∎

# Chapter 4

# BUDGET

# Budget

# President Submits Fiscal 2006 Plan: A Thousand Pages of Political Pain

PRESIDENT BUSH SENT LAWMAKERS the most austere fiscal blueprint of his presidency Feb. 7, a $2.55 trillion budget that called for the first nominal cut in domestic spending since fiscal 1996, when a confrontation between President Bill Clinton and the nascent GOP majority in Congress led to two government shutdowns. Bush also proposed the first reductions in politically sacrosanct entitlement programs such as Medicaid and crop subsidies since 1997. *(1996 Almanac, p. 2-4)*

The White House Office of Management and Budget (OMB) said the budget would produce a $390 billion deficit in fiscal 2006 and keep Bush on track to cut the annual deficit in half by 2009. However, Bush's budget did not include future costs of military activity in Iraq and Afghanistan beyond Sept. 30. It also left out the cost of widely expected legislation to modify the alternative minimum tax, as well as his proposal to overhaul Social Security — neither of which was enacted in 2005.

The budget relied almost entirely on domestic spending restraint to achieve the deficit reduction. Bush requested increases for defense and homeland security, and proposed $1.4 trillion in new tax cuts over 10 years.

Republican budget writers on Capitol Hill embraced Bush's call for domestic spending cuts, though they acknowledged the plan would be tough to implement. "Obviously, this is a budget which is going to cause some significant angst amongst my colleagues, to be kind," said Judd Gregg, R-N.H., chairman of the Senate Budget Committee. "But the fact that everyone's probably going to be upset by it, because everyone's ox gets gored, including defense, by the way . . . probably means they've done a good job."

Democrats generally blasted Bush for continuing to run up huge deficits through tax cuts while trying to slash domestic spending. John M. Spratt Jr. of South Carolina, ranking Democrat on the House Budget Committee, said domestic discretionary accounts represented less than 20 percent of the overall budget. "No one can argue that these programs are the source of the deficit, because they've barely increased over the last several years," Spratt said. "Cuts like this hurt, but in the end they barely make a dent in the deficit."

The Congressional Budget Office (CBO) published its annual recalculation of the president's budget in March. Congress traditionally used CBO's revised numbers in preparing its own budget resolution, although lawmakers said they were not required to do so.

## WHITE HOUSE PRIORITIES

- **Discretionary spending.** Bush called for capping discretionary spending — the money appropriators could allocate in the annual spending bills — at $804 billion in fiscal 2006, a 2.1 percent increase over the previous fiscal year not counting supplementary appropriations. Of that, he said, $419 billion would go to defense, $32 billion to homeland security and $389 billion to non-defense, non-homeland security.

CBO said Bush's proposals would cap discretionary spending at $843 billion, a 1.7 percent increase. Either way, the growth in discretionary accounts would be well below the projected 2.5 percent rate of inflation.

According to CBO, Bush's discretionary proposals included:

▶ $439 billion for defense, a 4.4 percent increase over fiscal 2005 spending but less than the 6.8 percent boost the Pentagon got the previous year. The extra funding was primarily for personnel and maintenance accounts, while the Pentagon's procurement budget would be frozen at existing levels. The president proposed average annual increases of 3.4 percent in defense funding for fiscal 2007 through 2010.

▶ A net total for homeland security of $29 billion, plus an additional $3 billion to $4 billion to be covered by offsetting user fees. Although most homeland accounts were slated for increases under the president's

## Fiscal 2006 Budget Totals

The following table shows President Bush's fiscal 2006 budget requests for budget authority, outlays and revenue, and the resulting deficit, as calculated by the White House Office of Management and Budget. The Congressional Budget Office issued its annual recalculation of the president's budget in March. CBO numbers for outlays, revenue and deficits, shown below, were subsequently used by Congress and the White House.

*(fiscal years, in billions of dollars)*

|  | Estimated 2005 | Proposed 2006 | 2007 | 2008 | 2009 | 2010 |
|---|---|---|---|---|---|---|
| **Budget Authority** | | | | | | |
| Bush | $2,477 | $2,548 | $2,662 | $2,787 | $2,925 | $3,064 |
| **Outlays** | | | | | | |
| Bush | 2,479 | 2,568 | 2,656 | 2,758 | 2,883 | 3,028 |
| CBO | 2,451 | 2,542 | 2,629 | 2,742 | 2,872 | 2,999 |
| **Revenue** | | | | | | |
| Bush | 2,053 | 2,178 | 2,344 | 2,507 | 2,650 | 2,821 |
| CBO | 2,057 | 2,210 | 2,350 | 2,492 | 2,625 | 2,770 |
| **Deficit** | | | | | | |
| Bush | −427 | −390 | −312 | −251 | −233 | −207 |
| CBO | −394 | −332 | −278 | −250 | −246 | −229 |

SOURCE: Office of Management and Budget, Congressional Budget Office

# Budget Proposals By Appropriations Panel

Following are President Bush's requests for discretionary fiscal 2006 budget authority for programs under the jurisdiction of the House and Senate Appropriations subcommittees. Subcommittee jurisdictions were subsequently changed.

| (in billions of dollars) | 2005 Enacted | 2006 Proposed | 2005-06 Percentage Change |
|---|---|---|---|
| Agriculture | $18.3 | $16.9 | -7.7% |
| Commerce, Justice, State | 40.8 | 44.1 | 8.1 |
| Defense | 390.4 | 407.6 | 4.4 |
| District of Columbia | 0.6 | 0.6 | 3.1 |
| Energy and Water development | 28.3 | 27.2 | -3.9 |
| Foreign Operations | 19.5 | 22.8 | 16.9 |
| Homeland Security | 29.0 | 29.3 | 1.0 |
| Interior | 20.2 | 19.7 | -2.5 |
| Labor, HHS, Education | 142.4 | 141.0 | -1.0 |
| Legislative Branch | 3.5 | 4.0 | 14.3 |
| Military Construction | 10.0 | 12.1 | 21.0 |
| Transportation, Treasury | 26.3 | 25.0 | -4.9 |
| VA, HUD, NASA and EPA | 93.5 | 90.5 | -3.2 |
| Allowances | —— | -0.4 | —— |
| TOTALS* | $822.7 | $840.3 | 2.1 |

\* Excludes $25 billion in supplemental budget authority for fiscal 2005 appropriated for military operations in Iraq and Afghanistan and an expected $80 billion in additional supplemental spending not yet requested.

NOTE: Figures may not add due to rounding          SOURCE: Office of Management and Budget

budget, the total was 4.9 percent below the previous year. That was mainly because Project Bioshield, a Bush administration initiative to bolster the nation's bioterror defenses, got a one-time infusion of $2.5 billion in fiscal 2005.

▶ $375 billion for non-defense, non-homeland security programs, a 0.7 percent cut from fiscal 2005 levels. Several accounts within this category were slated for increases, further reducing the funds that would be available for the remaining domestic programs. For example, Bush proposed what CBO said was an increase of $3.8 billion, or 12.8 percent, for international affairs, about $1.5 billion of which was for his Millennium Challenge Corporation. Medicare was expected to need a discretionary increase of $1.1 billion, or 26.5 percent, for the extra costs of administering the new prescription drug program.

Many of Bush's proposed cuts to discretionary programs — such as trimming Army Corps of Engineers water projects and eliminating $1.5 billion in anti-crime grants to state and local governments — had been tried before and ignored by a Republican Congress. The administration proposed eliminating 99 discretionary programs for a savings of $8.8 billion. Congress had rejected more than half those terminations before.

Bush counted on new user fees to offset some discretionary spending, though Congress had rejected many of these proposals in the past. The proposals included a $3 increase in the ticket tax paid by U.S. airline travelers that Bush said would generate $1.6 billion to help pay for airport screeners and new explosives-detection equipment. Other proposed revenue-raisers include a $250 annual enrollment fee for higher-income veterans to receive health benefits and an increase in prescription drug co-payments for veterans to $15 from $7.

● **Mandatory spending.** The budget also proposed net savings of $61.6 billion over five years and $137 billion over 10 years from entitlement programs. Later in the year, the White House said the budget would result in "gross" savings — not counting proposed increases in some mandatory programs — of $83.9 billion over five years and $187 billion over 10 years.

The differences with CBO also were more significant than in the case of discretionary programs. CBO said Bush's policy proposals would produce net savings of about $51 billion over five years and $140 billion over 10 years, if some refundable credits were not counted.

A major piece of the savings cited by the White House came from $60 billion in cuts from projected spending over 10 years for Medicaid, the joint federal-state health insurance program for the poor, which had been immune to budget cuts since 1997. The budget also proposed putting about $15 billion back into Medicaid and children's health programs, reducing the net savings to about $45 billion.

● **Taxes.** Bush called for a net total of $1.5 trillion in tax cuts in fiscal 2005 through 2014, according to the Joint Committee on Taxation, whose calculations were used by Congress and by CBO. Most of the estimated revenue loss was from Bush's proposal to make his earlier tax cuts permanent. The tax proposals in Bush's budget included:

▶ Permanent extension of the 2001 and 2003 tax cuts (PL 107-16, PL 108-27), which were scheduled to expire before, or by the end of, 2010, at a combined cost of $1.3 trillion over 10 years. (*2001 Almanac, p. 18-3; 2003 Almanac, p. 17-3*)

That included $147.8 billion to extend the 15 percent income tax rate for dividends and capital gains set to expire at the end of 2008. It also included the $609.6 billion cost of extending other income tax rate reductions, such as the existing 35 percent rate and the 10 percent rate bracket, that were set to expire after 2010. Extending repeal of the estate tax past 2010 was estimated to cost $289.9 billion through 2015. Other proposals included extending the treatment of taxes for married couples at a cost of $145.9 billion, and continuing the $1,000-per-child tax credit at a cost of $145.9 billion. Both were scheduled to expire after 2010. Bush also proposed to permanently allow small business to deduct up to $100,000, rather than $25,000, in the first year for new equipment purchases, at a cost of $191 billion. That provision was set to expire after 2007.

▶ New lifetime savings accounts that would allow tax-free earnings and withdrawals. Existing retirement savings programs, such as IRAs and 401(k)s, would be consolidated into two accounts: Retirement Savings Accounts and Employer Retirement Savings Accounts. The accounts were projected to bring in a net total of $12.3 billion over five years when deposits were being made, but over 10 years they were expected to cost $7.4 billion.

▶ Five new tax breaks for health care costs, including a refundable credit of up to $3,000 for health insurance premiums for taxpayers who were not covered through their employers, and a $500-per-employee small business credit for employer contributions to new Health Savings Accounts. The expected cost was $117.6 billion over 10 years.

▶ Permanent extension of a 20 percent tax credit for company research and development costs above a specified level. Congress had been renewing this credit annually since 1981. The estimated cost was $77.7 billion over 10 years.

● **Deficit.** The White House said the annual deficit would peak at $426.6 billion in fiscal 2005, going down to $390.1 billion in fiscal 2006 and $233 billion in 2009. Bush's promise to cut the deficit in half over five years was measured against OMB's initial fiscal 2004 deficit projection of $521 billion.

# Bush's Fiscal 2006 Proposal by Agency

Following are totals for new budget authority and expected outlays by fiscal year for 2004 through 2006 for Cabinet departments and major federal agencies. Totals include both discretionary and mandatory spending, some of which was permanently appropriated.

*(figures in millions of dollars)*

| | BUDGET AUTHORITY | | | OUTLAYS | | |
|---|---|---|---|---|---|---|
| | 2004 ACTUAL | 2005 ESTIMATE | 2006 PROPOSED | 2004 ACTUAL | 2005 ESTIMATE | 2006 PROPOSED |
| Legislative Branch | 3,932 | 3,905 | 4,412 | 3,885 | 4,083 | 4,356 |
| The Judiciary | 5,443 | 5,712 | 6,254 | 5,392 | 5,741 | 6,145 |
| Agriculture | 93,092 | 94,740 | 95,370 | 71,769 | 94,912 | 94,590 |
| Commerce | 5,898 | 6,456 | 9,523 | 5,850 | 6,278 | 6,500 |
| Defense - Military | 471,878 | 402,032 | 421,118 | 437,116 | 444,068 | 426,315 |
| Education | 67,200 | 71,478 | 68,804 | 62,816 | 70,953 | 64,272 |
| Energy | 22,068 | 21,507 | 21,239 | 19,972 | 22,178 | 21,969 |
| Health and Human Services | 556,712 | 581,673 | 662,119 | 543,389 | 585,772 | 643,886 |
| Homeland Security | 31,612 | 38,339 | 29,581 | 26,537 | 33,259 | 33,284 |
| Housing and Urban Development | 35,112 | 35,466 | 30,443 | 45,019 | 42,614 | 40,185 |
| Interior | 10,467 | 9,886 | 9,021 | 8,914 | 9,433 | 9,812 |
| Justice | 27,445 | 21,605 | 21,682 | 28,954 | 21,171 | 23,380 |
| Labor | 56,942 | 50,706 | 54,509 | 56,706 | 50,034 | 51,713 |
| State | 11,970 | 11,912 | 14,010 | 10,934 | 11,934 | 14,109 |
| Transportation | 60,523 | 60,833 | 58,807 | 54,547 | 58,215 | 60,585 |
| Treasury | 375,941 | 403,801 | 442,531 | 374,817 | 402,972 | 441,198 |
| Veterans Affairs | 60,279 | 67,487 | 68,226 | 59,554 | 68,046 | 68,281 |
| Corps of Engineers | 4,664 | 5,068 | 4,354 | 4,838 | 4,891 | 4,643 |
| Other Defense - Civil Programs | 41,850 | 43,599 | 44,628 | 41,730 | 43,460 | 44,489 |
| The EPA | 8,396 | 7,984 | 7,455 | 8,334 | 7,862 | 8,202 |
| Executive Office of the President | 18,763 | 404 | 329 | 3,308 | 5,765 | 7,192 |
| Foreign Assistance | 15,701 | 14,116 | 17,251 | 13,737 | 14,754 | 17,022 |
| General Services Administration | 69 | 293 | 71 | -403 | 459 | 54 |
| NASA | 15,379 | 16,197 | 16,457 | 15,189 | 15,719 | 15,744 |
| National Science Foundation | 5,615 | 5,598 | 5,731 | 5,118 | 5,641 | 5,666 |
| Office of Personnel Management | 59,920 | 63,932 | 67,219 | 56,535 | 60,964 | 64,259 |
| Small Business Administration | 4,222 | 3,344 | 636 | 4,075 | 3,036 | 790 |
| Social Security Administration | | | | | | |
| (On-budget) | 49,936 | 55,049 | 53,923 | 49,005 | 55,750 | 54,737 |
| (Off-budget) | 481,699 | 503,826 | 530,767 | 481,200 | 503,298 | 528,755 |
| Other Independent Agencies | | | | | | |
| (On-budget) | 15,187 | 16,950 | 19,007 | 10,034 | 20,681 | 18,544 |
| (Off-budget) | 2,057 | 884 | 3,774 | -4,130 | -1,010 | 4,063 |
| Allowances | — | 81,000 | -411 | — | 34,899 | 24,168 |
| Undistributed offsetting receipts | -212,526 | -228,428 | -241,291 | -212,526 | -228,428 | -241,291 |
| (On-budget) | (-114,967) | (-125,522) | (-131,790) | (-114,967) | (-125,522) | (-131,790) |
| (Off-budget) | (-97,559) | (-102,906) | (-109,501) | (-97,559) | (-102,906) | (-109,501) |
| TOTALS | $2,407,446 | $2,477,354 | $2,547,549 | $2,292,215 | $2,479,404 | $2,567,617 |

Figures may not add due to rounding.

SOURCE: Office of Management and Budget

# Bush's Fiscal 2006 Proposal by Function

A breakdown, in millions of dollars per fiscal year, of governmental spending by function rather than agency:

| | BUDGET AUTHORITY | | | OUTLAYS | | |
|---|---|---|---|---|---|---|
| | 2004 ACTUAL | 2005 ESTIMATE | 2006 PROPOSED | 2004 ACTUAL | 2005 ESTIMATE | 2006 PROPOSED |
| **NATIONAL DEFENSE** | | | | | | |
| Department of Defense — military | $471,001 | $402,032 | $421,118 | $436,521 | $443,897 | $426,286 |
| Atomic energy defense activities | 16,822 | 17,962 | 17,489 | 16,625 | 18,687 | 17,990 |
| Defense-related activities | 2,798 | 3,610 | 3,220 | 2,762 | 3,287 | 3,122 |
| Total, National defense | $490,621 | $423,604 | $441,827 | $455,908 | $465,871 | $447,398 |
| **INTERNATIONAL AFFAIRS** | | | | | | |
| International development and humanitarian assistance | 30,513 | 10,722 | 14,152 | 13,825 | 14,677 | 21,270 |
| International security assistance | 7,680 | 7,597 | 8,145 | 8,369 | 8,773 | 8,043 |
| Conduct of foreign affairs | 8,439 | 7,675 | 8,673 | 7,897 | 8,387 | 8,381 |
| Foreign information and exchange activities | 1,000 | 1,056 | 1,204 | 1,141 | 1,067 | 1,160 |
| International financial programs | –2,476 | –1,203 | –509 | –4,341 | –943 | –407 |
| Total, International affairs | $45,156 | $25,847 | $31,665 | $26,891 | $31,961 | $38,447 |
| **GENERAL SCIENCE, SPACE AND TECHNOLOGY** | | | | | | |
| General science and basic research | 9,070 | 9,130 | 9,126 | 8,416 | 9,174 | 9,062 |
| Space flight, research and supporting activities | 14,321 | 15,290 | 15,604 | 14,637 | 14,847 | 14,905 |
| Total, General science, space and technology | $23,391 | $24,420 | $24,730 | $23,053 | $24,021 | $23,967 |
| **ENERGY** | | | | | | |
| Energy supply | 1,843 | –84 | 279 | –1,555 | 50 | 725 |
| Energy conservation | 868 | 868 | 847 | 926 | 874 | 860 |
| Emergency energy preparedness | 176 | 175 | 166 | 158 | 174 | 174 |
| Energy information, policy, and regulation | 295 | 358 | 380 | 305 | 343 | 362 |
| Total, Energy | $3,182 | $1,317 | $1,672 | $–166 | $1,441 | $2,121 |
| **NATURAL RESOURCES AND ENVIRONMENT** | | | | | | |
| Water resources | 5,632 | 6,252 | 4,859 | 5,571 | 6,096 | 5,451 |
| Conservation and land management | 10,692 | 9,627 | 8,303 | 9,758 | 8,740 | 9,070 |
| Recreational resources | 2,988 | 3,028 | 2,926 | 2,963 | 3,189 | 3,123 |
| Pollution control and abatement | 8,557 | 8,138 | 7,667 | 8,485 | 8,030 | 8,418 |
| Other natural resources | 4,853 | 5,136 | 4,829 | 3,948 | 4,905 | 5,101 |
| Total, Natural resources and environment | $32,722 | $32,181 | $28,584 | $30,725 | $30,960 | $31,163 |
| **AGRICULTURE** | | | | | | |
| Farm income stabilization | 28,432 | 24,565 | 21,196 | 11,186 | 26,043 | 21,732 |
| Agricultural research and services | 4,298 | 4,549 | 4,036 | 4,254 | 4,461 | 4,288 |
| Total, Agriculture | $32,730 | $29,114 | $25,232 | $15,440 | $30,504 | $26,020 |
| **COMMERCE AND HOUSING CREDIT** | | | | | | |
| Mortgage credit | 17 | 506 | –536 | 2,659 | –1,027 | –4,286 |
| Postal Service | 2,117 | 1,452 | 1,885 | –4,070 | –442 | 2,174 |
| (On-budget) | (60) | (568) | (–1,889) | (60) | (568) | (–1,889) |
| (Off-budget) | (2,057) | (884) | (3,774) | (–4,130) | (–1,010) | (4,063) |
| Deposit insurance | 1 | 1 | 1 | –1,976 | –265 | –966 |
| Other advancement of commerce | 12,018 | 12,103 | 9,726 | 8,660 | 12,387 | 9,894 |
| Total, Commerce and housing credit | $14,153 | $14,062 | $11,076 | $5,273 | $10,653 | $6,816 |
| (On-budget) | (12,096) | (13,178) | (7,302) | (9,403) | (11,663) | (2,753) |
| (Off-budget) | (2,057) | (884) | (3,774) | (–4,130) | (–1,010) | (4,063) |
| **TRANSPORTATION** | | | | | | |
| Ground transportation | 45,229 | 45,668 | 44,672 | 40,743 | 43,694 | 45,625 |
| Air transportation | 18,330 | 18,507 | 16,441 | 16,743 | 17,951 | 17,258 |
| Water transportation | 7,200 | 7,033 | 7,900 | 6,898 | 6,371 | 7,368 |
| Other transportation | 301 | 365 | 421 | 242 | 470 | 422 |
| Total, Transportation | $71,060 | $71,573 | $69,434 | $64,626 | $68,486 | $70,673 |
| **COMMUNITY AND REGIONAL DEVELOPMENT** | | | | | | |
| Community development | 5,780 | 5,724 | 753 | 6,167 | 6,391 | 6,252 |
| Area and regional development | 2,535 | 2,905 | 5,419 | 2,329 | 2,969 | 2,855 |
| Disaster relief and insurance | 9,820 | 14,332 | 6,219 | 7,301 | 10,781 | 9,990 |
| Total, Community and regional development | $18,135 | $22,961 | $12,391 | $15,797 | $20,141 | $19,097 |
| **EDUCATION, TRAINING, EMPLOYMENT AND SOCIAL SERVICES** | | | | | | |
| Elementary, secondary and vocational education | 38,254 | 38,836 | 38,528 | 34,357 | 38,405 | 38,572 |
| Higher education | 25,602 | 29,212 | 26,894 | 25,264 | 28,766 | 22,269 |
| Research and general education aids | 3,061 | 3,186 | 3,068 | 3,005 | 3,349 | 3,246 |
| Training and employment | 7,255 | 7,456 | 7,241 | 7,912 | 7,384 | 6,876 |
| Other labor services | 1,610 | 1,635 | 1,564 | 1,552 | 1,661 | 1,603 |
| Social services | 16,210 | 16,548 | 15,906 | 15,855 | 16,689 | 16,137 |
| Total, Education, employment and social services | $91,992 | $96,873 | $93,201 | $87,945 | $96,254 | $88,703 |

| | BUDGET AUTHORITY | | | OUTLAYS | | |
|---|---|---|---|---|---|---|
| | 2004 ACTUAL | 2005 ESTIMATE | 2006 PROPOSED | 2004 ACTUAL | 2005 ESTIMATE | 2006 PROPOSED |
| **HEALTH** | | | | | | |
| Health care services | 219,540 | 223,475 | 257,112 | 210,092 | 226,315 | 236,027 |
| Health research and training | 28,932 | 29,501 | 29,338 | 27,099 | 28,257 | 29,362 |
| Consumer and occupational health and safety | 2,941 | 3,074 | 3,026 | 2,943 | 2,960 | 3,007 |
| Total, Health | $251,413 | $256,050 | $289,476 | $240,134 | $257,532 | $268,396 |
| **MEDICARE** | | | | | | |
| Total, Medicare | $271,656 | $294,282 | $345,861 | $269,360 | $295,432 | $345,746 |
| **INCOME SECURITY** | | | | | | |
| General retirement and disability insurance | 6,480 | 5,179 | 7,413 | 6,573 | 6,611 | 4,895 |
| Federal employee retirement and disability | 90,556 | 96,123 | 100,832 | 88,729 | 94,312 | 99,055 |
| Unemployment compensation | 45,596 | 38,235 | 39,312 | 44,994 | 38,066 | 39,330 |
| Housing assistance | 29,597 | 29,411 | 30,618 | 36,568 | 37,255 | 38,448 |
| Food and nutrition assistance | 48,582 | 53,427 | 60,253 | 46,012 | 53,103 | 56,877 |
| Other income security | 113,350 | 122,916 | 118,335 | 109,961 | 121,571 | 120,930 |
| Total, Income security | $334,161 | $345,291 | $356,763 | $332,837 | $350,918 | $359,535 |
| **SOCIAL SECURITY** | | | | | | |
| Total, Social Security | $496,047 | $520,213 | $546,832 | $495,548 | $519,686 | $544,821 |
| (On-budget) | (14,348) | (16,387) | (16,065) | (14,348) | (16,388) | (16,066) |
| (Off-budget) | (481,699) | (503,826) | (530,767) | (481,200) | (503,298) | (528,755) |
| **VETERANS' BENEFITS AND SERVICES** | | | | | | |
| Income security for veterans | 31,732 | 34,464 | 35,413 | 31,654 | 36,979 | 36,332 |
| Veterans' education, training and rehabilitation | 2,612 | 2,768 | 3,252 | 2,751 | 3,066 | 3,236 |
| Hospital and medical care for veterans | 27,342 | 28,797 | 28,901 | 26,783 | 26,579 | 28,099 |
| Veterans' housing | –1,941 | 798 | –49 | –1,980 | 790 | –55 |
| Other veterans' benefits and services | 735 | 777 | 818 | 571 | 747 | 778 |
| Total, Veterans' benefits and services | $60,480 | $67,604 | $68,335 | $59,779 | $68,161 | $68,390 |
| **ADMINISTRATION OF JUSTICE** | | | | | | |
| Federal law enforcement activities | 19,719 | 20,289 | 21,883 | 19,090 | 21,894 | 21,807 |
| Federal litigative and judicial activities | 9,525 | 9,880 | 10,561 | 9,685 | 9,937 | 10,914 |
| Federal correctional activities | 5,609 | 5,650 | 5,974 | 5,509 | 5,274 | 6,156 |
| Criminal justice assistance | 10,814 | 4,068 | 2,634 | 11,251 | 3,552 | 4,222 |
| Total, Administration of justice | $45,667 | $39,887 | $41,052 | $45,535 | $40,657 | $43,099 |
| **GENERAL GOVERNMENT** | | | | | | |
| Legislative functions | 3,166 | 3,190 | 3,632 | 3,187 | 3,425 | 3,671 |
| Executive direction and management | 580 | 633 | 560 | 510 | 634 | 572 |
| Central fiscal operations | 9,904 | 10,137 | 10,572 | 9,339 | 9,425 | 9,798 |
| General property and records management | 814 | 605 | 368 | 228 | 775 | 350 |
| Central personnel management | 207 | 237 | 212 | 217 | 241 | 218 |
| General purpose fiscal assistance | 7,702 | 3,424 | 3,190 | 7,675 | 3,421 | 3,187 |
| Other general government | 2,546 | 1,495 | 1,599 | 2,345 | 2,541 | 1,565 |
| Deductions for offsetting receipts | –1,679 | –1,607 | –1,607 | –1,679 | –1,607 | –1,607 |
| Total, General government | $23,240 | $18,114 | $18,526 | $21,822 | $18,855 | $17,754 |
| **NET INTEREST** | | | | | | |
| Interest on Treasury debt securities (gross) | 321,679 | 347,890 | 392,430 | 321,679 | 347,890 | 392,430 |
| Interest received by on-budget trust funds | –67,761 | –71,457 | –73,374 | –67,761 | –71,457 | –73,374 |
| Interest received by off-budget trust funds | –86,228 | –91,995 | –98,144 | –86,228 | –91,995 | –98,144 |
| Other interest | –4,541 | –4,704 | –8,641 | –4,473 | –4,693 | –8,641 |
| Other investment income | –2,972 | –1,797 | –1,195 | –2,972 | –1,797 | –1,195 |
| Total, Net interest | $160,177 | $177,937 | $211,076 | $160,245 | $177,948 | $211,076 |
| (On-budget) | (246,405) | (269,932) | (309,220) | (246,473) | (269,943) | (309,220) |
| (Off-budget) | (–86,228) | (–91,995) | (–98,144) | (–86,228) | (–91,995) | (–98,144) |
| **ALLOWANCES AND OFFSETTING RECEIPTS** | | | | | | |
| Total, Allowances | –– | $81,000 | –$411 | –– | $34,899 | $24,168 |
| Total, Undistributed offsetting receipts | –$58,537 | –$64,976 | –$69,773 | –$58,537 | –$64,976 | –$69,773 |
| (On-budget) | (–47,206) | (–54,065) | (–58,416) | (–47,206) | (–54,065) | (–58,416) |
| (Off-budget) | (–11,331) | (–10,911) | (–11,357) | (–11,331) | (–10,911) | (–11,357) |
| **TOTALS** | $2,407,446 | $2,477,354 | $2,547,549 | $2,292,215 | $2,479,404 | $2,567,617 |
| (On-budget) | (2,021,249) | (2,075,550) | (2,122,509) | (1,912,704) | (2,080,022) | (2,144,300) |
| (Off-budget) | (386,197) | (401,804) | (425,040) | (379,511) | (399,382) | (423,317) |

NOTE: Figures may not add due to rounding.

SOURCE: Office of Management and Budget

CBO said that under the president's budget, the deficit would fall to $394 billion in fiscal 2005, dropping to $332 billion in 2006 and $246 billion in 2009.

## ECONOMIC ASSUMPTIONS

The economic assumptions underpinning Bush's fiscal 2006 budget largely tracked the projections of congressional budget analysts and private forecasters.

The previous year, the White House had based its budget on an economic outlook that was significantly more conservative than that provided by CBO and the Blue Chip consensus forecast (an average based on the expectations of 50 private-sector economists). As a result, the administration's deficit projections for fiscal 2004 were unusually high. Critics said the White House overstated its projections with the intent of claiming progress toward cutting the deficit when the actual figures came in later in the year.

To avoid a repeat of such charges, the White House released its economic assumptions as soon as they were ready in December 2004. "The assumptions call for a continuation of the recent trends of strong, sustained growth, improving labor markets, low inflation, and, even allowing for a projected rise in the next few years, relatively low interest rates," OMB said in its budget documents.

The White House projected that gross domestic product (GDP), the total amount of goods and services produced inside the United States, would rise 3.6 percent in calendar 2005, a bit above the December projection of 3.5 percent and the same as the Blue Chip consensus. CBO projected a somewhat higher growth rate of 3.8 percent. All three forecasts were stronger than the historical long-term trend of roughly 3 percent annual GDP growth. *(Chart, this page)*

The administration assumed an unemployment rate of 5.3 percent for 2005, 0.1 percentage point higher than CBO and the Blue Chip consensus. OMB looked to business capital spending, net exports and consumer spending to drive an increase in the demand for labor in coming years.

The administration's five-year inflation estimate tracked the Blue Chip consensus forecast exactly and was at least two-tenths of a point higher than CBO's forecast. The White House predicted that inflation would average 2.4 percent in 2005, before dropping to 2.3 percent in 2006 and rising again and holding at 2.4 percent for the remainder of the five-year budget time frame. OMB noted that inflation had picked up in 2004 because of a surge in oil and other energy prices, but this trend was not expected to last. "With the recent easing of these prices, inflation is likely to be lower than in 2005," the budget said.

Some economists contended the projections of economic growth and tax receipts were understated. Indeed, there was a perception among some that the White House wanted to keep its estimates close to those in the private sector — even if those projections might be conservative — to avoid charges that it was relying too heavily on rosy economic growth forecasts to justify its tax cut policies. Over the past several years, top Republicans had argued that the best way to increase tax receipts and reduce the deficit was by cutting taxes to stimulate economic growth.

The White House's assumptions on interest rates were slightly lower than those from CBO and private economists. The interest rate forecast was also low by historical standards. For 91-day Treasury bills, the White House predicted an average 2.7 percent interest rate in 2005, three-tenths of a percentage point lower than the Blue Chip consensus and one-tenth of a point lower than CBO. The White House's estimates remained lower into the future. Likewise, for 10-year Treasury notes, the administration's forecast was lower than CBO's by two-tenths of a point and the private forecasters by one-tenth.

OMB included a traditional warning that even small errors in forecasting could have major consequences. If economic growth came in 1 percentage point less than forecast, sustained over the coming years, it would add $529 billion to the accumulated deficit. If growth were 1 percentage point lower than forecast in 2005 and the unemployment rate were to rise by one-half percentage point, that would add $200 billion to the deficit over five years. ∎

# Economic Forecasts Compared

| | 2005 | 2006 | 2007 | 2008 | 2009 | 2010 |
|---|---|---|---|---|---|---|
| **Real GDP growth** *(chain-weighted)* | | | | | | |
| Administration | 3.6% | 3.5% | 3.3% | 3.2% | 3.1% | 3.1% |
| Administration 2004 | 3.6 | 3.4 | 3.3 | 3.2 | 3.1 | 3.1 |
| CBO | 3.8 | 3.7 | 3.7 | 3.4 | 3.1 | 2.9 |
| Blue Chip | 3.6 | 3.4 | 3.2 | 3.2 | 3.1 | 3.3 |
| **Inflation** *(CPI)* | | | | | | |
| Administration | 2.4 | 2.3 | 2.4 | 2.4 | 2.4 | 2.4 |
| Administration 2004 | 1.5 | 1.8 | 2.1 | 2.4 | 2.5 | 2.5 |
| CBO | 2.4 | 1.9 | 2.1 | 2.2 | 2.2 | 2.2 |
| Blue Chip | 2.5 | 2.3 | 2.4 | 2.4 | 2.4 | 2.4 |
| **Unemployment** | | | | | | |
| Administration | 5.3 | 5.2 | 5.1 | 5.1 | 5.1 | 5.1 |
| Administration 2004 | 5.4 | 5.2 | 5.1 | 5.1 | 5.1 | 5.1 |
| CBO | 5.2 | 5.2 | 5.2 | 5.2 | 5.2 | 5.2 |
| Blue Chip | 5.2 | 5.2 | 5.1 | 5.1 | 5.1 | 5.1 |
| **91-day Treasury bills** | | | | | | |
| Administration | 2.7 | 3.5 | 3.8 | 4.0 | 4.1 | 4.2 |
| Administration 2004 | 2.4 | 3.3 | 4.0 | 4.3 | 4.4 | 4.4 |
| CBO | 2.8 | 4.0 | 4.6 | 4.6 | 4.6 | 4.6 |
| Blue Chip | 3.0 | 3.8 | 4.1 | 4.3 | 4.2 | 4.2 |
| **10-year Treasury notes** | | | | | | |
| Administration | 4.6 | 5.2 | 5.4 | 5.5 | 5.6 | 5.6 |
| Administration 2004 | 5.0 | 5.4 | 5.6 | 5.8 | 5.8 | 5.8 |
| CBO | 4.8 | 5.4 | 5.5 | 5.5 | 5.5 | 5.5 |
| Blue Chip | 4.7 | 5.3 | 5.6 | 5.6 | 5.6 | 5.6 |

This comparison of the forecasts from the administration, the Congressional Budget Office (CBO) and the Blue Chip consensus of private economists uses annual percentage changes in inflation-adjusted gross domestic product (GDP) and the consumer price index (CPI). The unemployment rate and the Treasury bill and note interest rates are annual averages. The administration forecast assumes enactment of the president's budget and therefore is not strictly comparable with those of CBO and the Blue Chip.

SOURCES: Office of Management and Budget, Congressional Budget Office, Blue Chip Economic Indicators

# Republicans Adopt Budget Resolution

CONGRESSIONAL REPUBLICANS produced a fiscal 2006 budget resolution that was adopted by slim margins in both chambers, without a single Democratic vote. The measure set an $843 billion fiscal 2006 cap on discretionary spending, including the first cut in non-defense discretionary programs since the Reagan administration. It also called for $34.7 billion in cuts from entitlement programs over five years — the first significant attempt to slow the growth in mandatory spending programs since a bipartisan budget-balancing deal was reached in 1997.

Adoption of the budget resolution (H Con Res 95) was a high priority for GOP leaders, who had been unable to complete a budget the previous year. Although they controlled both chambers, they had been unable to resolve an intraparty dispute over whether to reinstate so-called pay-as-you-go rules requiring that tax cuts or new entitlement spending be offset with other revenue or spending cuts. It was only the third time in 30 years that Congress had not completed a budget resolution. *(2004 Almanac, p. 4-9)*

The budget was a congressional document that did not go to the president for his signature, but it was important to the leadership because of the limit it set on discretionary spending and the special protection it could provide for subsequent bills to alter taxes and entitlement programs.

The limit on discretionary spending in the fiscal 2006 budget resolution mirrored President Bush's budget request, as calculated by the Congressional Budget Office (CBO). Any fiscal 2006 appropriations bill that exceeded the allocation would be subject to a point of order on the floor. In addition, the budget assumed that at least $50 billion in fiscal 2006 emergency funds would be appropriated for the wars in Iraq and Afghanistan; spending designated as an emergency was not subject to the cap. *(Bush budget, p. 4-3)*

The resolution instructed House and Senate authorizing committees to find specific savings to mandatory programs, which would be bundled together into a spending-cut reconciliation bill. It also called for two other reconciliation bills — one to reduce taxes by $70 billion and the other to increase the ceiling on federal borrowing. Reconciliation bills, which can only arise as a result of a budget resolution, are subject to special Senate rules that prohibit filibusters and bar amendments unrelated to the budget. The no-filibuster rule means that a reconciliation bill can be passed by a simple majority in the Senate, rather than requiring the 60 votes needed to halt a filibuster.

The central issue in House-Senate negotiations on a final budget resolution was how much to cut mandatory spending, especially Medicaid. To get a conference report on the budget through the Senate, House GOP leaders had to accept much less than the $69 billion in entitlement cuts that the House had initially passed. The final budget also included a Senate provision intended to pave the way for oil and gas drilling in portions of Alaska's Arctic National Wildlife Refuge (ANWR) — a GOP priority because it would allow such energy exploration to be part of a filibuster-proof reconciliation bill.

Republicans said the discretionary cap and entitlement cuts in the

**BOX SCORE**

**BILL:** H Con Res 95

**LEGISLATIVE ACTION:**

**House** adopted H Con Res 95 (H Rept 109-17), 218-214, on March 17.

**Senate** adopted S Con Res 18, 51-49, on March 17, and later inserted the text into H Con Res 95 and adopted it by voice vote.

**House** adopted the conference report (H Rept 109-62), 214-211, on April 28.

**Senate** adopted the conference report, 52-47, on April 28.

budget resolution would bring the deficit down fairly sharply to $211 billion in fiscal 2010. Democrats said the deficit would be worse than if the government ran on autopilot, because the budget called for $70 billion in tax cuts over five years while trimming mandatory spending programs by only $34.7 billion. Democrats also said future deficit calculations should include long-term costs for the Iraq war and other anticipated changes in law, such as reversing cuts to physicians' payments under Medicare and modifying the alternative minimum tax.

"When we add all of those things in and calculate their effect on the budget, here is what happens. ... The deficit never gets below $362 billion," said John M. Spratt Jr. of South Carolina, the ranking Democrat on the House Budget Committee.

## HIGHLIGHTS

Following are the main features of the fiscal 2006 budget resolution:

● **Discretionary spending.** A cap of $843 billion on discretionary spending, the one-third of the budget distributed annually through the appropriations bills. The budget recommended $438.9 billion for national defense, a 4 percent increase over fiscal 2005, and $29.1 billion for homeland security, a 4 percent increase. Appropriations outside of defense and homeland security would have to be cut by 1 percent for fiscal 2006 and would essentially be frozen through fiscal 2010. The overall cap was binding on appropriators, who would divide the funding into so-called 302(b) allocations for their subcommittees. Language in the budget stating how the funds should be allocated was only advisory, however.

● **Supplemental war spending.** An assumption that an additional $50 billion in fiscal 2006 discretionary funds would be needed for the wars in Iraq and Afghanistan, pending a larger supplemental spending request from the White House.

● **Mandatory spending cuts.** A net reduction of $34.7 billion over five years in the anticipated cost of entitlement programs, to be achieved through a reconciliation bill. Entitlement spending accounted for about 54 percent of the federal budget.

● **Tax cuts.** A total of $70 billion over five years in tax reductions, also to be achieved through a reconciliation bill. The budget resolution authorized an additional $36 billion in tax cuts, but did not protect them from a Senate filibuster.

● **Deficit.** An anticipated fiscal 2006 deficit of $382.7 billion, with declining deficits over the succeeding four years, reaching $254.4 billion in fiscal 2008 and $210.9 billion in fiscal 2010. That would beat by one year Bush's often-stated goal of cutting the deficit in half by 2009, using as a baseline the administration's initial fiscal 2004 deficit projection of $521 billion. If Social Security surpluses were not counted, however, the fiscal 2010 deficit was projected to reach $470.8 billion.

● **Debt limit increase.** Under the rules of the House, upon adoption of the budget by both chambers, the House was automatically considered to have passed a joint resolution increasing the statutory limit on the public debt, in this case from $8.184 trillion to $8.965 trillion, an increase of $781 million.

## LEGISLATIVE ACTION

### HOUSE COMMITTEE ACTION

Reflecting the influence of fiscal conservatives, the House Budget Committee approved a fiscal 2006 budget resolution (H Con Res 95 — H Rept 109-17) that called for $68.6 billion in cuts to mandatory programs over five years — about $18 billion more than Bush had requested in his budget. The resolution, drafted by Chairman Jim Nussle, R-Iowa, was approved, 22-15, on March 9.

The House resolution included:

● **Discretionary spending.** An $843 billion cap on discretionary appropriations, with $439 billion allocated for defense, $49.9 billion for homeland security activities spread through several agencies, and $404.1 billion, a decrease of 0.8 percent, for all other discretionary programs.

● **War spending.** An additional $50 billion in emergency fiscal 2006 funds in anticipation of a supplemental spending request from the White House.

● **Mandatory spending cuts.** Reconciliation instructions to nine authorizing committees to report legislation by Sept. 16 that would achieve $68.6 billion in net savings from entitlement programs over five years. Medicaid, education and pension law changes and the earned income tax credit were expected to produce most of the savings. While the resolution did not specifically mention Medicaid, it directed the Energy and Commerce Committee, whose jurisdiction included the program, to offer cuts totaling $20 billion, and it was assumed that most of the reduction would come from Medicaid.

● **Taxes.** Instructions to the Ways and Means Committee to report a reconciliation bill by June 24 that would cut taxes by $45 billion over five years. The resolution allowed for a total of $106 billion in tax cuts over five years, about $6 billion more than in Bush's budget, but only $45 billion would get reconciliation protection.

● **Deficit.** A projected deficit of $375.8 billion in fiscal 2006, falling to $229.4 billion in fiscal 2009, the year Bush vowed to halve the deficit.

The committee adopted one amendment, shifting $1.15 billion in discretionary budget authority from international affairs accounts to veterans' programs over five years. The proposal, adopted by voice vote, was offered by moderate Republican Jeb Bradley of New Hampshire.

The only Democratic amendment that found support on the GOP side was a proposal by the moderate-to-conservative Blue Dog Coalition that incorporated budget rules favored by conservatives. Among other things, it would have ended the House's automatic mechanism for approving an increase to the federal debt and required roll call votes on amendments that would cost at least $50 million. It failed on an 18-18 tie.

### HOUSE FLOOR ACTION

The House adopted the budget resolution March 17 by a narrow vote of 218-214, but only after GOP leaders had quelled a revolt by conservative members of the Republican Study Committee (RSC), who insisted on a new mechanism to stop spending bills that exceeded budget limits. *(House vote 88, p. H-30)*

The conservatives, led by RSC Chairman Mike Pence of Indiana, threatened to withhold their votes on the budget resolution unless they were satisfied. In the end, they settled for a promise from GOP leaders to amend House rules to create a new, though mostly redundant, point of order. It would apply when the House stripped fees or rescissions from a bill during floor debate, causing the remaining appropriation to exceed the discretionary allocation for the bill.

Some GOP authorizers expressed concern over the mandatory spending cuts that their committees were expected to deliver. Education and the Workforce Chairman John A. Boehner, R-Ohio, for example, acknowledged he would have difficulty producing the $21.4 billion in savings called for in the resolution. He was supposed to achieve a significant part of that through increases in premiums paid by companies to the financially troubled Pension Benefit Guaranty Corporation (PBGC).

Republicans defeated three Democratic substitutes. The Blue Dog Coalition, which usually offered a budget substitute, did not do so this time. The amendments were:

▸ A substitute by David R. Obey of Wisconsin, the ranking member on the Appropriations Committee, to increase the fiscal 2006 discretionary spending cap by $15.8 billion to allow extra funding for a variety of programs, including education, veterans and health care. The proposal was rejected, 180-242. *(House vote 82, p. H-28)*

▸ A Democratic substitute offered by Spratt to eliminate all mandatory spending cuts and increase taxes by $159 billion over five years, promising a balanced budget by 2012. It was rejected, 165-264. Illustrating divisions among Democrats, 36 members of the caucus voted against their leadership's alternative. *(House vote 87, p. H-30)*

▸ A substitute by the Congressional Black Caucus, which was rejected, 134-292. The amendment, offered by Melvin Watt of North Carolina, would have increased fiscal 2006 discretionary spending by $36.3 billion, focused mainly on education, job training, homeland security and veterans' programs, while rescinding tax cuts for wealthy individuals. *(House vote 85, p. H-28)*

### SENATE COMMITTEE ACTION

Across Capitol Hill, the Senate Budget Committee approved its version of the budget (S Con Res 18) by a vote of 12-10 on March 10, the day after the House committee acted. Unlike his House counterpart, newly installed Senate Budget Chairman Judd Gregg, R-N.H., had to work overtime to negotiate a plan that could appeal to moderate Republicans and win acceptance from GOP authorizers without completely alienating the fiscal conservatives. Powerful Republican committee chairmen, such as Saxby Chambliss, R-Ga., who ran the Agriculture Committee, and Michael B. Enzi, R-Wyo., chairman of the Senate Health, Education, Labor and Pensions panel, used their leverage to limit the demands upon them to produce savings.

The committee-approved resolution included:

● **Discretionary spending.** An $843.4 billion discretionary spending limit, $400 million higher than the House recommended. The resolution proposed to restore statutory "caps" on appropriated budget authority for three years — $843.4 billion in fiscal 2006, $868.5 billion in 2007, and $891.4 billion in 2008.

● **War spending.** An additional $50 billion in fiscal 2006 emergency spending for the war.

● **Mandatory spending cuts.** Instructions to eight authorizing committees to report proposals by June 6 that would save a total of $32 billion from entitlement programs over five years, significantly below the $51 billion sought by Bush and less than half the $68.6 billion proposed by the House. Gregg scaled back Bush's proposals to curb farm subsidies and raise PBGC premiums, but he stood firm on Medicaid, the federal-state health care plan for the poor and disabled, saying it was crucial for Congress to demonstrate a willingness to at least begin addressing the spiraling growth of entitlement programs. The resolution instructed the Finance Committee to find $15 billion in savings over five years, with the assumption that $14 billion of that would come from Medicaid.

# Debt Limit Increase Put Off Until 2006

THE HOUSE SENT the Senate a joint resolution in May to increase the statutory limit on the federal debt, but Congress took no further action. The Bush administration told lawmakers it did not expect to breach the existing debt limit until early 2006.

The limit applied to the government's outstanding public debt — in the form of Treasury securities, savings bonds and other government notes — and money borrowed from federal trust funds such as Social Security and Medicare.

Periodically, government borrowing came close to exceeding the debt ceiling. Congress then had no choice but to increase the limit — the government would default on its obligations otherwise — but the vote was often politically uncomfortable, particularly in times of rising deficits.

Early in the 109th Congress, it looked as though the Treasury Department would need more borrowing authority before the end of the year. Democrats tied the anticipated increase to the Bush administration's borrowing and tax cut policies. Republicans blamed the rise in debt on the bursting of the Internet stock market bubble, the Sept. 11, 2001, terrorist attacks and the subsequent military operations in Iraq and Afghanistan.

The House passed a debt limit increase automatically under a procedure known as the "Gephardt rule," which "deemed" that such a bill had been passed once both chambers adopted a budget resolution. The House and Senate both adopted the conference report on the fiscal 2006 budget resolution (H Con Res 95) on April 28. The resulting legislation (H J Res 47) proposed to increase the $8.18 trillion federal debt limit by $781 billion to nearly $9 trillion. (*Budget resolution, p. 4-9*)

The aim of the rule — named for its creator, former Rep. Richard A. Gephardt, D-Mo. (1977-2005) — was to get a debt limit increase through the House without forcing members to cast what could be a politically painful vote. Republicans renamed the procedure the "Hastert rule" after Speaker J. Dennis Hastert, R-Ill.

Republicans also gave themselves the option of moving a debt limit increase as a reconciliation bill. That would have helped in the Senate, where reconciliation bills are protected from filibusters, but the House would have had to vote on such a bill.

Congress put off action after the Treasury Department wrote lawmakers in August to say that a smaller-than-expected deficit attributed to a surge in federal tax revenue meant the debt ceiling did not have to be raised until sometime in the first quarter of 2006. The federal government ended fiscal 2005 with a deficit of $318.3 billion, about $100 billion less than projected at the start of the year.

Congress had last increased the debt ceiling in 2003. Republican congressional leaders delayed the vote until shortly after Election Day. The House passed the increase (PL 108-415) by a 208-204 vote. The margin in the Senate was 52-44, with both votes falling largely along party lines. The House cleared the legislation Nov. 18, the day the Treasury had set as the deadline for avoiding default. (*2003 Almanac, p. 5-12*)

● **ANWR.** As part of the reconciliation instructions, the resolution assumed the government would receive $2.4 billion in leasing revenues from drilling in ANWR.

● **Taxes.** Instructions to the Finance Committee to report a bill by Sept. 7 that would cut taxes by $70.2 billion over five years. Gregg said that tax-writers would be able to extend several tax cuts that were enacted in 2003 (PL 108-27) but slated to expire before 2010, including those on stock dividends, capital gains, small-business expensing, tuition costs and state and local sales taxes.

● **Deficit.** A projected $362 billion deficit for 2006, falling to $236 billion by 2009 and $232.3 billion in fiscal 2010.

## SENATE FLOOR ACTION

The Senate approved its budget resolution, 51-49, March 17, just hours after the House had acted. However, moderate Republicans teamed up with Democrats to shrink the mandatory spending cuts to $17 billion from the $32 billion approved by the committee — mainly by eliminating $14 billion in Medicaid reductions proposed by Bush. (*Senate vote 81, p. S-16*)

The Medicaid vote took some of the shine off two significant GOP wins by Gregg and Majority Leader Bill Frist, R-Tenn., on the divisive issues of pay-as-you-go rules and drilling in ANWR.

During a marathon session that featured voice or roll call votes on 59 amendments, the Senate:

▶ Adopted, 52-48, an amendment by Gordon H. Smith, R-Ore., to strip the reconciliation instructions to the Finance Committee. Instead, the amendment called for a presidentially appointed commission to study ways to overhaul Medicaid. (*Senate vote 58, p. S-13*)

The vote, which had the support of seven Republicans and all Senate Democrats, stung Gregg, who had made Medicaid cuts the centerpiece of his budget. A furious lobbying effort by Frist and administration officials failed to sway key moderates such as Susan Collins, R-Maine, who ended up as the decisive vote. "What we have said with this vote is that Congress is unwilling to curb spending in any of the areas where explosive growth is occurring," Gregg said. "We are effectively kicking the can down the road for maybe another decade, because I predict if we don't get these savings done this year, it will be a long time before we have another real opportunity."

The action also exasperated House Republicans, who wondered aloud how they could get the deep cuts they hoped for. "I'm not sure how we get a conference with the Senate," Nussle said. "This is going to be very difficult. Last year, they were at least trying. This year I think they almost gave up before they started the process."

▶ Adopted, 55-45, an amendment by Jim Bunning, R-Ky., to increase tax cuts protected in a reconciliation bill by $63.9 billion over five years — nearly double the amount in the original plan. Bunning's stated intent was to repeal a 1993 law (PL 103-66) that required some senior citizens to pay income tax on 85 percent of their Social Security benefits, but because any change in tax policy had to go through the Finance Committee, the only effect of the amendment was to increase the tax cut total protected from filibusters to $129 billion. Five Democrats, including three who faced re-election in 2006, voted for Bunning's amendment. (*Senate vote 74, p. S-15*)

Combined with the higher Medicaid spending, the additional tax cuts pushed the fiscal 2009 deficit under the budget resolution to about $255 billion — perilously close to breaking Bush's promise to cut the

deficit in half by that point.

▶ Adopted, 51-49, a proposal by Edward M. Kennedy, D-Mass., to raise the discretionary spending cap by $5.4 billion, to $848.8 billion, offset by a $5.4 billion reduction in the tax cut instructions, with the assumption that the extra funds would be dedicated to education. (*Senate vote 68, p. S-14*)

▶ Rejected, 49-51, an amendment by Maria Cantwell, D-Wash., to eliminate the ANWR provision. The vote was a reversal for drilling opponents, who had won a 52-48 vote to strike a similar provision in 2003. (*Senate vote 52, p. S-12; 2003 Almanac, p. 5-8*)

▶ Rejected, on a 50-50 tie, an attempt by Russ D. Feingold, D-Wis., to add pay-as-you-go budget language requiring that any tax cut or new entitlement spending proposal be fully offset or face a 60-vote point of order in the Senate. Feingold had succeeded, 51-48, on a similar amendment in 2004. (*Senate vote 53, p. S-13*)

Republicans Lincoln Chafee of Rhode Island, Olympia J. Snowe of Maine and George V. Voinovich of Ohio supported the PAYGO amendment and subsequently voted against the budget.

▶ Rejected, 46-54, an attempt by Max Baucus, D-Mont., to eliminate the $2.8 billion in cuts assigned to the Agriculture Committee. The Senate savings still fell far short of the $9 billion in agriculture cuts proposed by Bush and the $5.3 billion in the House version. (*Senate vote 69, p. S-15*)

▶ Adopted, 73-26, an amendment by Appropriations Chairman Thad Cochran, R-Miss., and ranking Democrat Robert C. Byrd of West Virginia to strike language that would have given the president new authority to determine which appropriations qualified as emergency spending. Under Gregg's original version, emergency spending would have counted against the appropriations cap for that fiscal year unless the president agreed with Congress and designated such spending an emergency. The vote to drop the language demonstrated the enduring clout of the Appropriations Committee. (*Senate vote 67, p. S-14*)

▶ Adopted a host of other amendments aimed at increasing funding for education, health care research and veterans' programs without increasing the overall cap. But as Gregg repeatedly reminded his colleagues, none of the language was binding on the appropriators.

## CONFERENCE/FINAL ACTION

The House adopted the conference report on the budget resolution (H Rept 109-62) by a vote of 214-211 on April 28; the Senate adopted the report, 52-47, later that day. (*House vote 149, p. H-48; Senate vote 114, p. S-22*)

The final budget closely resembled the version Gregg had put before his committee. The $34.7 billion in savings from mandatory programs over five years was only slightly larger than the $32 billion in the Senate bill but about half the $69 billion in the House version. The House agreed to take the Senate's proposal for a five-year, $70 billion tax cut reconciliation bill. Panels were told to report both the tax and spending cut bills in September.

An overriding desire to finish the budget resolution prompted House Republican leaders to make concessions to the small but well-positioned band of Senate GOP moderates who took a stand against future cuts in programs aimed at the poor or unemployed.

During several weeks of talks with the White House and Senate GOP leaders, Smith agreed to accept $10 billion in Medicaid cuts if a presidential study commission was created to recommend ways to wring savings from the program without hurting beneficiaries. But he balked when he discovered that budget negotiators also expected the Finance

Committee to propose an additional $6 billion in cuts coming from other programs such as Supplemental Security Income, which provides cash grants to the poorest of the poor.

In the end, Nussle and GOP leaders agreed to drop the extra $6 billion. They said taking the first step to cut mandatory spending was more important than standing firm on the higher figure. "The [budget] still maintains its basic integrity, which is the need to move forward to try to address major entitlements in the out years," said Gregg.

Senate GOP moderates were not the only ones to play a strong hand in limiting the entitlement cuts. Chambliss made it plain he would not accept significantly more than the $2.8 billion in cuts to farm subsidies and food stamp programs included in the Senate budget. Conferees settled on $3 billion. The House called for $9 billion.

Meanwhile, business groups lobbied hard to fend off an increase in PBGC premiums. Although the House proposed to raise $18 billion through such an increase, the final budget called for $6.6 billion in additional PBGC receipts.

The final budget instructed the House Resources and Senate Energy and Natural Resources committees to find $2.4 billion over five years for deficit reduction, with the assumption that the funding would come from leasing drilling rights in ANWR.

Despite the political pain encountered in even talking about entitlement cuts, the reductions assumed in the budget resolution amounted to just 0.4 percent of the $9.1 trillion total spending for such programs expected in fiscal 2006 through 2010. (*1997 Almanac, p. 2-47*)

## POSTSCRIPT

In the fall, Republican Speaker J. Dennis Hastert of Illinois called on the House to revise the budget resolution to require deeper cuts in mandatory spending and across-the-board reductions in discretionary programs. Hastert was reflecting a determined push by fiscal conservatives to offset a portion of the mounting relief and reconstruction costs following hurricanes Katrina and Rita in the Gulf Coast.

But Hastert and acting Majority Leader Roy Blunt, R-Mo., abandoned the idea after running into resistance from Republican moderates. The Senate leadership refused to consider such a change in their chamber, arguing that it was unnecessary and would take too much time. House leaders instead persuaded their authorizing committees to approve additional savings as part of a spending-cut reconciliation bill without relying on a new budget resolution.

● **Mandatory savings.** Before adjourning, Congress came close to clearing a reconciliation bill that would cut the expected growth of entitlement spending. Republican leaders had to strip out the ANWR provision to get the conference report through the House. Senate Democrats then raised procedural hurdles that forced a second House vote in 2006. The House cleared the bill — which CBO calculated would save $38.8 billion over five years — on Feb. 1, 2006 (PL 109-171). (*Budget reconciliation, p. 4-13*)

● **Tax cuts.** Republicans had less success on a tax reconciliation bill. The House and Senate passed markedly different tax cut packages in December (HR 4297, S 2020). In the early days of the second session, tax-writers remained unable to reconcile the demands of GOP conservatives to extend tax breaks for capital gains and dividends, and the insistence of moderate Republicans and Democrats that the bill modify the alternative minimum tax. (*Tax cut bill, p. 15-3*)

● **Debt limit.** Congress took no further action in the first session on legislation to increase the debt limit (H J Res 47). (*Debt limit, p. 4-11*) ■

# Mandatory Spending Cuts Clear in 2006

CONGRESS COMPLETED WORK on a budget reconciliation bill that promised to reduce spending on entitlement programs by $38.8 billion over five years — the first reduction in mandatory spending since 1997. The bill was a top priority for the Republican leadership and President Bush, but faced near-unanimous opposition from congressional Democrats. Though Democrats could not stop the bill, they raised a procedural hurdle at the last moment that forced final action on the measure into 2006. The bill cleared Feb. 1, 2006, and Bush signed it into law Feb. 8 (S 1932 — PL 109-171).

The biggest savings came from changes to federal student loan programs, Medicare and Medicaid. The bill also required higher premiums for the federal pension guarantee agency and counted on additional funds from auctioning portions of the electromagnetic spectrum. Those funds were used to offset some mandatory spending and to help pay for new expenditures that were included in the bill.

Republicans paved the way for the spending-cut package early in the year, when they adopted a fiscal 2006 budget resolution (H Con Res 95) that included instructions for a reconciliation bill that would reduce mandatory spending by $34.7 billion over five years. Reconciliation legislation has special protections in the Senate, where it is not subject to a filibuster. That meant that GOP leaders could count on passing the spending cuts with a simple majority, rather than the 60 votes that would be needed to cut off a filibuster. *(Budget resolution, p. 4-9)*

The leadership left the difficult work of actually putting such a bill together for the crowded end of the session. By that point Hurricane Katrina had altered the dynamic. The devastating storm generated new concern about the poor, whose suffering in New Orleans captured the nation's attention, but it also led fiscal conservatives to demand even deeper spending cuts to offset some of the tens of billions of dollars needed to cope with the Gulf Coast calamity. Within two weeks of the Aug. 29 storm, Congress had cleared $62.3 billion in emergency relief, and more was expected. *(Hurricane supplementals, p. 2-58)*

The Senate passed its reconciliation bill Nov. 3, proposing to cut entitlement spending by a net $35 billion over five years. Fiscal conservatives wanted deeper cuts, but influential Senate GOP moderates, including Gordon H. Smith of Oregon, refused to support more than $10 billion in cuts to Medicaid and held fast against other cuts to programs for the poor. The Senate bill included provisions to open a portion of Alaska's Arctic National Wildlife Refuge (ANWR) to oil and gas drilling.

Two weeks later, after repeated starts and stops, the House passed a bill that included $50 billion in net cuts to mandatory programs. When they returned from the Thanksgiving break, House and Senate negotiators managed to settle on a $38.8 billion five-year package. The ANWR language was removed, because House leaders concluded it was the only way they could get the conference report through their chamber. The provisions were attached to the fiscal 2006 Defense appropriations bill (PL 109-148) instead, but were ultimately dropped.

Democrats generally denounced the final bill, saying it would bring

## BOX SCORE

**BILL:**
S 1932 — PL 109-171

**LEGISLATIVE ACTION:**

**Senate** passed S 1932, 52-47, on Nov. 3.

**House** passed HR 4241 (H Rept 109-276), 217-215, on Nov. 18 and then inserted the text into S 1932.

**House** adopted the conference report on S 1932 (H Rept 109-362), 212-206, Dec. 19.

**Senate** rejected the conference report on procedural grounds Dec. 21 and approved an amended version of S 1932, 51-50.

**House** agreed to the amendment, 216-214, on Feb. 1, 2006, clearing the bill

**President** signed Feb. 8, 2006.

pain to the poor to help finance Republican tax cuts for the wealthy. No Democrat voted for the conference report in either chamber.

Republicans said they were doing the heavy lifting to overhaul mandatory spending programs such as Medicare, Medicaid and student loans that accounted for 55 percent of the budget and were growing on autopilot. They said their efforts were targeted at making the programs more efficient, with a minimal effect on beneficiaries.

However, Republicans included billions in new spending in the package in an effort to sway enough centrist votes to enact it. That reduced the net savings and drew the ire of GOP conservatives, who argued for omitting new spending provisions and concentrating on deficit reduction.

The final bill cut $5 billion more than required in the budget resolution and was expected to reduce federal spending by less than 0.3 percent over five years.

The package promised net savings of $4.7 billion over five years from projected spending on Medicaid, $6.4 billion from Medicare, $11.9 billion from mandatory student loan subsidies, $2.7 billion from farm programs and $1.5 billion from child support enforcement. New receipts included $3.6 billion from increased pension premiums and about $10 billion from auctioning off broadcast spectrum remaining from the transition to digital television.

Sweeteners added to gain votes included $7.3 billion to avert a scheduled 4.4 percent cut in doctors' Medicare reimbursements, about $1 billion to extend expired milk subsidies, $1 billion in budget authority for heating subsidies for the poor, $1 billion in budget authority for child care subsidies and $3.7 billion for new math, science and engineering scholarships. Last-minute deals to secure votes included removing any cuts to sugar subsidies and nixing a $1.9 billion cut to Medicare reimbursements for durable medical equipment. *(Provisions, p. 4-18)*

## HIGHLIGHTS

The following are major elements of the 2005 reconciliation law. Savings are in outlays over a five-year period (fiscal 2006 through 2010) as estimated by the Congressional Budget Office (CBO). The basis for comparison is a baseline projection issued by CBO in March that showed what existing programs would cost, adjusted for inflation.

● **Agriculture.** Net savings of $2.7 billion from reducing advances on direct subsidy payments to farmers, and reducing funding for mandatory conservation, research and rural development programs. The total included a two-year extension of the expired milk subsidy program, at a cost of $998 million.

● **Student loans.** Savings of more than $20 billion, combined with about $9.3 billion in new spending, resulting in net savings of $11.9 billion over five years. The biggest savings came from provisions that reduced yields for lenders, increased interest rates for parents' loans and eliminated mandatory funding for the administrative costs of student loan programs.

● **Medicaid.** A net reduction of $4.7 billion over five years from the

projected growth in spending for Medicaid, the federal-state health care program for the poor. CBO said the final bill included a net of $6.9 billion in Medicaid savings, but of that total, $2.1 billion was reallocated to help with Medicaid costs in states most affected by Katrina. The bill reduced the price Medicaid paid for prescription drugs by $3.9 billion; increased cost sharing for Medicaid beneficiaries and allowed states to reduce benefits, for a savings of $3.2 billion; tightened asset transfer rules to make it more difficult for people to qualify for long-term care coverage, for a savings of $2.4 billion. The law included about $3.6 billion in new Medicaid spending.

● **Medicare.** A net $6.4 billion reduction over five years in the growth of spending on Medicare, the federal health care program for the elderly and disabled. The biggest savings came from reducing Medicare payments for some imaging services, accelerating plans to charge premiums for some beneficiaries, reducing payments to home health care providers and reducing payments to "disproportionate share" hospitals, which have a large number of low-income patients.

The net savings were after a $7.3 billion provision that eliminated a scheduled 4.4 percent reduction in Medicare payments to physicians in 2006, instead freezing funding for one year at the 2005 level.

● **Child support.** $1.5 billion in savings over five years through changes to the child support enforcement program, mainly by eliminating federal matching funds to states in 2008 for the funds they use as incentive payments on child support enforcement.

● **Supplemental Security Income.** $712 million over five years from two changes in the Supplemental Security Income (SSI) program, which provides payments to poor, elderly and disabled individuals. The law required the Social Security Administration to review 20 percent of all favorable adult disability level determinations made by the states. It also required that more retroactive benefits be paid in installments.

● **Spectrum auction.** A net $7.4 billion from auctioning off analog frequencies vacated by television broadcasters as they switch to all-digital transmissions. That money was counted as an offset to entitlement spending. The law set Feb. 17, 2009, as the deadline for television stations to complete their transition from analog to digital transmission. The auction was expected to generate about $10 billion, but $2.6 billion was to be spent on other programs, including up to $1.4 billion in outlays to help consumers pay for equipment to keep their analog sets working after the digital transition and $1 billion to help first-responders acquire interoperable communications systems.

● **Pension insurance.** $3.6 billion over five years as a result of increased premiums paid by employers to the Pension Benefit Guaranty Corporation (PBGC), the federal agency that insures private pension plans. The annual flat-rate premiums paid by companies with pension plans increased to $30 from $19 per plan participant for single-employer plans and to $8 from $2.60 per worker for multi-employer plans. The law also established a new premium to be paid by companies that terminated their pension plans while in bankruptcy. Once the company emerged from bankruptcy, it was required to pay the PBGC $3,750 over three years for each plan participant.

● **Deposit insurance.** A net $250 million over five years from increasing the total premiums paid by banks and savings associations to the Federal Deposit Insurance Corporation (FDIC).

The law merged the FDIC's two deposit insurance funds — the Bank Insurance Fund and the Savings Association Insurance Fund — into a single fund, the Deposit Insurance Fund. It allowed risk-based premiums for insured institutions, and increased the amount covered in certain types of individual retirement accounts and 401(k)s to $250,000 from $100,000. The FDIC could increase the $100,000 deposit insurance available on most

bank accounts to compensate for inflation starting in 2010.

● **LIHEAP.** An additional $250 million in fiscal 2007 for the Low-Income Home Energy Assistance Program (LIHEAP), plus an extra $750 million for assistance to offset higher-than-anticipated energy costs caused by hurricanes Katrina and Rita. None of the money could be spent after the end of fiscal 2007.

● **TANF.** Reauthorization through fiscal 2010 of the welfare program known as Temporary Assistance for Needy Families (TANF) at the existing level of $16.6 billion a year for basic block grants. Supplemental grants were reauthorized for three years at the existing level of $319 million a year. The law also made some cuts, including eliminating bonuses that had been given to states for actions such as moving TANF recipients into jobs, saving $755 million over five years. A new grant program to promote healthy marriage was estimated to cost $604 million over five years. The net effect of all TANF provisions was a $374 million spending increase over five years.

● **Anti-dumping rule.** $300 million over five years from phasing out a trade law (PL 106-387) known as the Byrd amendment, under which anti-dumping and countervailing duties collected by the government were distributed to the domestic companies that were hurt by the imports. Instead, the funds were to be kept in the Treasury Department. The World Trade Organization had found that the Byrd amendment violated international trade laws.

## LEGISLATIVE ACTION

Under the fiscal 2006 budget resolution, House and Senate authorizers were instructed to submit mandatory savings provisions to their respective Budget committees by Sept. 16. The Budget panels were responsible for assembling the proposals and taking the resulting bill to the floor. In reality, the Senate bill was not introduced until Oct. 27. House Budget Chairman Jim Nussle of Iowa did not introduce his version until Nov. 7.

The House leadership had an especially difficult time. In an effort to quell a revolt by GOP conservatives over the mounting hurricane recovery costs, Speaker J. Dennis Hastert, R-Ill., called in early October for the first midsession amendment to a budget resolution since 1977. He said the leadership wanted to increase the requirement for mandatory savings to $50 billion and require across-the-board cuts in discretionary spending. But Hastert and Roy Blunt, R-Mo. — who had replaced Tom DeLay, R-Texas, as majority leader — ran into resistance from Republican moderates and ultimately abandoned the idea.

In the Senate, Budget Chairman Judd Gregg, R-N.H., and Majority Leader Bill Frist, R-Tenn., pressed ahead with plans to find hurricane offsets without trying to change the budget resolution. Frist called on the authorizers to make voluntary cuts beyond the required $34.7 billion, though most committees did not.

## SENATE COMMITTEE ACTION

The Senate Budget Committee voted 12-10 along party lines Oct. 26 to approve a bill (S 1932) that promised $39.1 billion in net savings over five years. The package included $71 billion in gross savings and $32 billion in new spending.

The bulk of the proposed savings were from Medicare, Medicaid and student loan programs, combined with new receipts from auctioning off analog spectrum and leasing drilling rights in parts of ANWR. The biggest controversies were over how much to cut from Medicare vs. Medicaid, and whether to include the ANWR provisions.

The Budget Committee compiled the bill from the proposals approved by the following eight Senate committees:

● **Agriculture.** The Agriculture, Nutrition and Forestry Committee

voted 11-9 on Oct. 19 to: Reduce commodity payments to farmers by $1.3 billion over five years; cut conservation programs by $1.1 billion. Reduce the maximum advance payments that farmers could receive to 40 percent from 50 percent for the 2006 crop year, and to 29 percent in crop years 2007 to 2011, saving almost $1 billion over five years. Plans to cut the food stamp program by $574 million were dropped. A two-year extension of the Milk Income Loss Contract was included at a cost of $998 million. (Savings: $3 billion, the same as required in the budget resolution)

● **Banking.** The Banking, Housing and Urban Affairs Committee voted 12-8 on Oct. 18 to: Retain the existing $100,000 limit on deposit insurance but adjust it for inflation starting in 2010. Allow more flexibility in determining whether to change bank premiums. Make a federal housing disposition program subject to annual appropriations. (Savings: $470 million, as in the budget resolution)

● **Commerce, Science and Transportation.** The committee voted 19-3 on Oct. 20 to: Set an April 2009 deadline for TV broadcasters to relinquish analog spectrum, which could then be auctioned by the government for an estimated $10 billion. Spend $3 billion to subsidize transition to digital for certain consumers. Money also would go for other purposes, including communications equipment for first-responders. (Receipts: $5 billion net; the budget required $4.8 billion)

● **Energy and Natural Resources.** The committee voted 13-9 on Oct. 19 to: Approve legislation that would generate federal revenue by leasing oil and gas drilling rights in sections of ANWR, authorizing the Interior Department to hold two lease sales by 2010. (Receipts: $2.5 billion; the budget resolution assumed $2.4 billion)

● **Environment and Public Works.** The panel by voice vote Oct. 18 recommended postponing until the end of 2008, a provision in the new highway law (PL 109-59) that exempted Alaska highway spending from federal obligation limits. (Savings: $27 million, same as in the budget)

● **Finance.** The committee voted 11-9 on Oct. 25 to: Save $18.6 billion from Medicare, coupled with $12.9 billion in additional spending, mainly to provide higher payments to doctors who served Medicare patients, for a net savings of $5.7 billion. Change the way Medicare paid for drugs, including the formula used to reimburse pharmacists. Eliminate a stabilization fund created by the 2003 Medicare drug law (PL 108-173) to entice preferred provider organizations to offer coverage in underserved regions. Reduce Medicaid spending by $4.3 billion. (Savings: $10 billion, same as in the budget)

● **Health, Education, Labor and Pensions.** The committee voted 15-5 on Oct. 18 to: Increase PBGC premiums bringing in $6.7 billion. Save a net $7 billion from student loan programs, mainly by reducing subsidies to lenders. CBO estimated that the education proposals would produce billions in savings beyond the $7 billion needed, but the committee used those savings for other education expenses. The bill called for two new mandatory grant programs to supplement Pell grants at a cost of $1.9 billion per year. (Savings: $13.7 billion net, the same as in the budget)

● **Judiciary.** The committee voted 14-2 on Oct. 20 to: Raise the minimum fee for non-immigrant L-1 visas by $750. Retrieve and reissue up to 30,000 unused H-1B visas from previous years with an added $500 fee. Retrieve and reissue unused immigrant work visas and increase the fee by $500. (Receipts: $565 million; the budget required $300 million)

## SENATE FLOOR ACTION

The Senate passed the bill, 52-47, on Nov. 3 after defeating an attempt to strip out the ANWR provisions. Before passage, the Senate adopted a series of amendments that added billions in new spending,

reducing the net savings to $35 billion from the $39.1 billion proposed by the authorizing committees. *(Senate vote 303, p. S-59)*

The leadership lost five moderate Republicans — Olympia J. Snowe and Susan Collins of Maine, Mike DeWine of Ohio, Norm Coleman of Minnesota and Lincoln Chafee of Rhode Island. Two moderate Democrats, Ben Nelson of Nebraska and Mary L. Landrieu of Louisiana, voted for the bill. Landrieu voted "yes" after billions of dollars in hurricane relief funds were added on the Senate floor.

Bush praised passage of the bill, though two days earlier the White House had issued a veto threat over the proposed elimination of the stabilization fund for the Medicare prescription drug program.

Gregg said it was "the first time in nearly a decade that we have succeeded in reviewing and reducing the federal rate of entitlement spending, which is rapidly outpacing the growth of our economy." Frist called the vote "a victory that we're going to relish here for a while."

Democratic leaders said the bill's savings would not even pay for a planned $70 billion tax cut package — the other half of Republicans' budget-reconciliation strategy — let alone make a dent in the budget deficit, which CBO estimated at $1.6 trillion over five years.

During the floor debate, the Senate:

▸ Rejected, 48-51, an attempt by Maria Cantwell, D-Wash., to strike the provisions that would open sections of ANWR to oil drilling. *(Senate vote 288, p. S-57)*

▸ Adopted by voice vote a proposal by Michael B. Enzi, R-Wyo., to add about $2.6 billion over five years in new education spending, including $1.7 billion in aid related to Katrina and $900 million in reduced fees on student loans.

▸ Adopted, by voice vote, an amendment by David Vitter, R-La., to provide $1.7 billion in contingent funding for coastal restoration in hurricane-damaged states and to upgrade communications for first-responders. The money was to come from spectrum sales, though only to the extent those sales generated more than $11 billion. However, generosity to the Gulf Coast had its limits. The Senate rejected, 48-51, a proposal by Blanche Lincoln, D-Ark., to add about $5 billion in Medicaid coverage for hurricane victims. *(Senate vote 285, p. S-56)*

▸ Adopted, 54-45, a proposal by Jeff Bingaman, D-N.M., to prevent scheduled reductions in certain Medicaid matching funds for some states for fiscal 2006, offset by extending prescription drug rebates in Medicaid managed care organizations. *(Senate vote 291, p. S-57)*

▸ Adopted by voice vote an amendment by Smith to allocate $450 million to states for a demonstration project providing Medicaid coverage to impoverished individuals with HIV.

▸ Adopted by voice vote an amendment by Max Baucus, D-Mont., to add $800 million to community pharmacy payments under Medicaid over five years, paid for by larger drug rebates.

▸ Rejected, 49-50, an attempt by Bill Nelson, D-Fla., to prevent a $1.3 billion increase in Medicare Part B premiums arising from the 1 percent increase in physicians' Medicare reimbursement rates. *(Senate vote 287, p. S-57)*

▸ Rejected an amendment by Snowe to allow the government to negotiate with pharmaceutical companies for less expensive Medicare drugs. Supporters failed, 51-48, to waive a point of order against the proposal; 60 votes were required. *(Senate vote 302, p. S-59)*

▸ Rejected a proposal by Kent Conrad of North Dakota, ranking Democrat on the Budget panel, to restore pay-as-you-go rules that would prevent passage of tax cuts or new mandatory spending without offsets. Supporters failed, 50-49, to waive a point of order. *(Senate vote 283, p. S-56)*

▸ Defeated, 46-53, an attempt by Finance Committee Chairman

Charles E. Grassley, R-Iowa, to cap commodity payments at $250,000 a year for married couples and $125,000 for individuals. The vote was a major win for large farms. The Senate adopted a similar provision in 2002, but it was stripped out later during conference with the House. *(Senate vote 290, p. S-57)*

▶ Rejected, 30-69, an amendment by John McCain, R-Ariz., to accelerate digital TV conversion by a year to April 7, 2008, to free up spectrum for use by public safety radios. *(Senate vote 293, p. S-58)*

▶ Agreed, 93-6, to an amendment by Trent Lott, R-Miss., that added language from a separate bill (S 1516) to restructure Amtrak and authorize more than $12 billion over six years for the nation's passenger rail service. *(Senate vote 292, p. S-57)*

## HOUSE COMMITTEE ACTION

Even as Senate leaders cheered their hard-fought win, House GOP leaders were scrambling to salvage their bolder budget-cutting plan in the face of a backlash by moderates.

The House Budget Committee approved a $53.9 billion savings package (HR 4241 — H Rept 109-276) Nov. 3 on a near party-line vote of 21-17. Nussle rejected Democrats' assertions that the cuts would cause significant pain, noting the savings would equal less than one-half of 1 percent of total mandatory spending over five years.

But before they could take the bill to the floor, Blunt and Hastert still had to negotiate changes to appease a group of moderates upset over oil drilling provisions as well as the cuts to Medicaid, food stamps, child-support enforcement and farm aid. Multiple closed-door meetings with rank-and-file members failed to yield the 218 votes needed for passage. "I fully expect we'll have 100 percent of Democrats voting against the reconciliation bill," said House Minority Leader Nancy Pelosi, D-Calif. "We'll make this budget very hot for the Republicans to handle."

The House bill differed from the Senate version in a number of major ways. Because House GOP conservatives refused to touch Medicare, their bill got all of its health-care savings from Medicaid ($9.5 billion). In the Senate, where GOP moderates insisted on avoiding changes that would affect Medicaid recipients, the bill split the savings between Medicaid ($4.3 billion) and Medicare ($5.7 billion).

As part of the Medicaid cuts, the House authorizers proposed giving states greater flexibility to impose cost sharing on Medicaid beneficiaries and to limit benefit packages. Moderates did score a victory in the House by scuttling a proposed increase in other co-pays from $3 to $5. The Senate bill included no changes to Medicaid cost sharing.

House authorizers did not include Senate provisions to eliminate the stabilization fund created under the Medicare law, or to allow an increase in the payment rate for Medicare doctors in 2006.

The Budget Committee compiled the recommendations approved by the following seven committees:

● **Agriculture.** The committee approved recommendations, 24-20, on Oct. 28 that would: Reduce commodity payments to farmers by $1 billion over five years, including a cut in the maximum advance payments from 50 percent to 40 percent for the 2006 and 2007 crop years. Cut food stamps by $794 million. Cut conservation programs by $760 million, cut research programs by $620 million and eliminate $446 million authorized for rural development programs. (Savings: $3.7 billion; the budget resolution called for $3 billion)

● **Education and the Workforce.** The committee agreed by voice vote Oct. 26 to increase PBGC premiums, which was expected to generate $6.2 billion. The panel agreed, 22-19, along party lines to save $14.3 billion over five years from student loan programs, mainly by higher inter-

est rates and lower lender subsidies. The proposal included some spending increases by phasing out student loan origination fees and increasing the borrowing limits. (Savings: More than $20 billion; the budget resolution called for $12.7 billion)

● **Energy and Commerce.** The committee agreed by voice vote Oct. 17 to approve provisions to: Reduce the growth of Medicaid spending by $9.4 billion. Change the way Medicaid paid for prescription drugs, allow states to increase cost sharing for some Medicaid beneficiaries, collect co-payments at emergency rooms and set stiffer guidelines for seniors who transferred assets to qualify for Medicaid coverage.

Set a Dec. 31, 2008, deadline for broadcasters to relinquish analog TV spectrum. Bring in $10 billion over five years by auctioning off the spectrum. Of the total, $1 billion would be used to subsidize consumers' transition to digital TV and $500 million to support emergency-responder communications upgrades. Increase LIHEAP funding by $1 billion. (Savings: $17 billion net; the budget called for $14.7 billion.)

● **Financial Services.** The committee's recommendations, approved by voice vote Oct. 27 would: Make changes to the federal deposit insurance system, generating $200 million; increase the limit on federally insured deposits to $130,000 and index it to inflation; allow risk-based premiums for insured institutions and double the coverage limits for certain types of individual retirement accounts and 401(k)s. Temporarily make a federal housing disposition program subject to annual appropriations, saving $270 million. (Savings: $470 million, as called for in the budget resolution)

● **Resources.** The committee voted 24-16 on Oct. 26 to allow the leasing of oil and gas rights in parts of ANWR, generating $2.5 billion, and to give states the option to allow offshore drilling, yielding more than $1.5 billion over five years. (Receipts: $3 billion; the budget called for $2.4 billion)

● **Transportation and Infrastructure.** The panel agreed by voice vote Oct. 26 to recommend an increase in tonnage fees on vessels arriving from foreign ports and on foreign-flagged vessels that leave from a U.S. port and return without stopping anywhere in between. (Receipts: $156 million; the budget called for $103 million)

● **Ways and Means.** The committee voted 22-17 on Oct. 26 to save an estimated $9 billion through actions such as repealing the Byrd amendment, and reducing the cost of federal programs for foster care, child support and aid to the disabled. The committee also added a bill (HR 240) to reauthorize the 1996 welfare law (PL 104-193) at a cost of $1 billion over five years. (Savings: $8 billion net; the budget called for $1 billion)

## HOUSE FLOOR ACTION

House GOP leaders eked out a narrow, 217-215, victory shortly before 2 a.m. Nov. 18 for a somewhat smaller $49.9 billion version of the bill. Passage was in doubt until the final moments. Republican leaders managed to corral just enough moderates with tweaks to the package, and persuaded conservatives to vote for it despite the removal of the ANWR provision. No amendments were allowed. *(House vote 601, p. H-190)*

Republican leaders agreed to a number of demands late Nov. 17 to win over the votes of leading GOP moderates such as Sherwood Boehlert of New York, who had derided the package as a recipe for the party to lose its majority in the House, and Delaware's Michael N. Castle. Boehlert said he also was promised that funding to revive the expired milk subsidy would be included in conference, along with additional home heating subsidies for the poor beyond the $1 billion included in

the House bill. "Moderates feel we have been heard, we have been listened to," Boehlert said.

The changes, which were made as part of the rule for floor debate:

▶ Eliminated the ANWR provisions, as well as provisions that would have allowed states to opt-out of the existing moratorium on new offshore oil and gas drilling.

▶ Allowed people with incomes up to 150 percent of the poverty level who were receiving non-cash aid under TANF to remain eligible for food stamps, and allowed children receiving such services to remain eligible for school lunch programs. Certain legal immigrants were exempted from a new seven-year waiting period for food stamps.

▶ Allowed seniors to retain up to $750,000 in home equity — up from $500,000 in the committee version — and still be entitled to Medicaid coverage for nursing home care.

▶ Dropped an attempt to increase to $5 from $3 the cap on Medicaid co-payments for individuals with incomes below the poverty line.

▶ Permitted the Department of Health and Human Services (HHS) to delay a reduction in reimbursements for prescription drugs required in the reported bill if the average prices pharmacies paid for the drugs were higher than the new amounts that HHS would pay.

An appeal to party loyalty also rounded up Republican votes. Steven C. LaTourette, R-Ohio, switched from "nay" to "yea." "As lousy as I thought this bill was, I am in the majority, and it's my responsibility to help the majority govern," LaTourette said. He said he was offered nothing in exchange for his support.

Jeff Flake of Arizona, a member of the conservative Republican Study Committee, said his group accepted the bill even though the cuts were slightly less than they asked for, and expressed hope that other parts of Hastert's plan for offsetting hurricane costs would be passed as well. "Our expectations are lowered these days," Flake said. "It was important to make this small step."

## CONFERENCE

With great difficulty, House and Senate negotiators managed in nearly three weeks of negotiations to bridge their differences and file a conference report (H Rept 109-362) in the early morning hours of Dec. 19.

The following are among the agreements reached in conference that allowed the bill to go forward:

● **ANWR.** The biggest change was an agreement by Sen. Ted Stevens, R-Alaska, to remove the Senate-passed ANWR provisions. House leaders said GOP moderates would reject the conference report if it included ANWR. Instead, the language was included in the fiscal 2006 Defense appropriations bill (HR 2863), though it ultimately was dropped from that bill as well. *(Defense appropriations, p. 2-14)*

● **Student loans.** Overall, student aid programs were sliced by about $11.9 billion, but the conference agreement included $3.7 billion in scholarships for low-income students who majored in math, science and foreign languages critical to U.S. security, delivered as an annual $4,000 grant to juniors and seniors, as well as grants for low-income students who took rigorous academic course loads. The Senate had sought $8 billion for new student grants. *(Higher education, p. 7-5)*

● **Medicare.** The influential doctors' lobby dodged a cut in Medicare payment rates, winning a freeze in reimbursement rates at 2005 levels rather than having them reduced by 4.4 percent as required under prior law. Negotiators also left intact the $10 billion stabilization fund for insurers involved in the new Medicare drug benefit.

● **Medicaid.** The $4.7 billion in net Medicaid savings was less than half what the House had sought. Conferees combined $6.9 billion in Medicaid savings with $2.1 billion in new Medicaid spending related to Hur-

ricane Katrina. *(Medicaid, p. 11-3)*

● **Child support.** A $1.5 billion cut in child support enforcement was retained, far less than the $4.9 billion reduction in the House version of the bill. Democrats charged that Republicans were helping deadbeat fathers, but Republicans countered that states were improperly using federal money as a state match to garner even more federal aid.

● **Welfare reauthorization.** The TANF reauthorization was not in either version and was added to the conference agreement, along with tougher requirements for states to move recipients into work programs starting in fiscal 2007. An extra $1 billion was included for child care payments for welfare mothers, well shy of the $6 billion sought by the Senate Finance Committee. *(Welfare, p. 10-7)*

● **Dumping duties.** Conferees agreed to repeal the law that channeled anti-dumping and countervailing duties to U.S. companies. But they phased out the law beginning Oct. 1, 2007, rather than eliminating it immediately as the House wanted. As a result, the change was expected to save $300 million instead of the $3.2 billion expected under the House bill.

Although most senators opposed the repeal, Grassley and some others pushed for it because of concern that foreign countries would retaliate with sanctions on U.S. exports, including farm products, if the law remained on the books.

● **Milk subsidy.** About $1 billion in extra spending was included to continue the Milk Income Loss Contract. The subsidy was important to dairy state lawmakers from the Northeast and Midwest, but opposed by Western lawmakers.

● **LIHEAP.** The final bill included $1 billion for low-income heating assistance in fiscal 2007. In an effort to win support for the ANWR provisions after they were inserted into the Defense appropriations bill, Stevens paired them with extra spending that included an additional $2 billion for LIHEAP. When the Senate dropped the ANWR provisions, the LIHEAP money was eliminated as well. Snowe, Collins and Coleman won an agreement from Frist that the Senate would consider a $2 billion supplemental spending bill for LIHEAP in 2006.

## FINAL ACTION

House leaders moved quickly once the conference report was filed, securing a 212-206 vote in favor of the agreement just after 6 a.m. on Dec. 19. *(House vote 670, p. H-212)*

But expectations of quick Senate action were dashed when Democrats in that chamber succeeded in stripping several provisions on procedural grounds. The Senate leadership managed to salvage the rest of the conference agreement, but only with the tie-breaking vote of Vice President Dick Cheney. That sent the measure back to the House for final approval in 2006.

Although the reconciliation bill was considered under special rules that protected it from a filibuster, Democrats managed to use another rule to halt action. On Dec. 21, Conrad raised objections that three provisions of the conference agreement violated the Byrd rule, a 1985 law that prohibits the inclusion in a reconciliation bill of provisions having only an incidental effect on the budget. One of the provisions would have made hospitals immune from malpractice liability if they refused to treat poor Medicaid recipients who could not afford a co-payment. The two others were technical in nature.

An attempt by Gregg to waive Conrad's objections failed on a 52-48 vote, well shy of the 60 votes needed. *(Senate vote 362, p. S-70)*

By upholding Conrad's objections, the Senate effectively nullified the conference report. To save the bill, Senate leaders managed to win a 51-50 vote in favor of an amendment to the House version of S 1932 that

# $318.3 Billion Deficit Is Third-Largest

THE FEDERAL DEFICIT FOR FISCAL 2005, which ended Sept. 30, came to $318.3 billion. That was lower than the peak of $412.7 billion reached the previous year, but it still was the third-largest deficit the federal government had ever run.

The Bush administration stressed that compared with the overall size of the economy, the fiscal 2005 deficit was a relatively modest 2.6 percent of the gross domestic product (GDP).

"As a percent of GDP, the 2005 deficit was lower than the deficits of 16 of the last 25 years," the Office of Management and Budget (OMB) and Treasury Department said in a report Oct. 14.

The final deficit was about $14.3 billion below the $333 billion OMB had projected in its July mid-session review of the budget. The improvement was due largely to higher-than-expected tax receipts. The government took in $15 billion more than anticipated, nearly $13 billion of it from corporate tax payments.

Treasury Secretary John W. Snow attributed the results to the administration's "lower taxes and pro-growth economic policies."

contained the conference report, minus the three struck provisions. Cheney returned from a trip to Pakistan to cast the tie-breaking vote. It was the seventh he had cast since the start of the Bush presidency in 2001. *(Senate vote 363, p. S-70)*

Five GOP moderates voted against the amendment: Smith, Snowe, Collins, Chafee and DeWine. Two other Republican moderates — Arlen Specter of Pennsylvania and Coleman — had signed a letter opposing cuts to Medicaid recipients, but voted for the measure.

The Senate action had the effect of returning the measure to the House for a final vote. House GOP leaders wanted to accomplish that without bringing all members — most of whom had already left for the holidays — back to the floor. But Pelosi demanded a roll call vote "in the light of day" — a reference to the pre-dawn House vote on the conference report — and that was not possible before the end of the year.

Bush congratulated both chambers on voting for the legislation in a Dec. 21 statement that did not mention that Congress failed to clear the measure before adjourning. "The Senate vote to reduce entitlement spending is a victory for taxpayers, fiscal restraint and responsible budgeting — and it will help keep us on track to cut the deficit in half by 2009," Bush said.

Although the measure was expected to clear when Congress reconvened in 2006, GOP leaders still had to work to round up the last few votes. The House narrowly cleared the bill, 216-214, on Feb. 1, 2006. ■

## [PROVISIONS]

# Budget Reconciliation Provisions

*Following are the main provisions of the budget reconciliation law (S 1932 — PL 109-171), which President Bush signed into law Feb. 8, 2006.*

## AGRICULTURE PROGRAMS

Changes to agriculture and rural development programs were expected to yield net savings of $2.7 billion over five years.

### COMMODITY PROGRAMS

● **Crop payments.** Advances to eligible farmers on their annual direct payments for certain crops were reduced to 40 percent in the 2006 crop year, down from 50 percent under prior law. The advance could be no more than 22 percent for 2007. The law affected only the timing of the direct payment, not the amount. (Savings: $1.5 billion in 2007)

● **Cotton subsidy.** The upland cotton Step-2 subsidy, which was successfully challenged by Brazil in the World Trade Organization, was eliminated. (Savings: $282 million over five years)

● **Milk Income Loss Contract.** The popular milk subsidy program, which primarily aided small- and medium-sized dairy farms, was extended through Sept. 30, 2007. (Cost: $998 million over five years)

### CONSERVATION

● **Watershed Rehabilitation Program.** The law limited funds for the Watershed Rehabilitation program, which provided aid to communities to rehabilitate aging local dams, and for the Natural Resources Conservation Service, which assisted projects to upgrade or remove dams. It prohibited the carryover of unused prior mandatory funding as of Oct. 1, 2006. (Savings: $210 million over five years)

● **Conservation Security Program.** The program, which provided financial and technical assistance to promote conservation on land used for agriculture production, was reauthorized through fiscal 2011, but the law limited spending to $2 billion for fiscal 2006 through 2010 and $5.7 billion for fiscal 2006 through 2015. (Savings: $649 million over five years)

● **Environmental Qualities Incentives Program.** The law extended the program through 2010 and limited payments to $450,000 in any six-year period. EQIP provides financial and technical aid to farmers and ranchers who follow conservation practices in areas where soil, water or other natural resources were threatened. (Savings: $75 million over five years)

### RURAL DEVELOPMENT, ENERGY AND RESEARCH

● **Rural development programs.** The law canceled unused funds from years prior to fiscal 2007 for rural development programs, including rural broadband grants, value-added agricultural product development grants, rural business grants and rural firefighter grants. It canceled fiscal 2007 funding for rural community grants. (Savings: $399 million over five years)

● **Research.** Funding for a competitive grant program that supported research, extension and education activities for U.S. agriculture was eliminated in fiscal 2007 through 2009. (Savings: $620 million over five years)

● **Energy programs.** Funding for a program that made loans and grants to farmers to purchase renewable energy systems or to make energy efficiency improvements was limited to $3 million in fiscal 2007. (Savings: $20 million over five years)

# DEPOSIT INSURANCE

Changes to the deposit insurance system that increased coverage for depositors and allowed the Federal Deposit Insurance Corporation (FDIC) to alter the premiums it charged banks and savings and loan associations were expected to produce a net savings of $250 million over the next five years. Most of the changes would have negligible effect until after 2010.

● **Merging BIF and SAIF.** The law required the FDIC to merge the separate funds that protected bank and savings and loan depositors no later than the start of the calendar quarter 90 days after enactment, which occurred Feb. 8. The assets and liabilities of the Bank Insurance Fund and the Savings Association Insurance Fund would be transferred to a new Deposit Insurance Fund that would cover all insured banks and thrifts.

● **Increase in deposit insurance amounts.** Beginning in April 2010 and every five years after, the FDIC was required to determine, together with the National Credit Union Administration (which insured credit union depositors) whether an increase in deposit insurance levels to cover inflation was warranted. The agencies would have to consider the financial health of the Deposit Insurance Fund, economic conditions and whether an increase would cause the amount of insurance fund reserves to fall below 1.15 percent of estimated insured deposits. If an increase was deemed warranted, it would be calculated by the change in the personal consumption expenditures price index published by the Commerce Department. The increase was to be limited to increments of $10,000 and applied to all covered accounts. The increase was to take effect Jan. 1 of the following year, unless Congress acts by July 1 to block it. (Cost: $50 million over five years.)

● **Deposit insurance for individual retirement accounts.** The law also increased deposit insurance coverage for individual retirement account holdings to $250,000 from $100,000, and permitted inflationary increases after 2010 for these accounts.

● **Deposit insurance premium assessments.** The FDIC was permitted to adjust collections of insurance premiums to keep the value of the Deposit Insurance Fund between 1.15 percent and 1.5 percent of estimated insured deposits (compared the previous requirement of a flat 1.25 percent ratio). In setting the insurance fund's ratio of assets to deposits, the FDIC was required to consider the potential for losses based on historical patterns and estimates for the future, and on general economic conditions. In setting premium assessments for banks and thrifts, including assessments based on the riskiness of specific institutions, the FDIC was authorized to consider the effect of assessment levels on the earnings and capital of insured institutions and any other factor deemed appropriate. The law allowed the FDIC to grant a one-time credit to banks and thrifts that paid assessments before 1997, which could be used to cover future assessments. (Savings: $300 million over five years.)

# DIGITAL TV

Provisions allowing the Federal Communications Commission (FCC) to auction analog spectrum vacated by television broadcasters were projected to bring in about $10 billion. The law directed $2.6 billion of the proceeds to other uses, leaving $7.4 billion over five years to be used for deficit reduction.

● **Reclaiming spectrum.** The law set a deadline of Feb. 17, 2009, for full-power television stations to return the frequencies used for analog broadcasts to the FCC. The stations had other spectrum for broadcasting digital signals.

● **Spectrum auctions.** The FCC was required to begin the process of auctioning off the reclaimed spectrum to wireless carriers and others by Jan. 28, 2008. The auction proceeds would be deposited in a newly created fund, the Digital Television Transition and Public Safety Fund, by June 30, 2008. On Sept. 30, 2009, $7.4 billion was to be transferred from the fund to the Treasury and treated as offsetting receipts.

● **Converter box subsidies.** Up to $1.5 billion in spectrum proceeds would be set aside to subsidize digital-to-analog converter boxes for the roughly 21 million Americans who still relied on over-the-air television broadcasts and would otherwise see their television screens go dark after the transition. The Commerce Department was authorized to distribute up to two $40 coupons per household to help cover the cost of converter boxes.

● **Public safety systems.** Up to $1 billion would be set aside for a grant program to help public safety agencies purchase and deploy interoperable communications systems.

● **Other uses of proceeds.** The law also allocated: up to $156 million to build a unified national emergency alert and tsunami warning system; $44 million to upgrade 911 emergency phone systems; $65 million to help eligible low-power television stations purchase equipment to upgrade from analog to digital operations; $10 million to help eligible low-power television stations purchase digital-to-analog conversion devices that would allow them to convert incoming digital signals to analog format.

It also allocated $30 million in fiscal 2007 and 2008 for a temporary digital television broadcast system to serve New York City until a permanent facility could be built atop the planned Freedom Tower. An additional $30 million would go to the Essential Air Service Program, which subsidizes commercial airline service in remote places, if funds appropriated to operate the program equaled or exceeded $110 million for that fiscal year.

● **Spectrum licenses.** The FCC was directed to assess $10 million in additional license fees in fiscal 2006, to be deposited in the Treasury.

# MEDICARE

Changes to Medicare, the federal health care program for the elderly and disabled, were projected to achieve $6.4 billion in net savings over five years. (Savings of less than $100 million are not indicated below.)

## MEDICARE PART A

● **Hospital quality improvement.** Hospitals that did not submit required quality data would get a lower increase in payments beginning in fiscal 2007. Their increase would drop by 2.0 percent, rather than 0.4 percent under previous law. (Savings: $300 million over five years)

● **Disproportionate share hospitals.** Inpatient hospital stays for patients who were covered by Medicaid for other services, but not for hospital inpatient services, would not count as Medicaid days for the purposes of calculating the additional payments Medicare made to hospitals that served a large number of low-income patients. (Savings: $1.2 billion over five years.)

● **Skilled nursing facilities.** Medicare was to reduce the percentage of its payments to skilled nursing facilities for uncollected debts from 100 percent to 70 percent. Unpaid debts incurred by beneficiaries eligible for both Medicare and Medicaid would be paid at 100 percent.

● **Inpatient rehabilitation facilities.** The "75 percent rule" — which requires that 75 percent of patients in a hospital classified as an "inpatient rehabilitation facility" have specified medical conditions — would begin in July 2008, instead of July 2007. In July 2006, a 60 percent threshold would be in place. In July 2007, it would increase to 65 percent. (Savings: $100 million over five years)

● **Gain-sharing demonstration.** Up to six demonstration programs would be created to evaluate gain-sharing agreements between hospitals and other providers beginning on Jan. 1, 2007. The practice allows doctors and hospitals to share the savings from treating patients more efficiently.

● **Specialty hospitals.** A moratorium on the enrollment of specialty hospitals in Medicare was extended for six months from the date of enactment or until the Health and Human Services (HHS) secretary issued a report containing a strategic plan on how to handle the issue of physicians' investments in such hospitals and how such hospitals would care for low-income patients. If the secretary did not issue the report within six months, the suspension would be extended two more months.

## MEDICARE PART B

● **Durable medical equipment.** Beneficiaries would be required to assume ownership of rental durable medical goods (excluding oxygen equipment) after 13 months of rental. For oxygen equipment, ownership would be required after 36 months. Medicaid could pay for service and maintenance if it was determined necessary. (Savings: $700 million over five years)

● **Imaging services.** The law reduced the reimbursement rate for imaging services by $2.8 billion over four years. Reimbursement rates for imaging services conducted in a physician's office could not be greater than the rate paid to hospitals for the same service. Savings from reduced rates for multiple images of contiguous body parts in 2006 and 2007 could be used to reduce overall spending. (Savings: $2.8 billion over five years)

● **Ambulatory surgical centers.** The law reduced Medicare payments to ambulatory care surgical centers to the rate Medicare paid to hospitals, if the hospital payment rates were lower. (Savings: $300 million over five years)

● **Physician payments.** The law froze Medicare payments to physicians at the 2005 level for 2006. Under prior law, the payments would have fallen by 4.4 percent as of January 2006. (Cost: $7.3 billion over five years)

● **Dialysis services.** The reimbursement rate for facilities providing end-stage renal disease services was increased by 1.6 percent in 2006. (Cost: $500 million over five years)

● **Means testing in Part B premiums.** The law accelerated the phase-in of a scheduled increase in Medicare Part B premiums for beneficiaries with incomes above certain levels. The phase-in was to begin in 2007 and be completed by 2009, instead of 2011. (Savings: $1.6 billion over five years)

● **Preventive screenings.** Screenings to detect abdominal aortic aneurysms would be covered as part of the physical exam for new Medicare beneficiaries who were at risk. The deductible in the Part B program would not apply to screenings for colorectal cancer. (Cost: $200 million over five years)

## PROVISIONS RELATED TO PART A AND B

● **Home health payments.** The law eliminated a scheduled 2.8 percent increase in home health care payments for 2006, although it provided for a one-year 5 percent additional payment to rural home health providers in 2006. Starting in 2007, home health care providers would have their payments reduced by 2 percentage points if they did not report required health care quality data to HHS.

● **Risk adjustment.** Starting in 2007, payments to Medicare Advantage plans would be altered to take into account the health status of the beneficiaries served in each plan, paying higher amounts for care of sicker patients. (Savings: $6.5 billion over five years)

## MEDICAID

Changes to Medicaid, the federal-state health program for the poor, were expected to reduce mandatory spending by a net $6.9 billion over five years, while paying for $3.6 billion in new spending.

## ASSET TRANSFERS

The law was projected to save $2.4 billion over five years by increasing the penalties on people who transferred their house or other assets for less than fair market value to qualify for nursing home care.

● **Five-year "look back."** States would look back five years, rather than three, when determining whether a senior applying for Medicaid-funded nursing home care had transferred assets below fair value to qualify for Medicaid.

● **Penalty.** Beneficiaries who made improper transfers would be penalized with a period of ineligibility for certain long-term care services beginning the month following the date of the asset transfer or the date the senior became eligible for Medicaid long-term care services, whichever was later.

● **Hardship waiver.** If the ineligibility period deprived an individual of medical care that would endanger their health or life, or deprive them of food or shelter, they could apply for a waiver of the penalty because of undue hardship.

● **Home equity.** The law excluded individuals with more than $500,000 in home equity from eligibility for nursing home or other long-term care coverage paid for by Medicaid. States could raise the limit to $750,000. Starting in 2011 the amount would increase each year based on the consumer price index.

## PRESCRIPTION DRUGS

Changes to payments for prescription drugs — mainly reducing Medicaid reimbursements to pharmacies — were expected to reduce spending by $3.9 billion over five years.

● **Limit on pharmacy reimbursement.** Medicaid would reimburse pharmacies for purchasing and dispensing multisource prescription drugs for up to 250 percent of the average sales price, known as the "average manufacturers price" (AMP). The AMP reimbursement rate takes into account the discounts and other savings that could be negotiated with manufacturers. Formerly, pharmacies were reimbursed for up to 150 percent of the average manufacturers' published price, known as "average wholesale price."

A "multisource" drug was defined as a drug that had at least one other drug on the market that was therapeutically equivalent.

● **Disclosure of AMP.** The HHS secretary was required to give states access to monthly AMP data, which was previously confidential.

## FRAUD, WASTE AND ABUSE

Provisions to reduce fraud, waste and abuse were expected to save $822 million over five years; $528 million of that was to be spent on education and other steps to improve the integrity of the program.

● **Third-party recovery.** The law required states to do more to find a party responsible for paying outstanding claims instead of relying on Medicaid as the payer of last resort.

● **State False Claims Act.** States with laws that met certain requirements for handling false claims were allowed to reduce by 10 percentage points the amount that they had to pay back to the federal government once the false claim was discovered.

● **Education.** States had to provide written explanations of fraud and whistleblower policies to providers that received more that $5 million a year from Medicaid.

● **Proof of citizenship.** The government would not reimburse states for a beneficiary who had not given a state proof of U.S. citizenship. Immigrants who were eligible for benefits were exempt from this provision.

● **Medicaid Integrity Program.** The HHS secretary could contract out duties such as reviewing audits, identifying overpayments and providing education on proper payments.

## COST SHARING AND BENEFIT REDUCTIONS

Allowing states to set higher premiums and cost-sharing payments and to offer limited benefits for some in Medicaid was projected to reduce outlays by $3.2 billion over five years

● **Premiums and cost sharing.** The law permitted states to charge premiums and require cost sharing by beneficiaries at or above the poverty level, with some restrictions. Under prior law, premiums and enrollment fees were generally prohibited and nominal cost sharing was limited to $3.

Under the new law, beneficiaries with incomes between 100 percent and 150 percent of the federal poverty line could not be charged a premium. cost sharing could not exceed 10 percent of the cost of the service for families with incomes between 100 percent and 150 percent of the poverty level, and 20 percent for families with incomes above 150 percent. Total payments for the year could not exceed 5 percent of the family income.

Certain groups could not be subject to cost sharing for some services, such as pregnancy-related care and preventive care for children under age 18.

● **Enforcement.** States could allow providers to refuse to offer service or dispense a drug if cost-sharing payments were not made at the time of service. If a beneficiary failed to pay premiums for 60 days, a state could terminate coverage.

● **Prescription drugs.** States were allowed to waive or lower co-payments for "preferred drugs" and could not require cost sharing from beneficiaries who otherwise were exempt from cost sharing. For drugs not designated as preferred drugs on a state's formulary, a state could set higher cost sharing and co-payments and could impose cost sharing on any beneficiary, even those who were otherwise exempt from cost sharing in the program. For beneficiaries with family incomes below 150 percent of poverty, cost sharing could not exceed a set nominal amount. For beneficiaries with family incomes above 150 percent of poverty, cost sharing could not exceed 20 percent of the cost of the drug.

● **Indexing.** The nominal rate for cost sharing, previously $3, would be indexed to the medical cost component of the consumer price index.

● **Emergency room.** States were allowed to increase cost sharing for certain beneficiaries who used the emergency room for non-urgent care. The law provided $50 million in mandatory funds for payments over four years to states to make non-emergency health services available and accessible.

● **Alternative benefit packages.** The law allowed states to replace the traditional Medicaid benefits package with a reduced-benefit, or "benchmark" plan, for certain populations. The plans had to provide basic services, such as physician and hospital coverage, and be actuarially equivalent to one of the following benchmarks: standard Blue Cross/Blue Shield Plan offered in the Federal Employees Health Benefit Plan, health coverage offered to state employees, coverage offered by the largest commercial health maintenance organization in the state or a different coverage plan approved by the HHS

States could not require certain beneficiaries to participate in the benchmark plans, including seniors who were poor enough to qualify

for Medicaid and who qualified for Medicare because they were over 65. Other exempted groups included pregnant women who had to be covered by state Medicaid programs, patients in Medicaid-funded hospice facilities or receiving long-term care, some children in foster care and blind or otherwise disabled individuals.

## STATE FINANCING

Changes to the rules for state financing of Medicaid programs, which affected the amount of federal grants, were estimated to save $1.2 billion over five years.

● **Restrictions on provider taxes.** The law required states that levied taxes on Medicaid managed care organizations and used the proceeds to help pay the state's share of Medicaid spending, to apply the tax to all managed care organizations, not just those that served Medicaid recipients. Generally, the organizations that paid the taxes got the money back in the form of increased Medicaid payments. But the increased payments also generated increased federal matching funds, and the states often kept the difference. The change was expected to save $435 over five years, and $2.9 billion over 10 years as states came under pressure to eliminate the taxes.

● **Case management costs.** States would only be able to charge Medicaid for case management services that were not covered under other programs such as foster care, saving a net $760 million over five years.

## SPENDING INCREASES

The law included a number of provisions that were projected to increase spending under Medicaid by a combined total of $3.6 billion over five years.

● **Medicaid buy-in.** Children with disabilities whose families earned more than the cut-off for Supplemental Social Security Income, but less than 300 percent of the poverty level, would be eligible for Medicaid benefits beginning in 2008. States choosing to offer these benefits were allowed to charge a premium and parents would be required to enroll in any available employer-sponsored coverage for themselves while the child was on Medicaid. (Cost: $1.4 billion over five years)

● **Home and community-based care.** Up to 10 states could participate in a five-year demonstration project to provide home and community-based services to children who would be hospitalized otherwise. (Cost: $766 million over five years)

● **Health information centers.** The law increased funding for health information centers that assisted families of children with special needs by a total of $22 million over five years.

● **"Money follows the person" demonstration.** The law authorized a demonstration project under which the federal government would pay a higher share of costs than under existing law for the first 12 months of long-term care services provided in the home or community for a person who was formerly in a nursing home. (Cost: $340 million over five years)

● **Health Opportunity Accounts.** Up to 10 states were allowed to participate in a demonstration program to set up health opportunity accounts that could be used by Medicaid beneficiaries who volunteered for the program to pay for medical treatment. Once a deductible was reached, beneficiaries would be covered under the state Medicaid program. States could not set a deductible that was higher than 110 percent of the state contribution to the account. States could contribute up to $2,500 for each adult and $1,000 for each child into a family's account. The programs had to disclose the cost of the care and encourage prevention and discourage overuse of health services.

If beneficiaries became ineligible for Medicaid, they could keep the

accounts for future health care costs. States could also choose to allow the beneficiaries to use the accounts to pay for job training.

● **Medicaid transformation grants.** The HHS secretary could provide extra funding to state Medicaid programs that adopted innovative methods for reducing medical errors; improving collection of payments and reducing fraud, waste and abuse; increasing the use of generic drugs; implementing a medication risk management program for beneficiaries who use a number of prescription drugs; and increasing the use university-based hospitals and clinics by the uninsured.

## KATRINA RELIEF

The law appropriated $2.1 billion to be used by the HHS secretary to help with health care costs for residents of states evacuated because of Hurricane Katrina.

## HUMAN RESOURCES

Changes in welfare law, child support and child welfare provisions added up to a net savings of $1.5 billion over five years.

### WELFARE

The law reauthorized the 1996 Temporary Assistance for Needy Families (TANF) law (PL 104-193) at a projected cost of $374 million over five years. Viewed over a 10-year period, however, the changes were projected to save $344 million.

● **TANF block grant.** The main TANF block grant to states was reauthorized through fiscal 2010 at the existing level of $16.5 billion per year. Supplemental grants were reauthorized through fiscal 2008 at $319 million per year.

● **Work requirements.** The law retained a 30-hour-per-week work requirement for individuals, but it altered what was known as the caseload reduction credit so that states would have to ensure that at least 50 percent of their welfare recipients were engaged in work. For the first time, the law applied work participation rules to state welfare programs that were funded entirely with state dollars, such as programs for people with disabilities or drug addictions and two-parent families.

● **Marriage promotion.** The law authorized grants of $150 million per year to states through fiscal 2010 for activities to promote "healthy marriage" and "responsible fatherhood."

● **Child care.** The law extended grants to states to provide child care subsidies to low-income families through 2010 and increased funding by a total of $1 billion over five years, for total funding of $2.9 billion per year.

### CHILD SUPPORT

Changes to child support enforcement were expected to save a net $1.5 billion over five years.

● **Federal matching payments.** The law barred states from using federal incentive payments to receive matching child support enforcement funds, beginning in 2008. States were still required to spend the incentive awards on child support services, but they could not also count the money as a match for additional federal funds. (Savings: a net $1.6 billion over five years)

● **Distribution of child support payments.** The law provided incentives to encourage states to give TANF families more of the child support payments collected on their behalf. Previously, families that applied for TANF had to allow the state to collect their child support payments; the money was divided between the state and federal government as partial repayment for the welfare assistance. The new law allowed states to pay up to $100 a month ($200 for families with two or more

children) of the child support collections to the TANF family. The federal government would compensate states for part of the funds they lost as a result. The law also simplified an existing requirement that states distribute to former TANF families child support arrearages from before and after the family was in the TANF program. (Combined cost: $423 million over five years)

● **New enforcement rules.** To increase collections, parents would be denied passports if they owed more than $2,500 in past-due child support payments, down from $5,000 under prior law. A triennial update of child support orders was required, and insurance payment data could be used as ammunition against non-custodial parents who owe child support.

● **Annual fee.** States were required to collect a new $25 annual fee from families that had never been on TANF but that had received at least $500 in child support services in a year. The states could retain part of the money.

● **Paternity tests.** The federal share of the cost for paternity tests dropped from 90 percent to 66 percent.

### CHILD WELFARE

Changes to child welfare programs were projected to save a net $320 million over five years. However, the law increased spending on two programs — funding for family courts and a program intended to keep troubled families together, or if that was impossible to promote adoption of abused and neglected children.

● **Limitation of matching funds.** The law limited states' claims to matching funds for administrative costs related to placing abused and neglected children in unlicensed foster homes. States had to license the home within 12 months of the placement. (Savings: $174 million over five years)

● **Eligibility for foster care aid.** The law limited eligibility for foster care and adoption assistance for about 4,000 children each month in nine Western states who would be subject to a 9th U.S. Circuit Court of Appeals ruling. The court had broadened those states' latitude to determine eligibility for such assistance in cases in which children lived with a relative outside the home from which they were removed. (Savings: $380 million over five years.)

● **Mandatory spending increases.** The law provided $20 million a year for new grants to improve the ability of state courts to track child abuse and neglect cases and train judges and other court personnel in child welfare law. Spending authority for the Safe and Stable Families program was increased. (Cost: $234 million over five years)

### SUPPLEMENTAL SECURITY INCOME

● **Disability reviews.** The Social Security Administration was directed to review at least 20 percent of disability claims approved by state-level Disability Determination Service offices in fiscal 2006, rising to 40 percent in fiscal 2007 and 50 percent in fiscal 2008. (Savings: $287 million)

● **Retroactive benefits.** The threshold for paying retroactive benefits owed to the disabled because of delays in approval was lowered. Any lump sum greater than three times the maximum monthly benefit would be subject to payments in installments, except under certain conditions, such as terminal illness. (Savings: $425 million)

### HIGHER EDUCATION

Changes to federal student loan programs were expected to save a net $11.9 billion over five years, mainly by reducing the amounts received by lenders and increasing some borrower costs.

● **Student loan reauthorization.** The law reauthorized the government's

two college loan programs through 2012. The Federal Family Education Loan program provided government guarantees for loans made by private lenders. The William D. Ford Direct Loan Program provided government loans to students and their families. So-called consolidation loans that enabled students to lock in prior year interest rates and combine multiple loans into a single payment were reauthorized through 2012.

● **Parent loan rate increase.** The fixed interest rate charged for guaranteed loans made to parents was changed to 8.5 percent starting in July 2006, rather than at 7.9 percent as under prior law.

● **"Excess interest."** Lenders earning more than the fair market return on student loans were required to rebate the "excess interest" paid by students and parents to the federal government. Prior law allowed the lender to receive the higher of the market rate or the amount paid by the borrower. (Combined savings under this and the parent loan rate provision: $14.3 billion over five years)

● **9.5 percent loans.** The law eliminated a provision of prior law that allowed lenders making loans backed by certain tax-exempt bonds to receive up to a 9.5 percent return from the government. An exception allowed nonprofit lenders with less than $100 million in outstanding 9.5 percent loans to make new loans under the system for five years. (Savings: $1.8 billion over five years)

● **Administrative costs.** The law eliminated mandatory funding for the costs of administering student loan programs beginning in fiscal 2007. After that, administrative costs would have to be paid through discretionary appropriations. (Savings: $2.2 billion over five years)

● **Guaranty agency fees.** Loan guaranty agencies were required to pay the government a 1 percent default insurance premium on guaranteed loans, which they could charge to student and parent borrowers. Previously, guaranty agencies had the option of charging such a fee, but they often waived it. (Savings: $1.5 billion over five years)

● **Federal lender insurance.** The law reduced the portion of a defaulted loan for which the lender was reimbursed to 97 percent from 98 percent for most lenders, and to 99 percent from 100 percent for "exceptional" lenders. (Savings: $505 million over five years)

● **Consolidation loans.** Borrowers would be able to get a direct loan from the government to consolidate existing loans only if the purpose was to enter into an income-contingent repayment plan. Also, the loan had to be submitted to a guaranty agency that counseled the borrower on rehabilitating the loan rather than defaulting. The government had to offer a direct consolidation loan to any borrower who defaulted or was rejected by a private lender. "In-school" consolidation was eliminated by prohibiting students from requesting early repayment of their loans. Married couples were prohibited from jointly consolidating their separate student loans. The government was required to establish regulations to preclude consolidation loans from being "an excessive proportion" of defaulted loans for which the government was required to reimburse guaranty agencies.

● **Guaranty agencies.** As of Oct. 1, the "collection cost" that a guaranty agency could charge a borrower for including a defaulted loan in a consolidation loan was limited to 18.5 percent of the outstanding principle and interest of the defaulted loan. The guaranty agency was required to remit part of the collection charges to the government immediately and remit the full amount of the charges by Oct. 1, 2009, if its proceeds from consolidating defaulted loans exceeded 45 percent of the agency's total collections of defaulted loans in a fiscal year.

● **Schools as lenders.** Colleges were prohibited from lending to undergraduates or to people who were not their students, and were limited to the loans they could make to their graduate students. Schools had to award contracts for financing, servicing or administering their loans on a competitive basis. Schools were required to offer lower interest rates or lower origination fees, or both, than either private lenders or the government can. The permissible default rate for a lending school was reduced to 10 percent from 15 percent. Annual audits had to be submitted to the government. Schools were required to use proceeds from interest paid by borrowers, subsidies from the government or sales of loans to increase need-based student grants. They were forbidden to use those proceeds to supplant federal grant money.

● **Increased loan limits.** The maximum amount of subsidized loans was increased to $3,500 from $2,625 for first-year students, and to $4,500 from $3,500 for second-year students, beginning in fiscal 2007. The limit for each year of graduate school was increased to $12,000 from $10,000. (Cost: $1.5 billion over five years)

● **Origination fees.** The 3 percent origination fee for Stafford loans would be phased out by 2010 for guaranteed loans and reduced to 1 percent by 2010 for direct loans. (Cost: $4 billion over five years)

● **New grant programs.** The law created two new mandatory grant programs for college students who were eligible for Pell grants. The first was available to first- and second-year college students who had completed a "rigorous" high school education. The second program aided third- and fourth-year students who were pursuing degrees in the physical, life or computer sciences, math, technology or engineering or one of several foreign languages considered critical for national security. The grants were $750 for a first-year student, $1,300 for a second-year student and $4,000 for third- and fourth-year students. The law appropriated $790 million in fiscal 2006 for the grants, rising to $1 billion in fiscal 2010. (Cost: $3.7 billion over five years)

● **Teacher loan forgiveness.** The law reauthorized an existing provision that allowed the government to forgive up to $5,000 in loans to highly qualified teachers of math, science or special education. Private school teachers who were exempt from state certification requirements could benefit from the provision in some cases.

## PENSION PLAN INSURANCE

An increase in the premiums that companies paid to the Pension Benefit Guaranty Corporation (PBGC), the federal agency that insured worker retirement plans, was expected to bring in a total of $3.6 billion over five years.

● **Single-employer plans.** Payments to the PBGC by individual corporations that offered their workers defined benefit pension plans — which pay retirees a set amount, usually based on years of service and earnings — were $30 per employee starting in 2006, an increase from $19. Future premium levels would be indexed to account for increases in average wages. (Receipts: $2.3 billion over five years)

● **Multi-employer plans.** Premiums paid to cover pension plans that applied to multiple employers were $8 per year for each participant, up from $2.60, beginning in 2006. After 2006, the premium would be increased to account for gains in average wages. (Receipts: $300 million over five years)

● **Termination premium.** Companies that attempted to terminate their pension plans while in bankruptcy between the end of 2005 and the start of 2011 would have to pay a special annual premium of $1,250 per participant for three years after the termination of the plan. The special premium also applied to cases in which the PBGC moved to terminate a plan. If a company was assessed the premium while in bankruptcy, it would not have to make the payment until after it exited from bankruptcy protection. The provision did not apply to companies that started bankruptcy proceedings prior to Oct. 18, 2005. (Receipts: $1 billion over five years)

## OTHER PROVISIONS

● **S-CHIP.** The law provided an additional $283 million in funds under the State Children's Health Insurance Program for states that faced funding shortfalls in 2006. No additional states were allowed to use S-CHIP funds to cover adults without children.

● **LIHEAP.** The law added $1 billion in fiscal 2007 to the Low Income Home Energy Assistance Program. Of that amount, $750 million was reserved for emergency needs. A law (PL 109-204) advancing that funding to fiscal 2007 was enacted in March 2006.

● **Anti-dumping duties.** The law phased out a 2000 statute that directed anti-dumping and countervailing duties, which were assessed as a trade penalty, to be distributed to the domestic companies that were hurt by the unfair trade. Starting in fiscal 2008, the revenue would begin staying in the Treasury instead. (Savings: $300 million over five years)

● **Vessel tonnage duties.** Tonnage fees would be increased by between 2 cents and 13.5 cents per ton depending on the location of the originating port. (Revenue: $156 million)

● **Civil filing fees.** U.S. District Court filing fees rose by $100 to $350. Appeals Court fees rose by $200 to $450. (Revenue: $167 million)

● **Bankruptcy fees.** Fees rose by $25 to $245 for Chapter 7 filings and by $85 to $235 for Chapter 13. A drafting error prevented an attempt to raise Chapter 11 filing fees by $1,750 to $2,750, which would have raised $68 million over five years. (Revenue: $307 million)

● **Housing.** A mandatory Federal Housing Administration program regarding rehabilitation grants and below-market sales of multifamily housing units became subject to annual appropriations. (Savings: $270 million) ■

**Chapter 5**

# CONGRESSIONAL AFFAIRS

# DeLay, Under Indictment in Texas, Resigns Leadership Post

HOUSE MAJORITY LEADER Tom DeLay, R-Texas, began 2005 as one of the most powerful figures on Capitol Hill. He ended it facing an indictment on felony money laundering charges in his home state, his bid for a 12th House term in serious jeopardy and his future very much in doubt.

At the start of the 109th Congress, DeLay appeared every bit as fearsome as his reputation and still sublimely confident of his authority over his troops. But a steady accumulation of questions and doubts about his ethics problems hung over the party, at a time when members were eager to move forward in the new Congress.

Not one of those problems on its own would have diminished DeLay's remarkable power, carefully cultivated over 11 years of GOP majority rule. But together and over time, they eroded the broad popularity DeLay enjoyed among the rank and file, particularly conservatives who dominated the Republican Conference. He gradually began to play less of a determining role in the party's legislative campaigns in the House, and by popular demand, lowered his profile in the national media.

Then in September, DeLay was indicted by a grand jury at the recommendation of Ronnie Earle, the district attorney in Travis County, Texas, who had an undisguised disdain for DeLay and the large footprint he had left on the state's political landscape. The charges set in motion the last act for DeLay. Compelled to give up his leadership post, at least temporarily, he stepped aside, handing over his duties as majority leader to Republican Whip Roy Blunt of Missouri, the third-ranking leader.

Though DeLay publicly proclaimed he would return to power once he cleared his name, he seemed more confident of that outcome than did many Republicans. By December, it was clear they were looking ahead to a future that did not necessarily include Tom DeLay.

## A ROUGH START TO THE 109TH

One of the first jobs faced in the new year by the Republican Conference — the group of all House Republicans — was to decide how to handle several rules changes the conference had agreed to in November 2004 at DeLay's insistence. Members particularly complained of being tarred in local newspapers and on talk radio for an internal conference decision to keep members of the GOP leadership in power even if they were indicted. The plan was meant to protect DeLay if he was indicted in Texas as part of a political fundraising investigation being led by Earle. (*2004 Almanac, p. 1-10*)

"There was a huge backlash," said a Republican leadership aide. "And a lot of it was from the party-base Republicans, the folks you never get criticism from. We got hammered on it."

DeLay agreed in early January to drop the plan because it was giving Democrats too much ammunition. Although Republican leaders pushed through several changes to House rules that affected the ethics committee, they also backed away from plans for a controversial change

that would have prohibited the committee from admonishing members for behavior that was unbecoming but that did not violate a specific written rule. (*Ethics committees, p. 5-6*)

When Speaker J. Dennis Hastert, R-Ill., announced the change of plans at a closed meeting of House Republicans, it was met by thunderous applause. "It's never a good idea to tie your shoelaces together right out of the gate," said J.D. Hayworth, R-Ariz., of the inauspicious start.

A senior Republican said afterward of DeLay: "He's going to be damaged by this. To put us through all of this was unnecessary. We had just won a resounding victory in the [2004] election. We did not need to go and change the caucus rules."

But to the lasting disappointment of the GOP rank and file, their efforts in the opening days of the session to turn the spotlight away from DeLay were unsuccessful.

In February, Hastert abruptly cleaned house at the Committee on Standards of Official Conduct, as the House ethics committee is formally known. Hastert removed the chairman and two Republican members and replaced them with loyalists in a move that was widely viewed as punishment for their decision in 2004 to admonish DeLay.

Joel Hefley, R-Colo. — who was replaced by Doc Hastings, R-Wash. — had been chairman in 2004 when the committee admonished DeLay for three ethics offenses. In one instance, the evenly divided panel said, DeLay improperly pressured a fellow Republican to vote for the 2003 Medicare prescription drug bill (PL 108-173) by promising to endorse the lawmaker's son in a House race. In a second, the panel took him to task for hosting a golf fundraiser with energy executives as Congress was working on a major energy bill.

And in a third, the 10 panel members determined it was wrong for DeLay to press the Federal Aviation Administration to use its resources to track down a group of Democratic state lawmakers who had fled Texas in 2003 rather than vote for a redistricting map engineered by DeLay. (*2004 Almanac, p. 5-4; 2003 Almanac, p. 14-6*)

## BAD NEWS KEEPS COMING

In the months that followed, Republicans endured a steady diet of negative revelations about their leader, some tying him to the shady practices of prominent GOP lobbyist Jack Abramoff and others raising questions about his fundraising machine in Texas.

A series of press reports in March and April described expensive trips DeLay had taken to golf resorts in Scotland and other places with lobbyist friends who had close ties to the organizations paying for the trips. Lawmakers were prohibited under House rules from accepting free trips from lobbyists.

In some cases, it appeared that DeLay's expenses were ultimately paid by Abramoff, who was under investigation for fraud in connection with a casino in Florida and multimillion-dollar contracts with Indian tribes on whose behalf he lobbied Congress. DeLay denied knowing his

expenses were covered by the lobbyist. The New York Times also reported that DeLay's wife and daughter had been paid $500,000 from his political action committees since 2001.

DeLay countered that the travel was tied to his work in Congress and to his fight for important causes, such as building the conservative movement in Great Britain. "The fact is that I have certain international responsibilities given to me by my leadership position but, more importantly, by my interests," he told the conservative-leaning Washington Times newspaper in April.

The criticism grew more serious when it started to bubble up from within. The normally friendly conservative editorial page of the Wall Street Journal sharply criticized DeLay in late March, saying, "Mr. DeLay, who rode to power in 1994 on a wave of revulsion at the everyday ways of big government, has become the living exemplar of some of its worst habits."

It did not take the political opposition long to detect a weakness in the Republican Party. Liberal groups including the labor-backed Campaign for America's Future picked up the theme of DeLay's ethics, spending thousands of dollars on ads in the districts of Republicans in swing districts.

Politically vulnerable Republicans began to distance themselves from DeLay. Rep. Christopher Shays of Connecticut, a moderate Republican in a Democrat-heavy district, suggested that the party might be better off without him. "He is an absolute embarrassment to me and to the Republican Party," Shays said. Public expressions of concern about the multiplying controversies also came from two senators facing re-election, Lincoln Chafee of Rhode Island, a moderate, and Rick Santorum, a conservative facing a tough re-election campaign in Pennsylvania. "You can't have your leader under a cloud," Chafee said. "It makes it difficult to run."

Stung by the criticism, DeLay made an unusual private appeal to GOP senators at a private luncheon April 12, asking them to hold their fire and give him a chance to make his case. He said publicly that he found the travel rules of the House "confusing," and suggested that the House ethics committee draft a more cogent policy for all members.

The ethics committee, however, had ceased to function. Democrats flatly refused to go along with ethics rules changes the Republicans had made in January and with staff changes demanded by the new leadership-picked Republicans on the committee. The panel's five Democrats blocked approval of the committee's operating rules, making it impossible for the 10-member panel to operate. The committee could accomplish only simple administrative duties.

Hastert rallied to the defense of his old friend and ally, suggesting at private meetings with Republicans that attacks on DeLay were tantamount to attacks on the majority. House Minority Leader Nancy Pelosi, D-Calif., scoffed at the notion that the majority's problems were created by the partisanship of Democrats. "Tom DeLay's own behavior is the source of these problems," she said. "We're not using the ethics process as a political tool."

## POPULARITY IN GOP ERODES

DeLay became more of a lightning rod when he jumped into the controversy over Terry Schiavo, a severely brain-damaged Florida woman whose fate was the subject of an intense debate over the right to die. In late March, he led a movement in Congress to intervene in the case, though ultimately a state court's decision to allow the woman's husband to remove her feeding tube prevailed. After Schiavo died March 31, DeLay fumed, "The time will come for the men responsible for this to answer for their behavior." A few days later, he apologized for

"inartful" remarks, which many perceived as a threat of retaliation against liberal judges. (Schiavo, p. 14-16)

In late April, DeLay complained about an unnamed "left wing syndicate" that was out to destroy his career.

By mid-spring, House Republicans were ready for a less visible majority leader. DeLay began spending less time in front of the cameras, letting Hastert and others in the top leadership speak for congressional Republicans at news conferences. But he remained a force behind the scenes, scheduling bills for floor action and mapping strategy to ensure their passage. Hastert continued to rely on his close political ally. The two had forged an interdependent relationship in the mid-1990s, when DeLay, then the GOP whip, made Hastert his chief deputy and later helped him become Speaker.

Conservative activists gave DeLay a much-needed boost in May, when the leaders of several prominent groups threw a formal dinner party for the majority leader to give him a highly visible showing of support. American Conservative Union Chairman David Keene described it as "a celebration to honor a conservative fighter." In remarks to the crowd, DeLay again blamed Democrats for his predicament. "Democrat leaders may wish we would just disappear, or that they could defeat us by some means other than the ballot box," he said. Democratic activists held an anti-DeLay demonstration outside the Capitol Hilton ballroom.

## POLITICAL PROBLEMS IN TEXAS

More trouble awaited DeLay in Texas, where state Democrats were mobilizing to take advantage of his weakened political condition. He attracted a highly motivated Democratic challenger, Nick Lampson, a seasoned political pro with money in his campaign treasury. Lampson had represented a district adjacent to DeLay's Houston-based 22nd District for eight years until he was swept out of office as a result of the redistricting that DeLay and his allies engineered in Austin.

In the redistricting, a confident DeLay had given up some of the Republican turf in his district; now, it improved opportunities for a Democrat to win it. Beginning in the spring and through the summer, DeLay began spending far more time in his district than he had had to before, attending the chicken dinners and ribbon-cuttings that he could no longer afford to skip.

After Hurricane Katrina hit the Gulf Coast at the end of August, DeLay was a fixture on the nightly local news as the Houston region began to accept thousands of evacuees from hard-hit New Orleans and other coastal cities. He also continued to be an impressive fundraiser, bringing in over $1 million in the first half of the year for his re-election campaign and raising twice as much money as Lampson.

## INDICTMENT FORCES DELAY TO STEP DOWN

But there were signs that legal cases involving a political action committee DeLay founded were coming to a head, with the promise of more negative headlines. On May 26, state District Judge Joseph Hart ruled in a civil case that Texans for a Republican Majority (TRMPAC) had failed to report $613,000 in contributions and $685,000 in expenditures as required by state law. DeLay was not named in the lawsuit, which was brought by Democrats, but three of his close associates who ran the committee were named in either the civil suit or a concurrent criminal case.

On Sept. 28, a Texas grand jury indicted DeLay in the fundraising scandal, a development that many Republicans had dreaded for months. He was charged with conspiracy to violate the state's campaign finance laws. Prosecutors alleged that he had a role in an

# Other Lawmakers Under Investigation

TOM DELAY, R-TEXAS, WAS the most visible, but not the only, member of Congress under criminal investigation in 2005. DeLay was forced to step down as House majority leader after he was indicted Sept. 28 for conspiracy to violate Texas campaign finance laws. Three other members of the House were being investigated in separate cases. (*DeLay, p. 5-3*)

The House ethics committee was not involved and conducted no investigations in 2005 because of partisan disputes over the rules and over who should work on the committee's staff. (*Ethics panels, p. 5-6*)

● **Cunningham.** Randy "Duke" Cunningham, R-Calif., resigned his seat Dec. 1 after pleading guilty to one count of bribery and one count of tax evasion. Cunningham had become an influential Republican voice on defense and intelligence policy during his 15 years in Congress. He admitted accepting at least $2.4 million in bribes, including about $1 million in cash as well as rugs, antiques, furniture, yacht club fees, boat repairs, moving costs and vacation expenses, in exchange for using his seat on the House Appropriations Committee to obtain earmarks on behalf of defense contractors.

"In my life, I have known great joy and great sorrow," Cunningham said tearfully outside a San Diego courthouse. "Now I know great shame."

Among the evidence prosecutors used was a "bribe menu" written on Cunningham's office stationery that sketched out for a contractor how much of a bribe he wanted based on the dollar value of earmarks the contractor sought in an appropriations bill.

Four months earlier, as details of the case began to become public, Cunningham announced that he would not seek re-election in 2006 so he could focus his energy on proving that he was innocent of any malfeasance.

The prosecutors' statements made apparent, and lawyers in the case confirmed, that the defense contractors were Brent Wilkes, head of the California-based ADCS Inc., which made software for digitizing documents and had won about $80 million in federal contracts since 1999; and Mitchell J. Wade, a founder of Washington-based MZM Inc., which had won $163 million in federal intelligence-gathering and analysis contracts in the previous three years. What first drew investigators' attention was Wade's purchase of Cunningham's home in Del Mar, Calif., for almost $1.7 million, and its subsequent sale at a $700,000 loss — along with the 42-foot yacht, which Wade named the *Duke-Stir*, made available rent-free as the congressman's Washington home.

Lawyers in the case said the other co-conspirators were Thomas Kontogiannis, a Long Island developer who sought Cunningham's help in trying to get a presidential pardon for a 2002 bribery conviction, and John T. Michael, a nephew of Kontogiannis' wife, who ran a mortgage company that financed Cunningham's purchases of a condominium in Arlington, Va., and a home in Rancho Santa Fe, Calif.

The eight-term congressman was subsequently sentenced March 3, 2006, to eight years and four months in prison. He was the first congressman to serve a prison term since Ohio Rep. James A. Traficant Jr. (1985-2002), a Democrat, was sentenced to eight years in prison and fined $150,000 on 10 counts of bribery, racketeering and tax evasion. (*2002 Almanac, p. 1-14*)

● **Ney.** House Administration Committee Chairman Bob Ney, R-Ohio, was implicated in a far-reaching Justice Department investigation of lobbyist Jack Abramoff, who gained notoriety from the more than $80 million he and his associates charged Indian tribes for their services. One of those associates, former DeLay press secretary Michael Scanlon, pleaded guilty Nov. 21 to conspiring to bribe Ney, identified in court documents as "Representative No. 1."

The congressman was not charged, and he insisted there was never any quid pro quo in his dealings with Abramoff. In 2002, Ney had tried to insert into an elections overhaul bill language that would have benefited an Indian gambling casino operated by an Abramoff client. Ney said he was duped by Abramoff.

Ney also placed statements into the Congressional Record in support of an Abramoff effort to buy a Florida gambling boat company. Ney and DeLay received golf trips to Scotland that were paid for by Abramoff, though the source of the financing was reported as being a charity founded by Abramoff.

On Jan. 15, 2006, Ney stepped down from his position as committee chairman under pressure from Speaker J. Dennis Hastert, R-Ill.

● **Jefferson.** Federal investigators worked throughout the year on a case involving allegations that Democratic Rep. William J. Jefferson of Louisiana took bribes to facilitate a deal between iGate Inc., a high-tech firm, and Nigeria. Some of Jefferson's aides were subpoenaed as part of that probe. On Aug. 3, federal agents raided Jefferson's homes in New Orleans and Washington, where they reportedly seized $90,000 in cash from Jefferson's freezer. Agents also searched offices of iGate Inc.

arrangement that passed at least $155,000 in corporate contributions from TRMPAC to the Republican National Committee, which then used the money to finance Republican state candidates. Under Texas law, corporate money could not be spent to influence state elections. A violation would be a third-degree felony, punishable by two to 10 years in jail and a fine of up to $10,000.

In keeping with Republican rules, DeLay temporarily stepped aside as majority leader the day he was indicted. He called Earle "an unabashed partisan zealot" and vowed to return to power after clearing his name of what he said were baseless charges. DeLay said that while he had been on the board of directors of the PAC, he left the day-to-day operations to others. "Let me be very, very clear," DeLay said. "I have done nothing wrong. I have violated no law, no regulation, no rule

of the House. I am innocent."

DeLay's indictment followed that of three close associates, who had set up TRMPAC at his direction — Jim Ellis, his longtime chief fundraiser; John Colyandro, executive director of TRMPAC; and Warren RoBold, a fundraiser for the committee.

Many House Republicans believed, as DeLay asserted, that the investigation was politically motivated, and they rallied to his defense. At a private meeting Sept. 28, the conference chose Blunt to act as the temporary majority leader while DeLay fought the charges. Blunt had been in the third-ranking leadership post since 2003.

With Hastert behind him, DeLay kept a substantial informal role in the leadership, continuing to be a force in decisions and strategy. Much of his staff was also left intact; so although Blunt held the

majority leader's title, he was surrounded by DeLay aides and loyalists who could watch him to make sure he did not get too settled in the job. The lobbyist community along Washington's K Street corridor also was reluctant to abandon DeLay, fearing that he would freeze out anyone who did not stick with him should he eventually recover all of his previous powers.

Still, DeLay's absence from the formal post had an immediate impact on the majority's productivity. Without his ability to bend the conference and individual members to his will — attributes that had earned him the nickname "the Hammer"— Republicans began to lose their cohesion.

In October, a GOP-drafted energy bill squeaked through, 212-210, but only after the balloting was extended for 40 minutes so DeLay could round up the final votes. In November, 22 Republicans staged a mini-revolt on the floor against a spending bill for labor and health programs. The bill failed, the first time Republican leaders lost a vote on a routine spending bill since the GOP took control of Congress in 1995.

On Dec. 12, the Supreme Court agreed to decide the validity of the congressional district map of Texas that had been drawn under DeLay's guidance. The court was expected to hear oral arguments in March 2006 from Hispanic, African-American, and Democratic plaintiffs and the county surrounding Austin. The plaintiffs planned to argue that the redistricting violated not only the Voting Rights Act, devoted to safeguarding the electoral influence of ethnic minorities, but also the constitutional requirement of "one person, one vote" for legislative districts. (Redistricting, p. 5-11)

In the closing weeks of the session, DeLay retained a devoted following among Republicans, but there was growing sentiment that change was in the offing. A few members privately encouraged Hastert to talk with DeLay to try to persuade him to give up his quest to return to power. Some even suggested that the Speaker call for new leadership elections to select a permanent replacement.

"The last thing anyone wants is to have a leadership team going through a tough election year with 'interim' behind its name," said Arizona's Jeff Flake, who predicted that there would be new leadership elections by February. ■

# House Ethics Panel Unable to Function

IN A YEAR DOMINATED BY SCANDAL in Congress, the House ethics committee ceased to function, as Republicans and Democrats fought to a standstill over rules and staffing and over which party would occupy the ethical high ground in the eyes of the public.

Republican leaders, fuming over the bipartisan committee's admonishments of Majority Leader Tom DeLay, R-Texas, for ethical lapses in 2004, tried to make it harder to bring and prosecute ethics cases. Democrats and outside watchdog groups reacted angrily, accusing them of tampering with the rules to protect the powerful Texan.

After a public backlash felt by GOP members in their districts, the leadership relented. But the Committee on Standards of Official Conduct, as the panel was formally known, remained dormant in the charged political environment in the House. It was unable to complete any investigations in 2005 in spite of several high profile cases of possible improprieties uncovered by the press and federal investigators.

In addition to the swirl of questions surrounding lavish trips abroad taken by DeLay with GOP lobbyist Jack Abramoff, California Republican Randy "Duke" Cunningham (1991-2005) resigned his seat Dec. 1 after pleading guilty to bribery and tax evasion. William J. Jefferson, D-La., was under federal investigation for allegedly accepting secret payments for helping a technology firm secure contracts in Nigeria. And though he had not been charged, House Administration Committee Chairman Bob Ney, R-Ohio, was implicated in a far-reaching Justice Department investigation of Abramoff. (DeLay, p. 5-3; investigations, p. 5-5)

The committee's predicament renewed the longstanding debate about whether Congress was capable of policing itself or whether the job should be taken over by an outside commission or group.

## CHANGING THE RULES

Bolstered by their victories in the November 2004 elections, House Republican leaders opened the 109th Congress by pushing through a set of rules changes (H Res 5) that affected how the ethics committee conducted business. The panel had angered the leadership in 2004 by admonishing DeLay, the second-ranking GOP leader, for three instances of inappropriate conduct that included hosting a fundraiser with energy industry lobbyists in 2002 while the House was crafting a major energy bill.

The House adopted the GOP leaders' rules package on a strict party-line vote of 220-195 on Jan. 4. (House vote 6, p. H-4)

The January ethics rules allowed a complaint against a House member to die after 45 days unless the chairman and ranking minority party member, or the committee as a whole, agreed it merited an investigation. "The rule gives them the right to stop anything from happening without even looking at the complaint," said Fred Wertheimer, president of the watchdog group Democracy 21. DeLay said the changes would make the process stronger by letting members have a presumption of innocence.

The new rules also gave a member the right to respond to the committee's conclusion before it was finalized or made public. The member also could submit a written response that the committee would have to disclose with any publicly released report or letter.

GOP leaders said this would protect members from being blindsided when ethics findings were released to the public. Critics said it would hamper the process by requiring the committee to hold a hearing before it could open a subcommittee investigation.

Another change codified what had been a common practice of allowing one attorney to represent multiple lawmakers involved in an ethics probe, a practice that critics said allowed the targets to compare their versions of events.

Republicans had agreed to the House rules changes after the November elections when they met to make plans for the 109th Congress, but the rules were not put in place until the House vote in January.

The GOP leadership had planned to go further, making two other changes specifically to protect DeLay. First, Republicans had approved an internal rule for their caucus that would have allowed a leader to remain in power even if he or she were indicted. Second, they planned to change House rules so that the ethics committee could not admonish a member for behavior that did not violate a specific rule but did

run afoul of the standard requiring that members and their employees conduct themselves at all times "in a manner which shall reflect creditably on the House of Representatives." That catchall provision was what the committee used to admonish DeLay in 2004, and it had been used against numerous other lawmakers. *(2004 Almanac, p. 1-10)*

But those proposals generated too much bad publicity and were dropped after rank-and-file Republicans complained they were being pilloried at home for altering the rules to protect DeLay.

Next, in a move widely viewed as punishment for the actions against DeLay, Speaker J. Dennis Hastert, R-Ill., in February cleaned house in the ethics panel. He removed ethics Chairman Joel Hefley, R-Colo., and two Republican members, replacing them with loyalists. Doc Hastings, R-Wash., took over as chairman and began to fire the panel's staff.

The changes set off a firestorm of criticism and led to the virtual shutdown of the committee. Led by ranking member Alan B. Mollohan of West Virginia, the panel's five Democrats blocked approval of the committee's operating rules, making it impossible for the 10-member, evenly divided panel to function. The panel could accomplish only simple administrative duties, while well-publicized cases of potential misconduct went unchecked.

Mollohan put additional pressure on the GOP by securing 208 cosponsors for a resolution (H Res 131) that would have amended or repealed the rules changes. Support crept upward toward the 218 signatures needed on a discharge petition, which would have forced a floor debate. Additional pressure from watchdog groups and increased home district press coverage also were factors that finally influenced Hastert to capitulate.

On April 27, the House voted overwhelmingly in favor of a resolution (H Res 240) that reversed all of the rules changes, so that the committee in effect reverted to the same standards it had operated under in previous congresses. The vote was 406-20. *(House vote 145, p. H-48)*

Even with that vote, the panel remained dormant because Mollohan and Hastings disagreed over who should be hired for chief counsel. They resolved that disagreement in June, but the committee did little for the rest of the year.

## SENATE ETHICS COMMITTEE

On the other side of the Capitol, the Senate Select Committee on Ethics took several small actions in 2005.

● **Frist.** Citizens for Responsibility and Ethics in Washington, a non-profit watchdog group, filed an ethics complaint against Senate Majority Leader Bill Frist, R-Tenn., questioning whether he violated Senate rules when he told managers of his family blind trusts to sell shares in hospital operator HCA Corp., a company co-founded by his father.

The panel normally responded to such complaints, but it was not expected to act until the Securities and Exchange Commission and the Justice Department finished separate probes of whether Frist's transactions violated insider-trading laws. Frist denied any wrongdoing and insisted that he got approval from the Ethics Committee before telling two trustees to sell shares of HCA stock held in his family's blind trusts. Senate rules required members to keep their hands off blind trusts, but Frist said he invoked an exemption that allowed members to intervene with trust managers if new responsibilities raised a potential conflict of interest.

● **Coburn.** The panel enforced a ban on outside compensation by ordering freshman Sen. Tom Coburn, R-Okla., to stop earning income from his medical practice. Coburn, an obstetrician, complied but then tried to add language overruling the Ethics panel as an amendment to the tax reconciliation bill (S 2020). He fell nine votes short of the 60 required to overcome a point of order. The vote Nov. 17 was 51-47. *(Senate vote 335, p. S-65)*

● **Shelby.** The committee also cleared Richard C. Shelby, R-Ala., the former vice chairman of the Select Intelligence Committee, of wrongdoing in connection with leaks to the media in 2002 of classified information gathered by U.S. intelligence agencies about the Sept. 11, 2001, terrorist attacks. The committee closed its probe of Shelby in November, telling the senator in a letter that federal investigators "produced evidence and information concerning your conduct in connection with the disclosure," which related to NSA intercepts, but said the case was closed without finding ethics violations. *(Shelby, 2004 Almanac, p. 5-5)* ■

# Continuity Plans Enacted for House

A PLAN TO QUICKLY RECONSTITUTE the House of Representatives in the wake of a terrorist attack or other catastrophe was put into law as part of the fiscal 2006 Legislative Branch appropriations bill. The need to ensure that the legislative branch would live on even if most of its members were killed or incapacitated had been a pressing issue since the Sept. 11, 2001, terrorist attacks. President Bush signed the bill into law Aug. 2 (HR 2985 — PL 109-55).

The measure established a process for states to hold special elections to fill vacancies if more than 100 House members could no longer perform their duties. The House had passed the provisions as a stand-alone bill (HR 841) by a vote of 329-68 on March 3. *(House vote 52, p. H-18)*

The House Appropriations Committee added the provisions to the Legislative Branch bill before approving the measure June 16. The amendment was offered by Chairman Jerry Lewis, R-Calif., as a way of prodding the Senate to approve the language. The House had passed a stand-alone "continuity of Congress" bill in 2004, but the Senate never took it up. *(2004 Almanac, p. 5-3)*

In the Senate, Robert C. Byrd of West Virginia, the ranking Democrat on the Appropriations Committee, struck the language from that chamber's version of the Legislative Branch bill. "Continuity of Congress is an issue of enormous consequence ... [and] not something to be decided by the House of Representatives alone," Byrd said. "I question the wisdom of using the Legislative Branch appropriations bills to ram this legislation through Congress."

But the longstanding tradition of allowing each chamber to decide its own fate prevailed when the bill went to a House-Senate conference. The House adopted the conference report on the bill (H Rept 109-189), 305-122, on July 28, and the Senate cleared the measure, 96-4, on July 29. *(House vote 451, p. H-140; Senate vote 211, p. S-42)*

Previously, it had been left up to the states to decide how to fill vacancies, though lawmakers did make some rules changes regarding continuity at the beginning of the 108th Congress. Among those: The House and Senate were allowed to convene outside Washington, and the Speaker could declare an emergency recess at any time. Speaker J. Dennis Hastert, R-Ill., regularly filed a secret list of temporary succes-

sors should he be incapacitated. A small cadre of members also went to a secure location whenever the president addressed a joint session of Congress.

On the Senate side, John Cornyn, R-Texas, continued to push for a constitutional amendment outlined in S J Res 6, which would require any procedures established in response to a widespread loss of lawmakers to expire after 120 days. However, it would permit 120-day extensions as long as one-fourth of the seats in either chamber remained vacant. Cornyn's proposal had run into opposition from House Republicans, and its prospects in either chamber were further dimmed by the enactment of the House continuity plan.

## HIGHLIGHTS

The legislative branch bill included the following provisions:

▶ States were required to hold special elections within 49 days following an announcement by the Speaker that more than 100 vacancies existed in the House. If a state had a regularly scheduled election to fill the seat within 75 days of the Speaker's announcement, it would not have to hold the special election.

▶ Candidates for the special elections had to be nominated no later than 10 days after the Speaker announced that the vacancies existed. The nomination could be made by the parties authorized by state law

to nominate candidates, or by any method the state determined was appropriate, including holding primary elections, as long as the method ensured that the special election would be held before the required deadline.

▶ Delegates from the District of Columbia and the territories as well as the resident commissioner from Puerto Rico were subject to the special election provisions of the bill. However, vacancies in those offices would not count toward the 100 vacancy threshold.

▶ States were required to ensure, to the greatest extent practicable, that absentee ballots for special elections were transmitted to military voters and overseas voters within 15 days of the Speaker's announcement. States had to accept and process otherwise valid ballots from such voters as long as they were received by the state election official no later than 45 days after the ballot was transmitted to the voter.

▶ Any challenge to the Speaker's announcement had to be filed within two days of the announcement in the federal district court with jurisdiction over that congressional district, and heard by a three-judge panel that would have to issue a final decision within three days of the filing. The governor of the state would have the right to intervene in support of, or in opposition to, the challenge. The decision of this three-judge panel was subject to further judicial review. ■

# Campaign Finance Bills Target 527s

HOUSE AND SENATE committees approved bills in the spring that were aimed at rewriting — or even rolling back — parts of the 2002 campaign finance law. But as the session wore on, Hurricane Katrina, budget woes, the war in Iraq and other issues pushed the matter to the back burner, and none of the campaign finance bills reached the floor in the first session. At year's end, an unfolding scandal involving Washington lobbyist Jack Abramoff and his connections with lawmakers spurred renewed interest in possible changes to lobbying and campaign finance rules in the second session.

The effort to revise campaign rules was driven mainly by Republicans who wanted to rein in certain tax-exempt groups — so-called 527 organizations — that had spent more than $400 million in "soft" or unregulated money trying to influence the 2004 elections. Unlike political campaigns or political action committees (PACs), these groups, named for the section of the tax code under which they operated, were able to accept unlimited contributions from wealthy individuals, unions and corporations. Among the frequently cited examples were Moveon.org and Swift Boat Veterans for Truth. While some of these groups financed GOP attack ads, Democrats were seen as the main beneficiaries of 527 fundraising.

Some Republicans, however, were interested less in writing new rules for 527s than in relaxing existing campaign finance restrictions. The 2002 law (PL 107-155) had banned previously unlimited "soft money" contributions to political parties and imposed curbs on the financing and placement of broadcast "issue" advertisements within 30 days of a primary or 60 days of a general election. Bob Ney of Ohio, chairman of the House Administration Committee, said the 2002 campaign law had trampled the

**BOX SCORE**

**BILLS:** HR 1316, HR 513, S 1053

**LEGISLATIVE ACTION:**

**Senate** Rules and Administration Committee approved S 1053 by voice vote on April 27.

**House** Administration Committee approved HR 1316 (H Rept 109-146), 6-3, on June 8.

**House** Administration Committee approved HR 513 (H Rept 109-181), 5-3, on June 29.

free-speech rights of individuals and associations with its many "onerous restrictions and harsh criminal penalties." *(2002 Almanac, p. 14-7)*

Reflecting the competing GOP priorities, the House Administration Committee marked up a pair of bills — one focused on tightening regulation of 527 groups, the other aimed at loosening existing restrictions on individuals, parties and PACs. The Senate Rules and Administration Committee approved a separate bill aimed at restricting 527s and making other changes in campaign finance law.

Under all the bills, 527 groups would have to comply with the same disclosure requirements and other restrictions that applied to political parties and political action committees. They would be considered "political committees," subject to limitations on soft money in the 2002 law, at least in so far as the groups were involved in activities aimed at affecting federal elections.

Most Democrats opposed all three bills, although each had a Democratic cosponsor. Party leaders said they wanted to give the 2002 law more time to work without interference, and that 527 groups were deliberately left unrestricted by that law to allow other avenues for election spending.

## LEGISLATIVE ACTION
### HOUSE COMMITTEE ACTION

The House Administration Committee considered rival campaign finance bills at separate markups in June.

● **Pence-Wynn.** The committee voted, 6-3, along party lines June 8 to approve a bill (HR 1316 — H Rept 109-146) aimed at strengthen-

ing the role of political parties and repealing sections of the 2002 campaign finance law and the Watergate-era laws that preceded it. Sponsors Mike Pence, R-Ind., and Albert R. Wynn, D-Md., said that reducing the regulation of hard and soft money would put other groups more on a par with 527 organizations.

However, the committee adopted, 6-3, a substitute amendment by Ney that added a provision requiring 527 groups to abide by Federal Election Commission (FEC) disclosure requirements. It also prohibited the FEC from regulating online communication, and allowed federal candidates to endorse state and local candidates without the endorsements being considered as coordinated contributions that had to be paid for with "hard" dollars.

As approved by the committee, the bill proposed to:

▶ Remove the aggregate $101,400 limit on contributions an individual could make to candidates and party committees in each two-year election cycle.

▶ Remove a cap on the amount party committees could spend on coordinated expenditures.

▶ Allow unlimited transfers from leadership PACs to party committees.

▶ Require 527 groups to file the same FEC reports as federal political committees.

▶ Allow state and local parties to spend non-federal dollars for voter registration and sample ballots.

▶ Exempt Internet communications from the definition of "public communications" regulated by the FEC, thereby settling an ongoing debate over FEC regulation of the political postings of "bloggers," Web writers and other Internet-publishing partisans.

Panel Democrats unanimously opposed the bill, saying it would roll back progress made by the 2002 campaign finance law and invoke the pre-Watergate days of scandal and corruption. "One of the good things that came out of Watergate is campaign finance reform. This bill brings us back to the pre-Watergate days," said Rep. Zoe Lofgren, D-Calif.

● **Shays-Meehan.** The committee voted, 5-3, on June 29 to send a rival bill (HR 513 — 109-181, Parts 1, 2) to the floor without recommendation. The bill was sponsored by Christopher Shays, R-Conn., and Martin T. Meehan, D-Mass., two of the chief architects of the 2002 campaign finance law. Shays and Meehan said 527 groups were operating as political committees but without the regulations that the 2002 law imposed on other political committees.

Under the Shays-Meehan bill, 527 groups would be required to:

▶ Register as political committees with the FEC and comply with federal campaign finance laws. Groups with annual receipts of less than $25,000 would be exempt.

▶ Use federal "hard money" contributions to finance ads that promoted or attacked federal candidates.

▶ Ensure that 50 percent of the money used to pay for voter mobilization activities or public communications affecting both federal and non-federal elections was hard money.

An amendment by Ney, adopted 5-3, added provisions to:

▶ Exempt 527 groups that worked only on behalf of non-federal officeholders.

▶ Exempt state PACs from having to register as a federal PAC if they were active only in a single state and did not have a candidate for federal office or a federal officeholder controlling or raising money for the organizations.

▶ Allow federal PACs to use non-federal money for expenditures designed only to assist state candidates even if they made an incidental reference to a federal candidate or political party.

During the somewhat acrimonious markup, panel Democrats, led by ranking member Juanita Millender-McDonald of California, strongly opposed the legislation, saying it would lower voter turnout, impede voter registration activities and violate independent groups' right to free speech.

The committee's majority blasted panel Democrats for their support of the 2002 campaign finance law criticized by its detractors for ultimately failing to halt the flow of soft money in federal elections. "527s are a curse to the political process," said Vernon J. Ehlers, R-Mich.

**SENATE COMMITTEE ACTION**

The Senate Rules and Administration Committee gave voice vote approval April 27 to a campaign finance bill (S 271) introduced by John McCain, R-Ariz., and Russ Feingold, D-Wis. — the two main Senate sponsors of the 2002 law — and by Chairman Trent Lott, R-Miss. The bill was introduced as a companion to HR 513, but the committee made a number of changes during the markup. Afterwards, Lott introduced it as a clean bill (S 1053).

The initial bill included provisions to:

▶ Require all 527s to register as political committees and comply with FEC rules unless they raised and spent money only for non-federal candidate elections, state or local ballot initiatives, or the nomination or confirmation of individuals to non-elected offices.

▶ Require that at least 50 percent of funds spent on voter mobilization activities affecting both federal and non-federal elections had to be hard money.

▶ Require that 527s maintaining a non-federal account accept no more than $25,000 per year per donor for that account. Corporations and labor unions could not contribute to those accounts.

"This legislation would not be necessary," McCain said when he introduced the bill, "if it weren't for the abject failure of the FEC to enforce existing law." McCain said the use of soft money by 527s to attack presidential candidates in the 2004 election was "clearly illegal under current statute, and the fact that they have been allowed to continue unchecked is unconscionable."

During the markup, the committee

▶ Adopted by voice vote a substitute by Lott that, among other things, exempted nonprofits that filed under section 501(c) of the tax code from the FEC restrictions. Also, 527 groups that received less than $25,000 a year would be exempt.

▶ Adopted a number of amendments by Robert F. Bennett, R-Utah, including a provision to prevent the FEC from regulating the Internet. Other Bennett amendments would allow trade associations to solicit campaign funds from member companies without prior written approval, raise the amounts PACs could receive and contribute to other PACs from $5,000 to $7,500, and allow unlimited transfers from leadership PACs to national parties.

▶ Approved two Democratic amendments. One, by Charles E. Schumer, D-N.Y., would exempt 527s that funded only non-broadcast voter registration and get-out-the-vote drives. The second, by Richard J. Durbin of Illinois, would require radio and television stations to sell advertising to candidates at the lowest rate available throughout the election cycle.

Schumer, however, removed his name from the list of bill cosponsors, accusing GOP leaders of preparing to use the measure "as an anti-campaign finance reform Trojan horse," to repeal changes made by the 2002 law once they were in conference with the House. ■

# House Majority Remains Unchanged

THREE SPECIAL ELECTIONS were held to fill House vacancies in 2005, but there were no partisan turnovers — the Republicans held two of the seats, the Democrats one. One Senate vacancy created during the year, when Jon Corzine was elected governor of New Jersey, was filled in early 2006 by a fellow Democrat.

In the only other gubernatorial race, Lt. Gov. Tim Kaine held the governorship of Virginia for the Democrats, taking 52 percent of the vote on Nov. 8 against Republican Jerry Kilgore, a former state attorney general. Because Virginia had been reliably Republican in recent years, Democrats hailed that outcome as a sign of the party's potential for good fortune nationally in the 2006 midterm election. But the state's recent political history offered a countervailing fact: In all eight gubernatorial elections since 1977, the winner had been from the party that did not hold the White House at the time.

● **New Jersey.** Corzine was elected governor after five years in the Senate and five years before that as the chairman and chief executive of the investment bank Goldman Sachs. He took 53 percent of the vote and won by a comfortable 9 percentage points against Republican businessman Doug Forrester, who also had lost a Senate race three years before to Democrat Frank R. Lautenberg.

Corzine was only the sixth person since 1913, when the direct election of senators began, to quit the Senate in the middle of his term to take up a governorship. The two most recent members of the group were Frank H. Murkowski of Alaska in 2002 and Pete Wilson of California in 1990. As a member of that tiny club, Corzine also had the extraordinary power under the Constitution to pick his own senatorial successor.

On Dec. 9, he announced that the final year of his term would be completed by Rep. Robert Menendez, a fellow liberal who had represented a district that hugged the Hudson River since 1993 and had been the chairman of the Democratic Caucus since 2003, a post that made him third in the party's House leadership hierarchy and the highest ranking Hispanic ever in Congress.

The appointment made some American political history: All of New Jersey's previous senators had been non-minority white men. When Menendez took office on Jan. 18, 2006, he became only the sixth Hispanic senator ever — although the third in the 109th Congress. Republican Mel Martinez of Florida and Democrat Ken Salazar of Colorado joined the Senate in 2005.

On Dec. 16, House Democrats elevated James E. Clyburn of South Carolina, who had been vice chairman for three years, to succeed Menendez as caucus chairman. Clyburn was not opposed for the job, which made him the highest-ranking African-American in Congress since William H. Gray III of Pennsylvania, who was the House Democratic whip from 1989-1991.

● **Ohio.** Republican Jean Schmidt won an Aug. 2 special election in the 2nd District of Ohio, which included eastern Cincinnati and the suburbs stretching along the Ohio River, with 52 percent against Democratic attorney Paul Hackett, a Marine Corps veteran of the Iraq War who sharply criticized Bush's handling of that conflict. Because the area had been so reliably Republican, Democrats viewed Schmidt's narrow victory as an indicator of weakening support for the president and his policies. The election of Schmidt, who had been president of Right to Life of Greater Cincinnati, brought the number of women in the House to 67, a record.

The seat had become vacant on April 29, when Rob Portman, who had held it since 1993, resigned upon his confirmation as the U.S. trade representative. *(Bush team, p. 10-3)*

● **California 48.** Republican John Campbell won a Dec. 6 special election in the 48th District, which included many of the southern Orange County suburbs of Los Angeles that he had represented in the state Senate for the rest of 2005 and in the state Assembly for the previous four years. Campbell won with just 45 percent of the vote, a relatively modest share in a district where Republicans regularly got at least two-thirds of the vote. But much of the GOP vote went to Jim Gilchrist, a co-founder of the Minuteman Project that solicited volunteers to conduct surveillance along the Mexican border. Gilchrist took 25 percent under the banner of the little-known American Independent Party. Democrat Steve Young, a lawyer, took 28 percent.

## Congress in Transition

**VACANCY (1)**

California 50 — Republican Rep. Randy "Duke" Cunningham resigned, effective Dec. 1, after pleading guilty to bribery and tax evasion.

**RETIRING SENATORS (1 R, 2 D, 1 I)**

Mark Dayton, D-Minn.
Bill Frist, R-Tenn.
James M. Jeffords, I-Vt.
Paul S. Sarbanes, D-Md.

**RETIRING HOUSE MEMBERS (3 R, 1 D)**

Michael Bilirakis, R-Fla. (9)
Henry J. Hyde, R-Ill. (6)
Major R. Owens, D-N.Y. (11)
Michael G. Oxley, R-Ohio (4)

**RUNNING FOR THE SENATE (2 R, 3 D, 1 I)**

Rep. Sherrod Brown, D-Ohio (13)
Rep. Benjamin L. Cardin, D-Md. (3)
Rep. Harold E. Ford Jr., D-Tenn. (9)
Rep. Katherine Harris, R-Fla. (13)
Rep. Mark Kennedy, R-Minn. (6)
Rep. Bernard Sanders, I-Vt. (At-large)

**RUNNING FOR GOVERNOR (7 R, 2 D)**

Rep. Bob Beauprez, R-Colo. (7)
Rep. Jim Davis, D-Fla. (11)
Rep. Jim Gibbons, R-Nev. (2)
Rep. Mark Green, R-Wis. (8)
Rep. Ernest Istook, R-Okla. (5)
Rep. Jim Nussle, R-Iowa (1)
Rep. Tom Osborne, R-Neb. (3)
Rep. C.L. "Butch" Otter, R-Idaho (1)
Rep. Ted Strickland, D-Ohio (6)

The seat became vacant Aug. 2 when Christopher Cox, who had held it since 1989 and had risen to become chairman of the House Homeland Security Committee, resigned after winning Senate confirmation to serve as chairman of the Securities and Exchange Commission.

● **California 5.** Democrat Doris Matsui won a March 8 special election with 69 percent of the vote against 11 opponents in the 5th District, centered in Sacramento. Her husband, Robert T. Matsui, had represented the district until his death Jan. 1, three days before he was to be sworn in for his 14th term. He died at age 63 from pneumonia result- ing from a rare stem cell disorder. Since 1988, Doris Matsui had been director of government relations for the Washington firm Collier Shannon Scott. She had served as a deputy director of public liaison in the Clinton administration, working on an array of domestic economic policy and trade initiatives.

Matsui became the 44th widow — 36 in the House and eight in the Senate — to directly succeed a spouse in Congress. Born in a World War II internment camp for Japanese-Americans, she also brought the number of Asian-Americans in the 109th Congress to six, a record. ∎

# Redistricting Has Mixed Results for GOP

THE UNPRECEDENTED DRIVE by Republicans to use middle-of-the-decade redistricting to boost their numbers in the House had mixed results in 2005. The newly installed GOP majority in Georgia's legislature redrew that state's congressional boundaries with the aim of picking up a seat or two in 2006. But the Supreme Court agreed to review the legality and constitutionality of the map drawn in Texas in 2003 that resulted in a net gain of six House seats for Republicans between the 2002 and 2004 election, casting some doubt on whether its boundaries would be used again in 2006.

Meanwhile, efforts to reopen congressional districting for the decade in New Mexico and Illinois, where Democrats had newly won control of state government, quickly came to naught. And in November voters in Ohio and California rejected proposals that would have taken redistricting power away from their states' legislatures — both of which had in recent decades drawn the boundaries mainly to protect congressional incumbents or benefit the party in power at the statehouse — and turn the process over to independent panels in the hope that their map-making would engender more competition.

## GEORGIA

Having won a majority of state House seats the previous fall, the Republican Party controlled both the General Assembly and the governorship in 2005 for the first time in modern times. On March 22, the legislature cleared a bill redrawing the boundaries of the state's 13 congressional districts. Gov. Sonny Perdue signed the measure May 3. The Justice Department endorsed, or "pre-cleared," the map Sept. 30. Under the Voting Rights Act (PL 89-110), Georgia was one of nine mostly Southern states with a history of racial discrimination that could not implement any changes in its electoral laws before obtaining a determination — either from Justice or a federal judge in Washington — that the change would not abridge, and was not designed to abridge, the political rights of ethnic minority groups. Democrats decided against challenging the map in court.

The map replaced one that had been drawn in 2001 by a Democratic-majority General Assembly and signed by Democratic Gov. Roy Barnes. Under reapportionment after the 2000 census, Georgia was awarded 13 House seats for the decade, an increase of two. In 2004, Republicans won seven of the seats, the Democrats six.

Republicans said that map split too many counties into different House districts and distributed voters in a way that unfairly benefited Democrats at a time when the state had trended steadily to the GOP. But their "re-redistricting" was much more modest in its partisan aims than that which occurred in Texas the previous year. The Republicans said they had two goals. The first was to secure the political for- tunes of one GOP incumbent, Phil Gingrey, by decreasing the number of African-American voters in the suburban 11th District near the state's northwestern corner. The second was to create politically competitive situations for GOP candidates in a pair of reconfigured districts that were to be defended by Democratic incumbents: Jim Marshall in the new 8th District, stretching from the exurbs of Atlanta south to near the Florida border, and John Barrow in the adjacent 12th District, which was redrawn to shed generally Democratic Athens.

## TEXAS

The Supreme Court agreed Dec. 12 to decide the validity of the Texas congressional district map. In so doing, the court inserted itself into one of the most consequential and bitter political fights in the country. It also returned to a question of constitutional law — how much partisanship may affect the drawing of electoral boundaries — on which the court essentially deadlocked just 20 months earlier.

Oral arguments were scheduled for March 1, 2006, in *League of United Latin American Citizens v. Perry*, a case consolidating challenges to the map brought by Hispanic, African-American and Democratic plaintiffs and the county surrounding the state capital of Austin. The four appellants offered a variety of rationales for striking down the map as violating not only the Voting Rights Act but also the constitutional requirement of "one person, one vote" for legislative districts.

The new lines were drawn in 2003, a year after Republicans won control of the state Legislature, with the express purpose of creating a GOP-majority Texas congressional delegation. It worked almost exactly as designed: The state elected 21 Republicans and 11 Democrats to the House in 2004; two years before, it had elected 15 Republicans and 17 Democrats. *(2003 Almanac, p. 14-6; 2004 Almanac, p. 18-18)*

The map produced intense enmity from Democrats at the Capitol because it was key to the GOP cushioning its relatively narrow majority in the House in 2004. It has stayed in the forefront of lawmakers' minds because its principal architect was Rep. Tom DeLay, who had been indicted in the fall for campaign finance activity related to his efforts to secure a Republican majority in the Texas state House so that the redistricting could occur. DeLay was compelled to step aside as majority leader in September. *(DeLay, p. 5-3)*

Still, the court's decision to look at the map generated widespread surprise. The Texas attorney general's office had waived its right to respond to the four appeals, which were filed after a special panel of three federal judges upheld the map in June. The court rarely takes a case without reading briefs filed by each side.

Earlier in December, the Justice Department acknowledged that in 2003 its staff lawyers and analysts had concluded unanimously that the

map should not be implemented because it would dilute the voting strength of Hispanics and African-Americans. But they were overruled by political appointees in the department and the map was given Justice's stamp of approval.

The judges who upheld the map in June said they examined it in light of the most recent Supreme Court case that addressed the limits of political gerrymandering, *Vieth v. Jubelirer*, from 2004. In that case, the court voted 5-4 to uphold a congressional map of Pennsylvania drawn with Republican dominance in mind and left the door open — just barely — to future challenges of congressional maps as excessively political. The narrow majority was unable to coalesce behind a single standard for deciding when the motives for congressional redistricting were too partisan. Four justices asserted that the question was not one for the federal courts to even entertain. *(2004 Almanac, p. 18-21)*

Two of those justices, however, no longer were on the court when the Texas case reached it: Chief Justice William H. Rehnquist died in August 2005, and Justice Sandra Day O'Connor' retirement took effect in January 2006 upon the confirmation of her successor, Samuel A. Alito Jr.

## STATE INITIATIVES

In California, a referendum that would have moved responsibility for redistricting from the Legislature to a panel of retired judges was rejected, 60 percent to 40 percent. The measure — known as Proposition 77 — was promoted by Republican Gov. Arnold Schwarzenegger. He argued that the Democratic-dominated legislature's control of redistricting had minimized electoral competition, while locking in what he and other Republicans viewed as a disproportionate advantage for the Democrats in the state's congressional and legislative seats.

In Ohio, a proposed state constitutional amendment, known as Issue 4, that would have transferred redistricting power from the General Assembly to a five-member commission, was rejected, 70 percent to 30 percent. The initiative was put on the ballot by Democrats, who had found themselves stuck in a minority position in the state in recent years. ■

**Chapter 6**

# DEFENSE

# Defense

# Bush Signs Defense Authorization Measure With Detainee Provision

THE SENATE CLEARED a $491.5 billion defense authorization bill four days before Christmas, bringing an end to more than six months of often rancorous debate in both chambers. As late as mid-December, the White House was threatening to veto the fiscal 2006 bill over a provision written by Sen. John McCain, R-Ariz., that prohibited "cruel, inhuman or degrading treatment" of detainees in U.S. custody. But the White House ultimately relented, and President Bush signed the bill into law Jan. 6, 2006 (HR 1815 – PL 109-163).

The final bill authorized $441.5 billion for the Pentagon and nuclear weapons programs under the Energy Department. The total was $1.8 billion, or 4 percent, more than provided in the fiscal 2005 law (PL 108-375), not counting emergency supplemental defense funds for operations in Iraq. It was about $290 million less than the president's request. *(2004 Almanac, p. 6-3)*

In addition, the bill authorized $50 billion in emergency funds for military operations in Iraq and Afghanistan as a "bridge" until Bush sent Congress another supplemental request for the war in early 2006. Aside from the $50 billion, the bill did not include funds for the wars.

Funds authorized by the bill were appropriated in three separate spending measures – those for Defense, Energy and Water and Military Construction and Veterans Affairs. *(Defense, p 2-14; Energy-Water, p. 2-22; Military Construction-VA, p. 2-43)*

Lawmakers used the bill to assert Congress' role in overseeing the war in Iraq and the treatment of detainees in U.S.-run prisons abroad. The measure required the president to submit quarterly reports on progress in the Iraq war and on benchmarks leading to a U.S. troop drawdown. In addition to McCain's provision on detainee abuse, the bill barred detainees held at Guantánamo Bay, Cuba, from suing for habeas corpus, though they gained a limited right to appeal their detention.

Congress increased servicemembers' pay by 3.1 percent and added other special payments and recruitment bonuses in an effort to keep the ranks filled. It also gave all reservists some access to the military's Tricare healthcare system.

Bush's $441.8 billion request focused the increases mainly on operations and maintenance and personnel. Congress chose to authorize more for weapons procurement and research and development, while providing about $1.2 billion less than Bush sought for operations and maintenance.

The final bill authorized:
- $125.7 billion for operations and maintenance.
- $108.9 billion for personnel.

- $77 billion for weapons procurement.
- $70.2 billion for research and development.
- $16.4 billion for Energy Department nuclear activities.
- $12.2 billion for military construction and family housing

While Congress authorized most of what Bush wanted for weapons, it made efforts to control costs and included provisions to rein in spending and check reported mismanagement in the Pentagon. The prices of several new ships—the DD(X) destroyer, the Virginia-class submarine and the Littoral Combat Ship – were capped. The Army had to justify more fully to Congress its plans for the Future Combat System before it could spend all the money appropriated for the program. The Pentagon was required to provide a comprehensive report on its plans to revamp its financial management systems before it could conduct any more financial audits.

The House passed its version of the bill in May, but the Senate did not vote until mid-November. The bill was further delayed while GOP leaders and the White House debated what to do about McCain's detainee amendment. Both chambers were overwhelmingly in favor of it, however, and once Bush relented, the authorization sailed through.

## HIGHLIGHTS

The fiscal 2006 defense authorization bill included the following components:

● **Prisoner abuse.** A prohibition on "cruel, inhuman or degrading treatment" of detainees in U.S. custody, regardless of where they were held. Military interrogators were required to follow standards set in an Army field manual that complied with the Geneva Conventions.

● **Iraq policy.** Language requiring the president to send Congress quarterly reports on military, political and economic progress in Iraq.

● **Missile defense.** $7.8 billion authorized for ballistic-missile defense programs – virtually the same as the administration's request but roughly $2 billion below fiscal 2005 spending.

● **Troop levels.** Authorization for an additional 10,000 personnel for the active-duty Army in fiscal 2006, for a new total of 512,400, and an additional 1,000 personnel for the Marine Corps, for a total of 179,000.

● **Navy shipbuilding.** $8.9 billion, $177 million more than requested. The total included $1.1 billion for research and development on the DD(X), the Navy's next-generation surface combat ship, and $766 million for procurement. Congress required the Pentagon to maintain 12 aircraft carriers, rather than 11 as the Navy wanted.

● **Aircraft.** $3.7 billion, as requested, for 24 F-22A Raptors, the Air Force's controversial fighter intended to replace the F-15. The bill also

authorized $4.9 billion for the Joint Strike Fighter, a next-generation multirole fighter aircraft for all services based on a common airframe. Another $2.8 billion was authorized to procure 38 Navy F/A-18E/F Super Hornet fighter jets.

● **Future Combat System.** $3.4 billion for the Future Combat System, the Army's next generation of combat vehicles and weapons systems.

● **Military pay raise and benefits.** An average 3.1 percent pay increase for military personnel in fiscal 2006, equal to the president's request, and a variety of benefits and incentives for active duty and reserve personnel.

## LEGISLATIVE ACTION
### HOUSE COMMITTEE ACTION

After more than 14 hours of debate, the House Armed Services Committee approved a $490.6 billion defense authorization bill (HR 1815 — H Rept 109-89) on May 19 by a vote of 61-1. The bill consisted of $441.6 billion for the Defense Department and $49.1 billion in emergency supplemental spending for the wars in Iraq and Afghanistan. The committee agreed to give the Pentagon much of what it wanted in the way of spending, but with guidelines on how the money should be used.

The panel's six subcommittees had approved portions of the authorization measure May 9-13.

Republicans included language in the committee report aimed at improving oversight of the military's accounting for big-ticket items. Beginning in fiscal 2006, the Pentagon would be required to evaluate and monitor changes to its initial cost estimates for major defense acquisition programs, and to provide Congress and the Defense secretary with alternatives if a program exceeded its original baseline cost by 15 percent or more.

The committee said programs were often allowed to get too far along before problems were acknowledged. "This committee strongly believes that Congress should be given alternatives to the traditional approach of either funding or terminating a program with significant cost overruns," the panel added.

The bill included:

● **Troop strength.** An increase of 10,000 Army and 1,000 Marine active duty personnel in fiscal 2006 to support the missions in Iraq and Afghanistan.

● **Pay and benefits.** A 3.1 percent pay increase, and a permanent increase from $12,420 to $100,000 in the death gratuity paid to the families of servicemembers killed in the line of duty.

● **Future Combat System.** $2.9 billion, $499 million less than Bush's $3.4 billion request.

● **Iraq supplemental.** $49.1 billion in emergency supplemental funding for ongoing operations in Iraq and Afghanistan. Of the total, $33.7 billion was allotted for operations and maintenance, $9.4 billion for personnel and $3.4 billion for additional procurement.

● **Aircraft.** $3.7 billion, as requested, for procurement of the F-22A Raptor; $4.9 billion, as requested for development of the Joint Strike Fighter and $152.4 million for advanced procurement.

● **Shipbuilding.** $10.8 billion, $2.1 billion more than Bush requested. The committee increased the number of ships to be purchased from four requested by Bush to seven, and proposed a major restructuring of the Navy's shipbuilding program. The committee proposed:

▸ A $1.7 billion per ship limit on future procurement costs for the DD(X) destroyer, which would effectively kill the program. The Navy expected to spend nearly twice that amount on the first ship. The committee zeroed out the $716 million in advanced procurement requested to begin construction of the first DD(X) destroyer, and authorized

$700 million of the $1.1 billion requested for continued research and development.

The committee said the cost of the ships had escalated to the point that it would be difficult, if not impossible, to fund construction of the existing ship design in quantities needed to meet force requirements. It recommended that the Navy establish a program for major surface combatant technology that would result in an affordable next-generation destroyer with capabilities equal to or greater than the existing *Arleigh Burke*-class guided-missile destroyer.

In the interim, the committee added $2.7 billion for the construction of two additional *Arleigh Burke*-class (DDG-51) destroyers, in part by using savings derived from its proposed cuts to the DD(X) program.

▸ $418 million, $268 million more than requested, to construct the LHA(R) amphibious assault ship.

▸ $765 million, an addition of $384 million, to buy two T-AKE dry cargo ships; the Pentagon requested one.

▸ A requirement that the Navy maintain no fewer than 11 aircraft carriers.

● **Space programs.** $436 million — $400 million less than the president sought — for the Transformational Communication Satellite program. The bill authorized $100 million — a $126 million cut — for the Space Radar program. Air Force officials had presented both programs as essential to future war fighting, but the committee expressed concerns that the programs were in danger of falling behind schedule and promising more than they could offer.

● **Nuclear weapon.** $4 million for Pentagon research on the Robust Nuclear Earth Penetrator, also known as the bunker buster, a weapon designed to burrow deep into the ground to strike hidden targets. The committee said the study would evaluate various options, "to include conventional as well as nuclear penetrator options." Although the administration insisted it only wanted research funds, Democrats had expressed fears that the program could trigger a new nuclear arms race or lower the threshold for use of a nuclear weapon. Bush requested the research funding for the Energy Department.

The committee also authorized $3.5 million, as requested, for an Air Force study to assess integrating the earth penetrator with the B-2 bomber.

During the markup, the committee:

▸ Adopted by voice vote as part of an en bloc amendment a provision by Chairman Duncan Hunter, R-Calif., to bar the Pentagon from procuring goods and services from foreign companies that received subsidies from their governments. The prohibition was aimed at the European Aeronautic Defense and Space Company (EADS), considered a major competitor of Boeing Co. to build the military's midair-refueling planes.

A second provision sought to bar the Pentagon from buying from foreign firms that sold items to China that were on the U.S. list of export-controlled defense hardware and services. If a foreign firm was banned from doing business with the Pentagon under the rule, the secretary of Defense would not be able to lift the ban for five years.

▸ Adopted by voice vote, an amendment by John M. McHugh, R-N.Y., to put into law an 11-year-old Pentagon policy restricting women from serving in direct ground combat or in units that had to accompany others into battle.

The Personnel Subcommittee, which McHugh chaired, had approved more restrictive language barring women from joining specific combat-support units in the Army. Hunter backed the tougher language, but House Democrats and Army officials strongly opposed it. "We're saying it's time for Congress to be more responsible" and take

a role in determining women's role in the military, McHugh said. Democrats opposed even McHugh's watered-down proposal, which they said could result in unnecessary restrictions at a time when recruiting and retention in the military was suffering.

▸ Rejected two attempts by Jeb Bradley, R-N.H., to halt the 2005 Base Realignment and Closure (BRAC) round. A proposal to terminate the process failed, 8-50. The committee rejected, 10-47, a second amendment, which would have delayed the BRAC round until several criteria were met, including the withdrawal of troops from Iraq. The White House had threatened to veto the fiscal 2005 bill if it contained a BRAC delay, and it renewed that threat later in May.

▸ Approved, 32-30, an amendment by Gene Taylor, D-Miss., to authorize $180 million for one year to extend the military's Tricare health care coverage to reservists who were not deployed. The cost would be offset by reducing money included in the bill for base closures. Under existing law, reservists only had access to Tricare when they were called to active duty. Seven Republicans supported the amendment, but McHugh opposed because of it's estimated price tag of $3.8 billion over five years. "We simply can't afford it," he said.

▸ Adopted by voice vote a proposal by Jo Ann Davis, R-Va., and Roscoe G. Bartlett, R-Md., adding $87 million to speed up by one year the delivery of the Navy's next-generation aircraft carrier. That brought the total for advance procurement to $652 million. The Navy would have to certify that the program would be on track to begin construction by 2007 instead of 2008 as planned.

▸ Rejected, 27-33, an attempt by Ellen O. Tauscher, D-Calif., to require the Pentagon's test and evaluation office to become more involved in overseeing testing of the nation's Ballistic Missile Defense program. The Missile Defense Agency wrote its own test plans for the system and relied on the Pentagon office for advice only.

▸ Rejected, 24-35, an amendment by Martin T. Meehan, D-Mass., to require the Pentagon to report on its long-term plan for maintaining facilities in Iraq.

## HOUSE FLOOR ACTION

The House passed the $490.6 billion bill by a vote of 390-39 on May 25. *(House vote 222, p. H-72)*

As passed, the bill called for:

▸ $124.3 billion for operations and maintenance, $2.6 billion less than Bush requested.

▸ $108.8 billion for personnel, $118 million less than requested.

▸ $79.1 billion for weapons procurement, $2.5 billion more than Bush requested.

▸ $69.5 billion for research and development, a $113 million boost.

▸ $16.4 billion, as requested, for Energy Department weapons and environmental-cleanup activities.

▸ $12.2 billion for military construction and family housing, about $160 million more than requested.

During the floor debate, the House:

● **Women in combat.** Adopted 428-1, a manager's amendment that allowed Hunter to sidestep a major controversy over the committee's language on the role of women in combat. Hunter substituted language calling on the Pentagon to review the matter and notify Congress within 60 legislative days if it planned to open jobs to women that were closed under existing policy. The notification period was later cut to 30 days in the conference report on the bill. *(House vote 217, p. H-70)*

● **Buy American.** Adopted by voice vote, as part of an en bloc amendment, a proposal by Donald Manzullo, R-Ill., to prohibit the secretary of Defense from waiving so-called Buy American provision that required that at least 50 percent of the cost of a military purchase consist of U.S.-built components.

● **Exit strategy.** Rejected, 128-300, an amendment by Lynn Woolsey, D-Calif., to express the sense of Congress that the president should develop a plan for withdrawing U.S. military forces from Iraq. *(House vote 220, p. H-70)*

● **Tricare for reservists.** Rejected, 211-218, a motion by Taylor to return the bill to committee to have his amendment extending Tricare health care to reservists restored. Although the amendment was adopted in committee, Hunter subsequently removed it on the grounds that its cost would push the bill over its allocation for mandatory spending. The Congressional Budget Office estimated the provision would cost the Pentagon $4.6 billion through 2010, assuming that many federal employees who were also reservists would abandon their health care plans and flock to Tricare because of lower premiums. Taylor insisted he could change his amendment to bar federal employees from signing up for Tricare, but stiff opposition from Hunter prevented the motion from receiving the necessary votes. *(House vote 221, p. H-72)*

● **Other amendments:**

▸ Adopted, 245-184, an amendment by Virgil H. Goode Jr., R-Va., to allow military personnel to assist in border security under certain circumstances. The provision was later dropped in conference on the bill. *(House vote 214, p. H-70)*

▸ Adopted, 336-92, an amendment by Cliff Stearns, R-Pa., expressing the sense of Congress that any college or university that discriminated against ROTC programs and military recruiters should be denied certain federal support, especially funding for military and defense programs. The final bill retained the provision. *(House vote 218, p. H-70)*

▸ Rejected, 194-233, an amendment by Susan A. Davis, D-Calif., to allow military personnel and their dependents overseas to use their own funds to obtain abortion services in overseas military hospitals. *(House vote 216, p. H-70)*

▸ Rejected, 112-316, an amendment by Bradley to postpone the 2005 BRAC recommendations until the Pentagon carried out plans to restructure overseas bases and a substantial number of troops returned from Iraq. The White House had warned that such an amendment would cause Defense Secretary Donald H. Rumsfeld and other senior advisors to recommend that Bush veto the bill. *(House vote 219, p. H-70)*

In a statement of administration policy issued the day of the House vote, the White House expressed strong opposition to bill provisions that would require a twelfth aircraft carrier, increase the minimum strength of the Army and Marine Corps and punish foreign suppliers who sold controlled items to China. It also objected to the Buy American provision and said the effort to set reporting requirements for major defense acquisition programs was "counterproductive congressional micromanagement."

## SENATE COMMITTEE ACTION

The Senate Armed Services Committee gave voice vote approval May 12 to a $491.6 billion version of the authorization bill (S 1042 — S Rept 109-69) that consisted of $441.6 billion in regular defense spending and $50 billion in emergency supplemental war funds.

The committee-approved authorization bill included:

● **Troop levels.** An increase of 20,000 in Army troop levels in fiscal 2006. The bill did not mention an increase in Marines.

● **Pay and benefits.** A 3.1 percent across-the-board pay raise for servicemembers, a permanent increase in gratuity payments to $100,000 and an increase in life insurance coverage from $250,000 to $400,000

for a servicemember whose death was combat-related.

● **Future Combat System.** $3.4 billion, as requested, $499 million more than in the House bill.

● **Shipbuilding.** $9.1 billion, $355 million above Bush's request, for Navy shipbuilding – a priority for committee Chairman John W. Warner, R-Va., a former Navy secretary whose state had one of the country's largest shipbuilding facilities. Unlike the House, the committee did not propose a major restructuring of shipbuilding programs. The committee also:

▸ Directed the Navy to retain 12 aircraft carriers until 180 days after completion of the Quadrennial Defense Review, expected in February 2006, and to take steps to extend the life of the carrier *USS John F. Kennedy*, which the Navy had planned to mothball.

▸ Added $50 million to Bush's request for the Navy's DD(X) destroyer program, bringing the total for advance procurement to $766 million, and added $10 million to Bush's $1.1 billion request for research and development. The committee required that the service maintain two shipyards to build the destroyers. The Navy wanted to hold a winner-take-all competition pitting General Dynamics' Bath Iron Works in Maine against Northrop Grumman Ship Systems' Ingalls Operations in Pascagoula, Miss. The Navy said it could save as much as $3 billion, but lawmakers from shipbuilding states banded together to prevent what they said could result in the closing of one of the shipyards.

▸ Added $25 million to the $225 million requested to modernize the *Arleigh Burke*–class destroyers. Unlike the House, the committee did not add funds for procurement.

▸ Provided $325 million for the LHA(R) amphibious assault ship, $175 million more than requested but $93 million less than in the House bill.

▸ Provided $380 million as requested for the T-AKE cargo ship, $384 million less than in the House version.

● **Aircraft.** $3.7 billion, the same as in the House bill, to procure 24 F-22A Raptors; $4.9 billion, as in the House bill, to develop the Joint Strike Fighter, with $152.4 million for advanced procurement.

● **Space programs.** $636 million — $200 million less than requested but $200 million more than in the House bill — for the Transformational Communications Satellite program. The committee recommended $151 million — $75 million below the request but $51 million more than in the House version — for the Space-Based Radar program.

● **Nuclear weapons.** $4.0 million, as requested, for the Energy Department to continue studying the nuclear bunker buster, but no funds for the Air Force to study integrating the weapon with the B-2 bomber.

● **Iraq War funding.** $50 billion in emergency supplemental funding for operations in Iraq and Afghanistan. The committee included $2.2 billion more than the House for personnel and $1.6 billion more for operations and maintenance, but $2.3 billion less for procurement.

## SENATE FLOOR ACTION

The Senate passed the bill, 98-0, on Nov. 15, then inserted the text into HR 1815 in preparation for a conference with the House. Before passing the bill, the Senate adopted a series of amendments aimed at forcefully asserting Congress' role in overseeing the war in Iraq and the treatment of detainees in U.S.-run prisons. *(Senate vote 326, p. S-64)*

As passed, the bill called for:

▸ $126.4 billion for operations and maintenance, $2.1 billion more than the House recommended.

▸ $109.2 billion for personnel, $355 million above the House bill.

▸ $78.2 billion for weapons procurement, $947 million less than in the House bill.

▸ $69.8 billion for research and development, $362 million more.

▸ $16.4 billion for Energy Department weapons and environmental-cleanup activities, the same as in the House bill.

▸ $12.1 billion for military construction and family housing, $102 million less.

The bill first came to the Senate floor in late July. But the number of amendments — and the volatility of several — led Majority Leader Bill Frist, R-Tenn., to put it on the back burner until an agreement could be reached on a limited number of relevant amendments. An attempt to invoke cloture, or limit debate, failed 50-48 on July 26. Sixty votes were required. *(Senate vote 205, p. S-40)*

By the time the Senate returned to the bill in early November, the public mood on the war had changed markedly. Domestic polls showed that nearly two-thirds of Americans disapproved of Bush's handling of the war, while international polls showed that reports of torture in U.S.-run jails abroad had hurt the nation's standing in the world.

● **Exit strategy.** Before passing the bill Nov. 15, the Senate voted 79-19 to add language requiring the president to send Congress quarterly unclassified reports on the course of the war and on progress toward drawing down U.S. forces. The proposal, offered by Frist and Warner, was the most powerful statement of congressional oversight on Iraq policy since the 2003 invasion. *(Senate vote 323, p. S-63)*

In its quarterly reports, the administration would be required to define the criteria for success in Iraq, including details on the number of Iraqi battalions that would have to be able to fight independently before U.S. troops could withdraw.

The proposal included non-binding "sense of the Senate" language declaring 2006 as the year that Iraqis should take the lead in their security. It called on the administration to tell Iraqis to make the compromises necessary for political progress and to explain the president's "strategy for success" to the American public.

The fiscal 2005 defense authorization had required progress reports on Iraq, but senators and aides said the new amendment would force the administration for the first time to spell out how conditions in Iraq were linked to goals for withdrawing U.S. troops. The fact that the reports would be unclassified was expected to give the public more of a window onto the debate.

The Frist-Warner amendment was offered as an alternative to a Democratic proposal that was nearly identical except for an additional provision requiring the Pentagon to set a schedule for a phased withdrawal from Iraq. "I don't want anything in this document relative to a timetable," Warner said. The Senate rejected the Democratic amendment, offered by Carl Levin, D-Mich., by a vote of 40-58. *(Senate vote 322, p. S-63)*

The political spin began immediately. Minority Leader Harry Reid, D-Nev., called the GOP amendment a "no-confidence" vote in the White House. Frist called it "a victory strategy" and said it was "absurd" to portray it as a repudiation of the White House or a call for a change in military strategy. Bush said he welcomed the vote.

● **Detainee abuse.** McCain won voice vote approval Nov. 4 for his amendment to bar "cruel, inhuman or degrading treatment or punishment" of detainees under U.S. custody, and requiring U.S. military personnel to abide by standards set in an Army field manual that complied with the Geneva Conventions. McCain's plan to add the language was one of the reasons Frist had pulled the bill in July. In a statement of administration policy issued July 21, the administration threatened to veto the bill if it included the McCain provision, saying it would tie the president's hands in the war on terror. Vice President Dick Cheney tried without success to persuade McCain to make an exemption for U.S. intelligence personnel. With the authorization bill stalled, McCain had turned to the Defense appropriations bill (HR 2863), and on Oct.

5, the Senate voted 90-9 to add the amendment to that measure. (Senate vote 249, p. S-49)

However, the Senate rejected, 43-55, a proposal by Levin to create an independent commission to investigate the treatment of detainees in the period since the Sept. 11, 2001, terrorist attacks. (Senate vote 309, p. S-60)

● **Detainee legal rights.** On Nov. 15 the Senate adopted an amendment by Lindsey Graham, R-S.C., along with Levin, and Jon Kyl, R-Ariz., to require the Defense secretary to report to Congress on procedures used by military tribunals in determining the status of alien inmates at Guantánamo Bay, Cuba. It required Senate confirmation of the civilian official overseeing the Combat Status Review Tribunals, and it prohibited the tribunals from using information obtained by "undue coercion." The proposal was adopted, 84-14. (Senate vote 325, p. S-63)

The amendment prohibited foreign detainees at Guantánamo to file habeas corpus suits in federal court, although they could go to the Circuit Court of Appeals for the District of Columbia to appeal the tribunal's determination of their status and any convictions by the tribunals. "We are going to make sure [enemy combatants] get due process accorded under international law and then some," Graham said, "and the Congress is going to watch what happens."

An attempt by Jeff Bingaman, D-N.M., to give detainees the right to petition for habeas corpus in the appeals court following a review tribunal was rejected, 44-54. (Senate vote 324, p. S-63)

● **Secret facilities.** In another sign the war was changing the political climate on Capitol Hill, the Senate on Nov. 10 adopted an amendment by John Kerry of Massachusetts, the Democrat's 2004 presidential candidate, to require the director of national intelligence to provide the House and Senate Intelligence committees with "a full accounting" of U.S.-run secret detention facilities. The secretary of Defense would also be required to report on what he knew about the facilities. The move came in response to a Washington Post report about a secret overseas system of CIA prisons for terrorists. The vote was 82-9. (Senate vote 318, p. S-62)

● **Benefits.** Among the changes to improve benefits, the Senate:

▶ Adopted by voice vote an amendment to extend military Tricare health care coverage to all reservists. Graham, who offered the amendment along with Hillary Rodham Clinton, D-N.Y., said it was necessary to make joining the National Guard or the military reserves more attractive. "This is the best money we can possibly spend," Graham said. "There's all kind of waste in the Pentagon that would more than pay for this."

He estimated the cost to be $3.8 billion over five years — less than past proposals to extend Tricare to reservists — because it would limit access to those on standby for deployment and charge covered reservists a significant premium. Existing law already extended Tricare to reservists who were called to active duty. "It's not possible" financially, said Ted Stevens, R-Alaska, chairman of the Senate Appropriations Defense Subcommittee. "They have to be notified to be called up as far as I'm concerned."

▶ Adopted by voice vote an amendment by Evan Bayh, D-Ind., to make up the income lost by reservists who experienced frequent or extended mobilizations.

● **Other amendments.** The Senate also:

▶ Rejected, 44-53, a proposal by Richard J. Durbin, D-Ill., to establish a special Senate committee to investigate the handling of contracts in Afghanistan and Iraq. (Senate vote 316, p. S-62)

▶ Adopted, 78-19, a proposal by Foreign Relations Chairman Richard G. Lugar, R-Ind., to lift restrictions on the Nunn-Lugar Cooperative Threat Reduction program, making it easier for the United States to work with Russia on non-proliferation activities. The amendment was retained in the final bill. (Senate vote 200, p. S-39)

▶ Adopted, 100-0, an amendment by Warner to designate $445 million out of the $50 billion war fund to buy additional heavily armored Humvees. (Senate vote 199, p. S-39)

▶ Rejected, 47-51, an amendment by Frank R. Lautenberg, D-N.J., to close a legal loophole that allowed foreign subsidiaries of U.S. companies to do business with countries such as Iran and Syria that were subject to U.S. sanctions. (Senate vote 203, p. S-40)

Lautenberg's amendment would have made those foreign subsidiaries subject to U.S. sanctions laws. It also would have required U.S. companies to disclose to shareholders any ownership stake of at least 10 percent in a foreign subsidiary that did business with sanctioned countries. The Senate instead adopted a less restrictive amendment by Susan Collins, R-Maine, to strengthen existing laws, including increasing fines and granting subpoena authority to investigate cases of U.S. companies engaging in business in sanctioned states. Her amendment was adopted, 98-0. (Senate vote 202, p. S-40)

When debate resumed in November, the Senate also:

▶ Adopted, 92-6, an amendment by Bill Nelson, D-Fla., to repeal a statutory requirement that survivor benefit annuities for widows and orphans of deceased or fully disabled military personnel be reduced by the amount of their dependency and indemnity compensation. (Senate vote 307, p. S-60)

▶ Adopted, 89-8, an amendment by Jim Talent, R-Mo., that would authorize the Air Force to keep production of the C-17 transport plane alive. The planes were built by the Boeing Co. in St. Louis, among other places, and Talent faced a tough re-election contest in 2006. The Air Force would be authorized to buy up to 42 C-17s. The service would have to keep the plane's production lines going at a minimum rate if it could not certify the reliability of another transport plane, Lockheed Martin Corp.'s C-5 Galaxy. The provision was retained, with certain conditions, in the final bill. (Senate vote 317, p. S-62)

▶ Adopted as part of a manager's amendment, proposals by Warner to enhance incentives used by the Pentagon to recruit and retain military personnel, including bonuses for re-enlistment and for recruiting others to join the military.

## CONFERENCE/FINAL ACTION

The bill was declared all-but-dead at several points, but once the dispute over McCain's amendment was resolved, House and Senate conferees were able to reach agreement Dec. 16. Before they could file the conference report, however, House GOP leaders insisted on adding a campaign finance provision to limit contributions to so-called 527 political groups. "There has got to come a time when conference reports are closed," Warner railed on the Senate floor. "I will not allow this to come to the floor with this provision in it."

House leaders backed down, paving the way for conferees to file their report Dec. 18. The House adopted the conference report (H Rept 109-360) by a vote of 374-41 the following day, and the Senate cleared the bill by voice vote Dec. 21. (House vote 665, p. H-210)

"This is a strong, bipartisan bill that serves the interests of the men and women of our armed forces, their families and our nation," said Warner. "It was essential that Congress include important provisions on detainee policy and on our operations in Iraq."

● **Detainee abuse.** By far the longest delay resulted from negotiations among McCain, the White House and Hunter over the detainee abuse provision. For months, Bush and Hunter flatly rejected the language.

# 2005 Base Closing List Takes Effect

A NEW ROUND OF BASE CLOSURES and realignments got under way in 2005, based on recommendations from a specially appointed commission. The 2005 Base Realignment and Closure (BRAC) Commission issued its report Sept. 8 after a series of reviews and public hearings. The purpose was to close or consolidate unneeded or redundant facilities.

The Defense Department estimated that about 18,000 civilian jobs would be lost. The biggest loser was Virginia, with a projected loss of about 10,840 jobs. The biggest winner was neighboring Maryland, which stood to gain about 7,770 jobs.

The 2005 round was the fifth to take place. Earlier rounds occurred in 1988, 1991, 1993 and 1995. The BRAC process, first enacted in 1988 (PL 100-456), was intended to insulate the decision making from congressional pressures.

Under BRAC, the Pentagon submitted a list of recommended closures and consolidations to a commission, which evaluated the proposals and submitted a final list to the president. The president could approve the list in its entirety and send it to Congress, or return it to the commission. If he sent it to Congress, it automatically became law unless Congress cleared a joint resolution blocking it. Congress would have 45 legislative days to clear the resolution, and it would require the president's signature to go into force.

The 2005 round took place as a result of a congressional directive enacted in 2001 (PL 107-107). According to the Defense Department, the final list included 22 major closures. Of 190 recommendations, the Pentagon said, the commission approved 119, accepted 45 with revisions, rejected 13, modified 13 and added five new ones.

The following are the major steps taken in 2005:

▸ March 15. President Bush appointed BRAC Commission.

▸ May 13. Pentagon announced its recommendations and sent them to the commission.

▸ Sept. 8. BRAC Commission sent its report to Bush.

▸ Sept. 15. Bush approved the recommendations and sent them to Congress.

▸ Oct. 27. House rejected a resolution of disapproval (H J Res 65), 85-324. (House vote 548, p. H-172)

▸ Nov. 9. Recommendations took effect, and the Pentagon was charged with developing plans to carry them out.

---

The turning point came Dec. 14 when the House endorsed the proposal by an overwhelming vote of 308-122. The following day Bush reversed course and accepted the language in an Oval Office meeting with McCain and Warner. McCain agreed to add certain protections for U.S. interrogators who might be prosecuted for actions that were "officially authorized and determined to be lawful at the time that they were conducted." Government personnel could use the fact they believed the acts were lawful as a defense, and the government could provide them with counsel. (House vote 630, p. H-202)

The rest of McCain's amendment remained intact. The same language was included in the Defense appropriations bill.

The final bill also required the Pentagon to ensure that all U.S.-trained Iraqi military personnel received training on internationally guaranteed human rights.

● **Detainee legal rights.** The conferees retained most of the Senate amendment limiting detainee legal rights. The final bill required a report to Congress on the procedures used by military tribunals in determining the status of detainees held at Guantánamo Bay. It barred detainees from filing habeas corpus suits contesting their treatment or detention, while giving them limited ability to appeal their detentions and certain sentences handed down by the tribunals. The civilian official overseeing the tribunals had to be confirmed by the Senate, and the tribunal was required to assess "to the extent practicable" whether statements were obtained under torture, though using such evidence was not ruled out.

Civil liberties groups argued that this could make certain statements obtained by torture admissible in court and would make the McCain ban on torture unenforceable.

The conference version added a requirement that the Defense secretary report on the procedures used to determine the status of detainees held by the U.S. military in Afghanistan and Iraq, and to report on the annual review process for those prisoners.

● **Secret facilities.** Conferees dropped the Senate's requirement that the administration report to Congress on secret CIA prisons overseas.

The House had voted, 228-187, on Dec. 16 to adopt a non-binding motion instructing House conferees to keep the amendment. (House vote 643, p. H-204)

● **Exit strategy.** Conferees retained most of the Warner-Frist amendment requiring the president to submit quarterly reports on progress in Iraq. However, where the Senate required a "schedule" for achieving the conditions necessary for a U.S. drawdown, conferees substituted the vaguer word "plan."

● **Acquisition oversight.** The House provision requiring an analysis of alternatives for any major weapons system that exceeded the original cost by 15 percent was modified to require a less formal analysis of such programs that exceeded the baseline by 50 percent.

● **Shipbuilding.** $8.9 billion, $177 million more than Bush requested but considerably less than the House wanted. Conferees rejected the House attempt to restructure the Navy shipbuilding program.

▸ Following the Senate's lead, conferees authorized $766 million for advance procurement of two DD(X) next-generation destroyers, and $1.1 billion for research and development. In place of the House effort to cap costs at $1.7 billion per ship, effectively halting the program, conferees set a limit of $2.3 billion. They dropped the House plan to authorize $2.5 billion for two additional Arleigh Burke-class destroyers. The final bill retained the Senate ban on selecting a single shipyard to build the next-generation destroyer.

▸ Although both chambers recommended more than doubling the $150 million requested for the LHA(R) amphibious assault ship, conferees reduced the final authorization to $50 million.

▸ Like the House, they added $384 million for a total of $764.5 million to buy two T-AKE dry cargo ships.

▸ Like both versions, the final bill added $87 million to the $565 million requested for advance procurement of a new carrier, but unlike the House bill it did not make the extra funding contingent on accelerating production from 2007 to 2008.

▸ The final bill required the Navy to maintain 12 aircraft carriers and authorized $288 million to extend the life of the USS John F. Kennedy.

● **Future Combat System.** Conferees dropped the House plan to cut $499 million from the request and restructure the program; instead, they authorized $3.4 billion, $50 million less than requested.

● **Space programs.** Agreeing with the House, conferees authorized $436 million, $400 million less than requested, for the Transformational Communications Satellite program. They authorized $100 million, $126 million less than requested for the Space-Based Radar program.

● **Pay and benefits.** In addition to the 3.1 percent pay increase, the bill provided improved benefits, including:

▸ A permanent increase in the death gratuity to $100,000 from $12,420, retroactive to Oct. 7, 2001.

▸ Authorization to pay for $150,000 in life insurance coverage for personnel serving in Iraq and Afghanistan. The bill authorized but did not require the Pentagon to pay for an additional $250,000 of coverage.

▸ Up to $750 per month in hardship duty pay, up from $300.

▸ Government-subsidized access to Tricare for all reserves who committed to continued services. It also authorized Tricare access for non-deployed reservists who were unemployed or ineligible for employer provided health insurance, and it extended authority for several special payments and bonuses for reserve personnel through Dec. 31, 2006.

▸ Payments of up to $3,000 per month to make up the income lost by reservists who were involuntarily mobilized and served for 18 continuous months or a similar extended period.

● **Recruitment.** The conference agreement increased the re-enlistment bonus for active-duty members to $90,000, from $60,000, and increased the enlistment bonus for new recruits to $40,000, from $20,000. It established a pilot program to grant $1,000 bonuses to servicemembers who encouraged new recruits to enlist.

The bill also increased the maximum enlistment age for active duty to 42, from 35.

● **Buy American.** Conferees dropped the House provisions that would have denied the Defense secretary waiver authority on Buy American requirements and would have prohibited purchases from foreign companies that were government subsidized or that sold restricted items to China.

● **Bunker buster.** Oct. 25, Sen. Pete V. Domenici, R-N.M., released a statement saying the administration wanted to focus on studying non-nuclear weapons for destroying deeply buried targets. The final bill authorized $4 million for the Pentagon to study "the physics of penetrating geologic media, to be completed by the end of fiscal year 2006." It did not authorize funds for an Energy Department study. ∎

**Chapter 7**

# EDUCATION

# Education

# Faith-Based Hiring an Issue In Debate Over Head Start Programs

PROSPECTS FOR CLEARING a bill to revamp and reauthorize Head Start, the preschool program for low-income children, appeared to improve in 2005 after Republicans dropped a controversial White House proposal to let some states take greater control of the program.

Head Start, a $6.8 billion federally funded program, was operated locally by nonprofit organizations and faith-based groups and served more than 900,000 low-income children. The last authorization, enacted in 1998 (PL 105-285), had expired at the end of fiscal 2003. The program had been extended by annual appropriations bills. *(1998 Almanac, p. 9-19)*

The reauthorization had been stalled for more than two years in a dispute over a Bush administration proposal to have as many as eight states take over their local Head Start programs to ensure coordination with state school curricula. That provision was contained in a 2003 House reauthorization bill that passed by a single vote but died in the Senate.

The House passed a revised bill in September 2005, after Republicans dropped the Bush administration plan in favor of new language that would require Head Start operators to bring their education programs into alignment with state school readiness standards. Most Democrats still opposed the bill because of a provision added on the floor to allow faith-based charities operating local Head Start programs to hire staff based on their religious preference. Republicans said this would ensure that religious groups did not have to change their character or mission to participate in Head Start. Democrats said it would allow faith-based groups to discriminate while using federal funds.

The Senate Health, Education, Labor and Pensions (HELP) Committee approved a reauthorization bill in May that contained many similar provisions, but not the faith-based hiring language. It also called for a bigger authorization — $7.2 billion for the program in fiscal 2006, and similar increases in subsequent years. The House bill called for $6.9 billion in 2006 and unspecified sums in later years.

Both bills included some safeguards backed by Democrats on a new standardized test used to measure the skills and progress of Head Start preschoolers.

## BACKGROUND

The Head Start program, which began in 1965 as part of President Lyndon B. Johnson's War on Poverty (PL 89-253), was designed to help break the cycle of poverty by providing children between the ages of 3 and 5 from low-income families with a comprehensive preschool program intended to prepare them for school. From the beginning, Head Start provided not just educational services, but also health, nutritional and other services to these children and their families.

**BOX SCORE**

**BILLS:** HR 2123, S 1107

**LEGISLATIVE ACTION:**

**House** passed HR 2123 (H Rept 109-136), 231-184, on Sept. 22.

**Senate** Health, Education, Labor and Pensions Committee approved S 1107 (S Rept 109-131) by voice vote May 25.

President Bush called for reshaping Head Start in early 2003 as part of his fiscal 2004 budget. He proposed giving states considerably more authority over the program and moving the administration from the Department of Health and Human Services (HHS) to the Department of Education as part of a plan to increase its emphasis on literacy.

The Bush administration and some congressional Republicans argued that allowing more state control of the federal-state program would ensure coordination with state school curricula. Democrats and the National Head Start Association, which represented 1,680 local operators, campaigned vigorously against the proposed change, arguing that it would eventually turn Head Start into a block grant program and erode its effectiveness in areas such as nutrition and health.

Anticipating stiff resistance to the plan, House Republicans introduced a five-year reauthorization bill in 2003 that dropped the idea of moving the program to the Education Department and replaced the shift of control to the states with a pilot program that would allow eight states to integrate their own preschool programs into Head Start. Head Start centers operated by church groups would have been allowed to hire staff on the basis of religious preferences.

A bill approved by the Senate Health, Education, Labor and Pensions Committee in 2003 left out the pilot projects and the faith-based hiring language because of significant opposition from Republicans on the panel. Democrats blocked the bill from reaching the Senate floor in 2004, because they feared that they would be shut out of a GOP-controlled conference committee and would be unable to influence the final version. *(2003 Almanac, p. 8-3; 2004 Almanac, p. 7-4)*

## LEGISLATIVE ACTION
### HOUSE COMMITTEE ACTION

The House Education and the Workforce Committee approved a new, six-year Head Start reauthorization bill (HR 2123 — H Rept 109-136) by a vote of 48-0 on May 18. The panel's Subcommittee on Education Reform approved the bill by voice vote May 11.

Subcommittee Chairman Michael N. Castle, R-Del., who had also written the 2003 bill, abandoned the controversial pilot projects. Instead, the bill required that Head Start operators work with local school districts to ensure that children entering kindergarten were well-prepared for academic work and that their programs were in line with state academic standards. Castle said this was a less contentious route toward Bush's goal of ensuring that children were academically prepared for elementary school.

The bill also included changes to prevent financial abuse in local programs. A report in the spring by Congress' Government Accountability Office (GAO) had found that 76 percent of local Head Start oper-

ators surveyed in 2000 had some form of financial irregularity. Operators would be required to establish a local governance board to monitor all program activities. Operators with program deficiencies would have to compete for grants.

Democrats thanked Castle for reaching out to them and removing the administration-backed pilot project, but they said they would like the bill to contain more funding for Head Start teachers.

The bill authorized $6.9 billion for the program in fiscal 2006 and "such sums as are necessary" in fiscal 2007 through 2011. Castle said he was "a little reluctant" to establish specific authorization levels because appropriators were never able to meet them and they could become a major source of contention.

### HOUSE FLOOR ACTION

The House passed the bill Sept. 22 on a largely party-line vote of 231-184. *(House vote 493, p. H-154)*

The most fractious debate surrounded an amendment, adopted 220-196, to allow faith-based charities operating local programs to hire staff based on their religious preference. *(House vote 492, p. H-154)*

John A. Boehner, R-Ohio, chairman of the Education and the Workforce Committee, offered the amendment. He argued that religious groups already had the authority to hire employees based on their religious beliefs under the 1964 Civil Rights Act (PL 88-352). But, he said, "too often, the federal government has ignored or impeded the efforts of faith-based organizations willing to lend a helping hand in providing critical services to the neediest in our communities."

Opponents said the amendment was unnecessary because more than 100 Head Start programs were already being run by faith-based providers without any problems.

"Faith-based organizations sponsor Head Start programs now. They have and they will continue to. My own church hosted a Head Start program," said Democrat Robert C. Scott of Virginia. "We are talking just about [hiring] discrimination."

The House also:

▸ Adopted by voice vote an amendment by Ron Kind, D-Wis., to suspend the Head Start National Reporting System, a new standardized test developed by the Bush administration that measured the skills and progress of more than 400,000 children ages 4 and 5 years old. A GAO study in May found that HHS had not demonstrated that the test would accurately measure the progress of Head Start children. Some program advocates were concerned that the testing would later be used to shut down operators whose students did not score well. Under the Kind amendment, the National Academy of Sciences would review the test and make recommendations.

▸ Adopted by voice vote an amendment by John L. Mica, R-Fla., to require HHS to use an outside consulting firm to help overhaul its management of Head Start.

▸ Rejected, 153-266, an amendment by Mark Souder, R-Ind., to retain the existing governance structure for Head Start and give councils of parents some authority over how local programs were operated. Castle's bill gave parent councils only an advisory role. *(House vote 488, p. H-154)*

▸ Rejected, 175-241, a proposal by Marilyn Musgrave, R-Colo., to allow for-profit providers participating in Head Start to make a profit. *(House vote 491, p. H-154)*

### SENATE COMMITTEE ACTION

The Senate Health, Education, Labor and Pensions Committee took less than half an hour May 25 to give voice vote approval to a five-year reauthorization bill (S 1107 — S Rept 109-131) that did not include the faith-based language.

The Senate bill called for a $300 million increase in authorized funding for each of the following three fiscal years, for a total of $7.2 billion in 2006, $7.5 billion in 2007 and $7.8 billion in 2008. Fiscal 2009 and 2010 would be funded with "such sums as necessary."

Some Democrats expressed concern about funding levels for teacher salaries. Under the bill, at least half of all Head Start teachers would have to have a bachelor's degree by 2011. Under existing law, half of all Head Start teachers had to have an associate's degree. Teachers were paid an average of $25,000 annually. Democrats said that with a college degree, those educators could easily earn more teaching elementary school. "We cannot put the qualifications out there and not provide the resources," said Patty Murray, D-Wash., a former preschool teacher.

Murray said she wanted a "trigger" that would delay the teacher qualification requirements unless Congress appropriated $7.2 billion annually for the program, but she agreed to work with Chairman Michael B. Enzi, R-Wyo., on a compromise before the bill reached the floor.

Senate Democrats also said that they would like stronger safeguards in the bill to monitor the Bush administration's new standardized test for preschool children. The Senate bill required that the National Academy of Sciences review all of the tests used in Head Start and within a year report its recommendations to improve the assessments.

The bill included two provisions to help the program reach more needy children. Head Start income eligibility requirements for families would be increased from 100 percent of the federal poverty level — nearly $19,000 annually for a family of four — to 130 percent. The legislation also would increase the funding for Early Head Start, which served children age 3 and younger, from 10 percent of Head Start's $6.8 billion overall funding to 18 percent by 2010.

Enzi also included more stringent standards for local operators applying to renew their grants, including allowing HHS to terminate a grant if a program was found to have multiple and recurring deficiencies. Enzi noted that under existing law some failing programs could operate almost two years before all appeals were exhausted. ∎

# Congress Revamps College Aid Program

CONGRESS REVISED and reauthorized part of the Higher Education Act, the nation's main federal college aid program, but left the rest to be completed in 2006.

A total of $73 billion in aid and subsidized loans to postsecondary students and schools was distributed under the education act in fiscal 2005. The law, last renewed in 1998 (PL 105-244), expired at the end of fiscal 2003. Since then, Congress had cleared a series of short-term extensions to keep the programs going while lawmakers worked on a multi-year reauthorization bill.

The House and Senate committees responsible for education programs approved versions of a long-term reauthorization, but neither measure reached the floor in 2005.

Instead, the two committees folded the provisions governing mandatory programs, such as guaranteed and direct student loans, into the budget reconciliation bill that cleared Feb. 2, 2006 (S 1932 — PL 109-171). The reconciliation bill, which was ordered under the fiscal 2006 budget resolution (H Con Res 95), was expected to cut the projected growth of student loan programs by a net $11.9 billion over five years. *(Budget reconciliation, p. 4-13)*

Lawmakers continued the discretionary programs under the Higher Education Act — such as Pell grants, teacher training, college access programs and aid to historically black colleges — through March 31 through another short-term extension (PL 109-150) to give lawmakers time to finish the reauthorization measure in the second session.

## LEGISLATIVE ACTION: REAUTHORIZATION
### HOUSE COMMITTEE ACTION

The House Education and the Workforce Committee approved a higher education reauthorization bill (HR 609 — H Rept 109-231) on July 22, following a three-day markup. The vote was 27-20. The panel's 21st Century Competitiveness Subcommittee approved the measure, 18-15, on July 14.

Sponsored by full committee Chairman John A. Boehner, R-Ohio, the six-year bill was expected to produce net savings of $8.7 billion from student loan entitlement programs in fiscal 2006 through 2010, mainly by increasing interest rates and fees paid by students and reducing subsidies to lenders. As approved by the committee, the bill included provisions to:

▶ Eliminate a 6.8 percent fixed rate for student loans that was scheduled to start in July 2006 under a 2002 law (PL 107-139). Instead, the bill would keep the existing variable rate, which was capped at 8.25 percent; the government paid the interest on subsidized loans while the student was in school.

Democrats complained that Republicans should have used the anticipated savings for additional student aid.

▶ Allow borrowers who wanted to consolidate their student loans to choose between a variable or a fixed rate, both capped at 8.25 percent. Under existing law, consolidated loans had a low fixed rate for up to 30 years, capped at 8.25 percent. The bill would require those choos-

---

**BOX SCORE**

**BILL:** S 1932 — PL 109-171

**LEGISLATIVE ACTION:**

**Senate** passed S 1932, which included parts of S 1614, 52-47, on Nov. 3.

**House** passed HR 4241, which included parts of HR 609, 217-215, on Nov. 18. It then inserted the text into S 1932.

**House** adopted the conference report on S 1932 (H Rept 109-362), 212-206, on Dec. 19.

**Senate** rejected the conference report and passed an amended version of S 1932, 51-50, on Dec. 21.

**House** agreed to the amendment, 216-214, on Feb. 1, 2006, clearing the bill.

**President** signed Feb. 8, 2006.

---

ing the fixed rate to pay a new 1 percent loan origination fee.

▶ Require lenders to rebate to the government income generated when the interest rate they charged to students was higher than what lenders were guaranteed to receive by the federal government.

▶ Eliminate a provision in existing law that allowed some lenders to receive interest payments totaling 9.5 percent on their federally backed loans, with the Education Department picking up the difference between that figure and the students' variable rate.

▶ Make it easier for private for-profit colleges to compete for federal aid by redefining the term "institute of higher education" to include accredited for-profit colleges. Public and non-profit universities argued that taxpayers should not be asked to subsidize for-profit schools. But Republicans said for-profit schools, which offered degree-granting courses in business, nursing and other specialty fields, were increasingly important for "non-traditional" students, especially those changing careers.

During the July 14 markup, the subcommittee:

▶ Adopted by a voice vote an amendment by Michael N. Castle, R-Del., to restore a rule requiring that at least 10 percent of a for-profit college's revenue be from sources other than federal aid and that it be applied to all colleges. Under Castle's proposal, students would not be immediately penalized with a loss of federal aid if their for-profit college violated the rule. Castle said his amendment was a "placeholder" to give lawmakers more time to work on a compromise.

"For-profit institutions by their very nature have profit as their bottom line. I think if they are receiving federal dollars, that money would supplant other money they don't have to spend," Castle said. "What do we have to fear allowing the for-profit sector the opportunity to compete?"

Boehner replied. "Competition makes all of us better."

▶ Adopted, 22-10, an amendment by Del. Luis Fortuño, R-Puerto Rico, to prohibit for-profit colleges from receiving funding for programs specifically designated for historically black colleges and Hispanic-serving institutions.

▶ Adopted by voice vote an amendment by Virginia Foxx, R-N.C., to prohibit the Education Department from creating a database to compile the personal information of college students.

The full Education and the Workforce Committee:

▶ Adopted, 26-20, an amendment by Tom Petri, R-Wis., to allow graduates who wanted to consolidate their federally subsidized students loans to choose between a variable or a fixed rate, both capped at 8.25 percent.

▶ Rejected, 17-26, a competing proposal by George Miller of California, the panel's ranking Democrat, to cap the variable or fixed rate on consolidated loans at 6.8 percent. It also would have increased the maximum Pell grant award by $500 over five years, to an overall total of $4,550.

▶ Adopted by voice vote an amendment by Castle to permit for-prof-

it colleges to compete for campus-based aid programs, but not for federal funding outside the bill's jurisdiction — such as grants from the National Science Foundation or the Department of Energy.

## SENATE COMMITTEE ACTION

The Senate Health, Education, Labor and Pensions Committee approved a five-year reauthorization bill (S 1614 — 109-218) by a vote of 20-0, on Sept. 8. The measure was the result of a bipartisan effort led by committee Chairman Michael B. Enzi, R-Wyo., and ranking Democrat Edward M. Kennedy of Massachusetts. As a result, no amendments were offered during the markup.

The bill was projected to reduce spending on mandatory student loan programs by a net $7 billion over five years as part of the committee's effort to comply with instructions in the budget resolution. But it also called for $8 billion in new money for student aid programs.

The bill would:

▶ Retain the scheduled change to a 6.8 percent fixed rate for student loans, saving students money if interest rates continued to rise.

▶ Require lenders to rebate to the government income generated when interest rates charged to students were higher than the guaranteed rate for lenders.

▶ Limit but not eliminate the ability of some lenders to charge a 9.5 percent interest rate.

▶ Set aside $4.5 billion over five years for a new entitlement program to give grants to low-income students to supplement Pell grant awards.

▶ Set aside $1 billion over five years for a new scholarship program for low-income students who majored in math and science fields.

## LEGISLATIVE ACTION: RECONCILIATION

Late in the session, authorizing committees in both chambers began working on a budget reconciliation package aimed at reducing the automatic annual growth in entitlement spending. The House and Senate committees sent their provisions to their respective Budget committees, which packaged them and took them to the floor.

## HOUSE COMMITTEE ACTION

The Education and the Workforce Committee agreed Oct. 26 to send the Budget Committee a package of cuts to mandatory student loan programs drawn from HR 609. The proposal, adopted 22-19 along party lines, would save an estimated $14.3 billion over five years, according to the Congressional Budget Office (CBO).

Boehner said none of the provisions would cost students directly, except one that would change the interest rate structure for graduates who consolidated their loans. He said most of the cuts would be borne by lenders, who would see decreases in federal subsidies. Democrats argued that lenders would cover their losses by passing the financial burden on to students.

The committee rejected, 20-27, a proposal by Miller to end the subsidy that allowed some lenders to earn a 9.5 percent return and use the savings to expand the Pell grant program.

The bill would increase the maximum amount of subsidized loans that students could borrow to $3,500 from $2,625 for first-year students, and to $4,500 from $3,500 for second-year students. The limit for unsubsidized loans for each year of graduate school would rise to $12,000 from $10,000. These changes were estimated to increase federal spending by $1.6 billion in fiscal 2007 through 2010.

The bill also included relief for student loan borrowers and institutions of higher education that were adversely affected by hurricanes Katrina and Rita. CBO said those provisions would cost $210 million in fiscal 2006, with no costs after that.

Boehner originally included a $2.5 billion education relief proposal that would have provided parents displaced by Hurricane Katrina with up to $6,700 per child to send their children to a public, private or religious school for one year. However, critics described it as a voucher plan which would use public funds to educate children in private schools, and the committee rejected it, 21-26, with four Republicans joining committee Democrats to defeat the amendment.

## SENATE COMMITTEE ACTION

On Oct. 18, the Health, Education, Labor and Pensions Committee approved, 15-5, a package that CBO said would cut mandatory spending on student loan programs by a net $8.5 billion over five years.

The committee adopted by voice vote a substitute by Enzi changing some of the provisions taken from S 1614. It increased the proposed low-income grant program from $4.5 billion to $6 billion, and increased the science and math grants from $1 billion to $2.3 billion. It proposed to reduce borrower origination fees on federally subsidized loans from 3 percent to 2.5 percent, and add $1.5 billion for financial relief to students affected by Hurricane Katrina.

## CONFERENCE/FINAL ACTION

The student loan provisions in the final budget reconciliation bill (S 1932 — H Rept 109-362) were expected to save a net $11.9 billion over five years, according to CBO. That was roughly halfway between the House and Senate proposals.

The House adopted the conference report on the bill, 212-206, on Dec. 19. But a successful procedural challenge in the Senate forced the House to vote again in 2006. On Feb. 1, the House agreed to a Senate change in the final bill, clearing the measure for the president. *(House vote 670, p. H-212)*

The major elements of the student loan section of the bill included:

▶ $14.3 billion in savings over five years by changing some interest rates and lender profits. The bill left in place the new 6.8 percent fixed rate for student loans scheduled for July 2006, but it increased the fixed rate for parent loans to 8.5 percent (the 2002 law had set it at 7.9 percent). Lenders were required to rebate to the government the difference between the minimum rate on student loans and any higher rate charged to borrowers.

▶ $1.8 billion in savings over five years by limiting the opportunity for lenders to get a 9.5 percent rate.

▶ $4 billion in additional outlays over five years from reducing or eliminating loan origination fees by 2010.

▶ $1.5 billion in new outlays over five years from increasing the maximum amount of subsidized loans to $3,500 from $2,625 for first-year students and to $4,500 from $3,500 for second-year students. The limit for unsubsidized loans for graduate school was increased to $12,000 per year from $10,000.

▶ $3.7 billion in new outlays over five years for new grants to low-income students and scholarships for science and math majors, as proposed by the Senate. ∎

# Vocational Ed Bills Stall

IN A REBUKE TO THE WHITE HOUSE, both chambers passed bills to reauthorize the 1998 Carl D. Perkins Vocational and Technical Education Act (PL 105-332) through 2011. President Bush wanted to eliminate the $1.3 billion program. However the bills went no further in the first session.

"There was a time in many schools when vocational education meant simply an extra class in shop," said Sen. Edward M. Kennedy, D-Mass., a sponsor of the Senate bill. "But today in Massachusetts, and many other states, we see the vital role that vocational education — now appropriately called career and technical education — can have in transforming the lives of students and workers, and in strengthening our economy."

The administration proposed killing the program, saying there was "little or no evidence of improved outcomes for students despite decades of federal investment." The White House wanted to use the money instead to extend the testing and standards required by the 2001 education law known as the No Child Left Behind Act (PL 107-110) into high schools.

Lawmakers rejected the president's proposal because of lobbying from businesses and vocational educators in their districts.

## LEGISLATIVE ACTION

The Senate passed its version of the bill, 99-0, on March 10, a day after it was reported out of committee. The Health, Education, Labor and Pensions Committee approved the measure (S 250 — S Rept 109-65) by voice vote March 9. Kennedy, the ranking Democrat on the committee, sponsored the measure with Michael B. Enzi, R-Wyo., the committee chairman. *(Senate vote 43, p. S-11)*

The House passed its version by a vote of 416-9 on May 4. The Education and the Workforce Committee had approved the measure (HR 366 — H Rept 109-25) by voice vote March 9. *(House vote 154, p. H-50)*

Both bills would authorize federal grants to states for supplemental programs, such as courses in emerging technologies, and sought to increase access to coursework for women and minorities.

The Senate bill would keep funding streams separate for the main Perkins grant program and the smaller Tech-Prep, a program that provided specialized math and science courses and gave vocational students a quicker way to earn a degree through a structured curriculum of two years in high school and two years at a community college.

The House bill, sponsored by Michael N. Castle, R-Del., proposed to merge the two. In fiscal 2005, Congress appropriated $1.2 billion for the Perkins grant program and $107 million for the Tech-Prep program.

The House on May 4 adopted by voice vote a Castle amendment that would require states to fund Tech-Prep activities at fiscal 2005 levels — an attempt to quell Democratic concerns that Tech-Prep would erode if the two programs were consolidated.

Under existing law, states could reserve up to 10 percent of Perkins grants for professional development and 5 percent for administrative activities. The House bill restricted states to using no more than 2 percent for administration. The Senate bill offered states more freedom to transfer funds between training and administrative accounts and proposed remove spending caps on non-traditional programs, such as prisoner retraining. The House measure would require states to use up to 2 percent of their grants for administrative purposes.

John A. Boehner, R-Ohio, chairman of the Education and the Workforce Committee, argued that the Senate bill would give states too much latitude and lead to more bureaucracy. "We've got too many former governors over there," he said of the Senate committee.

The two committees had approved versions of a reauthorization bill in 2004, but the legislation did not reach either floor because of the campaign-shortened legislative year. *(2004 Almanac, p. 7-5)* ■

**Chapter 8**

# ENERGY &
# ENVIRONMENT

# Energy Overhaul Includes Many Bush Priorities — But Not ANWR

After calling for a comprehensive overhaul of the nation's energy policies for more than four years, President Bush signed a new law on Aug. 8 that he said would achieve his goal of spurring domestic production of energy from both renewable and traditional sources (HR 6 — PL 109-58).

Congressional Republicans said the bill balanced incentives for new, "greener" alternatives, such as renewables and conservation, with the need to increase domestic production of more traditional resources, such as oil, nuclear power and coal.

Critics argued that the new law mainly subsidized traditional producers of oil and natural gas and would do little to help reduce the nation's appetite for fuel. Many Democrats were particularly unhappy that the measure did not set new vehicle fuel efficiency standards or require reductions in greenhouse-gas emissions, such as carbon dioxide, that scientists call a primary contributor to climate change.

The bill followed the general contours of the energy proposals that Bush first outlined in 2001, with its emphasis on greater production of oil, gas and coal. But the centerpiece of Bush's plan, and its most controversial proposal — drilling for oil in Alaska's Arctic National Wildlife Refuge (ANWR) — did not survive. *(ANWR, p. 8-18)*

The new law provided a package of tax breaks worth $14.6 billion over 11 years. Revenue-raising offsets were expected to reduce the net loss to the Treasury to $11.5 billion. The law also provided for $1.6 billion in new mandatory spending over 10 years that was not subject to the appropriations process and authorized tens of billions more that would be up to appropriators to provide.

The wide-ranging legislation addressed nearly every sector of the energy industry, providing incentives for coal producers, nuclear power, oil and gas companies, renewable power, energy efficiency and electric utilities. It called for extensive research and development and streamlined permitting processes, along with tax breaks and other strategies aimed at spurring new technologies, infrastructure and energy production. *(Provisions, p. 8-8)*

Republicans had written energy bills in the 107th and 108th Congresses, but disputes over issues such as fuel additives and oil exploration in Alaska prevented the massive legislation from becoming law. In 2003, the House adopted the conference report on an omnibus energy bill, but the measure collapsed in the Senate. *(2002 Almanac, p. 8-3; 2003 Almanac, p. 9-3; 2004 Almanac, p. 9-4)*

The House passed a bill in April 2005 that closely followed the Bush administration's priorities and the 2003 conference report. The Senate moved slower in an effort to draw bipartisan support. In late June, the Senate passed a bill that differed substantially from the House meas-

**BOX SCORE**

**BILL:** HR 6 — PL 109-58

**LEGISLATIVE ACTION:**

**House** passed HR 6, 249-183, on April 21.

**Senate** passed HR 6, amended, 85-12, on June 28.

**House** adopted conference report (H Rept 109-190), 275-156, on July 28.

**Senate** cleared the bill, 74-26, on July 29.

**President** signed Aug. 8.

ure, putting more emphasis on renewable fuels and technologies, and dropping several of the House's most controversial provisions.

House and Senate conferees completed negotiations on a final bill with surprising speed, reaching agreement in less than two weeks.

Lawmakers were eager to show they were taking action in the face of gasoline prices that had reached more than $2 per gallon. The president publicly called on Congress to send him a bill before leaving for the August recess. And top Republican energy negotiators — determined to avoid a repeat of their 2003 experience — were more willing to compromise.

Energy experts said the bill would have little or no effect on gas prices, which are governed by worldwide supply and demand. Nor would it reduce U.S. dependence on imported oil, though that was the administration's rationale for the legislation in the first place. By the time the bill was finished, Republicans instead were emphasizing its broader economic effects. "This bill will create jobs, job security and clean energy," said Pete V. Domenici, R-N.M., chairman of the Senate Energy and Natural Resources Committee.

To get the bill to Bush's desk, House GOP leaders agreed to drop two of the most contentious items: the plan to allow drilling for oil and natural gas in ANWR, and provisions to shield manufacturers of the fuel additive methyl tertiary butyl ether (MTBE) from most product liability suits associated with groundwater contamination.

The attempt to provide a liability waiver for MTBE producers had been a deal-killer in the 108th Congress. Like corn-based ethanol, MTBE was used to increase the oxygen content of gasoline so that it would burn more cleanly. But the additive also had been found to contaminate groundwater. Majority Leader Tom DeLay, R-Texas, insisted that the waiver be included in the 2003 energy bill conference report. More than half the country's MTBE producers had operations in his state. But GOP senators from the Northeast, whose states did not want to be stuck picking up the costly tab for MTBE cleanups, rejected the liability waiver and joined a Democratic filibuster that prevented the conference report from reaching the Senate floor.

Drilling advocates agreed to drop the ANWR provisions from the energy bill. They assumed they would be able to get them into law as part of a separate budget reconciliation package later in the year. However, drilling opponents were able to erect enough obstacles to defeat those plans as well.

## HIGHLIGHTS

The following are major components of the 2005 energy law:

● **Tax incentives and subsidies.** $14.6 billion in tax incentives and $3 billion in revenue-raising provisions, for a net reduction in federal

revenues of $11.5 billion in 2005 through 2015, according to Congress' Joint Committee on Taxation. Bush had requested $6.7 billion for energy-related tax incentives. The law included:

- $1.6 billion in tax credits for investment in clean-coal facilities.
- $2.7 billion to extend the renewable electricity production credit.
- $2.8 billion for domestic fossil fuel production.
- $1.3 billion for conservation and energy efficiency.
- $1.3 billion for alternative motor vehicles and fuels, including a tax credit of up to $3,400 for certain hybrid cars and trucks.

● **Ethanol.** A substantial increase in the amount of renewable fuels that refiners would have to add to gasoline, starting at an annual average of 4 billion gallons in 2006 and climbing to 7.5 billion gallons in 2012. Most producers were expected to use corn-based ethanol to reach this goal. The law eliminated the existing requirement that reformulated gasoline contain 2 percent oxygen by weight.

● **Electricity markets.** Overhaul of the nation's electricity markets, beginning with repeal of the 1935 Public Utility Holding Company Act (PUHCA), which restricted big power companies to certain geographic areas and lines of business in an effort to prevent monopolies. In place of those restrictions, the law strengthened the powers of the Federal Energy Regulatory Commission (FERC). It gave FERC the authority to enforce new mandatory reliability standards for electricity transmission networks and required FERC's approval for all mergers and all sales or leases of facilities valued in excess of $10 million. FERC, and to some degree state authorities, were authorized to examine the financial records of companies that owned or partly owned power plants. FERC was authorized to require any utility company transmitting electricity in multiple states to provide transmission services at rates comparable to those the utility charged itself.

FERC also was authorized to issue permits for construction of new power lines in areas of electricity congestion, regardless of state objections, and to use eminent domain to acquire the use of private property if necessary. When the proposed power line was to be on federal property, the Energy Department was to be the lead agency in coordinating all related federal authorizations, including environmental reviews.

● **LNG terminals.** Exclusive authority for FERC to approve the construction, expansion or operation of facilities that imported or processed liquefied natural gas (LNG). The effect was to strip state and local authorities of the power to block LNG terminals.

● **Nuclear energy.** Reauthorize the Price Anderson Act (PL 100-408) until 2025. The law had expired in 2003. Even without an extension, existing plants remained covered, but new plants would not be protected by liability limits. As a result, an extension was considered a prerequisite to any new nuclear power plant construction.

● **Offshore drilling.** Authority for the Interior Department to conduct an inventory of coastal oil and natural gas resources in the Outer Continental Shelf.

● **Auto fuel efficiency.** A requirement that the National Highway Traffic Safety Administration (NHTSA) conduct a study on the potential effects of significantly increasing fuel efficiency standards for cars by model year 2014. The study was to consider effects on the auto industry, gasoline supply and air quality.

● **Climate change.** A new cabinet-level advisory committee, charged with developing a national policy to address climate change and promote technologies to reduce greenhouse gas emissions. The policy was to be updated every five years. The Energy Department could authorize demonstration projects to test technology that limited harmful emissions.

● **Daylight-saving time.** A one-month extension of daylight-saving time beginning in 2007 aimed at conserving energy. Daylight-saving time would begin the second Sunday in March, instead of the first Sunday in April, and last through the first Sunday in November, instead of the last Sunday in October.

## HOUSE COMMITTEE ACTION

Four committees marked up portions of the House bill; all of them completed their work April 13. The measure largely mirrored the 2003 conference agreement, except that it included provisions to allow oil and gas production in ANWR. Research and development provisions — which the Science Committee had approved by voice vote Feb. 10 (HR 610 — H Rept 109-216) — were also added to the bill.

The Energy and Commerce Committee approved the core of the bill (HR 6) by a vote of 39-16 at the end of a marathon, three-day markup. The bill was drafted largely by Chairman Joe L. Barton, R-Texas. Though Democrats lost virtually every attempt to change the bill, Edward J. Markey, D-Mass., paid tribute to Barton for conducting a fair markup that allowed Democrats to offer their amendments and make their arguments.

The Ways and Means Committee approved a $8.1 billion package of energy tax breaks (HR 1541 — H Rept 109-45) on a 26-11 vote. Chairman Bill Thomas, R-Calif., indicated that the measure was essentially a bargaining tool to take to conference. His said his strategy was to load the House package with provisions that he did not expect the Senate to include in its bill.

Nearly all of the tax incentives were for traditional energy sources such as oil, natural gas, coal, nuclear power and electricity transmission. Only about 5 percent of the total was aimed at renewables and conservation. Democrats made two attempts to strike specific tax breaks for oil and coal, both of which failed. Several Republicans also voiced support for more incentives for renewables and energy conservation.

The Resources Committee gave voice vote approval to sections of HR 6 related to public lands, following an eight-hour session in which Democratic amendments were similarly rebuffed. The bill included drilling in ANWR and provisions to reduce regulations and provide incentives to promote energy production on public lands. "Energy continues to be the foundation and lifeblood of America's economy," said Chairman Richard W. Pombo, R-Calif. "But we have grown complacent. Our federal policies have lost sight of this simple yet critical fact."

The Government Reform Committee approved HR 1533, a small piece of the overall energy bill, by voice vote April 13. The provisions dealt with energy efficiency and conservation in the federal government.

The resulting House energy bill included provisions to:

● **ANWR.** Authorize the Interior Department to grant leases for oil and gas exploration, development and production on about 1.5 million acres of ANWR. Oil and gas exports from ANWR were barred.

The Resources Committee rejected, 13-30, an attempt by Markey to strike the provision. "My people, my state, the people who live on the land, want to do this," said Don Young, R-Alaska.

The panel also rejected, 16-31, an attempt by Raúl M. Grijalva, D-Ariz., to remove incentives for traditional oil and natural gas exploration on public lands. "These kickbacks are not needed," Grijalva said. "They are an insult to the American taxpayer."

● **MTBE.** Provide a "safe harbor" to protect U.S. manufacturers of MTBE against product liability for groundwater contamination, retroactive to Sept. 5, 2003. MTBE would be phased out as a gasoline additive, but would not be banned until 2015. The bill would authorize $250 million a year in fiscal 2005 through 2012 to help MTBE manufacturers convert their plants to produce other fuel additives.

The Energy and Commerce Committee rejected, 20-31, an attempt by Lois Capps, D-Calif., to strike the MTBE liability waiver. It rejected, 23-29, a Capps amendment to phase out the use of MTBE over four years and eliminate the transition assistance to MTBE manufacturers. Barton said he was holding "intense negotiations" on the MTBE dispute. "We will have the issue solved," he pledged, noting that the Republican majority in the Senate had grown. "We fully expect if there is a filibuster threat we'll have 60 votes for cloture. . . . I wouldn't be much of a chairman if I hadn't been working on this since last year."

● **Tax provisions.** Cut energy taxes by $8.1 billion over 11 years, with no revenue offsets. More than 90 percent of the tax breaks were aimed at domestic energy production and traditional energy sources such as oil, natural gas and electricity transmission.

● **Ethanol.** Require refiners to increase the amount of renewable fuels added to gasoline in the United States, starting with an annual average volume of 3.1 billion gallons in 2005, reaching 5 billion gallons in 2012. The requirement that reformulated gasoline contain 2 percent oxygen by weight would be eliminated.

● **Electricity.** Repeal PUHCA, and give FERC jurisdiction over reliability standards for electricity transmission networks. All mergers and all sales or leases of transmission facilities valued in excess of $10 million would have to be approved by FERC. The FERC would have the authority to issue permits for the construction of new power lines to relieve congestion over the objections of states, and could seek eminent domain right-of-way in federal court when necessary.

Republicans and some Democrats agreed that PUHCA was outdated and inhibited investment in the power industry, but many Democrats argued that the 1935 law should be replaced only if there was new oversight from the FERC to protect consumers from price spikes resulting from bad business deals. Republicans countered that further regulation would slow investment in the sector and unnecessarily obstruct market forces that they said would ultimately benefit consumers.

The Energy and Commerce Committee rejected, 22-27, an amendment by John D. Dingell of Michigan, ranking Democrat on the panel, to retain PUHCA and give FERC more power to punish fraud. The committee rejected, 13-31, a separate amendment to strike the provisions giving FERC the power to site power transmission lines on private lands.

● **LNG terminals.** Clarify that FERC, not state agencies, had final authority over the siting of LNG terminals. The question of whether FERC could override state objections to the sitings was the subject of a lawsuit by the state of California. Many localities had sought to block new LNG terminals over safety concerns, and opponents said the provision would allow FERC to ignore local objections.

Supporters argued that federal law already gave FERC the authority for siting and that the provision was needed to encourage a better investment climate for more natural gas import projects. "Since we're not producing more of our natural gas domestically, we need to site more of these import facilities," Barton said. He said he would work in conference "to perfect the language to make sure the states don't feel they're not being listened to."

Markey failed, 18-35, to strike the LNG siting provision during the Energy and Commerce markup.

● **Nuclear energy.** Reauthorize the Price-Anderson Act through 2025.

● **Hydrogen.** Authorize $4.1 billion over five years for Bush's initiative to develop hydrogen fuel cell cars.

● **Fuel efficiency.** Require the NHTSA to study the "feasibility and effects" of significantly reducing auto fuel consumption by model year 2014. The study would include alternatives to the existing system

of CAFE standards, and the effects of new standards on the automobile industry, vehicle safety and air quality. The NHTSA was responsible for setting corporate average fuel economy (CAFE) standards. The existing standards were 27.5 miles per gallon for passenger cars and 20.7 miles per gallon for light trucks and SUVs (22.7 miles per gallon for model year 2007).

The bill would authorize $2 million a year in fiscal 2005 through 2010 for the NHTSA to carry out these studies.

The Energy and Commerce Committee rejected, 10-36 an amendment by Markey to require that most cars get 33 miles to the gallon by 2014. "People want SUVs," countered Dingell. "This is a mandate with no incentives."

● **Daylight-saving time.** Extend daylight-saving time by two months, from the first Sunday in March through the last Sunday in November.

## HOUSE FLOOR ACTION

The House passed the bill April 21 by a vote of 249-183, with the support of 41 Democrats. *(House vote 132, p. H-42)*

The House made a number of changes to the bill, but Republicans were able to defeat a handful of high-profile amendments on issues such as ANWR, fuel economy standards and the siting of LNG terminals. In a move that took GOP leaders by surprise, Capps nearly succeeded in striking the MTBE liability protections.

Bush issued a statement praising the bill as "largely consistent with the key objectives of my comprehensive national energy policy," though he criticized the tax package saying he wanted more incentives for renewables and efficiency initiatives.

Democrats called the bill a windfall for the fossil fuel industry that would harm the environment and do little to lower consumer energy costs. They pointed in particular to the fact that the tax cuts were aimed almost entirely at traditional energy sectors and said the bill would shortchange alternative energy and conservation efforts, such as improved fuel efficiency, that were the cheapest and quickest ways to cut costs and reduce oil imports.

Among the dozens of amendments considered during the floor debate, the House:

▸ Rejected, by a narrow 213-219 vote, an amendment by Capps to strike the bill's liability protections for MTBE manufacturers. Capps read from a statement by the Congressional Budget Office (CBO) that concluded the waiver would impose an unfunded mandate on state and local governments by blocking them from suing MTBE makers to recover the costs of cleanup. Twenty-five Republicans backed the amendment. The rule for floor debate had denied Capps the right to offer an MTBE amendment, but it did not prohibit an amendment on unfunded mandates. *(House vote 129, p. H-42)*

▸ Rejected, 200-231, an attempt by Markey to strike the ANWR drilling provisions. *(House vote 122, p. H-40)*

▸ Rejected, 194-237, an amendment by Michael N. Castle, R-Del., to strike the provision giving FERC exclusive authority over the siting of LNG terminals. *(House vote 131, p. H-42)*

▸ Adopted, 259-172, an amendment by Mike Rogers, R-Mich., to require the EPA to update its test procedure for measuring fuel economy to reflect changed driving habits, such as higher speed limits, faster acceleration, differences between city and highway driving and air conditioning. *(House vote 119, p. H-40)*

▸ Rejected, 177-254, an amendment by Sherwood Boehlert, R-N.Y., to increase CAFE standards to 33 miles per gallon for cars manufactured by model year 2015. *(House vote 121, p. H-40)*

▸ Adopted by voice vote an amendment by Harold E. Ford Jr.,

D-Tenn., to require the EPA to set up a program to encourage the production of efficient hybrid and advanced diesel vehicles, and provide consumer incentives for buying the vehicles. The amendment authorized $300 million per year in fiscal 2006 through 2015 to carry out the program.

## SENATE COMMITTEE ACTION

The Senate Energy and Natural Resources Committee gave bipartisan support May 26 to the bulk of the Senate energy bill (S 10 — S Rept 109-78), which was assembled by Domenici. The 21-1 vote came at the end of five days of markups over two weeks.

The Environment and Public Works Committee had already given voice vote approval March 16 to a bill (S 606) requiring an increase in renewable fuel production to 6 billion gallons by 2012. The bill also required a halt to the production of MTBE within four years.

The Finance Committee gave voice vote approval June 16 to a package of energy tax incentives that focused heavily on renewable fuels, energy efficiency and conservation. The tax breaks were projected to have a net cost of $14.1 billion over 11 years.

Many committee Democrats thanked Chairman Charles E. Grassley, R-Iowa, for allowing bipartisan input on the bill. "The House bill heavily favors conventional sources of energy, such as oil, gas and electricity," said the ranking Democrat, Max Baucus of Montana. By contrast, he said, the Finance bill provided "a more balanced approach. It provides tax incentives needed to support and develop renewable energy sources." Democrat Charles E. Schumer of New York praised Grassley for how "green" the legislation was, saying the House-passed bill "didn't even seem to be the palest shade of green."

The resulting Senate energy bill included provisions to:

● **Tax provisions.** Cut energy taxes by a net $14.1 billion over 11 years. The package included a $4.6 billion extension of a credit for electricity produced from renewable sources, $2.3 billion for a clean coal tax credit, $3.8 billion for conservation and energy efficiency, $2.6 billion for alternative motor vehicles and fuels, and $2.8 billion for oil and gas producers.

● **Ethanol.** Require refiners to increase the amount of renewable fuels added to gasoline, starting with an annual average volume of 4 billion gallons in 2005, reaching 8 billion gallons in 2012, compared with 5 billion in the House bill. The bill would eliminate the 2 percent oxygen requirement for reformulated gasoline.

Dianne Feinstein, D-Calif., won a 12-10 vote in the Energy and Natural Resources Committee to exempt California from a requirement to use ethanol blended fuel all year long. The amendment would allow the state to use a different fuel during summer months. Feinstein said the emissions from ethanol could increase as the temperature increases making it less useful for improving air quality during hot weather.

● **MTBE.** Phase out the use of MTBE in fuel within four years and authorize $250 million a year in 2005 through 2008 to help MTBE manufacturers convert their facilities to produce other fuel additives.

● **Electricity.** Repeal PUHCA and replace it with language pushed by Democrats that would give FERC new authority over utility mergers. As in the House version, all mergers of electric utilities and all sales or leases valued in excess of $10 million would have to be approved by FERC. The Senate bill added the requirement that, when approving mergers, the commission consider cross-subsidization and whether it would be harmful to the consumer. In cross-subsidization, one company is charged higher prices so that a second company owned by the same parent company can get a lower rate.

Like the House bill, the measure gave FERC jurisdiction over relia-

bility standards for electricity transmission networks, as well as the authority to issue permits for the construction of new power lines over the objections of states and to use eminent domain to obtain rights-of-way when necessary.

The much-heralded compromise on PUHCA, which had been reached in the Energy and Natural Resource Committee, did not please everyone. "This is an unbelievable expansion of FERC authority," said Richard M. Burr, R-N.C., who joined several other Republicans in urging senators to reconsider the language before a floor vote.

● **Outer Continental Shelf.** Direct the Interior Department to conduct an inventory of oil and natural gas resources on the Outer Continental Shelf and report to Congress within six months of enactment.

After senators warned that any move to encourage offshore drilling could be a "poison pill," Domenici declined to offer an amendment in the Energy and Natural Resources Committee that would allow states to opt out of existing federal moratoriums on offshore drilling that covered most of the country's coastal areas. At the time, new leases were allowed only in parts of the Gulf Coast and off parts of Alaska.

● **LNG terminals.** Give FERC exclusive authority over the siting of LNG terminals.

● **Hydrogen.** Authorize $3.8 billion over five years for Bush's hydrogen initiative.

● **Nuclear energy.** Reauthorize the Price Anderson Act through 2025.

● **Energy efficiency.** Call for the president to take steps to cut oil consumption by 1 million barrels per day from the 25 million barrels-per-day demand projected for 2015. Democrats applauded the title as stronger than past Republican proposals.

● **Fuel economy.** Authorize $2 million per year in fiscal 2006 through 2010 for NHTSA rule-making on fuel efficiency and require the agency to report to Congress within a year on the potential impact of significantly increasing fuel efficiency standards for new cars by 2012. The study would include the effects on gasoline supplies, vehicle safety, sales of U.S. vehicles and air quality.

An amendment by Feinstein to require a 27.5 miles per gallon fuel-economy standard by 2011 for light trucks and SUVs, was rejected, 7-15, in the Energy and Natural Resources Committee. Republicans said the markets were already imposing greater fuel efficiency, pointing to plummeting sales of SUVs in response to high gas prices. They also argued that mandating tougher standards would threaten jobs and force manufacturers to produce lighter vehicles that would be less safe. Democrats cited a federal study showing that in many cases stricter fuel efficiency standards could be achieved by improving transmissions, which would not alter vehicle weight. They also said domestic automakers had been slow to respond to gasoline prices and the need to reduce U.S. dependency on imported oil.

## SENATE FLOOR ACTION

The Senate passed the bill, 85-12, on June 28 after completing work on it the week before. *(Senate vote 158, p. S-32)*

The bill had more bipartisan support than the House-passed version and was less friendly to oil, natural gas and coal producers. Senators, postponed the battles over ANWR and MTBE for the upcoming conference with the House.

The following are among the key amendments considered:

● **Renewable energy.** The Senate adopted, 52-48, a proposal by Jeff Bingaman, D-N.M., to establish a "renewable portfolio standard" that would require utilities to generate at least 10 percent of their electricity from renewable energy sources by 2020. Bingaman and Domenici had agreed not to debate the issue in committee because the panel was

so divided. *(Senate vote 141, p. S-28)*

● **Climate change.** Although the Senate cast a relatively strong vote against a detailed proposal to reduce greenhouse gases, the chamber went on record for the first time ever as recognizing that climate change was a significant problem and endorsing the need for mandatory emission limits. The Senate:

▶ Defeated, 38-60, an amendment by Joseph I. Lieberman, D-Conn., and John McCain, R-Ariz., to cap greenhouse gas emissions at 2000 levels by 2010 using a market-based program to cap overall pollution while allowing businesses to buy and sell permits to meet their obligations. The loss was more decisive than a 43-55 vote in 2003 rejecting similar legislation. However, the 2005 amendment included nuclear energy as an energy source that emits no greenhouse gases. Though the sponsors hoped that would attract more votes, it backfired, angering environmentalists and losing the support of several liberal Democrats. *(Senate vote 148, p. S-30)*

▶ Adopted by voice vote a non-binding "sense of the Senate" amendment by Bingaman stating that climate change was a problem and endorsing mandatory, market-based measures to "slow, stop and reverse" emissions. The amendment gained support from some senators who said they were ready to acknowledge global warming as a problem, but still could not sign on to the mandatory reductions sought by McCain and Lieberman. The amendment was adopted after a motion to table (kill) it, failed, 44-53. *(Senate vote 149, p. S-30)*

▶ Adopted, 66-29, an amendment by Chuck Hagel, R-Neb., to create a program of economic incentives — including direct loans, loan guarantees, lines of credit and production incentive payments — for businesses to reduce emissions of carbon dioxide and other greenhouse gases. *(Senate vote 144, p. S-29)*

▶ Rejected, 46-49, an amendment by John Kerry, D-Mass., calling for the United States to engage actively in international climate-change negotiations. *(Senate vote 151, p. S-30)*

● **Fuel economy.** On the issue of CAFE standards, the Senate:

▶ Adopted, 64-31, an amendment by Christopher S. Bond, R-Mo., to add several factors to be used in determining CAFE standards, including whether higher standards would divert resources from developing advanced technologies. The amendment also increased the authorization for NHTSA rule-making to $5 million a year in fiscal 2006 through 2010, and required the agency to issue new fuel economy standards for cars and light trucks within a few years. *(Senate vote 156, p. S-31)*

▶ Rejected, 28-67, a proposal by Richard J. Durbin, D-Ill., to increase fuel economy standards for passenger vehicles to 40 miles per gallon by model year 2016 and for light trucks to 27.5 miles per gallon. The White House said Bush was likely to veto a bill that set specific new CAFE standards. *(Senate vote 157, p. S-31)*

● **Energy efficiency.** The Senate rejected, 47-53, an amendment by Maria Cantwell, D-Wash., calling on the president to develop and implement measures to reduce petroleum imports by 40 percent by 2025. *(Senate vote 140, p. S-28)*

● **Offshore drilling.** Like the House bill, the measure did not seek to lift an existing ban on new federal offshore leases outside parts of the Gulf of Mexico and Alaska. On related issues, the Senate:

▶ Rejected, 44-52, an amendment by Republican Mel Martinez and Democrat Bill Nelson, both of Florida, to strike the provision authorizing an inventory of offshore oil and natural gas resources. *(Senate vote 143, p. S-29)*

▶ Adopted an amendment by Democrat Mary L. Landrieu and Republican David Vitter, both of Louisiana, to direct $1 billion over four years in federal oil and natural gas royalties to six states that allowed drilling along qualifying parts of their coastlines. Budget Committee Chairman Judd Gregg, R-N.H., said the amendment would create an entitlement program, but the Senate voted 69-26 to waive Gregg's budget point of order, then adopted the $1 billion coastal assistance program by voice vote. *(Senate vote 153, p. S-31)*

● **LNG terminals.** The Senate voted 52-45 to table an amendment by Feinstein that would have given states more authority in decisions to site LNG import facilities along their coasts. *(Senate vote 146, p. S-29)*

## CONFERENCE/FINAL ACTION

The House-Senate conference on the bill began July 14 and concluded July 26. The House adopted the conference report (H Rept 109-190) by a vote of 275-156 on July 28, and the Senate cleared the bill, 74-26, the next day. *(House vote 445, p. H-136; Senate vote 213, p. S-42)*

Negotiations before and during conference contrasted sharply with the bitter partnership of years past, when Republican leaders such as Billy Tauzin of Louisiana, Barton's predecessor as chairman of the House committee, and Frank H. Murkowski of Alaska, who preceded Domenici at the helm of the Senate panel, tried to force the legislation through. When Democrats briefly regained control of the Senate in 2001, they tried to rewrite the bill to their liking.

The difference this time, said Michigan Democrat Bart Stupak, a House conferee, was that Republicans "didn't shut us out." A turning point came in a closed-door meeting in June among Barton, Dingell, Domenici and Bingaman, where Barton pledged to have open discussions and allow input from Democrats. In exchange, the Democrats agreed not to stall the deliberations. Those promises of cooperation played out in a conference that involved intense, lengthy late-night trade-offs, but featured an inclusiveness between the parties that had not existed in the 2003 conference. "It's hard to sit there and negotiate when you know you have the votes" to win without the support of Democrats, Barton said. "But if you do that, at the end when it comes to the floor, everybody has a stake in it."

The following are among the main issues resolved by the conferees:

● **MTBE.** A chief obstacle to finishing the bill was removed when Barton and House GOP leaders gave up on the MTBE "safe harbor" provisions. Barton made one final try for a compromise that would have linked liability protection for the manufacturers with the creation of an $11.4 billion industry-government fund to pay to clean up MTBE-contaminated groundwater. But groups representing municipalities and water supplies, as well as senators from states with groundwater contamination, rejected the fund as inadequate. From the other side, the oil and natural gas industry balked at the cost. "There were certain parameters beyond which industry could not go," said Scott Segal, a lobbyist for some of the largest MTBE manufacturers.

Barton succeeded in winning a provision to allow future MTBE-related lawsuits to be moved to federal court. Business groups generally viewed federal courts as less sympathetic to plaintiffs than many state courts.

● **ANWR.** House Republican leaders also agreed to drop the ANWR drilling provisions, which were unlikely to survive a filibuster in the Senate. Drilling supporters thought they had a better chance of winning enactment as part of the budget reconciliation bill that would be assembled in the fall. Special rules prohibited filibusters on reconciliation bills, which meant the supporters would need only a majority, not the 60 votes required to limit debate. In the end, however, opponents succeeded in blocking the ANWR provisions on both the reconciliation bill and the Defense appropriations bill.

● **Renewable energy.** Conferees dropped the Senate's "renewable portfolio standards" that would have required utilities to generate at least 10 percent of their electricity from renewable energy sources.

● **Climate change.** The final bill created a new cabinet-level advisory committee to develop a national climate change policy and promote technologies to reduce greenhouse gas emissions. Conferees dropped the Senate amendment that would have created specific incentives for technologies to reduce greenhouse gases. The sense of the Senate resolution on climate change also was dropped.

● **Offshore drilling.** The final bill retained the Senate's proposal for an inventory of oil and natural gas resources on the Outer Continental Shelf. The bill also authorized reduced royalty payments for deep gas wells leased in shallow waters in parts of the Gulf of Mexico. States that allowed offshore oil and gas production would share $1 billion in mandatory funding for conservation and restoration projects related to coastal drilling.

● **LNG.** Efforts to give states more authority in siting LNG terminals failed. The final bill gave that power to FERC.

● **Fuel economy.** The final bill authorized $3.5 million a year, halfway between the amounts in the House and Senate bills, for NHTSA rule-making on fuel efficiency standards. It directed the NHTSA to study the potential effects of a significant increase in fuel efficiency standards by model year 2014 on the auto industry, the gasoline supply and the environment. The study was to include the examination of alternatives to the existing system, as the House wanted. The bill also included the House provision on expanding the factors used in determining fuel-efficiency.

Conferees dropped the Senate requirement that the NHTSA issue new car and light truck standards within a few years, as well as the Senate provision requiring that the United States reduce oil consumption by 1 million barrels a day by 2015.

● **Nuclear energy.** Incentives for constructing new nuclear power plants included production tax credits, loan guarantees, insurance against regulatory delays and extension of the Price-Anderson Act limiting liability. The bill authorized payments of up to $500 million for the first new reactor and up to $250 million for the next four if gov-

ernment delays in licensing caused cost overruns.

The bill directed the Energy Department to establish a Next Generation Nuclear Plant Project to design, build and operate a nuclear power plant that would generate electricity, hydrogen or both. The Idaho National Laboratory was named as the lead laboratory, and the bill authorized $1.3 billion for the project in fiscal 2006 through 2015. The House bill proposed $750 million in 2006 through 2010.

● **Taxes.** The $14.6 billion tax package in the final bill provided $2.8 billion in tax benefits for producers of fossil fuels. It had scaled-back versions of several Senate provisions including the $2.7 billion extension of a credit for electricity produced from renewable sources; $1.6 billion in credits for investment in "clean coal" facilities, mainly for producing electricity; $1.3 billion in tax breaks for conservation and energy efficiency and $1.3 billion for alternative motor vehicles and fuels.

The final bill included a new tax credit for purchasing gas-electric hybrid and "lean-burn" diesel-powered cars. The size of the credit would depend on the weight and fuel economy of the specific vehicle; the full credit would be available on 60,000 cars per manufacturer. The bill also established tax credits for investments in alternative fuel refueling stations and for manufacturers of energy-efficient dishwashers, washing machines and refrigerators.

Although the tax credits for oil and gas production were significantly less than the House wanted, the industry won a $974 million provision allowing companies to amortize over two years the geological and geophysical costs of oil and gas exploration in the United States.

Most of the $3 billion in revenue that brought the net total for the tax package to $11.5 billion came from reinstating a five-cents-per-barrel fee on crude oil to fund the Oil Spill Liability Trust Fund. That provision was expected to bring in $2.5 billion over 11 years.

● **Daylight-saving time.** The agreement extended daylight saving time by one month, instead of two as the House had wanted. Supporters said a longer extension would save energy and money and reduce crime. Farmers, airlines with international routes and religious groups concerned about the effect on their prayer schedules objected, as did the National PTA, which raised safety concerns about children walking to school in the dark. ■

---

[PROVISIONS]

# Details of the Energy Policy Overhaul

*Following are the main provisions of the energy policy overhaul law (HR 6 — PL 109-58), which President Bush signed into law Aug. 8.*

## ENERGY EFFICIENCY

● **Federal energy consumption.** The law requires reductions in energy consumed by federal buildings, starting in 2006. By fiscal 2015, agencies are to reduce consumption by 20 percent, relative to 2003 levels. When acquiring new equipment, agencies must purchase products designated as energy efficient by the Energy Star program or the Federal Energy Management Program.

Energy efficiency standards for new federal buildings will be set by the Energy Department within one year of enactment. The goal is for new buildings to use 30 percent less energy than the current standards. The Interior, Commerce and Agriculture departments are required to

use hybrid or other energy-efficient vehicles "to the extent practicable."

● **U.S. Capitol.** The Architect of the Capitol is required to develop, update and implement a conservation and management plan for all congressional facilities to meet the same standards as federal buildings. The law authorizes a total of $10 million in fiscal 2006 through 2010 for a study to evaluate the energy infrastructure of the Capitol.

● **Daylight-saving time.** Daylight-saving time will be extended by one month beginning in 2007. The start date will move from the first Sunday in April to the second Sunday of March; the end date will be the first Sunday of November instead of the last Sunday in October. By allowing one more hour of daylight in the evening, lawmakers hope to reduce energy needed for electric lighting.

The Energy Department is required to report to Congress within nine months on the impact on domestic energy consumption. After

reviewing the report, Congress could reinstate daylight-saving time to its current schedule.

● **Weatherization assistance.** The law reauthorizes the weatherization-assistance program, which provides grants to improve the energy efficiency of low-income homes. It authorizes a total of $1.8 billion in fiscal 2006 through 2008 for the purpose.

● **Low-Income Home Energy Assistance Program.** The law also reauthorizes the Low-Income Home Energy Assistance Program, which helps low-income consumers pay their energy bills. It authorizes a total of $15.3 billion for the program in fiscal 2005 through 2007.

● **State energy conservation programs.** The law authorizes a total of $325 million for state energy conservation programs in fiscal 2006 through 2008 and requires that states receiving the aid set a goal of reducing energy consumption by 25 percent from 1990 levels by 2012. In addition, a total of $150 million is authorized in fiscal 2006 through 2010 for grants to states to design energy-efficient buildings.

● **State appliance rebate program.** The law authorizes a total of $250 million in fiscal 2006 through 2010 to provide matching grants to states that establish or have programs to provide rebates to residential consumers for the purchase of Energy Star products.

● **Commercial products.** The law includes a number of provisions to increase the energy efficiency of commercial and industrial products, including establishing new standards for commercial refrigerators, freezers and clothes washers, and calling for studies of efficiency requirements for other products.

The General Services Administration is required to conduct a study on the use of intermittent escalators, which use sensors to stop when not in use, and specifies procedures to test the energy efficiency of illuminated exit signs, traffic signals and compact fluorescent lamps.

● **Energy reduction in public housing.** The Department of Housing and Urban Development is directed to develop a strategy for reducing utility expenses through conservation and efficiency in the design and construction of public housing.

## RENEWABLE ENERGY

● **Resource assessment.** The law authorizes a total of $50 million in fiscal 2006 through 2010 for the Energy Department to assess domestically available renewable energy resources, such as geothermal, wind and solar power.

● **Federal consumption.** The government is required to purchase at least 3 percent of its electricity from renewable sources in fiscal 2007, 5 percent in fiscal 2010 and 7.5 percent in fiscal 2013 and beyond. Sources can include solar, wind, biomass, landfill gas, geothermal, municipal solid waste or new hydroelectric generation capacity achieved from increased efficiency or additions of new capacity at an existing hydroelectric project.

● **Solar energy in public buildings.** The law authorizes a total of $250 million in fiscal 2006 through 2010 to enable federal officials to purchase and use solar electric systems in public buildings in an effort to accelerate the commercialization of the technology and reduce federal fossil-fuel consumption. Separately, the law authorizes $20 million for a solar electric system to be used in the Energy Department's Washington, D.C., headquarters, and a total of $50 million in fiscal 2006 through 2010 to evaluate the program.

● **Consumer rebates.** Consumers who install renewable power energy systems in their homes or small businesses can qualify for a rebate of up to $3,000 per unit. The law authorizes a total of $1 billion for the program from fiscal 2006 to 2010.

● **Sugar-cane ethanol.** The law authorizes $36 million for an EPA program to demonstrate the production of ethanol from sugar cane. The program is limited to producers in the states of Florida, Louisiana, Texas and Hawaii.

● **Biomass grants.** The law authorizes a total of $550 million in fiscal 2006 through 2016 for grants of up to $500,000 for the use of specific types of biomass materials for purposes such as electricity or fuel.

● **Geothermal leases.** Several provisions in the law are aimed at making geothermal energy more competitive with fossil fuels. While this energy can refer to any form of naturally occurring heat from the ground, steam is currently the most practical and common source used for generating electricity.

The Interior Department is required to hold a competitive lease sale every two years for areas that may produce geothermal energy. If the department receives no bids for a specific area, it can hold a non-competitive lease sale.

Under prior law, the Interior Department could issue geothermal leases on Forest Service land only with the consent of the Agriculture Department. However, there is no common procedure for the Agriculture Department to process such requests. The new law directs the departments to develop coordinated procedures for processing lease applications. The departments also must establish a program to reduce the backlog of applications for geothermal leases.

● **Hydroelectric licensing.** Under prior law, all applications to operate a hydroelectric facility were reviewed by federal environmental agencies, which could require the applicant to provide specified protections for water and wildlife as a condition for approval. Under the new law, applicants and other interested parties, such as environmental groups or Indian tribes, can offer alternatives to those government conditions. The federal agency must accept the alternative if it determines that it would provide adequate protection to water and wildlife and that it would cost less to implement than the initial proposed requirement or would result in improved operation of the project. Appeals may be heard by the Federal Energy Regulatory Commission (FERC).

● **Hydroelectric incentives.** The law authorizes a total of $100 million in fiscal 2006 through 2015 for incentive payments to hydroelectric facilities that begin operation within 10 years of enactment. Facilities are eligible for a sliding scale of payments, not to exceed $750,000 per year, based on their production.

In addition, a total of $100 million is authorized in fiscal 2006 through 2015 for incentives to existing hydroelectric facilities that improve their efficiency by at least 3 percent. The payments could not exceed 10 percent of the cost of the upgrade, or $750,000.

## OIL AND GAS

● **Strategic Petroleum Reserve.** The law directs the Energy Department, as soon as practical, to acquire oil to fill the reserve to its full capacity of 1 billion barrels. The department is required to establish guidelines for acquiring crude oil that maximize domestic supply, increase cost-effectiveness and protect national security.

● **Natural gas.** FERC is given exclusive authority to approve the construction, expansion or operation of liquefied natural gas (LNG) terminals. LNG is a compressed form of natural gas that is being shipped increasingly from overseas as demand rises. FERC is directed to consult with state governments about the safety of sites for liquefaction or gasification facilities, but the new law clarifies that the federal agency has final siting authority.

FERC can authorize a natural gas company to provide storage facilities for natural gas at market-based rates. The law also increases civil and criminal penalties to $1,000,000, from as low as $5,000, for indi-

viduals who knowingly violate laws regarding natural gas.

● **Hydraulic fracturing.** Hydraulic fracturing is the practice of injecting fluids or other agents into the ground to crack open underground areas for oil and gas exploration. The law exempts the practice, which environmentalists maintain contaminates groundwater, from review under the federal Safe Drinking Water Act (PL 93-523).

● **In-kind payments.** The Interior Department can require companies to pay royalties for drilling on federal lands in the form of oil or gas rather than cash. The department can then sell the oil or gas, or transport or process it. The department is prohibited from using funds from the sale of in-kind payments for personnel, travel or other administrative purposes. For each year of fiscal 2006 through 2015 in which the department receives in-kind royalty payments, it will have to report to Congress on the methods and impact of taking such payments.

● **Royalty rate reductions.** The law allows oil and gas companies to pay lower royalty fees for marginal gas and oil wells, or those that produce no more than 15 barrels per day of oil or gas. It also reduces royalty payments for deep gas wells leased in the shallow waters of the western and central areas of the Gulf of Mexico, and for drilling in deep water — more than 400 meters — of the Gulf. Companies also get royalty breaks for operations in which they inject captured carbon dioxide underground to help produce oil and gas. The practice is seen as a way to reduce emissions of the greenhouse gas.

● **Orphan wells.** Orphan wells are abandoned or capped wells that have no identifiable entity legally responsible for them or financially able to reclaim them. The Interior Department, in cooperation with the Agriculture Department, is required to establish a program to remediate, reclaim and close orphaned wells located on public lands. The Energy Department will provide technical and financial assistance to states to address orphan wells on state or private land. For the various orphan-well provisions, the measure authorizes a total of $125 million in fiscal 2006 through 2010, of which $25 million must be dedicated to assisting those who lease federal land for remediating and closing orphan wells on the property.

● **Outer Continental Shelf.** The Interior Department is authorized to conduct an inventory of oil and natural gas resources in the Outer Continental Shelf, a federally controlled area that in most states begins 3 miles offshore. The bill does not authorize new oil or gas production in parts of the Outer Continental Shelf where such production is currently prohibited, such as off the California and Florida coasts.

● **Permits for federal lands.** The law calls for federal agencies to speed up and better coordinate the permitting process for oil and gas development on federal lands, in some cases setting specific deadlines by which decisions on applications must be made. It also calls for agencies to designate corridors for infrastructure such as pipelines and electricity transmission lines.

● **Coastal impact assistance zones.** States that allow offshore production of oil and gas — a handful of Gulf states as well as Alaska — will share a total of $1 billion in fiscal 2007 through 2010 for conservation, protection or restoration projects that address the impacts of coastal drilling. The money is not subject to appropriations.

● **Great Lakes and Finger Lakes.** Oil or gas drilling is prohibited under any of the Great Lakes or Finger Lakes.

● **Refinery revitalization.** In an effort to address the need for new U.S. refinery capacity, the law authorizes the EPA, at the request of a governor, to establish a streamlined permit process that would coordinate state and federal processes.

● **National Petroleum Reserve.** The law directs the Interior Department to begin oil and gas exploration in the National Petroleum Reserve, which covers more than 23 million acres of public land on Alaska's North Slope. The oil and gas leases, issued by means of competitive bidding, would be for 10 years.

## COAL

● **Clean-coal initiative.** The clean-coal technology program, co-funded by the government and industry, is aimed at developing clean-coal technologies that reduce pollutants such as carbon dioxide, mercury and sulfur dioxide by specified amounts. The law authorizes a total of $1.8 billion in fiscal 2006 through 2014 for the project; 70 percent of the funding is to be used for gasification technology.

The law authorizes funds for an experimental clean-coal plant, creates grants to universities to establish clean-coal centers for excellence and authorizes loan guarantees for projects to cleanly produce energy from coal. It authorizes a demonstration project to produce energy from coal mined in the Western United States, and a program to evaluate the potential of advanced technology to produce energy from Illinois basin coal.

● **Clean air coal program.** A new program under the law is designed to encourage the production of power using clean-coal electric-generating equipment.

The law authorizes a total of $2.5 billion in fiscal 2007 through 2013 for the Energy Department to provide financial assistance, not to exceed 50 percent of the cost of any project, to aid the production of coal-based power using clean-coal electric-generating equipment that improves energy efficiency or reduces pollution but is not yet competitive. Between 25 percent and 75 percent of these projects must be for the sole purpose of generating electricity.

The law also authorizes a total of $500 million from fiscal 2007 through 2011 for projects at existing coal-based electricity generation plants that use advanced air pollution control equipment and processes. The goal is to reduce air pollution by encouraging industry to voluntarily exceed existing standards.

● **Coal on federal lands.** The law repeals the previous 160-acre cap on coal leases, allows for advanced payment of royalties from coal mines and requires an assessment of coal resources on federal lands other than national parks.

## INDIAN TRIBAL ENERGY DEVELOPMENT

● **Indian energy office.** A new Office of Indian Energy Policy and Programs within the Energy Department will coordinate the production of energy resources on Indian reservations.

● **Incentives.** A new Indian energy resource development program to be created within the Interior Department will provide grants and low-interest loans to tribes to develop energy resources. The Energy Department is authorized to provide loan guarantees — not to exceed a total of $2 billion at any given time — to spur energy production on reservations. Federal agencies purchasing energy can give preference to Indian-produced resources, as long as the price does not exceed the market price.

● **Development agreements/leases.** The law establishes guidelines allowing tribes to enter into business agreements or grant leases or rights-of-way expressly for the purpose of energy development or transmission. Specifically, tribes can submit an application to the Interior Department to enter into an energy-resource agreement with a separate entity. If the agreement is approved, the tribe can negotiate leases or other business deals related to energy on tribal lands without federal approval. Tribes are also allowed to grant leases or rights-of-way without federal approval if the terms do not exceed 30 years.

## NUCLEAR POWER

● **Price Anderson.** The law extends until 2025 the Price Anderson Act (PL 100-408), which limits nuclear power companies' liability for accidents. The act requires companies to purchase insurance coverage up to a certain amount, currently about $10 billion. The federal government is responsible for damages in excess of the cap, which is adjusted periodically.

The extension applies to new plants; coverage for existing plants would have continued even if the law were allowed to expire. Federal protection is considered necessary to encourage new nuclear power.

● **Antitrust review.** The law eliminates a previous requirement that a company's application to the Nuclear Regulatory Commission (NRC) to build or operate a nuclear plant be reviewed by the U.S. attorney general for antitrust concerns.

● **Whistleblowers.** The law expands whistleblower protections to federal contractors and subcontractors who work in nuclear energy.

● **Export of uranium for medical purposes.** Under certain conditions, the legislation allows the export of highly enriched uranium to Canada, Belgium, France, Germany and the Netherlands for the production of medical isotopes.

● **Export controls.** The law bars the sale, export or transfer of nuclear materials and "sensitive nuclear technology" to any nation the State Department has identified as a state sponsor of terrorist activities. The president may waive the ban if such a sale is vital to national security, or if it is certified that the country has not encouraged international proliferation of nuclear weapons within the previous 12 months.

● **Hydrogen production at nuclear plants.** The law authorizes $100 million for the Energy Department to establish two projects to demonstrate commercial production of hydrogen at nuclear plants.

● **Federal insurance for permitting delays.** A company that builds a new advanced nuclear reactor will be reimbursed for costs resulting from delays — for example, if the NRC misses schedules or deadlines or if litigation postpones completion of a project. The first two advanced reactors starting construction will be eligible for full reimbursement of such costs, up to $500 million each, while the next four will be covered for 50 percent of the costs, up to $250 million each.

● **Next Generation nuclear plant project.** The law authorizes $1.25 billion through 2015 and unspecified sums from fiscal 2016 through 2021 to develop a prototype "Next Generation" nuclear power plant by Sept. 30, 2021. The program is to be administered by the Energy Department.

● **Radiation source protection.** The law imposes new restrictions on the import and export of radioactive materials and calls on the NRC to establish a new tracking system for shipments of radioactive materials in the United States. It also calls for a task force that would report to Congress periodically with recommendations for new regulations or legislation regarding radioactive materials.

● **Reactor security.** The law calls for the NRC at least every three years to evaluate each nuclear plant's security procedures and the ability of their private security forces to defend against threats. The NRC also is instructed to study and possibly revise regulations regarding threats to nuclear plants, taking into account suicide attacks, water- and air-based threats, and the potential for attacks on spent-fuel shipments.

Before issuing a license for a nuclear power plant, the NRC must consult with the Department of Homeland Security regarding the vulnerability of the proposed location to terrorist attack. Nuclear power companies are required to fingerprint and conduct more extensive background checks on employees who have access to sensitive areas. The law also clarifies that security forces at nuclear facilities can carry certain firearms regardless of state laws restricting the firearms that can be used by private security forces.

## VEHICLES AND FUELS

● **Hybrid vehicles.** The Energy Department is directed to create a program to encourage domestic production and sales of efficient hybrid and advanced diesel vehicles and is authorized to make grants to domestic automakers for this purpose.

The law also authorizes $40 million for a new grant program to encourage the development of technologies for commercially viable hybrid/flexible fuel-cell vehicles. These cars would need to have a range of at least 250 miles, consume greatly reduced amounts of petroleum, and have commercial sales potential within five years.

● **State and local programs.** A pilot program, to be administered through the Energy Department's Clean Cities Program, is to provide up to 30 geographically dispersed grants to states, local governments or metropolitan transport authorities to acquire alternative-fueled passenger vehicles, motorized two-wheel bicycles, buses, delivery vehicles and airport ground-support vehicles. Along with purchasing vehicles, the money could be used for infrastructure, operations and maintenance costs. The law authorizes $200 million for the program, with the restriction that the federal money can make up no more than 50 percent of a specific project's cost; individual applicants are limited to a maximum grant of $15 million.

● **Fuel-cell transit bus initiative.** The Energy and Transportation departments are directed to create a demonstration program that awards competitive grants to five local projects involving the use of up to 25 fuel-cell buses. The law authorizes a total of $50 million in fiscal 2006 through 2010 for the program.

● **Clean school bus grants.** The EPA and the Energy Department are directed to establish a Clean School Bus program to help replace school buses manufactured prior to 1977 with alternative-fueled school buses — those which use natural gas, hydrogen, propane, methanol, ethanol or ultra-low-sulfur diesel. The grants could also be used to retrofit buses manufactured before 1991 with new, more efficient fuel technology. The program would pay up to 50 percent of the cost of a new bus, or up to 100 percent of the cost of a retrofit. The law authorizes a total of $110 million in fiscal 2006 and 2007, and unspecified sums through 2010 for the program.

The legislation also authorizes a total of $25 million in fiscal 2006 through 2009 for the Energy Department to cooperate with school bus companies in developing fuel-cell buses.

● **Diesel trucks.** The EPA and Energy Department are directed to create a similar program of grants to public agencies for retrofitting and modernizing diesel truck fleets, with the goal of reducing emissions. A total of $100 million is authorized in fiscal 2006 through 2008 .

● **Railroad efficiency.** The law calls for a partnership among the Energy and Transportation departments, the EPA, the railroad industry and locomotive manufacturers to develop train technologies that increase fuel economy, reduce emissions and lower costs. It authorizes a total of $65 million in fiscal 2006 through 2008 for the program.

● **Aviation fuel and emissions.** The Energy Department and NASA are directed to enter into a partnership to develop "ultra-efficient" engine technology for aircraft. The law authorizes a total of $250 million in fiscal 2006 through 2010 for the project.

● **Promoting bicycling.** The law authorizes $6.2 million for a new "Conserve by Bicycling" program that will involve 10 geographically diverse pilot projects designed to encourage bicycling in order to reduce the use of fuels.

● **Automobile fuel efficiency.** The law authorizes $17.5 million annually in fiscal 2006 through 2010 for the National Highway Traffic Safety Administration (NHTSA) to enforce existing corporate average fuel economy (CAFE) standards. Existing law requires automobile manufacturers to produce a product line with an average fuel economy of 27.5 miles per gallon for cars and a 20.7 mpg average for light trucks. The measure does not require an increase in vehicle-fuel economy.

The NHTSA is required to study the feasibility and potential effects of reducing fuel consumption for the model year 2014. The study, to be completed within one year, is to include consideration of alternatives to current CAFE standards, safety effects of greater efficiency and the impact on the automobile industry.

● **Federal procurement of fuel-cell technology.** Federal departments are required to begin using fuel-cell technologies within specific time frames. The law authorizes a total of $105 million from fiscal 2008 through 2010, and unspecified sums through 2015, for the purchase of fuel-cell vehicles or hydrogen energy systems by 2010. It also authorizes a total of $345 million in fiscal 2006 through 2010, and unspecified sums through 2015, for the purchase of stationary, portable or micro fuel cells for electricity generation by 2006.

● **Diesel emissions.** The law authorizes a total of $1 billion in fiscal 2007 through 2011 for an EPA program aimed at reducing diesel emissions. The money would go toward grants and low-interest loans to government agencies and nonprofit organizations for new engine configurations in truck fleets.

## HYDROGEN

● **Hydrogen and fuel-cell program.** Several provisions are aimed at developing technologies for producing hydrogen to be used as fuel with a goal of getting a commitment from automakers to offer hydrogen fuel-cell vehicles no later than 2015.

To ensure hydrogen production, storage and distribution, the law authorizes a total of $1.1 billion in fiscal 2006 through 2010, and unspecified sums through 2020.

To fund a limited number of Energy Department demonstration projects using hydrogen, the law authorizes a total of $1.3 billion in fiscal 2006 through 2010, and unspecified sums through 2020.

It also directs the Energy Department to provide grants or enter into contracts to develop safety codes and standards for fuel-cell vehicles and other hydrogen energy systems.

## RESEARCH AND DEVELOPMENT

The law authorizes billions of dollars for research and development programs to be administered by the Energy Department. The stated goal is to increase energy efficiency in all sectors, diversify energy supplies, reduce U.S. dependence on foreign energy sources, improve U.S. energy security and reduce the environmental impact of energy production. The authorizations include:

● **Energy efficiency.** A total of $2.8 billion in fiscal 2007 through 2013 for research on a range of topics, such as improved lighting and building efficiency.

● **Distributed energy and electric energy systems.** A total of $768 million in fiscal 2007 through 2009 for research in fields such as reliable electricity transmission and the efficient cooling of electronics.

● **Renewable energy.** A total of $2.2 billion in fiscal 2007 through 2009 for research on renewable energy technologies such as wind, solar and geothermal power.

● **Agricultural biomass.** A total of $2 billion in fiscal 2006 through 2015 for research on biofuels made from organic matter such as

plants and agricultural byproducts, with additional authorizations for specific programs.

● **Nuclear power.** A total of $2.3 billion in fiscal 2007 through 2009 for new technologies and programs to encourage the expansion of nuclear power — such as the Bush administration's Nuclear Power 2010 program, which aims to build a new U.S. nuclear power plant by 2010.

● **Fossil energy.** A total of nearly $1.9 billion in fiscal 2007 through 2009 for research activities involving fossil fuels. Much of the money is for coal research, including methods for improving existing plants but also new technologies such as gasification and sequestration, in which coal is converted into a gas and carbon is removed. Oil and gas development technologies, including methods for maximizing production from low-volume wells, are also to get a significant share of the funds. An additional $155 million is authorized for methane hydrate research and development. The Office of Arctic Energy is to get extended funding of $25 million per year in 2010 through 2012.

● **Science.** A total of $14 billion in fiscal 2007 through 2009 for energy-related research in fields such as physics, biology and environmental science, with additional funds for specific projects such as the rare isotope accelerator and the Spallation Neutron Source project.

● **International cooperation.** A total of $6 million in fiscal 2007 through 2010 for international energy training and outreach. The law also authorizes a total of $39 million in 2007 through 2009 to promote international cooperation on energy issues, with university participation. A "sense of Congress" clause urges cooperation with Israel.

● **Ultra-deep-water oil and gas.** A total of $550 million in direct spending in fiscal 2007 through 2017 for grants to encourage unconventional and new technologies in oil and gas exploration, such as ultra-deepwater drilling. The grants will be awarded to a private consortium selected by the Energy Department. In addition, the law authorizes the appropriation of a total of $1 billion in fiscal 2007 to 2016.

## ENERGY DEPARTMENT MANAGEMENT, TRAINING

To improve Energy Department management, the law calls for a new technology transfer coordinator to advise the department in transferring its work to the private sector and includes a "sense of Congress" clause directing the department to develop more stringent procurement and inventory controls.

The law authorizes a total of $60 million in fiscal 2006 through 2008 for the department to monitor workforce trends and establish training programs as necessary. It also calls for the department to establish educational programs in science and math, including programs to promote professional development for teachers.

## ELECTRICITY

● **Reliability standards.** The law calls for new mandatory reliability standards for electricity transmission networks and gives FERC jurisdiction to oversee and enforce them. FERC will certify electric reliability organizations (EROs) and grant them authority to create and enforce the standards. EROs would have to file reliability standards and any other changes with FERC, which could then approve or disapprove the standards.

All operators of bulk-electric power-generating systems are required to comply with the standards, which are to be designed to limit instability and cascading failures. EROs would have the authority to enforce penalties on any bulk-power operators that violate the standards. The measure also allows FERC to impose penalties if it finds violations.

Alaska and Hawaii are exempted from the provision.

● **Transmission facility siting.** The Energy Department is directed to

study congestion in the nation's electricity transmission system and designate troubled areas as "national interest" corridors. FERC would have new "backstop" authority to issue construction permits for transmission facilities in such corridors under certain conditions — for example, if FERC determines that the facility is in the public interest but a state commission has withheld approval.

Under certain conditions, electric companies can petition in district court for eminent domain to acquire right-of-way property for transmission facilities.

When the proposed power line is to be on federal property, the Energy Department is designated as the lead agency in coordinating all related federal authorizations. The department is responsible for producing a single environmental review to be used in all federal proceedings. In most cases, final permitting decisions must be made within one year, and federal agencies are required to communicate with applicants within 60 days on the likelihood of approval and key issues of concern.

If a permit is denied, the applicant has the right to appeal to the White House, which can overturn agency decisions.

The measure authorizes an internal review of existing rights-of-way on federal lands, including specifics about the status and time frame for individual applications. It also directs federal agencies involved in permitting transmission facilities to agree within one year to take steps to ensure "timely and coordinated" reviews of applications.

● **Transmission rates and incentives.** The Energy Department is authorized to establish an Advanced Power System Technology Incentive Program to provide incentive payments for utilities to employ new technologies to ensure reliability and efficiency and thereby reduce the cost of power. A total of $70 million is authorized in fiscal 2006 through 2012 for the payments, which are to be based on kilowatt-hours generated.

FERC is directed to establish incentive-based rates for interstate electricity transmission by public utilities within one year of enactment. This provision is intended to promote investment in electric transmission networks and technologies to ensure reliability. Additional incentives will be provided for participation in regional transmission organizations.

FERC may require any utility company that transmits electricity in multiple states to provide transmission services at rates comparable to the rates the utility company charges itself. FERC could exempt companies that sell fewer than 4 million megawatt hours of electricity per year, or do not operate a large-scale transmission system.

● **Electricity metering.** The law requires utilities to provide "net-metering" upon request to customers that use their own on-site power sources, such as solar panels or wind turbines. The metering would allow the electricity to be better accounted for on the customers' bills.

The electric utilities must provide customers, at their request, with "smart metering" service, giving customers a real-time schedule showing how the rates vary by the time of day, according to changes in wholesale power costs. The intent of the provision, which would take effect within 18 months of enactment, is to enable customers to manage energy use and cost by reducing demand during peak times.

The Energy Department is directed to educate consumers about the availability and benefits of advanced metering, and to work with states and energy companies to develop the smart-metering technologies.

● **PUHCA repeal.** The law repeals the 1935 Public Utility Holding Company Act (PUHCA), which restricted the ownership and operations of power companies and their ability to control energy prices. It replaces PUHCA with provisions designed to provide disclosure of power company finances. Specifically, it gives FERC — and, to a lesser extent, state authorities — the power to examine all relevant books, records, accounts and memorandums belonging to a company that owns or partly owns

a power facility to ensure that costs are allocated fairly to public utilities.

All sales or leases of facilities valued in excess of $10 million and all mergers must be approved by FERC.

● **Market transparency rules.** FERC is to establish rules to provide the public and the government with information to facilitate price transparency and participation in electricity markets. The rules must provide for the distribution of timely information about wholesale electric energy prices and transmission. The information is to be available to federal agencies, buyers and sellers of wholesale electricity, and the public. FERC must ensure that the disclosure of information would not harm the energy market or consumers.

The law also dramatically increases criminal penalties for market manipulation.

## MISCELLANEOUS
● **North American Energy Freedom commission.** The law establishes a commission of 16 members appointed by the president to develop a comprehensive national policy for achieving North American energy independence by 2025. The law authorizes $10 million over two years for the commission, which is scheduled to be appointed within 60 days of the bill's enactment and to submit its report within one year.

## ETHANOL AND MOTOR FUELS
● **Renewable fuels mandate.** Fuel refiners are required to roughly double the amount of biofuels used in the United States by 2012. The provision is most likely to result in the production of corn-based ethanol but also could include fuels derived from sewage waste, landfill or other organic matter. The annual average volume of renewable fuel is to increase incrementally, starting at 4 billion gallons in 2006 and reaching 7.5 billion gallons in 2012.

The EPA, in consultation with the Energy and Agriculture departments, can reduce or waive the requirement for a state, upon request. The requirement can be waived if it is determined that the mandate would have a significant adverse economic or environmental impact on the state or region, or that there is an inadequate renewable-fuel supply or distribution capacity to meet the requirement. Any waiver granted would last one year, but would be renewable. The Energy Department also can waive the requirement if it determines that the mandate would impose an economic hardship on a refinery.

The Federal Trade Commission is required to conduct an analysis within 180 days of enactment of the market concentration of ethanol and determine whether there is enough industry competition to avoid price-setting or other anti-competitive behavior.

● **Methyl tertiary butyl ether (MTBE).** MTBE is an oxygenate additive that produces cleaner-burning gasoline but has contaminated drinking water in communities across the country. A provision that would have provided limited liability protection to producers of MTBE was dropped, but the law allows any future lawsuits to be moved to federal district court.

● **Oxygenate requirement.** The law eliminates a 1990 requirement that reformulated gasoline contain at least 2 percent oxygen by weight, while calling for the EPA to establish standards to reduce toxic air pollutants from gasoline with fuel additives. It also requires the EPA to study the public health and environmental impacts of potential MTBE substitutes, including ethanol. Refiners had met the requirement by using more oxygenates, primarily MTBE but also ethanol, and MTBE producers had cited the requirement in defending themselves against lawsuits.

● **Market study.** The law calls for the EPA and Energy Department to conduct a study of the wide variety of federal, state and local fuel

requirements, including their effect on market supply, consumer prices, environmental goals and industry practices.

● **Incentives.** The law authorizes various grants and loan guarantees aimed at encouraging demonstration projects for the production of alternative fuels from sources such as biomass or sugar cane. Authorizations include:

A total of $650 million in fiscal 2006 and 2007 to provide grants for the construction of plants that produce cellulosic biomass ethanol from agricultural residues or municipal solid waste.

A total of $750 million in 2006 through 2008 for the production of ethanol and other renewable fuels derived from agricultural residues, wood residues, municipal solid waste or agricultural byproducts.

A total of $550 million in 2005 through 2009 for the EPA to fund demonstration projects of advanced biofuel technologies.

● **Underground storage tanks.** The Leaking Underground Storage Tank (LUST) Trust Fund is a federal program created by Congress in 1986 to finance the cleanup of sites where underground storage tanks have leaked petroleum or other hazardous substances. The fund is financed through a 0.1-cent-per-gallon tax on motor vehicle fuel sold in the United States.

The law requires the EPA to distribute at least 80 percent of the available funds each year to participating states for cleanup of hazardous sites or for enforcement activities. The remaining money — up to 20 percent of available funds — could be used to enforce regulations related to leaking storage tanks.

The measure requires extra leak-containment standards for underground tanks that are installed or replaced within 1,000 feet of a community drinking-water system or a potable drinking-water well. It requires manufacturers and installers of underground storage tanks to maintain evidence of financial responsibility in order to cover the costs of faulty manufacture or installation, and it requires more frequent inspections.

The law authorizes a total of $3 billion in fiscal 2005 through 2009 for the LUST fund and related activities.

● **Boutique fuels.** The EPA can waive individual state fuel-blending requirements for up to 20 days in "extreme and unusual" supply circumstances. The law also caps the number of special fuel blends, known as boutique fuels, that states can require at the number that existed on Sept. 1, 2004.

### CLIMATE CHANGE

● **Advisory committee.** The law creates a new Climate Change Technology Advisory Committee to coordinate federal activities and studies related to climate change in order to develop a national strategy to promote technologies for reducing greenhouse gas emissions. The law does not mandate specific reductions in such emissions.

The president is to appoint at least seven members to the committee, including the secretaries of Commerce, Agriculture, and Transportation and the EPA administrator. Within 18 months of enactment, the committee is to submit to the president and Congress a plan to reduce greenhouse gas emissions through commercial technologies.

● **Federal coordination.** A new Climate Change Technology Program will assist the committee by coordinating federal research and development efforts. The Energy Department can authorize demonstration projects relating to emissions-reducing technology.

● **Foreign policy.** The law directs the State Department to develop a policy to help developing countries reduce their greenhouse gas emissions. The department is required to report to Congress within 180 days of enactment on 25 developing countries that emit such gases. The department is to provide assistance in the form of bilateral agreements, private investments or the export of technologies that reduce greenhouse gases.

### INCENTIVES FOR INNOVATIVE TECHNOLOGIES

● **Loan guarantees.** Under a new Energy Department program, the federal government is authorized to provide loan guarantees for up to 80 percent of the cost of approved energy facilities. Projects eligible for the loan guarantees include renewable energy, advanced fossil energy, hydrogen fuel cells, advanced nuclear, carbon capture and sequestration, efficient electricity generation and distribution, production facilities for fuel-efficient vehicles, pollution-control equipment and refineries.

### STUDIES

The law calls for federal agencies to study a variety of energy-related issues and submit reports to Congress. Topics include oil and natural gas storage capacity and inventory, energy efficiency standards, telecommuting, the Low-Income Home Energy Assistance Program, oil bypass filtration technology, total integrated thermal systems, energy integration with Latin America, low-volume gas reservoir, gasoline markets and prices, progress on the Alaska natural gas pipeline, coal-bed methane, backup fuel capacity for industrial and power-generation facilities, Indian land rights-of-way, mobility of federal science and technology personnel, competition in the wholesale and retail electricity markets, rapid electrical grid restoration, distributed generation of electricity, natural gas supply shortage, hydrogen participation and employment, best management practices for the Energy Department, effect of electrical contaminant on energy production, alternative fuels, excessive charges for electricity, fuel-cell and hydrogen technology, links between energy security and increases in vehicle-miles traveled, cumulative impacts of offshore liquefied natural gas facilities, energy- and water-saving measures in congressional buildings, availability of skilled workers for energy and mineral security, impacts of the Energy Policy Act of 1992, benefits of utilities' economic dispatch, renewable energy on federal land, increased hydroelectric generation at existing federal facilities, split-estate federal oil and gas leasing and development practices, federal resource development conflicts in the Powder River Basin, national security review of international energy requirements, used oil refining, transmission system monitoring, and potential hydropower facilities.

### TAX PROVISIONS

Congress' Joint Committee on Taxation estimates that the new law will provide $14.6 billion in tax reductions and $3 billion in revenue increases, for a net reduction in federal revenues of $11.5 billion over the 11-year period of fiscal 2005 through 2015. All cost and revenue estimates are according to the committee.

### PRODUCTION AND SUPPLY INCENTIVES

● **Clean coal technology credit.** The law provides a 20 percent tax credit for the use of integrated gasification combined cycle (IGCC) generation technologies. It provides a 15 percent tax credit for other advanced clean coal projects producing electricity, and a 15 percent credit for certain industrial gasification projects that convert coal, petroleum residue, biomass or other materials recovered for their energy or feedstock value into a gas composed primarily of carbon monoxide and hydrogen for direct use or subsequent chemical or physical conversion. The Treasury secretary is directed to allocate up to $800 million in credits

to IGCC projects, up to $500 million in credits for other advanced clean coal projects and up to $350 million in credits to industrial gasification projects. (Cost: $1.6 billion over 11 years.)

● **Depreciation of electricity transmission property.** The law reduces the depreciation period for property used in the transmission of electricity for sale and related land improvements from 20 years to 15 years. The provision is effective for property placed in service after April 11, 2005. (Cost: $1.2 billion over 11 years.)

● **Production credit for wind energy and biomass electricity.** The tax credit allowed for the production of electricity from renewable resources is extended for two years and modified for certain facilities. Specifically, the placed-in-service date is extended through 2007 for "closed loop" biomass produced from plants grown specifically to produce electricity, "open loop" biomass (including agricultural livestock waste nutrients) facilities, geothermal energy facilities, small irrigation power facilities, landfill gas facilities and trash-combustion facilities. The placed-in-service dates for solar energy facilities, which expire Dec. 31, 2005, and refined coal facilities, which expire Dec. 31, 2008, are not extended.

Eligibility for the tax credit is to include electricity from hydropower and Indian coal. The credit is extended for 10 years for all renewable electricity sources under this provision, except Indian coal. The credit for Indian coal is available for seven years, beginning in 2006.

The credit is indexed for inflation and for 2005 is 0.9 cents per kilowatt-hour for open-loop biomass, small irrigation power facilities, landfill gas facilities and trash-combustion facilities, and 1.9 cents per kilowatt-hour for all other qualified renewable electricity.

The credit for wind and closed-loop biomass facilities placed in service by the end of 2005 is available for a 10-year period; the amount of the credit that may be claimed is phased out as the market price of electricity exceeds certain threshold levels. The credit is available for five years for the remaining facilities. The credit for refined coal in 2005 is $5.481 per ton and is available for 10 years.

The agreement also permits agricultural cooperatives to pass any portion of the credit through to their members.

● **Amortization for pollution control facilities in older plants.** Electric generation plants opened after 1975 can write off the cost of certified air-pollution-control facilities — but not water-pollution-control facilities — over a five-year period. The law provides a seven-year amortization period for air-pollution-control facilities used in connection with electric generation plants that are primarily coal-fired and placed in service after 1975.

Until now, the only electricity generation plants that could amortize the cost of certain air pollution control facilities over a five-year period were those placed in service before Jan. 1, 1976. A "certified pollution control facility" is defined as a treatment facility that controls water or air pollution, and that does not lead to a significant increase in output or capacity, to an extension of the useful life, to a reduction in total operating costs for the plant, or to an alteration in the nature of the manufacturing production process. (Cost: $1.1 billion over 11 years.)

● **Nuclear decommissioning costs.** The law modifies the tax rules governing the cost of decommissioning nuclear power plants. It repeals a "cost of service" requirement that previously limited the deductibility of contributions made by nuclear power plant owners to independent trust funds for the decommissioning of nuclear plants when they are retired. Under the law, regulated and unregulated contributors would qualify for the deduction.

A rule that prohibited these trust funds from accumulating more reserves than were needed to pay for decommissioning costs incurred after 1984 is also repealed. The law allows the trust funds to accumulate amounts sufficient to cover the present value of 100 percent of the estimated decommissioning costs. The provisions would be effective beginning in 2006. (Cost: $1.3 billion over 11 years.)

● **Clean renewable energy bonds.** The law allows a tax credit to holders of Clean Renewable Energy Bonds for bonds purchased before Dec. 31, 2007. (Cost: $411 million over 11 years.)

● **Income for rural electric cooperatives.** The law makes permanent recent changes designed to allow rural electric cooperatives to earn income from certain transactions with non-members of the cooperative tax-free. Currently, cooperatives are exempt from federal taxes as long as 85 percent of their annual income comes from members of the cooperative. (Cost: $277 million over 11 years.)

● **Credit for production from advanced nuclear power facilities.** A tax credit is created for electricity produced at advanced nuclear power facilities. A credit of 1.8 cents per kilowatt-hour will be allowed during the eight-year period beginning on the date the facility was placed in service. An advanced nuclear facility is defined as such if the reactor design was approved by the Nuclear Regulatory Commission after 1993 and it is placed in service by 2021. The total credit that could be claimed is subject to certain limitations. (Cost: $278 million over 11 years.)

● **Operating loss carryover for certain electric utility companies.** The law extends for five years the net operating loss (NOL) carryback period for taxable years 2003 through 2005 for certain electric utility companies. In general, the NOL — the amount by which a taxpayer's allowable deductions exceed gross income — may be carried back two years, or carried forward 20 years, to offset taxable income in those years.

Under the extension, refunds can be claimed only through 2008, and the amount of the NOL is limited to 20 percent of combined qualifying investment in transmission and pollution control equipment.

## DOMESTIC FOSSIL FUEL PROVISIONS

● **Non-conventional fuel production credit.** The law makes the credit for producing fuel from an unconventional source — such as oil produced from shale and tar sands — part of the general business credit. The credit is equal to $3 per barrel, or British thermal unit (BTU) oil barrel equivalent, adjusted for inflation. Unused credits can be carried back one year or carried forward up to 20 years. The provision is effective beginning in 2006, but no carryback of unused credits is permitted for taxes paid prior to 2006. The credit is set to expire in 2007. The law also allows a production credit for facilities that produce coke or coke gas. (Cost: $101 million over 11 years.)

● **Expensing for equipment used in refining liquid fuels.** Certain businesses are allowed to deduct 50 percent of the cost of liquid fuel refining equipment in the year the equipment is bought. The other 50 percent of the cost can be written off over a 10-year period, as was the case for all such costs before enactment. The new deduction applies to equipment placed in use after enactment and before 2012. (Cost: $406 million over 11 years.)

● **Depreciation of natural gas pipelines.** The law decreases the recovery, or depreciation, period for natural gas distribution pipelines from 20 years to 15 years. The provision applies to gas lines placed in service after April 11, 2005, and expires at the end of 2010. A seven-year depreciation period is allowed for natural gas-gathering lines. The allowable amount of depreciation can not be reduced by the alternative minimum tax. (Cost: $1 billion over 11 years.)

● **Natural gas prepayment exempt from arbitrage rules.** The measure exempts from arbitrage rules certain bond-financed prepayments by public utilities for natural gas, by creating an exception to the general rule that tax-exempt, bond-financed prepayments violate the arbi-

trage restrictions. (Cost: $53 million over 11 years.)

● **Geological and geophysical expenses.** Companies can amortize geological and geophysical costs incurred in connection with oil and gas exploration in the United States over two years. Previously, geological and geophysical costs were not deductible as ordinary business expenses in the year they occurred. (Cost: $974 million over 11 years.)

● **Small oil and gas producers.** The law allows more small oil and gas producers to take advantage of special tax breaks by changing the definition of "independent producer" from a producer that refines no more than 50,000 barrels a day to one that produces no more than 75,000 barrels a day. It allows the limit to be calculated on a yearly average basis, rather than on a daily basis as under prior law. (Cost: $158 million over 11 years.)

## CONSERVATION AND OTHER PROVISIONS

● **Deduction for energy-efficient commercial buildings.** The measure creates a deduction for energy-efficient commercial buildings that meet a 50 percent energy reduction standard. The maximum deduction is $1.80 per square foot of the building; the law also allows a 60-cents-per-square-foot deduction for building subsystems. The provision is effective beginning in 2006 and applies to property placed in service before 2008. (Cost: $243 million over 11 years.)

● **Business credit for construction of energy-efficient homes.** As part of the business tax credit, the law establishes a credit to contractors for the construction of new energy-efficient homes. Contractors can claim a $1,000 credit for construction that reduces energy consumption by 30 percent for manufactured homes, or $2,000 for homes with construction that reduces energy consumption by 50 percent. The provision applies to homes whose construction is "substantially" completed after 2005 and which are purchased prior to 2008. (Cost: $28 million over 11 years.)

● **Credit for improving energy efficiency.** The law establishes a 10 percent tax credit for the cost of certain energy-efficient improvements to existing homes, including improvements to insulation. It creates credits of up to $50 for the purchase of advanced main air-circulating fans, and up to $150 for natural gas, propane or oil furnaces or hot water boilers. The credit applies to improvements made in 2006 and 2007. (Cost: $556 million over three years.)

● **Credit for energy-efficient appliances.** A manufacturer tax credit is allowed for certain energy-efficient clothes washers, dishwashers and refrigerators. The amount of the credit depends on the appliance and its energy efficiency. The provision applies to appliances produced in 2006 and 2007; the manufacturer cannot claim credits in excess of $75 million for all taxable years. (Cost: $180 million over two years.)

● **Credit for energy-efficient equipment.** The law establishes a non-refundable 30 percent tax credit for the purchase of certain solar water-heating equipment, photovoltaic devices and fuel-cell equipment used exclusively for purposes other than heating swimming pools and hot tubs. The credit applies to purchases made in 2006 and 2007; the maximum credit for each of these systems is $2,000. (Cost: $31 million in fiscal 2006 through 2008.)

● **Business fuel cell investment credit.** The law creates a 30 percent tax credit for the installation of qualified fuel cells, and a 10 percent credit for the purchase of stationary microturbine power plants. The credit is available for 2006 and 2007. (Cost: $222 million over 11 years.)

● **R&D energy research credit.** The measure modifies the research and development tax credit and makes expenditures to certain research consortia for energy-related research eligible for the credit. (Cost: $92 million over 11 years.)

## ALTERNATIVE MOTOR VEHICLE AND FUELS INCENTIVES

● **Alternative power motor vehicle credit.** Under the law, tax credits will be allowed for the purchase of hybrid, fuel-cell, advanced "lean burn" technology and other alternative-power vehicles. The amount of the credit will vary based on the rated fuel economy of the vehicle and its estimated lifetime fuel savings. The credit ranges from $400 to $3,400 for hybrid cars and trucks; from $4,000 to $44,000 for fuel-cell vehicles; and from $4,000 to $32,000 for alternative-fuel vehicles. The credits are available for vehicles purchased in 2006 through 2014 for fuel-cell vehicles; before 2011 for hybrid cars, light trucks, advanced lean-burn technology vehicles and alternative-fuel motor vehicles; and before 2010 for hybrid medium and heavy trucks. The tax credit declines for hybrid vehicles in the quarter after a manufacturer's hybrid vehicle sales exceed 60,000. (Cost: $874 million over 11 years.)

● **Credit for installation of alternative fueling stations.** The law allows a 30 percent tax credit in the first year for the cost of equipment for refueling vehicles with alternative fuels, either at a business or a residence. To qualify, the fuels must be at least 85 percent ethanol, natural gas, liquefied natural gas, liquefied petroleum gas or hydrogen, or any mixture of diesel and biodiesel fuel containing at least 20 percent biodiesel. In the case of retail clean-fuel refueling equipment, the allowable maximum is $30,000; the maximum credit for residential use is $1,000. The credit is effective for equipment placed in service in 2006 and 2007. (Cost: $71 million over 11 years.)

● **Extension of income and excise tax credits for biodiesel fuel.** The law extends, from 2006 through 2008, the income tax credit and excise tax credit for biodiesel and biodiesel mixtures, and provides a similar income and excise tax credit for renewable diesel fuel. (Cost: $194 million over three years.)

● **Small-business agri-biodiesel producer credit.** The biodiesel fuels credit is expanded by the addition of a 10-cents-per-gallon credit for agri-biodiesel produced by small producers. The credit is available on the date of enactment and expires at the end of 2008. The limits on production capacity for small ethanol producers eligible for the credit is increased from 30 million to 60 million gallons. (Cost: $181 million over 11 years.)

## REVENUE-RAISING PROVISIONS

● **Oil Spill Liability Trust Fund.** The law reinstates, through 2014, the 5-cents-per-barrel Oil Spill Liability Trust Fund tax beginning in April 2006, or on the last day of any calendar quarter for which the Treasury Department estimates that the unobligated balance of the fund is less than $2 billion.

The tax, which is credited to the Oil Spill Liability Trust Fund, will be suspended during a quarter if the department estimates that the unobligated balance exceeds $2.7 billion.

The tax was imposed between 1990 and 1994 on imported petroleum products and crude oil received at a U.S. refinery, and any domestically produced crude oil exported from the United States if the crude oil had not been taxed before exportation. Taxes received were credited to the Oil Spill Liability Trust Fund. (Revenue: $2.5 billion over 11 years.)

● **Extend LUST tax.** Under the law, the LUST tax is extended through Sept. 30, 2011. Additionally, the tax is applied to dyed fuel. (Revenue: $349 million over 11 years.)

● **Modify recapture rules for amortization of intangible assets.** The law makes changes to the recapture rules for amortizing the cost of Section 197 intangibles, such as information base, licenses or permits issued by a government agency or a franchise, trademark or trade name. (Revenue: $171 million over 11 years.) ■

# Oil Refineries Bill Dropped in Senate

LESS THAN TWO MONTHS after President Bush signed a wide ranging energy package designed to boost domestic energy supplies and reduce the use of foreign oil (PL 109-58), House GOP leaders won passage of a new energy bill. This time the bill was designed to spur construction of oil refineries. Democrats and moderate Republicans lambasted the legislation, calling it a giveaway to the industry. A Senate committee rejected a similar bill.

Joe L. Barton, R-Texas, chairman of the House Energy and Commerce Committee, promoted the bill as a way to alleviate distribution bottlenecks of the kind that occurred in the Gulf Coast after hurricanes Katrina and Rita. The storms devastated much of the energy infrastructure in the Gulf of Mexico region, which contained 47 percent of the nation's oil refining capacity and 19 percent of the natural gas production. The national retail price for gasoline increased by 46 cents to $3.07 per gallon in the week after Hurricane Katrina.

Supporters stressed that no U.S. refineries had been built since 1976, and that the number of operating facilities had dropped by more than half since 1981. "We cannot stop hurricanes, but we can mitigate some of the . . . impacts," Barton said. "Now is the time to start to correct the problem and to build new refineries, in the United States."

The bill sought to put the Energy Department in charge of the permit process for new refineries, expedite court challenges and allow companies to petition the government for economic damages if their refinery projects were unnecessarily delayed. It called for limiting to six the number of specialty gasoline and diesel fuel blends that had to be produced to meet regional air pollution rules.

The bill also called for the president to designate potential new refinery sites on federal lands, including three on closed military bases.

In response to soaring gas prices, it specified that it was illegal for gasoline or diesel fuel vendors to engage in price-gouging in any region that had been declared a major disaster area, and required the Federal Trade Commission (FTC) to investigate and report to Congress on possible price-gouging after hurricanes Katrina and Rita.

The Congressional Budget Office calculated that the bill would increase direct spending by $3 billion over 10 years.

Most Democrats and a group of moderate Republicans said Barton was taking advantage of the national crisis created by Katrina and Rita to advance legislation that would undermine environmental safeguards to help an already profitable industry.

Before the floor debate, Barton dropped a contentious White House-backed provision that would have clarified for the courts an EPA rule designed to make it easier for power plants to upgrade their facilities without installing new equipment to reduce smokestack pollutants.

The Senate Environment and Public Works Committee tried to mark up a similar bill, but the measure was defeated on a 9-9 vote.

## LEGISLATIVE ACTION
### HOUSE COMMITTEE ACTION

The House Energy and Commerce Committee approved Barton's bill (HR 3893 — H Rept 109-244, Part 1) by voice vote Sept. 29 at the end of a 16-hour markup.

**BOX SCORE**

**BILLS:** HR 3893, S 1772

**LEGISLATIVE ACTION:**

**House** passed HR 3893 (H Rept 109-244, Part 1), 212-210 on Oct. 7.

**Senate** Environment and Public Works Committee rejected S 1772, 9-9, on Oct. 26.

Much of the debate was over a White House-backed provision to amend "new source review" language in the Clean Air Act that required industries upgrading their facilities to install modern anti-pollution controls unless the improvements were routine maintenance.

The bill proposed to codify a regulation issued by the Bush administration changing the definition of routine maintenance. That regulation was being challenged in court. Barton included the provision, which would shield the administration from such court challenges, at the administration's request. He said it was the White House's "top priority."

During the markup, the committee:

▸ Rejected, 16-24, an attempt to limit the new source review provision to oil and gas facilities.

▸ Agreed by voice vote to add language directing the FTC to crack down on alleged price gouging by gasoline and diesel fuel sellers, with penalties of up to $11,000 per day for violators.

▸ Defeated, 23-27, a Democratic substitute amendment that would have charged the Energy Department with constructing and operating a "strategic refining reserve" similar in concept to the Strategic Petroleum Reserve, the nation's crude oil stockpile. It also called for steeper fines and broader federal authority to investigate price-gouging throughout petroleum markets.

### HOUSE FLOOR ACTION

House Republican leaders eked out a 212-210 win for the bill Oct. 7, after holding the balloting open an extra 40 minutes while they persuaded two Republicans to change their "no" votes to "yes." Democrats chanted, "Shame! Shame! Shame!" when the gavel finally fell. *(House vote 519, p. H-164)*

The night before the vote, Barton dropped the new source review provisions at the request of the House leadership and the White House. The provisions had become a lightning rod for most Democrats and some moderate Republicans, who said the plan was the latest example of House GOP leaders using the hurricanes in the Gulf Coast as an excuse to try to get rid of environmental rules unpopular with energy companies. Barton said Speaker J. Dennis Hastert, R-Ill., and White House Chief of Staff Andrew H. Card Jr. decided late Oct. 6 that it would be wise to remove the provision from the bill, hold hearings and move it later as separate legislation.

That did not go far enough to satisfy bill critics, including a small band of moderate Republicans, who said the bill was fatally flawed because it would compromise too many existing environmental laws.

Democrats again offered their substitute, but the amendment was rejected, 199-222. *(House vote 517, p. H-164)*

At one point, sponsors had hoped to attach another bill that would have allowed energy leasing in protected coastal waters and the Arctic National Wildlife Refuge (ANWR). But Resources Chairman Richard W. Pombo, R-Calif., decided to hold off on that plan after the measure drew sharp criticism from Florida lawmakers and the state's Republican governor, Jeb Bush.

Pombo's original bill would have let coastal states choose to opt out of a federal moratorium on energy leasing on the Outer Continental

Shelf — already a tough sell in the Senate and with Florida lawmakers. But in marking up the bill, the Resources Committee went further, adopting an amendment to lift the moratorium outright for natural gas development, leaving states at the mercy of the federal government.

## SENATE COMMITTEE ACTION

The Senate Environment and Public Works Committee rejected a narrower refinery bill (S 1772) by a 9-9 vote, after moderate Republican Lincoln Chafee of Rhode Island joined Democrats in voting against the measure. Chafee said Congress should be addressing gasoline consumption as well as demand.

The measure, sponsored by Chairman James M. Inhofe, R-Okla.,

included provisions to reduce the number of "boutique" fuels used to meet air-quality regulations, allow states to opt into a new program streamlining the permitting process for new refinery projects, encourage the siting of new refineries on former military bases and authorize federal funding for state and local organizations working to redevelop those sites.

Opponents argued that the bill would lower environmental standards and authorize monetary aid for oil refiners that were already profiting from gasoline prices.

The committee rejected, 8-10, a Democratic substitute that would have directed the EPA to establish and run refineries as part of a Strategic Refinery Reserve similar to the Strategic Petroleum Reserve. ∎

# ANWR Drilling Proposal Blocked Again

REPUBLICAN LEADERS SAW 2005 as their best chance in years to win enactment of a law opening Alaska's Arctic National Wildlife Refuge (ANWR) to energy exploration. Republican gains in the November election seemed to put them within striking distance of achieving what had been the centerpiece of President Bush's energy policy since 2001.

But in the end, they came away empty-handed. It was the second time in less than three years that an ANWR drilling proposal died in a GOP-controlled Congress.

Early in the year, House Republicans succeeded in passing ANWR provisions as part of their energy overhaul bill, but they ultimately agreed to drop it to get the final measure through the Senate (PL 109-58).

Drilling supporters remained confident, however, that they could pass the proposal as part of a huge budget reconciliation bill expected in the fall. Such bills could not be filibustered in the Senate — which had been the graveyard for past ANWR proposals — so backers would only need a simple majority, not the 60 votes required to limit debate.

The Senate passed the budget reconciliation bill in November with the ANWR initiative intact. This time, however, the House proved to be the stumbling block. Enough GOP moderates opposed opening ANWR that House leaders conceded they could not win adoption of the conference report unless they removed the ANWR provisions.

Sen. Ted Stevens, R-Alaska, a tireless proponent of opening the wildlife refuge to drilling, agreed to move the provisions to the conference report on the fiscal 2006 Defense appropriations bill. That angered enough senators to halt work on the conference report, leaving the leadership with no choice but to drop the provisions. A bitter Stevens told his Senate colleagues, "I'm going to go to every one of your states, and I'm going to tell them what you've done."

Pete V. Domenici, chairman of the Senate Energy and Natural Resources Committee, vowed to return to the issue in 2006. "We will try again," said Domenici. "I will seek to include an ANWR provision in the budget resolution next spring just as we did this year. I will work to keep it in the budget reconciliation and hope for a more favorable outcome in the House."

## BACKGROUND

Environmentalists and those who wanted to open more public lands for energy development had been battling over ANWR for 25 years. The refuge, which totaled about 19 million acres, was estab-

lished in 1960 and expanded in 1980 under the Alaska National Interest Lands Conservation Act (PL 96-487), which reserved about 1.5 million acres of the coast for potential energy development. The Reagan administration first proposed opening the federal wildlife preserve for drilling in 1987. However, the 1980 law required a separate act of Congress to allow energy exploration, and the only such measure to pass both houses of Congress was vetoed by President Bill Clinton in 1995. *(1980 Almanac, p. 575; 1995 Almanac, p. 5-22)*

The U.S. Geological Survey estimated that the refuge could produce between 500,000 and 1.4 million barrels of crude oil a day at peak production. By comparison, the United States consumed some 20.4 million barrels a day, according to the Department of Energy.

Drilling advocates argued that the development of ANWR would reduce U.S. dependence on foreign oil, reduce gas prices and result in hundreds of thousands of new jobs. They said drilling and production would not harm wildlife, citing Alaska's nearby Prudhoe Bay as an example where oil development and wildlife co-existed and flourished. New, advanced technology, supporters said, made it easier to reap the maximum amount of fuel on less land and with fewer adverse effects on the environment.

Environmentalists argued that the area was unique and ecologically fragile, and that drilling would lay waste to vast areas of the tundra, its water sources and its wildlife. They noted that the amount of recoverable oil in ANWR was unknown and that it could take decades for production to be realized. Drilling in ANWR, they said, would have no effect on energy supplies or price.

## LEGISLATIVE ACTION
### ENERGY OVERHAUL

The House version of the energy policy overhaul bill, which passed 249-183 on April 21, included a section authorizing the Interior Department to grant leases for oil and gas exploration, development and production in 1.5 million acres of ANWR. The measure barred the export of oil or gas products from ANWR. *(House vote 132, p. H-42; energy overhaul, p. 8-3)*

The bill included provisions requiring the department to ensure that drilling and production in ANWR would have "no significant adverse effect" on fish and wildlife and their habitats, and banned above-ground surface occupancy by oil and gas producers in special areas. It required seasonal limits on oil and gas activities where necessary to avoid adverse effects during periods of concentrated fish and wildlife breeding, nesting and migration. The bill provided for expedited judi-

cial review of any actions taken in ANWR by the Interior Department.

Companies would pay royalties of at least 12.5 percent of the value of the oil or gas they removed. Half of the money would go to Alaska and half to the federal government.

The House rejected, 200-231, an attempt by Edward J. Markey, D-Mass., to strike the ANWR drilling provisions. *(House vote 122, p. H-40)*

The Senate bill did not include ANWR provisions. Knowing the proposal would trigger a filibuster, the two bill managers — Republican Domenici and Democrat Jeff Bingaman, both of New Mexico — left the issue out. Bingaman was the ranking member on the Energy and Natural Resources Committee.

When the bill went to conference, House leaders agreed to drop the section on ANWR, because supporters did not have the 60 votes to stop a filibuster. Their hopes lay instead with a reconciliation bill.

## BUDGET RESOLUTION

The first step toward including the ANWR provisions in the 2005 reconciliation bill came in April, when both chambers adopted a fiscal 2006 budget resolution (H Con Res 95) that assumed the federal government would generate $2.4 billion by leasing the drilling rights. That arcane step was crucial: It was the only way the ANWR proposal could be part of the filibuster-proof budget reconciliation package. *(Budget resolution, p. 4-9)*

The key vote came in the Senate on March 16, when GOP leaders succeeded in blocking a Democratic attempt to strike the drilling provisions from the budget resolution. The gain of four GOP seats in November provided the winning margin, allowing them to defeat the amendment by Maria Cantwell of Washington, 49-51. Seven Republicans voted to drop the ANWR provision, while three Democrats voted to keep the language. *(Senate vote 52, p. S-12)*

Two years before, the Senate had voted 52-48 to remove the provision from a budget resolution, a step that was the death knell for ANWR legislation for that session. *(2003 Almanac, p. 5-11)*

"The House has passed it a number of times; the hurdle was always the Senate," said Frank Maisano, a Washington energy lobbyist.

## BUDGET RECONCILIATION

When Congress began assembling the budget reconciliation bill in the fall, the Senate went first. The Energy and Natural Resources Committee approved language Oct. 19 to authorize the Interior Department to hold two lease sales for oil and gas drilling in ANWR by 2010. It said the leases would produce $2.5 billion in revenue over five years. *(Budget reconciliation, p. 4-13)*

The Senate passed the bill, 52-47, on Nov. 3, after again defeating an attempt by Cantwell to strip out the ANWR provision. Cantwell's amendment was rejected, 48-51. *(Senate votes 303, 288, pp. S-59, S-57)*

The Senate also adopted, 83-16, an amendment by Ron Wyden, D-Ore., and Jim Talent, R-Mo., to ban the export of oil or gas from ANWR. The proposal was consistent with House language, and Stevens said he backed it partly to boost ANWR leasing prospects in the other chamber. *(Senate vote 289, p. S-57)*

In the House, where GOP leaders were having a much more difficult time balancing the demands of moderates and conservatives in their caucus, the Resources Committee approved similar ANWR provisions Oct. 26. The leadership was having difficulty finding enough trade-offs

to win floor support for the budget reconciliation bill. On Nov. 8, 26 GOP lawmakers signed a letter urging leaders to drop ANWR drilling from the bill. The next day, following a meeting with House moderates, acting Majority Leader Roy Blunt, R-Mo., agreed to do so. With all House Democrats prepared to vote against the measure anyway — even a handful who in the past had supported ANWR drilling — GOP leaders had to get the moderates on board.

The House passed the bill, without the ANWR provisions, by a narrow vote of 217-215 on Nov. 18. *(House vote 601, p. H-190)*

For a number of GOP senators, including Stevens, Domenici and Lisa Murkowski of Alaska, ANWR drilling was by far the most important provision in the bill. Leaving it out also was a blow to the White House. But House leaders said they could not get the conference report through their chamber if it contained the provisions. Stevens, who chaired the Senate Defense Appropriations Subcommittee, agreed to move the proposal to the conference report on the Defense spending bill, where House leaders predicted it would have a better chance.

The House adopted the reconciliation conference report, 212-206, on Dec. 19, but the Senate raised other objections, forcing the House to vote again in 2006. The House cleared the bill, 216-214, on Feb. 1 (S 1932 — PL 109-171). *(House vote 670, p. H-212)*

## DEFENSE APPROPRIATIONS

By the time House and Senate conferees on the fiscal 2006 Defense spending bill met Dec. 18, the legislation had been selected to carry the ANWR drilling plan. In a bid to sweeten the deal, Stevens earmarked part of the future profits from ANWR drilling leases for additional aid to the Gulf Coast, which was suffering in the aftermath of hurricanes Katrina and Rita, as well as for border security. *(Defense appropriations, p. 2-15)*

The bill had to clear before lawmakers left for the holidays, especially because it included $50 billion in emergency funds that the Pentagon said were urgently needed to support operations in Iraq and Afghanistan. The House overwhelmingly adopted the conference report Dec. 19, with the ANWR provisions included. The vote was 308-106. *(House vote 669, p. H-212)*

But the ANWR add-on sparked a bitter dispute in the Senate. Stevens argued that the drilling was related to national security because it would reduce reliance on foreign oil supplies. Democrats accused Republicans of stretching Senate rules and playing politics with funding for the troops. Ranking Appropriations Democrat Robert C. Byrd of West Virginia, a longtime friend of Stevens, said, "I love this man, but I love the Senate more!" An attempt to cut off the debate failed, 56-44, four votes short of the number needed. *(Senate vote 364, p. S-71)*

Because most House members had already left for the year, Senate GOP leaders used an enrolling resolution to get rid of the ANWR provisions. The Senate adopted the resolution, 48-45, then cleared the Defense spending bill, 93-0. The House adopted the enrolling resolution by voice vote Dec. 22. *(Senate votes 365, 366, p. S-71)*

"This has been the saddest day of my life," Stevens said after the vote. "I am drawing the line now with a lot of people I have worked with before. I really am. I can't put in my mind the amount of time, the days I have spent with you working on your problems, and to know you said about me the things you said in the last two months. I say goodbye to the Senate tonight. Thank you very much." ∎

# Senate Delays on Endangered Species

THE HOUSE PASSED A BILL in September that called for sweeping changes to the 1973 Endangered Species Act, but the Senate took no action on the measure in the first session.

The House bill — written by Resources Chairman Richard W. Pombo, R-Calif. — proposed to revise scientific standards used in developing endangered species policies, end the federal government's power to protect critical habitats and compensate affected private property owners.

Pombo and his supporters said the bill would streamline the environmental law and enlist the help of landowners instead of penalizing them for having threatened or endangered species on their property.

The 1973 Endangered Species Law (PL 93-205) was enacted to protect wildlife at risk of extinction because of human development and pollution. It allowed the Fish and Wildlife Service and the National Marine Fisheries Service to designate species as endangered or threatened, and to issue regulations protecting their habitats to increase their numbers. There were nearly 1,300 domestic species listed as threatened or endangered. The law had not been reauthorized since 1992, but Congress had continued to appropriate money for the agencies to issue and enforce regulations.

There was broad agreement among lawmakers of both parties, ranchers and environmental groups that the law needed to be updated in light of new challenges. Only 17 species had increased their populations enough to be removed from endangered lists since the law's enactment, and the federal government faced numerous lawsuits over the status of critical habitat land.

But there was sharp disagreement over what should be done. The bill reflected the view of Pombo and many Republicans that the government should provide incentives for landowners to voluntarily conserve species on their land, instead of having mandatory restrictions placed on them. Many Democrats and lawmakers from more urban districts opposed Pombo's approach as providing a financial windfall for private interests and stripping away the environmental protections that were essential to restoring endangered species.

Lincoln Chafee, R-R.I., who chaired the Senate Environment and Public Works subcommittee with jurisdiction over endangered species, did not bring the bill up in 2005. Instead, Chafee and other senators requested a study of the critical habitat issue, which was not expected to be completed until early 2006.

## HIGHLIGHTS

The House-passed bill would:
- Reauthorize the Endangered Species Act through 2010.
- Eliminate the ability of federal officials to protect plant and animal species in danger of extinction by designating areas of "critical habitat" and placing restrictions on use of the land or water.
- Replace the critical habitat designation with a much-expanded recovery program to increase the populations of endangered species. Each recovery plan would have to contain measurable steps and identify areas of "special value" to the conservation of the species. These special value areas would replace the critical habitat designation for any species whose recovery plan was being developed shortly before the bill's enactment. The bill did not specify whether recovery plans would be legally binding.
- Authorize the Interior Department to enter into species recovery agreements with private landowners, in which the landowner would develop and carry out conservation plans and the government would provide grants to pay the costs of implementation. The grant money would have to be used to conserve a species by increasing its numbers.
- Require the federal government to compensate property owners who were adversely affected by a decision about an endangered species. The property owner would be reimbursed for the fair market value of the land use if no compromise could be reached to permit otherwise legal development.
- Change the standard for making decisions about endangered species to the "best available scientific data," defined as the best information available to the Interior Department at the time of a decision to protect a species. The information would have to come from peer-reviewed sources. The existing standard was the "best scientific and commercial data available."
- Expand the Interior Department's ability to enter into conservation agreements with states to protect species at risk of being threatened or endangered. Existing law allowed such agreements only for species already listed as endangered or threatened.

## LEGISLATIVE ACTION

As chairman of the House Resources Committee, Pombo spent several months negotiating with committee Democrats before releasing a detailed bill in September. The bipartisan effort paid off Sept. 22, when eight committee Democrats joined all but two Republicans to approve the measure, 26-12. (HR 3824— H Rept 109-237)

The House passed the bill, 229-193, on Sept. 29, after narrowly rejecting a Democratic substitute amendment. *(House vote 506, p. H-160)*

A group of 23 moderate Republican House members had urged Majority Leader Tom DeLay, R-Texas, not to rush the bill to the floor, saying it contained "perhaps the most profound changes to environmental law since the Clean Air Act Amendments of 1990."

A substitute, offered by George Miller, D-Calif., won support from 29 Republicans, but failed, 206-216. *(House vote 505, p. H-160)*

Supporters said the substitute would eliminate the "critical habitat" designation and rely instead on recovery plans. It also would offer new financial incentives and legal protections to landowners to save species and require greater state involvement in decision making. But they said the recovery plans would be enforceable, and the grants would be discretionary, not mandatory spending as under the bill.

Pombo succeeded in offsetting the Republican votes he lost with support from 36 Democrats, many from Western and Midwestern states. ∎

# Debate Over Corps Management Lingers

A BILL TO AUTHORIZE $11.6 billion in popular navigation, flood control and environmental projects passed in the House in July. The Senate Environment and Public Works Committee approved a similar bill in April, but the measure got no further in the first session.

The legislation would reauthorize the Water Resources Development Act (PL 106-541), which gives the Army Corps of Engineers the authority to carry out civilian water projects.

Farmers and other industries that depend on the nation's rivers to ship goods were particularly eager for the corps to get started on new projects, such as the replacement of locks and dams along the upper Mississippi and Illinois rivers. But Congress had been unable to renew the law since it expired in 2002 because of disagreements over how to improve the management of corps projects.

A coalition of environmental and taxpayer-watchdog groups wanted projects to undergo more stringent reviews and meet strict environmental restoration requirements. Lobbyists for shipbuilders, port authorities and others who benefited from the projects warned that new federal requirements would simply add to government waste by bogging down the system.

Supporters of the House bill said it would do more to improve corps operations than any previous legislation. But a White House statement of administration policy said the bill still "does not include much-needed policy and program reforms and has a significant overall cost."

Even critics of corps operations, however, were reluctant to stand in the way of a bill that had enthusiastic support from shippers, port authorities, and a range of governors and local officials seeking specific projects.

The largest project in both bills was a $3.6 billion plan to rebuild seven locks and dams along the upper Mississippi and Illinois rivers and to do related environmental rehabilitation. The bill also would authorize large flood control and environmental restoration projects along the Louisiana coast and in the Florida Everglades, and increase the federal share of the cost of deep-dredging ocean harbors, a major demand of shipping interests

## LEGISLATIVE ACTION
### HOUSE COMMITTEE, FLOOR ACTION

The House passed its water projects bill by a vote of 406-14 on July 14. The Transportation and Infrastructure Committee had given voice vote approval to the measure (HR 2864 — H Rept 109-154) on June 22. (*House vote 378, p. H-116*)

Sponsored by committee Chairman Don Young, R-Alaska, the bill provided for the corps to undertake nearly 700 projects and studies.

John J. "Jimmy" Duncan Jr., R-Tenn., chairman of the Water Resources and Environment Subcommittee, said the lengthy list of projects reflected pent-up demand caused by Congress' inability to clear a water development bill since 2000. Lawmakers typically reauthorized water projects every two years.

"This bill does more for corps reform than any bill in the history of the Congress," said Duncan. Under the bill, water projects costing $50 million or more would be subject to an independent peer review process. Smaller projects also would undergo peer review if they were

**BOX SCORE**

**BILLS:** HR 2864, S 728

**LEGISLATIVE ACTION:**

**House** passed HR 2864 (H Rept 109-154), 406-14, on July 14.

**Senate** Environment and Public Works Committee approved S 728 (S Rept 109-61) by voice vote April 13.

considered controversial. Peer review panels would be established by the National Academy of Sciences or a similar independent scientific organization.

For improvements to the Upper Mississippi River-Illinois Waterway System, the bill authorized $235 million for short-term navigation improvements, $1.8 billion for seven new locks and $1.6 billion for environmental restoration. That proposal survived an effort by Jeff Flake, R-Ariz., and Earl Blumenauer, D-Ore., to make the authorization contingent on an increase in barge traffic through the existing locks to an annual average of more than 35 million tons a year per lock for 2007 to 2009. According to the corps, the average was 28.8 million tons per lock in 2004.

Kenny Hulshof, R-Mo., said the reason for declining traffic passing through the Depression-era locks was precisely because of "the declining conditions of these locks and dams."

The bill also authorized about $1 billion each for the Louisiana coastal and Everglades projects.

### SENATE COMMITTEE ACTION

The Senate Environment and Public Works Committee approved its water projects bill (S 728 — S Rept 109-61) by voice vote April 13, but not before some committee members raised longstanding concerns that many corps projects were unnecessary and environmentally harmful.

The panel's ranking minority member, James M. Jeffords, I-Vt., said the measure retreated from a compromise worked out by committee members in 2004 that required the corps to perform more rigorous environmental reviews. "The simple fact is that we will only get a bill passed on the Senate floor and sent to the president if we aim for the center," responded the bill's sponsor, Christopher S. Bond, R-Mo. He said the bill failed to come to a vote in the Senate in 2004 because of industry opposition to the compromise language. "If we do what we did last year with policy issues, we will end up where we did last year, with no bill."

The bill required "major engineering, scientific and technical work products" related to corps projects to undergo a peer review, as long as the review did not delay the project or increase its cost. It also would give the corps the option of purchasing credits from a mitigation or conservation bank in lieu of taking action when it concluded that environmental restoration on a site would be too difficult. .

The 2003 bill had required peer review for a broader range of projects and provided for creation of a commission to investigate corps management and environmental practices and submit a report to Congress.

During the markup, the committee:

▸ Rejected by voice vote an amendment by Jeffords that would have required peer review of corps projects and established a Water Resources Planning Council to advise the corps on changing its planning process. Bond said the amendment would impose "significant, if not insurmountable, burdens" on corps projects.

▸ Adopted, 12-6, an amendment by David Vitter, R-La., to clarify the limits of corps jurisdiction over obstructions to maritime traffic on private property. Vitter and Bond said the corps had used a clause in the existing law to order changes on privately owned wetlands that, as Bond put it, "nobody in their right mind would want to navigate." ∎

**Chapter 9**

# FOREIGN POLICY &
# INTELLIGENCE

# Foreign Relations Bills Founder Under Weight of Amendments

**B**OTH CHAMBERS BEGAN work on versions of a foreign relations authorization bill, but prospects for completing the legislation appeared slim.

The House passed its bill by a comfortable margin in July, but the Senate's effort stalled on the floor in April. The bills were very different, and the House measure had at least a dozen provisions that the White House opposed. Congress regularly cleared stand-alone State Department authorization bills and smaller, targeted foreign policy measures, but no omnibus foreign affairs measure had become law in 20 years.

The House-passed bill proposed authorizing $20.8 billion for State Department operations and some foreign aid programs over two years. The Senate bill proposed $34 billion over two years for the State Department and for U.S. foreign aid programs, including many that were not in the House version.

The Senate bill won approval from the Foreign Relations Committee in March, but Chairman Richard G. Lugar, R-Ind., pulled it from the floor when he was unable to reach an agreement to limit debate or amendments. One amendment adopted before the bill was pulled called for lifting the so-called Mexico City policy, which barred U.S. aid to international organizations that performed abortions or provided consultations for abortion. The White House threatened to veto any legislation that lifted the ban.

In 2004, a similar bill was dropped from the Senate floor calendar due to fears that it could get bogged down in an unrelated debate, with Edward M. Kennedy, D-Mass., threatening to attach an amendment raising the minimum wage. Because foreign affairs authorizing bills seldom reached the Senate floor, much of the foreign aid clout in Congress had shifted to the appropriators rather than the authorizing committees. *(2004 Almanac, p. 11-16)*

## LEGISLATIVE ACTION
### SENATE COMMITTEE ACTION

The Senate Foreign Relations Committee approved a combined State Department and foreign aid authorization bill written by Lugar on a bipartisan vote of 18-0 on March 3 (S 600 — S Rept 109-35). The bill authorized $11.2 billion for State Department programs and $22.8 billion for foreign aid for fiscal 2006.

Approval only came after Republicans narrowly defeated a Democratic effort to reduce the $3 billion in the bill for President Bush's signature Millennium Challenge Account (MCA) in favor of shoring up more traditional aid programs. The MCA was created in 2003 (PL 108-199) to reward developing countries that held free elections, adopted good government programs and opened up their economic markets. It had not yet distributed any money, though State Department offi-

**BOX SCORE**

**BILLS:** HR 2601, S 600

**LEGISLATIVE ACTION:**

**Senate** Foreign Relations Committee approved S 600 (S Rept 109-35), 18-0, on March 3.

**Senate** bill pulled from floor April 6.

**House** passed HR 2601 (H Rept 109-168), 351-78, on July 20.

cials said it would do so soon. Republicans said the program gave developing countries not just a handout but an incentive to change their economies and government systems.

The committee rejected, 9-9, an attempt by Paul S. Sarbanes, D-Md., to restore about $700 million that Bush wanted to cut from traditional programs for children's health, UNICEF and other State Department-administered accounts. Sarbanes proposed to offset the extra funds by cutting $425 million from the MCA and trimming $275 million from other foreign aid, including assistance to Haiti, Sudan, Afghanistan and Ethiopia. "We were led to believe that the MCA would not come at the expense of . . . core humanitarian and development accounts," said Sarbanes. "It will be many more years before we begin seeing results [from the MCA]. These programs that are being cut, we know these programs."

### SENATE FLOOR ACTION

Although Lugar was eager for a chance to put his imprint on a range of U.S. foreign policy programs, he could not stop a deluge of floor amendments dealing with everything from abortion to trade with Cuba. After two days of debate, he pulled the bill April 6.

While the measure was on the floor, the Senate:

▶ Adopted, 52-46, an amendment by Barbara Boxer, D-Calif., to repeal the Mexico City policy. Under the amendment, organizations would receive U.S. aid if they used their own funds to provide health or medical services that did not violate federal law or the laws of the country in which they were being provided. *(Senate vote 83, p. S-17)*

▶ Adopted by voice vote a Lugar amendment to delete a provision in the underlying bill that would make permanent a 27.1 percent cap on U.S. contributions for United Nations peacekeeping. The Senate rejected, 40-57, an attempt by Joseph R. Biden Jr., D-Del., to maintain the cap for calendar years 2005 through 2007. The administration favored a two-year extension. *(Senate vote 84, p. S-17)*

▶ Agreed, 65-35, to table (kill) an amendment by Byron L. Dorgan, D-N.D., to reduce funding for international broadcasting operations from $641 million to $620 million and prohibit the use of funds for television broadcasts to Cuba. *(Senate vote 85, p. S-17)*

▶ Rejected, 33-67, a motion to table an amendment by Charles E. Schumer, D-N.Y., to impose a 27.5 percent duty on Chinese imports if China did not allow its currency to appreciate relative to the value of the U.S dollar. The president could delay implementing the tariffs and permit their removal if he certified that China had agreed to revalue its currency upward, at or near fair market value. The amendment was still pending when the debate was halted. *(Senate vote 86, p. S-17)*

Among the other pending amendments was a proposal to reverse a recent Treasury Department ruling that required advance payment for agricultural shipments to Cuba. Farm state senators such as Max Baucus, D-Mont., argued that the system was extremely burdensome and would hurt farm trade. Similar provisions had drawn veto threats.

John McCain, R-Ariz., wanted to lift Cold War-era trade restrictions on Ukraine. That stirred opposition in the Finance Committee, which wanted to consider the proposal first before the Senate voted.

### HOUSE COMMITTEE ACTION

The House International Relations Committee approved a two-year State Department authorization bill (HR 2601 — H Rept 109-168) on a 44-0 vote June 9. The panel's Subcommittee on Africa, Global Human Rights and International Operations had approved a draft of the measure by voice vote May 26.

The bill proposed authorizing $10.8 billion in fiscal 2006 and $10 billion in fiscal 2007 for the State Department, international broadcasting activities and various international assistance programs. It placed particular emphasis on security for U.S. diplomatic outposts abroad and included $1.5 billion for embassy improvements, $930 million for border security programs and $690 million to protect embassy personnel in fiscal 2006.

During the markup, the committee:

▶ Rejected, 14-29, an attempt by Darrell Issa, R-Calif., to strike a provision aimed at scaling back military aid to Egypt in favor of economic and educational assistance. The provision would cut $40 million from the $1.26 billion a year in U.S. military aid to Egypt and transfer the money to a new account. To receive the money, Egypt would have to produce plans for economic, political and educational change, as well as a strategy for fighting poverty. Supporters of the provision, including Tom Lantos of California, the committee's ranking Democrat, said the shift in money was needed to push for modernization in Egypt.

"We are the enablers of an Egyptian military buildup that is a horrendous misallocation of funds," Lantos said. "This makes a modest step in the right direction."

Republican Christopher H. Smith of New Jersey, who sponsored the authorization bill, said the funding transfer was a "serious wake-up call"for Egypt.

Issa argued that Egypt was an important partner in the war on terror and was instrumental in training Iraqi soldiers. Although he found support on both sides of the aisle, it was not enough to prevail.

▶ Adopted, 32-9, an amendment asking Bush to provide a plan for establishing a stable Iraqi government that would permit a U.S. drawdown there. The amendment, offered by Joseph Crowley, D-N.Y., was backed by 13 Republicans, including Chairman Henry J. Hyde, R-Ill.

▶ Rejected a pair of Iraq-related proposals by Barbara Lee, D-Calif. An amendment to express the sense of Congress that the president should develop and submit to Congress a plan for the withdrawal of U.S. military forces from Iraq was rejected, 12-33. A proposal to affirm that it was not the policy of the United States to maintain a permanent military presence in Iraq, including future bases, was defeated, 15-29.

### HOUSE FLOOR ACTION

The House voted, 351-78, on July 20 to pass the bill. *(House vote 399, p. H-122)*

A White House statement of administration policy, issued the day of the vote, opposed House passage of the bill. It criticized dozens of provisions, including proposals to shift money away from Egypt's military financing and to recognize Jerusalem as Israel's permanent capital, saying they would undermine the administration's foreign policy. Smith, the bill's sponsor, said he was unconcerned about the White House statement. "These aren't things that rise to the level of a veto threat," he said.

The debate often strayed far from State Department operations to the war in Iraq and the treatment of detained terror suspects.

During the floor debate, the House:

▶ Adopted, 226-195, an amendment by Hyde to withhold up to 50 percent of U.S. dues to the United Nations unless the secretary of State certified by Oct. 1, 2007, that the organization had complied with 32 of 39 changes in its operations. The list included more rigorous budget control, the creation of a U.N. independent oversight board and detailed financial disclosure for top U.N. officials. The House had passed similar provisions as a separate bill (HR 2745) by a vote of 221-184 on June 17. *(House vote 385, p. H-118; House vote 282, p. H-90)*

▶ Adopted by voice vote an amendment by Hyde to mandate sanctions against companies or countries in the arms business with China. The amendment was a toned-down version of a bill (HR 3100) that the House had rejected, 215-203, on July 14 under suspension of the rules, a special procedures that requires a two-thirds majority. The amendment would impose sanctions on governments or companies that knowingly sold military hardware or technology to China. *(House vote 374, p. H-114)*

▶ Adopted, 291-137, a non-binding amendment by Ileana Ros-Lehtinen, R-Fla., that opposed any "premature withdrawal" of U.S. troops from Iraq and warned that setting a date for withdrawal would "embolden" terrorists. "Incessant calls for an established date for withdrawal from Iraq have a negative effect," Ros-Lehtinen said. Democrats called the amendment "unnecessary and inflammatory" and "a Republican PR stunt," but failed in their bid to have it withdrawn and reintroduced as a stand-alone resolution. *(House vote 397, p. H-122)*

▶ Rejected, 203-227, a Democratic attempt to send the bill back to the International Relations Committee to add language asking the president to advise Congress on his benchmarks for a successful strategy in Iraq. The language also stated that it was U.S. policy: to devise a plan to bring stability to Iraq so that the responsibility for Iraq's security could be transferred to the Iraqi people as soon as possible, to provide adequate equipment for U.S. troops and to provide adequate healthcare benefits upon their return. *(House vote 398, p. H-122)*

▶ Adopted, 304-124, a non-binding amendment by Dana Rohrabacher, R-Calif., stating that the detention and interrogation of alleged terrorists at Guantánamo Bay, Cuba, was essential to winning the war against terrorism. *(House vote 396, p. H-122)* ■

# Lawmakers at Odds over DNI Powers

DISPUTES OVER THE BUSH administration's handling of intelligence and its treatment of foreign detainees prevented Congress from completing an intelligence authorization bill for fiscal 2006.

The largely secret annual bill set funding levels for intelligence programs and policy prescriptions for covert action, spy satellites and other intelligence activities. The holdup of the fiscal 2006 bill was not expected to interfere with U.S. intelligence activities, which were paid for in separate appropriations bills.

The House passed its version of the authorization (HR 2475) in June, and the Senate was on the verge of passing its bill (S 1803) in late December, when an unidentified Republican blocked further action, apparently to prevent consideration of several Democratic amendments.

Total spending for the nation's intelligence agencies was classified, but it was believed to be more than $40 billion for fiscal 2006. Both bills proposed scaling back some expensive spy satellite and airborne surveillance programs while expanding and upgrading human intelligence gathering, according to congressional aides. The legislation was the first authorization considered by Congress since it overhauled the intelligence community in 2004 (PL 108-458). *(2004 Almanac, p. 11-3)*

Although committee markups were closed, some of the issues that divided Congress in 2004 clearly resurfaced.

## LEGISLATIVE ACTION
### HOUSE COMMITTEE ACTION

The House Select Committee on Intelligence approved its version of the bill by voice vote May 24 (HR 2475 — H Rept 109-101). Chairman Peter Hoekstra, R-Mich., said the bill focused on improving human intelligence by increasing the number of spies and analysts, and by emphasizing training, especially in foreign languages. The Sept. 11 commission, which released its influential report in 2004, criticized U.S. intelligence agencies for having inadequate numbers of intelligence analysts and collectors with the right skills to penetrate Islamic terrorist cells. The bill reportedly recommended cuts to expensive satellite and surveillance systems. *(Sept. 11 commission, 2004 Almanac, p. 11-8)*

The main controversy in the closed-door markup was over a GOP-backed provision to limit the authority of the new director of national intelligence (DNI), created by the 2004 law. Under the bill, the DNI would be required to notify Congress and receive a response before transferring personnel to any of the new intelligence centers authorized under the 2004 overhaul. The provision had the backing of the Pentagon, which had been suspicious of the DNI's powers over military intelligence agencies from the outset.

The committee rejected an attempt by Jane Harman of California, the panel's top Democrat, to drop the language. The party-line vote was 9-12. Harman argued that the law was supposed to allow the DNI to handle personnel matters without interference from Congress, and that the provision would undermine his authority.

According to the committee report, the measure also ordered the DNI to give Congress a complete inventory of highly secretive "special access programs" operating at U.S. intelligence agencies. Few officials knew these programs existed or had access to the information. They

---

**BILLS:** HR 2475, S 1803

**LEGISLATIVE ACTION:**

**House** passed HR 2475 (H Rept 109-101), 409-16, on June 21.

**Senate** Select Intelligence approved S 1803 (S Rept 109-142), 15-0, on Sept. 22.

**Senate** Armed Services Committee approved S 1803 (S Rept 109-173) by voice vote Oct. 17.

---

existed outside of normal intelligence channels, and officials had to go through an approval process to be privy to the information. The highly compartmentalized programs were housed throughout the civilian and defense intelligence community and dealt with everything from human intelligence to technical tasks, such as surveillance operations.

The Bush administration opposed the creation of such an inventory.

Non-binding report language also called on the Department of Justice to be more aggressive in investigating and prosecuting leaks of classified materials. In its report, the panel expressed concern about fundamental holes in U.S. intelligence systems. The committee said that interception of satellite signals and blown cover among intelligence collectors and analysts had hurt U.S. intelligence operations in recent years. The panel wanted the Justice Department to investigate and prosecute those within the intelligence community who disclosed sources or released classified information.

### HOUSE FLOOR ACTION

The House passed the bill, 409-16, on June 21, despite White House objections that the measure would alter the administration's spending priorities by cutting expensive satellite and surveillance systems while boosting spending on human spies and language experts. *(House vote 290, p. H-92)*

Hoekstra said he expected the criticism. "We're clearly raising issues that people will be uncomfortable with," he said. "The bigger hits are clearly in space, but we have also modified other programs. Some are duplicative, and some don't work."

The rule governing floor action on the bill (H Res 331) automatically struck two provisions.

The first was the language requiring the DNI to get a "response" from Congress before transferring personnel within the intelligence system. Harman and John D. Negroponte, the DNI, strongly opposed the provision. Although Hoekstra backed the language in the committee, he said it had become too much of a distraction and agreed to submit a floor amendment striking it from the bill. Armed Services Chairman Duncan Hunter, R-Calif., objected and temporarily blocked the bill, but he relented after Negroponte paid a visit to his office and promised to consult on major personnel transfers if Hunter would allow the bill to go forward. "I've got his word on consultation," Hunter said. "That's as good as gold."

The second provision, which was removed at Hunter's behest, would have given the DNI the power to coordinate all overseas intelligence, including military intelligence operations. Hunter had fought against creating a DNI in the first place, and he opposed giving the position any power over military intelligence.

### SENATE COMMITTEE ACTION

The Senate version of the intelligence authorization (S 1803), was marked up by two panels.

● **Intelligence.** The Select Committee on Intelligence approved the bill, 15-0, in a closed session Sept. 22 (S 1803 — S Rept 109-142). The bill included provisions that would expand the authority of the DNI,

including giving him access to all information gathered by intelligence operatives throughout the federal government.

Non-classified portions of the bill and report were eventually released. They listed several changes made by the committee to the bill, including adoption, 8-7, of an amendment by Carl Levin, D-Mich., to require administration officials to comply with congressional requests for intelligence information within 15 days.

● **Armed Services.** The Armed Services Committee approved portions of the bill related to military intelligence in a unanimous roll call vote in a closed meeting Oct. 27 (S 1803 — S Rept 109-173). The panel amended the measure to preserve the independence of Defense Department operatives responsible for gathering the tactical intelligence used by troops in the field. The committee also specified that the DNI would not be allowed to bypass the armed forces' chain of command by seeking direct access to intelligence used to support military operations.

The bill provided for the creation of an inspector general for the intelligence community, but Armed Services added language to protect the authority of the Defense Department's own inspector general over investigations into military intelligence matters.

### SENATE FLOOR ACTION

The bill was scheduled for floor action Dec. 14, but an unidentified Republican member used senatorial prerogative to put a hold on the measure, preventing it from coming up for debate.

Democrats said the senator wanted to block consideration of three amendments that Select Intelligence Committee Chairman Pat Roberts, R-Kan., had agreed to allow.

Two of the amendments — by Edward M. Kennedy, D-Mass.— would have required the Bush administration to provide Congress with the president's daily intelligence briefings for the period preceding the 2003 invasion of Iraq, and called on the administration to submit periodic reports to the House and Senate intelligence committees on the health and status of suspected terrorists held by the CIA in any "clandestine prison or detention facility operated by the United States government." The Washington Post had reported in a front page story Nov. 2 that the CIA maintained a covert prison system abroad to hold terrorism suspects.

The third amendment, by John Kerry, D-Mass., would have required the Defense secretary and the DNI to submit a classified report to Congress within 60 days detailing the location and size of each facility, the number of detainees currently or formerly held there and plans for their future disposition.

The Bush administration had said that it considered the daily intelligence briefings privileged information and probably would veto any effort by Congress to secure access to them. Administration officials did not comment on secret CIA prisons abroad, the existence of which they had not confirmed. ■

**Chapter 10**

# GOVERNMENT OPERATIONS

# Government Operations

# President Makes Major Changes In Cabinet, Agency Leadership

PRESIDENT BUSH RECONFIGURED the top of his administration as his second term began in 2005, replacing nine of the 15 members of his Cabinet and installing new leadership in several other senior offices and agencies. Although such shifts were typical at the start of a second term, what was different in Bush's personnel choices, by historical standards, was the degree to which he avoided bringing new faces to his inner circle. Only two of his new Cabinet-level appointments were complete newcomers to the administration; the others had served elsewhere in the executive branch.

The Senate confirmed all of the president's picks except for John R. Bolton, whose nomination as ambassador to the United Nations failed to overcome a filibuster by Democrats concerned that the prospective envoy's combative, pre-emptory style was a poor match for a sensitive diplomatic post. After senators twice voted against invoking cloture to limit debate on Bolton's nomination, the president used his constitutional recess appointment powers to install Bolton at the United Nations during the Senate's August recess. *(Bolton, p. 10-4)*

Barbara Kellerman, research director at the Center for Public Leadership at Harvard's Kennedy School of Government, said Bush went beyond his predecessors in picking so many trusted team players and loyal stewards from his first administration. "This is par for the course, but Bush is taking it to a new extreme," she said. He "is appointing a real band of brothers — and sisters."

In addition, after four years in which discretion and loyalty emerged as the principal traits required to survive in Bush's inner circle, the president's choices for his second-term Cabinet plainly reflected his desire to reward those characteristics — and to avoid repeating any of the few irritations from the initial team he assembled. Bush's original core Cabinet — the 15 departmental secretaries in the presidential line of succession — remained the same throughout his first term with just two exceptions: Paul H. O'Neill, was forced out as Treasury secretary after two years on the job — in no small measure because his insistence on speaking his mind rather than cheerleading put him crosswise with both the White House and its Republican allies in Congress. And Mel Martinez resigned as secretary of Housing and Urban Development (HUD) at the end of 2003 to pursue his successful campaign for a Senate seat from Florida in 2004. (John W. Snow, the chairman of CSX Corp., was confirmed as Treasury secretary by voice vote in January 2003; Alphonso R. Jackson, the public housing authority director in Dallas, was confirmed as HUD secretary by voice vote in March 2004; both were retained by Bush at the start of his second term.)

Besides O'Neill, only two other member's of Bush's first-term top tier stood out as less than 100 percent loyal in public. Secretary of State Colin L. Powell, who as an Army general was chairman of the joint chiefs of staff under the president's father, did not ultimately conceal his role as a constant irritation to the White House, even if he ultimately supported the war in Iraq. He had no choice but to move on after the president won re-election. EPA Administrator Christine Todd Whitman, who was previously governor of New Jersey, was forced out in June 2003 because she allowed her disapproval of the president's environmental deregulatory desires to surface.

The following new Cabinet members were nominated by Bush and confirmed by the Senate:

## JUSTICE

Alberto R. Gonzales was confirmed as the nation's first Hispanic attorney general, 60-36, on Feb. 3 — the most votes cast against any of Bush's second-term Cabinet nominees. No Republican opposed him, but only six Democrats supported him. *(Senate vote 3, p. S-4)*

Gonzales, 49, who was the White House counsel in Bush's first term, was previously a justice of the Texas Supreme Court, a post to which Gov. Jeb Bush appointed him in 1999 after Gonzales served two years as Texas secretary of state and a turn as the governor's staff counsel. The son of Mexican immigrants, he was the first person in his family to go to college.

The confirmation vote came after three days of floor debate over Gonzales' qualifications. Gonzales spent eight hours before the Judiciary Committee Jan 6. His Democratic opponents generally cited what they characterized as Gonzales' evasive, legalistic answers to scores of questions during the confirmation process on issues such as federal sentencing guidelines, anti-terrorism laws and the use of torture in interrogating suspected terrorists. Gonzales mollified some of his critics by pledging to work collaboratively with Congress. That was seen as a marked contrast to the record of Bush's first-term attorney general, John Ashcroft, a former governor and senator from Missouri, who frustrated many lawmakers in both parties for his reluctance to testify or provide information.

## STATE

Condoleezza Rice, who had been Bush's closest foreign policy adviser since his first presidential campaign and was the White House national security adviser during the first term, was confirmed to succeed Powell as secretary of State, 85-13, after nine hours of debate Jan. 25. *(Senate vote 2, p. S-4)*

It was the most votes cast against a secretary of State nominee since Henry Clay was confirmed, 27-14, in 1825. The dozen Democrats and one independent who opposed Rice, 51, a former provost of Stanford University, acknowledged that her qualifications were above reproach and sought instead to turn the debate on her nomination into a referendum on the war in Iraq and Rice's role in formulating the administration's policy.

## HOMELAND SECURITY

Michael Chertoff was confirmed, 98-0, on Feb 15 to become the second head of the department, created a year after the Sept. 11 terrorist

# Bush Sidesteps Congress on Bolton

PRESIDENT BUSH USED a recess appointment to install John R. Bolton as his third ambassador to the United Nations, ending a five-month saga that divided senators largely along partisan lines. Bush said the post was too important to leave vacant at a time of war and debate about how to alter U.N. operations.

Democrats portrayed Bolton as an outspoken critic of multilateral organizations who was too abrasive to make a good diplomat, and they succeeded in a pair of floor votes to block a final roll call on his confirmation. Those cloture votes amounted to the most direct rejection of a Cabinet-level nominee since 1989, when the Senate voted against making John Tower Defense secretary. *(1989 Almanac, p. 403)*

Bush announced Bolton's nomination on March 7 to replace John C. Danforth, a former GOP senator from Missouri who had cited personal reasons in resigning in January after only seven months on the job. Danforth had succeeded Bush's initial U.N. envoy, John D. Negroponte. Bolton, 57, had been undersecretary of State for arms control and international security during Bush's first term. He was an assistant secretary of State in the first Bush administration and worked in the Justice Department and the U.S. Agency for International Development Under President Ronald Reagan.

Democrats immediately denounced the nomination, citing Bolton's reputation as an abrasive hard-liner who favored unilateral action over diplomacy. Secretary of State Condoleezza Rice countered that Bolton was the sort of "tough-minded diplomat" who was ideally suited to fight for the Bush administration's proposed U.N. "reform," which included measures to change the U.N. Human Rights Commission, create a stronger internal investigative division to combat corruption and create a mechanism for reviewing and eliminating obsolete mandates.

Personality became the main issue during Bolton's confirmation hearings before the Foreign Relations Committee in April, when some of Bolton's former government colleagues charged that he was abusive and tried to bully subordinates into altering intelligence to justify his ideological preconceptions. The investigation into

Bolton's career and confrontational management style involved interviews with 29 witnesses, 830 pages of documents and memos, and seven hours of questioning of the nominee, who also answered 100 written questions for the committee.

On May, 12, the committee voted 10-8 along party lines to send the nomination to the full Senate "without recommendation," only the third time in 22 years that the panel had forwarded a nominee without an endorsement. The neutral vote was the best GOP leaders could hope for after one Republican, George V. Voinovich, signaled he was ready to side with the Democrats — who wanted a negative recommendation — by delivering a scathing 15-minute rebuke of Bolton in which he labeled him "the poster child of what somebody in the diplomatic corps should not be."

On May 26, Republican leaders tried to win a cloture motion and shut off debate on the nomination but lost, 56-42, four votes short of the 60 votes required to invoke cloture *(Senate vote 129, p. S-26)*

Democrats denied they had filibustered the nomination, saying they wanted more information from the White House about how Bolton handled intelligence on Syria and top-secret National Security Agency documents while he was State's senior arms control official. Bolton's Senate GOP supporters said the request was a tactic to divert attention from the minority party's efforts to scuttle the nomination.

After some balky negotiations, the administration refused to turn over the information, and on June 20 the Republicans failed a second time to win cloture, 54-38. *(Senate vote 142, p. S-29)*

On Aug. 1, the first weekday after Congress began its summer break, Bush gave Bolton a recess appointment, a maneuver that allowed the president to bypass the Senate when it did not act on a nominee while in session. A few hours later, Bolton was at the United Nations in New York, shaking hands with his new diplomatic colleagues. Under the terms of a recess appointment, Bolton's U.N. service would end in January 2007, when he would have to be renominated for consideration by the 110th Congress.

attacks (PL 107-296), to oversee almost all the civilian federal government agencies working to combat terrorism. *(Senate vote 10, p. S-6)*

Chertoff, 51, had been a judge on the 3rd U.S. Circuit Court of Appeals since June and before that had been head of the criminal division in the Justice Department since the start of the Bush administration. Bush's initial choice to succeed Tom Ridge and become the department's second secretary was Bernard Kerik, a former New York City police chief, but he withdrew after eight days in late 2004 after a series of revelations about complications in his personal life and his financial arrangements with homeland security contractors.

## AGRICULTURE

Mike Johanns was confirmed by voice vote Jan. 20 to succeed Ann N. Veneman as secretary of Agriculture. Johanns, 55, grew up on an Iowa dairy farm and had a reputation as a careful politician, a strong conservative and an easygoing administrator as the governor of Nebraska since 1999. All of those characteristics came through in a confirmation hearing where he staked out no positions on the issues that senators raised.

## COMMERCE

Carlos Gutierrez was confirmed by voice vote Jan. 24 after Senate Democrats used the occasion to deride administration trade policies. The Commerce secretary's customary role is to advocate on behalf of U.S. businesses in international trade disputes. Gutierrez, 51, who served as Kellogg Co. chief executive since 1999, had no prior experience in public office before succeeding Donald L. Evans, another corporate executive who was one of the president's oldest friends from Texas. But members in both parties were drawn to Gutierrez's story of fleeing Cuba with his family at age 6 and beginning his career selling cereal from the back of a van in Mexico City.

## EDUCATION

Margaret Spellings, 47, was confirmed by voice vote Jan. 20 to succeed Rod Paige as Education secretary. After a turn at the Texas Association of School Boards, she had served as Bush's education adviser when he was governor of Texas and was the senior domestic policy adviser on the White House staff throughout Bush's first term. In that position she had a central role in writing the president's signature edu-

cation policy law (PL 107-110), known as No Child Left Behind. During her confirmation hearing she vowed to be open to the complaints of state, cities and congressional Democrats about the statute's implementation and federal funding levels.

## ENERGY

Samuel W. Bodman was confirmed by voice vote Jan. 31, succeeding Spencer Abraham at Energy. Bodman, 66, was a chemical engineer who rose to become chief executive officer of the chemical manufacturer Cabot Corp. before joining the administration as deputy Commerce secretary in 2001 and moving over to Treasury as deputy secretary in 2004. At his confirmation hearing, Bodman made it clear that he viewed his role as an administrator, not a policy maker, and that he would support existing Bush administration energy policies.

## HEALTH AND HUMAN SERVICES

Michael O. Leavitt was confirmed by voice vote Jan 26 as the successor to Tommy G. Thompson. Leavitt, 54, had spent the previous 14 months as the administrator of the EPA after Whitman's departure, and was hailed in both parties as having the political and administrative skills to implement the new Medicare prescription drug benefit. As governor of Utah for a decade before joining the administration, he raised some Democratic eyebrows by winning permission from the federal government to revamp the state's Medicaid program of medical coverage for the poor in a manner that increased the number of people covered but reduced some benefits.

## VETERANS AFFAIRS

Jim Nicholson was confirmed by voice vote Jan. 26, succeeding Anthony J. Principi at the VA. Principi served as chairman of the Republican National Committee from 1997 until 2001, then spent Bush's first term as ambassador to the Vatican. But what counted for veterans' groups was the eight years that Nicholson, 56, spent on active duty as an Army ranger, and his 22 subsequent years in the reserves.

## DIRECTOR OF NATIONAL INTELLIGENCE

John D. Negroponte, 66, a career diplomat who was Bush's first ambassador to the United Nations and then the envoy to Iraq for 14 months, was confirmed 98-2 on April 21 to lead the nation's spy agencies as the first director of national intelligence. *(Senate vote 107, p. S-21)*

Congress created the position under the 2004 intelligence overhaul law (PL 108-548) to coordinate and set budgets for the nation's far-flung intelligence activities. The position was also designed to become the new public face of U.S. intelligence, a position historically occupied by the director of the CIA. The Senate confirmed Air Force Lt. Gen. Michael V. Hayden, 50, by voice vote as deputy director of the new office. Hayden had been director of the National Security Agency since 1999. *(2004 Almanac, p. 11-3)*

## EPA

Stephen L. Johnson was confirmed by voice vote on April 29 to be the agency's third administrator under Bush. Earlier that day senators had voted, 61-37, to invoke cloture and thereby limit debate on the nominee. Johnson succeeded Leavitt, who had moved to HHS three months before. *(Senate vote 115, p. S-22)*

A group of Democratic senators had sought to block the nominee in an effort to compel the administration to turn over more information about its proposals for revamping federal clean air law . But the White House rebuffed them and the senators relented, saying they had no objection to the nominee. Johnson, 54, was a biologist with expertise in pesticide regulation. He had been at the EPA for 24 years, making him the first scientist and career agency employee in the top job.

## U.S. TRADE REPRESENTATIVE

Rep. Rob Portman of Ohio was confirmed by voice vote April 29 to be the president's principal trade negotiator, becoming the first member of Congress tapped for a job in the Bush administration. He succeeded Robert B. Zoellick, who became deputy secretary of State earlier in the year.

During a dozen years representing the Cincinnati area and in the House, Portman, 49, was a reliable vote for trade liberalization, both on the floor and in the Ways and Means Committee. Trade policy was not his emphasis, although he began his career as an international trade lawyer.

Since 2001, Portman had served as chairman of the Republican leadership — a position that Speaker J. Dennis Hastert, R-Ill., created to give Portman an insider's role in setting caucus policy and strategy. Portman also described himself as the president's "eyes and ears" in the House. As a trusted political adviser of Bush's, he played the roles of the possible Democratic vice presidential nominees in Dick Cheney's preparations for the debates in both 2000 and 2004. He also ran the office of legislative affairs in the George Bush administration

The president had said that he would only nominate members of Congress when he was confident that they would be replaced by fellow Republicans — and Portman was in August, although by a surprisingly close margin. *(Special elections, p. 5-10)* ■

# Bush Threatens to Veto USPS Overhaul

THE HOUSE PASSED THE FIRST comprehensive overhaul of the U.S. Postal Service in 35 years. A similar measure won approval from the Senate Homeland Security and Governmental Affairs Committee but went no further in the first session.

The legislation would allow the U.S. Postal Service to operate more like a private business by increasing its operational flexibility and its accountability. The agency, which had not been overhauled since 1970, had been in financial decline for years in the face of competition from private carriers, increased use of e-mail and the rising cost of employee benefits.

Both bills proposed the creation of a new regulatory commission. Both sought to give the postal service flexibility to adjust rates, especially on products that had to compete with private mail services such as FedEx Corp. and United Parcel Service Inc. And both would allow the agency to provide discounts to some private mailers that did part of the work, such as bar coding and sorting mail.

The legislation had bipartisan support and was backed by small businesses, bulk mailers, postal unions and even UPS.

However, Missouri Republican Christopher S. Bond put a hold on the bill in the Senate. Missouri-based Hallmark Cards Inc. was concerned because most of its customers used first-class postage and would be subject to rate increases, while bulk catalog companies, nonprofits and other bulk mailers would have decreased rates under the bill.

In addition, the White House threatened to veto the bill over two provisions it said would have an adverse effect on the federal budget. The first would eliminate a requirement that the Postal Service set aside $3 billion a year in an escrow account to cover retiree health benefits. Instead, both bills would allow the agency to use part of the money for operations, thereby avoiding the need to raise the price of postage in the short term to help cover day-to-day expenses.

The second was a proposal to make the Treasury, rather than the Postal Service, responsible for a $27 billion liability for benefits to military retirees who were Postal Service employees. The liability had been transferred from Treasury to the Postal Service in 2003 (PL 108-18). Leaving the pension responsibility with the Postal Service had the added effect of keeping the expenses "off-budget" and thus not counting them toward the deficit.

House and Senate committees approved similar legislation in 2004, but it died in the face of the same veto threats. *(2004 Almanac, p. 17-4)*

## LEGISLATIVE ACTION
### HOUSE COMMITTEE ACTION

The House Government Reform Committee approved the bill by a vote of 39-0 on April 13 (HR 22 — H Rept 109-66, Part 1). "In the 10 years that I have been working in Congress to enact postal reform, we have never had a more workable, effective piece of reform legislation on the table," said bill sponsor John M. McHugh, R-N.Y.

The committee gave voice-vote approval to an amendment by Steven C. LaTourette, R-Ohio, that removed a section of the bill opposed by the airlines. It would have allowed the Postal Service to contract with foreign airlines at prices negotiated by the service. Existing law required the Transportation Department to handle such negotiations. As

---

**BOX SCORE**

**BILLS:** S 662; HR 22

**LEGISLATIVE ACTION:**

**Senate** Homeland Security and Governmental Affairs Committee approved S 662, 15-1, on June 22.

**House** passed HR 22 (H Rept 109-66, Part 1), 410-20, on July 26.

---

amended, the bill called for the Government Accountability Office to conduct a one-year study of the effects of changing the procedure for using foreign airlines to transport U.S. mail.

The amendment also would give the Postal Service more flexibility to award bonuses to employees and require the service to file the same public financial statements and reports required of private companies.

To give the Postal Service more flexibility, the bill would allow the service to go to an 11-member board of governors when it wanted to propose a rate increase. The board would be able to act immediately. However, the increase could not exceed the annual change in the Consumer Price Index, a provision intended to ensure rate stability and predictability for consumers. Under existing law, the service had to get permission for a postage rate increase from the Postal Rate Commission — a process that could take more than a year.

The bill also proposed reconstituting the commission as the Postal Regulatory Commission with power to ensure that postal rates were properly set and that the Postal Service engaged in fair competition and thorough disclosure. The regulatory commission would have the authority to issue subpoenas and fines.

The Postal Service also would be required to file with the commission the same financial reports the Securities and Exchange Commission requires for private companies, a move aimed at increasing transparency and consumer confidence.

The measure proposed to introduce the concept of "pay for performance" into the Postal Service, which under existing law could not pay its top officials more than the government-capped salary for Cabinet secretaries — about $175,000. The House bill would allow the Postal Service to hire executives with salaries above that cap.

To help the Postal Service compete with the private sector, the legislation would allow it to give discounts to businesses that helped move bulk mail.

### HOUSE FLOOR ACTION

The House passed the bill July 26 by a vote of 410-20, despite a veto threat issued by the White House the same day. *(House vote 430, p. H-132)*

Thomas M. Davis III, R-Va., chairman of the Government Reform Committee, said rate increases, which would be necessary if the Postal Service had to put the $3 billion in escrow, would be "devastating." Davis said the Postal Service was falling into a "death spiral, where declining business leads to higher rates, which in turn leads to declining business."

The House rejected by voice vote an attempt by Jeb Hensarling, R-Texas, to remove the provisions that were opposed by the White House. His amendment would have required that all of the $3 billion in escrow be used to cover the Postal Service's unfunded health care liability. The amendment also would have struck the language permitting the Postal Service to shift $27 billion in pension benefits to the Treasury. "I, for one, do not want to go home in 2006 and say I voted for a rate increase," said Del. Eleanor Holmes Norton, D-D.C.

The House rejected, 82-345, an attempt by Mike Pence, R-Ind., to strike a provision in the bill that would alter the composition of the

board of governors. The existing board was made up of nine presidential appointees, the postmaster general and the deputy postmaster general. The bill would substitute a labor union representative for one of the appointees. (*House vote 428, p. H-132*)

### SENATE COMMITTEE ACTION

The Senate Homeland Security and Governmental Affairs Committee approved its bill (S 662) on June 22 by a vote of 15-1.

The committee gave voice vote approval to an amendment by Chairwoman Susan Collins, R-Maine, to strike the foreign airline provisions that were dropped in the House bill.

Postmaster General John E. Potter had told the committee in March

2004 that being able to negotiate rates with foreign airlines would help the struggling agency save more than $100 million each year.

The Senate bill would streamline the process for setting postal rates, linking them to the Consumer Price Index to allow the Postal Service to respond more quickly to changes in the market. It would grant a new Postal Regulatory Commission the power to institute emergency price increases in the event of "unexpected and extraordinary circumstances," such as the anthrax attacks in 2001.

Collins said her measure answered concerns raised in 2003 by a commission on postal reform created by Bush. "The financial and operational problems confronting the Postal Service are serious indeed," Collins said. ■

# TANF Grants Extended Through 2010

UNABLE TO AGREE on a major rewrite of the 1996 welfare overhaul, Congress opted to extend the law through fiscal 2010 with relatively modest changes. The reauthorization was part of the 2005 budget reconciliation bill, which was completed in December but did not clear until early 2006. President Bush signed the measure into law Feb. 8 (S 1932 – PL 109-171).

The landmark 1996 law (PL 104-193), which ended more than 60 years of guaranteed cash assistance to welfare beneficiaries, required adult recipients to work in exchange for benefits and gave states new flexibility to operate their programs. States received federal aid in the form of Temporary Assistance for Needy Families (TANF) block grants. The law originally was slated to expire in October 2002, but lawmakers temporarily extended the program 12 times while they tried to reach agreement on a broader bill. (*1996 Almanac, p. 6-3; 2003 Almanac, p. 16-3*)

The chief issues that separated the House and Senate concerned work rules for adult recipients and the level of funding for child care. The final bill did not change the individual work requirements, but most states had to ensure that more of their welfare recipients were meeting the law's work requirements.

Democrats and moderate Republicans said the bill imposed new requirements on states without providing additional money to meet them and that it did not include sufficient funds for government-subsidized child care programs that were essential to moving people into the workforce. House Republicans and the White House contended that tougher work requirements and programs promoting marriage were the best ways to help the 2 million families who relied on welfare assistance to escape poverty.

Supporters of the bill also said it would fix an accounting problem under the 1996 law. The 1996 law required states to make sure that at least 50 percent of their adult welfare recipients spent at least 30 hours a week engaged in activities considered "work." But the requirement came with an exception: The work-participation rate was reduced by 1 percentage point for every 1 percent that a state reduced its welfare caseloads.

By 2004, welfare caseloads had decreased by 56 percent nationwide, according to the Congressional Research Service. As a result, many states were not required to make any of their welfare recipients work at all. The rewrite in the budget bill revised the caseload reduction credit.

The Senate Finance Committee approved a reauthorization bill (S 667) in March, but the cost, particularly for child care subsidies, was

too high for many conservative Republicans, and the bill did not reach the floor. Two House panels marked up a separate a bill (HR 240) that required longer work hours and included less child care funding. A version of that measure was included in the budget reconciliation bill.

## HIGHLIGHTS

The welfare section of the budget reconciliation law:

● **Authorization.** Reauthorized TANF block grants for five years, through fiscal 2010, at the existing level of about $16.5 billion a year.

● **Work requirements.** Left the individual work requirement at 30 hours per week for adults receiving TANF funds. However, states were required to have 50 percent of their recipients engaged in work, and, starting in fiscal 2007, states could count only reductions since fiscal 2005.

● **State bonuses.** Eliminated two annual state bonuses – the $200 million "high performance" bonus and one of up to $100 million for the five states with the greatest percentage decrease in out-of-wedlock births and a decline from 1995 levels in abortion rates.

● **Child care.** Provided $2.9 billion per year in mandatory funding for child care subsidies – an increase of $1 billion over five years, or $200 million a year.

● **Marriage promotion.** Provided about $100 million a year over five years for grants to encourage "healthy marriage." Up to another $50 million per year was set aside for "responsible fatherhood" initiatives.

## LEGISLATIVE ACTION
### SENATE COMMITTEE ACTION

The Senate Finance Committee gave voice vote approval March 9 to a five-year reauthorization bill (S 667 – S Rept 109-151) sponsored by Grassley. The bill would have required welfare recipients to work 34 hours a week, up from 30 hours under the 1996 law, with 10 hours permitted for education and training. It retained a provision from existing law that allowed recipients to count vocational education and training as a core work activity for up to 12 months.

States would have to increase the portion of their welfare recipients engaged in work from 50 percent in 2006 to 70 percent in 2010.

The bill would have eliminated the bonus for reducing out-of-wedlock births and created a $100 million-a-year mandatory program to provide matching grants to states and Indian tribes to promote healthy marriage and fatherhood. In addition, it included $50 million a year in

mandatory grants to promote responsible fatherhood, another $26 million a year in discretionary funds for the same purpose and $100 million a year in research funds, 80 percent of which was to promote healthy marriage.

At the urging of Rick Santorum of Pennsylvania, chairman of the Senate Republican Conference, the bill would have authorized an increase of $1 billion over five years for the Social Services Block Grant, paid for by tightening eligibility standards for Supplemental Security Income beneficiaries. The existing block grant was funded at $1.7 billion annually.

Senate moderates, particularly Republican Olympia J. Snowe of Maine, played a major role in shaping the legislation. At Snowe's insistence, the bill called for increasing mandatory child care subsidies by a total of $6 billion over five years. Snowe and panel Democrats said a lack of affordable child care remained a major stumbling block to employment for many welfare recipients. Snowe said only one in seven children eligible for subsidized child care actually received such aid.

"I believe there shouldn't be any question of the need," she said.

Santorum voiced "serious concerns" about the $6 billion increase. "The issue of child care is a Washington-based issue. It is not an issue out in the states," Santorum said. He said the funds to encourage marriage and responsible fatherhood would do more to help children. However, he supported the Snowe provision because it would be funded by changing the eligibility standards for the earned income tax credit (EITC), a refundable tax credit for poor families whose wage earners made too little to owe income taxes.

Jeff Bingaman, D-N.M., opposed the offset, saying it would end the rights of some legal immigrant families to receive the EITC.

Grassley hoped to move the bill early in year with Democratic support so it would not get caught up in other partisan squabbles. But fiscal conservatives objected to the bill's cost: The Congressional Budget Offices said it would add about $10.8 billion in mandatory spending over five years. With the funding dispute unresolved, Senate GOP leaders did not try to bring the bill to the floor.

## HOUSE COMMITTEE ACTION

The Ways and Means Committee folded a GOP-backed welfare reauthorization bill (HR 240) into the House budget reconciliation package (HR 4241). The committee approved the provisions, 22-17, on Oct. 26. The panel's Human Resources Subcommittee had approved HR 240 by a vote of 7-4 on March 15. The House Education and the Workforce Committee also approved the bill, 23-20, on Oct. 20.

The measure, sponsored by Deborah Pryce, R-Ohio, had the support of the Bush administration. It called for adult recipients to work 40 hours a week, with 16 hours a week allowed for education and training. The other 24 hours would have to be devoted to direct work activities such as private or public employment, on-the-job training, or supervised community service. The bill proposed to increase federal child care subsidies by $1 billion over five years. The portion of recipients engaged in work would have to increase to 70 percent, as under the Senate bill.

The measure included proposals to promote healthy marriage that were similar to those in the Senate bill, and a $20-million-a-year discretionary program to encourage responsible fatherhood.

## FINAL ACTION

The House provisions were largely included in the conference report (H Rept 109-362) on the budget reconciliation bill. The House adopted the conference report, 212-206, Dec. 19. (House vote 670, p. H-212)

The Senate voted, 51-50, on Dec. 21 to approve the budget bill with three provisions unrelated to the welfare reauthorization stricken from the conference report, sending the bill back to the House for final action. The House agreed to the amended version by voice vote Feb. 1, 2006, clearing the bill. (Senate vote 363, p. S-70) ■

# Chapter 11

# HEALTH & SCIENCE

# Congress Cuts Medicaid Spending, Increases Co-Pays and Premiums

CONGRESS AGREED TO CUT the growth of spending on Medicaid as part of the $38.8 billion budget reconciliation bill that President Bush signed into law Feb. 8, 2006 (S 1932 – PL 109-171). The Medicaid savings – a net $4.7 billion over five years – was only a fraction of what conservatives in Congress had hoped for, but far more than most Democrats and a group of Republican moderates wanted.

Bush and his congressional allies had begun the year with bold plans to overhaul Medicaid, the jointly administered federal-state health care entitlement program for the poor, to significantly slow the program's soaring costs and give states more flexibility.

Medicaid spending had surged 63 percent over the previous five years and totaled more than $300 billion annually. The president called for $60 billion in savings from the program over 10 years as part of a broader drive to get control of entitlement spending, which consumed about 54 percent of the federal budget and continued to increase as if on autopilot. After putting $15 billion back into Medicaid and children's health programs, the net savings in Bush's plan came to $45 billion.

Bush called for reducing overpayments for prescription drugs, tightening restrictions on seniors who transferred their assets to qualify for Medicaid, and eliminating overpayments to the states. In a proposal that particularly alarmed his critics, Bush also wanted to give states more flexibility to tailor their Medicaid programs, which some saw as opening the door to setting spending caps.

The selection of Michael O. Leavitt, confirmed in January to head the Health and Human Services (HHS) Department, seemed to signal plans for big changes in the program. As governor of Utah, Leavitt had won permission from the U.S. government to finance an expansion of Medicaid coverage in his state by reducing benefits for some patients and increasing cost-sharing for low-income beneficiaries.

But moderate Republicans in both chambers managed to ratchet down Bush's plan, reducing the total cuts to Medicaid and instead getting a substantial share of the savings from Medicare, the federal health care program for the elderly and disabled.

Still, many of the Medicaid provisions that made it into the budget reconciliation bill reflected ideas championed by conservatives, such as increased co-payments and cost-sharing by Medicaid beneficiaries and flexibility for states to reduce benefits to some participants. *(Budget reconciliation, p. 4-13; provisions, p. 4-18 )*

The final bill also preserved a stabilization fund that was created by the 2003 Medicare drug law (PL 108-173) to entice preferred provider

**BILL:**
S 1932 — PL 109-171

**LEGISLATIVE ACTION:**

**Senate** passed S 1932, 52-47, on Nov. 3.

**House** passed HR 4241 (H Rept 109-276), 217-215, on Nov. 18 and then inserted the text into S 1932.

**House** adopted the conference report on S 1932 (H Rept 109-362), 212-206, Dec. 19.

**Senate** rejected the conference report on procedural grounds Dec. 21 and approved an amended version of S 1932, 51-50.

**House** agreed to the amendment, 216-214, on Feb. 1, 2006, clearing the bill

**President** signed Feb. 8, 2006.

organizations (PPOs) to offer coverage in underserved regions. The Senate proposed eliminating it for a savings of $5.4 billion over five years. The fund had been a key to gaining support for the 2003 bill from House conservatives, who saw it as a way to encourage more private sector involvement. The White House had warned that Bush was likely to veto a bill that killed the fund. *(2003 Almanac, p. 11-3)*

Republicans had tried to overhaul Medicaid twice in the previous decade. In 1995, the GOP sought to cut program spending by $163 billion over seven years, but the move was thwarted by President Bill Clinton, who said the cuts would force states to make untenable choices. President Bush made a more limited attempt in 2003, proposing to give states more flexibility in running the program in return for a capped allotment of money for optional Medicaid populations, which included some nursing home patients and certain low-income pregnant women and children in households not meeting criteria for mandatory coverage. That proposal also went nowhere in Congress.

## HIGHLIGHTS

The following are among the main components of the Medicaid and Medicare sections of the new law:

### MEDICAID

As calculated by the Congressional Budget Office, the Medicaid changes were expected to reduce mandatory spending by a net $4.7 billion over five years, after paying for $3.6 billion in new Medicaid spending and $2.1 billion in hurricane-related health care. The new law:

● **Asset transfers.** Increased penalties and tightened restrictions on individuals who transferred their assets at less than fair market value in order to qualify for Medicaid nursing home care. Individuals with more than $500,000 in home equity were ineligible for Medicaid nursing home benefits. (Savings: $2.4 billion over five years)

● **Prescription drugs.** Reduced payments for certain outpatient prescription drugs, mainly by reducing Medicaid reimbursements to pharmacies. (Savings: $3.9 billion over five years)

● **Cost-sharing and premiums.** Allowed states to charge premiums and require cost-sharing by beneficiaries at or above the poverty level, with some restrictions. Under prior law, premiums and enrollment fees generally were prohibited and nominal cost-sharing was limited to $3. The new law also allowed states to require cost-sharing by enrollees for certain prescription drugs. (Savings: $1.9 billion over five years)

● **State financing.** Altered some rules on state financing of Medicaid

programs that affected federal grants to the states. Changes included barring states from levying special taxes on Medicaid managed care organizations and using the proceeds to help pay the state's share of Medicaid. The organizations got the money back in the form of increased Medicaid payments, which also generated federal matching funds that the states often kept. (Savings: $1.2 billion over five years)

● **Alternative benefit packages.** Allowed states to replace the traditional Medicaid benefits package with a reduced-benefit, or "benchmark," plan for certain groups. The plans had to provide basic services, such as physician and hospital coverage. Certain beneficiaries could not be required to participate in these plans. (Savings: $1.3 billion over five years)

● **Fraud, waste and abuse.** Saved money through steps such as requiring states to do more to find parties responsible for paying outstanding claims instead of relying on Medicaid as the payer of last resort. (Savings: $822 million over five years, $528 million of which was to be spent on education and other steps to improve program integrity)

● **Medicaid buy-in.** Extended eligibility for Medicaid benefits to certain low-income children with disabilities, beginning in 2008. (Cost: $1.4 billion over five years)

● **Home and community-based care.** Allowed up to 10 states to participate in a five-year demonstration project to provide home and community-based services to children who would be hospitalized otherwise. (Cost: $766 million over five years)

● **Katrina relief.** Appropriated funds to help with health care costs for residents of states evacuated because of Hurricane Katrina. (Cost: $2.1 billion)

## MEDICARE

Changes to Medicare were projected to achieve $6.4 billion in net savings over five years. The law:

● **Payments for home health services.** Eliminated a scheduled 2.8 percent increase in home health care payments for 2006, although it provided for a one-year 5 percent additional payment to rural home health providers. Starting in 2007, payments to home health care providers would be reduced by 2 percentage points if they did not report required health care quality data to HHS. (Savings: $2 billion over five years)

● **Risk adjustment.** Altered payments to Medicare Advantage plans starting in 2006, to take into account the health status of the beneficiaries served. (Savings: $6.5 billion over five years)

● **Imaging services.** Reduced the reimbursement rate for imaging services. (Savings: $2.8 billion over five years)

● **Physician payments.** Froze Medicare payments to physicians at the 2005 level for 2006. Under prior law, the payments would have fallen by 4.4 percent as of January 2006. (Cost: $7.3 billion over five years)

## BUDGET RESOLUTION

The first round in the fight over Medicaid cuts took place when the House and Senate put together the fiscal 2006 budget resolution (H Con Res 95). The budget was important because it set the outlines of the later budget-reconciliation bill. *(Budget resolution, p. 4-9)*

The House adopted a budget resolution that instructed the Energy and Commerce Committee — the House panel with jurisdiction over Medicaid — to find a total of $20 billion in savings over five years. Leaders expected about $14 billion of that to come from Medicaid.

The Senate took up a version of the budget resolution (S Con Res 18) that called on the Finance Committee to find $15 billion in savings, with $14 billion expected to come from Medicaid.

But Republican Sen. Gordon H. Smith of Oregon upset the leader-ship plans with an amendment that stripped out the Finance Committee instructions and called for a commission to analyze the efficiency and effectiveness of the Medicaid program. "I don't know whether the proposed $14 billion cut is too large or too small. . . . But I know what it is going to mean. Another 60,000 Oregonians may be losing health care," Smith said.

Despite furious lobbying by GOP leaders, seven Republicans broke ranks in favor of their states and cast the deciding votes. The amendment was adopted, 52-48, on March 17. *(Senate vote 58, p. S-13)*

The vote stung Budget Committee Chairman Judd Gregg, R-N.H., who had made Medicaid cuts the centerpiece of his budget, and exasperated House Republicans. But it forced conferees on the budget resolution to walk a fine line between finding enough spending reductions to satisfy House conservatives and still reassuring just enough Senate GOP moderates that Medicaid would not take too big of a hit.

In talks with the White House and Senate GOP leaders over several weeks, Smith agreed to accept $10 billion in Medicaid cuts if a presidential study commission was created to recommend ways to wring savings from the program without hurting beneficiaries. None of the Medicaid savings would occur in the first year to give the commission time to report. But Smith said he would support the bill only if the conferees gave up plans to require Finance to produce an additional $6 billion in cuts from other programs for the poor.

Senate leaders, who needed Smith's vote and those of two or three moderates expected to vote with him, agreed to drop the extra $6 billion in cuts. House leaders accepted the decision, saying that taking the first steps to cut mandatory spending was more important than the exact amount.

The final budget resolution instructed the House Energy and Commerce Committee to save $14.7 billion.

## BUDGET RECONCILIATION

Republican leaders put off the task of finding the actual savings until the fall. By the time the authorizing committees started working on the budget reconciliation bill in October, the mood had changed considerably. Now they faced both the enormous costs of recovering from hurricanes Katrina and Rita, which devastated New Orleans and the Gulf Coast and the new sympathy for the poor and displaced that grew out of the tragedy.

For fiscal conservatives, the priority was finding more savings to offset the billions already appropriated for relief and recovery efforts. For Democrats and GOP moderates, it was preserving programs that helped the least fortunate. Both sides dug in.

● **Senate Finance Committee.** Senate Finance voted 11-9 along party lines Oct. 25 to approve a package of cuts that promised to save a net $9.9 billion. To secure the votes of GOP moderates Smith and Olympia J. Snowe of Maine, Chairman Charles E. Grassley, R-Iowa, split the cuts between Medicaid and Medicare. The panel proposed to save a net $4.3 billion from Medicaid and $5.7 billion from Medicare.

"We were supposed to use this process to reform Medicaid, and we've missed that opportunity," complained conservative Republican Jon Kyl of Arizona. He said that instead of making systemic changes to Medicaid to cut spending, the bill turned to pharmacies and the pharmaceutical industry for much of the savings. Bowing to pressure from moderates, the bill did not seek to increase Medicaid cost-sharing.

The panel rejected a series of Democratic amendments that included attempts to expand Medicaid eligibility to victims of Hurricane Katrina. The panel did insert $1.8 billion to reimburse states for providing health care services to those in the path of the storm.

The Finance Committee plan included:

▶ $6.3 billion in savings over five years from changes in the way Medicaid paid for drugs, including revisions in the formula used to reimburse pharmacists for drug costs and increased rebates paid to Medicaid by drug manufacturers.

▶ $1.8 billion for temporary aid in hurricane-affected areas.

▶ $5.4 billion in savings over five years from eliminating the stabilization fund created by the 2003 Medicare drug law. Democrats and some GOP moderates argued that the fund was superfluous since virtually every service region designated under the Medicare law was served by more than two private health plans. But conservatives said the government had to prove it could be a good business partner to health insurers and work hard to encourage more PPOs — which they said operated more efficiently and saved more money than the government — to sign on to offer Medicare benefits.

▶ $6.5 billion in savings over five years by giving higher Medicare payments to insurers who covered sicker patients and lower payments to those that enrolled healthier patients.

▶ $4.5 billion from linking payments to the quality of the providers.

▶ A 1 percent increase in Medicare physicians' fees in 2006. Under existing law, physicians were set to get a 4.4 percent reduction in fees for Medicare services in 2006. The doctors' lobby, the American Medical Association, was pushing hard for legislation to avoid the scheduled cut, saying it would lead more physicians to turn away from Medicare patients. The estimated cost was $10.8 billion over five years.

● **Senate floor action.** The Senate added billions in new spending, including some changes to Medicaid and Medicare, before passing the reconciliation bill, 52-47, on Nov. 3. The changes reduced the net savings to $35 billion from the $39.1 billion proposed by the Budget Committee. Savings from the Finance Committee Medicare and Medicaid provisions fell to $9.2 billion over five years. *(Senate vote 303, p. S-59)*

● **House Energy and Commerce.** House Republicans took a sharply different tack Oct. 28 by focusing exclusively on cuts to Medicaid and recommending no changes to Medicare. The Energy and Commerce Committee voted 28-22 along party lines to approve a $9.5 billion package of cuts to Medicaid. The proposal included:

▶ $1.2 billion in savings over five years from changing the way Medicaid paid for prescription drugs, including changing the formula for determining the cost of drugs to take into account factors such as bulk discounts.

▶ $2.7 billion in savings over five years by allowing states to increase some Medicaid beneficiaries' cost-sharing over a three-year period from $3 to $5 and allowing states to collect co-payments at emergency rooms. Conservatives, backed by Bush, argued that beneficiaries would take more control of their health care if they had a financial stake in it.

▶ $2.5 billion in savings over five years by putting in place stricter guidelines for seniors who transferred assets in order to qualify for Medicaid coverage.

▶ $2 billion in savings over five years from giving states the flexibility to structure their Medicaid coverage more like private health plans, including allowing co-payments on drugs for pregnant women and children.

▶ $2.5 billion for health care related to hurricane relief.

A rare break in the GOP ranks developed when Steve Buyer, R-Ind., offered an amendment to exempt mental health drugs from a provision that would allow states to create a Medicaid formula that would result in higher costs for non-preferred drugs. Nine Republicans joined 22 Democrats to adopt the amendment, 31-20, over the vehement objections of Chairman Joe L. Barton, R-Texas.

● **House floor action.** GOP leaders eked out a narrow, 217-215, victory on the bill (HR 4241) in the early morning hours of Nov. 18, after making a number of concessions to win over reluctant party moderates. The changes, made as part of the rule that governed floor debate on the bill, included significant changes in the Medicaid provisions. *(House vote 601, p. H-190)*

The revised provisions:

▶ Allowed seniors to retain up to $750,000 in home equity — up from $500,000 in the committee version — and still be entitled to Medicaid coverage for nursing home care.

▶ Dropped the attempt to increase from $3 to $5 the cap on Medicaid co-payments for individuals with incomes below the poverty line.

▶ Permitted HHS to delay a reduction in reimbursements for prescription drugs required in the committee version if the average prices pharmacies paid for the drugs were higher than the new amounts that HHS would pay.

● **Conference, final action.** Deciding how much to cut Medicaid and whether and how much to cut Medicare were among the biggest issues that faced conferees on the overall budget reconciliation bill.

Under persistent pressure from moderate Republicans in both chambers, GOP leaders pared back the Medicaid cuts to an amount relatively close to the Senate figure, making up the difference with Medicare cuts that conservatives had not planned to include in the reconciliation bill. The bill that emerged from conference cut a net $4.7 billion from Medicaid over five years — about 12 percent or $500 million more than the Senate had approved, but 50 percent or $4.7 billion less than the House wanted. Net Medicare cuts totaled $6.4 billion — about $1.4 billion more than in the Senate-passed bill. The House wanted no Medicare cuts at all.

At the last minute, after the conferees thought they were finished, House Speaker J. Dennis Hastert, R-Ill., and Senate negotiators had to give up $1.9 billion in anticipated cuts to secure the votes of Ohio lawmakers. The Ohioans threatened to scuttle the overall deal unless oxygen tank manufacturers, including a major Ohio company, were protected from planned cuts to Medicare.

Although the size of the Medicaid savings was reduced, conservatives prevailed on many of the decisions about how to cut the program. While the Senate would have gotten the lion's share of the savings from pharmacies and the pharmaceutical industry, the final bill looked as much to cost-sharing, reduced benefit packages and cracking down on seniors who disposed of assets to qualify for Medicaid nursing care.

The final bill got $3.6 billion in savings from Medicaid prescription drug programs, compared with $6.3 billion in the Senate bill and $1.9 billion in the House version. Conferees dropped the Senate plan to increase the rebates pharmaceutical companies paid to states under Medicaid. Instead, they got virtually all of the savings by changing the way pharmacists were reimbursed to more accurately reflect the actual costs pharmacists paid to acquire the drugs.

House conservatives also prevailed on the issue of tightening restrictions on seniors who transferred their assets to qualify for Medicaid, saving $2.4 billion over five years. The final bill limited home equity for individuals qualifying for nursing home care to $500,000, though states could change that to $750,000. The House had recommended $750,000. Prior law did not set a limit on home equity. The Senate bill would have made only minor changes to the asset-transfer rules.

Like the House bill, the final version allowed states to require co-payments and premiums for Medicaid recipients, saving $1.9 billion over five years. The House would have saved $2.7 billion; the Senate bill had no such provisions. States also got some flexibility in designing Med-

icaid benefit packages, a top conservative demand. The House would have saved $2 billion, the final bill $1.3 billion, from allowing states to offer reduced benefits.

Like the Senate bill, the conference report blocked the scheduled 4.4 percent cut in physicians' reimbursements, though it froze the existing rates rather than increasing them by 1 percent as the Senate wanted.

Like the Senate bill, the final measure saved $6.5 billion over five years by implementing a White House plan to give higher Medicare payments to insurers that covered sicker patients and lower payments to plans that enrolled healthier people. Conferees dropped the Senate plan to save $5.4 billion by eliminating the Medicare stabilization fund.

Some House Republicans had said that eliminating the fund was a "no-brainer" because of the amount it would save. But conservatives and the White House rejected a move they said would erode provisions in the law designed to increase competition and private sector involvement in the Medicare program.

The House adopted the conference report on S 1932 (H Rept 109-362), 212-206, on Dec. 19. The Senate rejected the conference report on procedural grounds Dec. 21, and then approved a slightly amended version of S 1932, 51-50. That sent the bill back to the House, which cleared it, 216-214, on Feb. 1, 2006. *(House vote 670, p. H-212; Senate vote 363, p. S-70)* ∎

# Law Establishes Medical Error Database

AFTER YEARS OF LABORIOUS negotiations, the House cleared legislation intended to reduce the number of fatalities from medical errors. The aim was to spot trends and patterns in order to help health care providers learn from mistakes without fear of liability. President Bush signed the bill into law July 29 (S 544 – PL 109-41).

The bill established a framework for voluntary, confidential reporting of medical errors, with feedback for health professionals and a national database to allow the identification of regional and national trends.

Enactment was the culmination of six years of effort in both chambers that began in 1999, when the Institute of Medicine, the health sciences arm of the National Academy of Sciences, issued a study on medical errors. The institute said as many as 98,000 patients died each year as a result of mistakes by health care professionals, making medical errors the eighth-leading cause of death in the United States. Many thousands more were injured, driving up health care costs, the institute said. The report offered several recommendations, including legislation to provide for the confidential reporting of medical errors and a subsequent analysis of the data to devise ways to improve patient safety.

Under the new law:

▶ The Department of Health and Human Services (HHS) would certify "patient safety organizations" based on criteria to be established by the department. The organizations were required to have appropriately qualified staff, including licensed or certified medical professionals.

▶ The organizations, run by private, state and local entities, would receive information on medical errors voluntarily reported by doctors and other health care providers. The organizations would analyze the information and then report back to providers on ways to improve patient safety and health care quality.

▶ All information reported to the organizations had to be kept confidential and could not identify any specific patient, health care provider or other person. Anyone who disclosed the information would be subject to a fine of $10,000 per violation. The data could not be used in malpractice suits, although the law did not shield information already available to lawyers for use in court cases.

▶ Employers were barred from taking any retaliatory job action

**BOX SCORE**

**BILL:**
S 544 – PL 109-41

**LEGISLATIVE ACTION:**

**Senate** passed S 544 by voice vote July 21.

**House** cleared S 544, 428-3, on July 27.

**President** signed July 29.

against an employee who reported patient safety information.

▶ HHS was required to establish a network of patient safety databases to collect reported, non-identifiable information concerning patient safety and analyze national and regional statistics on health care errors.

The House and Senate had passed separate bills dealing with medical errors in the 108th Congress, but the House never appointed conferees and the differences were not settled. Negotiators could not agree on how to reconcile the need for information on medical errors with the health care providers' fear of liability.

## LEGISLATIVE ACTION
### COMMITTEE ACTION

The Senate Health, Education, Labor and Pensions (HELP) Committee approved a bill (S 544) by voice vote March 9 that was identical to the chamber's 2004 measure.

The House Energy and Commerce committee approved a companion bill (HR 3205) by voice vote July 20. Supporters said the legislation would encourage health care providers to report medical errors by ensuring the data could not be used against them in liability cases. Chairman Joe L. Barton, R-Texas, said the bill language had been negotiated with Senate HELP Chairman Michael B. Enzi, R-Wyo., and Sen. Edward M. Kennedy, D-Mass., and would pass in both chambers.

### SENATE, HOUSE FLOOR ACTION

The Senate passed S 544 by voice vote July 21. The House cleared the bill by a vote of 428-3 on July 27. *(House vote 434, p. H-134)*

Kennedy, who had expressed concern that the bill not allow the concealment of criminal activity, voiced his satisfaction on the floor: "The bill is intended to make medical professionals feel secure in reporting errors without fear of punishment, and it is right to do so," Kennedy said. "But the bill tries to do so carefully, so that it does not accidentally shield persons who have negligently or intentionally caused harm to patients. The legislation also upholds existing state laws on reporting patient safety information." ∎

# Support Grows for Stem Cell Research

FIFTY HOUSE REPUBLICANS defied their leadership and the president in May to help pass a bill to expand federal funding of embryonic stem cell research. Senate Majority Leader Bill Frist, R-Tenn., shocked his colleagues in July by declaring his support for the bill, but he insisted on bringing it up in tandem with legislation backed by opponents of the research, and the debate never occurred.

Congress cleared a separate bill in December to fund research on umbilical cord blood cells. The measure had broad support in both chambers, and President Bush signed it into law Dec. 20 (HR 2520 – PL 109-129).

Under an executive order signed by Bush on Aug. 9, 2001, federal funding of stem cell research was restricted to the 78 stem cell lines that existed prior to that date. Critics said those existing lines were contaminated and not diverse enough. The National Institutes of Health estimated that only 22 of those lines were viable for human research.

Democrats and moderate Republicans had grown increasingly dissatisfied with the restrictions. Polls conducted the previous year showed broad support, even among Republican voters, for expanding federal funding for the research, which scientists hoped could lead to treatments for diseases such as Parkinson's, diabetes and some cancers. However, many conservatives remained staunchly opposed to embryonic stem cell research. They equated the destruction of embryos, which was necessary for the research, with abortion.

The use of stem cells from the umbilical cord, which was usually discarded following the birth of a baby, did not carry the same problems for conservatives. Like donated bone marrow, umbilical cord blood could be used to treat various genetic disorders. Supporters of its use as a source of stem cells contended that the cells could be used to reproduce human tissue for use in research. Some leading stem cell researchers, however, believed that embryonic stem cells were more capable of reproducing any type of human tissue for research purposes, and that cord blood stem cells, like adult stem cells, were of more limited use in research.

## STEM CELL RESEARCH
### HOUSE FLOOR ACTION

Pressed by constituents and buoyed by support from celebrities such as actor Michael J. Fox and former first lady Nancy Reagan, supporters of expanding embryonic stem cell research built enough momentum in Congress to secure promises from the leadership in March that they would get a floor vote on the issue.

On May 24, the House voted 238-194 to pass a bill (HR 810) that would allow federal funding of research on embryonic stem cell lines derived from surplus embryos at in vitro fertilization clinics that would otherwise be discarded. Donors would have to give consent for the research and could not accept payment. *(House vote 204, p. H-66)*

The Department of Health and Human Services (HHS) would have to issue ethical guidelines for federally funded researchers within 60 days of enactment.

The bill – sponsored by Michael N. Castle, R-Del., and Diana

**BOX SCORE**

**BILLS:** HR 2520 – PL 109-129; HR 810

**LEGISLATIVE ACTION:**

**House** passed HR 810, 238-194, on May 24.

**House** passed HR 2520, 431-1, on May 24.

**Senate** passed HR 2520, amended, by voice vote on Dec. 16.

**House** cleared HR 2520, 413-0, on Dec. 17.

**President** signed Dec. 20.

DeGette, D-Colo. – had more than 200 cosponsors. It was much narrower than other measures aimed at expanding stem cell research, a strategy backers hoped would garner support from members who might be uncomfortable voting for a broader bill.

House leaders tried to cast the cord blood bill as an alternative, but backers of the Castle-DeGette measure disputed that argument, saying more options should be available for scientific investigation.

The floor debate was emotional, with many of the 50 Republicans who supported the bill citing personal experiences – or those of close relatives – with illnesses such as diabetes, cancer and Parkinson's disease.

Joe L. Barton, R-Texas, who noted that his anti-abortion voting record previously stood at 100 percent, said he backed the bill because of his father, who had diabetes, and a brother, who had liver cancer. "Maybe the breakthrough will come in adult stem cells. I hope it does," said Barton, chairman of the House Energy and Commerce Committee. "But maybe, just maybe, it's going to come because of embryonic stem cells. Let's look at all avenues."

Jim Langevin, an anti-abortion Democrat from Rhode Island who was paralyzed as a teenager, also broke ranks. "What could be more life-affirming than using what would otherwise be discarded to save, extend and improve lives?" he said.

But abortion opponents maintained that destroying an embryo is akin to murder. "I believe that life begins at conception and that a human embryo is human life," said Mike Pence, R-Ind. "I believe it is morally wrong to take the tax dollars of millions of pro-life Americans, who believe that human life is sacred, and use it to fund the destruction of human embryos for research."

Bush reiterated his threat to veto an embryonic stem cell bill the day the measure passed. "This bill would take us across a critical ethical line by creating new incentives for the ongoing destruction of emerging human life," he said. "Crossing this line would be a great mistake."

The 238 votes in favor of the bill fell short of the 290 votes that would be needed to override a veto if all members of the House were present and voting, and House GOP leaders vowed to fight an override attempt if the bill landed back in their chamber. But supporters still were eager to see the Senate take up the bill.

### NO SENATE ACTION

Frist pledged to hold a Senate vote on the issue, but he spent much of July trying to figure out how to bring a series of bills to the floor to allow votes on a number of options. Arlen Specter, R-Pa., and Tom Harkin, D-Iowa, who had introduced a Senate version of the House bill (S 471), saw this as a strategy to siphon votes away from their legislation, and Frist could not get unanimous consent for his plan.

Then on July 29, the final day before the August recess, Frist unexpectedly went to the Senate floor and threw his support behind the House embryonic stem cell bill. "I believe the president's policy should be modified," Frist said. "We should expand federal funding ... carefully and thoughtfully staying within ethical bounds."

Frist said he had several problems with the House bill, including the

www.cq.com | 2005 CQ ALMANAC  **11-7**

potential for donors to be wooed by financial incentives for their embryos, but he said it was "fundamentally consistent" with his views. Supporters of the House bill said Frist's concerns easily could be addressed during the process of drawing up regulations and that the bill would not need to be amended.

Specter called Frist's speech "an earthquake," and said, "The majority leader has given cover to the entire Senate" to vote for the bill despite the veto threat.

Although Specter and others hoped Frist's support would add momentum to the bill, Frist continued to insist on bringing it to the floor in concert with other measures that addressed all sides of the debate. Democrats refused to agree, leading to a stalemate. Specter threatened to attach his measure to the spending bill for the departments of Labor, HHS and Education if he did not get a separate floor vote. But given the tight Senate schedule after Hurricane Katrina and the pressure to finish the appropriations bills, Frist and Specter agreed to table the issue until 2006.

### CORD BLOOD BILL

#### HIGHLIGHTS

The cord blood bill included provisions to:

● **Cord blood stem cell inventory.** Establish a new federal program to collect and store 150,000 units of human cord blood. The cord blood would be made available for transplantation, or if not appropriate for clinical use, for peer-reviewed research. The cord blood could be acquired only with the informed consent of the donor. The law authorized $79 million for fiscal 2007 through 2010 for the inventory.

● **Bone marrow program.** Authorize $158 million over five years for the National Bone Marrow Registry and expand it to deal with both bone marrow and cord blood transplants. The expanded program was renamed the C.W. Bill Young Cell Transplantation program.

● **Single access point.** Require the HHS secretary to establish an electronic database to give health care professionals and patients a single access point to search for cord blood and bone marrow matches.

#### HOUSE, SENATE ACTION

House leaders scheduled a vote on the cord blood bill for May 24 as an alternative to the embryonic stem cell measure being considered the same day. The House easily passed the cord blood bill (HR 2520), 431-1. Sponsored by Christopher H. Smith, R-N.J., the bill authorized funding for the less controversial practice of collecting and storing stem cells from umbilical cord blood. It also called for establishing a database to help physicians and researchers access the cells and bone marrow to use in treatment and research. *(House vote 205, p. H-66)*

On June 29, the Senate Health, Education, Labor and Pensions Committee gave voice vote approval to a similar bill (S 1317), after adopting a substitute amendment that incorporated language from the House measure on improvements in the bone marrow program. Sponsor Orrin G. Hatch, R-Utah, said the language was negotiated with the House and no conference would be needed.

Supporters of the Specter bill were reluctant to pass the cord blood measure unless it was paired with the more divisive embryonic stem cell legislation. But on Dec. 16, they relented, and the Senate passed an amended version of HR 2520 by voice vote. The House cleared the measure, 413-0, the next day. *(House vote 664, p. H-210)* ■

# NASA Reauthorization Aims for Mars

CONGRESS CLEARED A $36.6 billion bill to reauthorize NASA for two years, giving a congressional imprimatur to President Bush's plan to send astronauts back to the moon and on to Mars. The measure largely endorsed the president's ambitious plans for manned space exploration, but also addressed congressional concerns about the administration's plan to retire the space shuttle fleet in 2010. Bush signed the bill into law Dec. 30 (S 1281 — PL 109-155).

The measure authorized a total of $17.9 billion in fiscal 2007 and $18.7 billion in fiscal 2008. It directed NASA to continue work on the International Space Station, and urged a shuttle mission to repair the Hubble Space Telescope if it could be conducted safely. It also required NASA to dedicate 15 percent of its funding for space station research to subjects not related to human space exploration.

Congress had not enacted legislation reauthorizing the National Aeronautics and Space Administration since 2000 (PL 106-391), relying instead on authorizing language included in the annual appropriations bills. But authorizers wanted to pass a stand-alone bill in 2005 in light of the many challenges facing NASA, perhaps most significantly the debate about how and when to retire the decades-old shuttle fleet. In addition, NASA had to contend with budget cuts while trying to com-

**BOX SCORE**

**BILL:**
S 1281 — PL 109-155

**LEGISLATIVE ACTION:**

**House** passed HR 3070 (H Rept 109-173), 383-15, on July 22 and subsequently inserted the text into S 1281.

**Senate** passed S 1281 (S Rept 109-108) by voice vote Sept. 28.

**House** adopted the conference report (H Rept 109-354) by voice vote Dec. 17.

**Senate** cleared the bill by voice vote Dec. 22.

**President** signed Dec. 30.

plete expensive repairs to the Hubble Space Telescope and other infrastructure. *(2000 Almanac, p. 16-3)*

Bush's plan to return astronauts to the moon in preparation for a mission to Mars called for the space shuttle fleet to be retired in 2010 and for a new vehicle to be operational by 2014. The four-year gap in U.S. ability to send humans into space was partly responsible for scuttling a NASA authorization bill in the 108th Congress. Many lawmakers were loath to rely on Russia to get U.S. astronauts to and from the International Space Station. *(2004 Almanac, p. 17-3)*

While the new law did not set a specific date for retiring the shuttle fleet, it encouraged NASA to wait until a new vehicle that could transport humans was functional. NASA would have to report to Congress on any gap in the time the shuttle program retired and a new vehicle was ready. NASA had said it planned to have a new space vehicle operational by 2012, reducing to two years the gap in the ability to launch humans into space.

The new law also directed NASA to send Congress a schedule for dispatching a crew to repair the Hubble Telescope, providing the mission could be carried out safely. Without repairs, the telescope would fail when its gyroscopes and batteries wore out in a few years. The law stat-

ed the sense of Congress that the Hubble Space Telescope "is an extraordinary instrument that has provided, and should continue to provide, answers to profound scientific questions."

## LEGISLATIVE ACTION
### HOUSE COMMITTEE ACTION

The House Science Committee voted 36-0 on July 14 to approve a bill (HR 3070 — H Rept 109-173) that recommended a total of $33.4 billion for NASA in fiscal 2006 and 2007.

The bill encouraged, but did not require, a new space vehicle to be operational as close as possible to the shuttle fleet's scheduled retirement in 2010. Democrats were unsuccessful in winning language to prohibit NASA from grounding the shuttle fleet until a new spacecraft was ready to launch. However, they were able to win a two-year authorization in place of the one-year, $16.5 billion reauthorization approved by the panel's Space and Aeronautics Subcommittee. The subcommittee approved its draft, 10-0, on June 29.

"We had a rocky start, but I believe we have ended up with a good bill," said Bart Gordon, D-Tenn., the committee's ranking member.

The two-year authorization was part of an amendment by Chairman Chairman Sherwood Boehlert, R-N.Y, adopted by voice vote.

The committee rejected, 18-18, an amendment by Jerry F. Costello, D-Ill., to strike language allowing NASA to outsource certain federal jobs. Instead, the committee gave voice vote approval to an amendment that would require NASA to report on contracts performed overseas and on the purchases NASA made from foreign entities.

Along with the space shuttle retirement schedule, lawmakers also avoided addressing the problem of how the United States could pay Russia in the event that American astronauts had to hitch rides on their spacecraft past 2006. The Iran Nonproliferation Act (PL 106-178) banned U.S. payments to Russia in connection with the International Space Station, creating logistical problems for NASA. "We will be excluded from the space station after paying for it," warned Dana Rohrabacher, R-Calif. Boehlert said that an agreement on the issue would have to be a part of the final bill.

The House measure also required that several policies and strategies be included with NASA's budget requests for fiscal 2007, including a national aeronautics policy and a science policy to direct programs through 2020. The bill called for NASA to set a schedule for a shuttle mission to fix the ailing Hubble Space Telescope.

### HOUSE FLOOR ACTION

The House passed the two-year NASA reauthorization bill, 383-15, on July 22, after adopting an amendment requested by the White House that boosted the bill's space-exploration funding by at least $1.3 billion. *(House vote 416, p. H-128)*

Lawmakers gave voice vote approval to a manager's amendment that increased the exploration systems account to $8.4 billion — a move Boehlert said was necessary to garner White House support for the bill. The extra money brought the bill's total to about $34.7 billion.

### SENATE COMMITTEE ACTION

The Senate Commerce, Science and Transportation Committee approved an $87.7 billion five-year authorization bill (S 1281 — S Rept 109-108) by voice vote June 23. NASA would be authorized at $16.6 billion in fiscal 2006, rising to $18.5 billion in 2010.

The committee tacitly accepted Bush's plans to retire the space shuttle, but not before another vehicle was ready to replace it. The committee report said it was the intent of Congress "that there be no gap

# Iran, Syria Sanctions Tied to Space Travel

A BILL TO ALLOW THE United States to pay Russia for ferrying U.S. astronauts to the International Space Station solved a major problem for NASA. But it also served as a vehicle to broaden sanctions against Iran and apply them to Syria as well. Bush signed the bill into law Nov. 22 (S 1713 — PL 109-112).

The 2000 Iran Nonproliferation Act (PL 106-178) barred U.S. payments to Russia in connection with the International Space Station unless the president certified that Moscow was not helping Iran gain access to nuclear materials or other weapons of mass destruction. *(2000 Almanac, p. 11-10)*

But the United States needed transportation on the Russian Soyuz to get to and from the space station, especially after 2010. NASA was planning to retire the space shuttle fleet in that year, but it did not expect to have a new vehicle ready for use before 2012. *(NASA, p. 11-8)*

S 1713 essentially allowed NASA to ignore the Iran Nonproliferation Act for the purposes of sending astronauts to the space station until 2012. "We were able to get this legislation passed in time to prevent what would've been a major embarrassment," said Rep. Dana Rohrabacher, R-Calif. "Our space program would've been humiliated by the elimination of America's presence on the International Space Station."

The Senate passed S 1713 by voice vote Sept. 21. The House passed the bill by voice vote Oct. 26, after adding a section that expanded the sanctions in the Iran Nonproliferation Act. The sanctions originally applied to countries or companies that supplied materials, technology or services that helped Iran develop weapons of mass destruction. The amendment extended the sanctions to Syria and applied them to imports as well as exports of goods and services related to weapons of mass destruction.

The House was spurred to act against Syria by the assassination in February of Lebanon's former Prime Minister Rafik Hariri, an act that had been tied to Syrian and Lebanese officials.

The Senate cleared the amended bill by voice vote Nov. 8.

in the nation's ability to transport humans into space."

"We have added our bold vision to the president's bold vision," said Kay Bailey Hutchison, R-Texas, chairwoman of the subcommittee responsible for overseeing NASA.

The committee also differed with the White House on the types of research that would be performed on the space station. Bush wanted to restrict space station research to projects that supported space exploration. The Senate bill proposed to retain that emphasis but designate the space station as a national laboratory, which would expand the types of research that could be conducted on board.

Like the House bill, the measure required that the agency set a schedule for a shuttle mission to repair the Hubble Space Telescope.

### SENATE FLOOR ACTION

The Senate passed the bill by voice vote Sept. 28, after adopting a manager's amendment by Hutchison, also by voice vote. The amendment included language modifying the directive on retiring the space shuttle to encourage, but not require, NASA to keep it going until a new

vehicle to carry astronauts into space was operational.

The amendment required NASA to keep Congress informed on its progress and to give lawmakers a one-year notice if a replacement vehicle would not be ready before the final shuttle flight. NASA would have to report on the strategic risks associated with the gap, the estimated length of time during which the United States would not have independent human access to space, the steps that would be taken to shorten that length of time, and what other means would be used to allow human access to space during that period.

### CONFERENCE/FINAL ACTION

The House-Senate conference on the bill was relatively smooth, and the conference agreement was approved Dec. 15 with bipartisan sup-port. In preparation for conference, the House had passed S 1713 by voice vote Nov. 18 after substituting its own text.

The House adopted the conference report (H Rept 109-354) by voice vote Dec. 17, and the Senate cleared the bill by voice vote Dec. 22.

While largely endorsing Bush's blueprint for manned space exploration, the conference report included a number of directives requiring NASA to report to Congress on its progress toward meeting its space exploration goals.

Conferees did not have to address the Iran Non-Proliferation Act problem. On Nov. 22, Bush signed a bill (PL 109-112) that allowed NASA to ignore the Iran Nonproliferation Act in order to reimburse Russia for costs related to the International Space Station until 2012. *(Iran, Syria, p. 11-9)* ■

**Chapter 12**

# HOMELAND SECURITY

# Disputes Delay Reauthorization Of Anti-Terrorism Act Provisions

IN A SETBACK FOR THE Republican leadership, Congress was unable to agree on a plan to revise and reauthorize 16 expiring provisions of the 2001 anti-terrorism law known as the Patriot Act (PL 107-56). The House adopted the conference report on a reauthorization bill (HR 3199), but four Republicans joined nearly all the Senate Democrats to block final action in that chamber. With the provisions set to expire Dec. 31, Congress cleared a brief, five-week extension.

President Bush had won enactment of the Patriot Act shortly after the Sept. 11 terrorist attacks. The 16 expiring provisions gave the federal government enhanced authority to conduct searches and seizures and carry out electronic surveillance, including wiretaps and the interception and monitoring of e-mail and Internet communications. *(2001 Almanac, p. 14-3)*

The administration and its Republican allies wanted to make all sections of the law permanent and give law enforcement additional legal tools. But they came up against a bipartisan coalition of senators who wanted more protections for civil liberties and time limits on some of the most contentious provisions in the sweeping law. Republicans Larry E. Craig of Idaho, Lisa Murkowski of Alaska and John E. Sununu of New Hampshire joined repeatedly with Democrats Richard J. Durbin of Illinois, Russ Feingold of Wisconsin and Ken Salazar of Colorado to seek more limits on the powers conferred in the law.

The group succeeded in brokering a compromise bill sponsored by Judiciary Chairman Arlen Specter, R-Pa., which easily passed the Senate in July. The bill proposed four-year sunsets for two of the most controversial expiring provisions — giving the FBI power to seek "roving wiretaps" and get access to a wide array of business records — and further restrictions on the FBI's threshold for acquiring records and search warrants. The bill also included a four-year extension of a provision in the 2004 intelligence overhaul law (PL 108-458) that allowed law enforcement to seek warrants against "lone-wolf" terrorists who were not connected to a foreign power.

The White House fared better in the House, which passed a bill by Judiciary Chairman F. James Sensenbrenner Jr., R-Wis., which included 10-year authorizations for the two most controversial provisions and no sunset on the lone-wolf provision.

The House waited until mid-November to appoint conferees, leaving little time to work out a deal. Vermont Sen. Patrick J. Leahy, the ranking Democrat on the Senate Judiciary Committee, complained that Democrats were "shut out" of the conference and that the White House had stepped in to guide the legislation.

With time running out in the session, Specter and Sensenbrenner

| BOX SCORE | |
|---|---|
| **BILL:** HR 3199 | |

**LEGISLATIVE ACTION:**

**House** passed HR 3199 (H Rept 109-174, Parts 1, 2), 257-171, on July 21.

**Senate** passed HR 3199, amended (S 1389), by voice vote July 29.

**House** adopted the conference report (H Rept 109-333), 251-174, on Dec. 14.

**Senate** defeated cloture motion, 52-47, on Dec. 16 (60 votes required).

agreed to a compromise bill in December that included four-year extensions for the three provisions and some additional safeguards. The House adopted the conference report with a significant bloc of Democrats in support. But in the Senate, four Republicans aligned with 41 Democrats and the chamber's lone independent to defeat an attempt to limit debate on the conference report.

After the cloture motion was rejected, Leahy suggested a three-month extension of existing law to allow time for further negotiations. Although Senate Majority Leader Bill Frist, R-Tenn., and Bush insisted they would not support a short-term extension, they eventually backed down. The Senate passed a six-month extension, but the House reduced it to five weeks and the Senate concurred. Bush signed the measure into law Dec. 30 (S 2167 — PL 109-160), extending the anti-terrorism law until Feb. 3, 2006.

The provision in the 2001 anti-terrorism law that drew the most scrutiny was a section that allowed federal agents to get court orders for access to "any tangible thing" — mainly business records — related to an authorized terrorism investigation. The language amended the 1978 Foreign Intelligence Surveillance Act (PL 95-511), known as FISA, which was originally aimed at giving the government tools to combat foreign spying. *(1978 Almanac, p. 186)*

The provision drew fire from an unusual alliance of liberals and some conservatives who feared that it could be used to get access to a seemingly unlimited range of private records, including library and bookstore records. Librarians across the country vociferously opposed the language, saying it could be used for broad requests for their patron records. FBI Director Robert S. Mueller III assured lawmakers in April that the FBI had not used the provision to obtain library records because libraries had been voluntarily cooperating with requests for information.

In June, the House gave bipartisan support to an amendment by Vermont Independent Bernard Sanders that would have blocked the use of Justice Department funds to seek a FISA order for library circulation records, library patron lists, bookseller sales records or bookseller customer lists. Despite a veto warning, the vote was 238-187, with 38 Republicans — libertarians, moderates and conservatives — joining the majority. "That wasn't just about the libraries," said one House Republican who spoke on condition of anonymity. "That shows the mood of Congress." *(House vote 258, p. H-82)*

The Bush administration recommended that Congress modify the provision to give recipients of such orders the right to consult an attorney and challenge the orders in a FISA court. The anti-terrorism law barred the recipients from telling anyone at all.

## HIGHLIGHTS

The following are the main elements of the conference report on the reauthorization bill:

● **Temporary extensions.** Four-year reauthorization, through 2009, for provisions that:

▶ Allowed investigators to obtain orders for "roving wiretaps" to track a suspect by tapping multiple telephones, cellular phones or Internet connections. (Sec. 206)

▶ Allowed the FBI to obtain orders to seize business records, books and other documents related to an authorized investigation of international terrorism. (Sec. 215)

▶ Allowed investigators to seek warrants to conduct surveillance against rogue terrorist suspects, or "lone wolves," who were not connected with a foreign power or recognized organization.

● **Permanent extension.** Permanent authorization for 14 provisions, including sections that:

▶ Allowed law enforcement authorities to use wiretaps and other surveillance to investigate suspected acts of terrorism, including computer fraud. (Secs. 201, 202)

▶ Allowed law enforcement and intelligence officers to share information in matters of national security. (Secs. 203b, 203d)

▶ Made it easier under FISA to issue orders for pen register and trap-and-trace devices, which could be used to track telephone calls and Internet communications. (Secs. 204, 214)

▶ Extended the time duration of wiretaps and search warrants from 90 days to 120 days, with court ordered extensions of up to one year. (Sec. 207)

▶ Allowed the government to get access to voice mail by using search warrants rather than more difficult wiretap orders. (Sec. 209)

▶ Permitted Internet providers to disclose customer records to the government in an emergency. (Sec. 212)

▶ Allowed law enforcement agents to intercept electronic communications if the owner of a computer system or network believed someone was hacking into the system from the outside. (Sec. 217)

▶ Allowed the government to obtain FISA search warrants when "a significant purpose" was to investigate foreign intelligence activity — rather than "the" purpose, as under prior law. (Sec. 218)

▶ Allowed federal judges with jurisdiction over a particular investigation to issue search warrants for electronic evidence stored anywhere in the country. (Sec. 220)

▶ Provided for civil suits against unlawful disclosure of information obtained through the law's wiretapping authority, while giving immunity to those who assist in the carrying out of investigations under the law. (Secs 223, 225)

● **Added safeguards.** The conference report added provisions to:

▶ Require the FBI director or deputy to sign off on applications for court orders for library, bookstore, firearm sales, tax return, educational and medical records.

▶ Allow those ordered to turn over business records under a national security letter (Section 505) to contact an attorney and challenge the order in court. Such letters allowed the FBI to obtain records, credit reports and telephone records without the approval of a judge.

▶ Require the government to notify the subject of a "sneak and peek" search — conducted secretly without notifying the subject of the search warrant — within 30 days, with a possible 90-day extension. Previously, the notice could be delayed indefinitely. Authorities could no longer delay notification on the grounds that it would "unduly" delay a trial.

▶ Require that investigators seeking a roving wiretap order give the specific target or specific evidence of the need, and that they notify the court within 10 days after beginning surveillance of any new phone.

## LEGISLATIVE ACTION
### HOUSE COMMITTEE ACTION

The House Judiciary Committee amended and approved Sensenbrenner's bill (HR 3199 — H Rept 109-174, Part 1), on a 23-14 party-line vote July 13. As amended, the bill proposed to make 14 of the 16 provisions permanent and extend the roving wiretap and business records provisions for 10 years, through 2015.

The Intelligence Committee also amended and approved Sensenbrenner's bill July 13 (H Rept 109-174, Part 2).

Sensenbrenner's bill originally would have made all 16 provisions permanent, but he agreed to support an amendment by Dan Lungren, R-Calif., to set the two expiration dates. "I support, reluctantly, the longer sunset provision," Sensenbrenner said. The amendment was adopted, 26-2. Democratic attempts to terminate the provisions sooner — in 2009 or 2011 — were rejected.

The Judiciary-approved bill also proposed to:

▶ Require the FBI director to sign off on applications for court orders for library and bookseller records.

▶ Place new notification requirements on roving wiretaps.

▶ Allow recipients of a national security letter to contact an attorney and challenge the order in court. The judge would be given some discretion in dismissing the letter.

▶ Require investigators seeking business records to specify that the information being sought was "reasonably expected" to be relevant to a terrorism investigation.

The committee rejected nearly all of the more than 40 amendments offered by Democrats, many of them aimed at further restricting or demanding more information from law enforcement officers conducting surveillance, requesting records or entering homes without notifying the target of the investigation. A proposal by Jerrold Nadler, D-N.Y., to add sunsets to the other 14 expiring provisions, failed, 12-21. "The one thing sunsetting says is we should not get too comfortable with expanded police powers," Nadler said.

Democrats were not alone in their concerns. Republicans offered and won several new limitations.

The committee agreed to proposals by:

▶ Jeff Flake, R-Ariz., adopted by voice vote, to allow recipients of requests for information under the business records provision to consult with a lawyer and challenge the request in court.

▶ Darrell Issa, R-Calif., adopted, 34-0, to require investigators to notify a judge every time they planned to tap a new communications device, within 10 days of a new wiretap being approved.

▶ Lungren, adopted by voice vote, to require the attorney general to submit a report to Congress showing all cases in which communications service providers handed over records, such as e-mail.

▶ Zoe Lofgren, D-Calif., adopted, 34-0, to require the Justice Department to review the detention of material witnesses held without charges.

▶ Adam B. Schiff, D-Calif., adopted by voice vote to make it a federal crime to surveil, photograph, videotape, diagram or otherwise collect information with intent to plan or assist a terrorist attack against mass transit. Other Schiff amendments adopted by voice vote added to the list of crimes for which wiretaps could be authorized and property could be seized.

The Select Intelligence Committee approved the Sensenbrenner version of the bill on a voice vote, with one change: The committee added a sunset date of 2010 on the lone-wolf provision.

The committee adopted one other Democratic amendment, by Leonard L. Boswell of Iowa, to require the FBI to report back to a judge on what it was finding out from roving wiretaps.

## HOUSE FLOOR ACTION

The House passed the bill July 21 by a vote of 257-171. *(House vote 414, p. H-126)*

House Democrats tried to limit the expiration dates on all 16 provisions to just four years, but a motion to recommit the bill with instructions to do so was narrowly defeated, 209-218. Nine Republicans voted in favor of the motion. *(House vote 413, p. H-126)*

"Emergency powers should not become the standard once the threat is gone," said Dana Rohrabacher, R-Calif. "Let's stand up to the principles our Founding Fathers talked about: limiting government."

The White House issued a statement supporting the House bill but also expressed disappointment with the decision to include the expiration dates on the two provisions, calling the sunsets "unnecessary and detrimental."

"There's a delicate balance between security and liberty," said Democrat Jim McGovern of Massachusetts. "I believe this bill sacrifices too much of our liberty. Democracy takes courage — the courage to say to the terrorists, you will not change our way of life."

Sensenbrenner said he found no record of abuse of the law and therefore saw no need to put expiration dates on all 16 provisions. "Good oversight is done by congressional leaders, not sunsets," Sensenbrenner said.

The House considered 18 amendments during the 11-hour debate — far fewer than Democrats wanted — and adopted 17, most by wide margins. They included proposals by:

▶ Flake to require the approval of the FBI director for requests for library and bookstore records, adopted, 402-26. *(House vote 403, p. H-124)*

▶ Issa to require law enforcement officials using roving wiretaps to notify a judge within 15 days of tapping a new device, adopted, 406-21. *(House vote 404, p. H-124)*

▶ Shelley Moore Capito, R-W.Va., to create standard penalties for terrorist attacks and violence against railroad carriers and mass transportation systems, adopted 362-66. *(House vote 405, p. H-124)*

▶ Flake to allow recipients of national security letters to consult with an attorney and challenge the order in court. A judge could throw out the order "if compliance would be unreasonable or oppressive" to the recipient. The amendment was adopted 394-32. *(House vote 406, p. H-124)*

▶ Bill Delahunt, D-Mass., adopted 418-7, to allow the government to seize assets of those accused of the "federal crime of terrorism," rather than the existing provision which applied to those accused of "domestic terrorism," language that Delahunt said could include anti-abortion activists or environmental extremists. *(House vote 407, p. H-124)*

▶ Flake, adopted 407-21, to change the sneak and peek provisions so that authorities would no longer be allowed to delay notifying the subject of such a search because of concern that it would "unduly" delay a trial. *(House vote 408, p. H-126)*

▶ Howard L. Berman, D-Calif., to require federal agencies using data-mining technology to build databases to file reports on such activity to Congress. It was adopted, 261-165. *(House vote 409, p. H-126)*

▶ Schiff, to make it a crime to use a vessel to smuggle terrorists or dangerous materials into the United States, and make it a federal crime when a vessel operator failed to stop after being ordered to do so by a federal law enforcement officer. It was adopted, 381-45. *(House vote 410, p. H-126)*

▶ Melissa A. Hart, R-Pa., to increase fines from $11,000 to $50,000, and increase criminal penalties from 10 years to 20 years, for those who financed terrorism. It was adopted, 387-38. *(House vote 411, p. H-126)*

▶ Sheila Jackson-Lee, D-Texas, adopted 233-192, to allow families of victims of terrorism to seize assets in civil judgments against the terrorist. *(House vote 412, p. H-126)*

▶ Henry J. Hyde, R-Ill., adopted by voice vote, to make it a crime to sell or distribute drugs to finance terrorism and set a mandatory minimum of 20 years and a maximum life sentence for those found guilty.

▶ Pete Sessions, R-Texas, adopted by voice vote, to make it a crime, punishable by up to 20 years in prison, to interfere with anyone engaged in the authorized operation of an aircraft.

▶ Nita M. Lowey, D-N.Y., adopted by voice vote, to shift the distribution of certain first-responder grants by reducing the minimum amount each state received and distributing the rest based on risk.

## SENATE COMMITTEE ACTION

The Senate Judiciary Committee voted 18-0 on July 21 to approve a compromise bill (S 1389) that would make the same 14 sections permanent, but set four-year expiration dates on the roving wiretap and record search provisions. The committee also included a four-year sunset for the lone-wolf provision, which would be permanently reauthorized under the House bill.

The unanimous vote in the notoriously fractious committee signaled that the bill would go to the Senate floor with a built-in bipartisan unity that would be hard to break. The Senate panel had prepared dozens of amendments, and Specter and aides worked through the night before the markup to fashion a compromise the committee could accept. Specter hailed the eleventh-hour deal as "a very, very significant accomplishment."

The measure contained many of the same provisions that were added to the House bill, but it sometimes went further to curb government powers.

For instance, it required the FBI director or deputy director to sign off on any attempt to obtain medical or gun sales records, as well as records from libraries or booksellers. It proposed a higher threshold for business records searches, requiring authorities to demonstrate reasonable grounds, in a statement of fact, showing that the information sought was relevant to the activities of a foreign power, or that it pertained to an individual in contact with or known to a suspected agent of a foreign power.

Senators from both parties said they would keep pushing for more restrictions on law enforcement's powers. "There is still a lot of uneasiness about this legislation in middle America, and I think we need to pay attention to that," said Republican Tom Coburn of Oklahoma. Coburn favored making the entire anti-terrorism law, not just the 16 expiring provisions, temporary.

## SENATE FLOOR ACTION

In a striking contrast to the House, the Senate passed HR 3199 on July 29 without debate or roll call votes. Senators passed the bill by voice vote, after substituting the text of the Judiciary Committee measure.

Senators who had indicated that they would offer amendments on the floor, acquiesced in the unanimous consent necessary to consider the bill on short notice and pass it by voice vote.

"The alacrity of the bill's passage is a testament to the significant work that preceded its introduction and the intense efforts of many in the days that followed," Specter said. "The bill has been refined and improved to address the concerns of those on both sides of the political aisle."

## CONFERENCE

After numerous attempts at compromise, House and Senate conferees completed work on the bill Dec. 9. The House adopted the con-

ference report (H Rept 109-333), 251-174, on Dec. 14. But the Senate was not ready to go along. *(House vote 627, p. H-200)*

An attempt by Frist to secure the 60 votes needed to limit debate failed, 52-47, on Dec. 16. Four Republicans joined 41 Democrats and Vermont Independent James M. Jeffords in voting against cloture on the conference report. Frist changed his vote to "no" at the end to preserve his right to offer a motion to reconsider at a later date. *(Senate vote 358, p. S-69)*

Specter and Sensenbrenner had worked for weeks to try to find an acceptable compromise. "Everything is negotiable until everything is agreed on," Sensenbrenner said in November. "That is one of the unwritten rules of conference committees. When we reach an agreement on a package, we reach an agreement on all of the package."

A tentative deal reached just before Thanksgiving would have made the 14 provisions permanent, and set seven-year expiration dates for the roving wiretap and business records provisions, as well as for the lone-wolf provision. But Republicans Craig, Murkowski and Sununu, joined by Democrats Durbin, Feingold and Salazar, announced their opposition to the deal, sending the negotiators back to the table.

After that, the White House got more involved, and Vice President Dick Cheney entered the negotiations in early December. Within hours of Cheney joining the talks, Sensenbrenner agreed to the Senate's demand for four-year expirations on the roving wiretap and business records provisions, and the conference report was filed.

Despite five days of intense pressure from Senate Republican leaders and the White House, Craig, Murkowski and Sununu, along with Republican Chuck Hagel of Nebraska, refused to help the leadership invoke cloture and bring the conference report to a vote.

### SHORT-TERM EXTENSION

For nearly a week, Frist insisted that he and Bush would rather let the 2001 anti-terrorism law expire Dec. 31 than give in to demands for a short-term extension to break a bipartisan filibuster. But with the deadline looming and sentiment growing within the GOP caucus to protect the 16 provisions, Frist on Dec. 21 waved a white flag and supported a six-month extension (S 2167), which passed by voice vote.

However, Sensenbrenner objected to an extension that long, and with the agreement of the House leadership, he amended the bill to shorten the extension to five weeks. The House then passed the bill by voice vote Dec. 22.

With few good options left, the Senate cleared the revised bill a few hours later. John W. Warner, R-Va., was the only senator in the chamber to conduct what was the final legislative act of the session. ∎

# Coast Guard Bill Left Unfinished

THE HOUSE AND SENATE both passed legislation to reauthorize the Coast Guard, but they did not finalize the measure in the first session.

The House bill was a one-year, $8.7 billion authorization, while the Senate passed a two-year authorization of $8.2 billion in fiscal 2006 and $8.9 billion in fiscal 2007.

Beyond the money, the two chambers differed over the Coast Guard's Deepwater modernization program and whether foreign crews should be allowed to work on some U.S.-flagged vessels.

The Senate agreed to authorize $1.1 billion in fiscal 2006 and $1.2 billion in fiscal 2007 for Deepwater, the Coast Guard's long-term plan to update its fleet of cutters, aircraft, communication systems and other equipment. It also required that the Coast Guard complete the program in 10 to 15 years. The House bill included a $1.6 billion authorization for Deepwater in 2006 and included no specific timetable.

On the crew issue, Rep. Don Young, R-Alaska, championed a provision in the House bill to allow cruise and freighter operators to hire foreign workers for certain support positions such as wait staff, entertainment and maintenance. Unions that represented sailors and marine engineers argued that the provision would weaken national security because it would water down citizenship requirements for the crew. Proponents argued that it would simply codify existing practices. The Senate bill did not contain the worker provision.

### LEGISLATIVE ACTION
#### HOUSE COMMITTEE ACTION

The House Transportation and Infrastructure Committee approved a one-year reauthorization bill by voice vote May 18 (HR 889 — H Rept 109-204, Part 1) that recommended $8.7 billion

**BOX SCORE**

**BILL:** HR 889

**LEGISLATIVE ACTION:**

**House** passed HR 889 (H Rept 109-204, Part 1), 415-0, on Sept. 15.

**Senate** passed HR 889, amended (S 1280 — S Rept 109-114), by voice vote Oct. 27.

for the Coast Guard in fiscal 2006.

The committee approved a substitute amendment by Frank A. LoBiondo, R-N.J., the chairman of the panel's Coast Guard and Maritime Transportation Subcommittee, that increased the authorized funding level for the Deepwater program to $1.6 billion. The subcommittee's draft of the bill, approved April 13, included $1.1 billion for Deepwater, slightly above President Bush's request of $966 million.

The increase was intended to address concerns about a Coast Guard plan to stretch out the program from its 20-year schedule to as much as 25 years. Lawmakers said the longer timetable could result in construction of fewer vessels. The committee's total for Deepwater included $1.3 billion to acquire and build new vessels and aircraft and $284 million to maintain existing ones.

The bill also authorized $36 million for the Bridge Alteration Program, which redesigned or removed bridges that block navigation, and almost $5.6 billion for Coast Guard operations and maintenance. It authorized 45,500 active-duty personnel for the service in fiscal 2005 and fiscal 2006.

To help the Coast Guard maintain maritime security, the bill proposed redefining U.S. "navigable waters" to include territorial waters as far as 12 nautical miles offshore and allowing the Coast Guard to provide technical assistance to foreign maritime authorities.

### HOUSE FLOOR ACTION

The House passed the bill 415-0 on Sept. 15, after agreeing by voice vote to authorize an extra $60 million to reimburse the Coast Guard for the cost of saving and rescuing about 33,500 people stranded by Hurricane Katrina, which hit New Orleans and the Gulf Coast on Aug. 29. *(House vote 474, p. H-148)*

The bill also would temporarily extend existing mariners' licenses and vessel certificates, many of which had been left in the Coast Guard's New Orleans office. Coast Guard personnel affected by the hurricane also would be deemed eligible for property losses under the bill.

During the floor debate, the House:

▸ Adopted by voice vote Young's amendment to allow foreign workers to work in support jobs on U.S. cruise ships and freighters.

▸ Rejected, 163-254, an amendment by Edward J. Markey, D-Mass., to require the Coast Guard to review the security and safety records of any proposed liquefied natural gas terminals. LoBiondo opposed the amendment, saying it would add significantly to the Coast Guard's already heavy workload and that service members had no expertise to carry out such functions. *(House vote 473, p. H-148)*

▸ Adopted by voice vote an amendment by Vito J. Fossella, R-N.Y., to require ferries that carried more than 399 passengers to be equipped with a "black box" recording device similar to those on commercial airliners. The provision was in response to the 2003 crash of a Staten Island ferry in which 11 people died and 70 more were injured.

### SENATE COMMITTEE ACTION

The Senate Commerce, Science and Transportation Committee gave voice vote approval June 23 to a two-year bill (S 1280 – S Rept 109-114) that would authorize $8.2 billion in fiscal 2006 and $8.9 billion in fiscal 2007.

The committee rejected the Coast Guard's plan to stretch out the timetable for replacing aging ships and aircraft under its Deepwater program. "The Coast Guard's revised plan is falling far short of the mark," said Olympia J. Snowe, R-Maine. "We are putting our men and women in harm's way." Snowe said previous studies, including the Coast Guard's own figures, "do not buttress" the revised Deepwater plan. She complained that the agency had shown no methodology to back up its revised implementation plan.

The bill directed the Coast Guard to write a new plan that accelerated the completion date to between 10 and 15 years and to meet a number of new reporting requirements. The authorization included $1.1 billion in fiscal 2006 and $1.2 billion in fiscal 2007 for the program.

The bill also included $11.6 billion for operations and maintenance, $36 million for altering or removing bridges that obstructed navigation, and a force level of 45,500 active-duty personnel.

The committee proposed stiffer civil penalties for violating maritime laws and enhanced tools for the Coast Guard to enforce those laws. As recommended by the U.S. Commission on Ocean Policy, it directed the Coast Guard to develop a process for determining when damaged vessels could seek refuge in the United States. The bill also instructed the Coast Guard to take steps to improve the detection and interdiction of foreign vessels that violated fishing regulations.

### SENATE FLOOR ACTION

The Senate inserted its bill into HR 889 and passed the amended measure by voice vote Oct. 27. The Senate added language to extend annual leave for Coast Guard personnel who participated in the hurricane relief efforts and temporarily extend the expiration date of merchant marine licenses and vessel inspection certifications that were lost or damaged during hurricanes Katrina and Rita. ∎

# House Backs Homeland Reauthorization

THE HOUSE PASSED THE FIRST-EVER reauthorization bill for the Department of Homeland Security, but the committee responsible for the legislation in the Senate pushed consideration to 2006 because it was preoccupied with an investigation into the government's response to Hurricane Katrina.

The force behind passage of the reauthorization bill in the House (HR 1817) was Christopher Cox, R-Calif., who chaired the Homeland Security Committee until Aug. 2, when he resigned to become chairman of the Securities and Exchange Commission. Cox argued that by producing annual bills similar to those that authorize the Department of Defense, Congress would affirm the status of the three-year-old Homeland Security Department as an important part of the federal government's national security apparatus.

In the Senate, Susan Collins, R-Maine, who chaired the Homeland Security and Governmental Affairs Committee, started out with the intention of waiting until 2006 to mark up an authorization bill to give her panel time to study the issues. Then in July, Homeland Security Secretary Michael Chertoff announced plans for restructuring the department. Collins said she was inclined to move the timetable up a year to address elements of Chertoff's plan that needed congressional approval and to incorporate her own proposals on the structure and policies of the department. But Collins' plans were interrupted following Hurricane Katrina when Majority Leader Bill Frist, R-Tenn., tasked her committee to lead the Senate inquiry.

Meanwhile, House and Senate negotiators reached agreement on the fiscal 2006 Homeland Security appropriations bill (PL 109-90), which accommodated nearly all of Chertoff's restructuring proposals. These included the creation of a centralized intelligence office and a new consolidated preparedness division that would allow the Federal Emergency Management Agency to focus strictly on recovery and response to disasters. *(Appropriations, p. 2-28)*

Collins and Peter T. King, R-N.Y., who replaced Cox as chairman of the House committee, said they would push for an authorization bill in 2006.

### LEGISLATIVE ACTION
#### HOUSE COMMITTEE ACTION

In a testament to the tangle of overlapping responsibilities in Congress for authorizing and overseeing homeland security programs, the bill had to make its way through three House committees before going to the floor. Five other panels could have weighed in, but agreed not to.

● **Homeland Security.** Cox won approval from the Homeland Security Committee for his $34.2 billion authorization measure on April 27 (HR 1817 – H Rept 109-71, Part 1). The panel acted by voice vote.

The bill called for the hiring of 2,000 Border Patrol agents and included provisions to refine the department's much-maligned color-coded terror alert system, instructing the department to provide more-specific directions for responding to increases in the warning level. It also prescribed remedies to boost its frequently struggling intelligence wing. The authorization was in line with President Bush's budget request for the department.

Homeland Security had the fifth-highest discretionary budget in the

federal government, and Cox said it should be authorized annually, just like the Defense Department. But he also had another goal: sealing the legitimacy of the committee itself. The House rules package that made his committee permanent in January included language to allow chairmen of at least 10 other committees to claim jurisdiction over legislation that would affect various agencies and policies of the department.

To circumvent potential conflicts with other chairmen, Cox fended off most major amendments to the bill during the markup. Democrats initially sought an additional $7 billion, as well as language on port security, aviation security and other topics not covered by the legislation. In the end, Cox won their support.

● **Energy and Commerce.** The House Energy and Commerce Committee approved the bill by voice vote May 11 (H Rept 109-71, Part 2), after rewriting significant portions of a cybersecurity provision.

The panel agreed by voice vote to an amendment that would strip some of the new powers the Homeland Security Committee wanted to confer on the department's top cybersecurity official. Chairman Joe L. Barton, R-Texas, said he also wrote language to ensure that nothing in the bill would intrude on the powers of other agencies that protected computer networks.

The bill would create an assistant secretary for cybersecurity to oversee a National Cybersecurity Office and the National Communications System. Barton's amendment would leave in place the assistant secretary position but eliminate the National Cybersecurity Office and delete any new cybersecurity initiatives.

● **Judiciary.** The House Judiciary Committee approved the bill by voice vote May 12 (H Rept 109-71, Part 3), after adopting an amendment to clarify the definition of "terrorism prevention" to mean border and infrastructure security, information dissemination and first-responder preparedness.

### HOUSE FLOOR ACTION

The House passed the bill by a vote of 424-4 on May 18. *(House vote 189, p. H-62)*

Democrats, led by the ranking member on the Homeland Security Committee, Bennie Thompson of Mississippi, fought unsuccessfully to expand the scope of the measure with proposals that would have added $6.9 billion to the authorization and covered a broader sweep of homeland security. Their substitute amendment was rejected, 196-230. *(House vote 187, p. H-62)*

The House Rules Committee barred more than 60 amendments from coming to the floor, provoking complaints from lawmakers on both sides of the aisle who intended to offer changes. The House still considered two dozen amendments, and adopted more than half of them, including:

▶ A proposal by Cox and Judiciary Chairman F. James Sensenbrenner Jr., R-Wis., adopted by voice vote, to authorize $40 million to help state and local officials enforce federal immigration laws.

▶ An amendment by Charlie Norwood, R-Ga., adopted 242-185, to clarify the authority of state and local enforcement personnel to apprehend, detain, remove and transport illegal aliens in the routine course of duty. It also would require the department to provide training manuals on the detention of illegal immigrants. *(House vote 185, p. H-60)*

▶ An amendment by Darlene Hooley, D-Ore., adopted 363-65, to bar the use of an airline ticket fee increase proposed by Bush to fund anything authorized in the bill. *(House vote 184, p. H-60)*

Cox hailed the bill's passage as "historic," and said he hoped it would become an annual affair. He also said he might consider further authorizing bills during the session to address homeland security areas not covered by his legislation, including a possible bill to reflect changes sought by Chertoff. ∎

**Chapter 13**

# IMMIGRATION

# House-Passed 'Real ID Act' Folded Into Supplemental Spending Bill

HOUSE REPUBLICANS STARTED the year by winning quick enactment of legislation to crack down on illegal immigrants and tighten U.S. border security. The House passed the provisions in February as a separate bill, most of which became law as part of an $82 billion supplemental spending bill for operations in Iraq and Afghanistan. President Bush signed that bill May 11 (HR 1268 – PL 109-13).

The driving force behind the legislation was House Judiciary Committee Chairman F. James Sensenbrenner Jr., R-Wis., who said his intent was to "prevent another 9/11-type terrorist attack by disrupting terrorist travel."

The bill made it harder for illegal immigrants to seek asylum or get driver's licenses and removed some obstacles to the construction of physical barriers along portions of the U.S-Mexico border.

Most of the provisions had been included in the 2004 intelligence overhaul bill (PL 108-458), but House Republican leaders agreed to drop them as the price of getting the measure through the Senate. To placate an infuriated Sensenbrenner, they promised that the provisions would be included in the first must-move piece of legislation in 2005. (*2004 Almanac, p. 11-3*)

Senate Majority Leader Bill Frist, R-Tenn., tried to keep the immigration language out of the supplemental in his chamber for fear it would cause major delays. But House leaders were insistent, and the Senate ended up adding its own proposal to allow more temporary seasonal workers into the country.

Most of Sensenbrenner's language survived in the supplemental, though conferees tweaked some of the provisions to make them more acceptable in the Senate. The Senate amendment also was included. (*Provisions, p. 13-5*)

## HIGHLIGHTS

The immigration portion of the supplemental included provisions to:
● **Driver's licenses.** Require states to follow uniform national standards for issuing driver's licenses to be used for federal purposes, such as boarding airplanes. States could issue two tiers of driving documents: one for federal purposes, and a lower-tier document that would authorize driving for one year without proof of legal residency.

States also were required to share drivers' data among themselves and with the federal government.
● **Asylum.** Require all applicants for asylum to establish that race, religion, nationality, membership in a particular social group or political opinion was at least one "central reason" for their persecution.

Immigration judges could weigh the credibility of the applicant's testimony along with other evidence, and could consider the applicant's

**BOX SCORE**

**BILL:**
HR 1268 — PL 109-13

**LEGISLATIVE ACTION:**

**House** passed HR 418, 261-161, on Feb. 10.

**House** adopted the conference report on HR 1268 (H Rept 109-72), 368-58 on May 5.

**Senate** cleared HR 1268, 100-0, on May 10.

**President** signed May 11.

demeanor and the consistency between written or oral statements. The law removed a 10,000-per-year cap on the number of illegal immigrants granted asylum who could become legal permanent residents.

The law also lifted the cap on the number of H-2B visas for temporary seasonal workers.
● **Border fence.** Allow the Department of Homeland Security to pre-empt state and federal laws to build border fences, a provision aimed at completing a stalled fence project along the U.S.-Mexican border near San Diego.

## LEGISLATIVE ACTION
### HOUSE FLOOR ACTION

In one of its first major legislative actions of the year, the House passed Sensenbrenner's bill (HR 418), which he dubbed the Real ID Act, by a vote of 261-161 on Feb. 10. (*House vote 31, p. H-12*)

House GOP leaders planned to attach the provisions to an anticipated supplemental spending bill for Iraq and Afghanistan as soon as Bush requested the funds.

"This bill is about common sense. It is about protecting our borders and making our country safer," said Steve Chabot, R-Ohio. "We cannot continue to let our laws be exploited and circumvented by future terrorists to further their plans of violence, destruction and murder."

The White House issued a statement the day before the vote saying it "strongly" supported the Sensenbrenner asylum bill. Bush was promoting a policy that stressed border security and a guest-worker visa program that would allow immigrants to fill low-skill jobs. His support for the asylum bill was seen as part of his effort to woo reluctant Republicans who opposed any initiatives they saw as giving "amnesty" to lawbreakers
● **Asylum.** Under the legislation, applicants for asylum would be required to prove that race, religion, nationality, membership in a particular social group or political opinion was, or would be, a "central reason" for their persecution. In some cases, immigration judges could require applicants to provide corroborating evidence to back up their claims. There would be "no presumption of credibility" on the part of an asylum applicant, meaning the burden of proof would be on the person seeking asylum.

The legislation also would give immigration judges broader authority to weigh the credibility of people seeking asylum in the United States. Judges could determine credibility based on demeanor or the consistency of an applicant's written or oral statements — including those not made under oath.

Critics said the language would impose an unfairly high barrier for refugees seeking asylum, who might be forced to seek corroborating evidence from their persecutors. Religious organizations and human rights

groups said that judges might question an applicant's credibility based on cultural differences. For instance, an applicant might cast his or her eyes down and avoid eye contact as a sign of respect — an action that could lead a judge to question the refugee's honesty. Supporters responded that the bill would simply give immigration judges the discretion that judges in other civil and criminal proceedings already had.

The House rejected, 185-236, an attempt by Jerrold Nadler, D-N.Y., and Kendrick B. Meek, D-Fla., to strike the asylum provisions. (*House vote 28, p. H-12*)

● **Driver's licenses.** The National Conference of State Legislatures opposed the driver's license provisions, saying they would be costly and burdensome for states to implement. But many lawmakers, particularly those from states that would not see dramatic changes under the legislation, said the language made sense. Ten states did not require people to show they had a lawful presence in the United States before issuing them driver's licenses. An 11th state, Tennessee, issued separate driver's licenses and certificates for those who could prove legal residency and for those who could not.

● **Border fence.** Under the bill, the secretary of Homeland Security could waive all laws that impeded the construction of physical barriers and roads designed to curb illegal border crossings. Judicial review of the decision would not be allowed. The provision was designed to spur the completion of a fence on the border near San Diego, which had a three-mile gap near a canyon called "Smuggler's Gulch." The project had been delayed because of environmental concerns.

Critics said that while they did not necessarily object to completing the fence, the provisions were too broad. Under the language, any local, state or federal laws — whether governing child labor, competition for federal contracts or environmental protection — could be overruled to expedite physical barriers to curb illegal border crossings.

Jane Harman, D-Calif., said it would set a "dangerous precedent" by placing the secretary of Homeland Security "above all laws."

The House rejected, 179-243, an attempt by Sam Farr, D-Calif., to delete the border fence provisions. (*House vote 29, p. H-12*)

A month after the House passed Sensenbrenner's bill, GOP leaders added the immigration provisions to the supplemental (HR 1268) as part of the rule for floor debate (H Res 151). The rule was adopted by voice vote. The House passed the supplemental, 388-43 on March 16. (*House vote 77, p. H-26*)

Despite Frist's statements that he preferred to handle the crackdown on illegal immigrants in a separate bill, House Republicans said they were confident that the provisions would eventually be included in the supplemental sent to the president.

### SENATE FLOOR ACTION

Senate appropriators pointedly excluded immigration provisions from their version of the supplemental (HR 1268 — S Rept 109-52), but senators immediately began offering amendments once the bill reached the floor. The debate sidetracked action on the spending bill for nearly a week, but in the end the only major amendment adopted was a proposal to allow more seasonal workers into the country.

The amendment, by Barbara A. Mikulski, D-Md., exempted seasonal workers who had worked in the United States in previous years from a cap on the number of so-called H-2B visas issued nationwide. Amendment backers said the cap of 66,000 had been reached early in the fiscal year, leaving an insufficient workforce for the summer tourism and seafood harvesting seasons. Hotels, restaurants and the crab and lobster industries were particularly dependent on temporary immigrants. The amendment, adopted, 94-6, was not expected to complicate

negotiations with House Republicans. (*Senate vote 102, p. S-20*)

A separate amendment by Jon Kyl, R-Ariz., requiring the Department of Homeland Security to certify that the visa recipients were returning workers was adopted by voice vote.

The Senate also gave voice-vote approval to proposals to redirect unused visas toward foreign nurses and increase the number of visas available for highly skilled Australian workers.

The Senate was able to vote on Mikulski's amendment because supporters secured the 60 votes needed to cut off debate. Senators refused to limit debate on competing amendments addressing the legal status of temporary agricultural workers.

An amendment by Saxby Chambliss, R-Ga., would have created a temporary guest-worker program for farm laborers. Eligible workers could work in the United States for up to nine years, but could not obtain permanent resident status without returning home for at least a year and waiting in line with other applicants for green cards. A cloture motion on the amendment failed, 21-77. (*Senate vote 97, p. S-20*)

Larry E. Craig, R-Idaho, and Edward M. Kennedy, D-Mass., offered a competing amendment that would have created a two-step process for agricultural workers to apply for temporary and then permanent legal residency status. A cloture motion failed, 53-45, seven votes short of the 60 needed. (*Senate vote 98, p. S-20*)

The two guest-worker amendments, and another by Dianne Feinstein, D-Calif., that would have expressed the sense of the Senate that immigration provisions should not be included in the final bill, were all ruled non-germane and thrown out after the Senate voted 100-0 to cut off debate on the underlying bill. (*Senate vote 103, p. S-20*)

The Senate passed the supplemental, 99-0, on April 21. (*Senate vote 109, p. S-21*)

### CONFERENCE/FINAL ACTION

The conference agreement on the supplemental spending bill kept the House immigration provisions largely intact. Sensenbrenner credited the White House with ensuring that the language was included in the final bill. The House adopted the conference report (H Rept 109-72) by a vote of 368-58 on May 5. The Senate cleared the bill, 100-0, on May 10. (*House vote 161, p. H-52; Senate vote 117, p. S-23*)

Senate conferees won a few concessions that softened some House language, but sponsors and opponents agreed they made changes only at the margins. "Democrats were shut out of all negotiations in conference, and none of our concerns were addressed," said John Conyers Jr. of Michigan, the ranking Democrat on House Judiciary.

In the main changes, conferees agreed to:

▶ Remove language that would have allowed deportation of asylum applicants while their cases were pending in federal court.

▶ Modify the grounds for seeking asylum to state that the applicant had to establish that race, religion, nationality, membership in a particular social group, or political opinion was or would be "at least one central reason" for their persecution.

Critics of the original asylum language credited Sen. Sam Brownback, R-Kan., a conferee on the bill, for incorporating the changes.

▶ Allow federal district courts to hear claims that actions by the Homeland Security secretary in waiving existing laws to build the border fence were unconstitutional.

▶ Allow states to issue two tiers of driving documents: one for federal purposes, and a lower-tier document that would authorize driving for one year without proof of legal residency. The latter had to state that it was not acceptable by federal agencies and must have a unique design or color to alert federal agencies to that fact. ■

# [PROVISIONS]
# Details of New Immigration Law

*Following are the major asylum and border security provisions included in the supplemental legislation, which President Bush signed into law (HR 1268 — PL 109-13) May 11 :*

## ASYLUM

● **Central reasons.** Applicants for refugee status were required to establish that race, religion, nationality, membership in a particular social group, or political opinion was, or would be, at least one "central reason" for their persecution.

● **Corroboration.** The applicant's testimony alone without corroboration could be sufficient to satisfy this requirement if his testimony was credible, persuasive and referred to specific facts that demonstrate that he is a refugee.

● **Credibility.** In reviewing the application, the judge could weigh the credibility of the testimony along with other evidence. Among other factors, a judge could base his determination of credibility on the demeanor, candor or responsiveness of the applicant or witness, as well as the plausibility of the testimony and the consistency between written and oral statements. If the judge did make an adverse determination of credibility, there was a presumption of credibility upon appeal. Similar standards for credibility applied to immigrants seeking a stay of their deportation order.

● **Application.** Provisions related to conditions for granting asylum took effect on the date of enactment and applied only to individuals who applied on or after that date. Provisions regarding standards of review for reversing determinations took effect on the date of enactment and applied retroactively to all final deportation orders issued before or after that date.

● **Cap lifted.** The law lifted a cap that limited the number of people granted asylum in the United States who could have their status adjusted to permanent resident each year (10,000 in 2005) and removed a separate one entirely that limited the number of applicants who could be admitted for escaping coercive population-control methods.

## EXCLUSION & REMOVAL

● **Inadmissibility.** The terrorism-related justifications for denying admission to the United States under the Immigration and Nationality Act were expanded. Admission was now barred to any person who had engaged in or incited terrorist activity, was a representative of a terrorist organization or group that espoused terrorist activity, or endorsed or espoused terrorist activity or persuaded others to do so. Also denied admission were persons who had received military-type training from terrorist organizations, and the spouse and children of someone deemed inadmissible if the activity serving as the basis for the denial occurred within the five years prior to application.

● **Engaging in terrorist activities.** The measure expanded the definition of terrorist activities to include gathering information on potential targets; soliciting funds for terrorist activities and organizations; soliciting individuals to engage in conduct or membership in terrorist organizations; and providing material support, including safe houses, transportation, communications, funds, false documents, weapons or training. The provision narrowed an exception that previously protected those who did not know their actions would further a terrorist orga-

nization's goals. The exception was narrowed so that it protected only those who could demonstrate that they did not know and should not reasonably have known that it was a terrorist organization.

● **Terrorist organization.** The definition of a terrorist organization was expanded to include groups of two or more people, whether organized or not, who engaged in the terrorist activities, even if the group had not been designated by the State Department as a terrorist organization.

● **Waiver.** The secretary of State, in consultation with the attorney general and Homeland Security secretary, was given sole authority to waive the inadmissibility of people who represented political, social, or other groups that endorsed or espoused terrorist activity, those who endorsed or espoused terrorist activity or persuaded others to do so, or those who provided material support to organizations engaging in terrorist activities.

This waiver authority could not be exercised if removal proceedings had already been started against the person. The secretaries of State and Homeland Security were required to provide Congress a report identifying individual recipients of the waiver within 90 days of the fiscal year and within a week of waiving inadmissibility of a group.

● **Removal.** Any immigrant considered inadmissible would also be deportable on the same grounds as detailed above. This provision erased the previous distinction that made it easier to deny entry to those outside the country than remove those already in the United States legally.

● **Judicial review.** The new law aligned restrictions on judicial review of orders of removal with the Immigration and Nationality Act (INA) so that statutory and non-statutory habeas corpus review was barred wherever it was barred in the INA. There was an exception for judicial review of "constitutional claims or questions of law," but such cases could be brought only in a U.S. Court of Appeals rather than in lower federal district courts. All cases challenging removal orders that were pending in district courts the day the law was enacted were transferred to circuit courts.

## U.S.-MEXICO BORDER FENCE

● **Waiver.** The law gave the Homeland Security secretary the authority to waive all legal requirements in order to build barriers and roads.

● **Judicial review.** Legal challenges to the Homeland Security secretary's waiver decision had to allege constitutional violations and could be filed only in U.S. district courts. Under the new law, only the Supreme Court could opt to hear appeals, as the appeals courts were now excluded from review.

## DRIVER'S LICENSES

● **Federal use.** Beginning three years after enactment, driver's licenses that did not meet the requirements set out in the law would no longer be used by federal agencies for any official purpose. If a state issued a driver's license or identification card that did not satisfy the requirements, the license had to state on its face that it was not acceptable for federal identification or other purposes. Such licenses also had to use a unique design or color to indicate that they were not acceptable for federal purposes. The law did not set a time for states to comply with the new requirements, other than the three-year deadline.

● **License physical features.** Licenses had to include the driver's full legal name, date of birth, gender, driver's license or identification card number, digital photo, address of principal residence and signature. The licenses also had to have "physical security features" designed to prevent anyone from changing or duplicating them, and they had to use a common machine-readable technology.

● **Issuance requirements.** An applicant for a license had to present, and states had to verify the authenticity of, a photo identity document, documentation showing the applicant's date of birth, proof of a Social Security number, and documentation showing the applicant's name and address of principal residence.

Applicants had to provide valid documentary evidence that they were lawfully in the United States as citizens; that they were immigrants lawfully admitted for permanent or temporary residency; that they were recipients of or applicants for conditional permanent status, asylum or refugee status; or that they had a valid unexpired non-immigrant visa.

Applicants who had a pending asylum application or pending approval for temporary protected status, had approved deferred action status, or had a pending application for adjustment of status to permanent residency could be issued only a temporary driver's license or temporary identification card.

Temporary licenses and identification cards were valid only during the time the applicant was authorized to stay in the United States, or for one year in instances in which the period was indefinite. They could be renewed only if the applicant's stay was extended by the Department of Homeland Security. Licenses that were not temporary could not be valid for more than eight years.

● **Document verification.** Before issuing a license or identification card, states had to verify the validity and completeness of all documents with the agencies that issued them. States could not accept any foreign documents other than official passports. By Sept. 11, 2005, states were required to agree to routinely use an automated system, the Systematic Alien Verification for Entitlements, maintained by the Department of Homeland Security, to verify the legal presence of persons other than U.S. citizens. Applicants' Social Security numbers had to be confirmed with the Social Security Administration.

● **Record maintenance and access.** States were required to retain digital copies of documents presented by applicants and take digital pictures of them. The digital copies had to be retained for 10 years, or paper copies for seven years. States were required to provide other states with electronic access to their motor vehicle database that contained all the data printed on the driver's licenses or identification cards as well as the license holders' histories of violations and suspensions.

● **Counterfeits.** The law made it a crime to traffic in either false or actual authentication features used in false documents. Information about persons convicted of using false driver's licenses at airports would be included in aviation security screening databases.

● **Funding.** The Homeland Security secretary was authorized to make grants to help states conform to the new driver's license standards. The bill authorized "such sums as may be necessary to carry out this title," rather than delineating a specific dollar amount.

## BORDER INFRASTRUCTURE

● **Threat assessment.** The Homeland Security Department was directed to study "the technology, equipment, and personnel needed to address security vulnerabilities within the United States" for all Bureau of Customs and Border Protection field offices that had responsibility for border regions. Follow-up studies had to be conducted at least once every five years. The department was required to report its findings and conclusions, with legislative recommendations, to Congress.

● **Ground surveillance technologies.** The Homeland Security and Defense departments were directed to begin work on a pilot program within six months of enactment that would use ground surveillance technologies such as video cameras, sensors and motion detectors along the border, and then report the results to Congress.

● **Information sharing.** The Homeland Security Department was directed to begin work on a plan within six months of enactment to integrate communications among federal, state and local government agencies and Indian tribal agencies regarding border security, and then report the results to Congress.

## WORKER VISAS

● **Seasonal workers.** The law lifted the annual cap (66,000 in 2005) on the number of H-2B visas issued annually to people who had held temporary jobs in the United States for one of the three previous years.

● **Australia.** The law increased the number of visas available for highly skilled Australian workers to 10,500.

● **Nurses.** Up to 50,000 visas that were unused for other purposes between 2001 and 2004 were directed to foreign nurses. ■

# House Seeks to Tighten Borders

IN THE HECTIC FINAL DAYS OF THE SESSION, the House passed a bill to tighten border security and stiffen criminal penalties on illegal immigration. The bill — a late addition to the schedule — was the subject of a raucous floor debate and exposed deep divisions among Republicans on immigration.

House passage represented a win for the Immigration Reform Caucus, a group of more than 90 House conservatives led by Tom Tancredo, R-Colo. "For the first time in seven-and-a-half years, I'm going to be able to go out on the stump and talk about my party doing the right thing on immigration," said Tancredo. "And I feel good about it."

But the bill did not address an issue that many in both parties said was crucial to the debate: how to provide a pathway to legal residency for the millions of undocumented immigrants who were living and working in the United States, often in low-skilled, low-wage jobs. Senate leaders promised to take up immigration in 2006, and any Senate bill was likely to include some kind of "guest worker" visa program for illegal immigrants already in the country, a proposal that Tancredo's caucus said was unacceptable.

President Bush, as well as the U.S. Chamber of Commerce and Hispanic advocacy groups, called on Congress to create a guest-worker program that would allow illegal immigrants to become legal residents and eventually citizens. "We should not be content with laws that punish hard-working people who want only to provide for their families and deny businesses willing workers," Bush said Feb. 2 in his State of the Union address. *(Text, p. D-5)*

That position was supported by many Democrats and some moderate Republicans, but Tancredo and his bloc of House Republicans said it was a form of amnesty for people who broke the law by entering the country illegally. Tancredo introduced an overhaul bill in July (HR 3333) to make illegal entry a felony, with jail terms for employers who hired illegal immigrants.

The most controversial elements of the House-passed bill included provisions that would make it a crime to be in the United States illegally; require all employers to use a government system to check the immigration status of employees, including those already working for them, and punish those who helped illegal aliens, not only through smuggling, but also by assisting those already in the country.

## BACKGROUND

The nation's population of illegal immigrants was variously estimated at 10 million to 11 million, with several hundred thousand additional people crossing the Mexican border illegally each year. Illegal immigration was supposed to have at least slowed down after Congress passed the Immigration Reform and Control Act (PL 99-603) in 1986. That law granted amnesty to 2.7 million people living in the country illegally while imposing tough sanctions on employers who hired undocumented workers. But the law had never been strictly enforced. *(1986 Almanac, p. 61)*

The unspoken fact was that there were many beneficiaries of the status quo, including businesses and families that employed illegal labor, and the immigrants themselves, who wanted any job they could get. Consumers also benefited from the lower-priced goods and services that resulted from immigrant labor.

Immigration advocates argued that new arrivals filled the sorts of jobs Americans did not want or would be unable to fill as the workforce aged. However, some studies suggested that illegal immigration suppressed the wages of the least-skilled Americans.

There also was a mismatch between the costs and benefits of immigration at various levels of government. "The federal government sets immigration policy and reaps the benefits," said Princeton sociologist Douglas S. Massey, "but all the costs are paid at the state and local level."

The federal government collected income and payroll taxes from the 50 percent to 60 percent of illegal immigrants whose work was reported by businesses and individuals. Because illegal immigrants used fake Social Security numbers, their payroll taxes piled up in a fund for mismatched and invalid Social Security numbers that contained $463 billion as of 2002, according to the Economic Report of the President. The money served to offset other federal spending.

Meanwhile, state and local governments were footing most of the bill for health care, education and other services for illegal immigrants. They wanted the federal government to either reduce the flow of illegal immigration or help defray the costs. Though this still was an issue that mainly concerned border communities, the cost of illegal immigration was being felt in the Midwest and South as well.

## HIGHLIGHTS

The House-passed bill included provisions to:

● **Border security.** Require the Department of Homeland Security (DHS) to increase its "operational control" over U.S. borders within 18 months of enactment. The bill would require the construction of a double security fence — along with access roads, lighting, cameras and sensors — across several portions of the U.S-Mexico border. Fences would be built from Calexico, Calif., along most of the Arizona border; around Tecate, Calif., and El Paso, Texas; from Del Rio, Texas, to Eagle Pass, Texas; and from Laredo, Texas, to Brownsville, Texas. A study into the feasibility of a fence along the northern border with Canada also would be required.

● **Mandatory detention.** End a policy critics called "catch and release" that allowed apprehended illegals to be released with a promise to show up for a deportation hearing. Under the bill, all such illegals would be detained until they were deported or admitted into the country.

● **Expedited removal.** Allow non-Mexican aliens to be deported based on an order from an immigration official rather than an immigration judge. The expedited removal would apply to illegal aliens who had not been admitted or paroled and who had been apprehended within 14 days of entry and within 100 miles of an international border.

● **Cargo screening.** Require that radiation detectors be installed at all points of entry and that all cargo bound for the United States be screened for nuclear or radiological materials within one year of enactment.

● **Mandatory employee verification.** Require employers to use the Basic Pilot Employment Verification Program, a system run by the DHS, to screen employees' Social Security and foreign identification numbers. The mandatory system would be implemented in phases starting two years after enactment, when all employers would have to use the system for newly hired employees. Within three years, federal, state and local government and certain other private employers would

have to use the system to check the eligibility of all of their employees — both new hires and the existing workforce. Within six years of enactment, all other employers would have to do so for all of their workforce.

Employers who hired individuals who were ineligible to work in the United States would face minimum civil penalties ranging from $5,000 for a first offense to $25,000 to $40,000 per illegal employee for anything beyond the second offense. The existing range was $250 to $2,000 for a first offense and $3,000 to $10,000 per employee for a third offense.

● **Assisting illegal aliens.** Make it a crime to assist, encourage, direct or induce people to enter or remain in the country "knowing or in reckless disregard" of the fact that they were illegal immigrants. It would be a crime to transport such people into or within the country or conceal them from authorities.

● **Illegal presence.** Make it a criminal, rather than civil, violation to enter or reside in the country illegally, punishable by 366 days in prison.

● **Visa diversity.** Eliminate the visa diversity lottery, which provided about 50,000 permanent residency visas a year to people selected randomly from countries considered to be under-represented in the U.S. immigrant flow.

● **Local law enforcement.** Encourage local police to help enforce immigration law and withhold federal money from state and local governments that maintained policies preventing their police from reporting illegal immigrants to federal authorities or assisting in enforcement.

● **Terrorists and gangs.** Make it easier to deport illegal immigrants identified as terrorists and explicitly bar them from becoming citizens. The DHS could designate groups as criminal gangs, making it easier for their members to be detained and deported.

## LEGISLATIVE ACTION
### HOUSE COMMITTEE ACTION

Facing escalating pressure from Tancredo and others in the Republican Party to crack down on illegal immigrants, the House Judiciary Committee approved the bill (HR 4437 — H Rept 109-345, Part 1) on a 23-15 party-line vote Dec. 8.

Chairman F. James Sensenbrenner Jr., R-Wis., who sponsored the bill, combined most of the language from a border security bill that the House Homeland Security Committee had approved in November, with new provisions aimed at reducing incentives for people to migrate illegally to the United States.

Sensenbrenner's chief provision was the requirement that employers use Basic Pilot. Groups favoring reduced immigration said the program, which was voluntary, had worked well in trials. The U.S. Chamber of Commerce opposed making its use mandatory, saying it produced "false positive" results.

The bill for the first time would designate illegal immigration as a criminal, rather than a civil, offense and would increase penalties for a variety of immigration-related crimes.

The border security bill (HR 4312 — H Rept 109-329, Part 1), sponsored by Peter T. King, R-N.Y., required the government to create a comprehensive strategy for guarding the borders and called for adding police and surveillance equipment at the borders, particularly the porous boundary with Mexico.

Democrats supported King's bill, but they harshly criticized Sensenbrenner's version. "The majority's decision to bring forth, a week before we are about to leave, a border security bill can only be attributed to one of three things: stupidity, political panic or venality," said Howard L. Berman of California.

An amendment by Berman to add a guest-worker visa program was defeated 13-22. Republican Jeff Flake of Arizona, whose legislation was the model for Berman's amendment, voted "present" as a "gesture of appreciation" to the Democrat. But Flake said Berman's amendment did not include an important provision of his bill that would reduce a backlog of visa applications that forced many families to wait years for foreign relatives to receive permission to enter the United States.

Tancredo was not entirely satisfied with Sensenbrenner's bill. He and more than 20 members of his caucus sent a letter to House GOP leaders Dec. 5 asking them to allow votes on a series of floor amendments that would make the bill more restrictive. Among them was a proposal to end "birthright" citizenship — the constitutional guarantee that all children born on American soil, regardless of the immigration status of their parents, are citizens.

### HOUSE FLOOR ACTION

The House passed the bill by a vote of 239-182 on Dec. 16, after adopting two dozen amendments. Members had proposed about 128 amendments to the bill, evidence of the divisions over immigration and border security in the chamber and within the Republican Party itself. (House vote 661, p. H-210)

To the delight of Tancredo and his allies, the rule for floor debate did not allow a guest-worker program amendment, or even non-binding language proposed by Flake to express support for the principle behind guest-worker proposals.

Democrats opposed to the bill looked to the Senate to temper or strike many of the provisions. Speaking to Tancredo, Berman said on the floor: "I would bet these provisions which you like and which you think make this into an attractive proposition and a serious attempt will never be seen again."

Arizona Republican Jim Kolbe told reporters Dec. 15 that he would bet $100 the House immigration bill would never go to a conference committee with the Senate. "After we pass this, we send it off to the Senate, and that's the end of it," he said.

Lawmakers from Tancredo's caucus won two of their long-term goals: amendments to drop the diversity visa and to put pressure on local law enforcement to aid in cracking down on illegal immigrants. But they did not get a vote on an amendment to end "birthright" citizenship. Some in the caucus believed the children of illegal immigrants should not automatically be granted citizenship, calling them "anchor babies" that enabled whole families to immigrate to the United States.

During the debate, the House:

▶ Adopted, 273-148, an amendment by Robert W. Goodlatte, R-Va., to eliminate the visa diversity lottery. Many Republicans and some Democrats considered the lottery a security risk, susceptible to fraud and discriminatory toward others who had to claim work or family ties to the United States to qualify for immigration. (House vote 653, p. H-208)

▶ Adopted, 237-180, an amendment by Charlie Norwood, R-Ga., to encourage local police to help catch illegal immigrants. Federal money would be withheld from state and local governments that enacted policies forbidding their police to ask people about their immigration status, or otherwise preventing them from assisting in apprehending illegal immigrants. State and local officials and police had long protested such proposals, saying illegal immigrants would avoid reporting crimes to police if they believed they might be arrested for being in the country. (House vote 656, p. H-208)

▶ Rejected, 164-257, an amendment by Sensenbrenner to reduce the bill's criminal penalties for illegal immigrants — found either crossing the border or living in the country — from 366 days in prison to six

months. Sensenbrenner said the White House requested the change because the penalties in the bill would give the crimes felony status, entailing indictments and jury trials and discouraging prosecution. *(House vote 655, p. H-208)*

But many Republicans preferred the tougher penalties, and most Democrats were not going to help Sensenbrenner correct his bill, or be seen as voting for any criminal penalty for illegal immigrants. Most Democrats said it should not be a crime to reside in the country illegally, something considered only a civil violation under existing law.

▸ Adopted, 247-170, an amendment by Lynn Westmoreland, R-Ga., to cap penalties for companies caught hiring illegal immigrants. The amendment also would allow a company, on a first offense, to escape fines by claiming that it had made a good-faith effort to verify legality, and exempt companies from fines for hiring by their subcontractors. *(House vote 657, p. H-208)*

▸ Adopted, 260-159, an amendment by Duncan Hunter, R-Calif., to authorize extensive new fencing on the Mexican border. *(House vote 640, p. H-204)*

▸ Adopted by voice vote an amendment by Rick Renzi, R-Ariz., to require that Border Patrol uniforms be made in the United States. Renzi said the uniforms were being made in Mexico, presenting a security risk because people might steal them and sneak into the country posing as border agents.

For a time on Dec. 15, it appeared the legislation might not reach the floor. The day was marked by an emotional clash between rank-and-file Republicans and their leaders over the way the leadership planned to bring the bill to the floor and what amendments would be allowed. GOP leaders corralled their members for a private meeting in the basement of the Capitol in the early afternoon, where they explained a confusing set of rules governing debate and listened to several dozen lawmakers vent their concerns. "There were 35 or so speakers," said Kolbe, who was among them, "and there were at least 45 positions. Some people had two positions. There's just no consensus." ■

# Chapter 14

# LEGAL AFFAIRS

# Roberts Confirmed as Chief Justice Following Rehnquist's Death

JOHN G. ROBERTS JR. WAS confirmed Sept. 29 as the 17th chief justice of the United States. At age 50, Roberts was the youngest chief justice since John Marshall, who was nominated by President John Adams in 1801 and served for 34 years.

The Senate vote was somewhat of an anticlimax, as it had been clear for weeks that Roberts would win confirmation with a sizable majority. The Senate Judiciary Committee had approved the nomination, 13-5, a week earlier, following confirmation hearings where Roberts' performance awed even his toughest critics.

Roberts' smooth confirmation was a major victory for President Bush, as well as for Judiciary Committee Chairman Arlen Specter, R-Pa., who satisfied both conservatives and liberals with the way he presided over the four-day hearing and the nomination as a whole.

## ROBERTS NOMINATED TWICE

Bush first nominated Roberts on July 19 to succeed Justice Sandra Day O'Connor, who had announced her retirement 18 days earlier. But when Chief Justice William H. Rehnquist died Sept. 3 at age 80 after an 11-month battle with thyroid cancer, Bush quickly picked Roberts to head the high court. (O'Connor, p. 14-7; Rehnquist, p. 14-4)

Although the president had promised to consider ethnic, gender and occupational diversity in making his choice of a replacement for O'Connor, he ended up announcing the nomination of a white male judge well versed in establishment Washington — the profile of most of the sitting justices. The nomination came after two weeks of consultation with advisers and Senate leaders from both parties.

Roberts, who had sat on the U.S. Court of Appeals for the District of Columbia Circuit for only the previous two years, appeared to have won Bush's favor because his résumé offered a different sort of balance. He was reliably conservative enough to satisfy the Republican Party's social conservative base, but he lacked the lengthy paper trail of opinions, legal briefs and law review articles that could make him instantly objectionable to liberal interest groups and Senate Democrats.

The White House clearly gained the initial momentum, thanks in part to careful choreography. The president announced the nomination during a 9 p.m. press conference in the State Dining Room alongside Roberts, his wife and two young children.

Republicans stressed Roberts' gold-plated credentials: undergraduate and law degrees from Harvard, clerkships for both a renowned appeals court judge in New York and Rehnquist when he was an associate justice. After turns in the Justice Department and the White House counsel's office, Roberts argued 39 cases before the high court as a deputy solicitor general and as a partner in one of Washington's most prestigious law firms. He then took his seat on the federal appeals court in 2003, soon after he turned 48.

During the summer, Roberts paid one-on-one visits to senators' offices, impressing those on both sides of the aisles as intelligent and well spoken.

Liberal groups did their best to knock him down. People for the American Way, a coalition of gay rights groups, Alliance for Justice, and women's rights and civil rights organizations all came out against the nominee at a series of news conferences designed to build the appearance of momentum in the weeks prior to his confirmation hearings scheduled to start Sept. 6.

The liberal groups and their Democratic Senate allies tried without success to coax the White House into releasing documents from Roberts' most recent and highest-level executive branch position in the solicitor general's office during the administration of President George Bush. The White House contended that releasing the documents "would stifle the candid, honest and thorough advice that solicitor generals depend on from their attorneys."

Instead, in late July and mid-August, the administration released tens of thousands of pages of documents from 1981 to 1986. The most potentially damaging details were mostly two decades old, when issues such as pay equity and the Equal Rights Amendment were at the fore. Legal scholars and others said the material suggested that Roberts was a consistent advocate of judicial restraint, defending the idea that the federal courts could be prohibited from ordering busing to desegregate the schools, for example. He also advocated a limited role for both the courts and federal agencies in enforcing anti-discrimination laws.

Then on Sept. 3, three days before the Judiciary Committee was scheduled to begin Roberts' hearing, Rehnquist died. On Sept. 6, Bush withdrew Roberts' nomination to succeed O'Connor and nominated him instead to replace Rehnquist.

## JUDICIARY COMMITTEE HEARING

After a six-day delay, Roberts delivered a flawless performance at his confirmation hearing before the Senate Judiciary Committee, which commenced Sept. 12. Roberts brought no notes with him to the hearing room and took none once inside during a seamless performance full of answers that were off the cuff but so carefully constructed that Democrats were left all but powerless to alter the inevitability of his confirmation.

Nothing better symbolized Democrats' frustration than the moment on the second day of questioning when their most aggressive inquisitor, Joseph R. Biden Jr. of Delaware, shook his head, smiled his trademark broad, toothy grin and said, "You're good."

It was a backhanded compliment, and Biden later complained that Roberts was not forthcoming enough. "Without any knowledge of your understanding of the law, because you will not share it with us, we are rolling the dice with you, Judge," Biden said.

Republicans insisted that no nominee had ever been as forthcoming. "If people can't vote for you, then I doubt they can vote for any Republican nominee," Orrin G. Hatch, R-Utah, told Roberts.

What senators should ask and how much Roberts should answer were main points of contention as soon as the hearing got under way. Committee Democrats made it clear that they expected Roberts to

# Rehnquist Leaves Mark On the High Court

WHEN WILLIAM H. REHNQUIST began his lifetime appointment to the Supreme Court in January 1972, he was a lonely conservative voice on a predominately liberal court.

But by the 1990s, after he was joined by several more Republican-appointed justices, Rehnquist engineered a series of "federalism" decisions that curbed Congress' ability to pass broad regulatory statutes based on its constitutional authority to govern interstate commerce or enforce the 14th Amendment. Some considered this to be the greatest legacy for Rehnquist, who died Sept. 3 after being treated for about a year for thyroid cancer.

"There are a whole range of issues that conservatives have wanted to turn the … jurisprudence [of the court under chief justices Earl Warren and Warren E. Burger] around on," said Mark Tushnet, a Georgetown University law professor. "But federalism is one that's distinctively associated with Rehnquist."

Rehnquist's philosophy hinged on a strict interpretation of the Constitution. Even so, the decision for which his court was most likely to be remembered was its 2000 ruling in *Bush v. Gore*, which resulted in the election of George W. Bush. The 5-4 decision ended an intense legal battle over recounting presidential ballots in Flori-da, a political firestorm the Rehnquist court was reluctant to enter because of its fuzzy constitutional merits. *(2001 Almanac, p. 15-4)*

"None are more conscious of the vital limits on judicial authority than are the members of this Court, and none stand more in admiration of the Constitution's design to leave the selection of the President to the people, through their legislatures, and to the political sphere," said the unsigned opinion. "When contending parties invoke the process of the courts, however, it becomes our unsought responsibility to resolve the federal and constitutional issues the judicial system has been forced to confront."

Rehnquist did not participate in the only other case during his tenure that had a comparable effect on the presidency. The high court ruled 8-0 on July 24, 1974, in *United States v. Nixon*, that President Richard Nixon had to comply with a subpoena and turn over to a special prosecutor the White House tapes that implicated him and his aides in the Watergate conspiracy. Nixon resigned two weeks later, after the House Judiciary Committee approved articles of impeachment. Rehnquist had recused himself because of his previous work in Nixon's Justice Department. *(1974 Almanac, p. 890)*

## 'A GREEK TEMPLE'

Rehnquist began his Supreme Court journey in January 1952 as a clerk for Justice Robert H. Jackson. He arrived at the court build-

lay out his views about civil rights, privacy and the powers of Congress. Most Republicans on the panel said Roberts should be circumspect and refuse to answer any questions that would presage how he would lead the Supreme Court as its chief justice.

Playing the arbiter, Specter was careful not to side with either the conservatives to his right at the table or the Democrats to his left. "It has been my judgment, after participating in nine — this will be the 10th for me, personally — that nominees answer about as many questions as they think they have to in order to be confirmed," Specter said. "It's a subtle minuet."

In his opening statement spoken entirely from memory, Roberts compared the job of judge to being an umpire. "I will decide every case based on the record, according to the rule of law, without fear or favor, to the best of my ability," Roberts said. " And I will remember that it's my job to call balls and strikes and not to pitch or bat." *(Text, p. D-14)*

Neither the combativeness of Biden and Edward M. Kennedy, D-Mass., nor the patient questioning of Dianne Feinstein, D-Calif., could penetrate Roberts' circumspect style.

He repeatedly said he would not comment on any case likely to come before the court in the future, characterized his work in the Justice Department during the Reagan administration as that of a staff attorney rather than a decision maker, and defined his vision of the court — and himself — as "modest" and "limited." *(Excerpts, p. 14-6)*

The duty of judges "is to decide the cases before them. They're not to legislate. They're not to execute the laws," Roberts said.

Specter opened the first day of questioning with a line of inquiry on what could be considered Topic A in any Supreme Court nomination hearing: Abortion.

The chairman — the only Republican committee member who supported the 1973 decision in *Roe v. Wade* that established a woman's right to abortion — pressed Roberts vigorously on the topic. He quoted the Supreme Court's 1992 *Planned Parenthood of Southeastern Pa. v. Casey* deci-sion that expressly reaffirmed the central ruling of *Roe* by a 5-4 vote and noted that "people have organized intimate relationships" based on the decision for two decades.

"Well, senator," Roberts responded, "the importance of settled expectations in the application of stare decisis is a very important consideration," he said, referring to the legal principle of following judicial precedent. But citing the court's reasoning in *Casey*, he said other factors come into play as well, including "whether or not particular precedents have proven to be unworkable" and "whether the doctrinal basis of a decision had been eroded by subsequent developments."

Roberts did say he agreed with one privacy precedent, the Supreme Court's 1965 *Griswold v. Connecticut* decision "that marital privacy extends to contraception and availability of that." In the face of additional questions on privacy rights the next day, Roberts said he had no quarrel with the Supreme Court's conclusion in *Eisenstadt v. Baird*, a 1972 case that extended the right to contraceptives to unmarried people. Both decisions were precursors to *Roe v. Wade*.

But Roberts did not explicitly endorse *Roe*, and his general comments on privacy rights did not satisfy Democrats and liberal groups. In addition to abortion, many of the Democrats' questions centered on Roberts' writings during his tenure as a lawyer in the Justice Department under President Ronald Reagan and the White House counsel's office under President George Bush.

Kennedy repeatedly focused on Roberts' role in the Reagan administration's proposal for renewing the Voting Rights Act in 1982, but it was a line of questioning too esoteric to generate much new public outrage.

Roberts emphasized that he was a staff lawyer arguing the positions of his bosses, but he rarely backed away from the positions he once advocated. "It was the position of the Reagan administration, the position of the attorney general for whom I worked, that the Voting Rights Act should be extended for the longest extension in its history without change," Roberts said.

ing after a treacherous, wintry drive from his Wisconsin home in a 1941 Studebaker Champion with no heater. When he saw his new work site, the Supreme Court building, he thought it looked like "a magnificent Greek temple."

Rehnquist was born in Milwaukee, Wis., on Oct. 1, 1924, and was the son of a paper salesman. During World War II, he served in the Army Air Corps as a weather observer in North Africa. He attended college on the GI Bill, earning bachelor's and master's degrees in political science at Stanford University in 1948.

Rehnquist received a second master's degree, in government, from Harvard two years later. He entered Stanford Law School, where he graduated first in his class in 1951. The third-ranked student in his Stanford class, Sandra Day O'Connor, joined him on the Supreme Court in 1981 and eulogized him at his funeral Sept. 7. O'Connor had already announced her own plans to retire as soon as a successor was chosen and in place. (O'Connor, p. 14-7)

Twenty years after clerking for Jackson — and after a career as a private attorney in Phoenix and a stint at the Justice Department — Rehnquist joined the court. Nixon nominated him in 1971 to succeed John Marshall Harlan as an associate justice, and the Senate confirmed him by a vote of 68-26. In 1986, President Ronald Reagan nominated Rehnquist as chief justice to replace Warren E. Burger. He was confirmed to that position by a slightly narrower margin, 65-33. (1971 Almanac, p. 851; 1986 Almanac, p. 67)

One signal case in the court's evolution under Rehnquist came in 1995, when a five-justice majority struck down a 1990 law (PL 101-647) that had banned possession of a firearm in a school zone. Writing for the majority in the case, *United States v. Lopez*, Rehnquist rejected the government's rationale that Congress could regulate gun possession near schools because of the potential effects of violent crime on the national economy. "To uphold the Government's contentions here, we would have to pile inference upon inference in a manner that would bid fair to convert congressional authority under the Commerce Clause to a general police power of the sort retained by the States," Rehnquist wrote. (1995 Almanac, p. 6-40)

The other justices in the majority then were O'Connor, Anthony M. Kennedy, Antonin Scalia and Clarence Thomas — all appointed by GOP presidents.

In 2000, Rehnquist led the same group of five justices in striking down a 1994 law (PL 103-322) that had allowed victims of "a crime of violence motivated by gender," such as rape, to file civil lawsuits in federal courts against their attackers. Congress had asserted that such crimes hampered interstate commerce by deterring victims from crossing state lines. (2000 Almanac, p. 15-23)

"The regulation and punishment of intrastate violence that is not directed at the instrumentalities, channels, or goods involved in interstate commerce has always been the province of the States," Rehnquist wrote.

On the second day of questioning, he drew a distinction between how he handled matters as a Justice Department lawyer and what his role would be as a Supreme Court justice. "I would confront that as a judge and not as a staff attorney for an administration with a particular position on that issue," Roberts said.

He assured Charles E. Schumer, D-N.Y., simply that "I will be my own man on the Supreme Court."

Though he did not mention them by name, Roberts seemed to imply that there might be some distance between himself and conservative justices Scalia and Clarence Thomas on the question of determining the intent of the framers of the Constitution, saying he would "depart from some views of original intent."

Republicans other than Specter alternated between softball questions and defense of the nominee. By the second day of questioning, Republicans spoke as if Roberts' confirmation was a foregone conclusion. "I'm quite sure that the Senate is in fact going to confirm John Roberts, the man," said Mike DeWine, R-Ohio.

### THE COMMITTEE VOTE

The Senate Judiciary Committee set the stage for a lopsided floor vote when it voted 13-5 on Sept. 22 to recommend confirmation. A trio of Democrats, including, most surprisingly, the minority's ranking member, Patrick J. Leahy of Vermont, joined all 10 Republicans in supporting Roberts.

Leahy's announcement the day before the committee vote that he would endorse Roberts was a particular blow to liberal interest groups that had vociferously opposed the nomination. Ralph G. Neas, president of People for the American Way, said Leahy's "decision was inexplicable and deeply disappointing," and that his "support for Roberts will make him complicit" in rulings that Roberts would make on the high court.

Leahy and Wisconsin Sens. Russell D. Feingold and Herb Kohl, the

two other Judiciary Committee Democrats who voted for Roberts, were more equivocal in their praise than the panel's Republicans.

"We choose to take Judge Roberts at his word — and believe that those words will bind him throughout his tenure on the court," said Kohl. "Ultimately, Judge Roberts persuaded us that he will be the chief justice we saw this past week, not the chief justice that his critics see in his past."

### SENATE FLOOR ACTION

The Senate confirmed Roberts on Sept. 29 by a vote of 78-22. Twenty-two Democrats — exactly half the party's membership in the Senate — and independent James M. Jeffords of Vermont joined all 55 Republicans in supporting Roberts. (Senate vote 245, p. S-48)

The even split among the chamber's Democrats divided senators from Republican-dominated states and those with presidential ambitions in 2008.

Democrats Biden, Evan Bayh of Indiana and Hillary Rodham Clinton of New York — all viewed as potential contenders for their party's presidential nomination — voted against Roberts. Most red-state Democrats up for re-election in 2006, including Bill Nelson of Florida and Ben Nelson of Nebraska, voted for his confirmation.

Bush left an Oval Office meeting to watch the roll call vote with Roberts and a large crowd of his supporters in the Roosevelt Room of the White House. The assemblage broke into applause when Roberts received his 50th vote for confirmation, according to White House spokesman Scott McClellan. Roberts' wife watched the vote in person from the gallery above the Senate chamber floor.

The Supreme Court's senior justice, John Paul Stevens, administered the Article VI oath as required under the Constitution at a ceremony in the East Room of the White House a little more than three hours after the vote concluded. In brief remarks after taking the oath, Roberts said the bipartisan vote was "confirmation of what is for me a bedrock principle, that judging is different from politics." ■

# Roberts Speaks: Hearing Excerpts

FOR THREE DAYS, chief justice nominee John G. Roberts Jr. answered questions from the 18 members of the Senate Judiciary Committee. Following are excerpts from those answers on a variety of subjects:

**Stare decisis (judicial precedent):** "It's the notion that it's not enough that you might think that the precedent is flawed, that there are other considerations that enter into the calculus that have to be taken into account: the values of respect for precedent, evenhandedness, predictability, stability; the considerations on the other side, whether a precedent you think may be flawed is workable or not workable, whether it's been eroded."

"The court has frequently explained that stare decisis is strongest when you are dealing with a statutory decision. The theory is a very straightforward one, that if the court gets it wrong, Congress can fix it. And the Constitution, the court has explained, is different. Obviously, short of amendment, only the court can fix the constitutional precedents."

*Roe v. Wade:* "I know there are people who have strongly held views on both sides of the issue. I know that the responsibility of a judge confronting this issue is to decide the case according to the rule of law consistent with the precedents, not to take sides in a dispute as a matter of policy, but to decide it according to the law."

**Right to privacy:** "The right to privacy is protected under the Constitution in various ways. The court has . . . recognized that personal privacy is a component of the liberty protected by the due process clause. The court has explained that the liberty protected is not limited to freedom from physical restraint and that it's protected not simply procedurally, but as a substantive matter as well."

**Role of judges:** "Judges have to have the courage to make the unpopular decisions when they have to. That sometimes involves striking down acts of Congress. That sometimes involves ruling that acts of that executive are unconstitutional. That is a requirement of the judicial oath. You have to have that courage, but you also have to have the self-restraint to recognize that your role is limited to interpreting the law and does not include making the law."

"When it comes to interpreting of law, I go back to Marbury v. Madison. That is emphatically the province and duty of the judicial branch. We don't defer to the executive. We don't defer to the legislature in making that final decision about what the law is."

"Every day, judges put aside their personal views and beliefs and apply the law, whether the result is one they would agree with as a legislator or not agree with. The question is what the law is, not what they think it should be. I have seen that on the court of appeals. I have seen that as a practicing lawyer before the court. That is the ideal. I'm sure judges — I'm sure justices — don't always achieve it in every case because it is a human endeavor, and error is going to infect any human endeavor. But that is the ideal and I think good judges working hard cannot only achieve it, but also achieve it together in a collegial way and benefit from the insight and views of each other."

**Faith/religion:** "There's nothing in my personal views based on faith or other sources that would prevent me from applying the precedents of the court faithfully under principles of stare decisis.

"I do know this: That my faith and my religious beliefs do not play a role in judging. When it comes to judging, I look to the law books and always have. I don't look to the Bible or any other religious source.

"I think everyone would agree that the religion jurisprudence under the First Amendment, the establishment clause and the free exercise clause, could be clearer. . . . I think that both of those are animated by the principle that the framers intended the rights of full citizenship to be available to all citizens, without regard to their religious belief or lack of religious belief. That, I think, is the underlying principle, and hopefully the court's precedents over the years will continue to give life to that ideal."

**Civil rights:** "In the area of civil rights people have talked about memos I wrote about the administration's policy against busing or the administration's policy against quotas. Being against busing and being against quotas is not the same as being against civil rights. President [Ronald] Reagan was against busing, President Reagan was against quotas, but he was in favor of civil rights and that was the administration position that I was advancing in those memoranda."

"I would resist the suggestion that I'm racially insensitive. I know why the phrase 'Equal Justice Under Law' is carved in marble above the Supreme Court entrance. It is because of the fundamental commitment of the rule of law to ensure equal justice for all people without regard to their race or ethnic background or gender."

**Judicial checks and balances:** "I think the primary check is the same one that Alexander Hamilton talked about in the Federalist Papers because the exact argument was raised in the debates about the Constitution. People were concerned about a new judiciary. What was it going to do? They were concerned that it might deprive them of their rights. And, of course, Hamilton's famous answer was, the judiciary was going to be the least dangerous branch because it had no power. It didn't have the sword. It didn't have the purse. . . . I would say the primary check on the courts has always been judicial self-restraint and a recognition on the part of judges that they have a limited task, that they are insulated from the people. They're given life tenure . . . precisely because they're not shaping policy. They're not supposed to be responsive; they're supposed to just interpret the law."

**Answering questions:** "I've tried to share more of my views with respect to particular cases. I know other nominees have declined, for example, to comment on even a case like Marbury v. Madison because they thought as a theoretical matter it could come before the court. I tend to take a more practical and pragmatic approach to things, rather than a theoretical or ideological approach."

"I think I have been more forthcoming than any of the other nominees."

**Role of chief justice:** "I think one of the things that the chief justice should have as a top priority is to try to bring about a greater degree of coherence and consensus in the opinions of the court. . . . I actually believe that is something that should be a matter of concern for all of the justices, but as the chief, with responsibility for assigning opinions, I think he has greater scope for authority to exercise in that area and perhaps over time can develop greater persuasive authority to make the point."

"You don't, obviously, compromise strongly held views, but you do have to be open to the considered views of your colleagues."

"I will be my own man on the Supreme Court."

# Bush Drops Miers, Picks Alito for Court

PRESIDENT BUSH STUMBLED in his second try at replacing Supreme Court Justice Sandra Day O'Connor. Bush's first choice was John G. Roberts Jr., but when Chief Justice William H. Rehnquist died in September, the president chose Roberts to head the high court.

In early October, Bush nominated White House counsel Harriet Miers, to the great consternation of conservatives and their Senate Republican allies. Miers asked the president to withdraw her nomination and he did so later that month, after Senate Republican leaders told him the nomination was in very serious trouble.

After the president's closest political allies sank Miers' nomination, he assuaged them by tapping conservative federal appellate judge Samuel A. Alito Jr. in his third attempt to fill O'Connor's seat. Conservatives rejoiced; liberals promised to closely scrutinize Alito's lengthy legal record.

The White House pressured Judiciary Chairman Arlen Specter, R-Pa., to begin Alito's confirmation hearing soon, hoping for a vote late in the year. Specter announced instead that Alito's confirmation hearing would begin Jan. 9, 2006.

## MIERS' NOMINATION GETS LOW MARKS

Buffeted by low poll numbers and public dissatisfaction with his handling of the Iraq War and the aftermath of Hurricane Katrina in September, Bush settled on Miers, a lawyer with no national profile or constitutional law background, but with the same sort of path-breaking résumé that the woman she was picked to replace possessed before joining the court. Miers' history with Bush went back to the early days of his Texas political career.

When Bush announced Miers as his second choice to succeed O'Connor early on Oct. 3, conservative jaws dropped across the nation. "Disappointed, depressed and demoralized" was the reaction of William Kristol, editor of the influential conservative magazine The Weekly Standard. Even some Senate Republicans expressed concern: "I think there was some missed opportunity here, but I'm not throwing her out," said Sam Brownback of Kansas, a potential GOP presidential candidate in 2008.

The White House scrambled to reassure activists and GOP senators who feared Miers was another David H. Souter, the little-known federal appellate judge whom Bush's father picked for the high court in 1990 and who then drifted leftward once on the bench. Vice President Dick Cheney appeared that afternoon on two conservative radio talk shows, and the president called a news conference the next day to defend his choice. "I picked the best person I could find," Bush said. The president also dispatched Attorney General Alberto R. Gonzales to defend Miers on morning news shows as "uniquely qualified."

One of the few social conservative activists who publicly supported Miers was James Dobson, chairman of Focus on the Family, who hinted to reporters that he was privy to sensitive information that caused him to support her.

Dobson later explained on his radio show that he was referring to a conversation with White House Deputy Chief of Staff Karl Rove in which, Dobson said, Rove assured him that Miers was an evangelical Christian who would strictly interpret the Constitution. Dobson denied that he and Rove discussed how Miers viewed the high court's 1973 ruling in *Roe v. Wade* that established a woman's constitutional right to abortion.

For their part, Democrats mostly sat back and watched the show on

## O'Connor's Journey to The Center of the Bench

WHEN PRESIDENT RONALD REAGAN named Sandra Day O'Connor in 1981 to be the first woman on the Supreme Court, replacing Potter Stewart, she was known as a traditional conservative in her adopted home state of Arizona and was championed for the job by that state's Republican Sen. Barry Goldwater. *(1981 Almanac, p. 409)*

But as the court moved to the right over the next two decades, O'Connor came to be seen more as a moderate influence, and she often provided the deciding vote in 5-4 majorities, straddling the line between the conservative and liberal wings on the bench.

During 24 terms on the court, O'Connor consistently showed sensitivity to public opinion and political conditions, and a preference for narrow, one-step-at-a-time judicial decision making. That temperament may have been influenced by her service as a member of the Arizona State Senate and as its majority leader, the first woman to hold that position anywhere in the nation. O'Connor was the most recent justice to have served as an elected official.

Since 1994, when President Bill Clinton nominated Stephen G. Breyer to fill the last court vacancy, O'Connor more than any other justice had been responsible for unraveling Chief Justice William H. Rehnquist's conservative majorities.

In a 1992 case, *Planned Parenthood of Southeastern Pa. v. Casey*, she joined with Justices Anthony M. Kennedy and David H. Souter in writing the majority opinion in a 5-4 decision that, in essence, upheld the constitutional right to abortion. In 2000, in *Stenberg v. Carhart*, O'Connor cast a decisive fifth vote in a decision to strike down a Nebraska ban on a procedure its opponents called "partial birth" abortion.

More recently, in 2003, she joined with liberal Justice John Paul Stevens in *McConnell v. Federal Election Commission*, which upheld the McCain-Feingold campaign finance law, and in a 2004 case, *Hamdi v. Rumsfeld*, she fashioned the main opinion requiring some form of court-like hearings for U.S. citizens held as enemy combatants in the war on terror. Also in 2003, she cast her first vote to uphold a racial preference, in *Grutter v. Bollinger*, a 5-4 decision backing the affirmative-action policies of the University of Michigan law school.

In the year before her July 1 announcement that she would resign, she often found herself on the losing side of 5-4 decisions, including one at the end of the term, *Kelo v. City of New London*, that permitted state and local governments to use the doctrine of eminent domain to seize private property for use by private developers.

O'Connor's role as the pivotal vote on the Rehnquist Court was one of many ways in which her careers intersected with Rehnquist's. They graduated in the same class at Stanford Law School. She postponed her retirement when he died Sept. 3 to prevent a vacancy on the high court bench when its term began a month later. And she eulogized Rehnquist at his funeral Sept. 7.

the right. Sen. Charles E. Schumer of New York, expressing the need for caution, also let it be known that "it could have been a lot worse." And Minority Leader Harry Reid of Nevada — who had suggested to Bush at a Sept. 21 breakfast that he consider Miers — welcomed a nominee who hailed from somewhere other than a lower court. "In my view, the Supreme Court would benefit from the addition of a justice who has real experience as a practicing lawyer," Reid said.

The Senate Judiciary Committee sent Miers a lengthy questionnaire that reflected much of the conservative criticism of her nomination and dissatisfaction with the Bush administration's damage control effort. The committee asked Miers whether she had made "any representations to any individuals or interest groups" as to how she would rule on Supreme Court cases. Miers was asked to provide information about communications between Bush and his allies and "any individuals or interest groups with respect to how you would rule if confirmed."

Committee leaders said they found Miers' responses so "inadequate" they demanded she try again.

However, Specter openly bristled at attacks on Miers by right-wing critics on radio and television talk shows and the Internet, and he announced Oct. 19 that her confirmation hearing would begin Nov. 7. Democrats objected that they needed more time to vet her properly, but Specter said the hearing would last as long as necessary.

Senators from both parties demanded that Bush hand over documents related to Miers' White House tenure to help them understand her views on constitutional law questions. Bush adamantly refused to give the Senate such documents.

On Oct. 27, with the nomination clearly in deep trouble, Bush used the impasse over White House documents as a pretext to withdraw Miers' nomination. The White House released a letter to the president in which Miers wrote, "I am concerned that the confirmation process presents a burden for the White House and our staff that is not in the best interest of this country."

For Bush, already struggling to regain control of his second term in the face of low approval ratings, it was an embarrassing defeat. It was the most emphatic rejection yet from a Republican-run Congress that had mostly deferred to him and his agenda throughout his presidency. The implosion of Miers' nomination also revealed disarray and divisions within the broader GOP coalition, with Bush looking more and more like a lame duck.

### BUSH TURNS TO ALITO

The president wasted little time in deciding on his third choice to succeed O'Connor. On Oct. 31, Bush announced that he would nominate Alito, a judge on the U.S. Court of Appeals for the 3rd Circuit.

Unlike Harriet Miers, Alito had a lengthy and ideologically conservative paper trail, especially on the trigger issue of abortion. The National Archives released a 20-year-old memo in which Alito, then an assistant U.S. solicitor general, recommended that the government file a friend-of-the-court brief in a pending Supreme Court abortion case with the aim of weakening *Roe*.

"The court may be signaling an inclination to cut back," Alito wrote. "What can be made of this opportunity to advance the goals of bringing about the eventual overturning of *Roe v. Wade* and, in the meantime, of mitigating its effects?"

That memo, and other material in Alito's record, sparked an acrimonious partisan debate over whether he should be the one to replace O'Connor, a centrist linchpin on the court in preserving *Roe*. But that same record, which included a Yale law degree, 15 years on the 3rd Circuit, and respect from across the legal community, suggested that moderate Democrats would be unable to find the justification to sustain a filibuster to block his nomination. ∎

# 'Gang of 14' Averts Judicial Showdown

THE SENATE RENEWED ITS BATTLE over President Bush's judicial nominees at the start of the 109th Congress. For the first few months, lawmakers seemed headed toward a climactic showdown over Democratic filibusters of some appellate court nominees. But in May, seven Republicans and seven Democrats — who became known as the "Gang of 14" — seized control of the process, striking a deal on judicial nominees that averted the showdown.

Senate Majority Leader Bill Frist, R-Tenn., went to the Senate floor hours after the start of the session to warn that he would not hesitate to execute an arcane parliamentary move, dubbed the "nuclear option," to end minority filibusters of Bush's appellate court nominees. Democrats had filibustered 10 of Bush's nominees in the 108th Congress and threatened to block several more. *(2004 Almanac, p. 12-15)*

Emboldened by the four-seat increase in the Republican Senate majority after the November 2004 election, Frist said that if Democrats mounted another filibuster, he would use the nuclear option. In February, Bush renominated seven of 10 previously filibustered candidates, along with several others whom Democrats had threatened to block.

Although there was more than one possible sequence of moves, Frist was expected to break a filibuster by making a point of order that further debate on the nomination would be dilatory — in other words, intended only to indefinitely delay a vote. The presiding officer — probably Vice President Dick Cheney — would sustain Frist's point of order. That decision could be appealed, but if it were, Frist probably would move to table (kill) the appeal, a non-debatable motion that would require a simple majority of those present and voting to succeed.

Frist needed the support of 49 of his 54 fellow Republicans, assuming all 100 senators were present and voting and no one on the other side of the aisle joined the Republicans. Cheney would be on hand to break a tie. On April 22, Cheney announced he would back Frist from the presiding officer's chair if necessary. Senate Democrats threatened that they would retaliate by selectively hamstringing Senate business.

Although Frist took the Senate to the brink of confrontation, it was never clear that he had the votes needed to successfully execute the move. Republicans John McCain of Arizona, Lincoln Chafee of Rhode Island and Olympia J. Snowe of Maine all opposed the ploy. Three other Republicans — Judiciary Chairman Arlen Specter of Pennsylvania, John W. Warner of Virginia and Susan Collins of Maine — were publicly noncommittal, but clearly unenthusiastic about the prospect of the "nuclear option."

After Frist and Reid traded compromise proposals to no avail, Frist

scheduled the showdown for May 24. But on the evening of May 23, the 14 senators emerged from a meeting in McCain's Capitol Hill office with a "memorandum of understanding" that defused the crisis and averted the showdown.

The seven Democrats in the group agreed to vote to invoke cloture on three previously filibustered nominations, but made no specific commitments on four others. The Democrats also agreed that judicial nominees should be filibustered only under "extraordinary circumstances," though the definition of that term was left to each senator to decide.

In return, the seven Republicans agreed to oppose any change in Senate rules or procedures that would eliminate filibusters of judicial nominees. The Republicans retained the right to back Frist in the nuclear option if Democrats mounted a filibuster in what Republicans considered less than "extraordinary circumstances."

In the three weeks following the agreement, the Senate confirmed five of the seven previously filibustered judicial nominees. The five were:

- Priscilla Owen, confirmed to the U.S. Court of Appeals for the 5th Circuit, 55-34, on May 25. (*Senate vote 128, p. S-26*)
- Janice Rogers Brown, confirmed to the U.S. Court of Appeals for the D.C. Circuit, 56-43, on June 8. (*Senate vote 131, p. S-27*)
- William H. Pryor Jr., confirmed to the U.S. Court of Appeals for the 11th Circuit, 53-45, on June 9. (*Senate vote 133, p. S-27*)
- Richard A. Griffin, confirmed to the U.S. Court of Appeals for the 6th Circuit, 95-0, on June 9. (*Senate vote 134, p. S-27*)
- David W. McKeague, confirmed to the U.S. Court of Appeals for the 6th Circuit, 96-0, on June 9. (*Senate vote 135, p. S-27*)

The members of the Gang of 14 said they intended to continue to act in unison on judicial nominees for as long as possible. Members met after each of the president's three Supreme Court nominations to sound each other out, but the group's agreement never had to be put to the test. ■

# Senate Panel Approves Asbestos Bill

THE SENATE JUDICIARY COMMITTEE approved a bill to create a $140 billion trust fund to compensate people sickened by asbestos exposure, but that was as far as supporters could get in 2005. Majority Leader Bill Frist, R-Tenn., promised to make it the first piece of legislation taken up in 2006, but a range of outstanding questions made Senate passage unlikely in the 109th Congress.

The committee's approval of the bill (S 852) in May was a significant victory for Judiciary Chairman Arlen Specter, R-Pa., who struggled for months to draft legislation that would be acceptable to a majority of the committee members, as well as to the defendant companies and insurers that would pay into the fund and be shielded from further liability.

Dozens of companies had been driven into bankruptcy because of lawsuits brought by people exposed to asbestos, a fire-resistant, cancer-causing substance that was used in products such as insulation and automobile brake linings. Specter's bill aimed to end the litigation and channel victims' claims through a government office that would use specific criteria set in the law to determine compensation.

But senators on both sides of the aisle remained uneasy because no one knew how many claimants would qualify, which defendant companies and insurers would contribute to the fund, and how much each would owe. Perhaps the biggest challenge was easing conservatives' concerns that taxpayers could end up footing the bill if the trust fund was depleted before all the claims were paid. They also worried that defendant companies could pay billions into the fund and still end up with future lawsuits if the fund became insolvent.

Specter tried, unsuccessfully, to coax companies into revealing the extent of their liability, but the companies were unwilling to provide information that might make them targets for additional lawsuits if a trust fund were not created.

In August, the Congressional Budget Office (CBO) issued an analysis that showed a wide range of uncertainty about the costs of such a fund. CBO estimated the trust fund would collect a maximum of $140 billion, but would face claims of $120 billion to $150 billion. A study released in September by Bates White, a Washington national economics consulting firm, concluded the fund could quickly be overwhelmed by claims and run out of money.

Significant differences also remained among the companies and insurers that would pay into the trust fund. Smaller companies complained that larger ones would contribute less than their share based on potential liability. In addition, organized labor and trial lawyers, two major Democratic constituencies, attacked the trust fund's size as inadequate to compensate claimants fairly.

The most vocal supporters were coalitions of large companies that were defendants in asbestos suits, as well as the National Association of Manufacturers. Some veterans' organizations and unions also endorsed the bill.

In the House, fiscal conservatives preferred a much more limited approach that would keep asbestos cases in the court system and require plaintiffs to meet specific medical criteria.

Specter had taken on the job of trying to reconcile the needs of the various stakeholders when he became Judiciary chairman at the beginning of the year. He joked that he spent 12 hours a day focused on asbestos and the other 12 hours on judicial nominations.

Specter's predecessor as chairman, Orrin G. Hatch, R-Utah, had managed to usher asbestos legislation through the committee in 2003. But Frist, who later introduced a revised version of the bill on the floor, could not get the 60 votes needed to cut off debate in April 2004.

In the months of negotiations that followed, Frist and Minority Leader Tom Daschle, D-S.D. (1987-2005), managed to narrow their differences over the size of the fund but could not reach a deal before the November 2004 elections. (*2004 Almanac, p. 12-6*)

Specter introduced his bill in April, and by trying to please as many sides as possible, he eventually attracted six cosponsors on his committee, including Hatch.

## LEGISLATIVE ACTION
### SENATE COMMITTEE ACTION

After months of starts and stops, the Senate Judiciary Committee approved the bill (S 852 — S Rept 109-97) by a vote of 13-5 on May 26. However, three Republicans who voted for the bill made it clear they were only trying to advance the bill out of committee and that significant changes would have to be made during Senate floor consideration before they would vote to pass the bill. All five "no" votes were cast by Democrats. Democrats Dianne Feinstein of California, Herb Kohl of Wisconsin and Patrick J. Leahy of Vermont, the ranking member on the committee, voted for the bill.

During six markup sessions spanning four weeks, the panel debat-

# Medical Malpractice

A MEDICAL LIABILITY BILL THAT Republicans called an antidote to rising health care costs won House passage but went no further. The measure was part of GOP efforts to restrict lawsuits and cap jury awards, sometimes referred to as tort reform. Democrats decried the bill as a gift to the insurance and drug industries.

It was the eighth time the House had passed legislation to limit medical malpractice liability awards, but supporters had not been able to get enough support to get a vote in the Senate. (2004 Almanac, p. 12-12)

The House passed the bill (HR 5) by a vote of 230-194 on July 28. (House vote 449, p. H-138)

The measure proposed to cap non-economic damages awarded in medical malpractice suits for pain and suffering at $250,000, and limit punitive damages to two times the economic damages or $250,000, whichever was greater. It also would limit attorney fees.

In their effort to defeat the bill, opponents targeted a provision that would shield drug and medical device companies from most punitive damages if their products were approved by the Food and Drug Administration. The FDA approval process had come into question the previous two years after some popular painkillers such as Vioxx and Celebrex were found to increase the risk of heart attack, and some antidepressants were shown to increase the risk of suicide in children.

Sponsors of a Senate medical malpractice bill (S 354) removed the liability provision in the legislation they introduced this year.

Republicans argued that soaring malpractice awards were driving up health care costs, and that physicians' malpractice premiums were increasing to the point that some doctors were being forced out of business. Democrats countered that capping non-economic awards was unfair to injured plaintiffs. They contended that insurance companies were raising premiums to recoup investment losses, not because of litigation.

Capping malpractice damage awards was a prominent part of President Bush's health care platform, and he strongly supported the House bill.

ed dozens of amendments, many of them offered by Specter as he continued to tweak the bill to gain more support.

As approved by the committee, the bill included provisions to:
- Establish an Office of Asbestos Disease Compensation within the Labor Department that would be responsible for handling victims' claims and awarding damages.
- Establish an Asbestos Injury Claims Resolution Fund to pay for the awards. Companies that had been sued for asbestos-related injuries and the companies that insured them would be required to contribute a combined total of about $140 billion to the fund – up to $90 billion from the companies and $46 billion from their insurers.
- Move virtually all pending asbestos claims from the courts to the compensation office.
- Base awards on the seriousness of the person's asbestos-related disease or condition and their exposure to asbestos. The bill set criteria for nine levels of compensation. Awards would range from medical monitoring for someone with a non-malignant disease, to $1.1 million for a person with mesothelioma, a deadly form of lung cancer.
- Require that claims be filed within five years of getting the medical diagnosis. For those who had claims pending in court, the period

would be five years from enactment of the bill.
- Specify that if the fund ran out of money, it would sunset and any further claims would be handled in court.
- Require a general prohibition on the manufacturing or distribution of asbestos products, with an exception for uses considered critical to the Pentagon.

The amendments considered during the markup were a window into the myriad concerns and issues surrounding asbestos compensation.

In the course of the markups, the committee:
- Adopted a Specter amendment to allow insurers that covered a shortfall in the companies' contributions during the first five years to receive credits to reduce their later liability by an equal amount. Insurers had worried they could be stuck paying their share and part of the industry's. To allay concerns of another industry, Specter added language that would limit the financial obligations of wholesalers that were only conduits for products containing asbestos.
- Adopted by voice vote an amendment by Feinstein to give mesothelioma victims one lump-sum payment within 30 days from the date the claim was approved or six months from when the claim was filed, whichever was shorter. Feinstein had indicated that failure to guarantee that the sickest claimants would be paid first would be a "deal breaker" for her.
- Adopted by voice vote an amendment by Specter to exempt the Pentagon from the bill's ban on the sale and distribution of asbestos. Jon Kyl, R-Ariz., had worried the bill would be a burden on the Defense Department, which used asbestos in military hardware.

Other amendments in Specter's manager's package included one to allow for additional hardship adjustments for companies whose payments into the system might force them into bankruptcy, and another, requested by Sam Brownback, R-Kan., to ease the financial burden on smaller companies.
- Rejected, 5-12, an amendment by Edward M. Kennedy, D-Mass., that would have granted payment to smokers exposed to asbestos who did not show signs of asbestos-related disease, if an Institute of Medicine study showed such a link existed. Specter had excluded claims by smokers who showed no signs of asbestos-related disease in response to Republican concerns.
- Rejected an amendment by Lindsey Graham, R-S.C., and Kennedy that would have treated claimants living near other affected areas the same as residents near Libby, Mont., which was singled out for special treatment in the bill. Instead, the committee adopted a proposal by Specter and Leahy that called for a study of other potential exposure sites.

Specter acknowledged that he left some issues unresolved to move the bill out of committee before the Memorial Day recess in hopes of getting it to the floor during the summer.

One area of persistent disagreement was what would happen if the trust fund's administrators determined that it was running out of money. Kyl said he wanted concrete intermediate steps before the fund could sunset and claimants could return to the courts. The text of the bill remained vague about exactly how the administrator's recommendations for the fund would be considered by Congress.

Another sticking point was how to treat residents of areas near mines and processing plants that emitted asbestos fibers into the atmosphere.

Considerable resistance also remained from stakeholders who for years had taken the lead in negotiating the trust fund.

The AFL-CIO wrote in a May 24 letter to Specter and Leahy that it had "grave concerns" about many of the amendments to the bill that were adopted in earlier markups. Similarly, the American Insurance Association said in a statement after the committee's vote that it could not support the bill in its existing form. ∎

# Limits on Class Action Lawsuits Enacted

IN A MAJOR VICTORY for business, Congress cleared a bill early in the year aimed at limiting class action lawsuits — those that bring together the often small claims of a number of individual plaintiffs. The bill was a top priority for congressional Republicans and for President Bush, who signed the measure into law Feb. 18, less than 24 hours after it was cleared (S 5 — PL 109-2).

The legislation gave federal courts jurisdiction over class action lawsuits when the total amount in dispute exceeded $5 million and the defendant and a large portion of the plaintiffs lived in different states. As a result, federal courts for the first time were expected to hear large numbers of consumer protection cases.

Federal judges would use state consumer protection laws, but the cases would move forward using federal procedural law, often considered less friendly to plaintiffs.

Under previous law, class action suits could be heard in federal court only if each plaintiff stood to receive at least $75,000 and all the plaintiffs lived in different states from the defendants. As a result most class action cases were heard in state courts, and the standards used to determine whether a suit qualified as a class action varied from one state to another.

Business interests, led by the U.S. Chamber of Commerce, had spent six years and tens of millions of dollars lobbying for the bill's enactment. "America's employers and consumers are the big winners today," said Chamber President Thomas Donohue, who sat in the front row at the bill signing.

Supporters said the new law would help prevent "forum shopping," in which attorneys try to file their lawsuits in jurisdictions that are known for giving plaintiffs large awards, as well as "coupon settlements," which they said tended to benefit lawyers rather than aggrieved consumers.

Enactment was a significant defeat for consumer, civil rights and public interest groups, which said the measure would deprive seriously injured plaintiffs — ranging from mistreated foster children to drivers left paralyzed in accidents — of their day in court by shifting cases to the already overworked federal courts. Another loser was the Association of Trial Lawyers of America and the plaintiffs' attorneys it represented, most of whose political donations went to Democrats.

The House had approved similar class action bills in each of the previous three Congresses, most recently in June 2003. After failing to get the 60 votes needed to limit debate on the bill in 2003, Senate supporters agreed to several compromises that won additional Democratic support. The bill stalled again in 2004, however, when members in both parties tried to attach unrelated amendments on issues ranging from a minimum wage increase to global warming and immigration. *(2004 Almanac, p. 12-7; 2003 Almanac, p. 13-10)*

The GOP's increased majority in the Senate, where Republicans held 55 seats as a result of the 2004 elections, made the difference in 2005, enabling supporters to fight off five Democratic amendments and send the House a clean bill that it easily cleared.

The bill was the only piece of the Republican agenda for overhauling the civil justice system to be enacted in 2005.

---

**BOX SCORE**

**BILL:** S 5 — PL 109-2

**LEGISLATIVE ACTION:**
**Senate** passed S 5 (S Rept 109-14), 72-26, on Feb. 10.

**House** cleared S 5, 279-149, on Feb. 17.

**President** signed Feb. 18.

---

## HIGHLIGHTS

Following are highlights of the new law:

● **Federal jurisdiction.** Federal district courts were given jurisdiction over class action suits in which the amount in dispute exceeded $5 million, the class included 100 or more plaintiffs, and two-thirds or more of the plaintiffs lived in states other than that of the defendant.

● **Home state jurisdiction.** If two-thirds or more of the plaintiffs lived in the main defendant's home state, the case would remain in that state court. If between one-third and two-thirds of the defendants were citizens of the main defendant's home state, a federal district court judge would make the decision.

● **Plaintiff protection.** A federal judge could only approve a settlement that gave class members non-cash benefits, such as coupons for goods or services, after a hearing and a written finding that the terms were reasonable and fair to the plaintiffs. Attorney fees had to be proportional to the value of the coupons that plaintiffs actually redeemed, and they could not result in a net loss to the plaintiffs unless the judge determined that the plaintiffs' loss was outweighed by other, non-monetary benefits. A class action settlement could not give more to some plaintiffs just because they were geographically close to the court.

## LEGISLATIVE ACTION
### SENATE COMMITTEE ACTION

The Senate Judiciary Committee approved the bill Feb. 3 (S 5 — S Rept 109-14) by a 13-5 vote. Three Democrats — Dianne Feinstein of California, Herb Kohl of Wisconsin and Charles E. Schumer of New York — joined all 10 Republicans in voting for the measure.

The bill reflected the 2003 Senate compromise that brought several Democrats into the fold. Supporters said keeping the bill free of amendments was key to retaining the support of those Democrats and ensuring passage in the House, where GOP leaders said they were willing to take up the Senate version only if it remained clean. "We negotiated a pretty significant package," Christopher J. Dodd, D-Conn., said of the compromise. "If the bill changes, then all bets are off."

The committee rejected, 5-13, an amendment by ranking Democrat Patrick J. Leahy of Vermont that would have increased federal judges' salaries by 16.5 percent. Several Republicans said they supported the pay raise but considered the class action bill to be the wrong vehicle. "We cannot put it on this bill without undue complications," said Orrin G. Hatch, R-Utah.

Adding to the pressure for a clean bill, John Cornyn, R-Texas, indicated that if changes were made, he might introduce several proposals he said could make the bill stronger. Aides said Cornyn probably would not introduce the amendments unless Democrats pressed on with their additions. "If they place nice, we play nice," one Republican Senate staffer said.

### SENATE FLOOR ACTION

The Senate passed the bill without amendments Feb. 10. Supporters prevailed by a vote of 72-26, with the support of 18 Democrats and Independent James M. Jeffords of Vermont. *(Senate vote 9, p. S-5)*

During a week of floor debate, supporters defeated five Democrat-

ic amendments that might have complicated passage in the House. "My overriding concern is we not begin to pick apart this carefully balanced compromise," said longtime supporter Thomas R. Carper, D-Del.

Democratic and GOP backers insisted any tinkering would push the House to consider an even stricter version. The House had its own class action legislation (HR 516), which included provisions that were eliminated in the Senate bill, among them a ban on so-called bounty payments — disproportionate payments to named plaintiffs, those who actually testified and had their names appear on the class action suit.

The Senate:

▶ Rejected, 40-59, a proposal by Edward M. Kennedy, D-Mass., to exempt wage-and-hour and civil rights suits from the class action bill. (Senate vote 6, p. S-5)

▶ Rejected, 38-61, an amendment by Feinstein and Jeff Bingaman, D-N.M., to give federal judges more flexibility about which state consumer laws to apply in class action suits where plaintiffs were from multiple states. (Senate vote 7, p. S-5)

▶ Rejected, 37-61, a proposal by Russ Feingold, D-Wis., to place a 60-day limit on the amount of time federal judges would have to consider whether to send a class action case back to state court. (Senate vote 8, p. S-5)

▶ Agreed, 60-39, to table (kill) an amendment by Mark Pryor, D-Ark.,

to exempt suits brought by state attorneys. (Senate vote 5, p. S-5)

Feinstein and Bingaman ultimately voted for the final bill.

### HOUSE FLOOR ACTION

One week later, on Feb. 17, the House cleared the bill, 279-149. Fifty Democrats joined GOP colleagues in supporting the bill. Only one Republican — John T. Doolittle of California — voted against it. (House vote 38, p. H-14)

Before clearing the bill, the House:

▶ Rejected, 175-249, a motion by Sherrod Brown, D-Ohio, to send the bill back to committee to add an exemption for class action cases involving the arthritis drug Vioxx. The drug had been withdrawn from the market because of heart attack risks. On Feb. 18, a Food and Drug Administration panel ruled it suitable for sale, saying its benefits might outweigh the risks. (House vote 37, p. H-14)

▶ Rejected, 178-247, a substitute by John Conyers Jr. of Michigan, the Judiciary Committee's ranking Democrat, that incorporated amendments rejected or withdrawn in the Senate Feb. 10. The substitute included exemptions for civil rights and wage-and-hour lawsuits; suits initiated by state attorneys general; and "mass torts" involving physical injuries to a large number of people within a state, among other things. (House vote 36, p. H-14) ■

# Eminent Domain Ruling Draws Ire on Hill

THE HOUSE PASSED A BILL IN NOVEMBER aimed at limiting the effects of a controversial Supreme Court ruling on eminent domain. The bill proposed to bar states and local communities that received federal development funds from using eminent domain to seize private property for economic development.

Although the Senate did not take up the bill, senators indicated their opposition to the court ruling by voting to bar such use of eminent domain in transportation or housing projects funded in fiscal 2006.

In a 5-4 ruling June 23, the Supreme Court found in *Kelo v. City of New London* that New London, Conn., was allowed under state law to use its power of eminent domain to require several homeowners to vacate their properties to make way for commercial development. Writing for the majority, Justice John Paul Stevens said, "Promoting economic development is a traditional and long-accepted function of government."

Many lawmakers from both parties said the ruling was contrary to the Constitution's prohibition on government "takings" other than "for public use, with just compensation." The House adopted a resolution expressing its disapproval of the *Kelo* decision a week after the ruling. The measure (H Res 340) was adopted by an overwhelming vote of 365-33 on June 30. (House vote 361, p. H-110)

The House bill (HR 4128) was introduced by Judiciary Committee Chairman F. James Sensenbrenner Jr., R-Wis., and backed by the panel's ranking Democrat, John Conyers Jr. of Michigan. Its supporters ran the gamut from conservative Republican Tom DeLay of Texas, to liberal Democrat Maxine Waters of California. Opponents in both parties said the *Kelo* decision meant economically disadvantaged homeowners could be preyed upon by any state or local government that wanted to generate more revenue by transferring their property to commercial developers.

The Senate added language to the fiscal 2006 Transportation-

Treasury-Housing appropriations bill (HR 3058) that barred use of funds in the bill to support "any federal, state, or local projects that seek to use the power of eminent domain" for anything other than a public use. The amendment, by Christopher S. Bond, R-Mo., also directed the Government Accountability Office to send Congress a study within 12 months on the nationwide use of eminent domain and its impact. The Senate adopted Bond's amendment by voice vote, and conferees retained it in the final bill (PL 109-115). (Appropriations, p. 2-47)

### LEGISLATIVE ACTION
#### HOUSE COMMITTEE ACTION

The House Judiciary Committee approved the Sensenbrenner bill by a vote of 27-3 on Oct. 27 (HR 4128 — H Rept 109-262, Parts 1 and 2).

Under the terms of the bill:

▶ State and local governments that received federal economic development funds would be barred from using eminent domain to seize private land that was to be used for private economic development — or was subsequently used for such development. The bill defined "economic development" as private projects carried out for profit or to increase tax revenue, the tax base or jobs.

▶ State and local governments that violated the restrictions would be ineligible to receive federal economic development funds for two years.

▶ Any private property owner who suffered injury as a result of a state or local government violating these restrictions could bring a lawsuit against the government or seek a temporary restraining order or a preliminary injunction.

▶ The federal government would be similarly barred from using eminent domain to seize land for economic development.

▶ The prohibitions would not apply to the transfer of private property that had been abandoned or was considered an immediate threat to public health and safety, or that was going to be used for public-use

roads or hospitals, or for military bases.

The bill also contained a non-binding sense-of-Congress provision stating that it was "the policy of the United States to encourage, support, and promote the private ownership of property and to ensure that the constitutional and other legal rights of private property owners are protected by the federal government."

During the markup, the committee:

▶ Adopted by voice vote an amendment by Chris Cannon, R-Utah, to clarify that the bill's provisions should be construed as favoring broad protection of private property rights.

▶ Rejected by voice vote an amendment by Waters to prohibit the seizure of private property for any private use.

▶ Adopted by voice vote two Cannon amendments specifying that taking private property for use by a public utility was not prohibited.

### HOUSE FLOOR ACTION

The House passed the bill, 376-38, on Nov. 3. Two Republicans and 36 Democrats voted "no." *(House vote 568, p. H-178)*

"The House acted today to protect private property rights, a bold plan that enhances the penalty for states and localities that abuse their eminent domain power and defends the freedoms of private ownership," said acting Majority Leader Roy Blunt, R-Mo., after the vote.

Republicans allowed 10 amendments to be offered, an unusually high number that reflected GOP leaders' confidence that the legislation would sail through the chamber.

During the debate, the House:

▶ Rejected, 63-355, a proposal by Jerrold Nadler, D-N.Y., to allow a property owner to go to court to challenge the use of eminent domain to seize their property before any property was actually taken. The amendment would have dropped the two-year penalty on governments that violated restrictions in the bill. *(House vote 564, p. H-178)*

▶ Rejected, 49-368, a proposal by James P. Moran, D-Va., to narrow the definition of economic development to cover development undertaken for profit or where the primary purpose was to increase tax revenue, the tax base, jobs or economic development. Moran said that, as written, the definition was so broad as to include virtually every use of condemned property. Moran also proposed to remove the reference to future use of the property and to limit the time in which a suit could be filed to seven years from the time the property was finally condemned. Under the bill, it was seven years after the economic development was completed. *(House vote 565, p. H-178)*

▶ Rejected, 44-371, an amendment by Melvin Watt, D-N.C., to strike the text of the bill and retain only a provision expressing the sense of Congress recognizing the importance of property rights and stating that the *Kelo* decision could lead to abuses of eminent domain power. *(House vote 567, p. H-178)* ∎

# Republicans Victorious on Gun Liability

WITH FOUR ADDITIONAL SEATS in the Senate as a result of the 2004 elections, Republicans were able to clear legislation limiting the legal liability of firearms makers and dealers. Enactment was a victory for the National Rifle Association (NRA) and advocates of overhauling the civil justice system, who easily overcame Democratic resistance. President Bush strongly supported the bill and signed it into law Oct. 26 (S 397 – PL 109-92).

The debate over lawsuits against the firearms industry went back to 1998, when New Orleans led several cities in an effort to sue handgun manufacturers to pay for the cost of urban violence. Gun-rights lobbyists led by the NRA succeeded in enacting protections for the industry at the state level, but their efforts to change federal law took much longer because of resistance by Senate Democrats.

In the 108th Congress, Senate gun-control advocates halted action on a similar bill by attaching three amendments opposed by the bill's backers, including a renewal of the assault weapons ban (PL 103-322). As a result, Republicans — at the urging of the NRA — ended up voting down their own bill. *(2004 Almanac, p. 12-13)*

In 2005, Senate Majority Leader Bill Frist, R-Tenn., turned the tables on Democrats, using procedural maneuvers to control the amendments that could be offered. As a result, only three relatively non-controversial provisions were added.

Supporters of the legislation said allowing lawsuits against gunmakers was like taking car manufacturers to court when people drive drunk. They said the liability suits were often filed by anti-gun critics hoping to drive manufacturers out of business with exorbitant legal fees. House Judiciary Chairman F. James Sensenbrenner Jr., R-Wis., said

**BOX SCORE**

**BILL:**
S 397 – PL 109-92

**LEGISLATIVE ACTION:**

**Senate** passed S 397, 65-31, on July 29.

**House** cleared S 397, 283-144, on Oct. 20.

**President** signed Oct. 26.

such litigation threatened to "bankrupt the national firearms industry and deny all Americans their fundamental, constitutionally guaranteed right to bear arms."

Opponents said the law also would end up shielding gun dealers who sold weapons to criminals, although the statute did not preclude lawsuits against those who knowingly sold firearms that they knew would be used for a crime or when the firearm was defective.

### HIGHLIGHTS

The 2005 gun-liability law included provisions to:

● **Lawsuits.** Prohibit civil-liability actions from being brought in any state or federal court against manufacturers, distributors, dealers or importers of firearms and ammunition. Trade groups also were protected, and all pending legal action against gunmakers was dismissed.

● **Exceptions.** Exempt from liability protection anyone who sold or transferred a firearm knowing it was intended to be used for a crime of violence or drug trafficking, or anyone who knowingly violated state or federal laws applicable to the marketing or sale of firearms, when the violation resulted in harm.

The law also exempted cases in which proper use resulted in physical injury, death or property damage because of a defect in the firearm.

● **Gun safety.** Require importers, manufacturers and dealers to provide a secure gun storage or safety device for each handgun sold, delivered or transferred to any individual. Firearms sold to U.S. agencies, law enforcement officials and rail police officers were exempt from the requirement. Violators could have their licenses revoked or suspended for up to six months and also could be subject to a $2,500 fine.

● **Armor-piercing bullets.** Prohibit the manufacture or sale of armor-piercing ammunition — unless it was for use by the federal or state government, for export only or had been approved by the Justice Department for testing and experimentation uses.

● **Criminal penalties.** Increase penalties for individuals who used or carried armor-piercing ammunition in a violent or drug-trafficking crime. In addition to any sentences for the crime, the bill required a minimum prison sentence of 15 years, or if the crime resulted in death, a sentence of execution or life imprisonment.

● **Projectile testing.** Require the attorney general to conduct a study to determine whether a uniform standard for projectile testing against body armor was feasible and submit a report to Congress two years after enactment.

## LEGISLATIVE ACTION
### SENATE FLOOR ACTION

The Senate passed the gun-liability bill, which was sponsored by Larry E. Craig, R-Idaho, by a vote of 65-31 on July 29. (*Senate vote 219, p. S-43*)

Determined to avoid a replay of 2004, Frist took control of the debate from the beginning. On July 22, he filed a cloture motion to limit debate and bar non-germane amendments. He then filed a succession of amendments — a legislative procedure known as "filling the amendment tree" — that allowed him to control what amendments could be brought for debate. He allowed only those proposals he thought were harmless or easy to defeat, thus thwarting any potential Democratic efforts to add gun-control language.

The Senate approved Frist's cloture motion, 66-32, on July 26. The maneuvers gave Republicans relatively tight control of the floor debate and enabled bill supporters to direct the substance of the debate. (*Senate vote 206, p. S-41*)

Republicans then easily defeated Democratic amendments that would have allowed individuals, but not municipalities, to sue gunmakers; preserved the right of police officers or minors injured by firearms to sue for damages; and blocked the sale of so-called cop-killer bullets.

Passage was a victory for GOP leaders, who had promised to push the legislation through before the August recess. The 14 Democrats who voted for the bill were all from states with large rural areas where hunting was popular. Independent James M. Jeffords of Vermont also voted for the legislation, while two Republicans — Lincoln Chafee of Rhode Island and Mike DeWine of Ohio — voted against it.

During the floor debate, the Senate:

▶ Adopted, 70-30, a proposal by Herb Kohl, D-Wis., to require that child safety locks be sold with all handguns. The safety locks proposal was relatively non-controversial and received the same number of votes that it garnered when it was added to the 2004 bill. (*Senate vote 207, p. S-41*)

▶ Adopted, 72-26, an amendment by Craig to clarify that individuals under age 17 could recover damages authorized under federal and state law in a civil suit that met the existing exceptions in the bill. (*Senate vote 214, p. S-42*)

▶ Adopted, 87-11, a Craig amendment requiring the attorney general to commission a study to determine whether a uniform standard for the testing of projectiles against body armor was feasible. The amendment also increased to 15 years in prison the minimum penalty for violent or drug-trafficking crimes in which the perpetrator used or possessed armor-piercing ammunition. If use of such ammunition resulted in death, the person could face life in prison or the death penalty. (*Senate vote 216, p. S-43*)

### HOUSE FLOOR ACTION

The House cleared the bill by a vote of 283-144 on Oct. 20. (*House vote 534, p. S-168*)

The House Judiciary Committee had approved its version of the legislation (HR 800 — H Rept 109-124) by a vote of 22-12 on May 25. But leaders decided to bypass that measure and clear the Senate bill instead.

The rule for floor debate, approved by the Republican-controlled Rules Committee, barred any amendments. ■

# Flag-Burning Amendment Stalls in the Senate Again

THE HOUSE PASSED A PROPOSED constitutional amendment that would allow the enactment of federal laws to criminalize physical desecration of the American flag, but the resolution did not advance in the Senate.

Conservatives had been trying to win such a constitutional change since 1990, when the Supreme Court in *United States v. Eichman* struck down a federal law (PL 101-131) that banned flag desecration. That law had been enacted after the high court ruled in 1989 in *Texas v. Johnson* that a conviction under a Texas state law for desecration of the flag violated the First Amendment.

Supporters said the amendment was needed to protect a revered symbol. Critics said it would curtail freedom of expression.

The House passed the resolution (H J Res 10 — H Rept 109-131) by a vote of 286-130 on June 22, after rejecting, 129-279, a substitute by Melvin Watt, D-N.C., that would have required Congress to act in a manner consistent with the First Amendment. (*House votes 296, 293, pp. H-94, H-92*)

Gene Taylor, D-Miss., made two motions to recommit the resolution to the House Judiciary Committee with instructions to add language proposing a balanced budget amendment and the segregation of the Social Security trust fund from the federal budget. House Republicans employed parliamentary tactics to turn aside Taylor's motions.

This was the sixth time since 1995 that the necessary two-thirds of those present and voting in the House supported the constitutional change. But the tally in 2005 showed the lowest level of support yet for the amendment. In 2003, the last time the Senate had voted on such a resolution, 63 senators supported it. The resolution needed 67 votes (assuming all 100 senators were present and voting) to pass. If both chambers passed the proposed amendment, it would have to be ratified by three-quarters (38) of the states within seven years to become part of the Constitution. ■

# Parental Consent for Teen Abortions

THE HOUSE EASILY PASSED a bill to broaden the reach of state laws requiring parental consent or notification when a minor seeks an abortion. It was the fourth time the chamber had passed such a measure. Majority Leader Bill Frist, R-Tenn., said a companion Senate bill was among his top 10 priorities for the year, but he did not get to it in the first session.

The legislation (HR 748) was part of a strategy by anti-abortion lawmakers to offer a series of narrow bills to limit abortions, rather than to push for a constitutional amendment outlawing the procedure.

More than 30 states had parental involvement laws, and studies showed that passage of consent laws tended to be followed by an increase in the number of abortions in bordering states that did not have such laws.

The House passed similar parental notification legislation in 1998, 1999 and 2002, but the Senate did not act on any of those bills. Supporters hoped at the start of the 109th Congress that the tide had turned in the Senate as a result of the addition of several abortion opponents in the 2004 elections.

House sponsors, meanwhile, added language to the 2005 bill that made it somewhat less palatable in the Senate. The new provisions required that doctors notify parents in person or by certified mail of an out-of-state minor's request for an abortion. Parents or guardians of the minor would be able to sue doctors who did not comply.

## HIGHLIGHTS

The House-passed bill would:

● **Transporting a minor.** Make it a federal crime — punishable by a fine of up to $100,000 and up to one year in prison, or both — to knowingly take a minor across state lines with the intent that the minor have an abortion, if the minor lived in a state that had a parental notification law and no parental consent or notification was obtained.

▸ The bill included an exception if the abortion was necessary to save the minor's life, but not if it was to protect the pregnant minor's health. The minor and her parents would be exempt from prosecution.

▸ Individuals accused of violating this provision could defend themselves against civil and criminal actions by showing that they "reasonably believed" that parental consent or notification had been obtained, or they were presented with documents showing that a court in the minor's home state had waived any parental notification required under that state's laws.

● **Performing an abortion.** Make it a federal crime — punishable by a fine of up to $100,000 or a year in prison, or both — for a doctor to perform an abortion on a minor from another state in violation of the minor's home-state parental notification laws.

▸ A physician would be required to provide at least 24 hours notice directly to the minor's parent — either in writing or in person — before performing an abortion on a minor who was a resident of another state. Even if the parent accompanied the minor and consented to the abortion, there would still be a 24-hour waiting period. If such notice was not possible after a reasonable effort had been made, the physician would have to provide a 24-hour notice by certified mail, with return receipt requested. The notice would be considered delivered 48 hours from noon on the day after it was mailed.

▸ A doctor would be exempt from the bill's notification requirements if the abortion was necessary to save the minor's life; if it was performed in a state that had a law requiring parental notification or involvement and the doctor complied with that law; if the doctor was given documents showing with a reasonable degree of certainty that a court in the minor's home state waived any parental notification requirement; or, if the minor declared in a signed, written statement that she was the victim of sexual abuse, neglect or physical abuse by a parent. In the latter case, the doctor would have to notify the authorities in the minor's home state to receive any reports of abuse or neglect before performing the abortion.

## LEGISLATIVE ACTION
### HOUSE COMMITTEE ACTION

The House Judiciary Committee approved the bill (HR 748 — H Rept 109-51) by a vote of 20-13 on April 13. The panel's Subcommittee on the Constitution had approved the measure, 7-2, on March 17, after adopting language by Subcommittee Chairman Steve Chabot, R-Ohio, to clarify that defendants would be protected if they reasonably believed that parental consent had occurred, or if they had seen documents from a court in the minor's home state waiving the need for parental consent. The bill was sponsored by Ileana Ros-Lehtinen, R-Fla.

During the full committee markup, members:

▸ Rejected, 12-19, an amendment by Jerrold Nadler, D-N.Y., to exempt grandparents or adult siblings from being held criminally liable. "Congress shouldn't attempt to play doctor," Nadler said.

▸ Rejected, 12-18, a proposal by Robert C. Scott, D-Va., to exempt cab drivers, bus drivers and others who provide professional transportation.

▸ Rejected by voice vote an amendment by Maxine Waters, D-Calif., to make an exception for pregnancies resulting from sex with a parent, guardian or any household family member.

### HOUSE FLOOR ACTION

The House passed the bill by a vote of 270-157 on April 27. (House vote 144, p. H-46)

Republicans said they were trying to protect girls from men who were abusive or exerted undue influence. "When you have somebody secreting a girl to another state, that's an assault on family," said Chabot. "Parents are in the best position to determine what's best." Democrats said they too were trying to protect minors from abusive parents or situations of rape or incest, and that laws should not prevent girls from turning to trusted adults when they need help.

The House rejected several Democratic attempts to place additional limits on the bill, including:

▸ An amendment by Scott to exempt taxi, bus and ambulance drivers and doctors, nurses and other medical providers from penalties, which was rejected, 179-245. (House vote 141, p. H-46)

▸ A proposal by Sheila Jackson-Lee of Texas to exempt the minor's grandparents and members of the clergy from the terms of the legislation, which was defeated, 177-252. (House vote 142, p. H-46)

▸ A Democratic motion to recommit the bill with instructions to bar fathers from suing a doctor who performed an abortion on a daughter who had become pregnant by the father. It was defeated, 183-245. Republican F. James Sensenbrenner Jr. of Wisconsin, the Judiciary Committee's chairman, said evidence of a rape would come out in any such lawsuit and that the father would be punished

for the crime. *(House vote 143, p. H-46)*

Some of the most heated partisan exchanges occurred while the House was considering the rule (H Res 236) for floor debate. Democrats were furious over wording in the committee report on the bill. The report described several defeated Democratic amendments, intended to exempt certain classes of people from the law's penalties, as provisions that would have exempted "sexual predators from prosecution" if they fell into those classes.

Democrats, particularly Nadler, pointedly criticized Sensenbrenner for allowing the wording. But it took two tries for Democrats to persuade their Republican colleagues to revise the disputed language.

On May 3, John Conyers Jr. of Michigan, the ranking committee Democrat, brought a privileged resolution (H Res 253) to the floor to force revision of the report. After a sometimes emotional debate in which Democrats appealed to the comity of the House and Republicans advocated the need for exact language in legislation, the House tabled, or killed, the resolution, 220-196. *(House vote 151, p. H-50)*

Two days later, Nadler threatened to present a second privileged resolution and eat up more of the House's time.

In the end, the vehicle for resolving the dispute was the rule (H Res 258) for consideration of the fiscal 2005 supplemental appropriations bill for the wars in Iraq and Afghanistan (HR 1268). Adopted by voice vote, it included language calling for a revised report with neutral descriptions of Democratic amendments. ■

# Congress Intervenes in Schiavo Case

REPUBLICAN LEADERS spent a frantic week in March trying to intervene in the case of Terri Schiavo, a 41-year-old severely brain-damaged woman whose husband and parents had been battling since 1998 over whether to keep her alive through artificial means.

Schiavo had suffered severe brain damage in 1990 when her heart stopped for several minutes. Court-appointed doctors said she was in a persistent vegetative state. Her husband, Michael Schiavo, said she had told him she would not want to be kept alive artificially. Her parents, Bob and Mary Schindler, disputed that and insisted that she could get better with rehabilitative therapy. A Florida court had ruled that her feeding tube be removed March 18 in accordance with her husband's wishes.

According to a Florida appellate court, much of Terri Schiavo's cerebral cortex was gone. The court concluded that "unless an act of God, a true miracle, were to recreate her brain, [Schiavo] will always remain in an unconscious, reflexive state, totally dependent upon others to feed her and care for her most private needs."

The House passed a broadly worded bill March 16 to require a review by the federal courts in cases such as Schiavo's. The next day, the Senate passed a narrow private relief bill to allow Schiavo's parents to take their claim to federal court. The legislation said explicitly that it was not to be seen as a precedent for further legislation.

With House and Senate GOP leaders unable to agree on an approach, lawmakers issued subpoenas to Schiavo and her family in the hope of staving off the removal of the feeding tube. But the Florida trial judge who had long overseen Schiavo's case effectively ignored the subpoenas, and the tube was removed March 18.

At that point, Majority Leader Bill Frist, R-Tenn., and House Speaker J. Dennis Hastert, R-Ill., put aside their rare public feud over the legislation and agreed on a narrow bill that would enable the parents to go to federal court to try to have the feeding tube restored.

The Senate passed the bill in a Sunday session, the House cleared it the next day and President Bush quickly signed it into law (S 686 — PL 109-3). The effort proved futile, however. Federal courts rebuffed the Schindlers, and Schiavo died March 31.

The effort to save Schiavo was championed by Republican leaders and their conservative religious supporters. It sparked a national debate

**BOX SCORE**

**BILL:**
S 686 — PL 109-3

**LEGISLATIVE ACTION:**

**House** passed HR 1332 by voice vote March 16.

**Senate** passed S 653 by voice vote March 17.

**Senate** passed S 686 by voice vote March 20.

**House** cleared S 686, 203-58, March 21.

**President** signed March 21.

about end-of-life medical care and raised questions about the meaning of conservatism in national politics. Public opinion polls showed a majority of Americans opposed congressional intervention in the case.

## COMPETING BILLS

On Wednesday, March 16, the House passed a broadly worded bill (HR 1332) to authorize the transfer to federal courts — within 30 days after all state remedies were exhausted — of cases such as Schiavo's, that involved incapacitated people who had not executed an advance directive authorizing the withholding of sustenance.

The bill, drafted by Judiciary Committee Chairman F. James Sensenbrenner Jr., R-Wis., and Dave Weldon, R-Fla., passed by voice vote. "What Terri Schiavo and all disabled persons deserve is for justice to tilt toward life," Sensenbrenner said on the floor.

There was some disagreement on the floor. Alcee L. Hastings, D-Fla., said the decision to continue his mother's life support was one of the most difficult of his life. "There are certain things perhaps we ought not to legislate," he said. Jerrold Nadler, D-N.Y., called the bill "a dangerous, reckless way to deal with very serious issues."

In the Senate, Florida Republican Mel Martinez introduced a narrow private relief bill (S 653), and the Senate passed it by voice vote on Thursday, March 17.

House Republican leaders were preparing to leave Washington for a two-week spring recess, and they refused to take up the Senate bill, insisting that the Senate consider their broader measure instead. Sensenbrenner issued a statement after the Senate vote saying, "The House has completed its business and has adjourned." He said the Senate could pass the House bill "to ensure Terri Schiavo's civil rights are protected or it can allow Ms. Schiavo to starve to death."

House GOP leaders blamed Senate Democrats for the impasse, particularly Ron Wyden, D-Ore., who had indicated he would oppose any broader bill that might affect his state's assisted-suicide law. "As Terri Schiavo lays helpless in Florida, one day away from the unthinkable and unforgivable, the Senate Democrats refused to join Republicans to act on her behalf," Hastert and Majority Leader Tom DeLay, R-Texas, said in a joint statement.

That analysis was disputed, however, by the bill's strongest Repub-

lican supporters in both chambers, who said House GOP leaders were to blame. "There was broad opposition on both sides of the aisle" in the Senate to the House bill, said Rick Santorum of Pennsylvania, the chairman of the Senate Republican Conference.

Frist, a well-known heart surgeon before he joined the Senate, went to the floor late Thursday night for the second time in 12 hours to argue that Florida doctors had erred in saying Terri Schiavo was in a persistent vegetative state. "I question it based on a review of the video footage, which I spent an hour or so looking at last night in my office," Frist said. "She certainly seems to respond to visual stimuli." Critics said that in relying on family videotapes to challenge the diagnosis of doctors who had examined Schiavo, Frist was pandering to social conservatives rather than following his medical training.

### SUBPOENAS ISSUED; SPRING RECESS DELAYED

On Friday, March 18, the House and Senate delayed the start of their spring recess for one last effort to reach agreement on a bill.

"This act of barbarism must be prevented," DeLay told reporters. DeLay said lawmakers would work through the weekend to try to reconcile the competing House and Senate bills, but he assailed the Senate for refusing to accept the House approach. "All wisdom is not in the Senate," DeLay said.

House GOP leaders said the Senate bill would not guarantee that Schiavo's parents would be able to get a federal judge to hear their case. House supporters also insisted their broader approach was better because it would apply to all incapacitated people, not just Schiavo.

But Senate Republicans and Democrats were concerned the House bill would establish a dangerous precedent and clog courts with an untold number of such cases. They also feared it could interfere with state laws, such as Oregon's assisted-suicide statute. Privately, Senate Republicans also were seething that DeLay sent House lawmakers out of town March 17 before the Senate passed its bill.

In a last-ditch attempt to block removal of Schiavo's feeding tube, Thomas M. Davis III, R-Va., chairman of the House Government Reform Committee, subpoenaed Schiavo and her husband, Michael, to attend a March 25 hearing at the Florida hospice where Schiavo lived. The panel also subpoenaed two doctors treating Schiavo, as well as the hospice director. The committee instructed Michael Schiavo, the doctors and the hospice director to bring all the medical equipment used to provide nutrition and hydration to Schiavo in its "current and continuing state of operations" — language designed to prevent the removal of the feeding tube.

Henry A. Waxman of California, the ranking committee Democrat, denounced the subpoenas. "Congress has no authority to use subpoenas to tell doctors what treatment they can and cannot provide to any individual under their care," Waxman said. "These subpoenas were issued unilaterally by Tom Davis, acting at the request of the Republican leadership. There was no vote and no opportunity to debate the issue in committee."

Senate Republican leaders took a different approach, summoning Terri and Michael Schiavo to a March 28 Senate Health, Education, Labor and Pensions Committee hearing in Washington. They invoked federal criminal law that prohibited any attempt "to obstruct or impede" the attendance or testimony of a witness, which carried a penalty of up to five years in prison and a $100,000 fine, according to Senate Republican aides. They said the protection would extend to Terri Schiavo, even if her husband declined to appear, and even if Mrs. Schiavo did not appear.

Social conservatives praised the aggressive congressional moves. "Congress, and the Florida Legislature, must not let this travesty stand,"

said James C. Dobson, chairman of the advocacy group Focus on the Family. "They must continue to work to ensure that the weakest among us, who cannot speak for themselves, have the same legal rights and protections that even the most heinous criminals are afforded."

Some legal scholars were critical. "For Congress to reach out in a country of 300 million and intervene in a single case raises very disturbing questions of legitimacy," said Jonathan Turley, a George Washington University law professor.

A lawyer for the House of Representatives also filed a motion in a Florida state court to intervene in the case and modify a Florida judge's order that Schiavo's feeding tube be removed at 1 p.m.

But Florida Circuit Judge George Greer refused the request. "I have had no cogent reason why the [congressional] committee should intervene," Greer told attorneys in a conference call, adding that last-minute action by Congress did not invalidate years of court rulings.

### REPUBLICANS REACH AN AGREEMENT

Frist and Hastert agreed Saturday, March 19, on a narrow bill to give Schiavo's parents the right to file a lawsuit in the U.S. District Court for the Middle District of Florida, alleging that Schiavo's rights had been violated under the Constitution or federal law. The federal judge would be required to consider the Schindlers' allegations "de novo," that is, without taking into account any of the various Florida state court decisions that led to the removal of Schiavo's feeding tube. However, the law was silent on whether a federal judge should issue a temporary restraining order to force doctors to reinsert the feeding tube.

As part of the compromise, the new bill included a provision specifying that it did not "confer additional jurisdiction" on federal courts to hear any case related to a state law on assisted suicide. It also included a sense of Congress provision urging the 109th Congress to consider broader legislation dealing with similar cases.

On Sunday, March 20, the Senate passed the bill (S 686) by voice vote. The House voted, 203-58, early Monday to clear the legislation, with 156 Republicans voting in favor of the measure and five against. Democrats were almost evenly split, 47 for and 53 against. Bush signed the bill into law less than an hour later, and an attorney for Schiavo's parents quickly went to the federal district court in Tampa to file a request for an emergency injunction. *(House vote 90, p. H-30)*

Republicans expressed confidence that a federal judge would immediately order doctors to reinsert Schiavo's feeding tube. "I can't imagine that a judge that would legitimately take a case [under the bill] would allow the subject matter of the case to die," said Santorum, a driving force behind the bill. "That would be an irresponsible abuse of that judge's authority."

"She's not a vegetable. She's just handicapped, mentally challenged," DeLay said of Schiavo at a Sunday news conference.

### FEDERAL APPEALS DENIED

The Schindlers, however, had no more success with federal judges than they had had in the Florida courts. They met with a succession of rejections:

▶ March 22. U.S. District Judge James D. Whittemore denied the Schindlers' motion for a temporary restraining order to force doctors to reinsert Schiavo's feeding tube because the Schindlers did not meet the legal burden of proving they had a substantial likelihood of succeeding at trial.

▶ March 23. A three-judge panel of the U.S. Court of Appeals for the 11th Circuit affirmed Whittemore's decision. The two-to-one ruling expressed sympathy with the Schindlers but concluded that the law did

not support any of the parents' legal arguments. The full 11th Circuit declined to review the decision.

▸ March 24. The U.S. Supreme Court declined to hear the Schindlers' appeal. House GOP leaders had filed a friend-of-the-court brief arguing that Congress intended for a federal court to order doctors to reinsert Schiavo's feeding tube. DeLay and Sensenbrenner issued a joint statement after the court refused to hear the case, saying they "strongly believe that the court erred in reaching its conclusion and that once again they have chosen to ignore the clear intent of Congress."

▸ March 25. Whittemore rejected another motion by the Schindlers for a temporary restraining order, and a three-judge panel on the 11th Circuit affirmed that decision.

▸ March 30. The 11th Circuit denied the Schindlers' emergency petition for a rehearing by the full court. The U.S. Supreme Court once again refused to order Schiavo's feeding tube reinserted. It was the sixth time the high court had declined to intervene.

▸ March 31. Terri Schiavo died.

## AFTERWARD

In the immediate aftermath, angry Republican congressional leaders vowed to rein in the federal judiciary. In comments that generated widespread criticism, DeLay said after Schiavo's death that "this loss happened because our legal system did not protect the people who need protection most, and that will change. The time will come for the men responsible for this to answer for their behavior, but not today."

DeLay later apologized, saying April 13, "I said something in an inartful way. And I shouldn't have said it that way. And I apologize for saying it that way." But he said the judges' handling of the case still should be investigated.

Autopsy results, announced at a June 15 news conference in Largo, Fla., showed that Schiavo had massive and irreversible brain damage and was blind. The report said her brain was discolored and scarred, shriveled to half its normal size, and damaged in nearly all its regions, including the one responsible for vision. The autopsy could not determine what caused the original damage. ∎

# Chapter 15

# TAXES

# GOP Intraparty Dispute Pushes Tax Bill Into Next Session

REPUBLICAN LEADERS HOPED to send President Bush a package of up to $70 billion in tax cuts before the end of the year, but in the hectic weeks before adjournment they were unable to produce a compromise bill that satisfied both fiscal conservatives and moderates in their party. As a result, they planned to finish the job early in the second session.

The House and Senate passed markedly different tax cut packages late in the year, highlighting divisions over tax policy within the Republican Party.

The Senate bill, passed in November (S 2020), proposed $57.8 billion in net tax cuts over five years. The centerpiece was a set of provisions designed to keep more people from having to pay the alternative minimum tax (AMT). It also included extensions for a number of other expiring tax breaks, $7 billion in tax benefits for Gulf Coast hurricane victims, and a hefty set of revenue raisers to offset part of the cost. At the insistence of GOP moderates, the bill did not include provisions avidly sought by the House to extend reduced tax rates on capital gains and dividend income, which were not due to expire until 2008.

The House passed a measure in December (HR 4297) that had at its center a two-year extension of the capital gains and dividends tax reductions. The bill did not include an AMT provision. Ways and Means Chairman Bill Thomas, R-Calif., chose to advance that in separate legislation to leave room in the reconciliation bill for the capital gains and dividends provisions. The House subsequently passed the AMT bill (HR 4096). Congress cleared tax relief for the Gulf Coast area as a separate bill (PL 109-135) before adjourning.

Republicans had laid the groundwork for the tax cut package in April by adopting a fiscal 2006 budget resolution (H Con Res 95) that instructed the House and Senate tax-writing committees to propose $70 billion in revenue reductions over five years in the form of a tax-reconciliation bill. That was a critical step. Because a reconciliation bill was not subject to a filibuster in the Senate, it would allow GOP leaders to pass the tax cuts with a simple majority, rather than the 60 votes that would be needed to cut off a filibuster. *(Budget resolution, p. 4-9)*

Action on the tax cut bill was planned for the fall, but GOP leaders delayed it when Hurricane Katrina hit the Gulf Coast in late August. The mounting costs of recovery from the storm reinforced divisions within the GOP. Fiscal conservatives were intent on pushing ahead with their top tax priority, the capital gains and dividends cuts. Moderates became even more reluctant to extend a tax cut that was seen as primarily benefiting upper-income individuals. They were far more concerned about preventing the AMT — a levy designed to ensure that wealthy individuals paid at least some income tax — from hitting millions more middle-income taxpayers in 2006.

Also, Democrats did their best to make Republican moderates

**BOX SCORE**

**BILLS:** HR 4297, S 2020

**LEGISLATIVE ACTION:**

**Senate** passed S 2020, 64-33, on Nov. 18.

**House** passed HR 4297 (H Rept 109-304), 234-197, on Dec. 8.

uncomfortable over considering tax cuts at a time when their leaders also were pushing reductions in politically sensitive mandatory spending programs (S 1932).

GOP leaders decided the differences over the tax cuts were too great to resolve in the busy final weeks of the session and would have to be settled the following year.

## BACKGROUND

Both the House and Senate bills focused on extending provisions of the 2001 tax law (PL 107-16), the 2003 tax law (PL 108-27), and two 2004 tax laws (PL 108-311, PL 108-357). *(2001 Almanac, p. 18-3; 2003 Almanac, p. 17-3; 2004 Almanac, pp. 13-3, 13-8)*

● **AMT.** The alternative minimum tax was created in 1969 to ensure that high-income individuals and corporations could not use deductions, credits and other provisions to avoid paying at least some taxes. Taxpayers whose liability was greater under the AMT than under the regular tax system had to give up certain credits and deductions and so ended up paying higher taxes. To protect middle-income taxpayers from having to pay the alternative tax, the tax code exempted a certain amount of income from the AMT. But the levels were not adjusted for inflation, so a greater number of people were pushed into the AMT each year. According to the Joint Committee on Taxation , while fewer than 1 percent of taxpayers were subjected to the tax before 2000, it was projected to affect 29 million people, 20 percent of all taxpayers, by 2010.

To prevent more taxpayers from paying the AMT, Congress provided short-term increases to the exemption levels. Completely eliminating the AMT was considered too expensive. The Joint Tax Committee estimated it would cost nearly $611 billion over 10 years.

The 2001 tax law raised the exemption to $35,750 for single taxpayers (from $33,750) and $49,000 for joint filers (from $45,000); the provision expired at the end of 2003. The 2003 tax law extended the exemption for two years and increased it to $40,250 for individuals and $58,000 for married couples. A 2004 tax law (PL 108-311) extended those levels for an additional year, through 2005.

If the exemption levels were not extended, they would return to pre-2001 levels in 2006. According to the Joint Tax Committee, 19 million taxpayers, including a larger number of middle-income taxpayers, would be subject to the alternative tax. An estimated 3.6 million taxpayers were liable for the tax in 2005.

● **Capital gains and dividends.** The 2003 tax law reduced tax rates on capital gains — profits from the sale of assets — and dividends — corporate profits distributed to shareholders. It capped the rates for individuals at 15 percent. The rate for taxpayers in the two lowest brackets — the 10 percent and 15 percent brackets — was 5 percent through 2007, dropping to zero in 2008.

The provisions were due to expire after 2008. At that point, the max-

imum rate for capital gains would return to the pre-2003 level of 20 percent (10 percent for the lower brackets). Dividends would be taxed at the same rate as ordinary income.

## LEGISLATIVE ACTION
### SENATE COMMITTEE ACTION

The Senate Finance Committee approved a $59.6 billion tax cut package by a vote of 14-6 on Nov. 15, but only after conservatives agreed to drop a proposed extension of the capital gains and dividends tax breaks. The committee also voted to scale back proposed tax benefits for large oil companies. With those changes, three Democrats — ranking member Max Baucus of Montana, Blanche Lincoln of Arkansas and Charles E. Schumer of New York — joined in supporting the bill.

Finance Chairman Charles E. Grassley, R-Iowa, had postponed the session twice while he tried to secure enough votes to get the measure out of the committee. Grassley originally circulated a $68.8 billion, five-year package that would have extended the reduced rate on capital gains and dividends for one year, through 2009. Conservatives wanted to extend the break through 2010, but even Grassley's scaled-back version could not win the approval of Olympia J. Snowe of Maine, the moderate swing vote on the closely divided committee.

With Democrats expected to oppose any measure that included the investment tax break, Grassley had no votes to spare. Leaders considered skipping a markup and bringing the bill directly to the floor, but foresaw too many procedural difficulties.

By Nov. 15, conservatives had grudgingly agreed to allow the bill to proceed without the investment break. Snowe called the revised measure "a fiscally practical and responsible approach," given the size of the federal deficit and the cost of the hurricanes.

But several GOP conservatives on the panel — particularly Jon Kyl of Arizona, Michael D. Crapo of Idaho and Jim Bunning of Kentucky — made no secret that they would work to restore the capital gains break in conference. "We ought not to be doing the bill without that key element," Kyl said, arguing the provision was needed to spur investment. Majority Leader Bill Frist, R-Tenn., pledged that he would not bring a conference report back to the Senate without the capital gains and dividends language. "I will insist that negotiators include an extension of the capital gains and dividend tax relief," he said. However, Frist did not say that it had to be a two-year extension.

During the markup, the committee:

▶ Adopted by voice vote an amendment by Ron Wyden, D-Ore., to scale back a $1 billion tax break for oil and gas producers enacted in the 2005 energy law (PL 109-58). The law allowed companies to write off over two years the cost of geological and geophysical expenditures connected to oil and gas exploration in the United States. Wyden's amendment would prohibit certain large oil companies from receiving those tax benefits.

▶ Adopted by voice vote an amendment by Gordon H. Smith, R-Ore., to make private mortgage insurance premiums tax deductible.

▶ Rejected, on a 9-11 party-line vote, an amendment by Baucus and Kent Conrad, D-N.D., to scale back the bill to tax breaks that expired in 2005, expand the AMT exemption and offset the entire cost of the bill with revenue-raising provisions.

### SENATE FLOOR ACTION

The Senate passed the bill, 64-33, on Nov. 18. GOP leaders again insisted they would restore the extension of the capital gains and dividend rates when they negotiated a conference agreement with House Republicans. *(Senate vote 347, p. S-67)*

As passed, the bill provided about $76.5 billion in tax breaks over five years and included $18.8 billion in revenue-raising offsets for a net cost of $57.8 billion. Although the budget resolution allowed a $70 billion tax cut bill to move on the Senate floor under special reconciliation rules, it specified that a $35 billion package of mandatory spending cuts had to be cleared first. Until that happened, the Senate tax bill could not exceed a net cost of $60 billion. (The spending cut bill did not clear until 2006.) *(Budget reconciliation, p. 4-13)*

The Senate tax bill included:

● **Expiring tax provisions.** A $68.1 billion extension of expiring tax provisions. The biggest items on the list were:

▶ An extension of the AMT exemption through 2006, with the income level indexed for inflation. As amended on the floor, the bill also increased the exemption to $42,500 for individuals and $62,550 for joint returns. Senate aides said as a result the number of taxpayers subject to the AMT would not increase in 2006. (Cost: $30.5 billion)

▶ An extension through 2009 of a deduction for tuition and related higher-education expenses that was due to expire after 2005. (Cost: $7.4 billion)

▶ An extension through 2009 of a tax credit for voluntary IRA and other retirement savings contributions that was due to expire after 2006. (Cost: $4.1 billion)

▶ A one-year extension and expansion of the research and development credit for businesses that was due to expire after 2005. (Cost: $9.9 billion).

▶ A one-year extension of the deduction for state and local sales taxes in states that had no income tax, which was due to expire after 2005. (Cost: $2.6 billion)

▶ An extension through 2009 of a provision allowing small businesses to write off, or "expense," up to $100,000 in capital investments in the year they were made. The existing law was due to expire after 2007. (Cost: $7.3 billion)

● **Hurricane assistance.** $7 billion over five years in a series of tax incentives designed to spur economic activity on the hurricane-damaged Gulf Coast.

● **Charitable donations.** $637 million in net tax breaks to encourage charitable donations.

● **Revenue increases.** $14.5 billion in tax increases, used to offset some of the tax breaks. The revenue-raisers included:

▶ A provision, previously rejected by the House, to tighten the tax treatment of financial transactions that were deemed to have no "economic substance" — in other words, they were carried out primarily to reduce taxes. The proposal would raise $5.2 billion.

▶ A provision, inserted at the behest of Snowe and Schumer, to increase what constituted taxable income for large integrated oil companies, raising $4.3 billion. Western Republicans objected. "I'm very concerned that this is a backdoor attempt to place a windfall profits tax on oil companies," said Orrin G. Hatch, R-Utah. He said it would harm small oil companies, including three in Utah. The Senate kept the provision because the revenue was needed to comply with budget rules, but Grassley offered a manager's amendment, adopted by voice vote, that modified the provision so it would affect companies with worldwide production of at least 500,000 barrels of crude oil a day. The White House issued a statement saying Bush's advisers would recommend a veto if the provision remained in the final bill.

Senate GOP leaders beat back almost two dozen amendments, most offered by Democrats. However, the floor debate served as a forum for members of both parties to score political points at the expense of oil and gas companies, which were reaping huge profits amid high oil prices.

During the debate, the Senate:

▸ Rejected an amendment by Byron L. Dorgan, D-N.D., to impose a 50 percent excise tax on oil company profits when crude oil prices exceeded $40 per barrel, unless the company invested the profits in new production. The proceeds would be used for consumer rebates. The proposal drew fierce opposition from oil-state senators, who called it a disincentive to domestic oil production. It was struck down on a budget point of order after a 35-64 vote that fell well short of the 60 votes needed to waive the procedural barrier. *(Senate vote 331, p. S-64)*

▸ Defeated an amendment by Dianne Feinstein, D-Calif., to eliminate a tax break that allowed oil and gas companies to write off certain exploration and development costs in a single year. The amendment — which targeted ExxonMobil Corp., Shell Oil Co., ConocoPhillips, Chevron Corp. and BP — fell on a similar budget point of order, 48-51. *(Senate vote 332, p. S-65)*

▸ Rejected a series of Democratic amendments aimed at scaling back the size of the tax package or putting new hurdles in front of tax cuts. They included a proposal by Conrad to extend only those tax cuts that expired in 2005, expand the one-year AMT provision and provide tax incentives for Gulf Coast rebuilding. Unlike the underlying bill, the costs would have been offset by provisions cracking down on corporations that abused U.S. tax laws. The amendment was rejected, 44-55. *(Senate vote 330, p. S-64)*

▸ Rejected an amendment by Russ Feingold, D-Wis., to reinstate lapsed Senate pay-as-you-go rules that placed a 60-vote hurdle in front of mandatory spending increases and tax cuts that were not offset. Feingold failed, 50-48, to waive a 60-vote budget point of order. *(Senate vote 340, p. S-66)*

## HOUSE COMMITTEE ACTION

The House Ways and Means Committee voted 24-15 on Nov. 15 to approve a $56.1 billion tax bill (HR 4297 — H Rept 109-304), drafted by Thomas, that included no revenue offsets. But having just barely won a close floor victory on the mandatory spending cut bill, House GOP leaders postponed a floor vote on the tax cuts until lawmakers returned from the Thanksgiving recess the week of Dec. 5.

Unlike the Senate measure, the House bill included a two-year extension of the of the capital gains and dividends tax breaks, which cheered securities industry lobbyists and conservatives. It did not include the AMT extension — often called the AMT "patch" — a fact that made some House GOP moderates, such as Charles Bass of New Hampshire, wary.

Before the markup, Thomas deleted from his draft a series of popular tax break extensions that had bipartisan appeal, reducing the bill's net cost to $32 billion over five years. He then let members offer piecemeal amendments to add back the deleted provisions, or modified versions of them, and held roll call votes.

Thomas' approach allowed GOP members to take credit for various tax breaks and required Democrats to go on record as supporting many popular tax provisions, even though they opposed the overall measure. "Democrats voted in favor of the same tax relief they've built their careers on attacking," said a press release by the National Republican Congressional Committee.

## HOUSE FLOOR ACTION

The House passed the bill, 234-197, on Dec. 8, after passing separate bills earlier in the week to extend the AMT and provide tax relief to hurricane victims. *(House vote 621, p. H-198)*

As passed by the House, the bill included:

● **Capital gains and dividends.** A two-year extension, through 2010, of the reduced tax on dividends and capital gains. (Cost: $20.6 billion)

● **Other extensions:**

▸ A one-year extension and expansion of the research and development credit. (Cost: $9.2 billion)

▸ A one-year extension of the tuition deduction. (Cost: $1.7 billion)

▸ A one-year extension of the deduction for state and local sales taxes in states with no income tax. (Cost: $2.4 billion)

▸ An extension through 2008 of the tax credit for IRA and other voluntary retirement savings contributions. (Cost: $2.8 billion)

▸ An extension through 2008 of a provision that allowed corporations to exclude offshore "active financing" income from taxation. This provision was not in the Senate bill. (Cost: $4.8 billion)

▸ An extension through 2009 of increased expensing for small businesses. (Cost: $7.3 billion)

During the floor debate, the House:

▸ Rejected, 192-239, a Democratic substitute that would have eliminated the capital gains and dividends extensions, as well as extensions of tax cuts that were not due to expire in 2005, such as the active-financing exclusion and the higher expensing limits for small businesses. It would have eliminated individual tax liability for the AMT in fiscal 2006 for individual taxpayers with incomes below $100,000 ($200,000 for joint filers). *(House vote 619, p. H-198)*

▸ Rejected, 193-235, a motion by Charles B. Rangel of New York, ranking Democrat on Ways and Means, to send the bill back to the committee with instructions to strike the capital gains and dividend tax breaks and add a new section to provide AMT relief. *(House vote 620, p. H-198)*

## OTHER HOUSE BILLS

Before passing the tax reconciliation bill, the House passed two separate measures covering the AMT and tax relief for the Gulf Coast.

● **AMT.** On Dec. 7, the House passed a $31.2 billion one-year extension of the AMT exemption (HR 4096) that also would index the amount for inflation. The vote was an overwhelming 414-4. Rangel called the measure a "fig leaf" designed to cover up the GOP's lack of action on the issue, but he voted for the bill nonetheless. *(House vote 613, p. H-194)*

Senate Democrats worried, however, that if the AMT provision were taken out of the reconciliation bill and moved separately, it would leave plenty of room for House Republicans to include a two-year extension of the capital gains and dividends break. It also would lessen the need for billions of dollars in revenue-raising offsets proposed by the Senate but opposed by House GOP members.

● **Gulf Coast.** Also on Dec. 7, the House passed $7.1 billion worth of tax breaks for Gulf Coast rebuilding (HR 4440) by a vote of 415-4. That bill was cleared and became law. *(House vote 618, p. H-196; Hurricane relief, p. 15-6)* ■

# Hurricane Tax Relief Bills Enacted

CONGRESS CLEARED TWO bills to provide tax relief to the victims of Hurricane Katrina, which devastated the Louisiana, Mississippi and Alabama coasts the week of Aug. 29, and subsequent hurricanes Rita and Wilma that also hit the region.

The first, a $6.1 billion collection of provisions mainly to aid individuals and businesses hurt by Katrina, was enacted in September. The second, a $7.8 billion package of incentives for investment in the hurricane disaster zones, was signed in December.

## IMMEDIATE KATRINA RELIEF

Congress cleared a $6.1 billion package of tax breaks aimed at individuals and corporations in the hurricane-ravaged Gulf Coast region Sept. 21. President Bush signed the measure into law Sept. 23 (HR 3768 — PL 109-73).

The House and Senate passed slightly differing versions of the legislation by voice vote Sept. 15. After a brief tussle over the scope of tax breaks aimed at encouraging corporations to retain and hire victims of Katrina, and at spurring more charitable contributions, House and Senate tax writers resolved their differences Sept. 20, avoiding a drawn-out formal conference on the legislation.

The House adopted a special rule (H Res 454) by a vote of 422-0 on Sept. 21 that had the effect of amending and passing the bill, sending it back to the Senate. The Senate cleared the bill by voice vote that evening. (*House vote 480, p. H-150*)

The bill included provisions to:

▶ Allow individuals to withdraw up to $100,000 from their individual retirement accounts without paying the 10 percent federal penalty, provided they restored the funds to the account within three years.

▶ Allow Katrina victims to use their 2004 income in claiming the earned income tax credit or child tax credit on their 2005 tax returns. This was to ensure that those displaced by the hurricane did not lose benefits because of a change in their living situation.

▶ Allow firms with fewer than 200 employees to claim a 40 percent tax credit for up to $6,000 in wages paid to a worker between Aug. 28 and Dec. 31. This was a scaled-back version of a Senate provision aimed at encouraging businesses in the disaster area that could not operate to continue paying their workers.

▶ Make the "work opportunity" tax credit — used by employers of workers who received welfare benefits or food stamps — available for two years to those in disaster zones who hired people displaced by Katrina, and through the end of 2005 for employers outside the disaster area.

▶ Allow individuals in disaster zones to gain access to mortgage revenue bonds typically issued by state and local governments to help first-time homebuyers finance homes. Up to $150,000 of the proceeds from mortgage revenue bonds could be used to repair homes damaged by Hurricane Katrina.

▶ Allow S-corporations, partnerships and sole proprietorships to claim a deduction on charitable contributions of food inventory through the end of the year. It also allowed corporations to claim a

---

**BOX SCORE**

**BILLS:**
HR 3768 — PL 109-73;
HR 4440 — PL 109-135

**LEGISLATIVE ACTION:**

**House** passed HR 3768 by voice vote Sept. 15.

**Senate** passed HR 3768, amended, by voice vote Sept. 15.

**House** agreed to Senate amendment, with an amendment, 422-0, Sept. 21.

**Senate** cleared HR 3768 by voice vote Sept. 21.

**President** signed Sept. 23.

**House** passed HR 4440, 415-4, on Dec. 7.

**Senate** passed HR 4440, amended, by voice vote Dec. 16.

**House** cleared bill by voice vote Dec. 16.

**President** signed Dec. 22.

---

deduction through the end of 2005 for donations of educational books to public schools. This was a more limited version of a charitable deduction provision in the Senate bill.

▶ Temporarily increase deduction limits for cash donations made by individuals and corporations. The increased deduction for individuals applied to all charitable contributions, not just those related to Hurricane Katrina.

## STIMULATING INVESTMENT

Congress cleared a $7.8 billion package of tax incentives Dec. 16 that was intended to spur investment in the Gulf Coast region. Bush signed the measure into law Dec. 22 (HR 4440 — PL 109-135).

Final House and Senate passage marked a delayed victory for Louisiana and Mississippi lawmakers, who had worked for months to secure a second round of tax breaks to help rebuild their states. The bill was the product of a week of informal House-Senate negotiations that allowed tax writers to avoid a formal conference and expedite action as lawmakers prepared to leave for the holidays.

The centerpiece of the bill was the creation of "Gulf Opportunity Zones" to spur business investment in devastated areas of Alabama, Louisiana and Mississippi, with tax breaks and bond provisions that totaled $6.2 billion over five years. They included:

▶ A "bonus depreciation" deduction for businesses equal to 50 percent of the cost of new property investments made in the disaster zone. The cost to the Treasury would be $2 billion over five years.

▶ Additional tax-exempt bond authority for Louisiana, Mississippi and Alabama at a cost of $478 million over five years.

▶ A change in federal law to allow one additional "advance refunding" of debt for each state at a cost of $493 million over five years. Advance refunding allowed municipalities to issue new bonds to pay off outstanding bonds. Existing law allowed only one advance refunding of tax-exempt bonds.

▶ A 50 percent deduction for the costs of site cleanup and demolition from Aug. 27, 2005, through Dec. 31, 2007, at a cost of $121 million over five years.

▶ A 50 percent federal guarantee for up to $3 billion in bonds to aid local governments in Alabama, Louisiana and Mississippi that had lost revenue or lacked access to capital to help fund infrastructure projects or operating expenses.

The bill also expanded tax breaks enacted in the earlier hurricane tax relief law to apply to individuals and businesses affected by hurricanes Rita and Wilma, as well as Katrina.

## HOUSE ACTION

The House passed a $7.1 billion version of the bill, 415-4, on Dec. 7. (*House vote 618, p. H-196*)

The measure included a controversial provision to prohibit public and private golf courses, country clubs, massage parlors, hot tub facil-

ities, tanning salons, liquor stores, horse and dog racetracks and gambling facilities from taking advantage of any of the new tax benefits.

Ways and Means Chairman Bill Thomas, R-Calif., added the language at the insistence of a group of more than 30 social conservatives, led by Frank R. Wolf, R-Va. Thomas' decision won kudos from that group, but it drew a sharp rebuke from Mississippi Republican Trent Lott, a member of the Senate Finance Committee whose state's economy relied on casino revenue. Lott said he would not agree to a bill that did not benefit the gambling industry.

The White House agreed, saying tax benefits should be available to all industries.

The administration also did not like the 50 percent federal guarantee for up to $3 billion in bonds to aid local governments. A Treasury spokesman said "the cost of guarantees to taxpayers could far outweigh the value of the aid they provide to the people of the Gulf Coast; they would not benefit victims directly; and could have serious negative consequences on bond markets."

**SENATE/FINAL ACTION**

The Senate included a $7.1 billion package of Gulf Coast tax relief in its tax reconciliation bill (S 2020) passed Nov. 18, but House-Senate negotiations on that legislation were put off until 2006. *(Tax reconciliation, p. 15-3)*

After a week of House-Senate negotiations aimed at avoiding a formal conference, the Senate took up HR 4440 on Dec. 16, amended it with a compromise $7.8 billion tax cut package and passed it by voice vote. The House cleared the bill by voice vote later the same day.

The key sticking point in the negotiations was the House-passed language excluding country clubs, gambling facilities and other businesses from taking advantage of the new tax benefits. In the end, Senate tax writers engineered a complicated compromise that slightly watered down the House language. The final bill was written so that only the portion of gambling and racetrack facilities directly related to gambling room equipment and construction would be denied tax breaks.

The hotel and restaurant portions of casinos, for example, could still receive the benefit of the "bonus depreciation" deduction. Gambling facilities smaller than 100 square feet also would be afforded tax benefits — a provision that would ensure that stores with video gambling machines would not be denied the tax breaks.

Lott, who was intent on getting the tax breaks for his state before Congress adjourned, accepted the compromise, but vowed to repeal the provision in the next tax bill. ∎

# Katrina Knocks Estate Tax Off Agenda

REPUBLICANS WERE optimistic that their four-seat gain in the Senate in the 2004 elections would finally enable them to do away with the estate tax, or at least permanently reduce it. Hurricane Katrina canceled those plans.

Labeled the "death tax" by opponents, the estate tax was a perennial target of GOP tax cutters and their allies in the business community. The 2001 tax law (PL 107-16) set in motion a gradual phase-out of the tax, culminating in a full repeal in 2010. But because of budget constraints, the repeal was good for only one year and the estate tax was set to revert to the 2001 level in 2011. At that point, estates valued at more than $675,000 would be subject to a 55 percent tax when the owners died and the estates were passed on to heirs. *(2001 Almanac, p. 18-3)*

The House had voted three times since the 2001 law was enacted to extend the one-year repeal indefinitely, but each time the effort died in the Senate. GOP leaders said the "sunset" clause in the 2001 law was wreaking havoc with the ability of small-business owners to plan for the future. *(2002 Almanac, p, 16-5; 2003 Almanac, p. 17-15)*

On April 13, the House once again passed a bill to delete the sunset date, making the one-year repeal permanent. The bill (HR 8) passed 272-162, with 42 Democrats joining almost all Republicans present in supporting the repeal. The full repeal would cost $290 billion in its first 10 years, according to the Joint Committee on Taxation. *(House vote 102, p. H-34)*

Before passing the bill, the House rejected, 194-238, a Democratic alternative by Earl Pomeroy of North Dakota. It would have left the estate tax structure in place, but increased the exemption to $3 million for individuals and $6 million for married couples in 2006. In 2009, the exemption would have been increased to $3.5 million for individuals and $7 million for couples. *(House vote 101, p. H-34)*

Many Democrats argued that certain small businesses, including farms, should be exempt from the estate tax, but that the tax provided a badly needed source of federal revenue and should be left in place for the wealthiest Americans. Supporters of Pomeroy's substitute said it would cover 99.7 percent of estates while costing the Treasury only about $70 billion.

In the Senate, Majority Leader Bill Frist, R-Tenn., was under pressure from conservatives to hold a vote on the issue before senators left for the August recess. But Frist faced a crowded pre-recess agenda, plus resistance from the Senate's top GOP tax writer, Charles E. Grassley of Iowa. Grassley, chairman of the Finance Committee, said a rushed vote could doom compromise talks that were going on between the lead Senate supporter of a repeal, Republican Jon Kyl of Arizona, and Max Baucus of Montana, the top Democrat on the Finance Committee.

On July 29, as the Senate was wrapping up its work before the August recess, Frist filed a motion for cloture to limit debate on the House-passed estate tax repeal. The Senate was expected to vote on the issue as early as the evening of Sept. 6, although it was not clear whether Frist had the 60 votes needed to succeed. Still, the prospect of making Democrats choose between supporting a repeal of the tax on inherited wealth or alienating their business supporters back home was enough to make GOP leaders risk a loss on the procedural vote.

But the September cloture vote was never held. Before members returned from the recess, Hurricane Katrina devastated the Gulf Coast and totally revamped the congressional agenda. With hurricane victims suffering in Louisiana, Mississippi and Alabama, Senate GOP leaders canceled the estate tax vote. Meanwhile, Republican moderates were increasingly concerned about voting for more tax cuts at a time when Congress was considering cuts to mandatory programs and worrying about the enormous costs of the hurricane relief effort. The estate tax vanished from the congressional agenda for 2005. ∎

**Chapter 16**

# TECHNOLOGY & COMMUNICATIONS

# House Passes Tough Indecency Bill; Cable Question Stalls Senate Action

THE HOUSE PASSED A BILL TO INCREASE penalties on broadcasters for indecent programming, but the measure stalled in the Senate because of disagreements over whether to also regulate cable TV.

Ted Stevens, R-Alaska, who chaired the Senate Commerce, Science and Transportation Committee, favored the creation of a "family friendly" tier of programming on cable, as did several other senators. Sen. Ron Wyden, D-Ore., introduced a bill (S 946) to that effect. But Stevens also said he would prefer that the industry police itself.

Others wanted to mandate "a la carte" programming, which would allow consumers to pick and pay for only the channels they wanted, and still others favored applying Federal Communications Commission (FCC) regulations to cable and satellite operators (S 616).

Sen. Sam Brownback, R-Kan., introduced a bill similar to the House measure, though it did not apply to artists and performers. Like the House bill, it did not cover cable.

Hoping to avoid mandatory regulation, the National Cable and Telecommunications Association in April announced a $250 million campaign to educate consumers about the channel-blocking tools built into many cable set-top boxes. That was not enough to keep Congress at bay, however. In late November, the Senate Commerce Committee held a widely publicized forum on indecency, at which FCC Chairman Kevin J. Martin announced his support for a la carte programming and family tiers, reversing his agency's previous position.

With pressure from regulators and lawmakers growing, several major cable companies, including Comcast Corp. and Time Warner Inc., announced plans to offer family tiers. That was enough to keep the Senate from acting on indecency legislation before the end of the year.

Both chambers had passed indecency measures by overwhelming majorities in 2004, spurred on by Janet Jackson's famous "wardrobe malfunction" at the 2004 Super Bowl. But the Senate bill was derailed by a dispute over an unrelated provision on media ownership rules. *(2004 Almanac, p. 14-3)*

## LEGISLATIVE ACTION

On Feb. 9, the House Energy and Commerce Committee approved HR 310 (H Rept 109-5) by a vote of 46-2. "For those broadcasters who continue to act irresponsibly, the FCC needs adequate authority to enforce the law, and this bill would deliver that," said sponsor Fred Upton, R-Mich.

The bill, which mirrored the measure the House passed in 2004, included provisions to:

▸ Increase to $500,000 the ceiling on FCC fines for broadcasting indecent, obscene or profane material on radio or television programs, with no limit for repeat violations. Under existing law, broadcasters could be fined up to $32,500 per incident .

▸ Apply the same penalties to individuals who uttered obscene, indecent or profane material during a radio or television broadcast. Under existing law, artists could be fined only $11,000 under a process that had yet to be used.

▸ Require the FCC to consider whether the objectionable material was part of a live or recorded program and was scripted or unscripted; whether the broadcaster used a time delay to block objectionable material; whether there was reasonable opportunity to review the program or to believe that it might contain objectionable material; the size of the viewing audience; and whether the programming was part of a children's television program.

Network affiliates would not be liable for objectionable material in a network broadcast if they did not have the opportunity to review its content or did not have a reasonable basis to believe that the program would contain objectionable material.

▸ Require the FCC to consider revoking a station's broadcast license after three violations — known as the three-strikes provision.

▸ Instruct the FCC to consider violations and fines assessed against a broadcaster during license-renewal proceedings.

The committee defeated by voice vote an amendment by Jan Schakowsky, D-Ill., to protect artists from the proposed fine increase. "We are heading down a slippery slope when Big Brother decides what constitutes free speech and artistic expression," Schakowsky said.

## HOUSE FLOOR ACTION

The House passed the bill, 389-38, on Feb. 16. The White House issued a statement the day of the vote expressing strong support for the measure. *(House vote 35, p. H-14)*

"This legislation makes great strides in making it safe for families to come back again into their living rooms," said Joe L. Barton, R-Texas, chairman of the Energy and Commerce Committee. "For too long, broadcasters have pushed the envelope."

The House gave voice vote approval to a manager's amendment by Upton to clarify that the FCC could punish performers only if they intentionally violated indecency standards and knew the material would be broadcast. It also required the FCC to consider whether an individual was able to pay the fine.

Several Democrats said Washington was encouraging self-censorship in the media. Fourteen Democrats who supported similar legislation in 2004, as well as Vermont independent Bernard Sanders, voted against it this time. ■

# 'Spyware' Legislation Falters Again

PUBLIC CONCERN OVER "SPYWARE" — computer programs that surreptitiously access hard drives to collect personal data for third parties — forced Congress to take a serious look at anti-spyware proposals. But for the second straight year, disagreements over how to balance industry and consumer interests stalled the legislation. The House passed a pair of anti-spyware bills. In the Senate, a separate measure won committee approval but did not reach the floor.

The House passed the two bills by lopsided votes in May, after efforts to merge the proposals — one preventive, the other punitive — failed. Under the first bill (HR 29), sponsored by Mary Bono, R-Calif., software companies would have to get the computer user's permission before installing programs that could collect personal information. Some technology companies opposed Bono's approach, saying it could restrict legitimate interactive software and result in consumers being deluged with consent notices.

The second bill (HR 744), sponsored by Robert W. Goodlatte, R-Va., was more to the software industry's liking because it did not dictate specific technological requirements. Instead, it called for fines and prison sentences for individuals convicted of tapping into personal computers with the intent of committing fraud or damaging a machine.

A similar debate played out in the Senate Commerce, Science and Transportation Committee. In November, the panel approved legislation (S 687) sponsored by Conrad Burns, R-Mont., that was similar to Bono's effort to require the consumer's permission before companies could install software that could collect sensitive personal information. A rival bill (S 1004) sponsored by George Allen, R-Va., followed Goodlatte's approach of stiffer punishment for those that installed or used spyware.

The sequence of events in Congress was almost an exact repeat of what had occurred in 2004, when the House passed two competing spyware measures and the Senate Commerce, Science and Transportation Committee approved its own. None of those bills progressed any further. *(2004 Almanac, p. 14-9)*

Spyware programs, which are often transmitted to consumers without their consent, can track users' behavior on the Web, gather sensitive information about them and damage their machines.

## LEGISLATIVE ACTION
### HOUSE ENERGY AND COMMERCE COMMITTEE

The House Energy and Commerce Committee approved Bono's bill, 43-0, on March 9 (HR 29 — H Rept 109-32). The panel's Subcommittee on Commerce, Trade and Consumer Protection had approved it Feb. 16.

The measure, which closely resembled Bono's 2004 bill, had bipartisan support and the backing of companies such as Microsoft Corp., Yahoo! Inc., and eBay Inc.

It included provisions to bar anyone from installing an information-collection program on a computer without the user's consent. It outlawed a list of specific practices, including keystroke logging, computer hijacking and online advertisements that could not be closed. The Federal Trade Commission (FTC) would be able to seek civil penalties of up to $3 million for violations of those prohibitions.

Subcommittee Chairman Cliff Stearns, R-Fla., added language to

---

**BOX SCORE**

**BILLS:** HR 29, HR 744, S 687

**LEGISLATIVE ACTION:**

**House** passed HR 29 (H Rept 109-32), 393-4, on May 23.

**House** passed HR 744 (H Rept 109-93), 395-1, on May 23.

**Senate** Commerce, Science and Transportation Committee approved S 687, 14-8, on Nov. 17.

---

the 2005 bill to increase enforcement against "phishing" — the use of fake or "evil-twin" Web sites that resembled a legitimate site in order to collect personal information.

The subcommittee adopted an amendment by Stearns aimed at alleviating industry concerns that the bill was too broad. Among other things, the amendment clarified that the provisions would not apply to Internet "cookies," the strings of text saved in a browser when a computer user visited a Web site. Cookies were commonly used to store personal data, allowing companies to customize their Web sites for individual users. The amendment also stated that the bill was not meant to police computer users who voluntarily transmitted personal information to another party online.

But even with those changes, the measure ran into resistance from the Information Technology Association of America (ITAA). The trade group said the bill would impose excessive technical requirements on software developers, restrict interactive software programs, and constrain legitimate businesses that relied on "adware" programs to deliver targeted online advertising.

Committee Chairman Joe L. Barton, R-Texas, said he would "put considerable pressure on the Senate to act this year."

### HOUSE JUDICIARY COMMITTEE

The House Judiciary Committee gave voice vote approval May 18 to Goodlatte's bill (HR 744 — H Rept 109-33), which was backed by the ITAA.

Like the 2004 version, the bill sought to impose criminal penalties for accessing a computer to steal information or damage hardware. Goodlatte said he wanted to punish "bad actors" without stifling the growth of legitimate online businesses and new technologies.

The bill would make it a crime to use spyware to break the law, commit fraud or breach computer security. It called for fines or prison sentences of up to two years for intentionally gaining access to a computer without authorization and installing software to steal personal information with the intent to defraud, damage hardware or impair a security program. Using spyware as part of another criminal offense would bring fines or sentences of up to five years. States would be preempted from creating civil remedies based on violations of the bill.

### HOUSE FLOOR ACTION

Lawmakers gave up trying to meld the bills into a single measure that would protect consumers and still satisfy technology companies wary of government regulation. Instead, the House passed both bills May 23. Members voted 395-1 in favor of Goodlatte's bill, then passed the Bono bill, 393-4. *(House votes 200, 201, p. H-66)*

### SENATE COMMITTEE ACTION

The Commerce, Science and Transportation Committee approved Burns' bill (S 687), 14-8, on Nov. 17. Like the House Energy and Commerce measure, it sought to prohibit installation of software programs that automatically collected and transmitted personal information from computers without telling users.

The bill also would ban the installation of software that delivered online ads without identifying their source and would prohibit software that a user could not uninstall. Other provisions would outlaw "modem hijacking," which could leave victims saddled with unauthorized charges, and "denial of service" attacks, which could cripple Web sites by overloading them with traffic.

The committee rejected, 9-13, an amendment by Allen, who tried to substitute language from his own bill (S 1004) aimed at increasing civil and criminal penalties for using spyware to commit fraud or other crimes. Allen's amendment also would have given the FTC more resources to enforce the law.

Committee Chairman Ted Stevens, R-Alaska, said he was hopeful a compromise would be reached before a floor vote, but he set no specific timetable and the legislation never did go to the floor. ■

# Deadline Set for Digital TV Conversion

CONGRESS SET A HARD DEADLINE of Feb. 17, 2009, for broadcast television stations to fully convert to digital broadcasts and return their analog frequencies to the federal government. The legislation required that some of the freed-up frequencies be allocated to emergency responders. The rest were to be auctioned off for an estimated $10 billion. The law directed $2.6 billion of the proceeds to other uses, leaving $7.4 billion over five years for deficit reduction.

The legislation cleared Feb. 1, 2006, as part of the 2005 budget reconciliation bill, and President Bush signed the bill into law Feb. 8, 2006 (S 1932 — PL 109-171).

Enactment marked a major defeat for the powerful broadcasting lobby, which had fended off similar proposals for nearly a decade, and a victory for the wireless communications industry, which wanted access to the freed-up frequencies for a variety of innovative technologies.

Congress had taken the first real step under the 1996 telecommunications act (PL 104-104) by allowing the Federal Communications Commission (FCC) to give television stations a slice of free spectrum to use for digital broadcasting. A year later, lawmakers set a Dec. 31, 2006, deadline for broadcasters to convert all programming to digital and stop analog transmissions. But under intense pressure from the National Association of Broadcasters, Congress agreed to include a caveat: Stations were allowed to keep their analog frequencies until 85 percent of their market had equipment capable of viewing digital programming — a threshold that essentially allowed broadcasters to hang on to their old frequencies indefinitely. *(1996 Almanac, p. 3-43; 1997 Almanac, p. 3-34)*

By 2005 the chorus of calls to free up the TV spectrum for new uses was enough to overpower the broadcasters' protests. The calls were coming from the communications industry, which wanted access to the frequencies to bring a range of new wireless services to market. Signals on those frequencies, which were in the 700 MHz band, can pass through walls easily and travel long distances, making the spectrum perfect for a variety of wireless broadband services.

Congress, meanwhile, looked to the billions of dollars the federal government might reap by auctioning off the returned spectrum to help trim the budget deficit. And Hurricane Katrina, which left the Gulf Coast devastated in late August, highlighted weaknesses in emergency communications systems that prevented first-responders from being able to talk with one another — a problem that also had hampered lifesaving efforts after the Sept. 11, 2001, terrorist attacks.

Lawmakers were extremely sensitive to warnings, mainly from the broadcast industry, that setting a hard deadline for conversion to digital signals could leave millions of Americans without access to television. The Government Accountability Office said about 21 million Americans, many in low-income households, relied on over-the-air

analog programming. Congress' answer was to use part of the proceeds from auctioning the analog spectrum to subsidize set-top boxes that would convert digital signals to analog to keep old television sets working.

## HIGHLIGHTS

The budget reconciliation bill included provisions to:

● **Reclaiming spectrum.** Set Feb. 17, 2009, as the deadline for full-power television stations to return the frequencies used for analog broadcasts to the FCC.

● **Spectrum auctions.** Require the FCC to begin auctioning off the reclaimed spectrum to wireless carriers and others by Jan. 28, 2008. The auction proceeds were to be deposited in a newly created fund, the Digital Television Transition and Public Safety Fund. On Sept. 30, 2009, $7.4 billion from the proceeds would be transferred to the Treasury and treated as offsetting receipts.

● **Converter box subsidies.** Set aside up to $1.5 billion of the proceeds to subsidize digital-to-analog converter boxes for those who still relied on over-the-air television broadcasts and would otherwise see their television screens go dark after the transition.

● **Public safety systems.** Set aside up to $1 billion to help public safety agencies purchase and deploy interoperable communications systems. The law also allocated up to $156 million to build a unified national emergency alert and tsunami warning system and $44 million to upgrade 911 emergency phone systems.

● **Other uses of proceeds.** Allocate up to $65 million to help eligible low-power television stations purchase equipment to upgrade from analog to digital operations, and $10 million to help eligible low-power television stations purchase digital-to-analog conversion devices to convert incoming digital signals to analog format.

The law also allocated $30 million in fiscal 2007 and 2008 for a temporary digital television broadcast system to serve New York City until a permanent facility could be built atop the planned Freedom Tower. An additional $30 million would go to the Essential Air Service Program, which subsidized commercial airline service in remote places, if funds appropriated to operate the program equaled or exceeded $110 million for that fiscal year.

## LEGISLATIVE ACTION

The fiscal 2006 budget resolution (H Con Res 95) instructed specific authorizing committees in the House and Senate to prepare legislation that would contribute to an overall goal of reducing mandatory spending by $34.7 billion over five years. To reach their targets, the Senate Commerce, Science and Transportation Committee and the House Energy and Commerce Committee proposed requiring broadcasters to

return analog spectrum, which the government would auction for an estimated $10 billion. Both committees proposed that part of the proceeds go to other uses.

## SENATE COMMITTEE ACTION

The Senate Commerce, Science and Transportation Committee approved its spectrum provisions, 19-3, on Oct. 20. The committee proposed to:

▶ Set an April 7, 2009, deadline for TV broadcasters to relinquish analog spectrum.

▶ Set aside $3 billion of the proceeds for converter boxes, though the committee did not spell out how that money would be distributed other than to say it would be managed by the Commerce Department.

▶ Dedicate at least $5 billion from the spectrum auction to deficit reduction.

▶ Direct the FCC to collect $10 million in fees for licenses in 2006 to be used as offsetting receipts.

▶ Dedicate $1 billion to interoperable first-responder communications. An additional $250 million would be used to implement a national alert system, including a tsunami warning program.

▶ Allocate funds for other purposes, including $200 million to convert low-power television stations from analog to digital, $250 million for a program to upgrade emergency 911 phone systems and $250 million for hurricane relief. The bill listed a number of other uses for any funds that were left over.

The committee rejected, 5-17, an attempt by John McCain, R-Ariz., to advance the transition by two years to April 7, 2007, with the auction of recovered analog spectrum to begin Jan. 28, 2006, two years earlier than proposed in the bill. Senators worried that the earlier deadline might prevent millions of television viewers from watching the New Year's bowl games and holiday festivities, creating a political embarrassment.

The Senate Budget Committee packaged the spectrum provisions with those of seven other committees and approved the resulting budget reconciliation bill (S 1932), 12-10, on Oct. 26.

## HOUSE ACTION

The House Energy and Commerce Committee approved its spectrum proposal, 33-17, on Oct. 26. The provisions would:

▶ Set a Dec. 31, 2008, deadline for broadcasters to relinquish the spectrum.

▶ Devote $990 million to subsidize converter boxes. The committee proposed providing up to two coupons worth $40 each to households that requested them.

▶ Provide $500 million for first-responder communication efforts.

▶ Provide $30 million for New York transition and $3 million to aid low-power stations in converting digital to analog signals.

▶ Deposit the remainder of the proceeds from the spectrum auctions in the treasury.

▶ Allow cable and satellite operators to convert digital broadcasts into an analog-viewable format to avoid disrupting service.

▶ Require TV manufacturers to label analog sets with warnings that the equipment would not work after the digital switch.

The committee rejected, 21-28, an amendment by John D. Dingell, D-Mich., that would have delayed the hard deadline for digital conversion to April 7, 2009, and spent as much of the money from the spectrum sale as needed on consumer subsidies. Democrats estimated it would cost between $3.5 billion and $4 billion to ensure that no televisions went dark. The amendment would have dedicated $5.8 billion to increase interoperability among emergency responders.

The House Budget Committee combined the provisions with those of six other committees and approved its reconciliation bill (HR 4241 — H Rept 109-276), 21-17, on Nov. 3.

## FLOOR ACTION

The Senate passed its budget reconciliation bill, 52-47, on Nov. 3. During the floor debate, senators rejected, 30-69, an attempt by McCain to accelerate digital TV conversion by a year to April 7, 2008, to speed the availability of the spectrum for public safety radios. *(Senate votes 303, 293, pp. S-59, S-58)*

The House passed its version of the bill, 217-215, on Nov. 18. *(House vote 601, p. H-190)*

## CONFERENCE/FINAL ACTION

The House adopted the conference report on the reconciliation bill (H Rept 109-362), 212-206, on Dec. 19. *(House vote 670, p. H-212)*

The Senate approved an amended version of S 1932, 51-50, on Dec. 21 but refused to approve the conference report, sending it back to the House. The House cleared the bill by voice vote Feb. 1, 2006.

The conference report set the deadline for returning analog spectrum in February 2009, about halfway between the House and Senate proposals. Conferees agreed on a $1.5 billion subsidy for converter boxes, $500 million more than the House wanted but $1.5 billion less than the Senate proposed. They adopted the $40 coupon proposal passed by the House. The $1 billion for first interoperable emergency communications systems came after the Senate plan and was $500 million above the House figure.

To avoid running afoul of Senate rules barring items in reconciliation bills that do not affect government revenue, the conferees dropped several provisions from the House version, among them was language sought by the cable television industry to let cable providers convert high-definition digital signals to other formats. Also dropped were provisions aimed at preparing consumers for the digital transition, including the requirement that analog TV sets bear a notice that they would no longer work after the transition. Conferees provided $5 million for consumer education, but did not say how the money should be spent.

The unfinished business virtually guaranteed that Congress would have to revisit the digital transition in later legislation. ■

**Chapter 17**

# TRADE

# Trade

# Central American Trade Accord Just Squeaks Through

PARTISAN LOYALTY AND one-on-one negotiations enabled the White House and Republican leaders in Congress to win just enough votes to put the Central America Free Trade Agreement (CAFTA) into law. Congress cleared a bill implementing the pact July 28, and President Bush signed the measure into law Aug. 2 (HR 3283 — PL 109-53).

The agreement involved Costa Rica, El Salvador, Guatemala, Honduras and Nicaragua, and a linked accord with the Dominican Republic. It was completed in 2004, but opposition from U.S. labor groups and the sugar industry — and growing skepticism about the benefits of free trade — made passage a high-wire act for the administration.

The pact eliminated most tariffs and some other barriers to cross-border economic activity. It phased out customs duties on originating goods between participating countries over 10 years, while eliminating nearly all textile and clothing duties. It also eliminated export subsidies for agricultural goods traded among CAFTA nations. It specifically regulated the import of sugar into the United States, maintained the U.S. duty on sugar imports that exceeded a certain quota and allowed the United States to provide compensation to a participating nation in place of sugar imports.

The benefits to the United States were expected to be more political than economic. The six Central American and Caribbean economies together generated a little more than $200 billion a year, about the same as the economy of Missouri. Proponents mainly argued that CAFTA would have a positive effect on national security, immigration and regional stability.

The Office of the U.S. Trade Representative (USTR) also said that more than 80 percent of the imports from Central America and the Dominican Republic already entered the United States duty-free, so the agreement "levels the playing field for Americans."

Congress considered the bill to implement CAFTA under special fast-track procedures enacted in the 2002 Trade Promotion Authority Act (PL 107-210). Once the White House submitted the bill, lawmakers had 90 legislative days to consider it — 45 days for House committees, 15 days for House floor action, and 15 days each for Senate committee and floor votes. Congress could only accept or reject the bill; it could not amend it. The expedited process was intended to assure U.S. trade partners that lawmakers would not alter a trade agreement once it had been signed. In return, the administration was required to consult with Congress and keep the appropriate committees informed as it negotiated the pact and wrote the bill. *(2002 Almanac, 18-3)*

Supporters and foes of the administration's trade policy offered competing views of what the outcome meant for future trade pacts.

"The House rejected isolationism," said John Engler, president of the

**BOX SCORE**

**BILL:**
HR 3045 — PL 109-53

**LEGISLATIVE ACTION:**

**House** passed HR 3045 (H Rept 109-182), 217-215, July 28.

**Senate** cleared the bill, 55-45, on July 28.

**President** signed Aug. 2.

National Association of Manufacturers, in a statement. "It affirmed that America's economic future lies with open markets and a level playing field for international trade."

Opponents of administration policy portrayed the closeness of the vote and the degree to which the White House and GOP leaders had to scramble as evidence of a growing bipartisan bloc that was opposed to free trade for its own sake.

## HIGHLIGHTS

The target date for implementation of the trade agreement was Jan. 1, 2006. The following are highlights of the pact:

- **Manufactured goods.** The six countries agreed to eliminate tariffs immediately on about 80 percent of U.S.-made consumer and industrial goods. The remaining tariffs would be phased out over 10 years. Those on autos and auto parts would be phased out over five years.
- **Farm products.** Tariffs were to be eliminated immediately on about 50 percent of U.S. farm goods going to the six countries — particularly high-quality beef, soybeans, cotton and wheat. So-called sensitive agricultural products — corn, milk, potatoes and onions, for example — would be exempt from tariff reduction, or tariffs would be phased out over lengthy periods up to 20 years.
- **Textiles.** Textiles and apparel made in participating countries with U.S.-produced yarn and fabric could be shipped tariff-free to the United States, retroactive to Jan. 1, 2004. The region already was the second-largest consumer of U.S. yarn and fabric. Some Central American goods made with Canadian or Mexican yarn and fabric also would enter the United States tariff-free.
- **Sugar.** Quotas for U.S. sugar imports were to rise for CAFTA countries only, permitting increased imports from the region equal to about 1.2 percent of existing U.S. production in the first year, rising to about 1.7 percent in 15 years.
- **Services.** The six countries agreed to remove or reduce trade barriers in the fields of telecommunications, computers, package delivery, tourism, transportation, construction and engineering, financial services and insurance, and entertainment.
- **Intellectual property.** The Central American countries and the Dominican Republic agreed to increase patent, copyright and trademark protections for software, music, videos, written works and other intellectual property.
- **Government procurement.** The six countries agreed to enact anti-corruption measures for government contracting and permit U.S. companies to bid to provide a range of goods and services to those governments.
- **Worker rights.** The participants agreed to enforce their existing laws guaranteeing worker rights, but trade sanctions could not be used to

require compliance. The agreement did not require the countries to enact laws meeting International Labor Organization (ILO) standards.

● **Environment.** The participants agreed to enforce their existing environmental protection laws, but the agreement did not require changes and did not have a mechanism to require compliance.

## LEGISLATIVE ACTION

The congressional committees with jurisdiction over trade — House Ways and Means and Senate Finance — held informal mock markups of a draft administration bill the week of June 13. The sessions allowed members to recommend technical changes or signal concerns to the administration before it formally submitted the bill. Among the biggest issues were bipartisan worries among sugar-state lawmakers that their states would suffer from CAFTA's sugar provisions, concern from Democrats that CAFTA would not fully safeguard Central American workers' rights, and fears that CAFTA could cost U.S. jobs.

### SENATE COMMITTEE ACTION

The Senate Finance Committee approved its bill (S 1307 — S Rept 109-128), 11-9, on June 14. As late as the morning of the markup, the White House was unsure it could win approval without significant amendments that might require officials to renegotiate sections of the agreement.

The administration won a narrow victory by agreeing to continue talks with Sen. Craig Thomas, R-Wyo., other reluctant sugar-state lawmakers and sugar industry officials on strengthening the long-term global position of domestic sugar producers.

Kent Conrad, D-N.D., then dropped plans to offer as many as eight amendments to nullify or modify provisions that allowed increases in sugar imports from CAFTA countries. Republicans had worried that some of his proposals might be adopted because Conrad's views were shared by Max Baucus of Montana, the ranking committee Democrat, as well as by Thomas and Republican Michael D. Crapo of Idaho. Thomas gave his tentative support to the measure but said he might oppose it on the floor if the sugar talks yielded no results.

During the markup, the committee:

▶ Rejected on a 10-10 tie vote an amendment by John Kerry, D-Mass., that would have allowed the United States to impose sanctions if CAFTA countries failed to enforce labor laws.

▶ Adopted by voice vote a proposal by Ron Wyden, D-Ore., to expand Trade Adjustment Assistance (TAA) to include service-sector workers. Under existing law, TAA programs for workers who lost their jobs because of expanding trade was aimed primarily at manufacturing workers.

### HOUSE COMMITTEE ACTION

The House Ways and Means Committee approved an identical measure (HR 3045 — H Rept 109-182) June 15 on a 25-16 vote. Republicans insisted that CAFTA provided better worker protections than previous trade agreements and ruled out renegotiating sections of the pact.

Mark Foley, R-Fla., offered a qualification similar to Thomas' before casting a yes vote. "I am voting for this agreement at this meeting for the purpose of continuing debate," said Foley, whose state was home to major sugar cane producers.

During the markup, the committee:

▶ Agreed by voice vote to a substitute amendment by Chairman Bill Thomas, R-Calif., that was aimed at addressing labor concerns raised by many Democrats and some Republicans. The substitute called for a study of proposals to expand TAA to include service industry workers, and it drew on a proposal made by U.S. Trade Representative Rob Portman to create a way of monitoring CAFTA countries' progress in enforcing labor laws.

▶ Rejected, on a 17-24 party-line vote, a proposal by the panel's ranking Democrat, Charles B. Rangel of New York, to delay the trade pact from taking effect until CAFTA countries brought their labor standards in line with those of the ILO. It also would have made those standards enforceable with trade sanctions.

Rangel said the bill should be focused more on protecting "human rights and property rights." But E. Clay Shaw Jr., R-Fla., chairman of the Trade Subcommittee, argued that the CAFTA countries' laws, for the most part, already met ILO standards and that the amendment was "highly unnecessary."

▶ Rejected, 16-24, an amendment by Pete Stark, D-Calif., to revise patent protections favored by pharmaceutical companies. Stark said the provisions could restrict access to inexpensive drugs for people in Central America. Nancy L. Johnson, R-Conn., countered that the protections made it feasible for companies to develop drugs that were needed by developing countries.

▶ Rejected, 15-25, an amendment by Stephanie Tubbs Jones, D-Ohio, to double funding for the TAA to $519 million. Dave Camp, R-Mich., argued that state TAA accounts were running a cash surplus and had not requested additional funding.

### HOUSE, SENATE FLOOR ACTION

The House passed the bill early July 28 by a slim margin, 217-215. The roll call was held open for an hour and stretched after midnight as jockeying for votes continued. (House vote 443, p. H-136)

The Senate cleared the measure hours later by a 55-45 vote. Senators had already voted once on the pact, passing its identical but separate CAFTA bill (S 1307) by a 54-45 vote on June 30. To send the measure to the president, however, the Senate had to clear the House-passed bill. (Senate votes 209, 170, pp. S-41, S-34)

House GOP leaders had to cut numerous deals to win passage. Of the 217 "yes" votes, only 15 came from Democrats; 27 Republicans voted against the bill.

Opposition was especially strong in textile- and sugar-producing states, and not all Republicans from those districts were satisfied with administration pledges to contain CAFTA's potential effect on U.S. jobs. Phil English, R-Pa., pressed for floor action on a bill (HR 3283) aimed at China's alleged unfair trade practices. English said as many as 10 Republican lawmakers agreed to vote for CAFTA after the House passed the China bill July 27.

Bush made a rare appearance on Capitol Hill the morning of the House debate to rally rank-and-file Republicans. He challenged them to put aside parochial concerns in some cases and to seize what he argued was a unique opportunity to advance the cause of democracy in the hemisphere. Bush was joined at the rally by Vice President Dick Cheney, National Security Adviser Stephen J. Hadley and Portman. By the end of the day, Agriculture Secretary Mike Johanns and Commerce Secretary Carlos Gutierrez had also met with small groups of lawmakers off the floor as the debate unfolded.

GOP leaders still did not have the votes in hand when the electronic tally boards lit up in the House chamber shortly after 11 p.m. for a scheduled 15-minute vote. A half-hour later, the count was frozen at 214-211 in favor of the bill. Over the next half-hour, Portman said later, Republicans had to sort out "who gets to vote no," while still securing a victory for the party and the president.

Many undecided members finally relented to the arguments made by GOP leaders and administration officials about CAFTA's potential

effect on their districts.

For example, Robin Hayes, R-N.C., issued a statement after the vote saying he had decided that administration pledges to address concerns of textile makers were adequate. Earlier in the week, Portman promised to go back into the accord and amend three textile provisions to better ensure that U.S.-made fabric, not fabric from China, would be used in duty-free apparel assembled in Central America.

Robert B. Aderholt, R-Ala., was undecided until just before the vote because of concern for hosiery makers in his district. He received a letter from Portman and Gutierrez pledging that the administration would help protect sockmakers from import surges possible under CAFTA and other trade pacts.

Foley decided at the last minute to vote for the bill. "It was a gut wrencher," he said. "Each member of the leadership said they knew what an incredibly tough vote it was. And they assured me that tough nights like this would be remembered." ■

**Chapter 18**

# TRANSPORTATION & INFRASTRUCTURE

# Compromise Highway Bill Completed After Two-Year Clash

AFTER A LEGISLATIVE struggle that spanned two years and two Congresses, lawmakers cleared a $286.5 billion, six-year surface transportation bill in late July. President Bush signed the measure into law Aug. 10 at a ceremony in the district of House Speaker J. Dennis Hastert, R-Ill. (HR 3 — PL 109-59).

"Our economy depends on us having the most efficient, reliable transportation system in the world," Bush said at the signing ceremony. "If we want people working in America, we've got to make sure our highways and roads are modern. We've got to bring up this transportation system into the 21st century."

The bill — the Safe, Accountable, Flexible and Efficient Transportation Equity Act: A Legacy for Users, or SAFETEA-LU — authorized $244 billion for surface transportation programs in fiscal 2005 through 2009. Funding previously appropriated for fiscal 2004 brought the six-year total to $286.5 billion. The last authorization bill for highway, public transportation and traffic safety programs — the 1998 Transportation Equity Act for the 21st Century, or TEA-21 (PL 105-178) — expired Sept. 30, 2003. (1998 Almanac, p. 24-3)

The effort to write a new six-year highway bill was caught from the outset between record demands on the nation's transportation grid and White House insistence that the final bill not rely on a tax increase or spending beyond what was in the Highway Trust Fund, financed mainly through an excise tax on gasoline. In early 2003, Bush set a bottom line of $247 billion over six years; he increased it to $256 billion the following year.

The clash over total spending left several key Republicans in the unaccustomed position of leading the opposition against the administration's position. Republican Don Young of Alaska, chairman of the House Transportation and Infrastructure Committee, introduced an initial proposal in the fall of 2003 that called for $375 billion in transportation spending over six years, funded in part by an increase in the gasoline tax. That plan never saw serious consideration, but the House and Senate passed bills in 2004 that drew veto threats because they still called for for significantly more spending than Bush requested. The House bill totaled $283.2 billion; the Senate version reached $318.9 billion. (2004 Almanac, p. 16-3)

An even more difficult to resolve conflict pitted "donor" states — those that contributed significantly more in excise taxes to the Highway Trust Fund than they got back in highway aid — and "donee" or recipient states, which received more than they collected. House and Senate conferees labored for months in 2004 but could not come up with a plan that could satisfy the donor states — mainly fast-growing states in the South and Southwest — and still win even grudging

**BOX SCORE**

**BILL:** HR 3 — PL 109-59

**LEGISLATIVE ACTION:**

**House** passed HR 3 (H Rept 109-12, Parts 1, 2), 417-9, on March 10.

**Senate** passed HR 3, amended to include S 732 — S Rept 109-53, by 89-11, on May 17.

**House** adopted the conference report (H Rept 109-203), 412-8, on July 29.

**Senate** cleared the bill, 91-4 on July 29.

**President** signed Aug. 10.

acceptance from the other states and the White House. Donee states did not oppose a higher guarantee for donors as long as it did not reduce their highway funds. Under the 1998 law, all states were guaranteed a 90.5 percent rate of return. Donor states aimed to increase that to 95 percent.

In addition to the rate of return, donor states such as Arizona, California, Florida, North Carolina and Texas wanted to increase the scope of the guarantee — the range of programs to be included when calculating each state's share. The billions of dollars in projects requested by individual members were part of the calculation under the 1998 law, but the bill passed by the House in 2004 did not include them in the pot of money to be distributed by the formula.

A change in the tax treatment of ethanol fuels enacted in 2004 (PL 108-357) that was estimated to bring $18.9 billion into the Highway Trust Fund paved the way for the Bush administration to increase its bottom line for the bill in early 2005 to $283.9 billion over six years. The House passed a revised surface transportation bill in March that reflected the White House limit, but the Senate bill, passed in May, exceeded it by $11.1 billion. (Ethanol tax, 2004 Almanac, p. 13-3)

Congress had to pass six stopgap extensions of the 1998 law, on top of the six passed in 2004, to keep programs operating while a conference committee struggled to work out a compromise. The final bill authorized $2.5 billion more than the administration had said was acceptable, but much less than lawmakers, particularly in the Senate, wanted. The agreement guaranteed that by fiscal 2008 every state would get back at least 92 cents in federal highway funds for each dollar it paid into the Highway Trust Fund, and included members' projects as part of the calculation. (Provisions, p. 18-8)

Conferees agreed on changes in environmental reviews and planning procedures that proponents said would lead to faster, and sometimes less costly, completion of highway projects. The final legislation allowed more private sector involvement in financing, building and operating portions of the transportation grid, a key administration objective. Lawmakers devoted about 8 percent of the funding to more than 5,000 highway and transit projects in members' districts, far exceeding the earmarks in previous transportation bills.

"Every page of this bill has been built on accommodation and compromise," said Bill Thomas, R-Calif., chairman of the House Ways and Means Committee and a key broker in the conference negotiations.

Many transportation experts said the 2005 law could be the last of its kind. The law contained a mechanism through which Congress would get expert advice on the next authorization effort, which was expected to include recommendations on new ways to fund transportation projects and perhaps a new role for the federal government.

## HIGHLIGHTS

Out of the $286.5 billion authorization in the bill, $227.5 billion was allocated to the Federal Highway Administration, $52.6 billion to the Federal Transit Administration, $3.4 billion to the National Highway Traffic Safety Administration (NHTSA) and $2.9 billion to the Federal Motor Carrier Administration.

The following are some of the major components of the new law:
- **Highway programs.** A limit of $189.5 billion in obligational, or contract, authority for federal-aid highway programs in fiscal 2005 through 2009. Additional funding that was exempt from those obligation limits would also be available. Each state was allocated a specific amount of contract authority, which it could use to sign contracts for highway projects. When it was time to actually pay for the work, the state would draw the money from the Highway Trust Fund.
- **Minimum guarantee.** A new "equity bonus" program to ensure that each state received at least a 92 percent rate of return on its contribution to the trust fund by fiscal 2008, up from 90.5 percent under the 1998 law. All states would get more from the trust fund than they received over the life of the 1998 law. Each state's allocation was calculated based on a formula that took into account population, traffic and other factors, plus the equity bonus.
- **Members' projects.** More than 5,000 earmarks for highway and public transportation projects. Most were in the High Priority Projects program in the highway title and counted as part of the formula allocation for that state.
- **Projects of regional and national significance.** $1.8 billion for a new competitive grant program for projects that would have a significant impact on the movement of goods and people beyond an immediate area.
- **Toll roads.** Authority for states to charge tolls on newly constructed roads and on some existing roads as part of a demonstration project. States could allow reduced tolls or exemptions for vehicles such as gas-electric hybrids.
- **State project financing.** Continuation of a so-called innovative financing program to help states raise funds, often using unconventional means, for certain highway projects. The law also expanded a State Infrastructure Bank program that made loans for transportation projects, making it easier for states to collaborate with private entities to build and operate highways or public transportation lines.
- **Safety.** $5.6 billion for safety programs, including $3.1 billion for programs operated by the NHTSA and $2.5 billion for programs administered by the Federal Motor Carrier Safety Administration, which focused on large trucks and buses. The law included incentive grants for states to crack down on drivers who were caught not using seat belts and on repeat drunken driving offenders. The NHTSA was given tighter deadlines for issuing rules or reports on several pending safety issues, including vehicle rollover prevention and side impact protection.
- **Environment.** A new, consolidated planning process for highway and public transportation projects in metropolitan areas and states. The law for the first time designated the Transportation Department as the lead agency in conducting environmental impact reviews of transportation projects. It set new procedures aimed at expediting the review process, including a requirement that claims against a permit, license or approval be filed within 180 days of the issuance.
- **Public transportation.** $45.3 billion over five years to aid mass transit and public transportation programs. The law expanded a program that helped localities build light-rail and subway systems to include bus rapid transit lines. Private transit operators were eligible for grants.

Funding for transit in rural areas was expanded, and a "New Freedom Program" targeted funding for elderly and disabled populations.
- **Revenue.** Extension through 2011 of the six taxes that fed the Highway Trust Fund. The bill authorized the expenditure of money from the trust fund through fiscal 2009. The main funding source was the 18.4-cent per gallon federal tax on gasoline, of which 18.3 cents went to the trust fund. (The other 0.1 cent went to the Leaking Underground Storage Tank fund.) The other five taxes were excise taxes on diesel fuel and kerosene, and on special motor fuels, a retail sales tax on heavy highway vehicles, a manufacturers' excise tax on heavy vehicle tires and an annual use tax on heavy vehicles.

A new provision to combat fuel fraud was projected to increase revenue available in the Highway Trust Fund by almost $2 billion through 2009. It achieved this by taxing aviation-grade kerosene at the higher diesel fuel rate and crediting the initial tax receipts to the Highway Trust Fund, rather than to the Airport and Airway Trust Fund as in prior law.

The bill authorized $15 billion in tax-exempt bonds for highway projects or facilities to transfer freight between trucks and rail. It also included a series of unrelated special interest tax breaks, for groups such as liquor wholesalers and retailers.

## LEGISLATIVE ACTION
### HOUSE COMMITTEE ACTION

The House Transportation and Infrastructure Committee gave voice vote approval March 2 to a $283.9 billion surface transportation bill (HR 3 — H Rept 109-12, Parts 1, 2). With the benefit of nearly a year's worth of negotiations on many of the provisions in 2004, the markup proceeded quickly with only a few amendments offered. Because the committee and the White House had come to terms on the total in advance, the previous year's air of confrontation with the administration was no longer present.

However, Young was still not ready to put forward a formula for distributing highway money among the states. Majority Leader Tom DeLay, R-Texas, and other donor state lawmakers were pressing for a 95 percent rate of return. They also wanted Young to restore members' projects to the list of programs subject to the rate of return.

The committee bill retained the 90.5 percent rate of return, but it included a "re-opener" clause from the 2004 House bill that would force Congress to increase the rate shortly. The provision proposed to freeze highway funds at fiscal 2005 levels until Aug. 1, 2006, unless a new law was enacted that guaranteed a 92 percent return in fiscal 2006 rising to 95 percent in 2009.

As approved by the committee, the bill authorized:
- $225.5 billion for the Federal Highway Administration.
- $52.4 billion for the Federal Transit Administration.
- $3.2 billion for the NHTSA.
- $2.9 billion for the Federal Motor Carrier Safety Administration.

Those figures included about $86 billion already committed for fiscal 2004 and 2005 through various extensions to the 1998 law. They did not include additional contract authority to complete projects that were not finished by the end of fiscal 2009, which could make the eventual price tag closer to $300 billion.

The bill included a consolidated planning process for highways and public transportation projects for metropolitan areas and states, and a new process for environmental impact reviews on proposed transportation projects. It called for making the Transportation Department the lead agency in the review process, with tighter deadlines for public and agency comments, the resolution of disputes among agencies and judicial review.

Young won voice vote approval for a largely technical manager's amendment reflecting bipartisan consultations that added several new programs and inserted more than 3,315 highway and transit projects requested by members.

## HOUSE FLOOR ACTION

The House passed the bill by a vote of 417-9 on March 10. The nine "no" votes were almost all from Republican fiscal conservatives. *(House vote 65, p. H-22)*

Even as the debate began, Young was still trying to get enough support for an agreement to increase the minimum guarantee for each state. The resulting deal, which was added to the bill by voice vote as part of a manager's amendment, increased the amount of highway money to be distributed to states by formula to include about $11 billion in High Priority Projects earmarked by individual lawmakers.

Young left the actual rate of return to the House-Senate conference. "That figure is still floating," he said, adding that it would be "more than 90, less than 95." Even under the existing rate of 90.5 percent, however, the increased amount subject to the formula under his plan meant donor states would get more in highway funds than they did under the 1998 law.

Young's amendment also added tax and Highway Trust Fund provisions that the Ways and Means Committee had approved as a separate bill (HR 996 — H Rept 109-13) on March 3. The language extended the excise taxes that fed the trust fund through fiscal 2011.

Although the bill's bottom line was the same as the president's request, the White House issued a statement of administration policy March 8 warning that the re-opener clause would trigger a veto. "This provision would prevent states from obligating federal funds during the 2006 prime construction season and negate the stability and planning benefits of a long-term authorization bill," the statement said.

During the relatively short floor debate, the House:

▶ Rejected, 155-265, a proposal by Mark Kennedy, R-Minn., to make changes to the bill's toll provisions, allowing states to charge tolls on any existing toll road or newly constructed lane on the interstate system to manage congestion or reduce emissions. It also would permit an unlimited number of new express lanes where tolls could be charged. Kennedy said the tolls would help states raise an additional $50 billion for construction, while keeping "the trust of the driving public" by only charging for the cost of adding road capacity. *(House vote 59, p. H-20)*

▶ Agreed, 224-201, to strike language from the bill that would have required states that charged tolls on high-occupancy lanes to allow a reduced fee for low-income citizens. *(House vote 62, p. H-22)*

Amendment sponsor Thomas M. Davis III, R-Va., whose state was about to establish tolls on some major highways with fees pegged to traffic volume, said the requirement would be an administrative nightmare. James L. Oberstar, D-Minn., countered that with Davis' amendment, the well-off "will whiz through while the poor folk cannot afford to get through."

"Let me say to my friend," Davis, responded, "if you really want to help poor people, build additional lanes of traffic and get some of the traffic off the road so they can get onto the conventional lanes."

▶ Adopted by voice vote an amendment by three New Jersey lawmakers — Democrats Bill Pascrell Jr. and Robert Menendez and Republican Frank A. LoBiondo — to allow states to enact laws to prevent "pay-to-play" political contributions by contractors seeking state contracts. The Federal Highway Administration had threatened New Jersey with the loss of highway funds when the governor issued an executive order barring political contributions from contractors.

The administration said the order interfered with the principle of granting contracts to the lowest bidder, but Pascrell said that states should not be penalized for enacting anti-corruption laws.

▶ Adopted, 257-167, an amendment to expand the bill's exemptions from hours-of-service rules, which determined how long commercial truck drivers could stay on the road and when they could take mandated rest breaks. The bill exempted utility-truck operators and drivers who transported farm commodities and supplies or operated vehicles for the motion picture industry. *(House vote 57, p. H-20)*

## SENATE COMMITTEE ACTION

The Senate version of the bill was written by four committees in early March, with the Environment and Public Works Committee, chaired by James M. Inhofe, R-Okla., taking the lead. Although the chairmen made it clear that they favored higher spending, they complied with a leadership directive to keep the price tag below $283.9 billion. Majority Leader Bill Frist, R-Tenn., said if the bill exceeded that limit, he would not allow it onto the Senate floor. However, the chairmen indicated that once the bill reached the floor, all bets would be off.

● **Highway programs.** The Environment and Public Works Committee approved the core highway provisions by a vote of 17-1 on March 16 (S 732 — S Rept 109-53). The bill called for $191 billion in contract authority for highway programs in fiscal 2005 through 2009 — $227 billion when fiscal 2004 spending was counted. The provisions, with minor exceptions, were similar to those in the Senate's 2004 highway bill.

The bill proposed an "equity bonus" program to guarantee each state at least a 92 percent rate of return in fiscal 2005 through 2009 and to ensure that each state received at least 10 percent more funding over the life of the bill than it got under the 1988 law. The bill did not propose changing the scope of the program.

During the markup, the committee:

▶ Rejected, 5-13, an amendment by Hillary Rodham Clinton, D-N.Y., to guarantee each state a minimum 15 percent increase in funding over the 1998 law.

▶ Rejected by voice vote a "pay-to-play" contracting amendment offered by Frank R. Lautenberg, D-N.J.

● **Public transit.** The Banking, Housing and Urban Affairs Committee, chaired by Richard C. Shelby, R-Ala., approved $51.6 billion for public transit programs, an 18 percent share of total transportation funding. The provisions were approved by voice vote March 17. Transit advocates had fought for a 20 percent share, up from 18.8 percent in the 1998 law. But lobbyists said Inhofe used his position as de facto lead committee chairman on transportation issues to snare an additional $900 million for highways, leaving less for transit.

Paul S. Sarbanes of Maryland, the committee's ranking Democrat, considered offering an amendment to boost transit funding to $53.3 billion, restoring it to 18.8 percent of the total. But he said transit supporters did not want to hold up floor action on the bill or spark a fight with the highway lobby.

The transit section included provisions to allow the use of federal funds to pay private contractors for providing public transit services and to encourage agencies to set up bus rapid transit services instead of costlier, but more popular, light-rail lines.

● **Safety.** The Commerce, Science and Transportation Committee, which was responsible for safety provisions, approved its piece of the bill by voice vote April 14. The provisions included grants for a White House-backed program to reward states for passing "primary" seat belt laws that allowed police to pull drivers over for not wearing their seat

belts even if the police observed no other violations. Alternatively, states could get the grants if 90 percent of their drivers buckled up for two straight years. NHTSA chief Jeffrey Runge called the legislation "the single most important traffic safety measure" that Congress could pass.

But George Allen, R-Va., whose state imposed fines for not wearing seat belts only if the driver was pulled over for other offenses, said the bill smacked of "nanny government." The House-passed bill would give states money for achieving at least 85 percent seat belt usage, regardless of how they did it.

The committee gave the NHTSA deadlines for regulations on rollover prevention, occupant ejection prevention, roof strength, side-impact protection and the safety of 15-passenger vans that had been long sought by safety advocates.

● **Revenue.** The Finance Committee approved revenue provisions by voice vote April 19 that would pay for a $283.9 billion, six-year surface transportation bill. Chairman Charles E. Grassley, R-Iowa, said he was keeping his commitment to hold to $283.9 billion as the upper limit for the bill, but he told the committee he would seek additional revenue for the Highway Trust Fund once the bill reached the floor.

The provisions reauthorized the Highway Trust Fund through fiscal 2009 and extended the taxes that went into it through fiscal 2011. It also contained several non-transportation-related special-interest tax provisions from the Senate's 2004 surface transportation bill. They included a cap on the excise tax charged on fishing rods and poles, a repeal of occupational taxes on producers and marketers of alcoholic beverages and a tax exemption designed for custom firearms fabricators.

## SENATE FLOOR ACTION

The Senate passed a $295 billion version of the bill by a vote of 89-11 on May 17. The "nay" votes came from a small core of fiscal conservatives and from members who believed their states were being seriously shortchanged. (*Senate vote 125, p. S-25*)

Inhofe had added $11.1 billion to the authorization as part of a substitute amendment that was adopted by voice vote before the bill was passed. The increase allowed an additional $8.9 billion for highway programs and an extra $2.2 billion for transit. That brought the bill's authorization levels to $199.7 billion for highway programs and $46.5 billion for public transit. The amendment also included new revenue for the Highway Trust Fund that supporters said would make the increased spending "revenue neutral."

The revised bill posed a direct challenge to the White House, which had issued a statement of administration policy April 26 warning that if Congress broke the $283.9 billion mark, Bush's "senior advisers would recommend he veto the bill."

But without the extra funds, Inhofe could not come up with a formula for distributing highway money that could win majority support. The increase enabled him to raise the minimum rate of return for each state to 91 percent in fiscal 2006 and 92 percent by 2009. States that received more than they contributed to the trust fund would be guaranteed a 15 percent increase in funding over what they received under the 1998 law.

The revenue provisions, which were incorporated into the amendment with Inhofe's enthusiastic support, were written by Grassley and Max Baucus of Montana, the ranking Democrat on the Finance Committee. They included a proposed crackdown on fuel tax evasion schemes that would place more tax money in the Highway Trust Fund. Another provision would temporarily put revenue from a "gas guzzler" tax on cars getting less than 22.5 miles per gallon into the high-

way fund instead of the general treasury. The bill also included a repeal of the guzzler tax for limousines.

The largest revenue raiser was a proposal to tighten the tax treatment of financial transactions that were deemed to lack "economic substance" — meaning they were conducted primarily for the purpose of reducing taxes. The House had rejected the provision several times.

The Budget Committee put out a memo saying the Finance Committee was "rearranging paper entries on the government's books rather than increasing resources collected by the federal government." Budget Chairman Judd Gregg, R-N.H., objected that the manager's amendment violated budget rules, but the Senate voted 76-22 on May 11 to waive his point of order. (*Senate vote 118, p. S-23*)

The next day, the Senate agreed, 92-7, to limit debate on the Inhofe substitute, preventing the possibility of a filibuster. A subsequent attempt by Jeff Sessions, R-Ala., to reduce the authorization by $10.7 billion was rejected 16-84. (*Senate votes 122, 124, pp. S-24, S-25*)

The Senate had begun debating the bill in late April, just as more than 400 highway contractors from around the country descended on Capitol Hill as part of a previously scheduled "fly-in." The contractors fanned out to congressional offices, admonishing lawmakers that further legislative delays were hurting their industry. Senators said the fact was not lost on them, but that the issues that kept Congress from clearing the bill in 2004 had not become easier to resolve.

During the lengthy debate on the bill, the Senate:

▶ Rejected an attempt by Christopher S. Bond, R-Mo., to strike a provision in the bill requiring states to spend 2 percent of their highway construction money on alleviating pollution from storm water runoff. Bond said dropping the requirement would free an additional $900 million for road construction projects. Amendment opponents led by John W. Warner, R-Va., said the Clean Water Act required states to clean up contaminants that washed off roads into rivers, lakes and groundwater, and the states should be assured of federal funds to help pay the cost of compliance. The amendment was tabled (killed), 51-49, on April 28. (*Senate vote 113, p. S-22*)

▶ Adopted by voice vote May 10 an amendment by Kay Bailey Hutchison, R-Texas, to end a pilot program from the 1998 bill that allowed a select group of states to levy tolls on existing interstate highways. "To allow unelected transportation officials to simply install a toll booth on facilities already paid for by federal tax dollars is unacceptable," Hutchison said. The toll provision was one of several in which the Senate sought to define what tools states could use to augment their federal highway funding.

▶ Rejected an attempt by New Jersey senators Jon Corzine and Lautenberg, both Democrats, to add language similar to the House amendment limiting the ability of contractors seeking highway contracts to make campaign contributions to state lawmakers. The amendment was tabled, 57-40, on May 11. (*Senate vote 119, p. S-23*)

▶ Rejected another bid by Allen to revise the bill's seat belt incentive grants by substituting an 85 percent use rate for the requirement that qualifying states have either a primary safety belt law in effect or a safety belt use rate of 90 percent. The amendment was defeated, 14-86, on May 17. (*Senate vote 123, p. S-25*)

## CONFERENCE/FINAL ACTION

A 93-member conference committee held its first and only public meeting June 9, a few days after approving a 30-day extension of the 1998 surface transportation law. It was not until two and a half months later, with the August recess looming, that the conferees finished.

The House adopted the conference report (H Rept 109-203) by a vote

of 412-8 on July 29. The Senate cleared the bill, 91-4, later the same day. *(House vote 453, p. H-140; Senate vote 220, p. S-43)*

Two stopgap extensions of the 1988 law expired while conferees worked through June and July to resolve their differences. With the month-long August recess approaching, members and staff held marathon sessions to draft language, but frustrating snags seemed to pop up each time the bill drew close to final action. One of the last holdups was insistence by House GOP leaders that the conferees not file their report until after the House voted to approve the Central American Free Trade Agreement (PL 109-53), feeding speculation that they were using projects in the highway measure to drum up support for the pact. The conference report was filed July 28, about 19 hours after the House passed the trade bill. *(CAFTA, p. 17-3)*

The following are among the hundreds of decisions made by the conferees:

● **Equity bonus.** The bill created a new program, similar to that proposed by the Senate, to ensure that states received at least 92 percent of the money they contributed to the Highway Trust Fund by 2008. The guaranteed rate of return was 91.5 percent in fiscal 2007, and 92 percent in fiscal 2008 and 2009. States would receive an average of 17 percent more in fiscal 2006 than they did under the previous highway bill, rising to 21 percent in 2009. Conferees dropped the House re-opener clause. In a key concession to donor states, funds for members' projects were included in the pot of money that would be distributed by formula.

● **Members' projects.** The agreement authorized a total of $14.8 billion through fiscal 2009 for High Priority Projects, those earmarked by members. The conference agreement listed more than 5,000 individual highway projects and more than 1,000 projects in other categories of transportation funding, a record level of earmarking. Conferees agreed to provide 60 percent of the earmarks to the House and 40 percent to the Senate.

● **Toll and HOV lanes.** The agreement allowed states to establish high-occupancy toll (HOT) lane systems in which otherwise ineligible vehicles could use high-occupancy vehicle (HOV) lanes by paying a toll. States could reduce tolls, including charging no toll at all, for certain low-emission and energy-efficient vehicles, such as hybrid, gas/electric cars. The bill also authorized a pilot program to allow states to charge tolls for the use of interstate highways to manage congestion, reduce emissions in areas with air pollution or expand the highway to reduce congestion.

● **Safety.** Using elements of both bills, conferees agreed on one-time grants to states that had primary seat belt laws or that could show at least 85 percent seat belt use for two consecutive years. The final bill also included a House provision to authorize penalties and grants to encourage states to enact a 0.08 blood alcohol standard.

The NHTSA was given deadlines for establishing standards to reduce deaths and injuries associated with vehicle rollovers, side-impact crashes and vehicles backing up. The bill required safety switches on power windows and required rollover testing for 15-passenger vans.

● **Hours-of-service regulations.** The measure exempted certain drivers — including the operators of utility service vehicles, vehicles transmitting agricultural commodities and vehicles transporting equipment for the motion picture industry — from the maximum hours of service rules. The 2003 regulations had been thrown out by a court in

2004, but they were extended through Sept. 30, 2005, by one of the short-term highway law extensions (PL 108-310) to allow additional time to develop new rules. Conferees rejected an administration request to incorporate the 2003 rules into the conference agreement.

● **Tax provisions.** In addition to renewing through 2009 the six taxes that supported the Highway Trust Fund, the final bill included a number of the tax provisions added by the Senate. The Joint Committee on Taxation estimated these changes would increase revenue in the Highway Account of the Highway Trust Fund by a total of $1.8 billion in fiscal 2005 through 2009 and reduce revenue to the general treasury by $886 million. The main addition to the trust fund was the change in the taxation of aviation-grade kerosene, which contributed $1.7 billion. The provision was projected to reduce funds in the Airport and Airway Account by $1.8 billion in that period. Conferees dropped the Senate's "economic substance" provision, its proposal to repeal the gas guzzler tax on limousines and a provision that would have increased the amount of transit benefits that were exempt from taxation.

● **Other provisions.**

▶ Conferees dropped the House provision that would have allowed states to enact anti-corruption laws curbing the practice of "pay-to-play" contracting without losing their federal-aid highway dollars

▶ The bill included an $8.5 billion rescission of prior contact authority that would become available at the end of fiscal 2009, boosting the available contract authority at that point to $295 billion.

▶ The measure set tougher licensing standards for haulers of hazardous cargo.

▶ Negotiators stripped from the bill a House provision that would have added a fuel surcharge to the prices charged by motor carriers, brokers and freight forwarders when the price of fuel rose above a benchmark per gallon price. The surcharge requirement was sought by independent truckers competing against large carriers who could better absorb or avoid spikes in fuel prices.

While some fiscal conservatives and taxpayer watchdog groups denounced the final bill as a political grab-bag, lawmakers supporting it generally made no apology for fighting for their share of the funds.

The loudest protest arose over a pair of costly bridges in Alaska, inserted into the bill by Young, and dubbed "bridges to nowhere" because they connected to small, remote communities. When the appropriations bill that funded transportation projects came to the Senate floor in October, freshman Tom Coburn, R-Okla., a staunch fiscal conservative, proposed taking the $454 million for the bridges and spending it instead to reconstruct a Mississippi River bridge in New Orleans damaged by Hurricane Katrina. "People are fed up," Coburn told his colleagues. "All across the country, Americans are rising up against government overspending." *(Transportation-Treasury-Housing, p. 2-47)*

Sen. Ted Stevens, R-Alaska, former chairman of the Senate Appropriations Committee, was incensed at this challenge to the earmark system. "This amendment is an offense to me," Stevens thundered. "It is not only an offense to me, it is a threat to every person in my state . . . It is wrong to do this to any state." Most senators agreed, and Coburn's amendment was defeated, 15-82. *(Senate vote 262, p. S-52)*

Conferees on the appropriations bill (PL 109-115) quietly removed the specific funding for the two bridges, redirecting the money to a general fund that the state of Alaska could spend on transportation projects at its discretion — including on the two bridges, if it chose. ■

# Details of Surface Transportation Law

*Following are the main provisions of the surface transportation law (HR 3 — PL 109-59), which President Bush signed into law Aug. 10.*

## FEDERAL HIGHWAY PROGRAMS

The bill provides $189.5 billion in guaranteed spending for federal-aid highway programs in fiscal 2005 through 2009. The obligation limits are $34.4 billion for fiscal 2005, $36 billion for fiscal 2006, $38.2 billion for fiscal 2007, $39.6 billion for fiscal 2008 and $41.2 billion for fiscal 2009. The agreement also provides certain exemptions from these limits similar to those that were in the 1998 surface transportation law (PL 105-178), which it replaced. As a result, the total amount available was expected to exceed $189.5 billion.

## CORE HIGHWAY PROGRAMS

The vast majority of federal-aid highway funds are for six so-called core programs that are apportioned to the states under specified formulas. The new law authorizes:
- **Interstate maintenance program.** $25.2 billion for maintenance of the Interstate Highway System, including $500 million for the interstate-maintenance discretionary program.
- **National Highway System.** $30.5 billion for the nation's systems of interstate highways, major arterial routes and routes important to the national defense. It also increases the annual amount set aside for the Alaska Highway to $30 million. The annual amount set aside for U.S. territories is $40 million for fiscal 2005 and 2006, and $50 million for fiscal 2007 through 2009.
- **Surface Transportation Program.** $32.5 billion for this program, which provides states with flexible funding for projects on any federally funded highway. The law continues a requirement that states allocate a portion of their funds to urban areas with populations greater than 200,000. It also allows funds to be used for projects relating to intersections with high accident rates or high levels of congestion. It eliminates the set-asides for safety programs, since these are now funded through the core Highway Safety Improvement Program.

The law permits the use of funds under this program and the National Highway System Program to address environmental restoration, pollution abatement and control of certain noxious weeds.
- **Bridge program.** $21.6 billion over five years for the bridge replacement and rehabilitation program. The law requires that $100 million be set aside each year in fiscal 2006 through 2009 for designated projects, including $18.75 million annually for a bridge in Alaska and $12.5 million annually for the Golden Gate Bridge. It retains language from prior law that requires at least 15 percent of the funding in the program to be used on "off-system" bridges. The federal share for bridge projects can be up to 90 percent, and the federal role is expanded to include preventive maintenance, including the installation of measures to combat holes in sediment around the foundation of the bridge.
- **Congestion Mitigation and Air Quality Improvement Program.** $8.6 billion to be used by state and local governments on transportation projects that help meet the goals of the Clean Air Act. The law sets weighting factors for distributing funds based on whether an area is in compliance with EPA air quality standards.
- **Highway Safety Improvement Program.** A new, $5.1 billion program

to reduce traffic fatalities and injuries on public roads. The program replaces previous requirements that states set aside at least 10 percent of their funding from the Surface Transportation Program for safety purposes. Of the amounts authorized each year, the measure sets aside $220 million for the installation of protective devices at railway-highway crossings, $90 million for construction and operational improvements on rural roads deemed to be at high risk, and $560,000 for Operation Lifesaver. States have until Oct. 1, 2007, to develop state strategic highway safety plans. If a state fails to develop a plan by that date, its future apportionments are to be frozen at fiscal 2007 levels. If a state certifies that it has met certain requirements, it is to be given flexibility in using funds.

## OTHER HIGHWAY GRANT PROGRAMS

The law authorizes the following amounts for the remaining non-apportioned programs:
- **Appalachian Development Highway System Program.** $2.4 billion for the construction of Appalachian corridor highways in 13 states. Funds are distributed to the states based on latest cost to complete the system. State and local funds used to match the federal share of a project's costs cannot come from toll revenue.
- **Recreational trails.** $370 million to provide and maintain recreational trails for motorists, bicyclists and other users.
- **Federal lands.** $4.5 billion for public roads and transit facilities on federally owned and Indian lands.
- **National Corridor Infrastructure Program.** $1.9 billion for highway construction projects in corridors of national significance, such as routes with heavy interstate shipping traffic.
- **National scenic byways.** $175 million for maintaining and promoting a network of scenic roads, also called All-American Roads or America's Byways.
- **Ferry boats and ferry terminal facilities.** $285 million for construction of ferry boats and facilities. The law also codifies an existing ferry boat program.
- **Puerto Rico highways.** $665 million for a highway program in the commonwealth.
- **Projects of National and Regional Significance.** $1.8 billion for a new program to finance transportation projects that address critical national economic and transportation needs and cost at least $500 million, or 75 percent of a state's highway apportionment in the fiscal year prior to the state's application. Congress earmarked 25 projects for funding under this program.
- **High priority projects.** $14.8 billion for more than 5,100 specific projects designated by members. Of those, about 3,600 originated in the House; the remainder was added by the Senate.
- **Safe Routes to School.** $612 million for a new Safe Routes to School program aimed at making biking and walking to school safer and more appealing. The minimum allocation for a state is $1 million per year. Funds are to be distributed based on the proportion of elementary- and middle-school students in a state compared with the national total. State transportation departments can award project funds to agencies and nonprofit groups.
- **Maglev trains.** $90 million for two magnetic levitation (MAGLEV)

transportation projects, which are fixed guideway systems that allow for travel at speeds in excess of 240 miles per hour. One of the projects is to be located in Las Vegas, the second in an undetermined location in the eastern half of the country.

● **Corridor Planning and Development.** $140 million in only fiscal 2005 for this program.

● **Highways for LIFE.** $75 million for a new pilot program to encourage long-lasting, innovative, fast and efficient construction of roads through new techniques and materials.

● **Combating tax evasion.** $127 million for various state and federal efforts to crack down on schemes to avoid paying fuel taxes.

● **Other funding allocations and program changes.** Other specific apportionments in the bill include $1.9 billion for administrative expenses, $150 million for the Alaska Highway, $230 million for highways in U.S. territories and $52.8 million to reduce accidents at rail corridors. The bill authorizes general fund appropriations to pay for emergency road repairs that exceed $100 million in any year and sets aside $500 million for interstate discretionary projects.

States got an additional 25 years to complete construction of future interstate system routes before having to forfeit future interstate designation status. States were required to set aside 1.25 percent of the funding they receive for core highway programs for metropolitan planning activities.

The law extends the Transportation and Community and System Preservation pilot program through fiscal 2009, and authorizes $270 million for it. Under this program, states, local governments and metropolitan planning organizations are eligible for discretionary grants to plan and implement strategies that improve the efficiency of their transportation systems; reduce the environmental impacts; reduce the need for costly future public infrastructure investments; ensure efficient access to jobs, services, and centers of trade; and examine private sector development patterns and investments that support these goals.

### EQUITY BONUS

The law creates an Equity Bonus program, in place of the previous Minimum Guarantee program, to set the rate of return for each state on the money it contributes to the highway account of the Highway Trust Fund through gasoline taxes. The calculation is based on funding for 14 programs: the six core programs, the High Priority Projects program, the Equity Bonus program, the Appalachian Development Highway System program, the Recreational Trails program, the Safe Routes to School Program, the Metropolitan Planning Program, the Railway-Highway Crossings program and the Coordinated Border Infrastructure Program. The new Projects of Regional and National Significance program is not included.

The minimum rate of return, set at 90.5 percent in the 1998 law, is increased to 91.5 percent in fiscal 2007 and 92 percent in fiscal 2008 and 2009. The law also sets benchmarks for each year to ensure that states get more from the trust fund than they received during the life of the previous reauthorization measure. States are to receive 117 percent in fiscal 2005, 118 percent in 2006, 119 percent in 2007, 120 percent in 2008 and 121 percent in 2009. The law prevents states from receiving less money than under current law. The agreement authorizes such sums as may be necessary for the program.

### BUDGET AND CONTRACT AUTHORITY

● **RABA.** Revenue-aligned budget authority, or RABA, is extended through fiscal 2009. Under this mechanism, the budget authority available for highway programs is adjusted upward or downward based on revenues in the Highway Trust Fund. The law changes the basis for calculating available budget authority to a two-year rather than a one-year period to avoid drastic fluctuations in funding levels. It also prevents reductions in funding under RABA if the cash balance in the highway account of the Highway Trust Fund exceeds $6 billion on Oct. 1 of a fiscal year. A positive RABA adjustment is to be used to increase the rate of return for states where highway aid is less than 92 percent of the excise taxes they contribute to the highway account of the Highway Trust Fund. Any remaining funds are to be distributed proportionately.

● **Rescission of contract authority.** The law requires that $8.5 billion of the unobligated balances that have been apportioned to states for specified highway programs be rescinded Sept. 30, 2009. This rescission, which will affect each state in proportion to its share of highway program funds, will ensure that the net total contract authority does not exceed the bill's total funding level of $286.5 billion.

### TOLLS AND INNOVATIVE FINANCING

● **HOT lanes.** States are allowed to establish high-occupancy toll (HOT) lanes, which allow otherwise ineligible vehicles to use high-occupancy vehicle (HOV) lanes by paying a toll. To be eligible, state agencies must establish programs to inform motorists about the toll program, develop systems to automatically collect tolls and establish policies to adjust the toll amount to manage demand and to enforce violations. The law also continues a 15-site value-pricing toll program.

● **HOV restrictions.** States are permitted to change HOV lane restrictions for low-emission and energy-efficient vehicles. Vehicles deemed "inherently low-emission" under existing regulations can use the lanes if a state develops procedures for their use. Other low-emission and energy-efficient vehicles, which would be certified under regulations issued by the EPA, could use HOV lanes by paying tolls, although the tolls could be lower than those charged other vehicles, and states have the option of charging no toll at all. If a state agency collects more toll revenue than is needed to pay debt service on construction costs and "a reasonable rate of return on investment," the excess revenue may be used to develop or promote alternatives to single-occupancy vehicle travel or projects that improve safety.

● **Tolls for new roads.** A new pilot program, called EXPRESS Lanes, will allow 15 demonstration projects to collect tolls to finance additional interstate highway lanes, manage high levels of congestion to reduce emissions in areas designated as a "nonattainment" or "maintenance" under the Clean Air Act. Participating facilities can change variable tolls at different parts of the day; toll collection must be automated. The law also establishes a pilot program to allow the construction of three new interstate highway segments financed through toll collections.

● **TIFIA program.** The law authorizes $610 million for programs under the 1998 Transportation Infrastructure Finance and Innovation Act, which provides federal credit assistance for major investments in transportation. It modifies the programs, including extending eligibility for assistance to private rail facilities that serve a public benefit for highway users. It lowers to $50 million, from $100 million, the minimum cost for an eligible project and lowers to $15 million the minimum cost for an eligible intelligent transportation systems (ITS) project. Smaller states have the opportunity to participate.

● **State infrastructure banks.** The law codifies the existing State Infrastructure Bank program, which allows the Federal Highway Administration (FHWA) and states to enter into agreements to establish state infrastructure banks that make loans and provide other forms of credit assistance. The program is expanded to all 50 states. The law establishes funding requirements for the banks and sets limits on the

amount of federal funds that states can deposit in their highway, transit and rail accounts in the banks. Projects in areas with more than 200,000 people require approval from a metropolitan planning organization. The law also grants the consent of Congress for two or more states to enter into an agreement with the department to establish a multistate infrastructure bank.

## OTHER HIGHWAY PROVISIONS

● **Truck-parking facilities.** The law authorizes a pilot program to increase the number of available truck-parking facilities.

● **Intermodal pilot program.** The law creates a freight intermodal distribution pilot program and authorizes $5 million for each of six sites.

● **Delta region.** A $40 million program is authorized for multistate transportation projects in the eight-state Delta region (Alabama, Arkansas, Illinois, Kentucky, Louisiana, Mississippi, Missouri and Tennessee).

● **Work zone safety.** The Department of Transportation is directed to issue regulations requiring highway workers to wear high-visibility garments and has discretion to issue other rulings to enhance worker safety. The law authorizes safety training grants to nonprofit organizations and the creation of a work-zone safety information clearinghouse.

● **Roadway safety study.** The department is directed to contract with a nonprofit organization to promote pedestrian and bicycle safety.

● **Construction efficiency.** The law continues the department's authority to approve large "design-build" projects, in which one firm handles both design and construction responsibilities and can begin construction on one portion of a project before design work on the rest of the project is completed, as long as the project meets all National Environmental Policy Act requirements. Intermodal projects are included among those eligible for design-build.

● **State assumption of federal duties.** The law authorizes a pilot program in which five states can assume the department's responsibility for certain projects.

● **Real-time information.** A real-time system-management information program is to be established in all states to monitor traffic and travel conditions on major roads. States can obligate funds for real-time monitoring of traffic conditions, subject to approval by the Transportation Department.

● **Future interstate routes.** States were given 25 years, rather than the 12 years provided under prior law, to substantially complete construction of highways designated as future routes on the Interstate Highway System before they must forfeit that future status. The provision applies to both new and existing agreements.

● **Hybrid vehicle use.** It is the sense of Congress that the Transportation Department and the states should provide additional incentives, including the use of HOV lanes, for the purchase and use of hybrid and other fuel-efficient vehicles.

● **Transfer of highway and transit funds.** The law authorizes the transfer of highway funds to the Federal Transit Administration (FTA) for uses other than capital expenses on a transit project, provided the project is eligible for assistance under the highway title. States can request that funding be transferred to other states or to a federal agency. Any transferred funds must be used for the same purpose and in the same manner as originally authorized.

● **Small and minority-owned businesses.** At least 10 percent of the funding for specified programs must go to small businesses owned and controlled by socially and economically disadvantaged individuals.

● **Racial profiling.** The law authorizes $7.5 million per year through fiscal 2009 for a new grant program for states that enact laws prohibiting racial profiling by law enforcement personnel. The grants are to be used for analyzing data on traffic stops or for developing programs to reduce racial profiling.

● **Future surface transportation system needs.** A Surface Transportation Policy and Revenue Study Commission is to be created to determine the future needs of the surface transportation system and how those needs will be financed.

● **Road user fees.** The department is required to enter into an agreement with a university public-policy center for a long-term field test in which highway user fees are based on a vehicle's actual miles traveled as tracked by an onboard computer. A total of $12.5 million is authorized in fiscal 2006 through 2009 for the program.

● **Transportation improvements.** The law designates funding for 466 projects added in conference similar to projects in the high-priority program.

● **Services as part of matching share.** States were given additional flexibility in meeting their non-federal share requirements, including by counting the value of services donated by local government employees.

## HIGHWAY SAFETY PROGRAMS

The law provides a total of $3.1 billion through fiscal 2009 — all from the Highway Trust Fund — for highway safety programs operated by the National Highway and Traffic Safety Administration (NHTSA). The Transportation Department is allowed to transfer funds among incentive programs intended to encourage states to crack down on impaired driving, encourage safety belt usage and improve safety-information systems, so that states can receive as much as they were entitled under each program in each fiscal year. The law also requires NHTSA to review each state highway safety program every three years.

The law authorizes:

● **Highway safety grants.** $1.1 billion for "section 402" grants to state and local governments for highway safety programs. The law adds efforts to prevent aggressive, fatigued and distracted driving; requires states to encourage law enforcement agencies to follow guidelines for vehicular pursuits; and requires the department to develop a single application process for safety grant programs. Of the total, funding available to Indian tribes is increased to 2 percent, from .75 percent.

● **Safety research and outreach.** $502 million for the Highway Safety Research and Outreach Program for studies on topics such as the causes of traffic accidents, the impact of distracted and inattentive drivers, the effectiveness of various safety initiatives, pedestrian safety, the frequency that intoxication tests were refused, impaired motorcycle driving, and the effectiveness of advanced alcohol-detection technology to reduce alcohol-related crashes and fatalities.

● **Occupant protection incentive grants.** $120 million for a grant program for states that have laws or programs that promote the use of safety belts and child safety seats, such as a primary safety belt law that allows drivers to be stopped and fined for not wearing a safety belt even if they are not violating any other traffic laws. The funds can be used to implement or enforce such initiatives.

● **Safety belt use grants.** $498 million for grants to states that have either enacted a primary safety belt law since Dec. 31, 2002, or have a safety belt use rate after Dec. 31, 2005, of 85 percent or more for each of the two fiscal years prior to the year of the grant. The grants are to be used for safety purposes or for projects that correct road hazards or highway safety issues. A separate provision in the federal aid highways title authorizes $112 million in fiscal 2004 and 2005 for incentive grants for states that have met certain seat belt usage standards.

● **State traffic safety information improvements.** $138 million for a new grant program for states that improve the collection and sharing of safety-related information. The law authorizes $34.5 million annually in fiscal 2006 through 2009. Grants can be for $300,000 or more in the first year and $500,000 or more in succeeding years.

● **Alcohol-impaired driving.** $555 million over five years for incentive grants to states that implement programs to deter drunk driving. To be eligible, states must have an alcohol-related fatality rate at or below one death per 200 million vehicle miles traveled. Alternatively, they can have initiated a minimum number of programs or activities — three in fiscal 2006, four in 2007, and five in 2008 and 2009 — from a list that includes checkpoints; outreach efforts to judges to improve the prosecution of drunk-driving cases; increased blood alcohol content testing of drivers involved in fatal crashes; tougher sanctions against high-risk drivers; alcohol rehabilitation programs or specialized courts that closely supervise high-risk offenders; programs to deter underage drinking; administrative license revocation programs; and programs that use the proceeds from drunk-driving fines for drunk-driving programs.

A separate grant program is created to assist the 10 states with the highest impaired-driving fatality rates. To participate, the state must have an expenditure plan approved by NHTSA. Up to 15 percent of the total funding can be used for this purpose.

A separate provision in the federal aid highways title directs the department to withhold a portion of highway funds from states that have not enacted or enforced a 0.08 blood alcohol content law, while authorizing $110 million in incentive grants in fiscal 2004 and 2005 for states that have enacted such laws.

● **Motorcycle safety.** $25 million for a motorcycle safety incentive grant program for states that adopt and implement effective programs to reduce the number of crashes involving motorcycles. Grants may be used for motorcycle safety and awareness courses. A provision in the highways title establishes a committee, including representatives of motorcycling organizations, to advise the department on safety issues.

● **Child safety seat incentive program.** $25 million for a new grant program for states that have enacted a law requiring children in passenger vehicles to be secured in child safety seats or child booster seats that meet the requirements of "Anton's Law" (PL 107-318). Up to 50 percent of the funding can be used to purchase restraints for low-income families; the remainder is for enforcement, training or educational purposes.

● **Safety rulings and studies.** The law gives the NHTSA deadlines for completing a series of rules, standards and reports designed to reduce the incidence of vehicle rollovers, minimize deaths and injuries from side-impact crashes, prevent injuries caused by power windows, and prevent the use by schools of 15-passenger vans that have not passed a rollover test. The agency is also ordered to conduct studies on tire aging, vehicle backover avoidance technology, motor vehicle-related deaths and injuries in nontraffic incidents, and safety belt use technologies. A total of $586.1 million is designated for fiscal 2006 to fiscal 2009 to carry out the rule-makings and studies.

## PUBLIC TRANSPORTATION

The law authorizes $45.3 billion through fiscal 2009 for the FTA to assist public transportation activities. The total represents about 18.6 percent of the total surface transportation funding for fiscal 2005 through 2009, a slightly higher percentage than under the 1998 law. Of this amount, up to $37.2 billion (82 percent) is to be derived from the mass transit account of the Highway Trust Fund; the remaining $8.1 billion is to come from the general fund. The law discards the phrase "mass transit" in favor of the broader term "public transportation" to refer to rural and other nontraditional service areas as well as typical bus and light rail systems.

### TRANSPORTATION PLANNING

The agreement requires that FTA grants meet new state and metropolitan planning requirements, and requires the FTA to certify that planning organizations are carrying out their duties.

States and metropolitan planning organizations, representing areas of at least 50,000 people, are required to develop long-range transportation plans and transportation improvement programs for their service areas.

In writing their transportation plans, metropolitan planning organizations must consider proposals that meet several transportation and community objectives, such as improved mobility, promoting economic activity and increasing safety, over a 20-year forecast period. The organizations cannot be sued for the failure to consider a project in light of one or more of those objectives, and the decisions made by the Transportation Department regarding the suitability of a transportation plan or an improvement program is not challengeable as a federal action under the National Environmental Policy Act.

If the metropolitan planning organization represents an area found to be in non-attainment of ozone or carbon monoxide standards in the Clean Air Act, the organization must update its long-range transportation plan at least every four years; otherwise, the plan must be updated at least every five years. The transportation improvement programs, which outline the specific projects that will fulfill the goals of the long-range transportation plan, must be updated every four years. The requirements for state transportation plans and transportation improvement programs are similar to those for metropolitan areas.

The measure provides $487 million to assist in the development of transportation plans, project plans and designs and technical studies. Metropolitan planning organizations are slated to receive 83 percent of the grants, with four-fifths distributed based on population; states will receive 17 percent. States that receive grants have 30 days to distribute funds to the planning boards in the state.

### FORMULA GRANT PROGRAMS

The following amounts are authorized for formula grant programs:

● **Urban areas.** $19.1 billion over five years for formula grants to urban areas with 50,000 or more people. Urban grants for capital projects can cover 80 percent of the costs of a project. Grants for operating expenses, generally restricted to services in areas with fewer than 200,000 people, are limited to 50 percent of costs. The remaining project costs can come from undistributed reserves, service agreements or cash sources other than the government or transport revenues. Caps under previous law on the use of revenue from the sale of advertising and concessions are eliminated.

Urbanized areas — those that have more than 200,000 residents — are given an exemption from rules that prohibit such areas from using grants for operating expenses will see that exemption phased out by 2008. These areas are exempted because they are newly designated as urbanized under the 2000 census.

Grant recipients in areas of more than 200,000 people are required to expend 1 percent of the funds on projects that enhance public-transportation services and that are physically related to the service.

The measure created a new Small Transit Intensive Cities Formula, through which 1 percent of the total formula grant funding would be

dedicated to areas with fewer than 200,000 people that meet or exceed one or more measures of transit usage typical of areas that have populations of between 200,000 and 999,999 people.

● **Non-urban areas.** $1.9 billion over five years for grants to "other-than-urban" areas — those with fewer than 50,000 people. The grants can be used for capital projects, operating expenses or the acquisition of services, and can be issued to states or used to establish a rural transportation program. Funds can be distributed based on the relative population in the covered areas of each state with an adjustment for low-density areas to compensate for higher operating costs. The law also sets aside 2 percent of the funding for the rural transportation assistance program. A portion of the funding must be set aside for Indian tribes.

● **Growing and high-density states.** $1.7 billion over four years to growing and high-density states. The total is to be divided evenly with half the money going to states with growing populations, based on 15-year growth projections, and the other half going to states with population densities of more than 370 people per square mile. After these funds have been apportioned to the states under formulas, the remainder is to be added to the amounts available under the formula grant programs.

● **Job access grants.** $726 million over five years for the Job Access and Reverse Commute program, which the law converts into a formula grant program. The grants fund projects to ease travel to and from work for low-income individuals and welfare recipients. Grants also can be used for "reverse-commuting projects" that help transport urban residents to suburban and rural jobs. The law allocates 60 percent of the grants to urban areas with more than 200,000 people, 20 percent to urban areas with fewer than 200,000 people and 20 percent to non-urban areas.

● **New Freedom program.** $339 million over four years beginning in fiscal 2006 for the president's New Freedom program, which will provide public transportation grants to fund projects and services for the disabled that exceed the requirements of the Americans with Disabilities Act (PL 101-336), including transportation to work. Sixty percent of the funds are for areas with 200,000 or more people, 20 percent for areas with fewer than 200,000 people and 20 percent for non-urban areas. Projects will be selected on a competitive basis on the state and local levels.

● **Assisting the elderly and disabled.** $584 million over five years for existing formula grants to fund public-transportation projects that assist the elderly and the disabled. A pilot program in fiscal 2006 through 2009 in seven states will determine whether expanded authority to use grants for operating assistance improves service.

● **Bus accessibility.** $39 million over five years for the Over-the-Road Bus Accessibility program, which provides grants for the incremental costs of purchasing equipment to comply with the Americans with Disability Act. Of the total, 75 percent is for inter-city bus operators, and 25 percent to charter or other bus services. The federal share for grants is 90 percent.

## CAPITAL INVESTMENT GRANTS

The law authorizes funding for capital investment grants that go to states for specified projects. The fiscal 2005 funding is provided in accordance with the Consolidated Appropriations Act (PL 108-457). Beginning in fiscal 2006, the law changes the distribution, providing set amounts for the new starts program and the other amounts under a larger "Formula and Bus Grant" account.

● **New starts.** A total of $8 billion will be available over five years for Major Capital Investment grants — better known as "new starts" grants

— of $75 million or more for new, fixed-guideway transit systems or extensions to existing transit systems. New starts are to be carried out through an agreement guaranteeing full funding once a project is approved for final design and construction, and following an analysis of potential alternatives, project justification and local financial commitment. The law allows grants under the new starts program to cover 80 percent of the net cost of the project.

The law authorizes 31 projects reviewed by the FTA for final design and construction under existing full-funding agreements, 38 other projects for final design and construction, and 264 projects for preliminary engineering. It also provides specified funding for 52 individual projects. The Transportation Department is required to provide annual reports to Congress on new starts, and the Government Accountability Office (GAO) is required to conduct annual review.

The law authorizes a pilot program to establish three public-private partnerships for new fixed guideway projects. Four rail projects — in San Francisco; Santa Clara, Calif.; Washington County, Ore.; and the Virginia suburbs of Washington — are exempted from a requirement that they receive at least a "medium" cost-effectiveness rating to receive a funding recommendation from the FTA.

A separate alternative analysis program was created by the conference committee to pay up to 80 percent of the costs associated with studies of various options associated with a new starts project. A total of $18.9 million was authorized for 18 studies in fiscal 2006 and 2007.

● **Small starts.** The law creates a new "small starts" program for capital investment grants of under $75 million. Projects must have a total cost under $250 million, and the grants are subject to a streamlined and expedited evaluation process. Certain projects that do not involve fixed guideways, such as bus rapid transit lines, can get funds through the small starts program. The law sets aside $200 million a year from new starts funding in 2007 through 2009 for small starts grants.

● **Rail modernization.** The law authorizes $7.3 billion over the five-year period for grants to modernize existing fixed guideway systems, such as subways and light-rail systems.

● **Buses and bus facilities.** The law authorizes $4.3 billion over six years for grants to assist in procuring buses, or constructing or modernizing bus facilities. It earmarks funding from fiscal 2006 through 2009 for 665 specified projects, although 16 projects would be funded through the Clean Fuels Grants program. It sets aside $35 million annually for a new program for intermodal facilities proposed by the administration and $10 million annually from fiscal 2006 through 2009 for ferry boats. The age and condition of buses and facilities must be considered in making grants, and 5.5 percent of the grants each year must go to non-urban areas.

The law establishes a national program to develop fuel-cell bus technology, and authorizes grants, contracts and cooperative agreements with up to three nonprofit groups from geographically diverse areas, selected on a competitive basis. A total of $65 million is to be set aside from the total amount for these purposes. The law also requires the FTA to maintain a "new bus model" testing facility in Altoona, Pa.

## OTHER DISCRETIONARY GRANT PROGRAMS

● **Clean fuels grant program.** The law authorizes $238 million over five years for grants to cities of more than 200,000 people — or to the states for smaller areas — that are deemed to be in "non-attainment" or "maintenance" under the Clean Air Act. Distribution is to be based on the severity of ozone or carbon-monoxide levels. Two-thirds of the funds are to go to areas with more than 1 million people. The grants are for purchasing buses that use natural gas, biodiesel, alcohol-based fuels or

fuel cells, or are hybrid gas-electric vehicles. Up to 25 percent of the grant funding can be used for clean diesel buses. Funds can be used to construct or lease facilities for such buses, or to construct or improve public-transportation facilities to accommodate the buses. The grants can cover 90 percent of the costs of equipment needed to comply with the Clean Air Act.

● **Alternative transportation in national parks.** The Transportation Department will administer a new program for alternative transportation in national parks and on public lands, in consultation with the Interior Department. Alternative options include clean-fuel buses, rail, "innovative technologies or methods," and facilities for pedestrians, bicycles or non-motorized watercraft. The law authorizes a total of $97 million over four years for the program, which covers national parks, the National Wildlife Refuge System, recreational areas managed by the Bureau of Land Management and national forests.

## OTHER PROVISIONS

● **Worker issues.** Precedents in a 1994 Labor Department ruling must be applied when one contractor replaces another through competitive bidding, thus maintaining protections for employees. Two new programs — New Freedom and Alternative Transportation in Public Lands — are exempt from the labor protections. The law authorizes grants to states, local government and transit operators to provide fellowships for training personnel in managerial, technical and professional positions. It allows the department to apply a single agency's drug and alcohol testing regime if a particular provider is under the jurisdiction of more than one agency's rules.

● **Terrorist attacks on transit systems.** Prior law made it a crime to interfere with anyone dispatching, operating or maintaining a mass transportation vehicle or ferry. The new law amends the statute to specify that interfering with someone controlling such a vehicle also constitutes a federal crime. The change is meant to cover those who control the movement of rail cars from a central location.

● **Transportation benefits for federal workers.** Covered agencies in the Washington metropolitan area must implement a program that allows federal employees to receive tax-free transit benefits to cover commuting costs. This codifies an executive order and expands it to cover employees in the legislative and judicial branches, as well as independent agencies.

● **Private operators.** Private transit operators can be designated as subrecipients under certain programs, thus allowing them to receive financial assistance under federal grants provided to state and local agencies. The law also calls for other changes intended to increase private sector involvement in public transportation services.

● **Transit research.** The measure authorizes $314 million over five years for a variety of transit research activities, including those at university research centers and at a national transit institute at Rutgers University. A new fuel-cell bus technology competitive grant program is established. Other research projects include the use of public transportation facilities during an emergency, standards for transit-oriented development and the potential for using infrared audible signs to aid disabled people in using public transportation.

● **Expanded eligibility for capital projects.** The types of capital projects for which federal funding can be used are expanded to include intercity bus stations and terminals, crime-prevention security efforts and programs, the establishment of debt-service reserve funds, and mobility-management activities.

● **Safety and security.** The department is allowed to investigate safety hazards or security risks to establish the nature and extent of the risk and determine a course of action. Local authorities must submit a plan for correcting such hazards, and the department can withhold funds until the plan is submitted. States are required to establish safety program plans for rail-based "new start" projects. The law directs the Transportation and Homeland Security departments to define their respective roles in public transportation security and to conduct joint rule-making for public transportation security grants within 180 days of the law's enactment.

● **General provisions on financial assistance.** The law sets requirements for public hearings and notice for projects that will affect communities, permits bond proceeds to be used for local matching funds, and allows the FTA to assess fines or withhold grant funds if public transportation agencies violate the narrowly defined conditions under which public transportation providers can provide school bus transportation. It permits incidental use of alternative fueling facilities by non-transit users under specified conditions.

● **Capital projects.** Capital projects that obtain financial assistance must meet requirements in existing law that "ensure that people whose real property is acquired, or who move as a direct result of projects receiving federal funds, are treated fairly and equitably and receive assistance in moving from the property they occupy." The law also requires consultation with the Interior Department and the EPA to determine the potential economic, social and environmental impact of a project. The Transportation Department must certify that adequate opportunity was given to review the impact prior to approving an application for financial assistance. Acquisition of a railroad right of way may occur before environmental reviews are completed, as long as it is otherwise permitted under federal law.

● **'Buy America' requirements.** The law requires written justification for a waiver of "Buy America" requirements. It also requires the development of regulations that include a list of representative items subject to the requirements.

● **Contract requirements.** The law requires open and competitive contracting for procurement. Contracts for architecture, engineering and design must be competitive, and recipients must submit to an audit. The law spells out procurement practices for rolling stock, and allows the FTA and the GAO to examine all records for construction projects. Vehicles purchased through grants are excluded from state laws requiring that buses be obtained through in-state dealers. The law requires that contractors to public transportation agencies have adequate technical and financial capacity to carry out a proposed project.

● **Regulation prohibition.** The Transportation Department cannot regulate a public transportation provider's routes, operation or schedule, except during a regional or national emergency.

## MOTOR CARRIER SAFETY PROGRAMS

The law authorizes a total of $2.5 billion through fiscal 2009 for safety programs administered by the Federal Motor Carrier Safety Administration, which focuses on large trucks and buses. Of the total, $1.2 billion is for administrative expenses and $361 million is to be distributed through five grant programs: commercial driver's license program improvement, border enforcement, performance and registration information system management, commercial vehicle information systems and networks deployment, and safety data improvement.

● **Penalties.** The law doubles the punishment for commercial vehicle out-of-service violations, providing a 180-day suspension and a $2,500 fine for a first-time violator, and a two-year sentence and a $5,000 fine for a second-time offender. An employer who knowingly allows an employee to violate out-of-service orders is subject to a $25,000 fine and

a possible yearlong prison sentence.

The Federal Motor Carrier Safety Administration can suspend, amend or revoke the registration of a motor carrier company with a pattern of noncompliance. The law establishes a fine of $1,000 for each time that an uncooperative carrier or shipper denies an agency employee access to records or violates recordkeeping and reporting requirements, up to $10,000. It also allows the agency to ban a carrier from interstate commerce if it has been banned by the state in which it operates. The safety administration may consider an operator's safety record while operating in interstate, intrastate, Mexican and Canadian commerce, and its officers are allowed to stop trucks on the road for inspection; previously, only state officers were allowed to do so.

● **Vehicle towing.** States can require tow truck operators to have written authorization from a property owner to tow vehicles from the property; they also can require the owner or a designee to be on the property at the time the vehicle is being towed, a measure designed to curb "predatory" tow truck operators.

● **Motor carrier safety grants.** The law reauthorizes the Motor Carrier Safety Assistance Program and provides $984 million for it through fiscal 2009. It adds new requirements to a state's annual safety plan to tighten reporting, enforcement and oversight responsibilities. It expands a recipient's ability to use grants to enforce vehicle size and weight limitations other than at fixed weight facilities, to detect unlawful substances in commercial vehicles, or to enforce state traffic laws and regulations related to commercial vehicles. The law permits $15 million to be used annually for high-priority activities starting in fiscal 2006, and $29 million for audits of new entrant motor carriers. States are required to maintain a level of inspections equal to their average level in fiscal 2003 through 2005.

● **Border enforcement grants.** A new $128 million program will provide grants to states with international borders to carry out border-safety programs and related law enforcement activities.

● **Commercial driver's licenses.** The law requires individuals to pass a written test to obtain a commercial learner's permit; this information will be included in the commercial drivers' license information system. The law authorizes $100 million for a new grant program to help states to improve their commercial driver's license programs, including computer upgrades, publications, additional personnel, testing, training and quality control. It also requires a task force to study the commercial driver's license program's effectiveness.

● **Maximum hours of service.** The law provides exemptions from hours-of-service regulations — which limit the number of hours that truck drivers and commercial vehicle operators may drive — for utility-truck operators, operators transporting agricultural commodities and farm supplies, operators of vehicles transporting groundwater well-drilling rigs, and drivers who operate vehicles for the motion picture industry. It also provides a harvest-time exemption for drivers transporting grapes in parts of New York and for drivers responding to propane fuel or pipeline emergencies.

● **Unified carrier registration.** The Transportation Department is required to establish a Unified Carrier Registration System, an online federal registration system intended to serve as a clearinghouse and depository of information on motor carriers, brokers, freight forwarders and others required to register with the department. The provision is intended to replace the single-state registration system.

The law makes it an undue burden for states to impose, enact or enforce any requirement or charge any fee to register interstate operations with the state or complete other filing requirements if the carrier is registered with the safety agency and is in compliance with state laws.

### HOUSEHOLD-GOODS MOVERS

The law responds to the increased number of complaints against interstate movers received by the Federal Motor Carrier Safety Administration, including reports from consumers whose goods were held hostage pending payment of unexpected expenses.

● **Requirement to release goods upon payment.** The law codifies existing regulations that require movers to relinquish possession of household goods as long as the shipper pays 100 percent of a binding estimate or 110 percent of a non-binding estimate.

● **Requirements on movers and brokers.** The law requires a household-goods broker to provide prospective shippers with information about the motor carriers that the broker uses, the broker's Transportation Department identification number and a statement that it is not a motor carrier. Household-goods carriers must offer shippers arbitration on matters of loss or damage as well as over disputes about charges; the threshold for binding arbitration in such matters is raised to $10,000, from $5,000.

Movers must give consumers written estimates, as well as educational materials, such as the Department of Transportation pamphlets "Ready to Move?" and "Your Rights and Responsibilities When You Move."

● **Federal-state cooperation.** The law allows state agencies to enforce consumer protection laws and authorizes state attorneys general to file civil suits in behalf of their residents to compel a motor carrier to relinquish possession of a household goods shipment or to pay civil penalties. It creates a working group of state attorneys general, state consumer protection administrations, and federal and local law enforcement to develop uniform enforcement standards. The GAO is instructed to study the potential impact on motor carriers and shippers of allowing state attorneys general and consumer protection agencies to apply state laws and regulations to the interstate movement of household goods.

● **Penalties.** The law creates a civil penalty of at least $10,000 for household-goods brokers who provide consumers with an estimate before contracting with a household-goods mover. Anyone who transports household goods in interstate commerce without the proper authority will be subject to a fine of at least $25,000 per violation. The law creates civil penalties of not less than $10,000, and criminal penalties of up to two years imprisonment, for anyone who holds a person's goods hostage once full payment has been made.

● **Requirements for the department.** The agreement requires the Transportation Department to produce an electronic consumer's guide on its Web site to inform the public of its rights and responsibilities relating to household-goods movers. It requires the establishment of a database to track consumer complaints. The department also is required to review regulations about the insurance coverage provided by motor carriers to shippers.

### RESEARCH

The agreement authorizes $2.3 billion over five years for transportation research, education and technology deployment programs, and sets an annual obligation limit of $411 million per year. The law includes:

● **Research, technology and education.** Sets principles for research and technology spending, with an emphasis on fundamental, long-range research on gaps and emerging issues with national implications. It requires the department to develop a five-year transportation research and development strategic plan, to be reviewed by the National Academy of Sciences. In addition, the law authorizes $9.6 million a year for the National Highway Institute and $1.25 million a year for the creation of a program to focus on increasing the number of women and members of racial minorities in transportation-related engineering, tech-

nology and science fields.

● **Bridge programs.** Establishes three bridge research programs, including a 20-year, long-term bridge performance program. It also establishes the Innovative Bridge Research and Deployment Program to demonstrate and evaluate the use of innovative designs, materials and construction methods.

● **Technology deployment.** Establishes several technology deployment initiatives in areas such as new pavement materials, safety-related technology uses, wood composite materials, asphalt reclamation and the prevention of alkali silica reactivity.

● **Freight programs.** Creates a Freight Planning Capacity Building Program to improve the ability of metropolitan planning organizations and other planning bodies to plan for freight transportation. It also requires the establishment of a National Cooperative Freight Transportation Research Program, carried out through an agreement with the National Academy of Sciences, to develop improved ways to provide mobility for freight.

● **Environmental effects.** Authorizes $68 million through fiscal 2009 for a cooperative research program to examine the relationship between surface transportation and the environment.

● **Future research.** Creates a future strategic highway research program to be carried out by the National Academy of Sciences. The program will implement recommendations from a study required under the previous surface transportation bill and will focus on renewing aging highway infrastructure, human factors related to highway safety, reducing congestion, and planning and designing new capacity. The law authorizes $205 million through fiscal 2009 for the program.

● **Intelligent transportation systems.** Calls for the creation of a five-year National Intelligent Transportation System program plan, with goals that include speeding up the deployment of systems that use electronics, photonics, communications technologies or information processing technologies; improving understanding of the systems among transportation officials; and supporting their ongoing operation and maintenance. The program includes the development of "intelligent vehicles" and infrastructure, and promoting standards for the interoperability of various systems.

● **Other research programs.** Authorizes the establishment of a road weather research program and four "centers for surface transportation excellence." The law authorizes grants to transportation centers at several universities and research initiatives on traffic-related topics, as well as a two-year motorcycle crash causation study.

● **Bureau of Transportation Statistics.** Authorizes $27 million annually for the Bureau of Transportation Statistics. It allows the bureau to fine businesses, organizations and institutions up to $500 for refusing or neglecting to comply with a request for freight data. If false information is provided, the party will be liable for a fine of up to $10,000. The law allows access to information from other federal agencies, unless such sharing is prohibited by law or would impair the other agency's ability to carry out its functions. It limits the disclosure of certain information collected by the bureau.

## PLANNING AND ENVIRONMENTAL REVIEWS

The planning process for highway and public transportation projects is altered to create identical planning procedures for metropolitan and statewide planning. The law also sets forth procedures for expediting environmental reviews of projects.

● **Metropolitan planning.** Transportation planning in urban areas of 50,000 or more people must be carried out by a "metropolitan planning organization" designated by the governor and local officials. Under cer-

tain circumstances, more than one such organization can be established for an area. The metropolitan planning organization is responsible for developing a long-range transportation plan and a transportation improvement program, both of which must include all modes of transportation and integrated management of transportation systems.

The long-range plan should meet a list of transportation and community objectives — such as improved mobility, economic growth and increased safety — based on a 20-year forecast period. It is to include a financial plan indicating how programs would be implemented and what resources can be reasonably expected; it can also include additional projects that would be funded if additional funds were made available.

However, a metropolitan planning organization cannot be sued for failing to consider a project in light of one or more of those objectives, and the decisions made by the Transportation secretary regarding the suitability of a transportation plan or an improvement program is not challengeable under the National Environmental Policy Act.

For areas that were designated as in "attainment" under the Clean Air Act, such plans must be updated at least every five years; in "non-attainment" areas, updates are required at least every four years.

The transportation improvement program, which outlines the specific projects that will fulfill the goals of the long-range plan, must be updated at least every four years, rather than every two years as under previous law. The plans must contain a priority list of federally funded programs as well as a financial plan and a list of congestion-relief activities. A metropolitan planning area may develop an abbreviated plan if it meets Clean Air Act standards for ozone and carbon monoxide.

● **Larger metropolitan areas.** The Transportation secretary will designate areas with more than 200,000 people as "transportation management areas." Other areas also can be given this designation at the governor's request. Plans for these areas require cooperation with state and public transportation officials and must include congestion management provisions. Plans for transportation management areas must be certified every four years; otherwise, up to 20 percent of federal funds can be withheld. In most cases, projects will be selected by the metropolitan planning organization in consultation with the state. Transportation management areas that were in "non-attainment" under the Clean Air Act were barred from receiving funds for a highway project that would increase the number of single-occupant vehicles unless the project has a congestion management component.

● **Statewide planning.** In addition to the metropolitan planning requirements, the law requires states to develop long-range plans, with a 20-year horizon, and statewide transportation improvement programs that coordinate with the metropolitan plans and — where applicable and approved — with other states. Certain state laws and regulations on congestion management will satisfy federal requirements for these plans. The plans must be updated every four years, instead of the two years under prior law. The law requires states to consider the needs of rural areas and Indian tribes in developing their plans and to consult with local officials.

● **Funding.** The law authorizes $487 million to assist in the development of transportation plans, plans and designs for projects, or technical studies. Metropolitan planning organizations will receive 83 percent of the grants, with four-fifths distributed based on population; states will receive 17 percent. States that receive grants have 30 days to distribute funds to the planning boards in the state.

## ENVIRONMENTAL STREAMLINING

● **Lead agency and other participants.** The Transportation Department is to serve as the lead agency in the environmental review process

for any highway, transit or multimodal project that requires the department's approval. A state or local government agency sponsoring a project is to serve as joint lead agency and share in decision-making about the environmental review process. Other agencies that have an interest in the project will be invited to serve as "participating agencies."

The project sponsor must submit a notice to the department detailing the scope and location of the project, as well as a statement of the federal approvals that are believed necessary.

The lead agency, through consultation with the other participating agencies and the public, is responsible for defining the purpose and goals of the project and developing potential alternatives. The conference report on the bill specifies that the lead agency's definitions are "not binding on other agencies that have independent [environmental] responsibilities," but it says "other agencies shall show substantial deference to the purpose and need as defined by the lead agency."

Federal agencies are required to carry out concurrent reviews to the maximum extent practicable.

The lead agency is required to establish a plan for public and agency participation in the environmental review process. In establishing a schedule for completing the review, the lead agency must consider a number of factors, including the complexity of the project, the responsibilities of the participating agencies and the sensitivity of the natural and historical resources that could be affected by the project. The law states that nothing in these provisions can reduce time periods provided for public comment under existing federal law.

● **Deadlines.** Participating agencies and the public have a maximum of 60 days to review a draft environmental-impact statement. The law sets a 30-day review period for other documents. Both deadlines could be extended, and the provisions are not meant to reduce the time period provided under existing federal laws for public comments.

● **Dispute resolution.** The lead and participating agencies are required to work cooperatively to identify and resolve issues that could delay the process or result in a denial of the necessary approvals. If no resolution is reached within 30 days, and the lead agency determines that all needed information has been obtained, then the law requires that notification be provided to all participating parties and to Congress.

● **Judicial review.** The law establishes a 180-day period for filing any lawsuit challenging a permit, license or approval issued by a federal agency for a highway or transit project, unless another law allows a shorter period. The period starts when the lead agency gives public notice that a final decision has been issued. The law does not place a limit on filing claims against persons who have violated their permits, licenses or approvals. If new information warrants a supplemental environmental review, then a new 180-day period begins.

● **Delegation of authority.** The law authorizes a pilot program that will allow five designated states to assume the Department of Transportation's responsibility for conducting environmental reviews for a project, subject to audits by the department. The law also allows the department to assign responsibility to states for processing environmental reviews for projects designated as "categorical exclusions" under Council on Environmental Quality regulations, meaning they do not have a significant effect on the human environment. A third pilot program allows Alaska, California, Ohio, Oklahoma and Texas to assume federal responsibility for environmental reviews for one or more highway projects.

● **Protected areas and historic sites.** Transportation projects can go forward as long as they have minimal impact on protected parks, recreation areas, refuges and historic sites, and as long as the department has the concurrence of appropriate state or tribal officials. The Inter-

state Highway System cannot be considered a historic site for the purposes of certain historic preservation reviews, even if all or part of the system is on the National Register of Historic Places. There were exceptions for portions that contain an independently historic item, such as a bridge or engineering feature.

● **Categorical exclusions for ITS programs.** The department is required to issue rules to establish categorical exclusions from environmental review for activities that support the development of "intelligent transportation systems." The law also requires a nationwide agreement governing reviews of ITS activities under the National Historic Preservation Act.

## CLEAN AIR ACT COMPLIANCE

The measure changes planning requirements for areas that are in "non-attainment," meaning they fail to attain air-quality standards under the Clean Air Act. Under that law, such areas must demonstrate that transportation projects conform with State Implementation Plans, which outline how the area will attain the air-quality standards.

● **Planning updates and conformity demonstrations.** The law generally requires that updates to metropolitan transportation plans and transportation improvement programs, and to statewide transportation improvement programs, be made at least every four years in areas that are failing to meet Clean Air Act standards or are remediating a previous failure. The update may come sooner if the metropolitan planning organization is required to redetermine its conformity because of actions taken by the EPA. If the EPA acts, then conformity must be redetermined within two years, instead of 18 months as under prior law.

● **Time horizon.** The time horizon of state implementation plans for attaining air quality standards is changed from 20 years to the longest of 10 years, the latest year that a State Implementation Plan establishes an emissions budget, or the year after the completion of a regionally significant project that requires approval before the next determination is completed. The decision to change the time horizon would be made by a metropolitan planning organization, after consultation with the appropriate air control agency and with a period for public comment.

● **Conformity lapses.** If a nonattainment or maintenance area misses a conformity determination deadline, it has a 12-month grace period to come into compliance before a lapse is declared and the area is penalized.

● **Other clean air provisions.** The EPA is required to conduct a study to find a more accurate way to measure coarse particulate matter in the air, develop regulations for responding to air pollution created by an "exceptional event" and fully implement regulations that allow for the use of certain mineral wastes recovered from such sources as blast furnaces in concrete and granular mine tailings in asphalt. It authorizes $55 million annually in fiscal 2006 and 2007 and unspecified sums in fiscal 2008 through 2010 to promote the use of school buses that run on alternative or ultra-low sulfur diesel.

## HAZARDOUS MATERIALS

The law authorizes a total of $114 million from fiscal 2005 through 2008 for hazardous materials activities of the Pipeline and Hazardous Materials Safety Administration, and provides for the release of $111 million from the Hazardous Materials Emergency Preparedness Fund.

● **Jurisdiction.** The law stipulates the Transportation Department's authority over U.S.-registered aircraft that transport hazardous materials anywhere in the world, and clarifies the definition of "hazmat employee" and "hazmat employer."

● **List of hazardous materials.** The law updates the terminology used to describe hazardous materials and requires the Health and Human Services Department (HHS) to recommend any chemical and biological agents that should be regulated as hazardous materials.

● **Background checks.** The law eliminates redundant federal background checks for hazmat drivers. It permits the Federal Motor Carrier Safety Administration to engage in international activities to implement the North American Free Trade Agreement, and it subjects Canadian and Mexican drivers transporting hazardous materials to the same background checks as U.S. drivers. A state that has more stringent application requirements must offer an appeals process comparable to those available under federal law.

● **Special permits.** The department is authorized to issue special permits to any person who transports hazardous materials for commercial purposes. The initial permit is good for two years but can be renewed for four years. Special permits for the highway routing of hazardous materials are good for two years.

● **Registration requirements.** The department can require all persons who design or inspect packaging for the transporting of hazardous materials to register. The maximum registration fee is changed to $3,000 from $5,000. Each person who draws up shipping papers is required to make the disclosures required by law, and shipping papers for hazardous materials must be maintained for two years to facilitate investigations.

● **Civil and criminal penalties.** The maximum civil penalty in a hazardous materials accident is increased to $50,000, from $27,500; the fine can be increased to $100,000 if the incident results in death, serious illness or severe injury. Criminal penalties of up to five years are allowed in cases where an individual knowingly, recklessly or willingly violates the law. If an infraction results in death or bodily injury, the maximum sentence is increased to 10 years. Commercial truck owners and operators who continue to transport hazardous material more than 45 days after being declared unfit also are subject to the new criminal and civil penalties. An aggrieved party has 60 days to petition for a judicial review of actions taken by the department.

## RAIL TRANSPORTATION

On rail transportation, the new law:

● **High-speed rail corridor development.** Reauthorizes provisions of the Swift Act and authorizes $100 million annually in fiscal 2006 through 2013 — $70 million of it for high-speed rail corridor development and $30 million for technology deployment. The law authorizes the acquisition of track, signals, rail rolling stock and locomotives under the program.

● **Funds for rail improvement and relocation.** Authorizes $350 million annually from fiscal 2006 through 2009 for a grant program to provide financial assistance for local rail-line relocation and improvement. No more than 25 percent can be used on one project and at least half of the grants must be for $20 million or less. Authorized loan obligations under the Railroad Rehabilitation and Improvement Finance Program are increased to $35 billion, from $3.5 billion, and the amount that can be used for non-Class I railroad lines is increased to $7 billion from $1 billion. (Freight railroads were placed into classes based on their revenue. Class I railroads were the largest, with revenues in excess of $277.7 million as of 2004.)

● **Alaska Railroad.** Authorizes unspecified amounts for grants to the Alaska Railroad for capital rehabilitation and improvements for its passenger operations.

● **Other rail provisions.** Requires the Transportation Department to

study the effect of blocked highway-railroad grade crossings on emergency responders, develop rules to improve the safety of welded track and railroad tank cars, and contract with the National Academy of Science's Transportation Research Board for a comprehensive study of the nation's rail transportation system since the Staggers Rail Act of 1980.

## MISCELLANEOUS PROVISIONS

In addition, the law:

● **Emergency services coordination.** Calls for the creation of an interagency committee on emergency medical services to ensure coordination among federal agencies and other governmental entities that operate emergency medical services and 911 systems.

● **Gulf evacuation.** Requires the development of a comprehensive plan by the Transportation and Homeland Security departments for evacuating Gulf coastal areas during catastrophic hurricanes.

● **Car leasing liability.** Eliminates so-called vicarious liability under state law for motor vehicle rental and leasing companies, provided there is no negligence or criminal wrongdoing by the company. Vicarious liability laws impose unlimited liability on car and truck rental and leasing companies for injury and property damage caused by a vehicle solely because the company owns the vehicle, even if it had no involvement in the accident. Under the new law, the rental or leasing company must comply with state financial responsibility and insurance standards for each vehicle in the state law where the vehicle is registered. The provision takes effect on the date of enactment.

## HIGHWAY TRUST FUND AND TAXES

The law extends the authority to expend funds from the Highway Trust Fund through fiscal 2009. It extends the excise taxes used to finance that fund though fiscal 2011, including motor fuel taxes, such as the 18.3 cents-per-gallon tax on gasoline, the 24.3 cents-per-gallon tax on diesel fuels and three other excise taxes imposed on heavy highway vehicles or tires. (An additional 0.1 cent tax is also collected on those fuels and placed in the Leaking Underground Storage Tank trust fund.)

The Joint Committee on Taxation estimates that, overall, the tax provisions will reduce revenue to the federal government by $1.3 billion over 11 years, although provisions to reduce fuel fraud will increase the revenue available in the Highway Trust Fund by nearly $2 billion over the same period.

● **The 'Harry Byrd rule.'** A clause that reduces expenditures from the Highway Trust Fund to the states if the fund's current and expected balances fall below certain levels — known as the "Harry Byrd rule" — is modified to use a four-year projection of receipts instead of a two-year projection. State apportionments are reduced only if unfunded authorizations exceed four years of expected trust fund receipts.

### TRANSPORTATION EXCISE TAXES

● **Repeal of limousine tax.** The law repeals the so-called gas-guzzler tax on limousines that have an unloaded vehicle weight of more than 6,000 pounds. (Revenue loss: $46 million over 11 years.)

● **Exclusions from heavy-vehicle highway use tax.** A 12 percent excise tax on the first retail sale of heavy trucks and trailers will not apply to tractor-trailer trucks sold after Sept. 30, 2005, that are used chiefly for highway transportation in combination with a trailer or semitrailer. To qualify, the tractor must have a gross vehicle weight of 19,500 pounds or less. To be exempt, the gross combined weight of a tractor and a towed vehicle must be less than 33,000 pounds. (Revenue loss: $31 million over 11 years.)

● **Volumetric excise tax credit.** Several alternative fuels, most of which were previously allowed a reduced rate, are now subject to the full excise tax on fuel, calculated on the basis of the energy equivalent of a gallon of gasoline. However, the law also provides a 50 cents-per-gallon credit on the excise tax paid on such fuels through fiscal 2009. The provision covers natural gas, liquid petroleum gas, P-Series fuels, diesel from coal and liquid hydrocarbons derived from biomass. The provision applies to fuels that are sold, used or removed after Sept. 30, 2006. The provision is expected to add $466 million to the Highway Trust Fund through fiscal 2015, but that will be more than offset by the cost of the credit, which comes out of the general Treasury. (Net revenue loss: $44 million over 11 years.)

● **Consolidation of aquatic resources and sport fishing trust funds.** The law eliminates the Aquatic Resources Trust Fund and transforms the Sport Fish Restoration Account, previously part of the Aquatic Resources Trust Fund, into the Sport Fish Restoration and Boating Trust Fund. A portion of the excise taxes on special fuels and on gasoline used for motorboats and non-business use of small-engine outdoor equipment, as well as the excise tax on sport fishing equipment and duties on fishing tackle, yachts and pleasure cruises are to be deposited into the fund. Money in the trust fund is used to cover fish restoration, coastal wetlands protection, Clean Vessel Act programs and state boating safety programs. (The Congressional Budget Office estimates this will increase direct spending by $1.3 billion over 11 years.)

● **Repeal of export tax.** The law formally repeals a tax on the value of most commercial cargo exported from U.S. ports, which was ruled unconstitutional by the U.S. Supreme Court. The proceeds had been placed in the Harbor Maintenance Trust Fund. (No revenue effect.)

● **Aviation excise taxes.** The law continues an excise tax of 19.4 cents per gallon on aviation gasoline and a tax of 21.9 cents per gallon on jet fuel; all but 0.1 cent is dedicated to the Airport and Airways Trust Fund. In addition, air-passenger transportation is subjected to an excise tax equal to 7.5 percent of the amount paid by the passenger, plus $3.20 per domestic flight segment.

The law modifies some exemptions to the tax. An exemption for fuel used on a farm for farming purposes is extended to operators of crop dusters without a requirement for consent from the farm owner; the exemption covers fuel consumed when flying between farms where chemicals are applied, and to and from the airport. An exemption from the air-passenger tax for helicopters engaged in timber operations is extended to cover fixed-wing aircraft. The definition of rural airports is altered to include an airport that is not connected by paved roads to another airport and that has fewer than 100,000 commercial passengers departing on flight segments of at least 100 miles per year, thus affecting the flights eligible for the rural airport exemption from the excise tax on domestic flight segments. Seaplane trips are granted an exemption from the air passenger tax and from an air cargo tax of 6.25 percent, if the takeoff and landing occurs at a location that has not and does not receive assistance from the Airport and Airway Trust Fund. The measure clarifies that sightseeing flights are eligible for exemptions from the passenger taxes for small aircraft when those aircraft are not operating on "established lines." (Net revenue loss: $170 million over 11 years.)

## OTHER EXCISE TAX CHANGES

● **Occupational taxes on alcohol.** The law permanently eliminates special occupational taxes on producers and marketers of alcoholic beverages that had been suspended through June 2008 by the 2004 corporate tax overhaul (PL 108-357). It leaves intact registration,

recordkeeping and inspection rules in current law. (Revenue loss: $459 million over 11 years.)

● **Tax credit for alcohol inventories.** Wholesalers, distillers and importers of alcoholic beverages get a new income tax credit for the inventory costs associated with stock on which tax has already been paid at the point of purchase. (Revenue loss: $188 million.)

● **Quarterly filing requirements.** The law allows small domestic producers or importers of distilled spirits, wines and beer that have tax liability on alcohol of less than $50,000 to file quarterly returns within 14 days after the end of a calendar quarter, instead of on a semi-monthly basis. (Revenue loss: $6 million over 11 years.)

● **Exemption for custom gunsmiths.** The law exempts from a firearms excise tax — 10 percent or 11 percent of the price, depending on the type of gun — all firearms, pistols and revolvers that are made, produced or imported by a person who makes, produces or imports fewer than 50 such items per year. (Revenue loss: $8 million over 11 years.)

● **Tax limit on fishing equipment.** A $10 cap is placed on the excise tax that can be levied on fishing poles or rods. (Net revenue loss: $41 million over 11 years.)

## OTHER TAX PROVISIONS

● **Tax-exempt bonds.** The law provides authority to issue $15 billion in tax-exempt private activity bonds that can be used to finance highway projects or facilities for the transfer of freight between trains and trucks. The Transportation Department is given the discretion to allocate this authority to the states, and each state can receive up to $300 million. (Revenue loss: $738 million over 11 years.)

● **Studies and commissions.** A Motor Fuel Tax Enforcement Advisory Commission is established to review motor fuel tax collections and investigations, develop legislative proposals, monitor administrative regulations, and review cooperation between state and federal agencies, as well as among federal agencies. The commission would also review enforcement activities.

The law creates a National Surface Transportation Infrastructure Financing Commission to study the current state of the Highway Trust Fund and to consider alternative infrastructure funding approaches, including allowing states to opt out of the current federal fuel tax system. The Treasury Department is ordered to study the feasibility of exempting from excise taxes the motor fuel used in trucks for purposes other than the propulsion or movement of the vehicle. The IRS is ordered to report on new technologies that could be employed to improve the collection of excise taxes on diesel fuel.

● **Railroad real estate investment trusts.** A railroad real estate investment trust that becomes 100 percent state-owned can be taxed as though its income from the performance of essential government functions are accrued directly to the state. (Revenue loss: $2 million over 11 years.)

## FUEL FRAUD PREVENTION

● **Kerosene.** The principal source of additional revenue for the Highway Trust Fund among the tax changes is a requirement that kerosene — which can be used as both diesel and aviation fuel — be taxed at the diesel fuel rate of 24.3 cents per gallon. Previously, aviation fuel was taxed at a lower rate than diesel, which made it possible to purchase kerosene at the aviation-fuel rate and then use it for non-aviation purposes. The change applies to all kerosene except kerosene that is placed in the wing of a plane. Users of kerosene for aviation purposes are eligible for a tax credit or refund.

Tax receipts will go initially to the Highway Trust Fund, but 21.8 cents for each taxed gallon will be transferred to the Airport and Airway Trust

Fund if the kerosene is used for aviation purposes. The provision is expected to increase revenue in the Highway Trust Fund by $4.2 billion over 11 years, but cut the Airport and Airway Trust Fund by $4.3 billion over the same period. (Net revenue: $495 million over 11 years.)

● **Ultimate vendor rules.** The measure repeals a provision in prior law that allowed the final seller to administer refunds for the use of diesel fuel or kerosene used on farms. Farmers now must pay a tax when they buy the fuel, and then file a refund claim. (Negligible revenue.)

● **Refunds for excise tax purchased on credit cards.** Credit card companies that allow their cards to be used for tax-exempt fuel purchases must register with the IRS and are responsible for claiming tax refunds. (Negligible revenue.)

● **Re-registration.** Parties responsible for paying federal excise taxes on fuels, who must register with the IRS, are required to re-register if the firm changes ownership. (Revenue: $46 million over 11 years.)

● **Information sharing on imported taxable fuels.** The Homeland Security and Transportation departments are required to establish electronic means to provide the IRS with information about taxable fuels that are being imported into the United States. (Revenue: $41 million over 11 years.)

● **Registration requirements for deep-draft vessels.** Operators of deep-draft oceangoing vessels must register with the IRS to receive tax exemptions on bulk transfers of fuels. This overturns a Treasury Department regulation that exempted deep-draft vessels from the requirement, which applies to operators of pipelines, refineries and other vessels. The new law makes an exception for operators of vessels used exclusively to import taxable fuel. (Revenue: $26 million over 11 years.)

● **Penalties for adulterated fuels.** The law imposes a $10,000 fine for anyone who knowingly sells diesel fuel that does not comply with EPA regulations on sulfur content. This provision is intended to combat fuel tax evasion by individuals who mix untaxed fuel with fuel that should be taxed. ■

**Appendix A**

# CONGRESS &
# ITS MEMBERS

# Congress and Its Members
## A Touch of Gray on Capitol Hill

WHEN THE 109TH CONGRESS opened Jan. 4, the average age of senators was the highest ever, and the average House member was older than at any time in at least a century. The rise of the "citizen politician," heralded by the newly installed Republican majority a decade before, appeared no more: New House members tended to arrive with years of officeholding on their résumés — and a majority of senators had used the House as a steppingstone. Although gains in the congressional rosters of women and ethnic minorities were incremental since 2004, the totals set records nonetheless.

But the accelerating decline in military service among members was perhaps the most eye-catching statistic, given the prominent issues of war and security that this Congress faced.

In 1969, as Richard M. Nixon took office at the height of the Vietnam War, three of four members of Congress had been in the military. In 1991, when Congress authorized President George Bush to wage war to end Iraq's occupation of Kuwait, just more than half the members — 52 percent — were veterans.

But the 109th Congress, which would legislate on the nation's military campaigns in Iraq, Afghanistan and elsewhere in the war on terrorism, included just 140 veterans — 109 in the House and 31 in the Senate — barely one-quarter of the membership. That was a 9 percent decline just since the 108th Congress and a 49 percent drop since the Persian Gulf War 14 years ago.

The dwindling number of veterans in Congress was largely the result of the institution of an all-volunteer army in 1973 and the aging of the World War II generation. This was a concern for the most ardent defense hawks in Congress and for organizations that advocated for veterans. Their apprehensions were acute in a time of armed conflict and budgetary constraints that could pinch funding for veterans' health care.

"I think a veteran has a better understanding of what this country has to really deal with, what a soldier has to deal with, when we declare war on someone or we have to go to war," said Rep. John Salazar, a Democratic freshman from Colorado who served in the Army and had a son in the military.

Kentucky Republican Geoff Davis, another newly elected House member with an Army background, said military service "helps to bring into perspective the translation from theory to reality, which I think is often lost in legislation or policy that affects the military."

Some suggested that lawmakers might have demanded more oversight and answers about the Bush administration's Iraq policy if more of them had served in the armed forces. "There may have been some second-guessing as to whether going to war was the right thing to do, had we had more former service members," said Steve Robertson, the legislative director for the American Legion. "Because the last guy who wants to go to war is a veteran."

Yet, even some who lamented the decline of veterans on the con-

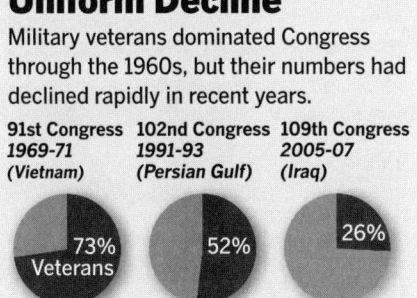

### Uniform Decline
Military veterans dominated Congress through the 1960s, but their numbers had declined rapidly in recent years.

**91st Congress 1969-71 (Vietnam)** — 73% Veterans — House: 320, Senate: 69

**102nd Congress 1991-93 (Persian Gulf)** — 52% — House: 208, Senate: 68

**109th Congress 2005-07 (Iraq)** — 26% — House: 109, Senate: 31

gressional rolls emphasized that military service was not a prerequisite to understanding defense policy or supporting veterans.

For example, veterans' groups were incensed when House Republican leaders replaced Christopher H. Smith, R-N.J. — a fervent supporter of increased federal spending on veterans' priorities — with Indiana Republican Steve Buyer, a conservative stalwart who favored the Bush administration's more frugal approach. Smith had no military experience; while Buyer did active duty in the Army during the 1980s and was still in the reserves.

"You don't have to be a veteran to love a vet," said Joe Davis, director of public affairs for the Veterans of Foreign Wars, although he added: "It does help to know what it is like to walk in a veteran's shoes."

### AGE AND THE SOCIAL SECURITY DEBATE

Passing up military service was a decision made years before for most lawmakers, given the increased "graying" of their ranks.

Many would be able to bring personal insight to the debate over another item on the legislative agenda: ensuring the solvency of Social Security. Its trustees said the program's trust funds would be drained in 2042 if no changes were made to policies for generating revenue and apportioning benefits. By that year, not one member of the 109th Congress would be below the retirement age; the youngest, 29-year-old Republican freshman Rep. Patrick T. McHenry of North Carolina, would turn 67 that fall. And, if the actuarial tables were correct, the vast majority of those in Congress in 2005 would be dead.

The average age of a senator in the 109th Congress was 60.4, a record. The oldest was 87- year-old West Virginia Democrat Robert C. Byrd — who also was the most senior lawmaker in either chamber, having entered his 47th year as senator and 53rd as a member of Congress. Byrd was set to pass South Carolina Republican Strom Thurmond as the longest-serving senator in June 2006, seven months before his eighth term expired.

Massachusetts Democrat John Kerry, still in the Senate after his unsuccessful challenge to President Bush in 2004, was 61, making him the 50th oldest senator. The youngest was 40-year-old New Hampshire Republican John E. Sununu.

The average age in the House was 55 — the highest since 1907, the earliest date for which the Congressional Research Service had data. The oldest member was 81-year-old Texas Republican Ralph M. Hall. McHenry was the only lawmaker in his 20s, though nine were younger than 35.

Of the 40 freshmen, eight Republicans and four Democrats were at least 55 years old. The oldest was 67-year-old Republican Joe Schwarz of Michigan. And their years came with sprinklings of added political seasoning. Twenty members of the Class of 2004 — fully half — arrived with at least a decade in elected office. Republican John R. "Randy" Kuhl Jr. of New York and California Democrat Jim Costa each served 24 years in the state legislature. Schwarz spent 15 years in the Michigan Senate.

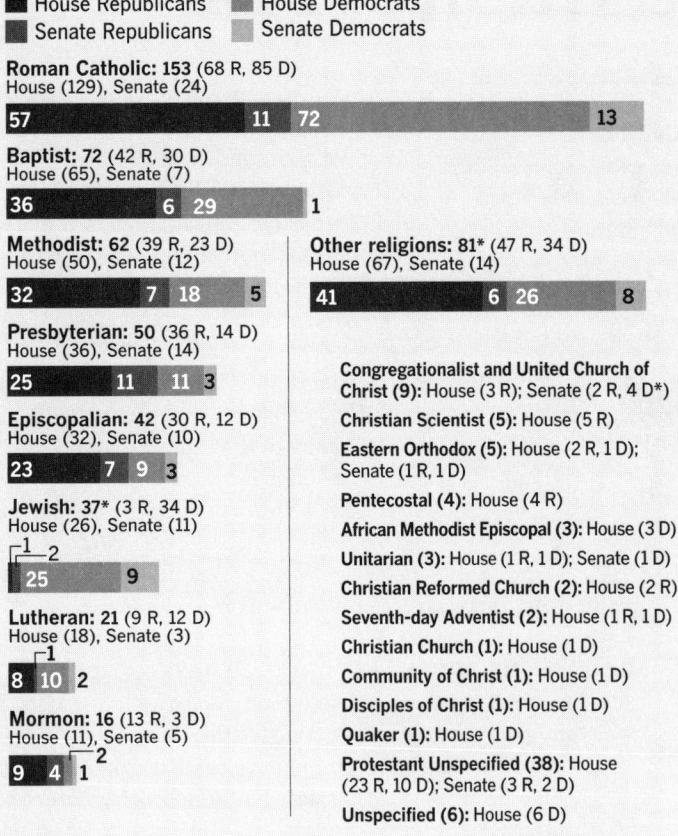

## Religious Affiliations

Almost all members make their religion public. Catholics had long been the biggest group, but Protestants combined were a solid majority.

■ House Republicans ■ House Democrats
■ Senate Republicans ■ Senate Democrats

**Roman Catholic: 153** (68 R, 85 D)
House (129), Senate (24)
57 | 11 | 72 | 13

**Baptist: 72** (42 R, 30 D)
House (65), Senate (7)
36 | 6 | 29 | 1

**Methodist: 62** (39 R, 23 D)
House (50), Senate (12)
32 | 7 | 18 | 5

**Presbyterian: 50** (36 R, 14 D)
House (36), Senate (14)
25 | 11 | 11 | 3

**Episcopalian: 42** (30 R, 12 D)
House (32), Senate (10)
23 | 7 | 9 | 3

**Jewish: 37*** (3 R, 34 D)
House (26), Senate (11)
1 | 2
25 | 9

**Lutheran: 21** (9 R, 12 D)
House (18), Senate (3)
1
8 | 10 | 2

**Mormon: 16** (13 R, 3 D)
House (11), Senate (5)
2
9 | 4 | 1

**Other religions: 81*** (47 R, 34 D)
House (67), Senate (14)
41 | 6 | 26 | 8

**Congregationalist and United Church of Christ (9):** House (3 R); Senate (2 R, 4 D*)
**Christian Scientist (5):** House (5 R)
**Eastern Orthodox (5):** House (2 R, 1 D); Senate (1 R, 1 D)
**Pentecostal (4):** House (4 R)
**African Methodist Episcopal (3):** House (3 D)
**Unitarian (3):** House (1 R, 1 D); Senate (1 D)
**Christian Reformed Church (2):** House (2 R)
**Seventh-day Adventist (2):** House (1 R, 1 D)
**Christian Church (1):** House (1 D)
**Community of Christ (1):** House (1 D)
**Disciples of Christ (1):** House (1 D)
**Quaker (1):** House (1 D)
**Protestant Unspecified (38):** House (23 R, 10 D); Senate (3 R, 2 D)
**Unspecified (6):** House (6 D)

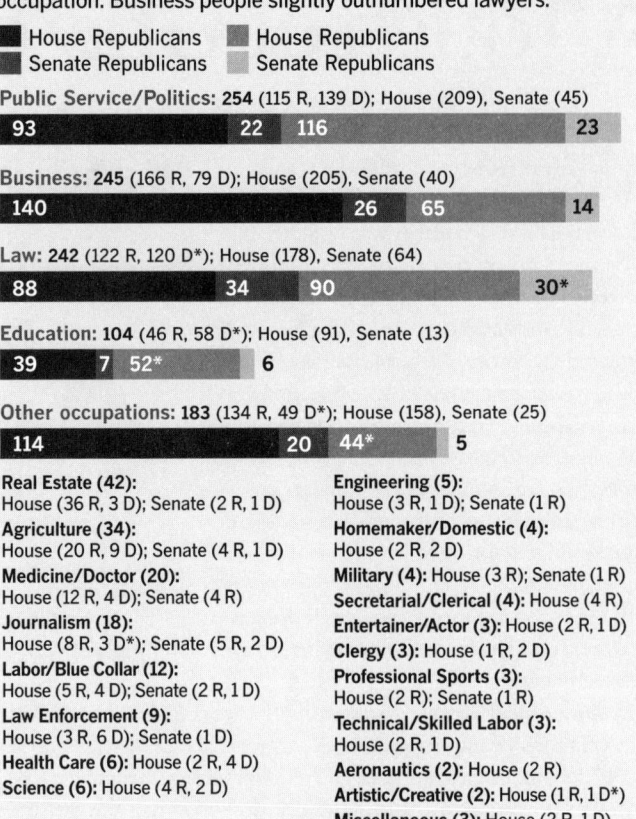

## Occupations

Many members had eclectic backgrounds and cited more than one occupation. Business people slightly outnumbered lawyers.

■ House Republicans ■ House Republicans
■ Senate Republicans ■ Senate Republicans

**Public Service/Politics: 254** (115 R, 139 D); House (209), Senate (45)
93 | 22 | 116 | 23

**Business: 245** (166 R, 79 D); House (205), Senate (40)
140 | 26 | 65 | 14

**Law: 242** (122 R, 120 D*); House (178), Senate (64)
88 | 34 | 90 | 30*

**Education: 104** (46 R, 58 D*); House (91), Senate (13)
39 | 7 | 52* | 6

**Other occupations: 183** (134 R, 49 D*); House (158), Senate (25)
114 | 20 | 44* | 5

**Real Estate (42):** House (36 R, 3 D); Senate (2 R, 1 D)
**Agriculture (34):** House (20 R, 9 D); Senate (4 R, 1 D)
**Medicine/Doctor (20):** House (12 R, 4 D); Senate (4 R)
**Journalism (18):** House (8 R, 3 D*); Senate (5 R, 2 D)
**Labor/Blue Collar (12):** House (5 R, 4 D); Senate (2 R, 1 D)
**Law Enforcement (9):** House (3 R, 6 D); Senate (1 D)
**Health Care (6):** House (2 R, 4 D)
**Science (6):** House (4 R, 2 D)

**Engineering (5):** House (3 R, 1 D); Senate (1 R)
**Homemaker/Domestic (4):** House (2 R, 2 D)
**Military (4):** House (3 R); Senate (1 R)
**Secretarial/Clerical (4):** House (4 R)
**Entertainer/Actor (3):** House (2 R, 1 D)
**Clergy (3):** House (1 R, 2 D)
**Professional Sports (3):** House (2 R); Senate (1 R)
**Technical/Skilled Labor (3):** House (2 R, 1 D)
**Aeronautics (2):** House (2 R)
**Artistic/Creative (2):** House (1 R, 1 D*)
**Miscellaneous (3):** House (2 R, 1 D)

* Figures include Congress' two independents, both from Vermont: Sen. James M. Jeffords and Rep. Bernard Sanders. Both caucus with the Democrats.

---

This contrasted sharply with the Class of 1994, the Republican-dominated group that swept into office on the "Contract With America" and heralded a GOP takeover after four decades in the House minority. Fewer than one in five of those freshmen had served at least 10 years in an elected office; many of them arrived declaring, prematurely, that political careerism was waning.

Political analysts said older candidates might fare better than younger ones because they had had more time to build a base of contacts and financial contributors — or possessed personal wealth that could finance a campaign.

"The increasing costs of campaigns in open seats and competitive incumbent-held seats puts a premium on candidates who have money or access to money as a consequence of their earlier careers," said Thomas E. Mann, a congressional scholar at the Brookings Institution.

The average age of Congress also had increased slightly because there was relatively low turnover in the 2004 election. Medical advances allowed people to live longer and maintain active lifestyles in their later years.

Moreover, several of those who departed in 2004 — either to pursue other offices or seek careers in the private sector — were on the young end of the congressional spectrum. Among the prominent mid-career "retirees" were Illinois Republican Peter G. Fitzgerald, just 44 when he retired from the Senate after one term; Louisiana Democrat John B. Breaux, who ended a 32-year congressional career at age 60; Oklahoma Republican Don Nickles, who left after four Senate terms and was only 56; and California Democrat Cal Dooley, 50, who left the House after 14 years to head the National Food Processors Association. Colorado

Republican Scott McInnis, 51, retired from the House after a dozen years to become a land use lobbyist; and Pennsylvania Republican James C. Greenwood, 53, also left the House after 12 years to head the Biotechnology Industry Organization.

Not all outgoing House members were taking their credentials to the private sector: Increasing numbers were making the short move to the other side of the Capitol.

For the first time in at least a half-century, most senators previously served in the House. The number of senators with House experience had risen in each of the past six elections, from 40 a decade ago to 52 in 2005.

### TRANSITIONAL POLITICS

This group included six of the nine senators first elected in 2004: Republicans Richard M. Burr of North Carolina, Jim DeMint of South Carolina, David Vitter of Louisiana, Johnny Isakson of Georgia, John Thune of South Dakota and Tom Coburn of Oklahoma. The first four segued directly from the House; Thune had left the House in 2002 to make his first Senate bid, while Coburn did not seek a fourth House term in 2000 to uphold a term limit pledge.

The attractions of serving in the Senate were obvious to many ambitious House members. One senator among 100 drew greater individual attention, served a longer term and routinely wielded more influence over the legislative process than one of 435 House members.

That was especially true for the more-junior House members, who had not accumulated seniority and who were more likely to run for the Senate than senior members in established positions of legislative power.

"Generally speaking, the House is not a very attractive place for a rank-and-file legislator," said Steven Smith, the director of the Weidenbaum Center on the Economy, Government, and Public Policy at Washington University in St. Louis. "You need substantial seniority to get up in the committee system and up in the party leadership to have much influence on matters in the House."

House rule changes instituted by the Republican majority, which tempered the benefits of seniority, also may have dampened members' desire to stay there.

"At one time, long-term House membership was a very attractive political career, and that may not satisfy people as much, especially when you have limited terms of committee chairs and where power no longer rests with committees the way it once did," said Bruce Oppenheimer, a political scientist at Vanderbilt University.

Gary C. Jacobson, a political scientist at the University of California at San Diego, attributed the escalation more to newfound opportunities for some House members to run for Senate — not to a magnified interest in serving on the Capitol's north side.

The political realignment of the South from a Democratic bastion to a Republican-leaning region provided ample opportunities for House Republicans. In 2004, the GOP won all six Southern Senate seats that incumbents were not defending; five were won by candidates with House experience.

Smith said that more muscular recruitment efforts by the Senate campaign committees also could explain why there were more senators with House experience.

Campaign committees, which once raised money for incumbents and did little else, had become sophisticated political organizations that made recruitment a top priority. And House members had proved proficient at winning elections and raising the millions of dollars needed in high-priced campaigns.

"It may be that House members are already well positioned, with the relationships they have with PACs doing business in Washington," Oppenheimer said. "Maybe they have an edge over people who are in other offices who might think about running for the Senate."

## RACE AND GENDER DYNAMICS

There were several ways of looking at the overall gender and racial demographics of Congress. On the one hand, they had changed only marginally: The congressional membership still had a disproportionate number of wealthy, well-educated, upper-middle-aged white men who came from backgrounds in law or business, with blacks, Hispanics and especially women represented in numbers lower than their percentages of the national population.

On the other hand, gains — steady, if slow — continued to be made in virtually every successive election cycle. There were more women in Congress at the outset of the 109th Congress than ever: 65 House members, plus the delegates from the District of Columbia, Guam and the Virgin Islands. That was an increase of five over the previous Congress.

Doris Matsui, a Democratic lobbyist, would soon fill the vacant seat created by the death of her husband, Robert, becoming the 67th

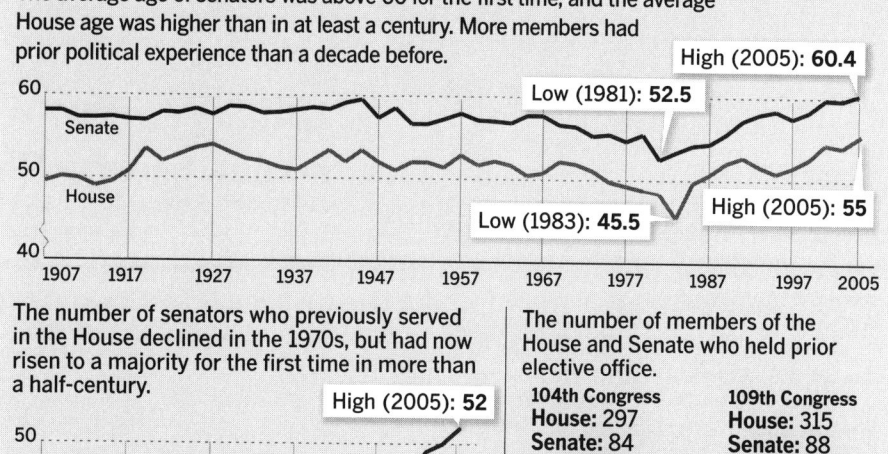

## Older . . . Wiser to Be Determined

The average age of senators was above 60 for the first time, and the average House age was higher than in at least a century. More members had prior political experience than a decade before.

High (2005): 60.4
Low (1981): 52.5
Senate
House
Low (1983): 45.5
High (2005): 55

1907 1917 1927 1937 1947 1957 1967 1977 1987 1997 2005

The number of senators who previously served in the House declined in the 1970s, but had now risen to a majority for the first time in more than a half-century.

High (2005): 52
Low (1979): 31

1955 1965 1975 1985 1995 2005

The number of members of the House and Senate who held prior elective office.

104th Congress
House: 297
Senate: 84
71%

109th Congress
House: 315
Senate: 88
75%

SOURCE: Statistics from before 1949 are from Congressional Research Service and Senate Historical Office.

woman in the House.

Prospects for increased representation of women in Congress appeared to be tied to their growing presence in state legislatures: Of the eight women freshmen in the House, all but one previously served as state lawmakers. Some saw an omen for the future in the fact that women hold 23 percent of all state legislative seats — a higher share than in the House (15 percent) or the Senate (14 percent). Women made up a greater share of the membership in 43 state legislatures than in Congress. Still, 51 percent of the U.S. population was female.

Women held their own in the Senate but gained no new ground. While all five women senators on the ballots won new terms, the five other women who were major party nominees were defeated.

Yet a woman's narrow loss was offset by a big advance for another group — Hispanics — in Florida, where Republican Mel Martinez edged Democrat Betty Castor by 1 percentage point. The elections of Martinez and Colorado Democrat Ken Salazar gave Hispanics their first Senate presence since Democrat Joseph M. Montoya of New Mexico left in 1977. This also was the first time there had been two Hispanic senators at the same time.

Adding to the Senate's diversity was the election of Barack Obama, the first black senator since another Illinois Democrat, Carol Moseley Braun, was defeated after one term in 1998 — and only the third ever popularly elected.

Although Hispanics were slightly more numerous than blacks in the population, they lagged in congressional representation: There were 40 blacks in the House (9 percent, as compared with 12.3 percent of the population) and 23 Hispanics (5 percent, vs. 12.5 percent of the population). Gains were slower for Hispanics largely because they were younger per capita and had lower levels of citizenship, voter registration and turnout than either blacks or non-Hispanic whites.

The number of black House members increased sharply in the early 1990s, when federal courts decreed that the Voting Rights Act required the drawing of heavily black House districts to remedy the effects of racial discrimination. But their numbers had increased only marginally in the past decade.

Success for African-American candidates was still typically found in

# Women and Minorities in the 109th Congress

Just 40 years earlier, women held a tiny share of the seats in Congress, and minorities had even fewer. The upward trend in their congressional ranks reflected tectonic shifts in American society in years since. Yet after a big spike in the early 1990s, gains for these groups had been gradual, and their representation in Congress remained below their proportions in the population at large. The most notable advances in the 2004 elections were in the Senate, which gained its first black member since 1999 and its first Hispanics since 1977.

## Blacks

**Senate (1 D)**
**Illinois:** Barack Obama, D

**House (40 D)**
**Alabama:** Artur Davis, D
**California:** Barbara Lee, D; Juanita Millender-McDonald, D; Maxine Waters, D; Diane Watson, D
**Florida:** Corinne Brown, D; Alcee L. Hastings, D; Kendrick B. Meek, D
**Georgia:** Sanford D. Bishop Jr., D; John Lewis, D; Cynthia A. McKinney, D; David Scott, D
**Illinois:** Danny K. Davis, D; Jesse L. Jackson Jr., D; Bobby L. Rush, D
**Indiana:** Julia Carson, D
**Louisiana:** William J. Jefferson, D
**Maryland:** Elijah E. Cummings, D; Albert R. Wynn, D
**Michigan:** John Conyers Jr., D; Carolyn Cheeks Kilpatrick, D
**Mississippi:** Bennie Thompson, D
**Missouri:** William Lacy Clay, D; Emanuel Cleaver II, D
**New Jersey:** Donald M. Payne, D
**New York:** Gregory W. Meeks, D; Major R. Owens, D; Charles B. Rangel, D; Edolphus Towns, D
**North Carolina:** G. K. Butterfield, D; Melvin Watt, D
**Ohio:** Stephanie Tubbs Jones, D
**Pennsylvania:** Chaka Fattah, D
**South Carolina:** James E. Clyburn, D
**Tennessee:** Harold E. Ford Jr., D
**Texas:** Al Green, D; Sheila Jackson-Lee, D; Eddie Bernice Johnson, D
**Virginia:** Robert C. Scott, D
**Wisconsin:** Gwen Moore, D

## Hispanics

**Senate (2; 1 R, 1 D)**
**Colorado:** Ken Salazar, D
**Florida:** Mel Martinez, R

**House (23; 19 D, 4 R)**
**Arizona:** Raúl M. Grijalva, D; Ed Pastor, D
**California:** Joe Baca, D; Xavier Becerra, D; Grace F. Napolitano, D; Lucille Roybal-Allard, D; Linda T. Sánchez, D; Loretta Sanchez, D; Hilda L. Solis, D
**Colorado:** John Salazar, D
**Florida:** Lincoln Diaz-Balart, R; Mario Diaz-Balart, R; Ileana Ros-Lehtinen, R
**Illinois:** Luis V. Gutierrez, D
**New Jersey:** Robert Menendez, D
**New York:** José E. Serrano, D; Nydia M. Velázquez, D
**Texas:** Henry Bonilla, R; Henry Cuellar, D; Charlie Gonzalez, D; Ruben Hinojosa, D; Solomon P. Ortiz, D; Silvestre Reyes, D

## Steady Gains, Seeking More

Women and minority members of the House and Senate, combined

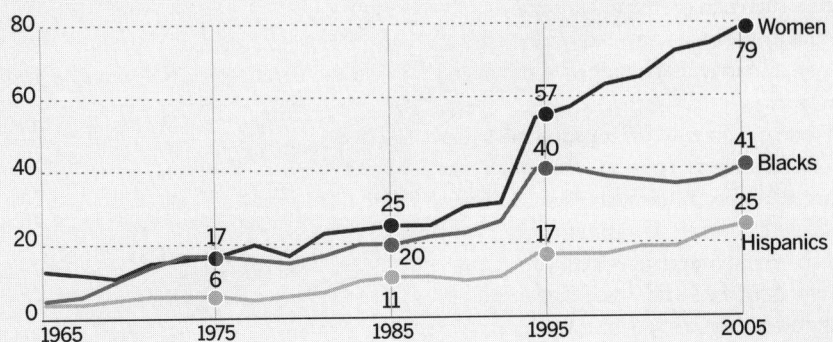

## Asians and Pacific Islanders

**Senate (2 D)**
**Hawaii:** Daniel K. Akaka, D; Daniel K. Inouye, D

**House (2 D)**
**California:** Michael M. Honda, D
**Oregon:** David Wu, D

## American Indians

**House (1 R)**
**Oklahoma:** Tom Cole, R

## Asian Indians

**House (1 R)**
**Louisiana:** Bobby Jindal, R

## Women

**Senate (14; 5 R, 9 D)**
**Alaska:** Lisa Murkowski, R
**Arkansas:** Blanche Lincoln, D
**California:** Barbara Boxer, D; Dianne Feinstein, D
**Louisiana:** Mary L. Landrieu, D
**Maine:** Susan Collins, R; Olympia J. Snowe, R
**Maryland:** Barbara A. Mikulski, D
**Michigan:** Debbie Stabenow, D
**New York:** Hillary Rodham Clinton, D
**North Carolina:** Elizabeth Dole, R
**Texas:** Kay Bailey Hutchison, R
**Washington:** Maria Cantwell, D; Patty Murray, D

**House (65; 23 R, 42 D)**
**California:** Mary Bono, R; Lois Capps, D; Susan A. Davis, D; Anna G. Eshoo, D; Jane Harman, D; Barbara Lee, D; Zoe Lofgren, D; Juanita Millender-McDonald, D; Grace F. Napolitano, D; Nancy Pelosi, D; Lucille Roybal-Allard, D; Linda T. Sánchez, D; Loretta Sanchez, D; Hilda L. Solis, D; Ellen O. Tauscher, D; Maxine Waters, D; Diane Watson, D; Lynn Woolsey, D
**Colorado:** Diana DeGette, D; Marilyn Musgrave, R
**Connecticut:** Rosa DeLauro, D; Nancy L. Johnson, R
**Florida:** Corinne Brown, D; Ginny Brown-Waite, R; Katherine Harris, R; Ileana Ros-Lehtinen, R Debbie Wasserman-Schultz, D
**Georgia:** Cynthia A. McKinney, D
**Illinois:** Melissa Bean, D; Judy Biggert, R; Jan Schakowsky, D
**Indiana:** Julia Carson, D
**Kentucky:** Anne M. Northup, R
**Michigan:** Carolyn Cheeks Kilpatrick, D; Candice S. Miller, R
**Minnesota:** Betty McCollum, D
**Missouri:** Jo Ann Emerson, R
**Nevada:** Shelley Berkley, D
**New Mexico:** Heather A. Wilson, R
**New York:** Sue W. Kelly, R; Nita M. Lowey, D; Carolyn B. Maloney, D; Carolyn McCarthy, D; Louise M. Slaughter, D; Nydia M. Velázquez, D
**North Carolina:** Virginia Foxx, R; Sue Myrick, R
**Ohio:** Stephanie Tubbs Jones, D; Marcy Kaptur, D; Deborah Pryce, R
**Oregon:** Darlene Hooley, D
**Pennsylvania:** Melissa A. Hart, R; Allyson Y. Schwartz, D
**South Dakota:** Stephanie Herseth, D
**Tennessee:** Marsha Blackburn, R
**Texas:** Kay Granger, R; Sheila Jackson-Lee, D; Eddie Bernice Johnson, D
**Virginia:** Jo Ann Davis, R; Thelma Drake, R
**Washington:** Cathy McMorris, R
**West Virginia:** Shelley Moore Capito, R
**Wisconsin:** Tammy Baldwin, D; Gwen Moore, D
**Wyoming:** Barbara Cubin, R

districts where they could tap a sizable black voter base. Black House members held all but four of the 37 House districts in which blacks made up at least one-third of the population — but just seven of the 398 other House seats across the nation.

Nonetheless, the 2004 election produced victories for a pair of big-city black Democrats whose districts did not have overwhelmingly minority populations. Democrat Emanuel Cleaver II, a former mayor of Kansas City, won in Missouri's 5th District, where the population was 24 percent black. There was precedent here: Black Democrat Alan Wheat held the Kansas City-based seat from 1983 to 1995.

Democrat Gwen Moore's victory in Wisconsin's 4th District was more of a breakthrough. She became Milwaukee's first black representative by winning in the open 4th District, where 33 percent of the residents were black. ∎

# Glossary of Congressional Terms

**Act** — The term for legislation once it has passed both chambers of Congress and has been signed by the president or passed over his veto, thus becoming law. Also used in parliamentary terminology for a bill that has been passed by one house and engrossed. (Also see engrossed bill.)

Adjournment sine die — Adjournment without a fixed day for reconvening — literally, "adjournment without a day." Usually used to connote the final adjournment of a session of Congress. A session can continue until noon Jan. 3 of the following year, when, under the 20th Amendment to the Constitution, it automatically terminates. Both chambers must agree to a concurrent resolution for either chamber to adjourn for more than three days.

**Adjournment to a day certain** — Adjournment under a motion or resolution that fixes the next time of meeting. Under the Constitution, neither chamber can adjourn for more than three days without the concurrence of the other. A session of Congress is not ended by adjournment to a day certain.

**Amendment** — A proposal by a member of Congress to alter the language, provisions or stipulations in a bill or in another amendment. An amendment usually is printed, debated and voted upon in the same manner as a bill.

Amendment in the nature of a substitute — Usually an amendment that seeks to replace the entire text of a bill by striking out everything after the enacting clause and inserting a new version of the bill. An amendment in the nature of a substitute can also refer to an amendment that replaces a large portion of the text of a bill.

**Appeal** — A member's challenge of a ruling or decision made by the presiding officer of the chamber. A senator can appeal to members of the Senate to override the decision. If carried by a majority vote, the appeal nullifies the chair's ruling. In the House, the decision of the Speaker traditionally has been final; seldom are there appeals to the members to reverse the Speaker's stand. To appeal a ruling is considered an attack on the Speaker.

**Appropriations bill** — A bill that gives legal authority to spend or obligate money from the Treasury. The Constitution disallows money to be drawn from the Treasury "but in Consequence of Appropriations made by Law."

By congressional custom, an appropriations bill originates in the House. It is not supposed to be considered by the full House or Senate until a related measure authorizing the funding is enacted. An appropriations bill grants the actual budget authority approved by the authorization bill, though not necessarily the full amount permissible under the authorization.

If the 11 regular appropriations bills are not enacted by the start of the fiscal year, Congress must pass a stopgap spending bill or the departments and agencies covered by the unfinished bills must shut down.

About half of all budget authority, notably that for Social Security and interest on the federal debt, does not require annual appropriations; those programs exist under permanent appropriations. (Also see authorization bill, budget authority, budget process and supplemental appropriations bill.)

**Authorization bill** — Basic, substantive legislation that establishes or continues the legal operation of a federal program or agency either indefinitely or for a specific period of time, or which sanctions a particular type of obligation or expenditure. Under the rules of both chambers, appropriations for a program or agency may not be considered until the program has been authorized, although this requirement is often waived.

An authorization sets the maximum amount of funds that can be given to a program or agency, although sometimes it merely authorizes "such sums as may be necessary." (Also see backdoor spending authority.)

**Backdoor spending authority** — Budget authority provided in legislation outside the normal appropriations process. The most common forms of backdoor spending are borrowing authority, contract authority, entitlements and loan guarantees that commit the government to payments of principal and interest on loans — such as guaranteed student loans — made by banks or other private lenders. Loan guarantees result in actual outlays only when there is a default by the borrower.

In some cases, such as interest on the public debt, a permanent appropriation is provided that becomes available without further action by Congress.

**Bills** — Most legislative proposals before Congress are in the form of bills and are designated according to the chamber in which they originate — HR in the House of Representatives or S in the Senate — and by a number assigned in the order in which they are introduced during the two-year period of a congressional term.

"Public bills" address general questions and become public laws if they are cleared by Congress and signed by the president. "Private bills" deal with individual matters, such as claims against the government, immigration and naturalization cases or land titles, and become private laws if approved and signed. (Also see private bills, resolution.)

**Bills introduced** — In both the House and Senate, any number of members may join in introducing a single bill or resolution. The first member listed is the sponsor of the bill, and all subsequent members listed are cosponsors.

Many bills are committee bills and are introduced under the name of the chairman of the committee or subcommittee. All appropriations bills fall into this category. A committee frequently holds hearings on a number of related bills and may agree to one of them or to an entirely new bill. (Also see clean bill.)

**Bills referred** — After a bill is introduced, it is referred to the committee or committees that have jurisdiction over the subject with which the bill is concerned. Under the standing rules of the House and Senate, bills are referred by the Speaker in the House and by the presiding officer in the Senate. In practice, the House and Senate parliamentarians act for these officials and refer the vast majority of bills. (Also see discharge a committee.)

**Borrowing authority** — Statutory authority that permits a federal agency to incur obligations and make payments for specified purposes with borrowed money.

**Budget** — The document sent to Congress by the president early each year estimating government revenue and expenditures for the ensuing fiscal year.

**Budget Act** — The common name for the Congressional Budget and Impoundment Control Act of 1974, which established the current budget process and created the Congressional Budget Office. The act also put limits on presidential authority to spend appropriated money. It has undergone several major revisions since 1974. *(Also see budget process, impoundments.)*

**Budget authority** — Authority for federal agencies to enter into obligations that result in immediate or future outlays. The basic forms of budget authority are appropriations, contract authority and borrowing authority. Budget authority may be classified by (1) the period of availability (one-year, multiple-year or without a time limitation), (2) the timing of congressional action (current or permanent) or (3) the manner of determining the amount available (definite or indefinite). *(Also see appropriations, outlays.)*

**Budget process** — The annual budget process was created by the Congressional Budget and Impoundment Control Act of 1974, with a timetable that was modified in 1990. Under the law, the president must submit his proposed budget by the first Monday in February. Congress is supposed to complete an annual budget resolution by April 15, setting guidelines for congressional action on spending and tax measures.

Budget rules enacted in the 1990 Budget Enforcement Act and updated in 1993 and 1997 set caps on discretionary spending through fiscal 2002. The caps could be adjusted annually to account for changes in the economy and other limited factors. In addition, pay-as-you-go (PAYGO) rules required that any tax cut, new entitlement program or expansion of existing entitlement benefits that would increase a deficit be offset by an increase in taxes or a cut in entitlement spending.

The rules held Congress harmless for budget-deficit increases that lawmakers did not explicitly cause — for example, increases due to a recession or to an expansion in the number of beneficiaries qualifying for Medicare or food stamps. PAYGO did not apply when there was a budget surplus.

If Congress exceeded the discretionary spending caps in its appropriations bills, the law required an across-the-board cut — known as a sequester — in non-exempt discretionary spending accounts. If Congress violated the PAYGO rules, entitlement programs were subject to a sequester. Supplemental appropriations were subject to similar controls, with the proviso that if both Congress and the president agreed, spending designated as an emergency could exceed the caps.

**Budget resolution** — A concurrent resolution that is passed by both chambers of Congress but does not require the president's signature. The measure sets a strict ceiling on discretionary budget authority, along with non-binding recommendations about how the spending should be allocated. The budget resolution may also contain "reconciliation instructions" requiring authorizing and tax-writing committees to propose changes in existing law to meet deficit-reduction goals. The Budget Committee in each chamber then bundles those proposals into a reconciliation bill and sends it to the floor. *(Also see reconciliation.)*

**By request** — A phrase used when a senator or representative introduces a bill at the request of an executive agency or private organization but does not necessarily endorse the legislation.

**Calendar** — An agenda or list of business awaiting possible action by each chamber. The House uses six legislative calendars. They are the Consent, Corrections, Discharge, House, Private and Union calendars. *(Also see individual listings.)*

In the Senate, all legislative matters reported from committee go on one calendar. They are listed there in the order in which committees report them or the Senate places them on the calendar, but they may be called up out of order by the majority leader, either by obtaining unanimous consent of the Senate or by a motion to call up a bill. The Senate also has one non-legislative calendar, which is used for treaties and nominations. *(Also see executive calendar.)*

**Call of the calendar** — Senate bills that are not brought up for debate by a motion, unanimous consent or a unanimous consent agreement are brought before the Senate for action when the calendar listing them is "called." Bills must be called in the order listed. Measures considered by this method usually are non-controversial, and debate on the bill and any proposed amendments is limited to five minutes for each senator.

**Chamber** — The meeting place for the membership of either the House or the Senate; also the membership of the House or Senate meeting as such.

**Clean bill** — Frequently after a committee has finished a major revision of a bill, one of the committee members, usually the chairman, will assemble the changes and what is left of the original bill into a new measure and introduce it as a "clean bill." The revised measure, which is given a new number, is referred back to the committee, which reports it to the floor for consideration. This often is a timesaver, as committee-recommended changes in a clean bill do not have to be considered and voted on by the chamber. Reporting a clean bill also protects committee amendments that could be subject to points of order concerning germaneness.

**Clerk of the House** — An officer of the House of Representatives who supervises its records and legislative business. Many former administrative duties were transferred in 1992 to a new position, the director of non-legislative and financial services.

**Cloture** — The process by which a filibuster can be ended in the Senate other than by unanimous consent. A motion for cloture can apply to any measure before the Senate, including a proposal to change the chamber's rules. A cloture motion requires the signatures of 16 senators to be introduced. To end a filibuster, the cloture motion must obtain the votes of three-fifths of the entire Senate membership (60 if there are no vacancies), except when the filibuster is against a proposal to amend the standing rules of the Senate and a two-thirds vote of senators present and voting is required.

The cloture request is put to a roll call vote one hour after the Senate meets on the second day following introduction of the motion. If approved, cloture limits each senator to one hour of debate. The bill or amendment in question comes to a final vote after 30 hours of consideration, including debate time and the time it takes to conduct roll calls, quorum calls and other procedural motions. *(Also see filibuster.)*

**Committee** — A division of the House or Senate that prepares legislation for action by the parent chamber or makes investigations as directed by the parent chamber.

There are several types of committees. Most standing committees are divided into subcommittees, which study legislation, hold hearings and report bills, with or without amendments, to the full committee. Only the full committee can report legislation for action by the House or Senate. *(Also see standing, oversight, select and special committees.)*

**Committee of the Whole** — The working title of what is formally "The Committee of the Whole House [of Representatives] on the State of the Union." The membership is composed of all House members sitting as a committee. Any 100 members who are present on the floor of the chamber to consider legislation comprise a quorum of the committee. Any legislation, however, must first have passed through the regular legislative or appropriations committee and have been placed on the calendar.

Technically, the Committee of the Whole considers only bills directly or indirectly appropriating money, authorizing appropriations or involving taxes or charges on the public. Because the Committee of the Whole need number only 100 representatives, a quorum is more readily attained and legislative business is expedited. Before 1971, members' positions were not individually recorded on votes taken in the Committee of the Whole.

When the full House resolves itself into the Committee of the Whole, it replaces the Speaker with a "chairman." A measure is debated and amendments may be proposed, with votes on amendments as needed. *(Also see five-minute rule.)*

When the committee completes its work on the measure, it dissolves itself by "rising." The Speaker returns, and the chairman of the Committee of the Whole reports to the House that the committee's work has been completed. At this time, members may demand a roll call vote on any amendment adopted in the Committee of the Whole. The final vote is on passage of the legislation.

In 1993 and 1994, the four delegates from the territories and the resident commissioner of Puerto Rico were allowed to vote on questions before the Committee of the Whole. If their votes were decisive in the outcome, however, the matter was automatically re-voted, with the delegates and resident commissioner ineligible. They could vote on final passage of bills or on separate votes demanded after the Committee of the Whole rises. This limited voting right was rescinded in 1995.

**Committee veto** — A requirement added to a few statutes directing that certain policy directives by an executive department or agency be reviewed by certain congressional committees before they are implemented. Under common practice, the government department or agency and the committees involved are expected to reach a consensus before the directives are carried out. *(Also see legislative veto.)*

**Concurrent resolution** — A concurrent resolution, designated H Con Res or S Con Res, must be adopted by both chambers, but it is not sent to the president for approval and, therefore, does not have the force of law. A concurrent resolution, for example, is used to fix the time for adjournment of a Congress. It is also used to express the sense of Congress on a foreign policy or domestic issue. The annual budget resolution is a concurrent resolution.

**Conference** — A meeting between representatives of the House and the Senate to reconcile differences between the two chambers on provisions of a bill. Members of the conference committee are appointed by the Speaker and the presiding officer of the Senate.

A majority of the conferees for each chamber must agree on a compromise, reflected in a "conference report" before the final bill can go back to both chambers for approval. When the conference report goes to the floor, it is difficult to amend. If it is not approved by both chambers, the bill may go back to conference under certain situations, or a new conference may be convened. Many rules and informal practices govern the conduct of conference committees.

Bills that are passed by both chambers with only minor differences need not be sent to conference. Either chamber may "concur" with the other's amendments, completing action on the legislation. Sometimes leaders of the committees of jurisdiction work out an informal compromise instead of having a formal conference. *(Also see custody of the papers.)*

**Confirmations** — *(See nominations.)*

**Congressional Record** — The daily, printed account of proceedings in both the House and Senate chambers, showing substantially verbatim debate, statements and a record of floor action. Highlights of legislative and committee action are given in a Daily Digest section of the Record, and members are entitled to have their extraneous remarks printed in an appendix known as "Extension of Remarks." Members may edit and revise remarks made on the floor during debate, although the House in 1995 limited members to technical or grammatical changes.

The Congressional Record provides a way to distinguish remarks spoken on the floor of the House and Senate from undelivered speeches. In the Senate, all speeches, articles and other matter that members insert in the Record without actually reading them on the floor are set off by large black dots, or bullets. However, a loophole allows a member to avoid the bulleting if he or she delivers any portion of the speech in person. In the House, undelivered speeches and other material are printed in a distinctive typeface. The record is also available in electronic form. *(Also see Journal.)*

**Congressional terms of office** — Terms normally begin on Jan. 3 of the year following a general election. Terms are two years for representatives and six years for senators. Representatives elected in special elections are sworn in for the remainder of a term. Under most state laws, a person may be appointed to fill a Senate vacancy and serve until a successor is elected; the successor serves until the end of the term applying to the vacant seat.

**Consent Calendar** — Members of the House may place on this calendar most bills on the Union or House Calendar that are considered non-controversial. Bills on the Consent Calendar normally are called on the first and third Mondays of each month. On the first occasion that a bill is called in this manner, consideration may be blocked by the objection of any member. The second time, if there are three objections, the bill is stricken from the Consent Calendar. If fewer than three members object, the bill is given immediate consideration.

A member may also postpone action on the bill by asking that the measure be passed over "without prejudice." In that case, no objection is recorded against the bill and its status on the Consent Calendar remains unchanged. A bill stricken from the Consent Calendar remains on the Union or House Calendar. The Consent Calendar has seldom been used in recent years.

**Continuing resolution** — A joint resolution, cleared by Congress and signed by the president, to provide new budget authority for federal

agencies and programs until the regular appropriations bills have been enacted. Also known as "CRs" or continuing appropriations, continuing resolutions are used to keep agencies operating when, as often happens, Congress fails to finish the regular appropriations process by the start of the new fiscal year.

The CR usually specifies a maximum rate at which an agency may incur obligations, based on the rate of the prior year, the president's budget request or an appropriations bill passed by either or both chambers of Congress but not yet enacted.

**Contract authority** — Budget authority contained in an authorization bill that permits the federal government to enter into contracts or other obligations for future payments from funds not yet appropriated by Congress. The assumption is that funds will be provided in a subsequent appropriations act. *(Also see budget authority.)*

**Corrections Calendar, Corrections Day** — A House calendar established in 1995 to speed consideration of bills aimed at eliminating burdensome or unnecessary regulations. Bills on the Corrections Calendar can be called up on the second and fourth Tuesday of each month, called Corrections Day. They are subject to one hour of debate without amendment, and require a three-fifths majority for passage. *(Also see calendar.)*

**Correcting recorded votes** — Rules prohibit members from changing their votes after the result has been announced. Occasionally, however, a member may announce hours, days or months after a vote has been taken that he or she was "incorrectly recorded." In the Senate, a request to change one's vote almost always receives unanimous consent, as long as it does not change the outcome. In the House, members are prohibited from changing votes if they were tallied by the electronic voting system.

**Cosponsor** — *(See bills introduced.)*

**Current services estimates** — Estimated budget authority and outlays for federal programs and operations for the forthcoming fiscal year based on continuation of existing levels of service without policy changes but with adjustments for inflation and for demographic changes that affect programs. These estimates, accompanied by the underlying economic and policy assumptions upon which they are based, are transmitted by the president to Congress when the budget is submitted.

**Custody of the papers** — To reconcile differences between the House and Senate versions of a bill, a conference may be arranged. The chamber with "custody of the papers" — the engrossed bill, engrossed amendments, messages of transmittal — is the only body empowered to request the conference. By custom, the chamber that asks for a conference is the last to act on the conference report.

Custody of the papers sometimes is manipulated to ensure that a particular chamber acts either first or last on the conference report. *(Also see conference.)*

**Deferral** — Executive branch action to defer, or delay, the spending of appropriated money. The 1974 Congressional Budget and Impoundment Control Act requires a special message from the president to Congress reporting a proposed deferral of spending. Deferrals may not extend beyond the end of the fiscal year in which the message is trans-

mitted. A federal district court in 1986 struck down the president's authority to defer spending for policy reasons; the ruling was upheld by a federal appeals court in 1987. Congress can prohibit proposed deferrals by enacting a law doing so; most often, cancellations of proposed deferrals are included in appropriations bills. *(Also see rescission.)*

**Dilatory motion** — A motion made for the purpose of killing time and preventing action on a bill or amendment. House rules outlaw dilatory motions, but enforcement is largely within the discretion of the Speaker or chairman of the Committee of the Whole. The Senate does not have a rule barring dilatory motions except under cloture.

**Discharge a committee** — Occasionally, attempts are made to relieve a committee of jurisdiction over a bill that is before it. This is attempted more often in the House than in the Senate, and the procedure rarely is successful.

In the House, if a committee does not report a bill within 30 days after the measure is referred to it, any member may file a discharge motion. Once offered, the motion is treated as a petition needing the signatures of a majority of members (218 if there are no vacancies). After the required signatures have been obtained, there is a delay of seven days.

Thereafter, on the second and fourth Mondays of each month, except during the last six days of a session, any member who has signed the petition must be recognized, if he or she so desires, to move that the committee be discharged. Debate on the motion to discharge is limited to 20 minutes. If the motion is carried, consideration of the bill becomes a matter of high privilege.

If a resolution to consider a bill is held up in the Rules Committee for more than seven legislative days, any member may enter a motion to discharge the committee. The motion is handled like any other discharge petition in the House. Occasionally, to expedite non-controversial legislative business, a committee is discharged by unanimous consent of the House, and a petition is not required. In 1993, the signatures on pending discharge petitions — previously kept secret — were made a matter of public record. *(For Senate procedure, see discharge resolution.)*

**Discharge Calendar** — The House calendar to which motions to discharge committees are referred when they have the required number of signatures (218) and are awaiting floor action. *(Also see calendar.)*

**Discharge petition** — *(See discharge a committee.)*

**Discharge resolution** — In the Senate, a special motion that any senator may introduce to relieve a committee from consideration of a bill before it. The resolution can be called up for Senate approval or disapproval in the same manner as any other Senate business. *(For House procedure, see discharge a committee.)*

**Discretionary spending caps** — *(See budget process.)*

**Division of a question for voting** — A practice that is more common in the Senate but also used in the House whereby a member may demand a division of an amendment or a motion for purposes of voting. Where an amendment or motion can be divided, the individual parts are voted on separately when a member demands a division. This procedure occurs most often during the consideration of conference reports.

**Enacting clause** — Key phrase in bills beginning, "Be it enacted by

the Senate and House of Representatives . . . ." A successful motion to strike it from legislation kills the measure.

**Engrossed bill** — The final copy of a bill as passed by one chamber, with the text as amended by floor action and certified by the clerk of the House or the secretary of the Senate.

**Enrolled bill** — The final copy of a bill that has been passed in identical form by both chambers. It is certified by an officer of the chamber of origin (clerk of the House or secretary of the Senate) and then sent on for the signatures of the House Speaker, the Senate president pro tempore and the president of the United States. An enrolled bill is printed on parchment.

**Entitlement program** — A federal program that guarantees a certain level of benefits to people or other entities who meet requirements set by law. Examples include Social Security and unemployment benefits. Some entitlements have permanent appropriations; others are funded under annual appropriations bills. In either case, it is mandatory for Congress to provide the money.

**Executive Calendar** — A non-legislative calendar in the Senate that lists presidential documents such as treaties and nominations. *(Also see calendar.)*

**Executive document** — A document, usually a treaty, sent to the Senate by the president for consideration or approval. Executive documents are referred to committee in the same manner as other measures. Unlike legislative documents, treaties do not die at the end of a Congress but remain "live" proposals until acted on by the Senate or withdrawn by the president.

**Executive session** — A meeting of a Senate or House committee (or occasionally of either chamber) that only its members may attend. Witnesses regularly appear at committee meetings in executive session — for example, Defense Department officials during presentations of classified defense information. Other members of Congress may be invited, but the public and news media are not allowed to attend.

**Filibuster** — A time-delaying tactic associated with the Senate and used by a minority in an effort to prevent a vote on a bill or amendment that probably would pass if voted upon directly. The most common method is to take advantage of the Senate's rules permitting unlimited debate, but other forms of parliamentary maneuvering may be used.

The stricter rules of the House make filibusters more difficult, but delaying tactics are employed occasionally through various procedural devices allowed by House rules. *(Also see cloture.)*

**Fiscal year** — Financial operations of the government are carried out in a 12-month fiscal year, beginning Oct. 1 and ending Sept. 30. The fiscal year carries the date of the calendar year in which it ends. (From fiscal 1844 to fiscal 1976, the fiscal year began July 1 and ended the following June 30.)

**Five-minute rule** — A debate-limiting rule of the House that is invoked when the House sits as the Committee of the Whole. Under the rule, a member offering an amendment and a member opposing it are each allowed to speak for five minutes. Debate is then closed. In practice, amendments regularly are debated for more than 10 minutes, with members gaining the floor by offering pro forma amendments or obtaining unanimous consent to speak longer than five minutes. *(Also see Committee of the Whole, hour rule, strike out the last word.)*

**Floor manager** — A member who has the task of steering legislation through floor debate and amendment to a final vote in the House or the Senate. Floor managers usually are chairmen or ranking members of the committee that reported the bill. Managers are responsible for apportioning the debate time granted to supporters of the bill. The ranking minority member of the committee normally apportions time for the minority party's participation in the debate.

**Frank** — A member's facsimile signature, which is used on envelopes in lieu of stamps for the member's official outgoing mail. The "franking privilege" is the right to send mail postage-free.

**Germane** — Pertaining to the subject matter of the measure at hand. All House amendments must be germane to the bill being considered. The Senate requires that amendments be germane when they are proposed to general appropriations bills or to bills being considered once cloture has been adopted or, frequently, when the Senate is proceeding under a unanimous consent agreement placing a time limit on consideration of a bill. The 1974 budget act also requires that amendments to concurrent budget resolutions be germane.

In the House, floor debate must be germane, and the first three hours of debate each day in the Senate must be germane to the pending business.

**Gramm-Rudman-Hollings Deficit Reduction Act** — *(See sequester.)*

**Grandfather clause** — A provision that exempts people or other entities already engaged in an activity from new rules or legislation affecting that activity.

**Hearings** — Committee sessions for taking testimony from witnesses. At hearings on legislation, witnesses usually include specialists, government officials and spokesmen for individuals or entities affected by the bill or bills under study. Hearings related to special investigations bring forth a variety of witnesses. Committees sometimes use their subpoena power to summon reluctant witnesses. The public and news media may attend open hearings but are barred from closed, or "executive," hearings. The vast majority of hearings are open to the public. *(Also see executive session.)*

**Hold-harmless clause** — A provision added to legislation to ensure that recipients of federal funds do not receive less in a future year than they did in the current year if a new formula for allocating funds authorized in the legislation would result in a reduction to the recipients. This clause has been used most often to soften the impact of sudden reductions in federal grants.

**Hopper** — Box on House clerk's desk into which members deposit bills and resolutions to introduce them.

**Hour rule** — A provision in the rules of the House that permits one hour of debate time for each member on amendments debated in the House of Representatives sitting as the House. Therefore, the House normally amends bills while sitting as the Committee of the Whole, where the five-minute rule on amendments operates.

**House as in the Committee of the Whole** — A procedure that can be used to expedite consideration of certain measures such as continuing resolutions and, when there is debate, private bills. The procedure can be invoked only with the unanimous consent of the House or a rule from the Rules Committee and has procedural elements of both the House sitting as the House of Representatives, such as the Speaker presiding and the previous question motion being in order, and the House sitting as the Committee of the Whole, with the five-minute rule being in order. *(See Committee of the Whole.)*

**House Calendar** — A listing for action by the House of public bills that do not directly or indirectly appropriate money or raise revenue. *(Also see calendar.)*

**Immunity** — The constitutional privilege of members of Congress to make verbal statements on the floor and in committee for which they cannot be sued or arrested for slander or libel. Also, freedom from arrest while traveling to or from sessions of Congress or on official business. Members in this status may only be arrested for treason, felonies or a breach of the peace, as defined by congressional manuals.

**Joint committee** — A committee composed of a specified number of members of both the House and Senate. A joint committee may be investigative or research-oriented, an example of the latter being the Joint Economic Committee. Others have housekeeping duties; examples include the joint committees on Printing and the Library of Congress.

**Joint resolution** — Like a bill, a joint resolution, designated H J Res or S J Res, requires the approval of both chambers and the signature of the president, and has the force of law if approved. There is no practical difference between a bill and a joint resolution. A joint resolution generally is used to address a limited matter such as a single appropriation.

Joint resolutions are also used to propose amendments to the Constitution. In that case, they require a two-thirds majority in both chambers. They do not require a presidential signature, but they must be ratified by three-fourths of the states to become a part of the Constitution. *(Also see concurrent resolution, resolution.)*

**Journal** — The official record of the proceedings of the House and Senate. The Journal records the actions taken in each chamber, but, unlike the Congressional Record, it does not include the substantially verbatim report of speeches, debates, statements and the like.

**Law** — An act of Congress that has been signed by the president or passed, over his veto, by Congress. Public bills, when signed, become public laws and are cited by the letters PL and a hyphenated number. The number before the hyphen corresponds to the Congress, and the one or more digits after the hyphen refer to the numerical sequence in which the president signed the bills during that Congress. Private bills, when signed, become private laws. *(Also see bills, private bills.)*

**Legislative day** — The "day" extending from the time either chamber meets after an adjournment until the time it next adjourns. Because the House normally adjourns from day to day, legislative days and calendar days usually coincide. But in the Senate, a legislative day may, and frequently does, extend over several calendar days. *(Also see recess.)*

**Line-item veto** — Presidential authority to strike individual items from appropriations bills, which presidents since Ulysses S. Grant have sought. Congress gave the president a form of the power in 1996 (PL 104-130), but this "enhanced rescission authority" was struck down by the Supreme Court in 1998 as unconstitutional because it allowed the president to change laws on his own.

**Loan guarantees** — Loans to third parties for which the federal government guarantees the repayment of principal or interest, in whole or in part, to the lender in the event of default.

**Lobby** — A group seeking to influence the passage or defeat of legislation. Originally the term referred to people frequenting the lobbies or corridors of legislative chambers to speak to lawmakers.

The definition of a lobby and the activity of lobbying is a matter of differing interpretation. By some definitions, lobbying is limited to direct attempts to influence lawmakers through personal interviews and persuasion. Under other definitions, lobbying includes attempts at indirect, or "grass-roots," influence, such as persuading members of a group to write or visit their district's representative and state's senators or attempting to create a climate of opinion favorable to a desired legislative goal.

The right to attempt to influence legislation is based on the First Amendment to the Constitution, which says Congress shall make no law abridging the right of the people "to petition the government for a redress of grievances."

**Majority leader** — Floor leader for the majority party in each chamber. In the Senate, in consultation with the minority leader, the majority leader directs the legislative schedule for the chamber. He or she is also his party's spokesman and chief strategist. In the House, the majority leader is second to the Speaker in the majority party's leadership and serves as the party's legislative strategist. *(Also see Speaker, whip.)*

**Manual** — The official handbook in each chamber prescribing in detail its organization, procedures and operations.

**Marking up a bill** — Going through the contents of a piece of legislation in committee or subcommittee to, for example, consider the provisions, act on amendments to provisions and proposed revisions to the language, and insert new sections and phraseology. If the bill is extensively amended, the committee's version may be introduced as a separate (or "clean") bill, with a new number, before being considered by the full House or Senate. *(Also see clean bill.)*

**Minority leader** — Floor leader for the minority party in each chamber.

**Morning hour** — The time set aside at the beginning of each legislative day for the consideration of regular, routine business. The "hour" is of indefinite duration in the House, where it is rarely used. In the Senate, it is the first two hours of a session following an adjournment, as distinguished from a recess. The morning hour can be terminated earlier if the morning business has been completed.

Business includes such matters as messages from the president, communications from the heads of departments, messages from the House, the presentation of petitions, reports of standing and select committees and the introduction of bills and resolutions.

During the first hour of the morning hour in the Senate, no motion to proceed to the consideration of any bill on the calendar is

in order except by unanimous consent. During the second hour, motions can be made but must be decided without debate. Senate committees may meet while the Senate conducts the morning hour.

**Motion** — In the House or Senate chamber, a request by a member to institute any one of a wide array of parliamentary actions. He or she "moves" for a certain procedure, such as the consideration of a measure. The precedence of motions, and whether they are debatable, is set forth in the House and Senate manuals.

**Nominations** — Presidential appointments to office subject to Senate confirmation. Although most nominations win quick Senate approval, some are controversial and become the topic of hearings and debate. Sometimes senators object to appointees for patronage reasons — for example, when a nomination to a local federal job is made without consulting the senators of the state concerned. In some situations a senator may object that the nominee is "personally obnoxious" to him. Usually other senators join in blocking such appointments out of courtesy to their colleagues. *(Also see senatorial courtesy.)*

**One-minute speeches** — Addresses by House members at the beginning of a legislative day. The speeches may cover any subject but are limited to one minute's duration.

**Outlays** — Actual spending that flows from the liquidation of budget authority. Outlays associated with appropriations bills and other legislation are estimates of future spending made by the Congressional Budget Office (CBO) and the White House's Office of Management and Budget (OMB). CBO's estimates govern bills for the purpose of congressional floor debate, while OMB's numbers govern when it comes to determining whether legislation exceeds spending caps.

Outlays in a given fiscal year may result from budget authority provided in the current year or in previous years. *(Also see budget authority, budget process.)*

**Override a veto** — If the president vetoes a bill and sends it back to Congress with his objections, Congress may try to override his veto and enact the bill into law. Neither chamber is required to attempt to override a veto. The override of a veto requires a recorded vote with a two-thirds majority of those present and voting in each chamber. The question put to each chamber is: "Shall the bill pass, the objections of the president to the contrary notwithstanding?" *(Also see pocket veto, veto.)*

**Oversight committee** — A congressional committee or designated subcommittee that is charged with general oversight of one or more federal agencies' programs and activities. Usually, the oversight panel for a particular agency is also the authorizing committee for that agency's programs and operations.

**Pair** — A voluntary, informal arrangement that two lawmakers, usually on opposite sides of an issue, make on recorded votes. In many cases, the result is to subtract a vote from each side, with no effect on the outcome.

Pairs are not authorized in the rules of either chamber, are not counted in tabulating the final result and have no official standing. However, members pairing are identified in the Congressional Record, along with their positions on such votes, if known. A member who expects to be absent for a vote can pair with a member who plans to vote, with the latter agreeing to withhold his or her vote.

There are three types of pairs:

(1) A live pair involves a member who is present for a vote and another who is absent. The member in attendance votes and then withdraws the vote, announcing that he or she has a live pair with colleague "X" and stating how the two members would have voted, one in favor, the other opposed. A live pair may affect the outcome of a closely contested vote, since it subtracts one "yea" or one "nay" from the final tally. A live pair may cover one or several specific issues.

(2) A general pair, widely used in the House, does not entail any arrangement between two members and does not affect the vote. Members who expect to be absent notify the clerk that they wish to make a general pair. Each member then is paired with another desiring a pair, and their names are listed in the Congressional Record. The member may or may not be paired with another taking the opposite position, and no indication of how the members would have voted is given.

(3) A specific pair is similar to a general pair, except that the opposing stands of the two members are identified and printed in the Congressional Record.

**Pay-as-you go (PAYGO) rules** — *(See budget process.)*

**Petition** — A request or plea sent to one or both chambers from an organization or private citizens' group seeking support for particular legislation or favorable consideration of a matter not yet receiving congressional attention. Petitions are referred to appropriate committees. In the House, a petition signed by a majority of members (218) can discharge a bill from a committee. *(Also see discharge a committee.)*

**Pocket veto** — The act of the president in withholding his approval of a bill after Congress has adjourned. When Congress is in session, a bill becomes law without the president's signature if he does not act upon it within 10 days, excluding Sundays, from the time he receives it. But if Congress adjourns sine die within that 10-day period, the bill, if unsigned, will die even if the president does not formally veto it.

The Supreme Court in 1986 agreed to decide whether the president could pocket veto a bill during recesses and between sessions of the same Congress or only between Congresses. The justices in 1987 declared the case moot, however, because the bill in question was invalid once the case reached the court. *(Also see adjournment sine die, veto.)*

**Point of order** — An objection raised by a member that the chamber is departing from rules governing its conduct of business. The objector cites the rule violated, with the chair sustaining his or her objection if correctly made. Order is restored by the chair's suspending proceedings of the chamber until it conforms to the prescribed "order of business."

Both chambers have procedures for overcoming a point of order, either by vote or, what is most common in the House, by including language in the rule for floor consideration that waives a point of order against a given bill. *(Also see rules.)*

**President of the Senate** — Under the Constitution, the vice president of the United States presides over the Senate. In his absence, the president pro tempore, or a senator designated by the president pro tempore, presides over the chamber.

**President pro tempore** — The chief officer of the Senate in the absence of the vice president — literally, but loosely, the president for a time. The president pro tempore is elected by his fellow senators.

Recent practice has been to elect the senator of the majority party with the longest period of continuous service.

**Previous question** — A motion for the previous question, when carried, has the effect of cutting off all debate, preventing the offering of further amendments and forcing a vote on the pending matter. In the House, a motion for the previous question is not permitted in the Committee of the Whole, unless a rule governing debate provides otherwise. The motion for the previous question is a debate-limiting device and is not in order in the Senate.

**Printed amendment** — A House rule guarantees five minutes of floor debate in support and five minutes in opposition, and no other debate time, on amendments printed in the Congressional Record at least one day prior to the amendment's consideration in the Committee of the Whole.

In the Senate, while amendments may be submitted for printing, they have no parliamentary standing or status. An amendment submitted for printing in the Senate, however, may be called up by any senator.

**Private bill** — A bill dealing with individual matters, such as claims against the government, immigration or land titles. When a private bill is before the chamber, two members may block its consideration, thereby recommitting the bill to committee. The backers still have recourse, however. The measure can be put into an "omnibus claims bill" — several private bills rolled into one. As with any bill, no part of an omnibus claims bill may be deleted without a vote. When the private bill goes back to the House floor in this form, it can be deleted from the omnibus bill only by majority vote.

**Private Calendar** — The House calendar for private bills. The Private Calendar must be called on the first Tuesday of each month, and the Speaker may call it on the third Tuesday of each month as well. *(Also see calendar, private bill.)*

**Privileged questions** — The order in which bills, motions and other legislative measures are considered on the floor of the Senate and House is governed by strict priorities. A motion to table, for instance, is more privileged than a motion to recommit. Thus, if a member moves to recommit a bill to committee for further consideration, another member can supersede the first action by moving to table it, and a vote will occur on the motion to table (or kill) before the motion to recommit. A motion to adjourn is considered "of the highest privilege" and must be considered before virtually any other motion.

**Pro forma amendment** — *(See strike out the last word.)*

**Public Laws** — *(See law.)*

**Questions of privilege** — These are matters affecting members of Congress individually or collectively. Matters affecting the rights, safety, dignity and integrity of proceedings of the House or Senate as a whole are questions of privilege in both chambers.

Questions involving individual members are called questions of "personal privilege." A member rising to ask a question of personal privilege is given precedence over almost all other proceedings. For instance, if a member feels that he or she has been improperly impugned in comments by another member, he or she can immediately demand to be heard on the floor on a question of personal privilege. An annotation

in the House rules points out that the privilege rests primarily on the Constitution, which gives members a conditional immunity from arrest and an unconditional freedom to speak in the House.

In 1993, the House changed its rules to allow the Speaker to delay for two legislative days the floor consideration of a question of the privileges of the House unless it is offered by the majority leader or minority leader.

**Quorum** — The number of members whose presence is necessary for the transaction of business. In the Senate and House, it is a majority of the membership. In the Committee of the Whole House, a quorum is 100. If a point of order is made that a quorum is not present, the only business that is in order is either a motion to adjourn or a motion to direct the sergeant-at-arms to request the attendance of absentees. In practice, however, both chambers conduct much of their business without a quorum present. *(Also see Committee of the Whole House.)*

**Reading of bills** — Traditional parliamentary procedure required bills to be read three times before they were passed. This custom is of little modern significance. Normally a bill is considered to have its first reading when it is introduced and printed, by title, in the Congressional Record. In the House, a bill's second reading comes when floor consideration begins. (The actual reading of a bill is most likely to occur at this point, if at all.) The second reading in the Senate is supposed to occur on the legislative day after the measure is introduced, but before it is referred to committee. The third reading (again, usually by title) takes place when floor action has been completed on amendments.

**Recess** — A recess, as distinguished from adjournment, does not end a legislative day and therefore does not interrupt unfinished business. (The rules in each chamber set forth certain matters to be taken up and disposed of at the beginning of each legislative day.) The House usually adjourns from day to day. The Senate often recesses, thus meeting on the same legislative day for several calendar days or even weeks at a time.

**Recognition** — The power of recognition of a member is lodged in the Speaker of the House and the presiding officer of the Senate. The presiding officer names the member to speak first when two or more members simultaneously request recognition. The order of recognition is governed by precedents and tradition for many situations. In the Senate, for instance, the majority leader has the right to be recognized first.

**Recommit to committee** — A motion, made on the floor after a bill has been debated, to return it to the committee that reported it. If agreed to, recommittal usually is considered a death blow to the bill. In the House, the right to offer a motion to recommit is guaranteed to the minority leader or someone he or she designates.

A motion to recommit may include instructions to the committee to report the bill again with specific amendments or by a certain date. Or the instructions may direct that a particular study be made, with no definite deadline for further action.

If the recommittal motion includes instructions to "report the bill back forthwith" and the motion is adopted, floor action on the bill continues with the changes directed by the instructions automatically incorporated into the bill; the committee does not actually reconsider the legislation.

**Reconciliation** — The 1974 budget act created a "reconciliation" procedure for bringing existing tax and spending laws into con-

formity with ceilings set in the congressional budget resolution. Under the procedure, the budget resolution sets specific deficit-reduction targets and instructs tax-writing and authorizing committees to propose changes in existing law to meet those targets. Those recommendations are consolidated without change by the Budget committees into an omnibus reconciliation bill, which then must be considered and approved by both chambers of Congress.

Special rules in the Senate limit debate on a reconciliation bill to 20 hours and bar extraneous or non-germane amendments. (Also see budget resolution, sequester.)

**Reconsider a vote** — Until it is disposed of, a motion to reconsider the vote by which an action was taken has the effect of putting the action in abeyance. In the Senate, the motion can be made only by a member who voted on the prevailing side of the original question or by a member who did not vote at all. In the House, it can be made only by a member on the prevailing side.

A common practice in the Senate after close votes on an issue is a motion to reconsider, followed by a motion to table the motion to reconsider. On this motion to table, senators vote as they voted on the original question, which allows the motion to table to prevail, assuming there are no switches. That closes the matter, and further motions to reconsider are not entertained.

In the House, as a routine precaution, a motion to reconsider usually is made every time a measure is passed. Such a motion almost always is tabled immediately, thus shutting off the possibility of future reconsideration except by unanimous consent.

Motions to reconsider must be entered in the Senate within the next two days the Senate is in session after the original vote has been taken. In the House, they must be entered either on the same day or on the next succeeding day the House is in session. Sometimes on a close vote, a member will switch his or her vote to be eligible to offer a motion to reconsider.

**Recorded vote** — A vote upon which each member's stand is individually made known. In the Senate, this is accomplished through a roll call of the entire membership, to which each senator on the floor must answer "yea," "nay" or "present." Since January 1973, the House has used an electronic voting system for recorded votes, including yea-and-nay votes formerly taken by roll calls.

When not required by the Constitution, a recorded vote can be obtained on questions in the House on the demand of one-fifth (44 members) of a quorum or one-fourth (25) of a quorum in the Committee of the Whole. Recorded votes are required in the House for appropriations, budget and tax bills. (Also see yeas and nays.)

**Report** — Both a verb and a noun as a congressional term. A committee that has been examining a bill referred to it by the parent chamber "reports" its findings and recommendations to the chamber when it completes consideration and returns the measure. The process is called "reporting" a bill. In some cases, a bill is reported without a written report.

A "report" is the document setting forth the committee's explanation of its action. Senate and House reports are numbered separately and are designated S Rept or H Rept. When a committee report is not unanimous, the dissenting committee members may file a statement of their views, called minority or dissenting views and referred to as a minority report. Members in disagreement with some provisions of a bill may file additional or supplementary views. Sometimes a bill is reported without a committee recommendation.

Legislative committees occasionally submit adverse reports. However, when a committee is opposed to a bill, it usually fails to report the bill at all. Some laws require that committee reports — favorable or adverse — be made.

**Rescission** — Cancellation of budget authority that was previously appropriated but has not yet been spent.

**Resolution** — A "simple" resolution, designated H Res or S Res, deals with matters entirely within the prerogatives of a single chamber. It requires neither passage by the other chamber nor approval by the president, and it does not have the force of law. Most resolutions deal with the rules or procedures of one chamber. They are also used to express the sentiments of a single chamber, such as condolences to the family of a deceased member, or to comment on foreign policy or executive business. A simple resolution is the vehicle for a "rule" from the House Rules Committee. (Also see concurrent and joint resolutions, rules.)

**Rider** — An amendment, usually not germane, that its sponsor hopes to get through more easily by including it in other legislation. A rider becomes law if the bill to which it is attached is enacted. Amendments providing legislative directives in appropriations bills are examples of riders, although technically legislation is banned from appropriations bills.

The House, unlike the Senate, has a strict germaneness rule; thus, riders usually are Senate devices to get legislation enacted quickly or to bypass lengthy House consideration and, possibly, opposition.

**Rules** — Each chamber has a body of rules and precedents that govern the conduct of business. These rules deal with issues such as duties of officers, the order of business, admission to the floor, parliamentary procedures on handling amendments and voting, and jurisdictions of committees. They are normally changed only at the start of each Congress.

In the House, a rule may also be a resolution reported by the Rules Committee to govern the handling of a particular bill on the floor. The committee may report a rule, also called a special order, in the form of a simple resolution. If the House adopts the resolution, the temporary rule becomes as valid as any standing rule and lapses only after action has been completed on the measure to which it pertains.

The rule sets the time limit on general debate. It may also waive points of order against provisions of the bill in question such as non-germane language or against certain amendments expected on the floor. It may even forbid all amendments or all amendments except those proposed by the legislative committee that handled the bill. In this instance, it is known as a "closed" rule as opposed to an "open" rule, which puts no limitation on floor amendments, thus leaving the bill completely open to alteration by the adoption of germane amendments. (Also see point of order.)

**Secretary of the Senate** — Chief administrative officer of the Senate, responsible for overseeing the duties of Senate employees, educating Senate pages, administering oaths, overseeing the registration of lobbyists and handling other tasks necessary for the continuing operation of the Senate. (Also see Clerk of the House.)

**Select or special committee** — A committee set up for a special purpose and, usually, for a limited time by resolution of either the House

or Senate. Most special committees are investigative and lack legislative authority: Legislation is not referred to them, and they cannot report bills to their parent chambers.

**Senatorial courtesy** — A general practice with no written rule — sometimes referred to as "the courtesy of the Senate" — applied to consideration of executive nominations. Generally, it means that nominations from a state are not to be confirmed unless they have been approved by the senators of the president's party of that state, with other senators following their colleagues' lead in the attitude they take toward consideration of such nominations. *(Also see nominations.)*

**Sequester** — Automatic, across-the-board spending cuts, generally triggered after the close of a session by a report issued by the Office of Management and Budget. Under the 1985 Gramm-Rudman-Hollings anti-deficit law, modified in 1987, a year-end sequester was triggered if the deficit exceeded a pre-set maximum. However, the Budget Enforcement Act of 1990, updated in 1993 and 1997, effectively replaced that procedure through fiscal 2002.

Instead, if Congress exceeded an annual cap on discretionary budget authority or outlays, a sequester was triggered for all eligible discretionary spending to make up the difference. If Congress violated pay-as-you-go rules by allowing the net effect of legislated changes in mandatory spending and taxes to increase the deficit, a sequester was triggered for all non-exempt entitlement programs. Similar procedures applied to supplemental appropriations bills. *(Also see budget process.)*

**Sine die** — *(See adjournment sine die.)*

**Speaker** — The presiding officer of the House of Representatives, selected by his party caucus and formally elected by the whole House. While both parties nominate candidates, choice by the majority party is tantamount to election. In 1995, House rules were changed to limit the Speaker to four consecutive terms.

**Special session** — A session of Congress after it has adjourned sine die, completing its regular session. Special sessions are convened by the president.

**Spending authority** — The 1974 budget act defines spending authority as borrowing authority, contract authority and entitlement authority for which budget authority is not provided in advance by appropriation acts.

**Sponsor** — *(See bills introduced.)*

**Standing committees** — Committees that are permanently established by House and Senate rules. The standing committees of the House were reorganized in 1974, with some changes in jurisdictions and titles made when Republicans took control of the House in 1995. The last major realignment of Senate committees was in 1977. The standing committees are legislative committees: Legislation may be referred to them, and they may report bills and resolutions to their parent chambers.

**Standing vote** — A non-recorded vote used in both the House and Senate. (A standing vote is also called a division vote.) Members in favor of a proposal stand and are counted by the presiding officer. Then members opposed stand and are counted. There is no record of how individual members voted.

**Statutes at large** — A chronological arrangement of the laws enacted in each session of Congress. Though indexed, the laws are not arranged by subject matter, and there is no indication of how they changed previously enacted laws. *(Also see law, U.S. Code.)*

**Strike from the Record** — A member of the House who is offended by remarks made on the House floor may move that the offending words be "taken down" for the Speaker's cognizance and then expunged from the debate as published in the Congressional Record.

**Strike out the last word** — A motion whereby a House member is entitled to speak for five minutes on an amendment then being debated by the chamber. A member gains recognition from the chair by moving to "strike out the last word" of the amendment or section of the bill under consideration. The motion is pro forma, requires no vote and does not change the amendment being debated. *(Also see five-minute rule.)*

**Substitute** — A motion, amendment or entire bill introduced in place of the pending legislative business. Passage of the substitute kills the original measure by supplanting it. The substitute may also be amended. *(Also see amendment in the nature of a substitute.)*

**Supplemental appropriations bill** — Legislation appropriating funds after the regular annual appropriations bill for a federal department or agency has been enacted. Supplemental appropriations bills often arrive about halfway through the fiscal year, when needs that Congress and the president did not anticipate (or may not have wanted to fund) become pressing. In recent years, supplementals have been driven by spending to help victims of natural disasters and to carry out peacekeeping commitments.

**Suspend the rules** — A time-saving procedure for passing bills in the House. The wording of the motion, which may be made by any member recognized by the Speaker, is: "I move to suspend the rules and pass the bill . . . ." A favorable vote by two-thirds of those present is required for passage. Debate is limited to 40 minutes, and no amendments from the floor are permitted. If a two-thirds favorable vote is not attained, the bill may be considered later under regular procedures. The suspension procedure is in order every Monday and Tuesday and is intended to be reserved for non-controversial bills.

**Table a bill** — Motions to table, or to "lay on the table," are used to block or kill amendments or other parliamentary questions. When approved, a tabling motion is considered the final disposition of that issue. One of the most widely used parliamentary procedures, the motion to table is not debatable, and adoption requires a simple majority vote.

In the Senate, however, different language sometimes is used. The motion may be worded to let a bill "lie on the table," perhaps for subsequent "picking up." This motion is more flexible, keeping the bill pending for later action, if desired. Tabling motions on amendments are effective debate-ending devices in the Senate.

**Treaties** — Executive proposals — in the form of resolutions of ratification — which must be submitted to the Senate for approval by two-thirds of the senators present. Treaties are normally sent to the Foreign Relations Committee for scrutiny before the Senate takes action. Foreign Relations has jurisdiction over all treaties, regardless of the subject matter. Treaties are read three times and debated on the floor in

much the same manner as legislative proposals. After approval by the Senate, treaties are formally ratified by the president.

**Trust funds** — Funds collected and used by the federal government for carrying out specific purposes and programs according to terms of a trust agreement or statute such as the Social Security and unemployment compensation trust funds. Such funds are administered by the government in a fiduciary capacity and are not available for the general purposes of the government.

**Unanimous consent** — A procedure used to expedite floor action. Proceedings of the House or Senate and action on legislation often take place upon the unanimous consent of the chamber, whether or not a rule of the chamber is being violated. It is frequently used in a routine fashion, such as by a senator requesting the unanimous consent of the Senate to have specified members of his or her staff present on the floor during debate on a specific amendment. A single member's objection blocks a unanimous consent request.

**Unanimous consent agreement** — A device used in the Senate to expedite legislation. Much of the Senate's legislative business, dealing with both minor and controversial issues, is conducted through unanimous consent or unanimous consent agreements. On major legislation, such agreements usually are printed and transmitted to all senators in advance of floor debate. Once agreed to, they are binding on all members unless the Senate, by unanimous consent, agrees to modify them. An agreement may list the order in which various bills are to be considered; specify the length of time for debate on bills and contested amendments and when they are to be voted upon; and, frequently, require that all amendments introduced be germane to the bill under consideration.

In this regard, unanimous consent agreements are similar to the "rules" issued by the House Rules Committee for bills pending in the House.

**Union Calendar** — Bills that directly or indirectly appropriate money or raise revenue are placed on this House calendar according to the date they are reported from committee. *(Also see calendar.)*

**U.S. Code** — A consolidation and codification of the general and permanent laws of the United States arranged by subject under 50 titles, the first six dealing with general or political subjects, and the other 44

alphabetically arranged from agriculture to war. The U.S. Code is updated annually, and a new set of bound volumes is published every six years. *(Also see law, statutes at large.)*

**Veto** — Disapproval by the president of a bill or joint resolution (other than one proposing an amendment to the Constitution). When Congress is in session, the president must veto a bill within 10 days, excluding Sundays, after he has received it; otherwise, it becomes law without his signature. When the president vetoes a bill, he returns it to the chamber of origin along with a message stating his objections. *(Also see pocket veto, override a veto.)*

**Voice vote** — In either the House or Senate, members answer "aye" or "no" in chorus, and the presiding officer decides the result. The term is also used loosely to indicate action by unanimous consent or without objection. *(Also see yeas and nays.)*

**Whip** — In effect, the assistant majority or minority leader, in either the House or Senate. His or her job is to help marshal votes in support of party strategy and legislation.

**Without objection** — Used in lieu of a vote on non-controversial motions, amendments or bills that may be passed in either chamber if no member voices an objection.

**Yeas and nays** — The Constitution requires that yea-and-nay votes be taken and recorded when requested by one-fifth of the members present. In the House, the Speaker determines whether one-fifth of the members present requested a vote. In the Senate, practice requires only 11 members. The Constitution requires the yeas and nays on a veto override attempt. *(Also see recorded vote.)*

**Yielding** — When a member has been recognized to speak, no other member may speak unless he or she obtains permission from the member recognized. This permission is called yielding and usually is requested in the form, "Will the gentleman (or gentlelady) yield to me?" While this activity occasionally is seen in the Senate, the Senate has no rule or practice to parcel out time.

In the House, the floor manager of a bill usually apportions debate time by yielding specific amounts of time to members who have requested it. ■

# Members of the 109th Congress, 1st Session . . .

*As of Dec. 22, 2005, when the Senate adjourned sine die.*

## Representatives
### R 231; D 202; I 1
### 1 vacancy

### — A —

Abercrombie, Neil, D-Hawaii (1)
Ackerman, Gary L., D-N.Y. (5)
Aderholt, Robert B., R-Ala. (4)
Akin, Todd, R-Mo. (2)
Alexander, Rodney, R-La. (5)
Allen, Tom, D-Maine (1)
Andrews, Robert E., D-N.J. (1)

### — B —

Baca, Joe, D-Calif. (43)
Bachus, Spencer, R-Ala. (6)
Baird, Brian, D-Wash. (3)
Baker, Richard H., R-La. (6)
Baldwin, Tammy, D-Wis. (2)
Barrett, J. Gresham, R-S.C. (3)
Barrow, John, D-Ga. (12)
Bartlett, Roscoe G., R-Md. (6)
Barton, Joe L., R-Texas (6)
Bass, Charles, R-N.H. (2)
Bean, Melissa, D-Ill. (8)
Beauprez, Bob, R-Colo. (7)
Becerra, Xavier, D-Calif. (31)
Berkley, Shelley, D-Nev. (1)
Berman, Howard L., D-Calif. (28)
Berry, Marion, D-Ark. (1)
Biggert, Judy, R-Ill. (13)
Bilirakis, Michael, R-Fla. (9)
Bishop, Rob, R-Utah (1)
Bishop, Sanford D. Jr., D-Ga. (2)
Bishop, Timothy H., D-N.Y. (1)
Blackburn, Marsha, R-Tenn. (7)
Blumenauer, Earl, D-Ore. (3)
Blunt, Roy, R-Mo. (7)
Boehlert, Sherwood, R-N.Y. (24)
Boehner, John A., R-Ohio (8)
Bonilla, Henry, R-Texas (23)
Bonner, Jo, R-Ala. (1)
Bono, Mary, R-Calif. (45)
Boozman, John, R-Ark. (3)
Boren, Dan, D-Okla. (2)
Boswell, Leonard L., D-Iowa (3)
Boucher, Rick, D-Va. (9)
Boustany, Charles Jr., R-La. (7)
Boyd, Allen, D-Fla. (2)
Bradley, Jeb, R-N.H. (1)
Brady, Kevin, R-Texas (8)
Brady, Robert A., D-Pa. (1)
Brown, Corrine, D-Fla. (3)
Brown, Henry E. Jr., R-S.C. (1)
Brown, Sherrod, D-Ohio (13)
Brown-Waite, Ginny, R-Fla. (5)
Burgess, Michael C., R-Texas (26)
Burton, Dan, R-Ind. (5)
Butterfield, G.K., D-N.C. (1)
Buyer, Steve, R-Ind. (4)

### — C —

Calvert, Ken, R-Calif. (44)
Camp, Dave, R-Mich. (4)
Campbell, John, R-Calif. (48)
Cannon, Chris, R-Utah (3)
Cantor, Eric, R-Va. (7)
Capito, Shelley Moore, R-W.Va. (2)
Capps, Lois, D-Calif. (23)
Capuano, Michael E., D-Mass. (8)
Cardin, Benjamin L., D-Md. (3)
Cardoza, Dennis, D-Calif. (18)
Carnahan, Russ, D-Mo. (3)
Carson, Julia, D-Ind. (7)
Carter, John, R-Texas (31)
Case, Ed, D-Hawaii (2)
Castle, Michael N., R-Del. (AL)
Chabot, Steve, R-Ohio (1)
Chandler, Ben, D-Ky. (6)
Chocola, Chris, R-Ind. (2)

Clay, William Lacy, D-Mo. (1)
Cleaver, Emanuel II, D-Mo. (5)
Clyburn, James E., D-S.C. (6)
Coble, Howard, R-N.C. (6)
Cole, Tom, R-Okla. (4)
Conaway, K. Michael, R-Texas (11)
Conyers, John Jr., D-Mich. (14)
Cooper, Jim, D-Tenn. (5)
Costa, Jim, D-Calif. (20)
Costello, Jerry F., D-Ill. (12)
Cramer, Robert E. "Bud," D-Ala. (5)
Crenshaw, Ander, R-Fla. (4)
Crowley, Joseph, D-N.Y. (7)
Cubin, Barbara, R-Wyo. (AL)
Cuellar, Henry, D-Texas (28)
Culberson, John, R-Texas (7)
Cummings, Elijah E., D-Md. (7)

### — D —

Davis, Artur, D-Ala. (7)
Davis, Danny K., D-Ill. (7)
Davis, Geoff, R-Ky. (4)
Davis, Jim, D-Fla. (11)
Davis, Jo Ann, R-Va. (1)
Davis, Lincoln, D-Tenn. (4)
Davis, Susan A., D-Calif. (53)
Davis, Thomas M. III, R-Va. (11)
Deal, Nathan, R-Ga. (10)
DeFazio, Peter A., D-Ore. (4)
DeGette, Diana, D-Colo. (1)
Delahunt, Bill, D-Mass. (10)
DeLauro, Rosa, D-Conn. (3)
DeLay, Tom, R-Texas (22)
Dent, Charlie, R-Pa. (15)
Diaz-Balart, Lincoln, R-Fla. (21)
Diaz-Balart, Mario, R-Fla. (25)
Dicks, Norm, D-Wash. (6)
Dingell, John D., D-Mich. (15)
Doggett, Lloyd, D-Texas (25)
Doolittle, John T., R-Calif. (4)
Doyle, Mike, D-Pa. (14)
Drake, Thelma, R-Va. (2)
Dreier, David, R-Calif. (26)
Duncan, John J. "Jimmy" Jr., R-Tenn. (2)

### — E —

Edwards, Chet, D-Texas (17)
Ehlers, Vernon J., R-Mich. (3)
Emanuel, Rahm, D-Ill. (5)
Emerson, Jo Ann, R-Mo. (8)
Engel, Eliot L., D-N.Y. (17)
English, Phil, R-Pa. (3)
Eshoo, Anna G., D-Calif. (14)
Etheridge, Bob, D-N.C. (2)
Evans, Lane, D-Ill. (17)
Everett, Terry, R-Ala. (2)

### — F —

Farr, Sam, D-Calif. (17)
Fattah, Chaka, D-Pa. (2)
Feeney, Tom, R-Fla. (24)
Ferguson, Mike, R-N.J. (7)
Filner, Bob, D-Calif. (51)
Fitzpatrick, Michael G., R-Pa. (8)
Flake, Jeff, R-Ariz. (6)
Foley, Mark, R-Fla. (16)
Forbes, J. Randy, R-Va. (4)
Ford, Harold E. Jr., D-Tenn. (9)
Fortenberry, Jeff, R-Neb. (1)
Fossella, Vito J., R-N.Y. (13)
Foxx, Virginia, R-N.C. (5)
Frank, Barney, D-Mass. (4)
Franks, Trent, R-Ariz. (2)
Frelinghuysen, Rodney, R-N.J. (11)

### — G —

Gallegly, Elton, R-Calif. (24)
Garrett, Scott, R-N.J. (5)
Gerlach, Jim, R-Pa. (6)
Gibbons, Jim, R-Nev. (2)
Gilchrest, Wayne T., R-Md. (1)
Gillmor, Paul E., R-Ohio (5)
Gingrey, Phil, R-Ga. (11)
Gohmert, Louie, R-Texas (1)
Gonzalez, Charlie, D-Texas (20)
Goode, Virgil H. Jr., R-Va. (5)
Goodlatte, Robert W., R-Va. (6)

Gordon, Bart, D-Tenn. (6)
Granger, Kay, R-Texas (12)
Graves, Sam, R-Mo. (6)
Green, Al, D-Texas (9)
Green, Gene, D-Texas (29)
Green, Mark, R-Wis. (8)
Grijalva, Raúl M., D-Ariz. (7)
Gutierrez, Luis V., D-Ill. (4)
Gutknecht, Gil, R-Minn. (1)

### — H —

Hall, Ralph M., R-Texas (4)
Harman, Jane, D-Calif. (36)
Harris, Katherine, R-Fla. (13)
Hart, Melissa A., R-Pa. (4)
Hastert, J. Dennis, R-Ill. (14)
Hastings, Alcee L., D-Fla. (23)
Hastings, Doc, R-Wash. (4)
Hayes, Robin, R-N.C. (8)
Hayworth, J.D., R-Ariz. (5)
Hefley, Joel, R-Colo. (5)
Hensarling, Jeb, R-Texas (5)
Herger, Wally, R-Calif. (2)
Herseth, Stephanie, D-S.D. (AL)
Higgins, Brian, D-N.Y. (27)
Hinchey, Maurice D., D-N.Y. (22)
Hinojosa, Rubén, D-Texas (15)
Hobson, David L., R-Ohio (7)
Hoekstra, Peter, R-Mich. (2)
Holden, Tim, D-Pa. (17)
Holt, Rush D., D-N.J. (12)
Honda, Michael M., D-Calif. (15)
Hooley, Darlene, D-Ore. (5)
Hostettler, John, R-Ind. (8)
Hoyer, Steny H., D-Md. (5)
Hulshof, Kenny, R-Mo. (9)
Hunter, Duncan, R-Calif. (52)
Hyde, Henry J., R-Ill. (6)

### — I, J —

Inglis, Bob, R-S.C. (4)
Inslee, Jay, D-Wash. (1)
Israel, Steve, D-N.Y. (2)
Issa, Darrell, R-Calif. (49)
Istook, Ernest, R-Okla. (5)
Jackson, Jesse L. Jr., D-Ill. (2)
Jackson-Lee, Sheila, D-Texas (18)
Jefferson, William J., D-La. (2)
Jindal, Bobby, R-La. (1)
Johnson, Eddie Bernice, D-Texas (30)
Johnson, Nancy L., R-Conn. (5)
Johnson, Sam, R-Texas (3)
Johnson, Timothy V., R-Ill. (15)
Jones, Stephanie Tubbs, D-Ohio (11)
Jones, Walter B., R-N.C. (3)

### — K —

Kanjorski, Paul E., D-Pa. (11)
Kaptur, Marcy, D-Ohio (9)
Keller, Ric, R-Fla. (8)
Kelly, Sue W., R-N.Y. (19)
Kennedy, Mark, R-Minn. (6)
Kennedy, Patrick J., D-R.I. (1)
Kildee, Dale E., D-Mich. (5)
Kilpatrick, Carolyn Cheeks, D-Mich. (13)
Kind, Ron, D-Wis. (3)
King, Peter T., R-N.Y. (3)
King, Steve, R-Iowa (5)
Kingston, Jack, R-Ga. (1)
Kirk, Mark Steven, R-Ill. (10)
Kline, John, R-Minn. (2)
Knollenberg, Joe, R-Mich. (9)
Kolbe, Jim, R-Ariz. (8)
Kucinich, Dennis J., D-Ohio (10)
Kuhl, John R. "Randy" Jr., R-N.Y. (29)

### — L —

LaHood, Ray, R-Ill. (18)
Langevin, Jim, D-R.I. (2)
Lantos, Tom, D-Calif. (12)
Larsen, Rick, D-Wash. (2)
Larson, John B., D-Conn. (1)
Latham, Tom, R-Iowa (4)
LaTourette, Steven C., R-Ohio (14)
Leach, Jim, R-Iowa (2)
Lee, Barbara, D-Calif. (9)
Levin, Sander M., D-Mich. (12)

Lewis, Jerry, R-Calif. (41)
Lewis, John, D-Ga. (5)
Lewis, Ron, R-Ky. (2)
Linder, John, R-Ga. (7)
Lipinski, Daniel, D-Ill. (3)
LoBiondo, Frank A., R-N.J. (2)
Lofgren, Zoe, D-Calif. (16)
Lowey, Nita M., D-N.Y. (18)
Lucas, Frank D., R-Okla. (3)
Lungren, Dan, R-Calif. (3)
Lynch, Stephen F., D-Mass. (9)

### — M —

Mack, Connie, R-Fla. (14)
Maloney, Carolyn B., D-N.Y. (14)
Manzullo, Donald, R-Ill. (16)
Marchant, Kenny, R-Texas (24)
Markey, Edward J., D-Mass. (7)
Marshall, Jim, D-Ga. (3)
Matheson, Jim, D-Utah (2)
Matsui, Doris, D-Calif. (5)
McCarthy, Carolyn, D-N.Y. (4)
McCaul, Michael, R-Texas (10)
McCollum, Betty, D-Minn. (4)
McCotter, Thaddeus, R-Mich. (11)
McCrery, Jim, R-La. (4)
McDermott, Jim, D-Wash. (7)
McGovern, Jim, D-Mass. (3)
McHenry, Patrick T., R-N.C. (10)
McHugh, John M., R-N.Y. (23)
McIntyre, Mike, D-N.C. (7)
McKeon, Howard P. "Buck," R-Calif. (25)
McKinney, Cynthia A., D-Ga. (4)
McMorris, Cathy, R-Wash. (5)
McNulty, Michael R., D-N.Y. (21)
Meehan, Martin T., D-Mass. (5)
Meek, Kendrick B., D-Fla. (17)
Meeks, Gregory W., D-N.Y. (6)
Melancon, Charlie, D-La. (3)
Menendez, Robert, D-N.J. (13)
Mica, John L., R-Fla. (7)
Michaud, Michael H., D-Maine (2)
Millender-McDonald, Juanita, D-Calif. (37)
Miller, Brad, D-N.C. (13)
Miller, Candice S., R-Mich. (10)
Miller, Gary G., R-Calif. (42)
Miller, George, D-Calif. (7)
Miller, Jeff, R-Fla. (1)
Mollohan, Alan B., D-W.Va. (1)
Moore, Dennis, D-Kan. (3)
Moore, Gwen, D-Wis. (4)
Moran, James P., D-Va. (8)
Moran, Jerry, R-Kan. (1)
Murphy, Tim, R-Pa. (18)
Murtha, John P., D-Pa. (12)
Musgrave, Marilyn, R-Colo. (4)
Myrick, Sue, R-N.C. (9)

### — N —

Nadler, Jerrold, D-N.Y. (8)
Napolitano, Grace F., D-Calif. (38)
Neal, Richard E., D-Mass. (2)
Neugebauer, Randy, R-Texas (19)
Ney, Bob, R-Ohio (18)
Northup, Anne M., R-Ky. (3)
Norwood, Charlie, R-Ga. (9)
Nunes, Devin, R-Calif. (21)
Nussle, Jim, R-Iowa (1)

### — O —

Oberstar, James L., D-Minn. (8)
Obey, David R., D-Wis. (7)
Olver, John W., D-Mass. (1)
Ortiz, Solomon P., D-Texas (27)
Osborne, Tom, R-Neb. (3)
Otter, C. L. "Butch," R-Idaho (1)
Owens, Major R., D-N.Y. (11)
Oxley, Michael G., R-Ohio (4)

### — P —

Pallone, Frank Jr., D-N.J. (6)
Pascrell, Bill Jr., D-N.J. (8)
Pastor, Ed, D-Ariz. (4)
Paul, Ron, R-Texas (14)
Payne, Donald M., D-N.J. (10)
Pearce, Steve, R-N.M. (2)
Pelosi, Nancy, D-Calif. (8)

# . . . Governors, Supreme Court, Cabinet-Rank Officers

Pence, Mike, R-Ind. (6)
Peterson, Collin C., D-Minn. (7)
Peterson, John E., R-Pa. (5)
Petri, Tom, R-Wis. (6)
Pickering, Charles W. "Chip" Jr., R-Miss. (3)
Pitts, Joe, R-Pa. (16)
Platts, Todd R., R-Pa. (19)
Poe, Ted, R-Texas (2)
Pombo, Richard W., R-Calif. (11)
Pomeroy, Earl, D-N.D. (AL)
Porter, Jon, R-Nev. (3)
Price, David E., D-N.C. (4)
Price, Tom, R-Ga. (6)
Pryce, Deborah, R-Ohio (15)
Putnam, Adam H., R-Fla. (12)

### — Q, R —

Radanovich, George P., R-Calif. (19)
Rahall, Nick J. II, D-W.Va. (3)
Ramstad, Jim, R-Minn. (3)
Rangel, Charles B., D-N.Y. (15)
Regula, Ralph, R-Ohio (16)
Rehberg, Denny, R-Mont. (AL)
Reichert, Dave, R-Wash. (8)
Renzi, Rick, R-Ariz. (1)
Reyes, Silvestre, D-Texas (16)
Reynolds, Thomas M., R-N.Y. (26)
Rogers, Harold, R-Ky. (5)
Rogers, Mike D., R-Ala. (3)
Rogers, Mike, R-Mich. (8)
Rohrabacher, Dana, R-Calif. (46)
Ros-Lehtinen, Ileana, R-Fla. (18)
Ross, Mike, D-Ark. (4)
Rothman, Steven R., D-N.J. (9)
Roybal-Allard, Lucille, D-Calif. (34)
Royce, Ed, R-Calif. (40)
Ruppersberger, C.A. Dutch, D-Md. (2)
Rush, Bobby L., D-Ill. (1)
Ryan, Paul D., R-Wis. (1)
Ryan, Tim, D-Ohio (17)
Ryun, Jim, R-Kan. (2)

### — S —

Sabo, Martin Olav, D-Minn. (5)
Salazar, John, D-Colo. (3)
Sánchez, Linda T., D-Calif. (39)
Sanchez, Loretta, D-Calif. (47)
Sanders, Bernard, I-Vt. (AL)
Saxton, H. James, R-N.J. (3)
Schakowsky, Jan, D-Ill. (9)
Schiff, Adam B., D-Calif. (29)
Schmidt, Jean, R-Ohio (2)
Schwartz, Allyson Y., D-Pa. (13)
Schwarz, Joe, R-Mich. (7)
Scott, David, D-Ga. (13)
Scott, Robert C., D-Va. (3)
Sensenbrenner, F. James Jr., R-Wis. (5)
Serrano, José E., D-N.Y. (16)
Sessions, Pete, R-Texas (32)
Shadegg, John, R-Ariz. (3)
Shaw, E. Clay Jr., R-Fla. (22)
Shays, Christopher, R-Conn. (4)
Sherman, Brad, D-Calif. (27)
Sherwood, Don, R-Pa. (10)
Shimkus, John, R-Ill. (19)
Shuster, Bill, R-Pa. (9)
Simmons, Rob, R-Conn. (2)
Simpson, Mike, R-Idaho (2)
Skelton, Ike, D-Mo. (4)
Slaughter, Louise M., D-N.Y. (28)
Smith, Adam, D-Wash. (9)
Smith, Christopher H., R-N.J. (4)
Smith, Lamar, R-Texas (21)
Snyder, Vic, D-Ark. (2)
Sodrel, Mike, R-Ind. (9)
Solis, Hilda L., D-Calif. (32)
Souder, Mark, R-Ind. (3)
Spratt, John M. Jr., D-S.C. (5)
Stark, Pete, D-Calif. (13)
Stearns, Cliff, R-Fla. (6)
Strickland, Ted, D-Ohio (6)
Stupak, Bart, D-Mich. (1)
Sullivan, John, R-Okla. (1)
Sweeney, John E., R-N.Y. (20)

### — T —

Tancredo, Tom, R-Colo. (6)
Tanner, John, D-Tenn. (8)
Tauscher, Ellen O., D-Calif. (10)
Taylor, Charles H., R-N.C. (11)
Taylor, Gene, D-Miss. (4)
Terry, Lee, R-Neb. (2)
Thomas, Bill, R-Calif. (22)
Thompson, Bennie, D-Miss. (2)
Thompson, Mike, D-Calif. (1)
Thornberry, William M. "Mac," R-Texas (13)
Tiahrt, Todd, R-Kan. (4)
Tiberi, Pat, R-Ohio (12)
Tierney, John F., D-Mass. (6)
Towns, Edolphus, D-N.Y. (10)
Turner, Michael R., R-Ohio (3)

### — U,V —

Udall, Mark, D-Colo. (2)
Udall, Tom, D-N.M. (3)
Upton, Fred, R-Mich. (6)
Van Hollen, Chris, D-Md. (8)
Velázquez, Nydia M., D-N.Y. (12)
Visclosky, Peter J., D-Ind. (1)

### — W —

Walden, Greg, R-Ore. (2)
Walsh, James T., R-N.Y. (25)
Wamp, Zach, R-Tenn. (3)
Wasserman-Schultz, Debbie, D-Fla. (20)
Waters, Maxine, D-Calif. (35)
Watson, Diane, D-Calif. (33)
Watt, Melvin, D-N.C. (12)
Waxman, Henry A., D-Calif. (30)
Weiner, Anthony, D-N.Y. (9)
Weldon, Curt, R-Pa. (7)
Weldon, Dave, R-Fla. (15)
Weller, Jerry, R-Ill. (11)
Westmoreland, Lynn, R-Ga. (8)
Wexler, Robert, D-Fla. (19)
Whitfield, Edward, R-Ky. (1)
Wicker, Roger, R-Miss. (1)
Wilson, Heather A., R-N.M. (1)
Wilson, Joe, R-S.C. (2)
Wolf, Frank R., R-Va. (10)
Woolsey, Lynn, D-Calif. (6)
Wu, David, D-Ore. (1)
Wynn, Albert R., D-Md. (4)

### — X, Y, Z —

Young, C.W. Bill, R-Fla. (10)
Young, Don, R-Alaska (AL)

## Delegates

Bordallo, Madeleine Z., D-Guam
Christensen, Donna M.C., D-Virgin Is.
Faleomavaega, Eni F.H., D-Am. Samoa
Fortuño, Luis, R-P.R.
Norton, Eleanor Holmes, D-D.C.

## Senators
### R 55; D 44; I 1

Akaka, Daniel K., D-Hawaii
Alexander, Lamar, R-Tenn.
Allard, Wayne, R-Colo.
Allen, George, R-Va.
Baucus, Max, D-Mont.
Bayh, Evan, D-Ind.
Bennett, Robert F., R-Utah
Biden, Joseph R. Jr., D-Del.
Bingaman, Jeff, D-N.M.
Bond, Christopher S., R-Mo.
Boxer, Barbara, D-Calif.
Brownback, Sam, R-Kan.
Bunning, Jim, R-Ky.
Burns, Conrad, R-Mont.
Burr, Richard M., R-N.C.
Byrd, Robert C., D-W.Va.
Cantwell, Maria, D-Wash.
Carper, Thomas R., D-Del.

Chafee, Lincoln, R-R.I.
Chambliss, Saxby, R-Ga.
Clinton, Hillary Rodham, D-N.Y.
Coburn, Tom, R-Okla.
Cochran, Thad, R-Miss.
Coleman, Norm, R-Minn.
Collins, Susan, R-Maine
Conrad, Kent, D-N.D.
Cornyn, John, R-Texas
Corzine, Jon, D-N.J.
Craig, Larry E., R-Idaho
Crapo, Michael D., R-Idaho
Dayton, Mark, D-Minn.
DeMint, Jim, R-S.C.
DeWine, Mike, R-Ohio
Dodd, Christopher J., D-Conn.
Dole, Elizabeth, R-N.C.
Domenici, Pete V., R-N.M.
Dorgan, Byron L., D-N.D.
Durbin, Richard J., D-Ill.
Ensign, John, R-Nev.
Enzi, Michael B., R-Wyo.
Feingold, Russell D., D-Wis.
Feinstein, Dianne, D-Calif.
Frist, Bill, R-Tenn.
Graham, Lindsey, R-S.C.
Grassley, Charles E., R-Iowa
Gregg, Judd, R-N.H.
Hagel, Chuck, R-Neb.
Harkin, Tom, D-Iowa
Hatch, Orrin G., R-Utah
Hutchison, Kay Bailey, R-Texas
Inhofe, James M., R-Okla.
Inouye, Daniel K., D-Hawaii
Isakson, Johnny, R-Ga.
Jeffords, James M., I-Vt.
Johnson, Tim, D-S.D.
Kennedy, Edward M., D-Mass.
Kerry, John, D-Mass.
Kohl, Herb, D-Wis.
Kyl, Jon, R-Ariz.
Landrieu, Mary L., D-La.
Lautenberg, Frank R., D-N.J.
Leahy, Patrick J., D-Vt.
Levin, Carl, D-Mich.
Lieberman, Joseph I., D-Conn.
Lincoln, Blanche, D-Ark.
Lott, Trent, R-Miss.
Lugar, Richard G., R-Ind.
Martinez, Mel, R-Fla.
McCain, John, R-Ariz.
McConnell, Mitch, R-Ky.
Mikulski, Barbara A., D-Md.
Murkowski, Lisa, R-Alaska
Murray, Patty, D-Wash.
Nelson, Ben, D-Neb.
Nelson, Bill, D-Fla.
Obama, Barack, D-Ill.
Pryor, Mark, D-Ark.
Reed, Jack, D-R.I.
Reid, Harry, D-Nev.
Roberts, Pat, R-Kan.
Rockefeller, John D. IV, D-W.Va.
Salazar, Ken, D-Colo.
Santorum, Rick, R-Pa.
Sarbanes, Paul S., D-Md.
Schumer, Charles E., D-N.Y.
Sessions, Jeff, R-Ala.
Shelby, Richard C., R-Ala.
Smith, Gordon H., R-Ore.
Snowe, Olympia J., R-Maine
Specter, Arlen, R-Pa.
Stabenow, Debbie, D-Mich.
Stevens, Ted, R-Alaska
Sununu, John E., R-N.H.
Talent, Jim, R-Mo.
Thomas, Craig, R-Wyo.
Thune, John, R-S.D.
Vitter, David, R-La.
Voinovich, George V., R-Ohio
Warner, John W., R-Va.
Wyden, Ron, D-Ore.

## Governors
### R 28; D 22

Ala. — Bob Riley, R
Alaska — Frank H. Murkowski, R
Ariz. — Janet Napolitano, D
Ark. — Mike Huckabee, R
Calif. — Arnold Schwarzenegger, R

Colo. — Bill Owens, R
Conn. — M. Jodi Rell, R
Del. — Ruth Ann Minner, D
Fla. — Jeb Bush, R
Ga. — Sonny Perdue, R
Hawaii — Linda Lingle, R
Idaho — Dirk Kempthorne, R
Ill. — Rod R. Blagojevich, D
Ind. — Mitch Daniels, R
Iowa — Tom Vilsack, D
Kan. — Kathleen Sebelius, D
Ky. — Ernie Fletcher, R
La. — Kathleen Babineaux Blanco, D
Maine — John Baldacci, D
Md. — Robert L. Ehrlich Jr., R
Mass. — Mitt Romney, R
Mich. — Jennifer M. Granholm, D
Minn. — Tim Pawlenty, R
Miss. — Haley Barbour, R
Mo. — Matt Blunt, R
Mont. — Brian Schweitzer, D
Neb. — Dave Heineman, R
Nev. — Kenny Guinn, R
N.H. — John Lynch, D
N.J. — Richard J. Codey, D (acting)
N.M. — Bill Richardson, D
N.Y. — George E. Pataki, R
N.C. — Michael F. Easley, D
N.D. — John Hoeven, R
Ohio — Bob Taft, R
Okla. — Brad Henry, D
Ore. — Theodore R. Kulongoski, D
Pa. — Edward G. Rendell, D
R.I. — Donald L. Carcieri, R
S.C. — Mark Sanford, R
S.D. — Michael Rounds, R
Tenn. — Phil Bredesen, D
Texas — Rick Perry, R
Utah — Jon Huntsman Jr., R
Vt. — Jim Douglas, R
Va. — Mark Warner, D
Wash. — Christine Gregoire, D
W.Va. — Joe Manchin III, D
Wis. — James E. Doyle, D
Wyo. — Dave Freudenthal, D

## Supreme Court

Roberts, John G. Jr. — Md., Chief Justice
Breyer, Stephen G. — Mass.
Ginsburg, Ruth Bader — N.Y.
Kennedy, Anthony M. — Calif.
O'Connor, Sandra Day — Ariz.
Scalia, Antonin — Va.
Souter, David H. — N.H.
Stevens, John Paul — Ill.
Thomas, Clarence — Ga.

## Cabinet

Bodman, Samuel W. — Energy
Chao, Elaine L. — Labor
Chertoff, Michael — Homeland Security
Gonzales, Alberto R. — Attorney General
Gutierrez, Carlos — Commerce
Jackson, Alphonso R. — Housing and Urban Development
Johanns, Mike — Agriculture
Leavitt, Michael O. — Health and Human Services
Mineta, Norman Y. — Transportation
Nicholson, Jim — Veterans Affairs
Norton, Gale A. — Interior
Rice, Condoleezza — State
Rumsfeld, Donald H. — Defense
Snow, John W. — Treasury
Spellings, Margaret — Education

## Other Executive Branch Officers

Cheney, Dick — Vice President
Bolten, Joshua B. — OMB Director
Card, Andrew H. Jr. — Chief of Staff
Hadley, Stephen J. — Assistant to the President for National Security Affairs
Hubbard, Al — Director, National Economic Council
Johnson, Stephen L. — EPA Administrator
Negroponte, John D. — Director of National Intelligence
Portman, Rob — U.S. Trade Representative

# Appendix B

# VOTE STUDIES

# Vote Studies

# Bush Boosts His Success Rate
# Even While Retreating on Key Issues

BY ONE MEASURE, President Bush can rightfully claim that 2005 was a successful year for getting his legislative agenda through Congress: He prevailed on 78 percent of the roll call votes on which his administration took a clear position. That is a strong statistic in any year, but even more noteworthy because it was logged during the fifth year of Bush's presidency.

Over the five decades that Congressional Quarterly has analyzed roll call votes in Congress, the longer presidents stay in office, generally the less well they have done at getting what they want.

Not so for Bush.

For the fifth year of a presidency, only the administration of Lyndon B. Johnson (who logged a 74.5 percent success rate) comes close to Bush's score. Even Ronald Reagan, in his fifth year in the White House, won on only 59.9 percent of the votes where he took a position. And Reagan's fellow Republicans voted against his positions about a fourth of the time.

This high presidential success score, though, is at odds with what is generally viewed as a complex relationship between Bush and the Republican-led Congress. The White House during 2005 often had to work hard to get its way against push-back from a unified wall of Democrats and defiant Republican dissenters.

While the president made sizable progress on his agenda early in the year, that was followed by a series of retreats and defeats — on treatment of military detainees, drilling in the Arctic, and renewal of the Patriot Act — late in the session. And there were some issues on Bush's agenda, such as a Social Security overhaul and another round of tax cuts, that didn't make it to a vote at all.

Finally, Bush's support in congressional voting is also based on an extraordinarily low number of votes on which the president could be seen as having a definitive position. Of 669 votes in the House, CQ could determine a Bush position for only 46 of them. That was true for just 45 of 366 votes in the Senate.

That is not because this administration does not have firm positions or convictions, but it does reflect a certain reluctance to get involved in the dirty details of legislative deal making. This has been the case for this administration for each of the five years of Bush's presidency, and it has been in stark contrast to his predecessor, Bill Clinton, who used the "statement of administration policy" more frequently as a tool to lay down markers for the GOP-led Congress. He also used the presidential veto 37 times in his two terms. Bush has not used it even once.

The fact that the administration's tentacles on the Hill are not very long or deep could combine with Bush's low approval rating as well as midterm election pressures to cause

more defections in the ranks, analysts say. Those defections are likely to come one issue at a time among those considered marginal allies of the president.

With many public opinion polls showing the president's popularity below 50 percent for much of the second half of the year, Republican lawmakers face a dilemma, said Paul S. Herrnson, director of the Center for American Politics and Citizenship at the University of Maryland.

"As the elections get closer, Republicans in close districts will have to vote against the president's policies when their constituents are strongly opposed," he said.

Said Daniel J. Mattoon, a GOP strategist with Podesta Mattoon in Washington: "I think you have a situation where members are going to start looking out for themselves."

At a time when the parties are jockeying for advantage, and seeking to present a unified front in advance of this fall's elections, the possibility of an every-man-for-himself environment will force House and Senate leaders to adopt what Mattoon calls "a more nuanced leadership."

Those potentially clashing impulses have already begun playing out on such issues as immigration reform, and will develop more fully if Congress decides to take on personal accounts or other major Social Security changes, he said.

## 'A GOOD RELATIONSHIP'

The legislative victories that made Bush's fifth year stand out from those of his modern White House predecessors were largely clustered in the early part of 2005, before Congress' attention became diverted by other demands: hurricane disaster relief; the Iraq death count and public questioning about whether the United States has an end game for the war; and the shakeup in House leadership following the September indictment of Majority Leader Tom DeLay on campaign finance-related charges in his home state of Texas.

The foundation of Bush's success score was built on enactment of long-sought limits on class action lawsuits and bankruptcy filings; an energy bill; a highway and transit bill that closely fit the administration's budget parameters; and the Central American Free Trade Agreement.

In addition, the Senate confirmed more of the judges that Bush wanted on the bench, and without much foot-dragging allowed John G. Roberts Jr. to become chief justice of the United States.

All of these, in addition to being tests of the president's clout, turned out to be picks by CQ's editors as "key votes" for the year. The

# Bush Continues His Run of Victories

Graph illustrates the percentage of the time in the past 53 years that the president won on roll call votes on which he took a clear position. Graph shows House and Senate figures combined. *(Data for each year, p. 86)*

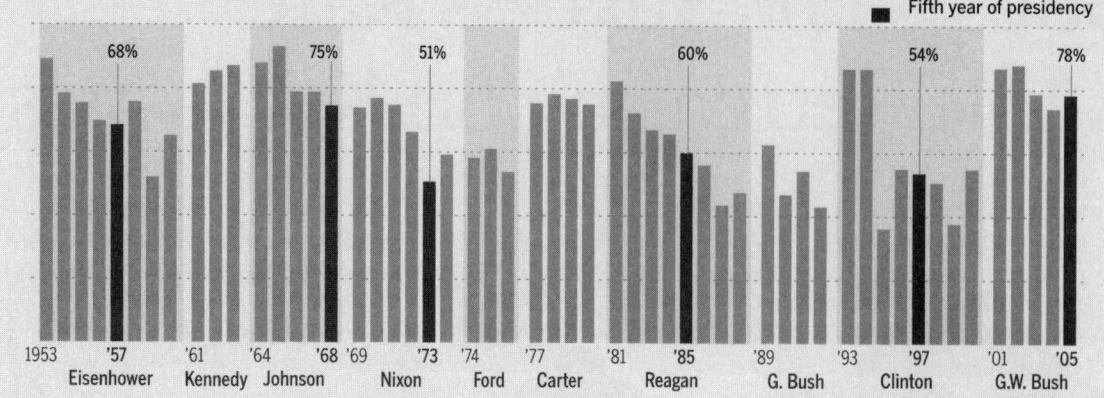

■ Fifth year of presidency

68%  75%  51%  60%  54%  78%

| 1953 | '57 | '61 | '64 | '68 | '69 | '73 | '74 | '77 | '81 | '85 | '89 | '93 | '97 | '01 | '05 |

Eisenhower  Kennedy  Johnson  Nixon  Ford  Carter  Reagan  G. Bush  Clinton  G.W. Bush

**2005 DATA**

**HOUSE TOTALS**

Defeats 10

36

Victories

**SENATE TOTALS**

35 victories 10 defeats

Nominations 2 / 19    Other issues 8 / 16

**BUSH SUCCESS RATE CONGRESSWIDE**

78%

| FOR MORE INFORMATION | |
|---|---|
| Top scorers | 85 |
| Background | 86 |
| List of votes | 87 |
| House members' scores | 88 |
| Senators' scores | 90 |

class action, bankruptcy and trade votes also show up as roll calls that pitted the two political parties against each other on Capitol Hill. *(Party unity, p. B-8; key votes, p. C-3)*

As far as congressional Republican leaders are concerned, backing up Bush on those major initiatives made 2005 a resoundingly successful year. Communication between the White House and Capitol Hill was constant, said House Republican Whip Roy Blunt of Missouri, who had at least temporarily taken the indicted DeLay's place.

And that paid off in major bills that became law, Blunt said. "Your study's indication that our support of the president's proposals is at least equal to what it was in 2004 is an indication that it continues to be a good relationship," he said.

Deborah Pryce of Ohio, chairwoman of the House Republican Conference, acknowledged that the relationship between GOP members and the White House "hasn't always been a bed of roses," but they shared a common goal, she said, and "those people appreciate what's at stake."

"I have seen the Speaker angry with the president. I have seen [White House Chief of Staff Andrew H. Card Jr.] get angry with the Speaker. But they work it out, and they don't do it on the front page, and that makes for trust," Pryce said.

Herrnson at the University of Maryland said the administration has shown that "Republicans can rule, in the sense that they have majorities in Congress and the White House and are pushing their agenda full-speed ahead, rather than governing democratically by reaching out to the other side."

House Speaker J. Dennis Hastert of Illinois has had a longstanding policy of trying to ensure that differences between the White House and lawmakers don't result in floor confrontations where either the Bush administration or GOP leaders lose face. That goes a long way toward shaping Bush's success in Congress.

"We are not going to play unless we play to win," said Ron Bonjean, Hastert's spokesman. "We want to have public discourse and debate, but we want our position to prevail."

In the case of the fiscal 2006 defense authorization bill, that meant keeping the legislation bottled up for months rather than risk a House floor vote on language — attached in the Senate by Arizona Republican John McCain — banning torture, or worse provoking the first presidential veto. Democrats protested loudly but to no avail.

"They are much more interested in partisan advantage than they are in substantial policy, and it is a shame because America is losing because of that," said House Democratic Whip Steny H. Hoyer of Maryland.

Early in the year, when it was clear that a majority of House Republicans were eager to follow the lead of Don Young of Alaska, chairman of the Transportation and Infrastructure Committee, and vote for a highway bill that would break the administration's spending limits, Hastert said he wouldn't allow such a bill onto the floor. Senate Majority Leader Bill Frist of Tennessee made the same commitment and Republicans had to amend the measure on the Senate floor to get around that line in the sand.

## RETREATS AND DEFEATS

Several significant legislative retreats not reflected in House or Senate votes came during a flurry of legislative horse-trading in the last days of the first session of the 109th Congress.

Bush found himself making an about-face and embracing compromise language on the use of torture against U.S. terrorist detainees after both the House and Senate — responding to reports of prisoner abuse at clandestine U.S. detention facilities — added language to the defense authorization bill calling on the administration to report to Congress on conditions in those facilities. And the Senate had added McCain's torture ban not only to the authorization measure but also to the more critical fiscal 2006 Defense spending bill.

House Republican leaders had also kept the conference report on the appropriations bill off the floor in order to avoid facing a vote on the language. But resistance proved to be futile, and on Dec. 15, Bush was standing in the Oval Office with his one-time rival McCain, saying, "We've been happy to work with him to achieve a common objective, and that is to make it clear to the world that this government does not torture and that we adhere to the international convention of torture, whether it be here, at home or abroad."

A day later, Bush retreated again when Congress didn't follow his script and failed to clear a bill that renewed expiring parts of the 2001 anti-terrorism law known as the Patriot Act. He was forced to sign a five-week extension of the expiring provisions that was passed by the House and Senate as Congress was about to adjourn for the year, and after insisting that he wanted a full renewal, not a stopgap of any length.

With the cameras rolling as Bush left the White House for his Christmas vacation, he chose to cast the extension vote as a win rather than a defeat. "It appears to me that Congress understands we've got to keep the Patriot Act in place, that we're still under threat," Bush told reporters.

That sound bite did not, and could not, convey the extent of White House resistance and how just two days earlier Bush's press secretary, Scott McClellan, had pointed a finger at "obstructionist politics" of Senate Democrats and equated their refusal to support a long-term renewal to "putting politics above our nation's security." Also left unsaid: Four Republican senators had voted with 41 Democrats against bringing to a vote the conference report that would reauthorize the law's provisions, and eight Republicans had undermined the president's position by signing a petition calling for a shorter-term extension.

Perhaps the year's biggest retreat was a tactical decision to scrap the Supreme Court nomination of White House Counsel Harriet Miers in the midst of loud outcries from conservatives. Withdrawing the nomination averted the possibility of an embarrassing loss on the Senate floor. And the move also made it impossible to include what clearly was an administration failure in the CQ presidential success scorecard.

Also not on the list of presidential defeats: Congress didn't complete work on a tax cut package — again in the face of bipartisan resistance — and it didn't make any headway on changing the Social Security system to create individual accounts, both White House priorities. Overhauling Social Security had been at the top of Bush's legislative to-do list as 2005 began, but with Democrats solidly united against the proposal and with Republicans not in agreement on whether to buck widespread public opposition, the plan was quietly shelved.

**VETO THREATS**

Even with leadership efforts to keep intraparty fights out of the public's eye, the White House intermittently chose to use the whip

## Senate Support, Minus Nominations

Graph shows the percentage of the time the president won on Senate roll call votes — other than nominations — on which he took a clear position. Data for this series is calculated dating back only to 1988.

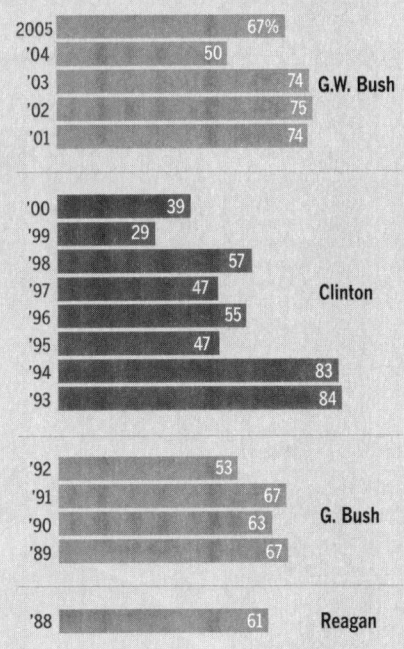

| Year | Value | President |
|---|---|---|
| 2005 | 67% | |
| '04 | 50 | |
| '03 | 74 | G.W. Bush |
| '02 | 75 | |
| '01 | 74 | |
| '00 | 39 | |
| '99 | 29 | |
| '98 | 57 | |
| '97 | 47 | Clinton |
| '96 | 55 | |
| '95 | 47 | |
| '94 | 83 | |
| '93 | 84 | |
| '92 | 53 | |
| '91 | 67 | G. Bush |
| '90 | 63 | |
| '89 | 67 | |
| '88 | 61 | Reagan |

of a veto threat.

The Bush administration issued 79 statements of administration policy during 2005, more than the 61 of a year earlier but fewer than the 90 issued in 2003. In 2005, those statements included a raft of veto threats including opposition to Medicare language in a spending cut bill, a bid to lift a ban on imported prescription drugs from Canada in the fiscal 2006 Agriculture appropriations bill, and a Defense department spending bill whose levels the administration deemed to be too low.

The White House also objected to three parts of the fiscal 2006 Transportation-Treasury-Housing spending bill — Amtrak funding, language that would lift a ban on travel to Cuba and an amendment that would restrict the administration's ability to "outsource" federal jobs to private companies. It threatened vetoes on language in the Senate's fiscal 2006 foreign aid spending bill that would overturn the administration's ban on the use of money for abortion counseling, and on a bill that would expand federally financed medical research using embryonic stem cells.

And the White House issued threats over a measure that would overturn the administration's easing of import restrictions on Canadian beef and over provisions in the highway bill.

In spite of those threats, the House defied the administration by supporting stem cell research and limits on federal job outsourcing. In the Senate, the administration lost votes on Canadian beef restrictions and on abortion counseling, often referred to as the "Mexico City policy."

Of the 46 roll call votes in the House and the 45 in the Senate on which the White House had expressed a clear position, according to CQ's editors, Bush lost on 20 — 10 in each chamber. Often, however, where lawmakers defied the administration's wishes and tempted a

---

# CQ Vote Study Guide

Congressional Quarterly has conducted studies analyzing the voting behavior of members of Congress since 1945. This is how the studies are carried out:

● **SELECTING VOTES.** CQ bases its vote studies on all roll call votes on which members were asked to vote "yea" or "nay." In 2005, there were 669 such votes in the House and 366 in the Senate. The totals exclude quorum calls (there were two in the House in 2005), because they require only that members vote "present."

The totals do include House votes to approve the Journal (eight in 2005) and Senate votes to instruct the sergeant at arms to request members' presence in the chamber (two in 2005).

The presidential support and party unity studies are based on votes selected from the total according to the criteria described on pages B-14 and B-19.

● **INDIVIDUAL SCORES.** Members' scores in the accompanying charts are based only on the votes each member actually cast. That has the effect of making individual support and opposition scores add to 100 percent. The same method is used for identifying the leading scorers on pages B-7 and B-11.

● **OVERALL SCORES.** For consistency with previous years, calculations of average scores by chamber, party and region are based on all eligible yea-or-nay votes, whether or not all members participated. As a result, a member's failure to vote reduces the average support and opposition scores. Therefore, averages are not strictly comparable to individual member scores. *(Methodology, 1987 Almanac, p. 22-C)*

● **ROUNDING.** Scores in the tables for the full House and Senate membership are rounded to the nearest percentage point, although rounding is not used to increase any score to 100 percent or to reduce any score to zero. Scores for party and chamber support and opposition leaders are reported to 1 decimal point to more precisely rank them.

# Frequency of Presidential Support Votes Remains Low

The House and Senate combined for 91 roll call votes in 2005 on which the editors of CQ Weekly determined that President Bush took a clear position. That exceeded the 84 so-called presidential support votes cast in 2004, which was the fewest since 1972.

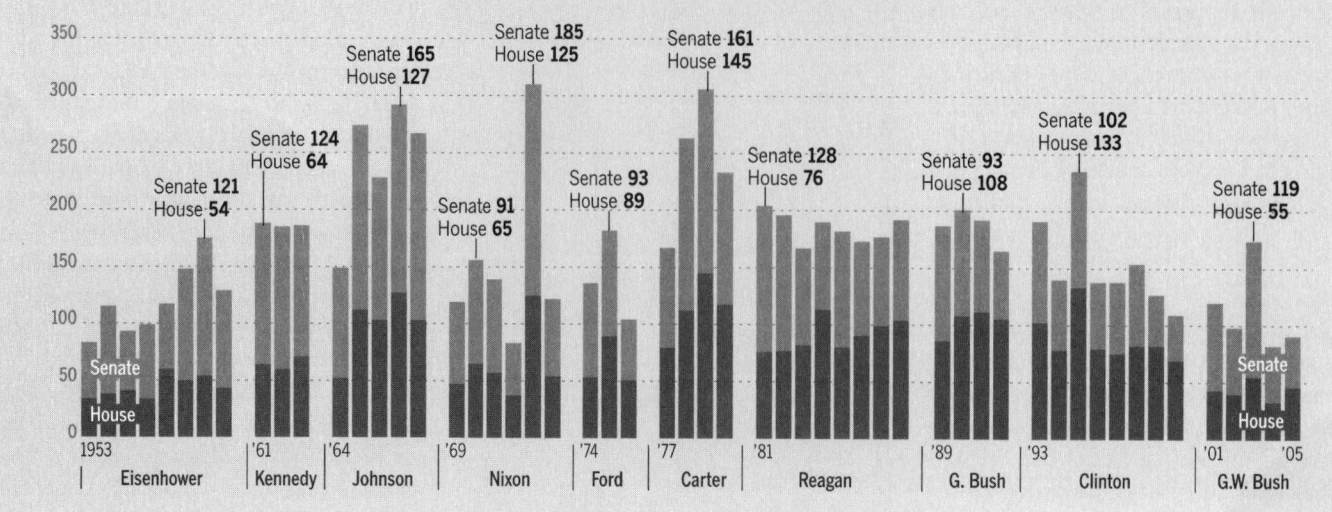

veto, the offending language died in a House-Senate conference committee, as with the outsourcing limits, or the administration was able to claim a compromise, as with the McCain anti-torture language.

"On the major issues, we have been in support of the president," Bonjean said. Where members will differ, he said, "is when it comes to parochial issues, the issues that are more below the radar."

The intraparty debate saw Republican divisions not only along regional lines, but also between groups of increasingly restless conservatives and moderates. Tensions exploded during the debate on the spending cut bill in both the House and Senate.

Congress' most fiscally conservative members began to openly criticize the White House and their Republican colleagues for allowing spending increases that helped widen the federal deficit, and GOP moderates balked at efforts by their partisan brethren to curb spending on such programs as heating assistance for the poor and student aid.

Still, for the most part, fiscal conservatives remained loyal to the White House.

Of Bush's most loyal House members — 13 who had presidential support scores of 93 percent or higher — 10 are publicly identified with the Republican Study Committee, a group of more than 100 lawmakers who champion reduced government spending, tax cuts and conservative social policies. The group claims 19 of the 34 members with support scores of 91 percent or higher. But five members of the group are among the 35 House Republicans who supported the president 75 percent of the time or less. That list includes Jeff Flake of Arizona, an outspoken critic of the administration's refusal to veto certain spending bills and an opponent of Bush's Cuba policy.

Eighteen of those House GOP lawmakers who were least supportive of the president belong to the Republican Main Street Partnership, a group of moderates who were swing votes in some of the administration's 2005 defeats, such as the May 24 vote on stem cells.

Conservatives can also be found at both ends of the spectrum in the Senate, with John Cornyn of Texas supporting the president on 44 of the 45 votes in 2005 on which Bush took a clear position, and Judd Gregg of New Hampshire, chairman of the Budget Committee and a consistent critic of government spending, among the 10 Republicans in the chamber who were least supportive.

Among those Senate Republicans with the lowest presidential support scores were four persistent administration critics: McCain, Susan Collins and Olympia J. Snowe of Maine, and Lincoln Chafee of Rhode Island.

## PARSING THE PERCENTAGES

Though the president set a new standard for fifth-year success, his percentage of winning votes in 2005 is less than it was during his first two years in office. He won on 86.7 percent of the roll call votes in 2001 on which he took a position and 87.8 percent in 2002.

Similarly, while Bush's average support score among House Republicans was 81 percent, a percentage point higher than the previous year, it was lower than any other year of his presidency. And the average Senate GOP support score of 86 percent is his lowest ever.

Democrats, meanwhile, sided with Bush less than ever, supporting his position 38 percent of the time in the Senate and 24 percent of the time in the House. During 2002, Bush's best year among Democrats, his Senate average support score was 71 percent and in the House it was 32 percent on votes where he took a position.

The lack of appeal to Democrats has been intentional. "The president decided after the last election to run an almost Republican-only strategy," said Mattoon.

One case in point was the reauthorization of the Patriot Act. Senate Democratic Whip Richard J. Durbin of Illinois said the administration and Senate GOP leaders might have won the Dec. 16 roll call in which they failed to get the 60 votes needed to invoke cloture and end the filibuster. All the White House had to do was make "a few strategic changes," Durbin said. "They wouldn't hear it. They just said take it or leave it."

## BIGGER FIGHTS, SMALLER VICTORIES

Whether by partisan design or political circumstance, the upshot is that the White House and Republican leaders have to fight harder and sometimes settle for narrower victories.

That was the case when the Senate on March 16 rejected, 49-51, an effort by Washington Democrat Maria Cantwell to strike procedural language in the budget resolution designed to make it more difficult to challenge legislation authorizing oil and natural gas drilling in part

# Leading Scorers: Presidential Support

**Support** indicates those who in 2005 voted most often for President Bush's position. **Opposition** shows those who voted most often against his position. Scores are based on actual votes cast. Members who missed half or more of the votes are not listed. Scores are rounded to 1 decimal point; those with identical scores are listed alphabetically. *(Complete scores, pp. B-16, B-18)*

## SUPPORT

| Republicans | | Democrats | |
|---|---|---|---|
| Cornyn, Texas | 97.8% | Nelson, Ben, Neb. | 75.6% |
| Allard, Colo. | 97.7 | Landrieu, La. | 64.4 |
| Allen, Va. | 95.6 | Pryor, Ark. | 57.8 |
| Cochran, Miss. | 95.6 | Lincoln, Ark. | 50.0 |
| Hutchison, Texas | 95.6 | Salazar, Colo. | 48.9 |
| Santorum, Pa. | 95.3 | Conrad, N.D. | 47.6 |
| Bond, Mo. | 93.3 | Nelson, Bill, Fla. | 46.5 |
| Brownback, Kan. | 93.3 | Lieberman, Conn. | 46.3 |
| Dole, N.C. | 93.3 | Johnson, S.D. | 45.5 |
| McConnell, Ky. | 93.3 | Kohl, Wis. | 45.5 |
| Bennett, Utah | 93.2 | Baucus, Mont. | 45.2 |
| Hatch, Utah | 93.2 | Byrd, W.Va. | 44.4 |

## OPPOSITION

| Republicans | | Democrats | |
|---|---|---|---|
| Chafee, R.I. | 44.4% | Wyden, Ore. | 74.4% |
| Collins, Maine | 37.8 | Kennedy, Mass. | 73.8 |
| Snowe, Maine | 33.3 | Harkin, Iowa | 72.7 |
| DeWine, Ohio | 24.4 | Lautenberg, N.J. | 72.7 |
| McCain, Ariz. | 22.5 | Biden, Del. | 72.5 |
| Smith, Ore. | 21.4 | Corzine, N.J. | 72.2 |
| Sununu, N.H. | 18.6 | Reed, R.I. | 71.1 |
| Gregg, N.H. | 18.2 | Boxer, Calif. | 70.5 |
| Craig, Idaho | 17.8 | Clinton, N.Y. | 68.9 |
| Coleman, Minn. | 16.3 | Dayton, Minn. | 68.9 |
| Enzi, Wyo. | 15.9 | Sarbanes, Md. | 68.9 |
| | | Schumer, N.Y. | 68.9 |

## SUPPORT

| Republicans | | Democrats | |
|---|---|---|---|
| Shadegg, Ariz. | 95.6% | Cramer, Ala. | 65.9% |
| Aderholt, Ala. | 93.5 | Boren, Okla. | 65.2 |
| Blackburn, Tenn. | 93.5 | Davis, Tenn. | 65.2 |
| Bonilla, Texas | 93.5 | Skelton, Mo. | 61.4 |
| Culberson, Texas | 93.5 | Marshall, Ga. | 58.7 |
| Hensarling, Texas | 93.5 | Cuellar, Texas | 57.1 |
| Barrett, S.C. | 93.3 | McIntyre, N.C. | 56.8 |
| Carter, Texas | 93.3 | Peterson, Minn. | 54.3 |
| Thornberry, Texas | 93.3 | Edwards, Texas | 52.2 |
| Johnson, Texas | 93.2 | Holden, Pa. | 52.2 |
| | | Melancon, La. | 52.2 |
| | | Chandler, Ky. | 50.0 |
| | | Ross, Ark. | 48.7 |

## OPPOSITION

| Republicans | | Democrats | |
|---|---|---|---|
| Paul, Texas | 62.2% | Brown, Ohio | 93.5% |
| Leach, Iowa | 51.1 | Payne, N.J. | 93.2 |
| Johnson, Ill. | 45.7 | DeLauro, Conn. | 91.3 |
| Shays, Conn. | 43.5 | Serrano, N.Y. | 91.3 |
| Johnson, Conn. | 41.3 | Delahunt, Mass. | 91.1 |
| Smith, N.J. | 40.0 | Watson, Calif. | 91.1 |
| Boehlert, N.Y. | 39.1 | Lewis, Ga. | 90.9 |
| Fitzpatrick, Pa. | 39.1 | Schakowsky, Ill. | 90.9 |
| Jones, N.C. | 38.6 | Capps, Calif. | 89.1 |
| Bartlett, Md. | 35.6 | Holt, N.J. | 89.1 |
| Simmons, Conn. | 34.9 | Kucinich, Ohio | 89.1 |
| Castle, Del. | 34.8 | McCollum, Minn. | 89.1 |
| Hostettler, Ind. | 33.3 | Owens, N.Y. | 89.1 |

of the Arctic National Wildlife Refuge (ANWR) in Alaska. Seven Republicans voted against the administration's position, while three Democrats voted with the president.

Then, in late December, the earlier narrow ANWR victory turned to defeat when the issue surfaced again on the fiscal 2006 Defense spending bill. That time, three Republicans voted against the president's position and refused to end a Democratic filibuster. And then seven Republicans again voted with all but one Democrat to strike the drilling language from the bill.

Just over 53 percent of the House is Republican, and on several close votes GOP leaders had to work extra hard to keep their members in line — as they did during a Nov. 18 vote on the spending cut bill — or woo Democrats to offset Republican defections, as during the July 28 vote on the Central American trade pact. To prevail on that vote, GOP leaders had to count on the votes of 15 Democrats to help offset 27 Republican defectors.

"They are still, at the end of the day, able to twist enough arms to pass their agenda," said House Minority Leader Nancy Pelosi of California. "It appears to be harder for them to do, but they prevail."

"What we are finding is that more and more Republicans are questioning some of the basic tenets of the Bush administration," Durbin said.

To the long-frustrated minority party, what seems to stand out about Bush's success with Congress over the year that just concluded is not how often Republicans had to scramble to deliver victories but how infrequently the president had to walk away empty-handed.

Hoyer expressed surprise that the president's success score wasn't higher. "This president is the first president that I know of who has never vetoed a bill," Hoyer said. "Why? Because this Congress is complacent and complicit and if [Bush] doesn't want it sent down there, if they [administration officials] don't want it passed, they don't pass it."

Bush does have that unbroken no-veto record. If it continues, he will be in the company of Thomas Jefferson, the only two-term president

never to return a bill to Congress.

During the 2006 congressional elections, Democrats want to turn that record into a liability for vulnerable Republicans. "What we'll say is if you want an independent representative for your district, vote Democratic. If you want a rubber stamp, vote Republican," Pelosi said.

Complaints of excess partisanship flow both ways and Republican leaders say that reaching out to Democrats is too often a waste of their time. After being repeatedly rebuffed across the aisle, several GOP leaders said, they became more determined to defend administration initiatives that might otherwise get a more critical reception.

"There has been an unusual and disappointing level of partisanship coming from the Democratic minority, and it has made it more difficult to bring issues together," said Bob Stevenson, a spokesman for

Frist. "In some ways that has galvanized the Republican majority."

Sen. Trent Lott agreed. "Every time Republicans get mad with the administration, the Democrats misplay or overplay their hand and make us mad and drive us right back into the arms of the president," the Mississippi Republican said.

That has been especially true on issues related to the administration's actions in Iraq and its anti-terrorism effort, Lott said. "They don't leave the Republicans any running room to maneuver away from what the president is trying to do," he said.

Whatever the causes, the effects are clear. "Especially in the House, Republicans understand that in order to pass major pieces of legislation, they need to stick together," said GOP strategist Mattoon. "They will get very little help from the Democrats." ■

# House Democrats Reach Record Unity

THERE WAS A TIME when to be a Democrat in Congress was akin to belonging to a luncheon club just so you could eat the food and enjoy the people. Staying for the program wasn't such a priority. No longer. Democrats on Capitol Hill are relying more on what has been the GOP political playbook, staying in step and sometimes getting tough with those who miss a beat.

A decade after Republicans determined there was value in strict adherence to party discipline, the message has sunk in on the other side of the aisle, and 2005 was a breakout year. Over the past half-century, Democrats in the House were never more unified, an analysis of roll call votes by Congressional Quarterly shows. And only twice before, in 1999 and 2001, were Senate Democrats more united than in 2005.

At the same time, House Republicans, who have played at this game much longer, increased their party loyalty a bit over 2004, though they didn't quite meet the record they set in 1995 — the year they took command of the chamber for the first time in four decades — and reached twice since in 2001 and 2003. Only Senate Republicans fell off the pace in 2005, dropping well below the level of partisan cohesion they reached in 2003. That year, in fact, still appears to have been the most partisan in Congress since World War II.

One manifestation of the leaders' demand for loyalty is a rising number of roll call votes on which a majority of Republicans line up against a majority of Democrats: These are party unity votes as defined by CQ. Almost half of the 669 recorded House votes in 2005 met this definition, as did almost two-thirds of the 366 Senate roll calls. Overall, party unity scores show Congress is becoming more divided on more issues more often, leaving little room for compromise on major issues.

Moreover, rising Democratic unity has forced the majority Republicans to work harder to win — and resulted in a few high-profile GOP defeats that also jeopardized the legislative agenda of President Bush.

An utter lack of Democratic support, for example, required Republican leaders to twist arms and make promises to preserve very narrow victories in both chambers on a spending cut bill that still must survive one more test in the House in 2006. Likewise, most Democrats refused to vote for the Central American Free Trade Agreement (CAFTA) — the centerpiece of Bush's trade agenda — leaving Republicans to scramble to win sufficient support from within their own ranks. And when House Democrats held tighter than the Republicans on a bill to permit federally financed medical research using embryonic stem cells, the GOP and the president both suffered a loss.

It's no coincidence that all three of those votes show up in a companion CQ analysis of the president's influence and were picked by CQ's editors as among the 28 "key votes" of 2005. (Presidential support, p. B-3; key votes, p. C-3)

"Democrats are emboldened," said Sarah Binder, a senior fellow at the Brookings Institution in Washington. "Democrats ... are going to be more cohesive when they're in the minority when they think they have an incentive to regain the majority."

House Democratic Leader Nancy Pelosi of California showed that she has learned from former House Majority Leader Tom DeLay of Texas and other GOP practitioners of strong-arm tactics to keep her caucus aligned. So serious have Democrats become about catching up — both at the ballot box and in party discipline — that in mid-December, Pelosi lambasted Edolphus Towns of New York for being absent during a crucial roll call on the spending cut bill that Republicans won by two votes.

Pelosi threatened to yank Towns' seat on the Energy and Commerce Committee, which would ordinarily be a high price to pay for a single missed roll call. But Towns was a repeat offender in Pelosi's book, having helped the opposition by voting in favor of the Central American trade pact in July. Then, as well, the GOP had prevailed by two votes.

"Traditionally we haven't been this unified," said Rep. Jim McDermott, D-Wash., who voted with his party colleagues 99 percent of the time in 2005.

He gave credit to Pelosi, a liberal Californian who critics said early on would be too out of step with the mainstream to be an effective leader. "It's primarily a reflection of Nancy's leadership as a persuasive voice to people all across the board," he said. "You can't dismiss her as some wild-eyed San Francisco liberal."

The evidence of rising unity is in the numbers: House Democrats voted with their party colleagues a record 88 percent of the time in 2005, just below the 90 percent average party support score House Republicans posted. The previous high for House Democrats was 87 percent in 2003; House Republicans reached 91 percent that year, in 2001 and in 1995.

In the Senate, both parties stuck together 88 percent of the time in 2005. For Democrats, that was a jump from an 83 percent average party support score in 2004, and just a hair below their record of 89 percent set in 1999 and 2001. For Senate Republicans, the drop in support from a record 94 percent in 2003 and a 90 percent score in 2004 helps

# Partisanship High as Democrats Still Lag Behind GOP

House Democrats were more unified than ever in 2005, voting on average with the party majority 88 percent of the time. House Republicans remained the most united group in Congress, with a 90 percent party unity score, close to an all-time high. In the Senate, Republicans supported the party position slightly less often than a year earlier, while Democrats rallied together more frequently.

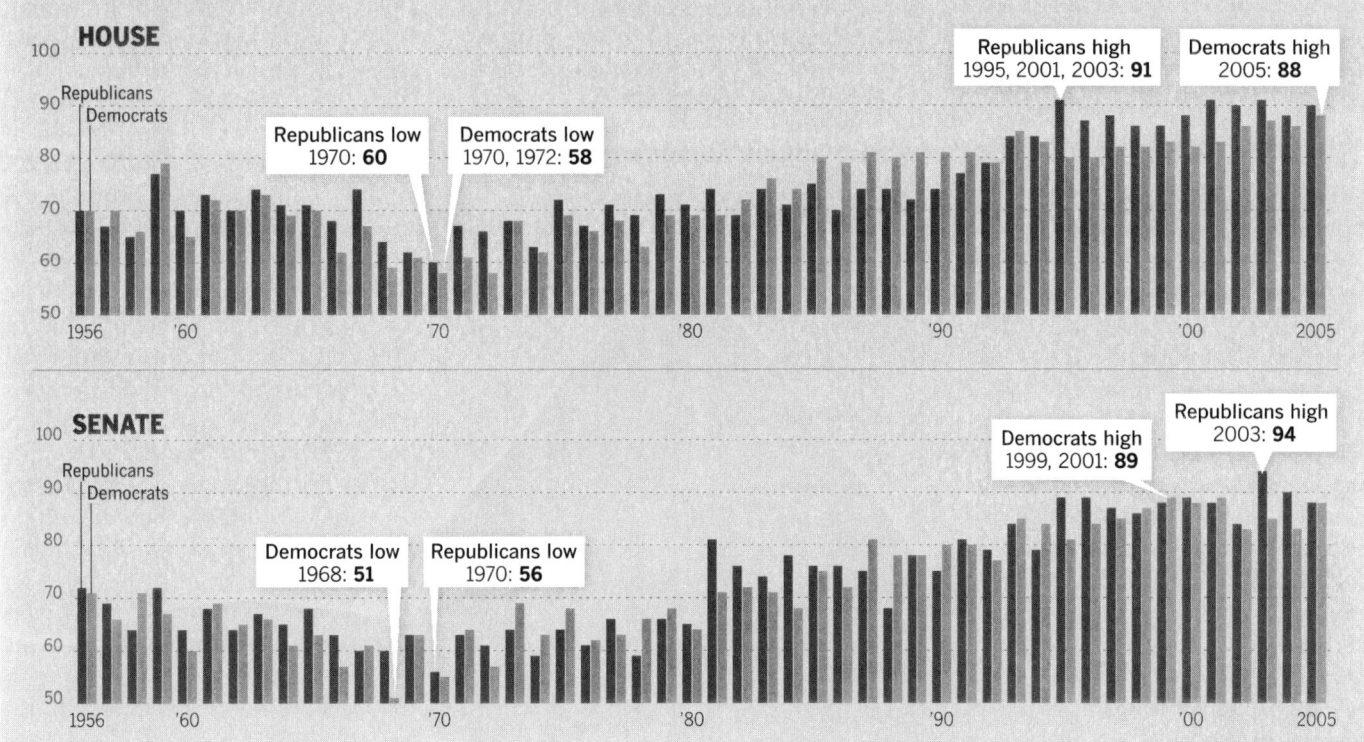

explain why they lost several critical votes in the days before Congress adjourned for the year.

"In the last six months, it's clearly been a more partisan place," said Todd Akin of Missouri, one of five House Republicans who voted with his party more than 99 percent of the time in 2005. "It's a precursor to a rigorous election season."

Still, GOP leaders scoff at the idea that Democrats are making any headway. And Republicans say they have remained remarkably unified considering the political pressures that accompany public sentiment about the war in Iraq and the task of running Congress in the face of increasingly aggressive tactics by the minority Democrats.

"On the issues that are most important to the American people, the Republicans have been united," said Amy Call, a spokeswoman for Senate Majority Leader Bill Frist of Tennessee, who at times has struggled to control his chamber.

## IT'S UNANIMOUS

Rising Democratic unity can also be seen in the frequency with which lawmakers voted unanimously on party unity roll calls. For years, GOP leader have managed often to squelch defections in their ranks — and in the notable partisan year of 2003, Republicans on both sides of the Capitol were unanimous on 239 party unity votes.

Democrats rose to the occasion, voting unanimously 82 times in the House and 69 times in the Senate. Those totals essentially matched the 91 times that Republicans voted unanimously in the House and the 59 times they did so in the Senate.

"I can't remember as many votes with 100 percent Democrats as we've had in the past couple of months," said House Minority Whip Steny H. Hoyer of Maryland.

Hoyer attributed the cohesion of his party's caucus to a coming of age of Pelosi's leadership — which has been under fire as Democrats struggled the past few years — and to what he termed "an exclusively partisan agenda" on the part of GOP leaders. "Whether you are conservative, liberal or moderate you find yourself disagreeing with the Republicans," he said.

He may have a point that is borne out in declining individual party unity scores for at least a dozen moderates in the Republican Party who feel alienated, as well as for some fiscal conservatives in the House who voted against Republican spending initiatives they thought were too expensive. At the same time, party unity scores for some moderate Democrats also fell in 2005, suggesting that disaffection with the deeper partisan strains of the leadership extends across the aisle.

The shift by moderates was especially evident among blue-state Republican senators, such as Susan Collins and Olympia J. Snowe of Maine, who have found it increasingly difficult to stick with their party on close votes. Collins' support score declined 19 points to 59 percent, and Snowe's score dropped 15 points to 56 percent.

Their defections, like that of Lincoln Cha-

## 2005 DATA
### AVERAGE PARTY UNITY SCORE

All Republicans: 90 percent
All Democrats: 88 percent

**HOUSE**
Republicans 90% — Democrats 88%

**SENATE**
Republicans 88% — Democrats 88%

**VOTES**

|  | SENATE | HOUSE |
|---|---|---|
| PARTISAN VOTES | 229 | 328 |
| TOTAL | 366 | 669 |
|  | 63% | 49% |

### FOR MORE INFORMATION

| | |
|---|---|
| Top scorers | 96 |
| Background | 97 |
| History | 98 |
| Senators' scores | 99 |
| House members' scores | 100 |

fee of Rhode Island, who backed his party less than half the time in 2005, will undoubtedly make it harder for Frist to accomplish his goals. Next year is Frist's last to make his mark as a legislator and a leader in preparation for a possible presidential run in 2008. He will not seek re-election to the Senate when his term ends in 2006.

Chafee, who represents a state that Democratic Sen. John Kerry carried by 20 points in the 2004 presidential election, says he isn't ashamed that he stayed with his party on only 47 percent of the party unity votes.

"I strive for consistency," he said with a chuckle when informed that his party support score was dead last among Republicans for the sixth straight year. "I would hope that consistency is there and that's what Rhode Islanders want."

Senate moderates have always been an important bloc in a chamber where the minority can block almost any legislation if they can muster 40 votes to sustain a filibuster. But over the past year, GOP moderates became a more significant voting bloc in the House, too.

Michael N. Castle of Delaware, Christopher Shays of Connecticut, Mark Steven Kirk of Illinois, Sherwood Boehlert of New York and Nancy L. Johnson of Connecticut are among a handful whose party support scores dropped. While moderates have often been ignored by conservative leaders in the House, their power was on display briefly when they blocked passage of the spending cut measure and demanded that a provision be removed that would have allowed oil and natural gas drilling in the Arctic National Wildlife Refuge.

"Moderate Republicans represent that old silent majority," said Wayne T. Gilchrest of Maryland, whose party support score dropped to 80 percent from 85 percent. "This is the dawning of a new day."

Some moderate Senate Democrats also shied from their party. Thomas R. Carper of Delaware, Mary L. Landrieu of Louisiana, Ben Nelson of Nebraska and Kent Conrad of North Dakota all voted with Republicans more often in 2005 than in 2004. Nelson was last among Democrats, voting with his party only 46 percent of the time.

### ELECTION WORRIES

And while Nelson's supporters in the strongly Republican state of Nebraska may remain comfortable with his record of defections, some GOP senators facing tough re-election fights in 2006 are finding similar reasons to occasionally abandon their party.

Mike DeWine of Ohio, who has trailed in his 2006 re-election campaign in some public opinion polls, saw his party support score drop to 70 percent from 79 percent. Chafee, who already has a primary challenger, dropped to 47 percent from 65 percent. Even the reliably conservative Rick Santorum, who trails in Pennsylvania surveys, dropped

## Unanimous Votes Are More Common

This graph shows the number of times that members of one party unanimously opposed a majority of the other party on roll call votes. Unanimous votes have become more frequent. That is especially true for Democrats, who recorded a record 151 unanimous roll calls in both chambers in 2005.

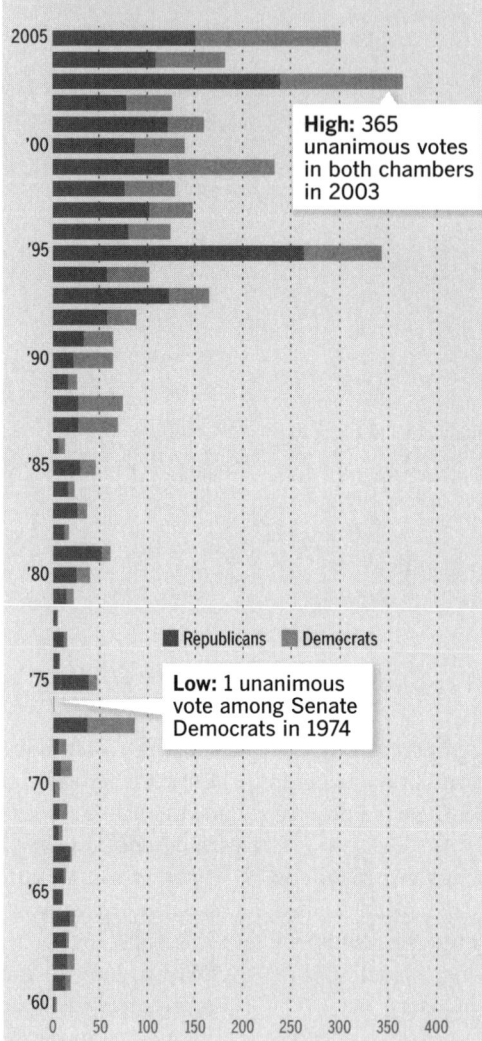

High: 365 unanimous votes in both chambers in 2003

Republicans  Democrats

Low: 1 unanimous vote among Senate Democrats in 1974

to 92 percent in his party support score from 96 percent. That put the chairman of the Republican Conference in the middle of the pack among fellow GOP senators.

Santorum dismissed his decline in party loyalty as having nothing to do with his election. "I'm sure it fluctuates every year," he said. "It just depends on what the votes are on."

And Jim Talent of Missouri, who trails in early public opinion surveys and whose party support score dropped to 84 percent from 96 percent, said he is willing to stand apart on core issues and that his overall loyalty to the GOP is not in question. "I'm not aware of the [party unity] scores, but I am aware when I'm disagreeing with my party or when I criticize the administration" on an issue, Talent said.

The impact of election-year politics wasn't limited to GOP senators. Democratic Rep. Harold E. Ford Jr. of Tennessee, who is running for Frist's Senate seat in a firmly Republican state, came across as more moderate in 2005, as his party support score dropped 7 points to 83 percent.

### OPTIMISTIC DEMOCRATS

Rising Democratic unity is boosting the confidence of the party's leaders. In the Senate, by banding together and winning a few GOP allies, Democrats derailed renewal of the 2001 anti-terrorism law known as the Patriot Act. In fact, they closed the year by winning seven of the last eight party unity votes.

In the House, Democrats rarely win major votes because they are badly outnumbered and the Republicans closely control the debate. But Pelosi has made her GOP counterparts work harder to win. "When I became leader, the Democrats were sort of a co-op. It was an amalgamation of ideas," Pelosi said. "We've decided to define ourselves and our priorities."

On the CAFTA vote, for example, House Republican leaders had to hold the roll call open after midnight July 27 while cajoling some of their more hesitant rank-and-file members to vote for the trade agreement. And on Nov. 17, the first time House leaders brought the conference agreement on the fiscal 2006 Labor/Health and Human Services spending bill up for a vote, all 201 Democrats voted against it, joined by 22 Republicans. Together, they temporarily killed the measure until it could be retooled and brought back to the House floor.

Republicans, meanwhile, have been working to instill party discipline in the next generation of House leaders — freshmen such as Patrick T. McHenry of North Carolina and Bobby Jindal of Louisiana. McHenry backed his party 99 percent of the time on party unity votes. Jindal voted with Republicans 97 percent of the time, and emphasized the few occasions he did not go along with party marching orders. "More important than the number is looking at the particular issue," Jindal said. "There have been times where I voted against the party, like CAFTA."

# Leading Scorers: Party Unity

**Support** indicates those who in 2005 voted most often with a majority of their party against a majority of the other party. **Opposition** shows those who voted most often against their party's majority on such party unity votes. Scores are based on actual votes cast. Members who missed half or more of the votes are not listed. Scores are rounded to 1 decimal point; those with identical scores are listed alphabetically. *(Complete scores, pp. B-21, B-22)*

| SUPPORT | | | OPPOSITION | | |
|---|---|---|---|---|---|
| **Republicans** | | **Democrats** | **Republicans** | | **Democrats** |
| McConnell, Ky. | 98.7% | Kennedy, Mass. 100.0% | Chafee, R.I. | 52.6% | Nelson, Ben, Neb. 53.9% |
| Bunning, Ky. | 98.2 | Boxer, Calif. 98.7 | Snowe, Maine | 44.1 | Baucus, Mont. 25.7 |
| Kyl, Ariz. | 97.8 | Durbin, Ill. 98.7 | Collins, Maine | 41.0 | Conrad, N.D. 23.6 |
| Allard, Colo. | 96.9 | Sarbanes, Md. 98.7 | Specter, Pa. | 31.4 | Landrieu, La. 23.5 |
| Cochran, Miss. | 96.9 | Lautenberg, N.J. 98.2 | DeWine, Ohio | 29.8 | Carper, Del. 23.1 |
| Sessions, Ala. | 96.9 | Mikulski, Md. 98.1 | Coleman, Minn. | 23.2 | Pryor, Ark. 19.7 |
| Brownback, Kan. | 96.5 | Harkin, Iowa 97.8 | Smith, Ore. | 17.8 | Lincoln, Ark. 18.8 |
| DeMint, S.C. | 96.5 | Reed, R.I. 97.8 | Talent, Mo. | 16.2 | Johnson, S.D. 17.0 |
| Frist, Tenn. | 96.5 | Kerry, Mass. 96.9 | McCain, Ariz. | 16.0 | Nelson, Bill, Fla. 16.2 |
| Bennett, Utah | 96.4 | Leahy, Vt. 96.9 | Voinovich, Ohio | 15.8 | Salazar, Colo. 16.2 |
| Grassley, Iowa | 95.6 | Levin, Mich. 96.9 | Lugar, Ind. | 15.6 | Byrd, W.Va. 15.9 |
| Hatch, Utah | 95.6 | Obama, Ill. 96.9 | Warner, Va. | 13.7 | Bingaman, N.M. 14.6 |

| SUPPORT | | | OPPOSITION | | |
|---|---|---|---|---|---|
| **Republicans** | | **Democrats** | **Republicans** | | **Democrats** |
| Akin, Mo. | 99.7% | Schakowsky, Ill. 99.7% | Leach, Iowa | 37.4% | Boren, Okla. 41.3% |
| Neugebauer, Texas | 99.4 | Miller, Calif. 99.4 | Shays, Conn. | 32.9 | Cramer, Ala. 40.5 |
| Blackburn, Tenn. | 99.1 | Lewis, Ga. 99.3 | Paul, Texas | 28.4 | Peterson, Minn. 36.0 |
| McHenry, N.C. | 99.1 | Payne, N.J. 99.3 | Simmons, Conn. | 25.6 | Taylor, Miss. 34.9 |
| Musgrave, Colo. | 99.1 | Meehan, Mass. 99.1 | Fitzpatrick, Pa. | 24.3 | Marshall, Ga. 33.3 |
| Barrett, S.C. | 99.0 | Van Hollen, Md. 99.1 | Castle, Del. | 23.6 | Davis, Tenn. 33.2 |
| Sessions, Texas | 99.0 | Becerra, Calif. 99.0 | Johnson, Ill. | 23.3 | Matheson, Utah 30.8 |
| Foxx, N.C. | 98.8 | McDermott, Wash. 99.0 | Boehlert, N.Y. | 23.1 | Cuellar, Texas 29.6 |
| Hayes, N.C. | 98.8 | Baldwin, Wis. 98.8 | Ehlers, Mich. | 21.6 | McIntyre, N.C. 29.5 |
| Cantor, Va. | 98.5 | McGovern, Mass. 98.8 | Smith, N.J. | 21.4 | Melancon, La. 29.2 |
| Franks, Ariz. | 98.5 | Pelosi, Calif. 98.8 | Johnson, Conn. | 20.9 | Tanner, Tenn. 26.5 |
| Garrett, N.J. | 98.5 | Sanchez, Linda, Calif. 98.8 | Ramstad, Minn. | 20.1 | Gordon, Tenn. 26.1 |
| King, Iowa | 98.5 | Woolsey, Calif. 98.8 | Gilchrest, Md. | 20.0 | Holden, Pa. 25.5 |
| Ryun, Kan. | 98.5 | | Kirk, Ill. | 19.6 | Edwards, Texas 25.2 |

## THE MORE THINGS CHANGE . . .

Despite a handful of significant partisan departures, several reliable trends continued in 2005.

For instance, Southern Democrats representing Republican states were the least loyal to their party, while Northern Republicans parted ways with the GOP more often than colleagues from other regions. And strong delegation-wide support for their parties was logged by Texas Republicans, California Democrats and Massachusetts Democrats.

There was no reason to expect the divisive atmosphere in either chamber would change in the second session, with an election coming up and Capitol Hill captivated by the latest installment in the saga of superlobbyist-turned-confessed-criminal Jack Abramoff, whose Jan. 3, 2006, guilty plea rattled the ranks of lawmakers and lobbyists alike.

"Parties aren't letting up," said Binder, the Brookings scholar. "They may look even more partisan in an election year. The minority won't have much incentive to hand victories to the majority."

The GOP majority, in turn, is likely to be highly motivated to stay unified as it strives to give its members opportunities to show a record of accomplishment to the voters who will decide how many Republicans return to Congress next year.

As 2005 wound down, Blunt reflected on the first session of the 109th Congress and public opinion polls showing a negative opinion of the legislative branch, and he professed to see a silver lining in those clouds: the expectation of a positive reaction to the session-closing votes to trim government spending, provide funding for military operations, and provide help for the states devastated by hurricanes Katrina and Rita.

"People's dissatisfaction with gas prices and the war has had an effect," he said. "What we've done over the last three weeks will have a positive impact on people's view of Congress." ■

# Second Most Roll Calls in a Decade

SENATORS AND HOUSE MEMBERS made more frequent appearances on the floors of their respective chambers in 2005 to cast "yea" or "nay" votes on the issue of the day than in any of the prior three years — reversing a recent trend of declining roll calls and diminished attendance.

House bells rang 669 times in 2005 signaling that members were being asked to cast a vote. That was just shy of the 675 roll calls in 2003 and the second most since 1995, when the House took 867 recorded votes. And while House members were being called to the floor more often, they were also more likely to show up. On average, House members actually cast votes 95.9 percent of the time — the highest percentage since 2001. Moreover, the voting percentage in the House was higher than the chamber's average for the past decade. The Senate was hardly less busy. On 366 occasions in 2005, the Senate clerk called the roll and recorded senators' positions. That was up from a 43-year low of 216 recorded votes in 2004 and a bit above the chamber's 50-year average. Senators, too, were more responsive than in the recent past, voting on average 97.4 percent of the time, above the 95.5 percent for 2004.

Still, while perfect attendance at roll calls is sometimes used by lawmakers as a badge of honor — and while overall the voting percentage for Congress is several percentage points higher during the last decade than it was in the previous 40 or so years — fewer and fewer members seem to make it to the floor for every vote. Only seven senators and nine House members cast ballots on every roll call in 2005, down from 18 senators and 11 House members the year before. Sen. Charles E. Grassley, R-Iowa, has the longest running perfect attendance record of any member of the 109th Congress; the last roll call he missed was in July 1993.

## Perfect Attendance

The following were the only lawmakers who cast "yea" or "nay" votes on every roll call ballot conducted in 2005:

### SENATE
**Republicans**
Susan Collins of Maine
Charles E. Grassley of Iowa
Olympia J. Snowe of Maine
Jim Talent of Missouri

**Democrats**
Thomas R. Carper of Delaware
Harry Reid of Nevada
Ken Salazar of Colorado

### HOUSE
**Republicans**
Robert B. Aderholt of Alabama
John J. "Jimmy" Duncan Jr. of Tennessee
Robert W. Goodlatte of Virginia
Mark Kennedy of Minnesota
John Kline of Minnesota
Ralph Regula of Ohio
Fred Upton of Michigan

**Democrats**
Dale E. Kildee of Michigan
Brad Miller of North Carolina

Congressional Quarterly gives lawmakers credit for voting only when they cast a "yea" or a "nay" during a roll call. Very occasionally, members will vote "present" either to avoid a perceived conflict of interest or to stage some form of protest. Often, these votes aren't explained, but regardless of explanation, members who vote present aren't counted by CQ as having participated in the vote.

For Congress as a whole, voting statistics for 2005 were exceptional. The 1,035 roll calls in both chambers made up the third highest total in a quarter-century, and the collective participation rate of 96.1 percent was the fourth highest in that time.

In part, the increase in roll call votes can be explained by a jump in work days. The House was in session 140 days, compared with 110 during the election year of 2004 and 133 in 2003. The Senate met on 159 calendar days in 2005, up from 133 the year before, though fewer than the 167 in 2003.

Especially for the House, sessions on the weekend, Monday or Friday were more prevalent than in the recent past. For several years, House leaders have regularly postponed floor votes for early in the week until after 6 p.m. on Tuesdays and have rarely scheduled Friday sessions, so members would have time to travel to their districts. The House met once on Saturday and twice on Sunday, the first time since 1995 there was more than one Sunday session in a year. Even so, the House met only 11 times on Friday all year long, and just 25 times on Monday.

The Senate, meantime, held two Saturday sessions and two on Sunday, the same as in 2004. ∎

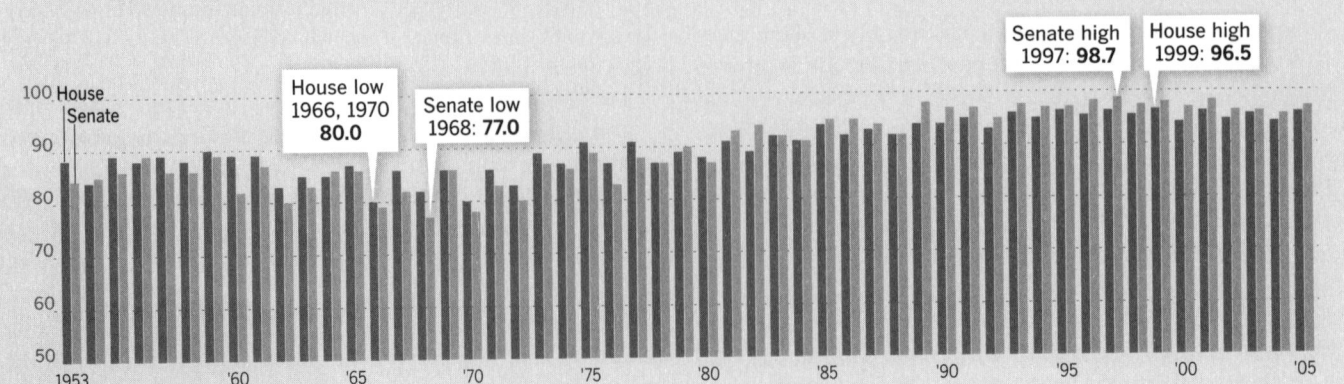

## Lawmakers Answer the Bell More Frequently

Lawmakers were more likely to show up on the floor and vote in 2005 than in the previous year, which was a 12-year low in voting participation for the Senate and matched a 12-year low for the House. Senators voted on average 97.4 percent of the time last year, and House members voted 95.9 percent of the time. For Congress as a whole, the participation rate was 96.1 percent, the highest in four years.

Senate high
1997: **98.7**

House high
1999: **96.5**

House low
1966, 1970
**80.0**

Senate low
1968: **77.0**

# Voting Participation History

These tables show the number of roll call votes and average participation rates for Congress as a whole and for each chamber since 1953.

| YEAR | ROLL CALLS | RATE | YEAR | ROLL CALLS | RATE | YEAR | ROLL CALLS | RATE |
|---|---|---|---|---|---|---|---|---|
| 2005 | 1,035 | 96.1% | 2005 | 669 | 95.9% | 2005 | 366 | 97.4% |
| 2004 | 759 | 94.2 | 2004 | 543 | 94.1 | 2004 | 216 | 95.5 |
| 2003 | 1,134 | 95.7 | 2003 | 675 | 95.6 | 2003 | 459 | 96.1 |
| 2002 | 736 | 94.8 | 2002 | 483 | 94.6 | 2002 | 253 | 96.3 |
| 2001 | 887 | 96.5 | 2001 | 507 | 96.2 | 2001 | 380 | 98.2 |
| 2000 | 898 | 94.4 | 2000 | 600 | 94.1 | 2000 | 298 | 96.9 |
| 1999 | 983 | 96.6 | 1999 | 609 | 96.5 | 1999 | 374 | 97.9 |
| 1998 | 847 | 95.7 | 1998 | 533 | 95.5 | 1998 | 314 | 97.4 |
| 1997 | 931 | 96.5 | 1997 | 633 | 96.3 | 1997 | 298 | 98.7 |
| 1996 | 760 | 95.8 | 1996 | 454 | 95.5 | 1996 | 306 | 98.2 |
| 1995 | 1,480 | 96.5 | 1995 | 867 | 96.4 | 1995 | 613 | 97.1 |
| 1994 | 826 | 95.0 | 1994 | 497 | 95.0 | 1994 | 329 | 97.0 |
| 1993 | 992 | 96.0 | 1993 | 597 | 96.0 | 1993 | 395 | 97.6 |
| 1992 | 743 | 93.4 | 1992 | 473 | 93.0 | 1992 | 270 | 95.0 |
| 1991 | 708 | 95.0 | 1991 | 428 | 95.0 | 1991 | 280 | 97.0 |
| 1990 | 862 | 95.0 | 1990 | 536 | 94.0 | 1990 | 326 | 97.0 |
| 1989 | 680 | 95.0 | 1989 | 368 | 94.0 | 1989 | 312 | 98.0 |
| 1988 | 830 | 92.0 | 1988 | 451 | 92.0 | 1988 | 379 | 92.0 |
| 1987 | 908 | 93.0 | 1987 | 488 | 93.0 | 1987 | 420 | 94.0 |
| 1986 | 805 | 93.0 | 1986 | 451 | 92.0 | 1986 | 354 | 95.0 |
| 1985 | 820 | 94.0 | 1985 | 439 | 94.0 | 1985 | 381 | 95.0 |
| 1984 | 683 | 91.0 | 1984 | 408 | 91.0 | 1984 | 275 | 91.0 |
| 1983 | 869 | 92.0 | 1983 | 498 | 92.0 | 1983 | 371 | 92.0 |
| 1982 | 924 | 90.0 | 1982 | 459 | 89.0 | 1982 | 465 | 94.0 |
| 1981 | 836 | 92.0 | 1981 | 353 | 91.0 | 1981 | 483 | 93.0 |
| 1980 | 1,135 | 87.0 | 1980 | 604 | 88.0 | 1980 | 531 | 87.0 |
| 1979 | 1,169 | 89.0 | 1979 | 672 | 89.0 | 1979 | 497 | 90.0 |
| 1978 | 1,350 | 87.0 | 1978 | 834 | 87.0 | 1978 | 516 | 87.0 |
| 1977 | 1,341 | 90.0 | 1977 | 706 | 91.0 | 1977 | 635 | 88.0 |
| 1976 | 1,349 | 86.0 | 1976 | 661 | 87.0 | 1976 | 688 | 83.0 |
| 1975 | 1,214 | 91.0 | 1975 | 612 | 91.0 | 1975 | 602 | 89.0 |
| 1974 | 1,081 | 87.0 | 1974 | 537 | 87.0 | 1974 | 544 | 86.0 |
| 1973 | 1,135 | 89.0 | 1973 | 541 | 89.0 | 1973 | 594 | 87.0 |
| 1972 | 861 | 82.0 | 1972 | 329 | 83.0 | 1972 | 532 | 80.0 |
| 1971 | 743 | 85.0 | 1971 | 320 | 86.0 | 1971 | 423 | 83.0 |
| 1970 | 684 | 79.0 | 1970 | 266 | 80.0 | 1970 | 418 | 78.0 |
| 1969 | 422 | 86.0 | 1969 | 177 | 86.0 | 1969 | 245 | 86.0 |
| 1968 | 514 | 80.0 | 1968 | 233 | 82.0 | 1968 | 281 | 77.0 |
| 1967 | 560 | 85.0 | 1967 | 245 | 86.0 | 1967 | 315 | 82.0 |
| 1966 | 428 | 79.0 | 1966 | 193 | 80.0 | 1966 | 235 | 79.0 |
| 1965 | 459 | 87.0 | 1965 | 201 | 87.0 | 1965 | 258 | 86.0 |
| 1964 | 418 | 85.0 | 1964 | 113 | 85.0 | 1964 | 305 | 86.0 |
| 1963 | 348 | 84.0 | 1963 | 119 | 85.0 | 1963 | 229 | 83.0 |
| 1962 | 348 | 82.0 | 1962 | 124 | 83.0 | 1962 | 224 | 80.0 |
| 1961 | 320 | 88.0 | 1961 | 116 | 89.0 | 1961 | 204 | 87.0 |
| 1960 | 300 | 87.0 | 1960 | 93 | 89.0 | 1960 | 207 | 82.0 |
| 1959 | 302 | 89.0 | 1959 | 87 | 90.0 | 1959 | 215 | 89.0 |
| 1958 | 293 | 87.0 | 1958 | 93 | 88.0 | 1958 | 200 | 86.0 |
| 1957 | 207 | 88.0 | 1957 | 100 | 89.0 | 1957 | 107 | 86.0 |
| 1956 | 203 | 88.0 | 1956 | 73 | 88.0 | 1956 | 130 | 89.0 |
| 1955 | 163 | 88.0 | 1955 | 76 | 89.0 | 1955 | 87 | 86.0 |
| 1954 | 247 | 84.0 | 1954 | 76 | 84.0 | 1954 | 171 | 85.0 |
| 1953 | 160 | 87.4 | 1953 | 71 | 88.2 | 1953 | 89 | 84.3 |

# Presidential Support Background

Congressional Quarterly selects the roll call votes used for its presidential support study based on explicit statements made by the president or his authorized spokesmen. **Support** scores show the percentage of roll calls on which members voted in agreement with the president. **Opposition** scores show the percentage of roll calls on which members voted against the president's position. **Success** shows the percentage of the selected votes on which the president prevailed. A member's failure to vote reduces the average scores for his party and chamber.

**Economic affairs** includes votes on trade and on omnibus and supplemental spending bills, which may fund both domestic and defense/foreign policy programs. **Confirmation** votes in the Senate are included only in chamber average scores.

| | Defense/Foreign Policy | | Domestic | | Economic Affairs | | Overall | |
|---|---|---|---|---|---|---|---|---|
| | 2005 | 2004 | 2005 | 2004 | 2005 | 2004 | 2005 | 2004 |
| Senate | 67% | 100% | 64% | 31% | 75% | 100% | 78% | 74% |
| House | 73 | 50 | 85 | 78 | 67 | 75 | 78 | 71 |
| Congress | 71 | 60 | 78 | 58 | 69 | 82 | 78 | 73 |

| | Support | | | | | Opposition | | | |
|---|---|---|---|---|---|---|---|---|---|
| | Republicans | | Democrats | | | Republicans | | Democrats | |
| | 2005 | 2004 | 2005 | 2004 | | 2005 | 2004 | 2005 | 2004 |
| Senate | 86% | 91% | 38% | 60% | Senate | 12% | 7% | 59% | 35% |
| House | 81 | 80 | 24 | 30 | House | 17 | 16 | 74 | 66 |

| | Support | | | | | | | | Opposition | | | | | | | |
|---|---|---|---|---|---|---|---|---|---|---|---|---|---|---|---|---|
| | East | | West | | South | | Midwest | | | East | | West | | South | | Midwest | |
| | 2005 | 2004 | 2005 | 2004 | 2005 | 2004 | 2005 | 2004 | | 2005 | 2004 | 2005 | 2004 | 2005 | 2004 | 2005 | 2004 |
| **Republicans** | | | | | | | | | **Republicans** | | | | | | | | |
| Senate | 73% | 85% | 85% | 91% | 90% | 93% | 87% | 91% | Senate | 24% | 12% | 12% | 6% | 8% | 6% | 12% | 7% |
| House | 75 | 74 | 83 | 82 | 83 | 82 | 79 | 81 | House | 24 | 18 | 15 | 14 | 14 | 12 | 18 | 16 |
| **Democrats** | | | | | | | | | | | | | | | | | |
| Senate | 32 | 56 | 31 | 59 | 54 | 64 | 39 | 62 | Senate | 63 | 35 | 59 | 37 | 44 | 27 | 58 | 38 |
| House | 20 | 26 | 19 | 26 | 33 | 39 | 24 | 28 | House | 79 | 70 | 78 | 70 | 63 | 56 | 75 | 67 |

Annual **success** rate combining the results of votes in both chambers of Congress

| Eisenhower | | Johnson | | Ford | | | | | |
|---|---|---|---|---|---|---|---|---|---|
| 1953 | 89.2% | 1964 | 87.9% | 1974 | 58.2% | 1984 | 65.8% | 1995 | 36.2% |
| 1954 | 78.3 | 1965 | 93.1 | 1975 | 61.0 | 1985 | 59.9 | 1996 | 55.1 |
| 1955 | 75.3 | 1966 | 78.9 | 1976 | 53.8 | 1986 | 56.1 | 1997 | 53.6 |
| 1956 | 69.7 | 1967 | 78.8 | | | 1987 | 43.5 | 1998 | 50.6 |
| 1957 | 68.4 | 1968 | 74.5 | Carter | | 1988 | 47.4 | 1999 | 37.8 |
| 1958 | 75.7 | | | 1977 | 75.4% | | | 2000 | 55.0 |
| 1959 | 52.0 | | | 1978 | 78.3 | G. Bush | | | |
| 1960 | 65.1 | Nixon | | 1979 | 76.8 | 1989 | 62.6% | G.W. Bush | |
| | | 1969 | 73.9% | 1980 | 75.1 | 1990 | 46.8 | 2001 | 86.7% |
| | | 1970 | 76.9 | | | 1991 | 54.2 | 2002 | 87.8 |
| Kennedy | | 1971 | 74.8 | Reagan | | 1992 | 43.0 | 2003 | 78.7 |
| 1961 | 81.4% | 1972 | 66.3 | 1981 | 82.4% | Clinton | | 2004 | 72.6 |
| 1962 | 85.4 | 1973 | 50.6 | 1982 | 72.4 | 1993 | 86.4% | 2005 | 78.0 |
| 1963 | 87.1 | 1974 | 59.6 | 1983 | 67.1 | 1994 | 86.4 | | |

* **Regions:** Congressional Quarterly defines regions of the United States as follows: **East:** Conn., Del., Maine, Md., Mass., N.H., N.J., N.Y., Pa., R.I., Vt., W.Va. **West:** Alaska, Ariz., Calif., Colo., Hawaii, Idaho, Mont., Nev., N.M., Ore., Utah, Wash., Wyo. **South:** Ala., Ark., Fla., Ga., Ky., La., Miss., N.C., Okla., S.C., Tenn., Texas, Va. **Midwest:** Ill., Ind., Iowa, Kan., Mich., Minn., Mo., Neb., N.D., Ohio, S.D., Wis.

# 2005 House Presidential Position Votes

Following is a list of 46 House roll call votes in 2005 on which the president took a clear position, based on his statements or those from authorized spokesmen. Votes are listed by roll call number in broad categories and identified by topic.

## Economic Affairs and Trade

| VOTE NUMBER | DESCRIPTION |
|---|---|
| **6 Victories** | |
| 102 | Estate tax repeal |
| 443 | Trade (Central America) |
| 601 | Spending cuts |
| 616 | Trade (Bahrain) |
| 621 | Tax cuts |
| 670 | Spending cuts |
| **3 Defeats** | |
| 430 | Postal Service |
| 547 | Financial regulation |
| 612 | Terrorism insurance |

## Defense and Foreign Policy

| VOTE NUMBER | DESCRIPTION |
|---|---|
| **8 Victories** | |
| 219 | Base closures |
| 254 | Cuba embargo |
| 326 | Aid to Egypt |
| 329 | Andean drug offensive |
| 345 | Cuba travel |
| 346 | Cuba travel |
| 348 | Cuba embargo |
| 548 | Base closures |
| **3 Defeats** | |
| 73 | Iraq embassy |
| 282 | U.N. overhaul |
| 630 | Detainee abuse |

## Domestic Policy

| VOTE NUMBER | DESCRIPTION |
|---|---|
| **22 Victories** | |
| 31 | Immigration |
| 35 | Broadcast indecency |
| 38 | Class action overhaul |
| 46 | Faith-based hiring |
| 121 | Auto fuel economy |
| 122 | ANWR oil drilling |
| 132 | Energy policy |
| 144 | Abortion notification |
| 205 | Stem cell research |
| 216 | Abortions (military) |
| 319 | Privacy (Medicare information-sharing) |
| 414 | Patriot Act renewal |
| 426 | Small-business health plans |
| 445 | Energy policy |
| 449 | Medical malpractice |
| 492 | Faith-based hiring |
| 493 | Head Start renewal |
| 533 | Food industry liability |
| 534 | Gunmaker liability |
| 553 | Frivolous lawsuits |
| 627 | Patriot Act renewal |
| 661 | Immigration |
| **4 Defeats** | |
| 204 | Stem cell research |
| 258 | Privacy (library records) |
| 347 | Federal outsourcing |
| 357 | Federal outsourcing |

### House Success Score

| | |
|---|---|
| Victories | 36 |
| Defeats | 10 |
| Total | 46 |
| Success rate | 78.3% |

# 2005 Senate Presidential Position Votes

The following is a list of 45 Senate roll call votes in 2005 on which the president took a clear position, based on his statements or those from authorized spokesmen. Votes are listed by roll call number in broad categories and identified by topic.

## Economic Affairs and Trade

| VOTE NUMBER | DESCRIPTION |
|---|---|
| **3 Victories** | |
| 170 | Trade (Central America) |
| 303 | Spending cuts |
| 363 | Spending cuts |
| **1 Defeat** | |
| 19 | Trade (Canada beef) |

## Defense and Foreign Policy

| VOTE NUMBER | DESCRIPTION |
|---|---|
| **4 Victories** | |
| 104 | Iraq embassy |
| 167 | Cuba travel |
| 171 | Nuclear weapons |
| 309 | Detainee abuse |
| **2 Defeats** | |
| 83 | International family planning |
| 249 | Detainee standards |

## Domestic Policy

| VOTE NUMBER | DESCRIPTION |
|---|---|
| **9 Victories** | |
| 9 | Class action overhaul |
| 52 | ANWR oil drilling |
| 148 | Climate Change |
| 157 | Auto fuel economy |
| 158 | Energy policy |
| 213 | Energy policy |
| 219 | Gunmaker liability |
| 225 | Mercury emissions |
| 288 | ANWR oil drilling |
| **5 Defeats** | |
| 125 | Highway spending |
| 149 | Climate change |
| 175 | First responder grants |
| 358 | Patriot Act renewal |
| 364 | ANWR oil drilling |

## Nominations

| VOTE NUMBER | DESCRIPTION |
|---|---|
| **19 Victories** | |
| 2 | Condoleezza Rice |
| 3 | Alberto R. Gonzales |
| 10 | Michael Chertoff |
| 87 | Paul A. Crotty |
| 107 | John D. Negroponte |
| 111 | J. Michael Seabright |
| 128 | Priscilla Owen |
| 131 | Janice Rogers Brown |
| 133 | William H. Pryor Jr. |
| 134 | Richard A. Griffin |
| 135 | David W. McKeague |
| 136 | Thomas B. Griffith |
| 190 | Lester M. Crawford |
| 198 | Thomas C. Dorr |
| 245 | John G. Roberts Jr. |
| 265 | Brian Edward Sandoval |
| 266 | Harry Sandlin Mattice Jr. |
| 276 | John Richard Smoak |
| 277 | Susan Bicke Neilson |

| VOTE NUMBER | DESCRIPTION |
|---|---|
| **2 Defeats** | |
| 129 | John R. Bolton (cloture) |
| 142 | John R. Bolton (cloture) |

### Senate Success Score

| | |
|---|---|
| Victories | 35 |
| Defeats | 10 |
| Total | 45 |
| Success rate | 77.8% |
| Success rate, minus nominations | 66.7% |

# HOUSE

**1. Presidential Support.** Percentage of recorded votes cast in 2005 on which President Bush took a position and on which the member voted "yea" or "nay" in agreement with the president's position. Failure to vote does not lower an individual's score.

**2. Presidential Opposition.** Percentage of recorded votes cast in 2005 on which President Bush took a position and on which the member voted "yea" or "nay" in disagreement with the president's position. Failure to vote does not lower an individual's score.

**3. Participation in Presidential Support Votes.** Percentage of the 46 recorded House votes on which President Bush took a position and on which the member was present and voted "yea" or "nay."

| | 1 | 2 | 3 |
|---|---|---|---|
| **ALABAMA** | | | |
| 1 Bonner | 83 | 17 | 100 |
| 2 Everett | 85 | 15 | 89 |
| 3 Rogers | 83 | 17 | 89 |
| 4 Aderholt | 93 | 7 | 89 |
| 5 Cramer | 66 | 34 | 89 |
| 6 Bachus | 88 | 12 | 89 |
| 7 Davis | 46 | 54 | 100 |
| **ALASKA** | | | |
| AL Young | 78 | 22 | 98 |
| **ARIZONA** | | | |
| 1 Renzi | 91 | 9 | 100 |
| 2 Franks | 91 | 9 | 98 |
| 3 Shadegg | 96 | 4 | 98 |
| 4 Pastor | 15 | 85 | 100 |
| 5 Hayworth | 85 | 15 | 100 |
| 6 Flake | 74 | 26 | 100 |
| 7 Grijalva | 13 | 87 | 100 |
| 8 Kolbe | 77 | 23 | 96 |
| **ARKANSAS** | | | |
| 1 Berry | 37 | 63 | 100 |
| 2 Snyder | 33 | 67 | 100 |
| 3 Boozman | 77 | 23 | 96 |
| 4 Ross | 49 | 51 | 85 |
| **CALIFORNIA** | | | |
| 1 Thompson | 18 | 82 | 98 |
| 2 Herger | 85 | 15 | 100 |
| 3 Lungren | 91 | 9 | 100 |
| 4 Doolittle | 86 | 14 | 96 |
| 5 Matsui, D.[1] | 14 | 86 | 100 |
| 6 Woolsey | 13 | 87 | 100 |
| 7 Miller, George | 16 | 84 | 98 |
| 8 Pelosi | 16 | 84 | 96 |
| 9 Lee | 13 | 87 | 100 |
| 10 Tauscher | 18 | 82 | 96 |
| 11 Pombo | 85 | 15 | 100 |
| 12 Lantos | 15 | 85 | 100 |
| 13 Stark | 11 | 89 | 98 |
| 14 Eshoo | 19 | 81 | 93 |
| 15 Honda | 18 | 82 | 98 |
| 16 Lofgren | 13 | 87 | 100 |
| 17 Farr | 18 | 82 | 98 |
| 18 Cardoza | 39 | 61 | 100 |
| 19 Radanovich | 86 | 14 | 96 |
| 20 Costa | 42 | 58 | 98 |
| 21 Nunes | 87 | 13 | 98 |
| 22 Thomas | 82 | 18 | 98 |
| 23 Capps | 11 | 89 | 100 |
| 24 Gallegly | 85 | 15 | 100 |
| 25 McKeon | 89 | 11 | 100 |
| 26 Dreier | 89 | 11 | 100 |
| 27 Sherman | 15 | 85 | 100 |
| 28 Berman | 18 | 82 | 98 |
| 29 Schiff | 24 | 76 | 89 |
| 30 Waxman | 16 | 84 | 96 |
| 31 Becerra | 16 | 84 | 98 |
| 32 Solis | 17 | 83 | 100 |
| 33 Watson | 9 | 91 | 98 |
| 34 Roybal-Allard | 15 | 85 | 87 |
| 35 Waters | 14 | 86 | 96 |
| 36 Harman | 26 | 74 | 93 |
| 37 Millender-McD. | 13 | 87 | 87 |
| 38 Napolitano | 14 | 86 | 96 |
| 39 Sánchez, Linda | 13 | 87 | 100 |
| 40 Royce | 89 | 11 | 98 |
| 41 Lewis | 89 | 11 | 100 |
| 42 Miller, Gary | 89 | 11 | 98 |
| 43 Baca | 34 | 66 | 96 |
| 44 Calvert | 89 | 11 | 100 |
| 45 Bono | 80 | 20 | 96 |
| 46 Rohrabacher | 80 | 20 | 100 |
| 47 Sanchez, Loretta | 24 | 76 | 98 |
| 48 Campbell[2] | 100 | 0 | 100 |
| 49 Issa | 89 | 11 | 98 |

| | 1 | 2 | 3 |
|---|---|---|---|
| 50 Cunningham[3] | 89 | 11 | 97 |
| 51 Filner | 15 | 85 | 100 |
| 52 Hunter | 89 | 11 | 98 |
| 53 Davis | 20 | 80 | 100 |
| **COLORADO** | | | |
| 1 DeGette | 16 | 84 | 98 |
| 2 Udall | 20 | 80 | 100 |
| 3 Salazar | 46 | 54 | 100 |
| 4 Musgrave | 89 | 11 | 98 |
| 5 Hefley | 84 | 16 | 96 |
| 6 Tancredo | 80 | 20 | 100 |
| 7 Beauprez | 87 | 13 | 100 |
| **CONNECTICUT** | | | |
| 1 Larson | 15 | 85 | 100 |
| 2 Simmons | 65 | 35 | 93 |
| 3 DeLauro | 9 | 91 | 100 |
| 4 Shays | 57 | 43 | 100 |
| 5 Johnson | 59 | 41 | 100 |
| **DELAWARE** | | | |
| AL Castle | 65 | 35 | 100 |
| **FLORIDA** | | | |
| 1 Miller | 85 | 15 | 100 |
| 2 Boyd | 42 | 58 | 98 |
| 3 Brown | 16 | 84 | 93 |
| 4 Crenshaw | 89 | 11 | 100 |
| 5 Brown-Waite | 83 | 17 | 87 |
| 6 Stearns | 87 | 13 | 98 |
| 7 Mica | 91 | 9 | 98 |
| 8 Keller | 84 | 16 | 96 |
| 9 Bilirakis | 84 | 16 | 98 |
| 10 Young | 82 | 18 | 98 |
| 11 Davis | 26 | 74 | 91 |
| 12 Putnam | 89 | 11 | 100 |
| 13 Harris | 79 | 21 | 91 |
| 14 Mack | 80 | 20 | 96 |
| 15 Weldon | 91 | 9 | 100 |
| 16 Foley | 79 | 21 | 93 |
| 17 Meek | 26 | 74 | 100 |
| 18 Ros-Lehtinen | 79 | 21 | 93 |
| 19 Wexler | 22 | 78 | 89 |
| 20 Wasserman-Schultz | 24 | 76 | 100 |
| 21 Diaz-Balart, L. | 81 | 19 | 93 |
| 22 Shaw | 81 | 19 | 93 |
| 23 Hastings | 21 | 79 | 93 |
| 24 Feeney | 89 | 11 | 96 |
| 25 Diaz-Balart, M. | 87 | 13 | 87 |
| **GEORGIA** | | | |
| 1 Kingston | 85 | 15 | 85 |
| 2 Bishop | 47 | 53 | 87 |
| 3 Marshall | 59 | 41 | 100 |
| 4 McKinney | 16 | 84 | 98 |
| 5 Lewis | 9 | 91 | 96 |
| 6 Price | 87 | 13 | 100 |
| 7 Linder | 89 | 11 | 98 |
| 8 Westmoreland | 90 | 10 | 89 |
| 9 Norwood | 85 | 15 | 100 |
| 10 Deal | 87 | 13 | 100 |
| 11 Gingrey | 87 | 13 | 98 |
| 12 Barrow | 47 | 53 | 98 |
| 13 Scott | 43 | 57 | 91 |
| **HAWAII** | | | |
| 1 Abercrombie | 15 | 85 | 100 |
| 2 Case | 48 | 52 | 100 |
| **IDAHO** | | | |
| 1 Otter | 70 | 30 | 100 |
| 2 Simpson | 91 | 9 | 100 |
| **ILLINOIS** | | | |
| 1 Rush | 20 | 80 | 100 |
| 2 Jackson | 13 | 87 | 100 |
| 3 Lipinski | 43 | 57 | 100 |
| 4 Gutierrez | 18 | 82 | 96 |
| 5 Emanuel | 24 | 76 | 91 |
| 6 Hyde | 90 | 10 | 87 |
| 7 Davis | 20 | 80 | 100 |
| 8 Bean | 48 | 52 | 100 |
| 9 Schakowsky | 9 | 91 | 96 |
| 10 Kirk | 67 | 33 | 100 |
| 11 Weller | 86 | 14 | 96 |
| 12 Costello | 37 | 63 | 100 |

[1] Rep. Doris Matsui, D-Calif., was sworn in March 10, 2005. The first vote for which she was eligible was vote 62. She was eligible for 42 presidential support votes in 2005.

[2] Rep. John Campbell, R-Calif., was sworn in Dec. 7, 2005, to replace Republican Christopher Cox, who resigned effective Aug. 2. The first vote for which Campbell was eligible was vote 619; he was eligible for five presidential support votes in 2005. The last vote for which Cox was eligible was vote 453; he was eligible for 31 presidential support votes in 2005. His presidential support score was 90 percent; presidential opposition score, 10 percent; participation rate, 94 percent.

[3] Rep. Randy "Duke" Cunningham, R-Calif., resigned effective Dec. 1, 2005. The last vote for which he was eligible was vote 608. He was eligible for 39 presidential support votes in 2005.

[4] The Speaker votes only at his discretion, usually to break a tie or to emphasize the importance of a matter.

[5] Rep. Jean Schmidt, R-Ohio, was sworn in Sept. 6, 2005, to replace Republican Rob Portman, who resigned effective April 29. The first vote for which Schmidt was eligible was vote 454; she was eligible for 15 presidential support votes in 2005. The last vote for which Portman was eligible was vote 150; he was eligible for 10 presidential support votes in 2005. His presidential support score was 100 percent; presidential opposition score, zero; participation rate, 100 percent.

**KEY**   Republicans   Democrats   *Independents*

| | 1 | 2 | 3 |
|---|---|---|---|
| 13 Biggert | 72 | 28 | 100 |
| 14 Hastert[4] | 100 | 0 | 28 |
| 15 Johnson | 54 | 46 | 100 |
| 16 Manzullo | 70 | 30 | 100 |
| 17 Evans | 11 | 89 | 98 |
| 18 LaHood | 69 | 31 | 98 |
| 19 Shimkus | 80 | 20 | 100 |
| **INDIANA** | | | |
| 1 Visclosky | 26 | 74 | 100 |
| 2 Chocola | 91 | 9 | 100 |
| 3 Souder | 87 | 13 | 100 |
| 4 Buyer | 86 | 14 | 93 |
| 5 Burton | 89 | 11 | 98 |
| 6 Pence | 91 | 9 | 96 |
| 7 Carson | 16 | 84 | 96 |
| 8 Hostettler | 67 | 33 | 98 |
| 9 Sodrel | 85 | 15 | 100 |
| **IOWA** | | | |
| 1 Nussle | 85 | 15 | 100 |
| 2 Leach | 49 | 51 | 98 |
| 3 Boswell | 39 | 61 | 83 |
| 4 Latham | 87 | 13 | 100 |
| 5 King | 87 | 13 | 100 |
| **KANSAS** | | | |
| 1 Moran | 76 | 24 | 100 |
| 2 Ryun | 87 | 13 | 100 |
| 3 Moore | 30 | 70 | 100 |
| 4 Tiahrt | 91 | 9 | 100 |
| **KENTUCKY** | | | |
| 1 Whitfield | 87 | 13 | 98 |
| 2 Lewis | 89 | 11 | 100 |
| 3 Northup | 87 | 13 | 100 |
| 4 Davis | 87 | 13 | 100 |
| 5 Rogers | 91 | 9 | 100 |
| 6 Chandler | 50 | 50 | 100 |
| **LOUISIANA** | | | |
| 1 Jindal | 85 | 15 | 100 |
| 2 Jefferson | 26 | 74 | 100 |
| 3 Melancon | 52 | 48 | 100 |
| 4 McCrery | 89 | 11 | 100 |
| 5 Alexander | 89 | 11 | 100 |
| 6 Baker | 91 | 9 | 93 |
| 7 Boustany | 86 | 14 | 96 |
| **MAINE** | | | |
| 1 Allen | 13 | 87 | 100 |
| 2 Michaud | 18 | 82 | 98 |
| **MARYLAND** | | | |
| 1 Gilchrest | 72 | 28 | 100 |
| 2 Ruppersberger | 35 | 65 | 100 |
| 3 Cardin | 22 | 78 | 100 |
| 4 Wynn | 27 | 73 | 98 |
| 5 Hoyer | 24 | 76 | 100 |
| 6 Bartlett | 64 | 36 | 98 |
| 7 Cummings | 17 | 83 | 100 |
| 8 Van Hollen | 15 | 85 | 100 |
| **MASSACHUSETTS** | | | |
| 1 Olver | 15 | 85 | 100 |
| 2 Neal | 15 | 85 | 100 |
| 3 McGovern | 15 | 85 | 100 |
| 4 Frank | 15 | 85 | 100 |
| 5 Meehan | 15 | 85 | 100 |
| 6 Tierney | 13 | 87 | 100 |
| 7 Markey | 15 | 85 | 100 |
| 8 Capuano | 17 | 83 | 100 |
| 9 Lynch | 16 | 84 | 93 |
| 10 Delahunt | 9 | 91 | 98 |
| **MICHIGAN** | | | |
| 1 Stupak | 28 | 72 | 93 |
| 2 Hoekstra | 91 | 9 | 100 |
| 3 Ehlers | 67 | 33 | 100 |
| 4 Camp | 83 | 17 | 91 |
| 5 Kildee | 22 | 78 | 100 |
| 6 Upton | 76 | 24 | 100 |
| 7 Schwarz | 72 | 28 | 100 |
| 8 Rogers | 87 | 13 | 100 |
| 9 Knollenberg | 89 | 11 | 100 |
| 10 Miller | 85 | 15 | 100 |
| 11 McCotter | 78 | 22 | 100 |
| 12 Levin | 20 | 80 | 100 |
| 13 Kilpatrick | 17 | 83 | 100 |
| 14 Conyers | 15 | 85 | 100 |
| 15 Dingell | 26 | 74 | 100 |

| | 1 | 2 | 3 |
|---|---|---|---|
| **MINNESOTA** | | | |
| 1 Gutknecht | 78 | 22 | 100 |
| 2 Kline | 89 | 11 | 100 |
| 3 Ramstad | 67 | 33 | 100 |
| 4 McCollum | 11 | 89 | 100 |
| 5 Sabo | 13 | 87 | 100 |
| 6 Kennedy | 87 | 13 | 100 |
| 7 Peterson | 54 | 46 | 100 |
| 8 Oberstar | 23 | 77 | 96 |
| **MISSISSIPPI** | | | |
| 1 Wicker | 84 | 16 | 98 |
| 2 Thompson | 17 | 83 | 100 |
| 3 Pickering | 82 | 18 | 98 |
| 4 Taylor | 45 | 55 | 96 |
| **MISSOURI** | | | |
| 1 Clay | 16 | 84 | 96 |
| 2 Akin | 91 | 9 | 100 |
| 3 Carnahan | 22 | 78 | 100 |
| 4 Skelton | 61 | 39 | 96 |
| 5 Cleaver | 22 | 78 | 98 |
| 6 Graves | 86 | 14 | 96 |
| 7 Blunt | 91 | 9 | 98 |
| 8 Emerson | 68 | 32 | 96 |
| 9 Hulshof | 83 | 17 | 100 |
| **MONTANA** | | | |
| AL Rehberg | 83 | 17 | 100 |
| **NEBRASKA** | | | |
| 1 Fortenberry | 87 | 13 | 100 |
| 2 Terry | 85 | 15 | 100 |
| 3 Osborne | 76 | 24 | 100 |
| **NEVADA** | | | |
| 1 Berkley | 28 | 72 | 100 |
| 2 Gibbons | 80 | 20 | 96 |
| 3 Porter | 80 | 20 | 100 |
| **NEW HAMPSHIRE** | | | |
| 1 Bradley | 70 | 30 | 100 |
| 2 Bass | 67 | 33 | 100 |
| **NEW JERSEY** | | | |
| 1 Andrews | 23 | 77 | 85 |
| 2 LoBiondo | 70 | 30 | 100 |
| 3 Saxton | 80 | 20 | 100 |
| 4 Smith | 60 | 40 | 98 |
| 5 Garrett | 84 | 16 | 96 |
| 6 Pallone | 17 | 83 | 100 |
| 7 Ferguson | 87 | 13 | 98 |
| 8 Pascrell | 15 | 85 | 100 |
| 9 Rothman | 29 | 71 | 98 |
| 10 Payne | 7 | 93 | 98 |
| 11 Frelinghuysen | 83 | 17 | 100 |
| 12 Holt | 11 | 89 | 100 |
| 13 Menendez | 24 | 76 | 100 |
| **NEW MEXICO** | | | |
| 1 Wilson | 70 | 30 | 96 |
| 2 Pearce | 87 | 13 | 100 |
| 3 Udall | 11 | 89 | 98 |
| **NEW YORK** | | | |
| 1 Bishop | 15 | 85 | 100 |
| 2 Israel | 24 | 76 | 100 |
| 3 King | 83 | 17 | 100 |
| 4 McCarthy | 22 | 78 | 98 |
| 5 Ackerman | 24 | 76 | 100 |
| 6 Meeks | 32 | 68 | 96 |
| 7 Crowley | 15 | 85 | 100 |
| 8 Nadler | 13 | 87 | 98 |
| 9 Weiner | 15 | 85 | 100 |
| 10 Towns | 33 | 67 | 98 |
| 11 Owens | 11 | 89 | 100 |
| 12 Velázquez | 18 | 82 | 98 |
| 13 Fossella | 83 | 17 | 100 |
| 14 Maloney | 17 | 83 | 100 |
| 15 Rangel | 16 | 84 | 96 |
| 16 Serrano | 9 | 91 | 100 |
| 17 Engel | 26 | 74 | 100 |
| 18 Lowey | 13 | 87 | 100 |
| 19 Kelly | 72 | 28 | 93 |
| 20 Sweeney | 82 | 18 | 96 |
| 21 McNulty | 26 | 74 | 100 |
| 22 Hinchey | 11 | 89 | 98 |
| 23 McHugh | 78 | 22 | 100 |
| 24 Boehlert | 61 | 39 | 100 |
| 25 Walsh | 86 | 14 | 96 |
| 26 Reynolds | 80 | 20 | 98 |
| 27 Higgins | 29 | 71 | 100 |
| 28 Slaughter | 14 | 86 | 96 |
| 29 Kuhl | 85 | 15 | 100 |

| | 1 | 2 | 3 |
|---|---|---|---|
| **NORTH CAROLINA** | | | |
| 1 Butterfield | 30 | 70 | 100 |
| 2 Etheridge | 24 | 76 | 98 |
| 3 Jones | 61 | 39 | 96 |
| 4 Price | 16 | 84 | 98 |
| 5 Foxx | 87 | 13 | 100 |
| 6 Coble | 78 | 22 | 100 |
| 7 McIntyre | 57 | 43 | 96 |
| 8 Hayes | 89 | 11 | 96 |
| 9 Myrick | 89 | 11 | 96 |
| 10 McHenry | 87 | 13 | 100 |
| 11 Taylor | 84 | 16 | 96 |
| 12 Watt | 16 | 84 | 98 |
| 13 Miller | 26 | 74 | 100 |
| **NORTH DAKOTA** | | | |
| AL Pomeroy | 41 | 59 | 100 |
| **OHIO** | | | |
| 1 Chabot | 89 | 11 | 100 |
| 2 Schmidt[5] | 87 | 13 | 100 |
| 3 Turner | 85 | 15 | 100 |
| 4 Oxley | 91 | 9 | 96 |
| 5 Gillmor | 88 | 12 | 93 |
| 6 Strickland | 22 | 78 | 100 |
| 7 Hobson | 87 | 13 | 100 |
| 8 Boehner | 91 | 9 | 96 |
| 9 Kaptur | 23 | 77 | 96 |
| 10 Kucinich | 11 | 89 | 100 |
| 11 Jones | 20 | 80 | 100 |
| 12 Tiberi | 71 | 29 | 98 |
| 13 Brown | 7 | 93 | 100 |
| 14 LaTourette | 71 | 29 | 98 |
| 15 Pryce | 84 | 16 | 98 |
| 16 Regula | 85 | 15 | 100 |
| 17 Ryan | 30 | 70 | 100 |
| 18 Ney | 72 | 28 | 100 |
| **OKLAHOMA** | | | |
| 1 Sullivan | 89 | 11 | 98 |
| 2 Boren | 65 | 35 | 100 |
| 3 Lucas | 87 | 13 | 100 |
| 4 Cole | 91 | 9 | 96 |
| 5 Istook | 89 | 11 | 96 |
| **OREGON** | | | |
| 1 Wu | 29 | 71 | 98 |
| 2 Walden | 80 | 20 | 100 |
| 3 Blumenauer | 11 | 89 | 96 |
| 4 DeFazio | 17 | 83 | 100 |
| 5 Hooley | 18 | 82 | 98 |
| **PENNSYLVANIA** | | | |
| 1 Brady | 18 | 82 | 98 |
| 2 Fattah | 11 | 89 | 98 |
| 3 English | 85 | 15 | 100 |
| 4 Hart | 89 | 11 | 100 |
| 5 Peterson | 83 | 17 | 87 |
| 6 Gerlach | 69 | 31 | 98 |
| 7 Weldon | 84 | 16 | 98 |
| 8 Fitzpatrick | 61 | 39 | 100 |
| 9 Shuster | 87 | 13 | 100 |
| 10 Sherwood | 87 | 13 | 100 |
| 11 Kanjorski | 39 | 61 | 100 |
| 12 Murtha | 38 | 62 | 98 |
| 13 Schwartz | 17 | 83 | 100 |
| 14 Doyle | 28 | 72 | 100 |
| 15 Dent | 78 | 22 | 100 |
| 16 Pitts | 85 | 15 | 100 |
| 17 Holden | 52 | 48 | 100 |
| 18 Murphy | 80 | 20 | 100 |
| 19 Platts | 80 | 20 | 100 |
| **RHODE ISLAND** | | | |
| 1 Kennedy | 22 | 78 | 98 |
| 2 Langevin | 20 | 80 | 100 |
| **SOUTH CAROLINA** | | | |
| 1 Brown | 83 | 17 | 91 |
| 2 Wilson | 91 | 9 | 100 |
| 3 Barrett | 93 | 7 | 98 |
| 4 Inglis | 76 | 24 | 100 |
| 5 Spratt | 27 | 73 | 98 |
| 6 Clyburn | 25 | 75 | 96 |
| **SOUTH DAKOTA** | | | |
| AL Herseth | 39 | 61 | 100 |
| **TENNESSEE** | | | |
| 1 Jenkins | 78 | 22 | 100 |
| 2 Duncan | 72 | 28 | 100 |

| | 1 | 2 | 3 |
|---|---|---|---|
| 3 Wamp | 87 | 13 | 100 |
| 4 Davis | 65 | 35 | 100 |
| 5 Cooper | 38 | 62 | 91 |
| 6 Gordon | 46 | 54 | 100 |
| 7 Blackburn | 93 | 7 | 100 |
| 8 Tanner | 38 | 62 | 98 |
| 9 Ford | 35 | 65 | 100 |
| **TEXAS** | | | |
| 1 Gohmert | 88 | 12 | 91 |
| 2 Poe | 81 | 19 | 93 |
| 3 Johnson, Sam | 93 | 7 | 96 |
| 4 Hall, R. | 84 | 16 | 96 |
| 5 Hensarling | 93 | 7 | 100 |
| 6 Barton | 87 | 13 | 98 |
| 7 Culberson | 93 | 7 | 100 |
| 8 Brady | 91 | 9 | 93 |
| 9 Green, A. | 20 | 80 | 100 |
| 10 McCaul | 85 | 15 | 100 |
| 11 Conaway | 87 | 13 | 100 |
| 12 Granger | 91 | 9 | 100 |
| 13 Thornberry | 93 | 7 | 98 |
| 14 Paul | 38 | 62 | 98 |
| 15 Hinojosa | 37 | 63 | 100 |
| 16 Reyes | 39 | 61 | 83 |
| 17 Edwards | 52 | 48 | 100 |
| 18 Jackson-Lee | 28 | 72 | 100 |
| 19 Neugebauer | 87 | 13 | 100 |
| 20 Gonzalez | 26 | 74 | 100 |
| 21 Smith | 89 | 11 | 100 |
| 22 DeLay | 91 | 9 | 93 |
| 23 Bonilla | 93 | 7 | 100 |
| 24 Marchant | 89 | 11 | 100 |
| 25 Doggett | 13 | 87 | 100 |
| 26 Burgess | 89 | 11 | 100 |
| 27 Ortiz | 45 | 55 | 87 |
| 28 Cuellar | 57 | 43 | 91 |
| 29 Green, G. | 35 | 65 | 93 |
| 30 Johnson, E.B. | 14 | 86 | 96 |
| 31 Carter | 93 | 7 | 98 |
| 32 Sessions | 90 | 10 | 91 |
| **UTAH** | | | |
| 1 Bishop | 78 | 22 | 98 |
| 2 Matheson | 43 | 57 | 100 |
| 3 Cannon | 87 | 13 | 100 |
| **VERMONT** | | | |
| AL Sanders | 15 | 85 | 100 |
| **VIRGINIA** | | | |
| 1 Davis, Jo Ann | 79 | 21 | 93 |
| 2 Drake | 89 | 11 | 100 |
| 3 Scott | 13 | 87 | 100 |
| 4 Forbes | 89 | 11 | 100 |
| 5 Goode | 84 | 16 | 98 |
| 6 Goodlatte | 85 | 15 | 100 |
| 7 Cantor | 89 | 11 | 100 |
| 8 Moran | 24 | 76 | 100 |
| 9 Boucher | 33 | 67 | 100 |
| 10 Wolf | 84 | 16 | 98 |
| 11 Davis, T. | 80 | 20 | 96 |
| **WASHINGTON** | | | |
| 1 Inslee | 17 | 83 | 100 |
| 2 Larsen | 28 | 72 | 100 |
| 3 Baird | 18 | 82 | 98 |
| 4 Hastings | 87 | 13 | 83 |
| 5 McMorris | 89 | 11 | 100 |
| 6 Dicks | 24 | 76 | 100 |
| 7 McDermott | 14 | 86 | 96 |
| 8 Reichert | 86 | 14 | 96 |
| 9 Smith | 24 | 76 | 100 |
| **WEST VIRGINIA** | | | |
| 1 Mollohan | 36 | 64 | 98 |
| 2 Capito | 75 | 25 | 96 |
| 3 Rahall | 33 | 67 | 98 |
| **WISCONSIN** | | | |
| 1 Ryan | 80 | 20 | 100 |
| 2 Baldwin | 13 | 87 | 100 |
| 3 Kind | 23 | 77 | 96 |
| 4 Moore | 11 | 89 | 98 |
| 5 Sensenbrenner | 81 | 19 | 93 |
| 6 Petri | 80 | 20 | 100 |
| 7 Obey | 18 | 82 | 96 |
| 8 Green | 85 | 15 | 100 |
| **WYOMING** | | | |
| AL Cubin | 80 | 20 | 100 |

## SENATE

**1. Presidential Support.** Percentage of recorded votes cast in 2005 on which President Bush took a position and on which the senator voted "yea" or "nay" in agreement with the president's position. Failure to vote does not lower an individual's score.

**2. Presidential Opposition.** Percentage of recorded votes cast in 2005 on which President Bush took a position and on which the senator voted "yea" or "nay" in disagreement with the president's position. Failure to vote does not lower an individual's score.

**3. Participation in Presidential Support Votes.** Percentage of the 45 recorded Senate votes on which President Bush took a position and on which the senator was present and voted "yea" or "nay."

| | 1 | 2 | 3 | | | 1 | 2 | 3 |
|---|---|---|---|---|---|---|---|---|
| **AMA** | | | | | **ONTANA** | | | |
| **Shelby** | 89 | 11 | 100 | | Baucus | 45 | 55 | 93 |
| **Sessions** | 90 | 10 | 93 | | **Burns** | 88 | 12 | 93 |
| **ALASKA** | | | | | **NEBRASKA** | | | |
| **Stevens** | 93 | 7 | 98 | | **Hagel** | 89 | 11 | 100 |
| **Murkowski** | 87 | 13 | 89 | | Nelson | 76 | 24 | 100 |
| **ARIZONA** | | | | | **NEVADA** | | | |
| **McCain** | 77 | 23 | 89 | | Reid | 38 | 62 | 100 |
| **Kyl** | 89 | 11 | 100 | | **Ensign** | 89 | 11 | 100 |
| **ARKANSAS** | | | | | **NEW HAMPSHIRE** | | | |
| Lincoln | 50 | 50 | 98 | | **Gregg** | 82 | 18 | 98 |
| Pryor | 58 | 42 | 100 | | **Sununu** | 81 | 19 | 96 |
| **CALIFORNIA** | | | | | **NEW JERSEY** | | | |
| Feinstein | 40 | 60 | 96 | | Corzine | 28 | 72 | 80 |
| Boxer | 30 | 70 | 98 | | Lautenberg | 27 | 73 | 98 |
| **COLORADO** | | | | | **NEW MEXICO** | | | |
| **Allard** | 98 | 2 | 98 | | **Domenici** | 89 | 11 | 98 |
| Salazar | 49 | 51 | 100 | | Bingaman | 43 | 57 | 98 |
| **CONNECTICUT** | | | | | **NEW YORK** | | | |
| Dodd | 33 | 67 | 93 | | Schumer | 31 | 69 | 100 |
| Lieberman | 46 | 54 | 91 | | Clinton | 31 | 69 | 100 |
| **DELAWARE** | | | | | **NORTH CAROLINA** | | | |
| Biden | 27 | 73 | 89 | | **Dole** | 93 | 7 | 100 |
| Carper | 38 | 62 | 100 | | **Burr** | 89 | 11 | 100 |
| **FLORIDA** | | | | | **NORTH DAKOTA** | | | |
| Nelson | 47 | 53 | 96 | | Conrad | 48 | 52 | 93 |
| **Martinez** | 91 | 9 | 98 | | Dorgan | 40 | 60 | 93 |
| **GEORGIA** | | | | | **OHIO** | | | |
| **Chambliss** | 91 | 9 | 100 | | **DeWine** | 76 | 24 | 100 |
| **Isakson** | 91 | 9 | 100 | | **Voinovich** | 87 | 13 | 100 |
| **HAWAII** | | | | | **OKLAHOMA** | | | |
| Inouye | 44 | 56 | 80 | | **Inhofe** | 91 | 9 | 100 |
| Akaka | 40 | 60 | 100 | | **Coburn** | 91 | 9 | 96 |
| **IDAHO** | | | | | **OREGON** | | | |
| **Craig** | 82 | 18 | 100 | | Wyden | 26 | 74 | 96 |
| **Crapo** | 84 | 16 | 100 | | **Smith** | 79 | 21 | 93 |
| **ILLINOIS** | | | | | **PENNSYLVANIA** | | | |
| Durbin | 33 | 67 | 100 | | **Specter** | 85 | 15 | 91 |
| Obama | 33 | 67 | 96 | | **Santorum** | 95 | 5 | 96 |
| **INDIANA** | | | | | **RHODE ISLAND** | | | |
| **Lugar** | 84 | 16 | 100 | | Reed | 29 | 71 | 100 |
| Bayh | 36 | 64 | 100 | | **Chafee** | 56 | 44 | 100 |
| **IOWA** | | | | | **SOUTH CAROLINA** | | | |
| **Grassley** | 89 | 11 | 100 | | **Graham** | 89 | 11 | 100 |
| Harkin | 27 | 73 | 98 | | **DeMint** | 91 | 9 | 100 |
| **KANSAS** | | | | | **SOUTH DAKOTA** | | | |
| **Brownback** | 93 | 7 | 100 | | Johnson | 45 | 55 | 98 |
| **Roberts** | 93 | 7 | 98 | | **Thune** | 86 | 14 | 96 |
| **KENTUCKY** | | | | | **TENNESSEE** | | | |
| **McConnell** | 93 | 7 | 100 | | **Frist** | 87 | 13 | 100 |
| **Bunning** | 91 | 9 | 98 | | **Alexander** | 88 | 12 | 96 |
| **LOUISIANA** | | | | | **TEXAS** | | | |
| Landrieu | 64 | 36 | 100 | | **Hutchison** | 96 | 4 | 100 |
| **Vitter** | 89 | 11 | 100 | | **Cornyn** | 98 | 2 | 100 |
| **MAINE** | | | | | **UTAH** | | | |
| **Snowe** | 67 | 33 | 100 | | **Hatch** | 93 | 7 | 98 |
| **Collins** | 62 | 38 | 100 | | **Bennett** | 93 | 7 | 98 |
| **MARYLAND** | | | | | **VERMONT** | | | |
| Sarbanes | 31 | 69 | 100 | | Leahy | 36 | 64 | 100 |
| Mikulski | 35 | 65 | 96 | | *Jeffords* | 36 | 64 | 87 |
| **MASSACHUSETTS** | | | | | **VIRGINIA** | | | |
| Kennedy | 26 | 74 | 93 | | **Warner** | 89 | 11 | 100 |
| Kerry | 34 | 66 | 98 | | **Allen** | 96 | 4 | 100 |
| **MICHIGAN** | | | | | **WASHINGTON** | | | |
| Levin | 41 | 59 | 98 | | Murray | 33 | 67 | 100 |
| Stabenow | 33 | 67 | 100 | | Cantwell | 36 | 64 | 100 |
| **MINNESOTA** | | | | | **WEST VIRGINIA** | | | |
| Dayton | 31 | 69 | 100 | | Byrd | 44 | 56 | 100 |
| **Coleman** | 84 | 16 | 96 | | Rockefeller | 40 | 60 | 93 |
| **MISSISSIPPI** | | | | | **WISCONSIN** | | | |
| **Cochran** | 96 | 4 | 100 | | Kohl | 45 | 55 | 98 |
| **Lott** | 93 | 7 | 96 | | Feingold | 37 | 63 | 96 |
| **MISSOURI** | | | | | **WYOMING** | | | |
| **Bond** | 93 | 7 | 100 | | **Thomas** | 84 | 16 | 100 |
| **Talent** | 91 | 9 | 100 | | **Enzi** | 84 | 16 | 98 |

**KEY**    **Republicans**    Democrats    *Independents*

# Party Unity Background

Roll call votes used for the party unity study are those on which a majority of voting Democrats opposed a majority of voting Republicans. **Support** indicates the percentage of the time that members voted in agreement with a majority of their party on party unity votes. **Opposition** indicates the percentage of the time members voted against a majority of their party. In calculating **average** scores by party, chamber and region, a member's failure to vote lowers the score for the group. The tables below also show the number of party unity votes on which each party was victorious, and the number of instances where each party voted unanimously.

## Average 2005 Party Unity Scores by Chamber

|  | HOUSE | | SENATE | | CONGRESS | |
|---|---|---|---|---|---|---|
|  | SUPPORT | OPPOSITION | SUPPORT | OPPOSITION | SUPPORT | OPPOSITION |
| Republicans | 90% | 7% | 88% | 10% | 90% | 7% |
| Democrats | 88 | 9 | 88 | 10 | 88 | 9 |

## Average 2005 Support/Opposition Scores by Party and Region

| SENATE | SUPPORT | OPPOSITION | HOUSE | SUPPORT | OPPOSITION |
|---|---|---|---|---|---|
| Northern Republicans | 85% | 13% | Northern Republicans | 89% | 8% |
| Southern Republicans | 93 | 6 | Southern Republicans | 92 | 4 |
| Northern Democrats | 88 | 9 | Northern Democrats | 90 | 7 |
| Southern Democrats | 80 | 19 | Southern Democrats | 81 | 15 |

* Southern Democrats and Southern Republicans are those from Ala., Ark., Fla., Ga., Ky., La., Miss., N.C., Okla., S.C., Tenn., Texas and Va. All others are considered Northern.

## Victories in Party Unity Votes

|  | HOUSE | | SENATE | | CONGRESS | |
|---|---|---|---|---|---|---|
|  | REPUBLICANS | DEMOCRATS | REPUBLICANS | DEMOCRATS | REPUBLICANS | DEMOCRATS |
| 2005 | 278 | 50 | 182 | 47 | 460 | 97 |
| 2004 | 213 | 42 | 85 | 28 | 298 | 70 |
| 2003 | 310 | 39 | 250 | 56 | 560 | 95 |
| 2002 | 170 | 39 | 73 | 42 | 243 | 81 |
| 2001 | 177 | 27 | 115 | 95 | 292 | 122 |
| 2000 | 182 | 77 | 114 | 31 | 296 | 108 |
| 1999 | 177 | 58 | 211 | 77 | 388 | 135 |
| 1998 | 216 | 80 | 114 | 61 | 330 | 141 |
| 1997 | 261 | 58 | 104 | 46 | 365 | 104 |
| 1996 | 208 | 48 | 132 | 59 | 340 | 107 |
| 1995 | 561 | 74 | 345 | 77 | 906 | 151 |
| 1994 | 50 | 257 | 41 | 129 | 91 | 386 |
| 1993 | 62 | 329 | 66 | 199 | 128 | 528 |
| 1992 | 54 | 251 | 61 | 82 | 115 | 333 |
| 1991 | 39 | 197 | 57 | 81 | 96 | 278 |

## Unanimous Voting by Parties

|  | HOUSE | | SENATE | | CONGRESS | |
|---|---|---|---|---|---|---|
|  | REPUBLICANS | DEMOCRATS | REPUBLICANS | DEMOCRATS | REPUBLICANS | DEMOCRATS |
| 2005 | 91 | 82 | 59 | 69 | 150 | 151 |
| 2004 | 77 | 70 | 31 | 3 | 108 | 73 |
| 2003 | 109 | 94 | 130 | 32 | 239 | 126 |
| 2002 | 54 | 37 | 23 | 12 | 77 | 49 |
| 2001 | 66 | 1 | 55 | 37 | 121 | 38 |
| 2000 | 67 | 1 | 19 | 52 | 86 | 53 |
| 1999 | 59 | 11 | 63 | 100 | 122 | 111 |
| 1998 | 42 | 8 | 33 | 46 | 75 | 54 |
| 1997 | 63 | 11 | 38 | 35 | 101 | 46 |
| 1996 | 32 | 10 | 47 | 35 | 79 | 45 |
| 1995 | 159 | 17 | 104 | 63 | 263 | 80 |
| 1994 | 38 | 7 | 19 | 37 | 57 | 44 |
| 1993 | 65 | 13 | 57 | 29 | 122 | 42 |
| 1992 | 47 | 18 | 10 | 12 | 57 | 30 |
| 1991 | 18 | 11 | 15 | 19 | 33 | 30 |

# Party Unity History

The table below shows how frequently during roll call votes a majority of Democrats aligns against a majority of Republicans. The tables in the center and at the right show the average party unity support score for each party in each chamber.

| Frequency of Unity Votes | | |
| --- | --- | --- |
| YEAR | HOUSE | SENATE |
| 2005 | 49.0% | 62.6% |
| 2004 | 47.0 | 52.3 |
| 2003 | 51.7 | 66.7 |
| 2002 | 43.3 | 45.5 |
| 2001 | 40.2 | 55.3 |
| 2000 | 43.2 | 48.7 |
| 1999 | 47.3 | 62.8 |
| 1998 | 55.5 | 55.7 |
| 1997 | 50.4 | 50.3 |
| 1996 | 56.4 | 62.4 |
| 1995 | 73.2 | 68.8 |
| 1994 | 61.8 | 51.7 |
| 1993 | 65.5 | 67.1 |
| 1992 | 64.5 | 53.0 |
| 1991 | 55.1 | 49.3 |
| 1990 | 49.1 | 54.3 |
| 1989 | 56.3 | 35.3 |
| 1988 | 47.0 | 42.5 |
| 1987 | 63.7 | 40.7 |
| 1986 | 56.5 | 52.3 |
| 1985 | 61.0 | 49.6 |
| 1984 | 47.1 | 40.0 |
| 1983 | 55.6 | 43.7 |
| 1982 | 36.4 | 43.4 |
| 1981 | 37.4 | 47.8 |
| 1980 | 37.6 | 45.8 |
| 1979 | 47.3 | 46.7 |
| 1978 | 33.2 | 45.2 |
| 1977 | 42.2 | 42.4 |
| 1976 | 35.9 | 37.2 |
| 1975 | 48.4 | 47.8 |
| 1974 | 29.4 | 44.3 |
| 1973 | 41.8 | 39.9 |
| 1972 | 27.1 | 36.5 |
| 1971 | 37.8 | 41.6 |
| 1970 | 27.1 | 35.2 |
| 1969 | 31.1 | 36.3 |
| 1968 | 35.2 | 32.0 |
| 1967 | 36.3 | 34.6 |
| 1966 | 41.5 | 50.2 |
| 1965 | 52.2 | 41.9 |
| 1964 | 54.9 | 35.7 |
| 1963 | 48.7 | 47.2 |
| 1962 | 46.0 | 41.1 |
| 1961 | 50.0 | 62.3 |
| 1960 | 52.7 | 36.7 |
| 1959 | 55.2 | 47.9 |
| 1958 | 39.8 | 43.5 |
| 1957 | 59.0 | 35.5 |
| 1956 | 43.8 | 53.1 |
| 1955 | 40.8 | 29.9 |
| 1954 | 38.2 | 48.0 |
| 1953 | 52.1 | 51.7 |

| House Average Scores | | |
| --- | --- | --- |
| YEAR | REPUBLICANS | DEMOCRATS |
| 2005 | 90% | 88% |
| 2004 | 88 | 86 |
| 2003 | 91 | 87 |
| 2002 | 90 | 86 |
| 2001 | 91 | 83 |
| 2000 | 88 | 82 |
| 1999 | 86 | 83 |
| 1998 | 86 | 82 |
| 1997 | 88 | 82 |
| 1996 | 87 | 80 |
| 1995 | 91 | 80 |
| 1994 | 84 | 83 |
| 1993 | 84 | 85 |
| 1992 | 79 | 79 |
| 1991 | 77 | 81 |
| 1990 | 74 | 81 |
| 1989 | 72 | 81 |
| 1988 | 74 | 80 |
| 1987 | 74 | 81 |
| 1986 | 70 | 79 |
| 1985 | 75 | 80 |
| 1984 | 71 | 74 |
| 1983 | 74 | 76 |
| 1982 | 69 | 72 |
| 1981 | 74 | 69 |
| 1980 | 71 | 69 |
| 1979 | 73 | 69 |
| 1978 | 69 | 63 |
| 1977 | 71 | 68 |
| 1976 | 67 | 66 |
| 1975 | 72 | 69 |
| 1974 | 63 | 62 |
| 1973 | 68 | 68 |
| 1972 | 66 | 58 |
| 1971 | 67 | 61 |
| 1970 | 60 | 58 |
| 1969 | 62 | 61 |
| 1968 | 64 | 59 |
| 1967 | 74 | 67 |
| 1966 | 68 | 62 |
| 1965 | 71 | 70 |
| 1964 | 71 | 69 |
| 1963 | 74 | 73 |
| 1962 | 70 | 70 |
| 1961 | 73 | 72 |
| 1960 | 70 | 65 |
| 1959 | 77 | 79 |
| 1958 | 65 | 66 |
| 1957 | 67 | 70 |
| 1956 | 70 | 70 |

| Senate Average Scores | | |
| --- | --- | --- |
| YEAR | REPUBLICANS | DEMOCRATS |
| 2005 | 88% | 88% |
| 2004 | 90 | 83 |
| 2003 | 94 | 85 |
| 2002 | 84 | 83 |
| 2001 | 88 | 89 |
| 2000 | 89 | 88 |
| 1999 | 88 | 89 |
| 1998 | 86 | 87 |
| 1997 | 87 | 85 |
| 1996 | 89 | 84 |
| 1995 | 89 | 81 |
| 1994 | 79 | 84 |
| 1993 | 84 | 85 |
| 1992 | 79 | 77 |
| 1991 | 81 | 80 |
| 1990 | 75 | 80 |
| 1989 | 78 | 78 |
| 1988 | 68 | 78 |
| 1987 | 75 | 81 |
| 1986 | 76 | 72 |
| 1985 | 76 | 75 |
| 1984 | 78 | 68 |
| 1983 | 74 | 71 |
| 1982 | 76 | 72 |
| 1981 | 81 | 71 |
| 1980 | 65 | 64 |
| 1979 | 66 | 68 |
| 1978 | 59 | 66 |
| 1977 | 66 | 63 |
| 1976 | 61 | 62 |
| 1975 | 64 | 68 |
| 1974 | 59 | 63 |
| 1973 | 64 | 69 |
| 1972 | 61 | 57 |
| 1971 | 63 | 64 |
| 1970 | 56 | 55 |
| 1969 | 63 | 63 |
| 1968 | 60 | 51 |
| 1967 | 60 | 61 |
| 1966 | 63 | 57 |
| 1965 | 68 | 63 |
| 1964 | 65 | 61 |
| 1963 | 67 | 66 |
| 1962 | 64 | 65 |
| 1961 | 68 | 69 |
| 1960 | 64 | 60 |
| 1959 | 72 | 67 |
| 1958 | 64 | 71 |
| 1957 | 69 | 66 |
| 1956 | 72 | 71 |

## Number of Party Unity Votes

In the House in 2005, the two parties aligned against each other on 328 of 669 roll call votes, or 49.0 percent. In the Senate, the parties opposed each other on 229 of 366 roll calls, or 62.6 percent. A list of roll call numbers that were party unity votes is available upon request from Congressional Quarterly.

Calculations of average scores by chamber, party and region are based on all eligible yea-or-nay votes, whether or not all members participated. As a result, a member's failure to vote reduces the average support and opposition scores. Therefore, averages are not strictly comparable to individual member scores.

Also, in the individual member score tables, Sen. James M. Jeffords, I-Vt., and Rep. Bernard Sanders, I-Vt., are treated as if they were Democrats in calculating their support and opposition scores. However, Jeffords' and Sanders' scores are not included in the Democratic Party averages for the Senate and House.

# SENATE

**1. Party Unity.** Percentage of recorded party unity votes in 2005 on which a senator voted "yea" or "nay" in agreement with a majority of his or her party. (Party unity roll calls are those on which a majority of voting Democrats opposed a majority of voting Republicans.) Percentages are based on votes cast; thus, failure to vote does not lower a member's score.

**2. Party Opposition.** Percentage of recorded party unity votes in 2005 on which a senator voted "yea" or "nay" in disagreement with a majority of his or her party. Percentages are based on votes cast; thus, failure to vote does not lower a member's score.

**3. Participation in Party Unity Votes.** Percentage of the 229 recorded Senate party unity votes in 2005 on which a senator was present and voted "yea" or "nay."

| | 1 | 2 | 3 | | 1 | 2 | 3 |
|---|---|---|---|---|---|---|---|
| **ALABAMA** | | | | **MONTANA** | | | |
| Shelby | 94 | 6 | 99 | Baucus | 74 | 26 | 99 |
| Sessions | 97 | 3 | 99 | Burns | 94 | 6 | 98 |
| **ALASKA** | | | | **NEBRASKA** | | | |
| Stevens | 95 | 5 | 99 | Hagel | 94 | 6 | 99 |
| Murkowski | 93 | 7 | 99 | Nelson | 46 | 54 | 99 |
| **ARIZONA** | | | | **NEVADA** | | | |
| McCain | 84 | 16 | 96 | Reid | 92 | 8 | 100 |
| Kyl | 98 | 2 | 99 | Ensign | 94 | 6 | 99 |
| **ARKANSAS** | | | | **NEW HAMPSHIRE** | | | |
| Lincoln | 81 | 19 | 100 | Gregg | 91 | 9 | 99 |
| Pryor | 80 | 20 | 99 | Sununu | 87 | 13 | 96 |
| **CALIFORNIA** | | | | **NEW JERSEY** | | | |
| Feinstein | 92 | 8 | 98 | Corzine | 97 | 3 | 65 |
| Boxer | 99 | 1 | 97 | Lautenberg | 98 | 2 | 99 |
| **COLORADO** | | | | **NEW MEXICO** | | | |
| Allard | 97 | 3 | 99 | Domenici | 93 | 7 | 96 |
| Salazar | 84 | 16 | 100 | Bingaman | 85 | 15 | 99 |
| **CONNECTICUT** | | | | **NEW YORK** | | | |
| Dodd | 94 | 6 | 97 | Schumer | 93 | 7 | 99 |
| Lieberman | 90 | 10 | 95 | Clinton | 96 | 4 | 96 |
| **DELAWARE** | | | | **NORTH CAROLINA** | | | |
| Biden | 89 | 11 | 96 | Dole | 93 | 7 | 100 |
| Carper | 77 | 23 | 100 | Burr | 95 | 5 | 99 |
| **FLORIDA** | | | | **NORTH DAKOTA** | | | |
| Nelson | 84 | 16 | 99 | Conrad | 76 | 24 | 96 |
| Martinez | 94 | 6 | 98 | Dorgan | 88 | 12 | 97 |
| **GEORGIA** | | | | **OHIO** | | | |
| Chambliss | 95 | 5 | 99 | DeWine | 70 | 30 | 99 |
| Isakson | 95 | 5 | 99 | Voinovich | 84 | 16 | 99 |
| **HAWAII** | | | | **OKLAHOMA** | | | |
| Inouye | 90 | 10 | 86 | Inhofe | 94 | 6 | 99 |
| Akaka | 96 | 4 | 100 | Coburn | 93 | 7 | 99 |
| **IDAHO** | | | | **OREGON** | | | |
| Craig | 93 | 7 | 99 | Wyden | 94 | 6 | 100 |
| Crapo | 95 | 5 | 99 | Smith | 82 | 18 | 98 |
| **ILLINOIS** | | | | **PENNSYLVANIA** | | | |
| Durbin | 99 | 1 | 99 | Specter | 69 | 31 | 97 |
| Obama | 97 | 3 | 99 | Santorum | 92 | 8 | 97 |
| **INDIANA** | | | | **RHODE ISLAND** | | | |
| Lugar | 84 | 16 | 98 | Reed | 98 | 2 | 99 |
| Bayh | 90 | 10 | 99 | Chafee | 47 | 53 | 99 |
| **IOWA** | | | | **SOUTH CAROLINA** | | | |
| Grassley | 96 | 4 | 100 | Graham | 92 | 8 | 99 |
| Harkin | 98 | 2 | 99 | DeMint | 96 | 4 | 99 |
| **KANSAS** | | | | **SOUTH DAKOTA** | | | |
| Brownback | 97 | 3 | 100 | Johnson | 83 | 17 | 98 |
| Roberts | 94 | 6 | 98 | Thune | 87 | 13 | 97 |
| **KENTUCKY** | | | | **TENNESSEE** | | | |
| McConnell | 99 | 1 | 99 | Frist | 97 | 3 | 100 |
| Bunning | 98 | 2 | 99 | Alexander | 92 | 8 | 98 |
| **LOUISIANA** | | | | **TEXAS** | | | |
| Landrieu | 76 | 24 | 97 | Hutchison | 90 | 10 | 100 |
| Vitter | 94 | 6 | 97 | Cornyn | 95 | 5 | 98 |
| **MAINE** | | | | **UTAH** | | | |
| Snowe | 56 | 44 | 100 | Hatch | 96 | 4 | 99 |
| Collins | 59 | 41 | 100 | Bennett | 96 | 4 | 97 |
| **MARYLAND** | | | | **VERMONT** | | | |
| Sarbanes | 99 | 1 | 100 | Leahy | 97 | 3 | 99 |
| Mikulski | 98 | 2 | 93 | *Jeffords* | 91 | 9 | 96 |
| **MASSACHUSETTS** | | | | **VIRGINIA** | | | |
| Kennedy | 100 | 0 | 98 | Warner | 86 | 14 | 99 |
| Kerry | 97 | 3 | 98 | Allen | 94 | 6 | 100 |
| **MICHIGAN** | | | | **WASHINGTON** | | | |
| Levin | 97 | 3 | 99 | Murray | 95 | 5 | 99 |
| Stabenow | 95 | 5 | 99 | Cantwell | 92 | 8 | 99 |
| **MINNESOTA** | | | | **WEST VIRGINIA** | | | |
| Dayton | 96 | 4 | 95 | Byrd | 84 | 16 | 99 |
| Coleman | 77 | 23 | 96 | Rockefeller | 93 | 7 | 95 |
| **MISSISSIPPI** | | | | **WISCONSIN** | | | |
| Cochran | 97 | 3 | 100 | Kohl | 89 | 11 | 99 |
| Lott | 95 | 5 | 88 | Feingold | 95 | 5 | 97 |
| **MISSOURI** | | | | **WYOMING** | | | |
| Bond | 94 | 6 | 99 | Thomas | 94 | 6 | 99 |
| Talent | 84 | 16 | 100 | Enzi | 94 | 6 | 99 |

**KEY**    **Republicans**    Democrats    *Independents*

# HOUSE

**1. Party Unity.** Percentage of recorded party unity votes in 2005 on which a member voted "yea" or "nay" in agreement with a majority of his or her party. (Party unity votes are those on which a majority of voting Democrats opposed a majority of voting Republicans.) Percentages are based on votes cast; thus, failure to vote does not lower a member's score.

**2. Party Opposition.** Percentage of recorded party unity votes in 2005 on which a member voted "yea" or "nay" in disagreement with a majority of his or her party. Percentages are based on votes cast; thus, failure to vote does not lower a member's score.

**3. Participation in Party Unity Votes.** Percentage of the 328 recorded House party unity votes in 2005 on which a member was present and voted "yea" or "nay."

| | 1 | 2 | 3 |
|---|---|---|---|
| **ALABAMA** | | | |
| 1 Bonner | 96 | 4 | 96 |
| 2 Everett | 96 | 4 | 95 |
| 3 Rogers | 94 | 6 | 94 |
| 4 Aderholt | 97 | 3 | 100 |
| 5 Cramer | 60 | 40 | 96 |
| 6 Bachus | 98 | 2 | 95 |
| 7 Davis | 83 | 17 | 99 |
| **ALASKA** | | | |
| AL Young | 91 | 9 | 92 |
| **ARIZONA** | | | |
| 1 Renzi | 92 | 8 | 100 |
| 2 Franks | 98 | 2 | 99 |
| 3 Shadegg | 98 | 2 | 94 |
| 4 Pastor | 93 | 7 | 99 |
| 5 Hayworth | 95 | 5 | 99 |
| 6 Flake | 91 | 9 | 97 |
| 7 Grijalva | 98 | 2 | 98 |
| 8 Kolbe | 90 | 10 | 96 |
| **ARKANSAS** | | | |
| 1 Berry | 75 | 25 | 100 |
| 2 Snyder | 86 | 14 | 99 |
| 3 Boozman | 96 | 4 | 96 |
| 4 Ross | 78 | 22 | 94 |
| **CALIFORNIA** | | | |
| 1 Thompson | 92 | 8 | 99 |
| 2 Herger | 97 | 3 | 99 |
| 3 Lungren | 97 | 3 | 99 |
| 4 Doolittle | 97 | 3 | 96 |
| 5 Matsui, D.[1] | 98 | 2 | 99 |
| 6 Woolsey | 99 | 1 | 98 |
| 7 Miller, George | 99 | 1 | 99 |
| 8 Pelosi | 99 | 1 | 98 |
| 9 Lee | 98 | 2 | 98 |
| 10 Tauscher | 95 | 5 | 98 |
| 11 Pombo | 96 | 4 | 97 |
| 12 Lantos | 96 | 4 | 97 |
| 13 Stark | 98 | 2 | 94 |
| 14 Eshoo | 97 | 3 | 96 |
| 15 Honda | 99 | 1 | 96 |
| 16 Lofgren | 97 | 3 | 99 |
| 17 Farr | 98 | 2 | 99 |
| 18 Cardoza | 79 | 21 | 98 |
| 19 Radanovich | 96 | 4 | 96 |
| 20 Costa | 79 | 21 | 97 |
| 21 Nunes | 96 | 4 | 98 |
| 22 Thomas | 92 | 8 | 93 |
| 23 Capps | 98 | 2 | 97 |
| 24 Gallegly | 97 | 3 | 96 |
| 25 McKeon | 97 | 3 | 99 |
| 26 Dreier | 96 | 4 | 100 |
| 27 Sherman | 95 | 5 | 99 |
| 28 Berman | 96 | 4 | 96 |
| 29 Schiff | 94 | 6 | 94 |
| 30 Waxman | 98 | 2 | 96 |
| 31 Becerra | 99 | 1 | 95 |
| 32 Solis | 99 | 1 | 97 |
| 33 Watson | 98 | 2 | 96 |
| 34 Roybal-Allard | 97 | 3 | 92 |
| 35 Waters | 96 | 4 | 93 |
| 36 Harman | 90 | 10 | 88 |
| 37 Millender-McD. | 98 | 2 | 84 |
| 38 Napolitano | 98 | 2 | 92 |
| 39 Sánchez, Linda | 99 | 1 | 99 |
| 40 Royce | 97 | 3 | 98 |
| 41 Lewis | 95 | 5 | 99 |
| 42 Miller, Gary | 98 | 2 | 96 |
| 43 Baca | 88 | 12 | 97 |
| 44 Calvert | 98 | 2 | 99 |
| 45 Bono | 93 | 7 | 94 |
| 46 Rohrabacher | 94 | 6 | 98 |
| 47 Sanchez, Loretta | 93 | 7 | 97 |
| 48 Campbell[2] | 100 | 0 | 100 |
| 49 Issa | 95 | 5 | 98 |

| | 1 | 2 | 3 |
|---|---|---|---|
| 50 Cunningham[3] | 95 | 5 | 95 |
| 51 Filner | 98 | 2 | 98 |
| 52 Hunter | 97 | 3 | 97 |
| 53 Davis | 96 | 4 | 99 |
| **COLORADO** | | | |
| 1 DeGette | 96 | 4 | 97 |
| 2 Udall | 91 | 9 | 99 |
| 3 Salazar | 81 | 19 | 99 |
| 4 Musgrave | 99 | 1 | 97 |
| 5 Hefley | 93 | 7 | 97 |
| 6 Tancredo | 93 | 7 | 95 |
| 7 Beauprez | 96 | 4 | 96 |
| **CONNECTICUT** | | | |
| 1 Larson | 98 | 2 | 91 |
| 2 Simmons | 74 | 26 | 95 |
| 3 DeLauro | 98 | 2 | 99 |
| 4 Shays | 67 | 33 | 95 |
| 5 Johnson | 79 | 21 | 99 |
| **DELAWARE** | | | |
| AL Castle | 76 | 24 | 99 |
| **FLORIDA** | | | |
| 1 Miller | 96 | 4 | 95 |
| 2 Boyd | 75 | 25 | 91 |
| 3 Brown | 96 | 4 | 91 |
| 4 Crenshaw | 97 | 3 | 99 |
| 5 Brown-Waite | 91 | 9 | 94 |
| 6 Stearns | 94 | 6 | 99 |
| 7 Mica | 97 | 3 | 99 |
| 8 Keller | 96 | 4 | 97 |
| 9 Bilirakis | 94 | 6 | 98 |
| 10 Young | 92 | 8 | 88 |
| 11 Davis | 89 | 11 | 91 |
| 12 Putnam | 97 | 3 | 99 |
| 13 Harris | 92 | 8 | 93 |
| 14 Mack | 96 | 4 | 98 |
| 15 Weldon | 95 | 5 | 98 |
| 16 Foley | 90 | 10 | 95 |
| 17 Meek | 93 | 7 | 98 |
| 18 Ros-Lehtinen | 91 | 9 | 95 |
| 19 Wexler | 97 | 3 | 94 |
| 20 Wasserman-Schultz | 94 | 6 | 98 |
| 21 Diaz-Balart, L. | 90 | 10 | 95 |
| 22 Shaw | 93 | 7 | 97 |
| 23 Hastings | 96 | 4 | 91 |
| 24 Feeney | 98 | 2 | 93 |
| 25 Diaz-Balart, M. | 94 | 6 | 88 |
| **GEORGIA** | | | |
| 1 Kingston | 98 | 2 | 94 |
| 2 Bishop | 77 | 23 | 96 |
| 3 Marshall | 67 | 33 | 99 |
| 4 McKinney | 97 | 3 | 98 |
| 5 Lewis | 99 | 1 | 83 |
| 6 Price | 97 | 3 | 99 |
| 7 Linder | 97 | 3 | 99 |
| 8 Westmoreland | 98 | 2 | 94 |
| 9 Norwood | 97 | 3 | 94 |
| 10 Deal | 98 | 2 | 98 |
| 11 Gingrey | 97 | 3 | 98 |
| 12 Barrow | 78 | 22 | 98 |
| 13 Scott | 79 | 21 | 96 |
| **HAWAII** | | | |
| 1 Abercrombie | 92 | 8 | 97 |
| 2 Case | 78 | 22 | 99 |
| **IDAHO** | | | |
| 1 Otter | 91 | 9 | 99 |
| 2 Simpson | 94 | 6 | 98 |
| **ILLINOIS** | | | |
| 1 Rush | 97 | 3 | 97 |
| 2 Jackson | 98 | 2 | 100 |
| 3 Lipinski | 86 | 14 | 99 |
| 4 Gutierrez | 98 | 2 | 90 |
| 5 Emanuel | 95 | 5 | 94 |
| 6 Hyde | 96 | 4 | 84 |
| 7 Davis | 97 | 3 | 98 |
| 8 Bean | 83 | 17 | 99 |
| 9 Schakowsky | 99 | 1 | 99 |
| 10 Kirk | 80 | 20 | 99 |
| 11 Weller | 94 | 6 | 97 |
| 12 Costello | 82 | 18 | 99 |

**KEY**   Republicans   Democrats   *Independents*

---

[1] Rep. Doris Matsui, D-Calif., was sworn in March 10, 2005. The first vote for which she was eligible was vote 62. She was eligible for 262 party unity votes in 2005.

[2] Rep. John Campbell, R-Calif., was sworn in Dec. 7, 2005, to replace Republican Christopher Cox, who resigned effective Aug. 2. The first vote for which Campbell was eligible was vote 619; he was eligible for 32 party unity votes in 2005. The last vote for which Cox was eligible was vote 453; he was eligible for 244 party unity votes in 2005. His party unity score was 95 percent; party opposition score, 5 percent; participation rate, 89 percent.

[3] Rep. Randy "Duke" Cunningham, R-Calif., resigned effective Dec. 1, 2005. The last vote for which he was eligible was vote 608. He was eligible for 295 party unity votes in 2005.

[4] The Speaker votes only at his discretion, usually to break a tie or to emphasize the importance of a matter.

[5] Rep. Jeanne Schmidt, R-Ohio, was sworn in Sept. 6, 2005, to replace Republican Rob Portman, who resigned effective April 29, 2005. The first vote for which Schmidt was eligible was vote 454; she was eligible for 84 party unity votes in 2005. The last vote for which Portman was eligible was vote 150; he was eligible for 86 party unity votes in 2005. His party unity score was 99 percent; party opposition score, 1 percent; participation rate, 91 percent.

| | 1 | 2 | 3 |
|---|---|---|---|
| 13 Biggert | 87 | 13 | 99 |
| 14 Hastert[4] | 100 | 0 | 13 |
| 15 Johnson | 77 | 23 | 99 |
| 16 Manzullo | 94 | 6 | 99 |
| 17 Evans | 98 | 2 | 98 |
| 18 LaHood | 89 | 11 | 93 |
| 19 Shimkus | 92 | 8 | 99 |
| **INDIANA** | | | |
| 1 Visclosky | 91 | 9 | 100 |
| 2 Chocola | 97 | 3 | 99 |
| 3 Souder | 97 | 3 | 97 |
| 4 Buyer | 98 | 2 | 96 |
| 5 Burton | 97 | 3 | 97 |
| 6 Pence | 98 | 2 | 98 |
| 7 Carson | 97 | 3 | 94 |
| 8 Hostettler | 91 | 9 | 98 |
| 9 Sodrel | 96 | 4 | 100 |
| **IOWA** | | | |
| 1 Nussle | 96 | 4 | 99 |
| 2 Leach | 63 | 37 | 95 |
| 3 Boswell | 82 | 18 | 86 |
| 4 Latham | 96 | 4 | 100 |
| 5 King | 98 | 2 | 100 |
| **KANSAS** | | | |
| 1 Moran | 92 | 8 | 98 |
| 2 Ryun | 98 | 2 | 99 |
| 3 Moore | 85 | 15 | 99 |
| 4 Tiahrt | 97 | 3 | 99 |
| **KENTUCKY** | | | |
| 1 Whitfield | 94 | 6 | 98 |
| 2 Lewis | 96 | 4 | 99 |
| 3 Northup | 96 | 4 | 97 |
| 4 Davis | 96 | 4 | 99 |
| 5 Rogers | 96 | 4 | 99 |
| 6 Chandler | 80 | 20 | 100 |
| **LOUISIANA** | | | |
| 1 Jindal | 97 | 3 | 98 |
| 2 Jefferson | 90 | 10 | 96 |
| 3 Melancon | 71 | 29 | 96 |
| 4 McCrery | 97 | 3 | 97 |
| 5 Alexander | 97 | 3 | 99 |
| 6 Baker | 98 | 2 | 97 |
| 7 Boustany | 96 | 4 | 97 |
| **MAINE** | | | |
| 1 Allen | 97 | 3 | 98 |
| 2 Michaud | 92 | 8 | 99 |
| **MARYLAND** | | | |
| 1 Gilchrest | 80 | 20 | 99 |
| 2 Ruppersberger | 89 | 11 | 99 |
| 3 Cardin | 95 | 5 | 97 |
| 4 Wynn | 87 | 13 | 99 |
| 5 Hoyer | 93 | 7 | 99 |
| 6 Bartlett | 89 | 11 | 98 |
| 7 Cummings | 97 | 3 | 97 |
| 8 Van Hollen | 99 | 1 | 99 |
| **MASSACHUSETTS** | | | |
| 1 Olver | 98 | 2 | 97 |
| 2 Neal | 97 | 3 | 96 |
| 3 McGovern | 99 | 1 | 99 |
| 4 Frank | 96 | 4 | 98 |
| 5 Meehan | 99 | 1 | 99 |
| 6 Tierney | 98 | 2 | 99 |
| 7 Markey | 98 | 2 | 99 |
| 8 Capuano | 96 | 4 | 99 |
| 9 Lynch | 92 | 8 | 97 |
| 10 Delahunt | 99 | 1 | 91 |
| **MICHIGAN** | | | |
| 1 Stupak | 87 | 13 | 95 |
| 2 Hoekstra | 96 | 4 | 99 |
| 3 Ehlers | 78 | 22 | 98 |
| 4 Camp | 95 | 5 | 95 |
| 5 Kildee | 91 | 9 | 100 |
| 6 Upton | 87 | 13 | 100 |
| 7 Schwarz | 85 | 15 | 98 |
| 8 Rogers | 94 | 6 | 97 |
| 9 Knollenberg | 95 | 5 | 98 |
| 10 Miller | 94 | 6 | 100 |
| 11 McCotter | 89 | 11 | 98 |
| 12 Levin | 95 | 5 | 100 |
| 13 Kilpatrick | 96 | 4 | 96 |
| 14 Conyers | 97 | 3 | 95 |
| 15 Dingell | 92 | 8 | 98 |

| | 1 | 2 | 3 |
|---|---|---|---|
| **MINNESOTA** | | | |
| 1 Gutknecht | 93 | 7 | 99 |
| 2 Kline | 97 | 3 | 100 |
| 3 Ramstad | 80 | 20 | 97 |
| 4 McCollum | 98 | 2 | 99 |
| 5 Sabo | 96 | 4 | 98 |
| 6 Kennedy | 92 | 8 | 100 |
| 7 Peterson | 64 | 36 | 98 |
| 8 Oberstar | 93 | 7 | 93 |
| **MISSISSIPPI** | | | |
| 1 Wicker | 97 | 3 | 97 |
| 2 Thompson | 93 | 7 | 100 |
| 3 Pickering | 94 | 6 | 94 |
| 4 Taylor | 65 | 35 | 94 |
| **MISSOURI** | | | |
| 1 Clay | 96 | 4 | 90 |
| 2 Akin | 99 | 1 | 97 |
| 3 Carnahan | 94 | 6 | 100 |
| 4 Skelton | 76 | 24 | 97 |
| 5 Cleaver | 96 | 4 | 98 |
| 6 Graves | 95 | 5 | 98 |
| 7 Blunt | 98 | 2 | 98 |
| 8 Emerson | 90 | 10 | 96 |
| 9 Hulshof | 93 | 7 | 99 |
| **MONTANA** | | | |
| AL Rehberg | 95 | 5 | 99 |
| **NEBRASKA** | | | |
| 1 Fortenberry | 95 | 5 | 99 |
| 2 Terry | 94 | 6 | 99 |
| 3 Osborne | 93 | 7 | 98 |
| **NEVADA** | | | |
| 1 Berkley | 92 | 8 | 95 |
| 2 Gibbons | 91 | 9 | 97 |
| 3 Porter | 90 | 10 | 99 |
| **NEW HAMPSHIRE** | | | |
| 1 Bradley | 87 | 13 | 99 |
| 2 Bass | 87 | 13 | 99 |
| **NEW JERSEY** | | | |
| 1 Andrews | 92 | 8 | 91 |
| 2 LoBiondo | 81 | 19 | 100 |
| 3 Saxton | 85 | 15 | 99 |
| 4 Smith | 79 | 21 | 98 |
| 5 Garrett | 98 | 2 | 98 |
| 6 Pallone | 97 | 3 | 99 |
| 7 Ferguson | 89 | 11 | 99 |
| 8 Pascrell | 93 | 7 | 98 |
| 9 Rothman | 93 | 7 | 92 |
| 10 Payne | 99 | 1 | 89 |
| 11 Frelinghuysen | 89 | 11 | 98 |
| 12 Holt | 97 | 3 | 99 |
| 13 Menendez | 93 | 7 | 95 |
| **NEW MEXICO** | | | |
| 1 Wilson | 82 | 18 | 95 |
| 2 Pearce | 96 | 4 | 97 |
| 3 Udall | 97 | 3 | 96 |
| **NEW YORK** | | | |
| 1 Bishop | 95 | 5 | 99 |
| 2 Israel | 94 | 6 | 98 |
| 3 King | 89 | 11 | 98 |
| 4 McCarthy | 93 | 7 | 95 |
| 5 Ackerman | 98 | 2 | 98 |
| 6 Meeks | 93 | 7 | 91 |
| 7 Crowley | 97 | 3 | 99 |
| 8 Nadler | 98 | 2 | 98 |
| 9 Weiner | 99 | 1 | 99 |
| 10 Towns | 93 | 7 | 94 |
| 11 Owens | 98 | 2 | 98 |
| 12 Velázquez | 98 | 2 | 97 |
| 13 Fossella | 90 | 10 | 98 |
| 14 Maloney | 98 | 2 | 98 |
| 15 Rangel | 98 | 2 | 95 |
| 16 Serrano | 96 | 4 | 98 |
| 17 Engel | 93 | 7 | 99 |
| 18 Lowey | 98 | 2 | 99 |
| 19 Kelly | 85 | 15 | 94 |
| 20 Sweeney | 88 | 12 | 92 |
| 21 McNulty | 93 | 7 | 98 |
| 22 Hinchey | 98 | 2 | 96 |
| 23 McHugh | 89 | 11 | 98 |
| 24 Boehlert | 77 | 23 | 98 |
| 25 Walsh | 92 | 8 | 96 |
| 26 Reynolds | 94 | 6 | 97 |
| 27 Higgins | 89 | 11 | 99 |
| 28 Slaughter | 97 | 3 | 95 |
| 29 Kuhl | 93 | 7 | 99 |

| | 1 | 2 | 3 |
|---|---|---|---|
| **NORTH CAROLINA** | | | |
| 1 Butterfield | 93 | 7 | 98 |
| 2 Etheridge | 88 | 12 | 99 |
| 3 Jones | 81 | 19 | 93 |
| 4 Price | 96 | 4 | 99 |
| 5 Foxx | 99 | 1 | 99 |
| 6 Coble | 94 | 6 | 99 |
| 7 McIntyre | 71 | 29 | 98 |
| 8 Hayes | 99 | 1 | 98 |
| 9 Myrick | 97 | 3 | 94 |
| 10 McHenry | 99 | 1 | 99 |
| 11 Taylor | 97 | 3 | 97 |
| 12 Watt | 98 | 2 | 98 |
| 13 Miller | 93 | 7 | 100 |
| **NORTH DAKOTA** | | | |
| AL Pomeroy | 80 | 20 | 97 |
| **OHIO** | | | |
| 1 Chabot | 95 | 5 | 99 |
| 2 Schmidt[5] | 98 | 2 | 100 |
| 3 Turner | 92 | 8 | 99 |
| 4 Oxley | 97 | 3 | 93 |
| 5 Gillmor | 94 | 6 | 94 |
| 6 Strickland | 91 | 9 | 95 |
| 7 Hobson | 94 | 6 | 98 |
| 8 Boehner | 97 | 3 | 98 |
| 9 Kaptur | 93 | 7 | 98 |
| 10 Kucinich | 98 | 2 | 98 |
| 11 Jones | 96 | 4 | 91 |
| 12 Tiberi | 95 | 5 | 97 |
| 13 Brown | 97 | 3 | 98 |
| 14 LaTourette | 86 | 14 | 94 |
| 15 Pryce | 94 | 6 | 99 |
| 16 Regula | 92 | 8 | 100 |
| 17 Ryan | 91 | 9 | 98 |
| 18 Ney | 91 | 9 | 97 |
| **OKLAHOMA** | | | |
| 1 Sullivan | 97 | 3 | 95 |
| 2 Boren | 59 | 41 | 99 |
| 3 Lucas | 97 | 3 | 97 |
| 4 Cole | 98 | 2 | 98 |
| 5 Istook | 98 | 2 | 90 |
| **OREGON** | | | |
| 1 Wu | 92 | 8 | 99 |
| 2 Walden | 92 | 8 | 99 |
| 3 Blumenauer | 97 | 3 | 97 |
| 4 DeFazio | 91 | 9 | 99 |
| 5 Hooley | 93 | 7 | 98 |
| **PENNSYLVANIA** | | | |
| 1 Brady | 93 | 7 | 95 |
| 2 Fattah | 96 | 4 | 95 |
| 3 English | 93 | 7 | 99 |
| 4 Hart | 96 | 4 | 100 |
| 5 Peterson | 95 | 5 | 92 |
| 6 Gerlach | 82 | 18 | 99 |
| 7 Weldon | 85 | 15 | 96 |
| 8 Fitzpatrick | 76 | 24 | 99 |
| 9 Shuster | 98 | 2 | 99 |
| 10 Sherwood | 95 | 5 | 99 |
| 11 Kanjorski | 80 | 20 | 99 |
| 12 Murtha | 76 | 24 | 96 |
| 13 Schwartz | 92 | 8 | 99 |
| 14 Doyle | 90 | 10 | 97 |
| 15 Dent | 89 | 11 | 100 |
| 16 Pitts | 97 | 3 | 99 |
| 17 Holden | 75 | 25 | 99 |
| 18 Murphy | 91 | 9 | 97 |
| 19 Platts | 84 | 16 | 97 |
| **RHODE ISLAND** | | | |
| 1 Kennedy | 96 | 4 | 98 |
| 2 Langevin | 92 | 8 | 100 |
| **SOUTH CAROLINA** | | | |
| 1 Brown | 96 | 4 | 93 |
| 2 Wilson | 97 | 3 | 99 |
| 3 Barrett | 99 | 1 | 96 |
| 4 Inglis | 93 | 7 | 99 |
| 5 Spratt | 88 | 12 | 99 |
| 6 Clyburn | 92 | 8 | 97 |
| **SOUTH DAKOTA** | | | |
| AL Herseth | 79 | 21 | 95 |
| **TENNESSEE** | | | |
| 1 Jenkins | 96 | 4 | 97 |
| 2 Duncan | 93 | 7 | 100 |

| | 1 | 2 | 3 |
|---|---|---|---|
| 3 Wamp | 94 | 6 | 98 |
| 4 Davis | 67 | 33 | 99 |
| 5 Cooper | 80 | 20 | 96 |
| 6 Gordon | 74 | 26 | 98 |
| 7 Blackburn | 99 | 1 | 99 |
| 8 Tanner | 74 | 26 | 98 |
| 9 Ford | 83 | 17 | 97 |
| **TEXAS** | | | |
| 1 Gohmert | 95 | 5 | 95 |
| 2 Poe | 94 | 6 | 96 |
| 3 Johnson, Sam | 98 | 2 | 97 |
| 4 Hall, R. | 96 | 4 | 97 |
| 5 Hensarling | 98 | 2 | 99 |
| 6 Barton | 96 | 4 | 89 |
| 7 Culberson | 98 | 2 | 97 |
| 8 Brady | 98 | 2 | 95 |
| 9 Green, A. | 93 | 7 | 100 |
| 10 McCaul | 96 | 4 | 97 |
| 11 Conaway | 96 | 4 | 96 |
| 12 Granger | 97 | 3 | 97 |
| 13 Thornberry | 98 | 2 | 99 |
| 14 Paul | 72 | 28 | 99 |
| 15 Hinojosa | 84 | 16 | 85 |
| 16 Reyes | 81 | 19 | 90 |
| 17 Edwards | 75 | 25 | 99 |
| 18 Jackson-Lee | 93 | 7 | 91 |
| 19 Neugebauer | 99 | 1 | 100 |
| 20 Gonzalez | 86 | 14 | 99 |
| 21 Smith | 98 | 2 | 97 |
| 22 DeLay | 98 | 2 | 95 |
| 23 Bonilla | 98 | 2 | 99 |
| 24 Marchant | 98 | 2 | 98 |
| 25 Doggett | 97 | 3 | 96 |
| 26 Burgess | 97 | 3 | 99 |
| 27 Ortiz | 78 | 22 | 94 |
| 28 Cuellar | 70 | 30 | 95 |
| 29 Green, G. | 82 | 18 | 96 |
| 30 Johnson, E.B. | 96 | 4 | 97 |
| 31 Carter | 98 | 2 | 95 |
| 32 Sessions | 99 | 1 | 92 |
| **UTAH** | | | |
| 1 Bishop | 97 | 3 | 97 |
| 2 Matheson | 69 | 31 | 100 |
| 3 Cannon | 96 | 4 | 98 |
| **VERMONT** | | | |
| AL *Sanders* | 97 | 3 | 99 |
| **VIRGINIA** | | | |
| 1 Davis, Jo Ann | 93 | 7 | 93 |
| 2 Drake | 98 | 2 | 100 |
| 3 Scott | 95 | 5 | 99 |
| 4 Forbes | 95 | 5 | 99 |
| 5 Goode | 93 | 7 | 98 |
| 6 Goodlatte | 96 | 4 | 100 |
| 7 Cantor | 98 | 2 | 99 |
| 8 Moran | 92 | 8 | 95 |
| 9 Boucher | 83 | 17 | 97 |
| 10 Wolf | 90 | 10 | 99 |
| 11 Davis, T. | 88 | 12 | 93 |
| **WASHINGTON** | | | |
| 1 Inslee | 97 | 3 | 99 |
| 2 Larsen | 93 | 7 | 98 |
| 3 Baird | 92 | 8 | 93 |
| 4 Hastings | 96 | 4 | 92 |
| 5 McMorris | 98 | 2 | 99 |
| 6 Dicks | 92 | 8 | 99 |
| 7 McDermott | 99 | 1 | 95 |
| 8 Reichert | 88 | 12 | 98 |
| 9 Smith | 90 | 10 | 99 |
| **WEST VIRGINIA** | | | |
| 1 Mollohan | 78 | 22 | 98 |
| 2 Capito | 90 | 10 | 97 |
| 3 Rahall | 87 | 13 | 98 |
| **WISCONSIN** | | | |
| 1 Ryan | 94 | 6 | 99 |
| 2 Baldwin | 99 | 1 | 100 |
| 3 Kind | 89 | 11 | 96 |
| 4 Moore | 97 | 3 | 97 |
| 5 Sensenbrenner | 93 | 7 | 98 |
| 6 Petri | 88 | 12 | 98 |
| 7 Obey | 95 | 5 | 95 |
| 8 Green | 89 | 11 | 100 |
| **WYOMING** | | | |
| AL Cubin | 94 | 6 | 94 |

# HOUSE

**1. Voting Participation.** Percentage of 669 recorded votes in 2005 on which a representative voted "yea" or "nay."

**2. Voting Participation (without Journal votes).** Percentage of 661 recorded votes in 2005 on which a member voted "yea" or "nay." In this version of the study, eight votes on approval of the House Journal were excluded.

*Absences because of illness.* Congressional Quarterly no longer designates members who missed votes because of illness. In the past, notations to that effect were based on official statements published in the Congressional Record, but these were found to be inconsistently used.

*Rounding.* Scores are rounded to the nearest percentage, except that no scores are rounded up to 100 percent. Members with a 100 percent score participated in all recorded votes for which they were eligible.

[1] Rep. Doris Matsui, D-Calif., was sworn in March 10, 2005. The first vote for which she was eligible was vote 62.

[2] Rep. John Campbell, R-Calif., was sworn in Dec. 7, 2005, to replace Republican Christopher Cox, who resigned effective Aug. 2. The first vote for which Campbell was eligible was vote 619. The last vote for which Cox was eligible was vote 453; his participation rate was 87 percent.

[3] Rep. Randy "Duke" Cunningham, R-Calif., resigned effective Dec. 1, 2005. The last vote for which he was eligible was vote 608.

[4] The Speaker votes only at his discretion, usually to break a tie or to emphasize the importance of a matter.

[5] Rep. Jean Schmidt, R-Ohio, was sworn in Sept. 6, 2005, to replace Republican Rob Portman, who resigned effective April 29. The first vote for which Schmidt was eligible was vote 454. The last vote for which Portman was eligible was vote 150; his participation rate was 91 percent.

| | 1 | 2 |
|---|---|---|
| **ALABAMA** | | |
| 1 Bonner | 97 | 97 |
| 2 Everett | 94 | 94 |
| 3 Rogers | 96 | 96 |
| 4 Aderholt | 100 | 100 |
| 5 Cramer | 95 | 95 |
| 6 Bachus | 95 | 95 |
| 7 Davis | 98 | 98 |
| **ALASKA** | | |
| AL Young | 90 | 90 |
| **ARIZONA** | | |
| 1 Renzi | 99 | 99 |
| 2 Franks | 99 | 98 |
| 3 Shadegg | 95 | 95 |
| 4 Pastor | 99 | 99 |
| 5 Hayworth | 99 | 99 |
| 6 Flake | 97 | 97 |
| 7 Grijalva | 97 | 98 |
| 8 Kolbe | 96 | 96 |
| **ARKANSAS** | | |
| 1 Berry | 99 | 99 |
| 2 Snyder | 99 | 99 |
| 3 Boozman | 97 | 97 |
| 4 Ross | 94 | 94 |
| **CALIFORNIA** | | |
| 1 Thompson | 99 | 99 |
| 2 Herger | 99 | 99 |
| 3 Lungren | 99 | 99 |
| 4 Doolittle | 94 | 94 |
| 5 Matsui, D.[1] | 99 | 99 |
| 6 Woolsey | 99 | 99 |
| 7 Miller, George | 97 | 97 |
| 8 Pelosi | 94 | 94 |
| 9 Lee | 96 | 96 |
| 10 Tauscher | 98 | 98 |
| 11 Pombo | 95 | 95 |
| 12 Lantos | 96 | 96 |
| 13 Stark | 87 | 87 |
| 14 Eshoo | 94 | 94 |
| 15 Honda | 96 | 96 |
| 16 Lofgren | 99 | 99 |
| 17 Farr | 99 | 98 |
| 18 Cardoza | 98 | 98 |
| 19 Radanovich | 94 | 94 |
| 20 Costa | 97 | 97 |
| 21 Nunes | 98 | 98 |
| 22 Thomas | 95 | 95 |
| 23 Capps | 96 | 96 |
| 24 Gallegly | 93 | 93 |
| 25 McKeon | 98 | 98 |
| 26 Dreier | 99 | 99 |
| 27 Sherman | 99 | 98 |
| 28 Berman | 92 | 92 |
| 29 Schiff | 93 | 93 |
| 30 Waxman | 96 | 96 |
| 31 Becerra | 93 | 93 |
| 32 Solis | 96 | 95 |
| 33 Watson | 94 | 94 |
| 34 Roybal-Allard | 90 | 90 |
| 35 Waters | 90 | 89 |
| 36 Harman | 89 | 89 |
| 37 Millender-McD. | 83 | 83 |
| 38 Napolitano | 93 | 93 |
| 39 Sánchez, Linda | 98 | 98 |
| 40 Royce | 97 | 97 |
| 41 Lewis | 99 | 99 |
| 42 Miller, Gary | 95 | 95 |
| 43 Baca | 96 | 96 |
| 44 Calvert | 97 | 97 |
| 45 Bono | 94 | 94 |
| 46 Rohrabacher | 98 | 98 |
| 47 Sanchez, Loretta | 95 | 95 |
| 48 Campbell[2] | 100 | 100 |
| 49 Issa | 97 | 97 |

| | 1 | 2 |
|---|---|---|
| 50 Cunningham[3] | 93 | 93 |
| 51 Filner | 97 | 97 |
| 52 Hunter | 94 | 94 |
| 53 Davis | 99 | 99 |
| **COLORADO** | | |
| 1 DeGette | 96 | 96 |
| 2 Udall | 98 | 98 |
| 3 Salazar | 99 | 99 |
| 4 Musgrave | 97 | 97 |
| 5 Hefley | 95 | 95 |
| 6 Tancredo | 94 | 95 |
| 7 Beauprez | 97 | 97 |
| **CONNECTICUT** | | |
| 1 Larson | 91 | 91 |
| 2 Simmons | 94 | 94 |
| 3 DeLauro | 99 | 99 |
| 4 Shays | 95 | 95 |
| 5 Johnson | 98 | 98 |
| **DELAWARE** | | |
| AL Castle | 99 | 99 |
| **FLORIDA** | | |
| 1 Miller | 94 | 94 |
| 2 Boyd | 92 | 92 |
| 3 Brown | 86 | 86 |
| 4 Crenshaw | 99 | 99 |
| 5 Brown-Waite | 88 | 89 |
| 6 Stearns | 99 | 99 |
| 7 Mica | 99 | 98 |
| 8 Keller | 96 | 96 |
| 9 Bilirakis | 97 | 97 |
| 10 Young | 85 | 85 |
| 11 Davis | 84 | 84 |
| 12 Putnam | 99 | 99 |
| 13 Harris | 91 | 91 |
| 14 Mack | 99 | 99 |
| 15 Weldon | 96 | 96 |
| 16 Foley | 95 | 95 |
| 17 Meek | 96 | 96 |
| 18 Ros-Lehtinen | 93 | 93 |
| 19 Wexler | 90 | 90 |
| 20 Wasserman-Schultz | 96 | 96 |
| 21 Diaz-Balart, L. | 91 | 91 |
| 22 Shaw | 96 | 96 |
| 23 Hastings | 87 | 87 |
| 24 Feeney | 92 | 92 |
| 25 Diaz-Balart, M. | 85 | 85 |
| **GEORGIA** | | |
| 1 Kingston | 92 | 92 |
| 2 Bishop | 95 | 95 |
| 3 Marshall | 98 | 98 |
| 4 McKinney | 96 | 96 |
| 5 Lewis | 86 | 86 |
| 6 Price | 99 | 99 |
| 7 Linder | 97 | 97 |
| 8 Westmoreland | 94 | 94 |
| 9 Norwood | 93 | 93 |
| 10 Deal | 97 | 97 |
| 11 Gingrey | 97 | 97 |
| 12 Barrow | 98 | 98 |
| 13 Scott | 96 | 96 |
| **HAWAII** | | |
| 1 Abercrombie | 97 | 97 |
| 2 Case | 98 | 98 |
| **IDAHO** | | |
| 1 Otter | 98 | 98 |
| 2 Simpson | 97 | 97 |
| **ILLINOIS** | | |
| 1 Rush | 91 | 91 |
| 2 Jackson | 99 | 99 |
| 3 Lipinski | 99 | 99 |
| 4 Gutierrez | 84 | 84 |
| 5 Emanuel | 95 | 95 |
| 6 Hyde | 87 | 87 |
| 7 Davis | 98 | 98 |
| 8 Bean | 99 | 99 |
| 9 Schakowsky | 97 | 97 |
| 10 Kirk | 97 | 97 |
| 11 Weller | 96 | 96 |
| 12 Costello | 97 | 97 |

**KEY**   Republicans   Democrats   *Independents*

| | 1 | 2 |
|---|---|---|
| 13 Biggert | 99 | 99 |
| 14 Hastert[4] | 9 | 9 |
| 15 Johnson | 98 | 98 |
| 16 Manzullo | 97 | 97 |
| 17 Evans | 97 | 97 |
| 18 LaHood | 93 | 93 |
| 19 Shimkus | 97 | 97 |
| **INDIANA** | | |
| 1 Visclosky | 99 | 99 |
| 2 Chocola | 99 | 99 |
| 3 Souder | 96 | 96 |
| 4 Buyer | 93 | 93 |
| 5 Burton | 96 | 96 |
| 6 Pence | 96 | 96 |
| 7 Carson | 93 | 93 |
| 8 Hostettler | 97 | 97 |
| 9 Sodrel | 99 | 99 |
| **IOWA** | | |
| 1 Nussle | 97 | 97 |
| 2 Leach | 95 | 95 |
| 3 Boswell | 79 | 79 |
| 4 Latham | 99 | 99 |
| 5 King | 99 | 99 |
| **KANSAS** | | |
| 1 Moran | 98 | 98 |
| 2 Ryun | 99 | 99 |
| 3 Moore | 99 | 99 |
| 4 Tiahrt | 98 | 98 |
| **KENTUCKY** | | |
| 1 Whitfield | 96 | 96 |
| 2 Lewis | 98 | 98 |
| 3 Northup | 97 | 97 |
| 4 Davis | 99 | 99 |
| 5 Rogers | 99 | 99 |
| 6 Chandler | 99 | 99 |
| **LOUISIANA** | | |
| 1 Jindal | 97 | 97 |
| 2 Jefferson | 95 | 95 |
| 3 Melancon | 95 | 95 |
| 4 McCrery | 96 | 96 |
| 5 Alexander | 99 | 99 |
| 6 Baker | 95 | 95 |
| 7 Boustany | 97 | 97 |
| **MAINE** | | |
| 1 Allen | 99 | 98 |
| 2 Michaud | 99 | 99 |
| **MARYLAND** | | |
| 1 Gilchrest | 98 | 98 |
| 2 Ruppersberger | 99 | 98 |
| 3 Cardin | 95 | 95 |
| 4 Wynn | 99 | 98 |
| 5 Hoyer | 99 | 98 |
| 6 Bartlett | 98 | 98 |
| 7 Cummings | 96 | 96 |
| 8 Van Hollen | 99 | 99 |
| **MASSACHUSETTS** | | |
| 1 Olver | 94 | 94 |
| 2 Neal | 93 | 94 |
| 3 McGovern | 99 | 99 |
| 4 Frank | 98 | 98 |
| 5 Meehan | 98 | 98 |
| 6 Tierney | 98 | 98 |
| 7 Markey | 99 | 99 |
| 8 Capuano | 97 | 97 |
| 9 Lynch | 95 | 95 |
| 10 Delahunt | 89 | 89 |
| **MICHIGAN** | | |
| 1 Stupak | 93 | 93 |
| 2 Hoekstra | 97 | 97 |
| 3 Ehlers | 97 | 97 |
| 4 Camp | 95 | 95 |
| 5 Kildee | 100 | 100 |
| 6 Upton | 100 | 100 |
| 7 Schwarz | 97 | 97 |
| 8 Rogers | 98 | 98 |
| 9 Knollenberg | 98 | 98 |
| 10 Miller | 99 | 99 |
| 11 McCotter | 98 | 98 |
| 12 Levin | 99 | 99 |
| 13 Kilpatrick | 93 | 93 |
| 14 Conyers | 95 | 95 |
| 15 Dingell | 96 | 96 |

| | 1 | 2 |
|---|---|---|
| **MINNESOTA** | | |
| 1 Gutknecht | 98 | 98 |
| 2 Kline | 100 | 100 |
| 3 Ramstad | 98 | 98 |
| 4 McCollum | 98 | 98 |
| 5 Sabo | 97 | 97 |
| 6 Kennedy | 100 | 100 |
| 7 Peterson | 98 | 98 |
| 8 Oberstar | 93 | 93 |
| **MISSISSIPPI** | | |
| 1 Wicker | 96 | 97 |
| 2 Thompson | 99 | 99 |
| 3 Pickering | 94 | 94 |
| 4 Taylor | 91 | 91 |
| **MISSOURI** | | |
| 1 Clay | 89 | 89 |
| 2 Akin | 98 | 98 |
| 3 Carnahan | 99 | 99 |
| 4 Skelton | 97 | 97 |
| 5 Cleaver | 98 | 98 |
| 6 Graves | 96 | 96 |
| 7 Blunt | 98 | 98 |
| 8 Emerson | 95 | 95 |
| 9 Hulshof | 97 | 97 |
| **MONTANA** | | |
| AL Rehberg | 99 | 99 |
| **NEBRASKA** | | |
| 1 Fortenberry | 99 | 99 |
| 2 Terry | 97 | 97 |
| 3 Osborne | 99 | 98 |
| **NEVADA** | | |
| 1 Berkley | 94 | 94 |
| 2 Gibbons | 95 | 95 |
| 3 Porter | 99 | 99 |
| **NEW HAMPSHIRE** | | |
| 1 Bradley | 99 | 99 |
| 2 Bass | 98 | 98 |
| **NEW JERSEY** | | |
| 1 Andrews | 89 | 89 |
| 2 LoBiondo | 99 | 99 |
| 3 Saxton | 99 | 99 |
| 4 Smith | 99 | 99 |
| 5 Garrett | 99 | 99 |
| 6 Pallone | 98 | 98 |
| 7 Ferguson | 98 | 98 |
| 8 Pascrell | 96 | 96 |
| 9 Rothman | 91 | 92 |
| 10 Payne | 86 | 87 |
| 11 Frelinghuysen | 98 | 98 |
| 12 Holt | 99 | 99 |
| 13 Menendez | 94 | 94 |
| **NEW MEXICO** | | |
| 1 Wilson | 97 | 97 |
| 2 Pearce | 97 | 97 |
| 3 Udall | 96 | 96 |
| **NEW YORK** | | |
| 1 Bishop | 99 | 99 |
| 2 Israel | 98 | 98 |
| 3 King | 98 | 98 |
| 4 McCarthy | 94 | 94 |
| 5 Ackerman | 96 | 95 |
| 6 Meeks | 90 | 90 |
| 7 Crowley | 96 | 96 |
| 8 Nadler | 97 | 97 |
| 9 Weiner | 94 | 94 |
| 10 Towns | 88 | 88 |
| 11 Owens | 96 | 96 |
| 12 Velázquez | 96 | 96 |
| 13 Fossella | 96 | 96 |
| 14 Maloney | 97 | 97 |
| 15 Rangel | 94 | 94 |
| 16 Serrano | 97 | 97 |
| 17 Engel | 98 | 98 |
| 18 Lowey | 99 | 99 |
| 19 Kelly | 96 | 96 |
| 20 Sweeney | 89 | 89 |
| 21 McNulty | 98 | 98 |
| 22 Hinchey | 94 | 94 |
| 23 McHugh | 97 | 97 |
| 24 Boehlert | 98 | 98 |
| 25 Walsh | 94 | 94 |
| 26 Reynolds | 96 | 96 |
| 27 Higgins | 96 | 97 |
| 28 Slaughter | 94 | 94 |
| 29 Kuhl | 99 | 99 |

| | 1 | 2 |
|---|---|---|
| **NORTH CAROLINA** | | |
| 1 Butterfield | 97 | 97 |
| 2 Etheridge | 97 | 97 |
| 3 Jones | 94 | 94 |
| 4 Price | 98 | 98 |
| 5 Foxx | 99 | 99 |
| 6 Coble | 97 | 97 |
| 7 McIntyre | 97 | 97 |
| 8 Hayes | 97 | 97 |
| 9 Myrick | 95 | 95 |
| 10 McHenry | 99 | 99 |
| 11 Taylor | 96 | 96 |
| 12 Watt | 96 | 96 |
| 13 Miller | 100 | 100 |
| **NORTH DAKOTA** | | |
| AL Pomeroy | 97 | 97 |
| **OHIO** | | |
| 1 Chabot | 99 | 99 |
| 2 Schmidt[5] | 100 | 100 |
| 3 Turner | 98 | 98 |
| 4 Oxley | 92 | 92 |
| 5 Gillmor | 94 | 94 |
| 6 Strickland | 90 | 90 |
| 7 Hobson | 97 | 97 |
| 8 Boehner | 97 | 97 |
| 9 Kaptur | 97 | 97 |
| 10 Kucinich | 98 | 98 |
| 11 Jones | 91 | 91 |
| 12 Tiberi | 97 | 97 |
| 13 Brown | 96 | 95 |
| 14 LaTourette | 94 | 94 |
| 15 Pryce | 96 | 96 |
| 16 Regula | 100 | 100 |
| 17 Ryan | 98 | 98 |
| 18 Ney | 97 | 97 |
| **OKLAHOMA** | | |
| 1 Sullivan | 95 | 95 |
| 2 Boren | 99 | 99 |
| 3 Lucas | 97 | 97 |
| 4 Cole | 97 | 98 |
| 5 Istook | 87 | 87 |
| **OREGON** | | |
| 1 Wu | 99 | 99 |
| 2 Walden | 99 | 98 |
| 3 Blumenauer | 95 | 95 |
| 4 DeFazio | 97 | 97 |
| 5 Hooley | 97 | 97 |
| **PENNSYLVANIA** | | |
| 1 Brady | 93 | 93 |
| 2 Fattah | 89 | 90 |
| 3 English | 98 | 98 |
| 4 Hart | 99 | 99 |
| 5 Peterson | 92 | 92 |
| 6 Gerlach | 98 | 98 |
| 7 Weldon | 95 | 95 |
| 8 Fitzpatrick | 99 | 99 |
| 9 Shuster | 99 | 99 |
| 10 Sherwood | 99 | 99 |
| 11 Kanjorski | 99 | 99 |
| 12 Murtha | 90 | 90 |
| 13 Schwartz | 99 | 99 |
| 14 Doyle | 96 | 96 |
| 15 Dent | 99 | 99 |
| 16 Pitts | 99 | 99 |
| 17 Holden | 99 | 98 |
| 18 Murphy | 97 | 97 |
| 19 Platts | 97 | 97 |
| **RHODE ISLAND** | | |
| 1 Kennedy | 96 | 96 |
| 2 Langevin | 99 | 99 |
| **SOUTH CAROLINA** | | |
| 1 Brown | 92 | 92 |
| 2 Wilson | 99 | 99 |
| 3 Barrett | 95 | 95 |
| 4 Inglis | 99 | 99 |
| 5 Spratt | 98 | 98 |
| 6 Clyburn | 96 | 96 |
| **SOUTH DAKOTA** | | |
| AL Herseth | 96 | 96 |
| **TENNESSEE** | | |
| 1 Jenkins | 92 | 92 |
| 2 Duncan | 100 | 100 |

| | 1 | 2 |
|---|---|---|
| 3 Wamp | 98 | 98 |
| 4 Davis | 98 | 98 |
| 5 Cooper | 96 | 96 |
| 6 Gordon | 97 | 97 |
| 7 Blackburn | 99 | 99 |
| 8 Tanner | 98 | 98 |
| 9 Ford | 92 | 92 |
| **TEXAS** | | |
| 1 Gohmert | 94 | 94 |
| 2 Poe | 96 | 96 |
| 3 Johnson, Sam | 96 | 96 |
| 4 Hall, R. | 97 | 97 |
| 5 Hensarling | 99 | 99 |
| 6 Barton | 91 | 91 |
| 7 Culberson | 96 | 96 |
| 8 Brady | 92 | 92 |
| 9 Green, A. | 99 | 99 |
| 10 McCaul | 98 | 98 |
| 11 Conaway | 94 | 94 |
| 12 Granger | 96 | 96 |
| 13 Thornberry | 99 | 99 |
| 14 Paul | 94 | 94 |
| 15 Hinojosa | 85 | 85 |
| 16 Reyes | 86 | 86 |
| 17 Edwards | 97 | 97 |
| 18 Jackson-Lee | 91 | 92 |
| 19 Neugebauer | 99 | 98 |
| 20 Gonzalez | 98 | 98 |
| 21 Smith | 97 | 97 |
| 22 DeLay | 95 | 95 |
| 23 Bonilla | 99 | 99 |
| 24 Marchant | 97 | 97 |
| 25 Doggett | 97 | 97 |
| 26 Burgess | 99 | 99 |
| 27 Ortiz | 92 | 92 |
| 28 Cuellar | 95 | 95 |
| 29 Green, G. | 96 | 97 |
| 30 Johnson, E.B. | 97 | 97 |
| 31 Carter | 96 | 96 |
| 32 Sessions | 90 | 90 |
| **UTAH** | | |
| 1 Bishop | 96 | 96 |
| 2 Matheson | 99 | 99 |
| 3 Cannon | 98 | 98 |
| **VERMONT** | | |
| AL Sanders | 97 | 97 |
| **VIRGINIA** | | |
| 1 Davis, Jo Ann | 93 | 93 |
| 2 Drake | 99 | 99 |
| 3 Scott | 97 | 97 |
| 4 Forbes | 99 | 99 |
| 5 Goode | 98 | 98 |
| 6 Goodlatte | 100 | 100 |
| 7 Cantor | 98 | 98 |
| 8 Moran | 95 | 95 |
| 9 Boucher | 96 | 96 |
| 10 Wolf | 99 | 99 |
| 11 Davis, T. | 94 | 94 |
| **WASHINGTON** | | |
| 1 Inslee | 99 | 99 |
| 2 Larsen | 97 | 97 |
| 3 Baird | 92 | 92 |
| 4 Hastings | 93 | 93 |
| 5 McMorris | 98 | 98 |
| 6 Dicks | 97 | 97 |
| 7 McDermott | 94 | 94 |
| 8 Reichert | 98 | 98 |
| 9 Smith | 98 | 98 |
| **WEST VIRGINIA** | | |
| 1 Mollohan | 97 | 97 |
| 2 Capito | 97 | 97 |
| 3 Rahall | 97 | 97 |
| **WISCONSIN** | | |
| 1 Ryan | 98 | 98 |
| 2 Baldwin | 99 | 99 |
| 3 Kind | 96 | 95 |
| 4 Moore | 97 | 97 |
| 5 Sensenbrenner | 98 | 98 |
| 6 Petri | 99 | 99 |
| 7 Obey | 95 | 95 |
| 8 Green | 99 | 99 |
| **WYOMING** | | |
| AL Cubin | 93 | 92 |

# SENATE

**1.** **Voting Participation.** Percentage of 366 recorded votes in 2005 on which a senator voted "yea" or "nay."

**2.** **Voting Participation (without motions to instruct).** Percentage of 364 recorded votes in 2005 on which a senator voted "yea" or "nay." In this version of the study, two votes to instruct the sergeant at arms to request the attendance of absent senators were excluded.

*Absences because of illness.* Congressional Quarterly no longer designates members who missed votes because of illness. In the past, notations to that effect were based on official statements published in the Congressional Record, but these were found to be inconsistently used.

*Rounding.* Scores are rounded to the nearest percentage point, except that no scores are rounded up to 100 percent. Senators with a 100 percent score participated in all recorded votes for which they were eligible.

| | 1 | 2 | | 1 | 2 |
|---|---|---|---|---|---|
| **ALABAMA** | | | **MONTANA** | | |
| Shelby | 99 | 99 | Baucus | 98 | 98 |
| Sessions | 98 | 98 | Burns | 97 | 97 |
| **ALASKA** | | | **NEBRASKA** | | |
| Stevens | 99 | 99 | Hagel | 99 | 99 |
| Murkowski | 96 | 96 | Nelson | 99 | 99 |
| **ARIZONA** | | | **NEVADA** | | |
| McCain | 91 | 91 | Reid | 100 | 100 |
| Kyl | 99 | 99 | Ensign | 98 | 98 |
| **ARKANSAS** | | | **NEW HAMPSHIRE** | | |
| Lincoln | 99 | 99 | Gregg | 98 | 98 |
| Pryor | 99 | 99 | Sununu | 96 | 96 |
| **CALIFORNIA** | | | **NEW JERSEY** | | |
| Feinstein | 98 | 98 | Corzine | 63 | 63 |
| Boxer | 96 | 96 | Lautenberg | 98 | 98 |
| **COLORADO** | | | **NEW MEXICO** | | |
| Allard | 99 | 99 | Domenici | 96 | 96 |
| Salazar | 100 | 100 | Bingaman | 99 | 99 |
| **CONNECTICUT** | | | **NEW YORK** | | |
| Dodd | 95 | 95 | Schumer | 99 | 99 |
| Lieberman | 94 | 94 | Clinton | 97 | 97 |
| **DELAWARE** | | | **NORTH CAROLINA** | | |
| Biden | 92 | 92 | Dole | 99 | 99 |
| Carper | 100 | 100 | Burr | 98 | 98 |
| **FLORIDA** | | | **NORTH DAKOTA** | | |
| Nelson | 99 | 99 | Conrad | 97 | 97 |
| Martinez | 96 | 96 | Dorgan | 97 | 97 |
| **GEORGIA** | | | **OHIO** | | |
| Chambliss | 97 | 97 | DeWine | 99 | 99 |
| Isakson | 99 | 99 | Voinovich | 99 | 99 |
| **HAWAII** | | | **OKLAHOMA** | | |
| Inouye | 86 | 87 | Inhofe | 98 | 98 |
| Akaka | 99 | 99 | Coburn | 99 | 99 |
| **IDAHO** | | | **OREGON** | | |
| Craig | 98 | 98 | Wyden | 99 | 99 |
| Crapo | 99 | 99 | Smith | 98 | 98 |
| **ILLINOIS** | | | **PENNSYLVANIA** | | |
| Durbin | 99 | 99 | Specter | 97 | 97 |
| Obama | 98 | 98 | Santorum | 96 | 96 |
| **INDIANA** | | | **RHODE ISLAND** | | |
| Lugar | 98 | 98 | Reed | 99 | 99 |
| Bayh | 98 | 98 | Chafee | 99 | 99 |
| **IOWA** | | | **SOUTH CAROLINA** | | |
| Grassley | 100 | 100 | Graham | 97 | 97 |
| Harkin | 98 | 98 | DeMint | 98 | 98 |
| **KANSAS** | | | **SOUTH DAKOTA** | | |
| Brownback | 99 | 99 | Johnson | 98 | 98 |
| Roberts | 98 | 98 | Thune | 96 | 96 |
| **KENTUCKY** | | | **TENNESSEE** | | |
| McConnell | 99 | 99 | Frist | 99 | 99 |
| Bunning | 99 | 99 | Alexander | 96 | 96 |
| **LOUISIANA** | | | **TEXAS** | | |
| Landrieu | 96 | 96 | Hutchison | 99 | 99 |
| Vitter | 95 | 95 | Cornyn | 98 | 98 |
| **MAINE** | | | **UTAH** | | |
| Snowe | 100 | 100 | Hatch | 99 | 99 |
| Collins | 100 | 100 | Bennett | 97 | 97 |
| **MARYLAND** | | | **VERMONT** | | |
| Sarbanes | 99 | 99 | Leahy | 99 | 99 |
| Mikulski | 93 | 93 | *Jeffords* | 96 | 96 |
| **MASSACHUSETTS** | | | **VIRGINIA** | | |
| Kennedy | 97 | 98 | Warner | 99 | 99 |
| Kerry | 98 | 98 | Allen | 99 | 99 |
| **MICHIGAN** | | | **WASHINGTON** | | |
| Levin | 99 | 99 | Murray | 99 | 99 |
| Stabenow | 99 | 99 | Cantwell | 98 | 98 |
| **MINNESOTA** | | | **WEST VIRGINIA** | | |
| Dayton | 95 | 96 | Byrd | 98 | 98 |
| Coleman | 97 | 97 | Rockefeller | 92 | 92 |
| **MISSISSIPPI** | | | **WISCONSIN** | | |
| Cochran | 99 | 99 | Kohl | 99 | 99 |
| Lott | 90 | 90 | Feingold | 98 | 98 |
| **MISSOURI** | | | **WYOMING** | | |
| Bond | 99 | 99 | Thomas | 98 | 98 |
| Talent | 100 | 100 | Enzi | 98 | 98 |

**KEY**    **Republicans**    Democrats    *Independents*

## Appendix C

# KEY VOTES

# Key Votes

# Votes Test Fealty Amid Quests To Further the GOP Agenda

IT IS TEMPTING TO SAY that the most important vote of 2005 occurred in November 2004 — when Americans went to the polls and handed congressional Republicans slightly bigger majorities in both the House and Senate. In particular, by increasing their Senate majority to a solid 55 from a tenuous 51, GOP leaders assumed they could more easily thwart a united phalanx of Democrats who had more and more been able to muster just enough votes to sidetrack prominent pieces of the Republican agenda.

On some level, it did work out that way. Bills restricting class action lawsuits, overhauling bankruptcy rules, granting liability protection to gunmakers and rewriting federal energy policy — all blocked by Senate Democrats in the past few years — became law in 2005.

Senate Republicans had to give up on a class action bill in July 2004 after they lost a vote on a motion to invoke cloture and break a Democratic filibuster. That roll call was deemed to have been one of two dozen "key votes" of that year. Some six months later, in February 2005, the Senate easily passed an almost identical bill as one of the first acts of the 109th Congress.

The editors of Congressional Quarterly selected 16 from among 366 roll calls in the Senate and and 12 from among 669 roll calls in the House as the key votes for 2005. For 60 years, this has been an annual exercise intended to illustrate legislative turning points and significant controversies, and to focus attention on how both the institution and the individual lawmakers acted.

Limiting plaintiffs from using multiple state courts to bring class action lawsuits had been a central component of the Republican "tort reform" agenda for years and was high on President Bush's second-term wish list from Congress. That made Senate passage of the bill a prime candidate to be picked as a key vote. The same can be said for bankruptcy overhaul, which became law after an eight-year effort.

Other easy selections included passage of the Central American

---

## How CQ Picks Key Votes

Since its founding in 1945, Congressional Quarterly has selected a series of key votes for both the House and Senate on major issues of the year.

A vote is judged to be key by the extent to which it represents:

- a matter of major controversy.
- a matter of presidential or political power.
- a matter of potentially great impact on the nation and lives of Americans.

For each group of related votes in each chamber on an issue, one key vote is usually chosen — one that, in the opinion of CQ editors, was the most important in determining the outcome of the issue for the year or best reflected the views of the individual members on that issue.

---

Free-Trade Agreement at a time of rising apprehension on Capitol Hill about globalization and weakening support for free-trade measures, enactment of a five-year highway and mass transit authorization after years of struggle over how to carve up a too-small pie among needy states, and confirmation of John G. Roberts Jr. as the first new chief justice of the United States in 19 years.

### INDEPENDENTLY INCLINED

On the other hand, if the president and his Republican allies thought the rightward shifting ideological sands that helped lead to swift enactment of the class action and bankruptcy laws portended sweeping success in 2005, they were very wrong. Two-thirds of the key votes of the year involved tests of the president's power to persuade Congress — and he lost on almost half of them. And that was as true in the typically lockstep House as it was in the more minority-friendly Senate.

Passage of the Republicans' marquee spending-cut package required careful vote counting and enforced party discipline in the House and the tie-breaking vote of Vice President Dick Cheney in the Senate. Rank-and-file GOP support for the president broke down over concern about the nation's standing in the world and protection of individual liberties. Both chambers stood up to White House pressure and insisted on clear standards for treatment of military detainees that barred torture, forcing Bush to cut a deal in order to save face. Both chambers insisted, over the president's objections, on limiting the reach of federal investigative powers. In the case of expiring parts of the anti-terrorism law known as the Patriot Act, he was compelled to accept the very sort of short-term extension that he had vowed to resist.

The House also dealt a blow to the president and the Republican majority leadership when it voted to permit limited federal research into the use of embryonic stem cells as a source of medical treatment. And the Senate took a step toward pushing the United States to impose limits on emissions of carbon dioxide and other greenhouse gases.

On the following pages are stories describing each of the key votes of 2005. They are listed in the order of their original vote numbers. ■

# SENATE VOTES

## 9 Class Action Lawsuits

**Passage of legislation to curb class action litigation by shifting jurisdiction over many such cases into federal court.**

For six years, business interests lobbied for restrictions on class action lawsuits, only to be thwarted by opponents in the Senate. But the 2004 elections, which boosted the number of Republicans in that chamber from 51 to 55, showed demonstrably that elections matter and that their outcome can change public policy.

When the new Congress convened, GOP leaders moved quickly to a class action bill that would give federal courts jurisdiction over cases involving at least 100 plaintiffs if at least $5 million was at stake and two-thirds of the plaintiffs lived in different states.

Majority Leader Bill Frist, R-Tenn., who is contemplating a 2008 presidential run, wanted an early victory to flex his political muscle and demonstrate that he could get things done. He had pulled the class action bill from the Senate floor in 2004 when a cloture motion fell 16 votes short of cutting off debate. Frist had some help. He had enough Democratic support that opponents could not mount a filibuster or use parliamentary delays to stop passage of the bill, as they have in past years.

Five Democratic amendments to the bill were defeated by wide margins. Supporters argued that adopting any of the amendments would derail the Senate compromise on the bill and complicate House passage. "We negotiated a pretty significant package," said Democrat Christopher J. Dodd of Connecticut. "If the bill changes, then all bets are off."

Democratic leaders were resigned to the fact that passage of the class action bill was not in doubt, but asserted that it would be the "high-water mark" for Republican efforts to change the civil justice system to limit some types of lawsuits, such as establishing an asbestos trust fund (S 852) and limiting damage awards in medical malpractice suits (HR 5). They proved to be mostly right. Those two bills could not get enough support to reach the Senate floor, but legislation (PL 109-92) to shield gun manufacturers and dealers from being sued when third parties misuse their products was cleared by Congress later in the year.

Without strong opposition from their leadership, 18 Democrats voted for the class action measure. No Republican voted against it. The bill was passed Feb. 10, 72-26: R 53-0; D 18-26 (ND 16-24, SD 2-2); I 1-0. The House easily cleared the measure the next week, giving President Bush his first major legislative accomplishment of his second term. *(Senate vote 9, p. C-26)*

Democratic supporters included Sen. Blanche Lincoln of Arkansas, home of retail giant Wal-Mart Stores Inc., which has been the defendant in major class action suits. Another key supporter was Dodd, whose home state is headquarters to many insurance companies.

In the aftermath of the vote, the Association of Trial Lawyers of America, a vocal opponent of the measure and a major source of campaign funds for Democratic candidates, ramped up its outreach efforts to Republican lawmakers.

## 28 Bankruptcy Law Overhaul

**Defeat of an amendment that would have prevented violent protesters from escaping court-ordered fines or judgments by filing for bankruptcy protection.**

With an increased majority in the Senate and several Democratic defections, Senate Republican leaders were able to defeat a controversial amendment that had become the critical obstacle to enacting a bankruptcy overhaul bill. The defeat of the amendment, offered by Democrat Charles E. Schumer of New York., all but guaranteed a victory for the banking and credit card industries and their congressional supporters, who had pushed for eight years to revamp the bankruptcy code.

The Senate passed the bill, 74-25, on March 10. The House followed suit on April 14, by a 302-126 vote.

That most likely would not have happened if Schumer had prevailed. House Republican leaders had made clear they would not take up the Senate-passed bankruptcy bill if it included the amendment, which would have prevented violent protesters from avoiding fines by filing for bankruptcy protection. In earlier versions, the amendment had specifically targeted anti-abortion protesters. In 2002, negotiations between Schumer and a group of House Republicans resulted in the language being changed to include all violent protesters, but the amendment was still anathema to conservative Republicans.

Worries that the Schumer amendment could stop the overhaul bill were not unfounded. During the 106th Congress, President Bill Clinton pocket vetoed a bankruptcy overhaul measure after the Schumer language was dropped from the bill. The amendment continued to plague overhaul advocates in the 107th and 108th Congresses. In 2004, Senate GOP leaders refused to bring the bill to the floor rather than risk having the language adopted.

Aware of the potential implications, Senate GOP leaders aggressively whipped their members to vote against the amendment. This time, Senate Republicans had more factors working in their favor. The most important was control of 55 seats in the chamber. That gave them greater leeway to allow some moderate caucus members to vote for the amendment without its defeat being jeopardized.

They also could rely on the support of the more conservative Democrats who oppose abortion rights and did not want to vote for a provision aimed at clamping down on abortion protesters. Finally, the clout of the credit card and finance industries, which donated $29.5 million to federal candidates during the eight years it took to enact the bankruptcy overhaul, could not have hurt.

Schumer called on the Senate not to "protect those who use violence," telling his colleagues that a vote against his proposal was a vote "against the rule of law." He stressed that the language would apply to any violent protester, not just those who oppose abortion rights. "If violent atheists burn down a church, it would apply to them," Schumer told his colleagues.

Senate Republicans attacked the amendment on two fronts. They said it was unnecessary and, more immediately, that it would once again prevent Congress from overhauling federal bankruptcy laws.

"Let's don't add this amendment, jeopardizing passage of this bill," Jeff Sessions, R-Ala., implored during the floor debate. He characterized the amendment as the "most perfect example of a poison pill" he had ever seen. Sessions was joined by Orrin G. Hatch, R-Utah, who argued that bankruptcy courts have made clear they will not allow

debtors to escape fines and judgments for willful, violent actions.

In the end, Republican efforts were enough to take down the amendment March 8. The Senate voted against it 46-53; R 4-51; D 41-2 (ND 37-2, SD 4-0); I 1-0. (*Senate vote 28, p. C-26*)

## 127 Confirmation of Judge Owen

**Vote to invoke cloture, or limit debate, on the nomination of Priscilla Owen to be a judge on the U.S. Court of Appeals for the 5th Circuit.**

Texas Supreme Court Justice Priscilla Owen was among the first candidates for the federal bench that President Bush submitted in 2001. But her nomination languished for more than four years before the Senate voted to confirm her in May.

Owen was perhaps the most ideologically controversial of the 10 appellate court nominees whom Democrats filibustered in the Republican-controlled Senate in the 108th Congress. Her opponents worried that she would be hostile to abortion rights as a federal judge. Bush renominated Owen and six of the other previously filibustered candidates in February. Still, the Senate Democratic caucus opposed an up-or-down vote until a group of senators — seven Republicans and seven Democrats — brokered a deal on judicial nominations in May, agreeing not to oppose cloture on the nomination.

A potential showdown over judicial nominations escalated in January, when Majority Leader Bill Frist, R-Tenn., went to the Senate floor on the first day of the 109th Congress to warn that he would not tolerate further Democratic filibusters of appellate court nominees. For the first few months of the year, Frist repeatedly threatened to execute an esoteric procedural gambit, dubbed the "nuclear option," to end minority filibusters of judicial nominees.

Frist and Minority Leader Harry Reid, D-Nev., exchanged half-hearted proposals and rhetorical potshots, to no avail. Finally, Frist scheduled a vote on cloture, which would cut off debate and lead to a vote on Owen's nomination, for May 24.

On May 23, Frist went before a battery of cameras outside the chamber to announce that if the cloture vote fell short of the 60-vote threshold for the motion to succeed, Vice President Dick Cheney would preside over the Senate while Frist made a point of order that there should be a finite amount of debate time for an appellate or a Supreme Court nominee. If Cheney upheld Frist's point of order and Democrats challenged the ruling, a simple majority was all Republicans would need to sustain Cheney's ruling.

Later that day, the group that became known as the "gang of 14" emerged from the Capitol Hill office of Arizona Republican John McCain with the deal that thwarted Frist, but also guaranteed the confirmation of Owen and several other contentious nominees. The 14 senators also agreed that judicial nominees should be filibustered only under "extraordinary circumstances," a term that was left to each group member to define.

The cloture vote on Owen the next day demonstrated that the 14 senators had defused what had promised to be a dramatic parliamentary showdown on judicial nominations, effectively taking control of the issue away from Senate leaders. The Senate agreed to the motion to invoke cloture on an 81-18 vote, which easily exceeded the 60 votes needed: R 55-0; D 26-17 (ND 23-16, SD 3-1); I 0-1. (*Senate vote 127, p. C-26*)

Owen was confirmed the next day with the support of only two Democrats. But the fact that more than half the Democrats had

voted to limit debate was a sign of their relief that the "gang of 14" had given the Senate a way to back away from a showdown over rules that could have fundamentally undermined the power of the minority party in the chamber.

## 129 Confirmation of Bolton as U.N. Ambassador

**Defeat of an attempt to invoke cloture and thereby move to a vote on the nomination of John R. Bolton to be U.S. ambassador to the United Nations.**

Bolton's nomination was in trouble from the moment President Bush announced him as his pick for the top job at the United Nations. Viewed as abrasive, confrontational and willing to run roughshod over his peers at the State Department while he was an undersecretary of State, Bolton faced serious opposition from Democrats and some moderate Republicans.

Several former colleagues testified against Bolton during his confirmation hearings. In public testimony, former State Department official Carl Ford Jr. provided the Senate Foreign Relations Committee with a damaging portrait of the nominee, describing him as a "quintessential kiss-up, kick down sort of guy." Bolton's nomination emerged from the committee in May "without recommendation" — not an outright rejection, but a cautionary message that the nominee would have trouble winning approval from the full Senate.

Democrats threatened to filibuster the Bolton nomination as it headed to the Senate floor. In public and private testimony, Bolton's critics accused him of verbally abusing subordinates and trying to manipulate intelligence appraised by State Department analysts regarding Iraq's weapons of mass destruction programs. In an attempt to end debate, Majority Leader Bill Frist, R-Tenn., made a motion to invoke cloture, which requires 60 votes.

But on May 26 the Senate rejected the motion, 56-42: R 53-1; D 3-40 (ND 1-38, SD 2-2); I 0-1. That was a major setback for the Bush administration and a blow to Bolton, who had routinely criticized the United Nations and vowed to push for changes at the institution. (*Senate vote 129, p. C-26*)

The cloture vote not only showed that Democrats were prepared to obstruct Bush's nominees; it also reflected the tenuous hold Republicans had on their majority in the Senate. Several moderate Republicans, such as Lincoln Chafee of Rhode Island, George V. Voinovich of Ohio and Chuck Hagel of Nebraska, remained undecided on Bolton throughout the nomination process, making it that much harder for Frist to bring home a victory for Bush on the controversial nomination.

Democrats contended that Bolton was unworthy of going to the United Nations to represent the U.S. government. They said they would allow a vote only if the White House released a series of intelligence documents showing how Bolton had handled information regarding Syria's weapons programs. Bolton was also accused of requesting National Security Agency intercepts so he could snoop on subordinates at the State Department.

The White House was not forthcoming with the documents, and Democrats refused to budge. The Senate held a second cloture vote June 20, but the result was so apparent that many senators skipped the vote, and cloture failed by even more votes than it did the first time, 54-38.

None of the Senate's parliamentary delays ended up mattering in the end. Bush bypassed the Senate and installed Bolton at the United Nations with a recess appointment on the first day of the August recess.

Bolton has been working at the United Nations for five months. His recess appointment will expire in January 2007, when he would have to be renominated.

## 149  Global Warming Policy

**Rejection of a motion to table a global warming resolution endorsing the need for mandatory federal greenhouse gas regulations, paving the way for adoption of the resolution.**

Since 1997, when the Senate voted 95-0 to condemn the international global warming agreement signed in Kyoto, Japan, Congress has resisted every effort to set mandatory limits on emissions of carbon dioxide and other gases that are widely blamed for contributing to worldwide climate change.

The Bush administration and, for the most part, Congress have argued that the Kyoto accord would hamstring the U.S. economy while letting off the hook developing nations that are projected to soon emit more greenhouse gases than the United States. There also remains a core of lawmakers who reject the premise of global warming, led by Senate Environment and Public Works Chairman James M. Inhofe, R-Okla., who has called climate change theories "phony science" and a "hoax."

An attempt in 2005 by Sens. John McCain, R-Ariz., and Joseph I. Lieberman, D-Conn., to mandate a reduction in greenhouse gas emissions to 2000 levels by 2010 actually lost ground, winning just 38 votes in favor after garnering 43 votes in 2003.

In a change from past practice, however, the Senate went on record for the first time ever as recognizing that climate change is a significant problem and endorsing the need for mandatory emission limits. While largely symbolic, the action, in support of a resolution offered by Jeff Bingaman, D-N.M., signaled a shift in the political landscape.

McCain and Lieberman offered their proposal in June to a comprehensive energy bill (HR 6). Their plan, which they had promoted for several years, would establish a domestic cap-and-trade model similar to the Kyoto approach. Such market-based programs cap overall pollution while allowing businesses to buy and sell permits in order to meet their obligations.

In a bid to attract more votes this time, senators embraced nuclear energy as an energy source that emits no greenhouse gases. The tactic backfired, angering environmentalists and losing the support of several liberal Democrats who had backed the legislation in 2003. The Senate did approve, 66-29, a separate amendment by Chuck Hagel, R-Neb., to offer economic incentives for businesses to reduce emissions of carbon dioxide and other greenhouse gases. The voluntary approach appealed to many Republicans, but critics derided it as inadequate.

Bingaman sought to bridge the gap between the McCain-Lieberman proposal to mandate a reduction in emissions and the laissez-faire model advanced by Hagel. He proposed tying emissions caps to economic growth and allowing the government to sell more permits to companies that failed to meet the targets once the market price for credits reached a certain level. This "safety valve" would give businesses economic certainty, but would allow emissions to rise in the future, albeit at a slower rate.

As the ranking Democrat on the Energy and Natural Resources Committee, Bingaman has a cooperative relationship with the panel's GOP chairman, fellow New Mexican Pete V. Domenici, and the two discussed the idea of jointly offering Bingaman's plan as an amendment to the energy bill. In the end, Domenici backed off, saying he feared splitting Republicans, alienating the White House and jeopardizing the

energy bill's prospects. But he agreed to hold hearings on the idea and to support an amendment expressing the sense of the Senate that climate change is a problem and endorsing mandatory, market-based measures to "slow, stop and reverse" emissions.

Inhofe moved to table Bingaman's resolution, sparking a showdown over the fundamental question of whether global warming is for real, and illustrating the shifting sentiments on the issue among some Republican senators.

"Climate change is here," said Mike DeWine, R-Ohio, who voted against the McCain-Lieberman amendment. "I am confident that we can draft a bill that will own up to our obligations to our children and our grandchildren and at the same time have dates that are practical." Domenici, who also had voted against McCain-Lieberman, also expressed his conviction that the science now shows that global warming is occurring and must be addressed.

Bingaman's resolution was adopted by voice vote June 22, after the Senate rejected Inhofe's motion to table the proposal 44-53; R 42-12; D 2-40 (ND 2-36, SD 0-4); I 0-1 *(Senate vote 149, p. C-26)*

In addition to the six Republicans who had voted for McCain-Lieberman, six more Republicans voted against the attempt to kill Bingaman's resolution. With that vote, 53 became a magic number in the Senate's global warming debate, offering a new baseline for potential support and a list of lawmakers who would, in principle, support climate change legislation. It also laid the groundwork for Bingaman, backed by Domenici, to pursue an alternative to the McCain-Lieberman plan in 2006.

## 170  Central American Trade Liberalization

**Passage of a bill to implement tariff reductions and other changes to U.S. trade law that were part of a free-trade agreement negotiated between the United States and five Central American countries, plus the Dominican Republic.**

President Bush has made expansion of trade with Western Hemisphere countries a hallmark of his administration from his first election. In 2004, after several fits and starts, his administration secured an agreement to relax trade barriers between the United States and Costa Rica, El Salvador, Guatemala, Honduras and Nicaragua. A parallel agreement was reached with the Dominican Republic.

The Constitution gives Congress explicit authority for trade pacts, but for several decades, lawmakers have allowed the president to negotiate agreements that are then sent to Congress for approval on up-or-down votes. Because no amendments are allowed in committee or on the floor, the White House often has to make side promises to lawmakers to win their votes on trade agreements.

That was the case with the Central American agreement, also known as CAFTA. The name evoked echoes of NAFTA, the 1993 North American Free-Trade Agreement with Mexico and Canada, which many members of the House and Senate thought had not been as beneficial for the United States as promised.

Since NAFTA (PL 103-182) was enacted, trade agreements have been an increasingly tough sell on Capitol Hill, and CAFTA was the first in more than a decade with low-wage countries that are seen as magnets for U.S. jobs. So supporters of the Central American pact decided to press for a vote first in the Senate, where its prospects were considered better than the House. In fact, House Republican leaders were uncertain they had the votes to win in that chamber, and it was hoped that a Senate vote to pass a bill implementing the agreement would give

the House an incentive to do the same.

Trade votes are generally easier in the Senate because senators have more diverse constituencies and the luxury of a six-year term to explain an unpopular vote. But even the Senate was reluctant to pass the CAFTA implementing bill (S 1307), and agreed to do so only after several weeks of administration efforts to address senators' concerns about sugar imports, labor rights in Central America and general uneasiness about the effects of globalization.

When the Senate finally voted late in the evening of June 30, as Congress was trying to get out of town for its July Fourth recess, the vote was an uncharacteristically tight 54-45: R 43-12; D 10-33 (ND 7-32, SD 3-1); I 1-0. (*Senate vote 170, p. C-26*)

The closeness of the vote illustrates a shift in sentiment among lawmakers of both parties on trade issues, though it is especially evident among Democrats, and may portend trouble for future accords.

To win Senate approval, the Bush administration first had to secure a majority in the Senate Finance Committee. Several of the panel's typically pro-trade members from both parties were concerned about the effect of the accord on jobs in their states from additional imports of sugar that would be permitted.

To address their concerns, U.S. Trade Representative Rob Portman and Agriculture Secretary Mike Johanns pledged to use provisions allowed under commodity trading rules to keep sugar imports permitted under CAFTA and other trade deals out of the U.S. market for the remaining two years of the current farm bill (PL 107-171). They also agreed to study the feasibility of government initiatives to spur production of ethanol made from sugar.

That helped win over Agriculture Chairman Saxby Chambliss, R-Ga., and Norm Coleman, R-Minn. But Max Baucus of Montana, the ranking Democrat on Finance, Idaho Republicans Michael D. Crapo and Larry E. Craig, and Conrad Burns R-Mont., were not convinced. They allowed the implementing bill to get out of committee on June 29, but voted against the measure on the floor the following day.

Faced with opposition from GOP sugar-state senators, the administration tried to entice wavering Democrats with a pledge of a multi-year commitment to beef up enforcement and monitoring of labor and environmental standards in Central America and to aid farmers in the region. That helped win the votes of Jeff Bingaman, D-N.M., and James M. Jeffords, I-Vt. But Christopher J. Dodd, D-Conn., who had hoped to support CAFTA, voted no with a "very, very heavy heart," citing concerns that labor protections in the agreement should have been stronger.

The Senate vote had the desired effect and gave impetus to the House, although that chamber came very close to rejecting the pact before voting yes in the end. The Senate had to vote again to clear the separate House-passed bill (HR 3045). The July 28 vote was almost identical to the early tally — 55-45. (*House CAFTA key vote, p. C-16*)

## 213 | Energy Policy Overhaul

**Final passage of legislation that includes incentives for greater domestic production of oil, gas, coal and nuclear power, encouragement for conservation and a reduction in regulation of the electric power industry.**

In the culmination of a four-year debate on energy policy, the Senate agreed to a compromise measure that followed the outlines of the energy plan President Bush proposed not long after taking office in 2001 but without the centerpiece of his proposal — drilling for oil and

gas in Alaska's Arctic National Wildlife Refuge (ANWR). That proved too difficult for Republican leaders to force through.

Negotiators also dropped from the final bill liability protection for companies that make the fuel additive methyl tertiary butyl ether (MTBE), an issue that prevented passage for two consecutive years.

The vote showed the broad support for energy legislation once ANWR and MTBE were set aside. More than half of the Senate's Democrats supported the final conference version, with only six Republicans opposed to it. The Senate easily cleared the measure July 29, 74-26: R 49-6; D 25-19 (ND 22-18, SD 3-1); I 0-1. (*Senate vote 213, p. C-27*)

The bill was a mixed success for the Bush administration and GOP leaders, who were intent on increasing domestic production of oil, gas and nuclear power as a way of reducing U.S. dependence on foreign fuels. They also opposed requiring Americans to conserve energy.

Opening the coastal plain of ANWR to energy exploration had been the main feature of Bush's energy plan but a rallying point for environmentalists trying to protect one of the nation's most pristine and remote wilderness areas. Dropping the provision was a GOP defeat.

Under pressure to deliver a bill, Republican leaders — particularly in the House — also had to give up on a contentious liability waiver for MTBE makers that had blocked final action on the bill in the Senate for two years. (*House energy key vote, p. C-16*)

The chemical, used at low levels since 1979, became more prevalent when refiners had to meet fuel standards established under the 1990 Clean Air Act amendments (PL 101-549) that aimed to reduce smog. But the additive had since been found to contaminate groundwater in some areas, including the Northeast and West Coast. Lawmakers from those areas worried that giving liability protection for manufacturers might leave states responsible for cleaning up MTBE in the ground

The new energy law (PL 109-58) includes tax incentives for both traditional and alternative energy producers. It authorizes $14.6 billion in tax breaks and credits between 2005 and 2015, including: $2.8 billion for fossil fuel production; $2.7 billion to extend the renewable electricity production credit; $1.6 billion for investments in plants designed to use cleaner-burning coal; $1.3 billion for conservation and energy efficiency; and $1.3 billion for alternative-fuel motor vehicles and fuels.

Some effects of the law might not be known for years. For instance, it makes major changes in the regulation of electricity markets, including repealing the 1935 Public Utility Holding Company Act, which has restricted many large power companies to certain geographic areas and lines of business. Lawmakers decided that the Federal Energy Regulatory Commission would be better able to examine electric utility books and have the power to block mergers. The new requirements will probably lead to a spate of mergers.

## 219 | Gun Industry Liability Shield

**Passage of legislation that protects gun manufacturers and dealers from being sued when third parties misuse their products.**

A priority of the National Rifle Association (NRA) and business groups that want to limit product liability lawsuits in general, legislation to protect gunmakers and dealers had previously stalled in the Senate because of Democratic opposition.

Majority Leader Bill Frist, R-Tenn., sought to avoid a replay of a sim-

ilar bill's fate in 2004 when Republicans spiked the entire measure rather than allow it to pass with three amendments attached by Democrats, including a renewal of the assault weapons ban.

When the new bill (S 397) reached the floor in July, Frist filed a succession of amendments — a legislative procedure known as "filling the amendment tree" — that allowed him to control what amendments could be brought up for debate. He allowed consideration only of those proposals he thought were harmless or easy to defeat on the floor, thus thwarting any potential Democratic efforts to add gun-control language.

Republicans easily defeated Democratic amendments that would have allowed individuals, but not municipalities, to sue gunmakers; preserved the right of police officers or minors injured by firearms to sue for damages; and blocked the sale of so-called cop-killer bullets. Instead, the Senate adopted a Republican alternative amendment requiring a study of a uniform standard for testing projectiles against body armor and increasing the penalties for violent or drug-trafficking crimes in which the perpetrator uses or possesses armor-piercing ammunition.

The Senate adopted only one Democratic amendment, by Herb Kohl of Wisconsin, to require that child safety locks be sold with all handguns.

The final vote July 29 was a victory for GOP leaders, who had promised to push the legislation through before the August recess, and showed the power of the gun rights lobby led by the NRA. The vote was 65-31: R 50-2; D 14-29 (ND 10-29, SD 4-0); I 1-0. *(Senate vote 219, p. C-27)*

The 14 Democrats who voted for the bill were all from states with large rural areas where hunting is popular. Independent James M. Jeffords of Vermont also voted for the legislation, while two Republicans — Lincoln Chafee of Rhode Island and Mike DeWine of Ohio — voted against it.

The House cleared the bill, 283-144, in October. The measure prohibits civil liability actions from being brought in any state or federal court against manufacturers, distributors, dealers or importers of firearms and ammunition. Trade groups also are protected, and all pending legal action against gunmakers will be dismissed.

The statute does not protect anyone who sells or transfers a firearm knowing it is intended to be used for a crime of violence or drug trafficking, or anyone who knowingly violates state or federal laws applicable to the marketing or sale of firearms, when the violation results in harm. It also exempts cases in which proper use results in physical injury, death or property damage because of a defect in the firearm.

## 220 Surface Transportation Spending

**Final passage of a six-year reauthorization of highway and transit programs that was more expensive than the Bush administration wanted but not as generous as many in Congress had demanded.**

For the second straight year, Majority Leader Bill Frist, R-Tenn., had to contain open defiance within his caucus at the administration's transportation spending policy. Even fiscal conservatives such as James M. Inhofe of Oklahoma, chairman of the Environment and Public Works Committee, and Charles E. Grassley of Iowa, who chairs the Finance Committee, wanted to spend more on highway programs than the administration said it would allow.

The long impasse and the vote accepting the eventual compromise showed the enduring power of public works projects for members of Congress, irrespective of their party. Frist was able to claim a victory of sorts for fiscal responsibility because the final conference version of the

bill (HR 3) exceeded the administration's request by just $2.5 billion. But the administration had made the task easier at the beginning of 2005 by increasing its request from $256 billion to $284 billion. Also, the bill included an $8.5 billion rescission of prior contract authority that becomes available at the end of fiscal 2009, boosting the available total contract authority at that point, and increasing the cost of the bill, to $295 billion. The authorization is good through fiscal 2009 and is retroactive to fiscal 2004.

Frist attempted to set the parameters early by saying that he stood by the administration's $284 billion request and threatening to bar anything more expensive from coming to the floor. But Inhofe said the nation's legitimate transportation needs required far more money and that transportation was one of the few areas where he, as a conservative, felt increased federal spending was justified. His committee sent to the floor a $284 billion package, but supported amending it to increase the authorization to $295 billion.

Grassley put together a package of tax changes and measures designed to crack down on fuel fraud that supporters claimed fully paid for the additional spending. Grassley's package came under immediate attack from other fiscal conservatives, such as Republican Judd Gregg of New Hampshire, the chairman of the Budget Committee, who said the administration's call for fiscal restraint was "being run over by a bulldozer."

Grassley's proposals also drew a veto threat from the White House and warnings from House Republican leaders that they would not survive conference negotiations.

Those negotiations were predictably difficult. The Senate took a different approach from the House in determining how much highway money each state would receive and in resolving longstanding complaints from the states that collect significantly more in gasoline taxes than they receive back from the government for transportation projects. The final bill was virtually the same as the Senate approach, guaranteeing each state a bonus to ensure by fiscal 2008 a return of at least 92 cents on each dollar contributed to the Highway Trust Fund.

Several senators were critical of the House for its long list of earmarks in the bill. The Senate version was more restrained. But once the measure went into conference, senators demanded the right to determine half of all "high-priority program" highway earmarks.

While it was generally understood that senators would be allocated some earmarks in conference, notwithstanding their public criticism, the scale of their demands in the context of the narrow fiscal margins negotiators were working with threw already difficult discussions into turmoil. It took marathon staff work and sometimes impromptu discussions among top conferees to reach agreement in the final moments before Congress departed for its summer recess.

The House adopted the conference report, 412-8, the morning of July 29 and sent it to the Senate. A little more than an hour later, the Senate cleared the measure 91-4: R 48-4; D 42-0 (ND 38-0, SD 4-0); I 1-0. *(Senate vote 220, p, C-27; House surface transportation key vote, p. C-17)*

## 245 Confirmation of Roberts as Chief Justice

**Confirmation of John G. Roberts Jr. as the 17th chief justice of the United States.**

After President Bush took office in 2001, conservative and liberal activists alike braced themselves for a cataclysmic Senate showdown over his first Supreme Court nominee.

But by the time the nomination of John G. Roberts Jr. to succeed William H. Rehnquist as chief justice reached the Senate floor in September, there was no suspense about the outcome.

Roberts, an accomplished appellate lawyer and federal appeals court judge, was originally nominated to replace centrist Justice Sandra Day O'Connor, who announced her retirement July 1 contingent upon her successor's confirmation. But after Rehnquist died Sept. 3, Bush instead nominated Roberts to succeed the chief justice.

Roberts performed brilliantly in his Senate Judiciary Committee confirmation hearing. Given that, and the fact that he was to replace the conservative Rehnquist, many Democrats chose not to heed the urging of liberal activists to vote against him.

The vote on Roberts marked a turning point in the judicial nomination war that had raged in the Senate since 2003. The filibuster-proof tally was a clear sign that many Senate Democrats lacked the appetite to oppose Bush's pick for the high court for ideological reasons.

Still, the Sept. 29 vote was historic, infused with more than a little sense of drama. It was the first Senate action on a chief justice nominee since 1986. Many senators had never voted on a Supreme Court nominee; the last high court vacancy occurred in 1994.

In recognition of the rarity of the moment, senators voted from their desks as the roll was called, rather than by their usual method of casting their votes in the well. Jane Roberts, the nominee's wife, watched from the gallery.

Robert C. Byrd, the 88-year-old West Virginia Democrat seeking a ninth term in 2006, walked to his desk with the aid of two canes. Judiciary Chairman Arlen Specter, R-Pa., took a seat next to his predecessor as committee chairman, Orrin G. Hatch, R-Utah. Hatch patted Specter on the back, and the two men shook hands.

Not all 100 senators were at their desks at the start of the roll call, however. A few stragglers — most notably New York Democrat Charles E. Schumer, one of Bush's main antagonists on judges — arrived late.

Twenty-two Democrats and Independent James M. Jeffords of Vermont joined all 55 Republicans in supporting Roberts. The vote was 78-22: R 55-0; D 22-22 (ND 18-22, SD 4-0); I 1-0. (*Senate vote 245, p. C-27*)

The 50-year-old Roberts, who is the youngest chief justice since John Marshall, was sworn in at the White House by Justice John Paul Stevens later the same day.

## 249 | Treatment of Military Detainees

**Adoption of an amendment to the fiscal 2006 Defense appropriations bill banning cruel, inhuman or degrading treatment of enemy combatants and requiring military interrogators to rely on an Army field manual that complies with the Geneva Conventions.**

No proposal caused more waves in Congress during the fall than legislation championed by John McCain, R-Ariz., to regulate the treatment of enemy combatants captured and detained by U.S. military forces or law enforcement. The proposal resulted in the delay of two major defense bills, a veto threat and frequent personal visits and phone calls to key lawmakers by Vice President Dick Cheney. The White House repeatedly told lawmakers they must not pass any legislation that would tie the president's hands in the war on terror.

The Republican-controlled Senate responded, but not with the outcome the White House wanted. On Oct. 5, the Senate adopted McCain's amendment 90-9; R 46-9; D 43-0 (ND 39-0; SD 4-0);

I 1-0. (*Senate vote 249, p. C-27*)

With such strong bipartisan support, the vote was the most direct slap to the administration on the moral conduct of the war on terrorism since it began four years ago. After a string of prison abuse scandals and questions over the legal rights of detainees, lawmakers agreed with McCain that the policy on handling military detainees should be decided by Congress.

McCain's amendment, adopted as part of the fiscal 2006 Defense appropriations bill (HR 2863), banned cruel, inhuman or degrading treatment of detainees. It also required military interrogators to use an Army field manual when trying to extract intelligence from suspects. The field manual, under revision at the time of the vote, outlines specific interrogation techniques that comply with the Geneva Conventions. President Bush has argued that the Geneva standards apply to state-sponsored, uniformed soldiers, but not to terrorists.

McCain, who as a Navy flier during the Vietnam War was shot down, captured and tortured for five and a half years, told his colleagues that banning the abuse of suspected terrorists was necessary. "They don't deserve our sympathy. But this isn't about who they are. This is about who we are. These are the values that distinguish us from our enemies." Terrorists do not adhere to anti-torture treaties, McCain said, "but "we're better than them, and we are the stronger for our faith."

A member of the Armed Services Committee, McCain initially proposed the language as an amendment to the fiscal 2006 defense authorization bill (S 1042), which was on the Senate floor in July. But Majority Leader Bill Frist, R-Tenn., pulled the authorization bill, citing more than 200 pending amendments. Frist said debate would take too long, and the Senate turned its attention to legislation that would shield gunmakers from liability lawsuits. McCain, however, insisted that his proposal was the primary reason the bill was pulled.

In October, McCain sought to attach the detainee requirements to the must-pass Defense appropriations bill. Frist was among the Republicans who voted in favor of the anti-abuse proposal. McCain subsequently won voice vote approval to add the language to the defense authorization bill as well.

After the House expressed strong support for the amendment in mid-December, Bush backed away from his veto threat. The amendment, with a relatively minor change, was cleared as part of both Defense bills. (*House detainee key vote, p. C-18*)

Democrats were quick to portray the move as a proxy vote on Bush's conduct of the war in Iraq. But Republicans — including McCain — were just as insistent that the vote contained no wider message.

"This does not have anything to do with [presidential] leadership," he said. "It has to do with treatment of [detainees] and human rights. And that message is wide enough."

## 262 | Redirection of Lawmakers' Earmarks

**Rejection of an amendment to the fiscal 2006 Transportation-Treasury-Housing spending bill that would have denied money for the construction of two "bridges to nowhere" in Alaska.**

The Senate was embarrassed by news coverage of its multimillion-dollar appropriations for "bridges to nowhere" on the coast of Alaska, but not enough to threaten the congressional tradition of members

earmarking federal projects and programs for their own states.

Not long after Rep. Don Young, R-Alaska, included the bridge projects at Ketchikan and Anchorage in a highway authorization bill (PL 109-59), someone noticed that they would connect to lightly settled areas — the Ketchikan bridge would link the town to an island with 50 residents and an airport — and dubbed them bridges to nowhere.

Freshman Republican Tom Coburn of Oklahoma, a staunch fiscal conservative, decided to take action when the fiscal 2006 Transportation-Treasury-Housing appropriations bill came to the Senate floor. "What I am here to tell you is that the rumble against spending is getting louder. People are fed up," Coburn told his colleagues. "All across the country, Americans are rising up against government overspending."

Coburn proposed removing the $454 million for the bridges and spending it instead to reconstruct a Mississippi River bridge in New Orleans damaged by Hurricane Katrina.

Alaska Republican Ted Stevens, former chairman of the Senate Appropriations Committee, was incensed at this challenge to the earmark system. "This amendment is an offense to me," Stevens thundered. "It is not only an offense to me, it is a threat to every person in my state. . . . It is wrong to do this to any state."

If Coburn's amendment were adopted, then money might be shifted from one state to another at will. "I will put the Senate on notice — and I don't kid people," Stevens said later. "If the Senate decides to discriminate against our state and take money only from our state, I will resign from this body. This is not the Senate I came to. This is not the Senate I devoted 37 years to. If one senator can decide he will take all the money from one state to solve a problem of another, that is not a union. That is not equality and is not treating my state the way I have seen it treated for 37 years."

The Senate agreed, and the Oct. 20 vote was a lopsided 15-82: R 11-43; D 4-38 (ND 3-35, SD 1-3); I 0-1. (Senate vote 262, p. C-28)

Although the amendment was defeated, it had at least in part the effect Coburn wanted. Media attention to the Alaska bridges increased the pressure on Congress to do something about them. Conferees on the appropriations bill quietly removed the specific funding for the two bridges as part of the final agreement. Instead, the conference report redirected the money to a general fund that the state of Alaska could spend on transportation projects at its discretion.

This achieved two goals: enabling Coburn and those who campaigned against such projects to declare a victory, while also allowing Stevens and his Alaskan colleagues to save face by keeping the money in their state.

There was nothing in the final bill that would prevent the state from simply deciding to allocate money to the two bridges.

## 323 | Conduct of the War in Iraq

**Adoption of an amendment to the fiscal 2006 defense authorization bill requiring the president to send Congress quarterly reports on progress toward meeting conditions for the withdrawal of U.S. forces from Iraq.**

More than any legislation passed since the invasion of Iraq in 2003, the Senate vote Nov. 15 sent a strong message to President Bush that Republicans were losing patience with his "stay the course" rhetoric and were watching the decline in public support for the war with increasing wariness as the 2006 midterm elections approached. The vote also represented Congress' most forceful assertion since the war began

that it has authority equal to the administration's in overseeing the conduct of the conflict.

The vote was on an amendment to the fiscal 2006 defense authorization bill (S 1042), offered by Majority Leader Bill Frist, R-Tenn., and John W. Warner, R-Va., chairman of the Armed Services Committee. Its stated purpose was "to clarify and recommend changes to the policy of the United States on Iraq and to require reports on certain matters related to Iraq."

The amendment, which was included in the final bill, requires the Bush administration to set a schedule for meeting preconditions for a pullout of U.S. troops from Iraq, such as the training of Iraqi security forces. It requires quarterly reports to Congress, in which the administration defines the criteria for success in Iraq, including details on the number of Iraqi battalions that must be able to fight independently before U.S. troops can withdraw.

In addition, in non-binding "sense of the Senate" language, the amendment declares 2006 as the year that Iraqis should take the lead on their security. It calls on the administration to tell Iraqi leaders to make the compromises necessary for political progress, and to explain to the American people what the president has called his "strategy for success." The Senate adopted the amendment 79-19: R 41-13; D 37-6. (ND 33-6, SD 4-0); I 1-0. (Senate vote 323, p. C-28)

Previous legislation had required the administration to provide Congress with reports on its progress in Iraq, but now the White House will have to describe — in unclassified reports that the public will be allowed to read — how conditions in Iraq are tied to goals for withdrawing U.S. troops. The measure also requires classified reports for lawmakers.

The GOP proposal was nearly identical to a Democratic plan sponsored by Carl Levin of Michigan, ranking member on Armed Services. The only significant difference was that Republicans rejected Democratic language that called for "estimated dates for the phased redeployment of the United States Armed Forces from Iraq." On Nov. 15, Republicans defeated Levin's version of the amendment, 40-58.

But given the public's growing disenchantment with the war, Republicans knew they could not just vote down the Democratic amendment without coming up with a solution of their own. "It's politically very difficult to say, 'I just voted against Levin,'" said Sen. Lincoln Chafee, R-R.I. "Now, you can say, 'But I voted for Warner.'"

Frist rejected as "absurd" the suggestion by some Democrats that his amendment represented a challenge to the president. But the vote did indicate a change in the political temperature — a shift driven by declining public support for the president's stewardship of the war, its rising costs and the more than 2,000 U.S. soldiers killed in the conflict so far. Members are feeling the heat, and they want to weigh in more aggressively on what we're doing," Rep. Curt Weldon, R-Pa., a senior member of the House Armed Services Committee, said of the Senate vote.

The vote on the Frist-Warner amendment came in the context of an increasingly fractious debate in Congress over how the war started and its possible denouement. That debate, which began after the 2004 presidential election, was rekindled in November, when Democrats accused Bush of misleading Congress and the nation about the intelligence he had cited to justify the Iraq war. Bush, backed by Republicans on Capitol Hill, responded that such charges were a partisan attempt to rewrite the Democrats' own history of support for the use of force against Iraq.

The Frist-Warner Iraq amendment avoided placing blame on the administration for its conduct of the war. But in its measured and subtle way, it indicated that Senate Republicans would no longer be acquiescent about the president's Iraq policy.

## 358 Anti-Terrorism Law Reauthorization

**Defeat of an effort to limit debate, and thereby move to a final vote, on the conference report on legislation extending 16 expiring provisions of the 2001 anti-terrorism law known as the Patriot Act.**

All year long, a small band of Senate Republicans worked closely with their Democratic colleagues to increase restrictions on surveillance powers granted to the executive branch under the 2001 anti-terrorism law (PL 107-56). But when it became clear that GOP leaders in the House and Senate, working with the White House, would not go far enough to satisfy critics' concerns about civil liberties protections, a nearly unanimous bloc of Democrats stuck with the small group of libertarian-leaning Republicans and refused to end a filibuster of the conference report on a bill (HR 3199) to reauthorize 16 provisions of the law that were set to expire Dec. 31.

On Dec. 16, two days after the House had adopted the conference report, the Senate defeated a motion to invoke cloture, or limit debate, on the report. The action forced President Bush and GOP leaders to do something they vowed they would never do: accept a short-term extension of the law to give negotiators more time to resolve their differences.

More telling, the vote illustrated that four years after the Sept. 11 terrorist attacks, the mood of lawmakers had shifted toward recognizing public concerns about civil liberties and the extent of police powers exercised in the fight against terrorism. The vote was taken on the same day The New York Times reported that Bush had authorized warrantless monitoring of international phone calls placed by U.S. citizens.

The motion to invoke cloture and limit debate on the conference report fell eight votes short of the 60 required for it to succeed. The vote was 52-47: R 50-5; D 2-41(ND 2-37, SD 0-4); I 0-1. Majority Leader Bill Frist, R-Tenn., switched his vote to "no" in a procedural tactic so he could move to reconsider the vote later. (*Senate vote 358, p. C-28*)

Republicans John E. Sununu of New Hampshire, Larry E. Craig of Idaho, Lisa Murkowski of Alaska and Chuck Hagel of Nebraska joined 41 Democrats and the Senate's lone independent, James M. Jeffords of Vermont, in voting against cloture.

Two Democrats — Ben Nelson of Nebraska and Tim Johnson of South Dakota — voted with the Republicans.

The House had adopted the conference report by a vote of 251-174, with the support of 44 Democrats.

After the cloture motion failed, Vermont Sen. Patrick J. Leahy, the ranking Democrat on the Judiciary Committee, immediately introduced a three-month extension of the current law with the intention of continuing negotiations so that additional restrictions might be placed on the expiring provisions. He wanted a bill that hewed closer to the one the Senate passed by voice vote in July.

Frist objected, saying he would not support a short-term extension and that Bush would not sign one. But as the days passed with no resolution in sight and senators anxious to close out the first session, Frist and Leahy came up with a last-minute compromise to extend the current law until July 1. The Senate passed that bill (S 2167) by voice vote Dec. 21.

The deal did not sit well with House Judiciary Chairman F. James Sensenbrenner Jr., R-Wis., who had fought any attempts at a short-term extension. He reduced the extension to five weeks, expiring on Feb. 3, and the Senate concurred. Bush signed the extension Dec. 30, while still urging Congress to reauthorize the law as soon as possible in 2006.

## 363 Cuts in Mandatory Spending

**Agreeing to a House amendment to a $38.8 billion budget savings package, with an amendment — an act that sent the bill back to the House.**

Clearing the $38.8 billion budget reconciliation package (S 1932) was a top priority for President Bush and Republican leaders of both chambers. The only thing standing in the way as the Senate entered the last real day of the session was adoption of the conference report. In the end, the spending-cut measure survived, more or less intact, although Vice President Dick Cheney had to cut short a trip to the Middle East to cast a tie-breaking vote.

But Democrats spoiled what Republicans had hoped would be a pre-adjournment victory on the first package of savings from entitlement programs such as Medicare, Medicaid and student loans since 1997. The measure was kicked back to the House, and final action was put off until after the first of the year.

Before the final Senate vote on the measure Dec. 21, Kent Conrad, D-N.D., frustrated GOP leaders and succeeded in deleting three minor provisions from the language of the conference agreement on the grounds that they violated the so-called Byrd Rule. That rule prohibits the inclusion of items in a reconciliation bill that have only an incidental budgetary effect, and 60 votes are required to override it. An attempt by Budget Chairman Judd Gregg, R-N.H., to waive the rule — and preserve the conference agreement without change — failed on a 52-48 vote.

But more important, once the Byrd Rule was invoked, the conference report was no longer valid for floor action, and the Senate was put in the unusual position of amending the bill and returning it to the House, which would then have to accept the Senate's changes in order to clear the measure for the president.

One of the stricken provisions would have granted hospitals immunity from malpractice lawsuits if they chose not to treat Medicaid recipients who could not afford co-payments. Two other provisions were essentially technical in nature.

The language of the conference agreement was virtually unchanged, but, in the House, Minority Leader Nancy Pelosi, D-Calif., insisted on a roll call vote. Because most House members had already headed home for the holidays, Republican leaders had little choice but to put off the vote on the slightly altered package until early 2006.

It was yet another obstacle in the path of a bill whose journey had been perilous from the outset. Still, House and Senate leaders thought they had successfully navigated all of the shoals.

They set the stage for the cuts in the fiscal 2006 budget resolution (H Con Res 95), which called for a reconciliation bill that would save $34.7 billion from mandatory spending programs over five years. That qualified the bill for special treatment in the Senate, allowing it to pass with 51 votes instead of the 60 typically needed when opponents threatened to mount a filibuster.

With fiscal conservatives demanding deeper cuts, and Democrats and some moderate Republicans trying to protect programs for the poor, GOP leaders put off the work of writing the bill until after the August recess. At that point the human and fiscal costs of Hurricane Katrina caused both sides to dig in.

By mid-November, the House had passed a $50 billion package, and the Senate had passed a $35 billion version. To get a conference report, GOP leaders had to bridge differences over spending and overcome dis-

agreements within Republican ranks over whether to allow drilling in Alaska's Arctic National Wildlife Refuge (ANWR), whether to cut Medicare, and how much to cut funds for Medicaid, student loans, food stamps and child support enforcement.

The way was cleared in the House when Sen. Ted Stevens, R-Alaska, agreed to remove the Senate's ANWR provisions and attach them instead to the final Defense appropriations bill. The House narrowly adopted the conference report, 212-206, on Dec. 19. *(Senate ANWR key vote, below; House mandatory cuts key vote, p. C-18)*

Conferees had made changes to satisfy Senate supporters as well. Majority Leader Bill Frist, R-Tenn., cut a deal with Norm Coleman, R-Minn., to remove cuts to sugar subsidies in conference. Coleman had voted against the original Senate bill.

Frist and House Speaker J. Dennis Hastert, R-Ill., also appeased Sen. George V. Voinovich, R-Ohio, by reducing planned cuts to Medicare equipment subsidies by $1.9 billion. That protected a major Ohio manufacturer of oxygen tanks for the elderly, but also reduced the planned savings for the entire package. The Coleman flip offset a switch from "yes" to "no" from Gordon H. Smith of Oregon, who along with four other moderate Senate Republicans — Olympia J. Snowe and Susan Collins of Maine, Mike DeWine of Ohio and Lincoln Chafee of Rhode Island — objected to increased costs for Medicaid recipients that were included in the conference agreement.

Before the vote could be held, however, Conrad raised his objections. Democrats had figured out that invoking the Byrd Rule was a means to sidetrack the bill even when they weren't permitted to mount a filibuster. Moreover, the Byrd Rule change gave opponents of the savings package yet another chance to modify or kill it.

The Senate adopted a motion to concur to the House version of the bill, with an amendment that amounted to the original conference agreement minus the three stricken provisions. The motion was agreed to, with Vice President Cheney casting a "yea" vote to break the tie, 50-50: R 50-5; D 0-44 (ND 0-40, SD 0-4); I 0-1. *(Senate vote 363, p. C-28)*

At a news conference afterward, Senate GOP leaders declared victory and vowed to continue their budget-cutting efforts in 2006. Frist dismissed the Democratic maneuver as a "a childish antic," but it denied Republicans the chance to attain their budget-cutting goal by year's end.

## 364 ANWR Oil Drilling

**Defeat of an effort to invoke cloture, thus limiting debate, on the 2006 Defense appropriations bill because of a controversial amendment that would have opened Alaska's Arctic National Wildlife Refuge to oil and gas exploration.**

Legislation enacted in 1980 (PL 96-487) left it up to Congress, not the White House, to decide whether to open part of the Arctic National Wildlife Refuge (ANWR) to oil and gas development. Lawmakers rejected ANWR drilling measures over the next several years, until a Republican-led Congress included a provision in a 1995 budget-saving measure to allow energy development in the area. President Bill Clinton vetoed the bill, and a decade later the fight over developing ANWR — fueled by record gasoline prices — was as fierce as ever.

In the past few years, the Senate has been the graveyard for any ANWR drilling efforts. But Republican gains in the November 2004 election provided the votes needed to keep an ANWR provision in

the fiscal 2006 budget resolution (H Con Res 95). A Democratic attempt to delete it was defeated 49-51 in March. That allowed Republicans to include ANWR drilling in a budget savings bill (S 1932) that was subject to special rules in the Senate. Those rules protect a so-called budget reconciliation bill from a filibuster, which means supporters need only 50 votes to prevail — not the 60 normally needed to overcome a filibuster.

"This is the first step," Sen. Ted Stevens, R-Alaska, said after the March vote. The 82-year-old chairman of the Senate Defense Appropriations Subcommittee has argued persistently that Alaskans know what is best for the remote wildlife refuge. "I've been on this track like a white rat for 24 years," he said at the time.

But this time, Stevens and fellow ANWR supporters ran into difficulty in the House, where moderates insisted the language be stripped out of that chamber's version of the reconciliation bill. House GOP leaders said they could not get enough votes for the conference report on the bill if the ANWR provision was included.

So Stevens agreed to include the provision in the separate conference report on the fiscal 2006 Defense spending bill (HR 2863). That measure, which provided $453.5 billion for military spending, including $50 billion for operations in Iraq and Afghanistan, was considered legislation Congress had to clear before adjourning for the year.

In a bid to ensure that the ANWR provision would stick, Stevens tied billions of dollars in expected revenue from ANWR to additional hurricane relief and homeland security programs. He dared Democrats, in effect, to vote against funding for the troops and other popular spending items. The House adopted the conference report, 308-106, on Dec. 19.

Many senators, though, were furious with the treatment given the appropriations bill in conference, where it gained not only the ANWR language, but a number of other provisions as well. Because it was no longer protected by Senate budget rules, the ANWR language was now vulnerable to a filibuster, and Democrats made it clear they would not accept it. So Majority Leader Bill Frist, R-Tenn., scheduled a vote to invoke cloture, or limit debate, on the measure.

The motion came up four votes short of the 60 required for it to succeed. The Dec. 21 vote was 56-44: R 52-3; D 4-40 (ND 3-37, SD 1-3); I 0-1. *(Senate vote 364, p. C-28)*

All but four Democrats — Hawaiians Daniel K. Akaka and Daniel K. Inouye; Mary L. Landrieu of Louisiana and Ben Nelson of Nebraska — voted against cloture. They were joined by Republicans Lincoln Chafee of Rhode Island and Mike DeWine of Ohio, as well as Frist, who changed his vote to "no" at the last minute to preserve the option of seeking reconsideration of the vote.

After an hours-long quorum call, during which leaders worked off the floor to come up with a way to complete work on the Defense bill, Frist announced a deal in which the Senate would clear the measure, but would also pass a separate enrolling resolution (S Con Res 74) under which the ANWR language would be removed from the bill. After adopting the resolution, 48-45, the Senate cleared the spending bill 93-0 on Dec. 21. President Bush signed the appropriations bill — without ANWR leasing language — into law Dec. 30.

"This has been the saddest day of my life," Stevens told his colleagues. "I'm going to go to every one of your states, and I'm going to tell them what you've done."

"This issue is too important to our consumers and our economy to accept defeat," said Pete V. Domenici, R-N.M., another drilling advocate. "We will try again."

# HOUSE VOTES

## 31 Immigration Policy Changes

**Passage of legislation making it more difficult for illegal immigrants to get driver's licenses and identity cards or to claim asylum, and authorizing the completion of a security fence along the border with Mexico near San Diego.**

Immigration emerged early as one of the year's biggest issues, and supporters of tighter borders won an early victory when House Judiciary Chairman F. James Sensenbrenner Jr., R-Wis., revived provisions dropped from intelligence overhaul legislation at the end of the 108th Congress and pushed them through to enactment.

That he did so with 42 House Democrats backing the measure was a demonstration that even with the Republicans split on some aspects of the immigration debate, the goal of securing the border was a relatively easy sell on both sides of the aisle.

To pass the bill (HR 418), which among other things imposed new requirements for those seeking driver's licenses and state ID cards, Republicans set aside their talk of states' rights, citing the higher priority of homeland security.

The driver's license provision and others were included in a version of an intelligence overhaul measure in the 108th Congress, but were dropped in conference. Sensenbrenner was the only House conferee not to sign the conference agreement, and he won assurances that the provisions would be among the first items of business in the 109th Congress — either as a stand-alone bill or attached to another measure.

In addition to the driver's license and asylum provisions, the immigration bill included language giving the secretary of Homeland Security the power to pre-empt state and federal laws if need be to construct physical barriers and roads designed to curb illegal border crossings. The provision was intended to spur completion of a fence along the U.S.-Mexico border near San Diego.

"We were able to win World War II quicker than we were able to complete this fence," Sensenbrenner quipped.

Critics said the provision was wildly out of proportion to the problem. The pre-emption applied to any local, state or federal laws — whether governing child labor, competition for federal contracts or environmental protection — that would impede physical barriers to curb illegal border crossings.

An attempt by Sam Farr, D-Calif., to remove the provision was rejected, 179-243.

Some members, echoing the concerns of state governors, also complained that the driver's license requirement was an unfunded mandate and would draw states into the expensive role of enforcing immigration laws.

But concerns for national security and outrage over the leaky southern border ruled the day. The House passed Sensenbrenner's bill, Feb. 10, 261-161: R 219-8; D 42-152 (ND 18-127; SD 24-25); I 0-1. Most of the measure was subsequently incorporated into the fiscal 2005 emergency supplemental appropriations bill (PL 109-13), which Bush signed into law in May. *(House vote 31, p. C-20)*

## 90 Federal Intervention in Schiavo Litigation

**Passage of legislation allowing the parents of Terri Schiavo, a brain-damaged Florida woman, access to federal courts to appeal state court decisions that allowed her husband to have her feeding tube removed.**

Three days into Congress' spring recess, House Speaker J. Dennis Hastert, R-Ill., summoned members back to Washington for a gut-wrenching vote that would become a touchstone in the culture war of social conservatives vs. liberals and libertarians. It also stoked public dissatisfaction with Congress.

In 1990, a Florida woman, Terri Schiavo, suffered severe brain damage after her heart briefly stopped. Doctors declared her to be in a persistent vegetative state, and her husband, Michael Schiavo, tried to stop life support, saying it was in accordance with her wishes.

But Terri Schiavo had left no living will, a document outlining her treatment preferences. A legal battle ensued between Michael Schiavo and his wife's parents, Robert and Mary Schindler, who believed she might recover. After various Florida courts considered and rejected the Schindlers' arguments over a seven-year span, Terri Schiavo's feeding tube was removed March 18.

But the case had become a cause célèbre for social conservatives. They argued that Schiavo, much like a fetus, was a person with a "right to life" but incapable of speaking for herself and deserving of the government's protection. Enter congressional Republicans.

As Schiavo's condition began to deteriorate after removal of her feeding tube, the Senate zipped through a bill (S 686) that would have given the Schindlers access to federal courts for a final consideration of their daughter's case. The Senate passed the bill by voice vote March 20 — which was Palm Sunday.

A handful of House Democrats, disgusted with Congress' intervention into what they saw as a family matter, objected to a voice vote in that chamber. Republican leaders called members back to town for a roll call vote the morning of March 21.

President Bush, expecting that the House would clear the bill, returned to Washington from his ranch in Crawford, Texas, to sign it, increasing the public focus.

As the vote neared its conclusion, Republican members clapped when the tally reached 218 — a quorum, ensuring that enough members were present to pass the bill. The final tally was 203-58: R 156-5; D 47-53 (ND 27-38, SD 20-15); I 0-0. Many Democrats, wary of the 2004 elections in which social issues such as gay marriage were perceived to have played a major role, voted for the bill while expressing discomfort with the precedent it set. *(House vote 90, p. C-20)*

Bush signed the bill into law (PL 109-3) an hour later. But the Republicans' effort would prove to be for naught — substantively and politically. Schiavo's case quickly made its way to the Supreme Court, which on March 24 declined to hear the case. She died a week later.

GOP leaders found themselves the focus of a political backlash. Senate Majority Leader Bill Frist, R-Tenn., had questioned Schiavo's diagnosis on the Senate floor after watching a videotape of her apparently responding to "visual stimuli" such as a floating balloon, but an autopsy confirmed that she was not only severely brain-damaged, but also blind.

Polls showed that most Americans, including a majority of Republicans, disapproved of Congress' action in the case.

## 145 House Ethics Regulations

**Adoption of a resolution to repeal three rules changes Republicans made at the start of the session giving House members new rights in ethics investigations.**

In an unusual retreat in the face of Democratic criticism, House Republicans on April 27 voted to reverse three changes in ethics rules they had pushed through on the opening day of the session. The changes had been made to help lawmakers such as Majority Leader Tom DeLay, R-Texas, who had been admonished three times by the ethics committee in the previous Congress. But it was the growing number of questions about DeLay's conduct, and the political damage it might cause his party, that led Republicans to reverse their decision.

The short-lived rules changes specified that any complaint against a House member would die after 45 days unless the committee had voted by then to proceed with an investigation. Previously, the ethics panel, known formally as the Committee on Standards of Official Conduct, had to make a decision on a complaint for it to either expire or proceed.

The House in January also gave members who were the object of an investigation the right to respond to the committee's conclusions before a decision was made final or publicly announced. Republicans said they devised this change to prevent the ethics committee from catching a member off-guard with an admonishment or other punishment.

A third change codified what had been an occasional practice of permitting one attorney to represent multiple members involved in an ethics case. Democrats on the committee wanted to prohibit such a move, saying it allowed the subject of a complaint to collaborate with witnesses via a single attorney and made it impossible for the panel to properly investigate a charge.

Democrats condemned the changes as soon as they were made in January, but Republicans largely ignored their objections.

Then, in March, Democrats on the evenly divided ethics committee refused to vote for a proposed set of procedural rules for the 109th Congress, leaving the panel in procedural limbo and unable to conduct investigations.

The committee's ranking Democrat, Alan B. Mollohan of West Virginia, had meanwhile gathered 208 co-sponsors, including three Republicans, for a resolution (H Res 131) to reverse the three ethics rule changes. Mollohan threatened to file a discharge petition that, if he could get 218 signatures, would bring his resolution directly to the floor.

At that point, Republican leaders decided the ethics impasse and bad publicity were not worth the fight. At a conference meeting with rank-and-file members the morning of April 27, House Speaker J. Dennis Hastert, R-Ill., defended the rules changes as "fair for all members," but said, "We need to move the ethics process forward." Republicans leaving the conference said Hastert told them the best course of action would be to reverse the rules changes.

Almost all of them ultimately agreed. Many said they simply followed the direction of Hastert, who told them it was time to end the stalemate. Other Republicans said they had come to oppose some or all of the rules changes.

By a vote of 406-20, the House adopted a resolution (H Res 241) governing floor debate on a second resolution (H Res 240) that actually rolled back the three rules changes: R 208-20; D 197-0 (ND 148-0, SD 49-0); I 1-0. *(House vote 145, p. C-20)*

The vote was one of the first of a series of strategic victories for Democrats. On June 30, they forced Republicans on the ethics committee to retreat once again on disputed staffing issues. Democrats prevailed in an effort to hire only nonpartisan professionals to work on the committee.

## 204 Federal Research on Stem Cells

**Passage of a bill that would expand federal funding for research on stem cells taken from surplus embryos at in vitro fertilization clinics.**

Republican moderates held Majority Leader Tom DeLay, R-Texas, to a promise that he would hold a vote before summer on a bill (HR 810) by Michael N. Castle, R-Del., to expand the number of stem cell lines available to federally funded researchers by allowing them to work on lines derived from surplus embryos at in vitro fertilization clinics.

An executive order issued by President Bush on Aug. 21, 2001, allows federally funded scientists to conduct research only on stem cell lines that existed before that date. The National Institutes of Health estimates 22 such lines are viable for research, though they are contaminated and probably would not be usable for medical treatments.

Supporters of the bill campaigned among their colleagues, stressing that days-old embryos, which have the ability to morph into almost any other kind of cell in the body, show great promise for cures for diseases such as Parkinson's and some cancers.

In an effort to derail the legislation, GOP leaders and conservatives who oppose the research because it requires the destruction of an embryo backed an alternative bill (HR 2520) by Christopher H. Smith, R-N.J. Smith's bill encouraged the use of stem cells, sometimes referred to as "adult stem cells," taken from umbilical cords after birth. Stem cells found in umbilical cord blood are less elastic because they come from specific tissue and are used mainly in treating blood disorders.

House leaders hoped Smith's bill would enable members who faced pressure from their constituents to cast a "pro-stem cell" vote without relaxing Bush's restrictions on research using embryos.

Backers of the Castle bill said they did not oppose Smith's measure, but that it did not address the need for funding research on embryonic cells. The moderate Republican Main Street Partnership launched a multimillion-dollar advertising campaign in support of Castle's bill that highlighted former first lady Nancy Reagan's support for embryonic research.

The floor debate May 24 showcased the emotion and personal experiences that influenced members' votes and led many Republicans to disregard their leadership and support Castle's bill.

Joe L. Barton, R-Texas, noted that his anti-abortion voting record stood at 100 percent until 2005, but said he backed the embryonic stem cell bill because of his father, who has diabetes, and a brother, who had liver cancer. "Maybe the breakthrough will come in adult stem cells. I hope it does. But maybe, just maybe, it's going to come because of embryonic stem cells. Let's look at all avenues."

Anti-abortion Democrat Jim Langevin of Rhode Island, who was paralyzed as a teenager, and Lane Evans, D-Ill., who has Parkinson's disease, made personal pleas to allow federal funding for embryonic research.

Opponents made equally emotional appeals. Twenty-one children were escorted around the Capitol to illustrate the use of surplus embryos to help infertile couples. The youths were born to mothers from surplus frozen embryos donated by other couples.

"The best one can say about embryonic stem cell research is it is a scientific exploration into the potential benefits of killing human

beings," said DeLay, who along with the rest of the House GOP leadership voted against Castle's bill.

Although Bush had reiterated his veto threat, Majority Whip Roy Blunt, R-Mo., said leaders wanted members to vote their consciences. When the vote was finished, 50 Republicans had broken with their leadership. The House passed Castle's bill, 238-194: R 50-180; D 187-14 (ND 140-10, SD 47-4); I 1-0. (*House vote 204, p. C-20*)

The tally fell short of the 290 votes that would be needed to override a veto if all members of the House were present and voting, but supporters expressed hope that a compromise could be reached.

Although the Senate did not take up the Castle bill in the first session, the cord blood bill was subsequently cleared (PL 109-129).

## 258 | Limits on Federal Search Powers

**Adoption of an amendment to the fiscal 2006 Commerce-Justice-Science spending bill to prohibit the FBI from gaining access to library and bookstore records under the 2001 anti-terrorism law known as the Patriot Act.**

Weeks before the House took up legislation to reauthorize expiring provisions of the Patriot Act (PL 107-56), a cadre of Republicans joined every House Democrat save one in making a bold — though ultimately symbolic — gesture toward limiting one of the law's most contentious provisions.

Section 215 of the Patriot Act allows FBI investigators to seize "any tangible things (including books, records, papers, documents and other items)" as part of a terrorism investigation once they get a warrant from a top-secret court established under the Foreign Intelligence Surveillance Act, or FISA (PL 95-511).

The section is one of 16 provisions of the anti-terrorism law that were scheduled to expire at the end of 2005. The White House pressed Congress to make all 16 permanent as part of a bill reauthorizing the act.

Civil liberties advocates, the American Conservative Union, librarians, doctors, business groups, gun rights advocates and former Georgia GOP Rep. Bob Barr (1995-2003) spent much of the year lobbying hard to keep the provision out of the Patriot Act reauthorization or, short of that, to exempt certain records and minimize access.

On June 15, the administration's effort suffered a bipartisan blow during House debate on the fiscal 2006 Commerce-Justice-Science appropriations bill (HR 2862). Not waiting for the Patriot Act debate, Vermont independent Bernard Sanders offered an amendment to bar use of money in the bill to seek a FISA court order to seize library circulation records, library patron lists, book sales records or book customer lists.

Defying a White House veto threat, 38 Republicans and 199 Democrats supported Sanders, pushing his amendment to adoption by a vote of 238-187: R 38-186; D 199-1(ND 150-0; SD 49-1); I 1-0. Dan Boren of Oklahoma was the only Democrat who voted against the amendment. (*House vote 258, p. C-22*)

Sanders garnered more votes than he had with a similar amendment the previous year, when he lost, 210-210. He noted that the 2004 amendment had drawn some opposition from members who did not like the fact that it would have barred FBI access to library Internet records. Sanders dropped that provision in the 2005 version.

The vote was perceived as a snub to the White House and a small victory for those arguing for more balance between the need to flush out terrorists and the desire to protect civil liberties. "A number of conservatives voted conservatively today, and 'conservative' means limited gov-

ernment," said Sanders, one of the most liberal members of the House, who pumped his arm in the air to applause as he left the chamber.

The provision was short-lived: When the House passed a bill (HR 3199) in July to renew the 16 expiring Patriotic Act provisions, the power to seize library and bookstore records was intact. It survived in conference, though the provision was one of two that were accorded a four-year extension; the rest were made permanent.

Still, the vote on Sanders' amendment was a clear indication that reauthorizing the Patriot Act would be no simple matter. With the conference report now stalled by a Senate filibuster, the portent proved accurate. (*Senate anti-terrorism act key vote, p. C-11*)

## 374 | Policy Toward China

**Defeat of a bill that would have imposed new trade restrictions on countries that allow the sale of arms and defense-related technology to China.**

The intense, last-minute lobbying around what had been a non-controversial bill to tighten sanctions on illegal arms sales to China highlighted Congress' continued dilemma on China policy: how to punish the Asian nation's anti-competitive business practices and arms trade while not jeopardizing U.S. commerce with it.

The bill (HR 3100) was designed to discourage European countries from lifting their embargoes on military trade with China. "The bill is not intended to be punitive; its primary purpose is deterrence," said Henry J. Hyde, R-Ill., chairman of the International Relations Committee and the bill's sponsor. It would have required the administration to annually report the names of countries that permit trade in military material with China and would have required an export license before any U.S. company could send military goods to such countries. The president could apply a range of sanctions against countries selling arms to China, including denying licenses for "dual use" goods — those that have both civilian and potential military applications — barring their participation in research projects or prohibiting them from owning U.S. defense companies.

Both Republicans and Democrats initially supported the legislation, and House leaders brought it to the floor under a suspension of the rules, a procedure used for non-controversial bills that requires a two-thirds vote for passage. Just two weeks earlier, the House had overwhelmingly adopted an amendment and a resolution expressing concern that the China National Offshore Oil Corp. Ltd. was trying to buy Unocal, a U.S. oil company, for $18.5 billion.

But House leaders underestimated the opposition from the defense industry, which has companies and manufacturing plants in many congressional districts. Defense manufacturers said the bill could end up punishing companies for selling dual-use products to China. Essentially, defense contractors such as Boeing Co. did not want to be punished for selling aircraft parts to commercial companies in China if those parts ended up on military jets.

When the roll call began July 14, the bill appeared headed for easy passage. But Donald Manzullo, R-Ill., the chairman of the Small Business Committee, was at work on the floor, trying to persuade his colleagues to change their votes.

Manzullo, whose district includes aircraft and machine parts manufacturers, worked both sides of the aisle, telling members that the legislation was a bad deal. He circulated a flyer drawn up by defense contractors saying "passage of this bill means that Boeing and other

aircraft manufacturers will sell fewer planes overseas."

In rapid sequence, dozens of lawmakers, worried that the bill could unintentionally punish defense contractors who do business with European companies that in turn sell to China, began to change their votes. What had been scheduled as a five-minute vote was held open for 23 minutes, but the measure failed to get the necessary two-thirds majority. The vote was 215-203: R 118-106; D 96-97 (ND 70-73, SD 26-24); I 1-0. *(House vote 374, p. C-22)*

A toned-down version of the measure was later attached to the State Department authorization bill (HR 2601) passed by the House in July. The amended version would still monitor European governments or companies that sell military hardware or technology to China, but would punish U.S. companies only if they knew their products would ultimately be used for military purposes. The bill went no further.

## 443 Central American Trade Liberalization

**Passage of a bill to implement tariff reductions and other changes to U.S. trade law that were part of a free-trade agreement negotiated between the United States and five Central American countries, plus the Dominican Republic.**

Hours before leaving for a monthlong August recess, the House voted to pass a bill implementing a free-trade accord between the United States and Costa Rica, El Salvador, Guatemala, Honduras and Nicaragua, plus a parallel agreement with the Dominican Republic.

The vote on the Central American accord, or CAFTA, was a referendum on U.S. trade policy, and a test both of the president's power and GOP party loyalty amid growing congressional partisanship and skepticism on trade.

Although the bill (HR 3045) was a marquee piece of President Bush's trade agenda, it took all of the wiles of then-Majority Leader Tom DeLay, R-Texas, to twist enough arms to eke out a two-vote victory margin. The close vote suggests that GOP members are increasingly wary about trade pacts, carefully weighing the potential impact on their own districts with the goals and desires of the president. Bush even made a rare appearance before the House Republican Conference the morning of the vote, and several members of the Cabinet spent part of the day on Capitol Hill helping to convince reluctant lawmakers.

Democratic support for CAFTA was all but non-existent, which many see as evidence of a backlash that Democrats have felt since a large number from their party supported NAFTA, the North American Free-Trade Agreement, in 1993 (PL 103-182).

The Senate had gone first to give momentum to the House, but even there the vote was a relatively close 54-45. *(Senate CAFTA key vote, p. C-6)*

The voting began in the House shortly after 11 p.m. on July 27, and did not end until well after midnight when the bill passed 217-215; R 202-27; D 15-187 (ND 7-144, SD 8-43); I 0-1. *(House vote 443, p. C-22)*

Almost until the end, a small but vital bloc of Republicans remained concerned that beleaguered domestic textile and apparel makers would be wiped out by imports of Chinese-made goods that they said could slip into the United States duty-free under CAFTA.

The administration had argued vigorously that, if anything, CAFTA would strengthen the bond between U.S. textile mills and Central American apparel factories. Just the same, U.S. Trade Representative Rob Portman promised to go back into the accord later to amend three textile provisions to prevent circumvention by the Chinese, winning over a handful of textile state members just days before the vote.

Additional maneuvering was required even as debate got under way. Robert B. Aderholt, R-Ala., received a letter from Portman and Commerce Secretary Carlos Gutierrez pledging administration help to protect sock makers from import surges possible under CAFTA and other trade pacts, support for an application by the Hosiery Technology Center for a Commerce Department export grant, and a commitment to work with the Pentagon to encourage purchase of U.S.-made socks only.

Another trouble spot was the concern that a modest increase in sugar imports permitted by CAFTA would undermine domestic producers and cost U.S. jobs. An administration proposal to use commodity swaps to contain additional sugar imports for the remaining two years of the current farm bill (PL 107-171) and to undertake a study of government initiatives to spur production of ethanol made from sugar helped win the votes of Dave Camp, R-Mich., Adam H. Putnam, R-Fla., and Mark Kennedy, R-Minn., among others. But Mark Foley, R-Fla., and several Louisiana lawmakers remained skeptical. Foley called his eventual decision to vote for the CAFTA bill a "gut wrencher."

One final issue involved demonstrating more resolve in countering unfair trade practices by China. Phil English, R-Pa., pressed for floor action on a bill (HR 3283) to strengthen U.S. enforcement of trade rules against China. He estimated that as many as 10 Republicans agreed to vote for CAFTA after the House passed the China bill earlier in the day.

A half-hour after the nominal 15-minute roll call vote on the CAFTA bill began, the count froze at 214-211 in favor. Eight Republicans who had either expressed opposition to CAFTA or said they were reluctant to support it had not cast their votes. About midnight, DeLay and GOP leaders persuaded Robin Hayes of North Carolina to switch his vote from no to yes. DeLay then persuaded two of the hesitant Republicans to vote for the trade agreement and allowed the rest to cast last-minute votes against it.

Only 15 Democrats voted yes, a sharp contrast to the 102 Democrats who had answered President Bill Clinton's call to vote for NAFTA more than a decade earlier. Democrats' opposition was based in part on their concerns about what they regarded as a lost opportunity to improve on the NAFTA model and raise labor and environmental standards in developing countries. But Republicans claimed that those "no" votes were simply a partisan effort to weaken Bush.

## 445 Energy Policy Overhaul

**Final passage of legislation that includes incentives for greater domestic production of oil, gas, coal and nuclear power, encouragement for conservation and a reduction in regulation of the electric power industry.**

It took four years, but record fuel prices gave Congress the motivation to pass energy legislation similar to what the Bush administration first proposed in 2001. The final bill (HR 6) emphasized greater production of domestic energy, as President Bush wanted. But to get the bill through the Senate, the White House had to forgo the centerpiece of its energy plan, drilling for oil and natural gas in Alaska's Arctic National Wildlife Refuge (ANWR). And House Republican leaders gave up one of their top priorities, liability protection for the oil companies that make the fuel additive MTBE (methyl tertiary buytl ether), which has been found to contaminate some groundwater.

For two years running, MTBE liability had defeated the energy bill

as House members from oil-producing states, led by then-Majority Leader Tom DeLay, R-Texas, demanded that it be included, while a coalition of Democrats and moderate Republicans demanded that it be dropped.

Though the administration lost on energy exploration in the Alaska wilderness, it was successful in reducing the cost of tax breaks and other incentives in the legislation to about half what GOP congressional leaders have sought in past years.

In one of the most significant energy votes in decades, the House adopted the conference report on the omnibus energy bill July 28, 275-156: R 200-31; D 75-124 (ND 41-107, SD 34-17); I 0-1. *(House vote 445, p. C-22)*

The House had passed other energy bills several times dating back to 2001 only to see them bog down in the Senate, where sponsors had trouble winning the 60 votes necessary to beat filibuster threats from senators upset by what they considered a bias in the legislation toward energy companies. *(Senate energy key vote, p. C-7)*

But this year DeLay and fellow Texas Republican Joe L. Barton, the chairman of the Energy and Commerce Committee, dropped their insistence that the bill include liability relief for the makers of MTBE, which has been used since the 1970s but became more prevalent after federal clean fuel requirements in the early 1990s. Like ethanol, MTBE helps gasoline burn more completely, helping to lower harmful tailpipe emissions. But it also has been found to contaminate groundwater where it has leaked from storage tanks. Some lawmakers, including northeastern Republicans, worried that the liability protection would leave their states to pay for the cleanup.

Unlike previous years, House leaders also won support for the measure by holding down the cost of its tax incentives, which in past years had exceeded $30 billion. That had been a point of criticism from fiscal conservatives and the White House this year. The conference agreement provides for $14.6 billion in tax breaks and credits between 2005 and 2015.

To help deliver the bill, House Republicans agreed to drop language that would have opened ANWR to energy exploration. GOP leaders shifted the provision to other legislation, first a spending-cut package (S 1932) and later a Defense appropriations bill (HR 2863), but those maneuvers also failed.

Even with the House vote and the subsequent Senate action, Congress may not be through with energy legislation. Just weeks after Bush signed the bill, energy supply disruptions from hurricanes Katrina and Rita triggered calls by some House GOP leaders, including Barton, for a new energy bill. On Oct. 7, the House narrowly passed a measure (HR 3893) that would ease environmental reviews and take other steps to encourage the construction of new or expanded refineries. The Senate did not take up the bill and is not expected to do so in 2006. Once again, it is opposed by a coalition of Democrats and moderate Republicans.

## 453 Surface Transportation Spending

**Final passage of a six-year reauthorization of highway and transit programs after more than two years of negotiations and concessions by the White House and Congress.**

It took more than two years and two Congresses, but the House on July 29 adopted the conference report on a bill (HR 3) reauthorizing the nation's highway and public transit programs. The House and Senate had reached the conference stage on a six-year reauthorization bill in 2004, but the negotiators could not get beyond disputes among mem-

bers over how to divide up highway money, and with the White House over the total cost of the bill.

In 2005, Congress finally settled for less money than it wanted; the Bush administration settled for more. The agreement gave a larger share of highway funds to fast-growing states, mainly in the South and Southwest, that argued they had been shortchanged by the previous highway law. In another victory for those states, the House agreed to deduct from each state's formula highway funds any money it received for earmarked projects — a blow to influential lawmakers such as Don Young, R-Alaska, the chairman of the Transportation and Infrastructure Committee — who are adroit at getting such projects for their states.

The final $286.5 billion bill contained more than 5,100 earmarks, demonstrating why highway spending is perennially popular among lawmakers. While the overwhelming majority were for road projects, some were for museums and other amenities not related to traffic. Watchdog groups and fiscal conservatives used the bill and the vote as symbols of the inability of either Republicans or Democrats to exercise self-restraint when it comes to home-state public works projects.

President Bush had for two years demanded that Congress authorize no more than $256 billion for surface transportation programs, while lawmakers were thinking more in the range of $319 billion to as much as $375 billion. The administration made a deal more realistic early in 2005 when it lifted its bottom-line demand to $284 billion — close to the compromise amount conferees had been negotiating in 2004 and just $2.5 billion away from the final figure.

Befitting the tortuous path the legislation had followed since the previous surface transportation law (PL 105-178) expired in September 2003, the final days of negotiations featured marathon sessions to draft language and frustrating snags that developed each time the bill drew close to final action.

Only eight dissidents were prepared to vote against the conference report when it reached the House floor July 29. Six of them were members of the Republican Study Committee, a group of fiscal and social conservatives frustrated with GOP leaders and the White House over spending issues The House adopted the conference report and sent it to the Senate, 412-8: R 217-8; D 194-0 (ND 144-0, SD 50-0); I 1-0. *(House vote 453, p. C-24; Senate transportation key vote, p. C-8)*

The dispute over earmarks resurfaced three months later. Bowing to public criticism of pork barrel spending in light of mounting hurricane-relief costs and pressure to rein in budget deficits, conferees on the transportation appropriations bill (HR 3058) redirected $454 million that had been earmarked in the highway bill for two bridges, dubbed "bridges to nowhere," in Alaska.

The action on the fiscal 2006 Transportation-Treasury-Housing spending bill was largely symbolic because Alaska will still get the money to use at its discretion. *(Senate earmarks key vote, p. C-9)*

## 506 Endangered Species Policy Rewrite

**Passage of a major revision of the 1973 Endangered Species Act that would remove a requirement that the government designate and protect habitat critical to threatened animal and plant species, which has been the source of frequent litigation.**

Rep. Richard W. Pombo, R-Calif., has been fighting environmentalists for years over the Endangered Species Act, arguing that it harms pri-

vate property owners while doing little to aid the recovery of threatened animal and plant species. In 2005, Pombo changed course somewhat and found a new, albeit limited, source of support among Democrats, many of them from Western states where the endangered species program has faced considerable opposition. As a result, Pombo persuaded the House to pass the most extensive changes to the species protection program since the law was reauthorized in 1988.

As chairman of the House Resources Committee, Pombo spent several months negotiating with committee Democrats before releasing a detailed bill (HR 3824) in September. The bipartisan effort paid off Sept. 22, when eight Democrats joined all but two Republicans to approve the bill in committee.

The bill would require the use of peer-reviewed science in federal regulatory decisions and require compensation for landowners affected by federal conservation efforts. It also would eliminate a requirement that the government designate and protect critical habitat for within a year of listing a species as endangered. Instead, the government would have to come up with a recovery plan, keeping in mind habitat and cost.

Opponents of the bill worry that the recovery plans might not be enforceable on private landowners or other government agencies. Environmental groups, which for years have sued the government for failing to designate critical habitat as required under current law, said habitat protection is a critical component of any long-term recovery plan. They declared the bill a frontal assault on a landmark law that, despite its problems, has kept alive most of the species it aims to protect.

Democrats attracted some bipartisan support for a substitute amendment that emphasized recovery planning on federal lands, while promoting technical assistance and grants for private property owners who cooperate on federal conservation programs. Twenty-nine Republicans joined Democrats on the vote, but the amendment failed, 206-216.

In the end, Pombo succeeded in offsetting the Republican votes he lost with support by 36 Democrats, many from Western and Midwestern states. The bill passed Sept. 29, 229-193: R 193-34; D 36-158 (ND 15-129, SD 21-29); I 0-1. *(House vote 506, p. C-24)*

The bill did not advance in the Senate. It was sent to an Environment and Public Works subcommittee chaired by Lincoln Chafee, a Rhode Island Republican who often sides with Democrats on environmental issues. Chafee chose to wait for the results of an independent study he and other senators had requested on the critical habitat question, expected in February.

## 630 Treatment of Military Detainees

**Agreement to a motion to instruct conferees on the fiscal 2006 Defense appropriations bill to support a Senate provision banning abusive treatment of detainees in U.S. custody.**

In an overwhelming vote Dec. 14, the House demonstrated its support for a proposal by Sen. John McCain, R-Ariz., to ban the use of torture on prisoners held in U.S. custody. The timing of the vote and the compelling margin of victory appeared to force President Bush to back down from his months-long opposition to McCain's initiative.

The president's compromise with McCain ended an internecine battle in Republican ranks over how to respond to reports of abuse that had tarnished America's image and complicated efforts to win the war of ideas against radical Islamic terrorists. The political conflict in

Washington pitted the president against lawmakers who ordinarily stood with him, including popular McCain, himself a victim of torture in Vietnam and the man Bush had defeated for the Republican nomination in the hard-fought primaries of 2000.

McCain's amendment banned "cruel, inhuman or degrading" treatment of detainees, and made an Army field manual on interrogations the standard for Defense Department handling of prisoners.

The House was voting on a "motion to instruct" its conferees on the fiscal 2006 Defense appropriations bill (HR 2863) to retain McCain's provision. Such motions are not binding, but the force of this one was undeniable. In a House where Republicans typically move in lockstep, more than 100 of them defied the president on the torture vote. The motion was agreed to 308-122: R 107-121; D 200-1 (ND 150-0, SD 50-1); I 1-0. *(House vote 630, p. C-24)*

McCain had won a 90-9 vote in early October to attach the language to the Senate version of the spending bill. For good measure, the Senate agreed by voice vote in early November to add it to the defense authorization bill (HR 1815) as well. *(Senate detainee key vote, p. C-9)*

Bush was so opposed to the amendment that he threatened to veto the two military bills in the middle of a bloody and costly war. Bush dispatched Vice President Dick Cheney to try to persuade McCain to create an exemption for the CIA, but the lobbying campaign backfired. It created the impression that the administration was in favor of torture, or at least opposed to Congress passing a law against it.

National Security Adviser Stephen J. Hadley soon replaced Cheney in the talks with McCain, and Bush spoke with the senator about the amendment on several occasions. Meanwhile, McCain negotiated with Duncan Hunter, R-Calif., chairman of the House Armed Services Committee, who sided with the administration and had his own ideas on changes he thought could improve McCain's amendment in the defense authorization bill.

With all of those talks, described by one aide as "a three-ring circus," going nowhere, the two massive defense bills were stalled going into December. On Dec. 14, House Republican leaders finally named conferees on the appropriations bill, clearing the way for John P. Murtha, D-Pa., to offer his motion to instruct the conferees.

The day after the highly publicized House vote, Bush invited McCain and Sen. John W. Warner, R-Va., to the White House to announce a compromise on the detainee amendment. McCain had not budged on his provision. But he agreed to additional language allowing U.S. interrogators—whether they work for the Defense Department, the CIA, the FBI or a contractor—to have the same legal protections that U.S. military personnel are accorded.

The language was cleared as part of both the defense spending and defense authorization bills.

## 670 Cuts in Mandatory Spending

**Adoption of the conference report on a $38.8 billion budget savings package.**

At the start of 2005, Republican leaders vowed to slow the growth of mandatory entitlement programs such as Medicare, Medicaid and student loans for the first time since 1997, and the House brought them close to achieving their goal. Despite having no Democratic support, they put themselves in position to clear a $38.8 billion savings package (S 1932) in early 2006.

The effort was hanging in the balance in the pre-dawn hours of

Dec. 19. House and Senate negotiators had labored into the night to reconcile a $35 billion Senate plan and a far different $50 billion House package. A deal was announced, then altered, as new objections arose and leaders sought to ensure they had enough support before a final vote.

Negotiations had been stalled for days because of an impasse over efforts to open Alaska's Arctic National Wildlife Refuge (ANWR) to drilling. House Republican moderates vowed to oppose any bill with the ANWR provision, and Sen. Ted Stevens, R-Alaska, a member of the conference committee, vowed to oppose any bill without it.

Stevens relented during a final weekend of negotiations once House and Senate leaders agreed to try to enact the ANWR provisions by attaching them to the fiscal 2006 Defense Appropriations bill (HR 2863) instead, a plan that ultimately failed. *(Senate ANWR key vote, p. C-12)*

On the evening of Dec. 18, House Speaker J. Dennis Hastert, R-Ill., announced that conferees had agreed on a $41.6 billion budget savings package. But after midnight, Hastert and Senate negotiators had to shrink the package to $38.8 billion to secure the votes of Ohio lawmakers who threatened to scuttle the overall deal unless oxygen tank manufacturers, including a major Ohio company, were protected from planned cuts to Medicare. The 774-page conference report was filed well after midnight. The vote came shortly after 6 a.m. on Dec. 19, with a number of lawmakers in both parties already having left town for the winter recess.

But with the backing of enough moderates, GOP leaders managed a 212-206 victory: R 212-9; D 0-196 (ND 0-146, SD 0-50); I 0-1. The vote turned out to be largely devoid of suspense, even though all of the Democrats who showed up voted no. *(House vote 670, p. C-24)*

House leaders had won a narrower 217-215 vote shortly before 2 a.m. Nov. 18 on their original package, which contained deeper cuts and fewer spending plums.

The final vote was a triumph for the House leadership team, which overcame months of doubt about its ability to deliver votes for the budget package in the face of the criminal indictment of former Majority Leader Tom DeLay, R-Texas, low poll ratings, carping by some moderates and unusually united Democratic opposition.

Yet the victory came at a cost, with House leaders unable to deliver on the $45 billion savings goal they had announced for the conference report. House and Senate moderates had forced leaders to abandon plans to cut off 250,000 recipients from food stamps, and to shrink cuts planned for child support enforcement and welfare. Meanwhile, House leaders refused to go along with a Senate plan to eliminate a $10 billion subsidy for companies included as part of the new Medicare drug benefit. The Senate cut had prompted a veto threat.

Alongside the budget cuts came a number of sweeteners to win votes, including $7.3 billion to prevent doctors from receiving a 4.4 percent Medicare pay cut, $2.1 billion to extend Medicaid to hurricane victims, $1 billion to continue a milk subsidy for two years, $1 billion in home heating subsidies for the poor, and $1.5 billion for digital television converters for analog televisions.

The bill did not clear, however. A procedural maneuver by Senate Democrats required an additional vote in the House. House Minority Leader Nancy Pelosi, D-Calif., refused a quick voice vote before the holidays, saying she wanted to force a vote "in the light of day." *(Senate budget key vote, p. C-11)*

Democrats and their allies vowed to renew pressure on House GOP moderates who supported the conference report to change their minds. Still, after a long night of waiting and deal making, GOP leaders declared victory and pledged to continue the belt-tightening in the new year. ■

# HOUSE 31, 90, 145, 204

**31.** **HR 418. Immigration Standards/Passage.** Passage of the bill that would tighten national standards for state driver's licenses and identity cards, make it more difficult for foreign nationals to claim asylum and authorize the completion of a security fence along the U.S.-Mexico border. It would allow immigration judges to weigh the credibility of asylum applicants in a variety of proceedings and remove the annual cap of 10,000 refugees who may become permanent residents. It also would require the Homeland Security Department to include in aviation security screening databases information on anyone convicted of using a false driver's license to board an airplane. Passed 261-161: R 219-8; D 42-152 (ND 18-127, SD 24-25); I 0-1. A "yea" was a vote in support of the president's position. Feb. 10, 2005. *(Story, p. C-13)*

**90.** **S 686. Schiavo Medical Care/Passage.** Sensenbrenner, R-Wis., motion to suspend the rules and pass the bill that would give the parents of Theresa Marie Schiavo, a severely brain-damaged Florida woman, the right to file a lawsuit in the U.S. District Court for the Middle District of Florida alleging that Schiavo's rights related to life-sustaining medical treatment have been violated under the Constitution or federal law. Motion agreed to, thus clearing the bill for the president, 203-58: R 156-5; D 47-53 (ND 27-38, SD 20-15); I 0-0. A two-thirds majority of those present and voting (174 in this case) is required for passage under suspension of the rules. March 21, 2005 (in the session that began and the Congressional Record dated March 20, 2005). *(Story, p. C-13)*

**145.** **H Res 240. House Rules/Adoption.** Adoption of the self-executing rule (H Res 241) under which the House would automatically adopt a resolution repealing three changes to the Rules of the House dealing with ethics committee procedures that were made at the start of the 109th Congress, including a rule that allowed the automatic dismissal of an ethics complaint that is not disposed of by the committee within 45 days. Adopted 406-20: R 208-20; D 197-0 (ND 148-0, SD 49-0); I 1-0. April 27, 2005. *(Story, p. C-14)*

**204.** **HR 810. Embryonic Stem Cell Research/Passage.** Passage of the bill that would allow the use of federal funds in research on embryonic stem cell lines derived from surplus embryos at invitro fertilization clinics, but only if donors give their consent and are not paid for the embryos. The bill would authorize the Health and Human Services Department to conduct and support research involving human embryonic stem cells that meet certain criteria, regardless of when the stem cells were derived from a human embryo. Passed 238-194: R 50-180; D 187-14 (ND 140-10, SD 47-4); I 1-0. A "nay" was a vote in support of the president's position. May 24, 2005. *(Story, p. C-14)*

[1] Rep. Doris Matsui, D-Calif., was sworn in March 10, 2005. The first vote for which she was eligible was vote 62.

[2] The Speaker votes only at his discretion, usually to break a tie or to emphasize the importance of a matter.

[3] Rep. Rob Portman, R-Ohio, resigned effective April 29. The last vote for which he was eligible was vote 150.

ND Northern Democrats, SD Southern Democrats
Southern states: Ala., Ark., Fla., Ga., Ky., La., Miss., N.C., Okla., S.C., Tenn., Texas, Va.

| | 31 | 90 | 145 | 204 |
|---|---|---|---|---|
| **ALABAMA** | | | | |
| 1 **Bonner** | Y | Y | Y | N |
| 2 **Everett** | Y | ? | Y | N |
| 3 **Rogers** | Y | Y | Y | N |
| 4 **Aderholt** | Y | Y | Y | N |
| 5 **Cramer** | Y | Y | Y | Y |
| 6 **Bachus** | Y | Y | Y | N |
| 7 Davis | Y | ? | Y | Y |
| **ALASKA** | | | | |
| AL **Young** | N | ? | Y | Y |
| **ARIZONA** | | | | |
| 1 **Renzi** | Y | Y | Y | N |
| 2 **Franks** | Y | Y | Y | N |
| 3 **Shadegg** | Y | ? | Y | N |
| 4 Pastor | N | ? | Y | Y |
| 5 **Hayworth** | Y | Y | Y | N |
| 6 **Flake** | Y | ? | Y | N |
| 7 Grijalva | N | ? | Y | Y |
| 8 **Kolbe** | Y | ? | Y | Y |
| **ARKANSAS** | | | | |
| 1 Berry | Y | Y | Y | Y |
| 2 Snyder | N | Y | Y | Y |
| 3 **Boozman** | Y | ? | Y | N |
| 4 Ross | Y | Y | Y | Y |
| **CALIFORNIA** | | | | |
| 1 Thompson | N | ? | Y | Y |
| 2 **Herger** | Y | ? | Y | N |
| 3 **Lungren** | Y | ? | Y | N |
| 4 **Doolittle** | Y | Y | Y | N |
| 5 Matsui,D.[1] | | N | Y | Y |
| 6 Woolsey | N | ? | Y | Y |
| 7 Miller, George | N | ? | Y | Y |
| 8 Pelosi | N | ? | Y | Y |
| 9 Lee | N | ? | ? | Y |
| 10 Tauscher | N | ? | Y | Y |
| 11 **Pombo** | N | ? | Y | N |
| 12 Lantos | N | ? | Y | Y |
| 13 Stark | N | ? | Y | Y |
| 14 Eshoo | ? | ? | Y | Y |
| 15 Honda | – | ? | Y | Y |
| 16 Lofgren | N | ? | Y | Y |
| 17 Farr | N | ? | Y | Y |
| 18 Cardoza | Y | ? | Y | Y |
| 19 **Radanovich** | Y | ? | Y | N |
| 20 Costa | Y | ? | Y | Y |
| 21 **Nunes** | Y | ? | Y | N |
| 22 **Thomas** | Y | ? | Y | N |
| 23 Capps | N | ? | Y | Y |
| 24 **Gallegly** | Y | ? | Y | N |
| 25 **McKeon** | Y | ? | Y | Y |
| 26 **Dreier** | Y | Y | Y | N |
| 27 Sherman | N | ? | Y | Y |
| 28 Berman | N | ? | Y | Y |
| 29 Schiff | N | N | Y | Y |
| 30 Waxman | N | ? | ? | Y |
| 31 Becerra | N | – | Y | Y |
| 32 Solis | N | ? | Y | Y |
| 33 Watson | N | ? | Y | Y |
| 34 Roybal-Allard | N | ? | Y | Y |
| 35 Waters | N | ? | Y | Y |
| 36 Harman | N | ? | Y | Y |
| 37 Millender-McD. | N | ? | Y | ? |
| 38 Napolitano | N | ? | Y | Y |
| 39 Sánchez, Linda | N | ? | Y | Y |
| 40 **Royce** | Y | ? | Y | N |
| 41 **Lewis** | Y | Y | Y | Y |
| 42 **Miller, Gary** | Y | ? | Y | N |
| 43 Baca | Y | Y | Y | Y |
| 44 **Calvert** | Y | Y | Y | Y |
| 45 **Bono** | Y | ? | Y | Y |
| 46 **Rohrabacher** | Y | ? | Y | Y |
| 47 Sanchez, Loretta | ? | ? | Y | Y |
| 48 **Cox** | Y | Y | Y | N |
| 49 **Issa** | Y | + | Y | Y |

| | 31 | 90 | 145 | 204 |
|---|---|---|---|---|
| 50 **Cunningham** | Y | ? | Y | Y |
| 51 Filner | N | ? | Y | Y |
| 52 **Hunter** | Y | ? | Y | N |
| 53 Davis | N | ? | Y | Y |
| **COLORADO** | | | | |
| 1 DeGette | N | ? | Y | Y |
| 2 Udall | N | ? | Y | Y |
| 3 Salazar | Y | ? | Y | Y |
| 4 **Musgrave** | Y | Y | Y | N |
| 5 **Hefley** | Y | Y | Y | N |
| 6 **Tancredo** | Y | Y | Y | N |
| 7 **Beauprez** | Y | Y | Y | N |
| **CONNECTICUT** | | | | |
| 1 Larson | N | N | Y | Y |
| 2 **Simmons** | Y | ? | Y | Y |
| 3 DeLauro | N | ? | Y | Y |
| 4 **Shays** | Y | N | Y | Y |
| 5 **Johnson** | Y | ? | Y | Y |
| **DELAWARE** | | | | |
| AL **Castle** | Y | N | Y | Y |
| **FLORIDA** | | | | |
| 1 **Miller** | Y | Y | Y | N |
| 2 Boyd | Y | ? | Y | Y |
| 3 Brown | N | ? | ? | Y |
| 4 **Crenshaw** | Y | Y | Y | N |
| 5 **Brown-Waite** | Y | N | Y | N |
| 6 **Stearns** | Y | ? | Y | N |
| 7 **Mica** | Y | ? | Y | N |
| 8 **Keller** | Y | ? | Y | N |
| 9 **Bilirakis** | Y | Y | Y | N |
| 10 **Young** | Y | ? | Y | Y |
| 11 Davis | Y | N | Y | Y |
| 12 **Putnam** | Y | Y | Y | N |
| 13 **Harris** | Y | Y | Y | N |
| 14 **Mack** | Y | Y | Y | N |
| 15 **Weldon** | Y | Y | N | N |
| 16 **Foley** | Y | Y | Y | Y |
| 17 Meek | N | Y | Y | Y |
| 18 **Ros-Lehtinen** | N | Y | Y | Y |
| 19 Wexler | N | N | Y | Y |
| 20 Wasserman-Schultz | N | N | Y | Y |
| 21 **Diaz-Balart, L.** | N | Y | Y | N |
| 22 **Shaw** | Y | ? | Y | Y |
| 23 Hastings | N | N | Y | Y |
| 24 **Feeney** | ? | Y | Y | N |
| 25 **Diaz-Balart, M.** | N | Y | Y | N |
| **GEORGIA** | | | | |
| 1 **Kingston** | Y | Y | Y | N |
| 2 Bishop | Y | Y | Y | Y |
| 3 Marshall | Y | Y | Y | N |
| 4 McKinney | N | N | Y | Y |
| 5 Lewis | N | N | Y | Y |
| 6 **Price** | Y | Y | N | N |
| 7 **Linder** | Y | Y | Y | N |
| 8 **Westmoreland** | Y | Y | – | N |
| 9 **Norwood** | Y | ? | Y | N |
| 10 **Deal** | Y | ? | Y | N |
| 11 **Gingrey** | Y | Y | Y | N |
| 12 Barrow | Y | Y | Y | Y |
| 13 Scott | Y | Y | Y | Y |
| **HAWAII** | | | | |
| 1 Abercrombie | N | ? | Y | Y |
| 2 Case | N | ? | Y | Y |
| **IDAHO** | | | | |
| 1 **Otter** | Y | Y | N | N |
| 2 **Simpson** | Y | Y | N | N |
| **ILLINOIS** | | | | |
| 1 Rush | N | ? | Y | Y |
| 2 Jackson | N | Y | Y | Y |
| 3 Lipinski | Y | Y | Y | N |
| 4 Gutierrez | N | N | Y | Y |
| 5 Emanuel | N | ? | Y | Y |
| 6 **Hyde** | Y | ? | Y | N |
| 7 Davis | N | ? | Y | Y |
| 8 Bean | Y | Y | Y | Y |
| 9 Schakowsky | N | ? | Y | Y |
| 10 **Kirk** | Y | Y | Y | Y |
| 11 **Weller** | Y | ? | Y | N |
| 12 Costello | Y | Y | Y | N |

### KEY Republicans Democrats *Independents*

| | | | | | |
|---|---|---|---|---|---|
| **Y** Voted for (yea) | | **X** Paired against | | **C** Voted "present" to avoid possible conflict of interest | |
| **#** Paired for | | **–** Announced against | | | |
| **+** Announced for | | **P** Voted "present" | | **?** Did not vote or otherwise make a position known | |
| **N** Voted against (nay) | | | | | |

| | 31 | 90 | 145 | 204 |
|---|---|---|---|---|
| 13 Biggert | Y | Y | Y | Y |
| 14 Hastert[2] | | Y | | N |
| 15 Johnson | Y | Y | Y | N |
| 16 Manzullo | Y | Y | Y | N |
| 17 Evans | N | N | Y | Y |
| 18 LaHood | Y | Y | Y | N |
| 19 Shimkus | Y | ? | Y | N |
| **INDIANA** | | | | |
| 1 Visclosky | N | N | Y | Y |
| 2 Chocola | Y | Y | Y | N |
| 3 Souder | Y | Y | P | N |
| 4 Buyer | Y | Y | N | N |
| 5 Burton | Y | Y | N | N |
| 6 Pence | Y | Y | N | N |
| 7 Carson | N | N | Y | Y |
| 8 Hostettler | Y | ? | Y | N |
| 9 Sodrel | Y | Y | Y | N |
| **IOWA** | | | | |
| 1 Nussle | Y | Y | Y | N |
| 2 Leach | Y | Y | Y | Y |
| 3 Boswell | N | ? | Y | Y |
| 4 Latham | Y | Y | Y | N |
| 5 King | Y | Y | N | N |
| **KANSAS** | | | | |
| 1 Moran | Y | ? | Y | N |
| 2 Ryun | Y | Y | Y | N |
| 3 Moore | N | - | Y | Y |
| 4 Tiahrt | Y | Y | N | N |
| **KENTUCKY** | | | | |
| 1 Whitfield | Y | Y | Y | N |
| 2 Lewis | Y | Y | Y | N |
| 3 Northup | Y | Y | Y | N |
| 4 Davis | Y | Y | Y | N |
| 5 Rogers | Y | ? | Y | N |
| 6 Chandler | Y | Y | Y | Y |
| **LOUISIANA** | | | | |
| 1 Jindal | Y | Y | Y | N |
| 2 Jefferson | N | ? | Y | Y |
| 3 Melancon | Y | Y | Y | Y |
| 4 McCrery | Y | ? | Y | N |
| 5 Alexander | Y | Y | Y | N |
| 6 Baker | Y | Y | Y | N |
| 7 Boustany | Y | ? | Y | N |
| **MAINE** | | | | |
| 1 Allen | N | ? | Y | Y |
| 2 Michaud | N | Y | Y | Y |
| **MARYLAND** | | | | |
| 1 Gilchrest | Y | Y | Y | Y |
| 2 Ruppersberger | N | ? | Y | Y |
| 3 Cardin | N | N | Y | Y |
| 4 Wynn | N | Y | Y | Y |
| 5 Hoyer | N | N | Y | Y |
| 6 Bartlett | ? | Y | Y | N |
| 7 Cummings | N | Y | Y | Y |
| 8 Van Hollen | N | N | Y | Y |
| **MASSACHUSETTS** | | | | |
| 1 Olver | N | N | Y | Y |
| 2 Neal | N | ? | Y | Y |
| 3 McGovern | N | ? | Y | Y |
| 4 Frank | N | N | Y | Y |
| 5 Meehan | N | ? | Y | Y |
| 6 Tierney | N | ? | Y | Y |
| 7 Markey | N | ? | Y | Y |
| 8 Capuano | N | N | Y | Y |
| 9 Lynch | N | Y | Y | Y |
| 10 Delahunt | N | ? | Y | Y |
| **MICHIGAN** | | | | |
| 1 Stupak | ? | Y | Y | N |
| 2 Hoekstra | Y | ? | Y | N |
| 3 Ehlers | Y | Y | Y | N |
| 4 Camp | Y | Y | Y | N |
| 5 Kildee | N | Y | Y | Y |
| 6 Upton | Y | Y | Y | Y |
| 7 Schwarz | Y | ? | Y | N |
| 8 Rogers | Y | Y | Y | N |
| 9 Knollenberg | Y | ? | Y | N |
| 10 Miller | Y | Y | Y | N |
| 11 McCotter | Y | Y | Y | N |
| 12 Levin | N | N | Y | Y |
| 13 Kilpatrick | N | ? | Y | Y |
| 14 Conyers | N | N | Y | Y |
| 15 Dingell | N | ? | Y | Y |

| | 31 | 90 | 145 | 204 |
|---|---|---|---|---|
| **MINNESOTA** | | | | |
| 1 Gutknecht | Y | ? | Y | N |
| 2 Kline | Y | Y | Y | N |
| 3 Ramstad | Y | Y | Y | Y |
| 4 McCollum | N | ? | Y | Y |
| 5 Sabo | N | ? | Y | Y |
| 6 Kennedy | Y | Y | Y | N |
| 7 Peterson | Y | ? | Y | N |
| 8 Oberstar | N | Y | Y | Y |
| **MISSISSIPPI** | | | | |
| 1 Wicker | Y | + | ? | N |
| 2 Thompson | N | N | Y | Y |
| 3 Pickering | Y | Y | Y | N |
| 4 Taylor | Y | ? | Y | N |
| **MISSOURI** | | | | |
| 1 Clay | N | N | Y | Y |
| 2 Akin | Y | Y | Y | N |
| 3 Carnahan | N | N | Y | Y |
| 4 Skelton | Y | Y | Y | Y |
| 5 Cleaver | N | N | Y | Y |
| 6 Graves | Y | Y | Y | N |
| 7 Blunt | Y | Y | Y | N |
| 8 Emerson | Y | Y | Y | Y |
| 9 Hulshof | Y | Y | Y | N |
| **MONTANA** | | | | |
| AL Rehberg | Y | Y | Y | N |
| **NEBRASKA** | | | | |
| 1 Fortenberry | Y | Y | Y | N |
| 2 Terry | Y | Y | Y | N |
| 3 Osborne | Y | ? | Y | N |
| **NEVADA** | | | | |
| 1 Berkley | N | N | Y | Y |
| 2 Gibbons | Y | ? | Y | Y |
| 3 Porter | Y | Y | Y | Y |
| **NEW HAMPSHIRE** | | | | |
| 1 Bradley | Y | ? | Y | Y |
| 2 Bass | Y | Y | Y | Y |
| **NEW JERSEY** | | | | |
| 1 Andrews | N | ? | Y | Y |
| 2 LoBiondo | Y | Y | Y | N |
| 3 Saxton | Y | Y | Y | N |
| 4 Smith | N | Y | Y | N |
| 5 Garrett | Y | Y | Y | N |
| 6 Pallone | N | N | Y | Y |
| 7 Ferguson | + | Y | Y | N |
| 8 Pascrell | N | N | Y | Y |
| 9 Rothman | N | N | ? | Y |
| 10 Payne | N | N | Y | Y |
| 11 Frelinghuysen | Y | ? | Y | Y |
| 12 Holt | N | N | Y | Y |
| 13 Menendez | N | ? | Y | Y |
| **NEW MEXICO** | | | | |
| 1 Wilson | N | ? | Y | Y |
| 2 Pearce | Y | Y | Y | N |
| 3 Udall | N | ? | Y | Y |
| **NEW YORK** | | | | |
| 1 Bishop | N | N | Y | Y |
| 2 Israel | N | N | Y | Y |
| 3 King | Y | ? | Y | N |
| 4 McCarthy | N | ? | Y | Y |
| 5 Ackerman | N | ? | Y | Y |
| 6 Meeks | N | ? | Y | Y |
| 7 Crowley | N | ? | Y | Y |
| 8 Nadler | N | N | Y | Y |
| 9 Weiner | N | N | Y | Y |
| 10 Towns | N | ? | Y | Y |
| 11 Owens | N | ? | Y | Y |
| 12 Velázquez | N | ? | Y | Y |
| 13 Fossella | Y | Y | Y | N |
| 14 Maloney | N | ? | Y | Y |
| 15 Rangel | N | ? | Y | Y |
| 16 Serrano | N | Y | Y | Y |
| 17 Engel | N | Y | Y | Y |
| 18 Lowey | N | ? | Y | Y |
| 19 Kelly | Y | Y | Y | Y |
| 20 Sweeney | Y | ? | Y | Y |
| 21 McNulty | Y | Y | Y | Y |
| 22 Hinchey | ? | ? | Y | Y |
| 23 McHugh | Y | Y | Y | N |
| 24 Boehlert | Y | ? | Y | Y |
| 25 Walsh | Y | Y | Y | Y |
| 26 Reynolds | Y | ? | Y | N |
| 27 Higgins | N | Y | Y | Y |
| 28 Slaughter | N | ? | Y | Y |
| 29 Kuhl | Y | Y | Y | N |

| | 31 | 90 | 145 | 204 |
|---|---|---|---|---|
| **CAROLINA** | | | | |
| 1 Butterfield | Y | N | Y | Y |
| 2 Etheridge | N | Y | Y | Y |
| 3 Jones | Y | Y | Y | N |
| 4 Price | N | N | Y | Y |
| 5 Foxx | Y | Y | Y | N |
| 6 Coble | Y | + | Y | Y |
| 7 McIntyre | Y | Y | Y | N |
| 8 Hayes | Y | Y | Y | N |
| 9 Myrick | Y | Y | Y | N |
| 10 McHenry | Y | Y | Y | N |
| 11 Taylor | Y | Y | Y | N |
| 12 Watt | N | N | Y | Y |
| 13 Miller | N | N | Y | Y |
| **NORTH DAKOTA** | | | | |
| AL Pomeroy | N | Y | Y | Y |
| **OHIO** | | | | |
| 1 Chabot | Y | Y | Y | N |
| 2 Portman[3] | Y | Y | Y | |
| 3 Turner | Y | Y | Y | N |
| 4 Oxley | Y | ? | Y | N |
| 5 Gillmor | Y | Y | N | N |
| 6 Strickland | Y | N | Y | Y |
| 7 Hobson | Y | Y | Y | N |
| 8 Boehner | Y | Y | Y | N |
| 9 Kaptur | N | N | Y | Y |
| 10 Kucinich | N | ? | Y | Y |
| 11 Jones | N | ? | Y | Y |
| 12 Tiberi | Y | Y | Y | N |
| 13 Brown | N | ? | Y | Y |
| 14 LaTourette | Y | ? | Y | Y |
| 15 Pryce | Y | Y | Y | N |
| 16 Regula | Y | Y | Y | Y |
| 17 Ryan | N | ? | Y | Y |
| 18 Ney | Y | Y | Y | N |
| **OKLAHOMA** | | | | |
| 1 Sullivan | Y | Y | Y | N |
| 2 Boren | Y | Y | Y | Y |
| 3 Lucas | Y | Y | Y | N |
| 4 Cole | Y | Y | Y | N |
| 5 Istook | Y | Y | Y | N |
| **OREGON** | | | | |
| 1 Wu | N | N | Y | Y |
| 2 Walden | Y | ? | Y | Y |
| 3 Blumenauer | N | ? | Y | Y |
| 4 DeFazio | Y | ? | Y | Y |
| 5 Hooley | Y | ? | Y | Y |
| **PENNSYLVANIA** | | | | |
| 1 Brady | N | Y | Y | Y |
| 2 Fattah | N | Y | Y | Y |
| 3 English | Y | Y | Y | N |
| 4 Hart | Y | Y | Y | N |
| 5 Peterson | Y | Y | Y | N |
| 6 Gerlach | Y | ? | Y | Y |
| 7 Weldon | Y | Y | Y | N |
| 8 Fitzpatrick | Y | Y | Y | N |
| 9 Shuster | Y | ? | Y | N |
| 10 Sherwood | Y | Y | Y | N |
| 11 Kanjorski | Y | Y | Y | Y |
| 12 Murtha | N | N | Y | Y |
| 13 Schwartz | N | N | Y | Y |
| 14 Doyle | N | N | Y | Y |
| 15 Dent | Y | N | Y | Y |
| 16 Pitts | Y | Y | Y | N |
| 17 Holden | Y | Y | Y | Y |
| 18 Murphy | Y | Y | Y | N |
| 19 Platts | Y | Y | Y | Y |
| **RHODE ISLAND** | | | | |
| 1 Kennedy | N | N | Y | Y |
| 2 Langevin | N | Y | Y | Y |
| **SOUTH CAROLINA** | | | | |
| 1 Brown | Y | ? | Y | N |
| 2 Wilson | Y | Y | Y | N |
| 3 Barrett | Y | Y | Y | N |
| 4 Inglis | Y | Y | Y | N |
| 5 Spratt | N | N | Y | Y |
| 6 Clyburn | N | N | Y | Y |
| **SOUTH DAKOTA** | | | | |
| AL Herseth | Y | Y | Y | Y |
| **TENNESSEE** | | | | |
| 1 Jenkins | Y | Y | Y | N |
| 2 Duncan | Y | Y | Y | N |

| | 31 | 90 | 145 | 204 |
|---|---|---|---|---|
| 3 Wamp | Y | Y | Y | N |
| 4 Davis | Y | Y | Y | N |
| 5 Cooper | Y | ? | Y | Y |
| 6 Gordon | Y | ? | Y | Y |
| 7 Blackburn | Y | Y | N | N |
| 8 Tanner | Y | Y | Y | Y |
| 9 Ford | Y | Y | Y | Y |
| **TEXAS** | | | | |
| 1 Gohmert | Y | Y | N | N |
| 2 Poe | Y | Y | N | N |
| 3 Johnson, Sam | Y | ? | Y | N |
| 4 Hall, R. | Y | Y | Y | N |
| 5 Hensarling | Y | Y | Y | N |
| 6 Barton | Y | Y | N | Y |
| 7 Culberson | Y | Y | N | N |
| 8 Brady | Y | ? | Y | N |
| 9 Green, A. | N | Y | Y | Y |
| 10 McCaul | Y | Y | Y | N |
| 11 Conaway | Y | Y | Y | N |
| 12 Granger | Y | ? | Y | Y |
| 13 Thornberry | Y | Y | N | N |
| 14 Paul | N | Y | N | N |
| 15 Hinojosa | - | ? | Y | Y |
| 16 Reyes | N | ? | Y | Y |
| 17 Edwards | Y | Y | Y | Y |
| 18 Jackson-Lee | N | ? | Y | Y |
| 19 Neugebauer | Y | Y | Y | N |
| 20 Gonzalez | N | ? | Y | Y |
| 21 Smith | Y | Y | Y | N |
| 22 DeLay | Y | Y | Y | N |
| 23 Bonilla | Y | Y | Y | N |
| 24 Marchant | Y | Y | Y | N |
| 25 Doggett | N | ? | Y | Y |
| 26 Burgess | Y | Y | N | N |
| 27 Ortiz | N | ? | Y | Y |
| 28 Cuellar | Y | Y | Y | Y |
| 29 Green, G. | ? | ? | Y | Y |
| 30 Johnson, E.B. | N | ? | Y | Y |
| 31 Carter | + | Y | N | N |
| 32 Sessions | Y | ? | Y | N |
| **UTAH** | | | | |
| 1 Bishop | Y | ? | Y | N |
| 2 Matheson | Y | Y | Y | Y |
| 3 Cannon | Y | Y | Y | N |
| **VERMONT** | | | | |
| AL Sanders | N | ? | Y | Y |
| **VIRGINIA** | | | | |
| 1 Davis, Jo Ann | Y | Y | Y | N |
| 2 Drake | Y | Y | Y | N |
| 3 Scott | N | N | Y | Y |
| 4 Forbes | Y | Y | Y | N |
| 5 Goode | Y | Y | Y | N |
| 6 Goodlatte | Y | Y | Y | N |
| 7 Cantor | Y | Y | Y | N |
| 8 Moran | N | N | Y | Y |
| 9 Boucher | Y | ? | Y | Y |
| 10 Wolf | Y | ? | Y | N |
| 11 Davis, T. | Y | Y | Y | Y |
| **WASHINGTON** | | | | |
| 1 Inslee | N | ? | Y | Y |
| 2 Larsen | N | ? | Y | Y |
| 3 Baird | N | Y | Y | Y |
| 4 Hastings | Y | Y | Y | ? |
| 5 McMorris | Y | ? | Y | Y |
| 6 Dicks | N | N | Y | Y |
| 7 McDermott | N | N | Y | Y |
| 8 Reichert | Y | Y | Y | Y |
| 9 Smith | N | ? | Y | Y |
| **WEST VIRGINIA** | | | | |
| 1 Mollohan | N | Y | Y | N |
| 2 Capito | Y | Y | Y | Y |
| 3 Rahall | N | ? | Y | N |
| **WISCONSIN** | | | | |
| 1 Ryan | Y | Y | Y | N |
| 2 Baldwin | N | N | Y | Y |
| 3 Kind | N | ? | Y | Y |
| 4 Moore | N | ? | Y | Y |
| 5 Sensenbrenner | Y | Y | Y | N |
| 6 Petri | Y | Y | Y | N |
| 7 Obey | N | Y | Y | Y |
| 8 Green | Y | Y | Y | N |
| **WYOMING** | | | | |
| AL Cubin | Y | ? | N | N |

# HOUSE 258, 374, 443, 445

**258.** HR 2862. Fiscal 2006 Commerce-Justice-Science Appropriations/ **Surveillance of Library Records.** Sanders, I-Vt., amendment that would prohibit the use of funds in the bill to make an application under the Foreign Intelligence Surveillance Act to acquire library circulation records, library patron lists, bookseller sales records or bookseller customer lists. Adopted 238-187: R 38-186; D 199-1 (ND 150-0, SD 49-1); I 1-0. A "nay" was a vote in support of the president's position. June 15, 2005. *(Story, p. C-15)*

**374.** HR 3100. **Arms Sales to China/Passage.** Hyde, R-Ill., motion to suspend the rules and pass the bill that would require the president to report to Congress 180 days after the bill's enactment, and yearly thereafter, identifying European or other entities that have exported any arms or dual-use technology to China for military use since Jan. 1, 2005. Motion rejected 215-203: R 118-106; D 96-97 (ND 70-73, SD 26-24); I 1-0. A two-thirds majority of those present and voting (279 in this case) is required for passage under suspension of the rules. July 14, 2005. *(Story, p. C-15)*

**443.** HR 3045. **Central American Free-Trade Agreement/Passage.** Passage of the bill that would implement a free-trade agreement between the United States and Costa Rica, El Salvador, Guatemala, Honduras and Nicaragua and a separate pact with the Dominican Republic. It also would eliminate customs duties on all originating goods traded among the participating nations within 10 days. Passed 217-215: R 202-27; D 15-187 (ND 7-144, SD 8-43); I 0-1. A "yea" was a vote in support of the president's position. July 28, 2005 (in the session that began and the Congressional Record dated July 27, 2005). *(Story, p. C-16)*

**445.** HR 6. **Energy Policy/Conference Report.** Adoption of the conference report on the bill that would overhaul the nation's energy policy and provide for $14.6 billion in energy-related tax incentives. It would allow lawsuits involving the gasoline additive methyl tertiary butyl ether to be moved to a federal district court and require refiners to annually use 7.5 billion gallons of renewable fuels by 2012. The measure would grant the Federal Energy Regulatory Commission (FERC) jurisdiction over reliability standards for electricity transmission networks and extend daylight-saving time by one month. It would allow FERC to approve the construction, expansion or operation of any facility that imports or processes natural gas, including liquefied natural gas. Adopted (thus sent to the Senate) 275-156: R 200-31; D 75-124 (ND 41-107, SD 34-17); I 0-1. A "yea" was a vote in support of the president's position. July 28, 2005. *(Story, p. C-16)*

\* The Speaker votes only at his discretion, usually to break a tie or to emphasize the importance of a matter.

ND Northern Democrats, SD Southern Democrats
Southern states: Ala., Ark., Fla., Ga., Ky., La., Miss., N.C., Okla., S.C., Tenn., Texas, Va.

| | 258 | 374 | 443 | 445 |
|---|---|---|---|---|
| **ALABAMA** | | | | |
| 1 Bonner | N | N | Y | N |
| 2 Everett | N | N | Y | Y |
| 3 Rogers | N | Y | Y | Y |
| 4 Aderholt | N | Y | Y | Y |
| 5 Cramer | Y | N | N | Y |
| 6 Bachus | N | Y | Y | Y |
| 7 Davis | Y | Y | N | Y |
| **ALASKA** | | | | |
| AL Young | Y | N | Y | Y |
| **ARIZONA** | | | | |
| 1 Renzi | N | N | Y | Y |
| 2 Franks | N | Y | Y | Y |
| 3 Shadegg | N | Y | Y | Y |
| 4 Pastor | Y | N | N | N |
| 5 Hayworth | N | Y | Y | Y |
| 6 Flake | Y | N | Y | N |
| 7 Grijalva | Y | Y | N | Y |
| 8 Kolbe | N | N | Y | Y |
| **ARKANSAS** | | | | |
| 1 Berry | Y | N | N | Y |
| 2 Snyder | Y | N | Y | Y |
| 3 Boozman | Y | Y | Y | Y |
| 4 Ross | Y | Y | N | Y |
| **CALIFORNIA** | | | | |
| 1 Thompson | Y | N | N | N |
| 2 Herger | N | Y | Y | Y |
| 3 Lungren | N | Y | Y | Y |
| 4 Doolittle | N | Y | Y | Y |
| 5 Matsui, D. | Y | Y | N | N |
| 6 Woolsey | Y | N | N | N |
| 7 Miller, George | Y | N | N | N |
| 8 Pelosi | Y | N | N | N |
| 9 Lee | Y | N | N | N |
| 10 Tauscher | Y | N | N | N |
| 11 Pombo | N | Y | Y | Y |
| 12 Lantos | Y | Y | N | N |
| 13 Stark | Y | N | N | N |
| 14 Eshoo | Y | N | N | N |
| 15 Honda | Y | N | N | N |
| 16 Lofgren | Y | N | N | N |
| 17 Farr | Y | Y | N | N |
| 18 Cardoza | Y | Y | N | Y |
| 19 Radanovich | N | Y | Y | Y |
| 20 Costa | Y | Y | N | Y |
| 21 Nunes | N | N | Y | Y |
| 22 Thomas | N | N | Y | Y |
| 23 Capps | Y | + | N | N |
| 24 Gallegly | N | + | Y | Y |
| 25 McKeon | N | N | Y | Y |
| 26 Dreier | N | N | Y | Y |
| 27 Sherman | Y | Y | N | N |
| 28 Berman | Y | N | N | N |
| 29 Schiff | Y | Y | N | N |
| 30 Waxman | Y | N | N | N |
| 31 Becerra | Y | N | N | N |
| 32 Solis | Y | N | N | N |
| 33 Watson | Y | Y | N | N |
| 34 Roybal-Allard | Y | Y | N | N |
| 35 Waters | Y | N | N | N |
| 36 Harman | Y | N | N | N |
| 37 Millender-McD. | Y | N | N | N |
| 38 Napolitano | Y | N | N | N |
| 39 Sánchez, Linda | Y | Y | N | N |
| 40 Royce | N | Y | Y | N |
| 41 Lewis | N | N | Y | Y |
| 42 Miller, Gary | N | Y | Y | Y |
| 43 Baca | Y | N | N | Y |
| 44 Calvert | N | N | Y | Y |
| 45 Bono | ? | Y | Y | Y |
| 46 Rohrabacher | N | Y | Y | N |
| 47 Sanchez, Loretta | Y | N | N | Y |
| 48 Cox | N | Y | Y | Y |
| 49 Issa | N | N | Y | Y |

| | 258 | 374 | 443 | 445 |
|---|---|---|---|---|
| 50 Cunningham | N | ? | Y | Y |
| 51 Filner | Y | Y | N | N |
| 52 Hunter | N | Y | N | Y |
| 53 Davis | Y | N | N | N |
| **COLORADO** | | | | |
| 1 DeGette | Y | Y | N | N |
| 2 Udall | Y | N | N | N |
| 3 Salazar | Y | Y | N | Y |
| 4 Musgrave | Y | Y | Y | Y |
| 5 Hefley | N | Y | Y | Y |
| 6 Tancredo | N | N | N | Y |
| 7 Beauprez | N | N | Y | Y |
| **CONNECTICUT** | | | | |
| 1 Larson | Y | Y | N | N |
| 2 Simmons | N | ? | N | Y |
| 3 DeLauro | Y | Y | N | N |
| 4 Shays | N | N | Y | N |
| 5 Johnson | N | N | Y | Y |
| **DELAWARE** | | | | |
| AL Castle | Y | Y | Y | N |
| **FLORIDA** | | | | |
| 1 Miller | Y | + | Y | N |
| 2 Boyd | Y | Y | N | N |
| 3 Brown | Y | Y | N | N |
| 4 Crenshaw | N | N | Y | N |
| 5 Brown-Waite | N | Y | Y | N |
| 6 Stearns | N | Y | Y | Y |
| 7 Mica | N | N | Y | Y |
| 8 Keller | N | Y | Y | N |
| 9 Bilirakis | N | Y | Y | N |
| 10 Young | N | ? | Y | N |
| 11 Davis | Y | Y | N | N |
| 12 Putnam | N | Y | Y | N |
| 13 Harris | Y | N | N | N |
| 14 Mack | N | Y | N | N |
| 15 Weldon | N | Y | Y | N |
| 16 Foley | N | Y | Y | N |
| 17 Meek | Y | N | N | N |
| 18 Ros-Lehtinen | N | Y | Y | N |
| 19 Wexler | Y | N | N | N |
| 20 Wasserman-Schultz | Y | Y | N | N |
| 21 Diaz-Balart, L. | N | Y | Y | N |
| 22 Shaw | N | Y | Y | N |
| 23 Hastings | Y | N | N | N |
| 24 Feeney | N | Y | Y | N |
| 25 Diaz-Balart, M. | N | Y | Y | N |
| **GEORGIA** | | | | |
| 1 Kingston | Y | N | Y | Y |
| 2 Bishop | Y | Y | N | Y |
| 3 Marshall | Y | N | N | Y |
| 4 McKinney | Y | N | N | N |
| 5 Lewis | Y | N | N | N |
| 6 Price | N | N | Y | Y |
| 7 Linder | N | Y | Y | Y |
| 8 Westmoreland | N | N | Y | Y |
| 9 Norwood | N | Y | Y | Y |
| 10 Deal | N | Y | Y | Y |
| 11 Gingrey | N | Y | Y | Y |
| 12 Barrow | Y | Y | N | Y |
| 13 Scott | Y | Y | N | Y |
| **HAWAII** | | | | |
| 1 Abercrombie | Y | Y | N | Y |
| 2 Case | Y | Y | N | N |
| **IDAHO** | | | | |
| 1 Otter | Y | N | N | Y |
| 2 Simpson | N | N | N | Y |
| **ILLINOIS** | | | | |
| 1 Rush | Y | N | N | Y |
| 2 Jackson | Y | N | N | N |
| 3 Lipinski | Y | N | N | Y |
| 4 Gutierrez | Y | + | N | N |
| 5 Emanuel | Y | N | N | N |
| 6 Hyde | - | Y | Y | Y |
| 7 Davis | Y | N | N | N |
| 8 Bean | Y | N | Y | Y |
| 9 Schakowsky | Y | N | N | ? |
| 10 Kirk | Y | N | Y | Y |
| 11 Weller | N | N | Y | Y |
| 12 Costello | Y | N | N | Y |

**KEY**    Republicans    Democrats    *Independents*

| | | | |
|---|---|---|---|
| Y | Voted for (yea) | X | Paired against |
| # | Paired for | - | Announced against |
| + | Announced for | P | Voted "present" |
| N | Voted against (nay) | | |
| C | Voted "present" to avoid possible conflict of interest | | |
| ? | Did not vote or otherwise make a position known | | |

| | 258 | 374 | 443 | 445 |
|---|---|---|---|---|
| 13 Biggert | N | N | Y | Y |
| 14 Hastert* | | | Y | Y |
| 15 Johnson | Y | Y | Y | Y |
| 16 Manzullo | Y | N | Y | Y |
| 17 Evans | Y | Y | N | Y |
| 18 LaHood | Y | N | Y | Y |
| 19 Shimkus | N | N | Y | Y |
| **INDIANA** | | | | |
| 1 Visclosky | Y | N | N | Y |
| 2 Chocola | N | Y | Y | Y |
| 3 Souder | N | Y | Y | Y |
| 4 Buyer | N | Y | Y | Y |
| 5 Burton | N | Y | Y | Y |
| 6 Pence | N | Y | Y | Y |
| 7 Carson | Y | ? | N | Y |
| 8 Hostettler | N | Y | N | Y |
| 9 Sodrel | N | N | Y | Y |
| **IOWA** | | | | |
| 1 Nussle | N | N | Y | Y |
| 2 Leach | Y | N | Y | Y |
| 3 Boswell | Y | N | N | Y |
| 4 Latham | N | N | Y | Y |
| 5 King | N | N | Y | Y |
| **KANSAS** | | | | |
| 1 Moran | Y | N | Y | Y |
| 2 Ryun | N | N | Y | Y |
| 3 Moore | Y | N | Y | Y |
| 4 Tiahrt | N | N | Y | Y |
| **KENTUCKY** | | | | |
| 1 Whitfield | Y | N | Y | Y |
| 2 Lewis | N | N | Y | Y |
| 3 Northup | N | Y | Y | Y |
| 4 Davis | N | N | Y | Y |
| 5 Rogers | N | Y | Y | Y |
| 6 Chandler | Y | Y | N | N |
| **LOUISIANA** | | | | |
| 1 Jindal | N | Y | N | Y |
| 2 Jefferson | Y | N | Y | Y |
| 3 Melancon | Y | Y | N | Y |
| 4 McCrery | N | N | Y | Y |
| 5 Alexander | N | Y | Y | Y |
| 6 Baker | N | N | Y | Y |
| 7 Boustany | N | N | N | Y |
| **MAINE** | | | | |
| 1 Allen | Y | Y | N | N |
| 2 Michaud | Y | Y | N | N |
| **MARYLAND** | | | | |
| 1 Gilchrest | N | N | Y | Y |
| 2 Ruppersberger | Y | N | N | Y |
| 3 Cardin | Y | ? | N | N |
| 4 Wynn | Y | N | N | Y |
| 5 Hoyer | Y | N | N | Y |
| 6 Bartlett | Y | N | Y | N |
| 7 Cummings | Y | Y | N | N |
| 8 Van Hollen | Y | N | N | N |
| **MASSACHUSETTS** | | | | |
| 1 Olver | Y | N | N | N |
| 2 Neal | Y | Y | N | N |
| 3 McGovern | Y | N | N | N |
| 4 Frank | Y | N | N | N |
| 5 Meehan | Y | N | N | N |
| 6 Tierney | Y | Y | N | N |
| 7 Markey | Y | N | N | N |
| 8 Capuano | Y | N | N | N |
| 9 Lynch | Y | N | N | N |
| 10 Delahunt | Y | N | N | N |
| **MICHIGAN** | | | | |
| 1 Stupak | Y | Y | N | Y |
| 2 Hoekstra | N | N | Y | Y |
| 3 Ehlers | Y | N | Y | Y |
| 4 Camp | N | Y | Y | Y |
| 5 Kildee | Y | Y | N | N |
| 6 Upton | N | N | Y | Y |
| 7 Schwarz | Y | Y | Y | Y |
| 8 Rogers | N | Y | Y | Y |
| 9 Knollenberg | N | Y | Y | Y |
| 10 Miller | N | Y | N | Y |
| 11 McCotter | N | Y | Y | Y |
| 12 Levin | Y | N | Y | N |
| 13 Kilpatrick | Y | + | N | N |
| 14 Conyers | Y | Y | N | N |
| 15 Dingell | Y | Y | N | N |

| | 258 | 374 | 443 | 445 |
|---|---|---|---|---|
| **MINNESOTA** | | | | |
| 1 Gutknecht | N | N | N | Y |
| 2 Kline | N | N | Y | Y |
| 3 Ramstad | N | Y | Y | Y |
| 4 McCollum | Y | N | N | N |
| 5 Sabo | Y | N | N | N |
| 6 Kennedy | N | N | Y | Y |
| 7 Peterson | Y | Y | N | Y |
| 8 Oberstar | + | ? | N | Y |
| **MISSISSIPPI** | | | | |
| 1 Wicker | N | Y | Y | Y |
| 2 Thompson | Y | Y | N | Y |
| 3 Pickering | N | Y | Y | Y |
| 4 Taylor | Y | Y | N | N |
| **MISSOURI** | | | | |
| 1 Clay | Y | N | N | Y |
| 2 Akin | N | Y | Y | Y |
| 3 Carnahan | Y | Y | N | N |
| 4 Skelton | Y | N | Y | Y |
| 5 Cleaver | Y | Y | N | N |
| 6 Graves | N | Y | Y | Y |
| 7 Blunt | N | Y | Y | Y |
| 8 Emerson | Y | Y | Y | Y |
| 9 Hulshof | N | N | Y | Y |
| **MONTANA** | | | | |
| AL Rehberg | Y | N | N | Y |
| **NEBRASKA** | | | | |
| 1 Fortenberry | N | Y | Y | Y |
| 2 Terry | N | Y | Y | Y |
| 3 Osborne | N | Y | Y | Y |
| **NEVADA** | | | | |
| 1 Berkley | Y | Y | N | N |
| 2 Gibbons | N | N | Y | Y |
| 3 Porter | Y | Y | Y | Y |
| **NEW HAMPSHIRE** | | | | |
| 1 Bradley | N | Y | Y | N |
| 2 Bass | N | N | Y | Y |
| **NEW JERSEY** | | | | |
| 1 Andrews | Y | Y | N | N |
| 2 LoBiondo | N | N | N | N |
| 3 Saxton | N | N | Y | N |
| 4 Smith | N | Y | N | N |
| 5 Garrett | - | N | N | N |
| 6 Pallone | Y | N | N | N |
| 7 Ferguson | N | Y | N | Y |
| 8 Pascrell | Y | Y | N | N |
| 9 Rothman | Y | Y | N | N |
| 10 Payne | Y | N | N | ? |
| 11 Frelinghuysen | N | N | Y | Y |
| 12 Holt | Y | N | N | N |
| 13 Menendez | Y | N | N | N |
| **NEW MEXICO** | | | | |
| 1 Wilson | N | N | Y | Y |
| 2 Pearce | N | Y | Y | Y |
| 3 Udall | Y | N | N | Y |
| **NEW YORK** | | | | |
| 1 Bishop | Y | Y | N | N |
| 2 Israel | Y | N | N | N |
| 3 King | N | Y | Y | Y |
| 4 McCarthy | Y | N | N | N |
| 5 Ackerman | Y | N | N | N |
| 6 Meeks | Y | N | Y | N |
| 7 Crowley | Y | N | N | N |
| 8 Nadler | Y | N | N | N |
| 9 Weiner | Y | ? | N | N |
| 10 Towns | Y | Y | Y | N |
| 11 Owens | Y | N | Y | N |
| 12 Velázquez | Y | N | N | N |
| 13 Fossella | N | N | Y | Y |
| 14 Maloney | Y | Y | N | N |
| 15 Rangel | Y | N | N | N |
| 16 Serrano | Y | N | N | N |
| 17 Engel | Y | Y | N | N |
| 18 Lowey | Y | N | N | N |
| 19 Kelly | N | Y | Y | Y |
| 20 Sweeney | N | N | Y | Y |
| 21 McNulty | Y | Y | N | N |
| 22 Hinchey | Y | N | N | N |
| 23 McHugh | N | N | Y | Y |
| 24 Boehlert | Y | N | Y | Y |
| 25 Walsh | N | Y | Y | Y |
| 26 Reynolds | N | Y | Y | Y |
| 27 Higgins | Y | Y | N | N |
| 28 Slaughter | Y | N | N | N |
| 29 Kuhl | N | Y | N | Y |

| | 258 | 374 | 443 | 445 |
|---|---|---|---|---|
| **NORTH CAROLINA** | | | | |
| 1 Butterfield | Y | Y | N | Y |
| 2 Etheridge | Y | N | Y | Y |
| 3 Jones | Y | Y | N | N |
| 4 Price | Y | N | N | N |
| 5 Foxx | N | Y | N | Y |
| 6 Coble | N | N | N | Y |
| 7 McIntyre | Y | ? | N | Y |
| 8 Hayes | N | Y | Y | Y |
| 9 Myrick | N | Y | Y | Y |
| 10 McHenry | N | Y | N | Y |
| 11 Taylor | Y | Y | - | Y |
| 12 Watt | Y | N | N | N |
| 13 Miller | Y | N | N | N |
| **NORTH DAKOTA** | | | | |
| AL Pomeroy | Y | N | N | Y |
| **OHIO** | | | | |
| 1 Chabot | N | Y | Y | Y |
| 2 Vacant | | | | |
| 3 Turner | N | N | Y | Y |
| 4 Oxley | N | Y | Y | Y |
| 5 Gillmor | Y | Y | Y | Y |
| 6 Strickland | Y | Y | N | Y |
| 7 Hobson | N | N | Y | Y |
| 8 Boehner | N | Y | N | Y |
| 9 Kaptur | Y | Y | N | N |
| 10 Kucinich | Y | Y | N | N |
| 11 Jones | Y | N | N | N |
| 12 Tiberi | N | N | Y | Y |
| 13 Brown | Y | Y | N | N |
| 14 LaTourette | Y | N | Y | Y |
| 15 Pryce | N | N | Y | Y |
| 16 Regula | N | N | Y | Y |
| 17 Ryan | Y | Y | N | Y |
| 18 Ney | Y | Y | N | Y |
| **OKLAHOMA** | | | | |
| 1 Sullivan | ? | N | Y | Y |
| 2 Boren | N | N | N | Y |
| 3 Lucas | N | Y | Y | Y |
| 4 Cole | N | Y | Y | Y |
| 5 Istook | N | Y | Y | Y |
| **OREGON** | | | | |
| 1 Wu | Y | Y | N | N |
| 2 Walden | Y | Y | Y | Y |
| 3 Blumenauer | Y | N | N | N |
| 4 DeFazio | Y | N | N | N |
| 5 Hooley | Y | N | N | N |
| **PENNSYLVANIA** | | | | |
| 1 Brady | Y | Y | N | ? |
| 2 Fattah | Y | Y | N | N |
| 3 English | N | N | Y | Y |
| 4 Hart | N | N | Y | Y |
| 5 Peterson | N | Y | Y | Y |
| 6 Gerlach | N | N | Y | Y |
| 7 Weldon | ? | Y | Y | Y |
| 8 Fitzpatrick | Y | Y | Y | N |
| 9 Shuster | N | N | Y | Y |
| 10 Sherwood | N | N | Y | Y |
| 11 Kanjorski | Y | Y | N | Y |
| 12 Murtha | Y | N | N | Y |
| 13 Schwartz | Y | Y | N | N |
| 14 Doyle | Y | Y | N | N |
| 15 Dent | N | Y | Y | Y |
| 16 Pitts | N | Y | Y | Y |
| 17 Holden | Y | Y | N | N |
| 18 Murphy | N | N | Y | Y |
| 19 Platts | N | Y | Y | Y |
| **RHODE ISLAND** | | | | |
| 1 Kennedy | Y | Y | N | N |
| 2 Langevin | Y | Y | N | N |
| **SOUTH CAROLINA** | | | | |
| 1 Brown | N | N | Y | Y |
| 2 Wilson | N | Y | Y | Y |
| 3 Barrett | N | Y | Y | Y |
| 4 Inglis | N | Y | Y | Y |
| 5 Spratt | Y | Y | N | Y |
| 6 Clyburn | Y | N | N | Y |
| **SOUTH DAKOTA** | | | | |
| AL Herseth | Y | N | N | Y |
| **TENNESSEE** | | | | |
| 1 Jenkins | N | N | Y | Y |
| 2 Duncan | Y | Y | Y | Y |

| | 258 | 374 | 443 | 445 |
|---|---|---|---|---|
| 3 Wamp | N | Y | Y | Y |
| 4 Davis | Y | Y | N | Y |
| 5 Cooper | Y | Y | Y | Y |
| 6 Gordon | Y | N | N | Y |
| 7 Blackburn | N | Y | Y | Y |
| 8 Tanner | Y | Y | Y | Y |
| 9 Ford | Y | Y | N | Y |
| **TEXAS** | | | | |
| 1 Gohmert | N | N | Y | Y |
| 2 Poe | Y | N | Y | Y |
| 3 Johnson, Sam | N | Y | Y | Y |
| 4 Hall, R. | N | N | Y | Y |
| 5 Hensarling | N | N | Y | Y |
| 6 Barton | N | Y | Y | Y |
| 7 Culberson | N | Y | Y | Y |
| 8 Brady | N | Y | Y | Y |
| 9 Green, A. | Y | Y | N | Y |
| 10 McCaul | N | Y | Y | Y |
| 11 Conaway | N | N | Y | Y |
| 12 Granger | N | Y | Y | Y |
| 13 Thornberry | N | N | Y | Y |
| 14 Paul | Y | N | N | N |
| 15 Hinojosa | Y | Y | Y | Y |
| 16 Reyes | Y | Y | N | Y |
| 17 Edwards | Y | Y | N | Y |
| 18 Jackson-Lee | Y | Y | N | Y |
| 19 Neugebauer | N | N | Y | Y |
| 20 Gonzalez | Y | N | N | Y |
| 21 Smith | N | N | Y | Y |
| 22 DeLay | N | Y | Y | Y |
| 23 Bonilla | N | N | Y | Y |
| 24 Marchant | N | N | Y | Y |
| 25 Doggett | Y | Y | N | N |
| 26 Burgess | Y | N | Y | Y |
| 27 Ortiz | Y | N | Y | Y |
| 28 Cuellar | ? | Y | N | Y |
| 29 Green, G. | Y | Y | N | Y |
| 30 Johnson, E.B. | Y | Y | N | Y |
| 31 Carter | N | N | Y | Y |
| 32 Sessions | ? | N | Y | Y |
| **UTAH** | | | | |
| 1 Bishop | Y | Y | Y | Y |
| 2 Matheson | Y | Y | Y | Y |
| 3 Cannon | N | N | Y | Y |
| **VERMONT** | | | | |
| AL Sanders | Y | Y | N | N |
| **VIRGINIA** | | | | |
| 1 Davis, Jo Ann | N | Y | - | Y |
| 2 Drake | N | Y | Y | Y |
| 3 Scott | Y | N | N | Y |
| 4 Forbes | N | Y | Y | Y |
| 5 Goode | N | Y | Y | Y |
| 6 Goodlatte | N | N | Y | Y |
| 7 Cantor | N | Y | Y | Y |
| 8 Moran | Y | N | Y | N |
| 9 Boucher | Y | N | N | Y |
| 10 Wolf | N | Y | Y | Y |
| 11 Davis, T. | N | N | Y | Y |
| **WASHINGTON** | | | | |
| 1 Inslee | Y | N | N | N |
| 2 Larsen | Y | N | N | N |
| 3 Baird | Y | N | N | N |
| 4 Hastings | N | Y | Y | Y |
| 5 McMorris | N | Y | Y | Y |
| 6 Dicks | Y | N | N | N |
| 7 McDermott | Y | N | N | N |
| 8 Reichert | N | N | Y | Y |
| 9 Smith | Y | N | N | N |
| **WEST VIRGINIA** | | | | |
| 1 Mollohan | Y | Y | N | Y |
| 2 Capito | N | Y | Y | Y |
| 3 Rahall | Y | N | N | Y |
| **WISCONSIN** | | | | |
| 1 Ryan | N | N | Y | Y |
| 2 Baldwin | Y | Y | N | N |
| 3 Kind | Y | N | N | N |
| 4 Moore | Y | N | N | N |
| 5 Sensenbrenner | N | Y | Y | Y |
| 6 Petri | Y | ? | N | Y |
| 7 Obey | Y | ? | N | N |
| 8 Green | N | Y | Y | Y |
| **WYOMING** | | | | |
| AL Cubin | Y | ? | N | Y |

# HOUSE 453, 506, 630, 670

## 453. HR 3. Surface Transportation Reauthorization/Conference Report.
Adoption of the conference report on the bill that would bring total authorization for federal highway, mass transit, safety and research programs, including fiscal 2004 funding, to $286.5 billion through 2009. The bill would increase the rate of return to states on their Highway Trust Fund contributions to 92 percent by fiscal 2008. It would make the Transportation Department the lead agency in the environmental review process for transportation projects. Adopted (thus sent to the Senate) 412-8: R 217-8; D 194-0 (ND 144-0, SD 50-0); I 1-0. July 29, 2005. *(Story, p. C-17)*

## 506. HR 3824. Endangered Species Act Overhaul/Passage.
Passage of the bill that would overhaul and reauthorize the Endangered Species Act through 2010. It would replace the critical habitat designation with expanded authority to develop recovery plans for species. The Interior Department would be required to reimburse landowners who are not allowed to develop their land because of protections for endangered species. It also would authorize grants for private landowners to protect endangered species. Passed 229-193: R 193-34; D 36-158 (ND 15-129, SD 21-29); I 0-1. Sept. 29, 2005. *(Story, p. C-17)*

## 630. HR 2863. Fiscal 2006 Defense Appropriations/Motion to Instruct.
Murtha, D-Pa., motion to instruct House conferees to include Senate-passed language that would establish the U.S. Army Field Manual on Intelligence Interrogation as the uniform standard for interrogating persons detained by the Department of Defense, and prohibit cruel, inhuman or degrading treatment of any prisoner detained by the U.S. government. Motion agreed to 308-122: R 107-121; D 200-1 (ND 150-0, SD 50-1); I 1-0. A "nay" was a vote in support of the president's position. Dec. 14, 2005. *(Story, p. C-18)*

## 670. S 1932. Budget Reconciliation/Conference Report.
Adoption of the conference report on the bill that would make changes to programs for a net savings of $38.8 billion over five years. The total includes savings of roughly $12.7 billion from the student loan program, $1.5 billion from aid to states to enforce child support payments and $4.8 billion from Medicaid. The bill would provide $2.1 billion in hurricane assistance, authorize an additional $1 billion for low-income energy assistance and provide $7.3 billion to avoid a scheduled Medicare reimbursement cut to physicians. Adopted (thus sent to the Senate) 212-206: R 212-9; D 0-196 (ND 0-146, SD 0-50); I 0-1. A "yea" was a vote in support of the president's position. Dec. 19, 2005 (in the session that began and the Congressional Record dated Dec. 18, 2005). *(Story, p. C-18)*

[1] Rep. John Campbell, R-Calif., was sworn in Dec. 7, 2005, to replace Republican Christopher Cox, who resigned effective Aug. 2. The first vote for which Campbell was eligible was vote 619. The last vote for which Cox was eligible was vote 453, on which he voted "yea."

[2] Rep. Randy "Duke" Cunningham, R-Calif., resigned effective Dec. 1, 2005. The last vote for which he was eligible was vote 608.

[3] The Speaker votes only at his discretion, usually to break a tie or to emphasize the importance of a matter.

[4] Rep. Jean Schmidt, R-Ohio, was sworn in Sept. 6, 2005, to replace Republican Rob Portman, who resigned effective April 29. The first vote for which Schmidt was eligible was vote 454.

ND Northern Democrats, SD Southern Democrats
Southern states: Ala., Ark., Fla., Ga., Ky., La., Miss., N.C., Okla., S.C., Tenn., Texas, Va.

| | 453 | 506 | 630 | 670 |
|---|---|---|---|---|
| **ALABAMA** | | | | |
| 1 Bonner | Y | Y | N | Y |
| 2 Everett | Y | Y | N | Y |
| 3 Rogers | Y | Y | N | Y |
| 4 Aderholt | Y | Y | N | Y |
| 5 Cramer | Y | Y | Y | N |
| 6 Bachus | Y | Y | Y | Y |
| 7 Davis | Y | Y | Y | N |
| **ALASKA** | | | | |
| AL Young | Y | Y | N | Y |
| **ARIZONA** | | | | |
| 1 Renzi | Y | Y | N | Y |
| 2 Franks | Y | Y | N | Y |
| 3 Shadegg | N | Y | N | Y |
| 4 Pastor | Y | N | Y | N |
| 5 Hayworth | Y | Y | N | Y |
| 6 Flake | N | Y | Y | Y |
| 7 Grijalva | Y | N | Y | N |
| 8 Kolbe | Y | Y | Y | ? |
| **ARKANSAS** | | | | |
| 1 Berry | Y | Y | Y | N |
| 2 Snyder | Y | N | Y | N |
| 3 Boozman | Y | Y | Y | Y |
| 4 Ross | Y | Y | Y | N |
| **CALIFORNIA** | | | | |
| 1 Thompson | Y | N | Y | N |
| 2 Herger | Y | Y | N | Y |
| 3 Lungren | Y | Y | N | Y |
| 4 Doolittle | Y | Y | N | Y |
| 5 Matsui, D. | Y | N | Y | N |
| 6 Woolsey | Y | N | Y | N |
| 7 Miller, George | ? | N | Y | N |
| 8 Pelosi | Y | N | Y | N |
| 9 Lee | Y | – | Y | N |
| 10 Tauscher | Y | N | Y | N |
| 11 Pombo | + | Y | Y | Y |
| 12 Lantos | Y | N | Y | N |
| 13 Stark | ? | N | Y | N |
| 14 Eshoo | Y | N | Y | N |
| 15 Honda | Y | N | Y | N |
| 16 Lofgren | Y | N | Y | N |
| 17 Farr | Y | N | Y | N |
| 18 Cardoza | Y | Y | Y | N |
| 19 Radanovich | Y | Y | N | ? |
| 20 Costa | Y | Y | + | N |
| 21 Nunes | Y | Y | N | Y |
| 22 Thomas | Y | Y | Y | Y |
| 23 Capps | + | N | Y | N |
| 24 Gallegly | Y | Y | N | Y |
| 25 McKeon | Y | Y | N | Y |
| 26 Dreier | Y | Y | N | Y |
| 27 Sherman | Y | N | Y | N |
| 28 Berman | Y | N | Y | N |
| 29 Schiff | Y | N | Y | N |
| 30 Waxman | Y | N | Y | N |
| 31 Becerra | Y | N | Y | N |
| 32 Solis | Y | N | Y | N |
| 33 Watson | Y | N | Y | N |
| 34 Roybal-Allard | Y | N | Y | ? |
| 35 Waters | Y | N | Y | N |
| 36 Harman | Y | – | Y | ? |
| 37 Millender-McD. | Y | N | Y | N |
| 38 Napolitano | Y | N | Y | N |
| 39 Sánchez, Linda | Y | N | Y | N |
| 40 Royce | N | Y | N | Y |
| 41 Lewis | Y | Y | N | Y |
| 42 Miller, Gary | Y | Y | N | ? |
| 43 Baca | Y | Y | Y | ? |
| 44 Calvert | Y | Y | N | Y |
| 45 Bono | Y | Y | N | Y |
| 46 Rohrabacher | Y | Y | N | Y |
| 47 Sanchez, Loretta | Y | N | Y | N |
| 48 Campbell[1] | | | N | Y |
| 49 Issa | Y | Y | Y | Y |

| | 453 | 506 | 630 | 670 |
|---|---|---|---|---|
| 50 Cunningham[2] | Y | Y | | |
| 51 Filner | Y | N | Y | N |
| 52 Hunter | Y | Y | N | Y |
| 53 Davis | Y | N | Y | N |
| **COLORADO** | | | | |
| 1 DeGette | Y | N | Y | N |
| 2 Udall | Y | N | Y | N |
| 3 Salazar | Y | Y | Y | N |
| 4 Musgrave | Y | Y | N | Y |
| 5 Hefley | Y | Y | N | Y |
| 6 Tancredo | Y | Y | N | Y |
| 7 Beauprez | Y | Y | Y | Y |
| **CONNECTICUT** | | | | |
| 1 Larson | Y | N | Y | N |
| 2 Simmons | Y | N | Y | Y |
| 3 DeLauro | Y | N | Y | N |
| 4 Shays | Y | N | Y | Y |
| 5 Johnson | Y | N | Y | Y |
| **DELAWARE** | | | | |
| AL Castle | Y | N | Y | Y |
| **FLORIDA** | | | | |
| 1 Miller | Y | Y | N | Y |
| 2 Boyd | Y | Y | Y | N |
| 3 Brown | Y | N | Y | N |
| 4 Crenshaw | Y | Y | N | Y |
| 5 Brown-Waite | Y | Y | Y | Y |
| 6 Stearns | Y | Y | Y | Y |
| 7 Mica | ? | Y | N | Y |
| 8 Keller | Y | Y | N | Y |
| 9 Bilirakis | Y | Y | N | Y |
| 10 Young | Y | Y | N | Y |
| 11 Davis | Y | ? | Y | N |
| 12 Putnam | Y | Y | N | Y |
| 13 Harris | Y | Y | N | Y |
| 14 Mack | Y | Y | Y | Y |
| 15 Weldon | Y | Y | N | Y |
| 16 Foley | Y | N | Y | Y |
| 17 Meek | Y | N | Y | N |
| 18 Ros-Lehtinen | Y | Y | N | Y |
| 19 Wexler | ? | N | Y | N |
| 20 Wasserman-Schultz | Y | N | Y | N |
| 21 Diaz-Balart, L. | Y | Y | N | Y |
| 22 Shaw | Y | Y | N | Y |
| 23 Hastings | Y | N | Y | N |
| 24 Feeney | Y | Y | N | Y |
| 25 Diaz-Balart, M. | Y | Y | + | Y |
| **GEORGIA** | | | | |
| 1 Kingston | Y | Y | N | Y |
| 2 Bishop | Y | Y | N | N |
| 3 Marshall | Y | N | N | N |
| 4 McKinney | Y | N | Y | N |
| 5 Lewis | Y | N | Y | N |
| 6 Price | Y | Y | N | Y |
| 7 Linder | Y | Y | N | Y |
| 8 Westmoreland | N | Y | N | Y |
| 9 Norwood | Y | Y | N | Y |
| 10 Deal | Y | Y | N | Y |
| 11 Gingrey | Y | Y | N | Y |
| 12 Barrow | Y | Y | Y | N |
| 13 Scott | Y | Y | Y | N |
| **HAWAII** | | | | |
| 1 Abercrombie | Y | Y | Y | N |
| 2 Case | Y | N | Y | N |
| **IDAHO** | | | | |
| 1 Otter | Y | Y | Y | Y |
| 2 Simpson | Y | Y | N | Y |
| **ILLINOIS** | | | | |
| 1 Rush | Y | N | Y | N |
| 2 Jackson | Y | N | Y | N |
| 3 Lipinski | Y | N | Y | N |
| 4 Gutierrez | Y | – | Y | ? |
| 5 Emanuel | Y | N | Y | N |
| 6 Hyde | Y | Y | + | ? |
| 7 Davis | Y | N | Y | N |
| 8 Bean | Y | N | Y | N |
| 9 Schakowsky | ? | N | Y | N |
| 10 Kirk | Y | N | Y | Y |
| 11 Weller | Y | Y | N | Y |
| 12 Costello | Y | Y | Y | N |

| KEY | Republicans | Democrats | Independents | |
|---|---|---|---|---|
| **Y** Voted for (yea) | | **X** Paired against | | **C** Voted "present" to avoid possible conflict of interest |
| **#** Paired for | | **–** Announced against | | Did not vote or otherwise make a position known |
| **+** Announced for | | **P** Voted "present" | | **?** |
| **N** Voted against (nay) | | | | |

| | 453 | 506 | 630 | 670 |
|---|---|---|---|---|
| 13 Biggert | Y | N | Y | Y |
| 14 Hastert[3] | Y | | | Y |
| 15 Johnson | Y | N | Y | N |
| 16 Manzullo | Y | Y | Y | Y |
| 17 Evans | Y | N | Y | N |
| 18 LaHood | Y | N | N | Y |
| 19 Shimkus | Y | Y | Y | Y |
| **INDIANA** | | | | |
| 1 Visclosky | Y | N | Y | N |
| 2 Chocola | Y | Y | Y | Y |
| 3 Souder | Y | Y | N | Y |
| 4 Buyer | Y | Y | N | N |
| 5 Burton | Y | Y | N | Y |
| 6 Pence | Y | Y | N | Y |
| 7 Carson | Y | N | Y | N |
| 8 Hostettler | Y | Y | N | ? |
| 9 Sodrel | Y | Y | Y | Y |
| **IOWA** | | | | |
| 1 Nussle | Y | Y | Y | Y |
| 2 Leach | Y | N | Y | N |
| 3 Boswell | Y | ? | Y | N |
| 4 Latham | Y | Y | Y | Y |
| 5 King | Y | Y | N | Y |
| **KANSAS** | | | | |
| 1 Moran | Y | Y | Y | Y |
| 2 Ryun | Y | Y | N | Y |
| 3 Moore | Y | N | Y | N |
| 4 Tiahrt | Y | Y | N | Y |
| **KENTUCKY** | | | | |
| 1 Whitfield | Y | Y | Y | Y |
| 2 Lewis | Y | Y | N | Y |
| 3 Northup | Y | Y | Y | Y |
| 4 Davis | Y | Y | Y | Y |
| 5 Rogers | Y | Y | N | Y |
| 6 Chandler | Y | N | Y | N |
| **LOUISIANA** | | | | |
| 1 Jindal | Y | Y | N | Y |
| 2 Jefferson | Y | N | Y | N |
| 3 Melancon | Y | Y | Y | N |
| 4 McCrery | Y | Y | Y | Y |
| 5 Alexander | Y | Y | Y | Y |
| 6 Baker | Y | Y | N | Y |
| 7 Boustany | Y | Y | Y | Y |
| **MAINE** | | | | |
| 1 Allen | Y | N | Y | N |
| 2 Michaud | Y | N | Y | N |
| **MARYLAND** | | | | |
| 1 Gilchrest | Y | N | Y | Y |
| 2 Ruppersberger | Y | N | Y | N |
| 3 Cardin | Y | N | Y | N |
| 4 Wynn | Y | Y | Y | N |
| 5 Hoyer | Y | N | Y | N |
| 6 Bartlett | Y | Y | Y | Y |
| 7 Cummings | Y | N | Y | N |
| 8 Van Hollen | Y | N | Y | N |
| **MASSACHUSETTS** | | | | |
| 1 Olver | Y | N | Y | N |
| 2 Neal | Y | N | Y | N |
| 3 McGovern | Y | N | Y | N |
| 4 Frank | Y | N | Y | N |
| 5 Meehan | Y | N | Y | N |
| 6 Tierney | Y | N | Y | N |
| 7 Markey | Y | N | Y | N |
| 8 Capuano | Y | N | Y | N |
| 9 Lynch | Y | N | Y | N |
| 10 Delahunt | ? | N | Y | N |
| **MICHIGAN** | | | | |
| 1 Stupak | Y | N | Y | N |
| 2 Hoekstra | Y | Y | N | Y |
| 3 Ehlers | Y | N | Y | Y |
| 4 Camp | Y | Y | Y | Y |
| 5 Kildee | Y | N | Y | N |
| 6 Upton | Y | N | Y | Y |
| 7 Schwarz | ? | N | Y | N |
| 8 Rogers | Y | Y | N | Y |
| 9 Knollenberg | Y | Y | Y | Y |
| 10 Miller | Y | Y | Y | Y |
| 11 McCotter | Y | Y | Y | Y |
| 12 Levin | Y | N | Y | N |
| 13 Kilpatrick | Y | N | Y | N |
| 14 Conyers | Y | N | Y | N |
| 15 Dingell | Y | N | Y | N |

| | 453 | 506 | 630 | 670 |
|---|---|---|---|---|
| **MINNESOTA** | | | | |
| 1 Gutknecht | Y | Y | Y | Y |
| 2 Kline | Y | Y | Y | Y |
| 3 Ramstad | Y | N | Y | Y |
| 4 McCollum | Y | N | Y | N |
| 5 Sabo | Y | N | Y | N |
| 6 Kennedy | Y | Y | Y | Y |
| 7 Peterson | Y | Y | Y | N |
| 8 Oberstar | Y | N | Y | N |
| **MISSISSIPPI** | | | | |
| 1 Wicker | Y | Y | N | Y |
| 2 Thompson | Y | Y | Y | N |
| 3 Pickering | Y | Y | Y | Y |
| 4 Taylor | Y | Y | Y | N |
| **MISSOURI** | | | | |
| 1 Clay | Y | N | Y | N |
| 2 Akin | Y | Y | N | Y |
| 3 Carnahan | Y | N | Y | N |
| 4 Skelton | Y | Y | Y | N |
| 5 Cleaver | Y | N | Y | N |
| 6 Graves | Y | Y | N | Y |
| 7 Blunt | Y | Y | N | Y |
| 8 Emerson | Y | Y | Y | Y |
| 9 Hulshof | Y | Y | Y | Y |
| **MONTANA** | | | | |
| AL Rehberg | Y | Y | N | Y |
| **NEBRASKA** | | | | |
| 1 Fortenberry | Y | Y | Y | Y |
| 2 Terry | Y | Y | N | Y |
| 3 Osborne | Y | Y | Y | Y |
| **NEVADA** | | | | |
| 1 Berkley | Y | N | Y | N |
| 2 Gibbons | Y | Y | Y | Y |
| 3 Porter | Y | Y | Y | Y |
| **NEW HAMPSHIRE** | | | | |
| 1 Bradley | Y | N | Y | Y |
| 2 Bass | Y | N | Y | Y |
| **NEW JERSEY** | | | | |
| 1 Andrews | Y | N | Y | N |
| 2 LoBiondo | Y | N | Y | Y |
| 3 Saxton | Y | N | Y | Y |
| 4 Smith | Y | N | Y | N |
| 5 Garrett | Y | Y | N | Y |
| 6 Pallone | Y | N | Y | N |
| 7 Ferguson | Y | N | Y | Y |
| 8 Pascrell | Y | N | Y | N |
| 9 Rothman | Y | N | Y | N |
| 10 Payne | Y | ? | Y | N |
| 11 Frelinghuysen | Y | N | N | Y |
| 12 Holt | Y | N | Y | N |
| 13 Menendez | Y | N | Y | N |
| **NEW MEXICO** | | | | |
| 1 Wilson | Y | Y | Y | N |
| 2 Pearce | Y | Y | N | Y |
| 3 Udall | Y | N | Y | N |
| **NEW YORK** | | | | |
| 1 Bishop | Y | N | Y | N |
| 2 Israel | Y | N | Y | N |
| 3 King | Y | Y | N | Y |
| 4 McCarthy | Y | N | Y | N |
| 5 Ackerman | Y | N | Y | N |
| 6 Meeks | Y | N | Y | N |
| 7 Crowley | Y | N | Y | N |
| 8 Nadler | Y | N | Y | N |
| 9 Weiner | Y | N | Y | N |
| 10 Towns | Y | ? | Y | N |
| 11 Owens | Y | N | Y | N |
| 12 Velázquez | Y | N | Y | N |
| 13 Fossella | Y | Y | N | Y |
| 14 Maloney | Y | N | Y | N |
| 15 Rangel | Y | N | Y | N |
| 16 Serrano | Y | N | Y | N |
| 17 Engel | Y | N | Y | N |
| 18 Lowey | Y | N | Y | N |
| 19 Kelly | Y | Y | Y | Y |
| 20 Sweeney | Y | Y | Y | N |
| 21 McNulty | Y | N | Y | N |
| 22 Hinchey | Y | N | Y | N |
| 23 McHugh | Y | Y | Y | N |
| 24 Boehlert | Y | N | Y | N |
| 25 Walsh | Y | Y | Y | Y |
| 26 Reynolds | Y | Y | Y | Y |
| 27 Higgins | Y | N | Y | N |
| 28 Slaughter | Y | N | Y | N |
| 29 Kuhl | Y | Y | Y | Y |

| | 453 | 506 | 630 | 670 |
|---|---|---|---|---|
| **NORTH CAROLINA** | | | | |
| 1 Butterfield | Y | N | Y | N |
| 2 Etheridge | Y | N | Y | N |
| 3 Jones | N | Y | Y | ? |
| 4 Price | Y | N | Y | N |
| 5 Foxx | Y | Y | N | Y |
| 6 Coble | Y | Y | N | Y |
| 7 McIntyre | Y | Y | Y | N |
| 8 Hayes | Y | Y | Y | Y |
| 9 Myrick | Y | Y | N | ? |
| 10 McHenry | Y | Y | N | Y |
| 11 Taylor | Y | Y | N | Y |
| 12 Watt | Y | N | Y | N |
| 13 Miller | Y | N | Y | N |
| **NORTH DAKOTA** | | | | |
| AL Pomeroy | Y | Y | Y | N |
| **OHIO** | | | | |
| 1 Chabot | Y | Y | N | Y |
| 2 Schmidt[4] | | Y | N | Y |
| 3 Turner | Y | Y | N | Y |
| 4 Oxley | Y | Y | N | Y |
| 5 Gillmor | Y | Y | N | Y |
| 6 Strickland | Y | N | Y | N |
| 7 Hobson | Y | ? | N | Y |
| 8 Boehner | N | N | N | Y |
| 9 Kaptur | Y | N | Y | N |
| 10 Kucinich | Y | N | Y | N |
| 11 Jones | Y | N | Y | N |
| 12 Tiberi | Y | Y | N | Y |
| 13 Brown | Y | N | Y | N |
| 14 LaTourette | Y | N | Y | N |
| 15 Pryce | Y | Y | Y | Y |
| 16 Regula | Y | Y | Y | Y |
| 17 Ryan | Y | N | Y | N |
| 18 Ney | Y | Y | N | Y |
| **OKLAHOMA** | | | | |
| 1 Sullivan | Y | Y | N | Y |
| 2 Boren | Y | Y | Y | N |
| 3 Lucas | Y | Y | N | Y |
| 4 Cole | Y | Y | N | Y |
| 5 Istook | Y | Y | N | ? |
| **OREGON** | | | | |
| 1 Wu | Y | N | Y | N |
| 2 Walden | Y | Y | Y | Y |
| 3 Blumenauer | Y | N | Y | N |
| 4 DeFazio | Y | N | Y | N |
| 5 Hooley | Y | N | Y | N |
| **PENNSYLVANIA** | | | | |
| 1 Brady | ? | N | Y | N |
| 2 Fattah | ? | - | Y | N |
| 3 English | Y | Y | Y | Y |
| 4 Hart | Y | N | Y | Y |
| 5 Peterson | Y | Y | Y | Y |
| 6 Gerlach | Y | N | Y | Y |
| 7 Weldon | Y | N | Y | Y |
| 8 Fitzpatrick | Y | N | Y | Y |
| 9 Shuster | Y | Y | Y | Y |
| 10 Sherwood | Y | Y | Y | Y |
| 11 Kanjorski | Y | N | Y | N |
| 12 Murtha | Y | N | Y | N |
| 13 Schwartz | Y | N | Y | N |
| 14 Doyle | Y | N | Y | N |
| 15 Dent | Y | Y | Y | Y |
| 16 Pitts | ? | Y | Y | Y |
| 17 Holden | Y | Y | Y | N |
| 18 Murphy | Y | Y | Y | Y |
| 19 Platts | Y | N | Y | Y |
| **RHODE ISLAND** | | | | |
| 1 Kennedy | Y | N | Y | N |
| 2 Langevin | Y | N | Y | N |
| **SOUTH CAROLINA** | | | | |
| 1 Brown | Y | Y | N | Y |
| 2 Wilson | Y | Y | N | Y |
| 3 Barrett | Y | Y | Y | Y |
| 4 Inglis | Y | Y | Y | Y |
| 5 Spratt | Y | N | Y | N |
| 6 Clyburn | Y | N | Y | N |
| **SOUTH DAKOTA** | | | | |
| AL Herseth | Y | Y | Y | N |
| **TENNESSEE** | | | | |
| 1 Jenkins | Y | Y | Y | Y |
| 2 Duncan | Y | Y | Y | Y |

| | 453 | 506 | 630 | 670 |
|---|---|---|---|---|
| 3 Wamp | Y | Y | Y | Y |
| 4 Davis | Y | Y | Y | N |
| 5 Cooper | Y | N | Y | N |
| 6 Gordon | Y | N | Y | N |
| 7 Blackburn | Y | Y | N | Y |
| 8 Tanner | Y | Y | Y | N |
| 9 Ford | Y | Y | Y | N |
| **TEXAS** | | | | |
| 1 Gohmert | Y | Y | N | Y |
| 2 Poe | Y | Y | N | Y |
| 3 Johnson, Sam | ? | Y | N | ? |
| 4 Hall, R. | Y | Y | N | Y |
| 5 Hensarling | N | Y | N | Y |
| 6 Barton | Y | Y | N | Y |
| 7 Culberson | Y | ? | N | Y |
| 8 Brady | Y | Y | N | Y |
| 9 Green, A. | Y | N | Y | N |
| 10 McCaul | Y | Y | N | Y |
| 11 Conaway | Y | Y | N | Y |
| 12 Granger | Y | Y | N | Y |
| 13 Thornberry | N | Y | N | Y |
| 14 Paul | ? | ? | Y | N |
| 15 Hinojosa | Y | Y | Y | N |
| 16 Reyes | Y | N | Y | ? |
| 17 Edwards | Y | Y | Y | N |
| 18 Jackson-Lee | Y | N | Y | N |
| 19 Neugebauer | Y | Y | N | Y |
| 20 Gonzalez | Y | N | Y | N |
| 21 Smith | Y | Y | N | Y |
| 22 DeLay | Y | Y | N | Y |
| 23 Bonilla | Y | Y | N | Y |
| 24 Marchant | Y | Y | N | Y |
| 25 Doggett | Y | N | Y | N |
| 26 Burgess | Y | Y | N | Y |
| 27 Ortiz | Y | Y | Y | N |
| 28 Cuellar | Y | Y | Y | N |
| 29 Green, G. | Y | N | Y | N |
| 30 Johnson, E.B. | Y | N | Y | N |
| 31 Carter | Y | Y | N | Y |
| 32 Sessions | Y | Y | N | Y |
| **UTAH** | | | | |
| 1 Bishop | Y | Y | N | Y |
| 2 Matheson | Y | Y | Y | N |
| 3 Cannon | Y | Y | N | Y |
| **VERMONT** | | | | |
| AL *Sanders* | Y | N | Y | N |
| **VIRGINIA** | | | | |
| 1 Davis, Jo Ann | Y | Y | Y | ? |
| 2 Drake | Y | Y | N | Y |
| 3 Scott | Y | N | Y | N |
| 4 Forbes | Y | Y | Y | Y |
| 5 Goode | Y | N | Y | Y |
| 6 Goodlatte | Y | Y | N | Y |
| 7 Cantor | Y | Y | N | Y |
| 8 Moran | Y | N | Y | N |
| 9 Boucher | Y | N | Y | N |
| 10 Wolf | Y | N | Y | Y |
| 11 Davis, T. | Y | N | Y | Y |
| **WASHINGTON** | | | | |
| 1 Inslee | Y | N | Y | N |
| 2 Larsen | Y | N | Y | N |
| 3 Baird | Y | N | Y | N |
| 4 Hastings | Y | Y | N | Y |
| 5 McMorris | Y | Y | Y | Y |
| 6 Dicks | Y | N | Y | N |
| 7 McDermott | Y | N | Y | N |
| 8 Reichert | Y | N | Y | N |
| 9 Smith | Y | N | Y | N |
| **WEST VIRGINIA** | | | | |
| 1 Mollohan | Y | Y | Y | N |
| 2 Capito | Y | Y | Y | Y |
| 3 Rahall | Y | N | Y | N |
| **WISCONSIN** | | | | |
| 1 Ryan | Y | Y | Y | Y |
| 2 Baldwin | Y | N | Y | N |
| 3 Kind | Y | N | Y | N |
| 4 Moore | Y | N | Y | N |
| 5 Sensenbrenner | N | Y | Y | Y |
| 6 Petri | Y | Y | Y | Y |
| 7 Obey | Y | N | Y | N |
| 8 Green | Y | Y | Y | Y |
| **WYOMING** | | | | |
| AL Cubin | Y | Y | N | Y |

# SENATE 9, 28, 127, 129, 149, 170

**9.** **S 5. Class Action Overhaul/Passage.** Passage of the bill that would give federal courts jurisdiction over class action cases involving at least 100 plaintiffs if at least $5 million was at stake and two-thirds of the plaintiffs lived in different states. It would require judges to review all non-cash settlements, such as coupons for goods and services, and limit attorney's fees paid in such settlements. It also would prohibit federal judges from approving a net loss settlement without finding that the loss is outweighed by non-monetary benefits. Passed 72-26: R 53-0; D 18-26 (ND 16-24, SD 2-2); I 1-0. A "yea" was a vote in support of the president's position. Feb. 10, 2005. (*Story, p. C-4*)

**28.** **S 256. Bankruptcy Overhaul/Violent Protesters.** Schumer, D-N.Y., amendment that would prohibit violent protesters, such as anti-abortion activists, from escaping court-ordered fines or judgments by filing for bankruptcy protection. It would bar such debtors from discharging debts, such as damages, court fines, penalties, citations or attorney fees, incurred from acts of violence or potential acts of violence. Rejected 46-53: R 4-51; D 41-2 (ND 37-2, SD 4-0); I 1-0. March 8, 2005. (*Story, p. C-4*)

**127.** **Owen Nomination/Cloture.** Motion to invoke cloture (thus limiting debate) on President Bush's nomination of Priscilla R. Owen of Texas to be a judge for the U.S. Court of Appeals for the 5th Circuit. Motion agreed to 81-18: R 55-0; D 26-17 (ND 23-16, SD 3-1); I 0-1. Three-fifths of the total Senate (60) is required to invoke cloture. May 24, 2005. (*Story, p. C-5*)

**129.** **Bolton Nomination/Cloture.** Motion to invoke cloture (thus limiting debate) on President Bush's nomination of John R. Bolton of Maryland to be the permanent U.S. representative to the United Nations. Motion rejected 56-42: R 53-1; D 3-40 (ND 1-38, SD 2-2); I 0-1. Three-fifths of the total Senate (60) is required to invoke cloture. A "yea" was a vote in support of the president's position. May 26, 2005. (*Story, p. C-5*)

**149.** **HR 6. Energy Policy/Climate Change.** Inhofe, R-Okla., motion to table (kill) the Bingaman, D-N.M., amendment that would express the sense of the Senate that Congress should enact a national program of mandatory, market-based limits and incentives on greenhouse gas emissions that slow, stop and reverse their growth at a rate that would not harm the economy, and would encourage comparable action by other nations. Motion rejected 44-53: R 42-12; D 2-40 (ND 2-36, SD 0-4); I 0-1. (Subsequently, the amendment was adopted by voice vote.) A "yea" was a vote in support of the president's position. June 22, 2005. (*Story, p. C-6*)

**170.** **S 1307. Central American Free-Trade Agreement/Passage.** Passage of the bill that would implement a free-trade agreement between the United States and Costa Rica, El Salvador, Guatemala, Honduras, Nicaragua and a separate pact with the Dominican Republic. It also would eliminate customs duties on all originating goods traded among the participating nations within 10 days. Passed 54-45: R 43-12; D 10-33 (ND 7-32, SD 3-1); I 1-0. A "yea" was a vote in support of the president's position. June 30, 2005. (*Story, p. C-6*)

ND Northern Democrats, SD Southern Democrats
Southern states: Ala., Ark., Fla., Ga., Ky., La., Miss., N.C., Okla., S.C., Tenn., Texas, Va.

| | 9 | 28 | 127 | 129 | 149 | 170 | | 9 | 28 | 127 | 129 | 149 | 170 |
|---|---|---|---|---|---|---|---|---|---|---|---|---|---|
| **ALABAMA** | | | | | | | **MONTANA** | | | | | | |
| Shelby | Y | N | Y | Y | Y | N | Baucus | N | Y | Y | N | Y | N |
| Sessions | Y | N | Y | Y | Y | Y | Burns | Y | N | Y | Y | Y | N |
| **ALASKA** | | | | | | | **NEBRASKA** | | | | | | |
| Stevens | Y | N | Y | Y | Y | Y | Hagel | Y | N | Y | Y | Y | Y |
| Murkowski | Y | N | Y | Y | Y | Y | Nelson | Y | N | Y | Y | Y | Y |
| **ARIZONA** | | | | | | | **NEVADA** | | | | | | |
| McCain | Y | N | Y | Y | N | Y | Reid | N | Y | Y | N | N | N |
| Kyl | Y | N | Y | Y | Y | Y | Ensign | Y | N | Y | Y | Y | Y |
| **ARKANSAS** | | | | | | | **NEW HAMPSHIRE** | | | | | | |
| Lincoln | Y | Y | N | N | N | Y | Gregg | Y | N | Y | Y | N | Y |
| Pryor | N | Y | Y | Y | N | Y | Sununu | ? | N | Y | Y | Y | Y |
| **CALIFORNIA** | | | | | | | **NEW JERSEY** | | | | | | |
| Feinstein | Y | Y | Y | N | N | Y | Corzine | N | ? | N | N | N | N |
| Boxer | N | Y | N | N | N | N | Lautenberg | N | Y | N | N | N | N |
| **COLORADO** | | | | | | | **NEW MEXICO** | | | | | | |
| Allard | Y | N | Y | Y | Y | Y | Domenici | Y | N | Y | N | Y | Y |
| Salazar | Y | Y | Y | N | N | N | Bingaman | Y | Y | Y | N | N | Y |
| **CONNECTICUT** | | | | | | | **NEW YORK** | | | | | | |
| Dodd | Y | Y | N | N | N | N | Schumer | Y | Y | Y | N | N | N |
| Lieberman | Y | Y | Y | N | N | ? | Clinton | N | Y | Y | N | N | N |
| **DELAWARE** | | | | | | | **NORTH CAROLINA** | | | | | | |
| Biden | N | Y | N | N | N | N | Dole | Y | N | Y | Y | Y | Y |
| Carper | Y | Y | Y | N | N | Y | Burr | Y | N | Y | Y | Y | Y |
| **FLORIDA** | | | | | | | **NORTH DAKOTA** | | | | | | |
| Nelson | N | Y | Y | Y | N | Y | Conrad | Y | Y | N | N | ? | Y |
| Martinez | Y | N | Y | Y | Y | Y | Dorgan | N | Y | N | N | ? | N |
| **GEORGIA** | | | | | | | **OHIO** | | | | | | |
| Chambliss | Y | N | Y | Y | Y | Y | DeWine | Y | N | Y | Y | Y | Y |
| Isakson | Y | N | Y | Y | Y | Y | Voinovich | Y | N | Y | Y | Y | Y |
| **HAWAII** | | | | | | | **OKLAHOMA** | | | | | | |
| Inouye | N | Y | ? | ? | N | N | Inhofe | Y | N | Y | Y | Y | Y |
| Akaka | N | Y | N | N | N | N | Coburn | Y | N | Y | Y | Y | Y |
| **IDAHO** | | | | | | | **OREGON** | | | | | | |
| Craig | Y | N | Y | Y | N | N | Wyden | N | Y | Y | N | N | Y |
| Crapo | Y | N | Y | Y | Y | Y | Smith | Y | N | Y | Y | Y | Y |
| **ILLINOIS** | | | | | | | **PENNSYLVANIA** | | | | | | |
| Durbin | N | Y | Y | N | N | N | Specter | Y | Y | Y | ? | N | N |
| Obama | Y | Y | Y | N | N | N | Santorum | ? | N | Y | Y | Y | Y |
| **INDIANA** | | | | | | | **RHODE ISLAND** | | | | | | |
| Lugar | Y | N | Y | Y | Y | Y | Reed | Y | Y | N | N | N | N |
| Bayh | Y | Y | Y | N | N | N | Chafee | Y | Y | Y | N | N | Y |
| **IOWA** | | | | | | | **SOUTH CAROLINA** | | | | | | |
| Grassley | Y | N | Y | Y | Y | Y | Graham | Y | N | Y | Y | N | Y |
| Harkin | N | Y | Y | N | N | N | DeMint | Y | N | Y | Y | Y | Y |
| **KANSAS** | | | | | | | **SOUTH DAKOTA** | | | | | | |
| Brownback | Y | N | Y | Y | Y | Y | Johnson | Y | Y | Y | N | N | N |
| Roberts | Y | N | Y | Y | Y | Y | Thune | Y | N | Y | Y | Y | N |
| **KENTUCKY** | | | | | | | **TENNESSEE** | | | | | | |
| McConnell | Y | N | Y | Y | Y | Y | Frist | Y | N | Y | N | Y | Y |
| Bunning | Y | N | Y | Y | Y | Y | Alexander | Y | N | Y | Y | N | Y |
| **LOUISIANA** | | | | | | | **TEXAS** | | | | | | |
| Landrieu | Y | Y | Y | Y | N | N | Hutchison | Y | N | Y | Y | Y | Y |
| Vitter | Y | N | Y | Y | N | Y | Cornyn | Y | N | Y | Y | Y | Y |
| **MAINE** | | | | | | | **UTAH** | | | | | | |
| Snowe | Y | Y | Y | N | N | N | Hatch | Y | N | Y | Y | Y | Y |
| Collins | Y | Y | Y | Y | N | N | Bennett | Y | N | Y | Y | Y | Y |
| **MARYLAND** | | | | | | | **VERMONT** | | | | | | |
| Sarbanes | N | Y | N | N | N | N | Leahy | N | Y | N | N | N | N |
| Mikulski | N | Y | N | N | N | N | Jeffords | Y | Y | N | N | N | Y |
| **MASSACHUSETTS** | | | | | | | **VIRGINIA** | | | | | | |
| Kennedy | N | Y | N | N | N | N | Warner | Y | N | Y | Y | N | Y |
| Kerry | N | Y | N | N | N | N | Allen | Y | N | Y | Y | Y | Y |
| **MICHIGAN** | | | | | | | **WASHINGTON** | | | | | | |
| Levin | N | Y | N | N | N | N | Murray | N | Y | N | N | N | Y |
| Stabenow | N | Y | N | N | N | N | Cantwell | Y | Y | N | N | N | Y |
| **MINNESOTA** | | | | | | | **WEST VIRGINIA** | | | | | | |
| Dayton | N | Y | N | N | N | N | Byrd | N | N | Y | N | N | N |
| Coleman | Y | N | Y | Y | – | Y | Rockefeller | Y | Y | N | N | N | N |
| **MISSISSIPPI** | | | | | | | **WISCONSIN** | | | | | | |
| Cochran | Y | N | Y | Y | Y | Y | Kohl | Y | Y | N | N | N | N |
| Lott | Y | N | Y | Y | Y | Y | Feingold | N | Y | N | N | N | N |
| **MISSOURI** | | | | | | | **WYOMING** | | | | | | |
| Bond | Y | N | Y | Y | Y | Y | Thomas | Y | N | Y | Y | Y | N |
| Talent | Y | N | Y | Y | Y | Y | Enzi | Y | N | Y | Y | Y | N |

**KEY**   Republicans   Democrats   *Independents*

| | | | | | |
|---|---|---|---|---|---|
| Y | Voted for (yea) | X | Paired against | C | Voted "present" to avoid possible conflict of interest |
| # | Paired for | – | Announced against | | |
| + | Announced for | P | Voted "present" | ? | Did not vote or otherwise make a position known |
| N | Voted against (nay) | | | | |

# SENATE 213, 219, 220, 245, 249

**213.** **HR 6. Energy Policy/Conference Report.** Adoption of the conference report on the bill that would overhaul the nation's energy policy and provide for $14.6 billion in energy-related tax incentives. It would allow lawsuits involving the gasoline additive methyl tertiary butyl ether (MTBE) to be moved to a federal district court and require refiners to annually use 7.5 billion gallons of renewable fuels by 2012. The measure would grant the Federal Energy Regulatory Commission (FERC) jurisdiction over reliability standards for electricity transmission networks and extend daylight-saving time by one month. It would allow FERC to approve the construction, expansion or operation of any facility that imports or processes natural gas, including liquefied natural gas. Adopted (thus cleared for the president) 74-26: R 49-6; D 25-19 (ND 22-18, SD 3-1); I 0-1. A "yea" was a vote in support of the president's position. July 29, 2005. *(Story, p. C-7)*

**219.** **S 397. Gun Liability/Passage.** Passage of the bill that would bar certain civil lawsuits against manufacturers, distributors, dealers and importers of firearms and ammunition, principally those lawsuits aimed at making them liable for gun violence. Trade groups also would be protected and all pending legal action against gunmakers would be dismissed. It also would, with certain exceptions, make it unlawful for licensed gun importers, manufacturers or dealers to sell, deliver or transfer handguns without a secure gun storage or safety device. Passed 65-31: R 50-2; D 14-29 (ND 10-29, SD 4-0); I 1-0. A "yea" was a vote in support of the president's position. July 29, 2005. *(Story, p. C-7)*

**220.** **HR 3. Fiscal 2006 Surface Transportation Reauthorization/Conference Report.** Adoption of the conference report on the bill that would bring total authorization for federal highway, mass transit, safety and research programs, including fiscal 2004 funding, to $286.5 billion through 2009. The bill would increase the rate of return to states on their Highway Trust Fund contributions to 92 percent by fiscal 2008. It would make the Transportation Department the lead agency in the environmental review process for transportation projects. Adopted (thus cleared for the president) 91-4: R 48-4; D 42-0 (ND 38-0, SD 4-0); I 1-0. July 29, 2005. *(Story, p. C-8)*

**245.** **Roberts Nomination/Confirmation.** Confirmation of President Bush's nomination of John G. Roberts Jr. of Maryland to be chief justice of the United States. Confirmed 78-22: R 55-0; D 22-22 (ND 18-22, SD 4-0); I 1-0. A "yea" was a vote in support of the president's position. Sept. 29, 2005. *(Story, p. C-8)*

**249.** **HR 2863. Fiscal 2006 Defense Appropriations/Detainee Standards.** McCain, R-Ariz., amendment that would establish the U.S. Army Field Manual on Intelligence Interrogation as the uniform standard for interrogating persons detained by the Department of Defense and prohibit cruel, inhuman or degrading treatment of any prisoner detained by the U.S. government. Adopted 90-9: R 46-9; D 43-0 (ND 39-0, SD 4-0); I 1-0. A "nay" was a vote in support of the president's position. Oct. 5, 2005. *(Story, p. C-9)*

ND Northern Democrats, SD Southern Democrats
Southern states: Ala., Ark., Fla., Ga., Ky., La., Miss., N.C., Okla., S.C., Tenn., Texas, Va.

| | 213 | 219 | 220 | 245 | 249 | | 213 | 219 | 220 | 245 | 249 |
|---|---|---|---|---|---|---|---|---|---|---|---|
| **ALABAMA** | | | | | | **MONTANA** | | | | | |
| Shelby | Y | Y | Y | Y | Y | Baucus | Y | Y | Y | Y | Y |
| Sessions | Y | Y | Y | Y | N | Burns | Y | Y | Y | Y | Y |
| **ALASKA** | | | | | | **NEBRASKA** | | | | | |
| Stevens | Y | Y | Y | Y | N | Hagel | Y | Y | Y | Y | Y |
| Murkowski | Y | Y | Y | Y | Y | Nelson | Y | Y | Y | Y | Y |
| **ARIZONA** | | | | | | **NEVADA** | | | | | |
| McCain | N | Y | N | Y | Y | Reid | N | Y | N | Y | Y |
| Kyl | N | Y | N | Y | Y | Ensign | Y | Y | Y | Y | Y |
| **ARKANSAS** | | | | | | **NEW HAMPSHIRE** | | | | | |
| Lincoln | Y | Y | Y | Y | Y | Gregg | N | Y | N | Y | Y |
| Pryor | Y | Y | Y | Y | Y | Sununu | N | ? | ? | Y | Y |
| **CALIFORNIA** | | | | | | **NEW JERSEY** | | | | | |
| Feinstein | N | – | + | N | Y | Corzine | N | N | Y | N | ? |
| Boxer | N | N | + | N | Y | Lautenberg | N | N | Y | N | Y |
| **COLORADO** | | | | | | **NEW MEXICO** | | | | | |
| Allard | Y | Y | Y | Y | N | Domenici | Y | Y | Y | Y | Y |
| Salazar | Y | Y | Y | Y | Y | Bingaman | Y | N | Y | Y | Y |
| **CONNECTICUT** | | | | | | **NEW YORK** | | | | | |
| Dodd | N | N | Y | Y | Y | Schumer | N | N | Y | N | Y |
| Lieberman | Y | N | Y | Y | Y | Clinton | N | N | Y | N | Y |
| **DELAWARE** | | | | | | **NORTH CAROLINA** | | | | | |
| Biden | N | N | Y | N | Y | Dole | Y | Y | Y | Y | Y |
| Carper | N | N | Y | Y | Y | Burr | Y | Y | Y | Y | Y |
| **FLORIDA** | | | | | | **NORTH DAKOTA** | | | | | |
| Nelson | N | Y | Y | Y | Y | Conrad | Y | Y | Y | Y | Y |
| Martinez | N | Y | Y | Y | Y | Dorgan | Y | Y | Y | Y | Y |
| **GEORGIA** | | | | | | **OHIO** | | | | | |
| Chambliss | Y | Y | Y | Y | Y | DeWine | N | Y | Y | Y | Y |
| Isakson | Y | Y | Y | Y | Y | Voinovich | Y | Y | Y | Y | Y |
| **HAWAII** | | | | | | **OKLAHOMA** | | | | | |
| Inouye | Y | N | Y | N | Y | Inhofe | Y | Y | Y | Y | N |
| Akaka | Y | N | Y | N | Y | Coburn | Y | Y | Y | Y | N |
| **IDAHO** | | | | | | **OREGON** | | | | | |
| Craig | Y | Y | Y | Y | Y | Wyden | N | N | Y | Y | Y |
| Crapo | Y | Y | Y | Y | Y | Smith | Y | + | + | Y | Y |
| **ILLINOIS** | | | | | | **PENNSYLVANIA** | | | | | |
| Durbin | Y | N | Y | N | Y | Specter | Y | Y | Y | Y | Y |
| Obama | Y | N | Y | N | Y | Santorum | Y | Y | Y | Y | Y |
| **INDIANA** | | | | | | **RHODE ISLAND** | | | | | |
| Lugar | Y | Y | Y | Y | Y | Reed | N | N | Y | N | Y |
| Bayh | Y | N | Y | N | Y | Chafee | N | N | Y | Y | Y |
| **IOWA** | | | | | | **SOUTH CAROLINA** | | | | | |
| Grassley | Y | Y | Y | Y | Y | Graham | Y | Y | Y | Y | Y |
| Harkin | Y | N | Y | N | Y | DeMint | Y | Y | Y | Y | Y |
| **KANSAS** | | | | | | **SOUTH DAKOTA** | | | | | |
| Brownback | Y | Y | Y | Y | Y | Johnson | Y | Y | Y | Y | Y |
| Roberts | Y | + | + | Y | N | Thune | Y | Y | Y | Y | Y |
| **KENTUCKY** | | | | | | **TENNESSEE** | | | | | |
| McConnell | Y | Y | Y | Y | Y | Frist | Y | Y | Y | Y | Y |
| Bunning | Y | Y | Y | Y | Y | Alexander | Y | Y | Y | Y | Y |
| **LOUISIANA** | | | | | | **TEXAS** | | | | | |
| Landrieu | Y | Y | Y | Y | Y | Hutchison | Y | Y | Y | Y | Y |
| Vitter | Y | Y | Y | Y | Y | Cornyn | Y | Y | N | Y | N |
| **MAINE** | | | | | | **UTAH** | | | | | |
| Snowe | Y | Y | Y | Y | Y | Hatch | Y | Y | Y | Y | Y |
| Collins | Y | Y | Y | Y | Y | Bennett | Y | Y | Y | Y | Y |
| **MARYLAND** | | | | | | **VERMONT** | | | | | |
| Sarbanes | N | N | Y | N | Y | Leahy | N | N | Y | Y | Y |
| Mikulski | Y | N | Y | N | Y | Jeffords | N | Y | Y | Y | Y |
| **MASSACHUSETTS** | | | | | | **VIRGINIA** | | | | | |
| Kennedy | N | N | Y | N | Y | Warner | Y | Y | Y | Y | Y |
| Kerry | N | N | Y | N | Y | Allen | Y | Y | Y | Y | Y |
| **MICHIGAN** | | | | | | **WASHINGTON** | | | | | |
| Levin | Y | N | Y | Y | Y | Murray | N | N | Y | Y | Y |
| Stabenow | Y | N | Y | N | Y | Cantwell | Y | N | Y | N | Y |
| **MINNESOTA** | | | | | | **WEST VIRGINIA** | | | | | |
| Dayton | Y | N | Y | N | Y | Byrd | Y | Y | Y | Y | Y |
| Coleman | Y | Y | Y | Y | Y | Rockefeller | Y | Y | Y | Y | Y |
| **MISSISSIPPI** | | | | | | **WISCONSIN** | | | | | |
| Cochran | Y | Y | Y | Y | N | Kohl | Y | Y | Y | Y | Y |
| Lott | Y | Y | Y | Y | Y | Feingold | N | N | Y | Y | Y |
| **MISSOURI** | | | | | | **WYOMING** | | | | | |
| Bond | Y | Y | Y | Y | N | Thomas | Y | Y | Y | Y | Y |
| Talent | Y | Y | Y | Y | Y | Enzi | Y | Y | Y | Y | Y |

| KEY | Republicans | Democrats | *Independents* |
|---|---|---|---|
| **Y** Voted for (yea) | | **X** Paired against | **C** Voted "present" to avoid possible conflict of interest |
| **#** Paired for | | **–** Announced against | |
| **+** Announced for | | **P** Voted "present" | **?** Did not vote or otherwise make a position known |
| **N** Voted against (nay) | | | |

# SENATE 262, 323, 358, 363, 364

**262.** HR 3058. Fiscal 2006 Transportation-Treasury-Housing Appropriations/Bridge Funding. Coburn, R-Okla., amendment that would transfer $125 million in funding from the Ketchikan-Gravina and Kink Arm bridge projects in Alaska to the reconstruction of the Twin Spans Bridge connecting New Orleans and Slidell, La. It would place remaining Alaska bridge funds into a general highway fund for Alaska. Rejected 15-82: R 11-43; D 4-38 (ND 3-35, SD 1-3); I 0-1. (By unanimous consent, the Senate agreed to raise the majority requirement for adoption of the Coburn amendment to 60 votes.) Oct. 20, 2005. *(Story, p. C-9)*

**323.** S 1042. Fiscal 2006 Defense Authorization/Iraq Withdrawal. Warner, R-Va., amendment that would require the president to submit an unclassified report to Congress 90 days after the bill's enactment and every three months thereafter on U.S. policy and operations in Iraq. It would also state that 2006 should be a period of significant transition to Iraqi sovereignty; that U.S. forces should not remain in Iraq any longer than necessary; and that the administration needs to explain to Congress and the American public the strategy for the completion of the Iraq mission. Adopted 79-19: R 41-13; D 37-6 (ND 33-6, SD 4-0); I 1-0. Nov. 15, 2005. *(Story, p. C-10)*

**358.** HR 3199. "Patriot Act" Reauthorization/Cloture. Motion to invoke cloture (thus limiting debate) on the conference report on the bill that would reauthorize the law known as the Patriot Act, and make permanent 14 of the 16 provisions of the act set to expire at the end of the year, and extend for four years the two provisions on access to business and other records and "roving" wiretaps. Motion rejected 52-47: R 50-5; D 2-41 (ND 2-37, SD 0-4); I 0-1. Three-fifths of the total Senate (60) is required to invoke cloture. A "yea" was a vote in support of the president's position. Dec. 16, 2005. *(Story, p. C-11)*

**363.** S 1932. Budget Reconciliation/Motion to Concur. Gregg, R-N.H., motion to concur in the House amendment with a Senate amendment on the bill that would make changes to programs for a net savings of $38.8 billion over five years. The Senate amendment would strike two reporting requirements and language that would allow for a Medicaid liability treatment provision regarding hospitals that deny treatment to low-income individuals unable to pay. Motion agreed to, with Vice President Cheney casting a "yea" vote to break the tie, 50-50: R 50-5; D 0-44 (ND 0-40, SD 0-4); I 0-1. A "yea" was a vote in support of the president's position. Dec. 21, 2005. *(Story, p. C-11)*

**364.** HR 2863. Fiscal 2006 Defense Appropriations/Cloture. Motion to invoke cloture (thus limiting debate) on the conference report on the bill that would appropriate $453.5 billion for Defense spending in fiscal 2006, including $50 billion for operations in Iraq and Afghanistan. It also would require a 1 percent across-the-board cut to all fiscal 2006 discretionary spending except Veterans Administration funding that was added to the legislation. It would provide $29 billion for disaster assistance to hurricane-damaged areas and $3.8 billion for flu preparedness. It would allow oil and gas leasing in the Arctic National Wildlife Refuge. Motion rejected 56-44: R 52-3; D 4-40 (ND 3-37, SD 1-3); I 0-1. Three-fifths of the total Senate (60) is required to invoke cloture. A "yea" was a vote in support of the president's position. Dec. 21, 2005. *(Story, p. C-12)*

ND Northern Democrats, SD Southern Democrats
Southern states: Ala., Ark., Fla., Ga., Ky., La., Miss., N.C., Okla., S.C., Tenn., Texas, Va.

| | 262 | 323 | 358 | 363 | 364 | | 262 | 323 | 358 | 363 | 364 |
|---|---|---|---|---|---|---|---|---|---|---|---|
| **ALABAMA** | | | | | | **MONTANA** | | | | | |
| Shelby | N | Y | Y | Y | Y | Baucus | N | Y | N | N | N |
| Sessions | Y | N | Y | Y | Y | Burns | N | Y | Y | Y | Y |
| **ALASKA** | | | | | | **NEBRASKA** | | | | | |
| Stevens | N | Y | Y | Y | Y | Hagel | N | Y | N | Y | Y |
| Murkowski | N | Y | N | Y | Y | Nelson | N | Y | Y | N | Y |
| **ARIZONA** | | | | | | **NEVADA** | | | | | |
| McCain | ? | N | Y | Y | Y | Reid | N | Y | N | N | N |
| Kyl | Y | N | Y | Y | Y | Ensign | N | Y | Y | Y | Y |
| **ARKANSAS** | | | | | | **NEW HAMPSHIRE** | | | | | |
| Lincoln | N | Y | N | N | N | Gregg | N | Y | Y | Y | Y |
| Pryor | N | Y | N | N | N | Sununu | Y | Y | Y | Y | Y |
| **CALIFORNIA** | | | | | | **NEW JERSEY** | | | | | |
| Feinstein | N | Y | N | N | N | Corzine | ? | ? | N | N | N |
| Boxer | N | Y | N | N | N | Lautenberg | N | Y | N | N | N |
| **COLORADO** | | | | | | **NEW MEXICO** | | | | | |
| Allard | Y | Y | Y | Y | Y | Domenici | N | Y | Y | Y | Y |
| Salazar | N | Y | N | N | N | Bingaman | N | Y | N | N | N |
| **CONNECTICUT** | | | | | | **NEW YORK** | | | | | |
| Dodd | N | Y | ? | N | N | Schumer | ? | Y | N | N | N |
| Lieberman | N | Y | N | N | N | Clinton | N | Y | N | N | N |
| **DELAWARE** | | | | | | **NORTH CAROLINA** | | | | | |
| Biden | N | Y | N | N | N | Dole | N | Y | Y | Y | Y |
| Carper | N | Y | N | N | N | Burr | Y | N | Y | Y | Y |
| **FLORIDA** | | | | | | **NORTH DAKOTA** | | | | | |
| Nelson | N | Y | N | N | N | Conrad | N | Y | N | N | N |
| Martinez | N | Y | Y | Y | Y | Dorgan | N | Y | N | N | N |
| **GEORGIA** | | | | | | **OHIO** | | | | | |
| Chambliss | N | N | Y | Y | Y | DeWine | Y | Y | Y | N | N |
| Isakson | N | N | Y | Y | Y | Voinovich | N | Y | Y | Y | Y |
| **HAWAII** | | | | | | **OKLAHOMA** | | | | | |
| Inouye | N | Y | N | N | Y | Inhofe | N | N | Y | Y | Y |
| Akaka | N | Y | N | N | Y | Coburn | Y | N | Y | Y | Y |
| **IDAHO** | | | | | | **OREGON** | | | | | |
| Craig | N | Y | N | Y | Y | Wyden | N | Y | N | N | N |
| Crapo | N | Y | Y | Y | Y | Smith | N | Y | N | N | Y |
| **ILLINOIS** | | | | | | **PENNSYLVANIA** | | | | | |
| Durbin | N | Y | N | N | N | Specter | N | Y | Y | Y | Y |
| Obama | N | Y | N | N | N | Santorum | N | Y | Y | Y | Y |
| **INDIANA** | | | | | | **RHODE ISLAND** | | | | | |
| Lugar | N | Y | Y | Y | Y | Reed | N | Y | N | N | N |
| Bayh | Y | Y | N | N | N | Chafee | N | Y | N | Y | N |
| **IOWA** | | | | | | **SOUTH CAROLINA** | | | | | |
| Grassley | N | Y | Y | Y | Y | Graham | Y | N | Y | Y | Y |
| Harkin | N | N | Y | Y | N | DeMint | Y | N | Y | Y | Y |
| **KANSAS** | | | | | | **SOUTH DAKOTA** | | | | | |
| Brownback | N | Y | Y | Y | Y | Johnson | N | Y | N | N | N |
| Roberts | N | Y | Y | Y | Y | Thune | N | N | Y | Y | Y |
| **KENTUCKY** | | | | | | **TENNESSEE** | | | | | |
| McConnell | N | Y | Y | Y | Y | Frist | N | Y | N | Y | N |
| Bunning | N | N | Y | Y | Y | Alexander | N | + | Y | Y | Y |
| **LOUISIANA** | | | | | | **TEXAS** | | | | | |
| Landrieu | Y | Y | N | N | Y | Hutchison | N | Y | Y | Y | Y |
| Vitter | Y | N | Y | Y | Y | Cornyn | N | Y | Y | Y | Y |
| **MAINE** | | | | | | **UTAH** | | | | | |
| Snowe | N | Y | Y | N | Y | Hatch | N | Y | Y | Y | Y |
| Collins | N | Y | Y | N | Y | Bennett | N | Y | Y | Y | Y |
| **MARYLAND** | | | | | | **VERMONT** | | | | | |
| Sarbanes | N | Y | N | N | N | Leahy | N | N | N | N | N |
| Mikulski | N | Y | N | N | N | Jeffords | N | Y | N | N | N |
| **MASSACHUSETTS** | | | | | | **VIRGINIA** | | | | | |
| Kennedy | N | N | N | N | N | Warner | N | Y | Y | Y | Y |
| Kerry | N | N | N | N | N | Allen | Y | Y | Y | Y | Y |
| **MICHIGAN** | | | | | | **WASHINGTON** | | | | | |
| Levin | N | Y | N | N | N | Murray | N | Y | N | N | N |
| Stabenow | N | Y | N | N | N | Cantwell | N | Y | N | N | N |
| **MINNESOTA** | | | | | | **WEST VIRGINIA** | | | | | |
| Dayton | N | Y | N | N | N | Byrd | N | N | N | N | N |
| Coleman | N | Y | Y | Y | Y | Rockefeller | N | Y | N | N | N |
| **MISSISSIPPI** | | | | | | **WISCONSIN** | | | | | |
| Cochran | N | Y | Y | Y | Y | Kohl | N | Y | N | N | N |
| Lott | N | Y | Y | Y | Y | Feingold | Y | Y | N | N | N |
| **MISSOURI** | | | | | | **WYOMING** | | | | | |
| Bond | N | Y | Y | Y | Y | Thomas | N | Y | Y | Y | Y |
| Talent | N | Y | Y | Y | Y | Enzi | N | Y | Y | Y | Y |

| **KEY** | **Republicans** | Democrats | *Independents* | |
|---|---|---|---|---|
| Y | Voted for (yea) | X | Paired against | C Voted "present" to avoid possible conflict of interest |
| # | Paired for | – | Announced against | |
| + | Announced for | P | Voted "present" | ? Did not vote or otherwise make a position known |
| N | Voted against (nay) | | | |

# Appendix D

# TEXTS

# President Ties 'Liberty in Our Land' To 'Success of Liberty in Other Lands'

*Following is the CQ Transcriptions transcript of George W. Bush's inaugural address from the West Front of the Capitol on Jan. 20, delivered just after he took the oath of office for his second term as president.*

VICE PRESIDENT CHENEY, Mr. Chief Justice, President Carter, President Bush, President Clinton, members of the United States Congress, Reverend, clergy, distinguished guests, fellow citizens:

On this day, prescribed by law and marked by ceremony, we celebrate the durable wisdom of our Constitution and recall the deep commitments that unite our country.

I am grateful for the honor of this hour, mindful of the consequential times in which we live and determined to fulfill the oath that I have sworn and you have witnessed.

At this second gathering, our duties are defined not by the words I use, but by the history we have seen together.

For a half a century, America defended our own freedom by standing watch on distant borders. After the shipwreck of communism came years of relative quiet, years of repose, years of sabbatical. And then there came a day of fire. We have seen our vulnerability and we have seen its deepest source.

For as long as whole regions of the world simmer in resentment and tyranny, prone to ideologies that feed hatred and excuse murder, violence will gather and multiply in destructive power and cross the most defended borders and raise a mortal threat.

There is only one force of history that can break the reign of hatred and resentment and expose the pretensions of tyrants and reward the hopes of the decent and tolerant, and that is the force of human freedom.

We are led, by events and common sense, to one conclusion: The survival of liberty in our land increasingly depends on the success of liberty in other lands. The best hope for peace in our world is the expansion of freedom in all the world.

America's vital interests and our deepest beliefs are now one. From the day of our founding, we have proclaimed that every man and woman on this earth has rights and dignity and matchless value, because they bear the image of the maker of heaven and Earth.

Across the generations, we have proclaimed the imperative of self-government, because no one is fit to be a master and no one deserves to be a slave.

## ENDING TYRANNY

Fancying these ideals is the mission that created our nation. It is the honorable achievement of our fathers. Now it is the urgent requirement of our nation's security and the calling of our time.

So it is the policy of the United States to seek and support the growth of democratic movements and institutions in every nation and culture, with the ultimate goal of ending tyranny in our world. This is not primarily the task of arms, though we will defend ourselves and our friends by force of arms when necessary.

Freedom, by its nature, must be chosen and defended by citizens and sustained by the rule of law and the protection of minorities. And when the soul of a nation finally speaks, the institutions that arise may reflect customs and traditions very different from our own.

America will not impose our own style of government on the unwilling. Our goal, instead, is to help others find their own voice, attain their own freedom and make their own way.

The great objective of ending tyranny is the concentrated work of generations. The difficulty of the task is no excuse for avoiding it.

America's influence is not unlimited. But, fortunately for the oppressed, America's influence is considerable, and we will use it confidently in freedom's cause.

My most solemn duty is to protect this nation and its people from further attacks and emerging threats. Some have unwisely chosen to test America's resolve and have found it firm. We will persistently clarify the choice before every ruler and every nation: the moral choice between oppression, which is always wrong, and freedom, which is eternally right.

America will not pretend that jailed dissidents prefer their chains, or that women welcome humiliation and servitude, or that any human being aspires to live at the mercy of bullies. We will encourage reform in other governments by making clear that success in our relations will require the decent treatment of their own people.

America's belief in human dignity will guide our policies, yet rights must be more than the grudging concessions of dictators. They are secured by free dissent and the participation of the governed.

In the long run, there is no justice without freedom, and there can be no human rights without human liberty.

Some, I know, have questioned the global appeal of liberty — though this time in history, four decades defined by the swiftest advance of freedom ever seen, is an odd time for doubt.

Americans, of all people, should never be surprised by the power of our ideals.

Eventually, the call of freedom comes to every mind and every soul. We do not accept the existence of permanent tyranny because we do not accept the possibility of permanent slavery. Liberty will come to those who love it.

Today, America speaks anew to the peoples of the world. All who live in tyranny and hopelessness can know the United States will not ignore your oppression, or excuse your oppressors. When you stand for your liberty, we will stand with you.

Democratic reformers facing repression, prison or exile can know America sees you for who you are, the future leaders of your free country.

The rulers of outlaw regimes can know that we still believe as Abraham Lincoln did: "Those who deny freedom to others deserve it not for themselves; and, under the rule of a just God, cannot long retain it."

The leaders of governments with long habits of control need to know: To serve your people you must learn to trust them. Start on this journey of progress and justice, and Amer-

ica will walk at your side.

And all the allies of the United States can know: We honor your friendship, we rely on your counsel and we depend on your help.

Division among free nations is a primary goal of freedom's enemies. The concerted effort of free nations to promote democracy is a prelude to our enemies' defeat.

Today, I also speak anew to my fellow citizens. From all of you, I have asked patience in the hard task of securing America, which you have granted in good measure.

Our country has accepted obligations that are difficult to fulfill and would be dishonorable to abandon. Yet because we have acted in the great liberating tradition of this nation, tens of millions have achieved their freedom. And as hope kindles hope, millions more will find it.

By our efforts we have lit a fire as well — a fire in the minds of men. It warms those who feel its power. It burns those who fight its progress. And one day this untamed fire of freedom will reach the darkest corners of our world.

A few Americans have accepted the hardest duties in this cause. In the quiet work of intelligence and diplomacy, the idealistic work of helping raise up free governments, the dangerous and necessary work of fighting our enemies, some have shown their devotion to our country in deaths that honored their whole lives. And we will always honor their names and their sacrifice.

All Americans have witnessed this idealism, and some for the first time. I ask our youngest citizens to believe the evidence of your eyes.

You have seen duty and allegiance in the determined faces of our soldiers. You have seen that life is fragile, and evil is real, and courage triumphs. Make the choice to serve in a cause larger than your wants, larger than yourself, and in your days you will add not just to the wealth of our country, but to its character.

## FREEDOM AT HOME

America has need of idealism and courage, because we have essential work at home: the unfinished work of American freedom.

In a world moving toward liberty, we are determined to show the meaning and promise of liberty.

In America's ideal of freedom, citizens find the dignity and security of economic independence, instead of laboring on the edge of subsistence. This is the broader definition of liberty that motivated the Homestead Act, the Social Security Act and the G.I. Bill of Rights.

And now we will extend this vision by reforming great institutions to serve the needs of our time.

To give every American a stake in the promise and future of our country, we will bring the highest standards to our schools and build an ownership society.

We will widen the ownership of homes and businesses, retirement savings and health insurance, preparing our people for the challenges of life in a free society.

By making every citizen an agent of his or her own destiny, we will give our fellow Americans greater freedom from want and fear, and make our society more prosperous and just and equal.

In America's ideal of freedom, the public interest depends on private character, on integrity, and tolerance toward others, and the rule of conscience in our own lives. Self-government relies, in the end, on the governing of the self.

That edifice of character is built in families, supported by communities with standards, and sustained in our national life by the truths of Sinai, the Sermon on the Mount, the words of the Koran, and the varied faiths of our people.

Americans move forward in every generation by reaffirming all that is good and true that came before: ideals of justice and conduct that are the same yesterday, today and forever.

In America's ideal of freedom, the exercise of rights is ennobled by service and mercy and a heart for the weak.

Liberty for all does not mean independence from one another. Our nation relies on men and women who look after a neighbor and surround the lost with love.

Americans at our best value the life we see in one another and must always remember that even the unwanted have worth.

And our country must abandon all the habits of racism because we cannot carry the message of freedom and the baggage of bigotry at the same time.

From the perspective of a single day, including this day of dedication, the issues and questions before our country are many.

From the viewpoint of centuries, the questions that come to us are narrowed and few. Did our generation advance the cause of freedom? And did our character bring credit to that cause?

These questions that judge us also unite us, because Americans of every party and background — Americans by choice and by birth —are bound to one another in the cause of freedom.

## HEALING DIVISIONS

We have known divisions, which must be healed to move forward in great purposes. And I will strive in good faith to heal them. Yet those divisions do not define America.

We felt the unity and fellowship of our nation when freedom came under attack, and our response came like a single hand over a single heart. And we can feel that same unity and pride whenever America acts for good, and the victims of disaster are given hope, and the unjust encounter justice, and the captives are set free.

We go forward with complete confidence in the eventual triumph of freedom. Not because history runs on the wheels of inevitability; it is human choices that move events. Not because we consider ourselves a chosen nation; God moves and chooses as he wills.

We have confidence because freedom is the permanent hope of mankind, the hunger in dark places, the longing of the soul.

When our founders declared a new order of the ages, when soldiers died in wave upon wave for a union based on liberty, when citizens marched in peaceful outrage under the banner "Freedom Now," they were acting on an ancient hope that is meant to be fulfilled.

History has an ebb and flow of justice, but history also has a visible direction, set by liberty and the author of liberty.

When the Declaration of Independence was first read in public and the Liberty Bell was sounded in celebration, a witness said: "It rang as if it meant something." In our time it means something still.

America, in this young century, proclaims liberty throughout all the world and to all the inhabitants thereof. Renewed in our strength, tested but not weary, we are ready for the greatest achievements in the history of freedom.

May God bless you, and may he watch over the United States of America. ■

# Bush's State of the Union Address

*Following is a transcript of President Bush's State of the Union address, delivered to a joint session of Congress on Feb. 2. Source: CQ Transcriptions.*

MR. SPEAKER, Vice President Cheney, members of Congress, fellow citizens: As a new Congress gathers, all of us in the elected branches of government share a great privilege: We've been placed in office by the votes of the people we serve. And tonight that is a privilege we share with newly elected leaders of Afghanistan, the Palestinian territories, Ukraine and a free and sovereign Iraq.

Two weeks ago, I stood on the steps of this Capitol and renewed the commitment of our nation to the guiding ideal of liberty for all. This evening I will set forth policies to advance that ideal at home and around the world.

Tonight, with a healthy, growing economy, with more Americans going back to work, with our nation an active force for good in the world, the state of our union is confident and strong.

Our generation has been blessed by the expansion of opportunity, by advances in medicine, by the security purchased by our parents' sacrifice. Now, as we see a little gray in the mirror — or a lot of gray — and we watch our children moving into adulthood, we ask the question: What will be the state of their union?

Members of Congress, the choices we make together will answer that question. Over the next several months, on issue after issue, let us do what Americans have always done and build a better world for our children and our grandchildren.

First, we must be good stewards of this economy and renew the great institutions on which millions of our fellow citizens rely.

America's economy is the fastest growing of any major industrialized nation. In the past four years, we have provided tax relief to every person who pays income taxes, overcome a recession, opened up new markets abroad, prosecuted corporate criminals, raised home ownership to its highest level in history. And in the last year alone, the United States has added 2.3 million new jobs. When action was needed, the Congress delivered, and the nation is grateful.

Now we must add to these achievements. By making our economy more flexible, more innovative and more competitive, we will keep America the economic leader of the world.

## DOMESTIC POLICY

America's prosperity requires restraining the spending appetite of the federal government. I welcome the bipartisan enthusiasm for spending discipline. I will send you a budget that holds the growth of discretionary spending below inflation, makes tax relief permanent and stays on track to cut the deficit in half by 2009.

My budget substantially reduces or eliminates more than 150 government programs that are not getting results or duplicate current efforts or do not fulfill essential priorities. The principle here is clear: Taxpayer dollars must be spent wisely or not at all.

To make our economy stronger and more dynamic, we must prepare a rising generation to fill the jobs of the 21st century.

Under the No Child Left Behind Act, standards are higher, test scores are on the rise and we're closing the achievement gap for minority students. Now we must demand better results from our high schools so every high school diploma is a ticket to success.

We will help an additional 200,000 workers to get training for a better career by reforming our job-training system and strengthening America's community colleges. And we will make it easier for Americans to afford a college education by increasing the size of Pell Grants.

To make our economy stronger and more competitive, America must reward, not punish, the efforts and dreams of entrepreneurs. Small business is the path of advancement, especially for women and minorities. So we must free small businesses from needless regulation and protect honest job creators from junk lawsuits.

Justice is distorted and our economy is held back by irresponsible class actions and frivolous asbestos claims. And I urge Congress to pass legal reforms this year.

To make our economy stronger and more productive, we must make health care more affordable and give families greater access to good coverage and more control over their health decisions. I ask Congress to move forward on a comprehensive health care agenda with tax credits to help low-income workers buy insurance; a community health center in every poor county; improved information technology to prevent medical error and needless costs; association health plans for small businesses and their employees . . . expanded health savings accounts . . . and medical liability reform that will reduce health care costs and make sure patients have the doctors and care they need.

To keep our economy growing, we also need reliable supplies of affordable, environmentally responsible energy. Nearly four years ago, I submitted a comprehensive energy strategy that encourages conservation, alternative sources, a modernized electricity grid and more production here at home, including safe, clean nuclear energy. My "Clear Skies" legislation will cut power-plant pollution and improve the health of our citizens. And my budget provides strong funding for leading-edge technology, from hydrogen-fueled cars to clean coal to renewable sources such as ethanol. Four years of debate is enough. I urge Congress to pass legislation that makes America more secure and less dependent on foreign energy.

All these proposals are essential to expand this economy and add new jobs, but they are just the beginning of our duty. To build the prosperity of future generations, we must update institutions that were created to meet the needs of an earlier time.

Year after year, Americans are burdened by an archaic, incoherent federal tax code. I've appointed a bipartisan panel to examine the tax code from top to bottom. And when their recommendations are delivered, you and I will work together to give this nation a tax code that is pro-growth, easy to understand and fair to all.

America's immigration system is also outdated — unsuited to the needs of our economy and to the values of our country. We should not be content with laws that punish hardworking people who want only to provide for their families and deny businesses willing workers, and invite chaos at our border. It is time for an immigration policy that permits temporary guest workers to fill jobs Americans will not take, that rejects amnesty, that tells us who is entering and leaving our country, and that closes the border to drug dealers and terrorists.

## SOCIAL SECURITY

One of America's most important institutions — a symbol of the trust between generations — is also in need of wise and effective reform. Social Security was a great moral success of the 20th century, and we must honor its great purposes in this new century. The system, however, on its current path, is headed toward bankruptcy. And so we must join together to strengthen and save Social Security.

Today, more than 45 million Americans receive Social Security benefits, and millions more are nearing retirement. And for them, the system is sound and fiscally strong. I have a message for every American who is 55 or older: Do not let anyone mislead you. For you, the Social Security system will not change in any way.

For younger workers, the Social Security system has serious problems that will grow worse with time. Social Security was created decades ago, for a very different era. In those days, people did not live as long, benefits were much lower than they are today, and a half-century ago, about 16 workers paid into the system for each person drawing benefits.

Our society has changed in ways the founders of Social Security could not have foreseen. In today's world, people are living longer and therefore drawing benefits longer. And those benefits are scheduled to rise dramatically over the next few decades. And instead of 16 workers paying in for every beneficiary, right now it's only about three workers. And over the next few decades, that number will fall to just two workers per beneficiary. With each passing year, fewer workers are paying ever-higher benefits to an ever-larger number of retirees.

So here is the result: Thirteen years from now, in 2018, Social Security will be paying out more than it takes in. And every year afterward will bring a new shortfall, bigger than the year before. For example, in the year 2027, the government will somehow have to come up with an extra $200 billion to keep the system afloat. And by 2033, the annual shortfall would be more than $300 billion. By the year 2042, the entire system would be exhausted and bankrupt.

If steps are not taken to avert that outcome, the only solutions would be dramatically higher taxes, massive new borrowing, or sudden and severe cuts in Social Security benefits or other government programs.

I recognize that 2018 and 2042 may seem a long way off. But those dates aren't so distant, as any parent will tell you. If you have a 5-year-old, you're already concerned about how you'll pay for college tuition 13 years down the road. If you've got children in their 20s, as some of us do, the idea of Social Security collapsing before they retire does not seem like a small matter. And it should not be a small matter to the United States Congress.

You and I share a responsibility. We must pass reforms that solve the financial problems of Social Security once and for all.

Fixing Social Security permanently will require an open, candid review of the options.

Some have suggested limiting benefits for wealthy retirees. Former Congressman Tim Penny has raised the possibility of indexing benefits to prices rather than wages. During the 1990s, my predecessor, President Clinton, spoke of increasing the retirement age. Former Sen. John Breaux suggested discouraging early collection of Social Security benefits. The late Sen. Daniel Patrick Moynihan recommended changing the way benefits are calculated. All these ideas are on the table.

I know that none of these reforms would be easy. But we have to move ahead with courage and honesty, because our children's retirement security is more important than partisan politics. I will work with members of Congress to find the most effective combination of reforms. I will listen to anyone who has a good idea to offer.

We must, however, be guided by some basic principles: We must make Social Security permanently sound, not leave that task for another day. We must not jeopardize our economic strength by increasing payroll taxes. We must ensure that lower-income Americans get the help they need to have dignity and peace of mind in their retirement. We must guarantee that there is no change for those now retired or nearing retirement. And we must take care that any changes in the system are gradual, so younger workers have years to prepare and plan for their future.

As we fix Social Security, we also have the responsibility to make the system a better deal for younger workers. And the best way to reach that goal is through voluntary personal retirement accounts.

Here is how the idea works: Right now, a set portion of the money you earn is taken out of your paycheck to pay for the Social Security benefits of today's retirees. If you're a younger worker, I believe you should be able to set aside part of that money in your own retirement account, so you can build a nest egg for your own future.

Here is why the personal accounts are a better deal: Your money will grow, over time, at a greater rate than anything the current system can deliver. And your account will provide money for retirement over and above the check you will receive from Social Security. In addition, you'll be able to pass along the money that accumulates in your personal account, if you wish, to your children — or grandchildren. And best of all, the money in the account is yours, and the government can never take it away.

The goal here is greater security in retirement, so we will set careful guidelines for personal accounts: We'll make sure the money

can only go into a conservative mix of bonds and stock funds. We'll make sure that your earnings are not eaten up by hidden Wall Street fees. We'll make sure there are good options to protect your investments from sudden market swings on the eve of your retirement. We'll make sure a personal account cannot be emptied out all at once, but rather paid out over time, as an addition to traditional Social Security benefits.

And we'll make sure this plan is fiscally responsible by starting personal retirement accounts gradually and raising the yearly limits on contributions over time, eventually permitting all workers to set aside 4 percentage points of their payroll taxes in their accounts.

Personal retirement accounts should be familiar to federal employees, because you already have something similar, called the Thrift Savings Plan, which lets workers deposit a portion of their paychecks into any of five different broadly based investment funds. It's time to extend the same security and choice and ownership to young Americans.

## A FREE SOCIETY

Our second great responsibility to our children and grandchildren is to honor and to pass along the values that sustain a free society. So many of my generation, after a long journey, have come home to family and faith, and are determined to bring up responsible, moral children. Government is not the source of these values, but government should never undermine them.

Because marriage is a sacred institution and the foundation of society, it should not be redefined by activist judges. For the good of families, children and society, I support a constitutional amendment to protect the institution of marriage.

Because a society is measured by how it treats the weak and vulnerable, we must strive to build a culture of life. Medical research can help us reach that goal, by developing treatments and cures that save lives and help people overcome disabilities. And I thank the Congress for doubling the funding of the National Institutes of Health.

To build a culture of life, we must also ensure that scientific advances always serve human dignity, not take advantage of some lives for the benefit of others. We should all be able to agree on some clear standards. I will work with Congress to ensure that human embryos are not created for experimentation or grown for body parts and that human life is never bought or sold as a commodity.

America will continue to lead the world in

medical research that is ambitious, aggressive and always ethical.

Because courts must always deliver impartial justice, judges have a duty to faithfully interpret the law, not legislate from the bench. As president, I have a constitutional responsibility to nominate men and women who understand the role of courts in our democracy and are well-qualified to serve on the bench, and I have done so. The Constitution also gives the Senate a responsibility: Every judicial nominee deserves an up-or-down vote.

Because one of the deepest values of our country is compassion, we must never turn away from any citizen who feels isolated from the opportunities of America. Our government will continue to support faith-based and community groups that bring hope to harsh places.

## GANG VIOLENCE

Now we need to focus on giving young people, especially young men in our cities, better options than apathy or gangs or jail. Tonight I propose a three-year initiative to help organizations keep young people out of gangs and show young men an ideal of manhood that respects women and rejects violence.

Taking on gang life will be one part of a broader outreach to at-risk youth, which involves parents and pastors, coaches and community leaders, in programs ranging from literacy to sports. And I am proud that the leader of this nationwide effort will be our first lady, Laura Bush.

Because HIV/AIDS brings suffering and fear into so many lives, I ask you to reauthorize the Ryan White Act to encourage prevention and provide care and treatment to the victims of that disease. And as we update this important law, we must focus our efforts on fellow citizens with the highest rates of new cases: African-American men and women.

Because one of the main sources of our national unity is our belief in equal justice, we need to make sure Americans of all races and backgrounds have confidence in the system that provides justice. In America we must make doubly sure no person is held to account for a crime he or she did not commit. So we are dramatically expanding the use of DNA evidence to prevent wrongful conviction. Soon I will send to Congress a proposal to fund special training for defense counsel in capital cases, because people on trial for their lives must have competent lawyers by their side.

## NATIONAL SECURITY

Our third responsibility to future generations is to leave them an America that is safe from danger and protected by peace. We will pass along to our children all the freedoms we enjoy. And chief among them is freedom from fear.

In the three and a half years since September the 11th, 2001, we've taken unprecedented actions to protect Americans.

We've created a new department of government to defend our homeland, focused the FBI on preventing terrorism, begun to reform our intelligence agencies, broken up terror cells across the country, expanded research on defenses against biological and chemical attack, improved border security, and trained more than a half-million first responders.

Police and firefighters, air marshals, researchers and so many others are working every day to make our homeland safer — and we thank them all.

Our nation, working with allies and friends, has also confronted the enemy abroad with measures that are determined, successful and continuing.

The al Qaeda terror network that attacked our country still has leaders, but many of its top commanders have been removed. There are still governments that sponsor and harbor terrorists, but their number has declined. There are still regimes seeking weapons of mass destruction, but no longer without attention and without consequence.

Our country is still the target of terrorists who want to kill many and intimidate us all. And we will stay on the offensive against them until the fight is won.

Pursuing our enemies is a vital commitment of the war on terror. And I thank the Congress for providing our service men and women with the resources they have needed. During this time of war, we must continue to support our military and give them the tools for victory.

Other nations around the globe have stood with us. In Afghanistan, an international force is helping provide security. In Iraq, 28 countries have troops on the ground, the United Nations and the European Union provided technical assistance for the elections, and NATO is leading a mission to help train Iraqi officers. We're cooperating with 60 governments in the Proliferation Security Initiative to detect and stop the transit of dangerous materials. We're working closely with the governments in Asia to convince North Korea to abandon its nuclear ambitions. Pakistan, Saudi Arabia and nine other countries have captured or detained al Qaeda terrorists.

In the next four years, my administration will continue to build the coalitions that will defeat the dangers of our time.

In the long term, the peace we seek will only be achieved by eliminating the conditions that feed radicalism and ideologies of murder. If whole regions of the world remain in despair and grow in hatred, they will be the recruiting grounds for terror, and that terror will stalk America and other free nations for decades.

The only force powerful enough to stop the rise of tyranny and terror, and replace hatred with hope is the force of human freedom.

Our enemies know this, and that is why the terrorist Zarqawi recently declared war on what he called the "evil principle" of democracy. And we've declared our own intention: America will stand with the allies of freedom to support democratic movements in the Middle East and beyond, with the ultimate goal of ending tyranny in our world.

The United States has no right, no desire and no intention to impose our form of government on anyone else. That is one of the main differences between us and our enemies. They seek to impose and expand an empire of oppression, in which a tiny group of brutal, self-appointed rulers control every aspect of every life.

Our aim is to build and preserve a community of free and independent nations, with governments that answer to their citizens and reflect their own cultures. And because democracies respect their own people and their neighbors, the advance of freedom will lead to peace.

That advance has great momentum in our time, shown by women voting in Afghanistan, and Palestinians choosing a new direction, and the people of Ukraine asserting their democratic rights and electing a president. We are witnessing landmark events in the history of liberty. And in the coming years, we will add to that story.

## THE MIDDLE EAST

The beginnings of reform and democracy in the Palestinian territories are now showing the power of freedom to break old patterns of violence and failure.

Tomorrow morning, Secretary of State Rice departs on a trip that will take her to Israel and the West Bank for meetings with Prime Minister Sharon and President Abbas. She will discuss with them how we and our friends can help the Palestinian people end terror and build the institutions of a peaceful, independent, democratic state.

To promote this democracy, I will ask Congress for $350 million to support Palestinian political, economic and security reforms. The

goal of two democratic states, Israel and Palestine, living side by side in peace is within reach, and America will help them achieve that goal.

To promote peace and stability in the broader Middle East, the United States will work with our friends in the region to fight the common threat of terror, while we encourage a higher standard of freedom.

Hopeful reform is already taking hold in an arc from Morocco to Jordan to Bahrain. The government of Saudi Arabia can demonstrate its leadership in the region by expanding the role of its people in determining their future. And the great and proud nation of Egypt, which showed the way toward peace in the Middle East, can now show the way toward democracy in the Middle East.

To promote peace in the broader Middle East, we must confront regimes that continue to harbor terrorists and pursue weapons of mass murder.

Syria still allows its territory and parts of Lebanon to be used by terrorists who seek to destroy every chance of peace in the region. You have passed, and we are applying, the Syrian Accountability Act. And we expect the Syrian government to end all support for terror and open the door to freedom.

Today, Iran remains the world's primary state sponsor of terror — pursuing nuclear weapons while depriving its people of the freedom they seek and deserve. We are working with European allies to make clear to the Iranian regime that it must give up its uranium enrichment program and any plutonium reprocessing and end its support for terror. And to the Iranian people, I say tonight: As you stand for your own liberty, America stands with you.

## IRAQ

Our generational commitment to the advance of freedom, especially in the Middle East, is now being tested and honored in Iraq. That country is a vital front in the war on terror, which is why the terrorists have chosen to make a stand there. Our men and women in uniform are fighting terrorists in Iraq so we do not have to face them here at home.

The victory of freedom in Iraq will strengthen a new ally in the war on terror, inspire democratic reformers from Damascus to Tehran, bring more hope and progress to a troubled region, and thereby lift a terrible threat from the lives of our children and grandchildren. We will succeed because the Iraqi people value their own liberty, as they showed the world last Sunday.

Across Iraq, often at great risk, millions of citizens went to the polls and elected 275 men and women to represent them in a new Transitional National Assembly.

A young woman in Baghdad told of waking to the sound of mortar fire on election day and wondering if it might be too dangerous to vote. She said, "Hearing those explosions, it occurred to me, the insurgents are weak, they are afraid of democracy, they are losing. So I got my husband, and I got my parents, and we all came out and voted together."

Americans recognize that spirit of liberty, because we share it. In any nation, casting your vote is an act of civic responsibility. For millions of Iraqis, it was also an act of personal courage, and they have earned the respect of us all.

One of Iraq's leading democracy and human rights advocates is Safia Taleb al-Suhail. She says of her country, "We were occupied for 35 years by Saddam Hussein. That was the real occupation. Thank you to the American people who paid the cost, but most of all to the soldiers."

Eleven years ago, Safia's father was assassinated by Saddam's intelligence service. Three days ago in Baghdad, Safia was finally able to vote for the leaders of her country. And we are honored that she is with us tonight.

The terrorists and insurgents are violently opposed to democracy and will continue to attack it. Yet the terrorists' most powerful myth is being destroyed. The whole world is seeing that the car bombers and assassins are not only fighting coalition forces, they are trying to destroy the hopes of Iraqis, expressed in free elections. And the whole world now knows that a small group of extremists will not overturn the will of the Iraqi people.

We will succeed in Iraq because Iraqis are determined to fight for their own freedom and to write their own history. As Prime Minister Allawi said in his speech to Congress last September, "Ordinary Iraqis are anxious to shoulder all the security burdens of our country as quickly as possible." That is the natural desire of an independent nation, and it also is the stated mission of our coalition in Iraq.

## SUPPORT FOR IRAQIS

The new political situation in Iraq opens a new phase of our work in that country. At the recommendation of our commanders on the ground and in consultation with the Iraqi government, we will increasingly focus our efforts on helping prepare more capable Iraqi security forces — forces with skilled officers and an effective command structure.

As those forces become more self-reliant and take on greater security responsibilities, America and its coalition partners will increasingly be in a supporting role. In the end, Iraqis must be able to defend their own country, and we will help that proud, new nation secure its liberty.

Recently an Iraqi interpreter said to a reporter, "Tell America not to abandon us." He and all Iraqis can be certain: While our military strategy is adapting to circumstances, our commitment remains firm and unchanging. We are standing for the freedom of our Iraqi friends, and freedom in Iraq will make America safer for generations to come.

We will not set an artificial timetable for leaving Iraq, because that would embolden the terrorists and make them believe they can wait us out. We are in Iraq to achieve a result: a country that is democratic, representative of all its people, at peace with its neighbors and able to defend itself.

And when that result is achieved, our men and women serving in Iraq will return home with the honor they have earned.

Right now, Americans in uniform are serving at posts across the world, often taking great risks on my orders. We have given them training and equipment. And they have given us an example of idealism and character that makes every American proud. The volunteers of our military are unrelenting in battle, unwavering in loyalty, unmatched in honor and decency; and every day they are making our nation more secure.

Some of our service men and women have survived terrible injuries, and this grateful country will do everything we can to help them recover. And we have said farewell to some very good men and women who died for our freedom and whose memory this nation will honor forever.

One name we honor is Marine Corps Sgt. Byron Norwood of Pflugerville, Texas, who was killed during the assault on Fallujah. His mom, Janet, sent me a letter and told me how much Byron loved being a Marine and how proud he was to be on the front line against terror. She wrote, "When Byron was home the last time, I said that I wanted to protect him like I had since he was born. He just hugged me and said, 'You've done your job, Mom. Now it is my turn to protect you.'"

Ladies and gentlemen, with grateful hearts, we honor freedom's defenders and our military families, represented here this evening by Sgt. Norwood's mom and dad, Janet and Bill Norwood.

In these four years, Americans have seen the unfolding of large events. We have known times of sorrow and hours of uncertainty and days of

victory. In all this history, even when we have disagreed, we have seen threads of purpose that unite us. The attack on freedom in our world has reaffirmed our confidence in freedom's power to change the world. We're all part of a great venture: to extend the promise of freedom in our country, to renew the values that sustain our liberty and to spread the peace that freedom brings.

As Franklin Roosevelt once reminded Americans, "Each age is a dream that is dying or one that is coming to birth."

And we live in the country where the biggest dreams are born. The abolition of slavery was only a dream — until it was fulfilled. The liberation of Europe from fascism was only a dream — until it was achieved. The fall of imperial communism was only a dream — until, one day, it was accomplished.

Our generation has dreams of its own, and we also go forward with confidence. The road of providence is uneven and unpredictable, yet we know where it leads: It leads to freedom.

Thank you. And may God bless America. ∎

# Democrats Respond

*Following is a transcript of the official Democratic response to President Bush's State of the Union address, which was delivered at the Capitol on Feb. 2 by the party's two congressional floor leaders. The first speaker was Senate Minority Leader Harry Reid of Nevada; the second speaker was House Minority Leader Nancy Pelosi of California. Source: CQ Transcriptions.*

NOW THAT YOU'VE HEARD from the president, I appreciate your taking a few minutes with us as we give our views on how we can live up to the American promise.

I was born and raised in the high desert of Nevada in a tiny town called Searchlight. My dad was a hard rock miner. My mom took in wash. I grew up around people of strong values, even if they rarely talked about them. They loved their country, worshiped God, never shunned hard work and never asked for special favors. My life has been very different from what I imagined growing up, but no matter how far I've traveled, Searchlight is still the place I go back to and still the place I call home.

A few weeks ago, I joined some friends of mine for a bite to eat at The Nugget, Searchlight's only restaurant. We were sitting down in a booth when a young boy, about 10 years old, named Devon, walked up to us. Carrying a skateboard under his arm, he said, Sen. Reid, when I grow up, I want to be just like you.

Well, the truth is, Devon could probably do a lot better. But the point still holds, and it's this: No one ever had to tell young Devon to dream big dreams. No one ever had to teach him that America is a place of possibility. He knows those things because they're borne deep in all Americans.

In the coming year, I believe we can make sure America lives up to its legacy as a land of opportunity if the president is willing to join hands and build from the center. It's important that we succeed. It's time that America's government lived up to the same values as America's families. It's time we invested in America's future and made sure our people have the skills to compete and thrive in a 21st century economy. That's what Democrats believe, and that's where we stand, and that's what we'll fight for.

Too many of the president's economic policies have left Americans and American companies struggling. And after we worked so hard to eliminate the deficit, his policies have added trillions to the debt — in effect, a birth tax of $36,000 on every child that is born.

**'MARSHALL PLAN FOR AMERICA'**

We Democrats have a different vision: spurring research and development in new technologies to help create the jobs of the future; rolling up our sleeves and fighting for today's jobs by ending the special tax breaks that encourage big corporations to ship jobs overseas; a trade policy that enforces the rules of the road so that we play to win in the global marketplace instead of sitting by and getting played for fools.

After World War II, through the Marshall Plan, we rebuilt Europe, and they went from poverty to an economic powerhouse. Today, we need to invest in our nation's future with a Marshall Plan for America to build the infrastructure our economy needs to go — and to grow. President Eisenhower did that in the 1950s with interstate highways. National investment created the Internet in the 1970s. We need to build the next economy, and we need to start now.

The 21st century economy holds great promise for our people. But unless we give all Americans the skills they need to succeed, countries like India and China will be taking our good-paying jobs that should be ours. From early childhood education to better elementary and high schools to making college more affordable to training workers so they can get better jobs, Democrats believe every American should have a world-class education and the skills they need in a worldwide economy.

Health care costs have shot up double dig-its year after year of the Bush administration, and that's costing us jobs, costing us our competitiveness and costing families their peace of mind. We need to make health care and prescription drugs affordable so that our families and our small businesses will no longer have to shoulder this dead weight.

Good, new jobs, world-class education, affordable health care: These things matter. Unfortunately, much of what the president offered weren't real answers.

You know, today is Groundhog Day. And what we saw and heard tonight was a little like the movie "Groundhog Day" — the same old ideology that we've heard before, over and over and over again. We can do better.

I want you to know that when we believe the president is on the right track, we won't let partisan interests get in the way of what's good for our country. We will be the first in line to work with him. But when he gets off-track, we will be there to hold him accountable. That's why we so strongly disagree with the president's plan to privatize Social Security.

Let me share with you why I believe the president's plan is so dangerous. There's a lot we can do to improve Americans' retirement security, but it's wrong to replace the guaranteed benefit that Americans have earned with a guaranteed benefit cut of up to 40 percent.

Make no mistake, that's exactly what President Bush is proposing. The Bush plan would take our already record-high $4.3 trillion national debt and put us another $2 trillion in the red. That's an immoral burden to place on the backs of the next generation.

But maybe most of all, the Bush plan isn't really Social Security reform; it's more like Social Security roulette. Democrats are all for giving Americans more of a say and more choices when it comes to their retirement savings, but that doesn't mean taking Social Security's guarantee and gambling with it. And that's coming from a senator who represents Las Vegas.

Sometimes important questions, like Social Security or the economy or education, get reduced to dollars and cents with the competing

policies of political parties. But really, these are questions about our old-fashioned moral values that don't get talked about much in Washington but matter so much to our country.

Are we willing to do right by our parents and take care of our children? Do we believe that big corporations with powerful lobbyists should get special favors and that the wealthiest should get special tax breaks? Or do we believe we are all God's children and that each of us should get a fair shot and a say in our future? Will we be able to tell young people, like Devon back in Searchlight, that America is still the land of the open road and that you can travel that open road to the place of your choice?

Even after the president's speech, the American people are still asking these questions. You can be sure that Democrats will continue to offer real answers in the months ahead. Now, I'd like to turn things over to my colleague, the great leader of the House Democrats, Nancy Pelosi.

THANK YOU, Sen. Reid. Throughout our nation's history, hope and optimism have defined the American spirit. With pride and determination, every generation has passed on a stronger America than the one it inherited. Our greatest responsibility is to leave our children a world that is a safer and more secure place.

As House Democratic leader, I want to speak with you this evening about an issue of grave concern: the national security of our country. Any discussion of our national security must begin with recognition and respect for our men and women in uniform. Whether they are fighting in Iraq and Afghanistan or delivering humanitarian aid to the victims of the tsunami in Asia, our troops have the gratitude of every American for their courage, their patriotism and the sacrifice that they are willing to make for our country.

I have seen that sacrifice up close. I've met with our troops in Iraq and Afghanistan, and I've visited our wounded in military hospitals here and overseas. Our troops not only defend us, they inspire us. They remind us of our responsibility to build a future worthy of their sacrifice.

Because of the courage of our servicemen and -women and the determination of the Iraqi people, Iraq's election on Sunday was a significant step toward Iraqis taking their future into their own hands. Now we must consider our future in Iraq.

We all know that the United States cannot stay in Iraq indefinitely and continue to be viewed as an occupying force; neither should we

slip out the back door, falsely declaring victory but leaving chaos. Despite the best efforts of our troops and their Iraqi counterparts, Iraq still faces a violent and persistent insurgency. And the chairman of the National Intelligence Council said in January that Iraq is now a magnet for international terrorists.

We have never heard a clear plan from this administration for ending our presence in Iraq. And we did not hear one tonight. Democrats believe a credible plan to bring our troops home and stabilizing Iraq must include three key elements.

First, responsibility for Iraqi security must be transferred to the Iraqis as soon as possible. This action is long overdue. The top priority for the U.S. military should have been for a long time now training the Iraqi army. We must not be lulled into a false sense of confidence by the administration's claim that a large number of security personnel have been trained. It simply hasn't happened. But it must.

Second, Iraq's economic development must be accelerated. Congress has provided billions of dollars for reconstruction, but little of that money has been spent effectively to put Iraqis to work rebuilding their country. Infrastructure improvements in Iraq are more than just projects; they give Iraqis hope for a better future and a stake in achieving it, and they contribute to Iraqi stability.

Third, regional diplomacy must be intensified. Diplomacy can lessen the political problems in Iraq, take pressure off of our troops and deprive the insurgency of the fuel of anti-Americanism on which it thrives.

If these three steps are taken, the next elections in Iraq, scheduled for December, can be held in a more secure atmosphere, with broader participation and a much smaller American presence.

## FUNDING FIRST-RESPONDERS

Just as we must transfer greater responsibility to the Iraqi people for their own security, we must embrace a renewed commitment to our security here at home.

It's been over three years since the attacks of Sept. 11. Our hopes and prayers will always be with the 9/11 families, who strengthen our resolve to win the war on terror. The pain and horror of that day will never be forgotten by any of us, yet the gaps in our security exposed by those attacks remain.

Despite the administration's rhetoric, airline cargo still goes uninspected, shipping containers go unscreened, and our railroads and power plants are not secure. Police officers and firefighters across America have

pleaded for the tools they need to prevent or respond to an attack, but the administration still hasn't delivered for our first-responders. The greatest threat to our homeland security are the tons of biological, chemical and even nuclear materials that are unaccounted for or unguarded.

The president says the right words about the threat, but he has failed to take action commensurate with it. We can, and we must, keep the world's most gruesome weapons out of the world's most dangerous hands. Nothing is more important to our homeland security and, indeed, to the safety of the world.

For three years, the president has failed to put together a comprehensive plan to protect America from terrorism, and we did not hear one tonight.

As we strive to close the gaps in our security here at home, we must do more to show our great strength as well as our greatness. We must extend the hand of friendship to our neighbors in Latin America. We must work to stop the genocide in Sudan. We must reinvigorate the Middle East peace process. And we must bring health and hope to people suffering from disease, devastation and the fury of despair.

We are called to do this and more by our faith and our common humanity, and also because these actions will enhance our national security. Democrats are committed to a strong national security that keeps America safe, that wins the war on terror and that never again sends our troops into harm's way without the equipment they need.

In our New Partnership for America's Future, House Democrats have made a commitment to guarantee a military second to none, to stop the spread of weapons of mass destruction, to build strong diplomatic alliances, to collect timely and reliable intelligence to keep us safe at home, and to honor our veterans and their families by making sure they have the health care and benefits they have earned.

For those returning from military service — our newest veterans — Democrats are calling for a G.I. bill of rights for the 21st century to guarantee access to education, health care and the opportunity for good jobs.

And we must protect and defend the American people. And we must also protect and defend our Constitution and the civil liberties contained therein. That is our oath of office.

A strong and secure America was our parents' gift to us. We owe our children and our grandchildren nothing less.

Thank you. Good night. And may God continue to bless the United States of America. ∎

# Bush Outlines Disaster Aid Program

*Following is the CQ Transcriptions transcript of the nationally televised address President Bush delivered from Jackson Square in New Orleans on Sept. 15:*

GOOD EVENING. I am speaking to you from the city of New Orleans — nearly empty, still partly under water, and waiting for life and hope to return.

Eastward from Lake Pontchartrain, across the Mississippi coast, to Alabama and into Florida, millions of lives were changed in a day by a cruel and wasteful storm. In the aftermath, we have seen fellow citizens left stunned and uprooted, searching for loved ones and grieving for the dead, and looking for meaning in a tragedy that seems so blind and random.

We have also witnessed the kind of desperation no citizen of this great and generous nation should ever have to know: fellow Americans calling out for food and water, vulnerable people left at the mercy of criminals who had no mercy, and the bodies of the dead lying uncovered and untended in the street.

These days of sorrow and outrage have also been marked by acts of courage and kindness that make all Americans proud.

Coast Guard and other personnel rescued tens of thousands of people from flooded neighborhoods. Religious congregations and families have welcomed strangers as brothers and sisters and neighbors. In the community of Chalmette, when two men tried to break into a home, the owner invited them to stay — and took in 15 other people who had no place to go. At Tulane Hospital for Children, doctors and nurses did not eat for days so patients could have food, and eventually carried the patients on their backs up eight flights of stairs to helicopters.

Many first-responders were victims themselves — wounded healers, with a sense of duty greater than their own suffering. When I met Steve Scott of the Biloxi Fire Department, he and his colleagues were conducting a house-to-house search for survivors. Steve told me this: "I lost my house and I lost my cars, but I still got my family and I still got my spirit."

Across the Gulf Coast, among people who have lost much and suffered much and given to the limit of their power, we are seeing that same spirit: a core of strength that survives all hurt, a faith in God no storm can take away, and a powerful American determination to clear the ruins and build better than before.

## RECOVERY AND REBUILDING

Tonight so many victims of the hurricane and the flood are far from home and friends and familiar things. You need to know that our whole nation cares about you, and in the journey ahead you are not alone.

To all who carry a burden of loss, I extend the deepest sympathy of our country. To every person who has served and sacrificed in this emergency, I offer the gratitude of our country.

And tonight I also offer this pledge of the American people: Throughout the area hit by the hurricane, we will do what it takes, we will stay as long as it takes, to help citizens rebuild their communities and their lives.

And all who question the future of the Crescent City need to know: There is no way to imagine America without New Orleans, and this great city will rise again.

The work of rescue is largely finished; the work of recovery is moving forward. In nearly all of Mississippi, electric power has been restored. Trade is starting to return to the port of New Orleans, and agricultural shipments are moving down the Mississippi River.

All major gasoline pipelines are now in operation, preventing the supply disruptions that many feared. The breaks in the levees have been closed, the pumps are running, and the water here in New Orleans is receding by the hour. Environmental officials are on the ground, taking water samples, identifying and dealing with hazardous debris, and working to get drinking water and wastewater treatment systems operating again. And some very sad duties are being carried out by professionals who gather the dead, treat them with respect, and prepare them for their rest.

In the task of recovery and rebuilding, some of the hardest work is still ahead. And it will require the creative skill and generosity of a united country.

## MEETING THE NEED

Our first commitment is to meet the immediate needs of those who had to flee their homes and leave all their possessions behind. For these Americans, every night brings uncertainty, every day requires new courage and, in the months to come, will bring more than their fair share of struggles.

The Department of Homeland Security is registering evacuees who are now in shelters, churches or private homes — whether in the Gulf region or far away.

I have signed an order providing immediate assistance to people from the disaster area. As of today, more than 500,000 evacuee families have gotten emergency help to pay for food, clothing and other essentials.

Evacuees who have not yet registered should contact FEMA or the Red Cross. We need to know who you are, because many of you will be eligible for broader assistance in the future.

Many families were separated during the evacuation, and we are working to help you reunite. Please call this number: 1-877-568-3317. That's 1-877-568-3317. And we will work to bring your family back together and pay for your travel to reach them.

In addition, we are taking steps to ensure that evacuees do not have to travel great distances or navigate bureaucracies to get the benefits that are there for them.

The Department of Health and Human Services has sent more than 1,500 health professionals, along with over 50 tons of medical supplies — including vaccines, antibiotics and medicines for people with chronic conditions, such as diabetes. The Social Security Administration is delivering checks. The Department of Labor is helping displaced persons apply for temporary jobs and unemployment benefits. And the Postal Service is registering new addresses so that people can get their mail.

To carry out the first stages of the relief effort and begin rebuilding at once, I have asked for, and the Congress has provided, more than $60 billion. This is an unprecedented response to an unprecedented crisis, which demonstrates the compassion and resolve of our nation.

## INFRASTRUCTURE

Our second commitment is to help the citizens of the Gulf Coast to overcome this disaster, put their lives back together and rebuild their communities.

Along this coast, for mile after mile, the wind and water swept the land clean. In Mississippi, many thousands of houses were damaged or destroyed. In New Orleans and surrounding parishes, more than a quarter-million houses are no longer safe to live in. Hundreds of thousands of people from across this region will need to find longer-term housing.

Our goal is to get people out of the shelters by the middle of October. So we are providing direct assistance to evacuees that allows them to rent apartments, and many are already moving into places of their own.

A number of states have taken in evacuees and shown them great compassion — admitting children to school and providing health care. So I will work with the Congress to ensure that states are reimbursed for these extra expenses.

In the disaster area and in cities that have received huge numbers of displaced people, we are beginning to bring in mobile homes and trailers for temporary use.

To relieve the burden on local health care facilities in the region, we are sending extra doctors and nurses to these areas. We're also providing money that can be used to cover overtime pay for police and fire departments while the cities and towns rebuild.

Near New Orleans, Biloxi and other cities, housing is urgently needed for police and firefighters, other service providers and the many workers who are going to rebuild these cities. Right now, many are sleeping on ships we have brought to the Port of New Orleans, and more ships are on their way to the region.

And we'll provide mobile homes and supply them with basic services, as close to construction areas as possible, so the rebuilding process can go forward as quickly as possible.

And the federal government will undertake a close partnership with the states of Louisiana and Mississippi, the city of New Orleans and other Gulf Coast cities, so they can rebuild in a sensible, well-planned way. Federal funds will cover the great majority of the costs of repairing public infrastructure in the disaster zone, from roads and bridges to schools and water systems.

Our goal is to get the work done quickly. And taxpayers expect this work to be done honestly and wisely. So we will have a team of inspectors general reviewing all expenditures.

In the rebuilding process, there will be many important decisions and many details to resolve. Yet we are moving forward according to some clear principles.

The federal government will be fully engaged in the mission, but Gov. [Haley] Barbour [of Mississippi], Gov. [Kathleen Babineaux] Blanco [of Louisiana], Mayor [C. Ray] Nagin [of New Orleans] and other state and local leaders will have the primary role in planning for their own future.

Clearly, communities will need to move decisively to change zoning laws and building codes, in order to avoid a repeat of what we

have seen. And in the work of rebuilding, as many jobs as possible should go to the men and women who live in Louisiana, Mississippi and Alabama.

## ANTI-POVERTY EFFORT

Our third commitment is this: When communities are rebuilt, they must be even better and stronger than before the storm.

Within the Gulf region are some of the most beautiful and historic places in America. As all of us saw on television, there is also some deep, persistent poverty in this region as well. That poverty has roots in a history of racial discrimination, which cut off generations from the opportunity of America. We have a duty to confront this poverty with bold action.

So let us restore all that we have cherished from yesterday, and let us rise above the legacy of inequality.

When the streets are rebuilt, there should be many new businesses, including minority-owned businesses, along those streets.

When the houses are rebuilt, more families should own, not rent, those houses.

When the regional economy revives, local people should be prepared for the jobs being created.

Americans want the Gulf Coast not just to survive, but to thrive; not just to cope, but to overcome. We want evacuees to come home, for the best of reasons — because they have a real chance at a better life in a place they love.

When one resident of this city who lost his home was asked by a reporter if he would relocate, he said, "No, I will rebuild, but I will build higher." That is our vision for the future in this city and beyond. We'll not just rebuild, we'll build higher and better.

To meet this goal, I will listen to good ideas from Congress and state and local officials and the private sector.

## SAFETY AND SECURITY

I believe we should start with three initiatives that the Congress should pass.

Tonight, I propose the creation of a Gulf opportunity zone, encompassing the region of the disaster in Louisiana and Mississippi and Alabama.

Within this zone, we should provide immediate incentives for job-creating investment; tax relief for small businesses; incentives to companies that create jobs; and loans and loan guarantees for small businesses, including minority-owned enterprises, to get them up and running again. It is entrepreneurship that creates jobs and opportunity. It is entre-

preneurship that helps break the cycle of poverty. And we will take the side of entrepreneurs as they lead the economic revival of the Gulf region.

I propose the creation of worker recovery accounts to help those evacuees who need extra help finding work. Under this plan, the federal government would provide accounts of up to $5,000, which these evacuees could draw upon for job training and education to help them get a good job and for child care expenses during their job search.

And to help lower-income citizens in the hurricane region build new and better lives, I also propose that Congress pass an Urban Homesteading Act.

Under this approach, we will identify property in the region owned by the federal government and provide building sites to low-income citizens free of charge, through a lottery. In return, they would pledge to build on the lot, with either a mortgage or help from a charitable organization like Habitat for Humanity.

Homeownership is one of the great strengths of any community, and it must be a central part of our vision for the revival of this region.

In the long run, the New Orleans area has a particular challenge, because much of the city lies below sea level. The people who call it home need to have reassurance that their lives will be safer in the years to come.

Protecting a city that sits lower than the water around it is not easy, but it can and has been done. City and parish officials in New Orleans and state officials in Louisiana will have a large part in the engineering decisions to come. And the Army Corps of Engineers will work at their side to make the flood-protection system stronger than it has ever been.

The work that has begun in the Gulf Coast region will be one of the largest reconstruction efforts the world has ever seen. When that job is done, all Americans will have something to be very proud of. And all Americans are needed in this common effort.

## ARMIES OF COMPASSION

It is the armies of compassion — charities and houses of worship and idealistic men and women — that give our reconstruction effort its humanity. They offer to those who hurt a friendly face, an arm around the shoulder and the reassurance that, in hard times, they can count on someone who cares.

By land, by sea and by air, good people wanting to make a difference deployed to the Gulf Coast. And they have been working

around the clock ever since.

The cash needed to support the armies of compassion is great, and Americans have given generously. For example, the private fundraising effort led by former Presidents [George] Bush and [Bill] Clinton has already received pledges of more than $100 million. Some of that money is going to the governors, to be used for immediate needs within their states. A portion will also be sent to local houses of worship, to help reimburse them for the expense of helping others.

This evening, the need is still urgent, and I ask the American people to continue donating to the Salvation Army, the Red Cross, other good charities and religious congregations in the region.

It is also essential for the many organizations of our country to reach out to your fellow citizens in the Gulf area. So I have asked USA Freedom Corps to create an information clearinghouse, available at usafreedomcorps.gov, so that families anywhere in the country can find opportunities to help families in the region or a school can support a school.

And I challenge existing organizations — churches and Scout troops or labor union locals — to get in touch with their counterparts in Mississippi, Louisiana or Alabama and learn what they can do to help.

In this great national enterprise, important work can be done by everyone, and everyone should find their role and do their part.

## LEARNING THE LESSON

The government of this nation will do its part as well. Our cities must have clear and up-to-date plans for responding to natural disasters and disease outbreaks or a terrorist attack, for evacuating large numbers of people in an emergency, and for providing the food and water and security they would need.

In a time of terror threats and weapons of mass destruction, the danger to our citizens reaches much wider than a fault line or a flood plain. I consider detailed emergency planning to be a national security priority.

And therefore, I have ordered the Department of Homeland Security to undertake an immediate review, in cooperation with local counterparts, of emergency plans in every major city in America.

I also want to know all the facts about the government response to Hurricane Katrina. The storm involved a massive flood, a major supply and security operation, and an evacuation order affecting more than a million people.

It was not a normal hurricane, and the normal disaster relief system was not equal to it.

Many of the men and women of the Coast Guard, the Federal Emergency Management Agency, the United States military, the National Guard, Homeland Security, and state and local governments performed skillfully under the worst conditions. Yet the system, at every level of government, was not well-coordinated and was overwhelmed in the first few days.

It is now clear that a challenge on this scale requires greater federal authority and a broader role for the armed forces, the institution of our government most capable of massive logistical operations on a moment's notice.

Four years after the frightening experience of September the 11th, Americans have every right to expect a more effective response in a time of emergency.

When the federal government fails to meet such an obligation, I as president am responsible for the problem and for the solution. So I have ordered every Cabinet secretary to participate in a comprehensive review of the government response to the hurricane.

This government will learn the lessons of Hurricane Katrina. We're going to review every action and make necessary changes so that we are better prepared for any challenge of nature or act of evil men that could threaten our people.

The United States Congress also has an important oversight function to perform. Congress is preparing an investigation, and I will work with members of both parties to make sure this effort is thorough.

## THE SECOND LINE

In the life of this nation, we have often been reminded that nature is an awesome force and that all life is fragile. We are the heirs of men and women who lived through those first terrible winters at Jamestown and Plymouth, who rebuilt Chicago after a great fire and San Francisco after a great earthquake, who reclaimed the prairie from the dust bowl of the 1930s.

Every time, the people of this land have come back from fire, flood and storm to build anew and to build better than what we had before. Americans have never left our destiny to the whims of nature, and we will not start now.

These trials have also reminded us that we are often stronger than we know — with the help of grace and one another. They remind us of a hope beyond all pain and death — a God who welcomes the lost to a house not made with hands. And they remind us that we are tied together in this life, in this nation, and that the despair of any touches us all.

I know that when you sit on the steps of a porch where a home once stood or sleep on a cot in a crowded shelter, it is hard to imagine a bright future. But that future will come.

The streets of Biloxi and Gulfport will again be filled with lovely homes and the sound of children playing. The churches of Alabama will have their broken steeples mended and their congregations whole. And here in New Orleans, the streetcars will once again rumble down St. Charles and the passionate soul of a great city will return.

In this place, there is a custom for the funerals of jazz musicians. The funeral procession parades slowly through the streets, followed by a band playing a mournful dirge as it moves to the cemetery. Once the casket has been laid in place, the band breaks into a joyful "second line," symbolizing the triumph of the spirit over death.

Tonight, the Gulf Coast is still coming through the dirge. Yet we will live to see the second line.

Thank you, and may God bless America. ■

# Roberts Opens With 'No Agenda'

*Following is the CQ Transcriptions transcript of John G. Roberts Jr.'s opening statement before the Senate Judiciary Committee on Sept. 12, the first day of hearings on Roberts' nomination to serve as chief justice of the United States:*

THANK YOU VERY MUCH, Mr. Chairman, Sen. Leahy, and members of the committee.

Let me begin by thanking Sens. Lugar and Warner and Bayh for their warm and generous introductions. And let me reiterate my thanks to the president for nominating me.

I'm humbled by his confidence, and, if confirmed, I will do everything I can to be worthy of the high trust he has placed in me.

Let me also thank you, Mr. Chairman, and the members of the committee for the many courtesies you've extended to me and my family over the past eight weeks.

I'm particularly grateful that members have been so accommodating in meeting with me personally. I have found those meetings very useful in better understanding the concerns of the committee as the committee undertakes its constitutional responsibility of advice and consent.

I know that I would not be here today were it not for the sacrifices and help over the years of my family, who you met earlier today, friends, mentors, teachers and colleagues — many of whom are here today.

Last week, one of those mentors and friends, Chief Justice William Rehnquist, was laid to rest. I talked last week with the nurses who helped care for him over the past year, and I was glad to hear from them that he was not a particularly good patient. He chafed at the limitations they tried to impose.

His dedication to duty over the past year was an inspiration to me and, I know, to many others. I will miss him.

My personal appreciation that I owe a great debt to others reinforces my view that a certain humility should characterize the judicial role.

Judges and justices are servants of the law, not the other way around. Judges are like umpires. Umpires don't make the rules; they apply them.

The role of an umpire and a judge is critical. They make sure everybody plays by the rules. But it is a limited role. Nobody ever went to a ball game to see the umpire.

Judges have to have the humility to recognize that they operate within a system of precedent, shaped by other judges equally striving to live up to the judicial oath.

And judges have to have the modesty to be open in the decisional process to the considered views of their colleagues on the bench.

Mr. Chairman, when I worked in the Department of Justice, in the office of the solicitor general, it was my job to argue cases for the United States before the Supreme Court.

I always found it very moving to stand before the justices and say, "I speak for my country."

But it was after I left the department and began arguing cases against the United States that I fully appreciated the importance of the Supreme Court and our constitutional system.

Here was the United States, the most powerful entity in the world, aligned against my client. And yet, all I had to do was convince the court that I was right on the law, and the government was wrong, and all that power and might would recede in deference to the rule of law.

That is a remarkable thing.

It is what we mean when we say that we are a government of laws and not of men. It is that rule of law that protects the rights and liberties of all Americans. It is the envy of the world. Because without the rule of law, any rights are meaningless.

President Ronald Reagan used to speak of the Soviet constitution, and he noted that it purported to grant wonderful rights of all sorts to people. But those rights were empty promises, because that system did not have an independent judiciary to uphold the rule of law and enforce those rights. We do, because of the wisdom of our founders and the sacrifices of our heroes over the generations to make their vision a reality.

Mr. Chairman, I come before the committee with no agenda. I have no platform. Judges are not politicians who can promise to do certain things in exchange for votes.

I have no agenda, but I do have a commitment. If I am confirmed, I will confront every case with an open mind. I will fully and fairly analyze the legal arguments that are presented. I will be open to the considered views of my colleagues on the bench. And I will decide every case based on the record, according to the rule of law, without fear or favor, to the best of my ability. And I will remember that it's my job to call balls and strikes and not to pitch or bat.

Sens. Lugar and Bayh talked of my boyhood back home in Indiana. I think all of us retain, from the days of our youth, certain enduring images. For me those images are of the endless fields of Indiana, stretching to the horizon, punctuated only by an isolated silo or a barn. And as I grew older, those endless fields came to represent for me the limitless possibilities of our great land.

Growing up, I never imagined that I would be here, in this historic room, nominated to be the chief justice. But now that I am here, I recall those endless fields with their promise of infinite possibilities, and that memory inspires in me a very profound commitment.

If I am confirmed, I will be vigilant to protect the independence and integrity of the Supreme Court, and I will work to ensure that it upholds the rule of law and safeguards those liberties that make this land one of endless possibilities for all Americans.

Thank you, Mr. Chairman. Thank you, members of the committee.

I look forward to your questions. ■

**Appendix E**

# PUBLIC LAWS

# Public Laws

# Laws Enacted in the First Session Of the 109th Congress

■ **PL 109-1** (HR 241) Accelerate the income tax benefits for charitable cash contributions for the relief of victims of the Dec. 26, 2004, tsunami in South Asia. Introduced by THOMAS, R-Calif., on Jan. 6, 2005. House Ways and Means discharged. House passed Jan. 6. Senate passed Jan. 6. President signed Jan. 7, 2005.

■ **PL 109-2** (S 5) Expand federal court jurisdiction over class action lawsuits, require courts to review non-cash settlements and limit attorney fees in such cases. Introduced by GRASSLEY, R-Iowa, on Jan. 25, 2005. Senate Judiciary reported Feb. 3 (S Rept 109-14). Senate passed Feb. 10. House passed Feb. 17. President signed Feb. 18, 2005.

■ **PL 109-3** (S 686) Provide for the relief of the parents of Theresa Marie Schiavo. Introduced by FRIST, R-Tenn., on March 20, 2005. Senate passed March 20. House passed, under suspension of the rules, March 21. President signed March 21, 2005.

■ **PL 109-4** (HR 1160) Reauthorize the Temporary Assistance for Needy Families block grant program through June 30, 2005. Introduced by HERGER, R-Calif., on March 8, 2005. House passed, under suspension of the rules, March 14. Senate passed March 15. President signed March 25, 2005.

■ **PL 109-5** (S 384) Extend the existence of the Nazi War Crimes and Japanese Imperial Government Records Interagency Working Group for two years. Introduced by DEWINE, R-Ohio, on Feb. 15, 2005. Senate passed Feb. 16. House Government Reform ordered reported March 10 (no written report). House passed, under suspension of the rules, March 14. President signed March 25, 2005.

■ **PL 109-6** (HR 1270) Amend the Internal Revenue Code of 1986 to extend the Leaking Underground Storage Tank Trust Fund financing rate. Introduced by THOMAS, R-Calif., on March 14, 2005. House passed, under suspension of the rules, March 16. Senate passed March 17. President signed March 31, 2005.

■ **PL 109-7** (HR 1134) Amend the Internal Revenue Code of 1986 to provide for the proper tax treatment of certain disaster mitigation payments. Introduced by FOLEY, R-Fla., on March 7, 2005. House passed, under suspension of the rules, March 14. Senate Finance discharged. Senate passed, with amendment, April 13. House agreed to Senate amendment April 14. President signed April 15, 2005.

■ **PL 109-8** (S 256) Amend Title 11 of the U.S. Code to make it more difficult for consumers to escape repaying debts through bankruptcy. Introduced by GRASSLEY, R-Iowa, on Feb. 1,

2005. Senate Judiciary reported, amended, Feb. 17 (no written report). Senate passed, amended, March 10. House Judiciary reported April 8 (H Rept 109-31, Part 1). House Financial Services discharged. Passed House April 14. President signed April 20, 2005.

■ **PL 109-9** (S 167) Provide intellectual property protection for movies, legalize movie-filtering technology, expand libraries' access to copyrighted works and reauthorize a Library of Congress film-preservation program. Introduced by HATCH, R-Utah, on Jan. 25, 2005. Senate Judiciary discharged. Senate passed, amended, Feb. 1. House Judiciary reported April 12 (H Rept 109-33, Part 1). House Administration discharged. House passed, under suspension of the rules, April 19. President signed April 27, 2005.

■ **PL 109-10** (HR 787) Designate the U.S. courthouse located at 501 I St., Sacramento, Calif., as the "Robert T. Matsui United States Courthouse." Introduced by THOMPSON, D-Calif., on Feb. 10, 2005. House passed, under suspension of the rules, April 13. Senate passed April 14. President signed April 29, 2005.

■ **PL 109-11** (H J Res 19) Appoint Shirley Ann Jackson as a citizen regent of the Board of Regents of the Smithsonian Institution. Introduced by JOHNSON, R-Texas, on Feb. 15, 2005. House passed, under suspension of the rules, April 19. Senate Rules and Administration discharged. Senate passed April 28. President signed May 5, 2005.

■ **PL 109-12** (H J Res 20) Appoint Robert P. Kogod as a citizen regent of the Board of Regents of the Smithsonian Institution. Introduced by JOHNSON, R-Texas, on Feb. 15, 2005. House passed, under suspension of the rules, April 19. Senate Rules and Administration Committee discharged. Senate passed April 28. President signed May 5, 2005.

■ **PL 109-13** (HR 1268) Make emergency supplemental appropriations for defense, the global war on terror and tsunami relief for the fiscal year ending Sept. 30, 2005. Introduced by LEWIS, R-Calif., on March 11, 2005. House Appropriations reported March 11 (H Rept 109-16). House passed, amended, March 16. Senate Appropriations reported, amended, April 6 (S Rept 109-52). Senate passed, amended, April 21. Conference report filed in the House May 3 (H Rept 109-72). House agreed to the conference report May 5. Senate agreed to the conference report May 10. President signed May 11, 2005.

■ **PL 109-14** (HR 2566). Extend highway, highway safety , motor safety, transit and other programs funded out of the Highway Trust Fund through July 1, 2005. Introduced by YOUNG, R-Alaska, on May 24, 2005. House passed, under suspension of

the rules, May 25. Senate passed May 26. President signed May 31, 2005.

■ **PL 109-15** (HR 1760) Designate the facility of the U.S. Postal Service located at 215 Martin Luther King, Jr. Blvd., Madison, Wis., as the "Robert M. La Follette, Sr. Post Office Building." Introduced by BALDWIN, D-Wis., on April 21, 2005. House Government Reform ordered reported May 5 (no written report). House passed, under suspension of the rules, May 16. Senate Homeland Security and Government Affairs discharged. Senate passed May 26. President signed June 17, 2005.

■ **PL 109-16** (HR 483) Designate a U.S. courthouse in Brownsville, Texas, as the "Reynaldo G. Garza and Filemon B. Vela United States Courthouse." Introduced by ORTIZ, D-Texas, on Feb. 1, 2005. House passed, under suspension of the rules, April 13. Senate Environment and Public Works reported June 9 (no written report). Senate passed June 15. President signed June 29, 2005.

■ **PL 109-17** (S 643) Amend the Agricultural Credit Act of 1987 to reauthorize state mediation programs through fiscal 2010. Introduced by ROBERTS, R-Kan., on March 16, 2005. Senate Agriculture, Nutrition and Forestry discharged. Senate passed April 21. House passed, under suspension of the rules, June 13. President signed June 29, 2005.

■ **PL 109-18** (HR 1812) Amend the Public Health Service Act to authorize grants through fiscal 2010 to develop and operate pilot "patient navigator" programs to improve patient-health outcomes. Introduced by MENENDEZ, D-N.J., on April 25, 2005. House Energy and Commerce reported June 7 (H Rept 109-104). House passed, amended, under suspension of the rules, June 13. Senate Health, Education, Labor and Pensions discharged. Senate passed June 22. President signed June 29, 2005.

■ **PL 109-19** (HR 3021) Reauthorize the Temporary Assistance for Needy Families block grant program through Sept. 30, 2005. Introduced by HERGER, R-Calif., on June 22, 2005. House passed, amended, under suspension of the rules, June 29. Senate passed June 30. President signed July 1, 2005.

■ **PL 109-20** (HR 3104) Extend highway, highway safety, motor carrier safety, transit and other programs funded out of the Highway Trust Fund through July 19, 2005. Introduced by YOUNG, R-Alaska, on June 29, 2005. House committees on Transportation, Ways and Means, Science, and Resources discharged. House passed June 30. Senate passed June 30. President signed July 1, 2005.

■ **PL 109-21** (S 714) Amend the Communications Act of 1934 to prohibit unsolicited advertisements by fax unless the sender has an "established business relationship" with the recipient, obtains the fax number either voluntarily through that relationship or from a publicly available source and provides an opt-out opportunity. Introduced by SMITH, R-Ore., on April 6, 2005. Senate Commerce, Science and Transportation reported, amended, June 7 (S Rept 109-76). Senate passed, amended, June 24. House passed, under suspension of the rules, June 28. President signed July 9, 2005.

■ **PL 109-22** (HR 120) Designate the facility of the U.S. Postal Service located at 30777 Rancho California Rd., Temecula, Calif., as the "Dalip Singh Saund Post Office Building." Introduced by ISSA, R-Calif., on Jan. 4, 2005. House passed, under suspension of the rules, Feb. 1. Senate Homeland Security and Governmental Affairs ordered reported June 22 (no written report). Senate passed June 29. President signed July 12, 2005.

■ **PL 109-23** (HR 289) Designate the facility of the U.S. Postal Service located at 8200 South Vermont Ave. in Los Angeles, Calif., as the "Sergeant First Class John Marshall Post Office Building." Introduced by WATERS, D-Calif., on Jan. 6, 2005. House passed, amended, under suspension of the rules, Feb. 1. Senate Homeland Security and Governmental Affairs ordered reported June 22 (no written report). Senate passed June 29. President signed July 12, 2005.

■ **PL 109-24** (HR 324) Designate the facility of the U.S. Postal Service located at 321 Montgomery Rd., Altamonte Springs, Fla., as the "Arthur Stacey Mastrapa Post Office Building." Introduced by FEENEY, R-Fla., on Jan. 25, 2005. House passed, under suspension of the rules, Feb. 15. Senate Homeland Security and Governmental Affairs ordered reported June 22 (no written report). Senate passed June 29. President signed July 12, 2005.

■ **PL 109-25** (HR 504) Designate the facility of the U.S. Postal Service located at 4960 West Washington Blvd., Los Angeles, Calif., as the "Ray Charles Post Office Building." Introduced by WATSON, D-Calif., on Feb. 1, 2005. House Government Reform ordered reported April 13 (no written report). House passed, under suspension of the rules, April 20. Senate Homeland Security and Governmental Affairs ordered reported June 22 (no written report). Senate passed June 29. President signed July 12, 2005.

■ **PL 109-26** (HR 627) Designate the facility of the U.S. Postal Service located at 40 Putnam Ave., Hamden, Conn., as the "Linda White-Epps Post Office." Introduced by DeLAURO, D-Conn., on Feb. 8, 2005. House Government Reform ordered reported May 5 (no written report). House passed, under suspension of the rules, May 16. Senate Homeland Security and Governmental Affairs ordered reported June 22 (no written report). Senate passed June 29. President signed July 12, 2005.

■ **PL 109-27** (HR 1072) Designate the facility of the U.S. Postal Service located at 151 West End St., Goliad, Texas, as the "Judge Emilio Vargas Post Office Building." Introduced by HINOJOSA, D-Texas, on March 3, 2005. House Government Reform ordered reported April 13 (no written report). House passed, under suspension of the rules, April 20. Senate Homeland Security and Governmental Affairs ordered reported June 22 (no written report). Senate passed June 29. President signed July 12, 2005.

■ **PL 109-28** (HR 1082) Designate the facility of the U.S. Postal Service located at 120 East Illinois Ave., Vinita, Okla., as the "Francis C. Goodpaster Post Office Building." Introduced by BOREN, D-Okla., on March 3, 2005. House Government Reform ordered reported April 13 (no written report). House passed, under suspension of the rules, May 4. Senate Homeland Security and Governmental Affairs ordered report-

ed June 22 (no written report). Senate passed June 29. President signed July 12, 2005.

■ **PL 109-29** (HR 1236) Designate the facility of the U.S. Postal Service located at 750 4th St., Sparks, Nev., as the "Mayor Tony Armstrong Memorial Post Office." Introduced by GIBBONS, R-Nev., on March 10, 2005. House Government Reform ordered reported April 13 (no written report). House passed, under suspension of the rules, April 26. Senate Homeland Security and Government Affairs ordered reported June 22 (no written report). Senate passed June 29. President signed July 12, 2005.

■ **PL 109-30** (HR 1460) Designate the facility of the U.S. Postal Service located at 6200 Rolling Rd., Springfield, Va., as the "Captain Mark Stubenhofer Post Office Building." Introduced by DAVIS, R-Va., on April 5, 2005. House passed, under suspension of the rules, April 6. Senate Homeland Security and Governmental Affairs ordered reported June 22 (no written report). Senate passed June 29. President signed July 12, 2005.

■ **PL 109-31** (HR 1524) Designate the facility of the U.S. Postal Service located at 12433 Antioch Rd., Overland Park, Kan., as the "Ed Eilert Post Office Building." Introduced by MOORE, D-Kan., on April 6, 2005. House Government Reform ordered reported April 13 (no written report). House passed, under suspension of the rules, April 26. Senate Homeland Security and Governmental Affairs ordered reported June 22 (no written report). Senate passed June 29. President signed July 12, 2005.

■ **PL 109-32** (HR 1542) Designate the facility of the U.S. Postal Service located at 695 Pleasant St., New Bedford, Mass., as the "Honorable Judge George N. Leighton Post Office Building." Introduced by FRANK, D-Mass., on April 12, 2005. House Government Reform ordered reported April 13 (no written report). House passed, under suspension of the rules, May 4. Senate Homeland Security and Governmental Affairs ordered reported June 22 (no written report). Senate passed June 29. President signed July 12, 2005.

■ **PL 109-33** (HR 2326) Designate the facility of the U.S. Postal Service located at 614 West Old County Rd., Belhaven, N.C., as the "Floyd Lupton Post Office." Introduced by JONES, R-N.C., on May 12, 2005. House Government Reform ordered reported May 26 (no written report). House passed, under suspension of the rules, June 13. Senate Homeland Security and Governmental Affairs ordered reported June 22 (no written report). Senate passed June 29. President signed July 12, 2005.

■ **PL 109-34** (S 1282) Amend the Communications Satellite Act of 1962 to strike the privatization criteria for INTELSAT separated entities, remove certain restrictions on separated and successor entities to INTELSAT and preserve the space segment of the Global Maritime Distress and Safety System. Introduced by BURNS, R-Mont., on June 21, 2005. Senate passed June 21. House Energy and Commerce discharged. House passed June 29. President signed July 12, 2005.

■ **PL 109-35** (HR 3332) Extend highway, highway safety, motor carrier safety, transit and other programs funded out of the Highway Trust Fund through July 21, 2005. Introduced by YOUNG, R-Alaska, on July 19, 2005. House committees on

Transportation and Infrastructure, Ways and Means, Science, and Resources discharged. House passed July 19. Senate passed July 19. President signed July 20, 2005.

■ **PL 109-36** (HR 1001) Designate the facility of the U.S. Postal Service located at 301 South Heatherwilde Blvd. in Pflugerville, Texas, as the "Sergeant Byron W. Norwood Post Office Building." Introduced by McCAUL, R-Texas, on March 1, 2005. House Government Reform ordered reported April 13 (no written report). House passed, under suspension of the rules, April 20. Senate Homeland Security and Governmental Affairs ordered reported June 22 (no written report). Senate passed June 29. President signed July 21, 2005.

■ **PL 109-37** (HR 3377) Extend highway, highway safety, motor carrier safety, transit and other programs funded out of the Highway Trust Fund through July 27, 2005. Introduced by YOUNG, R-Alaska, on July 21, 2005. House committees on Transportation and Infrastructure, Ways and Means, Science, and Resources discharged. House passed July 21. Senate passed July 21. President signed July 22, 2005.

■ **PL 109-38** (HR 3071) Permit the individuals currently serving as executive director, deputy executive directors, and general counsel of Congress' Office of Compliance to serve one additional term. Introduced by NEY, R-Ohio, on June 27, 2005. House Administration discharged. House passed June 30. Senate passed July 13. President signed July 27, 2005.

■ **PL 109-39** (H J RES 52) Approve the renewal of import restrictions contained in the Burmese Freedom and Democracy Act of 2003. Introduced by LANTOS, D-Calif., on May 26, 2005. House passed, under suspension of the rules, June 21. Senate passed July 19. President signed July 27, 2005.

■ **PL 109-40** (HR 3453) Extend highway, highway safety, motor carrier safety, transit and other programs funded out of the Highway Trust Fund through July 30, 2005. Introduced by YOUNG, R-Alaska, on July 27, 2005. House committees on Transportation and Infrastructure, Ways and Means, Science, and Resources discharged. House passed July 27. Senate passed July 27. President signed July 28, 2005.

■ **PL 109-41** (S 544) Establish procedures for voluntary confidential reporting of medical errors to independent patient safety organizations, which then would submit the information to a national database for analysis and recommendations on improving patient safety and reducing errors. Introduced by JEFFORDS, I-Vt., on March 8, 2005. Senate Health, Education, Labor and Pensions ordered reported March 9 (no written report). Senate passed, amended, July 21. House passed, under suspension of the rules, July 27. President signed July 29, 2005.

■ **PL 109-42** (HR 3512) Extend administrative expenses for highway, highway safety, motor carrier safety, transit and other programs funded out of the Highway Trust Fund through Aug. 14, 2005. Introduced by YOUNG, R-Alaska, on July 28, 2005. House committees on Transportation and Infrastructure, Ways and Means, Science, and Resources discharged. House passed July 29. Senate passed July 29. President signed July 30, 2005.

# PUBLIC LAWS

■ **PL 109-43** (HR 3423) Amend the Medical Device User Fee and Modernization Act to preserve fees paid by medical device manufacturers to help fund Food and Drug Administration reviews and speed up the approval process. Introduced by PITTS, R-Pa., on July 25, 2005. House Energy and Commerce discharged. House passed July 26. Senate passed July 27. President signed Aug. 1, 2005.

■ **PL 109-44** (HR 38) Designate a portion of the White Salmon River as a component of the National Wild and Scenic Rivers System. Introduced by BAIRD, D-Wash., on Jan. 4, 2005. House Resources reported June 14 (H Rept 109-125). House passed, amended, under suspension of the rules, June 27. Senate Energy and Natural Resources discharged. Senate passed July 26. President signed Aug. 2, 2005.

■ **PL 109-45** (HR 481) Authorize the Cheyenne and Arapaho Tribes of Oklahoma to convey approximately 1,465 acres to the secretary of the Interior to be held in trust for the tribes, and thus allow the National Park Service to formally establish the Sand Creek Massacre National Historic Site. Introduced by MUSGRAVE, R-Colo., on Feb. 1, 2005. House Resources reported, amended, June 8 (H Rept 109-107). House passed, amended, under suspension of the rules, June 27. Senate Energy and Natural Resources discharged. Senate passed July 26. President signed Aug. 2, 2005.

■ **PL 109-46** (HR 541) Direct the secretary of Agriculture to convey certain land to Lander County, Nev., and the secretary of the Interior to convey certain land to Eureka County, Nev., for continued use as cemeteries. Introduced by GIBBONS, R-Nev., on Feb. 2, 2005. House passed, under suspension of the rules, April 12. Senate Energy and Natural Resources discharged. Senate passed July 26. President signed Aug. 2, 2005.

■ **PL 109-47** (HR 794) Correct the south boundary of the Colorado River Indian Reservation in Arizona. Introduced by GRIJALVA, D-Ariz., on Feb. 14, 2005. House passed, under suspension of the rules, April 12. Senate Indian Affairs discharged. Senate passed July 26. President signed Aug. 2, 2005.

■ **PL 109-48** (HR 1046) Authorize the secretary of the Interior to contract with the city of Cheyenne, Wyo., for the storage of the city's water in the Kendrick Project in Wyoming. Introduced by CUBIN, R-Wyo., on March 2, 2005. House passed, under suspension of the rules, May 16. Senate passed July 26. President signed Aug. 2, 2005.

■ **PL 109-49** (H J RES 59) Express the sense of Congress that women suffragists should be revered and celebrated for working to ensure the right of women to vote in the United States. Introduced by BERKLEY, D-Nev., on July 14, 2005. House passed, amended, under suspension of the rules, July 25. Senate passed July 28. President signed Aug. 2, 2005.

■ **PL 109-50** (S 571) Designate the facility of the U.S. Postal Service located at 1915 Fulton St., Brooklyn, N.Y., as the "Congresswoman Shirley A. Chisholm Post Office Building." Introduced by SCHUMER, D-N.Y., on March 9, 2005. Senate Homeland Security and Governmental Affairs ordered reported June 22 (no written report). Senate passed June 29. House passed, under suspension of the rules, July 25. President signed Aug. 2, 2005.

■ **PL 109-51** (S 775) Designate the facility of the U.S. Postal Service located at 123 W. 7th St., Holdenville, Okla., as the "Boone Pickens Post Office." Introduced by INHOFE, R-Okla., on April 13, 2005. Senate Homeland Security and Governmental Affairs ordered reported June 22 (no written report). Senate passed June 29. House passed, under suspension of the rules, July 25. President signed Aug. 2, 2005.

■ **PL 109-52** (S 904) Designate the facility of the U.S. Postal Service located at 1560 Union Valley Rd., West Milford, N.J., as the "Brian P. Parrello Post Office Building." Introduced by LAUTENBERG, D-N.J., on April 26, 2005. Senate Homeland Security and Governmental Affairs ordered reported June 22 (no written report). Senate passed June 29. House passed, under suspension of the rules, July 26. President signed Aug. 2, 2005.

■ **PL 109-53** (HR 3045) Approve and implement the Central American Free Trade Agreement between the United States, Costa Rica, the Dominican Republic, El Salvador, Guatemala, Honduras, and Nicaragua — also known as CAFTA. Introduced by DeLAY, R-Texas, on June 23, 2005. House Ways and Means reported July 25 (H Rept 109-182). House passed July 28. Senate passed July 28. President signed Aug. 2, 2005.

■ **PL 109-54** (HR 2361) Make appropriations for the Interior Department, the EPA, and cultural programs and institutions for the fiscal year ending Sept. 30, 2006, and provide supplemental funding for veterans' health care. Introduced by TAYLOR, R-N.C., on May 13, 2005. House Appropriations reported May 13 (H Rept 109-80). House passed, amended, May 19. Senate Appropriations, reported, amended June 10 (S Rept 109-80). Senate passed, amended, June 29. Conference report filed in the House July 26 (H Rept 109-188). House agreed to the conference report July 28. Senate agreed to the conference report July 29. President signed Aug. 2, 2005.

■ **PL 109-55** (HR 2985) Make appropriations for the Legislative Branch, including the House of Representatives, the Senate and related agencies for the fiscal year ending Sept. 30, 2006. Introduced by LEWIS, R-Calif., on June 20, 2005. House Appropriations reported June 20 (H Rept 109-139). House passed, amended, June 22. Senate Appropriations reported, amended, June 24 (S Rept 109-89). Senate passed, amended, June 30. Conference report filed in the House on July 26 (H Rept 109-189). House agreed to the conference report July 28. Senate agreed to the conference report July 29. President signed Aug. 2, 2005.

■ **PL 109-56** (S 45) Amend the Controlled Substances Act to lift the patient limitation on prescribing drug addiction treatments by medical practitioners in group practices. Introduced by LEVIN, D-Mich., on Jan. 24, 2005. Senate committees on Health, Education, Labor and Pensions and the Judiciary discharged. Senate passed July 19. House passed, under suspension of the rules, July 27. President signed Aug. 2, 2005.

■ **PL 109-57** (S 1395) Amend the Controlled Substances Import and Export Act to provide authority for the attorney general to authorize the export of controlled substances from the United States to another country for subsequent export from that country to a second country, if certain conditions and safe-

guards are satisfied. Introduced by HATCH, R-Utah, on July 13, 2005. Senate passed July 13. House passed, under suspension of the rules, July 27. President signed Aug. 2, 2005.

■ **PL 109-58** (HR 6) Overhaul the nation's energy policies. Introduced by BARTON, R-Texas, on April 18, 2005. House passed, amended, April 21. Senate passed, amended, June 28. Conference report filed in the House July 27 (H Rept 109-190). House agreed to the conference report July 28. Senate agreed to the conference report July 29. President signed Aug. 8, 2005.

■ **PL 109-59** (HR 3) Authorize funds for federal aid highways, highway safety programs and transit programs. Introduced by YOUNG, R-Alaska, on Feb. 9, 2005. House Transportation and Infrastructure reported, amended, March 7 (H Rept 109-12, Part 1), and filed a supplemental report March 8 (H Rept 109-12, Part 2). House passed, amended, March 10. Senate passed, amended, May 17. Conference report filed in the House on July 28 (H Rept 109-203). House agreed to the conference report July 29. Senate agreed to the conference report July 29. President signed Aug. 10, 2005.

■ **PL 109-60** (HR 1132) Provide for the establishment of a controlled substance monitoring program in each state. Introduced by WHITFIELD, R-Ky., on March 3, 2005. House Energy and Commerce reported, amended, July 27 (H Rept 109-191). House passed, amended, under suspension of the rules, July 27. Senate passed July 29. President signed Aug. 11, 2005.

■ **PL 109-61** (HR 3645) Make emergency supplemental appropriations to meet immediate needs arising from the consequences of Hurricane Katrina, for the fiscal year ending Sept. 30, 2005. Introduced by LEWIS, R-Calif., on Sept. 2, 2005. House passed Sept. 2. Senate passed Sept. 2. President signed Sept. 2, 2005.

■ **PL 109-62** (HR 3673) Make further emergency supplemental appropriations to meet immediate needs arising from the consequences of Hurricane Katrina, for the fiscal year ending Sept. 30, 2005. Introduced by LEWIS, R-Calif., Sept. 7, 2005. House passed, under suspension of the rules, Sept. 8. Senate passed Sept. 8. President signed Sept. 8, 2005.

■ **PL 109-63** (HR 3650) Allow United States courts to conduct business during emergency conditions. Introduced by SENSENBRENNER, R-Wis., on Sept. 6, 2005. House passed, under suspension of the rules, Sept. 7. Senate passed Sept. 8. President signed Sept. 9, 2005.

■ **PL 109-64** (HR 804) Exclude from consideration as income certain payments under the national flood insurance program. Introduced by BAKER, R-La., on Feb. 15, 2005. House Financial Services reported, April 14 (H Rept 109-44). House passed, amended, under suspension of the rules, July 12. Senate Banking, Housing, and Urban Affairs reported, July 29 (no written report). Senate passed Sept. 8. President signed Sept. 20, 2005.

■ **PL 109-65** (HR 3669) Temporarily increase the borrowing authority of the Federal Emergency Management Agency for carrying out the national flood insurance program. Introduced by NEY, R-Ohio, on Sept. 7, 2005. House passed, under suspension of the rules, Sept. 8. Senate passed Sept. 12. President signed Sept. 20, 2005.

■ **PL 109-66** (HR 3169) Provide the secretary of Education with waiver authority for students eligible for Pell Grants who are adversely affected by a natural disaster. Introduced by KELLER, R-Fla., on June 30, 2005. House passed, amended, under suspension of the rules, Sept. 7. Senate passed Sept. 15. President signed Sept. 21, 2005.

■ **PL 109-67** (HR 3668) Provide the secretary of Education with waiver authority for students eligible for federal higher education grants who are adversely affected by a natural disaster. Introduced by JINDAL, R-La., on Sept. 7, 2005. House passed, amended, under suspension of the rules, Sept. 8. Senate passed Sept. 15. President signed Sept. 21, 2005.

■ **PL 109-68** (HR 3672) Provide assistance to families affected by Hurricane Katrina through the Temporary Assistance for Needy Families. Introduced by McCRERY, R-La., on Sept. 7, 2005. House passed, amended, under suspension of the rules, Sept. 8. Senate passed Sept. 15. President signed Sept. 21, 2005.

■ **PL 109-69** (S 252) Direct the secretary of the Interior to convey certain land in Washoe County, Nev., to the Board of Regents of the University and Community College System of Nevada. Introduced by REID, D-Nev., on Feb. 1, 2005. Senate Energy and Natural Resources reported March 14 (S Rept 109-38). Senate passed July 26. House passed, under suspension of the rules, Sept. 13. President signed Sept. 21, 2005.

■ **PL 109-70** (S 264) Amend the Reclamation Wastewater and Groundwater Study and Facilities Act to authorize certain projects in the state of Hawaii. Introduced by AKAKA, D-Hawaii, on Feb. 2, 2005. Senate Energy and Natural Resources reported March 10 (S Rept 109-33). Senate passed, amended, July 26. House passed, under suspension of the rules, Sept. 13. President signed Sept. 21, 2005.

■ **PL 109-71** (S 276) Revise the boundary of the Wind Cave National Park in South Dakota. Introduced by JOHNSON, D-S.D., on Feb. 3, 2005. Senate Energy and Natural Resources reported March 8 (S Rept 109-21). Senate passed July 26. House passed, under suspension of the rules, Sept. 13. President signed Sept. 21, 2005.

■ **PL 109-72** (HR 3761) Provide special rules for disaster relief employment under the 1988 Workforce Investment Act for individuals displaced by Hurricane Katrina. Introduced by BOUSTANY, R-La., on Sept. 14, 2005. House passed, amended, under suspension of the rules, Sept. 20. Senate passed Sept. 21. President signed Sept. 23, 2005.

■ **PL 109-73** (HR 3768) Provide emergency tax relief for persons affected by Hurricane Katrina. Introduced by McCRERY, R-La., on Sept. 14, 2005. House passed, amended, under suspension of the rules, Sept. 15. Senate passed, amended, Sept. 15. House agreed to Senate amendment with an amendment Sept. 21. Senate agreed to House amendment Sept. 21. President signed Sept. 23, 2005.

■ **PL 109-74** (HR 3649) Ensure funding for sportfishing and boating safety programs funded out of the Highway Trust Fund through the end of fiscal 2005. Introduced by YOUNG, R-Alaska, on Sept. 6, 2005. House passed, under suspension of

the rules, Sept. 13. Senate passed, amended, Sept. 15. House agreed to Senate amendment, under suspension of the rules, Sept. 20. President signed Sept. 29, 2005.

■ **PL 109-75** (S 1340) Amend the Pittman-Robertson Wildlife Restoration Act to extend the date after which surplus funds in the wildlife restoration fund become available for apportionment. Introduced by INHOFE, R-Okla., on June 30, 2005. Senate Environment and Public Works reported Aug. 31 (S Rept 109-125). Senate passed Sept. 9. House passed, under suspension of the rules, Sept. 20. President signed Sept. 29, 2005.

■ **PL 109-76** (S 1368) Extend the existence of the Parole Commission. Introduced by SPECTER, R-Pa., on July 1, 2005. Senate passed July 1. House passed, under suspension of the rules, Sept. 21. President signed Sept. 29, 2005.

■ **PL 109-77** (H J Res 68) Make continuing appropriations for fiscal 2006. Introduced by LEWIS, R-Calif., on Sept. 27, 2005. House passed Sept. 29. Senate passed Sept. 30. President signed Sept. 30, 2005.

■ **PL 109-78** (HR 2132) Extend the waiver authority of the secretary of Education with respect to student financial assistance during a war or other military operation or national emergency. Introduced by KLINE, R-Minn., on May 5, 2005. House passed, under suspension of the rules, Sept. 20. Senate Health, Education, Labor and Pensions Committee discharged. Senate passed Sept. 27. President signed Sept. 30, 2005.

■ **PL 109-79** (HR 2385) Extend for 10 years statutory authority for the secretary of Commerce, rather than the Federal Trade Commission, to produce the quarterly financial report. Introduced by TURNER, R-Ohio, on May 17, 2005. House Government Reform Committee reported, amended, July 12 (H Rept 109-164). Senate Commerce, Science, and Transportation Committee discharged. Senate Homeland Security and Governmental Affairs Committee discharged. Senate passed Sept. 26. President signed Sept. 30, 2005.

■ **PL 109-80** (HR 3200) Permanently increase, to $400,000, the maximum federally subsidized life insurance payment that families of military personnel may receive if a service member is killed in the line of duty. Introduced by MILLER, R-Fla., on July 11, 2005. House Committee on Veterans' Affairs reported July 20 (H Rept 109-177). House passed, under suspension of the rules, Sept 26. Senate Veteran's Affairs Committee discharged. Senate passed Sept. 27. President signed Sept. 30, 2005.

■ **PL 109-81** (HR 3784) Extend through Dec. 31, 2005, the authorization of appropriations for, and the duration of, each program authorized under the Higher Education Act of 1965. Introduced by BOEHNER, R-Ohio, on Sept. 15, 2005. House passed, amended, under suspension of the rules, Sept. 20. Senate Health, Education, Labor, and Pensions Committee discharged. Senate passed, amended, Sept. 26. House passed, under suspension of the rules, Sept. 28. President signed Sept. 30, 2005.

■ **PL 109-82** (HR 3864) Provide vocational rehabilitation services to individuals with disabilities affected by Hurricane Katrina or Hurricane Rita. Introduced by BOUSTANY, R-La.,

on Sept. 22, 2005. House passed, amended, under suspension of the rules, Sept. 28. Senate passed Sept. 28. President signed Sept. 30, 2005.

■ **PL 109-83** (S 1754) Extend the U.S. Grain Standards Act of 1916 (PL 64-190), which sets marketing and inspection standards for grains and oilseeds. Introduced by CHAMBLISS, R-Ga., on Sept. 22, 2005. Senate passed Sept. 22. House passed, under suspension of the rules, Sept. 28. President signed Sept. 30, 2005.

■ **PL 109-84** (HR 3667) Designate the facility of the U.S. Postal Service located at 200 South Barrington St., Los Angeles, as the "Karl Malden Station." Introduced by WAXMAN, D-Calif., on Sept. 7, 2005. House passed, under suspension of the rules, Sept. 21. Senate Homeland Security and Government Affairs discharged. Senate passed Sept. 27. President signed Oct. 4, 2005.

■ **PL 109-85** (HR 3767) Designate the facility of the U.S. Postal Service located at 2600 Oak St. in St. Charles, Ill., as the "Jacob L. Frazier Post Office Building." Introduced by HASTERT, R-Ill., on Sept. 14, 2005. House passed, under suspension of the rules, Sept. 21. Senate passed Sept. 27. President signed Oct. 4, 2005.

■ **PL 109-86** (HR 3863) Provide the secretary of Education with waiver authority for the reallocation rules in the Campus-Based Aid programs and extend the deadline by which funds have to be reallocated to institutions of higher education due to a natural disaster. Introduced by JINDAL, R-La., on Sept. 22, 2005. House passed, amended, under suspension of the rules, Sept. 27. Senate passed Sept. 30. President signed Oct. 7, 2005.

■ **PL 109-87** (S 1786) Authorize the secretary of Transportation to make emergency airport improvement project grants-in-aid under title 49, U.S. Code, for repairs and costs related to damage from hurricanes Katrina and Rita. Introduced by LOTT, R-Miss., on Sept. 28, 2005. Senate passed Sept. 28. House passed, under suspension of the rules, Oct. 6. President signed Oct. 7, 2005.

■ **PL 109-88** (S 1858) Permit use of $750 million for a program to lend money to local governments to maintain essential services in the aftermath of hurricanes Katrina and Rita. Introduced by VITTER, R-La., on Oct. 7, 2005. Senate passed Oct. 7. House passed Oct. 7. President signed Oct. 7, 2005.

■ **PL 109-89** (S 1413) Redesignate the Crowne Plaza in Kingston, Jamaica, as the Colin L. Powell Residential Plaza. Introduced by LUGAR, R-Ind., on July 15, 2005. Senate passed July 15. House passed, under suspension of the rules, Oct. 6. President signed Oct. 13, 2005.

■ **PL 109-90** (HR 2360) Make appropriations for the Department of Homeland Security for fiscal 2006. Introduced by ROGERS, R-Ky., on May 13, 2005. House Appropriations reported May 13 (H Rept 109-79). House passed, amended, May 17. Senate Appropriations reported, amended, June 16 (S Rept 109-83). Senate passed, amended, July 14. Conference report filed in the House Sept. 29 (H Rept 109-241). House agreed to the conference report Oct. 6. Senate agreed to the conference report Oct. 7. President signed Oct. 18, 2005.

■ **PL 109-91** (HR 3971) Provide assistance to individuals and states affected by Hurricane Katrina. Introduced by DEAL, R-Ga., on Oct. 6, 2005. House passed, under suspension of the rules, Oct. 6. Senate passed, amended, Oct. 7. House agreed to Senate amendment with amendments pursuant to H Res 501 on Oct. 19. Senate agreed to House amendments Oct. 19. President signed Oct. 20, 2005.

■ **PL 109-92** (S 397) Prohibit civil liability actions from being brought or continued against manufacturers, distributors, dealers or importers of firearms or ammunition for damages, injunctive or other relief resulting from the misuse of their products by others. Introduced by CRAIG, R-Idaho, on Feb. 16, 2005. Senate passed, amended, July 29. House passed Oct. 20. President signed Oct. 26, 2005.

■ **PL 109-93** (S 55) Adjust the boundary of Rocky Mountain National Park in Colorado to include 5.9 acres of non-federal land received in exchange for 70 acres of federal land. Introduced by ALLARD, R-Colo., on Jan. 24, 2005. Senate Energy and Natural Resources reported March 8 (S Rept 109-19). Senate passed July 26. House passed, under suspension of the rules, Oct. 18. President signed Oct. 26, 2005.

■ **PL 109-94** (S 156) Designate the 11,183 acres of the Ojito Wilderness Study Area in New Mexico as wilderness, take 11,514 acres of land into trust for the Pueblo of Zia. Introduced by BINGAMAN, D-N.M., on Jan. 25, 2005. Senate Energy and Natural Resources reported, amended, Feb. 28 (S Rept 109-13). Senate passed, amended, July 26. House passed, under suspension of the rules, Oct. 18. President signed Oct. 26, 2005.

■ **PL 109-95** (HR 1409) Amend the Foreign Assistance Act of 1961 to provide assistance for orphans and other vulnerable children in developing countries. Introduced by LEE, D-Calif., on March 17, 2005. House passed, amended, under suspension of the rules, Oct. 18. Senate passed Oct. 24. President signed Nov. 8, 2005.

■ **PL 109-96** (S 172) Amend the Federal Food, Drug and Cosmetic Act to provide for the regulation of all contact lenses as medical devices. Introduced by DeWINE, R-Ohio, on Jan. 26, 2005. Senate Health, Education, Labor, and Pensions reported, amended, July 27 (S Rept 109-110). Senate passed, amended, July 29. House passed, under suspension of the rules, Oct. 26. President signed Nov. 9, 2005.

■ **PL 109-97** (HR 2744) Make appropriations for Agriculture, Rural Development, Food and Drug Administration, and Related Agencies for fiscal 2006. Introduced by BONILLA, R-Texas, on June 3, 2005. House Appropriations reported June 2 (H Rept 109-102). House passed, amended, June 8. Senate Appropriations reported, amended, June 27 (S Rept 109-92). Senate passed, amended, Sept. 22. Conference report filed in the House Oct. 26 (H Rept 109-255). House agreed to the conference report Oct. 28. Senate agreed to the conference report Nov. 3. President signed Nov. 10, 2005.

■ **PL 109-98** (HR 2967) Designate the federal building located at 333 Mt. Elliott St. in Detroit as the "Rosa Parks Federal Building." Introduced by KILPATRICK, D-Mich., on June 17, 2005. House passed, under suspension of the rules, Oct. 26. Senate passed Nov. 1. President signed Nov. 11, 2005.

■ **PL 109-99** (HR 3765) Extend through March 31, 2006, the authority of the secretary of the Army to accept and expend funds contributed by non-federal public entities and to expedite the processing of permits. Introduced by BAIRD, D-Wash., on Sept. 14, 2005. House passed, under suspension of the rules, Sept. 20. Senate Environment and Public Works discharged. Senate passed, amended Oct. 7. House agreed to Senate amendments, under suspension of the rules, Oct. 18. President signed Nov. 11, 2005.

■ **PL 109-100** (S 37) Extend the special postage stamp for breast cancer research for two years. Introduced by FEINSTEIN, D-Calif., on Jan. 24, 2005. Senate Homeland Security and Governmental Affairs reported Sept. 26 (S Rept 109-140). Senate passed Sept. 27. House Government Reform, Energy and Commerce, and Armed Services discharged Oct. 27. House passed Oct. 27. President signed Nov. 11, 2005.

■ **PL 109-101** (S 1285) Designate the federal building located at 333 Mt. Elliott St. in Detroit as the "Rosa Parks Federal Building" and designate the annex located on the 200 block of 3rd St. NW in the District of Columbia as the "William B. Bryant Annex." Introduced by STABENOW, D-Mich., on June 22, 2005. Senate Environment and Public Works reported Oct. 26 (no written report). Senate passed, amended, Oct. 26. House passed, under suspension of the rules, Nov. 2. President signed Nov. 11, 2005.

■ **PL 109-102** (HR 3057) Make appropriations for foreign operations, export financing, and related programs for fiscal 2006. Introduced by KOLBE, R-Ariz., on June 24, 2005. House Appropriations reported June 24 (H Rept 109-152). House passed, amended, June 28. Senate Appropriations reported, amended, June 30 (S Rept 109-96). Senate passed, amended, July 20. Conference report filed in the House Nov. 2 (H Rept 109-265). House agreed to the conference report Nov. 4. Senate agreed to the conference report Nov. 10. President signed Nov. 14, 2005.

■ **PL 109-103** (HR 2419) Make appropriations for energy and water development for fiscal 2006. Introduced by HOBSON, R-Ohio, on May 18, 2005. House Appropriations reported May 18 (H Rept 109-86). House passed, amended, May 24. Senate Appropriations reported, amended, June 16 (S Rept 109-84). Senate passed, amended, July 1. Conference report filed in the House Nov. 7 (H Rept 109-275). House agreed to the conference report Nov. 9. Senate agreed to the conference report Nov. 14. President signed Nov. 19, 2005.

■ **PL 109-104** (HR 4326) Authorize the secretary of the Navy to enter into a contract for the nuclear refueling and complex overhaul of the *USS Carl Vinson* (CVN-70). Introduced by J. DAVIS, R-Va., on Nov. 15, 2005. House passed, under suspension of the rules, Nov. 16. Senate passed Nov. 18. President signed Nov. 19, 2005.

■ **PL 109-105** (H J Res 72) Make further continuing appropriations for fiscal 2006. Introduced by LEWIS, R-Calif., on Nov. 16, 2005. House passed Nov. 17. Senate passed Nov. 18. President signed Nov. 19, 2005.

■ **PL 109-106** (HR 4133) Temporarily increase the borrowing authority of the Federal Emergency Management Agency for

carrying out the national flood insurance program. Introduced by FITZPATRICK, R-Pa., on Oct. 25, 2005. House Financial Services reported Nov. 7 (H Rept 109-274). House passed, under suspension of the rules, Nov. 16. Senate passed, amended, Nov. 18. House agreed to Senate amendment Nov. 18. President signed Nov. 21, 2005.

■ **PL 109-107** (HR 2490) Designate the facility of the U.S. Postal Service located at 442 West Hamilton St., Allentown, Pa., as the "Mayor Joseph S. Daddona Memorial Post Office." Introduced by DENT, R-Pa., on May 19, 2005. House passed, under suspension of the rules, June 27. Senate Homeland Security and Governmental Affairs discharged. Senate passed Nov. 8. President signed Nov. 22, 2005.

■ **PL 109-108** (HR 2862) Make appropriations for science, the departments of State, Justice, and Commerce, and related agencies for fiscal 2006. Introduced by WOLF, R-Va., on June 10, 2005. House Appropriations reported June 10 (H Rept 109-118). House passed, amended, June 16. Senate Appropriations reported, amended June 23 (S Rept 109-88). Senate passed, amended, Sept. 15. Conference report filed in the House Nov. 7 (H Rept 109-272). House agreed to the conference report Nov. 9. Senate agreed to the conference report Nov. 16. President signed Nov. 22, 2005.

■ **PL 109-109** (HR 3339) To designate the facility of the U.S. Postal Service located at 2061 South Park Ave, in Buffalo, N.Y., as the "James T. Molloy Post Office Building." Introduced by HIGGINS, D-NY., on July 19, 2005. House passed, under suspension of the rules, July 26. Senate Homeland Security and Governmental Affairs discharged. Senate passed Nov. 8. President signed Nov. 22, 2005.

■ **PL 109-110** (S 161) Provide for a land exchange in the state of Arizona between the secretary of Agriculture and the Yavapai Ranch Limited Partnership. Introduced by McCAIN, R-Ariz., on Jan. 25, 2005. Senate Energy and Natural Resources reported March 16 (S Rept 109-40). Senate passed July 26. House passed, under suspension of the rules, Nov. 15. President signed Nov. 22, 2005.

■ **PL 109-111** (S 1234) Increase, effective Dec. 1, 2005, the rates of compensation for veterans with service-connected disabilities and the rates of dependency and indemnity compensation for survivors of certain disabled veterans. Introduced by CRAIG, R-Idaho, on June 14, 2005. Senate Veterans' Affairs reported Sept. 21 (S Rept 109-138). Senate passed, amended, Nov. 16. House passed Nov. 16. President signed Nov. 22, 2005.

■ **PL 109-112** (S 1713) Make amendments to the Iran Nonproliferation Act of 2000 related to International Space Station payments. Introduced by LUGAR, R-Ind., on Sept. 15, 2005. Senate Foreign Relations discharged. Senate passed Sept. 21. House passed, amended, under suspension of the rules, Oct. 26. Senate agreed to House amendments Nov. 8. President signed Nov. 22, 2005.

■ **PL 109-113** (S 1894) Amend part E of Title IV of the Social Security Act to allow foster care maintenance payments to private for-profit agencies. Introduced by INHOFE, R-Okla., on Oct. 19, 2005. Senate passed Oct. 19. House passed, under suspension of the rules, Nov. 8. President signed Nov. 22, 2005.

■ **PL 109-114** (HR 2528) Make appropriations for military quality of life functions of the Department of Defense, military construction, the Department of Veterans Affairs and related agencies for fiscal 2006. Introduced by WALSH, R-N.Y., on May 23, 2005. House Appropriations reported May 23 (H Rept 109-95). House passed, amended, May 26. Senate Appropriations reported, amended July 21 (S Rept 109-105). Senate passed, amended, Sept. 22. Conference report filed in the House Nov. 18 (H Rept 109-305). House agreed to the conference report Nov. 18. Senate agreed to the conference report Nov. 18. President signed Nov. 30, 2005.

■ **PL 109-115** (HR 3058) Make appropriations for the departments of Transportation, Treasury, and Housing and Urban Development, the Judiciary, District of Columbia and independent agencies for fiscal 2006. Introduced by KNOLLENBERG, R-Mich., on June 24, 2005. House Appropriations reported June 24 (H Rept 109-153). House passed, amended, June 30. Senate Appropriations reported, amended, July 26 (S Rept 109-109). Senate passed, amended, Oct. 20. Conference report filed in the House Nov. 18 (H Rept 109-307). House agreed to the conference report Nov. 18. Senate agreed to the conference report Nov. 21. President signed Nov. 30, 2005.

■ **PL 109-116** (HR 4145) Direct the Joint Committee on the Library to obtain a statue of Rosa Parks and place the statue in the National Statuary Hall of the U.S. Capitol. Introduced by JACKSON, D-Ill., on Oct. 26, 2005. House Administration discharged. House passed, amended, Nov. 18. Senate passed Nov. 18. President signed Dec. 1, 2005.

■ **PL 109-117** (HR 126) Amend public law 89-366 to allow for an adjustment in the number of free-roaming horses permitted in Cape Lookout National Seashore. Introduced by JONES, R-N.C., on Jan. 4, 2005. House passed, under suspension of the rules, March 14. Senate Energy and Natural Resources reported Oct. 19 (S Rept 109-154). Senate passed Nov. 16. President signed Dec. 1, 2005.

■ **PL 109-118** (HR 539) Designate certain National Forest System land in the Commonwealth of Puerto Rico as components of the National Wilderness Preservation System. Introduced by FORTUÑO, R-P.R., on Feb. 2, 2005. House Resources reported, amended, June 14 (H Rept 109-126). House passed, amended, under suspension of the rules, Sept. 13. Senate Energy and Natural Resources reported Oct. 19 (S Rept 109-155). Senate passed Nov. 16. President signed Dec. 1, 2005.

■ **PL 109-119** (HR 606) Authorize appropriations to the secretary of the Interior for the restoration of the Angel Island Immigration Station in California. Introduced by WOOLSEY, D-Calif., on Feb. 2, 2005. House passed, under suspension of the rules, May 23. Senate Energy and Natural Resources reported Oct. 19 (S Rept. 109-157). Senate passed Nov. 16. President signed Dec. 1, 2005.

■ **PL 109-120** (HR 1972) Direct the secretary of the Interior to conduct a special resource study to determine the suitability and feasibility of including in the National Park System certain sites in Williamson County, Tenn., relating to the Battle of Franklin. Introduced by BLACKBURN, R-Tenn., on April 28, 2005. House Resources reported, amended, Nov. 10

(H Rept 109-289). House passed, amended, under suspension of the rules, Nov. 15. Senate passed Nov. 16. President signed Dec. 1, 2005.

■ **PL 109-121** (HR 1973) Make access to safe water and sanitation for developing countries a specific policy objective of U.S. foreign assistance programs. Introduced by BLUMENAUER, D-Ore., on April 28, 2005. House International Relations reported, amended, Oct. 28 (H Rept 109-260). House passed, amended, under suspension of the rules, Nov. 7. Senate passed Nov. 16. President signed Dec. 1, 2005.

■ **PL 109-122** (HR 2062) Designate the facility of the U.S. Postal Service located at 57 West St. in Newville, Pa., as the "Randall D. Shughart Post Office Building." Introduced by SHUSTER, R-Pa., on May 3, 2005. House passed, under suspension of the rules, Sept. 27. Senate Homeland Security and Governmental Affairs discharged. Senate passed Nov. 18. President signed Dec. 1, 2005.

■ **PL 109-123** (HR 2183) Designate the facility of the U.S. Postal Service located at 567 Tompkins Ave. in Staten Island, N.Y., as the "Vincent Palladino Post Office." Introduced by FOSSELLA, R-N.Y., on May 5, 2005. House passed, under suspension of the rules, July 13. Senate Homeland Security and Governmental Affairs discharged. Senate passed Nov. 18. President signed Dec. 1, 2005.

■ **PL 109-124** (HR 3853) Designate the facility of the U.S. Postal Service located at 208 South Main St. in Parkdale, Ark., as the "Willie Vaughn Post Office." Introduced by ROSS, D-Ark., on Sept. 21, 2005. House passed, under suspension of the rules, Oct. 18. Senate Homeland Security and Governmental Affairs discharged. Senate passed Nov. 18. President signed Dec. 1, 2005.

■ **PL 109-125** (HR 584) Authorize the secretary of the Interior to recruit volunteers to assist with or facilitate the activities of various agencies and offices of the Department of the Interior. Introduced by POMBO, R-Calif., on Feb. 2, 2005. House passed, under suspension of the rules, March 14. Senate Energy and Natural Resources reported Oct. 19 (S Rept 109-156). Senate passed Nov. 16. President signed Dec. 7, 2005.

■ **PL 109-126** (HR 680) Direct the secretary of the Interior to convey certain land held in trust for the Paiute Indian Tribe of Utah to the City of Richfield, Utah. Introduced by CANNON, R-Utah, on Feb. 9, 2005. House passed, under suspension of the rules, March 14. Senate Indian Affairs reported Nov. 7 (S Rept 109-175). Senate passed Nov. 18, 2005. President signed Dec. 7, 2005.

■ **PL 109-127** (HR 1101) Revoke a public land order with respect to approximately 140 acres of lands erroneously included in the Cibola National Wildlife Refuge, Calif. Introduced by HUNTER, R-Calif., on March 3, 2005. House passed, under suspension of the rules, May 23. Senate Energy and Natural Resources reported Oct. 27 (S Rept 109-172). Senate passed Nov. 16. President signed Dec. 7, 2005.

■ **PL 109-128** (H J Res 75) Make further continuing appropriations for fiscal year 2006. Introduced by LEWIS, R-Calif., on Dec. 17, 2005. House passed, amended, under suspension of the rules, Dec. 17. Senate passed Dec. 17. President signed Dec. 18, 2005.

■ **PL 109-129** (HR 2520) Provide for the collection and maintenance of human cord blood stem cells for the treatment of patients and research, and amend the Public Health Service Act to authorize the C.W. Bill Young Cell Transplantation Program. Introduced by SMITH, R-N.J., on May 23, 2005. House passed, under suspension of the rules, May 24. Senate passed, amended, Dec. 16. House agreed to Senate amendment, under suspension of the rules, Dec. 17. President signed Dec. 20, 2005.

■ **PL 109-130** (S 52) Direct the secretary of the Interior to convey approximately 200 acres of real property to Beaver County, Utah. Introduced by HATCH, R-Utah, on Jan. 24, 2005. Senate Energy and Natural Resources reported March 30 (S Rept 109-43). Senate passed July 26. House passed, under suspension of the rules, Dec. 6. President signed Dec. 20, 2005.

■ **PL 109-131** (S 136) Authorize the secretary of the Interior to provide supplemental funding and other services that are necessary to assist certain local school districts in the state of California in providing education services for students attending schools located within Yosemite National Park. Also, authorize the secretary of the Interior to adjust the boundaries of the Golden Gate National Recreation Area and Redwood National Park. Introduced by FEINSTEIN, D-Calif., on Jan. 24, 2005. Senate Energy and Natural Resources reported, amended, April 28 (S Rept 109-63). Senate passed, amended, July 26. House passed, under suspension of the rules, Dec. 6. President signed Dec. 20, 2005.

■ **PL 109-132** (S 212) Amend the Valles Caldera Preservation Act to improve the preservation of the Valles Caldera. Introduced by DOMENICI, R-N.M., on Jan. 31, 2005. Senate Energy and Natural Resources reported Feb. 23 (S Rept 109-10). Senate passed July 26. House passed, under suspension of the rules, Dec. 6. President signed Dec. 20, 2005.

■ **PL 109-133** (S 279) Amend the Pueblo Land Act of 1924, to provide for the exercise of criminal jurisdiction. Introduced by DOMENICI, R-N.M., on Feb. 3, 2005. Senate Indian Affairs discharged. Senate passed, amended, July 26. House passed, under suspension of the rules, Dec. 6. President signed Dec. 20, 2005.

■ **PL 109-134** (S 1886) Authorize the transfer of naval vessels to certain foreign recipients. Introduced by LUGAR, R-Ind., on Oct. 18, 2005. Senate passed Oct. 18. House passed, under suspension of the rules, Dec. 6. President signed Dec. 20, 2005.

■ **PL 109-135** (HR 4440) Amend the Internal Revenue Code of 1986 to provide tax benefits for the Gulf Opportunity Zone and certain areas affected by hurricanes Rita and Wilma. Introduced by McCRERY, R-La., on Dec. 6, 2005. House passed, under suspension of the rules, Dec. 7. Senate passed, amended, Dec. 16. House agreed to Senate amendment Dec. 16. President signed Dec. 22, 2005.

■ **PL 109-136** (HR 797) Amend the Native American Housing Assistance and Self-Determination Act of 1996 and other acts to improve housing programs for Indians. Introduced by RENZI, R-Ariz., on Feb. 14, 2005. House passed, under suspension of the rules, April 6. Senate Indian Affairs reported Oct. 27 (S Rept 109-160). Senate passed, amended, Nov. 8. House agreed to Senate amendments, under suspension of the rules, Dec. 18. President signed Dec. 22, 2005.

■ **PL 109-137** (HR 3963) Amend the Federal Water Pollution Control Act to extend the authorization of appropriations for Long Island Sound. Introduced by SIMMONS, R-Conn., on Sept. 29, 2005. House Transportation and Infrastructure reported Nov. 14 (H Rept 109-293). House passed, under suspension of the rules, Dec. 7. Senate passed Dec. 16. President signed Dec. 22, 2005.

■ **PL 109-138** (HR 4195) Authorize early repayment of obligations to the Bureau of Reclamation within Rogue River Valley Irrigation District or within Medford Irrigation District. Introduced by WALDEN, R-Ore., on Nov. 1, 2005. House Resources reported Dec. 6 (H Rept 109-323). House passed, under suspension of the rules, Dec. 6. Senate Energy and Natural Resources discharged. Senate passed Dec. 16. President signed Dec. 22, 2005.

■ **PL 109-139** (HR 4324) Amend the Robert T. Stafford Disaster Relief and Emergency Assistance Act to reauthorize the predisaster mitigation program. Introduced by SHUSTER, R-Pa., on Nov. 15, 2005. House Transportation and Infrastructure discharged. House passed Nov. 18. Senate Homeland Security and Governmental Affairs discharged. Senate passed Dec. 15. President signed Dec. 22, 2005.

■ **PL 109-140** (HR 4436) Provide certain specific authorities for the Department of State. Introduced by SMITH, R-N.J., on Dec. 6, 2005. House passed, amended, under suspension of the rules, Dec. 14. Senate passed Dec. 15. President signed Dec. 22, 2005.

■ **PL 109-141** (HR 4508) Commend the outstanding efforts in response to Hurricane Katrina by members and employees of the Coast Guard and provide temporary relief for personnel and vessels affected by the hurricane. Introduced by YOUNG, R-Alaska, on Dec. 13, 2005. House passed, under suspension of the rules, Dec. 14. Senate passed Dec. 16. President signed Dec. 22, 2005.

■ **PL 109-142** (H J Res 38) Recognizing Commodore John Barry as the first flag officer of the United States Navy. Introduced by KING, R-N.Y., on March 17, 2005. House passed, under suspension of the rules, Dec. 14. Senate passed Dec. 16. President signed Dec. 22, 2005.

■ **PL 109-143** (S 335) Reauthorize the Congressional Award Act. Introduced by LIEBERMAN, D-Conn., on Feb. 9, 2005. Senate Homeland Security and Governmental Affairs reported June 23 (S Rept 109-87). Senate passed July 14. House passed, under suspension of the rules, Dec. 14. President signed Dec. 22, 2005.

■ **PL 109-144** (S 467) Extend the applicability of the Terrorism Risk Insurance Act of 2002. Introduced by DODD, D-Conn., on Feb. 18, 2005. Senate Banking, Housing and Urban Affairs reported, amended. Nov. 16 (no written report). Senate passed, amended, Nov. 18. House passed, amended, under suspension of the rules, Dec. 7. Senate agreed with amendment to the House amendment Dec. 16. House agreed to Senate amendment to House amendment under suspension of the rules Dec. 17. President signed Dec. 22, 2005.

■ **PL 109-145** (S 1047) Require the secretary of the Treasury to mint coins in commemoration of each of the past presidents and their spouses, respectively, improve circulation of the $1 coin and create a new bullion coin. Introduced by SUNUNU, R-N.H., on May 17, 2005. Senate Banking, Housing and Urban Affairs reported July 29 (no written report). Senate passed, amended Nov. 18. House passed, under suspension of the rules Dec. 13. President signed Dec. 22, 2005.

■ **PL 109-146** (HR 358) Require the secretary of the Treasury to mint coins in commemoration of the 50th anniversary of the desegregation of the Little Rock Central High School in Little Rock, Ark. Introduced by SNYDER, D-Ark., on Jan. 25, 2005. House Financial Services reported, amended, June 15, (H Rept 109-134, Part I). House Ways and Means discharged. House passed, amended, under suspension of the rules, June 27. Senate Banking, Housing and Urban Affairs discharged. Senate passed, amended, Nov. 18. House agreed to Senate amendment, under suspension of the rules, Dec. 18. President signed Dec. 22, 2005.

■ **PL 109-147** (HR 327) Allow binding arbitration clauses to be included in all contracts affecting land within the Gila River Indian Community Reservation. Introduced by GRIJALVA, D-Ariz., on Jan. 25, 2005. House passed, under suspension of the rules, Dec. 7. Senate passed Dec. 14. President signed Dec. 22, 2005.

■ **PL 109-148** (HR 2863) Make appropriations for the Department of Defense for fiscal 2006. Introduced by YOUNG, R-Fla., on June 10, 2005. House Appropriations reported June 10 (H Rept 109-119). House passed, amended, June 20. Senate Appropriations reported, amended, Sept. 29 (S Rept 109-141). Senate passed, amended, Oct. 7. Conference report filed in the House Dec. 18 (H Rept 109-359). House agreed to the conference report Dec. 19. Senate agreed to the conference report Dec. 21. President signed Dec. 30, 2005.

■ **PL 109-149** (HR 3010) Make appropriations for the departments of Labor, Health and Human Services, and Education, and related agencies for fiscal 2006. Introduced by REGULA, R-Ohio, on June 21, 2005. House Appropriations reported June 21 (H Rept 109-143). House passed, amended, June 24. Senate Appropriations reported, amended July 14 (S Rept 109-103). Senate passed, amended, Oct. 27. Conference report filed in the House Nov. 16 (H Rept 109-300). House rejected the conference report Nov. 17. New conference report filed in the House Dec. 13 (H Rept 109-337). House agreed to the conference report Dec. 14. Senate agreed to the conference report Dec. 21. President signed Dec. 30, 2005.

■ **PL 109-150** (HR 4525) Temporarily extend programs under the Higher Education Act of 1965. Introduced by BOEHNER, R-Ohio, on Dec. 14, 2005. House passed, amended, under suspension of the rules, Dec. 17. Senate passed Dec. 22. President signed Dec. 30, 2005.

■ **PL 109-151** (HR 4579) Amend Title I of the Employee Retirement Income Security Act of 1974, Title XXVII of the Public Health Service Act, and the Internal Revenue Code of 1986 to extend by one year provisions requiring parity in the application of certain limits to mental health benefits. Introduced by BOEHNER, R-Ohio, on Dec. 16, 2005. House passed, under suspension of the rules, Dec. 17. Senate passed Dec. 22. President signed Dec. 30, 2005.

■ **PL 109-152** (S 205) Authorize the American Battle Monuments Commission to establish in the state of Louisiana a memorial to honor the Buffalo Soldiers. Introduced by LANDRIEU, D-La., on Jan. 31, 2005. Senate Energy and Natural Resources reported, amended, March 9 (S Rept 109-24). Senate passed, amended July 26. House Resources discharged. House passed Dec. 19. President signed Dec. 30, 2005.

■ **PL 109-153** (S 652) Provide financial assistance for the rehabilitation of the Benjamin Franklin National Memorial in Philadel-

phia, Pa., and the development of an exhibit to commemorate the 300th anniversary of the birth of Benjamin Franklin. Introduced by SPECTER, R-Pa., on March 17, 2005. Senate Energy and Natural Resources reported Oct. 19 (S Rept 109-147). Senate passed Nov. 16. House Resources discharged. House passed Dec. 19. President signed Dec. 30, 2005.

■ **PL 109-154** (S 1238) Amend the Public Lands Corps Act of 1993 to provide for the conduct of projects that protect forests. Introduced by FEINSTEIN, D-Calif., on June 14, 2005. Senate Energy and Natural Resources reported, amended, Oct. 19 (S Rept 109-152). Senate passed, amended, Nov. 16. House passed Dec. 19. President signed Dec. 30, 2005.

■ **PL 109-155** (S 1281) Authorize appropriations for the National Aeronautics and Space Administration for science, aeronautics, exploration, exploration capabilities and the Inspector General, for fiscal years 2006, 2007, 2008, 2009 and 2010. Introduced by HUTCHISON, R-Texas, on June 21, 2005. Senate Commerce, Science and Transportation reported, amended, July 26 (S Rept 109-108). Senate passed, amended, Sept. 28. House passed, amended, Nov. 18. Conference report filed in the House Dec. 16 (H Rept 109-354). House agreed to the conference report, under suspension of the rules, Dec. 17. Senate agreed to the conference report Dec. 22. President signed Dec. 30, 2005.

■ **PL 109-156** (S 1310) Authorize the secretary of the Interior to allow the Columbia Gas Transmission Corp. to increase the diameter of a natural gas pipeline located in the Delaware Water Gap National Recreation Area. Introduced by SANTORUM, R-Pa., on June 24, 2005. Senate Energy and Natural Resources reported, amended, Dec. 8 (S Rept. 109-194). Senate passed, amended, Dec. 16. House passed Dec. 19. President signed Dec. 30, 2005.

■ **PL 109-157** (S 1481) Amend the Indian Land Consolidation Act to provide for probate reform. Introduced by McCAIN, R-Ariz., on July 26, 2005. Senate passed July 26. House Resources discharged. House passed Dec. 19. President signed Dec. 30, 2005.

■**PL 109-158** (S 1892) Amend Public Law 107-153 to modify a certain date. Introduced by McCAIN, R-Ariz., on Oct. 19, 2005. Senate Indian Affairs reported Dec. 8 (S Rept 109-201). Senate passed, amended, Dec. 16. House passed Dec. 19. President signed Dec. 30, 2005.

■ **PL 109-159** (S 1988) Authorize the transfer of items in the War Reserves Stockpile to the Republic of Korea. Introduced by LUGAR, R-Ind., on Nov. 9, 2005. Senate passed Nov. 9. House passed, under suspension of the rules, Dec. 18. President signed Dec. 30, 2005.

■ **PL 109-160** (S 2167) Amend the USA Patriot Act to extend to Feb. 3, 2006, the sunset of certain provisions of that act and the "lone wolf" provision of the Intelligence Reform and Terrorism Prevention Act of 2004. Introduced by SUNUNU, R-N.H., on Dec. 21, 2005. Senate passed Dec. 21. House passed, amended, Dec. 22, 2005. Senate agreed to House amendment Dec. 22, 2005. President signed Dec. 30, 2005.

■ **PL 109-161** (HR 4635) Reauthorize the Temporary Assistance for Needy Families block grant program through March 31, 2006. Introduced by HERGER, R-Calif., on Dec. 18, 2005. House Ways and Means discharged. House passed Dec. 19. Senate passed Dec. 22. President signed Dec. 30, 2005.

■ **PL 109-162** (HR 3402) Authorize appropriations for the Department of Justice for fiscal years 2006 through 2009. Introduced by SENSENBRENNER, R-Wis., on July 22, 2005. House Judiciary reported, amended, Sept. 22 (H Rept 109-233). House passed, amended, Sept. 28. Senate Judiciary discharged. Senate passed, amended, Dec. 16. House agreed to Senate amendment, under suspension of the rules, Dec. 17. President signed Jan. 5, 2006.

■ **PL 109-163** (HR 1815) Authorize appropriations for fiscal 2006 for military activities of the Department of Defense and prescribe military personnel strengths for fiscal 2006. Introduced by HUNTER, R-Calif., on April 26, 2005. House Armed Services reported, amended, May 20 (H Rept 109-89). House passed, amended, May 25. Senate Armed Services discharged. Senate passed, amended, Nov. 15. Conference report filed in the House Dec. 18 (H Rept 109-360). House agreed to conference report Dec. 19. Senate agreed to conference report Dec. 21. President signed Jan. 6, 2005.

■ **PL 109-164** (HR 972) Authorize appropriations for fiscal years 2006 and 2007 for the Trafficking Victims Protection Act of 2000. Introduced by SMITH, R-N.J., on Feb. 17, 2005. House International Relations reported, amended, Nov. 18 (H Rept 109-317, Part I). House Armed Services and House Energy and Commerce discharged. House Judiciary reported amended Dec. 8 (H Rept 109-317, Part II). House passed, amended, under suspension of the rules, Dec. 14. Senate passed Dec. 22. President signed Jan. 10, 2006.

■ **PL 109-165** (HR 2017) Amend the Torture Victims Relief Act of 1998 to authorize appropriations to provide assistance for domestic and foreign programs and centers for the treatment of victims of torture. Introduced by SMITH, R-N.J., on April 28, 2005. House passed, under suspension of the rules, Dec. 6. Senate passed Dec. 22. President signed Jan. 10, 2006.

■ **PL 109-166** (HR 3179) Reauthorize and amend the Junior Duck Stamp Conservation and Design Program Act of 1994. Introduced by ORTIZ, D-Texas, on June 30, 2005. House Resources discharged. House passed Dec. 19. Senate passed Dec. 22. President signed Jan. 10, 2006.

■ **PL 109-167** (HR 4501) Amend the Passport Act of June 4, 1920, to authorize the secretary of State to establish and collect a surcharge to cover the costs of meeting the increased demand for passports as a result of actions taken to comply with section 7209(b) of the Intelligence Reform and Terrorism Prevention Act of 2004. Introduced by HYDE, R-Ill., on Dec. 13, 2005. House passed, amended, under suspension of the rules, Dec. 18. Senate passed Dec. 22. President signed Jan 10, 2006.

■ **PL 109-168** (HR 4637) Make technical corrections in amendments made by the Energy Policy Act of 2005. Introduced by GILLMOR, R-Ohio, on Dec. 18, 2005. House Energy and Commerce discharged. House passed Dec. 19. Senate passed Dec. 22. President signed Jan 10, 2006.

■ **PL 109-169** (HR 4340) Implement the United States-Bahrain Free Trade Agreement. Introduced by BLUNT, R-Mo., on Nov. 16, 2005. House Ways and Means reported Dec. 6 (H Rept 109-318). House passed Dec. 7. Senate passed Dec. 13. President signed Jan. 11, 2006. ■

# HOUSE
# ROLL CALL
# VOTES

# House Roll Call Index
# By Bill Number

# IN THE HOUSE | By Vote Number

**1.*** **Quorum Call.** 424 members responded. Jan. 4, 2005.

**2.** **Election of the Speaker.** Nomination of J. Dennis Hastert, R-Ill., and Nancy Pelosi, D-Calif., for Speaker of the House of Representatives for the 109th Congress. Hastert elected, 226-199: R 226-0; D 0-198 (ND 0-148, SD 0-50); I 0-1. A "Y" on the chart represents a vote for Hastert; an "N" represents a vote for Pelosi, except in the case of Gene Taylor, D-Miss., who voted for John P. Murtha, D-Pa. A majority of the votes cast for a person by name (214 in this case) is needed for election. All members-elect are eligible to vote on the election of the Speaker. Jan. 4, 2005.

**3.** **H Res 5. House Organizing Resolution/Motion to Consider.** Baird, D-Wash., motion to consider the resolution that would set the rules for the 109th Congress. Motion agreed to 224-192: R 223-0; D 1-191 (ND 0-142, SD 1-49); I 0-1. Jan. 4, 2005.

**4.** **H Res 5. House Organizing Resolution/Previous Question.** Dreier, R-Calif., motion to order the previous question (thus ending debate and possibility of amendment) on adoption of the resolution that would set the rules for the 109th Congress. Motion agreed to 222-196: R 222-0; D 0-195 (ND 0-144, SD 0-51); I 0-1. Jan. 4, 2005.

**5.** **H Res 5. House Organizing Resolution/Motion to Commit.** Slaughter, D-N.Y., motion to commit the resolution that would set the rules for the 109th Congress to a select committee comprised of the majority and minority leader with instructions that it be reported back after adding sections that would set post-employment restrictions for members and require a two-thirds vote to waive the three day lay-over rule. Motion rejected 196-219: R 1-219; D 194-0 (ND 143-0, SD 51-0); I 1-0. Jan. 4, 2005.

**6.** **H Res 5. House Organizing Resolution/Adoption.** Adoption of the resolution that would set the rules for the 109th Congress. The rules would create a permanent Homeland Security Committee, allow lawmakers to pay for certain office-related expenses with campaign funds and outline procedures for operating with a provisional quorum after widespread death or incapacitation. Adopted 220-195: R 220-0; D 0-194 (ND 0-143, SD 0-51); I 0-1. Jan. 4, 2005.

**7.** **Electoral Vote Count.** Rep. Stephanie Tubbs Jones, D-Ohio, and Sen. Barbara Boxer, D-Calif., objection to the certification of the Ohio electoral votes to protest voting irregularities in that state. Rejected 31-267: R 0-178; D 31-88 (ND 23-60, SD 8-28); I 0-1. Jan. 6, 2005.

* CQ does not include quorum calls in its vote charts.

[1] Reps. Michael M. Honda, D-Calif.; Luis V. Gutierrez, D-Ill.; Tom Osborne, R-Neb.; and Chris Cannon, R-Utah, had not yet been sworn in, and thus were ineligible to vote except for the vote for Speaker. Reps. John Shadegg, R-Ariz., and Charlie Norwood, R-Ga., were sworn in Jan. 6, making them eligible for both the vote for Speaker and for vote 7.

[2] Rep. Robert T. Matsui, D-Calif., died Jan. 1, 2005. A special election for his replacement will be announced by Jan. 15.

[3] In the case of Rep. Gene Taylor, D-Miss., an "N" on vote 2 represents a vote for John P. Murtha, D-Pa.

ND Northern Democrats, SD Southern Democrats
Southern states: Ala., Ark., Fla., Ga., Ky., La., Miss., N.C., Okla., S.C., Tenn., Texas, Va.

| | 2 | 3 | 4 | 5 | 6 | 7 |
|---|---|---|---|---|---|---|
| **ALABAMA** | | | | | | |
| 1 **Bonner** | Y | Y | Y | N | Y | N |
| 2 **Everett** | Y | Y | Y | N | Y | ? |
| 3 **Rogers** | Y | Y | Y | N | Y | ? |
| 4 **Aderholt** | Y | Y | Y | N | Y | N |
| 5 **Cramer** | N | N | N | Y | N | N |
| 6 **Bachus** | Y | Y | Y | N | Y | N |
| 7 Davis | N | N | N | Y | N | N |
| **ALASKA** | | | | | | |
| AL **Young** | Y | Y | Y | N | Y | N |
| **ARIZONA** | | | | | | |
| 1 **Renzi** | Y | Y | Y | N | Y | N |
| 2 **Franks** | Y | Y | Y | N | Y | N |
| 3 **Shadegg**[1] | ? | I | I | I | I | N |
| 4 **Pastor** | N | N | N | Y | N | N |
| 5 **Hayworth** | Y | Y | Y | N | Y | N |
| 6 **Flake** | Y | Y | Y | N | Y | ? |
| 7 **Grijalva** | N | N | N | Y | N | Y |
| 8 **Kolbe** | Y | Y | Y | N | Y | ? |
| **ARKANSAS** | | | | | | |
| 1 **Berry** | N | N | N | Y | N | ? |
| 2 **Snyder** | N | N | N | Y | N | N |
| 3 **Boozman** | Y | Y | Y | N | Y | N |
| 4 **Ross** | N | N | N | Y | N | N |
| **CALIFORNIA** | | | | | | |
| 1 **Thompson** | N | N | N | Y | N | ? |
| 2 **Herger** | Y | Y | Y | N | Y | N |
| 3 **Lungren** | Y | Y | Y | N | Y | N |
| 4 **Doolittle** | Y | Y | Y | N | Y | ? |
| 5 Vacant[2] | | | | | | |
| 6 **Woolsey** | N | N | N | Y | N | Y |
| 7 **Miller, George** | N | N | N | Y | N | N |
| 8 **Pelosi** | N | N | N | Y | N | N |
| 9 **Lee** | N | N | N | Y | N | Y |
| 10 **Tauscher** | N | N | N | Y | N | N |
| 11 **Pombo** | Y | Y | Y | N | Y | N |
| 12 **Lantos** | N | N | N | Y | N | ? |
| 13 **Stark** | N | N | N | Y | N | ? |
| 14 **Eshoo** | N | N | N | Y | N | ? |
| 15 **Honda**[1] | ? | I | I | I | I | I |
| 16 **Lofgren** | N | N | N | Y | N | N |
| 17 **Farr** | N | N | N | Y | N | Y |
| 18 **Cardoza** | N | N | N | Y | N | ? |
| 19 **Radanovich** | Y | Y | Y | N | Y | N |
| 20 **Costa** | N | N | N | Y | N | N |
| 21 **Nunes** | Y | Y | Y | N | Y | N |
| 22 **Thomas** | Y | Y | Y | N | Y | N |
| 23 **Capps** | N | – | – | + | – | ? |
| 24 **Gallegly** | Y | Y | Y | N | Y | – |
| 25 **McKeon** | Y | Y | Y | N | Y | N |
| 26 **Dreier** | Y | Y | Y | N | Y | N |
| 27 **Sherman** | N | N | N | Y | N | – |
| 28 **Berman** | N | N | N | Y | N | N |
| 29 **Schiff** | N | N | N | Y | N | ? |
| 30 **Waxman** | N | N | N | Y | N | N |
| 31 **Becerra** | N | N | N | Y | N | ? |
| 32 **Solis** | N | – | N | Y | N | N |
| 33 **Watson** | N | N | ? | ? | ? | Y |
| 34 **Roybal-Allard** | N | N | N | Y | N | – |
| 35 **Waters** | N | N | N | Y | N | N |
| 36 **Harman** | N | N | N | Y | N | N |
| 37 **Millender-McD.** | N | ? | N | Y | N | ? |
| 38 **Napolitano** | N | N | N | Y | N | N |
| 39 **Sánchez, Linda** | N | N | N | Y | N | N |
| 40 **Royce** | Y | Y | Y | N | Y | N |
| 41 **Lewis** | Y | Y | Y | N | Y | N |
| 42 **Miller, Gary** | Y | Y | ? | ? | ? | ? |
| 43 **Baca** | N | N | N | Y | N | ? |
| 44 **Calvert** | Y | Y | Y | N | Y | N |
| 45 **Bono** | Y | Y | Y | N | Y | ? |
| 46 **Rohrabacher** | Y | P | Y | N | Y | ? |
| 47 **Sanchez, Loretta** | N | N | N | Y | N | ? |
| 48 **Cox** | + | Y | Y | N | Y | N |
| 49 **Issa** | Y | Y | Y | N | Y | N |

| | 2 | 3 | 4 | 5 | 6 | 7 |
|---|---|---|---|---|---|---|
| 50 **Cunningham** | Y | Y | N | Y | Y | ? |
| 51 **Filner** | N | N | N | Y | N | Y |
| 52 **Hunter** | Y | Y | Y | N | Y | N |
| 53 **Davis** | N | N | N | Y | N | N |
| **COLORADO** | | | | | | |
| 1 **DeGette** | N | N | N | Y | N | N |
| 2 **Udall** | N | N | N | Y | N | ? |
| 3 **Salazar** | N | N | N | Y | N | N |
| 4 **Musgrave** | Y | Y | Y | N | Y | N |
| 5 **Hefley** | Y | Y | Y | N | Y | ? |
| 6 **Tancredo** | Y | Y | Y | N | Y | ? |
| 7 **Beauprez** | Y | Y | Y | N | Y | N |
| **CONNECTICUT** | | | | | | |
| 1 **Larson** | N | N | N | Y | N | N |
| 2 **Simmons** | N | ? | Y | N | Y | N |
| 3 **DeLauro** | N | N | N | Y | N | N |
| 4 **Shays** | Y | Y | Y | N | Y | – |
| 5 **Johnson** | Y | ? | Y | N | Y | N |
| **DELAWARE** | | | | | | |
| AL **Castle** | Y | Y | Y | N | Y | N |
| **FLORIDA** | | | | | | |
| 1 **Miller** | Y | Y | Y | N | Y | ? |
| 2 **Boyd** | N | N | N | Y | N | ? |
| 3 **Brown** | N | N | N | Y | N | Y |
| 4 **Crenshaw** | Y | Y | Y | N | Y | N |
| 5 **Brown-Waite** | Y | Y | Y | N | Y | N |
| 6 **Stearns** | Y | Y | Y | N | Y | – |
| 7 **Mica** | Y | Y | Y | N | Y | – |
| 8 **Keller** | Y | Y | Y | N | Y | N |
| 9 **Bilirakis** | Y | Y | Y | N | Y | ? |
| 10 **Young** | Y | Y | Y | N | Y | N |
| 11 **Davis** | N | N | N | Y | N | N |
| 12 **Putnam** | Y | Y | Y | N | Y | N |
| 13 **Harris** | Y | Y | Y | N | Y | N |
| 14 **Mack** | Y | Y | Y | N | Y | N |
| 15 **Weldon** | Y | Y | Y | N | Y | N |
| 16 **Foley** | Y | Y | Y | N | Y | N |
| 17 **Meek** | N | N | N | Y | N | N |
| 18 **Ros-Lehtinen** | Y | Y | Y | N | Y | N |
| 19 **Wexler** | N | N | N | Y | N | ? |
| 20 Wasserman-Schultz | N | N | N | Y | N | N |
| 21 **Diaz-Balart, L.** | Y | Y | Y | N | Y | N |
| 22 **Shaw** | Y | Y | Y | N | Y | N |
| 23 **Hastings** | N | N | N | Y | N | Y |
| 24 **Feeney** | Y | ? | ? | ? | ? | N |
| 25 **Diaz-Balart, M.** | Y | Y | Y | N | Y | N |
| **GEORGIA** | | | | | | |
| 1 **Kingston** | Y | Y | Y | N | Y | N |
| 2 **Bishop** | N | N | N | Y | N | N |
| 3 **Marshall** | N | N | N | Y | N | N |
| 4 **McKinney** | N | N | N | Y | N | Y |
| 5 **Lewis** | N | N | N | Y | N | Y |
| 6 **Price** | Y | Y | Y | N | Y | N |
| 7 **Linder** | Y | Y | Y | N | Y | N |
| 8 **Westmoreland** | Y | Y | Y | N | Y | N |
| 9 **Norwood**[1] | ? | I | I | I | I | N |
| 10 **Deal** | Y | Y | Y | N | Y | N |
| 11 **Gingrey** | Y | Y | Y | N | Y | N |
| 12 **Barrow** | N | – | N | Y | N | N |
| 13 **Scott** | N | N | N | Y | N | N |
| **HAWAII** | | | | | | |
| 1 **Abercrombie** | N | N | N | Y | N | + |
| 2 **Case** | N | N | N | Y | N | N |
| **IDAHO** | | | | | | |
| 1 **Otter** | Y | Y | Y | N | Y | ? |
| 2 **Simpson** | Y | Y | Y | N | Y | N |
| **ILLINOIS** | | | | | | |
| 1 **Rush** | N | N | N | Y | N | ? |
| 2 **Jackson** | N | N | N | Y | N | Y |
| 3 **Lipinski** | N | N | N | Y | N | N |
| 4 **Gutierrez**[1] | ? | I | I | I | I | I |
| 5 **Emanuel** | N | N | N | Y | N | ? |
| 6 **Hyde** | Y | Y | Y | N | Y | N |
| 7 **Davis** | N | N | N | Y | N | N |
| 8 **Bean** | N | N | N | Y | N | N |
| 9 **Schakowsky** | N | N | N | Y | N | Y |
| 10 **Kirk** | Y | Y | Y | N | Y | N |
| 11 **Weller** | Y | Y | Y | N | Y | N |
| 12 **Costello** | N | N | N | Y | N | ? |

**KEY**  **Republicans**   Democrats   *Independents*

| | | | |
|---|---|---|---|
| **Y** | Voted for (yea) | **X** | Paired against |
| **#** | Paired for | **–** | Announced against |
| **+** | Announced for | **P** | Voted "present" |
| **N** | Voted against (nay) | | |
| **C** | Voted "present" to avoid possible conflict of interest | | |
| **?** | Did not vote or otherwise make a position known | | |

| | 2 | 3 | 4 | 5 | 6 | 7 |
|---|---|---|---|---|---|---|
| 13 **Biggert** | Y | Y | Y | N | Y | ? |
| 14 **Hastert** | | Y | | | | N |
| 15 **Johnson** | Y | Y | Y | N | Y | – |
| 16 **Manzullo** | Y | Y | Y | N | Y | N |
| 17 Evans | N | N | N | Y | N | Y |
| 18 **LaHood** | Y | Y | Y | N | Y | ? |
| 19 **Shimkus** | Y | Y | Y | N | Y | ? |
| **INDIANA** | | | | | | |
| 1 Visclosky | N | N | N | Y | N | N |
| 2 **Chocola** | Y | Y | Y | N | Y | N |
| 3 **Souder** | Y | Y | Y | N | Y | ? |
| 4 **Buyer** | Y | Y | Y | N | Y | N |
| 5 **Burton** | Y | Y | Y | N | Y | N |
| 6 **Pence** | Y | Y | Y | N | Y | N |
| 7 Carson | N | N | N | Y | N | Y |
| 8 **Hostettler** | Y | Y | Y | N | Y | N |
| 9 **Sodrel** | Y | Y | Y | N | Y | N |
| **IOWA** | | | | | | |
| 1 **Nussle** | Y | Y | Y | N | Y | N |
| 2 **Leach** | Y | Y | Y | N | Y | ? |
| 3 Boswell | N | N | N | Y | N | ? |
| 4 **Latham** | Y | Y | Y | N | Y | N |
| 5 **King** | Y | Y | Y | N | Y | N |
| **KANSAS** | | | | | | |
| 1 **Moran** | Y | Y | Y | N | Y | ? |
| 2 **Ryun** | Y | Y | Y | N | Y | N |
| 3 Moore | N | N | N | Y | N | N |
| 4 **Tiahrt** | Y | Y | Y | N | Y | N |
| **KENTUCKY** | | | | | | |
| 1 **Whitfield** | Y | Y | Y | N | Y | N |
| 2 **Lewis** | Y | Y | Y | N | Y | N |
| 3 **Northup** | + | Y | ? | ? | ? | N |
| 4 **Davis** | Y | Y | Y | N | Y | N |
| 5 **Rogers** | Y | Y | Y | N | Y | N |
| 6 Chandler | N | N | N | Y | N | N |
| **LOUISIANA** | | | | | | |
| 1 **Jindal** | Y | Y | Y | N | Y | N |
| 2 Jefferson | N | N | N | Y | N | ? |
| 3 Melancon | N | N | N | Y | N | N |
| 4 **McCrery** | Y | Y | Y | N | Y | N |
| 5 **Alexander** | Y | Y | Y | N | Y | N |
| 6 **Baker** | Y | Y | Y | N | Y | ? |
| 7 **Boustany** | Y | Y | Y | N | Y | N |
| **MAINE** | | | | | | |
| 1 Allen | N | N | N | Y | N | ? |
| 2 Michaud | N | N | N | Y | N | ? |
| **MARYLAND** | | | | | | |
| 1 **Gilchrest** | Y | Y | Y | N | Y | ? |
| 2 Ruppersberger | N | N | N | Y | N | ? |
| 3 Cardin | N | N | N | Y | N | ? |
| 4 Wynn | N | N | N | Y | N | ? |
| 5 Hoyer | N | N | N | Y | N | ? |
| 6 **Bartlett** | Y | Y | Y | N | Y | N |
| 7 Cummings | N | N | N | Y | N | N |
| 8 Van Hollen | N | N | N | Y | N | N |
| **MASSACHUSETTS** | | | | | | |
| 1 Olver | N | N | N | Y | N | Y |
| 2 Neal | N | N | N | Y | N | ? |
| 3 McGovern | N | N | N | Y | N | N |
| 4 Frank | N | N | N | Y | N | ? |
| 5 Meehan | N | N | N | Y | N | N |
| 6 Tierney | N | N | N | Y | N | N |
| 7 Markey | N | N | N | Y | N | Y |
| 8 Capuano | N | N | N | Y | N | ? |
| 9 Lynch | N | N | N | Y | N | ? |
| 10 Delahunt | N | N | N | Y | N | ? |
| **MICHIGAN** | | | | | | |
| 1 Stupak | N | N | N | Y | N | ? |
| 2 **Hoekstra** | Y | Y | Y | N | Y | N |
| 3 **Ehlers** | Y | Y | Y | N | Y | N |
| 4 **Camp** | Y | Y | Y | N | Y | N |
| 5 Kildee | N | N | N | Y | N | N |
| 6 **Upton** | Y | Y | Y | N | Y | N |
| 7 **Schwarz** | Y | Y | Y | N | Y | N |
| 8 **Rogers** | Y | Y | Y | N | Y | N |
| 9 **Knollenberg** | Y | Y | Y | N | Y | N |
| 10 **Miller** | Y | Y | Y | N | Y | N |
| 11 **McCotter** | Y | Y | Y | N | Y | N |
| 12 Levin | N | N | N | Y | N | N |
| 13 Kilpatrick | N | N | N | Y | N | Y |
| 14 Conyers | N | N | N | Y | N | Y |
| 15 Dingell | N | N | N | Y | N | N |
| **MINNESOTA** | | | | | | |
| 1 **Gutknecht** | Y | Y | Y | N | Y | ? |
| 2 **Kline** | Y | Y | Y | N | Y | N |
| 3 **Ramstad** | Y | Y | Y | N | Y | N |
| 4 McCollum | N | N | N | Y | N | N |
| 5 Sabo | N | N | N | Y | N | N |
| 6 **Kennedy** | Y | Y | Y | N | Y | N |
| 7 Peterson | N | N | N | Y | N | N |
| 8 Oberstar | N | N | N | Y | N | N |
| **MISSISSIPPI** | | | | | | |
| 1 **Wicker** | Y | Y | Y | N | Y | N |
| 2 Thompson | N | N | N | Y | N | Y |
| 3 **Pickering** | Y | Y | Y | N | Y | ? |
| 4 Taylor[3] | N | N | N | Y | N | N |
| **MISSOURI** | | | | | | |
| 1 Clay | N | N | N | Y | N | Y |
| 2 **Akin** | Y | Y | Y | N | Y | N |
| 3 Carnahan | N | N | N | Y | N | N |
| 4 Skelton | N | N | N | Y | N | ? |
| 5 Cleaver | N | N | N | Y | N | N |
| 6 **Graves** | Y | Y | Y | N | Y | – |
| 7 **Blunt** | Y | Y | Y | N | Y | N |
| 8 **Emerson** | Y | Y | Y | N | Y | N |
| 9 **Hulshof** | Y | Y | Y | N | Y | N |
| **MONTANA** | | | | | | |
| AL **Rehberg** | Y | Y | Y | N | Y | N |
| **NEBRASKA** | | | | | | |
| 1 **Fortenberry** | Y | Y | Y | – | Y | N |
| 2 **Terry** | Y | Y | Y | N | Y | ? |
| 3 **Osborne**[1] | Y | I | I | I | I | I |
| **NEVADA** | | | | | | |
| 1 Berkley | N | N | N | Y | N | ? |
| 2 **Gibbons** | Y | Y | Y | N | Y | N |
| 3 **Porter** | Y | Y | Y | N | Y | N |
| **NEW HAMPSHIRE** | | | | | | |
| 1 **Bradley** | Y | Y | Y | N | Y | N |
| 2 **Bass** | Y | Y | Y | N | Y | ? |
| **NEW JERSEY** | | | | | | |
| 1 Andrews | N | N | N | Y | N | N |
| 2 **LoBiondo** | Y | Y | Y | N | Y | N |
| 3 **Saxton** | Y | Y | Y | N | Y | N |
| 4 **Smith** | Y | Y | Y | N | Y | N |
| 5 **Garrett** | Y | Y | Y | N | Y | N |
| 6 Pallone | N | N | N | Y | N | Y |
| 7 **Ferguson** | Y | Y | Y | N | Y | N |
| 8 Pascrell | N | ? | N | Y | N | – |
| 9 Rothman | N | N | N | Y | N | N |
| 10 Payne | N | N | N | Y | N | Y |
| 11 **Frelinghuysen** | Y | Y | Y | N | Y | N |
| 12 Holt | N | N | N | Y | N | N |
| 13 Menendez | N | N | N | Y | N | – |
| **NEW MEXICO** | | | | | | |
| 1 **Wilson** | Y | Y | Y | N | Y | N |
| 2 **Pearce** | Y | Y | Y | N | Y | ? |
| 3 Udall | N | N | N | Y | N | N |
| **NEW YORK** | | | | | | |
| 1 Bishop | N | N | N | Y | N | ? |
| 2 Israel | N | N | N | Y | N | N |
| 3 **King** | Y | Y | Y | N | Y | N |
| 4 McCarthy | N | N | N | Y | N | – |
| 5 Ackerman | N | N | N | Y | N | ? |
| 6 Meeks | N | N | N | Y | N | ? |
| 7 Crowley | N | N | N | Y | N | ? |
| 8 Nadler | N | N | N | Y | N | N |
| 9 Weiner | N | N | N | Y | N | N |
| 10 Towns | N | N | N | Y | N | ? |
| 11 Owens | N | N | N | Y | N | Y |
| 12 Velázquez | N | N | N | Y | N | ? |
| 13 **Fossella** | Y | Y | Y | N | Y | ? |
| 14 Maloney | N | N | N | Y | N | ? |
| 15 Rangel | N | N | N | Y | N | ? |
| 16 Serrano | N | ? | ? | ? | ? | ? |
| 17 Engel | N | N | N | Y | N | N |
| 18 Lowey | N | N | N | Y | N | ? |
| 19 **Kelly** | Y | Y | Y | N | Y | ? |
| 20 **Sweeney** | Y | Y | Y | N | Y | ? |
| 21 McNulty | N | N | N | Y | N | N |
| 22 Hinchey | N | N | N | Y | N | Y |
| 23 **McHugh** | Y | Y | ? | ? | ? | N |
| 24 **Boehlert** | Y | Y | Y | N | Y | N |
| 25 **Walsh** | Y | Y | Y | N | Y | ? |
| 26 **Reynolds** | Y | Y | Y | N | Y | N |
| 27 Higgins | N | N | N | Y | N | ? |
| 28 Slaughter | N | N | N | Y | N | ? |
| 29 **Kuhl** | Y | Y | Y | N | Y | N |
| **NORTH CAROLINA** | | | | | | |
| 1 Butterfield | N | N | N | Y | N | N |
| 2 Etheridge | N | N | N | Y | N | N |
| 3 **Jones** | Y | Y | ? | ? | ? | ? |
| 4 Price | N | N | N | Y | N | N |
| 5 **Foxx** | Y | Y | Y | N | Y | N |
| 6 **Coble** | Y | Y | Y | N | Y | ? |
| 7 McIntyre | N | N | N | Y | N | ? |
| 8 **Hayes** | Y | Y | Y | N | Y | N |
| 9 **Myrick** | Y | Y | Y | N | Y | N |
| 10 **McHenry** | Y | Y | Y | N | Y | N |
| 11 **Taylor** | Y | Y | Y | N | Y | N |
| 12 Watt | N | N | N | Y | N | N |
| 13 Miller | N | Y | N | Y | N | N |
| **NORTH DAKOTA** | | | | | | |
| AL Pomeroy | N | N | N | Y | N | N |
| **OHIO** | | | | | | |
| 1 **Chabot** | Y | Y | Y | N | Y | N |
| 2 **Portman** | Y | Y | Y | N | Y | N |
| 3 **Turner** | Y | Y | Y | N | Y | N |
| 4 **Oxley** | Y | Y | Y | N | Y | N |
| 5 **Gillmor** | Y | Y | Y | N | Y | ? |
| 6 Strickland | N | N | N | Y | N | N |
| 7 **Hobson** | Y | Y | Y | N | Y | N |
| 8 **Boehner** | Y | Y | Y | N | Y | N |
| 9 Kaptur | N | N | N | Y | N | N |
| 10 Kucinich | N | N | N | Y | N | Y |
| 11 Jones | N | N | N | Y | N | Y |
| 12 **Tiberi** | Y | Y | Y | N | Y | N |
| 13 Brown | N | N | N | Y | N | N |
| 14 **LaTourette** | Y | Y | Y | N | Y | N |
| 15 **Pryce** | Y | Y | Y | N | Y | N |
| 16 **Regula** | Y | Y | Y | N | Y | N |
| 17 Ryan | N | N | N | Y | N | N |
| 18 **Ney** | Y | Y | Y | N | Y | N |
| **OKLAHOMA** | | | | | | |
| 1 **Sullivan** | Y | Y | Y | N | Y | ? |
| 2 Boren | N | N | N | Y | N | N |
| 3 **Lucas** | Y | Y | Y | N | Y | N |
| 4 **Cole** | Y | ? | Y | N | Y | N |
| 5 **Istook** | Y | Y | Y | N | Y | N |
| **OREGON** | | | | | | |
| 1 Wu | N | N | N | Y | N | N |
| 2 **Walden** | Y | Y | Y | N | Y | – |
| 3 Blumenauer | N | N | N | Y | N | ? |
| 4 DeFazio | N | N | N | Y | N | ? |
| 5 Hooley | N | N | N | Y | N | N |
| **PENNSYLVANIA** | | | | | | |
| 1 Brady | N | N | N | Y | N | ? |
| 2 Fattah | N | N | N | Y | N | ? |
| 3 **English** | Y | Y | Y | N | Y | N |
| 4 **Hart** | Y | Y | Y | N | Y | N |
| 5 **Peterson** | Y | Y | Y | ? | ? | N |
| 6 **Gerlach** | Y | Y | Y | N | Y | N |
| 7 **Weldon** | Y | Y | Y | N | Y | N |
| 8 **Fitzpatrick** | Y | Y | Y | N | Y | N |
| 9 **Shuster** | Y | Y | Y | N | Y | N |
| 10 **Sherwood** | Y | Y | Y | N | Y | N |
| 11 Kanjorski | N | N | N | Y | N | N |
| 12 Murtha | N | N | N | Y | N | N |
| 13 Schwartz | N | N | N | Y | N | N |
| 14 Doyle | N | N | N | ? | ? | ? |
| 15 **Dent** | Y | Y | Y | N | Y | N |
| 16 **Pitts** | Y | Y | Y | N | Y | N |
| 17 Holden | N | N | N | Y | N | ? |
| 18 **Murphy** | Y | Y | Y | N | Y | N |
| 19 **Platts** | Y | Y | Y | N | Y | N |
| **RHODE ISLAND** | | | | | | |
| 1 Kennedy | N | N | N | Y | N | N |
| 2 Langevin | N | N | N | Y | N | ? |
| **SOUTH CAROLINA** | | | | | | |
| 1 **Brown** | Y | Y | Y | N | Y | N |
| 2 **Wilson** | Y | Y | Y | N | Y | ? |
| 3 **Barrett** | Y | Y | Y | N | Y | N |
| 4 **Inglis** | Y | Y | Y | N | Y | N |
| 5 Spratt | N | N | N | Y | N | N |
| 6 Clyburn | N | N | N | Y | N | Y |
| **SOUTH DAKOTA** | | | | | | |
| AL Herseth | N | N | N | Y | N | N |
| **TENNESSEE** | | | | | | |
| 1 **Jenkins** | Y | Y | Y | N | Y | ? |
| 2 **Duncan** | Y | Y | Y | N | Y | N |
| 3 **Wamp** | Y | Y | Y | N | Y | N |
| 4 Davis | N | N | N | Y | N | ? |
| 5 Cooper | N | N | N | Y | N | ? |
| 6 Gordon | N | N | N | Y | N | N |
| 7 **Blackburn** | Y | Y | Y | N | Y | N |
| 8 Tanner | N | N | N | Y | N | ? |
| 9 Ford | N | N | N | Y | N | ? |
| **TEXAS** | | | | | | |
| 1 **Gohmert** | Y | Y | Y | N | Y | N |
| 2 **Poe** | Y | Y | Y | N | Y | N |
| 3 **Johnson, S.** | Y | Y | Y | N | Y | N |
| 4 **Hall** | Y | Y | Y | N | Y | N |
| 5 **Hensarling** | Y | Y | Y | N | Y | N |
| 6 **Barton** | Y | Y | Y | N | Y | N |
| 7 **Culberson** | Y | Y | Y | N | Y | N |
| 8 **Brady** | Y | Y | Y | N | Y | N |
| 9 Green, A. | N | N | N | Y | N | N |
| 10 **McCaul** | Y | Y | Y | N | Y | N |
| 11 **Conaway** | Y | Y | Y | N | Y | N |
| 12 **Granger** | Y | Y | Y | N | Y | ? |
| 13 **Thornberry** | Y | Y | Y | N | Y | N |
| 14 **Paul** | Y | Y | Y | N | Y | ? |
| 15 Hinojosa | N | N | N | Y | N | ? |
| 16 Reyes | N | N | N | Y | N | N |
| 17 Edwards | N | N | N | Y | N | ? |
| 18 Jackson-Lee | N | N | N | Y | N | Y |
| 19 **Neugebauer** | Y | Y | Y | N | Y | N |
| 20 Gonzalez | N | N | N | Y | N | ? |
| 21 **Smith** | Y | Y | Y | N | Y | N |
| 22 **DeLay** | Y | Y | Y | N | Y | N |
| 23 **Bonilla** | Y | Y | Y | N | Y | N |
| 24 **Marchant** | Y | Y | Y | N | Y | N |
| 25 Doggett | N | N | N | Y | N | ? |
| 26 **Burgess** | Y | Y | Y | N | Y | N |
| 27 Ortiz | N | N | N | Y | N | ? |
| 28 Cuellar | N | N | N | Y | N | N |
| 29 Green, G. | N | N | N | Y | N | N |
| 30 Johnson, E. | N | N | N | Y | N | Y |
| 31 **Carter** | Y | Y | Y | N | Y | N |
| 32 **Sessions** | Y | Y | Y | N | Y | N |
| **UTAH** | | | | | | |
| 1 **Bishop** | Y | Y | Y | N | Y | N |
| 2 Matheson | N | N | N | Y | N | ? |
| 3 **Cannon**[1] | ? | I | I | I | I | I |
| **VERMONT** | | | | | | |
| AL *Sanders* | N | N | N | Y | N | N |
| **VIRGINIA** | | | | | | |
| 1 **Davis, J.** | Y | Y | Y | N | Y | N |
| 2 **Drake** | Y | Y | Y | N | Y | N |
| 3 Scott | N | N | N | Y | N | N |
| 4 **Forbes** | Y | Y | Y | N | Y | ? |
| 5 **Goode** | Y | Y | Y | N | Y | ? |
| 6 **Goodlatte** | Y | Y | Y | N | Y | N |
| 7 **Cantor** | Y | Y | Y | N | Y | N |
| 8 Moran | N | N | N | Y | N | N |
| 9 Boucher | N | N | N | Y | N | ? |
| 10 **Wolf** | Y | Y | Y | N | Y | N |
| 11 **Davis, T.** | Y | Y | Y | N | Y | N |
| **WASHINGTON** | | | | | | |
| 1 Inslee | N | N | N | Y | N | ? |
| 2 Larsen | N | ? | ? | ? | ? | ? |
| 3 Baird | N | N | N | Y | N | ? |
| 4 **Hastings** | Y | Y | Y | N | ? | N |
| 5 **McMorris** | Y | Y | Y | N | Y | N |
| 6 Dicks | N | N | N | Y | N | N |
| 7 McDermott | N | N | N | Y | N | ? |
| 8 **Reichert** | Y | Y | Y | N | Y | N |
| 9 Smith | N | N | N | Y | N | ? |
| **WEST VIRGINIA** | | | | | | |
| 1 Mollohan | N | N | N | Y | N | N |
| 2 **Capito** | Y | Y | Y | N | Y | N |
| 3 Rahall | N | N | N | Y | N | N |
| **WISCONSIN** | | | | | | |
| 1 **Ryan** | Y | Y | Y | N | Y | N |
| 2 Baldwin | N | N | N | Y | N | ? |
| 3 Kind | N | N | N | Y | N | ? |
| 4 Moore | N | N | N | Y | N | N |
| 5 **Sensenbrenner** | Y | Y | Y | N | Y | N |
| 6 **Petri** | Y | Y | Y | N | Y | N |
| 7 Obey | N | N | N | Y | N | N |
| 8 **Green** | Y | Y | Y | N | Y | N |
| **WYOMING** | | | | | | |
| AL **Cubin** | Y | Y | Y | N | Y | N |

# IN THE HOUSE | By Vote Number

**8.** **H Con Res 16. Ukraine Elections/Adoption.** Hyde, R-Ill., motion to suspend the rules and adopt the concurrent resolution that would congratulate the people and government of Ukraine for ensuring a free and fair run-off presidential election Dec. 26, 2004. It also would express continuing support for the efforts of Ukraine to establish a full democracy, rule of law and respect for human rights. Motion agreed to 392-1: R 210-1; D 181-0 (ND 131-0, SD 50-0); I 1-0. A two-thirds majority of those present and voting (262 in this case) is required for adoption under suspension of the rules. Jan. 25, 2005.

**9.** **H Res 39. Liberation of Auschwitz 60th Anniversary/Adoption.** Hyde, R-Ill., motion to suspend the rules and adopt the resolution that would commend foreign countries, the United Nations and international organizations for marking the 60th anniversary of the liberation of Auschwitz on Jan. 27, 1945. Motion agreed to 393-0: R 211-0; D 181-0 (ND 132-0, SD 49-0); I 1-0. A two-thirds majority of those present and voting (262 in this case) is required for adoption under suspension of the rules. Jan. 25, 2005.

**10.** **HR 54. Congressional Gold Medals/Limit Increase.** Crowley, D-N.Y., amendment that would increase the limit on the number of congressional gold medals permitted under the bill from two per year to six per Congress, with no limit on how many of the six medals could be awarded in either year of a Congress. Rejected 189-212: R 1-209; D 187-3 (ND 139-2, SD 48-1); I 1-0. Jan. 26, 2005.

**11.** **HR 54. Congressional Gold Medals/Award Requirements.** Crowley, D-N.Y., amendment that would stipulate that no more than half of the congressional gold medals permitted under the bill could be awarded based on legislation sponsored by members of the same political party. Rejected 182-211: R 0-209; D 181-2 (ND 133-1, SD 48-1); I 1-0. Jan. 26, 2005.

**12.** **HR 54. Congressional Gold Medals/Recommit.** Crowley, D-N.Y., motion to recommit the bill to the Financial Services Committee with instructions to insert language preventing the Treasury secretary from striking a congressional gold medal for presentation posthumously in behalf of any individual except during the 20-year period beginning five years after the individual's death, unless the authorization for the medal was enacted before the individual's death. Motion rejected 187-217: R 0-215; D 186-2 (ND 137-2, SD 49-0); I 1-0. Jan. 26, 2005.

**13.** **HR 54. Congressional Gold Medals/Passage.** Passage of the bill that would limit the number of congressional gold medals that may be struck by the Treasury Department in any calendar year to two, effective as of the date of enactment. The medals could be awarded only to individuals, and could not be presented posthumously unless the recipient had been deceased for five years and then only for 20 years after that milestone. Passed 231-173: R 211-3; D 20-169 (ND 14-126, SD 6-43); I 0-1. Jan. 26, 2005.

| | 8 | 9 | 10 | 11 | 12 | 13 |
|---|---|---|---|---|---|---|
| **ALABAMA** | | | | | | |
| 1 Bonner | Y | Y | N | N | N | Y |
| 2 Everett | Y | Y | N | N | N | Y |
| 3 Rogers | Y | Y | N | N | N | Y |
| 4 Aderholt | Y | Y | N | N | N | Y |
| 5 Cramer | Y | Y | Y | Y | Y | N |
| 6 Bachus | Y | Y | N | N | N | Y |
| 7 Davis | Y | Y | Y | Y | Y | N |
| **ALASKA** | | | | | | |
| AL Young | Y | Y | N | N | N | Y |
| **ARIZONA** | | | | | | |
| 1 Renzi | Y | Y | N | N | N | Y |
| 2 Franks | Y | Y | N | N | N | Y |
| 3 Shadegg | Y | Y | N | N | N | Y |
| 4 Pastor | Y | Y | Y | Y | Y | N |
| 5 Hayworth | Y | Y | N | N | N | Y |
| 6 Flake | Y | Y | N | N | N | Y |
| 7 Grijalva | Y | Y | Y | ? | Y | N |
| 8 Kolbe | Y | Y | N | N | N | Y |
| **ARKANSAS** | | | | | | |
| 1 Berry | Y | Y | Y | Y | Y | N |
| 2 Snyder | Y | Y | Y | Y | Y | N |
| 3 Boozman | Y | Y | N | N | N | Y |
| 4 Ross | Y | Y | Y | Y | Y | N |
| **CALIFORNIA** | | | | | | |
| 1 Thompson | Y | Y | Y | Y | Y | N |
| 2 Herger | Y | Y | N | N | N | Y |
| 3 Lungren | Y | Y | N | N | N | Y |
| 4 Doolittle | Y | Y | N | N | N | Y |
| 5 Vacant | | | | | | |
| 6 Woolsey | Y | Y | Y | Y | Y | N |
| 7 Miller, George | Y | Y | Y | Y | Y | N |
| 8 Pelosi | Y | Y | Y | Y | Y | N |
| 9 Lee | + | + | Y | Y | Y | N |
| 10 Tauscher | Y | Y | Y | Y | Y | N |
| 11 Pombo | ? | ? | N | N | N | Y |
| 12 Lantos | + | + | ? | ? | ? | ? |
| 13 Stark | ? | ? | Y | Y | Y | N |
| 14 Eshoo | Y | Y | Y | Y | Y | N |
| 15 Honda | Y | Y | Y | Y | Y | N |
| 16 Lofgren | Y | Y | Y | Y | Y | N |
| 17 Farr | Y | Y | Y | Y | Y | N |
| 18 Cardoza | Y | Y | Y | Y | Y | N |
| 19 Radanovich | Y | Y | N | N | N | Y |
| 20 Costa | ? | ? | ? | ? | ? | ? |
| 21 Nunes | Y | Y | N | N | N | Y |
| 22 Thomas | Y | Y | N | N | N | Y |
| 23 Capps | Y | Y | Y | Y | Y | N |
| 24 Gallegly | ? | ? | ? | ? | ? | ? |
| 25 McKeon | Y | Y | N | N | N | Y |
| 26 Dreier | Y | Y | N | N | N | Y |
| 27 Sherman | Y | Y | Y | Y | Y | N |
| 28 Berman | Y | Y | Y | Y | Y | N |
| 29 Schiff | Y | Y | Y | + | + | N |
| 30 Waxman | Y | Y | Y | Y | Y | N |
| 31 Becerra | Y | Y | Y | Y | Y | N |
| 32 Solis | Y | Y | Y | Y | Y | N |
| 33 Watson | ? | ? | Y | Y | Y | N |
| 34 Roybal-Allard | ? | ? | ? | ? | ? | ? |
| 35 Waters | Y | Y | Y | ? | Y | N |
| 36 Harman | Y | Y | Y | ? | Y | N |
| 37 Millender-McD. | Y | Y | Y | Y | Y | N |
| 38 Napolitano | Y | Y | Y | Y | Y | N |
| 39 Sánchez, Linda | Y | Y | Y | Y | Y | N |
| 40 Royce | ? | ? | N | N | N | Y |
| 41 Lewis | Y | Y | N | N | N | Y |
| 42 Miller, Gary | Y | Y | N | ? | N | Y |
| 43 Baca | Y | Y | Y | Y | Y | N |
| 44 Calvert | Y | Y | N | N | N | Y |
| 45 Bono | ? | ? | ? | ? | ? | ? |
| 46 Rohrabacher | ? | ? | ? | ? | ? | ? |
| 47 Sanchez, Loretta | Y | Y | Y | Y | Y | N |
| 48 Cox | Y | Y | ? | N | N | Y |
| 49 Issa | Y | Y | N | N | N | Y |

| | 8 | 9 | 10 | 11 | 12 | 13 |
|---|---|---|---|---|---|---|
| 50 Cunningham | Y | Y | N | N | N | Y |
| 51 Filner | Y | Y | Y | Y | Y | N |
| 52 Hunter | ? | Y | N | N | N | Y |
| 53 Davis | Y | Y | Y | Y | Y | N |
| **COLORADO** | | | | | | |
| 1 DeGette | Y | Y | Y | Y | Y | N |
| 2 Udall | Y | Y | Y | Y | Y | N |
| 3 Salazar | Y | Y | Y | Y | Y | N |
| 4 Musgrave | Y | Y | N | N | N | Y |
| 5 Hefley | Y | Y | N | N | N | Y |
| 6 Tancredo | Y | Y | N | N | N | Y |
| 7 Beauprez | Y | Y | N | N | N | Y |
| **CONNECTICUT** | | | | | | |
| 1 Larson | Y | Y | Y | Y | Y | N |
| 2 Simmons | Y | Y | N | N | N | Y |
| 3 DeLauro | Y | Y | Y | Y | Y | N |
| 4 Shays | + | + | – | – | – | + |
| 5 Johnson | Y | Y | N | N | N | Y |
| **DELAWARE** | | | | | | |
| AL Castle | Y | Y | N | N | N | Y |
| **FLORIDA** | | | | | | |
| 1 Miller | Y | Y | N | N | N | Y |
| 2 Boyd | Y | Y | Y | Y | Y | Y |
| 3 Brown | ? | ? | Y | Y | Y | N |
| 4 Crenshaw | Y | Y | N | N | N | Y |
| 5 Brown-Waite | Y | Y | N | N | N | Y |
| 6 Stearns | Y | Y | N | N | N | Y |
| 7 Mica | Y | Y | N | N | N | Y |
| 8 Keller | Y | Y | N | N | N | Y |
| 9 Bilirakis | + | ? | ? | ? | ? | ? |
| 10 Young | Y | Y | N | N | N | Y |
| 11 Davis | Y | Y | ? | ? | ? | Y |
| 12 Putnam | Y | Y | N | N | N | Y |
| 13 Harris | Y | Y | N | N | N | Y |
| 14 Mack | Y | Y | N | N | N | Y |
| 15 Weldon | Y | Y | N | N | N | Y |
| 16 Foley | ? | ? | ? | ? | ? | ? |
| 17 Meek | Y | Y | Y | Y | Y | N |
| 18 Ros-Lehtinen | Y | Y | N | ? | N | Y |
| 19 Wexler | Y | Y | Y | Y | Y | N |
| 20 Wasserman-Schultz | Y | Y | Y | Y | Y | N |
| 21 Diaz-Balart, L. | Y | Y | N | N | N | Y |
| 22 Shaw | Y | Y | N | N | N | Y |
| 23 Hastings | Y | Y | Y | Y | Y | N |
| 24 Feeney | Y | Y | ? | N | N | Y |
| 25 Diaz-Balart, M. | Y | Y | N | N | N | Y |
| **GEORGIA** | | | | | | |
| 1 Kingston | Y | Y | N | N | N | Y |
| 2 Bishop | Y | Y | Y | Y | Y | N |
| 3 Marshall | Y | Y | N | N | Y | Y |
| 4 McKinney | Y | Y | Y | Y | Y | N |
| 5 Lewis | Y | Y | Y | Y | Y | N |
| 6 Price | Y | Y | N | N | N | Y |
| 7 Linder | Y | Y | N | N | N | Y |
| 8 Westmoreland | Y | Y | N | N | N | Y |
| 9 Norwood | Y | Y | N | N | N | Y |
| 10 Deal | Y | Y | N | N | N | Y |
| 11 Gingrey | Y | Y | N | N | N | Y |
| 12 Barrow | Y | Y | Y | Y | Y | N |
| 13 Scott | Y | Y | Y | Y | Y | N |
| **HAWAII** | | | | | | |
| 1 Abercrombie | Y | Y | Y | Y | Y | N |
| 2 Case | Y | Y | Y | Y | Y | Y |
| **IDAHO** | | | | | | |
| 1 Otter | Y | Y | N | N | N | Y |
| 2 Simpson | Y | Y | ? | ? | ? | ? |
| **ILLINOIS** | | | | | | |
| 1 Rush | ? | ? | Y | Y | Y | N |
| 2 Jackson | Y | Y | Y | Y | Y | N |
| 3 Lipinski | Y | Y | Y | Y | Y | N |
| 4 Gutierrez | Y | Y | Y | Y | Y | N |
| 5 Emanuel | Y | Y | Y | Y | Y | N |
| 6 Hyde | Y | Y | N | N | N | Y |
| 7 Davis | Y | Y | Y | Y | Y | N |
| 8 Bean | Y | Y | Y | Y | Y | N |
| 9 Schakowsky | Y | Y | Y | Y | Y | N |
| 10 Kirk | Y | Y | N | N | N | Y |
| 11 Weller | Y | Y | N | N | N | Y |
| 12 Costello | Y | Y | Y | Y | Y | N |

**KEY**    Republicans    Democrats    *Independents*

| | | | |
|---|---|---|---|
| **Y** Voted for (yea) | **X** Paired against | **C** Voted "present" to avoid possible conflict of interest |
| **#** Paired for | **–** Announced against | |
| **+** Announced for | **P** Voted "present" | **?** Did not vote or otherwise make a position known |
| **N** Voted against (nay) | | |

ND Northern Democrats, SD Southern Democrats
Southern states: Ala., Ark., Fla., Ga., Ky., La., Miss., N.C., Okla., S.C., Tenn., Texas, Va.

| | 8 | 9 | 10 | 11 | 12 | 13 |
|---|---|---|---|---|---|---|
| 13 **Biggert** | Y | Y | N | N | N | Y |
| 14 **Hastert** | | | | | | |
| 15 **Johnson** | Y | Y | N | N | N | Y |
| 16 **Manzullo** | ? | ? | ? | ? | ? | ? |
| 17 Evans | Y | Y | Y | Y | Y | N |
| 18 **LaHood** | Y | Y | N | N | N | Y |
| 19 **Shimkus** | Y | Y | N | N | N | Y |
| **INDIANA** | | | | | | |
| 1 Visclosky | Y | Y | Y | Y | Y | N |
| 2 **Chocola** | Y | Y | N | N | N | Y |
| 3 **Souder** | Y | Y | N | N | N | Y |
| 4 **Buyer** | Y | Y | N | N | N | Y |
| 5 **Burton** | ? | + | - | - | - | + |
| 6 **Pence** | Y | Y | N | N | N | Y |
| 7 Carson | Y | Y | Y | Y | Y | N |
| 8 **Hostettler** | Y | Y | N | N | N | Y |
| 9 **Sodrel** | Y | Y | N | N | N | Y |
| **IOWA** | | | | | | |
| 1 **Nussle** | Y | Y | N | N | N | Y |
| 2 **Leach** | Y | Y | N | N | N | Y |
| 3 Boswell | Y | Y | Y | Y | Y | N |
| 4 **Latham** | Y | Y | N | N | N | Y |
| 5 **King** | Y | Y | N | N | N | Y |
| **KANSAS** | | | | | | |
| 1 **Moran** | Y | Y | N | N | N | Y |
| 2 **Ryun** | Y | Y | N | N | N | Y |
| 3 Moore | Y | Y | Y | ? | Y | N |
| 4 **Tiahrt** | Y | Y | N | N | N | Y |
| **KENTUCKY** | | | | | | |
| 1 **Whitfield** | Y | Y | N | N | N | Y |
| 2 **Lewis** | Y | Y | N | N | N | Y |
| 3 **Northup** | Y | Y | N | N | N | Y |
| 4 **Davis** | Y | Y | N | N | N | Y |
| 5 **Rogers** | Y | Y | N | N | N | Y |
| 6 Chandler | Y | Y | Y | Y | Y | N |
| **LOUISIANA** | | | | | | |
| 1 **Jindal** | Y | Y | N | N | N | Y |
| 2 Jefferson | Y | Y | Y | Y | Y | N |
| 3 Melancon | Y | Y | Y | Y | Y | N |
| 4 **McCrery** | Y | Y | N | N | N | Y |
| 5 **Alexander** | Y | Y | N | N | N | Y |
| 6 **Baker** | Y | Y | N | N | N | Y |
| 7 **Boustany** | Y | Y | ? | ? | N | Y |
| **MAINE** | | | | | | |
| 1 Allen | Y | Y | Y | Y | Y | N |
| 2 Michaud | Y | Y | Y | Y | Y | N |
| **MARYLAND** | | | | | | |
| 1 **Gilchrest** | Y | Y | N | N | N | Y |
| 2 Ruppersberger | Y | Y | Y | Y | Y | N |
| 3 Cardin | Y | Y | Y | Y | Y | N |
| 4 Wynn | Y | Y | Y | Y | Y | N |
| 5 Hoyer | Y | Y | Y | Y | Y | N |
| 6 **Bartlett** | Y | Y | N | N | N | Y |
| 7 Cummings | Y | Y | Y | Y | N | N |
| 8 Van Hollen | Y | Y | Y | Y | Y | N |
| **MASSACHUSETTS** | | | | | | |
| 1 Olver | Y | Y | Y | Y | Y | N |
| 2 Neal | Y | Y | Y | Y | Y | N |
| 3 McGovern | Y | Y | Y | Y | Y | N |
| 4 Frank | ? | ? | ? | ? | ? | ? |
| 5 Meehan | Y | Y | Y | Y | Y | N |
| 6 Tierney | Y | Y | Y | Y | Y | N |
| 7 Markey | Y | Y | Y | Y | Y | N |
| 8 Capuano | Y | Y | Y | Y | Y | N |
| 9 Lynch | Y | Y | Y | Y | Y | N |
| 10 Delahunt | ? | ? | ? | ? | ? | ? |
| **MICHIGAN** | | | | | | |
| 1 Stupak | Y | Y | Y | Y | Y | Y |
| 2 **Hoekstra** | Y | Y | N | N | N | Y |
| 3 **Ehlers** | ? | ? | ? | ? | ? | ? |
| 4 **Camp** | Y | Y | N | N | N | Y |
| 5 Kildee | Y | Y | Y | Y | Y | N |
| 6 **Upton** | Y | Y | N | N | N | Y |
| 7 **Schwarz** | Y | Y | N | N | N | Y |
| 8 **Rogers** | Y | Y | N | N | N | Y |
| 9 **Knollenberg** | Y | Y | N | N | N | Y |
| 10 **Miller** | Y | Y | N | N | N | Y |
| 11 **McCotter** | ? | ? | ? | ? | ? | ? |
| 12 Levin | Y | Y | Y | Y | Y | N |
| 13 Kilpatrick | Y | Y | Y | Y | Y | N |
| 14 Conyers | Y | Y | Y | Y | Y | N |
| 15 Dingell | Y | Y | Y | Y | Y | N |

| | 8 | 9 | 10 | 11 | 12 | 13 |
|---|---|---|---|---|---|---|
| **MINNESOTA** | | | | | | |
| 1 **Gutknecht** | Y | Y | N | N | N | Y |
| 2 **Kline** | Y | Y | N | N | N | Y |
| 3 **Ramstad** | Y | Y | N | N | N | Y |
| 4 McCollum | ? | ? | Y | Y | Y | N |
| 5 Sabo | Y | Y | Y | Y | Y | N |
| 6 **Kennedy** | Y | Y | N | N | N | Y |
| 7 Peterson | Y | Y | Y | Y | Y | Y |
| 8 Oberstar | Y | Y | Y | Y | Y | N |
| **MISSISSIPPI** | | | | | | |
| 1 **Wicker** | Y | Y | N | N | N | Y |
| 2 Thompson | Y | Y | Y | Y | Y | N |
| 3 **Pickering** | Y | Y | N | N | N | Y |
| 4 Taylor | Y | Y | Y | Y | Y | Y |
| **MISSOURI** | | | | | | |
| 1 Clay | Y | Y | Y | Y | Y | N |
| 2 **Akin** | Y | Y | N | N | N | Y |
| 3 Carnahan | Y | Y | Y | Y | Y | N |
| 4 Skelton | Y | Y | Y | Y | Y | N |
| 5 Cleaver | Y | Y | Y | Y | Y | N |
| 6 **Graves** | ? | ? | ? | ? | ? | ? |
| 7 **Blunt** | Y | Y | N | N | N | Y |
| 8 **Emerson** | Y | Y | N | N | N | Y |
| 9 **Hulshof** | Y | Y | N | N | N | N |
| **MONTANA** | | | | | | |
| AL **Rehberg** | Y | Y | N | N | N | Y |
| **NEBRASKA** | | | | | | |
| 1 **Fortenberry** | Y | Y | N | N | N | Y |
| 2 **Terry** | Y | Y | N | N | N | Y |
| 3 **Osborne** | Y | Y | N | N | N | Y |
| **NEVADA** | | | | | | |
| 1 Berkley | + | + | + | + | + | + |
| 2 **Gibbons** | Y | Y | - | - | N | N |
| 3 **Porter** | Y | Y | N | N | N | Y |
| **NEW HAMPSHIRE** | | | | | | |
| 1 **Bradley** | Y | Y | N | N | N | Y |
| 2 **Bass** | Y | Y | N | N | N | Y |
| **NEW JERSEY** | | | | | | |
| 1 Andrews | Y | Y | Y | Y | Y | N |
| 2 **LoBiondo** | Y | Y | N | N | N | Y |
| 3 **Saxton** | Y | Y | N | N | N | Y |
| 4 **Smith** | Y | Y | N | N | N | Y |
| 5 **Garrett** | Y | Y | N | N | N | Y |
| 6 Pallone | Y | Y | Y | Y | Y | N |
| 7 **Ferguson** | Y | Y | N | N | N | Y |
| 8 Pascrell | Y | Y | Y | Y | Y | N |
| 9 Rothman | Y | Y | Y | Y | Y | N |
| 10 Payne | Y | Y | Y | Y | Y | N |
| 11 **Frelinghuysen** | Y | Y | N | N | N | Y |
| 12 Holt | Y | Y | N | Y | Y | Y |
| 13 Menendez | Y | Y | Y | Y | Y | N |
| **NEW MEXICO** | | | | | | |
| 1 **Wilson** | Y | Y | N | N | N | Y |
| 2 **Pearce** | Y | Y | N | N | N | Y |
| 3 Udall | Y | Y | Y | Y | Y | N |
| **NEW YORK** | | | | | | |
| 1 Bishop | Y | Y | Y | Y | Y | N |
| 2 Israel | ? | ? | ? | ? | ? | ? |
| 3 **King** | Y | Y | N | N | N | N |
| 4 McCarthy | Y | Y | Y | Y | Y | N |
| 5 Ackerman | Y | Y | Y | Y | Y | N |
| 6 Meeks | Y | Y | Y | Y | Y | N |
| 7 Crowley | Y | Y | Y | Y | Y | N |
| 8 Nadler | Y | Y | Y | Y | Y | N |
| 9 Weiner | Y | Y | Y | Y | Y | N |
| 10 Towns | ? | ? | Y | Y | Y | N |
| 11 Owens | Y | Y | Y | Y | Y | N |
| 12 Velázquez | Y | Y | Y | Y | Y | N |
| 13 **Fossella** | Y | Y | ? | N | N | Y |
| 14 Maloney | Y | Y | Y | Y | Y | N |
| 15 Rangel | Y | Y | Y | ? | Y | N |
| 16 Serrano | Y | Y | Y | Y | Y | N |
| 17 Engel | Y | Y | Y | Y | Y | N |
| 18 Lowey | Y | Y | Y | Y | Y | N |
| 19 **Kelly** | Y | Y | N | N | N | Y |
| 20 **Sweeney** | Y | Y | N | N | N | Y |
| 21 McNulty | Y | Y | Y | N | Y | N |
| 22 Hinchey | Y | Y | Y | Y | Y | N |
| 23 **McHugh** | Y | Y | N | N | N | Y |
| 24 **Boehlert** | Y | Y | N | N | N | Y |
| 25 **Walsh** | Y | Y | N | N | N | Y |
| 26 **Reynolds** | Y | Y | N | N | N | Y |
| 27 Higgins | Y | Y | Y | Y | Y | N |
| 28 Slaughter | Y | Y | Y | Y | Y | N |
| 29 **Kuhl** | Y | Y | N | N | N | Y |

| | 8 | 9 | 10 | 11 | 12 | 13 |
|---|---|---|---|---|---|---|
| **NORTH CAROLINA** | | | | | | |
| 1 Butterfield | Y | Y | Y | Y | Y | N |
| 2 Etheridge | Y | Y | Y | Y | Y | N |
| 3 **Jones** | Y | Y | N | N | N | Y |
| 4 Price | Y | Y | Y | Y | Y | N |
| 5 **Foxx** | Y | Y | N | N | N | Y |
| 6 **Coble** | Y | Y | N | N | N | Y |
| 7 McIntyre | Y | Y | Y | Y | Y | N |
| 8 **Hayes** | Y | Y | N | ? | N | Y |
| 9 **Myrick** | Y | Y | N | N | N | Y |
| 10 **McHenry** | Y | Y | N | N | N | Y |
| 11 **Taylor** | Y | Y | N | N | N | Y |
| 12 Watt | Y | ? | Y | Y | Y | N |
| 13 Miller | Y | Y | Y | Y | Y | N |
| **NORTH DAKOTA** | | | | | | |
| AL Pomeroy | Y | Y | Y | Y | N | N |
| **OHIO** | | | | | | |
| 1 **Chabot** | Y | Y | N | N | N | Y |
| 2 **Portman** | Y | Y | - | N | N | Y |
| 3 **Turner** | Y | Y | N | N | N | Y |
| 4 **Oxley** | Y | Y | N | N | N | Y |
| 5 **Gillmor** | Y | ? | N | N | N | Y |
| 6 Strickland | Y | Y | Y | Y | Y | N |
| 7 **Hobson** | Y | Y | N | N | N | Y |
| 8 **Boehner** | ? | ? | N | N | N | Y |
| 9 Kaptur | Y | Y | Y | Y | ? | Y |
| 10 Kucinich | Y | Y | Y | Y | Y | N |
| 11 Jones | Y | Y | Y | Y | Y | N |
| 12 **Tiberi** | Y | Y | N | N | N | Y |
| 13 Brown | Y | Y | Y | Y | Y | N |
| 14 **LaTourette** | Y | Y | N | N | N | Y |
| 15 **Pryce** | Y | Y | N | N | N | Y |
| 16 **Regula** | Y | Y | N | N | N | Y |
| 17 Ryan | ? | Y | Y | Y | Y | N |
| 18 **Ney** | Y | Y | N | N | N | Y |
| **OKLAHOMA** | | | | | | |
| 1 **Sullivan** | ? | ? | ? | ? | ? | ? |
| 2 Boren | Y | Y | Y | Y | Y | N |
| 3 **Lucas** | Y | Y | N | N | N | Y |
| 4 **Cole** | Y | Y | N | N | N | Y |
| 5 **Istook** | Y | Y | N | N | N | Y |
| **OREGON** | | | | | | |
| 1 Wu | Y | Y | Y | Y | Y | N |
| 2 **Walden** | Y | Y | N | N | N | Y |
| 3 Blumenauer | Y | Y | Y | Y | Y | N |
| 4 DeFazio | ? | ? | ? | ? | ? | ? |
| 5 Hooley | Y | Y | Y | Y | Y | N |
| **PENNSYLVANIA** | | | | | | |
| 1 Brady | Y | Y | Y | Y | Y | Y |
| 2 Fattah | ? | ? | Y | Y | Y | Y |
| 3 **English** | Y | Y | N | N | N | Y |
| 4 **Hart** | Y | Y | N | N | N | Y |
| 5 **Peterson** | Y | Y | N | N | N | Y |
| 6 **Gerlach** | Y | Y | N | N | N | Y |
| 7 **Weldon** | Y | Y | N | N | N | Y |
| 8 **Fitzpatrick** | Y | Y | N | N | N | Y |
| 9 **Shuster** | Y | Y | N | N | N | Y |
| 10 **Sherwood** | Y | Y | N | N | N | Y |
| 11 Kanjorski | Y | Y | Y | Y | Y | Y |
| 12 Murtha | ? | ? | Y | Y | Y | Y |
| 13 Schwartz | Y | Y | Y | Y | Y | Y |
| 14 Doyle | Y | Y | Y | Y | Y | N |
| 15 **Dent** | Y | Y | N | N | N | Y |
| 16 **Pitts** | Y | Y | N | N | N | Y |
| 17 Holden | Y | Y | Y | Y | Y | Y |
| 18 **Murphy** | Y | Y | N | N | N | Y |
| 19 **Platts** | ? | ? | N | N | N | Y |
| **RHODE ISLAND** | | | | | | |
| 1 Kennedy | Y | Y | Y | Y | Y | N |
| 2 Langevin | Y | Y | Y | Y | Y | N |
| **SOUTH CAROLINA** | | | | | | |
| 1 **Brown** | Y | Y | N | N | N | Y |
| 2 **Wilson** | Y | Y | N | N | N | Y |
| 3 **Barrett** | Y | Y | N | N | N | Y |
| 4 **Inglis** | Y | Y | N | N | N | Y |
| 5 Spratt | Y | Y | Y | Y | Y | N |
| 6 Clyburn | Y | Y | Y | Y | Y | N |
| **SOUTH DAKOTA** | | | | | | |
| AL Herseth | Y | Y | Y | Y | Y | N |
| **TENNESSEE** | | | | | | |
| 1 **Jenkins** | ? | ? | ? | ? | ? | ? |
| 2 **Duncan** | Y | Y | N | N | N | Y |

| | 8 | 9 | 10 | 11 | 12 | 13 |
|---|---|---|---|---|---|---|
| 3 **Wamp** | ? | ? | N | N | N | Y |
| 4 Davis | Y | Y | Y | Y | Y | Y |
| 5 Cooper | Y | Y | Y | Y | Y | N |
| 6 Gordon | Y | Y | Y | Y | Y | N |
| 7 **Blackburn** | Y | Y | N | N | - | Y |
| 8 Tanner | Y | Y | Y | Y | Y | N |
| 9 Ford | Y | Y | Y | Y | Y | N |
| **TEXAS** | | | | | | |
| 1 **Gohmert** | Y | Y | N | ? | N | Y |
| 2 **Poe** | Y | Y | N | N | N | Y |
| 3 **Johnson, S.** | Y | Y | N | N | N | Y |
| 4 **Hall** | Y | Y | N | N | N | Y |
| 5 **Hensarling** | Y | Y | N | N | N | Y |
| 6 **Barton** | Y | Y | N | N | N | Y |
| 7 **Culberson** | Y | Y | N | N | N | Y |
| 8 **Brady** | Y | Y | N | N | N | Y |
| 9 Green, A. | Y | Y | Y | Y | Y | N |
| 10 **McCaul** | Y | Y | N | N | N | Y |
| 11 **Conaway** | Y | Y | N | N | N | Y |
| 12 **Granger** | ? | ? | ? | ? | ? | ? |
| 13 **Thornberry** | Y | Y | N | N | N | Y |
| 14 **Paul** | N | Y | N | N | N | Y |
| 15 Hinojosa | Y | Y | Y | Y | Y | N |
| 16 Reyes | Y | Y | Y | Y | Y | N |
| 17 Edwards | Y | Y | Y | Y | Y | Y |
| 18 Jackson-Lee | Y | Y | Y | Y | Y | N |
| 19 **Neugebauer** | Y | Y | N | N | N | Y |
| 20 Gonzalez | Y | Y | Y | Y | Y | N |
| 21 **Smith** | Y | Y | N | N | N | Y |
| 22 **DeLay** | Y | Y | N | N | N | Y |
| 23 **Bonilla** | Y | Y | N | N | N | Y |
| 24 **Marchant** | Y | Y | N | N | N | Y |
| 25 Doggett | Y | Y | Y | Y | Y | N |
| 26 **Burgess** | Y | Y | N | N | N | Y |
| 27 Ortiz | Y | Y | Y | Y | Y | N |
| 28 Cuellar | Y | Y | Y | Y | Y | N |
| 29 Green, G. | Y | Y | Y | Y | Y | Y |
| 30 Johnson, E. | Y | Y | Y | Y | Y | N |
| 31 **Carter** | Y | Y | N | N | N | ? |
| 32 **Sessions** | Y | Y | N | N | N | Y |
| **UTAH** | | | | | | |
| 1 **Bishop** | Y | Y | N | N | N | Y |
| 2 Matheson | Y | Y | Y | Y | Y | N |
| 3 **Cannon** | Y | Y | N | N | N | Y |
| **VERMONT** | | | | | | |
| AL *Sanders* | Y | Y | Y | Y | Y | N |
| **VIRGINIA** | | | | | | |
| 1 **Davis, J.** | Y | Y | N | N | N | ? |
| 2 **Drake** | Y | Y | N | N | N | Y |
| 3 Scott | Y | Y | Y | Y | Y | N |
| 4 **Forbes** | Y | Y | N | N | N | Y |
| 5 **Goode** | Y | Y | N | N | N | Y |
| 6 **Goodlatte** | Y | Y | N | N | N | Y |
| 7 **Cantor** | Y | Y | N | N | N | Y |
| 8 Moran | Y | Y | ? | ? | ? | ? |
| 9 Boucher | Y | Y | Y | Y | Y | N |
| 10 **Wolf** | Y | Y | N | N | N | Y |
| 11 **Davis, T.** | Y | Y | N | N | N | Y |
| **WASHINGTON** | | | | | | |
| 1 Inslee | Y | Y | Y | Y | Y | N |
| 2 Larsen | Y | Y | Y | Y | Y | N |
| 3 Baird | Y | Y | ? | ? | ? | ? |
| 4 **Hastings** | Y | Y | N | N | N | Y |
| 5 **McMorris** | Y | Y | N | N | N | Y |
| 6 Dicks | Y | Y | Y | Y | Y | N |
| 7 McDermott | + | + | Y | Y | Y | N |
| 8 **Reichert** | Y | Y | N | N | N | Y |
| 9 Smith | Y | Y | Y | Y | Y | Y |
| **WEST VIRGINIA** | | | | | | |
| 1 Mollohan | Y | Y | Y | Y | Y | N |
| 2 **Capito** | Y | Y | N | N | N | Y |
| 3 Rahall | ? | ? | Y | Y | Y | N |
| **WISCONSIN** | | | | | | |
| 1 **Ryan** | Y | Y | N | N | N | Y |
| 2 Baldwin | Y | Y | Y | Y | Y | N |
| 3 Kind | Y | Y | Y | Y | Y | N |
| 4 Moore | Y | Y | Y | + | Y | N |
| 5 **Sensenbrenner** | Y | Y | N | N | N | Y |
| 6 **Petri** | Y | Y | N | N | N | Y |
| 7 Obey | Y | Y | Y | Y | Y | N |
| 8 **Green** | Y | Y | N | N | N | Y |
| **WYOMING** | | | | | | |
| AL **Cubin** | Y | Y | N | ? | N | Y |

# IN THE HOUSE | By Vote Number

**14.** **H Res 23. Catholic Schools Tribute/Adoption.** Boehner, R-Ohio, motion to suspend the rules and adopt the resolution that would express support for Catholic Schools Week and congratulate Catholic schools, students, parents and teachers for their roles in promoting a brighter and stronger future for the United States. Motion agreed to 408-0: R 218-0; D 189-0 (ND 143-0, SD 46-0); I 1-0. A two-thirds majority of those present and voting (272 in this case) is required for adoption under suspension of the rules. Feb. 1, 2005.

**15.** **HR 120. Dalip Singh Saund Post Office/Passage.** Issa, R-Calif., motion to suspend the rules and pass the bill that would designate a post office in Temecula, Calif., after former Rep. Dalip Singh Saund, D-Calif. (1957-63), the first Asian Indian-American elected to Congress. Motion agreed to 410-0: R 221-0; D 188-0 (ND 142-0, SD 46-0); I 1-0. A two-thirds majority of those present and voting (274 in this case) is required for passage under suspension of the rules. Feb. 1, 2005.

**16.** **H Con Res 36. Access for Military Recruiters/Adoption.** Adoption of the concurrent resolution that would express the sense of the Congress that the executive branch should aggressively challenge any decision that impedes the implementation of an existing ban on most federal funding for universities that do not grant equal access to military recruiters. Adopted 327-84: R 223-0; D 104-83 (ND 67-73, SD 37-10); I 0-1. Feb. 2, 2005.

**17.** **H Res 56. Palestinian Elections/Adoption.** Ros-Lehtinen, R-Fla., motion to suspend the rules and adopt the resolution that would commend the Palestinian people for conducting a free and fair presidential election on Jan. 9, 2005. It also would strongly condemn terrorism and urge the new president to take immediate steps to dismantle the Palestinian terrorist infrastructure. Motion agreed to 415-1: R 223-1; D 191-0 (ND 142-0, SD 49-0); I 1-0. A two-thirds majority of those present and voting (278 in this case) is required for adoption under suspension of the rules. Feb. 2, 2005.

**18.** **H Res 57. EU Arms Sales to China/Adoption.** Gallegly, R-Calif., motion to suspend the rules and adopt the resolution that would deplore the recent increase in arms sales by European Union (EU) member states to China, as well as the European Council's decision to lift its arms embargo on China. A two-thirds majority of those present and voting (276 in this case) is required for adoption under suspension of the rules. Motion agreed to 411-3: R 220-1; D 190-2 (ND 142-1, SD 48-1); I 1-0. Feb. 2, 2005.

**19.** **H Res 60. Iraqi Elections/Adoption.** Adoption of the resolution that would congratulate the Iraqi people for participating in the elections on Jan. 30, 2005. Adopted 404-9: R 223-1; D 180-8 (ND 134-7, SD 46-1); I 1-0. Feb. 2, 2005.

| | 14 | 15 | 16 | 17 | 18 | 19 |
|---|---|---|---|---|---|---|
| **ALABAMA** | | | | | | |
| 1 Bonner | Y | Y | Y | Y | Y | Y |
| 2 Everett | Y | Y | Y | Y | Y | Y |
| 3 Rogers | Y | Y | Y | Y | Y | Y |
| 4 Aderholt | Y | Y | Y | Y | Y | Y |
| 5 Cramer | Y | Y | Y | Y | Y | Y |
| 6 Bachus | ? | ? | Y | Y | Y | Y |
| 7 Davis | Y | Y | Y | Y | Y | Y |
| **ALASKA** | | | | | | |
| AL Young | Y | Y | Y | Y | Y | Y |
| **ARIZONA** | | | | | | |
| 1 Renzi | Y | Y | Y | Y | Y | Y |
| 2 Franks | Y | Y | Y | Y | Y | Y |
| 3 Shadegg | Y | Y | Y | Y | Y | Y |
| 4 Pastor | Y | Y | N | Y | Y | Y |
| 5 Hayworth | Y | Y | Y | Y | Y | Y |
| 6 Flake | Y | Y | Y | Y | Y | Y |
| 7 Grijalva | Y | Y | N | Y | Y | Y |
| 8 Kolbe | Y | Y | Y | Y | Y | Y |
| **ARKANSAS** | | | | | | |
| 1 Berry | Y | Y | Y | Y | Y | Y |
| 2 Snyder | Y | Y | Y | Y | Y | Y |
| 3 Boozman | Y | Y | Y | Y | Y | Y |
| 4 Ross | Y | Y | Y | Y | Y | Y |
| **CALIFORNIA** | | | | | | |
| 1 Thompson | Y | Y | N | Y | Y | Y |
| 2 Herger | Y | Y | Y | Y | Y | Y |
| 3 Lungren | Y | Y | Y | Y | Y | Y |
| 4 Doolittle | Y | Y | Y | Y | Y | Y |
| 5 Vacant | | | | | | |
| 6 Woolsey | Y | Y | N | Y | Y | N |
| 7 Miller, George | Y | Y | N | Y | Y | Y |
| 8 Pelosi | Y | Y | N | Y | Y | Y |
| 9 Lee | Y | Y | N | Y | Y | N |
| 10 Tauscher | Y | Y | Y | Y | Y | Y |
| 11 Pombo | Y | Y | Y | Y | Y | Y |
| 12 Lantos | Y | Y | Y | Y | Y | Y |
| 13 Stark | Y | Y | N | Y | Y | N |
| 14 Eshoo | ? | ? | ? | ? | ? | ? |
| 15 Honda | Y | Y | N | Y | Y | Y |
| 16 Lofgren | Y | Y | N | Y | Y | Y |
| 17 Farr | Y | Y | N | Y | Y | Y |
| 18 Cardoza | Y | Y | Y | Y | Y | Y |
| 19 Radanovich | Y | Y | Y | Y | Y | Y |
| 20 Costa | Y | Y | Y | Y | Y | Y |
| 21 Nunes | Y | Y | Y | Y | Y | Y |
| 22 Thomas | Y | Y | Y | Y | Y | Y |
| 23 Capps | Y | Y | N | Y | Y | Y |
| 24 Gallegly | Y | Y | Y | Y | Y | Y |
| 25 McKeon | Y | Y | Y | Y | Y | Y |
| 26 Dreier | Y | Y | Y | Y | Y | Y |
| 27 Sherman | Y | Y | Y | Y | Y | Y |
| 28 Berman | Y | Y | N | Y | Y | Y |
| 29 Schiff | Y | Y | Y | Y | Y | Y |
| 30 Waxman | Y | Y | N | Y | Y | Y |
| 31 Becerra | Y | Y | N | Y | Y | Y |
| 32 Solis | Y | Y | N | Y | Y | Y |
| 33 Watson | Y | Y | N | Y | Y | N |
| 34 Roybal-Allard | Y | Y | N | Y | Y | Y |
| 35 Waters | Y | Y | N | Y | Y | N |
| 36 Harman | Y | Y | Y | Y | Y | Y |
| 37 Millender-McD. | Y | Y | Y | Y | Y | Y |
| 38 Napolitano | Y | Y | Y | Y | Y | Y |
| 39 Sánchez, Linda | Y | Y | N | Y | Y | Y |
| 40 Royce | Y | Y | ? | Y | Y | Y |
| 41 Lewis | Y | Y | Y | Y | Y | Y |
| 42 Miller, Gary | Y | Y | Y | Y | Y | Y |
| 43 Baca | Y | Y | Y | Y | Y | Y |
| 44 Calvert | Y | Y | Y | Y | Y | Y |
| 45 Bono | Y | Y | Y | Y | Y | Y |
| 46 Rohrabacher | Y | Y | Y | Y | Y | Y |
| 47 Sanchez, Loretta | Y | Y | Y | Y | Y | Y |
| 48 Cox | ? | ? | Y | Y | Y | Y |
| 49 Issa | Y | Y | Y | Y | Y | Y |

| | 14 | 15 | 16 | 17 | 18 | 19 |
|---|---|---|---|---|---|---|
| 50 Cunningham | Y | Y | Y | Y | Y | Y |
| 51 Filner | Y | Y | N | Y | Y | Y |
| 52 Hunter | ? | ? | Y | Y | Y | Y |
| 53 Davis | Y | Y | Y | Y | Y | Y |
| **COLORADO** | | | | | | |
| 1 DeGette | Y | Y | N | Y | Y | Y |
| 2 Udall | Y | Y | Y | Y | Y | Y |
| 3 Salazar | Y | Y | Y | Y | Y | Y |
| 4 Musgrave | Y | Y | Y | Y | Y | Y |
| 5 Hefley | Y | Y | Y | Y | Y | Y |
| 6 Tancredo | Y | Y | Y | Y | Y | Y |
| 7 Beauprez | Y | Y | Y | Y | Y | Y |
| **CONNECTICUT** | | | | | | |
| 1 Larson | Y | Y | Y | Y | Y | Y |
| 2 Simmons | Y | Y | Y | Y | Y | Y |
| 3 DeLauro | Y | Y | N | Y | Y | Y |
| 4 Shays | Y | Y | Y | Y | Y | Y |
| 5 Johnson | Y | Y | Y | Y | Y | Y |
| **DELAWARE** | | | | | | |
| AL Castle | Y | Y | Y | Y | Y | Y |
| **FLORIDA** | | | | | | |
| 1 Miller | Y | Y | Y | Y | Y | Y |
| 2 Boyd | Y | Y | Y | Y | Y | Y |
| 3 Brown | ? | ? | ? | ? | ? | ? |
| 4 Crenshaw | Y | Y | Y | Y | Y | Y |
| 5 Brown-Waite | Y | Y | Y | Y | Y | Y |
| 6 Stearns | Y | Y | Y | Y | Y | Y |
| 7 Mica | Y | Y | Y | Y | Y | Y |
| 8 Keller | Y | Y | Y | Y | Y | Y |
| 9 Bilirakis | ? | ? | ? | ? | ? | ? |
| 10 Young | Y | Y | Y | Y | Y | Y |
| 11 Davis | Y | Y | Y | Y | Y | Y |
| 12 Putnam | Y | Y | Y | Y | Y | Y |
| 13 Harris | Y | Y | Y | Y | Y | Y |
| 14 Mack | Y | Y | Y | Y | Y | Y |
| 15 Weldon | ? | ? | Y | Y | Y | Y |
| 16 Foley | Y | Y | Y | Y | Y | Y |
| 17 Meek | Y | Y | Y | Y | Y | Y |
| 18 Ros-Lehtinen | Y | Y | Y | Y | Y | Y |
| 19 Wexler | Y | Y | N | Y | Y | Y |
| 20 Wasserman-Schultz | Y | Y | N | Y | Y | Y |
| 21 Diaz-Balart, L. | Y | Y | Y | Y | Y | Y |
| 22 Shaw | Y | Y | Y | Y | Y | Y |
| 23 Hastings | Y | Y | N | Y | Y | Y |
| 24 Feeney | Y | Y | Y | Y | Y | Y |
| 25 Diaz-Balart, M. | ? | ? | ? | ? | ? | ? |
| **GEORGIA** | | | | | | |
| 1 Kingston | Y | Y | Y | Y | Y | Y |
| 2 Bishop | Y | Y | Y | Y | Y | Y |
| 3 Marshall | Y | Y | Y | Y | Y | Y |
| 4 McKinney | Y | Y | N | Y | N | N |
| 5 Lewis | Y | Y | N | Y | Y | P |
| 6 Price | Y | Y | Y | Y | Y | Y |
| 7 Linder | Y | Y | Y | Y | Y | Y |
| 8 Westmoreland | Y | Y | Y | Y | Y | Y |
| 9 Norwood | Y | Y | Y | Y | Y | Y |
| 10 Deal | Y | Y | Y | Y | Y | Y |
| 11 Gingrey | Y | Y | Y | Y | Y | Y |
| 12 Barrow | Y | Y | Y | Y | Y | Y |
| 13 Scott | Y | Y | Y | Y | Y | Y |
| **HAWAII** | | | | | | |
| 1 Abercrombie | Y | Y | N | Y | Y | Y |
| 2 Case | Y | Y | Y | Y | Y | Y |
| **IDAHO** | | | | | | |
| 1 Otter | Y | Y | Y | Y | Y | Y |
| 2 Simpson | Y | Y | Y | Y | Y | Y |
| **ILLINOIS** | | | | | | |
| 1 Rush | ? | ? | ? | ? | ? | ? |
| 2 Jackson | Y | Y | N | Y | Y | Y |
| 3 Lipinski | Y | Y | Y | Y | Y | Y |
| 4 Gutierrez | Y | Y | N | Y | Y | Y |
| 5 Emanuel | Y | Y | N | Y | Y | Y |
| 6 Hyde | + | + | + | + | + | + |
| 7 Davis | Y | Y | N | Y | Y | Y |
| 8 Bean | Y | Y | Y | Y | Y | Y |
| 9 Schakowsky | Y | Y | N | Y | Y | Y |
| 10 Kirk | Y | Y | Y | Y | Y | Y |
| 11 Weller | Y | Y | Y | Y | Y | Y |
| 12 Costello | Y | Y | Y | Y | Y | Y |

**KEY**    **Republicans**    Democrats    *Independents*

| | | |
|---|---|---|
| **Y** Voted for (yea) | **X** Paired against | **C** Voted "present" to avoid possible conflict of interest |
| **#** Paired for | **–** Announced against | |
| **+** Announced for | **P** Voted "present" | **?** Did not vote or otherwise make a position known |
| **N** Voted against (nay) | | |

ND Northern Democrats, SD Southern Democrats
Southern states: Ala., Ark., Fla., Ga., Ky., La., Miss., N.C., Okla., S.C., Tenn., Texas, Va.

| | 14 | 15 | 16 | 17 | 18 | 19 |
|---|---|---|---|---|---|---|
| 13 **Biggert** | Y | Y | Y | Y | Y | Y |
| 14 **Hastert** | | | | | | Y |
| 15 **Johnson** | Y | Y | Y | Y | Y | Y |
| 16 **Manzullo** | ? | Y | Y | Y | ? | Y |
| 17 Evans | Y | Y | Y | Y | Y | Y |
| 18 **LaHood** | Y | Y | Y | Y | Y | Y |
| 19 **Shimkus** | Y | Y | Y | Y | Y | Y |
| INDIANA | | | | | | |
| 1 Visclosky | Y | Y | Y | Y | Y | Y |
| 2 **Chocola** | Y | Y | Y | Y | Y | Y |
| 3 **Souder** | Y | Y | Y | Y | Y | Y |
| 4 **Buyer** | Y | Y | Y | Y | Y | Y |
| 5 **Burton** | Y | Y | Y | Y | Y | Y |
| 6 **Pence** | Y | Y | Y | Y | Y | Y |
| 7 Carson | Y | Y | - | Y | Y | Y |
| 8 **Hostettler** | Y | Y | Y | Y | Y | Y |
| 9 **Sodrel** | Y | Y | Y | Y | Y | Y |
| IOWA | | | | | | |
| 1 **Nussle** | Y | Y | Y | Y | Y | Y |
| 2 **Leach** | Y | Y | Y | Y | Y | Y |
| 3 Boswell | Y | Y | Y | Y | Y | Y |
| 4 **Latham** | Y | Y | Y | Y | Y | Y |
| 5 **King** | Y | Y | Y | Y | Y | Y |
| KANSAS | | | | | | |
| 1 **Moran** | Y | Y | ? | ? | ? | ? |
| 2 **Ryun** | Y | Y | Y | Y | Y | Y |
| 3 Moore | Y | Y | Y | Y | Y | Y |
| 4 **Tiahrt** | Y | Y | Y | Y | + | Y |
| KENTUCKY | | | | | | |
| 1 **Whitfield** | Y | Y | Y | Y | Y | Y |
| 2 **Lewis** | Y | Y | Y | Y | Y | Y |
| 3 **Northup** | + | + | + | + | + | + |
| 4 **Davis** | Y | Y | Y | Y | + | Y |
| 5 **Rogers** | Y | Y | Y | Y | Y | Y |
| 6 Chandler | Y | Y | Y | Y | Y | Y |
| LOUISIANA | | | | | | |
| 1 **Jindal** | Y | Y | Y | Y | Y | Y |
| 2 Jefferson | Y | Y | Y | Y | Y | Y |
| 3 Melancon | Y | Y | Y | Y | Y | Y |
| 4 **McCrery** | Y | Y | Y | Y | Y | Y |
| 5 **Alexander** | Y | Y | Y | Y | Y | Y |
| 6 **Baker** | Y | Y | Y | Y | Y | Y |
| 7 **Boustany** | Y | Y | Y | Y | Y | Y |
| MAINE | | | | | | |
| 1 Allen | Y | Y | N | ? | Y | Y |
| 2 Michaud | Y | Y | N | Y | Y | Y |
| MARYLAND | | | | | | |
| 1 **Gilchrest** | Y | Y | Y | Y | Y | Y |
| 2 Ruppersberger | Y | Y | Y | Y | Y | Y |
| 3 Cardin | Y | Y | Y | Y | Y | Y |
| 4 Wynn | Y | Y | Y | Y | Y | Y |
| 5 Hoyer | Y | Y | Y | Y | Y | Y |
| 6 **Bartlett** | Y | Y | Y | Y | Y | Y |
| 7 Cummings | Y | Y | N | Y | Y | Y |
| 8 Van Hollen | Y | Y | Y | Y | Y | Y |
| MASSACHUSETTS | | | | | | |
| 1 Olver | Y | Y | N | Y | Y | Y |
| 2 Neal | Y | Y | N | Y | Y | Y |
| 3 McGovern | Y | Y | N | Y | Y | Y |
| 4 Frank | Y | Y | N | Y | Y | Y |
| 5 Meehan | Y | Y | N | Y | Y | Y |
| 6 Tierney | Y | Y | N | Y | Y | Y |
| 7 Markey | Y | Y | N | Y | Y | Y |
| 8 Capuano | Y | Y | N | Y | Y | Y |
| 9 Lynch | Y | Y | N | Y | Y | Y |
| 10 Delahunt | Y | Y | N | Y | Y | Y |
| MICHIGAN | | | | | | |
| 1 Stupak | ? | ? | ? | ? | ? | ? |
| 2 **Hoekstra** | Y | Y | Y | Y | Y | Y |
| 3 **Ehlers** | Y | Y | Y | Y | Y | Y |
| 4 **Camp** | Y | Y | Y | Y | Y | Y |
| 5 Kildee | Y | Y | Y | Y | Y | Y |
| 6 **Upton** | Y | Y | Y | Y | Y | Y |
| 7 **Schwarz** | Y | Y | Y | Y | Y | Y |
| 8 **Rogers** | Y | Y | Y | Y | + | Y |
| 9 **Knollenberg** | Y | Y | Y | Y | Y | Y |
| 10 **Miller** | Y | Y | Y | Y | Y | Y |
| 11 **McCotter** | Y | Y | Y | Y | Y | Y |
| 12 Levin | Y | Y | N | Y | Y | Y |
| 13 Kilpatrick | Y | Y | N | Y | Y | Y |
| 14 Conyers | Y | Y | N | Y | Y | Y |
| 15 Dingell | Y | Y | ? | ? | ? | ? |
| MINNESOTA | | | | | | |
| 1 **Gutknecht** | Y | Y | Y | Y | Y | Y |
| 2 **Kline** | Y | Y | Y | Y | Y | Y |
| 3 **Ramstad** | Y | Y | Y | Y | Y | Y |
| 4 McCollum | Y | Y | Y | Y | Y | Y |
| 5 Sabo | Y | Y | N | Y | Y | Y |
| 6 **Kennedy** | Y | Y | Y | Y | Y | Y |
| 7 Peterson | Y | Y | Y | Y | Y | Y |
| 8 Oberstar | Y | Y | N | Y | N | Y |
| MISSISSIPPI | | | | | | |
| 1 **Wicker** | Y | Y | Y | Y | Y | Y |
| 2 Thompson | Y | Y | Y | Y | Y | Y |
| 3 **Pickering** | Y | Y | Y | Y | Y | Y |
| 4 Taylor | Y | Y | Y | Y | Y | Y |
| MISSOURI | | | | | | |
| 1 Clay | Y | Y | N | Y | Y | Y |
| 2 **Akin** | Y | Y | Y | Y | Y | Y |
| 3 Carnahan | Y | Y | Y | Y | Y | Y |
| 4 Skelton | Y | Y | Y | Y | Y | Y |
| 5 Cleaver | Y | Y | Y | Y | Y | Y |
| 6 **Graves** | Y | Y | Y | Y | Y | Y |
| 7 **Blunt** | Y | Y | Y | Y | Y | Y |
| 8 **Emerson** | Y | Y | Y | Y | Y | Y |
| 9 **Hulshof** | Y | Y | Y | Y | Y | Y |
| MONTANA | | | | | | |
| AL **Rehberg** | Y | Y | Y | Y | Y | Y |
| NEBRASKA | | | | | | |
| 1 **Fortenberry** | Y | Y | Y | Y | Y | Y |
| 2 **Terry** | Y | Y | Y | Y | Y | Y |
| 3 **Osborne** | Y | Y | Y | Y | Y | Y |
| NEVADA | | | | | | |
| 1 Berkley | Y | Y | Y | Y | Y | Y |
| 2 **Gibbons** | Y | Y | Y | Y | Y | Y |
| 3 **Porter** | Y | Y | Y | Y | Y | Y |
| NEW HAMPSHIRE | | | | | | |
| 1 **Bradley** | Y | Y | Y | Y | Y | Y |
| 2 **Bass** | Y | Y | Y | Y | Y | Y |
| NEW JERSEY | | | | | | |
| 1 Andrews | Y | Y | Y | Y | Y | Y |
| 2 **LoBiondo** | Y | Y | Y | Y | Y | Y |
| 3 **Saxton** | Y | Y | Y | Y | Y | Y |
| 4 **Smith** | Y | Y | ? | Y | Y | Y |
| 5 **Garrett** | Y | Y | Y | Y | Y | Y |
| 6 Pallone | Y | Y | N | Y | Y | Y |
| 7 **Ferguson** | Y | Y | Y | Y | Y | Y |
| 8 Pascrell | Y | Y | N | Y | Y | Y |
| 9 Rothman | Y | Y | ? | ? | ? | ? |
| 10 Payne | Y | Y | N | Y | Y | P |
| 11 **Frelinghuysen** | Y | Y | Y | Y | Y | Y |
| 12 Holt | Y | Y | N | Y | Y | Y |
| 13 Menendez | Y | Y | Y | Y | Y | Y |
| NEW MEXICO | | | | | | |
| 1 **Wilson** | Y | Y | Y | Y | Y | Y |
| 2 **Pearce** | Y | Y | Y | Y | Y | Y |
| 3 Udall | ? | ? | ? | ? | ? | ? |
| NEW YORK | | | | | | |
| 1 Bishop | Y | Y | Y | Y | Y | Y |
| 2 Israel | Y | Y | Y | Y | Y | Y |
| 3 **King** | Y | Y | Y | Y | Y | Y |
| 4 McCarthy | Y | Y | Y | Y | Y | Y |
| 5 Ackerman | Y | Y | N | Y | Y | Y |
| 6 Meeks | ? | ? | N | Y | Y | Y |
| 7 Crowley | Y | Y | N | Y | Y | Y |
| 8 Nadler | Y | Y | N | Y | Y | Y |
| 9 Weiner | Y | Y | N | Y | Y | Y |
| 10 Towns | ? | ? | ? | ? | ? | ? |
| 11 Owens | Y | Y | N | Y | Y | P |
| 12 Velázquez | Y | Y | N | Y | Y | Y |
| 13 **Fossella** | Y | Y | Y | Y | Y | Y |
| 14 Maloney | Y | Y | N | Y | Y | Y |
| 15 Rangel | Y | Y | N | Y | Y | Y |
| 16 Serrano | Y | Y | N | Y | Y | Y |
| 17 Engel | Y | Y | N | Y | Y | Y |
| 18 Lowey | Y | Y | Y | Y | Y | Y |
| 19 **Kelly** | Y | Y | Y | Y | Y | ? |
| 20 **Sweeney** | ? | ? | Y | Y | Y | ? |
| 21 McNulty | Y | Y | Y | Y | Y | Y |
| 22 Hinchey | Y | Y | N | Y | Y | Y |
| 23 **McHugh** | Y | Y | Y | Y | Y | Y |
| 24 **Boehlert** | Y | Y | Y | Y | Y | Y |
| 25 **Walsh** | Y | Y | Y | Y | Y | Y |
| 26 **Reynolds** | Y | Y | Y | Y | Y | Y |
| 27 Higgins | Y | Y | Y | Y | Y | Y |
| 28 Slaughter | Y | Y | Y | Y | Y | Y |
| 29 **Kuhl** | Y | Y | Y | Y | Y | Y |
| NORTH CAROLINA | | | | | | |
| 1 Butterfield | Y | Y | Y | Y | Y | Y |
| 2 Etheridge | Y | Y | Y | Y | Y | Y |
| 3 **Jones** | Y | Y | Y | Y | Y | Y |
| 4 Price | Y | Y | Y | Y | Y | Y |
| 5 **Foxx** | Y | Y | Y | Y | Y | Y |
| 6 **Coble** | Y | Y | Y | Y | Y | Y |
| 7 McIntyre | Y | Y | Y | Y | Y | Y |
| 8 **Hayes** | Y | Y | Y | Y | Y | Y |
| 9 **Myrick** | Y | Y | Y | Y | Y | Y |
| 10 **McHenry** | Y | Y | Y | Y | Y | Y |
| 11 **Taylor** | Y | Y | Y | Y | Y | Y |
| 12 Watt | Y | Y | N | Y | Y | Y |
| 13 Miller | Y | Y | Y | Y | Y | Y |
| NORTH DAKOTA | | | | | | |
| AL Pomeroy | Y | Y | Y | Y | Y | Y |
| OHIO | | | | | | |
| 1 **Chabot** | Y | Y | Y | Y | Y | Y |
| 2 **Portman** | Y | Y | Y | Y | Y | Y |
| 3 **Turner** | Y | Y | Y | Y | Y | Y |
| 4 **Oxley** | Y | Y | Y | Y | Y | Y |
| 5 **Gillmor** | Y | Y | Y | Y | Y | Y |
| 6 Strickland | Y | Y | Y | Y | Y | Y |
| 7 **Hobson** | Y | Y | Y | Y | Y | Y |
| 8 **Boehner** | Y | Y | Y | Y | Y | Y |
| 9 Kaptur | Y | Y | Y | Y | Y | Y |
| 10 Kucinich | Y | Y | N | Y | Y | N |
| 11 Jones | Y | Y | Y | Y | Y | Y |
| 12 **Tiberi** | Y | Y | Y | Y | Y | Y |
| 13 Brown | Y | Y | N | Y | Y | Y |
| 14 **LaTourette** | Y | Y | Y | Y | Y | Y |
| 15 **Pryce** | Y | Y | Y | Y | Y | Y |
| 16 **Regula** | Y | Y | Y | Y | Y | Y |
| 17 Ryan | Y | Y | Y | Y | Y | Y |
| 18 **Ney** | Y | Y | Y | Y | Y | Y |
| OKLAHOMA | | | | | | |
| 1 **Sullivan** | Y | Y | Y | Y | Y | Y |
| 2 Boren | Y | Y | Y | Y | Y | Y |
| 3 **Lucas** | Y | Y | Y | Y | Y | Y |
| 4 **Cole** | Y | Y | Y | Y | Y | Y |
| 5 **Istook** | Y | Y | Y | Y | Y | Y |
| OREGON | | | | | | |
| 1 Wu | Y | Y | Y | Y | Y | Y |
| 2 **Walden** | Y | Y | Y | Y | Y | Y |
| 3 Blumenauer | Y | Y | N | Y | Y | Y |
| 4 DeFazio | Y | Y | Y | Y | Y | Y |
| 5 Hooley | Y | Y | Y | Y | Y | Y |
| PENNSYLVANIA | | | | | | |
| 1 Brady | Y | Y | N | Y | Y | Y |
| 2 Fattah | ? | ? | N | Y | Y | Y |
| 3 **English** | Y | Y | Y | Y | Y | Y |
| 4 **Hart** | Y | Y | Y | Y | Y | Y |
| 5 **Peterson** | ? | Y | Y | Y | Y | Y |
| 6 **Gerlach** | Y | Y | Y | Y | Y | Y |
| 7 **Weldon** | ? | ? | ? | ? | ? | ? |
| 8 **Fitzpatrick** | Y | Y | Y | Y | Y | Y |
| 9 **Shuster** | Y | Y | Y | Y | Y | Y |
| 10 **Sherwood** | Y | Y | Y | Y | Y | Y |
| 11 Kanjorski | Y | Y | Y | Y | Y | Y |
| 12 Murtha | Y | Y | Y | Y | Y | Y |
| 13 Schwartz | Y | Y | Y | Y | Y | Y |
| 14 Doyle | Y | Y | Y | Y | Y | Y |
| 15 **Dent** | + | Y | Y | Y | Y | Y |
| 16 **Pitts** | Y | Y | Y | Y | Y | Y |
| 17 Holden | Y | Y | Y | Y | Y | Y |
| 18 **Murphy** | Y | Y | Y | Y | Y | Y |
| 19 **Platts** | Y | Y | Y | Y | Y | Y |
| RHODE ISLAND | | | | | | |
| 1 Kennedy | Y | Y | Y | Y | Y | Y |
| 2 Langevin | Y | Y | Y | Y | Y | Y |
| SOUTH CAROLINA | | | | | | |
| 1 **Brown** | Y | Y | Y | Y | Y | Y |
| 2 **Wilson** | Y | Y | Y | Y | Y | Y |
| 3 **Barrett** | Y | Y | Y | Y | Y | Y |
| 4 **Inglis** | Y | Y | Y | Y | Y | Y |
| 5 Spratt | Y | Y | ? | Y | Y | Y |
| 6 Clyburn | Y | Y | Y | Y | Y | Y |
| SOUTH DAKOTA | | | | | | |
| AL Herseth | Y | Y | Y | Y | Y | Y |
| TENNESSEE | | | | | | |
| 1 **Jenkins** | Y | Y | Y | Y | Y | Y |
| 2 **Duncan** | Y | Y | Y | Y | Y | Y |
| 3 **Wamp** | Y | Y | Y | Y | Y | Y |
| 4 Davis | Y | Y | Y | Y | Y | Y |
| 5 Cooper | Y | Y | Y | Y | Y | Y |
| 6 Gordon | Y | Y | Y | Y | Y | ? |
| 7 **Blackburn** | Y | Y | Y | Y | Y | Y |
| 8 Tanner | Y | Y | Y | Y | Y | Y |
| 9 Ford | ? | ? | ? | Y | Y | Y |
| TEXAS | | | | | | |
| 1 **Gohmert** | Y | Y | Y | Y | Y | Y |
| 2 **Poe** | Y | Y | Y | Y | Y | Y |
| 3 **Johnson, Sam** | Y | Y | Y | Y | Y | Y |
| 4 **Hall, R.** | Y | Y | Y | Y | Y | Y |
| 5 **Hensarling** | Y | Y | Y | Y | Y | Y |
| 6 **Barton** | Y | Y | Y | Y | Y | Y |
| 7 **Culberson** | Y | Y | Y | Y | Y | Y |
| 8 **Brady** | Y | Y | Y | + | Y | Y |
| 9 Green, A. | Y | Y | N | Y | Y | Y |
| 10 **McCaul** | Y | Y | Y | Y | Y | Y |
| 11 **Conaway** | Y | Y | Y | Y | Y | Y |
| 12 **Granger** | Y | Y | Y | Y | Y | Y |
| 13 **Thornberry** | Y | Y | Y | Y | Y | Y |
| 14 **Paul** | Y | Y | Y | N | N | N |
| 15 Hinojosa | Y | Y | Y | Y | Y | Y |
| 16 Reyes | Y | Y | Y | Y | Y | Y |
| 17 Edwards | ? | ? | Y | Y | Y | Y |
| 18 Jackson-Lee | Y | Y | N | Y | Y | Y |
| 19 **Neugebauer** | Y | Y | Y | Y | Y | Y |
| 20 Gonzalez | Y | Y | Y | Y | Y | Y |
| 21 **Smith** | Y | Y | Y | Y | Y | Y |
| 22 **DeLay** | Y | Y | Y | Y | Y | Y |
| 23 **Bonilla** | Y | Y | Y | Y | Y | Y |
| 24 **Marchant** | Y | Y | Y | Y | Y | Y |
| 25 Doggett | Y | Y | Y | Y | Y | Y |
| 26 **Burgess** | Y | Y | Y | Y | Y | Y |
| 27 Ortiz | Y | Y | Y | Y | Y | Y |
| 28 Cuellar | Y | Y | Y | Y | Y | Y |
| 29 Green, G. | ? | ? | ? | ? | ? | ? |
| 30 Johnson, E.B. | Y | Y | N | Y | Y | Y |
| 31 **Carter** | Y | Y | Y | Y | Y | Y |
| 32 **Sessions** | Y | Y | Y | Y | Y | Y |
| UTAH | | | | | | |
| 1 **Bishop** | Y | Y | Y | Y | Y | Y |
| 2 Matheson | Y | Y | Y | Y | Y | Y |
| 3 **Cannon** | Y | Y | Y | Y | Y | Y |
| VERMONT | | | | | | |
| AL *Sanders* | Y | Y | N | Y | Y | Y |
| VIRGINIA | | | | | | |
| 1 **Davis, Jo Ann** | Y | Y | Y | Y | Y | Y |
| 2 **Drake** | Y | Y | Y | Y | Y | Y |
| 3 Scott | Y | Y | N | Y | Y | Y |
| 4 **Forbes** | Y | Y | Y | Y | Y | Y |
| 5 **Goode** | Y | Y | Y | Y | Y | Y |
| 6 **Goodlatte** | Y | Y | Y | Y | Y | Y |
| 7 **Cantor** | Y | Y | Y | Y | Y | Y |
| 8 Moran | Y | Y | Y | Y | Y | Y |
| 9 Boucher | ? | ? | Y | Y | Y | Y |
| 10 **Wolf** | Y | Y | Y | Y | Y | Y |
| 11 **Davis, T.** | Y | Y | Y | Y | Y | Y |
| WASHINGTON | | | | | | |
| 1 Inslee | Y | Y | Y | Y | Y | Y |
| 2 Larsen | Y | Y | Y | Y | Y | Y |
| 3 Baird | Y | Y | Y | Y | Y | Y |
| 4 **Hastings** | Y | Y | Y | Y | Y | Y |
| 5 **McMorris** | Y | Y | Y | Y | Y | Y |
| 6 Dicks | Y | Y | Y | Y | Y | Y |
| 7 McDermott | Y | Y | N | Y | Y | N |
| 8 **Reichert** | Y | Y | Y | Y | Y | Y |
| 9 Smith | Y | Y | Y | Y | Y | Y |
| WEST VIRGINIA | | | | | | |
| 1 Mollohan | Y | ? | N | Y | Y | Y |
| 2 **Capito** | Y | Y | Y | Y | Y | Y |
| 3 Rahall | Y | Y | N | Y | Y | Y |
| WISCONSIN | | | | | | |
| 1 **Ryan** | Y | Y | Y | Y | Y | Y |
| 2 Baldwin | Y | Y | N | Y | Y | Y |
| 3 Kind | Y | Y | Y | Y | Y | Y |
| 4 Moore | Y | Y | - | Y | Y | Y |
| 5 **Sensenbrenner** | Y | Y | Y | Y | Y | Y |
| 6 **Petri** | Y | Y | Y | Y | Y | Y |
| 7 Obey | Y | Y | ? | Y | Y | Y |
| 8 **Green** | Y | Y | Y | Y | Y | Y |
| WYOMING | | | | | | |
| AL **Cubin** | Y | Y | Y | Y | Y | Y |

# IN THE HOUSE | By Vote Number

**20.** **H Res 46. National Mentoring Month/Adoption.** Osborne, R-Neb., motion to suspend the rules and adopt the resolution that would support the goals and ideals of National Mentoring Month and praise the millions of adults who mentor children. Motion agreed to 414-0: R 227-0; D 186-0 (ND 139-0, SD 47-0); I 1-0. A two-thirds majority of those present and voting (276 in this case) is required for adoption under suspension of the rules. Feb. 8, 2005.

**21.** **HR 315. John Milton Bryan Simpson Courthouse/Passage.** Shuster, R-Pa., motion to suspend the rules and pass the bill that would name a federal courthouse in Jacksonville, Fla., after the late John Milton Bryan Simpson, a former judge who ordered the desegregation of public schools in Florida. Motion agreed to 412-0: R 225-0; D 186-0 (ND 138-0, SD 48-0); I 1-0. A two-thirds majority of those present and voting (275 in this case) is required for passage under suspension of the rules. Feb. 8, 2005.

**22.** **HR 548. Tony Hall Tribute/Passage.** Shuster, R-Pa., motion to suspend the rules and pass the bill that would name a federal building and courthouse in Dayton, Ohio, after former Rep. Tony P. Hall, D-Ohio (1979-2002). Motion agreed to 404-0: R 220-0; D 183-0 (ND 136-0, SD 47-0); I 1-0. A two-thirds majority of those present and voting (270 in this case) is required for passage under suspension of the rules. Feb. 8, 2005.

**23.** **HR 418. Immigration Standards/Question of Consideration.** Question of whether the House should consider the rule (H Res 71) to provide for House floor consideration of the bill that would tighten national standards for state driver's licenses and identity cards, make it more difficult for foreign nationals to claim asylum, and authorize the completion of a security fence on the U.S.-Mexico border. Agreed to consider 228-191: R 227-0; D 1-190 (ND 0-141, SD 1-49); I 0-1. (Jackson-Lee, D-Texas, had raised a point of order that the rule provided for an unfunded mandate in violation of section 426(a) of the Congressional Budget Act.) Feb. 9, 2005.

**24.** **H Con Res 6. Support of Boy Scouts/Adoption.** Hefley, R-Colo., motion to suspend the rules and adopt the concurrent resolution that would express the sense of Congress that the Defense Department should continue to support the activities of the Boy Scouts of America. Motion agreed to 418-7: R 229-0; D 188-7 (ND 139-7, SD 49-0); I 1-0. A two-thirds majority of those present and voting (284 in this case) is required for adoption under suspension of the rules. Feb. 9, 2005.

**25.** **H Con Res 26. Tuskegee Airmen Tribute/Adoption.** Rogers, R-Ala., motion to suspend the rules and adopt the concurrent resolution that would honor the Tuskegee Airmen, a group of African-American fighter pilots who fought in the U.S. Army Air Corps during World War II. Motion agreed to 423-0: R 228-0; D 194-0 (ND 146-0, SD 48-0); I 1-0. A two-thirds majority of those present and voting (282 in this case) is required for adoption under suspension of the rules. Feb. 9, 2005.

| | 20 | 21 | 22 | 23 | 24 | 25 |
|---|---|---|---|---|---|---|
| **ALABAMA** | | | | | | |
| 1 Bonner | Y | Y | Y | Y | Y | Y |
| 2 Everett | Y | Y | Y | Y | Y | Y |
| 3 Rogers | Y | Y | Y | Y | Y | Y |
| 4 Aderholt | Y | Y | Y | Y | Y | Y |
| 5 Cramer | Y | Y | Y | N | Y | Y |
| 6 Bachus | Y | Y | Y | Y | Y | Y |
| 7 Davis | Y | Y | Y | N | Y | Y |
| **ALASKA** | | | | | | |
| AL Young | Y | Y | Y | Y | Y | Y |
| **ARIZONA** | | | | | | |
| 1 Renzi | Y | Y | Y | Y | Y | Y |
| 2 Franks | Y | Y | Y | Y | Y | Y |
| 3 Shadegg | Y | Y | Y | Y | Y | Y |
| 4 Pastor | Y | Y | Y | N | Y | Y |
| 5 Hayworth | Y | Y | Y | Y | Y | Y |
| 6 Flake | Y | Y | Y | Y | Y | Y |
| 7 Grijalva | Y | Y | Y | N | Y | Y |
| 8 Kolbe | Y | Y | Y | Y | Y | Y |
| **ARKANSAS** | | | | | | |
| 1 Berry | Y | Y | Y | N | Y | Y |
| 2 Snyder | ? | ? | ? | ? | ? | ? |
| 3 Boozman | Y | Y | Y | Y | Y | Y |
| 4 Ross | Y | Y | Y | N | Y | Y |
| **CALIFORNIA** | | | | | | |
| 1 Thompson | Y | Y | Y | N | Y | Y |
| 2 Herger | Y | Y | Y | Y | Y | Y |
| 3 Lungren | Y | Y | Y | Y | Y | Y |
| 4 Doolittle | Y | Y | Y | Y | Y | |
| 5 Vacant | | | | | | |
| 6 Woolsey | Y | Y | Y | N | N | Y |
| 7 Miller, George | Y | Y | Y | N | Y | Y |
| 8 Pelosi | Y | Y | Y | N | Y | Y |
| 9 Lee | Y | Y | Y | N | N | Y |
| 10 Tauscher | Y | Y | Y | N | Y | Y |
| 11 Pombo | Y | Y | Y | Y | Y | Y |
| 12 Lantos | Y | Y | Y | N | Y | Y |
| 13 Stark | Y | Y | Y | N | N | Y |
| 14 Eshoo | ? | ? | ? | ? | ? | ? |
| 15 Honda | Y | Y | Y | N | Y | Y |
| 16 Lofgren | Y | Y | Y | N | Y | Y |
| 17 Farr | Y | Y | Y | N | Y | Y |
| 18 Cardoza | Y | Y | ? | N | Y | Y |
| 19 Radanovich | Y | Y | Y | Y | Y | Y |
| 20 Costa | Y | Y | Y | N | Y | Y |
| 21 Nunes | Y | Y | Y | Y | Y | Y |
| 22 Thomas | Y | Y | Y | Y | Y | Y |
| 23 Capps | Y | Y | Y | N | Y | Y |
| 24 Gallegly | Y | Y | Y | Y | Y | Y |
| 25 McKeon | Y | Y | Y | Y | Y | Y |
| 26 Dreier | Y | Y | Y | Y | Y | Y |
| 27 Sherman | Y | Y | Y | N | Y | Y |
| 28 Berman | Y | Y | Y | N | Y | Y |
| 29 Schiff | Y | Y | Y | – | Y | Y |
| 30 Waxman | Y | Y | Y | N | Y | Y |
| 31 Becerra | Y | Y | Y | N | Y | Y |
| 32 Solis | Y | Y | Y | N | Y | Y |
| 33 Watson | ? | ? | ? | N | Y | Y |
| 34 Roybal-Allard | Y | Y | Y | N | Y | Y |
| 35 Waters | Y | Y | Y | N | Y | Y |
| 36 Harman | Y | Y | Y | N | Y | Y |
| 37 Millender-McD. | Y | Y | Y | N | Y | Y |
| 38 Napolitano | Y | Y | ? | N | Y | Y |
| 39 Sánchez, Linda | Y | Y | Y | N | Y | Y |
| 40 Royce | Y | Y | Y | Y | Y | Y |
| 41 Lewis | Y | Y | Y | Y | Y | Y |
| 42 Miller, Gary | Y | Y | Y | Y | Y | Y |
| 43 Baca | Y | Y | Y | N | Y | Y |
| 44 Calvert | Y | Y | Y | Y | Y | Y |
| 45 Bono | Y | Y | Y | Y | Y | Y |
| 46 Rohrabacher | Y | Y | Y | Y | Y | Y |
| 47 Sanchez, Loretta | Y | Y | Y | N | Y | Y |
| 48 Cox | Y | Y | Y | Y | Y | Y |
| 49 Issa | Y | Y | Y | Y | Y | Y |

| | 20 | 21 | 22 | 23 | 24 | 25 |
|---|---|---|---|---|---|---|
| 50 Cunningham | Y | Y | Y | Y | Y | Y |
| 51 Filner | Y | Y | Y | N | Y | Y |
| 52 Hunter | Y | Y | Y | Y | Y | Y |
| 53 Davis | Y | Y | Y | N | Y | Y |
| **COLORADO** | | | | | | |
| 1 DeGette | ? | ? | ? | ? | Y | Y |
| 2 Udall | Y | Y | Y | N | Y | Y |
| 3 Salazar | Y | Y | Y | N | Y | Y |
| 4 Musgrave | Y | Y | Y | Y | Y | Y |
| 5 Hefley | Y | Y | Y | Y | Y | Y |
| 6 Tancredo | Y | Y | Y | Y | Y | Y |
| 7 Beauprez | Y | Y | Y | Y | Y | Y |
| **CONNECTICUT** | | | | | | |
| 1 Larson | Y | Y | Y | N | Y | Y |
| 2 Simmons | Y | Y | Y | Y | Y | Y |
| 3 DeLauro | Y | Y | Y | N | Y | Y |
| 4 Shays | Y | Y | Y | Y | Y | Y |
| 5 Johnson | Y | Y | Y | Y | Y | Y |
| **DELAWARE** | | | | | | |
| AL Castle | Y | Y | Y | Y | Y | Y |
| **FLORIDA** | | | | | | |
| 1 Miller | Y | Y | Y | Y | Y | Y |
| 2 Boyd | Y | Y | Y | N | Y | Y |
| 3 Brown | Y | Y | Y | N | Y | Y |
| 4 Crenshaw | Y | Y | Y | Y | Y | Y |
| 5 Brown-Waite | Y | Y | Y | Y | Y | Y |
| 6 Stearns | Y | Y | ? | Y | Y | Y |
| 7 Mica | Y | Y | Y | Y | Y | + |
| 8 Keller | Y | Y | Y | Y | Y | Y |
| 9 Bilirakis | Y | Y | Y | Y | Y | Y |
| 10 Young | Y | Y | Y | Y | Y | Y |
| 11 Davis | ? | Y | Y | N | Y | Y |
| 12 Putnam | Y | Y | Y | Y | Y | Y |
| 13 Harris | Y | Y | Y | Y | Y | Y |
| 14 Mack | Y | Y | Y | Y | Y | Y |
| 15 Weldon | Y | Y | Y | Y | Y | Y |
| 16 Foley | Y | Y | Y | Y | Y | Y |
| 17 Meek | Y | Y | Y | N | Y | Y |
| 18 Ros-Lehtinen | Y | Y | Y | Y | ? | ? |
| 19 Wexler | ? | ? | ? | N | Y | Y |
| 20 Wasserman-Schultz | Y | Y | Y | N | Y | Y |
| 21 Diaz-Balart, L. | Y | Y | Y | Y | Y | Y |
| 22 Shaw | Y | Y | Y | Y | Y | Y |
| 23 Hastings | Y | Y | Y | N | Y | Y |
| 24 Feeney | ? | ? | ? | ? | ? | ? |
| 25 Diaz-Balart, M. | Y | Y | Y | Y | Y | Y |
| **GEORGIA** | | | | | | |
| 1 Kingston | Y | Y | Y | Y | Y | Y |
| 2 Bishop | Y | Y | Y | N | Y | Y |
| 3 Marshall | Y | Y | Y | N | Y | Y |
| 4 McKinney | Y | Y | Y | N | Y | Y |
| 5 Lewis | Y | Y | Y | N | Y | Y |
| 6 Price | Y | Y | Y | Y | Y | Y |
| 7 Linder | Y | Y | Y | Y | Y | Y |
| 8 Westmoreland | Y | Y | Y | Y | Y | Y |
| 9 Norwood | Y | Y | Y | ? | Y | Y |
| 10 Deal | Y | Y | Y | Y | Y | Y |
| 11 Gingrey | Y | Y | Y | Y | Y | Y |
| 12 Barrow | Y | Y | Y | N | Y | Y |
| 13 Scott | Y | Y | Y | N | Y | Y |
| **HAWAII** | | | | | | |
| 1 Abercrombie | Y | Y | Y | N | Y | Y |
| 2 Case | Y | Y | Y | N | Y | Y |
| **IDAHO** | | | | | | |
| 1 Otter | Y | Y | Y | Y | Y | Y |
| 2 Simpson | Y | Y | Y | Y | Y | Y |
| **ILLINOIS** | | | | | | |
| 1 Rush | Y | Y | Y | N | ? | ? |
| 2 Jackson | Y | Y | Y | N | Y | Y |
| 3 Lipinski | Y | Y | Y | ? | Y | Y |
| 4 Gutierrez | + | + | + | N | Y | Y |
| 5 Emanuel | Y | Y | Y | N | Y | Y |
| 6 Hyde | Y | Y | Y | Y | Y | Y |
| 7 Davis | Y | Y | Y | ? | Y | Y |
| 8 Bean | Y | Y | Y | N | Y | Y |
| 9 Schakowsky | Y | Y | Y | N | Y | Y |
| 10 Kirk | Y | Y | ? | Y | Y | Y |
| 11 Weller | Y | Y | Y | Y | Y | Y |
| 12 Costello | Y | Y | Y | N | Y | Y |

| KEY | Republicans | Democrats | Independents | | |
|---|---|---|---|---|---|
| Y | Voted for (yea) | X | Paired against | C | Voted "present" to avoid possible conflict of interest |
| # | Paired for | – | Announced against | | |
| + | Announced for | P | Voted "present" | ? | Did not vote or otherwise make a position known |
| N | Voted against (nay) | | | | |

ND Northern Democrats, SD Southern Democrats
Southern states: Ala., Ark., Fla., Ga., Ky., La., Miss., N.C., Okla., S.C., Tenn., Texas, Va.

| | 20 | 21 | 22 | 23 | 24 | 25 |
|---|---|---|---|---|---|---|
| 13 **Biggert** | Y | Y | Y | Y | Y | Y |
| 14 **Hastert** | Y | | | | | |
| 15 **Johnson** | Y | Y | Y | Y | Y | Y |
| 16 **Manzullo** | Y | Y | Y | Y | Y | Y |
| 17 Evans | Y | Y | Y | N | Y | Y |
| 18 **LaHood** | Y | Y | Y | Y | Y | Y |
| 19 **Shimkus** | Y | Y | Y | Y | Y | Y |
| **INDIANA** | | | | | | |
| 1 Visclosky | Y | Y | Y | N | Y | Y |
| 2 **Chocola** | Y | Y | Y | Y | Y | Y |
| 3 **Souder** | Y | Y | Y | Y | Y | Y |
| 4 **Buyer** | Y | Y | Y | Y | Y | Y |
| 5 **Burton** | Y | Y | Y | Y | Y | Y |
| 6 **Pence** | Y | Y | Y | ? | Y | Y |
| 7 Carson | Y | Y | Y | N | Y | Y |
| 8 **Hostettler** | Y | Y | Y | Y | Y | Y |
| 9 **Sodrel** | Y | Y | Y | Y | Y | Y |
| **IOWA** | | | | | | |
| 1 **Nussle** | Y | Y | Y | Y | Y | Y |
| 2 **Leach** | Y | Y | Y | Y | Y | Y |
| 3 Boswell | Y | Y | Y | N | Y | Y |
| 4 **Latham** | Y | Y | Y | Y | Y | Y |
| 5 **King** | Y | Y | Y | Y | Y | Y |
| **KANSAS** | | | | | | |
| 1 **Moran** | Y | Y | Y | Y | Y | Y |
| 2 **Ryun** | Y | Y | Y | Y | Y | Y |
| 3 Moore | Y | Y | Y | N | Y | Y |
| 4 **Tiahrt** | Y | Y | Y | Y | Y | Y |
| **KENTUCKY** | | | | | | |
| 1 **Whitfield** | Y | Y | Y | Y | Y | Y |
| 2 **Lewis** | Y | Y | Y | Y | Y | Y |
| 3 **Northup** | Y | Y | Y | Y | Y | Y |
| 4 **Davis** | Y | Y | Y | Y | Y | Y |
| 5 **Rogers** | Y | Y | Y | Y | Y | Y |
| 6 Chandler | Y | Y | Y | N | Y | Y |
| **LOUISIANA** | | | | | | |
| 1 **Jindal** | Y | Y | Y | Y | Y | Y |
| 2 Jefferson | Y | Y | Y | N | Y | Y |
| 3 Melancon | Y | Y | Y | N | Y | Y |
| 4 **McCrery** | Y | Y | Y | Y | Y | Y |
| 5 **Alexander** | Y | Y | Y | Y | Y | Y |
| 6 **Baker** | Y | Y | Y | Y | Y | Y |
| 7 **Boustany** | Y | Y | Y | Y | Y | Y |
| **MAINE** | | | | | | |
| 1 Allen | Y | Y | Y | N | Y | Y |
| 2 Michaud | Y | Y | Y | N | Y | Y |
| **MARYLAND** | | | | | | |
| 1 **Gilchrest** | Y | Y | Y | Y | Y | Y |
| 2 Ruppersberger | Y | Y | Y | N | Y | Y |
| 3 Cardin | Y | Y | Y | N | Y | Y |
| 4 Wynn | Y | Y | Y | N | Y | Y |
| 5 Hoyer | Y | Y | Y | N | Y | Y |
| 6 **Bartlett** | Y | Y | Y | Y | Y | Y |
| 7 Cummings | Y | Y | Y | N | Y | Y |
| 8 Van Hollen | Y | Y | Y | N | Y | Y |
| **MASSACHUSETTS** | | | | | | |
| 1 Olver | Y | Y | Y | N | Y | Y |
| 2 Neal | Y | Y | Y | N | Y | Y |
| 3 McGovern | Y | Y | Y | N | Y | Y |
| 4 Frank | Y | Y | Y | N | N | Y |
| 5 Meehan | Y | Y | Y | N | Y | Y |
| 6 Tierney | Y | Y | Y | N | Y | Y |
| 7 Markey | Y | Y | Y | N | Y | Y |
| 8 Capuano | Y | Y | Y | N | Y | Y |
| 9 Lynch | ? | ? | ? | N | Y | Y |
| 10 Delahunt | Y | Y | Y | N | Y | Y |
| **MICHIGAN** | | | | | | |
| 1 Stupak | ? | ? | ? | ? | ? | ? |
| 2 **Hoekstra** | Y | Y | Y | Y | Y | Y |
| 3 **Ehlers** | Y | Y | Y | Y | Y | Y |
| 4 **Camp** | Y | Y | Y | Y | Y | Y |
| 5 Kildee | Y | Y | Y | N | Y | Y |
| 6 **Upton** | Y | Y | Y | Y | Y | Y |
| 7 **Schwarz** | Y | Y | Y | Y | Y | Y |
| 8 **Rogers** | Y | Y | Y | Y | Y | Y |
| 9 **Knollenberg** | Y | Y | Y | Y | Y | Y |
| 10 **Miller** | Y | Y | Y | Y | Y | Y |
| 11 **McCotter** | Y | Y | Y | Y | Y | Y |
| 12 Levin | Y | Y | Y | N | Y | Y |
| 13 Kilpatrick | Y | Y | Y | N | Y | Y |
| 14 Conyers | Y | Y | Y | N | Y | Y |
| 15 Dingell | Y | Y | Y | N | Y | Y |
| **MINNESOTA** | | | | | | |
| 1 **Gutknecht** | Y | Y | Y | Y | Y | Y |
| 2 **Kline** | Y | Y | Y | Y | Y | Y |
| 3 **Ramstad** | Y | Y | Y | Y | Y | Y |
| 4 McCollum | Y | Y | Y | N | Y | Y |
| 5 Sabo | ? | ? | ? | N | Y | Y |
| 6 **Kennedy** | Y | Y | Y | Y | Y | Y |
| 7 Peterson | Y | Y | Y | N | Y | Y |
| 8 Oberstar | Y | Y | Y | N | Y | Y |
| **MISSISSIPPI** | | | | | | |
| 1 **Wicker** | Y | Y | Y | Y | Y | Y |
| 2 Thompson | Y | Y | Y | N | Y | Y |
| 3 **Pickering** | Y | Y | Y | Y | Y | Y |
| 4 Taylor | Y | Y | Y | N | Y | Y |
| **MISSOURI** | | | | | | |
| 1 Clay | Y | Y | Y | N | Y | Y |
| 2 **Akin** | Y | Y | Y | Y | Y | Y |
| 3 Carnahan | Y | Y | Y | N | Y | Y |
| 4 Skelton | Y | Y | Y | N | Y | Y |
| 5 Cleaver | Y | Y | Y | N | Y | Y |
| 6 **Graves** | Y | Y | Y | Y | Y | Y |
| 7 **Blunt** | Y | Y | Y | Y | Y | Y |
| 8 **Emerson** | ? | ? | ? | Y | Y | Y |
| 9 **Hulshof** | Y | Y | Y | Y | Y | Y |
| **MONTANA** | | | | | | |
| AL **Rehberg** | Y | Y | Y | Y | Y | Y |
| **NEBRASKA** | | | | | | |
| 1 **Fortenberry** | Y | Y | Y | Y | Y | Y |
| 2 **Terry** | Y | Y | Y | Y | Y | Y |
| 3 **Osborne** | Y | Y | Y | Y | Y | Y |
| **NEVADA** | | | | | | |
| 1 Berkley | Y | Y | Y | N | Y | Y |
| 2 **Gibbons** | Y | Y | Y | Y | Y | Y |
| 3 **Porter** | Y | Y | Y | Y | Y | Y |
| **NEW HAMPSHIRE** | | | | | | |
| 1 **Bradley** | Y | Y | Y | Y | Y | Y |
| 2 **Bass** | Y | Y | Y | Y | Y | Y |
| **NEW JERSEY** | | | | | | |
| 1 Andrews | Y | Y | Y | N | Y | Y |
| 2 **LoBiondo** | + | + | + | Y | Y | Y |
| 3 **Saxton** | Y | Y | Y | Y | Y | Y |
| 4 **Smith** | Y | Y | Y | Y | Y | Y |
| 5 **Garrett** | Y | Y | Y | Y | Y | Y |
| 6 Pallone | Y | Y | Y | N | Y | Y |
| 7 **Ferguson** | Y | Y | Y | Y | Y | Y |
| 8 Pascrell | Y | Y | Y | N | Y | Y |
| 9 Rothman | Y | Y | Y | N | Y | Y |
| 10 Payne | ? | ? | ? | N | Y | Y |
| 11 **Frelinghuysen** | Y | Y | Y | Y | Y | Y |
| 12 Holt | Y | ? | ? | N | Y | Y |
| 13 Menendez | Y | Y | Y | N | Y | Y |
| **NEW MEXICO** | | | | | | |
| 1 **Wilson** | Y | Y | Y | Y | Y | Y |
| 2 **Pearce** | Y | Y | Y | Y | Y | Y |
| 3 Udall | Y | Y | Y | N | Y | Y |
| **NEW YORK** | | | | | | |
| 1 Bishop | Y | Y | Y | N | Y | Y |
| 2 Israel | Y | Y | Y | N | Y | Y |
| 3 **King** | Y | Y | Y | Y | Y | Y |
| 4 McCarthy | Y | Y | Y | N | Y | Y |
| 5 Ackerman | ? | ? | ? | N | Y | Y |
| 6 Meeks | Y | Y | Y | N | Y | Y |
| 7 Crowley | Y | Y | Y | N | Y | Y |
| 8 Nadler | Y | Y | Y | N | Y | Y |
| 9 Weiner | Y | Y | Y | N | Y | Y |
| 10 Towns | Y | Y | Y | N | Y | Y |
| 11 Owens | Y | Y | Y | N | Y | Y |
| 12 Velázquez | Y | Y | Y | N | Y | Y |
| 13 **Fossella** | Y | Y | Y | Y | Y | Y |
| 14 Maloney | Y | Y | Y | N | Y | Y |
| 15 Rangel | Y | Y | Y | N | Y | Y |
| 16 Serrano | Y | Y | Y | N | Y | Y |
| 17 Engel | Y | Y | Y | N | Y | Y |
| 18 Lowey | Y | Y | Y | N | Y | Y |
| 19 **Kelly** | Y | Y | Y | Y | Y | Y |
| 20 **Sweeney** | Y | Y | Y | Y | Y | Y |
| 21 McNulty | Y | Y | Y | N | Y | Y |
| 22 Hinchey | ? | ? | ? | ? | ? | ? |
| 23 **McHugh** | Y | Y | Y | Y | Y | Y |
| 24 **Boehlert** | Y | Y | Y | Y | Y | Y |
| 25 **Walsh** | Y | Y | Y | Y | Y | Y |
| 26 **Reynolds** | Y | Y | Y | Y | Y | Y |
| 27 Higgins | Y | Y | Y | N | Y | Y |
| 28 Slaughter | Y | Y | Y | N | Y | Y |
| 29 **Kuhl** | Y | Y | Y | Y | Y | Y |
| **NORTH CAROLINA** | | | | | | |
| 1 Butterfield | Y | Y | Y | N | Y | Y |
| 2 Etheridge | ? | ? | ? | N | Y | Y |
| 3 **Jones** | Y | Y | Y | ? | Y | Y |
| 4 Price | Y | Y | Y | N | Y | Y |
| 5 **Foxx** | Y | Y | Y | Y | Y | Y |
| 6 **Coble** | Y | Y | Y | Y | Y | Y |
| 7 McIntyre | Y | Y | Y | N | Y | Y |
| 8 **Hayes** | Y | Y | Y | Y | Y | Y |
| 9 **Myrick** | Y | Y | Y | Y | Y | Y |
| 10 **McHenry** | Y | Y | Y | Y | Y | Y |
| 11 **Taylor** | Y | Y | ? | Y | Y | Y |
| 12 Watt | Y | Y | Y | N | Y | Y |
| 13 Miller | Y | Y | Y | N | Y | Y |
| **NORTH DAKOTA** | | | | | | |
| AL Pomeroy | Y | Y | Y | N | Y | Y |
| **OHIO** | | | | | | |
| 1 **Chabot** | Y | Y | Y | Y | Y | Y |
| 2 **Portman** | Y | Y | Y | Y | Y | Y |
| 3 **Turner** | Y | Y | Y | Y | Y | Y |
| 4 **Oxley** | Y | Y | Y | Y | Y | Y |
| 5 **Gillmor** | Y | Y | Y | Y | Y | Y |
| 6 Strickland | Y | Y | Y | N | Y | Y |
| 7 **Hobson** | Y | Y | Y | Y | Y | Y |
| 8 **Boehner** | Y | Y | Y | Y | Y | Y |
| 9 Kaptur | Y | Y | Y | N | Y | Y |
| 10 Kucinich | Y | Y | Y | N | N | Y |
| 11 Jones | Y | Y | Y | N | Y | Y |
| 12 **Tiberi** | Y | Y | Y | Y | Y | Y |
| 13 Brown | Y | Y | Y | N | Y | Y |
| 14 **LaTourette** | Y | Y | Y | Y | Y | Y |
| 15 **Pryce** | Y | Y | Y | Y | Y | Y |
| 16 **Regula** | Y | Y | Y | Y | Y | Y |
| 17 Ryan | Y | Y | Y | N | Y | Y |
| 18 **Ney** | + | + | + | Y | Y | Y |
| **OKLAHOMA** | | | | | | |
| 1 **Sullivan** | Y | Y | Y | Y | Y | Y |
| 2 Boren | Y | Y | Y | N | Y | Y |
| 3 **Lucas** | Y | Y | Y | Y | Y | Y |
| 4 **Cole** | Y | Y | Y | Y | Y | Y |
| 5 **Istook** | Y | Y | Y | Y | Y | Y |
| **OREGON** | | | | | | |
| 1 Wu | Y | Y | Y | N | Y | Y |
| 2 **Walden** | Y | Y | Y | Y | Y | Y |
| 3 Blumenauer | Y | Y | Y | N | N | Y |
| 4 DeFazio | Y | Y | Y | N | Y | Y |
| 5 Hooley | Y | Y | Y | N | Y | Y |
| **PENNSYLVANIA** | | | | | | |
| 1 Brady | Y | Y | Y | N | Y | Y |
| 2 Fattah | Y | Y | Y | N | Y | Y |
| 3 **English** | Y | Y | Y | Y | Y | Y |
| 4 **Hart** | Y | Y | Y | Y | Y | Y |
| 5 **Peterson** | Y | Y | Y | Y | Y | Y |
| 6 **Gerlach** | Y | ? | ? | Y | Y | Y |
| 7 **Weldon** | Y | Y | Y | Y | Y | Y |
| 8 **Fitzpatrick** | Y | Y | Y | Y | Y | Y |
| 9 **Shuster** | Y | Y | Y | Y | Y | Y |
| 10 **Sherwood** | Y | Y | Y | Y | Y | Y |
| 11 Kanjorski | Y | Y | Y | N | Y | Y |
| 12 Murtha | Y | Y | Y | N | Y | Y |
| 13 Schwartz | Y | Y | Y | N | Y | Y |
| 14 Doyle | Y | Y | Y | N | Y | Y |
| 15 **Dent** | Y | Y | Y | Y | Y | Y |
| 16 **Pitts** | Y | Y | Y | Y | Y | Y |
| 17 Holden | Y | Y | Y | N | Y | Y |
| 18 **Murphy** | Y | Y | Y | Y | Y | Y |
| 19 **Platts** | Y | Y | Y | Y | Y | Y |
| **RHODE ISLAND** | | | | | | |
| 1 Kennedy | Y | Y | Y | N | Y | Y |
| 2 Langevin | Y | Y | Y | N | Y | Y |
| **SOUTH CAROLINA** | | | | | | |
| 1 **Brown** | Y | Y | Y | Y | Y | Y |
| 2 **Wilson** | Y | Y | ? | Y | Y | Y |
| 3 **Barrett** | Y | Y | Y | Y | Y | Y |
| 4 **Inglis** | Y | Y | Y | Y | Y | Y |
| 5 Spratt | Y | Y | Y | N | Y | Y |
| 6 Clyburn | Y | Y | ? | N | Y | Y |
| **SOUTH DAKOTA** | | | | | | |
| AL Herseth | Y | Y | Y | N | Y | Y |
| **TENNESSEE** | | | | | | |
| 1 **Jenkins** | Y | Y | Y | Y | Y | Y |
| 2 **Duncan** | Y | Y | Y | Y | Y | Y |
| 3 **Wamp** | Y | Y | Y | Y | Y | Y |
| 4 Davis | Y | Y | Y | Y | Y | Y |
| 5 Cooper | Y | Y | Y | N | Y | Y |
| 6 Gordon | Y | Y | Y | N | Y | ? |
| 7 **Blackburn** | Y | Y | Y | Y | Y | Y |
| 8 Tanner | Y | Y | Y | N | Y | Y |
| 9 Ford | Y | Y | Y | N | Y | Y |
| **TEXAS** | | | | | | |
| 1 **Gohmert** | Y | Y | Y | Y | Y | Y |
| 2 **Poe** | Y | Y | Y | Y | Y | Y |
| 3 **Johnson, S.** | Y | Y | Y | Y | Y | Y |
| 4 **Hall** | Y | Y | Y | Y | Y | Y |
| 5 **Hensarling** | Y | Y | Y | Y | Y | Y |
| 6 **Barton** | Y | Y | Y | Y | Y | Y |
| 7 **Culberson** | Y | Y | Y | Y | Y | Y |
| 8 **Brady** | Y | Y | Y | Y | Y | Y |
| 9 Green, A. | Y | Y | Y | N | Y | Y |
| 10 **McCaul** | Y | Y | Y | Y | Y | Y |
| 11 **Conaway** | Y | Y | Y | Y | Y | Y |
| 12 **Granger** | Y | Y | ? | Y | Y | Y |
| 13 **Thornberry** | Y | Y | Y | Y | Y | Y |
| 14 **Paul** | Y | Y | Y | Y | Y | Y |
| 15 Hinojosa | Y | Y | Y | N | + | + |
| 16 Reyes | Y | Y | Y | N | Y | Y |
| 17 Edwards | Y | Y | Y | N | Y | Y |
| 18 Jackson-Lee | Y | Y | Y | N | Y | Y |
| 19 **Neugebauer** | + | + | + | Y | Y | Y |
| 20 Gonzalez | Y | Y | Y | N | Y | Y |
| 21 **Smith** | Y | Y | Y | Y | Y | Y |
| 22 **DeLay** | Y | Y | Y | Y | Y | Y |
| 23 **Bonilla** | Y | Y | Y | Y | Y | Y |
| 24 **Marchant** | Y | Y | Y | Y | Y | Y |
| 25 Doggett | Y | Y | Y | N | Y | Y |
| 26 **Burgess** | Y | Y | Y | Y | Y | Y |
| 27 Ortiz | Y | Y | Y | N | Y | Y |
| 28 Cuellar | Y | Y | Y | N | Y | Y |
| 29 Green, G. | Y | Y | Y | N | Y | Y |
| 30 Johnson, E. | Y | Y | Y | N | Y | Y |
| 31 **Carter** | Y | Y | Y | Y | Y | Y |
| 32 **Sessions** | Y | Y | Y | Y | Y | Y |
| **UTAH** | | | | | | |
| 1 **Bishop** | Y | Y | Y | Y | Y | Y |
| 2 Matheson | Y | Y | Y | N | Y | Y |
| 3 **Cannon** | Y | Y | Y | Y | Y | Y |
| **VERMONT** | | | | | | |
| AL *Sanders* | Y | Y | Y | N | Y | Y |
| **VIRGINIA** | | | | | | |
| 1 **Davis, J.** | Y | Y | Y | Y | Y | Y |
| 2 **Drake** | Y | Y | Y | Y | Y | Y |
| 3 Scott | Y | Y | Y | N | Y | Y |
| 4 **Forbes** | Y | Y | Y | Y | Y | Y |
| 5 **Goode** | Y | Y | Y | Y | Y | Y |
| 6 **Goodlatte** | Y | Y | Y | Y | Y | Y |
| 7 **Cantor** | Y | Y | Y | Y | Y | Y |
| 8 Moran | Y | Y | Y | N | Y | Y |
| 9 Boucher | Y | Y | Y | N | Y | Y |
| 10 **Wolf** | Y | Y | Y | Y | Y | Y |
| 11 **Davis, T.** | Y | Y | Y | Y | Y | Y |
| **WASHINGTON** | | | | | | |
| 1 Inslee | Y | Y | Y | N | Y | Y |
| 2 Larsen | Y | Y | Y | N | Y | Y |
| 3 Baird | ? | ? | ? | N | Y | Y |
| 4 **Hastings** | Y | Y | Y | Y | Y | Y |
| 5 **McMorris** | Y | Y | Y | Y | Y | Y |
| 6 Dicks | Y | Y | Y | ? | Y | Y |
| 7 McDermott | Y | Y | Y | N | N | Y |
| 8 **Reichert** | Y | Y | Y | Y | Y | Y |
| 9 Smith | Y | Y | Y | N | Y | Y |
| **WEST VIRGINIA** | | | | | | |
| 1 Mollohan | Y | Y | Y | N | Y | Y |
| 2 **Capito** | Y | Y | Y | Y | Y | Y |
| 3 Rahall | Y | Y | Y | N | Y | Y |
| **WISCONSIN** | | | | | | |
| 1 **Ryan** | Y | Y | Y | Y | Y | Y |
| 2 Baldwin | Y | Y | Y | N | Y | Y |
| 3 Kind | Y | Y | Y | N | Y | Y |
| 4 Moore | Y | Y | Y | N | Y | Y |
| 5 **Sensenbrenner** | Y | Y | Y | Y | Y | Y |
| 6 **Petri** | Y | Y | Y | Y | Y | Y |
| 7 Obey | Y | Y | Y | ? | Y | Y |
| 8 **Green** | Y | Y | Y | Y | Y | Y |
| **WYOMING** | | | | | | |
| AL **Cubin** | Y | Y | Y | Y | Y | Y |

# IN THE HOUSE | By Vote Number

**26.** **H Con Res 30. National Black HIV/AIDS Awareness Day/Adoption.** Deal, R-Ga., motion to suspend the rules and adopt the concurrent resolution that would express congressional support for the goals and ideals of National Black HIV/AIDS Awareness Day and recognize its fifth anniversary. Motion agreed to 422-0: R 227-0; D 194-0 (ND 145-0, SD 49-0); I 1-0. A two-thirds majority of those present and voting (282 in this case) is required for adoption under suspension of the rules. Feb. 9, 2005.

**27.** **HR 418. Immigration Standards/Rule.** Adoption of the rule (H Res 75) to provide for further House floor consideration of the bill that would tighten national standards for state driver's licenses and identity cards, make it more difficult for foreign nationals to claim asylum, and authorize the completion of a security fence along the U.S.-Mexico border. Adopted 228-198: R 228-0; D 0-197 (ND 0-147, SD 0-50); I 0-1. Feb. 10, 2005.

**28.** **HR 418. Immigration Standards/Asylum Provisions.** Nadler, D-N.Y., amendment that would strike the section of the bill modifying conditions for granting asylum to foreign nationals. Rejected 185-236: R 10-216; D 174-20 (ND 140-5, SD 34-15); I 1-0. Feb. 10, 2005.

**29.** **HR 418. Immigration Standards/Border Security.** Farr, D-Calif., amendment that would strike language in the bill that would authorize the Homeland Security secretary to waive laws impeding construction of physical barriers and roads designed to curb illegal border crossings, including the completion of a fortified fence along the U.S.-Mexico border close to San Diego, Calif. Rejected 179-243: R 8-220; D 170-23 (ND 137-7, SD 33-16); I 1-0. Feb. 10, 2005.

**30.** **HR 418. Immigration Standards/Recommit.** Reyes, D-Texas, motion to recommit the bill to the Judiciary Committee with instructions to add language stating that a state's motor vehicle database could not include any information that would conflict with rights guaranteed under the First, Second or 14th Amendments. Motion rejected 195-229: R 2-227; D 192-2 (ND 144-1, SD 48-1); I 1-0. Feb. 10, 2005.

**31.** **HR 418. Immigration Standards/Passage.** Passage of the bill that would tighten national standards for state driver's licenses and identity cards, make it more difficult for foreign nationals to claim asylum, and authorize the completion of a security fence along the U.S.-Mexico border. It would allow immigration judges to weigh the credibility of asylum applicants in a variety of proceedings and remove the annual cap of 10,000 refugees who may become permanent residents. Passed 261-161: R 219-8; D 42-152 (ND 18-127, SD 24-25); I 0-1. A "yea" was a vote in support of the president's position. Feb. 10, 2005.

| | 26 | 27 | 28 | 29 | 30 | 31 |
|---|---|---|---|---|---|---|
| **ALABAMA** | | | | | | |
| 1 Bonner | Y | Y | N | N | N | Y |
| 2 Everett | Y | Y | N | N | N | Y |
| 3 Rogers | Y | Y | N | N | N | Y |
| 4 Aderholt | Y | Y | N | N | N | Y |
| 5 Cramer | Y | N | N | N | Y | Y |
| 6 Bachus | Y | Y | N | N | N | Y |
| 7 Davis | Y | N | Y | N | Y | Y |
| **ALASKA** | | | | | | |
| AL Young | Y | Y | N | N | N | N |
| **ARIZONA** | | | | | | |
| 1 Renzi | Y | Y | N | N | N | Y |
| 2 Franks | Y | Y | N | N | N | Y |
| 3 Shadegg | Y | Y | N | N | N | Y |
| 4 Pastor | Y | N | Y | Y | Y | N |
| 5 Hayworth | Y | Y | N | N | N | Y |
| 6 Flake | Y | Y | N | N | N | Y |
| 7 Grijalva | Y | N | Y | Y | Y | N |
| 8 Kolbe | Y | Y | N | N | N | Y |
| **ARKANSAS** | | | | | | |
| 1 Berry | Y | N | N | N | Y | Y |
| 2 Snyder | ? | N | Y | Y | Y | N |
| 3 Boozman | Y | Y | N | N | N | Y |
| 4 Ross | Y | N | Y | Y | Y | Y |
| **CALIFORNIA** | | | | | | |
| 1 Thompson | Y | N | Y | Y | Y | N |
| 2 Herger | Y | Y | N | N | N | Y |
| 3 Lungren | Y | Y | N | N | N | Y |
| 4 Doolittle | Y | Y | N | N | N | Y |
| 5 Vacant | | | | | | |
| 6 Woolsey | Y | N | Y | Y | Y | N |
| 7 Miller, George | Y | N | Y | Y | Y | N |
| 8 Pelosi | Y | N | Y | Y | Y | N |
| 9 Lee | Y | N | Y | Y | Y | N |
| 10 Tauscher | Y | N | Y | Y | Y | N |
| 11 Pombo | Y | Y | N | N | N | N |
| 12 Lantos | Y | N | Y | Y | Y | N |
| 13 Stark | Y | N | Y | Y | Y | N |
| 14 Eshoo | ? | ? | ? | ? | ? | ? |
| 15 Honda | Y | N | + | + | + | - |
| 16 Lofgren | Y | N | Y | Y | Y | N |
| 17 Farr | Y | N | Y | Y | Y | N |
| 18 Cardoza | Y | N | Y | Y | Y | N |
| 19 Radanovich | Y | ? | N | N | N | Y |
| 20 Costa | Y | N | Y | N | Y | N |
| 21 Nunes | Y | Y | N | N | N | Y |
| 22 Thomas | Y | Y | N | N | N | Y |
| 23 Capps | Y | N | Y | Y | Y | N |
| 24 Gallegly | Y | Y | N | N | N | Y |
| 25 McKeon | Y | Y | N | N | N | Y |
| 26 Dreier | Y | Y | N | N | N | Y |
| 27 Sherman | Y | N | Y | Y | Y | N |
| 28 Berman | Y | N | Y | Y | Y | N |
| 29 Schiff | Y | N | Y | Y | Y | N |
| 30 Waxman | Y | N | Y | Y | Y | N |
| 31 Becerra | Y | N | Y | Y | Y | N |
| 32 Solis | Y | N | Y | Y | Y | N |
| 33 Watson | Y | N | Y | Y | Y | N |
| 34 Roybal-Allard | Y | N | Y | Y | Y | N |
| 35 Waters | Y | N | Y | Y | Y | N |
| 36 Harman | Y | N | Y | Y | Y | N |
| 37 Millender-McD. | Y | N | Y | Y | Y | N |
| 38 Napolitano | Y | N | Y | Y | Y | N |
| 39 Sánchez, Linda | Y | N | Y | Y | Y | N |
| 40 Royce | Y | Y | N | N | N | Y |
| 41 Lewis | Y | Y | N | N | N | Y |
| 42 Miller, Gary | Y | Y | N | N | N | Y |
| 43 Baca | Y | N | Y | Y | Y | N |
| 44 Calvert | Y | Y | N | N | N | Y |
| 45 Bono | Y | Y | N | N | N | Y |
| 46 Rohrabacher | Y | Y | N | N | N | Y |
| 47 Sanchez, Loretta | Y | N | ? | ? | ? | ? |
| 48 Cox | Y | Y | N | N | N | Y |
| 49 Issa | Y | Y | N | N | N | Y |
| 50 Cunningham | Y | Y | N | N | N | Y |
| 51 Filner | Y | N | Y | Y | Y | N |
| 52 Hunter | Y | Y | N | N | N | Y |
| 53 Davis | Y | N | Y | Y | Y | N |
| **COLORADO** | | | | | | |
| 1 DeGette | Y | N | Y | Y | Y | N |
| 2 Udall | Y | N | Y | Y | Y | N |
| 3 Salazar | Y | N | Y | Y | Y | Y |
| 4 Musgrave | Y | Y | N | N | N | Y |
| 5 Hefley | Y | Y | N | N | N | Y |
| 6 Tancredo | Y | Y | N | N | N | Y |
| 7 Beauprez | Y | Y | N | N | N | Y |
| **CONNECTICUT** | | | | | | |
| 1 Larson | Y | N | Y | Y | Y | N |
| 2 Simmons | Y | Y | N | N | N | Y |
| 3 DeLauro | Y | N | Y | Y | Y | N |
| 4 Shays | Y | Y | N | N | N | Y |
| 5 Johnson | ? | Y | N | N | N | Y |
| **DELAWARE** | | | | | | |
| AL Castle | Y | Y | N | N | N | Y |
| **FLORIDA** | | | | | | |
| 1 Miller | Y | Y | N | N | N | Y |
| 2 Boyd | Y | N | Y | Y | Y | Y |
| 3 Brown | Y | N | Y | Y | Y | N |
| 4 Crenshaw | Y | Y | N | N | N | Y |
| 5 Brown-Waite | Y | Y | N | N | N | Y |
| 6 Stearns | Y | Y | N | N | N | Y |
| 7 Mica | Y | Y | N | N | N | Y |
| 8 Keller | Y | Y | N | N | N | Y |
| 9 Bilirakis | Y | Y | N | N | N | Y |
| 10 Young | Y | Y | N | N | N | Y |
| 11 Davis | Y | N | Y | Y | Y | N |
| 12 Putnam | Y | Y | N | N | N | Y |
| 13 Harris | Y | Y | N | N | N | Y |
| 14 Mack | Y | Y | N | N | N | Y |
| 15 Weldon | Y | Y | N | N | N | Y |
| 16 Foley | Y | Y | N | N | N | Y |
| 17 Meek | Y | N | Y | Y | Y | N |
| 18 Ros-Lehtinen | ? | Y | N | N | N | Y |
| 19 Wexler | Y | N | Y | Y | Y | N |
| 20 Wasserman-Schultz | Y | N | Y | Y | Y | N |
| 21 Diaz-Balart, L. | Y | Y | N | N | N | Y |
| 22 Shaw | Y | Y | N | N | N | Y |
| 23 Hastings | Y | N | Y | Y | Y | N |
| 24 Feeney | ? | ? | ? | ? | ? | ? |
| 25 Diaz-Balart, M. | Y | Y | N | N | N | Y |
| **GEORGIA** | | | | | | |
| 1 Kingston | Y | Y | N | N | N | Y |
| 2 Bishop | Y | N | Y | N | Y | Y |
| 3 Marshall | Y | N | N | N | Y | Y |
| 4 McKinney | Y | N | Y | Y | Y | N |
| 5 Lewis | Y | N | Y | Y | Y | N |
| 6 Price | Y | Y | N | N | N | Y |
| 7 Linder | Y | Y | N | N | N | Y |
| 8 Westmoreland | Y | Y | N | N | N | Y |
| 9 Norwood | Y | Y | N | N | N | Y |
| 10 Deal | Y | Y | N | N | N | Y |
| 11 Gingrey | Y | Y | N | N | N | Y |
| 12 Barrow | Y | N | N | N | Y | Y |
| 13 Scott | Y | N | Y | Y | Y | N |
| **HAWAII** | | | | | | |
| 1 Abercrombie | Y | N | Y | Y | Y | N |
| 2 Case | Y | N | N | Y | N | Y |
| **IDAHO** | | | | | | |
| 1 Otter | Y | Y | N | N | N | Y |
| 2 Simpson | Y | Y | N | N | N | Y |
| **ILLINOIS** | | | | | | |
| 1 Rush | Y | N | Y | Y | Y | N |
| 2 Jackson | Y | N | Y | Y | Y | N |
| 3 Lipinski | Y | N | Y | Y | Y | N |
| 4 Gutierrez | Y | N | Y | Y | Y | N |
| 5 Emanuel | Y | N | Y | Y | Y | N |
| 6 Hyde | Y | Y | N | N | N | Y |
| 7 Davis | Y | N | Y | Y | Y | N |
| 8 Bean | Y | Y | Y | N | Y | Y |
| 9 Schakowsky | Y | N | Y | Y | Y | N |
| 10 Kirk | Y | Y | N | N | N | Y |
| 11 Weller | Y | Y | N | N | N | Y |
| 12 Costello | Y | N | Y | Y | Y | N |

**KEY**  Republicans  Democrats  *Independents*

| | | | |
|---|---|---|---|
| Y | Voted for (yea) | X | Paired against |
| # | Paired for | - | Announced against |
| + | Announced for | P | Voted "present" |
| N | Voted against (nay) | C | Voted "present" to avoid possible conflict of interest |
| | | ? | Did not vote or otherwise make a position known |

ND Northern Democrats, SD Southern Democrats
Southern states: Ala., Ark., Fla., Ga., Ky., La., Miss., N.C., Okla., S.C., Tenn., Texas, Va.

| | 26 | 27 | 28 | 29 | 30 | 31 |
|---|---|---|---|---|---|---|
| 13 **Biggert** | Y | Y | N | N | N | Y |
| 14 **Hastert** | | | | | | |
| 15 **Johnson** | Y | Y | Y | Y | N | Y |
| 16 **Manzullo** | Y | Y | N | N | N | Y |
| 17 Evans | Y | N | Y | Y | Y | N |
| 18 **LaHood** | Y | Y | N | N | N | Y |
| 19 **Shimkus** | Y | Y | N | N | N | Y |
| **INDIANA** | | | | | | |
| 1 Visclosky | Y | N | Y | Y | Y | N |
| 2 **Chocola** | Y | Y | N | N | N | Y |
| 3 **Souder** | Y | Y | N | N | N | Y |
| 4 **Buyer** | Y | Y | N | N | N | Y |
| 5 **Burton** | Y | Y | N | N | N | Y |
| 6 **Pence** | Y | Y | N | N | N | Y |
| 7 Carson | Y | N | Y | Y | Y | N |
| 8 **Hostettler** | Y | Y | N | N | N | Y |
| 9 **Sodrel** | Y | Y | N | N | N | Y |
| **IOWA** | | | | | | |
| 1 **Nussle** | Y | Y | N | N | N | Y |
| 2 **Leach** | Y | Y | Y | N | N | Y |
| 3 Boswell | Y | N | Y | Y | Y | N |
| 4 **Latham** | Y | Y | N | N | N | Y |
| 5 **King** | Y | Y | N | N | N | Y |
| **KANSAS** | | | | | | |
| 1 **Moran** | Y | Y | N | N | N | Y |
| 2 **Ryun** | Y | Y | N | N | N | Y |
| 3 Moore | Y | N | Y | Y | Y | N |
| 4 **Tiahrt** | Y | Y | N | N | N | Y |
| **KENTUCKY** | | | | | | |
| 1 **Whitfield** | Y | Y | N | N | N | Y |
| 2 **Lewis** | Y | Y | N | N | N | Y |
| 3 **Northup** | Y | Y | N | N | N | Y |
| 4 **Davis** | Y | Y | N | N | N | Y |
| 5 **Rogers** | Y | Y | N | N | N | Y |
| 6 Chandler | Y | N | N | N | Y | Y |
| **LOUISIANA** | | | | | | |
| 1 **Jindal** | Y | Y | N | N | N | Y |
| 2 Jefferson | Y | N | N | Y | Y | N |
| 3 Melancon | Y | N | N | N | Y | Y |
| 4 **McCrery** | Y | Y | N | N | N | Y |
| 5 **Alexander** | Y | Y | N | N | N | Y |
| 6 **Baker** | Y | Y | N | N | N | Y |
| 7 **Boustany** | Y | Y | N | N | N | Y |
| **MAINE** | | | | | | |
| 1 Allen | Y | N | Y | Y | Y | N |
| 2 Michaud | Y | N | Y | Y | Y | N |
| **MARYLAND** | | | | | | |
| 1 **Gilchrest** | Y | Y | N | N | N | Y |
| 2 Ruppersberger | Y | N | Y | Y | Y | N |
| 3 Cardin | Y | N | Y | Y | Y | N |
| 4 Wynn | Y | N | Y | Y | Y | N |
| 5 Hoyer | Y | N | Y | Y | Y | N |
| 6 **Bartlett** | Y | Y | Y | N | N | ? |
| 7 Cummings | Y | N | Y | Y | Y | N |
| 8 Van Hollen | Y | N | Y | Y | Y | N |
| **MASSACHUSETTS** | | | | | | |
| 1 Olver | Y | N | Y | Y | Y | N |
| 2 Neal | Y | N | Y | Y | Y | N |
| 3 McGovern | Y | N | Y | Y | Y | N |
| 4 Frank | Y | N | Y | Y | Y | N |
| 5 Meehan | Y | N | Y | Y | Y | N |
| 6 Tierney | Y | N | Y | Y | Y | N |
| 7 Markey | Y | N | Y | Y | Y | N |
| 8 Capuano | Y | N | Y | Y | Y | N |
| 9 Lynch | Y | N | Y | Y | Y | N |
| 10 Delahunt | Y | N | Y | Y | Y | N |
| **MICHIGAN** | | | | | | |
| 1 Stupak | ? | ? | ? | ? | ? | ? |
| 2 **Hoekstra** | Y | Y | N | N | N | Y |
| 3 **Ehlers** | Y | Y | N | Y | N | Y |
| 4 **Camp** | Y | Y | N | N | N | Y |
| 5 Kildee | Y | N | Y | Y | Y | N |
| 6 **Upton** | Y | Y | N | N | N | Y |
| 7 **Schwarz** | Y | Y | N | N | N | Y |
| 8 **Rogers** | Y | Y | N | N | N | Y |
| 9 **Knollenberg** | Y | Y | N | N | N | Y |
| 10 **Miller** | Y | Y | N | N | N | Y |
| 11 **McCotter** | Y | Y | N | N | N | Y |
| 12 Levin | Y | N | Y | Y | Y | N |
| 13 Kilpatrick | Y | N | Y | Y | Y | N |
| 14 Conyers | Y | N | Y | Y | Y | N |
| 15 Dingell | Y | N | Y | Y | Y | N |

| | 26 | 27 | 28 | 29 | 30 | 31 |
|---|---|---|---|---|---|---|
| **MINNESOTA** | | | | | | |
| 1 **Gutknecht** | Y | Y | N | N | N | Y |
| 2 **Kline** | Y | Y | N | N | N | Y |
| 3 **Ramstad** | Y | Y | N | N | N | Y |
| 4 McCollum | Y | N | Y | Y | Y | N |
| 5 Sabo | Y | N | Y | Y | Y | N |
| 6 **Kennedy** | Y | Y | N | N | N | Y |
| 7 Peterson | Y | N | N | Y | Y | Y |
| 8 Oberstar | Y | N | Y | Y | Y | N |
| **MISSISSIPPI** | | | | | | |
| 1 **Wicker** | Y | Y | N | N | N | Y |
| 2 Thompson | Y | N | Y | Y | Y | N |
| 3 **Pickering** | Y | Y | ? | N | N | Y |
| 4 Taylor | Y | N | N | N | Y | Y |
| **MISSOURI** | | | | | | |
| 1 Clay | Y | N | Y | Y | Y | N |
| 2 **Akin** | Y | Y | N | N | N | Y |
| 3 Carnahan | Y | N | Y | Y | Y | N |
| 4 Skelton | Y | N | N | Y | Y | N |
| 5 Cleaver | Y | N | Y | Y | Y | N |
| 6 **Graves** | Y | Y | N | N | N | Y |
| 7 **Blunt** | Y | Y | N | N | N | Y |
| 8 **Emerson** | Y | Y | N | N | N | Y |
| 9 **Hulshof** | Y | Y | N | N | N | Y |
| **MONTANA** | | | | | | |
| AL **Rehberg** | Y | Y | N | N | N | Y |
| **NEBRASKA** | | | | | | |
| 1 **Fortenberry** | Y | Y | N | N | N | Y |
| 2 **Terry** | Y | Y | N | N | N | Y |
| 3 **Osborne** | Y | Y | N | N | N | Y |
| **NEVADA** | | | | | | |
| 1 Berkley | Y | N | Y | Y | Y | N |
| 2 **Gibbons** | Y | Y | N | N | N | Y |
| 3 **Porter** | Y | Y | N | N | N | Y |
| **NEW HAMPSHIRE** | | | | | | |
| 1 **Bradley** | Y | Y | N | N | N | Y |
| 2 **Bass** | Y | Y | – | N | N | Y |
| **NEW JERSEY** | | | | | | |
| 1 Andrews | Y | N | Y | Y | Y | N |
| 2 **LoBiondo** | Y | Y | N | Y | N | Y |
| 3 **Saxton** | Y | Y | N | Y | N | Y |
| 4 **Smith** | Y | Y | Y | N | N | N |
| 5 **Garrett** | Y | Y | N | N | N | Y |
| 6 Pallone | Y | N | Y | Y | Y | N |
| 7 **Ferguson** | Y | Y | N | N | N | + |
| 8 Pascrell | Y | N | Y | Y | Y | N |
| 9 Rothman | Y | N | Y | Y | Y | N |
| 10 Payne | Y | N | Y | Y | Y | N |
| 11 **Frelinghuysen** | Y | Y | N | N | N | Y |
| 12 Holt | Y | N | Y | Y | Y | N |
| 13 Menendez | Y | N | Y | Y | Y | N |
| **NEW MEXICO** | | | | | | |
| 1 **Wilson** | Y | Y | Y | Y | N | N |
| 2 **Pearce** | Y | Y | N | N | N | Y |
| 3 Udall | Y | N | Y | Y | Y | N |
| **NEW YORK** | | | | | | |
| 1 Bishop | Y | N | Y | Y | Y | N |
| 2 Israel | Y | N | Y | Y | Y | N |
| 3 **King** | Y | Y | N | N | N | Y |
| 4 McCarthy | Y | N | Y | Y | Y | N |
| 5 Ackerman | Y | N | Y | Y | Y | N |
| 6 Meeks | Y | N | Y | Y | Y | N |
| 7 Crowley | Y | N | Y | Y | Y | N |
| 8 Nadler | Y | N | Y | Y | Y | N |
| 9 Weiner | Y | N | Y | ? | Y | N |
| 10 Towns | Y | N | Y | Y | Y | N |
| 11 Owens | Y | N | Y | Y | Y | N |
| 12 Velázquez | Y | N | Y | Y | Y | N |
| 13 **Fossella** | Y | Y | N | N | N | Y |
| 14 Maloney | Y | N | Y | Y | Y | N |
| 15 Rangel | Y | N | Y | Y | Y | N |
| 16 Serrano | Y | N | Y | Y | Y | N |
| 17 Engel | Y | N | Y | Y | Y | N |
| 18 Lowey | Y | N | Y | Y | Y | N |
| 19 **Kelly** | Y | Y | N | N | N | Y |
| 20 **Sweeney** | Y | Y | N | N | N | Y |
| 21 McNulty | Y | N | Y | N | Y | Y |
| 22 Hinchey | ? | ? | ? | ? | ? | ? |
| 23 **McHugh** | ? | Y | N | N | N | Y |
| 24 **Boehlert** | Y | Y | N | Y | N | Y |
| 25 **Walsh** | Y | Y | Y | N | N | Y |
| 26 **Reynolds** | Y | Y | N | N | N | Y |
| 27 Higgins | Y | N | Y | Y | Y | N |
| 28 Slaughter | Y | N | Y | Y | Y | N |
| 29 **Kuhl** | Y | Y | N | N | N | Y |

| | 26 | 27 | 28 | 29 | 30 | 31 |
|---|---|---|---|---|---|---|
| **NORTH CAROLINA** | | | | | | |
| 1 Butterfield | Y | N | Y | Y | Y | Y |
| 2 Etheridge | Y | N | Y | Y | Y | N |
| 3 **Jones** | Y | Y | N | N | N | Y |
| 4 Price | Y | N | Y | Y | Y | N |
| 5 **Foxx** | Y | Y | N | N | N | Y |
| 6 **Coble** | Y | Y | N | N | N | Y |
| 7 McIntyre | Y | N | Y | N | Y | Y |
| 8 **Hayes** | Y | Y | N | N | N | Y |
| 9 **Myrick** | Y | Y | N | N | N | Y |
| 10 **McHenry** | Y | Y | N | N | N | Y |
| 11 **Taylor** | Y | Y | N | N | N | Y |
| 12 Watt | Y | N | Y | Y | Y | N |
| 13 Miller | Y | N | Y | Y | Y | N |
| **NORTH DAKOTA** | | | | | | |
| AL Pomeroy | Y | N | Y | Y | Y | N |
| **OHIO** | | | | | | |
| 1 **Chabot** | Y | Y | N | N | N | Y |
| 2 **Portman** | Y | Y | N | N | N | Y |
| 3 **Turner** | Y | Y | N | N | N | Y |
| 4 **Oxley** | Y | Y | ? | ? | N | Y |
| 5 **Gillmor** | Y | Y | N | N | N | Y |
| 6 Strickland | Y | N | Y | Y | Y | Y |
| 7 **Hobson** | Y | Y | N | N | N | Y |
| 8 **Boehner** | Y | Y | N | N | N | Y |
| 9 Kaptur | Y | N | Y | Y | Y | N |
| 10 Kucinich | ? | N | Y | Y | Y | N |
| 11 Jones | Y | N | Y | Y | Y | N |
| 12 **Tiberi** | Y | Y | N | N | N | Y |
| 13 Brown | Y | N | Y | Y | Y | N |
| 14 **LaTourette** | Y | Y | N | N | N | Y |
| 15 **Pryce** | Y | Y | N | N | N | Y |
| 16 **Regula** | Y | Y | N | N | N | Y |
| 17 Ryan | Y | N | Y | Y | Y | Y |
| 18 **Ney** | Y | Y | N | N | N | Y |
| **OKLAHOMA** | | | | | | |
| 1 **Sullivan** | Y | Y | N | N | N | Y |
| 2 Boren | Y | N | N | N | Y | Y |
| 3 **Lucas** | Y | Y | N | N | N | Y |
| 4 **Cole** | Y | Y | N | N | N | Y |
| 5 **Istook** | Y | Y | N | N | N | Y |
| **OREGON** | | | | | | |
| 1 Wu | Y | N | Y | Y | Y | N |
| 2 **Walden** | Y | Y | N | N | N | Y |
| 3 Blumenauer | Y | N | Y | Y | Y | N |
| 4 DeFazio | Y | N | Y | Y | Y | Y |
| 5 Hooley | Y | N | Y | Y | Y | Y |
| **PENNSYLVANIA** | | | | | | |
| 1 Brady | Y | N | Y | Y | Y | N |
| 2 Fattah | ? | N | Y | Y | Y | N |
| 3 **English** | Y | Y | N | N | N | Y |
| 4 **Hart** | Y | Y | N | N | N | Y |
| 5 **Peterson** | Y | Y | N | N | N | Y |
| 6 **Gerlach** | Y | Y | N | N | N | Y |
| 7 **Weldon** | Y | Y | N | N | N | Y |
| 8 **Fitzpatrick** | Y | Y | N | N | N | Y |
| 9 **Shuster** | Y | Y | N | N | N | Y |
| 10 **Sherwood** | Y | Y | N | N | N | Y |
| 11 Kanjorski | Y | N | Y | Y | Y | Y |
| 12 Murtha | Y | N | Y | Y | Y | N |
| 13 Schwartz | Y | N | Y | Y | Y | N |
| 14 Doyle | Y | N | Y | Y | Y | N |
| 15 **Dent** | Y | Y | N | N | N | Y |
| 16 **Pitts** | Y | Y | N | N | N | Y |
| 17 Holden | Y | N | N | N | Y | Y |
| 18 **Murphy** | Y | Y | N | N | N | Y |
| 19 **Platts** | Y | Y | N | N | N | Y |
| **RHODE ISLAND** | | | | | | |
| 1 Kennedy | Y | N | Y | Y | Y | N |
| 2 Langevin | Y | N | Y | Y | Y | N |
| **SOUTH CAROLINA** | | | | | | |
| 1 **Brown** | Y | Y | N | N | N | Y |
| 2 **Wilson** | Y | Y | N | N | N | Y |
| 3 **Barrett** | Y | Y | N | N | N | Y |
| 4 **Inglis** | Y | Y | N | N | N | Y |
| 5 Spratt | Y | N | Y | Y | Y | N |
| 6 Clyburn | Y | N | Y | Y | Y | N |
| **SOUTH DAKOTA** | | | | | | |
| AL Herseth | Y | N | Y | N | Y | Y |
| **TENNESSEE** | | | | | | |
| 1 **Jenkins** | Y | Y | N | N | N | Y |
| 2 **Duncan** | Y | Y | N | N | Y | Y |

| | 26 | 27 | 28 | 29 | 30 | 31 |
|---|---|---|---|---|---|---|
| 3 **Wamp** | Y | Y | N | N | N | Y |
| 4 Davis | Y | N | N | N | N | Y |
| 5 Cooper | Y | N | N | N | Y | Y |
| 6 Gordon | Y | N | N | Y | Y | Y |
| 7 **Blackburn** | Y | Y | N | N | N | Y |
| 8 Tanner | Y | N | N | Y | Y | Y |
| 9 Ford | Y | N | N | Y | Y | Y |
| **TEXAS** | | | | | | |
| 1 **Gohmert** | Y | Y | N | N | N | Y |
| 2 **Poe** | Y | Y | N | N | N | Y |
| 3 **Johnson, S.** | Y | Y | N | N | N | Y |
| 4 **Hall** | Y | Y | N | N | N | Y |
| 5 **Hensarling** | Y | Y | N | N | N | Y |
| 6 **Barton** | Y | Y | N | N | N | Y |
| 7 **Culberson** | Y | Y | N | N | N | Y |
| 8 **Brady** | Y | Y | N | N | N | Y |
| 9 Green, A. | Y | N | Y | Y | Y | N |
| 10 **McCaul** | Y | Y | N | N | N | Y |
| 11 **Conaway** | Y | Y | N | N | N | Y |
| 12 **Granger** | Y | Y | N | N | N | Y |
| 13 **Thornberry** | Y | Y | N | N | N | Y |
| 14 **Paul** | Y | Y | N | Y | Y | N |
| 15 Hinojosa | + | – | + | + | + | – |
| 16 Reyes | Y | N | Y | N | Y | N |
| 17 Edwards | Y | N | N | Y | Y | Y |
| 18 Jackson-Lee | Y | N | Y | Y | Y | N |
| 19 **Neugebauer** | Y | Y | N | N | N | Y |
| 20 Gonzalez | Y | N | Y | Y | Y | N |
| 21 **Smith** | Y | Y | N | N | N | Y |
| 22 **DeLay** | Y | Y | N | N | N | Y |
| 23 **Bonilla** | Y | Y | N | N | N | Y |
| 24 **Marchant** | Y | Y | N | N | N | Y |
| 25 Doggett | Y | N | Y | Y | Y | N |
| 26 **Burgess** | Y | Y | N | N | N | Y |
| 27 Ortiz | Y | N | Y | Y | Y | N |
| 28 Cuellar | Y | N | Y | Y | Y | Y |
| 29 Green, G. | Y | N | ? | ? | ? | ? |
| 30 Johnson, E. | Y | N | Y | Y | Y | N |
| 31 **Carter** | Y | ? | – | – | – | + |
| 32 **Sessions** | Y | Y | N | N | N | Y |
| **UTAH** | | | | | | |
| 1 **Bishop** | Y | Y | N | N | N | Y |
| 2 Matheson | Y | N | N | N | Y | Y |
| 3 **Cannon** | Y | Y | N | N | N | Y |
| **VERMONT** | | | | | | |
| AL *Sanders* | Y | N | Y | Y | Y | N |
| **VIRGINIA** | | | | | | |
| 1 **Davis, J.** | Y | Y | N | N | N | Y |
| 2 **Drake** | Y | Y | N | N | N | Y |
| 3 Scott | Y | N | Y | Y | Y | N |
| 4 **Forbes** | Y | Y | N | N | N | Y |
| 5 **Goode** | Y | Y | N | N | N | Y |
| 6 **Goodlatte** | Y | Y | N | N | N | Y |
| 7 **Cantor** | Y | Y | N | N | N | Y |
| 8 Moran | Y | N | Y | Y | Y | N |
| 9 Boucher | Y | N | Y | N | Y | Y |
| 10 **Wolf** | Y | Y | N | N | N | Y |
| 11 **Davis, T.** | Y | Y | N | N | N | Y |
| **WASHINGTON** | | | | | | |
| 1 Inslee | Y | N | Y | Y | Y | N |
| 2 Larsen | Y | N | Y | Y | Y | N |
| 3 Baird | Y | N | Y | Y | Y | N |
| 4 **Hastings** | Y | Y | N | N | N | Y |
| 5 **McMorris** | Y | Y | N | N | N | Y |
| 6 Dicks | Y | N | Y | Y | Y | N |
| 7 McDermott | Y | N | Y | Y | Y | N |
| 8 **Reichert** | Y | Y | N | N | N | Y |
| 9 Smith | Y | N | Y | Y | Y | N |
| **WEST VIRGINIA** | | | | | | |
| 1 Mollohan | Y | N | Y | Y | Y | N |
| 2 **Capito** | Y | Y | N | N | N | Y |
| 3 Rahall | Y | N | Y | Y | Y | N |
| **WISCONSIN** | | | | | | |
| 1 **Ryan** | Y | Y | N | N | N | Y |
| 2 Baldwin | Y | N | Y | Y | Y | N |
| 3 Kind | Y | N | Y | Y | Y | N |
| 4 Moore | Y | N | Y | Y | Y | N |
| 5 **Sensenbrenner** | Y | Y | N | N | N | Y |
| 6 **Petri** | Y | Y | N | N | N | Y |
| 7 Obey | Y | N | Y | Y | Y | N |
| 8 **Green** | Y | Y | N | N | N | Y |
| **WYOMING** | | | | | | |
| AL **Cubin** | Y | Y | N | N | N | Y |

# IN THE HOUSE | By Vote Number

**32.** **H Con Res 25. Greensboro Four Tribute/Adoption.** Dent, R-Pa., motion to suspend the rules and adopt the concurrent resolution that would applaud the valor and courage of four African-American college freshmen, known as the "Greensboro Four," who challenged segregation in Greensboro, N.C., on Feb. 1, 1960. Motion agreed to 424-0: R 228-0; D 195-0 (ND 144-0, SD 51-0); I 1-0. A two-thirds majority of those present and voting (283 in this case) is required for adoption under suspension of the rules. Feb. 15, 2005.

**33.** **HR 324. Arthur Stacey Mastrapa Post Office/Passage.** Dent, R-Pa., motion to suspend the rules and pass the bill that would designate a post office in Altamonte Springs, Fla., for Arthur Stacey Mastrapa, a postal worker and Army Reservist killed in Iraq. Motion agreed to 420-0: R 228-0; D 191-0 (ND 140-0, SD 51-0); I 1-0. A two-thirds majority of those present and voting (280 in this case) is required for passage under suspension of the rules. Feb. 15, 2005.

**34.** **HR 310. Broadcast Indecency/Previous Question.** Capito, R-W.Va., motion to order the previous question (thus ending debate and possibility of amendment) on adoption of the rule (H Res 95) to provide for House floor consideration of the bill that would increase the maximum fines for sexually explicit or vulgar broadcast programming. Motion agreed to 230-198: R 229-0; D 1-197 (ND 1-146, SD 0-51); I 0-1. Subsequently, the rule was adopted by voice vote. Feb. 16, 2005.

**35.** **HR 310. Broadcast Indecency/Passage.** Passage of the bill that would increase to $500,000 per violation the maximum fines that the Federal Communications Commission (FCC) could levy on broadcasters for airing indecent, obscene or profane material. The bill would require the FCC to consider revoking a license after three or more indecency-related offenses. Passed 389-38: R 228-1; D 161-36 (ND 114-32, SD 47-4); I 0-1. A "yea" was a vote in support of the president's position. Feb. 16, 2005.

**36** **S 5. Class Action Overhaul/Substitute.** Conyers, D-Mich., substitute amendment to the bill that would give federal courts jurisdiction over certain class action cases. It would allow for several exemptions and would prohibit federal district courts from denying certification of a class action suit if the laws of more than one state apply. Rejected 178-247: R 0-228; D 177-19 (ND 140-5, SD 37-14); I 1-0. Feb. 17, 2005.

**37.** **S 5. Class Action Overhaul/Motion to Commit.** Brown, D-Ohio, motion to commit the bill to the Judiciary Committee with instructions to add language specifying that the term "class action" does not include suits arising from the use of the drug Vioxx. Motion rejected 175-249: R 0-227; D 174-22 (ND 138-7, SD 36-15); I 1-0. Feb. 17, 2005.

**38.** **S 5. Class Action Overhaul/Passage.** Passage of the bill that would give federal courts jurisdiction over class action cases involving at least 100 plaintiffs if at least $5 million was at stake and two-thirds of the plaintiffs lived in different states. It would require judges to review all non-cash settlements and limit attorney's fees in such settlements. Passed 279-149: R 229-1; D 50-147 (ND 27-119, SD 23-28); I 0-1. A "yea" was a vote in support of the president's position. Feb. 17, 2005.

**39.** **H Res 91. Rafik Hariri Tribute/Adoption.** Issa, R-Calif., motion to suspend the rules and adopt the resolution that would condemn the killing of the former Lebanese prime minister in Beirut on Feb. 14, 2005. A two-thirds majority of those present and voting (273 in this case) is required for adoption under suspension of the rules. Motion agreed to 409-0: R 222-0; D 187-0 (ND 137-0, SD 50-0); I 0-0. Feb. 17, 2005.

ND Northern Democrats, SD Southern Democrats
Southern states: Ala., Ark., Fla., Ga., Ky., La., Miss., N.C., Okla., S.C., Tenn., Texas, Va.

| | 32 | 33 | 34 | 35 | 36 | 37 | 38 | 39 |
|---|---|---|---|---|---|---|---|---|
| **ALABAMA** | | | | | | | | |
| 1 Bonner | Y | Y | Y | Y | N | N | Y | Y |
| 2 Everett | Y | Y | Y | Y | N | N | Y | Y |
| 3 Rogers | Y | Y | Y | Y | N | N | Y | Y |
| 4 Aderholt | Y | Y | Y | Y | N | N | Y | Y |
| 5 Cramer | Y | Y | N | Y | N | N | Y | Y |
| 6 Bachus | Y | Y | Y | Y | N | N | Y | Y |
| 7 Davis | Y | Y | N | Y | Y | N | Y | Y |
| **ALASKA** | | | | | | | | |
| AL Young | Y | Y | Y | Y | N | N | Y | Y |
| **ARIZONA** | | | | | | | | |
| 1 Renzi | Y | Y | Y | Y | N | N | Y | Y |
| 2 Franks | Y | Y | Y | Y | N | N | Y | Y |
| 3 Shadegg | Y | Y | Y | Y | N | ? | Y | Y |
| 4 Pastor | Y | Y | N | Y | Y | Y | N | Y |
| 5 Hayworth | Y | Y | Y | Y | N | N | Y | Y |
| 6 Flake | Y | Y | Y | Y | N | N | Y | Y |
| 7 Grijalva | Y | Y | N | N | Y | Y | N | Y |
| 8 Kolbe | Y | Y | Y | Y | N | N | Y | Y |
| **ARKANSAS** | | | | | | | | |
| 1 Berry | Y | Y | N | Y | Y | Y | Y | Y |
| 2 Snyder | Y | Y | N | Y | Y | Y | N | Y |
| 3 Boozman | Y | Y | Y | Y | N | N | Y | Y |
| 4 Ross | Y | Y | N | Y | Y | Y | N | Y |
| **CALIFORNIA** | | | | | | | | |
| 1 Thompson | Y | Y | N | Y | Y | Y | N | Y |
| 2 Herger | Y | Y | Y | Y | N | N | Y | Y |
| 3 Lungren | Y | Y | Y | Y | N | N | Y | Y |
| 4 Doolittle | Y | Y | Y | Y | N | N | N | Y |
| 5 Vacant | | | | | | | | |
| 6 Woolsey | Y | Y | N | Y | Y | Y | N | Y |
| 7 Miller, George | Y | Y | N | Y | Y | Y | N | Y |
| 8 Pelosi | Y | Y | Y | Y | Y | Y | N | Y |
| 9 Lee | Y | Y | N | N | Y | Y | N | Y |
| 10 Tauscher | Y | Y | N | Y | Y | Y | N | Y |
| 11 Pombo | Y | Y | Y | Y | N | N | Y | Y |
| 12 Lantos | Y | Y | N | Y | Y | Y | N | Y |
| 13 Stark | ? | ? | N | N | Y | Y | N | Y |
| 14 Eshoo | ? | ? | ? | ? | ? | ? | ? | ? |
| 15 Honda | Y | Y | N | N | Y | Y | N | Y |
| 16 Lofgren | Y | Y | N | Y | Y | Y | N | Y |
| 17 Farr | Y | Y | N | N | ? | ? | ? | ? |
| 18 Cardoza | Y | Y | N | Y | Y | Y | N | Y |
| 19 Radanovich | Y | Y | Y | Y | N | N | Y | ? |
| 20 Costa | Y | Y | N | Y | Y | Y | Y | Y |
| 21 Nunes | Y | Y | Y | Y | N | N | Y | Y |
| 22 Thomas | Y | Y | Y | ? | N | N | Y | Y |
| 23 Capps | Y | Y | N | Y | Y | Y | N | Y |
| 24 Gallegly | Y | Y | Y | Y | N | N | Y | ? |
| 25 McKeon | Y | Y | Y | Y | N | N | Y | Y |
| 26 Dreier | Y | Y | Y | Y | N | N | Y | Y |
| 27 Sherman | Y | Y | N | Y | Y | Y | N | Y |
| 28 Berman | Y | Y | N | Y | Y | Y | N | Y |
| 29 Schiff | Y | Y | N | Y | Y | Y | N | Y |
| 30 Waxman | Y | Y | N | Y | Y | Y | N | Y |
| 31 Becerra | Y | Y | N | Y | Y | Y | N | Y |
| 32 Solis | Y | Y | N | Y | Y | Y | N | Y |
| 33 Watson | Y | Y | N | N | Y | Y | N | Y |
| 34 Roybal-Allard | Y | Y | N | Y | Y | Y | N | Y |
| 35 Waters | ? | ? | N | N | Y | Y | N | ? |
| 36 Harman | Y | Y | N | Y | Y | Y | Y | Y |
| 37 Millender-McD. | Y | Y | N | Y | Y | Y | N | Y |
| 38 Napolitano | Y | Y | N | Y | Y | Y | N | Y |
| 39 Sánchez, Linda | Y | Y | N | Y | Y | Y | N | Y |
| 40 Royce | Y | Y | Y | Y | N | N | Y | Y |
| 41 Lewis | Y | Y | Y | Y | N | N | Y | Y |
| 42 Miller, Gary | Y | Y | Y | Y | N | N | Y | Y |
| 43 Baca | Y | Y | N | Y | Y | Y | N | Y |
| 44 Calvert | Y | Y | Y | Y | N | N | Y | Y |
| 45 Bono | Y | Y | Y | Y | N | N | Y | Y |
| 46 Rohrabacher | Y | Y | Y | Y | N | N | Y | Y |
| 47 Sanchez, Loretta | Y | Y | N | Y | Y | Y | N | ? |
| 48 Cox | Y | Y | Y | N | ? | Y | Y | Y |
| 49 Issa | Y | Y | Y | Y | N | N | Y | Y |

| | 32 | 33 | 34 | 35 | 36 | 37 | 38 | 39 |
|---|---|---|---|---|---|---|---|---|
| 50 Cunningham | Y | Y | Y | Y | N | N | Y | Y |
| 51 Filner | Y | Y | N | Y | Y | Y | N | Y |
| 52 Hunter | Y | Y | Y | Y | N | N | Y | Y |
| 53 Davis | Y | Y | N | Y | Y | Y | N | Y |
| **COLORADO** | | | | | | | | |
| 1 DeGette | Y | ? | N | Y | Y | Y | N | Y |
| 2 Udall | Y | Y | N | Y | Y | N | N | Y |
| 3 Salazar | Y | Y | N | Y | Y | Y | N | Y |
| 4 Musgrave | Y | Y | Y | Y | N | N | Y | Y |
| 5 Hefley | Y | Y | Y | Y | N | N | Y | Y |
| 6 Tancredo | Y | Y | Y | Y | N | N | Y | Y |
| 7 Beauprez | Y | Y | Y | Y | N | N | Y | Y |
| **CONNECTICUT** | | | | | | | | |
| 1 Larson | Y | Y | N | Y | Y | Y | N | Y |
| 2 Simmons | Y | Y | N | Y | N | N | Y | Y |
| 3 DeLauro | Y | Y | N | Y | Y | Y | N | Y |
| 4 Shays | Y | Y | Y | Y | N | N | Y | Y |
| 5 Johnson | Y | Y | Y | Y | N | N | Y | Y |
| **DELAWARE** | | | | | | | | |
| AL Castle | Y | Y | Y | Y | N | N | Y | Y |
| **FLORIDA** | | | | | | | | |
| 1 Miller | ? | ? | Y | Y | N | N | Y | Y |
| 2 Boyd | Y | Y | N | Y | N | N | Y | Y |
| 3 Brown | Y | Y | N | Y | Y | Y | N | Y |
| 4 Crenshaw | Y | Y | Y | Y | N | N | Y | Y |
| 5 Brown-Waite | Y | Y | Y | Y | N | N | Y | Y |
| 6 Stearns | Y | Y | Y | Y | N | N | Y | Y |
| 7 Mica | Y | Y | Y | Y | N | N | Y | Y |
| 8 Keller | Y | Y | Y | Y | N | N | Y | Y |
| 9 Bilirakis | Y | Y | Y | N | N | N | Y | Y |
| 10 Young | Y | Y | Y | ? | N | N | Y | Y |
| 11 Davis | Y | Y | N | Y | Y | Y | N | Y |
| 12 Putnam | Y | Y | Y | Y | N | N | Y | Y |
| 13 Harris | Y | Y | Y | Y | N | N | Y | Y |
| 14 Mack | Y | Y | Y | Y | N | N | Y | Y |
| 15 Weldon | Y | Y | Y | Y | N | N | Y | Y |
| 16 Foley | Y | Y | Y | Y | N | N | Y | Y |
| 17 Meek | Y | Y | N | Y | Y | Y | N | Y |
| 18 Ros-Lehtinen | Y | Y | N | Y | N | N | Y | Y |
| 19 Wexler | Y | Y | N | Y | Y | Y | N | Y |
| 20 Wasserman-Schultz | Y | Y | N | N | Y | Y | N | Y |
| 21 Diaz-Balart, L. | Y | Y | Y | Y | N | N | Y | Y |
| 22 Shaw | Y | Y | Y | Y | N | N | Y | Y |
| 23 Hastings | Y | Y | N | N | Y | Y | N | Y |
| 24 Feeney | Y | Y | Y | Y | N | N | Y | ? |
| 25 Diaz-Balart, M. | Y | Y | Y | Y | N | N | Y | Y |
| **GEORGIA** | | | | | | | | |
| 1 Kingston | Y | Y | Y | Y | N | N | Y | Y |
| 2 Bishop | Y | Y | N | Y | Y | Y | N | Y |
| 3 Marshall | Y | Y | N | Y | N | N | Y | Y |
| 4 McKinney | Y | Y | Y | Y | Y | Y | N | Y |
| 5 Lewis | Y | Y | N | N | Y | Y | N | Y |
| 6 Price | Y | Y | Y | Y | N | N | Y | Y |
| 7 Linder | Y | Y | Y | Y | N | N | Y | Y |
| 8 Westmoreland | Y | Y | Y | Y | N | N | Y | Y |
| 9 Norwood | Y | Y | Y | Y | N | N | Y | Y |
| 10 Deal | Y | Y | Y | Y | N | N | Y | Y |
| 11 Gingrey | Y | Y | Y | Y | N | N | Y | Y |
| 12 Barrow | Y | Y | N | Y | Y | N | Y | Y |
| 13 Scott | Y | Y | N | Y | N | N | Y | Y |
| **HAWAII** | | | | | | | | |
| 1 Abercrombie | Y | Y | N | N | Y | Y | N | Y |
| 2 Case | Y | Y | N | Y | N | N | Y | Y |
| **IDAHO** | | | | | | | | |
| 1 Otter | Y | Y | Y | Y | N | N | Y | Y |
| 2 Simpson | Y | Y | Y | Y | N | N | Y | Y |
| **ILLINOIS** | | | | | | | | |
| 1 Rush | Y | Y | N | Y | Y | Y | N | Y |
| 2 Jackson | Y | Y | N | Y | Y | Y | N | Y |
| 3 Lipinski | Y | Y | Y | Y | Y | Y | N | Y |
| 4 Gutierrez | Y | Y | N | Y | Y | Y | N | Y |
| 5 Emanuel | Y | Y | N | Y | Y | Y | Y | Y |
| 6 Hyde | Y | Y | Y | Y | N | N | Y | Y |
| 7 Davis | Y | Y | N | Y | ? | Y | N | Y |
| 8 Bean | Y | Y | N | Y | N | N | Y | Y |
| 9 Schakowsky | Y | Y | N | N | Y | Y | N | Y |
| 10 Kirk | Y | Y | Y | Y | N | N | Y | ? |
| 11 Weller | Y | Y | Y | Y | N | N | Y | Y |
| 12 Costello | Y | Y | N | Y | Y | Y | Y | Y |

| | 32 | 33 | 34 | 35 | 36 | 37 | 38 | 39 |
|---|---|---|---|---|---|---|---|---|
| 13 **Biggert** | Y | Y | Y | Y | N | N | Y | Y |
| 14 **Hastert** | | | | | N | N | Y | |
| 15 **Johnson** | Y | Y | Y | Y | N | N | Y | Y |
| 16 **Manzullo** | Y | Y | Y | Y | N | N | Y | Y |
| 17 Evans | Y | Y | N | Y | Y | Y | N | Y |
| 18 **LaHood** | Y | Y | Y | Y | N | N | Y | Y |
| 19 **Shimkus** | Y | Y | Y | Y | N | N | Y | Y |
| **INDIANA** | | | | | | | | |
| 1 Visclosky | Y | Y | N | Y | Y | Y | N | Y |
| 2 **Chocola** | Y | Y | Y | Y | N | N | Y | Y |
| 3 **Souder** | Y | Y | Y | Y | N | N | Y | Y |
| 4 **Buyer** | Y | Y | Y | Y | N | ? | Y | Y |
| 5 **Burton** | Y | Y | Y | Y | N | N | Y | Y |
| 6 **Pence** | Y | Y | Y | Y | N | N | Y | Y |
| 7 Carson | Y | Y | N | Y | Y | Y | N | Y |
| 8 **Hostettler** | Y | Y | Y | Y | N | N | Y | Y |
| 9 **Sodrel** | Y | Y | Y | Y | N | N | Y | Y |
| **IOWA** | | | | | | | | |
| 1 **Nussle** | Y | Y | Y | Y | N | N | Y | Y |
| 2 **Leach** | Y | Y | Y | Y | N | N | Y | Y |
| 3 Boswell | Y | Y | N | Y | Y | Y | N | Y |
| 4 **Latham** | Y | Y | Y | Y | N | N | Y | Y |
| 5 **King** | Y | Y | Y | Y | N | N | Y | Y |
| **KANSAS** | | | | | | | | |
| 1 **Moran** | Y | Y | Y | Y | N | N | Y | Y |
| 2 **Ryun** | Y | Y | Y | Y | N | N | Y | Y |
| 3 Moore | Y | Y | N | Y | Y | Y | Y | Y |
| 4 **Tiahrt** | Y | Y | Y | Y | N | N | Y | Y |
| **KENTUCKY** | | | | | | | | |
| 1 **Whitfield** | Y | Y | Y | Y | N | N | Y | Y |
| 2 **Lewis** | Y | Y | Y | Y | N | N | Y | Y |
| 3 **Northup** | Y | Y | Y | Y | N | N | Y | Y |
| 4 **Davis** | Y | Y | Y | Y | N | N | Y | Y |
| 5 **Rogers** | Y | Y | Y | Y | N | N | Y | Y |
| 6 Chandler | Y | Y | N | Y | Y | Y | Y | Y |
| **LOUISIANA** | | | | | | | | |
| 1 **Jindal** | Y | Y | Y | Y | N | N | Y | Y |
| 2 Jefferson | Y | Y | N | Y | Y | Y | N | Y |
| 3 Melancon | Y | Y | N | Y | Y | Y | Y | Y |
| 4 **McCrery** | Y | Y | Y | Y | N | N | Y | Y |
| 5 **Alexander** | Y | Y | Y | Y | N | N | Y | Y |
| 6 **Baker** | Y | Y | Y | Y | N | N | ? | ? |
| 7 **Boustany** | Y | Y | Y | Y | N | N | Y | Y |
| **MAINE** | | | | | | | | |
| 1 Allen | Y | Y | N | Y | Y | Y | N | Y |
| 2 Michaud | Y | Y | N | Y | Y | Y | Y | Y |
| **MARYLAND** | | | | | | | | |
| 1 **Gilchrest** | Y | Y | Y | Y | N | N | Y | Y |
| 2 Ruppersberger | Y | Y | N | Y | Y | Y | Y | ? |
| 3 Cardin | Y | Y | N | Y | Y | Y | N | Y |
| 4 Wynn | Y | Y | ? | ? | Y | Y | N | Y |
| 5 Hoyer | Y | Y | N | Y | Y | Y | N | Y |
| 6 **Bartlett** | Y | Y | Y | Y | N | N | Y | Y |
| 7 Cummings | Y | Y | N | Y | Y | Y | N | Y |
| 8 Van Hollen | Y | Y | N | Y | Y | Y | N | Y |
| **MASSACHUSETTS** | | | | | | | | |
| 1 Olver | Y | Y | N | Y | Y | Y | N | Y |
| 2 Neal | Y | Y | N | Y | Y | Y | N | Y |
| 3 McGovern | Y | Y | N | Y | Y | Y | N | Y |
| 4 Frank | Y | Y | N | N | Y | Y | N | Y |
| 5 Meehan | Y | Y | N | Y | Y | Y | N | Y |
| 6 Tierney | Y | Y | N | Y | Y | Y | N | Y |
| 7 Markey | Y | Y | N | Y | Y | Y | N | Y |
| 8 Capuano | Y | Y | N | Y | Y | Y | N | Y |
| 9 Lynch | Y | Y | N | Y | Y | Y | N | Y |
| 10 Delahunt | Y | Y | N | N | Y | Y | N | Y |
| **MICHIGAN** | | | | | | | | |
| 1 Stupak | ? | ? | ? | ? | ? | ? | ? | ? |
| 2 **Hoekstra** | Y | Y | Y | Y | N | N | Y | Y |
| 3 **Ehlers** | Y | Y | Y | Y | N | N | Y | Y |
| 4 **Camp** | Y | Y | Y | Y | N | N | Y | Y |
| 5 Kildee | Y | Y | N | Y | Y | Y | N | Y |
| 6 **Upton** | Y | Y | Y | Y | N | N | Y | Y |
| 7 **Schwarz** | Y | Y | Y | Y | N | N | Y | Y |
| 8 **Rogers** | Y | Y | Y | Y | N | N | Y | Y |
| 9 **Knollenberg** | Y | Y | Y | Y | N | N | Y | Y |
| 10 **Miller** | Y | Y | Y | Y | N | N | Y | Y |
| 11 **McCotter** | Y | Y | Y | Y | N | N | Y | Y |
| 12 Levin | Y | Y | N | Y | Y | Y | N | Y |
| 13 Kilpatrick | Y | Y | N | Y | Y | Y | N | Y |
| 14 Conyers | Y | Y | N | N | Y | Y | N | Y |
| 15 Dingell | Y | Y | Y | Y | Y | Y | N | Y |

| | 32 | 33 | 34 | 35 | 36 | 37 | 38 | 39 |
|---|---|---|---|---|---|---|---|---|
| **MINNESOTA** | | | | | | | | |
| 1 **Gutknecht** | Y | Y | Y | Y | N | N | Y | Y |
| 2 **Kline** | Y | Y | Y | Y | N | N | Y | Y |
| 3 **Ramstad** | Y | Y | Y | Y | N | N | Y | Y |
| 4 McCollum | Y | Y | N | Y | Y | Y | N | Y |
| 5 Sabo | Y | Y | N | N | Y | Y | N | ? |
| 6 **Kennedy** | Y | Y | Y | Y | N | N | Y | Y |
| 7 Peterson | Y | Y | N | Y | N | N | Y | Y |
| 8 Oberstar | Y | Y | N | Y | Y | Y | N | Y |
| **MISSISSIPPI** | | | | | | | | |
| 1 **Wicker** | Y | Y | Y | Y | N | N | Y | Y |
| 2 Thompson | Y | Y | N | Y | Y | Y | N | Y |
| 3 **Pickering** | Y | Y | Y | Y | N | N | Y | Y |
| 4 Taylor | Y | Y | N | Y | N | Y | Y | Y |
| **MISSOURI** | | | | | | | | |
| 1 Clay | Y | Y | N | N | Y | Y | N | Y |
| 2 **Akin** | Y | Y | Y | Y | N | N | Y | Y |
| 3 Carnahan | Y | Y | N | Y | Y | Y | N | Y |
| 4 Skelton | Y | Y | N | Y | Y | Y | N | ? |
| 5 Cleaver | Y | Y | N | Y | Y | Y | N | Y |
| 6 **Graves** | Y | Y | Y | Y | N | N | Y | Y |
| 7 **Blunt** | Y | Y | Y | Y | N | N | Y | Y |
| 8 **Emerson** | Y | Y | Y | Y | N | N | Y | Y |
| 9 **Hulshof** | ? | ? | Y | Y | N | N | Y | Y |
| **MONTANA** | | | | | | | | |
| AL **Rehberg** | Y | Y | Y | Y | N | N | Y | Y |
| **NEBRASKA** | | | | | | | | |
| 1 **Fortenberry** | Y | Y | Y | Y | N | N | Y | Y |
| 2 **Terry** | Y | Y | Y | Y | N | N | Y | Y |
| 3 **Osborne** | Y | Y | Y | Y | N | N | Y | Y |
| **NEVADA** | | | | | | | | |
| 1 Berkley | Y | Y | N | Y | Y | Y | N | Y |
| 2 **Gibbons** | Y | Y | Y | Y | N | N | Y | Y |
| 3 **Porter** | Y | Y | Y | Y | N | N | Y | Y |
| **NEW HAMPSHIRE** | | | | | | | | |
| 1 **Bradley** | Y | Y | Y | Y | N | N | Y | Y |
| 2 **Bass** | Y | Y | Y | Y | N | N | Y | Y |
| **NEW JERSEY** | | | | | | | | |
| 1 Andrews | ? | ? | N | Y | Y | Y | N | Y |
| 2 **LoBiondo** | Y | Y | Y | Y | N | N | Y | Y |
| 3 **Saxton** | Y | Y | Y | Y | N | N | Y | Y |
| 4 **Smith** | Y | Y | Y | Y | N | N | Y | Y |
| 5 **Garrett** | Y | Y | Y | Y | N | N | Y | Y |
| 6 Pallone | Y | Y | N | Y | Y | Y | N | Y |
| 7 **Ferguson** | Y | Y | Y | Y | N | N | Y | Y |
| 8 Pascrell | Y | Y | N | Y | Y | Y | N | ? |
| 9 Rothman | Y | Y | N | Y | Y | Y | N | Y |
| 10 Payne | Y | Y | N | N | Y | Y | N | Y |
| 11 **Frelinghuysen** | Y | Y | Y | Y | N | N | Y | Y |
| 12 Holt | Y | Y | N | Y | Y | Y | N | Y |
| 13 Menendez | Y | Y | N | Y | Y | Y | N | Y |
| **NEW MEXICO** | | | | | | | | |
| 1 **Wilson** | Y | Y | Y | Y | N | N | Y | Y |
| 2 **Pearce** | Y | Y | Y | Y | N | N | Y | Y |
| 3 Udall | Y | Y | N | Y | Y | Y | N | Y |
| **NEW YORK** | | | | | | | | |
| 1 Bishop | Y | Y | N | Y | Y | Y | N | Y |
| 2 Israel | Y | Y | N | Y | Y | Y | N | Y |
| 3 **King** | Y | Y | Y | Y | N | N | Y | Y |
| 4 McCarthy | Y | Y | N | Y | Y | Y | N | Y |
| 5 Ackerman | Y | Y | N | N | Y | Y | N | Y |
| 6 Meeks | Y | Y | N | Y | Y | Y | Y | Y |
| 7 Crowley | Y | ? | N | Y | Y | Y | N | Y |
| 8 Nadler | Y | Y | N | N | Y | Y | N | Y |
| 9 Weiner | Y | Y | N | Y | Y | Y | N | Y |
| 10 Towns | Y | Y | N | Y | Y | Y | N | Y |
| 11 Owens | Y | Y | N | N | Y | Y | N | Y |
| 12 Velázquez | Y | Y | N | N | Y | Y | N | Y |
| 13 **Fossella** | Y | Y | Y | Y | N | N | Y | Y |
| 14 Maloney | Y | Y | N | Y | Y | Y | N | Y |
| 15 Rangel | Y | Y | N | Y | ? | ? | ? | ? |
| 16 Serrano | Y | Y | N | N | Y | Y | N | Y |
| 17 Engel | Y | Y | N | Y | Y | N | N | Y |
| 18 Lowey | Y | Y | N | Y | Y | Y | N | Y |
| 19 **Kelly** | Y | Y | Y | Y | N | N | Y | Y |
| 20 **Sweeney** | Y | Y | Y | Y | N | N | Y | Y |
| 21 McNulty | Y | Y | N | Y | Y | Y | N | Y |
| 22 Hinchey | Y | Y | N | N | Y | Y | N | Y |
| 23 **McHugh** | Y | Y | Y | Y | N | N | Y | Y |
| 24 **Boehlert** | Y | Y | Y | Y | N | N | Y | Y |
| 25 **Walsh** | Y | Y | Y | Y | N | N | Y | Y |
| 26 **Reynolds** | Y | Y | Y | Y | N | N | Y | Y |
| 27 Higgins | Y | Y | N | Y | Y | Y | Y | Y |
| 28 Slaughter | Y | Y | N | Y | Y | Y | N | Y |
| 29 **Kuhl** | Y | Y | Y | Y | N | N | Y | Y |

| | 32 | 33 | 34 | 35 | 36 | 37 | 38 | 39 |
|---|---|---|---|---|---|---|---|---|
| **NORTH CAROLINA** | | | | | | | | |
| 1 Butterfield | Y | Y | N | Y | Y | Y | N | Y |
| 2 Etheridge | Y | Y | N | Y | Y | Y | N | Y |
| 3 **Jones** | Y | Y | Y | Y | N | N | Y | Y |
| 4 Price | Y | Y | N | Y | Y | Y | N | Y |
| 5 **Foxx** | Y | Y | Y | Y | N | N | Y | Y |
| 6 **Coble** | Y | Y | Y | Y | N | N | Y | Y |
| 7 McIntyre | Y | Y | N | Y | Y | Y | N | ? |
| 8 **Hayes** | Y | Y | Y | Y | N | N | Y | Y |
| 9 **Myrick** | Y | Y | Y | Y | N | N | Y | Y |
| 10 **McHenry** | Y | Y | Y | Y | N | N | Y | Y |
| 11 **Taylor** | Y | Y | Y | Y | N | N | Y | ? |
| 12 Watt | Y | Y | N | Y | Y | Y | N | Y |
| 13 Miller | Y | Y | N | Y | Y | Y | N | Y |
| **NORTH DAKOTA** | | | | | | | | |
| AL Pomeroy | Y | Y | N | Y | Y | N | Y | Y |
| **OHIO** | | | | | | | | |
| 1 **Chabot** | Y | Y | Y | Y | N | N | Y | Y |
| 2 **Portman** | Y | Y | Y | Y | N | N | Y | Y |
| 3 **Turner** | Y | Y | Y | Y | N | N | Y | Y |
| 4 **Oxley** | Y | Y | ? | Y | N | N | Y | Y |
| 5 **Gillmor** | Y | Y | Y | Y | N | N | Y | Y |
| 6 Strickland | Y | Y | N | Y | Y | Y | N | Y |
| 7 **Hobson** | Y | Y | Y | Y | N | N | Y | Y |
| 8 **Boehner** | Y | Y | Y | Y | N | N | Y | ? |
| 9 Kaptur | Y | Y | N | ? | Y | Y | N | ? |
| 10 Kucinich | Y | Y | N | N | Y | Y | N | Y |
| 11 Jones | Y | Y | N | Y | Y | ? | N | Y |
| 12 **Tiberi** | Y | Y | Y | Y | N | N | Y | Y |
| 13 Brown | Y | Y | N | Y | Y | Y | N | Y |
| 14 **LaTourette** | Y | Y | Y | Y | N | N | Y | Y |
| 15 **Pryce** | Y | Y | Y | Y | N | N | Y | Y |
| 16 **Regula** | Y | Y | Y | Y | N | N | Y | Y |
| 17 Ryan | Y | Y | N | Y | Y | Y | N | Y |
| 18 **Ney** | Y | Y | Y | Y | N | N | Y | Y |
| **OKLAHOMA** | | | | | | | | |
| 1 **Sullivan** | Y | Y | Y | Y | ? | N | Y | Y |
| 2 Boren | Y | Y | N | Y | N | N | Y | Y |
| 3 **Lucas** | Y | Y | Y | Y | N | N | Y | Y |
| 4 **Cole** | Y | Y | Y | + | N | N | Y | Y |
| 5 **Istook** | Y | Y | Y | Y | N | N | Y | Y |
| **OREGON** | | | | | | | | |
| 1 Wu | Y | Y | N | Y | Y | Y | Y | Y |
| 2 **Walden** | Y | Y | Y | Y | N | N | Y | Y |
| 3 Blumenauer | Y | Y | N | Y | Y | Y | N | Y |
| 4 DeFazio | Y | Y | N | Y | Y | Y | N | Y |
| 5 Hooley | Y | Y | N | Y | Y | Y | N | Y |
| **PENNSYLVANIA** | | | | | | | | |
| 1 Brady | Y | Y | N | Y | Y | Y | N | Y |
| 2 Fattah | Y | ? | N | N | Y | Y | N | Y |
| 3 **English** | Y | Y | Y | Y | N | N | Y | Y |
| 4 **Hart** | Y | Y | Y | Y | N | N | Y | Y |
| 5 **Peterson** | Y | Y | Y | Y | N | N | Y | Y |
| 6 **Gerlach** | Y | Y | Y | Y | N | N | Y | Y |
| 7 **Weldon** | Y | Y | Y | Y | N | N | Y | Y |
| 8 **Fitzpatrick** | Y | Y | Y | Y | N | N | Y | Y |
| 9 **Shuster** | Y | Y | Y | Y | N | N | Y | Y |
| 10 **Sherwood** | Y | Y | Y | Y | N | N | Y | Y |
| 11 Kanjorski | Y | Y | N | Y | Y | Y | Y | Y |
| 12 Murtha | Y | ? | N | Y | N | N | Y | Y |
| 13 Schwartz | Y | Y | N | Y | Y | Y | N | Y |
| 14 Doyle | Y | Y | N | Y | Y | Y | N | Y |
| 15 **Dent** | Y | Y | Y | Y | N | N | Y | Y |
| 16 **Pitts** | Y | Y | Y | Y | N | N | Y | Y |
| 17 Holden | Y | Y | N | Y | N | N | Y | Y |
| 18 **Murphy** | Y | Y | Y | Y | N | N | Y | Y |
| 19 **Platts** | Y | Y | Y | Y | N | N | Y | Y |
| **RHODE ISLAND** | | | | | | | | |
| 1 Kennedy | Y | Y | N | Y | Y | Y | N | Y |
| 2 Langevin | Y | Y | N | Y | Y | Y | N | Y |
| **SOUTH CAROLINA** | | | | | | | | |
| 1 **Brown** | Y | Y | Y | Y | N | N | Y | Y |
| 2 **Wilson** | Y | Y | Y | Y | N | N | Y | Y |
| 3 **Barrett** | Y | Y | Y | Y | N | N | Y | Y |
| 4 **Inglis** | Y | Y | Y | Y | N | ? | Y | Y |
| 5 Spratt | Y | Y | N | Y | Y | N | N | Y |
| 6 Clyburn | Y | Y | N | Y | Y | Y | N | Y |
| **SOUTH DAKOTA** | | | | | | | | |
| AL Herseth | Y | Y | N | Y | Y | Y | N | Y |
| **TENNESSEE** | | | | | | | | |
| 1 **Jenkins** | Y | Y | Y | Y | N | N | Y | Y |
| 2 **Duncan** | Y | Y | Y | Y | N | N | Y | Y |

| | 32 | 33 | 34 | 35 | 36 | 37 | 38 | 39 |
|---|---|---|---|---|---|---|---|---|
| 3 **Wamp** | ? | ? | Y | Y | N | N | Y | Y |
| 4 Davis | Y | Y | N | Y | N | N | Y | Y |
| 5 Cooper | Y | Y | N | Y | N | N | Y | Y |
| 6 Gordon | Y | Y | N | Y | N | N | Y | Y |
| 7 **Blackburn** | Y | Y | Y | Y | N | N | Y | Y |
| 8 Tanner | Y | Y | N | Y | N | N | Y | Y |
| 9 Ford | Y | Y | N | Y | N | N | Y | Y |
| **TEXAS** | | | | | | | | |
| 1 **Gohmert** | Y | Y | Y | Y | N | N | Y | Y |
| 2 **Poe** | Y | Y | Y | Y | N | N | Y | Y |
| 3 **Johnson, S.** | Y | Y | Y | Y | N | N | Y | Y |
| 4 **Hall** | Y | Y | Y | Y | N | N | Y | Y |
| 5 **Hensarling** | Y | Y | Y | Y | N | N | Y | Y |
| 6 **Barton** | Y | Y | Y | Y | N | N | Y | Y |
| 7 **Culberson** | Y | Y | Y | Y | N | N | Y | Y |
| 8 **Brady** | Y | Y | Y | Y | N | N | Y | Y |
| 9 Green, A. | Y | Y | N | Y | Y | Y | N | Y |
| 10 **McCaul** | Y | Y | Y | Y | N | N | Y | Y |
| 11 **Conaway** | Y | Y | Y | Y | N | N | Y | Y |
| 12 **Granger** | Y | Y | Y | Y | N | N | Y | Y |
| 13 **Thornberry** | Y | Y | Y | Y | N | N | Y | Y |
| 14 **Paul** | Y | Y | Y | N | N | N | Y | Y |
| 15 Hinojosa | Y | Y | N | Y | Y | Y | Y | Y |
| 16 Reyes | Y | Y | N | Y | Y | Y | Y | Y |
| 17 Edwards | Y | Y | N | Y | Y | Y | Y | Y |
| 18 Jackson-Lee | Y | Y | N | Y | Y | Y | N | Y |
| 19 **Neugebauer** | Y | Y | Y | Y | N | N | Y | Y |
| 20 Gonzalez | Y | Y | N | Y | Y | Y | Y | Y |
| 21 **Smith** | Y | Y | Y | Y | N | N | Y | Y |
| 22 **DeLay** | Y | Y | Y | Y | N | N | Y | Y |
| 23 **Bonilla** | Y | Y | Y | Y | N | N | Y | Y |
| 24 **Marchant** | Y | Y | Y | Y | N | N | Y | Y |
| 25 Doggett | Y | Y | N | Y | Y | Y | N | Y |
| 26 **Burgess** | Y | Y | Y | Y | N | N | Y | Y |
| 27 Ortiz | Y | Y | N | Y | Y | Y | N | Y |
| 28 Cuellar | Y | Y | N | Y | N | N | Y | Y |
| 29 Green, G. | Y | Y | N | Y | Y | Y | N | Y |
| 30 Johnson, E. | Y | Y | N | Y | Y | Y | N | Y |
| 31 **Carter** | Y | Y | Y | Y | N | N | Y | Y |
| 32 **Sessions** | Y | Y | Y | Y | N | N | Y | Y |
| **UTAH** | | | | | | | | |
| 1 **Bishop** | Y | Y | Y | Y | N | N | Y | Y |
| 2 Matheson | Y | Y | N | Y | N | N | Y | Y |
| 3 **Cannon** | Y | Y | Y | Y | N | N | Y | Y |
| **VERMONT** | | | | | | | | |
| AL *Sanders* | Y | Y | N | N | Y | Y | N | ? |
| **VIRGINIA** | | | | | | | | |
| 1 **Davis, J.** | Y | Y | Y | Y | N | N | Y | Y |
| 2 **Drake** | Y | Y | Y | Y | N | N | Y | Y |
| 3 Scott | Y | Y | N | N | Y | Y | N | Y |
| 4 **Forbes** | Y | Y | Y | Y | N | N | Y | Y |
| 5 **Goode** | Y | Y | Y | Y | N | N | Y | Y |
| 6 **Goodlatte** | Y | Y | Y | Y | N | N | Y | Y |
| 7 **Cantor** | Y | Y | Y | Y | N | N | Y | Y |
| 8 Moran | Y | Y | N | Y | Y | Y | N | Y |
| 9 Boucher | Y | Y | N | Y | N | N | Y | Y |
| 10 **Wolf** | Y | Y | Y | Y | N | N | Y | Y |
| 11 **Davis, T.** | Y | Y | Y | Y | N | N | Y | Y |
| **WASHINGTON** | | | | | | | | |
| 1 Inslee | Y | Y | N | Y | Y | Y | N | Y |
| 2 Larsen | Y | Y | N | Y | Y | Y | Y | Y |
| 3 Baird | ? | ? | N | N | Y | Y | Y | Y |
| 4 **Hastings** | Y | Y | Y | Y | N | N | Y | Y |
| 5 **McMorris** | Y | Y | Y | Y | N | N | Y | Y |
| 6 Dicks | Y | Y | N | Y | Y | Y | N | Y |
| 7 McDermott | Y | Y | N | N | Y | Y | N | Y |
| 8 **Reichert** | Y | Y | ? | ? | ? | ? | + | + |
| 9 Smith | Y | Y | N | Y | Y | Y | Y | Y |
| **WEST VIRGINIA** | | | | | | | | |
| 1 Mollohan | Y | Y | N | Y | Y | Y | N | ? |
| 2 **Capito** | Y | Y | Y | Y | N | N | Y | ? |
| 3 Rahall | Y | Y | N | Y | Y | Y | Y | Y |
| **WISCONSIN** | | | | | | | | |
| 1 **Ryan** | Y | Y | Y | Y | N | N | Y | Y |
| 2 Baldwin | Y | Y | N | Y | Y | Y | N | Y |
| 3 Kind | Y | Y | N | Y | Y | Y | Y | ? |
| 4 Moore | Y | Y | N | Y | Y | Y | N | Y |
| 5 **Sensenbrenner** | Y | Y | Y | Y | N | N | Y | Y |
| 6 **Petri** | Y | Y | Y | Y | N | N | Y | Y |
| 7 Obey | Y | Y | N | Y | Y | Y | N | Y |
| 8 **Green** | Y | Y | Y | Y | N | N | Y | Y |
| **WYOMING** | | | | | | | | |
| AL **Cubin** | Y | Y | Y | Y | N | N | Y | Y |

# IN THE HOUSE | By Vote Number

**40.** **H Con Res 5. Sarah Winnemucca Statue/Adoption.** Ney, R-Ohio, motion to suspend the rules and adopt the concurrent resolution that would accept a statue of American Indian rights advocate Sarah Winnemucca into the National Statuary Hall in the Capitol. It also would authorize the state of Nevada to use the Capitol Rotunda for a presentation ceremony March 9, 2005. Motion agreed to 418-0: R 226-0; D 191-0 (ND 142-0, SD 49-0); I 1-0. A two-thirds majority of those present and voting (279 in this case) is required for adoption under suspension of the rules. March 1, 2005.

**41.** **H Con Res 63. Holocaust Remembrance/Adoption.** Ney, R-Ohio, motion to suspend the rules and adopt the concurrent resolution that would authorize the use of the Capitol Rotunda for a ceremony on May 5, 2005, to commemorate victims of the Holocaust. Motion agreed to 416-0: R 226-0; D 189-0 (ND 141-0, SD 48-0); I 1-0. A two-thirds majority of those present and voting (278 in this case) is required for adoption under suspension of the rules. March 1, 2005.

**42.** **HR 27. Job Training Reauthorization/Rule.** Adoption of the rule (H Res 126) to provide for House floor consideration of the bill that would reauthorize the Workforce Investment Act, consolidate several programs into block grants for states and allow faith-based providers of job training activities to use religion as a factor in hiring decisions. Adopted 227-191: R 226-0; D 1-191 (ND 0-141, SD 1-50); I 0-0. March 2, 2005.

**43.** **HR 912. Abuse Safeguards for Aid Organizations/Passage.** Smith, R-N.J., motion to suspend the rules and pass the bill that would require humanitarian aid organizations to adopt safeguards to protect women and children from sexual exploitation and abuse before receiving U.S. disaster assistance. The bill would require the president to provide Congress with a detailed report on the implementation of the bill. Motion agreed to 416-0: R 226-0; D 190-0 (ND 140-0, SD 50-0); I 0-0. A two-thirds majority of those present and voting (278 in this case) is required for passage under suspension of the rules. March 2, 2005.

**44.** **HR 27. Job Training Reauthorization/Youth Employment Programs.** Kildee, D-Mich., amendment that would strike the provision in the bill that would limit the portion of a state's funds used for youth employment programs to 30 percent of its allotment. Rejected 200-222: R 5-222; D 194-0 (ND 143-0, SD 51-0); I 1-0. March 2, 2005.

**45.** **HR 27. Job Training Reauthorization/Small Business Loans.** Velázquez, D-N.Y., amendment that would allow unemployed workers to use funds from personal re-employment accounts to cover the borrower guarantee costs of 7(a) loans used to start a small business. Rejected 202-221: R 8-219; D 193-2 (ND 142-2, SD 51-0); I 1-0. March 2, 2005.

**46.** **HR 27. Job Training Reauthorization/Religious Preferences.** Scott, D-Va., amendment that would strike the provision in the bill that would permit faith-based organizations to use religion as a factor in hiring decisions. Rejected 186-239: R 3-225; D 182-14 (ND 139-6, SD 43-8); I 1-0. A "nay" was a vote in support of the president's position. March 2, 2005.

| | 40 | 41 | 42 | 43 | 44 | 45 | 46 |
|---|---|---|---|---|---|---|---|
| **ALABAMA** | | | | | | | |
| 1 Bonner | Y | Y | Y | Y | N | N | N |
| 2 Everett | Y | Y | Y | Y | N | N | N |
| 3 Rogers | Y | Y | Y | Y | N | N | N |
| 4 Aderholt | Y | Y | Y | Y | N | N | N |
| 5 Cramer | Y | Y | N | Y | Y | Y | N |
| 6 Bachus | Y | Y | Y | Y | N | N | N |
| 7 Davis | Y | Y | N | Y | Y | Y | Y |
| **ALASKA** | | | | | | | |
| AL Young | Y | Y | Y | Y | N | N | N |
| **ARIZONA** | | | | | | | |
| 1 Renzi | Y | Y | Y | Y | N | Y | N |
| 2 Franks | Y | Y | Y | Y | N | N | N |
| 3 Shadegg | Y | Y | Y | Y | N | N | N |
| 4 Pastor | Y | Y | N | Y | Y | Y | Y |
| 5 Hayworth | Y | Y | Y | Y | N | N | N |
| 6 Flake | Y | Y | Y | Y | N | N | N |
| 7 Grijalva | Y | Y | N | Y | Y | Y | Y |
| 8 Kolbe | Y | Y | Y | Y | N | N | N |
| **ARKANSAS** | | | | | | | |
| 1 Berry | Y | Y | N | Y | Y | Y | Y |
| 2 Snyder | Y | Y | N | Y | Y | Y | Y |
| 3 Boozman | Y | Y | Y | Y | N | N | N |
| 4 Ross | Y | Y | N | Y | Y | Y | Y |
| **CALIFORNIA** | | | | | | | |
| 1 Thompson | Y | Y | N | Y | Y | Y | Y |
| 2 Herger | Y | Y | Y | Y | N | N | N |
| 3 Lungren | Y | Y | Y | Y | N | N | N |
| 4 Doolittle | Y | Y | Y | Y | N | N | N |
| 5 Vacant | | | | | | | |
| 6 Woolsey | Y | Y | N | Y | Y | Y | Y |
| 7 Miller, George | Y | Y | N | Y | Y | Y | Y |
| 8 Pelosi | Y | Y | N | Y | Y | Y | Y |
| 9 Lee | Y | Y | N | Y | Y | Y | Y |
| 10 Tauscher | Y | Y | N | Y | Y | Y | Y |
| 11 Pombo | Y | Y | Y | Y | N | N | N |
| 12 Lantos | Y | Y | N | Y | Y | Y | Y |
| 13 Stark | ? | ? | N | Y | Y | Y | Y |
| 14 Eshoo | Y | Y | N | Y | Y | Y | Y |
| 15 Honda | Y | Y | N | Y | Y | Y | Y |
| 16 Lofgren | Y | Y | N | Y | Y | Y | Y |
| 17 Farr | Y | Y | N | Y | Y | Y | Y |
| 18 Cardoza | Y | Y | N | Y | Y | Y | Y |
| 19 Radanovich | Y | Y | Y | Y | N | N | N |
| 20 Costa | Y | Y | N | Y | Y | Y | Y |
| 21 Nunes | Y | Y | Y | Y | N | N | N |
| 22 Thomas | Y | Y | Y | Y | N | N | N |
| 23 Capps | Y | Y | N | Y | Y | Y | Y |
| 24 Gallegly | Y | Y | Y | Y | N | N | N |
| 25 McKeon | Y | Y | Y | Y | N | N | N |
| 26 Dreier | Y | Y | Y | Y | N | N | N |
| 27 Sherman | Y | Y | N | Y | Y | Y | Y |
| 28 Berman | Y | Y | N | Y | Y | Y | Y |
| 29 Schiff | Y | Y | N | Y | Y | Y | Y |
| 30 Waxman | Y | Y | N | Y | Y | Y | Y |
| 31 Becerra | Y | Y | N | Y | Y | Y | Y |
| 32 Solis | Y | Y | N | Y | Y | Y | Y |
| 33 Watson | ? | Y | N | Y | Y | Y | Y |
| 34 Roybal-Allard | Y | Y | N | Y | Y | Y | Y |
| 35 Waters | Y | Y | N | Y | Y | Y | Y |
| 36 Harman | Y | Y | N | Y | Y | Y | Y |
| 37 Millender-McD. | ? | ? | ? | ? | ? | ? | ? |
| 38 Napolitano | ? | ? | ? | ? | ? | ? | ? |
| 39 Sánchez, Linda | Y | Y | N | Y | Y | Y | Y |
| 40 Royce | Y | Y | Y | Y | N | N | N |
| 41 Lewis | Y | Y | Y | Y | N | N | N |
| 42 Miller, Gary | Y | Y | Y | Y | N | N | N |
| 43 Baca | Y | Y | N | Y | Y | Y | Y |
| 44 Calvert | Y | Y | Y | Y | N | N | N |
| 45 Bono | Y | Y | Y | Y | N | N | N |
| 46 Rohrabacher | Y | Y | Y | Y | N | N | N |
| 47 Sanchez, Loretta | Y | Y | N | Y | Y | Y | Y |
| 48 Cox | Y | Y | Y | Y | N | N | N |
| 49 Issa | Y | Y | Y | Y | N | N | N |

| | 40 | 41 | 42 | 43 | 44 | 45 | 46 |
|---|---|---|---|---|---|---|---|
| 50 Cunningham | Y | Y | Y | Y | N | N | N |
| 51 Filner | Y | Y | Y | Y | N | N | N |
| 52 Hunter | Y | Y | Y | Y | N | N | N |
| 53 Davis | Y | Y | N | Y | Y | Y | Y |
| **COLORADO** | | | | | | | |
| 1 DeGette | Y | Y | N | Y | Y | Y | Y |
| 2 Udall | Y | Y | N | Y | Y | Y | Y |
| 3 Salazar | Y | Y | N | Y | Y | Y | Y |
| 4 Musgrave | Y | Y | Y | Y | N | N | N |
| 5 Hefley | Y | Y | Y | Y | N | N | N |
| 6 Tancredo | Y | Y | Y | Y | N | N | N |
| 7 Beauprez | Y | Y | Y | Y | N | N | N |
| **CONNECTICUT** | | | | | | | |
| 1 Larson | Y | Y | N | Y | Y | Y | Y |
| 2 Simmons | Y | Y | Y | Y | N | Y | Y |
| 3 DeLauro | Y | Y | N | Y | Y | Y | Y |
| 4 Shays | Y | Y | Y | Y | N | Y | Y |
| 5 Johnson | Y | Y | Y | Y | N | N | N |
| **DELAWARE** | | | | | | | |
| AL Castle | Y | Y | Y | Y | N | N | N |
| **FLORIDA** | | | | | | | |
| 1 Miller | Y | Y | Y | Y | N | N | N |
| 2 Boyd | Y | Y | N | Y | Y | Y | Y |
| 3 Brown | ? | ? | N | Y | Y | Y | Y |
| 4 Crenshaw | Y | Y | Y | Y | N | N | N |
| 5 Brown-Waite | Y | Y | Y | Y | N | N | N |
| 6 Stearns | Y | Y | Y | Y | N | N | N |
| 7 Mica | Y | Y | Y | Y | N | N | N |
| 8 Keller | Y | Y | Y | Y | N | N | N |
| 9 Bilirakis | Y | Y | Y | Y | N | N | N |
| 10 Young | Y | Y | Y | Y | N | N | N |
| 11 Davis | Y | Y | N | Y | Y | Y | Y |
| 12 Putnam | Y | Y | Y | Y | N | N | N |
| 13 Harris | ? | ? | ? | ? | ? | ? | ? |
| 14 Mack | Y | Y | Y | Y | N | N | N |
| 15 Weldon | Y | Y | Y | Y | N | N | N |
| 16 Foley | Y | Y | ? | ? | N | N | N |
| 17 Meek | Y | Y | N | Y | Y | Y | Y |
| 18 Ros-Lehtinen | Y | Y | Y | Y | N | N | N |
| 19 Wexler | Y | Y | N | Y | Y | Y | Y |
| 20 Wasserman-Schultz | Y | Y | N | Y | Y | Y | Y |
| 21 Diaz-Balart, L. | Y | Y | Y | Y | N | N | N |
| 22 Shaw | Y | Y | Y | Y | N | N | N |
| 23 Hastings | Y | Y | N | Y | Y | Y | Y |
| 24 Feeney | Y | Y | Y | Y | N | N | N |
| 25 Diaz-Balart, M. | Y | Y | Y | Y | N | N | N |
| **GEORGIA** | | | | | | | |
| 1 Kingston | ? | ? | Y | Y | N | N | N |
| 2 Bishop | Y | Y | N | Y | Y | Y | Y |
| 3 Marshall | Y | Y | N | Y | Y | Y | Y |
| 4 McKinney | Y | Y | N | Y | Y | Y | Y |
| 5 Lewis | Y | Y | N | Y | Y | Y | Y |
| 6 Price | Y | Y | Y | Y | N | N | N |
| 7 Linder | Y | Y | Y | Y | N | N | N |
| 8 Westmoreland | Y | Y | Y | Y | N | N | N |
| 9 Norwood | Y | Y | Y | Y | N | N | N |
| 10 Deal | Y | Y | Y | Y | N | N | N |
| 11 Gingrey | Y | Y | Y | Y | N | N | N |
| 12 Barrow | Y | Y | N | Y | Y | Y | N |
| 13 Scott | Y | Y | N | Y | Y | Y | Y |
| **HAWAII** | | | | | | | |
| 1 Abercrombie | Y | Y | N | Y | Y | Y | Y |
| 2 Case | Y | Y | N | Y | Y | Y | Y |
| **IDAHO** | | | | | | | |
| 1 Otter | Y | Y | Y | Y | N | N | N |
| 2 Simpson | Y | Y | Y | Y | N | N | N |
| **ILLINOIS** | | | | | | | |
| 1 Rush | ? | ? | N | Y | Y | Y | Y |
| 2 Jackson | Y | Y | N | Y | Y | Y | Y |
| 3 Lipinski | Y | Y | N | Y | Y | Y | Y |
| 4 Gutierrez | ? | ? | N | Y | Y | Y | Y |
| 5 Emanuel | Y | Y | N | Y | Y | Y | Y |
| 6 Hyde | Y | Y | Y | Y | N | N | N |
| 7 Davis | Y | Y | N | Y | Y | Y | Y |
| 8 Bean | Y | Y | N | Y | Y | Y | Y |
| 9 Schakowsky | Y | Y | N | Y | Y | Y | Y |
| 10 Kirk | Y | Y | Y | Y | N | N | N |
| 11 Weller | Y | Y | Y | Y | N | N | N |
| 12 Costello | Y | Y | N | Y | Y | Y | Y |

**KEY**   Republicans   Democrats   *Independents*

| | | | |
|---|---|---|---|
| Y | Voted for (yea) | X | Paired against |
| # | Paired for | – | Announced against |
| + | Announced for | P | Voted "present" |
| N | Voted against (nay) | C | Voted "present" to avoid possible conflict of interest |
| | | ? | Did not vote or otherwise make a position known |

ND Northern Democrats, SD Southern Democrats
Southern states: Ala., Ark., Fla., Ga., Ky., La., Miss., N.C., Okla., S.C., Tenn., Texas, Va.

| | 40 | 41 | 42 | 43 | 44 | 45 | 46 |
|---|---|---|---|---|---|---|---|
| 13 **Biggert** | Y | Y | Y | Y | N | N | N |
| 14 **Hastert** | | | | | | | |
| 15 **Johnson** | Y | Y | Y | Y | N | Y | N |
| 16 **Manzullo** | Y | Y | Y | Y | N | N | N |
| 17 Evans | Y | Y | N | Y | Y | Y | Y |
| 18 **LaHood** | Y | Y | Y | Y | N | N | N |
| 19 **Shimkus** | Y | Y | Y | Y | N | N | N |
| **INDIANA** | | | | | | | |
| 1 Visclosky | Y | Y | N | Y | Y | Y | Y |
| 2 **Chocola** | Y | Y | Y | Y | N | N | N |
| 3 **Souder** | Y | Y | Y | Y | N | N | N |
| 4 **Buyer** | Y | Y | Y | Y | N | N | N |
| 5 **Burton** | Y | Y | Y | Y | N | N | N |
| 6 **Pence** | Y | Y | Y | Y | N | N | N |
| 7 Carson | ? | ? | ? | ? | ? | ? | ? |
| 8 **Hostettler** | Y | Y | Y | Y | N | N | N |
| 9 **Sodrel** | Y | Y | Y | Y | N | N | N |
| **IOWA** | | | | | | | |
| 1 **Nussle** | Y | Y | Y | Y | N | N | N |
| 2 **Leach** | Y | Y | Y | Y | Y | N | N |
| 3 Boswell | Y | Y | N | Y | Y | Y | Y |
| 4 **Latham** | Y | Y | Y | Y | N | N | N |
| 5 **King** | Y | Y | Y | Y | N | N | N |
| **KANSAS** | | | | | | | |
| 1 **Moran** | Y | Y | Y | Y | N | N | N |
| 2 **Ryun** | Y | Y | Y | Y | N | N | N |
| 3 Moore | Y | Y | N | Y | Y | Y | Y |
| 4 **Tiahrt** | Y | Y | Y | Y | N | N | N |
| **KENTUCKY** | | | | | | | |
| 1 **Whitfield** | Y | Y | Y | Y | N | N | N |
| 2 **Lewis** | Y | Y | Y | Y | N | N | N |
| 3 **Northup** | Y | Y | Y | Y | N | N | N |
| 4 **Davis** | Y | Y | Y | Y | N | N | N |
| 5 **Rogers** | Y | Y | Y | Y | N | N | N |
| 6 Chandler | Y | Y | N | Y | Y | Y | N |
| **LOUISIANA** | | | | | | | |
| 1 **Jindal** | Y | Y | Y | Y | N | N | N |
| 2 Jefferson | Y | Y | N | Y | Y | Y | Y |
| 3 Melancon | Y | ? | N | Y | Y | Y | Y |
| 4 **McCrery** | Y | Y | Y | Y | ? | ? | N |
| 5 **Alexander** | Y | Y | Y | Y | N | N | N |
| 6 **Baker** | Y | Y | Y | Y | N | N | N |
| 7 **Boustany** | Y | Y | Y | Y | N | N | N |
| **MAINE** | | | | | | | |
| 1 Allen | Y | Y | N | ? | Y | Y | Y |
| 2 Michaud | Y | Y | N | Y | Y | Y | Y |
| **MARYLAND** | | | | | | | |
| 1 **Gilchrest** | Y | Y | Y | Y | N | N | N |
| 2 Ruppersberger | Y | Y | N | Y | Y | Y | Y |
| 3 Cardin | Y | Y | N | Y | Y | Y | Y |
| 4 Wynn | Y | Y | N | Y | Y | Y | Y |
| 5 Hoyer | Y | Y | N | Y | Y | Y | Y |
| 6 **Bartlett** | Y | Y | Y | Y | N | N | N |
| 7 Cummings | Y | Y | N | Y | Y | Y | Y |
| 8 Van Hollen | Y | Y | N | Y | Y | Y | Y |
| **MASSACHUSETTS** | | | | | | | |
| 1 Olver | Y | Y | N | Y | Y | Y | Y |
| 2 Neal | Y | Y | ? | Y | Y | Y | Y |
| 3 McGovern | Y | Y | ? | ? | Y | Y | Y |
| 4 Frank | Y | Y | N | Y | Y | Y | Y |
| 5 Meehan | Y | Y | N | Y | Y | Y | Y |
| 6 Tierney | Y | Y | N | Y | Y | Y | Y |
| 7 Markey | Y | Y | ? | ? | Y | Y | Y |
| 8 Capuano | Y | Y | ? | ? | Y | Y | Y |
| 9 Lynch | Y | Y | N | Y | Y | Y | Y |
| 10 Delahunt | Y | Y | N | Y | Y | Y | Y |
| **MICHIGAN** | | | | | | | |
| 1 Stupak | Y | Y | N | Y | Y | Y | Y |
| 2 **Hoekstra** | Y | Y | Y | Y | N | N | N |
| 3 **Ehlers** | Y | Y | Y | Y | N | N | N |
| 4 **Camp** | Y | Y | Y | Y | N | N | N |
| 5 Kildee | Y | Y | N | Y | Y | Y | Y |
| 6 **Upton** | Y | Y | Y | Y | N | N | N |
| 7 **Schwarz** | Y | Y | Y | Y | N | N | N |
| 8 **Rogers** | Y | Y | Y | Y | N | N | N |
| 9 **Knollenberg** | Y | Y | Y | ? | N | N | N |
| 10 **Miller** | Y | Y | Y | Y | N | N | N |
| 11 **McCotter** | Y | Y | Y | Y | N | N | N |
| 12 Levin | Y | Y | N | Y | Y | Y | Y |
| 13 Kilpatrick | Y | Y | N | Y | Y | Y | Y |
| 14 Conyers | Y | Y | N | Y | Y | Y | Y |
| 15 Dingell | Y | Y | N | Y | Y | Y | Y |
| **MINNESOTA** | | | | | | | |
| 1 **Gutknecht** | Y | Y | Y | Y | N | N | N |
| 2 **Kline** | Y | Y | Y | Y | N | N | N |
| 3 **Ramstad** | Y | Y | ? | Y | N | N | N |
| 4 McCollum | Y | Y | N | P | Y | Y | Y |
| 5 Sabo | Y | Y | N | Y | Y | Y | Y |
| 6 **Kennedy** | Y | Y | Y | Y | N | N | N |
| 7 Peterson | Y | Y | N | Y | Y | N | N |
| 8 Oberstar | Y | Y | N | Y | Y | Y | Y |
| **MISSISSIPPI** | | | | | | | |
| 1 **Wicker** | Y | Y | Y | Y | N | N | N |
| 2 Thompson | Y | Y | N | Y | Y | Y | Y |
| 3 **Pickering** | Y | Y | Y | Y | N | N | N |
| 4 Taylor | Y | Y | N | Y | Y | Y | N |
| **MISSOURI** | | | | | | | |
| 1 Clay | Y | Y | N | Y | Y | Y | Y |
| 2 **Akin** | Y | Y | Y | Y | N | N | N |
| 3 Carnahan | Y | Y | N | Y | Y | Y | Y |
| 4 Skelton | Y | Y | N | Y | Y | Y | N |
| 5 Cleaver | Y | Y | ? | ? | ? | ? | ? |
| 6 **Graves** | Y | Y | Y | Y | N | N | N |
| 7 **Blunt** | Y | Y | Y | Y | N | N | N |
| 8 **Emerson** | Y | Y | Y | Y | N | N | N |
| 9 **Hulshof** | Y | Y | Y | Y | N | N | N |
| **MONTANA** | | | | | | | |
| AL **Rehberg** | Y | Y | Y | Y | N | N | N |
| **NEBRASKA** | | | | | | | |
| 1 **Fortenberry** | Y | Y | Y | Y | N | N | N |
| 2 **Terry** | Y | Y | Y | Y | N | N | N |
| 3 **Osborne** | Y | Y | Y | Y | N | N | N |
| **NEVADA** | | | | | | | |
| 1 Berkley | Y | Y | N | Y | Y | Y | Y |
| 2 **Gibbons** | Y | Y | Y | Y | N | N | N |
| 3 **Porter** | Y | Y | Y | Y | N | N | N |
| **NEW HAMPSHIRE** | | | | | | | |
| 1 **Bradley** | Y | Y | Y | Y | N | N | N |
| 2 **Bass** | Y | Y | Y | Y | N | N | N |
| **NEW JERSEY** | | | | | | | |
| 1 Andrews | Y | Y | N | Y | Y | Y | Y |
| 2 **LoBiondo** | Y | Y | Y | Y | N | N | N |
| 3 **Saxton** | Y | Y | Y | Y | N | N | N |
| 4 **Smith** | Y | Y | Y | Y | N | N | N |
| 5 **Garrett** | Y | Y | Y | Y | N | N | N |
| 6 Pallone | Y | Y | N | Y | Y | Y | Y |
| 7 **Ferguson** | Y | Y | ? | ? | N | N | N |
| 8 Pascrell | Y | Y | N | Y | Y | Y | Y |
| 9 Rothman | Y | Y | N | Y | Y | Y | Y |
| 10 Payne | Y | Y | N | Y | Y | Y | Y |
| 11 **Frelinghuysen** | Y | Y | Y | Y | N | N | N |
| 12 Holt | Y | Y | N | Y | Y | Y | Y |
| 13 Menendez | Y | Y | N | Y | Y | Y | Y |
| **NEW MEXICO** | | | | | | | |
| 1 **Wilson** | Y | Y | Y | Y | N | N | N |
| 2 **Pearce** | Y | Y | Y | Y | N | Y | N |
| 3 Udall | Y | Y | N | Y | Y | Y | Y |
| **NEW YORK** | | | | | | | |
| 1 Bishop | Y | Y | N | Y | Y | Y | Y |
| 2 Israel | Y | Y | N | Y | Y | Y | Y |
| 3 **King** | Y | Y | Y | Y | N | N | N |
| 4 McCarthy | Y | Y | N | Y | Y | Y | Y |
| 5 Ackerman | Y | Y | N | Y | Y | Y | Y |
| 6 Meeks | ? | ? | ? | ? | ? | ? | ? |
| 7 Crowley | Y | Y | N | Y | Y | Y | Y |
| 8 Nadler | Y | Y | N | Y | Y | Y | Y |
| 9 Weiner | Y | Y | N | Y | Y | Y | Y |
| 10 Towns | Y | Y | N | Y | Y | Y | Y |
| 11 Owens | Y | Y | N | Y | Y | Y | Y |
| 12 Velázquez | Y | Y | N | Y | Y | Y | Y |
| 13 **Fossella** | Y | Y | Y | Y | N | Y | N |
| 14 Maloney | Y | Y | N | Y | Y | Y | Y |
| 15 Rangel | Y | Y | N | Y | Y | Y | Y |
| 16 Serrano | Y | Y | N | Y | Y | Y | Y |
| 17 Engel | Y | Y | N | Y | Y | Y | Y |
| 18 Lowey | Y | Y | N | Y | Y | Y | Y |
| 19 **Kelly** | Y | Y | Y | Y | N | N | N |
| 20 **Sweeney** | Y | ? | Y | Y | N | Y | N |
| 21 McNulty | Y | Y | N | Y | Y | Y | Y |
| 22 Hinchey | Y | Y | N | Y | Y | Y | Y |
| 23 **McHugh** | Y | Y | Y | Y | N | N | N |
| 24 **Boehlert** | Y | Y | Y | Y | N | N | N |
| 25 **Walsh** | Y | Y | Y | Y | N | N | N |
| 26 **Reynolds** | Y | Y | Y | Y | ? | ? | ? |
| 27 Higgins | Y | Y | N | Y | Y | Y | Y |
| 28 Slaughter | Y | Y | N | Y | Y | Y | Y |
| 29 **Kuhl** | Y | Y | Y | Y | N | N | N |
| **NORTH CAROLINA** | | | | | | | |
| 1 Butterfield | Y | Y | N | Y | Y | Y | Y |
| 2 Etheridge | Y | Y | N | Y | Y | Y | Y |
| 3 **Jones** | Y | Y | Y | Y | N | N | N |
| 4 Price | Y | Y | N | Y | Y | Y | Y |
| 5 **Foxx** | Y | Y | Y | Y | N | N | N |
| 6 **Coble** | Y | Y | Y | Y | N | N | N |
| 7 McIntyre | Y | Y | N | Y | Y | Y | N |
| 8 **Hayes** | Y | Y | Y | Y | N | N | N |
| 9 **Myrick** | Y | Y | Y | Y | N | N | N |
| 10 **McHenry** | Y | Y | Y | Y | N | N | N |
| 11 **Taylor** | Y | Y | Y | Y | N | N | N |
| 12 Watt | ? | ? | N | Y | Y | Y | Y |
| 13 Miller | Y | Y | N | Y | Y | Y | Y |
| **NORTH DAKOTA** | | | | | | | |
| AL Pomeroy | Y | Y | N | Y | Y | Y | Y |
| **OHIO** | | | | | | | |
| 1 **Chabot** | Y | Y | Y | Y | N | N | N |
| 2 **Portman** | Y | Y | Y | Y | N | N | N |
| 3 **Turner** | Y | Y | Y | Y | N | N | N |
| 4 **Oxley** | Y | Y | Y | Y | N | N | N |
| 5 **Gillmor** | ? | ? | ? | ? | ? | ? | ? |
| 6 Strickland | Y | Y | N | Y | Y | Y | Y |
| 7 **Hobson** | Y | Y | Y | Y | N | N | N |
| 8 **Boehner** | Y | Y | Y | Y | N | N | N |
| 9 Kaptur | Y | Y | N | Y | Y | Y | Y |
| 10 Kucinich | Y | Y | N | Y | Y | Y | Y |
| 11 Jones | Y | Y | N | Y | ? | ? | Y |
| 12 **Tiberi** | Y | Y | Y | Y | N | N | N |
| 13 Brown | Y | Y | N | Y | Y | Y | Y |
| 14 **LaTourette** | Y | Y | Y | Y | N | N | N |
| 15 **Pryce** | Y | Y | Y | Y | N | N | N |
| 16 **Regula** | Y | Y | Y | Y | N | N | N |
| 17 Ryan | Y | Y | N | Y | ? | Y | Y |
| 18 **Ney** | Y | Y | Y | Y | N | N | N |
| **OKLAHOMA** | | | | | | | |
| 1 **Sullivan** | Y | Y | Y | Y | N | N | N |
| 2 Boren | Y | Y | N | Y | Y | Y | Y |
| 3 **Lucas** | Y | Y | Y | Y | N | N | N |
| 4 **Cole** | Y | Y | Y | Y | N | N | N |
| 5 **Istook** | ? | Y | Y | Y | N | N | N |
| **OREGON** | | | | | | | |
| 1 Wu | Y | Y | N | Y | Y | Y | Y |
| 2 **Walden** | Y | Y | Y | Y | N | N | N |
| 3 Blumenauer | Y | Y | N | Y | Y | Y | Y |
| 4 DeFazio | Y | Y | N | Y | Y | N | Y |
| 5 Hooley | Y | Y | N | Y | Y | Y | Y |
| **PENNSYLVANIA** | | | | | | | |
| 1 Brady | Y | Y | N | Y | Y | Y | Y |
| 2 Fattah | Y | Y | N | Y | Y | Y | Y |
| 3 **English** | Y | Y | Y | Y | N | N | N |
| 4 **Hart** | Y | Y | Y | Y | N | N | N |
| 5 **Peterson** | ? | Y | Y | Y | N | N | N |
| 6 **Gerlach** | Y | Y | Y | Y | N | N | N |
| 7 **Weldon** | Y | Y | Y | Y | N | N | N |
| 8 **Fitzpatrick** | Y | Y | Y | Y | N | N | N |
| 9 **Shuster** | Y | Y | Y | Y | N | N | N |
| 10 **Sherwood** | Y | Y | Y | Y | N | N | N |
| 11 Kanjorski | Y | Y | N | Y | Y | Y | Y |
| 12 Murtha | Y | ? | N | Y | Y | Y | Y |
| 13 Schwartz | Y | Y | N | Y | Y | Y | Y |
| 14 Doyle | Y | Y | N | Y | Y | Y | Y |
| 15 **Dent** | Y | Y | Y | Y | N | N | N |
| 16 **Pitts** | Y | Y | Y | Y | N | N | N |
| 17 Holden | Y | Y | N | Y | Y | Y | Y |
| 18 **Murphy** | Y | Y | Y | Y | N | N | N |
| 19 **Platts** | Y | Y | Y | Y | N | N | N |
| **RHODE ISLAND** | | | | | | | |
| 1 Kennedy | Y | Y | N | Y | Y | Y | Y |
| 2 Langevin | Y | Y | N | Y | Y | Y | Y |
| **SOUTH CAROLINA** | | | | | | | |
| 1 **Brown** | Y | Y | Y | Y | N | N | N |
| 2 **Wilson** | Y | Y | Y | Y | N | N | N |
| 3 **Barrett** | Y | Y | Y | Y | N | N | N |
| 4 **Inglis** | Y | Y | Y | Y | N | N | N |
| 5 Spratt | Y | Y | N | Y | Y | Y | Y |
| 6 Clyburn | Y | Y | N | Y | Y | Y | Y |
| **SOUTH DAKOTA** | | | | | | | |
| AL Herseth | Y | Y | N | Y | Y | Y | N |
| **TENNESSEE** | | | | | | | |
| 1 **Jenkins** | Y | ? | Y | Y | N | N | N |
| 2 **Duncan** | Y | Y | Y | Y | N | N | N |
| 3 **Wamp** | Y | Y | Y | Y | N | N | N |
| 4 Davis | Y | Y | N | Y | Y | Y | N |
| 5 Cooper | Y | Y | N | Y | Y | Y | Y |
| 6 Gordon | Y | Y | N | Y | Y | Y | N |
| 7 **Blackburn** | Y | Y | Y | Y | N | N | N |
| 8 Tanner | Y | Y | N | Y | Y | Y | Y |
| 9 Ford | Y | Y | N | Y | Y | Y | Y |
| **TEXAS** | | | | | | | |
| 1 **Gohmert** | Y | Y | Y | Y | N | N | N |
| 2 **Poe** | Y | Y | Y | Y | N | N | N |
| 3 **Johnson, S.** | Y | Y | Y | Y | N | N | N |
| 4 **Hall** | Y | Y | Y | Y | N | N | N |
| 5 **Hensarling** | Y | Y | Y | Y | N | N | N |
| 6 **Barton** | Y | Y | Y | Y | N | N | N |
| 7 **Culberson** | Y | Y | Y | Y | N | N | N |
| 8 **Brady** | Y | Y | Y | Y | N | N | N |
| 9 Green | Y | Y | N | Y | Y | Y | Y |
| 10 **McCaul** | Y | Y | Y | Y | N | N | N |
| 11 **Conaway** | Y | Y | Y | Y | N | N | N |
| 12 **Granger** | Y | Y | Y | Y | N | N | N |
| 13 **Thornberry** | Y | Y | Y | Y | N | N | N |
| 14 **Paul** | Y | Y | Y | Y | Y | Y | N |
| 15 Hinojosa | Y | Y | Y | Y | Y | Y | Y |
| 16 Reyes | Y | Y | N | Y | Y | Y | Y |
| 17 Edwards | Y | Y | N | Y | Y | Y | Y |
| 18 Jackson-Lee | Y | Y | N | Y | Y | Y | Y |
| 19 **Neugebauer** | Y | Y | Y | Y | N | N | N |
| 20 Gonzalez | Y | Y | N | Y | Y | Y | Y |
| 21 **Smith** | Y | Y | Y | Y | N | N | N |
| 22 **DeLay** | Y | Y | Y | Y | N | N | N |
| 23 **Bonilla** | Y | Y | Y | Y | N | N | N |
| 24 **Marchant** | Y | Y | Y | Y | N | N | N |
| 25 Doggett | Y | Y | N | Y | Y | Y | Y |
| 26 **Burgess** | Y | Y | Y | Y | N | N | N |
| 27 Ortiz | Y | Y | N | Y | Y | Y | Y |
| 28 Cuellar | Y | Y | N | Y | Y | Y | Y |
| 29 Green | Y | Y | N | Y | Y | Y | Y |
| 30 Johnson, E. | Y | Y | N | Y | Y | Y | Y |
| 31 **Carter** | Y | Y | Y | Y | N | N | N |
| 32 **Sessions** | Y | Y | Y | Y | N | N | N |
| **UTAH** | | | | | | | |
| 1 **Bishop** | Y | Y | Y | Y | N | N | N |
| 2 Matheson | Y | Y | N | Y | Y | Y | Y |
| 3 **Cannon** | Y | Y | Y | Y | N | N | N |
| **VERMONT** | | | | | | | |
| AL *Sanders* | Y | Y | ? | ? | Y | Y | Y |
| **VIRGINIA** | | | | | | | |
| 1 **Davis, J.** | Y | Y | Y | Y | N | N | N |
| 2 **Drake** | Y | Y | Y | Y | N | N | N |
| 3 Scott | Y | Y | N | Y | Y | Y | Y |
| 4 **Forbes** | Y | Y | Y | Y | N | N | N |
| 5 **Goode** | Y | Y | Y | Y | N | N | N |
| 6 **Goodlatte** | Y | Y | Y | Y | N | N | N |
| 7 **Cantor** | Y | Y | Y | Y | N | N | N |
| 8 Moran | Y | Y | N | Y | Y | Y | Y |
| 9 Boucher | Y | Y | N | Y | Y | Y | Y |
| 10 **Wolf** | Y | Y | Y | Y | N | N | N |
| 11 **Davis, T.** | Y | Y | Y | Y | N | N | N |
| **WASHINGTON** | | | | | | | |
| 1 Inslee | Y | Y | N | Y | Y | Y | Y |
| 2 Larsen | Y | Y | N | Y | Y | Y | Y |
| 3 Baird | Y | Y | N | Y | Y | Y | Y |
| 4 **Hastings** | Y | Y | Y | Y | N | N | N |
| 5 **McMorris** | Y | Y | Y | Y | N | N | N |
| 6 Dicks | Y | Y | N | Y | Y | Y | Y |
| 7 McDermott | Y | Y | N | Y | Y | Y | Y |
| 8 **Reichert** | Y | Y | Y | Y | N | N | N |
| 9 Smith | Y | Y | N | Y | Y | Y | Y |
| **WEST VIRGINIA** | | | | | | | |
| 1 Mollohan | Y | Y | N | Y | Y | Y | N |
| 2 **Capito** | Y | Y | Y | Y | N | N | N |
| 3 Rahall | Y | Y | N | Y | Y | Y | N |
| **WISCONSIN** | | | | | | | |
| 1 **Ryan** | Y | Y | Y | Y | N | N | N |
| 2 Baldwin | Y | Y | N | Y | Y | Y | Y |
| 3 Kind | Y | Y | N | Y | Y | Y | Y |
| 4 Moore | Y | Y | N | Y | Y | Y | Y |
| 5 **Sensenbrenner** | Y | Y | Y | Y | N | N | N |
| 6 **Petri** | Y | Y | Y | Y | N | N | N |
| 7 Obey | Y | Y | N | Y | Y | Y | Y |
| 8 **Green** | Y | Y | Y | Y | N | N | N |
| **WYOMING** | | | | | | | |
| AL **Cubin** | Y | Y | Y | Y | N | N | N |

# IN THE HOUSE | By Vote Number

**47.** **HR 27. Job Training Reauthorization/Recommit.** Kildee, D-Mich., motion to recommit the bill to the Education and the Workforce Committee with instructions to add language that would provide financial assistance equal to the trade adjustment assistance program for job training, job searching or relocation costs for veterans returning from active duty in Iraq and to workers who are unemployed because their jobs were moved offshore. Motion rejected 197-228: R 0-228; D 196-0 (ND 145-0, SD 51-0); I 1-0. March 2, 2005.

**48.** **HR 27. Job Training Reauthorization/Passage.** Passage of a bill that would reauthorize the Workforce Investment Act, consolidate several programs into block grants for states and allow faith-based providers of job training activities to use religion as a factor in hiring decisions. It would combine the funding for adults, dislocated workers and employment services into a single $3 billion block grant program. The measure would authorize a demonstration program to create personal unemployment accounts under which an unemployed individual would receive a voucher worth up to $3,000 for job-training and other services. Passed 224-200: R 220-8; D 4-191 (ND 1-143, SD 3-48); I 0-1. March 2, 2005.

**49.** **HR 841. Continuity of Congress/Sixty-Day Election Deadline.** Millender-McDonald, D-Calif., amendment that would extend the deadline for conducting special elections under the bill from 45 days to 60 days after the Speaker's announcement. Rejected 192-229: R 1-225; D 190-4 (ND 142-3, SD 48-1); I 1-0. March 3, 2005.

**50.** **HR 841. Continuity of Congress/Lawsuit Deadline.** Jackson-Lee, D-Texas, amendment that would require that any lawsuit challenging the Speaker's announcement that more than 100 vacancies in the House exist must be filed within five days, rather than two days, of the announcement. It would allow any citizen of the district, or any group of citizens, to intervene in support or opposition to the challenge. Rejected 183-239: R 1-226; D 181-13 (ND 137-8, SD 44-5); I 1-0. March 3, 2005.

**51.** **HR 841. Continuity of Congress/Recommit.** Conyers, D-Mich., motion to recommit the bill to the House Administration Committee with instructions to add language that would require states to distribute election personnel and equipment equally when conducting special elections. Motion rejected 196-223: R 0-223; D 195-0 (ND 146-0, SD 49-0); I 1-0. March 3, 2005.

**52.** **HR 841. Continuity of Congress/Passage.** Passage of the bill that would require special elections to fill vacant House seats within 49 days of a catastrophe that kills at least 100 House members. If a regularly scheduled election is planned to fill a vacant House seat within 75 days of the House Speaker's announcement of the vacancies, then no special election for that seat is required. Parties would be required to nominate their candidates within 10 days of the House Speaker's announcement. Passed 329-68: R 206-3; D 122-65 (ND 88-52, SD 34-13); I 1-0. March 3, 2005.

| State / Member | 47 | 48 | 49 | 50 | 51 | 52 |
|---|---|---|---|---|---|---|
| **ALABAMA** | | | | | | |
| 1 Bonner | ? | ? | N | N | N | Y |
| 2 Everett | N | Y | N | N | N | ? |
| 3 Rogers | N | Y | N | N | N | Y |
| 4 Aderholt | N | Y | N | N | N | Y |
| 5 Cramer | Y | Y | Y | Y | Y | ? |
| 6 Bachus | N | Y | N | N | N | Y |
| 7 Davis | Y | N | Y | Y | Y | N |
| **ALASKA** | | | | | | |
| AL Young | N | Y | ? | ? | ? | ? |
| **ARIZONA** | | | | | | |
| 1 Renzi | N | Y | N | N | N | Y |
| 2 Franks | N | Y | N | N | N | Y |
| 3 Shadegg | N | Y | N | N | N | Y |
| 4 Pastor | Y | N | Y | Y | Y | Y |
| 5 Hayworth | N | Y | N | N | N | Y |
| 6 Flake | N | N | N | N | N | Y |
| 7 Grijalva | Y | N | Y | Y | Y | N |
| 8 Kolbe | N | Y | N | N | N | Y |
| **ARKANSAS** | | | | | | |
| 1 Berry | Y | N | Y | Y | Y | N |
| 2 Snyder | Y | N | Y | Y | Y | Y |
| 3 Boozman | N | Y | N | N | N | Y |
| 4 Ross | Y | N | Y | Y | Y | N |
| **CALIFORNIA** | | | | | | |
| 1 Thompson | Y | N | Y | N | Y | Y |
| 2 Herger | N | Y | N | N | N | Y |
| 3 Lungren | N | Y | N | N | N | Y |
| 4 Doolittle | N | Y | N | N | N | |
| 5 Vacant | | | | | | |
| 6 Woolsey | Y | N | Y | Y | Y | N |
| 7 Miller, George | Y | N | Y | Y | Y | Y |
| 8 Pelosi | Y | ? | Y | Y | Y | N |
| 9 Lee | Y | N | Y | Y | Y | N |
| 10 Tauscher | Y | N | Y | Y | Y | N |
| 11 Pombo | N | Y | N | N | N | ? |
| 12 Lantos | Y | N | Y | Y | Y | Y |
| 13 Stark | Y | N | Y | Y | Y | N |
| 14 Eshoo | Y | N | Y | Y | Y | N |
| 15 Honda | Y | N | Y | Y | Y | N |
| 16 Lofgren | Y | N | Y | Y | Y | Y |
| 17 Farr | Y | N | Y | Y | Y | N |
| 18 Cardoza | Y | N | Y | Y | Y | Y |
| 19 Radanovich | N | Y | N | N | N | Y |
| 20 Costa | Y | N | Y | Y | Y | Y |
| 21 Nunes | N | Y | N | N | N | Y |
| 22 Thomas | N | Y | N | N | N | Y |
| 23 Capps | Y | N | Y | Y | Y | Y |
| 24 Gallegly | N | Y | N | N | N | ? |
| 25 McKeon | N | Y | N | N | N | Y |
| 26 Dreier | N | Y | N | N | N | Y |
| 27 Sherman | Y | N | Y | Y | Y | Y |
| 28 Berman | Y | N | Y | Y | Y | Y |
| 29 Schiff | Y | N | Y | Y | Y | Y |
| 30 Waxman | Y | N | Y | Y | Y | Y |
| 31 Becerra | Y | N | Y | Y | Y | Y |
| 32 Solis | Y | N | Y | Y | Y | Y |
| 33 Watson | Y | N | Y | Y | Y | N |
| 34 Roybal-Allard | Y | N | Y | Y | Y | Y |
| 35 Waters | Y | N | Y | Y | Y | ? |
| 36 Harman | Y | N | Y | N | Y | Y |
| 37 Millender-McD. | ? | ? | Y | Y | Y | N |
| 38 Napolitano | ? | ? | ? | ? | ? | ? |
| 39 Sánchez, Linda | Y | N | Y | Y | Y | N |
| 40 Royce | N | Y | N | N | N | Y |
| 41 Lewis | N | Y | N | N | N | Y |
| 42 Miller, Gary | N | Y | N | N | N | Y |
| 43 Baca | Y | N | Y | Y | Y | Y |
| 44 Calvert | N | Y | N | N | N | Y |
| 45 Bono | N | Y | N | N | N | Y |
| 46 Rohrabacher | N | Y | N | N | N | N |
| 47 Sanchez, Loretta | Y | N | Y | N | Y | Y |
| 48 Cox | N | Y | N | N | N | Y |
| 49 Issa | N | Y | N | N | ? | ? |
| 50 Cunningham | N | Y | ? | ? | ? | ? |
| 51 Filner | Y | N | Y | Y | Y | N |
| 52 Hunter | N | Y | N | N | N | N |
| 53 Davis | Y | N | Y | Y | Y | N |
| **COLORADO** | | | | | | |
| 1 DeGette | Y | N | Y | Y | Y | Y |
| 2 Udall | Y | N | Y | Y | Y | Y |
| 3 Salazar | Y | N | Y | Y | Y | Y |
| 4 Musgrave | N | Y | N | N | N | Y |
| 5 Hefley | N | Y | Y | Y | N | Y |
| 6 Tancredo | N | N | N | N | N | Y |
| 7 Beauprez | N | Y | N | N | N | Y |
| **CONNECTICUT** | | | | | | |
| 1 Larson | Y | N | Y | Y | Y | N |
| 2 Simmons | N | Y | N | Y | Y | N |
| 3 DeLauro | Y | N | Y | Y | Y | N |
| 4 Shays | N | Y | N | N | N | Y |
| 5 Johnson | N | Y | N | N | N | Y |
| **DELAWARE** | | | | | | |
| AL Castle | N | Y | N | N | N | Y |
| **FLORIDA** | | | | | | |
| 1 Miller | N | Y | N | N | N | Y |
| 2 Boyd | Y | N | Y | Y | Y | Y |
| 3 Brown | Y | N | Y | Y | Y | Y |
| 4 Crenshaw | N | Y | N | N | N | Y |
| 5 Brown-Waite | N | Y | N | N | N | ? |
| 6 Stearns | N | Y | N | N | N | ? |
| 7 Mica | N | Y | N | N | N | ? |
| 8 Keller | N | Y | N | N | N | Y |
| 9 Bilirakis | N | Y | N | N | N | Y |
| 10 Young | N | Y | N | N | N | Y |
| 11 Davis | Y | N | Y | Y | Y | Y |
| 12 Putnam | N | Y | N | N | N | Y |
| 13 Harris | ? | ? | ? | ? | ? | ? |
| 14 Mack | N | Y | N | N | N | Y |
| 15 Weldon | N | Y | N | N | N | Y |
| 16 Foley | N | Y | N | N | N | Y |
| 17 Meek | Y | N | Y | Y | Y | N |
| 18 Ros-Lehtinen | N | Y | N | ? | ? | Y |
| 19 Wexler | Y | N | Y | Y | Y | N |
| 20 Wasserman-Schultz | Y | N | Y | Y | Y | N |
| 21 Diaz-Balart, L. | N | Y | N | N | N | Y |
| 22 Shaw | N | Y | N | N | N | Y |
| 23 Hastings | Y | N | Y | Y | Y | N |
| 24 Feeney | N | Y | N | N | N | ? |
| 25 Diaz-Balart, M. | N | Y | N | N | ? | ? |
| **GEORGIA** | | | | | | |
| 1 Kingston | N | Y | N | ? | ? | ? |
| 2 Bishop | Y | N | Y | Y | Y | Y |
| 3 Marshall | Y | Y | Y | Y | Y | Y |
| 4 McKinney | N | Y | Y | Y | Y | N |
| 5 Lewis | Y | N | ? | ? | ? | ? |
| 6 Price | N | Y | N | N | N | Y |
| 7 Linder | N | Y | N | N | N | Y |
| 8 Westmoreland | N | Y | N | N | N | Y |
| 9 Norwood | N | Y | N | N | N | Y |
| 10 Deal | N | Y | N | N | N | Y |
| 11 Gingrey | N | Y | N | N | N | Y |
| 12 Barrow | Y | N | Y | Y | Y | N |
| 13 Scott | Y | N | Y | Y | Y | ? |
| **HAWAII** | | | | | | |
| 1 Abercrombie | Y | N | Y | Y | Y | N |
| 2 Case | Y | N | Y | Y | Y | N |
| **IDAHO** | | | | | | |
| 1 Otter | N | Y | N | N | N | Y |
| 2 Simpson | N | Y | N | N | N | Y |
| **ILLINOIS** | | | | | | |
| 1 Rush | Y | N | Y | Y | Y | N |
| 2 Jackson | Y | N | Y | Y | Y | N |
| 3 Lipinski | Y | N | Y | Y | Y | Y |
| 4 Gutierrez | Y | N | Y | Y | Y | N |
| 5 Emanuel | Y | N | Y | Y | Y | N |
| 6 Hyde | N | Y | N | N | N | Y |
| 7 Davis | Y | N | Y | Y | Y | N |
| 8 Bean | Y | N | Y | Y | Y | N |
| 9 Schakowsky | Y | N | Y | Y | Y | N |
| 10 Kirk | N | Y | N | N | N | Y |
| 11 Weller | N | Y | N | N | N | Y |
| 12 Costello | Y | N | Y | Y | Y | N |

**KEY**    **Republicans**    Democrats    *Independents*

| | | |
|---|---|---|
| Y Voted for (yea) | X Paired against | C Voted "present" to avoid possible conflict of interest |
| # Paired for | − Announced against | |
| + Announced for | P Voted "present" | ? Did not vote or otherwise make a position known |
| N Voted against (nay) | | |

ND Northern Democrats, SD Southern Democrats
Southern states: Ala., Ark., Fla., Ga., Ky., La., Miss., N.C., Okla., S.C., Tenn., Texas, Va.

| | 47 | 48 | 49 | 50 | 51 | 52 |
|---|---|---|---|---|---|---|
| 13 **Biggert** | N | Y | N | N | N | Y |
| 14 **Hastert** | | | | | N | Y |
| 15 **Johnson** | N | Y | N | N | N | Y |
| 16 **Manzullo** | N | Y | N | N | N | Y |
| 17 Evans | Y | N | Y | Y | Y | Y |
| 18 **LaHood** | N | Y | N | N | N | Y |
| 19 **Shimkus** | N | Y | N | N | N | Y |
| **INDIANA** | | | | | | |
| 1 Visclosky | Y | N | Y | Y | Y | Y |
| 2 **Chocola** | N | Y | N | N | N | Y |
| 3 **Souder** | N | Y | N | N | N | Y |
| 4 **Buyer** | N | Y | N | N | N | Y |
| 5 **Burton** | N | Y | N | N | N | Y |
| 6 **Pence** | N | Y | N | N | N | Y |
| 7 Carson | ? | ? | ? | ? | ? | ? |
| 8 **Hostettler** | N | N | N | N | N | Y |
| 9 **Sodrel** | N | Y | N | N | N | Y |
| **IOWA** | | | | | | |
| 1 **Nussle** | N | Y | N | N | N | Y |
| 2 **Leach** | N | Y | ? | ? | ? | ? |
| 3 Boswell | Y | N | Y | Y | Y | Y |
| 4 **Latham** | N | Y | N | N | N | Y |
| 5 **King** | N | Y | N | N | N | Y |
| **KANSAS** | | | | | | |
| 1 **Moran** | N | Y | N | N | N | Y |
| 2 **Ryun** | N | Y | N | N | N | Y |
| 3 Moore | Y | N | Y | N | Y | Y |
| 4 **Tiahrt** | N | Y | N | N | N | Y |
| **KENTUCKY** | | | | | | |
| 1 **Whitfield** | N | Y | N | N | N | Y |
| 2 **Lewis** | N | Y | N | N | N | Y |
| 3 **Northup** | N | Y | N | N | N | Y |
| 4 **Davis** | N | Y | N | N | N | Y |
| 5 **Rogers** | N | Y | N | N | N | Y |
| 6 Chandler | Y | N | Y | Y | Y | Y |
| **LOUISIANA** | | | | | | |
| 1 **Jindal** | N | Y | N | N | N | Y |
| 2 Jefferson | Y | N | Y | Y | Y | N |
| 3 Melancon | Y | N | Y | Y | Y | Y |
| 4 **McCrery** | N | Y | N | N | N | Y |
| 5 **Alexander** | N | Y | N | N | N | Y |
| 6 **Baker** | N | Y | N | N | N | Y |
| 7 **Boustany** | N | Y | N | N | N | Y |
| **MAINE** | | | | | | |
| 1 Allen | Y | N | Y | Y | Y | Y |
| 2 Michaud | Y | N | N | Y | Y | Y |
| **MARYLAND** | | | | | | |
| 1 **Gilchrest** | N | Y | N | N | N | Y |
| 2 Ruppersberger | Y | N | Y | Y | Y | Y |
| 3 Cardin | Y | N | Y | Y | Y | Y |
| 4 Wynn | Y | N | Y | Y | Y | Y |
| 5 Hoyer | Y | N | Y | Y | Y | Y |
| 6 **Bartlett** | N | Y | N | N | N | Y |
| 7 Cummings | Y | N | Y | Y | Y | Y |
| 8 Van Hollen | Y | N | Y | Y | Y | N |
| **MASSACHUSETTS** | | | | | | |
| 1 Olver | Y | N | Y | Y | Y | N |
| 2 Neal | Y | N | Y | Y | Y | Y |
| 3 McGovern | Y | N | Y | Y | Y | N |
| 4 Frank | Y | N | Y | Y | Y | Y |
| 5 Meehan | Y | N | Y | Y | Y | ? |
| 6 Tierney | Y | N | Y | Y | Y | N |
| 7 Markey | Y | N | Y | Y | Y | N |
| 8 Capuano | Y | N | Y | Y | Y | Y |
| 9 Lynch | Y | N | Y | Y | Y | N |
| 10 Delahunt | Y | N | Y | Y | Y | ? |
| **MICHIGAN** | | | | | | |
| 1 Stupak | Y | N | Y | Y | Y | Y |
| 2 **Hoekstra** | N | Y | N | N | N | Y |
| 3 **Ehlers** | N | Y | N | N | N | Y |
| 4 **Camp** | N | Y | N | N | N | Y |
| 5 Kildee | Y | N | Y | Y | Y | Y |
| 6 **Upton** | N | Y | N | N | N | Y |
| 7 **Schwarz** | N | Y | N | N | N | Y |
| 8 **Rogers** | N | Y | N | N | N | Y |
| 9 **Knollenberg** | N | Y | N | N | N | Y |
| 10 **Miller** | N | Y | N | N | N | Y |
| 11 **McCotter** | N | Y | N | N | N | Y |
| 12 Levin | Y | N | Y | Y | Y | Y |
| 13 Kilpatrick | Y | N | Y | Y | Y | Y |
| 14 Conyers | Y | N | Y | Y | Y | N |
| 15 Dingell | Y | N | Y | Y | Y | Y |

| | 47 | 48 | 49 | 50 | 51 | 52 |
|---|---|---|---|---|---|---|
| **MINNESOTA** | | | | | | |
| 1 **Gutknecht** | N | Y | N | N | N | Y |
| 2 **Kline** | N | Y | N | N | N | Y |
| 3 **Ramstad** | N | Y | N | N | N | Y |
| 4 McCollum | Y | N | Y | Y | Y | N |
| 5 Sabo | Y | N | Y | Y | Y | Y |
| 6 **Kennedy** | N | Y | N | N | N | Y |
| 7 Peterson | Y | Y | Y | Y | Y | Y |
| 8 Oberstar | Y | N | Y | Y | Y | N |
| **MISSISSIPPI** | | | | | | |
| 1 **Wicker** | N | Y | N | N | N | Y |
| 2 Thompson | Y | N | Y | Y | Y | Y |
| 3 **Pickering** | N | Y | N | N | N | Y |
| 4 Taylor | Y | Y | Y | N | Y | N |
| **MISSOURI** | | | | | | |
| 1 Clay | Y | N | Y | Y | Y | Y |
| 2 **Akin** | N | Y | N | N | N | Y |
| 3 Carnahan | Y | N | Y | Y | Y | Y |
| 4 Skelton | Y | N | Y | Y | Y | Y |
| 5 Cleaver | ? | ? | Y | Y | Y | Y |
| 6 **Graves** | N | Y | N | N | N | ? |
| 7 **Blunt** | N | Y | N | N | N | Y |
| 8 **Emerson** | N | Y | N | N | N | ? |
| 9 **Hulshof** | N | Y | N | N | N | Y |
| **MONTANA** | | | | | | |
| AL **Rehberg** | N | Y | N | N | N | Y |
| **NEBRASKA** | | | | | | |
| 1 **Fortenberry** | N | Y | N | N | N | Y |
| 2 **Terry** | N | Y | N | N | N | ? |
| 3 **Osborne** | N | Y | N | N | N | Y |
| **NEVADA** | | | | | | |
| 1 Berkley | Y | N | Y | Y | Y | Y |
| 2 **Gibbons** | N | Y | N | N | N | Y |
| 3 **Porter** | N | Y | N | N | N | Y |
| **NEW HAMPSHIRE** | | | | | | |
| 1 **Bradley** | N | Y | N | N | N | Y |
| 2 **Bass** | N | Y | N | N | N | Y |
| **NEW JERSEY** | | | | | | |
| 1 Andrews | Y | N | Y | Y | Y | N |
| 2 **LoBiondo** | N | Y | N | N | N | Y |
| 3 **Saxton** | N | Y | N | N | N | Y |
| 4 **Smith** | N | Y | N | N | N | Y |
| 5 **Garrett** | N | Y | N | N | N | Y |
| 6 Pallone | Y | N | Y | Y | Y | N |
| 7 **Ferguson** | N | Y | N | N | N | Y |
| 8 Pascrell | Y | N | N | Y | Y | Y |
| 9 Rothman | Y | N | ? | ? | ? | ? |
| 10 Payne | Y | N | Y | Y | Y | N |
| 11 **Frelinghuysen** | N | Y | N | N | N | Y |
| 12 Holt | Y | N | Y | Y | Y | N |
| 13 Menendez | Y | N | Y | Y | Y | N |
| **NEW MEXICO** | | | | | | |
| 1 **Wilson** | N | Y | N | N | N | Y |
| 2 **Pearce** | N | Y | N | N | N | Y |
| 3 Udall | Y | N | Y | Y | Y | Y |
| **NEW YORK** | | | | | | |
| 1 Bishop | Y | N | Y | Y | Y | Y |
| 2 Israel | Y | N | Y | Y | Y | Y |
| 3 **King** | N | Y | N | N | N | Y |
| 4 McCarthy | Y | N | Y | Y | Y | Y |
| 5 Ackerman | Y | N | Y | Y | Y | Y |
| 6 Meeks | ? | ? | ? | ? | ? | ? |
| 7 Crowley | Y | N | Y | Y | Y | Y |
| 8 Nadler | Y | N | Y | Y | Y | N |
| 9 Weiner | Y | N | Y | Y | Y | Y |
| 10 Towns | Y | N | Y | Y | Y | Y |
| 11 Owens | Y | N | Y | Y | Y | Y |
| 12 Velázquez | Y | N | Y | Y | Y | Y |
| 13 **Fossella** | N | Y | N | N | N | Y |
| 14 Maloney | Y | N | Y | Y | Y | Y |
| 15 Rangel | Y | N | Y | Y | Y | Y |
| 16 Serrano | Y | N | Y | Y | Y | Y |
| 17 Engel | Y | N | Y | Y | Y | Y |
| 18 Lowey | Y | N | Y | Y | Y | Y |
| 19 **Kelly** | N | Y | N | N | N | Y |
| 20 **Sweeney** | N | Y | N | N | N | Y |
| 21 McNulty | Y | N | Y | N | Y | Y |
| 22 Hinchey | Y | N | Y | Y | Y | N |
| 23 **McHugh** | N | Y | N | N | N | Y |
| 24 **Boehlert** | N | Y | N | N | N | ? |
| 25 **Walsh** | N | Y | N | N | N | Y |
| 26 **Reynolds** | N | Y | N | N | N | Y |
| 27 Higgins | Y | N | N | Y | Y | Y |
| 28 Slaughter | Y | N | Y | Y | Y | ? |
| 29 **Kuhl** | N | Y | N | N | N | ? |

| | 47 | 48 | 49 | 50 | 51 | 52 |
|---|---|---|---|---|---|---|
| **NORTH CAROLINA** | | | | | | |
| 1 Butterfield | Y | N | Y | Y | Y | Y |
| 2 Etheridge | Y | N | Y | Y | Y | Y |
| 3 **Jones** | N | Y | N | N | N | N |
| 4 Price | Y | N | Y | Y | Y | Y |
| 5 **Foxx** | N | Y | N | N | N | Y |
| 6 **Coble** | N | Y | N | N | N | Y |
| 7 McIntyre | Y | N | Y | Y | Y | Y |
| 8 **Hayes** | N | Y | N | N | N | Y |
| 9 **Myrick** | N | Y | N | N | N | Y |
| 10 **McHenry** | N | Y | N | N | N | Y |
| 11 **Taylor** | N | Y | N | N | N | Y |
| 12 Watt | Y | N | Y | Y | Y | Y |
| 13 Miller | Y | N | Y | Y | Y | N |
| **NORTH DAKOTA** | | | | | | |
| AL Pomeroy | Y | N | Y | Y | Y | Y |
| **OHIO** | | | | | | |
| 1 **Chabot** | N | Y | N | N | N | Y |
| 2 **Portman** | N | Y | N | N | N | Y |
| 3 **Turner** | N | Y | N | N | N | Y |
| 4 **Oxley** | N | Y | N | N | N | Y |
| 5 **Gillmor** | ? | ? | N | N | N | Y |
| 6 Strickland | Y | N | Y | Y | Y | N |
| 7 **Hobson** | N | Y | N | N | N | Y |
| 8 **Boehner** | N | Y | N | N | N | Y |
| 9 Kaptur | Y | N | Y | Y | Y | Y |
| 10 Kucinich | Y | N | Y | Y | Y | N |
| 11 Jones | Y | N | Y | Y | Y | N |
| 12 **Tiberi** | N | Y | N | N | N | ? |
| 13 Brown | Y | N | ? | ? | Y | Y |
| 14 **LaTourette** | N | Y | N | N | N | ? |
| 15 **Pryce** | N | Y | N | N | N | Y |
| 16 **Regula** | N | Y | N | N | N | Y |
| 17 Ryan | Y | N | Y | Y | Y | N |
| 18 **Ney** | N | Y | N | N | N | Y |
| **OKLAHOMA** | | | | | | |
| 1 **Sullivan** | N | Y | N | N | N | Y |
| 2 Boren | Y | N | Y | N | Y | Y |
| 3 **Lucas** | N | Y | N | N | N | Y |
| 4 **Cole** | N | Y | N | N | N | Y |
| 5 **Istook** | N | Y | N | N | N | Y |
| **OREGON** | | | | | | |
| 1 Wu | Y | N | Y | Y | Y | Y |
| 2 **Walden** | N | Y | N | N | N | Y |
| 3 Blumenauer | Y | N | Y | Y | Y | Y |
| 4 DeFazio | Y | N | Y | Y | Y | Y |
| 5 Hooley | Y | N | Y | Y | Y | Y |
| **PENNSYLVANIA** | | | | | | |
| 1 Brady | Y | N | Y | Y | Y | Y |
| 2 Fattah | Y | N | Y | Y | Y | Y |
| 3 **English** | N | Y | N | N | N | Y |
| 4 **Hart** | N | Y | N | N | N | Y |
| 5 **Peterson** | N | Y | N | N | N | Y |
| 6 **Gerlach** | N | Y | N | N | N | Y |
| 7 **Weldon** | N | Y | N | N | N | ? |
| 8 **Fitzpatrick** | N | Y | N | N | N | Y |
| 9 **Shuster** | N | Y | N | N | N | Y |
| 10 **Sherwood** | N | Y | N | N | N | Y |
| 11 Kanjorski | Y | N | Y | Y | Y | Y |
| 12 Murtha | Y | N | Y | Y | Y | Y |
| 13 Schwartz | Y | N | Y | Y | Y | Y |
| 14 Doyle | Y | N | Y | Y | Y | Y |
| 15 **Dent** | N | Y | N | N | N | Y |
| 16 **Pitts** | N | Y | N | N | N | Y |
| 17 Holden | Y | N | Y | Y | Y | Y |
| 18 **Murphy** | N | Y | N | N | N | Y |
| 19 **Platts** | N | Y | N | N | N | Y |
| **RHODE ISLAND** | | | | | | |
| 1 Kennedy | Y | N | Y | Y | Y | N |
| 2 Langevin | Y | N | Y | Y | Y | N |
| **SOUTH CAROLINA** | | | | | | |
| 1 **Brown** | N | Y | N | N | N | Y |
| 2 **Wilson** | N | Y | N | N | N | Y |
| 3 **Barrett** | N | Y | N | N | N | Y |
| 4 **Inglis** | N | Y | ? | N | N | Y |
| 5 Spratt | Y | N | Y | Y | Y | ? |
| 6 Clyburn | Y | N | Y | Y | Y | N |
| **SOUTH DAKOTA** | | | | | | |
| AL Herseth | Y | N | Y | N | Y | Y |
| **TENNESSEE** | | | | | | |
| 1 **Jenkins** | N | Y | N | N | N | Y |
| 2 **Duncan** | N | N | N | N | N | N |

| | 47 | 48 | 49 | 50 | 51 | 52 |
|---|---|---|---|---|---|---|
| 3 **Wamp** | N | N | N | N | ? | ? |
| 4 Davis | Y | N | Y | N | Y | Y |
| 5 Cooper | Y | N | Y | Y | Y | Y |
| 6 Gordon | Y | N | Y | Y | Y | N |
| 7 **Blackburn** | N | Y | N | N | N | Y |
| 8 Tanner | Y | N | Y | Y | Y | Y |
| 9 Ford | Y | N | ? | ? | ? | ? |
| **TEXAS** | | | | | | |
| 1 **Gohmert** | N | Y | N | N | N | Y |
| 2 **Poe** | N | Y | N | N | N | Y |
| 3 **Johnson, S.** | N | Y | N | N | N | Y |
| 4 **Hall** | N | Y | N | N | N | Y |
| 5 **Hensarling** | N | N | N | N | N | Y |
| 6 **Barton** | N | Y | N | N | N | Y |
| 7 **Culberson** | N | Y | N | N | N | Y |
| 8 **Brady** | N | Y | N | N | N | Y |
| 9 Green, A. | Y | N | Y | Y | Y | Y |
| 10 **McCaul** | N | Y | N | N | N | Y |
| 11 **Conaway** | N | Y | N | N | N | Y |
| 12 **Granger** | N | Y | N | N | N | Y |
| 13 **Thornberry** | N | Y | N | N | N | Y |
| 14 **Paul** | N | N | N | N | N | Y |
| 15 Hinojosa | Y | N | Y | Y | Y | Y |
| 16 Reyes | Y | N | Y | Y | Y | Y |
| 17 Edwards | Y | N | Y | Y | Y | Y |
| 18 Jackson-Lee | Y | N | Y | Y | Y | N |
| 19 **Neugebauer** | N | Y | N | N | N | Y |
| 20 Gonzalez | Y | N | Y | Y | Y | N |
| 21 **Smith** | N | Y | N | N | N | Y |
| 22 **DeLay** | N | Y | N | N | N | Y |
| 23 **Bonilla** | N | Y | N | N | N | Y |
| 24 **Marchant** | N | Y | N | N | N | Y |
| 25 Doggett | Y | N | Y | Y | Y | Y |
| 26 **Burgess** | N | Y | N | N | N | Y |
| 27 Ortiz | Y | N | Y | Y | Y | Y |
| 28 Cuellar | Y | N | N | Y | Y | Y |
| 29 Green, G. | Y | N | Y | Y | Y | Y |
| 30 Johnson, E. | Y | N | Y | Y | Y | Y |
| 31 **Carter** | N | Y | N | N | N | Y |
| 32 **Sessions** | N | Y | N | N | N | Y |
| **UTAH** | | | | | | |
| 1 **Bishop** | N | Y | N | N | N | Y |
| 2 Matheson | Y | N | Y | N | Y | Y |
| 3 **Cannon** | N | Y | N | N | N | Y |
| **VERMONT** | | | | | | |
| AL *Sanders* | Y | N | Y | Y | Y | Y |
| **VIRGINIA** | | | | | | |
| 1 **Davis, J.** | N | Y | N | N | N | Y |
| 2 **Drake** | N | Y | N | N | N | Y |
| 3 Scott | Y | N | Y | Y | Y | N |
| 4 **Forbes** | N | Y | N | N | N | Y |
| 5 **Goode** | N | Y | N | N | N | Y |
| 6 **Goodlatte** | N | Y | N | N | N | Y |
| 7 **Cantor** | N | Y | N | N | N | Y |
| 8 Moran | Y | N | Y | Y | Y | N |
| 9 Boucher | Y | N | Y | Y | Y | Y |
| 10 **Wolf** | N | Y | N | N | N | Y |
| 11 **Davis, T.** | N | Y | N | N | N | Y |
| **WASHINGTON** | | | | | | |
| 1 Inslee | Y | N | Y | Y | Y | N |
| 2 Larsen | Y | N | Y | Y | Y | N |
| 3 Baird | Y | N | Y | Y | Y | N |
| 4 **Hastings** | N | Y | N | N | N | Y |
| 5 **McMorris** | N | Y | N | N | N | Y |
| 6 Dicks | Y | N | Y | Y | Y | N |
| 7 McDermott | Y | N | Y | Y | Y | ? |
| 8 **Reichert** | N | Y | N | N | N | Y |
| 9 Smith | Y | N | Y | Y | Y | Y |
| **WEST VIRGINIA** | | | | | | |
| 1 Mollohan | Y | N | Y | Y | Y | N |
| 2 **Capito** | N | Y | N | N | N | Y |
| 3 Rahall | Y | N | Y | Y | Y | Y |
| **WISCONSIN** | | | | | | |
| 1 **Ryan** | N | Y | N | N | N | Y |
| 2 Baldwin | Y | N | Y | Y | Y | N |
| 3 Kind | Y | N | Y | Y | Y | Y |
| 4 Moore | Y | N | Y | Y | Y | Y |
| 5 **Sensenbrenner** | N | N | N | N | N | Y |
| 6 **Petri** | N | Y | N | N | N | Y |
| 7 Obey | Y | N | Y | Y | Y | ? |
| 8 **Green** | N | Y | N | N | N | Y |
| **WYOMING** | | | | | | |
| AL **Cubin** | N | Y | N | N | N | Y |

# IN THE HOUSE | By Vote Number

**53. Procedural Motion/Journal.** Approval of the House Journal of Monday, March 7, 2005. Approved 378-29: R 220-8; D 157-21 (ND 112-18, SD 45-3); I 1-0. March 8, 2005.

**54. H Res 133. Committee Funding Extension/Adoption.** Ney, R-Ohio, motion to suspend the rules and adopt the resolution that would extend funding authority for House committees at current levels from April 1 through April 30. Motion agreed to 406-0: R 228-0; D 178-0 (ND 130-0, SD 48-0); I 0-0. A two-thirds majority of those present and voting (271 in this case) is required for adoption under suspension of the rules. March 8, 2005.

**55. H Res 122. Language Study/Adoption.** Porter, R-Nev., motion to suspend the rules and adopt the resolution that would express the sense of the House that language study contributes to the intellectual and social development of a student, as well as of the economy and security of the nation. Motion agreed to 396-0: R 223-0; D 173-0 (ND 126-0, SD 47-0); I 0-0. A two-thirds majority of those present and voting (264 in this case) is required for adoption under suspension of the rules. March 8, 2005.

**56. HR 3. Surface Transportation Reauthorization/Oil and Gas Hours-of-Service Exemptions.** Conaway, R-Texas, amendment that would exempt commercial drivers working in field operations for the natural gas and oil industry from hours-of-service rules issued by the Federal Motor Carrier Safety Administration in 2003. Rejected 198-226: R 185-43; D 13-182 (ND 6-139, SD 7-43); I 0-1. March 9, 2005.

**57. HR 3. Surface Transportation Reauthorization/Agriculture Hours-of-Service Exemptions.** Moran, R-Kan., amendment that would expand exemptions from hours-of-service rules for drivers of trucks transporting agricultural commodities to include livestock, food, feed, fiber and other farm products. Adopted 257-167: R 214-14; D 43-152 (ND 18-127, SD 25-25); I 0-1. March 9, 2005.

**58. HR 3. Surface Transportation Reauthorization/Vehicle Length Exemption.** Osborne, R-Neb., amendment that would exempt Nebraska from vehicle length restrictions of 65 feet and increase the limit to 81.5 feet for custom harvesters operating in the state during the harvesting of certain crops. Adopted 236-184: R 201-25; D 34-159 (ND 17-126, SD 17-33); I 1-0. March 9, 2005.

**59. HR 3. Surface Transportation Reauthorization/New Interstate Tolls.** Kennedy, R-Minn., amendment that would authorize new tolls on any existing toll road or newly constructed lane on the interstate system to manage congestion or address air pollution problems. It also would allow an unlimited number of new, toll-eligible express traffic lanes. Rejected 155-265: R 134-92; D 21-172 (ND 11-133, SD 10-39); I 0-1. March 9, 2005.

ND Northern Democrats, SD Southern Democrats
Southern states: Ala., Ark., Fla., Ga., Ky., La., Miss., N.C., Okla., S.C., Tenn., Texas, Va.

| | 53 | 54 | 55 | 56 | 57 | 58 | 59 |
|---|---|---|---|---|---|---|---|
| **ALABAMA** | | | | | | | |
| 1 Bonner | Y | Y | Y | Y | Y | Y | Y |
| 2 Everett | Y | Y | Y | Y | Y | Y | Y |
| 3 Rogers | Y | Y | Y | N | Y | Y | Y |
| 4 Aderholt | Y | Y | Y | Y | Y | Y | Y |
| 5 Cramer | Y | Y | Y | Y | Y | N | Y |
| 6 Bachus | Y | Y | Y | Y | Y | Y | N |
| 7 Davis | Y | Y | Y | N | Y | N | N |
| **ALASKA** | | | | | | | |
| AL Young | Y | Y | Y | N | N | N | N |
| **ARIZONA** | | | | | | | |
| 1 Renzi | Y | Y | Y | Y | Y | Y | Y |
| 2 Franks | Y | Y | Y | Y | Y | Y | Y |
| 3 Shadegg | Y | Y | Y | Y | Y | Y | Y |
| 4 Pastor | N | Y | Y | N | N | N | Y |
| 5 Hayworth | Y | Y | Y | Y | Y | Y | Y |
| 6 Flake | Y | Y | Y | Y | Y | Y | Y |
| 7 Grijalva | Y | Y | Y | N | N | N | N |
| 8 Kolbe | Y | Y | Y | Y | Y | Y | Y |
| **ARKANSAS** | | | | | | | |
| 1 Berry | Y | Y | Y | N | Y | N | N |
| 2 Snyder | Y | Y | Y | N | Y | N | N |
| 3 Boozman | Y | Y | Y | Y | Y | Y | Y |
| 4 Ross | Y | Y | Y | N | Y | N | N |
| **CALIFORNIA** | | | | | | | |
| 1 Thompson | Y | Y | Y | N | N | N | N |
| 2 Herger | Y | Y | Y | Y | Y | Y | N |
| 3 Lungren | Y | Y | Y | Y | Y | Y | N |
| 4 Doolittle | Y | Y | Y | Y | Y | Y | N |
| 5 Vacant | | | | | | | |
| 6 Woolsey | Y | Y | Y | N | N | N | N |
| 7 Miller, George | N | Y | Y | N | N | N | N |
| 8 Pelosi | Y | Y | Y | N | N | N | N |
| 9 Lee | ? | ? | ? | N | N | N | N |
| 10 Tauscher | Y | Y | Y | N | N | N | N |
| 11 Pombo | Y | Y | Y | Y | Y | Y | N |
| 12 Lantos | Y | Y | Y | N | N | N | N |
| 13 Stark | ? | ? | ? | N | N | N | N |
| 14 Eshoo | Y | Y | Y | N | N | N | N |
| 15 Honda | Y | Y | Y | N | N | N | N |
| 16 Lofgren | Y | Y | Y | N | N | N | N |
| 17 Farr | Y | Y | Y | N | N | N | N |
| 18 Cardoza | Y | Y | Y | N | Y | Y | Y |
| 19 Radanovich | Y | Y | Y | Y | Y | Y | N |
| 20 Costa | Y | Y | Y | N | Y | N | N |
| 21 Nunes | Y | Y | Y | Y | Y | Y | N |
| 22 Thomas | Y | Y | Y | Y | Y | Y | N |
| 23 Capps | Y | Y | Y | N | N | N | N |
| 24 Gallegly | Y | Y | Y | N | Y | Y | N |
| 25 McKeon | Y | Y | Y | Y | Y | Y | N |
| 26 Dreier | Y | Y | Y | Y | Y | Y | N |
| 27 Sherman | Y | Y | Y | N | N | N | N |
| 28 Berman | Y | Y | Y | N | N | N | N |
| 29 Schiff | Y | Y | Y | N | N | N | N |
| 30 Waxman | Y | Y | Y | N | N | Y | N |
| 31 Becerra | Y | Y | Y | N | N | N | N |
| 32 Solis | Y | Y | Y | N | N | N | N |
| 33 Watson | Y | Y | Y | N | N | Y | N |
| 34 Roybal-Allard | Y | Y | Y | N | N | N | N |
| 35 Waters | N | Y | Y | N | N | N | N |
| 36 Harman | Y | Y | Y | N | N | N | N |
| 37 Millender-McD. | Y | Y | Y | N | N | N | N |
| 38 Napolitano | Y | Y | Y | N | N | N | N |
| 39 Sánchez, Linda | Y | Y | Y | N | N | N | N |
| 40 Royce | Y | Y | Y | Y | Y | ? | Y |
| 41 Lewis | Y | Y | Y | Y | Y | Y | N |
| 42 Miller, Gary | Y | Y | Y | N | Y | Y | N |
| 43 Baca | Y | Y | Y | N | Y | N | N |
| 44 Calvert | Y | Y | Y | Y | Y | Y | N |
| 45 Bono | Y | Y | Y | Y | Y | Y | N |
| 46 Rohrabacher | Y | Y | Y | Y | Y | Y | Y |
| 47 Sanchez, Loretta | Y | Y | Y | N | N | N | N |
| 48 Cox | Y | Y | Y | Y | Y | Y | Y |
| 49 Issa | Y | Y | Y | Y | Y | Y | N |

| | 53 | 54 | 55 | 56 | 57 | 58 | 59 |
|---|---|---|---|---|---|---|---|
| 50 Cunningham | Y | Y | Y | Y | Y | Y | Y |
| 51 Filner | N | Y | Y | N | N | N | N |
| 52 Hunter | Y | Y | ? | Y | Y | Y | N |
| 53 Davis | Y | Y | Y | N | N | N | N |
| **COLORADO** | | | | | | | |
| 1 DeGette | Y | Y | Y | N | N | N | N |
| 2 Udall | N | Y | Y | Y | Y | Y | N |
| 3 Salazar | Y | Y | Y | Y | Y | Y | N |
| 4 Musgrave | Y | Y | Y | Y | Y | Y | Y |
| 5 Hefley | N | Y | Y | Y | Y | N | N |
| 6 Tancredo | Y | Y | Y | N | Y | Y | Y |
| 7 Beauprez | Y | Y | Y | Y | Y | Y | Y |
| **CONNECTICUT** | | | | | | | |
| 1 Larson | Y | Y | Y | N | N | N | N |
| 2 Simmons | Y | Y | Y | N | Y | Y | N |
| 3 DeLauro | Y | Y | Y | N | N | N | N |
| 4 Shays | Y | Y | Y | N | Y | Y | N |
| 5 Johnson | Y | Y | ? | N | Y | Y | N |
| **DELAWARE** | | | | | | | |
| AL Castle | Y | Y | Y | Y | Y | Y | N |
| **FLORIDA** | | | | | | | |
| 1 Miller | Y | Y | Y | Y | Y | Y | Y |
| 2 Boyd | Y | Y | N | Y | Y | Y | Y |
| 3 Brown | Y | Y | Y | N | N | N | N |
| 4 Crenshaw | Y | Y | Y | Y | Y | Y | Y |
| 5 Brown-Waite | Y | Y | Y | Y | Y | Y | Y |
| 6 Stearns | Y | Y | Y | Y | Y | Y | N |
| 7 Mica | Y | Y | Y | Y | Y | Y | N |
| 8 Keller | Y | Y | Y | Y | Y | Y | Y |
| 9 Bilirakis | Y | Y | Y | N | Y | N | N |
| 10 Young | Y | Y | Y | N | Y | Y | Y |
| 11 Davis | Y | Y | N | N | N | N | N |
| 12 Putnam | Y | Y | Y | Y | Y | Y | N |
| 13 Harris | Y | Y | Y | Y | Y | Y | Y |
| 14 Mack | Y | Y | Y | Y | Y | Y | Y |
| 15 Weldon | Y | Y | N | Y | Y | Y | Y |
| 16 Foley | Y | Y | Y | N | Y | Y | N |
| 17 Meek | Y | Y | Y | N | N | N | N |
| 18 Ros-Lehtinen | Y | Y | Y | N | N | N | N |
| 19 Wexler | Y | Y | Y | N | N | N | N |
| 20 Wasserman-Schultz | ? | ? | ? | N | N | N | N |
| 21 Diaz-Balart, L. | Y | Y | Y | Y | Y | Y | Y |
| 22 Shaw | Y | Y | Y | Y | Y | Y | N |
| 23 Hastings | N | Y | Y | N | N | N | N |
| 24 Feeney | Y | Y | Y | N | Y | Y | N |
| 25 Diaz-Balart, M. | Y | Y | Y | Y | Y | Y | Y |
| **GEORGIA** | | | | | | | |
| 1 Kingston | Y | Y | Y | Y | Y | Y | Y |
| 2 Bishop | Y | Y | Y | N | Y | Y | N |
| 3 Marshall | Y | Y | Y | N | Y | Y | N |
| 4 McKinney | Y | Y | Y | N | N | N | N |
| 5 Lewis | Y | Y | Y | N | N | N | N |
| 6 Price | Y | Y | Y | Y | Y | Y | N |
| 7 Linder | Y | Y | Y | Y | Y | Y | N |
| 8 Westmoreland | Y | Y | Y | Y | Y | Y | N |
| 9 Norwood | Y | Y | Y | Y | Y | Y | Y |
| 10 Deal | Y | Y | Y | Y | Y | Y | N |
| 11 Gingrey | Y | Y | Y | Y | Y | Y | N |
| 12 Barrow | ? | ? | ? | N | N | N | N |
| 13 Scott | Y | Y | Y | N | N | N | N |
| **HAWAII** | | | | | | | |
| 1 Abercrombie | Y | Y | Y | N | N | Y | N |
| 2 Case | Y | Y | Y | N | Y | N | N |
| **IDAHO** | | | | | | | |
| 1 Otter | N | Y | Y | Y | Y | Y | Y |
| 2 Simpson | Y | Y | ? | Y | Y | Y | Y |
| **ILLINOIS** | | | | | | | |
| 1 Rush | Y | Y | N | N | N | N | N |
| 2 Jackson | Y | Y | N | Y | N | N | N |
| 3 Lipinski | Y | Y | N | N | N | N | N |
| 4 Gutierrez | Y | Y | ? | N | N | N | N |
| 5 Emanuel | Y | Y | N | N | N | N | N |
| 6 Hyde | Y | Y | Y | Y | Y | Y | N |
| 7 Davis | Y | Y | N | N | N | N | N |
| 8 Bean | + | + | + | N | N | N | N |
| 9 Schakowsky | N | Y | ? | N | N | N | N |
| 10 Kirk | Y | Y | N | N | N | N | N |
| 11 Weller | N | Y | Y | Y | Y | Y | N |
| 12 Costello | Y | Y | N | Y | N | N | N |

**KEY**  Republicans    Democrats    *Independents*

| | | | |
|---|---|---|---|
| Y | Voted for (yea) | X | Paired against | C | Voted "present" to avoid possible conflict of interest |
| # | Paired for | – | Announced against | | |
| + | Announced for | P | Voted "present" | ? | Did not vote or otherwise make a position known |
| N | Voted against (nay) | | | | |

| | 53 | 54 | 55 | 56 | 57 | 58 | 59 |
|---|---|---|---|---|---|---|---|
| 13 **Biggert** | Y | Y | Y | N | N | N | N |
| 14 **Hastert** | | | | | | | |
| 15 **Johnson** | Y | Y | Y | Y | Y | Y | Y |
| 16 **Manzullo** | Y | Y | Y | Y | Y | Y | Y |
| 17 Evans | Y | Y | Y | N | N | N | N |
| 18 **LaHood** | Y | Y | Y | Y | Y | Y | Y |
| 19 **Shimkus** | Y | Y | Y | Y | Y | Y | Y |
| **INDIANA** | | | | | | | |
| 1 Visclosky | Y | Y | Y | N | N | N | N |
| 2 **Chocola** | Y | Y | Y | Y | Y | Y | N |
| 3 **Souder** | Y | Y | Y | Y | Y | Y | Y |
| 4 **Buyer** | Y | Y | Y | Y | Y | Y | Y |
| 5 **Burton** | Y | Y | Y | Y | Y | Y | Y |
| 6 **Pence** | Y | Y | Y | Y | Y | Y | Y |
| 7 Carson | ? | ? | ? | N | N | N | N |
| 8 **Hostettler** | Y | Y | Y | Y | Y | Y | Y |
| 9 **Sodrel** | Y | Y | Y | Y | Y | Y | N |
| **IOWA** | | | | | | | |
| 1 **Nussle** | Y | Y | Y | N | Y | Y | Y |
| 2 **Leach** | ? | ? | ? | N | Y | N | Y |
| 3 Boswell | Y | Y | Y | N | Y | Y | N |
| 4 **Latham** | N | Y | Y | Y | Y | Y | Y |
| 5 **King** | Y | Y | Y | Y | Y | Y | Y |
| **KANSAS** | | | | | | | |
| 1 **Moran** | Y | Y | Y | Y | Y | Y | Y |
| 2 **Ryun** | Y | Y | Y | Y | Y | Y | N |
| 3 Moore | Y | Y | Y | Y | Y | Y | Y |
| 4 **Tiahrt** | Y | Y | Y | Y | Y | Y | N |
| **KENTUCKY** | | | | | | | |
| 1 **Whitfield** | Y | Y | Y | Y | Y | Y | Y |
| 2 **Lewis** | Y | Y | Y | Y | Y | Y | N |
| 3 **Northup** | Y | Y | Y | Y | Y | Y | Y |
| 4 **Davis** | Y | Y | Y | Y | Y | Y | N |
| 5 **Rogers** | Y | Y | Y | Y | Y | Y | Y |
| 6 Chandler | Y | Y | Y | N | N | N | N |
| **LOUISIANA** | | | | | | | |
| 1 **Jindal** | Y | Y | Y | Y | Y | Y | Y |
| 2 Jefferson | Y | Y | Y | Y | N | N | ? |
| 3 Melancon | Y | Y | Y | Y | Y | Y | Y |
| 4 **McCrery** | Y | Y | Y | Y | Y | Y | N |
| 5 **Alexander** | Y | Y | Y | Y | Y | Y | Y |
| 6 **Baker** | Y | Y | Y | Y | Y | Y | N |
| 7 **Boustany** | Y | Y | Y | Y | Y | Y | Y |
| **MAINE** | | | | | | | |
| 1 Allen | Y | Y | Y | N | N | N | N |
| 2 Michaud | Y | Y | Y | N | N | N | Y |
| **MARYLAND** | | | | | | | |
| 1 **Gilchrest** | Y | Y | Y | N | Y | Y | N |
| 2 Ruppersberger | Y | Y | Y | N | Y | N | N |
| 3 Cardin | Y | Y | Y | N | N | N | N |
| 4 Wynn | Y | Y | ? | N | N | N | N |
| 5 Hoyer | Y | Y | Y | N | N | N | N |
| 6 **Bartlett** | Y | Y | Y | Y | Y | Y | N |
| 7 Cummings | Y | Y | Y | N | N | N | N |
| 8 Van Hollen | Y | Y | Y | N | N | N | N |
| **MASSACHUSETTS** | | | | | | | |
| 1 Olver | N | Y | Y | N | N | N | N |
| 2 Neal | Y | Y | Y | N | N | N | N |
| 3 McGovern | Y | Y | Y | N | N | N | N |
| 4 Frank | Y | Y | Y | N | N | Y | N |
| 5 Meehan | Y | Y | Y | N | N | N | N |
| 6 Tierney | Y | Y | Y | N | N | N | N |
| 7 Markey | Y | Y | Y | N | N | N | N |
| 8 Capuano | N | Y | Y | N | N | N | N |
| 9 Lynch | Y | Y | Y | N | N | Y | N |
| 10 Delahunt | Y | Y | Y | N | N | N | N |
| **MICHIGAN** | | | | | | | |
| 1 Stupak | ? | ? | ? | ? | ? | ? | ? |
| 2 **Hoekstra** | Y | Y | Y | N | Y | Y | Y |
| 3 **Ehlers** | Y | Y | Y | Y | Y | N | Y |
| 4 **Camp** | Y | Y | Y | Y | Y | Y | N |
| 5 Kildee | Y | Y | Y | N | N | N | N |
| 6 **Upton** | Y | Y | Y | N | Y | Y | Y |
| 7 **Schwarz** | Y | Y | Y | Y | Y | Y | N |
| 8 **Rogers** | Y | Y | Y | Y | Y | Y | N |
| 9 **Knollenberg** | Y | Y | Y | Y | Y | Y | Y |
| 10 **Miller** | Y | Y | Y | N | Y | Y | N |
| 11 **McCotter** | Y | Y | Y | N | N | N | Y |
| 12 Levin | Y | Y | Y | N | N | N | N |
| 13 Kilpatrick | Y | Y | Y | N | N | N | N |
| 14 Conyers | Y | Y | ? | N | N | N | N |
| 15 Dingell | Y | Y | Y | N | N | Y | N |

| | 53 | 54 | 55 | 56 | 57 | 58 | 59 |
|---|---|---|---|---|---|---|---|
| **MINNESOTA** | | | | | | | |
| 1 **Gutknecht** | N | Y | Y | Y | Y | Y | Y |
| 2 **Kline** | Y | Y | Y | Y | Y | Y | Y |
| 3 **Ramstad** | ? | ? | ? | ? | ? | ? | ? |
| 4 McCollum | Y | Y | Y | N | N | N | N |
| 5 Sabo | N | Y | Y | N | N | N | N |
| 6 **Kennedy** | Y | Y | Y | Y | Y | Y | Y |
| 7 Peterson | N | Y | Y | N | Y | Y | N |
| 8 Oberstar | N | Y | Y | N | N | N | N |
| **MISSISSIPPI** | | | | | | | |
| 1 **Wicker** | Y | Y | Y | Y | Y | Y | Y |
| 2 Thompson | N | Y | Y | N | N | N | N |
| 3 **Pickering** | Y | Y | Y | Y | Y | Y | Y |
| 4 Taylor | N | Y | Y | N | N | Y | N |
| **MISSOURI** | | | | | | | |
| 1 Clay | ? | ? | ? | ? | ? | ? | ? |
| 2 **Akin** | Y | Y | Y | Y | Y | Y | Y |
| 3 Carnahan | Y | Y | Y | N | N | N | N |
| 4 Skelton | Y | Y | Y | Y | Y | Y | N |
| 5 Cleaver | + | + | + | N | N | N | N |
| 6 **Graves** | Y | Y | Y | Y | Y | Y | N |
| 7 **Blunt** | Y | Y | Y | Y | Y | Y | Y |
| 8 **Emerson** | Y | Y | Y | Y | Y | Y | Y |
| 9 **Hulshof** | Y | Y | Y | Y | Y | Y | N |
| **MONTANA** | | | | | | | |
| AL **Rehberg** | Y | Y | Y | Y | Y | Y | Y |
| **NEBRASKA** | | | | | | | |
| 1 **Fortenberry** | Y | Y | Y | Y | Y | Y | N |
| 2 **Terry** | Y | Y | Y | Y | Y | Y | N |
| 3 **Osborne** | Y | Y | Y | Y | Y | Y | N |
| **NEVADA** | | | | | | | |
| 1 Berkley | ? | ? | ? | N | N | N | N |
| 2 **Gibbons** | Y | Y | Y | Y | Y | + | + |
| 3 **Porter** | Y | Y | Y | Y | Y | Y | N |
| **NEW HAMPSHIRE** | | | | | | | |
| 1 **Bradley** | Y | Y | Y | Y | Y | Y | Y |
| 2 **Bass** | ? | ? | ? | Y | N | Y | Y |
| **NEW JERSEY** | | | | | | | |
| 1 Andrews | Y | Y | Y | N | N | N | Y |
| 2 **LoBiondo** | N | Y | Y | N | Y | N | Y |
| 3 **Saxton** | Y | Y | Y | Y | Y | N | N |
| 4 **Smith** | Y | Y | Y | N | Y | N | Y |
| 5 **Garrett** | Y | Y | Y | Y | Y | Y | Y |
| 6 Pallone | Y | Y | Y | N | N | N | N |
| 7 **Ferguson** | Y | Y | Y | N | Y | N | Y |
| 8 Pascrell | Y | Y | Y | N | N | N | N |
| 9 Rothman | Y | Y | Y | ? | ? | ? | ? |
| 10 Payne | Y | Y | Y | N | N | ? | ? |
| 11 **Frelinghuysen** | Y | Y | Y | N | Y | Y | N |
| 12 Holt | Y | Y | Y | N | N | N | N |
| 13 Menendez | Y | Y | Y | N | N | N | N |
| **NEW MEXICO** | | | | | | | |
| 1 **Wilson** | Y | Y | Y | N | Y | Y | Y |
| 2 **Pearce** | Y | Y | Y | Y | Y | Y | Y |
| 3 Udall | N | Y | Y | Y | Y | N | N |
| **NEW YORK** | | | | | | | |
| 1 Bishop | Y | Y | Y | N | N | N | N |
| 2 Israel | Y | Y | Y | N | N | N | N |
| 3 **King** | Y | Y | Y | N | Y | Y | Y |
| 4 McCarthy | ? | ? | ? | N | N | N | N |
| 5 Ackerman | Y | Y | Y | N | N | N | N |
| 6 Meeks | ? | ? | ? | N | Y | N | Y |
| 7 Crowley | ? | ? | ? | N | N | N | N |
| 8 Nadler | Y | Y | Y | N | N | N | N |
| 9 Weiner | ? | ? | ? | N | N | N | N |
| 10 Towns | ? | ? | ? | N | N | N | N |
| 11 Owens | Y | Y | Y | N | N | N | N |
| 12 Velázquez | Y | Y | Y | N | N | N | N |
| 13 **Fossella** | N | Y | Y | N | Y | Y | Y |
| 14 Maloney | Y | Y | Y | N | N | N | N |
| 15 Rangel | Y | Y | Y | N | N | N | N |
| 16 Serrano | Y | Y | Y | N | N | N | N |
| 17 Engel | Y | Y | Y | N | N | N | N |
| 18 Lowey | Y | Y | Y | N | N | N | N |
| 19 **Kelly** | Y | Y | Y | N | Y | N | Y |
| 20 **Sweeney** | Y | Y | Y | N | Y | Y | Y |
| 21 McNulty | Y | Y | Y | N | N | N | N |
| 22 Hinchey | N | Y | Y | N | N | ? | N |
| 23 **McHugh** | Y | Y | Y | N | Y | Y | Y |
| 24 **Boehlert** | Y | Y | Y | Y | Y | N | Y |
| 25 **Walsh** | Y | Y | Y | N | Y | Y | N |
| 26 **Reynolds** | Y | Y | Y | N | Y | Y | Y |
| 27 Higgins | ? | ? | ? | N | N | N | N |
| 28 Slaughter | Y | Y | Y | N | N | Y | N |
| 29 **Kuhl** | Y | Y | Y | Y | Y | Y | N |

| | 53 | 54 | 55 | 56 | 57 | 58 | 59 |
|---|---|---|---|---|---|---|---|
| **NORTH CAROLINA** | | | | | | | |
| 1 Butterfield | Y | Y | Y | N | N | N | N |
| 2 Etheridge | Y | Y | Y | N | Y | Y | N |
| 3 **Jones** | Y | Y | Y | Y | Y | N | Y |
| 4 Price | Y | Y | Y | N | N | N | N |
| 5 **Foxx** | Y | Y | Y | Y | Y | Y | Y |
| 6 **Coble** | Y | Y | Y | N | Y | N | Y |
| 7 McIntyre | Y | Y | Y | Y | Y | Y | N |
| 8 **Hayes** | Y | Y | Y | Y | Y | Y | Y |
| 9 **Myrick** | Y | Y | Y | Y | Y | Y | N |
| 10 **McHenry** | Y | Y | Y | Y | Y | Y | Y |
| 11 **Taylor** | Y | Y | Y | Y | Y | Y | Y |
| 12 Watt | Y | Y | Y | N | N | N | N |
| 13 Miller | Y | Y | Y | N | N | N | N |
| **NORTH DAKOTA** | | | | | | | |
| AL Pomeroy | Y | Y | Y | N | Y | Y | N |
| **OHIO** | | | | | | | |
| 1 **Chabot** | Y | Y | Y | Y | Y | Y | Y |
| 2 **Portman** | Y | Y | Y | Y | Y | Y | Y |
| 3 **Turner** | Y | Y | Y | N | Y | Y | N |
| 4 **Oxley** | Y | Y | Y | Y | Y | Y | Y |
| 5 **Gillmor** | Y | Y | Y | N | Y | N | Y |
| 6 Strickland | Y | Y | Y | N | N | N | Y |
| 7 **Hobson** | Y | Y | Y | ? | ? | ? | ? |
| 8 **Boehner** | Y | Y | Y | Y | Y | Y | Y |
| 9 Kaptur | Y | Y | Y | N | N | N | N |
| 10 Kucinich | N | Y | Y | N | N | N | N |
| 11 Jones | Y | Y | Y | N | N | N | N |
| 12 **Tiberi** | Y | Y | Y | ? | ? | ? | ? |
| 13 Brown | Y | Y | Y | N | N | N | N |
| 14 **LaTourette** | Y | Y | Y | N | N | N | Y |
| 15 **Pryce** | Y | Y | Y | Y | Y | Y | Y |
| 16 **Regula** | Y | Y | Y | Y | Y | Y | N |
| 17 Ryan | Y | Y | Y | N | N | N | N |
| 18 **Ney** | Y | Y | Y | Y | Y | Y | Y |
| **OKLAHOMA** | | | | | | | |
| 1 **Sullivan** | Y | Y | Y | Y | Y | Y | Y |
| 2 Boren | Y | Y | Y | Y | Y | Y | Y |
| 3 **Lucas** | Y | Y | Y | Y | Y | Y | N |
| 4 **Cole** | Y | Y | Y | Y | Y | Y | Y |
| 5 **Istook** | Y | Y | Y | Y | Y | Y | Y |
| **OREGON** | | | | | | | |
| 1 Wu | Y | Y | Y | N | N | N | N |
| 2 **Walden** | Y | Y | ? | Y | Y | Y | N |
| 3 Blumenauer | Y | Y | ? | N | N | N | N |
| 4 DeFazio | Y | Y | Y | N | N | N | N |
| 5 Hooley | N | Y | Y | N | N | N | N |
| **PENNSYLVANIA** | | | | | | | |
| 1 Brady | ? | ? | ? | N | N | N | N |
| 2 Fattah | Y | Y | Y | N | N | N | N |
| 3 **English** | N | Y | Y | N | N | Y | Y |
| 4 **Hart** | Y | Y | Y | Y | N | Y | N |
| 5 **Peterson** | Y | Y | Y | Y | Y | Y | Y |
| 6 **Gerlach** | Y | Y | Y | N | Y | Y | N |
| 7 **Weldon** | Y | Y | Y | N | Y | N | Y |
| 8 **Fitzpatrick** | Y | Y | Y | N | Y | N | N |
| 9 **Shuster** | Y | Y | Y | Y | Y | Y | Y |
| 10 **Sherwood** | Y | Y | Y | Y | Y | Y | N |
| 11 Kanjorski | ? | ? | ? | N | N | N | N |
| 12 Murtha | Y | Y | Y | N | N | N | N |
| 13 Schwartz | Y | Y | Y | N | N | N | N |
| 14 Doyle | Y | Y | Y | N | N | N | N |
| 15 **Dent** | Y | Y | Y | Y | Y | Y | Y |
| 16 **Pitts** | Y | Y | Y | Y | Y | Y | Y |
| 17 Holden | Y | Y | Y | N | N | N | N |
| 18 **Murphy** | Y | Y | Y | N | N | N | N |
| 19 **Platts** | Y | Y | Y | N | Y | Y | Y |
| **RHODE ISLAND** | | | | | | | |
| 1 Kennedy | ? | ? | Y | N | N | Y | N |
| 2 Langevin | Y | Y | Y | N | N | N | N |
| **SOUTH CAROLINA** | | | | | | | |
| 1 **Brown** | Y | Y | Y | Y | Y | Y | Y |
| 2 **Wilson** | Y | Y | Y | Y | Y | Y | Y |
| 3 **Barrett** | Y | Y | Y | Y | Y | Y | Y |
| 4 **Inglis** | Y | Y | Y | Y | Y | Y | Y |
| 5 Spratt | Y | Y | Y | N | Y | N | N |
| 6 Clyburn | Y | Y | Y | N | N | N | N |
| **SOUTH DAKOTA** | | | | | | | |
| AL Herseth | ? | ? | ? | ? | ? | ? | ? |
| **TENNESSEE** | | | | | | | |
| 1 **Jenkins** | Y | Y | Y | Y | Y | Y | Y |
| 2 **Duncan** | Y | Y | Y | Y | Y | Y | Y |

| | 53 | 54 | 55 | 56 | 57 | 58 | 59 |
|---|---|---|---|---|---|---|---|
| 3 **Wamp** | Y | Y | Y | Y | Y | Y | Y |
| 4 Davis | Y | Y | Y | N | Y | Y | N |
| 5 Cooper | Y | Y | Y | N | Y | N | Y |
| 6 Gordon | Y | Y | Y | N | Y | Y | Y |
| 7 **Blackburn** | Y | Y | Y | Y | Y | Y | Y |
| 8 Tanner | Y | Y | Y | Y | Y | N | Y |
| 9 Ford | Y | Y | Y | N | Y | Y | N |
| **TEXAS** | | | | | | | |
| 1 **Gohmert** | Y | Y | Y | Y | Y | Y | N |
| 2 **Poe** | Y | Y | Y | Y | Y | Y | N |
| 3 **Johnson, S.** | Y | Y | Y | Y | Y | Y | N |
| 4 **Hall** | Y | Y | Y | Y | Y | Y | N |
| 5 **Hensarling** | Y | Y | Y | Y | Y | Y | Y |
| 6 **Barton** | Y | Y | Y | Y | Y | Y | N |
| 7 **Culberson** | Y | Y | Y | Y | Y | Y | N |
| 8 **Brady** | Y | Y | Y | Y | Y | Y | N |
| 9 Green, A. | Y | Y | Y | N | N | N | N |
| 10 **McCaul** | Y | Y | Y | Y | Y | Y | Y |
| 11 **Conaway** | Y | Y | Y | Y | Y | Y | N |
| 12 **Granger** | Y | Y | Y | Y | Y | Y | N |
| 13 **Thornberry** | Y | Y | Y | Y | Y | Y | Y |
| 14 **Paul** | Y | Y | Y | Y | Y | Y | Y |
| 15 Hinojosa | Y | Y | Y | N | Y | N | Y |
| 16 Reyes | Y | Y | Y | N | Y | N | Y |
| 17 Edwards | Y | Y | Y | N | Y | N | N |
| 18 Jackson-Lee | Y | Y | ? | ? | ? | ? | ? |
| 19 **Neugebauer** | Y | Y | Y | Y | Y | Y | Y |
| 20 Gonzalez | Y | Y | Y | N | N | Y | N |
| 21 **Smith** | Y | Y | Y | Y | Y | Y | Y |
| 22 **DeLay** | Y | Y | Y | Y | Y | Y | N |
| 23 **Bonilla** | Y | Y | Y | Y | Y | Y | N |
| 24 **Marchant** | Y | Y | Y | Y | Y | Y | N |
| 25 Doggett | Y | Y | Y | N | N | N | Y |
| 26 **Burgess** | Y | Y | Y | Y | Y | Y | N |
| 27 Ortiz | Y | Y | Y | N | Y | N | N |
| 28 Cuellar | Y | Y | Y | N | Y | Y | N |
| 29 Green, G. | Y | Y | Y | N | N | Y | N |
| 30 Johnson, E. | Y | Y | Y | N | N | N | N |
| 31 **Carter** | Y | Y | Y | Y | Y | Y | N |
| 32 **Sessions** | Y | Y | Y | Y | Y | Y | Y |
| **UTAH** | | | | | | | |
| 1 **Bishop** | Y | Y | Y | Y | Y | Y | ? |
| 2 Matheson | Y | Y | Y | Y | Y | N | N |
| 3 **Cannon** | Y | Y | Y | Y | Y | Y | Y |
| **VERMONT** | | | | | | | |
| AL *Sanders* | Y | ? | ? | N | N | Y | N |
| **VIRGINIA** | | | | | | | |
| 1 **Davis, J.** | Y | Y | Y | Y | N | Y | N |
| 2 **Drake** | Y | Y | Y | Y | Y | Y | Y |
| 3 Scott | Y | Y | Y | N | N | N | N |
| 4 **Forbes** | Y | Y | Y | Y | Y | Y | N |
| 5 **Goode** | Y | Y | Y | Y | Y | Y | Y |
| 6 **Goodlatte** | Y | Y | Y | Y | Y | Y | N |
| 7 **Cantor** | Y | Y | Y | Y | Y | Y | Y |
| 8 Moran | Y | Y | Y | N | N | N | N |
| 9 Boucher | ? | ? | ? | N | Y | Y | N |
| 10 **Wolf** | Y | Y | ? | N | N | N | N |
| 11 **Davis, T.** | Y | Y | Y | Y | Y | N | N |
| **WASHINGTON** | | | | | | | |
| 1 Inslee | Y | Y | Y | N | N | N | N |
| 2 Larsen | N | Y | Y | N | N | N | N |
| 3 Baird | ? | ? | ? | ? | ? | ? | ? |
| 4 **Hastings** | Y | Y | Y | Y | Y | Y | Y |
| 5 **McMorris** | Y | Y | Y | Y | Y | Y | Y |
| 6 Dicks | Y | Y | Y | N | N | N | N |
| 7 McDermott | N | Y | Y | N | N | N | N |
| 8 **Reichert** | Y | Y | Y | Y | Y | Y | N |
| 9 Smith | Y | Y | Y | N | N | N | Y |
| **WEST VIRGINIA** | | | | | | | |
| 1 Mollohan | Y | Y | Y | N | Y | N | Y |
| 2 **Capito** | Y | Y | Y | Y | Y | Y | N |
| 3 Rahall | Y | Y | Y | N | N | N | Y |
| **WISCONSIN** | | | | | | | |
| 1 **Ryan** | Y | Y | Y | Y | Y | Y | Y |
| 2 Baldwin | N | Y | Y | N | N | N | N |
| 3 Kind | Y | Y | Y | N | Y | Y | Y |
| 4 Moore | + | + | + | N | N | N | N |
| 5 **Sensenbrenner** | Y | Y | Y | Y | Y | N | Y |
| 6 **Petri** | Y | Y | Y | N | N | N | N |
| 7 Obey | Y | Y | Y | N | N | Y | N |
| 8 **Green** | Y | Y | Y | Y | Y | N | Y |
| **WYOMING** | | | | | | | |
| AL **Cubin** | Y | Y | Y | Y | Y | Y | Y |

# IN THE HOUSE | By Vote Number

**60.** HR 3. **Surface Transportation Reauthorization/Rental Company Liability.** Graves, R-Mo., amendment that would bar so-called vicarious liability under state law for car- and truck-rental companies for injuries and damage caused by vehicles they rent, provided there is no negligence or criminal wrong-doing by the company. Adopted 218-201: R 203-22; D 15-178 (ND 5-138, SD 10-40); I 0-1. March 9, 2005.

**61.** **Procedural Motion/Journal.** Approval of the House Journal of Wednesday, March 9, 2005. Approved 365-39: R 206-10; D 159-29 (ND 118-23, SD 41-6); I 0-0. March 10, 2005.

**62.** HR 3. **Surface Transportation Reauthorization/Low-Income Toll Reductions.** T. Davis, R-Va., amendment that would eliminate provisions in the bill that would require states to allow low-income individuals to pay reduced tolls on high-occupancy vehicle (HOV) lanes if they participate in HOV, congestion-pricing or construction toll programs. Adopted 224-201: R 214-11; D 10-189 (ND 4-144, SD 6-45); I 0-1. March 10, 2005.

**63.** HR 3. **Surface Transportation Reauthorization/Urban Area Grants.** Pitts, R-Pa., amendment that would authorize urban areas with populations that recently exceeded 200,000 to use grants under the Urbanized Area Formula Grants mass transit program to cover 50 percent of equipment and facilities operating costs in fiscal 2005 through 2007, and 25 percent for such costs in fiscal 2008 and 2009. Adopted 228-197: R 159-67; D 69-129 (ND 38-109, SD 31-20); I 0-1. March 10, 2005.

**64.** HR 3. **Surface Transportation Reauthorization/Recommit.** Higgins, D-N.Y., motion to recommit the bill to the House Transportation and Infrastructure and Ways and Means committees with instructions to add language that would increase funding in the bill to $318 billion, while providing offsets by eliminating certain tax provisions for companies that move jobs and operations offshore. Motion rejected 190-235: R 0-227; D 189-8 (ND 143-3, SD 46-5); I 1-0. March 10, 2005.

**65.** HR 3. **Surface Transportation Reauthorization/Passage.** Passage of the bill that would authorize $283.9 billion for federal aid highway, mass transit, safety and research programs from fiscal 2004 to 2009. The funding total includes $225.5 billion in guaranteed funding for highways, $52.4 billion for mass transit and other public transportation programs and $11.1 billion for members' projects. The bill, as amended, would include 92.6 percent of total highway funding in the calculation of a state's minimum guarantee of rate-of-return on their contributions to the Highway Trust Fund. Passed 417-9: R 218-9; D 198-0 (ND 147-0, SD 51-0); I 1-0. A "nay" was a vote in support of the president's position. March 10, 2005.

| | 60 | 61 | 62 | 63 | 64 | 65 |
|---|---|---|---|---|---|---|
| **ALABAMA** | | | | | | |
| 1 Bonner | Y | Y | Y | Y | N | Y |
| 2 Everett | Y | Y | N | Y | N | Y |
| 3 Rogers | N | ? | ? | ? | ? | ? |
| 4 Aderholt | Y | Y | Y | Y | N | Y |
| 5 Cramer | Y | Y | Y | Y | Y | Y |
| 6 Bachus | Y | ? | Y | N | N | Y |
| 7 Davis | N | Y | N | Y | N | Y |
| **ALASKA** | | | | | | |
| AL Young | N | Y | N | N | N | Y |
| **ARIZONA** | | | | | | |
| 1 Renzi | Y | Y | Y | Y | N | Y |
| 2 Franks | Y | Y | Y | Y | N | Y |
| 3 Shadegg | Y | Y | Y | Y | N | N |
| 4 Pastor | N | Y | N | N | Y | Y |
| 5 Hayworth | Y | Y | Y | Y | N | Y |
| 6 Flake | N | Y | Y | Y | N | N |
| 7 Grijalva | N | Y | N | N | Y | Y |
| 8 Kolbe | Y | Y | Y | Y | N | Y |
| **ARKANSAS** | | | | | | |
| 1 Berry | N | Y | N | N | Y | Y |
| 2 Snyder | N | Y | Y | N | N | Y |
| 3 Boozman | Y | Y | Y | Y | N | Y |
| 4 Ross | N | Y | N | N | Y | Y |
| **CALIFORNIA** | | | | | | |
| 1 Thompson | N | N | N | N | Y | Y |
| 2 Herger | Y | Y | ? | Y | N | Y |
| 3 Lungren | Y | Y | Y | N | N | Y |
| 4 Doolittle | N | Y | Y | N | N | Y |
| 5 Matsui, D.* | | | N | N | Y | Y |
| 6 Woolsey | N | Y | N | N | Y | Y |
| 7 Miller, George | N | Y | N | N | Y | Y |
| 8 Pelosi | N | Y | N | N | Y | Y |
| 9 Lee | N | Y | N | N | Y | Y |
| 10 Tauscher | N | Y | N | Y | Y | Y |
| 11 Pombo | Y | Y | Y | Y | N | Y |
| 12 Lantos | N | Y | N | N | Y | Y |
| 13 Stark | N | Y | N | N | Y | Y |
| 14 Eshoo | N | Y | N | N | Y | Y |
| 15 Honda | N | Y | N | N | Y | Y |
| 16 Lofgren | N | Y | N | N | Y | Y |
| 17 Farr | N | Y | N | N | Y | Y |
| 18 Cardoza | N | ? | N | N | Y | Y |
| 19 Radanovich | Y | Y | Y | Y | N | Y |
| 20 Costa | Y | Y | N | Y | Y | Y |
| 21 Nunes | Y | Y | Y | Y | N | Y |
| 22 Thomas | ? | Y | N | Y | N | Y |
| 23 Capps | N | Y | N | N | Y | Y |
| 24 Gallegly | Y | Y | Y | Y | N | Y |
| 25 McKeon | Y | Y | Y | Y | N | Y |
| 26 Dreier | Y | Y | Y | Y | N | Y |
| 27 Sherman | N | Y | N | N | Y | Y |
| 28 Berman | N | Y | N | N | Y | Y |
| 29 Schiff | N | Y | N | Y | Y | Y |
| 30 Waxman | N | Y | N | N | Y | Y |
| 31 Becerra | N | Y | N | N | Y | Y |
| 32 Solis | N | Y | N | N | Y | Y |
| 33 Watson | N | Y | N | Y | Y | Y |
| 34 Roybal-Allard | N | Y | N | N | Y | Y |
| 35 Waters | N | N | N | N | Y | Y |
| 36 Harman | N | Y | N | N | Y | Y |
| 37 Millender-McD. | N | Y | N | N | Y | Y |
| 38 Napolitano | N | Y | N | N | Y | Y |
| 39 Sánchez, Linda | N | Y | N | N | Y | Y |
| 40 Royce | Y | Y | Y | N | N | Y |
| 41 Lewis | Y | Y | Y | N | N | Y |
| 42 Miller, Gary | Y | Y | Y | N | N | Y |
| 43 Baca | N | Y | N | Y | Y | Y |
| 44 Calvert | Y | Y | Y | Y | N | Y |
| 45 Bono | Y | Y | Y | Y | N | Y |
| 46 Rohrabacher | Y | Y | Y | Y | N | Y |
| 47 Sanchez, Loretta | N | Y | N | N | Y | Y |
| 48 Cox | Y | ? | Y | N | Y | Y |
| 49 Issa | Y | Y | Y | Y | N | Y |

| | 60 | 61 | 62 | 63 | 64 | 65 |
|---|---|---|---|---|---|---|
| 50 Cunningham | Y | Y | Y | Y | N | Y |
| 51 Filner | N | N | N | N | Y | Y |
| 52 Hunter | Y | Y | Y | Y | N | Y |
| 53 Davis | N | Y | N | N | Y | Y |
| **COLORADO** | | | | | | |
| 1 DeGette | ? | Y | N | N | Y | Y |
| 2 Udall | N | N | N | Y | Y | Y |
| 3 Salazar | N | Y | N | N | Y | Y |
| 4 Musgrave | Y | Y | Y | Y | N | Y |
| 5 Hefley | Y | N | Y | N | N | Y |
| 6 Tancredo | N | P | Y | N | N | Y |
| 7 Beauprez | Y | Y | Y | Y | N | Y |
| **CONNECTICUT** | | | | | | |
| 1 Larson | N | Y | N | N | Y | Y |
| 2 Simmons | + | Y | Y | Y | N | Y |
| 3 DeLauro | N | Y | N | N | Y | Y |
| 4 Shays | Y | Y | Y | Y | N | Y |
| 5 Johnson | Y | Y | Y | Y | N | Y |
| **DELAWARE** | | | | | | |
| AL Castle | N | Y | N | N | N | N |
| **FLORIDA** | | | | | | |
| 1 Miller | Y | Y | Y | Y | N | Y |
| 2 Boyd | Y | Y | N | N | Y | Y |
| 3 Brown | N | Y | N | Y | Y | Y |
| 4 Crenshaw | Y | Y | Y | Y | N | Y |
| 5 Brown-Waite | Y | Y | Y | Y | N | Y |
| 6 Stearns | Y | Y | Y | Y | N | Y |
| 7 Mica | N | Y | Y | Y | N | Y |
| 8 Keller | Y | Y | Y | Y | N | Y |
| 9 Bilirakis | Y | Y | Y | Y | N | Y |
| 10 Young | N | Y | Y | Y | N | N |
| 11 Davis | N | Y | N | Y | Y | Y |
| 12 Putnam | Y | Y | Y | Y | N | Y |
| 13 Harris | Y | Y | Y | Y | N | Y |
| 14 Mack | Y | Y | Y | Y | N | Y |
| 15 Weldon | Y | Y | Y | Y | ? | Y |
| 16 Foley | Y | Y | Y | Y | N | Y |
| 17 Meek | N | Y | N | N | Y | Y |
| 18 Ros-Lehtinen | Y | Y | Y | N | N | Y |
| 19 Wexler | N | ? | N | N | Y | Y |
| 20 Wasserman-Schultz | N | Y | N | Y | N | Y |
| 21 Diaz-Balart, L. | N | Y | Y | N | N | Y |
| 22 Shaw | Y | Y | Y | N | N | Y |
| 23 Hastings | N | N | N | N | Y | Y |
| 24 Feeney | Y | Y | Y | Y | N | Y |
| 25 Diaz-Balart, M. | Y | Y | Y | Y | N | Y |
| **GEORGIA** | | | | | | |
| 1 Kingston | Y | Y | Y | Y | N | Y |
| 2 Bishop | N | Y | N | Y | Y | Y |
| 3 Marshall | N | N | N | Y | Y | Y |
| 4 McKinney | N | N | N | Y | Y | Y |
| 5 Lewis | N | N | N | Y | Y | Y |
| 6 Price | Y | Y | Y | Y | N | Y |
| 7 Linder | Y | Y | Y | Y | N | Y |
| 8 Westmoreland | Y | Y | Y | Y | N | N |
| 9 Norwood | Y | ? | Y | N | N | Y |
| 10 Deal | Y | Y | Y | N | N | Y |
| 11 Gingrey | Y | Y | Y | Y | N | Y |
| 12 Barrow | N | Y | N | N | Y | Y |
| 13 Scott | N | ? | N | N | Y | Y |
| **HAWAII** | | | | | | |
| 1 Abercrombie | N | Y | Y | N | Y | Y |
| 2 Case | N | Y | Y | N | Y | Y |
| **IDAHO** | | | | | | |
| 1 Otter | N | Y | Y | N | N | N |
| 2 Simpson | Y | Y | Y | N | N | N |
| **ILLINOIS** | | | | | | |
| 1 Rush | N | Y | N | N | Y | Y |
| 2 Jackson | N | Y | N | N | Y | Y |
| 3 Lipinski | N | Y | N | N | Y | Y |
| 4 Gutierrez | N | Y | N | N | Y | Y |
| 5 Emanuel | N | Y | N | N | Y | Y |
| 6 Hyde | Y | ? | Y | Y | N | Y |
| 7 Davis | N | Y | N | N | Y | Y |
| 8 Bean | N | Y | N | N | Y | Y |
| 9 Schakowsky | N | N | N | N | Y | Y |
| 10 Kirk | Y | Y | Y | N | N | Y |
| 11 Weller | Y | N | Y | Y | N | Y |
| 12 Costello | N | N | N | N | Y | Y |

**KEY** Republicans   Democrats   *Independents*

| | | | |
|---|---|---|---|
| **Y** Voted for (yea) | **X** Paired against | **C** Voted "present" to avoid possible conflict of interest |
| **#** Paired for | **–** Announced against | |
| **+** Announced for | **P** Voted "present" | **?** Did not vote or otherwise make a position known |
| **N** Voted against (nay) | | |

* Rep. Doris Matsui, D-Calif., was sworn in March 10, 2005. The first vote for which she was eligible was vote 62.

ND Northern Democrats, SD Southern Democrats
Southern states: Ala., Ark., Fla., Ga., Ky., La., Miss., N.C., Okla., S.C., Tenn., Texas, Va.

| | 60 | 61 | 62 | 63 | 64 | 65 |
|---|---|---|---|---|---|---|
| 13 **Biggert** | Y | Y | Y | N | N | Y |
| 14 **Hastert** | Y | | | | N | Y |
| 15 **Johnson** | N | Y | N | N | N | Y |
| 16 **Manzullo** | N | Y | Y | Y | N | Y |
| 17 Evans | N | Y | ? | ? | ? | ? |
| 18 **LaHood** | Y | Y | Y | Y | N | Y |
| 19 **Shimkus** | Y | Y | N | Y | N | Y |
| **INDIANA** | | | | | | |
| 1 Visclosky | N | Y | N | N | Y | Y |
| 2 **Chocola** | Y | Y | Y | Y | N | Y |
| 3 **Souder** | Y | Y | Y | Y | N | Y |
| 4 **Buyer** | Y | Y | Y | Y | N | Y |
| 5 **Burton** | Y | Y | Y | N | N | Y |
| 6 **Pence** | Y | Y | Y | Y | N | Y |
| 7 Carson | N | Y | N | N | Y | Y |
| 8 **Hostettler** | Y | Y | Y | Y | N | Y |
| 9 **Sodrel** | Y | Y | Y | N | N | Y |
| **IOWA** | | | | | | |
| 1 **Nussle** | Y | Y | Y | Y | N | Y |
| 2 **Leach** | Y | Y | Y | Y | N | Y |
| 3 Boswell | N | Y | N | N | Y | Y |
| 4 **Latham** | Y | N | Y | Y | N | Y |
| 5 **King** | Y | Y | Y | Y | N | Y |
| **KANSAS** | | | | | | |
| 1 **Moran** | Y | Y | Y | Y | N | Y |
| 2 **Ryun** | Y | Y | Y | Y | N | Y |
| 3 Moore | N | Y | N | Y | N | Y |
| 4 **Tiahrt** | Y | Y | Y | Y | N | Y |
| **KENTUCKY** | | | | | | |
| 1 **Whitfield** | Y | Y | Y | Y | N | Y |
| 2 **Lewis** | Y | Y | Y | Y | N | Y |
| 3 **Northup** | Y | ? | ? | ? | ? | ? |
| 4 **Davis** | Y | Y | Y | N | N | Y |
| 5 **Rogers** | Y | Y | Y | N | N | Y |
| 6 Chandler | N | Y | N | N | Y | Y |
| **LOUISIANA** | | | | | | |
| 1 **Jindal** | Y | Y | Y | Y | N | Y |
| 2 Jefferson | N | ? | N | Y | Y | Y |
| 3 Melancon | N | Y | N | Y | Y | Y |
| 4 **McCrery** | Y | Y | Y | N | N | Y |
| 5 **Alexander** | Y | Y | Y | Y | N | Y |
| 6 **Baker** | Y | Y | Y | Y | N | Y |
| 7 **Boustany** | Y | Y | Y | Y | N | Y |
| **MAINE** | | | | | | |
| 1 Allen | N | Y | N | N | Y | Y |
| 2 Michaud | N | Y | N | N | Y | Y |
| **MARYLAND** | | | | | | |
| 1 **Gilchrest** | Y | Y | Y | N | N | Y |
| 2 Ruppersberger | N | Y | N | Y | Y | Y |
| 3 Cardin | N | Y | N | Y | Y | Y |
| 4 Wynn | N | Y | N | Y | Y | Y |
| 5 Hoyer | N | Y | N | Y | Y | Y |
| 6 **Bartlett** | Y | Y | Y | Y | N | Y |
| 7 Cummings | N | ? | N | N | Y | Y |
| 8 Van Hollen | N | Y | N | N | Y | Y |
| **MASSACHUSETTS** | | | | | | |
| 1 Olver | N | N | N | Y | Y | Y |
| 2 Neal | N | Y | N | Y | Y | Y |
| 3 McGovern | N | N | N | Y | Y | Y |
| 4 Frank | N | Y | N | Y | Y | Y |
| 5 Meehan | N | Y | N | Y | Y | Y |
| 6 Tierney | N | ? | N | Y | Y | Y |
| 7 Markey | N | Y | N | Y | Y | Y |
| 8 Capuano | N | N | N | N | Y | Y |
| 9 Lynch | N | Y | N | Y | Y | Y |
| 10 Delahunt | N | ? | N | Y | Y | Y |
| **MICHIGAN** | | | | | | |
| 1 Stupak | ? | ? | ? | ? | ? | ? |
| 2 **Hoekstra** | Y | Y | Y | N | N | Y |
| 3 **Ehlers** | Y | Y | N | N | N | Y |
| 4 **Camp** | Y | Y | Y | N | N | Y |
| 5 Kildee | N | Y | N | N | Y | Y |
| 6 **Upton** | Y | Y | Y | N | N | Y |
| 7 **Schwarz** | Y | Y | Y | Y | N | Y |
| 8 **Rogers** | Y | Y | Y | Y | N | Y |
| 9 **Knollenberg** | N | Y | Y | N | N | Y |
| 10 **Miller** | Y | Y | Y | N | N | Y |
| 11 **McCotter** | Y | Y | Y | Y | N | Y |
| 12 Levin | N | Y | N | N | Y | Y |
| 13 Kilpatrick | N | Y | N | N | Y | Y |
| 14 Conyers | N | Y | N | N | Y | Y |
| 15 Dingell | N | Y | N | N | Y | Y |
| **MINNESOTA** | | | | | | |
| 1 **Gutknecht** | Y | N | Y | Y | N | Y |
| 2 **Kline** | Y | Y | Y | Y | N | Y |
| 3 **Ramstad** | ? | ? | ? | ? | ? | ? |
| 4 McCollum | N | Y | N | N | Y | Y |
| 5 Sabo | N | N | N | N | ? | Y |
| 6 **Kennedy** | Y | N | Y | Y | N | Y |
| 7 Peterson | Y | N | N | N | Y | Y |
| 8 Oberstar | N | N | N | N | Y | Y |
| **MISSISSIPPI** | | | | | | |
| 1 **Wicker** | Y | N | Y | N | N | Y |
| 2 Thompson | N | ? | N | N | Y | Y |
| 3 **Pickering** | Y | Y | Y | N | N | Y |
| 4 Taylor | N | N | N | Y | N | Y |
| **MISSOURI** | | | | | | |
| 1 Clay | ? | ? | N | Y | Y | Y |
| 2 **Akin** | Y | Y | Y | Y | N | Y |
| 3 Carnahan | N | Y | N | Y | Y | Y |
| 4 Skelton | N | Y | N | Y | Y | Y |
| 5 Cleaver | N | Y | N | Y | Y | Y |
| 6 **Graves** | Y | Y | Y | Y | N | Y |
| 7 **Blunt** | Y | Y | Y | Y | N | Y |
| 8 **Emerson** | Y | Y | Y | Y | N | Y |
| 9 **Hulshof** | Y | Y | Y | Y | N | Y |
| **MONTANA** | | | | | | |
| AL **Rehberg** | Y | Y | Y | Y | N | Y |
| **NEBRASKA** | | | | | | |
| 1 **Fortenberry** | Y | Y | Y | Y | N | Y |
| 2 **Terry** | N | Y | Y | Y | N | Y |
| 3 **Osborne** | Y | Y | Y | Y | N | Y |
| **NEVADA** | | | | | | |
| 1 Berkley | N | Y | N | N | Y | Y |
| 2 **Gibbons** | Y | N | Y | Y | N | Y |
| 3 **Porter** | Y | Y | Y | Y | N | Y |
| **NEW HAMPSHIRE** | | | | | | |
| 1 **Bradley** | Y | Y | Y | Y | N | Y |
| 2 **Bass** | Y | Y | Y | Y | N | Y |
| **NEW JERSEY** | | | | | | |
| 1 Andrews | N | Y | N | N | Y | Y |
| 2 **LoBiondo** | Y | N | Y | N | N | Y |
| 3 **Saxton** | ? | Y | Y | N | N | Y |
| 4 **Smith** | Y | Y | Y | N | N | Y |
| 5 **Garrett** | Y | Y | Y | Y | N | Y |
| 6 Pallone | N | Y | N | N | Y | Y |
| 7 **Ferguson** | Y | Y | Y | N | N | Y |
| 8 Pascrell | N | Y | N | N | Y | Y |
| 9 Rothman | ? | Y | N | N | Y | Y |
| 10 Payne | ? | ? | N | N | Y | Y |
| 11 **Frelinghuysen** | Y | Y | Y | Y | N | Y |
| 12 Holt | N | N | N | N | Y | Y |
| 13 Menendez | N | Y | N | N | Y | Y |
| **NEW MEXICO** | | | | | | |
| 1 **Wilson** | Y | Y | Y | Y | N | Y |
| 2 **Pearce** | Y | Y | Y | N | N | Y |
| 3 Udall | N | N | N | Y | Y | Y |
| **NEW YORK** | | | | | | |
| 1 Bishop | N | Y | N | N | Y | Y |
| 2 Israel | N | Y | N | N | Y | Y |
| 3 **King** | N | Y | Y | Y | N | Y |
| 4 McCarthy | N | Y | N | N | Y | Y |
| 5 Ackerman | N | Y | N | N | Y | Y |
| 6 Meeks | N | Y | N | N | Y | Y |
| 7 Crowley | N | Y | N | N | Y | Y |
| 8 Nadler | N | Y | N | N | Y | Y |
| 9 Weiner | N | Y | N | N | Y | Y |
| 10 Towns | N | Y | N | N | Y | Y |
| 11 Owens | N | Y | N | N | Y | Y |
| 12 Velázquez | N | Y | N | N | Y | Y |
| 13 **Fossella** | Y | ? | Y | Y | N | Y |
| 14 Maloney | N | Y | N | Y | Y | Y |
| 15 Rangel | N | Y | N | N | Y | Y |
| 16 Serrano | N | Y | N | N | Y | Y |
| 17 Engel | N | Y | N | Y | Y | Y |
| 18 Lowey | N | Y | N | Y | Y | Y |
| 19 **Kelly** | Y | Y | Y | Y | N | Y |
| 20 **Sweeney** | Y | Y | Y | Y | N | Y |
| 21 McNulty | N | N | N | N | Y | Y |
| 22 Hinchey | N | Y | N | N | Y | Y |
| 23 **McHugh** | Y | ? | Y | N | N | Y |
| 24 **Boehlert** | Y | Y | N | Y | N | Y |
| 25 **Walsh** | Y | Y | Y | N | N | Y |
| 26 **Reynolds** | Y | Y | Y | Y | N | Y |
| 27 Higgins | N | Y | N | N | Y | Y |
| 28 Slaughter | N | Y | N | ? | ? | ? |
| 29 **Kuhl** | Y | Y | Y | N | N | Y |
| **NORTH CAROLINA** | | | | | | |
| 1 Butterfield | N | Y | N | N | Y | Y |
| 2 Etheridge | N | Y | N | Y | Y | Y |
| 3 **Jones** | Y | Y | Y | Y | N | ? |
| 4 Price | N | Y | N | Y | Y | Y |
| 5 **Foxx** | Y | Y | Y | Y | N | Y |
| 6 **Coble** | Y | Y | Y | Y | N | Y |
| 7 McIntyre | Y | Y | N | Y | Y | Y |
| 8 **Hayes** | Y | Y | Y | Y | N | Y |
| 9 **Myrick** | Y | Y | Y | Y | N | Y |
| 10 **McHenry** | Y | ? | Y | Y | N | Y |
| 11 **Taylor** | Y | Y | Y | N | N | Y |
| 12 Watt | N | Y | N | Y | Y | Y |
| 13 Miller | N | Y | N | Y | Y | Y |
| **NORTH DAKOTA** | | | | | | |
| AL Pomeroy | N | Y | N | N | Y | Y |
| **OHIO** | | | | | | |
| 1 **Chabot** | Y | Y | Y | Y | N | Y |
| 2 **Portman** | Y | Y | Y | Y | N | Y |
| 3 **Turner** | N | Y | Y | Y | N | Y |
| 4 **Oxley** | Y | ? | Y | Y | N | Y |
| 5 **Gillmor** | Y | Y | Y | Y | N | Y |
| 6 Strickland | N | N | N | N | Y | Y |
| 7 **Hobson** | ? | Y | Y | N | N | Y |
| 8 **Boehner** | Y | Y | Y | Y | N | N |
| 9 Kaptur | N | Y | N | Y | Y | Y |
| 10 Kucinich | N | N | N | N | Y | Y |
| 11 Jones | N | Y | N | N | Y | Y |
| 12 **Tiberi** | ? | Y | Y | N | N | Y |
| 13 Brown | N | Y | N | Y | Y | Y |
| 14 **LaTourette** | N | Y | Y | N | N | Y |
| 15 **Pryce** | Y | Y | Y | N | N | Y |
| 16 **Regula** | Y | Y | Y | Y | N | Y |
| 17 Ryan | N | N | N | N | Y | Y |
| 18 **Ney** | Y | Y | Y | N | N | Y |
| **OKLAHOMA** | | | | | | |
| 1 **Sullivan** | Y | Y | Y | Y | N | Y |
| 2 Boren | Y | Y | Y | Y | N | Y |
| 3 **Lucas** | Y | Y | Y | Y | N | Y |
| 4 **Cole** | Y | + | Y | Y | N | Y |
| 5 **Istook** | N | Y | Y | Y | N | Y |
| **OREGON** | | | | | | |
| 1 Wu | N | N | N | Y | Y | Y |
| 2 **Walden** | Y | Y | Y | N | N | Y |
| 3 Blumenauer | N | Y | N | N | Y | Y |
| 4 DeFazio | N | Y | N | N | Y | Y |
| 5 Hooley | N | Y | N | Y | Y | Y |
| **PENNSYLVANIA** | | | | | | |
| 1 Brady | N | N | N | N | Y | Y |
| 2 Fattah | N | ? | N | N | Y | Y |
| 3 **English** | Y | N | Y | Y | N | Y |
| 4 **Hart** | Y | N | Y | Y | N | Y |
| 5 **Peterson** | Y | Y | Y | Y | N | Y |
| 6 **Gerlach** | Y | Y | Y | Y | N | Y |
| 7 **Weldon** | Y | Y | + | + | N | Y |
| 8 **Fitzpatrick** | N | Y | N | N | N | Y |
| 9 **Shuster** | Y | Y | Y | Y | N | Y |
| 10 **Sherwood** | Y | Y | Y | Y | N | Y |
| 11 Kanjorski | N | Y | N | N | Y | Y |
| 12 Murtha | N | Y | N | N | Y | Y |
| 13 Schwartz | N | Y | N | Y | Y | Y |
| 14 Doyle | N | Y | N | N | Y | Y |
| 15 **Dent** | Y | Y | Y | Y | N | Y |
| 16 **Pitts** | Y | Y | Y | Y | N | Y |
| 17 Holden | Y | Y | N | Y | Y | Y |
| 18 **Murphy** | Y | Y | Y | Y | N | Y |
| 19 **Platts** | Y | Y | Y | Y | N | Y |
| **RHODE ISLAND** | | | | | | |
| 1 Kennedy | N | Y | N | N | Y | Y |
| 2 Langevin | N | Y | N | N | Y | Y |
| **SOUTH CAROLINA** | | | | | | |
| 1 **Brown** | Y | Y | Y | N | N | Y |
| 2 **Wilson** | Y | Y | Y | N | N | Y |
| 3 **Barrett** | Y | Y | Y | N | N | Y |
| 4 **Inglis** | Y | Y | Y | N | N | Y |
| 5 Spratt | N | Y | N | N | Y | Y |
| 6 Clyburn | N | Y | N | N | Y | Y |
| **SOUTH DAKOTA** | | | | | | |
| AL Herseth | ? | Y | Y | N | Y | Y |
| **TENNESSEE** | | | | | | |
| 1 **Jenkins** | N | Y | Y | Y | N | Y |
| 2 **Duncan** | Y | Y | Y | Y | N | Y |
| 3 **Wamp** | Y | Y | Y | Y | N | Y |
| 4 Davis | Y | N | N | N | Y | Y |
| 5 Cooper | Y | N | N | Y | N | Y |
| 6 Gordon | Y | Y | N | N | Y | Y |
| 7 **Blackburn** | Y | Y | Y | N | N | Y |
| 8 Tanner | Y | Y | N | N | Y | Y |
| 9 Ford | N | Y | N | N | Y | Y |
| **TEXAS** | | | | | | |
| 1 **Gohmert** | Y | Y | Y | Y | N | Y |
| 2 **Poe** | Y | Y | Y | Y | N | Y |
| 3 **Johnson, S.** | Y | Y | Y | N | N | Y |
| 4 **Hall** | Y | Y | Y | Y | N | Y |
| 5 **Hensarling** | Y | Y | Y | Y | N | Y |
| 6 **Barton** | Y | Y | Y | Y | N | Y |
| 7 **Culberson** | Y | Y | Y | Y | N | Y |
| 8 **Brady** | Y | Y | Y | Y | N | Y |
| 9 Green, A. | N | Y | N | Y | Y | Y |
| 10 **McCaul** | Y | Y | Y | Y | N | Y |
| 11 **Conaway** | Y | ? | Y | N | N | Y |
| 12 **Granger** | Y | Y | Y | Y | N | Y |
| 13 **Thornberry** | Y | Y | Y | Y | N | N |
| 14 **Paul** | N | Y | Y | Y | N | N |
| 15 Hinojosa | N | Y | N | Y | Y | Y |
| 16 Reyes | N | Y | N | Y | Y | Y |
| 17 Edwards | N | Y | Y | Y | Y | Y |
| 18 Jackson-Lee | ? | Y | N | N | Y | Y |
| 19 **Neugebauer** | Y | Y | Y | Y | N | Y |
| 20 Gonzalez | N | Y | N | Y | Y | Y |
| 21 **Smith** | Y | Y | Y | Y | N | Y |
| 22 **DeLay** | Y | ? | ? | ? | ? | ? |
| 23 **Bonilla** | Y | Y | Y | Y | N | Y |
| 24 **Marchant** | Y | Y | Y | Y | N | Y |
| 25 Doggett | N | Y | N | Y | Y | Y |
| 26 **Burgess** | Y | Y | Y | Y | N | Y |
| 27 Ortiz | N | Y | N | Y | Y | Y |
| 28 Cuellar | Y | Y | N | Y | Y | Y |
| 29 Green, G. | N | Y | N | Y | Y | Y |
| 30 Johnson, E. | N | Y | N | N | Y | Y |
| 31 **Carter** | Y | Y | Y | Y | N | Y |
| 32 **Sessions** | Y | Y | Y | Y | N | Y |
| **UTAH** | | | | | | |
| 1 **Bishop** | ? | Y | Y | Y | N | Y |
| 2 Matheson | Y | Y | N | N | N | Y |
| 3 **Cannon** | Y | Y | Y | N | N | Y |
| **VERMONT** | | | | | | |
| AL *Sanders* | N | ? | N | N | Y | Y |
| **VIRGINIA** | | | | | | |
| 1 **Davis, J.** | Y | Y | Y | Y | N | Y |
| 2 **Drake** | Y | Y | Y | Y | N | Y |
| 3 Scott | N | Y | N | Y | Y | Y |
| 4 **Forbes** | Y | Y | Y | Y | N | Y |
| 5 **Goode** | Y | Y | Y | Y | N | Y |
| 6 **Goodlatte** | Y | Y | Y | Y | N | Y |
| 7 **Cantor** | Y | Y | Y | Y | N | Y |
| 8 Moran | N | Y | Y | N | Y | Y |
| 9 Boucher | Y | Y | N | N | Y | Y |
| 10 **Wolf** | Y | Y | Y | Y | N | Y |
| 11 **Davis, T.** | Y | Y | Y | Y | N | Y |
| **WASHINGTON** | | | | | | |
| 1 Inslee | N | Y | Y | Y | Y | Y |
| 2 Larsen | N | N | N | N | Y | Y |
| 3 Baird | ? | ? | ? | ? | ? | ? |
| 4 **Hastings** | Y | Y | Y | N | N | Y |
| 5 **McMorris** | Y | Y | Y | Y | N | Y |
| 6 Dicks | N | Y | N | N | Y | Y |
| 7 McDermott | N | N | N | N | Y | Y |
| 8 **Reichert** | Y | Y | N | N | N | Y |
| 9 Smith | N | Y | N | N | Y | Y |
| **WEST VIRGINIA** | | | | | | |
| 1 Mollohan | N | Y | N | N | Y | Y |
| 2 **Capito** | Y | Y | Y | N | N | Y |
| 3 Rahall | N | Y | N | N | Y | Y |
| **WISCONSIN** | | | | | | |
| 1 **Ryan** | Y | Y | Y | Y | N | Y |
| 2 Baldwin | N | N | N | Y | Y | Y |
| 3 Kind | N | Y | N | N | Y | Y |
| 4 Moore | N | Y | N | Y | Y | Y |
| 5 **Sensenbrenner** | Y | Y | Y | N | N | N |
| 6 **Petri** | N | Y | N | N | N | Y |
| 7 Obey | N | Y | N | N | Y | Y |
| 8 **Green** | Y | Y | Y | Y | N | Y |
| **WYOMING** | | | | | | |
| AL **Cubin** | Y | Y | Y | N | N | Y |

# IN THE HOUSE | By Vote Number

**66.** **H Res 135. Democracy Commission/Adoption.** Barrett, R-S.C., motion to suspend the rules and adopt the resolution that would establish the House Democracy Assistance Commission to provide advice to members and staff of newly formed parliaments in emerging democracies. Motion agreed to 386-2: R 208-1; D 177-1 (ND 133-0, SD 44-1); I 1-0. A two-thirds majority of those present and voting (259 in this case) is required for adoption under suspension of the rules. March 14, 2005.

**67.** **H Res 101. Hezbollah Terrorist Designation/Adoption.** Barrett, R-S.C., motion to suspend the rules and adopt the resolution that would urge the European Union to classify Hezbollah as a terrorist organization and prohibit funding to the group. Motion agreed to 380-3: R 208-1; D 171-2 (ND 126-2, SD 45-0); I 1-0. A two-thirds majority of those present and voting (259 in this case) is required for adoption under suspension of the rules. March 14, 2005.

**68.** **S 384. Interagency Working Group Extension/Passage.** Shays, R-Conn., motion to suspend the rules and pass the bill that would extend through December 2006 the term of the Nazi War Crimes and Japanese Imperial Government Records Interagency Working Group, which works to locate and declassify Nazi war criminal records. Motion agreed to 391-0: R 211-0; D 179-0 (ND 133-0, SD 46-0); I 1-0. A two-thirds majority of those present and voting (261 in this case) is required for passage under suspension of the rules. March 14, 2005.

**69.** **HR 1268. Fiscal 2005 Supplemental Appropriations/Previous Question.** Cole, R-Okla., motion to order the previous question (thus ending debate and possibility of amendment) on adoption of the rule (H Res 151) and a Cole amendment to the rule. The rule would provide for House floor consideration of the bill that would appropriate $81.3 billion in fiscal 2005 supplemental spending. The amendment would waive points of order against provisions on life insurance and death benefits for U.S. troops. Motion agreed to 220-195: R 220-1; D 0-193 (ND 0-144, SD 0-49); I 0-1. (Subsequently, the Cole amendment and the rule were adopted by voice vote.) March 15, 2005.

**70.** **H Res 153. Ethics Task Force/Motion to Table.** Lewis, R-Calif., motion to table (kill) the Pelosi, D-Calif., privileged resolution that would require the Speaker of the House to appoint a bipartisan task force, with equal representation of Republicans and Democrats, to make recommendations, by May 2, 2005, to restore public confidence in the House ethics process. Motion agreed to 223-194: R 223-1; D 0-192 (ND 0-145, SD 0-47); I 0-1. March 15, 2005.

**71.** **HR 1268. Fiscal 2005 Supplemental Appropriations/Ruling of the Chair.** Motion to sustain the ruling of the chair that upheld the Lewis, R-Calif., point of order against the Filner, D-Calif., amendment on grounds that it would constitute unauthorized legislation on an appropriations bill. The Filner amendment would provide an additional $3.1 billion for the Veterans Health Administration and designate it as emergency spending. Motion agreed to 224-200: R 223-0; D 1-199 (ND 1-148, SD 0-51); I 0-1. March 15, 2005.

**72.** **HR 1268. Fiscal 2005 Supplemental Appropriations/Contracting Investigation.** Tierney, D-Mass., amendment that would provide $5 million to establish a select committee to investigate reconstruction efforts in Iraq and Afghanistan. Rejected 191-236: R 0-226; D 190-10 (ND 140-9, SD 50-1); I 1-0. March 15, 2005.

**73.** **HR 1268. Fiscal 2005 Supplemental Appropriations/Embassy Funding.** Upton, R-Mich., amendment to prohibit use of funds in the bill for the security, construction and maintenance of U.S. embassies. The underlying bill would provide $592 million to construct a new embassy in Baghdad. Adopted 258-170: R 119-107; D 138-63 (ND 98-52, SD 40-11); I 1-0. A "nay" was a vote in support of the president's position. March 15, 2005.

ND Northern Democrats, SD Southern Democrats
Southern states: Ala., Ark., Fla., Ga., Ky., La., Miss., N.C., Okla., S.C., Tenn., Texas, Va.

| | 66 | 67 | 68 | 69 | 70 | 71 | 72 | 73 |
|---|---|---|---|---|---|---|---|---|
| **ALABAMA** | | | | | | | | |
| 1 Bonner | Y | Y | Y | Y | Y | Y | N | Y |
| 2 Everett | Y | Y | Y | Y | Y | Y | N | N |
| 3 Rogers | Y | Y | Y | Y | Y | Y | N | N |
| 4 Aderholt | Y | Y | Y | Y | Y | Y | N | N |
| 5 Cramer | ? | Y | Y | N | N | N | N | N |
| 6 Bachus | Y | Y | Y | Y | Y | Y | ? | ? |
| 7 Davis | ? | ? | ? | N | N | N | Y | N |
| **ALASKA** | | | | | | | | |
| AL Young | Y | Y | Y | Y | ? | Y | N | Y |
| **ARIZONA** | | | | | | | | |
| 1 Renzi | Y | Y | Y | Y | Y | N | N | N |
| 2 Franks | Y | ? | Y | Y | Y | Y | N | Y |
| 3 Shadegg | Y | Y | Y | Y | Y | Y | N | Y |
| 4 Pastor | Y | Y | Y | N | N | N | Y | Y |
| 5 Hayworth | Y | Y | Y | Y | Y | Y | N | Y |
| 6 Flake | ? | ? | ? | Y | Y | Y | N | Y |
| 7 Grijalva | Y | Y | Y | N | N | N | Y | Y |
| 8 Kolbe | Y | Y | Y | Y | Y | Y | N | N |
| **ARKANSAS** | | | | | | | | |
| 1 Berry | Y | Y | Y | N | N | N | Y | Y |
| 2 Snyder | Y | Y | Y | N | N | N | Y | N |
| 3 Boozman | Y | Y | Y | Y | Y | Y | N | N |
| 4 Ross | Y | Y | Y | N | N | N | Y | N |
| **CALIFORNIA** | | | | | | | | |
| 1 Thompson | Y | Y | Y | N | N | N | Y | Y |
| 2 Herger | Y | Y | Y | Y | Y | Y | N | N |
| 3 Lungren | Y | Y | Y | Y | Y | Y | N | N |
| 4 Doolittle | Y | Y | Y | Y | Y | Y | N | N |
| 5 Matsui, D. | Y | Y | Y | N | N | N | Y | Y |
| 6 Woolsey | Y | Y | Y | N | N | N | Y | Y |
| 7 Miller, George | ? | ? | ? | N | N | N | Y | Y |
| 8 Pelosi | ? | Y | Y | N | N | N | Y | N |
| 9 Lee | Y | Y | Y | N | N | N | Y | Y |
| 10 Tauscher | Y | Y | Y | N | N | N | Y | Y |
| 11 Pombo | Y | Y | Y | Y | Y | Y | N | Y |
| 12 Lantos | Y | Y | Y | N | N | N | Y | N |
| 13 Stark | Y | P | Y | N | N | N | Y | Y |
| 14 Eshoo | Y | Y | Y | N | N | N | Y | N |
| 15 Honda | Y | Y | Y | N | N | N | Y | Y |
| 16 Lofgren | Y | Y | Y | N | N | N | Y | Y |
| 17 Farr | Y | Y | Y | N | N | N | Y | Y |
| 18 Cardoza | Y | Y | Y | N | N | N | Y | Y |
| 19 Radanovich | Y | Y | Y | Y | Y | Y | N | Y |
| 20 Costa | Y | Y | Y | N | N | N | Y | Y |
| 21 Nunes | Y | Y | Y | Y | Y | Y | N | Y |
| 22 Thomas | Y | Y | Y | Y | Y | Y | N | N |
| 23 Capps | Y | Y | Y | N | N | N | Y | Y |
| 24 Gallegly | Y | Y | Y | Y | Y | Y | N | Y |
| 25 McKeon | Y | Y | Y | Y | Y | Y | N | N |
| 26 Dreier | Y | Y | Y | Y | Y | Y | N | N |
| 27 Sherman | Y | Y | Y | N | N | N | Y | Y |
| 28 Berman | Y | Y | Y | N | N | N | Y | N |
| 29 Schiff | Y | Y | Y | N | N | N | Y | Y |
| 30 Waxman | Y | ? | Y | N | N | N | Y | Y |
| 31 Becerra | ? | ? | ? | N | N | N | Y | Y |
| 32 Solis | Y | Y | Y | N | N | N | Y | Y |
| 33 Watson | Y | N | Y | N | N | N | Y | Y |
| 34 Roybal-Allard | Y | Y | Y | N | N | N | Y | Y |
| 35 Waters | Y | P | Y | ? | ? | ? | ? | ? |
| 36 Harman | Y | Y | Y | N | N | N | Y | N |
| 37 Millender-McD. | Y | Y | Y | N | N | ? | Y | Y |
| 38 Napolitano | Y | Y | Y | N | N | N | Y | Y |
| 39 Sánchez, Linda | ? | ? | ? | N | N | N | Y | Y |
| 40 Royce | Y | Y | Y | Y | Y | Y | N | Y |
| 41 Lewis | Y | Y | Y | Y | Y | Y | N | N |
| 42 Miller, Gary | Y | Y | Y | Y | Y | Y | N | Y |
| 43 Baca | Y | Y | Y | N | N | N | Y | Y |
| 44 Calvert | Y | Y | Y | Y | Y | Y | N | Y |
| 45 Bono | Y | Y | Y | Y | Y | Y | N | Y |
| 46 Rohrabacher | Y | Y | Y | Y | Y | Y | N | Y |
| 47 Sanchez, Loretta | Y | Y | Y | N | N | N | Y | Y |
| 48 Cox | Y | Y | Y | Y | Y | Y | N | N |
| 49 Issa | Y | Y | Y | Y | Y | Y | N | N |
| 50 Cunningham | Y | Y | Y | Y | Y | Y | N | N |
| 51 Filner | Y | Y | Y | N | N | N | Y | Y |
| 52 Hunter | ? | ? | ? | Y | Y | Y | N | N |
| 53 Davis | Y | Y | Y | N | N | N | Y | N |
| **COLORADO** | | | | | | | | |
| 1 DeGette | Y | Y | Y | N | N | N | Y | Y |
| 2 Udall | Y | Y | Y | N | N | N | Y | Y |
| 3 Salazar | Y | Y | Y | N | N | N | Y | Y |
| 4 Musgrave | Y | Y | Y | Y | Y | Y | N | Y |
| 5 Hefley | ? | ? | ? | Y | N | Y | N | Y |
| 6 Tancredo | Y | Y | Y | Y | Y | N | N | Y |
| 7 Beauprez | Y | Y | Y | Y | Y | Y | N | N |
| **CONNECTICUT** | | | | | | | | |
| 1 Larson | Y | Y | Y | N | N | N | Y | Y |
| 2 Simmons | Y | Y | Y | Y | Y | Y | N | Y |
| 3 DeLauro | Y | Y | Y | N | N | N | Y | Y |
| 4 Shays | Y | Y | Y | Y | Y | Y | N | N |
| 5 Johnson | Y | Y | Y | Y | Y | Y | N | N |
| **DELAWARE** | | | | | | | | |
| AL Castle | Y | Y | Y | Y | Y | Y | N | Y |
| **FLORIDA** | | | | | | | | |
| 1 Miller | Y | Y | Y | Y | Y | Y | N | Y |
| 2 Boyd | Y | Y | Y | Y | Y | Y | N | Y |
| 3 Brown | ? | ? | ? | ? | N | N | Y | Y |
| 4 Crenshaw | Y | Y | Y | Y | Y | Y | N | Y |
| 5 Brown-Waite | + | + | + | Y | Y | Y | N | Y |
| 6 Stearns | Y | Y | Y | Y | Y | Y | N | Y |
| 7 Mica | Y | Y | Y | Y | Y | Y | N | N |
| 8 Keller | Y | Y | Y | Y | Y | Y | N | Y |
| 9 Bilirakis | Y | Y | Y | Y | Y | Y | N | Y |
| 10 Young | Y | Y | Y | Y | Y | Y | N | N |
| 11 Davis | ? | ? | ? | N | ? | N | Y | Y |
| 12 Putnam | Y | Y | Y | Y | Y | Y | N | N |
| 13 Harris | Y | Y | Y | Y | Y | Y | N | Y |
| 14 Mack | Y | Y | Y | Y | Y | Y | N | Y |
| 15 Weldon | Y | Y | Y | Y | Y | Y | N | N |
| 16 Foley | Y | Y | Y | Y | Y | Y | N | Y |
| 17 Meek | Y | Y | Y | N | N | N | Y | Y |
| 18 Ros-Lehtinen | Y | Y | Y | Y | Y | Y | N | Y |
| 19 Wexler | ? | ? | ? | N | N | N | Y | Y |
| 20 Wasserman-Schultz | Y | Y | Y | N | N | N | Y | Y |
| 21 Diaz-Balart, L. | Y | Y | Y | Y | Y | Y | N | N |
| 22 Shaw | Y | Y | Y | ? | Y | Y | N | N |
| 23 Hastings | Y | Y | Y | N | N | N | Y | Y |
| 24 Feeney | ? | ? | ? | Y | Y | Y | N | N |
| 25 Diaz-Balart, M. | Y | Y | Y | Y | Y | Y | N | N |
| **GEORGIA** | | | | | | | | |
| 1 Kingston | Y | Y | Y | Y | Y | Y | N | Y |
| 2 Bishop | Y | Y | Y | N | N | N | Y | Y |
| 3 Marshall | Y | Y | Y | N | N | N | Y | Y |
| 4 McKinney | N | P | N | N | N | N | Y | Y |
| 5 Lewis | Y | Y | Y | N | N | N | Y | Y |
| 6 Price | Y | Y | Y | Y | Y | Y | N | N |
| 7 Linder | Y | Y | Y | Y | Y | Y | N | N |
| 8 Westmoreland | Y | Y | Y | ? | Y | Y | N | Y |
| 9 Norwood | Y | Y | Y | ? | ? | Y | N | Y |
| 10 Deal | Y | Y | Y | Y | Y | Y | N | Y |
| 11 Gingrey | Y | Y | Y | Y | Y | Y | N | Y |
| 12 Barrow | Y | Y | Y | N | N | N | Y | Y |
| 13 Scott | Y | Y | Y | N | N | N | Y | Y |
| **HAWAII** | | | | | | | | |
| 1 Abercrombie | Y | Y | Y | ? | N | N | Y | N |
| 2 Case | Y | Y | Y | N | N | N | Y | Y |
| **IDAHO** | | | | | | | | |
| 1 Otter | Y | Y | Y | Y | ? | Y | N | Y |
| 2 Simpson | ? | ? | ? | Y | Y | Y | N | N |
| **ILLINOIS** | | | | | | | | |
| 1 Rush | Y | Y | Y | N | N | N | Y | Y |
| 2 Jackson | Y | Y | Y | N | N | N | Y | N |
| 3 Lipinski | Y | Y | Y | N | N | N | Y | Y |
| 4 Gutierrez | ? | ? | ? | N | N | N | Y | Y |
| 5 Emanuel | Y | Y | Y | N | N | N | Y | Y |
| 6 Hyde | Y | Y | Y | Y | Y | ? | N | N |
| 7 Davis | Y | Y | Y | N | N | N | Y | Y |
| 8 Bean | Y | Y | Y | N | N | N | Y | Y |
| 9 Schakowsky | Y | Y | Y | N | N | N | Y | Y |
| 10 Kirk | Y | Y | Y | Y | Y | Y | N | N |
| 11 Weller | Y | Y | Y | Y | Y | Y | N | N |
| 12 Costello | Y | Y | Y | N | N | N | Y | Y |

**KEY** — Republicans — Democrats — *Independents*

| | | | |
|---|---|---|---|
| **Y** Voted for (yea) | **X** Paired against | **C** Voted "present" to avoid possible conflict of interest |
| **#** Paired for | **–** Announced against | |
| **+** Announced for | **P** Voted "present" | **?** Did not vote or otherwise make a position known |
| **N** Voted against (nay) | | |

| | 66 | 67 | 68 | 69 | 70 | 71 | 72 | 73 |
|---|---|---|---|---|---|---|---|---|
| 13 **Biggert** | Y | Y | Y | Y | Y | Y | N | N |
| 14 **Hastert** | | | | | | | | |
| 15 **Johnson** | Y | Y | Y | Y | Y | Y | N | N |
| 16 **Manzullo** | Y | Y | Y | Y | Y | Y | N | Y |
| 17 Evans | ? | ? | ? | N | N | N | Y | Y |
| 18 **LaHood** | ? | ? | ? | Y | Y | Y | N | N |
| 19 **Shimkus** | Y | Y | Y | Y | Y | Y | N | Y |
| **INDIANA** | | | | | | | | |
| 1 Visclosky | Y | Y | Y | N | N | N | Y | N |
| 2 **Chocola** | Y | Y | Y | Y | Y | Y | N | Y |
| 3 **Souder** | Y | Y | Y | Y | Y | Y | N | N |
| 4 **Buyer** | Y | Y | ? | Y | Y | Y | N | Y |
| 5 **Burton** | Y | Y | Y | Y | Y | Y | N | N |
| 6 **Pence** | ? | ? | ? | Y | Y | Y | N | Y |
| 7 Carson | Y | Y | Y | N | N | N | Y | Y |
| 8 **Hostettler** | Y | Y | Y | Y | Y | Y | N | Y |
| 9 **Sodrel** | Y | Y | Y | Y | Y | Y | N | Y |
| **IOWA** | | | | | | | | |
| 1 **Nussle** | ? | ? | ? | Y | Y | Y | N | Y |
| 2 **Leach** | Y | Y | Y | Y | Y | ? | ? | ? |
| 3 Boswell | ? | ? | ? | N | N | N | Y | N |
| 4 **Latham** | Y | Y | Y | Y | Y | Y | N | N |
| 5 **King** | Y | Y | Y | Y | Y | Y | N | Y |
| **KANSAS** | | | | | | | | |
| 1 **Moran** | Y | Y | Y | Y | Y | Y | N | Y |
| 2 **Ryun** | Y | Y | Y | Y | Y | Y | N | Y |
| 3 Moore | Y | Y | Y | N | N | N | Y | Y |
| 4 **Tiahrt** | Y | Y | Y | Y | Y | Y | N | N |
| **KENTUCKY** | | | | | | | | |
| 1 **Whitfield** | Y | Y | Y | Y | Y | Y | N | Y |
| 2 **Lewis** | Y | Y | Y | Y | Y | Y | N | N |
| 3 **Northup** | Y | Y | Y | Y | Y | Y | N | N |
| 4 **Davis** | Y | Y | Y | Y | Y | Y | N | N |
| 5 **Rogers** | Y | Y | Y | Y | Y | Y | N | N |
| 6 Chandler | Y | Y | Y | N | N | N | Y | Y |
| **LOUISIANA** | | | | | | | | |
| 1 **Jindal** | Y | Y | Y | Y | Y | Y | N | N |
| 2 Jefferson | Y | Y | Y | N | ? | N | Y | Y |
| 3 Melancon | Y | Y | Y | N | N | N | Y | Y |
| 4 **McCrery** | Y | Y | Y | Y | Y | Y | N | N |
| 5 **Alexander** | ? | ? | ? | Y | Y | Y | N | N |
| 6 **Baker** | Y | Y | Y | Y | Y | Y | N | N |
| 7 **Boustany** | ? | ? | ? | Y | Y | Y | N | N |
| **MAINE** | | | | | | | | |
| 1 Allen | Y | Y | Y | N | N | N | Y | N |
| 2 Michaud | Y | Y | Y | N | N | N | Y | Y |
| **MARYLAND** | | | | | | | | |
| 1 **Gilchrest** | Y | Y | Y | Y | Y | Y | N | N |
| 2 Ruppersberger | Y | Y | ? | ? | N | N | Y | N |
| 3 Cardin | Y | Y | Y | N | N | N | Y | Y |
| 4 Wynn | Y | Y | Y | N | N | N | Y | Y |
| 5 Hoyer | Y | Y | Y | N | N | N | Y | Y |
| 6 **Bartlett** | Y | Y | Y | Y | Y | Y | N | Y |
| 7 Cummings | Y | Y | Y | N | N | N | Y | Y |
| 8 Van Hollen | Y | ? | Y | N | N | N | Y | Y |
| **MASSACHUSETTS** | | | | | | | | |
| 1 Olver | Y | Y | Y | N | N | N | Y | Y |
| 2 Neal | Y | Y | Y | N | N | N | Y | Y |
| 3 McGovern | Y | Y | Y | N | N | N | Y | Y |
| 4 Frank | Y | Y | Y | N | N | N | Y | Y |
| 5 Meehan | Y | Y | Y | N | N | N | Y | Y |
| 6 Tierney | Y | Y | Y | N | N | N | Y | Y |
| 7 Markey | Y | Y | Y | N | N | N | Y | Y |
| 8 Capuano | ? | ? | ? | N | N | N | Y | N |
| 9 Lynch | Y | Y | Y | N | N | N | Y | Y |
| 10 Delahunt | Y | Y | Y | N | N | N | Y | Y |
| **MICHIGAN** | | | | | | | | |
| 1 Stupak | Y | Y | Y | N | N | N | Y | N |
| 2 **Hoekstra** | Y | Y | Y | Y | Y | Y | N | N |
| 3 **Ehlers** | Y | Y | Y | Y | Y | Y | N | Y |
| 4 **Camp** | Y | Y | Y | Y | Y | Y | N | Y |
| 5 Kildee | Y | Y | Y | N | N | N | Y | Y |
| 6 **Upton** | Y | Y | Y | Y | Y | Y | N | Y |
| 7 **Schwarz** | ? | Y | Y | Y | Y | Y | N | N |
| 8 **Rogers** | Y | Y | Y | + | Y | Y | N | Y |
| 9 **Knollenberg** | ? | ? | ? | ? | Y | Y | N | N |
| 10 **Miller** | Y | Y | Y | Y | Y | Y | N | Y |
| 11 **McCotter** | Y | Y | Y | Y | Y | Y | N | Y |
| 12 Levin | Y | Y | Y | N | N | N | Y | Y |
| 13 Kilpatrick | ? | ? | ? | N | N | N | Y | Y |
| 14 Conyers | Y | Y | Y | N | N | N | Y | Y |
| 15 Dingell | Y | Y | Y | N | N | N | Y | Y |
| **MINNESOTA** | | | | | | | | |
| 1 **Gutknecht** | Y | Y | Y | Y | Y | Y | N | Y |
| 2 **Kline** | Y | Y | Y | Y | Y | Y | N | N |
| 3 **Ramstad** | Y | Y | Y | Y | Y | Y | N | Y |
| 4 McCollum | Y | Y | Y | N | N | N | Y | Y |
| 5 Sabo | Y | Y | Y | N | N | N | Y | Y |
| 6 **Kennedy** | Y | Y | Y | Y | Y | Y | N | N |
| 7 Peterson | ? | ? | ? | N | N | N | N | Y |
| 8 Oberstar | Y | Y | Y | N | N | N | Y | Y |
| **MISSISSIPPI** | | | | | | | | |
| 1 **Wicker** | Y | Y | Y | Y | Y | Y | N | Y |
| 2 Thompson | Y | Y | Y | N | N | N | Y | Y |
| 3 **Pickering** | Y | Y | Y | Y | Y | Y | N | Y |
| 4 Taylor | Y | Y | Y | N | N | N | Y | Y |
| **MISSOURI** | | | | | | | | |
| 1 Clay | Y | Y | Y | ? | ? | N | Y | Y |
| 2 **Akin** | Y | Y | Y | Y | Y | Y | N | N |
| 3 Carnahan | Y | Y | Y | N | N | N | Y | Y |
| 4 Skelton | Y | Y | Y | N | N | N | Y | N |
| 5 Cleaver | Y | Y | Y | N | N | N | Y | Y |
| 6 **Graves** | Y | Y | Y | Y | Y | Y | N | N |
| 7 **Blunt** | Y | Y | Y | Y | Y | Y | N | N |
| 8 **Emerson** | ? | ? | ? | Y | Y | Y | N | N |
| 9 **Hulshof** | Y | Y | Y | Y | Y | Y | N | Y |
| **MONTANA** | | | | | | | | |
| AL **Rehberg** | Y | Y | Y | Y | ? | Y | N | N |
| **NEBRASKA** | | | | | | | | |
| 1 **Fortenberry** | Y | Y | Y | Y | Y | Y | N | N |
| 2 **Terry** | Y | Y | Y | Y | Y | ? | N | Y |
| 3 **Osborne** | Y | Y | Y | Y | Y | Y | N | Y |
| **NEVADA** | | | | | | | | |
| 1 Berkley | Y | Y | Y | N | N | N | Y | N |
| 2 **Gibbons** | Y | Y | Y | Y | Y | Y | N | Y |
| 3 **Porter** | Y | Y | Y | Y | Y | Y | N | Y |
| **NEW HAMPSHIRE** | | | | | | | | |
| 1 **Bradley** | Y | Y | Y | Y | Y | Y | N | Y |
| 2 **Bass** | Y | Y | Y | Y | Y | Y | N | Y |
| **NEW JERSEY** | | | | | | | | |
| 1 Andrews | Y | Y | Y | N | N | N | Y | Y |
| 2 **LoBiondo** | Y | Y | Y | Y | Y | Y | N | Y |
| 3 **Saxton** | Y | Y | Y | ? | Y | Y | N | N |
| 4 **Smith** | Y | Y | Y | Y | Y | Y | N | N |
| 5 **Garrett** | Y | Y | Y | Y | Y | Y | N | Y |
| 6 Pallone | ? | ? | ? | N | N | N | Y | Y |
| 7 **Ferguson** | Y | Y | Y | Y | Y | Y | N | N |
| 8 Pascrell | ? | ? | ? | ? | N | N | Y | N |
| 9 Rothman | Y | Y | Y | N | N | N | Y | N |
| 10 Payne | ? | ? | ? | N | N | N | Y | Y |
| 11 **Frelinghuysen** | Y | Y | Y | Y | Y | Y | N | N |
| 12 Holt | Y | Y | Y | N | N | N | Y | Y |
| 13 Menendez | + | + | + | N | N | N | Y | Y |
| **NEW MEXICO** | | | | | | | | |
| 1 **Wilson** | Y | Y | Y | N | Y | Y | N | Y |
| 2 **Pearce** | Y | Y | Y | Y | Y | Y | N | N |
| 3 Udall | Y | Y | Y | N | N | N | Y | Y |
| **NEW YORK** | | | | | | | | |
| 1 Bishop | Y | Y | Y | N | N | N | Y | Y |
| 2 Israel | Y | Y | Y | N | ? | N | Y | N |
| 3 **King** | Y | Y | Y | Y | Y | Y | N | N |
| 4 McCarthy | ? | ? | ? | N | N | N | Y | N |
| 5 Ackerman | Y | Y | Y | N | N | N | Y | N |
| 6 Meeks | Y | Y | Y | N | N | N | Y | Y |
| 7 Crowley | Y | Y | Y | N | N | N | Y | N |
| 8 Nadler | Y | Y | Y | N | N | N | Y | N |
| 9 Weiner | Y | Y | Y | N | N | N | Y | N |
| 10 Towns | Y | Y | Y | N | N | N | Y | Y |
| 11 Owens | Y | Y | Y | N | ? | N | Y | Y |
| 12 Velázquez | Y | Y | Y | N | N | N | Y | Y |
| 13 **Fossella** | Y | Y | Y | Y | Y | Y | N | Y |
| 14 Maloney | Y | Y | Y | N | N | N | Y | Y |
| 15 Rangel | ? | ? | ? | N | N | N | Y | Y |
| 16 Serrano | Y | Y | Y | N | N | N | Y | Y |
| 17 Engel | Y | Y | Y | N | N | N | Y | N |
| 18 Lowey | Y | Y | Y | N | N | N | Y | Y |
| 19 **Kelly** | ? | ? | ? | Y | Y | Y | N | N |
| 20 **Sweeney** | Y | Y | Y | ? | ? | ? | ? | ? |
| 21 McNulty | Y | Y | Y | N | N | N | Y | N |
| 22 Hinchey | Y | P | Y | N | N | N | Y | N |
| 23 **McHugh** | Y | Y | Y | Y | Y | Y | N | N |
| 24 **Boehlert** | Y | Y | Y | ? | Y | Y | N | Y |
| 25 **Walsh** | ? | ? | ? | ? | ? | ? | ? | ? |
| 26 **Reynolds** | Y | Y | Y | Y | Y | Y | N | N |
| 27 Higgins | Y | Y | Y | N | N | N | Y | N |
| 28 Slaughter | Y | Y | Y | N | N | N | Y | Y |
| 29 **Kuhl** | Y | Y | Y | Y | Y | Y | N | Y |
| **NORTH CAROLINA** | | | | | | | | |
| 1 Butterfield | Y | Y | Y | N | N | N | Y | Y |
| 2 Etheridge | Y | Y | Y | N | N | N | Y | Y |
| 3 **Jones** | Y | Y | Y | Y | Y | Y | N | Y |
| 4 Price | Y | Y | Y | N | N | N | Y | Y |
| 5 **Foxx** | Y | Y | Y | Y | Y | Y | N | Y |
| 6 **Coble** | Y | Y | Y | Y | Y | Y | N | Y |
| 7 McIntyre | Y | Y | Y | N | N | N | Y | Y |
| 8 **Hayes** | Y | Y | Y | Y | Y | Y | N | N |
| 9 **Myrick** | Y | Y | Y | Y | Y | Y | N | N |
| 10 **McHenry** | Y | Y | Y | Y | Y | Y | N | N |
| 11 **Taylor** | ? | Y | Y | Y | Y | Y | N | N |
| 12 Watt | Y | Y | Y | N | N | N | Y | Y |
| 13 Miller | Y | Y | Y | N | N | N | Y | Y |
| **NORTH DAKOTA** | | | | | | | | |
| AL Pomeroy | Y | Y | Y | N | N | N | Y | N |
| **OHIO** | | | | | | | | |
| 1 **Chabot** | Y | ? | Y | Y | ? | Y | N | Y |
| 2 **Portman** | Y | Y | Y | Y | Y | Y | N | N |
| 3 **Turner** | Y | Y | Y | Y | Y | Y | N | Y |
| 4 **Oxley** | Y | Y | Y | Y | Y | ? | N | N |
| 5 **Gillmor** | Y | Y | Y | Y | Y | Y | N | N |
| 6 Strickland | Y | Y | Y | N | N | N | Y | Y |
| 7 **Hobson** | Y | Y | Y | Y | Y | Y | N | N |
| 8 **Boehner** | Y | Y | Y | Y | Y | Y | N | Y |
| 9 Kaptur | Y | Y | Y | N | N | N | Y | N |
| 10 Kucinich | Y | Y | Y | N | N | N | Y | Y |
| 11 Jones | ? | ? | ? | ? | ? | N | Y | N |
| 12 **Tiberi** | Y | Y | Y | Y | Y | Y | N | Y |
| 13 Brown | Y | Y | Y | N | N | N | Y | Y |
| 14 **LaTourette** | Y | Y | Y | Y | Y | Y | N | Y |
| 15 **Pryce** | ? | ? | ? | Y | Y | Y | N | N |
| 16 **Regula** | Y | Y | Y | Y | Y | Y | N | N |
| 17 Ryan | Y | Y | Y | N | N | N | Y | N |
| 18 **Ney** | Y | Y | Y | Y | Y | Y | N | Y |
| **OKLAHOMA** | | | | | | | | |
| 1 **Sullivan** | Y | Y | Y | Y | Y | ? | N | Y |
| 2 Boren | Y | Y | Y | N | N | N | Y | N |
| 3 **Lucas** | Y | Y | Y | Y | Y | Y | N | N |
| 4 **Cole** | Y | Y | Y | Y | Y | Y | N | N |
| 5 **Istook** | Y | Y | Y | Y | Y | ? | N | Y |
| **OREGON** | | | | | | | | |
| 1 Wu | Y | Y | Y | N | N | N | Y | Y |
| 2 **Walden** | Y | Y | Y | Y | Y | Y | N | Y |
| 3 Blumenauer | Y | Y | Y | N | N | N | Y | Y |
| 4 DeFazio | Y | Y | Y | N | N | N | Y | Y |
| 5 Hooley | Y | Y | Y | N | N | N | Y | Y |
| **PENNSYLVANIA** | | | | | | | | |
| 1 Brady | Y | Y | Y | N | N | N | N | N |
| 2 Fattah | Y | Y | Y | N | N | N | Y | N |
| 3 **English** | Y | Y | Y | Y | Y | Y | N | N |
| 4 **Hart** | Y | Y | Y | Y | Y | Y | N | N |
| 5 **Peterson** | ? | ? | ? | Y | Y | Y | N | Y |
| 6 **Gerlach** | Y | Y | Y | Y | Y | Y | N | N |
| 7 **Weldon** | Y | Y | Y | Y | Y | Y | N | N |
| 8 **Fitzpatrick** | Y | Y | Y | Y | Y | Y | N | Y |
| 9 **Shuster** | Y | Y | Y | Y | Y | Y | N | Y |
| 10 **Sherwood** | Y | Y | Y | Y | Y | Y | N | N |
| 11 Kanjorski | Y | Y | Y | N | N | N | Y | N |
| 12 Murtha | Y | Y | Y | N | N | N | Y | N |
| 13 Schwartz | Y | Y | Y | N | N | N | Y | N |
| 14 Doyle | Y | Y | Y | N | N | N | N | N |
| 15 **Dent** | Y | Y | Y | Y | Y | Y | N | Y |
| 16 **Pitts** | Y | Y | Y | Y | Y | Y | N | Y |
| 17 Holden | Y | Y | Y | N | N | N | N | N |
| 18 **Murphy** | Y | Y | Y | Y | Y | Y | N | Y |
| 19 **Platts** | Y | Y | Y | Y | Y | Y | N | Y |
| **RHODE ISLAND** | | | | | | | | |
| 1 Kennedy | Y | Y | Y | N | N | N | ? | N |
| 2 Langevin | Y | Y | Y | N | N | N | Y | Y |
| **SOUTH CAROLINA** | | | | | | | | |
| 1 **Brown** | Y | Y | Y | Y | Y | Y | N | Y |
| 2 **Wilson** | Y | Y | Y | Y | Y | Y | N | N |
| 3 **Barrett** | Y | Y | Y | Y | Y | Y | N | N |
| 4 **Inglis** | Y | Y | Y | Y | Y | Y | N | Y |
| 5 Spratt | Y | Y | Y | N | N | N | Y | Y |
| 6 Clyburn | Y | Y | Y | N | N | N | Y | Y |
| **SOUTH DAKOTA** | | | | | | | | |
| AL Herseth | Y | Y | Y | N | N | N | Y | N |
| **TENNESSEE** | | | | | | | | |
| 1 **Jenkins** | Y | Y | Y | Y | Y | Y | N | Y |
| 2 **Duncan** | Y | Y | Y | Y | Y | Y | N | Y |
| 3 **Wamp** | Y | Y | Y | Y | Y | Y | N | N |
| 4 Davis | Y | Y | Y | N | N | N | Y | N |
| 5 Cooper | Y | Y | Y | N | N | N | Y | Y |
| 6 Gordon | Y | Y | Y | N | N | N | Y | Y |
| 7 **Blackburn** | ? | ? | ? | Y | Y | Y | N | Y |
| 8 Tanner | Y | Y | Y | N | N | N | Y | Y |
| 9 Ford | Y | Y | Y | N | N | N | Y | N |
| **TEXAS** | | | | | | | | |
| 1 **Gohmert** | Y | Y | Y | Y | Y | Y | N | Y |
| 2 **Poe** | Y | Y | Y | Y | Y | Y | N | Y |
| 3 **Johnson, S.** | Y | Y | Y | Y | Y | Y | N | Y |
| 4 **Hall** | Y | Y | Y | Y | Y | Y | N | Y |
| 5 **Hensarling** | Y | Y | Y | Y | Y | Y | N | Y |
| 6 **Barton** | Y | Y | Y | Y | Y | Y | N | Y |
| 7 **Culberson** | ? | ? | ? | Y | Y | Y | N | N |
| 8 **Brady** | Y | Y | Y | Y | Y | Y | N | Y |
| 9 Green, A. | Y | Y | Y | N | N | N | Y | Y |
| 10 **McCaul** | Y | Y | Y | Y | Y | Y | N | Y |
| 11 **Conaway** | Y | Y | Y | Y | Y | Y | N | Y |
| 12 **Granger** | Y | Y | Y | Y | Y | Y | N | N |
| 13 **Thornberry** | Y | Y | Y | Y | Y | Y | ? | ? |
| 14 **Paul** | N | N | Y | Y | Y | Y | N | Y |
| 15 Hinojosa | ? | ? | ? | – | – | N | Y | Y |
| 16 Reyes | Y | Y | Y | N | ? | N | Y | Y |
| 17 Edwards | Y | Y | Y | N | N | N | Y | N |
| 18 Jackson-Lee | Y | Y | Y | N | N | N | Y | N |
| 19 **Neugebauer** | Y | Y | Y | Y | Y | Y | N | Y |
| 20 Gonzalez | Y | Y | Y | N | N | N | Y | Y |
| 21 **Smith** | Y | Y | Y | Y | Y | Y | N | Y |
| 22 **DeLay** | Y | Y | Y | Y | Y | Y | N | N |
| 23 **Bonilla** | Y | Y | Y | Y | Y | Y | N | N |
| 24 **Marchant** | Y | Y | Y | Y | Y | Y | N | Y |
| 25 Doggett | Y | Y | Y | N | N | N | Y | Y |
| 26 **Burgess** | Y | Y | Y | ? | Y | Y | N | Y |
| 27 Ortiz | Y | Y | Y | N | N | N | Y | Y |
| 28 Cuellar | Y | Y | Y | N | N | N | Y | Y |
| 29 Green, G. | Y | Y | Y | N | N | N | Y | Y |
| 30 Johnson, E. | Y | Y | Y | N | N | N | Y | Y |
| 31 **Carter** | Y | Y | Y | Y | Y | Y | N | N |
| 32 **Sessions** | ? | ? | Y | Y | Y | Y | N | Y |
| **UTAH** | | | | | | | | |
| 1 **Bishop** | Y | Y | Y | Y | Y | Y | N | N |
| 2 Matheson | Y | Y | Y | N | N | N | Y | Y |
| 3 **Cannon** | Y | Y | Y | Y | Y | Y | N | Y |
| **VERMONT** | | | | | | | | |
| AL *Sanders* | Y | Y | Y | N | N | N | Y | Y |
| **VIRGINIA** | | | | | | | | |
| 1 **Davis, J.** | Y | Y | Y | Y | Y | Y | N | Y |
| 2 **Drake** | Y | Y | Y | Y | Y | Y | N | N |
| 3 Scott | Y | Y | Y | N | N | N | Y | Y |
| 4 **Forbes** | Y | Y | Y | Y | Y | Y | N | N |
| 5 **Goode** | Y | Y | Y | Y | Y | Y | N | Y |
| 6 **Goodlatte** | Y | Y | Y | Y | Y | Y | N | Y |
| 7 **Cantor** | Y | Y | Y | Y | Y | Y | N | N |
| 8 Moran | Y | Y | Y | N | N | N | Y | Y |
| 9 Boucher | Y | Y | Y | N | N | N | Y | Y |
| 10 **Wolf** | Y | Y | Y | Y | Y | Y | N | Y |
| 11 **Davis, T.** | Y | Y | Y | Y | Y | Y | N | N |
| **WASHINGTON** | | | | | | | | |
| 1 Inslee | Y | Y | Y | N | N | N | Y | Y |
| 2 Larsen | Y | Y | Y | N | N | N | Y | Y |
| 3 Baird | ? | ? | ? | ? | ? | N | Y | Y |
| 4 **Hastings** | Y | Y | Y | Y | Y | Y | N | N |
| 5 **McMorris** | Y | Y | Y | Y | Y | Y | N | N |
| 6 Dicks | Y | Y | Y | N | N | N | Y | N |
| 7 McDermott | Y | P | Y | N | N | N | Y | Y |
| 8 **Reichert** | Y | Y | Y | Y | Y | Y | N | Y |
| 9 Smith | Y | Y | Y | N | N | N | Y | N |
| **WEST VIRGINIA** | | | | | | | | |
| 1 Mollohan | Y | Y | Y | N | N | N | N | N |
| 2 **Capito** | Y | Y | Y | Y | Y | Y | N | N |
| 3 Rahall | Y | N | Y | N | N | N | N | N |
| **WISCONSIN** | | | | | | | | |
| 1 **Ryan** | Y | Y | Y | Y | Y | Y | N | Y |
| 2 Baldwin | Y | Y | Y | N | N | N | Y | Y |
| 3 Kind | Y | Y | Y | N | N | N | Y | Y |
| 4 Moore | Y | Y | Y | N | N | N | Y | Y |
| 5 **Sensenbrenner** | Y | Y | Y | Y | Y | Y | N | Y |
| 6 **Petri** | Y | Y | Y | Y | Y | Y | N | Y |
| 7 Obey | Y | Y | Y | N | N | N | Y | Y |
| 8 **Green** | Y | Y | Y | Y | Y | Y | N | Y |
| **WYOMING** | | | | | | | | |
| AL **Cubin** | Y | Y | Y | Y | Y | Y | N | N |

# IN THE HOUSE | By Vote Number

**74. HR 1268. Fiscal 2005 Supplemental Appropriations/Aid for Saudi Arabia.** Weiner, D-N.Y., amendment that would prohibit the use of funds in the bill for assistance to Saudi Arabia. Rejected 196-231: R 39-187; D 156-44 (ND 121-28, SD 35-16); I 1-0. March 15, 2005.

**75. HR 1268. Fiscal 2005 Supplemental Appropriations/Torture Policy.** Markey, D-Mass., amendment that would prohibit the use of funds in the bill to contravene U.S. laws implementing the U.N. Convention Against Torture. Adopted 420-2: R 222-2; D 197-0 (ND 148-0, SD 49-0); I 1-0. March 16, 2005.

**76. HR 1268. Fiscal 2005 Supplemental Appropriations/Recommit.** Hooley, D-Ore., motion to recommit the bill to the Appropriations Committee with instructions to add language that would increase funding for military health care by $100 million and for transitional job training for military personnel by $50 million. Motion rejected 200-229: R 2-226; D 197-3 (ND 146-3, SD 51-0); I 1-0. March 16, 2005.

**77. HR 1268. Fiscal 2005 Supplemental Appropriations/Passage.** Passage of the bill that would appropriate $81.4 billion in fiscal 2005 supplemental spending for military operations and reconstruction in Iraq and Afghanistan and for disaster assistance to victims of the December 2004 tsunami in South Asia. The bill would provide $15.5 billion for military personnel, $37.5 billion for operations and maintenance, $18.2 billion for procurement, $1.3 billion for reconstruction in Afghanistan and $4.6 billion for new combat brigades under the Army's force-restructuring plan. It also would provide $656 million for tsunami relief and recovery, and $222 million to reimburse the U.S. military for its tsunami-relief operations. Passed 388-43: R 226-3; D 162-39 (ND 115-35, SD 47-4); I 0-1. March 16, 2005.

**78. H Con Res 95. Fiscal 2006 Budget Resolution/Previous Question.** Putnam, R-Fla., motion to order the previous question (thus ending debate and possibility of amendment) on adoption of the rule (H Res 154) to provide for House floor consideration of the concurrent resolution that would set broad spending and revenue targets over the next five years. Motion agreed to 230-202: R 229-0; D 1-201 (ND 0-151, SD 1-50); I 0-1. March 16, 2005.

**79. H Con Res 95. Fiscal 2006 Budget Resolution/Rule.** Adoption of the rule (H Res 154) to provide for House floor consideration of the concurrent resolution that would set broad spending and revenue targets over the next five years. Adopted 228-196: R 227-0; D 1-195 (ND 1-147, SD 0-48); I 0-1. March 16, 2005.

**80. HR 1270. Leaking Underground Storage Tanks/Passage.** Chocola, R-Ind., motion to suspend the rules and pass the bill that would extend the 0.1-cent tax rate on motor vehicle fuels sold in the United States to fund the Leaking Underground Storage Tank Trust Fund through Oct. 1, 2005. Motion agreed to 431-1: R 228-1; D 202-0 (ND 151-0, SD 51-0); I 1-0. A two-thirds majority of those present and voting (288 in this case) is required for passage under suspension of the rules. March 16, 2005.

**81. H Con Res 98. China-Taiwan Relations/Adoption.** Smith, R-N.J., motion to suspend the rules and adopt the concurrent resolution that would express the sense of Congress that the March 14, 2005, passage of an anti-secession law by China is of grave concern to the United States because it provides a legal justification for the use of force against Taiwan. Motion agreed to 424-4: R 226-1; D 197-3 (ND 147-3, SD 50-0); I 1-0. A two-thirds majority of those present and voting (286 in this case) is required for adoption under suspension of the rules. March 16, 2005.

ND Northern Democrats, SD Southern Democrats
Southern states: Ala., Ark., Fla., Ga., Ky., La., Miss., N.C., Okla., S.C., Tenn., Texas, Va.

| | 74 | 75 | 76 | 77 | 78 | 79 | 80 | 81 |
|---|---|---|---|---|---|---|---|---|
| **ALABAMA** | | | | | | | | |
| 1 Bonner | N | Y | N | Y | Y | Y | Y | Y |
| 2 Everett | N | Y | N | Y | Y | Y | Y | Y |
| 3 Rogers | Y | Y | N | Y | Y | Y | Y | Y |
| 4 Aderholt | N | Y | N | Y | Y | Y | Y | Y |
| 5 Cramer | Y | Y | Y | Y | N | N | Y | Y |
| 6 Bachus | ? | Y | N | Y | Y | Y | Y | Y |
| 7 Davis | N | Y | Y | N | N | N | Y | Y |
| **ALASKA** | | | | | | | | |
| AL Young | N | Y | N | Y | Y | Y | Y | Y |
| **ARIZONA** | | | | | | | | |
| 1 Renzi | N | Y | N | Y | Y | Y | Y | Y |
| 2 Franks | N | Y | N | Y | Y | Y | Y | Y |
| 3 Shadegg | N | Y | N | Y | Y | Y | Y | Y |
| 4 Pastor | N | Y | Y | N | Y | N | Y | Y |
| 5 Hayworth | Y | Y | N | Y | Y | Y | Y | Y |
| 6 Flake | N | Y | N | Y | Y | Y | Y | Y |
| 7 Grijalva | Y | Y | N | N | N | N | Y | Y |
| 8 Kolbe | N | Y | N | Y | Y | Y | Y | Y |
| **ARKANSAS** | | | | | | | | |
| 1 Berry | Y | Y | Y | Y | N | N | Y | Y |
| 2 Snyder | N | Y | Y | N | N | N | Y | Y |
| 3 Boozman | N | Y | N | Y | Y | Y | Y | Y |
| 4 Ross | Y | Y | Y | Y | N | N | Y | Y |
| **CALIFORNIA** | | | | | | | | |
| 1 Thompson | Y | Y | Y | N | N | N | Y | Y |
| 2 Herger | N | Y | N | Y | Y | Y | Y | Y |
| 3 Lungren | N | Y | N | Y | Y | Y | Y | Y |
| 4 Doolittle | N | Y | N | Y | Y | Y | Y | Y |
| 5 Matsui, D. | Y | Y | Y | N | N | N | Y | Y |
| 6 Woolsey | Y | Y | Y | N | N | N | Y | Y |
| 7 Miller, George | Y | Y | Y | N | N | N | Y | Y |
| 8 Pelosi | Y | Y | Y | N | N | N | Y | Y |
| 9 Lee | Y | Y | Y | N | N | N | Y | Y |
| 10 Tauscher | Y | Y | Y | N | N | N | Y | Y |
| 11 Pombo | N | Y | N | Y | Y | Y | Y | Y |
| 12 Lantos | Y | Y | Y | N | N | N | Y | Y |
| 13 Stark | N | Y | Y | N | N | N | Y | Y |
| 14 Eshoo | Y | Y | Y | N | N | N | Y | Y |
| 15 Honda | Y | Y | Y | N | ? | N | Y | Y |
| 16 Lofgren | Y | Y | Y | N | N | N | Y | Y |
| 17 Farr | Y | Y | Y | N | N | N | Y | Y |
| 18 Cardoza | Y | Y | Y | N | N | N | Y | Y |
| 19 Radanovich | N | Y | N | Y | ? | ? | Y | Y |
| 20 Costa | Y | Y | Y | N | N | N | Y | Y |
| 21 Nunes | N | Y | N | Y | Y | Y | Y | Y |
| 22 Thomas | N | Y | N | Y | Y | Y | Y | Y |
| 23 Capps | Y | Y | Y | N | N | N | Y | Y |
| 24 Gallegly | N | Y | N | Y | Y | Y | Y | Y |
| 25 McKeon | N | Y | N | Y | Y | Y | Y | Y |
| 26 Dreier | N | Y | N | Y | Y | Y | Y | Y |
| 27 Sherman | Y | Y | Y | N | N | N | Y | Y |
| 28 Berman | Y | Y | Y | N | N | N | Y | Y |
| 29 Schiff | Y | Y | Y | N | N | N | Y | Y |
| 30 Waxman | Y | Y | Y | N | N | N | Y | Y |
| 31 Becerra | Y | Y | Y | N | N | N | Y | Y |
| 32 Solis | Y | Y | Y | N | N | N | Y | Y |
| 33 Watson | Y | Y | Y | N | N | ? | Y | Y |
| 34 Roybal-Allard | N | ? | ? | N | N | N | Y | Y |
| 35 Waters | ? | Y | Y | N | N | N | Y | Y |
| 36 Harman | Y | Y | Y | N | N | N | Y | Y |
| 37 Millender-McD. | Y | Y | Y | N | N | N | Y | Y |
| 38 Napolitano | Y | Y | Y | N | N | N | Y | Y |
| 39 Sánchez, Linda | Y | Y | Y | N | N | N | Y | Y |
| 40 Royce | Y | Y | N | Y | Y | Y | Y | Y |
| 41 Lewis | N | Y | N | Y | Y | Y | Y | Y |
| 42 Miller, Gary | N | Y | N | Y | Y | Y | Y | Y |
| 43 Baca | Y | Y | Y | N | N | N | Y | Y |
| 44 Calvert | N | Y | N | Y | Y | Y | Y | Y |
| 45 Bono | N | Y | N | Y | Y | Y | Y | Y |
| 46 Rohrabacher | Y | P | N | Y | Y | Y | Y | Y |
| 47 Sanchez, Loretta | Y | Y | Y | N | N | N | Y | Y |
| 48 Cox | Y | Y | N | Y | Y | Y | Y | Y |
| 49 Issa | N | Y | N | Y | Y | Y | Y | Y |

| | 74 | 75 | 76 | 77 | 78 | 79 | 80 | 81 |
|---|---|---|---|---|---|---|---|---|
| 50 Cunningham | N | Y | N | Y | Y | Y | Y | Y |
| 51 Filner | Y | Y | Y | N | N | N | Y | Y |
| 52 Hunter | N | Y | N | Y | Y | Y | Y | Y |
| 53 Davis | Y | Y | Y | Y | N | N | Y | Y |
| **COLORADO** | | | | | | | | |
| 1 DeGette | N | Y | Y | N | N | N | Y | Y |
| 2 Udall | Y | Y | Y | Y | N | N | Y | Y |
| 3 Salazar | Y | Y | Y | N | N | N | Y | Y |
| 4 Musgrave | N | Y | N | Y | Y | Y | Y | Y |
| 5 Hefley | N | Y | N | Y | Y | Y | Y | Y |
| 6 Tancredo | N | Y | N | Y | Y | Y | Y | Y |
| 7 Beauprez | N | Y | N | Y | Y | Y | Y | Y |
| **CONNECTICUT** | | | | | | | | |
| 1 Larson | Y | Y | Y | N | N | N | Y | Y |
| 2 Simmons | Y | Y | Y | N | Y | Y | Y | Y |
| 3 DeLauro | Y | Y | Y | N | N | N | Y | Y |
| 4 Shays | N | Y | N | Y | Y | Y | Y | Y |
| 5 Johnson | N | Y | N | Y | Y | Y | Y | Y |
| **DELAWARE** | | | | | | | | |
| AL Castle | N | Y | N | Y | Y | Y | Y | Y |
| **FLORIDA** | | | | | | | | |
| 1 Miller | N | Y | N | Y | Y | Y | Y | Y |
| 2 Boyd | Y | Y | Y | Y | N | Y | Y | Y |
| 3 Brown | Y | Y | Y | N | N | Y | Y | Y |
| 4 Crenshaw | N | Y | N | Y | Y | Y | Y | Y |
| 5 Brown-Waite | Y | Y | N | Y | Y | Y | Y | Y |
| 6 Stearns | Y | Y | N | Y | Y | Y | Y | Y |
| 7 Mica | N | Y | N | Y | Y | Y | Y | Y |
| 8 Keller | N | Y | N | Y | Y | Y | Y | Y |
| 9 Bilirakis | Y | Y | N | Y | Y | Y | Y | Y |
| 10 Young | N | Y | N | Y | Y | Y | Y | Y |
| 11 Davis | Y | Y | Y | Y | N | N | Y | Y |
| 12 Putnam | N | Y | N | Y | Y | Y | Y | Y |
| 13 Harris | N | Y | N | Y | Y | Y | Y | Y |
| 14 Mack | N | Y | N | Y | Y | Y | Y | Y |
| 15 Weldon | N | Y | N | Y | ? | Y | Y | Y |
| 16 Foley | N | Y | N | Y | Y | Y | Y | Y |
| 17 Meek | Y | Y | Y | N | N | N | Y | Y |
| 18 Ros-Lehtinen | Y | Y | N | Y | Y | Y | Y | Y |
| 19 Wexler | Y | Y | Y | N | N | ? | Y | Y |
| 20 Wasserman-Schultz | Y | Y | Y | N | N | N | Y | Y |
| 21 Diaz-Balart, L. | N | Y | N | Y | Y | Y | Y | Y |
| 22 Shaw | N | Y | N | Y | Y | Y | Y | Y |
| 23 Hastings | Y | Y | Y | N | N | N | Y | Y |
| 24 Feeney | N | Y | N | Y | Y | Y | Y | Y |
| 25 Diaz-Balart, M. | N | Y | N | Y | Y | Y | Y | Y |
| **GEORGIA** | | | | | | | | |
| 1 Kingston | N | Y | N | Y | Y | Y | Y | Y |
| 2 Bishop | N | Y | Y | N | N | N | Y | Y |
| 3 Marshall | Y | Y | Y | Y | N | N | Y | Y |
| 4 McKinney | N | ? | N | N | N | N | Y | Y |
| 5 Lewis | Y | Y | Y | N | N | N | Y | Y |
| 6 Price | N | P | N | Y | Y | Y | Y | Y |
| 7 Linder | N | Y | N | Y | Y | Y | Y | Y |
| 8 Westmoreland | N | P | N | Y | Y | Y | Y | Y |
| 9 Norwood | N | Y | N | Y | Y | Y | Y | Y |
| 10 Deal | N | Y | N | Y | Y | Y | Y | Y |
| 11 Gingrey | N | Y | N | Y | Y | Y | Y | Y |
| 12 Barrow | Y | Y | Y | N | N | N | Y | Y |
| 13 Scott | N | Y | Y | N | N | N | Y | Y |
| **HAWAII** | | | | | | | | |
| 1 Abercrombie | N | Y | N | Y | N | N | Y | Y |
| 2 Case | N | Y | Y | N | N | N | Y | Y |
| **IDAHO** | | | | | | | | |
| 1 Otter | Y | Y | N | Y | Y | Y | Y | Y |
| 2 Simpson | N | Y | N | Y | Y | Y | Y | Y |
| **ILLINOIS** | | | | | | | | |
| 1 Rush | N | Y | Y | Y | N | ? | Y | Y |
| 2 Jackson | N | Y | Y | N | N | N | Y | Y |
| 3 Lipinski | Y | Y | Y | N | N | N | Y | Y |
| 4 Gutierrez | Y | Y | Y | N | N | N | Y | Y |
| 5 Emanuel | N | Y | Y | N | N | N | Y | Y |
| 6 Hyde | N | Y | N | Y | Y | Y | Y | Y |
| 7 Davis | Y | Y | Y | N | N | N | Y | Y |
| 8 Bean | Y | Y | Y | Y | N | N | Y | Y |
| 9 Schakowsky | Y | Y | Y | N | N | N | Y | Y |
| 10 Kirk | N | Y | N | Y | Y | Y | Y | Y |
| 11 Weller | N | Y | N | Y | Y | Y | Y | Y |
| 12 Costello | N | Y | Y | Y | N | N | Y | Y |

**KEY**    **Republicans**    Democrats    *Independents*

| | | | |
|---|---|---|---|
| Y | Voted for (yea) | X | Paired against |
| # | Paired for | – | Announced against |
| + | Announced for | P | Voted "present" |
| N | Voted against (nay) | C | Voted "present" to avoid possible conflict of interest |
| | | ? | Did not vote or otherwise make a position known |

| | 74 | 75 | 76 | 77 | 78 | 79 | 80 | 81 |
|---|---|---|---|---|---|---|---|---|
| 13 **Biggert** | N | Y | N | Y | Y | Y | Y | Y |
| 14 **Hastert** | | | | | | | | |
| 15 **Johnson** | Y | Y | N | Y | Y | Y | Y | Y |
| 16 **Manzullo** | N | Y | N | Y | Y | Y | Y | Y |
| 17 Evans | Y | Y | Y | Y | N | N | Y | Y |
| 18 **LaHood** | N | Y | N | Y | Y | Y | Y | Y |
| 19 **Shimkus** | N | Y | N | Y | Y | Y | Y | Y |
| **INDIANA** | | | | | | | | |
| 1 Visclosky | N | Y | Y | Y | N | N | Y | Y |
| 2 **Chocola** | N | Y | N | Y | Y | Y | Y | Y |
| 3 **Souder** | Y | N | N | Y | Y | Y | Y | Y |
| 4 **Buyer** | N | Y | N | Y | Y | Y | Y | Y |
| 5 **Burton** | Y | Y | N | Y | Y | Y | Y | Y |
| 6 **Pence** | Y | Y | N | Y | Y | Y | Y | Y |
| 7 Carson | Y | Y | Y | Y | N | N | Y | Y |
| 8 **Hostettler** | Y | Y | N | Y | Y | ? | ? | Y |
| 9 **Sodrel** | N | Y | N | Y | Y | Y | Y | Y |
| **IOWA** | | | | | | | | |
| 1 **Nussle** | N | Y | N | Y | Y | Y | Y | Y |
| 2 **Leach** | ? | Y | N | Y | Y | Y | Y | Y |
| 3 Boswell | Y | Y | Y | Y | N | N | Y | Y |
| 4 **Latham** | N | Y | N | Y | Y | Y | Y | Y |
| 5 **King** | N | Y | N | Y | Y | Y | Y | Y |
| **KANSAS** | | | | | | | | |
| 1 **Moran** | Y | Y | N | Y | Y | Y | Y | Y |
| 2 **Ryun** | Y | Y | N | Y | Y | Y | Y | Y |
| 3 Moore | Y | Y | Y | Y | N | N | Y | Y |
| 4 **Tiahrt** | N | Y | N | Y | Y | Y | Y | ? |
| **KENTUCKY** | | | | | | | | |
| 1 **Whitfield** | N | Y | N | Y | Y | Y | Y | Y |
| 2 **Lewis** | N | Y | N | Y | Y | Y | Y | Y |
| 3 **Northup** | N | Y | N | Y | Y | Y | Y | Y |
| 4 **Davis** | N | Y | N | Y | Y | Y | Y | Y |
| 5 **Rogers** | N | Y | N | Y | Y | Y | Y | Y |
| 6 Chandler | Y | Y | Y | Y | N | N | Y | Y |
| **LOUISIANA** | | | | | | | | |
| 1 **Jindal** | N | Y | N | Y | Y | Y | Y | Y |
| 2 Jefferson | Y | Y | Y | Y | N | ? | Y | Y |
| 3 Melancon | Y | Y | Y | Y | N | ? | Y | ? |
| 4 **McCrery** | N | Y | N | Y | Y | Y | Y | Y |
| 5 **Alexander** | N | Y | N | Y | Y | Y | Y | Y |
| 6 **Baker** | N | ? | N | Y | Y | Y | Y | Y |
| 7 **Boustany** | N | Y | N | Y | Y | Y | Y | Y |
| **MAINE** | | | | | | | | |
| 1 Allen | N | Y | Y | Y | N | N | Y | Y |
| 2 Michaud | Y | Y | Y | Y | N | N | Y | Y |
| **MARYLAND** | | | | | | | | |
| 1 **Gilchrest** | N | Y | N | Y | Y | Y | Y | ? |
| 2 Ruppersberger | N | Y | Y | Y | N | N | Y | Y |
| 3 Cardin | Y | Y | Y | Y | N | N | Y | Y |
| 4 Wynn | Y | Y | Y | Y | N | N | Y | Y |
| 5 Hoyer | Y | Y | Y | Y | N | N | Y | Y |
| 6 **Bartlett** | N | Y | N | Y | Y | Y | Y | Y |
| 7 Cummings | Y | Y | Y | Y | N | N | Y | Y |
| 8 Van Hollen | Y | Y | Y | Y | N | N | Y | Y |
| **MASSACHUSETTS** | | | | | | | | |
| 1 Olver | Y | Y | Y | Y | N | N | Y | Y |
| 2 Neal | Y | Y | Y | Y | N | N | Y | ? |
| 3 McGovern | Y | Y | Y | N | N | N | Y | Y |
| 4 Frank | Y | Y | Y | N | N | N | Y | Y |
| 5 Meehan | Y | Y | Y | N | N | N | Y | Y |
| 6 Tierney | Y | Y | Y | N | N | N | Y | Y |
| 7 Markey | Y | Y | Y | N | N | N | Y | Y |
| 8 Capuano | Y | Y | Y | N | N | N | Y | Y |
| 9 Lynch | Y | Y | Y | Y | N | N | Y | Y |
| 10 Delahunt | Y | Y | Y | Y | N | N | Y | Y |
| **MICHIGAN** | | | | | | | | |
| 1 Stupak | Y | Y | Y | Y | N | N | Y | Y |
| 2 **Hoekstra** | N | Y | N | Y | Y | Y | Y | Y |
| 3 **Ehlers** | N | Y | N | Y | Y | Y | Y | Y |
| 4 **Camp** | N | Y | N | Y | Y | Y | Y | Y |
| 5 Kildee | N | Y | Y | Y | N | N | Y | Y |
| 6 **Upton** | N | Y | N | Y | Y | Y | Y | Y |
| 7 **Schwarz** | N | Y | N | Y | Y | Y | Y | Y |
| 8 **Rogers** | Y | Y | N | Y | Y | Y | Y | Y |
| 9 **Knollenberg** | N | Y | N | Y | Y | Y | Y | Y |
| 10 **Miller** | N | Y | N | Y | Y | Y | Y | Y |
| 11 **McCotter** | Y | Y | N | Y | Y | Y | Y | Y |
| 12 Levin | Y | Y | Y | Y | N | N | Y | Y |
| 13 Kilpatrick | N | Y | Y | Y | N | N | Y | Y |
| 14 Conyers | Y | Y | Y | Y | N | N | Y | Y |
| 15 Dingell | N | Y | Y | Y | N | N | Y | Y |

| | 74 | 75 | 76 | 77 | 78 | 79 | 80 | 81 |
|---|---|---|---|---|---|---|---|---|
| **MINNESOTA** | | | | | | | | |
| 1 **Gutknecht** | N | Y | N | Y | Y | Y | Y | Y |
| 2 **Kline** | N | Y | N | Y | Y | Y | Y | Y |
| 3 **Ramstad** | Y | Y | N | Y | Y | Y | Y | Y |
| 4 McCollum | Y | Y | Y | N | N | N | Y | N |
| 5 Sabo | Y | Y | Y | Y | N | N | Y | Y |
| 6 **Kennedy** | Y | Y | N | Y | Y | Y | Y | Y |
| 7 Peterson | Y | Y | Y | Y | N | N | Y | Y |
| 8 Oberstar | Y | Y | Y | Y | N | N | Y | N |
| **MISSISSIPPI** | | | | | | | | |
| 1 **Wicker** | N | Y | N | Y | Y | Y | Y | Y |
| 2 Thompson | N | Y | Y | Y | N | N | Y | Y |
| 3 **Pickering** | N | Y | N | Y | Y | Y | Y | Y |
| 4 Taylor | N | Y | Y | Y | N | N | Y | Y |
| **MISSOURI** | | | | | | | | |
| 1 Clay | Y | Y | Y | N | N | N | Y | Y |
| 2 **Akin** | N | Y | N | Y | Y | Y | Y | Y |
| 3 Carnahan | Y | Y | Y | Y | N | N | Y | Y |
| 4 Skelton | N | Y | Y | Y | N | N | Y | Y |
| 5 Cleaver | Y | Y | Y | Y | N | N | Y | Y |
| 6 **Graves** | Y | Y | N | Y | Y | Y | Y | Y |
| 7 **Blunt** | N | Y | N | Y | Y | Y | Y | Y |
| 8 **Emerson** | N | Y | N | Y | Y | Y | Y | Y |
| 9 **Hulshof** | N | Y | N | Y | Y | Y | Y | Y |
| **MONTANA** | | | | | | | | |
| AL **Rehberg** | N | Y | N | Y | Y | Y | Y | Y |
| **NEBRASKA** | | | | | | | | |
| 1 **Fortenberry** | N | Y | N | Y | Y | Y | Y | Y |
| 2 **Terry** | N | Y | N | Y | Y | Y | Y | Y |
| 3 **Osborne** | N | Y | N | Y | Y | Y | Y | Y |
| **NEVADA** | | | | | | | | |
| 1 Berkley | Y | Y | Y | Y | N | N | Y | Y |
| 2 **Gibbons** | N | Y | N | Y | Y | Y | Y | Y |
| 3 **Porter** | Y | Y | N | Y | Y | Y | Y | Y |
| **NEW HAMPSHIRE** | | | | | | | | |
| 1 **Bradley** | N | Y | N | Y | Y | Y | Y | Y |
| 2 **Bass** | N | Y | N | Y | Y | Y | Y | Y |
| **NEW JERSEY** | | | | | | | | |
| 1 Andrews | Y | Y | Y | Y | N | N | Y | Y |
| 2 **LoBiondo** | N | Y | N | Y | Y | Y | Y | Y |
| 3 **Saxton** | N | Y | N | Y | Y | Y | Y | Y |
| 4 **Smith** | N | Y | ? | Y | Y | Y | Y | Y |
| 5 **Garrett** | N | Y | N | Y | Y | Y | Y | Y |
| 6 Pallone | Y | Y | Y | N | N | N | Y | Y |
| 7 **Ferguson** | Y | Y | N | Y | Y | Y | Y | Y |
| 8 Pascrell | Y | Y | Y | Y | N | N | Y | Y |
| 9 Rothman | Y | Y | Y | Y | N | N | Y | Y |
| 10 Payne | Y | Y | Y | N | N | N | Y | Y |
| 11 **Frelinghuysen** | N | Y | N | Y | Y | Y | Y | Y |
| 12 Holt | Y | Y | Y | N | N | N | Y | Y |
| 13 Menendez | Y | Y | Y | Y | N | N | Y | Y |
| **NEW MEXICO** | | | | | | | | |
| 1 **Wilson** | N | Y | N | Y | Y | Y | Y | Y |
| 2 **Pearce** | N | Y | N | Y | Y | Y | Y | Y |
| 3 Udall | Y | Y | Y | Y | N | N | Y | Y |
| **NEW YORK** | | | | | | | | |
| 1 Bishop | Y | Y | Y | Y | N | N | Y | Y |
| 2 Israel | Y | Y | Y | Y | N | N | Y | Y |
| 3 **King** | N | Y | N | Y | Y | Y | Y | Y |
| 4 McCarthy | Y | Y | Y | Y | N | N | Y | Y |
| 5 Ackerman | N | Y | Y | Y | N | N | Y | Y |
| 6 Meeks | Y | Y | Y | Y | N | N | Y | Y |
| 7 Crowley | Y | Y | Y | Y | N | N | Y | Y |
| 8 Nadler | Y | Y | Y | Y | N | N | Y | Y |
| 9 Weiner | Y | Y | Y | N | N | N | Y | Y |
| 10 Towns | Y | Y | Y | N | N | N | Y | Y |
| 11 Owens | Y | Y | Y | N | N | N | Y | Y |
| 12 Velázquez | Y | Y | Y | N | N | N | Y | Y |
| 13 **Fossella** | N | Y | N | Y | Y | Y | Y | Y |
| 14 Maloney | Y | Y | Y | N | N | N | Y | Y |
| 15 Rangel | Y | Y | Y | N | N | N | Y | Y |
| 16 Serrano | Y | Y | Y | N | N | N | Y | Y |
| 17 Engel | Y | Y | Y | Y | N | N | Y | Y |
| 18 Lowey | Y | Y | Y | Y | N | N | Y | Y |
| 19 **Kelly** | N | Y | N | Y | Y | Y | Y | Y |
| 20 **Sweeney** | ? | ? | ? | ? | Y | Y | Y | Y |
| 21 McNulty | Y | Y | Y | Y | N | N | Y | Y |
| 22 Hinchey | Y | Y | Y | N | N | N | Y | Y |
| 23 **McHugh** | N | Y | N | Y | Y | Y | Y | Y |
| 24 **Boehlert** | N | Y | N | Y | Y | Y | Y | Y |
| 25 **Walsh** | ? | Y | N | Y | Y | Y | Y | Y |
| 26 **Reynolds** | N | Y | N | Y | Y | Y | Y | Y |
| 27 Higgins | Y | Y | Y | Y | N | N | Y | Y |
| 28 Slaughter | Y | Y | Y | Y | N | N | Y | Y |
| 29 **Kuhl** | N | Y | N | Y | Y | Y | Y | Y |

| | 74 | 75 | 76 | 77 | 78 | 79 | 80 | 81 |
|---|---|---|---|---|---|---|---|---|
| **NORTH CAROLINA** | | | | | | | | |
| 1 Butterfield | Y | Y | Y | Y | N | N | Y | Y |
| 2 Etheridge | N | Y | Y | Y | N | N | Y | Y |
| 3 **Jones** | Y | Y | Y | Y | Y | Y | Y | Y |
| 4 Price | N | Y | Y | Y | N | N | Y | Y |
| 5 **Foxx** | N | Y | N | Y | Y | Y | Y | Y |
| 6 **Coble** | N | Y | N | N | Y | Y | Y | Y |
| 7 McIntyre | Y | Y | Y | Y | N | N | Y | Y |
| 8 **Hayes** | N | N | N | Y | Y | Y | Y | Y |
| 9 **Myrick** | N | Y | N | Y | Y | Y | Y | Y |
| 10 **McHenry** | N | Y | N | Y | Y | Y | Y | Y |
| 11 **Taylor** | N | Y | N | Y | Y | Y | Y | Y |
| 12 Watt | Y | Y | Y | Y | N | ? | Y | Y |
| 13 Miller | Y | Y | Y | Y | N | N | Y | Y |
| **NORTH DAKOTA** | | | | | | | | |
| AL Pomeroy | N | Y | Y | Y | N | N | Y | Y |
| **OHIO** | | | | | | | | |
| 1 **Chabot** | Y | Y | N | Y | Y | Y | Y | Y |
| 2 **Portman** | N | ? | N | Y | Y | Y | Y | Y |
| 3 **Turner** | N | Y | N | Y | Y | Y | Y | Y |
| 4 **Oxley** | N | Y | N | Y | Y | Y | Y | Y |
| 5 **Gillmor** | N | Y | N | Y | Y | Y | Y | Y |
| 6 Strickland | Y | Y | Y | Y | N | N | Y | Y |
| 7 **Hobson** | N | Y | N | Y | Y | Y | Y | Y |
| 8 **Boehner** | N | Y | N | Y | Y | Y | Y | Y |
| 9 Kaptur | N | Y | Y | Y | N | N | Y | Y |
| 10 Kucinich | N | Y | Y | N | N | N | Y | Y |
| 11 Jones | Y | Y | Y | Y | N | N | Y | Y |
| 12 **Tiberi** | N | Y | N | Y | Y | Y | Y | Y |
| 13 Brown | Y | Y | Y | Y | N | N | Y | Y |
| 14 **LaTourette** | N | Y | N | Y | Y | Y | Y | Y |
| 15 **Pryce** | N | Y | N | Y | Y | Y | Y | Y |
| 16 **Regula** | N | Y | N | Y | Y | Y | Y | Y |
| 17 Ryan | Y | Y | Y | Y | N | N | Y | Y |
| 18 **Ney** | N | Y | N | Y | Y | Y | Y | Y |
| **OKLAHOMA** | | | | | | | | |
| 1 **Sullivan** | Y | Y | N | Y | Y | Y | Y | Y |
| 2 Boren | Y | Y | Y | Y | N | N | Y | Y |
| 3 **Lucas** | N | Y | N | Y | Y | Y | Y | Y |
| 4 **Cole** | N | Y | N | Y | Y | Y | Y | Y |
| 5 **Istook** | N | Y | N | Y | Y | Y | Y | Y |
| **OREGON** | | | | | | | | |
| 1 Wu | Y | Y | Y | Y | N | N | Y | Y |
| 2 **Walden** | N | Y | N | Y | Y | Y | Y | Y |
| 3 Blumenauer | Y | Y | Y | N | N | N | Y | Y |
| 4 DeFazio | Y | Y | Y | Y | N | N | Y | Y |
| 5 Hooley | Y | Y | Y | Y | N | N | Y | Y |
| **PENNSYLVANIA** | | | | | | | | |
| 1 Brady | Y | Y | N | Y | N | N | Y | Y |
| 2 Fattah | Y | Y | Y | Y | N | N | Y | Y |
| 3 **English** | N | Y | N | Y | Y | Y | Y | Y |
| 4 **Hart** | N | Y | N | Y | Y | Y | Y | Y |
| 5 **Peterson** | N | Y | N | Y | Y | Y | Y | Y |
| 6 **Gerlach** | N | Y | N | Y | Y | Y | Y | Y |
| 7 **Weldon** | N | Y | N | Y | Y | Y | Y | Y |
| 8 **Fitzpatrick** | N | Y | N | Y | Y | Y | Y | Y |
| 9 **Shuster** | N | Y | N | Y | Y | Y | Y | Y |
| 10 **Sherwood** | N | Y | N | Y | Y | Y | Y | Y |
| 11 Kanjorski | N | Y | N | Y | N | N | Y | Y |
| 12 Murtha | N | Y | N | Y | N | N | Y | Y |
| 13 Schwartz | Y | Y | Y | Y | N | N | Y | Y |
| 14 Doyle | N | Y | Y | Y | N | N | Y | Y |
| 15 **Dent** | Y | Y | N | Y | Y | Y | Y | Y |
| 16 **Pitts** | N | Y | N | Y | Y | Y | Y | Y |
| 17 Holden | Y | Y | Y | Y | N | N | Y | Y |
| 18 **Murphy** | N | Y | N | Y | Y | Y | Y | Y |
| 19 **Platts** | Y | Y | N | Y | Y | Y | Y | Y |
| **RHODE ISLAND** | | | | | | | | |
| 1 Kennedy | Y | Y | Y | Y | N | N | Y | Y |
| 2 Langevin | Y | Y | Y | Y | N | N | Y | Y |
| **SOUTH CAROLINA** | | | | | | | | |
| 1 **Brown** | Y | Y | N | Y | Y | Y | Y | Y |
| 2 **Wilson** | N | Y | N | Y | Y | Y | Y | Y |
| 3 **Barrett** | N | Y | N | Y | Y | Y | Y | Y |
| 4 **Inglis** | N | Y | N | Y | Y | Y | Y | Y |
| 5 Spratt | Y | Y | Y | Y | N | N | Y | Y |
| 6 Clyburn | Y | Y | Y | Y | N | N | Y | Y |
| **SOUTH DAKOTA** | | | | | | | | |
| AL Herseth | Y | Y | Y | Y | N | N | Y | Y |
| **TENNESSEE** | | | | | | | | |
| 1 **Jenkins** | N | Y | N | Y | Y | Y | Y | Y |
| 2 **Duncan** | N | Y | N | N | Y | Y | Y | Y |

| | 74 | 75 | 76 | 77 | 78 | 79 | 80 | 81 |
|---|---|---|---|---|---|---|---|---|
| 3 **Wamp** | N | Y | N | Y | Y | Y | Y | Y |
| 4 Davis | Y | Y | Y | Y | N | N | Y | Y |
| 5 Cooper | Y | Y | Y | Y | N | N | Y | Y |
| 6 Gordon | Y | Y | Y | Y | N | N | Y | Y |
| 7 **Blackburn** | N | Y | N | Y | Y | Y | Y | Y |
| 8 Tanner | N | Y | Y | Y | N | N | Y | Y |
| 9 Ford | Y | Y | Y | Y | N | N | Y | Y |
| **TEXAS** | | | | | | | | |
| 1 **Gohmert** | N | Y | N | Y | Y | Y | Y | Y |
| 2 **Poe** | N | Y | N | Y | Y | Y | Y | Y |
| 3 **Johnson, S.** | N | Y | N | Y | Y | Y | Y | ? |
| 4 **Hall** | Y | Y | N | Y | Y | Y | Y | Y |
| 5 **Hensarling** | N | Y | N | Y | Y | Y | Y | Y |
| 6 **Barton** | N | Y | N | Y | Y | Y | Y | Y |
| 7 **Culberson** | N | Y | N | Y | Y | Y | Y | Y |
| 8 **Brady** | N | Y | N | Y | Y | Y | Y | Y |
| 9 Green, A. | Y | Y | Y | Y | N | N | Y | Y |
| 10 **McCaul** | N | Y | N | Y | Y | Y | Y | Y |
| 11 **Conaway** | N | Y | N | Y | Y | Y | Y | Y |
| 12 **Granger** | N | Y | N | Y | Y | Y | Y | Y |
| 13 **Thornberry** | ? | Y | N | Y | Y | Y | Y | Y |
| 14 **Paul** | Y | Y | Y | N | Y | Y | N | N |
| 15 Hinojosa | N | Y | Y | Y | N | N | Y | Y |
| 16 Reyes | Y | Y | Y | Y | N | N | Y | Y |
| 17 Edwards | Y | Y | Y | Y | N | N | Y | Y |
| 18 Jackson-Lee | N | Y | Y | N | N | N | Y | Y |
| 19 **Neugebauer** | N | Y | N | Y | Y | Y | Y | Y |
| 20 Gonzalez | N | Y | Y | Y | N | N | Y | Y |
| 21 **Smith** | N | Y | N | Y | Y | Y | Y | Y |
| 22 **DeLay** | N | Y | N | Y | Y | Y | Y | Y |
| 23 **Bonilla** | N | Y | N | Y | Y | Y | Y | Y |
| 24 **Marchant** | N | Y | N | Y | Y | Y | Y | Y |
| 25 Doggett | Y | Y | Y | Y | N | N | Y | Y |
| 26 **Burgess** | N | Y | N | Y | Y | Y | Y | Y |
| 27 Ortiz | Y | Y | Y | Y | N | N | Y | Y |
| 28 Cuellar | N | Y | Y | Y | N | N | Y | Y |
| 29 Green, G. | Y | Y | Y | Y | N | N | Y | Y |
| 30 Johnson, E. | Y | Y | Y | Y | N | N | Y | Y |
| 31 **Carter** | N | Y | N | Y | Y | Y | Y | Y |
| 32 **Sessions** | N | Y | N | Y | Y | Y | Y | Y |
| **UTAH** | | | | | | | | |
| 1 **Bishop** | N | Y | N | Y | Y | Y | Y | Y |
| 2 Matheson | Y | Y | Y | Y | N | N | Y | Y |
| 3 **Cannon** | N | Y | N | Y | Y | Y | Y | Y |
| **VERMONT** | | | | | | | | |
| AL *Sanders* | Y | Y | Y | N | N | N | Y | Y |
| **VIRGINIA** | | | | | | | | |
| 1 **Davis, J.** | Y | Y | N | Y | Y | Y | Y | Y |
| 2 **Drake** | N | Y | N | Y | Y | Y | Y | Y |
| 3 Scott | Y | Y | Y | Y | N | N | Y | Y |
| 4 **Forbes** | N | Y | N | Y | Y | Y | Y | Y |
| 5 **Goode** | Y | Y | N | Y | Y | Y | Y | Y |
| 6 **Goodlatte** | N | Y | N | Y | Y | Y | Y | Y |
| 7 **Cantor** | N | Y | N | Y | Y | Y | Y | Y |
| 8 Moran | N | Y | Y | Y | N | N | Y | Y |
| 9 Boucher | N | ? | Y | Y | N | N | Y | Y |
| 10 **Wolf** | N | Y | N | Y | Y | Y | Y | Y |
| 11 **Davis, T.** | N | Y | N | Y | Y | Y | Y | Y |
| **WASHINGTON** | | | | | | | | |
| 1 Inslee | Y | Y | Y | Y | N | N | Y | Y |
| 2 Larsen | Y | ? | Y | Y | N | N | Y | Y |
| 3 Baird | Y | ? | ? | ? | N | N | Y | Y |
| 4 **Hastings** | N | Y | N | Y | Y | Y | Y | Y |
| 5 **McMorris** | N | Y | N | Y | Y | Y | Y | Y |
| 6 Dicks | Y | Y | Y | Y | N | N | Y | Y |
| 7 McDermott | Y | Y | Y | N | N | N | Y | N |
| 8 **Reichert** | N | Y | N | Y | Y | Y | Y | Y |
| 9 Smith | ? | Y | Y | Y | N | N | Y | Y |
| **WEST VIRGINIA** | | | | | | | | |
| 1 Mollohan | N | Y | Y | Y | N | N | Y | Y |
| 2 **Capito** | N | Y | N | Y | Y | Y | Y | Y |
| 3 Rahall | N | Y | Y | Y | N | N | Y | Y |
| **WISCONSIN** | | | | | | | | |
| 1 **Ryan** | N | Y | N | Y | Y | Y | Y | Y |
| 2 Baldwin | N | Y | Y | N | N | N | Y | Y |
| 3 Kind | Y | Y | Y | Y | N | N | Y | Y |
| 4 Moore | Y | Y | Y | Y | N | N | Y | Y |
| 5 **Sensenbrenner** | Y | Y | N | Y | Y | Y | Y | Y |
| 6 **Petri** | Y | Y | N | Y | Y | Y | Y | Y |
| 7 Obey | N | Y | Y | Y | N | Y | Y | Y |
| 8 **Green** | Y | Y | N | Y | Y | Y | Y | Y |
| **WYOMING** | | | | | | | | |
| AL **Cubin** | N | ? | ? | ? | ? | ? | ? | ? |

# IN THE HOUSE | By Vote Number

## 82. H Con Res 95. Fiscal 2006 Budget Resolution/Increased Spending.
Obey, D-Wis., amendment that would increase fiscal 2006 spending by a total of $15.8 billion, including $8 billion for education, training and social services programs, $2 billion for health care, and $2.9 billion for veterans' health care. It also would increase fiscal 2006 revenue by $25.8 billion by reducing tax cuts for those earning more than $1 million. Rejected 180-242: R 3-218; D 176-24 (ND 137-12, SD 39-12); I 1-0. March 17, 2005.

## 83. H Con Res 95. Fiscal 2006 Budget Resolution/Republican Study Committee Substitute. Hensarling, R-Texas, substitute that would call for an extra $58 billion in mandatory spending cuts over five years. It would reduce non-defense and non-homeland discretionary spending by 2 percent. It would provide reconciliation protection for $106 billion in tax cuts, establish new budgetary points of order and require roll call votes on legislation authorizing or appropriating more than $50 million. Rejected 102-320: R 101-122; D 1-197 (ND 1-148, SD 0-49); I 0-1. March 17, 2005.

## 84. H Con Res 32. Syrian Occupation of Lebanon/Adoption. Ros-Lehtinen, R-Fla., motion to suspend the rules and adopt the concurrent resolution that would express the sense of Congress that Lebanon is a captive country and that its occupation by Syria represents a long-term threat to the security of the Middle East. Motion agreed to 419-1: R 221-1; D 197-0 (ND 147-0, SD 50-0); I 1-0. A two-thirds majority of those present and voting (280 in this case) is required for adoption under suspension of the rules. March 17, 2005.

## 85. H Con Res 95. Fiscal 2006 Budget Resolution/Congressional Black Caucus Substitute. Watt, D-N.C., substitute that would increase fiscal 2006 spending by $36.3 billion, including $23.9 billion for education and job training and $7.8 billion for homeland security and veterans' programs. It would call for action to rescind tax cuts for wealthy individuals, close several tax loopholes and reduce funding for the ballistic missile defense program. Rejected 134-292: R 1-225; D 132-67 (ND 104-45, SD 28-22); I 1-0. March 17, 2005.

## 86. H Con Res 95. Fiscal 2006 Budget Resolution/Motion to Rise.
Blumenauer, D-Ore., motion to rise from the Committee of the Whole. Motion rejected 101-313: R 0-224; D 100-89 (ND 83-58, SD 17-31); I 1-0. March 17, 2005.

| | 82 | 83 | 84 | 85 | 86 |
|---|---|---|---|---|---|
| **ALABAMA** | | | | | |
| 1 Bonner | N | Y | Y | N | N |
| 2 Everett | N | N | Y | N | N |
| 3 Rogers | N | N | Y | N | N |
| 4 Aderholt | N | N | Y | N | N |
| 5 Cramer | N | N | Y | N | N |
| 6 Bachus | N | N | Y | N | N |
| 7 Davis | Y | N | Y | Y | Y |
| **ALASKA** | | | | | |
| AL Young | N | N | Y | N | N |
| **ARIZONA** | | | | | |
| 1 Renzi | N | N | Y | N | N |
| 2 Franks | N | Y | Y | N | N |
| 3 Shadegg | N | Y | Y | N | N |
| 4 Pastor | Y | N | Y | Y | Y |
| 5 Hayworth | N | Y | Y | N | N |
| 6 Flake | N | Y | Y | N | N |
| 7 Grijalva | Y | N | Y | Y | Y |
| 8 Kolbe | N | N | Y | N | N |
| **ARKANSAS** | | | | | |
| 1 Berry | Y | N | Y | N | Y |
| 2 Snyder | Y | N | Y | N | N |
| 3 Boozman | N | Y | Y | N | N |
| 4 Ross | Y | N | Y | N | N |
| **CALIFORNIA** | | | | | |
| 1 Thompson | N | N | Y | N | N |
| 2 Herger | N | Y | Y | N | N |
| 3 Lungren | N | Y | Y | N | N |
| 4 Doolittle | N | N | Y | N | ? |
| 5 Matsui, D. | Y | N | Y | Y | Y |
| 6 Woolsey | Y | N | Y | Y | Y |
| 7 Miller, George | Y | N | Y | Y | Y |
| 8 Pelosi | Y | N | Y | Y | Y |
| 9 Lee | Y | N | Y | Y | Y |
| 10 Tauscher | Y | N | Y | N | N |
| 11 Pombo | N | Y | Y | N | N |
| 12 Lantos | Y | N | Y | Y | N |
| 13 Stark | Y | N | Y | Y | ? |
| 14 Eshoo | Y | N | Y | Y | Y |
| 15 Honda | Y | N | Y | Y | Y |
| 16 Lofgren | Y | N | Y | Y | N |
| 17 Farr | Y | N | Y | Y | Y |
| 18 Cardoza | N | N | Y | N | ? |
| 19 Radanovich | N | Y | Y | N | N |
| 20 Costa | N | N | Y | N | N |
| 21 Nunes | N | N | Y | N | N |
| 22 Thomas | N | N | Y | N | N |
| 23 Capps | Y | N | Y | N | N |
| 24 Gallegly | N | N | Y | N | N |
| 25 McKeon | N | N | Y | N | N |
| 26 Dreier | N | N | Y | N | N |
| 27 Sherman | Y | N | Y | Y | Y |
| 28 Berman | Y | N | Y | N | N |
| 29 Schiff | Y | N | Y | N | N |
| 30 Waxman | Y | N | Y | N | ? |
| 31 Becerra | Y | N | Y | Y | Y |
| 32 Solis | Y | N | Y | Y | Y |
| 33 Watson | Y | N | Y | Y | Y |
| 34 Roybal-Allard | Y | N | Y | Y | Y |
| 35 Waters | Y | N | Y | Y | N |
| 36 Harman | Y | N | Y | N | N |
| 37 Millender-McD. | Y | N | Y | Y | Y |
| 38 Napolitano | Y | N | Y | Y | Y |
| 39 Sánchez, Linda | Y | N | Y | Y | Y |
| 40 Royce | N | Y | Y | N | N |
| 41 Lewis | N | N | Y | N | N |
| 42 Miller, Gary | N | Y | Y | N | N |
| 43 Baca | Y | N | Y | N | N |
| 44 Calvert | N | N | Y | N | N |
| 45 Bono | N | N | Y | N | N |
| 46 Rohrabacher | N | Y | Y | N | N |
| 47 Sanchez, Loretta | Y | N | Y | N | N |
| 48 Cox | N | Y | Y | N | N |
| 49 Issa | N | N | Y | N | N |

| | 82 | 83 | 84 | 85 | 86 |
|---|---|---|---|---|---|
| 50 Cunningham | N | N | Y | N | N |
| 51 Filner | Y | N | Y | Y | Y |
| 52 Hunter | N | Y | Y | N | N |
| 53 Davis | Y | N | Y | N | N |
| **COLORADO** | | | | | |
| 1 DeGette | Y | N | Y | N | N |
| 2 Udall | Y | N | Y | N | Y |
| 3 Salazar | N | N | Y | N | N |
| 4 Musgrave | N | Y | Y | N | N |
| 5 Hefley | N | N | Y | N | N |
| 6 Tancredo | N | N | Y | N | N |
| 7 Beauprez | N | Y | Y | N | N |
| **CONNECTICUT** | | | | | |
| 1 Larson | ? | ? | Y | Y | Y |
| 2 Simmons | N | N | Y | N | N |
| 3 DeLauro | Y | N | Y | Y | Y |
| 4 Shays | N | N | Y | N | N |
| 5 Johnson | N | N | Y | N | N |
| **DELAWARE** | | | | | |
| AL Castle | N | N | Y | N | N |
| **FLORIDA** | | | | | |
| 1 Miller | N | Y | Y | N | N |
| 2 Boyd | Y | N | Y | N | Y |
| 3 Brown | Y | N | Y | Y | Y |
| 4 Crenshaw | N | N | Y | N | N |
| 5 Brown-Waite | N | Y | Y | N | N |
| 6 Stearns | N | Y | Y | N | N |
| 7 Mica | N | Y | Y | N | N |
| 8 Keller | N | Y | Y | N | N |
| 9 Bilirakis | Y | N | Y | N | N |
| 10 Young | ? | ? | ? | ? | ? |
| 11 Davis | Y | N | Y | Y | Y |
| 12 Putnam | N | N | Y | N | N |
| 13 Harris | N | Y | Y | N | N |
| 14 Mack | N | N | Y | N | N |
| 15 Weldon | N | N | Y | N | N |
| 16 Foley | – | – | + | Y | N |
| 17 Meek | Y | N | Y | Y | Y |
| 18 Ros-Lehtinen | N | N | Y | N | N |
| 19 Wexler | Y | N | Y | Y | Y |
| 20 Wasserman-Schultz | Y | N | Y | Y | Y |
| 21 Diaz-Balart, L. | ? | ? | Y | N | N |
| 22 Shaw | N | N | Y | N | N |
| 23 Hastings | Y | N | Y | Y | Y |
| 24 Feeney | N | Y | Y | N | N |
| 25 Diaz-Balart, M. | ? | Y | Y | N | N |
| **GEORGIA** | | | | | |
| 1 Kingston | N | N | Y | N | N |
| 2 Bishop | Y | N | Y | N | N |
| 3 Marshall | N | N | Y | N | N |
| 4 McKinney | Y | N | P | Y | Y |
| 5 Lewis | Y | N | Y | Y | Y |
| 6 Price | N | Y | Y | N | N |
| 7 Linder | N | Y | Y | N | N |
| 8 Westmoreland | N | Y | Y | N | N |
| 9 Norwood | N | Y | Y | N | N |
| 10 Deal | N | N | Y | N | N |
| 11 Gingrey | N | Y | Y | N | N |
| 12 Barrow | N | N | Y | N | N |
| 13 Scott | Y | N | Y | N | N |
| **HAWAII** | | | | | |
| 1 Abercrombie | Y | N | Y | Y | Y |
| 2 Case | N | Y | Y | N | N |
| **IDAHO** | | | | | |
| 1 Otter | N | Y | Y | N | N |
| 2 Simpson | N | N | Y | N | N |
| **ILLINOIS** | | | | | |
| 1 Rush | Y | N | Y | Y | Y |
| 2 Jackson | Y | N | Y | Y | Y |
| 3 Lipinski | Y | N | Y | Y | N |
| 4 Gutierrez | Y | N | Y | Y | Y |
| 5 Emanuel | Y | N | Y | Y | Y |
| 6 Hyde | N | N | Y | N | N |
| 7 Davis | Y | N | Y | Y | Y |
| 8 Bean | N | N | Y | N | N |
| 9 Schakowsky | Y | N | Y | Y | Y |
| 10 Kirk | N | N | Y | N | N |
| 11 Weller | N | Y | Y | N | N |
| 12 Costello | Y | N | Y | Y | Y |

**KEY**  Republicans  Democrats  *Independents*

| | | | |
|---|---|---|---|
| **Y** Voted for (yea) | **X** Paired against | **C** Voted "present" to avoid possible conflict of interest |
| **#** Paired for | **–** Announced against | |
| **+** Announced for | **P** Voted "present" | **?** Did not vote or otherwise make a position known |
| **N** Voted against (nay) | | |

ND Northern Democrats, SD Southern Democrats
Southern states: Ala., Ark., Fla., Ga., Ky., La., Miss., N.C., Okla., S.C., Tenn., Texas, Va.

| | | 82 | 83 | 84 | 85 | 86 |
|---|---|---|---|---|---|---|
| 13 | Biggert | N | N | Y | N | N |
| 14 | Hastert | | | | | |
| 15 | Johnson | N | N | Y | N | N |
| 16 | Manzullo | N | Y | Y | N | N |
| 17 | Evans | Y | N | Y | Y | Y |
| 18 | LaHood | N | N | Y | N | N |
| 19 | Shimkus | N | Y | Y | N | N |
| **INDIANA** | | | | | | |
| 1 | Visclosky | Y | N | Y | N | N |
| 2 | Chocola | N | Y | Y | N | N |
| 3 | Souder | N | N | Y | N | N |
| 4 | Buyer | N | N | Y | N | N |
| 5 | Burton | N | N | Y | N | N |
| 6 | Pence | N | Y | Y | N | N |
| 7 | Carson | Y | N | Y | Y | Y |
| 8 | Hostettler | N | Y | Y | N | N |
| 9 | Sodrel | N | Y | Y | N | N |
| **IOWA** | | | | | | |
| 1 | Nussle | N | N | Y | N | N |
| 2 | Leach | N | N | Y | N | N |
| 3 | Boswell | N | N | Y | N | N |
| 4 | Latham | N | N | Y | N | N |
| 5 | King | N | Y | Y | N | N |
| **KANSAS** | | | | | | |
| 1 | Moran | N | Y | Y | N | N |
| 2 | Ryun | N | Y | Y | N | N |
| 3 | Moore | N | N | Y | N | N |
| 4 | Tiahrt | N | Y | Y | N | N |
| **KENTUCKY** | | | | | | |
| 1 | Whitfield | N | N | Y | N | N |
| 2 | Lewis | N | N | Y | N | N |
| 3 | Northup | N | N | Y | N | N |
| 4 | Davis | N | N | Y | N | N |
| 5 | Rogers | N | N | Y | N | N |
| 6 | Chandler | Y | N | Y | N | N |
| **LOUISIANA** | | | | | | |
| 1 | Jindal | N | Y | Y | N | N |
| 2 | Jefferson | Y | ? | Y | Y | N |
| 3 | Melancon | N | ? | Y | N | N |
| 4 | McCrery | N | N | Y | N | N |
| 5 | Alexander | N | N | Y | N | N |
| 6 | Baker | N | N | Y | N | N |
| 7 | Boustany | N | N | Y | N | N |
| **MAINE** | | | | | | |
| 1 | Allen | Y | N | Y | N | Y |
| 2 | Michaud | Y | N | Y | N | N |
| **MARYLAND** | | | | | | |
| 1 | Gilchrest | N | N | Y | N | N |
| 2 | Ruppersberger | Y | N | Y | Y | N |
| 3 | Cardin | Y | N | Y | Y | N |
| 4 | Wynn | Y | N | Y | Y | N |
| 5 | Hoyer | Y | N | Y | Y | N |
| 6 | Bartlett | N | Y | Y | N | N |
| 7 | Cummings | Y | N | Y | Y | ? |
| 8 | Van Hollen | Y | N | Y | Y | Y |
| **MASSACHUSETTS** | | | | | | |
| 1 | Olver | Y | N | Y | Y | ? |
| 2 | Neal | Y | N | Y | Y | Y |
| 3 | McGovern | Y | N | Y | Y | Y |
| 4 | Frank | Y | N | Y | Y | Y |
| 5 | Meehan | Y | N | Y | Y | Y |
| 6 | Tierney | Y | N | Y | Y | Y |
| 7 | Markey | Y | N | Y | Y | Y |
| 8 | Capuano | Y | N | Y | P | Y |
| 9 | Lynch | Y | N | Y | Y | N |
| 10 | Delahunt | ? | ? | ? | ? | ? |
| **MICHIGAN** | | | | | | |
| 1 | Stupak | Y | N | Y | N | N |
| 2 | Hoekstra | N | Y | Y | N | N |
| 3 | Ehlers | N | N | Y | N | N |
| 4 | Camp | N | N | Y | N | N |
| 5 | Kildee | Y | N | Y | N | N |
| 6 | Upton | N | N | Y | N | N |
| 7 | Schwarz | N | N | Y | N | N |
| 8 | Rogers | N | N | Y | N | N |
| 9 | Knollenberg | N | N | Y | N | N |
| 10 | Miller | N | N | Y | N | N |
| 11 | McCotter | N | Y | Y | N | ? |
| 12 | Levin | Y | N | Y | Y | N |
| 13 | Kilpatrick | Y | N | Y | Y | N |
| 14 | Conyers | Y | N | Y | Y | Y |
| 15 | Dingell | Y | N | Y | Y | N |

| | | 82 | 83 | 84 | 85 | 86 |
|---|---|---|---|---|---|---|
| **MINNESOTA** | | | | | | |
| 1 | Gutknecht | N | Y | Y | N | N |
| 2 | Kline | N | Y | Y | N | N |
| 3 | Ramstad | N | N | Y | N | N |
| 4 | McCollum | Y | N | Y | Y | N |
| 5 | Sabo | Y | N | Y | Y | Y |
| 6 | Kennedy | N | N | Y | N | N |
| 7 | Peterson | N | N | Y | N | N |
| 8 | Oberstar | Y | N | Y | Y | N |
| **MISSISSIPPI** | | | | | | |
| 1 | Wicker | N | N | Y | N | N |
| 2 | Thompson | Y | N | Y | Y | Y |
| 3 | Pickering | N | N | Y | N | N |
| 4 | Taylor | N | N | Y | N | Y |
| **MISSOURI** | | | | | | |
| 1 | Clay | Y | N | Y | Y | Y |
| 2 | Akin | N | Y | Y | N | N |
| 3 | Carnahan | Y | N | Y | N | Y |
| 4 | Skelton | N | N | Y | N | N |
| 5 | Cleaver | Y | N | Y | Y | Y |
| 6 | Graves | N | N | Y | N | N |
| 7 | Blunt | N | Y | Y | N | N |
| 8 | Emerson | N | N | Y | N | N |
| 9 | Hulshof | N | N | Y | N | N |
| **MONTANA** | | | | | | |
| AL | Rehberg | N | N | Y | N | N |
| **NEBRASKA** | | | | | | |
| 1 | Fortenberry | N | N | Y | N | N |
| 2 | Terry | N | Y | Y | N | N |
| 3 | Osborne | N | N | Y | N | N |
| **NEVADA** | | | | | | |
| 1 | Berkley | Y | N | Y | N | Y |
| 2 | Gibbons | N | Y | Y | N | N |
| 3 | Porter | N | N | Y | N | N |
| **NEW HAMPSHIRE** | | | | | | |
| 1 | Bradley | N | N | Y | N | N |
| 2 | Bass | N | N | Y | N | N |
| **NEW JERSEY** | | | | | | |
| 1 | Andrews | Y | N | Y | Y | Y |
| 2 | LoBiondo | N | N | Y | N | N |
| 3 | Saxton | N | N | Y | N | N |
| 4 | Smith | N | N | Y | N | N |
| 5 | Garrett | N | Y | Y | N | N |
| 6 | Pallone | Y | N | Y | N | N |
| 7 | Ferguson | N | N | Y | N | N |
| 8 | Pascrell | Y | N | Y | Y | N |
| 9 | Rothman | Y | N | Y | Y | Y |
| 10 | Payne | Y | N | Y | Y | Y |
| 11 | Frelinghuysen | N | N | Y | N | N |
| 12 | Holt | Y | N | Y | Y | Y |
| 13 | Menendez | Y | N | Y | Y | N |
| **NEW MEXICO** | | | | | | |
| 1 | Wilson | Y | N | Y | N | N |
| 2 | Pearce | N | N | Y | N | N |
| 3 | Udall | Y | N | Y | Y | N |
| **NEW YORK** | | | | | | |
| 1 | Bishop | Y | N | Y | Y | Y |
| 2 | Israel | Y | N | Y | N | Y |
| 3 | King | ? | ? | ? | N | N |
| 4 | McCarthy | Y | N | Y | N | N |
| 5 | Ackerman | Y | N | Y | Y | Y |
| 6 | Meeks | Y | N | Y | Y | Y |
| 7 | Crowley | Y | N | Y | Y | Y |
| 8 | Nadler | Y | N | Y | Y | Y |
| 9 | Weiner | Y | N | Y | Y | N |
| 10 | Towns | Y | N | Y | Y | Y |
| 11 | Owens | Y | N | Y | Y | Y |
| 12 | Velázquez | Y | N | Y | Y | Y |
| 13 | Fossella | N | N | Y | N | N |
| 14 | Maloney | Y | N | Y | Y | Y |
| 15 | Rangel | Y | N | Y | Y | Y |
| 16 | Serrano | Y | N | Y | Y | Y |
| 17 | Engel | Y | N | Y | Y | N |
| 18 | Lowey | Y | N | Y | Y | N |
| 19 | Kelly | N | N | Y | N | N |
| 20 | Sweeney | N | N | Y | N | N |
| 21 | McNulty | Y | N | Y | Y | N |
| 22 | Hinchey | Y | N | P | Y | Y |
| 23 | McHugh | N | N | Y | N | N |
| 24 | Boehlert | N | N | Y | N | N |
| 25 | Walsh | N | N | Y | N | N |
| 26 | Reynolds | ? | Y | Y | N | N |
| 27 | Higgins | Y | N | Y | Y | Y |
| 28 | Slaughter | Y | N | Y | Y | Y |
| 29 | Kuhl | N | Y | Y | N | N |

| | | 82 | 83 | 84 | 85 | 86 |
|---|---|---|---|---|---|---|
| **NORTH CAROLINA** | | | | | | |
| 1 | Butterfield | Y | N | Y | Y | Y |
| 2 | Etheridge | Y | N | Y | Y | Y |
| 3 | Jones | Y | N | Y | N | N |
| 4 | Price | Y | N | Y | Y | N |
| 5 | Foxx | N | Y | Y | N | N |
| 6 | Coble | - | + | + | - | - |
| 7 | McIntyre | N | N | Y | N | N |
| 8 | Hayes | N | N | Y | N | N |
| 9 | Myrick | N | Y | Y | N | N |
| 10 | McHenry | N | Y | Y | N | N |
| 11 | Taylor | N | N | Y | N | N |
| 12 | Watt | Y | N | Y | Y | ? |
| 13 | Miller | Y | N | Y | Y | N |
| **NORTH DAKOTA** | | | | | | |
| AL | Pomeroy | Y | N | Y | N | N |
| **OHIO** | | | | | | |
| 1 | Chabot | N | Y | Y | N | N |
| 2 | Portman | ? | ? | ? | N | N |
| 3 | Turner | N | N | Y | N | N |
| 4 | Oxley | N | N | Y | N | N |
| 5 | Gillmor | N | N | Y | N | N |
| 6 | Strickland | Y | N | Y | N | Y |
| 7 | Hobson | N | N | Y | N | N |
| 8 | Boehner | N | Y | Y | N | ? |
| 9 | Kaptur | Y | N | Y | Y | Y |
| 10 | Kucinich | Y | N | P | Y | Y |
| 11 | Jones | Y | N | Y | Y | Y |
| 12 | Tiberi | N | N | ? | N | N |
| 13 | Brown | Y | N | Y | Y | Y |
| 14 | LaTourette | N | N | Y | N | N |
| 15 | Pryce | N | N | Y | N | N |
| 16 | Regula | N | N | Y | N | N |
| 17 | Ryan | Y | N | Y | Y | Y |
| 18 | Ney | N | N | Y | N | ? |
| **OKLAHOMA** | | | | | | |
| 1 | Sullivan | N | Y | Y | N | ? |
| 2 | Boren | N | N | Y | N | N |
| 3 | Lucas | N | Y | Y | N | N |
| 4 | Cole | N | Y | Y | N | N |
| 5 | Istook | N | Y | Y | N | N |
| **OREGON** | | | | | | |
| 1 | Wu | Y | N | Y | N | N |
| 2 | Walden | N | Y | Y | N | N |
| 3 | Blumenauer | Y | N | Y | Y | Y |
| 4 | DeFazio | Y | N | Y | Y | Y |
| 5 | Hooley | Y | N | Y | Y | Y |
| **PENNSYLVANIA** | | | | | | |
| 1 | Brady | Y | N | Y | Y | N |
| 2 | Fattah | Y | N | Y | Y | Y |
| 3 | English | N | N | Y | N | N |
| 4 | Hart | N | N | Y | N | N |
| 5 | Peterson | N | N | Y | N | N |
| 6 | Gerlach | N | N | Y | N | N |
| 7 | Weldon | N | N | Y | N | N |
| 8 | Fitzpatrick | N | N | Y | N | N |
| 9 | Shuster | N | Y | Y | N | N |
| 10 | Sherwood | N | N | Y | N | N |
| 11 | Kanjorski | Y | N | Y | Y | N |
| 12 | Murtha | Y | N | Y | N | N |
| 13 | Schwartz | Y | N | Y | Y | N |
| 14 | Doyle | Y | N | Y | Y | N |
| 15 | Dent | N | N | Y | N | N |
| 16 | Pitts | N | Y | Y | N | N |
| 17 | Holden | Y | N | Y | Y | N |
| 18 | Murphy | N | N | Y | N | N |
| 19 | Platts | N | N | Y | N | N |
| **RHODE ISLAND** | | | | | | |
| 1 | Kennedy | Y | N | Y | Y | Y |
| 2 | Langevin | Y | N | Y | N | N |
| **SOUTH CAROLINA** | | | | | | |
| 1 | Brown | N | N | Y | N | N |
| 2 | Wilson | N | Y | Y | N | N |
| 3 | Barrett | N | Y | Y | N | N |
| 4 | Inglis | N | Y | Y | N | N |
| 5 | Spratt | Y | N | Y | Y | N |
| 6 | Clyburn | Y | N | Y | Y | N |
| **SOUTH DAKOTA** | | | | | | |
| AL | Herseth | Y | N | Y | N | N |
| **TENNESSEE** | | | | | | |
| 1 | Jenkins | N | Y | Y | N | N |
| 2 | Duncan | N | Y | Y | N | N |

| | | 82 | 83 | 84 | 85 | 86 |
|---|---|---|---|---|---|---|
| 3 | Wamp | N | Y | Y | N | N |
| 4 | Davis | N | N | Y | N | N |
| 5 | Cooper | N | N | Y | N | N |
| 6 | Gordon | N | N | Y | N | Y |
| 7 | Blackburn | N | Y | Y | N | N |
| 8 | Tanner | N | N | Y | N | N |
| 9 | Ford | N | N | Y | P | N |
| **TEXAS** | | | | | | |
| 1 | Gohmert | N | Y | Y | ? | N |
| 2 | Poe | N | Y | Y | N | N |
| 3 | Johnson, S. | N | Y | Y | N | N |
| 4 | Hall | N | Y | Y | N | N |
| 5 | Hensarling | N | Y | Y | N | N |
| 6 | Barton | N | N | Y | N | N |
| 7 | Culberson | N | N | Y | N | N |
| 8 | Brady | N | Y | Y | N | N |
| 9 | Green, A. | Y | N | Y | Y | Y |
| 10 | McCaul | N | Y | Y | N | N |
| 11 | Conaway | N | N | Y | N | N |
| 12 | Granger | N | N | Y | N | N |
| 13 | Thornberry | N | N | Y | N | N |
| 14 | Paul | N | Y | N | N | N |
| 15 | Hinojosa | Y | N | Y | Y | ? |
| 16 | Reyes | Y | N | Y | N | N |
| 17 | Edwards | Y | N | Y | N | N |
| 18 | Jackson-Lee | Y | N | Y | Y | ? |
| 19 | Neugebauer | N | Y | Y | N | N |
| 20 | Gonzalez | Y | N | Y | Y | Y |
| 21 | Smith | N | N | Y | N | N |
| 22 | DeLay | N | N | ? | N | N |
| 23 | Bonilla | N | N | Y | N | N |
| 24 | Marchant | N | Y | Y | N | N |
| 25 | Doggett | Y | N | Y | Y | Y |
| 26 | Burgess | N | Y | Y | N | N |
| 27 | Ortiz | Y | N | Y | Y | N |
| 28 | Cuellar | Y | N | Y | Y | N |
| 29 | Green, G. | Y | N | Y | Y | N |
| 30 | Johnson, E. | Y | N | Y | Y | Y |
| 31 | Carter | N | N | Y | N | N |
| 32 | Sessions | N | Y | Y | N | N |
| **UTAH** | | | | | | |
| 1 | Bishop | N | Y | Y | N | N |
| 2 | Matheson | N | N | Y | N | N |
| 3 | Cannon | N | Y | Y | N | N |
| **VERMONT** | | | | | | |
| AL | *Sanders* | Y | N | Y | Y | Y |
| **VIRGINIA** | | | | | | |
| 1 | Davis, J. | N | N | Y | P | N |
| 2 | Drake | N | Y | Y | N | N |
| 3 | Scott | Y | N | Y | Y | Y |
| 4 | Forbes | ? | ? | ? | N | N |
| 5 | Goode | N | N | Y | N | N |
| 6 | Goodlatte | N | Y | Y | N | N |
| 7 | Cantor | N | Y | Y | N | N |
| 8 | Moran | Y | N | Y | Y | N |
| 9 | Boucher | Y | N | Y | N | N |
| 10 | Wolf | N | N | Y | N | N |
| 11 | Davis, T. | N | N | Y | N | N |
| **WASHINGTON** | | | | | | |
| 1 | Inslee | Y | N | Y | N | Y |
| 2 | Larsen | Y | N | Y | N | ? |
| 3 | Baird | Y | N | Y | N | Y |
| 4 | Hastings | N | N | Y | N | N |
| 5 | McMorris | N | Y | Y | N | N |
| 6 | Dicks | Y | N | Y | N | N |
| 7 | McDermott | Y | N | P | Y | ? |
| 8 | Reichert | N | N | Y | N | N |
| 9 | Smith | Y | N | Y | N | Y |
| **WEST VIRGINIA** | | | | | | |
| 1 | Mollohan | Y | N | Y | N | N |
| 2 | Capito | N | N | Y | N | N |
| 3 | Rahall | Y | N | Y | N | N |
| **WISCONSIN** | | | | | | |
| 1 | Ryan | N | N | Y | N | N |
| 2 | Baldwin | Y | N | Y | Y | Y |
| 3 | Kind | Y | N | Y | Y | N |
| 4 | Moore | Y | N | Y | Y | N |
| 5 | Sensenbrenner | N | N | Y | N | N |
| 6 | Petri | N | N | Y | N | N |
| 7 | Obey | Y | N | Y | Y | P |
| 8 | Green | N | N | Y | N | N |
| **WYOMING** | | | | | | |
| AL | Cubin | ? | ? | ? | ? | N |

# IN THE HOUSE | By Vote Number

**87.** **H Con Res 95. Fiscal 2006 Budget Resolution/Democratic Substitute.** Spratt, D-S.C., substitute that would institute pay-as-you-go rules requiring tax cuts and mandatory spending increases be offset, while eliminating $68.6 billion in cuts to mandatory spending. It would add $4.5 billion more for education and training, $1.6 billion for veterans and $2.9 billion for environmental protection and conservation. It also would call for spending levels that produce a balanced budget by fiscal 2012. Rejected 165-264: R 0-228; D 164-36 (ND 130-19, SD 34-17); I 1-0. March 17, 2005.

**88.** **H Con Res 95. Fiscal 2006 Budget Resolution/Adoption.** Adoption of the concurrent resolution that would allow up to $843 billion in discretionary spending in fiscal 2006, plus $50 billion for operations in Iraq. It would call for mandatory spending cuts of $68.6 billion over five years and tax cuts totaling $106 billion, $45 billion of it protected by reconciliation rules. Defense spending would increase by 4 percent over fiscal 2005, to $439 billion, and non-defense spending would be cut by 1 percent, to $404 billion. Adopted 218-214: R 218-12; D 0-201 (ND 0-150, SD 0-51); I 0-1. March 17, 2005.

**89.** **H Con Res 18. Syrian Human Rights Abuses/Adoption.** Smith, R-N.J., motion to suspend the rules and adopt the concurrent resolution that would condemn the Syrian government for gross violations of internationally recognized human rights. Motion agreed to 402-3: R 217-1; D 184-2 (ND 135-1, SD 49-1); I 1-0. A two-thirds majority of those present and voting (270 in this case) is required for adoption under suspension of the rules. March 17, 2005.

**90.** **S 686. Schiavo Medical Care/Passage.** Sensenbrenner, R-Wis., motion to suspend the rules and pass the bill that would give the parents of Theresa Marie Schiavo, a severely brain-damaged Florida woman, the right to file a lawsuit in the U.S. District Court for the Middle District of Florida alleging that Schiavo's rights related to life-sustaining medical treatment have been violated under the Constitution or federal law. Motion agreed to, thus cleared for the president, 203-58: R 156-5; D 47-53 (ND 28-37, SD 19-16); I 0-0. A two-thirds majority of those present and voting (174 in this case) is required for passage under suspension of the rules. March 21, 2005 (in the session that began and the Congressional Record dated March 20, 2005).

ND Northern Democrats, SD Southern Democrats
Southern states: Ala., Ark., Fla., Ga., Ky., La., Miss., N.C., Okla., S.C., Tenn., Texas, Va.

| | 87 | 88 | 89 | 90 |
|---|---|---|---|---|
| **ALABAMA** | | | | |
| 1 Bonner | N | Y | Y | Y |
| 2 Everett | N | Y | Y | ? |
| 3 Rogers | N | Y | Y | Y |
| 4 Aderholt | N | Y | Y | Y |
| 5 Cramer | N | N | Y | Y |
| 6 Bachus | N | Y | Y | Y |
| 7 Davis | Y | N | Y | ? |
| **ALASKA** | | | | |
| AL Young | N | Y | Y | ? |
| **ARIZONA** | | | | |
| 1 Renzi | N | Y | Y | Y |
| 2 Franks | N | Y | Y | Y |
| 3 Shadegg | N | Y | Y | ? |
| 4 Pastor | Y | N | Y | ? |
| 5 Hayworth | N | Y | Y | Y |
| 6 Flake | N | Y | Y | ? |
| 7 Grijalva | Y | N | Y | ? |
| 8 Kolbe | N | Y | Y | ? |
| **ARKANSAS** | | | | |
| 1 Berry | N | N | Y | Y |
| 2 Snyder | Y | N | Y | Y |
| 3 Boozman | N | Y | Y | ? |
| 4 Ross | N | N | Y | Y |
| **CALIFORNIA** | | | | |
| 1 Thompson | N | N | ? | ? |
| 2 Herger | N | Y | Y | ? |
| 3 Lungren | N | Y | Y | ? |
| 4 Doolittle | N | Y | Y | Y |
| 5 Matsui, D. | Y | N | Y | N |
| 6 Woolsey | N | N | Y | ? |
| 7 Miller, George | Y | N | Y | ? |
| 8 Pelosi | Y | N | Y | ? |
| 9 Lee | N | N | Y | ? |
| 10 Tauscher | Y | N | Y | ? |
| 11 Pombo | N | Y | Y | ? |
| 12 Lantos | Y | N | Y | ? |
| 13 Stark | N | N | Y | ? |
| 14 Eshoo | Y | N | Y | ? |
| 15 Honda | Y | N | Y | ? |
| 16 Lofgren | Y | N | ? | ? |
| 17 Farr | Y | N | Y | ? |
| 18 Cardoza | N | N | Y | ? |
| 19 Radanovich | N | Y | Y | ? |
| 20 Costa | N | N | Y | ? |
| 21 Nunes | N | Y | Y | ? |
| 22 Thomas | N | Y | Y | ? |
| 23 Capps | Y | N | ? | ? |
| 24 Gallegly | N | Y | ? | ? |
| 25 McKeon | N | Y | Y | ? |
| 26 Dreier | N | Y | Y | Y |
| 27 Sherman | Y | N | Y | ? |
| 28 Berman | Y | N | ? | ? |
| 29 Schiff | Y | N | Y | N |
| 30 Waxman | Y | N | Y | ? |
| 31 Becerra | Y | N | ? | – |
| 32 Solis | Y | N | Y | ? |
| 33 Watson | Y | N | Y | ? |
| 34 Roybal-Allard | Y | N | Y | ? |
| 35 Waters | Y | N | Y | ? |
| 36 Harman | Y | N | Y | ? |
| 37 Millender-McD. | Y | N | Y | ? |
| 38 Napolitano | Y | N | ? | ? |
| 39 Sánchez, Linda | Y | N | Y | ? |
| 40 Royce | N | Y | Y | ? |
| 41 Lewis | N | Y | Y | Y |
| 42 Miller, Gary | N | Y | ? | ? |
| 43 Baca | Y | N | ? | Y |
| 44 Calvert | N | Y | ? | Y |
| 45 Bono | N | Y | ? | ? |
| 46 Rohrabacher | N | Y | ? | ? |
| 47 Sanchez, Loretta | N | N | Y | ? |
| 48 Cox | N | Y | Y | Y |
| 49 Issa | N | Y | Y | + |

| | 87 | 88 | 89 | 90 |
|---|---|---|---|---|
| 50 Cunningham | N | Y | Y | ? |
| 51 Filner | N | N | Y | ? |
| 52 Hunter | N | Y | Y | ? |
| 53 Davis | Y | N | Y | ? |
| **COLORADO** | | | | |
| 1 DeGette | Y | N | ? | ? |
| 2 Udall | Y | N | Y | ? |
| 3 Salazar | N | N | Y | ? |
| 4 Musgrave | N | Y | Y | Y |
| 5 Hefley | N | Y | Y | Y |
| 6 Tancredo | N | Y | Y | Y |
| 7 Beauprez | N | Y | Y | Y |
| **CONNECTICUT** | | | | |
| 1 Larson | Y | N | Y | N |
| 2 Simmons | N | N | Y | ? |
| 3 DeLauro | Y | N | Y | ? |
| 4 Shays | N | N | Y | N |
| 5 Johnson | N | Y | Y | ? |
| **DELAWARE** | | | | |
| AL Castle | N | Y | Y | N |
| **FLORIDA** | | | | |
| 1 Miller | N | Y | Y | Y |
| 2 Boyd | N | N | Y | ? |
| 3 Brown | Y | N | Y | ? |
| 4 Crenshaw | N | Y | Y | ? |
| 5 Brown-Waite | N | Y | ? | N |
| 6 Stearns | N | Y | Y | ? |
| 7 Mica | N | Y | ? | ? |
| 8 Keller | N | Y | Y | Y |
| 9 Bilirakis | N | Y | Y | Y |
| 10 Young | ? | ? | ? | ? |
| 11 Davis | Y | N | Y | N |
| 12 Putnam | N | Y | Y | Y |
| 13 Harris | N | Y | ? | Y |
| 14 Mack | N | Y | Y | Y |
| 15 Weldon | N | Y | Y | Y |
| 16 Foley | N | Y | Y | Y |
| 17 Meek | Y | N | Y | ? |
| 18 Ros-Lehtinen | N | Y | Y | Y |
| 19 Wexler | Y | N | Y | N |
| 20 Wasserman-Schultz | Y | N | Y | N |
| 21 Diaz-Balart, L. | N | Y | Y | Y |
| 22 Shaw | N | Y | Y | ? |
| 23 Hastings | Y | N | Y | N |
| 24 Feeney | N | Y | Y | Y |
| 25 Diaz-Balart, M. | N | Y | Y | Y |
| **GEORGIA** | | | | |
| 1 Kingston | N | Y | Y | Y |
| 2 Bishop | Y | N | Y | Y |
| 3 Marshall | N | N | Y | Y |
| 4 McKinney | Y | N | N | N |
| 5 Lewis | Y | N | Y | N |
| 6 Price | N | Y | Y | Y |
| 7 Linder | N | Y | Y | Y |
| 8 Westmoreland | N | Y | Y | Y |
| 9 Norwood | N | Y | Y | ? |
| 10 Deal | N | Y | Y | Y |
| 11 Gingrey | N | Y | Y | Y |
| 12 Barrow | N | N | Y | Y |
| 13 Scott | Y | N | Y | Y |
| **HAWAII** | | | | |
| 1 Abercrombie | Y | N | Y | ? |
| 2 Case | N | N | Y | ? |
| **IDAHO** | | | | |
| 1 Otter | N | Y | Y | Y |
| 2 Simpson | N | Y | Y | Y |
| **ILLINOIS** | | | | |
| 1 Rush | Y | N | Y | ? |
| 2 Jackson | Y | N | Y | Y |
| 3 Lipinski | N | N | Y | Y |
| 4 Gutierrez | Y | N | Y | N |
| 5 Emanuel | Y | N | Y | ? |
| 6 Hyde | N | Y | Y | ? |
| 7 Davis | Y | N | Y | ? |
| 8 Bean | N | N | Y | Y |
| 9 Schakowsky | Y | N | Y | ? |
| 10 Kirk | N | Y | Y | ? |
| 11 Weller | N | Y | Y | ? |
| 12 Costello | Y | N | Y | Y |

**KEY**  Republicans  Democrats  *Independents*

| | | |
|---|---|---|
| Y Voted for (yea) | X Paired against | C Voted "present" to avoid possible conflict of interest |
| # Paired for | – Announced against | |
| + Announced for | P Voted "present" | ? Did not vote or otherwise make a position known |
| N Voted against (nay) | | |

| | 87 | 88 | 89 | 90 |
|---|---|---|---|---|
| 13 Biggert | N | Y | Y | Y |
| 14 Hastert | | Y | | Y |
| 15 Johnson | N | N | Y | Y |
| 16 Manzullo | N | Y | Y | Y |
| 17 Evans | Y | N | ? | N |
| 18 LaHood | N | Y | Y | Y |
| 19 Shimkus | N | Y | Y | ? |
| **INDIANA** | | | | |
| 1 Visclosky | Y | N | Y | N |
| 2 Chocola | N | Y | Y | Y |
| 3 Souder | N | Y | Y | Y |
| 4 Buyer | N | Y | Y | Y |
| 5 Burton | N | Y | Y | Y |
| 6 Pence | N | Y | Y | Y |
| 7 Carson | Y | N | Y | N |
| 8 Hostettler | N | N | Y | ? |
| 9 Sodrel | N | Y | Y | Y |
| **IOWA** | | | | |
| 1 Nussle | N | Y | Y | Y |
| 2 Leach | N | Y | ? | Y |
| 3 Boswell | N | N | Y | ? |
| 4 Latham | N | Y | Y | Y |
| 5 King | N | Y | Y | Y |
| **KANSAS** | | | | |
| 1 Moran | N | Y | Y | ? |
| 2 Ryun | - | Y | Y | Y |
| 3 Moore | N | N | Y | - |
| 4 Tiahrt | N | Y | Y | Y |
| **KENTUCKY** | | | | |
| 1 Whitfield | N | Y | Y | Y |
| 2 Lewis | N | Y | Y | Y |
| 3 Northup | N | Y | Y | Y |
| 4 Davis | N | Y | Y | Y |
| 5 Rogers | N | Y | Y | ? |
| 6 Chandler | N | N | Y | Y |
| **LOUISIANA** | | | | |
| 1 Jindal | N | Y | Y | Y |
| 2 Jefferson | Y | N | Y | ? |
| 3 Melancon | N | N | Y | Y |
| 4 McCrery | N | Y | Y | ? |
| 5 Alexander | N | Y | Y | Y |
| 6 Baker | N | Y | Y | Y |
| 7 Boustany | N | Y | Y | ? |
| **MAINE** | | | | |
| 1 Allen | Y | N | Y | ? |
| 2 Michaud | N | N | Y | Y |
| **MARYLAND** | | | | |
| 1 Gilchrest | N | Y | Y | Y |
| 2 Ruppersberger | Y | N | Y | ? |
| 3 Cardin | Y | N | Y | N |
| 4 Wynn | Y | N | Y | Y |
| 5 Hoyer | Y | N | Y | N |
| 6 Bartlett | N | Y | Y | Y |
| 7 Cummings | Y | N | Y | Y |
| 8 Van Hollen | Y | N | Y | N |
| **MASSACHUSETTS** | | | | |
| 1 Olver | Y | N | Y | N |
| 2 Neal | Y | N | Y | ? |
| 3 McGovern | Y | N | Y | ? |
| 4 Frank | Y | N | Y | N |
| 5 Meehan | Y | N | Y | ? |
| 6 Tierney | Y | N | Y | ? |
| 7 Markey | Y | N | ? | ? |
| 8 Capuano | P | N | Y | N |
| 9 Lynch | Y | N | Y | Y |
| 10 Delahunt | ? | ? | ? | ? |
| **MICHIGAN** | | | | |
| 1 Stupak | Y | N | Y | Y |
| 2 Hoekstra | N | Y | Y | ? |
| 3 Ehlers | N | Y | Y | Y |
| 4 Camp | N | Y | Y | Y |
| 5 Kildee | Y | N | Y | Y |
| 6 Upton | N | Y | Y | Y |
| 7 Schwarz | N | Y | Y | Y |
| 8 Rogers | N | Y | Y | ? |
| 9 Knollenberg | N | Y | Y | ? |
| 10 Miller | N | Y | Y | Y |
| 11 McCotter | N | Y | Y | Y |
| 12 Levin | Y | N | Y | N |
| 13 Kilpatrick | Y | N | Y | ? |
| 14 Conyers | Y | N | Y | N |
| 15 Dingell | Y | N | Y | ? |

| | 87 | 88 | 89 | 90 |
|---|---|---|---|---|
| **MINNESOTA** | | | | |
| 1 Gutknecht | N | N | Y | ? |
| 2 Kline | N | Y | Y | Y |
| 3 Ramstad | N | Y | Y | Y |
| 4 McCollum | Y | N | Y | ? |
| 5 Sabo | Y | N | Y | ? |
| 6 Kennedy | N | Y | Y | Y |
| 7 Peterson | N | N | Y | ? |
| 8 Oberstar | Y | N | Y | Y |
| **MISSISSIPPI** | | | | |
| 1 Wicker | N | Y | Y | + |
| 2 Thompson | Y | N | Y | N |
| 3 Pickering | N | Y | Y | Y |
| 4 Taylor | N | N | Y | ? |
| **MISSOURI** | | | | |
| 1 Clay | Y | N | Y | N |
| 2 Akin | N | Y | Y | Y |
| 3 Carnahan | Y | N | Y | N |
| 4 Skelton | Y | N | Y | N |
| 5 Cleaver | Y | N | Y | N |
| 6 Graves | N | Y | Y | Y |
| 7 Blunt | N | Y | Y | Y |
| 8 Emerson | N | N | Y | Y |
| 9 Hulshof | N | Y | Y | Y |
| **MONTANA** | | | | |
| AL Rehberg | N | Y | Y | Y |
| **NEBRASKA** | | | | |
| 1 Fortenberry | N | Y | Y | Y |
| 2 Terry | N | Y | Y | Y |
| 3 Osborne | N | Y | Y | ? |
| **NEVADA** | | | | |
| 1 Berkley | Y | N | Y | N |
| 2 Gibbons | N | Y | Y | ? |
| 3 Porter | N | Y | Y | Y |
| **NEW HAMPSHIRE** | | | | |
| 1 Bradley | N | Y | Y | ? |
| 2 Bass | N | Y | Y | Y |
| **NEW JERSEY** | | | | |
| 1 Andrews | Y | N | Y | ? |
| 2 LoBiondo | N | Y | Y | Y |
| 3 Saxton | N | Y | Y | Y |
| 4 Smith | N | N | Y | Y |
| 5 Garrett | N | Y | ? | Y |
| 6 Pallone | Y | N | Y | N |
| 7 Ferguson | N | Y | Y | Y |
| 8 Pascrell | Y | N | Y | N |
| 9 Rothman | Y | N | Y | N |
| 10 Payne | Y | N | Y | N |
| 11 Frelinghuysen | N | Y | ? | ? |
| 12 Holt | Y | N | Y | N |
| 13 Menendez | Y | N | Y | ? |
| **NEW MEXICO** | | | | |
| 1 Wilson | N | Y | Y | ? |
| 2 Pearce | N | Y | Y | Y |
| 3 Udall | Y | N | Y | ? |
| **NEW YORK** | | | | |
| 1 Bishop | Y | N | Y | N |
| 2 Israel | Y | N | Y | N |
| 3 King | N | Y | Y | ? |
| 4 McCarthy | Y | N | Y | ? |
| 5 Ackerman | Y | N | Y | ? |
| 6 Meeks | Y | N | Y | ? |
| 7 Crowley | Y | N | Y | ? |
| 8 Nadler | Y | N | ? | N |
| 9 Weiner | Y | N | Y | N |
| 10 Towns | Y | N | Y | ? |
| 11 Owens | Y | N | Y | ? |
| 12 Velázquez | Y | N | Y | ? |
| 13 Fossella | N | Y | Y | Y |
| 14 Maloney | Y | N | Y | ? |
| 15 Rangel | Y | N | Y | ? |
| 16 Serrano | Y | N | Y | Y |
| 17 Engel | Y | N | Y | Y |
| 18 Lowey | Y | N | Y | ? |
| 19 Kelly | N | Y | Y | ? |
| 20 Sweeney | N | Y | Y | ? |
| 21 McNulty | Y | N | Y | Y |
| 22 Hinchey | Y | N | ? | ? |
| 23 McHugh | N | Y | Y | ? |
| 24 Boehlert | N | Y | Y | ? |
| 25 Walsh | N | Y | Y | ? |
| 26 Reynolds | N | Y | Y | ? |
| 27 Higgins | Y | N | Y | ? |
| 28 Slaughter | Y | N | Y | ? |
| 29 Kuhl | N | Y | Y | Y |

| | 87 | 88 | 89 | 90 |
|---|---|---|---|---|
| **NORTH CAROLINA** | | | | |
| 1 Butterfield | Y | N | Y | N |
| 2 Etheridge | Y | N | Y | Y |
| 3 Jones | N | N | Y | Y |
| 4 Price | Y | N | Y | N |
| 5 Foxx | N | Y | Y | Y |
| 6 Coble | - | + | + | + |
| 7 McIntyre | N | N | Y | Y |
| 8 Hayes | N | Y | Y | Y |
| 9 Myrick | N | Y | Y | Y |
| 10 McHenry | N | Y | Y | Y |
| 11 Taylor | N | Y | Y | Y |
| 12 Watt | Y | N | Y | N |
| 13 Miller | Y | N | Y | N |
| **NORTH DAKOTA** | | | | |
| AL Pomeroy | Y | N | Y | Y |
| **OHIO** | | | | |
| 1 Chabot | N | Y | Y | Y |
| 2 Portman | N | Y | ? | Y |
| 3 Turner | N | Y | Y | Y |
| 4 Oxley | N | Y | Y | ? |
| 5 Gillmor | N | Y | Y | Y |
| 6 Strickland | Y | N | Y | N |
| 7 Hobson | N | Y | Y | Y |
| 8 Boehner | N | Y | Y | Y |
| 9 Kaptur | Y | N | Y | N |
| 10 Kucinich | N | N | N | ? |
| 11 Jones | Y | N | Y | ? |
| 12 Tiberi | N | Y | Y | Y |
| 13 Brown | Y | N | Y | ? |
| 14 LaTourette | N | Y | Y | ? |
| 15 Pryce | N | Y | Y | Y |
| 16 Regula | N | Y | Y | Y |
| 17 Ryan | Y | N | Y | ? |
| 18 Ney | N | Y | Y | Y |
| **OKLAHOMA** | | | | |
| 1 Sullivan | N | Y | Y | Y |
| 2 Boren | N | N | Y | Y |
| 3 Lucas | N | Y | Y | Y |
| 4 Cole | N | Y | Y | Y |
| 5 Istook | N | Y | Y | Y |
| **OREGON** | | | | |
| 1 Wu | Y | N | Y | N |
| 2 Walden | N | Y | Y | ? |
| 3 Blumenauer | Y | N | Y | ? |
| 4 DeFazio | Y | N | Y | ? |
| 5 Hooley | Y | N | Y | ? |
| **PENNSYLVANIA** | | | | |
| 1 Brady | Y | N | Y | Y |
| 2 Fattah | Y | N | Y | Y |
| 3 English | N | Y | Y | Y |
| 4 Hart | N | Y | Y | Y |
| 5 Peterson | N | Y | Y | Y |
| 6 Gerlach | N | Y | Y | ? |
| 7 Weldon | N | Y | Y | Y |
| 8 Fitzpatrick | N | Y | Y | Y |
| 9 Shuster | N | Y | Y | ? |
| 10 Sherwood | N | Y | Y | Y |
| 11 Kanjorski | N | Y | Y | Y |
| 12 Murtha | N | N | Y | N |
| 13 Schwartz | Y | N | Y | N |
| 14 Doyle | Y | N | Y | N |
| 15 Dent | N | Y | Y | N |
| 16 Pitts | N | Y | Y | Y |
| 17 Holden | Y | N | Y | N |
| 18 Murphy | N | Y | Y | Y |
| 19 Platts | N | Y | Y | Y |
| **RHODE ISLAND** | | | | |
| 1 Kennedy | Y | N | Y | N |
| 2 Langevin | Y | N | Y | Y |
| **SOUTH CAROLINA** | | | | |
| 1 Brown | N | Y | Y | ? |
| 2 Wilson | N | Y | Y | Y |
| 3 Barrett | N | Y | Y | Y |
| 4 Inglis | N | Y | Y | Y |
| 5 Spratt | Y | N | Y | N |
| 6 Clyburn | Y | N | Y | N |
| **SOUTH DAKOTA** | | | | |
| AL Herseth | N | N | Y | Y |
| **TENNESSEE** | | | | |
| 1 Jenkins | N | Y | Y | Y |
| 2 Duncan | N | Y | Y | Y |

| | 87 | 88 | 89 | 90 |
|---|---|---|---|---|
| 3 Wamp | N | Y | Y | Y |
| 4 Davis | N | N | Y | Y |
| 5 Cooper | N | N | Y | ? |
| 6 Gordon | N | N | Y | ? |
| 7 Blackburn | N | Y | Y | Y |
| 8 Tanner | N | Y | Y | Y |
| 9 Ford | N | N | Y | Y |
| **TEXAS** | | | | |
| 1 Gohmert | N | Y | Y | Y |
| 2 Poe | N | Y | Y | Y |
| 3 Johnson, S. | N | Y | Y | ? |
| 4 Hall | N | Y | Y | Y |
| 5 Hensarling | N | Y | Y | Y |
| 6 Barton | N | Y | Y | ? |
| 7 Culberson | N | Y | Y | Y |
| 8 Brady | N | Y | Y | ? |
| 9 Green, A. | Y | N | Y | Y |
| 10 McCaul | N | Y | Y | Y |
| 11 Conaway | N | Y | Y | Y |
| 12 Granger | N | Y | Y | ? |
| 13 Thornberry | N | Y | Y | Y |
| 14 Paul | N | N | N | ? |
| 15 Hinojosa | Y | N | Y | ? |
| 16 Reyes | Y | N | Y | ? |
| 17 Edwards | Y | N | Y | ? |
| 18 Jackson-Lee | Y | N | Y | ? |
| 19 Neugebauer | N | Y | Y | Y |
| 20 Gonzalez | Y | N | Y | ? |
| 21 Smith | N | Y | Y | Y |
| 22 DeLay | N | Y | Y | Y |
| 23 Bonilla | N | Y | Y | ? |
| 24 Marchant | N | Y | Y | Y |
| 25 Doggett | Y | N | Y | ? |
| 26 Burgess | N | Y | Y | Y |
| 27 Ortiz | Y | N | Y | ? |
| 28 Cuellar | Y | N | Y | Y |
| 29 Green, G. | Y | N | Y | ? |
| 30 Johnson, E. | Y | N | Y | ? |
| 31 Carter | N | Y | Y | Y |
| 32 Sessions | N | Y | Y | Y |
| **UTAH** | | | | |
| 1 Bishop | N | Y | Y | ? |
| 2 Matheson | N | N | Y | Y |
| 3 Cannon | N | Y | Y | Y |
| **VERMONT** | | | | |
| AL *Sanders* | Y | N | Y | ? |
| **VIRGINIA** | | | | |
| 1 Davis, J. | N | Y | ? | Y |
| 2 Drake | N | Y | Y | Y |
| 3 Scott | Y | N | Y | N |
| 4 Forbes | N | Y | Y | Y |
| 5 Goode | N | Y | Y | Y |
| 6 Goodlatte | N | Y | Y | Y |
| 7 Cantor | N | Y | Y | Y |
| 8 Moran | Y | N | Y | N |
| 9 Boucher | Y | N | ? | ? |
| 10 Wolf | N | Y | Y | ? |
| 11 Davis, T. | N | Y | Y | Y |
| **WASHINGTON** | | | | |
| 1 Inslee | Y | N | Y | ? |
| 2 Larsen | Y | N | Y | ? |
| 3 Baird | Y | N | Y | Y |
| 4 Hastings | N | Y | Y | Y |
| 5 McMorris | N | Y | Y | ? |
| 6 Dicks | Y | N | ? | N |
| 7 McDermott | Y | N | Y | N |
| 8 Reichert | N | Y | Y | N |
| 9 Smith | Y | N | ? | ? |
| **WEST VIRGINIA** | | | | |
| 1 Mollohan | Y | N | Y | Y |
| 2 Capito | N | Y | Y | Y |
| 3 Rahall | Y | N | Y | ? |
| **WISCONSIN** | | | | |
| 1 Ryan | N | Y | Y | Y |
| 2 Baldwin | Y | N | Y | N |
| 3 Kind | Y | N | Y | N |
| 4 Moore | Y | N | Y | N |
| 5 Sensenbrenner | N | Y | Y | Y |
| 6 Petri | N | Y | Y | ? |
| 7 Obey | Y | N | Y | ? |
| 8 Green | N | Y | Y | Y |
| **WYOMING** | | | | |
| AL Cubin | N | Y | Y | ? |

# IN THE HOUSE | By Vote Number

**91.** **H Res 108. Zurab Zhvania Tribute/Adoption.** McCotter, R-Mich., motion to suspend the rules and adopt the resolution that would express the sympathy of the House of Representatives to the family of Zurab Zhvania and the people of the Republic of Georgia for the death of their prime minister. Motion agreed to 402-0: R 214-0; D 187-0 (ND 138-0, SD 49-0); I 1-0. A two-thirds majority of those present and voting (268 in this case) is required for adoption under suspension of the rules. April 5, 2005.

**92.** **H Res 120. Tsunami Response/Adoption.** McCotter, R-Mich., motion to suspend the rules and adopt the resolution commending the efforts by the armed forces and civilian employees of the State Department and the U.S. Agency for International Development in response to the earthquake and tsunami in South Asia of Dec. 26, 2004. Motion agreed to 401-0: R 214-0; D 186-0 (ND 138-0, SD 48-0); I 1-0. A two-thirds majority of those present and voting (268 in this case) is required for adoption under suspension of the rules. April 5, 2005.

**93.** **H Con Res 34. Yogi Bhajan Tribute/Adoption.** McCotter, R-Mich., motion to suspend the rules and adopt the concurrent resolution that would honor the life and contributions of Yogi Bhajan, a leader of Sikhs, and would express condolences to the Sikh community on his death. Motion agreed to 405-0: R 215-0; D 189-0 (ND 141-0, SD 48-0); I 1-0. A two-thirds majority of those present and voting (270 in this case) is required for adoption under suspension of the rules. April 5, 2005.

**94.** **H Res 190. Pope John Paul II Tribute/Adoption.** Adoption of a resolution that would honor the life and achievements of Pope John Paul II and express profound sorrow on his death. Adopted 415-0: R 222-0; D 192-0 (ND 142-0, SD 50-0); I 1-0. April 6, 2005.

**95.** **H Res 148. Financial Literacy Month/Adoption.** Gutknecht, R-Minn., motion to suspend the rules and adopt the resolution that would express support for the goals and ideals of Financial Literacy Month. Motion agreed to 409-2: R 216-2; D 192-0 (ND 143-0, SD 49-0); I 1-0. A two-thirds majority of those present and voting (274 in this case) is required for adoption under suspension of the rules. April 6, 2005.

| | 91 | 92 | 93 | 94 | 95 |
|---|---|---|---|---|---|
| **ALABAMA** | | | | | |
| 1 Bonner | Y | Y | Y | Y | Y |
| 2 Everett | Y | Y | Y | Y | Y |
| 3 Rogers | Y | Y | Y | Y | Y |
| 4 Aderholt | Y | Y | Y | Y | Y |
| 5 Cramer | Y | Y | Y | Y | Y |
| 6 Bachus | Y | Y | Y | Y | Y |
| 7 Davis | Y | Y | Y | Y | Y |
| **ALASKA** | | | | | |
| AL Young | Y | Y | Y | Y | Y |
| **ARIZONA** | | | | | |
| 1 Renzi | Y | Y | ? | Y | Y |
| 2 Franks | Y | Y | Y | Y | Y |
| 3 Shadegg | Y | Y | Y | Y | Y |
| 4 Pastor | Y | Y | Y | Y | Y |
| 5 Hayworth | Y | Y | Y | Y | Y |
| 6 Flake | Y | Y | Y | Y | N |
| 7 Grijalva | ? | Y | Y | Y | Y |
| 8 Kolbe | Y | Y | Y | Y | Y |
| **ARKANSAS** | | | | | |
| 1 Berry | Y | Y | Y | Y | Y |
| 2 Snyder | Y | Y | Y | Y | Y |
| 3 Boozman | Y | Y | Y | Y | Y |
| 4 Ross | Y | Y | Y | Y | Y |
| **CALIFORNIA** | | | | | |
| 1 Thompson | Y | Y | Y | Y | Y |
| 2 Herger | Y | Y | Y | Y | Y |
| 3 Lungren | Y | Y | Y | Y | Y |
| 4 Doolittle | Y | Y | Y | Y | Y |
| 5 Matsui, D. | Y | Y | Y | Y | Y |
| 6 Woolsey | Y | Y | Y | Y | Y |
| 7 Miller, George | Y | Y | Y | Y | Y |
| 8 Pelosi | Y | Y | Y | Y | Y |
| 9 Lee | Y | Y | Y | Y | Y |
| 10 Tauscher | Y | Y | Y | Y | Y |
| 11 Pombo | Y | Y | Y | Y | Y |
| 12 Lantos | Y | Y | Y | Y | Y |
| 13 Stark | Y | Y | Y | Y | Y |
| 14 Eshoo | Y | Y | Y | Y | Y |
| 15 Honda | Y | Y | Y | Y | Y |
| 16 Lofgren | Y | Y | Y | Y | Y |
| 17 Farr | Y | Y | Y | Y | Y |
| 18 Cardoza | Y | Y | Y | Y | Y |
| 19 Radanovich | Y | Y | Y | Y | Y |
| 20 Costa | ? | Y | Y | Y | Y |
| 21 Nunes | Y | Y | Y | Y | Y |
| 22 Thomas | Y | Y | Y | Y | Y |
| 23 Capps | Y | Y | Y | Y | Y |
| 24 Gallegly | Y | Y | Y | Y | Y |
| 25 McKeon | Y | Y | Y | Y | Y |
| 26 Dreier | Y | Y | Y | Y | Y |
| 27 Sherman | Y | Y | Y | Y | Y |
| 28 Berman | Y | ? | Y | Y | Y |
| 29 Schiff | Y | Y | Y | Y | Y |
| 30 Waxman | Y | Y | Y | Y | Y |
| 31 Becerra | Y | Y | Y | Y | Y |
| 32 Solis | Y | Y | Y | Y | Y |
| 33 Watson | ? | ? | ? | ? | ? |
| 34 Roybal-Allard | Y | Y | Y | Y | Y |
| 35 Waters | ? | ? | ? | ? | ? |
| 36 Harman | Y | ? | Y | Y | Y |
| 37 Millender-McD. | ? | ? | ? | ? | ? |
| 38 Napolitano | Y | Y | Y | + | Y |
| 39 Sánchez, Linda | Y | Y | Y | Y | Y |
| 40 Royce | Y | Y | Y | Y | Y |
| 41 Lewis | Y | Y | Y | Y | Y |
| 42 Miller, Gary | Y | Y | Y | Y | Y |
| 43 Baca | Y | Y | Y | Y | Y |
| 44 Calvert | ? | ? | ? | Y | Y |
| 45 Bono | Y | Y | Y | Y | Y |
| 46 Rohrabacher | Y | Y | Y | Y | Y |
| 47 Sanchez, Loretta | Y | Y | Y | Y | Y |
| 48 Cox | Y | Y | Y | Y | Y |
| 49 Issa | Y | Y | Y | Y | Y |

| | 91 | 92 | 93 | 94 | 95 |
|---|---|---|---|---|---|
| 50 Cunningham | Y | Y | Y | Y | Y |
| 51 Filner | Y | Y | Y | Y | Y |
| 52 Hunter | ? | ? | ? | Y | Y |
| 53 Davis | Y | Y | Y | Y | Y |
| **COLORADO** | | | | | |
| 1 DeGette | Y | Y | Y | Y | Y |
| 2 Udall | Y | Y | Y | Y | Y |
| 3 Salazar | Y | Y | Y | Y | Y |
| 4 Musgrave | Y | Y | Y | Y | Y |
| 5 Hefley | Y | Y | Y | Y | Y |
| 6 Tancredo | Y | Y | Y | Y | Y |
| 7 Beauprez | Y | Y | Y | Y | Y |
| **CONNECTICUT** | | | | | |
| 1 Larson | Y | Y | Y | Y | Y |
| 2 Simmons | Y | Y | Y | Y | Y |
| 3 DeLauro | Y | Y | Y | Y | Y |
| 4 Shays | Y | Y | Y | Y | ? |
| 5 Johnson | Y | Y | Y | Y | Y |
| **DELAWARE** | | | | | |
| AL Castle | Y | Y | Y | Y | Y |
| **FLORIDA** | | | | | |
| 1 Miller | Y | Y | Y | Y | Y |
| 2 Boyd | Y | Y | Y | Y | Y |
| 3 Brown | Y | Y | Y | Y | Y |
| 4 Crenshaw | Y | Y | Y | Y | Y |
| 5 Brown-Waite | Y | Y | Y | Y | Y |
| 6 Stearns | Y | Y | Y | Y | Y |
| 7 Mica | Y | Y | Y | Y | Y |
| 8 Keller | Y | ? | Y | Y | Y |
| 9 Bilirakis | Y | Y | Y | Y | Y |
| 10 Young | ? | ? | ? | ? | ? |
| 11 Davis | Y | Y | Y | Y | Y |
| 12 Putnam | Y | Y | Y | Y | Y |
| 13 Harris | Y | Y | Y | Y | Y |
| 14 Mack | Y | Y | Y | Y | Y |
| 15 Weldon | Y | Y | Y | Y | Y |
| 16 Foley | Y | Y | Y | Y | Y |
| 17 Meek | Y | Y | Y | Y | Y |
| 18 Ros-Lehtinen | Y | Y | Y | Y | Y |
| 19 Wexler | Y | Y | Y | Y | Y |
| 20 Wasserman-Schultz | Y | Y | Y | Y | Y |
| 21 Diaz-Balart, L. | Y | Y | Y | Y | Y |
| 22 Shaw | Y | Y | Y | Y | Y |
| 23 Hastings | Y | Y | Y | Y | Y |
| 24 Feeney | Y | Y | Y | Y | Y |
| 25 Diaz-Balart, M. | Y | Y | Y | Y | Y |
| **GEORGIA** | | | | | |
| 1 Kingston | Y | Y | Y | ? | ? |
| 2 Bishop | Y | Y | Y | Y | Y |
| 3 Marshall | Y | Y | Y | Y | Y |
| 4 McKinney | Y | Y | Y | Y | Y |
| 5 Lewis | Y | Y | Y | Y | Y |
| 6 Price | Y | Y | Y | Y | Y |
| 7 Linder | Y | Y | Y | Y | Y |
| 8 Westmoreland | Y | Y | Y | Y | Y |
| 9 Norwood | Y | Y | Y | Y | Y |
| 10 Deal | Y | Y | Y | Y | Y |
| 11 Gingrey | Y | Y | Y | Y | Y |
| 12 Barrow | Y | Y | P | Y | Y |
| 13 Scott | Y | ? | Y | Y | Y |
| **HAWAII** | | | | | |
| 1 Abercrombie | Y | Y | Y | Y | Y |
| 2 Case | Y | Y | Y | Y | Y |
| **IDAHO** | | | | | |
| 1 Otter | Y | Y | Y | Y | ? |
| 2 Simpson | Y | Y | Y | Y | Y |
| **ILLINOIS** | | | | | |
| 1 Rush | Y | Y | Y | Y | Y |
| 2 Jackson | Y | Y | Y | Y | Y |
| 3 Lipinski | Y | Y | Y | Y | + |
| 4 Gutierrez | Y | Y | Y | + | + |
| 5 Emanuel | Y | Y | Y | Y | Y |
| 6 Hyde | Y | Y | Y | Y | Y |
| 7 Davis | Y | Y | Y | Y | Y |
| 8 Bean | Y | Y | Y | Y | Y |
| 9 Schakowsky | Y | Y | Y | Y | Y |
| 10 Kirk | Y | ? | Y | Y | Y |
| 11 Weller | Y | Y | Y | Y | Y |
| 12 Costello | ? | ? | ? | Y | Y |

**KEY**   Republicans   Democrats   *Independents*

| | | | |
|---|---|---|---|
| Y | Voted for (yea) | X | Paired against |
| # | Paired for | – | Announced against |
| + | Announced for | P | Voted "present" |
| N | Voted against (nay) | C | Voted "present" to avoid possible conflict of interest |
| | | ? | Did not vote or otherwise make a position known |

ND Northern Democrats, SD Southern Democrats
Southern states: Ala., Ark., Fla., Ga., Ky., La., Miss., N.C., Okla., S.C., Tenn., Texas, Va.

| | | 91 | 92 | 93 | 94 | 95 |
|---|---|---|---|---|---|---|
| 13 | Biggert | Y | Y | Y | Y | Y |
| 14 | Hastert | | | | | |
| 15 | Johnson | Y | Y | Y | Y | Y |
| 16 | Manzullo | Y | Y | Y | Y | Y |
| 17 | Evans | ? | Y | Y | Y | ? |
| 18 | LaHood | Y | Y | Y | Y | Y |
| 19 | Shimkus | ? | ? | ? | ? | ? |
| **INDIANA** | | | | | | |
| 1 | Visclosky | Y | Y | Y | Y | Y |
| 2 | Chocola | Y | Y | Y | Y | Y |
| 3 | Souder | ? | ? | ? | ? | ? |
| 4 | Buyer | Y | Y | Y | Y | Y |
| 5 | Burton | Y | Y | Y | Y | Y |
| 6 | Pence | Y | Y | Y | Y | Y |
| 7 | Carson | Y | Y | Y | Y | Y |
| 8 | Hostettler | ? | ? | ? | Y | Y |
| 9 | Sodrel | Y | Y | Y | Y | Y |
| **IOWA** | | | | | | |
| 1 | Nussle | Y | Y | Y | Y | Y |
| 2 | Leach | Y | Y | Y | Y | Y |
| 3 | Boswell | Y | Y | Y | Y | Y |
| 4 | Latham | Y | Y | Y | Y | Y |
| 5 | King | Y | Y | Y | Y | Y |
| **KANSAS** | | | | | | |
| 1 | Moran | Y | Y | Y | Y | Y |
| 2 | Ryun | Y | Y | Y | Y | Y |
| 3 | Moore | Y | Y | Y | Y | Y |
| 4 | Tiahrt | Y | Y | Y | Y | Y |
| **KENTUCKY** | | | | | | |
| 1 | Whitfield | Y | Y | Y | Y | Y |
| 2 | Lewis | + | + | + | Y | Y |
| 3 | Northup | Y | Y | Y | Y | Y |
| 4 | Davis | Y | Y | Y | Y | Y |
| 5 | Rogers | Y | Y | Y | Y | Y |
| 6 | Chandler | Y | Y | Y | Y | Y |
| **LOUISIANA** | | | | | | |
| 1 | Jindal | Y | Y | Y | Y | Y |
| 2 | Jefferson | Y | Y | Y | Y | ? |
| 3 | Melancon | Y | Y | Y | Y | Y |
| 4 | McCrery | Y | Y | Y | Y | Y |
| 5 | Alexander | ? | ? | ? | Y | Y |
| 6 | Baker | Y | Y | Y | Y | Y |
| 7 | Boustany | Y | Y | Y | Y | Y |
| **MAINE** | | | | | | |
| 1 | Allen | Y | Y | Y | Y | Y |
| 2 | Michaud | Y | Y | Y | Y | Y |
| **MARYLAND** | | | | | | |
| 1 | Gilchrest | Y | Y | Y | Y | Y |
| 2 | Ruppersberger | Y | Y | Y | Y | Y |
| 3 | Cardin | Y | Y | Y | Y | Y |
| 4 | Wynn | Y | Y | Y | Y | Y |
| 5 | Hoyer | Y | Y | Y | Y | Y |
| 6 | Bartlett | Y | Y | Y | Y | Y |
| 7 | Cummings | Y | Y | Y | Y | Y |
| 8 | Van Hollen | Y | Y | Y | Y | Y |
| **MASSACHUSETTS** | | | | | | |
| 1 | Olver | Y | Y | Y | Y | Y |
| 2 | Neal | Y | Y | Y | Y | Y |
| 3 | McGovern | Y | Y | Y | Y | Y |
| 4 | Frank | Y | Y | Y | Y | Y |
| 5 | Meehan | Y | Y | Y | Y | Y |
| 6 | Tierney | Y | Y | Y | Y | Y |
| 7 | Markey | Y | Y | Y | Y | Y |
| 8 | Capuano | Y | Y | Y | Y | Y |
| 9 | Lynch | Y | Y | Y | ? | Y |
| 10 | Delahunt | Y | Y | Y | Y | Y |
| **MICHIGAN** | | | | | | |
| 1 | Stupak | Y | ? | Y | Y | Y |
| 2 | Hoekstra | ? | ? | ? | ? | ? |
| 3 | Ehlers | ? | ? | ? | Y | Y |
| 4 | Camp | Y | Y | Y | Y | Y |
| 5 | Kildee | Y | Y | Y | Y | Y |
| 6 | Upton | Y | Y | Y | Y | Y |
| 7 | Schwarz | Y | Y | Y | Y | Y |
| 8 | Rogers | Y | Y | Y | Y | Y |
| 9 | Knollenberg | Y | Y | Y | Y | Y |
| 10 | Miller | Y | Y | Y | Y | Y |
| 11 | McCotter | Y | Y | Y | Y | Y |
| 12 | Levin | Y | Y | Y | Y | Y |
| 13 | Kilpatrick | Y | Y | ? | Y | Y |
| 14 | Conyers | Y | ? | Y | Y | Y |
| 15 | Dingell | Y | Y | Y | Y | Y |

| | | 91 | 92 | 93 | 94 | 95 |
|---|---|---|---|---|---|---|
| **MINNESOTA** | | | | | | |
| 1 | Gutknecht | Y | Y | Y | Y | Y |
| 2 | Kline | Y | Y | Y | Y | Y |
| 3 | Ramstad | Y | Y | Y | Y | Y |
| 4 | McCollum | Y | Y | Y | Y | Y |
| 5 | Sabo | Y | Y | Y | Y | Y |
| 6 | Kennedy | Y | Y | Y | Y | Y |
| 7 | Peterson | Y | Y | Y | Y | Y |
| 8 | Oberstar | Y | Y | Y | Y | |
| **MISSISSIPPI** | | | | | | |
| 1 | Wicker | Y | Y | Y | Y | Y |
| 2 | Thompson | Y | Y | Y | Y | Y |
| 3 | Pickering | Y | Y | Y | Y | Y |
| 4 | Taylor | Y | Y | Y | Y | Y |
| **MISSOURI** | | | | | | |
| 1 | Clay | Y | Y | Y | Y | Y |
| 2 | Akin | Y | Y | Y | Y | Y |
| 3 | Carnahan | Y | Y | Y | Y | Y |
| 4 | Skelton | Y | Y | Y | Y | Y |
| 5 | Cleaver | Y | Y | Y | Y | Y |
| 6 | Graves | Y | Y | Y | Y | Y |
| 7 | Blunt | Y | Y | Y | Y | Y |
| 8 | Emerson | Y | Y | Y | Y | Y |
| 9 | Hulshof | Y | Y | Y | Y | Y |
| **MONTANA** | | | | | | |
| AL | Rehberg | Y | Y | Y | Y | Y |
| **NEBRASKA** | | | | | | |
| 1 | Fortenberry | Y | Y | Y | Y | Y |
| 2 | Terry | Y | Y | Y | Y | Y |
| 3 | Osborne | Y | Y | Y | Y | Y |
| **NEVADA** | | | | | | |
| 1 | Berkley | Y | Y | Y | Y | Y |
| 2 | Gibbons | Y | Y | Y | Y | Y |
| 3 | Porter | Y | Y | Y | Y | Y |
| **NEW HAMPSHIRE** | | | | | | |
| 1 | Bradley | Y | Y | Y | Y | Y |
| 2 | Bass | Y | Y | Y | Y | Y |
| **NEW JERSEY** | | | | | | |
| 1 | Andrews | Y | Y | Y | Y | Y |
| 2 | LoBiondo | Y | Y | Y | Y | Y |
| 3 | Saxton | Y | Y | Y | Y | Y |
| 4 | Smith | Y | Y | Y | Y | Y |
| 5 | Garrett | Y | Y | Y | Y | Y |
| 6 | Pallone | Y | Y | Y | Y | Y |
| 7 | Ferguson | ? | ? | ? | Y | Y |
| 8 | Pascrell | Y | Y | Y | Y | Y |
| 9 | Rothman | Y | Y | Y | Y | Y |
| 10 | Payne | ? | ? | ? | Y | Y |
| 11 | Frelinghuysen | Y | Y | Y | Y | Y |
| 12 | Holt | Y | Y | Y | Y | Y |
| 13 | Menendez | Y | Y | Y | Y | Y |
| **NEW MEXICO** | | | | | | |
| 1 | Wilson | Y | Y | Y | Y | Y |
| 2 | Pearce | Y | Y | Y | Y | Y |
| 3 | Udall | Y | Y | Y | Y | Y |
| **NEW YORK** | | | | | | |
| 1 | Bishop | Y | Y | Y | Y | Y |
| 2 | Israel | Y | Y | Y | Y | Y |
| 3 | King | Y | Y | Y | Y | Y |
| 4 | McCarthy | Y | Y | Y | Y | Y |
| 5 | Ackerman | Y | Y | Y | Y | Y |
| 6 | Meeks | Y | Y | Y | Y | Y |
| 7 | Crowley | Y | Y | Y | Y | Y |
| 8 | Nadler | Y | Y | Y | Y | Y |
| 9 | Weiner | Y | Y | Y | Y | Y |
| 10 | Towns | Y | Y | Y | Y | Y |
| 11 | Owens | Y | Y | Y | Y | Y |
| 12 | Velázquez | Y | Y | Y | Y | Y |
| 13 | Fossella | Y | Y | Y | Y | Y |
| 14 | Maloney | Y | Y | Y | Y | Y |
| 15 | Rangel | ? | ? | ? | ? | ? |
| 16 | Serrano | Y | Y | Y | Y | Y |
| 17 | Engel | Y | Y | Y | Y | Y |
| 18 | Lowey | Y | Y | Y | Y | Y |
| 19 | Kelly | Y | Y | Y | Y | Y |
| 20 | Sweeney | Y | Y | Y | Y | Y |
| 21 | McNulty | Y | Y | Y | Y | Y |
| 22 | Hinchey | Y | Y | Y | Y | Y |
| 23 | McHugh | Y | Y | Y | Y | Y |
| 24 | Boehlert | Y | Y | Y | Y | Y |
| 25 | Walsh | Y | Y | Y | Y | Y |
| 26 | Reynolds | Y | Y | Y | Y | Y |
| 27 | Higgins | Y | Y | Y | Y | Y |
| 28 | Slaughter | Y | Y | Y | Y | Y |
| 29 | Kuhl | Y | Y | Y | Y | Y |

| | | 91 | 92 | 93 | 94 | 95 |
|---|---|---|---|---|---|---|
| **NORTH CAROLINA** | | | | | | |
| 1 | Butterfield | Y | Y | Y | Y | Y |
| 2 | Etheridge | Y | Y | Y | Y | Y |
| 3 | Jones | Y | Y | Y | Y | ? |
| 4 | Price | Y | Y | Y | Y | Y |
| 5 | Foxx | Y | Y | Y | Y | Y |
| 6 | Coble | ? | ? | ? | Y | Y |
| 7 | McIntyre | Y | Y | Y | Y | Y |
| 8 | Hayes | Y | Y | Y | Y | Y |
| 9 | Myrick | Y | Y | Y | Y | Y |
| 10 | McHenry | Y | Y | Y | Y | Y |
| 11 | Taylor | Y | Y | Y | Y | Y |
| 12 | Watt | Y | Y | Y | Y | Y |
| 13 | Miller | Y | Y | Y | Y | |
| **NORTH DAKOTA** | | | | | | |
| AL | Pomeroy | Y | Y | Y | Y | Y |
| **OHIO** | | | | | | |
| 1 | Chabot | Y | Y | Y | Y | Y |
| 2 | Portman | Y | Y | Y | Y | Y |
| 3 | Turner | Y | Y | Y | Y | Y |
| 4 | Oxley | Y | Y | Y | Y | Y |
| 5 | Gillmor | Y | Y | Y | Y | Y |
| 6 | Strickland | Y | Y | Y | Y | Y |
| 7 | Hobson | Y | Y | Y | ? | ? |
| 8 | Boehner | ? | ? | ? | Y | Y |
| 9 | Kaptur | Y | Y | Y | Y | Y |
| 10 | Kucinich | Y | Y | Y | Y | Y |
| 11 | Jones | Y | Y | Y | Y | Y |
| 12 | Tiberi | Y | Y | Y | Y | Y |
| 13 | Brown | ? | ? | ? | ? | ? |
| 14 | LaTourette | ? | ? | ? | Y | Y |
| 15 | Pryce | Y | Y | Y | Y | Y |
| 16 | Regula | Y | Y | Y | Y | Y |
| 17 | Ryan | ? | ? | ? | Y | Y |
| 18 | Ney | Y | Y | Y | Y | Y |
| **OKLAHOMA** | | | | | | |
| 1 | Sullivan | Y | Y | Y | Y | Y |
| 2 | Boren | Y | Y | Y | Y | Y |
| 3 | Lucas | Y | Y | Y | Y | Y |
| 4 | Cole | Y | Y | Y | Y | Y |
| 5 | Istook | Y | Y | Y | + | Y |
| **OREGON** | | | | | | |
| 1 | Wu | Y | Y | Y | Y | Y |
| 2 | Walden | Y | Y | Y | Y | Y |
| 3 | Blumenauer | Y | Y | Y | Y | Y |
| 4 | DeFazio | Y | Y | Y | Y | Y |
| 5 | Hooley | Y | Y | Y | Y | Y |
| **PENNSYLVANIA** | | | | | | |
| 1 | Brady | Y | Y | Y | Y | Y |
| 2 | Fattah | ? | ? | ? | Y | Y |
| 3 | English | Y | Y | Y | Y | Y |
| 4 | Hart | Y | Y | Y | Y | Y |
| 5 | Peterson | Y | Y | Y | Y | Y |
| 6 | Gerlach | Y | Y | Y | Y | Y |
| 7 | Weldon | Y | Y | Y | Y | Y |
| 8 | Fitzpatrick | Y | Y | Y | Y | Y |
| 9 | Shuster | Y | Y | Y | Y | Y |
| 10 | Sherwood | Y | Y | Y | Y | Y |
| 11 | Kanjorski | Y | Y | Y | Y | Y |
| 12 | Murtha | Y | Y | Y | Y | Y |
| 13 | Schwartz | Y | Y | Y | Y | Y |
| 14 | Doyle | Y | Y | Y | Y | Y |
| 15 | Dent | Y | Y | Y | Y | Y |
| 16 | Pitts | Y | Y | Y | Y | Y |
| 17 | Holden | Y | Y | Y | Y | Y |
| 18 | Murphy | Y | Y | Y | Y | Y |
| 19 | Platts | ? | Y | Y | Y | Y |
| **RHODE ISLAND** | | | | | | |
| 1 | Kennedy | Y | Y | Y | Y | Y |
| 2 | Langevin | Y | Y | Y | Y | Y |
| **SOUTH CAROLINA** | | | | | | |
| 1 | Brown | Y | Y | Y | Y | Y |
| 2 | Wilson | Y | Y | Y | Y | Y |
| 3 | Barrett | Y | Y | Y | Y | Y |
| 4 | Inglis | Y | Y | Y | Y | Y |
| 5 | Spratt | Y | Y | Y | Y | Y |
| 6 | Clyburn | Y | Y | Y | ? | ? |
| **SOUTH DAKOTA** | | | | | | |
| AL | Herseth | Y | Y | Y | Y | Y |
| **TENNESSEE** | | | | | | |
| 1 | Jenkins | Y | Y | Y | Y | Y |
| 2 | Duncan | Y | Y | Y | Y | Y |

| | | 91 | 92 | 93 | 94 | 95 |
|---|---|---|---|---|---|---|
| 3 | Wamp | Y | Y | Y | Y | Y |
| 4 | Davis | Y | Y | Y | Y | Y |
| 5 | Cooper | Y | Y | Y | Y | Y |
| 6 | Gordon | Y | Y | Y | Y | Y |
| 7 | Blackburn | Y | Y | Y | Y | Y |
| 8 | Tanner | Y | Y | Y | Y | Y |
| 9 | Ford | Y | Y | Y | Y | Y |
| **TEXAS** | | | | | | |
| 1 | Gohmert | Y | Y | ? | Y | ? |
| 2 | Poe | Y | Y | Y | Y | Y |
| 3 | Johnson, S. | Y | Y | Y | Y | Y |
| 4 | Hall | Y | Y | Y | Y | Y |
| 5 | Hensarling | Y | Y | Y | Y | Y |
| 6 | Barton | Y | Y | Y | Y | Y |
| 7 | Culberson | ? | Y | Y | Y | Y |
| 8 | Brady | Y | Y | Y | Y | Y |
| 9 | Green | Y | Y | Y | Y | Y |
| 10 | McCaul | Y | Y | Y | Y | Y |
| 11 | Conaway | Y | Y | Y | Y | Y |
| 12 | Granger | ? | ? | ? | Y | Y |
| 13 | Thornberry | Y | Y | Y | Y | Y |
| 14 | Paul | Y | Y | Y | Y | N |
| 15 | Hinojosa | Y | Y | Y | Y | Y |
| 16 | Reyes | Y | Y | Y | Y | Y |
| 17 | Edwards | Y | Y | Y | Y | Y |
| 18 | Jackson-Lee | + | + | + | Y | Y |
| 19 | Neugebauer | + | + | + | Y | Y |
| 20 | Gonzalez | Y | Y | Y | Y | Y |
| 21 | Smith | Y | Y | Y | Y | Y |
| 22 | DeLay | Y | Y | Y | Y | ? |
| 23 | Bonilla | Y | Y | Y | Y | Y |
| 24 | Marchant | Y | Y | Y | Y | Y |
| 25 | Doggett | Y | Y | Y | Y | Y |
| 26 | Burgess | Y | Y | Y | Y | Y |
| 27 | Ortiz | Y | Y | Y | Y | Y |
| 28 | Cuellar | Y | Y | Y | Y | Y |
| 29 | Green | Y | Y | Y | Y | Y |
| 30 | Johnson, E. | Y | Y | Y | Y | Y |
| 31 | Carter | Y | Y | Y | Y | Y |
| 32 | Sessions | Y | Y | Y | Y | Y |
| **UTAH** | | | | | | |
| 1 | Bishop | Y | Y | Y | Y | Y |
| 2 | Matheson | Y | Y | Y | Y | Y |
| 3 | Cannon | Y | Y | Y | Y | Y |
| **VERMONT** | | | | | | |
| AL | *Sanders* | Y | Y | Y | Y | Y |
| **VIRGINIA** | | | | | | |
| 1 | Davis, J. | Y | Y | Y | Y | Y |
| 2 | Drake | Y | Y | Y | Y | Y |
| 3 | Scott | ? | ? | ? | Y | Y |
| 4 | Forbes | Y | Y | Y | ? | ? |
| 5 | Goode | Y | Y | Y | Y | Y |
| 6 | Goodlatte | Y | Y | Y | Y | Y |
| 7 | Cantor | Y | Y | Y | Y | Y |
| 8 | Moran | Y | Y | Y | Y | Y |
| 9 | Boucher | Y | Y | Y | Y | Y |
| 10 | Wolf | Y | Y | Y | Y | Y |
| 11 | Davis, T. | Y | Y | Y | Y | Y |
| **WASHINGTON** | | | | | | |
| 1 | Inslee | Y | Y | Y | Y | Y |
| 2 | Larsen | Y | Y | Y | Y | Y |
| 3 | Baird | ? | ? | ? | ? | ? |
| 4 | Hastings | Y | Y | Y | Y | Y |
| 5 | McMorris | Y | Y | Y | Y | Y |
| 6 | Dicks | Y | Y | Y | Y | Y |
| 7 | McDermott | Y | Y | Y | Y | Y |
| 8 | Reichert | Y | Y | Y | Y | Y |
| 9 | Smith | Y | Y | Y | Y | Y |
| **WEST VIRGINIA** | | | | | | |
| 1 | Mollohan | Y | Y | Y | Y | Y |
| 2 | Capito | Y | Y | Y | Y | Y |
| 3 | Rahall | Y | Y | Y | Y | Y |
| **WISCONSIN** | | | | | | |
| 1 | Ryan | Y | Y | Y | Y | Y |
| 2 | Baldwin | Y | Y | Y | Y | Y |
| 3 | Kind | Y | Y | Y | Y | Y |
| 4 | Moore | Y | Y | Y | Y | Y |
| 5 | Sensenbrenner | Y | Y | Y | Y | Y |
| 6 | Petri | Y | Y | Y | Y | Y |
| 7 | Obey | Y | Y | Y | Y | Y |
| 8 | Green | Y | Y | Y | Y | Y |
| **WYOMING** | | | | | | |
| AL | Cubin | Y | Y | Y | ? | ? |

# IN THE HOUSE | By Vote Number

**96.** **HR 135. Water Commission/Passage.** Duncan, R-Tenn., motion to suspend the rules and pass the bill that would authorize $9 million to establish the 21st Century Water Commission, responsible for projecting future water supply and demand as well as studying current public and private water management programs, and developing recommendations for a comprehensive water strategy. Motion agreed to 402-22: R 204-22; D 197-0 (ND 148-0, SD 49-0); I 1-0. A two-thirds majority of those present and voting (283 in this case) is required for passage under suspension of the rules. April 12, 2005.

**97.** **HR 541. Nevada Land Conveyance/Passage.** Duncan, R-Tenn., motion to suspend the rules and pass the bill that would convey 8.75 acres from Kingston Cemetery to go to Lander County, Nev., and 10 acres from Maiden's Grave Cemetery to Eureka County, Nev., and would require that the land be used as a cemetery. Motion agreed to 423-0: R 225-0; D 197-0 (ND 148-0, SD 49-0); I 1-0. A two-thirds majority of those present and voting (282 in this case) is required for passage under suspension of the rules. April 12, 2005.

**98.** **HR 1463. Justin W. Williams Tribute/Passage.** Shuster, R-Pa., motion to suspend the rules and pass the bill that would designate a portion of a federal building in Alexandria, Va., after the late Justin W. Williams, an attorney who worked in the Justice Department for many years. Motion agreed to 427-0: R 227-0; D 199-0 (ND 149-0, SD 50-0); I 1-0. A two-thirds majority of those present and voting (285 in this case) is required for passage under suspension of the rules. April 13, 2005.

**99.** **HR 787. Robert T. Matsui Courthouse/Passage.** Shuster, R-Pa., motion to suspend the rules and pass the bill that would name a federal courthouse in Sacramento, Calif., after former Rep. Robert T. Matsui, D-Calif. (1979-2005), who died Jan. 1 after 26 years in office. Motion agreed to 426-0: R 225-0; D 200-0 (ND 150-0, SD 50-0); I 1-0. A two-thirds majority of those present and voting (284 in this case) is required for passage under suspension of the rules. April 13, 2005.

**100.** **HR 8. Estate Tax Permanent Repeal/Previous Question.** Hastings, R-Wash., motion to order the previous question (thus ending debate and possibility of amendment) on adoption of the rule (H Res 202) to provide for House floor consideration of the bill that would permanently repeal the estate tax. Motion agreed to 237-195: R 230-0; D 7-194 (ND 3-147, SD 4-47); I 0-1. (Subsequently, the rule was adopted by voice vote.) April 13, 2005.

**101.** **HR 8. Estate Tax Permanent Repeal/Democratic Substitute.** Pomeroy, D-N.D., substitute amendment that would increase the estate tax exemption to $3 million for individuals and $6 million for married couples in 2006. In 2009, the exemption would increase to $3.5 million for individuals and $7 million for married couples. The substitute would freeze the maximum estate tax at the current rate of 47 percent and reinstate the 5 percent surtax on estates valued at more than $10 million that was repealed under the 2001 tax law. Rejected 194-238: R 1-228; D 193-9 (ND 145-6, SD 48-3); I 0-1. April 13, 2005.

**102.** **HR 8. Estate Tax Permanent Repeal/Passage.** Passage of the bill that would make permanent the repeal of the estate tax contained in the 2001 tax cut law (PL 107-16) and which is set to expire after 2010. Passed 272-162: R 230-1; D 42-160 (ND 23-128, SD 19-32); I 0-1. A "yea" was a vote in support of the president's position. April 13, 2005.

ND Northern Democrats, SD Southern Democrats
Southern states: Ala., Ark., Fla., Ga., Ky., La., Miss., N.C., Okla., S.C., Tenn., Texas, Va.

| | 96 | 97 | 98 | 99 | 100 | 101 | 102 |
|---|---|---|---|---|---|---|---|
| **ALABAMA** | | | | | | | |
| 1 Bonner | Y | Y | Y | Y | Y | N | Y |
| 2 Everett | Y | Y | Y | Y | Y | N | Y |
| 3 Rogers | Y | Y | Y | Y | Y | N | Y |
| 4 Aderholt | Y | Y | Y | Y | Y | N | Y |
| 5 Cramer | Y | Y | Y | Y | Y | N | Y |
| 6 Bachus | Y | Y | Y | Y | Y | N | Y |
| 7 Davis | Y | Y | Y | Y | N | Y | N |
| **ALASKA** | | | | | | | |
| AL Young | Y | Y | Y | Y | Y | N | Y |
| **ARIZONA** | | | | | | | |
| 1 Renzi | Y | Y | Y | Y | Y | N | Y |
| 2 Franks | Y | Y | Y | Y | Y | N | Y |
| 3 Shadegg | Y | Y | Y | Y | Y | N | Y |
| 4 Pastor | Y | Y | Y | N | N | Y | N |
| 5 Hayworth | Y | Y | Y | Y | Y | N | Y |
| 6 Flake | N | Y | Y | Y | Y | N | Y |
| 7 Grijalva | Y | Y | Y | Y | N | Y | N |
| 8 Kolbe | Y | Y | Y | Y | Y | N | Y |
| **ARKANSAS** | | | | | | | |
| 1 Berry | Y | Y | Y | Y | N | Y | Y |
| 2 Snyder | Y | Y | Y | Y | N | Y | N |
| 3 Boozman | Y | Y | Y | Y | Y | N | Y |
| 4 Ross | Y | Y | Y | Y | N | Y | Y |
| **CALIFORNIA** | | | | | | | |
| 1 Thompson | Y | Y | Y | Y | N | Y | N |
| 2 Herger | Y | Y | Y | Y | Y | N | Y |
| 3 Lungren | Y | Y | Y | Y | Y | N | Y |
| 4 Doolittle | Y | Y | + | + | Y | N | Y |
| 5 Matsui, D. | Y | Y | Y | Y | N | Y | N |
| 6 Woolsey | Y | Y | Y | Y | N | Y | N |
| 7 Miller, George | Y | ? | Y | Y | N | Y | N |
| 8 Pelosi | Y | Y | Y | Y | N | Y | N |
| 9 Lee | Y | Y | Y | Y | N | Y | N |
| 10 Tauscher | Y | Y | Y | Y | N | Y | N |
| 11 Pombo | Y | Y | Y | Y | Y | N | Y |
| 12 Lantos | Y | Y | Y | Y | N | Y | N |
| 13 Stark | ? | ? | Y | Y | N | Y | N |
| 14 Eshoo | Y | Y | Y | Y | N | Y | N |
| 15 Honda | Y | Y | Y | Y | N | Y | N |
| 16 Lofgren | Y | Y | Y | Y | N | Y | N |
| 17 Farr | Y | Y | Y | Y | N | Y | Y |
| 18 Cardoza | Y | Y | Y | Y | N | Y | Y |
| 19 Radanovich | Y | Y | Y | Y | Y | N | Y |
| 20 Costa | Y | Y | Y | Y | N | Y | Y |
| 21 Nunes | Y | Y | Y | Y | Y | N | Y |
| 22 Thomas | Y | Y | Y | Y | Y | N | Y |
| 23 Capps | Y | Y | Y | Y | N | Y | N |
| 24 Gallegly | Y | Y | Y | Y | Y | N | Y |
| 25 McKeon | Y | Y | Y | Y | Y | N | Y |
| 26 Dreier | Y | Y | Y | Y | Y | N | Y |
| 27 Sherman | Y | Y | Y | Y | N | Y | N |
| 28 Berman | Y | Y | Y | Y | N | Y | N |
| 29 Schiff | Y | Y | Y | Y | N | Y | N |
| 30 Waxman | Y | Y | Y | Y | N | Y | N |
| 31 Becerra | Y | Y | Y | Y | N | Y | N |
| 32 Solis | Y | Y | Y | Y | N | Y | N |
| 33 Watson | Y | Y | Y | Y | N | Y | N |
| 34 Roybal-Allard | Y | Y | Y | Y | N | Y | N |
| 35 Waters | Y | Y | Y | Y | N | Y | N |
| 36 Harman | Y | Y | Y | Y | Y | Y | N |
| 37 Millender-McD. | Y | Y | Y | Y | N | Y | N |
| 38 Napolitano | Y | Y | Y | Y | N | Y | N |
| 39 Sánchez, Linda | Y | Y | Y | Y | N | Y | N |
| 40 Royce | Y | Y | Y | Y | Y | N | Y |
| 41 Lewis | Y | Y | Y | Y | Y | N | Y |
| 42 Miller, Gary | Y | Y | Y | Y | Y | N | Y |
| 43 Baca | Y | Y | Y | Y | N | Y | N |
| 44 Calvert | Y | Y | Y | ? | Y | N | Y |
| 45 Bono | Y | Y | Y | Y | Y | N | Y |
| 46 Rohrabacher | Y | Y | Y | Y | Y | N | Y |
| 47 Sanchez, Loretta | Y | Y | Y | Y | N | Y | N |
| 48 Cox | Y | Y | Y | Y | Y | N | Y |
| 49 Issa | Y | Y | Y | Y | Y | N | Y |
| 50 Cunningham | Y | Y | Y | Y | N | Y | |
| 51 Filner | Y | Y | Y | Y | N | Y | Y |
| 52 Hunter | Y | Y | ? | Y | Y | N | Y |
| 53 Davis | Y | Y | Y | Y | N | Y | N |
| **COLORADO** | | | | | | | |
| 1 DeGette | Y | Y | Y | Y | N | Y | N |
| 2 Udall | Y | Y | Y | Y | N | Y | N |
| 3 Salazar | Y | Y | Y | Y | N | Y | N |
| 4 Musgrave | Y | Y | Y | Y | Y | N | Y |
| 5 Hefley | Y | Y | Y | Y | Y | N | Y |
| 6 Tancredo | Y | Y | Y | Y | Y | N | Y |
| 7 Beauprez | Y | Y | Y | Y | Y | N | Y |
| **CONNECTICUT** | | | | | | | |
| 1 Larson | Y | Y | Y | Y | N | Y | N |
| 2 Simmons | Y | Y | Y | Y | Y | N | Y |
| 3 DeLauro | Y | Y | Y | Y | N | Y | N |
| 4 Shays | Y | Y | Y | Y | N | Y | N |
| 5 Johnson | Y | Y | Y | Y | Y | N | Y |
| **DELAWARE** | | | | | | | |
| AL Castle | Y | Y | Y | Y | Y | Y | Y |
| **FLORIDA** | | | | | | | |
| 1 Miller | N | Y | Y | Y | Y | N | Y |
| 2 Boyd | Y | Y | Y | Y | N | Y | N |
| 3 Brown | Y | Y | Y | Y | N | Y | N |
| 4 Crenshaw | Y | Y | Y | Y | Y | N | Y |
| 5 Brown-Waite | Y | Y | Y | Y | Y | N | Y |
| 6 Stearns | Y | Y | Y | Y | Y | N | Y |
| 7 Mica | Y | Y | Y | Y | Y | N | Y |
| 8 Keller | Y | Y | Y | ? | Y | N | Y |
| 9 Bilirakis | Y | Y | Y | Y | Y | N | Y |
| 10 Young | Y | Y | Y | Y | Y | N | Y |
| 11 Davis | Y | Y | Y | Y | N | Y | N |
| 12 Putnam | Y | Y | Y | Y | Y | N | Y |
| 13 Harris | Y | Y | Y | Y | Y | N | Y |
| 14 Mack | Y | Y | Y | Y | Y | N | Y |
| 15 Weldon | Y | Y | Y | Y | Y | N | Y |
| 16 Foley | Y | Y | Y | Y | Y | N | Y |
| 17 Meek | Y | Y | Y | Y | N | Y | N |
| 18 Ros-Lehtinen | Y | Y | Y | Y | Y | N | Y |
| 19 Wexler | Y | Y | Y | Y | N | Y | N |
| 20 Wasserman-Schultz | Y | Y | Y | Y | N | Y | N |
| 21 Diaz-Balart, L. | Y | Y | Y | Y | Y | N | Y |
| 22 Shaw | Y | Y | Y | Y | Y | N | Y |
| 23 Hastings | Y | Y | Y | Y | N | Y | N |
| 24 Feeney | Y | Y | Y | Y | Y | N | Y |
| 25 Diaz-Balart, M. | Y | Y | Y | Y | Y | N | Y |
| **GEORGIA** | | | | | | | |
| 1 Kingston | Y | Y | Y | Y | Y | N | Y |
| 2 Bishop | Y | Y | Y | Y | N | Y | Y |
| 3 Marshall | Y | Y | Y | Y | N | Y | N |
| 4 McKinney | Y | Y | Y | Y | N | Y | N |
| 5 Lewis | Y | Y | Y | Y | N | Y | N |
| 6 Price | Y | Y | Y | Y | Y | N | Y |
| 7 Linder | Y | Y | Y | Y | Y | N | Y |
| 8 Westmoreland | Y | Y | Y | Y | Y | N | Y |
| 9 Norwood | Y | Y | Y | Y | Y | N | Y |
| 10 Deal | Y | Y | Y | ? | Y | N | Y |
| 11 Gingrey | Y | Y | Y | Y | Y | N | Y |
| 12 Barrow | Y | Y | Y | Y | N | Y | Y |
| 13 Scott | Y | Y | Y | Y | N | Y | Y |
| **HAWAII** | | | | | | | |
| 1 Abercrombie | Y | Y | Y | Y | N | N | N |
| 2 Case | Y | Y | Y | Y | N | N | N |
| **IDAHO** | | | | | | | |
| 1 Otter | N | Y | Y | Y | Y | N | Y |
| 2 Simpson | Y | Y | Y | Y | Y | N | Y |
| **ILLINOIS** | | | | | | | |
| 1 Rush | Y | Y | Y | Y | N | Y | N |
| 2 Jackson | Y | Y | Y | Y | N | Y | N |
| 3 Lipinski | Y | Y | Y | Y | N | Y | N |
| 4 Gutierrez | Y | Y | Y | Y | N | Y | N |
| 5 Emanuel | Y | Y | Y | Y | N | Y | N |
| 6 Hyde | Y | Y | Y | Y | Y | N | Y |
| 7 Davis | Y | Y | Y | Y | N | Y | N |
| 8 Bean | Y | Y | Y | Y | N | Y | Y |
| 9 Schakowsky | Y | Y | Y | Y | N | Y | N |
| 10 Kirk | Y | Y | Y | Y | Y | N | Y |
| 11 Weller | Y | Y | Y | Y | Y | N | Y |
| 12 Costello | Y | Y | Y | Y | N | Y | Y |

**KEY**  Republicans   Democrats   *Independents*

| | | | |
|---|---|---|---|
| Y | Voted for (yea) | X Paired against | C Voted "present" to avoid possible conflict of interest |
| # | Paired for | – Announced against | |
| + | Announced for | P Voted "present" | ? Did not vote or otherwise make a position known |
| N | Voted against (nay) | | |

| | 96 | 97 | 98 | 99 | 100 | 101 | 102 |
|---|---|---|---|---|---|---|---|
| 13 **Biggert** | Y | Y | Y | Y | Y | N | Y |
| 14 **Hastert** | | | | | | | Y |
| 15 **Johnson** | Y | Y | Y | Y | Y | N | Y |
| 16 **Manzullo** | N | Y | Y | Y | Y | N | Y |
| 17 Evans | Y | Y | Y | Y | N | Y | N |
| 18 **LaHood** | N | Y | Y | Y | Y | N | Y |
| 19 **Shimkus** | Y | Y | Y | Y | Y | N | Y |
| **INDIANA** | | | | | | | |
| 1 Visclosky | Y | Y | Y | Y | N | Y | N |
| 2 **Chocola** | Y | Y | Y | ? | Y | N | Y |
| 3 **Souder** | Y | Y | Y | Y | Y | N | Y |
| 4 **Buyer** | Y | Y | Y | Y | Y | N | Y |
| 5 **Burton** | Y | Y | Y | Y | Y | N | Y |
| 6 **Pence** | N | Y | Y | Y | Y | N | Y |
| 7 Carson | Y | Y | Y | Y | N | Y | N |
| 8 **Hostettler** | Y | Y | Y | Y | Y | N | Y |
| 9 **Sodrel** | Y | Y | Y | Y | Y | N | Y |
| **IOWA** | | | | | | | |
| 1 **Nussle** | Y | Y | Y | Y | Y | N | Y |
| 2 **Leach** | Y | Y | Y | Y | Y | N | N |
| 3 Boswell | Y | Y | Y | Y | N | Y | Y |
| 4 **Latham** | Y | Y | Y | Y | Y | N | Y |
| 5 **King** | Y | Y | Y | Y | Y | N | Y |
| **KANSAS** | | | | | | | |
| 1 **Moran** | Y | Y | Y | Y | Y | N | Y |
| 2 **Ryun** | Y | Y | Y | Y | Y | N | Y |
| 3 Moore | Y | Y | Y | Y | N | Y | N |
| 4 **Tiahrt** | Y | Y | Y | Y | Y | N | Y |
| **KENTUCKY** | | | | | | | |
| 1 **Whitfield** | Y | Y | Y | Y | Y | N | Y |
| 2 **Lewis** | + | + | Y | Y | Y | N | Y |
| 3 **Northup** | Y | Y | Y | Y | Y | N | Y |
| 4 **Davis** | Y | Y | Y | Y | Y | N | Y |
| 5 **Rogers** | Y | Y | Y | Y | Y | N | Y |
| 6 Chandler | Y | Y | Y | Y | N | Y | Y |
| **LOUISIANA** | | | | | | | |
| 1 **Jindal** | Y | Y | Y | Y | Y | – | Y |
| 2 Jefferson | Y | Y | Y | Y | N | Y | Y |
| 3 Melancon | Y | Y | Y | Y | N | Y | Y |
| 4 **McCrery** | Y | Y | Y | Y | Y | N | Y |
| 5 **Alexander** | Y | Y | Y | Y | Y | N | Y |
| 6 **Baker** | Y | Y | Y | Y | Y | N | Y |
| 7 **Boustany** | Y | Y | Y | Y | Y | N | Y |
| **MAINE** | | | | | | | |
| 1 Allen | Y | Y | Y | Y | N | Y | N |
| 2 Michaud | Y | Y | Y | Y | N | Y | N |
| **MARYLAND** | | | | | | | |
| 1 **Gilchrest** | Y | Y | Y | Y | Y | N | Y |
| 2 Ruppersberger | Y | Y | Y | Y | N | Y | Y |
| 3 Cardin | Y | Y | Y | Y | N | Y | N |
| 4 Wynn | Y | Y | Y | Y | N | Y | Y |
| 5 Hoyer | Y | Y | Y | Y | N | Y | N |
| 6 **Bartlett** | Y | Y | Y | Y | Y | N | Y |
| 7 Cummings | Y | Y | Y | Y | N | Y | N |
| 8 Van Hollen | Y | Y | Y | Y | N | Y | N |
| **MASSACHUSETTS** | | | | | | | |
| 1 Olver | Y | Y | Y | Y | N | N | N |
| 2 Neal | Y | Y | Y | Y | N | Y | N |
| 3 McGovern | Y | Y | Y | Y | N | Y | N |
| 4 Frank | Y | Y | Y | Y | N | Y | N |
| 5 Meehan | Y | Y | Y | Y | N | Y | N |
| 6 Tierney | Y | Y | Y | Y | N | Y | N |
| 7 Markey | Y | Y | Y | Y | N | Y | N |
| 8 Capuano | Y | Y | Y | Y | N | Y | N |
| 9 Lynch | Y | Y | Y | Y | N | Y | N |
| 10 Delahunt | Y | Y | Y | Y | N | Y | N |
| **MICHIGAN** | | | | | | | |
| 1 Stupak | Y | Y | Y | Y | N | Y | N |
| 2 **Hoekstra** | Y | Y | Y | Y | Y | N | Y |
| 3 **Ehlers** | Y | Y | Y | Y | Y | N | Y |
| 4 **Camp** | Y | Y | Y | Y | Y | N | Y |
| 5 Kildee | Y | Y | Y | Y | N | Y | N |
| 6 **Upton** | Y | Y | Y | Y | Y | N | Y |
| 7 **Schwarz** | Y | Y | Y | Y | Y | N | Y |
| 8 **Rogers** | Y | Y | Y | Y | Y | N | Y |
| 9 **Knollenberg** | Y | Y | Y | Y | Y | N | Y |
| 10 **Miller** | N | Y | Y | Y | Y | N | Y |
| 11 **McCotter** | Y | Y | Y | Y | Y | N | Y |
| 12 Levin | Y | Y | Y | Y | N | Y | N |
| 13 Kilpatrick | Y | Y | Y | Y | N | Y | N |
| 14 Conyers | Y | Y | Y | Y | N | Y | N |
| 15 Dingell | Y | Y | Y | Y | N | Y | N |

| | 96 | 97 | 98 | 99 | 100 | 101 | 102 |
|---|---|---|---|---|---|---|---|
| **MINNESOTA** | | | | | | | |
| 1 **Gutknecht** | N | Y | Y | Y | Y | N | Y |
| 2 **Kline** | Y | Y | Y | Y | Y | N | Y |
| 3 **Ramstad** | Y | Y | Y | Y | Y | N | Y |
| 4 McCollum | Y | Y | Y | Y | N | Y | N |
| 5 Sabo | Y | Y | Y | Y | N | Y | N |
| 6 **Kennedy** | Y | Y | Y | Y | Y | N | Y |
| 7 Peterson | Y | Y | Y | Y | N | Y | Y |
| 8 Oberstar | Y | Y | Y | Y | N | Y | N |
| **MISSISSIPPI** | | | | | | | |
| 1 **Wicker** | Y | Y | Y | Y | Y | N | Y |
| 2 Thompson | Y | Y | Y | Y | N | Y | N |
| 3 **Pickering** | Y | Y | Y | Y | Y | N | Y |
| 4 Taylor | Y | Y | Y | Y | N | Y | N |
| **MISSOURI** | | | | | | | |
| 1 Clay | Y | Y | Y | Y | N | Y | Y |
| 2 **Akin** | Y | Y | Y | Y | Y | N | Y |
| 3 Carnahan | Y | Y | Y | Y | N | Y | N |
| 4 Skelton | Y | Y | Y | Y | N | Y | Y |
| 5 Cleaver | Y | Y | Y | Y | N | Y | N |
| 6 **Graves** | Y | Y | Y | Y | Y | N | Y |
| 7 **Blunt** | Y | Y | Y | Y | Y | N | Y |
| 8 **Emerson** | N | Y | Y | Y | Y | N | Y |
| 9 **Hulshof** | Y | Y | Y | Y | Y | N | Y |
| **MONTANA** | | | | | | | |
| AL **Rehberg** | Y | Y | Y | Y | Y | N | Y |
| **NEBRASKA** | | | | | | | |
| 1 **Fortenberry** | Y | Y | Y | Y | Y | N | Y |
| 2 **Terry** | Y | Y | Y | Y | Y | N | Y |
| 3 **Osborne** | Y | Y | Y | Y | Y | N | Y |
| **NEVADA** | | | | | | | |
| 1 Berkley | Y | Y | Y | Y | N | Y | Y |
| 2 **Gibbons** | Y | Y | Y | Y | Y | N | Y |
| 3 **Porter** | Y | Y | Y | Y | Y | N | Y |
| **NEW HAMPSHIRE** | | | | | | | |
| 1 **Bradley** | Y | Y | Y | Y | Y | N | Y |
| 2 **Bass** | Y | Y | Y | Y | Y | N | Y |
| **NEW JERSEY** | | | | | | | |
| 1 Andrews | Y | Y | Y | Y | N | Y | N |
| 2 **LoBiondo** | Y | Y | Y | Y | Y | N | Y |
| 3 **Saxton** | Y | Y | Y | Y | Y | N | Y |
| 4 **Smith** | Y | Y | Y | Y | Y | N | Y |
| 5 **Garrett** | Y | Y | Y | Y | Y | N | Y |
| 6 Pallone | Y | Y | Y | Y | N | Y | N |
| 7 **Ferguson** | Y | Y | Y | Y | Y | N | Y |
| 8 Pascrell | Y | Y | Y | Y | N | Y | N |
| 9 Rothman | Y | Y | Y | Y | N | Y | N |
| 10 Payne | Y | Y | Y | Y | N | Y | N |
| 11 **Frelinghuysen** | Y | Y | ? | Y | Y | N | Y |
| 12 Holt | Y | Y | Y | Y | N | Y | N |
| 13 Menendez | Y | Y | Y | Y | N | Y | N |
| **NEW MEXICO** | | | | | | | |
| 1 **Wilson** | Y | Y | Y | Y | Y | N | Y |
| 2 **Pearce** | Y | Y | Y | Y | Y | N | Y |
| 3 Udall | Y | Y | Y | Y | N | Y | N |
| **NEW YORK** | | | | | | | |
| 1 Bishop | Y | Y | Y | Y | N | Y | N |
| 2 Israel | Y | Y | Y | Y | N | Y | Y |
| 3 **King** | Y | Y | Y | Y | Y | N | Y |
| 4 McCarthy | Y | Y | Y | Y | N | Y | Y |
| 5 Ackerman | Y | Y | Y | Y | N | Y | N |
| 6 Meeks | Y | Y | ? | Y | N | Y | N |
| 7 Crowley | Y | Y | Y | Y | N | Y | N |
| 8 Nadler | Y | Y | Y | Y | N | Y | N |
| 9 Weiner | Y | Y | Y | Y | N | Y | N |
| 10 Towns | Y | Y | Y | Y | N | Y | N |
| 11 Owens | Y | Y | Y | Y | N | Y | N |
| 12 Velázquez | Y | Y | Y | Y | N | Y | N |
| 13 **Fossella** | Y | Y | Y | Y | Y | N | Y |
| 14 Maloney | Y | Y | Y | Y | N | Y | N |
| 15 Rangel | Y | Y | Y | Y | N | Y | N |
| 16 Serrano | Y | Y | Y | Y | N | Y | N |
| 17 Engel | Y | Y | Y | Y | N | Y | N |
| 18 Lowey | Y | Y | Y | Y | N | Y | N |
| 19 **Kelly** | Y | Y | Y | Y | Y | N | Y |
| 20 **Sweeney** | Y | Y | Y | Y | Y | N | Y |
| 21 McNulty | Y | Y | Y | Y | N | Y | N |
| 22 Hinchey | Y | Y | Y | Y | N | Y | N |
| 23 **McHugh** | Y | Y | Y | Y | Y | N | Y |
| 24 **Boehlert** | Y | Y | Y | Y | Y | N | Y |
| 25 **Walsh** | Y | Y | Y | Y | Y | N | Y |
| 26 **Reynolds** | Y | Y | Y | Y | Y | N | Y |
| 27 Higgins | Y | Y | Y | Y | N | Y | N |
| 28 Slaughter | Y | Y | Y | Y | N | Y | N |
| 29 **Kuhl** | Y | Y | Y | Y | Y | N | Y |

| | 96 | 97 | 98 | 99 | 100 | 101 | 102 |
|---|---|---|---|---|---|---|---|
| **NORTH CAROLINA** | | | | | | | |
| 1 Butterfield | Y | Y | Y | Y | N | Y | Y |
| 2 Etheridge | Y | Y | Y | Y | N | Y | N |
| 3 **Jones** | N | Y | Y | Y | Y | N | Y |
| 4 Price | Y | Y | Y | Y | N | Y | N |
| 5 **Foxx** | N | Y | Y | Y | Y | N | Y |
| 6 **Coble** | N | Y | Y | Y | Y | N | Y |
| 7 McIntyre | Y | Y | Y | Y | N | Y | Y |
| 8 **Hayes** | Y | Y | Y | Y | Y | N | Y |
| 9 **Myrick** | N | Y | Y | Y | Y | N | Y |
| 10 **McHenry** | Y | Y | Y | Y | Y | N | Y |
| 11 **Taylor** | Y | Y | Y | Y | Y | N | Y |
| 12 Watt | Y | Y | Y | Y | N | Y | N |
| 13 Miller | Y | Y | Y | Y | N | Y | N |
| **NORTH DAKOTA** | | | | | | | |
| AL Pomeroy | Y | Y | Y | Y | N | Y | N |
| **OHIO** | | | | | | | |
| 1 **Chabot** | Y | Y | Y | Y | Y | N | Y |
| 2 **Portman** | Y | Y | Y | Y | Y | N | Y |
| 3 **Turner** | Y | Y | Y | Y | Y | N | Y |
| 4 **Oxley** | Y | Y | Y | Y | Y | N | Y |
| 5 **Gillmor** | ? | ? | ? | ? | ? | ? | ? |
| 6 Strickland | Y | Y | Y | Y | N | Y | N |
| 7 **Hobson** | Y | Y | Y | Y | Y | N | Y |
| 8 **Boehner** | Y | Y | Y | Y | Y | N | Y |
| 9 Kaptur | Y | Y | Y | Y | N | Y | N |
| 10 Kucinich | Y | Y | Y | Y | N | Y | N |
| 11 Jones | Y | Y | Y | Y | N | Y | N |
| 12 **Tiberi** | Y | Y | Y | Y | Y | N | Y |
| 13 Brown | Y | Y | Y | Y | N | Y | N |
| 14 **LaTourette** | Y | Y | Y | Y | Y | N | Y |
| 15 **Pryce** | Y | Y | Y | Y | Y | N | Y |
| 16 **Regula** | Y | Y | Y | Y | Y | N | Y |
| 17 Ryan | Y | Y | Y | Y | N | Y | Y |
| 18 **Ney** | Y | Y | Y | Y | Y | N | Y |
| **OKLAHOMA** | | | | | | | |
| 1 **Sullivan** | Y | Y | Y | Y | Y | N | Y |
| 2 Boren | Y | Y | Y | Y | N | Y | Y |
| 3 **Lucas** | Y | Y | Y | Y | Y | N | Y |
| 4 **Cole** | Y | Y | Y | Y | Y | N | Y |
| 5 **Istook** | N | Y | Y | Y | Y | N | Y |
| **OREGON** | | | | | | | |
| 1 Wu | Y | Y | Y | Y | N | Y | N |
| 2 **Walden** | Y | Y | Y | Y | Y | N | Y |
| 3 Blumenauer | Y | Y | Y | Y | N | Y | N |
| 4 DeFazio | Y | Y | Y | Y | N | Y | N |
| 5 Hooley | Y | Y | Y | Y | N | Y | Y |
| **PENNSYLVANIA** | | | | | | | |
| 1 Brady | Y | Y | Y | Y | N | N | N |
| 2 Fattah | ? | Y | Y | Y | N | Y | N |
| 3 **English** | Y | Y | Y | Y | Y | N | Y |
| 4 **Hart** | Y | Y | Y | Y | Y | N | Y |
| 5 **Peterson** | Y | Y | Y | Y | Y | N | Y |
| 6 **Gerlach** | Y | Y | Y | Y | Y | N | Y |
| 7 **Weldon** | Y | Y | Y | Y | Y | N | Y |
| 8 **Fitzpatrick** | Y | Y | Y | Y | Y | N | Y |
| 9 **Shuster** | Y | Y | Y | Y | Y | N | Y |
| 10 **Sherwood** | Y | Y | Y | Y | Y | N | Y |
| 11 Kanjorski | Y | Y | Y | Y | N | Y | N |
| 12 Murtha | Y | Y | Y | Y | N | N | N |
| 13 Schwartz | Y | Y | Y | Y | N | Y | N |
| 14 Doyle | Y | Y | Y | Y | N | Y | N |
| 15 **Dent** | Y | Y | Y | Y | Y | N | Y |
| 16 **Pitts** | Y | Y | Y | Y | Y | N | Y |
| 17 Holden | Y | Y | Y | Y | N | Y | N |
| 18 **Murphy** | Y | Y | Y | Y | Y | N | Y |
| 19 **Platts** | Y | Y | Y | Y | Y | N | Y |
| **RHODE ISLAND** | | | | | | | |
| 1 Kennedy | Y | Y | Y | Y | N | Y | N |
| 2 Langevin | Y | Y | Y | Y | N | Y | N |
| **SOUTH CAROLINA** | | | | | | | |
| 1 **Brown** | Y | Y | Y | Y | Y | N | Y |
| 2 **Wilson** | Y | Y | Y | Y | Y | N | Y |
| 3 **Barrett** | Y | Y | Y | Y | Y | N | Y |
| 4 **Inglis** | ? | ? | Y | Y | Y | N | Y |
| 5 Spratt | Y | Y | Y | Y | N | Y | N |
| 6 Clyburn | Y | Y | Y | Y | N | Y | N |
| **SOUTH DAKOTA** | | | | | | | |
| AL Herseth | Y | Y | Y | Y | N | Y | N |
| **TENNESSEE** | | | | | | | |
| 1 **Jenkins** | ? | ? | Y | Y | Y | N | Y |
| 2 **Duncan** | Y | Y | Y | Y | Y | N | Y |

| | 96 | 97 | 98 | 99 | 100 | 101 | 102 |
|---|---|---|---|---|---|---|---|
| 3 **Wamp** | Y | Y | Y | Y | Y | N | Y |
| 4 Davis | Y | Y | ? | Y | N | Y | Y |
| 5 Cooper | Y | Y | Y | Y | N | Y | N |
| 6 Gordon | Y | Y | Y | Y | Y | N | Y |
| 7 **Blackburn** | N | Y | Y | Y | Y | N | Y |
| 8 Tanner | Y | Y | Y | Y | N | N | N |
| 9 Ford | ? | ? | Y | Y | N | Y | N |
| **TEXAS** | | | | | | | |
| 1 **Gohmert** | Y | Y | Y | Y | Y | N | Y |
| 2 **Poe** | Y | Y | Y | Y | Y | N | Y |
| 3 **Johnson, S.** | N | Y | Y | Y | Y | N | Y |
| 4 **Hall** | Y | Y | Y | Y | Y | N | Y |
| 5 **Hensarling** | N | Y | Y | Y | Y | N | Y |
| 6 **Barton** | Y | Y | Y | Y | Y | N | Y |
| 7 **Culberson** | N | Y | Y | Y | Y | N | Y |
| 8 **Brady** | Y | Y | Y | Y | Y | N | Y |
| 9 Green | Y | Y | Y | Y | N | Y | N |
| 10 **McCaul** | Y | Y | Y | Y | Y | N | Y |
| 11 **Conaway** | Y | Y | Y | Y | Y | N | Y |
| 12 **Granger** | Y | Y | Y | Y | Y | N | Y |
| 13 **Thornberry** | Y | ? | Y | Y | Y | N | Y |
| 14 **Paul** | N | Y | Y | Y | Y | N | Y |
| 15 Hinojosa | Y | Y | Y | Y | N | Y | Y |
| 16 Reyes | Y | Y | Y | ? | N | Y | N |
| 17 Edwards | ? | ? | Y | Y | N | Y | Y |
| 18 Jackson-Lee | Y | Y | Y | Y | N | Y | Y |
| 19 **Neugebauer** | Y | Y | Y | Y | Y | N | Y |
| 20 Gonzalez | Y | Y | Y | Y | N | Y | N |
| 21 **Smith** | Y | Y | Y | Y | Y | N | Y |
| 22 **DeLay** | Y | Y | Y | Y | Y | N | Y |
| 23 **Bonilla** | Y | Y | Y | Y | Y | N | Y |
| 24 **Marchant** | Y | Y | Y | Y | Y | N | Y |
| 25 Doggett | Y | Y | Y | Y | N | Y | N |
| 26 **Burgess** | Y | Y | Y | Y | Y | N | Y |
| 27 Ortiz | Y | Y | Y | Y | N | Y | Y |
| 28 Cuellar | Y | Y | Y | Y | N | Y | Y |
| 29 Green | Y | Y | Y | Y | N | Y | N |
| 30 Johnson, E. | Y | Y | Y | Y | N | Y | N |
| 31 **Carter** | + | + | Y | Y | Y | N | Y |
| 32 **Sessions** | Y | Y | Y | Y | Y | N | Y |
| **UTAH** | | | | | | | |
| 1 **Bishop** | Y | Y | Y | Y | Y | N | Y |
| 2 Matheson | Y | Y | Y | Y | N | Y | Y |
| 3 **Cannon** | Y | Y | Y | Y | Y | N | Y |
| **VERMONT** | | | | | | | |
| AL *Sanders* | Y | Y | Y | Y | N | N | N |
| **VIRGINIA** | | | | | | | |
| 1 **Davis, J.** | N | Y | Y | Y | Y | N | Y |
| 2 **Drake** | Y | Y | Y | Y | Y | N | Y |
| 3 Scott | Y | Y | Y | Y | N | Y | N |
| 4 **Forbes** | Y | Y | Y | Y | Y | N | Y |
| 5 **Goode** | N | Y | Y | Y | Y | N | Y |
| 6 **Goodlatte** | Y | Y | Y | Y | Y | N | Y |
| 7 **Cantor** | Y | Y | Y | Y | Y | N | Y |
| 8 Moran | Y | Y | Y | Y | N | Y | N |
| 9 Boucher | Y | Y | Y | Y | N | Y | Y |
| 10 **Wolf** | Y | Y | Y | Y | Y | N | Y |
| 11 **Davis, T.** | Y | Y | Y | Y | Y | N | Y |
| **WASHINGTON** | | | | | | | |
| 1 Inslee | Y | Y | Y | Y | N | Y | N |
| 2 Larsen | Y | Y | Y | Y | N | Y | Y |
| 3 Baird | Y | Y | ? | ? | ? | Y | N |
| 4 **Hastings** | Y | Y | Y | Y | Y | N | Y |
| 5 **McMorris** | Y | Y | Y | Y | Y | N | Y |
| 6 Dicks | Y | Y | Y | Y | N | Y | N |
| 7 McDermott | Y | Y | Y | Y | N | Y | N |
| 8 **Reichert** | Y | Y | Y | Y | Y | N | Y |
| 9 Smith | ? | ? | Y | Y | N | Y | N |
| **WEST VIRGINIA** | | | | | | | |
| 1 Mollohan | Y | Y | Y | Y | N | Y | N |
| 2 **Capito** | Y | Y | Y | Y | Y | N | Y |
| 3 Rahall | Y | Y | Y | Y | Y | Y | Y |
| **WISCONSIN** | | | | | | | |
| 1 **Ryan** | Y | Y | Y | Y | Y | N | Y |
| 2 Baldwin | Y | Y | Y | Y | N | Y | N |
| 3 Kind | Y | Y | Y | Y | N | Y | N |
| 4 Moore | Y | Y | Y | Y | N | Y | N |
| 5 **Sensenbrenner** | Y | Y | Y | Y | Y | N | Y |
| 6 **Petri** | Y | Y | Y | Y | Y | N | Y |
| 7 Obey | Y | Y | Y | Y | N | Y | N |
| 8 **Green** | Y | Y | Y | Y | Y | N | Y |
| **WYOMING** | | | | | | | |
| AL **Cubin** | N | Y | Y | Y | Y | N | Y |

# IN THE HOUSE | By Vote Number

**103. Procedural Motion/Adjourn.** Woolsey, D-Calif., motion to adjourn. Motion rejected 49-371: R 1-220; D 48-150 (ND 40-107, SD 8-43); I 0-1. April 14, 2005.

**104. S 256. Bankruptcy Overhaul/Previous Question.** Gingrey, R-Ga., motion to order the previous question (thus ending debate and possibility of amendment) on adoption of the rule (H Res 211) to provide for House floor consideration of the bill that would overhaul bankruptcy laws. Motion agreed to 227-199: R 227-0; D 0-198 (ND 0-148, SD 0-50); I 0-1. April 14, 2005.

**105. S 256. Bankruptcy Overhaul/Rule.** Adoption of the rule (H Res 211) to provide for House floor consideration of the bill that would overhaul bankruptcy laws. Adopted 227-196: R 225-0; D 2-195 (ND 1-147, SD 1-48); I 0-1. April 14, 2005.

**106. H Res 213. Ethics Task Force/Motion to Table.** Sensenbrenner, R-Wis., motion to table (kill) the Pelosi, D-Calif., privileged resolution that would require the Speaker of the House to appoint a bipartisan task force, with equal representation of Republicans and Democrats, to make recommendations, by June 1, 2005, to restore public confidence in the House ethics process. Motion agreed to 218-195: R 218-2; D 0-192 (ND 0-144, SD 0-48); I 0-1. April 14, 2005.

**107. S 256. Bankruptcy Overhaul/Recommit.** Schakowsky, D-Ill., motion to recommit the bill to the House Judiciary Committee with instructions to exempt members of the National Guard and Reserve from the means test in the bill if their debt was a result of active duty service or was incurred within two years of returning home from their service. Motion rejected 200-229: R 1-228; D 198-1 (ND 148-0, SD 50-1); I 1-0. April 14, 2005.

**108. S 256. Bankruptcy Overhaul/Passage.** Passage of the bill that would create a means test tied to the median incomes of individual states to determine whether personal bankruptcy filers were able to repay some or all of their debts. Those deemed able to pay would be pushed into Chapter 13 bankruptcy, which results in a court-ordered repayment plan; those with insufficient assets would be allowed to file under Chapter 7, which erases debts after the forfeiture of certain assets. The bill would exempt disabled veterans from the means test if their debts were incurred primarily when they were on active duty or performing homeland defense duties. It also would make a number of debts non-dischargeable, including student loans, child support, alimony and luxury payments over $500 made within three months of a bankruptcy filing. Passed (thus cleared for the president) 302-126: R 229-0; D 73-125 (ND 41-106, SD 32-19); I 0-1. April 14, 2005.

ND Northern Democrats, SD Southern Democrats
Southern states: Ala., Ark., Fla., Ga., Ky., La., Miss., N.C., Okla., S.C., Tenn., Texas, Va.

| | 103 | 104 | 105 | 106 | 107 | 108 |
|---|---|---|---|---|---|---|
| **ALABAMA** | | | | | | |
| 1 Bonner | N | Y | Y | Y | N | Y |
| 2 Everett | N | Y | Y | Y | N | Y |
| 3 Rogers | N | Y | Y | Y | N | Y |
| 4 Aderholt | N | Y | Y | Y | N | Y |
| 5 Cramer | N | N | N | N | Y | Y |
| 6 Bachus | N | Y | Y | Y | N | Y |
| 7 Davis | N | N | N | N | Y | Y |
| **ALASKA** | | | | | | |
| AL Young | N | Y | Y | ? | N | Y |
| **ARIZONA** | | | | | | |
| 1 Renzi | N | Y | Y | Y | N | Y |
| 2 Franks | N | Y | Y | Y | N | Y |
| 3 Shadegg | N | Y | Y | Y | N | Y |
| 4 Pastor | N | N | N | N | Y | Y |
| 5 Hayworth | N | Y | Y | Y | N | Y |
| 6 Flake | N | Y | Y | Y | N | Y |
| 7 Grijalva | N | N | N | N | Y | N |
| 8 Kolbe | N | Y | Y | Y | N | Y |
| **ARKANSAS** | | | | | | |
| 1 Berry | N | N | N | N | Y | Y |
| 2 Snyder | N | N | N | N | Y | Y |
| 3 Boozman | N | Y | Y | Y | N | Y |
| 4 Ross | N | N | N | N | Y | Y |
| **CALIFORNIA** | | | | | | |
| 1 Thompson | N | N | N | N | Y | Y |
| 2 Herger | ? | Y | Y | Y | N | Y |
| 3 Lungren | N | Y | Y | Y | N | Y |
| 4 Doolittle | N | Y | Y | Y | N | Y |
| 5 Matsui, D. | N | N | N | N | Y | N |
| 6 Woolsey | Y | N | N | N | Y | N |
| 7 Miller, George | Y | N | N | N | Y | N |
| 8 Pelosi | N | N | N | N | Y | N |
| 9 Lee | Y | N | N | N | Y | N |
| 10 Tauscher | N | N | N | N | Y | Y |
| 11 Pombo | N | Y | Y | Y | N | Y |
| 12 Lantos | N | N | N | N | Y | ? |
| 13 Stark | Y | N | N | N | Y | N |
| 14 Eshoo | N | N | N | N | Y | N |
| 15 Honda | N | N | N | N | Y | N |
| 16 Lofgren | N | N | N | – | Y | N |
| 17 Farr | N | N | N | N | Y | N |
| 18 Cardoza | N | N | N | N | Y | Y |
| 19 Radanovich | N | Y | Y | Y | N | Y |
| 20 Costa | N | N | N | N | Y | Y |
| 21 Nunes | N | Y | Y | Y | N | Y |
| 22 Thomas | ? | Y | Y | Y | N | Y |
| 23 Capps | Y | N | N | N | Y | N |
| 24 Gallegly | N | Y | Y | Y | N | Y |
| 25 McKeon | N | Y | Y | Y | N | Y |
| 26 Dreier | N | Y | Y | Y | N | Y |
| 27 Sherman | N | N | N | N | Y | N |
| 28 Berman | Y | N | N | N | Y | N |
| 29 Schiff | N | N | N | N | Y | N |
| 30 Waxman | Y | N | N | N | Y | N |
| 31 Becerra | N | N | N | N | Y | N |
| 32 Solis | + | – | – | – | + | – |
| 33 Watson | N | N | N | N | Y | N |
| 34 Roybal-Allard | N | N | N | N | Y | N |
| 35 Waters | Y | N | N | N | Y | N |
| 36 Harman | N | N | N | N | Y | N |
| 37 Millender-McD. | N | N | N | N | Y | N |
| 38 Napolitano | N | N | N | N | Y | N |
| 39 Sánchez, Linda | Y | N | N | N | Y | N |
| 40 Royce | N | Y | Y | Y | N | Y |
| 41 Lewis | N | Y | Y | Y | N | Y |
| 42 Miller, Gary | N | Y | Y | Y | N | Y |
| 43 Baca | N | N | N | N | Y | Y |
| 44 Calvert | N | Y | Y | Y | N | Y |
| 45 Bono | N | Y | Y | Y | N | Y |
| 46 Rohrabacher | N | Y | Y | Y | N | Y |
| 47 Sanchez, Loretta | N | N | N | N | Y | N |
| 48 Cox | N | Y | Y | Y | N | Y |
| 49 Issa | N | Y | Y | Y | N | Y |

| | 103 | 104 | 105 | 106 | 107 | 108 |
|---|---|---|---|---|---|---|
| 50 Cunningham | N | Y | Y | Y | N | Y |
| 51 Filner | Y | N | N | N | Y | N |
| 52 Hunter | N | Y | Y | Y | N | Y |
| 53 Davis | N | N | N | N | Y | N |
| **COLORADO** | | | | | | |
| 1 DeGette | N | N | N | N | Y | N |
| 2 Udall | N | N | N | N | Y | N |
| 3 Salazar | N | N | N | N | Y | Y |
| 4 Musgrave | N | Y | Y | Y | N | Y |
| 5 Hefley | N | Y | Y | Y | N | Y |
| 6 Tancredo | N | Y | Y | ? | N | Y |
| 7 Beauprez | N | Y | Y | Y | N | Y |
| **CONNECTICUT** | | | | | | |
| 1 Larson | N | N | N | N | Y | N |
| 2 Simmons | N | Y | Y | Y | N | Y |
| 3 DeLauro | Y | N | N | N | Y | N |
| 4 Shays | N | Y | Y | Y | N | Y |
| 5 Johnson | N | Y | Y | Y | N | Y |
| **DELAWARE** | | | | | | |
| AL Castle | N | Y | Y | Y | N | Y |
| **FLORIDA** | | | | | | |
| 1 Miller | N | Y | Y | Y | N | Y |
| 2 Boyd | N | N | N | N | Y | Y |
| 3 Brown | N | N | N | ? | Y | N |
| 4 Crenshaw | N | Y | Y | Y | N | Y |
| 5 Brown-Waite | N | Y | Y | Y | N | Y |
| 6 Stearns | N | Y | Y | Y | N | Y |
| 7 Mica | N | Y | Y | Y | N | Y |
| 8 Keller | N | Y | Y | Y | N | Y |
| 9 Bilirakis | ? | Y | Y | Y | N | Y |
| 10 Young | N | Y | Y | Y | N | Y |
| 11 Davis | N | N | N | N | Y | Y |
| 12 Putnam | N | Y | Y | Y | N | Y |
| 13 Harris | N | Y | Y | Y | N | Y |
| 14 Mack | N | Y | Y | Y | N | Y |
| 15 Weldon | N | Y | Y | Y | ? | ? |
| 16 Foley | N | Y | Y | Y | N | Y |
| 17 Meek | N | N | N | N | Y | Y |
| 18 Ros-Lehtinen | N | Y | Y | Y | N | Y |
| 19 Wexler | N | N | N | N | Y | N |
| 20 Wasserman-Schultz | N | N | N | N | Y | N |
| 21 Diaz-Balart, L. | N | Y | Y | Y | N | Y |
| 22 Shaw | N | Y | Y | Y | N | Y |
| 23 Hastings | N | N | N | N | Y | N |
| 24 Feeney | N | Y | ? | Y | N | Y |
| 25 Diaz-Balart, M. | N | Y | Y | Y | N | Y |
| **GEORGIA** | | | | | | |
| 1 Kingston | N | Y | Y | Y | N | Y |
| 2 Bishop | N | N | N | N | Y | Y |
| 3 Marshall | N | N | N | N | Y | N |
| 4 McKinney | Y | N | N | N | Y | N |
| 5 Lewis | N | N | N | N | Y | N |
| 6 Price | N | Y | Y | Y | N | Y |
| 7 Linder | N | Y | Y | Y | N | Y |
| 8 Westmoreland | N | Y | Y | Y | N | Y |
| 9 Norwood | N | Y | Y | ? | N | Y |
| 10 Deal | N | Y | Y | Y | N | Y |
| 11 Gingrey | N | Y | Y | Y | N | Y |
| 12 Barrow | N | N | N | N | Y | N |
| 13 Scott | N | N | N | N | Y | Y |
| **HAWAII** | | | | | | |
| 1 Abercrombie | N | N | N | N | Y | N |
| 2 Case | N | N | N | N | Y | Y |
| **IDAHO** | | | | | | |
| 1 Otter | N | Y | Y | Y | N | Y |
| 2 Simpson | N | Y | Y | Y | N | Y |
| **ILLINOIS** | | | | | | |
| 1 Rush | N | N | N | N | Y | N |
| 2 Jackson | N | N | N | N | Y | N |
| 3 Lipinski | N | N | N | N | Y | N |
| 4 Gutierrez | N | N | N | ? | ? | ? |
| 5 Emanuel | N | N | N | N | Y | N |
| 6 Hyde | N | Y | Y | ? | N | Y |
| 7 Davis | N | N | N | N | Y | N |
| 8 Bean | N | N | N | N | Y | Y |
| 9 Schakowsky | Y | N | N | N | Y | N |
| 10 Kirk | N | Y | Y | Y | N | Y |
| 11 Weller | N | Y | Y | Y | N | Y |
| 12 Costello | N | N | N | N | Y | N |

**KEY**

| Republicans | Democrats | Independents |
|---|---|---|

| | | |
|---|---|---|
| Y Voted for (yea) | X Paired against | C Voted "present" to avoid possible conflict of interest |
| # Paired for | – Announced against | |
| + Announced for | P Voted "present" | ? Did not vote or otherwise make a position known |
| N Voted against (nay) | | |

| | 103 | 104 | 105 | 106 | 107 | 108 |
|---|---|---|---|---|---|---|
| 13 **Biggert** | N | Y | Y | Y | N | Y |
| 14 **Hastert** | | | | | N | Y |
| 15 **Johnson** | N | Y | Y | Y | Y | Y |
| 16 **Manzullo** | ? | Y | Y | Y | N | Y |
| 17 Evans | Y | N | N | ? | Y | N |
| 18 **LaHood** | N | ? | ? | ? | ? | ? |
| 19 **Shimkus** | N | Y | Y | Y | N | Y |
| **INDIANA** | | | | | | |
| 1 Visclosky | N | N | N | N | Y | N |
| 2 **Chocola** | N | Y | Y | Y | N | Y |
| 3 **Souder** | N | Y | Y | ? | N | Y |
| 4 **Buyer** | ? | Y | Y | Y | N | Y |
| 5 **Burton** | N | Y | Y | Y | N | Y |
| 6 **Pence** | N | Y | Y | Y | N | Y |
| 7 Carson | N | N | N | N | Y | N |
| 8 **Hostettler** | N | Y | Y | Y | N | Y |
| 9 **Sodrel** | N | Y | Y | Y | N | Y |
| **IOWA** | | | | | | |
| 1 **Nussle** | N | Y | Y | Y | N | Y |
| 2 **Leach** | N | Y | Y | N | N | Y |
| 3 Boswell | N | N | N | N | Y | Y |
| 4 **Latham** | N | Y | Y | Y | N | Y |
| 5 **King** | N | Y | Y | Y | N | Y |
| **KANSAS** | | | | | | |
| 1 **Moran** | N | Y | Y | Y | N | Y |
| 2 **Ryun** | N | Y | Y | Y | N | Y |
| 3 Moore | N | N | N | N | Y | Y |
| 4 **Tiahrt** | N | Y | Y | Y | N | Y |
| **KENTUCKY** | | | | | | |
| 1 **Whitfield** | N | Y | Y | Y | N | Y |
| 2 **Lewis** | N | Y | Y | Y | N | Y |
| 3 **Northup** | N | Y | Y | Y | N | Y |
| 4 **Davis** | N | Y | Y | Y | N | Y |
| 5 **Rogers** | N | Y | Y | Y | N | Y |
| 6 Chandler | N | N | N | N | Y | Y |
| **LOUISIANA** | | | | | | |
| 1 **Jindal** | N | Y | Y | Y | N | Y |
| 2 Jefferson | N | N | N | N | Y | Y |
| 3 Melancon | N | N | N | N | Y | Y |
| 4 **McCrery** | ? | Y | Y | Y | N | Y |
| 5 **Alexander** | N | Y | Y | Y | N | Y |
| 6 **Baker** | N | Y | Y | Y | N | Y |
| 7 **Boustany** | N | Y | Y | Y | N | Y |
| **MAINE** | | | | | | |
| 1 Allen | Y | N | N | ? | Y | N |
| 2 Michaud | N | N | N | N | Y | Y |
| **MARYLAND** | | | | | | |
| 1 **Gilchrest** | N | Y | Y | Y | N | Y |
| 2 Ruppersberger | N | N | N | N | Y | Y |
| 3 Cardin | N | N | N | N | Y | N |
| 4 Wynn | N | N | N | N | Y | N |
| 5 Hoyer | N | N | N | N | Y | Y |
| 6 **Bartlett** | N | Y | Y | Y | N | Y |
| 7 Cummings | N | N | N | N | Y | N |
| 8 Van Hollen | N | N | N | N | Y | N |
| **MASSACHUSETTS** | | | | | | |
| 1 Olver | Y | N | N | ? | Y | N |
| 2 Neal | N | N | N | N | Y | N |
| 3 McGovern | Y | N | N | N | Y | N |
| 4 Frank | Y | N | N | N | Y | N |
| 5 Meehan | N | N | N | N | Y | N |
| 6 Tierney | Y | N | N | N | Y | N |
| 7 Markey | Y | N | N | N | Y | N |
| 8 Capuano | Y | N | N | N | Y | N |
| 9 Lynch | N | N | N | N | Y | N |
| 10 Delahunt | Y | N | N | N | Y | N |
| **MICHIGAN** | | | | | | |
| 1 Stupak | N | N | N | N | Y | N |
| 2 **Hoekstra** | N | Y | Y | Y | N | Y |
| 3 **Ehlers** | N | Y | Y | Y | N | Y |
| 4 **Camp** | N | Y | Y | Y | N | Y |
| 5 Kildee | N | N | N | N | Y | N |
| 6 **Upton** | N | Y | Y | Y | N | Y |
| 7 **Schwarz** | N | Y | Y | Y | N | Y |
| 8 **Rogers** | N | Y | Y | Y | N | Y |
| 9 **Knollenberg** | N | Y | Y | Y | N | Y |
| 10 **Miller** | N | Y | Y | Y | N | Y |
| 11 **McCotter** | N | Y | Y | Y | N | Y |
| 12 Levin | N | N | N | N | Y | N |
| 13 Kilpatrick | Y | N | N | N | Y | N |
| 14 Conyers | Y | N | N | N | Y | N |
| 15 Dingell | Y | N | N | N | Y | N |
| **MINNESOTA** | | | | | | |
| 1 **Gutknecht** | N | Y | ? | Y | N | Y |
| 2 **Kline** | N | Y | Y | Y | N | Y |
| 3 **Ramstad** | N | Y | Y | Y | N | Y |
| 4 McCollum | N | N | N | N | Y | N |
| 5 Sabo | N | N | N | N | Y | N |
| 6 **Kennedy** | N | Y | Y | Y | N | Y |
| 7 Peterson | N | N | Y | N | Y | Y |
| 8 Oberstar | Y | N | N | N | Y | N |
| **MISSISSIPPI** | | | | | | |
| 1 **Wicker** | N | Y | Y | Y | N | Y |
| 2 Thompson | Y | N | N | N | Y | N |
| 3 **Pickering** | N | Y | Y | Y | N | Y |
| 4 Taylor | N | N | N | N | Y | Y |
| **MISSOURI** | | | | | | |
| 1 Clay | Y | N | N | N | Y | N |
| 2 **Akin** | N | Y | Y | Y | N | Y |
| 3 Carnahan | N | N | N | N | Y | N |
| 4 Skelton | N | N | N | N | Y | Y |
| 5 Cleaver | N | N | N | N | Y | Y |
| 6 **Graves** | N | Y | Y | Y | N | Y |
| 7 **Blunt** | N | Y | Y | Y | N | Y |
| 8 **Emerson** | N | Y | Y | Y | N | Y |
| 9 **Hulshof** | N | Y | Y | Y | N | Y |
| **MONTANA** | | | | | | |
| AL **Rehberg** | N | Y | Y | Y | N | Y |
| **NEBRASKA** | | | | | | |
| 1 **Fortenberry** | N | Y | Y | Y | N | Y |
| 2 **Terry** | N | Y | Y | Y | N | Y |
| 3 **Osborne** | N | Y | Y | Y | N | Y |
| **NEVADA** | | | | | | |
| 1 Berkley | ? | ? | ? | ? | ? | ? |
| 2 **Gibbons** | N | Y | Y | Y | N | Y |
| 3 **Porter** | N | Y | Y | Y | N | Y |
| **NEW HAMPSHIRE** | | | | | | |
| 1 **Bradley** | N | Y | Y | Y | N | Y |
| 2 **Bass** | N | Y | Y | Y | N | Y |
| **NEW JERSEY** | | | | | | |
| 1 Andrews | N | N | N | N | Y | Y |
| 2 **LoBiondo** | N | Y | Y | Y | N | Y |
| 3 **Saxton** | N | Y | Y | Y | N | Y |
| 4 **Smith** | N | Y | Y | Y | N | Y |
| 5 **Garrett** | N | Y | Y | Y | N | Y |
| 6 Pallone | N | N | N | N | Y | N |
| 7 **Ferguson** | N | Y | Y | Y | N | Y |
| 8 Pascrell | N | N | N | N | Y | N |
| 9 Rothman | N | N | N | N | Y | Y |
| 10 Payne | Y | ? | N | N | Y | N |
| 11 **Frelinghuysen** | N | Y | Y | Y | N | Y |
| 12 Holt | Y | N | N | N | Y | N |
| 13 Menendez | N | N | N | N | Y | Y |
| **NEW MEXICO** | | | | | | |
| 1 **Wilson** | N | Y | Y | Y | N | Y |
| 2 **Pearce** | N | Y | Y | Y | N | Y |
| 3 Udall | N | N | N | N | Y | N |
| **NEW YORK** | | | | | | |
| 1 Bishop | N | N | N | N | Y | N |
| 2 Israel | N | N | N | N | Y | Y |
| 3 **King** | N | Y | Y | Y | N | Y |
| 4 McCarthy | N | N | N | N | Y | Y |
| 5 Ackerman | N | N | N | N | Y | N |
| 6 Meeks | N | N | N | N | Y | Y |
| 7 Crowley | N | N | N | N | Y | Y |
| 8 Nadler | Y | N | N | N | Y | N |
| 9 Weiner | N | N | N | N | Y | N |
| 10 Towns | ? | N | N | N | Y | N |
| 11 Owens | Y | N | N | N | Y | N |
| 12 Velázquez | N | N | N | N | Y | N |
| 13 **Fossella** | N | Y | Y | Y | N | Y |
| 14 Maloney | N | N | N | N | Y | N |
| 15 Rangel | Y | N | ? | ? | Y | N |
| 16 Serrano | ? | N | N | N | Y | N |
| 17 Engel | N | N | N | N | Y | N |
| 18 Lowey | N | N | N | N | Y | N |
| 19 **Kelly** | N | Y | Y | Y | N | Y |
| 20 **Sweeney** | N | Y | Y | Y | N | Y |
| 21 McNulty | N | N | N | N | Y | N |
| 22 Hinchey | Y | N | N | N | Y | N |
| 23 **McHugh** | N | Y | Y | Y | N | Y |
| 24 **Boehlert** | N | Y | Y | Y | N | Y |
| 25 **Walsh** | N | Y | Y | Y | N | Y |
| 26 **Reynolds** | N | Y | Y | Y | N | Y |
| 27 Higgins | N | N | N | N | Y | Y |
| 28 Slaughter | N | N | N | N | Y | N |
| 29 **Kuhl** | N | Y | Y | Y | N | Y |
| **NORTH CAROLINA** | | | | | | |
| 1 Butterfield | Y | N | N | N | Y | N |
| 2 Etheridge | N | N | N | N | Y | Y |
| 3 **Jones** | N | Y | Y | Y | N | Y |
| 4 Price | N | N | N | N | Y | Y |
| 5 **Foxx** | N | Y | Y | Y | N | Y |
| 6 **Coble** | N | Y | Y | Y | N | Y |
| 7 McIntyre | N | N | N | N | Y | Y |
| 8 **Hayes** | N | Y | Y | ? | N | Y |
| 9 **Myrick** | N | Y | Y | ? | N | Y |
| 10 **McHenry** | N | Y | Y | Y | N | Y |
| 11 **Taylor** | N | Y | Y | ? | N | Y |
| 12 Watt | N | N | N | N | Y | N |
| 13 Miller | N | N | N | N | Y | N |
| **NORTH DAKOTA** | | | | | | |
| AL Pomeroy | N | N | N | N | Y | Y |
| **OHIO** | | | | | | |
| 1 **Chabot** | N | Y | Y | Y | N | Y |
| 2 **Portman** | N | Y | Y | Y | N | Y |
| 3 **Turner** | N | Y | Y | Y | N | Y |
| 4 **Oxley** | N | Y | Y | ? | N | Y |
| 5 **Gillmor** | ? | ? | ? | ? | ? | ? |
| 6 Strickland | N | N | N | N | Y | Y |
| 7 **Hobson** | N | Y | Y | Y | N | Y |
| 8 **Boehner** | N | Y | Y | Y | N | Y |
| 9 Kaptur | Y | N | N | N | Y | N |
| 10 Kucinich | Y | N | N | N | Y | N |
| 11 Jones | Y | N | N | N | Y | N |
| 12 **Tiberi** | N | Y | Y | Y | N | Y |
| 13 Brown | N | N | N | N | Y | N |
| 14 **LaTourette** | N | Y | Y | Y | N | Y |
| 15 **Pryce** | N | Y | Y | Y | N | Y |
| 16 **Regula** | N | Y | Y | Y | N | Y |
| 17 Ryan | N | N | N | N | Y | N |
| 18 **Ney** | N | Y | Y | Y | N | Y |
| **OKLAHOMA** | | | | | | |
| 1 **Sullivan** | N | Y | Y | Y | N | Y |
| 2 Boren | N | N | N | N | Y | Y |
| 3 **Lucas** | N | Y | Y | Y | N | Y |
| 4 **Cole** | N | Y | Y | Y | N | Y |
| 5 **Istook** | ? | Y | Y | Y | N | Y |
| **OREGON** | | | | | | |
| 1 Wu | N | N | N | N | Y | Y |
| 2 **Walden** | N | Y | Y | Y | N | Y |
| 3 Blumenauer | N | N | N | N | Y | N |
| 4 DeFazio | N | N | N | N | Y | N |
| 5 Hooley | N | N | N | N | Y | Y |
| **PENNSYLVANIA** | | | | | | |
| 1 Brady | Y | N | N | N | Y | N |
| 2 Fattah | Y | N | N | N | Y | N |
| 3 **English** | N | Y | Y | Y | N | Y |
| 4 **Hart** | N | Y | Y | Y | N | Y |
| 5 **Peterson** | N | Y | Y | Y | N | Y |
| 6 **Gerlach** | N | Y | Y | Y | N | Y |
| 7 **Weldon** | N | Y | Y | Y | N | Y |
| 8 **Fitzpatrick** | N | Y | Y | Y | N | Y |
| 9 **Shuster** | N | Y | Y | Y | N | Y |
| 10 **Sherwood** | N | Y | Y | Y | N | Y |
| 11 Kanjorski | N | N | N | N | Y | N |
| 12 Murtha | N | N | N | N | Y | Y |
| 13 Schwartz | N | N | N | N | Y | Y |
| 14 Doyle | N | N | N | N | Y | N |
| 15 **Dent** | N | Y | Y | Y | N | Y |
| 16 **Pitts** | N | Y | Y | Y | N | Y |
| 17 Holden | N | N | N | N | Y | Y |
| 18 **Murphy** | N | Y | Y | Y | N | Y |
| 19 **Platts** | N | Y | Y | Y | N | Y |
| **RHODE ISLAND** | | | | | | |
| 1 Kennedy | Y | N | N | N | Y | N |
| 2 Langevin | N | N | N | N | Y | N |
| **SOUTH CAROLINA** | | | | | | |
| 1 **Brown** | N | Y | Y | Y | N | Y |
| 2 **Wilson** | N | Y | Y | Y | N | Y |
| 3 **Barrett** | N | Y | Y | Y | N | Y |
| 4 **Inglis** | N | Y | Y | Y | N | Y |
| 5 Spratt | N | N | N | N | Y | Y |
| 6 Clyburn | Y | N | N | N | Y | N |
| **SOUTH DAKOTA** | | | | | | |
| AL Herseth | N | N | N | N | Y | Y |
| **TENNESSEE** | | | | | | |
| 1 **Jenkins** | N | Y | ? | Y | N | Y |
| 2 **Duncan** | N | Y | Y | Y | N | Y |
| 3 **Wamp** | ? | ? | Y | Y | N | Y |
| 4 Davis | N | N | N | N | Y | Y |
| 5 Cooper | Y | ? | ? | N | Y | Y |
| 6 Gordon | N | N | ? | ? | Y | Y |
| 7 **Blackburn** | N | Y | Y | Y | N | Y |
| 8 Tanner | N | N | N | N | Y | Y |
| 9 Ford | N | N | N | N | Y | Y |
| **TEXAS** | | | | | | |
| 1 **Gohmert** | N | Y | Y | Y | N | Y |
| 2 **Poe** | N | Y | Y | Y | N | Y |
| 3 **Johnson, S.** | N | Y | Y | Y | N | Y |
| 4 **Hall** | N | Y | Y | Y | N | Y |
| 5 **Hensarling** | N | Y | Y | Y | N | Y |
| 6 **Barton** | N | Y | Y | Y | N | Y |
| 7 **Culberson** | N | Y | Y | Y | N | Y |
| 8 **Brady** | N | Y | Y | Y | N | Y |
| 9 Green | Y | N | N | N | Y | Y |
| 10 **McCaul** | N | Y | Y | Y | N | Y |
| 11 **Conaway** | N | Y | Y | Y | N | Y |
| 12 **Granger** | N | Y | Y | Y | N | Y |
| 13 **Thornberry** | N | Y | Y | Y | N | Y |
| 14 **Paul** | Y | Y | Y | Y | N | Y |
| 15 Hinojosa | N | N | N | N | Y | Y |
| 16 Reyes | N | N | N | N | Y | Y |
| 17 Edwards | N | N | N | N | Y | Y |
| 18 Jackson-Lee | Y | N | N | N | Y | N |
| 19 **Neugebauer** | N | Y | Y | Y | N | Y |
| 20 Gonzalez | N | N | N | N | Y | Y |
| 21 **Smith** | N | Y | Y | Y | N | Y |
| 22 **DeLay** | N | Y | Y | Y | N | Y |
| 23 **Bonilla** | N | Y | Y | Y | N | Y |
| 24 **Marchant** | N | Y | Y | Y | N | Y |
| 25 Doggett | Y | N | N | N | Y | N |
| 26 **Burgess** | N | Y | Y | Y | N | Y |
| 27 Ortiz | N | N | N | N | Y | Y |
| 28 Cuellar | N | N | N | N | Y | Y |
| 29 Green | N | N | N | N | Y | N |
| 30 Johnson, E. | N | N | N | ? | Y | N |
| 31 **Carter** | N | Y | Y | Y | N | Y |
| 32 **Sessions** | N | Y | Y | Y | N | Y |
| **UTAH** | | | | | | |
| 1 **Bishop** | N | Y | Y | Y | N | Y |
| 2 Matheson | N | N | N | N | Y | Y |
| 3 **Cannon** | N | Y | Y | Y | N | Y |
| **VERMONT** | | | | | | |
| AL *Sanders* | N | N | N | N | Y | N |
| **VIRGINIA** | | | | | | |
| 1 **Davis, J.** | N | Y | Y | Y | N | Y |
| 2 **Drake** | N | Y | Y | Y | N | Y |
| 3 Scott | N | N | N | N | Y | N |
| 4 **Forbes** | N | Y | Y | Y | N | Y |
| 5 **Goode** | N | Y | Y | Y | N | Y |
| 6 **Goodlatte** | N | Y | Y | Y | N | Y |
| 7 **Cantor** | N | Y | Y | Y | N | Y |
| 8 Moran | N | N | N | N | Y | Y |
| 9 Boucher | N | N | N | N | Y | Y |
| 10 **Wolf** | N | Y | Y | Y | N | Y |
| 11 **Davis, T.** | ? | ? | ? | Y | N | Y |
| **WASHINGTON** | | | | | | |
| 1 Inslee | N | N | N | N | Y | N |
| 2 Larsen | N | N | N | N | Y | Y |
| 3 Baird | N | N | N | N | Y | Y |
| 4 **Hastings** | N | Y | Y | Y | N | Y |
| 5 **McMorris** | N | Y | Y | Y | N | Y |
| 6 Dicks | N | N | N | N | Y | N |
| 7 McDermott | Y | N | N | N | Y | N |
| 8 **Reichert** | N | Y | Y | Y | N | Y |
| 9 Smith | N | N | N | N | Y | N |
| **WEST VIRGINIA** | | | | | | |
| 1 Mollohan | N | N | N | N | Y | Y |
| 2 **Capito** | N | Y | Y | Y | N | Y |
| 3 Rahall | N | N | N | N | Y | Y |
| **WISCONSIN** | | | | | | |
| 1 **Ryan** | N | Y | Y | Y | N | Y |
| 2 Baldwin | Y | N | N | N | Y | N |
| 3 Kind | N | N | N | N | Y | Y |
| 4 Moore | N | N | N | N | Y | N |
| 5 **Sensenbrenner** | N | Y | Y | Y | N | Y |
| 6 **Petri** | N | Y | Y | Y | N | Y |
| 7 Obey | N | N | N | N | Y | N |
| 8 **Green** | N | Y | Y | Y | N | Y |
| **WYOMING** | | | | | | |
| AL **Cubin** | N | Y | Y | Y | N | Y |

# IN THE HOUSE | By Vote Number

**109.** **HR 683. Trademark Protection/Passage.** Sensenbrenner, R-Wis., motion to suspend the rules and pass the bill that would allow trademark owners to seek an injunction against the use of similar trademarks that might harm a company's reputation or confuse consumers. Motion agreed to 411-8: R 220-3; D 190-5 (ND 140-5, SD 50-0); I 1-0. A two-thirds majority of those present and voting (280 in this case) is required for passage under suspension of the rules. April 19, 2005.

**110.** **H J Res 19. Citizen Regent For Smithsonian Institution/Passage.** Ney, R-Ohio, motion to suspend the rules and pass the joint resolution that would appoint Shirley Ann Jackson of New York as a citizen regent of the Smithsonian Institution. Motion agreed to 417-0: R 222-0; D 194-0 (ND 144-0, SD 50-0); I 1-0. A two-thirds majority of those present and voting (278 in this case) is required for passage under suspension of the rules. April 19, 2005.

**111.** **H J Res 20. Citizen Regent For Smithsonian Institution/Passage.** Ney, R-Ohio, motion to suspend the rules and pass the joint resolution that would appoint Robert P. Kogod of the District of Columbia as a citizen regent of the Smithsonian Institution. Motion agreed to 412-0: R 222-0; D 190-0 (ND 141-0, SD 49-0); I 0-0. A two-thirds majority of those present and voting (275 in this case) is required for passage under suspension of the rules. April 19, 2005.

**112.** **HR 6. Energy Policy/Question of Consideration.** Question of whether the House should consider the rule (H Res 219) to provide for House floor consideration of the bill that would overhaul the nation's energy policy. Agreed to consider 231-193: R 224-0; D 7-192 (ND 1-147, SD 6-45); I 0-1. (McGovern, D-Mass., had raised a point of order that the rule would waive points of order against an unfunded mandate in the bill in violation of section 426(a) of the Congressional Budget Act.) April 20, 2005.

**113.** **H Con Res 126. Red Lake School Shooting/Adoption.** Kline, R-Minn., motion to suspend the rules and adopt the concurrent resolution that would express condolences to the families and friends of victims of the school shootings in Red Lake, Minn. Motion agreed to 424-0: R 224-0; D 199-0 (ND 148-0, SD 51-0); I 1-0. A two-thirds majority of those present and voting (283 in this case) is required for adoption under suspension of the rules. April 20, 2005.

**114.** **H Res 208. Polio Vaccine Anniversary/Adoption.** Murphy, R-Pa., motion to suspend the rules and adopt the resolution to recognize the University of Pittsburgh, Dr. Jonas Salk and others on the 50th anniversary of the discovery of the polio vaccine. Motion agreed to 422-0: R 223-0; D 198-0 (ND 147-0, SD 51-0); I 1-0. A two-thirds majority of those present and voting (282 in this case) is required for adoption under suspension of the rules. April 20, 2005.

**115.** **HR 6. Energy Policy/Refinery Approval Process.** Solis, D-Calif., amendment that would strike a provision in the bill that would allow an expedited review and approval process to open refineries in areas that have experienced manufacturing-sector layoffs and have unemployment rates that exceed the national average by at least 10 percent. Rejected 182-248: R 15-215; D 166-33 (ND 137-11, SD 29-22); I 1-0. April 20, 2005.

**116.** **HR 6. Energy Policy/Strategic Petroleum Reserve.** Kaptur, D-Ohio, amendment that would rename the Strategic Petroleum Reserve the Strategic Fuels Reserve, and would give the Energy Department authority to include alternate fuels, such as ethanol and biodiesel, in the reserve. Rejected 186-239: R 12-214; D 173-25 (ND 139-8, SD 34-17); I 1-0. April 20, 2005.

ND Northern Democrats, SD Southern Democrats
Southern states: Ala., Ark., Fla., Ga., Ky., La., Miss., N.C., Okla., S.C., Tenn., Texas, Va.

| | 109 | 110 | 111 | 112 | 113 | 114 | 115 | 116 |
|---|---|---|---|---|---|---|---|---|
| **ALABAMA** | | | | | | | | |
| 1 Bonner | Y | Y | Y | Y | Y | Y | N | N |
| 2 Everett | Y | Y | Y | Y | Y | Y | N | N |
| 3 Rogers | Y | Y | Y | Y | Y | Y | N | N |
| 4 Aderholt | Y | Y | Y | Y | Y | Y | N | N |
| 5 Cramer | Y | Y | Y | N | Y | Y | N | N |
| 6 Bachus | Y | Y | Y | Y | ? | ? | N | ? |
| 7 Davis | Y | Y | Y | N | Y | Y | Y | N |
| **ALASKA** | | | | | | | | |
| AL Young | ? | ? | ? | Y | Y | ? | N | N |
| **ARIZONA** | | | | | | | | |
| 1 Renzi | Y | Y | Y | Y | Y | Y | N | N |
| 2 Franks | Y | Y | Y | Y | Y | Y | N | N |
| 3 Shadegg | Y | Y | Y | Y | Y | Y | N | N |
| 4 Pastor | Y | Y | Y | N | Y | Y | Y | Y |
| 5 Hayworth | Y | Y | Y | Y | Y | Y | N | N |
| 6 Flake | N | Y | Y | Y | Y | Y | N | N |
| 7 Grijalva | Y | Y | Y | N | Y | Y | Y | ? |
| 8 Kolbe | Y | Y | Y | Y | Y | Y | N | N |
| **ARKANSAS** | | | | | | | | |
| 1 Berry | Y | Y | Y | N | Y | Y | N | Y |
| 2 Snyder | Y | Y | Y | N | Y | Y | Y | Y |
| 3 Boozman | Y | Y | Y | Y | Y | Y | N | N |
| 4 Ross | Y | Y | Y | N | Y | Y | N | Y |
| **CALIFORNIA** | | | | | | | | |
| 1 Thompson | Y | Y | Y | N | Y | Y | Y | Y |
| 2 Herger | Y | Y | Y | Y | Y | Y | N | N |
| 3 Lungren | Y | Y | Y | Y | Y | Y | N | N |
| 4 Doolittle | ? | ? | ? | Y | Y | Y | N | N |
| 5 Matsui, D. | Y | Y | Y | N | Y | Y | Y | Y |
| 6 Woolsey | Y | Y | Y | N | Y | Y | Y | Y |
| 7 Miller, George | Y | Y | Y | N | Y | Y | Y | Y |
| 8 Pelosi | Y | Y | Y | N | Y | Y | Y | Y |
| 9 Lee | Y | Y | Y | N | Y | Y | Y | Y |
| 10 Tauscher | Y | Y | Y | N | Y | Y | Y | Y |
| 11 Pombo | Y | Y | Y | Y | Y | Y | N | N |
| 12 Lantos | Y | Y | Y | N | Y | Y | Y | Y |
| 13 Stark | Y | Y | Y | N | Y | Y | Y | Y |
| 14 Eshoo | Y | Y | ? | N | Y | Y | Y | Y |
| 15 Honda | Y | Y | Y | N | Y | Y | Y | Y |
| 16 Lofgren | Y | Y | Y | N | Y | Y | Y | Y |
| 17 Farr | Y | Y | Y | N | Y | Y | Y | Y |
| 18 Cardoza | Y | Y | Y | N | Y | Y | N | N |
| 19 Radanovich | Y | Y | Y | Y | Y | Y | N | N |
| 20 Costa | Y | Y | Y | N | Y | Y | N | Y |
| 21 Nunes | Y | Y | Y | Y | Y | Y | N | N |
| 22 Thomas | Y | Y | Y | Y | Y | Y | N | N |
| 23 Capps | Y | Y | Y | N | Y | Y | Y | Y |
| 24 Gallegly | Y | Y | Y | Y | Y | Y | N | N |
| 25 McKeon | Y | Y | Y | Y | Y | Y | N | N |
| 26 Dreier | Y | Y | Y | Y | Y | Y | N | N |
| 27 Sherman | Y | Y | Y | N | Y | Y | Y | Y |
| 28 Berman | Y | Y | Y | N | Y | Y | Y | Y |
| 29 Schiff | Y | Y | Y | N | Y | Y | Y | Y |
| 30 Waxman | Y | Y | Y | N | Y | Y | Y | Y |
| 31 Becerra | Y | Y | Y | N | Y | Y | Y | Y |
| 32 Solis | Y | Y | Y | N | Y | Y | Y | Y |
| 33 Watson | Y | Y | Y | N | Y | Y | Y | Y |
| 34 Roybal-Allard | Y | Y | Y | N | Y | Y | Y | Y |
| 35 Waters | Y | Y | Y | N | Y | Y | Y | Y |
| 36 Harman | Y | Y | Y | N | Y | Y | N | Y |
| 37 Millender-McD. | Y | Y | Y | N | Y | Y | Y | Y |
| 38 Napolitano | Y | Y | Y | N | Y | Y | Y | Y |
| 39 Sánchez, Linda | Y | Y | Y | N | Y | Y | Y | Y |
| 40 Royce | Y | Y | Y | Y | Y | Y | N | N |
| 41 Lewis | Y | Y | Y | Y | Y | Y | N | N |
| 42 Miller, Gary | Y | Y | Y | Y | Y | Y | N | N |
| 43 Baca | Y | Y | Y | N | Y | Y | N | N |
| 44 Calvert | Y | Y | Y | Y | Y | Y | N | N |
| 45 Bono | Y | Y | Y | Y | Y | Y | N | N |
| 46 Rohrabacher | Y | Y | Y | Y | Y | Y | N | N |
| 47 Sanchez, Loretta | Y | Y | Y | N | Y | Y | N | Y |
| 48 Cox | Y | Y | Y | Y | Y | Y | N | Y |
| 49 Issa | Y | Y | Y | Y | Y | Y | N | N |

| | 109 | 110 | 111 | 112 | 113 | 114 | 115 | 116 |
|---|---|---|---|---|---|---|---|---|
| 50 Cunningham | Y | Y | Y | Y | Y | Y | N | N |
| 51 Filner | N | Y | Y | N | Y | Y | Y | Y |
| 52 Hunter | Y | Y | Y | Y | Y | Y | N | ? |
| 53 Davis | Y | Y | Y | N | Y | Y | Y | Y |
| **COLORADO** | | | | | | | | |
| 1 DeGette | ? | ? | ? | ? | ? | ? | Y | Y |
| 2 Udall | Y | Y | Y | N | Y | Y | Y | Y |
| 3 Salazar | Y | Y | Y | N | Y | Y | N | N |
| 4 Musgrave | Y | Y | Y | Y | Y | Y | N | N |
| 5 Hefley | Y | Y | Y | Y | Y | Y | N | N |
| 6 Tancredo | Y | Y | Y | Y | Y | Y | N | N |
| 7 Beauprez | Y | Y | Y | Y | Y | Y | N | N |
| **CONNECTICUT** | | | | | | | | |
| 1 Larson | Y | Y | Y | N | Y | Y | Y | Y |
| 2 Simmons | Y | Y | Y | N | Y | Y | Y | N |
| 3 DeLauro | Y | Y | Y | N | Y | Y | Y | Y |
| 4 Shays | Y | Y | Y | Y | Y | Y | Y | Y |
| 5 Johnson | Y | Y | Y | Y | Y | Y | N | N |
| **DELAWARE** | | | | | | | | |
| AL Castle | Y | Y | Y | Y | Y | Y | Y | N |
| **FLORIDA** | | | | | | | | |
| 1 Miller | Y | Y | Y | Y | Y | Y | N | N |
| 2 Boyd | Y | Y | Y | N | Y | Y | N | Y |
| 3 Brown | Y | Y | Y | N | Y | Y | Y | Y |
| 4 Crenshaw | Y | Y | Y | Y | Y | Y | N | N |
| 5 Brown-Waite | Y | Y | Y | Y | Y | Y | N | N |
| 6 Stearns | Y | Y | Y | Y | Y | Y | N | N |
| 7 Mica | Y | Y | Y | Y | Y | Y | N | N |
| 8 Keller | Y | Y | Y | Y | Y | Y | N | N |
| 9 Bilirakis | Y | Y | Y | Y | Y | Y | N | N |
| 10 Young | ? | ? | ? | ? | ? | ? | N | N |
| 11 Davis | Y | Y | Y | N | Y | Y | Y | Y |
| 12 Putnam | Y | Y | Y | Y | Y | Y | N | N |
| 13 Harris | Y | Y | Y | Y | Y | Y | N | N |
| 14 Mack | Y | Y | Y | Y | Y | Y | N | N |
| 15 Weldon | Y | Y | Y | Y | Y | Y | N | N |
| 16 Foley | Y | Y | Y | Y | Y | Y | N | N |
| 17 Meek | Y | Y | Y | N | Y | Y | Y | Y |
| 18 Ros-Lehtinen | Y | Y | Y | Y | Y | Y | N | N |
| 19 Wexler | ? | ? | ? | N | Y | Y | Y | Y |
| 20 Wasserman-Schultz | Y | Y | Y | N | Y | Y | Y | N |
| 21 Diaz-Balart, L. | ? | ? | ? | ? | ? | ? | N | N |
| 22 Shaw | Y | Y | Y | Y | Y | Y | N | N |
| 23 Hastings | Y | Y | Y | N | Y | Y | Y | Y |
| 24 Feeney | Y | Y | Y | Y | Y | Y | N | N |
| 25 Diaz-Balart, M. | Y | Y | Y | Y | Y | Y | N | N |
| **GEORGIA** | | | | | | | | |
| 1 Kingston | Y | Y | Y | Y | Y | Y | N | N |
| 2 Bishop | Y | Y | Y | N | Y | Y | N | Y |
| 3 Marshall | Y | Y | Y | N | Y | Y | Y | Y |
| 4 McKinney | Y | Y | Y | N | Y | Y | Y | Y |
| 5 Lewis | Y | Y | Y | N | Y | Y | Y | Y |
| 6 Price | Y | Y | Y | Y | Y | Y | N | N |
| 7 Linder | Y | Y | Y | Y | Y | Y | N | N |
| 8 Westmoreland | Y | Y | Y | Y | Y | Y | N | N |
| 9 Norwood | Y | Y | Y | Y | Y | Y | N | N |
| 10 Deal | ? | ? | ? | Y | Y | Y | N | N |
| 11 Gingrey | Y | Y | Y | Y | Y | Y | N | N |
| 12 Barrow | Y | Y | Y | N | Y | Y | N | Y |
| 13 Scott | Y | Y | ? | N | Y | Y | N | Y |
| **HAWAII** | | | | | | | | |
| 1 Abercrombie | Y | Y | Y | N | Y | Y | Y | Y |
| 2 Case | Y | Y | Y | ? | ? | ? | Y | Y |
| **IDAHO** | | | | | | | | |
| 1 Otter | Y | Y | Y | Y | Y | Y | N | N |
| 2 Simpson | Y | Y | Y | Y | Y | Y | N | N |
| **ILLINOIS** | | | | | | | | |
| 1 Rush | ? | ? | ? | N | Y | Y | Y | Y |
| 2 Jackson | Y | Y | Y | N | Y | Y | Y | Y |
| 3 Lipinski | Y | Y | Y | N | Y | Y | Y | Y |
| 4 Gutierrez | Y | Y | Y | N | Y | Y | Y | Y |
| 5 Emanuel | Y | Y | Y | N | Y | Y | ? | ? |
| 6 Hyde | Y | Y | Y | Y | Y | Y | N | N |
| 7 Davis | Y | Y | Y | N | Y | Y | Y | Y |
| 8 Bean | Y | Y | Y | N | Y | Y | Y | Y |
| 9 Schakowsky | Y | Y | Y | N | Y | Y | Y | Y |
| 10 Kirk | Y | Y | Y | Y | Y | Y | N | N |
| 11 Weller | Y | Y | Y | Y | ? | Y | N | N |
| 12 Costello | N | Y | Y | N | Y | N | N | Y |

| | 109 | 110 | 111 | 112 | 113 | 114 | 115 | 116 |
|---|---|---|---|---|---|---|---|---|
| 13 **Biggert** | Y | Y | Y | Y | Y | Y | N | N |
| 14 **Hastert** | | | | | | | | |
| 15 **Johnson** | Y | Y | Y | Y | Y | Y | Y | N |
| 16 **Manzullo** | Y | Y | Y | Y | Y | Y | N | N |
| 17 Evans | Y | Y | ? | N | Y | Y | Y | Y |
| 18 **LaHood** | Y | Y | Y | Y | Y | Y | N | N |
| 19 **Shimkus** | Y | Y | Y | Y | Y | Y | N | N |
| **INDIANA** | | | | | | | | |
| 1 Visclosky | Y | Y | Y | N | Y | Y | Y | Y |
| 2 **Chocola** | Y | Y | ? | Y | Y | Y | N | N |
| 3 **Souder** | Y | Y | Y | Y | Y | Y | N | Y |
| 4 **Buyer** | Y | Y | Y | Y | Y | Y | N | N |
| 5 **Burton** | Y | Y | Y | Y | Y | Y | N | N |
| 6 **Pence** | Y | Y | Y | Y | Y | Y | N | N |
| 7 Carson | Y | Y | Y | N | Y | Y | Y | Y |
| 8 **Hostettler** | Y | Y | Y | Y | Y | Y | N | Y |
| 9 **Sodrel** | Y | Y | Y | Y | Y | Y | N | N |
| **IOWA** | | | | | | | | |
| 1 **Nussle** | Y | Y | ? | Y | Y | Y | N | Y |
| 2 **Leach** | Y | Y | Y | Y | Y | Y | Y | Y |
| 3 Boswell | Y | Y | Y | N | Y | Y | N | Y |
| 4 **Latham** | Y | Y | Y | Y | Y | Y | N | N |
| 5 **King** | Y | Y | Y | Y | Y | Y | N | N |
| **KANSAS** | | | | | | | | |
| 1 **Moran** | Y | Y | Y | Y | Y | Y | N | N |
| 2 **Ryun** | Y | Y | Y | Y | Y | Y | N | N |
| 3 Moore | Y | Y | Y | N | Y | Y | Y | Y |
| 4 **Tiahrt** | Y | Y | Y | Y | Y | Y | N | N |
| **KENTUCKY** | | | | | | | | |
| 1 **Whitfield** | Y | Y | Y | Y | Y | Y | N | N |
| 2 **Lewis** | Y | Y | Y | Y | Y | Y | N | N |
| 3 **Northup** | Y | Y | Y | Y | Y | Y | N | N |
| 4 **Davis** | Y | Y | Y | Y | Y | Y | N | N |
| 5 **Rogers** | Y | Y | Y | Y | Y | Y | N | N |
| 6 Chandler | Y | Y | Y | N | Y | Y | Y | Y |
| **LOUISIANA** | | | | | | | | |
| 1 **Jindal** | Y | Y | Y | Y | Y | Y | N | N |
| 2 Jefferson | Y | Y | Y | N | Y | Y | Y | N |
| 3 Melancon | Y | Y | Y | Y | Y | Y | N | N |
| 4 **McCrery** | Y | Y | Y | Y | Y | Y | N | N |
| 5 **Alexander** | Y | Y | Y | Y | Y | Y | N | N |
| 6 **Baker** | Y | Y | Y | Y | Y | Y | N | N |
| 7 **Boustany** | Y | Y | Y | Y | Y | Y | N | N |
| **MAINE** | | | | | | | | |
| 1 Allen | Y | Y | Y | N | Y | Y | Y | N |
| 2 Michaud | Y | Y | Y | N | Y | Y | Y | Y |
| **MARYLAND** | | | | | | | | |
| 1 **Gilchrest** | Y | Y | Y | Y | Y | Y | Y | Y |
| 2 Ruppersberger | Y | Y | Y | N | Y | Y | N | Y |
| 3 Cardin | Y | Y | Y | N | Y | Y | Y | Y |
| 4 Wynn | Y | Y | Y | N | Y | Y | Y | Y |
| 5 Hoyer | Y | Y | Y | N | Y | Y | Y | Y |
| 6 **Bartlett** | Y | Y | Y | Y | Y | Y | N | N |
| 7 Cummings | Y | Y | Y | N | Y | Y | Y | Y |
| 8 Van Hollen | Y | Y | Y | N | Y | Y | Y | Y |
| **MASSACHUSETTS** | | | | | | | | |
| 1 Olver | Y | Y | Y | N | Y | Y | Y | Y |
| 2 Neal | Y | Y | Y | N | Y | Y | Y | Y |
| 3 McGovern | Y | Y | Y | N | Y | Y | Y | Y |
| 4 Frank | Y | Y | Y | N | Y | Y | Y | Y |
| 5 Meehan | Y | Y | Y | N | Y | Y | Y | Y |
| 6 Tierney | Y | Y | Y | N | Y | Y | Y | Y |
| 7 Markey | Y | Y | Y | N | Y | Y | Y | Y |
| 8 Capuano | Y | Y | Y | N | Y | Y | Y | Y |
| 9 Lynch | Y | Y | Y | N | Y | Y | Y | Y |
| 10 Delahunt | Y | Y | Y | N | Y | Y | ? | Y |
| **MICHIGAN** | | | | | | | | |
| 1 Stupak | Y | Y | Y | N | Y | Y | Y | Y |
| 2 **Hoekstra** | Y | Y | Y | Y | Y | Y | N | N |
| 3 **Ehlers** | Y | Y | Y | Y | Y | Y | Y | Y |
| 4 **Camp** | Y | Y | Y | Y | Y | Y | N | N |
| 5 Kildee | Y | Y | Y | N | Y | Y | Y | Y |
| 6 **Upton** | Y | Y | Y | Y | Y | Y | N | N |
| 7 **Schwarz** | Y | Y | Y | Y | Y | Y | N | N |
| 8 **Rogers** | Y | Y | Y | Y | Y | Y | N | N |
| 9 **Knollenberg** | Y | Y | Y | Y | Y | Y | N | N |
| 10 **Miller** | Y | Y | Y | Y | Y | Y | N | N |
| 11 **McCotter** | Y | Y | Y | Y | Y | Y | N | N |
| 12 Levin | Y | Y | Y | N | Y | Y | Y | N |
| 13 Kilpatrick | Y | Y | Y | N | Y | Y | Y | Y |
| 14 Conyers | Y | Y | Y | N | Y | Y | Y | Y |
| 15 Dingell | Y | Y | Y | N | Y | Y | Y | N |
| **MINNESOTA** | | | | | | | | |
| 1 **Gutknecht** | Y | Y | Y | Y | Y | Y | N | Y |
| 2 **Kline** | Y | Y | Y | Y | Y | Y | N | N |
| 3 **Ramstad** | Y | Y | Y | Y | Y | Y | Y | N |
| 4 McCollum | Y | Y | Y | N | Y | Y | Y | Y |
| 5 Sabo | Y | Y | Y | N | Y | Y | Y | Y |
| 6 **Kennedy** | Y | Y | Y | Y | Y | Y | N | Y |
| 7 Peterson | Y | Y | Y | N | Y | Y | N | Y |
| 8 Oberstar | Y | Y | Y | N | Y | Y | Y | Y |
| **MISSISSIPPI** | | | | | | | | |
| 1 **Wicker** | Y | Y | Y | Y | Y | Y | N | N |
| 2 Thompson | Y | Y | Y | N | Y | Y | Y | Y |
| 3 **Pickering** | Y | Y | Y | Y | Y | Y | N | ? |
| 4 Taylor | Y | Y | Y | N | Y | Y | N | Y |
| **MISSOURI** | | | | | | | | |
| 1 Clay | Y | Y | Y | N | Y | Y | Y | Y |
| 2 **Akin** | Y | Y | Y | Y | Y | Y | N | N |
| 3 Carnahan | Y | Y | Y | N | Y | Y | Y | Y |
| 4 Skelton | Y | Y | Y | N | Y | Y | Y | Y |
| 5 Cleaver | Y | Y | Y | N | Y | Y | Y | Y |
| 6 **Graves** | Y | Y | Y | Y | Y | Y | N | N |
| 7 **Blunt** | Y | Y | Y | Y | Y | Y | N | N |
| 8 **Emerson** | Y | Y | Y | Y | Y | Y | N | Y |
| 9 **Hulshof** | Y | Y | Y | Y | Y | Y | N | N |
| **MONTANA** | | | | | | | | |
| AL **Rehberg** | Y | Y | Y | Y | Y | Y | N | N |
| **NEBRASKA** | | | | | | | | |
| 1 **Fortenberry** | Y | Y | Y | Y | Y | Y | N | N |
| 2 **Terry** | Y | Y | Y | Y | Y | Y | N | N |
| 3 **Osborne** | Y | Y | Y | Y | Y | Y | N | N |
| **NEVADA** | | | | | | | | |
| 1 Berkley | Y | Y | Y | N | Y | Y | Y | Y |
| 2 **Gibbons** | Y | Y | Y | Y | Y | Y | N | N |
| 3 **Porter** | Y | Y | Y | Y | Y | Y | N | N |
| **NEW HAMPSHIRE** | | | | | | | | |
| 1 **Bradley** | Y | + | Y | Y | Y | Y | N | N |
| 2 **Bass** | Y | Y | Y | Y | Y | Y | N | N |
| **NEW JERSEY** | | | | | | | | |
| 1 Andrews | Y | Y | Y | N | Y | Y | ? | ? |
| 2 **LoBiondo** | Y | Y | Y | Y | Y | Y | Y | N |
| 3 **Saxton** | Y | Y | Y | Y | Y | Y | Y | N |
| 4 **Smith** | Y | Y | Y | Y | Y | Y | Y | N |
| 5 **Garrett** | Y | Y | Y | Y | Y | Y | N | N |
| 6 Pallone | ? | ? | ? | N | Y | Y | Y | Y |
| 7 **Ferguson** | Y | Y | Y | Y | Y | Y | N | N |
| 8 Pascrell | Y | Y | ? | N | Y | Y | Y | Y |
| 9 Rothman | Y | Y | Y | N | Y | Y | Y | Y |
| 10 Payne | Y | Y | Y | N | Y | Y | Y | Y |
| 11 **Frelinghuysen** | Y | Y | Y | Y | Y | Y | N | N |
| 12 Holt | Y | Y | Y | N | Y | Y | Y | Y |
| 13 Menendez | + | + | + | N | Y | Y | Y | Y |
| **NEW MEXICO** | | | | | | | | |
| 1 **Wilson** | Y | Y | Y | Y | Y | Y | Y | N |
| 2 **Pearce** | Y | Y | Y | Y | Y | Y | N | N |
| 3 Udall | Y | Y | Y | N | Y | Y | Y | Y |
| **NEW YORK** | | | | | | | | |
| 1 Bishop | Y | Y | Y | N | Y | Y | Y | Y |
| 2 Israel | Y | Y | Y | N | Y | Y | Y | Y |
| 3 **King** | Y | Y | Y | Y | Y | Y | N | N |
| 4 McCarthy | Y | Y | Y | N | Y | Y | Y | Y |
| 5 Ackerman | Y | Y | Y | N | Y | Y | Y | Y |
| 6 Meeks | Y | Y | Y | N | Y | Y | Y | Y |
| 7 Crowley | Y | Y | Y | N | Y | Y | Y | Y |
| 8 Nadler | Y | Y | Y | N | Y | Y | Y | Y |
| 9 Weiner | Y | Y | Y | N | Y | Y | Y | Y |
| 10 Towns | Y | Y | Y | N | Y | Y | Y | N |
| 11 Owens | Y | Y | Y | N | Y | Y | Y | Y |
| 12 Velázquez | Y | Y | Y | N | Y | Y | Y | Y |
| 13 **Fossella** | + | Y | Y | Y | Y | Y | N | N |
| 14 Maloney | Y | Y | Y | N | Y | Y | Y | Y |
| 15 Rangel | Y | Y | Y | N | Y | Y | Y | Y |
| 16 Serrano | Y | Y | Y | N | Y | Y | Y | Y |
| 17 Engel | Y | Y | Y | N | Y | Y | Y | Y |
| 18 Lowey | Y | Y | Y | N | Y | Y | Y | Y |
| 19 **Kelly** | Y | Y | Y | ? | ? | ? | ? | ? |
| 20 **Sweeney** | Y | Y | Y | ? | ? | ? | N | N |
| 21 McNulty | Y | Y | Y | N | Y | Y | Y | Y |
| 22 Hinchey | Y | Y | Y | N | Y | Y | Y | Y |
| 23 **McHugh** | Y | Y | Y | Y | Y | Y | N | N |
| 24 **Boehlert** | Y | Y | Y | Y | Y | Y | Y | N |
| 25 **Walsh** | Y | Y | Y | Y | Y | Y | N | N |
| 26 **Reynolds** | Y | Y | Y | Y | Y | Y | N | N |
| 27 Higgins | Y | Y | Y | N | Y | Y | Y | Y |
| 28 Slaughter | Y | Y | Y | N | Y | Y | Y | Y |
| 29 **Kuhl** | Y | Y | Y | ? | Y | Y | N | N |
| **NORTH CAROLINA** | | | | | | | | |
| 1 Butterfield | Y | Y | Y | N | Y | Y | Y | Y |
| 2 Etheridge | Y | Y | Y | N | Y | Y | Y | Y |
| 3 **Jones** | Y | Y | Y | Y | Y | Y | N | N |
| 4 Price | Y | Y | Y | N | Y | Y | Y | Y |
| 5 **Foxx** | Y | Y | Y | + | + | Y | N | N |
| 6 **Coble** | Y | Y | Y | Y | Y | Y | N | N |
| 7 McIntyre | Y | Y | Y | N | Y | Y | Y | Y |
| 8 **Hayes** | Y | Y | Y | Y | Y | Y | N | N |
| 9 **Myrick** | Y | Y | Y | Y | Y | Y | N | N |
| 10 **McHenry** | Y | Y | Y | Y | Y | Y | N | N |
| 11 **Taylor** | Y | Y | Y | Y | Y | Y | N | N |
| 12 Watt | Y | Y | Y | N | Y | Y | Y | Y |
| 13 Miller | Y | Y | Y | N | Y | Y | Y | Y |
| **NORTH DAKOTA** | | | | | | | | |
| AL Pomeroy | Y | Y | Y | N | Y | Y | N | Y |
| **OHIO** | | | | | | | | |
| 1 **Chabot** | Y | Y | Y | Y | Y | Y | N | N |
| 2 **Portman** | Y | Y | Y | ? | Y | Y | N | N |
| 3 **Turner** | Y | Y | Y | Y | Y | Y | N | N |
| 4 **Oxley** | Y | Y | Y | Y | Y | Y | N | N |
| 5 **Gillmor** | Y | Y | Y | Y | Y | Y | N | N |
| 6 Strickland | Y | Y | Y | N | Y | ? | Y | Y |
| 7 **Hobson** | Y | Y | Y | Y | Y | Y | N | N |
| 8 **Boehner** | Y | Y | Y | Y | Y | Y | N | N |
| 9 Kaptur | Y | Y | Y | N | Y | Y | Y | Y |
| 10 Kucinich | Y | Y | Y | N | Y | Y | Y | Y |
| 11 Jones | Y | Y | Y | N | Y | Y | Y | Y |
| 12 **Tiberi** | Y | Y | Y | Y | Y | Y | N | N |
| 13 Brown | Y | Y | Y | N | Y | Y | Y | Y |
| 14 **LaTourette** | Y | Y | Y | Y | Y | Y | N | Y |
| 15 **Pryce** | Y | Y | Y | Y | Y | Y | N | N |
| 16 **Regula** | Y | Y | Y | Y | Y | Y | N | N |
| 17 Ryan | Y | Y | Y | N | Y | Y | Y | Y |
| 18 **Ney** | Y | Y | Y | Y | Y | Y | N | N |
| **OKLAHOMA** | | | | | | | | |
| 1 **Sullivan** | Y | Y | Y | Y | Y | Y | N | N |
| 2 Boren | Y | Y | Y | N | Y | Y | N | N |
| 3 **Lucas** | Y | Y | Y | Y | Y | Y | N | N |
| 4 **Cole** | Y | Y | Y | Y | Y | Y | N | N |
| 5 **Istook** | ? | ? | ? | Y | Y | Y | N | N |
| **OREGON** | | | | | | | | |
| 1 Wu | N | Y | Y | N | Y | Y | Y | Y |
| 2 **Walden** | Y | Y | Y | Y | Y | Y | N | N |
| 3 Blumenauer | Y | Y | Y | N | Y | Y | Y | Y |
| 4 DeFazio | N | Y | Y | N | Y | Y | Y | Y |
| 5 Hooley | Y | Y | Y | N | Y | Y | Y | Y |
| **PENNSYLVANIA** | | | | | | | | |
| 1 Brady | Y | Y | Y | N | Y | Y | Y | Y |
| 2 Fattah | ? | ? | ? | N | Y | Y | Y | Y |
| 3 **English** | Y | Y | Y | Y | Y | Y | N | N |
| 4 **Hart** | Y | Y | Y | Y | Y | Y | N | N |
| 5 **Peterson** | Y | Y | Y | Y | Y | Y | N | N |
| 6 **Gerlach** | Y | ? | Y | Y | Y | Y | Y | N |
| 7 **Weldon** | Y | Y | Y | Y | Y | Y | N | N |
| 8 **Fitzpatrick** | Y | Y | Y | Y | Y | Y | Y | N |
| 9 **Shuster** | Y | Y | Y | Y | Y | Y | N | N |
| 10 **Sherwood** | Y | Y | Y | Y | Y | Y | N | N |
| 11 Kanjorski | Y | Y | Y | N | Y | Y | Y | Y |
| 12 Murtha | Y | ? | ? | N | Y | Y | Y | Y |
| 13 Schwartz | Y | Y | Y | N | Y | Y | Y | Y |
| 14 Doyle | Y | Y | Y | N | Y | Y | Y | Y |
| 15 **Dent** | Y | Y | Y | Y | Y | Y | N | N |
| 16 **Pitts** | Y | Y | Y | Y | Y | Y | N | N |
| 17 Holden | Y | Y | Y | N | Y | Y | Y | Y |
| 18 **Murphy** | Y | Y | Y | Y | Y | Y | N | N |
| 19 **Platts** | Y | Y | Y | Y | Y | Y | N | N |
| **RHODE ISLAND** | | | | | | | | |
| 1 Kennedy | ? | ? | ? | ? | ? | ? | Y | Y |
| 2 Langevin | Y | Y | Y | N | Y | Y | Y | Y |
| **SOUTH CAROLINA** | | | | | | | | |
| 1 **Brown** | Y | Y | Y | Y | Y | Y | N | N |
| 2 **Wilson** | Y | Y | Y | Y | Y | Y | N | N |
| 3 **Barrett** | Y | Y | Y | Y | Y | Y | N | N |
| 4 **Inglis** | Y | Y | Y | Y | Y | Y | N | N |
| 5 Spratt | Y | Y | Y | N | Y | Y | Y | Y |
| 6 Clyburn | Y | Y | Y | N | Y | Y | Y | Y |
| **SOUTH DAKOTA** | | | | | | | | |
| AL Herseth | Y | Y | Y | N | Y | Y | N | Y |
| **TENNESSEE** | | | | | | | | |
| 1 **Jenkins** | ? | ? | ? | Y | Y | Y | N | N |
| 2 **Duncan** | N | Y | Y | Y | Y | Y | N | N |
| 3 **Wamp** | Y | Y | Y | Y | Y | Y | N | N |
| 4 Davis | Y | Y | Y | N | Y | Y | N | Y |
| 5 Cooper | Y | Y | Y | N | Y | Y | N | N |
| 6 Gordon | Y | Y | Y | N | Y | Y | N | Y |
| 7 **Blackburn** | Y | Y | Y | Y | Y | Y | N | N |
| 8 Tanner | Y | Y | Y | N | Y | Y | N | Y |
| 9 Ford | Y | Y | Y | N | Y | Y | N | Y |
| **TEXAS** | | | | | | | | |
| 1 **Gohmert** | Y | Y | Y | Y | Y | + | N | ? |
| 2 **Poe** | Y | Y | Y | Y | Y | Y | N | N |
| 3 **Johnson, S.** | Y | Y | Y | Y | Y | Y | N | N |
| 4 **Hall** | Y | Y | Y | Y | Y | Y | N | N |
| 5 **Hensarling** | Y | Y | Y | Y | Y | Y | N | N |
| 6 **Barton** | Y | Y | Y | Y | Y | Y | N | N |
| 7 **Culberson** | Y | Y | Y | Y | Y | Y | N | N |
| 8 **Brady** | Y | Y | Y | Y | Y | Y | N | N |
| 9 Green | Y | Y | Y | N | Y | Y | Y | N |
| 10 **McCaul** | Y | Y | Y | Y | Y | Y | N | N |
| 11 **Conaway** | Y | Y | Y | Y | Y | Y | N | N |
| 12 **Granger** | Y | Y | Y | Y | Y | Y | N | N |
| 13 **Thornberry** | Y | Y | Y | Y | Y | Y | N | N |
| 14 **Paul** | N | Y | Y | Y | Y | Y | N | N |
| 15 Hinojosa | Y | Y | Y | Y | Y | Y | N | N |
| 16 Reyes | Y | Y | Y | Y | Y | Y | N | N |
| 17 Edwards | Y | Y | Y | N | Y | Y | N | N |
| 18 Jackson-Lee | Y | Y | Y | N | Y | Y | Y | N |
| 19 **Neugebauer** | Y | Y | Y | Y | Y | Y | N | N |
| 20 Gonzalez | Y | Y | Y | Y | Y | Y | Y | N |
| 21 **Smith** | Y | Y | Y | Y | Y | Y | N | N |
| 22 **DeLay** | Y | Y | Y | Y | Y | Y | N | N |
| 23 **Bonilla** | Y | Y | Y | Y | Y | Y | N | N |
| 24 **Marchant** | Y | Y | Y | Y | Y | Y | N | N |
| 25 Doggett | Y | Y | Y | N | Y | Y | Y | N |
| 26 **Burgess** | Y | Y | Y | Y | Y | Y | N | N |
| 27 Ortiz | Y | Y | Y | Y | Y | Y | N | N |
| 28 Cuellar | Y | Y | Y | N | Y | Y | N | N |
| 29 Green | Y | Y | Y | Y | Y | Y | N | N |
| 30 Johnson, E. | Y | Y | Y | N | Y | Y | Y | N |
| 31 **Carter** | Y | Y | Y | Y | Y | Y | N | N |
| 32 **Sessions** | Y | Y | Y | Y | ? | Y | N | N |
| **UTAH** | | | | | | | | |
| 1 **Bishop** | Y | Y | Y | Y | Y | Y | N | N |
| 2 Matheson | Y | Y | Y | N | Y | Y | N | N |
| 3 **Cannon** | Y | Y | Y | Y | Y | Y | N | N |
| **VERMONT** | | | | | | | | |
| AL *Sanders* | Y | Y | ? | N | Y | Y | Y | Y |
| **VIRGINIA** | | | | | | | | |
| 1 **Davis, J.** | Y | Y | Y | Y | Y | Y | N | N |
| 2 **Drake** | Y | Y | Y | Y | Y | Y | N | N |
| 3 Scott | Y | Y | Y | N | Y | Y | Y | Y |
| 4 **Forbes** | Y | Y | Y | Y | Y | Y | N | N |
| 5 **Goode** | Y | Y | Y | Y | Y | Y | N | N |
| 6 **Goodlatte** | Y | Y | Y | Y | Y | Y | N | N |
| 7 **Cantor** | Y | Y | Y | Y | Y | Y | N | N |
| 8 Moran | Y | Y | Y | N | Y | Y | Y | Y |
| 9 Boucher | Y | Y | Y | N | Y | Y | N | Y |
| 10 **Wolf** | Y | Y | Y | Y | Y | Y | N | N |
| 11 **Davis, T.** | Y | Y | Y | Y | Y | Y | N | N |
| **WASHINGTON** | | | | | | | | |
| 1 Inslee | Y | Y | Y | N | Y | Y | Y | Y |
| 2 Larsen | Y | Y | Y | N | Y | Y | Y | Y |
| 3 Baird | Y | Y | Y | N | Y | Y | Y | Y |
| 4 **Hastings** | Y | Y | Y | Y | Y | Y | N | N |
| 5 **McMorris** | Y | Y | Y | Y | Y | Y | N | N |
| 6 Dicks | Y | Y | Y | N | Y | Y | Y | Y |
| 7 McDermott | Y | Y | Y | N | Y | Y | Y | Y |
| 8 **Reichert** | Y | Y | Y | Y | Y | Y | N | N |
| 9 Smith | Y | Y | Y | N | Y | Y | Y | Y |
| **WEST VIRGINIA** | | | | | | | | |
| 1 Mollohan | Y | Y | Y | N | Y | Y | Y | ? |
| 2 **Capito** | Y | Y | Y | Y | Y | Y | N | N |
| 3 Rahall | Y | Y | Y | N | Y | Y | Y | Y |
| **WISCONSIN** | | | | | | | | |
| 1 **Ryan** | Y | Y | Y | Y | Y | Y | N | N |
| 2 Baldwin | Y | Y | Y | N | Y | Y | Y | Y |
| 3 Kind | Y | Y | Y | N | Y | Y | Y | Y |
| 4 Moore | N | Y | Y | N | Y | Y | Y | Y |
| 5 **Sensenbrenner** | Y | Y | Y | Y | Y | Y | N | N |
| 6 **Petri** | Y | Y | Y | Y | Y | Y | N | N |
| 7 Obey | Y | Y | Y | N | Y | Y | Y | Y |
| 8 **Green** | Y | Y | Y | Y | Y | Y | N | Y |
| **WYOMING** | | | | | | | | |
| AL **Cubin** | Y | Y | Y | Y | Y | Y | N | N |

# IN THE HOUSE | By Vote Number

**117.** **HR 6. Energy Policy/Oil Demand Reduction.** Waxman, D-Calif., amendment that would require federal agencies to develop steps to reduce demand for oil by 1 million barrels per day by 2013. Rejected 166-262: R 18-210; D 147-52 (ND 123-25, SD 24-27); I 1-0. April 20, 2005.

**118.** **HR 6. Energy Policy/Energy Dependence Reduction.** Bishop, D-N.Y., amendment that would require electric utility companies to reduce dependence on non-renewable energy sources and authorize $50 million over 10 years for the development of new electricity reliability standards for bulk-power. It would provide tax benefits for energy-efficient homes and other energy-efficient buildings, and prohibit oil and gas drilling in the Great Lakes. Rejected 170-259: R 4-226; D 165-33 (ND 137-10, SD 28-23); I 1-0. April 20, 2005.

**119.** **HR 6. Energy Policy/Fuel Economy Testing.** Rogers, R-Mich., amendment to the Johnson, R-Conn., amendment. The Rogers amendment would direct the EPA to revise certain federal vehicle fuel-economy measure-ment standards to factor in higher speed limits, variations in temperature and other fuel-depleting features to provide consumers with accurate fuel economy data on new vehicle labels. The Johnson amendment would require the EPA's fuel economy test procedures to reflect current driving patterns and conditions, and provide consumers with fuel economy information. Adopted 259-172: R 189-41; D 70-130 (ND 38-111, SD 32-19); I 0-1. April 20, 2005.

**120.** **HR 6. Energy Policy/Fuel Economy Testing.** Johnson, R-Conn., amendment to direct the EPA to revise certain federal vehicle fuel-economy measurement standards to factor in higher speed limits, variations in temperature and other fuel-depleting features to provide consumers with accurate fuel economy data on new vehicle labels. Adopted 346-85: R 225-5; D 121-79 (ND 74-75, SD 47-4); I 0-1. April 20, 2005.

**121.** **HR 6 Energy Policy/CAFE Standards.** Boehlert, R-N.Y., amendment to require the Transportation Department to issue regulations by model year 2007 that would increase fuel efficiency standards to at least 33 miles per gallon in automobiles manufactured by model year 2015. Rejected 177-254: R 36-194; D 140-60 (ND 118-31, SD 22-29); I 1-0. A "nay" was a vote in support of the president's position. April 20, 2005.

**122.** **HR 6. Energy Policy/ANWR Drilling.** Markey, D-Mass., amendment to strike the provision in the bill that would allow leases for oil and gas exploration, development and production in Alaska's Arctic National Wildlife Refuge. Rejected 200-231: R 29-201; D 170-30 (ND 138-11, SD 32-19); I 1-0. A "nay" was a vote in support of the president's position. April 20, 2005.

**123.** **HR 6. Energy Policy/Power Act Violations.** Dingell, D-Mich., amendment to authorize the Federal Energy Regulatory Commission to refund electricity overcharges and increase the penalties for violations of the Federal Power Act. It would strike a provision in the bill repealing the Public Utility Holding Company Act (PUHCA), and direct the Securities and Exchange Commission to review utility companies' compliance with PUHCA. Rejected 188-243: R 6-224; D 181-19 (ND 143-6, SD 38-13); I 1-0. April 20, 2005.

**124.** **HR 6. Energy Policy/Uranium Mining.** Udall, D-N.M., amendment to strike the provision in the bill that would authorize $10 million annually from fiscal 2006-08 for a program to seek improved technologies for mining uranium and for environmental restoration of uranium-mine sites. Rejected 204-225: R 24-202; D 179-23 (ND 143-8, SD 36-15); I 1-0. April 21, 2005.

ND Northern Democrats, SD Southern Democrats
Southern states: Ala., Ark., Fla., Ga., Ky., La., Miss., N.C., Okla., S.C., Tenn., Texas, Va.

| Member | 117 | 118 | 119 | 120 | 121 | 122 | 123 | 124 |
|---|---|---|---|---|---|---|---|---|
| **ALABAMA** | | | | | | | | |
| 1 Bonner | N | N | Y | Y | N | N | N | N |
| 2 Everett | N | N | Y | Y | N | N | N | N |
| 3 Rogers | N | N | Y | Y | N | N | N | N |
| 4 Aderholt | N | N | Y | Y | N | N | N | N |
| 5 Cramer | N | N | Y | Y | N | N | Y | N |
| 6 Bachus | ? | N | Y | Y | N | N | N | N |
| 7 Davis | Y | Y | Y | Y | N | N | N | Y |
| **ALASKA** | | | | | | | | |
| AL Young | N | N | Y | Y | N | N | N | N |
| **ARIZONA** | | | | | | | | |
| 1 Renzi | N | N | Y | Y | N | N | N | Y |
| 2 Franks | N | N | Y | Y | N | N | N | ? |
| 3 Shadegg | N | N | Y | Y | N | N | N | N |
| 4 Pastor | Y | Y | Y | Y | Y | Y | Y | Y |
| 5 Hayworth | N | N | Y | Y | N | N | N | Y |
| 6 Flake | N | N | Y | Y | N | N | N | Y |
| 7 Grijalva | Y | Y | N | N | Y | Y | Y | Y |
| 8 Kolbe | N | N | N | Y | N | N | N | N |
| **ARKANSAS** | | | | | | | | |
| 1 Berry | N | N | Y | Y | N | N | Y | N |
| 2 Snyder | Y | Y | N | Y | Y | Y | Y | Y |
| 3 Boozman | N | N | Y | Y | N | N | N | N |
| 4 Ross | N | N | Y | Y | N | N | Y | N |
| **CALIFORNIA** | | | | | | | | |
| 1 Thompson | Y | Y | N | N | Y | Y | Y | Y |
| 2 Herger | N | N | Y | Y | N | N | N | N |
| 3 Lungren | N | N | Y | Y | N | N | N | N |
| 4 Doolittle | N | N | Y | Y | N | N | N | N |
| 5 Matsui, D. | Y | Y | N | N | Y | Y | Y | Y |
| 6 Woolsey | Y | Y | N | N | Y | Y | Y | Y |
| 7 Miller, George | Y | Y | N | N | Y | Y | Y | Y |
| 8 Pelosi | Y | Y | N | N | Y | Y | Y | Y |
| 9 Lee | Y | Y | N | N | Y | Y | Y | Y |
| 10 Tauscher | Y | Y | N | N | Y | Y | Y | Y |
| 11 Pombo | N | N | Y | Y | N | N | N | N |
| 12 Lantos | Y | Y | N | N | Y | Y | Y | Y |
| 13 Stark | Y | Y | N | N | Y | Y | Y | Y |
| 14 Eshoo | Y | Y | N | N | Y | Y | Y | Y |
| 15 Honda | Y | Y | N | N | Y | Y | Y | Y |
| 16 Lofgren | Y | Y | N | Y | Y | Y | Y | Y |
| 17 Farr | Y | Y | N | N | Y | Y | Y | Y |
| 18 Cardoza | Y | N | Y | N | Y | N | Y | Y |
| 19 Radanovich | N | N | Y | N | N | N | N | N |
| 20 Costa | Y | N | N | Y | N | Y | N | Y |
| 21 Nunes | N | N | Y | N | N | N | N | N |
| 22 Thomas | N | N | Y | Y | N | N | N | N |
| 23 Capps | Y | Y | N | Y | Y | Y | Y | Y |
| 24 Gallegly | N | N | Y | Y | N | N | N | N |
| 25 McKeon | N | N | Y | Y | N | N | N | N |
| 26 Dreier | N | N | Y | Y | N | N | N | N |
| 27 Sherman | Y | Y | N | N | Y | Y | Y | Y |
| 28 Berman | Y | Y | N | N | Y | Y | Y | Y |
| 29 Schiff | Y | Y | N | N | Y | Y | Y | Y |
| 30 Waxman | Y | Y | N | N | Y | Y | Y | Y |
| 31 Becerra | Y | Y | N | N | Y | Y | Y | Y |
| 32 Solis | Y | Y | N | N | Y | Y | Y | Y |
| 33 Watson | Y | Y | N | N | Y | Y | Y | Y |
| 34 Roybal-Allard | Y | Y | N | N | Y | Y | Y | Y |
| 35 Waters | Y | Y | N | N | Y | Y | Y | Y |
| 36 Harman | Y | Y | Y | Y | Y | Y | Y | Y |
| 37 Millender-McD. | Y | Y | N | N | Y | Y | Y | Y |
| 38 Napolitano | Y | Y | N | N | Y | Y | Y | Y |
| 39 Sánchez, Linda | Y | Y | N | N | Y | Y | Y | Y |
| 40 Royce | N | N | Y | N | N | N | N | N |
| 41 Lewis | N | N | Y | Y | N | N | N | N |
| 42 Miller, Gary | N | N | Y | Y | N | N | N | N |
| 43 Baca | N | Y | Y | N | N | Y | Y | Y |
| 44 Calvert | N | N | Y | Y | N | N | N | N |
| 45 Bono | N | N | Y | Y | N | N | N | N |
| 46 Rohrabacher | N | N | Y | Y | N | N | N | Y |
| 47 Sanchez, Loretta | Y | Y | N | Y | Y | Y | Y | Y |
| 48 Cox | N | N | Y | N | N | N | N | N |
| 49 Issa | N | N | Y | Y | N | N | N | N |
| 50 Cunningham | N | N | Y | Y | N | N | N | N |
| 51 Filner | Y | Y | N | Y | Y | Y | Y | Y |
| 52 Hunter | N | N | Y | Y | N | N | N | N |
| 53 Davis | Y | Y | N | N | Y | Y | Y | Y |
| **COLORADO** | | | | | | | | |
| 1 DeGette | Y | Y | N | Y | Y | Y | Y | Y |
| 2 Udall | Y | Y | N | N | Y | Y | Y | Y |
| 3 Salazar | N | Y | Y | N | Y | N | Y | Y |
| 4 Musgrave | N | N | Y | Y | N | N | N | N |
| 5 Hefley | N | N | N | Y | N | N | N | N |
| 6 Tancredo | N | N | Y | Y | N | N | N | Y |
| 7 Beauprez | N | N | Y | Y | N | N | N | N |
| **CONNECTICUT** | | | | | | | | |
| 1 Larson | Y | Y | N | Y | Y | Y | Y | Y |
| 2 Simmons | N | Y | N | N | Y | N | Y | Y |
| 3 DeLauro | Y | Y | N | Y | Y | Y | Y | Y |
| 4 Shays | Y | Y | N | Y | Y | Y | Y | Y |
| 5 Johnson | N | N | N | Y | Y | Y | N | N |
| **DELAWARE** | | | | | | | | |
| AL Castle | N | N | N | Y | N | Y | N | Y |
| **FLORIDA** | | | | | | | | |
| 1 Miller | N | N | Y | Y | N | N | N | N |
| 2 Boyd | N | N | Y | Y | N | N | N | Y |
| 3 Brown | Y | Y | N | Y | Y | Y | Y | Y |
| 4 Crenshaw | N | N | Y | N | N | N | N | N |
| 5 Brown-Waite | N | N | Y | Y | N | N | N | N |
| 6 Stearns | N | N | Y | Y | N | N | N | N |
| 7 Mica | N | N | Y | Y | N | N | N | N |
| 8 Keller | N | N | Y | Y | N | N | N | N |
| 9 Bilirakis | N | N | Y | Y | Y | N | N | N |
| 10 Young | N | N | Y | Y | N | N | N | ? |
| 11 Davis | Y | Y | N | Y | Y | Y | Y | Y |
| 12 Putnam | N | N | Y | N | N | N | N | N |
| 13 Harris | N | N | Y | Y | N | N | N | N |
| 14 Mack | N | N | Y | Y | N | N | N | N |
| 15 Weldon | N | N | Y | Y | N | N | N | N |
| 16 Foley | N | N | N | Y | N | N | N | N |
| 17 Meek | N | Y | Y | N | Y | N | Y | Y |
| 18 Ros-Lehtinen | N | N | Y | Y | N | N | N | N |
| 19 Wexler | Y | Y | Y | Y | Y | Y | Y | Y |
| 20 Wasserman-Schultz | Y | Y | N | N | Y | Y | Y | Y |
| 21 Diaz-Balart, L. | N | N | Y | Y | N | N | N | N |
| 22 Shaw | N | N | Y | Y | N | N | N | N |
| 23 Hastings | N | Y | Y | Y | Y | Y | Y | Y |
| 24 Feeney | N | N | Y | Y | N | N | N | N |
| 25 Diaz-Balart, M. | N | N | Y | Y | N | N | N | N |
| **GEORGIA** | | | | | | | | |
| 1 Kingston | N | N | Y | Y | N | N | N | N |
| 2 Bishop | N | Y | Y | N | N | N | N | Y |
| 3 Marshall | N | N | Y | N | N | Y | Y | N |
| 4 McKinney | Y | Y | Y | Y | Y | Y | Y | Y |
| 5 Lewis | Y | Y | N | N | Y | Y | Y | Y |
| 6 Price | N | N | Y | Y | N | N | N | N |
| 7 Linder | N | N | Y | Y | N | N | N | N |
| 8 Westmoreland | N | N | Y | Y | N | N | N | N |
| 9 Norwood | N | N | Y | Y | N | N | N | N |
| 10 Deal | N | N | Y | Y | N | N | N | N |
| 11 Gingrey | N | N | Y | Y | N | N | N | N |
| 12 Barrow | Y | Y | Y | Y | Y | Y | Y | Y |
| 13 Scott | N | N | Y | Y | N | Y | N | N |
| **HAWAII** | | | | | | | | |
| 1 Abercrombie | Y | Y | N | N | Y | Y | Y | Y |
| 2 Case | Y | Y | N | Y | Y | Y | Y | Y |
| **IDAHO** | | | | | | | | |
| 1 Otter | N | N | Y | Y | N | N | N | N |
| 2 Simpson | N | N | Y | Y | N | N | N | N |
| **ILLINOIS** | | | | | | | | |
| 1 Rush | Y | Y | Y | Y | Y | Y | Y | Y |
| 2 Jackson | Y | Y | N | Y | Y | Y | Y | Y |
| 3 Lipinski | Y | Y | N | Y | Y | Y | Y | Y |
| 4 Gutierrez | Y | Y | N | Y | Y | Y | Y | Y |
| 5 Emanuel | ? | ? | ? | ? | ? | ? | ? | ? |
| 6 Hyde | N | N | Y | Y | N | N | N | N |
| 7 Davis | Y | Y | Y | Y | Y | Y | Y | Y |
| 8 Bean | Y | Y | N | Y | Y | Y | Y | Y |
| 9 Schakowsky | Y | Y | N | N | Y | Y | Y | Y |
| 10 Kirk | Y | Y | N | Y | Y | Y | N | Y |
| 11 Weller | N | N | Y | Y | N | N | N | N |
| 12 Costello | Y | N | Y | Y | Y | Y | Y | Y |

**KEY** Republicans  Democrats  *Independents*

| | | | |
|---|---|---|---|
| Y | Voted for (yea) | X | Paired against |
| # | Paired for | – | Announced against |
| + | Announced for | P | Voted "present" |
| N | Voted against (nay) | C | Voted "present" to avoid possible conflict of interest |
| | | ? | Did not vote or otherwise make a position known |

| | 117 | 118 | 119 | 120 | 121 | 122 | 123 | 124 |
|---|---|---|---|---|---|---|---|---|
| 13 **Biggert** | N | N | N | Y | Y | N | N | N |
| 14 **Hastert** | | | | | | | | |
| 15 **Johnson** | Y | N | N | Y | Y | Y | N | Y |
| 16 **Manzullo** | N | N | Y | Y | N | N | N | N |
| 17 Evans | Y | Y | N | N | Y | Y | Y | Y |
| 18 **LaHood** | N | N | N | Y | Y | N | N | N |
| 19 **Shimkus** | N | N | Y | Y | N | N | N | N |
| **INDIANA** | | | | | | | | |
| 1 Visclosky | N | Y | Y | Y | N | Y | N | Y |
| 2 **Chocola** | N | N | Y | Y | N | N | N | N |
| 3 **Souder** | N | N | Y | Y | N | N | N | N |
| 4 **Buyer** | N | N | Y | Y | N | N | N | N |
| 5 **Burton** | N | N | Y | Y | N | N | N | N |
| 6 **Pence** | N | N | Y | Y | N | N | N | N |
| 7 Carson | Y | Y | Y | Y | Y | Y | Y | Y |
| 8 **Hostettler** | N | N | Y | Y | N | N | N | N |
| 9 **Sodrel** | N | N | Y | Y | N | N | N | N |
| **IOWA** | | | | | | | | |
| 1 **Nussle** | N | N | Y | Y | N | N | N | N |
| 2 **Leach** | Y | N | N | Y | Y | Y | N | Y |
| 3 Boswell | N | Y | Y | Y | N | Y | N | Y |
| 4 **Latham** | N | N | Y | Y | N | N | N | N |
| 5 **King** | N | N | Y | Y | N | N | N | N |
| **KANSAS** | | | | | | | | |
| 1 **Moran** | N | N | Y | Y | N | N | N | N |
| 2 **Ryun** | N | N | Y | Y | N | N | N | N |
| 3 Moore | N | Y | N | Y | N | Y | Y | Y |
| 4 **Tiahrt** | N | N | Y | Y | N | N | N | N |
| **KENTUCKY** | | | | | | | | |
| 1 **Whitfield** | N | N | Y | Y | N | N | N | N |
| 2 **Lewis** | N | N | Y | Y | N | N | N | N |
| 3 **Northup** | N | N | Y | Y | N | N | N | N |
| 4 **Davis** | N | N | Y | Y | N | N | N | N |
| 5 **Rogers** | N | N | Y | Y | N | N | N | N |
| 6 Chandler | N | Y | Y | Y | N | Y | N | Y |
| **LOUISIANA** | | | | | | | | |
| 1 **Jindal** | N | N | Y | Y | N | N | N | N |
| 2 Jefferson | N | Y | Y | Y | N | N | Y | Y |
| 3 Melancon | N | N | Y | Y | N | N | N | N |
| 4 **McCrery** | N | N | Y | Y | N | N | N | N |
| 5 **Alexander** | N | N | Y | Y | N | N | N | N |
| 6 **Baker** | N | N | Y | N | N | N | N | N |
| 7 **Boustany** | N | N | Y | Y | N | N | N | N |
| **MAINE** | | | | | | | | |
| 1 Allen | Y | Y | N | N | Y | Y | Y | Y |
| 2 Michaud | Y | Y | N | Y | Y | Y | Y | Y |
| **MARYLAND** | | | | | | | | |
| 1 **Gilchrest** | Y | N | N | Y | Y | Y | N | Y |
| 2 Ruppersberger | N | Y | Y | Y | N | Y | Y | Y |
| 3 Cardin | Y | Y | N | Y | Y | Y | Y | Y |
| 4 Wynn | N | Y | Y | Y | N | Y | Y | N |
| 5 Hoyer | Y | Y | Y | Y | N | Y | Y | Y |
| 6 **Bartlett** | Y | N | N | Y | Y | Y | N | N |
| 7 Cummings | Y | Y | Y | Y | N | Y | Y | Y |
| 8 Van Hollen | Y | Y | N | N | Y | Y | Y | Y |
| **MASSACHUSETTS** | | | | | | | | |
| 1 Olver | Y | Y | N | N | Y | Y | Y | Y |
| 2 Neal | Y | Y | N | N | Y | Y | Y | Y |
| 3 McGovern | Y | Y | N | N | Y | Y | Y | Y |
| 4 Frank | Y | Y | N | N | Y | Y | Y | Y |
| 5 Meehan | Y | Y | N | N | Y | Y | Y | Y |
| 6 Tierney | Y | Y | N | N | Y | Y | Y | Y |
| 7 Markey | Y | Y | N | N | Y | Y | Y | Y |
| 8 Capuano | Y | Y | N | N | Y | Y | Y | Y |
| 9 Lynch | Y | Y | N | Y | Y | Y | Y | Y |
| 10 Delahunt | Y | Y | N | Y | Y | Y | Y | Y |
| **MICHIGAN** | | | | | | | | |
| 1 Stupak | N | Y | Y | Y | N | Y | Y | N |
| 2 **Hoekstra** | N | N | Y | Y | N | N | N | N |
| 3 **Ehlers** | Y | N | N | Y | Y | Y | Y | Y |
| 4 **Camp** | N | N | Y | Y | N | N | N | N |
| 5 Kildee | N | Y | Y | Y | N | Y | Y | Y |
| 6 **Upton** | N | N | Y | Y | N | N | N | N |
| 7 **Schwarz** | N | N | Y | Y | N | Y | N | N |
| 8 **Rogers** | N | N | Y | Y | N | N | N | N |
| 9 **Knollenberg** | N | N | Y | Y | N | N | N | N |
| 10 **Miller** | N | N | Y | Y | N | N | N | N |
| 11 **McCotter** | N | N | Y | Y | N | N | N | N |
| 12 Levin | N | Y | Y | Y | N | Y | Y | Y |
| 13 Kilpatrick | Y | Y | Y | Y | N | Y | Y | Y |
| 14 Conyers | Y | Y | Y | Y | N | Y | Y | Y |
| 15 Dingell | N | Y | Y | Y | N | Y | Y | Y |

| | 117 | 118 | 119 | 120 | 121 | 122 | 123 | 124 |
|---|---|---|---|---|---|---|---|---|
| **MINNESOTA** | | | | | | | | |
| 1 **Gutknecht** | N | N | Y | Y | Y | N | N | N |
| 2 **Kline** | N | N | Y | Y | N | N | N | N |
| 3 **Ramstad** | Y | N | N | Y | Y | Y | N | N |
| 4 McCollum | Y | Y | N | N | Y | Y | Y | Y |
| 5 Sabo | Y | Y | N | Y | Y | Y | Y | Y |
| 6 **Kennedy** | N | N | Y | Y | N | Y | N | N |
| 7 Peterson | N | N | Y | Y | Y | N | Y | Y |
| 8 Oberstar | Y | Y | N | Y | Y | Y | Y | Y |
| **MISSISSIPPI** | | | | | | | | |
| 1 **Wicker** | N | N | Y | Y | N | N | N | N |
| 2 Thompson | Y | Y | Y | Y | N | Y | Y | Y |
| 3 **Pickering** | N | N | Y | Y | N | N | N | N |
| 4 Taylor | Y | N | Y | Y | Y | N | Y | Y |
| **MISSOURI** | | | | | | | | |
| 1 Clay | N | ? | Y | Y | N | Y | Y | Y |
| 2 **Akin** | N | N | Y | Y | N | N | N | N |
| 3 Carnahan | Y | Y | N | Y | Y | Y | Y | Y |
| 4 Skelton | Y | N | N | Y | Y | N | Y | Y |
| 5 Cleaver | N | Y | Y | Y | N | Y | Y | Y |
| 6 **Graves** | N | N | Y | Y | N | N | Y | N |
| 7 **Blunt** | N | N | Y | Y | N | N | N | N |
| 8 **Emerson** | N | N | Y | Y | N | N | N | N |
| 9 **Hulshof** | N | N | Y | Y | N | N | N | N |
| **MONTANA** | | | | | | | | |
| AL **Rehberg** | N | N | Y | Y | N | N | N | N |
| **NEBRASKA** | | | | | | | | |
| 1 **Fortenberry** | N | N | Y | Y | N | N | N | N |
| 2 **Terry** | N | N | Y | Y | N | N | N | N |
| 3 **Osborne** | N | N | Y | Y | N | N | N | N |
| **NEVADA** | | | | | | | | |
| 1 Berkley | Y | Y | N | Y | Y | Y | Y | Y |
| 2 **Gibbons** | N | N | Y | Y | N | N | N | N |
| 3 **Porter** | N | N | Y | Y | N | N | N | N |
| **NEW HAMPSHIRE** | | | | | | | | |
| 1 **Bradley** | Y | N | N | Y | N | Y | N | N |
| 2 **Bass** | Y | N | Y | Y | N | Y | N | N |
| **NEW JERSEY** | | | | | | | | |
| 1 Andrews | ? | ? | ? | ? | ? | ? | ? | Y |
| 2 **LoBiondo** | Y | N | N | N | Y | Y | N | Y |
| 3 **Saxton** | Y | N | N | N | Y | Y | N | Y |
| 4 **Smith** | Y | N | N | N | Y | Y | N | Y |
| 5 **Garrett** | N | N | N | Y | N | N | N | N |
| 6 Pallone | Y | Y | N | N | Y | Y | Y | Y |
| 7 **Ferguson** | N | N | N | Y | N | Y | N | N |
| 8 Pascrell | Y | Y | N | N | Y | Y | Y | Y |
| 9 Rothman | Y | Y | N | Y | Y | Y | Y | Y |
| 10 Payne | Y | Y | N | N | Y | Y | Y | Y |
| 11 **Frelinghuysen** | N | N | N | Y | Y | Y | N | N |
| 12 Holt | Y | Y | N | N | Y | Y | Y | Y |
| 13 Menendez | Y | Y | N | N | Y | Y | Y | Y |
| **NEW MEXICO** | | | | | | | | |
| 1 **Wilson** | N | N | Y | Y | N | N | N | Y |
| 2 **Pearce** | N | N | Y | Y | N | N | N | N |
| 3 Udall | Y | Y | N | N | Y | Y | Y | Y |
| **NEW YORK** | | | | | | | | |
| 1 Bishop | Y | Y | N | N | Y | Y | Y | Y |
| 2 Israel | Y | Y | N | N | Y | Y | Y | Y |
| 3 **King** | N | N | N | Y | Y | N | N | N |
| 4 McCarthy | Y | Y | N | N | Y | Y | Y | Y |
| 5 Ackerman | Y | Y | N | N | Y | Y | Y | Y |
| 6 Meeks | N | N | Y | N | N | Y | Y | Y |
| 7 Crowley | Y | Y | Y | Y | Y | Y | Y | Y |
| 8 Nadler | Y | Y | N | N | Y | Y | Y | Y |
| 9 Weiner | Y | Y | N | N | Y | Y | Y | Y |
| 10 Towns | N | N | N | Y | N | N | Y | Y |
| 11 Owens | Y | Y | N | Y | Y | Y | Y | Y |
| 12 Velázquez | Y | Y | N | N | Y | Y | Y | Y |
| 13 **Fossella** | N | N | N | Y | N | N | N | N |
| 14 Maloney | Y | Y | N | N | Y | Y | Y | Y |
| 15 Rangel | Y | Y | N | Y | Y | Y | Y | Y |
| 16 Serrano | Y | Y | N | Y | Y | Y | Y | Y |
| 17 Engel | Y | Y | N | N | Y | Y | Y | Y |
| 18 Lowey | Y | Y | N | N | Y | Y | Y | Y |
| 19 **Kelly** | ? | ? | ? | ? | ? | ? | ? | ? |
| 20 **Sweeney** | N | N | N | Y | N | N | N | N |
| 21 McNulty | Y | Y | N | N | Y | Y | Y | Y |
| 22 Hinchey | Y | Y | N | N | Y | Y | Y | Y |
| 23 **McHugh** | N | N | Y | Y | N | N | N | N |
| 24 **Boehlert** | Y | N | N | Y | Y | Y | Y | Y |
| 25 **Walsh** | Y | N | Y | Y | N | Y | N | N |
| 26 **Reynolds** | N | N | Y | Y | Y | N | N | N |
| 27 Higgins | Y | Y | N | N | Y | Y | Y | Y |
| 28 Slaughter | ? | Y | N | N | Y | Y | Y | Y |
| 29 **Kuhl** | N | N | Y | Y | N | N | N | N |

| | 117 | 118 | 119 | 120 | 121 | 122 | 123 | 124 |
|---|---|---|---|---|---|---|---|---|
| **NORTH CAROLINA** | | | | | | | | |
| 1 Butterfield | Y | Y | N | Y | Y | Y | Y | Y |
| 2 Etheridge | Y | Y | N | Y | Y | Y | Y | Y |
| 3 **Jones** | N | N | Y | Y | N | N | N | N |
| 4 Price | Y | Y | N | Y | Y | Y | Y | Y |
| 5 **Foxx** | N | N | Y | Y | N | N | N | N |
| 6 **Coble** | N | N | Y | Y | N | N | N | N |
| 7 McIntyre | Y | N | Y | Y | N | Y | N | Y |
| 8 **Hayes** | N | N | Y | Y | N | N | N | N |
| 9 **Myrick** | N | N | Y | Y | N | N | N | N |
| 10 **McHenry** | N | N | Y | Y | N | N | N | N |
| 11 **Taylor** | N | N | Y | Y | N | N | N | N |
| 12 Watt | Y | Y | Y | Y | Y | Y | Y | Y |
| 13 Miller | Y | Y | N | N | Y | Y | Y | Y |
| **NORTH DAKOTA** | | | | | | | | |
| AL Pomeroy | Y | N | N | Y | N | Y | N | Y |
| **OHIO** | | | | | | | | |
| 1 **Chabot** | N | N | Y | Y | N | N | N | Y |
| 2 **Portman** | N | N | Y | Y | N | N | N | ? |
| 3 **Turner** | N | N | Y | Y | N | N | N | N |
| 4 **Oxley** | N | N | Y | Y | N | N | N | N |
| 5 **Gillmor** | N | N | Y | Y | N | N | N | N |
| 6 Strickland | N | Y | Y | Y | N | Y | Y | Y |
| 7 **Hobson** | N | N | Y | Y | N | N | N | N |
| 8 **Boehner** | N | N | Y | Y | N | N | N | N |
| 9 Kaptur | Y | Y | N | Y | N | Y | Y | Y |
| 10 Kucinich | Y | Y | N | N | Y | Y | Y | Y |
| 11 Jones | Y | Y | Y | Y | N | Y | Y | Y |
| 12 **Tiberi** | N | N | Y | Y | Y | N | N | N |
| 13 Brown | Y | Y | N | Y | Y | Y | Y | Y |
| 14 **LaTourette** | ? | Y | Y | Y | Y | N | N | N |
| 15 **Pryce** | N | N | Y | Y | N | N | N | N |
| 16 **Regula** | N | N | N | Y | N | N | N | N |
| 17 Ryan | Y | Y | Y | Y | Y | Y | Y | Y |
| 18 **Ney** | N | N | Y | Y | N | N | N | N |
| **OKLAHOMA** | | | | | | | | |
| 1 **Sullivan** | N | N | Y | Y | N | N | N | N |
| 2 Boren | N | N | Y | Y | N | N | N | N |
| 3 **Lucas** | N | N | Y | Y | N | N | N | N |
| 4 **Cole** | N | N | Y | Y | N | N | N | N |
| 5 **Istook** | N | N | Y | Y | N | N | N | N |
| **OREGON** | | | | | | | | |
| 1 Wu | Y | Y | N | Y | Y | Y | Y | Y |
| 2 **Walden** | N | N | Y | Y | N | N | N | N |
| 3 Blumenauer | Y | Y | N | N | Y | Y | Y | Y |
| 4 DeFazio | Y | Y | N | N | Y | Y | Y | Y |
| 5 Hooley | Y | Y | N | Y | Y | Y | Y | Y |
| **PENNSYLVANIA** | | | | | | | | |
| 1 Brady | N | Y | Y | Y | Y | N | Y | Y |
| 2 Fattah | Y | Y | N | Y | Y | Y | Y | Y |
| 3 **English** | N | N | N | Y | N | N | N | N |
| 4 **Hart** | N | N | Y | Y | N | N | N | N |
| 5 **Peterson** | N | N | N | Y | N | N | N | N |
| 6 **Gerlach** | N | N | N | Y | Y | Y | N | N |
| 7 **Weldon** | N | N | N | Y | Y | N | N | N |
| 8 **Fitzpatrick** | Y | N | N | Y | Y | Y | N | Y |
| 9 **Shuster** | N | N | Y | Y | N | N | N | N |
| 10 **Sherwood** | N | N | N | Y | N | N | N | N |
| 11 Kanjorski | N | Y | Y | Y | N | N | N | N |
| 12 Murtha | N | Y | Y | Y | N | N | Y | N |
| 13 Schwartz | Y | Y | N | N | Y | Y | Y | Y |
| 14 Doyle | N | Y | Y | Y | N | Y | Y | N |
| 15 **Dent** | N | N | Y | Y | N | N | N | N |
| 16 **Pitts** | N | N | Y | Y | N | N | N | N |
| 17 Holden | N | Y | Y | Y | N | Y | N | N |
| 18 **Murphy** | N | N | Y | Y | N | N | N | N |
| 19 **Platts** | Y | Y | N | Y | Y | N | N | ? |
| **RHODE ISLAND** | | | | | | | | |
| 1 Kennedy | Y | Y | N | N | Y | Y | Y | Y |
| 2 Langevin | Y | Y | N | N | Y | Y | Y | Y |
| **SOUTH CAROLINA** | | | | | | | | |
| 1 **Brown** | N | N | Y | Y | N | N | N | N |
| 2 **Wilson** | N | N | Y | Y | N | N | N | N |
| 3 **Barrett** | N | N | Y | Y | N | N | N | N |
| 4 **Inglis** | N | N | Y | Y | Y | Y | N | N |
| 5 Spratt | Y | Y | N | Y | Y | Y | Y | Y |
| 6 Clyburn | Y | Y | Y | Y | N | Y | Y | Y |
| **SOUTH DAKOTA** | | | | | | | | |
| AL Herseth | Y | N | Y | Y | Y | N | N | N |
| **TENNESSEE** | | | | | | | | |
| 1 **Jenkins** | N | N | Y | Y | N | N | N | N |
| 2 **Duncan** | N | N | Y | Y | N | N | N | N |

| | 117 | 118 | 119 | 120 | 121 | 122 | 123 | 124 |
|---|---|---|---|---|---|---|---|---|
| 3 **Wamp** | N | N | N | Y | N | N | N | N |
| 4 Davis | N | N | Y | Y | N | N | Y | Y |
| 5 Cooper | Y | Y | N | Y | Y | Y | Y | Y |
| 6 Gordon | N | N | Y | Y | N | Y | Y | N |
| 7 **Blackburn** | N | N | Y | Y | N | N | N | N |
| 8 Tanner | N | N | Y | Y | N | N | Y | Y |
| 9 Ford | Y | Y | N | Y | Y | Y | Y | Y |
| **TEXAS** | | | | | | | | |
| 1 **Gohmert** | N | N | Y | Y | N | N | N | N |
| 2 **Poe** | N | N | Y | Y | N | N | N | N |
| 3 **Johnson, S.** | N | N | Y | Y | N | N | N | N |
| 4 **Hall** | N | N | Y | Y | N | N | N | N |
| 5 **Hensarling** | N | N | Y | Y | N | N | N | N |
| 6 **Barton** | N | N | Y | Y | N | N | N | N |
| 7 **Culberson** | N | N | Y | Y | N | N | N | N |
| 8 **Brady** | N | N | Y | Y | N | N | N | N |
| 9 Green | N | N | Y | Y | N | N | Y | Y |
| 10 **McCaul** | N | N | Y | Y | N | N | N | N |
| 11 **Conaway** | N | N | Y | Y | N | N | N | N |
| 12 **Granger** | N | N | Y | Y | N | N | N | N |
| 13 **Thornberry** | N | N | Y | Y | N | N | N | N |
| 14 **Paul** | N | N | Y | Y | N | N | N | Y |
| 15 Hinojosa | N | N | N | Y | N | N | N | N |
| 16 Reyes | N | N | Y | Y | N | N | N | N |
| 17 Edwards | N | N | Y | Y | N | N | N | N |
| 18 Jackson-Lee | N | N | Y | Y | N | Y | Y | Y |
| 19 **Neugebauer** | N | N | Y | Y | N | N | N | N |
| 20 Gonzalez | N | N | Y | Y | N | Y | Y | N |
| 21 **Smith** | N | N | Y | Y | N | N | N | N |
| 22 **DeLay** | N | N | Y | Y | N | N | N | N |
| 23 **Bonilla** | N | N | Y | Y | N | N | N | N |
| 24 **Marchant** | N | N | Y | Y | N | N | N | N |
| 25 Doggett | Y | Y | N | N | Y | Y | Y | Y |
| 26 **Burgess** | N | N | Y | Y | N | N | N | N |
| 27 Ortiz | N | N | Y | Y | N | N | N | N |
| 28 Cuellar | N | N | Y | Y | N | N | N | N |
| 29 Green | N | N | Y | Y | N | N | N | Y |
| 30 Johnson, E. | N | Y | Y | Y | Y | Y | Y | Y |
| 31 **Carter** | N | N | Y | Y | N | N | N | N |
| 32 **Sessions** | N | N | Y | Y | N | N | N | N |
| **UTAH** | | | | | | | | |
| 1 **Bishop** | N | N | Y | Y | N | N | N | N |
| 2 Matheson | N | N | N | Y | Y | Y | Y | Y |
| 3 **Cannon** | N | N | Y | Y | N | N | N | N |
| **VERMONT** | | | | | | | | |
| AL *Sanders* | Y | Y | N | N | Y | Y | Y | Y |
| **VIRGINIA** | | | | | | | | |
| 1 **Davis, J.** | N | N | Y | Y | N | N | N | N |
| 2 **Drake** | N | N | Y | Y | N | N | N | N |
| 3 Scott | Y | Y | Y | Y | N | Y | Y | Y |
| 4 **Forbes** | N | N | Y | Y | N | N | N | N |
| 5 **Goode** | N | N | Y | Y | N | N | N | N |
| 6 **Goodlatte** | N | N | Y | Y | N | N | N | N |
| 7 **Cantor** | N | N | Y | Y | N | N | N | N |
| 8 Moran | Y | Y | N | Y | Y | Y | Y | Y |
| 9 Boucher | N | N | Y | Y | N | N | Y | N |
| 10 **Wolf** | N | N | N | N | Y | N | N | N |
| 11 **Davis, T.** | Y | N | N | Y | Y | Y | N | N |
| **WASHINGTON** | | | | | | | | |
| 1 Inslee | Y | Y | N | N | Y | Y | Y | Y |
| 2 Larsen | Y | Y | N | N | Y | Y | Y | Y |
| 3 Baird | Y | Y | N | Y | Y | Y | Y | Y |
| 4 **Hastings** | N | N | Y | Y | N | N | N | N |
| 5 **McMorris** | N | N | Y | Y | N | N | N | N |
| 6 Dicks | Y | Y | N | Y | Y | Y | Y | Y |
| 7 McDermott | Y | ? | N | N | Y | Y | Y | Y |
| 8 **Reichert** | N | N | Y | Y | N | Y | N | N |
| 9 Smith | Y | Y | N | Y | Y | Y | Y | Y |
| **WEST VIRGINIA** | | | | | | | | |
| 1 Mollohan | N | Y | Y | Y | N | N | Y | N |
| 2 **Capito** | N | N | Y | Y | N | N | N | N |
| 3 Rahall | N | Y | Y | Y | N | Y | Y | Y |
| **WISCONSIN** | | | | | | | | |
| 1 **Ryan** | N | N | Y | Y | N | N | N | N |
| 2 Baldwin | Y | Y | N | N | Y | Y | Y | Y |
| 3 Kind | Y | Y | N | N | Y | Y | Y | Y |
| 4 Moore | Y | Y | N | N | Y | Y | Y | Y |
| 5 **Sensenbrenner** | N | N | Y | Y | N | N | Y | Y |
| 6 **Petri** | N | N | N | Y | Y | Y | Y | Y |
| 7 Obey | Y | Y | N | N | Y | Y | Y | Y |
| 8 **Green** | N | N | Y | Y | N | N | N | Y |
| **WYOMING** | | | | | | | | |
| AL **Cubin** | N | N | Y | Y | N | N | N | N |

# IN THE HOUSE | By Vote Number

**125.** **HR 6. Energy Policy/Renewable Fuels.** Engel, D-N.Y., amendment that would make producers of all renewable fuels approved by the Energy Department eligible for grants to build renewable fuel production facilities. Adopted 239-190: R 45-181; D 193-9 (ND 147-4, SD 46-5); I 1-0. April 21, 2005.

**126.** **HR 6. Energy Policy/Gas Company Consolidation.** Israel, D-N.Y., amendment that would direct the comptroller general to study and report to Congress within one year on the impact of the consolidation of gasoline refiners, importers, producers, and wholesalers on the retail gasoline market. Adopted 302-128: R 102-126; D 199-2 (ND 150-0, SD 49-2); I 1-0. April 21, 2005.

**127.** **HR 6. Energy Policy/Mustard Seed Feasibility.** Kucinich, D-Ohio, amendment that would authorize a study by the National Academy of Sciences on the feasibility of mustard seed as a feedstock for biodiesel. Adopted 259-171: R 68-161; D 190-10 (ND 144-5, SD 46-5); I 1-0. April 21, 2005.

**128.** **HR 6. Energy Policy/Royalty Payments.** Grijalva, D-Ariz., amendment that would strike a provision in the bill authorizing the Interior Department to suspend collection of royalties for certain gas wells leased in the deep waters of the Gulf of Mexico. Rejected 203-227: R 29-200; D 173-27 (ND 141-9, SD 32-18); I 1-0. April 21, 2005.

**129.** **HR 6. Energy Policy/MTBE Liability.** Capps, D-Calif., motion to strike a provision in the bill that would provide liability protection for manufacturers of the gasoline additive methyl tertiary butyl ether (MTBE). Motion rejected 213-219: R 25-205; D 187-14 (ND 148-2, SD 39-12); I 1-0. April 21, 2005.

**130.** **HR 6. Energy Policy/Environmental Justice.** Hastings, D-Fla., amendment that would expand the definition of environmental justice, direct each federal agency to establish an office of environmental justice and re-establish the interagency federal working group on environmental justice. Rejected 185-243: R 2-224; D 182-19 (ND 143-7, SD 39-12); I 1-0. April 21, 2005.

**131.** **HR 6. Energy Policy/Natural Gas Facilities.** Castle, R-Del., amendment that would strike a provision in the bill specifying that the Federal Energy Regulatory Commission, instead of state agencies, would have the authority to approve the construction, expansion or operation of any facility that imports or processes natural gas, including liquefied natural gas. Rejected 194-237: R 35-194; D 158-43 (ND 132-18, SD 26-25); I 1-0. April 21, 2005.

**132.** **HR 6. Energy Policy/Passage.** Passage of the bill that would overhaul the nation's energy policy and provide for approximately $8 billion in energy-related tax incentives. It also would authorize the Interior Department to hold a lease sale for oil and gas exploration, development, and production in the Arctic National Wildlife Refuge in Alaska, on a total of about 1.6 million acres. Makers of the gasoline additive methyl tertiary butyl ether would be protected from liability, but would have to cease production of the additive by 2015. The bill would grant the Federal Energy Regulatory Commission jurisdiction over reliability standards for electricity transmission networks and extend daylight-saving time by two months. Passed 249-183: R 208-22; D 41-160 (ND 20-130, SD 21-30); I 0-1. A "yea" was a vote in support of the president's position. April 21, 2005.

ND Northern Democrats, SD Southern Democrats
Southern states: Ala., Ark., Fla., Ga., Ky., La., Miss., N.C., Okla., S.C., Tenn., Texas, Va.

| | 125 | 126 | 127 | 128 | 129 | 130 | 131 | 132 |
|---|---|---|---|---|---|---|---|---|
| **ALABAMA** | | | | | | | | |
| 1 Bonner | N | Y | N | N | N | N | Y |
| 2 Everett | N | Y | N | N | N | N | Y |
| 3 Rogers | N | N | Y | N | N | N | Y |
| 4 Aderholt | N | Y | N | N | N | N | Y |
| 5 Cramer | Y | Y | N | N | N | N | Y |
| 6 Bachus | N | N | N | N | N | N | Y |
| 7 Davis | Y | Y | Y | Y | Y | N | Y |
| **ALASKA** | | | | | | | | |
| AL Young | N | N | N | N | N | N | Y |
| **ARIZONA** | | | | | | | | |
| 1 Renzi | N | Y | Y | N | N | N | Y |
| 2 Franks | ? | N | N | N | N | N | Y |
| 3 Shadegg | N | N | N | N | N | N | Y |
| 4 Pastor | Y | Y | Y | Y | Y | Y | N |
| 5 Hayworth | N | Y | N | N | N | N | Y |
| 6 Flake | N | N | N | N | N | N | N |
| 7 Grijalva | Y | Y | Y | Y | Y | Y | N |
| 8 Kolbe | N | Y | N | N | N | N | Y |
| **ARKANSAS** | | | | | | | | |
| 1 Berry | Y | Y | Y | Y | Y | N | N |
| 2 Snyder | Y | Y | Y | Y | Y | N | N |
| 3 Boozman | N | N | N | N | N | N | Y |
| 4 Ross | Y | Y | N | N | Y | N | Y |
| **CALIFORNIA** | | | | | | | | |
| 1 Thompson | Y | Y | N | Y | Y | Y | N |
| 2 Herger | N | N | N | N | N | N | Y |
| 3 Lungren | N | Y | N | N | N | N | Y |
| 4 Doolittle | N | N | Y | N | N | N | Y |
| 5 Matsui, D. | Y | Y | Y | Y | Y | Y | N |
| 6 Woolsey | Y | Y | Y | Y | Y | Y | N |
| 7 Miller, George | Y | Y | Y | Y | Y | Y | N |
| 8 Pelosi | Y | Y | Y | Y | Y | Y | N |
| 9 Lee | Y | Y | Y | Y | Y | Y | N |
| 10 Tauscher | Y | Y | Y | Y | Y | Y | N |
| 11 Pombo | N | Y | N | N | N | N | Y |
| 12 Lantos | Y | Y | Y | Y | Y | Y | N |
| 13 Stark | Y | Y | Y | Y | Y | Y | N |
| 14 Eshoo | Y | Y | Y | Y | Y | Y | N |
| 15 Honda | Y | Y | Y | Y | Y | Y | N |
| 16 Lofgren | Y | Y | N | Y | Y | Y | N |
| 17 Farr | Y | Y | Y | Y | Y | Y | N |
| 18 Cardoza | Y | Y | N | Y | N | Y | N |
| 19 Radanovich | N | N | N | N | N | N | Y |
| 20 Costa | N | Y | N | Y | N | Y | N |
| 21 Nunes | N | N | N | N | N | N | Y |
| 22 Thomas | N | N | N | N | N | N | Y |
| 23 Capps | Y | Y | Y | Y | Y | Y | N |
| 24 Gallegly | N | N | N | N | N | N | Y |
| 25 McKeon | N | N | N | N | N | N | Y |
| 26 Dreier | N | N | N | N | N | N | Y |
| 27 Sherman | Y | Y | Y | Y | Y | Y | N |
| 28 Berman | Y | Y | ? | Y | Y | Y | N |
| 29 Schiff | Y | Y | Y | Y | Y | Y | N |
| 30 Waxman | Y | Y | Y | Y | Y | Y | N |
| 31 Becerra | Y | Y | Y | Y | Y | Y | N |
| 32 Solis | Y | Y | Y | Y | Y | Y | N |
| 33 Watson | Y | Y | Y | Y | Y | Y | N |
| 34 Roybal-Allard | Y | Y | Y | Y | Y | Y | N |
| 35 Waters | Y | Y | Y | Y | Y | Y | N |
| 36 Harman | Y | Y | Y | Y | Y | Y | N |
| 37 Millender-McD. | Y | Y | Y | Y | Y | Y | N |
| 38 Napolitano | Y | Y | Y | Y | Y | Y | N |
| 39 Sánchez, Linda | Y | Y | Y | Y | Y | Y | N |
| 40 Royce | N | Y | N | N | N | N | N |
| 41 Lewis | N | N | N | N | N | N | Y |
| 42 Miller, Gary | N | N | N | N | N | N | Y |
| 43 Baca | Y | Y | Y | Y | Y | Y | Y |
| 44 Calvert | N | N | N | N | N | Y | Y |
| 45 Bono | Y | Y | N | N | N | N | Y |
| 46 Rohrabacher | N | Y | N | N | N | Y | Y |
| 47 Sanchez, Loretta | Y | Y | Y | Y | Y | Y | N |
| 48 Cox | N | Y | N | N | N | N | Y |
| 49 Issa | Y | Y | N | N | N | N | Y |
| **COLORADO** | | | | | | | | |
| 1 DeGette | Y | Y | Y | Y | Y | Y | N |
| 2 Udall | Y | Y | Y | Y | Y | Y | N |
| 3 Salazar | Y | Y | Y | Y | Y | Y | N |
| 4 Musgrave | N | N | N | N | N | N | Y |
| 5 Hefley | N | N | N | N | N | N | Y |
| 6 Tancredo | N | Y | N | N | N | N | Y |
| 7 Beauprez | N | N | N | N | N | N | Y |
| **CONNECTICUT** | | | | | | | | |
| 1 Larson | Y | Y | Y | Y | Y | Y | N |
| 2 Simmons | Y | Y | Y | Y | N | Y | Y |
| 3 DeLauro | Y | Y | Y | Y | Y | Y | N |
| 4 Shays | Y | Y | N | Y | + | Y | N |
| 5 Johnson | Y | Y | Y | Y | N | Y | N |
| **DELAWARE** | | | | | | | | |
| AL Castle | Y | Y | N | Y | Y | N | Y | N |
| **FLORIDA** | | | | | | | | |
| 1 Miller | Y | N | N | N | N | N | Y |
| 2 Boyd | N | Y | Y | Y | Y | Y | N |
| 3 Brown | Y | Y | Y | ? | Y | Y | N |
| 4 Crenshaw | N | N | N | N | N | N | Y |
| 5 Brown-Waite | Y | Y | N | N | N | N | Y |
| 6 Stearns | N | Y | N | N | N | N | Y |
| 7 Mica | N | N | N | ? | N | N | Y |
| 8 Keller | N | N | N | ? | N | Y | Y |
| 9 Bilirakis | N | Y | Y | N | N | N | Y |
| 10 Young | ? | Y | Y | N | N | N | Y |
| 11 Davis | Y | Y | Y | N | Y | Y | N |
| 12 Putnam | N | Y | N | N | N | N | Y |
| 13 Harris | Y | Y | N | N | N | N | Y |
| 14 Mack | N | N | N | N | N | N | Y |
| 15 Weldon | N | N | N | N | N | N | Y |
| 16 Foley | N | N | N | N | N | N | Y |
| 17 Meek | Y | Y | Y | Y | Y | Y | N |
| 18 Ros-Lehtinen | N | N | N | N | N | N | Y |
| 19 Wexler | Y | Y | Y | Y | Y | Y | N |
| 20 Wasserman-Schultz | Y | Y | Y | Y | Y | Y | N |
| 21 Diaz-Balart, L. | N | N | N | N | N | N | Y |
| 22 Shaw | N | Y | N | N | N | N | Y |
| 23 Hastings | Y | Y | Y | Y | Y | Y | N |
| 24 Feeney | N | N | N | N | N | N | Y |
| 25 Diaz-Balart, M. | N | N | N | N | N | N | Y |
| **GEORGIA** | | | | | | | | |
| 1 Kingston | N | Y | N | N | N | N | Y |
| 2 Bishop | N | Y | N | Y | N | Y | Y |
| 3 Marshall | N | Y | Y | Y | N | N | N |
| 4 McKinney | Y | Y | Y | Y | Y | N | N |
| 5 Lewis | Y | Y | Y | Y | Y | Y | N |
| 6 Price | N | N | N | N | N | N | Y |
| 7 Linder | N | N | N | N | N | N | Y |
| 8 Westmoreland | N | N | N | N | N | N | Y |
| 9 Norwood | N | N | N | N | N | N | Y |
| 10 Deal | N | N | N | N | N | N | Y |
| 11 Gingrey | N | Y | N | N | N | N | Y |
| 12 Barrow | Y | Y | Y | Y | Y | Y | Y |
| 13 Scott | N | Y | Y | N | Y | N | Y |
| **HAWAII** | | | | | | | | |
| 1 Abercrombie | Y | Y | Y | N | Y | Y | N |
| 2 Case | Y | Y | Y | Y | N | Y | N |
| **IDAHO** | | | | | | | | |
| 1 Otter | N | N | Y | N | N | N | Y |
| 2 Simpson | N | N | Y | N | N | N | Y |
| **ILLINOIS** | | | | | | | | |
| 1 Rush | Y | Y | Y | Y | Y | N | Y |
| 2 Jackson | Y | Y | Y | Y | Y | Y | N |
| 3 Lipinski | Y | Y | Y | Y | Y | Y | Y |
| 4 Gutierrez | Y | Y | Y | Y | Y | Y | Y |
| 5 Emanuel | Y | Y | Y | Y | Y | Y | N |
| 6 Hyde | N | N | N | N | N | N | Y |
| 7 Davis | Y | Y | Y | Y | Y | Y | N |
| 8 Bean | Y | Y | Y | Y | Y | Y | N |
| 9 Schakowsky | Y | Y | Y | Y | Y | Y | N |
| 10 Kirk | Y | Y | Y | Y | Y | Y | N |
| 11 Weller | N | N | Y | N | N | N | Y |
| 12 Costello | Y | Y | Y | Y | Y | Y | Y |
| **50 Cunningham** | Y | N | Y | N | N | N | Y |
| **51 Filner** | Y | Y | Y | Y | Y | Y | N |
| **52 Hunter** | N | Y | Y | N | N | N | Y |
| **53 Davis** | Y | Y | Y | Y | Y | Y | N |

| KEY | Republicans | Democrats | *Independents* |
|---|---|---|---|

| Y | Voted for (yea) | X | Paired against | C | Voted "present" to avoid possible conflict of interest |
|---|---|---|---|---|---|
| # | Paired for | – | Announced against | | |
| + | Announced for | P | Voted "present" | ? | Did not vote or otherwise make a position known |
| N | Voted against (nay) | | | | |

| | 125 | 126 | 127 | 128 | 129 | 130 | 131 | 132 |
|---|---|---|---|---|---|---|---|---|
| 13 **Biggert** | N | N | N | N | N | N | N | Y |
| 14 **Hastert** | | | | | N | | | Y |
| 15 **Johnson** | N | Y | N | Y | Y | Y | N | Y |
| 16 **Manzullo** | N | Y | Y | N | N | N | N | Y |
| 17 Evans | Y | Y | Y | Y | Y | Y | Y | N |
| 18 **LaHood** | Y | Y | Y | Y | N | N | N | Y |
| 19 **Shimkus** | N | Y | Y | N | N | N | N | Y |
| **INDIANA** | | | | | | | | |
| 1 Visclosky | Y | Y | Y | Y | Y | Y | N | Y |
| 2 **Chocola** | N | Y | N | N | N | N | N | Y |
| 3 **Souder** | N | N | N | N | N | N | ? | Y |
| 4 **Buyer** | N | N | N | N | N | N | N | Y |
| 5 **Burton** | N | N | Y | N | N | N | N | Y |
| 6 **Pence** | N | N | N | N | N | N | N | Y |
| 7 Carson | Y | Y | Y | N | Y | Y | Y | N |
| 8 **Hostettler** | N | Y | N | N | N | N | N | Y |
| 9 **Sodrel** | N | N | N | N | N | N | N | Y |
| **IOWA** | | | | | | | | |
| 1 **Nussle** | N | N | N | N | N | N | N | Y |
| 2 **Leach** | N | Y | Y | Y | Y | N | N | N |
| 3 Boswell | Y | Y | Y | N | Y | Y | N | Y |
| 4 **Latham** | N | N | N | N | N | N | N | Y |
| 5 **King** | N | N | N | N | N | N | N | Y |
| **KANSAS** | | | | | | | | |
| 1 **Moran** | N | Y | N | N | N | N | N | Y |
| 2 **Ryun** | N | N | N | N | N | N | N | Y |
| 3 Moore | Y | Y | Y | Y | Y | Y | Y | N |
| 4 **Tiahrt** | N | N | Y | N | N | N | N | Y |
| **KENTUCKY** | | | | | | | | |
| 1 **Whitfield** | N | N | N | N | N | N | N | Y |
| 2 **Lewis** | N | Y | N | N | N | N | N | Y |
| 3 **Northup** | N | Y | N | N | N | N | N | Y |
| 4 **Davis** | N | N | Y | N | N | N | N | Y |
| 5 **Rogers** | N | N | N | N | N | N | N | Y |
| 6 Chandler | Y | Y | Y | Y | Y | Y | Y | N |
| **LOUISIANA** | | | | | | | | |
| 1 **Jindal** | N | N | N | N | N | N | N | Y |
| 2 Jefferson | Y | Y | Y | N | Y | Y | N | Y |
| 3 Melancon | Y | Y | Y | N | N | Y | N | Y |
| 4 **McCrery** | N | N | N | N | N | N | N | Y |
| 5 **Alexander** | N | N | N | N | N | N | N | Y |
| 6 **Baker** | N | N | N | N | N | N | N | Y |
| 7 **Boustany** | N | N | N | N | N | N | N | Y |
| **MAINE** | | | | | | | | |
| 1 Allen | Y | Y | Y | Y | Y | Y | Y | N |
| 2 Michaud | Y | Y | Y | Y | Y | Y | Y | N |
| **MARYLAND** | | | | | | | | |
| 1 **Gilchrest** | Y | Y | Y | N | Y | N | Y | N |
| 2 Ruppersberger | Y | Y | Y | Y | Y | Y | Y | N |
| 3 Cardin | Y | Y | Y | Y | Y | Y | Y | N |
| 4 Wynn | Y | Y | Y | Y | Y | Y | N | Y |
| 5 Hoyer | Y | Y | Y | Y | Y | Y | Y | N |
| 6 **Bartlett** | Y | Y | Y | N | N | N | N | N |
| 7 Cummings | Y | Y | Y | Y | Y | Y | N | N |
| 8 Van Hollen | Y | Y | Y | Y | Y | Y | Y | N |
| **MASSACHUSETTS** | | | | | | | | |
| 1 Olver | Y | Y | Y | Y | Y | Y | Y | N |
| 2 Neal | Y | Y | Y | Y | Y | Y | Y | N |
| 3 McGovern | Y | Y | Y | Y | Y | Y | Y | N |
| 4 Frank | Y | Y | Y | Y | Y | Y | Y | N |
| 5 Meehan | Y | Y | Y | Y | Y | Y | Y | N |
| 6 Tierney | Y | Y | Y | Y | Y | Y | Y | N |
| 7 Markey | Y | Y | Y | Y | Y | Y | Y | N |
| 8 Capuano | Y | Y | N | Y | Y | Y | Y | N |
| 9 Lynch | Y | Y | N | Y | Y | Y | Y | N |
| 10 Delahunt | Y | Y | Y | Y | Y | Y | Y | N |
| **MICHIGAN** | | | | | | | | |
| 1 Stupak | N | Y | Y | Y | Y | Y | Y | N |
| 2 **Hoekstra** | Y | Y | N | N | N | N | N | Y |
| 3 **Ehlers** | N | Y | N | Y | N | N | Y | N |
| 4 **Camp** | N | Y | N | N | N | N | N | Y |
| 5 Kildee | Y | Y | Y | Y | Y | Y | Y | N |
| 6 **Upton** | N | Y | Y | Y | N | N | N | Y |
| 7 **Schwarz** | N | Y | Y | N | N | N | N | N |
| 8 **Rogers** | Y | Y | Y | N | N | N | N | Y |
| 9 **Knollenberg** | N | N | N | N | N | N | N | Y |
| 10 **Miller** | N | Y | Y | N | N | N | N | Y |
| 11 **McCotter** | Y | Y | Y | N | N | N | N | Y |
| 12 Levin | Y | Y | Y | Y | Y | Y | Y | N |
| 13 Kilpatrick | Y | Y | Y | Y | Y | Y | N | N |
| 14 Conyers | Y | Y | Y | Y | Y | Y | Y | N |
| 15 Dingell | Y | Y | Y | Y | Y | Y | Y | N |

| | 125 | 126 | 127 | 128 | 129 | 130 | 131 | 132 |
|---|---|---|---|---|---|---|---|---|
| **MINNESOTA** | | | | | | | | |
| 1 **Gutknecht** | N | Y | N | N | N | N | Y | Y |
| 2 **Kline** | N | N | N | N | N | N | N | Y |
| 3 **Ramstad** | Y | Y | Y | Y | Y | N | Y | Y |
| 4 McCollum | Y | Y | Y | Y | Y | Y | Y | N |
| 5 Sabo | Y | Y | Y | Y | Y | Y | Y | N |
| 6 **Kennedy** | N | Y | Y | Y | N | N | N | Y |
| 7 Peterson | Y | Y | Y | N | Y | N | N | Y |
| 8 Oberstar | Y | Y | Y | Y | Y | Y | Y | N |
| **MISSISSIPPI** | | | | | | | | |
| 1 **Wicker** | Y | Y | N | N | N | N | N | Y |
| 2 Thompson | Y | Y | Y | Y | Y | Y | Y | N |
| 3 **Pickering** | N | Y | N | N | N | N | N | Y |
| 4 Taylor | Y | Y | Y | Y | Y | N | Y | N |
| **MISSOURI** | | | | | | | | |
| 1 Clay | Y | Y | Y | Y | Y | Y | Y | N |
| 2 **Akin** | N | N | N | N | N | N | N | Y |
| 3 Carnahan | Y | Y | Y | Y | Y | N | Y | N |
| 4 Skelton | Y | Y | Y | Y | Y | N | N | Y |
| 5 Cleaver | Y | Y | Y | Y | Y | Y | Y | N |
| 6 **Graves** | Y | N | N | N | N | N | N | Y |
| 7 **Blunt** | N | N | N | N | N | N | N | Y |
| 8 **Emerson** | N | Y | Y | N | N | N | Y | Y |
| 9 **Hulshof** | N | Y | Y | N | N | N | N | Y |
| **MONTANA** | | | | | | | | |
| AL **Rehberg** | N | N | N | N | N | N | N | Y |
| **NEBRASKA** | | | | | | | | |
| 1 **Fortenberry** | N | Y | Y | N | N | N | N | Y |
| 2 **Terry** | N | N | N | N | N | N | N | Y |
| 3 **Osborne** | N | N | Y | N | N | N | N | Y |
| **NEVADA** | | | | | | | | |
| 1 Berkley | Y | Y | Y | Y | Y | Y | Y | N |
| 2 **Gibbons** | N | Y | Y | N | N | N | N | Y |
| 3 **Porter** | N | Y | Y | N | N | N | N | Y |
| **NEW HAMPSHIRE** | | | | | | | | |
| 1 **Bradley** | N | Y | N | Y | Y | N | N | N |
| 2 **Bass** | N | Y | N | Y | N | N | N | Y |
| **NEW JERSEY** | | | | | | | | |
| 1 Andrews | Y | Y | Y | Y | Y | Y | Y | N |
| 2 **LoBiondo** | Y | Y | Y | Y | Y | N | Y | N |
| 3 **Saxton** | Y | Y | Y | Y | Y | N | Y | N |
| 4 **Smith** | Y | Y | Y | Y | Y | N | Y | N |
| 5 **Garrett** | N | N | N | N | N | N | N | Y |
| 6 Pallone | Y | Y | Y | Y | Y | Y | Y | N |
| 7 **Ferguson** | Y | N | Y | Y | N | N | N | Y |
| 8 Pascrell | Y | Y | Y | Y | Y | Y | Y | N |
| 9 Rothman | Y | Y | Y | Y | Y | Y | Y | N |
| 10 Payne | Y | Y | Y | Y | Y | Y | Y | N |
| 11 **Frelinghuysen** | Y | N | Y | Y | Y | N | Y | Y |
| 12 Holt | Y | Y | Y | Y | Y | Y | Y | N |
| 13 Menendez | Y | Y | Y | Y | Y | Y | Y | N |
| **NEW MEXICO** | | | | | | | | |
| 1 **Wilson** | N | Y | Y | N | N | Y | N | Y |
| 2 **Pearce** | N | N | N | N | N | N | N | Y |
| 3 Udall | Y | Y | Y | Y | Y | Y | Y | N |
| **NEW YORK** | | | | | | | | |
| 1 Bishop | Y | Y | Y | Y | Y | Y | Y | N |
| 2 Israel | Y | Y | Y | Y | Y | Y | Y | N |
| 3 **King** | Y | Y | N | N | N | N | Y | Y |
| 4 McCarthy | Y | Y | Y | Y | Y | Y | Y | N |
| 5 Ackerman | Y | Y | Y | Y | Y | Y | Y | N |
| 6 Meeks | Y | Y | Y | Y | Y | Y | Y | Y |
| 7 Crowley | Y | Y | Y | Y | Y | Y | Y | N |
| 8 Nadler | Y | Y | Y | Y | Y | Y | Y | N |
| 9 Weiner | Y | Y | Y | Y | Y | Y | Y | N |
| 10 Towns | Y | Y | Y | N | Y | Y | N | Y |
| 11 Owens | Y | Y | Y | Y | Y | Y | N | N |
| 12 Velázquez | Y | Y | ? | ? | ? | ? | ? | ? |
| 13 **Fossella** | Y | Y | ? | N | N | N | Y | Y |
| 14 Maloney | Y | Y | Y | Y | Y | Y | Y | N |
| 15 Rangel | Y | Y | Y | Y | Y | Y | Y | N |
| 16 Serrano | Y | Y | Y | Y | Y | Y | Y | N |
| 17 Engel | Y | Y | Y | Y | Y | Y | Y | N |
| 18 Lowey | Y | Y | Y | Y | Y | Y | Y | N |
| 19 **Kelly** | ? | ? | ? | ? | ? | ? | ? | ? |
| 20 **Sweeney** | Y | Y | Y | N | Y | N | N | Y |
| 21 McNulty | Y | Y | Y | Y | Y | Y | Y | N |
| 22 Hinchey | Y | Y | Y | Y | Y | Y | Y | N |
| 23 **McHugh** | Y | Y | Y | N | N | N | N | Y |
| 24 **Boehlert** | Y | Y | Y | Y | Y | N | Y | N |
| 25 **Walsh** | Y | N | N | N | N | N | N | Y |
| 26 **Reynolds** | Y | Y | N | N | N | N | N | Y |
| 27 Higgins | Y | Y | Y | Y | Y | Y | Y | N |
| 28 Slaughter | Y | Y | Y | Y | Y | Y | Y | N |
| 29 **Kuhl** | N | N | N | N | N | N | N | Y |

| | 125 | 126 | 127 | 128 | 129 | 130 | 131 | 132 |
|---|---|---|---|---|---|---|---|---|
| **NORTH CAROLINA** | | | | | | | | |
| 1 Butterfield | Y | Y | Y | Y | Y | Y | Y | N |
| 2 Etheridge | Y | Y | Y | Y | Y | Y | Y | N |
| 3 **Jones** | N | Y | N | N | N | N | Y | N |
| 4 Price | Y | Y | Y | Y | Y | Y | Y | N |
| 5 **Foxx** | N | N | N | N | N | N | N | Y |
| 6 **Coble** | N | N | Y | N | N | N | N | Y |
| 7 McIntyre | Y | Y | Y | Y | Y | Y | N | N |
| 8 **Hayes** | N | N | N | N | N | N | N | Y |
| 9 **Myrick** | N | N | N | N | N | N | N | Y |
| 10 **McHenry** | N | N | N | N | N | N | N | Y |
| 11 **Taylor** | N | N | Y | N | N | N | N | Y |
| 12 Watt | Y | Y | Y | Y | Y | Y | Y | N |
| 13 Miller | Y | Y | Y | Y | Y | Y | Y | N |
| **NORTH DAKOTA** | | | | | | | | |
| AL Pomeroy | N | Y | Y | Y | Y | N | N | Y |
| **OHIO** | | | | | | | | |
| 1 **Chabot** | N | Y | N | N | N | N | N | Y |
| 2 **Portman** | ? | ? | Y | N | N | N | N | Y |
| 3 **Turner** | N | Y | N | N | N | N | N | Y |
| 4 **Oxley** | N | ? | N | N | N | N | N | Y |
| 5 **Gillmor** | N | N | N | N | N | N | N | Y |
| 6 Strickland | N | Y | Y | Y | Y | Y | Y | N |
| 7 **Hobson** | N | Y | N | N | N | N | N | Y |
| 8 **Boehner** | N | N | N | N | N | N | N | Y |
| 9 Kaptur | Y | Y | Y | Y | Y | Y | Y | N |
| 10 Kucinich | Y | Y | Y | Y | Y | Y | Y | N |
| 11 Jones | Y | Y | Y | Y | Y | Y | N | N |
| 12 **Tiberi** | N | Y | N | N | N | N | N | Y |
| 13 Brown | Y | Y | Y | Y | Y | Y | Y | N |
| 14 **LaTourette** | Y | Y | Y | N | N | N | N | Y |
| 15 **Pryce** | N | Y | N | N | N | N | N | Y |
| 16 **Regula** | Y | Y | Y | N | N | N | N | Y |
| 17 Ryan | Y | Y | Y | Y | Y | Y | Y | N |
| 18 **Ney** | Y | Y | N | N | N | N | N | Y |
| **OKLAHOMA** | | | | | | | | |
| 1 **Sullivan** | N | N | Y | N | N | N | N | Y |
| 2 Boren | Y | N | N | N | N | N | N | Y |
| 3 **Lucas** | N | N | N | N | N | N | N | Y |
| 4 **Cole** | N | N | N | N | N | N | N | Y |
| 5 **Istook** | N | N | N | N | N | N | N | Y |
| **OREGON** | | | | | | | | |
| 1 Wu | Y | Y | Y | Y | Y | Y | Y | N |
| 2 **Walden** | N | Y | Y | N | N | N | N | Y |
| 3 Blumenauer | Y | Y | Y | Y | Y | Y | Y | N |
| 4 DeFazio | Y | Y | Y | Y | Y | Y | Y | N |
| 5 Hooley | Y | Y | Y | Y | Y | Y | Y | N |
| **PENNSYLVANIA** | | | | | | | | |
| 1 Brady | Y | Y | Y | Y | Y | Y | Y | Y |
| 2 Fattah | Y | Y | Y | Y | Y | Y | Y | N |
| 3 **English** | Y | Y | N | N | N | ? | N | Y |
| 4 **Hart** | N | N | N | N | N | N | N | Y |
| 5 **Peterson** | N | Y | N | N | N | N | N | Y |
| 6 **Gerlach** | Y | Y | Y | Y | N | N | Y | N |
| 7 **Weldon** | Y | Y | Y | Y | Y | N | Y | Y |
| 8 **Fitzpatrick** | Y | Y | Y | Y | Y | N | N | N |
| 9 **Shuster** | N | N | Y | N | N | N | N | Y |
| 10 **Sherwood** | N | Y | N | N | N | N | N | Y |
| 11 Kanjorski | Y | Y | Y | Y | Y | Y | N | N |
| 12 Murtha | Y | Y | Y | Y | Y | Y | N | Y |
| 13 Schwartz | Y | Y | Y | Y | Y | Y | Y | N |
| 14 Doyle | Y | Y | Y | Y | Y | Y | N | Y |
| 15 **Dent** | N | Y | Y | N | N | N | N | Y |
| 16 **Pitts** | N | N | N | N | N | N | N | Y |
| 17 Holden | Y | Y | Y | Y | Y | Y | N | Y |
| 18 **Murphy** | N | Y | Y | N | N | N | N | Y |
| 19 **Platts** | Y | Y | Y | Y | Y | N | Y | Y |
| **RHODE ISLAND** | | | | | | | | |
| 1 Kennedy | Y | Y | Y | Y | Y | Y | Y | N |
| 2 Langevin | Y | Y | Y | Y | Y | Y | Y | N |
| **SOUTH CAROLINA** | | | | | | | | |
| 1 **Brown** | N | N | N | N | N | N | Y | Y |
| 2 **Wilson** | N | N | N | N | N | N | N | Y |
| 3 **Barrett** | N | N | N | N | N | N | N | Y |
| 4 **Inglis** | N | N | N | Y | N | N | N | N |
| 5 Spratt | Y | Y | Y | Y | Y | Y | Y | N |
| 6 Clyburn | Y | Y | Y | Y | Y | Y | Y | N |
| **SOUTH DAKOTA** | | | | | | | | |
| AL Herseth | Y | Y | Y | Y | Y | Y | N | Y |
| **TENNESSEE** | | | | | | | | |
| 1 **Jenkins** | N | N | N | N | N | N | Y | Y |
| 2 **Duncan** | N | N | N | N | N | N | N | Y |

| | 125 | 126 | 127 | 128 | 129 | 130 | 131 | 132 |
|---|---|---|---|---|---|---|---|---|
| 3 **Wamp** | Y | N | Y | N | N | N | N | N |
| 4 Davis | Y | Y | Y | Y | Y | N | N | Y |
| 5 Cooper | Y | Y | N | Y | Y | N | N | N |
| 6 Gordon | Y | Y | Y | Y | Y | N | N | Y |
| 7 **Blackburn** | N | N | N | N | N | N | N | Y |
| 8 Tanner | Y | Y | Y | Y | Y | N | Y | N |
| 9 Ford | Y | Y | Y | Y | Y | Y | Y | Y |
| **TEXAS** | | | | | | | | |
| 1 **Gohmert** | Y | N | N | N | N | N | N | Y |
| 2 **Poe** | N | N | N | N | N | N | N | Y |
| 3 **Johnson, S.** | N | N | N | N | N | N | N | Y |
| 4 **Hall** | N | N | Y | N | N | ? | N | Y |
| 5 **Hensarling** | N | N | N | N | N | N | N | Y |
| 6 **Barton** | N | N | Y | N | N | N | N | Y |
| 7 **Culberson** | N | N | N | N | N | N | N | Y |
| 8 **Brady** | N | N | Y | N | N | N | N | Y |
| 9 Green | Y | Y | Y | N | N | Y | N | Y |
| 10 **McCaul** | Y | N | N | N | N | N | N | Y |
| 11 **Conaway** | N | N | N | N | N | N | N | Y |
| 12 **Granger** | N | N | N | N | N | N | N | Y |
| 13 **Thornberry** | N | N | N | N | N | N | N | Y |
| 14 **Paul** | N | N | N | N | N | N | Y | N |
| 15 Hinojosa | Y | Y | Y | N | N | Y | N | Y |
| 16 Reyes | Y | Y | Y | N | N | Y | N | Y |
| 17 Edwards | Y | Y | Y | N | N | N | N | Y |
| 18 Jackson-Lee | Y | Y | Y | N | N | Y | N | Y |
| 19 **Neugebauer** | N | N | N | N | N | N | N | Y |
| 20 Gonzalez | Y | Y | Y | N | N | Y | N | Y |
| 21 **Smith** | N | N | N | N | N | N | N | Y |
| 22 **DeLay** | N | N | Y | N | N | N | N | Y |
| 23 **Bonilla** | N | N | N | N | N | N | N | Y |
| 24 **Marchant** | N | N | N | N | N | N | N | Y |
| 25 Doggett | Y | Y | N | Y | Y | Y | Y | N |
| 26 **Burgess** | N | N | Y | N | N | N | N | Y |
| 27 Ortiz | Y | Y | Y | N | N | Y | N | Y |
| 28 Cuellar | Y | N | Y | N | N | Y | N | Y |
| 29 Green | N | Y | Y | N | N | Y | N | Y |
| 30 Johnson, E. | Y | Y | Y | Y | Y | Y | Y | N |
| 31 **Carter** | N | N | N | N | N | N | N | Y |
| 32 **Sessions** | N | N | N | N | N | N | N | ? |
| **UTAH** | | | | | | | | |
| 1 **Bishop** | N | N | N | N | N | N | N | Y |
| 2 Matheson | Y | Y | N | N | Y | Y | N | Y |
| 3 **Cannon** | ? | N | N | N | N | N | N | Y |
| **VERMONT** | | | | | | | | |
| AL *Sanders* | Y | Y | Y | Y | Y | Y | Y | N |
| **VIRGINIA** | | | | | | | | |
| 1 **Davis, J.** | N | Y | N | N | N | N | Y | Y |
| 2 **Drake** | N | Y | N | N | N | N | N | Y |
| 3 Scott | Y | Y | Y | Y | Y | Y | Y | N |
| 4 **Forbes** | N | Y | N | N | N | N | N | Y |
| 5 **Goode** | N | Y | N | N | Y | N | N | Y |
| 6 **Goodlatte** | N | Y | N | N | N | N | N | Y |
| 7 **Cantor** | N | N | N | N | N | N | N | Y |
| 8 Moran | Y | Y | Y | Y | Y | Y | N | N |
| 9 Boucher | Y | Y | Y | N | Y | N | N | Y |
| 10 **Wolf** | N | Y | N | N | Y | N | Y | Y |
| 11 **Davis, T.** | N | Y | N | N | Y | N | N | Y |
| **WASHINGTON** | | | | | | | | |
| 1 Inslee | Y | Y | Y | Y | Y | Y | Y | N |
| 2 Larsen | Y | Y | Y | Y | Y | Y | Y | N |
| 3 Baird | Y | ? | Y | Y | Y | Y | Y | N |
| 4 **Hastings** | N | N | N | N | N | N | N | Y |
| 5 **McMorris** | N | N | N | N | N | N | N | Y |
| 6 Dicks | Y | Y | Y | Y | Y | Y | Y | N |
| 7 McDermott | Y | Y | Y | Y | Y | Y | Y | N |
| 8 **Reichert** | N | N | N | N | Y | N | N | Y |
| 9 Smith | Y | Y | Y | Y | Y | Y | Y | N |
| **WEST VIRGINIA** | | | | | | | | |
| 1 Mollohan | Y | Y | Y | N | Y | Y | Y | Y |
| 2 **Capito** | Y | Y | N | N | N | N | N | Y |
| 3 Rahall | Y | Y | Y | Y | Y | Y | Y | N |
| **WISCONSIN** | | | | | | | | |
| 1 **Ryan** | N | N | N | N | Y | N | N | Y |
| 2 Baldwin | Y | Y | Y | Y | Y | Y | Y | N |
| 3 Kind | Y | Y | Y | Y | Y | Y | Y | N |
| 4 Moore | Y | Y | Y | Y | Y | Y | Y | N |
| 5 **Sensenbrenner** | N | Y | N | Y | Y | N | N | Y |
| 6 **Petri** | N | Y | N | Y | N | N | N | Y |
| 7 Obey | Y | Y | Y | Y | Y | Y | Y | N |
| 8 **Green** | N | Y | N | Y | Y | N | N | Y |
| **WYOMING** | | | | | | | | |
| AL **Cubin** | N | N | N | N | N | ? | N | Y |

# IN THE HOUSE | By Vote Number

**133.** **HR 1268. Fiscal 2005 Supplemental Appropriations/Motion to Instruct.** Obey, D-Wis., motion to instruct House conferees to insist on a conference report that would include the highest possible funding for additional border patrol agents and increase funds for other immigration and law-enforcement programs, and accept the Senate provision that future funding for military operations in Afghanistan and Iraq be included in the president's annual budget. Motion agreed to 417-4: R 220-4; D 196-0 (ND 146-0, SD 50-0); I 1-0. April 26, 2005.

**134.** **H Con Res 95. Fiscal 2006 Budget Resolution/Motion to Instruct.** Herseth, D-S.D., motion to instruct House conferees to insist on a conference report that would reject cuts to the Medicaid program and instruct conferees to include a $1.5 million reserve fund for the creation of a bipartisan Medicaid commission. Motion agreed to 348-72: R 152-72; D 195-0 (ND 145-0, SD 50-0); I 1-0. April 26, 2005.

**135.** **Procedural Motion/Journal.** Approval of the House Journal of Tuesday, April 26, 2005. Approved 371-47: R 213-12; D 157-35 (ND 115-28, SD 42-7); I 1-0. April 27, 2005.

**136.** **HR 902. Commemorative Coins/Passage.** Castle, R-Del., motion to suspend the rules and pass the bill that would authorize the U.S. Mint to issue a new $1 coin to commemorate U.S. presidents and a series of $10 gold bullion coins to honor first ladies. It also would authorize the Mint to redesign the back of the penny that will be issued in 2009 to commemorate the 200th anniversary of President Abraham Lincoln's birth. Motion agreed to 422-6: R 226-2; D 195-4 (ND 145-4, SD 50-0); I 1-0. A two-thirds majority of those present and voting (286 in this case) is required for passage under suspension of the rules. April 27, 2005.

**137.** **H Con Res 81. Cuba Human Rights Condemnation/Adoption.** Smith, R-N.J., motion to suspend the rules and adopt the concurrent resolution that would condemn the arrest of more than 75 journalists, labor union organizers, civic leaders, librarians and human rights activists as Cuban political prisoners in March 2003. Motion agreed to 398-27: R 226-1; D 171-26 (ND 125-23, SD 46-3); I 1-0. A two-thirds majority of those present and voting (284 in this case) is required for passage under suspension of the rules. April 27, 2005.

**138.** **H Res 235. Small Business Bill of Rights/Previous Question.** Capito, R-W.Va., motion to order the previous question (thus ending debate and possibility of amendment) on adoption of the rule (H Res 235) to provide for House floor consideration of the bill that would express the sense of the House that small businesses should have a bill of rights. Motion agreed to 228-201: R 228-0; D 0-200 (ND 0-150, SD 0-50); I 0-1. (Subsequently, the rule was adopted by voice vote.) April 27, 2005.

| | 133 | 134 | 135 | 136 | 137 | 138 |
|---|---|---|---|---|---|---|
| **ALABAMA** | | | | | | |
| 1 Bonner | Y | Y | Y | Y | Y | Y |
| 2 Everett | Y | Y | Y | Y | Y | Y |
| 3 Rogers | Y | Y | Y | Y | Y | Y |
| 4 Aderholt | Y | Y | Y | Y | Y | Y |
| 5 Cramer | Y | Y | Y | Y | Y | N |
| 6 Bachus | Y | Y | Y | Y | ? | Y |
| 7 Davis | Y | Y | Y | Y | Y | N |
| **ALASKA** | | | | | | |
| AL Young | Y | Y | Y | Y | Y | Y |
| **ARIZONA** | | | | | | |
| 1 Renzi | Y | Y | Y | Y | Y | Y |
| 2 Franks | Y | N | Y | Y | Y | Y |
| 3 Shadegg | Y | N | Y | Y | Y | Y |
| 4 Pastor | Y | Y | Y | Y | Y | N |
| 5 Hayworth | Y | N | Y | Y | Y | Y |
| 6 Flake | Y | N | Y | Y | Y | Y |
| 7 Grijalva | Y | Y | N | Y | N | N |
| 8 Kolbe | Y | N | Y | Y | Y | Y |
| **ARKANSAS** | | | | | | |
| 1 Berry | Y | Y | Y | Y | Y | N |
| 2 Snyder | Y | Y | Y | Y | Y | Y |
| 3 Boozman | Y | Y | Y | Y | Y | Y |
| 4 Ross | Y | Y | Y | Y | Y | N |
| **CALIFORNIA** | | | | | | |
| 1 Thompson | Y | Y | N | Y | Y | N |
| 2 Herger | Y | N | Y | Y | Y | Y |
| 3 Lungren | Y | Y | Y | Y | Y | Y |
| 4 Doolittle | Y | Y | Y | Y | Y | Y |
| 5 Matsui, D. | Y | Y | Y | Y | Y | N |
| 6 Woolsey | Y | Y | Y | Y | N | N |
| 7 Miller, George | Y | Y | N | Y | N | N |
| 8 Pelosi | Y | Y | Y | Y | Y | N |
| 9 Lee | + | + | Y | Y | N | N |
| 10 Tauscher | Y | Y | Y | Y | Y | N |
| 11 Pombo | Y | Y | Y | Y | Y | Y |
| 12 Lantos | Y | Y | Y | Y | Y | N |
| 13 Stark | Y | Y | Y | Y | N | N |
| 14 Eshoo | Y | Y | Y | Y | Y | N |
| 15 Honda | Y | Y | Y | Y | Y | N |
| 16 Lofgren | Y | Y | Y | Y | Y | N |
| 17 Farr | Y | Y | Y | Y | N | N |
| 18 Cardoza | Y | Y | Y | Y | Y | N |
| 19 Radanovich | Y | N | Y | Y | Y | Y |
| 20 Costa | Y | Y | Y | Y | Y | N |
| 21 Nunes | Y | N | Y | Y | Y | Y |
| 22 Thomas | Y | N | Y | Y | Y | Y |
| 23 Capps | Y | Y | Y | Y | Y | N |
| 24 Gallegly | Y | Y | Y | Y | Y | Y |
| 25 McKeon | Y | Y | Y | Y | Y | Y |
| 26 Dreier | Y | Y | Y | Y | Y | Y |
| 27 Sherman | Y | Y | Y | Y | Y | N |
| 28 Berman | Y | Y | Y | N | Y | N |
| 29 Schiff | Y | Y | Y | Y | Y | N |
| 30 Waxman | Y | Y | Y | Y | Y | N |
| 31 Becerra | Y | Y | Y | Y | Y | N |
| 32 Solis | Y | Y | Y | Y | Y | N |
| 33 Watson | Y | Y | ? | Y | Y | N |
| 34 Roybal-Allard | Y | Y | Y | Y | Y | N |
| 35 Waters | Y | Y | N | Y | N | N |
| 36 Harman | Y | Y | Y | Y | Y | N |
| 37 Millender-McD. | Y | Y | Y | Y | Y | N |
| 38 Napolitano | Y | Y | Y | Y | Y | N |
| 39 Sánchez, Linda | Y | Y | Y | Y | Y | N |
| 40 Royce | Y | N | Y | Y | Y | Y |
| 41 Lewis | Y | Y | Y | Y | Y | Y |
| 42 Miller, Gary | Y | Y | Y | Y | Y | Y |
| 43 Baca | Y | Y | Y | Y | Y | N |
| 44 Calvert | Y | Y | Y | Y | Y | Y |
| 45 Bono | Y | Y | Y | Y | Y | Y |
| 46 Rohrabacher | Y | N | Y | Y | Y | Y |
| 47 Sanchez, Loretta | Y | Y | N | Y | Y | N |
| 48 Cox | Y | N | Y | Y | Y | Y |
| 49 Issa | Y | Y | Y | Y | Y | Y |
| 50 Cunningham | Y | Y | Y | Y | Y | Y |
| 51 Filner | Y | Y | N | Y | Y | N |
| 52 Hunter | Y | N | ? | Y | Y | Y |
| 53 Davis | Y | Y | Y | Y | Y | N |
| **COLORADO** | | | | | | |
| 1 DeGette | Y | Y | Y | Y | Y | N |
| 2 Udall | Y | Y | N | Y | Y | N |
| 3 Salazar | Y | Y | Y | Y | Y | N |
| 4 Musgrave | Y | N | Y | Y | Y | Y |
| 5 Hefley | Y | Y | N | Y | Y | Y |
| 6 Tancredo | Y | N | P | Y | Y | Y |
| 7 Beauprez | Y | Y | Y | Y | Y | Y |
| **CONNECTICUT** | | | | | | |
| 1 Larson | Y | Y | N | Y | Y | N |
| 2 Simmons | Y | Y | Y | Y | Y | N |
| 3 DeLauro | Y | Y | Y | Y | Y | N |
| 4 Shays | Y | Y | Y | Y | Y | N |
| 5 Johnson | Y | Y | Y | Y | Y | Y |
| **DELAWARE** | | | | | | |
| AL Castle | Y | Y | Y | Y | Y | Y |
| **FLORIDA** | | | | | | |
| 1 Miller | Y | N | Y | Y | Y | Y |
| 2 Boyd | Y | Y | Y | Y | Y | N |
| 3 Brown | ? | ? | ? | ? | ? | ? |
| 4 Crenshaw | Y | Y | Y | Y | Y | Y |
| 5 Brown-Waite | Y | Y | Y | Y | Y | Y |
| 6 Stearns | Y | N | Y | Y | Y | Y |
| 7 Mica | Y | Y | Y | Y | Y | Y |
| 8 Keller | Y | Y | Y | Y | Y | Y |
| 9 Bilirakis | Y | Y | Y | Y | Y | Y |
| 10 Young | Y | Y | ? | Y | Y | Y |
| 11 Davis | Y | Y | Y | Y | Y | N |
| 12 Putnam | Y | Y | Y | Y | Y | Y |
| 13 Harris | ? | ? | Y | Y | Y | Y |
| 14 Mack | Y | N | Y | N | Y | Y |
| 15 Weldon | Y | N | Y | Y | Y | Y |
| 16 Foley | Y | Y | Y | Y | Y | Y |
| 17 Meek | Y | Y | Y | Y | Y | N |
| 18 Ros-Lehtinen | Y | Y | Y | Y | Y | Y |
| 19 Wexler | Y | Y | Y | Y | Y | N |
| 20 Wasserman-Schultz | Y | Y | Y | Y | Y | N |
| 21 Diaz-Balart, L. | ? | ? | Y | Y | Y | Y |
| 22 Shaw | Y | Y | Y | Y | Y | Y |
| 23 Hastings | Y | Y | N | Y | Y | N |
| 24 Feeney | N | N | Y | Y | Y | Y |
| 25 Diaz-Balart, M. | ? | ? | Y | Y | Y | Y |
| **GEORGIA** | | | | | | |
| 1 Kingston | Y | N | Y | Y | Y | Y |
| 2 Bishop | Y | Y | Y | Y | Y | N |
| 3 Marshall | Y | Y | N | Y | Y | N |
| 4 McKinney | Y | Y | Y | Y | N | N |
| 5 Lewis | Y | Y | Y | Y | N | N |
| 6 Price | Y | N | Y | Y | Y | Y |
| 7 Linder | Y | N | Y | Y | Y | Y |
| 8 Westmoreland | ? | ? | ? | ? | ? | ? |
| 9 Norwood | Y | N | Y | Y | Y | Y |
| 10 Deal | Y | N | Y | Y | Y | Y |
| 11 Gingrey | Y | N | Y | Y | Y | Y |
| 12 Barrow | Y | Y | Y | Y | Y | N |
| 13 Scott | Y | Y | Y | Y | Y | N |
| **HAWAII** | | | | | | |
| 1 Abercrombie | Y | Y | Y | Y | Y | N |
| 2 Case | Y | Y | Y | Y | Y | N |
| **IDAHO** | | | | | | |
| 1 Otter | Y | N | Y | Y | Y | Y |
| 2 Simpson | Y | Y | Y | Y | Y | Y |
| **ILLINOIS** | | | | | | |
| 1 Rush | Y | Y | Y | Y | N | N |
| 2 Jackson | Y | Y | Y | Y | N | N |
| 3 Lipinski | Y | Y | Y | Y | Y | N |
| 4 Gutierrez | + | + | ? | Y | Y | N |
| 5 Emanuel | Y | Y | Y | Y | Y | N |
| 6 Hyde | Y | Y | Y | Y | Y | Y |
| 7 Davis | Y | Y | Y | Y | N | N |
| 8 Bean | Y | Y | Y | Y | Y | N |
| 9 Schakowsky | Y | Y | N | Y | N | N |
| 10 Kirk | Y | Y | Y | Y | Y | Y |
| 11 Weller | Y | Y | N | Y | Y | Y |
| 12 Costello | Y | Y | N | Y | Y | N |

**KEY**  Republicans  Democrats  *Independents*

| | | |
|---|---|---|
| **Y** Voted for (yea) | **X** Paired against | **C** Voted "present" to avoid possible conflict of interest |
| **#** Paired for | **–** Announced against | |
| **+** Announced for | **P** Voted "present" | **?** Did not vote or otherwise make a position known |
| **N** Voted against (nay) | | |

ND Northern Democrats, SD Southern Democrats
Southern states: Ala., Ark., Fla., Ga., Ky., La., Miss., N.C., Okla., S.C., Tenn., Texas, Va.

| | 133 | 134 | 135 | 136 | 137 | 138 |
|---|---|---|---|---|---|---|
| 13 **Biggert** | Y | Y | Y | Y | Y | Y |
| 14 **Hastert** | | | | | | |
| 15 **Johnson** | Y | Y | Y | Y | Y | Y |
| 16 **Manzullo** | Y | Y | Y | Y | Y | Y |
| 17 Evans | Y | Y | Y | Y | Y | N |
| 18 **LaHood** | Y | Y | Y | Y | Y | Y |
| 19 **Shimkus** | Y | Y | Y | Y | Y | Y |
| **INDIANA** | | | | | | |
| 1 Visclosky | Y | Y | Y | Y | Y | N |
| 2 **Chocola** | Y | Y | Y | Y | Y | Y |
| 3 **Souder** | Y | N | Y | Y | Y | Y |
| 4 **Buyer** | Y | N | Y | Y | Y | Y |
| 5 **Burton** | Y | Y | Y | Y | Y | Y |
| 6 **Pence** | Y | N | Y | Y | Y | Y |
| 7 Carson | Y | Y | Y | Y | N | N |
| 8 **Hostettler** | Y | N | Y | Y | Y | Y |
| 9 **Sodrel** | Y | Y | Y | Y | Y | Y |
| **IOWA** | | | | | | |
| 1 **Nussle** | Y | Y | Y | Y | Y | Y |
| 2 **Leach** | Y | Y | Y | Y | Y | Y |
| 3 Boswell | Y | Y | Y | Y | Y | N |
| 4 **Latham** | Y | Y | N | Y | Y | Y |
| 5 **King** | Y | N | Y | Y | Y | Y |
| **KANSAS** | | | | | | |
| 1 **Moran** | Y | Y | N | Y | Y | Y |
| 2 **Ryun** | Y | Y | Y | Y | Y | Y |
| 3 Moore | Y | Y | Y | Y | Y | N |
| 4 **Tiahrt** | N | N | Y | Y | Y | Y |
| **KENTUCKY** | | | | | | |
| 1 **Whitfield** | Y | Y | N | Y | Y | Y |
| 2 **Lewis** | Y | Y | Y | Y | Y | Y |
| 3 **Northup** | Y | Y | Y | Y | Y | Y |
| 4 **Davis** | Y | Y | Y | Y | Y | Y |
| 5 **Rogers** | Y | Y | Y | Y | Y | Y |
| 6 Chandler | Y | Y | Y | Y | Y | N |
| **LOUISIANA** | | | | | | |
| 1 **Jindal** | Y | Y | Y | Y | Y | Y |
| 2 Jefferson | Y | Y | Y | Y | Y | N |
| 3 Melancon | Y | Y | Y | Y | Y | N |
| 4 **McCrery** | Y | Y | Y | Y | Y | Y |
| 5 **Alexander** | Y | Y | Y | Y | Y | Y |
| 6 **Baker** | Y | N | Y | Y | Y | Y |
| 7 **Boustany** | Y | N | Y | Y | Y | Y |
| **MAINE** | | | | | | |
| 1 Allen | Y | Y | Y | Y | Y | N |
| 2 Michaud | Y | Y | Y | Y | Y | N |
| **MARYLAND** | | | | | | |
| 1 **Gilchrest** | Y | Y | Y | Y | Y | Y |
| 2 Ruppersberger | Y | Y | Y | Y | Y | N |
| 3 Cardin | Y | Y | Y | Y | Y | N |
| 4 Wynn | Y | Y | Y | Y | N | N |
| 5 Hoyer | Y | Y | Y | Y | Y | N |
| 6 **Bartlett** | Y | N | Y | Y | Y | Y |
| 7 Cummings | Y | Y | Y | Y | Y | N |
| 8 Van Hollen | Y | Y | Y | Y | Y | N |
| **MASSACHUSETTS** | | | | | | |
| 1 Olver | Y | Y | Y | Y | N | N |
| 2 Neal | Y | Y | Y | Y | Y | N |
| 3 McGovern | Y | Y | Y | Y | Y | N |
| 4 Frank | Y | Y | Y | Y | Y | N |
| 5 Meehan | Y | Y | Y | Y | Y | N |
| 6 Tierney | Y | Y | Y | Y | Y | N |
| 7 Markey | Y | Y | Y | Y | Y | N |
| 8 Capuano | Y | Y | N | N | Y | N |
| 9 Lynch | Y | Y | Y | Y | Y | N |
| 10 Delahunt | Y | Y | Y | Y | Y | N |
| **MICHIGAN** | | | | | | |
| 1 Stupak | Y | Y | N | Y | Y | N |
| 2 **Hoekstra** | Y | Y | Y | Y | Y | Y |
| 3 **Ehlers** | Y | Y | Y | Y | Y | Y |
| 4 **Camp** | Y | Y | Y | Y | Y | Y |
| 5 Kildee | Y | Y | Y | Y | Y | N |
| 6 **Upton** | Y | Y | Y | Y | Y | Y |
| 7 **Schwarz** | Y | Y | Y | Y | Y | Y |
| 8 **Rogers** | Y | N | Y | Y | Y | Y |
| 9 **Knollenberg** | Y | Y | Y | Y | Y | Y |
| 10 **Miller** | Y | Y | Y | Y | Y | Y |
| 11 **McCotter** | Y | Y | N | Y | Y | Y |
| 12 Levin | Y | Y | Y | Y | Y | N |
| 13 Kilpatrick | Y | ? | Y | Y | N | N |
| 14 Conyers | Y | Y | Y | Y | Y | N |
| 15 Dingell | Y | Y | Y | Y | Y | N |

| | 133 | 134 | 135 | 136 | 137 | 138 |
|---|---|---|---|---|---|---|
| **MINNESOTA** | | | | | | |
| 1 **Gutknecht** | Y | N | N | Y | Y | Y |
| 2 **Kline** | Y | Y | Y | Y | Y | Y |
| 3 **Ramstad** | Y | Y | N | Y | Y | Y |
| 4 McCollum | Y | Y | Y | Y | Y | N |
| 5 Sabo | Y | Y | N | Y | Y | N |
| 6 **Kennedy** | Y | Y | Y | Y | Y | Y |
| 7 Peterson | Y | Y | N | Y | Y | N |
| 8 Oberstar | Y | Y | N | Y | Y | N |
| **MISSISSIPPI** | | | | | | |
| 1 **Wicker** | ? | ? | ? | ? | ? | ? |
| 2 Thompson | Y | Y | N | Y | N | N |
| 3 **Pickering** | Y | Y | Y | Y | Y | Y |
| 4 Taylor | Y | Y | N | Y | Y | N |
| **MISSOURI** | | | | | | |
| 1 Clay | Y | Y | Y | Y | N | N |
| 2 **Akin** | Y | N | Y | Y | Y | Y |
| 3 Carnahan | Y | Y | Y | Y | Y | N |
| 4 Skelton | Y | Y | Y | Y | Y | N |
| 5 Cleaver | Y | Y | Y | Y | Y | N |
| 6 **Graves** | Y | Y | Y | Y | Y | Y |
| 7 **Blunt** | Y | Y | Y | Y | Y | Y |
| 8 **Emerson** | Y | Y | Y | Y | Y | Y |
| 9 **Hulshof** | Y | Y | Y | Y | Y | Y |
| **MONTANA** | | | | | | |
| AL **Rehberg** | Y | Y | Y | Y | Y | Y |
| **NEBRASKA** | | | | | | |
| 1 **Fortenberry** | Y | Y | Y | Y | Y | Y |
| 2 **Terry** | Y | N | Y | Y | Y | Y |
| 3 **Osborne** | Y | Y | Y | Y | Y | Y |
| **NEVADA** | | | | | | |
| 1 Berkley | Y | Y | Y | Y | Y | N |
| 2 **Gibbons** | Y | Y | Y | Y | Y | Y |
| 3 **Porter** | Y | Y | Y | Y | Y | Y |
| **NEW HAMPSHIRE** | | | | | | |
| 1 **Bradley** | Y | Y | Y | Y | Y | Y |
| 2 **Bass** | Y | Y | Y | Y | Y | Y |
| **NEW JERSEY** | | | | | | |
| 1 Andrews | Y | Y | Y | Y | Y | N |
| 2 **LoBiondo** | Y | Y | N | Y | Y | Y |
| 3 **Saxton** | Y | Y | Y | Y | Y | Y |
| 4 **Smith** | Y | Y | Y | Y | Y | Y |
| 5 **Garrett** | Y | N | Y | Y | Y | Y |
| 6 Pallone | Y | Y | Y | Y | Y | N |
| 7 **Ferguson** | Y | N | Y | Y | Y | Y |
| 8 Pascrell | Y | Y | Y | Y | Y | N |
| 9 Rothman | ? | ? | ? | ? | ? | ? |
| 10 Payne | Y | Y | Y | Y | N | N |
| 11 **Frelinghuysen** | Y | Y | Y | Y | Y | Y |
| 12 Holt | Y | Y | N | Y | Y | N |
| 13 Menendez | Y | Y | ? | Y | Y | N |
| **NEW MEXICO** | | | | | | |
| 1 **Wilson** | Y | Y | Y | Y | Y | Y |
| 2 **Pearce** | Y | N | Y | Y | Y | Y |
| 3 Udall | Y | Y | N | Y | Y | N |
| **NEW YORK** | | | | | | |
| 1 Bishop | Y | Y | Y | Y | Y | N |
| 2 Israel | Y | Y | Y | Y | Y | N |
| 3 **King** | Y | Y | Y | Y | Y | Y |
| 4 McCarthy | Y | Y | Y | Y | Y | N |
| 5 Ackerman | Y | Y | Y | Y | Y | N |
| 6 Meeks | Y | Y | Y | Y | N | N |
| 7 Crowley | Y | Y | Y | Y | Y | N |
| 8 Nadler | Y | Y | N | Y | Y | N |
| 9 Weiner | Y | Y | Y | Y | Y | N |
| 10 Towns | Y | Y | Y | Y | N | N |
| 11 Owens | Y | Y | Y | Y | Y | N |
| 12 Velázquez | Y | Y | ? | Y | N | N |
| 13 **Fossella** | Y | Y | N | Y | Y | Y |
| 14 Maloney | Y | Y | Y | Y | Y | N |
| 15 Rangel | Y | Y | Y | Y | N | N |
| 16 Serrano | Y | Y | Y | Y | N | N |
| 17 Engel | Y | Y | Y | Y | Y | N |
| 18 Lowey | Y | Y | Y | Y | Y | N |
| 19 **Kelly** | Y | Y | Y | Y | Y | Y |
| 20 **Sweeney** | Y | Y | Y | Y | Y | Y |
| 21 McNulty | Y | Y | Y | Y | Y | N |
| 22 Hinchey | Y | Y | N | Y | N | N |
| 23 **McHugh** | Y | Y | Y | Y | Y | Y |
| 24 **Boehlert** | Y | Y | Y | Y | Y | Y |
| 25 **Walsh** | Y | Y | Y | Y | Y | Y |
| 26 **Reynolds** | Y | Y | Y | Y | Y | Y |
| 27 Higgins | Y | Y | Y | Y | Y | N |
| 28 Slaughter | Y | Y | Y | Y | Y | N |
| 29 **Kuhl** | Y | Y | Y | Y | Y | Y |

| | 133 | 134 | 135 | 136 | 137 | 138 |
|---|---|---|---|---|---|---|
| **NORTH CAROLINA** | | | | | | |
| 1 Butterfield | Y | Y | Y | Y | Y | N |
| 2 Etheridge | Y | Y | Y | Y | Y | N |
| 3 **Jones** | Y | Y | Y | Y | Y | Y |
| 4 Price | Y | Y | Y | Y | Y | N |
| 5 **Foxx** | Y | N | Y | Y | Y | Y |
| 6 **Coble** | N | Y | Y | Y | Y | Y |
| 7 McIntyre | Y | Y | Y | Y | Y | N |
| 8 **Hayes** | Y | Y | Y | Y | Y | Y |
| 9 **Myrick** | Y | N | Y | Y | Y | Y |
| 10 **McHenry** | Y | N | Y | Y | Y | Y |
| 11 **Taylor** | Y | N | Y | Y | Y | Y |
| 12 Watt | Y | Y | Y | Y | P | N |
| 13 Miller | Y | Y | Y | Y | Y | N |
| **NORTH DAKOTA** | | | | | | |
| AL Pomeroy | Y | Y | Y | Y | Y | N |
| **OHIO** | | | | | | |
| 1 **Chabot** | Y | N | Y | Y | Y | Y |
| 2 **Portman** | Y | Y | Y | + | + | + |
| 3 **Turner** | Y | Y | Y | Y | Y | Y |
| 4 **Oxley** | Y | Y | Y | Y | Y | Y |
| 5 **Gillmor** | Y | Y | Y | Y | Y | Y |
| 6 Strickland | Y | Y | N | N | Y | N |
| 7 **Hobson** | Y | Y | Y | Y | Y | Y |
| 8 **Boehner** | Y | Y | Y | Y | Y | Y |
| 9 Kaptur | Y | Y | Y | Y | Y | N |
| 10 Kucinich | Y | Y | N | Y | N | N |
| 11 Jones | Y | Y | Y | Y | ? | N |
| 12 **Tiberi** | N | N | N | Y | Y | Y |
| 13 Brown | Y | Y | Y | Y | Y | N |
| 14 **LaTourette** | Y | Y | Y | Y | Y | Y |
| 15 **Pryce** | Y | Y | Y | Y | Y | Y |
| 16 **Regula** | Y | Y | Y | Y | Y | Y |
| 17 Ryan | Y | Y | Y | Y | Y | N |
| 18 **Ney** | Y | Y | Y | Y | Y | Y |
| **OKLAHOMA** | | | | | | |
| 1 **Sullivan** | Y | Y | Y | Y | Y | Y |
| 2 Boren | Y | Y | Y | Y | Y | N |
| 3 **Lucas** | Y | Y | Y | Y | Y | Y |
| 4 **Cole** | Y | Y | Y | Y | Y | Y |
| 5 **Istook** | Y | N | Y | Y | Y | Y |
| **OREGON** | | | | | | |
| 1 Wu | Y | Y | N | Y | Y | N |
| 2 **Walden** | Y | Y | Y | Y | Y | Y |
| 3 Blumenauer | Y | Y | Y | Y | Y | N |
| 4 DeFazio | Y | Y | N | N | P | N |
| 5 Hooley | ? | ? | ? | Y | Y | N |
| **PENNSYLVANIA** | | | | | | |
| 1 Brady | Y | Y | N | Y | Y | N |
| 2 Fattah | Y | Y | ? | Y | Y | N |
| 3 **English** | Y | Y | ? | Y | Y | Y |
| 4 **Hart** | Y | Y | N | Y | Y | Y |
| 5 **Peterson** | Y | Y | Y | Y | Y | Y |
| 6 **Gerlach** | Y | Y | Y | Y | Y | Y |
| 7 **Weldon** | Y | Y | Y | Y | Y | Y |
| 8 **Fitzpatrick** | Y | Y | Y | Y | Y | Y |
| 9 **Shuster** | Y | Y | Y | Y | Y | Y |
| 10 **Sherwood** | Y | Y | Y | Y | Y | Y |
| 11 Kanjorski | Y | Y | Y | Y | Y | N |
| 12 Murtha | ? | ? | Y | Y | Y | N |
| 13 Schwartz | Y | Y | Y | Y | Y | N |
| 14 Doyle | Y | Y | Y | Y | Y | N |
| 15 **Dent** | Y | Y | Y | Y | Y | Y |
| 16 **Pitts** | Y | N | Y | Y | Y | Y |
| 17 Holden | Y | Y | Y | Y | Y | N |
| 18 **Murphy** | Y | N | Y | Y | Y | Y |
| 19 **Platts** | Y | Y | Y | Y | Y | Y |
| **RHODE ISLAND** | | | | | | |
| 1 Kennedy | Y | Y | ? | Y | Y | N |
| 2 Langevin | Y | Y | Y | Y | Y | N |
| **SOUTH CAROLINA** | | | | | | |
| 1 **Brown** | Y | Y | Y | Y | Y | Y |
| 2 **Wilson** | Y | Y | Y | Y | Y | Y |
| 3 **Barrett** | Y | N | Y | Y | Y | Y |
| 4 **Inglis** | Y | N | Y | Y | Y | Y |
| 5 Spratt | Y | Y | ? | Y | Y | N |
| 6 Clyburn | Y | Y | Y | Y | Y | N |
| **SOUTH DAKOTA** | | | | | | |
| AL Herseth | Y | Y | Y | Y | Y | N |
| **TENNESSEE** | | | | | | |
| 1 **Jenkins** | ? | ? | Y | Y | Y | Y |
| 2 **Duncan** | Y | N | Y | Y | Y | Y |

| | 133 | 134 | 135 | 136 | 137 | 138 |
|---|---|---|---|---|---|---|
| 3 **Wamp** | Y | N | Y | Y | Y | Y |
| 4 Davis | Y | Y | Y | Y | Y | N |
| 5 Cooper | Y | Y | Y | Y | Y | N |
| 6 Gordon | Y | Y | Y | Y | Y | N |
| 7 **Blackburn** | Y | N | Y | Y | Y | Y |
| 8 Tanner | Y | Y | N | Y | Y | N |
| 9 Ford | Y | Y | N | Y | Y | N |
| **TEXAS** | | | | | | |
| 1 **Gohmert** | Y | Y | Y | Y | Y | Y |
| 2 **Poe** | Y | N | Y | N | Y | Y |
| 3 **Johnson, S.** | Y | N | Y | Y | Y | Y |
| 4 **Hall** | Y | Y | Y | Y | Y | Y |
| 5 **Hensarling** | Y | N | Y | Y | Y | Y |
| 6 **Barton** | Y | N | Y | Y | Y | Y |
| 7 **Culberson** | Y | N | Y | Y | Y | Y |
| 8 **Brady** | + | – | Y | Y | Y | Y |
| 9 Green | Y | Y | Y | Y | Y | N |
| 10 **McCaul** | Y | Y | Y | Y | Y | Y |
| 11 **Conaway** | Y | N | Y | Y | Y | Y |
| 12 **Granger** | Y | Y | Y | Y | Y | Y |
| 13 **Thornberry** | Y | N | Y | Y | Y | Y |
| 14 **Paul** | Y | N | Y | Y | N | Y |
| 15 Hinojosa | Y | Y | Y | Y | Y | N |
| 16 Reyes | Y | Y | Y | Y | Y | N |
| 17 Edwards | Y | Y | Y | Y | Y | N |
| 18 Jackson-Lee | Y | Y | Y | Y | Y | N |
| 19 **Neugebauer** | Y | N | Y | Y | Y | Y |
| 20 Gonzalez | Y | Y | Y | Y | Y | N |
| 21 **Smith** | Y | Y | Y | Y | Y | Y |
| 22 **DeLay** | Y | Y | Y | Y | Y | Y |
| 23 **Bonilla** | Y | N | Y | Y | Y | Y |
| 24 **Marchant** | Y | N | Y | Y | Y | Y |
| 25 Doggett | Y | Y | Y | Y | Y | N |
| 26 **Burgess** | Y | N | Y | Y | Y | Y |
| 27 Ortiz | Y | Y | Y | Y | Y | N |
| 28 Cuellar | Y | Y | Y | Y | Y | N |
| 29 Green | Y | Y | N | Y | Y | N |
| 30 Johnson, E. | Y | Y | Y | Y | N | N |
| 31 **Carter** | Y | N | Y | Y | Y | Y |
| 32 **Sessions** | Y | N | Y | Y | Y | Y |
| **UTAH** | | | | | | |
| 1 **Bishop** | Y | N | Y | Y | Y | Y |
| 2 Matheson | Y | Y | Y | Y | Y | N |
| 3 **Cannon** | Y | N | Y | Y | Y | Y |
| **VERMONT** | | | | | | |
| AL *Sanders* | Y | Y | Y | Y | Y | N |
| **VIRGINIA** | | | | | | |
| 1 **Davis, J.** | Y | Y | Y | Y | Y | Y |
| 2 **Drake** | Y | Y | Y | Y | Y | Y |
| 3 Scott | Y | Y | Y | Y | Y | N |
| 4 **Forbes** | Y | Y | Y | Y | Y | Y |
| 5 **Goode** | Y | Y | Y | Y | Y | Y |
| 6 **Goodlatte** | Y | Y | Y | Y | Y | Y |
| 7 **Cantor** | Y | Y | Y | Y | Y | Y |
| 8 Moran | Y | Y | Y | Y | Y | N |
| 9 Boucher | Y | Y | Y | Y | Y | N |
| 10 **Wolf** | Y | Y | Y | Y | Y | Y |
| 11 **Davis, T.** | Y | Y | Y | Y | Y | Y |
| **WASHINGTON** | | | | | | |
| 1 Inslee | Y | Y | Y | Y | Y | N |
| 2 Larsen | Y | Y | N | Y | Y | N |
| 3 Baird | Y | Y | N | Y | Y | N |
| 4 **Hastings** | Y | Y | Y | Y | Y | Y |
| 5 **McMorris** | Y | Y | Y | Y | Y | Y |
| 6 Dicks | Y | Y | Y | Y | Y | N |
| 7 McDermott | Y | Y | N | Y | N | N |
| 8 **Reichert** | Y | Y | Y | Y | Y | Y |
| 9 Smith | Y | Y | Y | ? | Y | N |
| **WEST VIRGINIA** | | | | | | |
| 1 Mollohan | Y | Y | Y | Y | Y | N |
| 2 **Capito** | Y | Y | Y | Y | Y | Y |
| 3 Rahall | Y | Y | Y | Y | Y | N |
| **WISCONSIN** | | | | | | |
| 1 **Ryan** | Y | Y | Y | Y | Y | Y |
| 2 Baldwin | Y | Y | N | Y | Y | N |
| 3 Kind | Y | Y | Y | Y | Y | N |
| 4 Moore | Y | Y | Y | Y | Y | N |
| 5 **Sensenbrenner** | Y | Y | Y | Y | Y | Y |
| 6 **Petri** | Y | Y | Y | Y | Y | Y |
| 7 Obey | Y | Y | Y | Y | Y | N |
| 8 **Green** | Y | Y | Y | Y | Y | Y |
| **WYOMING** | | | | | | |
| AL **Cubin** | Y | Y | Y | Y | Y | Y |

# IN THE HOUSE | By Vote Number

**139.** HR 748. **Abortion Notification/Previous Question.** Gingrey, R-Ga., motion to order the previous question (thus ending debate and possibility of amendment) on adoption of the rule (H Res 236) to provide for House floor consideration of the bill that would make it a crime to transport a minor across state lines with the intent to obtain an abortion and circumvent state parental-consent laws. Motion agreed to 234-192: R 226-0; D 8-191 (ND 4-145, SD 4-46); I 0-1. (Subsequently, the rule was adopted by voice vote.) April 27, 2005.

**140.** H Res 22. **"Small Business Bill of Rights"/Recommit.** Velázquez, D-N.Y., motion to recommit the resolution to the House Small Business Committee. Motion rejected 188-222: R 0-212; D 187-10 (ND 141-8, SD 46-2); I 1-0. (Subsequently, the resolution was adopted by voice vote.) April 27, 2005.

**141.** HR 748. **Abortion Notification/Professional Transportation and Medical Provider Exemption.** Scott, D-Va., amendment that would exempt taxicab drivers, bus drivers and others in the professional transportation business, as well as doctors, nurses and other medical providers or their staff from criminal liability under the transportation provisions in the bill. Rejected 179-245: R 15-211; D 163-34 (ND 129-19, SD 34-15); I 1-0. April 27, 2005.

**142.** HR 748. **Abortion Notification/Grandparent and Clergy Exemption.** Jackson-Lee, D-Texas., amendment that would exempt from prosecution the grandparents of the minor or a member of the clergy who transports a minor across state lines for the purposes of obtaining an abortion. Rejected 177-252: R 13-215; D 163-37 (ND 129-21, SD 34-16); I 1-0. April 27, 2005.

**143.** HR 748. **Abortion Notification/Recommit.** Nadler, D-N.Y., motion to recommit the bill to the House Judiciary Committee with instructions to include language which would bar fathers who have committed rape or incest against a minor that resulted in a pregnancy from being able to sue the doctor who performed the abortion. Motion rejected 183-245: R 10-218; D 172-27 (ND 135-15, SD 37-12); I 1-0. April 27, 2005.

**144.** HR 748. **Abortion Notification/Passage.** Passage of the bill that would bar the transportation of a minor girl across state lines to obtain an abortion without the consent of a parent, guardian or judge. The bill would authorize fines and/or up to a year in prison for individuals who transport a minor to a state without a parental consent law in an attempt to circumvent parents' involvement. Doctors who perform such abortions also would be subject to the penalties. Abortion providers in states without parental consent laws would be required to try to notify a parent or legal guardian, either personally or by certified mail, before performing an abortion on a minor who was a resident of another state. Passed 270-157: R 216-11; D 54-145 (ND 27-122, SD 27-23); I 0-1. A "yea" was a vote in support of the president's position. April 27, 2005.

| | 139 | 140 | 141 | 142 | 143 | 144 |
|---|---|---|---|---|---|---|
| **ALABAMA** | | | | | | |
| 1 **Bonner** | Y | N | N | N | N | Y |
| 2 **Everett** | Y | N | N | N | N | Y |
| 3 **Rogers** | Y | N | N | N | N | Y |
| 4 **Aderholt** | Y | N | N | N | N | Y |
| 5 **Cramer** | N | Y | N | N | N | Y |
| 6 **Bachus** | Y | N | N | N | N | Y |
| 7 Davis | N | Y | Y | Y | Y | N |
| **ALASKA** | | | | | | |
| AL **Young** | Y | N | N | N | N | Y |
| **ARIZONA** | | | | | | |
| 1 **Renzi** | Y | N | N | N | N | Y |
| 2 **Franks** | Y | N | N | N | N | Y |
| 3 **Shadegg** | Y | ? | N | N | N | Y |
| 4 Pastor | N | Y | Y | Y | Y | N |
| 5 **Hayworth** | Y | N | N | N | N | Y |
| 6 **Flake** | Y | ? | N | N | N | Y |
| 7 Grijalva | N | Y | ? | Y | Y | N |
| 8 Kolbe | Y | N | Y | N | Y | Y |
| **ARKANSAS** | | | | | | |
| 1 Berry | Y | Y | N | N | N | Y |
| 2 Snyder | N | Y | N | N | Y | Y |
| 3 **Boozman** | Y | N | N | N | N | Y |
| 4 Ross | N | Y | Y | Y | Y | Y |
| **CALIFORNIA** | | | | | | |
| 1 Thompson | N | Y | Y | Y | Y | N |
| 2 **Herger** | Y | N | N | N | N | Y |
| 3 **Lungren** | Y | N | N | N | N | Y |
| 4 **Doolittle** | Y | ? | N | N | N | Y |
| 5 Matsui, D. | N | Y | Y | Y | Y | N |
| 6 Woolsey | N | Y | Y | Y | Y | N |
| 7 Miller, George | N | Y | Y | Y | Y | N |
| 8 Pelosi | N | Y | Y | Y | Y | N |
| 9 Lee | N | Y | Y | Y | Y | N |
| 10 Tauscher | N | Y | Y | Y | Y | N |
| 11 **Pombo** | Y | N | N | N | N | Y |
| 12 Lantos | N | Y | Y | Y | Y | N |
| 13 Stark | N | Y | Y | Y | Y | N |
| 14 Eshoo | N | Y | Y | Y | Y | N |
| 15 Honda | N | Y | Y | Y | Y | N |
| 16 Lofgren | N | Y | Y | Y | Y | N |
| 17 Farr | N | Y | Y | Y | Y | N |
| 18 Cardoza | N | Y | Y | Y | Y | Y |
| 19 **Radanovich** | Y | N | N | N | N | Y |
| 20 Costa | N | N | Y | Y | Y | Y |
| 21 **Nunes** | Y | N | N | N | N | Y |
| 22 **Thomas** | Y | N | N | N | N | Y |
| 23 Capps | N | Y | Y | Y | Y | N |
| 24 **Gallegly** | Y | N | N | N | N | Y |
| 25 **McKeon** | Y | N | N | N | N | Y |
| 26 **Dreier** | Y | N | N | N | N | Y |
| 27 Sherman | N | Y | Y | Y | Y | N |
| 28 Berman | N | Y | Y | Y | Y | N |
| 29 Schiff | N | Y | Y | Y | Y | N |
| 30 Waxman | N | Y | Y | Y | Y | N |
| 31 Becerra | N | Y | Y | Y | Y | N |
| 32 Solis | N | Y | Y | Y | Y | N |
| 33 Watson | N | Y | Y | Y | Y | N |
| 34 Roybal-Allard | N | Y | Y | Y | Y | N |
| 35 Waters | N | Y | Y | Y | Y | N |
| 36 Harman | N | Y | Y | Y | Y | N |
| 37 Millender-McD. | N | Y | Y | Y | Y | N |
| 38 Napolitano | N | Y | Y | Y | Y | N |
| 39 Sánchez, Linda | N | Y | Y | Y | Y | N |
| 40 **Royce** | Y | N | N | N | N | Y |
| 41 **Lewis** | Y | N | N | N | N | Y |
| 42 **Miller, Gary** | Y | N | N | N | N | Y |
| 43 Baca | N | Y | Y | Y | Y | Y |
| 44 **Calvert** | Y | N | N | N | N | Y |
| 45 **Bono** | Y | N | N | N | N | Y |
| 46 **Rohrabacher** | Y | N | N | N | N | Y |
| 47 Sanchez, Loretta | N | Y | Y | Y | Y | N |
| 48 **Cox** | Y | N | N | N | N | Y |
| 49 **Issa** | Y | N | N | N | N | Y |

| | 139 | 140 | 141 | 142 | 143 | 144 |
|---|---|---|---|---|---|---|
| 50 **Cunningham** | Y | N | N | N | N | Y |
| 51 Filner | N | Y | Y | Y | Y | N |
| 52 **Hunter** | Y | N | N | N | N | Y |
| 53 Davis | N | Y | Y | Y | Y | N |
| **COLORADO** | | | | | | |
| 1 DeGette | N | Y | Y | Y | Y | N |
| 2 Udall | N | Y | Y | Y | Y | N |
| 3 Salazar | N | N | Y | N | Y | Y |
| 4 **Musgrave** | Y | ? | N | N | N | Y |
| 5 **Hefley** | Y | N | N | N | N | Y |
| 6 **Tancredo** | Y | N | N | N | N | Y |
| 7 **Beauprez** | Y | N | N | N | N | Y |
| **CONNECTICUT** | | | | | | |
| 1 Larson | N | Y | Y | Y | Y | N |
| 2 **Simmons** | Y | N | Y | N | Y | N |
| 3 DeLauro | N | Y | Y | Y | Y | N |
| 4 **Shays** | Y | N | Y | N | Y | N |
| 5 Johnson | Y | N | Y | N | Y | N |
| **DELAWARE** | | | | | | |
| AL **Castle** | Y | N | Y | Y | Y | N |
| **FLORIDA** | | | | | | |
| 1 **Miller** | Y | N | N | N | N | Y |
| 2 Boyd | N | Y | Y | Y | Y | Y |
| 3 Brown | ? | ? | ? | ? | ? | ? |
| 4 **Crenshaw** | Y | N | N | N | N | Y |
| 5 **Brown-Waite** | Y | ? | ? | N | N | Y |
| 6 **Stearns** | Y | N | N | N | N | Y |
| 7 **Mica** | Y | N | N | N | N | Y |
| 8 **Keller** | Y | N | N | N | N | Y |
| 9 **Bilirakis** | Y | N | N | N | N | Y |
| 10 **Young** | Y | N | N | N | N | Y |
| 11 Davis | N | Y | Y | Y | Y | N |
| 12 **Putnam** | Y | N | N | N | N | Y |
| 13 **Harris** | Y | N | N | N | N | Y |
| 14 **Mack** | Y | N | N | N | N | Y |
| 15 **Weldon** | Y | N | N | N | N | Y |
| 16 **Foley** | Y | N | N | N | N | Y |
| 17 Meek | N | Y | Y | Y | Y | N |
| 18 **Ros-Lehtinen** | Y | N | N | N | N | Y |
| 19 Wexler | N | Y | Y | Y | Y | N |
| 20 Wasserman-Schultz | N | Y | Y | Y | Y | N |
| 21 **Diaz-Balart, L.** | Y | N | N | N | N | Y |
| 22 **Shaw** | Y | N | N | N | N | Y |
| 23 Hastings | N | Y | Y | Y | Y | N |
| 24 **Feeney** | Y | ? | N | N | N | Y |
| 25 **Diaz-Balart, M.** | Y | N | N | N | N | Y |
| **GEORGIA** | | | | | | |
| 1 **Kingston** | Y | N | N | N | N | Y |
| 2 Bishop | N | Y | Y | Y | ? | Y |
| 3 Marshall | N | Y | N | N | Y | Y |
| 4 McKinney | N | Y | Y | Y | Y | N |
| 5 Lewis | N | Y | Y | Y | Y | N |
| 6 **Price** | Y | N | N | N | N | Y |
| 7 **Linder** | Y | N | N | N | N | Y |
| 8 **Westmoreland** | ? | ? | ? | ? | ? | ? |
| 9 **Norwood** | Y | N | N | N | N | Y |
| 10 **Deal** | Y | N | N | N | N | Y |
| 11 **Gingrey** | Y | N | N | N | N | Y |
| 12 Barrow | N | Y | Y | Y | Y | Y |
| 13 Scott | N | ? | Y | Y | Y | N |
| **HAWAII** | | | | | | |
| 1 Abercrombie | N | Y | Y | Y | Y | N |
| 2 Case | N | N | Y | Y | Y | N |
| **IDAHO** | | | | | | |
| 1 **Otter** | Y | N | N | N | N | Y |
| 2 **Simpson** | Y | N | N | N | N | Y |
| **ILLINOIS** | | | | | | |
| 1 Rush | N | Y | Y | Y | Y | N |
| 2 Jackson | N | Y | Y | Y | Y | N |
| 3 Lipinski | Y | Y | N | N | N | Y |
| 4 Gutierrez | N | Y | Y | Y | Y | N |
| 5 Emanuel | N | Y | Y | Y | Y | Y |
| 6 **Hyde** | Y | N | N | N | N | Y |
| 7 Davis | N | Y | Y | Y | Y | N |
| 8 Bean | N | Y | Y | Y | Y | Y |
| 9 Schakowsky | N | Y | Y | Y | Y | N |
| 10 **Kirk** | Y | N | Y | Y | Y | N |
| 11 **Weller** | Y | N | N | N | N | Y |
| 12 Costello | Y | N | N | N | N | Y |

**KEY** Republicans Democrats *Independents*

| | | | | | |
|---|---|---|---|---|---|
| **Y** | Voted for (yea) | **X** | Paired against | **C** | Voted "present" to avoid possible conflict of interest |
| **#** | Paired for | **–** | Announced against | | |
| **+** | Announced for | **P** | Voted "present" | **?** | Did not vote or otherwise make a position known |
| **N** | Voted against (nay) | | | | |

ND Northern Democrats, SD Southern Democrats
Southern states: Ala., Ark., Fla., Ga., Ky., La., Miss., N.C., Okla., S.C., Tenn., Texas, Va.

| | 139 | 140 | 141 | 142 | 143 | 144 |
|---|---|---|---|---|---|---|
| 13 **Biggert** | Y | N | Y | Y | N | N |
| 14 **Hastert** | | | | | | |
| 15 **Johnson** | Y | N | N | N | N | Y |
| 16 **Manzullo** | Y | N | N | N | N | Y |
| 17 Evans | N | Y | Y | Y | Y | N |
| 18 **LaHood** | Y | N | N | N | N | Y |
| 19 **Shimkus** | Y | N | N | N | N | Y |
| **INDIANA** | | | | | | |
| 1 Visclosky | N | Y | Y | Y | Y | N |
| 2 **Chocola** | Y | N | N | N | N | Y |
| 3 **Souder** | Y | ? | N | N | N | Y |
| 4 **Buyer** | Y | N | N | N | N | Y |
| 5 **Burton** | Y | ? | N | N | N | Y |
| 6 **Pence** | Y | ? | N | N | N | Y |
| 7 Carson | N | Y | Y | Y | Y | N |
| 8 **Hostettler** | Y | N | N | N | N | Y |
| 9 **Sodrel** | Y | N | N | N | N | Y |
| **IOWA** | | | | | | |
| 1 **Nussle** | Y | N | N | N | N | Y |
| 2 **Leach** | Y | N | Y | Y | Y | Y |
| 3 Boswell | N | Y | Y | Y | Y | Y |
| 4 **Latham** | Y | N | N | N | N | Y |
| 5 **King** | Y | N | N | N | N | Y |
| **KANSAS** | | | | | | |
| 1 **Moran** | Y | N | N | N | N | Y |
| 2 **Ryun** | Y | N | N | N | N | Y |
| 3 Moore | N | Y | Y | N | Y | N |
| 4 **Tiahrt** | Y | N | N | N | N | Y |
| **KENTUCKY** | | | | | | |
| 1 **Whitfield** | Y | N | N | N | N | Y |
| 2 **Lewis** | Y | N | N | N | N | Y |
| 3 **Northup** | Y | N | N | N | N | Y |
| 4 **Davis** | Y | N | N | N | N | Y |
| 5 **Rogers** | Y | N | N | N | N | Y |
| 6 Chandler | N | Y | N | N | Y | Y |
| **LOUISIANA** | | | | | | |
| 1 **Jindal** | Y | N | N | N | N | Y |
| 2 Jefferson | N | Y | Y | Y | Y | N |
| 3 Melancon | N | Y | N | N | N | Y |
| 4 **McCrery** | Y | N | N | N | N | Y |
| 5 **Alexander** | Y | N | N | N | N | Y |
| 6 **Baker** | Y | N | N | N | N | Y |
| 7 **Boustany** | Y | N | N | N | N | Y |
| **MAINE** | | | | | | |
| 1 Allen | N | Y | Y | Y | Y | N |
| 2 Michaud | N | Y | Y | Y | Y | N |
| **MARYLAND** | | | | | | |
| 1 **Gilchrest** | Y | N | N | Y | N | N |
| 2 Ruppersberger | N | Y | Y | Y | Y | N |
| 3 Cardin | N | Y | Y | Y | Y | N |
| 4 Wynn | N | Y | Y | Y | Y | N |
| 5 Hoyer | N | Y | Y | Y | Y | N |
| 6 **Bartlett** | Y | N | N | N | N | Y |
| 7 Cummings | N | Y | Y | Y | Y | N |
| 8 Van Hollen | N | Y | Y | Y | Y | N |
| **MASSACHUSETTS** | | | | | | |
| 1 Olver | N | Y | + | Y | Y | N |
| 2 Neal | N | Y | Y | Y | Y | N |
| 3 McGovern | N | Y | Y | Y | Y | N |
| 4 Frank | N | Y | Y | Y | Y | N |
| 5 Meehan | N | Y | Y | Y | Y | N |
| 6 Tierney | N | Y | Y | Y | Y | N |
| 7 Markey | N | Y | Y | Y | Y | N |
| 8 Capuano | N | Y | Y | Y | Y | N |
| 9 Lynch | N | ? | Y | N | Y | Y |
| 10 Delahunt | N | Y | Y | Y | Y | N |
| **MICHIGAN** | | | | | | |
| 1 Stupak | Y | Y | N | N | N | Y |
| 2 **Hoekstra** | Y | N | N | N | N | Y |
| 3 **Ehlers** | Y | N | N | N | Y | Y |
| 4 **Camp** | Y | N | N | N | N | ? |
| 5 Kildee | N | N | N | N | N | Y |
| 6 **Upton** | Y | N | N | N | N | Y |
| 7 **Schwarz** | Y | N | Y | N | N | Y |
| 8 **Rogers** | Y | N | N | N | N | Y |
| 9 **Knollenberg** | Y | N | N | N | N | Y |
| 10 **Miller** | Y | N | N | N | N | Y |
| 11 **McCotter** | Y | N | N | N | N | Y |
| 12 Levin | N | Y | Y | Y | Y | N |
| 13 Kilpatrick | N | Y | Y | Y | Y | N |
| 14 Conyers | N | N | Y | Y | Y | N |
| 15 Dingell | N | Y | Y | Y | Y | N |
| **MINNESOTA** | | | | | | |
| 1 **Gutknecht** | Y | N | N | N | N | Y |
| 2 **Kline** | Y | N | N | N | N | Y |
| 3 **Ramstad** | Y | N | N | N | N | Y |
| 4 McCollum | N | Y | Y | Y | Y | N |
| 5 Sabo | N | Y | Y | Y | Y | N |
| 6 **Kennedy** | Y | N | N | N | N | Y |
| 7 Peterson | N | Y | N | N | N | Y |
| 8 Oberstar | N | Y | N | N | N | Y |
| **MISSISSIPPI** | | | | | | |
| 1 **Wicker** | ? | ? | ? | ? | ? | ? |
| 2 Thompson | N | Y | Y | Y | Y | N |
| 3 **Pickering** | Y | N | N | N | N | Y |
| 4 Taylor | Y | N | N | N | N | Y |
| **MISSOURI** | | | | | | |
| 1 Clay | N | Y | Y | Y | Y | Y |
| 2 **Akin** | Y | N | N | N | N | Y |
| 3 Carnahan | N | Y | Y | Y | Y | N |
| 4 Skelton | N | Y | N | N | N | Y |
| 5 Cleaver | N | Y | Y | Y | Y | N |
| 6 **Graves** | Y | N | N | N | N | Y |
| 7 **Blunt** | Y | N | N | N | N | Y |
| 8 **Emerson** | Y | N | N | N | N | Y |
| 9 **Hulshof** | Y | N | N | N | N | Y |
| **MONTANA** | | | | | | |
| AL **Rehberg** | Y | N | N | N | N | Y |
| **NEBRASKA** | | | | | | |
| 1 **Fortenberry** | Y | N | N | N | N | Y |
| 2 **Terry** | Y | N | N | N | N | Y |
| 3 **Osborne** | Y | N | N | N | N | Y |
| **NEVADA** | | | | | | |
| 1 Berkley | N | Y | Y | Y | Y | N |
| 2 **Gibbons** | Y | N | N | N | N | Y |
| 3 **Porter** | Y | N | N | N | N | Y |
| **NEW HAMPSHIRE** | | | | | | |
| 1 **Bradley** | Y | N | N | N | N | Y |
| 2 **Bass** | Y | N | Y | Y | Y | N |
| **NEW JERSEY** | | | | | | |
| 1 Andrews | N | Y | Y | Y | Y | N |
| 2 **LoBiondo** | Y | N | N | N | N | Y |
| 3 **Saxton** | Y | N | N | N | N | Y |
| 4 **Smith** | Y | N | N | N | N | Y |
| 5 **Garrett** | Y | N | N | N | N | Y |
| 6 Pallone | N | Y | Y | Y | Y | N |
| 7 **Ferguson** | Y | N | N | N | N | Y |
| 8 Pascrell | N | Y | N | N | Y | N |
| 9 Rothman | ? | ? | ? | ? | ? | ? |
| 10 Payne | N | Y | Y | Y | Y | N |
| 11 **Frelinghuysen** | Y | N | N | N | N | Y |
| 12 Holt | N | Y | Y | Y | Y | N |
| 13 Menendez | N | Y | Y | Y | Y | N |
| **NEW MEXICO** | | | | | | |
| 1 **Wilson** | ? | N | N | N | N | ? |
| 2 **Pearce** | Y | N | ? | N | N | Y |
| 3 Udall | N | Y | Y | Y | Y | N |
| **NEW YORK** | | | | | | |
| 1 Bishop | N | Y | Y | Y | Y | N |
| 2 Israel | N | Y | Y | Y | Y | N |
| 3 **King** | Y | N | N | N | N | Y |
| 4 McCarthy | N | Y | Y | Y | Y | N |
| 5 Ackerman | N | Y | Y | Y | Y | N |
| 6 Meeks | N | Y | Y | Y | Y | N |
| 7 Crowley | N | Y | Y | Y | Y | N |
| 8 Nadler | N | Y | Y | Y | Y | N |
| 9 Weiner | N | Y | Y | Y | Y | N |
| 10 Towns | N | Y | Y | Y | Y | N |
| 11 Owens | N | Y | Y | Y | Y | N |
| 12 Velázquez | N | Y | Y | Y | Y | N |
| 13 **Fossella** | Y | N | N | N | N | Y |
| 14 Maloney | N | Y | Y | Y | Y | N |
| 15 Rangel | N | Y | Y | Y | Y | N |
| 16 Serrano | N | Y | Y | Y | Y | N |
| 17 Engel | N | Y | Y | Y | Y | N |
| 18 Lowey | N | Y | Y | Y | Y | N |
| 19 **Kelly** | Y | N | Y | N | N | Y |
| 20 **Sweeney** | Y | N | Y | N | N | Y |
| 21 McNulty | N | Y | N | N | Y | Y |
| 22 Hinchey | N | Y | Y | Y | Y | N |
| 23 **McHugh** | Y | N | N | N | N | Y |
| 24 **Boehlert** | Y | N | Y | Y | Y | N |
| 25 **Walsh** | Y | N | N | N | N | Y |
| 26 **Reynolds** | Y | N | N | N | N | Y |
| 27 Higgins | N | Y | Y | Y | Y | N |
| 28 Slaughter | N | Y | Y | Y | Y | N |
| 29 **Kuhl** | Y | N | N | N | N | Y |
| **NORTH CAROLINA** | | | | | | |
| 1 Butterfield | N | Y | Y | Y | Y | N |
| 2 Etheridge | N | Y | Y | Y | Y | Y |
| 3 **Jones** | Y | N | N | N | N | Y |
| 4 Price | N | Y | Y | Y | Y | N |
| 5 **Foxx** | Y | N | N | N | N | Y |
| 6 **Coble** | Y | N | N | N | N | Y |
| 7 McIntyre | N | Y | N | N | N | Y |
| 8 **Hayes** | Y | N | N | N | N | Y |
| 9 **Myrick** | Y | ? | N | N | N | Y |
| 10 **McHenry** | Y | N | N | N | N | Y |
| 11 **Taylor** | Y | N | N | N | N | Y |
| 12 Watt | N | Y | Y | Y | Y | N |
| 13 Miller | N | Y | Y | Y | Y | N |
| **NORTH DAKOTA** | | | | | | |
| AL Pomeroy | N | Y | N | N | N | Y |
| **OHIO** | | | | | | |
| 1 **Chabot** | Y | N | N | N | N | Y |
| 2 **Portman** | + | N | N | N | N | Y |
| 3 **Turner** | Y | N | N | N | N | Y |
| 4 **Oxley** | Y | N | N | N | N | Y |
| 5 **Gillmor** | Y | N | N | N | N | Y |
| 6 Strickland | N | Y | Y | N | Y | Y |
| 7 **Hobson** | Y | N | N | N | N | Y |
| 8 **Boehner** | Y | N | N | N | N | Y |
| 9 Kaptur | N | Y | Y | Y | Y | N |
| 10 Kucinich | N | Y | Y | Y | Y | N |
| 11 Jones | N | Y | Y | Y | Y | N |
| 12 **Tiberi** | Y | N | N | N | N | Y |
| 13 Brown | N | Y | Y | Y | Y | N |
| 14 **LaTourette** | Y | N | N | N | N | Y |
| 15 **Pryce** | Y | N | N | N | N | Y |
| 16 **Regula** | Y | N | N | N | N | Y |
| 17 Ryan | N | Y | N | N | N | Y |
| 18 **Ney** | Y | N | N | N | N | Y |
| **OKLAHOMA** | | | | | | |
| 1 **Sullivan** | Y | N | N | N | N | Y |
| 2 Boren | Y | N | N | N | N | Y |
| 3 **Lucas** | Y | N | N | N | N | Y |
| 4 **Cole** | Y | N | N | N | N | Y |
| 5 **Istook** | Y | ? | N | ? | N | Y |
| **OREGON** | | | | | | |
| 1 Wu | N | Y | Y | Y | Y | N |
| 2 **Walden** | Y | N | N | N | N | Y |
| 3 Blumenauer | N | Y | Y | Y | Y | ? |
| 4 DeFazio | N | Y | Y | Y | Y | N |
| 5 Hooley | N | Y | Y | Y | Y | N |
| **PENNSYLVANIA** | | | | | | |
| 1 Brady | N | Y | Y | Y | Y | N |
| 2 Fattah | N | Y | Y | Y | Y | N |
| 3 **English** | Y | N | ? | N | N | Y |
| 4 **Hart** | Y | N | N | N | N | Y |
| 5 **Peterson** | Y | N | N | N | N | Y |
| 6 **Gerlach** | Y | N | N | N | N | Y |
| 7 **Weldon** | Y | N | N | N | N | Y |
| 8 **Fitzpatrick** | Y | N | N | N | N | Y |
| 9 **Shuster** | Y | N | N | N | N | Y |
| 10 **Sherwood** | Y | N | N | N | N | Y |
| 11 Kanjorski | N | Y | N | Y | N | Y |
| 12 Murtha | N | Y | N | N | N | Y |
| 13 Schwartz | N | Y | Y | Y | Y | N |
| 14 Doyle | N | Y | N | Y | Y | Y |
| 15 **Dent** | Y | N | Y | Y | N | Y |
| 16 **Pitts** | Y | ? | N | N | N | Y |
| 17 Holden | Y | Y | N | N | N | Y |
| 18 **Murphy** | Y | N | N | N | N | N |
| 19 **Platts** | Y | N | N | N | N | Y |
| **RHODE ISLAND** | | | | | | |
| 1 Kennedy | N | Y | Y | Y | Y | N |
| 2 Langevin | Y | Y | N | N | Y | Y |
| **SOUTH CAROLINA** | | | | | | |
| 1 **Brown** | Y | N | N | N | N | Y |
| 2 **Wilson** | Y | N | N | N | N | Y |
| 3 **Barrett** | Y | N | N | N | N | Y |
| 4 **Inglis** | Y | N | N | N | N | Y |
| 5 Spratt | N | Y | Y | Y | Y | Y |
| 6 Clyburn | N | Y | Y | Y | Y | N |
| **SOUTH DAKOTA** | | | | | | |
| AL Herseth | N | Y | Y | Y | Y | N |
| **TENNESSEE** | | | | | | |
| 1 **Jenkins** | Y | N | N | N | N | Y |
| 2 **Duncan** | Y | N | N | N | N | Y |
| 3 **Wamp** | Y | N | N | N | N | Y |
| 4 Davis | Y | Y | N | N | N | Y |
| 5 Cooper | N | Y | Y | Y | Y | Y |
| 6 Gordon | N | Y | N | N | N | Y |
| 7 **Blackburn** | Y | N | N | N | N | Y |
| 8 Tanner | N | Y | N | Y | N | Y |
| 9 Ford | N | Y | Y | Y | N | Y |
| **TEXAS** | | | | | | |
| 1 **Gohmert** | Y | N | N | N | N | Y |
| 2 **Poe** | Y | N | N | N | N | Y |
| 3 **Johnson, S.** | Y | ? | N | N | N | Y |
| 4 **Hall** | Y | N | N | N | N | Y |
| 5 **Hensarling** | Y | ? | N | N | N | Y |
| 6 **Barton** | Y | N | N | Y | N | Y |
| 7 **Culberson** | Y | N | N | N | N | Y |
| 8 **Brady** | Y | – | N | N | ? | Y |
| 9 Green | N | Y | Y | Y | Y | N |
| 10 **McCaul** | Y | N | N | N | N | Y |
| 11 **Conaway** | Y | N | N | N | N | Y |
| 12 **Granger** | Y | N | N | N | N | Y |
| 13 **Thornberry** | Y | N | N | N | N | Y |
| 14 **Paul** | Y | N | Y | Y | N | N |
| 15 Hinojosa | N | + | Y | Y | Y | Y |
| 16 Reyes | N | Y | Y | N | Y | Y |
| 17 Edwards | N | Y | N | N | Y | Y |
| 18 Jackson-Lee | N | Y | Y | Y | Y | N |
| 19 **Neugebauer** | Y | N | N | N | N | Y |
| 20 Gonzalez | N | Y | Y | Y | Y | N |
| 21 **Smith** | ? | N | N | N | N | Y |
| 22 **DeLay** | Y | N | N | N | N | Y |
| 23 **Bonilla** | Y | N | N | N | N | Y |
| 24 **Marchant** | Y | N | N | N | N | Y |
| 25 Doggett | N | Y | Y | Y | Y | N |
| 26 **Burgess** | Y | N | N | N | N | Y |
| 27 Ortiz | N | Y | N | N | N | Y |
| 28 Cuellar | N | Y | N | N | N | Y |
| 29 Green | N | Y | ? | Y | Y | N |
| 30 Johnson, E. | N | Y | Y | Y | Y | N |
| 31 **Carter** | Y | N | N | N | N | Y |
| 32 **Sessions** | Y | N | N | N | N | Y |
| **UTAH** | | | | | | |
| 1 **Bishop** | Y | N | N | N | N | Y |
| 2 Matheson | N | Y | N | N | Y | Y |
| 3 **Cannon** | Y | N | N | N | N | Y |
| **VERMONT** | | | | | | |
| AL *Sanders* | N | Y | Y | Y | Y | N |
| **VIRGINIA** | | | | | | |
| 1 **Davis, J.** | Y | N | N | N | N | Y |
| 2 **Drake** | Y | N | N | N | N | Y |
| 3 Scott | N | Y | Y | Y | Y | N |
| 4 **Forbes** | Y | N | N | N | N | Y |
| 5 **Goode** | Y | N | N | N | N | Y |
| 6 **Goodlatte** | Y | N | N | N | N | Y |
| 7 **Cantor** | Y | N | N | N | N | Y |
| 8 Moran | N | Y | Y | Y | Y | N |
| 9 Boucher | N | Y | Y | Y | Y | N |
| 10 **Wolf** | Y | N | N | N | N | Y |
| 11 **Davis, T.** | Y | N | N | N | N | Y |
| **WASHINGTON** | | | | | | |
| 1 Inslee | N | Y | Y | Y | Y | N |
| 2 Larsen | N | Y | Y | Y | Y | N |
| 3 Baird | N | Y | Y | Y | Y | N |
| 4 **Hastings** | Y | N | N | N | N | Y |
| 5 **McMorris** | Y | N | N | N | N | Y |
| 6 Dicks | N | Y | Y | Y | Y | N |
| 7 McDermott | ? | Y | Y | Y | Y | N |
| 8 **Reichert** | Y | N | N | N | N | Y |
| 9 Smith | N | Y | Y | Y | Y | N |
| **WEST VIRGINIA** | | | | | | |
| 1 Mollohan | N | Y | N | N | N | Y |
| 2 **Capito** | Y | N | N | N | N | Y |
| 3 Rahall | N | N | N | N | N | Y |
| **WISCONSIN** | | | | | | |
| 1 **Ryan** | Y | – | N | N | N | Y |
| 2 Baldwin | N | Y | Y | Y | Y | N |
| 3 Kind | N | N | Y | Y | Y | N |
| 4 Moore | N | Y | Y | Y | Y | N |
| 5 **Sensenbrenner** | Y | N | N | N | N | Y |
| 6 **Petri** | Y | N | N | N | N | Y |
| 7 Obey | N | N | Y | Y | Y | Y |
| 8 **Green** | Y | N | N | N | N | Y |
| **WYOMING** | | | | | | |
| AL **Cubin** | Y | ? | N | N | N | Y |

# IN THE HOUSE | By Vote Number

**145.** **H Res 240. House Rules/Adoption.** Adoption of the self-executing rule (H Res 241) under which the House would automatically adopt a resolution repealing three changes to the Rules of the House dealing with ethics committee procedures that were made at the start of the 109th Congress, including a rule that allowed the automatic dismissal of an ethics complaint that is not disposed of by the committee within 45 days. Adopted 406-20: R 208-20; D 197-0 (ND 148-0, SD 49-0); I 1-0. April 27, 2005.

**146.** **H Con Res 95. Fiscal 2006 Budget Resolution/Same-Day Consideration.** Adoption of the resolution (H Res 242) that would waive the two-thirds majority vote requirement for same- day consideration of the rule to provide for House floor consideration of the conference report on the fiscal 2006 budget resolution (H Con Res 95). Adopted 230-199: R 230-0; D 0-198 (ND 0-149, SD 0-49); I 0-1. April 28, 2005.

**147.** **H Con Res 95 . Fiscal 2006 Budget Resolution/Previous Question.** Putnam, R-Fla., motion to order the previous question (thus ending debate and possibility of amendment) on adoption of the rule (H Res 248) to provide for House floor consideration of the conference report on the concurrent resolution that would set broad spending and revenue targets over the next five years. Motion agreed to 228-196: R 228-0; D 0-195 (ND 0-148, SD 0-47); I 0-1. (Subsequently, the rule was adopted by voice vote.) April 28, 2005.

**148.** **Procedural Motion/Journal.** Approval of the House Journal of Wednesday April 27, 2005. Approved 345-75: R 201-23; D 143-52 (ND 105-43, SD 38-9); I 1-0. April 28, 2005.

**149.** **H Con Res 95. Fiscal 2006 Budget Resolution/Conference Report.** Adoption of the conference report on the concurrent resolution that would set broad spending and revenue targets for five years, limit discretionary spending to $843 billion in fiscal 2006, and provide instructions for reconciliation bills that would achieve $70 billion in tax cuts and $34.7 billion in savings to mandatory programs, including $10 billion in Medicaid savings. Adopted (thus sent to the Senate) 214-211: R 214-15; D 0-195 (ND 0-148, SD 0-47); I 0-1. April 28, 2005.

**150.** **H Res 210. Intellectual Property Day/Adoption.** Sensenbrenner, R-Wis., motion to suspend the rules and adopt the resolution that would support the goals of World Intellectual Property Day, to promote, inform and teach the importance of intellectual property. Motion agreed to 315-0: R 176-0; D 139-0 (ND 107-0, SD 32-0); I 0-0. A two-thirds majority of those present and voting (210 in this case) is required for adoption under suspension of the rules. April 28, 2005.

| | 145 | 146 | 147 | 148 | 149 | 150 |
|---|---|---|---|---|---|---|
| **ALABAMA** | | | | | | |
| 1 Bonner | Y | Y | Y | Y | Y | ? |
| 2 Everett | Y | Y | Y | Y | Y | ? |
| 3 Rogers | Y | Y | Y | Y | Y | ? |
| 4 Aderholt | Y | Y | Y | Y | Y | Y |
| 5 Cramer | Y | N | N | Y | N | Y |
| 6 Bachus | Y | Y | Y | Y | Y | Y |
| 7 Davis | Y | N | N | Y | N | Y |
| **ALASKA** | | | | | | |
| AL Young | Y | Y | Y | Y | Y | Y |
| **ARIZONA** | | | | | | |
| 1 Renzi | Y | Y | Y | Y | Y | Y |
| 2 Franks | Y | Y | Y | Y | Y | Y |
| 3 Shadegg | Y | Y | Y | Y | Y | ? |
| 4 Pastor | Y | N | N | Y | N | Y |
| 5 Hayworth | Y | Y | Y | Y | Y | Y |
| 6 Flake | Y | Y | ? | ? | ? | ? |
| 7 Grijalva | Y | N | N | N | N | Y |
| 8 Kolbe | Y | Y | Y | Y | Y | Y |
| **ARKANSAS** | | | | | | |
| 1 Berry | Y | N | N | N | N | Y |
| 2 Snyder | Y | N | N | Y | N | Y |
| 3 Boozman | Y | Y | Y | Y | Y | Y |
| 4 Ross | Y | N | N | Y | N | Y |
| **CALIFORNIA** | | | | | | |
| 1 Thompson | Y | N | N | N | N | Y |
| 2 Herger | Y | Y | Y | Y | Y | Y |
| 3 Lungren | Y | Y | Y | Y | Y | Y |
| 4 Doolittle | Y | Y | Y | Y | Y | Y |
| 5 Matsui, D. | Y | N | N | Y | N | Y |
| 6 Woolsey | Y | N | N | Y | N | Y |
| 7 Miller, George | Y | N | N | Y | N | Y |
| 8 Pelosi | Y | N | N | Y | N | ? |
| 9 Lee | ? | N | N | Y | N | Y |
| 10 Tauscher | Y | N | N | N | N | Y |
| 11 Pombo | Y | Y | Y | Y | Y | Y |
| 12 Lantos | Y | N | N | Y | N | Y |
| 13 Stark | Y | ? | N | N | N | ? |
| 14 Eshoo | Y | N | N | Y | N | Y |
| 15 Honda | Y | N | N | Y | N | Y |
| 16 Lofgren | Y | N | N | Y | N | Y |
| 17 Farr | Y | N | N | Y | N | Y |
| 18 Cardoza | Y | N | N | Y | N | Y |
| 19 Radanovich | Y | Y | Y | Y | Y | ? |
| 20 Costa | Y | N | N | Y | N | Y |
| 21 Nunes | Y | Y | Y | Y | Y | ? |
| 22 Thomas | Y | Y | Y | Y | Y | Y |
| 23 Capps | Y | N | N | Y | N | ? |
| 24 Gallegly | Y | Y | Y | Y | Y | ? |
| 25 McKeon | Y | Y | Y | Y | Y | ? |
| 26 Dreier | Y | Y | Y | Y | Y | Y |
| 27 Sherman | Y | N | N | Y | N | Y |
| 28 Berman | Y | N | N | Y | N | ? |
| 29 Schiff | Y | N | N | Y | N | Y |
| 30 Waxman | ? | N | N | Y | N | Y |
| 31 Becerra | Y | N | N | N | N | Y |
| 32 Solis | Y | N | N | Y | N | Y |
| 33 Watson | Y | N | N | Y | N | Y |
| 34 Roybal-Allard | Y | N | N | Y | N | Y |
| 35 Waters | Y | N | N | N | N | Y |
| 36 Harman | Y | N | N | Y | N | Y |
| 37 Millender-McD. | Y | N | N | Y | N | Y |
| 38 Napolitano | Y | N | N | Y | N | Y |
| 39 Sánchez, Linda | Y | N | N | Y | N | Y |
| 40 Royce | Y | Y | Y | Y | Y | Y |
| 41 Lewis | Y | Y | Y | Y | Y | Y |
| 42 Miller, Gary | Y | Y | Y | Y | Y | ? |
| 43 Baca | Y | N | N | Y | N | ? |
| 44 Calvert | Y | Y | Y | Y | Y | Y |
| 45 Bono | Y | Y | Y | Y | Y | Y |
| 46 Rohrabacher | Y | Y | Y | Y | Y | Y |
| 47 Sanchez, Loretta | Y | N | N | N | N | ? |
| 48 Cox | Y | Y | Y | Y | Y | ? |
| 49 Issa | Y | Y | Y | N | Y | Y |
| 50 Cunningham | Y | Y | ? | ? | ? | ? |
| 51 Filner | Y | N | – | – | – | + |
| 52 Hunter | Y | Y | Y | Y | Y | Y |
| 53 Davis | Y | N | N | Y | N | Y |
| **COLORADO** | | | | | | |
| 1 DeGette | Y | N | N | Y | N | Y |
| 2 Udall | Y | N | N | N | N | Y |
| 3 Salazar | Y | N | N | Y | N | Y |
| 4 Musgrave | Y | Y | Y | Y | Y | Y |
| 5 Hefley | Y | Y | Y | N | Y | Y |
| 6 Tancredo | Y | Y | Y | P | Y | Y |
| 7 Beauprez | Y | Y | Y | Y | Y | Y |
| **CONNECTICUT** | | | | | | |
| 1 Larson | Y | N | N | N | N | ? |
| 2 Simmons | Y | Y | Y | N | N | ? |
| 3 DeLauro | Y | N | N | Y | N | ? |
| 4 Shays | Y | Y | Y | Y | N | ? |
| 5 Johnson | Y | Y | Y | N | N | ? |
| **DELAWARE** | | | | | | |
| AL Castle | Y | Y | Y | N | Y | Y |
| **FLORIDA** | | | | | | |
| 1 Miller | Y | Y | Y | Y | Y | Y |
| 2 Boyd | Y | N | N | Y | N | ? |
| 3 Brown | ? | ? | N | N | N | Y |
| 4 Crenshaw | Y | Y | Y | Y | Y | Y |
| 5 Brown-Waite | Y | Y | Y | Y | Y | Y |
| 6 Stearns | Y | Y | Y | Y | Y | Y |
| 7 Mica | Y | Y | Y | Y | Y | Y |
| 8 Keller | Y | Y | Y | Y | Y | Y |
| 9 Bilirakis | Y | Y | Y | Y | Y | Y |
| 10 Young | Y | Y | Y | Y | Y | Y |
| 11 Davis | Y | N | N | Y | N | ? |
| 12 Putnam | Y | Y | Y | Y | Y | ? |
| 13 Harris | Y | Y | Y | Y | Y | Y |
| 14 Mack | Y | Y | Y | Y | Y | Y |
| 15 Weldon | N | Y | Y | Y | Y | Y |
| 16 Foley | Y | Y | Y | Y | Y | Y |
| 17 Meek | Y | N | N | Y | N | Y |
| 18 Ros-Lehtinen | Y | Y | Y | Y | Y | Y |
| 19 Wexler | Y | N | N | Y | N | Y |
| 20 Wasserman-Schultz | Y | N | N | Y | N | Y |
| 21 Diaz-Balart, L. | Y | Y | Y | Y | Y | Y |
| 22 Shaw | Y | Y | Y | Y | Y | ? |
| 23 Hastings | Y | N | N | N | N | Y |
| 24 Feeney | Y | Y | Y | Y | Y | Y |
| 25 Diaz-Balart, M. | Y | Y | Y | Y | Y | Y |
| **GEORGIA** | | | | | | |
| 1 Kingston | Y | Y | Y | Y | Y | Y |
| 2 Bishop | Y | N | N | Y | N | ? |
| 3 Marshall | Y | N | N | N | N | ? |
| 4 McKinney | Y | N | N | Y | N | ? |
| 5 Lewis | Y | N | N | Y | N | ? |
| 6 Price | N | Y | Y | Y | Y | Y |
| 7 Linder | Y | Y | Y | Y | Y | Y |
| 8 Westmoreland | ? | Y | Y | Y | Y | Y |
| 9 Norwood | Y | Y | Y | N | Y | ? |
| 10 Deal | Y | Y | Y | Y | Y | ? |
| 11 Gingrey | Y | Y | Y | Y | Y | ? |
| 12 Barrow | Y | N | N | Y | N | Y |
| 13 Scott | Y | N | N | Y | N | ? |
| **HAWAII** | | | | | | |
| 1 Abercrombie | Y | N | N | Y | N | Y |
| 2 Case | Y | N | N | Y | N | Y |
| **IDAHO** | | | | | | |
| 1 Otter | N | Y | Y | N | Y | Y |
| 2 Simpson | N | Y | Y | Y | Y | Y |
| **ILLINOIS** | | | | | | |
| 1 Rush | Y | N | N | Y | N | Y |
| 2 Jackson | Y | N | N | Y | N | Y |
| 3 Lipinski | Y | N | N | Y | N | Y |
| 4 Gutierrez | Y | N | N | Y | N | Y |
| 5 Emanuel | Y | N | N | Y | N | ? |
| 6 Hyde | Y | ? | Y | Y | Y | Y |
| 7 Davis | Y | N | N | Y | N | Y |
| 8 Bean | Y | N | N | Y | N | Y |
| 9 Schakowsky | Y | N | N | N | N | ? |
| 10 Kirk | Y | Y | Y | Y | Y | Y |
| 11 Weller | Y | Y | Y | N | Y | ? |
| 12 Costello | Y | N | N | N | N | Y |

**KEY**   **Republicans**   Democrats   *Independents*

| | | | |
|---|---|---|---|
| Y | Voted for (yea) | X | Paired against | C | Voted "present" to avoid possible conflict of interest |
| # | Paired for | – | Announced against | | |
| + | Announced for | P | Voted "present" | ? | Did not vote or otherwise make a position known |
| N | Voted against (nay) | | | | |

ND Northern Democrats, SD Southern Democrats
Southern states: Ala., Ark., Fla., Ga., Ky., La., Miss., N.C., Okla., S.C., Tenn., Texas, Va.

| | 145 | 146 | 147 | 148 | 149 | 150 |
|---|---|---|---|---|---|---|
| 13 **Biggert** | Y | Y | Y | Y | Y | Y |
| 14 **Hastert** | | | | Y | Y | |
| 15 **Johnson** | Y | Y | Y | Y | N | ? |
| 16 **Manzullo** | Y | Y | Y | Y | Y | Y |
| 17 Evans | Y | N | N | Y | N | Y |
| 18 **LaHood** | Y | Y | Y | Y | Y | ? |
| 19 **Shimkus** | Y | Y | Y | Y | Y | Y |
| **INDIANA** | | | | | | |
| 1 Visclosky | Y | N | N | N | N | Y |
| 2 **Chocola** | Y | Y | Y | Y | Y | Y |
| 3 **Souder** | P | Y | Y | Y | Y | Y |
| 4 **Buyer** | N | Y | Y | Y | Y | ? |
| 5 **Burton** | N | Y | Y | Y | Y | ? |
| 6 **Pence** | N | Y | Y | Y | Y | Y |
| 7 Carson | Y | N | N | Y | N | Y |
| 8 **Hostettler** | Y | Y | Y | Y | Y | Y |
| 9 **Sodrel** | Y | Y | Y | Y | Y | Y |
| **IOWA** | | | | | | |
| 1 **Nussle** | Y | Y | Y | Y | Y | Y |
| 2 **Leach** | Y | Y | Y | Y | N | Y |
| 3 Boswell | Y | N | N | Y | N | Y |
| 4 **Latham** | Y | Y | Y | N | Y | Y |
| 5 **King** | N | Y | Y | Y | Y | Y |
| **KANSAS** | | | | | | |
| 1 **Moran** | Y | Y | Y | Y | Y | Y |
| 2 **Ryun** | Y | Y | Y | Y | Y | Y |
| 3 Moore | Y | N | N | N | N | Y |
| 4 **Tiahrt** | N | Y | Y | Y | Y | Y |
| **KENTUCKY** | | | | | | |
| 1 **Whitfield** | Y | Y | Y | Y | Y | Y |
| 2 **Lewis** | Y | Y | Y | Y | Y | Y |
| 3 **Northup** | Y | Y | Y | Y | Y | ? |
| 4 **Davis** | Y | Y | Y | Y | Y | Y |
| 5 **Rogers** | Y | Y | Y | Y | Y | ? |
| 6 Chandler | Y | N | N | Y | N | ? |
| **LOUISIANA** | | | | | | |
| 1 **Jindal** | Y | Y | Y | Y | Y | Y |
| 2 Jefferson | Y | N | N | ? | ? | ? |
| 3 Melancon | Y | N | N | Y | N | Y |
| 4 **McCrery** | Y | Y | Y | Y | Y | Y |
| 5 **Alexander** | Y | Y | Y | Y | Y | Y |
| 6 **Baker** | Y | Y | Y | Y | Y | ? |
| 7 **Boustany** | Y | Y | Y | Y | Y | Y |
| **MAINE** | | | | | | |
| 1 Allen | Y | N | N | Y | N | ? |
| 2 Michaud | Y | N | N | Y | N | Y |
| **MARYLAND** | | | | | | |
| 1 **Gilchrest** | Y | Y | Y | Y | Y | Y |
| 2 Ruppersberger | Y | N | N | Y | N | Y |
| 3 Cardin | Y | N | N | Y | N | Y |
| 4 Wynn | Y | N | N | Y | N | Y |
| 5 Hoyer | Y | N | N | Y | N | Y |
| 6 **Bartlett** | Y | Y | Y | Y | Y | Y |
| 7 Cummings | Y | N | N | Y | N | Y |
| 8 Van Hollen | Y | N | N | Y | N | Y |
| **MASSACHUSETTS** | | | | | | |
| 1 Olver | Y | N | N | N | N | ? |
| 2 Neal | Y | N | N | N | N | ? |
| 3 McGovern | Y | N | N | N | N | Y |
| 4 Frank | Y | N | N | Y | N | Y |
| 5 Meehan | Y | N | N | Y | N | ? |
| 6 Tierney | Y | N | N | Y | N | ? |
| 7 Markey | Y | N | N | N | N | Y |
| 8 Capuano | Y | N | N | N | N | ? |
| 9 Lynch | Y | N | N | Y | N | ? |
| 10 Delahunt | Y | N | N | Y | N | ? |
| **MICHIGAN** | | | | | | |
| 1 Stupak | Y | N | N | N | N | Y |
| 2 **Hoekstra** | Y | Y | Y | Y | Y | Y |
| 3 **Ehlers** | Y | Y | Y | Y | Y | Y |
| 4 **Camp** | Y | Y | Y | Y | Y | Y |
| 5 Kildee | Y | N | N | Y | N | Y |
| 6 **Upton** | Y | Y | Y | Y | Y | Y |
| 7 **Schwarz** | Y | Y | Y | Y | Y | Y |
| 8 **Rogers** | Y | Y | Y | Y | Y | Y |
| 9 **Knollenberg** | Y | Y | Y | Y | Y | Y |
| 10 **Miller** | Y | Y | Y | Y | Y | Y |
| 11 **McCotter** | Y | Y | Y | N | Y | Y |
| 12 Levin | Y | N | N | N | N | Y |
| 13 Kilpatrick | Y | N | N | Y | N | Y |
| 14 Conyers | Y | N | N | Y | N | Y |
| 15 Dingell | Y | N | N | Y | N | Y |
| **MINNESOTA** | | | | | | |
| 1 **Gutknecht** | Y | Y | Y | N | N | Y |
| 2 **Kline** | Y | Y | Y | Y | Y | Y |
| 3 **Ramstad** | Y | Y | Y | N | N | Y |
| 4 McCollum | Y | N | N | Y | N | Y |
| 5 Sabo | Y | N | N | N | N | Y |
| 6 **Kennedy** | Y | Y | Y | N | Y | Y |
| 7 Peterson | Y | N | N | N | Y | Y |
| 8 Oberstar | Y | N | N | N | N | Y |
| **MISSISSIPPI** | | | | | | |
| 1 **Wicker** | ? | Y | Y | Y | Y | Y |
| 2 Thompson | Y | N | N | N | N | Y |
| 3 **Pickering** | Y | Y | Y | Y | Y | Y |
| 4 Taylor | Y | N | N | N | N | Y |
| **MISSOURI** | | | | | | |
| 1 Clay | Y | N | N | Y | N | ? |
| 2 **Akin** | Y | Y | Y | Y | Y | Y |
| 3 Carnahan | Y | N | N | Y | N | Y |
| 4 Skelton | Y | N | N | Y | N | Y |
| 5 Cleaver | Y | N | N | Y | N | Y |
| 6 **Graves** | Y | Y | Y | N | Y | ? |
| 7 **Blunt** | Y | Y | Y | Y | Y | Y |
| 8 **Emerson** | Y | Y | Y | Y | Y | Y |
| 9 **Hulshof** | Y | Y | Y | N | Y | Y |
| **MONTANA** | | | | | | |
| AL **Rehberg** | Y | Y | Y | Y | Y | Y |
| **NEBRASKA** | | | | | | |
| 1 **Fortenberry** | Y | Y | Y | Y | Y | Y |
| 2 **Terry** | Y | Y | Y | Y | Y | Y |
| 3 **Osborne** | Y | Y | Y | Y | Y | Y |
| **NEVADA** | | | | | | |
| 1 Berkley | Y | N | N | ? | N | ? |
| 2 **Gibbons** | Y | Y | Y | N | Y | Y |
| 3 **Porter** | Y | Y | Y | Y | Y | Y |
| **NEW HAMPSHIRE** | | | | | | |
| 1 **Bradley** | Y | Y | Y | Y | Y | Y |
| 2 **Bass** | Y | Y | Y | Y | N | ? |
| **NEW JERSEY** | | | | | | |
| 1 Andrews | Y | N | N | Y | N | Y |
| 2 **LoBiondo** | Y | Y | Y | N | N | Y |
| 3 **Saxton** | Y | Y | Y | Y | N | Y |
| 4 **Smith** | Y | Y | Y | Y | Y | Y |
| 5 **Garrett** | Y | Y | Y | Y | Y | Y |
| 6 Pallone | Y | N | N | Y | N | Y |
| 7 **Ferguson** | Y | Y | Y | Y | Y | Y |
| 8 Pascrell | Y | N | N | Y | N | Y |
| 9 Rothman | ? | ? | ? | ? | ? | ? |
| 10 Payne | Y | N | N | Y | N | Y |
| 11 **Frelinghuysen** | Y | Y | Y | Y | Y | Y |
| 12 Holt | Y | N | N | Y | N | Y |
| 13 Menendez | Y | N | N | Y | N | ? |
| **NEW MEXICO** | | | | | | |
| 1 **Wilson** | Y | Y | Y | Y | Y | Y |
| 2 **Pearce** | Y | Y | Y | Y | Y | ? |
| 3 Udall | Y | N | N | N | N | Y |
| **NEW YORK** | | | | | | |
| 1 Bishop | Y | N | N | Y | N | ? |
| 2 Israel | Y | N | N | Y | N | ? |
| 3 **King** | Y | Y | Y | ? | Y | ? |
| 4 McCarthy | Y | N | N | N | N | Y |
| 5 Ackerman | Y | N | N | Y | N | ? |
| 6 Meeks | Y | N | ? | Y | N | ? |
| 7 Crowley | Y | N | N | Y | N | ? |
| 8 Nadler | Y | N | N | N | N | ? |
| 9 Weiner | Y | N | N | N | N | ? |
| 10 Towns | Y | N | N | Y | ? | ? |
| 11 Owens | Y | N | N | Y | N | Y |
| 12 Velázquez | Y | N | N | Y | N | ? |
| 13 **Fossella** | Y | Y | Y | N | Y | Y |
| 14 Maloney | Y | N | N | Y | N | ? |
| 15 Rangel | Y | N | N | Y | N | ? |
| 16 Serrano | Y | N | N | Y | N | Y |
| 17 Engel | Y | N | N | Y | N | Y |
| 18 Lowey | Y | N | N | Y | N | ? |
| 19 **Kelly** | Y | Y | Y | N | Y | Y |
| 20 **Sweeney** | Y | Y | Y | Y | Y | Y |
| 21 McNulty | Y | N | N | N | N | Y |
| 22 Hinchey | Y | N | N | N | N | ? |
| 23 **McHugh** | Y | Y | Y | Y | Y | ? |
| 24 **Boehlert** | Y | Y | Y | Y | N | ? |
| 25 **Walsh** | Y | Y | Y | Y | Y | ? |
| 26 **Reynolds** | Y | Y | Y | Y | Y | Y |
| 27 Higgins | Y | N | N | Y | N | Y |
| 28 Slaughter | Y | N | N | N | N | ? |
| 29 **Kuhl** | Y | Y | Y | Y | Y | Y |
| **NORTH CAROLINA** | | | | | | |
| 1 Butterfield | Y | N | N | Y | N | ? |
| 2 Etheridge | Y | N | N | Y | N | ? |
| 3 **Jones** | Y | Y | Y | N | N | Y |
| 4 Price | Y | N | N | Y | N | ? |
| 5 **Foxx** | Y | Y | Y | Y | Y | Y |
| 6 **Coble** | Y | Y | Y | Y | Y | Y |
| 7 McIntyre | Y | N | N | Y | N | Y |
| 8 **Hayes** | Y | Y | Y | Y | Y | ? |
| 9 **Myrick** | Y | Y | Y | Y | Y | Y |
| 10 **McHenry** | N | Y | Y | Y | Y | Y |
| 11 **Taylor** | Y | Y | Y | Y | Y | ? |
| 12 Watt | Y | N | N | Y | N | ? |
| 13 Miller | Y | N | N | Y | N | Y |
| **NORTH DAKOTA** | | | | | | |
| AL Pomeroy | Y | N | N | Y | N | Y |
| **OHIO** | | | | | | |
| 1 **Chabot** | Y | Y | Y | Y | Y | Y |
| 2 **Portman** | Y | Y | Y | Y | Y | Y |
| 3 **Turner** | Y | Y | Y | Y | Y | ? |
| 4 **Oxley** | Y | Y | Y | Y | Y | ? |
| 5 **Gillmor** | N | Y | Y | Y | Y | Y |
| 6 Strickland | Y | N | N | N | N | ? |
| 7 **Hobson** | Y | Y | Y | Y | Y | Y |
| 8 **Boehner** | Y | Y | Y | ? | Y | Y |
| 9 Kaptur | Y | N | N | Y | N | Y |
| 10 Kucinich | Y | N | N | N | N | Y |
| 11 Jones | Y | N | N | Y | N | ? |
| 12 **Tiberi** | Y | Y | Y | N | Y | ? |
| 13 Brown | Y | N | N | Y | N | ? |
| 14 **LaTourette** | Y | Y | Y | Y | Y | Y |
| 15 **Pryce** | Y | Y | Y | N | Y | Y |
| 16 **Regula** | Y | Y | Y | Y | Y | Y |
| 17 Ryan | Y | N | N | Y | N | ? |
| 18 **Ney** | Y | Y | Y | Y | Y | Y |
| **OKLAHOMA** | | | | | | |
| 1 **Sullivan** | Y | Y | Y | ? | Y | Y |
| 2 Boren | Y | N | N | Y | N | Y |
| 3 **Lucas** | Y | Y | Y | Y | Y | Y |
| 4 **Cole** | Y | Y | Y | Y | Y | Y |
| 5 **Istook** | Y | Y | Y | Y | Y | Y |
| **OREGON** | | | | | | |
| 1 Wu | Y | N | N | N | N | Y |
| 2 **Walden** | Y | Y | Y | Y | Y | Y |
| 3 Blumenauer | Y | N | N | Y | N | Y |
| 4 DeFazio | Y | N | N | N | N | ? |
| 5 Hooley | Y | N | N | Y | N | Y |
| **PENNSYLVANIA** | | | | | | |
| 1 Brady | Y | N | N | N | N | Y |
| 2 Fattah | Y | N | N | Y | N | Y |
| 3 **English** | Y | Y | Y | Y | Y | Y |
| 4 **Hart** | Y | Y | Y | N | Y | Y |
| 5 **Peterson** | Y | Y | Y | Y | Y | ? |
| 6 **Gerlach** | Y | Y | Y | Y | Y | Y |
| 7 **Weldon** | Y | Y | Y | Y | Y | Y |
| 8 **Fitzpatrick** | Y | Y | Y | N | Y | Y |
| 9 **Shuster** | Y | Y | Y | Y | Y | Y |
| 10 **Sherwood** | Y | Y | Y | Y | Y | Y |
| 11 Kanjorski | Y | N | N | Y | N | Y |
| 12 Murtha | Y | N | N | Y | N | Y |
| 13 Schwartz | Y | N | N | Y | N | Y |
| 14 Doyle | Y | N | N | Y | N | ? |
| 15 **Dent** | Y | Y | Y | Y | Y | Y |
| 16 **Pitts** | Y | Y | Y | Y | Y | Y |
| 17 Holden | Y | N | N | Y | N | Y |
| 18 **Murphy** | Y | Y | Y | Y | Y | ? |
| 19 **Platts** | Y | Y | Y | N | Y | Y |
| **RHODE ISLAND** | | | | | | |
| 1 Kennedy | Y | N | N | N | N | Y |
| 2 Langevin | Y | N | N | Y | N | Y |
| **SOUTH CAROLINA** | | | | | | |
| 1 **Brown** | Y | Y | Y | Y | Y | ? |
| 2 **Wilson** | Y | Y | Y | Y | Y | Y |
| 3 **Barrett** | Y | Y | Y | Y | Y | ? |
| 4 **Inglis** | Y | Y | Y | Y | Y | ? |
| 5 Spratt | Y | N | N | Y | N | Y |
| 6 Clyburn | Y | N | ? | ? | ? | ? |
| **SOUTH DAKOTA** | | | | | | |
| AL Herseth | Y | N | N | Y | N | Y |
| **TENNESSEE** | | | | | | |
| 1 **Jenkins** | Y | Y | Y | Y | Y | Y |
| 2 **Duncan** | Y | Y | Y | Y | Y | Y |
| 3 **Wamp** | Y | Y | Y | Y | Y | ? |
| 4 Davis | Y | N | N | Y | N | ? |
| 5 Cooper | Y | N | N | Y | N | ? |
| 6 Gordon | Y | N | N | Y | N | ? |
| 7 **Blackburn** | N | Y | Y | Y | Y | Y |
| 8 Tanner | Y | N | N | N | N | Y |
| 9 Ford | Y | ? | ? | ? | ? | ? |
| **TEXAS** | | | | | | |
| 1 **Gohmert** | N | Y | Y | Y | Y | Y |
| 2 **Poe** | N | Y | Y | Y | Y | Y |
| 3 **Johnson, S.** | Y | Y | Y | Y | Y | Y |
| 4 **Hall** | Y | Y | Y | Y | Y | Y |
| 5 **Hensarling** | Y | Y | Y | Y | Y | Y |
| 6 **Barton** | N | Y | Y | Y | Y | Y |
| 7 **Culberson** | N | Y | Y | Y | Y | Y |
| 8 **Brady** | Y | Y | Y | Y | Y | Y |
| 9 Green | Y | N | N | Y | N | Y |
| 10 **McCaul** | Y | Y | Y | Y | Y | Y |
| 11 **Conaway** | Y | Y | Y | Y | Y | Y |
| 12 **Granger** | Y | Y | Y | Y | Y | Y |
| 13 **Thornberry** | N | Y | Y | Y | Y | Y |
| 14 **Paul** | Y | Y | ? | ? | ? | ? |
| 15 Hinojosa | Y | N | N | Y | N | Y |
| 16 Reyes | Y | N | N | Y | N | ? |
| 17 Edwards | Y | N | N | Y | N | Y |
| 18 Jackson-Lee | Y | N | N | N | N | Y |
| 19 **Neugebauer** | Y | Y | Y | Y | Y | ? |
| 20 Gonzalez | Y | N | N | Y | N | Y |
| 21 **Smith** | Y | Y | Y | Y | Y | Y |
| 22 **DeLay** | Y | Y | Y | Y | Y | Y |
| 23 **Bonilla** | Y | Y | Y | ? | Y | Y |
| 24 **Marchant** | Y | Y | Y | Y | Y | Y |
| 25 Doggett | Y | N | ? | ? | ? | ? |
| 26 **Burgess** | N | Y | Y | Y | Y | Y |
| 27 Ortiz | Y | N | N | Y | N | Y |
| 28 Cuellar | Y | N | N | Y | N | Y |
| 29 Green | Y | N | N | N | N | Y |
| 30 Johnson, E. | Y | N | N | Y | N | Y |
| 31 **Carter** | N | Y | Y | Y | Y | Y |
| 32 **Sessions** | Y | Y | Y | Y | Y | Y |
| **UTAH** | | | | | | |
| 1 **Bishop** | Y | Y | Y | Y | Y | Y |
| 2 Matheson | Y | N | N | Y | N | Y |
| 3 **Cannon** | Y | Y | Y | Y | Y | ? |
| **VERMONT** | | | | | | |
| AL *Sanders* | Y | N | N | Y | N | ? |
| **VIRGINIA** | | | | | | |
| 1 **Davis, J.** | Y | Y | Y | Y | Y | ? |
| 2 **Drake** | Y | Y | Y | Y | Y | Y |
| 3 Scott | Y | N | N | N | N | Y |
| 4 **Forbes** | Y | Y | Y | Y | Y | Y |
| 5 **Goode** | Y | Y | Y | Y | N | ? |
| 6 **Goodlatte** | Y | Y | Y | Y | Y | Y |
| 7 **Cantor** | Y | Y | Y | Y | Y | Y |
| 8 Moran | Y | N | – | Y | N | Y |
| 9 Boucher | ? | N | N | Y | N | Y |
| 10 **Wolf** | Y | Y | Y | Y | Y | Y |
| 11 **Davis, T.** | Y | Y | Y | Y | Y | ? |
| **WASHINGTON** | | | | | | |
| 1 Inslee | Y | N | N | Y | N | Y |
| 2 Larsen | Y | N | N | N | N | ? |
| 3 Baird | Y | N | N | N | N | Y |
| 4 **Hastings** | Y | Y | Y | Y | Y | Y |
| 5 **McMorris** | Y | Y | Y | Y | Y | Y |
| 6 Dicks | Y | N | N | Y | N | ? |
| 7 McDermott | Y | N | N | N | N | Y |
| 8 **Reichert** | Y | Y | Y | Y | Y | Y |
| 9 Smith | Y | N | N | Y | N | Y |
| **WEST VIRGINIA** | | | | | | |
| 1 Mollohan | Y | N | N | Y | N | Y |
| 2 **Capito** | Y | Y | Y | Y | Y | ? |
| 3 Rahall | Y | N | N | Y | N | Y |
| **WISCONSIN** | | | | | | |
| 1 **Ryan** | Y | Y | Y | Y | Y | ? |
| 2 Baldwin | Y | N | N | N | N | Y |
| 3 Kind | Y | N | N | N | N | Y |
| 4 Moore | Y | N | N | N | N | Y |
| 5 **Sensenbrenner** | Y | Y | Y | Y | Y | Y |
| 6 **Petri** | Y | Y | Y | Y | Y | Y |
| 7 Obey | Y | N | N | Y | N | Y |
| 8 **Green** | Y | Y | Y | Y | N | Y |
| **WYOMING** | | | | | | |
| AL **Cubin** | N | Y | Y | Y | Y | Y |

# IN THE HOUSE | By Vote Number

**151.** **HR 748. House Judiciary Committee Report/Motion to Table.**
Sensenbrenner, R-Wis., motion to table (kill) the Conyers, D-Mich., privileged resolution (H Res 253) that would direct the chairman of the Judiciary Committee to provide a supplement to the committee report that would describe Democratic committee amendments with objective language for the interstate abortion notification bill. Motion agreed to 220-196: R 220-0; D 0-195 (ND 0-146, SD 0-49); I 0-1. May 3, 2005.

**152.** **H Res 228. Vietnamese Americans Tribute/Adoption.** Fortenberry, R-Neb., motion to suspend the rules and adopt the resolution that would celebrate the contributions of Vietnamese Americans, honor all members of the U.S. and South Vietnamese armed forces who fought in the Vietnam conflict and observe the 30th anniversary of the fall of the Republic of Vietnam to the Communist forces of North Vietnam on April 30, 1975. Motion agreed to 416-0: R 222-0; D 193-0 (ND 145-0, SD 48-0); I 1-0. A two-thirds majority of those present and voting (278 in this case) is required for adoption under suspension of the rules. May 3, 2005.

**153.** **HR 366. Vocational and Technical Education/Recommit.** Miller, D-Calif., motion to recommit the bill to the House Education and the Workforce Committee with instructions to include language that would bar the use of Education Department funds to pay journalists or commentators to espouse points of view and would require on-air disclosure if prepackaged news segments were paid for with federal funds. Motion rejected 197-224: R 1-223; D 195-1 (ND 146-1, SD 49-0); I 1-0. May 4, 2005.

**154.** **HR 366. Vocational and Technical Education/Passage.** Passage of the bill that would reauthorize the Perkins vocational and technical education program for $1.3 billion in fiscal 2006 and such funds as necessary in fiscal 2007-11. The bill would merge Perkins funding with Tech-Prep, a program that provides specialized math and science courses to ease the transition of high school students to vocational school or community college. It also would provide federal grants to states for supplemental programs, such as courses in emerging technologies. Passed 416-9: R 218-9; D 197-0 (ND 147-0, SD 50-0); I 1-0. May 4, 2005.

**155.** **H Con Res 127. Charles Ghankay Taylor Condemnation/Adoption.**
Smith, R-N.J., motion to suspend the rules and adopt the concurrent resolution that would call on the government of Nigeria to transfer Charles Ghankay Taylor, former president of Liberia, to a United Nations special court to be tried for war crimes and other violations of international humanitarian law. Motion agreed to 421-1: R 223-1; D 197-0 (ND 148-0, SD 49-0); I 1-0. A two-thirds majority of those present and voting (282 in this case) is required for adoption under suspension of the rules. May 4, 2005.

**156.** **H Res 195. Victory in Europe Anniversary/Adoption.** Smith, R-N.J., motion to suspend the rules and adopt the resolution that would recognize the 60th anniversary of the liberation of Western Bohemia by Allied military forces, and honor those individuals who gave their lives during the liberation. Motion agreed to 419-0: R 224-0; D 194-0 (ND 145-0, SD 49-0); I 1-0. A two-thirds majority of those present and voting (280 in this case) is required for adoption under suspension of the rules. May 4, 2005.

*Rep. Rob Portman, R-Ohio, resigned effective April 29, 2005. The last vote for which he was eligible was vote 150.

ND Northern Democrats, SD Southern Democrats
Southern states: Ala., Ark., Fla., Ga., Ky., La., Miss., N.C., Okla., S.C., Tenn., Texas, Va.

| | 151 | 152 | 153 | 154 | 155 | 156 |
|---|---|---|---|---|---|---|
| **ALABAMA** | | | | | | |
| 1 Bonner | Y | Y | N | Y | Y | Y |
| 2 Everett | Y | Y | N | Y | Y | Y |
| 3 Rogers | Y | Y | N | Y | Y | Y |
| 4 Aderholt | Y | Y | N | Y | Y | Y |
| 5 Cramer | N | Y | Y | Y | Y | Y |
| 6 Bachus | Y | Y | N | Y | Y | Y |
| 7 Davis | N | Y | Y | Y | Y | Y |
| **ALASKA** | | | | | | |
| AL Young | Y | Y | N | Y | Y | Y |
| **ARIZONA** | | | | | | |
| 1 Renzi | Y | Y | N | Y | Y | Y |
| 2 Franks | Y | Y | N | N | Y | Y |
| 3 Shadegg | Y | Y | N | Y | Y | Y |
| 4 Pastor | N | Y | Y | Y | Y | Y |
| 5 Hayworth | Y | Y | N | Y | Y | Y |
| 6 Flake | Y | Y | N | Y | Y | Y |
| 7 Grijalva | N | Y | Y | Y | Y | Y |
| 8 Kolbe | Y | Y | N | Y | Y | Y |
| **ARKANSAS** | | | | | | |
| 1 Berry | N | ? | Y | Y | Y | Y |
| 2 Snyder | N | Y | Y | Y | Y | Y |
| 3 Boozman | Y | Y | N | Y | Y | Y |
| 4 Ross | N | Y | Y | Y | Y | Y |
| **CALIFORNIA** | | | | | | |
| 1 Thompson | N | Y | Y | Y | Y | Y |
| 2 Herger | Y | Y | N | Y | Y | Y |
| 3 Lungren | Y | Y | N | Y | Y | Y |
| 4 Doolittle | Y | Y | N | Y | Y | Y |
| 5 Matsui, D. | N | Y | Y | Y | Y | Y |
| 6 Woolsey | N | Y | Y | Y | Y | Y |
| 7 Miller, George | N | Y | Y | Y | Y | ? |
| 8 Pelosi | N | Y | Y | Y | Y | Y |
| 9 Lee | N | Y | Y | Y | Y | Y |
| 10 Tauscher | N | Y | Y | Y | Y | Y |
| 11 Pombo | Y | Y | N | Y | Y | Y |
| 12 Lantos | N | Y | Y | Y | Y | Y |
| 13 Stark | N | Y | Y | Y | Y | Y |
| 14 Eshoo | N | Y | Y | Y | Y | Y |
| 15 Honda | N | Y | Y | Y | Y | Y |
| 16 Lofgren | N | Y | Y | Y | Y | Y |
| 17 Farr | N | Y | Y | Y | Y | Y |
| 18 Cardoza | N | Y | Y | Y | Y | Y |
| 19 Radanovich | Y | Y | N | Y | Y | Y |
| 20 Costa | N | Y | Y | Y | Y | Y |
| 21 Nunes | Y | Y | N | Y | Y | Y |
| 22 Thomas | Y | Y | N | Y | Y | Y |
| 23 Capps | N | Y | Y | Y | Y | Y |
| 24 Gallegly | Y | Y | N | Y | Y | Y |
| 25 McKeon | Y | Y | N | Y | Y | Y |
| 26 Dreier | Y | Y | N | Y | Y | Y |
| 27 Sherman | N | Y | Y | Y | Y | Y |
| 28 Berman | N | Y | Y | Y | Y | Y |
| 29 Schiff | N | Y | Y | Y | Y | Y |
| 30 Waxman | N | Y | Y | Y | Y | Y |
| 31 Becerra | N | Y | Y | Y | Y | Y |
| 32 Solis | N | Y | Y | Y | Y | Y |
| 33 Watson | N | Y | Y | Y | Y | Y |
| 34 Roybal-Allard | N | Y | Y | Y | Y | Y |
| 35 Waters | N | Y | Y | Y | Y | Y |
| 36 Harman | N | Y | Y | Y | Y | Y |
| 37 Millender-McD. | N | Y | Y | Y | Y | Y |
| 38 Napolitano | N | Y | Y | Y | Y | Y |
| 39 Sánchez, Linda | N | Y | Y | Y | Y | Y |
| 40 Royce | Y | Y | N | N | Y | Y |
| 41 Lewis | Y | Y | N | Y | Y | Y |
| 42 Miller, Gary | Y | Y | N | Y | Y | Y |
| 43 Baca | N | Y | Y | Y | Y | Y |
| 44 Calvert | Y | Y | N | Y | Y | Y |
| 45 Bono | Y | Y | N | Y | Y | Y |
| 46 Rohrabacher | Y | Y | N | Y | Y | Y |
| 47 Sanchez, Loretta | N | Y | + | Y | Y | Y |
| 48 Cox | Y | Y | N | Y | Y | Y |
| 49 Issa | Y | Y | N | Y | Y | Y |

| | 151 | 152 | 153 | 154 | 155 | 156 |
|---|---|---|---|---|---|---|
| 50 Cunningham | Y | Y | N | Y | Y | Y |
| 51 Filner | N | Y | Y | Y | Y | Y |
| 52 Hunter | Y | Y | N | Y | Y | Y |
| 53 Davis | N | Y | Y | Y | Y | Y |
| **COLORADO** | | | | | | |
| 1 DeGette | N | Y | Y | Y | Y | Y |
| 2 Udall | N | Y | Y | Y | Y | Y |
| 3 Salazar | N | Y | Y | Y | Y | Y |
| 4 Musgrave | Y | Y | N | Y | Y | Y |
| 5 Hefley | Y | Y | N | Y | Y | Y |
| 6 Tancredo | Y | Y | N | Y | Y | Y |
| 7 Beauprez | Y | Y | N | Y | Y | Y |
| **CONNECTICUT** | | | | | | |
| 1 Larson | – | + | + | + | + | + |
| 2 Simmons | Y | Y | N | Y | Y | Y |
| 3 DeLauro | N | Y | Y | Y | Y | Y |
| 4 Shays | ? | Y | N | Y | Y | Y |
| 5 Johnson | ? | Y | N | Y | Y | Y |
| **DELAWARE** | | | | | | |
| AL Castle | Y | Y | N | Y | Y | Y |
| **FLORIDA** | | | | | | |
| 1 Miller | Y | Y | N | Y | Y | Y |
| 2 Boyd | N | Y | Y | Y | Y | Y |
| 3 Brown | N | Y | Y | Y | Y | Y |
| 4 Crenshaw | Y | Y | N | Y | Y | Y |
| 5 Brown-Waite | Y | Y | N | Y | Y | Y |
| 6 Stearns | Y | Y | N | Y | Y | Y |
| 7 Mica | Y | Y | N | Y | Y | Y |
| 8 Keller | Y | Y | N | Y | Y | Y |
| 9 Bilirakis | Y | Y | N | Y | Y | Y |
| 10 Young | Y | Y | N | Y | Y | Y |
| 11 Davis | ? | ? | Y | Y | Y | Y |
| 12 Putnam | Y | Y | N | Y | Y | Y |
| 13 Harris | Y | Y | N | Y | Y | Y |
| 14 Mack | Y | Y | N | Y | Y | Y |
| 15 Weldon | ? | ? | N | Y | Y | Y |
| 16 Foley | Y | Y | N | Y | Y | Y |
| 17 Meek | N | Y | Y | Y | Y | Y |
| 18 Ros-Lehtinen | Y | Y | N | Y | Y | Y |
| 19 Wexler | N | Y | Y | Y | Y | Y |
| 20 Wasserman-Schultz | N | Y | Y | Y | Y | Y |
| 21 Diaz-Balart, L. | ? | ? | ? | ? | ? | ? |
| 22 Shaw | Y | Y | N | Y | Y | Y |
| 23 Hastings | N | Y | Y | Y | Y | Y |
| 24 Feeney | Y | Y | N | N | Y | Y |
| 25 Diaz-Balart, M. | ? | ? | ? | ? | ? | ? |
| **GEORGIA** | | | | | | |
| 1 Kingston | Y | Y | N | Y | Y | Y |
| 2 Bishop | N | Y | Y | Y | Y | Y |
| 3 Marshall | N | Y | Y | Y | Y | Y |
| 4 McKinney | N | Y | Y | Y | Y | Y |
| 5 Lewis | N | Y | Y | Y | Y | Y |
| 6 Price | Y | Y | N | Y | Y | Y |
| 7 Linder | Y | Y | N | Y | Y | Y |
| 8 Westmoreland | Y | Y | N | Y | Y | Y |
| 9 Norwood | Y | Y | N | Y | Y | Y |
| 10 Deal | Y | Y | N | Y | Y | Y |
| 11 Gingrey | Y | Y | N | Y | Y | Y |
| 12 Barrow | N | Y | Y | Y | Y | Y |
| 13 Scott | N | Y | Y | Y | Y | Y |
| **HAWAII** | | | | | | |
| 1 Abercrombie | N | Y | Y | Y | Y | ? |
| 2 Case | N | Y | Y | Y | Y | Y |
| **IDAHO** | | | | | | |
| 1 Otter | ? | ? | N | Y | Y | Y |
| 2 Simpson | ? | ? | N | Y | Y | Y |
| **ILLINOIS** | | | | | | |
| 1 Rush | N | Y | Y | Y | Y | Y |
| 2 Jackson | N | Y | Y | Y | Y | Y |
| 3 Lipinski | N | Y | Y | Y | Y | Y |
| 4 Gutierrez | N | Y | Y | Y | Y | Y |
| 5 Emanuel | N | Y | Y | Y | Y | Y |
| 6 Hyde | Y | Y | N | Y | Y | Y |
| 7 Davis | N | Y | Y | Y | Y | Y |
| 8 Bean | N | Y | Y | Y | Y | Y |
| 9 Schakowsky | N | Y | Y | Y | Y | Y |
| 10 Kirk | Y | Y | N | Y | ? | ? |
| 11 Weller | Y | Y | N | Y | Y | Y |
| 12 Costello | N | Y | Y | Y | Y | Y |

| KEY | Republicans | Democrats | Independents |
|---|---|---|---|

| | | | |
|---|---|---|---|
| Y | Voted for (yea) | X Paired against | C Voted "present" to avoid possible conflict of interest |
| # | Paired for | – Announced against | ? Did not vote or otherwise make a position known |
| + | Announced for | P Voted "present" | |
| N | Voted against (nay) | | |

| | 151 | 152 | 153 | 154 | 155 | 156 |
|---|---|---|---|---|---|---|
| 13 **Biggert** | ? | Y | N | Y | Y | Y |
| 14 **Hastert** | | | | | | |
| 15 **Johnson** | Y | Y | N | Y | Y | Y |
| 16 **Manzullo** | Y | Y | N | Y | Y | Y |
| 17 Evans | N | Y | Y | Y | Y | Y |
| 18 **LaHood** | Y | Y | N | Y | Y | Y |
| 19 **Shimkus** | Y | Y | N | Y | Y | Y |
| **INDIANA** | | | | | | |
| 1 Visclosky | N | Y | Y | Y | Y | Y |
| 2 **Chocola** | Y | Y | N | Y | Y | Y |
| 3 **Souder** | Y | Y | N | Y | Y | Y |
| 4 **Buyer** | Y | Y | N | Y | Y | Y |
| 5 **Burton** | Y | Y | N | Y | Y | Y |
| 6 **Pence** | Y | Y | N | Y | Y | Y |
| 7 Carson | N | Y | Y | Y | Y | Y |
| 8 **Hostettler** | Y | Y | N | N | Y | Y |
| 9 **Sodrel** | Y | Y | N | Y | Y | Y |
| **IOWA** | | | | | | |
| 1 **Nussle** | Y | Y | N | Y | Y | Y |
| 2 **Leach** | Y | Y | N | Y | Y | Y |
| 3 Boswell | N | Y | Y | Y | Y | Y |
| 4 **Latham** | Y | Y | N | Y | Y | Y |
| 5 **King** | Y | Y | N | Y | Y | Y |
| **KANSAS** | | | | | | |
| 1 **Moran** | Y | Y | N | Y | Y | Y |
| 2 **Ryun** | Y | Y | N | Y | Y | Y |
| 3 Moore | N | Y | Y | Y | Y | ? |
| 4 **Tiahrt** | Y | Y | N | Y | Y | Y |
| **KENTUCKY** | | | | | | |
| 1 **Whitfield** | Y | Y | N | Y | Y | ? |
| 2 **Lewis** | Y | Y | N | Y | Y | Y |
| 3 **Northup** | Y | Y | N | Y | Y | Y |
| 4 **Davis** | Y | Y | N | Y | Y | Y |
| 5 **Rogers** | Y | Y | N | Y | Y | Y |
| 6 Chandler | N | Y | Y | Y | Y | Y |
| **LOUISIANA** | | | | | | |
| 1 **Jindal** | Y | Y | N | Y | Y | Y |
| 2 Jefferson | N | Y | Y | Y | Y | Y |
| 3 Melancon | N | Y | ? | Y | Y | Y |
| 4 **McCrery** | Y | Y | N | Y | Y | Y |
| 5 **Alexander** | Y | Y | N | Y | Y | Y |
| 6 **Baker** | Y | Y | N | Y | Y | Y |
| 7 **Boustany** | Y | Y | N | Y | Y | Y |
| **MAINE** | | | | | | |
| 1 Allen | N | Y | Y | Y | Y | Y |
| 2 Michaud | N | Y | Y | Y | Y | Y |
| **MARYLAND** | | | | | | |
| 1 **Gilchrest** | Y | Y | N | Y | Y | Y |
| 2 Ruppersberger | N | Y | Y | Y | Y | Y |
| 3 Cardin | N | Y | Y | Y | Y | Y |
| 4 Wynn | N | Y | Y | Y | Y | Y |
| 5 Hoyer | ? | ? | Y | Y | Y | Y |
| 6 **Bartlett** | Y | Y | N | N | Y | Y |
| 7 Cummings | N | Y | Y | Y | Y | Y |
| 8 Van Hollen | N | Y | Y | Y | Y | Y |
| **MASSACHUSETTS** | | | | | | |
| 1 Olver | N | Y | Y | Y | Y | Y |
| 2 Neal | N | Y | Y | Y | Y | Y |
| 3 McGovern | N | Y | Y | Y | Y | Y |
| 4 Frank | N | Y | Y | Y | Y | Y |
| 5 Meehan | N | Y | Y | Y | Y | Y |
| 6 Tierney | N | Y | Y | Y | Y | Y |
| 7 Markey | N | Y | Y | Y | Y | Y |
| 8 Capuano | N | Y | Y | Y | Y | Y |
| 9 Lynch | N | Y | Y | Y | Y | Y |
| 10 Delahunt | N | Y | Y | Y | Y | Y |
| **MICHIGAN** | | | | | | |
| 1 Stupak | N | Y | Y | Y | Y | Y |
| 2 **Hoekstra** | Y | Y | N | Y | Y | Y |
| 3 **Ehlers** | Y | Y | N | Y | Y | Y |
| 4 **Camp** | Y | Y | N | Y | Y | Y |
| 5 Kildee | N | Y | Y | Y | Y | Y |
| 6 **Upton** | Y | Y | N | Y | Y | Y |
| 7 **Schwarz** | Y | Y | N | Y | Y | Y |
| 8 **Rogers** | Y | Y | ? | Y | Y | Y |
| 9 **Knollenberg** | Y | Y | N | Y | Y | Y |
| 10 **Miller** | Y | Y | N | Y | Y | Y |
| 11 **McCotter** | Y | Y | N | Y | Y | Y |
| 12 Levin | N | Y | Y | Y | Y | Y |
| 13 Kilpatrick | N | Y | Y | Y | Y | Y |
| 14 Conyers | N | Y | Y | Y | Y | Y |
| 15 Dingell | N | Y | Y | Y | Y | Y |

| | 151 | 152 | 153 | 154 | 155 | 156 |
|---|---|---|---|---|---|---|
| **MINNESOTA** | | | | | | |
| 1 **Gutknecht** | Y | Y | ? | Y | Y | Y |
| 2 **Kline** | Y | Y | N | Y | Y | Y |
| 3 **Ramstad** | Y | Y | Y | Y | Y | Y |
| 4 McCollum | N | Y | Y | Y | Y | Y |
| 5 Sabo | N | Y | Y | Y | Y | Y |
| 6 **Kennedy** | Y | Y | N | Y | Y | Y |
| 7 Peterson | N | Y | Y | Y | Y | Y |
| 8 Oberstar | N | Y | Y | Y | Y | Y |
| **MISSISSIPPI** | | | | | | |
| 1 **Wicker** | Y | Y | N | Y | Y | Y |
| 2 Thompson | N | Y | Y | Y | Y | Y |
| 3 **Pickering** | Y | Y | N | Y | Y | Y |
| 4 Taylor | N | Y | Y | Y | Y | Y |
| **MISSOURI** | | | | | | |
| 1 Clay | ? | ? | Y | Y | Y | Y |
| 2 **Akin** | Y | Y | N | Y | Y | Y |
| 3 Carnahan | N | Y | Y | Y | Y | Y |
| 4 Skelton | N | Y | Y | Y | Y | Y |
| 5 Cleaver | N | Y | Y | Y | Y | Y |
| 6 **Graves** | Y | Y | N | Y | Y | Y |
| 7 **Blunt** | Y | Y | N | Y | Y | Y |
| 8 **Emerson** | Y | Y | N | Y | Y | Y |
| 9 **Hulshof** | Y | Y | N | Y | Y | Y |
| **MONTANA** | | | | | | |
| AL **Rehberg** | Y | Y | N | Y | Y | Y |
| **NEBRASKA** | | | | | | |
| 1 **Fortenberry** | Y | Y | N | Y | Y | Y |
| 2 **Terry** | Y | Y | N | Y | Y | Y |
| 3 **Osborne** | Y | Y | N | Y | Y | Y |
| **NEVADA** | | | | | | |
| 1 Berkley | N | Y | Y | Y | Y | Y |
| 2 **Gibbons** | Y | Y | N | Y | Y | Y |
| 3 **Porter** | Y | Y | N | Y | Y | Y |
| **NEW HAMPSHIRE** | | | | | | |
| 1 **Bradley** | Y | Y | N | Y | Y | Y |
| 2 **Bass** | Y | Y | N | Y | Y | Y |
| **NEW JERSEY** | | | | | | |
| 1 Andrews | N | Y | N | Y | Y | Y |
| 2 **LoBiondo** | Y | Y | N | Y | Y | Y |
| 3 **Saxton** | Y | Y | N | Y | Y | Y |
| 4 **Smith** | Y | Y | N | Y | Y | Y |
| 5 **Garrett** | Y | Y | N | N | Y | Y |
| 6 Pallone | N | Y | Y | Y | Y | Y |
| 7 **Ferguson** | Y | Y | N | Y | Y | Y |
| 8 Pascrell | N | Y | Y | Y | Y | Y |
| 9 Rothman | N | Y | Y | Y | Y | Y |
| 10 Payne | N | Y | Y | Y | Y | Y |
| 11 **Frelinghuysen** | Y | Y | N | Y | Y | Y |
| 12 Holt | N | Y | Y | Y | Y | Y |
| 13 Menendez | N | Y | Y | Y | Y | Y |
| **NEW MEXICO** | | | | | | |
| 1 **Wilson** | Y | Y | N | Y | Y | Y |
| 2 **Pearce** | Y | Y | N | Y | Y | Y |
| 3 Udall | N | Y | Y | Y | Y | Y |
| **NEW YORK** | | | | | | |
| 1 Bishop | N | Y | Y | Y | Y | Y |
| 2 Israel | N | Y | Y | Y | Y | Y |
| 3 **King** | Y | Y | N | Y | Y | Y |
| 4 McCarthy | N | Y | Y | Y | Y | Y |
| 5 Ackerman | N | Y | Y | Y | Y | Y |
| 6 Meeks | N | Y | Y | Y | Y | Y |
| 7 Crowley | N | Y | Y | Y | Y | Y |
| 8 Nadler | N | Y | Y | Y | Y | Y |
| 9 Weiner | N | Y | ? | Y | ? | ? |
| 10 Towns | N | Y | Y | ? | Y | Y |
| 11 Owens | N | Y | Y | Y | Y | Y |
| 12 Velázquez | N | Y | Y | Y | Y | Y |
| 13 **Fossella** | Y | Y | N | Y | Y | Y |
| 14 Maloney | N | Y | Y | Y | Y | Y |
| 15 Rangel | N | Y | Y | Y | Y | Y |
| 16 Serrano | N | Y | Y | Y | Y | Y |
| 17 Engel | N | Y | Y | Y | Y | Y |
| 18 Lowey | N | Y | Y | Y | Y | Y |
| 19 **Kelly** | Y | Y | N | Y | Y | Y |
| 20 **Sweeney** | Y | Y | N | Y | Y | Y |
| 21 McNulty | N | Y | Y | Y | Y | Y |
| 22 Hinchey | N | Y | Y | Y | Y | Y |
| 23 **McHugh** | Y | Y | N | Y | Y | Y |
| 24 **Boehlert** | Y | Y | N | Y | Y | Y |
| 25 **Walsh** | ? | ? | N | Y | Y | Y |
| 26 **Reynolds** | Y | Y | N | Y | Y | Y |
| 27 Higgins | N | Y | Y | Y | Y | Y |
| 28 Slaughter | N | Y | Y | Y | Y | Y |
| 29 **Kuhl** | Y | Y | N | Y | Y | Y |

| | 151 | 152 | 153 | 154 | 155 | 156 |
|---|---|---|---|---|---|---|
| **NORTH CAROLINA** | | | | | | |
| 1 Butterfield | N | Y | Y | Y | Y | Y |
| 2 Etheridge | N | Y | Y | Y | Y | Y |
| 3 **Jones** | Y | Y | N | Y | Y | Y |
| 4 Price | N | Y | Y | Y | Y | Y |
| 5 **Foxx** | Y | Y | N | Y | Y | Y |
| 6 **Coble** | Y | Y | N | Y | Y | Y |
| 7 McIntyre | N | Y | Y | Y | Y | Y |
| 8 **Hayes** | Y | Y | N | Y | Y | Y |
| 9 **Myrick** | Y | Y | N | Y | Y | Y |
| 10 **McHenry** | Y | Y | N | Y | Y | Y |
| 11 **Taylor** | Y | Y | N | Y | Y | Y |
| 12 Watt | N | Y | Y | Y | Y | Y |
| 13 Miller | N | Y | Y | Y | Y | Y |
| **NORTH DAKOTA** | | | | | | |
| AL Pomeroy | N | Y | Y | Y | Y | Y |
| **OHIO** | | | | | | |
| 1 **Chabot** | Y | Y | N | Y | Y | Y |
| 2 Vacant* | | | | | | |
| 3 **Turner** | Y | Y | N | Y | Y | Y |
| 4 **Oxley** | Y | Y | N | Y | Y | Y |
| 5 **Gillmor** | Y | Y | N | Y | Y | Y |
| 6 Strickland | N | Y | Y | Y | Y | Y |
| 7 **Hobson** | Y | Y | N | Y | Y | Y |
| 8 **Boehner** | Y | Y | N | Y | Y | Y |
| 9 Kaptur | N | Y | Y | Y | Y | Y |
| 10 Kucinich | N | Y | Y | Y | Y | Y |
| 11 Jones | N | Y | Y | Y | Y | Y |
| 12 **Tiberi** | Y | Y | N | Y | Y | Y |
| 13 Brown | ? | ? | ? | ? | ? | ? |
| 14 **LaTourette** | Y | Y | N | Y | Y | Y |
| 15 **Pryce** | Y | Y | N | Y | Y | Y |
| 16 **Regula** | Y | Y | N | Y | Y | Y |
| 17 Ryan | N | Y | Y | Y | Y | Y |
| 18 **Ney** | Y | Y | N | Y | Y | Y |
| **OKLAHOMA** | | | | | | |
| 1 **Sullivan** | Y | ? | N | Y | ? | Y |
| 2 Boren | N | Y | Y | Y | Y | Y |
| 3 **Lucas** | Y | Y | N | Y | Y | Y |
| 4 **Cole** | Y | Y | N | Y | Y | Y |
| 5 **Istook** | Y | Y | N | Y | Y | Y |
| **OREGON** | | | | | | |
| 1 Wu | N | Y | Y | Y | Y | Y |
| 2 **Walden** | Y | Y | N | Y | Y | Y |
| 3 Blumenauer | N | Y | Y | Y | Y | Y |
| 4 DeFazio | N | Y | Y | Y | Y | Y |
| 5 Hooley | N | Y | Y | Y | Y | Y |
| **PENNSYLVANIA** | | | | | | |
| 1 Brady | N | Y | Y | Y | Y | Y |
| 2 Fattah | ? | ? | Y | Y | Y | Y |
| 3 **English** | Y | Y | N | Y | Y | Y |
| 4 **Hart** | Y | Y | N | Y | Y | Y |
| 5 **Peterson** | Y | Y | N | Y | Y | Y |
| 6 **Gerlach** | Y | Y | N | Y | Y | Y |
| 7 **Weldon** | Y | Y | – | + | + | + |
| 8 **Fitzpatrick** | Y | Y | N | Y | Y | Y |
| 9 **Shuster** | Y | Y | N | Y | Y | Y |
| 10 **Sherwood** | Y | Y | N | Y | Y | Y |
| 11 Kanjorski | N | Y | Y | Y | Y | Y |
| 12 Murtha | N | ? | Y | Y | Y | Y |
| 13 Schwartz | N | Y | Y | Y | Y | Y |
| 14 Doyle | N | Y | Y | Y | Y | Y |
| 15 **Dent** | Y | Y | N | Y | Y | Y |
| 16 **Pitts** | Y | Y | N | Y | Y | Y |
| 17 Holden | N | Y | Y | Y | Y | Y |
| 18 **Murphy** | Y | Y | N | Y | Y | Y |
| 19 **Platts** | Y | Y | N | Y | Y | Y |
| **RHODE ISLAND** | | | | | | |
| 1 Kennedy | N | Y | Y | Y | Y | Y |
| 2 Langevin | N | Y | Y | Y | Y | Y |
| **SOUTH CAROLINA** | | | | | | |
| 1 **Brown** | Y | Y | N | Y | Y | Y |
| 2 **Wilson** | Y | Y | N | Y | Y | Y |
| 3 **Barrett** | Y | Y | N | Y | Y | Y |
| 4 **Inglis** | Y | Y | N | Y | Y | Y |
| 5 Spratt | N | Y | Y | Y | Y | Y |
| 6 Clyburn | N | Y | Y | Y | Y | Y |
| **SOUTH DAKOTA** | | | | | | |
| AL Herseth | N | Y | Y | Y | Y | Y |
| **TENNESSEE** | | | | | | |
| 1 **Jenkins** | Y | Y | N | Y | Y | Y |
| 2 **Duncan** | Y | Y | N | Y | Y | Y |

| | 151 | 152 | 153 | 154 | 155 | 156 |
|---|---|---|---|---|---|---|
| 3 **Wamp** | Y | Y | N | Y | Y | Y |
| 4 Davis | N | Y | Y | Y | Y | Y |
| 5 Cooper | N | Y | Y | Y | Y | Y |
| 6 Gordon | N | Y | Y | Y | Y | ? |
| 7 **Blackburn** | Y | Y | N | Y | Y | Y |
| 8 Tanner | N | Y | Y | Y | Y | Y |
| 9 Ford | N | Y | Y | Y | Y | Y |
| **TEXAS** | | | | | | |
| 1 **Gohmert** | Y | Y | N | Y | Y | Y |
| 2 **Poe** | Y | Y | N | Y | Y | Y |
| 3 **Johnson, S.** | Y | Y | N | Y | Y | Y |
| 4 **Hall** | Y | Y | N | Y | Y | Y |
| 5 **Hensarling** | Y | Y | N | N | Y | Y |
| 6 **Barton** | Y | Y | N | Y | Y | Y |
| 7 **Culberson** | ? | ? | N | Y | Y | Y |
| 8 **Brady** | Y | Y | N | Y | Y | Y |
| 9 Green | N | Y | Y | Y | Y | Y |
| 10 **McCaul** | Y | Y | N | Y | Y | Y |
| 11 **Conaway** | Y | Y | N | Y | Y | Y |
| 12 **Granger** | Y | Y | N | Y | Y | Y |
| 13 **Thornberry** | Y | Y | N | Y | Y | Y |
| 14 **Paul** | Y | Y | N | N | N | Y |
| 15 Hinojosa | N | Y | Y | Y | Y | Y |
| 16 Reyes | N | Y | Y | Y | Y | Y |
| 17 Edwards | ? | ? | Y | Y | Y | Y |
| 18 Jackson-Lee | N | Y | Y | Y | ? | Y |
| 19 **Neugebauer** | Y | Y | N | Y | ? | Y |
| 20 Gonzalez | N | Y | Y | Y | Y | Y |
| 21 **Smith** | Y | Y | ? | Y | Y | Y |
| 22 **DeLay** | Y | Y | N | Y | Y | Y |
| 23 **Bonilla** | Y | Y | N | Y | Y | Y |
| 24 **Marchant** | Y | Y | N | Y | Y | Y |
| 25 Doggett | N | Y | Y | Y | Y | Y |
| 26 **Burgess** | Y | Y | N | Y | Y | Y |
| 27 Ortiz | N | Y | Y | Y | Y | Y |
| 28 Cuellar | N | Y | Y | Y | Y | Y |
| 29 Green | N | Y | Y | Y | Y | Y |
| 30 Johnson, E. | N | Y | Y | Y | Y | Y |
| 31 **Carter** | Y | Y | N | Y | Y | Y |
| 32 **Sessions** | Y | Y | N | Y | Y | Y |
| **UTAH** | | | | | | |
| 1 **Bishop** | Y | Y | N | Y | Y | Y |
| 2 Matheson | N | Y | Y | Y | Y | Y |
| 3 **Cannon** | Y | Y | N | Y | Y | Y |
| **VERMONT** | | | | | | |
| AL *Sanders* | N | Y | Y | Y | Y | Y |
| **VIRGINIA** | | | | | | |
| 1 **Davis, J.** | Y | Y | N | Y | Y | Y |
| 2 **Drake** | Y | Y | N | Y | Y | Y |
| 3 Scott | N | Y | ? | ? | ? | ? |
| 4 **Forbes** | Y | Y | N | Y | Y | Y |
| 5 **Goode** | Y | Y | N | Y | Y | Y |
| 6 **Goodlatte** | Y | Y | N | Y | Y | Y |
| 7 **Cantor** | Y | Y | N | Y | Y | Y |
| 8 Moran | N | Y | Y | Y | Y | Y |
| 9 Boucher | N | Y | Y | Y | Y | Y |
| 10 **Wolf** | Y | Y | N | Y | Y | Y |
| 11 **Davis, T.** | Y | Y | N | Y | Y | Y |
| **WASHINGTON** | | | | | | |
| 1 Inslee | N | Y | Y | Y | Y | Y |
| 2 Larsen | N | Y | Y | Y | Y | Y |
| 3 Baird | N | Y | Y | Y | Y | Y |
| 4 **Hastings** | Y | Y | N | Y | Y | Y |
| 5 **McMorris** | Y | Y | N | Y | Y | ? |
| 6 Dicks | N | Y | Y | Y | Y | Y |
| 7 McDermott | N | Y | Y | Y | Y | Y |
| 8 **Reichert** | Y | Y | N | Y | Y | Y |
| 9 Smith | N | Y | Y | Y | Y | Y |
| **WEST VIRGINIA** | | | | | | |
| 1 Mollohan | N | Y | Y | Y | Y | Y |
| 2 **Capito** | Y | Y | N | Y | Y | Y |
| 3 Rahall | N | Y | Y | Y | Y | Y |
| **WISCONSIN** | | | | | | |
| 1 **Ryan** | Y | Y | N | Y | Y | Y |
| 2 Baldwin | N | Y | Y | Y | Y | Y |
| 3 Kind | N | Y | Y | Y | Y | Y |
| 4 Moore | N | Y | Y | Y | Y | Y |
| 5 **Sensenbrenner** | Y | Y | N | N | Y | Y |
| 6 **Petri** | Y | Y | N | Y | Y | Y |
| 7 Obey | N | Y | Y | Y | Y | Y |
| 8 **Green** | Y | Y | N | Y | Y | Y |
| **WYOMING** | | | | | | |
| AL **Cubin** | Y | Y | N | Y | Y | Y |

# IN THE HOUSE | By Vote Number

**157.** **HR 1185. Federal Deposit Insurance Limit/Passage.** Passage of the bill that would increase to $130,000 from $100,000 the ceiling on bank deposits guaranteed by the Federal Deposit Insurance Corporation and index the limit to inflation thereafter. It would merge the FDIC's Bank Insurance Fund and the Savings Association Insurance Fund. The FDIC would be able to set risk-based premiums for insured institutions and double to $260,000 the coverage limits for certain types of retirement accounts. Passed 413-10: R 219-5; D 194-4 (ND 147-2, SD 47-2); I 0-1. May 4, 2005.

**158.** **H Res 233. Victory in Europe Anniversary/Adoption.** Smith, R-N.J., motion to suspend the rules and adopt the resolution that would recognize the 60th anniversary of the end of World War II in Europe and that would express respect and appreciation to the men and women who served in Europe during World War II. Motion agreed to 423-0: R 225-0; D 197-0 (ND 148-0, SD 49-0); I 1-0. A two-thirds majority of those present and voting (282 in this case) is required for adoption under suspension of the rules. May 4, 2005.

**159.** **HR 1268. Fiscal 2005 Supplemental Appropriations/Previous Question.** Cole, R-Okla., motion to order the previous question (thus ending debate and possibility of amendment) on adoption of the rule (H Res 258) to provide for House floor consideration of the conference report on the bill that would appropriate $82 billion in fiscal 2005 supplemental spending for military operations and reconstruction in Iraq and Afghanistan and for disaster assistance to victims of the December 2004 tsunami. The rule also would allow for the chairman of the Judiciary Committee to file a supplemental report to the interstate abortion notification bill (HR 748). Motion agreed to 224-196: R 224-1; D 0-194 (ND 0-144, SD 0-50); I 0-1. (Subsequently, the rule was adopted by voice vote.) May 5, 2005.

**160.** **HR 1268. Fiscal 2005 Supplemental Appropriations/Recommit.** Obey, D-Wis., motion to recommit the bill to the conference committee with instructions to include Senate language that would provide for the highest levels of funding for immigration and customs enforcement. Motion rejected 201-225: R 2-225; D 198-0 (ND 147-0, SD 51-0); I 1-0. May 5, 2005.

**161.** **HR 1268. Fiscal 2005 Supplemental Appropriations/Adoption.** Adoption of the conference report on the bill that would appropriate $82 billion in fiscal 2005 supplemental spending for military operations and reconstruction in Iraq and Afghanistan and for disaster assistance to victims of the December 2004 tsunami. It also would establish national driver's license standards, stiffen asylum requirements and speed completion of a fence on the U.S.-Mexico border. Adopted (thus sent to the Senate) 368-58: R 225-3; D 143-54 (ND 98-48, SD 45-6); I 0-1. May 5, 2005.

ND Northern Democrats, SD Southern Democrats
Southern states: Ala., Ark., Fla., Ga., Ky., La., Miss., N.C., Okla., S.C., Tenn., Texas, Va.

| | 157 | 158 | 159 | 160 | 161 |
|---|---|---|---|---|---|
| **ALABAMA** | | | | | |
| 1 Bonner | Y | Y | Y | N | Y |
| 2 Everett | Y | Y | Y | N | Y |
| 3 Rogers | Y | Y | Y | N | Y |
| 4 Aderholt | Y | Y | Y | N | Y |
| 5 Cramer | Y | Y | N | Y | Y |
| 6 Bachus | Y | Y | Y | N | Y |
| 7 Davis | Y | Y | N | Y | Y |
| **ALASKA** | | | | | |
| AL Young | Y | Y | Y | N | Y |
| **ARIZONA** | | | | | |
| 1 Renzi | Y | Y | Y | N | Y |
| 2 Franks | + | + | Y | N | Y |
| 3 Shadegg | Y | Y | Y | N | Y |
| 4 Pastor | Y | Y | N | Y | N |
| 5 Hayworth | Y | Y | Y | N | Y |
| 6 Flake | N | Y | Y | N | Y |
| 7 Grijalva | Y | Y | N | Y | N |
| 8 Kolbe | Y | Y | Y | N | Y |
| **ARKANSAS** | | | | | |
| 1 Berry | Y | Y | N | Y | Y |
| 2 Snyder | Y | Y | N | Y | N |
| 3 Boozman | Y | Y | Y | N | Y |
| 4 Ross | Y | Y | N | Y | Y |
| **CALIFORNIA** | | | | | |
| 1 Thompson | Y | Y | N | Y | N |
| 2 Herger | + | Y | Y | N | Y |
| 3 Lungren | Y | Y | Y | N | Y |
| 4 Doolittle | Y | Y | Y | ? | Y |
| 5 Matsui, D. | Y | Y | N | Y | P |
| 6 Woolsey | Y | Y | N | Y | N |
| 7 Miller, George | Y | Y | N | Y | N |
| 8 Pelosi | Y | Y | N | Y | Y |
| 9 Lee | Y | Y | N | Y | N |
| 10 Tauscher | Y | Y | N | Y | Y |
| 11 Pombo | Y | Y | Y | N | Y |
| 12 Lantos | Y | Y | N | + | + |
| 13 Stark | N | Y | N | Y | N |
| 14 Eshoo | Y | Y | N | Y | Y |
| 15 Honda | Y | Y | N | Y | Y |
| 16 Lofgren | Y | Y | N | Y | Y |
| 17 Farr | Y | Y | N | Y | N |
| 18 Cardoza | Y | Y | N | Y | Y |
| 19 Radanovich | Y | Y | Y | N | Y |
| 20 Costa | Y | Y | N | Y | Y |
| 21 Nunes | Y | Y | Y | N | Y |
| 22 Thomas | Y | Y | Y | N | Y |
| 23 Capps | Y | Y | – | + | + |
| 24 Gallegly | Y | Y | Y | N | Y |
| 25 McKeon | Y | Y | Y | N | Y |
| 26 Dreier | Y | Y | Y | N | Y |
| 27 Sherman | Y | Y | N | Y | Y |
| 28 Berman | Y | Y | N | Y | Y |
| 29 Schiff | Y | Y | N | Y | Y |
| 30 Waxman | Y | Y | N | Y | Y |
| 31 Becerra | Y | Y | N | Y | N |
| 32 Solis | Y | Y | ? | Y | Y |
| 33 Watson | Y | Y | N | Y | N |
| 34 Roybal-Allard | Y | Y | N | Y | Y |
| 35 Waters | Y | Y | N | Y | N |
| 36 Harman | Y | Y | N | Y | Y |
| 37 Millender-McD. | Y | Y | N | Y | Y |
| 38 Napolitano | Y | Y | N | Y | N |
| 39 Sánchez, Linda | Y | Y | N | Y | N |
| 40 Royce | N | Y | Y | N | Y |
| 41 Lewis | Y | Y | Y | N | Y |
| 42 Miller, Gary | Y | Y | Y | N | Y |
| 43 Baca | Y | Y | N | Y | Y |
| 44 Calvert | Y | Y | Y | N | Y |
| 45 Bono | Y | Y | Y | N | Y |
| 46 Rohrabacher | N | Y | Y | N | Y |
| 47 Sanchez, Loretta | Y | Y | N | Y | Y |
| 48 Cox | Y | Y | Y | N | Y |
| 49 Issa | Y | Y | Y | N | Y |

| | 157 | 158 | 159 | 160 | 161 |
|---|---|---|---|---|---|
| 50 Cunningham | Y | Y | Y | N | Y |
| 51 Filner | Y | Y | N | Y | N |
| 52 Hunter | Y | Y | Y | N | Y |
| 53 Davis | Y | Y | N | Y | Y |
| **COLORADO** | | | | | |
| 1 DeGette | Y | Y | N | Y | Y |
| 2 Udall | Y | Y | N | Y | Y |
| 3 Salazar | Y | Y | N | Y | Y |
| 4 Musgrave | Y | Y | Y | N | Y |
| 5 Hefley | Y | Y | Y | N | Y |
| 6 Tancredo | Y | ? | Y | N | Y |
| 7 Beauprez | Y | Y | Y | N | Y |
| **CONNECTICUT** | | | | | |
| 1 Larson | + | + | – | + | + |
| 2 Simmons | Y | Y | N | Y | Y |
| 3 DeLauro | Y | Y | N | Y | Y |
| 4 Shays | Y | Y | Y | N | Y |
| 5 Johnson | Y | Y | Y | N | Y |
| **DELAWARE** | | | | | |
| AL Castle | Y | Y | Y | N | Y |
| **FLORIDA** | | | | | |
| 1 Miller | Y | Y | Y | N | Y |
| 2 Boyd | Y | Y | N | Y | Y |
| 3 Brown | Y | Y | N | Y | Y |
| 4 Crenshaw | Y | Y | Y | N | Y |
| 5 Brown-Waite | Y | Y | Y | N | Y |
| 6 Stearns | Y | Y | Y | N | Y |
| 7 Mica | Y | Y | Y | N | Y |
| 8 Keller | Y | Y | Y | N | Y |
| 9 Bilirakis | Y | Y | Y | N | Y |
| 10 Young | Y | Y | Y | N | Y |
| 11 Davis | Y | Y | N | Y | Y |
| 12 Putnam | Y | Y | Y | N | Y |
| 13 Harris | Y | Y | Y | N | Y |
| 14 Mack | Y | Y | Y | N | Y |
| 15 Weldon | Y | Y | Y | N | Y |
| 16 Foley | Y | Y | Y | N | Y |
| 17 Meek | Y | Y | N | Y | Y |
| 18 Ros-Lehtinen | Y | Y | Y | N | Y |
| 19 Wexler | Y | Y | N | Y | N |
| 20 Wasserman-Schultz | Y | Y | N | Y | Y |
| 21 Diaz-Balart, L. | ? | ? | ? | ? | ? |
| 22 Shaw | Y | Y | Y | N | Y |
| 23 Hastings | Y | Y | N | Y | Y |
| 24 Feeney | Y | Y | Y | N | Y |
| 25 Diaz-Balart, M. | ? | ? | ? | ? | ? |
| **GEORGIA** | | | | | |
| 1 Kingston | Y | Y | Y | N | Y |
| 2 Bishop | Y | Y | N | Y | Y |
| 3 Marshall | Y | Y | N | Y | Y |
| 4 McKinney | Y | Y | N | Y | N |
| 5 Lewis | Y | Y | N | Y | N |
| 6 Price | Y | Y | Y | N | Y |
| 7 Linder | Y | Y | Y | N | Y |
| 8 Westmoreland | Y | Y | Y | N | Y |
| 9 Norwood | Y | Y | Y | N | Y |
| 10 Deal | Y | Y | Y | N | Y |
| 11 Gingrey | Y | Y | Y | N | Y |
| 12 Barrow | Y | Y | N | Y | Y |
| 13 Scott | Y | Y | N | Y | Y |
| **HAWAII** | | | | | |
| 1 Abercrombie | Y | Y | N | Y | N |
| 2 Case | Y | Y | N | Y | Y |
| **IDAHO** | | | | | |
| 1 Otter | Y | Y | Y | N | Y |
| 2 Simpson | Y | Y | Y | N | Y |
| **ILLINOIS** | | | | | |
| 1 Rush | Y | Y | N | Y | Y |
| 2 Jackson | Y | Y | N | Y | Y |
| 3 Lipinski | Y | Y | N | Y | Y |
| 4 Gutierrez | Y | Y | N | Y | N |
| 5 Emanuel | Y | Y | N | Y | Y |
| 6 Hyde | Y | Y | ? | N | Y |
| 7 Davis | Y | Y | N | Y | N |
| 8 Bean | Y | Y | N | Y | Y |
| 9 Schakowsky | Y | Y | N | Y | N |
| 10 Kirk | Y | Y | Y | N | Y |
| 11 Weller | Y | Y | Y | N | Y |
| 12 Costello | Y | Y | N | Y | Y |

**KEY**   Republicans   Democrats   *Independents*

| | | |
|---|---|---|
| Y Voted for (yea) | X Paired against | C Voted "present" to avoid possible conflict of interest |
| # Paired for | – Announced against | |
| + Announced for | P Voted "present" | ? Did not vote or otherwise make a position known |
| N Voted against (nay) | | |

| | 157 | 158 | 159 | 160 | 161 |
|---|---|---|---|---|---|
| 13 Biggert | Y | Y | Y | N | Y |
| 14 Hastert | | | | | |
| 15 Johnson | Y | Y | Y | N | Y |
| 16 Manzullo | Y | Y | Y | N | Y |
| 17 Evans | Y | Y | N | Y | Y |
| 18 LaHood | Y | Y | Y | N | Y |
| 19 Shimkus | Y | Y | Y | N | Y |
| **INDIANA** | | | | | |
| 1 Visclosky | Y | Y | N | Y | Y |
| 2 Chocola | Y | Y | Y | N | Y |
| 3 Souder | Y | Y | Y | N | Y |
| 4 Buyer | Y | Y | Y | N | Y |
| 5 Burton | Y | Y | Y | N | Y |
| 6 Pence | Y | Y | Y | N | Y |
| 7 Carson | Y | Y | N | Y | N |
| 8 Hostettler | Y | Y | Y | N | Y |
| 9 Sodrel | Y | Y | Y | N | Y |
| **IOWA** | | | | | |
| 1 Nussle | Y | Y | Y | N | Y |
| 2 Leach | Y | Y | N | N | Y |
| 3 Boswell | Y | Y | N | Y | Y |
| 4 Latham | Y | Y | Y | N | Y |
| 5 King | Y | Y | Y | N | Y |
| **KANSAS** | | | | | |
| 1 Moran | Y | Y | Y | N | Y |
| 2 Ryun | Y | Y | Y | N | Y |
| 3 Moore | Y | Y | N | Y | Y |
| 4 Tiahrt | Y | Y | Y | N | Y |
| **KENTUCKY** | | | | | |
| 1 Whitfield | Y | Y | Y | N | Y |
| 2 Lewis | Y | Y | Y | N | Y |
| 3 Northup | Y | Y | Y | N | Y |
| 4 Davis | Y | Y | Y | N | Y |
| 5 Rogers | Y | Y | Y | N | Y |
| 6 Chandler | Y | Y | N | Y | Y |
| **LOUISIANA** | | | | | |
| 1 Jindal | Y | Y | Y | N | Y |
| 2 Jefferson | Y | Y | N | Y | Y |
| 3 Melancon | Y | Y | N | Y | Y |
| 4 McCrery | Y | Y | Y | N | Y |
| 5 Alexander | Y | Y | Y | N | Y |
| 6 Baker | Y | Y | Y | N | Y |
| 7 Boustany | Y | Y | Y | N | Y |
| **MAINE** | | | | | |
| 1 Allen | Y | Y | N | Y | Y |
| 2 Michaud | Y | Y | N | Y | Y |
| **MARYLAND** | | | | | |
| 1 Gilchrest | Y | Y | Y | N | Y |
| 2 Ruppersberger | Y | Y | N | Y | Y |
| 3 Cardin | Y | Y | N | Y | Y |
| 4 Wynn | Y | Y | N | Y | Y |
| 5 Hoyer | Y | Y | N | Y | Y |
| 6 Bartlett | Y | Y | Y | N | Y |
| 7 Cummings | Y | Y | N | Y | Y |
| 8 Van Hollen | Y | Y | N | Y | Y |
| **MASSACHUSETTS** | | | | | |
| 1 Olver | Y | Y | N | Y | N |
| 2 Neal | Y | Y | N | Y | Y |
| 3 McGovern | Y | Y | N | Y | N |
| 4 Frank | Y | Y | N | Y | N |
| 5 Meehan | Y | Y | N | Y | N |
| 6 Tierney | Y | Y | N | Y | N |
| 7 Markey | Y | Y | N | Y | N |
| 8 Capuano | Y | Y | N | Y | N |
| 9 Lynch | Y | Y | N | Y | Y |
| 10 Delahunt | Y | Y | N | Y | N |
| **MICHIGAN** | | | | | |
| 1 Stupak | Y | Y | N | Y | Y |
| 2 Hoekstra | Y | Y | Y | N | Y |
| 3 Ehlers | Y | Y | Y | N | Y |
| 4 Camp | Y | Y | Y | N | Y |
| 5 Kildee | Y | Y | N | Y | Y |
| 6 Upton | Y | Y | Y | N | Y |
| 7 Schwarz | Y | Y | Y | N | Y |
| 8 Rogers | Y | Y | Y | N | Y |
| 9 Knollenberg | Y | Y | Y | N | Y |
| 10 Miller | Y | Y | Y | N | Y |
| 11 McCotter | Y | Y | Y | N | Y |
| 12 Levin | Y | Y | N | Y | Y |
| 13 Kilpatrick | Y | Y | N | Y | Y |
| 14 Conyers | Y | Y | N | Y | N |
| 15 Dingell | Y | Y | N | Y | Y |

| | 157 | 158 | 159 | 160 | 161 |
|---|---|---|---|---|---|
| **MINNESOTA** | | | | | |
| 1 Gutknecht | Y | Y | Y | N | Y |
| 2 Kline | Y | Y | Y | N | Y |
| 3 Ramstad | Y | Y | Y | N | Y |
| 4 McCollum | Y | Y | N | Y | N |
| 5 Sabo | Y | Y | N | Y | Y |
| 6 Kennedy | Y | Y | Y | N | Y |
| 7 Peterson | Y | Y | N | Y | Y |
| 8 Oberstar | Y | Y | N | Y | N |
| **MISSISSIPPI** | | | | | |
| 1 Wicker | Y | Y | Y | N | Y |
| 2 Thompson | Y | Y | N | Y | Y |
| 3 Pickering | Y | Y | Y | N | Y |
| 4 Taylor | N | Y | N | Y | Y |
| **MISSOURI** | | | | | |
| 1 Clay | Y | Y | ? | Y | N |
| 2 Akin | Y | Y | Y | N | Y |
| 3 Carnahan | Y | Y | N | Y | Y |
| 4 Skelton | Y | Y | N | Y | Y |
| 5 Cleaver | Y | Y | N | Y | Y |
| 6 Graves | Y | Y | Y | N | Y |
| 7 Blunt | Y | Y | Y | N | Y |
| 8 Emerson | Y | Y | Y | N | Y |
| 9 Hulshof | Y | Y | Y | N | Y |
| **MONTANA** | | | | | |
| AL Rehberg | Y | Y | Y | N | Y |
| **NEBRASKA** | | | | | |
| 1 Fortenberry | Y | Y | Y | N | Y |
| 2 Terry | Y | Y | Y | N | Y |
| 3 Osborne | Y | Y | Y | N | Y |
| **NEVADA** | | | | | |
| 1 Berkley | Y | Y | N | Y | Y |
| 2 Gibbons | Y | Y | Y | N | Y |
| 3 Porter | Y | Y | Y | N | Y |
| **NEW HAMPSHIRE** | | | | | |
| 1 Bradley | Y | Y | Y | N | Y |
| 2 Bass | Y | Y | Y | N | Y |
| **NEW JERSEY** | | | | | |
| 1 Andrews | Y | Y | N | Y | Y |
| 2 LoBiondo | Y | Y | Y | N | Y |
| 3 Saxton | Y | Y | Y | N | Y |
| 4 Smith | Y | Y | Y | N | Y |
| 5 Garrett | Y | Y | Y | N | Y |
| 6 Pallone | Y | Y | N | Y | N |
| 7 Ferguson | Y | Y | Y | N | Y |
| 8 Pascrell | Y | Y | N | Y | Y |
| 9 Rothman | Y | Y | N | Y | Y |
| 10 Payne | Y | Y | N | Y | N |
| 11 Frelinghuysen | Y | Y | Y | N | Y |
| 12 Holt | Y | Y | N | Y | N |
| 13 Menendez | Y | Y | N | Y | Y |
| **NEW MEXICO** | | | | | |
| 1 Wilson | Y | Y | Y | N | Y |
| 2 Pearce | Y | Y | Y | N | Y |
| 3 Udall | Y | Y | N | Y | Y |
| **NEW YORK** | | | | | |
| 1 Bishop | Y | Y | N | Y | Y |
| 2 Israel | Y | Y | N | Y | Y |
| 3 King | Y | Y | Y | N | Y |
| 4 McCarthy | Y | Y | N | Y | Y |
| 5 Ackerman | Y | Y | N | Y | Y |
| 6 Meeks | Y | Y | N | Y | N |
| 7 Crowley | Y | Y | N | Y | Y |
| 8 Nadler | Y | Y | N | Y | N |
| 9 Weiner | Y | Y | N | Y | N |
| 10 Towns | Y | Y | N | Y | N |
| 11 Owens | Y | Y | N | Y | N |
| 12 Velázquez | Y | Y | N | Y | N |
| 13 Fossella | Y | Y | Y | N | Y |
| 14 Maloney | Y | Y | N | Y | N |
| 15 Rangel | Y | Y | N | Y | N |
| 16 Serrano | Y | Y | N | Y | N |
| 17 Engel | Y | Y | N | Y | Y |
| 18 Lowey | Y | Y | N | Y | Y |
| 19 Kelly | Y | Y | Y | N | Y |
| 20 Sweeney | Y | Y | Y | N | Y |
| 21 McNulty | Y | Y | N | Y | Y |
| 22 Hinchey | Y | Y | N | Y | N |
| 23 McHugh | Y | Y | Y | N | Y |
| 24 Boehlert | Y | Y | Y | N | Y |
| 25 Walsh | Y | Y | Y | N | Y |
| 26 Reynolds | Y | Y | Y | N | Y |
| 27 Higgins | Y | Y | N | Y | Y |
| 28 Slaughter | Y | Y | N | Y | N |
| 29 Kuhl | Y | Y | Y | N | Y |

| | 157 | 158 | 159 | 160 | 161 |
|---|---|---|---|---|---|
| **NORTH CAROLINA** | | | | | |
| 1 Butterfield | Y | Y | N | Y | Y |
| 2 Etheridge | Y | Y | N | Y | Y |
| 3 Jones | Y | Y | Y | Y | Y |
| 4 Price | Y | Y | N | Y | Y |
| 5 Foxx | Y | Y | Y | N | Y |
| 6 Coble | Y | Y | Y | N | N |
| 7 McIntyre | Y | Y | N | Y | Y |
| 8 Hayes | Y | Y | Y | N | Y |
| 9 Myrick | Y | Y | Y | N | Y |
| 10 McHenry | Y | Y | Y | N | Y |
| 11 Taylor | Y | Y | Y | N | Y |
| 12 Watt | Y | Y | N | Y | N |
| 13 Miller | Y | Y | N | Y | Y |
| **NORTH DAKOTA** | | | | | |
| AL Pomeroy | Y | Y | N | Y | Y |
| **OHIO** | | | | | |
| 1 Chabot | Y | Y | Y | N | Y |
| 2 Vacant | | | | | |
| 3 Turner | Y | Y | Y | N | Y |
| 4 Oxley | Y | Y | Y | N | Y |
| 5 Gillmor | Y | Y | Y | N | Y |
| 6 Strickland | Y | Y | N | Y | Y |
| 7 Hobson | Y | Y | Y | N | Y |
| 8 Boehner | Y | Y | Y | N | Y |
| 9 Kaptur | Y | ? | ? | Y | Y |
| 10 Kucinich | Y | Y | N | Y | N |
| 11 Jones | Y | Y | ? | Y | N |
| 12 Tiberi | Y | Y | Y | N | Y |
| 13 Brown | ? | ? | ? | ? | ? |
| 14 LaTourette | Y | Y | Y | N | Y |
| 15 Pryce | Y | Y | Y | N | Y |
| 16 Regula | Y | Y | Y | N | Y |
| 17 Ryan | Y | Y | N | Y | Y |
| 18 Ney | Y | Y | Y | N | Y |
| **OKLAHOMA** | | | | | |
| 1 Sullivan | Y | Y | Y | N | Y |
| 2 Boren | Y | Y | N | Y | Y |
| 3 Lucas | Y | Y | Y | N | Y |
| 4 Cole | Y | Y | Y | N | Y |
| 5 Istook | Y | Y | ? | N | Y |
| **OREGON** | | | | | |
| 1 Wu | Y | Y | N | Y | Y |
| 2 Walden | Y | Y | Y | N | Y |
| 3 Blumenauer | Y | Y | N | Y | Y |
| 4 DeFazio | N | Y | N | Y | Y |
| 5 Hooley | Y | Y | N | Y | Y |
| **PENNSYLVANIA** | | | | | |
| 1 Brady | Y | Y | N | Y | Y |
| 2 Fattah | Y | Y | N | Y | Y |
| 3 English | Y | Y | Y | N | Y |
| 4 Hart | Y | Y | Y | N | Y |
| 5 Peterson | Y | Y | Y | N | Y |
| 6 Gerlach | Y | Y | Y | N | Y |
| 7 Weldon | Y | Y | Y | N | Y |
| 8 Fitzpatrick | Y | Y | Y | N | Y |
| 9 Shuster | Y | Y | Y | N | Y |
| 10 Sherwood | Y | Y | Y | N | Y |
| 11 Kanjorski | Y | Y | N | Y | Y |
| 12 Murtha | Y | Y | N | Y | Y |
| 13 Schwartz | Y | Y | N | Y | Y |
| 14 Doyle | Y | Y | N | Y | Y |
| 15 Dent | Y | Y | Y | N | Y |
| 16 Pitts | Y | Y | Y | N | Y |
| 17 Holden | Y | Y | N | Y | Y |
| 18 Murphy | Y | Y | Y | N | Y |
| 19 Platts | Y | Y | ? | N | Y |
| **RHODE ISLAND** | | | | | |
| 1 Kennedy | Y | Y | N | Y | Y |
| 2 Langevin | Y | Y | N | Y | Y |
| **SOUTH CAROLINA** | | | | | |
| 1 Brown | Y | Y | Y | N | Y |
| 2 Wilson | Y | Y | Y | N | Y |
| 3 Barrett | Y | Y | Y | N | Y |
| 4 Inglis | Y | Y | Y | N | Y |
| 5 Spratt | Y | Y | N | Y | Y |
| 6 Clyburn | Y | Y | N | Y | Y |
| **SOUTH DAKOTA** | | | | | |
| AL Herseth | Y | Y | N | Y | Y |
| **TENNESSEE** | | | | | |
| 1 Jenkins | Y | Y | Y | N | Y |
| 2 Duncan | Y | Y | Y | N | N |

| | 157 | 158 | 159 | 160 | 161 |
|---|---|---|---|---|---|
| 3 Wamp | Y | Y | N | Y | Y |
| 4 Davis | Y | Y | N | Y | Y |
| 5 Cooper | N | Y | N | Y | Y |
| 6 Gordon | Y | Y | ? | Y | N |
| 7 Blackburn | Y | Y | Y | N | Y |
| 8 Tanner | Y | Y | N | Y | Y |
| 9 Ford | Y | Y | N | Y | Y |
| **TEXAS** | | | | | |
| 1 Gohmert | Y | Y | Y | N | Y |
| 2 Poe | Y | Y | Y | N | Y |
| 3 Johnson, S. | Y | Y | Y | N | Y |
| 4 Hall | Y | Y | Y | N | Y |
| 5 Hensarling | Y | Y | Y | N | Y |
| 6 Barton | Y | Y | Y | N | Y |
| 7 Culberson | Y | Y | Y | N | Y |
| 8 Brady | Y | Y | Y | N | Y |
| 9 Green | Y | Y | N | Y | Y |
| 10 McCaul | Y | Y | Y | N | Y |
| 11 Conaway | Y | Y | Y | N | Y |
| 12 Granger | Y | Y | Y | N | Y |
| 13 Thornberry | Y | Y | Y | N | Y |
| 14 Paul | N | Y | Y | N | N |
| 15 Hinojosa | Y | Y | N | Y | Y |
| 16 Reyes | Y | Y | N | Y | Y |
| 17 Edwards | Y | Y | N | Y | Y |
| 18 Jackson-Lee | + | + | N | Y | N |
| 19 Neugebauer | Y | Y | Y | N | Y |
| 20 Gonzalez | Y | Y | N | Y | Y |
| 21 Smith | Y | Y | Y | N | Y |
| 22 DeLay | Y | Y | Y | N | Y |
| 23 Bonilla | Y | Y | Y | N | Y |
| 24 Marchant | Y | Y | Y | N | Y |
| 25 Doggett | Y | Y | N | Y | Y |
| 26 Burgess | Y | Y | Y | N | Y |
| 27 Ortiz | Y | Y | N | Y | Y |
| 28 Cuellar | Y | Y | N | Y | Y |
| 29 Green | Y | Y | N | Y | Y |
| 30 Johnson, E. | Y | Y | N | Y | Y |
| 31 Carter | Y | Y | Y | N | Y |
| 32 Sessions | Y | Y | Y | N | Y |
| **UTAH** | | | | | |
| 1 Bishop | Y | Y | Y | N | Y |
| 2 Matheson | Y | Y | N | Y | Y |
| 3 Cannon | Y | Y | Y | N | Y |
| **VERMONT** | | | | | |
| AL *Sanders* | N | Y | N | Y | N |
| **VIRGINIA** | | | | | |
| 1 Davis, J. | N | Y | Y | N | Y |
| 2 Drake | + | Y | Y | N | Y |
| 3 Scott | ? | ? | N | Y | Y |
| 4 Forbes | Y | Y | Y | N | Y |
| 5 Goode | Y | Y | Y | N | Y |
| 6 Goodlatte | Y | Y | Y | N | Y |
| 7 Cantor | Y | Y | Y | N | Y |
| 8 Moran | Y | Y | N | Y | Y |
| 9 Boucher | Y | Y | N | Y | Y |
| 10 Wolf | Y | Y | Y | N | Y |
| 11 Davis, T. | Y | Y | Y | N | Y |
| **WASHINGTON** | | | | | |
| 1 Inslee | Y | Y | N | Y | Y |
| 2 Larsen | Y | Y | N | Y | Y |
| 3 Baird | Y | Y | N | Y | Y |
| 4 Hastings | ? | ? | Y | N | Y |
| 5 McMorris | Y | Y | Y | N | Y |
| 6 Dicks | Y | Y | N | Y | Y |
| 7 McDermott | Y | Y | N | Y | N |
| 8 Reichert | Y | Y | Y | N | Y |
| 9 Smith | Y | Y | N | Y | Y |
| **WEST VIRGINIA** | | | | | |
| 1 Mollohan | Y | Y | N | Y | Y |
| 2 Capito | Y | Y | Y | N | Y |
| 3 Rahall | Y | Y | N | Y | Y |
| **WISCONSIN** | | | | | |
| 1 Ryan | Y | Y | Y | N | Y |
| 2 Baldwin | Y | Y | N | Y | N |
| 3 Kind | Y | Y | N | Y | Y |
| 4 Moore | Y | Y | N | Y | N |
| 5 Sensenbrenner | Y | Y | Y | N | Y |
| 6 Petri | Y | Y | Y | N | Y |
| 7 Obey | Y | Y | N | Y | Y |
| 8 Green | Y | Y | Y | N | Y |
| **WYOMING** | | | | | |
| AL Cubin | Y | Y | Y | N | Y |

# IN THE HOUSE | By Vote Number

**162.** **H Res 193. Democracy in Cuba/Adoption.** Ros-Lehtinen, R-Fla., motion to suspend the rules and adopt the resolution that would ask the international community to support the Assembly to Promote the Civil Society in Cuba's mission to bring democracy to that country and would urge the administration and international community to actively oppose any attempts by the Castro regime to repress or punish the organizers of and participants in the assembly. Motion agreed to 392-22: R 223-1; D 169-21 (ND 120-20, SD 49-1); I 0-0. A two-thirds majority of those present and voting (276 in this case) is required for adoption under suspension of the rules. May 10, 2005.

**163.** **H Res 142. Rotary International Tribute/Adoption.** Ros-Lehtinen, R-Fla., motion to suspend the rules and adopt the resolution that would recognize Rotary International on its Feb. 23, 2005, anniversary for 100 years of service throughout the world. Motion agreed to 413-0: R 223-0; D 190-0 (ND 140-0, SD 50-0); I 0-0. A two-thirds majority of those present and voting (276 in this case) is required for adoption under suspension of the rules. May 10, 2005.

**164.** **HR 1279. Gang Deterrence/Previous Question.** Gingrey, R-Ga., motion to order the previous question (thus ending debate and possibility of amendment) on adoption of the rule (H Res 268) to provide for House floor consideration of the bill that would create new federal criminal penalties for crimes committed by gang members and increase criminal penalties for certain violent crimes. Motion agreed to 227-198: R 227-0; D 0-197 (ND 0-148, SD 0-49); I 0-1. (Subsequently, the rule was adopted by voice vote.) May 11, 2005.

**165.** **HR 1279. Gang Deterrence/Illegal Aliens.** Goodlatte, R-Va., amendment that would add five years to any sentence for violent crime or drug trafficking when the offender is an illegal alien. It would add 15 years to a sentence if the alien has previously been deported for criminal offenses and has re-entered the country. Adopted 266-159: R 215-13; D 51-145 (ND 31-117, SD 20-28); I 0-1. May 11, 2005.

**166.** **HR 1279. Gang Deterrence/Gang Membership Study.** Norwood, R-Ga., amendment that would require the Justice and Homeland Security departments to conduct a joint study and report to Congress within one year on the connection between illegal immigration and gang membership. Adopted 395-31: R 229-0; D 165-31 (ND 118-30, SD 47-1); I 1-0. May 11, 2005.

| | 162 | 163 | 164 | 165 | 166 |
|---|---|---|---|---|---|
| **ALABAMA** | | | | | |
| 1 Bonner | Y | Y | Y | Y | Y |
| 2 Everett | Y | Y | Y | Y | Y |
| 3 Rogers | Y | Y | Y | Y | Y |
| 4 Aderholt | Y | Y | Y | Y | Y |
| 5 Cramer | Y | Y | N | Y | Y |
| 6 Bachus | Y | ? | Y | Y | Y |
| 7 Davis | Y | Y | N | N | Y |
| **ALASKA** | | | | | |
| AL Young | Y | Y | Y | Y | Y |
| **ARIZONA** | | | | | |
| 1 Renzi | Y | Y | Y | Y | Y |
| 2 Franks | Y | Y | Y | Y | Y |
| 3 Shadegg | Y | Y | Y | Y | Y |
| 4 Pastor | Y | Y | N | N | Y |
| 5 Hayworth | Y | Y | Y | Y | Y |
| 6 Flake | Y | Y | Y | N | Y |
| 7 Grijalva | Y | Y | N | N | N |
| 8 Kolbe | Y | Y | Y | Y | Y |
| **ARKANSAS** | | | | | |
| 1 Berry | Y | Y | N | Y | Y |
| 2 Snyder | Y | Y | N | Y | Y |
| 3 Boozman | Y | Y | Y | Y | Y |
| 4 Ross | Y | Y | N | Y | Y |
| **CALIFORNIA** | | | | | |
| 1 Thompson | Y | Y | N | N | Y |
| 2 Herger | Y | Y | Y | Y | Y |
| 3 Lungren | Y | Y | Y | Y | Y |
| 4 Doolittle | Y | Y | Y | Y | Y |
| 5 Matsui, D. | Y | Y | N | N | Y |
| 6 Woolsey | N | Y | N | N | Y |
| 7 Miller, George | N | Y | N | N | Y |
| 8 Pelosi | Y | Y | N | N | Y |
| 9 Lee | N | Y | N | N | N |
| 10 Tauscher | Y | Y | N | N | Y |
| 11 Pombo | Y | Y | Y | Y | Y |
| 12 Lantos | ? | ? | N | N | Y |
| 13 Stark | N | Y | N | N | N |
| 14 Eshoo | Y | Y | N | N | Y |
| 15 Honda | Y | Y | N | N | Y |
| 16 Lofgren | Y | Y | N | N | Y |
| 17 Farr | N | Y | N | N | Y |
| 18 Cardoza | Y | Y | N | Y | Y |
| 19 Radanovich | Y | Y | Y | Y | Y |
| 20 Costa | Y | Y | N | Y | Y |
| 21 Nunes | Y | Y | Y | Y | Y |
| 22 Thomas | Y | Y | Y | Y | Y |
| 23 Capps | Y | Y | N | N | Y |
| 24 Gallegly | Y | Y | Y | Y | Y |
| 25 McKeon | Y | Y | Y | Y | Y |
| 26 Dreier | Y | Y | Y | Y | Y |
| 27 Sherman | Y | Y | N | N | Y |
| 28 Berman | Y | Y | N | N | Y |
| 29 Schiff | ? | ? | N | N | Y |
| 30 Waxman | Y | Y | N | N | Y |
| 31 Becerra | Y | Y | N | N | Y |
| 32 Solis | Y | Y | N | N | N |
| 33 Watson | Y | Y | N | N | Y |
| 34 Roybal-Allard | Y | Y | N | N | Y |
| 35 Waters | N | Y | N | N | Y |
| 36 Harman | Y | Y | N | Y | Y |
| 37 Millender-McD. | ? | ? | ? | ? | ? |
| 38 Napolitano | Y | Y | N | N | Y |
| 39 Sánchez, Linda | Y | Y | N | N | N |
| 40 Royce | Y | Y | Y | Y | Y |
| 41 Lewis | Y | Y | Y | Y | Y |
| 42 Miller, Gary | Y | Y | Y | Y | Y |
| 43 Baca | Y | Y | N | N | Y |
| 44 Calvert | Y | Y | Y | Y | Y |
| 45 Bono | Y | Y | Y | Y | Y |
| 46 Rohrabacher | Y | Y | Y | Y | Y |
| 47 Sanchez, Loretta | Y | Y | N | N | Y |
| 48 Cox | Y | Y | Y | Y | Y |
| 49 Issa | Y | Y | Y | Y | Y |
| 50 Cunningham | Y | Y | Y | Y | Y |
| 51 Filner | Y | Y | N | N | N |
| 52 Hunter | Y | Y | Y | Y | Y |
| 53 Davis | Y | Y | N | N | Y |
| **COLORADO** | | | | | |
| 1 DeGette | Y | Y | N | N | Y |
| 2 Udall | Y | Y | N | Y | Y |
| 3 Salazar | Y | Y | N | N | Y |
| 4 Musgrave | ? | ? | ? | ? | ? |
| 5 Hefley | Y | Y | Y | Y | Y |
| 6 Tancredo | Y | Y | Y | Y | Y |
| 7 Beauprez | Y | Y | Y | Y | Y |
| **CONNECTICUT** | | | | | |
| 1 Larson | + | + | – | – | + |
| 2 Simmons | Y | Y | Y | Y | Y |
| 3 DeLauro | Y | Y | N | N | Y |
| 4 Shays | Y | Y | Y | Y | Y |
| 5 Johnson | Y | Y | Y | Y | Y |
| **DELAWARE** | | | | | |
| AL Castle | Y | Y | Y | N | Y |
| **FLORIDA** | | | | | |
| 1 Miller | Y | Y | Y | Y | Y |
| 2 Boyd | Y | Y | N | Y | Y |
| 3 Brown | Y | Y | N | N | Y |
| 4 Crenshaw | Y | Y | Y | Y | Y |
| 5 Brown-Waite | Y | Y | Y | Y | Y |
| 6 Stearns | Y | Y | Y | Y | Y |
| 7 Mica | Y | Y | Y | Y | Y |
| 8 Keller | ? | Y | Y | Y | Y |
| 9 Bilirakis | Y | Y | Y | Y | Y |
| 10 Young | Y | Y | Y | Y | Y |
| 11 Davis | Y | Y | N | N | Y |
| 12 Putnam | Y | Y | Y | Y | Y |
| 13 Harris | Y | ? | Y | Y | Y |
| 14 Mack | Y | Y | Y | Y | Y |
| 15 Weldon | Y | Y | Y | Y | Y |
| 16 Foley | Y | Y | Y | Y | Y |
| 17 Meek | Y | Y | N | N | Y |
| 18 Ros-Lehtinen | Y | Y | Y | Y | Y |
| 19 Wexler | Y | Y | N | N | Y |
| 20 Wasserman-Schultz | Y | Y | N | ? | ? |
| 21 Diaz-Balart, L. | Y | Y | Y | N | Y |
| 22 Shaw | Y | Y | Y | Y | Y |
| 23 Hastings | ? | ? | ? | ? | ? |
| 24 Feeney | Y | Y | Y | Y | Y |
| 25 Diaz-Balart, M. | Y | Y | Y | N | Y |
| **GEORGIA** | | | | | |
| 1 Kingston | Y | Y | Y | Y | Y |
| 2 Bishop | Y | Y | N | N | Y |
| 3 Marshall | Y | Y | N | Y | Y |
| 4 McKinney | N | Y | N | N | N |
| 5 Lewis | Y | Y | N | N | N |
| 6 Price | Y | Y | Y | Y | Y |
| 7 Linder | Y | Y | Y | Y | Y |
| 8 Westmoreland | Y | Y | Y | Y | Y |
| 9 Norwood | Y | Y | Y | Y | Y |
| 10 Deal | Y | Y | Y | Y | Y |
| 11 Gingrey | Y | Y | Y | Y | Y |
| 12 Barrow | Y | Y | N | Y | Y |
| 13 Scott | Y | Y | N | Y | Y |
| **HAWAII** | | | | | |
| 1 Abercrombie | Y | Y | N | Y | N |
| 2 Case | Y | Y | N | Y | Y |
| **IDAHO** | | | | | |
| 1 Otter | ? | ? | Y | Y | Y |
| 2 Simpson | Y | Y | Y | Y | Y |
| **ILLINOIS** | | | | | |
| 1 Rush | Y | Y | N | N | Y |
| 2 Jackson | Y | Y | N | N | Y |
| 3 Lipinski | Y | Y | N | Y | Y |
| 4 Gutierrez | ? | ? | N | N | N |
| 5 Emanuel | Y | Y | N | N | Y |
| 6 Hyde | Y | Y | ? | Y | Y |
| 7 Davis | Y | Y | N | N | N |
| 8 Bean | Y | Y | N | Y | Y |
| 9 Schakowsky | Y | Y | N | N | N |
| 10 Kirk | Y | Y | Y | Y | Y |
| 11 Weller | Y | Y | Y | Y | Y |
| 12 Costello | ? | Y | N | Y | Y |

| KEY | Republicans | Democrats | Independents | | |
|---|---|---|---|---|---|
| Y | Voted for (yea) | X | Paired against | C | Voted "present" to avoid possible conflict of interest |
| # | Paired for | – | Announced against | | |
| + | Announced for | P | Voted "present" | ? | Did not vote or otherwise make a position known |
| N | Voted against (nay) | | | | |

ND Northern Democrats, SD Southern Democrats
Southern states: Ala., Ark., Fla., Ga., Ky., La., Miss., N.C., Okla., S.C., Tenn., Texas, Va.

| | 162 | 163 | 164 | 165 | 166 |
|---|---|---|---|---|---|
| 13 Biggert | Y | Y | Y | Y | Y |
| 14 Hastert | | | | | |
| 15 Johnson | Y | Y | Y | Y | Y |
| 16 Manzullo | Y | Y | Y | Y | Y |
| 17 Evans | Y | Y | N | N | Y |
| 18 LaHood | Y | Y | Y | Y | Y |
| 19 Shimkus | Y | Y | Y | Y | Y |
| **INDIANA** | | | | | |
| 1 Visclosky | Y | Y | N | N | Y |
| 2 Chocola | Y | Y | Y | Y | Y |
| 3 Souder | Y | Y | Y | Y | Y |
| 4 Buyer | Y | Y | Y | Y | Y |
| 5 Burton | Y | Y | Y | Y | Y |
| 6 Pence | Y | Y | Y | Y | Y |
| 7 Carson | Y | Y | N | N | Y |
| 8 Hostettler | Y | Y | Y | Y | Y |
| 9 Sodrel | Y | Y | Y | Y | Y |
| **IOWA** | | | | | |
| 1 Nussle | Y | Y | Y | Y | Y |
| 2 Leach | Y | Y | Y | N | Y |
| 3 Boswell | Y | Y | N | Y | Y |
| 4 Latham | Y | Y | Y | Y | Y |
| 5 King | Y | Y | Y | Y | Y |
| **KANSAS** | | | | | |
| 1 Moran | Y | Y | Y | Y | Y |
| 2 Ryun | Y | Y | Y | Y | Y |
| 3 Moore | Y | Y | N | Y | Y |
| 4 Tiahrt | Y | Y | Y | Y | Y |
| **KENTUCKY** | | | | | |
| 1 Whitfield | Y | Y | Y | Y | Y |
| 2 Lewis | Y | Y | Y | Y | Y |
| 3 Northup | Y | Y | Y | Y | Y |
| 4 Davis | Y | Y | Y | Y | Y |
| 5 Rogers | Y | Y | Y | Y | Y |
| 6 Chandler | Y | Y | N | Y | Y |
| **LOUISIANA** | | | | | |
| 1 Jindal | Y | Y | Y | Y | Y |
| 2 Jefferson | Y | Y | N | N | Y |
| 3 Melancon | Y | Y | N | Y | Y |
| 4 McCrery | Y | Y | Y | Y | Y |
| 5 Alexander | Y | Y | Y | Y | Y |
| 6 Baker | Y | Y | Y | Y | Y |
| 7 Boustany | Y | Y | Y | Y | Y |
| **MAINE** | | | | | |
| 1 Allen | Y | Y | N | N | Y |
| 2 Michaud | Y | Y | N | Y | Y |
| **MARYLAND** | | | | | |
| 1 Gilchrest | Y | ? | Y | Y | Y |
| 2 Ruppersberger | Y | Y | N | N | Y |
| 3 Cardin | Y | Y | N | N | Y |
| 4 Wynn | Y | Y | N | N | Y |
| 5 Hoyer | Y | Y | N | N | Y |
| 6 Bartlett | Y | Y | Y | Y | Y |
| 7 Cummings | Y | Y | N | N | Y |
| 8 Van Hollen | Y | Y | N | N | Y |
| **MASSACHUSETTS** | | | | | |
| 1 Olver | N | Y | N | N | N |
| 2 Neal | Y | Y | N | N | Y |
| 3 McGovern | Y | Y | N | N | N |
| 4 Frank | Y | ? | N | N | Y |
| 5 Meehan | Y | Y | N | N | Y |
| 6 Tierney | ? | ? | N | N | Y |
| 7 Markey | Y | Y | N | N | Y |
| 8 Capuano | Y | Y | N | N | Y |
| 9 Lynch | Y | Y | N | N | Y |
| 10 Delahunt | Y | Y | N | N | N |
| **MICHIGAN** | | | | | |
| 1 Stupak | Y | Y | N | N | Y |
| 2 Hoekstra | Y | Y | Y | Y | Y |
| 3 Ehlers | Y | Y | Y | Y | Y |
| 4 Camp | Y | Y | Y | Y | Y |
| 5 Kildee | Y | Y | N | N | Y |
| 6 Upton | Y | Y | Y | Y | Y |
| 7 Schwarz | Y | Y | Y | Y | Y |
| 8 Rogers | Y | Y | Y | Y | Y |
| 9 Knollenberg | Y | Y | Y | Y | Y |
| 10 Miller | Y | Y | Y | Y | Y |
| 11 McCotter | Y | Y | Y | Y | Y |
| 12 Levin | Y | Y | N | N | Y |
| 13 Kilpatrick | N | Y | N | N | N |
| 14 Conyers | N | ? | N | N | N |
| 15 Dingell | ? | ? | N | N | Y |

| | 162 | 163 | 164 | 165 | 166 |
|---|---|---|---|---|---|
| **MINNESOTA** | | | | | |
| 1 Gutknecht | Y | Y | Y | Y | Y |
| 2 Kline | Y | Y | Y | Y | Y |
| 3 Ramstad | Y | Y | Y | Y | Y |
| 4 McCollum | Y | Y | N | N | Y |
| 5 Sabo | Y | Y | N | N | Y |
| 6 Kennedy | Y | Y | Y | Y | Y |
| 7 Peterson | Y | Y | N | Y | Y |
| 8 Oberstar | Y | Y | N | N | N |
| **MISSISSIPPI** | | | | | |
| 1 Wicker | Y | Y | Y | Y | Y |
| 2 Thompson | Y | Y | N | N | Y |
| 3 Pickering | Y | Y | Y | Y | Y |
| 4 Taylor | Y | Y | N | Y | Y |
| **MISSOURI** | | | | | |
| 1 Clay | Y | Y | N | N | Y |
| 2 Akin | Y | Y | Y | Y | Y |
| 3 Carnahan | Y | Y | N | N | Y |
| 4 Skelton | Y | Y | N | Y | Y |
| 5 Cleaver | Y | Y | N | N | Y |
| 6 Graves | Y | Y | Y | Y | Y |
| 7 Blunt | Y | Y | Y | Y | Y |
| 8 Emerson | Y | Y | Y | Y | Y |
| 9 Hulshof | ? | ? | Y | Y | Y |
| **MONTANA** | | | | | |
| AL Rehberg | Y | Y | Y | Y | Y |
| **NEBRASKA** | | | | | |
| 1 Fortenberry | Y | Y | Y | Y | Y |
| 2 Terry | Y | Y | Y | Y | Y |
| 3 Osborne | Y | Y | Y | Y | Y |
| **NEVADA** | | | | | |
| 1 Berkley | ? | ? | ? | ? | ? |
| 2 Gibbons | Y | Y | Y | Y | Y |
| 3 Porter | Y | Y | Y | Y | Y |
| **NEW HAMPSHIRE** | | | | | |
| 1 Bradley | Y | Y | Y | Y | Y |
| 2 Bass | Y | Y | Y | Y | Y |
| **NEW JERSEY** | | | | | |
| 1 Andrews | Y | Y | N | N | Y |
| 2 LoBiondo | Y | Y | Y | Y | Y |
| 3 Saxton | Y | Y | Y | Y | Y |
| 4 Smith | Y | Y | Y | Y | Y |
| 5 Garrett | Y | Y | Y | Y | Y |
| 6 Pallone | Y | Y | N | N | Y |
| 7 Ferguson | ? | Y | Y | Y | Y |
| 8 Pascrell | Y | Y | N | N | Y |
| 9 Rothman | Y | Y | N | N | Y |
| 10 Payne | N | N | N | N | N |
| 11 Frelinghuysen | Y | Y | Y | Y | Y |
| 12 Holt | Y | Y | N | N | N |
| 13 Menendez | Y | Y | N | N | Y |
| **NEW MEXICO** | | | | | |
| 1 Wilson | Y | Y | N | Y | Y |
| 2 Pearce | Y | Y | Y | Y | Y |
| 3 Udall | N | Y | N | N | Y |
| **NEW YORK** | | | | | |
| 1 Bishop | Y | Y | N | Y | Y |
| 2 Israel | Y | Y | N | Y | Y |
| 3 King | Y | Y | Y | Y | Y |
| 4 McCarthy | Y | Y | N | Y | Y |
| 5 Ackerman | Y | Y | N | N | Y |
| 6 Meeks | N | Y | N | N | Y |
| 7 Crowley | Y | Y | N | N | Y |
| 8 Nadler | Y | Y | N | N | N |
| 9 Weiner | ? | ? | N | N | Y |
| 10 Towns | N | Y | N | N | Y |
| 11 Owens | Y | Y | N | N | Y |
| 12 Velázquez | N | Y | N | N | Y |
| 13 Fossella | Y | Y | Y | Y | Y |
| 14 Maloney | Y | Y | N | N | Y |
| 15 Rangel | Y | Y | N | N | N |
| 16 Serrano | N | Y | N | N | Y |
| 17 Engel | Y | Y | N | Y | Y |
| 18 Lowey | Y | Y | N | N | Y |
| 19 Kelly | Y | Y | Y | Y | Y |
| 20 Sweeney | Y | Y | Y | Y | Y |
| 21 McNulty | Y | Y | N | N | Y |
| 22 Hinchey | N | Y | N | N | Y |
| 23 McHugh | Y | Y | Y | Y | Y |
| 24 Boehlert | Y | Y | Y | Y | Y |
| 25 Walsh | Y | Y | Y | Y | Y |
| 26 Reynolds | Y | Y | Y | Y | Y |
| 27 Higgins | Y | Y | N | Y | Y |
| 28 Slaughter | Y | Y | N | N | Y |
| 29 Kuhl | Y | Y | Y | Y | Y |

| | 162 | 163 | 164 | 165 | 166 |
|---|---|---|---|---|---|
| **NORTH CAROLINA** | | | | | |
| 1 Butterfield | Y | Y | N | N | Y |
| 2 Etheridge | Y | Y | N | Y | Y |
| 3 Jones | Y | Y | Y | N | Y |
| 4 Price | Y | Y | N | N | Y |
| 5 Foxx | Y | Y | Y | Y | Y |
| 6 Coble | Y | Y | Y | Y | Y |
| 7 McIntyre | Y | Y | N | Y | Y |
| 8 Hayes | Y | Y | Y | Y | Y |
| 9 Myrick | Y | Y | Y | Y | Y |
| 10 McHenry | Y | Y | Y | Y | Y |
| 11 Taylor | Y | Y | Y | Y | Y |
| 12 Watt | Y | N | N | N | Y |
| 13 Miller | Y | Y | N | N | Y |
| **NORTH DAKOTA** | | | | | |
| AL Pomeroy | Y | Y | N | Y | Y |
| **OHIO** | | | | | |
| 1 Chabot | Y | Y | Y | Y | Y |
| 2 Vacant | | | | | |
| 3 Turner | Y | Y | Y | Y | Y |
| 4 Oxley | Y | Y | Y | Y | Y |
| 5 Gillmor | Y | Y | Y | Y | Y |
| 6 Strickland | Y | Y | N | N | Y |
| 7 Hobson | Y | Y | Y | Y | Y |
| 8 Boehner | Y | Y | Y | Y | Y |
| 9 Kaptur | Y | Y | N | N | Y |
| 10 Kucinich | N | Y | N | N | N |
| 11 Jones | N | Y | N | N | Y |
| 12 Tiberi | Y | Y | Y | Y | Y |
| 13 Brown | Y | Y | N | N | Y |
| 14 LaTourette | Y | Y | Y | N | Y |
| 15 Pryce | Y | Y | Y | Y | Y |
| 16 Regula | Y | Y | Y | Y | Y |
| 17 Ryan | Y | Y | N | N | Y |
| 18 Ney | Y | Y | Y | Y | Y |
| **OKLAHOMA** | | | | | |
| 1 Sullivan | Y | Y | Y | Y | Y |
| 2 Boren | Y | Y | N | Y | Y |
| 3 Lucas | Y | Y | Y | Y | Y |
| 4 Cole | Y | Y | Y | Y | Y |
| 5 Istook | Y | Y | Y | Y | Y |
| **OREGON** | | | | | |
| 1 Wu | Y | Y | N | Y | Y |
| 2 Walden | Y | Y | Y | Y | Y |
| 3 Blumenauer | Y | Y | N | N | Y |
| 4 DeFazio | Y | Y | N | N | Y |
| 5 Hooley | Y | Y | N | N | Y |
| **PENNSYLVANIA** | | | | | |
| 1 Brady | Y | Y | N | N | Y |
| 2 Fattah | Y | Y | N | N | Y |
| 3 English | Y | Y | Y | Y | Y |
| 4 Hart | Y | Y | Y | Y | Y |
| 5 Peterson | Y | Y | Y | Y | Y |
| 6 Gerlach | Y | Y | Y | Y | Y |
| 7 Weldon | Y | Y | Y | Y | Y |
| 8 Fitzpatrick | Y | Y | Y | Y | Y |
| 9 Shuster | Y | Y | Y | Y | Y |
| 10 Sherwood | Y | Y | Y | Y | Y |
| 11 Kanjorski | Y | Y | N | N | Y |
| 12 Murtha | Y | Y | N | N | Y |
| 13 Schwartz | Y | Y | N | N | Y |
| 14 Doyle | Y | Y | N | N | Y |
| 15 Dent | Y | Y | Y | Y | Y |
| 16 Pitts | Y | Y | Y | Y | Y |
| 17 Holden | Y | Y | N | Y | Y |
| 18 Murphy | Y | Y | Y | Y | Y |
| 19 Platts | Y | Y | Y | Y | Y |
| **RHODE ISLAND** | | | | | |
| 1 Kennedy | Y | Y | N | Y | Y |
| 2 Langevin | Y | Y | N | N | Y |
| **SOUTH CAROLINA** | | | | | |
| 1 Brown | Y | Y | Y | Y | Y |
| 2 Wilson | + | + | Y | Y | Y |
| 3 Barrett | Y | Y | Y | Y | Y |
| 4 Inglis | Y | Y | Y | Y | Y |
| 5 Spratt | Y | Y | N | Y | Y |
| 6 Clyburn | Y | Y | N | N | Y |
| **SOUTH DAKOTA** | | | | | |
| AL Herseth | Y | Y | N | Y | Y |
| **TENNESSEE** | | | | | |
| 1 Jenkins | Y | Y | Y | Y | Y |
| 2 Duncan | Y | Y | Y | Y | Y |

| | 162 | 163 | 164 | 165 | 166 |
|---|---|---|---|---|---|
| 3 Wamp | Y | Y | Y | Y | Y |
| 4 Davis | Y | Y | N | Y | Y |
| 5 Cooper | Y | Y | N | N | Y |
| 6 Gordon | Y | Y | N | Y | Y |
| 7 Blackburn | Y | Y | Y | Y | Y |
| 8 Tanner | Y | Y | N | Y | Y |
| 9 Ford | Y | Y | N | N | Y |
| **TEXAS** | | | | | |
| 1 Gohmert | Y | Y | Y | Y | Y |
| 2 Poe | Y | Y | Y | Y | Y |
| 3 Johnson, S. | Y | Y | Y | Y | Y |
| 4 Hall | Y | Y | Y | Y | Y |
| 5 Hensarling | Y | Y | Y | Y | Y |
| 6 Barton | Y | Y | Y | Y | Y |
| 7 Culberson | Y | Y | Y | Y | Y |
| 8 Brady | Y | Y | Y | Y | Y |
| 9 Green | Y | Y | N | N | Y |
| 10 McCaul | Y | Y | Y | Y | Y |
| 11 Conaway | Y | Y | Y | Y | Y |
| 12 Granger | Y | Y | Y | Y | Y |
| 13 Thornberry | Y | Y | Y | Y | Y |
| 14 Paul | N | Y | N | N | Y |
| 15 Hinojosa | Y | Y | N | N | Y |
| 16 Reyes | Y | Y | N | N | Y |
| 17 Edwards | Y | Y | N | Y | Y |
| 18 Jackson-Lee | Y | Y | N | N | Y |
| 19 Neugebauer | Y | Y | N | N | Y |
| 20 Gonzalez | Y | Y | N | N | Y |
| 21 Smith | Y | Y | Y | Y | Y |
| 22 DeLay | Y | Y | Y | Y | Y |
| 23 Bonilla | Y | Y | Y | Y | Y |
| 24 Marchant | Y | Y | Y | Y | Y |
| 25 Doggett | Y | Y | N | N | Y |
| 26 Burgess | Y | Y | Y | Y | Y |
| 27 Ortiz | Y | Y | N | N | Y |
| 28 Cuellar | Y | Y | N | N | Y |
| 29 Green | Y | Y | N | N | Y |
| 30 Johnson, E. | Y | Y | N | N | Y |
| 31 Carter | Y | Y | Y | Y | Y |
| 32 Sessions | Y | Y | Y | Y | Y |
| **UTAH** | | | | | |
| 1 Bishop | Y | Y | Y | ? | Y |
| 2 Matheson | Y | Y | N | Y | Y |
| 3 Cannon | Y | Y | Y | Y | Y |
| **VERMONT** | | | | | |
| AL *Sanders* | ? | ? | N | N | Y |
| **VIRGINIA** | | | | | |
| 1 Davis, J. | Y | Y | Y | Y | Y |
| 2 Drake | Y | Y | Y | Y | Y |
| 3 Scott | Y | Y | N | N | Y |
| 4 Forbes | Y | Y | Y | Y | Y |
| 5 Goode | Y | Y | ? | Y | Y |
| 6 Goodlatte | Y | Y | Y | Y | Y |
| 7 Cantor | Y | Y | Y | Y | Y |
| 8 Moran | Y | Y | ? | ? | ? |
| 9 Boucher | Y | Y | N | N | Y |
| 10 Wolf | Y | Y | Y | Y | Y |
| 11 Davis, T. | Y | Y | Y | Y | Y |
| **WASHINGTON** | | | | | |
| 1 Inslee | Y | Y | N | N | Y |
| 2 Larsen | Y | Y | N | Y | Y |
| 3 Baird | Y | Y | N | Y | Y |
| 4 Hastings | Y | Y | Y | Y | Y |
| 5 McMorris | Y | Y | Y | Y | Y |
| 6 Dicks | Y | Y | N | N | Y |
| 7 McDermott | N | Y | N | N | N |
| 8 Reichert | Y | Y | N | Y | Y |
| 9 Smith | Y | Y | N | Y | Y |
| **WEST VIRGINIA** | | | | | |
| 1 Mollohan | Y | Y | N | N | Y |
| 2 Capito | Y | Y | Y | Y | Y |
| 3 Rahall | Y | Y | N | N | Y |
| **WISCONSIN** | | | | | |
| 1 Ryan | Y | Y | Y | Y | Y |
| 2 Baldwin | Y | Y | N | N | N |
| 3 Kind | Y | Y | N | N | Y |
| 4 Moore | P | Y | N | N | Y |
| 5 Sensenbrenner | Y | Y | Y | Y | Y |
| 6 Petri | Y | Y | Y | Y | Y |
| 7 Obey | Y | Y | N | N | Y |
| 8 Green | Y | Y | Y | Y | Y |
| **WYOMING** | | | | | |
| AL Cubin | Y | Y | Y | Y | Y |

# IN THE HOUSE | By Vote Number

**167.** **HR 1279. Gang Deterrence/Recommit.** Tierney, D-Mass., motion to recommit the bill to the House Judiciary Committee with instructions to include language that would prohibit profiteering and fraud in connection with the war and reconstruction efforts in Iraq. Motion rejected 198-227: R 2-227; D 195-0 (ND 147-0, SD 48-0); I 1-0. May 11, 2005.

**168.** **HR 1279. Gang Deterrence/Passage.** Passage of the bill that would increase penalties for crimes committed by "criminal street gangs." Certain gang-related offenses would be subject to mandatory minimum sentences, including 30 years or more in prison for cases of kidnapping, aggravated sexual assault or maiming. It would authorize $438 million over five years for federal, state and local law enforcement efforts against violent gangs and for law enforcement efforts to share intelligence and jointly investigate violent gangs. The bill would also add 94 assistant U.S. attorneys, 100 inspectors and 100 agents to work on gang activity. Passed 279-144: R 208-20; D 71-123 (ND 44-102, SD 27-21); I 0-1. May 11, 2005.

**169.** **HR 1544. First-Responder Funding/Urban Area Security Initiative.** Weiner, D-N.Y., amendment that would limit to 50 the number of grants provided under the Urban Area Security Initiative. Rejected 88-331: R 0-228; D 88-102 (ND 80-60, SD 8-42); I 0-1. May 12, 2005.

**170.** **HR 1544. First-Responder Funding/Passage.** Passage of the bill that would change the distribution of certain first-responder grants provided by the Homeland Security Department to require that grants be distributed primarily based on threat levels. Each state would be guaranteed at least 0.25 percent of the total funding available, or 0.45 percent for states that have an international border or that are on a body of water with an international border. It also would require state governments to develop three-year homeland security plans for enhancing their preparedness and response capabilities. Passed 409-10: R 227-1; D 181-9 (ND 134-6, SD 47-3); I 1-0. May 12, 2005.

| | 167 | 168 | 169 | 170 |
|---|---|---|---|---|
| **ALABAMA** | | | | |
| 1 Bonner | N | Y | N | Y |
| 2 Everett | N | Y | N | Y |
| 3 Rogers | N | Y | N | Y |
| 4 Aderholt | N | Y | N | Y |
| 5 Cramer | Y | Y | N | Y |
| 6 Bachus | N | Y | N | Y |
| 7 Davis | Y | Y | N | N |
| **ALASKA** | | | | |
| AL Young | N | Y | N | Y |
| **ARIZONA** | | | | |
| 1 Renzi | N | Y | N | Y |
| 2 Franks | N | Y | N | Y |
| 3 Shadegg | N | N | N | Y |
| 4 Pastor | Y | N | N | Y |
| 5 Hayworth | N | Y | N | Y |
| 6 Flake | N | N | N | Y |
| 7 Grijalva | Y | N | N | Y |
| 8 Kolbe | N | Y | N | Y |
| **ARKANSAS** | | | | |
| 1 Berry | Y | Y | N | N |
| 2 Snyder | Y | N | N | Y |
| 3 Boozman | N | Y | N | Y |
| 4 Ross | Y | Y | N | N |
| **CALIFORNIA** | | | | |
| 1 Thompson | Y | N | N | Y |
| 2 Herger | N | Y | N | Y |
| 3 Lungren | N | Y | N | Y |
| 4 Doolittle | N | Y | N | Y |
| 5 Matsui, D. | Y | N | N | Y |
| 6 Woolsey | Y | N | Y | Y |
| 7 Miller, George | Y | N | Y | Y |
| 8 Pelosi | Y | N | Y | Y |
| 9 Lee | Y | N | Y | Y |
| 10 Tauscher | Y | N | Y | Y |
| 11 Pombo | N | Y | N | Y |
| 12 Lantos | Y | Y | Y | Y |
| 13 Stark | Y | N | Y | Y |
| 14 Eshoo | Y | N | Y | Y |
| 15 Honda | Y | N | ? | Y |
| 16 Lofgren | Y | N | N | Y |
| 17 Farr | Y | N | Y | Y |
| 18 Cardoza | Y | Y | N | Y |
| 19 Radanovich | N | Y | N | Y |
| 20 Costa | Y | Y | N | Y |
| 21 Nunes | N | Y | N | Y |
| 22 Thomas | N | Y | N | Y |
| 23 Capps | Y | N | Y | Y |
| 24 Gallegly | N | Y | N | Y |
| 25 McKeon | N | Y | N | Y |
| 26 Dreier | N | Y | N | Y |
| 27 Sherman | Y | N | Y | Y |
| 28 Berman | Y | N | ? | ? |
| 29 Schiff | Y | N | Y | Y |
| 30 Waxman | Y | N | ? | ? |
| 31 Becerra | Y | N | ? | ? |
| 32 Solis | Y | N | + | + |
| 33 Watson | Y | Y | ? | ? |
| 34 Roybal-Allard | Y | N | ? | ? |
| 35 Waters | Y | N | Y | Y |
| 36 Harman | Y | Y | N | Y |
| 37 Millender-McD. | ? | ? | ? | ? |
| 38 Napolitano | Y | N | Y | Y |
| 39 Sánchez, Linda | Y | N | N | Y |
| 40 Royce | N | Y | N | Y |
| 41 Lewis | N | Y | N | Y |
| 42 Miller, Gary | N | Y | N | Y |
| 43 Baca | Y | Y | N | Y |
| 44 Calvert | N | Y | N | Y |
| 45 Bono | N | Y | N | Y |
| 46 Rohrabacher | N | Y | N | Y |
| 47 Sanchez, Loretta | Y | N | – | + |
| 48 Cox | N | Y | N | Y |
| 49 Issa | N | Y | N | Y |

| | 167 | 168 | 169 | 170 |
|---|---|---|---|---|
| 50 Cunningham | N | Y | N | Y |
| 51 Filner | Y | N | Y | Y |
| 52 Hunter | N | Y | N | Y |
| 53 Davis | Y | N | Y | Y |
| **COLORADO** | | | | |
| 1 DeGette | Y | N | N | Y |
| 2 Udall | Y | N | Y | Y |
| 3 Salazar | Y | Y | N | Y |
| 4 Musgrave | ? | ? | ? | ? |
| 5 Hefley | N | Y | N | Y |
| 6 Tancredo | N | Y | N | Y |
| 7 Beauprez | N | Y | N | Y |
| **CONNECTICUT** | | | | |
| 1 Larson | + | – | – | + |
| 2 Simmons | N | Y | N | Y |
| 3 DeLauro | Y | N | N | Y |
| 4 Shays | N | Y | N | Y |
| 5 Johnson | N | Y | N | Y |
| **DELAWARE** | | | | |
| AL Castle | N | Y | N | Y |
| **FLORIDA** | | | | |
| 1 Miller | N | Y | N | Y |
| 2 Boyd | Y | Y | N | Y |
| 3 Brown | Y | N | Y | Y |
| 4 Crenshaw | N | Y | N | Y |
| 5 Brown-Waite | N | Y | N | Y |
| 6 Stearns | N | Y | N | Y |
| 7 Mica | N | Y | N | Y |
| 8 Keller | N | Y | N | Y |
| 9 Bilirakis | N | Y | N | Y |
| 10 Young | N | Y | N | Y |
| 11 Davis | Y | Y | N | Y |
| 12 Putnam | N | Y | N | Y |
| 13 Harris | N | Y | N | Y |
| 14 Mack | N | Y | N | Y |
| 15 Weldon | N | Y | N | Y |
| 16 Foley | N | Y | N | Y |
| 17 Meek | Y | Y | N | Y |
| 18 Ros-Lehtinen | N | Y | N | Y |
| 19 Wexler | Y | N | Y | Y |
| 20 Wasserman-Schultz | ? | ? | N | Y |
| 21 Diaz-Balart, L. | N | Y | N | Y |
| 22 Shaw | N | Y | N | Y |
| 23 Hastings | ? | ? | ? | ? |
| 24 Feeney | N | ? | N | Y |
| 25 Diaz-Balart, M. | N | Y | N | Y |
| **GEORGIA** | | | | |
| 1 Kingston | N | Y | ? | ? |
| 2 Bishop | Y | Y | N | Y |
| 3 Marshall | Y | Y | N | Y |
| 4 McKinney | Y | N | Y | Y |
| 5 Lewis | Y | N | Y | Y |
| 6 Price | N | Y | N | Y |
| 7 Linder | N | Y | N | Y |
| 8 Westmoreland | N | Y | N | Y |
| 9 Norwood | N | Y | N | Y |
| 10 Deal | N | Y | N | Y |
| 11 Gingrey | N | Y | N | Y |
| 12 Barrow | Y | Y | Y | Y |
| 13 Scott | Y | Y | Y | Y |
| **HAWAII** | | | | |
| 1 Abercrombie | Y | N | Y | Y |
| 2 Case | Y | Y | N | Y |
| **IDAHO** | | | | |
| 1 Otter | N | Y | N | Y |
| 2 Simpson | N | Y | N | Y |
| **ILLINOIS** | | | | |
| 1 Rush | Y | N | Y | Y |
| 2 Jackson | Y | N | Y | Y |
| 3 Lipinski | Y | Y | Y | Y |
| 4 Gutierrez | Y | N | Y | Y |
| 5 Emanuel | Y | Y | Y | Y |
| 6 Hyde | N | Y | N | Y |
| 7 Davis | Y | N | Y | Y |
| 8 Bean | Y | Y | Y | Y |
| 9 Schakowsky | Y | N | Y | Y |
| 10 Kirk | N | Y | N | Y |
| 11 Weller | N | Y | N | Y |
| 12 Costello | Y | Y | Y | Y |

ND Northern Democrats, SD Southern Democrats
Southern states: Ala., Ark., Fla., Ga., Ky., La., Miss., N.C., Okla., S.C., Tenn., Texas, Va.

| | 167 | 168 | 169 | 170 |
|---|---|---|---|---|
| 13 Biggert | N | Y | N | Y |
| 14 Hastert | | | | |
| 15 Johnson | N | Y | N | Y |
| 16 Manzullo | N | N | N | Y |
| 17 Evans | Y | ? | N | Y |
| 18 LaHood | N | Y | N | Y |
| 19 Shimkus | N | Y | N | Y |
| **INDIANA** | | | | |
| 1 Visclosky | Y | Y | N | Y |
| 2 Chocola | N | Y | N | Y |
| 3 Souder | N | Y | N | Y |
| 4 Buyer | N | Y | N | Y |
| 5 Burton | N | Y | N | Y |
| 6 Pence | N | Y | N | Y |
| 7 Carson | Y | N | N | Y |
| 8 Hostettler | N | N | N | Y |
| 9 Sodrel | N | Y | N | Y |
| **IOWA** | | | | |
| 1 Nussle | N | Y | N | Y |
| 2 Leach | Y | Y | N | Y |
| 3 Boswell | Y | Y | N | Y |
| 4 Latham | N | Y | N | Y |
| 5 King | N | Y | N | Y |
| **KANSAS** | | | | |
| 1 Moran | N | Y | N | Y |
| 2 Ryun | N | Y | N | Y |
| 3 Moore | Y | Y | Y | Y |
| 4 Tiahrt | N | Y | N | Y |
| **KENTUCKY** | | | | |
| 1 Whitfield | N | Y | N | Y |
| 2 Lewis | N | Y | N | Y |
| 3 Northup | N | Y | N | Y |
| 4 Davis | N | Y | N | Y |
| 5 Rogers | N | Y | N | Y |
| 6 Chandler | Y | Y | N | Y |
| **LOUISIANA** | | | | |
| 1 Jindal | N | Y | N | Y |
| 2 Jefferson | Y | N | N | Y |
| 3 Melancon | Y | Y | Y | Y |
| 4 McCrery | N | Y | N | Y |
| 5 Alexander | N | Y | N | Y |
| 6 Baker | N | Y | N | Y |
| 7 Boustany | N | Y | N | Y |
| **MAINE** | | | | |
| 1 Allen | Y | N | N | N |
| 2 Michaud | Y | N | N | N |
| **MARYLAND** | | | | |
| 1 Gilchrest | N | Y | N | Y |
| 2 Ruppersberger | Y | Y | Y | Y |
| 3 Cardin | Y | Y | Y | Y |
| 4 Wynn | Y | Y | N | Y |
| 5 Hoyer | Y | Y | Y | Y |
| 6 Bartlett | N | N | N | Y |
| 7 Cummings | Y | N | N | Y |
| 8 Van Hollen | Y | Y | Y | Y |
| **MASSACHUSETTS** | | | | |
| 1 Olver | Y | N | Y | Y |
| 2 Neal | Y | N | Y | Y |
| 3 McGovern | Y | N | Y | Y |
| 4 Frank | Y | N | Y | Y |
| 5 Meehan | Y | N | Y | Y |
| 6 Tierney | Y | N | Y | Y |
| 7 Markey | Y | N | Y | Y |
| 8 Capuano | Y | N | Y | Y |
| 9 Lynch | Y | N | Y | Y |
| 10 Delahunt | Y | N | Y | Y |
| **MICHIGAN** | | | | |
| 1 Stupak | Y | Y | N | Y |
| 2 Hoekstra | N | Y | N | Y |
| 3 Ehlers | N | N | N | Y |
| 4 Camp | N | Y | N | Y |
| 5 Kildee | Y | Y | N | Y |
| 6 Upton | N | Y | N | Y |
| 7 Schwarz | N | Y | N | Y |
| 8 Rogers | N | Y | N | Y |
| 9 Knollenberg | N | Y | N | Y |
| 10 Miller | N | Y | N | Y |
| 11 McCotter | N | Y | N | Y |
| 12 Levin | Y | Y | N | Y |
| 13 Kilpatrick | Y | Y | N | Y |
| 14 Conyers | Y | Y | N | Y |
| 15 Dingell | Y | N | N | Y |

| | 167 | 168 | 169 | 170 |
|---|---|---|---|---|
| **MINNESOTA** | | | | |
| 1 Gutknecht | N | N | N | Y |
| 2 Kline | N | Y | N | Y |
| 3 Ramstad | N | Y | N | Y |
| 4 McCollum | Y | N | N | Y |
| 5 Sabo | Y | N | Y | N |
| 6 Kennedy | N | Y | N | Y |
| 7 Peterson | Y | Y | N | Y |
| 8 Oberstar | Y | N | N | Y |
| **MISSISSIPPI** | | | | |
| 1 Wicker | N | Y | N | Y |
| 2 Thompson | Y | N | N | Y |
| 3 Pickering | N | Y | N | Y |
| 4 Taylor | Y | Y | N | Y |
| **MISSOURI** | | | | |
| 1 Clay | Y | N | Y | Y |
| 2 Akin | N | Y | N | Y |
| 3 Carnahan | Y | N | N | Y |
| 4 Skelton | Y | Y | Y | Y |
| 5 Cleaver | Y | N | N | Y |
| 6 Graves | N | Y | N | Y |
| 7 Blunt | N | Y | N | Y |
| 8 Emerson | N | Y | N | Y |
| 9 Hulshof | N | Y | N | Y |
| **MONTANA** | | | | |
| AL Rehberg | N | Y | N | Y |
| **NEBRASKA** | | | | |
| 1 Fortenberry | N | Y | N | Y |
| 2 Terry | N | Y | N | Y |
| 3 Osborne | N | Y | N | Y |
| **NEVADA** | | | | |
| 1 Berkley | ? | ? | ? | ? |
| 2 Gibbons | N | Y | N | Y |
| 3 Porter | N | Y | N | Y |
| **NEW HAMPSHIRE** | | | | |
| 1 Bradley | N | Y | N | Y |
| 2 Bass | N | Y | N | Y |
| **NEW JERSEY** | | | | |
| 1 Andrews | Y | N | Y | Y |
| 2 LoBiondo | N | Y | N | Y |
| 3 Saxton | N | Y | N | Y |
| 4 Smith | N | Y | N | Y |
| 5 Garrett | N | N | N | Y |
| 6 Pallone | Y | N | Y | Y |
| 7 Ferguson | N | Y | N | Y |
| 8 Pascrell | Y | Y | N | Y |
| 9 Rothman | Y | N | Y | Y |
| 10 Payne | Y | N | Y | Y |
| 11 Frelinghuysen | N | Y | N | Y |
| 12 Holt | Y | N | Y | Y |
| 13 Menendez | Y | N | Y | Y |
| **NEW MEXICO** | | | | |
| 1 Wilson | N | Y | N | Y |
| 2 Pearce | N | Y | N | Y |
| 3 Udall | Y | N | N | Y |
| **NEW YORK** | | | | |
| 1 Bishop | Y | Y | Y | Y |
| 2 Israel | Y | Y | Y | Y |
| 3 King | N | Y | N | Y |
| 4 McCarthy | Y | Y | N | Y |
| 5 Ackerman | Y | N | Y | Y |
| 6 Meeks | ? | ? | Y | Y |
| 7 Crowley | Y | N | Y | Y |
| 8 Nadler | Y | N | Y | Y |
| 9 Weiner | Y | N | Y | Y |
| 10 Towns | Y | N | Y | Y |
| 11 Owens | Y | N | Y | Y |
| 12 Velázquez | Y | N | Y | Y |
| 13 Fossella | N | Y | N | Y |
| 14 Maloney | Y | N | Y | Y |
| 15 Rangel | Y | N | Y | Y |
| 16 Serrano | Y | N | Y | Y |
| 17 Engel | Y | N | Y | Y |
| 18 Lowey | Y | N | Y | Y |
| 19 Kelly | N | Y | N | Y |
| 20 Sweeney | N | N | N | Y |
| 21 McNulty | Y | Y | Y | Y |
| 22 Hinchey | Y | N | Y | Y |
| 23 McHugh | N | Y | N | Y |
| 24 Boehlert | N | Y | N | Y |
| 25 Walsh | N | Y | N | Y |
| 26 Reynolds | N | Y | N | Y |
| 27 Higgins | Y | Y | Y | Y |
| 28 Slaughter | Y | Y | Y | Y |
| 29 Kuhl | N | Y | N | Y |

| | 167 | 168 | 169 | 170 |
|---|---|---|---|---|
| **NORTH CAROLINA** | | | | |
| 1 Butterfield | Y | N | N | Y |
| 2 Etheridge | Y | Y | N | Y |
| 3 Jones | N | Y | N | Y |
| 4 Price | Y | N | N | Y |
| 5 Foxx | N | Y | N | Y |
| 6 Coble | N | Y | N | Y |
| 7 McIntyre | Y | Y | N | Y |
| 8 Hayes | N | Y | N | Y |
| 9 Myrick | N | Y | N | Y |
| 10 McHenry | N | N | N | Y |
| 11 Taylor | N | Y | N | Y |
| 12 Watt | Y | N | N | Y |
| 13 Miller | Y | Y | N | Y |
| **NORTH DAKOTA** | | | | |
| AL Pomeroy | Y | Y | N | Y |
| **OHIO** | | | | |
| 1 Chabot | N | Y | N | Y |
| 2 Vacant | | | | |
| 3 Turner | N | Y | N | Y |
| 4 Oxley | N | Y | N | Y |
| 5 Gillmor | N | Y | N | Y |
| 6 Strickland | Y | N | N | Y |
| 7 Hobson | N | Y | N | Y |
| 8 Boehner | N | Y | N | Y |
| 9 Kaptur | Y | Y | N | Y |
| 10 Kucinich | Y | N | N | Y |
| 11 Jones | Y | N | N | Y |
| 12 Tiberi | N | Y | N | Y |
| 13 Brown | Y | N | N | Y |
| 14 LaTourette | N | N | N | Y |
| 15 Pryce | N | Y | N | Y |
| 16 Regula | N | Y | N | Y |
| 17 Ryan | Y | Y | N | Y |
| 18 Ney | N | Y | N | Y |
| **OKLAHOMA** | | | | |
| 1 Sullivan | N | Y | N | Y |
| 2 Boren | Y | Y | N | Y |
| 3 Lucas | N | Y | N | Y |
| 4 Cole | N | Y | N | Y |
| 5 Istook | N | Y | N | Y |
| **OREGON** | | | | |
| 1 Wu | Y | Y | Y | Y |
| 2 Walden | N | Y | N | Y |
| 3 Blumenauer | Y | N | Y | Y |
| 4 DeFazio | Y | Y | N | Y |
| 5 Hooley | Y | Y | N | Y |
| **PENNSYLVANIA** | | | | |
| 1 Brady | Y | N | Y | Y |
| 2 Fattah | Y | N | Y | Y |
| 3 English | N | Y | N | Y |
| 4 Hart | N | Y | N | Y |
| 5 Peterson | N | Y | N | Y |
| 6 Gerlach | N | Y | N | Y |
| 7 Weldon | N | Y | N | Y |
| 8 Fitzpatrick | N | Y | N | Y |
| 9 Shuster | N | Y | N | Y |
| 10 Sherwood | N | N | N | Y |
| 11 Kanjorski | Y | Y | N | Y |
| 12 Murtha | Y | Y | N | Y |
| 13 Schwartz | Y | Y | Y | Y |
| 14 Doyle | Y | Y | Y | Y |
| 15 Dent | N | Y | N | Y |
| 16 Pitts | N | N | N | Y |
| 17 Holden | Y | Y | N | Y |
| 18 Murphy | N | Y | N | Y |
| 19 Platts | N | Y | N | Y |
| **RHODE ISLAND** | | | | |
| 1 Kennedy | Y | N | N | Y |
| 2 Langevin | Y | Y | N | Y |
| **SOUTH CAROLINA** | | | | |
| 1 Brown | N | Y | N | Y |
| 2 Wilson | N | Y | N | Y |
| 3 Barrett | N | Y | N | Y |
| 4 Inglis | N | N | N | Y |
| 5 Spratt | Y | Y | N | Y |
| 6 Clyburn | Y | N | N | Y |
| **SOUTH DAKOTA** | | | | |
| AL Herseth | Y | Y | N | N |
| **TENNESSEE** | | | | |
| 1 Jenkins | N | Y | N | Y |
| 2 Duncan | N | N | N | Y |

| | 167 | 168 | 169 | 170 |
|---|---|---|---|---|
| 3 Wamp | N | N | N | Y |
| 4 Davis | Y | Y | N | Y |
| 5 Cooper | Y | N | N | Y |
| 6 Gordon | Y | Y | N | Y |
| 7 Blackburn | N | Y | N | Y |
| 8 Tanner | Y | N | N | Y |
| 9 Ford | Y | Y | N | Y |
| **TEXAS** | | | | |
| 1 Gohmert | N | Y | N | Y |
| 2 Poe | N | Y | N | Y |
| 3 Johnson, S. | N | Y | N | Y |
| 4 Hall | N | Y | N | Y |
| 5 Hensarling | N | N | N | Y |
| 6 Barton | N | Y | N | Y |
| 7 Culberson | N | Y | N | Y |
| 8 Brady | N | Y | N | Y |
| 9 Green | Y | N | Y | Y |
| 10 McCaul | N | Y | N | Y |
| 11 Conaway | N | Y | N | Y |
| 12 Granger | N | Y | N | Y |
| 13 Thornberry | N | Y | N | Y |
| 14 Paul | N | N | N | Y |
| 15 Hinojosa | Y | N | N | Y |
| 16 Reyes | Y | Y | N | Y |
| 17 Edwards | Y | Y | N | Y |
| 18 Jackson-Lee | Y | N | N | Y |
| 19 Neugebauer | N | Y | N | Y |
| 20 Gonzalez | Y | N | Y | Y |
| 21 Smith | N | Y | N | Y |
| 22 DeLay | N | Y | N | Y |
| 23 Bonilla | N | Y | N | Y |
| 24 Marchant | N | Y | N | Y |
| 25 Doggett | Y | N | N | Y |
| 26 Burgess | N | Y | N | Y |
| 27 Ortiz | Y | Y | N | Y |
| 28 Cuellar | Y | Y | N | Y |
| 29 Green | Y | N | Y | Y |
| 30 Johnson, E. | Y | N | N | Y |
| 31 Carter | N | Y | N | Y |
| 32 Sessions | N | Y | N | Y |
| **UTAH** | | | | |
| 1 Bishop | N | Y | N | Y |
| 2 Matheson | Y | Y | N | Y |
| 3 Cannon | N | Y | N | Y |
| **VERMONT** | | | | |
| AL Sanders | Y | N | N | Y |
| **VIRGINIA** | | | | |
| 1 Davis, J. | N | Y | N | Y |
| 2 Drake | N | Y | N | Y |
| 3 Scott | Y | N | N | Y |
| 4 Forbes | N | Y | N | Y |
| 5 Goode | N | Y | N | Y |
| 6 Goodlatte | N | Y | N | Y |
| 7 Cantor | N | Y | N | Y |
| 8 Moran | ? | ? | Y | Y |
| 9 Boucher | Y | Y | N | Y |
| 10 Wolf | N | Y | N | Y |
| 11 Davis, T. | N | Y | N | Y |
| **WASHINGTON** | | | | |
| 1 Inslee | Y | N | N | Y |
| 2 Larsen | Y | N | N | Y |
| 3 Baird | Y | N | N | Y |
| 4 Hastings | N | Y | N | Y |
| 5 McMorris | N | Y | N | Y |
| 6 Dicks | Y | N | N | Y |
| 7 McDermott | Y | N | Y | N |
| 8 Reichert | N | Y | N | Y |
| 9 Smith | Y | N | Y | Y |
| **WEST VIRGINIA** | | | | |
| 1 Mollohan | Y | N | N | Y |
| 2 Capito | N | Y | N | Y |
| 3 Rahall | Y | N | N | Y |
| **WISCONSIN** | | | | |
| 1 Ryan | N | Y | N | Y |
| 2 Baldwin | Y | N | N | Y |
| 3 Kind | Y | N | N | Y |
| 4 Moore | Y | N | N | N |
| 5 Sensenbrenner | N | Y | N | Y |
| 6 Petri | N | Y | N | Y |
| 7 Obey | Y | N | N | Y |
| 8 Green | Y | N | N | Y |
| **WYOMING** | | | | |
| AL Cubin | N | N | N | N |

# IN THE HOUSE | By Vote Number

**171.** **HR 627. Linda White-Epps Post Office/Passage.** Miller, R-Mich., motion to suspend the rules and pass the bill that would name a post office in Hamden, Conn., for Linda White-Epps, who founded the cancer-survivor support group "Sisters' Journey" in Connecticut. Motion agreed to 390-0: R 213-0; D 176-0 (ND 134-0, SD 42-0); I 1-0. A two-thirds majority of those present and voting (260 in this case) is required for passage under suspension of the rules. May 16, 2005.

**172.** **H Res 266. Peace Officers Memorial Day/Adoption.** Miller, R-Mich., motion to suspend the rules and adopt the resolution that would support the goals and ideals of Peace Officers Memorial Day and ask the public to observe the day with appropriate ceremonies and respect. Motion agreed to 391-0: R 213-0; D 177-0 (ND 135-0, SD 42-0); I 1-0. A two-thirds majority of those present and voting (261 in this case) is required for adoption under suspension of the rules. May 16, 2005.

**173.** **HR 2107. Law Enforcement Officers Memorial Fund/Passage.** Renzi, R-Ariz., motion to suspend the rules and pass the bill that would transfer control of the National Law Enforcement Memorial Maintenance Fund from the National Park Service to the National Law Enforcement Officers Memorial Fund Inc., a nonprofit corporation that operates and maintains the National Law Enforcement Officers Memorial. Motion agreed to 392-0: R 214-0; D 177-0 (ND 135-0, SD 42-0); I 1-0. A two-thirds majority of those present and voting (262 in this case) is required for passage under suspension of the rules. May 16, 2005.

**174.** **HR 2360. Fiscal 2006 Homeland Security Appropriations/Previous Question.** Sessions, R-Texas, motion to order the previous question (thus ending debate and possibility of further amendment) on adoption of the rule (H Res 278) to provide for House floor consideration of the bill that would appropriate $31.9 billion in fiscal 2006 for the Department of Homeland Security. Motion agreed to 223-185: R 223-0; D 0-184 (ND 0-134, SD 0-50); I 0-1. May 17, 2005.

**175.** **HR 2360. Fiscal 2006 Homeland Security Appropriations/Rule.** Adoption of the rule (H Res 278), as amended, to provide for House floor consideration of the bill that would appropriate $31.9 billion in fiscal 2006 for the Department of Homeland Security. Adopted 222-185: R 221-1; D 1-183 (ND 1-134, SD 0-49); I 0-1. May 17, 2005.

**176.** **HR 2360. Fiscal 2006 Homeland Security Appropriations/Chemical Plant Security.** Menendez, D-N.J., amendment that would increase funding by $50 million for state and local grant programs to improve security of chemical plants. The amendment would be offset by a $50 million cut to the Office of the Undersecretary for Management. Adopted 225-198: R 35-193; D 189-5 (ND 142-3, SD 47-2); I 1-0. May 17, 2005.

**177.** **HR 2360. Fiscal 2006 Homeland Security Appropriations/Immigration.** Tancredo, R-Colo., amendment that would prohibit the use of funds to assist state or local governments that have restrictions on exchanging information with the Bureau of Immigration and Customs Enforcement on an individual's citizenship or immigration status. Rejected 165-258: R 163-65; D 2-192 (ND 0-145, SD 2-47); I 0-1. May 17, 2005.

ND Northern Democrats, SD Southern Democrats
Southern states: Ala., Ark., Fla., Ga., Ky., La., Miss., N.C., Okla., S.C., Tenn., Texas, Va.

| | 171 | 172 | 173 | 174 | 175 | 176 | 177 |
|---|---|---|---|---|---|---|---|
| **ALABAMA** | | | | | | | |
| 1 Bonner | Y | Y | Y | Y | Y | N | Y |
| 2 Everett | Y | Y | Y | Y | Y | N | Y |
| 3 Rogers | Y | Y | Y | Y | Y | N | Y |
| 4 Aderholt | Y | Y | Y | Y | Y | N | Y |
| 5 Cramer | Y | Y | Y | N | N | Y | Y |
| 6 Bachus | Y | Y | Y | Y | Y | N | Y |
| 7 Davis | ? | ? | ? | N | N | Y | N |
| **ALASKA** | | | | | | | |
| AL Young | Y | Y | Y | Y | Y | N | N |
| **ARIZONA** | | | | | | | |
| 1 Renzi | Y | Y | Y | Y | Y | N | Y |
| 2 Franks | Y | Y | Y | Y | Y | N | Y |
| 3 Shadegg | Y | Y | Y | Y | Y | N | Y |
| 4 Pastor | Y | Y | Y | N | N | Y | N |
| 5 Hayworth | Y | Y | Y | Y | Y | N | Y |
| 6 Flake | Y | Y | Y | Y | Y | N | Y |
| 7 Grijalva | Y | Y | Y | N | N | Y | N |
| 8 Kolbe | Y | Y | Y | Y | Y | N | Y |
| **ARKANSAS** | | | | | | | |
| 1 Berry | Y | Y | Y | N | N | Y | N |
| 2 Snyder | Y | Y | Y | N | N | Y | N |
| 3 Boozman | Y | Y | Y | Y | Y | N | Y |
| 4 Ross | Y | Y | Y | N | N | Y | N |
| **CALIFORNIA** | | | | | | | |
| 1 Thompson | Y | Y | Y | N | N | Y | N |
| 2 Herger | Y | Y | Y | Y | Y | N | Y |
| 3 Lungren | Y | Y | Y | Y | Y | N | Y |
| 4 Doolittle | Y | Y | Y | Y | Y | N | Y |
| 5 Matsui, D. | Y | Y | Y | N | N | Y | N |
| 6 Woolsey | Y | Y | Y | N | N | Y | N |
| 7 Miller, George | Y | Y | Y | N | N | Y | N |
| 8 Pelosi | Y | Y | Y | N | N | Y | N |
| 9 Lee | Y | Y | Y | N | N | Y | N |
| 10 Tauscher | Y | Y | Y | N | N | Y | N |
| 11 Pombo | Y | Y | Y | Y | Y | N | Y |
| 12 Lantos | ? | ? | ? | N | N | Y | N |
| 13 Stark | Y | Y | Y | N | N | Y | N |
| 14 Eshoo | Y | Y | Y | N | N | Y | N |
| 15 Honda | Y | Y | Y | N | ? | Y | N |
| 16 Lofgren | Y | Y | Y | N | N | Y | N |
| 17 Farr | Y | Y | Y | N | N | Y | N |
| 18 Cardoza | Y | Y | Y | N | N | Y | N |
| 19 Radanovich | Y | Y | Y | Y | Y | N | Y |
| 20 Costa | + | Y | Y | N | N | Y | N |
| 21 Nunes | Y | Y | Y | Y | Y | N | Y |
| 22 Thomas | Y | Y | Y | ? | Y | N | Y |
| 23 Capps | Y | Y | ? | N | N | Y | N |
| 24 Gallegly | Y | Y | Y | Y | Y | N | Y |
| 25 McKeon | Y | Y | Y | Y | Y | N | Y |
| 26 Dreier | Y | Y | Y | Y | Y | N | Y |
| 27 Sherman | Y | Y | Y | N | N | Y | N |
| 28 Berman | Y | Y | Y | N | N | Y | N |
| 29 Schiff | Y | Y | Y | N | N | Y | N |
| 30 Waxman | Y | Y | Y | N | N | Y | N |
| 31 Becerra | Y | Y | Y | N | N | Y | N |
| 32 Solis | Y | Y | Y | N | N | Y | N |
| 33 Watson | Y | Y | Y | N | N | Y | N |
| 34 Roybal-Allard | Y | Y | Y | N | N | Y | N |
| 35 Waters | ? | ? | ? | ? | ? | Y | N |
| 36 Harman | Y | Y | Y | N | N | Y | N |
| 37 Millender-McD. | ? | ? | ? | ? | ? | ? | ? |
| 38 Napolitano | Y | Y | Y | N | N | Y | N |
| 39 Sánchez, Linda | Y | Y | Y | N | N | Y | N |
| 40 Royce | Y | Y | Y | Y | Y | N | Y |
| 41 Lewis | Y | Y | Y | Y | Y | N | Y |
| 42 Miller, Gary | Y | Y | Y | Y | Y | N | Y |
| 43 Baca | Y | Y | Y | N | N | Y | N |
| 44 Calvert | Y | Y | Y | Y | Y | N | Y |
| 45 Bono | Y | Y | Y | Y | Y | N | Y |
| 46 Rohrabacher | Y | Y | Y | Y | Y | N | Y |
| 47 Sanchez, Loretta | Y | Y | Y | N | N | Y | N |
| 48 Cox | Y | Y | Y | Y | Y | N | Y |
| 49 Issa | Y | Y | Y | Y | Y | N | Y |
| 50 Cunningham | Y | Y | Y | Y | Y | N | Y |
| 51 Filner | Y | Y | Y | N | N | Y | N |
| 52 Hunter | Y | Y | Y | Y | Y | N | Y |
| 53 Davis | Y | Y | Y | N | N | Y | N |
| **COLORADO** | | | | | | | |
| 1 DeGette | Y | Y | Y | N | N | Y | N |
| 2 Udall | Y | Y | Y | N | N | Y | N |
| 3 Salazar | Y | Y | Y | N | N | Y | N |
| 4 Musgrave | Y | Y | Y | Y | Y | N | Y |
| 5 Hefley | Y | Y | Y | Y | Y | N | Y |
| 6 Tancredo | Y | Y | Y | Y | Y | N | Y |
| 7 Beauprez | Y | Y | Y | Y | Y | N | Y |
| **CONNECTICUT** | | | | | | | |
| 1 Larson | ? | ? | ? | – | – | + | N |
| 2 Simmons | Y | Y | Y | Y | Y | Y | N |
| 3 DeLauro | Y | Y | Y | N | N | Y | N |
| 4 Shays | Y | Y | Y | Y | Y | N | Y |
| 5 Johnson | Y | Y | Y | Y | Y | N | N |
| **DELAWARE** | | | | | | | |
| AL Castle | Y | Y | Y | Y | Y | N | N |
| **FLORIDA** | | | | | | | |
| 1 Miller | Y | Y | Y | Y | Y | – | + |
| 2 Boyd | Y | Y | Y | N | N | Y | N |
| 3 Brown | ? | ? | ? | N | N | Y | N |
| 4 Crenshaw | Y | Y | Y | Y | Y | N | Y |
| 5 Brown-Waite | Y | Y | Y | Y | Y | N | Y |
| 6 Stearns | Y | Y | Y | Y | Y | N | Y |
| 7 Mica | Y | Y | Y | Y | Y | N | Y |
| 8 Keller | Y | Y | Y | Y | Y | N | Y |
| 9 Bilirakis | Y | Y | Y | Y | Y | N | Y |
| 10 Young | ? | ? | ? | ? | ? | ? | ? |
| 11 Davis | Y | Y | Y | N | N | Y | N |
| 12 Putnam | Y | Y | Y | Y | Y | N | Y |
| 13 Harris | Y | Y | Y | Y | Y | N | Y |
| 14 Mack | Y | Y | Y | Y | Y | N | Y |
| 15 Weldon | ? | ? | ? | Y | Y | N | Y |
| 16 Foley | Y | Y | Y | Y | Y | N | Y |
| 17 Meek | ? | ? | ? | N | N | Y | N |
| 18 Ros-Lehtinen | ? | ? | ? | Y | Y | Y | Y |
| 19 Wexler | ? | ? | ? | N | N | ? | ? |
| 20 Wasserman-Schultz | ? | ? | ? | N | N | Y | N |
| 21 Diaz-Balart, L. | ? | ? | ? | Y | Y | Y | Y |
| 22 Shaw | Y | Y | Y | Y | Y | N | Y |
| 23 Hastings | Y | Y | Y | N | N | Y | N |
| 24 Feeney | Y | Y | Y | Y | Y | N | Y |
| 25 Diaz-Balart, M. | ? | ? | Y | Y | Y | N | Y |
| **GEORGIA** | | | | | | | |
| 1 Kingston | Y | Y | Y | Y | Y | N | Y |
| 2 Bishop | Y | Y | Y | N | N | Y | N |
| 3 Marshall | ? | ? | ? | N | N | Y | N |
| 4 McKinney | Y | Y | Y | N | N | Y | N |
| 5 Lewis | ? | ? | Y | N | N | ? | ? |
| 6 Price | Y | Y | Y | Y | Y | N | Y |
| 7 Linder | Y | Y | Y | Y | Y | N | Y |
| 8 Westmoreland | Y | Y | Y | Y | Y | N | Y |
| 9 Norwood | Y | Y | Y | Y | Y | N | Y |
| 10 Deal | Y | Y | Y | Y | Y | N | Y |
| 11 Gingrey | Y | Y | Y | Y | Y | N | Y |
| 12 Barrow | Y | Y | Y | N | Y | Y | N |
| 13 Scott | Y | Y | Y | N | N | Y | N |
| **HAWAII** | | | | | | | |
| 1 Abercrombie | Y | Y | Y | N | N | Y | N |
| 2 Case | Y | Y | Y | N | N | Y | N |
| **IDAHO** | | | | | | | |
| 1 Otter | Y | Y | Y | Y | Y | N | Y |
| 2 Simpson | Y | Y | Y | Y | Y | N | Y |
| **ILLINOIS** | | | | | | | |
| 1 Rush | Y | Y | Y | N | N | Y | N |
| 2 Jackson | Y | Y | Y | Y | N | Y | N |
| 3 Lipinski | Y | Y | Y | N | N | Y | N |
| 4 Gutierrez | + | + | + | N | N | Y | N |
| 5 Emanuel | Y | Y | Y | N | N | Y | N |
| 6 Hyde | Y | Y | Y | Y | Y | N | Y |
| 7 Davis | ? | ? | ? | ? | ? | Y | N |
| 8 Bean | Y | Y | Y | N | N | Y | N |
| 9 Schakowsky | Y | Y | Y | N | N | Y | N |
| 10 Kirk | Y | Y | Y | Y | Y | N | N |
| 11 Weller | Y | Y | Y | Y | Y | N | N |
| 12 Costello | Y | Y | Y | N | N | Y | N |

**KEY** **Republicans** Democrats *Independents*

| | | | |
|---|---|---|---|
| Y | Voted for (yea) | X Paired against | C Voted "present" to avoid possible conflict of interest |
| # | Paired for | – Announced against | |
| + | Announced for | P Voted "present" | ? Did not vote or otherwise make a position known |
| N | Voted against (nay) | | |

| | 171 | 172 | 173 | 174 | 175 | 176 | 177 |
|---|---|---|---|---|---|---|---|
| 13 **Biggert** | Y | Y | Y | Y | Y | N | N |
| 14 **Hastert** | | | | | | | |
| 15 **Johnson** | Y | Y | Y | Y | Y | N | N |
| 16 **Manzullo** | ? | ? | ? | Y | Y | N | Y |
| 17 Evans | Y | Y | Y | N | N | Y | N |
| 18 **LaHood** | Y | Y | Y | Y | Y | N | N |
| 19 **Shimkus** | Y | Y | Y | Y | Y | N | Y |
| **INDIANA** | | | | | | | |
| 1 Visclosky | Y | Y | Y | N | N | N | N |
| 2 **Chocola** | Y | Y | Y | Y | Y | N | N |
| 3 **Souder** | ? | ? | ? | Y | Y | N | Y |
| 4 **Buyer** | Y | Y | Y | Y | Y | N | Y |
| 5 **Burton** | + | + | + | ? | ? | N | Y |
| 6 **Pence** | Y | Y | Y | Y | Y | N | Y |
| 7 Carson | ? | ? | ? | ? | ? | Y | N |
| 8 **Hostettler** | Y | Y | Y | Y | Y | Y | Y |
| 9 **Sodrel** | Y | Y | Y | Y | Y | N | Y |
| **IOWA** | | | | | | | |
| 1 **Nussle** | Y | Y | Y | Y | Y | N | Y |
| 2 **Leach** | Y | Y | Y | Y | Y | Y | N |
| 3 Boswell | Y | Y | Y | N | N | Y | N |
| 4 **Latham** | Y | Y | Y | Y | Y | N | N |
| 5 **King** | Y | Y | Y | Y | Y | N | Y |
| **KANSAS** | | | | | | | |
| 1 **Moran** | Y | Y | Y | Y | Y | N | Y |
| 2 **Ryun** | Y | Y | Y | Y | Y | N | Y |
| 3 Moore | Y | Y | Y | N | N | Y | N |
| 4 **Tiahrt** | Y | Y | Y | Y | Y | N | Y |
| **KENTUCKY** | | | | | | | |
| 1 **Whitfield** | Y | Y | Y | Y | Y | N | Y |
| 2 **Lewis** | Y | Y | Y | Y | Y | N | Y |
| 3 **Northup** | Y | Y | Y | Y | Y | N | N |
| 4 **Davis** | Y | Y | Y | Y | Y | N | Y |
| 5 **Rogers** | Y | Y | Y | Y | Y | N | Y |
| 6 Chandler | Y | Y | Y | N | N | Y | N |
| **LOUISIANA** | | | | | | | |
| 1 **Jindal** | Y | Y | Y | Y | Y | N | Y |
| 2 Jefferson | Y | Y | Y | N | N | Y | N |
| 3 Melancon | Y | Y | Y | N | N | Y | N |
| 4 **McCrery** | Y | Y | Y | Y | Y | N | Y |
| 5 **Alexander** | Y | Y | Y | Y | Y | N | Y |
| 6 **Baker** | Y | Y | Y | Y | Y | N | Y |
| 7 **Boustany** | Y | Y | Y | Y | Y | N | Y |
| **MAINE** | | | | | | | |
| 1 Allen | Y | Y | Y | N | N | Y | N |
| 2 Michaud | Y | Y | Y | N | N | Y | N |
| **MARYLAND** | | | | | | | |
| 1 **Gilchrest** | ? | ? | ? | Y | Y | Y | N |
| 2 Ruppersberger | Y | Y | Y | N | N | Y | N |
| 3 Cardin | Y | Y | Y | N | N | Y | N |
| 4 Wynn | Y | Y | Y | N | N | Y | N |
| 5 Hoyer | Y | Y | Y | N | N | Y | N |
| 6 **Bartlett** | Y | Y | Y | Y | Y | N | Y |
| 7 Cummings | Y | Y | Y | N | N | Y | N |
| 8 Van Hollen | Y | Y | Y | N | N | Y | N |
| **MASSACHUSETTS** | | | | | | | |
| 1 Olver | Y | Y | Y | N | N | Y | N |
| 2 Neal | ? | ? | ? | ? | ? | Y | N |
| 3 McGovern | Y | Y | Y | N | N | Y | N |
| 4 Frank | Y | Y | Y | N | N | Y | N |
| 5 Meehan | Y | Y | Y | N | N | Y | N |
| 6 Tierney | Y | Y | Y | N | N | Y | N |
| 7 Markey | Y | Y | Y | N | N | Y | N |
| 8 Capuano | Y | Y | Y | N | N | Y | N |
| 9 Lynch | Y | Y | Y | N | N | Y | N |
| 10 Delahunt | Y | Y | Y | N | N | Y | N |
| **MICHIGAN** | | | | | | | |
| 1 Stupak | Y | Y | Y | N | N | Y | N |
| 2 **Hoekstra** | Y | Y | Y | Y | Y | N | Y |
| 3 **Ehlers** | Y | Y | Y | Y | Y | N | N |
| 4 **Camp** | Y | Y | Y | Y | Y | N | Y |
| 5 Kildee | Y | Y | Y | N | N | Y | N |
| 6 **Upton** | Y | Y | Y | Y | Y | N | N |
| 7 **Schwarz** | Y | Y | Y | Y | Y | Y | N |
| 8 **Rogers** | Y | Y | Y | Y | Y | N | Y |
| 9 **Knollenberg** | Y | Y | Y | Y | Y | N | N |
| 10 **Miller** | Y | Y | Y | Y | Y | N | Y |
| 11 **McCotter** | Y | Y | Y | Y | Y | N | Y |
| 12 Levin | Y | Y | Y | N | N | Y | N |
| 13 Kilpatrick | + | + | + | – | – | + | – |
| 14 Conyers | Y | Y | Y | N | N | Y | N |
| 15 Dingell | Y | Y | Y | ? | ? | Y | N |

| | 171 | 172 | 173 | 174 | 175 | 176 | 177 |
|---|---|---|---|---|---|---|---|
| **MINNESOTA** | | | | | | | |
| 1 **Gutknecht** | Y | Y | Y | Y | Y | N | Y |
| 2 **Kline** | Y | Y | Y | Y | Y | N | Y |
| 3 **Ramstad** | Y | Y | Y | Y | Y | Y | Y |
| 4 McCollum | Y | Y | Y | N | N | Y | N |
| 5 Sabo | Y | Y | Y | N | N | N | N |
| 6 **Kennedy** | Y | Y | Y | Y | Y | N | N |
| 7 Peterson | Y | Y | Y | ? | N | N | N |
| 8 Oberstar | Y | Y | Y | N | N | Y | N |
| **MISSISSIPPI** | | | | | | | |
| 1 **Wicker** | ? | ? | ? | ? | ? | N | Y |
| 2 Thompson | Y | Y | Y | N | N | Y | N |
| 3 **Pickering** | Y | Y | Y | Y | Y | N | Y |
| 4 Taylor | ? | ? | ? | N | N | Y | Y |
| **MISSOURI** | | | | | | | |
| 1 Clay | ? | ? | ? | N | N | Y | N |
| 2 **Akin** | Y | Y | Y | Y | Y | N | Y |
| 3 Carnahan | Y | Y | Y | N | N | Y | N |
| 4 Skelton | Y | Y | Y | N | N | Y | N |
| 5 Cleaver | Y | Y | Y | N | N | Y | N |
| 6 **Graves** | + | + | + | Y | Y | N | Y |
| 7 **Blunt** | Y | Y | Y | Y | Y | N | N |
| 8 **Emerson** | Y | Y | Y | Y | P | N | Y |
| 9 **Hulshof** | Y | Y | Y | Y | Y | N | Y |
| **MONTANA** | | | | | | | |
| AL **Rehberg** | Y | Y | Y | Y | Y | N | Y |
| **NEBRASKA** | | | | | | | |
| 1 **Fortenberry** | Y | Y | Y | Y | Y | N | N |
| 2 **Terry** | Y | Y | Y | Y | Y | N | N |
| 3 **Osborne** | Y | Y | Y | Y | Y | N | N |
| **NEVADA** | | | | | | | |
| 1 Berkley | Y | Y | Y | N | N | Y | N |
| 2 **Gibbons** | Y | Y | Y | Y | Y | N | Y |
| 3 **Porter** | Y | Y | Y | Y | Y | Y | N |
| **NEW HAMPSHIRE** | | | | | | | |
| 1 **Bradley** | Y | Y | Y | Y | Y | Y | Y |
| 2 **Bass** | Y | Y | Y | Y | Y | Y | Y |
| **NEW JERSEY** | | | | | | | |
| 1 Andrews | Y | Y | Y | N | N | Y | N |
| 2 **LoBiondo** | Y | Y | Y | Y | Y | Y | N |
| 3 **Saxton** | Y | Y | Y | Y | Y | Y | N |
| 4 **Smith** | Y | Y | Y | Y | Y | Y | N |
| 5 **Garrett** | Y | Y | Y | Y | Y | N | Y |
| 6 Pallone | Y | Y | Y | N | N | Y | N |
| 7 **Ferguson** | Y | Y | Y | Y | Y | Y | N |
| 8 Pascrell | Y | Y | Y | N | N | Y | N |
| 9 Rothman | Y | Y | Y | N | N | Y | N |
| 10 Payne | Y | Y | Y | N | N | ? | ? |
| 11 **Frelinghuysen** | Y | Y | Y | Y | Y | N | N |
| 12 Holt | Y | Y | Y | N | N | Y | N |
| 13 Menendez | Y | Y | Y | N | N | Y | N |
| **NEW MEXICO** | | | | | | | |
| 1 **Wilson** | Y | Y | Y | Y | Y | Y | N |
| 2 **Pearce** | Y | Y | Y | Y | Y | N | N |
| 3 Udall | Y | Y | Y | N | N | Y | N |
| **NEW YORK** | | | | | | | |
| 1 Bishop | Y | Y | Y | N | N | Y | N |
| 2 Israel | Y | Y | Y | N | N | Y | N |
| 3 **King** | Y | Y | Y | Y | Y | Y | N |
| 4 McCarthy | Y | Y | Y | N | N | Y | N |
| 5 Ackerman | ? | ? | ? | ? | ? | ? | ? |
| 6 Meeks | Y | Y | Y | N | N | Y | N |
| 7 Crowley | Y | Y | Y | N | N | Y | N |
| 8 Nadler | Y | Y | Y | N | N | Y | N |
| 9 Weiner | Y | Y | Y | N | N | Y | N |
| 10 Towns | Y | Y | Y | N | N | Y | N |
| 11 Owens | Y | Y | Y | ? | ? | Y | N |
| 12 Velázquez | Y | Y | Y | N | N | Y | N |
| 13 **Fossella** | Y | Y | Y | Y | Y | Y | N |
| 14 Maloney | Y | Y | Y | N | N | Y | N |
| 15 Rangel | Y | Y | Y | N | N | Y | N |
| 16 Serrano | Y | Y | Y | N | N | Y | N |
| 17 Engel | Y | Y | Y | N | N | Y | N |
| 18 Lowey | Y | Y | Y | N | N | Y | N |
| 19 **Kelly** | Y | Y | Y | Y | Y | Y | N |
| 20 **Sweeney** | ? | ? | ? | ? | ? | N | Y |
| 21 McNulty | Y | Y | Y | N | N | Y | N |
| 22 Hinchey | Y | Y | Y | N | N | Y | N |
| 23 **McHugh** | Y | Y | Y | Y | Y | N | Y |
| 24 **Boehlert** | Y | Y | Y | Y | Y | N | N |
| 25 **Walsh** | Y | Y | Y | Y | Y | N | N |
| 26 **Reynolds** | Y | Y | Y | Y | Y | N | N |
| 27 Higgins | Y | Y | Y | N | N | Y | N |
| 28 Slaughter | Y | Y | Y | – | N | Y | N |
| 29 **Kuhl** | Y | Y | Y | Y | Y | N | N |

| | 171 | 172 | 173 | 174 | 175 | 176 | 177 |
|---|---|---|---|---|---|---|---|
| **NORTH CAROLINA** | | | | | | | |
| 1 Butterfield | Y | Y | Y | N | N | Y | N |
| 2 Etheridge | Y | Y | Y | N | N | Y | N |
| 3 **Jones** | Y | Y | Y | Y | Y | N | Y |
| 4 Price | Y | Y | Y | N | N | Y | N |
| 5 **Foxx** | Y | Y | Y | Y | Y | N | Y |
| 6 **Coble** | Y | Y | Y | Y | Y | N | Y |
| 7 McIntyre | Y | Y | Y | N | N | Y | N |
| 8 **Hayes** | Y | Y | Y | Y | Y | N | Y |
| 9 **Myrick** | Y | Y | Y | Y | Y | N | Y |
| 10 **McHenry** | Y | Y | Y | Y | Y | N | Y |
| 11 **Taylor** | Y | Y | Y | Y | Y | N | Y |
| 12 Watt | Y | Y | Y | N | N | Y | N |
| 13 Miller | Y | Y | Y | N | N | Y | N |
| **NORTH DAKOTA** | | | | | | | |
| AL Pomeroy | Y | Y | Y | N | N | Y | N |
| **OHIO** | | | | | | | |
| 1 **Chabot** | Y | Y | Y | Y | Y | N | Y |
| 2 Vacant | | | | | | | |
| 3 **Turner** | Y | Y | Y | Y | Y | N | N |
| 4 **Oxley** | Y | Y | Y | Y | Y | N | N |
| 5 **Gillmor** | Y | Y | Y | Y | Y | N | Y |
| 6 Strickland | Y | Y | Y | N | N | Y | N |
| 7 **Hobson** | Y | Y | Y | Y | Y | N | N |
| 8 **Boehner** | Y | Y | Y | Y | Y | N | Y |
| 9 Kaptur | Y | ? | Y | N | N | Y | N |
| 10 Kucinich | Y | Y | Y | N | N | Y | N |
| 11 Jones | Y | Y | Y | N | N | Y | N |
| 12 **Tiberi** | Y | Y | Y | Y | Y | N | N |
| 13 Brown | Y | Y | Y | N | N | Y | N |
| 14 **LaTourette** | Y | Y | Y | Y | Y | N | N |
| 15 **Pryce** | ? | ? | ? | Y | Y | N | N |
| 16 **Regula** | Y | Y | Y | Y | Y | N | N |
| 17 Ryan | Y | Y | Y | N | N | Y | N |
| 18 **Ney** | Y | Y | Y | Y | Y | N | Y |
| **OKLAHOMA** | | | | | | | |
| 1 **Sullivan** | Y | Y | Y | Y | Y | N | Y |
| 2 Boren | Y | Y | Y | N | N | Y | N |
| 3 **Lucas** | Y | Y | Y | Y | Y | N | Y |
| 4 **Cole** | Y | Y | Y | Y | Y | N | N |
| 5 **Istook** | ? | ? | ? | Y | P | N | Y |
| **OREGON** | | | | | | | |
| 1 Wu | Y | Y | Y | N | N | Y | N |
| 2 **Walden** | Y | Y | Y | Y | Y | N | Y |
| 3 Blumenauer | Y | Y | Y | N | N | Y | N |
| 4 DeFazio | Y | Y | Y | N | N | Y | N |
| 5 Hooley | Y | Y | Y | N | N | Y | N |
| **PENNSYLVANIA** | | | | | | | |
| 1 Brady | Y | Y | Y | ? | ? | ? | ? |
| 2 Fattah | Y | Y | Y | ? | ? | Y | N |
| 3 **English** | Y | Y | Y | Y | Y | N | N |
| 4 **Hart** | Y | Y | Y | Y | Y | N | N |
| 5 **Peterson** | Y | Y | Y | Y | Y | N | Y |
| 6 **Gerlach** | Y | Y | Y | Y | Y | Y | N |
| 7 **Weldon** | Y | Y | Y | Y | Y | Y | Y |
| 8 **Fitzpatrick** | Y | Y | Y | Y | Y | Y | N |
| 9 **Shuster** | Y | Y | Y | Y | Y | N | Y |
| 10 **Sherwood** | Y | Y | Y | Y | Y | N | N |
| 11 Kanjorski | ? | ? | ? | ? | ? | Y | N |
| 12 Murtha | Y | Y | Y | N | N | Y | N |
| 13 Schwartz | Y | Y | Y | N | N | Y | N |
| 14 Doyle | ? | ? | ? | ? | ? | Y | N |
| 15 **Dent** | Y | Y | Y | Y | Y | Y | Y |
| 16 **Pitts** | Y | Y | Y | Y | Y | N | Y |
| 17 Holden | ? | ? | ? | N | N | Y | N |
| 18 **Murphy** | Y | Y | Y | Y | Y | Y | N |
| 19 **Platts** | Y | Y | Y | Y | Y | Y | Y |
| **RHODE ISLAND** | | | | | | | |
| 1 Kennedy | Y | Y | Y | N | N | Y | N |
| 2 Langevin | Y | Y | Y | N | N | Y | N |
| **SOUTH CAROLINA** | | | | | | | |
| 1 **Brown** | Y | Y | Y | Y | Y | N | Y |
| 2 **Wilson** | Y | Y | Y | Y | Y | N | Y |
| 3 **Barrett** | + | + | + | Y | Y | N | Y |
| 4 **Inglis** | Y | Y | Y | Y | Y | N | Y |
| 5 Spratt | Y | Y | Y | N | N | Y | N |
| 6 Clyburn | Y | Y | Y | N | N | Y | N |
| **SOUTH DAKOTA** | | | | | | | |
| AL Herseth | Y | Y | Y | N | N | Y | N |
| **TENNESSEE** | | | | | | | |
| 1 **Jenkins** | Y | Y | Y | Y | Y | N | Y |
| 2 **Duncan** | Y | Y | Y | Y | Y | N | Y |

| | 171 | 172 | 173 | 174 | 175 | 176 | 177 |
|---|---|---|---|---|---|---|---|
| 3 **Wamp** | Y | Y | Y | Y | Y | N | Y |
| 4 Davis | Y | Y | Y | N | N | Y | N |
| 5 Cooper | Y | Y | Y | N | N | Y | N |
| 6 Gordon | Y | Y | Y | N | N | Y | N |
| 7 **Blackburn** | Y | Y | Y | Y | Y | N | Y |
| 8 Tanner | Y | Y | Y | N | N | Y | N |
| 9 Ford | Y | Y | ? | N | N | Y | N |
| **TEXAS** | | | | | | | |
| 1 **Gohmert** | ? | ? | ? | ? | ? | N | Y |
| 2 **Poe** | Y | Y | Y | Y | Y | N | Y |
| 3 **Johnson, S.** | Y | Y | Y | Y | Y | N | Y |
| 4 **Hall** | Y | Y | Y | Y | Y | N | Y |
| 5 **Hensarling** | Y | Y | Y | Y | Y | N | N |
| 6 **Barton** | Y | Y | Y | Y | Y | N | Y |
| 7 **Culberson** | Y | Y | Y | Y | Y | N | Y |
| 8 **Brady** | ? | ? | ? | Y | Y | N | Y |
| 9 Green | Y | Y | Y | N | N | Y | N |
| 10 **McCaul** | Y | Y | Y | Y | Y | N | Y |
| 11 **Conaway** | Y | Y | Y | Y | Y | N | Y |
| 12 **Granger** | Y | Y | Y | Y | Y | Y | Y |
| 13 **Thornberry** | Y | Y | Y | Y | Y | N | Y |
| 14 **Paul** | Y | Y | Y | Y | Y | N | Y |
| 15 Hinojosa | Y | Y | Y | N | N | Y | N |
| 16 Reyes | Y | Y | Y | N | N | Y | N |
| 17 Edwards | Y | Y | Y | N | N | N | N |
| 18 Jackson-Lee | Y | Y | Y | N | N | Y | N |
| 19 **Neugebauer** | Y | Y | Y | Y | Y | N | Y |
| 20 Gonzalez | Y | Y | Y | N | N | Y | N |
| 21 **Smith** | Y | Y | Y | Y | Y | N | Y |
| 22 **DeLay** | Y | Y | Y | Y | Y | N | Y |
| 23 **Bonilla** | Y | Y | Y | Y | Y | N | Y |
| 24 **Marchant** | Y | Y | Y | Y | Y | N | Y |
| 25 Doggett | Y | Y | Y | N | N | Y | N |
| 26 **Burgess** | Y | Y | Y | Y | Y | N | Y |
| 27 Ortiz | Y | Y | Y | N | N | Y | N |
| 28 Cuellar | Y | Y | Y | N | N | Y | N |
| 29 Green | Y | Y | Y | N | N | Y | N |
| 30 Johnson, E. | Y | Y | Y | N | N | Y | N |
| 31 **Carter** | Y | Y | Y | Y | Y | N | Y |
| 32 **Sessions** | Y | Y | Y | Y | Y | N | Y |
| **UTAH** | | | | | | | |
| 1 **Bishop** | Y | Y | Y | Y | Y | N | Y |
| 2 Matheson | Y | Y | Y | N | N | Y | N |
| 3 **Cannon** | Y | Y | Y | Y | Y | N | N |
| **VERMONT** | | | | | | | |
| AL *Sanders* | Y | Y | Y | N | N | Y | N |
| **VIRGINIA** | | | | | | | |
| 1 **Davis, J.** | Y | Y | Y | Y | Y | N | Y |
| 2 **Drake** | Y | Y | Y | Y | Y | N | Y |
| 3 Scott | Y | Y | Y | N | ? | Y | N |
| 4 **Forbes** | Y | Y | Y | Y | Y | N | Y |
| 5 **Goode** | Y | Y | Y | Y | Y | N | Y |
| 6 **Goodlatte** | Y | Y | Y | Y | Y | N | Y |
| 7 **Cantor** | Y | Y | Y | Y | Y | N | Y |
| 8 Moran | ? | ? | ? | N | N | N | N |
| 9 Boucher | Y | Y | Y | ? | ? | Y | N |
| 10 **Wolf** | Y | Y | Y | Y | Y | N | N |
| 11 **Davis, T.** | Y | Y | Y | Y | Y | N | N |
| **WASHINGTON** | | | | | | | |
| 1 Inslee | Y | Y | Y | N | N | Y | N |
| 2 Larsen | ? | ? | ? | N | N | Y | N |
| 3 Baird | Y | Y | Y | ? | ? | Y | N |
| 4 **Hastings** | Y | Y | Y | Y | Y | N | N |
| 5 **McMorris** | Y | Y | Y | Y | Y | N | N |
| 6 Dicks | Y | Y | Y | N | N | Y | N |
| 7 McDermott | Y | Y | Y | N | N | Y | N |
| 8 **Reichert** | Y | Y | Y | Y | Y | N | N |
| 9 Smith | ? | Y | Y | N | N | Y | N |
| **WEST VIRGINIA** | | | | | | | |
| 1 Mollohan | Y | Y | Y | N | N | Y | N |
| 2 **Capito** | Y | Y | Y | Y | Y | Y | N |
| 3 Rahall | Y | Y | Y | N | N | Y | N |
| **WISCONSIN** | | | | | | | |
| 1 **Ryan** | Y | Y | Y | Y | Y | Y | N |
| 2 Baldwin | Y | Y | Y | N | N | Y | N |
| 3 Kind | Y | Y | Y | N | N | Y | N |
| 4 Moore | Y | Y | Y | N | N | Y | N |
| 5 **Sensenbrenner** | Y | Y | Y | Y | Y | N | Y |
| 6 **Petri** | Y | Y | Y | Y | Y | N | N |
| 7 Obey | Y | Y | Y | N | N | Y | N |
| 8 **Green** | Y | Y | Y | Y | Y | Y | N |
| **WYOMING** | | | | | | | |
| AL **Cubin** | Y | Y | Y | ? | ? | N | Y |

# IN THE HOUSE | By Vote Number

**178.** HR 2360. Fiscal 2006 Homeland Security Appropriations/ **Detention Centers.** Meeks, D-N.Y., amendment that would prohibit the use of funds in the bill to close any detention facility operated by or on behalf of U.S. Immigration and Customs Enforcement that has been operational in 2005. Rejected 199-223: R 22-205; D 176-18 (ND 133-12, SD 43-6); I 1-0. May 17, 2005.

**179.** HR 2360. Fiscal 2006 Homeland Security Appropriations/Driver's **License Standards.** Obey, D-Wis., amendment that would provide $100 million for states to comply with new national driver's license standards, offset with cuts spread through the bill. Adopted 226-198: R 32-196; D 193-2 (ND 144-2, SD 49-0); I 1-0. May 17, 2005.

**180.** HR 2360. Fiscal 2006 Homeland Security Appropriations/Passage. Passage of the bill that would provide $31.9 billion in fiscal 2006 for the Homeland Security Department, including $22 billion for security, enforcement and investigation activities; $5.7 billion for the Transportation Security Administration, and $3.6 billion for state and local grant programs. It would withhold more than $310 million pending improvements in air cargo screening and deployment of more explosive-detection technologies at airports. Passed 424-1: R 229-1; D 194-0 (ND 145-0, SD 49-0); I 1-0. May 17, 2005.

**181.** HR 1817. Fiscal 2006 Homeland Security Authorization/Previous **Question.** Sessions, R-Texas, motion to order the previous question (thus ending debate and possibility of amendment) on adoption of the rule (H Res 283) that would provide for House floor consideration of the bill that would authorize $34.2 billion in fiscal 2006 for the Department of Homeland Security. Motion agreed to 226-199: R 226-0; D 0-198 (ND 0-148, SD 0-50); I 0-1. May 18, 2005.

**182.** HR 1817. Fiscal 2006 Homeland Security Authorization/Rule. Adoption of the rule (H Res 283) to provide for House floor consideration of the bill that would authorize $34.2 billion in fiscal 2006 for the Department of Homeland Security. Adopted 284-124: R 221-0; D 63-124 (ND 43-96, SD 20-28); I 0-0. May 18, 2005.

**183.** HR 1817. Fiscal 2006 Homeland Security Authorization/Inspector **General Funding.** Meek, D-Fla., amendment that would increase funding for the Department of Homeland Security Office of Inspector General to $200 million. Rejected 184-244: R 2-226; D 181-18 (ND 136-13, SD 45-5); I 1-0. May 18, 2005.

**184.** HR 1817. Fiscal 2006 Homeland Security Authorization/Airline **Passenger Fees.** Hooley, D-Ore., amendment that would bar any funds authorized by the bill to come from an increase in the aviation security passenger fee. Adopted 363-65: R 176-52; D 186-13 (ND 141-8, SD 45-5); I 1-0. May 18, 2005.

**185.** HR 1817. Fiscal 2006 Homeland Security Authorization/State and **Local Law Enforcement Duties.** Norwood, R-Ga., amendment that would clarify the existing authority for state and local enforcement personnel to apprehend, detain, remove and transport illegal aliens in the routine course of duty. It also would require the Homeland Security Department to establish a manual for training personnel to enforce immigration laws and set guidelines for making the training available. Adopted 242-185: R 216-11; D 26-173 (ND 14-135, SD 12-38); I 0-1. May 18, 2005.

ND Northern Democrats, SD Southern Democrats
Southern states: Ala., Ark., Fla., Ga., Ky., La., Miss., N.C., Okla., S.C., Tenn., Texas, Va.

| | 178 | 179 | 180 | 181 | 182 | 183 | 184 | 185 |
|---|---|---|---|---|---|---|---|---|
| **ALABAMA** | | | | | | | | |
| 1 Bonner | N | N | Y | Y | Y | N | Y | Y |
| 2 Everett | N | Y | Y | Y | Y | N | N | Y |
| 3 Rogers | N | N | Y | Y | Y | N | Y | Y |
| 4 Aderholt | N | N | Y | Y | Y | N | Y | Y |
| 5 Cramer | N | Y | Y | N | Y | N | Y | Y |
| 6 Bachus | N | N | Y | Y | Y | N | Y | Y |
| 7 Davis | Y | Y | Y | N | N | Y | N | Y |
| **ALASKA** | | | | | | | | |
| AL Young | N | Y | Y | Y | Y | N | N | Y |
| **ARIZONA** | | | | | | | | |
| 1 Renzi | N | N | Y | Y | Y | N | Y | Y |
| 2 Franks | N | N | Y | Y | Y | N | N | Y |
| 3 Shadegg | N | N | Y | Y | Y | N | Y | Y |
| 4 Pastor | Y | Y | Y | N | N | Y | N | N |
| 5 Hayworth | N | N | Y | Y | Y | N | Y | Y |
| 6 Flake | N | N | Y | Y | Y | N | N | Y |
| 7 Grijalva | N | Y | Y | N | N | Y | Y | N |
| 8 Kolbe | N | N | Y | Y | Y | N | Y | Y |
| **ARKANSAS** | | | | | | | | |
| 1 Berry | Y | Y | Y | N | Y | Y | N | N |
| 2 Snyder | Y | Y | Y | N | N | Y | Y | N |
| 3 Boozman | N | N | Y | Y | Y | N | Y | Y |
| 4 Ross | Y | Y | Y | N | Y | Y | N | Y |
| **CALIFORNIA** | | | | | | | | |
| 1 Thompson | Y | Y | Y | N | N | Y | N | N |
| 2 Herger | N | N | Y | Y | Y | N | Y | Y |
| 3 Lungren | N | N | Y | Y | Y | N | N | Y |
| 4 Doolittle | Y | N | Y | Y | Y | N | Y | Y |
| 5 Matsui, D. | Y | Y | Y | N | N | Y | Y | N |
| 6 Woolsey | Y | Y | Y | N | N | Y | Y | N |
| 7 Miller, George | Y | Y | Y | N | ? | Y | Y | N |
| 8 Pelosi | Y | Y | Y | N | N | Y | Y | N |
| 9 Lee | Y | Y | Y | N | N | Y | Y | N |
| 10 Tauscher | Y | Y | Y | N | N | Y | Y | N |
| 11 Pombo | N | N | Y | Y | Y | N | Y | Y |
| 12 Lantos | Y | Y | Y | N | N | Y | Y | N |
| 13 Stark | Y | Y | Y | N | ? | Y | Y | N |
| 14 Eshoo | Y | Y | Y | N | ? | Y | Y | N |
| 15 Honda | Y | Y | Y | N | N | Y | Y | N |
| 16 Lofgren | N | Y | Y | N | N | Y | Y | N |
| 17 Farr | Y | Y | Y | N | N | Y | Y | N |
| 18 Cardoza | Y | Y | Y | N | ? | Y | Y | N |
| 19 Radanovich | N | N | Y | Y | Y | N | N | Y |
| 20 Costa | N | Y | Y | N | Y | N | N | N |
| 21 Nunes | N | N | Y | Y | Y | N | N | Y |
| 22 Thomas | N | N | Y | Y | Y | N | N | Y |
| 23 Capps | Y | Y | Y | N | N | Y | Y | N |
| 24 Gallegly | N | N | Y | Y | Y | N | Y | Y |
| 25 McKeon | N | N | Y | Y | ? | N | Y | Y |
| 26 Dreier | N | N | Y | Y | Y | N | Y | Y |
| 27 Sherman | N | Y | Y | N | N | Y | Y | N |
| 28 Berman | N | Y | Y | N | ? | Y | Y | N |
| 29 Schiff | N | Y | Y | N | N | Y | Y | N |
| 30 Waxman | Y | Y | Y | N | N | Y | Y | N |
| 31 Becerra | Y | Y | Y | N | ? | Y | Y | N |
| 32 Solis | N | Y | Y | N | N | Y | Y | N |
| 33 Watson | Y | Y | Y | N | N | Y | Y | N |
| 34 Roybal-Allard | Y | Y | Y | N | N | Y | Y | N |
| 35 Waters | Y | Y | Y | N | N | Y | Y | N |
| 36 Harman | Y | Y | Y | N | N | Y | Y | N |
| 37 Millender-McD. | ? | ? | ? | ? | ? | ? | ? | ? |
| 38 Napolitano | Y | Y | Y | N | ? | Y | Y | N |
| 39 Sánchez, Linda | Y | Y | Y | N | Y | Y | Y | N |
| 40 Royce | N | Y | Y | Y | Y | N | Y | Y |
| 41 Lewis | N | N | Y | Y | Y | N | Y | Y |
| 42 Miller, Gary | N | N | Y | Y | Y | N | Y | Y |
| 43 Baca | Y | Y | Y | N | Y | Y | Y | N |
| 44 Calvert | N | N | Y | Y | Y | N | Y | Y |
| 45 Bono | N | N | Y | Y | Y | N | Y | Y |
| 46 Rohrabacher | N | N | Y | Y | Y | N | N | Y |
| 47 Sanchez, Loretta | Y | Y | Y | N | N | Y | Y | N |
| 48 Cox | N | N | Y | Y | Y | N | Y | Y |
| 49 Issa | N | N | Y | Y | Y | N | Y | Y |

| | 178 | 179 | 180 | 181 | 182 | 183 | 184 | 185 |
|---|---|---|---|---|---|---|---|---|
| 50 Cunningham | N | N | Y | Y | Y | N | Y | Y |
| 51 Filner | Y | Y | Y | N | N | Y | Y | N |
| 52 Hunter | N | N | Y | Y | Y | N | Y | Y |
| 53 Davis | Y | Y | Y | N | N | Y | Y | N |
| **COLORADO** | | | | | | | | |
| 1 DeGette | Y | Y | Y | N | N | Y | Y | N |
| 2 Udall | Y | Y | Y | N | N | Y | Y | N |
| 3 Salazar | Y | Y | Y | N | N | Y | Y | N |
| 4 Musgrave | N | N | Y | Y | Y | N | Y | Y |
| 5 Hefley | N | N | Y | Y | Y | N | Y | Y |
| 6 Tancredo | N | N | Y | ? | ? | ? | ? | ? |
| 7 Beauprez | N | N | Y | Y | Y | N | Y | Y |
| **CONNECTICUT** | | | | | | | | |
| 1 Larson | + | + | + | – | – | + | + | – |
| 2 Simmons | N | N | Y | Y | Y | N | Y | Y |
| 3 DeLauro | Y | Y | Y | N | N | Y | Y | N |
| 4 Shays | N | N | Y | Y | Y | N | N | Y |
| 5 Johnson | N | N | Y | Y | Y | Y | N | Y |
| **DELAWARE** | | | | | | | | |
| AL Castle | N | N | Y | Y | Y | N | Y | Y |
| **FLORIDA** | | | | | | | | |
| 1 Miller | – | N | Y | Y | Y | N | Y | Y |
| 2 Boyd | Y | Y | Y | N | Y | Y | Y | Y |
| 3 Brown | Y | Y | Y | N | N | Y | Y | N |
| 4 Crenshaw | N | N | Y | Y | Y | N | Y | Y |
| 5 Brown-Waite | N | N | Y | Y | Y | N | Y | Y |
| 6 Stearns | N | N | Y | Y | Y | N | Y | Y |
| 7 Mica | N | N | Y | Y | Y | N | N | Y |
| 8 Keller | N | N | Y | Y | Y | N | Y | Y |
| 9 Bilirakis | N | N | Y | Y | Y | N | Y | Y |
| 10 Young | ? | ? | Y | Y | Y | N | Y | Y |
| 11 Davis | Y | Y | Y | N | Y | Y | N | N |
| 12 Putnam | N | N | Y | Y | Y | N | Y | Y |
| 13 Harris | N | N | Y | Y | Y | N | Y | Y |
| 14 Mack | N | N | Y | Y | Y | N | N | Y |
| 15 Weldon | N | N | Y | Y | Y | N | Y | Y |
| 16 Foley | N | Y | ? | ? | N | Y | Y | Y |
| 17 Meek | Y | Y | Y | N | N | Y | Y | N |
| 18 Ros-Lehtinen | N | N | Y | Y | Y | N | N | N |
| 19 Wexler | ? | ? | ? | N | Y | Y | Y | N |
| 20 Wasserman-Schultz | Y | Y | Y | N | N | Y | Y | N |
| 21 Diaz-Balart, L. | N | N | Y | Y | Y | N | N | N |
| 22 Shaw | N | N | Y | Y | Y | N | N | N |
| 23 Hastings | Y | Y | Y | N | Y | Y | Y | N |
| 24 Feeney | N | N | Y | Y | Y | N | Y | N |
| 25 Diaz-Balart, M. | N | N | Y | Y | Y | N | N | N |
| **GEORGIA** | | | | | | | | |
| 1 Kingston | N | N | Y | Y | Y | N | N | Y |
| 2 Bishop | Y | Y | Y | N | Y | Y | N | Y |
| 3 Marshall | N | Y | Y | N | Y | Y | Y | Y |
| 4 McKinney | N | Y | Y | N | N | Y | N | N |
| 5 Lewis | ? | ? | ? | ? | ? | ? | ? | ? |
| 6 Price | N | N | Y | Y | Y | N | N | Y |
| 7 Linder | Y | N | Y | Y | Y | N | N | Y |
| 8 Westmoreland | N | N | Y | Y | Y | N | N | Y |
| 9 Norwood | N | N | Y | Y | Y | N | N | Y |
| 10 Deal | N | N | Y | Y | Y | N | N | Y |
| 11 Gingrey | N | N | Y | Y | Y | N | N | Y |
| 12 Barrow | Y | Y | Y | N | Y | Y | Y | Y |
| 13 Scott | Y | Y | Y | N | Y | Y | Y | Y |
| **HAWAII** | | | | | | | | |
| 1 Abercrombie | Y | Y | Y | N | Y | Y | Y | N |
| 2 Case | N | Y | Y | N | ? | Y | Y | N |
| **IDAHO** | | | | | | | | |
| 1 Otter | N | N | Y | Y | Y | N | N | Y |
| 2 Simpson | N | N | Y | Y | Y | N | Y | Y |
| **ILLINOIS** | | | | | | | | |
| 1 Rush | Y | Y | Y | N | N | Y | Y | N |
| 2 Jackson | Y | Y | Y | N | N | Y | Y | N |
| 3 Lipinski | Y | Y | Y | N | N | Y | Y | N |
| 4 Gutierrez | Y | N | Y | N | N | Y | Y | N |
| 5 Emanuel | Y | Y | Y | N | N | Y | Y | N |
| 6 Hyde | N | Y | Y | ? | ? | N | Y | Y |
| 7 Davis | Y | Y | Y | N | N | Y | Y | N |
| 8 Bean | Y | Y | Y | N | N | Y | Y | N |
| 9 Schakowsky | Y | Y | Y | N | N | Y | Y | N |
| 10 Kirk | N | N | Y | Y | Y | N | Y | Y |
| 11 Weller | N | N | Y | Y | Y | N | N | Y |
| 12 Costello | Y | Y | Y | N | N | Y | Y | N |

**KEY**

| Republicans | Democrats | Independents |
|---|---|---|

| | | | |
|---|---|---|---|
| Y | Voted for (yea) | X | Paired against |
| # | Paired for | – | Announced against |
| + | Announced for | P | Voted "present" |
| N | Voted against (nay) | C | Voted "present" to avoid possible conflict of interest |
| | | ? | Did not vote or otherwise make a position known |

| | 178 | 179 | 180 | 181 | 182 | 183 | 184 | 185 |
|---|---|---|---|---|---|---|---|---|
| 13 **Biggert** | N | N | Y | Y | Y | N | Y | Y |
| 14 **Hastert** | | | | | | | | |
| 15 **Johnson** | N | Y | Y | Y | Y | N | Y | Y |
| 16 **Manzullo** | N | N | Y | Y | Y | N | Y | Y |
| 17 Evans | Y | Y | Y | N | Y | N | Y | N |
| 18 **LaHood** | N | N | Y | Y | Y | N | Y | Y |
| 19 **Shimkus** | N | N | Y | Y | Y | N | Y | Y |
| **INDIANA** | | | | | | | | |
| 1 Visclosky | Y | Y | Y | N | N | Y | Y | N |
| 2 **Chocola** | N | N | Y | Y | Y | N | Y | Y |
| 3 **Souder** | Y | N | Y | Y | Y | N | N | Y |
| 4 **Buyer** | N | N | Y | Y | ? | N | N | Y |
| 5 **Burton** | Y | N | Y | Y | Y | N | Y | Y |
| 6 **Pence** | N | N | Y | Y | Y | N | N | Y |
| 7 Carson | Y | Y | Y | N | N | Y | Y | N |
| 8 **Hostettler** | Y | Y | Y | Y | Y | N | Y | Y |
| 9 **Sodrel** | N | N | Y | Y | Y | N | Y | Y |
| **IOWA** | | | | | | | | |
| 1 **Nussle** | N | N | Y | Y | Y | N | Y | Y |
| 2 **Leach** | N | N | Y | Y | Y | N | Y | Y |
| 3 Boswell | Y | Y | Y | N | N | Y | Y | Y |
| 4 **Latham** | N | N | Y | Y | Y | N | Y | Y |
| 5 **King** | N | N | Y | Y | Y | N | N | Y |
| **KANSAS** | | | | | | | | |
| 1 **Moran** | N | N | Y | Y | Y | N | N | Y |
| 2 **Ryun** | N | N | Y | Y | Y | N | N | Y |
| 3 Moore | Y | Y | Y | N | N | Y | Y | N |
| 4 **Tiahrt** | N | N | Y | Y | Y | N | Y | Y |
| **KENTUCKY** | | | | | | | | |
| 1 **Whitfield** | N | N | Y | Y | Y | N | N | Y |
| 2 **Lewis** | N | N | Y | Y | Y | N | Y | Y |
| 3 **Northup** | N | N | Y | Y | Y | N | Y | Y |
| 4 **Davis** | N | N | Y | Y | Y | N | Y | Y |
| 5 **Rogers** | N | N | Y | Y | Y | N | Y | Y |
| 6 Chandler | Y | Y | Y | N | Y | Y | Y | Y |
| **LOUISIANA** | | | | | | | | |
| 1 **Jindal** | N | N | Y | Y | Y | N | Y | Y |
| 2 Jefferson | Y | Y | Y | N | ? | Y | Y | N |
| 3 Melancon | Y | Y | Y | N | Y | Y | Y | N |
| 4 **McCrery** | N | N | Y | Y | Y | N | Y | Y |
| 5 **Alexander** | N | N | Y | Y | Y | N | Y | Y |
| 6 **Baker** | N | N | Y | Y | Y | N | Y | Y |
| 7 **Boustany** | N | N | Y | Y | Y | N | N | Y |
| **MAINE** | | | | | | | | |
| 1 Allen | Y | Y | Y | N | Y | Y | Y | N |
| 2 Michaud | Y | Y | Y | N | Y | Y | Y | N |
| **MARYLAND** | | | | | | | | |
| 1 **Gilchrest** | N | N | Y | Y | Y | N | Y | Y |
| 2 Ruppersberger | Y | Y | Y | N | Y | Y | Y | Y |
| 3 Cardin | Y | Y | Y | N | Y | Y | Y | N |
| 4 Wynn | Y | Y | Y | N | N | Y | Y | N |
| 5 Hoyer | Y | Y | Y | N | N | Y | Y | N |
| 6 **Bartlett** | N | N | Y | Y | Y | N | N | Y |
| 7 Cummings | Y | Y | Y | N | N | Y | Y | N |
| 8 Van Hollen | Y | Y | Y | N | N | Y | Y | N |
| **MASSACHUSETTS** | | | | | | | | |
| 1 Olver | Y | Y | Y | N | N | Y | Y | N |
| 2 Neal | Y | Y | Y | N | N | Y | Y | N |
| 3 McGovern | Y | Y | Y | N | N | Y | Y | N |
| 4 Frank | Y | Y | Y | N | N | Y | N | N |
| 5 Meehan | Y | Y | Y | N | N | Y | Y | N |
| 6 Tierney | Y | Y | Y | N | N | N | N | N |
| 7 Markey | Y | Y | Y | ? | N | Y | Y | N |
| 8 Capuano | N | Y | Y | N | Y | Y | Y | N |
| 9 Lynch | Y | Y | Y | N | N | Y | Y | N |
| 10 Delahunt | Y | Y | Y | N | N | Y | Y | N |
| **MICHIGAN** | | | | | | | | |
| 1 Stupak | Y | Y | Y | N | Y | Y | Y | N |
| 2 **Hoekstra** | N | N | Y | Y | Y | N | N | Y |
| 3 **Ehlers** | N | Y | Y | Y | Y | N | N | N |
| 4 **Camp** | N | Y | Y | Y | Y | N | Y | Y |
| 5 Kildee | Y | Y | Y | N | N | Y | Y | N |
| 6 **Upton** | N | N | Y | Y | Y | N | Y | Y |
| 7 **Schwarz** | N | N | Y | Y | Y | N | Y | Y |
| 8 **Rogers** | N | N | Y | Y | Y | N | Y | Y |
| 9 **Knollenberg** | N | N | Y | Y | ? | N | Y | Y |
| 10 **Miller** | N | N | Y | Y | Y | N | N | Y |
| 11 **McCotter** | N | Y | Y | Y | Y | N | Y | Y |
| 12 Levin | Y | Y | Y | N | Y | Y | Y | N |
| 13 Kilpatrick | + | + | + | N | N | Y | Y | N |
| 14 Conyers | Y | Y | Y | N | Y | Y | Y | N |
| 15 Dingell | Y | Y | Y | N | N | Y | Y | N |
| **MINNESOTA** | | | | | | | | |
| 1 **Gutknecht** | N | N | Y | Y | Y | N | N | Y |
| 2 **Kline** | N | N | Y | Y | Y | N | Y | Y |
| 3 **Ramstad** | N | N | Y | Y | Y | N | Y | Y |
| 4 McCollum | Y | Y | Y | N | ? | Y | Y | N |
| 5 Sabo | Y | Y | Y | N | N | Y | N | N |
| 6 **Kennedy** | N | N | Y | Y | Y | N | Y | Y |
| 7 Peterson | Y | Y | Y | N | Y | Y | N | Y |
| 8 Oberstar | Y | Y | Y | N | N | Y | Y | N |
| **MISSISSIPPI** | | | | | | | | |
| 1 **Wicker** | N | N | Y | Y | Y | N | N | Y |
| 2 Thompson | Y | Y | Y | N | N | Y | Y | N |
| 3 **Pickering** | N | N | Y | Y | Y | N | Y | Y |
| 4 Taylor | N | Y | Y | N | N | N | N | Y |
| **MISSOURI** | | | | | | | | |
| 1 Clay | Y | Y | Y | N | N | Y | Y | N |
| 2 **Akin** | N | ? | Y | Y | Y | N | Y | Y |
| 3 Carnahan | Y | Y | Y | N | Y | Y | Y | N |
| 4 Skelton | N | Y | Y | N | Y | N | Y | Y |
| 5 Cleaver | Y | Y | Y | N | N | Y | Y | N |
| 6 **Graves** | N | N | Y | Y | Y | N | Y | Y |
| 7 **Blunt** | N | N | Y | Y | Y | N | N | Y |
| 8 **Emerson** | N | N | Y | Y | Y | N | Y | Y |
| 9 **Hulshof** | N | N | Y | Y | Y | N | Y | Y |
| **MONTANA** | | | | | | | | |
| AL **Rehberg** | N | N | Y | Y | Y | N | Y | Y |
| **NEBRASKA** | | | | | | | | |
| 1 **Fortenberry** | N | N | Y | Y | Y | N | Y | Y |
| 2 **Terry** | Y | N | Y | Y | Y | N | Y | Y |
| 3 **Osborne** | Y | N | Y | Y | Y | N | Y | Y |
| **NEVADA** | | | | | | | | |
| 1 Berkley | Y | Y | Y | N | N | Y | Y | N |
| 2 **Gibbons** | N | N | Y | Y | Y | N | Y | Y |
| 3 **Porter** | N | N | Y | Y | Y | N | Y | Y |
| **NEW HAMPSHIRE** | | | | | | | | |
| 1 **Bradley** | N | N | Y | Y | Y | N | Y | Y |
| 2 **Bass** | N | N | Y | Y | Y | N | Y | Y |
| **NEW JERSEY** | | | | | | | | |
| 1 Andrews | Y | Y | Y | N | N | Y | Y | N |
| 2 **LoBiondo** | N | Y | Y | Y | Y | N | Y | Y |
| 3 **Saxton** | N | N | Y | Y | Y | N | Y | Y |
| 4 **Smith** | N | Y | Y | Y | Y | N | Y | Y |
| 5 **Garrett** | N | N | Y | Y | Y | N | Y | Y |
| 6 Pallone | Y | Y | Y | N | N | Y | Y | N |
| 7 **Ferguson** | N | N | Y | Y | Y | N | Y | Y |
| 8 Pascrell | Y | Y | Y | N | - | Y | Y | N |
| 9 Rothman | Y | Y | Y | N | N | Y | Y | N |
| 10 Payne | ? | ? | ? | N | N | Y | Y | N |
| 11 **Frelinghuysen** | N | N | Y | Y | Y | N | Y | N |
| 12 Holt | Y | Y | Y | N | Y | Y | Y | N |
| 13 Menendez | Y | Y | Y | N | N | Y | Y | N |
| **NEW MEXICO** | | | | | | | | |
| 1 **Wilson** | N | N | Y | Y | Y | N | Y | N |
| 2 **Pearce** | N | N | Y | Y | Y | N | Y | Y |
| 3 Udall | Y | Y | Y | N | N | Y | Y | N |
| **NEW YORK** | | | | | | | | |
| 1 Bishop | Y | Y | Y | N | Y | Y | Y | Y |
| 2 Israel | Y | Y | Y | N | N | Y | Y | Y |
| 3 **King** | Y | N | Y | Y | Y | N | Y | Y |
| 4 McCarthy | Y | Y | Y | N | Y | Y | Y | Y |
| 5 Ackerman | ? | Y | Y | N | Y | Y | Y | N |
| 6 Meeks | Y | Y | Y | N | N | Y | Y | N |
| 7 Crowley | Y | Y | Y | N | N | Y | Y | N |
| 8 Nadler | Y | Y | Y | N | N | Y | N | N |
| 9 Weiner | Y | Y | Y | N | N | Y | Y | N |
| 10 Towns | Y | Y | Y | N | N | Y | Y | N |
| 11 Owens | Y | Y | Y | N | N | Y | Y | N |
| 12 Velázquez | Y | Y | Y | N | N | Y | Y | N |
| 13 **Fossella** | Y | N | Y | Y | Y | N | Y | Y |
| 14 Maloney | Y | Y | Y | N | N | Y | Y | N |
| 15 Rangel | Y | Y | Y | N | N | Y | Y | N |
| 16 Serrano | Y | Y | Y | N | N | Y | Y | N |
| 17 Engel | Y | Y | Y | N | N | Y | Y | N |
| 18 Lowey | Y | Y | Y | N | N | Y | Y | N |
| 19 **Kelly** | Y | N | Y | Y | Y | N | Y | Y |
| 20 **Sweeney** | Y | N | Y | Y | Y | N | Y | Y |
| 21 McNulty | Y | Y | Y | N | N | Y | Y | N |
| 22 Hinchey | Y | Y | Y | N | N | Y | Y | N |
| 23 **McHugh** | Y | Y | Y | Y | Y | N | Y | Y |
| 24 **Boehlert** | N | N | Y | Y | Y | N | Y | Y |
| 25 **Walsh** | Y | N | Y | Y | Y | N | Y | Y |
| 26 **Reynolds** | Y | N | Y | Y | Y | N | Y | Y |
| 27 Higgins | Y | Y | Y | N | N | Y | Y | Y |
| 28 Slaughter | Y | Y | Y | N | N | Y | Y | N |
| 29 **Kuhl** | N | Y | Y | Y | Y | N | Y | Y |
| **NORTH CAROLINA** | | | | | | | | |
| 1 Butterfield | Y | Y | Y | N | N | Y | Y | N |
| 2 Etheridge | Y | Y | Y | N | N | Y | Y | N |
| 3 **Jones** | N | Y | Y | Y | Y | N | Y | Y |
| 4 Price | Y | Y | Y | N | N | Y | Y | N |
| 5 **Foxx** | N | N | Y | Y | Y | N | Y | Y |
| 6 **Coble** | N | N | Y | Y | Y | N | Y | Y |
| 7 McIntyre | Y | Y | Y | N | Y | Y | Y | Y |
| 8 **Hayes** | N | N | Y | Y | Y | N | N | Y |
| 9 **Myrick** | N | Y | Y | Y | ? | N | Y | Y |
| 10 **McHenry** | N | N | Y | Y | Y | N | Y | Y |
| 11 **Taylor** | N | N | Y | Y | Y | N | Y | N |
| 12 Watt | Y | Y | Y | N | N | Y | Y | N |
| 13 Miller | Y | Y | Y | N | N | Y | Y | N |
| **NORTH DAKOTA** | | | | | | | | |
| AL Pomeroy | Y | Y | Y | N | N | Y | Y | N |
| **OHIO** | | | | | | | | |
| 1 **Chabot** | N | N | Y | Y | Y | N | Y | Y |
| 2 Vacant | | | | | | | | |
| 3 **Turner** | N | N | Y | Y | ? | N | Y | Y |
| 4 **Oxley** | N | N | Y | Y | Y | N | Y | Y |
| 5 **Gillmor** | N | Y | Y | Y | Y | N | N | Y |
| 6 Strickland | Y | Y | Y | N | Y | Y | Y | N |
| 7 **Hobson** | N | N | Y | Y | Y | N | Y | Y |
| 8 **Boehner** | N | N | Y | Y | Y | N | Y | Y |
| 9 Kaptur | Y | Y | Y | N | N | Y | Y | N |
| 10 Kucinich | Y | Y | Y | N | N | Y | Y | N |
| 11 Jones | Y | Y | Y | N | N | Y | Y | N |
| 12 **Tiberi** | N | N | Y | Y | Y | N | Y | Y |
| 13 Brown | Y | Y | Y | N | Y | Y | Y | N |
| 14 **LaTourette** | N | N | Y | Y | Y | N | N | Y |
| 15 **Pryce** | N | N | Y | Y | Y | N | Y | Y |
| 16 **Regula** | N | N | Y | Y | Y | N | Y | Y |
| 17 Ryan | Y | Y | Y | N | Y | Y | Y | N |
| 18 **Ney** | N | N | Y | Y | Y | N | N | Y |
| **OKLAHOMA** | | | | | | | | |
| 1 **Sullivan** | Y | N | Y | Y | Y | N | Y | ? |
| 2 Boren | Y | Y | Y | N | Y | N | Y | Y |
| 3 **Lucas** | N | N | Y | Y | Y | ? | ? | ? |
| 4 **Cole** | N | N | Y | Y | Y | N | N | Y |
| 5 **Istook** | N | N | Y | Y | Y | N | N | Y |
| **OREGON** | | | | | | | | |
| 1 Wu | Y | Y | Y | N | Y | Y | Y | N |
| 2 **Walden** | N | N | Y | Y | Y | N | Y | Y |
| 3 Blumenauer | N | Y | Y | N | Y | Y | Y | N |
| 4 DeFazio | Y | Y | Y | N | Y | Y | Y | Y |
| 5 Hooley | Y | Y | Y | N | Y | Y | Y | Y |
| **PENNSYLVANIA** | | | | | | | | |
| 1 Brady | ? | ? | ? | N | Y | Y | Y | N |
| 2 Fattah | Y | Y | Y | N | Y | Y | Y | N |
| 3 **English** | N | N | Y | Y | Y | N | N | Y |
| 4 **Hart** | N | N | Y | Y | Y | N | Y | Y |
| 5 **Peterson** | N | N | Y | Y | Y | N | Y | Y |
| 6 **Gerlach** | N | Y | Y | Y | Y | N | Y | Y |
| 7 **Weldon** | N | N | Y | Y | Y | N | Y | Y |
| 8 **Fitzpatrick** | N | Y | Y | ? | Y | N | Y | Y |
| 9 **Shuster** | N | N | Y | Y | Y | N | N | Y |
| 10 **Sherwood** | N | N | Y | Y | Y | N | Y | Y |
| 11 Kanjorski | Y | Y | Y | N | N | Y | Y | N |
| 12 Murtha | Y | Y | Y | N | Y | Y | Y | N |
| 13 Schwartz | Y | Y | Y | N | Y | Y | Y | N |
| 14 Doyle | Y | Y | Y | N | Y | Y | Y | N |
| 15 **Dent** | N | Y | Y | Y | Y | N | Y | Y |
| 16 **Pitts** | Y | N | Y | Y | Y | N | Y | Y |
| 17 Holden | Y | Y | Y | N | Y | Y | Y | Y |
| 18 **Murphy** | N | Y | Y | Y | Y | N | Y | Y |
| 19 **Platts** | N | Y | Y | Y | Y | N | N | Y |
| **RHODE ISLAND** | | | | | | | | |
| 1 Kennedy | Y | Y | Y | N | N | Y | Y | N |
| 2 Langevin | Y | Y | Y | N | N | Y | Y | N |
| **SOUTH CAROLINA** | | | | | | | | |
| 1 **Brown** | N | N | Y | Y | Y | N | Y | Y |
| 2 **Wilson** | N | N | Y | Y | Y | N | Y | Y |
| 3 **Barrett** | N | N | Y | Y | Y | N | Y | Y |
| 4 **Inglis** | N | N | Y | Y | Y | N | Y | Y |
| 5 Spratt | Y | Y | Y | N | Y | Y | Y | N |
| 6 Clyburn | Y | Y | Y | N | N | Y | Y | N |
| **SOUTH DAKOTA** | | | | | | | | |
| AL Herseth | Y | Y | Y | N | N | Y | Y | N |
| **TENNESSEE** | | | | | | | | |
| 1 **Jenkins** | N | N | Y | Y | Y | N | Y | Y |
| 2 **Duncan** | N | N | Y | Y | Y | N | Y | Y |
| 3 **Wamp** | N | N | Y | Y | Y | N | Y | Y |
| 4 Davis | N | Y | Y | N | N | Y | Y | Y |
| 5 Cooper | Y | Y | Y | N | N | Y | N | N |
| 6 Gordon | Y | Y | Y | N | N | Y | Y | Y |
| 7 **Blackburn** | N | N | Y | Y | Y | N | Y | Y |
| 8 Tanner | N | Y | Y | N | Y | Y | Y | Y |
| 9 Ford | Y | Y | Y | N | N | Y | N | N |
| **TEXAS** | | | | | | | | |
| 1 **Gohmert** | Y | Y | Y | Y | Y | N | Y | Y |
| 2 **Poe** | N | N | Y | Y | Y | N | Y | Y |
| 3 **Johnson, S.** | N | N | Y | Y | Y | N | N | Y |
| 4 **Hall** | Y | N | Y | Y | Y | N | Y | Y |
| 5 **Hensarling** | N | N | Y | Y | Y | N | N | Y |
| 6 **Barton** | N | N | Y | Y | Y | N | Y | Y |
| 7 **Culberson** | N | N | Y | Y | Y | N | Y | Y |
| 8 **Brady** | N | N | Y | Y | Y | N | Y | Y |
| 9 Green | Y | Y | Y | N | N | Y | Y | N |
| 10 **McCaul** | N | Y | Y | Y | Y | N | Y | Y |
| 11 **Conaway** | N | N | Y | Y | Y | N | Y | Y |
| 12 **Granger** | N | N | Y | Y | Y | N | Y | Y |
| 13 **Thornberry** | N | N | Y | Y | Y | N | N | Y |
| 14 **Paul** | Y | N | N | Y | Y | N | Y | Y |
| 15 Hinojosa | Y | Y | Y | N | Y | Y | Y | N |
| 16 Reyes | Y | Y | Y | N | Y | Y | Y | N |
| 17 Edwards | Y | Y | Y | N | N | Y | Y | N |
| 18 Jackson-Lee | Y | Y | Y | N | N | Y | Y | N |
| 19 **Neugebauer** | N | N | Y | Y | Y | N | Y | Y |
| 20 Gonzalez | Y | Y | Y | N | N | Y | Y | N |
| 21 **Smith** | N | N | Y | Y | Y | N | N | Y |
| 22 **DeLay** | N | N | Y | Y | Y | N | Y | Y |
| 23 **Bonilla** | ? | N | Y | Y | Y | N | N | Y |
| 24 **Marchant** | N | N | Y | Y | ? | N | N | Y |
| 25 Doggett | Y | Y | Y | N | N | Y | Y | N |
| 26 **Burgess** | N | N | Y | Y | Y | N | Y | Y |
| 27 Ortiz | Y | Y | Y | N | Y | Y | Y | N |
| 28 Cuellar | Y | Y | Y | N | Y | Y | Y | N |
| 29 Green | Y | Y | Y | N | N | Y | Y | N |
| 30 Johnson, E. | Y | Y | Y | N | Y | Y | Y | N |
| 31 **Carter** | N | N | Y | Y | Y | N | Y | Y |
| 32 **Sessions** | Y | N | Y | Y | Y | N | N | Y |
| **UTAH** | | | | | | | | |
| 1 **Bishop** | N | N | Y | Y | Y | N | Y | Y |
| 2 Matheson | Y | Y | Y | N | Y | N | Y | Y |
| 3 **Cannon** | N | N | Y | Y | Y | N | N | N |
| **VERMONT** | | | | | | | | |
| AL *Sanders* | Y | Y | Y | N | ? | Y | Y | N |
| **VIRGINIA** | | | | | | | | |
| 1 **Davis, J.** | N | Y | Y | Y | Y | N | Y | Y |
| 2 **Drake** | N | N | Y | Y | Y | N | Y | Y |
| 3 Scott | Y | Y | Y | N | Y | Y | Y | N |
| 4 **Forbes** | N | N | Y | Y | Y | N | Y | Y |
| 5 **Goode** | N | N | Y | Y | Y | N | Y | Y |
| 6 **Goodlatte** | N | N | Y | Y | Y | N | Y | Y |
| 7 **Cantor** | N | N | Y | Y | Y | N | N | Y |
| 8 Moran | Y | Y | Y | N | N | Y | Y | N |
| 9 Boucher | Y | Y | Y | N | ? | N | Y | N |
| 10 **Wolf** | N | N | Y | Y | Y | N | Y | Y |
| 11 **Davis, T.** | N | N | Y | Y | Y | N | Y | Y |
| **WASHINGTON** | | | | | | | | |
| 1 Inslee | Y | Y | Y | N | N | Y | Y | N |
| 2 Larsen | Y | Y | Y | N | Y | Y | Y | N |
| 3 Baird | Y | Y | Y | N | N | N | N | N |
| 4 **Hastings** | N | N | Y | Y | Y | N | Y | Y |
| 5 **McMorris** | N | N | Y | Y | Y | N | Y | Y |
| 6 Dicks | Y | Y | Y | N | N | Y | Y | N |
| 7 McDermott | Y | Y | Y | N | N | Y | Y | N |
| 8 **Reichert** | N | N | Y | Y | Y | N | Y | N |
| 9 Smith | Y | Y | ? | N | N | Y | Y | N |
| **WEST VIRGINIA** | | | | | | | | |
| 1 Mollohan | Y | Y | Y | N | Y | N | Y | N |
| 2 **Capito** | N | Y | Y | Y | Y | N | Y | Y |
| 3 Rahall | Y | Y | Y | N | Y | Y | Y | N |
| **WISCONSIN** | | | | | | | | |
| 1 **Ryan** | N | Y | Y | Y | Y | N | N | Y |
| 2 Baldwin | Y | Y | Y | N | N | Y | Y | N |
| 3 Kind | Y | Y | Y | N | Y | Y | Y | N |
| 4 Moore | N | Y | Y | N | N | Y | Y | N |
| 5 **Sensenbrenner** | Y | Y | Y | Y | Y | N | N | Y |
| 6 **Petri** | Y | Y | Y | Y | Y | N | N | Y |
| 7 Obey | Y | Y | Y | N | N | Y | N | N |
| 8 **Green** | N | Y | Y | Y | Y | N | Y | Y |
| **WYOMING** | | | | | | | | |
| AL **Cubin** | N | N | Y | Y | Y | N | Y | Y |

# IN THE HOUSE | By Vote Number

**186.** HR 1817. Fiscal 2006 Homeland Security Authorization/Border **Violence Activity.** Jackson-Lee, D-Texas, amendment that would require the Homeland Security secretary to submit a report to Congress on border violence activity that includes the number and types of activities that have occurred, a description of victim categories and a description of the steps the agency is taking and plans to prevent these activities. Rejected 182-245: R 2-225; D 179-20 (ND 136-13, SD 43-7); I 1-0. May 18, 2005.

**187.** HR 1817. Fiscal 2006 Homeland Security Authorization/Democratic **Substitute.** Thompson, D-Miss., substitute amendment that would authorize $41 billion in fiscal 2006 for the Department of Homeland Security, including $6.5 billion for grants to state and local governments, $1.8 billion for science and technology programs and $3.3 billion for emergency preparedness and response activities. The substitute also would authorize $2.8 billion for a three-year grant program to reduce the vulnerability of transit systems to terrorist attacks and more than $1 billion for rail security. It would require that 100 percent of air cargo on passenger planes be screened within three years. Rejected 196-230: R 1-227; D 194-3 (ND 147-0, SD 47-3); I 1-0. May 8, 2005.

**188.** HR 1817. Fiscal 2006 Homeland Security Authorization/Recommit. Thompson, D-Miss., motion to recommit the bill to the House Homeland Security Committee with instructions to include language that would authorize $400 million in fiscal 2006 for in-line checked baggage screening system installations as well as require that all air cargo on passenger planes be screened within three years. Motion rejected 199-228: R 1-226; D 197-2 (ND 147-2, SD 50-0); I 1-0. May 18, 2005.

**189.** HR 1817. Fiscal 2006 Homeland Security Authorization/Passage. Passage of the bill that would authorize $34.2 billion in fiscal 2006 for the Department of Homeland Security, including $6.9 billion for Customs and Border Protection and $2 billion for grants to state and local governments for terrorism preparedness. It also would authorize the hiring of 2,000 new border patrol agents and create an assistant secretary for cybersecurity to oversee the National Cyber Security Division and the National Communications System. The bill would refine the color-coded threat alert system by requiring any alerts or advisories to include information on appropriate protective measures and limit the scope to a specific region, locality, or economic sector. Passed 424-4: R 227-1; D 196-3 (ND 146-3, SD 50-0); I 1-0. May 18, 2005.

**190.** HR 2361. Fiscal 2006 Interior and Environment Appropriations/ **Previous Question.** Bishop, R-Utah, motion to order the previous question (thus ending debate and possibility of amendment) on adoption of the rule H Res 287) to provide for House floor consideration of the bill that would appropriate $26.2 billion in fiscal 2006 for the Department of Interior, the EPA and related agencies. Motion agreed to 215-194: R 215-0; D 0-193 (ND 0-144, SD 0-49); I 0-1. Subsequently, the rule was adopted by voice vote. May 19, 2005.

**191.** HR 2361. Fiscal 2006 Interior and Environment Appropriations/ **Payments in Lieu of Taxes.** Hefley, R-Colo., amendment that would increase the bill's appropriations by $4.8 million for payments in lieu of taxes while reducing funding for the National Endowment for the Arts by $15 million. Rejected 109-311: R 102-121; D 7-189 (ND 5-142, SD 2-47); I 0-1. May 19, 2005.

ND Northern Democrats, SD Southern Democrats
Southern states: Ala., Ark., Fla., Ga., Ky., La., Miss., N.C., Okla., S.C., Tenn., Texas, Va.

| | 186 | 187 | 188 | 189 | 190 | 191 |
|---|---|---|---|---|---|---|
| **ALABAMA** | | | | | | |
| 1 Bonner | N | N | N | Y | Y | Y |
| 2 Everett | N | N | N | Y | Y | Y |
| 3 Rogers | N | N | N | Y | Y | N |
| 4 Aderholt | N | N | N | Y | Y | N |
| 5 Cramer | N | Y | Y | Y | N | N |
| 6 Bachus | N | N | N | Y | Y | Y |
| 7 Davis | Y | Y | Y | Y | N | N |
| **ALASKA** | | | | | | |
| AL Young | N | N | N | Y | Y | Y |
| **ARIZONA** | | | | | | |
| 1 Renzi | N | N | N | Y | Y | N |
| 2 Franks | N | N | N | Y | Y | Y |
| 3 Shadegg | N | N | N | Y | Y | Y |
| 4 Pastor | Y | Y | N | Y | N | N |
| 5 Hayworth | N | N | N | Y | Y | Y |
| 6 Flake | N | N | N | Y | Y | Y |
| 7 Grijalva | Y | Y | Y | Y | N | N |
| 8 Kolbe | N | N | N | Y | Y | N |
| **ARKANSAS** | | | | | | |
| 1 Berry | N | Y | Y | Y | N | N |
| 2 Snyder | Y | Y | Y | Y | N | N |
| 3 Boozman | N | N | N | Y | Y | N |
| 4 Ross | Y | Y | Y | Y | N | N |
| **CALIFORNIA** | | | | | | |
| 1 Thompson | N | Y | Y | Y | N | N |
| 2 Herger | N | N | N | Y | Y | N |
| 3 Lungren | N | N | N | Y | Y | Y |
| 4 Doolittle | N | N | N | Y | Y | Y |
| 5 Matsui, D. | Y | Y | Y | Y | ? | N |
| 6 Woolsey | Y | Y | Y | Y | N | N |
| 7 Miller, George | Y | Y | Y | Y | N | N |
| 8 Pelosi | Y | Y | Y | Y | N | N |
| 9 Lee | Y | Y | Y | Y | N | N |
| 10 Tauscher | Y | Y | Y | Y | N | N |
| 11 Pombo | N | N | N | Y | Y | Y |
| 12 Lantos | Y | Y | Y | Y | N | N |
| 13 Stark | Y | Y | Y | Y | N | N |
| 14 Eshoo | Y | Y | Y | Y | N | N |
| 15 Honda | Y | Y | Y | Y | N | N |
| 16 Lofgren | Y | Y | Y | Y | N | N |
| 17 Farr | Y | Y | Y | Y | N | N |
| 18 Cardoza | N | Y | Y | Y | N | N |
| 19 Radanovich | N | N | N | Y | Y | Y |
| 20 Costa | N | Y | Y | Y | N | N |
| 21 Nunes | N | N | N | Y | Y | Y |
| 22 Thomas | N | N | N | Y | Y | N |
| 23 Capps | Y | Y | Y | Y | N | N |
| 24 Gallegly | N | N | N | Y | Y | Y |
| 25 McKeon | N | N | N | Y | Y | N |
| 26 Dreier | N | N | N | Y | Y | N |
| 27 Sherman | Y | Y | Y | Y | N | N |
| 28 Berman | Y | Y | Y | Y | N | N |
| 29 Schiff | Y | Y | Y | Y | N | N |
| 30 Waxman | Y | Y | Y | Y | N | N |
| 31 Becerra | Y | Y | Y | Y | N | N |
| 32 Solis | Y | Y | Y | Y | N | N |
| 33 Watson | Y | Y | Y | Y | N | N |
| 34 Roybal-Allard | Y | Y | Y | Y | N | N |
| 35 Waters | Y | Y | Y | Y | N | N |
| 36 Harman | Y | Y | Y | Y | ? | ? |
| 37 Millender-McD. | ? | ? | ? | ? | ? | ? |
| 38 Napolitano | Y | Y | Y | Y | N | N |
| 39 Sánchez, Linda | Y | Y | Y | Y | N | N |
| 40 Royce | N | N | N | Y | Y | Y |
| 41 Lewis | N | N | N | Y | Y | N |
| 42 Miller, Gary | N | N | N | Y | Y | Y |
| 43 Baca | Y | Y | Y | Y | N | N |
| 44 Calvert | N | N | N | Y | Y | N |
| 45 Bono | N | N | N | Y | Y | N |
| 46 Rohrabacher | N | N | N | Y | Y | Y |
| 47 Sanchez, Loretta | Y | Y | Y | Y | N | N |
| 48 Cox | N | N | N | Y | Y | N |
| 49 Issa | N | N | N | Y | Y | N |
| **50 Cunningham** | N | N | N | Y | Y | N |
| 51 Filner | Y | Y | Y | Y | N | N |
| 52 Hunter | N | N | N | Y | Y | Y |
| 53 Davis | Y | Y | Y | Y | N | N |
| **COLORADO** | | | | | | |
| 1 DeGette | Y | Y | Y | Y | N | N |
| 2 Udall | Y | Y | Y | Y | ? | N |
| 3 Salazar | Y | Y | Y | Y | N | Y |
| 4 Musgrave | N | N | N | Y | Y | Y |
| 5 Hefley | N | N | N | Y | Y | Y |
| 6 Tancredo | ? | ? | ? | ? | ? | ? |
| 7 Beauprez | N | N | N | Y | Y | Y |
| **CONNECTICUT** | | | | | | |
| 1 Larson | + | + | + | + | − | − |
| 2 Simmons | N | N | N | Y | Y | N |
| 3 DeLauro | Y | Y | Y | Y | N | N |
| 4 Shays | N | Y | Y | Y | ? | Y |
| 5 Johnson | N | N | N | Y | Y | N |
| **DELAWARE** | | | | | | |
| AL Castle | N | N | N | Y | Y | N |
| **FLORIDA** | | | | | | |
| 1 Miller | N | N | N | Y | Y | Y |
| 2 Boyd | N | Y | Y | Y | N | N |
| 3 Brown | Y | Y | Y | Y | N | N |
| 4 Crenshaw | N | N | N | Y | Y | N |
| 5 Brown-Waite | N | N | N | Y | Y | Y |
| 6 Stearns | N | N | N | Y | Y | Y |
| 7 Mica | N | N | N | Y | Y | N |
| 8 Keller | N | N | N | Y | ? | N |
| 9 Bilirakis | N | N | N | Y | Y | N |
| 10 Young | N | N | N | Y | Y | N |
| 11 Davis | Y | Y | Y | Y | N | N |
| 12 Putnam | N | N | N | Y | Y | Y |
| 13 Harris | N | N | N | Y | Y | N |
| 14 Mack | N | N | N | Y | Y | Y |
| 15 Weldon | N | N | N | Y | Y | Y |
| 16 Foley | N | N | N | Y | Y | N |
| 17 Meek | Y | Y | Y | Y | N | N |
| 18 Ros-Lehtinen | N | N | N | Y | Y | N |
| 19 Wexler | Y | Y | Y | Y | N | N |
| 20 Wasserman-Schultz | Y | Y | Y | Y | N | N |
| 21 Diaz-Balart, L. | N | N | N | Y | Y | N |
| 22 Shaw | N | N | N | Y | Y | N |
| 23 Hastings | Y | Y | Y | Y | N | N |
| 24 Feeney | N | N | ? | Y | Y | Y |
| 25 Diaz-Balart, M. | N | N | N | Y | Y | Y |
| **GEORGIA** | | | | | | |
| 1 Kingston | N | N | N | Y | Y | N |
| 2 Bishop | Y | Y | Y | Y | N | N |
| 3 Marshall | Y | Y | Y | Y | N | N |
| 4 McKinney | Y | Y | Y | Y | N | N |
| 5 Lewis | ? | ? | ? | ? | ? | ? |
| 6 Price | N | N | N | Y | Y | N |
| 7 Linder | N | N | N | Y | Y | Y |
| 8 Westmoreland | N | N | N | Y | Y | Y |
| 9 Norwood | N | N | N | Y | Y | Y |
| 10 Deal | N | N | N | Y | Y | N |
| 11 Gingrey | N | N | N | Y | ? | Y |
| 12 Barrow | Y | Y | Y | Y | N | N |
| 13 Scott | N | Y | Y | Y | N | N |
| **HAWAII** | | | | | | |
| 1 Abercrombie | Y | Y | Y | Y | N | N |
| 2 Case | Y | Y | Y | Y | N | N |
| **IDAHO** | | | | | | |
| 1 Otter | N | N | N | Y | Y | Y |
| 2 Simpson | N | N | N | Y | ? | N |
| **ILLINOIS** | | | | | | |
| 1 Rush | Y | Y | Y | Y | N | N |
| 2 Jackson | Y | Y | Y | Y | N | N |
| 3 Lipinski | Y | Y | Y | Y | N | N |
| 4 Gutierrez | Y | Y | Y | N | N | N |
| 5 Emanuel | Y | Y | Y | Y | N | N |
| 6 Hyde | N | N | N | Y | Y | N |
| 7 Davis | Y | Y | Y | Y | N | N |
| 8 Bean | Y | Y | Y | Y | N | N |
| 9 Schakowsky | Y | Y | Y | Y | N | N |
| 10 Kirk | N | N | N | Y | Y | N |
| 11 Weller | N | N | N | Y | Y | Y |
| 12 Costello | Y | Y | Y | Y | N | N |

**KEY**   Republicans   Democrats   *Independents*

| | | | |
|---|---|---|---|
| Y | Voted for (yea) | X | Paired against |
| # | Paired for | − | Announced against |
| + | Announced for | P | Voted "present" |
| N | Voted against (nay) | | |

| | |
|---|---|
| C | Voted "present" to avoid possible conflict of interest |
| ? | Did not vote or otherwise make a position known |

| | 186 | 187 | 188 | 189 | 190 | 191 |
|---|---|---|---|---|---|---|
| 13 **Biggert** | N | N | N | Y | Y | N |
| 14 **Hastert** | | | | | | |
| 15 **Johnson** | N | N | N | Y | Y | N |
| 16 **Manzullo** | N | N | N | Y | Y | Y |
| 17 Evans | Y | Y | Y | Y | N | N |
| 18 **LaHood** | N | N | N | Y | Y | N |
| 19 **Shimkus** | N | N | N | Y | Y | N |
| **INDIANA** | | | | | | |
| 1 Visclosky | Y | Y | Y | Y | N | N |
| 2 **Chocola** | N | N | N | Y | Y | N |
| 3 **Souder** | N | N | N | Y | Y | N |
| 4 **Buyer** | N | N | N | Y | Y | Y |
| 5 **Burton** | N | N | N | Y | Y | Y |
| 6 **Pence** | N | N | N | Y | Y | Y |
| 7 Carson | Y | Y | Y | Y | N | N |
| 8 **Hostettler** | Y | N | N | Y | Y | Y |
| 9 **Sodrel** | N | N | N | Y | Y | N |
| **IOWA** | | | | | | |
| 1 **Nussle** | N | N | N | Y | Y | N |
| 2 **Leach** | Y | N | N | Y | Y | ? |
| 3 Boswell | Y | Y | Y | Y | N | N |
| 4 **Latham** | N | N | N | Y | Y | N |
| 5 **King** | N | N | N | Y | Y | Y |
| **KANSAS** | | | | | | |
| 1 **Moran** | N | N | N | Y | Y | N |
| 2 **Ryun** | N | N | N | Y | Y | Y |
| 3 Moore | Y | Y | Y | Y | N | N |
| 4 **Tiahrt** | N | N | N | Y | ? | Y |
| **KENTUCKY** | | | | | | |
| 1 **Whitfield** | N | N | N | Y | Y | N |
| 2 **Lewis** | N | N | N | Y | Y | Y |
| 3 **Northup** | N | N | N | Y | Y | N |
| 4 **Davis** | N | N | N | Y | Y | N |
| 5 **Rogers** | N | N | N | Y | Y | N |
| 6 Chandler | Y | Y | Y | Y | N | N |
| **LOUISIANA** | | | | | | |
| 1 **Jindal** | N | N | N | Y | Y | N |
| 2 Jefferson | Y | Y | Y | Y | N | N |
| 3 Melancon | Y | Y | Y | Y | N | N |
| 4 **McCrery** | N | N | N | Y | Y | N |
| 5 **Alexander** | N | N | N | Y | Y | N |
| 6 **Baker** | N | N | N | Y | Y | N |
| 7 **Boustany** | N | N | N | Y | ? | N |
| **MAINE** | | | | | | |
| 1 Allen | Y | Y | Y | Y | N | N |
| 2 Michaud | Y | Y | Y | Y | N | N |
| **MARYLAND** | | | | | | |
| 1 **Gilchrest** | N | N | N | Y | Y | N |
| 2 Ruppersberger | Y | Y | Y | Y | N | N |
| 3 Cardin | Y | Y | Y | Y | N | N |
| 4 Wynn | Y | Y | Y | Y | N | N |
| 5 Hoyer | Y | Y | Y | Y | N | N |
| 6 **Bartlett** | N | N | N | Y | Y | Y |
| 7 Cummings | Y | Y | Y | Y | N | N |
| 8 Van Hollen | Y | Y | Y | Y | N | N |
| **MASSACHUSETTS** | | | | | | |
| 1 Olver | Y | Y | Y | Y | N | N |
| 2 Neal | Y | Y | Y | Y | N | N |
| 3 McGovern | Y | Y | Y | Y | N | N |
| 4 Frank | Y | Y | Y | Y | N | N |
| 5 Meehan | Y | Y | Y | Y | N | N |
| 6 Tierney | N | Y | Y | Y | N | N |
| 7 Markey | Y | Y | Y | N | N | N |
| 8 Capuano | Y | Y | Y | Y | N | N |
| 9 Lynch | Y | Y | Y | Y | N | N |
| 10 Delahunt | Y | Y | Y | Y | N | N |
| **MICHIGAN** | | | | | | |
| 1 Stupak | Y | Y | Y | Y | N | N |
| 2 **Hoekstra** | N | N | N | Y | Y | Y |
| 3 **Ehlers** | N | N | N | Y | Y | N |
| 4 **Camp** | N | N | N | Y | Y | N |
| 5 Kildee | Y | Y | Y | Y | N | N |
| 6 **Upton** | N | N | N | Y | Y | N |
| 7 **Schwarz** | N | N | N | Y | Y | N |
| 8 **Rogers** | N | N | N | Y | Y | N |
| 9 **Knollenberg** | N | N | N | Y | Y | N |
| 10 **Miller** | N | N | N | Y | Y | N |
| 11 **McCotter** | N | N | N | Y | Y | N |
| 12 Levin | Y | Y | Y | Y | N | N |
| 13 Kilpatrick | Y | Y | Y | Y | N | N |
| 14 Conyers | Y | Y | Y | Y | N | N |
| 15 Dingell | Y | Y | Y | Y | N | N |
| **MINNESOTA** | | | | | | |
| 1 **Gutknecht** | N | N | N | Y | Y | Y |
| 2 **Kline** | N | N | N | Y | Y | Y |
| 3 **Ramstad** | N | N | N | Y | Y | N |
| 4 McCollum | Y | Y | Y | Y | N | N |
| 5 Sabo | Y | Y | Y | Y | N | N |
| 6 **Kennedy** | N | N | N | Y | Y | N |
| 7 Peterson | N | Y | Y | Y | N | Y |
| 8 Oberstar | Y | Y | Y | Y | N | N |
| **MISSISSIPPI** | | | | | | |
| 1 **Wicker** | N | N | N | Y | Y | N |
| 2 Thompson | Y | Y | Y | Y | N | N |
| 3 **Pickering** | N | N | N | Y | Y | N |
| 4 Taylor | N | N | Y | Y | N | Y |
| **MISSOURI** | | | | | | |
| 1 Clay | Y | Y | Y | Y | N | N |
| 2 **Akin** | N | N | N | Y | Y | Y |
| 3 Carnahan | Y | Y | Y | Y | N | N |
| 4 Skelton | N | Y | Y | Y | N | Y |
| 5 Cleaver | Y | Y | Y | Y | N | N |
| 6 **Graves** | N | N | N | Y | Y | Y |
| 7 **Blunt** | N | N | N | Y | Y | Y |
| 8 **Emerson** | N | N | N | Y | Y | Y |
| 9 **Hulshof** | N | N | N | Y | Y | Y |
| **MONTANA** | | | | | | |
| AL **Rehberg** | N | N | N | Y | Y | N |
| **NEBRASKA** | | | | | | |
| 1 **Fortenberry** | N | N | N | Y | Y | N |
| 2 **Terry** | N | N | N | Y | Y | N |
| 3 **Osborne** | N | N | N | Y | Y | N |
| **NEVADA** | | | | | | |
| 1 Berkley | Y | Y | Y | Y | N | Y |
| 2 **Gibbons** | N | N | N | Y | Y | Y |
| 3 **Porter** | N | N | N | Y | Y | N |
| **NEW HAMPSHIRE** | | | | | | |
| 1 **Bradley** | N | N | N | Y | Y | N |
| 2 **Bass** | N | N | N | Y | Y | N |
| **NEW JERSEY** | | | | | | |
| 1 Andrews | Y | Y | Y | Y | N | N |
| 2 **LoBiondo** | N | N | N | Y | Y | N |
| 3 **Saxton** | N | N | N | Y | Y | N |
| 4 **Smith** | N | N | N | Y | Y | N |
| 5 **Garrett** | N | N | N | Y | Y | Y |
| 6 Pallone | Y | Y | Y | Y | N | N |
| 7 **Ferguson** | N | N | N | Y | Y | N |
| 8 Pascrell | Y | Y | Y | Y | N | N |
| 9 Rothman | Y | Y | Y | Y | N | N |
| 10 Payne | Y | Y | Y | Y | N | N |
| 11 **Frelinghuysen** | N | N | N | Y | Y | N |
| 12 Holt | Y | Y | Y | Y | N | N |
| 13 Menendez | Y | Y | Y | Y | N | N |
| **NEW MEXICO** | | | | | | |
| 1 **Wilson** | N | N | N | Y | Y | Y |
| 2 **Pearce** | N | N | N | Y | Y | N |
| 3 Udall | Y | Y | Y | Y | N | N |
| **NEW YORK** | | | | | | |
| 1 Bishop | Y | Y | Y | Y | N | N |
| 2 Israel | Y | Y | Y | Y | N | N |
| 3 **King** | N | N | N | Y | Y | N |
| 4 McCarthy | Y | Y | Y | Y | N | N |
| 5 Ackerman | Y | Y | Y | Y | N | N |
| 6 Meeks | Y | Y | Y | Y | N | N |
| 7 Crowley | Y | Y | Y | Y | N | N |
| 8 Nadler | Y | Y | Y | Y | N | N |
| 9 Weiner | Y | Y | Y | Y | N | N |
| 10 Towns | Y | Y | Y | Y | N | N |
| 11 Owens | Y | Y | Y | Y | N | N |
| 12 Velázquez | Y | Y | Y | Y | N | N |
| 13 **Fossella** | N | N | N | Y | Y | N |
| 14 Maloney | Y | Y | Y | Y | N | N |
| 15 Rangel | Y | Y | Y | Y | N | N |
| 16 Serrano | Y | Y | Y | Y | N | N |
| 17 Engel | Y | Y | Y | Y | N | N |
| 18 Lowey | Y | Y | Y | Y | N | N |
| 19 **Kelly** | N | N | N | Y | Y | N |
| 20 **Sweeney** | N | N | N | Y | Y | N |
| 21 McNulty | Y | Y | Y | Y | N | N |
| 22 Hinchey | Y | Y | Y | Y | N | N |
| 23 **McHugh** | N | N | N | Y | Y | N |
| 24 **Boehlert** | N | N | N | Y | Y | N |
| 25 **Walsh** | N | N | N | Y | Y | N |
| 26 **Reynolds** | N | N | N | Y | Y | N |
| 27 Higgins | Y | Y | Y | Y | N | N |
| 28 Slaughter | Y | Y | Y | Y | N | N |
| 29 **Kuhl** | N | N | N | Y | Y | Y |
| **NORTH CAROLINA** | | | | | | |
| 1 Butterfield | Y | Y | Y | Y | N | N |
| 2 Etheridge | Y | Y | Y | Y | N | N |
| 3 **Jones** | N | N | N | Y | Y | Y |
| 4 Price | Y | Y | Y | Y | N | N |
| 5 **Foxx** | N | N | N | Y | Y | Y |
| 6 **Coble** | N | N | N | Y | Y | N |
| 7 McIntyre | Y | Y | Y | Y | N | N |
| 8 **Hayes** | N | N | N | Y | Y | N |
| 9 **Myrick** | N | N | N | Y | Y | Y |
| 10 **McHenry** | N | N | N | Y | Y | Y |
| 11 **Taylor** | ? | N | N | Y | Y | N |
| 12 Watt | Y | Y | Y | Y | N | N |
| 13 Miller | Y | Y | Y | Y | N | N |
| **NORTH DAKOTA** | | | | | | |
| AL Pomeroy | N | Y | Y | Y | N | Y |
| **OHIO** | | | | | | |
| 1 **Chabot** | N | N | N | Y | Y | Y |
| 2 Vacant | | | | | | |
| 3 **Turner** | N | N | N | Y | Y | N |
| 4 **Oxley** | N | N | N | Y | Y | N |
| 5 **Gillmor** | N | N | N | Y | Y | N |
| 6 Strickland | N | Y | Y | Y | ? | ? |
| 7 **Hobson** | N | N | N | Y | Y | N |
| 8 **Boehner** | N | N | N | Y | Y | Y |
| 9 Kaptur | Y | ? | Y | Y | N | N |
| 10 Kucinich | Y | Y | Y | Y | N | N |
| 11 Jones | Y | Y | Y | Y | N | N |
| 12 **Tiberi** | N | N | N | Y | Y | N |
| 13 Brown | Y | Y | Y | Y | N | N |
| 14 **LaTourette** | N | N | N | Y | Y | ? |
| 15 **Pryce** | N | N | N | Y | Y | N |
| 16 **Regula** | N | N | N | Y | Y | N |
| 17 Ryan | Y | Y | Y | Y | N | N |
| 18 **Ney** | N | N | N | Y | ? | N |
| **OKLAHOMA** | | | | | | |
| 1 **Sullivan** | N | N | N | Y | ? | Y |
| 2 Boren | N | N | Y | Y | N | N |
| 3 **Lucas** | ? | ? | ? | ? | ? | ? |
| 4 **Cole** | N | N | N | Y | Y | N |
| 5 **Istook** | N | N | N | Y | Y | Y |
| **OREGON** | | | | | | |
| 1 Wu | Y | Y | Y | Y | N | N |
| 2 **Walden** | N | N | N | Y | Y | N |
| 3 Blumenauer | N | Y | Y | Y | N | N |
| 4 DeFazio | Y | Y | Y | Y | N | N |
| 5 Hooley | Y | Y | Y | Y | N | N |
| **PENNSYLVANIA** | | | | | | |
| 1 Brady | Y | Y | Y | Y | N | N |
| 2 Fattah | Y | Y | Y | Y | ? | N |
| 3 **English** | N | N | N | Y | Y | N |
| 4 **Hart** | N | N | N | Y | Y | N |
| 5 **Peterson** | N | N | N | Y | Y | N |
| 6 **Gerlach** | N | N | N | Y | Y | N |
| 7 **Weldon** | N | N | N | Y | ? | ? |
| 8 **Fitzpatrick** | N | N | N | Y | Y | N |
| 9 **Shuster** | N | N | N | Y | Y | Y |
| 10 **Sherwood** | N | N | N | Y | Y | N |
| 11 Kanjorski | Y | Y | Y | Y | N | N |
| 12 Murtha | N | Y | Y | Y | N | N |
| 13 Schwartz | Y | Y | Y | Y | N | N |
| 14 Doyle | Y | Y | Y | Y | N | N |
| 15 **Dent** | N | N | N | Y | Y | N |
| 16 **Pitts** | N | N | N | Y | Y | Y |
| 17 Holden | Y | Y | Y | Y | N | N |
| 18 **Murphy** | N | N | N | Y | Y | N |
| 19 **Platts** | N | N | N | Y | Y | N |
| **RHODE ISLAND** | | | | | | |
| 1 Kennedy | Y | Y | Y | Y | N | N |
| 2 Langevin | Y | Y | Y | Y | N | N |
| **SOUTH CAROLINA** | | | | | | |
| 1 **Brown** | N | N | N | Y | Y | N |
| 2 **Wilson** | N | N | N | Y | Y | Y |
| 3 **Barrett** | N | N | N | Y | Y | Y |
| 4 **Inglis** | N | N | N | Y | Y | N |
| 5 Spratt | Y | Y | Y | Y | N | N |
| 6 Clyburn | Y | Y | Y | Y | N | N |
| **SOUTH DAKOTA** | | | | | | |
| AL Herseth | N | Y | Y | Y | N | N |
| **TENNESSEE** | | | | | | |
| 1 **Jenkins** | N | N | N | Y | Y | Y |
| 2 **Duncan** | N | N | N | Y | Y | N |
| 3 **Wamp** | N | N | N | Y | Y | N |
| 4 Davis | Y | Y | Y | Y | N | N |
| 5 Cooper | Y | Y | Y | Y | N | N |
| 6 Gordon | Y | Y | Y | Y | N | N |
| 7 **Blackburn** | N | N | N | Y | Y | Y |
| 8 Tanner | N | Y | Y | Y | N | Y |
| 9 Ford | Y | Y | Y | Y | N | N |
| **TEXAS** | | | | | | |
| 1 **Gohmert** | N | N | N | Y | Y | Y |
| 2 **Poe** | N | N | N | Y | Y | Y |
| 3 **Johnson, S.** | N | N | N | Y | Y | Y |
| 4 **Hall** | N | N | N | Y | Y | Y |
| 5 **Hensarling** | N | N | N | Y | Y | Y |
| 6 **Barton** | N | N | N | Y | Y | Y |
| 7 **Culberson** | N | N | N | Y | Y | Y |
| 8 **Brady** | N | N | N | Y | Y | Y |
| 9 Green | Y | Y | Y | Y | N | N |
| 10 **McCaul** | N | N | N | Y | Y | N |
| 11 **Conaway** | N | N | N | Y | Y | + |
| 12 **Granger** | N | N | N | Y | Y | N |
| 13 **Thornberry** | N | N | N | Y | Y | Y |
| 14 **Paul** | N | N | N | N | Y | Y |
| 15 Hinojosa | Y | Y | Y | Y | N | N |
| 16 Reyes | Y | Y | Y | Y | N | N |
| 17 Edwards | Y | Y | Y | Y | N | N |
| 18 Jackson-Lee | Y | Y | Y | Y | ? | ? |
| 19 **Neugebauer** | N | N | N | Y | Y | Y |
| 20 Gonzalez | Y | Y | Y | Y | N | N |
| 21 **Smith** | N | N | N | Y | Y | N |
| 22 **DeLay** | N | N | N | Y | Y | Y |
| 23 **Bonilla** | N | N | N | Y | Y | N |
| 24 **Marchant** | N | N | N | Y | Y | Y |
| 25 Doggett | Y | Y | Y | Y | N | N |
| 26 **Burgess** | N | N | N | Y | ? | Y |
| 27 Ortiz | Y | Y | Y | Y | N | N |
| 28 Cuellar | Y | Y | Y | Y | N | N |
| 29 Green | Y | N | Y | Y | N | N |
| 30 Johnson, E. | Y | Y | Y | Y | N | N |
| 31 **Carter** | N | N | N | Y | Y | N |
| 32 **Sessions** | N | N | N | Y | Y | Y |
| **UTAH** | | | | | | |
| 1 **Bishop** | N | N | N | Y | Y | Y |
| 2 Matheson | Y | Y | Y | Y | N | N |
| 3 **Cannon** | N | N | N | Y | Y | Y |
| **VERMONT** | | | | | | |
| AL *Sanders* | Y | Y | Y | Y | N | N |
| **VIRGINIA** | | | | | | |
| 1 **Davis, J.** | N | N | N | Y | Y | Y |
| 2 **Drake** | N | N | N | Y | Y | N |
| 3 Scott | Y | Y | Y | Y | N | N |
| 4 **Forbes** | N | N | N | Y | Y | Y |
| 5 **Goode** | N | N | N | Y | Y | Y |
| 6 **Goodlatte** | N | N | N | Y | Y | Y |
| 7 **Cantor** | N | N | N | Y | ? | N |
| 8 Moran | Y | Y | Y | Y | N | N |
| 9 Boucher | Y | Y | Y | Y | N | N |
| 10 **Wolf** | N | N | N | Y | Y | N |
| 11 **Davis, T.** | N | N | N | Y | Y | N |
| **WASHINGTON** | | | | | | |
| 1 Inslee | Y | Y | Y | Y | N | N |
| 2 Larsen | Y | Y | Y | Y | N | N |
| 3 Baird | Y | Y | N | Y | N | N |
| 4 **Hastings** | N | N | N | Y | Y | Y |
| 5 **McMorris** | N | N | N | Y | Y | Y |
| 6 Dicks | Y | Y | Y | Y | N | N |
| 7 McDermott | Y | ? | Y | Y | N | N |
| 8 **Reichert** | N | N | N | Y | Y | N |
| 9 Smith | Y | Y | Y | Y | N | N |
| **WEST VIRGINIA** | | | | | | |
| 1 Mollohan | N | Y | Y | Y | N | N |
| 2 **Capito** | N | N | N | Y | Y | N |
| 3 Rahall | N | Y | Y | Y | N | N |
| **WISCONSIN** | | | | | | |
| 1 **Ryan** | N | N | N | Y | ? | Y |
| 2 Baldwin | Y | Y | Y | Y | N | N |
| 3 Kind | Y | Y | Y | Y | N | N |
| 4 Moore | Y | Y | Y | Y | N | N |
| 5 **Sensenbrenner** | N | N | N | Y | Y | Y |
| 6 **Petri** | N | N | N | Y | Y | Y |
| 7 Obey | Y | Y | Y | N | N | N |
| 8 **Green** | N | N | N | Y | Y | Y |
| **WYOMING** | | | | | | |
| AL **Cubin** | N | N | N | Y | Y | Y |

# IN THE HOUSE | By Vote Number

**192.** HR 2361. Fiscal 2006 Interior and Environment Appropriations/ **Natural Gas Moratorium.** Peterson, R-Pa., amendment that would lift the moratorium on natural gas production in the Outer Continental Shelf. Rejected 157-262: R 130-93; D 27-168 (ND 8-138, SD 19-30); I 0-1. May 19, 2005.

**193.** HR 2361. Fiscal 2006 Interior and Environment Appropriations/ **Hazardous Substance Superfund.** Terry, R-Neb., amendment that would increase funding for the superfund hazardous waste cleanup program by $130 million, offset by a cut in the EPA's Science and Technology account. Rejected 76-344: R 42-181; D 34-162 (ND 28-119, SD 6-43); I 0-1. May 19, 2005.

**194.** HR 2361. Fiscal 2006 Interior and Environment Appropriations/ **Clean Water Revolving Fund.** Obey, D-Wis., amendment that would increase the Clean Water State Revolving Fund by $100 million, offset by a cut in state and tribal assistance grants. Rejected 186-235: R 6-218; D 179-17 (ND 133-14, SD 46-3); I 1-0. May 19, 2005.

**195.** HR 2361. Fiscal 2006 Interior and Environment Appropriations/ **Forest Service Funding.** Beauprez, R-Colo., amendment that would increase funding for the Forest Service by $27.5 million, offset by reducing funds for the National Endowment for the Arts by $30 million. Rejected 122-298: R 116-108; D 6-189 (ND 4-143, SD 2-46); I 0-1. May 19, 2005.

**196.** HR 2361. Fiscal 2006 Interior and Environment Appropriations/ **Wild Horses and Burros.** Rahall, D-W.Va., amendment that would prohibit the use of funds in the bill for the sale or slaughter of wild horses and burros. Adopted 249-159: R 78-140; D 170-19 (ND 132-11, SD 38-8); I 1-0. May 19, 2005.

**197.** HR 2361. Fiscal 2006 Interior and Environment Appropriations/ **Across-the-Board Cut.** Hefley, R-Colo., amendment that would require a 1 percent across-the-board cut to discretionary spending. Rejected 90-326: R 87-134; D 3-191 (ND 1-144, SD 2-47); I 0-1. May 19, 2005.

**198.** HR 2361. Fiscal 2006 Interior and Environment Appropriations/ **Recommit.** Obey, D-Wis., motion to recommit the bill to the House Appropriations Committee with instructions to include language that would add $242 million for the Clean Water State Revolving Fund and $110 million for State and Tribal Assistance Grants. Motion rejected 191-228: R 0-223; D 190-5 (ND 141-5, SD 49-0); I 1-0. May 19, 2005.

**199.** HR 2361. Fiscal 2006 Interior and Environment Appropriations/ **Passage.** Passage of the bill that would provide $26.2 billion in fiscal 2006 for the Department of Interior, the EPA and related agencies. The bill would provide $9.8 billion for the Interior Department, $7.7 billion for the EPA, $4.2 billion for the Forest Service and $3.1 billion for the Indian Health Service. The National Endowment for the Arts would receive $131 million and the National Endowment for the Humanities would be funded at $143 million. It would maintain the moratorium on natural gas production in the Outer Continental Shelf. Passed 329-89: R 214-8; D 115-80 (ND 75-71, SD 40-9); I 0-1. May 19, 2005.

| | 192 | 193 | 194 | 195 | 196 | 197 | 198 | 199 |
|---|---|---|---|---|---|---|---|---|
| **ALABAMA** | | | | | | | | |
| 1 Bonner | Y | N | N | N | N | N | N | Y |
| 2 Everett | Y | N | N | Y | Y | Y | N | Y |
| 3 Rogers | N | N | N | Y | N | N | N | Y |
| 4 Aderholt | Y | N | N | N | N | N | N | Y |
| 5 Cramer | Y | N | Y | N | Y | N | Y | Y |
| 6 Bachus | Y | N | N | Y | N | N | N | Y |
| 7 Davis | N | N | Y | N | Y | N | Y | Y |
| **ALASKA** | | | | | | | | |
| AL Young | Y | N | N | Y | ? | ? | ? | ? |
| **ARIZONA** | | | | | | | | |
| 1 Renzi | Y | N | N | Y | N | N | N | Y |
| 2 Franks | Y | N | N | Y | Y | Y | N | N |
| 3 Shadegg | Y | N | N | Y | N | Y | N | Y |
| 4 Pastor | N | N | Y | N | Y | N | Y | N |
| 5 Hayworth | Y | Y | N | Y | N | N | N | Y |
| 6 Flake | Y | Y | N | Y | N | Y | N | N |
| 7 Grijalva | N | N | Y | N | Y | N | Y | N |
| 8 Kolbe | Y | ? | N | N | N | N | N | Y |
| **ARKANSAS** | | | | | | | | |
| 1 Berry | Y | N | Y | N | Y | N | Y | N |
| 2 Snyder | N | N | Y | N | Y | N | Y | Y |
| 3 Boozman | Y | N | N | N | N | N | N | Y |
| 4 Ross | Y | N | Y | N | N | N | Y | Y |
| **CALIFORNIA** | | | | | | | | |
| 1 Thompson | N | N | Y | N | Y | N | Y | Y |
| 2 Herger | Y | N | N | Y | N | Y | N | Y |
| 3 Lungren | Y | N | N | Y | N | N | N | Y |
| 4 Doolittle | Y | N | N | Y | N | N | N | Y |
| 5 Matsui, D. | N | Y | Y | N | Y | N | Y | N |
| 6 Woolsey | N | N | Y | N | Y | N | Y | N |
| 7 Miller, George | N | N | Y | N | Y | N | Y | N |
| 8 Pelosi | N | N | Y | N | Y | N | Y | N |
| 9 Lee | N | N | Y | N | Y | N | Y | N |
| 10 Tauscher | N | N | Y | N | Y | N | Y | N |
| 11 Pombo | N | N | N | Y | N | N | N | Y |
| 12 Lantos | N | N | Y | N | Y | N | Y | N |
| 13 Stark | N | N | Y | N | Y | N | Y | N |
| 14 Eshoo | N | N | Y | N | Y | N | Y | N |
| 15 Honda | N | N | Y | N | Y | N | Y | N |
| 16 Lofgren | N | N | Y | N | Y | N | Y | N |
| 17 Farr | N | N | Y | N | Y | N | Y | Y |
| 18 Cardoza | N | N | Y | N | N | N | Y | Y |
| 19 Radanovich | N | N | N | N | ? | ? | ? | ? |
| 20 Costa | N | N | Y | N | N | N | Y | Y |
| 21 Nunes | Y | N | N | Y | N | N | N | Y |
| 22 Thomas | Y | N | N | N | N | N | N | Y |
| 23 Capps | N | N | Y | N | Y | N | Y | N |
| 24 Gallegly | N | N | N | Y | Y | N | N | Y |
| 25 McKeon | N | N | N | Y | N | N | N | Y |
| 26 Dreier | N | N | N | Y | N | N | N | Y |
| 27 Sherman | N | N | Y | N | Y | N | Y | N |
| 28 Berman | N | N | Y | N | Y | N | Y | N |
| 29 Schiff | N | N | Y | N | Y | N | Y | Y |
| 30 Waxman | N | N | Y | N | Y | N | Y | N |
| 31 Becerra | N | N | Y | N | Y | N | Y | N |
| 32 Solis | N | N | Y | N | Y | N | Y | N |
| 33 Watson | N | N | Y | N | Y | N | Y | N |
| 34 Roybal-Allard | N | N | Y | N | Y | N | Y | N |
| 35 Waters | N | N | Y | N | Y | N | Y | N |
| 36 Harman | ? | ? | ? | ? | ? | ? | ? | ? |
| 37 Millender-McD. | ? | ? | ? | ? | ? | ? | ? | ? |
| 38 Napolitano | N | N | N | N | Y | N | Y | N |
| 39 Sánchez, Linda | N | N | Y | N | Y | N | Y | N |
| 40 Royce | N | N | Y | N | Y | N | N | Y |
| 41 Lewis | N | N | Y | N | N | N | N | Y |
| 42 Miller, Gary | Y | Y | N | Y | N | Y | N | Y |
| 43 Baca | N | N | Y | N | Y | N | Y | Y |
| 44 Calvert | N | N | Y | N | N | N | N | Y |
| 45 Bono | N | N | N | N | N | N | N | Y |
| 46 Rohrabacher | Y | N | N | Y | N | Y | N | N |
| 47 Sanchez, Loretta | N | N | Y | N | Y | N | Y | N |
| 48 Cox | N | N | Y | N | ? | N | N | Y |
| 49 Issa | N | N | N | Y | Y | Y | N | Y |

| | 192 | 193 | 194 | 195 | 196 | 197 | 198 | 199 |
|---|---|---|---|---|---|---|---|---|
| 50 Cunningham | N | N | N | Y | N | N | N | Y |
| 51 Filner | N | N | Y | N | Y | N | Y | Y |
| 52 Hunter | Y | N | N | Y | N | Y | N | Y |
| 53 Davis | N | N | Y | N | Y | N | Y | Y |
| **COLORADO** | | | | | | | | |
| 1 DeGette | N | N | Y | N | Y | N | Y | N |
| 2 Udall | N | N | Y | Y | Y | N | Y | N |
| 3 Salazar | Y | Y | Y | Y | N | N | Y | N |
| 4 Musgrave | Y | Y | N | Y | N | Y | N | Y |
| 5 Hefley | Y | N | N | Y | N | Y | N | Y |
| 6 Tancredo | ? | ? | ? | ? | ? | ? | ? | ? |
| 7 Beauprez | Y | N | N | Y | N | Y | N | Y |
| **CONNECTICUT** | | | | | | | | |
| 1 Larson | – | – | + | – | + | – | + | – |
| 2 Simmons | N | N | N | N | Y | N | Y | Y |
| 3 DeLauro | N | N | Y | N | Y | N | Y | N |
| 4 Shays | ? | ? | ? | ? | ? | ? | ? | ? |
| 5 Johnson | Y | N | Y | N | Y | N | N | Y |
| **DELAWARE** | | | | | | | | |
| AL Castle | N | N | N | N | Y | N | N | Y |
| **FLORIDA** | | | | | | | | |
| 1 Miller | N | Y | N | Y | N | Y | N | Y |
| 2 Boyd | N | N | Y | N | N | N | N | Y |
| 3 Brown | N | N | Y | N | Y | N | Y | N |
| 4 Crenshaw | N | N | N | N | N | N | N | Y |
| 5 Brown-Waite | N | N | Y | Y | N | Y | N | N |
| 6 Stearns | N | N | Y | N | N | N | N | Y |
| 7 Mica | Y | N | N | N | N | N | N | Y |
| 8 Keller | N | N | N | Y | Y | Y | N | Y |
| 9 Bilirakis | N | N | N | Y | Y | N | N | Y |
| 10 Young | N | N | N | N | N | N | N | Y |
| 11 Davis | N | Y | Y | N | N | N | N | Y |
| 12 Putnam | N | N | N | N | N | N | N | Y |
| 13 Harris | N | N | N | Y | Y | N | N | Y |
| 14 Mack | N | N | N | Y | N | Y | N | Y |
| 15 Weldon | N | N | N | Y | N | N | N | Y |
| 16 Foley | N | N | N | N | Y | Y | N | Y |
| 17 Meek | N | N | Y | N | Y | N | Y | Y |
| 18 Ros-Lehtinen | N | N | N | Y | N | N | N | Y |
| 19 Wexler | N | N | Y | N | Y | N | Y | N |
| 20 Wasserman-Schultz | N | N | Y | N | Y | N | Y | N |
| 21 Diaz-Balart, L. | N | N | N | Y | N | N | N | Y |
| 22 Shaw | N | N | N | N | N | N | N | Y |
| 23 Hastings | N | N | Y | N | Y | N | Y | N |
| 24 Feeney | N | N | N | Y | N | Y | N | Y |
| 25 Diaz-Balart, M. | N | N | N | Y | Y | Y | N | Y |
| **GEORGIA** | | | | | | | | |
| 1 Kingston | N | N | Y | N | Y | N | N | Y |
| 2 Bishop | N | N | Y | N | Y | N | Y | Y |
| 3 Marshall | Y | N | N | N | N | Y | Y | Y |
| 4 McKinney | N | Y | Y | N | Y | N | Y | N |
| 5 Lewis | ? | ? | ? | ? | ? | ? | ? | ? |
| 6 Price | Y | N | N | Y | N | Y | N | Y |
| 7 Linder | Y | N | N | Y | N | Y | N | Y |
| 8 Westmoreland | Y | N | N | Y | N | Y | N | Y |
| 9 Norwood | Y | Y | N | Y | Y | Y | N | Y |
| 10 Deal | Y | Y | N | Y | Y | N | N | Y |
| 11 Gingrey | Y | N | N | Y | N | Y | N | Y |
| 12 Barrow | N | Y | Y | N | + | N | Y | Y |
| 13 Scott | N | N | N | N | Y | N | Y | Y |
| **HAWAII** | | | | | | | | |
| 1 Abercrombie | Y | N | N | N | Y | N | N | Y |
| 2 Case | N | N | Y | N | Y | N | N | Y |
| **IDAHO** | | | | | | | | |
| 1 Otter | Y | N | N | Y | N | Y | N | Y |
| 2 Simpson | Y | N | N | N | N | N | N | Y |
| **ILLINOIS** | | | | | | | | |
| 1 Rush | N | N | Y | N | Y | N | Y | Y |
| 2 Jackson | N | N | Y | N | Y | N | Y | N |
| 3 Lipinski | N | N | Y | N | Y | N | Y | N |
| 4 Gutierrez | ? | Y | Y | N | Y | N | Y | N |
| 5 Emanuel | N | N | Y | N | Y | N | Y | N |
| 6 Hyde | Y | N | N | N | N | N | N | Y |
| 7 Davis | N | N | Y | N | Y | N | Y | N |
| 8 Bean | N | Y | Y | Y | Y | Y | Y | Y |
| 9 Schakowsky | N | N | Y | N | Y | N | Y | N |
| 10 Kirk | N | N | Y | N | N | N | N | Y |
| 11 Weller | Y | Y | N | Y | Y | N | N | Y |
| 12 Costello | N | Y | Y | N | Y | N | Y | N |

ND Northern Democrats, SD Southern Democrats
Southern states: Ala., Ark., Fla., Ga., Ky., La., Miss., N.C., Okla., S.C., Tenn., Texas, Va.

| | 192 | 193 | 194 | 195 | 196 | 197 | 198 | 199 |
|---|---|---|---|---|---|---|---|---|
| 13 **Biggert** | N | N | N | N | Y | N | N | Y |
| 14 **Hastert** | | | | | | | | |
| 15 **Johnson** | N | N | Y | N | Y | N | N | Y |
| 16 **Manzullo** | Y | N | N | Y | N | Y | N | Y |
| 17 Evans | N | N | Y | N | Y | N | Y | Y |
| 18 **LaHood** | N | N | N | N | N | N | N | Y |
| 19 **Shimkus** | Y | Y | N | Y | N | Y | N | Y |
| **INDIANA** | | | | | | | | |
| 1 Visclosky | N | N | Y | N | Y | N | Y | Y |
| 2 **Chocola** | Y | Y | N | N | N | Y | N | Y |
| 3 **Souder** | Y | N | N | Y | N | N | N | Y |
| 4 **Buyer** | Y | N | N | Y | N | Y | N | Y |
| 5 **Burton** | Y | N | N | Y | N | Y | N | Y |
| 6 **Pence** | Y | Y | N | Y | Y | Y | N | Y |
| 7 Carson | N | N | Y | N | Y | N | Y | Y |
| 8 **Hostettler** | Y | Y | N | Y | Y | Y | N | N |
| 9 **Sodrel** | Y | N | N | N | N | N | N | Y |
| **IOWA** | | | | | | | | |
| 1 **Nussle** | N | N | N | Y | N | N | N | Y |
| 2 **Leach** | ? | ? | ? | ? | ? | ? | ? | ? |
| 3 Boswell | N | N | Y | N | N | N | Y | Y |
| 4 **Latham** | N | N | N | Y | N | N | N | Y |
| 5 **King** | Y | Y | N | Y | N | Y | N | Y |
| **KANSAS** | | | | | | | | |
| 1 **Moran** | Y | Y | N | N | N | Y | N | Y |
| 2 **Ryun** | Y | N | N | Y | N | Y | N | Y |
| 3 Moore | N | N | Y | N | Y | N | Y | Y |
| 4 **Tiahrt** | Y | N | N | Y | N | N | N | Y |
| **KENTUCKY** | | | | | | | | |
| 1 **Whitfield** | N | N | N | N | Y | N | N | Y |
| 2 **Lewis** | Y | N | N | Y | N | Y | N | Y |
| 3 **Northup** | Y | N | N | N | N | N | N | Y |
| 4 **Davis** | N | N | N | N | N | N | N | Y |
| 5 **Rogers** | Y | N | N | N | N | N | N | Y |
| 6 Chandler | N | N | Y | N | N | N | Y | N |
| **LOUISIANA** | | | | | | | | |
| 1 **Jindal** | Y | Y | N | N | N | Y | N | Y |
| 2 Jefferson | Y | N | Y | N | Y | N | Y | Y |
| 3 Melancon | Y | N | Y | N | N | N | Y | Y |
| 4 **McCrery** | Y | N | N | N | N | N | N | Y |
| 5 **Alexander** | Y | N | N | N | N | N | N | Y |
| 6 **Baker** | Y | N | N | N | N | Y | N | Y |
| 7 **Boustany** | Y | N | N | Y | N | N | N | Y |
| **MAINE** | | | | | | | | |
| 1 Allen | N | N | Y | N | Y | N | Y | N |
| 2 Michaud | N | N | Y | N | Y | N | Y | N |
| **MARYLAND** | | | | | | | | |
| 1 **Gilchrest** | N | N | N | N | N | N | N | Y |
| 2 Ruppersberger | N | Y | Y | N | Y | N | Y | Y |
| 3 Cardin | N | N | Y | N | Y | N | Y | N |
| 4 Wynn | N | Y | Y | N | Y | N | Y | Y |
| 5 Hoyer | N | N | Y | N | Y | N | Y | N |
| 6 **Bartlett** | N | N | N | Y | Y | Y | N | Y |
| 7 Cummings | N | N | Y | N | Y | N | Y | Y |
| 8 Van Hollen | N | N | Y | N | Y | N | Y | N |
| **MASSACHUSETTS** | | | | | | | | |
| 1 Olver | N | N | N | N | Y | N | Y | Y |
| 2 Neal | N | N | Y | N | Y | N | Y | N |
| 3 McGovern | N | N | Y | N | Y | N | Y | N |
| 4 Frank | N | Y | Y | N | ? | N | Y | N |
| 5 Meehan | N | N | Y | N | Y | N | Y | Y |
| 6 Tierney | N | N | Y | N | Y | N | Y | N |
| 7 Markey | N | Y | Y | N | Y | N | Y | N |
| 8 Capuano | N | Y | N | N | Y | N | N | Y |
| 9 Lynch | N | N | Y | N | ? | N | Y | Y |
| 10 Delahunt | N | N | Y | N | Y | N | Y | Y |
| **MICHIGAN** | | | | | | | | |
| 1 Stupak | N | Y | N | N | Y | N | Y | Y |
| 2 **Hoekstra** | Y | N | N | Y | N | Y | N | Y |
| 3 **Ehlers** | N | N | N | N | Y | N | N | Y |
| 4 **Camp** | N | Y | N | N | N | N | N | Y |
| 5 Kildee | N | N | Y | N | Y | N | Y | Y |
| 6 **Upton** | Y | N | N | N | Y | N | N | Y |
| 7 **Schwarz** | N | N | N | N | N | N | N | Y |
| 8 **Rogers** | N | N | N | N | Y | Y | N | Y |
| 9 **Knollenberg** | N | N | N | N | N | N | N | Y |
| 10 **Miller** | N | N | N | N | Y | N | N | Y |
| 11 **McCotter** | N | N | N | N | Y | Y | N | Y |
| 12 Levin | N | N | Y | N | Y | N | Y | Y |
| 13 Kilpatrick | N | N | Y | N | Y | N | Y | Y |
| 14 Conyers | N | N | Y | N | Y | N | Y | N |
| 15 Dingell | N | Y | Y | N | N | N | Y | N |
| **MINNESOTA** | | | | | | | | |
| 1 **Gutknecht** | Y | N | N | Y | N | Y | N | Y |
| 2 **Kline** | Y | N | N | Y | N | N | N | Y |
| 3 **Ramstad** | N | Y | Y | N | Y | Y | N | Y |
| 4 McCollum | N | N | Y | N | Y | N | Y | N |
| 5 Sabo | Y | N | Y | N | N | N | Y | Y |
| 6 **Kennedy** | N | Y | Y | Y | Y | Y | N | Y |
| 7 Peterson | Y | N | Y | N | N | N | Y | Y |
| 8 Oberstar | Y | N | Y | N | N | N | Y | N |
| **MISSISSIPPI** | | | | | | | | |
| 1 **Wicker** | Y | N | N | Y | N | N | N | Y |
| 2 Thompson | N | N | Y | N | Y | N | Y | Y |
| 3 **Pickering** | Y | N | N | Y | N | N | N | Y |
| 4 Taylor | Y | Y | Y | Y | Y | Y | Y | N |
| **MISSOURI** | | | | | | | | |
| 1 Clay | N | N | Y | N | ? | ? | ? | ? |
| 2 **Akin** | Y | Y | N | Y | N | Y | N | Y |
| 3 Carnahan | N | N | Y | N | Y | N | Y | Y |
| 4 Skelton | N | N | Y | N | Y | N | Y | Y |
| 5 Cleaver | N | N | Y | N | Y | N | Y | Y |
| 6 **Graves** | Y | N | N | Y | N | Y | N | Y |
| 7 **Blunt** | N | N | N | N | N | N | N | Y |
| 8 **Emerson** | Y | N | N | Y | N | N | N | Y |
| 9 **Hulshof** | Y | N | N | N | N | N | N | Y |
| **MONTANA** | | | | | | | | |
| AL **Rehberg** | N | N | N | N | N | N | N | Y |
| **NEBRASKA** | | | | | | | | |
| 1 **Fortenberry** | Y | Y | N | N | N | N | N | Y |
| 2 **Terry** | Y | Y | N | N | N | Y | N | Y |
| 3 **Osborne** | Y | Y | N | N | N | N | N | Y |
| **NEVADA** | | | | | | | | |
| 1 Berkley | N | N | Y | N | Y | N | Y | N |
| 2 **Gibbons** | Y | N | N | Y | N | Y | N | Y |
| 3 **Porter** | Y | N | N | Y | N | N | N | Y |
| **NEW HAMPSHIRE** | | | | | | | | |
| 1 **Bradley** | N | Y | N | N | Y | N | N | Y |
| 2 **Bass** | N | N | N | N | Y | N | N | Y |
| **NEW JERSEY** | | | | | | | | |
| 1 Andrews | N | N | Y | N | Y | N | Y | Y |
| 2 **LoBiondo** | N | Y | N | N | Y | N | N | Y |
| 3 **Saxton** | N | Y | N | N | Y | N | N | Y |
| 4 **Smith** | N | N | N | N | Y | N | N | Y |
| 5 **Garrett** | Y | N | N | Y | N | Y | N | Y |
| 6 Pallone | N | Y | Y | N | Y | N | Y | N |
| 7 **Ferguson** | N | N | N | N | Y | N | N | Y |
| 8 Pascrell | N | Y | Y | N | Y | N | Y | N |
| 9 Rothman | N | N | Y | N | Y | N | Y | Y |
| 10 Payne | N | N | Y | N | Y | N | Y | N |
| 11 **Frelinghuysen** | N | N | N | N | Y | N | N | Y |
| 12 Holt | N | N | Y | N | Y | N | Y | N |
| 13 Menendez | N | Y | Y | N | Y | N | Y | N |
| **NEW MEXICO** | | | | | | | | |
| 1 **Wilson** | Y | N | N | Y | Y | N | N | Y |
| 2 **Pearce** | Y | Y | N | N | N | N | N | Y |
| 3 Udall | N | N | Y | N | Y | N | Y | Y |
| **NEW YORK** | | | | | | | | |
| 1 Bishop | N | N | Y | N | Y | N | Y | N |
| 2 Israel | N | N | Y | N | Y | N | Y | N |
| 3 **King** | Y | N | N | N | Y | N | N | Y |
| 4 McCarthy | N | N | Y | N | Y | N | Y | N |
| 5 Ackerman | N | N | Y | N | Y | N | Y | N |
| 6 Meeks | N | N | Y | N | Y | N | Y | Y |
| 7 Crowley | N | N | Y | N | Y | N | Y | Y |
| 8 Nadler | N | Y | Y | N | Y | N | Y | N |
| 9 Weiner | N | N | Y | N | Y | N | Y | Y |
| 10 Towns | N | N | Y | N | Y | N | Y | Y |
| 11 Owens | N | N | Y | N | Y | N | Y | N |
| 12 Velázquez | N | N | Y | N | Y | N | Y | N |
| 13 **Fossella** | N | N | N | N | Y | N | N | Y |
| 14 Maloney | N | Y | Y | N | Y | N | Y | Y |
| 15 Rangel | N | N | Y | N | Y | N | Y | Y |
| 16 Serrano | N | N | Y | N | Y | N | Y | Y |
| 17 Engel | N | N | Y | N | Y | N | Y | Y |
| 18 Lowey | N | N | N | N | Y | N | Y | Y |
| 19 **Kelly** | N | Y | Y | N | Y | N | N | Y |
| 20 **Sweeney** | N | N | N | N | Y | N | N | Y |
| 21 McNulty | N | N | Y | N | Y | N | Y | Y |
| 22 Hinchey | N | Y | Y | N | Y | N | Y | Y |
| 23 **McHugh** | Y | N | N | N | Y | N | N | Y |
| 24 **Boehlert** | N | N | N | N | N | N | N | Y |
| 25 **Walsh** | N | N | N | N | N | N | N | Y |
| 26 **Reynolds** | N | N | N | N | Y | N | N | Y |
| 27 Higgins | N | N | Y | N | Y | N | Y | Y |
| 28 Slaughter | N | N | Y | N | Y | N | Y | Y |
| 29 **Kuhl** | Y | N | N | Y | Y | N | N | Y |
| **NORTH CAROLINA** | | | | | | | | |
| 1 Butterfield | N | N | Y | ? | Y | N | Y | Y |
| 2 Etheridge | N | N | Y | N | Y | N | Y | N |
| 3 **Jones** | N | N | N | Y | Y | Y | N | N |
| 4 Price | N | N | Y | N | Y | N | Y | Y |
| 5 **Foxx** | Y | N | N | Y | N | Y | N | Y |
| 6 **Coble** | Y | N | N | Y | N | N | N | Y |
| 7 McIntyre | N | N | N | N | N | N | Y | Y |
| 8 **Hayes** | Y | N | N | Y | N | N | N | Y |
| 9 **Myrick** | Y | N | N | Y | Y | Y | N | Y |
| 10 **McHenry** | Y | N | N | Y | N | Y | N | Y |
| 11 **Taylor** | N | N | N | N | N | N | N | Y |
| 12 Watt | N | N | Y | N | Y | N | Y | Y |
| 13 Miller | N | N | Y | N | Y | N | Y | Y |
| **NORTH DAKOTA** | | | | | | | | |
| AL Pomeroy | N | N | Y | N | N | N | Y | Y |
| **OHIO** | | | | | | | | |
| 1 **Chabot** | N | N | N | Y | Y | Y | N | Y |
| 2 Vacant | | | | | | | | |
| 3 **Turner** | N | N | N | N | Y | N | N | Y |
| 4 **Oxley** | Y | N | N | N | N | N | N | Y |
| 5 **Gillmor** | N | N | N | N | N | N | N | Y |
| 6 Strickland | ? | ? | ? | ? | ? | ? | ? | ? |
| 7 **Hobson** | N | N | N | N | Y | N | N | Y |
| 8 **Boehner** | Y | Y | N | Y | N | N | N | Y |
| 9 Kaptur | N | N | Y | N | Y | N | Y | Y |
| 10 Kucinich | N | N | Y | N | Y | N | Y | N |
| 11 Jones | N | N | N | N | Y | ? | Y | N |
| 12 **Tiberi** | Y | N | N | N | N | N | N | Y |
| 13 Brown | N | N | Y | N | ? | N | Y | N |
| 14 **LaTourette** | ? | ? | ? | ? | ? | ? | ? | ? |
| 15 **Pryce** | N | N | N | N | N | N | N | Y |
| 16 **Regula** | Y | N | N | N | N | N | N | Y |
| 17 Ryan | N | N | Y | N | Y | N | Y | N |
| 18 **Ney** | Y | N | N | Y | N | N | N | Y |
| **OKLAHOMA** | | | | | | | | |
| 1 **Sullivan** | Y | N | ? | Y | N | Y | N | Y |
| 2 Boren | Y | Y | Y | Y | N | N | Y | Y |
| 3 **Lucas** | ? | ? | ? | ? | ? | ? | ? | ? |
| 4 **Cole** | Y | N | N | Y | N | N | N | Y |
| 5 **Istook** | Y | N | N | Y | N | ? | N | Y |
| **OREGON** | | | | | | | | |
| 1 Wu | N | Y | Y | N | Y | N | Y | Y |
| 2 **Walden** | N | N | N | N | N | N | N | Y |
| 3 Blumenauer | N | N | Y | N | Y | N | Y | N |
| 4 DeFazio | N | Y | Y | Y | Y | N | Y | Y |
| 5 Hooley | N | N | Y | N | Y | N | Y | Y |
| **PENNSYLVANIA** | | | | | | | | |
| 1 Brady | N | Y | N | N | Y | N | Y | Y |
| 2 Fattah | N | Y | Y | N | Y | N | Y | Y |
| 3 **English** | Y | N | N | N | Y | N | N | Y |
| 4 **Hart** | Y | N | N | N | N | Y | N | Y |
| 5 **Peterson** | Y | ? | N | N | N | N | N | Y |
| 6 **Gerlach** | N | Y | N | N | ? | N | N | Y |
| 7 **Weldon** | ? | N | N | N | Y | N | N | Y |
| 8 **Fitzpatrick** | N | Y | N | N | Y | N | N | Y |
| 9 **Shuster** | Y | Y | N | Y | N | Y | N | Y |
| 10 **Sherwood** | Y | N | N | N | N | N | N | Y |
| 11 Kanjorski | N | Y | N | N | Y | N | N | Y |
| 12 Murtha | N | N | N | N | Y | N | N | Y |
| 13 Schwartz | N | Y | N | N | Y | N | Y | Y |
| 14 Doyle | Y | Y | N | N | Y | N | Y | Y |
| 15 **Dent** | Y | N | N | N | Y | N | N | Y |
| 16 **Pitts** | Y | Y | N | Y | Y | Y | N | Y |
| 17 Holden | Y | Y | N | N | Y | N | N | Y |
| 18 **Murphy** | Y | Y | N | N | Y | N | N | Y |
| 19 **Platts** | N | N | N | N | Y | N | N | Y |
| **RHODE ISLAND** | | | | | | | | |
| 1 Kennedy | N | N | Y | N | Y | N | Y | Y |
| 2 Langevin | N | N | Y | N | Y | N | Y | Y |
| **SOUTH CAROLINA** | | | | | | | | |
| 1 **Brown** | Y | N | N | N | N | N | N | Y |
| 2 **Wilson** | Y | N | N | Y | N | Y | N | Y |
| 3 **Barrett** | Y | N | N | Y | N | Y | N | Y |
| 4 **Inglis** | N | N | N | N | N | Y | N | Y |
| 5 Spratt | N | N | Y | N | Y | N | Y | Y |
| 6 Clyburn | N | N | Y | N | Y | N | Y | Y |
| **SOUTH DAKOTA** | | | | | | | | |
| AL Herseth | N | N | Y | Y | Y | N | Y | Y |
| **TENNESSEE** | | | | | | | | |
| 1 **Jenkins** | Y | Y | N | N | N | Y | N | Y |
| 2 **Duncan** | Y | N | N | N | N | Y | N | Y |
| 3 **Wamp** | N | N | N | N | Y | N | N | Y |
| 4 Davis | Y | N | Y | N | Y | N | Y | Y |
| 5 Cooper | Y | N | Y | N | Y | N | Y | Y |
| 6 Gordon | N | N | Y | N | Y | N | Y | Y |
| 7 **Blackburn** | Y | N | N | Y | N | Y | N | Y |
| 8 Tanner | Y | N | Y | N | Y | Y | Y | N |
| 9 Ford | N | N | Y | N | Y | N | Y | Y |
| **TEXAS** | | | | | | | | |
| 1 **Gohmert** | Y | N | N | Y | N | N | N | Y |
| 2 **Poe** | N | Y | N | Y | ? | Y | N | Y |
| 3 **Johnson, S.** | Y | Y | N | Y | N | Y | N | Y |
| 4 **Hall** | Y | Y | N | Y | Y | Y | N | Y |
| 5 **Hensarling** | Y | Y | N | Y | N | Y | N | Y |
| 6 **Barton** | Y | N | N | N | Y | Y | N | Y |
| 7 **Culberson** | Y | N | N | Y | ? | N | N | Y |
| 8 **Brady** | Y | N | N | Y | N | Y | N | Y |
| 9 Green | Y | N | Y | N | Y | N | Y | Y |
| 10 **McCaul** | Y | N | N | Y | Y | N | N | Y |
| 11 **Conaway** | + | N | N | N | N | N | N | Y |
| 12 **Granger** | Y | N | N | N | N | N | N | Y |
| 13 **Thornberry** | Y | N | N | Y | N | Y | N | Y |
| 14 **Paul** | Y | N | N | Y | ? | Y | N | N |
| 15 Hinojosa | Y | N | Y | N | – | N | Y | Y |
| 16 Reyes | Y | N | Y | N | Y | N | Y | Y |
| 17 Edwards | Y | N | N | N | Y | N | Y | Y |
| 18 Jackson-Lee | ? | ? | ? | ? | ? | ? | ? | ? |
| 19 **Neugebauer** | Y | N | N | Y | N | Y | N | Y |
| 20 Gonzalez | Y | N | Y | N | Y | N | Y | Y |
| 21 **Smith** | Y | N | N | N | N | N | N | Y |
| 22 **DeLay** | N | N | N | Y | N | N | N | Y |
| 23 **Bonilla** | Y | N | N | Y | N | N | N | Y |
| 24 **Marchant** | Y | N | N | Y | ? | N | N | ? |
| 25 Doggett | N | Y | Y | N | Y | N | Y | Y |
| 26 **Burgess** | Y | N | N | Y | Y | Y | N | Y |
| 27 Ortiz | Y | N | Y | N | Y | N | Y | Y |
| 28 Cuellar | Y | N | Y | N | Y | N | Y | Y |
| 29 Green | Y | Y | Y | N | Y | N | Y | Y |
| 30 Johnson, E. | N | N | Y | N | Y | N | Y | Y |
| 31 **Carter** | Y | N | N | Y | N | N | N | Y |
| 32 **Sessions** | Y | N | N | Y | N | Y | N | Y |
| **UTAH** | | | | | | | | |
| 1 **Bishop** | Y | Y | N | ? | N | N | N | Y |
| 2 Matheson | N | N | Y | N | N | N | Y | N |
| 3 **Cannon** | Y | Y | N | Y | N | Y | N | Y |
| **VERMONT** | | | | | | | | |
| AL *Sanders* | N | N | Y | N | Y | N | Y | N |
| **VIRGINIA** | | | | | | | | |
| 1 **Davis, J.** | N | N | N | Y | Y | Y | N | Y |
| 2 **Drake** | N | N | N | N | N | N | N | Y |
| 3 Scott | N | N | Y | N | Y | N | Y | Y |
| 4 **Forbes** | N | N | N | N | Y | N | N | Y |
| 5 **Goode** | Y | N | N | Y | Y | N | N | Y |
| 6 **Goodlatte** | Y | N | N | Y | N | Y | N | Y |
| 7 **Cantor** | N | N | N | Y | N | N | N | Y |
| 8 Moran | N | N | Y | N | + | N | Y | Y |
| 9 Boucher | N | N | Y | N | Y | N | Y | Y |
| 10 **Wolf** | N | N | N | N | N | N | N | Y |
| 11 **Davis, T.** | N | N | N | N | Y | N | N | Y |
| **WASHINGTON** | | | | | | | | |
| 1 Inslee | N | N | Y | N | Y | N | Y | N |
| 2 Larsen | N | N | Y | N | Y | N | Y | Y |
| 3 Baird | N | N | N | N | Y | N | Y | N |
| 4 **Hastings** | Y | N | N | Y | N | N | N | Y |
| 5 **McMorris** | Y | N | N | Y | N | N | N | Y |
| 6 Dicks | N | N | Y | N | Y | N | Y | Y |
| 7 McDermott | N | N | Y | N | Y | N | Y | N |
| 8 **Reichert** | N | N | N | N | N | N | N | Y |
| 9 Smith | N | Y | Y | N | Y | N | Y | Y |
| **WEST VIRGINIA** | | | | | | | | |
| 1 Mollohan | Y | N | N | N | Y | N | N | Y |
| 2 **Capito** | N | N | N | N | Y | N | N | Y |
| 3 Rahall | N | N | Y | N | Y | N | Y | N |
| **WISCONSIN** | | | | | | | | |
| 1 **Ryan** | N | Y | N | Y | N | Y | N | Y |
| 2 Baldwin | N | N | Y | N | Y | N | Y | N |
| 3 Kind | N | N | Y | N | Y | N | Y | N |
| 4 Moore | N | Y | Y | N | Y | N | Y | N |
| 5 **Sensenbrenner** | Y | N | N | Y | N | Y | N | Y |
| 6 **Petri** | N | N | N | Y | N | Y | N | Y |
| 7 Obey | N | N | Y | N | Y | N | Y | N |
| 8 **Green** | N | N | Y | Y | Y | Y | N | Y |
| **WYOMING** | | | | | | | | |
| AL **Cubin** | Y | Y | N | Y | N | Y | N | Y |

# IN THE HOUSE | By Vote Number

**200.** HR 744. "Spyware" Programs/Passage. Sensenbrenner, R-Wis., motion to suspend the rules and pass the bill that would establish criminal penalties, including up to two years in prison, for intentionally gaining unauthorized access to a computer to steal information or damage the machine. Intentionally gaining access in furtherance of a federal crime could mean up to five years in prison. Motion agreed to 395-1: R 207-1; D 187-0 (ND 137-0, SD 50-0); I 1-0. A two-thirds majority of those present and voting (264 in this case) is required for passage under suspension of the rules. May 23, 2005.

**201.** HR 29. "Spyware" Programs/Passage. Barton, R-Texas., motion to suspend the rules and pass the bill that would require software companies to obtain permission from computer users before installing programs that can collect personal information and distribute it to third parties. Violators would be subject to fines of up to $3 million. Motion agreed to 393-4: R 207-1; D 185-3 (ND 136-2, SD 49-1); I 1-0. A two-thirds majority of those present and voting (265 in this case) is required for passage under suspension of the rules. May 23, 2005.

**202.** H Con Res 149. Israel Independence Tribute/Adoption. Ros-Lehtinen, R-Fla., motion to suspend the rules and adopt the concurrent resolution that would recognize that Israel's independence provided a refuge and homeland for the Jewish people and congratulate the Israeli people on the country's 57th anniversary of independence. Motion agreed to 397-0: R 208-0; D 188-0 (ND 138-0, SD 50-0); I 1-0. A two-thirds majority of those present and voting (265 in this case) is required for adoption under suspension of the rules. May 23, 2005.

**203.** HR 2419. Fiscal 2006 Energy and Water Appropriations/Previous Question. L. Diaz-Balart, R-Fla., motion to order the previous question (thus ending debate and possibility of amendment) on adoption of the rule (H Res 291) to provide for House floor consideration of the bill that would appropriate $29.7 billion in fiscal 2006 for energy and water development projects. Motion agreed to 219-190: R 218-0; D 1-189 (ND 1-141, SD 0-48); I 0-1. (Subsequently, the rule was adopted by voice vote.) May 24, 2005.

**204.** HR 810. Embryonic Stem Cell Research/Passage. Passage of the bill to allow the use of federal funds in research on embryonic stem cell lines derived from surplus embryos at in-vitro fertilization clinics, but only if donors give their consent and are not paid for the embryos. The bill would authorize the Health and Human Services Department to conduct and support research involving human embryonic stem cells that meet certain criteria, regardless of when the stem cells were derived from a human embryo. Passed 238-194: R 50-180; D 187-14 (ND 140-10, SD 47-4); I 1-0. A "nay" was a vote in support of the president's position. May 24, 2005.

**205.** HR 2520. Cord Blood Stem Cell Research/Passage. Barton, R-Texas, motion to suspend the rules and pass the bill to create a new federal program to collect and store umbilical-cord-blood stem cells. The bill would reauthorize and expand the current bone-marrow registry program to both bone-marrow and cord-blood transplants. It would authorize $156 million over five years for the program. Motion agreed to 431-1: R 229-1; D 201-0 (ND 150-0, SD 51-0); I 1-0. A two-thirds majority of those present and voting (288 in this case) is required for passage under suspension of the rules. A "yea" was a vote in support of the president's position. May 24, 2005.

ND Northern Democrats, SD Southern Democrats
Southern states: Ala., Ark., Fla., Ga., Ky., La., Miss., N.C., Okla., S.C., Tenn., Texas, Va.

| | 200 | 201 | 202 | 203 | 204 | 205 |
|---|---|---|---|---|---|---|
| **ALABAMA** | | | | | | |
| 1 Bonner | Y | Y | Y | Y | N | Y |
| 2 Everett | Y | Y | Y | Y | N | Y |
| 3 Rogers | Y | Y | Y | Y | N | Y |
| 4 Aderholt | Y | Y | Y | Y | N | Y |
| 5 Cramer | Y | Y | Y | N | Y | Y |
| 6 Bachus | Y | Y | Y | Y | N | Y |
| 7 Davis | ? | ? | ? | N | Y | Y |
| **ALASKA** | | | | | | |
| AL Young | ? | ? | ? | Y | Y | Y |
| **ARIZONA** | | | | | | |
| 1 Renzi | Y | Y | Y | Y | N | Y |
| 2 Franks | Y | Y | Y | Y | N | Y |
| 3 Shadegg | Y | Y | Y | Y | N | Y |
| 4 Pastor | Y | Y | Y | N | Y | Y |
| 5 Hayworth | Y | Y | Y | Y | N | Y |
| 6 Flake | Y | Y | Y | Y | N | Y |
| 7 Grijalva | Y | Y | Y | N | Y | Y |
| 8 Kolbe | Y | Y | Y | Y | Y | Y |
| **ARKANSAS** | | | | | | |
| 1 Berry | Y | Y | Y | N | Y | Y |
| 2 Snyder | Y | Y | Y | N | Y | Y |
| 3 Boozman | Y | Y | Y | Y | N | Y |
| 4 Ross | Y | Y | Y | N | Y | Y |
| **CALIFORNIA** | | | | | | |
| 1 Thompson | Y | Y | Y | N | Y | Y |
| 2 Herger | Y | Y | Y | Y | N | Y |
| 3 Lungren | Y | Y | Y | Y | N | Y |
| 4 Doolittle | Y | Y | Y | Y | N | Y |
| 5 Matsui, D. | Y | Y | Y | N | Y | Y |
| 6 Woolsey | Y | Y | Y | N | Y | Y |
| 7 Miller, George | Y | Y | Y | N | Y | Y |
| 8 Pelosi | Y | Y | Y | N | Y | Y |
| 9 Lee | Y | Y | Y | N | Y | Y |
| 10 Tauscher | Y | Y | Y | N | Y | Y |
| 11 Pombo | Y | Y | Y | Y | N | Y |
| 12 Lantos | Y | Y | Y | N | Y | Y |
| 13 Stark | ? | ? | ? | N | Y | Y |
| 14 Eshoo | Y | Y | Y | N | Y | Y |
| 15 Honda | Y | Y | Y | N | Y | Y |
| 16 Lofgren | Y | N | Y | N | Y | Y |
| 17 Farr | Y | Y | Y | N | Y | Y |
| 18 Cardoza | Y | Y | Y | ? | Y | Y |
| 19 Radanovich | Y | Y | Y | Y | N | Y |
| 20 Costa | Y | Y | Y | N | Y | Y |
| 21 Nunes | Y | Y | Y | Y | N | Y |
| 22 Thomas | Y | Y | Y | Y | N | Y |
| 23 Capps | Y | Y | Y | N | Y | Y |
| 24 Gallegly | + | + | + | Y | N | Y |
| 25 McKeon | Y | Y | Y | Y | N | Y |
| 26 Dreier | Y | Y | Y | Y | N | Y |
| 27 Sherman | Y | Y | Y | N | Y | Y |
| 28 Berman | Y | Y | Y | N | Y | Y |
| 29 Schiff | Y | Y | Y | N | Y | Y |
| 30 Waxman | Y | Y | Y | N | Y | Y |
| 31 Becerra | ? | ? | ? | N | Y | Y |
| 32 Solis | Y | Y | Y | N | Y | Y |
| 33 Watson | Y | Y | Y | N | Y | Y |
| 34 Roybal-Allard | Y | Y | Y | N | Y | Y |
| 35 Waters | Y | Y | Y | N | Y | Y |
| 36 Harman | Y | Y | Y | N | Y | Y |
| 37 Millender-McD. | ? | ? | ? | ? | ? | ? |
| 38 Napolitano | Y | Y | Y | N | Y | Y |
| 39 Sánchez, Linda | Y | Y | Y | N | Y | Y |
| 40 Royce | Y | Y | Y | Y | N | Y |
| 41 Lewis | Y | Y | Y | Y | Y | Y |
| 42 Miller, Gary | Y | Y | Y | Y | N | Y |
| 43 Baca | Y | Y | Y | N | Y | Y |
| 44 Calvert | Y | Y | Y | Y | Y | Y |
| 45 Bono | Y | Y | Y | Y | Y | Y |
| 46 Rohrabacher | Y | Y | Y | Y | Y | Y |
| 47 Sanchez, Loretta | ? | ? | ? | ? | Y | Y |
| 48 Cox | Y | Y | Y | Y | N | Y |
| 49 Issa | Y | Y | Y | Y | Y | Y |
| 50 Cunningham | Y | Y | Y | Y | Y | Y |
| 51 Filner | Y | Y | Y | N | Y | Y |
| 52 Hunter | Y | Y | Y | Y | N | Y |
| 53 Davis | Y | Y | Y | N | Y | Y |
| **COLORADO** | | | | | | |
| 1 DeGette | Y | Y | Y | N | Y | Y |
| 2 Udall | Y | Y | Y | N | Y | Y |
| 3 Salazar | Y | Y | Y | N | Y | Y |
| 4 Musgrave | Y | Y | Y | Y | N | Y |
| 5 Hefley | Y | Y | Y | Y | N | Y |
| 6 Tancredo | Y | Y | Y | Y | N | Y |
| 7 Beauprez | Y | Y | Y | Y | N | Y |
| **CONNECTICUT** | | | | | | |
| 1 Larson | Y | Y | Y | N | Y | Y |
| 2 Simmons | Y | Y | Y | Y | Y | Y |
| 3 DeLauro | Y | Y | Y | N | Y | Y |
| 4 Shays | + | + | + | Y | Y | Y |
| 5 Johnson | Y | Y | Y | Y | Y | Y |
| **DELAWARE** | | | | | | |
| AL Castle | Y | Y | Y | Y | Y | Y |
| **FLORIDA** | | | | | | |
| 1 Miller | Y | Y | Y | Y | N | Y |
| 2 Boyd | Y | Y | Y | N | Y | Y |
| 3 Brown | Y | Y | Y | N | Y | Y |
| 4 Crenshaw | Y | Y | Y | Y | N | Y |
| 5 Brown-Waite | Y | Y | Y | Y | Y | Y |
| 6 Stearns | Y | Y | Y | Y | N | Y |
| 7 Mica | Y | Y | Y | Y | N | Y |
| 8 Keller | Y | Y | Y | Y | N | Y |
| 9 Bilirakis | Y | Y | Y | Y | N | Y |
| 10 Young | Y | Y | Y | Y | Y | Y |
| 11 Davis | Y | Y | Y | N | Y | Y |
| 12 Putnam | Y | Y | Y | Y | N | Y |
| 13 Harris | Y | Y | Y | Y | Y | Y |
| 14 Mack | Y | Y | Y | Y | Y | Y |
| 15 Weldon | Y | Y | Y | Y | N | Y |
| 16 Foley | Y | Y | Y | Y | Y | Y |
| 17 Meek | Y | Y | Y | ? | Y | Y |
| 18 Ros-Lehtinen | Y | Y | Y | N | Y | Y |
| 19 Wexler | Y | Y | Y | ? | Y | Y |
| 20 Wasserman-Schultz | Y | Y | Y | N | Y | Y |
| 21 Diaz-Balart, L. | Y | Y | Y | Y | Y | Y |
| 22 Shaw | ? | ? | ? | Y | Y | Y |
| 23 Hastings | Y | Y | Y | N | Y | Y |
| 24 Feeney | Y | Y | Y | Y | N | Y |
| 25 Diaz-Balart, M. | Y | Y | Y | Y | N | Y |
| **GEORGIA** | | | | | | |
| 1 Kingston | ? | ? | ? | Y | N | Y |
| 2 Bishop | Y | Y | Y | N | Y | Y |
| 3 Marshall | Y | Y | Y | N | Y | Y |
| 4 McKinney | Y | Y | Y | N | Y | Y |
| 5 Lewis | Y | Y | Y | N | Y | Y |
| 6 Price | Y | Y | Y | Y | N | Y |
| 7 Linder | Y | Y | Y | Y | N | Y |
| 8 Westmoreland | Y | Y | Y | Y | N | Y |
| 9 Norwood | Y | Y | Y | Y | N | Y |
| 10 Deal | Y | Y | Y | Y | N | Y |
| 11 Gingrey | Y | Y | Y | Y | N | Y |
| 12 Barrow | Y | Y | Y | N | Y | Y |
| 13 Scott | Y | Y | Y | N | Y | Y |
| **HAWAII** | | | | | | |
| 1 Abercrombie | Y | Y | Y | N | Y | Y |
| 2 Case | Y | Y | Y | N | Y | Y |
| **IDAHO** | | | | | | |
| 1 Otter | Y | Y | Y | Y | N | Y |
| 2 Simpson | Y | Y | Y | Y | N | Y |
| **ILLINOIS** | | | | | | |
| 1 Rush | ? | ? | ? | ? | Y | Y |
| 2 Jackson | Y | Y | Y | N | Y | Y |
| 3 Lipinski | Y | Y | Y | N | Y | Y |
| 4 Gutierrez | Y | Y | Y | N | Y | Y |
| 5 Emanuel | Y | Y | Y | N | Y | Y |
| 6 Hyde | Y | Y | Y | Y | N | Y |
| 7 Davis | Y | Y | Y | N | Y | Y |
| 8 Bean | Y | Y | Y | N | Y | Y |
| 9 Schakowsky | Y | Y | Y | N | Y | Y |
| 10 Kirk | Y | Y | Y | Y | Y | Y |
| 11 Weller | Y | Y | Y | Y | N | Y |
| 12 Costello | Y | Y | Y | N | N | Y |

| KEY | Republicans | Democrats | Independents |
|---|---|---|---|

| | | |
|---|---|---|
| Y Voted for (yea) | X Paired against | C Voted "present" to avoid possible conflict of interest |
| # Paired for | – Announced against | |
| + Announced for | P Voted "present" | ? Did not vote or otherwise make a position known |
| N Voted against (nay) | | |

| | 200 | 201 | 202 | 203 | 204 | 205 |
|---|---|---|---|---|---|---|
| 13 **Biggert** | Y | Y | Y | Y | Y | Y |
| 14 **Hastert** | | | | | N | Y |
| 15 **Johnson** | Y | Y | Y | Y | N | Y |
| 16 **Manzullo** | Y | Y | Y | Y | N | Y |
| 17 Evans | Y | Y | Y | N | Y | Y |
| 18 **LaHood** | Y | Y | Y | Y | N | Y |
| 19 **Shimkus** | ? | ? | ? | Y | N | Y |
| **INDIANA** | | | | | | |
| 1 Visclosky | Y | Y | Y | N | Y | Y |
| 2 **Chocola** | Y | Y | Y | Y | N | Y |
| 3 **Souder** | Y | Y | Y | Y | N | Y |
| 4 **Buyer** | ? | ? | ? | Y | N | Y |
| 5 **Burton** | + | + | + | ? | N | Y |
| 6 **Pence** | Y | Y | Y | Y | N | Y |
| 7 Carson | Y | Y | Y | N | Y | Y |
| 8 **Hostettler** | Y | Y | Y | Y | N | Y |
| 9 **Sodrel** | Y | Y | Y | Y | N | Y |
| **IOWA** | | | | | | |
| 1 **Nussle** | Y | Y | Y | Y | N | Y |
| 2 **Leach** | Y | Y | Y | Y | Y | Y |
| 3 Boswell | Y | Y | Y | N | Y | Y |
| 4 **Latham** | Y | Y | Y | Y | N | Y |
| 5 **King** | Y | Y | Y | Y | N | Y |
| **KANSAS** | | | | | | |
| 1 **Moran** | Y | Y | Y | Y | N | Y |
| 2 **Ryun** | Y | Y | Y | Y | N | Y |
| 3 Moore | ? | Y | Y | N | Y | Y |
| 4 **Tiahrt** | Y | Y | Y | Y | N | Y |
| **KENTUCKY** | | | | | | |
| 1 **Whitfield** | Y | Y | Y | Y | N | Y |
| 2 **Lewis** | Y | Y | Y | Y | N | Y |
| 3 **Northup** | Y | Y | Y | Y | N | Y |
| 4 **Davis** | Y | Y | Y | Y | N | Y |
| 5 **Rogers** | Y | Y | Y | Y | N | Y |
| 6 Chandler | Y | Y | Y | N | Y | Y |
| **LOUISIANA** | | | | | | |
| 1 **Jindal** | Y | Y | Y | Y | N | Y |
| 2 Jefferson | Y | Y | Y | N | Y | Y |
| 3 Melancon | Y | Y | Y | N | Y | Y |
| 4 **McCrery** | ? | ? | ? | Y | N | Y |
| 5 **Alexander** | Y | Y | Y | Y | N | Y |
| 6 **Baker** | Y | Y | Y | Y | N | Y |
| 7 **Boustany** | Y | Y | Y | Y | N | Y |
| **MAINE** | | | | | | |
| 1 Allen | Y | Y | Y | N | Y | Y |
| 2 Michaud | Y | Y | Y | N | Y | Y |
| **MARYLAND** | | | | | | |
| 1 **Gilchrest** | Y | Y | Y | Y | Y | Y |
| 2 Ruppersberger | Y | Y | Y | N | Y | Y |
| 3 Cardin | Y | Y | Y | N | Y | Y |
| 4 Wynn | Y | Y | Y | N | Y | Y |
| 5 Hoyer | Y | Y | Y | N | Y | Y |
| 6 **Bartlett** | Y | Y | Y | Y | N | Y |
| 7 Cummings | Y | Y | Y | N | Y | Y |
| 8 Van Hollen | Y | Y | Y | N | Y | Y |
| **MASSACHUSETTS** | | | | | | |
| 1 Olver | Y | Y | Y | N | Y | Y |
| 2 Neal | Y | Y | Y | N | Y | Y |
| 3 McGovern | Y | Y | Y | N | Y | Y |
| 4 Frank | Y | Y | Y | N | Y | Y |
| 5 Meehan | Y | Y | Y | N | Y | Y |
| 6 Tierney | Y | Y | Y | N | Y | Y |
| 7 Markey | Y | Y | Y | N | Y | Y |
| 8 Capuano | Y | Y | Y | N | Y | Y |
| 9 Lynch | ? | ? | ? | N | Y | Y |
| 10 Delahunt | ? | ? | ? | ? | Y | Y |
| **MICHIGAN** | | | | | | |
| 1 Stupak | Y | Y | Y | N | N | Y |
| 2 **Hoekstra** | Y | Y | Y | Y | N | Y |
| 3 **Ehlers** | Y | Y | Y | Y | N | Y |
| 4 **Camp** | Y | Y | Y | Y | N | Y |
| 5 Kildee | Y | Y | Y | N | N | Y |
| 6 **Upton** | Y | Y | Y | Y | Y | Y |
| 7 **Schwarz** | Y | Y | Y | Y | Y | Y |
| 8 **Rogers** | Y | Y | Y | Y | N | Y |
| 9 **Knollenberg** | Y | Y | Y | Y | N | Y |
| 10 **Miller** | ? | ? | ? | Y | N | Y |
| 11 **McCotter** | Y | Y | Y | Y | N | Y |
| 12 Levin | Y | Y | Y | N | Y | Y |
| 13 Kilpatrick | Y | Y | Y | N | Y | Y |
| 14 Conyers | Y | Y | Y | N | Y | Y |
| 15 Dingell | Y | Y | Y | ? | Y | Y |

| | 200 | 201 | 202 | 203 | 204 | 205 |
|---|---|---|---|---|---|---|
| **MINNESOTA** | | | | | | |
| 1 **Gutknecht** | Y | Y | Y | Y | N | Y |
| 2 **Kline** | Y | Y | Y | Y | N | Y |
| 3 **Ramstad** | Y | Y | Y | Y | Y | Y |
| 4 McCollum | Y | Y | Y | N | Y | Y |
| 5 Sabo | Y | Y | Y | N | Y | Y |
| 6 **Kennedy** | Y | Y | Y | Y | N | Y |
| 7 Peterson | Y | Y | Y | Y | N | Y |
| 8 Oberstar | Y | Y | Y | N | N | Y |
| **MISSISSIPPI** | | | | | | |
| 1 **Wicker** | Y | Y | Y | Y | N | Y |
| 2 Thompson | Y | Y | Y | N | Y | Y |
| 3 **Pickering** | Y | Y | Y | Y | N | Y |
| 4 Taylor | Y | Y | Y | N | N | Y |
| **MISSOURI** | | | | | | |
| 1 Clay | ? | ? | ? | N | Y | Y |
| 2 **Akin** | Y | Y | Y | Y | N | Y |
| 3 Carnahan | Y | Y | Y | N | Y | Y |
| 4 Skelton | Y | Y | Y | N | Y | Y |
| 5 Cleaver | Y | Y | Y | N | Y | Y |
| 6 **Graves** | Y | Y | Y | Y | N | Y |
| 7 **Blunt** | Y | Y | Y | Y | N | Y |
| 8 **Emerson** | Y | Y | Y | Y | Y | Y |
| 9 **Hulshof** | Y | Y | Y | Y | N | Y |
| **MONTANA** | | | | | | |
| AL **Rehberg** | Y | Y | Y | Y | N | Y |
| **NEBRASKA** | | | | | | |
| 1 **Fortenberry** | Y | Y | Y | Y | N | Y |
| 2 **Terry** | Y | Y | Y | Y | N | Y |
| 3 **Osborne** | Y | Y | Y | Y | N | Y |
| **NEVADA** | | | | | | |
| 1 Berkley | Y | Y | Y | N | Y | Y |
| 2 **Gibbons** | + | + | + | Y | Y | Y |
| 3 **Porter** | Y | Y | Y | Y | Y | Y |
| **NEW HAMPSHIRE** | | | | | | |
| 1 **Bradley** | Y | Y | Y | Y | Y | Y |
| 2 **Bass** | Y | Y | Y | Y | Y | Y |
| **NEW JERSEY** | | | | | | |
| 1 Andrews | Y | Y | Y | N | Y | Y |
| 2 **LoBiondo** | Y | Y | Y | Y | N | Y |
| 3 **Saxton** | Y | Y | Y | Y | N | Y |
| 4 **Smith** | Y | Y | Y | Y | N | Y |
| 5 **Garrett** | Y | Y | Y | Y | N | Y |
| 6 Pallone | Y | Y | Y | N | Y | Y |
| 7 **Ferguson** | ? | ? | ? | Y | N | Y |
| 8 Pascrell | Y | Y | Y | N | Y | Y |
| 9 Rothman | Y | Y | Y | N | Y | Y |
| 10 Payne | Y | Y | Y | N | Y | Y |
| 11 **Frelinghuysen** | Y | Y | Y | Y | Y | Y |
| 12 Holt | Y | Y | Y | N | Y | Y |
| 13 Menendez | Y | Y | Y | N | Y | Y |
| **NEW MEXICO** | | | | | | |
| 1 **Wilson** | Y | Y | Y | Y | Y | Y |
| 2 **Pearce** | Y | Y | Y | Y | N | Y |
| 3 Udall | Y | Y | Y | N | Y | Y |
| **NEW YORK** | | | | | | |
| 1 Bishop | Y | Y | Y | N | Y | Y |
| 2 Israel | Y | Y | Y | N | Y | Y |
| 3 **King** | Y | Y | Y | Y | N | Y |
| 4 McCarthy | Y | Y | Y | N | Y | Y |
| 5 Ackerman | Y | Y | Y | N | Y | Y |
| 6 Meeks | ? | ? | ? | ? | Y | Y |
| 7 Crowley | Y | Y | Y | N | Y | Y |
| 8 Nadler | Y | Y | Y | N | Y | Y |
| 9 Weiner | Y | Y | Y | N | Y | Y |
| 10 Towns | Y | Y | Y | N | Y | Y |
| 11 Owens | Y | Y | Y | N | Y | Y |
| 12 Velázquez | ? | ? | ? | N | Y | Y |
| 13 **Fossella** | Y | Y | Y | Y | Y | Y |
| 14 Maloney | Y | Y | Y | N | Y | Y |
| 15 Rangel | Y | Y | Y | N | Y | Y |
| 16 Serrano | Y | Y | Y | N | Y | Y |
| 17 Engel | Y | Y | Y | N | Y | Y |
| 18 Lowey | Y | Y | Y | N | Y | Y |
| 19 **Kelly** | Y | Y | Y | Y | Y | Y |
| 20 **Sweeney** | Y | Y | Y | Y | Y | Y |
| 21 McNulty | Y | Y | Y | N | Y | Y |
| 22 Hinchey | Y | Y | Y | N | Y | Y |
| 23 **McHugh** | Y | Y | Y | Y | N | Y |
| 24 **Boehlert** | Y | Y | Y | ? | Y | Y |
| 25 **Walsh** | Y | Y | Y | ? | N | Y |
| 26 **Reynolds** | Y | Y | Y | ? | N | Y |
| 27 Higgins | Y | Y | Y | N | Y | Y |
| 28 Slaughter | Y | Y | Y | N | Y | Y |
| 29 **Kuhl** | Y | Y | Y | ? | N | Y |

| | 200 | 201 | 202 | 203 | 204 | 205 |
|---|---|---|---|---|---|---|
| **NORTH CAROLINA** | | | | | | |
| 1 Butterfield | Y | Y | Y | N | Y | Y |
| 2 Etheridge | Y | Y | Y | N | Y | Y |
| 3 **Jones** | Y | Y | Y | ? | N | Y |
| 4 Price | Y | Y | Y | N | Y | Y |
| 5 **Foxx** | Y | Y | Y | Y | N | Y |
| 6 **Coble** | Y | Y | Y | Y | Y | Y |
| 7 McIntyre | Y | Y | Y | N | N | Y |
| 8 **Hayes** | Y | Y | Y | Y | N | Y |
| 9 **Myrick** | Y | Y | Y | Y | N | Y |
| 10 **McHenry** | Y | Y | Y | Y | N | Y |
| 11 **Taylor** | Y | Y | Y | Y | N | Y |
| 12 Watt | Y | Y | Y | ? | Y | Y |
| 13 Miller | Y | Y | Y | N | Y | Y |
| **NORTH DAKOTA** | | | | | | |
| AL Pomeroy | Y | Y | Y | N | Y | Y |
| **OHIO** | | | | | | |
| 1 **Chabot** | Y | Y | Y | Y | N | Y |
| 2 Vacant | | | | | | |
| 3 **Turner** | Y | Y | Y | Y | N | Y |
| 4 **Oxley** | Y | Y | Y | Y | N | Y |
| 5 **Gillmor** | Y | Y | Y | Y | N | Y |
| 6 Strickland | Y | Y | Y | N | Y | Y |
| 7 **Hobson** | Y | Y | Y | Y | N | Y |
| 8 **Boehner** | Y | Y | Y | Y | N | Y |
| 9 Kaptur | Y | Y | Y | N | N | Y |
| 10 Kucinich | Y | Y | Y | N | Y | Y |
| 11 Jones | Y | Y | Y | N | Y | Y |
| 12 **Tiberi** | Y | Y | Y | Y | N | Y |
| 13 Brown | ? | ? | ? | N | Y | Y |
| 14 **LaTourette** | ? | ? | ? | Y | Y | Y |
| 15 **Pryce** | ? | ? | ? | ? | Y | Y |
| 16 **Regula** | Y | Y | Y | Y | Y | Y |
| 17 Ryan | Y | Y | Y | N | Y | Y |
| 18 **Ney** | Y | Y | Y | Y | N | Y |
| **OKLAHOMA** | | | | | | |
| 1 **Sullivan** | Y | Y | Y | Y | N | Y |
| 2 Boren | Y | Y | Y | N | Y | Y |
| 3 **Lucas** | Y | Y | Y | Y | N | Y |
| 4 **Cole** | Y | Y | Y | Y | N | Y |
| 5 **Istook** | ? | ? | ? | ? | N | Y |
| **OREGON** | | | | | | |
| 1 Wu | Y | N | Y | ? | Y | Y |
| 2 **Walden** | Y | Y | Y | Y | Y | Y |
| 3 Blumenauer | Y | Y | Y | N | Y | Y |
| 4 DeFazio | Y | Y | Y | N | Y | Y |
| 5 Hooley | Y | Y | Y | N | Y | Y |
| **PENNSYLVANIA** | | | | | | |
| 1 Brady | Y | Y | Y | N | Y | Y |
| 2 Fattah | ? | ? | ? | N | Y | Y |
| 3 **English** | ? | ? | ? | Y | N | Y |
| 4 **Hart** | Y | Y | Y | Y | N | Y |
| 5 **Peterson** | Y | Y | Y | Y | N | Y |
| 6 **Gerlach** | Y | Y | Y | Y | Y | Y |
| 7 **Weldon** | Y | Y | Y | Y | N | Y |
| 8 **Fitzpatrick** | Y | Y | Y | Y | N | Y |
| 9 **Shuster** | Y | Y | Y | Y | N | Y |
| 10 **Sherwood** | Y | Y | Y | Y | N | Y |
| 11 Kanjorski | Y | Y | Y | N | Y | Y |
| 12 Murtha | Y | Y | Y | N | Y | Y |
| 13 Schwartz | Y | Y | Y | N | Y | Y |
| 14 Doyle | Y | Y | Y | N | Y | Y |
| 15 **Dent** | Y | Y | Y | Y | Y | Y |
| 16 **Pitts** | Y | Y | Y | Y | N | Y |
| 17 Holden | Y | Y | Y | N | N | Y |
| 18 **Murphy** | Y | Y | Y | Y | N | Y |
| 19 **Platts** | Y | Y | Y | Y | Y | Y |
| **RHODE ISLAND** | | | | | | |
| 1 Kennedy | + | + | + | N | Y | Y |
| 2 Langevin | Y | Y | Y | N | Y | Y |
| **SOUTH CAROLINA** | | | | | | |
| 1 **Brown** | Y | Y | Y | Y | N | Y |
| 2 **Wilson** | Y | Y | Y | Y | N | Y |
| 3 **Barrett** | + | + | + | Y | N | Y |
| 4 **Inglis** | Y | Y | Y | Y | N | Y |
| 5 Spratt | Y | Y | Y | N | Y | Y |
| 6 Clyburn | Y | Y | Y | N | Y | Y |
| **SOUTH DAKOTA** | | | | | | |
| AL Herseth | Y | Y | Y | N | Y | Y |
| **TENNESSEE** | | | | | | |
| 1 **Jenkins** | Y | Y | Y | Y | N | Y |
| 2 **Duncan** | Y | Y | Y | Y | N | Y |

| | 200 | 201 | 202 | 203 | 204 | 205 |
|---|---|---|---|---|---|---|
| 3 **Wamp** | Y | Y | Y | Y | N | Y |
| 4 Davis | Y | Y | Y | N | N | Y |
| 5 Cooper | Y | Y | Y | N | Y | Y |
| 6 Gordon | Y | Y | Y | N | Y | Y |
| 7 **Blackburn** | Y | Y | Y | Y | N | Y |
| 8 Tanner | Y | Y | Y | N | Y | Y |
| 9 Ford | Y | Y | Y | N | Y | Y |
| **TEXAS** | | | | | | |
| 1 **Gohmert** | ? | ? | ? | ? | N | Y |
| 2 **Poe** | + | + | + | + | N | Y |
| 3 **Johnson, S.** | Y | Y | Y | Y | N | Y |
| 4 **Hall** | Y | Y | Y | Y | N | Y |
| 5 **Hensarling** | Y | Y | Y | Y | N | Y |
| 6 **Barton** | Y | Y | Y | Y | Y | Y |
| 7 **Culberson** | Y | Y | Y | Y | N | Y |
| 8 **Brady** | Y | Y | Y | ? | N | Y |
| 9 Green | Y | Y | Y | N | Y | Y |
| 10 **McCaul** | Y | Y | Y | Y | N | Y |
| 11 **Conaway** | Y | Y | Y | Y | N | Y |
| 12 **Granger** | Y | Y | Y | Y | Y | Y |
| 13 **Thornberry** | Y | Y | Y | Y | N | Y |
| 14 **Paul** | N | N | Y | Y | N | N |
| 15 Hinojosa | Y | Y | Y | N | Y | Y |
| 16 Reyes | Y | Y | Y | N | Y | Y |
| 17 Edwards | Y | Y | Y | N | Y | Y |
| 18 Jackson-Lee | Y | N | Y | N | Y | Y |
| 19 **Neugebauer** | Y | Y | Y | Y | N | Y |
| 20 Gonzalez | Y | Y | Y | N | Y | Y |
| 21 **Smith** | Y | Y | Y | Y | N | Y |
| 22 **DeLay** | Y | Y | Y | Y | N | Y |
| 23 **Bonilla** | Y | Y | Y | Y | N | Y |
| 24 **Marchant** | Y | Y | Y | Y | N | Y |
| 25 Doggett | Y | Y | Y | N | Y | Y |
| 26 **Burgess** | Y | Y | Y | Y | N | Y |
| 27 Ortiz | Y | Y | Y | N | Y | Y |
| 28 Cuellar | Y | Y | Y | N | Y | Y |
| 29 Green | Y | Y | Y | N | Y | Y |
| 30 Johnson, E. | Y | Y | Y | N | Y | Y |
| 31 **Carter** | Y | Y | Y | Y | N | Y |
| 32 **Sessions** | ? | ? | ? | Y | N | Y |
| **UTAH** | | | | | | |
| 1 **Bishop** | Y | Y | Y | Y | N | Y |
| 2 Matheson | Y | Y | Y | N | Y | Y |
| 3 **Cannon** | Y | Y | Y | Y | N | Y |
| **VERMONT** | | | | | | |
| AL *Sanders* | Y | Y | Y | N | Y | Y |
| **VIRGINIA** | | | | | | |
| 1 **Davis, J.** | Y | Y | Y | Y | N | Y |
| 2 **Drake** | Y | Y | Y | Y | N | Y |
| 3 Scott | Y | Y | Y | N | Y | Y |
| 4 **Forbes** | Y | Y | Y | Y | N | Y |
| 5 **Goode** | Y | Y | Y | Y | N | Y |
| 6 **Goodlatte** | Y | Y | Y | Y | N | Y |
| 7 **Cantor** | Y | Y | Y | Y | N | Y |
| 8 Moran | Y | Y | Y | N | Y | Y |
| 9 Boucher | Y | Y | Y | N | Y | Y |
| 10 **Wolf** | Y | Y | Y | Y | N | Y |
| 11 **Davis, T.** | Y | Y | Y | Y | Y | Y |
| **WASHINGTON** | | | | | | |
| 1 Inslee | Y | Y | Y | N | Y | Y |
| 2 Larsen | Y | Y | Y | N | Y | Y |
| 3 Baird | Y | Y | Y | N | Y | Y |
| 4 **Hastings** | ? | ? | ? | ? | ? | ? |
| 5 **McMorris** | Y | Y | Y | Y | N | Y |
| 6 Dicks | Y | Y | Y | N | Y | Y |
| 7 McDermott | Y | Y | Y | ? | Y | Y |
| 8 **Reichert** | Y | Y | Y | Y | N | Y |
| 9 Smith | Y | Y | Y | N | Y | Y |
| **WEST VIRGINIA** | | | | | | |
| 1 Mollohan | Y | Y | Y | N | N | Y |
| 2 **Capito** | Y | Y | Y | Y | Y | Y |
| 3 Rahall | Y | Y | Y | N | N | Y |
| **WISCONSIN** | | | | | | |
| 1 **Ryan** | Y | Y | Y | Y | N | Y |
| 2 Baldwin | Y | Y | Y | N | Y | Y |
| 3 Kind | Y | Y | Y | N | Y | Y |
| 4 Moore | Y | Y | Y | N | Y | Y |
| 5 **Sensenbrenner** | Y | Y | Y | Y | N | Y |
| 6 **Petri** | Y | Y | Y | Y | N | Y |
| 7 Obey | Y | Y | Y | N | Y | Y |
| 8 **Green** | Y | Y | Y | Y | N | Y |
| **WYOMING** | | | | | | |
| AL **Cubin** | ? | ? | ? | Y | N | Y |

# IN THE HOUSE | By Vote Number

**206.** **HR 1224. Business Checking Accounts/Passage.** Kelly, R-N.Y., motion to suspend the rules and pass the bill that would allow banks, thrifts and certain industrial loan companies to pay interest on balances held in business checking accounts. Motion agreed to 424-1: R 226-0; D 197-1 (ND 146-1, SD 51-0); I 1-0. A two-thirds majority of those present and voting (284 in this case) is required for passage under suspension of the rules. May 24, 2005.

**207.** **HR 2419. Fiscal 2006 Energy and Water Appropriations/Energy Efficiency and Conservation.** Markey, D-Mass., amendment that would transfer $15.5 million from interim storage and reprocessing and direct the funds towards energy efficiency and conservation. Rejected 110-312: R 1-223; D 108-89 (ND 96-51, SD 12-38); I 1-0. May 24, 2005.

**208.** **HR 2419. Fiscal 2006 Energy and Water Appropriations/Army Corps of Engineers Funding.** Jones, R-N.C., amendment that would increase funding for the Army Corps of Engineers by $20 million, offset by an equal cut for the Energy Department's administration account. Rejected 152-275: R 43-183; D 109-91 (ND 81-68, SD 28-23); I 0-1. May 24, 2005.

**209.** **HR 2419. Fiscal 2006 Energy and Water Appropriations/Strategic Petroleum Reserve.** Stupak, D-Mich., amendment that would bar the use of funds in the bill to accept oil deliveries to the Strategic Petroleum Reserve. Rejected 174-253: R 12-215; D 161-38 (ND 132-16, SD 29-22); I 1-0. May 24, 2005.

**210.** **HR 2419. Fiscal 2006 Energy and Water Appropriations/Recommit.** Etheridge, D-N.C., motion to recommit the bill to the Appropriations Committee with instructions to include language that would direct $500,000 toward a study on imported oil and provide $1 million for the Energy secretary to conduct a conference with OPEC nations on oil prices. Motion rejected 167-261: R 1-226; D 165-35 (ND 125-24, SD 40-11); I 1-0. May 24, 2005.

**211.** **HR 2419. Fiscal 2006 Energy and Water Appropriations/Passage.** Passage of the bill that would provide $29.7 billion in fiscal 2006 for energy and water development projects, including $4.7 billion for the Army Corps of Engineers and $8.8 billion for the National Nuclear Security Administration. It also would provide $661 million for the Yucca Mountain nuclear waste repository, including $10 million for the department to begin accepting waste for interim storage at one or more facilities by fiscal 2006. Passed 416-13: R 219-8; D 196-5 (ND 146-4, SD 50-1); I 1-0. May 24, 2005.

**212.** **HR 1815. Fiscal 2006 Defense Authorization/Previous Question.** Cole, R-Okla., motion to order the previous question (thus ending debate and possibility of amendment) on adoption of the rule (H Res 293) to provide for House floor consideration of the bill that would authorize $441.6 billion in fiscal 2006 for the Department of Defense and an additional $49.1 billion in emergency supplemental spending. Motion agreed to 225-200: R 225-0; D 0-199 (ND 0-148, SD 0-51); I 0-1. May 25, 2005.

**213.** **HR 1815. Fiscal 2006 Defense Authorization/Rule.** Adoption of the rule (H Res 293) to provide for House floor consideration of the bill that would authorize $441.6 billion in fiscal 2006 for the Department of Defense and $49.1 billion in emergency supplemental spending. Adopted 225-198: R 223-0; D 2-197 (ND 2-146, SD 0-51); I 0-1. May 25, 2005.

ND Northern Democrats, SD Southern Democrats
Southern states: Ala., Ark., Fla., Ga., Ky., La., Miss., N.C., Okla., S.C., Tenn., Texas, Va.

| | 206 | 207 | 208 | 209 | 210 | 211 | 212 | 213 |
|---|---|---|---|---|---|---|---|---|
| **ALABAMA** | | | | | | | | |
| 1 Bonner | Y | N | N | N | N | Y | Y | Y |
| 2 Everett | Y | N | N | N | N | Y | Y | Y |
| 3 Rogers | Y | N | Y | N | N | Y | Y | Y |
| 4 Aderholt | Y | N | N | N | N | Y | Y | Y |
| 5 Cramer | Y | N | N | N | N | Y | N | N |
| 6 Bachus | Y | N | N | N | N | Y | Y | Y |
| 7 Davis | Y | N | N | Y | Y | Y | N | N |
| **ALASKA** | | | | | | | | |
| AL Young | Y | ? | ? | ? | ? | ? | Y | Y |
| **ARIZONA** | | | | | | | | |
| 1 Renzi | Y | N | Y | N | N | Y | Y | Y |
| 2 Franks | Y | N | N | N | N | N | Y | Y |
| 3 Shadegg | Y | N | N | N | N | Y | Y | Y |
| 4 Pastor | Y | N | N | + | Y | N | N | N |
| 5 Hayworth | Y | N | Y | N | N | Y | Y | Y |
| 6 Flake | Y | N | N | N | N | N | Y | Y |
| 7 Grijalva | Y | Y | Y | Y | Y | Y | N | N |
| 8 Kolbe | Y | N | N | N | N | Y | Y | Y |
| **ARKANSAS** | | | | | | | | |
| 1 Berry | Y | N | N | N | N | Y | N | N |
| 2 Snyder | Y | N | N | N | N | Y | N | N |
| 3 Boozman | Y | N | N | N | N | Y | Y | Y |
| 4 Ross | Y | N | Y | N | Y | Y | N | N |
| **CALIFORNIA** | | | | | | | | |
| 1 Thompson | Y | Y | Y | Y | Y | Y | N | N |
| 2 Herger | Y | N | N | N | N | Y | Y | Y |
| 3 Lungren | Y | N | Y | N | N | Y | Y | Y |
| 4 Doolittle | Y | N | N | N | N | Y | Y | Y |
| 5 Matsui, D. | Y | N | Y | Y | Y | Y | N | N |
| 6 Woolsey | Y | Y | Y | Y | Y | Y | N | N |
| 7 Miller, George | Y | Y | N | Y | Y | Y | N | N |
| 8 Pelosi | Y | Y | N | Y | Y | Y | N | N |
| 9 Lee | Y | Y | Y | ? | Y | Y | N | N |
| 10 Tauscher | Y | N | N | Y | Y | Y | N | N |
| 11 Pombo | Y | N | N | N | N | Y | Y | Y |
| 12 Lantos | Y | Y | N | Y | Y | Y | N | N |
| 13 Stark | Y | Y | Y | Y | Y | Y | N | N |
| 14 Eshoo | Y | Y | Y | Y | Y | Y | N | N |
| 15 Honda | Y | Y | Y | Y | Y | Y | N | N |
| 16 Lofgren | Y | Y | N | Y | Y | Y | N | N |
| 17 Farr | Y | Y | N | Y | Y | Y | N | N |
| 18 Cardoza | Y | N | Y | Y | Y | Y | N | N |
| 19 Radanovich | Y | N | N | N | N | Y | Y | Y |
| 20 Costa | Y | N | Y | Y | Y | Y | N | N |
| 21 Nunes | Y | N | N | N | N | Y | Y | Y |
| 22 Thomas | Y | N | N | N | N | Y | Y | Y |
| 23 Capps | Y | Y | Y | Y | Y | Y | N | N |
| 24 Gallegly | Y | N | N | N | N | Y | Y | Y |
| 25 McKeon | Y | N | N | N | N | Y | Y | Y |
| 26 Dreier | Y | N | N | N | N | Y | Y | Y |
| 27 Sherman | Y | Y | Y | Y | Y | N | N | N |
| 28 Berman | Y | Y | N | Y | Y | Y | N | N |
| 29 Schiff | Y | Y | N | Y | Y | Y | N | N |
| 30 Waxman | Y | Y | Y | Y | Y | Y | N | N |
| 31 Becerra | Y | Y | Y | Y | Y | Y | N | N |
| 32 Solis | Y | Y | N | Y | Y | Y | N | N |
| 33 Watson | Y | Y | Y | Y | Y | Y | N | N |
| 34 Roybal-Allard | Y | Y | Y | Y | Y | Y | N | N |
| 35 Waters | Y | N | N | Y | Y | Y | N | N |
| 36 Harman | Y | Y | N | Y | Y | Y | N | N |
| 37 Millender-McD. | ? | ? | ? | ? | ? | ? | ? | ? |
| 38 Napolitano | Y | Y | Y | Y | Y | Y | N | N |
| 39 Sánchez, Linda | Y | Y | Y | Y | Y | Y | N | N |
| 40 Royce | Y | N | N | N | N | Y | Y | Y |
| 41 Lewis | Y | N | N | N | N | Y | Y | Y |
| 42 Miller, Gary | Y | N | Y | N | N | Y | Y | Y |
| 43 Baca | Y | N | Y | Y | Y | Y | N | N |
| 44 Calvert | Y | N | N | N | N | Y | Y | Y |
| 45 Bono | Y | N | N | N | N | Y | Y | Y |
| 46 Rohrabacher | Y | N | N | N | N | Y | Y | Y |
| 47 Sanchez, Loretta | Y | Y | N | Y | Y | Y | N | N |
| 48 Cox | Y | N | N | N | N | Y | Y | Y |
| 49 Issa | Y | N | N | N | N | Y | Y | ? |
| 50 Cunningham | Y | N | N | N | Y | Y | Y | Y |
| 51 Filner | Y | Y | N | Y | Y | Y | N | N |
| 52 Hunter | Y | N | N | N | N | Y | Y | Y |
| 53 Davis | Y | Y | Y | Y | Y | Y | N | N |
| **COLORADO** | | | | | | | | |
| 1 DeGette | Y | Y | Y | Y | Y | Y | N | N |
| 2 Udall | Y | Y | Y | Y | N | Y | N | N |
| 3 Salazar | Y | N | Y | Y | Y | Y | N | N |
| 4 Musgrave | Y | N | N | N | N | Y | Y | ? |
| 5 Hefley | Y | N | N | N | N | Y | Y | Y |
| 6 Tancredo | Y | N | N | N | N | Y | Y | Y |
| 7 Beauprez | Y | N | N | N | N | Y | Y | Y |
| **CONNECTICUT** | | | | | | | | |
| 1 Larson | Y | Y | N | Y | Y | Y | N | N |
| 2 Simmons | Y | N | N | N | N | Y | Y | Y |
| 3 DeLauro | Y | Y | N | Y | Y | Y | N | N |
| 4 Shays | Y | N | N | N | N | Y | Y | Y |
| 5 Johnson | Y | N | N | N | N | Y | Y | Y |
| **DELAWARE** | | | | | | | | |
| AL Castle | Y | N | N | N | N | Y | ? | Y |
| **FLORIDA** | | | | | | | | |
| 1 Miller | Y | N | N | N | N | Y | Y | Y |
| 2 Boyd | Y | N | N | N | N | Y | N | N |
| 3 Brown | Y | Y | Y | Y | Y | Y | N | N |
| 4 Crenshaw | Y | N | N | N | N | Y | Y | Y |
| 5 Brown-Waite | Y | N | Y | N | N | Y | Y | Y |
| 6 Stearns | Y | N | N | N | N | Y | Y | Y |
| 7 Mica | Y | N | N | N | N | Y | Y | Y |
| 8 Keller | Y | N | N | N | N | Y | Y | Y |
| 9 Bilirakis | Y | N | N | N | N | Y | Y | Y |
| 10 Young | Y | N | N | N | N | Y | Y | Y |
| 11 Davis | Y | N | N | N | Y | N | N | N |
| 12 Putnam | Y | N | N | N | N | Y | Y | Y |
| 13 Harris | Y | N | N | N | N | Y | Y | Y |
| 14 Mack | Y | N | N | N | N | Y | Y | Y |
| 15 Weldon | Y | N | N | N | N | Y | Y | Y |
| 16 Foley | Y | N | N | N | N | Y | Y | Y |
| 17 Meek | Y | N | Y | Y | Y | Y | N | N |
| 18 Ros-Lehtinen | Y | N | N | N | N | Y | Y | Y |
| 19 Wexler | Y | Y | Y | Y | Y | Y | N | N |
| 20 Wasserman-Schultz | Y | Y | Y | Y | Y | Y | N | N |
| 21 Diaz-Balart, L. | Y | N | N | N | N | Y | Y | Y |
| 22 Shaw | Y | N | Y | N | N | Y | Y | Y |
| 23 Hastings | Y | Y | Y | Y | Y | Y | N | N |
| 24 Feeney | Y | N | N | N | N | Y | Y | Y |
| 25 Diaz-Balart, M. | Y | N | N | N | N | Y | Y | Y |
| **GEORGIA** | | | | | | | | |
| 1 Kingston | Y | N | N | N | N | Y | Y | Y |
| 2 Bishop | Y | N | N | Y | Y | Y | N | N |
| 3 Marshall | Y | N | Y | N | Y | Y | N | N |
| 4 McKinney | Y | Y | Y | Y | Y | Y | N | N |
| 5 Lewis | Y | Y | Y | Y | Y | Y | N | N |
| 6 Price | Y | N | N | N | N | Y | Y | Y |
| 7 Linder | ? | N | N | N | N | Y | Y | Y |
| 8 Westmoreland | Y | N | N | N | N | Y | Y | Y |
| 9 Norwood | Y | N | N | N | N | Y | Y | Y |
| 10 Deal | Y | N | N | N | N | Y | Y | Y |
| 11 Gingrey | Y | N | N | N | N | Y | ? | Y |
| 12 Barrow | Y | Y | Y | Y | Y | Y | N | N |
| 13 Scott | Y | N | N | Y | Y | Y | N | N |
| **HAWAII** | | | | | | | | |
| 1 Abercrombie | Y | Y | Y | N | Y | N | N | N |
| 2 Case | Y | N | Y | N | Y | Y | N | N |
| **IDAHO** | | | | | | | | |
| 1 Otter | Y | N | N | N | Y | Y | Y | Y |
| 2 Simpson | Y | N | N | N | N | Y | Y | Y |
| **ILLINOIS** | | | | | | | | |
| 1 Rush | Y | N | Y | Y | Y | Y | N | N |
| 2 Jackson | Y | Y | N | Y | Y | Y | N | N |
| 3 Lipinski | Y | Y | Y | Y | Y | Y | N | N |
| 4 Gutierrez | Y | N | Y | Y | Y | Y | N | N |
| 5 Emanuel | Y | N | Y | Y | Y | Y | N | N |
| 6 Hyde | Y | N | N | N | Y | N | Y | Y |
| 7 Davis | Y | N | Y | Y | Y | Y | N | N |
| 8 Bean | Y | – | Y | N | Y | Y | N | N |
| 9 Schakowsky | Y | N | N | Y | Y | Y | N | N |
| 10 Kirk | Y | N | N | N | N | Y | Y | Y |
| 11 Weller | Y | N | N | N | N | Y | Y | Y |
| 12 Costello | Y | N | Y | N | Y | N | N | N |

## KEY

| | Republicans | Democrats | Independents | | |
|---|---|---|---|---|---|
| **Y** | Voted for (yea) | | **X** | Paired against | **C** Voted "present" to avoid possible conflict of interest |
| **#** | Paired for | | **–** | Announced against | |
| **+** | Announced for | | **P** | Voted "present" | **?** Did not vote or otherwise make a position known |
| **N** | Voted against (nay) | | | | |

| | 206 | 207 | 208 | 209 | 210 | 211 | 212 | 213 |
|---|---|---|---|---|---|---|---|---|
| 13 **Biggert** | Y | N | N | N | N | Y | Y | Y |
| 14 **Hastert** | | | | | | | | |
| 15 **Johnson** | Y | N | Y | Y | N | Y | Y | Y |
| 16 **Manzullo** | Y | N | N | N | N | Y | Y | Y |
| 17 Evans | Y | Y | Y | Y | Y | Y | N | N |
| 18 **LaHood** | Y | N | N | N | N | Y | Y | Y |
| 19 **Shimkus** | Y | N | Y | N | N | Y | Y | Y |
| **INDIANA** | | | | | | | | |
| 1 Visclosky | Y | N | N | Y | N | Y | N | N |
| 2 **Chocola** | Y | N | N | N | N | Y | Y | Y |
| 3 **Souder** | Y | N | N | N | N | Y | Y | Y |
| 4 **Buyer** | Y | N | N | N | N | Y | Y | Y |
| 5 **Burton** | Y | N | N | N | N | Y | Y | Y |
| 6 **Pence** | Y | ? | N | N | N | Y | Y | Y |
| 7 Carson | Y | Y | Y | Y | Y | Y | N | N |
| 8 **Hostettler** | Y | N | Y | N | N | Y | Y | Y |
| 9 **Sodrel** | Y | N | N | N | N | Y | Y | Y |
| **IOWA** | | | | | | | | |
| 1 **Nussle** | Y | N | Y | N | N | Y | Y | Y |
| 2 **Leach** | Y | N | Y | Y | N | Y | Y | Y |
| 3 Boswell | ? | Y | Y | Y | Y | Y | N | N |
| 4 **Latham** | Y | N | N | N | N | Y | Y | Y |
| 5 **King** | Y | N | N | N | N | Y | Y | Y |
| **KANSAS** | | | | | | | | |
| 1 **Moran** | Y | N | N | N | N | Y | Y | Y |
| 2 **Ryun** | Y | N | N | N | N | Y | Y | Y |
| 3 Moore | Y | N | Y | Y | Y | Y | N | N |
| 4 **Tiahrt** | Y | N | N | N | N | Y | Y | Y |
| **KENTUCKY** | | | | | | | | |
| 1 **Whitfield** | Y | N | N | N | N | Y | Y | Y |
| 2 **Lewis** | Y | N | N | N | N | Y | Y | Y |
| 3 **Northup** | Y | N | N | N | N | Y | Y | Y |
| 4 **Davis** | Y | N | N | N | N | Y | Y | Y |
| 5 **Rogers** | Y | N | N | N | N | Y | Y | Y |
| 6 Chandler | Y | Y | Y | Y | Y | Y | N | N |
| **LOUISIANA** | | | | | | | | |
| 1 **Jindal** | Y | N | N | N | N | Y | Y | Y |
| 2 Jefferson | Y | N | Y | N | Y | Y | N | N |
| 3 Melancon | Y | N | Y | N | Y | Y | N | N |
| 4 **McCrery** | Y | ? | N | N | N | Y | Y | Y |
| 5 **Alexander** | Y | N | N | N | N | Y | Y | Y |
| 6 **Baker** | Y | N | N | N | N | Y | Y | Y |
| 7 **Boustany** | Y | N | N | N | N | Y | Y | Y |
| **MAINE** | | | | | | | | |
| 1 Allen | Y | + | + | + | Y | Y | N | N |
| 2 Michaud | Y | Y | Y | Y | Y | Y | N | N |
| **MARYLAND** | | | | | | | | |
| 1 **Gilchrest** | Y | N | N | N | N | Y | Y | Y |
| 2 Ruppersberger | Y | N | Y | Y | Y | Y | N | N |
| 3 Cardin | Y | N | N | Y | Y | Y | N | N |
| 4 Wynn | Y | N | Y | Y | Y | Y | N | N |
| 5 Hoyer | Y | N | N | Y | Y | Y | N | N |
| 6 **Bartlett** | Y | N | Y | N | N | Y | Y | Y |
| 7 Cummings | Y | N | Y | Y | Y | Y | N | N |
| 8 Van Hollen | Y | Y | N | Y | Y | Y | N | N |
| **MASSACHUSETTS** | | | | | | | | |
| 1 Olver | Y | Y | N | Y | Y | Y | N | N |
| 2 Neal | Y | Y | Y | Y | Y | Y | N | N |
| 3 McGovern | Y | Y | Y | Y | Y | Y | N | N |
| 4 Frank | Y | Y | Y | Y | Y | Y | N | N |
| 5 Meehan | Y | Y | Y | Y | Y | Y | N | N |
| 6 Tierney | Y | Y | Y | Y | N | Y | N | N |
| 7 Markey | Y | Y | Y | Y | Y | Y | N | N |
| 8 Capuano | Y | Y | N | Y | N | Y | N | N |
| 9 Lynch | Y | Y | Y | Y | N | Y | N | N |
| 10 Delahunt | Y | Y | Y | Y | Y | Y | N | N |
| **MICHIGAN** | | | | | | | | |
| 1 Stupak | Y | N | N | Y | N | Y | N | N |
| 2 **Hoekstra** | Y | N | N | N | N | Y | Y | Y |
| 3 **Ehlers** | Y | N | N | N | N | Y | Y | Y |
| 4 **Camp** | Y | N | N | N | N | Y | Y | Y |
| 5 Kildee | Y | N | Y | Y | Y | Y | N | N |
| 6 **Upton** | Y | N | N | N | N | Y | Y | Y |
| 7 **Schwarz** | Y | N | N | N | N | Y | Y | Y |
| 8 **Rogers** | Y | N | N | N | N | Y | Y | Y |
| 9 **Knollenberg** | Y | N | N | N | N | Y | Y | Y |
| 10 **Miller** | Y | N | N | N | N | Y | Y | Y |
| 11 **McCotter** | Y | N | N | N | N | Y | Y | Y |
| 12 Levin | Y | N | N | Y | Y | Y | N | N |
| 13 Kilpatrick | Y | N | N | Y | Y | Y | N | N |
| 14 Conyers | Y | Y | Y | Y | Y | Y | N | N |
| 15 Dingell | ? | N | N | N | Y | Y | N | N |

| | 206 | 207 | 208 | 209 | 210 | 211 | 212 | 213 |
|---|---|---|---|---|---|---|---|---|
| **MINNESOTA** | | | | | | | | |
| 1 **Gutknecht** | Y | N | Y | Y | N | Y | Y | Y |
| 2 **Kline** | Y | N | N | N | N | Y | Y | Y |
| 3 **Ramstad** | Y | N | N | N | N | Y | Y | Y |
| 4 McCollum | Y | Y | N | Y | Y | Y | N | N |
| 5 Sabo | Y | Y | N | N | N | Y | N | N |
| 6 **Kennedy** | Y | N | N | N | N | Y | Y | Y |
| 7 Peterson | Y | N | Y | Y | N | Y | N | N |
| 8 Oberstar | Y | Y | Y | Y | N | Y | N | N |
| **MISSISSIPPI** | | | | | | | | |
| 1 **Wicker** | ? | N | N | N | N | Y | Y | Y |
| 2 Thompson | Y | N | N | N | Y | Y | N | N |
| 3 **Pickering** | Y | ? | ? | ? | ? | ? | ? | ? |
| 4 Taylor | Y | N | Y | Y | N | Y | N | N |
| **MISSOURI** | | | | | | | | |
| 1 Clay | Y | Y | Y | Y | Y | Y | ? | ? |
| 2 **Akin** | Y | N | N | N | N | Y | Y | Y |
| 3 Carnahan | Y | N | Y | Y | Y | Y | N | N |
| 4 Skelton | Y | N | Y | N | Y | Y | N | N |
| 5 Cleaver | Y | N | N | Y | Y | Y | N | N |
| 6 **Graves** | Y | N | N | N | N | Y | Y | Y |
| 7 **Blunt** | Y | N | N | N | N | Y | Y | Y |
| 8 **Emerson** | Y | N | N | N | N | Y | ? | ? |
| 9 **Hulshof** | Y | N | Y | N | N | Y | Y | Y |
| **MONTANA** | | | | | | | | |
| AL **Rehberg** | Y | N | N | N | N | Y | Y | Y |
| **NEBRASKA** | | | | | | | | |
| 1 **Fortenberry** | Y | N | Y | N | N | Y | Y | Y |
| 2 **Terry** | Y | N | Y | Y | N | Y | Y | Y |
| 3 **Osborne** | ? | N | N | N | N | Y | Y | Y |
| **NEVADA** | | | | | | | | |
| 1 Berkley | Y | Y | Y | Y | N | N | N | N |
| 2 **Gibbons** | Y | Y | Y | N | N | N | Y | Y |
| 3 **Porter** | Y | N | Y | N | N | N | Y | Y |
| **NEW HAMPSHIRE** | | | | | | | | |
| 1 **Bradley** | Y | N | N | N | N | Y | Y | Y |
| 2 **Bass** | Y | N | N | N | N | Y | Y | Y |
| **NEW JERSEY** | | | | | | | | |
| 1 Andrews | Y | N | N | Y | Y | Y | N | Y |
| 2 **LoBiondo** | Y | N | N | N | N | Y | Y | Y |
| 3 **Saxton** | Y | N | N | N | N | Y | Y | Y |
| 4 **Smith** | Y | N | N | N | N | Y | Y | Y |
| 5 **Garrett** | Y | N | N | N | N | Y | Y | Y |
| 6 Pallone | Y | Y | Y | Y | Y | Y | N | N |
| 7 **Ferguson** | Y | N | N | N | N | Y | Y | Y |
| 8 Pascrell | Y | N | N | Y | Y | Y | N | N |
| 9 Rothman | Y | N | N | Y | Y | Y | N | N |
| 10 Payne | Y | Y | Y | Y | Y | Y | N | N |
| 11 **Frelinghuysen** | Y | N | N | N | N | Y | Y | Y |
| 12 Holt | Y | Y | N | Y | N | Y | N | N |
| 13 Menendez | Y | Y | Y | Y | Y | Y | N | N |
| **NEW MEXICO** | | | | | | | | |
| 1 **Wilson** | Y | N | N | N | N | Y | Y | Y |
| 2 **Pearce** | Y | N | N | N | N | Y | Y | Y |
| 3 Udall | Y | Y | Y | Y | N | Y | N | N |
| **NEW YORK** | | | | | | | | |
| 1 Bishop | Y | Y | Y | Y | Y | Y | N | N |
| 2 Israel | Y | Y | Y | Y | Y | Y | N | N |
| 3 **King** | Y | N | Y | N | N | Y | Y | Y |
| 4 McCarthy | Y | N | N | Y | Y | Y | N | N |
| 5 Ackerman | Y | Y | Y | Y | Y | Y | N | N |
| 6 Meeks | ? | N | N | Y | Y | Y | N | N |
| 7 Crowley | Y | Y | N | Y | Y | Y | N | N |
| 8 Nadler | Y | Y | N | Y | Y | Y | N | N |
| 9 Weiner | Y | Y | Y | Y | Y | Y | N | N |
| 10 Towns | Y | N | Y | Y | Y | Y | N | N |
| 11 Owens | Y | Y | N | Y | Y | Y | N | N |
| 12 Velázquez | Y | Y | N | Y | Y | Y | N | N |
| 13 **Fossella** | Y | N | Y | N | N | Y | Y | Y |
| 14 Maloney | Y | Y | Y | Y | Y | Y | N | N |
| 15 Rangel | Y | Y | Y | Y | Y | Y | N | N |
| 16 Serrano | Y | Y | N | Y | Y | Y | N | N |
| 17 Engel | Y | N | Y | Y | Y | Y | N | N |
| 18 Lowey | Y | Y | Y | Y | Y | Y | N | N |
| 19 **Kelly** | Y | N | N | Y | N | Y | Y | Y |
| 20 **Sweeney** | Y | N | N | N | N | Y | Y | Y |
| 21 McNulty | Y | Y | N | Y | Y | Y | N | N |
| 22 Hinchey | Y | Y | N | Y | N | Y | N | N |
| 23 **McHugh** | Y | N | N | N | N | Y | Y | Y |
| 24 **Boehlert** | Y | N | N | N | N | Y | Y | Y |
| 25 **Walsh** | Y | N | N | N | N | Y | Y | Y |
| 26 **Reynolds** | Y | N | N | N | N | Y | Y | Y |
| 27 Higgins | Y | N | Y | Y | Y | Y | N | N |
| 28 Slaughter | Y | Y | Y | Y | Y | Y | N | N |
| 29 **Kuhl** | Y | N | N | N | N | Y | Y | Y |

| | 206 | 207 | 208 | 209 | 210 | 211 | 212 | 213 |
|---|---|---|---|---|---|---|---|---|
| **NORTH CAROLINA** | | | | | | | | |
| 1 Butterfield | Y | N | Y | Y | Y | Y | N | N |
| 2 Etheridge | Y | N | Y | Y | Y | N | N | N |
| 3 **Jones** | Y | N | Y | Y | Y | Y | Y | ? |
| 4 Price | Y | N | Y | Y | Y | Y | N | N |
| 5 **Foxx** | Y | N | N | N | N | Y | Y | Y |
| 6 **Coble** | Y | N | Y | N | N | Y | Y | Y |
| 7 McIntyre | Y | N | Y | Y | Y | Y | N | N |
| 8 **Hayes** | Y | N | N | N | N | Y | Y | Y |
| 9 **Myrick** | Y | N | N | N | N | Y | Y | Y |
| 10 **McHenry** | Y | N | N | N | N | Y | Y | Y |
| 11 **Taylor** | Y | N | N | N | N | Y | Y | Y |
| 12 Watt | Y | N | Y | Y | Y | Y | N | N |
| 13 Miller | Y | N | N | Y | Y | Y | N | N |
| **NORTH DAKOTA** | | | | | | | | |
| AL Pomeroy | Y | N | Y | Y | Y | Y | N | N |
| **OHIO** | | | | | | | | |
| 1 **Chabot** | Y | N | N | N | N | Y | Y | Y |
| 2 Vacant | | | | | | | | |
| 3 **Turner** | Y | N | N | N | N | Y | Y | Y |
| 4 **Oxley** | Y | N | N | N | N | Y | Y | Y |
| 5 **Gillmor** | Y | N | N | N | N | Y | Y | Y |
| 6 Strickland | Y | N | Y | Y | Y | Y | N | N |
| 7 **Hobson** | Y | N | N | N | N | Y | Y | Y |
| 8 **Boehner** | Y | N | Y | N | N | Y | Y | Y |
| 9 Kaptur | Y | N | N | N | N | Y | N | N |
| 10 Kucinich | Y | Y | Y | Y | Y | N | N | N |
| 11 Jones | Y | N | N | Y | Y | Y | N | N |
| 12 **Tiberi** | Y | N | N | N | N | Y | Y | Y |
| 13 Brown | Y | Y | Y | Y | Y | Y | N | N |
| 14 **LaTourette** | Y | N | N | N | N | Y | Y | Y |
| 15 **Pryce** | Y | N | N | N | N | Y | Y | Y |
| 16 **Regula** | Y | N | N | N | N | Y | Y | Y |
| 17 Ryan | Y | Y | N | Y | Y | Y | N | N |
| 18 **Ney** | Y | N | N | N | N | Y | Y | Y |
| **OKLAHOMA** | | | | | | | | |
| 1 **Sullivan** | Y | N | N | N | N | Y | Y | Y |
| 2 Boren | Y | N | N | N | N | Y | N | N |
| 3 **Lucas** | Y | N | N | N | N | Y | Y | Y |
| 4 **Cole** | Y | N | N | N | N | Y | Y | Y |
| 5 **Istook** | Y | N | N | N | N | Y | Y | Y |
| **OREGON** | | | | | | | | |
| 1 Wu | Y | Y | N | Y | Y | Y | N | N |
| 2 **Walden** | Y | N | N | N | N | Y | Y | Y |
| 3 Blumenauer | Y | Y | N | N | N | Y | N | N |
| 4 DeFazio | N | Y | Y | Y | Y | Y | N | N |
| 5 Hooley | Y | Y | Y | Y | Y | Y | N | N |
| **PENNSYLVANIA** | | | | | | | | |
| 1 Brady | Y | N | N | Y | Y | Y | N | N |
| 2 Fattah | Y | N | N | Y | Y | Y | N | N |
| 3 **English** | Y | N | N | N | N | Y | Y | Y |
| 4 **Hart** | Y | N | N | N | N | Y | Y | Y |
| 5 **Peterson** | Y | N | N | N | N | Y | Y | Y |
| 6 **Gerlach** | Y | N | Y | N | N | Y | Y | Y |
| 7 **Weldon** | Y | N | N | N | N | Y | Y | Y |
| 8 **Fitzpatrick** | Y | N | N | N | N | Y | Y | Y |
| 9 **Shuster** | Y | N | N | N | N | Y | Y | Y |
| 10 **Sherwood** | Y | N | N | N | N | Y | Y | Y |
| 11 Kanjorski | Y | N | N | N | N | Y | N | N |
| 12 Murtha | Y | N | N | N | N | Y | ? | ? |
| 13 Schwartz | Y | Y | N | Y | Y | Y | N | N |
| 14 Doyle | Y | N | N | Y | Y | Y | N | N |
| 15 **Dent** | Y | N | N | N | N | Y | Y | Y |
| 16 **Pitts** | Y | N | N | N | N | Y | Y | Y |
| 17 Holden | Y | N | N | Y | N | Y | N | N |
| 18 **Murphy** | Y | N | Y | N | N | Y | Y | Y |
| 19 **Platts** | Y | N | N | N | N | Y | Y | Y |
| **RHODE ISLAND** | | | | | | | | |
| 1 Kennedy | Y | Y | Y | Y | Y | Y | N | N |
| 2 Langevin | Y | Y | Y | Y | Y | Y | N | N |
| **SOUTH CAROLINA** | | | | | | | | |
| 1 **Brown** | Y | N | N | N | N | Y | Y | Y |
| 2 **Wilson** | Y | N | Y | N | N | Y | Y | Y |
| 3 **Barrett** | Y | N | N | N | N | Y | Y | Y |
| 4 **Inglis** | Y | N | N | N | N | Y | Y | Y |
| 5 Spratt | Y | Y | N | Y | Y | Y | N | N |
| 6 Clyburn | Y | N | N | N | Y | Y | N | N |
| **SOUTH DAKOTA** | | | | | | | | |
| AL Herseth | Y | N | Y | Y | Y | Y | N | N |
| **TENNESSEE** | | | | | | | | |
| 1 **Jenkins** | Y | N | Y | N | N | Y | Y | Y |
| 2 **Duncan** | Y | N | Y | N | N | Y | Y | Y |

| | 206 | 207 | 208 | 209 | 210 | 211 | 212 | 213 |
|---|---|---|---|---|---|---|---|---|
| 3 **Wamp** | Y | ? | ? | N | N | Y | Y | Y |
| 4 Davis | Y | N | Y | N | Y | Y | N | N |
| 5 Cooper | Y | Y | N | N | Y | Y | N | N |
| 6 Gordon | Y | N | N | Y | Y | Y | N | N |
| 7 **Blackburn** | Y | N | N | N | N | Y | Y | Y |
| 8 Tanner | Y | N | Y | Y | Y | Y | N | N |
| 9 Ford | Y | Y | Y | N | Y | Y | N | N |
| **TEXAS** | | | | | | | | |
| 1 **Gohmert** | Y | N | N | N | N | Y | Y | Y |
| 2 **Poe** | Y | N | Y | N | N | Y | Y | Y |
| 3 **Johnson, S.** | Y | N | Y | N | N | Y | Y | Y |
| 4 **Hall** | Y | N | N | N | N | Y | Y | Y |
| 5 **Hensarling** | Y | N | N | N | N | Y | Y | Y |
| 6 **Barton** | Y | N | N | N | N | Y | Y | Y |
| 7 **Culberson** | Y | N | N | N | N | Y | Y | Y |
| 8 **Brady** | Y | N | N | N | N | Y | Y | Y |
| 9 Green | Y | N | Y | Y | Y | Y | N | N |
| 10 **McCaul** | Y | N | Y | N | N | Y | Y | Y |
| 11 **Conaway** | Y | N | N | N | N | Y | Y | Y |
| 12 **Granger** | Y | N | N | N | N | Y | Y | Y |
| 13 **Thornberry** | Y | N | N | N | N | Y | Y | Y |
| 14 **Paul** | Y | N | Y | Y | N | N | Y | Y |
| 15 Hinojosa | Y | N | Y | N | Y | Y | N | N |
| 16 Reyes | Y | N | Y | N | N | Y | N | N |
| 17 Edwards | Y | N | N | Y | N | Y | N | N |
| 18 Jackson-Lee | Y | N | Y | Y | Y | Y | N | N |
| 19 **Neugebauer** | Y | N | N | N | N | Y | Y | Y |
| 20 Gonzalez | Y | N | Y | N | N | Y | N | N |
| 21 **Smith** | Y | N | N | N | N | Y | Y | Y |
| 22 **DeLay** | Y | N | N | N | N | Y | Y | Y |
| 23 **Bonilla** | Y | N | N | N | N | Y | Y | Y |
| 24 **Marchant** | Y | N | N | N | N | Y | Y | Y |
| 25 Doggett | Y | ? | N | Y | Y | Y | N | N |
| 26 **Burgess** | Y | N | N | N | N | Y | Y | Y |
| 27 Ortiz | Y | N | Y | N | N | Y | N | N |
| 28 Cuellar | Y | N | N | N | Y | Y | N | N |
| 29 Green | Y | N | Y | N | N | Y | N | N |
| 30 Johnson, E. | Y | Y | Y | Y | Y | Y | N | N |
| 31 **Carter** | Y | N | N | N | N | Y | Y | Y |
| 32 **Sessions** | Y | N | Y | N | N | Y | Y | Y |
| **UTAH** | | | | | | | | |
| 1 **Bishop** | Y | N | Y | N | N | Y | Y | Y |
| 2 Matheson | Y | Y | Y | Y | Y | N | N | N |
| 3 **Cannon** | Y | N | Y | N | N | Y | Y | Y |
| **VERMONT** | | | | | | | | |
| AL *Sanders* | Y | Y | N | Y | Y | Y | N | N |
| **VIRGINIA** | | | | | | | | |
| 1 **Davis, J.** | Y | N | Y | Y | N | Y | Y | Y |
| 2 **Drake** | Y | N | N | N | N | Y | Y | Y |
| 3 Scott | Y | N | Y | Y | Y | Y | N | N |
| 4 **Forbes** | Y | N | Y | Y | N | Y | Y | Y |
| 5 **Goode** | Y | N | Y | N | N | Y | Y | Y |
| 6 **Goodlatte** | Y | N | N | Y | N | Y | Y | Y |
| 7 **Cantor** | Y | N | N | N | N | Y | Y | Y |
| 8 Moran | Y | N | Y | Y | Y | Y | N | N |
| 9 Boucher | Y | N | N | Y | Y | Y | N | N |
| 10 **Wolf** | Y | N | N | N | N | Y | Y | Y |
| 11 **Davis, T.** | Y | N | N | N | N | Y | Y | Y |
| **WASHINGTON** | | | | | | | | |
| 1 Inslee | Y | Y | Y | Y | Y | N | N | N |
| 2 Larsen | Y | Y | Y | Y | Y | Y | N | N |
| 3 Baird | Y | Y | Y | Y | Y | Y | N | N |
| 4 **Hastings** | ? | ? | ? | ? | ? | ? | ? | ? |
| 5 **McMorris** | Y | N | N | N | N | Y | Y | Y |
| 6 Dicks | Y | Y | N | Y | Y | Y | N | N |
| 7 McDermott | Y | Y | Y | Y | N | Y | N | N |
| 8 **Reichert** | Y | N | N | N | N | Y | Y | Y |
| 9 Smith | Y | Y | Y | N | N | Y | N | N |
| **WEST VIRGINIA** | | | | | | | | |
| 1 Mollohan | Y | N | N | N | N | Y | N | N |
| 2 **Capito** | Y | N | N | N | N | Y | Y | Y |
| 3 Rahall | Y | Y | Y | Y | Y | Y | N | N |
| **WISCONSIN** | | | | | | | | |
| 1 **Ryan** | Y | N | N | N | N | Y | Y | Y |
| 2 Baldwin | Y | Y | N | Y | Y | Y | N | N |
| 3 Kind | Y | N | Y | Y | N | Y | N | N |
| 4 Moore | Y | + | Y | Y | Y | Y | N | N |
| 5 **Sensenbrenner** | Y | N | N | N | N | N | Y | Y |
| 6 **Petri** | Y | N | Y | N | N | Y | Y | Y |
| 7 Obey | Y | Y | N | Y | Y | Y | N | N |
| 8 **Green** | Y | N | Y | Y | N | N | Y | Y |
| **WYOMING** | | | | | | | | |
| AL **Cubin** | Y | N | N | N | N | Y | Y | Y |

# IN THE HOUSE | By Vote Number

**214.** **HR 1815. Fiscal 2006 Defense Authorization/Border Security.**
Goode, R-Va., amendment that would authorize the Defense secretary to assign military personnel to assist the Homeland Security Department with border security under certain circumstances. Adopted 245-184: R 214-13; D 31-170 (ND 15-135, SD 16-35); I 0-1. May 25, 2005.

**215.** **HR 1815. Fiscal 2006 Defense Authorization/Boy Scouts.** J. Davis, R-Va., amendment that would require the Defense Department to provide the minimum level of support it provided the Boy Scouts and similar youth groups in the previous four fiscal years. Support would be defined as holding meetings, camping events, or other activities on Defense property and hosting any official event of the youth organization. Adopted 413-16: R 227-0; D 185-16 (ND 135-15, SD 50-1); I 1-0. May 25, 2005.

**216.** **HR 1815. Fiscal 2006 Defense Authorization/Abortion at Military Facilities.** Davis, D-Calif., amendment that would allow overseas military facilities to provide privately funded abortions for women who are in the military or are military dependents. Rejected 194-233: R 22-203; D 171-30 (ND 131-19, SD 40-11); I 1-0. A "nay" was a vote in support of the president's position. May 25, 2005.

**217.** **HR 1815. Fiscal 2006 Defense Authorization/Women in Combat.**
Hunter, R-Calif., amendment that would require the Defense Department to provide Congress with a detailed report on policy regarding women in combat by March 31, 2006. The Pentagon would be required to give Congress at least 60 legislative days advance notice before opening or closing any jobs to women. It would extend veterans' preference to individuals who served on active duty in the armed forces for more than 180 consecutive days between Sept. 11, 2001, and the end of Operation Iraqi Freedom and who were discharged under honorable conditions. Adopted 428-1: R 227-0; D 200-1 (ND 149-1, SD 51-0); I 1-0. May 25, 2005.

**218.** **HR 1815. Fiscal 2006 Defense Authorization/ROTC Programs.**
Stearns, R-Fla., amendment that would express the sense of Congress that any college or university that denies equal access or discriminates against Reserve Officer Training Corps (ROTC) programs or military recruiters should be denied certain federal taxpayer support, especially funding for military and defense programs. The amendment would require the Defense secretary to report to Congress on the colleges and universities that are denying equal access to military recruiters and ROTC programs. Adopted 336-92: R 227-0; D 109-91 (ND 70-80, SD 39-11); I 0-1. May 25, 2005.

**219.** **HR 1815. Fiscal 2006 Defense Authorization/BRAC Closures.** Bradley, R-N.H., amendment that would postpone the 2005 Base Realignment and Closure recommendations until one year after the Defense secretary has implemented recommendations of the Review of Overseas Military Facility Structure; a substantial number of U.S. troops return from Iraq; congressional committees receive the quadrennial defense review; the National Maritime Security Strategy is implemented; and the Homeland Defense and Civil Support Directive is implemented. Rejected 112-316: R 40-186; D 72-129 (ND 49-101, SD 23-28); I 0-1. A "nay" was a vote in support of the president's position. May 25, 2005.

**220.** **HR 1815. Fiscal 2006 Defense Authorization/Withdrawal From Iraq.**
Woolsey, D-Calif., amendment to express the sense of Congress that the president should develop a plan for withdrawing U.S. military forces from Iraq and submit it to the appropriate congressional committees. Rejected 128-300: R 5-221; D 122-79 (ND 101-49, SD 21-30); I 1-0. May 25, 2005.

ND Northern Democrats, SD Southern Democrats
Southern states: Ala., Ark., Fla., Ga., Ky., La., Miss., N.C., Okla., S.C., Tenn., Texas, Va.

| | 214 | 215 | 216 | 217 | 218 | 219 | 220 |
|---|---|---|---|---|---|---|---|
| **ALABAMA** | | | | | | | |
| 1 Bonner | Y | Y | N | Y | Y | N | N |
| 2 Everett | Y | Y | N | Y | Y | N | N |
| 3 Rogers | Y | Y | N | Y | Y | N | N |
| 4 Aderholt | Y | Y | N | Y | Y | N | N |
| 5 Cramer | Y | Y | Y | Y | Y | N | N |
| 6 Bachus | Y | Y | N | Y | Y | N | N |
| 7 Davis | N | Y | Y | Y | Y | Y | N |
| **ALASKA** | | | | | | | |
| AL Young | Y | Y | N | Y | Y | N | N |
| **ARIZONA** | | | | | | | |
| 1 Renzi | Y | Y | N | Y | Y | N | N |
| 2 Franks | Y | Y | N | Y | Y | N | N |
| 3 Shadegg | Y | Y | N | Y | Y | N | N |
| 4 Pastor | N | Y | Y | Y | N | N | Y |
| 5 Hayworth | Y | Y | N | Y | Y | N | N |
| 6 Flake | N | Y | N | Y | Y | N | N |
| 7 Grijalva | N | Y | Y | Y | N | N | Y |
| 8 Kolbe | N | Y | Y | Y | Y | N | N |
| **ARKANSAS** | | | | | | | |
| 1 Berry | N | Y | N | Y | Y | N | N |
| 2 Snyder | N | Y | Y | Y | Y | N | N |
| 3 Boozman | Y | Y | N | Y | Y | Y | N |
| 4 Ross | N | Y | N | Y | Y | Y | N |
| **CALIFORNIA** | | | | | | | |
| 1 Thompson | N | Y | Y | Y | N | N | Y |
| 2 Herger | Y | Y | N | Y | Y | N | N |
| 3 Lungren | Y | Y | N | Y | Y | N | N |
| 4 Doolittle | Y | Y | N | Y | Y | N | N |
| 5 Matsui, D. | N | Y | Y | Y | N | N | Y |
| 6 Woolsey | N | N | Y | Y | N | N | Y |
| 7 Miller, George | N | Y | Y | Y | N | N | Y |
| 8 Pelosi | N | Y | Y | Y | N | N | N |
| 9 Lee | N | N | Y | Y | N | N | Y |
| 10 Tauscher | N | Y | Y | Y | Y | N | N |
| 11 Pombo | Y | Y | N | Y | Y | N | N |
| 12 Lantos | N | Y | Y | Y | N | N | Y |
| 13 Stark | N | N | Y | Y | N | N | Y |
| 14 Eshoo | N | Y | Y | Y | N | N | Y |
| 15 Honda | N | Y | Y | Y | N | N | Y |
| 16 Lofgren | N | Y | Y | Y | N | N | Y |
| 17 Farr | N | Y | Y | Y | N | N | Y |
| 18 Cardoza | N | Y | Y | Y | Y | Y | N |
| 19 Radanovich | Y | Y | N | Y | Y | N | N |
| 20 Costa | N | Y | Y | Y | Y | N | N |
| 21 Nunes | Y | Y | N | Y | Y | N | N |
| 22 Thomas | Y | Y | Y | Y | Y | N | N |
| 23 Capps | N | Y | Y | Y | N | Y | Y |
| 24 Gallegly | Y | Y | N | Y | Y | N | N |
| 25 McKeon | Y | Y | N | Y | Y | N | N |
| 26 Dreier | N | Y | N | Y | Y | N | N |
| 27 Sherman | N | Y | Y | Y | Y | N | Y |
| 28 Berman | N | Y | Y | Y | Y | N | N |
| 29 Schiff | N | Y | Y | Y | Y | N | N |
| 30 Waxman | N | Y | Y | Y | N | N | Y |
| 31 Becerra | N | Y | Y | Y | N | N | Y |
| 32 Solis | N | N | Y | Y | N | N | Y |
| 33 Watson | N | Y | Y | Y | N | Y | Y |
| 34 Roybal-Allard | N | Y | Y | Y | N | N | N |
| 35 Waters | N | Y | Y | Y | N | N | Y |
| 36 Harman | N | Y | Y | Y | Y | N | N |
| 37 Millender-McD. | ? | ? | ? | ? | ? | ? | ? |
| 38 Napolitano | N | Y | Y | Y | N | N | Y |
| 39 Sánchez, Linda | N | N | Y | Y | N | N | Y |
| 40 Royce | Y | Y | N | Y | Y | N | N |
| 41 Lewis | Y | Y | N | Y | Y | N | N |
| 42 Miller, Gary | Y | Y | N | Y | Y | N | N |
| 43 Baca | N | Y | Y | Y | Y | N | N |
| 44 Calvert | Y | Y | N | Y | Y | N | N |
| 45 Bono | Y | Y | Y | Y | Y | N | N |
| 46 Rohrabacher | Y | Y | N | Y | Y | N | N |
| 47 Sanchez, Loretta | N | Y | Y | Y | Y | N | N |
| 48 Cox | Y | Y | N | Y | Y | N | N |
| 49 Issa | Y | Y | N | Y | Y | N | N |

| | 214 | 215 | 216 | 217 | 218 | 219 | 220 |
|---|---|---|---|---|---|---|---|
| 50 Cunningham | Y | Y | N | Y | Y | N | N |
| 51 Filner | N | Y | Y | Y | N | N | Y |
| 52 Hunter | Y | Y | N | Y | Y | N | N |
| 53 Davis | N | Y | Y | Y | Y | N | N |
| **COLORADO** | | | | | | | |
| 1 DeGette | N | Y | Y | Y | N | N | Y |
| 2 Udall | Y | Y | Y | Y | Y | N | N |
| 3 Salazar | N | Y | N | Y | Y | N | N |
| 4 Musgrave | Y | Y | N | Y | Y | N | N |
| 5 Hefley | Y | Y | N | Y | Y | N | N |
| 6 Tancredo | Y | Y | N | Y | Y | N | N |
| 7 Beauprez | Y | Y | N | Y | Y | N | N |
| **CONNECTICUT** | | | | | | | |
| 1 Larson | N | Y | Y | Y | N | Y | Y |
| 2 Simmons | N | Y | Y | Y | Y | Y | Y |
| 3 DeLauro | N | Y | Y | Y | N | Y | Y |
| 4 Shays | Y | Y | Y | Y | Y | Y | Y |
| 5 Johnson | Y | Y | Y | Y | Y | Y | Y |
| **DELAWARE** | | | | | | | |
| AL Castle | Y | Y | Y | Y | Y | N | N |
| **FLORIDA** | | | | | | | |
| 1 Miller | Y | Y | N | Y | Y | N | N |
| 2 Boyd | Y | Y | Y | Y | Y | N | N |
| 3 Brown | N | Y | Y | Y | Y | N | N |
| 4 Crenshaw | Y | Y | N | Y | Y | N | N |
| 5 Brown-Waite | Y | Y | N | Y | Y | Y | N |
| 6 Stearns | Y | Y | N | Y | Y | N | N |
| 7 Mica | Y | Y | – | Y | Y | N | N |
| 8 Keller | Y | Y | N | Y | Y | N | N |
| 9 Bilirakis | Y | Y | N | Y | Y | N | N |
| 10 Young | Y | Y | N | Y | Y | N | N |
| 11 Davis | N | Y | Y | Y | Y | N | N |
| 12 Putnam | N | Y | N | Y | Y | N | N |
| 13 Harris | Y | Y | N | Y | Y | N | N |
| 14 Mack | Y | Y | N | Y | Y | N | N |
| 15 Weldon | Y | Y | N | Y | Y | Y | N |
| 16 Foley | Y | Y | N | Y | Y | N | N |
| 17 Meek | N | Y | Y | Y | N | N | N |
| 18 Ros-Lehtinen | Y | Y | Y | Y | Y | N | N |
| 19 Wexler | N | Y | Y | Y | N | N | Y |
| 20 Wasserman-Schultz | N | N | Y | Y | N | Y | Y |
| 21 Diaz-Balart, L. | Y | Y | N | Y | Y | N | N |
| 22 Shaw | Y | Y | Y | Y | Y | N | N |
| 23 Hastings | N | Y | Y | Y | N | Y | Y |
| 24 Feeney | Y | Y | N | Y | Y | N | N |
| 25 Diaz-Balart, M. | Y | Y | N | Y | Y | N | N |
| **GEORGIA** | | | | | | | |
| 1 Kingston | Y | Y | N | Y | Y | N | N |
| 2 Bishop | Y | Y | Y | Y | Y | N | N |
| 3 Marshall | Y | Y | N | Y | Y | N | N |
| 4 McKinney | N | Y | Y | Y | N | N | Y |
| 5 Lewis | N | Y | Y | Y | N | Y | Y |
| 6 Price | Y | Y | N | Y | Y | N | N |
| 7 Linder | Y | Y | N | Y | Y | N | N |
| 8 Westmoreland | Y | Y | N | Y | Y | N | N |
| 9 Norwood | Y | Y | N | Y | Y | N | N |
| 10 Deal | Y | Y | N | Y | Y | N | N |
| 11 Gingrey | Y | Y | N | Y | Y | N | N |
| 12 Barrow | Y | Y | Y | Y | Y | Y | N |
| 13 Scott | N | Y | Y | Y | Y | Y | N |
| **HAWAII** | | | | | | | |
| 1 Abercrombie | N | Y | Y | Y | Y | Y | Y |
| 2 Case | Y | Y | Y | Y | Y | N | N |
| **IDAHO** | | | | | | | |
| 1 Otter | Y | Y | N | Y | Y | N | N |
| 2 Simpson | Y | Y | N | Y | Y | N | N |
| **ILLINOIS** | | | | | | | |
| 1 Rush | N | Y | Y | Y | N | N | Y |
| 2 Jackson | N | Y | Y | Y | N | N | Y |
| 3 Lipinski | N | Y | N | Y | Y | N | Y |
| 4 Gutierrez | N | N | Y | Y | N | N | Y |
| 5 Emanuel | N | Y | Y | Y | N | N | Y |
| 6 Hyde | Y | Y | N | Y | Y | N | N |
| 7 Davis | N | Y | Y | Y | N | N | Y |
| 8 Bean | N | Y | Y | Y | Y | N | N |
| 9 Schakowsky | N | N | Y | Y | N | Y | Y |
| 10 Kirk | Y | Y | Y | Y | Y | N | N |
| 11 Weller | Y | Y | N | Y | Y | N | N |
| 12 Costello | Y | Y | N | Y | Y | N | Y |

**KEY** Republicans    Democrats    *Independents*

| | | |
|---|---|---|
| Y Voted for (yea) | X Paired against | C Voted "present" to avoid possible conflict of interest |
| # Paired for | – Announced against | |
| + Announced for | P Voted "present" | ? Did not vote or otherwise make a position known |
| N Voted against (nay) | | |

| | 214 | 215 | 216 | 217 | 218 | 219 | 220 |
|---|---|---|---|---|---|---|---|
| 13 **Biggert** | Y | Y | Y | Y | Y | N | N |
| 14 **Hastert** | | | | | | | |
| 15 **Johnson** | Y | Y | N | Y | Y | N | N |
| 16 **Manzullo** | Y | Y | N | Y | Y | Y | N |
| 17 Evans | N | Y | Y | Y | Y | Y | Y |
| 18 **LaHood** | Y | Y | N | Y | Y | Y | N |
| 19 **Shimkus** | Y | Y | N | Y | Y | Y | N |
| **INDIANA** | | | | | | | |
| 1 Visclosky | N | Y | Y | Y | Y | N | N |
| 2 **Chocola** | Y | Y | N | Y | Y | N | N |
| 3 **Souder** | N | Y | N | Y | Y | N | N |
| 4 **Buyer** | N | Y | ? | Y | Y | N | N |
| 5 **Burton** | Y | Y | N | Y | Y | N | N |
| 6 **Pence** | Y | Y | N | Y | Y | N | N |
| 7 Carson | N | Y | Y | Y | N | N | Y |
| 8 **Hostettler** | Y | Y | N | Y | Y | N | N |
| 9 **Sodrel** | Y | Y | N | Y | Y | N | N |
| **IOWA** | | | | | | | |
| 1 **Nussle** | Y | Y | N | Y | Y | N | N |
| 2 **Leach** | Y | Y | Y | Y | Y | N | Y |
| 3 Boswell | Y | Y | Y | Y | Y | N | Y |
| 4 **Latham** | Y | Y | N | Y | Y | N | N |
| 5 **King** | Y | Y | N | Y | Y | N | N |
| **KANSAS** | | | | | | | |
| 1 **Moran** | Y | Y | N | Y | Y | N | N |
| 2 **Ryun** | Y | Y | N | Y | Y | N | N |
| 3 Moore | Y | Y | Y | Y | Y | N | N |
| 4 **Tiahrt** | Y | Y | N | Y | Y | N | N |
| **KENTUCKY** | | | | | | | |
| 1 **Whitfield** | Y | Y | N | Y | Y | N | N |
| 2 **Lewis** | Y | Y | N | Y | Y | N | N |
| 3 **Northup** | Y | Y | N | Y | Y | N | N |
| 4 **Davis** | Y | Y | N | Y | Y | N | N |
| 5 **Rogers** | Y | Y | N | Y | Y | N | N |
| 6 Chandler | Y | Y | Y | Y | ? | N | N |
| **LOUISIANA** | | | | | | | |
| 1 **Jindal** | Y | Y | N | Y | Y | Y | N |
| 2 Jefferson | N | Y | Y | Y | Y | Y | Y |
| 3 Melancon | N | Y | N | Y | N | Y | Y |
| 4 **McCrery** | Y | Y | N | Y | Y | N | N |
| 5 **Alexander** | Y | Y | N | Y | Y | N | N |
| 6 **Baker** | Y | Y | N | Y | Y | N | N |
| 7 **Boustany** | Y | Y | N | Y | Y | N | N |
| **MAINE** | | | | | | | |
| 1 Allen | N | Y | Y | Y | N | Y | Y |
| 2 Michaud | N | Y | N | Y | N | Y | Y |
| **MARYLAND** | | | | | | | |
| 1 **Gilchrest** | Y | Y | Y | Y | Y | N | N |
| 2 Ruppersberger | N | Y | Y | Y | Y | N | N |
| 3 Cardin | N | Y | Y | Y | Y | N | N |
| 4 Wynn | N | Y | Y | Y | Y | N | Y |
| 5 Hoyer | N | Y | Y | Y | Y | N | N |
| 6 **Bartlett** | Y | Y | N | Y | Y | N | N |
| 7 Cummings | N | Y | Y | Y | Y | N | Y |
| 8 Van Hollen | N | Y | Y | Y | Y | N | Y |
| **MASSACHUSETTS** | | | | | | | |
| 1 Olver | N | Y | Y | Y | N | N | Y |
| 2 Neal | N | Y | Y | Y | N | N | Y |
| 3 McGovern | N | Y | Y | Y | N | N | Y |
| 4 Frank | N | N | Y | Y | N | N | Y |
| 5 Meehan | N | Y | Y | Y | N | N | Y |
| 6 Tierney | N | Y | Y | Y | N | N | Y |
| 7 Markey | N | Y | Y | Y | N | N | Y |
| 8 Capuano | N | Y | Y | Y | Y | N | Y |
| 9 Lynch | N | Y | N | Y | Y | Y | Y |
| 10 Delahunt | N | Y | Y | Y | Y | Y | Y |
| **MICHIGAN** | | | | | | | |
| 1 Stupak | N | Y | N | Y | Y | N | N |
| 2 **Hoekstra** | Y | Y | N | Y | Y | N | N |
| 3 **Ehlers** | N | Y | N | Y | Y | Y | N |
| 4 **Camp** | Y | Y | N | Y | Y | N | N |
| 5 Kildee | N | Y | N | Y | Y | N | N |
| 6 **Upton** | Y | Y | N | Y | Y | N | N |
| 7 **Schwarz** | Y | Y | N | Y | Y | Y | N |
| 8 **Rogers** | Y | Y | N | Y | Y | N | N |
| 9 **Knollenberg** | Y | Y | N | Y | Y | N | N |
| 10 **Miller** | Y | Y | N | Y | Y | N | N |
| 11 **McCotter** | Y | Y | N | Y | Y | Y | N |
| 12 Levin | N | Y | Y | Y | N | N | N |
| 13 Kilpatrick | N | Y | Y | Y | N | N | Y |
| 14 Conyers | N | N | Y | Y | N | N | Y |
| 15 Dingell | N | Y | Y | Y | N | N | N |

| | 214 | 215 | 216 | 217 | 218 | 219 | 220 |
|---|---|---|---|---|---|---|---|
| **MINNESOTA** | | | | | | | |
| 1 **Gutknecht** | Y | Y | N | Y | Y | N | N |
| 2 **Kline** | N | Y | N | Y | Y | N | N |
| 3 **Ramstad** | Y | Y | Y | Y | Y | N | N |
| 4 McCollum | N | Y | Y | Y | N | Y | Y |
| 5 Sabo | N | Y | Y | Y | Y | N | Y |
| 6 **Kennedy** | Y | Y | N | Y | Y | N | N |
| 7 Peterson | Y | Y | N | Y | Y | N | N |
| 8 Oberstar | N | Y | N | Y | N | Y | Y |
| **MISSISSIPPI** | | | | | | | |
| 1 **Wicker** | Y | Y | N | Y | Y | Y | N |
| 2 Thompson | N | Y | Y | Y | Y | Y | Y |
| 3 **Pickering** | Y | Y | N | Y | Y | Y | N |
| 4 Taylor | Y | Y | N | Y | Y | Y | N |
| **MISSOURI** | | | | | | | |
| 1 Clay | N | Y | Y | Y | Y | Y | Y |
| 2 **Akin** | Y | Y | N | Y | Y | N | N |
| 3 Carnahan | N | Y | Y | Y | Y | N | Y |
| 4 Skelton | N | Y | N | Y | Y | N | N |
| 5 Cleaver | N | Y | Y | Y | Y | N | Y |
| 6 **Graves** | Y | Y | N | Y | Y | N | N |
| 7 **Blunt** | Y | Y | N | Y | Y | N | N |
| 8 **Emerson** | ? | ? | ? | ? | ? | ? | ? |
| 9 **Hulshof** | Y | Y | N | Y | Y | N | N |
| **MONTANA** | | | | | | | |
| AL **Rehberg** | Y | Y | N | Y | Y | Y | N |
| **NEBRASKA** | | | | | | | |
| 1 **Fortenberry** | Y | Y | N | Y | Y | N | N |
| 2 **Terry** | Y | Y | N | Y | Y | N | N |
| 3 **Osborne** | Y | Y | N | Y | Y | N | N |
| **NEVADA** | | | | | | | |
| 1 Berkley | N | Y | Y | Y | Y | N | N |
| 2 **Gibbons** | Y | Y | N | Y | Y | Y | N |
| 3 **Porter** | Y | Y | N | Y | Y | N | ? |
| **NEW HAMPSHIRE** | | | | | | | |
| 1 **Bradley** | Y | Y | Y | Y | Y | Y | N |
| 2 **Bass** | Y | Y | Y | Y | Y | Y | N |
| **NEW JERSEY** | | | | | | | |
| 1 Andrews | N | Y | Y | Y | Y | N | N |
| 2 **LoBiondo** | Y | Y | N | Y | Y | N | N |
| 3 **Saxton** | Y | Y | N | Y | Y | N | N |
| 4 **Smith** | Y | Y | N | Y | Y | Y | N |
| 5 **Garrett** | Y | Y | N | Y | Y | N | N |
| 6 Pallone | N | Y | Y | Y | N | Y | Y |
| 7 **Ferguson** | Y | Y | N | Y | Y | N | N |
| 8 Pascrell | N | Y | Y | Y | N | Y | Y |
| 9 Rothman | N | Y | Y | Y | N | Y | Y |
| 10 Payne | N | Y | Y | Y | N | Y | Y |
| 11 **Frelinghuysen** | Y | Y | Y | Y | Y | N | N |
| 12 Holt | N | Y | Y | Y | N | Y | Y |
| 13 Menendez | N | Y | Y | Y | Y | Y | Y |
| **NEW MEXICO** | | | | | | | |
| 1 **Wilson** | N | Y | N | Y | Y | Y | N |
| 2 **Pearce** | N | Y | N | Y | Y | Y | N |
| 3 Udall | N | Y | Y | Y | N | Y | Y |
| **NEW YORK** | | | | | | | |
| 1 Bishop | Y | Y | Y | Y | Y | N | N |
| 2 Israel | Y | Y | Y | Y | Y | N | N |
| 3 **King** | Y | Y | N | Y | Y | N | N |
| 4 McCarthy | Y | Y | Y | Y | Y | N | N |
| 5 Ackerman | N | N | Y | Y | N | N | N |
| 6 Meeks | N | Y | Y | Y | N | N | Y |
| 7 Crowley | N | Y | Y | Y | N | Y | N |
| 8 Nadler | N | Y | Y | Y | N | N | Y |
| 9 Weiner | N | Y | Y | Y | N | N | Y |
| 10 Towns | N | Y | Y | Y | N | Y | N |
| 11 Owens | N | Y | Y | Y | N | Y | Y |
| 12 Velázquez | N | Y | Y | Y | N | Y | Y |
| 13 **Fossella** | Y | Y | N | Y | Y | N | N |
| 14 Maloney | N | Y | Y | N | N | N | Y |
| 15 Rangel | N | Y | Y | Y | N | N | Y |
| 16 Serrano | N | Y | Y | Y | N | Y | Y |
| 17 Engel | N | Y | Y | Y | Y | N | N |
| 18 Lowey | N | Y | Y | Y | N | Y | N |
| 19 **Kelly** | Y | Y | Y | Y | Y | N | N |
| 20 **Sweeney** | Y | Y | N | Y | Y | N | N |
| 21 McNulty | N | Y | N | Y | N | Y | Y |
| 22 Hinchey | N | Y | Y | Y | N | Y | Y |
| 23 **McHugh** | Y | Y | N | Y | Y | N | N |
| 24 **Boehlert** | Y | Y | Y | Y | Y | N | N |
| 25 **Walsh** | Y | Y | N | Y | Y | N | N |
| 26 **Reynolds** | Y | Y | N | Y | Y | Y | N |
| 27 Higgins | N | Y | Y | Y | Y | Y | N |
| 28 Slaughter | N | Y | Y | Y | N | Y | Y |
| 29 **Kuhl** | Y | Y | N | Y | Y | N | N |

| | 214 | 215 | 216 | 217 | 218 | 219 | 220 |
|---|---|---|---|---|---|---|---|
| **NORTH CAROLINA** | | | | | | | |
| 1 Butterfield | N | Y | N | Y | Y | N | N |
| 2 Etheridge | Y | Y | Y | Y | Y | N | N |
| 3 **Jones** | Y | Y | N | Y | Y | Y | Y |
| 4 Price | N | Y | Y | Y | Y | N | Y |
| 5 **Foxx** | Y | Y | N | Y | Y | N | N |
| 6 **Coble** | Y | Y | N | Y | Y | N | Y |
| 7 McIntyre | Y | Y | N | Y | Y | N | N |
| 8 **Hayes** | Y | Y | N | Y | Y | N | N |
| 9 **Myrick** | Y | Y | N | Y | Y | N | N |
| 10 **McHenry** | Y | Y | N | Y | Y | N | N |
| 11 **Taylor** | Y | Y | N | Y | Y | N | N |
| 12 Watt | N | Y | Y | Y | N | N | Y |
| 13 Miller | N | Y | Y | Y | Y | N | Y |
| **NORTH DAKOTA** | | | | | | | |
| AL Pomeroy | Y | Y | Y | Y | Y | N | N |
| **OHIO** | | | | | | | |
| 1 **Chabot** | Y | Y | N | Y | Y | N | N |
| 2 Vacant | | | | | | | |
| 3 **Turner** | Y | Y | N | Y | Y | N | N |
| 4 **Oxley** | Y | Y | N | Y | Y | N | N |
| 5 **Gillmor** | Y | Y | N | Y | Y | N | N |
| 6 Strickland | N | Y | Y | Y | Y | Y | Y |
| 7 **Hobson** | Y | Y | N | Y | Y | N | N |
| 8 **Boehner** | Y | Y | N | Y | Y | N | N |
| 9 Kaptur | N | Y | Y | Y | N | N | Y |
| 10 Kucinich | N | N | Y | Y | N | Y | Y |
| 11 Jones | N | Y | Y | Y | N | Y | Y |
| 12 **Tiberi** | Y | Y | N | Y | Y | N | N |
| 13 Brown | N | Y | Y | Y | N | Y | Y |
| 14 **LaTourette** | Y | Y | N | Y | Y | Y | N |
| 15 **Pryce** | Y | Y | Y | Y | Y | N | N |
| 16 **Regula** | Y | Y | N | Y | Y | N | N |
| 17 Ryan | Y | Y | N | Y | Y | N | Y |
| 18 **Ney** | Y | Y | N | Y | Y | N | N |
| **OKLAHOMA** | | | | | | | |
| 1 **Sullivan** | Y | Y | N | Y | Y | N | N |
| 2 Boren | Y | Y | N | Y | Y | N | N |
| 3 **Lucas** | Y | Y | N | Y | Y | N | N |
| 4 **Cole** | Y | Y | N | Y | Y | N | N |
| 5 **Istook** | Y | Y | N | Y | Y | N | N |
| **OREGON** | | | | | | | |
| 1 Wu | N | Y | Y | Y | N | Y | Y |
| 2 **Walden** | Y | Y | Y | Y | Y | N | N |
| 3 Blumenauer | N | N | Y | Y | N | N | Y |
| 4 DeFazio | Y | Y | Y | Y | Y | Y | Y |
| 5 Hooley | Y | Y | Y | Y | Y | Y | Y |
| **PENNSYLVANIA** | | | | | | | |
| 1 Brady | N | Y | Y | Y | N | Y | Y |
| 2 Fattah | N | Y | Y | Y | Y | Y | Y |
| 3 **English** | Y | Y | N | Y | Y | Y | N |
| 4 **Hart** | Y | Y | N | Y | Y | Y | N |
| 5 **Peterson** | Y | Y | N | Y | Y | N | N |
| 6 **Gerlach** | Y | Y | N | Y | Y | Y | N |
| 7 **Weldon** | Y | Y | N | Y | Y | N | N |
| 8 **Fitzpatrick** | Y | Y | N | Y | Y | Y | N |
| 9 **Shuster** | Y | Y | N | Y | Y | N | N |
| 10 **Sherwood** | Y | Y | N | Y | Y | N | N |
| 11 Kanjorski | N | Y | N | Y | Y | N | N |
| 12 Murtha | N | Y | N | Y | Y | Y | N |
| 13 Schwartz | N | Y | Y | Y | Y | Y | Y |
| 14 Doyle | N | Y | Y | Y | Y | Y | Y |
| 15 **Dent** | Y | Y | Y | Y | Y | N | N |
| 16 **Pitts** | Y | Y | N | Y | Y | N | N |
| 17 Holden | N | Y | N | Y | Y | N | N |
| 18 **Murphy** | Y | Y | N | Y | Y | Y | N |
| 19 **Platts** | Y | Y | N | Y | Y | N | N |
| **RHODE ISLAND** | | | | | | | |
| 1 Kennedy | N | Y | Y | Y | Y | N | N |
| 2 Langevin | N | Y | N | Y | Y | Y | N |
| **SOUTH CAROLINA** | | | | | | | |
| 1 **Brown** | ? | ? | ? | ? | ? | ? | ? |
| 2 **Wilson** | Y | Y | N | Y | Y | N | N |
| 3 **Barrett** | Y | Y | N | Y | Y | N | N |
| 4 **Inglis** | Y | Y | N | Y | Y | N | N |
| 5 Spratt | Y | Y | Y | Y | Y | N | N |
| 6 Clyburn | N | Y | Y | Y | Y | N | Y |
| **SOUTH DAKOTA** | | | | | | | |
| AL Herseth | N | Y | Y | Y | Y | Y | N |
| **TENNESSEE** | | | | | | | |
| 1 **Jenkins** | Y | Y | N | Y | Y | Y | N |
| 2 **Duncan** | Y | Y | N | Y | Y | N | Y |

| | 214 | 215 | 216 | 217 | 218 | 219 | 220 |
|---|---|---|---|---|---|---|---|
| 3 **Wamp** | Y | Y | N | Y | Y | N | N |
| 4 Davis | Y | Y | N | Y | Y | N | N |
| 5 Cooper | N | Y | Y | Y | Y | N | N |
| 6 Gordon | Y | Y | Y | Y | Y | Y | Y |
| 7 **Blackburn** | Y | Y | N | Y | Y | Y | N |
| 8 Tanner | Y | Y | Y | Y | Y | N | N |
| 9 Ford | Y | Y | Y | Y | Y | Y | N |
| **TEXAS** | | | | | | | |
| 1 **Gohmert** | Y | Y | N | Y | Y | Y | N |
| 2 **Poe** | Y | Y | N | Y | Y | N | N |
| 3 **Johnson, S.** | Y | Y | N | Y | Y | N | N |
| 4 **Hall** | Y | Y | N | Y | Y | Y | N |
| 5 **Hensarling** | Y | Y | N | Y | Y | N | N |
| 6 **Barton** | Y | Y | N | Y | Y | N | N |
| 7 **Culberson** | Y | Y | N | Y | Y | N | N |
| 8 **Brady** | Y | Y | N | Y | Y | N | N |
| 9 Green | N | Y | Y | Y | N | Y | Y |
| 10 **McCaul** | Y | Y | N | Y | Y | N | N |
| 11 **Conaway** | Y | Y | N | Y | Y | N | N |
| 12 **Granger** | Y | Y | N | Y | Y | N | N |
| 13 **Thornberry** | N | Y | N | Y | Y | N | N |
| 14 **Paul** | N | Y | N | Y | Y | Y | Y |
| 15 Hinojosa | N | Y | Y | Y | Y | Y | Y |
| 16 Reyes | N | Y | Y | Y | Y | N | N |
| 17 Edwards | N | Y | Y | Y | Y | N | N |
| 18 Jackson-Lee | N | Y | Y | Y | N | Y | Y |
| 19 **Neugebauer** | Y | Y | N | Y | Y | N | N |
| 20 Gonzalez | N | Y | Y | Y | Y | Y | N |
| 21 **Smith** | Y | Y | N | Y | Y | N | N |
| 22 **DeLay** | Y | Y | N | Y | Y | N | N |
| 23 **Bonilla** | Y | Y | N | Y | Y | N | N |
| 24 **Marchant** | Y | Y | N | Y | Y | N | N |
| 25 Doggett | N | Y | Y | Y | Y | N | Y |
| 26 **Burgess** | Y | Y | N | Y | Y | N | N |
| 27 Ortiz | N | Y | N | Y | Y | Y | N |
| 28 Cuellar | N | Y | N | Y | Y | Y | N |
| 29 Green | N | Y | Y | Y | Y | Y | Y |
| 30 Johnson, E. | N | Y | Y | Y | Y | N | Y |
| 31 **Carter** | Y | Y | N | Y | Y | N | N |
| 32 **Sessions** | Y | Y | N | Y | Y | N | N |
| **UTAH** | | | | | | | |
| 1 **Bishop** | Y | Y | N | Y | Y | ? | N |
| 2 Matheson | Y | Y | Y | Y | Y | N | N |
| 3 **Cannon** | Y | Y | N | Y | Y | N | N |
| **VERMONT** | | | | | | | |
| AL *Sanders* | N | Y | Y | Y | N | N | Y |
| **VIRGINIA** | | | | | | | |
| 1 **Davis, J.** | Y | Y | N | Y | Y | Y | N |
| 2 **Drake** | Y | Y | N | Y | Y | N | N |
| 3 Scott | N | Y | Y | Y | N | Y | Y |
| 4 **Forbes** | Y | Y | N | Y | Y | N | N |
| 5 **Goode** | Y | Y | N | Y | Y | N | N |
| 6 **Goodlatte** | Y | Y | N | Y | Y | N | N |
| 7 **Cantor** | Y | Y | N | Y | Y | N | N |
| 8 Moran | N | Y | Y | Y | N | Y | Y |
| 9 Boucher | Y | Y | Y | Y | Y | N | N |
| 10 **Wolf** | Y | Y | N | Y | Y | Y | N |
| 11 **Davis, T.** | Y | Y | N | Y | Y | Y | N |
| **WASHINGTON** | | | | | | | |
| 1 Inslee | N | Y | Y | Y | Y | N | Y |
| 2 Larsen | N | Y | Y | Y | Y | N | N |
| 3 Baird | N | Y | Y | Y | Y | Y | Y |
| 4 **Hastings** | ? | ? | ? | ? | ? | ? | ? |
| 5 **McMorris** | Y | Y | N | Y | Y | N | N |
| 6 Dicks | N | Y | Y | Y | Y | N | N |
| 7 McDermott | N | N | Y | Y | N | N | Y |
| 8 **Reichert** | Y | Y | N | Y | Y | N | N |
| 9 Smith | N | Y | Y | Y | Y | N | N |
| **WEST VIRGINIA** | | | | | | | |
| 1 Mollohan | N | Y | N | Y | N | Y | N |
| 2 **Capito** | Y | Y | Y | Y | Y | Y | N |
| 3 Rahall | N | Y | N | Y | N | Y | Y |
| **WISCONSIN** | | | | | | | |
| 1 **Ryan** | Y | Y | N | Y | Y | N | N |
| 2 Baldwin | N | N | Y | Y | N | N | Y |
| 3 Kind | Y | Y | Y | Y | Y | N | N |
| 4 Moore | N | N | Y | Y | N | Y | Y |
| 5 **Sensenbrenner** | Y | Y | N | Y | Y | N | N |
| 6 **Petri** | Y | Y | N | Y | Y | N | N |
| 7 Obey | N | Y | Y | Y | N | N | Y |
| 8 **Green** | Y | Y | N | Y | Y | N | N |
| **WYOMING** | | | | | | | |
| AL **Cubin** | Y | Y | N | Y | Y | N | N |

# IN THE HOUSE | By Vote Number

**221.** **HR 1815. Fiscal 2006 Defense Authorization/Recommit.** Taylor, D-Miss., motion to recommit the bill to the House Armed Services Committee with instructions to extend access to the military's Tricare health insurance program to all reservists and National Guard members. Motion rejected 211-218: R 9-218; D 201-0 (ND 150-0, SD 51-0); I 1-0. May 25, 2005.

**222.** **HR 1815. Fiscal 2006 Defense Authorization/Passage.** Passage of the bill that would authorize $441.6 billion for defense programs and $49.1 billion in emergency supplemental spending for fiscal 2006. The Pentagon would be required to notify Congress within 60 consecutive legislative days if it intends to open to women military jobs closed under a 1994 policy that restricts women from serving in units that are sent into direct ground combat, such as infantry, armor and special forces. Passed 390-39: R 225-2; D 164-37 (ND 117-33, SD 47-4); I 1-0. May 25, 2005.

**223.** **HR 2528 Fiscal 2006 Military Quality of Life and Veterans Affairs Appropriations/Previous Question.** Gingrey, R-Ga., motion to order the previous question (thus ending debate and possibility of amendment) on adoption of the rule (H Res 298) to provide for House floor consideration of the bill that would appropriate $121.8 billion in fiscal 2006 for the Department of Veterans Affairs, military construction and military housing. Motion agreed to 223-194: R 223-0; D 0-193 (ND 0-144, SD 0-49); I 0-1. Subsequently, the rule was adopted by voice vote. May 26, 2005.

**224.** **HR 2528. Fiscal 2006 Military Quality of Life and Veterans Affairs Appropriations/Veterans Health.** Melancon, D-La., amendment that would add $53 million for veterans' health care and to process claims for compensation and pensions. It would be offset by a $169 million cut to the 2005 Base Realignment and Closure account. Rejected 213-214: R 19-210; D 193-4 (ND 145-2, SD 48-2); I 1-0. May 26, 2005.

**225.** **HR 2528. Fiscal 2006 Military Quality of Life and Veterans Affairs Appropriations/Environmental Remediation.** Blumenauer, D-Ore., amendment to add $351 million to complete all environmental remediation at bases closed during the 1988 round of base closings, offset by a $351 million cut to the 2005 Base Realignment and Closure account. Rejected 171-254: R 13-214; D 157-40 (ND 128-19, SD 29-21); I 1-0. May 26, 2005.

**226.** **HR 2528. Fiscal 2006 Military Quality of Life and Veterans Affairs Appropriations/Passage.** Passage of the bill that would provide $121.8 billion in fiscal 2006 for the Department of Veterans Affairs, military construction and military housing. The bill would provide $68.1 billion for the Department of Veterans Affairs, including $28.8 billion for the Veterans' Health Administration. It also would provide $5.8 billion for military construction, $4.2 billion for military family housing and $1.6 billion for the latest round of base closures. Passed 425-1: R 228-0; D 196-1 (ND 146-1, SD 50-0); I 1-0. May 26, 2005.

**227.** **HR 3. Surface Transportation Reauthorization/Motion to Instruct.** Oberstar, D-Minn., motion to instruct House conferees to insist on a conference report that would authorize additional funds for highway, transit and safety programs to increase the guaranteed rate of return for states to at least 92 percent, without reducing the amount each state was provided by the $283.9 billion, six-year bill. Motion rejected 189-223: R 2-222; D 186-1 (ND 138-1, SD 48-0); I 1-0. May 26, 2005.

| | 221 | 222 | 223 | 224 | 225 | 226 | 227 |
|---|---|---|---|---|---|---|---|
| **ALABAMA** | | | | | | | |
| 1 Bonner | N | Y | Y | N | N | Y | N |
| 2 Everett | N | Y | Y | N | N | Y | N |
| 3 Rogers | N | Y | Y | N | N | Y | N |
| 4 Aderholt | N | Y | Y | N | N | Y | N |
| 5 Cramer | Y | Y | N | N | N | Y | ? |
| 6 Bachus | N | Y | Y | N | N | Y | N |
| 7 Davis | Y | Y | N | Y | N | Y | Y |
| **ALASKA** | | | | | | | |
| AL Young | N | Y | Y | N | N | Y | N |
| **ARIZONA** | | | | | | | |
| 1 Renzi | N | Y | Y | N | N | Y | N |
| 2 Franks | N | Y | Y | N | N | Y | N |
| 3 Shadegg | N | Y | Y | N | N | Y | N |
| 4 Pastor | Y | Y | N | Y | N | Y | Y |
| 5 Hayworth | N | Y | Y | N | N | Y | N |
| 6 Flake | N | Y | Y | N | N | Y | N |
| 7 Grijalva | Y | N | N | Y | Y | Y | Y |
| 8 Kolbe | N | Y | Y | N | N | Y | N |
| **ARKANSAS** | | | | | | | |
| 1 Berry | Y | Y | N | Y | N | Y | Y |
| 2 Snyder | Y | Y | N | Y | N | Y | Y |
| 3 Boozman | N | Y | Y | N | N | Y | N |
| 4 Ross | Y | Y | N | Y | N | Y | Y |
| **CALIFORNIA** | | | | | | | |
| 1 Thompson | Y | Y | N | Y | Y | Y | Y |
| 2 Herger | N | Y | Y | N | N | Y | N |
| 3 Lungren | N | Y | Y | N | N | Y | N |
| 4 Doolittle | N | Y | Y | N | N | Y | N |
| 5 Matsui, D. | Y | Y | N | Y | Y | Y | Y |
| 6 Woolsey | Y | N | N | Y | Y | Y | Y |
| 7 Miller, George | Y | Y | N | Y | Y | Y | Y |
| 8 Pelosi | Y | Y | N | Y | Y | Y | Y |
| 9 Lee | Y | Y | N | Y | Y | Y | Y |
| 10 Tauscher | Y | Y | N | Y | Y | Y | Y |
| 11 Pombo | N | Y | Y | N | N | Y | N |
| 12 Lantos | Y | Y | N | Y | Y | Y | Y |
| 13 Stark | Y | N | N | Y | Y | N | Y |
| 14 Eshoo | Y | Y | N | Y | Y | Y | Y |
| 15 Honda | Y | Y | N | Y | Y | Y | Y |
| 16 Lofgren | Y | Y | N | Y | Y | Y | Y |
| 17 Farr | Y | Y | N | Y | Y | Y | Y |
| 18 Cardoza | Y | Y | N | Y | Y | Y | Y |
| 19 Radanovich | N | Y | Y | N | N | Y | N |
| 20 Costa | Y | Y | N | Y | Y | Y | Y |
| 21 Nunes | N | Y | Y | N | N | Y | N |
| 22 Thomas | N | Y | Y | N | N | Y | N |
| 23 Capps | Y | Y | N | Y | Y | Y | Y |
| 24 Gallegly | N | Y | Y | N | N | Y | N |
| 25 McKeon | N | Y | Y | N | N | Y | N |
| 26 Dreier | N | Y | Y | N | N | Y | N |
| 27 Sherman | Y | Y | N | Y | Y | Y | Y |
| 28 Berman | Y | Y | N | Y | Y | Y | Y |
| 29 Schiff | Y | Y | N | Y | Y | Y | Y |
| 30 Waxman | Y | Y | N | Y | Y | Y | Y |
| 31 Becerra | Y | Y | N | Y | Y | Y | Y |
| 32 Solis | Y | N | N | Y | Y | Y | Y |
| 33 Watson | Y | Y | N | Y | Y | Y | Y |
| 34 Roybal-Allard | Y | Y | N | Y | Y | Y | Y |
| 35 Waters | Y | N | N | Y | Y | Y | Y |
| 36 Harman | Y | Y | N | Y | Y | Y | Y |
| 37 Millender-McD. | ? | ? | ? | ? | ? | ? | ? |
| 38 Napolitano | Y | Y | N | Y | Y | Y | Y |
| 39 Sánchez, Linda | Y | Y | N | Y | Y | Y | Y |
| 40 Royce | N | Y | Y | N | N | Y | N |
| 41 Lewis | N | Y | Y | N | N | Y | N |
| 42 Miller, Gary | N | Y | Y | N | N | Y | N |
| 43 Baca | Y | Y | N | Y | Y | Y | Y |
| 44 Calvert | N | Y | Y | N | N | Y | N |
| 45 Bono | N | Y | Y | N | N | Y | N |
| 46 Rohrabacher | N | Y | Y | N | N | Y | N |
| 47 Sanchez, Loretta | Y | Y | N | Y | Y | Y | Y |
| 48 Cox | N | Y | Y | N | ? | N | Y |
| 49 Issa | N | Y | Y | N | N | Y | N |
| 50 Cunningham | N | Y | Y | N | N | Y | ? |
| 51 Filner | Y | N | – | + | + | – | + |
| 52 Hunter | N | Y | Y | N | N | Y | N |
| 53 Davis | Y | Y | N | Y | N | Y | Y |
| **COLORADO** | | | | | | | |
| 1 DeGette | Y | Y | N | Y | Y | Y | Y |
| 2 Udall | Y | Y | N | Y | Y | Y | Y |
| 3 Salazar | Y | Y | N | Y | Y | Y | Y |
| 4 Musgrave | N | Y | Y | N | N | Y | N |
| 5 Hefley | N | Y | Y | N | N | Y | N |
| 6 Tancredo | N | Y | Y | N | N | Y | N |
| 7 Beauprez | N | Y | Y | N | N | Y | N |
| **CONNECTICUT** | | | | | | | |
| 1 Larson | Y | Y | N | Y | Y | Y | Y |
| 2 Simmons | N | Y | Y | N | Y | Y | N |
| 3 DeLauro | Y | Y | N | Y | Y | Y | Y |
| 4 Shays | Y | Y | N | Y | N | Y | N |
| 5 Johnson | N | Y | Y | N | N | Y | N |
| **DELAWARE** | | | | | | | |
| AL Castle | N | Y | Y | N | N | Y | N |
| **FLORIDA** | | | | | | | |
| 1 Miller | N | Y | Y | N | N | Y | N |
| 2 Boyd | Y | Y | N | Y | N | Y | Y |
| 3 Brown | Y | Y | N | Y | Y | Y | Y |
| 4 Crenshaw | N | Y | Y | N | N | Y | N |
| 5 Brown-Waite | Y | Y | Y | N | N | Y | N |
| 6 Stearns | N | Y | Y | N | N | Y | N |
| 7 Mica | N | Y | Y | N | N | Y | N |
| 8 Keller | N | Y | Y | N | N | Y | N |
| 9 Bilirakis | N | Y | Y | N | N | Y | N |
| 10 Young | N | Y | ? | N | N | Y | N |
| 11 Davis | Y | Y | N | Y | N | Y | Y |
| 12 Putnam | N | Y | Y | N | N | Y | N |
| 13 Harris | N | Y | Y | N | N | Y | N |
| 14 Mack | N | Y | Y | N | N | Y | N |
| 15 Weldon | N | Y | Y | N | N | Y | N |
| 16 Foley | N | Y | Y | N | N | Y | N |
| 17 Meek | Y | Y | N | Y | Y | Y | Y |
| 18 Ros-Lehtinen | N | Y | Y | N | Y | Y | N |
| 19 Wexler | Y | Y | N | Y | Y | Y | Y |
| 20 Wasserman-Schultz | Y | Y | N | Y | Y | Y | Y |
| 21 Diaz-Balart, L. | N | Y | Y | N | N | Y | N |
| 22 Shaw | N | Y | Y | N | N | Y | N |
| 23 Hastings | Y | N | N | Y | Y | Y | Y |
| 24 Feeney | N | Y | Y | N | N | Y | N |
| 25 Diaz-Balart, M. | N | Y | Y | N | N | Y | N |
| **GEORGIA** | | | | | | | |
| 1 Kingston | N | Y | Y | N | N | Y | N |
| 2 Bishop | Y | Y | N | Y | N | Y | Y |
| 3 Marshall | Y | Y | N | Y | N | Y | Y |
| 4 McKinney | Y | N | ? | Y | Y | Y | Y |
| 5 Lewis | N | N | Y | Y | Y | Y | Y |
| 6 Price | N | Y | Y | N | N | Y | N |
| 7 Linder | N | Y | Y | N | N | Y | N |
| 8 Westmoreland | N | Y | Y | N | N | Y | N |
| 9 Norwood | N | Y | ? | N | N | Y | N |
| 10 Deal | N | Y | Y | N | N | Y | ? |
| 11 Gingrey | N | Y | Y | N | N | Y | N |
| 12 Barrow | Y | Y | N | Y | Y | Y | Y |
| 13 Scott | Y | Y | N | Y | Y | Y | Y |
| **HAWAII** | | | | | | | |
| 1 Abercrombie | Y | Y | N | Y | Y | Y | Y |
| 2 Case | Y | Y | N | Y | Y | Y | Y |
| **IDAHO** | | | | | | | |
| 1 Otter | N | Y | Y | N | N | Y | N |
| 2 Simpson | N | Y | Y | N | N | Y | N |
| **ILLINOIS** | | | | | | | |
| 1 Rush | Y | N | N | Y | Y | Y | Y |
| 2 Jackson | Y | N | N | Y | Y | Y | Y |
| 3 Lipinski | Y | Y | N | Y | Y | Y | Y |
| 4 Gutierrez | Y | N | N | Y | Y | Y | Y |
| 5 Emanuel | Y | Y | N | Y | Y | Y | Y |
| 6 Hyde | N | Y | ? | N | N | Y | N |
| 7 Davis | Y | N | N | Y | Y | Y | Y |
| 8 Bean | Y | Y | N | Y | Y | Y | Y |
| 9 Schakowsky | Y | N | N | Y | Y | Y | Y |
| 10 Kirk | N | Y | Y | N | N | Y | N |
| 11 Weller | N | Y | Y | N | N | Y | N |
| 12 Costello | Y | Y | N | Y | Y | Y | Y |

ND Northern Democrats, SD Southern Democrats
Southern states: Ala., Ark., Fla., Ga., Ky., La., Miss., N.C., Okla., S.C., Tenn., Texas, Va.

| | 221 | 222 | 223 | 224 | 225 | 226 | 227 |
|---|---|---|---|---|---|---|---|
| 13 **Biggert** | N | Y | Y | N | N | Y | N |
| 14 **Hastert** | | | | N | | | |
| 15 **Johnson** | N | Y | Y | N | Y | Y | N |
| 16 **Manzullo** | N | Y | Y | N | Y | Y | N |
| 17 Evans | Y | Y | N | Y | Y | Y | Y |
| 18 **LaHood** | N | Y | Y | N | N | Y | N |
| 19 **Shimkus** | N | Y | Y | N | N | Y | N |
| **INDIANA** | | | | | | | |
| 1 Visclosky | Y | Y | N | Y | N | Y | Y |
| 2 **Chocola** | N | Y | Y | N | N | Y | N |
| 3 **Souder** | N | Y | Y | N | N | Y | N |
| 4 **Buyer** | N | Y | Y | N | N | Y | N |
| 5 **Burton** | N | Y | Y | N | N | Y | N |
| 6 **Pence** | N | Y | Y | N | N | Y | N |
| 7 Carson | Y | Y | N | Y | Y | Y | Y |
| 8 **Hostettler** | N | Y | Y | N | N | Y | N |
| 9 **Sodrel** | N | Y | Y | N | Y | Y | N |
| **IOWA** | | | | | | | |
| 1 **Nussle** | N | Y | Y | N | N | Y | N |
| 2 **Leach** | Y | Y | Y | Y | N | Y | N |
| 3 Boswell | Y | Y | N | Y | Y | Y | Y |
| 4 **Latham** | Y | Y | Y | N | N | Y | N |
| 5 **King** | N | Y | Y | N | N | Y | N |
| **KANSAS** | | | | | | | |
| 1 **Moran** | N | Y | Y | N | N | Y | N |
| 2 **Ryun** | N | Y | Y | N | N | Y | N |
| 3 Moore | Y | Y | N | Y | Y | Y | Y |
| 4 **Tiahrt** | N | Y | Y | N | N | Y | N |
| **KENTUCKY** | | | | | | | |
| 1 **Whitfield** | N | Y | Y | N | N | Y | N |
| 2 **Lewis** | N | Y | Y | N | N | Y | N |
| 3 **Northup** | N | Y | Y | N | N | Y | N |
| 4 **Davis** | N | Y | Y | N | N | Y | N |
| 5 **Rogers** | N | Y | Y | N | N | Y | N |
| 6 Chandler | Y | Y | N | Y | Y | Y | Y |
| **LOUISIANA** | | | | | | | |
| 1 **Jindal** | N | Y | Y | N | N | Y | N |
| 2 Jefferson | Y | Y | N | Y | Y | Y | Y |
| 3 Melancon | Y | Y | N | Y | Y | Y | Y |
| 4 **McCrery** | N | Y | Y | N | N | Y | N |
| 5 **Alexander** | N | Y | Y | N | N | Y | N |
| 6 **Baker** | N | Y | Y | N | N | Y | N |
| 7 **Boustany** | N | Y | Y | N | N | Y | N |
| **MAINE** | | | | | | | |
| 1 Allen | Y | Y | N | Y | Y | Y | Y |
| 2 Michaud | Y | Y | N | Y | N | Y | Y |
| **MARYLAND** | | | | | | | |
| 1 **Gilchrest** | N | Y | Y | N | N | Y | N |
| 2 Ruppersberger | Y | Y | N | Y | Y | Y | Y |
| 3 Cardin | Y | Y | N | Y | Y | Y | Y |
| 4 Wynn | Y | Y | N | Y | Y | Y | Y |
| 5 Hoyer | Y | Y | N | Y | N | Y | Y |
| 6 **Bartlett** | N | Y | Y | N | N | Y | N |
| 7 Cummings | Y | Y | N | Y | Y | Y | Y |
| 8 Van Hollen | Y | Y | N | Y | Y | Y | Y |
| **MASSACHUSETTS** | | | | | | | |
| 1 Olver | Y | N | N | Y | Y | Y | Y |
| 2 Neal | Y | Y | N | Y | Y | Y | Y |
| 3 McGovern | Y | N | N | Y | Y | Y | Y |
| 4 Frank | Y | N | N | Y | N | Y | Y |
| 5 Meehan | Y | Y | N | Y | Y | Y | Y |
| 6 Tierney | Y | N | N | Y | Y | Y | Y |
| 7 Markey | Y | Y | N | Y | Y | Y | Y |
| 8 Capuano | Y | Y | N | Y | Y | Y | Y |
| 9 Lynch | Y | Y | N | Y | Y | Y | Y |
| 10 Delahunt | Y | N | N | Y | Y | Y | ? |
| **MICHIGAN** | | | | | | | |
| 1 Stupak | Y | Y | N | Y | Y | Y | Y |
| 2 **Hoekstra** | N | Y | Y | N | N | Y | N |
| 3 **Ehlers** | N | Y | Y | N | Y | Y | N |
| 4 **Camp** | N | Y | Y | N | N | Y | N |
| 5 Kildee | Y | Y | N | Y | Y | Y | Y |
| 6 **Upton** | N | Y | Y | N | N | Y | N |
| 7 **Schwarz** | N | Y | Y | N | N | Y | N |
| 8 **Rogers** | N | Y | Y | N | N | Y | N |
| 9 **Knollenberg** | N | Y | Y | N | N | Y | N |
| 10 **Miller** | N | Y | Y | N | N | Y | N |
| 11 **McCotter** | N | Y | Y | N | N | Y | N |
| 12 Levin | Y | Y | N | Y | N | Y | Y |
| 13 Kilpatrick | Y | N | N | Y | Y | Y | Y |
| 14 Conyers | Y | N | N | Y | Y | Y | Y |
| 15 Dingell | Y | Y | N | Y | Y | Y | Y |

| | 221 | 222 | 223 | 224 | 225 | 226 | 227 |
|---|---|---|---|---|---|---|---|
| **MINNESOTA** | | | | | | | |
| 1 **Gutknecht** | N | Y | Y | N | N | Y | N |
| 2 **Kline** | N | Y | Y | N | N | Y | N |
| 3 **Ramstad** | Y | Y | Y | Y | N | Y | N |
| 4 McCollum | Y | Y | N | Y | Y | Y | Y |
| 5 Sabo | Y | Y | N | Y | Y | Y | Y |
| 6 **Kennedy** | N | Y | Y | Y | N | Y | N |
| 7 Peterson | Y | Y | N | Y | N | Y | Y |
| 8 Oberstar | Y | N | N | Y | Y | Y | Y |
| **MISSISSIPPI** | | | | | | | |
| 1 **Wicker** | N | Y | Y | N | N | Y | N |
| 2 Thompson | Y | Y | N | Y | Y | Y | Y |
| 3 **Pickering** | N | Y | Y | N | N | Y | N |
| 4 Taylor | Y | Y | N | Y | Y | Y | ? |
| **MISSOURI** | | | | | | | |
| 1 Clay | Y | Y | N | Y | Y | Y | Y |
| 2 **Akin** | N | Y | Y | N | N | Y | N |
| 3 Carnahan | Y | Y | N | Y | Y | Y | Y |
| 4 Skelton | Y | Y | N | Y | N | Y | Y |
| 5 Cleaver | Y | Y | N | Y | Y | Y | Y |
| 6 **Graves** | N | Y | Y | N | N | Y | N |
| 7 **Blunt** | N | Y | Y | N | N | Y | N |
| 8 **Emerson** | ? | ? | ? | ? | ? | ? | ? |
| 9 **Hulshof** | N | Y | Y | N | N | Y | N |
| **MONTANA** | | | | | | | |
| AL **Rehberg** | N | Y | Y | N | N | Y | N |
| **NEBRASKA** | | | | | | | |
| 1 **Fortenberry** | N | Y | Y | N | N | Y | N |
| 2 **Terry** | N | Y | Y | N | N | Y | N |
| 3 **Osborne** | N | Y | Y | N | N | Y | N |
| **NEVADA** | | | | | | | |
| 1 Berkley | Y | Y | N | Y | Y | Y | ? |
| 2 **Gibbons** | N | Y | Y | Y | N | Y | N |
| 3 **Porter** | N | Y | Y | Y | N | Y | N |
| **NEW HAMPSHIRE** | | | | | | | |
| 1 **Bradley** | N | Y | Y | N | N | Y | N |
| 2 **Bass** | N | Y | Y | N | N | Y | N |
| **NEW JERSEY** | | | | | | | |
| 1 Andrews | Y | Y | N | Y | Y | Y | Y |
| 2 **LoBiondo** | N | Y | Y | N | N | Y | N |
| 3 **Saxton** | N | Y | Y | N | N | Y | N |
| 4 **Smith** | N | Y | Y | Y | N | Y | N |
| 5 **Garrett** | N | Y | Y | N | N | Y | N |
| 6 Pallone | Y | Y | N | Y | Y | Y | Y |
| 7 **Ferguson** | N | Y | Y | N | N | Y | N |
| 8 Pascrell | Y | Y | N | Y | Y | Y | Y |
| 9 Rothman | Y | Y | N | Y | Y | Y | Y |
| 10 Payne | Y | N | N | Y | Y | Y | Y |
| 11 **Frelinghuysen** | N | Y | ? | N | N | Y | N |
| 12 Holt | Y | Y | N | Y | Y | Y | Y |
| 13 Menendez | Y | Y | ? | ? | ? | ? | ? |
| **NEW MEXICO** | | | | | | | |
| 1 **Wilson** | Y | Y | Y | Y | Y | Y | N |
| 2 **Pearce** | N | Y | Y | N | N | Y | N |
| 3 Udall | Y | Y | N | Y | Y | Y | Y |
| **NEW YORK** | | | | | | | |
| 1 Bishop | Y | Y | N | Y | Y | Y | Y |
| 2 Israel | Y | Y | N | Y | Y | Y | Y |
| 3 **King** | N | Y | Y | N | N | Y | N |
| 4 McCarthy | Y | Y | N | Y | Y | Y | ? |
| 5 Ackerman | Y | Y | N | Y | Y | Y | Y |
| 6 Meeks | Y | Y | N | Y | Y | Y | Y |
| 7 Crowley | Y | Y | N | Y | Y | Y | Y |
| 8 Nadler | Y | Y | N | Y | Y | Y | Y |
| 9 Weiner | Y | Y | N | Y | Y | Y | Y |
| 10 Towns | Y | Y | N | Y | Y | Y | Y |
| 11 Owens | Y | N | N | Y | Y | Y | Y |
| 12 Velázquez | Y | N | N | Y | Y | Y | Y |
| 13 **Fossella** | N | Y | Y | Y | N | Y | N |
| 14 Maloney | Y | Y | N | Y | Y | Y | Y |
| 15 Rangel | Y | N | N | Y | Y | Y | Y |
| 16 Serrano | Y | N | N | Y | Y | Y | Y |
| 17 Engel | Y | Y | N | Y | Y | Y | Y |
| 18 Lowey | Y | Y | N | Y | Y | Y | Y |
| 19 **Kelly** | N | Y | Y | N | N | Y | N |
| 20 **Sweeney** | N | Y | ? | N | N | Y | N |
| 21 McNulty | Y | Y | N | Y | Y | Y | ? |
| 22 Hinchey | Y | N | N | Y | Y | Y | Y |
| 23 **McHugh** | N | Y | Y | N | N | Y | N |
| 24 **Boehlert** | N | Y | Y | N | N | Y | N |
| 25 **Walsh** | N | Y | Y | N | N | Y | N |
| 26 **Reynolds** | N | Y | Y | N | N | Y | N |
| 27 Higgins | Y | Y | N | Y | Y | Y | Y |
| 28 Slaughter | Y | Y | N | Y | Y | Y | Y |
| 29 **Kuhl** | N | Y | Y | N | N | Y | N |

| | 221 | 222 | 223 | 224 | 225 | 226 | 227 |
|---|---|---|---|---|---|---|---|
| **NORTH CAROLINA** | | | | | | | |
| 1 Butterfield | Y | Y | N | Y | Y | Y | Y |
| 2 Etheridge | Y | Y | N | Y | Y | Y | Y |
| 3 **Jones** | Y | Y | Y | Y | N | Y | N |
| 4 Price | Y | Y | N | Y | Y | Y | Y |
| 5 **Foxx** | N | Y | Y | N | N | Y | N |
| 6 **Coble** | N | Y | Y | N | N | Y | N |
| 7 McIntyre | Y | Y | N | Y | N | Y | Y |
| 8 **Hayes** | N | Y | Y | N | N | Y | N |
| 9 **Myrick** | N | Y | Y | N | N | Y | N |
| 10 **McHenry** | N | Y | Y | N | N | Y | N |
| 11 **Taylor** | N | Y | Y | N | N | Y | N |
| 12 Watt | Y | N | N | Y | Y | Y | Y |
| 13 Miller | Y | Y | N | Y | Y | Y | Y |
| **NORTH DAKOTA** | | | | | | | |
| AL Pomeroy | Y | Y | N | Y | N | Y | Y |
| **OHIO** | | | | | | | |
| 1 **Chabot** | N | Y | Y | N | N | Y | N |
| 2 Vacant | | | | | | | |
| 3 **Turner** | N | Y | Y | N | N | Y | N |
| 4 **Oxley** | N | Y | Y | N | N | Y | N |
| 5 **Gillmor** | N | Y | Y | N | N | Y | N |
| 6 Strickland | Y | Y | N | Y | Y | Y | Y |
| 7 **Hobson** | N | Y | Y | N | N | Y | N |
| 8 **Boehner** | N | Y | Y | N | N | Y | N |
| 9 Kaptur | Y | Y | N | Y | Y | Y | Y |
| 10 Kucinich | Y | N | N | Y | Y | Y | Y |
| 11 Jones | Y | N | ? | Y | Y | Y | Y |
| 12 **Tiberi** | N | Y | Y | N | N | Y | N |
| 13 Brown | Y | Y | N | Y | Y | Y | Y |
| 14 **LaTourette** | N | Y | Y | N | N | Y | N |
| 15 **Pryce** | N | Y | Y | N | N | Y | N |
| 16 **Regula** | N | Y | Y | N | N | Y | N |
| 17 Ryan | Y | Y | N | Y | Y | Y | Y |
| 18 **Ney** | N | Y | Y | N | N | Y | N |
| **OKLAHOMA** | | | | | | | |
| 1 **Sullivan** | N | Y | Y | N | N | Y | N |
| 2 Boren | Y | Y | N | Y | N | Y | Y |
| 3 **Lucas** | N | Y | Y | N | N | Y | N |
| 4 **Cole** | N | Y | Y | N | N | Y | N |
| 5 **Istook** | N | Y | Y | N | N | Y | N |
| **OREGON** | | | | | | | |
| 1 Wu | Y | N | N | Y | Y | Y | Y |
| 2 **Walden** | N | Y | Y | N | Y | Y | N |
| 3 Blumenauer | Y | N | N | Y | Y | Y | Y |
| 4 DeFazio | Y | Y | N | Y | Y | Y | Y |
| 5 Hooley | Y | Y | N | Y | Y | Y | Y |
| **PENNSYLVANIA** | | | | | | | |
| 1 Brady | Y | Y | N | Y | Y | Y | Y |
| 2 Fattah | Y | Y | N | Y | Y | Y | N |
| 3 **English** | N | Y | Y | N | N | Y | N |
| 4 **Hart** | N | Y | Y | N | N | Y | N |
| 5 **Peterson** | N | Y | Y | N | N | Y | N |
| 6 **Gerlach** | N | Y | Y | Y | N | Y | N |
| 7 **Weldon** | N | Y | Y | N | N | Y | ? |
| 8 **Fitzpatrick** | N | Y | Y | Y | N | Y | N |
| 9 **Shuster** | N | Y | Y | N | N | Y | N |
| 10 **Sherwood** | N | Y | Y | N | N | Y | N |
| 11 Kanjorski | Y | Y | N | Y | N | Y | Y |
| 12 Murtha | Y | Y | ? | N | N | Y | Y |
| 13 Schwartz | Y | Y | N | Y | Y | Y | Y |
| 14 Doyle | Y | Y | ? | ? | ? | ? | ? |
| 15 **Dent** | N | Y | Y | Y | N | Y | N |
| 16 **Pitts** | N | Y | Y | N | N | Y | N |
| 17 Holden | Y | Y | N | Y | N | Y | ? |
| 18 **Murphy** | N | Y | Y | N | N | Y | N |
| 19 **Platts** | N | Y | Y | N | N | Y | N |
| **RHODE ISLAND** | | | | | | | |
| 1 Kennedy | Y | Y | N | Y | N | Y | Y |
| 2 Langevin | Y | Y | N | Y | Y | Y | Y |
| **SOUTH CAROLINA** | | | | | | | |
| 1 **Brown** | ? | ? | Y | N | N | Y | N |
| 2 **Wilson** | N | Y | Y | N | N | Y | N |
| 3 **Barrett** | N | Y | Y | N | N | Y | N |
| 4 **Inglis** | N | Y | Y | N | N | Y | N |
| 5 Spratt | Y | Y | N | Y | N | Y | Y |
| 6 Clyburn | Y | Y | N | Y | Y | Y | Y |
| **SOUTH DAKOTA** | | | | | | | |
| AL Herseth | Y | Y | ? | Y | N | Y | Y |
| **TENNESSEE** | | | | | | | |
| 1 **Jenkins** | N | Y | Y | N | N | Y | ? |
| 2 **Duncan** | N | N | Y | N | N | Y | N |

| | 221 | 222 | 223 | 224 | 225 | 226 | 227 |
|---|---|---|---|---|---|---|---|
| 3 **Wamp** | N | Y | Y | N | N | Y | N |
| 4 Davis | Y | Y | N | Y | N | Y | Y |
| 5 Cooper | Y | Y | N | Y | N | Y | Y |
| 6 Gordon | Y | Y | N | Y | Y | Y | Y |
| 7 **Blackburn** | N | Y | Y | N | N | Y | N |
| 8 Tanner | Y | Y | N | Y | N | Y | Y |
| 9 Ford | Y | Y | N | Y | Y | Y | Y |
| **TEXAS** | | | | | | | |
| 1 **Gohmert** | N | Y | Y | N | N | Y | N |
| 2 **Poe** | N | Y | Y | Y | N | Y | N |
| 3 **Johnson, S.** | N | Y | Y | N | N | Y | N |
| 4 **Hall** | N | Y | Y | Y | Y | Y | N |
| 5 **Hensarling** | N | Y | Y | N | N | Y | N |
| 6 **Barton** | N | Y | Y | N | N | Y | N |
| 7 **Culberson** | N | Y | Y | N | N | Y | N |
| 8 **Brady** | N | Y | Y | N | N | Y | N |
| 9 Green | Y | Y | N | Y | Y | Y | Y |
| 10 **McCaul** | N | Y | Y | N | N | Y | N |
| 11 **Conaway** | N | Y | Y | N | N | Y | N |
| 12 **Granger** | N | Y | Y | N | N | Y | N |
| 13 **Thornberry** | N | Y | Y | N | N | Y | N |
| 14 **Paul** | Y | N | Y | Y | Y | Y | Y |
| 15 Hinojosa | Y | Y | N | Y | Y | Y | Y |
| 16 Reyes | Y | Y | N | Y | N | Y | Y |
| 17 Edwards | Y | Y | N | Y | Y | Y | Y |
| 18 Jackson-Lee | Y | Y | N | Y | Y | Y | Y |
| 19 **Neugebauer** | N | Y | Y | N | N | Y | N |
| 20 Gonzalez | Y | Y | N | Y | Y | Y | Y |
| 21 **Smith** | N | Y | Y | N | N | Y | N |
| 22 **DeLay** | N | Y | Y | N | N | Y | N |
| 23 **Bonilla** | N | Y | Y | N | N | Y | N |
| 24 **Marchant** | N | Y | Y | N | N | Y | N |
| 25 Doggett | Y | Y | N | Y | Y | Y | Y |
| 26 **Burgess** | N | Y | Y | N | N | Y | N |
| 27 Ortiz | Y | Y | N | N | N | Y | Y |
| 28 Cuellar | Y | Y | N | Y | N | Y | Y |
| 29 Green | Y | Y | N | Y | N | Y | ? |
| 30 Johnson, E. | Y | Y | – | + | + | + | Y |
| 31 **Carter** | N | Y | Y | N | N | Y | N |
| 32 **Sessions** | N | Y | Y | N | N | Y | N |
| **UTAH** | | | | | | | |
| 1 **Bishop** | N | Y | Y | N | N | Y | N |
| 2 Matheson | Y | Y | N | Y | Y | Y | Y |
| 3 **Cannon** | N | Y | Y | N | N | Y | N |
| **VERMONT** | | | | | | | |
| AL *Sanders* | Y | Y | N | Y | Y | Y | Y |
| **VIRGINIA** | | | | | | | |
| 1 **Davis, J.** | N | Y | Y | Y | Y | Y | N |
| 2 **Drake** | N | Y | Y | N | N | Y | N |
| 3 Scott | Y | Y | N | Y | N | Y | Y |
| 4 **Forbes** | N | Y | Y | N | N | Y | N |
| 5 **Goode** | Y | Y | Y | N | N | Y | N |
| 6 **Goodlatte** | N | Y | Y | N | N | Y | N |
| 7 **Cantor** | N | Y | Y | N | N | Y | N |
| 8 Moran | Y | Y | N | Y | Y | Y | Y |
| 9 Boucher | Y | Y | N | Y | N | Y | Y |
| 10 **Wolf** | N | Y | Y | N | N | Y | N |
| 11 **Davis, T.** | N | Y | Y | N | N | Y | Y |
| **WASHINGTON** | | | | | | | |
| 1 Inslee | Y | Y | N | Y | Y | Y | Y |
| 2 Larsen | Y | Y | N | Y | N | Y | Y |
| 3 Baird | Y | Y | N | Y | Y | Y | Y |
| 4 **Hastings** | ? | ? | ? | ? | ? | ? | ? |
| 5 **McMorris** | N | Y | Y | N | N | Y | N |
| 6 Dicks | Y | Y | N | Y | N | Y | Y |
| 7 McDermott | Y | N | N | Y | Y | Y | ? |
| 8 **Reichert** | N | Y | Y | Y | N | Y | N |
| 9 Smith | Y | Y | N | Y | Y | Y | ? |
| **WEST VIRGINIA** | | | | | | | |
| 1 Mollohan | Y | Y | N | N | N | Y | Y |
| 2 **Capito** | N | Y | Y | Y | N | Y | N |
| 3 Rahall | Y | Y | N | Y | Y | Y | Y |
| **WISCONSIN** | | | | | | | |
| 1 **Ryan** | N | Y | Y | N | N | Y | N |
| 2 Baldwin | Y | N | N | Y | Y | Y | Y |
| 3 Kind | Y | Y | N | Y | Y | Y | ? |
| 4 Moore | Y | N | N | Y | Y | Y | Y |
| 5 **Sensenbrenner** | N | Y | Y | N | N | Y | N |
| 6 **Petri** | N | Y | Y | N | N | Y | N |
| 7 Obey | Y | Y | N | Y | Y | Y | Y |
| 8 **Green** | N | Y | Y | Y | N | Y | N |
| **WYOMING** | | | | | | | |
| AL **Cubin** | N | Y | Y | N | N | Y | N |

# IN THE HOUSE | By Vote Number

**228.** **H Con Res 44. Cinco de Mayo Tribute/Adoption.** Ros-Lehtinen, R-Fla., motion to suspend the rules and adopt the concurrent resolution that would recognize Mexico's struggle for independence from European control and would request the president to issue a proclamation recognizing the fight for Mexican independence. Motion agreed to 405-0: R 220-0; D 184-0 (ND 137-0, SD 47-0); I 1-0. A two-thirds majority of those present and voting (270 in this case) is required for adoption under suspension of the rules. June 7, 2005.

**229.** **H Res 282. Condemnation of Anti-Semitic Statements/Adoption.** Ros-Lehtinen, R-Fla., motion to suspend the rules and adopt the resolution that would call on the United Nations to officially and publicly condemn anti-Semitic statements made at U.N. meetings and by U.N. member states. Motion agreed to 409-2: R 222-1; D 186-1 (ND 141-0, SD 45-1); I 1-0. A two-thirds majority of those present and voting (274 in this case) is required for adoption under suspension of the rules. June 7, 2005.

**230.** **HR 2744. Fiscal 2006 Agriculture Appropriations/Animal and Plant Health Inspection Service.** Weiner, D-N.Y., amendment that would increase funding by $19 million for the Animal and Plant Health Inspection Service, to be offset by a $21 million reduction to the Agriculture Department common computing environment account. Adopted 226-201: R 40-188; D 185-13 (ND 145-4, SD 40-9); I 1-0. June 8, 2005.

**231.** **HR 2744. Fiscal 2006 Agriculture Appropriations/Country-of-Origin Labels.** Rehberg, R-Mont., amendment that would strike a provision that would prohibit the Agriculture Department from using funds in the bill to enforce country-of-origin labels for meat and meat products. Rejected 187-240: R 41-188; D 145-52 (ND 130-19, SD 15-33); I 1-0. June 8, 2005.

**232.** **HR 2744. Fiscal 2006 Agriculture Appropriations/Conflict of Interest Requirement.** Hinchey, D-N.Y., amendment that would prohibit the use of funds in the bill to grant a waiver of financial conflict of interest requirements for a voting member of an advisory committee or panel of the Food and Drug Administration. Adopted 218-210: R 32-198; D 185-12 (ND 143-5, SD 42-7); I 1-0. June 8, 2005.

**233.** **HR 2744. Fiscal 2006 Agriculture Appropriations/Wild Horses.** Sweeney, R-N.Y., amendment that would prohibit use of funds in the bill to pay salaries or expenses of employees to inspect horses and regulate transportation of horses intended for slaughter, including for meat, under the Federal Meat Inspection Act or the Federal Agriculture Improvement and Reform Act. Adopted 269-158: R 104-125; D 164-33 (ND 132-16, SD 32-17); I 1-0. June 8, 2005.

**234.** **HR 2744. Fiscal 2006 Agriculture Appropriations/Sugar Program.** Blumenauer, D-Ore., amendment that would bar use of funds in the bill for salaries or expenses of personnel who make loans in excess of 17 cents per pound for domestically grown raw sugar cane or 21.6 cents per pound for refined beet sugar from domestically grown beets. Rejected 146-280: R 81-148; D 65-131 (ND 57-91, SD 8-40); I 0-1. June 8, 2005.

ND Northern Democrats, SD Southern Democrats
Southern states: Ala., Ark., Fla., Ga., Ky., La., Miss., N.C., Okla., S.C., Tenn., Texas, Va.

| | 228 | 229 | 230 | 231 | 232 | 233 | 234 |
|---|---|---|---|---|---|---|---|
| **ALABAMA** | | | | | | | |
| 1 Bonner | Y | Y | N | Y | N | N | N |
| 2 Everett | Y | Y | N | Y | N | N | N |
| 3 Rogers | Y | Y | N | Y | N | N | N |
| 4 Aderholt | Y | Y | N | N | N | Y | N |
| 5 Cramer | Y | Y | N | Y | N | N | N |
| 6 Bachus | Y | Y | N | N | N | Y | N |
| 7 Davis | Y | Y | Y | Y | Y | Y | N |
| **ALASKA** | | | | | | | |
| AL Young | ? | ? | N | Y | N | N | N |
| **ARIZONA** | | | | | | | |
| 1 Renzi | Y | Y | Y | N | N | Y | N |
| 2 Franks | Y | Y | N | N | N | N | N |
| 3 Shadegg | Y | Y | N | N | N | N | Y |
| 4 Pastor | Y | Y | N | N | Y | N | N |
| 5 Hayworth | Y | Y | N | N | N | Y | Y |
| 6 Flake | Y | Y | N | N | N | N | N |
| 7 Grijalva | Y | Y | Y | Y | Y | Y | Y |
| 8 Kolbe | Y | Y | N | N | N | N | Y |
| **ARKANSAS** | | | | | | | |
| 1 Berry | Y | Y | N | N | Y | N | N |
| 2 Snyder | Y | Y | Y | N | Y | N | N |
| 3 Boozman | Y | Y | N | N | N | Y | N |
| 4 Ross | Y | Y | N | Y | N | N | N |
| **CALIFORNIA** | | | | | | | |
| 1 Thompson | Y | Y | Y | Y | Y | Y | Y |
| 2 Herger | Y | Y | Y | N | N | Y | Y |
| 3 Lungren | Y | Y | N | N | N | Y | N |
| 4 Doolittle | Y | Y | N | N | N | N | N |
| 5 Matsui, D. | Y | Y | Y | Y | Y | Y | Y |
| 6 Woolsey | Y | Y | Y | Y | Y | Y | Y |
| 7 Miller, George | Y | Y | Y | Y | Y | Y | Y |
| 8 Pelosi | Y | Y | Y | Y | Y | Y | Y |
| 9 Lee | Y | Y | Y | Y | Y | Y | Y |
| 10 Tauscher | Y | Y | Y | Y | Y | Y | Y |
| 11 Pombo | Y | Y | N | N | N | N | N |
| 12 Lantos | Y | Y | Y | Y | Y | Y | Y |
| 13 Stark | ? | ? | Y | Y | Y | Y | Y |
| 14 Eshoo | Y | Y | Y | Y | Y | Y | Y |
| 15 Honda | + | + | Y | Y | Y | N | N |
| 16 Lofgren | Y | Y | Y | Y | Y | Y | Y |
| 17 Farr | Y | Y | N | N | Y | N | N |
| 18 Cardoza | Y | Y | N | N | N | N | N |
| 19 Radanovich | Y | Y | N | N | N | N | N |
| 20 Costa | Y | Y | Y | N | N | N | N |
| 21 Nunes | Y | Y | N | N | N | N | N |
| 22 Thomas | Y | Y | N | N | N | N | N |
| 23 Capps | Y | Y | Y | Y | Y | Y | Y |
| 24 Gallegly | Y | Y | N | N | N | Y | Y |
| 25 McKeon | Y | Y | N | N | N | N | N |
| 26 Dreier | Y | Y | N | N | Y | N | N |
| 27 Sherman | Y | Y | Y | Y | Y | Y | Y |
| 28 Berman | Y | Y | Y | Y | Y | Y | Y |
| 29 Schiff | + | Y | Y | Y | Y | Y | Y |
| 30 Waxman | Y | Y | Y | Y | Y | Y | Y |
| 31 Becerra | Y | Y | Y | Y | Y | Y | Y |
| 32 Solis | Y | Y | Y | Y | Y | Y | Y |
| 33 Watson | Y | Y | Y | Y | Y | Y | Y |
| 34 Roybal-Allard | Y | Y | Y | Y | Y | Y | Y |
| 35 Waters | Y | Y | Y | Y | Y | Y | Y |
| 36 Harman | Y | Y | Y | Y | Y | Y | Y |
| 37 Millender-McD. | Y | Y | Y | Y | Y | Y | Y |
| 38 Napolitano | Y | Y | Y | Y | Y | Y | N |
| 39 Sánchez, Linda | Y | Y | Y | Y | Y | Y | Y |
| 40 Royce | Y | Y | N | N | N | N | Y |
| 41 Lewis | Y | Y | N | N | N | N | N |
| 42 Miller, Gary | Y | Y | N | N | N | N | N |
| 43 Baca | Y | Y | N | N | Y | N | N |
| 44 Calvert | Y | Y | N | N | N | N | N |
| 45 Bono | Y | Y | N | Y | N | Y | N |
| 46 Rohrabacher | Y | Y | N | N | N | Y | N |
| 47 Sanchez, Loretta | + | + | Y | Y | Y | Y | N |
| 48 Cox | Y | Y | ? | ? | ? | ? | ? |
| 49 Issa | Y | Y | N | N | N | Y | N |

| | 228 | 229 | 230 | 231 | 232 | 233 | 234 |
|---|---|---|---|---|---|---|---|
| 50 Cunningham | Y | Y | N | N | N | Y | N |
| 51 Filner | Y | Y | Y | N | Y | Y | Y |
| 52 Hunter | Y | Y | N | Y | N | Y | N |
| 53 Davis | Y | Y | Y | Y | Y | Y | Y |
| **COLORADO** | | | | | | | |
| 1 DeGette | Y | Y | Y | Y | Y | Y | Y |
| 2 Udall | Y | Y | Y | Y | Y | Y | N |
| 3 Salazar | Y | Y | Y | Y | Y | N | N |
| 4 Musgrave | Y | Y | N | N | N | N | N |
| 5 Hefley | Y | Y | N | Y | N | Y | N |
| 6 Tancredo | Y | Y | N | N | N | Y | Y |
| 7 Beauprez | Y | Y | N | N | N | N | N |
| **CONNECTICUT** | | | | | | | |
| 1 Larson | Y | Y | Y | Y | Y | Y | ? |
| 2 Simmons | Y | Y | Y | Y | N | Y | Y |
| 3 DeLauro | Y | Y | Y | Y | Y | Y | N |
| 4 Shays | Y | Y | Y | Y | Y | Y | Y |
| 5 Johnson | Y | Y | N | Y | N | Y | N |
| **DELAWARE** | | | | | | | |
| AL Castle | Y | Y | N | N | N | Y | Y |
| **FLORIDA** | | | | | | | |
| 1 Miller | Y | Y | N | Y | N | N | N |
| 2 Boyd | Y | Y | N | N | Y | N | N |
| 3 Brown | ? | ? | Y | Y | Y | Y | N |
| 4 Crenshaw | Y | Y | N | Y | N | N | N |
| 5 Brown-Waite | Y | Y | N | Y | N | N | N |
| 6 Stearns | Y | Y | N | N | N | N | N |
| 7 Mica | Y | Y | N | N | N | N | N |
| 8 Keller | Y | Y | N | N | N | Y | Y |
| 9 Bilirakis | Y | Y | N | N | N | Y | Y |
| 10 Young | Y | Y | N | Y | N | Y | Y |
| 11 Davis | Y | Y | Y | Y | Y | N | N |
| 12 Putnam | Y | Y | N | N | N | Y | N |
| 13 Harris | Y | Y | N | N | N | N | N |
| 14 Mack | Y | Y | N | N | N | N | N |
| 15 Weldon | Y | Y | N | Y | N | N | N |
| 16 Foley | Y | Y | Y | N | Y | N | N |
| 17 Meek | Y | Y | Y | Y | Y | Y | N |
| 18 Ros-Lehtinen | Y | Y | N | N | Y | N | N |
| 19 Wexler | Y | Y | N | Y | N | N | N |
| 20 Wasserman-Schultz | Y | Y | Y | Y | N | N | N |
| 21 Diaz-Balart, L. | Y | Y | N | N | N | N | N |
| 22 Shaw | Y | Y | N | Y | N | Y | Y |
| 23 Hastings | ? | ? | ? | ? | ? | ? | ? |
| 24 Feeney | Y | Y | N | N | N | N | N |
| 25 Diaz-Balart, M. | Y | Y | N | N | N | Y | N |
| **GEORGIA** | | | | | | | |
| 1 Kingston | Y | Y | N | N | N | Y | N |
| 2 Bishop | Y | Y | N | Y | Y | Y | N |
| 3 Marshall | Y | Y | N | N | Y | Y | N |
| 4 McKinney | Y | N | Y | Y | Y | N | Y |
| 5 Lewis | Y | Y | Y | Y | Y | Y | Y |
| 6 Price | Y | Y | N | N | N | N | N |
| 7 Linder | Y | Y | N | N | N | N | N |
| 8 Westmoreland | Y | Y | N | N | N | N | N |
| 9 Norwood | Y | Y | Y | N | N | N | N |
| 10 Deal | Y | Y | N | N | N | Y | N |
| 11 Gingrey | Y | Y | N | N | N | Y | Y |
| 12 Barrow | Y | Y | Y | Y | Y | Y | N |
| 13 Scott | ? | ? | N | Y | N | N | N |
| **HAWAII** | | | | | | | |
| 1 Abercrombie | Y | Y | N | N | Y | Y | N |
| 2 Case | Y | Y | Y | N | Y | Y | N |
| **IDAHO** | | | | | | | |
| 1 Otter | ? | ? | N | N | N | N | N |
| 2 Simpson | Y | Y | N | N | N | N | N |
| **ILLINOIS** | | | | | | | |
| 1 Rush | ? | ? | ? | ? | ? | ? | ? |
| 2 Jackson | Y | Y | Y | Y | Y | Y | Y |
| 3 Lipinski | Y | Y | Y | Y | Y | Y | N |
| 4 Gutierrez | ? | ? | Y | Y | Y | Y | Y |
| 5 Emanuel | Y | Y | Y | Y | Y | Y | Y |
| 6 Hyde | + | + | N | N | N | Y | N |
| 7 Davis | Y | Y | Y | Y | Y | Y | Y |
| 8 Bean | Y | Y | Y | Y | Y | Y | Y |
| 9 Schakowsky | Y | Y | Y | Y | Y | Y | N |
| 10 Kirk | Y | Y | N | N | Y | Y | N |
| 11 Weller | Y | Y | N | N | N | Y | N |
| 12 Costello | Y | Y | Y | N | Y | Y | N |

**KEY** Republicans Democrats *Independents*

| | | | |
|---|---|---|---|
| Y | Voted for (yea) | X | Paired against |
| # | Paired for | – | Announced against |
| + | Announced for | P | Voted "present" |
| N | Voted against (nay) | C | Voted "present" to avoid possible conflict of interest |
| | | ? | Did not vote or otherwise make a position known |

| | 228 | 229 | 230 | 231 | 232 | 233 | 234 |
|---|---|---|---|---|---|---|---|
| 13 **Biggert** | Y | Y | Y | N | N | Y | Y |
| 14 **Hastert** | | | | | N | | |
| 15 **Johnson** | Y | Y | N | N | N | Y | N |
| 16 **Manzullo** | Y | Y | N | N | N | N | Y |
| 17 Evans | Y | Y | Y | Y | Y | Y | N |
| 18 **LaHood** | Y | Y | N | N | N | N | N |
| 19 **Shimkus** | Y | Y | N | N | N | N | N |
| **INDIANA** | | | | | | | |
| 1 Visclosky | Y | Y | Y | N | Y | Y | N |
| 2 **Chocola** | Y | Y | N | N | N | N | Y |
| 3 **Souder** | Y | Y | Y | N | N | N | Y |
| 4 **Buyer** | Y | Y | N | N | N | N | N |
| 5 **Burton** | Y | Y | N | N | Y | Y | Y |
| 6 **Pence** | Y | Y | N | N | N | Y | Y |
| 7 Carson | Y | Y | Y | Y | Y | N | Y |
| 8 **Hostettler** | Y | Y | N | N | N | Y | Y |
| 9 **Sodrel** | Y | Y | N | N | N | N | N |
| **IOWA** | | | | | | | |
| 1 **Nussle** | ? | ? | N | N | N | N | N |
| 2 **Leach** | Y | Y | N | N | Y | N | N |
| 3 Boswell | Y | Y | Y | Y | Y | N | N |
| 4 **Latham** | Y | Y | N | N | N | N | N |
| 5 **King** | Y | Y | N | N | N | N | N |
| **KANSAS** | | | | | | | |
| 1 **Moran** | Y | Y | N | N | Y | N | N |
| 2 **Ryun** | Y | Y | N | N | N | N | N |
| 3 Moore | Y | Y | Y | N | Y | Y | Y |
| 4 **Tiahrt** | Y | Y | N | N | N | Y | N |
| **KENTUCKY** | | | | | | | |
| 1 **Whitfield** | Y | Y | N | N | N | Y | N |
| 2 **Lewis** | Y | Y | N | N | Y | Y | N |
| 3 **Northup** | Y | Y | N | N | Y | N | N |
| 4 **Davis** | Y | Y | N | N | N | Y | N |
| 5 **Rogers** | Y | Y | N | N | Y | Y | N |
| 6 Chandler | Y | Y | Y | N | Y | Y | N |
| **LOUISIANA** | | | | | | | |
| 1 **Jindal** | Y | Y | Y | N | Y | Y | N |
| 2 Jefferson | Y | Y | Y | N | N | Y | N |
| 3 Melancon | Y | Y | Y | Y | Y | N | N |
| 4 **McCrery** | Y | Y | N | N | N | N | N |
| 5 **Alexander** | Y | Y | N | N | N | N | N |
| 6 **Baker** | Y | Y | N | N | N | N | N |
| 7 **Boustany** | Y | Y | N | N | N | N | N |
| **MAINE** | | | | | | | |
| 1 Allen | Y | Y | Y | Y | Y | Y | Y |
| 2 Michaud | Y | Y | Y | Y | Y | Y | N |
| **MARYLAND** | | | | | | | |
| 1 **Gilchrest** | Y | Y | Y | N | N | Y | N |
| 2 Ruppersberger | Y | Y | Y | Y | Y | Y | N |
| 3 Cardin | Y | Y | Y | Y | Y | Y | N |
| 4 Wynn | Y | Y | Y | N | Y | Y | N |
| 5 Hoyer | Y | Y | Y | Y | Y | Y | N |
| 6 **Bartlett** | Y | Y | N | Y | N | Y | Y |
| 7 Cummings | Y | Y | N | Y | Y | Y | N |
| 8 Van Hollen | Y | Y | Y | Y | Y | Y | Y |
| **MASSACHUSETTS** | | | | | | | |
| 1 Olver | Y | Y | Y | Y | Y | Y | N |
| 2 Neal | Y | Y | Y | Y | Y | Y | N |
| 3 McGovern | Y | Y | Y | Y | Y | Y | N |
| 4 Frank | Y | Y | Y | Y | Y | Y | Y |
| 5 Meehan | Y | Y | Y | Y | Y | Y | Y |
| 6 Tierney | Y | Y | Y | Y | Y | Y | Y |
| 7 Markey | Y | Y | Y | Y | Y | Y | Y |
| 8 Capuano | Y | Y | Y | Y | Y | Y | Y |
| 9 Lynch | Y | Y | Y | Y | Y | Y | N |
| 10 Delahunt | ? | Y | Y | Y | Y | N | Y |
| **MICHIGAN** | | | | | | | |
| 1 Stupak | Y | Y | Y | Y | Y | Y | N |
| 2 **Hoekstra** | Y | Y | Y | N | N | N | N |
| 3 **Ehlers** | Y | Y | Y | Y | Y | Y | Y |
| 4 **Camp** | Y | Y | Y | N | N | N | N |
| 5 Kildee | Y | Y | Y | Y | Y | Y | N |
| 6 **Upton** | Y | Y | Y | Y | N | Y | Y |
| 7 **Schwarz** | Y | Y | Y | N | N | Y | N |
| 8 **Rogers** | Y | Y | Y | N | N | Y | N |
| 9 **Knollenberg** | Y | Y | N | N | N | N | N |
| 10 **Miller** | Y | Y | Y | N | N | N | N |
| 11 **McCotter** | Y | Y | Y | N | N | Y | N |
| 12 Levin | Y | Y | Y | Y | Y | Y | N |
| 13 Kilpatrick | Y | Y | Y | Y | Y | Y | N |
| 14 Conyers | ? | Y | Y | Y | Y | Y | Y |
| 15 Dingell | Y | Y | Y | Y | Y | N | N |
| **MINNESOTA** | | | | | | | |
| 1 **Gutknecht** | Y | Y | N | N | Y | Y | N |
| 2 **Kline** | Y | Y | N | N | N | Y | N |
| 3 **Ramstad** | Y | Y | Y | N | N | Y | Y |
| 4 McCollum | ? | ? | Y | Y | Y | Y | N |
| 5 Sabo | Y | Y | Y | Y | Y | Y | N |
| 6 **Kennedy** | Y | Y | N | N | N | Y | N |
| 7 Peterson | Y | Y | Y | Y | N | N | N |
| 8 Oberstar | Y | Y | Y | Y | Y | N | N |
| **MISSISSIPPI** | | | | | | | |
| 1 **Wicker** | Y | Y | N | N | N | N | N |
| 2 Thompson | Y | Y | Y | N | Y | Y | N |
| 3 **Pickering** | Y | Y | N | Y | N | Y | N |
| 4 Taylor | Y | Y | Y | Y | Y | Y | N |
| **MISSOURI** | | | | | | | |
| 1 Clay | Y | Y | Y | N | Y | Y | N |
| 2 **Akin** | Y | Y | ? | N | N | N | Y |
| 3 Carnahan | Y | Y | Y | N | Y | Y | N |
| 4 Skelton | Y | Y | Y | N | Y | N | N |
| 5 Cleaver | Y | Y | Y | N | Y | Y | N |
| 6 **Graves** | Y | Y | N | N | N | N | N |
| 7 **Blunt** | Y | Y | N | N | N | N | N |
| 8 **Emerson** | Y | Y | N | N | Y | N | N |
| 9 **Hulshof** | Y | Y | N | N | Y | N | N |
| **MONTANA** | | | | | | | |
| AL **Rehberg** | Y | Y | N | Y | N | N | N |
| **NEBRASKA** | | | | | | | |
| 1 **Fortenberry** | Y | Y | N | Y | N | N | N |
| 2 **Terry** | Y | Y | N | N | N | N | N |
| 3 **Osborne** | Y | Y | N | Y | N | N | N |
| **NEVADA** | | | | | | | |
| 1 Berkley | Y | Y | Y | Y | Y | Y | Y |
| 2 **Gibbons** | Y | Y | Y | N | N | Y | Y |
| 3 **Porter** | Y | Y | Y | N | N | Y | Y |
| **NEW HAMPSHIRE** | | | | | | | |
| 1 **Bradley** | Y | Y | Y | N | Y | Y | Y |
| 2 **Bass** | Y | Y | Y | N | Y | Y | Y |
| **NEW JERSEY** | | | | | | | |
| 1 Andrews | + | + | Y | N | Y | Y | Y |
| 2 **LoBiondo** | Y | Y | Y | Y | N | Y | Y |
| 3 **Saxton** | Y | Y | N | Y | N | Y | N |
| 4 **Smith** | Y | Y | Y | Y | N | Y | Y |
| 5 **Garrett** | Y | Y | N | N | N | N | Y |
| 6 Pallone | Y | Y | Y | Y | Y | Y | Y |
| 7 **Ferguson** | Y | Y | Y | N | N | Y | Y |
| 8 Pascrell | Y | Y | Y | Y | Y | Y | Y |
| 9 Rothman | ? | ? | Y | Y | Y | Y | N |
| 10 Payne | ? | ? | Y | Y | Y | Y | Y |
| 11 **Frelinghuysen** | Y | Y | N | N | N | Y | Y |
| 12 Holt | Y | Y | Y | Y | Y | Y | Y |
| 13 Menendez | Y | Y | ? | ? | ? | ? | ? |
| **NEW MEXICO** | | | | | | | |
| 1 **Wilson** | Y | Y | Y | Y | N | N | N |
| 2 **Pearce** | Y | Y | N | Y | N | N | N |
| 3 Udall | Y | Y | Y | Y | Y | Y | Y |
| **NEW YORK** | | | | | | | |
| 1 Bishop | Y | Y | Y | Y | Y | Y | Y |
| 2 Israel | Y | Y | Y | Y | Y | Y | N |
| 3 **King** | Y | Y | Y | Y | N | Y | N |
| 4 McCarthy | Y | Y | Y | Y | Y | Y | N |
| 5 Ackerman | Y | Y | Y | Y | Y | Y | N |
| 6 Meeks | Y | Y | Y | N | N | Y | Y |
| 7 Crowley | Y | Y | Y | Y | Y | Y | N |
| 8 Nadler | Y | Y | Y | Y | Y | Y | N |
| 9 Weiner | Y | Y | Y | Y | Y | Y | Y |
| 10 Towns | Y | Y | Y | Y | N | Y | N |
| 11 Owens | Y | Y | Y | Y | Y | Y | Y |
| 12 Velázquez | Y | Y | Y | Y | Y | Y | Y |
| 13 **Fossella** | Y | Y | Y | N | N | Y | Y |
| 14 Maloney | Y | Y | Y | Y | Y | Y | N |
| 15 Rangel | Y | Y | Y | Y | Y | N | N |
| 16 Serrano | Y | Y | Y | Y | Y | Y | N |
| 17 Engel | Y | Y | Y | Y | Y | Y | N |
| 18 Lowey | Y | Y | Y | Y | Y | Y | Y |
| 19 **Kelly** | Y | Y | Y | Y | Y | Y | N |
| 20 **Sweeney** | Y | Y | Y | N | N | Y | Y |
| 21 McNulty | Y | Y | Y | N | Y | Y | Y |
| 22 Hinchey | Y | Y | Y | Y | Y | Y | N |
| 23 **McHugh** | Y | Y | N | Y | Y | N | N |
| 24 **Boehlert** | Y | Y | N | Y | Y | Y | Y |
| 25 **Walsh** | Y | Y | N | N | N | N | N |
| 26 **Reynolds** | Y | Y | N | N | N | N | N |
| 27 Higgins | Y | Y | Y | Y | Y | Y | N |
| 28 Slaughter | Y | Y | Y | N | + | + | N |
| 29 **Kuhl** | Y | Y | N | N | N | Y | Y |
| **NORTH CAROLINA** | | | | | | | |
| 1 Butterfield | Y | Y | Y | N | Y | Y | N |
| 2 Etheridge | Y | Y | Y | N | N | Y | N |
| 3 **Jones** | Y | Y | N | Y | Y | Y | N |
| 4 Price | Y | Y | Y | N | N | Y | N |
| 5 **Foxx** | Y | Y | N | N | N | N | N |
| 6 **Coble** | Y | Y | N | N | N | N | N |
| 7 McIntyre | Y | Y | N | N | Y | Y | N |
| 8 **Hayes** | Y | Y | N | N | N | N | N |
| 9 **Myrick** | Y | Y | N | Y | N | Y | Y |
| 10 **McHenry** | Y | Y | N | N | N | N | Y |
| 11 **Taylor** | Y | Y | N | N | N | N | N |
| 12 Watt | Y | Y | Y | Y | Y | N | N |
| 13 Miller | Y | Y | Y | N | N | Y | N |
| **NORTH DAKOTA** | | | | | | | |
| AL Pomeroy | Y | Y | Y | Y | Y | N | N |
| **OHIO** | | | | | | | |
| 1 **Chabot** | Y | Y | N | N | N | Y | Y |
| 2 Vacant | | | | | | | |
| 3 **Turner** | Y | Y | N | N | N | Y | N |
| 4 **Oxley** | + | + | N | N | N | N | N |
| 5 **Gillmor** | Y | Y | N | N | N | N | N |
| 6 Strickland | Y | Y | Y | Y | Y | Y | N |
| 7 **Hobson** | Y | Y | N | N | N | N | N |
| 8 **Boehner** | Y | Y | N | N | N | N | N |
| 9 Kaptur | ? | Y | Y | Y | Y | Y | N |
| 10 Kucinich | Y | Y | Y | Y | Y | Y | N |
| 11 Jones | Y | Y | Y | Y | Y | Y | N |
| 12 **Tiberi** | Y | Y | N | N | N | N | Y |
| 13 Brown | Y | Y | Y | Y | Y | Y | N |
| 14 **LaTourette** | Y | Y | N | N | N | Y | N |
| 15 **Pryce** | Y | Y | N | N | N | Y | N |
| 16 **Regula** | Y | Y | N | Y | N | N | N |
| 17 Ryan | Y | Y | Y | Y | Y | Y | N |
| 18 **Ney** | Y | Y | N | N | N | Y | Y |
| **OKLAHOMA** | | | | | | | |
| 1 **Sullivan** | Y | Y | N | N | N | N | N |
| 2 Boren | Y | Y | N | N | Y | N | N |
| 3 **Lucas** | ? | Y | N | N | N | N | N |
| 4 **Cole** | Y | Y | N | N | N | N | N |
| 5 **Istook** | Y | Y | N | Y | N | N | Y |
| **OREGON** | | | | | | | |
| 1 Wu | Y | Y | Y | Y | Y | Y | N |
| 2 **Walden** | Y | Y | N | Y | N | N | N |
| 3 Blumenauer | Y | Y | Y | Y | Y | Y | Y |
| 4 DeFazio | Y | Y | Y | Y | Y | Y | N |
| 5 Hooley | Y | Y | Y | Y | Y | Y | N |
| **PENNSYLVANIA** | | | | | | | |
| 1 Brady | Y | Y | Y | Y | Y | Y | Y |
| 2 Fattah | Y | Y | Y | Y | Y | Y | Y |
| 3 **English** | Y | Y | N | N | N | Y | Y |
| 4 **Hart** | Y | Y | N | N | N | N | Y |
| 5 **Peterson** | Y | Y | N | N | Y | N | Y |
| 6 **Gerlach** | Y | Y | N | N | N | Y | Y |
| 7 **Weldon** | ? | Y | Y | Y | Y | Y | N |
| 8 **Fitzpatrick** | Y | Y | Y | N | Y | Y | Y |
| 9 **Shuster** | Y | Y | N | N | N | N | Y |
| 10 **Sherwood** | Y | Y | N | N | N | N | N |
| 11 Kanjorski | Y | Y | Y | N | Y | Y | Y |
| 12 Murtha | Y | Y | Y | Y | Y | Y | N |
| 13 Schwartz | Y | Y | Y | Y | Y | Y | Y |
| 14 Doyle | Y | Y | Y | Y | Y | Y | Y |
| 15 **Dent** | Y | Y | N | N | N | Y | Y |
| 16 **Pitts** | Y | Y | N | N | N | Y | Y |
| 17 Holden | Y | Y | Y | Y | Y | Y | N |
| 18 **Murphy** | Y | Y | N | N | N | N | Y |
| 19 **Platts** | ? | ? | N | N | Y | Y | Y |
| **RHODE ISLAND** | | | | | | | |
| 1 Kennedy | + | + | Y | Y | Y | Y | Y |
| 2 Langevin | Y | Y | Y | Y | Y | Y | Y |
| **SOUTH CAROLINA** | | | | | | | |
| 1 **Brown** | Y | Y | N | N | Y | Y | Y |
| 2 **Wilson** | Y | Y | N | N | N | Y | Y |
| 3 **Barrett** | Y | Y | N | N | N | N | N |
| 4 **Inglis** | Y | Y | N | N | N | Y | Y |
| 5 Spratt | Y | Y | Y | N | Y | Y | N |
| 6 Clyburn | Y | Y | Y | N | N | Y | N |
| **SOUTH DAKOTA** | | | | | | | |
| AL Herseth | Y | Y | Y | Y | Y | Y | N |
| **TENNESSEE** | | | | | | | |
| 1 **Jenkins** | ? | ? | N | N | Y | N | N |
| 2 **Duncan** | Y | Y | N | N | Y | N | Y |
| 3 **Wamp** | Y | Y | N | N | Y | Y | Y |
| 4 Davis | Y | Y | N | N | Y | N | N |
| 5 Cooper | Y | Y | Y | N | N | N | Y |
| 6 Gordon | Y | Y | Y | N | Y | Y | Y |
| 7 **Blackburn** | Y | Y | N | N | N | N | Y |
| 8 Tanner | Y | Y | Y | N | Y | Y | N |
| 9 Ford | Y | Y | Y | ? | Y | Y | N |
| **TEXAS** | | | | | | | |
| 1 **Gohmert** | Y | Y | N | N | N | Y | N |
| 2 **Poe** | Y | Y | Y | N | N | Y | Y |
| 3 **Johnson, S.** | Y | Y | N | N | N | N | Y |
| 4 **Hall** | Y | Y | N | N | N | Y | N |
| 5 **Hensarling** | Y | Y | N | N | N | N | Y |
| 6 **Barton** | Y | Y | N | N | N | N | N |
| 7 **Culberson** | Y | Y | N | N | N | N | N |
| 8 **Brady** | Y | Y | N | N | N | N | N |
| 9 Green | Y | Y | Y | Y | Y | Y | N |
| 10 **McCaul** | Y | Y | Y | N | N | Y | N |
| 11 **Conaway** | Y | Y | N | N | N | N | N |
| 12 **Granger** | Y | Y | N | N | N | N | N |
| 13 **Thornberry** | Y | Y | N | N | N | N | N |
| 14 **Paul** | Y | N | Y | Y | Y | Y | Y |
| 15 Hinojosa | Y | Y | Y | N | Y | N | – |
| 16 Reyes | Y | Y | Y | N | Y | N | N |
| 17 Edwards | Y | Y | Y | N | Y | N | N |
| 18 Jackson-Lee | ? | ? | ? | ? | ? | ? | ? |
| 19 **Neugebauer** | Y | Y | N | N | N | N | N |
| 20 Gonzalez | Y | Y | Y | N | Y | Y | N |
| 21 **Smith** | Y | Y | N | N | N | N | N |
| 22 **DeLay** | Y | Y | N | N | N | N | N |
| 23 **Bonilla** | Y | Y | N | N | N | N | N |
| 24 **Marchant** | Y | Y | N | N | N | N | N |
| 25 Doggett | Y | Y | Y | Y | Y | Y | Y |
| 26 **Burgess** | Y | Y | N | N | N | Y | Y |
| 27 Ortiz | Y | Y | N | N | Y | Y | N |
| 28 Cuellar | Y | Y | Y | N | Y | N | N |
| 29 Green | Y | ? | N | Y | Y | Y | N |
| 30 Johnson, E. | Y | Y | Y | Y | Y | Y | N |
| 31 **Carter** | Y | Y | N | N | N | N | N |
| 32 **Sessions** | Y | Y | N | N | N | N | Y |
| **UTAH** | | | | | | | |
| 1 **Bishop** | Y | Y | N | N | N | N | N |
| 2 Matheson | Y | Y | Y | Y | N | N | Y |
| 3 **Cannon** | Y | Y | N | N | N | N | N |
| **VERMONT** | | | | | | | |
| AL *Sanders* | Y | Y | Y | Y | Y | Y | N |
| **VIRGINIA** | | | | | | | |
| 1 **Davis, J.** | Y | Y | N | Y | N | Y | Y |
| 2 **Drake** | Y | Y | N | N | N | N | N |
| 3 Scott | Y | Y | Y | Y | Y | Y | Y |
| 4 **Forbes** | Y | Y | N | N | N | Y | Y |
| 5 **Goode** | Y | Y | N | N | N | Y | N |
| 6 **Goodlatte** | Y | Y | N | N | N | N | N |
| 7 **Cantor** | Y | Y | N | N | N | N | N |
| 8 Moran | Y | Y | Y | N | Y | Y | Y |
| 9 Boucher | Y | Y | Y | N | Y | N | Y |
| 10 **Wolf** | Y | Y | N | N | N | Y | N |
| 11 **Davis, T.** | Y | Y | N | N | N | Y | Y |
| **WASHINGTON** | | | | | | | |
| 1 Inslee | Y | Y | Y | Y | Y | Y | Y |
| 2 Larsen | Y | Y | Y | N | Y | Y | N |
| 3 Baird | Y | Y | Y | Y | Y | Y | N |
| 4 **Hastings** | Y | Y | N | N | N | N | N |
| 5 **McMorris** | Y | Y | N | Y | N | N | N |
| 6 Dicks | Y | Y | Y | Y | Y | Y | N |
| 7 McDermott | Y | Y | Y | Y | Y | Y | Y |
| 8 **Reichert** | Y | Y | N | N | N | Y | N |
| 9 Smith | Y | Y | Y | Y | Y | N | Y |
| **WEST VIRGINIA** | | | | | | | |
| 1 Mollohan | Y | Y | Y | Y | Y | Y | N |
| 2 **Capito** | Y | Y | N | Y | N | Y | N |
| 3 Rahall | Y | Y | Y | Y | Y | Y | N |
| **WISCONSIN** | | | | | | | |
| 1 **Ryan** | Y | Y | N | N | N | N | Y |
| 2 Baldwin | Y | Y | Y | Y | Y | Y | Y |
| 3 Kind | Y | Y | Y | Y | Y | Y | Y |
| 4 Moore | Y | Y | Y | Y | Y | Y | Y |
| 5 **Sensenbrenner** | Y | Y | N | Y | N | Y | Y |
| 6 **Petri** | Y | Y | N | N | N | N | Y |
| 7 Obey | Y | Y | Y | Y | Y | Y | N |
| 8 **Green** | Y | Y | Y | N | N | Y | Y |
| **WYOMING** | | | | | | | |
| AL **Cubin** | + | Y | Y | Y | N | N | N |

# IN THE HOUSE | By Vote Number

**235.** HR 2744. Fiscal 2006 Agriculture Appropriations/Market Access Program. Chabot, R-Ohio, amendment that would prohibit the use of funds in the bill to carry out activities of the Market Access Program, which helps fund advertising and marketing for agricultural exports. Rejected 66-356: R 48-178; D 18-177 (ND 16-131, SD 2-46); I 0-1. June 8, 2005.

**236.** HR 2744. Fiscal 2006 Agriculture Appropriations/Across-the-Board Cut. Hefley, R-Colo., amendment that would require a 1 percent across-the-board cut in discretionary spending. Rejected 80-335: R 76-144; D 4-190 (ND 2-146, SD 2-44); I 0-1. June 8, 2005.

**237.** HR 2744. Fiscal 2006 Agriculture Appropriations/Food Stamps. Garrett, R-N.J., amendment that would prohibit the use of funds under the food stamp program to contravene existing immigration law requiring that sponsors of legal aliens be financially liable for government benefits provided to the aliens. Rejected 169-258: R 162-66; D 7-191 (ND 2-148, SD 5-43); I 0-1. June 8, 2005.

**238.** HR 2744. Fiscal 2006 Agriculture Appropriations/Passage. Passage of the bill that would provide $100.3 billion in fiscal 2006 for the Department of Agriculture and related agencies, such as the Food and Drug Administration (FDA). The bill would fund the food stamp program at $40.7 billion and the child nutrition program at $12.4 billion. It would provide $25.7 billion for the Commodity Credit Corporation, $5.3 billion for the Women, Infants and Children program and $1.5 billion for the FDA. Passed 408-18: R 215-13; D 192-5 (ND 145-4, SD 47-1); I 1-0. June 8, 2005.

**239.** H J Res 27. World Trade Organization Withdrawal/Passage. Passage of the joint resolution that would withdraw congressional approval of the agreement establishing the World Trade Organization. Rejected 86-338: R 39-185; D 46-153 (ND 39-110, SD 7-43); I 1-0. June 9, 2005.

**240.** H Res 310. Ethics Committee Staff/Motion to Table. Blunt, R-Mo., motion to table (kill) the Pelosi, D-Calif., privileged resolution that would direct the Committee on Standards of Official Conduct to appoint a nonpartisan professional staff if a majority of the committee agrees to do so. Motion agreed to 219-199: R 219-0; D 0-198 (ND 0-148, SD 0-50); I 0-1. June 9, 2005.

| | 235 | 236 | 237 | 238 | 239 | 240 |
|---|---|---|---|---|---|---|
| **ALABAMA** | | | | | | |
| 1 Bonner | N | N | Y | Y | N | Y |
| 2 Everett | N | Y | Y | Y | Y | ? |
| 3 Rogers | N | N | Y | Y | N | Y |
| 4 Aderholt | N | N | Y | Y | N | Y |
| 5 Cramer | N | N | Y | Y | N | N |
| 6 Bachus | Y | N | Y | Y | N | Y |
| 7 Davis | N | N | N | Y | N | N |
| **ALASKA** | | | | | | |
| AL Young | N | ? | ? | ? | N | Y |
| **ARIZONA** | | | | | | |
| 1 Renzi | N | N | Y | Y | N | Y |
| 2 Franks | Y | Y | Y | N | Y | Y |
| 3 Shadegg | Y | Y | Y | N | Y | Y |
| 4 Pastor | N | N | N | Y | Y | N |
| 5 Hayworth | Y | Y | Y | N | N | Y |
| 6 Flake | Y | Y | Y | N | N | Y |
| 7 Grijalva | N | N | N | Y | Y | N |
| 8 Kolbe | N | N | Y | Y | N | N |
| **ARKANSAS** | | | | | | |
| 1 Berry | N | N | N | Y | N | N |
| 2 Snyder | N | N | N | Y | N | N |
| 3 Boozman | N | N | Y | N | Y | Y |
| 4 Ross | N | N | N | Y | N | N |
| **CALIFORNIA** | | | | | | |
| 1 Thompson | N | N | N | Y | N | N |
| 2 Herger | N | Y | Y | Y | N | Y |
| 3 Lungren | N | Y | Y | Y | N | Y |
| 4 Doolittle | N | N | Y | Y | N | Y |
| 5 Matsui, D. | N | N | N | Y | N | N |
| 6 Woolsey | N | N | N | Y | N | N |
| 7 Miller, George | N | N | N | Y | N | N |
| 8 Pelosi | N | N | N | Y | N | N |
| 9 Lee | N | N | N | Y | Y | N |
| 10 Tauscher | N | N | N | Y | N | N |
| 11 Pombo | N | N | N | Y | Y | Y |
| 12 Lantos | N | N | N | Y | N | N |
| 13 Stark | N | N | N | N | N | N |
| 14 Eshoo | N | N | N | Y | N | N |
| 15 Honda | N | N | N | Y | N | N |
| 16 Lofgren | N | N | N | Y | N | N |
| 17 Farr | N | N | N | Y | N | N |
| 18 Cardoza | N | N | N | Y | Y | N |
| 19 Radanovich | N | Y | Y | Y | N | Y |
| 20 Costa | N | N | N | Y | Y | N |
| 21 Nunes | N | N | N | Y | N | Y |
| 22 Thomas | N | N | N | Y | N | N |
| 23 Capps | N | N | N | Y | N | N |
| 24 Gallegly | N | N | Y | Y | N | Y |
| 25 McKeon | N | N | N | Y | N | Y |
| 26 Dreier | N | N | Y | Y | N | Y |
| 27 Sherman | N | N | N | Y | N | N |
| 28 Berman | N | N | N | Y | N | N |
| 29 Schiff | N | N | N | Y | N | N |
| 30 Waxman | Y | N | N | Y | N | N |
| 31 Becerra | N | N | N | Y | N | N |
| 32 Solis | N | N | N | Y | N | N |
| 33 Watson | N | N | N | Y | N | N |
| 34 Roybal-Allard | N | N | N | Y | N | N |
| 35 Waters | N | N | N | Y | Y | N |
| 36 Harman | N | N | N | Y | N | N |
| 37 Millender-McD. | N | N | N | Y | N | N |
| 38 Napolitano | N | N | N | Y | Y | N |
| 39 Sánchez, Linda | N | N | N | Y | Y | N |
| 40 Royce | Y | Y | Y | N | N | Y |
| 41 Lewis | N | N | N | Y | N | N |
| 42 Miller, Gary | Y | Y | Y | N | N | Y |
| 43 Baca | N | N | N | Y | N | N |
| 44 Calvert | N | N | Y | Y | N | Y |
| 45 Bono | N | N | Y | Y | N | ? |
| 46 Rohrabacher | Y | Y | Y | N | N | Y |
| 47 Sanchez, Loretta | N | N | N | Y | N | N |
| 48 Cox | ? | Y | Y | Y | ? | ? |
| 49 Issa | N | Y | Y | Y | N | Y |

| | 235 | 236 | 237 | 238 | 239 | 240 |
|---|---|---|---|---|---|---|
| 50 Cunningham | N | N | Y | N | Y | Y |
| 51 Filner | N | N | Y | N | N | N |
| 52 Hunter | N | Y | Y | Y | Y | Y |
| 53 Davis | N | N | N | Y | N | N |
| **COLORADO** | | | | | | |
| 1 DeGette | Y | N | N | Y | N | N |
| 2 Udall | N | N | Y | N | N | N |
| 3 Salazar | N | N | N | Y | N | N |
| 4 Musgrave | N | N | Y | Y | N | Y |
| 5 Hefley | N | Y | Y | Y | N | Y |
| 6 Tancredo | Y | Y | Y | Y | N | Y |
| 7 Beauprez | N | Y | Y | Y | N | Y |
| **CONNECTICUT** | | | | | | |
| 1 Larson | N | N | N | Y | N | N |
| 2 Simmons | N | N | Y | Y | N | Y |
| 3 DeLauro | N | N | N | Y | N | N |
| 4 Shays | Y | Y | Y | N | N | Y |
| 5 Johnson | N | N | Y | Y | N | Y |
| **DELAWARE** | | | | | | |
| AL Castle | Y | N | N | Y | N | Y |
| **FLORIDA** | | | | | | |
| 1 Miller | N | Y | Y | Y | Y | Y |
| 2 Boyd | N | N | N | Y | N | N |
| 3 Brown | N | N | N | Y | N | N |
| 4 Crenshaw | ? | N | N | Y | N | Y |
| 5 Brown-Waite | N | Y | Y | Y | N | Y |
| 6 Stearns | N | Y | Y | Y | Y | Y |
| 7 Mica | N | Y | Y | Y | N | Y |
| 8 Keller | N | Y | Y | Y | N | Y |
| 9 Bilirakis | N | N | Y | Y | Y | Y |
| 10 Young | N | N | Y | Y | N | Y |
| 11 Davis | N | N | N | Y | N | N |
| 12 Putnam | N | Y | Y | Y | N | Y |
| 13 Harris | N | Y | Y | Y | N | Y |
| 14 Mack | N | Y | Y | Y | N | Y |
| 15 Weldon | N | Y | Y | Y | N | Y |
| 16 Foley | N | N | Y | Y | N | Y |
| 17 Meek | N | N | N | Y | N | N |
| 18 Ros-Lehtinen | N | N | N | Y | N | Y |
| 19 Wexler | N | N | Y | Y | N | N |
| 20 Wasserman-Schultz | N | ? | N | Y | N | N |
| 21 Diaz-Balart, L. | N | N | Y | Y | N | Y |
| 22 Shaw | N | Y | Y | Y | N | Y |
| 23 Hastings | ? | ? | ? | ? | ? | ? |
| 24 Feeney | Y | Y | Y | N | Y | Y |
| 25 Diaz-Balart, M. | N | Y | N | Y | N | Y |
| **GEORGIA** | | | | | | |
| 1 Kingston | N | N | Y | Y | N | Y |
| 2 Bishop | N | ? | Y | Y | Y | N |
| 3 Marshall | N | ? | Y | Y | Y | N |
| 4 McKinney | Y | N | N | Y | Y | N |
| 5 Lewis | N | N | N | Y | N | N |
| 6 Price | Y | Y | Y | Y | N | Y |
| 7 Linder | Y | Y | Y | Y | N | Y |
| 8 Westmoreland | N | Y | Y | Y | Y | Y |
| 9 Norwood | N | Y | Y | Y | N | Y |
| 10 Deal | N | Y | Y | Y | Y | Y |
| 11 Gingrey | N | Y | Y | Y | N | Y |
| 12 Barrow | N | N | Y | Y | N | N |
| 13 Scott | N | N | N | Y | N | N |
| **HAWAII** | | | | | | |
| 1 Abercrombie | N | N | N | Y | Y | N |
| 2 Case | N | N | N | Y | N | N |
| **IDAHO** | | | | | | |
| 1 Otter | N | N | Y | Y | Y | Y |
| 2 Simpson | N | N | N | Y | N | Y |
| **ILLINOIS** | | | | | | |
| 1 Rush | ? | ? | N | Y | N | N |
| 2 Jackson | N | N | N | Y | Y | N |
| 3 Lipinski | Y | N | N | Y | P | N |
| 4 Gutierrez | N | N | N | Y | N | N |
| 5 Emanuel | N | N | N | Y | N | N |
| 6 Hyde | Y | N | Y | Y | N | Y |
| 7 Davis | N | N | N | Y | Y | N |
| 8 Bean | N | Y | N | N | N | N |
| 9 Schakowsky | Y | N | N | Y | N | N |
| 10 Kirk | N | N | N | Y | N | Y |
| 11 Weller | N | N | N | Y | N | Y |
| 12 Costello | N | N | N | Y | N | N |

**KEY**   Republicans   Democrats   *Independents*

| | | | |
|---|---|---|---|
| **Y** Voted for (yea) | **X** Paired against | **C** Voted "present" to avoid possible conflict of interest |
| **#** Paired for | **–** Announced against | |
| **+** Announced for | **P** Voted "present" | **?** Did not vote or otherwise make a position known |
| **N** Voted against (nay) | | |

ND Northern Democrats, SD Southern Democrats
Southern states: Ala., Ark., Fla., Ga., Ky., La., Miss., N.C., Okla., S.C., Tenn., Texas, Va.

| | 235 | 236 | 237 | 238 | 239 | 240 |
|---|---|---|---|---|---|---|
| 13 **Biggert** | N | N | N | Y | N | Y |
| 14 **Hastert** | | | | | | |
| 15 **Johnson** | N | N | N | Y | N | Y |
| 16 **Manzullo** | Y | Y | Y | Y | N | Y |
| 17 Evans | N | N | N | Y | Y | N |
| 18 **LaHood** | N | N | N | Y | ? | ? |
| 19 **Shimkus** | N | Y | N | Y | N | Y |
| **INDIANA** | | | | | | |
| 1 Visclosky | N | N | N | Y | Y | N |
| 2 **Chocola** | N | Y | Y | Y | N | Y |
| 3 **Souder** | N | N | Y | Y | N | Y |
| 4 **Buyer** | N | Y | N | Y | N | Y |
| 5 **Burton** | N | N | Y | Y | N | Y |
| 6 **Pence** | Y | Y | Y | Y | N | Y |
| 7 Carson | Y | N | N | Y | N | N |
| 8 **Hostettler** | Y | Y | Y | Y | Y | Y |
| 9 **Sodrel** | N | N | Y | Y | N | Y |
| **IOWA** | | | | | | |
| 1 **Nussle** | N | N | Y | Y | N | Y |
| 2 **Leach** | N | N | N | Y | N | Y |
| 3 Boswell | N | N | N | Y | N | N |
| 4 **Latham** | N | N | N | Y | N | Y |
| 5 **King** | N | ? | Y | Y | N | Y |
| **KANSAS** | | | | | | |
| 1 **Moran** | N | N | Y | Y | N | Y |
| 2 **Ryun** | N | N | Y | Y | N | Y |
| 3 Moore | ? | N | N | Y | N | N |
| 4 **Tiahrt** | N | N | Y | Y | N | Y |
| **KENTUCKY** | | | | | | |
| 1 **Whitfield** | N | N | Y | Y | Y | Y |
| 2 **Lewis** | N | N | Y | Y | N | Y |
| 3 **Northup** | N | N | Y | Y | N | Y |
| 4 **Davis** | N | N | Y | Y | N | Y |
| 5 **Rogers** | N | N | Y | Y | N | Y |
| 6 Chandler | N | N | N | Y | N | N |
| **LOUISIANA** | | | | | | |
| 1 **Jindal** | N | N | Y | Y | N | Y |
| 2 Jefferson | N | N | N | Y | N | N |
| 3 Melancon | N | N | N | Y | N | N |
| 4 **McCrery** | N | N | Y | Y | N | Y |
| 5 **Alexander** | N | N | N | Y | N | Y |
| 6 **Baker** | N | Y | Y | Y | N | Y |
| 7 **Boustany** | N | N | N | Y | N | Y |
| **MAINE** | | | | | | |
| 1 Allen | N | N | N | Y | N | N |
| 2 Michaud | N | N | N | Y | N | N |
| **MARYLAND** | | | | | | |
| 1 **Gilchrest** | N | N | N | Y | N | Y |
| 2 Ruppersberger | N | N | N | Y | N | N |
| 3 Cardin | N | N | N | Y | N | N |
| 4 Wynn | N | N | N | Y | N | N |
| 5 Hoyer | N | N | N | Y | N | N |
| 6 **Bartlett** | Y | Y | Y | Y | Y | Y |
| 7 Cummings | N | N | N | Y | N | N |
| 8 Van Hollen | Y | N | N | Y | N | N |
| **MASSACHUSETTS** | | | | | | |
| 1 Olver | N | N | N | Y | N | N |
| 2 Neal | N | N | N | Y | N | N |
| 3 McGovern | N | N | N | Y | N | N |
| 4 Frank | N | N | N | Y | Y | N |
| 5 Meehan | N | N | N | Y | N | N |
| 6 Tierney | Y | N | N | Y | Y | N |
| 7 Markey | Y | N | N | Y | N | N |
| 8 Capuano | Y | N | N | Y | N | N |
| 9 Lynch | N | N | N | Y | Y | N |
| 10 Delahunt | N | N | N | Y | N | N |
| **MICHIGAN** | | | | | | |
| 1 Stupak | N | N | N | Y | Y | N |
| 2 **Hoekstra** | N | N | Y | Y | N | Y |
| 3 **Ehlers** | Y | N | N | Y | N | Y |
| 4 **Camp** | ? | N | Y | Y | N | Y |
| 5 Kildee | N | N | N | Y | Y | N |
| 6 **Upton** | N | N | Y | Y | N | Y |
| 7 **Schwarz** | N | N | N | Y | N | Y |
| 8 **Rogers** | N | Y | Y | Y | N | Y |
| 9 **Knollenberg** | N | N | N | Y | N | Y |
| 10 **Miller** | N | N | Y | Y | N | Y |
| 11 **McCotter** | N | Y | Y | Y | Y | Y |
| 12 Levin | N | N | N | Y | N | N |
| 13 Kilpatrick | N | N | N | Y | N | N |
| 14 Conyers | N | N | N | Y | N | N |
| 15 Dingell | N | N | N | Y | N | N |

| | 235 | 236 | 237 | 238 | 239 | 240 |
|---|---|---|---|---|---|---|
| **MINNESOTA** | | | | | | |
| 1 **Gutknecht** | N | Y | Y | Y | N | Y |
| 2 **Kline** | N | N | Y | Y | N | Y |
| 3 **Ramstad** | Y | Y | Y | Y | N | Y |
| 4 McCollum | N | N | N | Y | N | N |
| 5 Sabo | N | N | N | Y | Y | N |
| 6 **Kennedy** | N | N | Y | Y | N | Y |
| 7 Peterson | N | N | N | Y | N | N |
| 8 Oberstar | N | N | N | Y | Y | N |
| **MISSISSIPPI** | | | | | | |
| 1 **Wicker** | N | N | Y | Y | N | Y |
| 2 Thompson | N | N | N | Y | N | N |
| 3 **Pickering** | N | – | + | Y | N | Y |
| 4 Taylor | N | Y | Y | N | Y | N |
| **MISSOURI** | | | | | | |
| 1 Clay | N | N | N | Y | N | N |
| 2 **Akin** | Y | Y | Y | Y | N | Y |
| 3 Carnahan | N | N | N | Y | N | N |
| 4 Skelton | N | N | N | Y | N | N |
| 5 Cleaver | N | N | N | Y | N | N |
| 6 **Graves** | N | Y | Y | Y | N | Y |
| 7 **Blunt** | N | N | Y | Y | N | Y |
| 8 **Emerson** | N | N | Y | Y | N | Y |
| 9 **Hulshof** | N | N | N | Y | ? | ? |
| **MONTANA** | | | | | | |
| AL **Rehberg** | N | N | N | Y | N | Y |
| **NEBRASKA** | | | | | | |
| 1 **Fortenberry** | N | N | N | Y | N | Y |
| 2 **Terry** | N | Y | N | Y | N | ? |
| 3 **Osborne** | N | N | N | Y | N | Y |
| **NEVADA** | | | | | | |
| 1 Berkley | Y | N | N | Y | N | N |
| 2 **Gibbons** | Y | Y | Y | Y | Y | Y |
| 3 **Porter** | N | N | N | Y | N | Y |
| **NEW HAMPSHIRE** | | | | | | |
| 1 **Bradley** | Y | Y | Y | N | N | Y |
| 2 **Bass** | Y | Y | Y | N | N | Y |
| **NEW JERSEY** | | | | | | |
| 1 Andrews | Y | N | N | Y | N | N |
| 2 **LoBiondo** | Y | N | N | Y | N | Y |
| 3 **Saxton** | N | N | N | Y | N | Y |
| 4 **Smith** | Y | N | N | Y | N | Y |
| 5 **Garrett** | Y | Y | Y | Y | Y | Y |
| 6 Pallone | N | N | N | Y | Y | N |
| 7 **Ferguson** | Y | N | N | Y | N | Y |
| 8 Pascrell | N | N | N | Y | Y | N |
| 9 Rothman | N | N | N | Y | N | N |
| 10 Payne | N | ? | N | Y | Y | N |
| 11 **Frelinghuysen** | Y | N | Y | Y | N | Y |
| 12 Holt | N | N | N | Y | N | N |
| 13 Menendez | ? | ? | ? | ? | ? | ? |
| **NEW MEXICO** | | | | | | |
| 1 **Wilson** | N | N | N | Y | N | Y |
| 2 **Pearce** | N | N | Y | Y | N | Y |
| 3 Udall | N | N | N | Y | N | N |
| **NEW YORK** | | | | | | |
| 1 Bishop | N | N | N | Y | N | N |
| 2 Israel | N | N | N | Y | N | N |
| 3 **King** | N | N | N | Y | N | ? |
| 4 McCarthy | N | N | N | Y | N | N |
| 5 Ackerman | N | N | N | Y | N | N |
| 6 Meeks | N | N | N | Y | N | N |
| 7 Crowley | N | N | N | Y | N | N |
| 8 Nadler | N | N | N | Y | N | N |
| 9 Weiner | N | N | N | Y | N | N |
| 10 Towns | N | N | N | Y | N | N |
| 11 Owens | N | N | N | ? | Y | N |
| 12 Velázquez | N | N | N | Y | N | N |
| 13 **Fossella** | Y | Y | Y | N | N | Y |
| 14 Maloney | N | N | N | Y | N | N |
| 15 Rangel | N | N | N | Y | N | N |
| 16 Serrano | N | N | N | Y | N | N |
| 17 Engel | N | N | N | Y | N | N |
| 18 Lowey | N | N | N | Y | N | N |
| 19 **Kelly** | N | N | N | Y | N | Y |
| 20 **Sweeney** | N | N | Y | Y | N | ? |
| 21 McNulty | N | N | N | Y | N | N |
| 22 Hinchey | N | N | N | Y | Y | N |
| 23 **McHugh** | N | N | Y | Y | N | Y |
| 24 **Boehlert** | N | N | N | Y | N | Y |
| 25 **Walsh** | N | N | N | Y | N | Y |
| 26 **Reynolds** | N | ? | N | Y | N | Y |
| 27 Higgins | N | N | N | Y | N | N |
| 28 Slaughter | ? | N | N | Y | N | N |
| 29 **Kuhl** | N | N | Y | Y | N | Y |

| | 235 | 236 | 237 | 238 | 239 | 240 |
|---|---|---|---|---|---|---|
| **NORTH CAROLINA** | | | | | | |
| 1 Butterfield | N | N | N | Y | N | N |
| 2 Etheridge | N | N | N | Y | N | N |
| 3 **Jones** | N | Y | Y | Y | Y | Y |
| 4 Price | N | N | N | Y | N | N |
| 5 **Foxx** | N | Y | Y | Y | Y | Y |
| 6 **Coble** | N | Y | Y | Y | Y | Y |
| 7 McIntyre | N | N | Y | Y | Y | N |
| 8 **Hayes** | N | N | Y | Y | N | Y |
| 9 **Myrick** | Y | Y | Y | Y | N | Y |
| 10 **McHenry** | Y | + | Y | Y | N | Y |
| 11 **Taylor** | N | N | Y | Y | Y | Y |
| 12 Watt | N | N | N | Y | N | N |
| 13 Miller | N | N | N | Y | N | N |
| **NORTH DAKOTA** | | | | | | |
| AL Pomeroy | N | N | N | Y | N | N |
| **OHIO** | | | | | | |
| 1 **Chabot** | Y | Y | Y | Y | N | Y |
| 2 Vacant | | | | | | |
| 3 **Turner** | N | N | N | Y | N | Y |
| 4 **Oxley** | N | N | N | Y | N | Y |
| 5 **Gillmor** | N | N | Y | Y | N | Y |
| 6 Strickland | N | N | N | Y | Y | ? |
| 7 **Hobson** | N | N | N | Y | ? | ? |
| 8 **Boehner** | N | N | N | Y | N | Y |
| 9 Kaptur | N | N | N | Y | Y | N |
| 10 Kucinich | Y | N | N | N | Y | N |
| 11 Jones | N | N | N | Y | Y | N |
| 12 **Tiberi** | Y | N | Y | Y | ? | ? |
| 13 Brown | Y | N | N | Y | Y | N |
| 14 **LaTourette** | N | N | N | Y | Y | Y |
| 15 **Pryce** | N | N | N | Y | N | Y |
| 16 **Regula** | N | N | N | Y | N | Y |
| 17 Ryan | N | N | N | Y | Y | N |
| 18 **Ney** | N | N | Y | Y | Y | Y |
| **OKLAHOMA** | | | | | | |
| 1 **Sullivan** | ? | Y | Y | Y | Y | Y |
| 2 Boren | N | N | N | Y | N | N |
| 3 **Lucas** | N | N | N | Y | N | Y |
| 4 **Cole** | N | N | Y | Y | N | Y |
| 5 **Istook** | Y | ? | Y | Y | Y | Y |
| **OREGON** | | | | | | |
| 1 Wu | N | N | N | Y | N | N |
| 2 **Walden** | N | N | Y | Y | N | Y |
| 3 Blumenauer | N | N | N | Y | N | N |
| 4 DeFazio | N | N | Y | Y | Y | N |
| 5 Hooley | N | N | N | Y | N | N |
| **PENNSYLVANIA** | | | | | | |
| 1 Brady | N | N | N | Y | N | N |
| 2 Fattah | N | N | N | Y | N | N |
| 3 **English** | Y | N | N | Y | N | Y |
| 4 **Hart** | N | N | N | Y | N | Y |
| 5 **Peterson** | N | N | N | Y | N | Y |
| 6 **Gerlach** | N | N | N | Y | N | Y |
| 7 **Weldon** | N | N | N | Y | N | Y |
| 8 **Fitzpatrick** | Y | N | N | Y | N | Y |
| 9 **Shuster** | N | Y | Y | Y | N | Y |
| 10 **Sherwood** | N | N | N | Y | N | Y |
| 11 Kanjorski | N | N | N | Y | N | N |
| 12 Murtha | N | N | N | Y | N | ? |
| 13 Schwartz | N | N | N | Y | N | N |
| 14 Doyle | N | N | N | Y | Y | N |
| 15 **Dent** | Y | Y | Y | Y | N | Y |
| 16 **Pitts** | N | Y | Y | Y | N | Y |
| 17 Holden | N | N | N | Y | N | N |
| 18 **Murphy** | N | N | Y | Y | N | Y |
| 19 **Platts** | N | N | Y | Y | N | Y |
| **RHODE ISLAND** | | | | | | |
| 1 Kennedy | N | N | N | Y | Y | N |
| 2 Langevin | N | N | N | Y | N | N |
| **SOUTH CAROLINA** | | | | | | |
| 1 **Brown** | N | N | Y | Y | N | Y |
| 2 **Wilson** | Y | Y | Y | Y | N | Y |
| 3 **Barrett** | Y | Y | Y | Y | N | Y |
| 4 **Inglis** | Y | Y | Y | Y | N | Y |
| 5 Spratt | ? | N | N | Y | N | N |
| 6 Clyburn | N | N | N | Y | N | N |
| **SOUTH DAKOTA** | | | | | | |
| AL Herseth | N | N | N | Y | N | N |
| **TENNESSEE** | | | | | | |
| 1 **Jenkins** | N | Y | Y | Y | Y | Y |
| 2 **Duncan** | Y | Y | Y | Y | Y | Y |

| | 235 | 236 | 237 | 238 | 239 | 240 |
|---|---|---|---|---|---|---|
| 3 **Wamp** | N | Y | Y | Y | Y | Y |
| 4 Davis | N | N | N | Y | Y | N |
| 5 Cooper | N | N | N | Y | N | N |
| 6 Gordon | N | ? | ? | ? | N | N |
| 7 **Blackburn** | N | Y | Y | Y | N | Y |
| 8 Tanner | N | Y | N | Y | N | N |
| 9 Ford | N | N | N | Y | N | N |
| **TEXAS** | | | | | | |
| 1 **Gohmert** | N | ? | Y | Y | Y | Y |
| 2 **Poe** | N | N | Y | Y | N | Y |
| 3 **Johnson, S.** | N | ? | Y | Y | N | Y |
| 4 **Hall** | N | N | Y | Y | N | Y |
| 5 **Hensarling** | Y | Y | Y | Y | N | Y |
| 6 **Barton** | N | N | N | Y | N | Y |
| 7 **Culberson** | N | ? | Y | Y | N | Y |
| 8 **Brady** | N | Y | Y | Y | N | Y |
| 9 Green | N | N | N | Y | N | N |
| 10 **McCaul** | N | N | Y | Y | N | Y |
| 11 **Conaway** | N | N | Y | Y | N | Y |
| 12 **Granger** | N | N | Y | Y | N | ? |
| 13 **Thornberry** | N | N | N | Y | N | Y |
| 14 **Paul** | Y | Y | Y | N | Y | Y |
| 15 Hinojosa | N | N | N | Y | N | N |
| 16 Reyes | N | N | N | Y | N | N |
| 17 Edwards | N | N | N | Y | N | N |
| 18 Jackson-Lee | ? | ? | ? | ? | N | N |
| 19 **Neugebauer** | N | N | Y | Y | N | Y |
| 20 Gonzalez | N | N | N | Y | N | N |
| 21 **Smith** | N | N | Y | ? | N | Y |
| 22 **DeLay** | N | N | Y | Y | N | Y |
| 23 **Bonilla** | N | N | N | Y | N | Y |
| 24 **Marchant** | N | N | Y | Y | N | Y |
| 25 Doggett | Y | N | N | Y | N | N |
| 26 **Burgess** | Y | Y | Y | Y | N | Y |
| 27 Ortiz | N | N | N | Y | N | N |
| 28 Cuellar | N | N | N | Y | N | N |
| 29 Green | N | N | N | Y | Y | N |
| 30 Johnson, E. | N | N | N | Y | N | N |
| 31 **Carter** | N | N | Y | Y | N | Y |
| 32 **Sessions** | N | Y | Y | Y | N | Y |
| **UTAH** | | | | | | |
| 1 **Bishop** | N | Y | Y | Y | Y | Y |
| 2 Matheson | Y | Y | Y | Y | N | N |
| 3 **Cannon** | N | ? | N | Y | N | Y |
| **VERMONT** | | | | | | |
| AL *Sanders* | N | N | N | Y | Y | N |
| **VIRGINIA** | | | | | | |
| 1 **Davis, J.** | Y | Y | Y | Y | ? | Y |
| 2 **Drake** | N | N | Y | Y | N | Y |
| 3 Scott | N | N | N | Y | N | N |
| 4 **Forbes** | N | N | Y | Y | N | Y |
| 5 **Goode** | N | N | Y | Y | Y | Y |
| 6 **Goodlatte** | N | N | Y | Y | N | Y |
| 7 **Cantor** | N | N | N | Y | N | Y |
| 8 Moran | N | N | N | Y | N | N |
| 9 Boucher | N | N | N | Y | N | N |
| 10 **Wolf** | N | N | N | Y | N | Y |
| 11 **Davis, T.** | N | Y | N | Y | N | Y |
| **WASHINGTON** | | | | | | |
| 1 Inslee | N | N | N | Y | N | N |
| 2 Larsen | N | N | N | Y | N | N |
| 3 Baird | N | N | N | Y | N | N |
| 4 **Hastings** | N | N | N | Y | N | Y |
| 5 **McMorris** | N | N | N | Y | N | Y |
| 6 Dicks | N | N | N | Y | N | N |
| 7 McDermott | Y | N | N | N | N | N |
| 8 **Reichert** | N | N | Y | Y | N | Y |
| 9 Smith | N | N | N | Y | N | N |
| **WEST VIRGINIA** | | | | | | |
| 1 Mollohan | N | N | N | Y | Y | N |
| 2 **Capito** | N | N | Y | Y | N | Y |
| 3 Rahall | N | N | N | Y | Y | N |
| **WISCONSIN** | | | | | | |
| 1 **Ryan** | N | Y | Y | Y | N | Y |
| 2 Baldwin | N | N | N | Y | Y | N |
| 3 Kind | N | N | N | Y | N | N |
| 4 Moore | Y | N | N | Y | N | N |
| 5 **Sensenbrenner** | Y | Y | Y | N | Y | Y |
| 6 **Petri** | N | Y | Y | Y | N | Y |
| 7 Obey | N | N | N | Y | Y | N |
| 8 **Green** | N | N | Y | Y | N | Y |
| **WYOMING** | | | | | | |
| AL **Cubin** | N | Y | Y | Y | N | Y |

# IN THE HOUSE | By Vote Number

**241.** **S 643. State Mediation Programs/Passage.** Lucas, R-Okla., motion to suspend the rules and pass the bill that would authorize $7.5 million in each of fiscal 2006 through 2010 for grants for state agricultural mediation programs. Motion agreed to 371-2: R 205-2; D 165-0 (ND 120-0, SD 45-0); I 1-0. A two-thirds majority of those present and voting (249 in this case) is required for passage under suspension of the rules. June 13, 2005.

**242.** **HR 2326. Floyd Lupton Post Office/Passage.** Duncan, R-Tenn., motion to suspend the rules and pass the bill that would designate a post office in Belhaven, N.C., after Floyd Lupton, who served as chief of staff to the late Rep. Walter B. Jones Sr., D-N.C. (1966-92), for 26 years. Motion agreed to 370-0: R 204-0; D 165-0 (ND 120-0, SD 45-0); I 1-0. A two-thirds majority of those present and voting (247 in this case) is required for passage under suspension of the rules. June 13, 2005.

**243.** **HR 2862. Fiscal 2006 Commerce-Justice-Science Appropriations/ Previous Question.** Gingrey, R-Ga., motion to order the previous question (thus ending debate and possibility of amendment) on adoption of the rule (H Res 314) to provide for House floor consideration of the bill that would appropriate $57.8 billion in fiscal 2006 for the departments of Commerce, Justice and State, as well as various science and other related agencies. Motion agreed to 222-190: R 220-0; D 2-189 (ND 0-142, SD 2-47); I 0-1. (Subsequently, the rule was adopted by voice vote.) June 14, 2005.

**244.** **HR 2862. Fiscal 2006 Commerce-Justice-Science Appropriations/ State and Local Law Enforcement Funding.** Obey, D-Wis., amendment that would add $100 million for justice assistance grants to state and local law enforcement and $100 million for law enforcement grants under the Community Oriented Policing Services program, offset by a $200 million decrease for NASA. Rejected 196-230: R 21-206; D 174-24 (ND 137-11, SD 37-13); I 1-0. June 14, 2005.

**245.** **HR 2862. Fiscal 2006 Commerce-Justice-Science Appropriations/ Justice Assistance Grants.** Terry, R-Neb., amendment that would increase funding for Justice Assistance Grants by $286 million, offset with a 0.448 percent across-the-board cut in discretionary spending. Rejected 175-252: R 91-137; D 84-114 (ND 64-84, SD 20-30); I 0-1. June 14, 2005.

**246.** **HR 2862. Fiscal 2006 Commerce-Justice-Science Appropriations/ Small Business Loan Program.** Velázquez, D-N.Y., amendment that would provide $79 million for the Small Business Administration's 7(a) small business loan program offset by various cuts in the bill. Adopted 234-189: R 36-189; D 197-0 (ND 147-0, SD 50-0); I 1-0. June 14, 2005.

**247.** **HR 2862. Fiscal 2006 Commerce-Justice-Science Appropriations/ Law Enforcement Funding.** Reichert, R-Wash., amendment that would increase funding by $78.3 million for Community Oriented Policing Services programs. It would be offset by reducing funds for salaries and expenses at the FBI and the Drug Enforcement Administration, and reducing funds for international broadcasting operations. Rejected 130-297: R 55-173; D 75-123 (ND 61-87, SD 14-36); I 0-1. June 14, 2005.

| | 241 | 242 | 243 | 244 | 245 | 246 | 247 |
|---|---|---|---|---|---|---|---|
| **ALABAMA** | | | | | | | |
| 1 Bonner | Y | Y | Y | N | N | N | N |
| 2 Everett | Y | Y | ? | N | N | N | N |
| 3 Rogers | Y | Y | Y | N | Y | N | N |
| 4 Aderholt | Y | Y | Y | N | N | N | N |
| 5 Cramer | Y | Y | N | N | N | Y | N |
| 6 Bachus | Y | Y | Y | N | Y | N | Y |
| 7 Davis | Y | Y | N | N | N | Y | N |
| **ALASKA** | | | | | | | |
| AL Young | Y | Y | Y | N | N | N | Y |
| **ARIZONA** | | | | | | | |
| 1 Renzi | Y | Y | Y | Y | Y | Y | Y |
| 2 Franks | Y | Y | Y | N | N | N | N |
| 3 Shadegg | Y | Y | Y | N | N | N | N |
| 4 Pastor | Y | Y | N | Y | Y | Y | Y |
| 5 Hayworth | Y | Y | Y | N | N | N | N |
| 6 Flake | N | Y | Y | N | N | N | N |
| 7 Grijalva | Y | Y | N | Y | Y | Y | Y |
| 8 Kolbe | Y | Y | Y | N | N | N | N |
| **ARKANSAS** | | | | | | | |
| 1 Berry | Y | Y | N | Y | N | Y | N |
| 2 Snyder | Y | Y | N | Y | N | Y | N |
| 3 Boozman | Y | + | Y | N | Y | N | N |
| 4 Ross | Y | Y | N | Y | N | Y | N |
| **CALIFORNIA** | | | | | | | |
| 1 Thompson | Y | Y | N | Y | Y | Y | N |
| 2 Herger | Y | Y | Y | N | Y | N | N |
| 3 Lungren | Y | Y | Y | Y | N | N | N |
| 4 Doolittle | Y | Y | Y | N | N | N | N |
| 5 Matsui, D. | Y | Y | N | Y | Y | Y | Y |
| 6 Woolsey | Y | Y | N | Y | N | Y | Y |
| 7 Miller, George | Y | Y | N | Y | N | Y | N |
| 8 Pelosi | Y | Y | N | Y | N | Y | N |
| 9 Lee | + | + | N | Y | Y | Y | Y |
| 10 Tauscher | Y | Y | N | Y | Y | Y | N |
| 11 Pombo | Y | Y | Y | N | N | N | N |
| 12 Lantos | Y | Y | N | Y | N | Y | N |
| 13 Stark | ? | ? | ? | Y | N | Y | Y |
| 14 Eshoo | Y | Y | N | Y | N | Y | N |
| 15 Honda | Y | Y | N | Y | N | Y | N |
| 16 Lofgren | Y | Y | N | Y | N | Y | N |
| 17 Farr | Y | Y | N | Y | N | Y | N |
| 18 Cardoza | ? | ? | N | Y | Y | Y | N |
| 19 Radanovich | ? | ? | N | Y | N | N | N |
| 20 Costa | Y | Y | N | N | Y | Y | N |
| 21 Nunes | Y | Y | Y | N | N | N | N |
| 22 Thomas | Y | Y | ? | N | N | N | N |
| 23 Capps | Y | Y | N | Y | N | Y | N |
| 24 Gallegly | Y | Y | N | Y | N | N | N |
| 25 McKeon | Y | Y | Y | N | N | N | N |
| 26 Dreier | Y | Y | Y | N | N | N | N |
| 27 Sherman | Y | Y | N | Y | N | Y | N |
| 28 Berman | Y | Y | N | Y | N | Y | N |
| 29 Schiff | Y | Y | N | Y | N | Y | N |
| 30 Waxman | Y | Y | N | Y | N | Y | N |
| 31 Becerra | Y | Y | N | Y | N | Y | N |
| 32 Solis | Y | Y | N | Y | N | Y | Y |
| 33 Watson | Y | Y | N | Y | N | Y | Y |
| 34 Roybal-Allard | Y | Y | N | Y | N | Y | N |
| 35 Waters | ? | ? | N | N | Y | Y | Y |
| 36 Harman | Y | Y | N | Y | N | Y | N |
| 37 Millender-McD. | Y | Y | N | Y | N | Y | N |
| 38 Napolitano | Y | Y | N | Y | Y | Y | Y |
| 39 Sánchez, Linda | + | + | N | Y | N | Y | Y |
| 40 Royce | Y | Y | Y | N | N | N | N |
| 41 Lewis | Y | Y | Y | N | N | N | N |
| 42 Miller, Gary | Y | Y | Y | N | N | N | N |
| 43 Baca | Y | Y | N | Y | Y | Y | N |
| 44 Calvert | Y | Y | Y | N | N | N | N |
| 45 Bono | Y | Y | Y | N | Y | N | N |
| 46 Rohrabacher | Y | Y | Y | N | N | N | N |
| 47 Sanchez, Loretta | ? | ? | N | Y | N | Y | N |
| 48 Cox | Y | Y | Y | ? | ? | ? | ? |
| 49 Issa | Y | Y | Y | N | N | N | N |
| 50 Cunningham | Y | Y | Y | N | N | N | N |
| 51 Filner | Y | Y | N | Y | N | Y | N |
| 52 Hunter | Y | Y | Y | N | N | N | N |
| 53 Davis | Y | Y | N | Y | N | Y | N |
| **COLORADO** | | | | | | | |
| 1 DeGette | Y | Y | N | Y | Y | Y | Y |
| 2 Udall | + | + | N | N | Y | Y | N |
| 3 Salazar | Y | Y | N | N | Y | Y | N |
| 4 Musgrave | Y | Y | Y | N | Y | N | Y |
| 5 Hefley | Y | Y | Y | N | N | N | N |
| 6 Tancredo | Y | Y | Y | N | N | ? | N |
| 7 Beauprez | Y | Y | Y | N | N | Y | N |
| **CONNECTICUT** | | | | | | | |
| 1 Larson | Y | Y | – | Y | N | Y | N |
| 2 Simmons | ? | ? | Y | Y | N | Y | Y |
| 3 DeLauro | Y | Y | N | Y | N | Y | Y |
| 4 Shays | ? | ? | Y | Y | N | N | N |
| 5 Johnson | Y | Y | Y | N | N | N | N |
| **DELAWARE** | | | | | | | |
| AL Castle | Y | Y | Y | N | N | N | N |
| **FLORIDA** | | | | | | | |
| 1 Miller | Y | Y | Y | N | N | N | N |
| 2 Boyd | Y | Y | N | Y | N | Y | N |
| 3 Brown | Y | Y | N | Y | N | Y | N |
| 4 Crenshaw | Y | Y | Y | N | N | N | N |
| 5 Brown-Waite | Y | Y | Y | N | Y | N | Y |
| 6 Stearns | Y | Y | Y | N | N | N | N |
| 7 Mica | Y | Y | Y | N | N | N | N |
| 8 Keller | ? | ? | Y | N | N | N | Y |
| 9 Bilirakis | Y | Y | Y | N | N | N | N |
| 10 Young | ? | ? | ? | N | N | N | N |
| 11 Davis | ? | ? | N | Y | N | Y | N |
| 12 Putnam | Y | Y | Y | N | N | N | N |
| 13 Harris | Y | Y | Y | N | N | N | N |
| 14 Mack | Y | Y | ? | N | N | N | N |
| 15 Weldon | Y | Y | Y | N | N | N | N |
| 16 Foley | Y | Y | N | N | N | N | N |
| 17 Meek | ? | ? | N | Y | N | Y | Y |
| 18 Ros-Lehtinen | ? | ? | N | Y | N | N | N |
| 19 Wexler | Y | Y | N | Y | N | Y | N |
| 20 Wasserman-Schultz | Y | Y | N | Y | N | Y | N |
| 21 Diaz-Balart, L. | Y | Y | Y | N | N | N | N |
| 22 Shaw | Y | Y | Y | N | N | N | N |
| 23 Hastings | Y | Y | N | Y | N | Y | N |
| 24 Feeney | Y | Y | Y | N | N | N | N |
| 25 Diaz-Balart, M. | Y | Y | Y | N | N | N | N |
| **GEORGIA** | | | | | | | |
| 1 Kingston | Y | Y | Y | N | N | N | N |
| 2 Bishop | Y | Y | Y | Y | N | Y | N |
| 3 Marshall | Y | Y | Y | Y | Y | Y | N |
| 4 McKinney | Y | Y | N | N | Y | N | Y |
| 5 Lewis | ? | ? | N | Y | Y | Y | Y |
| 6 Price | Y | Y | Y | N | N | N | N |
| 7 Linder | Y | Y | Y | N | N | N | N |
| 8 Westmoreland | Y | Y | Y | N | N | N | N |
| 9 Norwood | Y | Y | Y | N | N | N | N |
| 10 Deal | Y | Y | Y | N | N | N | N |
| 11 Gingrey | Y | ? | Y | N | N | N | N |
| 12 Barrow | Y | Y | Y | Y | Y | Y | N |
| 13 Scott | Y | Y | N | Y | Y | Y | N |
| **HAWAII** | | | | | | | |
| 1 Abercrombie | Y | Y | N | Y | N | Y | N |
| 2 Case | ? | ? | N | Y | N | Y | N |
| **IDAHO** | | | | | | | |
| 1 Otter | Y | Y | Y | N | N | N | Y |
| 2 Simpson | Y | Y | Y | N | N | N | N |
| **ILLINOIS** | | | | | | | |
| 1 Rush | ? | ? | N | Y | Y | Y | N |
| 2 Jackson | Y | Y | N | Y | Y | Y | N |
| 3 Lipinski | Y | Y | N | Y | N | Y | Y |
| 4 Gutierrez | + | + | N | Y | N | Y | N |
| 5 Emanuel | Y | Y | N | Y | N | Y | N |
| 6 Hyde | Y | Y | Y | N | N | N | N |
| 7 Davis | Y | Y | N | Y | Y | Y | N |
| 8 Bean | Y | Y | N | Y | N | Y | N |
| 9 Schakowsky | Y | Y | N | Y | N | Y | N |
| 10 Kirk | Y | Y | Y | N | N | N | N |
| 11 Weller | Y | Y | Y | N | N | N | N |
| 12 Costello | Y | Y | N | Y | Y | Y | Y |

| KEY | Republicans | Democrats | *Independents* |
|---|---|---|---|

| | | | |
|---|---|---|---|
| Y | Voted for (yea) | X Paired against | C Voted "present" to avoid possible conflict of interest |
| # | Paired for | – Announced against | ? Did not vote or otherwise make a position known |
| + | Announced for | P Voted "present" | |
| N | Voted against (nay) | | |

ND Northern Democrats, SD Southern Democrats
Southern states: Ala., Ark., Fla., Ga., Ky., La., Miss., N.C., Okla., S.C., Tenn., Texas, Va.

| | 241 | 242 | 243 | 244 | 245 | 246 | 247 |
|---|---|---|---|---|---|---|---|
| 13 **Biggert** | Y | Y | Y | N | N | N | N |
| 14 **Hastert** | | | | | | | |
| 15 **Johnson** | Y | Y | Y | N | Y | N | Y |
| 16 **Manzullo** | Y | Y | Y | N | N | N | N |
| 17 Evans | Y | Y | N | Y | N | Y | Y |
| 18 **LaHood** | ? | ? | Y | N | N | N | N |
| 19 **Shimkus** | ? | ? | Y | N | Y | N | Y |
| **INDIANA** | | | | | | | |
| 1 Visclosky | Y | Y | N | Y | N | Y | N |
| 2 **Chocola** | Y | Y | Y | N | Y | N | Y |
| 3 **Souder** | Y | Y | Y | N | Y | N | Y |
| 4 **Buyer** | ? | ? | ? | N | N | N | N |
| 5 **Burton** | Y | Y | Y | N | Y | N | N |
| 6 **Pence** | Y | ? | Y | N | Y | N | N |
| 7 Carson | Y | Y | N | Y | Y | Y | N |
| 8 **Hostettler** | Y | Y | Y | N | N | N | N |
| 9 **Sodrel** | Y | Y | Y | N | N | N | N |
| **IOWA** | | | | | | | |
| 1 **Nussle** | Y | Y | Y | N | Y | N | N |
| 2 **Leach** | Y | Y | Y | N | Y | Y | N |
| 3 Boswell | ? | ? | N | Y | Y | Y | N |
| 4 **Latham** | Y | Y | Y | Y | Y | N | N |
| 5 **King** | Y | Y | Y | N | Y | N | Y |
| **KANSAS** | | | | | | | |
| 1 **Moran** | Y | Y | Y | N | Y | Y | Y |
| 2 **Ryun** | Y | Y | Y | N | N | N | N |
| 3 Moore | Y | Y | N | Y | Y | Y | N |
| 4 **Tiahrt** | Y | Y | Y | N | N | N | N |
| **KENTUCKY** | | | | | | | |
| 1 **Whitfield** | Y | Y | Y | N | N | Y | N |
| 2 **Lewis** | Y | Y | Y | N | Y | N | N |
| 3 **Northup** | Y | Y | Y | N | N | N | N |
| 4 **Davis** | Y | Y | Y | N | N | N | Y |
| 5 **Rogers** | Y | Y | Y | N | N | N | N |
| 6 Chandler | Y | Y | N | Y | Y | Y | Y |
| **LOUISIANA** | | | | | | | |
| 1 **Jindal** | Y | Y | Y | N | Y | N | N |
| 2 Jefferson | Y | Y | N | Y | N | Y | Y |
| 3 Melancon | Y | Y | N | Y | Y | Y | Y |
| 4 **McCrery** | Y | Y | ? | Y | Y | ? | Y |
| 5 **Alexander** | Y | Y | Y | N | N | N | N |
| 6 **Baker** | ? | ? | Y | N | Y | N | N |
| 7 **Boustany** | Y | Y | Y | N | Y | N | N |
| **MAINE** | | | | | | | |
| 1 Allen | Y | Y | N | Y | N | Y | Y |
| 2 Michaud | Y | Y | N | Y | N | Y | Y |
| **MARYLAND** | | | | | | | |
| 1 **Gilchrest** | Y | Y | Y | N | N | N | N |
| 2 Ruppersberger | Y | Y | N | Y | Y | Y | N |
| 3 Cardin | Y | Y | N | Y | Y | Y | N |
| 4 Wynn | Y | Y | N | Y | Y | Y | N |
| 5 Hoyer | ? | ? | N | Y | N | Y | N |
| 6 **Bartlett** | Y | Y | Y | N | N | N | N |
| 7 Cummings | Y | Y | ? | Y | Y | Y | N |
| 8 Van Hollen | Y | Y | N | Y | Y | Y | N |
| **MASSACHUSETTS** | | | | | | | |
| 1 Olver | Y | Y | N | Y | N | Y | Y |
| 2 Neal | ? | ? | N | Y | N | Y | Y |
| 3 McGovern | Y | Y | N | Y | N | Y | N |
| 4 Frank | Y | Y | N | Y | N | Y | Y |
| 5 Meehan | Y | Y | N | Y | Y | Y | Y |
| 6 Tierney | Y | Y | N | Y | N | Y | Y |
| 7 Markey | Y | Y | N | Y | N | Y | N |
| 8 Capuano | Y | Y | N | Y | Y | Y | N |
| 9 Lynch | Y | Y | N | Y | Y | Y | N |
| 10 Delahunt | ? | ? | N | Y | Y | Y | N |
| **MICHIGAN** | | | | | | | |
| 1 Stupak | Y | Y | N | Y | Y | Y | N |
| 2 **Hoekstra** | Y | Y | Y | N | N | N | N |
| 3 **Ehlers** | + | + | Y | N | N | N | Y |
| 4 **Camp** | Y | Y | Y | Y | N | N | N |
| 5 Kildee | Y | Y | N | Y | N | Y | N |
| 6 **Upton** | Y | Y | Y | Y | Y | N | Y |
| 7 **Schwarz** | Y | Y | Y | N | N | N | N |
| 8 **Rogers** | Y | Y | Y | N | Y | N | N |
| 9 **Knollenberg** | + | + | + | N | N | N | N |
| 10 **Miller** | Y | Y | Y | N | N | N | N |
| 11 **McCotter** | Y | Y | Y | N | Y | Y | N |
| 12 Levin | Y | Y | N | Y | N | Y | N |
| 13 Kilpatrick | + | + | N | Y | N | Y | N |
| 14 Conyers | Y | Y | N | Y | N | ? | Y |
| 15 Dingell | ? | ? | N | Y | N | Y | N |

| | 241 | 242 | 243 | 244 | 245 | 246 | 247 |
|---|---|---|---|---|---|---|---|
| **MINNESOTA** | | | | | | | |
| 1 **Gutknecht** | Y | Y | Y | N | Y | N | N |
| 2 **Kline** | Y | Y | Y | N | Y | Y | N |
| 3 **Ramstad** | Y | Y | Y | Y | Y | Y | Y |
| 4 McCollum | Y | Y | N | Y | N | Y | N |
| 5 Sabo | Y | Y | N | Y | N | Y | N |
| 6 **Kennedy** | Y | Y | Y | N | Y | Y | Y |
| 7 Peterson | Y | Y | N | Y | N | Y | Y |
| 8 Oberstar | ? | ? | ? | ? | ? | ? | ? |
| **MISSISSIPPI** | | | | | | | |
| 1 **Wicker** | Y | Y | Y | N | N | N | N |
| 2 Thompson | Y | Y | N | Y | N | Y | N |
| 3 **Pickering** | Y | Y | Y | N | N | N | N |
| 4 Taylor | Y | Y | N | N | Y | Y | N |
| **MISSOURI** | | | | | | | |
| 1 Clay | Y | Y | N | Y | N | Y | Y |
| 2 **Akin** | Y | Y | Y | N | N | N | N |
| 3 Carnahan | Y | Y | N | Y | Y | Y | Y |
| 4 Skelton | Y | Y | N | Y | Y | Y | N |
| 5 Cleaver | Y | Y | N | Y | N | Y | N |
| 6 **Graves** | Y | Y | Y | N | Y | Y | N |
| 7 **Blunt** | Y | Y | Y | N | N | N | N |
| 8 **Emerson** | Y | Y | Y | N | Y | N | N |
| 9 **Hulshof** | ? | ? | Y | N | Y | Y | N |
| **MONTANA** | | | | | | | |
| AL **Rehberg** | Y | Y | Y | N | N | N | N |
| **NEBRASKA** | | | | | | | |
| 1 **Fortenberry** | Y | Y | Y | N | Y | N | Y |
| 2 **Terry** | Y | Y | Y | N | Y | N | Y |
| 3 **Osborne** | Y | Y | Y | N | Y | N | Y |
| **NEVADA** | | | | | | | |
| 1 Berkley | ? | ? | N | Y | N | Y | N |
| 2 **Gibbons** | Y | Y | Y | Y | Y | N | N |
| 3 **Porter** | Y | Y | Y | N | Y | Y | Y |
| **NEW HAMPSHIRE** | | | | | | | |
| 1 **Bradley** | Y | Y | Y | N | N | Y | N |
| 2 **Bass** | Y | Y | Y | N | N | N | N |
| **NEW JERSEY** | | | | | | | |
| 1 Andrews | Y | Y | N | Y | N | Y | N |
| 2 **LoBiondo** | Y | Y | Y | N | Y | Y | Y |
| 3 **Saxton** | Y | Y | Y | N | N | N | N |
| 4 **Smith** | Y | Y | Y | Y | N | N | N |
| 5 **Garrett** | Y | Y | Y | N | N | N | N |
| 6 Pallone | Y | Y | N | Y | Y | Y | Y |
| 7 **Ferguson** | Y | Y | Y | N | N | N | N |
| 8 Pascrell | ? | ? | ? | Y | Y | Y | N |
| 9 Rothman | ? | ? | ? | ? | ? | ? | ? |
| 10 Payne | ? | ? | N | Y | N | Y | Y |
| 11 **Frelinghuysen** | Y | Y | Y | N | N | N | N |
| 12 Holt | Y | Y | N | Y | N | Y | N |
| 13 Menendez | Y | Y | N | Y | N | Y | N |
| **NEW MEXICO** | | | | | | | |
| 1 **Wilson** | Y | Y | Y | Y | N | Y | N |
| 2 **Pearce** | Y | Y | Y | N | N | N | N |
| 3 Udall | Y | Y | N | Y | Y | Y | N |
| **NEW YORK** | | | | | | | |
| 1 Bishop | Y | Y | N | Y | Y | Y | Y |
| 2 Israel | Y | Y | N | Y | Y | Y | N |
| 3 **King** | Y | Y | Y | Y | Y | Y | N |
| 4 McCarthy | Y | Y | N | Y | Y | Y | N |
| 5 Ackerman | Y | Y | N | Y | Y | Y | Y |
| 6 Meeks | Y | Y | N | Y | Y | Y | Y |
| 7 Crowley | ? | ? | N | Y | Y | Y | Y |
| 8 Nadler | ? | ? | N | Y | Y | Y | Y |
| 9 Weiner | Y | Y | N | Y | Y | Y | Y |
| 10 Towns | ? | ? | N | Y | Y | Y | Y |
| 11 Owens | ? | ? | ? | Y | N | Y | Y |
| 12 Velázquez | Y | Y | N | Y | N | Y | Y |
| 13 **Fossella** | + | + | Y | Y | Y | N | N |
| 14 Maloney | Y | Y | N | Y | Y | Y | N |
| 15 Rangel | Y | Y | N | Y | N | Y | N |
| 16 Serrano | Y | Y | N | Y | N | Y | N |
| 17 Engel | Y | Y | N | Y | Y | Y | Y |
| 18 Lowey | Y | Y | N | Y | N | Y | N |
| 19 **Kelly** | Y | Y | Y | N | Y | Y | Y |
| 20 **Sweeney** | ? | ? | ? | N | N | N | N |
| 21 McNulty | Y | Y | N | Y | Y | Y | Y |
| 22 Hinchey | Y | Y | N | Y | Y | Y | N |
| 23 **McHugh** | Y | Y | Y | N | N | N | N |
| 24 **Boehlert** | Y | Y | Y | N | N | N | N |
| 25 **Walsh** | Y | Y | Y | N | N | N | N |
| 26 **Reynolds** | Y | Y | Y | N | N | N | Y |
| 27 Higgins | Y | Y | N | Y | N | Y | N |
| 28 Slaughter | Y | Y | N | Y | N | Y | Y |
| 29 **Kuhl** | Y | Y | Y | N | N | Y | N |

| | 241 | 242 | 243 | 244 | 245 | 246 | 247 |
|---|---|---|---|---|---|---|---|
| **NORTH CAROLINA** | | | | | | | |
| 1 Butterfield | Y | Y | N | Y | N | Y | N |
| 2 Etheridge | Y | Y | N | Y | Y | Y | Y |
| 3 **Jones** | Y | Y | Y | N | Y | N | Y |
| 4 Price | Y | Y | N | Y | N | Y | N |
| 5 **Foxx** | Y | Y | Y | N | Y | N | N |
| 6 **Coble** | Y | Y | Y | N | Y | N | N |
| 7 McIntyre | Y | Y | N | Y | Y | Y | N |
| 8 **Hayes** | Y | Y | Y | N | N | Y | Y |
| 9 **Myrick** | Y | Y | Y | N | N | N | Y |
| 10 **McHenry** | Y | Y | Y | N | Y | N | Y |
| 11 **Taylor** | Y | Y | Y | N | N | N | N |
| 12 Watt | Y | Y | N | Y | Y | Y | N |
| 13 Miller | Y | Y | N | N | N | Y | N |
| **NORTH DAKOTA** | | | | | | | |
| AL Pomeroy | Y | Y | N | Y | Y | Y | Y |
| **OHIO** | | | | | | | |
| 1 **Chabot** | Y | Y | Y | Y | Y | N | N |
| 2 Vacant | | | | | | | |
| 3 **Turner** | Y | Y | Y | N | N | Y | N |
| 4 **Oxley** | ? | ? | Y | N | N | N | N |
| 5 **Gillmor** | Y | Y | Y | N | N | N | N |
| 6 Strickland | ? | ? | ? | ? | ? | ? | ? |
| 7 **Hobson** | Y | Y | Y | N | N | N | N |
| 8 **Boehner** | Y | Y | Y | N | N | N | N |
| 9 Kaptur | Y | Y | N | Y | Y | Y | Y |
| 10 Kucinich | Y | Y | N | N | N | Y | N |
| 11 Jones | Y | Y | ? | N | Y | Y | N |
| 12 **Tiberi** | Y | Y | Y | N | N | N | N |
| 13 Brown | Y | Y | N | Y | Y | Y | Y |
| 14 **LaTourette** | Y | Y | Y | N | N | Y | N |
| 15 **Pryce** | Y | Y | Y | N | N | N | N |
| 16 **Regula** | Y | Y | Y | N | N | N | N |
| 17 Ryan | Y | Y | N | Y | Y | Y | N |
| 18 **Ney** | Y | Y | Y | N | Y | Y | N |
| **OKLAHOMA** | | | | | | | |
| 1 **Sullivan** | ? | ? | Y | N | Y | N | N |
| 2 Boren | Y | Y | N | N | Y | Y | N |
| 3 **Lucas** | Y | Y | Y | N | N | N | N |
| 4 **Cole** | Y | Y | Y | N | N | Y | N |
| 5 **Istook** | ? | ? | Y | N | N | N | N |
| **OREGON** | | | | | | | |
| 1 Wu | Y | Y | N | Y | Y | Y | N |
| 2 **Walden** | Y | Y | Y | N | Y | N | Y |
| 3 Blumenauer | Y | Y | N | Y | N | Y | N |
| 4 DeFazio | Y | Y | N | Y | Y | Y | N |
| 5 Hooley | Y | Y | N | Y | Y | Y | Y |
| **PENNSYLVANIA** | | | | | | | |
| 1 Brady | Y | Y | N | N | N | Y | Y |
| 2 Fattah | ? | ? | N | Y | N | Y | Y |
| 3 **English** | Y | Y | Y | N | N | N | Y |
| 4 **Hart** | Y | Y | Y | N | N | N | N |
| 5 **Peterson** | ? | ? | ? | ? | Y | N | N |
| 6 **Gerlach** | Y | Y | Y | N | Y | N | Y |
| 7 **Weldon** | Y | Y | Y | N | N | Y | N |
| 8 **Fitzpatrick** | Y | Y | Y | Y | Y | N | Y |
| 9 **Shuster** | Y | Y | Y | N | Y | N | N |
| 10 **Sherwood** | Y | Y | Y | N | N | N | N |
| 11 Kanjorski | Y | Y | N | N | N | Y | Y |
| 12 Murtha | ? | ? | N | N | N | Y | Y |
| 13 Schwartz | Y | Y | N | Y | N | Y | Y |
| 14 Doyle | Y | Y | N | N | Y | Y | Y |
| 15 **Dent** | Y | Y | Y | Y | N | N | N |
| 16 **Pitts** | Y | Y | Y | N | N | N | N |
| 17 Holden | Y | Y | N | Y | Y | Y | Y |
| 18 **Murphy** | Y | Y | Y | N | N | Y | N |
| 19 **Platts** | Y | Y | Y | Y | Y | Y | Y |
| **RHODE ISLAND** | | | | | | | |
| 1 Kennedy | + | + | N | Y | N | Y | N |
| 2 Langevin | Y | Y | N | Y | N | Y | N |
| **SOUTH CAROLINA** | | | | | | | |
| 1 **Brown** | Y | Y | Y | N | N | N | Y |
| 2 **Wilson** | Y | Y | Y | N | N | N | N |
| 3 **Barrett** | Y | Y | Y | N | Y | N | N |
| 4 **Inglis** | Y | Y | Y | N | N | N | N |
| 5 Spratt | Y | Y | N | Y | N | Y | N |
| 6 Clyburn | ? | ? | N | Y | N | Y | N |
| **SOUTH DAKOTA** | | | | | | | |
| AL Herseth | Y | Y | N | Y | Y | Y | N |
| **TENNESSEE** | | | | | | | |
| 1 **Jenkins** | ? | ? | Y | N | Y | N | N |
| 2 **Duncan** | Y | Y | Y | N | Y | N | Y |

| | 241 | 242 | 243 | 244 | 245 | 246 | 247 |
|---|---|---|---|---|---|---|---|
| 3 **Wamp** | Y | Y | Y | N | Y | N | Y |
| 4 Davis | Y | Y | N | N | N | Y | N |
| 5 Cooper | ? | ? | N | Y | Y | Y | N |
| 6 Gordon | Y | Y | N | N | N | Y | N |
| 7 **Blackburn** | Y | Y | Y | Y | Y | N | N |
| 8 Tanner | Y | Y | N | Y | Y | Y | Y |
| 9 Ford | Y | Y | N | Y | N | Y | Y |
| **TEXAS** | | | | | | | |
| 1 **Gohmert** | Y | Y | Y | Y | Y | Y | N |
| 2 **Poe** | Y | Y | Y | N | Y | N | Y |
| 3 **Johnson, S.** | Y | Y | Y | N | Y | N | N |
| 4 **Hall** | Y | Y | Y | N | N | N | N |
| 5 **Hensarling** | Y | Y | Y | N | N | N | N |
| 6 **Barton** | Y | Y | Y | N | Y | N | N |
| 7 **Culberson** | Y | Y | Y | N | N | N | N |
| 8 **Brady** | Y | Y | Y | N | N | N | N |
| 9 Green, A. | Y | Y | N | N | N | Y | Y |
| 10 **McCaul** | Y | Y | Y | N | N | N | N |
| 11 **Conaway** | Y | Y | Y | N | N | Y | N |
| 12 **Granger** | Y | Y | Y | N | N | N | N |
| 13 **Thornberry** | Y | Y | Y | N | N | N | N |
| 14 **Paul** | N | Y | Y | N | N | Y | Y |
| 15 Hinojosa | ? | ? | ? | ? | ? | ? | ? |
| 16 Reyes | Y | Y | N | N | Y | Y | N |
| 17 Edwards | Y | Y | N | Y | N | Y | N |
| 18 Jackson-Lee | Y | Y | N | N | N | Y | N |
| 19 **Neugebauer** | Y | Y | Y | N | N | N | N |
| 20 Gonzalez | Y | Y | N | N | Y | Y | N |
| 21 **Smith** | Y | Y | Y | N | N | N | N |
| 22 **DeLay** | Y | Y | Y | N | N | N | N |
| 23 **Bonilla** | Y | Y | Y | N | N | N | N |
| 24 **Marchant** | Y | ? | Y | N | Y | Y | N |
| 25 Doggett | Y | Y | N | Y | Y | Y | N |
| 26 **Burgess** | Y | Y | Y | N | N | N | Y |
| 27 Ortiz | Y | Y | N | N | Y | Y | N |
| 28 Cuellar | Y | Y | N | Y | Y | Y | N |
| 29 Green, G. | Y | Y | N | N | Y | Y | Y |
| 30 Johnson, E. | Y | Y | N | Y | N | Y | N |
| 31 **Carter** | Y | Y | Y | N | N | N | N |
| 32 **Sessions** | ? | ? | ? | ? | ? | ? | ? |
| **UTAH** | | | | | | | |
| 1 **Bishop** | Y | Y | Y | N | Y | N | Y |
| 2 Matheson | Y | Y | N | Y | Y | Y | Y |
| 3 **Cannon** | Y | Y | Y | N | Y | N | N |
| **VERMONT** | | | | | | | |
| AL *Sanders* | Y | Y | N | Y | N | Y | N |
| **VIRGINIA** | | | | | | | |
| 1 **Davis, J.** | Y | Y | Y | N | N | N | N |
| 2 **Drake** | Y | Y | Y | N | N | N | N |
| 3 Scott | Y | Y | N | Y | N | Y | N |
| 4 **Forbes** | Y | Y | Y | N | N | N | N |
| 5 **Goode** | Y | Y | Y | N | N | N | N |
| 6 **Goodlatte** | Y | Y | Y | N | N | N | N |
| 7 **Cantor** | Y | Y | Y | N | N | N | N |
| 8 Moran | Y | Y | N | Y | N | Y | Y |
| 9 Boucher | Y | Y | ? | Y | Y | Y | Y |
| 10 **Wolf** | Y | Y | Y | N | N | N | N |
| 11 **Davis, T.** | Y | Y | Y | N | N | N | N |
| **WASHINGTON** | | | | | | | |
| 1 Inslee | Y | Y | N | Y | Y | Y | Y |
| 2 Larsen | ? | ? | N | Y | Y | Y | Y |
| 3 Baird | Y | Y | N | Y | Y | Y | N |
| 4 **Hastings** | Y | Y | Y | N | N | N | Y |
| 5 **McMorris** | Y | Y | Y | N | Y | N | Y |
| 6 Dicks | Y | Y | N | Y | N | Y | N |
| 7 McDermott | Y | Y | N | Y | N | Y | N |
| 8 **Reichert** | Y | Y | Y | N | Y | N | Y |
| 9 Smith | Y | Y | N | Y | Y | Y | Y |
| **WEST VIRGINIA** | | | | | | | |
| 1 Mollohan | Y | Y | N | N | N | Y | N |
| 2 **Capito** | ? | ? | Y | N | N | Y | N |
| 3 Rahall | Y | Y | N | Y | N | Y | Y |
| **WISCONSIN** | | | | | | | |
| 1 **Ryan** | Y | Y | Y | N | Y | ? | Y |
| 2 Baldwin | Y | Y | N | Y | Y | Y | Y |
| 3 Kind | Y | Y | N | Y | N | Y | N |
| 4 Moore | ? | ? | N | Y | Y | Y | Y |
| 5 **Sensenbrenner** | Y | Y | Y | N | Y | N | N |
| 6 **Petri** | Y | Y | Y | N | Y | N | Y |
| 7 Obey | Y | Y | N | Y | N | Y | N |
| 8 **Green** | + | + | Y | Y | Y | Y | Y |
| **WYOMING** | | | | | | | |
| AL **Cubin** | Y | Y | Y | N | Y | Y | Y |

# IN THE HOUSE | By Vote Number

**248.** HR 2862. Fiscal 2006 Commerce-Justice-Science Appropriations/ **Law and Drug Enforcement Funding.** Baird, D-Wash., amendment that would increase funding for Community Oriented Policing Services programs by $10 million and the Drug Enforcement Administration by $10 million. It would be offset by a $10 million cut in funding for the 2010 decennial census and a $10 million decrease for salaries and expenses at the Bureau of the Census. Adopted 260-168: R 96-133; D 163-35 (ND 122-26, SD 41-9); I 1-0. June 14, 2005.

**249.** HR 2862. Fiscal 2006 Commerce-Justice-Science Appropriations/ **Justice Assistance Grants.** Stearns, R-Fla., amendment that would increase funding for Justice Assistance Grants by $10 million, offset by a reduction for the Legal Services Corporation. Rejected 112-316: R 109-120; D 3-195 (ND 0-148, SD 3-47); I 0-1. June 14, 2005.

**250.** HR 2862. Fiscal 2006 Commerce-Justice-Science Appropriations/ **State Criminal Alien Assistance Program.** Dreier, R-Calif., amendment that would increase funding for the State Criminal Alien Assistance Program by $50 million, offset by a reduction for operations, research and facilities at the National Oceanic and Atmospheric Administration. Adopted 231-195: R 178-50; D 53-144 (ND 40-107, SD 13-37); I 0-1. June 14, 2005.

**251.** HR 2862. Fiscal 2006 Commerce-Justice-Science Appropriations/ **Community Oriented Policing Services.** Weiner, D-N.Y., amendment that would increase funding for the Community Oriented Policing Services program by $126.2 million, offset with cuts to the National Science Foundation. Rejected 31-396: R 6-221; D 25-174 (ND 21-129, SD 4-45); I 0-1. June 15, 2005.

**252.** HR 2862. Fiscal 2006 Commerce-Justice-Science Appropriations/ **NOAA Funding.** Inslee, D-Wash., amendment that would increase funding for the National Oceanic and Atmospheric Administration Operations, Research and Facilities account by $5 million, offset by reductions related to export control functions at the Department of Commerce. Rejected 177-248: R 26-200; D 150-48 (ND 117-31, SD 33-17); I 1-0. June 15, 2005.

**253** HR 2862. Fiscal 2006 Commerce-Justice-Science Appropriations/ **U.N. Contribution Decrease.** Hayworth, R-Ariz., amendment that would cut the U.S. contribution to the United Nations by $218 million. Rejected 124-304: R 120-107; D 4-196 (ND 1-149, SD 3-47); I 0-1. June 15. 2005.

**254.** HR 2862. Fiscal 2006 Commerce-Justice-Science Appropriations/ **Cuban Gift and Humanitarian Donations.** Flake, R-Ariz., amendment that would prohibit the use of funds in the bill to implement, administer or enforce regulations related to license exemptions for gift parcels and humanitarian donations for Cuba. Rejected 210-216: R 35-190; D 174-26 (ND 134-16, SD 40-10); I 1-0. A "nay" was a vote in support of the president's position. June 15, 2005.

| | 248 | 249 | 250 | 251 | 252 | 253 | 254 |
|---|---|---|---|---|---|---|---|
| **ALABAMA** | | | | | | | |
| 1 Bonner | Y | N | N | N | N | Y | Y |
| 2 Everett | Y | Y | N | N | N | Y | Y |
| 3 Rogers | Y | N | Y | N | N | Y | N |
| 4 Aderholt | N | Y | N | N | N | N | N |
| 5 Cramer | N | N | N | N | Y | N | Y |
| 6 Bachus | N | N | ? | N | ? | Y | N |
| 7 Davis | Y | N | N | N | N | N | N |
| **ALASKA** | | | | | | | |
| AL Young | N | N | Y | N | N | Y | N |
| **ARIZONA** | | | | | | | |
| 1 Renzi | Y | N | Y | Y | N | Y | N |
| 2 Franks | N | Y | Y | N | N | Y | N |
| 3 Shadegg | Y | Y | Y | N | N | Y | N |
| 4 Pastor | Y | N | N | N | N | N | Y |
| 5 Hayworth | Y | N | N | N | N | Y | N |
| 6 Flake | N | Y | Y | N | N | N | Y |
| 7 Grijalva | Y | N | N | Y | N | N | Y |
| 8 Kolbe | N | N | Y | N | N | N | Y |
| **ARKANSAS** | | | | | | | |
| 1 Berry | N | N | N | N | N | N | Y |
| 2 Snyder | Y | N | N | N | N | N | Y |
| 3 Boozman | Y | Y | Y | N | N | Y | Y |
| 4 Ross | Y | N | N | N | N | N | Y |
| **CALIFORNIA** | | | | | | | |
| 1 Thompson | Y | N | N | N | Y | N | Y |
| 2 Herger | Y | Y | Y | N | N | Y | N |
| 3 Lungren | N | Y | Y | N | N | N | N |
| 4 Doolittle | N | Y | Y | N | N | N | N |
| 5 Matsui, D. | Y | N | N | N | Y | N | Y |
| 6 Woolsey | Y | N | N | N | Y | N | Y |
| 7 Miller, George | Y | N | N | N | Y | N | Y |
| 8 Pelosi | Y | N | N | N | Y | N | Y |
| 9 Lee | N | N | N | Y | N | N | Y |
| 10 Tauscher | Y | N | N | N | Y | N | Y |
| 11 Pombo | Y | Y | Y | N | N | Y | N |
| 12 Lantos | Y | N | N | N | Y | N | Y |
| 13 Stark | N | N | Y | N | Y | N | Y |
| 14 Eshoo | Y | N | N | N | Y | N | Y |
| 15 Honda | Y | N | N | N | Y | N | Y |
| 16 Lofgren | Y | N | N | N | Y | N | Y |
| 17 Farr | Y | N | N | N | Y | N | Y |
| 18 Cardoza | Y | N | Y | N | ? | N | N |
| 19 Radanovich | Y | Y | Y | N | N | N | N |
| 20 Costa | Y | N | Y | N | N | N | Y |
| 21 Nunes | N | Y | Y | N | N | N | N |
| 22 Thomas | N | N | Y | N | N | N | N |
| 23 Capps | N | N | N | Y | N | N | Y |
| 24 Gallegly | N | Y | Y | N | N | N | N |
| 25 McKeon | N | N | Y | N | N | N | N |
| 26 Dreier | N | N | Y | N | N | N | N |
| 27 Sherman | Y | N | N | N | N | N | Y |
| 28 Berman | Y | N | Y | N | Y | N | N |
| 29 Schiff | Y | N | Y | N | Y | N | N |
| 30 Waxman | Y | N | N | N | Y | N | Y |
| 31 Becerra | Y | N | Y | N | Y | N | Y |
| 32 Solis | Y | N | Y | N | Y | N | Y |
| 33 Watson | N | N | N | N | Y | N | Y |
| 34 Roybal-Allard | N | N | Y | N | Y | N | Y |
| 35 Waters | N | N | N | N | Y | N | Y |
| 36 Harman | Y | N | N | Y | N | N | Y |
| 37 Millender-McD. | Y | N | N | N | Y | N | Y |
| 38 Napolitano | N | N | N | Y | N | N | Y |
| 39 Sánchez, Linda | Y | N | N | N | Y | N | Y |
| 40 Royce | N | Y | Y | N | N | Y | N |
| 41 Lewis | N | N | Y | N | N | N | N |
| 42 Miller, Gary | N | N | Y | N | N | Y | N |
| 43 Baca | Y | N | Y | N | Y | N | Y |
| 44 Calvert | N | N | Y | N | N | Y | N |
| 45 Bono | N | N | Y | N | N | Y | Y |
| 46 Rohrabacher | N | Y | Y | N | N | Y | N |
| 47 Sanchez, Loretta | N | N | N | N | N | N | Y |
| 48 Cox | N | Y | Y | N | ? | N | N |
| 49 Issa | N | Y | Y | N | N | N | N |

| | 248 | 249 | 250 | 251 | 252 | 253 | 254 |
|---|---|---|---|---|---|---|---|
| 50 Cunningham | N | Y | Y | N | N | Y | N |
| 51 Filner | Y | N | N | N | Y | N | Y |
| 52 Hunter | N | Y | Y | N | N | Y | N |
| 53 Davis | Y | N | Y | N | Y | N | Y |
| **COLORADO** | | | | | | | |
| 1 DeGette | Y | N | N | N | Y | N | Y |
| 2 Udall | Y | N | N | N | N | N | Y |
| 3 Salazar | Y | N | N | N | N | N | Y |
| 4 Musgrave | Y | Y | Y | N | N | Y | N |
| 5 Hefley | Y | Y | N | N | Y | Y | N |
| 6 Tancredo | N | Y | Y | N | N | Y | N |
| 7 Beauprez | Y | N | N | N | N | N | N |
| **CONNECTICUT** | | | | | | | |
| 1 Larson | Y | N | N | N | Y | N | Y |
| 2 Simmons | Y | N | N | N | Y | N | Y |
| 3 DeLauro | Y | N | N | N | Y | N | Y |
| 4 Shays | N | N | N | Y | N | Y | Y |
| 5 Johnson | N | N | Y | N | Y | N | Y |
| **DELAWARE** | | | | | | | |
| AL Castle | Y | N | N | N | Y | N | Y |
| **FLORIDA** | | | | | | | |
| 1 Miller | N | Y | Y | – | N | Y | N |
| 2 Boyd | Y | N | N | N | Y | N | N |
| 3 Brown | N | N | N | N | N | N | N |
| 4 Crenshaw | N | Y | N | N | N | N | N |
| 5 Brown-Waite | Y | N | Y | N | Y | Y | N |
| 6 Stearns | Y | Y | Y | N | N | Y | N |
| 7 Mica | Y | Y | Y | N | N | Y | N |
| 8 Keller | Y | Y | N | N | N | Y | N |
| 9 Bilirakis | Y | Y | N | N | Y | Y | Y |
| 10 Young | N | N | N | N | Y | Y | N |
| 11 Davis | Y | N | N | N | Y | N | Y |
| 12 Putnam | N | Y | Y | N | N | Y | N |
| 13 Harris | Y | N | Y | N | Y | N | Y |
| 14 Mack | N | Y | Y | N | Y | Y | Y |
| 15 Weldon | N | N | N | N | N | N | N |
| 16 Foley | Y | Y | N | N | N | Y | Y |
| 17 Meek | Y | Y | N | N | Y | N | Y |
| 18 Ros-Lehtinen | N | N | Y | N | N | N | N |
| 19 Wexler | Y | N | N | N | Y | N | Y |
| 20 Wasserman-Schultz | Y | N | N | N | Y | N | N |
| 21 Diaz-Balart, L. | N | N | Y | N | N | N | N |
| 22 Shaw | Y | N | N | N | N | Y | N |
| 23 Hastings | Y | N | N | Y | N | N | Y |
| 24 Feeney | N | Y | N | N | Y | Y | N |
| 25 Diaz-Balart, M. | N | N | Y | N | N | N | N |
| **GEORGIA** | | | | | | | |
| 1 Kingston | Y | N | Y | N | N | Y | N |
| 2 Bishop | N | N | N | N | N | N | Y |
| 3 Marshall | Y | N | N | N | Y | N | Y |
| 4 McKinney | N | N | N | N | Y | N | Y |
| 5 Lewis | Y | N | N | N | Y | N | Y |
| 6 Price | Y | Y | Y | N | N | Y | N |
| 7 Linder | N | Y | Y | N | N | Y | N |
| 8 Westmoreland | N | Y | Y | N | N | Y | N |
| 9 Norwood | Y | Y | Y | N | N | Y | N |
| 10 Deal | Y | Y | Y | N | N | Y | N |
| 11 Gingrey | Y | Y | Y | N | N | Y | N |
| 12 Barrow | Y | Y | Y | Y | Y | N | Y |
| 13 Scott | Y | N | N | N | Y | N | Y |
| **HAWAII** | | | | | | | |
| 1 Abercrombie | Y | N | N | N | N | N | Y |
| 2 Case | Y | N | N | N | Y | N | N |
| **IDAHO** | | | | | | | |
| 1 Otter | N | Y | Y | N | N | Y | Y |
| 2 Simpson | N | N | Y | N | N | N | N |
| **ILLINOIS** | | | | | | | |
| 1 Rush | Y | N | N | N | Y | N | Y |
| 2 Jackson | Y | N | N | N | Y | N | Y |
| 3 Lipinski | Y | N | Y | N | Y | N | Y |
| 4 Gutierrez | N | N | + | N | Y | N | Y |
| 5 Emanuel | Y | N | N | N | Y | N | Y |
| 6 Hyde | N | Y | Y | ? | ? | ? | ? |
| 7 Davis | Y | N | N | Y | N | N | Y |
| 8 Bean | Y | N | N | N | Y | N | Y |
| 9 Schakowsky | N | N | N | N | Y | N | Y |
| 10 Kirk | N | N | N | N | N | N | N |
| 11 Weller | N | N | Y | N | N | N | N |
| 12 Costello | Y | N | Y | N | Y | N | Y |

**KEY**    Republicans    Democrats    *Independents*

| | | | |
|---|---|---|---|
| Y | Voted for (yea) | X | Paired against |
| # | Paired for | – | Announced against |
| + | Announced for | P | Voted "present" |
| N | Voted against (nay) | | |

| | |
|---|---|
| C | Voted "present" to avoid possible conflict of interest |
| ? | Did not vote or otherwise make a position known |

ND Northern Democrats, SD Southern Democrats
Southern states: Ala., Ark., Fla., Ga., Ky., La., Miss., N.C., Okla., S.C., Tenn., Texas, Va.

| | 248 | 249 | 250 | 251 | 252 | 253 | 254 |
|---|---|---|---|---|---|---|---|
| 13 **Biggert** | N | N | N | N | N | N | Y |
| 14 **Hastert** | | | | | | | |
| 15 **Johnson** | Y | N | N | N | N | N | Y |
| 16 **Manzullo** | N | N | Y | N | N | Y | N |
| 17 Evans | Y | N | Y | N | N | N | Y |
| 18 **LaHood** | Y | N | Y | N | N | N | Y |
| 19 **Shimkus** | Y | Y | Y | N | ? | N | Y |
| **INDIANA** | | | | | | | |
| 1 Visclosky | N | N | N | N | N | N | Y |
| 2 **Chocola** | Y | Y | Y | N | N | N | N |
| 3 **Souder** | Y | Y | Y | N | N | Y | N |
| 4 **Buyer** | N | Y | Y | N | N | Y | N |
| 5 **Burton** | N | Y | Y | N | N | Y | N |
| 6 **Pence** | N | Y | N | N | N | N | N |
| 7 Carson | Y | N | N | Y | N | N | Y |
| 8 **Hostettler** | N | Y | Y | N | N | Y | Y |
| 9 **Sodrel** | N | Y | N | N | N | Y | N |
| **IOWA** | | | | | | | |
| 1 **Nussle** | Y | Y | Y | N | N | Y | N |
| 2 **Leach** | Y | N | N | N | N | N | Y |
| 3 Boswell | Y | N | Y | Y | N | N | Y |
| 4 **Latham** | N | N | Y | N | N | N | N |
| 5 **King** | Y | Y | Y | N | N | Y | N |
| **KANSAS** | | | | | | | |
| 1 **Moran** | Y | N | N | N | N | Y | Y |
| 2 **Ryun** | N | Y | Y | N | N | N | N |
| 3 Moore | Y | N | Y | N | N | N | Y |
| 4 **Tiahrt** | N | N | Y | N | N | N | N |
| **KENTUCKY** | | | | | | | |
| 1 **Whitfield** | N | Y | Y | N | N | Y | N |
| 2 **Lewis** | Y | Y | Y | N | N | Y | N |
| 3 **Northup** | N | N | Y | N | N | N | N |
| 4 **Davis** | Y | Y | Y | N | N | Y | N |
| 5 **Rogers** | N | N | Y | N | N | N | N |
| 6 Chandler | Y | N | Y | N | N | N | N |
| **LOUISIANA** | | | | | | | |
| 1 **Jindal** | Y | Y | N | N | Y | Y | N |
| 2 Jefferson | N | N | N | N | Y | N | Y |
| 3 Melancon | Y | N | N | - | Y | N | N |
| 4 **McCrery** | Y | N | Y | N | N | N | N |
| 5 **Alexander** | N | N | N | N | N | N | N |
| 6 **Baker** | N | N | N | N | N | Y | N |
| 7 **Boustany** | N | N | N | N | N | N | N |
| **MAINE** | | | | | | | |
| 1 Allen | Y | N | N | N | Y | N | Y |
| 2 Michaud | Y | N | N | N | Y | N | Y |
| **MARYLAND** | | | | | | | |
| 1 **Gilchrest** | N | N | N | N | N | N | N |
| 2 Ruppersberger | Y | N | N | N | Y | N | Y |
| 3 Cardin | N | N | N | N | Y | N | Y |
| 4 Wynn | N | N | N | N | Y | N | Y |
| 5 Hoyer | N | N | N | N | Y | N | Y |
| 6 **Bartlett** | Y | Y | Y | N | N | Y | N |
| 7 Cummings | Y | N | N | N | Y | N | Y |
| 8 Van Hollen | Y | N | N | N | Y | N | Y |
| **MASSACHUSETTS** | | | | | | | |
| 1 Olver | Y | N | N | N | Y | N | Y |
| 2 Neal | Y | N | N | N | Y | N | Y |
| 3 McGovern | Y | N | N | N | Y | N | Y |
| 4 Frank | Y | N | N | N | Y | N | Y |
| 5 Meehan | Y | N | N | N | Y | N | Y |
| 6 Tierney | Y | N | N | N | Y | N | Y |
| 7 Markey | Y | N | N | N | N | N | Y |
| 8 Capuano | Y | N | N | N | Y | N | Y |
| 9 Lynch | Y | N | N | N | N | N | Y |
| 10 Delahunt | Y | N | N | N | Y | N | Y |
| **MICHIGAN** | | | | | | | |
| 1 Stupak | Y | N | N | N | Y | N | Y |
| 2 **Hoekstra** | N | N | Y | N | N | N | N |
| 3 **Ehlers** | Y | N | N | N | Y | N | Y |
| 4 **Camp** | N | Y | Y | N | N | N | Y |
| 5 Kildee | Y | N | N | N | Y | N | Y |
| 6 **Upton** | Y | N | N | N | N | Y | Y |
| 7 **Schwarz** | Y | N | N | N | N | N | Y |
| 8 **Rogers** | N | Y | Y | N | N | N | N |
| 9 **Knollenberg** | N | N | Y | N | N | N | N |
| 10 **Miller** | N | N | Y | N | Y | N | N |
| 11 **McCotter** | Y | N | Y | N | N | Y | N |
| 12 Levin | Y | N | N | N | Y | N | Y |
| 13 Kilpatrick | Y | N | N | N | N | N | Y |
| 14 Conyers | N | N | N | Y | Y | N | Y |
| 15 Dingell | Y | N | N | N | Y | N | Y |

| | 248 | 249 | 250 | 251 | 252 | 253 | 254 |
|---|---|---|---|---|---|---|---|
| **MINNESOTA** | | | | | | | |
| 1 **Gutknecht** | Y | Y | N | N | N | Y | N |
| 2 **Kline** | Y | Y | Y | N | Y | N | N |
| 3 **Ramstad** | Y | N | Y | Y | N | Y | Y |
| 4 McCollum | Y | N | N | N | Y | N | Y |
| 5 Sabo | Y | N | N | N | N | N | Y |
| 6 **Kennedy** | Y | Y | Y | N | Y | N | N |
| 7 Peterson | Y | N | Y | N | Y | Y | Y |
| 8 Oberstar | ? | ? | ? | ? | ? | ? | ? |
| **MISSISSIPPI** | | | | | | | |
| 1 **Wicker** | N | N | Y | N | N | N | N |
| 2 Thompson | Y | N | Y | N | N | N | Y |
| 3 **Pickering** | Y | N | Y | N | N | N | N |
| 4 Taylor | Y | N | N | N | Y | Y | Y |
| **MISSOURI** | | | | | | | |
| 1 Clay | N | N | N | N | Y | N | Y |
| 2 **Akin** | N | Y | Y | N | N | Y | N |
| 3 Carnahan | Y | N | Y | N | N | N | N |
| 4 Skelton | Y | N | N | N | Y | N | N |
| 5 Cleaver | Y | N | N | N | Y | N | N |
| 6 **Graves** | Y | Y | Y | N | N | Y | Y |
| 7 **Blunt** | N | N | Y | N | N | N | N |
| 8 **Emerson** | Y | N | Y | N | N | Y | Y |
| 9 **Hulshof** | Y | N | Y | N | N | Y | N |
| **MONTANA** | | | | | | | |
| AL **Rehberg** | N | N | Y | N | N | N | N |
| **NEBRASKA** | | | | | | | |
| 1 **Fortenberry** | Y | Y | Y | N | N | N | N |
| 2 **Terry** | Y | Y | N | N | N | Y | N |
| 3 **Osborne** | Y | N | Y | N | N | N | Y |
| **NEVADA** | | | | | | | |
| 1 Berkley | Y | N | N | N | N | N | N |
| 2 **Gibbons** | Y | Y | Y | N | N | Y | N |
| 3 **Porter** | N | Y | Y | Y | N | N | N |
| **NEW HAMPSHIRE** | | | | | | | |
| 1 **Bradley** | Y | N | N | Y | Y | N | N |
| 2 **Bass** | N | N | Y | N | Y | N | Y |
| **NEW JERSEY** | | | | | | | |
| 1 Andrews | N | N | N | N | Y | N | N |
| 2 **LoBiondo** | Y | Y | Y | N | Y | Y | N |
| 3 **Saxton** | N | N | N | N | N | N | N |
| 4 **Smith** | Y | N | Y | N | N | Y | N |
| 5 **Garrett** | N | Y | Y | N | N | Y | ? |
| 6 Pallone | Y | N | N | Y | Y | N | N |
| 7 **Ferguson** | Y | N | Y | N | N | N | N |
| 8 Pascrell | N | N | N | Y | Y | N | N |
| 9 Rothman | ? | ? | N | Y | Y | N | N |
| 10 Payne | N | N | N | Y | Y | N | Y |
| 11 **Frelinghuysen** | N | N | Y | N | N | N | N |
| 12 Holt | Y | N | N | N | Y | N | Y |
| 13 Menendez | N | N | N | Y | Y | N | N |
| **NEW MEXICO** | | | | | | | |
| 1 **Wilson** | Y | N | Y | N | N | N | N |
| 2 **Pearce** | N | N | Y | N | N | N | N |
| 3 Udall | Y | N | Y | N | Y | N | Y |
| **NEW YORK** | | | | | | | |
| 1 Bishop | Y | N | N | Y | Y | N | Y |
| 2 Israel | Y | N | N | Y | Y | N | Y |
| 3 **King** | Y | N | Y | N | N | N | N |
| 4 McCarthy | Y | N | N | N | Y | N | Y |
| 5 Ackerman | Y | N | N | Y | Y | N | Y |
| 6 Meeks | Y | N | N | N | Y | N | Y |
| 7 Crowley | Y | N | N | N | Y | N | Y |
| 8 Nadler | Y | N | Y | N | Y | N | Y |
| 9 Weiner | Y | N | Y | Y | Y | N | Y |
| 10 Towns | Y | N | N | Y | Y | N | Y |
| 11 Owens | N | N | N | Y | N | N | Y |
| 12 Velázquez | Y | N | N | Y | Y | N | Y |
| 13 **Fossella** | Y | N | Y | N | Y | Y | N |
| 14 Maloney | N | N | N | N | Y | N | Y |
| 15 Rangel | N | N | N | N | Y | N | Y |
| 16 Serrano | N | N | N | N | N | N | Y |
| 17 Engel | Y | N | Y | N | Y | N | N |
| 18 Lowey | Y | N | N | Y | Y | N | Y |
| 19 **Kelly** | N | N | Y | Y | Y | Y | N |
| 20 **Sweeney** | N | N | Y | N | N | N | N |
| 21 McNulty | Y | N | Y | N | Y | N | Y |
| 22 Hinchey | Y | N | N | N | Y | N | Y |
| 23 **McHugh** | Y | N | Y | N | N | N | N |
| 24 **Boehlert** | Y | N | N | N | N | N | Y |
| 25 **Walsh** | N | N | Y | N | N | N | N |
| 26 **Reynolds** | N | Y | Y | N | N | N | N |
| 27 Higgins | Y | N | Y | Y | Y | N | Y |
| 28 Slaughter | Y | N | N | N | Y | N | Y |
| 29 **Kuhl** | Y | Y | Y | N | N | Y | N |

| | 248 | 249 | 250 | 251 | 252 | 253 | 254 |
|---|---|---|---|---|---|---|---|
| **NORTH CAROLINA** | | | | | | | |
| 1 Butterfield | Y | N | N | N | Y | N | Y |
| 2 Etheridge | Y | N | N | N | N | N | Y |
| 3 **Jones** | Y | Y | Y | N | N | Y | N |
| 4 Price | Y | N | N | N | Y | N | Y |
| 5 **Foxx** | N | N | Y | N | N | Y | N |
| 6 **Coble** | Y | Y | N | N | N | Y | N |
| 7 McIntyre | Y | N | Y | Y | Y | Y | N |
| 8 **Hayes** | N | N | Y | N | N | Y | N |
| 9 **Myrick** | N | Y | Y | N | N | N | N |
| 10 **McHenry** | N | Y | Y | N | N | Y | N |
| 11 **Taylor** | N | N | N | N | N | Y | N |
| 12 Watt | N | N | N | N | Y | N | Y |
| 13 Miller | Y | N | N | N | Y | N | Y |
| **NORTH DAKOTA** | | | | | | | |
| AL Pomeroy | Y | N | N | N | Y | N | Y |
| **OHIO** | | | | | | | |
| 1 **Chabot** | Y | Y | Y | N | N | Y | N |
| 2 Vacant | | | | | | | |
| 3 **Turner** | N | N | Y | N | N | N | N |
| 4 **Oxley** | N | N | Y | N | N | N | N |
| 5 **Gillmor** | N | N | Y | N | N | N | Y |
| 6 Strickland | ? | ? | ? | Y | Y | N | Y |
| 7 **Hobson** | N | N | Y | N | N | N | N |
| 8 **Boehner** | N | Y | N | N | N | N | N |
| 9 Kaptur | Y | N | N | N | Y | N | Y |
| 10 Kucinich | N | N | N | Y | Y | N | Y |
| 11 Jones | Y | N | N | N | ? | N | Y |
| 12 **Tiberi** | N | N | N | N | N | Y | ? |
| 13 Brown | Y | N | Y | N | Y | N | Y |
| 14 **LaTourette** | N | N | N | N | N | N | N |
| 15 **Pryce** | N | N | Y | N | N | N | N |
| 16 **Regula** | N | N | Y | N | N | N | N |
| 17 Ryan | Y | N | Y | N | Y | N | Y |
| 18 **Ney** | Y | N | Y | N | N | Y | Y |
| **OKLAHOMA** | | | | | | | |
| 1 **Sullivan** | N | Y | Y | N | N | N | N |
| 2 Boren | Y | Y | N | N | N | N | Y |
| 3 **Lucas** | N | Y | N | N | N | Y | N |
| 4 **Cole** | N | Y | N | N | N | N | N |
| 5 **Istook** | N | Y | N | N | N | Y | N |
| **OREGON** | | | | | | | |
| 1 Wu | Y | N | N | N | Y | N | N |
| 2 **Walden** | Y | N | Y | N | N | N | N |
| 3 Blumenauer | Y | N | N | N | Y | N | Y |
| 4 DeFazio | Y | N | Y | N | Y | N | Y |
| 5 Hooley | Y | N | N | N | Y | N | Y |
| **PENNSYLVANIA** | | | | | | | |
| 1 Brady | Y | N | N | N | N | N | Y |
| 2 Fattah | Y | N | ? | N | Y | N | Y |
| 3 **English** | N | N | Y | N | N | N | N |
| 4 **Hart** | N | N | Y | N | N | Y | N |
| 5 **Peterson** | Y | N | Y | N | N | Y | Y |
| 6 **Gerlach** | Y | N | Y | N | Y | N | N |
| 7 **Weldon** | Y | N | N | N | Y | N | N |
| 8 **Fitzpatrick** | Y | N | N | N | Y | N | N |
| 9 **Shuster** | N | N | Y | N | N | Y | N |
| 10 **Sherwood** | N | N | Y | N | N | N | N |
| 11 Kanjorski | Y | N | N | N | N | N | Y |
| 12 Murtha | N | N | N | N | N | N | N |
| 13 Schwartz | Y | N | Y | N | Y | N | Y |
| 14 Doyle | Y | N | N | N | Y | N | Y |
| 15 **Dent** | Y | N | Y | N | N | N | N |
| 16 **Pitts** | N | Y | N | N | N | N | N |
| 17 Holden | Y | N | N | Y | N | N | Y |
| 18 **Murphy** | Y | N | Y | Y | N | Y | N |
| 19 **Platts** | Y | N | N | N | Y | Y | N |
| **RHODE ISLAND** | | | | | | | |
| 1 Kennedy | Y | N | N | N | Y | N | Y |
| 2 Langevin | Y | N | N | N | Y | N | Y |
| **SOUTH CAROLINA** | | | | | | | |
| 1 **Brown** | N | N | N | N | N | Y | Y |
| 2 **Wilson** | N | Y | Y | N | N | N | N |
| 3 **Barrett** | N | Y | N | N | N | Y | N |
| 4 **Inglis** | N | N | N | N | N | N | Y |
| 5 Spratt | N | N | N | N | Y | N | Y |
| 6 Clyburn | Y | N | N | N | N | N | Y |
| **SOUTH DAKOTA** | | | | | | | |
| AL Herseth | Y | N | Y | N | N | N | Y |
| **TENNESSEE** | | | | | | | |
| 1 **Jenkins** | N | N | Y | N | N | Y | N |
| 2 **Duncan** | N | Y | Y | N | N | Y | N |

| | 248 | 249 | 250 | 251 | 252 | 253 | 254 |
|---|---|---|---|---|---|---|---|
| 3 **Wamp** | Y | N | Y | N | N | Y | N |
| 4 Davis | Y | Y | N | N | N | N | Y |
| 5 Cooper | Y | N | N | N | N | N | Y |
| 6 Gordon | Y | N | N | N | Y | N | Y |
| 7 **Blackburn** | N | N | Y | N | N | N | N |
| 8 Tanner | Y | N | N | N | Y | N | Y |
| 9 Ford | Y | N | N | N | Y | N | Y |
| **TEXAS** | | | | | | | |
| 1 **Gohmert** | Y | Y | Y | N | N | Y | N |
| 2 **Poe** | Y | Y | Y | N | Y | Y | N |
| 3 **Johnson, S.** | N | Y | Y | N | N | Y | N |
| 4 **Hall** | N | Y | Y | N | N | Y | N |
| 5 **Hensarling** | N | Y | Y | N | N | Y | N |
| 6 **Barton** | N | Y | Y | N | N | Y | N |
| 7 **Culberson** | N | N | Y | N | N | N | N |
| 8 **Brady** | N | Y | Y | N | N | N | ? |
| 9 Green, A. | Y | N | N | N | Y | N | Y |
| 10 **McCaul** | Y | Y | Y | N | Y | Y | N |
| 11 **Conaway** | N | N | Y | N | N | N | N |
| 12 **Granger** | N | N | Y | N | N | N | N |
| 13 **Thornberry** | Y | Y | Y | N | N | Y | N |
| 14 **Paul** | Y | Y | Y | N | N | Y | Y |
| 15 Hinojosa | ? | ? | ? | N | N | N | Y |
| 16 Reyes | Y | N | Y | N | N | N | Y |
| 17 Edwards | Y | N | N | N | Y | N | Y |
| 18 Jackson-Lee | Y | N | N | N | Y | N | Y |
| 19 **Neugebauer** | N | Y | Y | N | N | Y | N |
| 20 Gonzalez | N | N | Y | N | Y | N | Y |
| 21 **Smith** | N | N | Y | N | N | Y | N |
| 22 **DeLay** | N | Y | Y | N | N | N | N |
| 23 **Bonilla** | N | N | Y | N | N | Y | N |
| 24 **Marchant** | N | Y | Y | N | N | Y | N |
| 25 Doggett | Y | N | Y | N | Y | N | Y |
| 26 **Burgess** | N | N | Y | N | N | Y | N |
| 27 Ortiz | Y | N | Y | N | Y | N | Y |
| 28 Cuellar | Y | N | Y | ? | ? | ? | ? |
| 29 Green, G. | Y | N | Y | Y | Y | Y | Y |
| 30 Johnson, E. | N | N | Y | N | Y | N | Y |
| 31 **Carter** | N | N | Y | N | N | Y | N |
| 32 **Sessions** | ? | ? | ? | ? | ? | ? | ? |
| **UTAH** | | | | | | | |
| 1 **Bishop** | N | Y | Y | N | N | Y | N |
| 2 Matheson | Y | N | N | N | N | N | Y |
| 3 **Cannon** | N | N | Y | N | N | Y | N |
| **VERMONT** | | | | | | | |
| AL *Sanders* | Y | N | N | N | Y | N | Y |
| **VIRGINIA** | | | | | | | |
| 1 **Davis, J.** | Y | Y | Y | N | N | Y | N |
| 2 **Drake** | Y | Y | Y | N | N | Y | N |
| 3 Scott | Y | N | N | N | Y | N | Y |
| 4 **Forbes** | Y | Y | Y | N | N | Y | N |
| 5 **Goode** | N | Y | Y | N | N | Y | N |
| 6 **Goodlatte** | N | Y | Y | N | N | Y | N |
| 7 **Cantor** | N | N | Y | N | N | N | N |
| 8 Moran | N | N | N | N | N | N | Y |
| 9 Boucher | Y | N | N | N | Y | N | Y |
| 10 **Wolf** | N | N | Y | N | N | N | N |
| 11 **Davis, T.** | N | N | Y | N | N | N | N |
| **WASHINGTON** | | | | | | | |
| 1 Inslee | Y | N | N | N | Y | N | Y |
| 2 Larsen | Y | N | Y | N | Y | N | Y |
| 3 Baird | Y | N | N | N | Y | N | Y |
| 4 **Hastings** | Y | Y | Y | N | N | Y | N |
| 5 **McMorris** | Y | N | Y | N | N | Y | N |
| 6 Dicks | Y | N | N | N | Y | N | Y |
| 7 McDermott | Y | N | N | N | Y | N | Y |
| 8 **Reichert** | Y | N | N | N | N | N | N |
| 9 Smith | Y | N | Y | N | Y | N | Y |
| **WEST VIRGINIA** | | | | | | | |
| 1 Mollohan | N | N | N | N | N | N | Y |
| 2 **Capito** | Y | N | Y | N | N | N | N |
| 3 Rahall | Y | N | N | N | N | N | Y |
| **WISCONSIN** | | | | | | | |
| 1 **Ryan** | Y | Y | Y | N | N | N | Y |
| 2 Baldwin | Y | N | N | N | Y | N | Y |
| 3 Kind | Y | N | N | N | Y | N | Y |
| 4 Moore | Y | N | N | N | Y | N | Y |
| 5 **Sensenbrenner** | N | Y | Y | N | N | Y | N |
| 6 **Petri** | N | Y | Y | N | N | Y | N |
| 7 Obey | Y | N | N | N | N | N | Y |
| 8 **Green** | Y | Y | Y | N | N | Y | N |
| **WYOMING** | | | | | | | |
| AL **Cubin** | Y | Y | Y | N | N | Y | Y |

# IN THE HOUSE | By Vote Number

**255.** HR 2862. Fiscal 2006 Commerce-Justice-Science Appropriations/ **Medical Marijuana.** Hinchey, D-N.Y., amendment that would prohibit the use of funds in the bill to prevent the implementation of state laws authorizing the use of marijuana for medical reasons in Alaska, California, Colorado, Hawaii, Maine, Montana, Nevada, Oregon, Vermont or Washington state. Rejected 161-264: R 15-210; D 145-54 (ND 123-26, SD 22-28); I 1-0. June 15, 2005.

**256.** HR 2862. Fiscal 2006 Commerce-Justice-Science Appropriations/ **Equal Employment Opportunity Commission.** Jones, D-Ohio, amendment that would prohibit use of funds in the bill to close or consolidate any office of the Equal Employment Opportunity Commission or make any reductions in the number of full-time officers or employees in any commission office as part of workforce repositioning, restructuring or reorganizing. Rejected 201-222: R 2-221; D 198-1 (ND 148-1, SD 50-0); I 1-0. June 15, 2005.

**257.** HR 2862. Fiscal 2006 Commerce-Justice-Science Appropriations/ **Ten Commandments Court Ruling.** Hostettler, R-Ind., amendment that would prohibit the use of funds in the bill to enforce a ruling by the U.S. District Court for the Southern District of Indiana that a monument representing the Ten Commandments must be removed from the county courthouse. Adopted 242-182: R 204-20; D 38-161 (ND 17-133, SD 21-28); I 0-1. June 15, 2005.

**258.** HR 2862. Fiscal 2006 Commerce-Justice-Science Appropriations/ **Surveillance of Library Records.** Sanders, I-Vt., amendment that would prohibit the use of funds in the bill to make an application under the Foreign Intelligence Surveillance Act to acquire library circulation records, library patron lists, bookseller sales records or bookseller customer lists. Adopted 238-187: R 38-186; D 199-1 (ND 150-0, SD 49-1); I 1-0. A "nay" was a vote in support of the president's position. June 15, 2005.

**259.** HR 2862. Fiscal 2006 Commerce-Justice-Science Appropriations/ **U.N. Funding.** Paul, R-Texas, amendment that would prohibit the use of funds in the bill to pay any U.S. contribution to the United Nations or any affiliated agency of the United Nations. Rejected 65-357: R 64-160; D 1-196 (ND 0-149, SD 1-47); I 0-1. June 16, 2005.

**260.** HR 2862. Fiscal 2006 Commerce-Justice-Science Appropriations/ **Across-the-Board Cut.** Hefley, R-Colo., amendment that would require an approximate 1 percent across-the-board cut in discretionary spending. Rejected 91-336: R 87-140; D 4-195 (ND 2-147, SD 2-48); I 0-1. June 16, 2005.

**261.** HR 2862. Fiscal 2006 Commerce-Justice-Science Appropriations/ **U.S. Commitment Against Torture.** Markey, D-Mass., amendment that would reaffirm the U.S. commitment to the U.N. Convention Against Torture. Adopted 415-8: R 215-8; D 199-0 (ND 149-0, SD 50-0); I 1-0. June 16, 2005.

| | 255 | 256 | 257 | 258 | 259 | 260 | 261 |
|---|---|---|---|---|---|---|---|
| **ALABAMA** | | | | | | | |
| 1 Bonner | N | N | Y | N | Y | N | Y |
| 2 Everett | N | N | Y | N | Y | Y | Y |
| 3 Rogers | N | N | Y | N | Y | N | Y |
| 4 Aderholt | N | N | Y | N | N | N | Y |
| 5 Cramer | N | Y | Y | Y | N | N | Y |
| 6 Bachus | N | N | Y | N | Y | Y | Y |
| 7 Davis | N | Y | N | Y | N | N | Y |
| **ALASKA** | | | | | | | |
| AL Young | N | N | Y | Y | N | N | Y |
| **ARIZONA** | | | | | | | |
| 1 Renzi | N | N | Y | N | N | N | Y |
| 2 Franks | N | N | Y | N | Y | Y | Y |
| 3 Shadegg | N | N | Y | N | N | Y | Y |
| 4 Pastor | Y | Y | N | Y | N | N | Y |
| 5 Hayworth | N | N | Y | N | Y | N | P |
| 6 Flake | Y | N | Y | N | N | N | Y |
| 7 Grijalva | Y | Y | N | Y | N | N | Y |
| 8 Kolbe | N | N | N | N | N | N | Y |
| **ARKANSAS** | | | | | | | |
| 1 Berry | N | Y | Y | Y | N | N | Y |
| 2 Snyder | N | Y | N | Y | N | N | Y |
| 3 Boozman | N | N | Y | N | Y | N | Y |
| 4 Ross | N | Y | Y | Y | N | N | Y |
| **CALIFORNIA** | | | | | | | |
| 1 Thompson | Y | Y | N | Y | N | N | Y |
| 2 Herger | N | N | Y | N | Y | Y | Y |
| 3 Lungren | N | N | Y | N | N | Y | Y |
| 4 Doolittle | N | N | Y | N | Y | N | Y |
| 5 Matsui, D. | Y | Y | N | Y | N | N | Y |
| 6 Woolsey | Y | Y | N | Y | ? | N | Y |
| 7 Miller, George | Y | Y | N | Y | N | N | Y |
| 8 Pelosi | Y | Y | N | Y | N | N | Y |
| 9 Lee | Y | Y | N | Y | N | N | Y |
| 10 Tauscher | Y | Y | N | Y | N | N | Y |
| 11 Pombo | N | N | Y | N | Y | N | Y |
| 12 Lantos | Y | Y | N | Y | N | N | Y |
| 13 Stark | Y | Y | N | Y | N | N | Y |
| 14 Eshoo | Y | Y | N | Y | N | N | Y |
| 15 Honda | Y | Y | N | Y | N | N | Y |
| 16 Lofgren | Y | Y | N | Y | N | N | Y |
| 17 Farr | Y | Y | N | Y | N | N | Y |
| 18 Cardoza | N | Y | Y | Y | N | N | Y |
| 19 Radanovich | N | N | Y | N | N | Y | Y |
| 20 Costa | Y | Y | N | Y | N | N | Y |
| 21 Nunes | N | N | Y | N | N | N | Y |
| 22 Thomas | N | N | Y | N | N | N | Y |
| 23 Capps | Y | Y | N | Y | N | N | Y |
| 24 Gallegly | N | N | Y | N | N | N | Y |
| 25 McKeon | N | N | Y | N | N | N | Y |
| 26 Dreier | N | N | Y | N | N | N | Y |
| 27 Sherman | Y | Y | N | Y | N | N | Y |
| 28 Berman | Y | Y | N | Y | N | N | Y |
| 29 Schiff | Y | Y | N | Y | N | N | Y |
| 30 Waxman | Y | Y | N | Y | N | N | Y |
| 31 Becerra | Y | Y | N | Y | N | N | Y |
| 32 Solis | Y | Y | N | Y | N | N | Y |
| 33 Watson | Y | Y | N | Y | N | N | Y |
| 34 Roybal-Allard | Y | Y | N | Y | N | N | Y |
| 35 Waters | Y | Y | N | Y | N | N | ? |
| 36 Harman | Y | Y | N | Y | N | N | Y |
| 37 Millender-McD. | Y | Y | N | Y | N | N | Y |
| 38 Napolitano | Y | + | N | Y | N | N | Y |
| 39 Sánchez, Linda | Y | Y | N | Y | N | N | Y |
| 40 Royce | Y | N | Y | N | N | Y | Y |
| 41 Lewis | N | N | N | N | N | N | Y |
| 42 Miller, Gary | N | N | Y | N | N | Y | Y |
| 43 Baca | Y | Y | N | Y | N | N | Y |
| 44 Calvert | N | N | Y | N | N | N | Y |
| 45 Bono | N | ? | ? | ? | ? | ? | ? |
| 46 Rohrabacher | Y | N | Y | N | Y | Y | Y |
| 47 Sanchez, Loretta | Y | Y | N | Y | N | N | Y |
| 48 Cox | ? | N | Y | N | ? | Y | Y |
| 49 Issa | N | N | Y | N | N | Y | Y |
| 50 Cunningham | N | N | Y | N | N | N | Y |
| 51 Filner | Y | Y | N | Y | N | N | Y |
| 52 Hunter | N | N | Y | N | Y | N | Y |
| 53 Davis | Y | Y | N | Y | N | N | Y |
| **COLORADO** | | | | | | | |
| 1 DeGette | Y | Y | N | Y | N | N | Y |
| 2 Udall | Y | Y | N | Y | N | N | Y |
| 3 Salazar | Y | Y | Y | Y | N | N | Y |
| 4 Musgrave | N | N | Y | Y | Y | Y | Y |
| 5 Hefley | N | N | Y | N | Y | Y | Y |
| 6 Tancredo | N | Y | N | Y | N | Y | Y |
| 7 Beauprez | Y | N | Y | N | N | N | Y |
| **CONNECTICUT** | | | | | | | |
| 1 Larson | Y | Y | N | Y | N | N | Y |
| 2 Simmons | Y | Y | N | Y | N | N | Y |
| 3 DeLauro | Y | Y | N | Y | N | N | Y |
| 4 Shays | N | N | N | N | N | N | Y |
| 5 Johnson | Y | N | N | N | N | N | Y |
| **DELAWARE** | | | | | | | |
| AL Castle | N | N | Y | N | N | N | Y |
| **FLORIDA** | | | | | | | |
| 1 Miller | N | N | Y | Y | Y | Y | Y |
| 2 Boyd | N | Y | Y | Y | N | N | Y |
| 3 Brown | Y | Y | N | Y | N | N | Y |
| 4 Crenshaw | N | N | Y | N | N | N | Y |
| 5 Brown-Waite | N | N | Y | N | N | Y | Y |
| 6 Stearns | N | N | Y | N | Y | Y | Y |
| 7 Mica | N | N | Y | N | N | Y | N |
| 8 Keller | N | N | Y | N | Y | Y | Y |
| 9 Bilirakis | N | N | Y | N | Y | Y | Y |
| 10 Young | N | N | Y | N | Y | Y | Y |
| 11 Davis | Y | Y | N | Y | N | N | Y |
| 12 Putnam | N | N | Y | N | N | Y | Y |
| 13 Harris | N | N | Y | N | Y | N | Y |
| 14 Mack | N | N | Y | N | N | Y | Y |
| 15 Weldon | N | N | Y | N | Y | N | Y |
| 16 Foley | N | N | Y | N | Y | N | Y |
| 17 Meek | Y | Y | N | Y | N | N | Y |
| 18 Ros-Lehtinen | N | N | Y | N | N | N | Y |
| 19 Wexler | Y | Y | N | Y | N | N | Y |
| 20 Wasserman-Schultz | N | Y | N | Y | N | N | Y |
| 21 Diaz-Balart, L. | N | N | Y | N | N | N | Y |
| 22 Shaw | N | N | Y | N | N | N | Y |
| 23 Hastings | Y | Y | N | Y | N | N | Y |
| 24 Feeney | ? | N | Y | N | Y | Y | N |
| 25 Diaz-Balart, M. | N | N | Y | N | N | N | Y |
| **GEORGIA** | | | | | | | |
| 1 Kingston | N | N | N | Y | N | N | Y |
| 2 Bishop | Y | Y | Y | Y | N | N | Y |
| 3 Marshall | N | Y | Y | Y | N | N | Y |
| 4 McKinney | Y | Y | N | Y | ? | N | Y |
| 5 Lewis | Y | Y | N | Y | N | N | Y |
| 6 Price | N | N | Y | N | Y | Y | Y |
| 7 Linder | N | N | Y | N | Y | N | Y |
| 8 Westmoreland | N | N | Y | N | Y | Y | N |
| 9 Norwood | N | N | Y | N | Y | N | Y |
| 10 Deal | N | N | Y | N | Y | N | Y |
| 11 Gingrey | N | N | Y | N | Y | N | Y |
| 12 Barrow | N | Y | Y | Y | N | N | Y |
| 13 Scott | Y | Y | Y | Y | N | N | Y |
| **HAWAII** | | | | | | | |
| 1 Abercrombie | Y | Y | N | Y | N | N | Y |
| 2 Case | Y | Y | N | Y | N | N | Y |
| **IDAHO** | | | | | | | |
| 1 Otter | Y | N | Y | Y | Y | Y | Y |
| 2 Simpson | Y | N | Y | N | Y | N | Y |
| **ILLINOIS** | | | | | | | |
| 1 Rush | Y | Y | N | Y | N | N | Y |
| 2 Jackson | Y | Y | N | Y | N | N | Y |
| 3 Lipinski | N | Y | Y | Y | N | N | Y |
| 4 Gutierrez | Y | Y | N | Y | N | N | Y |
| 5 Emanuel | Y | Y | N | Y | N | N | Y |
| 6 Hyde | ? | ? | ? | ? | N | N | Y |
| 7 Davis | Y | Y | N | Y | N | N | Y |
| 8 Bean | N | Y | N | Y | N | Y | Y |
| 9 Schakowsky | Y | Y | N | Y | N | N | Y |
| 10 Kirk | N | N | N | N | N | N | + |
| 11 Weller | N | N | Y | N | N | N | Y |
| 12 Costello | N | Y | Y | Y | N | N | Y |

**KEY**    Republicans    Democrats    *Independents*

| | | |
|---|---|---|
| **Y** Voted for (yea) | **X** Paired against | **C** Voted "present" to avoid possible conflict of interest |
| **#** Paired for | **–** Announced against | |
| **+** Announced for | **P** Voted "present" | **?** Did not vote or otherwise make a position known |
| **N** Voted against (nay) | | |

ND Northern Democrats, SD Southern Democrats
Southern states: Ala., Ark., Fla., Ga., Ky., La., Miss., N.C., Okla., S.C., Tenn., Texas, Va.

| | 255 | 256 | 257 | 258 | 259 | 260 | 261 |
|---|---|---|---|---|---|---|---|
| 13 **Biggert** | N | N | Y | N | N | N | Y |
| 14 **Hastert** | | | | | | | |
| 15 **Johnson** | Y | N | Y | Y | N | N | Y |
| 16 **Manzullo** | N | N | Y | Y | Y | Y | Y |
| 17 Evans | Y | Y | N | Y | N | N | Y |
| 18 **LaHood** | N | N | Y | Y | N | N | Y |
| 19 **Shimkus** | N | Y | Y | N | N | Y | Y |
| **INDIANA** | | | | | | | |
| 1 Visclosky | N | Y | N | Y | N | N | Y |
| 2 **Chocola** | N | N | Y | N | N | Y | Y |
| 3 **Souder** | N | N | Y | N | N | N | Y |
| 4 **Buyer** | N | N | Y | N | N | Y | ? |
| 5 **Burton** | N | N | Y | N | Y | Y | Y |
| 6 **Pence** | N | N | Y | N | N | Y | Y |
| 7 Carson | Y | Y | N | Y | N | N | Y |
| 8 **Hostettler** | N | N | Y | N | Y | Y | Y |
| 9 **Sodrel** | N | N | Y | N | N | Y | Y |
| **IOWA** | | | | | | | |
| 1 **Nussle** | N | N | Y | N | N | N | Y |
| 2 **Leach** | N | N | Y | Y | N | N | Y |
| 3 Boswell | N | Y | Y | Y | N | N | Y |
| 4 **Latham** | N | N | Y | N | N | N | Y |
| 5 **King** | N | N | Y | N | Y | Y | Y |
| **KANSAS** | | | | | | | |
| 1 **Moran** | N | N | Y | Y | Y | Y | Y |
| 2 **Ryun** | N | N | Y | N | Y | Y | Y |
| 3 Moore | N | Y | Y | Y | N | N | Y |
| 4 **Tiahrt** | N | N | Y | N | N | N | Y |
| **KENTUCKY** | | | | | | | |
| 1 **Whitfield** | N | N | Y | Y | N | N | Y |
| 2 **Lewis** | N | N | Y | N | Y | Y | Y |
| 3 **Northup** | N | ? | Y | N | N | N | Y |
| 4 **Davis** | N | N | Y | N | Y | N | N |
| 5 **Rogers** | N | N | Y | N | N | N | Y |
| 6 Chandler | N | Y | Y | Y | ? | N | Y |
| **LOUISIANA** | | | | | | | |
| 1 **Jindal** | N | N | Y | N | Y | Y | Y |
| 2 Jefferson | Y | Y | N | Y | N | N | Y |
| 3 Melancon | Y | Y | Y | Y | N | N | Y |
| 4 **McCrery** | N | N | Y | N | ? | N | Y |
| 5 **Alexander** | N | N | Y | N | N | N | Y |
| 6 **Baker** | N | N | Y | N | N | Y | Y |
| 7 **Boustany** | N | N | Y | N | N | N | Y |
| **MAINE** | | | | | | | |
| 1 Allen | Y | Y | N | Y | N | N | Y |
| 2 Michaud | Y | Y | N | Y | N | N | Y |
| **MARYLAND** | | | | | | | |
| 1 **Gilchrest** | Y | N | N | N | N | N | Y |
| 2 Ruppersberger | Y | Y | N | Y | N | N | Y |
| 3 Cardin | Y | Y | N | Y | N | N | Y |
| 4 Wynn | Y | Y | Y | Y | N | N | Y |
| 5 Hoyer | Y | Y | N | Y | N | N | Y |
| 6 **Bartlett** | Y | N | Y | Y | Y | Y | Y |
| 7 Cummings | N | Y | N | Y | N | N | Y |
| 8 Van Hollen | Y | Y | N | Y | N | N | Y |
| **MASSACHUSETTS** | | | | | | | |
| 1 Olver | Y | Y | N | Y | N | N | Y |
| 2 Neal | Y | Y | N | Y | N | N | Y |
| 3 McGovern | Y | Y | N | Y | N | N | Y |
| 4 Frank | Y | Y | N | Y | N | N | Y |
| 5 Meehan | Y | Y | N | Y | N | N | Y |
| 6 Tierney | Y | Y | N | Y | N | N | Y |
| 7 Markey | Y | Y | N | Y | N | N | Y |
| 8 Capuano | Y | Y | N | Y | N | N | Y |
| 9 Lynch | N | Y | Y | Y | N | N | Y |
| 10 Delahunt | Y | Y | N | Y | N | N | Y |
| **MICHIGAN** | | | | | | | |
| 1 Stupak | N | Y | N | Y | N | N | Y |
| 2 **Hoekstra** | N | N | Y | N | N | N | Y |
| 3 **Ehlers** | N | N | Y | Y | N | N | Y |
| 4 **Camp** | N | N | Y | N | N | N | Y |
| 5 Kildee | Y | Y | N | Y | N | N | Y |
| 6 **Upton** | N | N | Y | N | N | N | Y |
| 7 **Schwarz** | N | N | Y | Y | N | N | Y |
| 8 **Rogers** | N | N | Y | N | N | Y | ? |
| 9 **Knollenberg** | N | N | N | N | N | N | Y |
| 10 **Miller** | N | N | Y | N | N | N | Y |
| 11 **McCotter** | N | Y | Y | N | N | Y | Y |
| 12 Levin | N | Y | N | Y | N | N | Y |
| 13 Kilpatrick | Y | Y | N | Y | N | N | Y |
| 14 Conyers | ? | Y | N | Y | N | ? | Y |
| 15 Dingell | N | Y | N | Y | N | N | Y |
| **MINNESOTA** | | | | | | | |
| 1 **Gutknecht** | N | N | Y | N | N | Y | Y |
| 2 **Kline** | N | N | Y | N | N | N | Y |
| 3 **Ramstad** | N | N | Y | N | N | Y | Y |
| 4 McCollum | Y | Y | N | Y | N | N | Y |
| 5 Sabo | Y | Y | N | Y | N | N | Y |
| 6 **Kennedy** | N | N | Y | N | N | N | Y |
| 7 Peterson | N | N | Y | Y | N | N | Y |
| 8 Oberstar | ? | ? | ? | ? | ? | ? | ? |
| **MISSISSIPPI** | | | | | | | |
| 1 **Wicker** | N | N | Y | N | N | N | Y |
| 2 Thompson | N | Y | N | Y | N | N | Y |
| 3 **Pickering** | N | N | Y | N | N | N | Y |
| 4 Taylor | N | Y | Y | Y | Y | Y | Y |
| **MISSOURI** | | | | | | | |
| 1 Clay | Y | Y | N | Y | N | N | Y |
| 2 **Akin** | N | N | Y | N | Y | Y | Y |
| 3 Carnahan | Y | Y | N | Y | N | N | Y |
| 4 Skelton | N | Y | Y | Y | N | N | Y |
| 5 Cleaver | Y | Y | N | Y | N | N | Y |
| 6 **Graves** | N | N | Y | N | N | Y | N |
| 7 **Blunt** | N | N | Y | N | N | N | N |
| 8 **Emerson** | N | N | Y | Y | N | N | Y |
| 9 **Hulshof** | N | N | Y | N | Y | N | Y |
| **MONTANA** | | | | | | | |
| AL **Rehberg** | Y | N | Y | Y | N | N | Y |
| **NEBRASKA** | | | | | | | |
| 1 **Fortenberry** | N | N | Y | N | N | N | Y |
| 2 **Terry** | N | N | Y | N | N | N | Y |
| 3 **Osborne** | N | N | Y | N | N | N | Y |
| **NEVADA** | | | | | | | |
| 1 Berkley | Y | Y | N | Y | N | N | Y |
| 2 **Gibbons** | N | N | Y | N | Y | Y | Y |
| 3 **Porter** | Y | N | Y | Y | N | N | Y |
| **NEW HAMPSHIRE** | | | | | | | |
| 1 **Bradley** | N | N | Y | N | N | N | Y |
| 2 **Bass** | N | N | Y | N | N | Y | Y |
| **NEW JERSEY** | | | | | | | |
| 1 Andrews | Y | Y | N | Y | N | N | Y |
| 2 **LoBiondo** | N | N | Y | N | N | N | Y |
| 3 **Saxton** | N | N | Y | N | N | N | Y |
| 4 **Smith** | N | N | Y | N | N | N | Y |
| 5 **Garrett** | ? | ? | ? | ? | Y | Y | Y |
| 6 Pallone | Y | Y | N | Y | N | N | Y |
| 7 **Ferguson** | N | N | Y | N | N | N | Y |
| 8 Pascrell | Y | Y | N | Y | N | N | Y |
| 9 Rothman | Y | Y | N | Y | N | N | Y |
| 10 Payne | Y | Y | N | Y | N | N | Y |
| 11 **Frelinghuysen** | N | N | Y | N | N | N | Y |
| 12 Holt | Y | Y | N | Y | N | N | Y |
| 13 Menendez | Y | Y | N | Y | N | N | Y |
| **NEW MEXICO** | | | | | | | |
| 1 **Wilson** | N | N | N | N | N | N | Y |
| 2 **Pearce** | N | N | Y | N | N | N | Y |
| 3 Udall | Y | Y | N | Y | N | N | Y |
| **NEW YORK** | | | | | | | |
| 1 Bishop | Y | Y | N | Y | N | N | Y |
| 2 Israel | Y | Y | N | Y | N | N | Y |
| 3 **King** | N | N | Y | N | N | N | Y |
| 4 McCarthy | Y | Y | N | Y | N | N | Y |
| 5 Ackerman | Y | Y | N | Y | N | N | Y |
| 6 Meeks | Y | Y | N | Y | N | N | Y |
| 7 Crowley | Y | Y | N | Y | N | N | Y |
| 8 Nadler | Y | Y | N | Y | N | N | Y |
| 9 Weiner | Y | Y | N | Y | N | N | Y |
| 10 Towns | Y | Y | N | Y | N | N | Y |
| 11 Owens | Y | Y | N | Y | N | N | Y |
| 12 Velázquez | Y | Y | N | Y | N | N | Y |
| 13 **Fossella** | N | N | Y | N | N | Y | Y |
| 14 Maloney | Y | Y | N | Y | N | N | Y |
| 15 Rangel | Y | Y | N | Y | N | N | Y |
| 16 Serrano | Y | Y | N | Y | N | N | Y |
| 17 Engel | Y | Y | N | Y | N | N | Y |
| 18 Lowey | Y | Y | N | Y | N | N | Y |
| 19 **Kelly** | N | N | Y | N | N | N | Y |
| 20 **Sweeney** | N | N | N | N | N | N | Y |
| 21 McNulty | Y | Y | N | Y | N | N | Y |
| 22 Hinchey | Y | Y | N | Y | N | N | Y |
| 23 **McHugh** | N | N | N | N | N | N | Y |
| 24 **Boehlert** | N | N | N | Y | N | N | Y |
| 25 **Walsh** | N | N | Y | N | N | N | Y |
| 26 **Reynolds** | N | N | Y | N | N | N | Y |
| 27 Higgins | Y | Y | Y | Y | N | N | Y |
| 28 Slaughter | Y | Y | N | Y | N | N | Y |
| 29 **Kuhl** | N | N | Y | N | N | N | Y |
| **NORTH CAROLINA** | | | | | | | |
| 1 Butterfield | Y | Y | N | Y | N | N | Y |
| 2 Etheridge | N | Y | Y | Y | N | N | Y |
| 3 **Jones** | N | N | Y | Y | Y | Y | Y |
| 4 Price | Y | Y | N | Y | N | N | Y |
| 5 **Foxx** | N | N | Y | N | Y | Y | Y |
| 6 **Coble** | N | N | Y | N | Y | Y | Y |
| 7 McIntyre | N | Y | Y | Y | N | N | Y |
| 8 **Hayes** | N | N | Y | N | N | N | N |
| 9 **Myrick** | N | N | Y | N | N | Y | Y |
| 10 **McHenry** | N | N | Y | N | Y | Y | Y |
| 11 **Taylor** | N | N | Y | Y | N | N | Y |
| 12 Watt | Y | Y | N | Y | N | N | Y |
| 13 Miller | N | Y | N | Y | N | N | Y |
| **NORTH DAKOTA** | | | | | | | |
| AL Pomeroy | N | Y | Y | Y | N | N | Y |
| **OHIO** | | | | | | | |
| 1 **Chabot** | N | N | Y | N | N | Y | Y |
| 2 Vacant | | | | | | | |
| 3 **Turner** | N | N | Y | N | N | N | Y |
| 4 **Oxley** | N | N | Y | N | N | N | Y |
| 5 **Gillmor** | N | N | Y | Y | N | N | Y |
| 6 Strickland | Y | Y | N | Y | N | N | Y |
| 7 **Hobson** | N | N | Y | N | N | N | Y |
| 8 **Boehner** | N | N | Y | N | N | N | Y |
| 9 Kaptur | Y | Y | Y | Y | N | N | Y |
| 10 Kucinich | Y | Y | N | Y | N | N | Y |
| 11 Jones | Y | Y | N | Y | N | N | Y |
| 12 **Tiberi** | N | N | Y | N | Y | N | Y |
| 13 Brown | Y | Y | N | Y | N | N | Y |
| 14 **LaTourette** | N | N | Y | Y | N | N | Y |
| 15 **Pryce** | N | N | Y | N | ? | N | Y |
| 16 **Regula** | N | N | Y | N | N | N | Y |
| 17 Ryan | Y | Y | N | Y | N | N | Y |
| 18 **Ney** | N | N | Y | Y | Y | N | Y |
| **OKLAHOMA** | | | | | | | |
| 1 **Sullivan** | N | ? | ? | ? | N | N | Y |
| 2 Boren | N | Y | Y | N | N | N | Y |
| 3 **Lucas** | N | N | Y | N | N | N | Y |
| 4 **Cole** | N | N | Y | N | N | N | Y |
| 5 **Istook** | N | N | Y | N | N | N | Y |
| **OREGON** | | | | | | | |
| 1 Wu | Y | Y | N | Y | N | N | Y |
| 2 **Walden** | N | N | Y | Y | N | N | Y |
| 3 Blumenauer | Y | Y | N | Y | N | N | Y |
| 4 DeFazio | Y | Y | N | Y | N | N | Y |
| 5 Hooley | Y | Y | N | Y | N | N | Y |
| **PENNSYLVANIA** | | | | | | | |
| 1 Brady | Y | Y | N | Y | N | N | Y |
| 2 Fattah | Y | Y | N | Y | N | N | Y |
| 3 **English** | N | N | Y | N | N | N | Y |
| 4 **Hart** | N | N | Y | N | N | Y | Y |
| 5 **Peterson** | N | N | Y | Y | Y | N | Y |
| 6 **Gerlach** | N | N | Y | N | N | N | Y |
| 7 **Weldon** | N | ? | ? | ? | N | N | Y |
| 8 **Fitzpatrick** | N | N | Y | Y | N | N | Y |
| 9 **Shuster** | N | N | Y | N | Y | Y | Y |
| 10 **Sherwood** | N | N | Y | N | N | N | Y |
| 11 Kanjorski | Y | Y | N | Y | N | N | Y |
| 12 Murtha | N | Y | N | Y | N | N | Y |
| 13 Schwartz | N | Y | N | Y | N | N | Y |
| 14 Doyle | Y | Y | N | Y | N | N | Y |
| 15 **Dent** | N | N | N | N | N | N | Y |
| 16 **Pitts** | N | N | Y | N | N | ? | Y |
| 17 Holden | N | Y | N | Y | N | N | Y |
| 18 **Murphy** | N | N | Y | N | N | N | Y |
| 19 **Platts** | N | N | Y | N | Y | N | Y |
| **RHODE ISLAND** | | | | | | | |
| 1 Kennedy | Y | Y | N | Y | N | N | Y |
| 2 Langevin | N | Y | Y | Y | N | N | Y |
| **SOUTH CAROLINA** | | | | | | | |
| 1 **Brown** | N | N | Y | N | N | N | Y |
| 2 **Wilson** | N | N | Y | N | Y | Y | Y |
| 3 **Barrett** | N | N | Y | N | Y | Y | Y |
| 4 **Inglis** | N | N | Y | N | N | Y | Y |
| 5 Spratt | N | Y | N | Y | N | N | Y |
| 6 Clyburn | N | Y | N | Y | N | N | Y |
| **SOUTH DAKOTA** | | | | | | | |
| AL Herseth | N | Y | Y | Y | N | N | Y |
| **TENNESSEE** | | | | | | | |
| 1 **Jenkins** | N | N | Y | N | N | Y | Y |
| 2 **Duncan** | N | N | Y | Y | Y | Y | Y |
| 3 **Wamp** | N | N | Y | N | Y | N | Y |
| 4 Davis | N | Y | Y | Y | N | N | Y |
| 5 Cooper | N | Y | N | Y | N | N | Y |
| 6 Gordon | N | Y | Y | Y | N | N | Y |
| 7 **Blackburn** | N | N | Y | N | N | Y | Y |
| 8 Tanner | N | Y | Y | Y | N | Y | Y |
| 9 Ford | N | Y | N | Y | N | N | Y |
| **TEXAS** | | | | | | | |
| 1 **Gohmert** | N | N | Y | N | N | Y | Y |
| 2 **Poe** | N | N | Y | Y | N | Y | Y |
| 3 **Johnson, S.** | N | N | Y | N | Y | Y | Y |
| 4 **Hall** | N | N | Y | N | N | Y | Y |
| 5 **Hensarling** | N | N | Y | N | N | Y | Y |
| 6 **Barton** | N | N | Y | N | N | Y | Y |
| 7 **Culberson** | N | N | Y | N | N | N | Y |
| 8 **Brady** | N | N | Y | N | N | Y | Y |
| 9 Green, A. | Y | Y | N | Y | N | N | Y |
| 10 **McCaul** | N | N | Y | N | N | N | Y |
| 11 **Conaway** | N | N | Y | N | N | N | Y |
| 12 **Granger** | N | N | N | N | N | N | Y |
| 13 **Thornberry** | N | N | Y | N | N | N | Y |
| 14 **Paul** | Y | N | Y | Y | Y | Y | Y |
| 15 Hinojosa | N | Y | Y | Y | N | N | Y |
| 16 Reyes | N | Y | Y | Y | N | N | Y |
| 17 Edwards | N | Y | N | Y | N | N | Y |
| 18 Jackson-Lee | Y | Y | N | Y | N | N | Y |
| 19 **Neugebauer** | N | N | Y | N | Y | Y | Y |
| 20 Gonzalez | Y | Y | N | Y | N | N | Y |
| 21 **Smith** | N | N | Y | N | N | N | Y |
| 22 **DeLay** | N | N | Y | N | N | N | Y |
| 23 **Bonilla** | N | N | Y | N | N | N | N |
| 24 **Marchant** | N | N | Y | N | N | N | Y |
| 25 Doggett | Y | Y | N | Y | N | N | Y |
| 26 **Burgess** | N | N | Y | Y | Y | N | Y |
| 27 Ortiz | N | Y | Y | Y | N | N | Y |
| 28 Cuellar | ? | ? | ? | ? | ? | ? | ? |
| 29 Green, G. | N | Y | Y | Y | N | N | Y |
| 30 Johnson, E. | Y | Y | N | Y | N | N | Y |
| 31 **Carter** | N | N | Y | N | N | N | Y |
| 32 **Sessions** | ? | ? | ? | ? | ? | ? | ? |
| **UTAH** | | | | | | | |
| 1 **Bishop** | N | N | Y | Y | Y | Y | Y |
| 2 Matheson | N | Y | Y | Y | N | N | Y |
| 3 **Cannon** | N | N | Y | N | Y | Y | Y |
| **VERMONT** | | | | | | | |
| AL *Sanders* | Y | Y | N | Y | N | N | Y |
| **VIRGINIA** | | | | | | | |
| 1 **Davis, J.** | N | N | Y | N | Y | N | Y |
| 2 **Drake** | N | N | Y | N | N | N | Y |
| 3 Scott | Y | Y | N | Y | N | N | Y |
| 4 **Forbes** | N | N | Y | N | Y | N | Y |
| 5 **Goode** | N | N | Y | N | Y | N | Y |
| 6 **Goodlatte** | N | N | Y | N | N | N | Y |
| 7 **Cantor** | N | N | Y | N | N | N | ? |
| 8 Moran | Y | Y | N | Y | N | N | Y |
| 9 Boucher | Y | Y | ? | Y | N | N | Y |
| 10 **Wolf** | N | N | N | N | N | N | Y |
| 11 **Davis, T.** | N | N | N | N | ? | N | Y |
| **WASHINGTON** | | | | | | | |
| 1 Inslee | Y | Y | N | Y | N | N | Y |
| 2 Larsen | N | Y | N | Y | N | N | Y |
| 3 Baird | Y | Y | N | Y | N | N | Y |
| 4 **Hastings** | N | N | Y | N | N | N | Y |
| 5 **McMorris** | N | N | Y | N | N | Y | Y |
| 6 Dicks | N | Y | N | Y | N | N | Y |
| 7 McDermott | Y | Y | N | Y | N | N | Y |
| 8 **Reichert** | N | N | Y | N | N | N | Y |
| 9 Smith | Y | Y | N | Y | N | N | Y |
| **WEST VIRGINIA** | | | | | | | |
| 1 Mollohan | N | Y | N | Y | N | N | Y |
| 2 **Capito** | N | N | Y | N | N | N | Y |
| 3 Rahall | N | Y | Y | Y | N | N | Y |
| **WISCONSIN** | | | | | | | |
| 1 **Ryan** | N | N | Y | N | N | Y | Y |
| 2 Baldwin | Y | Y | N | Y | N | N | Y |
| 3 Kind | Y | Y | N | Y | N | N | Y |
| 4 Moore | Y | Y | N | Y | N | N | Y |
| 5 **Sensenbrenner** | N | N | Y | N | N | Y | Y |
| 6 **Petri** | N | N | Y | Y | N | Y | Y |
| 7 Obey | Y | Y | N | Y | N | N | Y |
| 8 **Green** | N | N | Y | N | N | N | Y |
| **WYOMING** | | | | | | | |
| AL **Cubin** | N | N | Y | Y | Y | Y | Y |

# IN THE HOUSE | By Vote Number

**262.** HR 2862. Fiscal 2006 Commerce-Justice-Science Appropriations/ **Immigration Standards.** Tancredo, R-Colo., amendment that would prohibit the use of funds for the State Criminal Alien Assistance Program by any state or local government entity that restricts its officials from transmitting information regarding an individual's citizenship or immigration status to the Department of Homeland Security. Rejected 204-222: R 189-37; D 15-184 (ND 7-142, SD 8-42); I 0-1. June 16, 2005.

**263.** HR 2862. Fiscal 2006 Commerce-Justice-Science Appropriations/ **Immigration and Trade Agreements.** Tancredo, R-Colo., amendment that would prohibit the use of funds in the bill to include provisions in any trade agreement that would increase the number of aliens permitted into the United States as non-immigrants or permanent residents. Rejected 106-322: R 89-139; D 17-182 (ND 11-138, SD 6-44); I 0-1. June 16, 2005.

**264.** HR 2862. Fiscal 2006 Commerce-Justice-Science Appropriations/ **Racial Conviction Distribution.** Jackson-Lee, D-Texas, amendment that would prohibit funds in the bill to be used to fund state or local anti-drug task forces that do not collect and make available data on the racial distribution of convictions. Rejected 183-244: R 2-226; D 180-18 (ND 137-11, SD 43-7); I 1-0. June 16, 2005.

**265.** HR 2862. Fiscal 2006 Commerce-Justice-Science Appropriations/ **Firearms Exportation.** Moran, D-Va., amendment that would prohibit the use of funds in the bill to license the export of non-automatic or semiautomatic .50 caliber firearms. Rejected 149-278: R 15-212; D 134-65 (ND 114-36, SD 20-29); I 0-1. June 16, 2005.

**266.** HR 2862. Fiscal 2006 Commerce-Justice-Science Appropriations/ **U.N. Population Fund.** Maloney, D-N.Y., amendment that would prohibit the use of funds in the bill to enforce any provision of law that restricts or prohibits funding for the U.N. Population Fund. Rejected 192-233: R 19-209; D 172-24 (ND 132-15, SD 40-9); I 1-0. June 16, 2005.

**267.** HR 2862. Fiscal 2006 Commerce-Justice-Science Appropriations/ **Illegal Immigration.** King, R-Iowa, amendment that would increase by $1 million funds for provisions in current law that allow state or local officials to transmit information regarding an individual's citizenship or immigration status to the Homeland Security Department. It would be offset by a reduction in salaries, expenses and general legal activities at the Justice Department. Adopted 218-208: R 208-20; D 10-187 (ND 3-144, SD 7-43); I 0-1. June 16, 2005.

| | 262 | 263 | 264 | 265 | 266 | 267 |
|---|---|---|---|---|---|---|
| **ALABAMA** | | | | | | |
| 1 Bonner | Y | N | N | N | N | Y |
| 2 Everett | Y | N | N | N | N | Y |
| 3 Rogers | Y | Y | N | N | N | Y |
| 4 Aderholt | Y | Y | N | N | N | Y |
| 5 Cramer | Y | N | N | N | Y | N |
| 6 Bachus | Y | N | N | N | N | Y |
| 7 Davis | N | N | Y | N | Y | N |
| **ALASKA** | | | | | | |
| AL Young | N | N | N | N | N | N |
| **ARIZONA** | | | | | | |
| 1 Renzi | Y | Y | N | N | N | Y |
| 2 Franks | Y | Y | N | N | N | Y |
| 3 Shadegg | Y | N | N | N | N | Y |
| 4 Pastor | N | N | Y | Y | Y | N |
| 5 Hayworth | Y | Y | N | N | N | Y |
| 6 Flake | Y | N | N | N | N | N |
| 7 Grijalva | N | N | Y | Y | Y | N |
| 8 Kolbe | Y | N | N | N | N | Y |
| **ARKANSAS** | | | | | | |
| 1 Berry | N | N | Y | N | Y | N |
| 2 Snyder | N | N | Y | N | Y | N |
| 3 Boozman | Y | Y | N | N | N | Y |
| 4 Ross | N | N | Y | N | N | N |
| **CALIFORNIA** | | | | | | |
| 1 Thompson | N | N | Y | N | Y | N |
| 2 Herger | Y | N | N | N | N | Y |
| 3 Lungren | Y | N | N | N | N | Y |
| 4 Doolittle | Y | N | N | N | N | Y |
| 5 Matsui, D. | N | N | Y | Y | Y | N |
| 6 Woolsey | N | N | Y | Y | Y | N |
| 7 Miller, George | N | N | Y | Y | Y | N |
| 8 Pelosi | N | N | Y | Y | Y | N |
| 9 Lee | N | N | Y | Y | Y | N |
| 10 Tauscher | N | N | Y | Y | Y | N |
| 11 Pombo | Y | Y | N | N | N | Y |
| 12 Lantos | N | N | Y | Y | Y | N |
| 13 Stark | N | N | Y | Y | Y | N |
| 14 Eshoo | N | N | Y | Y | Y | N |
| 15 Honda | N | N | Y | Y | Y | N |
| 16 Lofgren | N | N | Y | Y | Y | N |
| 17 Farr | N | N | Y | Y | Y | N |
| 18 Cardoza | N | N | Y | N | Y | N |
| 19 Radanovich | Y | N | N | N | N | Y |
| 20 Costa | Y | N | N | N | Y | N |
| 21 Nunes | Y | N | N | N | N | Y |
| 22 Thomas | Y | N | N | N | N | Y |
| 23 Capps | N | N | Y | Y | Y | N |
| 24 Gallegly | Y | N | N | N | N | Y |
| 25 McKeon | Y | N | N | N | N | Y |
| 26 Dreier | Y | N | N | N | N | Y |
| 27 Sherman | N | N | Y | Y | Y | N |
| 28 Berman | N | N | Y | Y | Y | N |
| 29 Schiff | N | N | Y | Y | Y | N |
| 30 Waxman | N | N | Y | Y | Y | N |
| 31 Becerra | N | N | Y | Y | Y | N |
| 32 Solis | N | N | Y | Y | Y | N |
| 33 Watson | N | N | Y | Y | Y | N |
| 34 Roybal-Allard | N | N | Y | Y | Y | N |
| 35 Waters | N | N | Y | Y | Y | ? |
| 36 Harman | N | N | Y | Y | Y | N |
| 37 Millender-McD. | N | N | Y | Y | Y | N |
| 38 Napolitano | N | N | Y | Y | Y | N |
| 39 Sánchez, Linda | N | N | Y | Y | Y | N |
| 40 Royce | Y | Y | N | N | N | Y |
| 41 Lewis | N | N | N | N | N | N |
| 42 Miller, Gary | Y | Y | N | N | N | Y |
| 43 Baca | N | N | Y | N | Y | N |
| 44 Calvert | Y | N | N | N | N | Y |
| 45 Bono | ? | ? | ? | ? | ? | ? |
| 46 Rohrabacher | Y | Y | N | N | N | Y |
| 47 Sanchez, Loretta | N | N | Y | Y | Y | N |
| 48 Cox | Y | Y | N | N | N | Y |
| 49 Issa | Y | N | N | N | N | Y |

| | 262 | 263 | 264 | 265 | 266 | 267 |
|---|---|---|---|---|---|---|
| 50 Cunningham | Y | N | N | N | N | Y |
| 51 Filner | N | N | Y | Y | Y | N |
| 52 Hunter | ? | Y | N | N | N | Y |
| 53 Davis | N | N | Y | Y | Y | N |
| **COLORADO** | | | | | | |
| 1 DeGette | N | N | Y | Y | Y | N |
| 2 Udall | N | N | Y | N | Y | N |
| 3 Salazar | N | N | Y | N | Y | N |
| 4 Musgrave | Y | N | N | N | N | Y |
| 5 Hefley | Y | Y | N | N | N | Y |
| 6 Tancredo | Y | Y | N | N | N | Y |
| 7 Beauprez | Y | N | N | N | N | Y |
| **CONNECTICUT** | | | | | | |
| 1 Larson | N | N | Y | Y | Y | N |
| 2 Simmons | N | N | N | N | Y | Y |
| 3 DeLauro | N | N | Y | Y | Y | N |
| 4 Shays | Y | N | Y | Y | Y | Y |
| 5 Johnson | Y | N | Y | Y | Y | Y |
| **DELAWARE** | | | | | | |
| AL Castle | N | N | N | Y | Y | Y |
| **FLORIDA** | | | | | | |
| 1 Miller | Y | Y | N | N | N | Y |
| 2 Boyd | N | N | N | N | Y | N |
| 3 Brown | N | N | Y | Y | Y | N |
| 4 Crenshaw | Y | Y | N | N | N | Y |
| 5 Brown-Waite | Y | Y | N | N | N | Y |
| 6 Stearns | Y | Y | N | N | N | Y |
| 7 Mica | Y | Y | N | N | N | Y |
| 8 Keller | Y | Y | N | N | N | Y |
| 9 Bilirakis | Y | Y | N | N | N | Y |
| 10 Young | Y | Y | N | N | N | Y |
| 11 Davis | N | N | Y | Y | Y | N |
| 12 Putnam | Y | Y | N | N | N | Y |
| 13 Harris | Y | Y | N | N | N | Y |
| 14 Mack | Y | Y | N | N | N | Y |
| 15 Weldon | Y | Y | N | N | N | Y |
| 16 Foley | + | N | N | N | Y | N |
| 17 Meek | N | N | Y | Y | Y | N |
| 18 Ros-Lehtinen | N | N | N | N | N | Y |
| 19 Wexler | N | N | Y | Y | Y | N |
| 20 Wasserman-Schultz | N | N | Y | Y | Y | N |
| 21 Diaz-Balart, L. | N | N | N | N | N | N |
| 22 Shaw | Y | N | N | N | N | Y |
| 23 Hastings | N | N | Y | Y | Y | N |
| 24 Feeney | Y | Y | N | N | N | Y |
| 25 Diaz-Balart, M. | N | N | N | N | N | N |
| **GEORGIA** | | | | | | |
| 1 Kingston | Y | N | N | N | N | Y |
| 2 Bishop | N | N | N | Y | N | N |
| 3 Marshall | Y | Y | Y | N | N | Y |
| 4 McKinney | N | N | Y | Y | Y | N |
| 5 Lewis | N | N | Y | Y | Y | N |
| 6 Price | Y | N | N | N | N | Y |
| 7 Linder | Y | N | N | N | N | Y |
| 8 Westmoreland | Y | N | N | N | N | Y |
| 9 Norwood | Y | Y | N | N | N | Y |
| 10 Deal | Y | Y | N | N | N | Y |
| 11 Gingrey | Y | Y | N | N | N | Y |
| 12 Barrow | Y | Y | Y | N | Y | N |
| 13 Scott | N | N | Y | Y | Y | N |
| **HAWAII** | | | | | | |
| 1 Abercrombie | N | Y | Y | Y | Y | N |
| 2 Case | Y | Y | N | Y | Y | Y |
| **IDAHO** | | | | | | |
| 1 Otter | Y | N | N | N | N | Y |
| 2 Simpson | Y | Y | N | N | N | Y |
| **ILLINOIS** | | | | | | |
| 1 Rush | N | N | ? | Y | Y | N |
| 2 Jackson | N | N | Y | Y | Y | N |
| 3 Lipinski | N | N | Y | Y | Y | N |
| 4 Gutierrez | N | N | Y | Y | Y | N |
| 5 Emanuel | N | N | Y | Y | Y | N |
| 6 Hyde | Y | N | N | N | N | Y |
| 7 Davis | N | N | Y | Y | Y | N |
| 8 Bean | N | N | Y | Y | Y | N |
| 9 Schakowsky | N | N | Y | Y | Y | N |
| 10 Kirk | N | N | N | Y | Y | N |
| 11 Weller | N | N | N | N | N | Y |
| 12 Costello | N | N | Y | N | N | N |

ND Northern Democrats, SD Southern Democrats
Southern states: Ala., Ark., Fla., Ga., Ky., La., Miss., N.C., Okla., S.C., Tenn., Texas, Va.

| | 262 | 263 | 264 | 265 | 266 | 267 |
|---|---|---|---|---|---|---|
| 13 **Biggert** | N | N | N | N | Y | N |
| 14 **Hastert** | | | | | | |
| 15 **Johnson** | N | N | N | N | N | Y |
| 16 **Manzullo** | Y | Y | N | N | N | Y |
| 17 Evans | N | N | Y | Y | Y | N |
| 18 **LaHood** | Y | N | N | N | N | Y |
| 19 **Shimkus** | Y | N | N | N | N | Y |
| **INDIANA** | | | | | | |
| 1 Visclosky | N | N | Y | N | Y | N |
| 2 **Chocola** | Y | N | N | N | N | Y |
| 3 **Souder** | Y | N | N | N | N | Y |
| 4 **Buyer** | Y | N | N | N | N | Y |
| 5 **Burton** | Y | N | N | N | N | Y |
| 6 **Pence** | Y | Y | N | N | N | Y |
| 7 Carson | N | N | Y | Y | Y | N |
| 8 **Hostettler** | Y | Y | N | N | N | Y |
| 9 **Sodrel** | Y | Y | N | N | N | Y |
| **IOWA** | | | | | | |
| 1 **Nussle** | Y | N | N | N | N | Y |
| 2 **Leach** | N | N | N | Y | Y | Y |
| 3 Boswell | N | N | N | N | Y | N |
| 4 **Latham** | Y | N | N | N | N | Y |
| 5 **King** | Y | Y | N | N | N | Y |
| **KANSAS** | | | | | | |
| 1 **Moran** | Y | Y | N | N | N | Y |
| 2 **Ryun** | Y | Y | N | N | N | Y |
| 3 Moore | N | N | Y | Y | Y | N |
| 4 **Tiahrt** | Y | N | N | N | N | Y |
| **KENTUCKY** | | | | | | |
| 1 **Whitfield** | Y | Y | N | N | N | Y |
| 2 **Lewis** | Y | N | N | N | N | Y |
| 3 **Northup** | Y | N | N | N | N | Y |
| 4 **Davis** | Y | N | N | N | N | Y |
| 5 **Rogers** | Y | N | N | N | N | Y |
| 6 Chandler | N | N | N | N | Y | Y |
| **LOUISIANA** | | | | | | |
| 1 **Jindal** | Y | N | N | N | N | Y |
| 2 Jefferson | N | N | Y | N | Y | N |
| 3 Melancon | N | Y | N | N | N | N |
| 4 **McCrery** | Y | N | N | N | N | Y |
| 5 **Alexander** | Y | N | N | N | N | Y |
| 6 **Baker** | Y | N | N | N | N | Y |
| 7 **Boustany** | Y | N | N | N | N | Y |
| **MAINE** | | | | | | |
| 1 Allen | N | N | Y | Y | Y | N |
| 2 Michaud | N | N | Y | N | Y | N |
| **MARYLAND** | | | | | | |
| 1 **Gilchrest** | N | N | N | Y | Y | N |
| 2 Ruppersberger | N | N | Y | N | Y | N |
| 3 Cardin | N | N | Y | Y | Y | N |
| 4 Wynn | N | N | Y | Y | Y | N |
| 5 Hoyer | N | N | Y | Y | Y | N |
| 6 **Bartlett** | Y | Y | N | N | N | Y |
| 7 Cummings | N | N | Y | Y | Y | N |
| 8 Van Hollen | N | N | Y | Y | Y | N |
| **MASSACHUSETTS** | | | | | | |
| 1 Olver | N | N | Y | Y | Y | N |
| 2 Neal | N | N | Y | Y | Y | N |
| 3 McGovern | N | N | Y | Y | Y | N |
| 4 Frank | N | N | Y | Y | Y | N |
| 5 Meehan | N | N | Y | Y | Y | N |
| 6 Tierney | ? | N | Y | Y | Y | N |
| 7 Markey | N | N | Y | Y | Y | N |
| 8 Capuano | N | N | Y | Y | Y | N |
| 9 Lynch | N | N | Y | Y | Y | N |
| 10 Delahunt | N | ? | Y | Y | ? | N |
| **MICHIGAN** | | | | | | |
| 1 Stupak | N | N | Y | N | N | N |
| 2 **Hoekstra** | Y | N | N | N | N | Y |
| 3 **Ehlers** | N | N | N | Y | N | N |
| 4 **Camp** | Y | N | N | N | N | Y |
| 5 Kildee | N | N | Y | N | N | N |
| 6 **Upton** | Y | N | N | N | N | Y |
| 7 **Schwarz** | N | N | N | N | N | Y |
| 8 **Rogers** | Y | Y | N | N | N | Y |
| 9 **Knollenberg** | N | N | N | N | N | N |
| 10 **Miller** | Y | Y | N | N | N | Y |
| 11 **McCotter** | Y | Y | N | N | N | Y |
| 12 Levin | N | N | Y | Y | Y | N |
| 13 Kilpatrick | N | N | Y | Y | Y | N |
| 14 Conyers | N | N | Y | Y | ? | N |
| 15 Dingell | N | N | Y | N | Y | N |

| | 262 | 263 | 264 | 265 | 266 | 267 |
|---|---|---|---|---|---|---|
| **MINNESOTA** | | | | | | |
| 1 **Gutknecht** | Y | Y | N | N | N | Y |
| 2 **Kline** | Y | N | N | N | N | Y |
| 3 **Ramstad** | Y | N | N | Y | Y | Y |
| 4 McCollum | N | N | Y | Y | Y | N |
| 5 Sabo | N | N | Y | Y | Y | N |
| 6 **Kennedy** | Y | N | N | N | N | Y |
| 7 Peterson | Y | Y | N | N | N | Y |
| 8 Oberstar | ? | ? | ? | ? | ? | ? |
| **MISSISSIPPI** | | | | | | |
| 1 **Wicker** | Y | N | N | N | N | Y |
| 2 Thompson | N | N | Y | Y | Y | N |
| 3 **Pickering** | Y | N | N | N | N | Y |
| 4 Taylor | Y | Y | N | N | N | Y |
| **MISSOURI** | | | | | | |
| 1 Clay | N | N | Y | Y | Y | N |
| 2 **Akin** | Y | Y | N | N | N | Y |
| 3 Carnahan | N | N | Y | Y | Y | N |
| 4 Skelton | Y | Y | Y | N | N | N |
| 5 Cleaver | N | N | Y | Y | Y | N |
| 6 **Graves** | Y | Y | N | N | N | Y |
| 7 **Blunt** | Y | N | N | N | N | Y |
| 8 **Emerson** | Y | Y | N | N | N | Y |
| 9 **Hulshof** | Y | N | N | N | N | Y |
| **MONTANA** | | | | | | |
| AL **Rehberg** | Y | Y | N | N | N | Y |
| **NEBRASKA** | | | | | | |
| 1 **Fortenberry** | Y | N | N | N | N | Y |
| 2 **Terry** | N | N | N | N | N | Y |
| 3 **Osborne** | Y | N | N | N | N | Y |
| **NEVADA** | | | | | | |
| 1 Berkley | N | N | Y | Y | Y | N |
| 2 **Gibbons** | Y | Y | N | N | N | Y |
| 3 **Porter** | N | N | N | N | N | N |
| **NEW HAMPSHIRE** | | | | | | |
| 1 **Bradley** | Y | Y | N | N | Y | Y |
| 2 **Bass** | Y | N | N | N | Y | Y |
| **NEW JERSEY** | | | | | | |
| 1 Andrews | N | N | Y | Y | Y | N |
| 2 **LoBiondo** | N | Y | N | Y | N | Y |
| 3 **Saxton** | N | N | N | N | N | Y |
| 4 **Smith** | Y | N | N | N | N | Y |
| 5 **Garrett** | Y | Y | N | N | N | Y |
| 6 Pallone | N | N | Y | Y | Y | N |
| 7 **Ferguson** | N | N | N | Y | N | N |
| 8 Pascrell | N | Y | Y | Y | Y | N |
| 9 Rothman | N | N | Y | Y | Y | N |
| 10 Payne | N | N | Y | Y | Y | N |
| 11 **Frelinghuysen** | N | N | N | N | Y | Y |
| 12 Holt | N | N | Y | Y | Y | N |
| 13 Menendez | N | N | Y | Y | Y | N |
| **NEW MEXICO** | | | | | | |
| 1 **Wilson** | N | N | N | N | N | N |
| 2 **Pearce** | Y | N | N | N | N | Y |
| 3 Udall | N | N | Y | Y | Y | N |
| **NEW YORK** | | | | | | |
| 1 Bishop | N | N | Y | Y | Y | N |
| 2 Israel | N | N | Y | Y | Y | N |
| 3 **King** | Y | N | N | N | N | Y |
| 4 McCarthy | N | N | Y | Y | Y | N |
| 5 Ackerman | N | N | Y | N | Y | N |
| 6 Meeks | N | N | Y | Y | Y | N |
| 7 Crowley | N | N | Y | N | Y | N |
| 8 Nadler | N | N | Y | Y | Y | N |
| 9 Weiner | N | N | Y | Y | Y | N |
| 10 Towns | N | N | Y | Y | Y | N |
| 11 Owens | N | N | Y | Y | Y | N |
| 12 Velázquez | N | N | Y | Y | Y | N |
| 13 **Fossella** | N | N | N | N | N | Y |
| 14 Maloney | N | N | Y | Y | Y | N |
| 15 Rangel | N | N | Y | Y | Y | N |
| 16 Serrano | N | N | Y | Y | Y | N |
| 17 Engel | N | N | Y | Y | Y | N |
| 18 Lowey | N | N | Y | Y | Y | N |
| 19 **Kelly** | N | N | N | N | Y | Y |
| 20 **Sweeney** | Y | Y | N | N | N | Y |
| 21 McNulty | N | N | Y | N | Y | N |
| 22 Hinchey | N | N | Y | Y | ? | ? |
| 23 **McHugh** | Y | Y | N | N | N | Y |
| 24 **Boehlert** | N | N | N | N | Y | Y |
| 25 **Walsh** | Y | N | N | N | N | N |
| 26 **Reynolds** | N | N | N | N | N | Y |
| 27 Higgins | N | N | Y | Y | Y | N |
| 28 Slaughter | N | N | Y | Y | Y | N |
| 29 **Kuhl** | N | N | N | N | N | Y |

| | 262 | 263 | 264 | 265 | 266 | 267 |
|---|---|---|---|---|---|---|
| **NORTH CAROLINA** | | | | | | |
| 1 Butterfield | N | N | Y | N | Y | N |
| 2 Etheridge | N | N | Y | N | Y | N |
| 3 **Jones** | Y | Y | N | N | N | Y |
| 4 Price | N | N | Y | Y | Y | N |
| 5 **Foxx** | Y | Y | N | N | N | Y |
| 6 **Coble** | Y | Y | N | N | N | Y |
| 7 McIntyre | N | N | Y | N | N | Y |
| 8 **Hayes** | Y | Y | N | N | N | Y |
| 9 **Myrick** | Y | N | N | N | N | Y |
| 10 **McHenry** | Y | Y | N | N | N | Y |
| 11 **Taylor** | Y | Y | N | N | N | Y |
| 12 Watt | N | N | Y | Y | Y | N |
| 13 Miller | N | N | Y | Y | Y | N |
| **NORTH DAKOTA** | | | | | | |
| AL Pomeroy | N | N | N | N | Y | N |
| **OHIO** | | | | | | |
| 1 **Chabot** | Y | Y | N | N | N | Y |
| 2 Vacant | | | | | | |
| 3 **Turner** | Y | N | N | N | N | Y |
| 4 **Oxley** | Y | N | N | ? | N | Y |
| 5 **Gillmor** | Y | Y | N | N | N | Y |
| 6 Strickland | N | Y | Y | N | Y | N |
| 7 **Hobson** | Y | N | N | N | N | Y |
| 8 **Boehner** | Y | N | N | N | N | Y |
| 9 Kaptur | N | Y | Y | N | N | N |
| 10 Kucinich | N | N | Y | Y | Y | N |
| 11 Jones | N | N | Y | Y | Y | N |
| 12 **Tiberi** | Y | N | N | N | N | Y |
| 13 Brown | N | N | Y | Y | Y | N |
| 14 **LaTourette** | Y | N | N | N | N | Y |
| 15 **Pryce** | Y | N | N | N | N | Y |
| 16 **Regula** | Y | N | N | Y | N | Y |
| 17 Ryan | N | Y | Y | N | N | N |
| 18 **Ney** | Y | Y | N | N | N | Y |
| **OKLAHOMA** | | | | | | |
| 1 **Sullivan** | Y | Y | N | N | N | Y |
| 2 Boren | N | Y | Y | N | N | Y |
| 3 **Lucas** | Y | N | N | N | N | Y |
| 4 **Cole** | Y | N | N | N | N | Y |
| 5 **Istook** | Y | Y | N | N | N | Y |
| **OREGON** | | | | | | |
| 1 Wu | N | N | Y | N | Y | N |
| 2 **Walden** | Y | N | N | N | N | Y |
| 3 Blumenauer | N | N | Y | Y | Y | N |
| 4 DeFazio | N | Y | Y | N | Y | N |
| 5 Hooley | N | N | Y | Y | Y | N |
| **PENNSYLVANIA** | | | | | | |
| 1 Brady | N | N | Y | Y | Y | N |
| 2 Fattah | N | N | Y | Y | Y | N |
| 3 **English** | Y | N | N | N | N | Y |
| 4 **Hart** | Y | N | N | N | N | Y |
| 5 **Peterson** | Y | Y | N | N | N | Y |
| 6 **Gerlach** | Y | N | N | N | Y | Y |
| 7 **Weldon** | Y | Y | N | Y | N | Y |
| 8 **Fitzpatrick** | Y | N | N | Y | N | Y |
| 9 **Shuster** | Y | Y | N | N | N | Y |
| 10 **Sherwood** | Y | N | N | N | N | Y |
| 11 Kanjorski | Y | N | N | N | N | N |
| 12 Murtha | Y | N | N | N | N | N |
| 13 Schwartz | N | N | Y | Y | Y | N |
| 14 Doyle | N | N | Y | Y | N | N |
| 15 **Dent** | Y | N | N | N | Y | Y |
| 16 **Pitts** | Y | Y | N | N | N | Y |
| 17 Holden | Y | Y | Y | N | N | N |
| 18 **Murphy** | N | Y | N | N | N | Y |
| 19 **Platts** | Y | Y | N | N | N | Y |
| **RHODE ISLAND** | | | | | | |
| 1 Kennedy | N | N | Y | Y | Y | N |
| 2 Langevin | N | N | Y | Y | Y | N |
| **SOUTH CAROLINA** | | | | | | |
| 1 **Brown** | Y | N | N | N | N | Y |
| 2 **Wilson** | Y | Y | N | N | N | Y |
| 3 **Barrett** | Y | Y | N | N | N | Y |
| 4 **Inglis** | Y | N | N | N | N | Y |
| 5 Spratt | N | N | Y | Y | Y | N |
| 6 Clyburn | N | N | Y | Y | Y | N |
| **SOUTH DAKOTA** | | | | | | |
| AL Herseth | N | Y | N | N | Y | N |
| **TENNESSEE** | | | | | | |
| 1 **Jenkins** | Y | N | N | N | N | Y |
| 2 **Duncan** | Y | Y | N | N | N | Y |

| | 262 | 263 | 264 | 265 | 266 | 267 |
|---|---|---|---|---|---|---|
| 3 **Wamp** | Y | Y | N | N | N | Y |
| 4 Davis | Y | Y | N | N | N | N |
| 5 Cooper | N | N | Y | N | Y | N |
| 6 Gordon | Y | N | Y | N | Y | N |
| 7 **Blackburn** | Y | N | N | N | N | Y |
| 8 Tanner | Y | N | N | N | Y | Y |
| 9 Ford | N | N | Y | N | Y | N |
| **TEXAS** | | | | | | |
| 1 **Gohmert** | Y | Y | N | N | N | Y |
| 2 **Poe** | Y | N | N | N | N | Y |
| 3 **Johnson, S.** | Y | N | N | N | N | Y |
| 4 **Hall** | Y | Y | N | N | N | Y |
| 5 **Hensarling** | Y | N | N | N | N | Y |
| 6 **Barton** | Y | Y | N | N | N | Y |
| 7 **Culberson** | Y | N | N | N | N | Y |
| 8 **Brady** | Y | Y | N | N | N | Y |
| 9 Green, A. | N | N | Y | Y | Y | N |
| 10 **McCaul** | Y | N | N | N | N | Y |
| 11 **Conaway** | Y | N | N | N | N | Y |
| 12 **Granger** | Y | N | N | N | N | Y |
| 13 **Thornberry** | Y | N | N | N | N | Y |
| 14 **Paul** | Y | Y | Y | N | N | Y |
| 15 Hinojosa | N | N | Y | N | Y | N |
| 16 Reyes | N | N | Y | N | Y | N |
| 17 Edwards | N | N | Y | N | Y | N |
| 18 Jackson-Lee | N | N | Y | Y | ? | N |
| 19 **Neugebauer** | Y | N | N | N | N | Y |
| 20 Gonzalez | N | N | Y | N | Y | N |
| 21 **Smith** | Y | Y | N | N | N | Y |
| 22 **DeLay** | Y | N | N | N | N | Y |
| 23 **Bonilla** | Y | N | N | N | N | Y |
| 24 **Marchant** | Y | Y | N | N | N | Y |
| 25 Doggett | N | N | Y | Y | Y | N |
| 26 **Burgess** | Y | Y | N | N | N | Y |
| 27 Ortiz | N | N | Y | N | N | N |
| 28 Cuellar | ? | ? | ? | ? | ? | ? |
| 29 Green, G. | N | N | Y | ? | Y | N |
| 30 Johnson, E. | N | N | Y | Y | Y | N |
| 31 **Carter** | Y | N | N | N | N | Y |
| 32 **Sessions** | ? | ? | ? | ? | ? | ? |
| **UTAH** | | | | | | |
| 1 **Bishop** | Y | N | N | N | N | Y |
| 2 Matheson | N | N | N | N | Y | Y |
| 3 **Cannon** | N | N | N | N | N | Y |
| **VERMONT** | | | | | | |
| AL *Sanders* | N | N | Y | N | Y | N |
| **VIRGINIA** | | | | | | |
| 1 **Davis, J.** | Y | Y | N | N | N | Y |
| 2 **Drake** | Y | Y | N | N | N | Y |
| 3 Scott | N | N | Y | Y | Y | N |
| 4 **Forbes** | Y | Y | N | N | N | Y |
| 5 **Goode** | Y | Y | N | N | N | Y |
| 6 **Goodlatte** | Y | Y | N | N | N | Y |
| 7 **Cantor** | Y | N | N | N | N | Y |
| 8 Moran | N | N | Y | Y | Y | N |
| 9 Boucher | Y | N | Y | N | Y | N |
| 10 **Wolf** | Y | Y | N | Y | N | Y |
| 11 **Davis, T.** | Y | N | N | Y | N | Y |
| **WASHINGTON** | | | | | | |
| 1 Inslee | N | N | Y | Y | Y | N |
| 2 Larsen | N | N | Y | N | Y | N |
| 3 Baird | N | N | N | Y | Y | N |
| 4 **Hastings** | N | N | N | N | N | Y |
| 5 **McMorris** | Y | Y | N | N | N | Y |
| 6 Dicks | N | N | N | Y | Y | N |
| 7 McDermott | N | N | ? | Y | Y | ? |
| 8 **Reichert** | N | N | N | N | N | N |
| 9 Smith | N | N | Y | N | Y | N |
| **WEST VIRGINIA** | | | | | | |
| 1 Mollohan | N | N | Y | N | N | N |
| 2 **Capito** | N | N | N | N | Y | Y |
| 3 Rahall | N | N | N | N | N | N |
| **WISCONSIN** | | | | | | |
| 1 **Ryan** | N | N | N | N | N | Y |
| 2 Baldwin | N | N | Y | Y | Y | N |
| 3 Kind | N | N | Y | N | Y | N |
| 4 Moore | N | N | Y | Y | Y | N |
| 5 **Sensenbrenner** | Y | Y | N | N | N | Y |
| 6 **Petri** | Y | Y | N | N | N | Y |
| 7 Obey | N | N | Y | N | N | N |
| 8 **Green** | N | Y | N | N | N | Y |
| **WYOMING** | | | | | | |
| AL **Cubin** | Y | N | N | N | N | Y |

# IN THE HOUSE | By Vote Number

**268.** **HR 2862. Fiscal 2006 Commerce-Justice-Science Appropriations/ Passage.** Passage of the bill that would provide $57.8 billion in fiscal 2006 for the Departments of Commerce, Justice and State as well as various science and other related agencies. It would provide $21.8 billion for the Justice Department, $5.8 billion for the Commerce Department, $9.7 billion for the State Department and international broadcasting agencies, $16.5 billion for NASA, and $5.6 billion for the National Science Foundation. It would block the Office of the U.S. Trade Representative from enforcing language in future trade agreements that would make it more difficult to import prescription drugs from the specific countries involved. Passed 418-7: R 221-5; D 196-2 (ND 147-1, SD 49-1); I 1-0. June 16, 2005.

**269.** **HR 2863. Fiscal 2006 Defense Appropriations/Previous Question.** Cole, R-Okla., motion to order the previous question (thus ending debate and possibility of amendment) on adoption of the rule (H Res 315) to provide for House floor consideration of the bill that would appropriate $408.9 billion in fiscal 2006 for the Defense Department. Motion agreed to 223-200: R 223-1; D 0-198 (ND 0-148, SD 0-50); I 0-1. (Subsequently, the rule was adopted by voice vote.) June 16, 2005.

**270.** **HR 2745. U.N. Overhaul/Immunity for U.N. Officials.** King, R-N.Y., amendment that would instruct the president to direct the U.S. permanent representative to the United Nations to ensure that the Secretary General exercises the right and duty to waive immunity of any U.N. official who is under investigation for, or is charged with, committing a serious criminal offense. Adopted 405-13: R 224-0; D 180-13 (ND 134-10, SD 46-3); I 1-0. June 16, 2005.

**271.** **HR 2745. U.N. Overhaul/U.S. Contributions to the United Nations.** Poe, R-Texas, amendment that would require the Office of Management and Budget to submit a report to the House International Relations Committee on the U.S. contributions to the United Nations, including assessed, voluntary and in-kind contributions. Adopted 402-14: R 223-0; D 178-14 (ND 131-12, SD 47-2); I 1-0. June 16, 2005.

**272.** **HR 2745. U.N. Overhaul/IAEA Resolution.** Cantor, R-Va., amendment that would direct the U.S. permanent representative to the International Atomic Energy Agency to ensure that the IAEA adopts a resolution making Iran ineligible to receive any nuclear material, technology, equipment or assistance from any IAEA member state until it is in full compliance with the agency. Adopted 411-9: R 223-1; D 187-8 (ND 139-7, SD 48-1); I 1-0. June 16, 2005.

**273.** **H Res 324. House Judiciary Committee Hearing/Motion to Table.** DeLay, R-Texas, motion to table (kill) the Nadler, D-N.Y., privileged resolution that would condemn the breaking of House rules by the chairman of the Judiciary Committee during a hearing on the law known as the Patriot Act on June 10, 2005. It would instruct the chairman, in consultation with the ranking Democrat, to schedule another day of hearings with witnesses requested by the minority. Motion agreed to 222-191: R 222-0; D 0-190 (ND 0-142, SD 0-48); I 0-1. June 16, 2005.

ND Northern Democrats, SD Southern Democrats
Southern states: Ala., Ark., Fla., Ga., Ky., La., Miss., N.C., Okla., S.C., Tenn., Texas, Va.

| | 268 | 269 | 270 | 271 | 272 | 273 |
|---|---|---|---|---|---|---|
| **ALABAMA** | | | | | | |
| 1 Bonner | Y | Y | Y | Y | Y | Y |
| 2 Everett | Y | Y | Y | Y | Y | Y |
| 3 Rogers | Y | Y | Y | Y | Y | Y |
| 4 Aderholt | Y | Y | Y | Y | Y | Y |
| 5 Cramer | Y | N | Y | Y | Y | N |
| 6 Bachus | Y | Y | Y | Y | Y | Y |
| 7 Davis | Y | N | Y | Y | Y | N |
| **ALASKA** | | | | | | |
| AL Young | Y | Y | ? | ? | ? | ? |
| **ARIZONA** | | | | | | |
| 1 Renzi | Y | Y | Y | Y | Y | Y |
| 2 Franks | Y | Y | Y | Y | Y | Y |
| 3 Shadegg | Y | Y | Y | Y | Y | Y |
| 4 Pastor | Y | N | Y | Y | Y | N |
| 5 Hayworth | Y | Y | Y | Y | Y | Y |
| 6 Flake | N | Y | Y | Y | Y | Y |
| 7 Grijalva | Y | N | Y | Y | Y | N |
| 8 Kolbe | Y | Y | Y | Y | Y | Y |
| **ARKANSAS** | | | | | | |
| 1 Berry | Y | N | Y | Y | Y | N |
| 2 Snyder | Y | N | Y | Y | Y | N |
| 3 Boozman | Y | Y | Y | Y | Y | Y |
| 4 Ross | Y | N | Y | Y | Y | N |
| **CALIFORNIA** | | | | | | |
| 1 Thompson | Y | N | Y | Y | Y | N |
| 2 Herger | Y | Y | Y | Y | Y | Y |
| 3 Lungren | Y | Y | Y | Y | Y | Y |
| 4 Doolittle | Y | Y | Y | Y | Y | Y |
| 5 Matsui, D. | Y | N | Y | Y | Y | N |
| 6 Woolsey | Y | N | N | N | Y | N |
| 7 Miller, George | Y | N | Y | Y | Y | ? |
| 8 Pelosi | Y | N | ? | ? | ? | ? |
| 9 Lee | ? | N | N | N | N | N |
| 10 Tauscher | Y | N | Y | Y | Y | N |
| 11 Pombo | Y | Y | Y | Y | Y | Y |
| 12 Lantos | Y | N | Y | Y | Y | N |
| 13 Stark | Y | N | N | N | N | N |
| 14 Eshoo | Y | N | Y | Y | Y | N |
| 15 Honda | Y | N | N | Y | Y | N |
| 16 Lofgren | Y | N | Y | Y | Y | N |
| 17 Farr | Y | N | Y | Y | Y | N |
| 18 Cardoza | Y | N | Y | Y | Y | N |
| 19 Radanovich | Y | Y | Y | Y | Y | Y |
| 20 Costa | Y | N | Y | Y | Y | N |
| 21 Nunes | Y | Y | Y | Y | Y | Y |
| 22 Thomas | Y | ? | Y | Y | Y | Y |
| 23 Capps | Y | N | Y | Y | Y | N |
| 24 Gallegly | Y | Y | Y | Y | Y | Y |
| 25 McKeon | Y | Y | Y | Y | Y | Y |
| 26 Dreier | Y | Y | Y | Y | Y | Y |
| 27 Sherman | Y | N | Y | Y | Y | N |
| 28 Berman | Y | N | Y | Y | Y | ? |
| 29 Schiff | Y | N | Y | Y | Y | N |
| 30 Waxman | Y | N | Y | Y | Y | N |
| 31 Becerra | Y | N | Y | Y | Y | N |
| 32 Solis | Y | N | Y | Y | Y | N |
| 33 Watson | Y | N | Y | Y | Y | N |
| 34 Roybal-Allard | Y | N | Y | Y | Y | N |
| 35 Waters | Y | N | P | Y | Y | N |
| 36 Harman | Y | N | Y | Y | Y | N |
| 37 Millender-McD. | Y | N | ? | ? | ? | ? |
| 38 Napolitano | Y | N | Y | Y | Y | N |
| 39 Sánchez, Linda | Y | N | Y | Y | Y | N |
| 40 Royce | Y | Y | Y | Y | Y | Y |
| 41 Lewis | Y | Y | Y | Y | Y | Y |
| 42 Miller, Gary | Y | Y | Y | Y | Y | Y |
| 43 Baca | Y | N | Y | Y | Y | N |
| 44 Calvert | Y | Y | Y | Y | Y | Y |
| 45 Bono | ? | ? | ? | ? | ? | ? |
| 46 Rohrabacher | Y | Y | Y | Y | Y | Y |
| 47 Sanchez, Loretta | Y | N | Y | Y | Y | N |
| 48 Cox | Y | Y | ? | ? | ? | ? |
| 49 Issa | Y | Y | Y | Y | Y | Y |

| | 268 | 269 | 270 | 271 | 272 | 273 |
|---|---|---|---|---|---|---|
| 50 Cunningham | Y | Y | Y | Y | Y | Y |
| 51 Filner | Y | N | Y | Y | Y | N |
| 52 Hunter | Y | Y | Y | Y | Y | Y |
| 53 Davis | Y | N | Y | Y | Y | N |
| **COLORADO** | | | | | | |
| 1 DeGette | Y | N | Y | Y | Y | N |
| 2 Udall | Y | N | Y | Y | Y | N |
| 3 Salazar | Y | N | Y | Y | Y | N |
| 4 Musgrave | Y | Y | Y | Y | Y | Y |
| 5 Hefley | N | Y | Y | Y | Y | Y |
| 6 Tancredo | Y | Y | Y | Y | Y | Y |
| 7 Beauprez | Y | Y | Y | Y | Y | Y |
| **CONNECTICUT** | | | | | | |
| 1 Larson | Y | N | Y | Y | Y | N |
| 2 Simmons | Y | Y | Y | Y | Y | Y |
| 3 DeLauro | Y | N | Y | Y | Y | N |
| 4 Shays | Y | Y | Y | Y | Y | Y |
| 5 Johnson | Y | Y | Y | Y | Y | Y |
| **DELAWARE** | | | | | | |
| AL Castle | Y | Y | Y | Y | Y | Y |
| **FLORIDA** | | | | | | |
| 1 Miller | N | Y | Y | Y | Y | Y |
| 2 Boyd | Y | N | Y | Y | Y | N |
| 3 Brown | Y | N | Y | Y | Y | N |
| 4 Crenshaw | Y | Y | Y | Y | Y | Y |
| 5 Brown-Waite | Y | Y | Y | Y | Y | Y |
| 6 Stearns | Y | Y | Y | Y | Y | Y |
| 7 Mica | Y | Y | Y | Y | Y | Y |
| 8 Keller | Y | Y | Y | Y | Y | Y |
| 9 Bilirakis | Y | Y | Y | Y | Y | Y |
| 10 Young | Y | Y | Y | Y | Y | Y |
| 11 Davis | Y | N | Y | Y | Y | N |
| 12 Putnam | Y | Y | Y | Y | Y | Y |
| 13 Harris | Y | Y | Y | Y | Y | Y |
| 14 Mack | Y | Y | Y | Y | Y | Y |
| 15 Weldon | Y | Y | Y | Y | Y | Y |
| 16 Foley | Y | Y | Y | Y | Y | Y |
| 17 Meek | Y | N | Y | Y | Y | N |
| 18 Ros-Lehtinen | Y | Y | Y | Y | Y | Y |
| 19 Wexler | Y | N | Y | Y | Y | N |
| 20 Wasserman-Schultz | Y | N | Y | Y | Y | N |
| 21 Diaz-Balart, L. | Y | Y | Y | Y | Y | Y |
| 22 Shaw | Y | Y | Y | Y | Y | Y |
| 23 Hastings | Y | N | N | N | Y | N |
| 24 Feeney | Y | Y | Y | Y | Y | Y |
| 25 Diaz-Balart, M. | Y | Y | Y | Y | Y | Y |
| **GEORGIA** | | | | | | |
| 1 Kingston | Y | Y | Y | Y | Y | Y |
| 2 Bishop | Y | N | Y | Y | Y | N |
| 3 Marshall | Y | N | Y | Y | Y | N |
| 4 McKinney | Y | N | N | N | N | N |
| 5 Lewis | Y | N | Y | Y | Y | N |
| 6 Price | Y | Y | Y | Y | Y | Y |
| 7 Linder | Y | Y | Y | Y | Y | Y |
| 8 Westmoreland | Y | Y | Y | Y | Y | Y |
| 9 Norwood | Y | Y | Y | Y | Y | Y |
| 10 Deal | Y | Y | Y | Y | Y | Y |
| 11 Gingrey | Y | Y | Y | Y | Y | Y |
| 12 Barrow | Y | N | Y | Y | Y | N |
| 13 Scott | Y | N | Y | Y | Y | N |
| **HAWAII** | | | | | | |
| 1 Abercrombie | Y | N | Y | Y | N | N |
| 2 Case | Y | N | Y | Y | Y | N |
| **IDAHO** | | | | | | |
| 1 Otter | Y | Y | Y | Y | Y | Y |
| 2 Simpson | Y | Y | Y | Y | Y | Y |
| **ILLINOIS** | | | | | | |
| 1 Rush | Y | N | Y | Y | Y | N |
| 2 Jackson | Y | N | Y | N | Y | N |
| 3 Lipinski | Y | N | Y | Y | Y | N |
| 4 Gutierrez | Y | N | Y | Y | Y | N |
| 5 Emanuel | Y | N | Y | Y | Y | N |
| 6 Hyde | Y | Y | Y | Y | Y | Y |
| 7 Davis | Y | N | Y | Y | Y | N |
| 8 Bean | Y | N | Y | Y | Y | N |
| 9 Schakowsky | Y | N | Y | Y | Y | N |
| 10 Kirk | Y | Y | Y | Y | Y | Y |
| 11 Weller | Y | Y | Y | Y | Y | Y |
| 12 Costello | Y | N | Y | Y | Y | N |

**KEY**  Republicans   Democrats   *Independents*

| | | | |
|---|---|---|---|
| **Y** | Voted for (yea) | **X** Paired against | **C** Voted "present" to avoid possible conflict of interest |
| **#** | Paired for | **–** Announced against | |
| **+** | Announced for | **P** Voted "present" | **?** Did not vote or otherwise make a position known |
| **N** | Voted against (nay) | | |

| | 268 | 269 | 270 | 271 | 272 | 273 |
|---|---|---|---|---|---|---|
| 13 **Biggert** | Y | Y | Y | Y | Y | Y |
| 14 **Hastert** | | | | | | |
| 15 **Johnson** | Y | Y | Y | Y | Y | Y |
| 16 **Manzullo** | Y | Y | Y | Y | Y | Y |
| 17 Evans | Y | N | Y | Y | Y | N |
| 18 **LaHood** | Y | Y | Y | Y | Y | Y |
| 19 **Shimkus** | Y | Y | Y | Y | Y | Y |
| **INDIANA** | | | | | | |
| 1 Visclosky | Y | N | Y | Y | Y | N |
| 2 **Chocola** | Y | Y | Y | Y | Y | Y |
| 3 **Souder** | Y | Y | Y | Y | Y | Y |
| 4 **Buyer** | Y | Y | Y | ? | Y | Y |
| 5 **Burton** | Y | Y | Y | Y | Y | Y |
| 6 **Pence** | Y | Y | Y | Y | Y | Y |
| 7 Carson | Y | N | Y | N | Y | N |
| 8 **Hostettler** | Y | N | Y | Y | Y | Y |
| 9 **Sodrel** | Y | Y | Y | Y | Y | Y |
| **IOWA** | | | | | | |
| 1 **Nussle** | Y | Y | Y | Y | Y | Y |
| 2 **Leach** | Y | Y | Y | Y | Y | Y |
| 3 Boswell | Y | N | Y | Y | Y | N |
| 4 **Latham** | Y | Y | Y | Y | Y | Y |
| 5 **King** | Y | Y | Y | Y | Y | Y |
| **KANSAS** | | | | | | |
| 1 **Moran** | Y | Y | Y | Y | Y | Y |
| 2 **Ryun** | Y | Y | Y | Y | Y | Y |
| 3 Moore | Y | N | Y | Y | Y | N |
| 4 **Tiahrt** | Y | Y | Y | Y | Y | Y |
| **KENTUCKY** | | | | | | |
| 1 **Whitfield** | ? | Y | Y | Y | Y | Y |
| 2 **Lewis** | Y | Y | Y | Y | Y | Y |
| 3 **Northup** | Y | Y | Y | Y | Y | Y |
| 4 **Davis** | Y | Y | Y | Y | Y | Y |
| 5 **Rogers** | Y | Y | Y | Y | Y | Y |
| 6 Chandler | Y | N | Y | Y | Y | N |
| **LOUISIANA** | | | | | | |
| 1 **Jindal** | Y | Y | Y | Y | Y | Y |
| 2 Jefferson | Y | N | Y | Y | Y | N |
| 3 Melancon | Y | N | Y | Y | Y | N |
| 4 **McCrery** | Y | Y | Y | Y | Y | Y |
| 5 **Alexander** | Y | Y | Y | Y | Y | Y |
| 6 **Baker** | Y | Y | Y | Y | Y | Y |
| 7 **Boustany** | Y | Y | Y | Y | Y | Y |
| **MAINE** | | | | | | |
| 1 Allen | Y | N | Y | Y | Y | N |
| 2 Michaud | Y | N | Y | Y | Y | N |
| **MARYLAND** | | | | | | |
| 1 **Gilchrest** | Y | Y | Y | Y | Y | Y |
| 2 Ruppersberger | Y | N | Y | Y | Y | N |
| 3 Cardin | Y | N | ? | ? | Y | N |
| 4 Wynn | Y | N | Y | Y | Y | N |
| 5 Hoyer | Y | N | Y | Y | Y | N |
| 6 **Bartlett** | Y | Y | Y | Y | Y | Y |
| 7 Cummings | Y | N | Y | Y | Y | N |
| 8 Van Hollen | Y | N | Y | Y | Y | N |
| **MASSACHUSETTS** | | | | | | |
| 1 Olver | Y | N | Y | Y | Y | N |
| 2 Neal | Y | N | Y | Y | Y | N |
| 3 McGovern | Y | N | Y | N | Y | N |
| 4 Frank | Y | N | Y | N | Y | N |
| 5 Meehan | Y | N | Y | Y | Y | N |
| 6 Tierney | Y | N | Y | Y | Y | N |
| 7 Markey | Y | N | Y | Y | Y | N |
| 8 Capuano | Y | N | N | Y | Y | N |
| 9 Lynch | Y | N | Y | Y | Y | N |
| 10 Delahunt | ? | N | Y | Y | Y | ? |
| **MICHIGAN** | | | | | | |
| 1 Stupak | Y | N | Y | Y | Y | N |
| 2 **Hoekstra** | Y | Y | Y | Y | Y | Y |
| 3 **Ehlers** | Y | Y | Y | Y | Y | Y |
| 4 **Camp** | Y | Y | Y | Y | Y | Y |
| 5 Kildee | Y | N | Y | Y | Y | N |
| 6 **Upton** | Y | Y | Y | Y | Y | Y |
| 7 **Schwarz** | Y | Y | Y | Y | Y | Y |
| 8 **Rogers** | Y | Y | Y | Y | Y | Y |
| 9 **Knollenberg** | Y | Y | Y | Y | Y | Y |
| 10 **Miller** | Y | Y | Y | Y | Y | Y |
| 11 **McCotter** | Y | Y | Y | Y | Y | Y |
| 12 Levin | Y | N | Y | Y | Y | N |
| 13 Kilpatrick | Y | N | Y | Y | Y | N |
| 14 Conyers | Y | N | N | ? | N | N |
| 15 Dingell | Y | N | Y | Y | Y | N |

| | 268 | 269 | 270 | 271 | 272 | 273 |
|---|---|---|---|---|---|---|
| **MINNESOTA** | | | | | | |
| 1 **Gutknecht** | Y | Y | Y | Y | Y | Y |
| 2 **Kline** | Y | Y | Y | Y | Y | Y |
| 3 **Ramstad** | Y | Y | Y | Y | Y | Y |
| 4 McCollum | Y | N | Y | Y | Y | N |
| 5 Sabo | Y | N | Y | Y | Y | N |
| 6 **Kennedy** | Y | Y | Y | Y | Y | Y |
| 7 Peterson | Y | N | Y | Y | Y | N |
| 8 Oberstar | ? | ? | ? | ? | ? | ? |
| **MISSISSIPPI** | | | | | | |
| 1 **Wicker** | Y | Y | Y | Y | Y | Y |
| 2 Thompson | Y | N | Y | Y | Y | N |
| 3 **Pickering** | Y | Y | Y | Y | Y | Y |
| 4 Taylor | Y | N | Y | Y | Y | N |
| **MISSOURI** | | | | | | |
| 1 Clay | Y | N | Y | Y | Y | N |
| 2 **Akin** | Y | Y | Y | Y | Y | Y |
| 3 Carnahan | Y | N | Y | Y | Y | N |
| 4 Skelton | Y | N | Y | Y | Y | N |
| 5 Cleaver | Y | N | Y | Y | Y | N |
| 6 **Graves** | Y | Y | Y | Y | Y | Y |
| 7 **Blunt** | Y | Y | Y | Y | Y | Y |
| 8 **Emerson** | Y | Y | Y | Y | Y | Y |
| 9 **Hulshof** | Y | Y | Y | Y | Y | Y |
| **MONTANA** | | | | | | |
| AL **Rehberg** | Y | Y | Y | Y | Y | Y |
| **NEBRASKA** | | | | | | |
| 1 **Fortenberry** | Y | Y | Y | Y | Y | Y |
| 2 **Terry** | Y | Y | Y | Y | Y | Y |
| 3 **Osborne** | Y | Y | Y | Y | Y | Y |
| **NEVADA** | | | | | | |
| 1 Berkley | Y | N | Y | Y | Y | N |
| 2 **Gibbons** | Y | Y | Y | Y | Y | Y |
| 3 **Porter** | Y | Y | Y | Y | Y | Y |
| **NEW HAMPSHIRE** | | | | | | |
| 1 **Bradley** | Y | Y | Y | Y | Y | Y |
| 2 **Bass** | Y | Y | Y | Y | Y | Y |
| **NEW JERSEY** | | | | | | |
| 1 Andrews | Y | N | Y | Y | Y | N |
| 2 **LoBiondo** | Y | Y | Y | Y | Y | Y |
| 3 **Saxton** | Y | Y | Y | Y | Y | Y |
| 4 **Smith** | Y | Y | Y | Y | Y | Y |
| 5 **Garrett** | Y | Y | Y | Y | Y | Y |
| 6 Pallone | Y | N | Y | Y | Y | N |
| 7 **Ferguson** | Y | Y | Y | Y | Y | Y |
| 8 Pascrell | Y | N | Y | Y | Y | N |
| 9 Rothman | Y | N | Y | Y | Y | N |
| 10 Payne | Y | N | Y | N | Y | N |
| 11 **Frelinghuysen** | Y | Y | Y | Y | Y | Y |
| 12 Holt | Y | N | Y | Y | Y | N |
| 13 Menendez | Y | N | Y | Y | Y | N |
| **NEW MEXICO** | | | | | | |
| 1 **Wilson** | Y | Y | Y | Y | Y | Y |
| 2 **Pearce** | Y | Y | Y | Y | Y | Y |
| 3 Udall | Y | N | Y | Y | Y | N |
| **NEW YORK** | | | | | | |
| 1 Bishop | Y | N | Y | Y | Y | N |
| 2 Israel | Y | N | Y | Y | Y | N |
| 3 **King** | Y | Y | Y | Y | Y | Y |
| 4 McCarthy | Y | N | Y | Y | Y | N |
| 5 Ackerman | Y | N | Y | Y | Y | N |
| 6 Meeks | Y | N | Y | Y | Y | N |
| 7 Crowley | Y | N | Y | Y | Y | N |
| 8 Nadler | Y | N | Y | Y | Y | N |
| 9 Weiner | Y | N | Y | Y | Y | N |
| 10 Towns | Y | N | Y | Y | Y | N |
| 11 Owens | Y | N | Y | Y | Y | N |
| 12 Velázquez | Y | N | Y | Y | Y | N |
| 13 **Fossella** | Y | Y | Y | Y | Y | Y |
| 14 Maloney | Y | N | Y | Y | Y | N |
| 15 Rangel | Y | N | N | Y | Y | N |
| 16 Serrano | Y | N | Y | Y | Y | N |
| 17 Engel | Y | N | Y | Y | Y | N |
| 18 Lowey | Y | N | Y | Y | Y | N |
| 19 **Kelly** | Y | Y | Y | Y | Y | Y |
| 20 **Sweeney** | Y | Y | Y | Y | Y | Y |
| 21 McNulty | Y | N | Y | Y | Y | N |
| 22 Hinchey | Y | N | N | Y | Y | N |
| 23 **McHugh** | Y | Y | Y | Y | Y | Y |
| 24 **Boehlert** | Y | Y | Y | Y | Y | Y |
| 25 **Walsh** | Y | Y | Y | Y | Y | Y |
| 26 **Reynolds** | Y | Y | Y | Y | Y | Y |
| 27 Higgins | Y | N | Y | Y | Y | N |
| 28 Slaughter | Y | N | Y | Y | Y | N |
| 29 **Kuhl** | Y | Y | Y | Y | Y | Y |

| | 268 | 269 | 270 | 271 | 272 | 273 |
|---|---|---|---|---|---|---|
| **NORTH CAROLINA** | | | | | | |
| 1 Butterfield | Y | N | Y | Y | Y | N |
| 2 Etheridge | Y | N | Y | Y | Y | N |
| 3 **Jones** | Y | Y | Y | Y | Y | Y |
| 4 Price | Y | N | Y | Y | Y | N |
| 5 **Foxx** | Y | Y | Y | Y | Y | Y |
| 6 **Coble** | Y | Y | Y | Y | Y | Y |
| 7 McIntyre | Y | N | Y | Y | Y | N |
| 8 **Hayes** | Y | Y | Y | Y | Y | Y |
| 9 **Myrick** | Y | Y | Y | Y | Y | Y |
| 10 **McHenry** | Y | Y | Y | Y | Y | Y |
| 11 **Taylor** | Y | Y | Y | Y | Y | Y |
| 12 Watt | Y | N | Y | N | Y | N |
| 13 Miller | Y | N | Y | Y | Y | N |
| **NORTH DAKOTA** | | | | | | |
| AL Pomeroy | Y | N | Y | Y | Y | N |
| **OHIO** | | | | | | |
| 1 **Chabot** | Y | Y | Y | Y | Y | Y |
| 2 Vacant | | | | | | |
| 3 **Turner** | Y | Y | Y | Y | Y | Y |
| 4 **Oxley** | Y | Y | Y | Y | Y | ? |
| 5 **Gillmor** | Y | Y | ? | ? | ? | ? |
| 6 Strickland | Y | N | Y | Y | Y | N |
| 7 **Hobson** | Y | Y | Y | Y | Y | Y |
| 8 **Boehner** | Y | Y | Y | Y | Y | Y |
| 9 Kaptur | Y | N | Y | Y | Y | N |
| 10 Kucinich | Y | N | N | N | N | N |
| 11 Jones | Y | ? | N | Y | Y | N |
| 12 **Tiberi** | Y | Y | Y | Y | Y | Y |
| 13 Brown | Y | N | Y | Y | Y | N |
| 14 **LaTourette** | Y | Y | Y | Y | Y | ? |
| 15 **Pryce** | Y | Y | Y | Y | Y | Y |
| 16 **Regula** | Y | Y | Y | Y | Y | Y |
| 17 Ryan | Y | N | Y | Y | Y | N |
| 18 **Ney** | Y | Y | Y | Y | Y | Y |
| **OKLAHOMA** | | | | | | |
| 1 **Sullivan** | Y | Y | Y | Y | Y | Y |
| 2 Boren | Y | N | Y | Y | Y | N |
| 3 **Lucas** | Y | Y | Y | Y | Y | Y |
| 4 **Cole** | Y | Y | Y | Y | Y | Y |
| 5 **Istook** | Y | Y | Y | Y | Y | Y |
| **OREGON** | | | | | | |
| 1 Wu | Y | N | Y | Y | Y | N |
| 2 **Walden** | Y | Y | Y | Y | Y | Y |
| 3 Blumenauer | Y | N | ? | ? | ? | ? |
| 4 DeFazio | Y | N | Y | Y | Y | N |
| 5 Hooley | Y | N | ? | ? | ? | ? |
| **PENNSYLVANIA** | | | | | | |
| 1 Brady | Y | N | Y | Y | Y | N |
| 2 Fattah | Y | N | Y | Y | Y | N |
| 3 **English** | Y | ? | Y | Y | Y | Y |
| 4 **Hart** | Y | Y | Y | Y | Y | Y |
| 5 **Peterson** | Y | Y | Y | Y | Y | Y |
| 6 **Gerlach** | Y | Y | Y | Y | Y | Y |
| 7 **Weldon** | Y | Y | Y | Y | Y | Y |
| 8 **Fitzpatrick** | Y | Y | Y | Y | Y | Y |
| 9 **Shuster** | Y | Y | Y | Y | Y | Y |
| 10 **Sherwood** | Y | Y | Y | Y | Y | Y |
| 11 Kanjorski | Y | N | Y | Y | Y | N |
| 12 Murtha | Y | N | Y | Y | Y | N |
| 13 Schwartz | Y | N | Y | Y | Y | N |
| 14 Doyle | Y | N | Y | Y | Y | N |
| 15 **Dent** | Y | Y | Y | Y | Y | Y |
| 16 **Pitts** | Y | Y | Y | Y | Y | Y |
| 17 Holden | Y | N | Y | Y | Y | N |
| 18 **Murphy** | Y | Y | Y | Y | Y | Y |
| 19 **Platts** | Y | Y | Y | Y | Y | Y |
| **RHODE ISLAND** | | | | | | |
| 1 Kennedy | Y | ? | Y | Y | Y | N |
| 2 Langevin | Y | N | Y | Y | Y | N |
| **SOUTH CAROLINA** | | | | | | |
| 1 **Brown** | Y | Y | Y | Y | Y | Y |
| 2 **Wilson** | Y | Y | Y | Y | Y | Y |
| 3 **Barrett** | Y | Y | Y | Y | Y | Y |
| 4 **Inglis** | Y | Y | Y | Y | Y | Y |
| 5 Spratt | Y | N | Y | Y | Y | N |
| 6 Clyburn | Y | N | Y | Y | Y | N |
| **SOUTH DAKOTA** | | | | | | |
| AL Herseth | Y | N | Y | Y | Y | N |
| **TENNESSEE** | | | | | | |
| 1 **Jenkins** | Y | Y | Y | Y | Y | Y |
| 2 **Duncan** | N | Y | Y | Y | Y | Y |

| | 268 | 269 | 270 | 271 | 272 | 273 |
|---|---|---|---|---|---|---|
| 3 **Wamp** | Y | Y | Y | Y | Y | Y |
| 4 Davis | Y | N | Y | Y | Y | N |
| 5 Cooper | N | N | Y | Y | Y | N |
| 6 Gordon | Y | N | Y | Y | Y | N |
| 7 **Blackburn** | Y | Y | Y | Y | Y | Y |
| 8 Tanner | Y | N | Y | Y | Y | N |
| 9 Ford | Y | N | Y | Y | Y | N |
| **TEXAS** | | | | | | |
| 1 **Gohmert** | Y | Y | Y | Y | Y | Y |
| 2 **Poe** | Y | Y | Y | Y | Y | Y |
| 3 **Johnson, S.** | Y | Y | Y | Y | Y | Y |
| 4 **Hall** | Y | Y | Y | Y | Y | Y |
| 5 **Hensarling** | Y | Y | Y | Y | Y | Y |
| 6 **Barton** | + | Y | Y | Y | Y | Y |
| 7 **Culberson** | Y | Y | Y | Y | Y | Y |
| 8 **Brady** | Y | Y | Y | Y | Y | Y |
| 9 Green, A. | Y | N | Y | Y | Y | N |
| 10 **McCaul** | Y | Y | Y | Y | Y | Y |
| 11 **Conaway** | Y | Y | Y | Y | Y | Y |
| 12 **Granger** | Y | ? | Y | Y | Y | Y |
| 13 **Thornberry** | Y | Y | Y | Y | Y | Y |
| 14 **Paul** | N | Y | Y | Y | N | Y |
| 15 Hinojosa | Y | N | Y | Y | Y | N |
| 16 Reyes | Y | N | ? | ? | ? | ? |
| 17 Edwards | Y | N | Y | Y | Y | N |
| 18 Jackson-Lee | Y | N | Y | Y | Y | N |
| 19 **Neugebauer** | Y | Y | Y | Y | Y | Y |
| 20 Gonzalez | Y | N | Y | Y | Y | N |
| 21 **Smith** | Y | Y | Y | Y | Y | Y |
| 22 **DeLay** | Y | Y | Y | Y | Y | Y |
| 23 **Bonilla** | Y | Y | Y | Y | Y | Y |
| 24 **Marchant** | Y | Y | Y | Y | Y | Y |
| 25 Doggett | Y | N | Y | Y | Y | N |
| 26 **Burgess** | Y | Y | Y | Y | Y | Y |
| 27 Ortiz | Y | N | Y | Y | Y | N |
| 28 Cuellar | ? | ? | ? | ? | ? | ? |
| 29 Green, G. | Y | N | Y | Y | Y | N |
| 30 Johnson, E. | Y | N | Y | Y | Y | N |
| 31 **Carter** | Y | Y | Y | Y | Y | Y |
| 32 **Sessions** | ? | ? | ? | ? | ? | ? |
| **UTAH** | | | | | | |
| 1 **Bishop** | Y | Y | Y | Y | Y | Y |
| 2 Matheson | N | N | Y | Y | Y | N |
| 3 **Cannon** | Y | Y | Y | Y | Y | Y |
| **VERMONT** | | | | | | |
| AL *Sanders* | Y | N | Y | Y | Y | N |
| **VIRGINIA** | | | | | | |
| 1 **Davis, J.** | Y | Y | Y | Y | Y | Y |
| 2 **Drake** | Y | Y | Y | Y | Y | Y |
| 3 Scott | Y | N | N | Y | Y | N |
| 4 **Forbes** | Y | Y | Y | Y | Y | Y |
| 5 **Goode** | Y | Y | Y | Y | Y | Y |
| 6 **Goodlatte** | Y | Y | Y | Y | Y | Y |
| 7 **Cantor** | Y | Y | Y | Y | Y | Y |
| 8 Moran | Y | N | Y | Y | Y | N |
| 9 Boucher | Y | N | Y | Y | Y | ? |
| 10 **Wolf** | Y | Y | Y | Y | Y | Y |
| 11 **Davis, T.** | Y | ? | ? | ? | ? | ? |
| **WASHINGTON** | | | | | | |
| 1 Inslee | Y | N | Y | ? | Y | N |
| 2 Larsen | Y | N | Y | Y | Y | N |
| 3 Baird | Y | N | Y | Y | Y | N |
| 4 **Hastings** | Y | Y | Y | Y | Y | Y |
| 5 **McMorris** | Y | Y | Y | Y | Y | Y |
| 6 Dicks | Y | N | Y | Y | Y | ? |
| 7 McDermott | Y | N | N | N | N | N |
| 8 **Reichert** | Y | Y | Y | Y | Y | Y |
| 9 Smith | Y | N | Y | Y | Y | N |
| **WEST VIRGINIA** | | | | | | |
| 1 Mollohan | Y | N | Y | Y | Y | N |
| 2 **Capito** | Y | Y | Y | Y | Y | Y |
| 3 Rahall | Y | N | Y | Y | Y | N |
| **WISCONSIN** | | | | | | |
| 1 **Ryan** | Y | Y | Y | Y | Y | Y |
| 2 Baldwin | Y | N | Y | Y | Y | N |
| 3 Kind | Y | N | Y | Y | Y | N |
| 4 Moore | Y | N | Y | N | N | N |
| 5 **Sensenbrenner** | Y | Y | Y | Y | Y | Y |
| 6 **Petri** | Y | Y | Y | Y | Y | Y |
| 7 Obey | Y | N | Y | Y | Y | N |
| 8 **Green** | Y | Y | Y | Y | Y | Y |
| **WYOMING** | | | | | | |
| AL **Cubin** | Y | Y | Y | Y | Y | Y |

# IN THE HOUSE | By Vote Number

**274.** HR 2745. U.N. Overhaul/Country-Specific Resolutions. Royce, R-Calif., amendment that would add a statement barring the elimination of country-specific resolutions to the list of changes required of the United Nations in the area of human rights overhaul. Adopted 373-32: R 218-1; D 154-31 (ND 115-25, SD 39-6); I 1-0. June 17, 2005.

**275.** HR 2745. U.N. Overhaul/Suspension of Member State. Fortenberry, R-Neb., amendment to direct the U.S. representative to seek the adoption and use of mechanisms to suspend a member state if its government is engaged in, or complicit in, acts of genocide, war crimes or crimes against humanity; to impose an arms and trade embargo, travel restrictions and asset freezes on groups or individuals responsible for such actions; and to deploy peacekeeping forces to halt such actions. Adopted 375-29: R 218-1; D 156-28 (ND 118-22, SD 38-6); I 1-0. June 17, 2005.

**276.** HR 2745. U.N. Overhaul/Oil-for-Food Program. Flake, R-Ariz., amendment to require the United Nations to release documents about the Oil-for-Food Program upon request by member states and to waive U.S. immunity of U.N. officials for civil or criminal acts under federal or state law that transpired in the United States in connection with the program. Adopted 366-38: R 220-0; D 145-38 (ND 106-32, SD 39-6); I 1-0. June 17, 2005.

**277.** HR 2745. U.N. Overhaul/Anti-Semitic Statements. Chabot, R-Ohio, amendment that would direct the U.S. ambassador to the United Nations to oppose anti-Semitic statements and anti-Israel resolutions in the United Nations. Adopted 405-2: R 219-1; D 185-1 (ND 140-0, SD 45-1); I 1-0. June 17, 2005.

**278.** HR 2745. U.N. Overhaul/U.N. Assessment Levels. Pence, R-Ind., amendment to direct the U.S. representative to ensure that the scale of assessments for a permanent member of the Security Council is no more than five times that for any other permanent member. If a permanent member is not in compliance, the U.N. representative would seek to deny that member the use of its veto in the Security Council. Adopted 281-126: R 211-8; D 70-117 (ND 48-93, SD 22-24); I 0-1. June 17, 2005.

**279.** HR 2745. U.N. Overhaul/U.S. Foreign Assistance. Gohmert, R-Texas, amendment to bar U.S. aid to countries that oppose the U.S. position on more than 50 percent of U.N. votes. Rejected 108-297: R 106-112; D 2-184 (ND 0-140, SD 2-44); I 0-1. June 17, 2005.

**280.** HR 2745. U.N. Overhaul/Increase in U.S. Withheld Dues. Stearns, R-Fla., amendment to increase the amount of regular U.S. dues withheld under the bill to 75 percent, from 50 percent. Rejected 100-306: R 97-122; D 3-183 (ND 1-139, SD 2-44); I 0-1. June 17, 2005.

**281.** HR 2745. U.N. Overhaul/Democratic Substitute. Lantos, D-Calif., substitute amendment that would give the secretary of State authority to withhold up to 50 percent of U.S. dues unless the United Nations has complied with 32 of 39 changes by Oct. 1, 2007. The United States also could withhold up to 50 percent of its dues if member states do not make substantial progress in raising voluntary contributions for some programs. Rejected 190-216: R 9-211; D 180-5 (ND 136-3, SD 44-2); I 1-0. June 17, 2005.

| | 274 | 275 | 276 | 277 | 278 | 279 | 280 | 281 |
|---|---|---|---|---|---|---|---|---|
| **ALABAMA** | | | | | | | | |
| 1 Bonner | Y | Y | Y | Y | Y | N | N | N |
| 2 Everett | Y | Y | Y | Y | Y | N | N | N |
| 3 Rogers | Y | Y | Y | Y | Y | N | Y | N |
| 4 Aderholt | Y | Y | Y | Y | Y | N | Y | N |
| 5 Cramer | Y | Y | Y | Y | Y | N | N | Y |
| 6 Bachus | Y | Y | Y | Y | Y | N | N | N |
| 7 Davis | Y | Y | Y | Y | Y | N | N | Y |
| **ALASKA** | | | | | | | | |
| AL Young | Y | Y | Y | Y | Y | Y | N | N |
| **ARIZONA** | | | | | | | | |
| 1 Renzi | Y | Y | Y | Y | Y | N | Y | N |
| 2 Franks | Y | Y | Y | Y | Y | Y | Y | N |
| 3 Shadegg | Y | Y | Y | Y | Y | Y | Y | N |
| 4 Pastor | Y | Y | Y | N | N | N | N | Y |
| 5 Hayworth | Y | Y | Y | Y | Y | Y | Y | N |
| 6 Flake | Y | Y | Y | Y | N | N | N | N |
| 7 Grijalva | N | N | N | Y | N | N | N | Y |
| 8 Kolbe | Y | Y | Y | Y | N | N | N | Y |
| **ARKANSAS** | | | | | | | | |
| 1 Berry | Y | Y | Y | Y | Y | N | N | Y |
| 2 Snyder | Y | Y | Y | Y | N | N | N | Y |
| 3 Boozman | Y | Y | Y | Y | Y | N | Y | N |
| 4 Ross | Y | Y | Y | Y | Y | N | N | Y |
| **CALIFORNIA** | | | | | | | | |
| 1 Thompson | Y | Y | Y | Y | Y | N | N | Y |
| 2 Herger | Y | Y | Y | Y | Y | Y | Y | N |
| 3 Lungren | Y | Y | Y | Y | Y | Y | Y | N |
| 4 Doolittle | Y | Y | Y | Y | Y | Y | Y | N |
| 5 Matsui, D. | Y | Y | Y | Y | Y | N | N | Y |
| 6 Woolsey | N | N | N | Y | N | N | N | Y |
| 7 Miller, George | Y | N | N | Y | N | N | N | Y |
| 8 Pelosi | ? | ? | ? | ? | ? | ? | ? | ? |
| 9 Lee | N | N | N | Y | N | N | N | Y |
| 10 Tauscher | Y | Y | Y | Y | N | N | N | Y |
| 11 Pombo | Y | Y | Y | Y | Y | Y | Y | N |
| 12 Lantos | Y | Y | Y | Y | N | N | N | Y |
| 13 Stark | ? | ? | ? | ? | ? | ? | ? | ? |
| 14 Eshoo | Y | Y | Y | Y | N | N | N | Y |
| 15 Honda | Y | Y | N | Y | N | N | N | Y |
| 16 Lofgren | Y | Y | Y | Y | N | N | N | Y |
| 17 Farr | Y | Y | N | Y | N | N | N | Y |
| 18 Cardoza | Y | Y | Y | Y | Y | N | N | Y |
| 19 Radanovich | Y | Y | Y | Y | Y | N | Y | N |
| 20 Costa | Y | Y | Y | Y | N | N | N | Y |
| 21 Nunes | Y | Y | Y | Y | Y | N | N | N |
| 22 Thomas | Y | Y | Y | Y | Y | N | N | N |
| 23 Capps | Y | Y | Y | Y | N | N | N | Y |
| 24 Gallegly | Y | Y | Y | Y | Y | N | N | Y |
| 25 McKeon | Y | Y | Y | Y | Y | Y | Y | N |
| 26 Dreier | Y | Y | Y | Y | Y | N | N | N |
| 27 Sherman | Y | Y | Y | Y | N | N | N | Y |
| 28 Berman | Y | Y | Y | Y | N | N | N | Y |
| 29 Schiff | Y | Y | Y | Y | N | N | N | Y |
| 30 Waxman | ? | ? | ? | ? | ? | ? | ? | ? |
| 31 Becerra | Y | Y | Y | Y | N | N | N | Y |
| 32 Solis | N | N | N | Y | N | N | N | Y |
| 33 Watson | N | N | N | Y | N | N | N | Y |
| 34 Roybal-Allard | Y | Y | Y | Y | N | N | N | Y |
| 35 Waters | N | N | Y | Y | N | N | N | Y |
| 36 Harman | Y | Y | Y | Y | N | N | N | Y |
| 37 Millender-McD. | ? | ? | ? | ? | ? | ? | ? | ? |
| 38 Napolitano | Y | Y | Y | Y | N | N | N | Y |
| 39 Sánchez, Linda | Y | Y | Y | Y | N | N | N | Y |
| 40 Royce | Y | Y | Y | Y | Y | Y | Y | N |
| 41 Lewis | Y | Y | Y | Y | Y | N | N | N |
| 42 Miller, Gary | Y | Y | Y | Y | Y | Y | Y | N |
| 43 Baca | Y | Y | Y | Y | N | N | N | Y |
| 44 Calvert | Y | Y | Y | Y | Y | N | N | N |
| 45 Bono | ? | ? | ? | ? | ? | ? | ? | ? |
| 46 Rohrabacher | Y | Y | Y | Y | Y | Y | Y | N |
| 47 Sanchez, Loretta | Y | Y | Y | Y | N | N | N | Y |
| 48 Cox | Y | Y | Y | Y | N | N | N | N |
| 49 Issa | + | + | + | + | – | – | – | – |
| **50 Cunningham** | Y | Y | Y | Y | Y | N | N | N |
| 51 Filner | Y | Y | Y | N | N | N | N | Y |
| 52 Hunter | Y | Y | Y | Y | Y | N | Y | N |
| 53 Davis | Y | Y | Y | Y | N | N | N | Y |
| **COLORADO** | | | | | | | | |
| 1 DeGette | Y | N | N | Y | N | N | N | Y |
| 2 Udall | Y | Y | Y | Y | N | N | N | Y |
| 3 Salazar | Y | Y | Y | Y | N | N | N | Y |
| 4 Musgrave | Y | Y | Y | Y | Y | Y | Y | N |
| 5 Hefley | Y | Y | Y | Y | Y | Y | Y | N |
| 6 Tancredo | Y | Y | Y | Y | Y | Y | Y | N |
| 7 Beauprez | Y | Y | Y | Y | N | Y | N | N |
| **CONNECTICUT** | | | | | | | | |
| 1 Larson | N | N | N | Y | N | N | N | Y |
| 2 Simmons | ? | ? | ? | ? | ? | ? | ? | ? |
| 3 DeLauro | Y | Y | Y | Y | N | N | N | Y |
| 4 Shays | Y | Y | Y | Y | N | N | N | Y |
| 5 Johnson | Y | Y | Y | Y | N | N | N | Y |
| **DELAWARE** | | | | | | | | |
| AL Castle | Y | Y | Y | Y | Y | N | N | Y |
| **FLORIDA** | | | | | | | | |
| 1 Miller | Y | Y | Y | Y | Y | N | Y | N |
| 2 Boyd | Y | Y | Y | Y | N | N | N | Y |
| 3 Brown | ? | ? | ? | ? | ? | ? | ? | ? |
| 4 Crenshaw | Y | Y | Y | Y | N | N | N | N |
| 5 Brown-Waite | Y | Y | Y | Y | Y | N | Y | N |
| 6 Stearns | Y | Y | Y | Y | Y | Y | Y | N |
| 7 Mica | Y | Y | Y | Y | Y | N | N | N |
| 8 Keller | Y | Y | Y | Y | Y | N | N | N |
| 9 Bilirakis | Y | Y | Y | Y | Y | N | N | N |
| 10 Young | Y | Y | Y | Y | Y | N | N | N |
| 11 Davis | Y | Y | Y | Y | N | N | N | Y |
| 12 Putnam | Y | Y | Y | Y | Y | N | N | N |
| 13 Harris | Y | Y | Y | Y | N | N | N | N |
| 14 Mack | Y | Y | Y | Y | N | N | N | N |
| 15 Weldon | Y | Y | Y | Y | Y | Y | Y | N |
| 16 Foley | Y | Y | Y | Y | Y | Y | N | N |
| 17 Meek | Y | N | N | Y | N | N | N | Y |
| 18 Ros-Lehtinen | Y | Y | Y | Y | N | N | N | N |
| 19 Wexler | Y | Y | Y | Y | N | N | N | Y |
| 20 Wasserman-Schultz | Y | Y | Y | Y | N | N | N | Y |
| 21 Diaz-Balart, L. | Y | Y | Y | Y | ? | N | N | N |
| 22 Shaw | Y | Y | Y | Y | N | N | N | N |
| 23 Hastings | N | N | N | Y | N | N | N | Y |
| 24 Feeney | Y | Y | Y | Y | Y | Y | Y | N |
| 25 Diaz-Balart, M. | Y | Y | Y | Y | Y | Y | Y | N |
| **GEORGIA** | | | | | | | | |
| 1 Kingston | Y | Y | Y | Y | Y | Y | Y | N |
| 2 Bishop | ? | ? | ? | ? | ? | ? | ? | ? |
| 3 Marshall | Y | Y | Y | Y | N | N | N | Y |
| 4 McKinney | N | Y | N | N | N | N | N | Y |
| 5 Lewis | N | N | N | Y | N | N | N | Y |
| 6 Price | Y | Y | Y | Y | Y | Y | Y | N |
| 7 Linder | Y | Y | Y | Y | Y | Y | Y | N |
| 8 Westmoreland | Y | Y | Y | Y | Y | Y | Y | N |
| 9 Norwood | Y | Y | Y | Y | Y | Y | Y | N |
| 10 Deal | Y | Y | Y | Y | Y | Y | Y | N |
| 11 Gingrey | ? | ? | ? | ? | ? | ? | ? | ? |
| 12 Barrow | Y | Y | Y | Y | N | N | N | Y |
| 13 Scott | Y | Y | Y | Y | N | N | N | Y |
| **HAWAII** | | | | | | | | |
| 1 Abercrombie | Y | Y | Y | Y | N | N | N | Y |
| 2 Case | Y | Y | Y | Y | N | N | N | Y |
| **IDAHO** | | | | | | | | |
| 1 Otter | Y | Y | Y | Y | Y | Y | Y | N |
| 2 Simpson | Y | Y | Y | Y | Y | N | N | N |
| **ILLINOIS** | | | | | | | | |
| 1 Rush | Y | Y | N | Y | N | N | N | Y |
| 2 Jackson | N | N | N | Y | N | N | N | Y |
| 3 Lipinski | Y | Y | Y | Y | N | N | N | Y |
| 4 Gutierrez | N | N | N | Y | N | N | N | Y |
| 5 Emanuel | Y | Y | Y | Y | N | N | N | Y |
| 6 Hyde | Y | Y | Y | Y | Y | N | N | N |
| 7 Davis | Y | Y | Y | Y | N | N | N | Y |
| 8 Bean | Y | Y | Y | Y | N | N | N | Y |
| 9 Schakowsky | N | N | N | Y | N | N | N | Y |
| 10 Kirk | Y | Y | Y | Y | N | N | N | N |
| 11 Weller | Y | Y | Y | Y | N | N | N | N |
| 12 Costello | Y | Y | Y | Y | N | N | N | Y |

ND Northern Democrats, SD Southern Democrats
Southern states: Ala., Ark., Fla., Ga., Ky., La., Miss., N.C., Okla., S.C., Tenn., Texas, Va.

| | 274 | 275 | 276 | 277 | 278 | 279 | 280 | 281 |
|---|---|---|---|---|---|---|---|---|
| 13 **Biggert** | Y | Y | Y | Y | N | N | ? | N |
| 14 **Hastert** | | | | | | | | |
| 15 **Johnson** | Y | Y | Y | Y | N | N | N | N |
| 16 **Manzullo** | Y | Y | Y | Y | Y | Y | Y | N |
| 17 Evans | Y | Y | Y | Y | N | N | N | Y |
| 18 **LaHood** | Y | Y | Y | Y | Y | N | N | Y |
| 19 **Shimkus** | Y | Y | Y | Y | Y | N | N | N |
| **INDIANA** | | | | | | | | |
| 1 Visclosky | Y | Y | Y | Y | Y | N | N | Y |
| 2 **Chocola** | Y | Y | Y | Y | ? | N | N | N |
| 3 **Souder** | Y | Y | Y | Y | Y | N | Y | N |
| 4 **Buyer** | Y | Y | Y | Y | Y | Y | Y | N |
| 5 **Burton** | Y | Y | Y | Y | Y | Y | Y | N |
| 6 **Pence** | Y | Y | Y | Y | Y | N | N | N |
| 7 Carson | Y | Y | Y | Y | N | N | N | Y |
| 8 **Hostettler** | Y | Y | Y | Y | Y | Y | Y | N |
| 9 **Sodrel** | Y | Y | Y | Y | Y | Y | N | N |
| **IOWA** | | | | | | | | |
| 1 **Nussle** | Y | Y | Y | Y | Y | N | N | N |
| 2 **Leach** | Y | Y | Y | Y | N | N | N | Y |
| 3 Boswell | Y | Y | Y | Y | N | N | N | Y |
| 4 **Latham** | Y | Y | Y | Y | Y | N | N | N |
| 5 **King** | Y | Y | Y | Y | Y | Y | Y | N |
| **KANSAS** | | | | | | | | |
| 1 **Moran** | Y | Y | Y | Y | Y | Y | Y | N |
| 2 **Ryun** | Y | Y | Y | Y | Y | Y | Y | N |
| 3 Moore | Y | Y | Y | Y | Y | N | N | Y |
| 4 **Tiahrt** | Y | Y | Y | Y | Y | Y | Y | N |
| **KENTUCKY** | | | | | | | | |
| 1 **Whitfield** | Y | Y | Y | Y | Y | N | N | N |
| 2 **Lewis** | Y | Y | Y | Y | Y | Y | Y | N |
| 3 **Northup** | Y | Y | Y | Y | Y | N | N | N |
| 4 **Davis** | Y | Y | Y | Y | Y | Y | N | N |
| 5 **Rogers** | Y | Y | Y | Y | Y | N | N | N |
| 6 Chandler | Y | Y | Y | Y | Y | N | N | Y |
| **LOUISIANA** | | | | | | | | |
| 1 **Jindal** | Y | Y | Y | Y | Y | N | Y | N |
| 2 Jefferson | Y | Y | Y | Y | N | N | N | Y |
| 3 Melancon | Y | Y | Y | Y | Y | N | N | Y |
| 4 **McCrery** | Y | Y | Y | Y | Y | Y | Y | N |
| 5 **Alexander** | Y | Y | Y | Y | Y | Y | Y | N |
| 6 **Baker** | Y | Y | Y | Y | Y | Y | Y | N |
| 7 **Boustany** | Y | Y | Y | Y | Y | N | Y | N |
| **MAINE** | | | | | | | | |
| 1 Allen | Y | Y | Y | Y | N | N | N | Y |
| 2 Michaud | Y | Y | Y | Y | N | N | N | Y |
| **MARYLAND** | | | | | | | | |
| 1 **Gilchrest** | Y | Y | Y | Y | N | N | N | N |
| 2 Ruppersberger | Y | Y | Y | Y | Y | N | N | Y |
| 3 Cardin | Y | Y | Y | Y | Y | N | N | Y |
| 4 Wynn | Y | Y | Y | Y | Y | N | N | Y |
| 5 Hoyer | Y | Y | Y | Y | Y | N | N | Y |
| 6 **Bartlett** | Y | Y | Y | Y | Y | Y | Y | N |
| 7 Cummings | Y | Y | Y | Y | N | N | N | Y |
| 8 Van Hollen | Y | Y | Y | Y | N | N | N | Y |
| **MASSACHUSETTS** | | | | | | | | |
| 1 Olver | N | Y | N | Y | N | N | N | Y |
| 2 Neal | Y | Y | Y | Y | N | N | N | Y |
| 3 McGovern | N | Y | N | Y | N | N | N | Y |
| 4 Frank | Y | Y | Y | Y | Y | N | N | Y |
| 5 Meehan | Y | Y | Y | Y | N | N | N | Y |
| 6 Tierney | Y | Y | N | Y | N | N | N | Y |
| 7 Markey | N | Y | Y | Y | N | N | N | Y |
| 8 Capuano | N | Y | N | Y | N | N | N | Y |
| 9 Lynch | Y | Y | ? | Y | Y | N | Y | Y |
| 10 Delahunt | N | N | N | Y | N | N | N | Y |
| **MICHIGAN** | | | | | | | | |
| 1 Stupak | Y | Y | Y | Y | N | N | N | Y |
| 2 **Hoekstra** | Y | Y | Y | Y | Y | N | N | N |
| 3 **Ehlers** | Y | Y | Y | Y | Y | N | N | Y |
| 4 **Camp** | Y | Y | Y | Y | Y | N | N | N |
| 5 Kildee | Y | Y | Y | Y | N | N | N | Y |
| 6 **Upton** | Y | Y | Y | Y | Y | N | N | N |
| 7 **Schwarz** | Y | Y | Y | Y | Y | N | N | N |
| 8 **Rogers** | Y | Y | Y | Y | Y | N | N | N |
| 9 **Knollenberg** | Y | Y | Y | Y | Y | N | N | N |
| 10 **Miller** | Y | Y | Y | Y | Y | Y | Y | N |
| 11 **McCotter** | Y | Y | Y | Y | Y | N | N | N |
| 12 Levin | Y | Y | Y | Y | N | N | N | Y |
| 13 Kilpatrick | Y | N | N | Y | N | N | N | Y |
| 14 Conyers | N | N | N | Y | N | N | N | Y |
| 15 Dingell | Y | N | N | Y | N | N | N | Y |

| | 274 | 275 | 276 | 277 | 278 | 279 | 280 | 281 |
|---|---|---|---|---|---|---|---|---|
| **MINNESOTA** | | | | | | | | |
| 1 **Gutknecht** | Y | Y | Y | Y | Y | N | N | N |
| 2 **Kline** | Y | Y | Y | Y | Y | N | N | N |
| 3 **Ramstad** | Y | Y | Y | Y | Y | N | N | N |
| 4 McCollum | Y | Y | N | Y | N | N | N | Y |
| 5 Sabo | Y | Y | N | Y | N | N | N | Y |
| 6 **Kennedy** | Y | Y | Y | Y | Y | N | N | N |
| 7 Peterson | Y | Y | Y | Y | Y | N | N | ? |
| 8 Oberstar | Y | Y | N | Y | N | N | N | Y |
| **MISSISSIPPI** | | | | | | | | |
| 1 **Wicker** | Y | Y | Y | Y | Y | N | N | N |
| 2 Thompson | N | Y | N | Y | N | N | N | Y |
| 3 **Pickering** | Y | Y | Y | Y | Y | Y | N | N |
| 4 Taylor | ? | ? | ? | Y | Y | Y | Y | N |
| **MISSOURI** | | | | | | | | |
| 1 Clay | Y | Y | Y | Y | N | N | N | Y |
| 2 **Akin** | Y | Y | Y | Y | Y | Y | Y | N |
| 3 Carnahan | Y | Y | Y | Y | Y | N | N | Y |
| 4 Skelton | ? | ? | ? | ? | ? | ? | ? | ? |
| 5 Cleaver | Y | Y | Y | Y | N | N | N | Y |
| 6 **Graves** | ? | ? | ? | ? | ? | ? | ? | ? |
| 7 **Blunt** | Y | Y | Y | Y | Y | Y | N | N |
| 8 **Emerson** | Y | Y | Y | Y | Y | Y | Y | N |
| 9 **Hulshof** | Y | Y | Y | Y | Y | Y | Y | N |
| **MONTANA** | | | | | | | | |
| AL **Rehberg** | Y | Y | Y | Y | Y | Y | Y | N |
| **NEBRASKA** | | | | | | | | |
| 1 **Fortenberry** | Y | Y | Y | Y | Y | N | N | N |
| 2 **Terry** | Y | Y | Y | Y | Y | N | Y | N |
| 3 **Osborne** | Y | Y | Y | Y | Y | N | N | N |
| **NEVADA** | | | | | | | | |
| 1 Berkley | Y | Y | Y | Y | Y | N | N | Y |
| 2 **Gibbons** | Y | Y | Y | Y | Y | Y | Y | N |
| 3 **Porter** | Y | Y | Y | Y | Y | N | N | N |
| **NEW HAMPSHIRE** | | | | | | | | |
| 1 **Bradley** | Y | Y | Y | Y | Y | N | N | N |
| 2 **Bass** | Y | Y | Y | Y | Y | N | N | Y |
| **NEW JERSEY** | | | | | | | | |
| 1 Andrews | ? | ? | ? | ? | ? | ? | ? | ? |
| 2 **LoBiondo** | Y | Y | Y | Y | Y | N | N | N |
| 3 **Saxton** | Y | Y | Y | Y | Y | N | N | N |
| 4 **Smith** | Y | Y | Y | Y | Y | N | N | N |
| 5 **Garrett** | Y | Y | Y | Y | Y | Y | Y | N |
| 6 Pallone | Y | Y | Y | Y | N | N | N | Y |
| 7 **Ferguson** | Y | Y | Y | Y | Y | N | N | N |
| 8 Pascrell | N | N | Y | Y | N | N | N | Y |
| 9 Rothman | Y | Y | Y | Y | N | N | N | Y |
| 10 Payne | N | N | N | Y | N | N | N | Y |
| 11 **Frelinghuysen** | Y | Y | Y | Y | Y | N | N | N |
| 12 Holt | Y | Y | Y | Y | N | N | N | Y |
| 13 Menendez | Y | Y | Y | Y | Y | N | N | Y |
| **NEW MEXICO** | | | | | | | | |
| 1 **Wilson** | Y | Y | Y | Y | N | N | N | N |
| 2 **Pearce** | Y | Y | Y | Y | Y | N | N | N |
| 3 Udall | Y | Y | Y | Y | Y | N | N | Y |
| **NEW YORK** | | | | | | | | |
| 1 Bishop | Y | Y | Y | Y | N | N | N | Y |
| 2 Israel | Y | Y | Y | Y | N | N | N | Y |
| 3 **King** | Y | Y | Y | Y | Y | N | N | N |
| 4 McCarthy | Y | Y | Y | Y | Y | N | N | Y |
| 5 Ackerman | Y | Y | Y | Y | N | N | N | Y |
| 6 Meeks | N | N | Y | Y | N | N | N | Y |
| 7 Crowley | Y | Y | Y | Y | N | N | N | Y |
| 8 Nadler | Y | Y | N | Y | N | N | N | Y |
| 9 Weiner | Y | Y | Y | Y | N | N | N | Y |
| 10 Towns | Y | N | Y | Y | N | N | N | Y |
| 11 Owens | Y | Y | N | Y | N | N | N | Y |
| 12 Velázquez | Y | Y | Y | ? | N | N | N | Y |
| 13 **Fossella** | + | Y | Y | Y | Y | N | N | N |
| 14 Maloney | Y | Y | Y | Y | N | N | N | Y |
| 15 Rangel | N | Y | Y | Y | N | N | N | Y |
| 16 Serrano | N | N | N | Y | N | N | N | Y |
| 17 Engel | Y | Y | Y | Y | N | N | N | Y |
| 18 Lowey | Y | Y | Y | Y | N | N | N | Y |
| 19 **Kelly** | Y | Y | Y | Y | Y | Y | N | N |
| 20 **Sweeney** | Y | Y | Y | Y | Y | N | N | N |
| 21 McNulty | Y | Y | Y | Y | N | N | N | Y |
| 22 Hinchey | Y | Y | Y | Y | N | N | N | Y |
| 23 **McHugh** | Y | Y | Y | Y | Y | N | N | N |
| 24 **Boehlert** | Y | Y | Y | Y | Y | N | N | Y |
| 25 **Walsh** | ? | ? | ? | ? | ? | ? | ? | ? |
| 26 **Reynolds** | Y | Y | Y | Y | Y | N | N | N |
| 27 Higgins | Y | Y | Y | Y | Y | N | N | Y |
| 28 Slaughter | Y | Y | Y | Y | N | N | N | Y |
| 29 **Kuhl** | Y | Y | Y | Y | Y | N | N | N |

| | 274 | 275 | 276 | 277 | 278 | 279 | 280 | 281 |
|---|---|---|---|---|---|---|---|---|
| **NORTH CAROLINA** | | | | | | | | |
| 1 Butterfield | Y | Y | Y | Y | Y | N | N | Y |
| 2 Etheridge | Y | Y | Y | Y | Y | N | N | Y |
| 3 **Jones** | Y | Y | Y | Y | Y | Y | Y | N |
| 4 Price | Y | Y | Y | Y | N | N | N | Y |
| 5 **Foxx** | Y | Y | Y | Y | Y | Y | Y | N |
| 6 **Coble** | Y | Y | Y | Y | Y | Y | Y | N |
| 7 McIntyre | Y | Y | Y | Y | Y | N | N | Y |
| 8 **Hayes** | Y | Y | Y | Y | Y | Y | Y | N |
| 9 **Myrick** | Y | Y | Y | Y | Y | Y | Y | N |
| 10 **McHenry** | Y | Y | Y | Y | Y | Y | Y | N |
| 11 **Taylor** | Y | Y | Y | Y | Y | Y | N | N |
| 12 Watt | Y | ? | N | Y | N | N | N | Y |
| 13 Miller | Y | Y | Y | Y | N | N | N | Y |
| **NORTH DAKOTA** | | | | | | | | |
| AL Pomeroy | Y | Y | Y | Y | Y | N | N | Y |
| **OHIO** | | | | | | | | |
| 1 **Chabot** | Y | Y | Y | Y | Y | Y | Y | N |
| 2 Vacant | | | | | | | | |
| 3 **Turner** | Y | Y | Y | Y | Y | N | N | N |
| 4 **Oxley** | Y | Y | Y | Y | Y | N | N | N |
| 5 **Gillmor** | ? | ? | ? | ? | ? | ? | ? | ? |
| 6 Strickland | Y | Y | Y | Y | Y | N | N | Y |
| 7 **Hobson** | Y | Y | Y | Y | Y | N | N | N |
| 8 **Boehner** | ? | ? | ? | ? | ? | ? | ? | ? |
| 9 Kaptur | Y | Y | ? | Y | N | N | N | Y |
| 10 Kucinich | N | Y | N | Y | N | N | N | Y |
| 11 Jones | N | Y | N | Y | N | N | N | Y |
| 12 **Tiberi** | Y | Y | Y | Y | Y | Y | Y | N |
| 13 Brown | Y | Y | Y | Y | N | N | N | Y |
| 14 **LaTourette** | Y | Y | Y | Y | N | Y | N | N |
| 15 **Pryce** | Y | Y | Y | Y | Y | N | N | N |
| 16 **Regula** | Y | Y | Y | Y | Y | N | N | N |
| 17 Ryan | Y | Y | Y | Y | Y | N | N | Y |
| 18 **Ney** | Y | Y | Y | Y | Y | Y | Y | N |
| **OKLAHOMA** | | | | | | | | |
| 1 **Sullivan** | Y | Y | Y | Y | Y | Y | Y | N |
| 2 Boren | Y | Y | Y | Y | Y | N | N | Y |
| 3 **Lucas** | Y | Y | Y | Y | Y | Y | Y | N |
| 4 **Cole** | Y | Y | Y | Y | Y | N | N | N |
| 5 **Istook** | Y | Y | Y | Y | Y | ? | Y | N |
| **OREGON** | | | | | | | | |
| 1 Wu | Y | Y | Y | Y | Y | N | N | Y |
| 2 **Walden** | Y | Y | Y | Y | Y | N | N | N |
| 3 Blumenauer | + | - | - | + | - | - | - | + |
| 4 DeFazio | Y | Y | Y | Y | Y | N | N | Y |
| 5 Hooley | ? | ? | ? | ? | ? | ? | ? | ? |
| **PENNSYLVANIA** | | | | | | | | |
| 1 Brady | Y | Y | Y | Y | N | N | N | Y |
| 2 Fattah | Y | Y | Y | Y | N | N | N | Y |
| 3 **English** | Y | Y | Y | Y | Y | N | N | N |
| 4 **Hart** | Y | Y | Y | Y | Y | Y | N | N |
| 5 **Peterson** | Y | Y | Y | Y | Y | Y | N | N |
| 6 **Gerlach** | Y | Y | Y | Y | Y | N | N | N |
| 7 **Weldon** | Y | ? | Y | Y | Y | N | N | N |
| 8 **Fitzpatrick** | Y | Y | Y | Y | Y | N | N | N |
| 9 **Shuster** | Y | Y | Y | Y | Y | Y | Y | N |
| 10 **Sherwood** | Y | Y | Y | Y | Y | N | N | N |
| 11 Kanjorski | N | N | Y | Y | N | N | N | Y |
| 12 Murtha | N | N | Y | Y | N | N | N | N |
| 13 Schwartz | Y | Y | Y | Y | Y | N | N | Y |
| 14 Doyle | Y | Y | Y | Y | Y | N | N | Y |
| 15 **Dent** | Y | Y | Y | Y | Y | N | N | N |
| 16 **Pitts** | Y | Y | Y | Y | Y | Y | Y | N |
| 17 Holden | Y | Y | Y | Y | Y | N | N | Y |
| 18 **Murphy** | Y | Y | Y | Y | Y | N | N | N |
| 19 **Platts** | Y | Y | Y | Y | Y | N | N | N |
| **RHODE ISLAND** | | | | | | | | |
| 1 Kennedy | Y | Y | Y | Y | N | ? | ? | ? |
| 2 Langevin | Y | Y | Y | Y | Y | N | N | Y |
| **SOUTH CAROLINA** | | | | | | | | |
| 1 **Brown** | Y | Y | Y | Y | Y | Y | Y | N |
| 2 **Wilson** | Y | Y | Y | Y | Y | Y | Y | N |
| 3 **Barrett** | Y | Y | Y | Y | Y | Y | Y | N |
| 4 **Inglis** | Y | Y | Y | Y | Y | N | N | Y |
| 5 Spratt | Y | Y | Y | Y | Y | N | N | Y |
| 6 Clyburn | N | N | Y | Y | N | N | N | Y |
| **SOUTH DAKOTA** | | | | | | | | |
| AL Herseth | Y | Y | Y | Y | Y | N | N | Y |
| **TENNESSEE** | | | | | | | | |
| 1 **Jenkins** | Y | Y | Y | Y | Y | Y | Y | N |
| 2 **Duncan** | Y | Y | Y | Y | Y | Y | Y | N |

| | 274 | 275 | 276 | 277 | 278 | 279 | 280 | 281 |
|---|---|---|---|---|---|---|---|---|
| 3 **Wamp** | Y | Y | Y | Y | Y | Y | Y | N |
| 4 Davis | Y | Y | Y | Y | Y | N | N | Y |
| 5 Cooper | Y | Y | Y | Y | N | N | N | Y |
| 6 Gordon | Y | Y | Y | Y | N | N | N | Y |
| 7 **Blackburn** | Y | Y | Y | Y | Y | N | Y | N |
| 8 Tanner | Y | Y | Y | Y | Y | N | N | Y |
| 9 Ford | Y | Y | Y | Y | Y | N | N | Y |
| **TEXAS** | | | | | | | | |
| 1 **Gohmert** | Y | Y | Y | Y | Y | Y | Y | N |
| 2 **Poe** | Y | Y | Y | Y | Y | Y | N | N |
| 3 **Johnson, S.** | Y | Y | Y | Y | Y | Y | Y | N |
| 4 **Hall** | Y | Y | Y | Y | Y | Y | N | N |
| 5 **Hensarling** | Y | Y | Y | Y | Y | N | N | N |
| 6 **Barton** | Y | Y | Y | Y | Y | Y | Y | N |
| 7 **Culberson** | Y | Y | Y | Y | Y | Y | N | N |
| 8 **Brady** | Y | Y | Y | Y | Y | Y | N | N |
| 9 Green, A. | N | Y | Y | Y | N | N | N | Y |
| 10 **McCaul** | Y | Y | Y | Y | Y | Y | Y | N |
| 11 **Conaway** | Y | Y | Y | Y | Y | Y | N | N |
| 12 **Granger** | Y | Y | Y | Y | Y | N | N | N |
| 13 **Thornberry** | Y | Y | Y | Y | Y | N | N | N |
| 14 **Paul** | N | N | Y | N | N | Y | Y | N |
| 15 Hinojosa | Y | Y | Y | Y | N | N | N | Y |
| 16 Reyes | ? | ? | ? | ? | ? | ? | ? | ? |
| 17 Edwards | Y | Y | Y | Y | Y | N | N | Y |
| 18 Jackson-Lee | Y | Y | Y | Y | N | N | N | Y |
| 19 **Neugebauer** | Y | Y | Y | Y | Y | Y | Y | N |
| 20 Gonzalez | Y | Y | Y | Y | N | N | N | Y |
| 21 **Smith** | Y | Y | Y | Y | Y | Y | N | N |
| 22 **DeLay** | Y | Y | Y | Y | Y | Y | N | N |
| 23 **Bonilla** | Y | Y | Y | Y | Y | N | N | N |
| 24 **Marchant** | Y | Y | Y | Y | Y | Y | Y | N |
| 25 Doggett | Y | Y | Y | Y | N | N | N | Y |
| 26 **Burgess** | Y | Y | Y | Y | Y | Y | Y | N |
| 27 Ortiz | Y | Y | Y | Y | N | N | N | Y |
| 28 Cuellar | ? | ? | ? | ? | ? | ? | ? | ? |
| 29 Green, G. | Y | Y | Y | Y | Y | Y | Y | Y |
| 30 Johnson, E. | + | + | + | + | - | - | - | + |
| 31 **Carter** | Y | Y | Y | Y | Y | Y | Y | N |
| 32 **Sessions** | ? | ? | ? | ? | ? | ? | ? | ? |
| **UTAH** | | | | | | | | |
| 1 **Bishop** | Y | Y | Y | Y | Y | Y | Y | N |
| 2 Matheson | Y | Y | Y | Y | Y | N | N | Y |
| 3 **Cannon** | Y | Y | Y | Y | Y | Y | Y | N |
| **VERMONT** | | | | | | | | |
| AL *Sanders* | Y | Y | Y | Y | N | N | N | Y |
| **VIRGINIA** | | | | | | | | |
| 1 **Davis, J.** | Y | Y | Y | Y | Y | Y | Y | N |
| 2 **Drake** | Y | Y | Y | Y | Y | Y | Y | N |
| 3 Scott | N | N | N | Y | N | N | N | Y |
| 4 **Forbes** | Y | Y | Y | Y | Y | Y | Y | N |
| 5 **Goode** | Y | Y | Y | Y | Y | Y | Y | N |
| 6 **Goodlatte** | Y | Y | Y | Y | Y | Y | N | N |
| 7 **Cantor** | Y | Y | Y | Y | Y | Y | N | N |
| 8 Moran | Y | Y | Y | Y | N | N | N | Y |
| 9 Boucher | Y | Y | Y | Y | N | N | N | Y |
| 10 **Wolf** | Y | Y | Y | Y | Y | N | N | N |
| 11 **Davis, T.** | ? | ? | ? | ? | ? | ? | ? | ? |
| **WASHINGTON** | | | | | | | | |
| 1 Inslee | Y | Y | Y | Y | N | N | N | Y |
| 2 Larsen | Y | Y | Y | Y | N | N | N | Y |
| 3 Baird | ? | ? | ? | ? | ? | ? | ? | ? |
| 4 **Hastings** | Y | Y | Y | Y | Y | N | N | N |
| 5 **McMorris** | Y | Y | Y | Y | Y | Y | Y | N |
| 6 Dicks | Y | Y | Y | Y | N | N | N | Y |
| 7 McDermott | ? | ? | ? | ? | ? | ? | ? | ? |
| 8 **Reichert** | Y | Y | Y | Y | Y | N | N | N |
| 9 Smith | ? | ? | Y | Y | N | N | N | Y |
| **WEST VIRGINIA** | | | | | | | | |
| 1 Mollohan | Y | Y | Y | Y | Y | N | N | Y |
| 2 **Capito** | Y | Y | Y | Y | Y | Y | Y | N |
| 3 Rahall | Y | N | Y | Y | N | N | N | Y |
| **WISCONSIN** | | | | | | | | |
| 1 **Ryan** | Y | Y | Y | Y | Y | N | N | N |
| 2 Baldwin | Y | Y | Y | Y | N | N | N | Y |
| 3 Kind | Y | Y | Y | Y | N | N | N | Y |
| 4 Moore | Y | Y | Y | Y | N | N | N | Y |
| 5 **Sensenbrenner** | Y | Y | Y | Y | Y | Y | Y | N |
| 6 **Petri** | Y | Y | Y | Y | Y | N | Y | N |
| 7 Obey | Y | Y | ? | Y | N | N | N | Y |
| 8 **Green** | Y | Y | Y | Y | Y | N | Y | N |
| **WYOMING** | | | | | | | | |
| AL **Cubin** | Y | Y | Y | Y | Y | N | N | N |

# IN THE HOUSE | By Vote Number

**282.** HR 2745. U.N. Overhaul/Passage. Passage of the bill that would withhold up to 50 percent of U.S. dues to the United Nations unless the secretary of State certifies by Oct. 1, 2007, that the United Nations has complied with 32 of 39 changes in its operations, 14 of them mandatory. Overall U.S. contributions would be capped at 22 percent of the regular (non-peacekeeping) U.N. budget. Passed 221-184: R 213-7; D 8-176 (ND 3-136, SD 5-40); I 0-1. A "nay" was a vote in support of the president's position. June 17, 2005.

**283.** HR 2863. Fiscal 2006 Defense Appropriations/Religious Proselytizing. Obey, D-Wis., amendment to the Hunter, R-Calif., amendment. The Obey amendment would express the sense of Congress that coercive and abusive religious proselytizing at the Air Force Academy is inconsistent with academy standards. The Hunter amendment would strike similar language in the underlying bill and express the sense of Congress that expression of personal religious faith is welcome in the military and that the Air Force should review issues of religious tolerance at the academy and issue a report. Rejected 198-210: R 8-207; D 189-3 (ND 143-1, SD 46-2); I 1-0. (Subsequently, the Hunter amendment was adopted by voice vote.) June 20, 2005.

**284.** HR 2863. Fiscal 2006 Defense Appropriations/Uzbekistan. Doggett, D-Texas, amendment that would prohibit use of funds in the bill for activities in Uzbekistan. Rejected 84-329: R 1-217; D 82-112 (ND 76-71, SD 6-41); I 1-0. June 20, 2005.

**285.** HR 2863. Fiscal 2006 Defense Appropriations/Military Action Against Rogue Nations. DeFazio, D-Ore., amendment to prohibit the administration from initiating military operations without authorization from Congress. Rejected 136-280: R 3-218; D 132-62 (ND 107-40, SD 25-22); I 1-0. June 20, 2005.

**286.** HR 2863. Fiscal 2006 Defense Appropriations/Small Business Procurement. Velázquez, D-N.Y., amendment to bar use of funds in the bill for certain procurement policies that effectively exclude small businesses. Rejected 180-235: R 2-219; D 177-16 (ND 138-9, SD 39-7); I 1-0. June 20, 2005.

**287.** HR 2863. Fiscal 2006 Defense Appropriations/Passage. Passage of the bill that would appropriate $408.9 billion for the Department of Defense, including $45.3 billion for operations in Iraq and Afghanistan. The total includes $116.1 billion for operations and maintenance, $76.8 billion for procurement and $71.7 billion for research and development. Passed 398-19: R 219-2; D 178-17 (ND 133-14, SD 45-3); I 1-0. June 20, 2005.

**288.** HR 2475 Fiscal 2006 Intelligence Authorization/Previous Question. Putnam, R-Fla., motion to order the previous question (thus ending debate and the possibility of amendment) on adoption of the rule (H Res 331) to provide for House floor consideration of the intelligence authorization bill. Motion agreed to 224-201: R 224-0; D 0-200 (ND 0-150, SD 0-50); I 0-1. (Subsequently, the rule was adopted by voice vote.) June 21, 2005.

**289.** HR 2475. Fiscal 2006 Intelligence Authorization/Recommit. Waxman, D-Calif., motion to recommit the bill to the House Intelligence Committee with instructions to include language that would establish a bipartisan independent commission to investigate the detainee abuses at Abu Ghraib prison and other facilities. Motion rejected 197-228: R 1-223; D 195-5 (ND 148-2, SD 47-3); I 1-0. June 21, 2005.

ND Northern Democrats, SD Southern Democrats
Southern states: Ala., Ark., Fla., Ga., Ky., La., Miss., N.C., Okla., S.C., Tenn., Texas, Va.

| | 282 | 283 | 284 | 285 | 286 | 287 | 288 | 289 |
|---|---|---|---|---|---|---|---|---|
| **ALABAMA** | | | | | | | | |
| 1 Bonner | Y | N | N | N | N | Y | Y | N |
| 2 Everett | Y | N | N | N | N | Y | Y | N |
| 3 Rogers | Y | – | N | N | N | Y | Y | N |
| 4 Aderholt | Y | N | N | N | N | Y | Y | N |
| 5 Cramer | N | Y | N | N | Y | Y | N | N |
| 6 Bachus | Y | N | N | N | N | Y | Y | N |
| 7 Davis | N | Y | N | N | Y | Y | N | Y |
| **ALASKA** | | | | | | | | |
| AL Young | Y | N | N | N | N | Y | Y | N |
| **ARIZONA** | | | | | | | | |
| 1 Renzi | Y | N | N | N | N | Y | Y | N |
| 2 Franks | Y | N | N | N | N | Y | Y | N |
| 3 Shadegg | Y | N | N | N | N | Y | Y | N |
| 4 Pastor | N | Y | Y | Y | Y | Y | N | Y |
| 5 Hayworth | Y | N | N | N | N | Y | Y | N |
| 6 Flake | Y | ? | ? | ? | ? | ? | Y | N |
| 7 Grijalva | N | Y | Y | Y | Y | Y | N | Y |
| 8 Kolbe | Y | N | N | N | N | Y | Y | N |
| **ARKANSAS** | | | | | | | | |
| 1 Berry | N | Y | N | Y | Y | Y | N | Y |
| 2 Snyder | N | Y | N | N | Y | Y | N | Y |
| 3 Boozman | Y | N | N | N | N | Y | Y | N |
| 4 Ross | N | Y | N | N | Y | Y | N | Y |
| **CALIFORNIA** | | | | | | | | |
| 1 Thompson | N | Y | Y | Y | Y | Y | N | Y |
| 2 Herger | Y | N | N | N | N | Y | Y | N |
| 3 Lungren | Y | N | N | N | N | Y | Y | N |
| 4 Doolittle | Y | N | N | N | N | Y | Y | N |
| 5 Matsui, D. | N | Y | N | Y | Y | Y | N | Y |
| 6 Woolsey | N | Y | Y | Y | Y | N | N | Y |
| 7 Miller, George | N | Y | Y | Y | Y | Y | N | Y |
| 8 Pelosi | ? | Y | Y | Y | Y | Y | N | Y |
| 9 Lee | N | Y | Y | Y | Y | N | N | Y |
| 10 Tauscher | N | Y | N | Y | Y | Y | N | Y |
| 11 Pombo | Y | N | N | N | N | Y | Y | N |
| 12 Lantos | N | ? | N | Y | Y | Y | N | Y |
| 13 Stark | ? | Y | Y | Y | Y | N | N | Y |
| 14 Eshoo | N | Y | Y | Y | Y | Y | N | Y |
| 15 Honda | N | Y | Y | Y | Y | Y | N | Y |
| 16 Lofgren | N | Y | Y | Y | Y | Y | N | Y |
| 17 Farr | N | Y | Y | Y | Y | Y | N | Y |
| 18 Cardoza | N | Y | N | Y | Y | Y | N | Y |
| 19 Radanovich | Y | N | N | N | Y | Y | Y | N |
| 20 Costa | N | Y | N | N | Y | Y | N | Y |
| 21 Nunes | Y | N | N | N | N | Y | Y | N |
| 22 Thomas | Y | N | N | N | N | Y | Y | N |
| 23 Capps | N | Y | Y | Y | Y | Y | N | Y |
| 24 Gallegly | Y | N | N | N | N | Y | Y | N |
| 25 McKeon | Y | N | N | N | N | Y | Y | N |
| 26 Dreier | Y | N | N | N | N | Y | Y | N |
| 27 Sherman | N | Y | N | Y | Y | Y | N | Y |
| 28 Berman | N | Y | N | Y | Y | Y | N | Y |
| 29 Schiff | N | Y | N | Y | Y | Y | N | Y |
| 30 Waxman | ? | ? | ? | ? | ? | ? | N | Y |
| 31 Becerra | N | Y | Y | Y | Y | Y | N | Y |
| 32 Solis | N | Y | Y | Y | Y | Y | N | Y |
| 33 Watson | N | Y | Y | Y | Y | Y | N | Y |
| 34 Roybal-Allard | N | Y | Y | Y | Y | Y | N | Y |
| 35 Waters | N | Y | Y | N | Y | N | N | Y |
| 36 Harman | N | Y | N | Y | Y | Y | N | Y |
| 37 Millender-McD. | ? | Y | Y | Y | Y | Y | N | Y |
| 38 Napolitano | N | Y | Y | Y | Y | Y | N | Y |
| 39 Sánchez, Linda | N | Y | Y | Y | Y | Y | N | Y |
| 40 Royce | Y | N | N | N | N | Y | Y | N |
| 41 Lewis | Y | N | N | N | N | Y | Y | N |
| 42 Miller, Gary | Y | N | N | N | N | Y | Y | N |
| 43 Baca | N | Y | N | Y | Y | Y | N | Y |
| 44 Calvert | Y | N | N | N | N | Y | Y | N |
| 45 Bono | ? | N | N | N | N | Y | Y | N |
| 46 Rohrabacher | Y | N | N | N | N | Y | Y | N |
| 47 Sanchez, Loretta | N | Y | Y | Y | Y | Y | N | Y |
| 48 Cox | Y | N | N | N | N | Y | Y | N |
| 49 Issa | + | N | N | N | N | Y | Y | N |

| | 282 | 283 | 284 | 285 | 286 | 287 | 288 | 289 |
|---|---|---|---|---|---|---|---|---|
| 50 Cunningham | Y | N | N | N | N | Y | Y | N |
| 51 Filner | N | Y | Y | Y | Y | N | N | Y |
| 52 Hunter | Y | N | N | N | N | Y | Y | N |
| 53 Davis | N | Y | N | N | Y | Y | N | Y |
| **COLORADO** | | | | | | | | |
| 1 DeGette | N | Y | Y | Y | Y | Y | N | Y |
| 2 Udall | N | Y | Y | Y | Y | Y | N | Y |
| 3 Salazar | N | Y | N | N | Y | Y | N | Y |
| 4 Musgrave | Y | N | N | N | N | Y | Y | N |
| 5 Hefley | Y | N | N | N | N | Y | Y | N |
| 6 Tancredo | Y | N | N | N | N | Y | Y | N |
| 7 Beauprez | Y | N | N | N | N | Y | Y | N |
| **CONNECTICUT** | | | | | | | | |
| 1 Larson | N | Y | N | Y | Y | Y | N | Y |
| 2 Simmons | + | N | N | N | N | Y | Y | N |
| 3 DeLauro | N | Y | Y | Y | Y | Y | N | Y |
| 4 Shays | N | N | N | N | N | Y | Y | N |
| 5 Johnson | Y | N | N | N | N | Y | Y | N |
| **DELAWARE** | | | | | | | | |
| AL Castle | N | N | N | N | N | Y | Y | N |
| **FLORIDA** | | | | | | | | |
| 1 Miller | Y | N | N | N | N | Y | Y | N |
| 2 Boyd | N | Y | ? | ? | ? | ? | N | Y |
| 3 Brown | ? | ? | ? | ? | ? | ? | N | Y |
| 4 Crenshaw | Y | N | ? | ? | ? | Y | Y | N |
| 5 Brown-Waite | Y | N | N | N | N | Y | Y | N |
| 6 Stearns | Y | N | N | N | N | Y | Y | N |
| 7 Mica | Y | N | N | N | N | Y | Y | N |
| 8 Keller | Y | N | N | N | N | Y | Y | N |
| 9 Bilirakis | Y | N | N | N | N | Y | Y | N |
| 10 Young | Y | N | N | N | Y | ? | ? | ? |
| 11 Davis | N | Y | N | Y | Y | Y | N | Y |
| 12 Putnam | Y | N | N | N | N | Y | Y | N |
| 13 Harris | Y | – | – | – | – | + | Y | N |
| 14 Mack | Y | N | N | N | N | Y | Y | N |
| 15 Weldon | Y | N | N | N | N | Y | Y | N |
| 16 Foley | Y | N | N | N | N | Y | Y | N |
| 17 Meek | N | Y | N | Y | Y | Y | N | Y |
| 18 Ros-Lehtinen | Y | N | N | N | N | Y | Y | N |
| 19 Wexler | N | ? | ? | ? | ? | ? | N | Y |
| 20 Wasserman-Schultz | N | ? | ? | ? | ? | Y | N | Y |
| 21 Diaz-Balart, L. | Y | N | N | N | N | Y | Y | N |
| 22 Shaw | Y | N | N | N | N | Y | Y | N |
| 23 Hastings | N | Y | N | N | Y | Y | N | Y |
| 24 Feeney | Y | N | N | N | N | Y | Y | N |
| 25 Diaz-Balart, M. | Y | N | N | N | N | Y | Y | N |
| **GEORGIA** | | | | | | | | |
| 1 Kingston | Y | N | N | N | N | Y | Y | N |
| 2 Bishop | ? | Y | N | Y | Y | Y | N | Y |
| 3 Marshall | N | N | N | Y | Y | Y | N | N |
| 4 McKinney | N | Y | Y | Y | N | N | N | Y |
| 5 Lewis | N | Y | Y | Y | Y | N | ? | ? |
| 6 Price | Y | N | N | N | N | Y | Y | N |
| 7 Linder | Y | N | N | N | N | Y | Y | N |
| 8 Westmoreland | Y | N | N | N | N | Y | Y | N |
| 9 Norwood | Y | N | N | N | N | Y | Y | N |
| 10 Deal | Y | N | N | N | N | Y | Y | N |
| 11 Gingrey | Y | N | N | N | N | Y | Y | N |
| 12 Barrow | ? | N | N | N | Y | Y | N | Y |
| 13 Scott | N | Y | N | Y | Y | Y | N | Y |
| **HAWAII** | | | | | | | | |
| 1 Abercrombie | N | Y | Y | Y | Y | Y | N | Y |
| 2 Case | N | Y | N | Y | Y | Y | N | Y |
| **IDAHO** | | | | | | | | |
| 1 Otter | Y | N | N | N | N | Y | Y | N |
| 2 Simpson | Y | N | N | N | N | Y | Y | N |
| **ILLINOIS** | | | | | | | | |
| 1 Rush | N | Y | Y | Y | Y | Y | N | Y |
| 2 Jackson | N | Y | Y | Y | Y | N | N | Y |
| 3 Lipinski | N | Y | N | Y | Y | Y | N | Y |
| 4 Gutierrez | N | Y | Y | Y | Y | Y | N | Y |
| 5 Emanuel | N | Y | N | Y | Y | Y | N | Y |
| 6 Hyde | Y | N | N | N | N | Y | Y | N |
| 7 Davis | N | Y | Y | Y | Y | N | N | Y |
| 8 Bean | N | Y | N | N | Y | Y | N | Y |
| 9 Schakowsky | N | Y | Y | Y | Y | N | N | Y |
| 10 Kirk | Y | Y | N | N | N | Y | Y | N |
| 11 Weller | Y | N | – | N | N | Y | Y | N |
| 12 Costello | Y | Y | N | Y | Y | Y | N | Y |

**KEY**  Republicans  Democrats  *Independents*

| Y | Voted for (yea) | X | Paired against | C | Voted "present" to avoid possible conflict of interest |
|---|---|---|---|---|---|
| # | Paired for | – | Announced against | | |
| + | Announced for | P | Voted "present" | ? | Did not vote or otherwise make a position known |
| N | Voted against (nay) | | | | |

| | 282 | 283 | 284 | 285 | 286 | 287 | 288 | 289 |
|---|---|---|---|---|---|---|---|---|
| 13 **Biggert** | Y | Y | N | N | N | Y | Y | N |
| 14 **Hastert** | | | | | | | | |
| 15 **Johnson** | Y | N | N | N | N | Y | Y | N |
| 16 **Manzullo** | Y | N | N | N | N | Y | Y | N |
| 17 Evans | N | Y | Y | Y | Y | Y | N | Y |
| 18 **LaHood** | Y | N | N | N | N | Y | Y | N |
| 19 **Shimkus** | Y | ? | N | N | N | Y | Y | N |
| **INDIANA** | | | | | | | | |
| 1 Visclosky | N | Y | N | N | Y | Y | N | Y |
| 2 **Chocola** | Y | N | N | N | N | Y | Y | N |
| 3 **Souder** | Y | ? | ? | ? | ? | ? | Y | N |
| 4 **Buyer** | Y | N | N | N | N | Y | Y | N |
| 5 **Burton** | Y | N | N | N | N | Y | Y | N |
| 6 **Pence** | Y | N | N | N | N | Y | Y | – |
| 7 Carson | N | Y | Y | Y | Y | Y | N | Y |
| 8 **Hostettler** | Y | N | N | N | N | Y | Y | N |
| 9 **Sodrel** | Y | N | N | N | N | Y | Y | N |
| **IOWA** | | | | | | | | |
| 1 **Nussle** | Y | N | N | N | N | Y | Y | N |
| 2 **Leach** | N | Y | N | Y | Y | Y | Y | Y |
| 3 Boswell | N | Y | N | Y | N | Y | N | Y |
| 4 **Latham** | Y | N | N | N | N | Y | Y | N |
| 5 **King** | Y | N | N | N | N | Y | Y | N |
| **KANSAS** | | | | | | | | |
| 1 **Moran** | Y | N | N | N | N | Y | Y | N |
| 2 **Ryun** | Y | N | N | N | N | Y | Y | N |
| 3 Moore | N | Y | N | N | Y | Y | N | Y |
| 4 **Tiahrt** | Y | N | N | N | N | Y | Y | N |
| **KENTUCKY** | | | | | | | | |
| 1 **Whitfield** | Y | N | N | N | N | Y | ? | N |
| 2 **Lewis** | Y | ? | ? | ? | ? | ? | Y | N |
| 3 **Northup** | Y | N | N | N | N | Y | Y | N |
| 4 **Davis** | Y | N | N | N | N | Y | Y | N |
| 5 **Rogers** | Y | N | N | N | N | Y | Y | N |
| 6 Chandler | N | Y | N | Y | Y | Y | N | Y |
| **LOUISIANA** | | | | | | | | |
| 1 **Jindal** | Y | N | N | N | N | Y | Y | N |
| 2 Jefferson | N | Y | N | N | N | Y | N | Y |
| 3 Melancon | N | Y | N | N | N | Y | N | Y |
| 4 **McCrery** | Y | N | N | N | N | Y | Y | N |
| 5 **Alexander** | Y | N | N | N | N | Y | Y | N |
| 6 **Baker** | Y | ? | ? | ? | ? | ? | Y | N |
| 7 **Boustany** | Y | N | N | N | N | Y | Y | N |
| **MAINE** | | | | | | | | |
| 1 Allen | N | Y | Y | N | Y | Y | N | Y |
| 2 Michaud | N | Y | N | Y | Y | Y | N | Y |
| **MARYLAND** | | | | | | | | |
| 1 **Gilchrest** | Y | N | N | N | N | Y | Y | N |
| 2 Ruppersberger | N | Y | N | N | Y | Y | N | Y |
| 3 Cardin | N | Y | Y | Y | Y | Y | N | Y |
| 4 Wynn | N | Y | N | Y | Y | Y | N | Y |
| 5 Hoyer | N | Y | N | N | Y | Y | N | Y |
| 6 **Bartlett** | Y | N | N | N | N | Y | Y | N |
| 7 Cummings | N | Y | N | Y | Y | Y | N | Y |
| 8 Van Hollen | N | Y | Y | Y | Y | Y | N | Y |
| **MASSACHUSETTS** | | | | | | | | |
| 1 Olver | N | Y | Y | Y | Y | Y | N | Y |
| 2 Neal | N | Y | Y | Y | Y | Y | N | Y |
| 3 McGovern | N | Y | Y | Y | Y | Y | N | Y |
| 4 Frank | N | Y | Y | Y | Y | Y | N | Y |
| 5 Meehan | N | Y | Y | Y | Y | Y | N | Y |
| 6 Tierney | N | Y | Y | Y | Y | Y | N | Y |
| 7 Markey | N | Y | Y | Y | Y | Y | N | Y |
| 8 Capuano | N | Y | N | Y | Y | Y | N | Y |
| 9 Lynch | N | Y | N | N | Y | Y | N | Y |
| 10 Delahunt | N | Y | Y | Y | Y | Y | N | Y |
| **MICHIGAN** | | | | | | | | |
| 1 Stupak | N | Y | N | N | Y | Y | N | Y |
| 2 **Hoekstra** | Y | N | N | N | Y | Y | Y | N |
| 3 **Ehlers** | Y | – | N | N | N | Y | Y | N |
| 4 **Camp** | Y | N | N | N | N | Y | Y | N |
| 5 Kildee | N | Y | N | Y | Y | Y | N | Y |
| 6 **Upton** | Y | N | N | N | N | Y | Y | N |
| 7 **Schwarz** | Y | ? | ? | ? | ? | ? | Y | N |
| 8 **Rogers** | Y | N | N | N | N | Y | Y | N |
| 9 **Knollenberg** | Y | ? | N | N | N | Y | Y | N |
| 10 **Miller** | Y | N | N | N | N | Y | Y | N |
| 11 **McCotter** | Y | N | N | N | N | Y | Y | N |
| 12 Levin | N | Y | N | Y | Y | Y | N | Y |
| 13 Kilpatrick | N | ? | N | Y | N | Y | N | Y |
| 14 Conyers | N | ? | Y | Y | Y | N | N | Y |
| 15 Dingell | N | Y | N | Y | Y | Y | N | Y |
| **MINNESOTA** | | | | | | | | |
| 1 **Gutknecht** | Y | N | N | N | N | Y | Y | N |
| 2 **Kline** | Y | N | N | N | N | Y | Y | N |
| 3 **Ramstad** | Y | N | N | N | N | Y | Y | N |
| 4 McCollum | N | Y | Y | Y | Y | Y | N | Y |
| 5 Sabo | N | Y | Y | Y | Y | Y | N | Y |
| 6 **Kennedy** | Y | N | N | N | N | Y | Y | N |
| 7 Peterson | N | N | N | N | N | Y | N | Y |
| 8 Oberstar | N | Y | Y | Y | Y | Y | N | Y |
| **MISSISSIPPI** | | | | | | | | |
| 1 **Wicker** | Y | N | N | N | N | Y | Y | N |
| 2 Thompson | N | Y | N | Y | N | Y | N | Y |
| 3 **Pickering** | Y | N | N | N | N | Y | Y | N |
| 4 Taylor | Y | N | N | N | Y | Y | N | Y |
| **MISSOURI** | | | | | | | | |
| 1 Clay | N | Y | Y | Y | Y | Y | N | Y |
| 2 **Akin** | Y | N | N | N | N | Y | Y | N |
| 3 Carnahan | N | Y | N | Y | Y | Y | N | Y |
| 4 Skelton | ? | Y | N | N | Y | Y | N | Y |
| 5 Cleaver | N | Y | N | Y | Y | Y | N | Y |
| 6 **Graves** | + | N | N | N | N | Y | Y | N |
| 7 **Blunt** | Y | N | N | N | N | Y | Y | N |
| 8 **Emerson** | Y | N | N | N | N | Y | Y | N |
| 9 **Hulshof** | Y | N | N | N | N | Y | Y | N |
| **MONTANA** | | | | | | | | |
| AL **Rehberg** | Y | N | N | N | N | Y | Y | N |
| **NEBRASKA** | | | | | | | | |
| 1 **Fortenberry** | Y | N | N | N | N | Y | Y | N |
| 2 **Terry** | Y | N | N | N | N | Y | Y | N |
| 3 **Osborne** | Y | N | N | N | N | Y | Y | N |
| **NEVADA** | | | | | | | | |
| 1 Berkley | Y | Y | Y | Y | Y | Y | N | Y |
| 2 **Gibbons** | Y | N | N | N | N | Y | Y | N |
| 3 **Porter** | Y | N | N | N | N | Y | Y | N |
| **NEW HAMPSHIRE** | | | | | | | | |
| 1 **Bradley** | Y | N | N | N | N | Y | Y | N |
| 2 **Bass** | Y | N | N | N | N | Y | Y | N |
| **NEW JERSEY** | | | | | | | | |
| 1 Andrews | – | Y | N | Y | Y | Y | N | Y |
| 2 **LoBiondo** | Y | N | N | N | N | Y | Y | N |
| 3 **Saxton** | Y | N | N | N | N | Y | Y | N |
| 4 **Smith** | Y | N | N | N | N | Y | Y | N |
| 5 **Garrett** | Y | N | N | N | N | Y | Y | N |
| 6 Pallone | N | Y | Y | Y | Y | Y | N | Y |
| 7 **Ferguson** | Y | N | N | N | N | Y | Y | N |
| 8 Pascrell | N | Y | N | Y | Y | Y | N | Y |
| 9 Rothman | N | Y | N | Y | Y | Y | N | Y |
| 10 Payne | N | Y | Y | Y | Y | N | N | Y |
| 11 **Frelinghuysen** | Y | N | N | N | N | Y | Y | N |
| 12 Holt | N | Y | Y | Y | Y | Y | N | Y |
| 13 Menendez | N | Y | N | Y | Y | Y | N | Y |
| **NEW MEXICO** | | | | | | | | |
| 1 **Wilson** | Y | Y | N | N | N | Y | Y | N |
| 2 **Pearce** | Y | N | N | N | N | Y | Y | N |
| 3 Udall | N | Y | Y | Y | Y | Y | N | Y |
| **NEW YORK** | | | | | | | | |
| 1 Bishop | N | Y | N | N | Y | Y | N | Y |
| 2 Israel | N | Y | N | N | Y | Y | N | Y |
| 3 **King** | Y | N | N | N | N | Y | Y | N |
| 4 McCarthy | N | Y | N | N | Y | Y | N | Y |
| 5 Ackerman | N | Y | N | Y | Y | Y | N | Y |
| 6 Meeks | N | Y | Y | Y | Y | Y | N | Y |
| 7 Crowley | N | Y | N | Y | Y | Y | N | Y |
| 8 Nadler | N | Y | Y | Y | Y | Y | N | Y |
| 9 Weiner | N | Y | Y | Y | Y | Y | N | Y |
| 10 Towns | N | ? | ? | ? | ? | ? | N | Y |
| 11 Owens | N | Y | Y | Y | Y | N | N | Y |
| 12 Velázquez | N | Y | Y | Y | Y | Y | N | Y |
| 13 **Fossella** | Y | N | N | N | N | Y | Y | N |
| 14 Maloney | N | Y | N | Y | Y | Y | N | Y |
| 15 Rangel | N | Y | N | Y | Y | N | N | Y |
| 16 Serrano | N | Y | Y | Y | Y | Y | N | Y |
| 17 Engel | N | Y | N | Y | Y | Y | N | Y |
| 18 Lowey | N | Y | N | N | Y | Y | N | Y |
| 19 **Kelly** | Y | N | N | N | N | Y | Y | N |
| 20 **Sweeney** | Y | N | N | N | N | Y | Y | N |
| 21 McNulty | N | Y | Y | Y | Y | Y | N | Y |
| 22 Hinchey | N | Y | Y | Y | Y | N | N | Y |
| 23 **McHugh** | Y | N | N | N | N | Y | Y | N |
| 24 **Boehlert** | N | N | N | N | N | Y | Y | N |
| 25 **Walsh** | ? | N | N | N | N | Y | Y | N |
| 26 **Reynolds** | Y | ? | ? | N | N | Y | Y | N |
| 27 Higgins | N | Y | N | Y | Y | Y | N | Y |
| 28 Slaughter | ? | Y | Y | Y | Y | Y | N | Y |
| 29 **Kuhl** | Y | N | N | N | N | Y | Y | N |
| **NORTH CAROLINA** | | | | | | | | |
| 1 Butterfield | N | Y | N | N | Y | Y | N | Y |
| 2 Etheridge | N | Y | N | N | Y | Y | N | Y |
| 3 **Jones** | Y | N | N | Y | N | Y | Y | N |
| 4 Price | N | Y | N | Y | Y | Y | N | Y |
| 5 **Foxx** | Y | N | N | N | N | Y | Y | N |
| 6 **Coble** | Y | N | N | N | N | Y | Y | N |
| 7 McIntyre | Y | Y | N | N | Y | Y | N | Y |
| 8 **Hayes** | Y | N | N | N | N | Y | Y | N |
| 9 **Myrick** | Y | N | N | N | N | Y | Y | N |
| 10 **McHenry** | Y | N | N | N | N | Y | Y | N |
| 11 **Taylor** | Y | N | N | N | N | Y | Y | N |
| 12 Watt | N | Y | N | Y | Y | N | N | Y |
| 13 Miller | N | Y | N | N | Y | Y | N | Y |
| **NORTH DAKOTA** | | | | | | | | |
| AL Pomeroy | N | Y | Y | N | Y | Y | N | Y |
| **OHIO** | | | | | | | | |
| 1 **Chabot** | Y | N | N | N | N | Y | Y | N |
| 2 Vacant | | | | | | | | |
| 3 **Turner** | Y | N | N | N | N | Y | Y | N |
| 4 **Oxley** | Y | N | N | N | N | Y | Y | N |
| 5 **Gillmor** | ? | N | N | N | N | Y | Y | N |
| 6 Strickland | N | Y | Y | Y | Y | Y | N | Y |
| 7 **Hobson** | Y | N | N | N | N | Y | Y | N |
| 8 **Boehner** | ? | N | N | N | N | Y | Y | N |
| 9 Kaptur | N | Y | N | N | Y | Y | N | Y |
| 10 Kucinich | N | Y | Y | Y | Y | N | N | Y |
| 11 Jones | N | Y | N | N | N | Y | N | Y |
| 12 **Tiberi** | Y | N | N | N | N | Y | Y | N |
| 13 Brown | N | Y | Y | Y | Y | Y | N | Y |
| 14 **LaTourette** | Y | N | N | N | N | Y | Y | N |
| 15 **Pryce** | Y | N | N | N | N | Y | Y | N |
| 16 **Regula** | Y | N | N | N | N | Y | Y | N |
| 17 Ryan | N | Y | N | N | N | Y | N | Y |
| 18 **Ney** | Y | N | N | N | N | Y | Y | N |
| **OKLAHOMA** | | | | | | | | |
| 1 **Sullivan** | Y | N | N | N | N | Y | Y | N |
| 2 Boren | N | Y | N | N | Y | Y | N | Y |
| 3 **Lucas** | Y | N | N | N | N | Y | Y | N |
| 4 **Cole** | Y | N | N | N | N | Y | Y | N |
| 5 **Istook** | Y | ? | ? | ? | ? | ? | Y | N |
| **OREGON** | | | | | | | | |
| 1 Wu | N | Y | N | Y | Y | Y | N | Y |
| 2 **Walden** | Y | N | N | N | N | Y | ? | N |
| 3 Blumenauer | ? | Y | Y | Y | Y | Y | N | Y |
| 4 DeFazio | N | Y | Y | Y | Y | Y | N | Y |
| 5 Hooley | ? | Y | Y | Y | Y | Y | N | Y |
| **PENNSYLVANIA** | | | | | | | | |
| 1 Brady | N | Y | N | N | Y | Y | N | Y |
| 2 Fattah | N | Y | N | N | Y | Y | N | Y |
| 3 **English** | Y | N | N | N | N | Y | Y | N |
| 4 **Hart** | Y | N | N | N | N | Y | Y | N |
| 5 **Peterson** | Y | N | N | N | N | Y | Y | N |
| 6 **Gerlach** | Y | N | N | N | N | Y | Y | N |
| 7 **Weldon** | Y | N | N | N | N | Y | Y | N |
| 8 **Fitzpatrick** | Y | N | N | N | N | Y | Y | N |
| 9 **Shuster** | Y | N | N | N | N | Y | Y | N |
| 10 **Sherwood** | Y | N | N | N | N | Y | Y | N |
| 11 Kanjorski | N | Y | N | N | Y | Y | N | Y |
| 12 Murtha | N | Y | N | N | Y | Y | N | Y |
| 13 Schwartz | N | Y | N | N | Y | Y | N | Y |
| 14 Doyle | N | Y | N | N | Y | Y | N | Y |
| 15 **Dent** | Y | Y | N | N | N | Y | Y | N |
| 16 **Pitts** | Y | N | N | N | N | Y | Y | N |
| 17 Holden | N | Y | N | N | Y | Y | N | Y |
| 18 **Murphy** | Y | N | N | N | N | Y | + | – |
| 19 **Platts** | Y | ? | N | N | N | Y | Y | N |
| **RHODE ISLAND** | | | | | | | | |
| 1 Kennedy | ? | Y | N | N | Y | Y | N | Y |
| 2 Langevin | N | Y | N | N | Y | Y | N | Y |
| **SOUTH CAROLINA** | | | | | | | | |
| 1 **Brown** | Y | N | N | N | N | Y | Y | N |
| 2 **Wilson** | Y | N | N | N | N | Y | Y | N |
| 3 **Barrett** | Y | N | N | N | N | Y | Y | N |
| 4 **Inglis** | Y | N | N | N | N | Y | Y | N |
| 5 Spratt | N | Y | N | N | Y | Y | N | Y |
| 6 Clyburn | N | Y | N | Y | N | Y | N | Y |
| **SOUTH DAKOTA** | | | | | | | | |
| AL Herseth | N | ? | ? | ? | ? | ? | ? | ? |
| **TENNESSEE** | | | | | | | | |
| 1 **Jenkins** | Y | N | N | N | N | Y | Y | N |
| 2 **Duncan** | Y | N | N | N | N | N | Y | N |
| 3 **Wamp** | Y | – | – | N | N | Y | Y | N |
| 4 Davis | N | Y | N | N | N | Y | N | N |
| 5 Cooper | N | Y | N | N | Y | Y | N | Y |
| 6 Gordon | N | Y | N | N | Y | Y | N | Y |
| 7 **Blackburn** | Y | N | N | N | N | Y | Y | N |
| 8 Tanner | ? | Y | N | N | Y | Y | N | Y |
| 9 Ford | N | Y | N | N | Y | Y | N | Y |
| **TEXAS** | | | | | | | | |
| 1 **Gohmert** | Y | N | N | N | N | Y | Y | N |
| 2 **Poe** | Y | N | N | N | N | Y | Y | N |
| 3 **Johnson, S.** | Y | N | N | N | N | Y | Y | N |
| 4 **Hall** | Y | N | N | N | N | Y | Y | N |
| 5 **Hensarling** | Y | N | N | N | N | Y | Y | N |
| 6 **Barton** | Y | N | N | N | N | Y | Y | N |
| 7 **Culberson** | Y | N | N | N | N | Y | Y | N |
| 8 **Brady** | Y | N | N | N | N | Y | Y | N |
| 9 Green, A. | N | Y | N | Y | Y | Y | N | Y |
| 10 **McCaul** | Y | N | N | N | N | Y | Y | N |
| 11 **Conaway** | Y | N | N | N | N | Y | Y | ? |
| 12 **Granger** | Y | ? | ? | ? | ? | ? | Y | N |
| 13 **Thornberry** | Y | N | N | N | N | Y | Y | N |
| 14 **Paul** | N | N | Y | Y | N | N | Y | N |
| 15 Hinojosa | N | Y | N | Y | Y | Y | N | Y |
| 16 Reyes | ? | Y | N | Y | Y | Y | N | Y |
| 17 Edwards | N | Y | N | Y | Y | Y | N | Y |
| 18 Jackson-Lee | N | Y | Y | Y | Y | Y | N | Y |
| 19 **Neugebauer** | Y | N | N | N | N | Y | Y | N |
| 20 Gonzalez | N | Y | N | Y | Y | Y | N | Y |
| 21 **Smith** | Y | N | N | N | N | Y | Y | N |
| 22 **DeLay** | Y | N | N | N | N | Y | Y | N |
| 23 **Bonilla** | Y | N | N | N | N | Y | Y | N |
| 24 **Marchant** | Y | N | N | N | N | Y | Y | N |
| 25 Doggett | N | Y | Y | Y | Y | Y | N | Y |
| 26 **Burgess** | Y | N | N | N | N | Y | Y | N |
| 27 Ortiz | N | Y | N | Y | Y | Y | N | Y |
| 28 Cuellar | ? | Y | N | N | Y | Y | N | Y |
| 29 Green, G. | Y | Y | N | Y | Y | Y | N | Y |
| 30 Johnson, E. | – | Y | Y | Y | Y | Y | N | Y |
| 31 **Carter** | Y | N | N | N | N | Y | + | – |
| 32 **Sessions** | ? | N | N | N | N | Y | ? | ? |
| **UTAH** | | | | | | | | |
| 1 **Bishop** | Y | N | N | N | N | Y | Y | N |
| 2 Matheson | N | Y | N | N | N | Y | N | N |
| 3 **Cannon** | Y | N | N | N | N | Y | Y | N |
| **VERMONT** | | | | | | | | |
| AL *Sanders* | N | Y | Y | Y | Y | Y | N | Y |
| **VIRGINIA** | | | | | | | | |
| 1 **Davis, J.** | Y | N | N | N | N | Y | Y | N |
| 2 **Drake** | Y | N | N | N | N | Y | Y | N |
| 3 Scott | N | Y | N | Y | N | Y | N | Y |
| 4 **Forbes** | Y | N | N | N | N | Y | Y | N |
| 5 **Goode** | N | N | N | N | N | Y | Y | N |
| 6 **Goodlatte** | Y | N | N | N | N | Y | Y | N |
| 7 **Cantor** | Y | N | N | N | N | Y | Y | N |
| 8 Moran | N | Y | Y | Y | Y | Y | N | Y |
| 9 Boucher | N | Y | N | Y | N | Y | N | Y |
| 10 **Wolf** | Y | N | N | N | N | Y | Y | N |
| 11 **Davis, T.** | ? | N | N | N | N | Y | Y | N |
| **WASHINGTON** | | | | | | | | |
| 1 Inslee | N | Y | Y | Y | Y | Y | N | Y |
| 2 Larsen | N | Y | Y | Y | Y | Y | N | Y |
| 3 Baird | ? | Y | Y | Y | Y | Y | N | Y |
| 4 **Hastings** | Y | N | N | N | N | Y | Y | N |
| 5 **McMorris** | Y | N | N | N | N | Y | Y | N |
| 6 Dicks | N | Y | N | N | Y | Y | N | Y |
| 7 McDermott | – | Y | Y | Y | Y | N | N | Y |
| 8 **Reichert** | N | N | N | N | N | Y | Y | N |
| 9 Smith | N | Y | Y | Y | N | Y | N | Y |
| **WEST VIRGINIA** | | | | | | | | |
| 1 Mollohan | Y | Y | N | N | Y | Y | N | Y |
| 2 **Capito** | Y | N | N | N | N | Y | Y | N |
| 3 Rahall | N | Y | N | Y | Y | Y | N | Y |
| **WISCONSIN** | | | | | | | | |
| 1 **Ryan** | Y | N | N | N | N | Y | Y | N |
| 2 Baldwin | N | Y | Y | Y | Y | N | N | Y |
| 3 Kind | N | Y | N | Y | Y | Y | N | Y |
| 4 Moore | N | ? | ? | ? | ? | ? | N | Y |
| 5 **Sensenbrenner** | Y | Y | N | N | N | Y | Y | N |
| 6 **Petri** | Y | N | N | N | N | Y | Y | N |
| 7 Obey | N | Y | N | Y | Y | Y | N | Y |
| 8 **Green** | Y | N | N | N | N | Y | Y | N |
| **WYOMING** | | | | | | | | |
| AL **Cubin** | Y | N | N | N | N | Y | Y | N |

# IN THE HOUSE | By Vote Number

## 290. HR 2475. Fiscal 2006 Intelligence Authorization/Passage.
Passage of the bill that would authorize classified amounts in fiscal 2006 for U.S. intelligence activities and agencies including the CIA, the National Security Agency and the Defense Intelligence Agency. Passed 409-16: R 222-2; D 186-14 (ND 137-13, SD 49-1); I 1-0. June 21, 2005.

## 291. H J Res 52. Myanmar Sanctions/Passage.
Shaw, R-Fla., motion to suspend the rules and pass the joint resolution that would extend for one year import restrictions on products from Myanmar, formerly known as Burma, until the president certifies that the Myanmar government has made significant progress in democracy and human rights. Motion agreed to 423-2: R 222-2; D 200-0 (ND 150-0, SD 50-0); I 1-0. A two-thirds majority of those present and voting (284 in this case) is required for passage under suspension of the rules. June 21, 2005.

## 292. H Con Res 160. Juneteenth Independence Day Tribute/Adoption.
Brown-Waite, R-Fla., motion to suspend the rules and adopt the concurrent resolution to recognize the historical significance and back the celebration of June 19, 1865, as "Juneteenth," and urge the president to call for the public to observe the day. Motion agreed to 425-0: R 224-0; D 200-0 (ND 150-0, SD 50-0); I 1-0. A two-thirds majority of those present and voting (284 in this case) is required for adoption under suspension of the rules. June 21, 2005.

## 293. H J Res 10. Flag Desecration Constitutional Amendment/Democratic Substitute.
Watt, D-N.C., substitute amendment that would grant Congress the power to prohibit the physical desecration of the U.S. flag but only if that is consistent with the First Amendment of the Constitution. Rejected 129-279: R 3-213; D 125-66 (ND 101-44, SD 24-22); I 1-0. June 22, 2005.

## 294. H J Res 10. Flag Desecration Constitutional Amendment/Appeal Ruling of the Chair.
Sensenbrenner, R-Wis., motion to table (kill) the Taylor, D-Miss., appeal of the ruling of the chair that the Taylor motion to recommit was not germane. The Taylor motion would recommit the bill to the Judiciary Committee with instructions to add language proposing a balanced-budget constitutional amendment. Motion agreed to 222-194: R 221-0; D 1-193 (ND 1-147, SD 0-46); I 0-1. June 22, 2005.

## 295. H J Res 10. Flag Desecration Constitutional Amendment/Appeal Ruling of the Chair.
Sensenbrenner, R-Wis., motion to table (kill) the Taylor, D-Miss., appeal of the ruling of the chair that the Taylor motion to recommit was not germane. The Taylor motion would recommit the bill to the Judiciary Committee to add language proposing a constitutional amendment to segregate several trust funds from the federal budget. Motion agreed to 222-190: R 220-0; D 2-189 (ND 2-143, SD 0-46); I 0-1. June 22, 2005.

ND Northern Democrats, SD Southern Democrats
Southern states: Ala., Ark., Fla., Ga., Ky., La., Miss., N.C., Okla., S.C., Tenn., Texas, Va.

| | 290 | 291 | 292 | 293 | 294 | 295 |
|---|---|---|---|---|---|---|
| **ALABAMA** | | | | | | |
| 1 Bonner | Y | Y | Y | ? | ? | ? |
| 2 Everett | Y | Y | Y | N | Y | Y |
| 3 Rogers | Y | Y | Y | N | Y | Y |
| 4 Aderholt | Y | Y | Y | N | Y | Y |
| 5 Cramer | Y | Y | Y | N | N | N |
| 6 Bachus | Y | Y | Y | N | Y | Y |
| 7 Davis | Y | Y | Y | Y | N | N |
| **ALASKA** | | | | | | |
| AL Young | Y | Y | Y | N | Y | Y |
| **ARIZONA** | | | | | | |
| 1 Renzi | Y | Y | Y | N | Y | Y |
| 2 Franks | Y | Y | Y | N | Y | Y |
| 3 Shadegg | Y | Y | Y | N | Y | Y |
| 4 Pastor | Y | Y | Y | Y | N | N |
| 5 Hayworth | Y | Y | Y | N | Y | Y |
| 6 Flake | Y | N | Y | N | Y | Y |
| 7 Grijalva | Y | Y | Y | Y | N | N |
| 8 Kolbe | Y | Y | Y | N | Y | Y |
| **ARKANSAS** | | | | | | |
| 1 Berry | Y | Y | Y | N | N | N |
| 2 Snyder | Y | Y | Y | N | N | N |
| 3 Boozman | Y | Y | Y | N | Y | Y |
| 4 Ross | Y | Y | Y | N | N | N |
| **CALIFORNIA** | | | | | | |
| 1 Thompson | Y | Y | Y | Y | N | N |
| 2 Herger | Y | Y | Y | N | Y | Y |
| 3 Lungren | Y | Y | Y | N | Y | Y |
| 4 Doolittle | Y | Y | Y | N | Y | Y |
| 5 Matsui, D. | Y | Y | Y | Y | N | N |
| 6 Woolsey | N | Y | Y | N | N | N |
| 7 Miller, George | Y | Y | Y | Y | N | N |
| 8 Pelosi | Y | Y | Y | Y | N | N |
| 9 Lee | N | Y | N | N | N | N |
| 10 Tauscher | Y | Y | Y | Y | N | N |
| 11 Pombo | Y | Y | Y | N | Y | Y |
| 12 Lantos | Y | Y | Y | N | N | N |
| 13 Stark | N | Y | Y | N | N | N |
| 14 Eshoo | Y | Y | Y | Y | N | N |
| 15 Honda | Y | Y | Y | Y | N | N |
| 16 Lofgren | Y | Y | Y | Y | N | N |
| 17 Farr | Y | Y | Y | Y | N | N |
| 18 Cardoza | Y | Y | Y | N | N | N |
| 19 Radanovich | Y | Y | Y | N | Y | Y |
| 20 Costa | Y | Y | Y | Y | N | N |
| 21 Nunes | Y | Y | Y | N | Y | Y |
| 22 Thomas | Y | Y | Y | ? | ? | ? |
| 23 Capps | Y | Y | Y | Y | N | N |
| 24 Gallegly | Y | Y | Y | N | Y | Y |
| 25 McKeon | Y | Y | Y | N | Y | Y |
| 26 Dreier | Y | Y | Y | N | Y | Y |
| 27 Sherman | Y | Y | Y | N | N | N |
| 28 Berman | Y | Y | Y | Y | N | N |
| 29 Schiff | Y | Y | Y | Y | N | N |
| 30 Waxman | Y | Y | Y | Y | N | N |
| 31 Becerra | Y | Y | Y | + | N | N |
| 32 Solis | Y | Y | Y | Y | N | N |
| 33 Watson | N | Y | Y | Y | N | N |
| 34 Roybal-Allard | Y | Y | Y | Y | N | N |
| 35 Waters | N | Y | Y | N | N | N |
| 36 Harman | Y | Y | Y | N | N | N |
| 37 Millender-McD. | Y | Y | Y | Y | N | N |
| 38 Napolitano | Y | Y | Y | Y | N | N |
| 39 Sánchez, Linda | Y | Y | Y | Y | N | N |
| 40 Royce | Y | Y | Y | N | Y | Y |
| 41 Lewis | Y | Y | Y | N | Y | Y |
| 42 Miller, Gary | Y | Y | Y | N | Y | Y |
| 43 Baca | Y | Y | Y | N | N | N |
| 44 Calvert | Y | Y | Y | N | Y | Y |
| 45 Bono | Y | Y | Y | N | Y | Y |
| 46 Rohrabacher | Y | Y | Y | N | Y | Y |
| 47 Sanchez, Loretta | Y | Y | Y | N | N | N |
| 48 Cox | Y | Y | Y | N | Y | ? |
| 49 Issa | Y | Y | Y | N | Y | Y |

| | 290 | 291 | 292 | 293 | 294 | 295 |
|---|---|---|---|---|---|---|
| 50 Cunningham | Y | Y | Y | N | Y | Y |
| 51 Filner | Y | Y | Y | Y | N | N |
| 52 Hunter | Y | Y | Y | N | Y | Y |
| 53 Davis | Y | Y | Y | Y | N | N |
| **COLORADO** | | | | | | |
| 1 DeGette | Y | Y | Y | N | N | N |
| 2 Udall | Y | Y | Y | N | N | N |
| 3 Salazar | Y | Y | Y | N | N | N |
| 4 Musgrave | Y | Y | Y | N | Y | Y |
| 5 Hefley | Y | Y | Y | N | Y | Y |
| 6 Tancredo | Y | Y | Y | N | Y | Y |
| 7 Beauprez | Y | Y | Y | N | Y | Y |
| **CONNECTICUT** | | | | | | |
| 1 Larson | Y | Y | Y | Y | N | N |
| 2 Simmons | Y | Y | Y | N | Y | Y |
| 3 DeLauro | Y | Y | Y | Y | N | N |
| 4 Shays | Y | Y | Y | N | Y | Y |
| 5 Johnson | Y | Y | Y | N | Y | Y |
| **DELAWARE** | | | | | | |
| AL Castle | Y | Y | Y | N | Y | Y |
| **FLORIDA** | | | | | | |
| 1 Miller | Y | Y | Y | N | Y | Y |
| 2 Boyd | Y | Y | Y | ? | ? | ? |
| 3 Brown | Y | Y | Y | Y | N | N |
| 4 Crenshaw | Y | Y | Y | N | Y | Y |
| 5 Brown-Waite | Y | Y | Y | ? | Y | Y |
| 6 Stearns | Y | Y | Y | N | Y | Y |
| 7 Mica | Y | Y | Y | N | Y | Y |
| 8 Keller | Y | Y | Y | N | Y | Y |
| 9 Bilirakis | Y | Y | Y | N | Y | Y |
| 10 Young | ? | ? | ? | N | Y | Y |
| 11 Davis | Y | Y | Y | N | N | N |
| 12 Putnam | Y | Y | Y | N | Y | Y |
| 13 Harris | Y | Y | Y | N | Y | Y |
| 14 Mack | Y | Y | Y | N | Y | Y |
| 15 Weldon | Y | Y | Y | N | Y | Y |
| 16 Foley | Y | Y | Y | N | Y | Y |
| 17 Meek | Y | Y | Y | Y | N | N |
| 18 Ros-Lehtinen | Y | Y | Y | N | Y | Y |
| 19 Wexler | Y | Y | Y | Y | N | N |
| 20 Wasserman-Schultz | Y | Y | Y | Y | N | N |
| 21 Diaz-Balart, L. | Y | Y | Y | N | Y | Y |
| 22 Shaw | Y | Y | Y | N | Y | Y |
| 23 Hastings | Y | Y | Y | Y | N | N |
| 24 Feeney | Y | Y | Y | N | Y | Y |
| 25 Diaz-Balart, M. | Y | Y | Y | N | Y | Y |
| **GEORGIA** | | | | | | |
| 1 Kingston | Y | Y | Y | N | Y | Y |
| 2 Bishop | Y | Y | Y | N | N | N |
| 3 Marshall | Y | Y | Y | N | N | N |
| 4 McKinney | N | Y | Y | N | N | N |
| 5 Lewis | ? | ? | ? | ? | ? | ? |
| 6 Price | Y | Y | Y | N | Y | Y |
| 7 Linder | Y | Y | Y | N | Y | Y |
| 8 Westmoreland | Y | Y | Y | N | Y | Y |
| 9 Norwood | Y | Y | Y | N | Y | Y |
| 10 Deal | Y | ? | ? | N | Y | Y |
| 11 Gingrey | Y | Y | Y | N | Y | Y |
| 12 Barrow | Y | Y | Y | N | N | N |
| 13 Scott | Y | Y | Y | N | N | N |
| **HAWAII** | | | | | | |
| 1 Abercrombie | Y | Y | Y | Y | N | N |
| 2 Case | Y | Y | Y | N | N | N |
| **IDAHO** | | | | | | |
| 1 Otter | Y | Y | Y | N | Y | Y |
| 2 Simpson | Y | Y | Y | N | Y | Y |
| **ILLINOIS** | | | | | | |
| 1 Rush | Y | Y | Y | N | N | N |
| 2 Jackson | N | Y | Y | N | N | N |
| 3 Lipinski | Y | Y | Y | N | N | N |
| 4 Gutierrez | Y | Y | Y | N | N | N |
| 5 Emanuel | Y | Y | Y | N | N | N |
| 6 Hyde | Y | Y | Y | N | Y | Y |
| 7 Davis | Y | Y | Y | Y | N | N |
| 8 Bean | Y | Y | Y | N | N | N |
| 9 Schakowsky | Y | Y | Y | N | N | N |
| 10 Kirk | Y | Y | Y | N | Y | Y |
| 11 Weller | Y | Y | Y | N | Y | Y |
| 12 Costello | Y | Y | Y | N | N | N |

| | 290 | 291 | 292 | 293 | 294 | 295 |
|---|---|---|---|---|---|---|
| 13 **Biggert** | Y | Y | Y | N | Y | Y |
| 14 **Hastert** | | | | | | |
| 15 **Johnson** | Y | Y | Y | N | Y | Y |
| 16 **Manzullo** | Y | Y | Y | N | Y | Y |
| 17 Evans | Y | Y | Y | Y | N | N |
| 18 **LaHood** | Y | Y | Y | N | Y | Y |
| 19 **Shimkus** | Y | Y | Y | N | Y | Y |
| **INDIANA** | | | | | | |
| 1 Visclosky | Y | Y | Y | Y | N | N |
| 2 **Chocola** | Y | Y | Y | N | Y | Y |
| 3 **Souder** | Y | Y | Y | N | Y | Y |
| 4 **Buyer** | Y | Y | Y | N | Y | Y |
| 5 **Burton** | Y | Y | Y | N | Y | Y |
| 6 **Pence** | + | Y | Y | N | Y | Y |
| 7 Carson | Y | Y | Y | Y | N | N |
| 8 **Hostettler** | Y | Y | Y | N | Y | Y |
| 9 **Sodrel** | Y | Y | Y | N | Y | Y |
| **IOWA** | | | | | | |
| 1 **Nussle** | Y | Y | Y | N | Y | Y |
| 2 **Leach** | Y | Y | Y | Y | Y | Y |
| 3 Boswell | Y | Y | Y | N | N | N |
| 4 **Latham** | Y | Y | Y | N | Y | Y |
| 5 **King** | Y | Y | Y | N | Y | Y |
| **KANSAS** | | | | | | |
| 1 **Moran** | Y | Y | Y | N | Y | Y |
| 2 **Ryun** | Y | Y | Y | N | Y | Y |
| 3 Moore | Y | Y | Y | Y | N | N |
| 4 **Tiahrt** | Y | Y | Y | N | Y | Y |
| **KENTUCKY** | | | | | | |
| 1 **Whitfield** | Y | Y | Y | N | Y | Y |
| 2 **Lewis** | Y | Y | Y | N | Y | Y |
| 3 **Northup** | Y | Y | Y | N | Y | Y |
| 4 **Davis** | Y | Y | Y | N | Y | Y |
| 5 **Rogers** | Y | Y | Y | N | Y | Y |
| 6 Chandler | Y | Y | Y | N | N | N |
| **LOUISIANA** | | | | | | |
| 1 **Jindal** | Y | Y | Y | N | Y | Y |
| 2 Jefferson | Y | Y | Y | Y | N | N |
| 3 Melancon | Y | Y | Y | N | N | N |
| 4 **McCrery** | Y | Y | Y | N | Y | Y |
| 5 **Alexander** | Y | Y | Y | N | Y | Y |
| 6 **Baker** | Y | Y | Y | N | Y | Y |
| 7 **Boustany** | Y | Y | Y | N | Y | Y |
| **MAINE** | | | | | | |
| 1 Allen | Y | Y | Y | Y | N | N |
| 2 Michaud | Y | Y | Y | N | N | N |
| **MARYLAND** | | | | | | |
| 1 **Gilchrest** | Y | Y | Y | Y | Y | Y |
| 2 Ruppersberger | Y | Y | Y | Y | N | N |
| 3 Cardin | Y | Y | Y | Y | N | N |
| 4 Wynn | Y | Y | Y | N | N | N |
| 5 Hoyer | Y | Y | Y | N | N | N |
| 6 **Bartlett** | Y | Y | Y | N | Y | Y |
| 7 Cummings | Y | Y | Y | Y | N | N |
| 8 Van Hollen | Y | Y | Y | Y | N | N |
| **MASSACHUSETTS** | | | | | | |
| 1 Olver | Y | Y | Y | Y | N | N |
| 2 Neal | Y | Y | Y | Y | N | N |
| 3 McGovern | Y | Y | Y | Y | N | N |
| 4 Frank | Y | Y | Y | ? | N | Y |
| 5 Meehan | Y | Y | Y | Y | N | N |
| 6 Tierney | Y | Y | Y | Y | N | N |
| 7 Markey | Y | Y | Y | N | N | N |
| 8 Capuano | Y | Y | Y | Y | N | N |
| 9 Lynch | Y | Y | Y | N | N | N |
| 10 Delahunt | Y | Y | Y | Y | N | N |
| **MICHIGAN** | | | | | | |
| 1 Stupak | Y | Y | Y | N | N | N |
| 2 **Hoekstra** | Y | Y | Y | N | Y | Y |
| 3 **Ehlers** | Y | Y | Y | N | Y | Y |
| 4 **Camp** | Y | Y | Y | N | Y | Y |
| 5 Kildee | Y | Y | Y | N | N | N |
| 6 **Upton** | Y | Y | Y | N | Y | Y |
| 7 **Schwarz** | Y | Y | Y | N | Y | Y |
| 8 **Rogers** | Y | Y | Y | N | Y | Y |
| 9 **Knollenberg** | Y | Y | Y | N | Y | Y |
| 10 **Miller** | Y | Y | Y | N | Y | Y |
| 11 **McCotter** | Y | Y | Y | N | Y | Y |
| 12 Levin | Y | Y | Y | N | N | N |
| 13 Kilpatrick | Y | Y | Y | Y | N | N |
| 14 Conyers | N | Y | Y | Y | N | N |
| 15 Dingell | Y | Y | Y | Y | N | N |
| **MINNESOTA** | | | | | | |
| 1 **Gutknecht** | Y | Y | Y | N | Y | Y |
| 2 **Kline** | Y | Y | Y | N | Y | Y |
| 3 **Ramstad** | Y | Y | Y | N | Y | Y |
| 4 McCollum | Y | Y | Y | Y | N | N |
| 5 Sabo | Y | Y | Y | Y | Y | Y |
| 6 **Kennedy** | Y | Y | Y | N | Y | Y |
| 7 Peterson | Y | Y | Y | N | N | N |
| 8 Oberstar | N | Y | Y | Y | N | N |
| **MISSISSIPPI** | | | | | | |
| 1 **Wicker** | Y | Y | Y | N | Y | Y |
| 2 Thompson | Y | Y | Y | Y | N | N |
| 3 **Pickering** | Y | Y | Y | ? | Y | Y |
| 4 Taylor | Y | Y | Y | N | N | N |
| **MISSOURI** | | | | | | |
| 1 Clay | Y | Y | Y | Y | N | N |
| 2 **Akin** | Y | Y | Y | N | Y | Y |
| 3 Carnahan | Y | Y | Y | Y | N | N |
| 4 Skelton | Y | Y | Y | N | N | N |
| 5 Cleaver | Y | Y | Y | Y | N | N |
| 6 **Graves** | Y | Y | Y | N | Y | Y |
| 7 **Blunt** | Y | Y | Y | N | Y | Y |
| 8 **Emerson** | Y | Y | Y | N | Y | Y |
| 9 **Hulshof** | Y | Y | Y | N | Y | Y |
| **MONTANA** | | | | | | |
| AL **Rehberg** | Y | Y | Y | N | Y | Y |
| **NEBRASKA** | | | | | | |
| 1 **Fortenberry** | Y | Y | Y | N | Y | Y |
| 2 **Terry** | Y | Y | Y | N | Y | Y |
| 3 **Osborne** | Y | Y | Y | N | Y | Y |
| **NEVADA** | | | | | | |
| 1 Berkley | Y | Y | Y | N | N | N |
| 2 **Gibbons** | Y | Y | Y | N | Y | Y |
| 3 **Porter** | Y | Y | Y | N | Y | Y |
| **NEW HAMPSHIRE** | | | | | | |
| 1 **Bradley** | Y | Y | Y | N | Y | Y |
| 2 **Bass** | Y | Y | Y | N | Y | Y |
| **NEW JERSEY** | | | | | | |
| 1 Andrews | Y | Y | Y | Y | N | N |
| 2 **LoBiondo** | Y | Y | Y | N | Y | Y |
| 3 **Saxton** | Y | Y | Y | N | Y | Y |
| 4 **Smith** | Y | Y | Y | N | Y | Y |
| 5 **Garrett** | Y | Y | Y | N | Y | Y |
| 6 Pallone | Y | Y | Y | Y | N | N |
| 7 **Ferguson** | Y | Y | Y | N | Y | Y |
| 8 Pascrell | Y | Y | Y | N | N | N |
| 9 Rothman | Y | Y | Y | N | N | N |
| 10 Payne | N | Y | Y | Y | N | ? |
| 11 **Frelinghuysen** | Y | Y | Y | N | Y | Y |
| 12 Holt | Y | Y | Y | Y | N | N |
| 13 Menendez | Y | Y | Y | N | N | N |
| **NEW MEXICO** | | | | | | |
| 1 **Wilson** | Y | Y | Y | N | Y | Y |
| 2 **Pearce** | Y | Y | Y | N | Y | Y |
| 3 Udall | Y | Y | Y | Y | N | N |
| **NEW YORK** | | | | | | |
| 1 Bishop | Y | Y | Y | N | N | N |
| 2 Israel | Y | Y | Y | Y | N | N |
| 3 **King** | Y | Y | Y | N | Y | Y |
| 4 McCarthy | Y | Y | Y | N | N | N |
| 5 Ackerman | Y | Y | Y | Y | N | N |
| 6 Meeks | Y | Y | Y | Y | N | N |
| 7 Crowley | Y | Y | Y | N | N | N |
| 8 Nadler | Y | Y | Y | Y | N | N |
| 9 Weiner | Y | Y | Y | Y | N | ? |
| 10 Towns | Y | Y | Y | Y | N | N |
| 11 Owens | N | Y | Y | Y | N | N |
| 12 Velázquez | Y | Y | Y | Y | N | N |
| 13 **Fossella** | Y | Y | Y | N | Y | Y |
| 14 Maloney | Y | Y | Y | Y | N | N |
| 15 Rangel | N | Y | Y | ? | ? | ? |
| 16 Serrano | Y | Y | Y | N | N | N |
| 17 Engel | Y | Y | Y | Y | N | N |
| 18 Lowey | Y | Y | Y | Y | N | N |
| 19 **Kelly** | Y | Y | Y | N | Y | Y |
| 20 **Sweeney** | Y | Y | Y | N | Y | Y |
| 21 McNulty | Y | Y | Y | Y | N | N |
| 22 Hinchey | Y | Y | Y | Y | N | N |
| 23 **McHugh** | Y | Y | Y | N | Y | Y |
| 24 **Boehlert** | Y | Y | Y | N | Y | Y |
| 25 **Walsh** | Y | Y | Y | N | Y | Y |
| 26 **Reynolds** | Y | Y | Y | N | Y | Y |
| 27 Higgins | Y | Y | Y | N | N | N |
| 28 Slaughter | Y | Y | Y | Y | N | N |
| 29 **Kuhl** | Y | Y | Y | N | Y | Y |
| **NORTH CAROLINA** | | | | | | |
| 1 Butterfield | Y | Y | Y | Y | N | N |
| 2 Etheridge | Y | Y | Y | Y | N | N |
| 3 **Jones** | Y | Y | Y | N | Y | Y |
| 4 Price | Y | Y | Y | Y | N | N |
| 5 **Foxx** | Y | Y | Y | N | Y | Y |
| 6 **Coble** | Y | Y | Y | N | Y | Y |
| 7 McIntyre | Y | Y | Y | N | N | N |
| 8 **Hayes** | Y | Y | Y | N | Y | Y |
| 9 **Myrick** | Y | Y | Y | N | Y | Y |
| 10 **McHenry** | Y | Y | Y | N | Y | Y |
| 11 **Taylor** | Y | Y | Y | N | Y | Y |
| 12 Watt | Y | Y | Y | Y | N | N |
| 13 Miller | Y | Y | Y | Y | N | N |
| **NORTH DAKOTA** | | | | | | |
| AL Pomeroy | Y | Y | Y | ? | ? | ? |
| **OHIO** | | | | | | |
| 1 **Chabot** | Y | Y | Y | N | Y | Y |
| 2 Vacant | | | | | | |
| 3 **Turner** | Y | Y | Y | N | Y | Y |
| 4 **Oxley** | Y | Y | Y | ? | ? | ? |
| 5 **Gillmor** | Y | Y | Y | N | Y | Y |
| 6 Strickland | Y | Y | Y | N | N | N |
| 7 **Hobson** | Y | Y | Y | N | Y | Y |
| 8 **Boehner** | Y | Y | Y | N | Y | Y |
| 9 Kaptur | Y | Y | Y | Y | N | N |
| 10 Kucinich | N | Y | Y | N | N | N |
| 11 Jones | Y | Y | Y | Y | N | N |
| 12 **Tiberi** | Y | Y | Y | N | Y | Y |
| 13 Brown | Y | Y | Y | N | N | N |
| 14 **LaTourette** | Y | Y | Y | N | Y | Y |
| 15 **Pryce** | Y | Y | Y | N | Y | Y |
| 16 **Regula** | Y | Y | Y | N | Y | Y |
| 17 Ryan | Y | Y | Y | Y | N | N |
| 18 **Ney** | Y | Y | Y | ? | ? | ? |
| **OKLAHOMA** | | | | | | |
| 1 **Sullivan** | Y | Y | Y | N | Y | Y |
| 2 Boren | Y | Y | Y | N | N | N |
| 3 **Lucas** | Y | Y | Y | N | Y | Y |
| 4 **Cole** | Y | Y | Y | N | Y | Y |
| 5 **Istook** | Y | Y | Y | N | Y | Y |
| **OREGON** | | | | | | |
| 1 Wu | Y | Y | Y | Y | N | N |
| 2 **Walden** | Y | Y | Y | N | Y | Y |
| 3 Blumenauer | Y | Y | Y | Y | N | N |
| 4 DeFazio | Y | Y | Y | Y | N | N |
| 5 Hooley | Y | Y | Y | Y | N | N |
| **PENNSYLVANIA** | | | | | | |
| 1 Brady | Y | Y | Y | Y | N | N |
| 2 Fattah | Y | Y | Y | Y | N | N |
| 3 **English** | Y | Y | Y | N | Y | Y |
| 4 **Hart** | Y | Y | Y | N | Y | Y |
| 5 **Peterson** | Y | Y | Y | N | Y | Y |
| 6 **Gerlach** | Y | Y | Y | N | Y | Y |
| 7 **Weldon** | Y | Y | Y | N | Y | Y |
| 8 **Fitzpatrick** | Y | Y | Y | N | Y | Y |
| 9 **Shuster** | Y | Y | Y | N | Y | Y |
| 10 **Sherwood** | Y | Y | Y | N | Y | Y |
| 11 Kanjorski | Y | Y | Y | N | N | N |
| 12 Murtha | Y | Y | Y | ? | N | ? |
| 13 Schwartz | Y | Y | Y | N | N | N |
| 14 Doyle | Y | Y | Y | Y | N | N |
| 15 **Dent** | Y | Y | Y | N | Y | Y |
| 16 **Pitts** | Y | Y | Y | N | Y | Y |
| 17 Holden | Y | Y | Y | N | N | N |
| 18 **Murphy** | + | + | ? | N | Y | Y |
| 19 **Platts** | Y | Y | Y | N | Y | Y |
| **RHODE ISLAND** | | | | | | |
| 1 Kennedy | Y | Y | Y | Y | N | N |
| 2 Langevin | Y | Y | Y | N | N | N |
| **SOUTH CAROLINA** | | | | | | |
| 1 **Brown** | Y | Y | Y | N | Y | Y |
| 2 **Wilson** | Y | Y | Y | N | Y | Y |
| 3 **Barrett** | Y | Y | Y | N | Y | Y |
| 4 **Inglis** | Y | Y | Y | N | Y | Y |
| 5 Spratt | Y | Y | Y | Y | N | N |
| 6 Clyburn | Y | Y | Y | Y | N | N |
| **SOUTH DAKOTA** | | | | | | |
| AL Herseth | ? | ? | ? | ? | ? | ? |
| **TENNESSEE** | | | | | | |
| 1 **Jenkins** | Y | Y | Y | N | Y | Y |
| 2 **Duncan** | N | Y | Y | N | Y | Y |
| 3 **Wamp** | Y | Y | Y | N | Y | Y |
| 4 Davis | Y | Y | Y | N | N | N |
| 5 Cooper | Y | Y | Y | Y | N | N |
| 6 Gordon | Y | Y | Y | N | N | N |
| 7 **Blackburn** | Y | Y | Y | N | Y | Y |
| 8 Tanner | Y | Y | Y | Y | N | N |
| 9 Ford | Y | Y | Y | N | N | N |
| **TEXAS** | | | | | | |
| 1 **Gohmert** | Y | Y | Y | – | Y | Y |
| 2 **Poe** | Y | Y | Y | N | Y | Y |
| 3 **Johnson, S.** | Y | Y | Y | N | Y | Y |
| 4 **Hall** | Y | Y | Y | N | Y | Y |
| 5 **Hensarling** | Y | Y | Y | N | Y | Y |
| 6 **Barton** | Y | Y | Y | ? | ? | ? |
| 7 **Culberson** | Y | Y | Y | N | Y | Y |
| 8 **Brady** | Y | Y | Y | N | Y | Y |
| 9 Green, A. | Y | Y | Y | Y | N | N |
| 10 **McCaul** | Y | Y | Y | ? | ? | ? |
| 11 **Conaway** | + | ? | + | ? | ? | ? |
| 12 **Granger** | Y | Y | Y | N | Y | Y |
| 13 **Thornberry** | Y | Y | Y | N | Y | Y |
| 14 **Paul** | N | N | Y | Y | Y | Y |
| 15 Hinojosa | Y | Y | Y | ? | ? | ? |
| 16 Reyes | Y | Y | Y | N | N | N |
| 17 Edwards | Y | Y | Y | N | N | N |
| 18 Jackson-Lee | Y | Y | Y | ? | ? | ? |
| 19 **Neugebauer** | Y | Y | Y | N | Y | Y |
| 20 Gonzalez | Y | Y | Y | Y | N | N |
| 21 **Smith** | Y | Y | Y | ? | ? | ? |
| 22 **DeLay** | Y | Y | Y | ? | Y | Y |
| 23 **Bonilla** | Y | Y | Y | N | Y | Y |
| 24 **Marchant** | Y | Y | Y | ? | Y | Y |
| 25 Doggett | Y | Y | Y | ? | ? | ? |
| 26 **Burgess** | Y | Y | Y | N | Y | Y |
| 27 Ortiz | Y | Y | Y | N | N | N |
| 28 Cuellar | Y | Y | Y | N | N | N |
| 29 Green, G. | Y | Y | Y | N | N | N |
| 30 Johnson, E. | Y | Y | Y | Y | N | N |
| 31 **Carter** | + | + | + | ? | ? | ? |
| 32 **Sessions** | ? | ? | ? | N | Y | Y |
| **UTAH** | | | | | | |
| 1 **Bishop** | Y | Y | Y | N | Y | Y |
| 2 Matheson | Y | Y | Y | Y | N | N |
| 3 **Cannon** | Y | Y | Y | N | Y | Y |
| **VERMONT** | | | | | | |
| AL *Sanders* | Y | Y | Y | Y | N | N |
| **VIRGINIA** | | | | | | |
| 1 **Davis, J.** | Y | Y | Y | N | Y | Y |
| 2 **Drake** | Y | Y | Y | N | Y | Y |
| 3 Scott | Y | Y | Y | Y | N | N |
| 4 **Forbes** | Y | Y | Y | N | Y | Y |
| 5 **Goode** | Y | Y | Y | N | Y | Y |
| 6 **Goodlatte** | Y | Y | Y | N | Y | Y |
| 7 **Cantor** | Y | Y | Y | N | Y | Y |
| 8 Moran | Y | Y | Y | Y | N | N |
| 9 Boucher | Y | Y | Y | Y | N | N |
| 10 **Wolf** | Y | Y | Y | N | Y | Y |
| 11 **Davis, T.** | Y | Y | Y | N | Y | Y |
| **WASHINGTON** | | | | | | |
| 1 Inslee | Y | Y | Y | Y | N | N |
| 2 Larsen | Y | Y | Y | Y | N | N |
| 3 Baird | Y | Y | Y | Y | N | N |
| 4 **Hastings** | Y | Y | Y | N | Y | Y |
| 5 **McMorris** | Y | Y | Y | N | Y | Y |
| 6 Dicks | Y | Y | Y | Y | N | N |
| 7 McDermott | N | Y | Y | Y | N | N |
| 8 **Reichert** | Y | Y | Y | N | Y | Y |
| 9 Smith | Y | Y | Y | N | N | N |
| **WEST VIRGINIA** | | | | | | |
| 1 Mollohan | Y | Y | Y | N | N | N |
| 2 **Capito** | Y | Y | Y | N | Y | Y |
| 3 Rahall | Y | Y | Y | N | N | N |
| **WISCONSIN** | | | | | | |
| 1 **Ryan** | Y | Y | Y | N | Y | Y |
| 2 Baldwin | Y | Y | Y | Y | N | N |
| 3 Kind | Y | Y | Y | Y | N | N |
| 4 Moore | Y | Y | Y | N | N | N |
| 5 **Sensenbrenner** | Y | Y | Y | N | Y | Y |
| 6 **Petri** | Y | Y | Y | N | Y | Y |
| 7 Obey | Y | Y | Y | Y | N | N |
| 8 **Green** | Y | Y | Y | N | Y | Y |
| **WYOMING** | | | | | | |
| AL **Cubin** | Y | Y | Y | N | Y | Y |

# IN THE HOUSE | By Vote Number

**296.** **H J Res 10. Flag Desecration Constitutional Amendment/ Passage.** Passage of the joint resolution to propose a constitutional amendment to state that Congress shall have the power to prohibit the physical desecration of the flag of the United States. Passed 286-130: R 209-12; D 77-117 (ND 50-98, SD 27-19); I 0-1. A two-thirds majority vote of those present and voting (278 in this case) is required to pass a joint resolution proposing a constitutional amendment. June 22, 2005.

**297.** **HR 2985. Fiscal 2006 Legislative Branch Appropriations/ Previous Question.** L. Diaz-Balart, R-Fla., motion to order the previous question (thus ending debate and the possibility of amendment) on adoption of the rule (H Res 334) to provide for House floor consideration of the legislative branch spending bill. Motion agreed to 219-196: R 219-1; D 0-194 (ND 0-148, SD 0-46); I 0-1. June 22, 2005.

**298.** **HR 2985. Fiscal 2006 Legislative Branch Appropriations/Rule.** Adoption of the rule (H Res 334) to provide for House floor consideration of the bill that would appropriate $2.9 billion in fiscal 2006 for legislative branch operations, excluding funds for Senate operations. Adopted 220-192: R 220-0; D 0-191 (ND 0-147, SD 0-44); I 0-1. June 22, 2005.

**299.** **HR 2985. Fiscal 2006 Legislative Branch Appropriations/ Continuity of Congress.** Baird, D-Wash., amendment that would strike language in the bill that would require states to hold special elections within 49 days to fill open House seats if more than 100 vacancies occur due to a terrorist attack or other catastrophe. Rejected 143-268: R 1-218; D 141-50 (ND 113-33, SD 28-17); I 1-0. June 22, 2005.

**300.** **HR 2985. Fiscal 2006 Legislative Branch Appropriations/Capitol Police Horses.** J. Davis, R-Va., amendment that would strike provisions in the bill that would prohibit the Capitol Police from operating a mounted horse unit and require the transfer of the horses and equipment to the U.S. Park Police. Rejected 185-226: R 63-155; D 121-71 (ND 93-54, SD 28-17); I 1-0. June 22, 2005.

**301.** **HR 2985. Fiscal 2006 Legislative Branch Appropriations/ Across-the-Board Cut.** Hefley, R-Colo., amendment that would reduce all discretionary spending in the bill by 1 percent. Rejected 114-294: R 91-125; D 23-168 (ND 14-132, SD 9-36); I 0-1. June 22, 2005.

| Member | 296 | 297 | 298 | 299 | 300 | 301 |
|---|---|---|---|---|---|---|
| **ALABAMA** | | | | | | |
| 1 Bonner | ? | ? | ? | ? | ? | ? |
| 2 Everett | Y | Y | Y | N | N | Y |
| 3 Rogers | Y | Y | Y | N | N | N |
| 4 Aderholt | Y | Y | Y | N | N | N |
| 5 Cramer | Y | N | N | N | N | N |
| 6 Bachus | Y | Y | Y | N | N | ? |
| 7 Davis | N | N | ? | Y | N | N |
| **ALASKA** | | | | | | |
| AL Young | Y | Y | Y | N | Y | N |
| **ARIZONA** | | | | | | |
| 1 Renzi | Y | Y | Y | N | N | N |
| 2 Franks | Y | Y | Y | N | Y | Y |
| 3 Shadegg | N | Y | Y | N | Y | Y |
| 4 Pastor | N | N | N | Y | N | N |
| 5 Hayworth | Y | Y | Y | N | N | Y |
| 6 Flake | N | Y | Y | N | N | Y |
| 7 Grijalva | N | N | N | Y | Y | N |
| 8 Kolbe | N | Y | Y | N | N | N |
| **ARKANSAS** | | | | | | |
| 1 Berry | Y | N | N | Y | N | Y |
| 2 Snyder | N | N | N | N | N | Y |
| 3 Boozman | Y | Y | Y | N | Y | N |
| 4 Ross | Y | N | N | Y | Y | Y |
| **CALIFORNIA** | | | | | | |
| 1 Thompson | N | N | N | Y | Y | N |
| 2 Herger | Y | Y | Y | N | N | Y |
| 3 Lungren | Y | Y | Y | N | N | N |
| 4 Doolittle | Y | Y | Y | N | N | N |
| 5 Matsui, D. | N | N | N | Y | N | N |
| 6 Woolsey | N | N | N | Y | Y | N |
| 7 Miller, George | N | N | N | Y | N | N |
| 8 Pelosi | N | N | N | Y | Y | N |
| 9 Lee | N | N | N | Y | Y | N |
| 10 Tauscher | N | N | N | Y | Y | N |
| 11 Pombo | Y | Y | Y | N | N | N |
| 12 Lantos | Y | N | N | Y | Y | N |
| 13 Stark | N | N | N | N | Y | N |
| 14 Eshoo | N | N | N | Y | N | N |
| 15 Honda | N | N | N | Y | Y | N |
| 16 Lofgren | N | N | N | Y | Y | N |
| 17 Farr | N | N | N | Y | N | ? |
| 18 Cardoza | Y | N | N | N | N | Y |
| 19 Radanovich | Y | Y | Y | N | Y | N |
| 20 Costa | Y | N | N | N | N | N |
| 21 Nunes | Y | Y | Y | N | N | N |
| 22 Thomas | ? | ? | ? | ? | ? | ? |
| 23 Capps | Y | N | N | Y | N | N |
| 24 Gallegly | Y | Y | Y | N | N | N |
| 25 McKeon | Y | Y | Y | N | N | N |
| 26 Dreier | N | Y | Y | N | N | N |
| 27 Sherman | Y | N | N | Y | N | N |
| 28 Berman | N | N | N | Y | N | N |
| 29 Schiff | N | N | N | Y | N | N |
| 30 Waxman | N | N | N | Y | Y | N |
| 31 Becerra | N | N | N | Y | Y | N |
| 32 Solis | N | N | N | Y | Y | N |
| 33 Watson | N | N | N | ? | Y | N |
| 34 Roybal-Allard | N | N | N | N | N | N |
| 35 Waters | N | N | N | Y | Y | N |
| 36 Harman | Y | N | N | Y | Y | N |
| 37 Millender-McD. | N | N | N | Y | Y | N |
| 38 Napolitano | N | N | N | Y | Y | N |
| 39 Sánchez, Linda | N | N | N | Y | Y | N |
| 40 Royce | Y | Y | Y | N | N | Y |
| 41 Lewis | Y | Y | Y | N | N | N |
| 42 Miller, Gary | Y | Y | Y | N | N | Y |
| 43 Baca | Y | N | N | N | N | N |
| 44 Calvert | Y | Y | Y | N | N | N |
| 45 Bono | Y | Y | Y | N | N | N |
| 46 Rohrabacher | Y | Y | Y | N | N | Y |
| 47 Sanchez, Loretta | Y | N | N | N | N | N |
| 48 Cox | Y | Y | Y | N | N | N |
| 49 Issa | Y | Y | Y | N | N | Y |
| 50 Cunningham | Y | Y | Y | N | Y | N |
| 51 Filner | N | N | N | Y | Y | N |
| 52 Hunter | Y | Y | Y | N | Y | N |
| 53 Davis | N | N | N | Y | N | N |
| **COLORADO** | | | | | | |
| 1 DeGette | N | N | N | Y | Y | Y |
| 2 Udall | N | N | N | Y | Y | Y |
| 3 Salazar | Y | N | N | Y | Y | N |
| 4 Musgrave | Y | Y | Y | N | N | Y |
| 5 Hefley | Y | Y | Y | N | Y | Y |
| 6 Tancredo | Y | Y | Y | N | N | Y |
| 7 Beauprez | Y | Y | Y | N | N | Y |
| **CONNECTICUT** | | | | | | |
| 1 Larson | N | N | N | Y | Y | N |
| 2 Simmons | Y | Y | Y | N | Y | N |
| 3 DeLauro | N | N | N | Y | Y | N |
| 4 Shays | N | Y | Y | N | Y | N |
| 5 Johnson | Y | Y | Y | N | N | N |
| **DELAWARE** | | | | | | |
| AL Castle | Y | Y | Y | N | N | N |
| **FLORIDA** | | | | | | |
| 1 Miller | Y | Y | Y | N | Y | Y |
| 2 Boyd | ? | ? | ? | ? | ? | ? |
| 3 Brown | Y | N | N | Y | Y | N |
| 4 Crenshaw | Y | Y | Y | N | N | N |
| 5 Brown-Waite | Y | Y | Y | N | N | Y |
| 6 Stearns | Y | Y | Y | N | Y | Y |
| 7 Mica | Y | Y | Y | N | N | N |
| 8 Keller | Y | Y | Y | N | N | N |
| 9 Bilirakis | Y | Y | Y | N | N | N |
| 10 Young | Y | N | N | N | N | N |
| 11 Davis | N | N | N | Y | N | N |
| 12 Putnam | Y | Y | Y | N | N | N |
| 13 Harris | Y | Y | Y | N | N | N |
| 14 Mack | Y | Y | Y | N | N | Y |
| 15 Weldon | Y | Y | Y | N | N | N |
| 16 Foley | Y | Y | Y | N | N | N |
| 17 Meek | N | N | N | Y | Y | N |
| 18 Ros-Lehtinen | Y | Y | Y | N | Y | N |
| 19 Wexler | N | N | N | Y | Y | N |
| 20 Wasserman-Schultz | N | N | N | Y | Y | N |
| 21 Diaz-Balart, L. | Y | Y | Y | N | N | N |
| 22 Shaw | Y | Y | Y | N | N | N |
| 23 Hastings | N | N | N | Y | Y | N |
| 24 Feeney | Y | Y | Y | N | N | Y |
| 25 Diaz-Balart, M. | Y | Y | Y | N | Y | N |
| **GEORGIA** | | | | | | |
| 1 Kingston | Y | Y | Y | N | N | N |
| 2 Bishop | Y | N | N | N | N | N |
| 3 Marshall | N | N | N | Y | N | N |
| 4 McKinney | N | N | N | Y | Y | N |
| 5 Lewis | ? | ? | ? | ? | ? | ? |
| 6 Price | Y | Y | Y | N | N | Y |
| 7 Linder | Y | Y | Y | N | N | N |
| 8 Westmoreland | Y | Y | Y | N | Y | Y |
| 9 Norwood | Y | Y | Y | N | N | Y |
| 10 Deal | Y | Y | Y | N | N | Y |
| 11 Gingrey | Y | Y | Y | N | N | Y |
| 12 Barrow | N | N | N | Y | Y | N |
| 13 Scott | Y | N | N | Y | Y | N |
| **HAWAII** | | | | | | |
| 1 Abercrombie | N | N | N | Y | Y | N |
| 2 Case | N | N | N | Y | Y | N |
| **IDAHO** | | | | | | |
| 1 Otter | Y | Y | Y | N | Y | Y |
| 2 Simpson | Y | Y | Y | N | Y | N |
| **ILLINOIS** | | | | | | |
| 1 Rush | N | N | N | Y | Y | N |
| 2 Jackson | N | N | N | Y | Y | N |
| 3 Lipinski | N | N | N | Y | Y | N |
| 4 Gutierrez | N | N | N | Y | Y | N |
| 5 Emanuel | N | N | N | Y | Y | N |
| 6 Hyde | Y | Y | Y | N | Y | N |
| 7 Davis | N | N | N | Y | Y | N |
| 8 Bean | Y | N | N | N | N | Y |
| 9 Schakowsky | N | N | N | Y | Y | N |
| 10 Kirk | Y | Y | Y | N | Y | N |
| 11 Weller | Y | Y | Y | N | Y | N |
| 12 Costello | Y | N | N | N | Y | N |

**KEY**  Republicans  Democrats  *Independents*

| | | | |
|---|---|---|---|
| Y | Voted for (yea) | X | Paired against |
| # | Paired for | – | Announced against |
| + | Announced for | P | Voted "present" |
| N | Voted against (nay) | C | Voted "present" to avoid possible conflict of interest |
| | | ? | Did not vote or otherwise make a position known |

ND Northern Democrats, SD Southern Democrats
Southern states: Ala., Ark., Fla., Ga., Ky., La., Miss., N.C., Okla., S.C., Tenn., Texas, Va.

| | 296 | 297 | 298 | 299 | 300 | 301 |
|---|---|---|---|---|---|---|
| 13 **Biggert** | Y | Y | Y | N | N | Y |
| 14 **Hastert** | Y | | | N | | |
| 15 **Johnson** | Y | Y | Y | N | N | N |
| 16 **Manzullo** | Y | Y | Y | N | N | Y |
| 17 Evans | N | N | N | Y | Y | N |
| 18 **LaHood** | Y | Y | Y | N | N | N |
| 19 **Shimkus** | Y | Y | Y | N | N | Y |
| **INDIANA** | | | | | | |
| 1 Visclosky | N | N | N | Y | N | N |
| 2 **Chocola** | Y | Y | Y | N | N | Y |
| 3 **Souder** | Y | Y | Y | N | N | N |
| 4 **Buyer** | Y | Y | Y | N | Y | ? |
| 5 **Burton** | Y | Y | Y | N | Y | Y |
| 6 **Pence** | Y | Y | Y | N | N | Y |
| 7 Carson | N | N | N | Y | N | N |
| 8 **Hostettler** | Y | Y | Y | N | Y | Y |
| 9 **Sodrel** | Y | Y | Y | N | Y | N |
| **IOWA** | | | | | | |
| 1 **Nussle** | Y | Y | Y | N | N | N |
| 2 **Leach** | N | N | Y | N | N | N |
| 3 Boswell | Y | N | N | Y | Y | N |
| 4 **Latham** | Y | Y | Y | N | N | N |
| 5 **King** | Y | Y | Y | N | N | Y |
| **KANSAS** | | | | | | |
| 1 **Moran** | Y | Y | Y | N | N | Y |
| 2 **Ryun** | Y | Y | Y | N | Y | Y |
| 3 Moore | N | N | N | Y | N | N |
| 4 **Tiahrt** | Y | Y | Y | N | N | N |
| **KENTUCKY** | | | | | | |
| 1 **Whitfield** | Y | Y | Y | N | Y | Y |
| 2 **Lewis** | Y | Y | Y | N | N | Y |
| 3 **Northup** | Y | Y | Y | N | N | N |
| 4 **Davis** | Y | Y | Y | N | N | N |
| 5 **Rogers** | Y | Y | Y | N | N | N |
| 6 Chandler | Y | N | N | Y | Y | Y |
| **LOUISIANA** | | | | | | |
| 1 **Jindal** | Y | Y | Y | N | N | Y |
| 2 Jefferson | Y | N | N | Y | Y | N |
| 3 Melancon | Y | N | N | N | Y | N |
| 4 **McCrery** | Y | Y | Y | N | N | N |
| 5 **Alexander** | Y | Y | Y | N | N | N |
| 6 **Baker** | Y | Y | Y | N | N | N |
| 7 **Boustany** | Y | Y | Y | N | Y | N |
| **MAINE** | | | | | | |
| 1 Allen | N | N | N | N | N | N |
| 2 Michaud | Y | N | N | N | Y | Y |
| **MARYLAND** | | | | | | |
| 1 **Gilchrest** | N | Y | Y | N | Y | N |
| 2 Ruppersberger | Y | N | N | Y | Y | N |
| 3 Cardin | N | N | N | N | Y | N |
| 4 Wynn | Y | N | N | N | Y | N |
| 5 Hoyer | N | N | N | Y | N | N |
| 6 **Bartlett** | Y | Y | Y | N | N | Y |
| 7 Cummings | N | N | N | Y | N | N |
| 8 Van Hollen | N | N | N | Y | Y | N |
| **MASSACHUSETTS** | | | | | | |
| 1 Olver | N | N | N | Y | N | N |
| 2 Neal | Y | N | N | N | N | N |
| 3 McGovern | Y | N | N | Y | N | N |
| 4 Frank | N | N | N | Y | N | N |
| 5 Meehan | N | N | N | Y | Y | N |
| 6 Tierney | N | N | N | Y | Y | N |
| 7 Markey | N | N | N | N | Y | N |
| 8 Capuano | N | N | N | Y | Y | N |
| 9 Lynch | Y | N | N | Y | Y | N |
| 10 Delahunt | Y | N | N | N | Y | N |
| **MICHIGAN** | | | | | | |
| 1 Stupak | Y | N | N | N | Y | N |
| 2 **Hoekstra** | N | Y | Y | N | N | N |
| 3 **Ehlers** | N | Y | Y | N | N | N |
| 4 **Camp** | Y | Y | Y | N | N | N |
| 5 Kildee | Y | N | N | Y | N | N |
| 6 **Upton** | Y | Y | Y | N | N | N |
| 7 **Schwarz** | N | Y | Y | N | Y | N |
| 8 **Rogers** | Y | Y | Y | N | N | N |
| 9 **Knollenberg** | Y | Y | Y | N | N | N |
| 10 **Miller** | Y | Y | Y | N | Y | N |
| 11 **McCotter** | Y | Y | Y | N | Y | Y |
| 12 Levin | N | N | N | Y | N | N |
| 13 Kilpatrick | N | N | N | Y | N | N |
| 14 Conyers | N | N | N | Y | N | N |
| 15 Dingell | N | N | N | Y | Y | N |

| | 296 | 297 | 298 | 299 | 300 | 301 |
|---|---|---|---|---|---|---|
| **MINNESOTA** | | | | | | |
| 1 **Gutknecht** | Y | Y | Y | N | N | Y |
| 2 **Kline** | Y | Y | Y | N | N | N |
| 3 **Ramstad** | Y | Y | Y | N | Y | Y |
| 4 McCollum | N | N | N | Y | Y | N |
| 5 Sabo | N | N | ? | Y | N | N |
| 6 **Kennedy** | Y | Y | Y | N | N | Y |
| 7 Peterson | Y | N | N | N | Y | N |
| 8 Oberstar | N | N | N | Y | N | N |
| **MISSISSIPPI** | | | | | | |
| 1 **Wicker** | Y | Y | Y | N | N | N |
| 2 Thompson | Y | N | N | Y | Y | N |
| 3 **Pickering** | Y | Y | Y | N | Y | N |
| 4 Taylor | Y | N | N | Y | N | Y |
| **MISSOURI** | | | | | | |
| 1 Clay | N | N | N | Y | Y | N |
| 2 **Akin** | Y | ? | Y | N | N | Y |
| 3 Carnahan | Y | N | N | Y | Y | N |
| 4 Skelton | Y | N | N | N | Y | N |
| 5 Cleaver | N | N | N | Y | Y | N |
| 6 **Graves** | Y | Y | Y | N | N | Y |
| 7 **Blunt** | Y | Y | Y | N | N | N |
| 8 **Emerson** | Y | Y | Y | N | N | N |
| 9 **Hulshof** | Y | Y | Y | N | N | Y |
| **MONTANA** | | | | | | |
| AL **Rehberg** | Y | Y | Y | N | N | N |
| **NEBRASKA** | | | | | | |
| 1 **Fortenberry** | Y | Y | Y | N | N | N |
| 2 **Terry** | Y | Y | Y | N | N | Y |
| 3 **Osborne** | Y | Y | Y | N | N | N |
| **NEVADA** | | | | | | |
| 1 Berkley | Y | N | N | Y | N | N |
| 2 **Gibbons** | Y | Y | Y | N | N | Y |
| 3 **Porter** | Y | Y | Y | N | Y | N |
| **NEW HAMPSHIRE** | | | | | | |
| 1 **Bradley** | Y | Y | Y | N | N | Y |
| 2 **Bass** | Y | Y | Y | N | N | Y |
| **NEW JERSEY** | | | | | | |
| 1 Andrews | Y | N | N | Y | N | N |
| 2 **LoBiondo** | Y | Y | Y | N | N | Y |
| 3 **Saxton** | Y | Y | Y | N | Y | Y |
| 4 **Smith** | Y | Y | Y | N | Y | N |
| 5 **Garrett** | Y | Y | Y | N | N | Y |
| 6 Pallone | Y | N | N | Y | N | N |
| 7 **Ferguson** | Y | Y | Y | N | N | N |
| 8 Pascrell | Y | N | N | Y | Y | N |
| 9 Rothman | Y | N | N | Y | Y | N |
| 10 Payne | N | N | N | Y | Y | N |
| 11 **Frelinghuysen** | Y | Y | Y | N | N | N |
| 12 Holt | N | N | N | Y | Y | N |
| 13 Menendez | Y | N | N | Y | N | N |
| **NEW MEXICO** | | | | | | |
| 1 **Wilson** | Y | Y | Y | N | N | N |
| 2 **Pearce** | Y | Y | Y | N | N | N |
| 3 Udall | N | N | N | Y | Y | Y |
| **NEW YORK** | | | | | | |
| 1 Bishop | Y | N | N | Y | N | N |
| 2 Israel | N | N | N | N | Y | N |
| 3 **King** | Y | Y | Y | N | Y | N |
| 4 McCarthy | Y | N | N | Y | Y | N |
| 5 Ackerman | N | N | N | Y | Y | N |
| 6 Meeks | N | N | N | Y | Y | N |
| 7 Crowley | Y | N | N | Y | Y | N |
| 8 Nadler | N | N | N | Y | Y | N |
| 9 Weiner | N | N | N | Y | Y | N |
| 10 Towns | Y | N | N | Y | Y | N |
| 11 Owens | N | N | N | Y | Y | N |
| 12 Velázquez | N | N | N | Y | Y | N |
| 13 **Fossella** | Y | Y | Y | N | Y | Y |
| 14 Maloney | N | N | N | Y | Y | Y |
| 15 Rangel | ? | ? | ? | ? | ? | ? |
| 16 Serrano | N | N | N | Y | Y | N |
| 17 Engel | N | N | N | N | Y | N |
| 18 Lowey | N | N | N | Y | Y | N |
| 19 **Kelly** | Y | Y | Y | N | N | N |
| 20 **Sweeney** | Y | Y | Y | N | N | N |
| 21 McNulty | Y | N | N | N | Y | N |
| 22 Hinchey | N | N | N | Y | Y | N |
| 23 **McHugh** | Y | Y | Y | N | N | N |
| 24 **Boehlert** | Y | Y | Y | N | N | N |
| 25 **Walsh** | Y | Y | Y | N | N | N |
| 26 **Reynolds** | Y | Y | Y | N | N | N |
| 27 Higgins | Y | N | N | Y | N | N |
| 28 Slaughter | N | N | N | Y | N | N |
| 29 **Kuhl** | Y | Y | Y | N | N | N |

| | 296 | 297 | 298 | 299 | 300 | 301 |
|---|---|---|---|---|---|---|
| **NORTH CAROLINA** | | | | | | |
| 1 Butterfield | N | N | N | Y | N | N |
| 2 Etheridge | Y | N | N | Y | Y | N |
| 3 **Jones** | Y | Y | Y | N | Y | Y |
| 4 Price | N | N | N | Y | N | N |
| 5 **Foxx** | Y | Y | Y | N | N | Y |
| 6 **Coble** | Y | Y | Y | N | N | Y |
| 7 McIntyre | Y | N | N | N | Y | N |
| 8 **Hayes** | Y | Y | Y | N | N | N |
| 9 **Myrick** | Y | Y | Y | N | N | Y |
| 10 **McHenry** | Y | Y | Y | N | N | Y |
| 11 **Taylor** | Y | Y | Y | N | N | N |
| 12 Watt | N | N | N | Y | N | N |
| 13 Miller | N | N | N | Y | N | N |
| **NORTH DAKOTA** | | | | | | |
| AL Pomeroy | ? | ? | ? | ? | ? | ? |
| **OHIO** | | | | | | |
| 1 **Chabot** | Y | Y | Y | N | Y | Y |
| 2 Vacant | | | | | | |
| 3 **Turner** | Y | Y | Y | N | Y | N |
| 4 **Oxley** | ? | ? | ? | ? | ? | ? |
| 5 **Gillmor** | Y | Y | Y | N | N | N |
| 6 Strickland | Y | N | N | Y | Y | N |
| 7 **Hobson** | Y | Y | Y | N | N | N |
| 8 **Boehner** | Y | Y | Y | N | N | N |
| 9 Kaptur | Y | N | N | Y | Y | N |
| 10 Kucinich | N | ? | ? | ? | ? | ? |
| 11 Jones | N | N | N | ? | ? | ? |
| 12 **Tiberi** | Y | Y | Y | ? | ? | ? |
| 13 Brown | Y | N | N | Y | Y | Y |
| 14 **LaTourette** | Y | Y | Y | ? | ? | ? |
| 15 **Pryce** | Y | Y | Y | N | N | N |
| 16 **Regula** | Y | Y | Y | N | N | N |
| 17 Ryan | N | N | N | Y | Y | N |
| 18 **Ney** | ? | ? | ? | ? | ? | ? |
| **OKLAHOMA** | | | | | | |
| 1 **Sullivan** | Y | Y | Y | N | N | Y |
| 2 Boren | Y | N | N | Y | Y | N |
| 3 **Lucas** | Y | Y | Y | N | N | N |
| 4 **Cole** | Y | Y | Y | ? | ? | ? |
| 5 **Istook** | Y | Y | Y | N | N | N |
| **OREGON** | | | | | | |
| 1 Wu | N | N | N | Y | Y | N |
| 2 **Walden** | Y | Y | Y | N | N | N |
| 3 Blumenauer | N | N | N | Y | N | N |
| 4 DeFazio | N | N | N | Y | Y | N |
| 5 Hooley | N | N | N | Y | N | Y |
| **PENNSYLVANIA** | | | | | | |
| 1 Brady | N | N | N | Y | Y | N |
| 2 Fattah | N | N | N | N | Y | N |
| 3 **English** | Y | Y | Y | N | N | N |
| 4 **Hart** | Y | Y | Y | N | N | Y |
| 5 **Peterson** | Y | Y | Y | N | Y | N |
| 6 **Gerlach** | Y | Y | Y | N | Y | N |
| 7 **Weldon** | Y | Y | Y | N | Y | N |
| 8 **Fitzpatrick** | Y | Y | Y | N | Y | N |
| 9 **Shuster** | Y | Y | Y | N | N | Y |
| 10 **Sherwood** | Y | Y | Y | N | N | N |
| 11 Kanjorski | Y | N | N | N | Y | N |
| 12 Murtha | Y | N | N | N | Y | N |
| 13 Schwartz | N | N | N | N | N | N |
| 14 Doyle | Y | N | N | N | Y | N |
| 15 **Dent** | Y | Y | Y | N | N | N |
| 16 **Pitts** | Y | Y | Y | N | Y | Y |
| 17 Holden | Y | N | N | N | Y | N |
| 18 **Murphy** | Y | Y | Y | N | N | N |
| 19 **Platts** | Y | Y | Y | N | Y | N |
| **RHODE ISLAND** | | | | | | |
| 1 Kennedy | N | N | N | Y | Y | N |
| 2 Langevin | Y | N | N | Y | Y | N |
| **SOUTH CAROLINA** | | | | | | |
| 1 **Brown** | Y | Y | Y | N | N | N |
| 2 **Wilson** | Y | Y | Y | N | Y | Y |
| 3 **Barrett** | Y | Y | Y | N | N | Y |
| 4 **Inglis** | Y | Y | Y | N | Y | Y |
| 5 Spratt | Y | N | N | Y | Y | N |
| 6 Clyburn | Y | N | N | Y | Y | N |
| **SOUTH DAKOTA** | | | | | | |
| AL Herseth | ? | N | N | N | Y | Y |
| **TENNESSEE** | | | | | | |
| 1 **Jenkins** | Y | Y | Y | N | N | Y |
| 2 **Duncan** | Y | Y | Y | N | N | Y |

| | 296 | 297 | 298 | 299 | 300 | 301 |
|---|---|---|---|---|---|---|
| 3 **Wamp** | Y | Y | Y | N | N | N |
| 4 Davis | Y | N | N | ? | ? | ? |
| 5 Cooper | N | N | N | N | Y | Y |
| 6 Gordon | Y | N | N | Y | Y | N |
| 7 **Blackburn** | Y | Y | Y | N | N | Y |
| 8 Tanner | N | N | N | N | N | Y |
| 9 Ford | Y | N | N | N | N | N |
| **TEXAS** | | | | | | |
| 1 **Gohmert** | Y | Y | Y | N | N | Y |
| 2 **Poe** | Y | Y | Y | N | Y | Y |
| 3 **Johnson, S.** | Y | Y | Y | N | N | N |
| 4 **Hall** | Y | Y | Y | N | N | N |
| 5 **Hensarling** | Y | Y | Y | N | Y | Y |
| 6 **Barton** | ? | ? | ? | ? | ? | ? |
| 7 **Culberson** | Y | Y | Y | N | N | N |
| 8 **Brady** | ? | Y | Y | N | N | Y |
| 9 Green, A. | N | N | N | Y | Y | N |
| 10 **McCaul** | ? | ? | ? | ? | ? | ? |
| 11 **Conaway** | + | ? | ? | ? | ? | ? |
| 12 **Granger** | Y | Y | Y | N | N | N |
| 13 **Thornberry** | Y | Y | Y | N | Y | N |
| 14 **Paul** | N | Y | Y | N | N | Y |
| 15 Hinojosa | ? | ? | ? | ? | ? | ? |
| 16 Reyes | Y | N | N | N | Y | N |
| 17 Edwards | Y | N | N | Y | N | Y |
| 18 Jackson-Lee | ? | ? | ? | ? | ? | ? |
| 19 **Neugebauer** | Y | Y | Y | N | N | Y |
| 20 Gonzalez | N | N | N | N | Y | N |
| 21 **Smith** | ? | ? | ? | ? | ? | ? |
| 22 **DeLay** | Y | Y | Y | N | N | N |
| 23 **Bonilla** | Y | Y | Y | N | N | N |
| 24 **Marchant** | Y | Y | Y | N | N | N |
| 25 Doggett | ? | ? | ? | ? | ? | ? |
| 26 **Burgess** | Y | Y | Y | N | N | Y |
| 27 Ortiz | Y | N | N | N | Y | N |
| 28 Cuellar | Y | N | N | N | Y | N |
| 29 Green, G. | Y | N | N | Y | Y | N |
| 30 Johnson, E. | N | N | N | Y | N | N |
| 31 **Carter** | ? | ? | ? | ? | ? | ? |
| 32 **Sessions** | Y | Y | Y | N | N | Y |
| **UTAH** | | | | | | |
| 1 **Bishop** | Y | Y | Y | N | Y | N |
| 2 Matheson | N | N | N | Y | N | Y |
| 3 **Cannon** | Y | Y | Y | N | N | Y |
| **VERMONT** | | | | | | |
| AL *Sanders* | N | N | N | Y | Y | N |
| **VIRGINIA** | | | | | | |
| 1 **Davis, J.** | Y | Y | Y | N | Y | Y |
| 2 **Drake** | Y | Y | Y | N | Y | Y |
| 3 Scott | N | N | N | Y | N | N |
| 4 **Forbes** | Y | Y | Y | N | Y | Y |
| 5 **Goode** | Y | Y | Y | N | Y | N |
| 6 **Goodlatte** | Y | Y | Y | N | Y | N |
| 7 **Cantor** | Y | Y | Y | N | N | N |
| 8 Moran | N | N | N | Y | N | N |
| 9 Boucher | N | N | ? | Y | Y | N |
| 10 **Wolf** | Y | Y | Y | N | N | N |
| 11 **Davis, T.** | Y | Y | ? | N | Y | N |
| **WASHINGTON** | | | | | | |
| 1 Inslee | N | N | N | Y | Y | Y |
| 2 Larsen | N | N | N | Y | Y | N |
| 3 Baird | Y | N | N | Y | N | N |
| 4 **Hastings** | Y | Y | Y | N | N | N |
| 5 **McMorris** | Y | Y | Y | N | N | Y |
| 6 Dicks | N | N | N | Y | N | N |
| 7 McDermott | N | N | N | Y | N | N |
| 8 **Reichert** | Y | Y | Y | N | Y | N |
| 9 Smith | Y | N | N | Y | N | Y |
| **WEST VIRGINIA** | | | | | | |
| 1 Mollohan | Y | N | N | N | Y | N |
| 2 **Capito** | Y | Y | Y | N | N | N |
| 3 Rahall | Y | N | N | N | Y | N |
| **WISCONSIN** | | | | | | |
| 1 **Ryan** | Y | Y | Y | N | N | Y |
| 2 Baldwin | N | N | N | Y | Y | N |
| 3 Kind | N | N | N | Y | N | Y |
| 4 Moore | N | N | N | N | N | N |
| 5 **Sensenbrenner** | Y | Y | Y | N | N | Y |
| 6 **Petri** | N | Y | Y | N | Y | Y |
| 7 Obey | N | N | N | Y | N | N |
| 8 **Green** | Y | Y | Y | N | N | Y |
| **WYOMING** | | | | | | |
| AL **Cubin** | Y | Y | Y | N | N | Y |

# IN THE HOUSE | By Vote Number

**302.** **HR 2985. Fiscal 2006 Legislative Branch Appropriations/
Recommit.** Obey, D-Wis., motion to recommit the bill to the House Appropriations Committee. Motion rejected 180-232: R 0-219; D 179-13 (ND 135-12, SD 44-1); I 1-0. June 22, 2005.

**303.** **HR 2985. Fiscal 2006 Legislative Branch Appropriations/
Passage.** Passage of the bill that would appropriate $2.9 billion in fiscal 2006 for legislative branch operations, excluding funds for Senate operations. It would provide $1.1 billion for operations of the House of Representatives, $543 million for the Library of Congress, $482 million for the Government Accountability Office, $317 million for the Architect of the Capitol and $123 million for the Government Printing Office. Passed 330-82: R 205-14; D 125-67 (ND 96-51, SD 29-16); I 0-1. June 22, 2005.

**304.** **HR 3010. Fiscal 2006 Labor-HHS-Education Appropriations/
Previous Question.** Capito, R-W.Va., motion to order the previous question (thus ending debate and the possibility of amendment) on adoption of the rule (H Res 337) to provide for House floor consideration of the bill that would appropriate $602 billion in fiscal 2006 for the departments of Labor, Health and Human Services and Education and for other various agencies and programs. Motion agreed to 225-194: R 224-0; D 1-193 (ND 0-145, SD 1-48); I 0-1. (Subsequently, the rule was adopted by voice vote.) June 23, 2005.

**305.** **HR 3010. Fiscal 2006 Labor-HHS-Education Appropriations/
Corporation for Public Broadcasting.** Obey, D-Wis., amendment that would add $100 million for the Corporation for Public Broadcasting, offset with cuts to the Department of Labor departmental management and pilot programs, Health Resources and Services Administration program management and Department of Education departmental management and demonstration projects. Adopted 284-140: R 87-140; D 196-0 (ND 148-0, SD 48-0); I 1-0. June 23, 2005.

**306.** **HR 3010. Fiscal 2006 Labor-HHS-Education Appropriations/
Respirator Testing.** Owens, D-N.Y., amendment that would strike a provision in the bill that would bar funds from enforcing an Occupational Safety and Health Administration requirement that hospitals conduct annual testing of respirators for tuberculosis exposure. Rejected 206-216: R 12-214; D 193-2 (ND 147-1, SD 46-1); I 1-0. June 23, 2005.

**307.** **HR 3010. Fiscal 2006 Labor-HHS-Education Appropriations/
Special Education Funding.** Bradley, R-N.H., amendment that would increase funds for special education by $50 million, offset with reductions to the Occupational Safety and Health Administration and Education Department program administration accounts. Rejected 161-262: R 115-111; D 46-150 (ND 30-119, SD 16-31); I 0-1. June 23, 2005.

| | 302 | 303 | 304 | 305 | 306 | 307 |
|---|---|---|---|---|---|---|
| **ALABAMA** | | | | | | |
| 1 Bonner | ? | ? | Y | N | N | N |
| 2 Everett | N | Y | Y | N | N | Y |
| 3 Rogers | N | Y | Y | Y | N | N |
| 4 Aderholt | N | Y | Y | Y | N | N |
| 5 Cramer | Y | Y | N | Y | Y | N |
| 6 Bachus | N | Y | Y | N | N | N |
| 7 Davis | Y | Y | N | Y | Y | N |
| **ALASKA** | | | | | | |
| AL Young | N | Y | Y | Y | N | Y |
| **ARIZONA** | | | | | | |
| 1 Renzi | N | Y | Y | Y | N | Y |
| 2 Franks | N | Y | Y | N | N | Y |
| 3 Shadegg | N | Y | Y | N | N | Y |
| 4 Pastor | Y | N | N | Y | Y | Y |
| 5 Hayworth | N | Y | Y | Y | N | Y |
| 6 Flake | N | N | Y | N | N | Y |
| 7 Grijalva | Y | N | N | Y | Y | N |
| 8 Kolbe | N | Y | Y | N | N | N |
| **ARKANSAS** | | | | | | |
| 1 Berry | Y | N | N | Y | Y | N |
| 2 Snyder | Y | N | N | Y | Y | N |
| 3 Boozman | N | Y | Y | Y | N | Y |
| 4 Ross | N | N | N | Y | Y | N |
| **CALIFORNIA** | | | | | | |
| 1 Thompson | Y | N | N | Y | Y | N |
| 2 Herger | N | Y | Y | N | N | Y |
| 3 Lungren | N | Y | Y | N | N | Y |
| 4 Doolittle | Y | Y | Y | N | N | N |
| 5 Matsui, D. | Y | Y | N | Y | Y | N |
| 6 Woolsey | Y | Y | N | Y | Y | N |
| 7 Miller, George | Y | N | N | Y | Y | N |
| 8 Pelosi | Y | Y | N | Y | Y | N |
| 9 Lee | Y | N | N | Y | Y | N |
| 10 Tauscher | Y | Y | N | Y | Y | N |
| 11 Pombo | N | Y | Y | N | N | N |
| 12 Lantos | Y | Y | N | Y | Y | N |
| 13 Stark | Y | N | N | Y | Y | N |
| 14 Eshoo | Y | Y | N | Y | Y | N |
| 15 Honda | Y | N | N | Y | Y | N |
| 16 Lofgren | Y | Y | N | Y | Y | N |
| 17 Farr | Y | Y | N | Y | Y | N |
| 18 Cardoza | Y | N | N | Y | Y | N |
| 19 Radanovich | N | Y | Y | N | N | N |
| 20 Costa | Y | Y | N | Y | Y | N |
| 21 Nunes | N | Y | Y | Y | N | N |
| 22 Thomas | ? | ? | Y | Y | N | N |
| 23 Capps | Y | Y | N | Y | Y | N |
| 24 Gallegly | N | Y | Y | N | N | Y |
| 25 McKeon | N | Y | Y | N | N | N |
| 26 Dreier | N | Y | Y | N | N | N |
| 27 Sherman | Y | N | N | Y | Y | N |
| 28 Berman | Y | Y | N | Y | Y | N |
| 29 Schiff | Y | Y | N | Y | Y | N |
| 30 Waxman | Y | Y | N | Y | Y | N |
| 31 Becerra | Y | Y | N | Y | Y | N |
| 32 Solis | Y | Y | N | Y | Y | N |
| 33 Watson | Y | N | N | Y | Y | N |
| 34 Roybal-Allard | Y | Y | N | Y | Y | N |
| 35 Waters | Y | Y | N | Y | Y | N |
| 36 Harman | Y | Y | N | ? | ? | ? |
| 37 Millender-McD. | Y | Y | N | Y | Y | N |
| 38 Napolitano | Y | Y | N | Y | Y | N |
| 39 Sánchez, Linda | Y | Y | N | Y | Y | N |
| 40 Royce | N | Y | Y | N | N | N |
| 41 Lewis | N | Y | Y | N | N | N |
| 42 Miller, Gary | N | Y | Y | N | N | N |
| 43 Baca | Y | Y | N | Y | Y | N |
| 44 Calvert | N | Y | Y | N | N | N |
| 45 Bono | N | Y | Y | Y | N | N |
| 46 Rohrabacher | N | Y | Y | N | N | Y |
| 47 Sanchez, Loretta | Y | Y | N | Y | Y | N |
| 48 Cox | N | Y | Y | N | N | N |
| 49 Issa | N | Y | Y | N | N | N |

| | 302 | 303 | 304 | 305 | 306 | 307 |
|---|---|---|---|---|---|---|
| 50 Cunningham | N | Y | Y | Y | N | N |
| 51 Filner | Y | N | N | Y | Y | N |
| 52 Hunter | N | Y | ? | N | N | Y |
| 53 Davis | Y | N | N | Y | Y | Y |
| **COLORADO** | | | | | | |
| 1 DeGette | Y | Y | N | Y | Y | N |
| 2 Udall | Y | N | N | Y | Y | Y |
| 3 Salazar | Y | N | N | Y | Y | N |
| 4 Musgrave | N | Y | Y | N | N | Y |
| 5 Hefley | N | N | Y | N | N | Y |
| 6 Tancredo | N | N | Y | N | N | Y |
| 7 Beauprez | N | Y | Y | N | N | Y |
| **CONNECTICUT** | | | | | | |
| 1 Larson | Y | Y | N | Y | Y | N |
| 2 Simmons | N | Y | Y | Y | N | Y |
| 3 DeLauro | Y | N | N | Y | Y | N |
| 4 Shays | N | N | Y | Y | Y | Y |
| 5 Johnson | N | Y | Y | Y | N | Y |
| **DELAWARE** | | | | | | |
| AL Castle | N | Y | Y | Y | N | N |
| **FLORIDA** | | | | | | |
| 1 Miller | N | Y | Y | Y | N | Y |
| 2 Boyd | ? | ? | ? | ? | ? | ? |
| 3 Brown | Y | Y | N | Y | Y | N |
| 4 Crenshaw | N | Y | Y | N | N | N |
| 5 Brown-Waite | N | Y | Y | N | N | N |
| 6 Stearns | N | N | N | N | N | N |
| 7 Mica | N | Y | Y | N | N | N |
| 8 Keller | N | Y | Y | N | N | N |
| 9 Bilirakis | N | Y | Y | N | N | Y |
| 10 Young | N | Y | Y | N | N | N |
| 11 Davis | Y | Y | N | Y | Y | N |
| 12 Putnam | N | Y | Y | N | N | N |
| 13 Harris | N | Y | Y | N | N | N |
| 14 Mack | N | Y | Y | N | N | N |
| 15 Weldon | N | Y | Y | N | N | N |
| 16 Foley | Y | Y | Y | Y | N | Y |
| 17 Meek | Y | Y | N | ? | ? | ? |
| 18 Ros-Lehtinen | N | Y | Y | N | N | Y |
| 19 Wexler | Y | Y | N | Y | Y | N |
| 20 Wasserman-Schultz | Y | N | N | Y | Y | N |
| 21 Diaz-Balart, L. | N | Y | Y | N | N | N |
| 22 Shaw | N | Y | Y | N | N | N |
| 23 Hastings | Y | N | N | Y | Y | N |
| 24 Feeney | N | Y | Y | N | N | Y |
| 25 Diaz-Balart, M. | N | Y | Y | N | N | N |
| **GEORGIA** | | | | | | |
| 1 Kingston | N | Y | Y | N | N | N |
| 2 Bishop | Y | N | N | Y | Y | N |
| 3 Marshall | Y | N | N | Y | Y | N |
| 4 McKinney | Y | Y | N | Y | Y | N |
| 5 Lewis | ? | ? | ? | ? | ? | ? |
| 6 Price | N | Y | Y | N | N | N |
| 7 Linder | N | Y | Y | N | N | N |
| 8 Westmoreland | N | Y | Y | N | N | N |
| 9 Norwood | N | Y | Y | N | N | N |
| 10 Deal | N | Y | Y | N | N | N |
| 11 Gingrey | N | Y | Y | N | N | N |
| 12 Barrow | Y | N | N | Y | Y | N |
| 13 Scott | Y | Y | N | Y | Y | N |
| **HAWAII** | | | | | | |
| 1 Abercrombie | N | Y | N | Y | Y | N |
| 2 Case | N | Y | N | Y | Y | N |
| **IDAHO** | | | | | | |
| 1 Otter | N | N | Y | N | N | Y |
| 2 Simpson | N | Y | Y | N | N | Y |
| **ILLINOIS** | | | | | | |
| 1 Rush | Y | Y | N | Y | Y | N |
| 2 Jackson | Y | N | N | Y | Y | N |
| 3 Lipinski | Y | N | N | Y | Y | N |
| 4 Gutierrez | Y | Y | N | Y | Y | N |
| 5 Emanuel | Y | Y | N | Y | Y | N |
| 6 Hyde | N | Y | ? | N | N | N |
| 7 Davis | Y | Y | N | Y | Y | N |
| 8 Bean | N | Y | N | Y | Y | N |
| 9 Schakowsky | Y | N | N | Y | Y | N |
| 10 Kirk | N | Y | Y | Y | N | N |
| 11 Weller | N | Y | Y | N | N | Y |
| 12 Costello | Y | Y | N | Y | Y | N |

**KEY**    Republicans    Democrats    *Independents*

| | | | |
|---|---|---|---|
| Y | Voted for (yea) | X | Paired against |
| # | Paired for | – | Announced against |
| + | Announced for | P | Voted "present" |
| N | Voted against (nay) | | |

C   Voted "present" to avoid possible conflict of interest

?   Did not vote or otherwise make a position known

ND Northern Democrats, SD Southern Democrats
Southern states: Ala., Ark., Fla., Ga., Ky., La., Miss., N.C., Okla., S.C., Tenn., Texas, Va.

| | 302 | 303 | 304 | 305 | 306 | 307 |
|---|---|---|---|---|---|---|
| 13 **Biggert** | N | Y | Y | Y | N | Y |
| 14 **Hastert** | N | Y | | | | |
| 15 **Johnson** | N | Y | Y | Y | Y | Y |
| 16 **Manzullo** | N | Y | Y | N | N | Y |
| 17 Evans | Y | Y | N | Y | Y | N |
| 18 **LaHood** | N | Y | Y | Y | Y | N |
| 19 **Shimkus** | N | Y | Y | Y | Y | N |
| **INDIANA** | | | | | | |
| 1 Visclosky | Y | Y | N | Y | Y | N |
| 2 **Chocola** | N | Y | Y | N | N | Y |
| 3 **Souder** | N | Y | Y | N | N | Y |
| 4 **Buyer** | N | Y | ? | N | N | N |
| 5 **Burton** | N | Y | Y | N | N | Y |
| 6 **Pence** | N | Y | Y | N | N | Y |
| 7 Carson | Y | Y | N | Y | Y | N |
| 8 **Hostettler** | N | Y | Y | N | N | Y |
| 9 **Sodrel** | N | Y | Y | Y | N | N |
| **IOWA** | | | | | | |
| 1 **Nussle** | N | Y | Y | N | N | Y |
| 2 **Leach** | N | Y | Y | Y | N | Y |
| 3 Boswell | Y | N | N | Y | Y | N |
| 4 **Latham** | N | Y | Y | Y | N | Y |
| 5 **King** | N | Y | Y | N | N | Y |
| **KANSAS** | | | | | | |
| 1 **Moran** | N | Y | Y | Y | N | Y |
| 2 **Ryun** | N | Y | Y | N | N | Y |
| 3 Moore | Y | N | N | Y | Y | Y |
| 4 **Tiahrt** | N | Y | Y | N | N | N |
| **KENTUCKY** | | | | | | |
| 1 **Whitfield** | N | Y | Y | Y | N | N |
| 2 **Lewis** | N | Y | Y | Y | N | Y |
| 3 **Northup** | N | Y | Y | N | N | N |
| 4 **Davis** | N | Y | Y | N | N | N |
| 5 **Rogers** | N | Y | Y | Y | N | N |
| 6 Chandler | Y | N | N | Y | Y | Y |
| **LOUISIANA** | | | | | | |
| 1 **Jindal** | N | Y | Y | N | N | Y |
| 2 Jefferson | Y | Y | N | Y | Y | N |
| 3 Melancon | Y | N | N | Y | Y | N |
| 4 **McCrery** | N | Y | Y | N | N | Y |
| 5 **Alexander** | N | Y | Y | Y | N | N |
| 6 **Baker** | N | Y | Y | N | N | N |
| 7 **Boustany** | N | Y | Y | N | N | N |
| **MAINE** | | | | | | |
| 1 Allen | Y | Y | N | Y | Y | N |
| 2 Michaud | Y | Y | N | Y | Y | N |
| **MARYLAND** | | | | | | |
| 1 **Gilchrest** | N | Y | Y | Y | N | N |
| 2 Ruppersberger | Y | Y | N | Y | Y | N |
| 3 Cardin | Y | Y | N | Y | Y | N |
| 4 Wynn | Y | Y | N | Y | Y | N |
| 5 Hoyer | Y | Y | N | Y | Y | N |
| 6 **Bartlett** | N | Y | Y | N | N | N |
| 7 Cummings | Y | Y | N | Y | Y | N |
| 8 Van Hollen | Y | Y | N | Y | Y | N |
| **MASSACHUSETTS** | | | | | | |
| 1 Olver | Y | N | N | Y | Y | N |
| 2 Neal | Y | Y | N | Y | Y | N |
| 3 McGovern | Y | N | N | Y | Y | N |
| 4 Frank | Y | N | N | Y | Y | Y |
| 5 Meehan | Y | N | N | Y | Y | Y |
| 6 Tierney | Y | N | N | Y | Y | Y |
| 7 Markey | Y | Y | N | Y | Y | Y |
| 8 Capuano | Y | Y | N | Y | Y | N |
| 9 Lynch | Y | Y | N | Y | Y | N |
| 10 Delahunt | Y | Y | N | Y | Y | N |
| **MICHIGAN** | | | | | | |
| 1 Stupak | Y | N | N | Y | Y | N |
| 2 **Hoekstra** | N | Y | Y | N | N | Y |
| 3 **Ehlers** | N | Y | Y | Y | N | N |
| 4 **Camp** | N | Y | Y | Y | N | Y |
| 5 Kildee | Y | N | N | Y | Y | N |
| 6 **Upton** | N | Y | Y | Y | N | Y |
| 7 **Schwarz** | N | Y | Y | Y | N | N |
| 8 **Rogers** | N | Y | Y | N | N | N |
| 9 **Knollenberg** | N | Y | Y | N | N | N |
| 10 **Miller** | N | Y | Y | Y | N | Y |
| 11 **McCotter** | N | Y | Y | Y | Y | Y |
| 12 Levin | Y | Y | N | Y | Y | N |
| 13 Kilpatrick | Y | Y | N | Y | Y | N |
| 14 Conyers | Y | N | N | Y | Y | N |
| 15 Dingell | Y | Y | N | Y | Y | N |
| **MINNESOTA** | | | | | | |
| 1 **Gutknecht** | N | Y | Y | N | N | Y |
| 2 **Kline** | N | Y | Y | N | N | Y |
| 3 **Ramstad** | N | Y | Y | Y | N | Y |
| 4 McCollum | Y | N | N | Y | Y | Y |
| 5 Sabo | Y | Y | N | Y | Y | N |
| 6 **Kennedy** | N | N | Y | Y | N | Y |
| 7 Peterson | Y | Y | ? | Y | N | Y |
| 8 Oberstar | Y | N | N | Y | Y | N |
| **MISSISSIPPI** | | | | | | |
| 1 **Wicker** | N | Y | Y | N | N | N |
| 2 Thompson | Y | Y | N | Y | Y | N |
| 3 **Pickering** | N | Y | Y | Y | N | Y |
| 4 Taylor | Y | N | N | Y | Y | N |
| **MISSOURI** | | | | | | |
| 1 Clay | Y | Y | N | Y | Y | N |
| 2 **Akin** | N | Y | Y | N | N | Y |
| 3 Carnahan | Y | Y | N | Y | Y | N |
| 4 Skelton | Y | Y | N | Y | Y | N |
| 5 Cleaver | Y | N | N | Y | Y | Y |
| 6 **Graves** | N | N | Y | N | N | Y |
| 7 **Blunt** | N | Y | Y | N | N | N |
| 8 **Emerson** | N | Y | Y | N | N | N |
| 9 **Hulshof** | N | N | Y | N | N | Y |
| **MONTANA** | | | | | | |
| AL **Rehberg** | N | Y | Y | N | N | N |
| **NEBRASKA** | | | | | | |
| 1 **Fortenberry** | N | Y | Y | N | N | Y |
| 2 **Terry** | N | Y | Y | N | Y | Y |
| 3 **Osborne** | N | Y | Y | N | N | Y |
| **NEVADA** | | | | | | |
| 1 Berkley | Y | Y | N | Y | Y | N |
| 2 **Gibbons** | N | Y | Y | Y | N | Y |
| 3 **Porter** | N | Y | Y | Y | N | Y |
| **NEW HAMPSHIRE** | | | | | | |
| 1 **Bradley** | N | Y | Y | Y | N | Y |
| 2 **Bass** | N | Y | Y | ? | ? | ? |
| **NEW JERSEY** | | | | | | |
| 1 Andrews | Y | N | N | Y | Y | N |
| 2 **LoBiondo** | N | Y | Y | N | Y | N |
| 3 **Saxton** | N | Y | Y | N | N | N |
| 4 **Smith** | N | Y | Y | Y | N | N |
| 5 **Garrett** | N | Y | Y | N | N | Y |
| 6 Pallone | Y | N | N | Y | Y | N |
| 7 **Ferguson** | N | Y | Y | Y | Y | Y |
| 8 Pascrell | N | Y | N | Y | Y | N |
| 9 Rothman | Y | Y | N | Y | Y | N |
| 10 Payne | Y | N | N | Y | Y | N |
| 11 **Frelinghuysen** | N | Y | Y | Y | N | N |
| 12 Holt | Y | Y | N | Y | Y | N |
| 13 Menendez | Y | N | N | Y | Y | N |
| **NEW MEXICO** | | | | | | |
| 1 **Wilson** | N | Y | Y | ? | ? | ? |
| 2 **Pearce** | N | Y | Y | N | N | Y |
| 3 Udall | Y | N | N | ? | ? | ? |
| **NEW YORK** | | | | | | |
| 1 Bishop | Y | Y | N | Y | Y | Y |
| 2 Israel | Y | Y | N | Y | Y | N |
| 3 **King** | N | Y | Y | Y | N | N |
| 4 McCarthy | Y | Y | N | Y | Y | N |
| 5 Ackerman | Y | Y | N | Y | Y | N |
| 6 Meeks | Y | Y | N | Y | ? | N |
| 7 Crowley | Y | Y | N | Y | Y | N |
| 8 Nadler | Y | Y | N | Y | Y | N |
| 9 Weiner | Y | Y | N | Y | Y | Y |
| 10 Towns | Y | Y | N | Y | Y | N |
| 11 Owens | Y | N | N | Y | Y | N |
| 12 Velázquez | Y | Y | N | Y | Y | N |
| 13 **Fossella** | N | Y | Y | Y | N | Y |
| 14 Maloney | Y | N | N | Y | Y | N |
| 15 Rangel | ? | ? | N | Y | Y | N |
| 16 Serrano | Y | Y | N | Y | Y | N |
| 17 Engel | Y | Y | N | Y | Y | N |
| 18 Lowey | Y | N | N | Y | Y | N |
| 19 **Kelly** | N | Y | Y | Y | N | Y |
| 20 **Sweeney** | N | Y | Y | Y | N | N |
| 21 McNulty | Y | Y | N | Y | Y | N |
| 22 Hinchey | Y | Y | N | Y | Y | N |
| 23 **McHugh** | N | Y | Y | Y | N | N |
| 24 **Boehlert** | N | Y | Y | Y | N | N |
| 25 **Walsh** | N | Y | Y | Y | N | N |
| 26 **Reynolds** | N | Y | Y | Y | N | N |
| 27 Higgins | Y | N | N | Y | Y | N |
| 28 Slaughter | Y | Y | N | Y | Y | N |
| 29 **Kuhl** | N | Y | Y | Y | N | Y |
| **NORTH CAROLINA** | | | | | | |
| 1 Butterfield | Y | Y | N | Y | Y | Y |
| 2 Etheridge | Y | N | N | Y | Y | Y |
| 3 **Jones** | N | N | Y | N | ? | Y |
| 4 Price | Y | Y | N | Y | Y | Y |
| 5 **Foxx** | N | Y | Y | N | N | Y |
| 6 **Coble** | N | Y | Y | Y | N | Y |
| 7 McIntyre | Y | Y | N | Y | Y | Y |
| 8 **Hayes** | N | Y | Y | N | N | Y |
| 9 **Myrick** | N | Y | Y | N | N | N |
| 10 **McHenry** | N | Y | Y | N | N | Y |
| 11 **Taylor** | N | Y | Y | N | N | Y |
| 12 Watt | Y | N | N | Y | Y | N |
| 13 Miller | Y | Y | N | Y | Y | Y |
| **NORTH DAKOTA** | | | | | | |
| AL Pomeroy | ? | ? | ? | Y | Y | Y |
| **OHIO** | | | | | | |
| 1 **Chabot** | N | Y | Y | N | N | N |
| 2 Vacant | | | | | | |
| 3 **Turner** | N | Y | Y | N | N | N |
| 4 **Oxley** | ? | ? | Y | N | N | N |
| 5 **Gillmor** | N | Y | Y | Y | N | N |
| 6 Strickland | Y | Y | N | Y | Y | N |
| 7 **Hobson** | N | Y | Y | N | N | N |
| 8 **Boehner** | N | Y | Y | N | N | N |
| 9 Kaptur | N | Y | N | Y | Y | N |
| 10 Kucinich | ? | ? | ? | Y | Y | N |
| 11 Jones | ? | ? | ? | Y | Y | N |
| 12 **Tiberi** | ? | ? | Y | Y | N | N |
| 13 Brown | Y | N | N | Y | Y | N |
| 14 **LaTourette** | ? | ? | ? | Y | Y | N |
| 15 **Pryce** | N | Y | Y | Y | N | N |
| 16 **Regula** | N | Y | Y | N | N | N |
| 17 Ryan | Y | Y | ? | ? | Y | Y |
| 18 **Ney** | ? | ? | Y | Y | N | N |
| **OKLAHOMA** | | | | | | |
| 1 **Sullivan** | N | Y | Y | N | N | N |
| 2 Boren | Y | Y | N | Y | Y | Y |
| 3 **Lucas** | N | Y | Y | N | N | N |
| 4 **Cole** | ? | ? | Y | N | N | Y |
| 5 **Istook** | N | Y | Y | N | N | N |
| **OREGON** | | | | | | |
| 1 Wu | Y | N | N | Y | Y | Y |
| 2 **Walden** | N | Y | Y | Y | N | Y |
| 3 Blumenauer | Y | Y | N | Y | Y | Y |
| 4 DeFazio | Y | Y | N | Y | Y | N |
| 5 Hooley | Y | Y | N | Y | Y | Y |
| **PENNSYLVANIA** | | | | | | |
| 1 Brady | N | Y | N | Y | Y | N |
| 2 Fattah | Y | Y | N | Y | Y | N |
| 3 **English** | N | Y | Y | Y | N | Y |
| 4 **Hart** | N | Y | Y | Y | N | Y |
| 5 **Peterson** | N | Y | Y | Y | N | N |
| 6 **Gerlach** | N | Y | Y | Y | N | Y |
| 7 **Weldon** | N | Y | Y | Y | Y | Y |
| 8 **Fitzpatrick** | N | Y | Y | Y | N | Y |
| 9 **Shuster** | N | Y | Y | N | N | N |
| 10 **Sherwood** | N | Y | Y | Y | N | N |
| 11 Kanjorski | N | Y | N | Y | Y | N |
| 12 Murtha | N | Y | N | Y | Y | N |
| 13 Schwartz | Y | Y | N | Y | Y | N |
| 14 Doyle | N | Y | N | Y | Y | N |
| 15 **Dent** | N | Y | Y | Y | N | N |
| 16 **Pitts** | N | Y | Y | N | N | Y |
| 17 Holden | N | Y | N | Y | Y | N |
| 18 **Murphy** | N | Y | Y | Y | Y | Y |
| 19 **Platts** | N | Y | ? | Y | Y | Y |
| **RHODE ISLAND** | | | | | | |
| 1 Kennedy | Y | Y | N | Y | Y | Y |
| 2 Langevin | Y | Y | N | Y | Y | Y |
| **SOUTH CAROLINA** | | | | | | |
| 1 **Brown** | N | Y | Y | N | N | Y |
| 2 **Wilson** | N | Y | Y | N | N | N |
| 3 **Barrett** | N | Y | Y | N | N | ? |
| 4 **Inglis** | N | Y | Y | Y | N | N |
| 5 Spratt | Y | Y | N | Y | Y | N |
| 6 Clyburn | Y | Y | N | Y | Y | N |
| **SOUTH DAKOTA** | | | | | | |
| AL Herseth | Y | N | N | Y | Y | Y |
| **TENNESSEE** | | | | | | |
| 1 **Jenkins** | N | Y | Y | Y | N | Y |
| 2 **Duncan** | N | N | Y | Y | N | Y |
| 3 **Wamp** | N | Y | Y | Y | N | N |
| 4 Davis | Y | Y | N | Y | Y | Y |
| 5 Cooper | Y | N | N | Y | Y | Y |
| 6 Gordon | ? | ? | N | Y | Y | Y |
| 7 **Blackburn** | N | Y | Y | N | N | N |
| 8 Tanner | Y | N | N | Y | Y | Y |
| 9 Ford | Y | Y | N | Y | Y | Y |
| **TEXAS** | | | | | | |
| 1 **Gohmert** | N | Y | Y | N | N | Y |
| 2 **Poe** | N | Y | Y | N | N | Y |
| 3 **Johnson, S.** | N | Y | Y | N | N | N |
| 4 **Hall** | N | Y | Y | N | N | N |
| 5 **Hensarling** | N | Y | Y | N | N | Y |
| 6 **Barton** | ? | ? | Y | N | N | N |
| 7 **Culberson** | N | Y | Y | N | N | N |
| 8 **Brady** | N | Y | Y | N | N | Y |
| 9 Green, A. | Y | Y | N | Y | Y | Y |
| 10 **McCaul** | ? | ? | Y | Y | N | Y |
| 11 **Conaway** | ? | ? | Y | N | N | N |
| 12 **Granger** | N | Y | Y | N | N | N |
| 13 **Thornberry** | N | Y | Y | N | N | N |
| 14 **Paul** | N | N | Y | Y | N | Y |
| 15 Hinojosa | ? | ? | N | Y | Y | N |
| 16 Reyes | Y | Y | N | Y | ? | ? |
| 17 Edwards | Y | Y | N | Y | Y | Y |
| 18 Jackson-Lee | ? | ? | N | Y | Y | N |
| 19 **Neugebauer** | N | Y | Y | N | N | Y |
| 20 Gonzalez | Y | Y | N | Y | Y | N |
| 21 **Smith** | ? | ? | Y | N | N | N |
| 22 **DeLay** | N | Y | Y | N | N | N |
| 23 **Bonilla** | N | Y | Y | N | N | N |
| 24 **Marchant** | N | Y | Y | Y | N | N |
| 25 Doggett | ? | ? | N | Y | Y | N |
| 26 **Burgess** | N | Y | Y | N | N | N |
| 27 Ortiz | Y | Y | N | Y | Y | N |
| 28 Cuellar | Y | Y | N | Y | Y | N |
| 29 Green, G. | Y | N | N | Y | Y | N |
| 30 Johnson, E. | Y | Y | N | Y | Y | N |
| 31 **Carter** | ? | ? | Y | N | N | N |
| 32 **Sessions** | N | Y | Y | N | N | Y |
| **UTAH** | | | | | | |
| 1 **Bishop** | N | Y | Y | N | N | Y |
| 2 Matheson | Y | N | N | Y | Y | Y |
| 3 **Cannon** | N | Y | Y | N | N | Y |
| **VERMONT** | | | | | | |
| AL *Sanders* | Y | N | N | Y | Y | N |
| **VIRGINIA** | | | | | | |
| 1 **Davis, J.** | N | N | Y | Y | N | Y |
| 2 **Drake** | N | Y | Y | Y | N | Y |
| 3 Scott | Y | N | N | Y | Y | N |
| 4 **Forbes** | N | Y | Y | N | N | Y |
| 5 **Goode** | N | N | Y | N | N | N |
| 6 **Goodlatte** | N | Y | Y | N | N | N |
| 7 **Cantor** | N | Y | Y | N | N | N |
| 8 Moran | Y | Y | N | Y | Y | N |
| 9 Boucher | Y | Y | N | Y | Y | N |
| 10 **Wolf** | N | Y | Y | Y | N | N |
| 11 **Davis, T.** | N | Y | ? | ? | ? | ? |
| **WASHINGTON** | | | | | | |
| 1 Inslee | Y | N | N | Y | Y | Y |
| 2 Larsen | Y | Y | N | Y | Y | N |
| 3 Baird | Y | N | N | Y | Y | N |
| 4 **Hastings** | N | Y | Y | N | N | N |
| 5 **McMorris** | N | Y | Y | N | N | Y |
| 6 Dicks | Y | Y | N | Y | Y | N |
| 7 McDermott | Y | N | N | Y | Y | N |
| 8 **Reichert** | N | Y | Y | Y | N | Y |
| 9 Smith | Y | N | N | Y | Y | Y |
| **WEST VIRGINIA** | | | | | | |
| 1 Mollohan | N | Y | N | Y | Y | N |
| 2 **Capito** | N | Y | Y | Y | N | Y |
| 3 Rahall | N | Y | N | Y | Y | N |
| **WISCONSIN** | | | | | | |
| 1 **Ryan** | N | Y | Y | N | N | Y |
| 2 Baldwin | Y | N | N | Y | Y | N |
| 3 Kind | Y | N | N | Y | Y | Y |
| 4 Moore | Y | Y | ? | Y | Y | N |
| 5 **Sensenbrenner** | N | Y | Y | N | N | Y |
| 6 **Petri** | N | Y | Y | Y | N | Y |
| 7 Obey | Y | N | N | Y | Y | N |
| 8 **Green** | N | N | Y | N | N | Y |
| **WYOMING** | | | | | | |
| AL **Cubin** | N | Y | Y | Y | N | Y |

# IN THE HOUSE | By Vote Number

**308.** **HR 3010. Fiscal 2006 Labor-HHS-Education Appropriations/ AmeriCorps Funding.** Price, R-Ga., amendment that would add $70 million to the Teacher Incentive Fund, offset by a cut in operations funding for AmeriCorps grants. Rejected 102-298: R 101-114; D 1-183 (ND 0-138, SD 1-45); I 0-1. June 24, 2005.

**309.** **HR 3010. Fiscal 2006 Labor-HHS-Education Appropriations/ United Airlines Pensions.** Miller, D-Calif., amendment that would prohibit the use of funds to terminate the United Airlines employees' pension plan. Adopted 219-185: R 31-185; D 187-0 (ND 140-0, SD 47-0); I 1-0. June 24, 2005.

**310.** **HR 3010. Fiscal 2006 Labor-HHS-Education Appropriations/ Medicaid Commission.** Brown, D-Ohio, amendment that would prohibit the use of funds in the bill for the operations of the Medicaid Commission. Rejected 170-237: R 1-218; D 168-19 (ND 128-12, SD 40-7); I 1-0. June 24, 2005.

**311.** **HR 3010. Fiscal 2006 Labor-HHS-Education Appropriations/ Social Security Numbers.** Filner, D-Calif., amendment that would prohibit the use of funds in the bill to place Social Security numbers on identification cards issued to Medicare beneficiaries. Adopted 314-94: R 128-92; D 185-2 (ND 138-2, SD 47-0); I 1-0. June 24, 2005.

**312.** **HR 3010. Fiscal 2006 Labor-HHS-Education Appropriations/ Impotence Prescription Drugs.** King, R-Iowa, amendment that would prohibit the use of funds in the bill to pay for drugs prescribed for the treatment of impotence. Adopted 285-121: R 185-33; D 100-87 (ND 68-72, SD 32-15); I 0-1. June 24, 2005.

**313.** **HR 3010. Fiscal 2006 Labor-HHS-Education Appropriations/ Discretionary Spending Cut.** Hefley, R-Colo., amendment that would reduce discretionary spending in the bill by 1 percent. Rejected 84-323: R 82-137; D 2-185 (ND 1-139, SD 1-46); I 0-1. June 24, 2005.

**314.** **HR 3010. Fiscal 2006 Labor-HHS-Education Appropriations/ Corporation for Public Broadcasting Content.** Hinchey, D-N.Y., amendment that would prohibit the use of funds by any federal department, agency, officer or employee to exercise any direction, supervision, or control over the content or distribution of public telecommunications programs and services. Rejected 187-218: R 3-216; D 183-2 (ND 137-2, SD 46-0); I 1-0. June 24, 2005.

**315.** **HR 3010. Fiscal 2006 Labor-HHS-Education Appropriations/ Tribal Labor Standards.** Hayworth, R-Ariz., amendment that would prohibit the use of funds in the bill for the National Labor Relations Board to exert jurisdiction over tribally owned or operated enterprises on tribal land. Rejected 146-256: R 142-74; D 4-181 (ND 3-135, SD 1-46); I 0-1. June 24, 2005.

| Member | 308 | 309 | 310 | 311 | 312 | 313 | 314 | 315 |
|---|---|---|---|---|---|---|---|---|
| **ALABAMA** | | | | | | | | |
| 1 Bonner | N | N | N | Y | Y | N | N | Y |
| 2 Everett | N | N | N | N | Y | N | N | Y |
| 3 Rogers | ? | ? | ? | ? | ? | ? | ? | ? |
| 4 Aderholt | N | N | N | N | Y | N | N | Y |
| 5 Cramer | N | Y | N | Y | Y | N | Y | N |
| 6 Bachus | N | N | N | N | N | Y | N | Y |
| 7 Davis | N | Y | N | Y | Y | N | Y | N |
| **ALASKA** | | | | | | | | |
| AL Young | N | N | N | Y | N | N | N | N |
| **ARIZONA** | | | | | | | | |
| 1 Renzi | Y | N | N | Y | Y | N | N | Y |
| 2 Franks | Y | N | N | Y | Y | Y | N | Y |
| 3 Shadegg | N | N | N | Y | Y | Y | N | Y |
| 4 Pastor | N | Y | Y | Y | N | N | Y | N |
| 5 Hayworth | Y | N | N | Y | Y | N | N | Y |
| 6 Flake | Y | N | N | Y | Y | Y | N | Y |
| 7 Grijalva | N | Y | Y | Y | N | N | Y | N |
| 8 Kolbe | N | N | N | N | Y | N | N | Y |
| **ARKANSAS** | | | | | | | | |
| 1 Berry | N | Y | Y | Y | Y | N | Y | N |
| 2 Snyder | N | Y | Y | Y | N | N | Y | N |
| 3 Boozman | ? | ? | ? | ? | ? | ? | ? | ? |
| 4 Ross | N | Y | Y | Y | Y | N | Y | N |
| **CALIFORNIA** | | | | | | | | |
| 1 Thompson | N | Y | Y | Y | Y | N | Y | N |
| 2 Herger | Y | N | N | Y | Y | Y | N | Y |
| 3 Lungren | Y | N | N | Y | Y | Y | N | Y |
| 4 Doolittle | N | N | N | Y | Y | N | N | Y |
| 5 Matsui, D. | N | Y | Y | Y | Y | N | Y | N |
| 6 Woolsey | N | Y | Y | Y | N | N | Y | N |
| 7 Miller, George | N | Y | Y | Y | N | N | Y | N |
| 8 Pelosi | N | Y | Y | Y | N | N | Y | N |
| 9 Lee | N | Y | Y | Y | N | N | Y | N |
| 10 Tauscher | N | Y | Y | Y | Y | N | Y | N |
| 11 Pombo | Y | N | N | Y | Y | N | N | N |
| 12 Lantos | N | Y | Y | Y | Y | N | Y | N |
| 13 Stark | N | Y | Y | Y | Y | N | Y | N |
| 14 Eshoo | N | Y | Y | Y | Y | N | Y | N |
| 15 Honda | ? | Y | Y | Y | Y | N | Y | N |
| 16 Lofgren | N | Y | Y | Y | Y | N | Y | N |
| 17 Farr | N | Y | Y | Y | Y | N | Y | N |
| 18 Cardoza | N | Y | Y | Y | Y | N | Y | N |
| 19 Radanovich | Y | N | N | N | Y | N | N | Y |
| 20 Costa | N | Y | Y | Y | Y | N | Y | N |
| 21 Nunes | N | N | N | N | Y | ? | ? | ? |
| 22 Thomas | N | N | N | N | N | N | N | N |
| 23 Capps | N | Y | Y | Y | N | N | Y | N |
| 24 Gallegly | Y | N | N | Y | Y | N | N | Y |
| 25 McKeon | Y | N | N | Y | Y | N | N | Y |
| 26 Dreier | N | N | N | N | Y | N | N | Y |
| 27 Sherman | N | Y | Y | Y | N | N | N | N |
| 28 Berman | N | Y | Y | Y | N | N | Y | N |
| 29 Schiff | N | Y | Y | Y | Y | N | Y | N |
| 30 Waxman | N | Y | Y | Y | N | N | Y | N |
| 31 Becerra | - | + | + | + | + | - | + | - |
| 32 Solis | N | Y | Y | Y | Y | N | Y | N |
| 33 Watson | N | Y | Y | Y | N | N | Y | ? |
| 34 Roybal-Allard | N | Y | Y | Y | N | N | Y | N |
| 35 Waters | N | Y | Y | Y | N | N | Y | N |
| 36 Harman | ? | ? | ? | ? | ? | ? | ? | ? |
| 37 Millender-McD. | N | Y | Y | Y | N | N | Y | N |
| 38 Napolitano | N | Y | Y | Y | N | N | Y | N |
| 39 Sánchez, Linda | N | Y | Y | Y | N | N | Y | N |
| 40 Royce | Y | N | N | N | Y | Y | N | Y |
| 41 Lewis | N | N | N | N | Y | N | N | Y |
| 42 Miller, Gary | Y | N | N | N | Y | N | N | Y |
| 43 Baca | N | Y | Y | Y | Y | N | Y | ? |
| 44 Calvert | Y | N | N | N | Y | N | N | Y |
| 45 Bono | N | Y | N | N | N | N | N | Y |
| 46 Rohrabacher | Y | N | N | N | Y | N | N | Y |
| 47 Sanchez, Loretta | N | Y | Y | Y | N | N | Y | N |
| 48 Cox | Y | ? | N | Y | Y | Y | N | N |
| 49 Issa | N | N | N | N | Y | Y | N | Y |
| 50 Cunningham | N | N | N | Y | N | N | N | Y |
| 51 Filner | N | Y | Y | Y | N | N | Y | N |
| 52 Hunter | N | N | N | N | Y | N | N | Y |
| 53 Davis | N | Y | Y | Y | N | N | N | Y |
| **COLORADO** | | | | | | | | |
| 1 DeGette | N | Y | Y | Y | N | N | Y | N |
| 2 Udall | N | Y | Y | Y | Y | N | Y | N |
| 3 Salazar | N | Y | N | Y | Y | N | Y | N |
| 4 Musgrave | Y | N | N | Y | Y | Y | N | Y |
| 5 Hefley | N | N | N | Y | Y | Y | N | Y |
| 6 Tancredo | Y | Y | N | Y | Y | Y | N | Y |
| 7 Beauprez | Y | N | N | Y | Y | Y | N | Y |
| **CONNECTICUT** | | | | | | | | |
| 1 Larson | N | Y | Y | Y | N | N | Y | N |
| 2 Simmons | - | + | - | + | - | - | - | N |
| 3 DeLauro | N | Y | Y | Y | N | N | Y | N |
| 4 Shays | N | Y | N | N | N | Y | N | Y |
| 5 Johnson | Y | N | N | N | N | N | N | N |
| **DELAWARE** | | | | | | | | |
| AL Castle | N | N | N | Y | N | N | N | Y |
| **FLORIDA** | | | | | | | | |
| 1 Miller | Y | Y | N | Y | Y | Y | N | Y |
| 2 Boyd | ? | ? | ? | ? | ? | ? | ? | ? |
| 3 Brown | N | Y | Y | Y | N | N | Y | N |
| 4 Crenshaw | N | N | N | N | Y | N | N | Y |
| 5 Brown-Waite | Y | N | N | N | Y | N | N | Y |
| 6 Stearns | Y | Y | N | Y | Y | Y | N | Y |
| 7 Mica | Y | N | N | N | Y | N | N | Y |
| 8 Keller | N | N | N | N | Y | N | N | Y |
| 9 Bilirakis | Y | Y | N | N | Y | N | N | + |
| 10 Young | ? | ? | ? | ? | ? | ? | ? | ? |
| 11 Davis | N | Y | Y | Y | N | N | Y | N |
| 12 Putnam | N | N | N | Y | N | N | N | Y |
| 13 Harris | N | N | N | N | Y | N | N | ? |
| 14 Mack | Y | N | N | N | Y | N | N | Y |
| 15 Weldon | Y | N | N | N | Y | N | N | Y |
| 16 Foley | Y | N | N | Y | Y | N | N | Y |
| 17 Meek | N | Y | Y | Y | N | N | Y | N |
| 18 Ros-Lehtinen | N | N | N | N | Y | N | N | ? |
| 19 Wexler | ? | Y | Y | Y | Y | N | Y | N |
| 20 Wasserman-Schultz | N | Y | Y | Y | N | N | Y | N |
| 21 Diaz-Balart, L. | Y | N | N | Y | Y | N | N | Y |
| 22 Shaw | N | N | N | N | Y | N | N | Y |
| 23 Hastings | N | Y | Y | Y | N | N | Y | N |
| 24 Feeney | N | Y | N | Y | Y | N | N | Y |
| 25 Diaz-Balart, M. | Y | N | N | N | Y | N | N | Y |
| **GEORGIA** | | | | | | | | |
| 1 Kingston | ? | ? | N | N | Y | N | N | Y |
| 2 Bishop | N | Y | N | Y | Y | N | Y | N |
| 3 Marshall | N | Y | N | Y | N | N | Y | N |
| 4 McKinney | N | Y | Y | Y | N | N | Y | N |
| 5 Lewis | ? | ? | ? | ? | ? | ? | ? | ? |
| 6 Price | Y | N | N | N | Y | Y | N | Y |
| 7 Linder | Y | N | N | N | Y | N | N | Y |
| 8 Westmoreland | Y | N | N | N | Y | Y | N | Y |
| 9 Norwood | Y | N | N | N | N | N | N | Y |
| 10 Deal | Y | N | N | N | N | N | N | Y |
| 11 Gingrey | Y | N | N | N | Y | N | N | Y |
| 12 Barrow | N | Y | Y | Y | N | N | Y | N |
| 13 Scott | N | Y | Y | Y | N | N | Y | N |
| **HAWAII** | | | | | | | | |
| 1 Abercrombie | N | Y | Y | Y | N | N | Y | N |
| 2 Case | N | Y | Y | Y | N | N | Y | N |
| **IDAHO** | | | | | | | | |
| 1 Otter | Y | Y | N | Y | Y | Y | N | Y |
| 2 Simpson | N | N | N | Y | Y | N | N | Y |
| **ILLINOIS** | | | | | | | | |
| 1 Rush | N | Y | Y | Y | N | N | Y | N |
| 2 Jackson | N | Y | Y | Y | N | N | Y | N |
| 3 Lipinski | N | Y | Y | Y | N | N | Y | N |
| 4 Gutierrez | ? | ? | ? | ? | ? | ? | ? | ? |
| 5 Emanuel | N | Y | Y | Y | N | N | Y | N |
| 6 Hyde | N | Y | N | N | Y | N | N | Y |
| 7 Davis | N | Y | Y | Y | N | N | Y | N |
| 8 Bean | N | Y | N | Y | N | Y | N | Y |
| 9 Schakowsky | N | Y | Y | Y | Y | N | Y | N |
| 10 Kirk | N | N | N | Y | Y | N | N | Y |
| 11 Weller | N | N | N | Y | Y | N | N | Y |
| 12 Costello | N | Y | Y | Y | Y | N | Y | N |

**KEY**   Republicans   Democrats   *Independents*

| | | | |
|---|---|---|---|
| **Y** Voted for (yea) | **X** Paired against | **C** Voted "present" to avoid possible conflict of interest |
| **#** Paired for | **-** Announced against | |
| **+** Announced for | **P** Voted "present" | **?** Did not vote or otherwise make a position known |
| **N** Voted against (nay) | | |

ND Northern Democrats, SD Southern Democrats
Southern states: Ala., Ark., Fla., Ga., Ky., La., Miss., N.C., Okla., S.C., Tenn., Texas, Va.

| | 308 | 309 | 310 | 311 | 312 | 313 | 314 | 315 |
|---|---|---|---|---|---|---|---|---|
| 13 **Biggert** | N | N | N | N | Y | N | N | Y |
| 14 **Hastert** | | | | | | | | |
| 15 **Johnson** | N | N | N | Y | Y | N | Y | N |
| 16 **Manzullo** | N | N | N | N | Y | Y | N | N |
| 17 Evans | ? | Y | Y | Y | N | N | Y | N |
| 18 **LaHood** | N | Y | N | Y | Y | N | N | N |
| 19 **Shimkus** | N | Y | Y | Y | Y | Y | N | N |
| **INDIANA** | | | | | | | | |
| 1 Visclosky | N | Y | Y | Y | Y | N | Y | N |
| 2 **Chocola** | Y | N | N | N | Y | Y | N | Y |
| 3 **Souder** | Y | N | N | N | Y | N | N | N |
| 4 **Buyer** | Y | N | N | Y | N | Y | N | Y |
| 5 **Burton** | Y | N | N | N | Y | Y | N | Y |
| 6 **Pence** | Y | N | N | Y | Y | Y | N | Y |
| 7 Carson | N | Y | Y | Y | Y | N | Y | N |
| 8 **Hostettler** | Y | N | N | N | Y | Y | N | Y |
| 9 **Sodrel** | Y | N | N | N | Y | N | N | Y |
| **IOWA** | | | | | | | | |
| 1 **Nussle** | N | N | N | Y | Y | N | N | N |
| 2 **Leach** | N | N | N | Y | Y | N | Y | N |
| 3 Boswell | N | Y | Y | Y | Y | N | Y | N |
| 4 **Latham** | N | N | N | Y | N | N | N | Y |
| 5 **King** | Y | N | N | N | Y | Y | N | Y |
| **KANSAS** | | | | | | | | |
| 1 **Moran** | N | N | N | Y | Y | Y | N | N |
| 2 **Ryun** | Y | N | N | Y | Y | Y | N | Y |
| 3 Moore | N | Y | N | Y | Y | N | Y | N |
| 4 **Tiahrt** | Y | N | N | N | Y | N | N | N |
| **KENTUCKY** | | | | | | | | |
| 1 **Whitfield** | ? | ? | N | N | N | N | N | Y |
| 2 **Lewis** | Y | N | N | Y | Y | Y | N | Y |
| 3 **Northup** | N | N | N | Y | Y | N | N | Y |
| 4 **Davis** | Y | N | N | N | Y | N | N | Y |
| 5 **Rogers** | Y | N | N | Y | Y | N | N | Y |
| 6 Chandler | N | Y | Y | Y | Y | N | Y | N |
| **LOUISIANA** | | | | | | | | |
| 1 **Jindal** | Y | N | N | N | Y | Y | N | Y |
| 2 Jefferson | N | Y | Y | Y | N | N | Y | N |
| 3 Melancon | N | Y | Y | Y | Y | N | Y | N |
| 4 **McCrery** | N | N | N | N | N | N | N | Y |
| 5 **Alexander** | N | N | N | N | Y | N | N | N |
| 6 **Baker** | N | N | N | N | Y | N | N | Y |
| 7 **Boustany** | N | N | N | N | Y | N | N | Y |
| **MAINE** | | | | | | | | |
| 1 Allen | N | Y | Y | Y | Y | N | Y | N |
| 2 Michaud | N | Y | Y | Y | Y | N | Y | N |
| **MARYLAND** | | | | | | | | |
| 1 **Gilchrest** | N | N | N | N | N | N | N | Y |
| 2 Ruppersberger | N | Y | Y | Y | N | N | Y | N |
| 3 Cardin | N | Y | Y | Y | Y | N | Y | N |
| 4 Wynn | N | Y | N | Y | N | N | Y | N |
| 5 Hoyer | N | Y | Y | Y | N | N | Y | N |
| 6 **Bartlett** | ? | ? | ? | ? | ? | Y | N | Y |
| 7 Cummings | N | Y | Y | Y | Y | N | Y | N |
| 8 Van Hollen | N | Y | Y | Y | Y | N | Y | N |
| **MASSACHUSETTS** | | | | | | | | |
| 1 Olver | N | Y | Y | Y | Y | N | Y | N |
| 2 Neal | N | Y | Y | Y | N | N | Y | N |
| 3 McGovern | N | Y | Y | Y | Y | N | Y | N |
| 4 Frank | N | Y | Y | Y | Y | N | Y | N |
| 5 Meehan | N | Y | Y | Y | N | N | Y | N |
| 6 Tierney | N | Y | Y | Y | Y | N | Y | N |
| 7 Markey | N | Y | Y | Y | N | N | Y | N |
| 8 Capuano | N | Y | Y | Y | N | N | Y | N |
| 9 Lynch | N | Y | N | Y | N | N | Y | N |
| 10 Delahunt | ? | ? | ? | ? | ? | ? | ? | ? |
| **MICHIGAN** | | | | | | | | |
| 1 Stupak | N | Y | Y | Y | Y | N | Y | N |
| 2 **Hoekstra** | N | N | N | Y | Y | N | N | N |
| 3 **Ehlers** | N | N | N | N | N | N | N | N |
| 4 **Camp** | N | N | N | Y | Y | N | N | ? |
| 5 Kildee | N | Y | Y | Y | N | N | Y | N |
| 6 **Upton** | N | N | N | Y | Y | N | N | N |
| 7 **Schwarz** | N | N | N | Y | N | N | N | N |
| 8 **Rogers** | Y | N | N | Y | Y | Y | N | Y |
| 9 **Knollenberg** | N | N | N | N | Y | N | N | N |
| 10 **Miller** | N | N | N | Y | Y | N | N | N |
| 11 **McCotter** | N | Y | N | Y | Y | Y | N | Y |
| 12 Levin | N | Y | Y | Y | N | N | Y | N |
| 13 Kilpatrick | N | Y | Y | Y | N | N | Y | N |
| 14 Conyers | N | Y | Y | Y | Y | N | Y | N |
| 15 Dingell | N | Y | Y | Y | Y | N | Y | N |
| **MINNESOTA** | | | | | | | | |
| 1 **Gutknecht** | Y | N | N | N | Y | Y | N | Y |
| 2 **Kline** | Y | N | N | N | Y | N | N | Y |
| 3 **Ramstad** | Y | N | N | Y | Y | N | N | Y |
| 4 McCollum | N | Y | Y | Y | N | N | Y | N |
| 5 Sabo | N | Y | Y | N | N | N | Y | N |
| 6 **Kennedy** | Y | N | N | Y | Y | N | N | Y |
| 7 Peterson | N | Y | N | Y | Y | N | Y | Y |
| 8 Oberstar | N | Y | Y | Y | Y | N | Y | N |
| **MISSISSIPPI** | | | | | | | | |
| 1 **Wicker** | ? | N | N | Y | Y | N | N | Y |
| 2 Thompson | N | Y | Y | Y | Y | N | Y | N |
| 3 **Pickering** | N | ? | N | Y | Y | N | N | Y |
| 4 Taylor | ? | ? | ? | ? | ? | ? | ? | ? |
| **MISSOURI** | | | | | | | | |
| 1 Clay | N | Y | Y | Y | N | N | Y | ? |
| 2 **Akin** | Y | N | N | N | Y | Y | N | Y |
| 3 Carnahan | N | Y | Y | Y | N | N | Y | N |
| 4 Skelton | N | Y | N | Y | Y | N | Y | N |
| 5 Cleaver | N | Y | Y | Y | Y | N | Y | N |
| 6 **Graves** | Y | N | N | Y | Y | Y | N | N |
| 7 **Blunt** | N | N | N | Y | Y | N | N | ? |
| 8 **Emerson** | Y | N | N | Y | Y | N | N | N |
| 9 **Hulshof** | Y | N | N | N | N | N | N | Y |
| **MONTANA** | | | | | | | | |
| AL **Rehberg** | N | N | N | Y | Y | N | N | Y |
| **NEBRASKA** | | | | | | | | |
| 1 **Fortenberry** | Y | N | N | Y | Y | N | N | Y |
| 2 **Terry** | Y | N | N | Y | Y | Y | N | N |
| 3 **Osborne** | N | N | N | N | N | N | N | N |
| **NEVADA** | | | | | | | | |
| 1 Berkley | N | Y | Y | Y | N | N | Y | N |
| 2 **Gibbons** | Y | Y | N | Y | Y | N | N | N |
| 3 **Porter** | N | N | N | N | Y | N | N | N |
| **NEW HAMPSHIRE** | | | | | | | | |
| 1 **Bradley** | N | N | N | Y | Y | N | N | Y |
| 2 **Bass** | N | N | N | N | Y | Y | N | Y |
| **NEW JERSEY** | | | | | | | | |
| 1 Andrews | ? | ? | ? | ? | ? | ? | ? | ? |
| 2 **LoBiondo** | N | Y | N | Y | Y | N | N | N |
| 3 **Saxton** | N | N | N | N | Y | N | N | N |
| 4 **Smith** | N | Y | N | Y | Y | N | N | N |
| 5 **Garrett** | Y | N | N | Y | Y | Y | N | Y |
| 6 Pallone | N | Y | Y | Y | N | N | Y | N |
| 7 **Ferguson** | N | N | N | Y | N | N | N | N |
| 8 Pascrell | N | Y | Y | Y | Y | N | Y | N |
| 9 Rothman | N | Y | Y | Y | N | N | Y | N |
| 10 Payne | N | Y | Y | Y | N | N | Y | N |
| 11 **Frelinghuysen** | N | N | N | Y | Y | N | N | Y |
| 12 Holt | N | Y | Y | Y | N | N | Y | N |
| 13 Menendez | N | Y | Y | Y | N | N | Y | N |
| **NEW MEXICO** | | | | | | | | |
| 1 **Wilson** | ? | ? | ? | ? | ? | ? | ? | ? |
| 2 **Pearce** | Y | Y | N | N | Y | N | N | Y |
| 3 Udall | ? | ? | ? | ? | ? | ? | ? | ? |
| **NEW YORK** | | | | | | | | |
| 1 Bishop | N | Y | Y | Y | Y | N | Y | N |
| 2 Israel | N | Y | Y | Y | Y | N | Y | N |
| 3 **King** | N | N | N | Y | N | N | N | N |
| 4 McCarthy | N | Y | Y | Y | Y | N | Y | N |
| 5 Ackerman | N | Y | Y | Y | N | N | Y | N |
| 6 Meeks | ? | ? | ? | ? | ? | ? | ? | ? |
| 7 Crowley | N | Y | Y | Y | Y | N | Y | N |
| 8 Nadler | N | Y | Y | Y | N | N | Y | N |
| 9 Weiner | N | Y | Y | Y | Y | N | Y | N |
| 10 Towns | ? | ? | ? | ? | ? | ? | ? | N |
| 11 Owens | N | Y | Y | Y | N | N | Y | N |
| 12 Velázquez | N | Y | Y | Y | N | N | Y | N |
| 13 **Fossella** | Y | Y | N | Y | N | Y | N | N |
| 14 Maloney | N | Y | Y | Y | N | N | Y | N |
| 15 Rangel | N | Y | Y | Y | N | N | Y | N |
| 16 Serrano | N | Y | Y | Y | N | N | Y | N |
| 17 Engel | N | Y | Y | Y | N | N | Y | N |
| 18 Lowey | N | Y | Y | Y | N | N | Y | N |
| 19 **Kelly** | Y | N | N | Y | Y | N | N | Y |
| 20 **Sweeney** | N | Y | N | N | N | N | N | N |
| 21 McNulty | N | Y | Y | Y | N | N | Y | N |
| 22 Hinchey | N | Y | Y | Y | N | N | Y | N |
| 23 **McHugh** | N | Y | N | Y | N | N | N | N |
| 24 **Boehlert** | N | Y | N | Y | N | N | N | N |
| 25 **Walsh** | N | N | N | Y | N | N | N | N |
| 26 **Reynolds** | N | N | N | Y | Y | N | N | N |
| 27 Higgins | N | Y | Y | Y | Y | N | Y | N |
| 28 Slaughter | N | Y | N | Y | Y | N | Y | ? |
| 29 **Kuhl** | N | Y | N | Y | Y | N | N | N |
| **NORTH CAROLINA** | | | | | | | | |
| 1 Butterfield | N | Y | Y | Y | N | N | Y | N |
| 2 Etheridge | N | Y | Y | Y | Y | N | Y | N |
| 3 **Jones** | ? | ? | ? | ? | ? | ? | ? | ? |
| 4 Price | N | Y | Y | Y | N | N | Y | N |
| 5 **Foxx** | Y | N | N | Y | Y | Y | N | Y |
| 6 **Coble** | Y | N | N | N | Y | Y | N | Y |
| 7 McIntyre | N | Y | N | Y | Y | N | Y | N |
| 8 **Hayes** | Y | N | N | N | Y | N | N | Y |
| 9 **Myrick** | N | N | N | N | Y | Y | N | N |
| 10 **McHenry** | Y | N | N | N | Y | Y | N | Y |
| 11 **Taylor** | ? | N | N | N | Y | N | N | Y |
| 12 Watt | N | Y | Y | Y | N | N | Y | N |
| 13 Miller | N | Y | Y | Y | N | N | Y | N |
| **NORTH DAKOTA** | | | | | | | | |
| AL Pomeroy | N | Y | N | Y | Y | N | Y | Y |
| **OHIO** | | | | | | | | |
| 1 **Chabot** | ? | N | N | Y | Y | Y | N | Y |
| 2 Vacant | | | | | | | | |
| 3 **Turner** | N | N | N | Y | Y | N | N | N |
| 4 **Oxley** | N | N | N | N | Y | N | N | N |
| 5 **Gillmor** | N | N | N | Y | Y | N | N | N |
| 6 Strickland | N | Y | Y | Y | Y | N | Y | N |
| 7 **Hobson** | N | N | N | N | Y | N | N | N |
| 8 **Boehner** | N | N | N | Y | Y | N | N | Y |
| 9 Kaptur | N | Y | Y | Y | Y | N | ? | N |
| 10 Kucinich | N | Y | Y | Y | Y | N | Y | N |
| 11 Jones | N | Y | Y | Y | Y | N | Y | N |
| 12 **Tiberi** | N | N | N | N | Y | N | N | Y |
| 13 Brown | N | Y | Y | Y | N | N | Y | N |
| 14 **LaTourette** | N | Y | N | N | ? | ? | ? | ? |
| 15 **Pryce** | N | N | N | N | Y | N | N | N |
| 16 **Regula** | N | N | N | N | Y | N | N | N |
| 17 Ryan | N | Y | Y | Y | Y | N | Y | ? |
| 18 **Ney** | Y | N | N | Y | Y | N | N | Y |
| **OKLAHOMA** | | | | | | | | |
| 1 **Sullivan** | Y | N | N | N | Y | Y | N | Y |
| 2 Boren | N | Y | N | Y | Y | N | Y | Y |
| 3 **Lucas** | N | N | N | Y | Y | N | N | Y |
| 4 **Cole** | N | N | N | Y | Y | N | N | Y |
| 5 **Istook** | Y | N | N | N | Y | N | N | Y |
| **OREGON** | | | | | | | | |
| 1 Wu | N | Y | Y | Y | Y | N | Y | N |
| 2 **Walden** | N | N | N | N | N | N | N | Y |
| 3 Blumenauer | N | Y | Y | Y | N | N | Y | N |
| 4 DeFazio | N | Y | Y | Y | Y | N | Y | N |
| 5 Hooley | N | Y | Y | Y | N | N | Y | N |
| **PENNSYLVANIA** | | | | | | | | |
| 1 Brady | N | Y | Y | Y | Y | N | Y | N |
| 2 Fattah | ? | ? | ? | ? | ? | ? | ? | ? |
| 3 **English** | Y | N | N | Y | Y | N | N | Y |
| 4 **Hart** | N | N | N | N | Y | Y | N | Y |
| 5 **Peterson** | N | N | N | Y | Y | N | N | N |
| 6 **Gerlach** | N | Y | N | Y | Y | N | N | N |
| 7 **Weldon** | N | N | N | Y | Y | N | N | N |
| 8 **Fitzpatrick** | N | Y | N | Y | Y | N | N | N |
| 9 **Shuster** | N | N | N | N | Y | N | N | Y |
| 10 **Sherwood** | N | N | N | N | Y | N | N | N |
| 11 Kanjorski | N | Y | Y | N | Y | N | Y | N |
| 12 Murtha | N | Y | Y | Y | Y | N | Y | N |
| 13 Schwartz | N | Y | Y | Y | Y | N | Y | N |
| 14 Doyle | N | Y | Y | Y | Y | N | Y | N |
| 15 **Dent** | N | N | N | Y | Y | N | N | N |
| 16 **Pitts** | Y | N | N | N | Y | Y | N | Y |
| 17 Holden | N | Y | Y | Y | Y | N | Y | N |
| 18 **Murphy** | Y | N | N | Y | Y | N | N | N |
| 19 **Platts** | N | N | N | Y | Y | N | N | N |
| **RHODE ISLAND** | | | | | | | | |
| 1 Kennedy | N | Y | Y | Y | N | N | Y | N |
| 2 Langevin | N | Y | Y | Y | N | N | Y | N |
| **SOUTH CAROLINA** | | | | | | | | |
| 1 **Brown** | N | N | N | N | Y | N | N | Y |
| 2 **Wilson** | Y | N | N | N | Y | Y | N | Y |
| 3 **Barrett** | Y | N | N | Y | Y | Y | N | Y |
| 4 **Inglis** | Y | N | N | N | N | Y | N | N |
| 5 Spratt | N | Y | Y | Y | Y | N | Y | N |
| 6 Clyburn | N | Y | Y | Y | Y | N | Y | N |
| **SOUTH DAKOTA** | | | | | | | | |
| AL Herseth | N | Y | N | Y | Y | N | Y | Y |
| **TENNESSEE** | | | | | | | | |
| 1 **Jenkins** | N | N | N | Y | Y | Y | N | Y |
| 2 **Duncan** | N | N | N | Y | Y | Y | N | Y |
| 3 **Wamp** | N | N | N | Y | Y | N | N | Y |
| 4 Davis | N | Y | Y | Y | Y | N | Y | N |
| 5 Cooper | N | Y | Y | Y | Y | N | Y | N |
| 6 Gordon | N | Y | N | Y | Y | N | Y | N |
| 7 **Blackburn** | Y | N | N | Y | Y | Y | N | Y |
| 8 Tanner | N | Y | Y | Y | Y | Y | Y | N |
| 9 Ford | N | Y | Y | Y | Y | N | Y | N |
| **TEXAS** | | | | | | | | |
| 1 **Gohmert** | ? | ? | ? | ? | ? | ? | ? | ? |
| 2 **Poe** | N | Y | N | Y | Y | Y | N | N |
| 3 **Johnson, S.** | N | N | N | Y | Y | N | N | N |
| 4 **Hall** | Y | N | N | Y | Y | N | N | Y |
| 5 **Hensarling** | N | N | N | Y | Y | Y | N | Y |
| 6 **Barton** | N | N | N | Y | N | Y | N | Y |
| 7 **Culberson** | Y | N | N | Y | Y | N | N | Y |
| 8 **Brady** | Y | N | N | N | Y | Y | N | Y |
| 9 Green, A. | N | Y | Y | Y | Y | N | Y | N |
| 10 **McCaul** | Y | N | N | Y | Y | N | N | Y |
| 11 **Conaway** | N | N | N | Y | Y | N | N | Y |
| 12 **Granger** | N | N | N | Y | Y | N | N | N |
| 13 **Thornberry** | Y | N | N | Y | Y | Y | N | Y |
| 14 **Paul** | Y | Y | N | Y | Y | Y | N | Y |
| 15 Hinojosa | N | Y | Y | Y | Y | N | Y | N |
| 16 Reyes | ? | ? | ? | ? | ? | ? | ? | ? |
| 17 Edwards | N | Y | Y | Y | Y | N | Y | N |
| 18 Jackson-Lee | N | Y | Y | Y | N | N | Y | N |
| 19 **Neugebauer** | Y | N | N | Y | Y | Y | N | Y |
| 20 Gonzalez | N | Y | Y | Y | N | N | Y | N |
| 21 **Smith** | Y | N | N | N | Y | N | N | Y |
| 22 **DeLay** | N | N | N | N | Y | N | N | Y |
| 23 **Bonilla** | N | N | N | N | ? | N | N | N |
| 24 **Marchant** | Y | N | ? | Y | Y | N | N | Y |
| 25 Doggett | N | Y | Y | Y | Y | N | Y | N |
| 26 **Burgess** | N | N | N | Y | N | N | N | Y |
| 27 Ortiz | N | Y | Y | Y | N | N | Y | N |
| 28 Cuellar | Y | Y | Y | Y | Y | N | Y | N |
| 29 Green, G. | N | Y | Y | Y | Y | N | Y | N |
| 30 Johnson, E. | N | Y | Y | Y | Y | N | Y | N |
| 31 **Carter** | Y | N | N | Y | Y | N | N | Y |
| 32 **Sessions** | Y | N | N | Y | Y | Y | N | Y |
| **UTAH** | | | | | | | | |
| 1 **Bishop** | N | N | N | Y | Y | Y | N | N |
| 2 Matheson | N | Y | N | Y | Y | N | Y | N |
| 3 **Cannon** | Y | N | N | Y | Y | Y | N | N |
| **VERMONT** | | | | | | | | |
| AL *Sanders* | N | Y | Y | Y | N | N | Y | N |
| **VIRGINIA** | | | | | | | | |
| 1 **Davis, J.** | Y | N | N | Y | Y | Y | N | Y |
| 2 **Drake** | N | N | N | Y | Y | N | N | Y |
| 3 Scott | N | Y | Y | Y | N | N | ? | N |
| 4 **Forbes** | Y | N | N | Y | Y | N | N | Y |
| 5 **Goode** | Y | Y | N | Y | Y | N | N | Y |
| 6 **Goodlatte** | Y | N | N | Y | Y | Y | N | Y |
| 7 **Cantor** | N | N | N | N | Y | N | N | Y |
| 8 Moran | N | Y | Y | Y | Y | N | Y | N |
| 9 Boucher | N | Y | Y | Y | Y | N | Y | N |
| 10 **Wolf** | N | Y | N | N | Y | N | N | N |
| 11 **Davis, T.** | ? | ? | ? | ? | ? | ? | ? | ? |
| **WASHINGTON** | | | | | | | | |
| 1 Inslee | N | Y | Y | Y | N | N | Y | N |
| 2 Larsen | N | Y | Y | Y | Y | N | Y | N |
| 3 Baird | N | Y | Y | Y | N | N | N | N |
| 4 **Hastings** | N | N | N | N | Y | N | N | Y |
| 5 **McMorris** | N | N | N | Y | N | N | N | Y |
| 6 Dicks | N | Y | Y | Y | N | N | Y | N |
| 7 McDermott | N | Y | Y | Y | N | N | Y | N |
| 8 **Reichert** | N | Y | N | Y | Y | N | N | Y |
| 9 Smith | N | Y | Y | Y | Y | N | Y | N |
| **WEST VIRGINIA** | | | | | | | | |
| 1 Mollohan | ? | ? | ? | ? | ? | ? | ? | N |
| 2 **Capito** | ? | ? | ? | ? | ? | ? | ? | ? |
| 3 Rahall | – | + | + | + | + | – | + | N |
| **WISCONSIN** | | | | | | | | |
| 1 **Ryan** | Y | N | N | Y | Y | Y | N | Y |
| 2 Baldwin | N | Y | Y | Y | Y | N | Y | N |
| 3 Kind | N | Y | N | Y | Y | N | Y | N |
| 4 Moore | N | Y | Y | Y | N | N | Y | N |
| 5 **Sensenbrenner** | Y | Y | N | Y | Y | Y | N | N |
| 6 **Petri** | Y | N | N | Y | Y | Y | N | N |
| 7 Obey | N | Y | Y | Y | Y | N | Y | N |
| 8 **Green** | Y | Y | N | Y | Y | N | N | Y |
| **WYOMING** | | | | | | | | |
| AL **Cubin** | N | N | N | Y | N | Y | N | N |

# IN THE HOUSE | By Vote Number

**316.** HR 3010. Fiscal 2006 Labor-HHS-Education Appropriations/ **Student Loans.** Van Hollen, D-Md., amendment that would prohibit the use of funds in the bill to pay certain lenders a rate of return on student loans that is 6 percent higher than the return lenders receive on regular student loans. Adopted 224-178: R 42-175; D 181-3 (ND 135-2, SD 46-1); I 1-0. June 24, 2005.

**317.** HR 3010. Fiscal 2006 Labor-HHS-Education Appropriations/ **Mental Health Screening.** Paul, R-Texas, amendment that would prohibit the use of funds in the bill to create or implement any universal mental health screening program. Rejected 97-304: R 93-124; D 4-179 (ND 2-135, SD 2-44); I 0-1. June 24, 2005.

**318.** HR 3010. Fiscal 2006 Labor-HHS-Education Appropriations/ **Wal-Mart Labor Agreement.** DeLauro, D-Conn., amendment that would prohibit use of funds in the bill to carry out a settlement agreement between the Labor Department and Wal-Mart, which would provide Wal-Mart with 15 days' advance notice of any investigation or audit of possible child labor violations. Rejected 165-234: R 3-212; D 161-22 (ND 129-8, SD 32-14); I 1-0. June 24, 2005.

**319.** HR 3010. Fiscal 2006 Labor-HHS-Education Appropriations/ **Beneficiary Personal Information.** Hinchey, D-N.Y., amendment that would prohibit the use of funds in the bill to distribute the personal information of Medicare and Medicaid beneficiaries to private companies for marketing purposes. Rejected 192-210: R 9-207; D 182-3 (ND 137-1, SD 45-2); I 1-0. A "nay" was a vote in support of the president's position. June 24, 2005.

**320.** HR 3010. Fiscal 2006 Labor-HHS-Education Appropriations/ **Recommit.** Obey, D-Wis., motion to recommit the bill to the Appropriations Committee. Motion rejected 185-216: R 0-216; D 184-0 (ND 138-0, SD 46-0); I 1-0. June 24, 2005.

**321.** HR 3010. Fiscal 2006 Labor-HHS-Education Appropriations/ **Passage.** Passage of the bill that would appropriate $601.6 billion in fiscal 2006, including $143 billion in discretionary spending, for the Labor, Health and Human Services, and Education departments and related agencies. The bill would provide $63.7 billion for the Education Department, $14.8 billion for the Labor Department, and $473.8 billion for Health and Human Services. Passed 250-151: R 206-10; D 44-140 (ND 32-106, SD 12-34); I 0-1. June 24, 2005.

**322.** H Res 199. Srebrenica Massacre Remembrance/Adoption. Smith, R-N.J., motion to suspend the rules and adopt the resolution that would express the sense of the House that the victims of the massacre at Srebrenica should be honored and remembered and that the actions of the Serbian forces in Bosnia between 1992 and 1995 meet the criteria of genocide. Motion agreed to 370-1: R 199-1; D 170-0 (ND 128-0, SD 42-0); I 1-0. A two-thirds majority of those present and voting (248 in this case) is required for adoption under suspension of the rules. June 27, 2005.

**323.** H Con Res 155. Albania Parliamentary Elections/Adoption. Smith, R-N.J., motion to suspend the rules and adopt the concurrent resolution that would urge the government of Albania to conduct fair elections in which observers are given unobstructed access to all aspects of the election process. Motion agreed to 369-1: R 200-1; D 168-0 (ND 126-0, SD 42-0); I 1-0. A two-thirds majority of those present and voting (247 in this case) is required for adoption under suspension of the rules. June 27, 2005.

ND Northern Democrats, SD Southern Democrats
Southern states: Ala., Ark., Fla., Ga., Ky., La., Miss., N.C., Okla., S.C., Tenn., Texas, Va.

| | 316 | 317 | 318 | 319 | 320 | 321 | 322 | 323 |
|---|---|---|---|---|---|---|---|---|
| **ALABAMA** | | | | | | | | |
| 1 Bonner | N | N | N | N | N | Y | Y | Y |
| 2 Everett | N | Y | N | N | N | Y | Y | Y |
| 3 Rogers | ? | ? | ? | ? | ? | Y | ? | Y |
| 4 Aderholt | N | Y | N | N | N | Y | Y | Y |
| 5 Cramer | Y | N | N | Y | Y | Y | Y | Y |
| 6 Bachus | N | N | N | N | N | Y | Y | Y |
| 7 Davis | Y | N | N | Y | Y | N | Y | Y |
| **ALASKA** | | | | | | | | |
| AL Young | N | N | N | N | N | Y | Y | Y |
| **ARIZONA** | | | | | | | | |
| 1 Renzi | Y | N | N | N | N | Y | Y | Y |
| 2 Franks | N | Y | N | N | N | Y | Y | Y |
| 3 Shadegg | Y | Y | N | N | N | Y | Y | Y |
| 4 Pastor | Y | N | Y | Y | Y | N | Y | Y |
| 5 Hayworth | N | N | N | N | N | Y | Y | Y |
| 6 Flake | N | Y | N | N | N | N | Y | Y |
| 7 Grijalva | Y | N | Y | Y | Y | N | Y | Y |
| 8 Kolbe | N | N | N | N | N | Y | Y | Y |
| **ARKANSAS** | | | | | | | | |
| 1 Berry | N | N | N | Y | N | Y | Y | Y |
| 2 Snyder | Y | N | N | Y | N | Y | Y | Y |
| 3 Boozman | ? | ? | ? | ? | ? | Y | Y | Y |
| 4 Ross | Y | N | N | Y | N | ? | ? | |
| **CALIFORNIA** | | | | | | | | |
| 1 Thompson | Y | N | N | Y | Y | Y | Y | Y |
| 2 Herger | N | Y | N | N | N | Y | Y | Y |
| 3 Lungren | N | N | N | N | N | Y | Y | Y |
| 4 Doolittle | N | N | N | N | N | Y | Y | Y |
| 5 Matsui, D. | Y | N | Y | Y | Y | Y | + | + |
| 6 Woolsey | Y | N | Y | Y | Y | N | Y | Y |
| 7 Miller, George | Y | N | Y | Y | Y | N | Y | Y |
| 8 Pelosi | Y | N | Y | Y | Y | N | Y | Y |
| 9 Lee | Y | N | Y | Y | Y | N | Y | Y |
| 10 Tauscher | Y | N | Y | Y | Y | N | Y | Y |
| 11 Pombo | N | N | N | N | N | Y | Y | Y |
| 12 Lantos | Y | N | Y | Y | Y | N | Y | Y |
| 13 Stark | Y | N | Y | Y | Y | N | ? | ? |
| 14 Eshoo | Y | N | Y | Y | Y | N | ? | ? |
| 15 Honda | Y | N | Y | Y | Y | N | ? | ? |
| 16 Lofgren | Y | N | Y | Y | Y | N | Y | Y |
| 17 Farr | Y | N | Y | Y | Y | Y | Y | Y |
| 18 Cardoza | Y | N | Y | Y | Y | N | Y | Y |
| 19 Radanovich | N | N | N | N | N | Y | Y | Y |
| 20 Costa | Y | N | ? | Y | Y | N | Y | Y |
| 21 Nunes | ? | ? | ? | ? | ? | ? | Y | Y |
| 22 Thomas | ? | N | N | N | N | Y | Y | Y |
| 23 Capps | Y | N | Y | Y | Y | N | Y | Y |
| 24 Gallegly | N | Y | N | N | N | Y | Y | Y |
| 25 McKeon | N | N | N | N | N | Y | Y | Y |
| 26 Dreier | N | N | N | N | N | Y | Y | Y |
| 27 Sherman | Y | N | Y | Y | Y | N | Y | Y |
| 28 Berman | Y | N | Y | ? | ? | ? | Y | Y |
| 29 Schiff | Y | N | Y | Y | Y | N | Y | Y |
| 30 Waxman | Y | N | Y | Y | Y | N | Y | Y |
| 31 Becerra | + | – | + | + | + | – | Y | Y |
| 32 Solis | Y | N | Y | Y | Y | N | Y | Y |
| 33 Watson | ? | ? | ? | ? | ? | ? | Y | Y |
| 34 Roybal-Allard | Y | N | Y | Y | Y | N | Y | Y |
| 35 Waters | Y | N | Y | Y | Y | N | Y | Y |
| 36 Harman | ? | ? | ? | ? | ? | ? | Y | Y |
| 37 Millender-McD. | Y | N | Y | Y | Y | N | Y | Y |
| 38 Napolitano | Y | N | Y | Y | Y | N | Y | Y |
| 39 Sánchez, Linda | Y | N | Y | Y | Y | N | Y | Y |
| 40 Royce | N | Y | N | N | N | Y | Y | Y |
| 41 Lewis | N | N | N | N | N | Y | Y | Y |
| 42 Miller, Gary | N | Y | N | N | N | Y | Y | Y |
| 43 Baca | ? | ? | ? | ? | ? | ? | Y | Y |
| 44 Calvert | N | N | N | N | N | Y | Y | Y |
| 45 Bono | N | N | N | N | N | Y | Y | Y |
| 46 Rohrabacher | N | Y | N | N | N | Y | ? | ? |
| 47 Sanchez, Loretta | Y | N | Y | Y | Y | N | Y | Y |
| 48 Cox | N | Y | N | N | N | Y | Y | Y |
| 49 Issa | N | N | N | N | N | Y | Y | Y |

| | 316 | 317 | 318 | 319 | 320 | 321 | 322 | 323 |
|---|---|---|---|---|---|---|---|---|
| 50 Cunningham | N | N | N | N | N | Y | + | + |
| 51 Filner | Y | N | Y | Y | Y | N | + | + |
| 52 Hunter | N | N | N | N | Y | ? | ? | ? |
| 53 Davis | Y | N | Y | Y | Y | N | Y | Y |
| **COLORADO** | | | | | | | | |
| 1 DeGette | Y | N | Y | Y | Y | N | Y | Y |
| 2 Udall | Y | N | Y | Y | Y | N | Y | Y |
| 3 Salazar | Y | N | Y | Y | Y | N | Y | Y |
| 4 Musgrave | N | Y | N | N | N | Y | Y | Y |
| 5 Hefley | N | Y | N | N | N | Y | Y | Y |
| 6 Tancredo | N | Y | N | N | N | Y | Y | Y |
| 7 Beauprez | N | N | N | N | N | Y | Y | Y |
| **CONNECTICUT** | | | | | | | | |
| 1 Larson | Y | N | Y | Y | Y | N | Y | Y |
| 2 Simmons | Y | N | Y | N | N | Y | Y | Y |
| 3 DeLauro | Y | N | Y | Y | Y | N | Y | Y |
| 4 Shays | Y | N | Y | N | N | Y | Y | Y |
| 5 Johnson | Y | N | N | N | N | Y | Y | Y |
| **DELAWARE** | | | | | | | | |
| AL Castle | N | N | N | N | N | Y | Y | Y |
| **FLORIDA** | | | | | | | | |
| 1 Miller | N | Y | N | N | N | Y | Y | Y |
| 2 Boyd | ? | ? | ? | ? | ? | ? | Y | Y |
| 3 Brown | Y | N | Y | Y | N | ? | ? | ? |
| 4 Crenshaw | N | N | N | N | N | Y | Y | Y |
| 5 Brown-Waite | Y | Y | N | N | N | Y | Y | Y |
| 6 Stearns | Y | Y | N | N | N | Y | Y | Y |
| 7 Mica | N | N | N | N | N | Y | Y | Y |
| 8 Keller | N | N | N | Y | N | Y | Y | Y |
| 9 Bilirakis | + | + | – | – | N | Y | Y | Y |
| 10 Young | N | N | N | N | Y | ? | ? | ? |
| 11 Davis | Y | N | Y | Y | Y | N | ? | ? |
| 12 Putnam | N | N | N | N | N | Y | Y | Y |
| 13 Harris | ? | ? | ? | ? | ? | ? | ? | ? |
| 14 Mack | N | Y | N | N | N | Y | Y | Y |
| 15 Weldon | N | Y | N | N | N | Y | Y | Y |
| 16 Foley | Y | N | N | N | N | Y | Y | Y |
| 17 Meek | Y | ? | Y | Y | Y | N | Y | Y |
| 18 Ros-Lehtinen | N | N | N | N | N | Y | Y | Y |
| 19 Wexler | Y | Y | Y | Y | Y | N | Y | Y |
| 20 Wasserman-Schultz | Y | N | Y | Y | Y | N | Y | Y |
| 21 Diaz-Balart, L. | N | N | N | N | N | Y | ? | ? |
| 22 Shaw | N | N | N | N | N | Y | Y | Y |
| 23 Hastings | Y | N | Y | Y | Y | N | Y | Y |
| 24 Feeney | N | Y | N | N | N | Y | Y | Y |
| 25 Diaz-Balart, M. | N | N | N | N | N | Y | ? | ? |
| **GEORGIA** | | | | | | | | |
| 1 Kingston | N | Y | N | N | N | Y | ? | ? |
| 2 Bishop | Y | N | N | Y | Y | Y | Y | Y |
| 3 Marshall | Y | N | Y | Y | Y | N | Y | Y |
| 4 McKinney | Y | Y | Y | Y | Y | N | Y | Y |
| 5 Lewis | ? | ? | ? | ? | ? | ? | Y | Y |
| 6 Price | N | Y | N | N | N | Y | Y | Y |
| 7 Linder | N | Y | N | N | N | Y | Y | Y |
| 8 Westmoreland | N | Y | N | N | N | Y | Y | Y |
| 9 Norwood | N | Y | N | N | N | Y | Y | Y |
| 10 Deal | N | N | N | N | N | Y | Y | Y |
| 11 Gingrey | Y | Y | N | N | N | Y | Y | Y |
| 12 Barrow | Y | N | Y | Y | Y | N | Y | Y |
| 13 Scott | Y | N | Y | Y | Y | Y | Y | Y |
| **HAWAII** | | | | | | | | |
| 1 Abercrombie | Y | N | Y | Y | Y | ? | ? | ? |
| 2 Case | Y | N | Y | Y | Y | N | Y | Y |
| **IDAHO** | | | | | | | | |
| 1 Otter | Y | Y | N | Y | N | N | Y | Y |
| 2 Simpson | Y | Y | N | N | N | Y | ? | ? |
| **ILLINOIS** | | | | | | | | |
| 1 Rush | Y | N | Y | Y | Y | Y | Y | Y |
| 2 Jackson | Y | N | Y | Y | Y | N | Y | Y |
| 3 Lipinski | Y | N | Y | Y | Y | N | Y | Y |
| 4 Gutierrez | + | – | + | + | + | – | + | + |
| 5 Emanuel | Y | N | Y | Y | Y | N | Y | Y |
| 6 Hyde | N | N | N | N | N | Y | Y | Y |
| 7 Davis | Y | N | Y | Y | Y | N | Y | Y |
| 8 Bean | Y | N | Y | Y | Y | Y | Y | Y |
| 9 Schakowsky | Y | N | Y | Y | Y | N | Y | Y |
| 10 Kirk | N | N | N | N | N | Y | + | + |
| 11 Weller | Y | Y | N | N | N | Y | Y | Y |
| 12 Costello | Y | N | Y | Y | Y | Y | Y | Y |

**KEY**　　Republicans　　Democrats　　*Independents*

| | | | |
|---|---|---|---|
| Y | Voted for (yea) | X | Paired against |
| # | Paired for | – | Announced against |
| + | Announced for | P | Voted "present" |
| N | Voted against (nay) | C | Voted "present" to avoid possible conflict of interest |
| | | ? | Did not vote or otherwise make a position known |

| | 316 | 317 | 318 | 319 | 320 | 321 | 322 | 323 |
|---|---|---|---|---|---|---|---|---|
| 13 **Biggert** | N | Y | N | N | N | Y | Y | Y |
| 14 **Hastert** | | | | | | | | |
| 15 **Johnson** | N | Y | Y | N | N | Y | Y | Y |
| 16 **Manzullo** | N | Y | N | N | N | Y | Y | Y |
| 17 Evans | Y | N | Y | Y | Y | Y | Y | Y |
| 18 **LaHood** | N | N | N | N | N | Y | Y | Y |
| 19 **Shimkus** | Y | Y | N | N | N | Y | ? | ? |
| **INDIANA** | | | | | | | | |
| 1 Visclosky | Y | N | Y | Y | Y | Y | Y | Y |
| 2 **Chocola** | N | Y | N | N | N | Y | Y | Y |
| 3 **Souder** | N | Y | N | N | N | Y | ? | ? |
| 4 **Buyer** | N | N | N | N | N | Y | Y | Y |
| 5 **Burton** | N | Y | N | N | N | Y | + | + |
| 6 **Pence** | N | Y | N | N | N | Y | Y | Y |
| 7 Carson | Y | N | Y | Y | Y | N | + | + |
| 8 **Hostettler** | N | Y | N | Y | N | Y | Y | Y |
| 9 **Sodrel** | N | Y | N | N | N | Y | ? | ? |
| **IOWA** | | | | | | | | |
| 1 **Nussle** | N | N | N | N | N | Y | Y | Y |
| 2 **Leach** | N | N | N | Y | N | Y | Y | Y |
| 3 Boswell | Y | N | Y | Y | Y | Y | Y | Y |
| 4 **Latham** | N | N | N | N | N | Y | Y | Y |
| 5 **King** | N | Y | N | N | N | Y | Y | Y |
| **KANSAS** | | | | | | | | |
| 1 **Moran** | N | Y | N | N | ? | ? | Y | Y |
| 2 **Ryun** | N | Y | N | N | N | Y | Y | Y |
| 3 Moore | Y | N | N | Y | Y | N | Y | Y |
| 4 **Tiahrt** | N | N | N | N | N | Y | Y | Y |
| **KENTUCKY** | | | | | | | | |
| 1 **Whitfield** | N | N | N | N | N | Y | Y | Y |
| 2 **Lewis** | N | Y | N | N | N | Y | Y | Y |
| 3 **Northup** | Y | N | N | N | N | Y | Y | Y |
| 4 **Davis** | Y | Y | N | N | N | Y | Y | Y |
| 5 **Rogers** | N | N | N | N | N | Y | Y | Y |
| 6 Chandler | Y | N | Y | Y | Y | N | Y | Y |
| **LOUISIANA** | | | | | | | | |
| 1 **Jindal** | N | Y | N | N | N | Y | Y | Y |
| 2 Jefferson | Y | N | ? | Y | Y | N | ? | ? |
| 3 Melancon | Y | N | Y | Y | Y | N | Y | Y |
| 4 **McCrery** | N | N | N | N | N | Y | Y | Y |
| 5 **Alexander** | N | N | N | N | N | Y | Y | Y |
| 6 **Baker** | N | N | N | N | N | Y | Y | Y |
| 7 **Boustany** | N | N | N | N | N | Y | Y | Y |
| **MAINE** | | | | | | | | |
| 1 Allen | Y | N | Y | Y | Y | N | Y | Y |
| 2 Michaud | Y | N | Y | Y | Y | N | ? | ? |
| **MARYLAND** | | | | | | | | |
| 1 **Gilchrest** | N | N | N | N | N | Y | Y | Y |
| 2 Ruppersberger | Y | N | Y | Y | Y | Y | ? | ? |
| 3 Cardin | Y | N | Y | Y | Y | N | ? | ? |
| 4 Wynn | Y | N | N | Y | Y | Y | Y | ? |
| 5 Hoyer | Y | N | Y | Y | Y | N | Y | Y |
| 6 **Bartlett** | N | Y | N | N | N | Y | Y | Y |
| 7 Cummings | Y | N | Y | Y | Y | N | Y | Y |
| 8 Van Hollen | Y | N | Y | Y | Y | N | Y | Y |
| **MASSACHUSETTS** | | | | | | | | |
| 1 Olver | Y | N | Y | Y | Y | N | Y | Y |
| 2 Neal | Y | N | Y | Y | Y | Y | Y | Y |
| 3 McGovern | Y | N | Y | Y | Y | N | Y | Y |
| 4 Frank | Y | N | Y | Y | Y | N | Y | Y |
| 5 Meehan | Y | N | Y | Y | Y | Y | Y | Y |
| 6 Tierney | Y | N | Y | Y | Y | N | Y | Y |
| 7 Markey | Y | N | Y | Y | Y | N | Y | Y |
| 8 Capuano | Y | N | Y | Y | Y | N | Y | Y |
| 9 Lynch | Y | N | Y | Y | Y | N | Y | Y |
| 10 Delahunt | ? | ? | ? | ? | ? | ? | Y | Y |
| **MICHIGAN** | | | | | | | | |
| 1 Stupak | Y | N | Y | Y | Y | N | Y | Y |
| 2 **Hoekstra** | N | Y | N | N | N | Y | Y | Y |
| 3 **Ehlers** | N | N | N | N | N | Y | Y | Y |
| 4 **Camp** | ? | ? | ? | ? | ? | ? | Y | Y |
| 5 Kildee | Y | N | Y | Y | Y | Y | Y | Y |
| 6 **Upton** | Y | Y | N | N | N | Y | Y | Y |
| 7 **Schwarz** | Y | N | N | N | N | Y | Y | Y |
| 8 **Rogers** | Y | Y | N | N | N | Y | Y | Y |
| 9 **Knollenberg** | N | N | N | N | N | Y | Y | Y |
| 10 **Miller** | Y | N | N | N | N | Y | Y | Y |
| 11 **McCotter** | Y | Y | N | N | N | Y | Y | Y |
| 12 Levin | Y | N | Y | Y | Y | N | Y | Y |
| 13 Kilpatrick | Y | N | Y | Y | Y | N | + | + |
| 14 Conyers | Y | N | Y | Y | Y | N | Y | Y |
| 15 Dingell | Y | N | Y | Y | Y | N | Y | Y |

| | 316 | 317 | 318 | 319 | 320 | 321 | 322 | 323 |
|---|---|---|---|---|---|---|---|---|
| **MINNESOTA** | | | | | | | | |
| 1 **Gutknecht** | N | Y | N | N | N | Y | Y | Y |
| 2 **Kline** | N | Y | N | N | N | Y | Y | Y |
| 3 **Ramstad** | Y | N | N | N | N | N | Y | Y |
| 4 McCollum | Y | N | Y | Y | Y | N | Y | Y |
| 5 Sabo | Y | N | Y | Y | Y | N | Y | Y |
| 6 **Kennedy** | N | Y | N | N | N | Y | Y | Y |
| 7 Peterson | Y | N | Y | Y | Y | N | Y | Y |
| 8 Oberstar | Y | N | Y | Y | Y | N | Y | Y |
| **MISSISSIPPI** | | | | | | | | |
| 1 **Wicker** | N | N | N | N | N | Y | Y | Y |
| 2 Thompson | Y | N | N | Y | Y | Y | Y | Y |
| 3 **Pickering** | Y | N | N | N | N | Y | Y | Y |
| 4 Taylor | + | + | - | + | + | - | + | + |
| **MISSOURI** | | | | | | | | |
| 1 Clay | ? | ? | ? | Y | Y | N | Y | Y |
| 2 **Akin** | N | Y | N | N | N | Y | Y | Y |
| 3 Carnahan | Y | N | Y | Y | Y | N | Y | Y |
| 4 Skelton | ? | ? | ? | ? | ? | ? | Y | Y |
| 5 Cleaver | Y | N | Y | Y | Y | N | Y | Y |
| 6 **Graves** | Y | Y | N | N | N | Y | Y | Y |
| 7 **Blunt** | N | N | ? | N | N | Y | Y | Y |
| 8 **Emerson** | Y | N | N | N | N | Y | Y | Y |
| 9 **Hulshof** | Y | N | N | N | N | Y | Y | Y |
| **MONTANA** | | | | | | | | |
| AL **Rehberg** | N | N | N | N | N | Y | Y | Y |
| **NEBRASKA** | | | | | | | | |
| 1 **Fortenberry** | N | N | N | N | N | Y | Y | Y |
| 2 **Terry** | N | Y | N | N | N | Y | ? | ? |
| 3 **Osborne** | N | N | N | N | N | Y | Y | Y |
| **NEVADA** | | | | | | | | |
| 1 Berkley | Y | N | Y | Y | Y | N | Y | Y |
| 2 **Gibbons** | N | N | N | N | N | N | Y | Y |
| 3 **Porter** | N | N | N | N | N | Y | Y | Y |
| **NEW HAMPSHIRE** | | | | | | | | |
| 1 **Bradley** | Y | N | N | N | N | Y | Y | Y |
| 2 **Bass** | Y | N | N | N | N | Y | Y | Y |
| **NEW JERSEY** | | | | | | | | |
| 1 Andrews | + | - | + | + | + | - | Y | Y |
| 2 **LoBiondo** | Y | N | N | N | N | Y | Y | Y |
| 3 **Saxton** | N | N | N | N | N | Y | Y | Y |
| 4 **Smith** | Y | N | N | N | N | Y | Y | Y |
| 5 **Garrett** | N | Y | N | N | N | Y | Y | Y |
| 6 Pallone | Y | N | Y | Y | Y | N | Y | Y |
| 7 **Ferguson** | Y | N | N | N | N | Y | Y | Y |
| 8 Pascrell | Y | N | Y | Y | Y | Y | Y | Y |
| 9 Rothman | Y | N | Y | Y | Y | Y | Y | Y |
| 10 Payne | Y | N | Y | Y | Y | N | ? | ? |
| 11 **Frelinghuysen** | N | N | N | N | N | Y | Y | Y |
| 12 Holt | Y | N | Y | Y | Y | Y | Y | Y |
| 13 Menendez | Y | N | Y | Y | Y | N | Y | Y |
| **NEW MEXICO** | | | | | | | | |
| 1 **Wilson** | ? | ? | ? | ? | ? | - | Y | Y |
| 2 **Pearce** | N | N | N | N | N | Y | Y | Y |
| 3 Udall | ? | ? | ? | ? | ? | ? | Y | Y |
| **NEW YORK** | | | | | | | | |
| 1 Bishop | Y | N | Y | Y | Y | N | + | + |
| 2 Israel | Y | N | Y | Y | Y | N | ? | ? |
| 3 **King** | N | N | N | N | N | Y | Y | Y |
| 4 McCarthy | Y | N | Y | Y | Y | N | Y | Y |
| 5 Ackerman | Y | N | Y | Y | Y | N | Y | Y |
| 6 Meeks | ? | ? | ? | ? | ? | ? | Y | Y |
| 7 Crowley | Y | N | Y | Y | Y | N | Y | Y |
| 8 Nadler | Y | N | Y | Y | Y | N | Y | Y |
| 9 Weiner | Y | N | Y | Y | Y | N | ? | ? |
| 10 Towns | Y | N | N | N | Y | Y | Y | Y |
| 11 Owens | Y | N | Y | Y | Y | N | Y | Y |
| 12 Velázquez | Y | N | Y | Y | Y | N | Y | Y |
| 13 **Fossella** | N | N | N | N | N | Y | + | + |
| 14 Maloney | Y | N | Y | Y | Y | N | Y | Y |
| 15 Rangel | Y | N | Y | Y | Y | N | Y | Y |
| 16 Serrano | Y | N | Y | Y | Y | Y | Y | Y |
| 17 Engel | Y | N | Y | Y | Y | Y | Y | Y |
| 18 Lowey | Y | N | Y | Y | Y | N | Y | Y |
| 19 **Kelly** | Y | N | N | N | N | Y | Y | Y |
| 20 **Sweeney** | N | N | N | N | N | Y | ? | ? |
| 21 McNulty | Y | N | Y | Y | Y | N | Y | Y |
| 22 Hinchey | Y | Y | Y | Y | Y | N | Y | Y |
| 23 **McHugh** | Y | N | N | N | N | Y | ? | ? |
| 24 **Boehlert** | Y | N | N | N | N | Y | ? | ? |
| 25 **Walsh** | N | N | N | N | N | Y | Y | Y |
| 26 **Reynolds** | N | N | N | N | N | Y | ? | ? |
| 27 Higgins | Y | N | Y | Y | Y | Y | ? | ? |
| 28 Slaughter | + | - | + | + | + | - | + | + |
| 29 **Kuhl** | Y | N | N | N | N | Y | Y | Y |

| | 316 | 317 | 318 | 319 | 320 | 321 | 322 | 323 |
|---|---|---|---|---|---|---|---|---|
| **NORTH CAROLINA** | | | | | | | | |
| 1 Butterfield | Y | N | N | Y | Y | N | Y | Y |
| 2 Etheridge | Y | N | Y | Y | Y | N | + | + |
| 3 **Jones** | ? | ? | ? | ? | ? | ? | Y | Y |
| 4 Price | Y | N | Y | Y | Y | N | Y | Y |
| 5 **Foxx** | N | Y | N | N | N | Y | Y | Y |
| 6 **Coble** | N | N | N | N | N | Y | Y | Y |
| 7 McIntyre | Y | N | Y | Y | Y | N | Y | Y |
| 8 **Hayes** | N | Y | N | N | N | Y | Y | Y |
| 9 **Myrick** | N | Y | N | N | N | Y | Y | Y |
| 10 **McHenry** | N | Y | N | N | N | Y | Y | Y |
| 11 **Taylor** | N | N | ? | ? | ? | ? | Y | Y |
| 12 Watt | Y | N | Y | Y | Y | N | Y | Y |
| 13 Miller | Y | N | Y | Y | Y | N | Y | Y |
| **NORTH DAKOTA** | | | | | | | | |
| AL Pomeroy | N | N | Y | Y | Y | Y | Y | Y |
| **OHIO** | | | | | | | | |
| 1 **Chabot** | Y | Y | N | Y | N | Y | Y | Y |
| 2 Vacant | | | | | | | | |
| 3 **Turner** | Y | N | N | N | N | Y | ? | ? |
| 4 **Oxley** | N | N | N | N | N | Y | + | + |
| 5 **Gillmor** | N | N | N | N | N | Y | Y | Y |
| 6 Strickland | Y | N | Y | Y | Y | N | ? | ? |
| 7 **Hobson** | N | N | N | N | N | Y | ? | ? |
| 8 **Boehner** | N | N | N | N | N | Y | Y | Y |
| 9 Kaptur | Y | N | Y | Y | Y | N | Y | Y |
| 10 Kucinich | Y | N | Y | Y | Y | N | ? | ? |
| 11 Jones | Y | N | Y | Y | Y | N | ? | ? |
| 12 **Tiberi** | N | N | N | N | N | Y | Y | Y |
| 13 Brown | Y | N | Y | Y | Y | N | Y | Y |
| 14 **LaTourette** | ? | ? | ? | ? | ? | ? | ? | ? |
| 15 **Pryce** | N | N | N | N | N | Y | ? | ? |
| 16 **Regula** | N | N | N | N | N | Y | Y | Y |
| 17 Ryan | ? | ? | Y | Y | Y | N | Y | Y |
| 18 **Ney** | N | N | N | N | N | Y | Y | Y |
| **OKLAHOMA** | | | | | | | | |
| 1 **Sullivan** | N | N | N | N | N | Y | Y | Y |
| 2 Boren | Y | N | N | Y | Y | Y | Y | Y |
| 3 **Lucas** | N | N | N | N | N | Y | Y | Y |
| 4 **Cole** | N | Y | N | N | N | Y | Y | Y |
| 5 **Istook** | N | Y | N | N | N | Y | ? | ? |
| **OREGON** | | | | | | | | |
| 1 Wu | Y | N | Y | Y | Y | N | Y | Y |
| 2 **Walden** | N | N | N | N | N | Y | ? | ? |
| 3 Blumenauer | Y | N | Y | Y | Y | N | Y | Y |
| 4 DeFazio | Y | N | Y | Y | Y | N | Y | Y |
| 5 Hooley | Y | N | Y | Y | Y | N | Y | Y |
| **PENNSYLVANIA** | | | | | | | | |
| 1 Brady | Y | N | Y | Y | Y | Y | ? | ? |
| 2 Fattah | ? | ? | ? | ? | ? | ? | ? | ? |
| 3 **English** | N | N | N | N | N | Y | Y | Y |
| 4 **Hart** | N | Y | N | N | N | Y | Y | Y |
| 5 **Peterson** | Y | ? | N | N | N | Y | Y | Y |
| 6 **Gerlach** | N | N | N | N | N | Y | Y | Y |
| 7 **Weldon** | N | N | N | N | N | Y | Y | Y |
| 8 **Fitzpatrick** | N | N | N | Y | N | Y | Y | Y |
| 9 **Shuster** | N | N | N | N | N | Y | Y | Y |
| 10 **Sherwood** | N | N | N | N | N | Y | Y | Y |
| 11 Kanjorski | Y | N | Y | Y | Y | N | Y | Y |
| 12 Murtha | Y | N | Y | Y | Y | Y | Y | ? |
| 13 Schwartz | Y | N | Y | Y | Y | N | Y | Y |
| 14 Doyle | Y | N | Y | Y | Y | Y | Y | Y |
| 15 **Dent** | N | N | N | N | N | Y | Y | Y |
| 16 **Pitts** | Y | Y | N | N | N | Y | Y | Y |
| 17 Holden | Y | N | Y | Y | Y | Y | Y | Y |
| 18 **Murphy** | Y | N | N | N | N | Y | Y | Y |
| 19 **Platts** | N | N | N | N | N | Y | Y | Y |
| **RHODE ISLAND** | | | | | | | | |
| 1 Kennedy | Y | N | Y | Y | Y | N | Y | Y |
| 2 Langevin | Y | N | Y | Y | Y | N | Y | Y |
| **SOUTH CAROLINA** | | | | | | | | |
| 1 **Brown** | N | N | N | N | N | Y | Y | Y |
| 2 **Wilson** | N | N | N | N | N | Y | Y | Y |
| 3 **Barrett** | N | Y | N | N | N | Y | Y | Y |
| 4 **Inglis** | N | N | N | N | N | Y | Y | Y |
| 5 Spratt | Y | N | Y | Y | Y | N | Y | Y |
| 6 Clyburn | Y | N | N | N | Y | N | Y | Y |
| **SOUTH DAKOTA** | | | | | | | | |
| AL Herseth | Y | N | Y | Y | Y | N | Y | Y |
| **TENNESSEE** | | | | | | | | |
| 1 **Jenkins** | N | Y | N | N | N | Y | ? | ? |
| 2 **Duncan** | N | Y | N | N | N | Y | Y | Y |

| | 316 | 317 | 318 | 319 | 320 | 321 | 322 | 323 |
|---|---|---|---|---|---|---|---|---|
| 3 **Wamp** | N | N | N | N | N | Y | Y | Y |
| 4 Davis | Y | N | Y | Y | Y | Y | Y | Y |
| 5 Cooper | Y | N | Y | Y | Y | N | Y | Y |
| 6 Gordon | Y | N | Y | Y | Y | Y | ? | ? |
| 7 **Blackburn** | N | Y | N | N | N | Y | Y | Y |
| 8 Tanner | Y | N | N | Y | ? | ? | Y | Y |
| 9 Ford | Y | N | N | Y | Y | N | ? | ? |
| **TEXAS** | | | | | | | | |
| 1 **Gohmert** | ? | ? | ? | ? | ? | ? | Y | Y |
| 2 **Poe** | N | Y | N | N | N | Y | Y | Y |
| 3 **Johnson, S.** | N | N | N | N | N | Y | Y | Y |
| 4 **Hall** | N | N | N | N | N | Y | Y | Y |
| 5 **Hensarling** | N | Y | N | N | N | Y | Y | Y |
| 6 **Barton** | N | N | N | N | N | Y | Y | Y |
| 7 **Culberson** | N | Y | N | N | N | Y | ? | ? |
| 8 **Brady** | N | Y | N | N | N | Y | Y | Y |
| 9 Green, A. | Y | N | Y | Y | Y | N | Y | Y |
| 10 **McCaul** | N | N | N | N | N | Y | Y | Y |
| 11 **Conaway** | N | N | N | N | N | Y | Y | Y |
| 12 **Granger** | N | N | N | N | N | Y | Y | Y |
| 13 **Thornberry** | N | Y | N | N | N | Y | Y | Y |
| 14 **Paul** | N | Y | N | Y | N | N | N | N |
| 15 Hinojosa | Y | N | Y | Y | Y | Y | Y | Y |
| 16 Reyes | ? | ? | ? | ? | ? | ? | Y | Y |
| 17 Edwards | Y | N | Y | Y | Y | N | Y | Y |
| 18 Jackson-Lee | Y | N | Y | Y | Y | N | Y | Y |
| 19 **Neugebauer** | N | Y | N | N | N | Y | Y | Y |
| 20 Gonzalez | Y | N | N | Y | Y | Y | + | + |
| 21 **Smith** | N | N | N | N | N | Y | Y | Y |
| 22 **DeLay** | N | Y | N | N | N | Y | Y | Y |
| 23 **Bonilla** | N | N | N | N | N | Y | Y | Y |
| 24 **Marchant** | N | Y | N | N | N | Y | Y | Y |
| 25 Doggett | Y | N | Y | Y | Y | N | Y | Y |
| 26 **Burgess** | N | N | N | N | N | Y | Y | Y |
| 27 Ortiz | Y | N | Y | Y | Y | Y | Y | Y |
| 28 Cuellar | Y | N | N | Y | Y | N | Y | Y |
| 29 Green, G. | Y | N | Y | Y | Y | N | Y | Y |
| 30 Johnson, E. | Y | N | Y | Y | Y | N | Y | Y |
| 31 **Carter** | N | N | N | N | N | Y | Y | Y |
| 32 **Sessions** | N | Y | N | N | N | Y | Y | Y |
| **UTAH** | | | | | | | | |
| 1 **Bishop** | N | N | N | N | N | Y | Y | Y |
| 2 Matheson | N | N | N | Y | Y | N | Y | Y |
| 3 **Cannon** | N | Y | N | N | N | Y | Y | Y |
| **VERMONT** | | | | | | | | |
| AL *Sanders* | Y | N | Y | Y | Y | N | Y | Y |
| **VIRGINIA** | | | | | | | | |
| 1 **Davis, J.** | N | Y | N | Y | N | Y | Y | Y |
| 2 **Drake** | N | Y | N | N | N | Y | Y | Y |
| 3 Scott | Y | N | Y | Y | Y | N | Y | Y |
| 4 **Forbes** | N | Y | N | N | N | Y | Y | Y |
| 5 **Goode** | Y | Y | ? | ? | ? | ? | Y | Y |
| 6 **Goodlatte** | N | Y | N | N | N | Y | Y | Y |
| 7 **Cantor** | N | N | N | N | N | Y | Y | Y |
| 8 Moran | Y | N | Y | Y | Y | N | Y | Y |
| 9 Boucher | Y | N | Y | Y | Y | Y | Y | Y |
| 10 **Wolf** | N | N | N | N | N | Y | Y | Y |
| 11 **Davis, T.** | ? | ? | ? | ? | ? | ? | ? | ? |
| **WASHINGTON** | | | | | | | | |
| 1 Inslee | Y | N | Y | Y | Y | N | Y | Y |
| 2 Larsen | Y | N | Y | Y | Y | N | Y | Y |
| 3 Baird | Y | N | Y | Y | Y | N | Y | Y |
| 4 **Hastings** | N | N | N | N | N | Y | Y | Y |
| 5 **McMorris** | N | Y | N | N | N | Y | Y | Y |
| 6 Dicks | Y | N | Y | Y | Y | Y | Y | Y |
| 7 McDermott | Y | N | Y | Y | Y | N | Y | Y |
| 8 **Reichert** | N | N | N | N | N | Y | Y | Y |
| 9 Smith | Y | N | Y | Y | Y | N | Y | Y |
| **WEST VIRGINIA** | | | | | | | | |
| 1 Mollohan | Y | N | Y | Y | Y | Y | Y | Y |
| 2 **Capito** | ? | ? | ? | ? | ? | ? | Y | Y |
| 3 Rahall | Y | N | Y | Y | Y | Y | + | + |
| **WISCONSIN** | | | | | | | | |
| 1 **Ryan** | N | Y | N | N | N | Y | Y | Y |
| 2 Baldwin | Y | N | Y | Y | Y | N | Y | Y |
| 3 Kind | Y | N | N | Y | Y | N | Y | Y |
| 4 Moore | Y | Y | Y | Y | Y | N | Y | Y |
| 5 **Sensenbrenner** | N | Y | N | N | N | Y | Y | Y |
| 6 **Petri** | Y | Y | N | N | N | Y | Y | Y |
| 7 Obey | Y | N | Y | Y | Y | N | Y | Y |
| 8 **Green** | Y | Y | N | N | N | Y | + | Y |
| **WYOMING** | | | | | | | | |
| AL **Cubin** | N | Y | N | N | N | Y | Y | Y |

# IN THE HOUSE | By Vote Number

**324.** **HR 458. Military Personnel Financial Services/Passage.** Davis, R-Ky., motion to suspend the rules and pass the bill that would ban all future sales of contractual plan mutual funds, require greater regulation of insurance sales on military bases and establish requirements for certain loans to service members. Motion agreed to 405-2: R 217-2; D 187-0 (ND 144-0, SD 43-0); I 1-0. A two-thirds majority of those present and voting (272 in this case) is required for passage under suspension of the rules. June 28, 2005.

**325.** **HR 3057. Fiscal 2006 Foreign Operations Appropriations/Previous Question.** L. Diaz-Balart, R-Fla., motion to order the previous question (thus ending debate and the possibility of amendment) on adoption of the rule (H Res 341) to provide for House floor consideration of the bill that would appropriate $20.3 billion in fiscal 2006 for foreign aid and economic assistance. Motion agreed to 217-189: R 217-0; D 0-188 (ND 0-145, SD 0-43); I 0-1. (Subsequently, the rule was adopted by voice vote.) June 28, 2005.

**326.** **HR 3057. Fiscal 2006 Foreign Operations Appropriations/Aid to Egypt.** Pitts, R-Pa., amendment that would transfer $750 million of military aid for Egypt to programs for malaria in Africa. Rejected 87-326: R 53-168; D 34-157 (ND 29-118, SD 5-39); I 0-1. A "nay" was a vote in support of the president's position. June 28, 2005.

**327.** **HR 3058 Fiscal 2006 Transportation-Treasury-Housing Appropriations/Previous Question.** L. Diaz-Balart, R-Fla., motion to order the previous question (thus ending debate and the possibility of amendment) on adoption of the rule (H Res 342) to provide for House floor consideration of the bill that would provide $139.1 billion in fiscal 2006 for the departments of Transportation, Treasury, and Housing and Urban Development as well as the judiciary and the District of Columbia. Motion agreed to 263-152: R 136-87; D 127-64 (ND 101-46, SD 26-18); I 0-1. June 28, 2005.

**328.** **HR 3058. Fiscal 2006 Transportation-Treasury-Housing Appropriations/Rule.** Adoption of the rule (H Res 342) that would provide for House floor consideration of the bill that would provide $139.1 billion in fiscal 2006 for the Departments of Transportation, Treasury, and Housing and Urban Development as well as the judiciary and the District of Columbia. Adopted 219-193: R 219-2; D 0-190 (ND 0-146, SD 0-44); I 0-1. June 28, 2005.

**329.** **HR 3057. Fiscal 2006 Foreign Operations Appropriations/Andean Counterdrug Initiative.** McGovern, D-Mass., amendment that would reduce by $100 million funds for the Andean Counterdrug Initiative. Rejected 189-234: R 19-207; D 169-27 (ND 134-16, SD 35-11); I 1-0. A "nay" was a vote in support of the president's position. June 28, 2005.

**330.** **HR 3057. Fiscal 2006 Foreign Operations Appropriations/Limitation on Foreign Assistance.** Beauprez, R-Colo., amendment that would limit assistance to foreign countries that refuse to extradite to the United States any individual accused in the United States of killing a law enforcement officer. Adopted 327-98: R 208-18; D 119-79 (ND 82-68, SD 37-11); I 0-1. June 28, 2005.

**331.** **HR 3057. Fiscal 2006 Foreign Operations Appropriations/Aid for Saudi Arabia.** Weiner, D-N.Y., amendment that would prohibit use of funds in the bill for assistance to Saudi Arabia. Adopted 293-132: R 121-105; D 171-27 (ND 132-18, SD 39-9); I 1-0. June 28, 2005.

| Member | 324 | 325 | 326 | 327 | 328 | 329 | 330 | 331 |
|---|---|---|---|---|---|---|---|---|
| **ALABAMA** | | | | | | | | |
| 1 Bonner | Y | Y | N | Y | Y | N | Y | N |
| 2 Everett | Y | Y | N | Y | Y | N | Y | N |
| 3 Rogers | Y | Y | Y | N | Y | N | Y | Y |
| 4 Aderholt | Y | Y | N | N | Y | N | Y | N |
| 5 Cramer | N | N | Y | N | N | N | N | Y |
| 6 Bachus | Y | Y | N | Y | N | Y | N | Y |
| 7 Davis | Y | N | N | Y | N | Y | Y | Y |
| **ALASKA** | | | | | | | | |
| AL Young | Y | Y | N | Y | Y | N | Y | N |
| **ARIZONA** | | | | | | | | |
| 1 Renzi | Y | Y | N | N | Y | N | Y | Y |
| 2 Franks | Y | Y | Y | Y | Y | N | Y | Y |
| 3 Shadegg | Y | Y | N | Y | Y | N | Y | Y |
| 4 Pastor | Y | N | N | Y | N | Y | N | N |
| 5 Hayworth | Y | Y | Y | Y | Y | N | Y | Y |
| 6 Flake | N | Y | N | N | Y | Y | Y | Y |
| 7 Grijalva | Y | N | N | Y | N | Y | N | Y |
| 8 Kolbe | Y | Y | N | Y | Y | N | N | N |
| **ARKANSAS** | | | | | | | | |
| 1 Berry | Y | N | Y | N | N | N | Y | Y |
| 2 Snyder | Y | N | N | N | N | N | N | Y |
| 3 Boozman | Y | Y | N | N | Y | N | Y | Y |
| 4 Ross | ? | ? | ? | ? | ? | ? | ? | ? |
| **CALIFORNIA** | | | | | | | | |
| 1 Thompson | Y | N | N | Y | N | Y | Y | Y |
| 2 Herger | ? | Y | N | Y | Y | N | Y | Y |
| 3 Lungren | Y | Y | N | Y | N | Y | N | Y |
| 4 Doolittle | ? | ? | ? | ? | ? | ? | ? | ? |
| 5 Matsui, D. | Y | N | N | Y | N | Y | N | Y |
| 6 Woolsey | Y | N | N | Y | N | Y | N | Y |
| 7 Miller, George | Y | N | N | Y | N | Y | N | Y |
| 8 Pelosi | Y | N | N | Y | N | Y | N | Y |
| 9 Lee | Y | N | N | Y | N | Y | N | Y |
| 10 Tauscher | Y | N | N | Y | N | Y | N | Y |
| 11 Pombo | Y | Y | N | Y | Y | N | Y | Y |
| 12 Lantos | Y | N | Y | Y | Y | Y | Y | Y |
| 13 Stark | Y | N | N | ? | Y | N | N | |
| 14 Eshoo | Y | N | N | Y | N | Y | N | Y |
| 15 Honda | Y | N | N | Y | N | Y | N | Y |
| 16 Lofgren | Y | N | N | N | N | Y | N | Y |
| 17 Farr | Y | N | N | Y | N | Y | N | Y |
| 18 Cardoza | Y | N | Y | N | N | N | Y | Y |
| 19 Radanovich | Y | Y | N | Y | Y | N | Y | N |
| 20 Costa | Y | N | N | Y | N | Y | N | Y |
| 21 Nunes | Y | Y | N | Y | Y | N | Y | N |
| 22 Thomas | Y | Y | N | Y | Y | N | N | N |
| 23 Capps | Y | N | N | N | N | Y | N | Y |
| 24 Gallegly | Y | Y | N | Y | Y | N | Y | Y |
| 25 McKeon | Y | Y | N | Y | Y | N | Y | N |
| 26 Dreier | Y | Y | N | Y | Y | N | N | Y |
| 27 Sherman | Y | N | Y | N | Y | N | Y | Y |
| 28 Berman | Y | N | N | Y | N | Y | N | Y |
| 29 Schiff | Y | N | N | N | N | Y | N | Y |
| 30 Waxman | Y | N | N | Y | N | Y | N | Y |
| 31 Becerra | Y | N | N | N | N | Y | N | Y |
| 32 Solis | Y | N | N | Y | N | Y | N | Y |
| 33 Watson | Y | N | Y | Y | N | Y | N | Y |
| 34 Roybal-Allard | Y | N | N | Y | N | Y | N | Y |
| 35 Waters | Y | N | N | Y | N | Y | N | Y |
| 36 Harman | Y | N | N | Y | N | Y | N | Y |
| 37 Millender-McD. | Y | N | N | Y | N | Y | N | Y |
| 38 Napolitano | Y | N | N | Y | N | Y | N | Y |
| 39 Sánchez, Linda | Y | N | N | Y | N | Y | N | Y |
| 40 Royce | Y | Y | Y | N | Y | N | Y | Y |
| 41 Lewis | Y | Y | Y | Y | Y | N | N | N |
| 42 Miller, Gary | Y | Y | N | Y | Y | N | Y | Y |
| 43 Baca | Y | N | N | Y | N | Y | N | Y |
| 44 Calvert | Y | Y | N | Y | Y | N | Y | Y |
| 45 Bono | Y | Y | Y | Y | Y | N | Y | Y |
| 46 Rohrabacher | Y | Y | N | Y | Y | Y | N | Y |
| 47 Sanchez, Loretta | Y | N | N | N | N | Y | N | Y |
| 48 Cox | Y | Y | N | Y | Y | ? | Y | Y |
| 49 Issa | Y | Y | N | Y | Y | N | Y | Y |
| 50 Cunningham | Y | Y | N | Y | N | Y | N | Y |
| 51 Filner | Y | N | N | N | N | Y | N | Y |
| 52 Hunter | Y | Y | ? | Y | Y | N | Y | N |
| 53 Davis | Y | N | N | N | N | Y | Y | Y |
| **COLORADO** | | | | | | | | |
| 1 DeGette | Y | N | N | N | N | Y | N | Y |
| 2 Udall | Y | N | N | N | N | Y | N | Y |
| 3 Salazar | Y | N | N | N | N | Y | Y | Y |
| 4 Musgrave | Y | Y | N | Y | N | Y | Y | Y |
| 5 Hefley | Y | Y | Y | Y | N | Y | Y | Y |
| 6 Tancredo | Y | Y | Y | Y | Y | Y | Y | Y |
| 7 Beauprez | Y | ? | Y | Y | Y | N | Y | Y |
| **CONNECTICUT** | | | | | | | | |
| 1 Larson | Y | N | N | Y | N | Y | N | Y |
| 2 Simmons | Y | Y | N | N | Y | N | Y | Y |
| 3 DeLauro | Y | N | N | Y | N | Y | N | Y |
| 4 Shays | ? | ? | N | Y | Y | N | N | ? |
| 5 Johnson | Y | Y | N | N | Y | N | N | N |
| **DELAWARE** | | | | | | | | |
| AL Castle | Y | Y | N | N | Y | N | Y | N |
| **FLORIDA** | | | | | | | | |
| 1 Miller | Y | Y | N | Y | N | Y | N | Y |
| 2 Boyd | Y | N | N | Y | N | Y | Y | Y |
| 3 Brown | Y | N | N | N | Y | N | Y | Y |
| 4 Crenshaw | Y | Y | N | Y | N | Y | N | Y |
| 5 Brown-Waite | Y | Y | N | Y | N | Y | N | Y |
| 6 Stearns | Y | Y | N | Y | N | Y | N | Y |
| 7 Mica | Y | Y | N | Y | N | Y | N | Y |
| 8 Keller | Y | Y | N | Y | N | Y | N | Y |
| 9 Bilirakis | Y | Y | N | Y | N | Y | Y | Y |
| 10 Young | Y | Y | N | Y | N | Y | N | Y |
| 11 Davis | Y | N | N | N | N | N | N | Y |
| 12 Putnam | Y | Y | N | Y | N | Y | N | N |
| 13 Harris | Y | Y | Y | Y | N | Y | Y | Y |
| 14 Mack | Y | Y | Y | Y | N | Y | Y | Y |
| 15 Weldon | Y | Y | N | Y | N | Y | Y | Y |
| 16 Foley | Y | Y | N | Y | N | Y | N | N |
| 17 Meek | Y | N | N | Y | N | N | Y | Y |
| 18 Ros-Lehtinen | Y | Y | N | Y | N | Y | N | Y |
| 19 Wexler | Y | N | N | Y | N | Y | N | Y |
| 20 Wasserman-Schultz | Y | N | N | Y | N | Y | Y | Y |
| 21 Diaz-Balart, L. | Y | Y | N | Y | N | ? | N | |
| 22 Shaw | Y | Y | N | Y | N | Y | N | Y |
| 23 Hastings | Y | N | N | Y | N | Y | N | Y |
| 24 Feeney | Y | Y | Y | Y | Y | Y | Y | Y |
| 25 Diaz-Balart, M. | Y | Y | Y | Y | N | Y | N | Y |
| **GEORGIA** | | | | | | | | |
| 1 Kingston | ? | ? | ? | ? | ? | ? | ? | ? |
| 2 Bishop | Y | N | N | Y | N | N | Y | N |
| 3 Marshall | Y | N | N | N | N | N | Y | N |
| 4 McKinney | Y | N | N | N | N | ? | N | N |
| 5 Lewis | Y | N | Y | Y | N | Y | N | Y |
| 6 Price | Y | Y | Y | Y | N | Y | N | Y |
| 7 Linder | Y | Y | ? | ? | ? | N | Y | Y |
| 8 Westmoreland | Y | Y | N | Y | N | Y | N | Y |
| 9 Norwood | Y | Y | Y | Y | N | Y | Y | Y |
| 10 Deal | Y | Y | Y | N | Y | N | Y | Y |
| 11 Gingrey | Y | Y | N | Y | N | ? | N | Y |
| 12 Barrow | Y | N | N | N | N | Y | Y | Y |
| 13 Scott | Y | N | N | N | N | Y | N | Y |
| **HAWAII** | | | | | | | | |
| 1 Abercrombie | Y | N | N | Y | N | Y | N | Y |
| 2 Case | Y | N | N | N | N | N | Y | Y |
| **IDAHO** | | | | | | | | |
| 1 Otter | Y | Y | N | Y | N | Y | N | Y |
| 2 Simpson | Y | Y | N | N | Y | N | Y | N |
| **ILLINOIS** | | | | | | | | |
| 1 Rush | Y | N | N | Y | N | Y | N | Y |
| 2 Jackson | Y | N | N | Y | N | Y | N | Y |
| 3 Lipinski | Y | N | N | Y | N | Y | N | Y |
| 4 Gutierrez | Y | N | N | Y | N | Y | N | Y |
| 5 Emanuel | Y | N | N | Y | N | Y | N | Y |
| 6 Hyde | Y | Y | N | Y | Y | N | N | N |
| 7 Davis | Y | N | N | Y | N | Y | N | Y |
| 8 Bean | Y | N | N | N | N | Y | Y | Y |
| 9 Schakowsky | Y | N | N | Y | N | Y | N | Y |
| 10 Kirk | Y | Y | N | Y | N | Y | N | Y |
| 11 Weller | Y | Y | Y | Y | N | Y | N | Y |
| 12 Costello | Y | N | N | Y | N | Y | Y | Y |

**KEY**    Republicans    Democrats    *Independents*

| | | | |
|---|---|---|---|
| **Y** | Voted for (yea) | **X** Paired against | **C** Voted "present" to avoid possible conflict of interest |
| **#** | Paired for | **–** Announced against | |
| **+** | Announced for | **P** Voted "present" | **?** Did not vote or otherwise make a position known |
| **N** | Voted against (nay) | | |

ND Northern Democrats, SD Southern Democrats
Southern states: Ala., Ark., Fla., Ga., Ky., La., Miss., N.C., Okla., S.C., Tenn., Texas, Va.

| | 324 | 325 | 326 | 327 | 328 | 329 | 330 | 331 |
|---|---|---|---|---|---|---|---|---|
| 13 **Biggert** | Y | Y | N | Y | Y | N | Y | N |
| 14 **Hastert** | | | | | | | | |
| 15 **Johnson** | Y | Y | Y | N | Y | N | Y | Y |
| 16 **Manzullo** | Y | Y | N | N | Y | N | Y | Y |
| 17 Evans | Y | N | N | N | N | Y | Y | Y |
| 18 **LaHood** | Y | Y | N | N | Y | N | Y | N |
| 19 **Shimkus** | Y | Y | N | N | Y | N | Y | N |
| **INDIANA** | | | | | | | | |
| 1 Visclosky | Y | N | N | Y | N | Y | Y | Y |
| 2 **Chocola** | Y | Y | N | N | Y | N | Y | Y |
| 3 **Souder** | Y | Y | Y | Y | Y | N | Y | Y |
| 4 **Buyer** | Y | Y | N | Y | Y | N | Y | N |
| 5 **Burton** | Y | Y | Y | Y | Y | N | Y | Y |
| 6 **Pence** | Y | Y | Y | Y | Y | N | Y | Y |
| 7 Carson | Y | N | Y | N | N | Y | Y | Y |
| 8 **Hostettler** | Y | Y | Y | Y | Y | N | Y | Y |
| 9 **Sodrel** | Y | Y | N | N | Y | N | Y | Y |
| **IOWA** | | | | | | | | |
| 1 **Nussle** | Y | Y | N | N | Y | N | Y | N |
| 2 **Leach** | Y | Y | N | Y | Y | Y | Y | N |
| 3 Boswell | Y | N | N | N | N | Y | Y | Y |
| 4 **Latham** | Y | Y | N | N | Y | N | Y | N |
| 5 **King** | Y | Y | Y | Y | Y | N | Y | Y |
| **KANSAS** | | | | | | | | |
| 1 **Moran** | Y | Y | N | N | Y | N | Y | Y |
| 2 **Ryun** | Y | Y | Y | N | Y | N | Y | Y |
| 3 Moore | Y | N | N | N | N | Y | Y | Y |
| 4 **Tiahrt** | Y | Y | N | Y | Y | N | Y | N |
| **KENTUCKY** | | | | | | | | |
| 1 **Whitfield** | Y | Y | N | Y | Y | N | Y | Y |
| 2 **Lewis** | Y | Y | N | Y | ? | N | Y | Y |
| 3 **Northup** | Y | Y | Y | N | Y | N | Y | N |
| 4 **Davis** | Y | Y | N | Y | Y | N | Y | Y |
| 5 **Rogers** | Y | Y | N | Y | Y | N | N | N |
| 6 Chandler | Y | N | N | N | N | Y | Y | Y |
| **LOUISIANA** | | | | | | | | |
| 1 **Jindal** | Y | Y | N | N | Y | N | Y | Y |
| 2 Jefferson | ? | ? | N | Y | N | Y | N | N |
| 3 Melancon | Y | N | Y | N | N | N | Y | Y |
| 4 **McCrery** | Y | Y | N | Y | Y | N | N | N |
| 5 **Alexander** | Y | Y | N | Y | Y | N | Y | Y |
| 6 **Baker** | Y | Y | N | Y | Y | N | Y | Y |
| 7 **Boustany** | Y | Y | N | N | Y | N | Y | N |
| **MAINE** | | | | | | | | |
| 1 Allen | Y | N | N | N | N | Y | Y | N |
| 2 Michaud | ? | ? | ? | ? | ? | Y | Y | Y |
| **MARYLAND** | | | | | | | | |
| 1 **Gilchrest** | Y | Y | N | Y | Y | N | Y | N |
| 2 Ruppersberger | Y | N | N | Y | N | N | Y | N |
| 3 Cardin | Y | N | N | Y | N | Y | Y | Y |
| 4 Wynn | Y | N | N | Y | N | Y | Y | Y |
| 5 Hoyer | Y | N | N | Y | N | Y | Y | Y |
| 6 **Bartlett** | Y | Y | Y | N | Y | Y | Y | N |
| 7 Cummings | Y | N | N | Y | N | Y | N | Y |
| 8 Van Hollen | Y | N | N | Y | N | Y | Y | Y |
| **MASSACHUSETTS** | | | | | | | | |
| 1 Olver | Y | N | N | Y | N | Y | N | Y |
| 2 Neal | Y | N | N | Y | N | Y | Y | Y |
| 3 McGovern | Y | N | N | Y | N | Y | N | Y |
| 4 Frank | Y | N | Y | Y | N | N | N | Y |
| 5 Meehan | Y | N | N | Y | N | Y | Y | ? |
| 6 Tierney | Y | N | N | Y | N | Y | N | Y |
| 7 Markey | Y | N | N | Y | N | Y | Y | Y |
| 8 Capuano | Y | N | N | Y | N | Y | Y | Y |
| 9 Lynch | Y | N | N | Y | N | ? | ? | Y |
| 10 Delahunt | Y | N | N | Y | N | Y | Y | N |
| **MICHIGAN** | | | | | | | | |
| 1 Stupak | Y | N | N | N | N | Y | Y | Y |
| 2 **Hoekstra** | Y | Y | N | Y | Y | N | Y | N |
| 3 **Ehlers** | Y | Y | N | Y | Y | Y | N | N |
| 4 **Camp** | Y | Y | N | Y | Y | N | Y | N |
| 5 Kildee | Y | N | N | N | N | Y | N | Y |
| 6 **Upton** | Y | Y | N | Y | Y | Y | Y | N |
| 7 **Schwarz** | Y | Y | N | Y | Y | N | Y | N |
| 8 **Rogers** | Y | Y | N | N | Y | N | Y | N |
| 9 **Knollenberg** | Y | Y | N | Y | Y | N | N | N |
| 10 **Miller** | Y | Y | N | Y | Y | N | Y | Y |
| 11 **McCotter** | Y | Y | N | Y | Y | N | Y | Y |
| 12 Levin | Y | N | N | Y | N | Y | N | Y |
| 13 Kilpatrick | + | – | N | Y | N | Y | N | N |
| 14 Conyers | Y | N | N | Y | N | Y | N | N |
| 15 Dingell | Y | N | N | Y | N | Y | N | N |
| **MINNESOTA** | | | | | | | | |
| 1 **Gutknecht** | Y | Y | Y | Y | Y | Y | Y | Y |
| 2 **Kline** | Y | Y | N | Y | Y | N | Y | N |
| 3 **Ramstad** | Y | Y | N | N | Y | Y | Y | Y |
| 4 McCollum | Y | N | Y | N | N | Y | N | Y |
| 5 Sabo | Y | N | N | Y | N | Y | N | N |
| 6 **Kennedy** | Y | Y | N | N | Y | N | Y | N |
| 7 Peterson | Y | N | Y | N | N | N | Y | Y |
| 8 Oberstar | Y | N | N | Y | N | Y | N | N |
| **MISSISSIPPI** | | | | | | | | |
| 1 **Wicker** | Y | Y | N | Y | Y | N | Y | N |
| 2 Thompson | Y | N | N | Y | N | Y | Y | Y |
| 3 **Pickering** | Y | Y | N | N | Y | N | Y | Y |
| 4 Taylor | + | – | N | N | N | Y | Y | N |
| **MISSOURI** | | | | | | | | |
| 1 Clay | Y | N | Y | Y | N | Y | Y | Y |
| 2 **Akin** | Y | Y | Y | Y | Y | N | Y | Y |
| 3 Carnahan | Y | N | N | N | N | Y | Y | Y |
| 4 Skelton | Y | N | N | Y | N | Y | Y | N |
| 5 Cleaver | + | – | N | Y | N | Y | Y | Y |
| 6 **Graves** | Y | Y | N | N | Y | N | Y | Y |
| 7 **Blunt** | Y | Y | N | Y | Y | N | Y | N |
| 8 **Emerson** | Y | Y | N | N | Y | N | Y | Y |
| 9 **Hulshof** | Y | Y | N | N | Y | Y | Y | Y |
| **MONTANA** | | | | | | | | |
| AL **Rehberg** | Y | Y | N | Y | Y | N | Y | N |
| **NEBRASKA** | | | | | | | | |
| 1 **Fortenberry** | Y | Y | N | Y | Y | N | Y | Y |
| 2 **Terry** | Y | Y | N | Y | Y | N | Y | Y |
| 3 **Osborne** | Y | Y | N | N | Y | N | Y | Y |
| **NEVADA** | | | | | | | | |
| 1 Berkley | Y | N | Y | N | N | Y | Y | Y |
| 2 **Gibbons** | Y | Y | Y | N | Y | N | Y | Y |
| 3 **Porter** | Y | Y | N | N | Y | N | Y | Y |
| **NEW HAMPSHIRE** | | | | | | | | |
| 1 **Bradley** | Y | Y | Y | N | Y | N | Y | N |
| 2 **Bass** | Y | Y | N | Y | Y | N | Y | Y |
| **NEW JERSEY** | | | | | | | | |
| 1 Andrews | Y | N | N | Y | N | Y | Y | Y |
| 2 **LoBiondo** | Y | Y | Y | N | Y | N | Y | Y |
| 3 **Saxton** | Y | Y | N | Y | Y | N | Y | N |
| 4 **Smith** | Y | ? | N | Y | Y | N | Y | Y |
| 5 **Garrett** | Y | Y | Y | Y | Y | N | Y | Y |
| 6 Pallone | Y | N | N | Y | N | Y | Y | Y |
| 7 **Ferguson** | Y | Y | N | Y | Y | N | Y | Y |
| 8 Pascrell | Y | N | N | Y | N | Y | Y | Y |
| 9 Rothman | Y | N | N | Y | N | N | Y | Y |
| 10 Payne | ? | ? | Y | Y | N | Y | N | Y |
| 11 **Frelinghuysen** | Y | Y | N | Y | Y | N | Y | Y |
| 12 Holt | Y | N | N | N | N | Y | N | Y |
| 13 Menendez | Y | N | N | Y | N | N | Y | Y |
| **NEW MEXICO** | | | | | | | | |
| 1 **Wilson** | Y | Y | N | Y | Y | N | Y | N |
| 2 **Pearce** | Y | Y | N | N | Y | N | Y | N |
| 3 Udall | Y | N | Y | N | N | Y | N | Y |
| **NEW YORK** | | | | | | | | |
| 1 Bishop | Y | N | N | N | N | Y | Y | Y |
| 2 Israel | Y | N | N | Y | N | Y | Y | Y |
| 3 **King** | Y | Y | N | Y | Y | N | Y | Y |
| 4 McCarthy | Y | N | N | Y | N | Y | Y | Y |
| 5 Ackerman | Y | N | N | Y | N | Y | N | Y |
| 6 Meeks | Y | N | N | Y | N | Y | N | Y |
| 7 Crowley | Y | N | Y | Y | N | N | Y | Y |
| 8 Nadler | Y | N | Y | Y | N | Y | N | Y |
| 9 Weiner | Y | N | Y | Y | N | Y | Y | Y |
| 10 Towns | Y | N | Y | Y | N | Y | N | Y |
| 11 Owens | Y | N | N | Y | N | Y | Y | Y |
| 12 Velázquez | Y | N | N | Y | N | Y | N | Y |
| 13 **Fossella** | + | + | Y | N | Y | N | Y | Y |
| 14 Maloney | Y | N | Y | N | N | N | N | Y |
| 15 Rangel | Y | N | N | Y | N | Y | Y | Y |
| 16 Serrano | Y | N | Y | Y | N | Y | N | Y |
| 17 Engel | ? | N | N | Y | N | Y | Y | Y |
| 18 Lowey | Y | N | N | Y | N | Y | N | Y |
| 19 **Kelly** | Y | Y | N | N | Y | Y | Y | N |
| 20 **Sweeney** | ? | ? | N | Y | Y | N | N | N |
| 21 McNulty | Y | N | N | Y | N | Y | Y | Y |
| 22 Hinchey | Y | N | Y | Y | N | Y | N | Y |
| 23 **McHugh** | ? | ? | ? | ? | ? | N | Y | N |
| 24 **Boehlert** | Y | Y | N | Y | Y | N | Y | Y |
| 25 **Walsh** | Y | ? | N | Y | Y | N | Y | N |
| 26 **Reynolds** | Y | Y | N | Y | Y | N | Y | N |
| 27 Higgins | ? | ? | ? | ? | ? | Y | Y | Y |
| 28 Slaughter | Y | N | N | Y | N | Y | N | Y |
| 29 **Kuhl** | Y | Y | N | N | Y | N | Y | Y |
| **NORTH CAROLINA** | | | | | | | | |
| 1 Butterfield | Y | N | N | Y | N | Y | Y | Y |
| 2 Etheridge | + | – | – | – | – | Y | Y | N |
| 3 **Jones** | ? | ? | Y | N | Y | Y | Y | Y |
| 4 Price | ? | ? | ? | ? | ? | Y | Y | N |
| 5 **Foxx** | Y | Y | Y | N | Y | N | Y | Y |
| 6 **Coble** | Y | Y | Y | N | Y | N | Y | Y |
| 7 McIntyre | Y | N | + | + | – | – | + | + |
| 8 **Hayes** | Y | Y | – | – | + | – | + | – |
| 9 **Myrick** | Y | Y | Y | Y | Y | N | Y | Y |
| 10 **McHenry** | Y | Y | Y | N | Y | N | Y | Y |
| 11 **Taylor** | Y | Y | N | Y | Y | N | Y | N |
| 12 Watt | Y | N | N | Y | N | Y | N | Y |
| 13 Miller | Y | N | N | N | N | Y | Y | Y |
| **NORTH DAKOTA** | | | | | | | | |
| AL Pomeroy | Y | N | N | N | N | Y | Y | Y |
| **OHIO** | | | | | | | | |
| 1 **Chabot** | Y | Y | N | N | N | N | Y | Y |
| 2 Vacant | | | | | | | | |
| 3 **Turner** | Y | Y | N | Y | Y | N | Y | N |
| 4 **Oxley** | Y | Y | N | Y | Y | N | N | N |
| 5 **Gillmor** | Y | Y | N | Y | Y | N | N | Y |
| 6 Strickland | Y | N | Y | N | N | Y | Y | Y |
| 7 **Hobson** | Y | Y | N | Y | Y | N | N | N |
| 8 **Boehner** | Y | Y | N | Y | Y | N | Y | N |
| 9 Kaptur | Y | N | N | N | N | Y | Y | Y |
| 10 Kucinich | Y | N | N | N | N | Y | N | Y |
| 11 Jones | Y | N | N | Y | N | Y | N | Y |
| 12 **Tiberi** | Y | Y | Y | Y | Y | N | Y | Y |
| 13 Brown | Y | N | Y | N | N | Y | Y | Y |
| 14 **LaTourette** | Y | Y | N | Y | Y | N | Y | Y |
| 15 **Pryce** | Y | Y | N | Y | Y | N | Y | N |
| 16 **Regula** | Y | Y | N | Y | Y | N | Y | N |
| 17 Ryan | Y | N | N | N | N | Y | Y | Y |
| 18 **Ney** | Y | Y | N | Y | Y | N | Y | N |
| **OKLAHOMA** | | | | | | | | |
| 1 **Sullivan** | Y | Y | N | Y | Y | N | Y | Y |
| 2 Boren | Y | N | N | N | N | Y | Y | Y |
| 3 **Lucas** | Y | Y | N | Y | Y | N | Y | Y |
| 4 **Cole** | Y | Y | N | Y | Y | N | Y | N |
| 5 **Istook** | Y | Y | N | Y | Y | N | Y | N |
| **OREGON** | | | | | | | | |
| 1 Wu | Y | N | N | N | N | Y | Y | Y |
| 2 **Walden** | Y | Y | N | N | Y | N | Y | Y |
| 3 Blumenauer | Y | N | Y | Y | N | Y | N | Y |
| 4 DeFazio | Y | N | Y | N | N | Y | Y | Y |
| 5 Hooley | Y | N | N | N | N | Y | Y | Y |
| **PENNSYLVANIA** | | | | | | | | |
| 1 Brady | Y | N | N | Y | N | Y | Y | Y |
| 2 Fattah | Y | N | N | Y | N | Y | Y | Y |
| 3 **English** | Y | Y | N | N | Y | N | Y | Y |
| 4 **Hart** | Y | Y | N | N | Y | N | Y | N |
| 5 **Peterson** | ? | ? | N | N | Y | N | N | N |
| 6 **Gerlach** | Y | Y | Y | N | Y | N | Y | Y |
| 7 **Weldon** | Y | Y | N | Y | Y | N | Y | Y |
| 8 **Fitzpatrick** | Y | Y | N | N | Y | N | Y | Y |
| 9 **Shuster** | Y | Y | N | N | Y | N | Y | Y |
| 10 **Sherwood** | Y | Y | N | N | Y | N | N | N |
| 11 Kanjorski | Y | N | N | Y | N | N | Y | N |
| 12 Murtha | ? | ? | N | Y | N | N | Y | N |
| 13 Schwartz | Y | N | N | N | N | Y | Y | Y |
| 14 Doyle | Y | N | N | Y | N | Y | Y | Y |
| 15 **Dent** | Y | Y | N | N | Y | N | Y | Y |
| 16 **Pitts** | Y | Y | Y | N | Y | Y | Y | Y |
| 17 Holden | Y | N | N | N | N | Y | Y | Y |
| 18 **Murphy** | Y | Y | N | N | Y | N | Y | N |
| 19 **Platts** | Y | Y | Y | N | Y | N | Y | Y |
| **RHODE ISLAND** | | | | | | | | |
| 1 Kennedy | Y | N | Y | Y | N | N | Y | Y |
| 2 Langevin | Y | N | N | N | N | Y | Y | Y |
| **SOUTH CAROLINA** | | | | | | | | |
| 1 **Brown** | + | + | – | + | + | N | Y | Y |
| 2 **Wilson** | Y | Y | N | Y | Y | N | Y | N |
| 3 **Barrett** | Y | Y | N | N | Y | N | Y | Y |
| 4 **Inglis** | Y | Y | N | Y | Y | N | Y | N |
| 5 Spratt | ? | ? | ? | ? | ? | Y | Y | Y |
| 6 Clyburn | ? | ? | ? | ? | ? | Y | Y | Y |
| **SOUTH DAKOTA** | | | | | | | | |
| AL Herseth | Y | N | Y | N | N | Y | Y | Y |
| **TENNESSEE** | | | | | | | | |
| 1 **Jenkins** | + | + | Y | N | Y | N | Y | Y |
| 2 **Duncan** | Y | Y | Y | N | Y | Y | Y | Y |
| 3 **Wamp** | Y | Y | N | N | Y | N | Y | Y |
| 4 Davis | Y | N | N | N | N | Y | Y | Y |
| 5 Cooper | Y | N | N | Y | N | Y | Y | Y |
| 6 Gordon | Y | N | Y | N | N | Y | Y | Y |
| 7 **Blackburn** | Y | Y | N | N | Y | N | Y | N |
| 8 Tanner | Y | N | N | N | N | Y | Y | Y |
| 9 Ford | Y | N | N | N | N | Y | Y | Y |
| **TEXAS** | | | | | | | | |
| 1 **Gohmert** | Y | Y | Y | Y | Y | N | Y | Y |
| 2 **Poe** | Y | Y | Y | Y | Y | N | Y | Y |
| 3 **Johnson, S.** | Y | Y | N | Y | Y | N | Y | Y |
| 4 **Hall** | Y | Y | N | Y | Y | Y | Y | Y |
| 5 **Hensarling** | Y | Y | N | N | Y | N | Y | N |
| 6 **Barton** | Y | Y | Y | Y | Y | N | Y | N |
| 7 **Culberson** | Y | Y | N | Y | Y | N | Y | Y |
| 8 **Brady** | Y | Y | N | Y | Y | N | Y | N |
| 9 Green, A. | Y | N | N | Y | N | Y | Y | Y |
| 10 **McCaul** | Y | Y | N | N | Y | N | Y | N |
| 11 **Conaway** | Y | Y | N | Y | Y | N | Y | Y |
| 12 **Granger** | Y | Y | N | Y | Y | N | Y | N |
| 13 **Thornberry** | Y | Y | N | Y | Y | N | Y | N |
| 14 **Paul** | N | Y | Y | N | N | Y | Y | Y |
| 15 Hinojosa | Y | N | N | Y | N | + | Y | Y |
| 16 Reyes | Y | N | N | Y | N | Y | Y | Y |
| 17 Edwards | Y | N | N | N | N | N | Y | Y |
| 18 Jackson-Lee | Y | N | N | Y | N | Y | Y | Y |
| 19 **Neugebauer** | Y | Y | Y | N | Y | N | Y | Y |
| 20 Gonzalez | Y | N | N | Y | N | N | Y | Y |
| 21 **Smith** | Y | Y | N | Y | Y | N | Y | N |
| 22 **DeLay** | Y | Y | N | Y | Y | N | Y | N |
| 23 **Bonilla** | Y | Y | N | Y | Y | N | Y | N |
| 24 **Marchant** | Y | Y | N | Y | Y | N | Y | Y |
| 25 Doggett | Y | N | Y | N | N | Y | Y | Y |
| 26 **Burgess** | Y | Y | N | N | Y | N | Y | N |
| 27 Ortiz | + | – | – | + | – | – | + | + |
| 28 Cuellar | Y | N | N | N | N | Y | Y | Y |
| 29 Green, G. | Y | N | N | Y | N | N | Y | Y |
| 30 Johnson, E. | Y | N | N | Y | N | Y | N | Y |
| 31 **Carter** | Y | Y | N | Y | Y | N | Y | N |
| 32 **Sessions** | Y | Y | N | Y | Y | N | Y | N |
| **UTAH** | | | | | | | | |
| 1 **Bishop** | Y | Y | Y | Y | Y | N | Y | N |
| 2 Matheson | Y | N | Y | N | N | N | Y | Y |
| 3 **Cannon** | Y | Y | Y | Y | Y | N | Y | N |
| **VERMONT** | | | | | | | | |
| AL *Sanders* | Y | N | N | N | N | Y | N | Y |
| **VIRGINIA** | | | | | | | | |
| 1 **Davis, J.** | Y | Y | N | N | Y | N | Y | Y |
| 2 **Drake** | Y | Y | N | N | Y | N | Y | Y |
| 3 Scott | Y | N | N | Y | N | Y | N | Y |
| 4 **Forbes** | Y | Y | N | N | Y | N | Y | Y |
| 5 **Goode** | Y | Y | Y | N | Y | N | Y | Y |
| 6 **Goodlatte** | Y | Y | Y | Y | Y | N | Y | Y |
| 7 **Cantor** | Y | Y | Y | Y | Y | N | Y | N |
| 8 Moran | Y | N | N | Y | N | N | Y | Y |
| 9 Boucher | Y | N | N | Y | N | Y | N | N |
| 10 **Wolf** | Y | Y | – | Y | Y | N | Y | N |
| 11 **Davis, T.** | Y | Y | N | Y | Y | N | Y | Y |
| **WASHINGTON** | | | | | | | | |
| 1 Inslee | Y | N | N | N | N | Y | Y | Y |
| 2 Larsen | Y | N | N | Y | N | Y | N | Y |
| 3 Baird | Y | N | N | N | N | Y | N | Y |
| 4 **Hastings** | Y | Y | N | Y | Y | N | Y | N |
| 5 **McMorris** | Y | Y | N | N | Y | N | Y | N |
| 6 Dicks | Y | N | N | Y | N | Y | Y | Y |
| 7 McDermott | Y | N | N | Y | N | Y | N | N |
| 8 **Reichert** | Y | Y | N | N | Y | N | Y | N |
| 9 Smith | Y | N | N | N | N | Y | N | Y |
| **WEST VIRGINIA** | | | | | | | | |
| 1 Mollohan | Y | N | ? | ? | ? | N | Y | N |
| 2 **Capito** | Y | Y | ? | ? | ? | N | Y | N |
| 3 Rahall | Y | N | ? | ? | ? | Y | Y | N |
| **WISCONSIN** | | | | | | | | |
| 1 **Ryan** | Y | Y | N | N | Y | N | Y | N |
| 2 Baldwin | Y | N | N | Y | N | Y | N | N |
| 3 Kind | Y | N | N | N | N | Y | Y | Y |
| 4 Moore | Y | N | N | Y | N | Y | Y | Y |
| 5 **Sensenbrenner** | Y | Y | Y | N | Y | Y | Y | Y |
| 6 **Petri** | Y | Y | Y | N | Y | N | Y | Y |
| 7 Obey | Y | N | N | N | N | Y | Y | N |
| 8 **Green** | Y | Y | N | N | Y | N | Y | Y |
| **WYOMING** | | | | | | | | |
| AL **Cubin** | Y | Y | N | Y | Y | N | Y | Y |

# IN THE HOUSE | By Vote Number

**332.** HR 3057. Fiscal 2006 Foreign Operations Appropriations/Nuclear Power Plants in China. Sanders, I-Vt., amendment that would bar the Export-Import Bank from using funds in the bill to approve federal loans or loan guarantees for the construction of nuclear power plants in China. Adopted 313-114: R 139-88; D 173-26 (ND 136-15, SD 37-11); I 1-0. June 28, 2005.

**333.** HR 3057. Fiscal 2006 Foreign Operations Appropriations/Foreign Assistance Limit. Deal, R-Ga., amendment that would prohibit the State Department from using funds in the bill to provide aid to any country that has an extradition treaty with the United States but refuses to extradite individuals accused of a crime punishable by imprisonment. The restriction would not affect funds for international narcotics control and law enforcement. Adopted 294-132: R 184-43; D 109-89 (ND 80-71, SD 29-18); I 1-0. June 28, 2005.

**334.** HR 3057. Fiscal 2006 Foreign Operations Appropriations/Discretionary Spending Cut. Hefley, R-Colo., amendment that would reduce discretionary spending in the bill by 1 percent. Rejected 117-309: R 105-122; D 12-186 (ND 8-142, SD 4-44); I 0-1. June 28, 2005.

**335.** HR 3057. Fiscal 2006 Foreign Operations Appropriations/Passage. Passage of the bill that would appropriate $20.3 billion in fiscal 2006 for foreign operations and economic assistance, including $2.7 billion for programs to combat HIV/AIDS and related diseases, and $1.75 billion for the Millennium Challenge Corporation. Passed 393-32: R 199-27; D 193-5 (ND 148-2, SD 45-3); I 1-0. June 28, 2005.

**336.** HR 3058. Fiscal 2006 Transportation-Treasury-Housing Appropriations/Amtrak Routes. Brown, D-Fla., amendment that would eliminate language in the bill that would prohibit the use of federal funds for 18 specified Amtrak routes, all of which require federal subsidies of more than $30 per passenger. Adopted 269-152: R 73-151; D 195-1 (ND 148-0, SD 47-1); I 1-0. June 29, 2005.

**337.** HR 3058. Fiscal 2006 Transportation-Treasury-Housing Appropriations/Homeless Assistance Grants. Kennedy, R-Minn., amendment that would increase homeless-assistance grants by $100 million, offset with a reduction to Amtrak. Rejected 59-362: R 57-168; D 2-193 (ND 0-147, SD 2-46); I 0-1. June 29, 2005.

**338.** HR 3058. Fiscal 2006 Transportation-Treasury-Housing Appropriations/Fair Housing Programs. A. Green, D-Texas, amendment that would increase funding for Fair Housing programs by $7.7 million, offset by a cut to the IRS information systems account. Adopted 231-191: R 35-191; D 195-0 (ND 147-0, SD 48-0); I 1-0. June 29, 2005.

**339.** HR 3058. Fiscal 2006 Transportation-Treasury-Housing Appropriations/Housing Vouchers. Nadler, D-N.Y., amendment that would provide an additional $100 million for Section 8 housing vouchers, offset by a $120 million decrease to the working capital fund from the Housing and Urban Development management and administration account. Adopted 225-194: R 30-193; D 194-1 (ND 147-1, SD 47-0); I 1-0. June 29, 2005.

| | 332 | 333 | 334 | 335 | 336 | 337 | 338 | 339 |
|---|---|---|---|---|---|---|---|---|
| **ALABAMA** | | | | | | | | |
| 1 Bonner | Y | Y | Y | Y | N | N | N | N |
| 2 Everett | Y | Y | Y | Y | N | N | N | N |
| 3 Rogers | Y | Y | N | Y | N | N | N | N |
| 4 Aderholt | Y | Y | N | Y | N | N | N | N |
| 5 Cramer | N | Y | N | Y | Y | N | Y | Y |
| 6 Bachus | Y | Y | N | Y | N | N | N | ? |
| 7 Davis | Y | N | N | Y | Y | N | Y | Y |
| **ALASKA** | | | | | | | | |
| AL Young | Y | Y | N | Y | Y | N | N | N |
| **ARIZONA** | | | | | | | | |
| 1 Renzi | Y | N | N | Y | Y | Y | Y | Y |
| 2 Franks | Y | Y | Y | N | N | Y | N | Y |
| 3 Shadegg | Y | Y | Y | Y | N | Y | N | N |
| 4 Pastor | Y | N | N | Y | Y | N | Y | Y |
| 5 Hayworth | Y | Y | Y | Y | N | Y | N | N |
| 6 Flake | Y | Y | Y | N | N | Y | N | N |
| 7 Grijalva | Y | N | N | Y | Y | N | Y | Y |
| 8 Kolbe | N | N | N | Y | N | N | N | N |
| **ARKANSAS** | | | | | | | | |
| 1 Berry | Y | Y | Y | N | Y | N | Y | Y |
| 2 Snyder | N | N | N | Y | Y | N | Y | Y |
| 3 Boozman | Y | Y | N | Y | N | N | N | N |
| 4 Ross | ? | ? | ? | ? | ? | ? | ? | ? |
| **CALIFORNIA** | | | | | | | | |
| 1 Thompson | Y | N | N | Y | Y | N | Y | Y |
| 2 Herger | Y | Y | Y | Y | N | N | N | N |
| 3 Lungren | N | Y | Y | Y | N | N | N | N |
| 4 Doolittle | ? | ? | ? | ? | N | N | N | N |
| 5 Matsui, D. | Y | N | N | Y | Y | N | Y | Y |
| 6 Woolsey | Y | N | N | Y | Y | N | Y | Y |
| 7 Miller, George | Y | N | N | Y | Y | ? | ? | Y |
| 8 Pelosi | Y | N | N | Y | Y | N | Y | Y |
| 9 Lee | Y | N | N | Y | Y | N | Y | Y |
| 10 Tauscher | N | N | N | Y | Y | N | Y | Y |
| 11 Pombo | Y | Y | Y | N | N | N | N | N |
| 12 Lantos | Y | Y | N | Y | Y | N | Y | Y |
| 13 Stark | Y | N | N | N | Y | ? | ? | ? |
| 14 Eshoo | Y | N | N | Y | Y | N | Y | Y |
| 15 Honda | Y | N | N | Y | Y | N | Y | Y |
| 16 Lofgren | N | Y | N | Y | Y | N | Y | Y |
| 17 Farr | Y | N | N | Y | Y | N | Y | Y |
| 18 Cardoza | Y | Y | Y | Y | Y | N | Y | Y |
| 19 Radanovich | N | Y | Y | N | N | N | N | N |
| 20 Costa | Y | Y | Y | Y | Y | N | Y | Y |
| 21 Nunes | Y | N | N | Y | N | N | N | N |
| 22 Thomas | N | N | N | Y | N | N | N | N |
| 23 Capps | Y | N | N | Y | Y | N | Y | Y |
| 24 Gallegly | Y | Y | Y | Y | N | N | N | N |
| 25 McKeon | Y | Y | N | Y | N | N | N | N |
| 26 Dreier | N | N | N | Y | N | N | N | N |
| 27 Sherman | Y | Y | N | Y | Y | N | Y | Y |
| 28 Berman | Y | N | N | Y | Y | N | Y | Y |
| 29 Schiff | Y | N | N | Y | Y | N | Y | Y |
| 30 Waxman | Y | N | N | Y | Y | N | Y | Y |
| 31 Becerra | Y | N | N | Y | Y | N | Y | Y |
| 32 Solis | Y | N | N | Y | Y | N | Y | Y |
| 33 Watson | Y | N | N | Y | Y | N | Y | Y |
| 34 Roybal-Allard | Y | N | N | Y | Y | N | Y | Y |
| 35 Waters | Y | N | ? | Y | Y | N | Y | Y |
| 36 Harman | Y | Y | N | Y | Y | N | Y | Y |
| 37 Millender-McD. | Y | Y | N | Y | Y | N | Y | Y |
| 38 Napolitano | Y | N | N | Y | Y | N | Y | Y |
| 39 Sánchez, Linda | Y | N | N | Y | Y | N | Y | Y |
| 40 Royce | Y | Y | Y | Y | N | N | N | N |
| 41 Lewis | N | N | N | ? | N | N | N | N |
| 42 Miller, Gary | Y | Y | Y | Y | N | N | N | N |
| 43 Baca | Y | Y | N | Y | Y | N | Y | Y |
| 44 Calvert | Y | Y | N | Y | N | N | N | N |
| 45 Bono | Y | Y | N | Y | N | N | N | N |
| 46 Rohrabacher | Y | Y | Y | N | N | N | N | N |
| 47 Sanchez, Loretta | Y | N | N | Y | N | Y | Y | Y |
| 48 Cox | Y | Y | Y | Y | N | ? | ? | ? |
| 49 Issa | Y | Y | Y | Y | N | N | N | N |
| **50 Cunningham** | Y | Y | N | Y | N | N | N | N |
| 51 Filner | Y | Y | N | Y | N | Y | N | Y |
| 52 Hunter | Y | Y | N | Y | N | Y | N | N |
| 53 Davis | Y | Y | N | Y | Y | N | Y | Y |
| **COLORADO** | | | | | | | | |
| 1 DeGette | Y | N | N | Y | Y | N | Y | Y |
| 2 Udall | Y | N | N | Y | Y | N | Y | Y |
| 3 Salazar | Y | N | N | Y | Y | N | Y | Y |
| 4 Musgrave | Y | Y | Y | Y | N | Y | N | N |
| 5 Hefley | Y | Y | N | Y | N | Y | N | N |
| 6 Tancredo | Y | Y | N | N | N | Y | N | N |
| 7 Beauprez | N | Y | Y | N | N | N | Y | N |
| **CONNECTICUT** | | | | | | | | |
| 1 Larson | Y | N | N | Y | Y | N | Y | Y |
| 2 Simmons | Y | Y | N | Y | Y | N | Y | Y |
| 3 DeLauro | Y | N | N | Y | Y | N | Y | Y |
| 4 Shays | N | N | N | Y | N | N | Y | Y |
| 5 Johnson | N | Y | N | Y | Y | N | N | Y |
| **DELAWARE** | | | | | | | | |
| AL Castle | N | N | N | Y | Y | N | N | Y |
| **FLORIDA** | | | | | | | | |
| 1 Miller | Y | Y | N | N | N | Y | N | N |
| 2 Boyd | Y | Y | N | Y | Y | N | Y | Y |
| 3 Brown | Y | N | N | Y | Y | N | Y | Y |
| 4 Crenshaw | N | N | N | Y | N | N | N | N |
| 5 Brown-Waite | Y | Y | Y | Y | N | N | N | N |
| 6 Stearns | Y | Y | Y | N | N | N | N | N |
| 7 Mica | N | Y | Y | N | N | N | N | N |
| 8 Keller | N | Y | N | Y | N | N | N | N |
| 9 Bilirakis | N | Y | Y | Y | Y | N | N | N |
| 10 Young | N | Y | N | Y | N | N | N | N |
| 11 Davis | Y | N | N | Y | Y | N | Y | Y |
| 12 Putnam | N | N | N | Y | N | N | N | N |
| 13 Harris | Y | Y | Y | Y | Y | N | N | N |
| 14 Mack | N | Y | N | N | N | N | N | N |
| 15 Weldon | N | N | N | Y | N | N | N | N |
| 16 Foley | Y | N | N | Y | N | N | N | ? |
| 17 Meek | Y | N | N | Y | Y | N | Y | Y |
| 18 Ros-Lehtinen | N | N | N | Y | N | N | N | N |
| 19 Wexler | N | N | N | Y | N | N | Y | Y |
| 20 Wasserman-Schultz | Y | Y | N | Y | Y | N | Y | Y |
| 21 Diaz-Balart, L. | Y | N | N | Y | ? | N | N | N |
| 22 Shaw | Y | Y | N | Y | N | N | N | N |
| 23 Hastings | Y | N | N | Y | Y | N | Y | Y |
| 24 Feeney | N | Y | Y | N | N | Y | N | N |
| 25 Diaz-Balart, M. | Y | N | Y | Y | ? | N | N | N |
| **GEORGIA** | | | | | | | | |
| 1 Kingston | ? | ? | ? | ? | N | N | N | N |
| 2 Bishop | Y | Y | N | Y | Y | N | Y | Y |
| 3 Marshall | Y | N | Y | Y | N | Y | N | Y |
| 4 McKinney | Y | N | N | Y | Y | N | Y | Y |
| 5 Lewis | Y | N | N | Y | ? | ? | ? | ? |
| 6 Price | N | Y | Y | N | N | Y | N | N |
| 7 Linder | Y | Y | Y | N | N | N | N | N |
| 8 Westmoreland | Y | Y | Y | N | N | Y | N | N |
| 9 Norwood | Y | Y | N | N | N | N | N | N |
| 10 Deal | Y | Y | Y | N | N | N | N | N |
| 11 Gingrey | Y | Y | N | N | N | N | N | N |
| 12 Barrow | Y | Y | N | Y | Y | N | Y | ? |
| 13 Scott | Y | Y | N | Y | ? | ? | ? | Y |
| **HAWAII** | | | | | | | | |
| 1 Abercrombie | Y | Y | N | Y | Y | N | Y | Y |
| 2 Case | N | Y | N | Y | Y | N | Y | Y |
| **IDAHO** | | | | | | | | |
| 1 Otter | N | Y | Y | N | N | N | N | N |
| 2 Simpson | N | Y | N | Y | N | N | N | N |
| **ILLINOIS** | | | | | | | | |
| 1 Rush | Y | N | N | Y | Y | N | Y | Y |
| 2 Jackson | Y | N | N | Y | Y | N | Y | Y |
| 3 Lipinski | Y | Y | N | Y | Y | N | Y | Y |
| 4 Gutierrez | Y | N | N | Y | Y | N | Y | Y |
| 5 Emanuel | Y | N | N | Y | Y | N | Y | Y |
| 6 Hyde | Y | Y | N | Y | N | N | N | N |
| 7 Davis | Y | N | N | Y | Y | N | Y | Y |
| 8 Bean | Y | Y | Y | Y | Y | N | Y | Y |
| 9 Schakowsky | Y | N | N | Y | Y | N | Y | Y |
| 10 Kirk | N | N | N | Y | N | N | N | N |
| 11 Weller | N | Y | N | Y | N | N | N | N |
| 12 Costello | Y | Y | Y | Y | Y | N | Y | Y |

ND Northern Democrats, SD Southern Democrats
Southern states: Ala., Ark., Fla., Ga., Ky., La., Miss., N.C., Okla., S.C., Tenn., Texas, Va.

| | 332 | 333 | 334 | 335 | 336 | 337 | 338 | 339 |
|---|---|---|---|---|---|---|---|---|
| 13 **Biggert** | N | N | N | Y | N | Y | Y | N |
| 14 **Hastert** | | | | | | | | |
| 15 **Johnson** | Y | Y | N | Y | N | N | N | Y |
| 16 **Manzullo** | N | Y | Y | Y | N | N | N | N |
| 17 Evans | Y | N | N | Y | Y | N | Y | Y |
| 18 **LaHood** | N | Y | N | Y | N | N | N | N |
| 19 **Shimkus** | N | Y | Y | Y | N | N | Y | N |
| **INDIANA** | | | | | | | | |
| 1 Visclosky | Y | Y | N | Y | Y | N | Y | Y |
| 2 **Chocola** | N | Y | Y | Y | N | Y | N | N |
| 3 **Souder** | Y | N | N | Y | Y | N | N | N |
| 4 **Buyer** | Y | Y | Y | Y | N | N | N | N |
| 5 **Burton** | Y | Y | Y | Y | N | N | N | N |
| 6 **Pence** | Y | Y | Y | Y | N | Y | N | N |
| 7 Carson | Y | N | N | Y | Y | N | Y | Y |
| 8 **Hostettler** | Y | Y | Y | N | N | Y | N | N |
| 9 **Sodrel** | Y | Y | N | Y | N | N | N | N |
| **IOWA** | | | | | | | | |
| 1 **Nussle** | Y | Y | N | Y | Y | N | N | ? |
| 2 **Leach** | Y | Y | N | Y | Y | N | Y | Y |
| 3 Boswell | Y | Y | N | Y | Y | N | Y | Y |
| 4 **Latham** | N | N | N | Y | Y | N | N | N |
| 5 **King** | Y | Y | Y | Y | N | N | N | N |
| **KANSAS** | | | | | | | | |
| 1 **Moran** | N | Y | Y | Y | Y | N | Y | Y |
| 2 **Ryun** | N | Y | Y | N | N | Y | N | N |
| 3 Moore | Y | Y | N | Y | Y | N | Y | Y |
| 4 **Tiahrt** | N | Y | N | Y | N | N | N | N |
| **KENTUCKY** | | | | | | | | |
| 1 **Whitfield** | N | Y | N | Y | Y | N | N | N |
| 2 **Lewis** | Y | Y | Y | Y | N | N | Y | N |
| 3 **Northup** | Y | Y | N | Y | N | N | N | N |
| 4 **Davis** | N | N | N | Y | N | N | N | N |
| 5 **Rogers** | Y | Y | N | Y | N | N | N | N |
| 6 Chandler | Y | Y | N | Y | Y | N | Y | Y |
| **LOUISIANA** | | | | | | | | |
| 1 **Jindal** | Y | Y | Y | Y | Y | Y | N | N |
| 2 Jefferson | N | N | N | Y | Y | N | Y | Y |
| 3 Melancon | Y | Y | N | Y | Y | N | Y | Y |
| 4 **McCrery** | N | N | N | Y | N | Y | N | N |
| 5 **Alexander** | N | Y | N | Y | N | N | N | N |
| 6 **Baker** | Y | Y | Y | Y | N | N | N | N |
| 7 **Boustany** | N | Y | N | Y | Y | N | N | Y |
| **MAINE** | | | | | | | | |
| 1 Allen | Y | N | N | Y | Y | N | Y | Y |
| 2 Michaud | Y | Y | N | Y | Y | N | Y | Y |
| **MARYLAND** | | | | | | | | |
| 1 **Gilchrest** | N | N | N | Y | Y | N | N | N |
| 2 Ruppersberger | N | Y | N | Y | Y | N | Y | Y |
| 3 Cardin | Y | Y | N | Y | Y | N | Y | Y |
| 4 Wynn | Y | Y | N | Y | Y | N | Y | Y |
| 5 Hoyer | Y | Y | N | Y | Y | N | Y | Y |
| 6 **Bartlett** | N | Y | Y | N | N | N | N | N |
| 7 Cummings | Y | N | N | Y | Y | N | Y | Y |
| 8 Van Hollen | Y | Y | N | Y | Y | N | Y | Y |
| **MASSACHUSETTS** | | | | | | | | |
| 1 Olver | Y | N | N | Y | Y | N | Y | Y |
| 2 Neal | Y | Y | N | Y | ? | ? | ? | ? |
| 3 McGovern | Y | N | N | Y | Y | N | Y | Y |
| 4 Frank | Y | N | N | Y | Y | N | Y | Y |
| 5 Meehan | Y | N | N | Y | Y | N | Y | Y |
| 6 Tierney | Y | N | N | Y | Y | N | Y | Y |
| 7 Markey | Y | N | N | Y | Y | N | Y | Y |
| 8 Capuano | Y | N | N | Y | Y | N | Y | Y |
| 9 Lynch | Y | Y | N | Y | Y | N | Y | Y |
| 10 Delahunt | Y | N | N | Y | Y | N | Y | Y |
| **MICHIGAN** | | | | | | | | |
| 1 Stupak | Y | Y | N | Y | Y | N | Y | Y |
| 2 **Hoekstra** | N | N | N | Y | N | N | N | N |
| 3 **Ehlers** | N | N | N | Y | Y | N | Y | N |
| 4 **Camp** | Y | Y | N | Y | Y | N | N | N |
| 5 Kildee | Y | Y | N | Y | Y | N | Y | Y |
| 6 **Upton** | N | Y | Y | Y | Y | N | N | N |
| 7 **Schwarz** | N | N | N | Y | Y | N | Y | N |
| 8 **Rogers** | Y | Y | Y | Y | Y | N | N | N |
| 9 **Knollenberg** | N | N | N | Y | N | N | N | N |
| 10 **Miller** | N | Y | N | Y | N | N | N | N |
| 11 **McCotter** | Y | Y | Y | Y | Y | Y | N | N |
| 12 Levin | N | Y | N | Y | Y | N | Y | Y |
| 13 Kilpatrick | Y | N | N | Y | Y | N | Y | Y |
| 14 Conyers | Y | N | N | Y | ? | ? | Y | Y |
| 15 Dingell | Y | N | N | Y | Y | N | Y | Y |
| **MINNESOTA** | | | | | | | | |
| 1 **Gutknecht** | Y | Y | Y | Y | N | N | N | N |
| 2 **Kline** | N | N | N | Y | N | Y | N | N |
| 3 **Ramstad** | Y | Y | N | Y | N | Y | Y | Y |
| 4 McCollum | Y | Y | N | Y | Y | N | Y | Y |
| 5 Sabo | Y | N | N | Y | Y | N | Y | Y |
| 6 **Kennedy** | Y | Y | Y | Y | N | Y | Y | Y |
| 7 Peterson | Y | Y | Y | Y | Y | N | Y | Y |
| 8 Oberstar | N | N | N | Y | Y | N | Y | Y |
| **MISSISSIPPI** | | | | | | | | |
| 1 **Wicker** | N | Y | N | Y | Y | N | N | N |
| 2 Thompson | Y | Y | N | Y | Y | N | Y | Y |
| 3 **Pickering** | Y | Y | N | Y | Y | N | Y | N |
| 4 Taylor | Y | Y | Y | N | Y | N | Y | Y |
| **MISSOURI** | | | | | | | | |
| 1 Clay | Y | N | N | Y | ? | ? | ? | ? |
| 2 **Akin** | Y | Y | Y | Y | - | - | - | - |
| 3 Carnahan | Y | Y | N | Y | Y | N | Y | Y |
| 4 Skelton | Y | Y | N | Y | Y | N | Y | Y |
| 5 Cleaver | Y | N | N | Y | Y | N | Y | Y |
| 6 **Graves** | N | Y | Y | Y | N | Y | N | N |
| 7 **Blunt** | Y | N | N | Y | N | N | N | N |
| 8 **Emerson** | Y | Y | N | Y | N | N | Y | N |
| 9 **Hulshof** | N | Y | Y | N | N | N | Y | N |
| **MONTANA** | | | | | | | | |
| AL **Rehberg** | N | N | N | Y | Y | N | N | N |
| **NEBRASKA** | | | | | | | | |
| 1 **Fortenberry** | Y | Y | N | Y | Y | N | N | N |
| 2 **Terry** | Y | Y | Y | Y | N | N | N | N |
| 3 **Osborne** | Y | Y | N | Y | Y | N | N | N |
| **NEVADA** | | | | | | | | |
| 1 Berkley | Y | Y | N | Y | Y | N | Y | Y |
| 2 **Gibbons** | Y | Y | Y | N | Y | N | Y | N |
| 3 **Porter** | Y | Y | N | Y | Y | Y | N | N |
| **NEW HAMPSHIRE** | | | | | | | | |
| 1 **Bradley** | N | Y | Y | Y | N | Y | Y | Y |
| 2 **Bass** | Y | Y | Y | Y | N | N | N | N |
| **NEW JERSEY** | | | | | | | | |
| 1 Andrews | Y | Y | N | Y | Y | N | Y | Y |
| 2 **LoBiondo** | Y | Y | N | Y | Y | N | N | N |
| 3 **Saxton** | Y | Y | N | Y | Y | N | N | N |
| 4 **Smith** | Y | N | N | Y | Y | N | N | Y |
| 5 **Garrett** | Y | Y | Y | Y | N | N | N | N |
| 6 Pallone | Y | Y | N | Y | Y | N | Y | Y |
| 7 **Ferguson** | Y | Y | N | Y | N | N | N | N |
| 8 Pascrell | Y | N | N | Y | Y | N | Y | Y |
| 9 Rothman | Y | Y | N | Y | Y | N | Y | Y |
| 10 Payne | Y | N | N | Y | Y | N | Y | Y |
| 11 **Frelinghuysen** | N | N | N | Y | N | N | N | N |
| 12 Holt | Y | N | N | Y | Y | N | Y | Y |
| 13 Menendez | Y | Y | N | Y | Y | N | Y | Y |
| **NEW MEXICO** | | | | | | | | |
| 1 **Wilson** | Y | Y | N | Y | Y | Y | Y | Y |
| 2 **Pearce** | N | Y | N | Y | N | Y | N | N |
| 3 Udall | Y | N | N | Y | Y | N | Y | Y |
| **NEW YORK** | | | | | | | | |
| 1 Bishop | Y | Y | N | Y | Y | N | Y | Y |
| 2 Israel | Y | Y | N | Y | Y | N | Y | Y |
| 3 **King** | N | Y | N | Y | N | N | N | N |
| 4 McCarthy | Y | Y | N | Y | Y | N | Y | Y |
| 5 Ackerman | Y | N | N | Y | Y | N | Y | Y |
| 6 Meeks | Y | N | N | Y | Y | N | Y | Y |
| 7 Crowley | N | Y | N | Y | Y | N | Y | Y |
| 8 Nadler | Y | N | N | Y | Y | N | Y | Y |
| 9 Weiner | Y | Y | N | Y | Y | N | Y | Y |
| 10 Towns | Y | N | N | Y | Y | N | Y | Y |
| 11 Owens | Y | Y | N | Y | Y | N | Y | Y |
| 12 Velázquez | Y | N | N | Y | Y | N | Y | Y |
| 13 **Fossella** | Y | Y | Y | Y | N | N | N | Y |
| 14 Maloney | Y | N | N | Y | Y | N | Y | Y |
| 15 Rangel | Y | Y | N | Y | Y | N | Y | Y |
| 16 Serrano | Y | N | N | Y | Y | N | Y | Y |
| 17 Engel | Y | Y | N | Y | Y | N | Y | Y |
| 18 Lowey | Y | N | N | Y | Y | N | Y | Y |
| 19 **Kelly** | Y | Y | N | Y | Y | N | Y | Y |
| 20 **Sweeney** | N | N | N | Y | N | N | N | N |
| 21 McNulty | Y | Y | Y | Y | Y | N | Y | Y |
| 22 Hinchey | Y | Y | N | Y | Y | N | Y | Y |
| 23 **McHugh** | Y | Y | N | Y | N | N | N | Y |
| 24 **Boehlert** | Y | Y | N | Y | Y | N | N | N |
| 25 **Walsh** | Y | N | N | Y | N | N | N | N |
| 26 **Reynolds** | Y | Y | N | Y | N | N | N | N |
| 27 Higgins | Y | Y | N | Y | Y | N | Y | Y |
| 28 Slaughter | Y | Y | N | Y | Y | N | Y | Y |
| 29 **Kuhl** | N | Y | N | Y | Y | N | N | Y |
| **NORTH CAROLINA** | | | | | | | | |
| 1 Butterfield | Y | N | N | Y | Y | N | Y | Y |
| 2 Etheridge | N | N | N | Y | Y | N | Y | Y |
| 3 **Jones** | Y | Y | Y | N | N | Y | Y | Y |
| 4 Price | N | N | N | Y | Y | N | Y | Y |
| 5 **Foxx** | Y | Y | Y | Y | N | Y | N | N |
| 6 **Coble** | Y | Y | Y | Y | N | N | N | N |
| 7 McIntyre | + | + | - | + | Y | N | Y | Y |
| 8 **Hayes** | + | + | + | - | N | N | N | N |
| 9 **Myrick** | N | Y | Y | Y | N | Y | N | N |
| 10 **McHenry** | Y | Y | Y | Y | N | Y | N | N |
| 11 **Taylor** | Y | Y | N | Y | N | N | N | N |
| 12 Watt | Y | N | N | Y | Y | N | Y | Y |
| 13 Miller | N | Y | N | Y | Y | N | Y | Y |
| **NORTH DAKOTA** | | | | | | | | |
| AL Pomeroy | N | Y | N | Y | Y | N | Y | Y |
| **OHIO** | | | | | | | | |
| 1 **Chabot** | Y | Y | Y | Y | N | Y | N | N |
| 2 Vacant | | | | | | | | |
| 3 **Turner** | Y | Y | N | Y | Y | N | N | N |
| 4 **Oxley** | N | N | N | Y | N | N | N | N |
| 5 **Gillmor** | Y | Y | N | Y | N | N | N | N |
| 6 Strickland | Y | Y | N | Y | Y | N | Y | Y |
| 7 **Hobson** | N | N | N | Y | N | N | N | N |
| 8 **Boehner** | Y | Y | N | Y | N | N | N | N |
| 9 Kaptur | Y | Y | N | Y | Y | N | Y | Y |
| 10 Kucinich | Y | N | N | Y | Y | N | Y | Y |
| 11 Jones | Y | N | N | Y | Y | N | Y | Y |
| 12 **Tiberi** | Y | Y | Y | Y | Y | Y | N | N |
| 13 Brown | Y | Y | N | Y | Y | N | Y | Y |
| 14 **LaTourette** | Y | Y | N | Y | Y | N | N | N |
| 15 **Pryce** | N | N | N | Y | N | N | N | N |
| 16 **Regula** | N | N | N | Y | Y | N | N | N |
| 17 Ryan | Y | Y | N | Y | Y | N | Y | Y |
| 18 **Ney** | Y | Y | N | Y | Y | N | Y | N |
| **OKLAHOMA** | | | | | | | | |
| 1 **Sullivan** | N | Y | N | Y | N | N | N | N |
| 2 Boren | Y | Y | N | Y | Y | N | Y | Y |
| 3 **Lucas** | Y | Y | N | N | N | N | N | N |
| 4 **Cole** | N | Y | N | Y | N | N | N | N |
| 5 **Istook** | Y | Y | N | Y | N | ? | N | N |
| **OREGON** | | | | | | | | |
| 1 Wu | Y | Y | N | Y | Y | N | Y | Y |
| 2 **Walden** | Y | Y | Y | Y | Y | N | N | N |
| 3 Blumenauer | Y | N | N | Y | Y | N | Y | Y |
| 4 DeFazio | Y | Y | Y | Y | Y | N | Y | Y |
| 5 Hooley | Y | N | N | Y | Y | N | Y | Y |
| **PENNSYLVANIA** | | | | | | | | |
| 1 Brady | Y | Y | N | Y | Y | N | Y | Y |
| 2 Fattah | Y | Y | N | Y | Y | N | Y | Y |
| 3 **English** | Y | Y | N | Y | Y | N | N | N |
| 4 **Hart** | N | Y | Y | Y | Y | N | N | N |
| 5 **Peterson** | N | N | N | Y | ? | ? | ? | ? |
| 6 **Gerlach** | Y | Y | N | Y | Y | N | Y | N |
| 7 **Weldon** | Y | Y | N | Y | Y | N | N | N |
| 8 **Fitzpatrick** | Y | Y | N | Y | Y | N | Y | Y |
| 9 **Shuster** | Y | Y | Y | Y | Y | N | N | N |
| 10 **Sherwood** | N | N | N | Y | N | N | N | N |
| 11 Kanjorski | Y | Y | N | Y | Y | N | Y | Y |
| 12 Murtha | N | Y | N | Y | Y | N | Y | Y |
| 13 Schwartz | Y | Y | N | Y | Y | N | Y | N |
| 14 Doyle | N | Y | N | Y | Y | N | Y | Y |
| 15 **Dent** | Y | Y | N | Y | Y | N | Y | N |
| 16 **Pitts** | Y | Y | Y | Y | N | N | N | N |
| 17 Holden | Y | Y | N | Y | Y | N | Y | Y |
| 18 **Murphy** | N | Y | N | Y | + | N | Y | Y |
| 19 **Platts** | Y | Y | Y | Y | Y | N | Y | N |
| **RHODE ISLAND** | | | | | | | | |
| 1 Kennedy | Y | Y | N | Y | Y | N | Y | Y |
| 2 Langevin | Y | Y | N | Y | Y | N | Y | Y |
| **SOUTH CAROLINA** | | | | | | | | |
| 1 **Brown** | Y | Y | N | Y | N | N | N | N |
| 2 **Wilson** | N | Y | Y | Y | N | Y | N | N |
| 3 **Barrett** | Y | Y | Y | Y | N | Y | N | N |
| 4 **Inglis** | N | Y | Y | Y | N | N | N | N |
| 5 Spratt | N | Y | N | Y | Y | N | Y | Y |
| 6 Clyburn | Y | Y | N | Y | Y | N | Y | Y |
| **SOUTH DAKOTA** | | | | | | | | |
| AL Herseth | Y | Y | N | Y | Y | N | Y | Y |
| **TENNESSEE** | | | | | | | | |
| 1 **Jenkins** | Y | Y | Y | N | N | N | N | N |
| 2 **Duncan** | Y | Y | Y | N | N | N | N | N |
| 3 **Wamp** | N | Y | N | Y | N | N | N | N |
| 4 Davis | Y | Y | N | Y | Y | Y | Y | Y |
| 5 Cooper | N | N | N | Y | N | Y | Y | Y |
| 6 Gordon | Y | Y | N | Y | Y | N | Y | Y |
| 7 **Blackburn** | Y | Y | Y | Y | N | Y | N | N |
| 8 Tanner | Y | Y | Y | N | Y | N | Y | Y |
| 9 Ford | Y | Y | N | Y | Y | N | Y | Y |
| **TEXAS** | | | | | | | | |
| 1 **Gohmert** | Y | Y | Y | Y | N | N | N | N |
| 2 **Poe** | Y | Y | Y | Y | N | Y | Y | N |
| 3 **Johnson, S.** | Y | Y | Y | Y | N | ? | ? | ? |
| 4 **Hall** | N | Y | N | Y | Y | N | N | N |
| 5 **Hensarling** | Y | Y | Y | Y | N | Y | N | N |
| 6 **Barton** | N | Y | Y | Y | N | N | N | N |
| 7 **Culberson** | Y | Y | N | Y | ? | N | N | N |
| 8 **Brady** | N | Y | Y | Y | N | Y | N | N |
| 9 Green, A. | Y | Y | N | Y | Y | N | Y | Y |
| 10 **McCaul** | Y | Y | N | Y | Y | N | Y | N |
| 11 **Conaway** | N | Y | N | Y | N | N | Y | N |
| 12 **Granger** | N | N | N | Y | N | N | N | N |
| 13 **Thornberry** | N | N | N | Y | N | Y | N | N |
| 14 **Paul** | Y | Y | Y | N | N | Y | Y | Y |
| 15 Hinojosa | Y | Y | N | Y | Y | N | Y | Y |
| 16 Reyes | Y | Y | N | Y | Y | N | Y | Y |
| 17 Edwards | N | Y | N | Y | Y | N | Y | Y |
| 18 Jackson-Lee | Y | - | N | Y | Y | N | Y | Y |
| 19 **Neugebauer** | Y | Y | Y | Y | N | Y | N | N |
| 20 Gonzalez | Y | Y | N | Y | Y | N | Y | Y |
| 21 **Smith** | Y | Y | N | Y | N | N | N | N |
| 22 **DeLay** | N | N | N | Y | N | N | N | N |
| 23 **Bonilla** | N | N | N | Y | N | N | N | N |
| 24 **Marchant** | Y | Y | Y | Y | N | N | N | N |
| 25 Doggett | Y | Y | N | Y | Y | N | Y | Y |
| 26 **Burgess** | Y | Y | Y | Y | N | Y | N | N |
| 27 Ortiz | + | + | - | + | Y | N | Y | Y |
| 28 Cuellar | Y | Y | N | Y | Y | N | Y | Y |
| 29 Green, G. | Y | Y | Y | Y | Y | N | Y | Y |
| 30 Johnson, E. | Y | N | N | Y | Y | N | Y | Y |
| 31 **Carter** | N | N | N | Y | N | N | N | N |
| 32 **Sessions** | N | Y | Y | Y | N | Y | N | N |
| **UTAH** | | | | | | | | |
| 1 **Bishop** | Y | Y | Y | Y | N | N | N | Y |
| 2 Matheson | Y | Y | N | Y | Y | N | Y | Y |
| 3 **Cannon** | N | Y | Y | Y | N | N | N | N |
| **VERMONT** | | | | | | | | |
| AL *Sanders* | Y | Y | N | Y | Y | N | Y | Y |
| **VIRGINIA** | | | | | | | | |
| 1 **Davis, J.** | Y | Y | Y | N | Y | N | N | N |
| 2 **Drake** | Y | Y | N | Y | Y | N | N | N |
| 3 Scott | Y | N | N | Y | Y | N | Y | Y |
| 4 **Forbes** | Y | Y | Y | Y | Y | N | N | N |
| 5 **Goode** | Y | Y | Y | N | Y | N | N | N |
| 6 **Goodlatte** | N | Y | Y | N | Y | N | N | N |
| 7 **Cantor** | N | N | N | Y | N | N | N | N |
| 8 Moran | Y | Y | N | Y | Y | N | Y | Y |
| 9 Boucher | N | N | N | Y | Y | N | Y | Y |
| 10 **Wolf** | Y | Y | N | Y | N | N | N | N |
| 11 **Davis, T.** | N | N | N | Y | N | N | N | N |
| **WASHINGTON** | | | | | | | | |
| 1 Inslee | Y | Y | N | Y | Y | N | Y | Y |
| 2 Larsen | N | N | N | Y | Y | N | Y | Y |
| 3 Baird | Y | Y | N | Y | Y | N | Y | Y |
| 4 **Hastings** | Y | Y | N | Y | Y | N | N | N |
| 5 **McMorris** | N | Y | Y | Y | Y | N | N | N |
| 6 Dicks | N | Y | N | Y | Y | N | Y | Y |
| 7 McDermott | Y | N | N | Y | Y | N | Y | Y |
| 8 **Reichert** | N | Y | N | Y | N | Y | Y | Y |
| 9 Smith | N | N | N | Y | Y | N | Y | Y |
| **WEST VIRGINIA** | | | | | | | | |
| 1 Mollohan | Y | Y | N | ? | Y | N | Y | Y |
| 2 **Capito** | Y | Y | N | Y | Y | N | Y | Y |
| 3 Rahall | Y | Y | Y | N | Y | N | Y | Y |
| **WISCONSIN** | | | | | | | | |
| 1 **Ryan** | N | Y | Y | Y | N | Y | N | N |
| 2 Baldwin | Y | N | N | Y | Y | N | Y | Y |
| 3 Kind | N | Y | N | Y | Y | N | Y | Y |
| 4 Moore | Y | Y | N | Y | Y | N | Y | Y |
| 5 **Sensenbrenner** | Y | Y | Y | N | N | Y | N | N |
| 6 **Petri** | Y | Y | Y | N | N | N | N | N |
| 7 Obey | Y | N | N | Y | Y | N | Y | Y |
| 8 **Green** | Y | Y | Y | Y | Y | Y | N | Y |
| **WYOMING** | | | | | | | | |
| AL **Cubin** | N | Y | Y | N | N | Y | N | N |

# IN THE HOUSE | By Vote Number

**340.** HR 3058. Fiscal 2006 Transportation-Treasury-Housing Appropriations/HOPE VI Housing. Davis, D-Ala., amendment to increase HOPE VI housing grants by $60 million, offset by a decrease in the General Services Administration Federal Buildings Fund. Adopted 248-173: R 59-166; D 188-7 (ND 143-5, SD 45-2); I 1-0. June 29, 2005.

**341.** HR 3058. Fiscal 2006 Transportation-Treasury-Housing Appropriations/Supreme Court Funding. King, R-Iowa, amendment that would reduce by $1.5 million salaries and expenses for the U.S. Supreme Court. Rejected 42-374: R 40-184; D 2-189 (ND 0-147, SD 2-42); I 0-1. June 29, 2005.

**342.** HR 3058. Fiscal 2006 Transportation-Treasury-Housing Appropriations/Federal Judiciary Funding. Herseth, D-S.D., amendment that would increase funding for the salaries and expenses of the Courts of Appeals, district courts and other judicial services by $6.9 million, offset by a reduction in the Federal Buildings Fund. Rejected 188-232: R 10-215; D 177-17 (ND 136-13, SD 41-4); I 1-0. June 29, 2005.

**343.** HR 3058. Fiscal 2006 Transportation-Treasury-Housing Appropriations/Drug Trafficking. Hooley, D-Ore., amendment that would add $9 million to the High Intensity Drug Trafficking Areas Program, offset by a cut in Office of Management and Budget salaries and expenses. Adopted 315-103: R 124-100; D 190-3 (ND 145-3, SD 45-0); I 1-0. June 29, 2005.

**344.** HR 3058. Fiscal 2006 Transportation-Treasury-Housing Appropriations/Youth Anti-Drug Campaign. Souder, R-Ind., amendment that would increase by $25 million funding for the National Youth Anti-Drug Media Campaign, offset by a decrease in the Federal Buildings Fund. Adopted 268-151: R 136-88; D 131-63 (ND 100-49, SD 31-14); I 1-0. June 29, 2005.

**345.** HR 3058. Fiscal 2006 Transportation-Treasury-Housing Appropriations/Cuban Travel Restrictions. Davis, D-Fla., amendment that would prohibit use of funds in the bill to implement, administer or enforce administration restrictions on travel to Cuba that allow individuals to visit immediate relatives there once every three years for a maximum of two consecutive weeks. Rejected 208-211: R 32-192; D 175-19 (ND 138-11, SD 37-8); I 1-0. A "nay" was a vote in support of the president's position. June 30, 2005.

**346.** HR 3058. Fiscal 2006 Transportation-Treasury-Housing Appropriations/Cuban Educational Travel. Lee, D-Calif., amendment that would prohibit use of funds in the bill to enforce regulations preventing travel to Cuba by academic institutions. Rejected 187-233: R 20-203; D 166-30 (ND 134-16, SD 32-14); I 1-0. A "nay" was a vote in support of the president's position. June 30, 2005.

**347.** HR 3058. Fiscal 2006 Transportation-Treasury-Housing Appropriations/Flight Service Stations. Sanders, I-Vt., amendment that would prohibit use of funds in the bill for the competitive sourcing of flight service stations. The amendment would nullify a $1.9 billion contract awarded to Lockheed Martin Corp. in February. Adopted 238-177: R 48-175; D 189-2 (ND 149-0, SD 40-2); I 1-0. A "nay" was a vote in support of the president's position. June 30, 2005.

ND Northern Democrats, SD Southern Democrats
Southern states: Ala., Ark., Fla., Ga., Ky., La., Miss., N.C., Okla., S.C., Tenn., Texas, Va.

| | 340 | 341 | 342 | 343 | 344 | 345 | 346 | 347 |
|---|---|---|---|---|---|---|---|---|
| **ALABAMA** | | | | | | | | |
| 1 Bonner | Y | N | N | N | Y | N | N | Y |
| 2 Everett | N | N | N | N | Y | ? | ? | ? |
| 3 Rogers | Y | N | N | N | Y | ? | ? | ? |
| 4 Aderholt | N | N | N | N | N | N | N | N |
| 5 Cramer | Y | N | N | Y | Y | ? | ? | ? |
| 6 Bachus | ? | ? | ? | ? | ? | ? | ? | ? |
| 7 Davis | Y | N | Y | Y | Y | Y | Y | Y |
| **ALASKA** | | | | | | | | |
| AL Young | N | ? | ? | ? | ? | N | N | N |
| **ARIZONA** | | | | | | | | |
| 1 Renzi | Y | Y | N | Y | Y | N | N | N |
| 2 Franks | N | Y | N | Y | Y | N | N | N |
| 3 Shadegg | N | N | Y | N | Y | N | N | N |
| 4 Pastor | Y | N | Y | N | Y | Y | Y | Y |
| 5 Hayworth | Y | Y | Y | N | Y | N | N | N |
| 6 Flake | N | N | N | N | Y | N | N | N |
| 7 Grijalva | Y | N | Y | Y | N | Y | Y | Y |
| 8 Kolbe | N | N | N | N | Y | Y | N | N |
| **ARKANSAS** | | | | | | | | |
| 1 Berry | Y | N | Y | Y | Y | Y | Y | Y |
| 2 Snyder | Y | N | Y | Y | Y | Y | Y | Y |
| 3 Boozman | N | N | N | N | Y | ? | N | Y |
| 4 Ross | ? | ? | ? | ? | ? | ? | ? | ? |
| **CALIFORNIA** | | | | | | | | |
| 1 Thompson | Y | N | Y | Y | Y | Y | Y | Y |
| 2 Herger | N | Y | N | Y | Y | N | N | Y |
| 3 Lungren | N | N | Y | N | N | N | N | N |
| 4 Doolittle | N | N | N | N | N | N | N | N |
| 5 Matsui, D. | Y | N | Y | Y | Y | Y | Y | Y |
| 6 Woolsey | Y | N | Y | Y | Y | Y | Y | Y |
| 7 Miller, George | Y | N | Y | N | Y | Y | Y | Y |
| 8 Pelosi | Y | N | Y | N | Y | Y | Y | Y |
| 9 Lee | Y | N | Y | N | Y | Y | Y | Y |
| 10 Tauscher | Y | N | Y | Y | Y | Y | Y | Y |
| 11 Pombo | N | Y | N | Y | N | N | N | N |
| 12 Lantos | Y | N | Y | Y | Y | Y | Y | Y |
| 13 Stark | ? | ? | ? | ? | ? | Y | Y | Y |
| 14 Eshoo | Y | N | Y | Y | Y | Y | Y | Y |
| 15 Honda | Y | N | Y | Y | Y | Y | Y | Y |
| 16 Lofgren | Y | N | Y | Y | Y | Y | Y | Y |
| 17 Farr | Y | N | Y | Y | Y | Y | Y | Y |
| 18 Cardoza | Y | N | Y | Y | N | Y | Y | Y |
| 19 Radanovich | N | N | N | Y | Y | N | N | N |
| 20 Costa | Y | N | Y | Y | Y | Y | Y | Y |
| 21 Nunes | N | N | N | Y | N | N | N | N |
| 22 Thomas | N | ? | ? | ? | ? | N | N | N |
| 23 Capps | Y | N | Y | Y | Y | Y | Y | Y |
| 24 Gallegly | N | N | Y | N | N | N | N | N |
| 25 McKeon | N | N | N | N | N | N | N | N |
| 26 Dreier | N | N | Y | N | N | N | N | N |
| 27 Sherman | Y | N | Y | N | Y | N | Y | Y |
| 28 Berman | Y | N | Y | ? | Y | Y | Y | Y |
| 29 Schiff | Y | N | Y | Y | Y | ? | ? | ? |
| 30 Waxman | Y | N | Y | Y | Y | Y | Y | Y |
| 31 Becerra | Y | N | Y | N | Y | Y | Y | Y |
| 32 Solis | Y | N | Y | N | Y | Y | Y | Y |
| 33 Watson | Y | N | Y | N | Y | Y | Y | Y |
| 34 Roybal-Allard | Y | N | Y | N | Y | Y | Y | Y |
| 35 Waters | Y | N | Y | Y | Y | Y | Y | Y |
| 36 Harman | Y | N | Y | Y | Y | Y | Y | Y |
| 37 Millender-McD. | Y | N | Y | N | Y | Y | Y | Y |
| 38 Napolitano | Y | N | Y | Y | Y | Y | Y | Y |
| 39 Sánchez, Linda | Y | N | Y | N | Y | Y | Y | Y |
| 40 Royce | N | N | N | N | N | N | N | N |
| 41 Lewis | N | N | N | N | N | N | N | N |
| 42 Miller, Gary | N | N | N | N | N | N | N | N |
| 43 Baca | Y | N | Y | Y | Y | Y | Y | Y |
| 44 Calvert | N | N | Y | N | N | N | N | N |
| 45 Bono | N | N | N | N | Y | N | N | N |
| 46 Rohrabacher | Y | Y | N | N | N | N | N | N |
| 47 Sanchez, Loretta | Y | N | Y | Y | Y | Y | Y | Y |
| 48 Cox | ? | N | N | N | N | Y | N | N |
| 49 Issa | N | N | N | Y | N | N | N | N |
| 50 Cunningham | N | N | N | N | N | N | N | N |
| 51 Filner | Y | N | Y | Y | Y | Y | Y | Y |
| 52 Hunter | N | N | N | N | N | N | N | N |
| 53 Davis | Y | N | Y | N | Y | Y | Y | Y |
| **COLORADO** | | | | | | | | |
| 1 DeGette | Y | N | Y | N | Y | Y | Y | Y |
| 2 Udall | Y | N | Y | Y | Y | Y | Y | Y |
| 3 Salazar | Y | N | Y | Y | N | N | N | N |
| 4 Musgrave | N | Y | N | Y | N | N | N | N |
| 5 Hefley | N | Y | N | Y | N | N | N | N |
| 6 Tancredo | N | N | Y | Y | N | N | N | N |
| 7 Beauprez | Y | N | N | N | Y | N | N | N |
| **CONNECTICUT** | | | | | | | | |
| 1 Larson | Y | N | Y | N | Y | Y | Y | Y |
| 2 Simmons | Y | Y | N | Y | N | N | N | Y |
| 3 DeLauro | Y | N | Y | N | Y | Y | Y | Y |
| 4 Shays | Y | N | Y | N | Y | Y | Y | Y |
| 5 Johnson | Y | N | N | N | N | Y | Y | Y |
| **DELAWARE** | | | | | | | | |
| AL Castle | Y | N | N | Y | N | Y | Y | N |
| **FLORIDA** | | | | | | | | |
| 1 Miller | N | Y | N | N | N | N | N | N |
| 2 Boyd | Y | N | Y | Y | Y | N | Y | N |
| 3 Brown | Y | N | Y | Y | Y | N | N | ? |
| 4 Crenshaw | N | N | N | N | N | N | N | N |
| 5 Brown-Waite | N | N | N | N | N | N | N | N |
| 6 Stearns | N | N | Y | N | Y | N | N | – |
| 7 Mica | N | N | Y | N | N | N | N | N |
| 8 Keller | N | N | N | Y | Y | N | N | N |
| 9 Bilirakis | N | N | Y | N | N | N | N | Y |
| 10 Young | N | N | N | N | N | N | N | N |
| 11 Davis | Y | N | Y | Y | Y | Y | Y | Y |
| 12 Putnam | N | N | Y | Y | N | N | N | N |
| 13 Harris | Y | Y | N | Y | Y | N | N | N |
| 14 Mack | N | Y | N | N | N | N | N | N |
| 15 Weldon | N | N | N | Y | N | N | N | N |
| 16 Foley | N | N | N | Y | N | N | N | Y |
| 17 Meek | Y | N | Y | Y | Y | Y | Y | Y |
| 18 Ros-Lehtinen | N | N | N | N | N | N | N | N |
| 19 Wexler | Y | N | Y | Y | Y | N | N | Y |
| 20 Wasserman-Schultz | Y | N | Y | Y | N | N | N | Y |
| 21 Diaz-Balart, L. | N | N | N | N | N | N | N | N |
| 22 Shaw | N | N | Y | N | N | N | N | N |
| 23 Hastings | Y | N | Y | N | Y | N | N | Y |
| 24 Feeney | N | N | Y | N | N | N | N | N |
| 25 Diaz-Balart, M. | N | N | N | N | N | N | N | N |
| **GEORGIA** | | | | | | | | |
| 1 Kingston | N | N | N | N | ? | ? | ? | ? |
| 2 Bishop | Y | ? | ? | ? | ? | ? | ? | ? |
| 3 Marshall | Y | N | Y | Y | Y | Y | Y | Y |
| 4 McKinney | Y | N | Y | Y | Y | Y | Y | Y |
| 5 Lewis | ? | ? | ? | ? | ? | Y | Y | Y |
| 6 Price | N | N | N | Y | N | N | N | N |
| 7 Linder | N | N | Y | N | N | N | N | N |
| 8 Westmoreland | Y | ? | ? | ? | ? | ? | ? | ? |
| 9 Norwood | N | N | N | N | N | N | N | N |
| 10 Deal | N | N | N | N | N | N | N | N |
| 11 Gingrey | N | Y | N | Y | N | N | N | N |
| 12 Barrow | ? | ? | ? | ? | ? | N | N | ? |
| 13 Scott | ? | ? | ? | ? | ? | ? | ? | ? |
| **HAWAII** | | | | | | | | |
| 1 Abercrombie | Y | N | Y | Y | Y | Y | Y | Y |
| 2 Case | Y | N | Y | Y | N | N | N | Y |
| **IDAHO** | | | | | | | | |
| 1 Otter | N | N | N | Y | Y | Y | Y | N |
| 2 Simpson | N | N | Y | N | N | N | N | N |
| **ILLINOIS** | | | | | | | | |
| 1 Rush | Y | N | Y | N | Y | Y | Y | Y |
| 2 Jackson | Y | N | Y | N | Y | Y | Y | Y |
| 3 Lipinski | Y | N | Y | Y | Y | Y | Y | Y |
| 4 Gutierrez | Y | N | Y | N | Y | Y | Y | Y |
| 5 Emanuel | Y | N | Y | Y | Y | Y | Y | Y |
| 6 Hyde | N | N | N | N | N | N | N | N |
| 7 Davis | Y | N | Y | Y | Y | Y | Y | Y |
| 8 Bean | Y | N | Y | Y | Y | Y | Y | Y |
| 9 Schakowsky | Y | N | Y | Y | Y | Y | Y | Y |
| 10 Kirk | N | N | N | Y | N | N | N | Y |
| 11 Weller | N | N | Y | N | N | N | N | N |
| 12 Costello | Y | N | Y | Y | Y | Y | Y | Y |

## KEY — Republicans — Democrats — Independents

| | | |
|---|---|---|
| **Y** Voted for (yea) | **X** Paired against | **C** Voted "present" to avoid possible conflict of interest |
| **#** Paired for | **–** Announced against | **?** Did not vote or otherwise make a position known |
| **+** Announced for | **P** Voted "present" | |
| **N** Voted against (nay) | | |

| | 340 | 341 | 342 | 343 | 344 | 345 | 346 | 347 |
|---|---|---|---|---|---|---|---|---|
| 13 **Biggert** | N | N | Y | Y | Y | Y | Y | N |
| 14 **Hastert** | | | | | | | | |
| 15 **Johnson** | N | Y | N | Y | N | Y | Y | Y |
| 16 **Manzullo** | N | N | N | Y | Y | N | N | N |
| 17 Evans | Y | N | Y | Y | N | Y | Y | Y |
| 18 **LaHood** | N | N | N | Y | Y | Y | N | Y |
| 19 **Shimkus** | N | N | N | Y | N | N | N | N |
| INDIANA | | | | | | | | |
| 1 Visclosky | Y | N | Y | Y | N | Y | Y | Y |
| 2 **Chocola** | Y | N | N | N | Y | N | N | N |
| 3 **Souder** | N | N | N | Y | Y | N | N | N |
| 4 **Buyer** | N | N | N | ? | Y | N | N | N |
| 5 **Burton** | Y | N | N | N | Y | N | N | N |
| 6 **Pence** | N | N | N | N | Y | N | N | N |
| 7 Carson | Y | N | N | Y | N | Y | Y | Y |
| 8 **Hostettler** | N | N | N | N | Y | Y | Y | Y |
| 9 **Sodrel** | Y | N | N | N | Y | N | N | Y |
| IOWA | | | | | | | | |
| 1 **Nussle** | N | N | N | Y | Y | N | N | Y |
| 2 **Leach** | Y | N | N | Y | N | Y | N | Y |
| 3 Boswell | Y | N | Y | Y | Y | Y | Y | Y |
| 4 **Latham** | N | N | N | Y | Y | N | N | Y |
| 5 **King** | N | Y | N | Y | Y | N | N | N |
| KANSAS | | | | | | | | |
| 1 **Moran** | Y | N | N | Y | Y | Y | Y | N |
| 2 **Ryun** | N | N | N | N | N | N | N | N |
| 3 Moore | Y | N | Y | Y | Y | Y | Y | Y |
| 4 **Tiahrt** | N | N | N | N | N | N | N | N |
| KENTUCKY | | | | | | | | |
| 1 **Whitfield** | N | N | N | Y | N | N | N | N |
| 2 **Lewis** | Y | Y | N | Y | Y | N | N | N |
| 3 **Northup** | N | N | N | N | N | N | N | N |
| 4 **Davis** | N | N | N | Y | Y | N | N | Y |
| 5 **Rogers** | N | N | N | N | Y | N | N | N |
| 6 Chandler | Y | N | Y | Y | Y | N | N | Y |
| LOUISIANA | | | | | | | | |
| 1 **Jindal** | Y | N | N | Y | N | N | N | N |
| 2 Jefferson | Y | N | Y | Y | Y | Y | Y | Y |
| 3 Melancon | Y | N | Y | Y | Y | N | N | Y |
| 4 **McCrery** | N | N | N | N | N | N | N | N |
| 5 **Alexander** | N | N | N | Y | Y | N | N | N |
| 6 **Baker** | N | N | N | N | Y | N | N | N |
| 7 **Boustany** | Y | N | N | Y | Y | N | N | N |
| MAINE | | | | | | | | |
| 1 Allen | Y | N | Y | Y | N | Y | Y | Y |
| 2 Michaud | N | N | N | Y | N | Y | Y | Y |
| MARYLAND | | | | | | | | |
| 1 **Gilchrest** | Y | N | N | Y | Y | Y | Y | N |
| 2 Ruppersberger | Y | N | Y | Y | Y | Y | Y | Y |
| 3 Cardin | Y | N | Y | Y | Y | Y | Y | Y |
| 4 Wynn | Y | N | Y | Y | N | Y | Y | Y |
| 5 Hoyer | Y | N | Y | Y | N | Y | Y | Y |
| 6 **Bartlett** | Y | N | N | N | Y | N | N | N |
| 7 Cummings | Y | N | Y | Y | Y | Y | Y | Y |
| 8 Van Hollen | Y | N | Y | Y | Y | Y | Y | Y |
| MASSACHUSETTS | | | | | | | | |
| 1 Olver | Y | N | Y | Y | N | Y | Y | Y |
| 2 Neal | ? | ? | ? | ? | ? | Y | Y | Y |
| 3 McGovern | Y | N | Y | Y | N | Y | Y | Y |
| 4 Frank | Y | N | N | N | N | Y | Y | Y |
| 5 Meehan | Y | N | Y | Y | Y | Y | Y | Y |
| 6 Tierney | Y | N | Y | Y | N | Y | Y | Y |
| 7 Markey | Y | N | Y | Y | N | Y | Y | Y |
| 8 Capuano | Y | N | Y | Y | N | Y | Y | Y |
| 9 Lynch | Y | N | Y | Y | Y | Y | Y | Y |
| 10 Delahunt | Y | N | Y | Y | Y | Y | Y | Y |
| MICHIGAN | | | | | | | | |
| 1 Stupak | Y | N | Y | Y | Y | Y | Y | Y |
| 2 **Hoekstra** | N | N | N | N | N | N | N | N |
| 3 **Ehlers** | N | N | N | N | Y | Y | N | N |
| 4 **Camp** | N | N | N | Y | Y | N | N | N |
| 5 Kildee | Y | N | Y | Y | N | Y | Y | Y |
| 6 **Upton** | Y | N | N | Y | Y | N | N | N |
| 7 **Schwarz** | N | N | N | Y | Y | N | N | Y |
| 8 **Rogers** | N | N | N | N | Y | N | N | Y |
| 9 **Knollenberg** | N | N | N | N | N | N | N | N |
| 10 **Miller** | N | N | N | N | Y | N | N | N |
| 11 **McCotter** | N | N | N | Y | Y | N | N | Y |
| 12 Levin | Y | N | Y | Y | Y | Y | Y | Y |
| 13 Kilpatrick | Y | N | N | Y | N | Y | Y | Y |
| 14 Conyers | Y | N | Y | Y | Y | Y | Y | Y |
| 15 Dingell | Y | N | Y | Y | Y | Y | Y | Y |

| | 340 | 341 | 342 | 343 | 344 | 345 | 346 | 347 |
|---|---|---|---|---|---|---|---|---|
| MINNESOTA | | | | | | | | |
| 1 **Gutknecht** | Y | Y | N | N | Y | N | N | N |
| 2 **Kline** | Y | N | N | Y | Y | N | N | N |
| 3 **Ramstad** | Y | N | N | Y | Y | Y | Y | N |
| 4 McCollum | Y | N | Y | Y | Y | Y | Y | Y |
| 5 Sabo | Y | N | Y | Y | N | Y | Y | Y |
| 6 **Kennedy** | Y | N | N | Y | Y | N | N | N |
| 7 Peterson | Y | N | Y | Y | Y | Y | Y | Y |
| 8 Oberstar | N | N | Y | Y | Y | Y | Y | Y |
| MISSISSIPPI | | | | | | | | |
| 1 **Wicker** | Y | N | N | N | N | N | N | N |
| 2 Thompson | Y | N | Y | Y | N | Y | Y | Y |
| 3 **Pickering** | Y | N | N | Y | Y | N | N | N |
| 4 Taylor | Y | Y | Y | Y | Y | Y | Y | Y |
| MISSOURI | | | | | | | | |
| 1 Clay | ? | N | Y | Y | N | Y | Y | Y |
| 2 **Akin** | – | Y | N | N | Y | N | N | N |
| 3 Carnahan | Y | N | Y | Y | Y | Y | N | Y |
| 4 Skelton | Y | N | Y | Y | Y | N | N | Y |
| 5 Cleaver | Y | N | Y | Y | N | Y | Y | Y |
| 6 **Graves** | Y | N | N | Y | Y | Y | Y | N |
| 7 **Blunt** | N | N | N | N | N | N | N | N |
| 8 **Emerson** | N | N | N | Y | N | Y | Y | Y |
| 9 **Hulshof** | Y | N | N | Y | Y | N | N | N |
| MONTANA | | | | | | | | |
| AL **Rehberg** | N | N | N | N | N | N | N | Y |
| NEBRASKA | | | | | | | | |
| 1 **Fortenberry** | N | N | N | Y | Y | N | N | Y |
| 2 **Terry** | Y | N | N | Y | Y | N | N | N |
| 3 **Osborne** | N | N | N | Y | Y | Y | Y | Y |
| NEVADA | | | | | | | | |
| 1 Berkley | Y | N | Y | Y | Y | N | N | Y |
| 2 **Gibbons** | Y | Y | N | Y | Y | N | N | Y |
| 3 **Porter** | N | N | Y | Y | Y | N | N | Y |
| NEW HAMPSHIRE | | | | | | | | |
| 1 **Bradley** | N | N | N | Y | N | N | N | N |
| 2 **Bass** | N | N | N | Y | Y | Y | Y | Y |
| NEW JERSEY | | | | | | | | |
| 1 Andrews | Y | N | Y | Y | Y | Y | N | Y |
| 2 **LoBiondo** | Y | N | N | Y | Y | N | N | Y |
| 3 **Saxton** | N | N | N | N | N | N | N | N |
| 4 **Smith** | Y | N | N | Y | Y | N | N | Y |
| 5 **Garrett** | N | N | N | N | N | Y | N | N |
| 6 Pallone | Y | N | Y | Y | Y | N | N | Y |
| 7 **Ferguson** | N | N | N | N | N | N | N | N |
| 8 Pascrell | Y | N | Y | Y | N | Y | N | Y |
| 9 Rothman | Y | N | Y | Y | Y | N | N | Y |
| 10 Payne | Y | N | Y | Y | Y | Y | Y | Y |
| 11 **Frelinghuysen** | N | N | N | N | N | N | N | N |
| 12 Holt | Y | N | Y | Y | Y | Y | Y | Y |
| 13 Menendez | Y | N | Y | Y | Y | N | N | Y |
| NEW MEXICO | | | | | | | | |
| 1 **Wilson** | Y | N | N | Y | Y | N | N | N |
| 2 **Pearce** | N | Y | N | N | N | N | N | N |
| 3 Udall | Y | N | Y | Y | Y | Y | Y | Y |
| NEW YORK | | | | | | | | |
| 1 Bishop | Y | N | Y | Y | Y | Y | Y | Y |
| 2 Israel | Y | N | Y | Y | Y | Y | Y | Y |
| 3 **King** | N | N | N | Y | Y | N | N | Y |
| 4 McCarthy | Y | N | Y | Y | Y | Y | Y | Y |
| 5 Ackerman | Y | N | Y | Y | Y | N | N | Y |
| 6 Meeks | Y | N | Y | Y | Y | Y | Y | Y |
| 7 Crowley | Y | N | Y | Y | Y | Y | Y | Y |
| 8 Nadler | Y | N | Y | Y | Y | Y | Y | Y |
| 9 Weiner | Y | N | Y | Y | Y | Y | Y | Y |
| 10 Towns | Y | N | Y | Y | N | Y | Y | Y |
| 11 Owens | Y | N | Y | Y | Y | Y | Y | Y |
| 12 Velázquez | Y | N | Y | Y | Y | Y | Y | Y |
| 13 **Fossella** | N | N | N | Y | Y | N | N | Y |
| 14 Maloney | Y | N | Y | Y | N | Y | Y | Y |
| 15 Rangel | Y | ? | N | Y | Y | Y | Y | Y |
| 16 Serrano | Y | N | Y | Y | Y | Y | Y | Y |
| 17 Engel | Y | N | Y | Y | Y | N | N | Y |
| 18 Lowey | Y | N | Y | Y | N | Y | Y | Y |
| 19 **Kelly** | Y | Y | Y | Y | Y | N | N | Y |
| 20 **Sweeney** | N | N | N | N | Y | N | N | Y |
| 21 McNulty | Y | N | Y | Y | Y | Y | Y | Y |
| 22 Hinchey | Y | N | Y | Y | Y | Y | Y | Y |
| 23 **McHugh** | N | N | N | Y | N | N | N | Y |
| 24 **Boehlert** | Y | N | N | Y | N | Y | Y | Y |
| 25 **Walsh** | N | N | N | N | N | N | N | Y |
| 26 **Reynolds** | N | N | N | N | N | N | N | Y |
| 27 Higgins | Y | ? | Y | Y | Y | Y | N | Y |
| 28 Slaughter | Y | N | Y | Y | Y | Y | Y | Y |
| 29 **Kuhl** | N | N | N | Y | Y | N | N | N |

| | 340 | 341 | 342 | 343 | 344 | 345 | 346 | 347 |
|---|---|---|---|---|---|---|---|---|
| NORTH CAROLINA | | | | | | | | |
| 1 Butterfield | Y | N | Y | Y | Y | Y | Y | Y |
| 2 Etheridge | Y | N | Y | Y | Y | Y | Y | Y |
| 3 **Jones** | Y | N | N | Y | Y | N | N | N |
| 4 Price | Y | N | Y | Y | Y | Y | Y | Y |
| 5 **Foxx** | N | Y | N | N | Y | N | N | N |
| 6 **Coble** | Y | N | Y | Y | Y | N | N | N |
| 7 McIntyre | Y | Y | Y | Y | Y | N | N | Y |
| 8 **Hayes** | N | N | N | N | N | N | N | N |
| 9 **Myrick** | N | Y | N | N | Y | N | N | N |
| 10 **McHenry** | N | Y | N | Y | Y | N | N | N |
| 11 **Taylor** | N | N | N | Y | N | N | N | N |
| 12 Watt | Y | ? | Y | Y | N | Y | Y | Y |
| 13 Miller | Y | N | Y | Y | Y | N | N | Y |
| NORTH DAKOTA | | | | | | | | |
| AL Pomeroy | Y | N | Y | Y | Y | Y | Y | Y |
| OHIO | | | | | | | | |
| 1 **Chabot** | N | Y | N | Y | Y | N | N | N |
| 2 Vacant | | | | | | | | |
| 3 **Turner** | Y | N | N | N | N | N | N | Y |
| 4 **Oxley** | N | N | N | Y | N | N | N | N |
| 5 **Gillmor** | N | N | N | Y | Y | N | N | N |
| 6 Strickland | Y | N | Y | Y | Y | Y | Y | Y |
| 7 **Hobson** | N | N | N | N | N | N | N | N |
| 8 **Boehner** | N | N | N | Y | Y | N | N | N |
| 9 Kaptur | Y | N | N | Y | Y | Y | Y | ? |
| 10 Kucinich | Y | N | Y | Y | N | Y | Y | Y |
| 11 Jones | Y | N | Y | Y | N | Y | Y | Y |
| 12 **Tiberi** | Y | N | N | Y | Y | Y | Y | Y |
| 13 Brown | Y | N | Y | Y | N | Y | Y | Y |
| 14 **LaTourette** | N | N | N | Y | N | N | N | Y |
| 15 **Pryce** | N | N | N | N | N | N | N | N |
| 16 **Regula** | N | N | N | N | N | N | N | Y |
| 17 Ryan | Y | N | Y | Y | N | Y | Y | Y |
| 18 **Ney** | Y | ? | N | Y | Y | Y | N | N |
| OKLAHOMA | | | | | | | | |
| 1 **Sullivan** | N | N | N | N | N | N | N | N |
| 2 Boren | Y | N | Y | Y | Y | Y | N | Y |
| 3 **Lucas** | N | N | N | Y | Y | N | N | N |
| 4 **Cole** | N | N | N | N | N | N | N | N |
| 5 **Istook** | N | N | N | N | ? | N | N | N |
| OREGON | | | | | | | | |
| 1 Wu | Y | N | Y | Y | Y | N | N | Y |
| 2 **Walden** | N | N | N | Y | Y | N | N | N |
| 3 Blumenauer | Y | N | Y | Y | N | Y | Y | Y |
| 4 DeFazio | N | N | N | Y | Y | Y | Y | Y |
| 5 Hooley | Y | N | Y | Y | Y | Y | Y | Y |
| PENNSYLVANIA | | | | | | | | |
| 1 Brady | Y | N | Y | Y | Y | Y | Y | Y |
| 2 Fattah | Y | N | Y | Y | Y | Y | Y | Y |
| 3 **English** | N | N | N | N | Y | N | N | Y |
| 4 **Hart** | N | Y | N | N | Y | N | N | N |
| 5 **Peterson** | ? | ? | ? | ? | ? | ? | ? | ? |
| 6 **Gerlach** | Y | N | N | Y | Y | N | N | Y |
| 7 **Weldon** | Y | N | N | Y | Y | Y | N | N |
| 8 **Fitzpatrick** | Y | N | Y | Y | Y | N | N | Y |
| 9 **Shuster** | N | Y | N | Y | N | N | N | Y |
| 10 **Sherwood** | N | N | N | Y | N | N | N | N |
| 11 Kanjorski | Y | N | Y | Y | N | Y | Y | Y |
| 12 Murtha | Y | N | Y | Y | Y | Y | Y | Y |
| 13 Schwartz | Y | N | Y | Y | Y | Y | Y | Y |
| 14 Doyle | Y | N | Y | Y | Y | Y | Y | Y |
| 15 **Dent** | Y | N | N | Y | Y | N | N | N |
| 16 **Pitts** | N | Y | N | N | Y | N | N | N |
| 17 Holden | N | N | Y | Y | Y | Y | Y | Y |
| 18 **Murphy** | Y | N | N | Y | Y | N | N | Y |
| 19 **Platts** | Y | N | N | N | Y | N | N | N |
| RHODE ISLAND | | | | | | | | |
| 1 Kennedy | Y | N | Y | Y | Y | Y | N | Y |
| 2 Langevin | Y | N | Y | Y | Y | Y | Y | Y |
| SOUTH CAROLINA | | | | | | | | |
| 1 **Brown** | Y | N | N | N | N | N | N | N |
| 2 **Wilson** | Y | Y | N | N | Y | N | N | N |
| 3 **Barrett** | Y | N | N | N | Y | N | N | N |
| 4 **Inglis** | N | N | N | N | N | N | N | N |
| 5 Spratt | Y | N | Y | Y | Y | Y | Y | Y |
| 6 Clyburn | Y | N | Y | Y | N | Y | Y | Y |
| SOUTH DAKOTA | | | | | | | | |
| AL Herseth | Y | N | Y | Y | Y | Y | Y | Y |
| TENNESSEE | | | | | | | | |
| 1 **Jenkins** | Y | N | N | Y | Y | N | N | N |
| 2 **Duncan** | Y | Y | N | Y | Y | Y | N | N |

| | 340 | 341 | 342 | 343 | 344 | 345 | 346 | 347 |
|---|---|---|---|---|---|---|---|---|
| 3 **Wamp** | N | N | N | Y | Y | N | N | N |
| 4 Davis | Y | N | N | Y | Y | Y | Y | Y |
| 5 Cooper | Y | ? | ? | ? | ? | ? | ? | ? |
| 6 Gordon | Y | N | Y | Y | Y | Y | Y | Y |
| 7 **Blackburn** | N | Y | N | Y | Y | N | N | N |
| 8 Tanner | Y | N | Y | Y | Y | Y | Y | Y |
| 9 Ford | Y | N | Y | Y | Y | Y | Y | Y |
| TEXAS | | | | | | | | |
| 1 **Gohmert** | Y | Y | Y | Y | Y | N | N | N |
| 2 **Poe** | N | Y | N | Y | Y | N | N | N |
| 3 **Johnson, S.** | ? | N | N | N | Y | N | N | N |
| 4 **Hall** | N | N | N | N | Y | N | N | N |
| 5 **Hensarling** | N | N | N | N | N | N | N | N |
| 6 **Barton** | N | N | N | Y | Y | N | N | N |
| 7 **Culberson** | N | N | N | N | N | N | N | N |
| 8 **Brady** | N | N | N | N | N | N | N | N |
| 9 Green, A. | Y | N | Y | Y | Y | Y | Y | Y |
| 10 **McCaul** | N | N | N | N | Y | N | N | N |
| 11 **Conaway** | N | N | N | Y | Y | N | N | Y |
| 12 **Granger** | N | N | N | N | N | N | N | N |
| 13 **Thornberry** | N | N | N | N | Y | N | N | N |
| 14 **Paul** | N | Y | N | N | N | Y | Y | N |
| 15 Hinojosa | Y | N | Y | Y | N | Y | Y | Y |
| 16 Reyes | Y | N | Y | Y | N | ? | Y | Y |
| 17 Edwards | Y | N | Y | Y | Y | Y | Y | Y |
| 18 Jackson-Lee | Y | N | Y | Y | N | Y | Y | Y |
| 19 **Neugebauer** | N | Y | N | N | Y | N | N | N |
| 20 Gonzalez | N | N | N | Y | N | Y | Y | Y |
| 21 **Smith** | N | N | Y | N | N | N | N | N |
| 22 **DeLay** | N | N | N | N | N | N | N | N |
| 23 **Bonilla** | N | N | N | N | N | N | N | N |
| 24 **Marchant** | N | N | N | N | Y | N | N | N |
| 25 Doggett | Y | N | Y | Y | N | Y | Y | Y |
| 26 **Burgess** | N | N | N | Y | N | N | N | N |
| 27 Ortiz | Y | N | Y | Y | Y | N | N | ? |
| 28 Cuellar | Y | N | Y | Y | Y | Y | N | Y |
| 29 Green, G. | N | N | Y | Y | N | Y | N | N |
| 30 Johnson, E. | Y | N | Y | Y | N | Y | Y | ? |
| 31 **Carter** | N | N | N | N | N | N | N | N |
| 32 **Sessions** | N | N | N | N | Y | N | N | N |
| UTAH | | | | | | | | |
| 1 **Bishop** | N | Y | N | Y | Y | N | N | N |
| 2 Matheson | Y | N | Y | Y | Y | Y | Y | Y |
| 3 **Cannon** | N | N | N | Y | Y | N | N | N |
| VERMONT | | | | | | | | |
| AL *Sanders* | Y | N | Y | Y | Y | Y | Y | Y |
| VIRGINIA | | | | | | | | |
| 1 **Davis, J.** | N | Y | N | Y | Y | N | N | N |
| 2 **Drake** | N | Y | N | Y | N | N | N | N |
| 3 Scott | Y | N | N | Y | N | Y | Y | Y |
| 4 **Forbes** | N | N | N | Y | Y | N | N | N |
| 5 **Goode** | N | Y | N | Y | N | N | N | N |
| 6 **Goodlatte** | N | N | Y | Y | Y | N | N | N |
| 7 **Cantor** | N | N | N | N | N | N | N | N |
| 8 Moran | Y | N | Y | Y | N | Y | Y | N |
| 9 Boucher | Y | N | Y | Y | N | Y | Y | Y |
| 10 **Wolf** | N | N | N | N | N | N | N | N |
| 11 **Davis, T.** | N | N | N | Y | Y | N | N | N |
| WASHINGTON | | | | | | | | |
| 1 Inslee | Y | N | Y | Y | Y | Y | Y | Y |
| 2 Larsen | Y | N | Y | Y | Y | Y | Y | Y |
| 3 Baird | N | N | N | Y | Y | Y | Y | Y |
| 4 **Hastings** | N | N | N | N | N | N | N | N |
| 5 **McMorris** | N | N | N | Y | Y | N | N | N |
| 6 Dicks | Y | N | Y | Y | Y | Y | Y | Y |
| 7 McDermott | Y | N | Y | Y | Y | Y | Y | Y |
| 8 **Reichert** | Y | N | N | Y | Y | N | N | N |
| 9 Smith | Y | N | Y | Y | Y | Y | Y | Y |
| WEST VIRGINIA | | | | | | | | |
| 1 Mollohan | Y | N | N | N | N | Y | Y | Y |
| 2 **Capito** | Y | N | N | Y | Y | N | N | Y |
| 3 Rahall | Y | N | Y | Y | Y | Y | Y | Y |
| WISCONSIN | | | | | | | | |
| 1 **Ryan** | N | N | N | N | Y | Y | Y | N |
| 2 Baldwin | Y | N | Y | Y | Y | Y | Y | Y |
| 3 Kind | Y | N | Y | Y | Y | Y | Y | Y |
| 4 Moore | Y | N | Y | N | Y | – | Y | Y |
| 5 **Sensenbrenner** | N | N | N | Y | Y | N | N | N |
| 6 **Petri** | Y | N | N | Y | N | N | N | N |
| 7 Obey | Y | N | Y | Y | N | Y | Y | Y |
| 8 **Green** | N | N | N | Y | Y | N | N | Y |
| WYOMING | | | | | | | | |
| AL **Cubin** | Y | Y | N | Y | Y | Y | N | Y |

# IN THE HOUSE | By Vote Number

**348.** HR 3058. Fiscal 2006 Transportation-Treasury-Housing Appropriations/Cuba Economic Embargo. Rangel, D-N.Y., amendment that would prohibit the use of funds to implement, administer or enforce the economic embargo of Cuba. Rejected 169-250: R 20-203; D 148-47 (ND 122-27, SD 26-20); I 1-0. A "nay" was a vote in support of the president's position. June 30, 2005.

**349.** HR 3058. Fiscal 2006 Transportation-Treasury-Housing Appropriations/D.C. Firearm Laws. Souder, R-Ind., amendment that would prohibit the use of funds in the bill to enforce District of Columbia laws requiring that a registered firearm be kept unloaded and disassembled, or with the trigger locked, unless it is kept at a place of business or used for lawful recreation. Adopted 259-161: R 209-15; D 50-145 (ND 27-122, SD 23-23); I 0-1. June 30, 2005.

**350.** HR 3058. Fiscal 2006 Transportation-Treasury-Housing Appropriations/Eminent Domain. Garrett, R-N.J., amendment that would prohibit the use of funds in the bill to improve or construct infrastructure support on private property obtained through the power of eminent domain for private development. Adopted 231-189: R 192-31; D 39-157 (ND 23-127, SD 16-30); I 0-1. June 30, 2005.

**351.** HR 3058. Fiscal 2006 Transportation-Treasury-Housing Appropriations/Offshore Contracts. DeLauro, D-Conn., amendment that would prohibit the use of funds in the bill to carry out contracts with a U.S. company that is incorporated or chartered in Bermuda, Barbados, the Cayman Islands, Antigua or Panama to avoid U.S. taxes. Rejected 190-231: R 20-203; D 169-28 (ND 137-13, SD 32-15); I 1-0. June 30, 2005.

**352.** HR 3058. Fiscal 2006 Transportation-Treasury-Housing Appropriations/Discretionary Spending Cut. Hefley, R-Colo., amendment that would reduce discretionary spending in the bill by 1 percent. Rejected 88-338: R 83-144; D 5-193 (ND 2-146, SD 3-47); I 0-1. June 30, 2005.

**353.** HR 3058. Fiscal 2006 Transportation-Treasury-Housing Appropriations/Sale of Unocal Corp. Kilpatrick, D-Mich., amendment that would prohibit the use of funds by the Treasury Department to make a favorable recommendation of the sale of Unocal Corporation to the China National Offshore Oil Corporation. Adopted 333-92: R 155-71; D 177-21 (ND 132-16, SD 45-5); I 1-0. June 30, 2005.

**354.** HR 3058. Fiscal 2006 Transportation-Treasury-Housing Appropriations/Congressional Testimony. Obey, D-Wis., amendment that would prohibit the use of funds in the bill to contravene an Office of Management and Budget regulation that requires administration officials to give frank and complete answers to all questions when testifying before congressional committees or communicating with members of Congress. Rejected 208-215: R 9-215; D 198-0 (ND 148-0, SD 50-0); I 1-0. June 30, 2005.

**355.** HR 3058. Fiscal 2006 Transportation-Treasury-Housing Appropriations/Prescription Drug Costs. Brown, D-Ohio, amendment that would prohibit the use of funds in the bill by the Council of Economic Advisers to produce an Economic Report of the President estimating that the average cost of developing and introducing a new prescription drug to the market would be $800 million or more. Rejected 141-284: R 15-212; D 125-72 (ND 100-47, SD 25-25); I 1-0. June 30, 2005.

ND Northern Democrats, SD Southern Democrats
Southern states: Ala., Ark., Fla., Ga., Ky., La., Miss., N.C., Okla., S.C., Tenn., Texas, Va.

| | 348 | 349 | 350 | 351 | 352 | 353 | 354 | 355 |
|---|---|---|---|---|---|---|---|---|
| **ALABAMA** | | | | | | | | |
| 1 Bonner | N | Y | Y | N | N | Y | N | N |
| 2 Everett | ? | ? | ? | ? | ? | ? | ? | ? |
| 3 Rogers | ? | ? | ? | ? | N | Y | N | N |
| 4 Aderholt | N | Y | Y | N | N | Y | N | N |
| 5 Cramer | ? | ? | ? | ? | N | Y | Y | N |
| 6 Bachus | ? | ? | ? | ? | Y | N | N | N |
| 7 Davis | N | Y | N | Y | N | Y | Y | N |
| **ALASKA** | | | | | | | | |
| AL Young | N | Y | Y | N | N | N | N | N |
| **ARIZONA** | | | | | | | | |
| 1 Renzi | N | Y | Y | N | Y | Y | N | N |
| 2 Franks | N | Y | Y | N | Y | N | N | N |
| 3 Shadegg | ? | Y | Y | N | Y | N | N | N |
| 4 Pastor | Y | N | Y | N | Y | Y | Y | Y |
| 5 Hayworth | N | Y | Y | N | Y | Y | N | N |
| 6 Flake | Y | Y | Y | N | Y | N | N | N |
| 7 Grijalva | Y | N | N | Y | N | Y | Y | Y |
| 8 Kolbe | Y | Y | N | N | N | N | N | N |
| **ARKANSAS** | | | | | | | | |
| 1 Berry | Y | Y | Y | Y | N | Y | Y | Y |
| 2 Snyder | Y | N | N | N | N | Y | N | Y |
| 3 Boozman | Y | Y | Y | N | N | Y | N | N |
| 4 Ross | ? | ? | ? | ? | ? | ? | ? | ? |
| **CALIFORNIA** | | | | | | | | |
| 1 Thompson | Y | N | N | N | N | Y | Y | N |
| 2 Herger | Y | Y | Y | N | Y | Y | N | N |
| 3 Lungren | N | Y | Y | N | Y | N | N | N |
| 4 Doolittle | N | Y | Y | N | Y | N | N | N |
| 5 Matsui, D. | Y | N | N | N | N | Y | Y | Y |
| 6 Woolsey | Y | N | Y | N | N | Y | Y | Y |
| 7 Miller, George | Y | N | N | Y | N | Y | Y | Y |
| 8 Pelosi | Y | N | N | Y | N | Y | Y | Y |
| 9 Lee | Y | N | N | Y | N | Y | Y | Y |
| 10 Tauscher | Y | N | Y | N | Y | Y | Y | Y |
| 11 Pombo | N | Y | Y | N | N | Y | N | N |
| 12 Lantos | N | N | N | N | N | Y | Y | Y |
| 13 Stark | Y | N | N | N | N | Y | Y | Y |
| 14 Eshoo | Y | N | N | N | Y | Y | Y | N |
| 15 Honda | Y | N | Y | N | N | Y | Y | N |
| 16 Lofgren | Y | N | N | N | N | Y | Y | N |
| 17 Farr | Y | N | Y | N | N | Y | Y | Y |
| 18 Cardoza | N | Y | N | N | N | Y | Y | Y |
| 19 Radanovich | N | Y | Y | Y | Y | Y | N | N |
| 20 Costa | N | Y | N | Y | N | Y | Y | N |
| 21 Nunes | N | Y | Y | N | Y | Y | N | N |
| 22 Thomas | N | Y | N | N | N | N | N | N |
| 23 Capps | Y | N | N | N | Y | Y | Y | Y |
| 24 Gallegly | N | Y | N | N | N | Y | N | N |
| 25 McKeon | N | Y | Y | N | Y | Y | N | N |
| 26 Dreier | N | Y | Y | N | N | N | N | N |
| 27 Sherman | N | N | N | Y | N | Y | Y | N |
| 28 Berman | N | N | N | N | N | Y | Y | Y |
| 29 Schiff | ? | ? | ? | ? | ? | ? | ? | ? |
| 30 Waxman | Y | N | N | N | N | Y | Y | Y |
| 31 Becerra | Y | N | N | Y | N | Y | Y | Y |
| 32 Solis | Y | N | N | N | N | Y | Y | Y |
| 33 Watson | Y | N | N | Y | N | Y | Y | Y |
| 34 Roybal-Allard | Y | N | N | Y | N | Y | Y | Y |
| 35 Waters | Y | N | Y | N | ? | ? | ? | ? |
| 36 Harman | Y | N | N | Y | ? | ? | ? | ? |
| 37 Millender-McD. | Y | N | N | Y | N | Y | Y | Y |
| 38 Napolitano | Y | N | N | Y | N | Y | Y | Y |
| 39 Sánchez, Linda | Y | N | N | Y | N | Y | Y | Y |
| 40 Royce | N | Y | Y | N | Y | Y | N | N |
| 41 Lewis | N | Y | N | N | N | Y | N | N |
| 42 Miller, Gary | N | Y | Y | N | Y | N | N | N |
| 43 Baca | Y | Y | N | Y | N | Y | Y | N |
| 44 Calvert | N | Y | Y | N | N | Y | N | N |
| 45 Bono | Y | N | N | N | N | Y | N | N |
| 46 Rohrabacher | N | Y | Y | Y | Y | Y | N | N |
| 47 Sanchez, Loretta | Y | N | N | Y | N | Y | Y | N |
| 48 Cox | N | Y | Y | N | Y | ? | N | N |
| 49 Issa | N | Y | Y | N | N | Y | N | N |
| **COLORADO** | | | | | | | | |
| 50 Cunningham | N | Y | Y | N | N | Y | N | N |
| 51 Filner | Y | N | N | Y | N | Y | N | N |
| 52 Hunter | N | Y | Y | N | Y | N | N | N |
| 53 Davis | N | N | N | Y | N | Y | Y | N |
| 1 DeGette | Y | N | N | Y | N | Y | Y | N |
| 2 Udall | Y | N | N | Y | N | Y | Y | Y |
| 3 Salazar | N | Y | Y | Y | N | Y | Y | Y |
| 4 Musgrave | N | Y | Y | N | Y | Y | N | N |
| 5 Hefley | N | Y | Y | N | Y | Y | N | Y |
| 6 Tancredo | N | Y | Y | N | Y | Y | N | Y |
| 7 Beauprez | N | Y | Y | N | Y | N | N | N |
| **CONNECTICUT** | | | | | | | | |
| 1 Larson | Y | N | N | Y | N | Y | Y | Y |
| 2 Simmons | N | Y | Y | N | Y | Y | Y | N |
| 3 DeLauro | N | N | N | Y | N | Y | Y | Y |
| 4 Shays | N | N | N | N | N | N | N | N |
| 5 Johnson | Y | N | Y | N | N | N | N | N |
| **DELAWARE** | | | | | | | | |
| AL Castle | N | N | N | N | N | Y | N | N |
| **FLORIDA** | | | | | | | | |
| 1 Miller | N | Y | Y | N | Y | Y | N | N |
| 2 Boyd | N | Y | Y | N | N | Y | Y | N |
| 3 Brown | N | Y | N | Y | N | Y | Y | Y |
| 4 Crenshaw | N | Y | Y | N | N | Y | N | N |
| 5 Brown-Waite | N | Y | N | Y | N | Y | N | N |
| 6 Stearns | N | Y | Y | N | Y | N | N | N |
| 7 Mica | N | Y | Y | N | Y | Y | N | N |
| 8 Keller | N | Y | Y | N | N | Y | N | N |
| 9 Bilirakis | N | Y | Y | N | N | Y | N | N |
| 10 Young | N | N | Y | N | N | Y | N | N |
| 11 Davis | N | N | N | Y | N | Y | Y | Y |
| 12 Putnam | N | Y | Y | N | N | Y | N | N |
| 13 Harris | N | Y | Y | N | N | Y | N | N |
| 14 Mack | N | Y | Y | Y | Y | N | N | N |
| 15 Weldon | N | Y | N | N | N | Y | N | N |
| 16 Foley | N | N | Y | N | N | N | N | N |
| 17 Meek | N | Y | N | Y | N | Y | Y | N |
| 18 Ros-Lehtinen | N | Y | N | N | Y | N | N | N |
| 19 Wexler | N | N | N | Y | N | Y | Y | Y |
| 20 Wasserman-Schultz | N | N | N | Y | N | Y | Y | Y |
| 21 Diaz-Balart, L. | N | Y | Y | N | Y | N | N | N |
| 22 Shaw | N | Y | N | N | N | N | N | N |
| 23 Hastings | N | N | N | Y | N | Y | Y | Y |
| 24 Feeney | N | Y | Y | N | Y | N | N | N |
| 25 Diaz-Balart, M. | N | Y | Y | N | Y | N | N | N |
| **GEORGIA** | | | | | | | | |
| 1 Kingston | ? | ? | ? | ? | ? | ? | ? | ? |
| 2 Bishop | ? | ? | ? | Y | N | Y | Y | Y |
| 3 Marshall | N | Y | Y | N | N | Y | Y | Y |
| 4 McKinney | Y | N | N | Y | N | Y | Y | Y |
| 5 Lewis | Y | N | N | N | N | Y | Y | Y |
| 6 Price | N | Y | Y | N | Y | N | N | N |
| 7 Linder | N | Y | Y | N | Y | N | N | N |
| 8 Westmoreland | ? | ? | ? | ? | Y | Y | N | N |
| 9 Norwood | N | Y | N | Y | N | Y | N | N |
| 10 Deal | N | Y | Y | N | Y | N | N | N |
| 11 Gingrey | N | Y | Y | N | Y | N | N | N |
| 12 Barrow | N | Y | Y | N | Y | Y | Y | Y |
| 13 Scott | ? | ? | ? | ? | N | Y | Y | Y |
| **HAWAII** | | | | | | | | |
| 1 Abercrombie | Y | N | Y | N | Y | N | Y | Y |
| 2 Case | N | N | N | Y | N | Y | Y | Y |
| **IDAHO** | | | | | | | | |
| 1 Otter | Y | Y | Y | N | Y | N | N | Y |
| 2 Simpson | N | Y | N | N | N | Y | N | N |
| **ILLINOIS** | | | | | | | | |
| 1 Rush | Y | N | N | N | N | Y | Y | N |
| 2 Jackson | Y | N | N | Y | N | Y | Y | Y |
| 3 Lipinski | N | N | N | Y | N | Y | Y | Y |
| 4 Gutierrez | Y | N | N | Y | N | Y | Y | Y |
| 5 Emanuel | Y | N | N | N | N | Y | Y | Y |
| 6 Hyde | N | Y | N | N | N | Y | N | N |
| 7 Davis | Y | N | N | Y | N | Y | Y | Y |
| 8 Bean | Y | N | N | N | N | Y | Y | N |
| 9 Schakowsky | Y | N | N | Y | N | Y | Y | Y |
| 10 Kirk | N | N | N | N | N | N | N | N |
| 11 Weller | N | Y | Y | N | Y | Y | N | N |
| 12 Costello | Y | Y | Y | Y | N | Y | Y | Y |

**KEY**    Republicans    Democrats    *Independents*

| | | | |
|---|---|---|---|
| **Y** Voted for (yea) | **X** Paired against | **C** Voted "present" to avoid possible conflict of interest |
| **#** Paired for | **–** Announced against | |
| **+** Announced for | **P** Voted "present" | **?** Did not vote or otherwise make a position known |
| **N** Voted against (nay) | | |

| | 348 | 349 | 350 | 351 | 352 | 353 | 354 | 355 |
|---|---|---|---|---|---|---|---|---|
| 13 **Biggert** | Y | Y | Y | N | N | N | N | N |
| 14 **Hastert** | | | | | | | | |
| 15 **Johnson** | Y | Y | Y | N | N | N | N | N |
| 16 **Manzullo** | Y | Y | Y | N | Y | Y | N | Y |
| 17 Evans | ? | N | N | Y | N | Y | Y | Y |
| 18 **LaHood** | Y | Y | Y | N | N | Y | N | N |
| 19 **Shimkus** | N | Y | Y | N | Y | Y | N | N |
| **INDIANA** | | | | | | | | |
| 1 Visclosky | Y | N | N | Y | N | Y | Y | Y |
| 2 **Chocola** | N | Y | Y | N | Y | N | N | N |
| 3 **Souder** | N | Y | Y | N | N | Y | Y | N |
| 4 **Buyer** | N | Y | Y | N | Y | Y | N | N |
| 5 **Burton** | N | Y | Y | N | Y | Y | N | Y |
| 6 **Pence** | N | Y | Y | N | Y | Y | N | N |
| 7 Carson | Y | N | N | Y | N | Y | Y | Y |
| 8 **Hostettler** | N | Y | Y | N | Y | Y | N | N |
| 9 **Sodrel** | N | Y | Y | N | N | Y | N | N |
| **IOWA** | | | | | | | | |
| 1 **Nussle** | N | Y | Y | N | N | Y | N | N |
| 2 **Leach** | Y | N | Y | N | N | N | Y | N |
| 3 Boswell | Y | Y | N | N | N | Y | Y | Y |
| 4 **Latham** | N | Y | N | N | N | N | N | N |
| 5 **King** | N | Y | Y | N | Y | Y | N | Y |
| **KANSAS** | | | | | | | | |
| 1 **Moran** | Y | Y | Y | Y | N | Y | N | N |
| 2 **Ryun** | N | Y | Y | N | Y | Y | N | N |
| 3 Moore | Y | N | N | N | N | Y | Y | N |
| 4 **Tiahrt** | N | Y | + | N | N | Y | Y | N |
| **KENTUCKY** | | | | | | | | |
| 1 **Whitfield** | N | Y | Y | N | N | Y | N | N |
| 2 **Lewis** | N | Y | Y | N | Y | Y | N | N |
| 3 **Northup** | N | Y | Y | Y | N | Y | N | Y |
| 4 **Davis** | N | Y | Y | N | N | N | N | N |
| 5 **Rogers** | N | Y | Y | N | N | Y | N | N |
| 6 Chandler | N | Y | Y | Y | N | Y | Y | Y |
| **LOUISIANA** | | | | | | | | |
| 1 **Jindal** | N | Y | Y | N | Y | N | N | N |
| 2 Jefferson | Y | Y | N | N | N | Y | Y | N |
| 3 Melancon | N | Y | Y | N | N | Y | Y | N |
| 4 **McCrery** | N | Y | Y | N | N | N | N | N |
| 5 **Alexander** | N | Y | Y | N | N | N | N | N |
| 6 **Baker** | N | Y | Y | N | N | N | N | N |
| 7 **Boustany** | N | Y | Y | N | N | N | N | N |
| **MAINE** | | | | | | | | |
| 1 Allen | Y | N | N | Y | N | Y | Y | Y |
| 2 Michaud | Y | Y | N | Y | N | Y | Y | Y |
| **MARYLAND** | | | | | | | | |
| 1 **Gilchrest** | N | N | Y | N | N | N | N | N |
| 2 Ruppersberger | Y | N | Y | Y | N | Y | Y | Y |
| 3 Cardin | N | N | N | Y | N | Y | Y | Y |
| 4 Wynn | Y | N | N | Y | N | Y | Y | Y |
| 5 Hoyer | Y | N | N | Y | N | Y | Y | Y |
| 6 **Bartlett** | N | Y | Y | N | Y | N | N | Y |
| 7 Cummings | Y | N | N | Y | N | Y | Y | Y |
| 8 Van Hollen | Y | N | N | Y | N | Y | Y | Y |
| **MASSACHUSETTS** | | | | | | | | |
| 1 Olver | Y | N | N | Y | N | Y | Y | Y |
| 2 Neal | Y | N | N | Y | N | Y | Y | Y |
| 3 McGovern | Y | N | N | Y | N | Y | Y | N |
| 4 Frank | Y | N | N | Y | N | Y | Y | N |
| 5 Meehan | Y | N | N | Y | N | Y | Y | Y |
| 6 Tierney | Y | N | N | Y | N | Y | Y | Y |
| 7 Markey | Y | N | N | Y | N | Y | Y | N |
| 8 Capuano | Y | N | N | Y | N | Y | Y | N |
| 9 Lynch | Y | N | Y | Y | N | Y | Y | Y |
| 10 Delahunt | Y | N | N | Y | N | N | Y | Y |
| **MICHIGAN** | | | | | | | | |
| 1 Stupak | Y | Y | N | Y | N | Y | Y | Y |
| 2 **Hoekstra** | N | Y | Y | N | Y | N | N | Y |
| 3 **Ehlers** | N | Y | N | N | N | N | N | N |
| 4 **Camp** | N | Y | Y | N | N | Y | N | N |
| 5 Kildee | Y | N | N | Y | N | Y | Y | Y |
| 6 **Upton** | Y | Y | Y | Y | N | N | Y | N |
| 7 **Schwarz** | N | Y | N | N | N | Y | N | N |
| 8 **Rogers** | N | Y | Y | N | Y | Y | N | N |
| 9 **Knollenberg** | N | Y | N | N | N | N | N | N |
| 10 **Miller** | N | Y | Y | N | N | Y | N | N |
| 11 **McCotter** | N | Y | Y | N | N | Y | N | N |
| 12 Levin | Y | N | N | Y | N | N | Y | Y |
| 13 Kilpatrick | Y | N | N | Y | N | Y | Y | Y |
| 14 Conyers | Y | N | Y | Y | N | Y | Y | Y |
| 15 Dingell | Y | Y | N | Y | N | Y | Y | N |

| | 348 | 349 | 350 | 351 | 352 | 353 | 354 | 355 |
|---|---|---|---|---|---|---|---|---|
| **MINNESOTA** | | | | | | | | |
| 1 **Gutknecht** | N | Y | Y | N | Y | Y | N | Y |
| 2 **Kline** | N | Y | Y | N | N | Y | N | N |
| 3 **Ramstad** | Y | N | Y | N | N | Y | Y | N |
| 4 McCollum | Y | N | N | Y | N | Y | Y | Y |
| 5 Sabo | Y | N | N | Y | N | Y | Y | Y |
| 6 **Kennedy** | N | Y | Y | N | N | Y | N | N |
| 7 Peterson | Y | Y | Y | Y | N | Y | Y | N |
| 8 Oberstar | Y | Y | N | Y | N | Y | Y | Y |
| **MISSISSIPPI** | | | | | | | | |
| 1 **Wicker** | N | Y | Y | N | N | Y | N | N |
| 2 Thompson | Y | N | Y | Y | N | Y | Y | N |
| 3 **Pickering** | N | Y | Y | N | N | Y | N | N |
| 4 Taylor | Y | Y | Y | Y | Y | Y | Y | Y |
| **MISSOURI** | | | | | | | | |
| 1 Clay | Y | N | Y | Y | N | Y | Y | N |
| 2 **Akin** | N | Y | Y | N | Y | Y | N | N |
| 3 Carnahan | N | N | N | Y | N | Y | Y | Y |
| 4 Skelton | N | Y | N | Y | N | Y | Y | N |
| 5 Cleaver | Y | N | N | Y | N | Y | Y | N |
| 6 **Graves** | N | Y | Y | N | Y | N | N | N |
| 7 **Blunt** | N | Y | Y | N | N | N | N | N |
| 8 **Emerson** | Y | Y | Y | N | N | Y | N | Y |
| 9 **Hulshof** | N | Y | Y | N | N | N | N | N |
| **MONTANA** | | | | | | | | |
| AL **Rehberg** | N | Y | Y | N | N | Y | N | N |
| **NEBRASKA** | | | | | | | | |
| 1 **Fortenberry** | N | Y | Y | N | N | Y | N | N |
| 2 **Terry** | N | Y | Y | N | Y | Y | N | N |
| 3 **Osborne** | Y | Y | Y | N | N | Y | N | N |
| **NEVADA** | | | | | | | | |
| 1 Berkley | N | N | N | Y | N | Y | Y | Y |
| 2 **Gibbons** | N | Y | Y | N | Y | Y | N | Y |
| 3 **Porter** | N | Y | Y | N | N | Y | N | N |
| **NEW HAMPSHIRE** | | | | | | | | |
| 1 **Bradley** | N | Y | Y | Y | N | Y | N | N |
| 2 **Bass** | N | Y | Y | Y | Y | Y | N | N |
| **NEW JERSEY** | | | | | | | | |
| 1 Andrews | N | N | N | Y | Y | Y | Y | N |
| 2 **LoBiondo** | N | Y | Y | N | N | Y | N | N |
| 3 **Saxton** | N | Y | Y | N | N | Y | N | N |
| 4 **Smith** | N | Y | Y | Y | N | Y | N | N |
| 5 **Garrett** | N | Y | Y | N | Y | N | N | N |
| 6 Pallone | N | N | Y | Y | N | Y | Y | Y |
| 7 **Ferguson** | N | N | Y | N | N | Y | N | N |
| 8 Pascrell | N | N | N | Y | N | Y | Y | N |
| 9 Rothman | N | N | N | Y | N | Y | Y | N |
| 10 Payne | Y | N | N | Y | N | Y | Y | Y |
| 11 **Frelinghuysen** | N | N | Y | N | N | N | N | N |
| 12 Holt | N | N | N | Y | N | Y | Y | N |
| 13 Menendez | N | N | N | Y | N | Y | Y | N |
| **NEW MEXICO** | | | | | | | | |
| 1 **Wilson** | N | Y | Y | N | N | Y | N | N |
| 2 **Pearce** | N | Y | Y | N | N | Y | N | N |
| 3 Udall | Y | N | N | Y | N | Y | Y | Y |
| **NEW YORK** | | | | | | | | |
| 1 Bishop | Y | N | N | Y | N | Y | Y | Y |
| 2 Israel | Y | N | N | Y | N | Y | Y | Y |
| 3 **King** | N | N | N | N | N | N | N | N |
| 4 McCarthy | Y | N | N | Y | N | Y | Y | Y |
| 5 Ackerman | N | N | N | Y | N | Y | Y | Y |
| 6 Meeks | Y | N | N | Y | N | Y | Y | N |
| 7 Crowley | Y | N | N | Y | N | Y | Y | Y |
| 8 Nadler | Y | N | N | Y | N | Y | Y | Y |
| 9 Weiner | Y | N | N | Y | N | Y | Y | Y |
| 10 Towns | Y | N | N | Y | N | Y | Y | N |
| 11 Owens | Y | N | N | Y | N | Y | Y | Y |
| 12 Velázquez | Y | N | N | Y | N | Y | Y | Y |
| 13 **Fossella** | N | Y | Y | N | Y | Y | N | N |
| 14 Maloney | Y | N | N | Y | N | Y | Y | Y |
| 15 Rangel | Y | N | N | Y | N | Y | Y | Y |
| 16 Serrano | Y | N | N | Y | N | Y | Y | Y |
| 17 Engel | N | N | N | Y | N | Y | Y | N |
| 18 Lowey | Y | N | N | Y | N | Y | Y | Y |
| 19 **Kelly** | N | Y | Y | N | N | Y | N | N |
| 20 **Sweeney** | N | Y | Y | N | N | Y | N | N |
| 21 McNulty | Y | N | Y | Y | N | Y | Y | Y |
| 22 Hinchey | Y | N | Y | Y | N | Y | Y | Y |
| 23 **McHugh** | N | Y | Y | N | N | Y | N | N |
| 24 **Boehlert** | N | Y | N | N | N | N | N | N |
| 25 **Walsh** | N | Y | N | N | N | N | N | N |
| 26 **Reynolds** | N | Y | N | N | N | Y | N | N |
| 27 Higgins | N | Y | Y | Y | N | Y | Y | Y |
| 28 Slaughter | Y | N | Y | Y | N | Y | Y | Y |
| 29 **Kuhl** | N | Y | Y | N | N | Y | N | N |

| | 348 | 349 | 350 | 351 | 352 | 353 | 354 | 355 |
|---|---|---|---|---|---|---|---|---|
| **NORTH CAROLINA** | | | | | | | | |
| 1 Butterfield | N | N | N | N | N | Y | Y | Y |
| 2 Etheridge | N | N | N | N | N | Y | Y | N |
| 3 **Jones** | N | Y | Y | Y | Y | Y | Y | Y |
| 4 Price | Y | N | N | N | N | N | Y | N |
| 5 **Foxx** | N | Y | Y | N | Y | Y | N | N |
| 6 **Coble** | N | Y | Y | N | Y | Y | N | N |
| 7 McIntyre | N | Y | Y | Y | N | Y | Y | N |
| 8 **Hayes** | N | Y | N | Y | N | N | N | N |
| 9 **Myrick** | N | Y | Y | N | Y | Y | N | N |
| 10 **McHenry** | N | Y | Y | N | Y | Y | N | N |
| 11 **Taylor** | N | Y | Y | N | N | Y | N | N |
| 12 Watt | Y | N | N | N | N | Y | Y | Y |
| 13 Miller | N | N | N | N | N | Y | Y | Y |
| **NORTH DAKOTA** | | | | | | | | |
| AL Pomeroy | Y | Y | Y | N | N | Y | Y | Y |
| **OHIO** | | | | | | | | |
| 1 **Chabot** | N | Y | Y | N | Y | Y | N | N |
| 2 Vacant | | | | | | | | |
| 3 **Turner** | N | Y | N | N | N | Y | N | N |
| 4 **Oxley** | N | Y | N | N | N | N | N | N |
| 5 **Gillmor** | N | Y | Y | ? | N | Y | N | N |
| 6 Strickland | Y | Y | N | Y | N | Y | Y | Y |
| 7 **Hobson** | N | Y | N | N | N | Y | N | N |
| 8 **Boehner** | N | Y | Y | N | N | N | N | N |
| 9 Kaptur | Y | N | N | Y | N | Y | Y | N |
| 10 Kucinich | Y | N | N | Y | N | Y | Y | Y |
| 11 Jones | Y | N | N | Y | N | Y | Y | Y |
| 12 **Tiberi** | Y | Y | Y | N | N | Y | N | N |
| 13 Brown | Y | N | N | Y | N | Y | Y | Y |
| 14 **LaTourette** | N | Y | N | N | N | Y | N | N |
| 15 **Pryce** | N | Y | Y | N | N | N | N | N |
| 16 **Regula** | N | Y | N | N | N | Y | N | N |
| 17 Ryan | Y | Y | N | Y | N | Y | Y | Y |
| 18 **Ney** | N | Y | Y | N | N | Y | N | N |
| **OKLAHOMA** | | | | | | | | |
| 1 **Sullivan** | N | Y | Y | N | N | Y | ? | N |
| 2 Boren | Y | Y | Y | N | N | Y | Y | N |
| 3 **Lucas** | N | Y | Y | N | N | Y | N | N |
| 4 **Cole** | N | Y | Y | N | N | N | N | N |
| 5 **Istook** | N | Y | Y | N | N | N | N | N |
| **OREGON** | | | | | | | | |
| 1 Wu | N | Y | N | Y | N | Y | Y | N |
| 2 **Walden** | N | Y | Y | N | N | Y | N | N |
| 3 Blumenauer | Y | N | N | N | N | N | Y | Y |
| 4 DeFazio | Y | Y | Y | Y | N | Y | Y | Y |
| 5 Hooley | Y | N | Y | N | N | Y | Y | N |
| **PENNSYLVANIA** | | | | | | | | |
| 1 Brady | Y | N | N | Y | N | Y | Y | Y |
| 2 Fattah | Y | N | N | Y | N | Y | Y | Y |
| 3 **English** | N | Y | N | N | N | Y | N | N |
| 4 **Hart** | N | Y | Y | N | Y | Y | N | N |
| 5 **Peterson** | ? | ? | ? | ? | ? | ? | ? | ? |
| 6 **Gerlach** | N | Y | Y | N | N | Y | N | N |
| 7 **Weldon** | N | Y | Y | N | N | N | N | N |
| 8 **Fitzpatrick** | N | Y | Y | Y | N | Y | N | N |
| 9 **Shuster** | N | Y | Y | N | N | Y | ? | N |
| 10 **Sherwood** | N | Y | N | Y | N | N | ? | N |
| 11 Kanjorski | Y | Y | N | Y | N | Y | Y | N |
| 12 Murtha | N | Y | N | N | N | N | Y | N |
| 13 Schwartz | Y | N | N | Y | N | Y | Y | N |
| 14 Doyle | Y | N | N | Y | N | Y | Y | N |
| 15 **Dent** | N | Y | Y | N | N | Y | N | N |
| 16 **Pitts** | N | Y | Y | N | Y | Y | N | N |
| 17 Holden | N | Y | N | Y | N | Y | Y | N |
| 18 **Murphy** | N | Y | Y | N | N | Y | N | N |
| 19 **Platts** | N | Y | Y | Y | N | Y | N | N |
| **RHODE ISLAND** | | | | | | | | |
| 1 Kennedy | N | N | N | Y | N | Y | Y | Y |
| 2 Langevin | Y | N | N | Y | N | Y | Y | Y |
| **SOUTH CAROLINA** | | | | | | | | |
| 1 **Brown** | N | Y | Y | N | N | Y | N | N |
| 2 **Wilson** | N | Y | Y | N | Y | N | N | N |
| 3 **Barrett** | N | Y | Y | N | Y | Y | N | N |
| 4 **Inglis** | N | Y | N | N | Y | Y | N | N |
| 5 Spratt | N | N | N | N | N | Y | Y | N |
| 6 Clyburn | Y | N | Y | Y | N | Y | Y | N |
| **SOUTH DAKOTA** | | | | | | | | |
| AL Herseth | Y | Y | Y | Y | N | Y | Y | Y |
| **TENNESSEE** | | | | | | | | |
| 1 **Jenkins** | N | Y | Y | Y | Y | Y | N | N |
| 2 **Duncan** | N | Y | Y | Y | Y | Y | N | N |

| | 348 | 349 | 350 | 351 | 352 | 353 | 354 | 355 |
|---|---|---|---|---|---|---|---|---|
| 3 **Wamp** | N | Y | Y | Y | N | Y | N | N |
| 4 Davis | Y | Y | Y | Y | Y | Y | Y | N |
| 5 Cooper | ? | ? | ? | ? | N | N | Y | N |
| 6 Gordon | Y | Y | Y | Y | N | Y | Y | N |
| 7 **Blackburn** | N | Y | Y | N | Y | Y | N | N |
| 8 Tanner | Y | Y | Y | N | Y | Y | Y | N |
| 9 Ford | Y | Y | N | Y | N | Y | Y | Y |
| **TEXAS** | | | | | | | | |
| 1 **Gohmert** | N | Y | Y | N | Y | Y | N | N |
| 2 **Poe** | N | Y | Y | N | Y | Y | N | N |
| 3 **Johnson, S.** | N | Y | Y | N | Y | Y | N | N |
| 4 **Hall** | N | Y | Y | N | N | N | N | N |
| 5 **Hensarling** | N | Y | Y | N | Y | N | N | N |
| 6 **Barton** | N | Y | Y | N | Y | N | N | N |
| 7 **Culberson** | N | Y | Y | N | N | Y | N | N |
| 8 **Brady** | N | Y | Y | N | Y | N | N | N |
| 9 Green, A. | Y | N | N | Y | N | Y | Y | Y |
| 10 **McCaul** | N | Y | Y | N | N | Y | N | N |
| 11 **Conaway** | N | Y | Y | N | N | N | N | N |
| 12 **Granger** | N | Y | N | N | N | N | N | N |
| 13 **Thornberry** | N | Y | Y | N | Y | N | N | N |
| 14 **Paul** | Y | Y | Y | Y | Y | N | Y | Y |
| 15 Hinojosa | Y | N | N | Y | N | Y | Y | Y |
| 16 Reyes | Y | Y | N | Y | N | Y | Y | N |
| 17 Edwards | Y | Y | N | Y | N | Y | Y | Y |
| 18 Jackson-Lee | Y | N | Y | Y | N | Y | Y | Y |
| 19 **Neugebauer** | N | Y | Y | N | Y | N | N | N |
| 20 Gonzalez | Y | N | N | Y | N | Y | Y | N |
| 21 **Smith** | N | Y | Y | N | N | N | N | N |
| 22 **DeLay** | N | Y | Y | N | N | Y | N | N |
| 23 **Bonilla** | N | Y | Y | N | N | N | N | N |
| 24 **Marchant** | N | Y | Y | N | N | Y | N | N |
| 25 Doggett | Y | N | N | Y | N | N | Y | Y |
| 26 **Burgess** | N | Y | Y | N | N | N | N | N |
| 27 Ortiz | N | Y | N | Y | N | Y | Y | Y |
| 28 Cuellar | N | Y | Y | Y | N | Y | Y | N |
| 29 Green, G. | N | Y | N | N | N | Y | Y | Y |
| 30 Johnson, E. | Y | N | N | Y | N | Y | Y | Y |
| 31 **Carter** | N | Y | Y | N | N | N | N | N |
| 32 **Sessions** | N | Y | Y | N | Y | N | N | N |
| **UTAH** | | | | | | | | |
| 1 **Bishop** | N | Y | Y | N | N | Y | N | N |
| 2 Matheson | Y | Y | Y | N | N | Y | Y | N |
| 3 **Cannon** | N | Y | Y | N | Y | N | N | N |
| **VERMONT** | | | | | | | | |
| AL *Sanders* | Y | N | N | Y | N | Y | Y | Y |
| **VIRGINIA** | | | | | | | | |
| 1 **Davis, J.** | N | Y | Y | N | Y | Y | N | N |
| 2 **Drake** | N | Y | Y | N | N | Y | N | N |
| 3 Scott | Y | N | N | N | N | Y | Y | N |
| 4 **Forbes** | N | Y | Y | N | N | Y | N | N |
| 5 **Goode** | N | Y | Y | N | N | Y | N | N |
| 6 **Goodlatte** | N | Y | Y | N | N | Y | N | N |
| 7 **Cantor** | N | Y | Y | N | N | N | N | N |
| 8 Moran | Y | N | N | N | N | N | Y | Y |
| 9 Boucher | Y | Y | N | Y | N | Y | Y | N |
| 10 **Wolf** | N | N | N | N | N | Y | N | N |
| 11 **Davis, T.** | N | N | N | N | N | N | N | N |
| **WASHINGTON** | | | | | | | | |
| 1 Inslee | Y | N | N | Y | N | N | Y | N |
| 2 Larsen | Y | N | N | Y | N | N | Y | Y |
| 3 Baird | Y | Y | N | Y | N | N | Y | N |
| 4 **Hastings** | N | Y | N | N | N | N | N | N |
| 5 **McMorris** | N | Y | Y | N | Y | N | N | N |
| 6 Dicks | Y | N | N | N | N | N | Y | N |
| 7 McDermott | Y | N | N | Y | N | N | Y | Y |
| 8 **Reichert** | N | Y | N | N | N | Y | N | Y |
| 9 Smith | Y | N | N | Y | N | N | Y | N |
| **WEST VIRGINIA** | | | | | | | | |
| 1 Mollohan | Y | Y | Y | Y | N | Y | Y | Y |
| 2 **Capito** | N | Y | Y | N | N | Y | N | N |
| 3 Rahall | Y | Y | N | Y | N | Y | Y | N |
| **WISCONSIN** | | | | | | | | |
| 1 **Ryan** | Y | Y | Y | N | Y | N | N | N |
| 2 Baldwin | Y | N | N | Y | N | Y | Y | Y |
| 3 Kind | Y | Y | N | Y | N | Y | Y | N |
| 4 Moore | Y | N | N | Y | N | Y | Y | N |
| 5 **Sensenbrenner** | N | Y | Y | N | Y | Y | N | N |
| 6 **Petri** | N | Y | Y | N | Y | N | N | N |
| 7 Obey | Y | P | N | Y | N | Y | Y | ? |
| 8 **Green** | N | Y | Y | Y | N | Y | N | N |
| **WYOMING** | | | | | | | | |
| AL **Cubin** | N | Y | Y | N | Y | Y | N | N |

# IN THE HOUSE | By Vote Number

**356.** HR 3058. Fiscal 2006 Transportation-Treasury-Housing Appropriations/Travel Service Program. Velázquez, D-N.Y., amendment that would prohibit use of funds in the bill for the General Services Administration to carry out the eTravel Service program. Adopted 233-192: R 39-187; D 193-5 (ND 143-5, SD 50-0); I 1-0. June 30, 2005.

**357.** HR 3058. Fiscal 2006 Transportation-Treasury-Housing Appropriations/Federal Job Outsourcing. Van Hollen, D-Md., amendment that would prohibit use of funds in the bill to implement a May 29, 2003, Office of Management and Budget rule streamlining the outsourcing of work by federal agencies. Adopted 222-203: R 24-202; D 197-1 (ND 147-1, SD 50-0); I 1-0. A "nay" was a vote in support of the president's position. June 30, 2005.

**358.** HR 3058. Fiscal 2006 Transportation-Treasury-Housing Appropriations/Passage. Passage of the bill that would appropriate $139.1 billion in fiscal 2006, including $66.9 billion in discretionary spending, for the departments of Housing and Urban Development, Treasury and Transportation, and related agencies. The bill includes $603 million for the District of Columbia. Passed 405-18: R 216-9; D 188-9 (ND 140-7, SD 48-2); I 1-0. June 30, 2005.

**359.** H Res 345. Suspension Motions/Previous Question. Putnam, R-Fla., motion to order the previous question (thus ending debate and possibility of amendment) on adoption of the resolution to provide for House floor consideration of bills under suspension of the rules on June 30, 2005. Motion agreed to 216-191: R 216-0; D 0-190 (ND 0-142, SD 0-48); I 0-1. (Subsequently, the rule was adopted by voice vote.) June 30, 2005.

**360.** H Res 344. Review of Sale of Unocal/Adoption. Ney, R-Ohio, motion to suspend the rules and adopt the resolution that would state if the Unocal Corporation enters into an agreement of acquisition, merger, or takeover by the China National Offshore Oil Corporation, the president should immediately start a thorough review of the action. Motion agreed to 398-15: R 216-6; D 181-9 (ND 133-8, SD 48-1); I 1-0. A two-thirds majority of those present and voting (276 in this case) is required for adoption under suspension of the rules. June 30, 2005.

**361.** H Res 340. Eminent Domain Ruling/Adoption. Sensenbrenner, R-Wis., motion to suspend the rules and adopt the resolution that would note the House of Representatives disagrees with the majority opinion in *Kelo v. City of New London* and its holdings, and agrees with the dissenting opinion in its upholding of the historical interpretation of the takings clause and its deference to the rights of individuals and their property. Motion agreed to 365-33: R 220-1; D 144-32 (ND 101-28, SD 43-4); I 1-0. A two-thirds majority of those present and voting (266 in this case) is required for adoption under suspension of the rules. June 30, 2005.

**362.** HR 3130. Fiscal 2005 Veterans' Supplemental Appropriations/Passage. Walsh, R-N.Y., motion to suspend the rules and pass the bill that would provide $975 million in supplemental fiscal 2005 funding for veterans' medical care. Motion agreed to 419-0: R 227-0; D 191-0 (ND 142-0, SD 49-0); I 1-0. A two-thirds majority of those present and voting (280 in this case) is required for passage under suspension of the rules. June 30, 2005.

| Member | 356 | 357 | 358 | 359 | 360 | 361 | 362 |
|---|---|---|---|---|---|---|---|
| **ALABAMA** | | | | | | | |
| 1 Bonner | N | N | Y | Y | Y | Y | Y |
| 2 Everett | ? | ? | ? | ? | ? | ? | ? |
| 3 Rogers | N | Y | Y | Y | Y | Y | Y |
| 4 Aderholt | N | N | Y | Y | Y | Y | Y |
| 5 Cramer | Y | Y | Y | ? | ? | ? | ? |
| 6 Bachus | N | N | Y | Y | Y | Y | Y |
| 7 Davis | Y | Y | Y | Y | Y | Y | Y |
| **ALASKA** | | | | | | | |
| AL Young | N | N | Y | Y | Y | Y | Y |
| **ARIZONA** | | | | | | | |
| 1 Renzi | Y | N | Y | Y | Y | Y | Y |
| 2 Franks | N | N | N | Y | Y | Y | Y |
| 3 Shadegg | N | N | Y | Y | Y | Y | Y |
| 4 Pastor | Y | Y | N | Y | N | Y | Y |
| 5 Hayworth | Y | N | Y | Y | Y | Y | Y |
| 6 Flake | N | N | N | Y | Y | Y | Y |
| 7 Grijalva | Y | Y | Y | N | Y | N | Y |
| 8 Kolbe | N | N | Y | Y | Y | Y | Y |
| **ARKANSAS** | | | | | | | |
| 1 Berry | Y | Y | Y | N | Y | Y | Y |
| 2 Snyder | Y | Y | Y | N | Y | P | Y |
| 3 Boozman | ? | N | Y | Y | Y | Y | Y |
| 4 Ross | ? | ? | ? | ? | ? | ? | ? |
| **CALIFORNIA** | | | | | | | |
| 1 Thompson | Y | Y | Y | N | Y | Y | Y |
| 2 Herger | N | N | Y | Y | Y | Y | Y |
| 3 Lungren | N | N | Y | Y | N | Y | Y |
| 4 Doolittle | N | N | Y | Y | Y | Y | Y |
| 5 Matsui, D. | Y | Y | Y | N | Y | N | Y |
| 6 Woolsey | Y | Y | Y | N | Y | N | Y |
| 7 Miller, George | Y | Y | Y | N | Y | Y | Y |
| 8 Pelosi | Y | Y | Y | N | ? | ? | ? |
| 9 Lee | Y | Y | Y | N | Y | Y | Y |
| 10 Tauscher | Y | Y | Y | N | Y | Y | Y |
| 11 Pombo | N | N | Y | Y | Y | Y | Y |
| 12 Lantos | Y | Y | Y | N | Y | Y | Y |
| 13 Stark | Y | Y | N | N | N | N | Y |
| 14 Eshoo | Y | Y | Y | N | Y | Y | Y |
| 15 Honda | Y | Y | Y | N | Y | Y | Y |
| 16 Lofgren | Y | Y | Y | N | Y | Y | Y |
| 17 Farr | Y | Y | Y | N | Y | Y | Y |
| 18 Cardoza | Y | Y | Y | N | Y | Y | Y |
| 19 Radanovich | N | N | Y | ? | Y | Y | Y |
| 20 Costa | Y | Y | Y | N | Y | Y | Y |
| 21 Nunes | N | N | Y | Y | Y | Y | Y |
| 22 Thomas | N | N | Y | Y | N | Y | Y |
| 23 Capps | Y | Y | Y | N | Y | Y | Y |
| 24 Gallegly | N | N | Y | Y | Y | Y | Y |
| 25 McKeon | N | N | Y | Y | Y | Y | Y |
| 26 Dreier | N | N | Y | Y | Y | Y | Y |
| 27 Sherman | Y | Y | Y | N | Y | N | Y |
| 28 Berman | Y | Y | Y | ? | ? | ? | ? |
| 29 Schiff | ? | ? | ? | ? | ? | ? | ? |
| 30 Waxman | Y | Y | Y | N | Y | N | Y |
| 31 Becerra | Y | Y | Y | N | Y | Y | Y |
| 32 Solis | Y | Y | Y | - | + | + | + |
| 33 Watson | Y | Y | Y | N | Y | N | Y |
| 34 Roybal-Allard | Y | Y | Y | N | Y | Y | Y |
| 35 Waters | ? | ? | ? | ? | ? | ? | ? |
| 36 Harman | ? | ? | ? | ? | ? | ? | ? |
| 37 Millender-McD. | Y | Y | Y | N | Y | Y | Y |
| 38 Napolitano | Y | Y | Y | N | Y | Y | Y |
| 39 Sánchez, Linda | Y | Y | Y | N | Y | Y | Y |
| 40 Royce | N | N | Y | Y | Y | Y | Y |
| 41 Lewis | N | N | Y | Y | Y | Y | Y |
| 42 Miller, Gary | N | N | Y | Y | Y | Y | Y |
| 43 Baca | Y | Y | Y | N | Y | Y | Y |
| 44 Calvert | N | N | Y | Y | Y | Y | Y |
| 45 Bono | N | N | Y | Y | Y | Y | Y |
| 46 Rohrabacher | N | N | Y | Y | Y | Y | Y |
| 47 Sanchez, Loretta | Y | Y | Y | N | Y | P | Y |
| 48 Cox | N | ? | Y | ? | Y | Y | Y |
| 49 Issa | N | N | Y | Y | Y | Y | Y |

| Member | 356 | 357 | 358 | 359 | 360 | 361 | 362 |
|---|---|---|---|---|---|---|---|
| 50 Cunningham | N | N | Y | Y | Y | Y | Y |
| 51 Filner | Y | Y | Y | N | Y | Y | Y |
| 52 Hunter | N | N | Y | Y | Y | Y | Y |
| 53 Davis | Y | Y | Y | N | Y | Y | Y |
| **COLORADO** | | | | | | | |
| 1 DeGette | Y | Y | Y | N | Y | N | Y |
| 2 Udall | Y | Y | Y | N | Y | Y | Y |
| 3 Salazar | Y | Y | Y | N | Y | Y | Y |
| 4 Musgrave | N | N | Y | ? | Y | Y | Y |
| 5 Hefley | N | N | N | Y | Y | Y | Y |
| 6 Tancredo | N | N | N | Y | Y | Y | Y |
| 7 Beauprez | N | N | Y | Y | Y | Y | Y |
| **CONNECTICUT** | | | | | | | |
| 1 Larson | Y | Y | Y | N | Y | Y | Y |
| 2 Simmons | Y | Y | Y | Y | Y | Y | Y |
| 3 DeLauro | Y | Y | Y | N | Y | Y | Y |
| 4 Shays | Y | N | Y | N | Y | Y | Y |
| 5 Johnson | N | N | Y | Y | Y | Y | Y |
| **DELAWARE** | | | | | | | |
| AL Castle | N | N | Y | Y | Y | Y | Y |
| **FLORIDA** | | | | | | | |
| 1 Miller | N | N | N | Y | Y | Y | Y |
| 2 Boyd | Y | Y | Y | N | Y | Y | Y |
| 3 Brown | Y | Y | Y | N | Y | Y | Y |
| 4 Crenshaw | N | N | Y | Y | Y | Y | Y |
| 5 Brown-Waite | N | N | Y | Y | Y | Y | Y |
| 6 Stearns | N | N | Y | Y | Y | Y | Y |
| 7 Mica | N | N | Y | Y | Y | Y | Y |
| 8 Keller | N | N | Y | ? | Y | Y | Y |
| 9 Bilirakis | Y | N | Y | Y | Y | Y | Y |
| 10 Young | N | Y | Y | Y | Y | Y | Y |
| 11 Davis | Y | Y | Y | N | Y | Y | Y |
| 12 Putnam | N | N | Y | Y | Y | Y | Y |
| 13 Harris | N | N | Y | Y | Y | Y | Y |
| 14 Mack | N | N | Y | Y | Y | Y | Y |
| 15 Weldon | N | N | Y | Y | Y | Y | Y |
| 16 Foley | N | N | Y | Y | Y | Y | Y |
| 17 Meek | Y | Y | Y | N | Y | Y | Y |
| 18 Ros-Lehtinen | Y | Y | Y | N | Y | Y | Y |
| 19 Wexler | Y | Y | Y | N | Y | Y | Y |
| 20 Wasserman-Schultz | Y | Y | Y | N | Y | Y | Y |
| 21 Diaz-Balart, L. | Y | N | Y | Y | Y | Y | Y |
| 22 Shaw | N | N | Y | Y | Y | Y | Y |
| 23 Hastings | Y | Y | Y | N | Y | N | Y |
| 24 Feeney | N | N | Y | Y | Y | Y | Y |
| 25 Diaz-Balart, M. | N | N | Y | Y | Y | Y | Y |
| **GEORGIA** | | | | | | | |
| 1 Kingston | ? | ? | ? | ? | ? | ? | ? |
| 2 Bishop | Y | Y | Y | N | Y | Y | Y |
| 3 Marshall | Y | Y | Y | N | Y | Y | Y |
| 4 McKinney | Y | Y | Y | N | Y | Y | Y |
| 5 Lewis | Y | Y | Y | N | Y | Y | Y |
| 6 Price | N | N | Y | Y | Y | Y | Y |
| 7 Linder | N | N | Y | Y | Y | Y | Y |
| 8 Westmoreland | N | N | Y | ? | Y | Y | Y |
| 9 Norwood | N | N | Y | Y | Y | Y | Y |
| 10 Deal | N | N | Y | Y | Y | Y | Y |
| 11 Gingrey | N | N | Y | Y | Y | Y | Y |
| 12 Barrow | Y | Y | Y | N | Y | Y | Y |
| 13 Scott | Y | Y | Y | N | Y | Y | Y |
| **HAWAII** | | | | | | | |
| 1 Abercrombie | Y | Y | Y | N | Y | Y | Y |
| 2 Case | Y | Y | Y | N | Y | N | Y |
| **IDAHO** | | | | | | | |
| 1 Otter | N | N | N | Y | Y | Y | Y |
| 2 Simpson | N | N | Y | Y | Y | Y | Y |
| **ILLINOIS** | | | | | | | |
| 1 Rush | Y | Y | Y | N | Y | Y | Y |
| 2 Jackson | Y | Y | Y | N | Y | N | Y |
| 3 Lipinski | Y | Y | Y | N | Y | Y | Y |
| 4 Gutierrez | Y | Y | Y | N | Y | Y | Y |
| 5 Emanuel | Y | Y | Y | N | Y | Y | Y |
| 6 Hyde | N | N | Y | Y | Y | Y | Y |
| 7 Davis | Y | Y | Y | N | Y | Y | Y |
| 8 Bean | Y | Y | Y | N | Y | Y | Y |
| 9 Schakowsky | Y | Y | Y | N | Y | P | Y |
| 10 Kirk | N | N | Y | Y | Y | N | Y |
| 11 Weller | N | N | Y | Y | Y | Y | Y |
| 12 Costello | Y | Y | Y | N | Y | Y | Y |

**KEY**   Republicans   Democrats   *Independents*

| | | | |
|---|---|---|---|
| **Y** Voted for (yea) | **X** Paired against | **C** Voted "present" to avoid possible conflict of interest |
| **#** Paired for | **–** Announced against | |
| **+** Announced for | **P** Voted "present" | **?** Did not vote or otherwise make a position known |
| **N** Voted against (nay) | | |

ND Northern Democrats, SD Southern Democrats
Southern states: Ala., Ark., Fla., Ga., Ky., La., Miss., N.C., Okla., S.C., Tenn., Texas, Va.

| | 356 | 357 | 358 | 359 | 360 | 361 | 362 |
|---|---|---|---|---|---|---|---|
| 13 **Biggert** | N | N | Y | Y | Y | Y | Y |
| 14 **Hastert** | | | | | | | |
| 15 **Johnson** | Y | Y | Y | Y | Y | Y | Y |
| 16 **Manzullo** | Y | N | Y | Y | Y | Y | Y |
| 17 Evans | Y | Y | Y | N | Y | Y | Y |
| 18 **LaHood** | N | N | Y | Y | Y | Y | Y |
| 19 **Shimkus** | N | Y | Y | Y | Y | Y | Y |
| **INDIANA** | | | | | | | |
| 1 Visclosky | Y | Y | Y | N | Y | Y | Y |
| 2 **Chocola** | N | N | Y | Y | Y | Y | Y |
| 3 **Souder** | N | N | Y | Y | Y | Y | Y |
| 4 **Buyer** | N | N | Y | Y | Y | Y | Y |
| 5 **Burton** | N | N | Y | Y | Y | Y | Y |
| 6 **Pence** | N | N | Y | Y | Y | Y | Y |
| 7 Carson | Y | Y | N | N | Y | Y | Y |
| 8 **Hostettler** | N | Y | Y | Y | Y | N | Y |
| 9 **Sodrel** | N | N | Y | Y | Y | Y | Y |
| **IOWA** | | | | | | | |
| 1 **Nussle** | N | N | Y | Y | Y | Y | Y |
| 2 **Leach** | N | N | Y | Y | Y | Y | Y |
| 3 Boswell | Y | Y | Y | N | Y | Y | Y |
| 4 **Latham** | N | N | Y | Y | Y | Y | Y |
| 5 **King** | Y | N | Y | Y | Y | Y | Y |
| **KANSAS** | | | | | | | |
| 1 **Moran** | Y | N | Y | Y | Y | Y | Y |
| 2 **Ryun** | N | N | Y | Y | Y | Y | Y |
| 3 Moore | Y | Y | Y | N | Y | Y | Y |
| 4 **Tiahrt** | N | N | Y | Y | Y | Y | Y |
| **KENTUCKY** | | | | | | | |
| 1 **Whitfield** | N | N | Y | Y | Y | Y | Y |
| 2 **Lewis** | N | Y | Y | Y | Y | Y | Y |
| 3 **Northup** | N | N | Y | Y | Y | Y | Y |
| 4 **Davis** | N | N | Y | Y | Y | Y | Y |
| 5 **Rogers** | N | N | Y | ? | Y | Y | Y |
| 6 Chandler | Y | Y | Y | N | Y | Y | Y |
| **LOUISIANA** | | | | | | | |
| 1 **Jindal** | N | N | Y | Y | Y | Y | Y |
| 2 Jefferson | Y | Y | Y | N | Y | Y | Y |
| 3 Melancon | Y | Y | Y | N | Y | Y | Y |
| 4 **McCrery** | N | N | ? | Y | Y | Y | Y |
| 5 **Alexander** | N | N | Y | Y | Y | Y | Y |
| 6 **Baker** | N | N | Y | Y | Y | Y | Y |
| 7 **Boustany** | N | N | + | Y | Y | Y | Y |
| **MAINE** | | | | | | | |
| 1 Allen | Y | Y | Y | N | Y | N | Y |
| 2 Michaud | Y | Y | Y | N | Y | Y | Y |
| **MARYLAND** | | | | | | | |
| 1 **Gilchrest** | N | N | Y | Y | Y | Y | Y |
| 2 Ruppersberger | Y | Y | Y | N | Y | Y | Y |
| 3 Cardin | Y | Y | Y | ? | Y | Y | Y |
| 4 Wynn | Y | Y | Y | N | Y | N | Y |
| 5 Hoyer | Y | Y | Y | N | Y | Y | Y |
| 6 **Bartlett** | N | N | Y | Y | Y | Y | Y |
| 7 Cummings | Y | Y | Y | N | Y | Y | Y |
| 8 Van Hollen | Y | Y | Y | N | Y | Y | Y |
| **MASSACHUSETTS** | | | | | | | |
| 1 Olver | Y | Y | Y | N | Y | P | Y |
| 2 Neal | Y | Y | Y | N | Y | P | Y |
| 3 McGovern | Y | Y | Y | N | Y | Y | Y |
| 4 Frank | Y | Y | Y | N | Y | Y | Y |
| 5 Meehan | Y | Y | Y | N | Y | Y | Y |
| 6 Tierney | Y | Y | Y | N | Y | P | Y |
| 7 Markey | Y | Y | Y | N | Y | Y | Y |
| 8 Capuano | N | Y | Y | N | Y | P | Y |
| 9 Lynch | Y | Y | Y | N | Y | Y | Y |
| 10 Delahunt | Y | Y | Y | N | Y | Y | Y |
| **MICHIGAN** | | | | | | | |
| 1 Stupak | Y | Y | Y | N | Y | Y | Y |
| 2 **Hoekstra** | N | N | Y | Y | Y | Y | Y |
| 3 **Ehlers** | N | N | Y | Y | Y | Y | Y |
| 4 **Camp** | N | N | Y | Y | Y | Y | Y |
| 5 Kildee | Y | Y | Y | N | Y | Y | Y |
| 6 **Upton** | N | N | Y | Y | Y | Y | Y |
| 7 **Schwarz** | N | N | Y | Y | Y | Y | Y |
| 8 **Rogers** | N | N | Y | ? | Y | Y | Y |
| 9 **Knollenberg** | N | N | Y | Y | Y | Y | Y |
| 10 **Miller** | N | N | Y | Y | Y | Y | Y |
| 11 **McCotter** | Y | Y | Y | Y | Y | Y | Y |
| 12 Levin | Y | Y | Y | N | Y | N | Y |
| 13 Kilpatrick | Y | Y | Y | N | Y | N | Y |
| 14 Conyers | Y | Y | N | N | Y | Y | Y |
| 15 Dingell | Y | Y | Y | N | Y | N | Y |

| | 356 | 357 | 358 | 359 | 360 | 361 | 362 |
|---|---|---|---|---|---|---|---|
| **MINNESOTA** | | | | | | | |
| 1 **Gutknecht** | N | Y | Y | Y | Y | Y | Y |
| 2 **Kline** | N | N | Y | Y | Y | Y | Y |
| 3 **Ramstad** | Y | N | Y | Y | Y | Y | Y |
| 4 McCollum | Y | Y | Y | N | Y | P | Y |
| 5 Sabo | N | Y | Y | N | Y | P | Y |
| 6 **Kennedy** | N | N | Y | Y | Y | Y | Y |
| 7 Peterson | N | Y | Y | N | Y | Y | Y |
| 8 Oberstar | N | Y | Y | ? | Y | N | Y |
| **MISSISSIPPI** | | | | | | | |
| 1 **Wicker** | N | N | Y | ? | Y | Y | Y |
| 2 Thompson | Y | Y | Y | N | Y | Y | Y |
| 3 **Pickering** | Y | N | Y | Y | Y | Y | Y |
| 4 Taylor | Y | Y | N | N | Y | Y | Y |
| **MISSOURI** | | | | | | | |
| 1 Clay | Y | Y | Y | N | ? | ? | ? |
| 2 **Akin** | N | N | Y | Y | Y | Y | Y |
| 3 Carnahan | Y | Y | Y | N | Y | Y | Y |
| 4 Skelton | Y | Y | Y | N | Y | Y | Y |
| 5 Cleaver | Y | Y | Y | N | Y | Y | Y |
| 6 **Graves** | Y | N | Y | Y | Y | Y | Y |
| 7 **Blunt** | N | N | Y | Y | Y | Y | Y |
| 8 **Emerson** | N | Y | Y | Y | Y | Y | Y |
| 9 **Hulshof** | Y | N | Y | Y | Y | Y | Y |
| **MONTANA** | | | | | | | |
| AL **Rehberg** | N | N | Y | Y | Y | Y | Y |
| **NEBRASKA** | | | | | | | |
| 1 **Fortenberry** | Y | N | Y | Y | Y | Y | Y |
| 2 **Terry** | Y | N | Y | Y | Y | Y | Y |
| 3 **Osborne** | Y | N | Y | Y | Y | Y | Y |
| **NEVADA** | | | | | | | |
| 1 Berkley | Y | Y | Y | N | Y | Y | Y |
| 2 **Gibbons** | Y | N | Y | Y | Y | Y | Y |
| 3 **Porter** | Y | N | Y | Y | Y | Y | Y |
| **NEW HAMPSHIRE** | | | | | | | |
| 1 **Bradley** | N | N | Y | Y | Y | Y | Y |
| 2 **Bass** | N | N | Y | Y | Y | Y | Y |
| **NEW JERSEY** | | | | | | | |
| 1 Andrews | Y | Y | Y | N | Y | Y | Y |
| 2 **LoBiondo** | N | Y | Y | Y | Y | Y | Y |
| 3 **Saxton** | N | N | Y | Y | Y | Y | Y |
| 4 **Smith** | Y | Y | Y | ? | Y | Y | Y |
| 5 **Garrett** | N | N | Y | Y | Y | Y | Y |
| 6 Pallone | Y | Y | Y | N | Y | Y | Y |
| 7 **Ferguson** | N | N | Y | Y | Y | Y | Y |
| 8 Pascrell | Y | Y | Y | N | Y | Y | Y |
| 9 Rothman | Y | Y | Y | N | Y | N | Y |
| 10 Payne | Y | Y | Y | N | Y | N | Y |
| 11 **Frelinghuysen** | N | N | Y | Y | Y | Y | Y |
| 12 Holt | Y | Y | Y | N | Y | P | Y |
| 13 Menendez | Y | Y | Y | N | Y | Y | Y |
| **NEW MEXICO** | | | | | | | |
| 1 **Wilson** | N | N | Y | Y | Y | Y | Y |
| 2 **Pearce** | Y | N | Y | Y | Y | Y | Y |
| 3 Udall | Y | Y | Y | N | Y | Y | Y |
| **NEW YORK** | | | | | | | |
| 1 Bishop | Y | Y | Y | N | Y | Y | Y |
| 2 Israel | Y | Y | Y | N | Y | Y | Y |
| 3 **King** | Y | N | Y | Y | Y | Y | Y |
| 4 McCarthy | Y | Y | Y | N | Y | Y | Y |
| 5 Ackerman | Y | Y | Y | N | Y | P | Y |
| 6 Meeks | Y | Y | Y | N | Y | Y | Y |
| 7 Crowley | Y | Y | Y | N | Y | Y | Y |
| 8 Nadler | Y | Y | Y | N | Y | N | Y |
| 9 Weiner | Y | Y | Y | N | Y | Y | Y |
| 10 Towns | Y | Y | Y | N | Y | Y | Y |
| 11 Owens | Y | Y | Y | N | Y | Y | Y |
| 12 Velázquez | Y | Y | Y | N | Y | Y | Y |
| 13 **Fossella** | N | N | Y | Y | Y | Y | Y |
| 14 Maloney | Y | Y | Y | N | Y | Y | Y |
| 15 Rangel | Y | Y | ? | N | Y | Y | Y |
| 16 Serrano | Y | Y | Y | N | Y | Y | Y |
| 17 Engel | Y | Y | Y | N | Y | Y | Y |
| 18 Lowey | Y | Y | Y | N | Y | N | Y |
| 19 **Kelly** | Y | Y | Y | Y | Y | Y | Y |
| 20 **Sweeney** | N | N | Y | Y | Y | Y | Y |
| 21 McNulty | Y | Y | Y | N | Y | Y | Y |
| 22 Hinchey | Y | Y | Y | N | Y | Y | Y |
| 23 **McHugh** | N | Y | Y | Y | Y | Y | Y |
| 24 **Boehlert** | N | N | Y | Y | Y | Y | Y |
| 25 **Walsh** | N | N | Y | Y | Y | Y | Y |
| 26 **Reynolds** | N | N | Y | Y | Y | + | Y |
| 27 Higgins | Y | Y | Y | ? | ? | ? | ? |
| 28 Slaughter | Y | Y | Y | N | Y | Y | Y |
| 29 **Kuhl** | N | Y | Y | Y | Y | Y | Y |

| | 356 | 357 | 358 | 359 | 360 | 361 | 362 |
|---|---|---|---|---|---|---|---|
| **NORTH CAROLINA** | | | | | | | |
| 1 Butterfield | Y | Y | Y | ? | Y | Y | Y |
| 2 Etheridge | Y | Y | Y | N | Y | Y | Y |
| 3 **Jones** | N | Y | N | Y | Y | Y | Y |
| 4 Price | Y | Y | Y | N | Y | Y | Y |
| 5 **Foxx** | N | N | Y | Y | Y | Y | Y |
| 6 **Coble** | Y | N | Y | Y | Y | Y | Y |
| 7 McIntyre | Y | Y | Y | N | Y | Y | Y |
| 8 **Hayes** | N | N | Y | Y | Y | Y | Y |
| 9 **Myrick** | N | N | Y | Y | Y | Y | Y |
| 10 **McHenry** | N | N | Y | Y | Y | Y | Y |
| 11 **Taylor** | Y | N | Y | Y | Y | Y | Y |
| 12 Watt | Y | Y | Y | N | Y | P | Y |
| 13 Miller | Y | Y | Y | N | Y | N | Y |
| **NORTH DAKOTA** | | | | | | | |
| AL Pomeroy | Y | Y | Y | N | Y | Y | Y |
| **OHIO** | | | | | | | |
| 1 **Chabot** | N | N | Y | Y | Y | Y | Y |
| 2 Vacant | | | | | | | |
| 3 **Turner** | N | N | Y | Y | Y | P | Y |
| 4 **Oxley** | N | N | Y | Y | Y | Y | Y |
| 5 **Gillmor** | N | N | Y | Y | Y | Y | Y |
| 6 Strickland | Y | Y | Y | N | Y | Y | Y |
| 7 **Hobson** | N | N | Y | Y | Y | Y | Y |
| 8 **Boehner** | N | N | Y | ? | Y | Y | Y |
| 9 Kaptur | Y | Y | Y | N | Y | P | Y |
| 10 Kucinich | Y | Y | Y | N | Y | Y | Y |
| 11 Jones | Y | Y | Y | N | Y | N | Y |
| 12 **Tiberi** | N | N | Y | Y | Y | Y | Y |
| 13 Brown | Y | Y | Y | N | Y | Y | Y |
| 14 **LaTourette** | N | Y | Y | Y | Y | Y | Y |
| 15 **Pryce** | N | N | Y | Y | Y | Y | Y |
| 16 **Regula** | N | N | Y | Y | Y | Y | Y |
| 17 Ryan | Y | Y | Y | N | Y | Y | Y |
| 18 **Ney** | N | N | Y | Y | Y | Y | Y |
| **OKLAHOMA** | | | | | | | |
| 1 **Sullivan** | N | N | Y | Y | Y | Y | Y |
| 2 Boren | Y | Y | Y | N | Y | Y | Y |
| 3 **Lucas** | N | N | Y | Y | Y | Y | Y |
| 4 **Cole** | N | N | Y | Y | ? | Y | Y |
| 5 **Istook** | N | N | Y | Y | Y | Y | Y |
| **OREGON** | | | | | | | |
| 1 Wu | Y | Y | Y | N | Y | P | Y |
| 2 **Walden** | N | N | Y | Y | Y | Y | Y |
| 3 Blumenauer | Y | Y | Y | N | N | P | Y |
| 4 DeFazio | Y | Y | Y | N | Y | Y | Y |
| 5 Hooley | Y | Y | Y | N | Y | Y | Y |
| **PENNSYLVANIA** | | | | | | | |
| 1 Brady | Y | Y | Y | N | Y | Y | Y |
| 2 Fattah | Y | Y | Y | N | ? | N | Y |
| 3 **English** | N | N | Y | ? | Y | Y | Y |
| 4 **Hart** | N | N | Y | Y | Y | Y | Y |
| 5 **Peterson** | ? | ? | ? | ? | ? | ? | ? |
| 6 **Gerlach** | Y | Y | Y | Y | ? | Y | Y |
| 7 **Weldon** | Y | N | Y | Y | Y | Y | Y |
| 8 **Fitzpatrick** | Y | Y | Y | Y | Y | Y | Y |
| 9 **Shuster** | Y | N | Y | Y | Y | Y | Y |
| 10 **Sherwood** | N | N | Y | Y | Y | Y | Y |
| 11 Kanjorski | Y | Y | Y | N | Y | Y | Y |
| 12 Murtha | Y | Y | Y | N | ? | ? | ? |
| 13 Schwartz | Y | Y | Y | N | Y | Y | Y |
| 14 Doyle | Y | Y | Y | N | Y | Y | Y |
| 15 **Dent** | Y | Y | Y | Y | Y | Y | Y |
| 16 **Pitts** | N | N | Y | Y | Y | Y | Y |
| 17 Holden | Y | Y | Y | N | Y | Y | Y |
| 18 **Murphy** | N | N | Y | Y | Y | Y | Y |
| 19 **Platts** | Y | Y | Y | Y | Y | Y | Y |
| **RHODE ISLAND** | | | | | | | |
| 1 Kennedy | Y | Y | Y | N | Y | Y | Y |
| 2 Langevin | Y | Y | Y | N | Y | Y | Y |
| **SOUTH CAROLINA** | | | | | | | |
| 1 **Brown** | N | N | Y | Y | Y | Y | Y |
| 2 **Wilson** | N | N | Y | Y | Y | Y | Y |
| 3 **Barrett** | N | N | Y | Y | Y | Y | Y |
| 4 **Inglis** | N | N | Y | Y | Y | Y | Y |
| 5 Spratt | Y | Y | Y | N | Y | Y | Y |
| 6 Clyburn | Y | Y | Y | N | Y | Y | Y |
| **SOUTH DAKOTA** | | | | | | | |
| AL Herseth | Y | Y | Y | N | Y | Y | Y |
| **TENNESSEE** | | | | | | | |
| 1 **Jenkins** | N | N | Y | Y | Y | Y | Y |
| 2 **Duncan** | N | N | Y | Y | Y | Y | Y |

| | 356 | 357 | 358 | 359 | 360 | 361 | 362 |
|---|---|---|---|---|---|---|---|
| 3 **Wamp** | N | N | Y | Y | Y | Y | Y |
| 4 Davis | Y | Y | Y | N | Y | Y | Y |
| 5 Cooper | Y | Y | N | N | Y | Y | Y |
| 6 Gordon | Y | Y | Y | N | Y | Y | Y |
| 7 **Blackburn** | N | N | Y | Y | Y | Y | Y |
| 8 Tanner | Y | Y | Y | N | Y | Y | Y |
| 9 Ford | Y | Y | Y | N | Y | Y | Y |
| **TEXAS** | | | | | | | |
| 1 **Gohmert** | N | N | Y | Y | Y | Y | Y |
| 2 **Poe** | Y | N | Y | Y | Y | Y | Y |
| 3 **Johnson, S.** | N | N | Y | Y | ? | ? | Y |
| 4 **Hall** | Y | N | Y | Y | Y | Y | Y |
| 5 **Hensarling** | N | N | Y | Y | Y | Y | Y |
| 6 **Barton** | N | N | Y | Y | Y | Y | Y |
| 7 **Culberson** | N | N | Y | Y | Y | Y | Y |
| 8 **Brady** | N | N | Y | Y | Y | Y | Y |
| 9 Green, A. | Y | Y | Y | N | Y | N | Y |
| 10 **McCaul** | N | N | Y | Y | ? | ? | Y |
| 11 **Conaway** | N | N | Y | Y | Y | Y | Y |
| 12 **Granger** | N | N | Y | Y | Y | P | Y |
| 13 **Thornberry** | N | N | Y | Y | Y | Y | Y |
| 14 **Paul** | N | Y | N | ? | N | P | Y |
| 15 Hinojosa | Y | Y | Y | N | Y | Y | Y |
| 16 Reyes | Y | Y | Y | N | Y | Y | Y |
| 17 Edwards | Y | Y | Y | N | Y | Y | Y |
| 18 Jackson-Lee | Y | Y | Y | N | Y | Y | Y |
| 19 **Neugebauer** | N | N | Y | Y | Y | Y | Y |
| 20 Gonzalez | Y | Y | Y | N | Y | Y | Y |
| 21 **Smith** | N | N | Y | Y | Y | Y | Y |
| 22 **DeLay** | N | N | Y | Y | Y | Y | Y |
| 23 **Bonilla** | N | N | Y | Y | Y | Y | Y |
| 24 **Marchant** | N | N | Y | Y | Y | Y | Y |
| 25 Doggett | Y | Y | Y | N | Y | Y | Y |
| 26 **Burgess** | N | N | Y | Y | Y | Y | Y |
| 27 Ortiz | Y | Y | Y | N | Y | Y | Y |
| 28 Cuellar | Y | Y | Y | N | Y | Y | Y |
| 29 Green, G. | Y | Y | Y | N | Y | Y | Y |
| 30 Johnson, E. | Y | Y | Y | N | Y | Y | Y |
| 31 **Carter** | N | N | Y | Y | Y | Y | Y |
| 32 **Sessions** | N | N | Y | Y | Y | Y | Y |
| **UTAH** | | | | | | | |
| 1 **Bishop** | N | Y | Y | Y | Y | Y | Y |
| 2 Matheson | Y | Y | N | N | Y | Y | Y |
| 3 **Cannon** | N | N | Y | Y | Y | Y | Y |
| **VERMONT** | | | | | | | |
| AL *Sanders* | Y | Y | Y | N | Y | Y | Y |
| **VIRGINIA** | | | | | | | |
| 1 **Davis, J.** | Y | Y | Y | Y | Y | Y | Y |
| 2 **Drake** | N | N | Y | Y | Y | Y | Y |
| 3 Scott | Y | Y | Y | N | Y | Y | Y |
| 4 **Forbes** | Y | N | Y | Y | Y | Y | Y |
| 5 **Goode** | Y | N | Y | Y | Y | Y | Y |
| 6 **Goodlatte** | N | N | Y | Y | Y | Y | Y |
| 7 **Cantor** | N | N | Y | Y | Y | Y | Y |
| 8 Moran | Y | Y | Y | N | N | N | Y |
| 9 Boucher | Y | Y | Y | N | Y | Y | Y |
| 10 **Wolf** | N | N | Y | Y | Y | Y | Y |
| 11 **Davis, T.** | N | N | Y | Y | N | Y | Y |
| **WASHINGTON** | | | | | | | |
| 1 Inslee | Y | Y | Y | N | N | N | Y |
| 2 Larsen | Y | Y | Y | N | N | N | Y |
| 3 Baird | Y | Y | Y | N | N | N | Y |
| 4 **Hastings** | N | N | Y | Y | Y | Y | Y |
| 5 **McMorris** | N | N | Y | Y | Y | Y | Y |
| 6 Dicks | Y | Y | Y | N | N | N | Y |
| 7 McDermott | Y | Y | Y | N | N | N | Y |
| 8 **Reichert** | Y | N | Y | Y | Y | Y | Y |
| 9 Smith | N | N | Y | N | N | Y | Y |
| **WEST VIRGINIA** | | | | | | | |
| 1 Mollohan | Y | Y | Y | N | Y | Y | Y |
| 2 **Capito** | N | Y | Y | Y | Y | Y | Y |
| 3 Rahall | Y | Y | Y | - | Y | Y | Y |
| **WISCONSIN** | | | | | | | |
| 1 **Ryan** | N | N | Y | Y | Y | Y | Y |
| 2 Baldwin | Y | Y | N | N | Y | Y | Y |
| 3 Kind | Y | Y | N | N | Y | Y | Y |
| 4 Moore | Y | Y | Y | N | Y | Y | Y |
| 5 **Sensenbrenner** | N | N | N | Y | Y | Y | Y |
| 6 **Petri** | N | N | Y | Y | Y | Y | Y |
| 7 Obey | Y | Y | N | N | Y | Y | Y |
| 8 **Green** | N | N | Y | Y | Y | Y | Y |
| **WYOMING** | | | | | | | |
| AL **Cubin** | N | N | Y | Y | Y | Y | Y |

# IN THE HOUSE | By Vote Number

**363.** **H Con Res 168. North Korea Kidnapping Condemnation/Adoption.** Smith, R-N.J., motion to suspend the rules and adopt the concurrent resolution that would condemn and call upon the North Korean government to immediately cease and desist in the abduction and continued captivity of citizens of South Korea and Japan. Motion agreed to 362-1: R 201-1; D 160-0 (ND 122-0, SD 38-0); I 1-0. A two-thirds majority of those present and voting (242 in this case) is required for adoption under suspension of the rules. July 11, 2005.

**364.** **H Res 333. Weekend of Prayer for Darfur/Adoption.** Smith, R-N.J., motion to suspend the rules and adopt the resolution that would support a National Weekend of Prayer and Reflection for Darfur, Sudan. Motion agreed to 364-2: R 203-1; D 160-1 (ND 120-1, SD 40-0); I 1-0. A two-thirds majority of those present and voting (244 in this case) is required for adoption under suspension of the rules. July 11, 2005.

**365.** **HR 739, HR 740, HR 741, HR 742. OSHA Bills/Previous Question.** Bishop, R-Utah, motion to order the previous question (thus ending debate and possibility of amendment) on adoption of the rule (H Res 351) to provide for House floor consideration of four Occupational Safety and Health Administration (OSHA)-related bills. Motion agreed to 223-191: R 222-1; D 1-189 (ND 1-142, SD 0-47); I 0-1. July 12, 2005.

**366.** **HR 739, HR 740, HR 741, HR 742. OSHA Bills/Rule.** Adoption of the rule (H Res 351) that would provide for House consideration of four OSHA-related bills. The rule specifies that if more than one bill passes the House, the text of those bills will be combined into one measure. Adopted 224-189: R 224-0; D 0-188 (ND 0-142, SD 0-46); I 0-1. July 12, 2005.

**367.** **H Res 352. Barriers to U.S. Economic Competitiveness/Adoption.** Boustany, R-La., motion to suspend the rules and adopt the resolution that would recognize that to improve U.S. competitiveness, congressional action is needed to remove barriers — ranging from tax law and trade restrictions to health care security — to keeping and creating jobs. Motion rejected 242-177: R 225-0; D 17-176 (ND 7-139, SD 10-37); I 0-1. A two-thirds majority of those present and voting (280 in this case) is required for adoption under suspension of the rules. July 12, 2005.

**368.** **H Res 343. Women's Political Rights in Kuwait/Adoption.** Smith, R-N.J., motion to suspend the rules and adopt the resolution that would commend the government of Kuwait for providing female citizens the right to vote and hold public office and urge the full participation of Kuwaiti women in the political life of their country. Motion agreed to 420-0: R 226-0; D 193-0 (ND 146-0, SD 47-0); I 1-0. A two-thirds majority of those present and voting (280 in this case) is required for adoption under suspension of the rules. July 12, 2005.

ND Northern Democrats, SD Southern Democrats
Southern states: Ala., Ark., Fla., Ga., Ky., La., Miss., N.C., Okla., S.C., Tenn., Texas, Va.

| | 363 | 364 | 365 | 366 | 367 | 368 |
|---|---|---|---|---|---|---|
| **ALABAMA** | | | | | | |
| 1 Bonner | + | + | Y | Y | Y | Y |
| 2 Everett | ? | ? | Y | Y | Y | Y |
| 3 Rogers | Y | Y | Y | Y | Y | Y |
| 4 Aderholt | Y | Y | Y | Y | Y | Y |
| 5 Cramer | Y | Y | N | N | Y | Y |
| 6 Bachus | Y | Y | Y | Y | Y | Y |
| 7 Davis | Y | Y | N | N | N | Y |
| **ALASKA** | | | | | | |
| AL Young | Y | Y | Y | Y | Y | Y |
| **ARIZONA** | | | | | | |
| 1 Renzi | Y | Y | Y | Y | Y | Y |
| 2 Franks | Y | Y | Y | Y | Y | Y |
| 3 Shadegg | ? | ? | ? | ? | ? | ? |
| 4 Pastor | Y | Y | N | N | N | Y |
| 5 Hayworth | Y | Y | Y | Y | Y | Y |
| 6 Flake | Y | Y | Y | Y | Y | Y |
| 7 Grijalva | Y | Y | N | N | N | Y |
| 8 Kolbe | Y | Y | Y | Y | Y | Y |
| **ARKANSAS** | | | | | | |
| 1 Berry | Y | Y | N | N | N | Y |
| 2 Snyder | Y | Y | N | N | N | Y |
| 3 Boozman | ? | ? | Y | Y | Y | Y |
| 4 Ross | Y | Y | N | N | N | Y |
| **CALIFORNIA** | | | | | | |
| 1 Thompson | Y | Y | N | N | N | Y |
| 2 Herger | Y | Y | Y | Y | Y | Y |
| 3 Lungren | Y | Y | Y | Y | Y | Y |
| 4 Doolittle | Y | Y | Y | Y | Y | Y |
| 5 Matsui, D. | Y | Y | N | N | N | Y |
| 6 Woolsey | Y | Y | N | N | N | Y |
| 7 Miller, George | ? | ? | N | N | N | Y |
| 8 Pelosi | Y | Y | N | N | N | Y |
| 9 Lee | + | + | N | N | N | Y |
| 10 Tauscher | Y | Y | N | N | N | Y |
| 11 Pombo | + | + | ? | ? | ? | ? |
| 12 Lantos | Y | Y | N | N | N | Y |
| 13 Stark | Y | Y | N | N | N | Y |
| 14 Eshoo | + | + | N | N | N | Y |
| 15 Honda | Y | Y | N | N | N | Y |
| 16 Lofgren | Y | Y | N | N | N | Y |
| 17 Farr | ? | ? | N | N | N | Y |
| 18 Cardoza | Y | Y | N | N | N | Y |
| 19 Radanovich | Y | Y | Y | Y | Y | Y |
| 20 Costa | Y | Y | N | N | N | Y |
| 21 Nunes | Y | Y | Y | Y | Y | Y |
| 22 Thomas | Y | Y | Y | Y | Y | Y |
| 23 Capps | Y | Y | N | N | N | Y |
| 24 Gallegly | + | + | Y | Y | Y | Y |
| 25 McKeon | Y | Y | Y | Y | Y | Y |
| 26 Dreier | Y | Y | Y | Y | Y | Y |
| 27 Sherman | Y | Y | N | N | N | Y |
| 28 Berman | Y | Y | N | N | N | Y |
| 29 Schiff | Y | Y | N | N | N | Y |
| 30 Waxman | Y | Y | N | N | N | Y |
| 31 Becerra | ? | ? | N | N | N | Y |
| 32 Solis | Y | Y | N | N | N | Y |
| 33 Watson | Y | Y | N | N | N | Y |
| 34 Roybal-Allard | Y | Y | N | N | N | Y |
| 35 Waters | ? | ? | N | N | N | Y |
| 36 Harman | Y | Y | N | N | N | Y |
| 37 Millender-McD. | Y | Y | N | N | N | Y |
| 38 Napolitano | Y | Y | N | N | N | Y |
| 39 Sánchez, Linda | + | + | N | N | N | Y |
| 40 Royce | Y | Y | Y | Y | Y | Y |
| 41 Lewis | Y | Y | Y | Y | Y | Y |
| 42 Miller, Gary | Y | Y | Y | Y | Y | Y |
| 43 Baca | Y | Y | N | N | N | Y |
| 44 Calvert | Y | Y | Y | Y | Y | Y |
| 45 Bono | Y | Y | Y | Y | Y | Y |
| 46 Rohrabacher | Y | Y | Y | Y | Y | Y |
| 47 Sanchez, Loretta | Y | Y | N | N | N | Y |
| 48 Cox | Y | Y | Y | Y | Y | Y |
| 49 Issa | Y | Y | Y | Y | Y | Y |
| 50 Cunningham | Y | Y | Y | Y | Y | Y |
| 51 Filner | ? | + | N | N | N | Y |
| 52 Hunter | ? | ? | Y | Y | Y | Y |
| 53 Davis | Y | Y | N | N | N | Y |
| **COLORADO** | | | | | | |
| 1 DeGette | Y | Y | N | N | N | Y |
| 2 Udall | Y | Y | N | N | N | Y |
| 3 Salazar | Y | Y | N | N | N | Y |
| 4 Musgrave | Y | Y | Y | Y | Y | Y |
| 5 Hefley | Y | Y | Y | Y | Y | Y |
| 6 Tancredo | Y | Y | Y | Y | Y | Y |
| 7 Beauprez | Y | Y | Y | Y | Y | Y |
| **CONNECTICUT** | | | | | | |
| 1 Larson | Y | Y | N | N | N | Y |
| 2 Simmons | Y | Y | Y | Y | Y | Y |
| 3 DeLauro | Y | Y | N | N | N | Y |
| 4 Shays | Y | Y | Y | Y | Y | Y |
| 5 Johnson | Y | Y | Y | Y | Y | Y |
| **DELAWARE** | | | | | | |
| AL Castle | Y | Y | Y | Y | Y | Y |
| **FLORIDA** | | | | | | |
| 1 Miller | ? | ? | ? | ? | ? | ? |
| 2 Boyd | Y | Y | N | N | N | Y |
| 3 Brown | ? | ? | ? | ? | ? | ? |
| 4 Crenshaw | Y | Y | Y | Y | Y | Y |
| 5 Brown-Waite | Y | Y | Y | Y | Y | Y |
| 6 Stearns | Y | Y | Y | Y | Y | Y |
| 7 Mica | Y | Y | Y | Y | Y | Y |
| 8 Keller | Y | Y | Y | Y | Y | Y |
| 9 Bilirakis | Y | Y | Y | Y | Y | Y |
| 10 Young | Y | Y | Y | Y | Y | Y |
| 11 Davis | Y | Y | N | N | N | Y |
| 12 Putnam | Y | Y | Y | Y | Y | Y |
| 13 Harris | Y | Y | Y | Y | Y | Y |
| 14 Mack | Y | Y | Y | Y | Y | Y |
| 15 Weldon | Y | Y | Y | Y | Y | Y |
| 16 Foley | Y | Y | Y | Y | Y | Y |
| 17 Meek | Y | Y | N | N | N | Y |
| 18 Ros-Lehtinen | Y | Y | Y | Y | Y | Y |
| 19 Wexler | Y | Y | N | N | N | Y |
| 20 Wasserman-Schultz | ? | ? | N | N | N | Y |
| 21 Diaz-Balart, L. | Y | Y | Y | Y | Y | Y |
| 22 Shaw | Y | Y | Y | Y | Y | Y |
| 23 Hastings | Y | Y | N | N | N | Y |
| 24 Feeney | Y | Y | Y | Y | Y | Y |
| 25 Diaz-Balart, M. | Y | Y | Y | Y | Y | Y |
| **GEORGIA** | | | | | | |
| 1 Kingston | ? | ? | Y | Y | Y | Y |
| 2 Bishop | Y | Y | N | N | N | Y |
| 3 Marshall | Y | Y | N | N | Y | Y |
| 4 McKinney | ? | ? | N | N | N | Y |
| 5 Lewis | Y | Y | N | N | N | Y |
| 6 Price | Y | Y | Y | ? | Y | Y |
| 7 Linder | Y | Y | Y | Y | Y | Y |
| 8 Westmoreland | Y | Y | Y | Y | Y | Y |
| 9 Norwood | Y | Y | Y | Y | Y | Y |
| 10 Deal | Y | Y | Y | Y | Y | Y |
| 11 Gingrey | Y | Y | Y | Y | Y | Y |
| 12 Barrow | Y | Y | N | N | Y | Y |
| 13 Scott | Y | Y | N | N | N | Y |
| **HAWAII** | | | | | | |
| 1 Abercrombie | Y | Y | - | - | - | + |
| 2 Case | Y | Y | N | N | Y | Y |
| **IDAHO** | | | | | | |
| 1 Otter | Y | Y | Y | Y | Y | Y |
| 2 Simpson | Y | Y | Y | Y | Y | Y |
| **ILLINOIS** | | | | | | |
| 1 Rush | ? | ? | N | N | N | Y |
| 2 Jackson | Y | Y | N | N | N | Y |
| 3 Lipinski | Y | Y | N | N | Y | Y |
| 4 Gutierrez | + | + | N | N | N | Y |
| 5 Emanuel | Y | Y | N | N | N | Y |
| 6 Hyde | Y | Y | Y | Y | Y | Y |
| 7 Davis | Y | Y | N | N | N | Y |
| 8 Bean | Y | Y | N | N | Y | Y |
| 9 Schakowsky | Y | Y | N | N | N | Y |
| 10 Kirk | Y | Y | Y | Y | Y | Y |
| 11 Weller | Y | Y | Y | Y | Y | Y |
| 12 Costello | ? | ? | N | N | N | Y |

**KEY**    **Republicans**    Democrats    *Independents*

| | | |
|---|---|---|
| Y Voted for (yea) | X Paired against | C Voted "present" to avoid possible conflict of interest |
| # Paired for | – Announced against | |
| + Announced for | P Voted "present" | ? Did not vote or otherwise make a position known |
| N Voted against (nay) | | |

| | 363 | 364 | 365 | 366 | 367 | 368 |
|---|---|---|---|---|---|---|
| 13 **Biggert** | Y | Y | Y | Y | Y | Y |
| 14 **Hastert** | | | | | | |
| 15 **Johnson** | + | + | Y | Y | + | Y |
| 16 **Manzullo** | Y | Y | Y | Y | Y | Y |
| 17 Evans | Y | Y | N | N | N | Y |
| 18 **LaHood** | ? | ? | Y | Y | Y | Y |
| 19 **Shimkus** | ? | ? | Y | Y | Y | Y |
| **INDIANA** | | | | | | |
| 1 Visclosky | Y | Y | N | N | N | Y |
| 2 **Chocola** | Y | Y | Y | Y | Y | Y |
| 3 **Souder** | Y | Y | Y | Y | Y | Y |
| 4 **Buyer** | Y | Y | Y | Y | Y | Y |
| 5 **Burton** | Y | Y | Y | Y | Y | Y |
| 6 **Pence** | Y | Y | Y | Y | Y | Y |
| 7 Carson | Y | Y | - | N | N | Y |
| 8 **Hostettler** | Y | Y | Y | Y | Y | Y |
| 9 **Sodrel** | Y | Y | Y | Y | Y | Y |
| **IOWA** | | | | | | |
| 1 **Nussle** | Y | Y | Y | Y | Y | Y |
| 2 **Leach** | Y | Y | Y | Y | Y | Y |
| 3 Boswell | Y | Y | N | N | N | Y |
| 4 **Latham** | Y | Y | Y | Y | Y | Y |
| 5 **King** | Y | Y | Y | Y | Y | Y |
| **KANSAS** | | | | | | |
| 1 **Moran** | Y | Y | Y | Y | Y | Y |
| 2 **Ryun** | Y | Y | Y | Y | Y | Y |
| 3 Moore | Y | Y | N | N | N | Y |
| 4 **Tiahrt** | Y | Y | Y | Y | Y | Y |
| **KENTUCKY** | | | | | | |
| 1 **Whitfield** | Y | Y | Y | Y | Y | Y |
| 2 **Lewis** | Y | Y | Y | Y | Y | Y |
| 3 **Northup** | Y | Y | Y | Y | Y | Y |
| 4 **Davis** | Y | Y | Y | Y | Y | Y |
| 5 **Rogers** | Y | Y | Y | Y | Y | Y |
| 6 Chandler | Y | Y | N | N | Y | Y |
| **LOUISIANA** | | | | | | |
| 1 **Jindal** | Y | Y | Y | Y | Y | Y |
| 2 Jefferson | Y | Y | N | N | N | Y |
| 3 Melancon | Y | Y | N | N | Y | Y |
| 4 **McCrery** | Y | Y | Y | Y | Y | Y |
| 5 **Alexander** | Y | Y | Y | Y | Y | Y |
| 6 **Baker** | ? | ? | Y | Y | Y | Y |
| 7 **Boustany** | Y | Y | Y | Y | Y | Y |
| **MAINE** | | | | | | |
| 1 Allen | Y | Y | N | N | N | Y |
| 2 Michaud | Y | Y | N | N | N | Y |
| **MARYLAND** | | | | | | |
| 1 **Gilchrest** | Y | Y | Y | Y | Y | Y |
| 2 Ruppersberger | Y | Y | N | N | N | Y |
| 3 Cardin | Y | Y | N | N | N | Y |
| 4 Wynn | Y | Y | N | N | N | Y |
| 5 Hoyer | Y | Y | N | N | N | Y |
| 6 **Bartlett** | P | Y | Y | Y | Y | Y |
| 7 Cummings | Y | Y | N | N | N | Y |
| 8 Van Hollen | Y | Y | N | N | N | Y |
| **MASSACHUSETTS** | | | | | | |
| 1 Olver | Y | Y | N | N | N | Y |
| 2 Neal | ? | ? | N | N | N | Y |
| 3 McGovern | Y | Y | N | N | N | Y |
| 4 Frank | Y | Y | N | ? | N | Y |
| 5 Meehan | Y | Y | N | N | N | Y |
| 6 Tierney | ? | ? | N | N | N | Y |
| 7 Markey | Y | Y | N | N | N | Y |
| 8 Capuano | Y | Y | N | N | N | Y |
| 9 Lynch | Y | Y | N | N | N | Y |
| 10 Delahunt | Y | Y | ? | ? | N | Y |
| **MICHIGAN** | | | | | | |
| 1 Stupak | ? | ? | N | N | N | Y |
| 2 **Hoekstra** | Y | Y | Y | Y | Y | Y |
| 3 **Ehlers** | Y | Y | + | Y | Y | Y |
| 4 **Camp** | ? | ? | Y | Y | Y | Y |
| 5 Kildee | Y | Y | N | N | N | Y |
| 6 **Upton** | Y | Y | Y | Y | Y | Y |
| 7 **Schwarz** | Y | Y | Y | Y | Y | Y |
| 8 **Rogers** | Y | Y | Y | Y | Y | Y |
| 9 **Knollenberg** | Y | Y | Y | Y | Y | Y |
| 10 **Miller** | Y | Y | Y | Y | Y | Y |
| 11 **McCotter** | Y | Y | Y | Y | Y | Y |
| 12 Levin | Y | Y | N | N | N | Y |
| 13 Kilpatrick | + | + | N | N | N | Y |
| 14 Conyers | + | + | - | - | - | + |
| 15 Dingell | Y | Y | N | N | N | Y |

| | 363 | 364 | 365 | 366 | 367 | 368 |
|---|---|---|---|---|---|---|
| **MINNESOTA** | | | | | | |
| 1 **Gutknecht** | Y | Y | Y | Y | Y | Y |
| 2 **Kline** | Y | Y | Y | Y | Y | Y |
| 3 **Ramstad** | Y | Y | Y | Y | Y | Y |
| 4 McCollum | Y | Y | N | N | N | Y |
| 5 Sabo | Y | Y | N | N | N | Y |
| 6 **Kennedy** | Y | Y | Y | Y | Y | Y |
| 7 Peterson | Y | Y | N | N | N | Y |
| 8 Oberstar | Y | Y | N | N | N | Y |
| **MISSISSIPPI** | | | | | | |
| 1 **Wicker** | Y | Y | Y | Y | Y | Y |
| 2 Thompson | Y | Y | N | N | N | Y |
| 3 **Pickering** | ? | ? | Y | Y | Y | Y |
| 4 Taylor | Y | Y | N | N | Y | Y |
| **MISSOURI** | | | | | | |
| 1 Clay | ? | ? | ? | ? | ? | ? |
| 2 **Akin** | Y | Y | Y | Y | Y | Y |
| 3 Carnahan | Y | Y | N | N | N | Y |
| 4 Skelton | Y | Y | N | N | Y | Y |
| 5 Cleaver | Y | Y | N | N | N | Y |
| 6 **Graves** | Y | Y | Y | Y | Y | Y |
| 7 **Blunt** | Y | Y | Y | Y | Y | Y |
| 8 **Emerson** | Y | Y | Y | Y | Y | Y |
| 9 **Hulshof** | ? | ? | Y | Y | Y | Y |
| **MONTANA** | | | | | | |
| AL **Rehberg** | Y | Y | Y | Y | Y | Y |
| **NEBRASKA** | | | | | | |
| 1 **Fortenberry** | Y | Y | Y | Y | Y | Y |
| 2 **Terry** | Y | Y | Y | Y | Y | Y |
| 3 **Osborne** | Y | Y | Y | Y | Y | Y |
| **NEVADA** | | | | | | |
| 1 Berkley | Y | Y | N | N | N | Y |
| 2 **Gibbons** | Y | Y | Y | Y | Y | Y |
| 3 **Porter** | Y | Y | Y | Y | Y | Y |
| **NEW HAMPSHIRE** | | | | | | |
| 1 **Bradley** | Y | Y | Y | Y | Y | Y |
| 2 **Bass** | Y | Y | Y | Y | Y | Y |
| **NEW JERSEY** | | | | | | |
| 1 Andrews | Y | Y | N | N | N | Y |
| 2 **LoBiondo** | Y | Y | Y | Y | Y | Y |
| 3 **Saxton** | Y | Y | Y | Y | Y | Y |
| 4 **Smith** | Y | Y | Y | Y | Y | Y |
| 5 **Garrett** | Y | Y | Y | Y | Y | Y |
| 6 Pallone | Y | Y | N | N | N | Y |
| 7 **Ferguson** | Y | Y | Y | Y | Y | Y |
| 8 Pascrell | Y | Y | N | N | N | Y |
| 9 Rothman | Y | Y | N | N | N | Y |
| 10 Payne | Y | Y | N | N | N | Y |
| 11 **Frelinghuysen** | Y | Y | Y | Y | Y | Y |
| 12 Holt | + | + | N | N | N | Y |
| 13 Menendez | Y | Y | N | N | N | Y |
| **NEW MEXICO** | | | | | | |
| 1 **Wilson** | Y | Y | Y | Y | Y | Y |
| 2 **Pearce** | Y | Y | Y | Y | Y | Y |
| 3 Udall | Y | Y | N | N | N | Y |
| **NEW YORK** | | | | | | |
| 1 Bishop | Y | Y | N | N | N | Y |
| 2 Israel | Y | Y | N | N | N | Y |
| 3 **King** | Y | Y | Y | Y | Y | Y |
| 4 McCarthy | Y | Y | N | N | N | Y |
| 5 Ackerman | Y | N | N | N | N | Y |
| 6 Meeks | Y | Y | N | N | N | Y |
| 7 Crowley | Y | Y | N | N | N | Y |
| 8 Nadler | Y | Y | N | N | N | Y |
| 9 Weiner | ? | ? | N | N | N | Y |
| 10 Towns | ? | ? | N | N | N | Y |
| 11 Owens | Y | Y | N | N | N | Y |
| 12 Velázquez | Y | Y | N | N | N | Y |
| 13 **Fossella** | Y | Y | Y | Y | Y | Y |
| 14 Maloney | Y | Y | N | N | N | Y |
| 15 Rangel | Y | Y | N | N | N | Y |
| 16 Serrano | Y | Y | N | N | N | Y |
| 17 Engel | Y | Y | N | N | N | Y |
| 18 Lowey | Y | Y | N | N | N | Y |
| 19 **Kelly** | Y | Y | Y | Y | Y | Y |
| 20 **Sweeney** | ? | ? | Y | Y | Y | Y |
| 21 McNulty | Y | Y | N | N | N | Y |
| 22 Hinchey | ? | ? | N | N | N | Y |
| 23 **McHugh** | Y | Y | Y | Y | Y | Y |
| 24 **Boehlert** | Y | Y | Y | Y | Y | Y |
| 25 **Walsh** | Y | Y | Y | Y | Y | Y |
| 26 **Reynolds** | Y | Y | Y | Y | Y | Y |
| 27 Higgins | Y | Y | N | N | N | Y |
| 28 Slaughter | Y | Y | N | N | N | Y |
| 29 **Kuhl** | Y | Y | Y | Y | Y | Y |

| | 363 | 364 | 365 | 366 | 367 | 368 |
|---|---|---|---|---|---|---|
| **NORTH CAROLINA** | | | | | | |
| 1 Butterfield | Y | Y | N | N | N | Y |
| 2 Etheridge | Y | Y | N | N | N | Y |
| 3 **Jones** | Y | Y | Y | Y | Y | Y |
| 4 Price | ? | ? | N | N | N | Y |
| 5 **Foxx** | Y | + | Y | Y | Y | Y |
| 6 **Coble** | Y | Y | Y | Y | Y | Y |
| 7 McIntyre | Y | Y | N | N | N | Y |
| 8 **Hayes** | Y | Y | Y | Y | Y | Y |
| 9 **Myrick** | ? | ? | ? | ? | ? | ? |
| 10 **McHenry** | Y | Y | Y | Y | Y | Y |
| 11 **Taylor** | ? | ? | Y | Y | Y | Y |
| 12 Watt | ? | ? | N | ? | N | Y |
| 13 Miller | Y | Y | N | N | N | Y |
| **NORTH DAKOTA** | | | | | | |
| AL Pomeroy | Y | Y | N | N | N | Y |
| **OHIO** | | | | | | |
| 1 **Chabot** | Y | Y | Y | Y | Y | Y |
| 2 Vacant | | | | | | |
| 3 **Turner** | Y | Y | Y | Y | Y | Y |
| 4 **Oxley** | Y | Y | Y | Y | Y | Y |
| 5 **Gillmor** | Y | Y | Y | Y | Y | Y |
| 6 Strickland | ? | ? | N | N | N | Y |
| 7 **Hobson** | Y | Y | Y | Y | Y | Y |
| 8 **Boehner** | Y | Y | Y | Y | Y | Y |
| 9 Kaptur | Y | Y | N | N | N | Y |
| 10 Kucinich | Y | Y | N | N | N | Y |
| 11 Jones | ? | ? | ? | ? | ? | ? |
| 12 **Tiberi** | Y | Y | Y | Y | Y | Y |
| 13 Brown | Y | Y | N | N | N | Y |
| 14 **LaTourette** | Y | Y | Y | Y | Y | Y |
| 15 **Pryce** | ? | ? | Y | Y | Y | Y |
| 16 **Regula** | Y | Y | Y | Y | Y | Y |
| 17 Ryan | Y | Y | N | N | N | Y |
| 18 **Ney** | Y | Y | Y | Y | Y | Y |
| **OKLAHOMA** | | | | | | |
| 1 **Sullivan** | Y | Y | Y | Y | Y | Y |
| 2 Boren | Y | Y | N | N | Y | Y |
| 3 **Lucas** | Y | Y | Y | Y | Y | Y |
| 4 **Cole** | Y | Y | Y | Y | Y | Y |
| 5 **Istook** | Y | Y | Y | Y | Y | Y |
| **OREGON** | | | | | | |
| 1 Wu | Y | Y | N | N | N | Y |
| 2 **Walden** | Y | Y | Y | Y | Y | Y |
| 3 Blumenauer | Y | Y | N | N | N | Y |
| 4 DeFazio | ? | ? | N | N | N | Y |
| 5 Hooley | Y | Y | N | N | N | Y |
| **PENNSYLVANIA** | | | | | | |
| 1 Brady | ? | ? | N | N | N | Y |
| 2 Fattah | ? | ? | N | N | N | Y |
| 3 **English** | ? | ? | Y | Y | Y | Y |
| 4 **Hart** | Y | Y | Y | Y | Y | Y |
| 5 **Peterson** | Y | Y | Y | Y | Y | Y |
| 6 **Gerlach** | Y | Y | Y | Y | Y | Y |
| 7 **Weldon** | ? | Y | Y | Y | Y | Y |
| 8 **Fitzpatrick** | Y | Y | Y | Y | Y | Y |
| 9 **Shuster** | Y | Y | Y | Y | Y | Y |
| 10 **Sherwood** | Y | Y | Y | Y | Y | Y |
| 11 Kanjorski | Y | Y | N | N | N | Y |
| 12 Murtha | ? | ? | N | N | N | Y |
| 13 Schwartz | Y | Y | N | N | N | Y |
| 14 Doyle | Y | Y | N | N | N | Y |
| 15 **Dent** | Y | Y | Y | Y | Y | Y |
| 16 **Pitts** | Y | Y | Y | Y | Y | Y |
| 17 Holden | Y | Y | N | N | Y | Y |
| 18 **Murphy** | Y | Y | Y | Y | Y | Y |
| 19 **Platts** | Y | Y | Y | Y | Y | Y |
| **RHODE ISLAND** | | | | | | |
| 1 Kennedy | Y | Y | N | - | N | Y |
| 2 Langevin | Y | Y | N | N | N | Y |
| **SOUTH CAROLINA** | | | | | | |
| 1 **Brown** | Y | Y | Y | Y | Y | Y |
| 2 **Wilson** | Y | Y | Y | Y | Y | Y |
| 3 **Barrett** | Y | Y | Y | Y | Y | Y |
| 4 **Inglis** | Y | Y | Y | Y | Y | Y |
| 5 Spratt | ? | Y | N | N | N | Y |
| 6 Clyburn | Y | Y | N | N | N | Y |
| **SOUTH DAKOTA** | | | | | | |
| AL Herseth | Y | Y | N | N | N | Y |
| **TENNESSEE** | | | | | | |
| 1 **Jenkins** | ? | ? | Y | Y | Y | Y |
| 2 **Duncan** | Y | Y | Y | Y | Y | Y |

| | 363 | 364 | 365 | 366 | 367 | 368 |
|---|---|---|---|---|---|---|
| 3 **Wamp** | Y | Y | Y | Y | Y | Y |
| 4 Davis | Y | Y | N | N | N | Y |
| 5 Cooper | Y | Y | N | N | N | Y |
| 6 Gordon | Y | Y | N | N | N | Y |
| 7 **Blackburn** | Y | Y | Y | Y | Y | Y |
| 8 Tanner | Y | Y | N | N | Y | Y |
| 9 Ford | Y | Y | N | N | N | Y |
| **TEXAS** | | | | | | |
| 1 **Gohmert** | Y | Y | Y | Y | Y | Y |
| 2 **Poe** | Y | Y | Y | ? | Y | Y |
| 3 **Johnson, S.** | Y | Y | Y | Y | Y | Y |
| 4 **Hall** | Y | Y | Y | Y | Y | Y |
| 5 **Hensarling** | Y | Y | Y | Y | Y | Y |
| 6 **Barton** | Y | Y | Y | Y | Y | Y |
| 7 **Culberson** | Y | Y | Y | Y | Y | Y |
| 8 **Brady** | ? | Y | Y | Y | Y | Y |
| 9 Green, A. | Y | Y | N | N | N | Y |
| 10 **McCaul** | Y | Y | Y | Y | Y | Y |
| 11 **Conaway** | Y | Y | Y | Y | Y | Y |
| 12 **Granger** | Y | Y | Y | Y | Y | Y |
| 13 **Thornberry** | ? | ? | Y | Y | Y | Y |
| 14 **Paul** | N | N | Y | Y | Y | Y |
| 15 Hinojosa | + | + | - | - | - | + |
| 16 Reyes | ? | ? | N | N | N | Y |
| 17 Edwards | ? | ? | N | N | N | Y |
| 18 Jackson-Lee | ? | ? | N | N | N | Y |
| 19 **Neugebauer** | + | + | Y | Y | Y | Y |
| 20 Gonzalez | + | + | - | - | - | + |
| 21 **Smith** | Y | Y | Y | Y | Y | Y |
| 22 **DeLay** | Y | Y | ? | Y | Y | Y |
| 23 **Bonilla** | Y | Y | Y | Y | Y | Y |
| 24 **Marchant** | ? | ? | ? | Y | Y | Y |
| 25 Doggett | Y | Y | N | N | N | Y |
| 26 **Burgess** | Y | Y | Y | Y | Y | Y |
| 27 Ortiz | + | + | - | - | - | + |
| 28 Cuellar | Y | Y | N | N | Y | Y |
| 29 Green, G. | Y | Y | N | N | N | Y |
| 30 Johnson, E. | Y | Y | N | N | N | Y |
| 31 **Carter** | Y | Y | Y | Y | Y | Y |
| 32 **Sessions** | Y | Y | Y | Y | Y | Y |
| **UTAH** | | | | | | |
| 1 **Bishop** | Y | Y | Y | Y | Y | Y |
| 2 Matheson | Y | Y | N | N | Y | Y |
| 3 **Cannon** | Y | Y | Y | Y | Y | Y |
| **VERMONT** | | | | | | |
| AL *Sanders* | Y | Y | N | N | N | Y |
| **VIRGINIA** | | | | | | |
| 1 **Davis, J.** | Y | Y | Y | Y | Y | Y |
| 2 **Drake** | Y | Y | Y | Y | Y | Y |
| 3 Scott | ? | ? | N | N | N | Y |
| 4 **Forbes** | Y | Y | Y | Y | Y | Y |
| 5 **Goode** | Y | Y | Y | Y | Y | Y |
| 6 **Goodlatte** | Y | Y | Y | Y | Y | Y |
| 7 **Cantor** | Y | Y | Y | Y | Y | Y |
| 8 Moran | Y | Y | N | N | N | Y |
| 9 Boucher | Y | Y | N | N | N | Y |
| 10 **Wolf** | Y | Y | Y | Y | Y | Y |
| 11 **Davis, T.** | Y | Y | Y | Y | Y | Y |
| **WASHINGTON** | | | | | | |
| 1 Inslee | Y | Y | N | N | N | Y |
| 2 Larsen | Y | Y | N | N | N | Y |
| 3 Baird | Y | Y | N | N | N | Y |
| 4 **Hastings** | Y | Y | Y | Y | Y | Y |
| 5 **McMorris** | Y | Y | Y | Y | Y | Y |
| 6 Dicks | Y | ? | N | N | N | Y |
| 7 McDermott | Y | Y | N | N | N | Y |
| 8 **Reichert** | Y | Y | Y | Y | Y | Y |
| 9 Smith | Y | Y | N | N | N | Y |
| **WEST VIRGINIA** | | | | | | |
| 1 Mollohan | Y | Y | N | N | N | Y |
| 2 **Capito** | Y | Y | Y | Y | Y | Y |
| 3 Rahall | Y | Y | N | N | N | Y |
| **WISCONSIN** | | | | | | |
| 1 **Ryan** | Y | Y | Y | Y | Y | Y |
| 2 Baldwin | Y | Y | N | N | N | Y |
| 3 Kind | Y | Y | N | N | N | Y |
| 4 Moore | + | + | N | N | N | Y |
| 5 **Sensenbrenner** | Y | Y | Y | Y | Y | Y |
| 6 **Petri** | Y | Y | Y | Y | Y | Y |
| 7 Obey | ? | ? | ? | ? | ? | ? |
| 8 **Green** | Y | Y | Y | Y | Y | Y |
| **WYOMING** | | | | | | |
| AL **Cubin** | Y | Y | Y | Y | Y | Y |

# IN THE HOUSE | By Vote Number

**369.** **HR 739. Workplace Safety Citation Appeals/Passage.** Passage of the bill that would allow the Occupational Safety and Health Review Commission to make exceptions to the 15-day deadline for employers to respond to an OSHA citation. Passed 256-164: R 225-0; D 31-163 (ND 15-130, SD 16-33); I 0-1. July 12, 2005.

**370.** **HR 740. Occupational Safety and Health Review Commission/Passage.** Passage of the bill that would expand the membership of the Occupational Safety and Health Review Commission from three to five. Passed 234-185: R 226-0; D 8-184 (ND 2-141, SD 6-43); I 0-1. July 12, 2005.

**371.** **HR 741. Occupational Safety and Health Review Commission Rulings/Passage.** Passage of the bill that would require courts and judges to defer to Occupational Safety and Health Review Commission rulings when interpreting questions of law. The commission hears appeals of Occupational Safety and Health Administration violations. Passed 226-197: R 217-9; D 9-187 (ND 2-144, SD 7-43); I 0-1. July 12, 2005.

**372.** **HR 742. Small Business Attorneys' Fees/Passage.** Passage of the bill that would allow courts to reimburse small businesses for their attorney fees if they successfully contest an OSHA ruling. Current law permits such reimbursement only if the court finds that OSHA was not "substantially justified" in its ruling. Passed 235-187: R 218-8; D 17-178 (ND 5-140, SD 12-38); I 0-1. July 12, 2005.

**373.** **HR 6. Energy Policy/Motion to Instruct.** Capps, D-Calif., motion to instruct House conferees to reject the inclusion of any provisions in the conference report that would provide liability protection for manufacturers of the gasoline additive methyl tertiary butyl ether. Motion rejected 201-217: R 21-204; D 179-13 (ND 141-1, SD 38-12); I 1-0. July 14, 2005.

**374.** **HR 3100. Arms Sales to China/Passage.** Hyde, R-Ill., motion to suspend the rules and pass the bill that would require the president to report to Congress 180 days after the bill's enactment, and yearly thereafter, identifying European or other entities that have exported any arms or dual-use technology to China for military use since Jan. 1, 2005. Motion rejected 215-203: R 118-106; D 96-97 (ND 70-73, SD 26-24); I 1-0. A two-thirds majority of those present and voting (279 in this case) is required for passage under suspension of the rules. July 14, 2005.

| | 369 | 370 | 371 | 372 | 373 | 374 |
|---|---|---|---|---|---|---|
| **ALABAMA** | | | | | | |
| 1 Bonner | Y | Y | Y | Y | N | N |
| 2 Everett | Y | Y | Y | Y | N | N |
| 3 Rogers | Y | Y | Y | Y | N | Y |
| 4 Aderholt | Y | Y | Y | Y | N | Y |
| 5 Cramer | Y | Y | Y | Y | N | Y |
| 6 Bachus | Y | Y | Y | Y | N | Y |
| 7 Davis | N | N | N | N | Y | Y |
| **ALASKA** | | | | | | |
| AL Young | Y | Y | Y | Y | N | N |
| **ARIZONA** | | | | | | |
| 1 Renzi | Y | Y | Y | Y | N | N |
| 2 Franks | Y | Y | Y | Y | N | Y |
| 3 Shadegg | ? | ? | ? | ? | N | Y |
| 4 Pastor | N | N | N | N | Y | N |
| 5 Hayworth | Y | Y | Y | Y | N | N |
| 6 Flake | Y | Y | Y | Y | N | N |
| 7 Grijalva | N | N | N | N | Y | Y |
| 8 Kolbe | Y | Y | Y | Y | N | N |
| **ARKANSAS** | | | | | | |
| 1 Berry | N | N | N | N | Y | N |
| 2 Snyder | N | N | N | N | Y | N |
| 3 Boozman | Y | Y | Y | Y | N | Y |
| 4 Ross | N | N | N | N | Y | Y |
| **CALIFORNIA** | | | | | | |
| 1 Thompson | N | N | N | N | Y | N |
| 2 Herger | Y | Y | Y | Y | N | Y |
| 3 Lungren | Y | Y | Y | Y | N | Y |
| 4 Doolittle | Y | Y | Y | Y | N | N |
| 5 Matsui, D. | N | N | N | N | Y | N |
| 6 Woolsey | N | N | N | N | Y | N |
| 7 Miller, George | N | N | N | N | Y | N |
| 8 Pelosi | N | N | N | N | Y | Y |
| 9 Lee | N | N | N | N | Y | N |
| 10 Tauscher | N | N | N | N | Y | N |
| 11 Pombo | + | + | + | + | N | N |
| 12 Lantos | N | N | N | N | Y | Y |
| 13 Stark | N | N | N | N | Y | N |
| 14 Eshoo | N | N | N | N | Y | N |
| 15 Honda | N | N | N | N | Y | N |
| 16 Lofgren | N | N | N | N | Y | N |
| 17 Farr | N | N | N | N | Y | Y |
| 18 Cardoza | N | N | N | N | Y | N |
| 19 Radanovich | Y | Y | Y | Y | N | N |
| 20 Costa | Y | Y | Y | Y | Y | Y |
| 21 Nunes | Y | Y | Y | Y | N | N |
| 22 Thomas | Y | Y | Y | Y | N | N |
| 23 Capps | N | N | N | N | + | N |
| 24 Gallegly | Y | Y | Y | Y | ? | ? |
| 25 McKeon | Y | Y | Y | Y | N | N |
| 26 Dreier | Y | Y | Y | Y | N | N |
| 27 Sherman | N | N | N | N | Y | N |
| 28 Berman | N | N | N | N | Y | N |
| 29 Schiff | N | N | N | N | Y | Y |
| 30 Waxman | N | N | N | N | Y | Y |
| 31 Becerra | N | N | N | N | Y | Y |
| 32 Solis | N | N | N | N | Y | Y |
| 33 Watson | N | N | N | N | Y | Y |
| 34 Roybal-Allard | N | N | N | N | Y | Y |
| 35 Waters | N | N | N | N | Y | Y |
| 36 Harman | Y | N | N | N | Y | N |
| 37 Millender-McD. | N | N | N | N | Y | Y |
| 38 Napolitano | N | N | N | N | Y | Y |
| 39 Sánchez, Linda | N | N | N | N | Y | Y |
| 40 Royce | Y | Y | Y | Y | N | N |
| 41 Lewis | Y | Y | Y | Y | N | N |
| 42 Miller, Gary | Y | Y | Y | Y | N | N |
| 43 Baca | N | N | N | N | Y | N |
| 44 Calvert | Y | Y | Y | Y | N | N |
| 45 Bono | Y | Y | Y | Y | N | N |
| 46 Rohrabacher | Y | Y | Y | Y | N | N |
| 47 Sanchez, Loretta | N | N | N | N | Y | N |
| 48 Cox | ? | Y | Y | Y | N | N |
| 49 Issa | Y | Y | Y | Y | N | N |
| 50 Cunningham | Y | Y | Y | Y | ? | ? |
| 51 Filner | N | N | N | N | Y | Y |
| 52 Hunter | Y | Y | Y | Y | N | Y |
| 53 Davis | N | N | N | N | Y | N |
| **COLORADO** | | | | | | |
| 1 DeGette | N | N | N | N | Y | Y |
| 2 Udall | Y | N | N | N | Y | N |
| 3 Salazar | Y | N | N | N | Y | Y |
| 4 Musgrave | Y | Y | Y | Y | N | Y |
| 5 Hefley | Y | Y | Y | Y | N | Y |
| 6 Tancredo | Y | Y | Y | Y | N | N |
| 7 Beauprez | Y | Y | Y | Y | N | N |
| **CONNECTICUT** | | | | | | |
| 1 Larson | N | N | N | N | Y | Y |
| 2 Simmons | Y | Y | N | Y | ? | ? |
| 3 DeLauro | N | N | N | N | Y | Y |
| 4 Shays | Y | Y | Y | Y | N | N |
| 5 Johnson | Y | Y | Y | Y | N | N |
| **DELAWARE** | | | | | | |
| AL Castle | Y | Y | Y | Y | Y | Y |
| **FLORIDA** | | | | | | |
| 1 Miller | ? | ? | ? | ? | ? | ? |
| 2 Boyd | Y | Y | Y | Y | Y | Y |
| 3 Brown | ? | ? | ? | ? | Y | Y |
| 4 Crenshaw | Y | Y | Y | Y | N | N |
| 5 Brown-Waite | Y | Y | Y | Y | N | N |
| 6 Stearns | Y | Y | Y | Y | N | N |
| 7 Mica | Y | Y | Y | Y | N | N |
| 8 Keller | Y | Y | Y | Y | N | N |
| 9 Bilirakis | Y | Y | Y | Y | N | N |
| 10 Young | Y | Y | Y | Y | ? | ? |
| 11 Davis | Y | N | N | N | Y | Y |
| 12 Putnam | Y | Y | Y | Y | N | N |
| 13 Harris | Y | Y | Y | Y | N | N |
| 14 Mack | Y | Y | Y | Y | N | N |
| 15 Weldon | Y | Y | Y | Y | N | N |
| 16 Foley | Y | Y | Y | Y | N | N |
| 17 Meek | N | N | N | N | Y | N |
| 18 Ros-Lehtinen | Y | Y | Y | Y | N | N |
| 19 Wexler | N | N | N | N | Y | Y |
| 20 Wasserman-Schultz | N | N | N | N | Y | Y |
| 21 Diaz-Balart, L. | Y | Y | Y | Y | N | N |
| 22 Shaw | Y | Y | Y | Y | N | N |
| 23 Hastings | N | N | N | N | Y | Y |
| 24 Feeney | Y | Y | Y | Y | N | N |
| 25 Diaz-Balart, M. | Y | Y | Y | Y | N | N |
| **GEORGIA** | | | | | | |
| 1 Kingston | Y | Y | Y | Y | N | N |
| 2 Bishop | Y | N | N | N | Y | Y |
| 3 Marshall | Y | N | N | N | Y | N |
| 4 McKinney | N | N | N | N | Y | Y |
| 5 Lewis | N | N | N | N | Y | Y |
| 6 Price | Y | Y | Y | Y | N | N |
| 7 Linder | Y | Y | Y | Y | N | N |
| 8 Westmoreland | Y | Y | Y | Y | N | N |
| 9 Norwood | Y | Y | Y | Y | N | N |
| 10 Deal | Y | Y | Y | Y | N | Y |
| 11 Gingrey | Y | Y | Y | Y | N | N |
| 12 Barrow | N | N | N | N | Y | Y |
| 13 Scott | N | N | N | N | Y | Y |
| **HAWAII** | | | | | | |
| 1 Abercrombie | - | - | - | - | N | Y |
| 2 Case | Y | Y | Y | Y | Y | Y |
| **IDAHO** | | | | | | |
| 1 Otter | Y | Y | Y | Y | N | N |
| 2 Simpson | Y | Y | Y | Y | N | N |
| **ILLINOIS** | | | | | | |
| 1 Rush | N | N | N | N | Y | N |
| 2 Jackson | N | N | N | N | Y | N |
| 3 Lipinski | N | N | N | N | Y | N |
| 4 Gutierrez | N | ? | N | N | + | + |
| 5 Emanuel | N | N | N | N | Y | N |
| 6 Hyde | Y | Y | Y | Y | N | Y |
| 7 Davis | N | N | N | N | Y | N |
| 8 Bean | Y | N | N | N | Y | N |
| 9 Schakowsky | N | N | N | N | Y | N |
| 10 Kirk | Y | Y | Y | Y | N | N |
| 11 Weller | Y | Y | Y | Y | N | N |
| 12 Costello | N | N | N | N | Y | N |

| KEY | Republicans | Democrats | Independents |
|---|---|---|---|

| Y | Voted for (yea) | X | Paired against | C | Voted "present" to avoid possible conflict of interest |
|---|---|---|---|---|---|
| # | Paired for | - | Announced against | | |
| + | Announced for | P | Voted "present" | ? | Did not vote or otherwise make a position known |
| N | Voted against (nay) | | | | |

ND Northern Democrats, SD Southern Democrats
Southern states: Ala., Ark., Fla., Ga., Ky., La., Miss., N.C., Okla., S.C., Tenn., Texas, Va.

| | 369 | 370 | 371 | 372 | 373 | 374 |
|---|---|---|---|---|---|---|
| 13 **Biggert** | Y | Y | Y | Y | N | N |
| 14 **Hastert** | | | | | N | |
| 15 **Johnson** | Y | Y | Y | Y | Y | Y |
| 16 **Manzullo** | Y | Y | Y | Y | N | N |
| 17 Evans | N | N | N | N | Y | Y |
| 18 **LaHood** | Y | Y | Y | Y | N | N |
| 19 **Shimkus** | Y | Y | Y | Y | N | N |
| **INDIANA** | | | | | | |
| 1 Visclosky | N | N | N | N | Y | N |
| 2 **Chocola** | Y | Y | Y | Y | N | Y |
| 3 **Souder** | Y | Y | Y | Y | N | Y |
| 4 **Buyer** | Y | Y | Y | Y | N | Y |
| 5 **Burton** | Y | Y | Y | Y | N | Y |
| 6 **Pence** | Y | Y | Y | Y | N | Y |
| 7 Carson | N | N | N | N | ? | ? |
| 8 **Hostettler** | Y | Y | Y | Y | N | Y |
| 9 **Sodrel** | Y | Y | Y | Y | N | N |
| **IOWA** | | | | | | |
| 1 **Nussle** | Y | Y | Y | Y | N | N |
| 2 **Leach** | Y | Y | Y | Y | Y | N |
| 3 Boswell | N | N | N | N | Y | N |
| 4 **Latham** | Y | Y | Y | Y | N | N |
| 5 **King** | Y | Y | Y | Y | N | N |
| **KANSAS** | | | | | | |
| 1 **Moran** | Y | Y | Y | Y | N | N |
| 2 **Ryun** | Y | Y | Y | Y | N | N |
| 3 Moore | N | N | N | N | Y | N |
| 4 **Tiahrt** | Y | Y | Y | Y | N | N |
| **KENTUCKY** | | | | | | |
| 1 **Whitfield** | Y | Y | Y | Y | N | N |
| 2 **Lewis** | Y | Y | Y | Y | N | N |
| 3 **Northup** | Y | Y | Y | Y | N | Y |
| 4 **Davis** | Y | Y | Y | Y | N | N |
| 5 **Rogers** | Y | Y | Y | Y | N | Y |
| 6 Chandler | N | N | N | N | Y | Y |
| **LOUISIANA** | | | | | | |
| 1 **Jindal** | Y | Y | Y | Y | N | Y |
| 2 Jefferson | N | N | N | N | Y | N |
| 3 Melancon | N | N | N | N | N | Y |
| 4 **McCrery** | Y | Y | Y | Y | N | N |
| 5 **Alexander** | Y | Y | Y | Y | N | Y |
| 6 **Baker** | Y | Y | Y | Y | N | N |
| 7 **Boustany** | Y | Y | Y | Y | N | N |
| **MAINE** | | | | | | |
| 1 Allen | N | N | N | N | Y | Y |
| 2 Michaud | N | N | N | N | Y | Y |
| **MARYLAND** | | | | | | |
| 1 **Gilchrest** | Y | Y | Y | Y | N | N |
| 2 Ruppersberger | N | N | N | N | Y | N |
| 3 Cardin | ? | ? | ? | ? | ? | ? |
| 4 Wynn | Y | N | N | Y | Y | N |
| 5 Hoyer | N | N | N | N | Y | N |
| 6 **Bartlett** | Y | Y | Y | Y | N | N |
| 7 Cummings | N | N | N | N | Y | Y |
| 8 Van Hollen | N | N | N | N | Y | N |
| **MASSACHUSETTS** | | | | | | |
| 1 Olver | N | N | N | N | Y | N |
| 2 Neal | N | N | N | N | Y | Y |
| 3 McGovern | N | N | N | N | Y | N |
| 4 Frank | N | N | N | N | Y | Y |
| 5 Meehan | N | N | N | N | Y | N |
| 6 Tierney | N | N | N | N | Y | Y |
| 7 Markey | N | N | N | N | Y | Y |
| 8 Capuano | N | N | N | N | Y | N |
| 9 Lynch | N | N | N | N | Y | N |
| 10 Delahunt | N | N | N | N | Y | N |
| **MICHIGAN** | | | | | | |
| 1 Stupak | N | N | N | N | Y | Y |
| 2 **Hoekstra** | Y | Y | Y | Y | N | N |
| 3 **Ehlers** | Y | Y | Y | Y | N | N |
| 4 **Camp** | Y | Y | Y | Y | N | N |
| 5 Kildee | N | N | N | N | Y | Y |
| 6 **Upton** | Y | Y | Y | Y | N | N |
| 7 **Schwarz** | Y | Y | Y | Y | N | Y |
| 8 **Rogers** | Y | Y | Y | Y | N | Y |
| 9 **Knollenberg** | Y | Y | Y | Y | N | Y |
| 10 **Miller** | Y | Y | Y | Y | N | Y |
| 11 **McCotter** | Y | Y | Y | Y | N | Y |
| 12 Levin | N | N | N | N | Y | N |
| 13 Kilpatrick | N | N | N | N | + | + |
| 14 Conyers | – | – | – | – | Y | Y |
| 15 Dingell | N | N | N | N | Y | Y |
| **MINNESOTA** | | | | | | |
| 1 **Gutknecht** | Y | Y | Y | Y | N | N |
| 2 **Kline** | Y | Y | Y | Y | N | N |
| 3 **Ramstad** | Y | Y | Y | Y | Y | Y |
| 4 McCollum | N | N | N | N | Y | N |
| 5 Sabo | N | N | N | N | Y | N |
| 6 **Kennedy** | Y | Y | Y | Y | N | N |
| 7 Peterson | N | N | N | N | Y | Y |
| 8 Oberstar | N | N | N | N | ? | ? |
| **MISSISSIPPI** | | | | | | |
| 1 **Wicker** | Y | Y | Y | Y | N | Y |
| 2 Thompson | N | N | N | N | Y | Y |
| 3 **Pickering** | Y | Y | Y | Y | N | Y |
| 4 Taylor | Y | Y | Y | Y | Y | Y |
| **MISSOURI** | | | | | | |
| 1 Clay | N | N | N | N | Y | N |
| 2 **Akin** | Y | Y | Y | Y | N | Y |
| 3 Carnahan | N | N | N | N | Y | Y |
| 4 Skelton | Y | N | N | N | Y | N |
| 5 Cleaver | N | N | N | N | Y | Y |
| 6 **Graves** | Y | Y | Y | Y | N | Y |
| 7 **Blunt** | Y | Y | Y | Y | N | Y |
| 8 **Emerson** | Y | Y | Y | Y | N | Y |
| 9 **Hulshof** | Y | Y | Y | Y | N | N |
| **MONTANA** | | | | | | |
| AL **Rehberg** | Y | Y | Y | Y | N | N |
| **NEBRASKA** | | | | | | |
| 1 **Fortenberry** | Y | Y | Y | Y | N | Y |
| 2 **Terry** | Y | Y | Y | Y | N | Y |
| 3 **Osborne** | Y | Y | Y | Y | N | Y |
| **NEVADA** | | | | | | |
| 1 Berkley | N | N | N | N | Y | Y |
| 2 **Gibbons** | Y | Y | Y | Y | N | N |
| 3 **Porter** | Y | Y | Y | Y | N | Y |
| **NEW HAMPSHIRE** | | | | | | |
| 1 **Bradley** | Y | Y | Y | Y | Y | Y |
| 2 **Bass** | Y | Y | Y | Y | N | N |
| **NEW JERSEY** | | | | | | |
| 1 Andrews | N | N | N | N | Y | Y |
| 2 **LoBiondo** | Y | Y | N | N | Y | N |
| 3 **Saxton** | Y | Y | N | N | Y | N |
| 4 **Smith** | Y | Y | N | N | Y | Y |
| 5 **Garrett** | Y | Y | Y | Y | N | N |
| 6 Pallone | N | N | N | N | Y | N |
| 7 **Ferguson** | Y | Y | Y | Y | N | N |
| 8 Pascrell | N | N | N | N | Y | Y |
| 9 Rothman | N | N | N | N | Y | Y |
| 10 Payne | N | N | N | N | Y | N |
| 11 **Frelinghuysen** | Y | Y | Y | Y | Y | N |
| 12 Holt | N | N | N | N | Y | N |
| 13 Menendez | N | N | N | – | Y | N |
| **NEW MEXICO** | | | | | | |
| 1 **Wilson** | Y | Y | Y | Y | Y | N |
| 2 **Pearce** | Y | Y | Y | Y | N | Y |
| 3 Udall | N | N | N | N | Y | N |
| **NEW YORK** | | | | | | |
| 1 Bishop | N | N | N | N | Y | Y |
| 2 Israel | N | N | N | N | Y | N |
| 3 **King** | Y | Y | N | Y | N | Y |
| 4 McCarthy | N | N | N | N | Y | N |
| 5 Ackerman | N | N | N | N | Y | Y |
| 6 Meeks | N | N | N | N | Y | N |
| 7 Crowley | N | N | N | N | Y | Y |
| 8 Nadler | N | N | N | N | Y | Y |
| 9 Weiner | N | N | N | N | ? | ? |
| 10 Towns | ? | ? | N | N | Y | Y |
| 11 Owens | N | N | N | N | Y | Y |
| 12 Velázquez | Y | N | N | Y | Y | N |
| 13 **Fossella** | Y | Y | Y | Y | N | N |
| 14 Maloney | N | N | N | N | Y | Y |
| 15 Rangel | N | ? | N | N | Y | N |
| 16 Serrano | N | N | N | N | Y | Y |
| 17 Engel | N | N | N | N | Y | Y |
| 18 Lowey | N | N | N | N | Y | Y |
| 19 **Kelly** | Y | Y | Y | Y | Y | Y |
| 20 **Sweeney** | Y | Y | N | Y | Y | N |
| 21 McNulty | N | N | N | N | Y | Y |
| 22 Hinchey | N | N | N | N | Y | N |
| 23 **McHugh** | Y | Y | N | Y | N | N |
| 24 **Boehlert** | Y | Y | Y | N | Y | N |
| 25 **Walsh** | Y | Y | Y | Y | N | Y |
| 26 **Reynolds** | Y | Y | Y | Y | N | Y |
| 27 Higgins | N | N | N | N | Y | Y |
| 28 Slaughter | N | N | N | N | Y | N |
| 29 **Kuhl** | Y | Y | Y | Y | N | N |
| **NORTH CAROLINA** | | | | | | |
| 1 Butterfield | N | N | N | N | Y | Y |
| 2 Etheridge | N | N | N | N | Y | N |
| 3 **Jones** | Y | Y | Y | Y | N | Y |
| 4 Price | N | N | N | N | Y | N |
| 5 **Foxx** | Y | Y | Y | Y | N | Y |
| 6 **Coble** | Y | Y | Y | Y | N | N |
| 7 McIntyre | Y | N | N | N | ? | ? |
| 8 **Hayes** | Y | Y | Y | Y | N | Y |
| 9 **Myrick** | ? | ? | ? | ? | N | Y |
| 10 **McHenry** | Y | Y | Y | Y | N | Y |
| 11 **Taylor** | Y | Y | Y | Y | N | Y |
| 12 Watt | N | ? | N | N | Y | N |
| 13 Miller | N | N | N | N | Y | N |
| **NORTH DAKOTA** | | | | | | |
| AL Pomeroy | N | N | N | N | Y | N |
| **OHIO** | | | | | | |
| 1 **Chabot** | Y | Y | Y | Y | N | Y |
| 2 Vacant | | | | | | |
| 3 **Turner** | Y | Y | Y | Y | N | N |
| 4 **Oxley** | Y | Y | Y | Y | N | Y |
| 5 **Gillmor** | Y | Y | Y | Y | N | Y |
| 6 Strickland | N | N | N | N | ? | Y |
| 7 **Hobson** | Y | Y | Y | Y | N | N |
| 8 **Boehner** | Y | Y | Y | Y | N | N |
| 9 Kaptur | N | N | N | N | Y | Y |
| 10 Kucinich | N | N | N | N | Y | Y |
| 11 Jones | ? | ? | ? | ? | Y | N |
| 12 **Tiberi** | Y | Y | Y | Y | N | N |
| 13 Brown | N | N | N | N | Y | Y |
| 14 **LaTourette** | Y | Y | Y | N | N | N |
| 15 **Pryce** | Y | Y | Y | Y | N | N |
| 16 **Regula** | Y | Y | Y | Y | N | N |
| 17 Ryan | N | N | N | N | Y | Y |
| 18 **Ney** | Y | Y | Y | Y | N | Y |
| **OKLAHOMA** | | | | | | |
| 1 **Sullivan** | Y | Y | Y | Y | N | N |
| 2 Boren | Y | Y | Y | Y | N | N |
| 3 **Lucas** | Y | Y | Y | Y | N | Y |
| 4 **Cole** | Y | Y | Y | Y | N | Y |
| 5 **Istook** | Y | Y | Y | Y | N | Y |
| **OREGON** | | | | | | |
| 1 Wu | N | N | N | N | Y | Y |
| 2 **Walden** | Y | Y | Y | Y | N | Y |
| 3 Blumenauer | N | N | N | N | Y | N |
| 4 DeFazio | N | N | N | N | Y | Y |
| 5 Hooley | N | N | N | N | Y | N |
| **PENNSYLVANIA** | | | | | | |
| 1 Brady | N | N | N | N | Y | Y |
| 2 Fattah | N | N | N | N | Y | Y |
| 3 **English** | Y | Y | Y | Y | N | N |
| 4 **Hart** | Y | Y | Y | Y | N | N |
| 5 **Peterson** | Y | Y | Y | Y | N | Y |
| 6 **Gerlach** | Y | Y | Y | Y | N | Y |
| 7 **Weldon** | Y | Y | Y | N | N | Y |
| 8 **Fitzpatrick** | Y | Y | N | N | Y | Y |
| 9 **Shuster** | Y | Y | Y | Y | N | N |
| 10 **Sherwood** | Y | Y | Y | Y | N | Y |
| 11 Kanjorski | N | N | N | N | Y | Y |
| 12 Murtha | N | N | N | N | Y | N |
| 13 Schwartz | N | N | N | N | Y | Y |
| 14 Doyle | N | N | N | N | Y | Y |
| 15 **Dent** | Y | Y | Y | Y | N | Y |
| 16 **Pitts** | Y | Y | Y | Y | N | Y |
| 17 Holden | N | N | N | N | Y | Y |
| 18 **Murphy** | Y | Y | Y | Y | N | N |
| 19 **Platts** | Y | Y | Y | Y | N | Y |
| **RHODE ISLAND** | | | | | | |
| 1 Kennedy | N | N | N | N | Y | Y |
| 2 Langevin | N | N | N | N | Y | Y |
| **SOUTH CAROLINA** | | | | | | |
| 1 **Brown** | Y | Y | Y | Y | N | N |
| 2 **Wilson** | Y | Y | Y | Y | N | Y |
| 3 **Barrett** | Y | Y | Y | Y | N | Y |
| 4 **Inglis** | Y | Y | Y | Y | N | Y |
| 5 Spratt | N | N | N | N | Y | Y |
| 6 Clyburn | N | N | N | N | Y | N |
| **SOUTH DAKOTA** | | | | | | |
| AL Herseth | Y | N | N | N | Y | N |
| **TENNESSEE** | | | | | | |
| 1 **Jenkins** | Y | Y | Y | Y | N | N |
| 2 **Duncan** | Y | Y | Y | Y | N | Y |
| 3 **Wamp** | Y | Y | Y | Y | N | Y |
| 4 Davis | Y | N | Y | Y | Y | Y |
| 5 Cooper | Y | N | N | Y | Y | Y |
| 6 Gordon | Y | Y | N | N | Y | N |
| 7 **Blackburn** | Y | Y | Y | Y | N | Y |
| 8 Tanner | Y | N | N | Y | Y | Y |
| 9 Ford | Y | N | N | Y | Y | Y |
| **TEXAS** | | | | | | |
| 1 **Gohmert** | Y | Y | Y | Y | N | N |
| 2 **Poe** | Y | Y | Y | Y | N | N |
| 3 **Johnson, S.** | Y | Y | Y | Y | N | Y |
| 4 **Hall** | Y | Y | Y | Y | N | N |
| 5 **Hensarling** | Y | Y | Y | Y | N | N |
| 6 **Barton** | Y | Y | Y | Y | N | Y |
| 7 **Culberson** | Y | Y | Y | Y | N | Y |
| 8 **Brady** | Y | Y | Y | Y | N | N |
| 9 Green, A. | N | N | N | N | N | Y |
| 10 **McCaul** | Y | Y | Y | Y | N | Y |
| 11 **Conaway** | Y | Y | Y | Y | N | N |
| 12 **Granger** | Y | Y | Y | Y | N | Y |
| 13 **Thornberry** | Y | Y | Y | Y | N | N |
| 14 **Paul** | Y | Y | N | Y | N | N |
| 15 Hinojosa | – | N | N | N | N | Y |
| 16 Reyes | N | N | N | N | N | N |
| 17 Edwards | Y | N | N | Y | N | Y |
| 18 Jackson-Lee | N | N | N | N | N | Y |
| 19 **Neugebauer** | Y | Y | Y | Y | N | N |
| 20 Gonzalez | Y | N | N | Y | N | N |
| 21 **Smith** | Y | Y | Y | Y | N | N |
| 22 **DeLay** | Y | Y | Y | Y | N | Y |
| 23 **Bonilla** | Y | Y | Y | Y | N | N |
| 24 **Marchant** | Y | Y | Y | Y | N | N |
| 25 Doggett | N | N | N | N | Y | Y |
| 26 **Burgess** | Y | Y | Y | Y | N | N |
| 27 Ortiz | N | N | N | N | N | N |
| 28 Cuellar | Y | Y | Y | Y | N | N |
| 29 Green, G. | N | N | N | N | N | Y |
| 30 Johnson, E. | N | N | N | N | Y | Y |
| 31 **Carter** | Y | Y | Y | Y | N | N |
| 32 **Sessions** | Y | Y | Y | Y | N | N |
| **UTAH** | | | | | | |
| 1 **Bishop** | Y | Y | Y | Y | N | Y |
| 2 Matheson | Y | Y | Y | Y | Y | Y |
| 3 **Cannon** | Y | Y | Y | Y | N | N |
| **VERMONT** | | | | | | |
| AL *Sanders* | N | N | N | N | Y | Y |
| **VIRGINIA** | | | | | | |
| 1 **Davis, J.** | Y | Y | Y | Y | N | Y |
| 2 **Drake** | Y | Y | Y | Y | N | Y |
| 3 Scott | N | N | N | N | Y | N |
| 4 **Forbes** | Y | Y | Y | Y | N | Y |
| 5 **Goode** | Y | Y | Y | Y | N | Y |
| 6 **Goodlatte** | Y | Y | Y | Y | N | N |
| 7 **Cantor** | Y | Y | Y | Y | N | Y |
| 8 Moran | N | N | N | N | Y | N |
| 9 Boucher | N | N | N | N | Y | N |
| 10 **Wolf** | Y | Y | Y | Y | Y | Y |
| 11 **Davis, T.** | Y | Y | Y | Y | Y | N |
| **WASHINGTON** | | | | | | |
| 1 Inslee | N | N | N | N | Y | N |
| 2 Larsen | N | N | N | N | Y | N |
| 3 Baird | Y | N | N | N | Y | N |
| 4 **Hastings** | Y | Y | Y | Y | N | Y |
| 5 **McMorris** | Y | Y | Y | Y | N | Y |
| 6 Dicks | N | N | N | N | Y | N |
| 7 McDermott | N | N | N | N | Y | N |
| 8 **Reichert** | Y | Y | Y | Y | Y | N |
| 9 Smith | N | N | N | N | Y | N |
| **WEST VIRGINIA** | | | | | | |
| 1 Mollohan | Y | N | N | N | Y | Y |
| 2 **Capito** | Y | Y | Y | Y | N | Y |
| 3 Rahall | Y | N | N | N | Y | N |
| **WISCONSIN** | | | | | | |
| 1 **Ryan** | Y | Y | Y | Y | N | N |
| 2 Baldwin | N | N | N | N | Y | Y |
| 3 Kind | N | N | N | N | Y | N |
| 4 Moore | N | N | N | N | Y | Y |
| 5 **Sensenbrenner** | Y | Y | Y | Y | Y | N |
| 6 **Petri** | Y | Y | Y | Y | N | N |
| 7 Obey | ? | ? | ? | ? | ? | ? |
| 8 **Green** | Y | Y | Y | Y | Y | Y |
| **WYOMING** | | | | | | |
| AL **Cubin** | Y | Y | Y | Y | ? | ? |

# IN THE HOUSE | By Vote Number

**375.** **H Res 356. London Bombings Condemnation/Adoption.** Hyde, R-Ill., motion to suspend the rules and adopt the resolution that would condemn the London terrorist attacks on July 7, 2005, and express condolences to the families and friends of those killed in the attacks and sympathies to those injured. Motion agreed to 416-0: R 224-0; D 191-0 (ND 142-0, SD 49-0); I 1-0. A two-thirds majority of those present and voting (278 in this case) is required for adoption under suspension of the rules. July 14, 2005.

**376.** **HR 2864. Water Resources Development/Tonnage Fees.** Rohrabacher, R-Calif., amendment that would permit ports to impose container fees in addition to tonnage fees and currently allowed fees on imports. It would also expand the allowed use of collected fees to include construction, operation and maintenance of infrastructure and security services related to the port that levies the fee. Rejected 111-310: R 57-167; D 53-143 (ND 46-100, SD 7-43); I 1-0. July 14, 2005.

**377.** **HR 2864. Water Resources Development/Upper Mississippi River and Illinois Waterway System.** Flake, R-Ariz., amendment that would allow the Army Corps of Engineers to proceed with seven new locks authorized in the bill on the Mississippi and Illinois rivers only if more than an average of 35 million tons of commodities per lock are processed in 2007 through 2009. It would also require the Corps to implement an appointment system to schedule and prioritize barge traffic and prepare two reports to evaluate any project that goes forward. Rejected 105-315: R 46-179; D 59-136 (ND 51-94, SD 8-42); I 0-0. July 14, 2005.

**378.** **HR 2864. Water Resources Development/Passage.** Passage of the bill that would authorize $11.6 billion for more than 700 water resource development projects and studies by the Army Corps of Engineers for flood control, navigation, beach erosion control and environmental restoration. Certain water development projects that exceed $50 million would receive an independent review. The bill would authorize $3.4 billion for a system of new locks and dams and environmental restoration for the Upper Mississippi River and Illinois waterway system. Passed 406-14: R 211-13; D 194-1 (ND 145-0, SD 49-1); I 1-0. July 14, 2005.

**379.** **H Con Res 191. Victory in Japan Day Tribute/Adoption.** Hyde, R-Ill., motion to suspend the rules and adopt the concurrent resolution that would honor all veterans of World War II on the 60th anniversary of the war's end and call upon the public to commemorate Sept. 2, 2005, as a day of remembrance and appreciation. Motion agreed to 399-0: R 213-0; D 186-0 (ND 140-0, SD 46-0); I 0-0. A two-thirds majority of those present and voting (266 in this case) is required for adoption under suspension of the rules. July 14, 2005.

| | 375 | 376 | 377 | 378 | 379 |
|---|---|---|---|---|---|
| **ALABAMA** | | | | | |
| 1 Bonner | Y | N | N | Y | Y |
| 2 Everett | Y | N | N | Y | ? |
| 3 Rogers | Y | N | N | Y | Y |
| 4 Aderholt | Y | N | N | Y | Y |
| 5 Cramer | Y | N | N | Y | Y |
| 6 Bachus | Y | Y | N | Y | Y |
| 7 Davis | Y | N | N | Y | Y |
| **ALASKA** | | | | | |
| AL Young | Y | N | N | Y | Y |
| **ARIZONA** | | | | | |
| 1 Renzi | Y | Y | N | Y | Y |
| 2 Franks | ? | Y | Y | N | Y |
| 3 Shadegg | Y | Y | Y | N | Y |
| 4 Pastor | Y | N | N | Y | Y |
| 5 Hayworth | Y | Y | Y | Y | Y |
| 6 Flake | Y | Y | Y | N | Y |
| 7 Grijalva | Y | N | N | Y | Y |
| 8 Kolbe | Y | N | Y | Y | Y |
| **ARKANSAS** | | | | | |
| 1 Berry | Y | N | N | Y | Y |
| 2 Snyder | Y | N | N | Y | Y |
| 3 Boozman | Y | N | N | Y | Y |
| 4 Ross | Y | N | N | Y | Y |
| **CALIFORNIA** | | | | | |
| 1 Thompson | Y | N | N | Y | Y |
| 2 Herger | Y | Y | N | Y | Y |
| 3 Lungren | Y | Y | N | Y | Y |
| 4 Doolittle | Y | Y | N | Y | Y |
| 5 Matsui, D. | Y | N | N | Y | Y |
| 6 Woolsey | Y | N | Y | Y | Y |
| 7 Miller, George | Y | N | Y | Y | Y |
| 8 Pelosi | Y | N | ? | ? | Y |
| 9 Lee | Y | N | N | Y | Y |
| 10 Tauscher | Y | N | N | Y | Y |
| 11 Pombo | Y | Y | N | Y | Y |
| 12 Lantos | Y | N | N | Y | Y |
| 13 Stark | Y | N | Y | Y | Y |
| 14 Eshoo | Y | N | Y | Y | Y |
| 15 Honda | Y | N | Y | Y | Y |
| 16 Lofgren | Y | N | Y | Y | Y |
| 17 Farr | Y | Y | Y | Y | Y |
| 18 Cardoza | Y | N | N | Y | Y |
| 19 Radanovich | Y | N | N | Y | Y |
| 20 Costa | Y | Y | N | Y | Y |
| 21 Nunes | Y | N | N | Y | Y |
| 22 Thomas | Y | N | N | Y | Y |
| 23 Capps | + | - | + | + | + |
| 24 Gallegly | ? | ? | ? | ? | ? |
| 25 McKeon | Y | N | N | Y | Y |
| 26 Dreier | Y | N | N | Y | Y |
| 27 Sherman | Y | Y | Y | Y | Y |
| 28 Berman | Y | N | N | Y | Y |
| 29 Schiff | Y | N | N | Y | Y |
| 30 Waxman | Y | N | Y | Y | Y |
| 31 Becerra | Y | N | N | Y | Y |
| 32 Solis | Y | N | N | Y | Y |
| 33 Watson | Y | N | Y | Y | Y |
| 34 Roybal-Allard | Y | N | N | Y | Y |
| 35 Waters | Y | N | N | Y | Y |
| 36 Harman | Y | Y | Y | Y | Y |
| 37 Millender-McD. | Y | N | N | Y | Y |
| 38 Napolitano | Y | Y | N | Y | Y |
| 39 Sánchez, Linda | Y | N | N | Y | Y |
| 40 Royce | Y | Y | Y | N | Y |
| 41 Lewis | Y | N | N | Y | Y |
| 42 Miller, Gary | Y | N | N | Y | Y |
| 43 Baca | Y | N | N | Y | Y |
| 44 Calvert | Y | Y | N | Y | Y |
| 45 Bono | Y | Y | Y | Y | Y |
| 46 Rohrabacher | Y | Y | Y | Y | Y |
| 47 Sanchez, Loretta | Y | Y | Y | Y | Y |
| 48 Cox | Y | N | N | Y | Y |
| 49 Issa | Y | Y | N | Y | Y |
| 50 Cunningham | ? | ? | ? | ? | ? |
| 51 Filner | Y | N | N | Y | Y |
| 52 Hunter | Y | Y | N | Y | Y |
| 53 Davis | Y | N | Y | Y | Y |
| **COLORADO** | | | | | |
| 1 DeGette | Y | Y | Y | Y | Y |
| 2 Udall | Y | Y | Y | Y | Y |
| 3 Salazar | Y | N | N | Y | Y |
| 4 Musgrave | Y | N | N | Y | ? |
| 5 Hefley | Y | Y | N | Y | Y |
| 6 Tancredo | Y | Y | Y | N | Y |
| 7 Beauprez | Y | N | N | Y | Y |
| **CONNECTICUT** | | | | | |
| 1 Larson | Y | Y | N | Y | Y |
| 2 Simmons | Y | N | N | Y | Y |
| 3 DeLauro | Y | Y | Y | Y | Y |
| 4 Shays | Y | N | Y | Y | Y |
| 5 Johnson | Y | N | Y | Y | Y |
| **DELAWARE** | | | | | |
| AL Castle | Y | N | Y | Y | Y |
| **FLORIDA** | | | | | |
| 1 Miller | ? | ? | ? | ? | ? |
| 2 Boyd | Y | N | N | Y | ? |
| 3 Brown | Y | N | N | Y | Y |
| 4 Crenshaw | Y | N | N | Y | Y |
| 5 Brown-Waite | Y | Y | N | Y | Y |
| 6 Stearns | Y | Y | Y | N | Y |
| 7 Mica | Y | N | Y | Y | Y |
| 8 Keller | Y | N | N | Y | Y |
| 9 Bilirakis | Y | N | N | Y | ? |
| 10 Young | ? | ? | ? | ? | ? |
| 11 Davis | Y | N | N | Y | Y |
| 12 Putnam | Y | N | N | Y | Y |
| 13 Harris | Y | N | N | Y | Y |
| 14 Mack | Y | N | N | Y | Y |
| 15 Weldon | Y | N | N | Y | Y |
| 16 Foley | Y | N | N | Y | Y |
| 17 Meek | Y | N | N | Y | Y |
| 18 Ros-Lehtinen | Y | N | N | Y | Y |
| 19 Wexler | Y | N | N | Y | Y |
| 20 Wasserman-Schultz | Y | N | N | Y | Y |
| 21 Diaz-Balart, L. | Y | N | N | Y | Y |
| 22 Shaw | Y | N | N | Y | Y |
| 23 Hastings | Y | N | Y | Y | Y |
| 24 Feeney | Y | Y | Y | Y | Y |
| 25 Diaz-Balart, M. | Y | N | N | Y | Y |
| **GEORGIA** | | | | | |
| 1 Kingston | Y | N | N | Y | Y |
| 2 Bishop | Y | N | N | Y | Y |
| 3 Marshall | Y | Y | Y | Y | ? |
| 4 McKinney | Y | Y | Y | Y | Y |
| 5 Lewis | Y | N | N | Y | Y |
| 6 Price | Y | N | N | Y | Y |
| 7 Linder | Y | N | N | Y | Y |
| 8 Westmoreland | Y | N | N | Y | Y |
| 9 Norwood | Y | N | N | Y | Y |
| 10 Deal | Y | N | N | Y | Y |
| 11 Gingrey | Y | N | Y | Y | Y |
| 12 Barrow | Y | Y | N | Y | Y |
| 13 Scott | Y | Y | N | Y | Y |
| **HAWAII** | | | | | |
| 1 Abercrombie | ? | Y | N | Y | Y |
| 2 Case | Y | Y | N | Y | Y |
| **IDAHO** | | | | | |
| 1 Otter | Y | Y | Y | Y | Y |
| 2 Simpson | Y | N | N | Y | Y |
| **ILLINOIS** | | | | | |
| 1 Rush | Y | N | N | Y | Y |
| 2 Jackson | Y | N | N | Y | Y |
| 3 Lipinski | Y | N | N | Y | Y |
| 4 Gutierrez | Y | N | N | Y | Y |
| 5 Emanuel | Y | N | N | Y | Y |
| 6 Hyde | Y | N | N | Y | Y |
| 7 Davis | Y | N | N | Y | Y |
| 8 Bean | Y | N | N | Y | Y |
| 9 Schakowsky | Y | N | N | Y | Y |
| 10 Kirk | Y | N | N | Y | Y |
| 11 Weller | Y | N | N | Y | Y |
| 12 Costello | Y | Y | N | Y | Y |

| KEY | Republicans | Democrats | *Independents* |
|---|---|---|---|
| **Y** Voted for (yea) | **X** Paired against | **C** Voted "present" to avoid possible conflict of interest |
| **#** Paired for | **-** Announced against | |
| **+** Announced for | **P** Voted "present" | **?** Did not vote or otherwise make a position known |
| **N** Voted against (nay) | | |

ND Northern Democrats, SD Southern Democrats
Southern states: Ala., Ark., Fla., Ga., Ky., La., Miss., N.C., Okla., S.C., Tenn., Texas, Va.

| | 375 | 376 | 377 | 378 | 379 |
|---|---|---|---|---|---|
| 13 Biggert | Y | N | N | Y | Y |
| 14 Hastert | Y | | | | |
| 15 Johnson | Y | N | N | Y | Y |
| 16 Manzullo | Y | N | N | Y | Y |
| 17 Evans | Y | Y | N | Y | Y |
| 18 LaHood | Y | N | N | Y | Y |
| 19 Shimkus | Y | N | N | Y | Y |
| **INDIANA** | | | | | |
| 1 Visclosky | Y | N | N | Y | Y |
| 2 Chocola | Y | N | Y | Y | Y |
| 3 Souder | Y | Y | N | Y | Y |
| 4 Buyer | Y | Y | N | Y | Y |
| 5 Burton | Y | Y | Y | Y | Y |
| 6 Pence | Y | Y | Y | Y | Y |
| 7 Carson | ? | ? | ? | ? | ? |
| 8 Hostettler | Y | Y | N | Y | Y |
| 9 Sodrel | Y | Y | N | Y | Y |
| **IOWA** | | | | | |
| 1 Nussle | Y | N | N | Y | Y |
| 2 Leach | Y | N | N | Y | Y |
| 3 Boswell | Y | N | N | Y | Y |
| 4 Latham | Y | N | N | Y | Y |
| 5 King | Y | Y | N | Y | Y |
| **KANSAS** | | | | | |
| 1 Moran | Y | N | N | Y | Y |
| 2 Ryun | Y | N | N | Y | Y |
| 3 Moore | Y | N | N | Y | Y |
| 4 Tiahrt | Y | N | N | Y | Y |
| **KENTUCKY** | | | | | |
| 1 Whitfield | Y | N | N | Y | Y |
| 2 Lewis | Y | N | N | Y | Y |
| 3 Northup | Y | N | N | Y | Y |
| 4 Davis | Y | N | N | Y | Y |
| 5 Rogers | Y | N | N | Y | Y |
| 6 Chandler | Y | N | N | Y | Y |
| **LOUISIANA** | | | | | |
| 1 Jindal | Y | N | N | Y | Y |
| 2 Jefferson | Y | N | N | Y | Y |
| 3 Melancon | Y | N | N | Y | Y |
| 4 McCrery | Y | N | N | Y | Y |
| 5 Alexander | Y | N | N | Y | Y |
| 6 Baker | Y | N | N | Y | Y |
| 7 Boustany | Y | N | N | Y | Y |
| **MAINE** | | | | | |
| 1 Allen | Y | N | N | Y | Y |
| 2 Michaud | Y | N | Y | Y | Y |
| **MARYLAND** | | | | | |
| 1 Gilchrest | Y | N | N | Y | Y |
| 2 Ruppersberger | Y | N | N | Y | Y |
| 3 Cardin | ? | ? | ? | ? | ? |
| 4 Wynn | Y | N | N | Y | Y |
| 5 Hoyer | Y | N | N | Y | Y |
| 6 Bartlett | Y | Y | Y | Y | Y |
| 7 Cummings | Y | N | N | Y | Y |
| 8 Van Hollen | Y | N | Y | Y | Y |
| **MASSACHUSETTS** | | | | | |
| 1 Olver | Y | Y | Y | Y | ? |
| 2 Neal | Y | N | N | Y | Y |
| 3 McGovern | Y | Y | Y | Y | Y |
| 4 Frank | Y | Y | N | Y | Y |
| 5 Meehan | Y | N | N | Y | ? |
| 6 Tierney | Y | N | Y | Y | Y |
| 7 Markey | Y | Y | N | Y | Y |
| 8 Capuano | Y | N | N | Y | Y |
| 9 Lynch | Y | N | N | Y | Y |
| 10 Delahunt | Y | Y | N | Y | ? |
| **MICHIGAN** | | | | | |
| 1 Stupak | Y | N | N | Y | Y |
| 2 Hoekstra | Y | N | Y | Y | Y |
| 3 Ehlers | Y | N | N | Y | Y |
| 4 Camp | Y | N | N | Y | Y |
| 5 Kildee | Y | N | N | Y | Y |
| 6 Upton | Y | N | N | Y | Y |
| 7 Schwarz | Y | Y | N | Y | Y |
| 8 Rogers | Y | Y | N | Y | Y |
| 9 Knollenberg | Y | N | N | Y | Y |
| 10 Miller | Y | Y | N | Y | Y |
| 11 McCotter | Y | Y | Y | Y | Y |
| 12 Levin | Y | N | N | Y | Y |
| 13 Kilpatrick | + | + | + | + | + |
| 14 Conyers | Y | N | N | Y | Y |
| 15 Dingell | Y | Y | Y | Y | Y |

| | 375 | 376 | 377 | 378 | 379 |
|---|---|---|---|---|---|
| **MINNESOTA** | | | | | |
| 1 Gutknecht | Y | Y | N | Y | Y |
| 2 Kline | Y | N | N | Y | Y |
| 3 Ramstad | Y | N | Y | Y | Y |
| 4 McCollum | Y | Y | Y | Y | Y |
| 5 Sabo | Y | N | N | Y | Y |
| 6 Kennedy | Y | N | N | Y | Y |
| 7 Peterson | Y | Y | N | Y | Y |
| 8 Oberstar | ? | ? | ? | ? | ? |
| **MISSISSIPPI** | | | | | |
| 1 Wicker | Y | N | N | Y | Y |
| 2 Thompson | Y | N | N | Y | Y |
| 3 Pickering | Y | N | N | Y | Y |
| 4 Taylor | Y | Y | N | Y | |
| **MISSOURI** | | | | | |
| 1 Clay | Y | N | N | Y | Y |
| 2 Akin | Y | Y | N | Y | Y |
| 3 Carnahan | Y | N | N | Y | Y |
| 4 Skelton | Y | N | N | Y | Y |
| 5 Cleaver | Y | N | N | Y | Y |
| 6 Graves | Y | N | N | Y | Y |
| 7 Blunt | Y | Y | N | Y | Y |
| 8 Emerson | Y | Y | N | Y | Y |
| 9 Hulshof | Y | N | N | Y | Y |
| **MONTANA** | | | | | |
| AL Rehberg | Y | N | N | Y | Y |
| **NEBRASKA** | | | | | |
| 1 Fortenberry | Y | Y | N | Y | Y |
| 2 Terry | Y | N | N | Y | ? |
| 3 Osborne | Y | N | N | Y | ? |
| **NEVADA** | | | | | |
| 1 Berkley | Y | N | Y | Y | Y |
| 2 Gibbons | Y | N | Y | Y | Y |
| 3 Porter | Y | N | N | Y | Y |
| **NEW HAMPSHIRE** | | | | | |
| 1 Bradley | Y | N | Y | Y | Y |
| 2 Bass | Y | N | Y | Y | Y |
| **NEW JERSEY** | | | | | |
| 1 Andrews | Y | N | Y | Y | Y |
| 2 LoBiondo | Y | N | N | Y | Y |
| 3 Saxton | Y | N | Y | Y | ? |
| 4 Smith | Y | N | N | Y | Y |
| 5 Garrett | Y | N | Y | Y | Y |
| 6 Pallone | Y | N | N | Y | Y |
| 7 Ferguson | Y | N | N | Y | Y |
| 8 Pascrell | Y | N | N | Y | Y |
| 9 Rothman | Y | N | N | Y | Y |
| 10 Payne | Y | N | N | Y | Y |
| 11 Frelinghuysen | Y | N | N | Y | ? |
| 12 Holt | Y | N | N | Y | Y |
| 13 Menendez | Y | N | N | Y | + |
| **NEW MEXICO** | | | | | |
| 1 Wilson | Y | N | N | Y | Y |
| 2 Pearce | ? | N | N | Y | Y |
| 3 Udall | Y | Y | Y | Y | Y |
| **NEW YORK** | | | | | |
| 1 Bishop | Y | N | N | Y | Y |
| 2 Israel | Y | N | N | Y | Y |
| 3 King | Y | N | N | Y | Y |
| 4 McCarthy | Y | N | N | Y | Y |
| 5 Ackerman | Y | N | N | Y | Y |
| 6 Meeks | Y | N | N | Y | Y |
| 7 Crowley | Y | N | Y | Y | Y |
| 8 Nadler | Y | N | N | Y | Y |
| 9 Weiner | ? | N | N | Y | Y |
| 10 Towns | Y | N | N | Y | Y |
| 11 Owens | Y | N | N | Y | Y |
| 12 Velázquez | Y | N | N | Y | Y |
| 13 Fossella | Y | N | N | Y | Y |
| 14 Maloney | Y | N | Y | Y | Y |
| 15 Rangel | Y | N | N | Y | Y |
| 16 Serrano | Y | N | N | Y | Y |
| 17 Engel | Y | N | N | Y | Y |
| 18 Lowey | Y | N | N | Y | Y |
| 19 Kelly | Y | N | N | Y | Y |
| 20 Sweeney | Y | N | N | Y | Y |
| 21 McNulty | Y | Y | Y | Y | Y |
| 22 Hinchey | Y | N | N | Y | ? |
| 23 McHugh | Y | N | N | Y | Y |
| 24 Boehlert | Y | N | Y | Y | Y |
| 25 Walsh | Y | N | N | Y | Y |
| 26 Reynolds | Y | N | N | Y | Y |
| 27 Higgins | Y | N | N | Y | Y |
| 28 Slaughter | Y | N | N | Y | Y |
| 29 Kuhl | Y | N | Y | Y | Y |

| | 375 | 376 | 377 | 378 | 379 |
|---|---|---|---|---|---|
| **NORTH CAROLINA** | | | | | |
| 1 Butterfield | ? | Y | N | Y | Y |
| 2 Etheridge | Y | N | N | Y | Y |
| 3 Jones | Y | Y | N | Y | Y |
| 4 Price | Y | N | N | Y | Y |
| 5 Foxx | Y | Y | N | Y | Y |
| 6 Coble | Y | Y | N | Y | Y |
| 7 McIntyre | ? | ? | ? | ? | ? |
| 8 Hayes | Y | N | N | Y | Y |
| 9 Myrick | Y | Y | Y | Y | Y |
| 10 McHenry | Y | Y | Y | Y | Y |
| 11 Taylor | Y | Y | N | Y | Y |
| 12 Watt | Y | N | N | Y | Y |
| 13 Miller | Y | N | N | Y | Y |
| **NORTH DAKOTA** | | | | | |
| AL Pomeroy | Y | N | N | Y | Y |
| **OHIO** | | | | | |
| 1 Chabot | Y | N | Y | Y | Y |
| 2 Vacant | | | | | |
| 3 Turner | Y | N | N | Y | ? |
| 4 Oxley | Y | N | N | Y | Y |
| 5 Gillmor | Y | N | N | Y | Y |
| 6 Strickland | Y | N | Y | Y | Y |
| 7 Hobson | Y | N | N | Y | ? |
| 8 Boehner | Y | N | N | N | Y |
| 9 Kaptur | Y | N | N | Y | Y |
| 10 Kucinich | Y | Y | Y | Y | Y |
| 11 Jones | Y | N | N | Y | Y |
| 12 Tiberi | Y | N | N | Y | ? |
| 13 Brown | Y | Y | Y | Y | Y |
| 14 LaTourette | Y | N | N | Y | Y |
| 15 Pryce | Y | N | N | Y | Y |
| 16 Regula | Y | N | N | Y | Y |
| 17 Ryan | Y | Y | Y | Y | Y |
| 18 Ney | Y | N | N | Y | Y |
| **OKLAHOMA** | | | | | |
| 1 Sullivan | Y | N | N | Y | Y |
| 2 Boren | Y | N | N | Y | Y |
| 3 Lucas | Y | N | N | Y | Y |
| 4 Cole | Y | N | N | Y | Y |
| 5 Istook | Y | Y | N | Y | Y |
| **OREGON** | | | | | |
| 1 Wu | Y | N | Y | Y | Y |
| 2 Walden | Y | N | Y | Y | ? |
| 3 Blumenauer | Y | N | Y | Y | Y |
| 4 DeFazio | Y | N | N | Y | Y |
| 5 Hooley | Y | Y | Y | Y | Y |
| **PENNSYLVANIA** | | | | | |
| 1 Brady | Y | N | N | Y | Y |
| 2 Fattah | Y | N | N | Y | Y |
| 3 English | Y | N | N | Y | Y |
| 4 Hart | Y | N | N | Y | Y |
| 5 Peterson | Y | N | N | Y | Y |
| 6 Gerlach | Y | N | N | Y | Y |
| 7 Weldon | Y | N | N | Y | Y |
| 8 Fitzpatrick | Y | Y | N | Y | Y |
| 9 Shuster | Y | N | N | Y | Y |
| 10 Sherwood | Y | N | N | Y | Y |
| 11 Kanjorski | Y | N | N | Y | Y |
| 12 Murtha | Y | N | N | Y | Y |
| 13 Schwartz | Y | N | N | Y | Y |
| 14 Doyle | Y | N | N | Y | Y |
| 15 Dent | Y | N | N | Y | Y |
| 16 Pitts | Y | N | N | Y | Y |
| 17 Holden | Y | N | N | Y | Y |
| 18 Murphy | Y | N | N | Y | Y |
| 19 Platts | Y | ? | N | Y | Y |
| **RHODE ISLAND** | | | | | |
| 1 Kennedy | Y | Y | Y | Y | Y |
| 2 Langevin | Y | Y | Y | Y | Y |
| **SOUTH CAROLINA** | | | | | |
| 1 Brown | Y | N | N | Y | ? |
| 2 Wilson | Y | N | Y | Y | Y |
| 3 Barrett | Y | N | Y | Y | Y |
| 4 Inglis | Y | N | Y | N | Y |
| 5 Spratt | Y | N | N | Y | Y |
| 6 Clyburn | Y | N | N | Y | Y |
| **SOUTH DAKOTA** | | | | | |
| AL Herseth | Y | Y | N | Y | Y |
| **TENNESSEE** | | | | | |
| 1 Jenkins | Y | N | N | Y | Y |
| 2 Duncan | Y | Y | N | Y | Y |

| | 375 | 376 | 377 | 378 | 379 |
|---|---|---|---|---|---|
| 3 Wamp | Y | N | N | Y | Y |
| 4 Davis | Y | N | N | Y | Y |
| 5 Cooper | Y | N | Y | N | Y |
| 6 Gordon | Y | N | N | Y | ? |
| 7 Blackburn | Y | N | Y | Y | Y |
| 8 Tanner | Y | N | N | Y | Y |
| 9 Ford | Y | N | N | Y | Y |
| **TEXAS** | | | | | |
| 1 Gohmert | Y | Y | Y | Y | Y |
| 2 Poe | Y | Y | N | Y | Y |
| 3 Johnson, S. | Y | Y | N | Y | Y |
| 4 Hall | Y | N | N | ? | Y |
| 5 Hensarling | Y | N | Y | N | Y |
| 6 Barton | Y | N | N | Y | Y |
| 7 Culberson | Y | N | N | Y | Y |
| 8 Brady | Y | N | N | Y | Y |
| 9 Green, A. | Y | N | N | Y | Y |
| 10 McCaul | Y | N | N | Y | Y |
| 11 Conaway | Y | N | N | Y | Y |
| 12 Granger | Y | N | N | Y | Y |
| 13 Thornberry | Y | N | N | Y | Y |
| 14 Paul | Y | Y | N | N | Y |
| 15 Hinojosa | Y | N | N | Y | Y |
| 16 Reyes | Y | N | N | Y | Y |
| 17 Edwards | Y | N | N | Y | Y |
| 18 Jackson-Lee | Y | N | N | Y | Y |
| 19 Neugebauer | Y | N | N | Y | Y |
| 20 Gonzalez | Y | N | N | Y | Y |
| 21 Smith | Y | N | N | Y | Y |
| 22 DeLay | Y | N | N | Y | Y |
| 23 Bonilla | Y | N | N | Y | Y |
| 24 Marchant | Y | N | Y | Y | Y |
| 25 Doggett | Y | N | N | Y | Y |
| 26 Burgess | Y | Y | N | Y | Y |
| 27 Ortiz | Y | N | N | Y | Y |
| 28 Cuellar | Y | N | N | Y | Y |
| 29 Green, G. | Y | N | N | Y | Y |
| 30 Johnson, E. | Y | N | N | Y | Y |
| 31 Carter | Y | N | N | Y | Y |
| 32 Sessions | Y | N | N | Y | Y |
| **UTAH** | | | | | |
| 1 Bishop | Y | N | N | Y | Y |
| 2 Matheson | Y | N | N | Y | Y |
| 3 Cannon | Y | N | N | Y | Y |
| **VERMONT** | | | | | |
| AL Sanders | Y | Y | ? | Y | ? |
| **VIRGINIA** | | | | | |
| 1 Davis, J. | Y | N | N | N | Y |
| 2 Drake | Y | N | N | Y | Y |
| 3 Scott | Y | N | N | Y | Y |
| 4 Forbes | Y | N | N | Y | Y |
| 5 Goode | Y | Y | Y | Y | Y |
| 6 Goodlatte | Y | N | N | Y | Y |
| 7 Cantor | Y | N | N | Y | Y |
| 8 Moran | Y | N | Y | Y | Y |
| 9 Boucher | Y | N | N | Y | Y |
| 10 Wolf | Y | N | N | Y | Y |
| 11 Davis, T. | Y | N | Y | N | Y |
| **WASHINGTON** | | | | | |
| 1 Inslee | Y | N | Y | Y | Y |
| 2 Larsen | Y | N | N | Y | Y |
| 3 Baird | Y | N | N | Y | Y |
| 4 Hastings | Y | N | N | Y | Y |
| 5 McMorris | Y | N | N | Y | Y |
| 6 Dicks | Y | N | N | Y | Y |
| 7 McDermott | Y | Y | N | Y | Y |
| 8 Reichert | Y | N | N | Y | Y |
| 9 Smith | Y | N | Y | Y | Y |
| **WEST VIRGINIA** | | | | | |
| 1 Mollohan | ? | N | N | Y | Y |
| 2 Capito | Y | N | N | Y | Y |
| 3 Rahall | Y | N | N | Y | Y |
| **WISCONSIN** | | | | | |
| 1 Ryan | Y | N | N | Y | Y |
| 2 Baldwin | Y | Y | Y | Y | Y |
| 3 Kind | Y | N | Y | Y | Y |
| 4 Moore | Y | Y | Y | Y | Y |
| 5 Sensenbrenner | Y | N | N | Y | Y |
| 6 Petri | Y | N | N | Y | Y |
| 7 Obey | ? | N | Y | Y | Y |
| 8 Green | Y | N | N | Y | Y |
| **WYOMING** | | | | | |
| AL Cubin | ? | ? | ? | ? | ? |

# IN THE HOUSE | By Vote Number

**380.** H Res 328. Polish Workers Strike Anniversary/Adoption.
Ros-Lehtinen, R-Fla., motion to suspend the rules and adopt the resolution that would recognize the 25th anniversary of the strikes that led to the formation of Poland's Solidarity trade union and the fall of communism in Poland. Motion agreed to 385-0: R 213-0; D 171-0 (ND 127-0, SD 44-0); I 1-0. A two-thirds majority of those present and voting (257 in this case) is required for adoption under suspension of the rules. July 18, 2005.

**381.** H Con Res 175. Tribute to Slave Trade Descendants/Adoption.
Ros-Lehtinen, R-Fla., motion to suspend the rules and adopt the concurrent resolution that would recognize the injustices suffered by African descendants of the trans-Atlantic slave trade in Latin America and the Caribbean. Motion agreed to 382-6: R 206-6; D 175-0 (ND 130-0, SD 45-0); I 1-0. A two-thirds majority of those present and voting (259 in this case) is required for adoption under suspension of the rules. July 18, 2005.

**382.** H Res 364. U.S.-India Relations/Adoption. Ros-Lehtinen, R-Fla., motion to suspend the rules and adopt the resolution that would commend the continuing improvement of relations between the United States and India. Motion agreed to 388-0: R 211-0; D 176-0 (ND 131-0, SD 45-0); I 1-0. A two-thirds majority of those present and voting (259 in this case) is required for adoption under suspension of the rules. July 18, 2005.

**383.** HR 2601. State Department Authorization/Previous Question.
Bishop, R-Utah, motion to order the previous question (thus ending debate and the possibility of amendment) on adoption of the rule (H Res 365) and a Bishop amendment to the rule. The rule would provide for House floor consideration of the bill that would authorize $20.8 billion in appropriations through fiscal 2007 for the Department of State and foreign aid programs. The Bishop amendment would clarify the debate time for certain amendments. Motion agreed to 226-196: R 224-0; D 2-195 (ND 0-148, SD 2-47); I 0-1. (Subsequently, the Bishop amendment was adopted by voice vote.) July 19, 2005.

**384.** HR 2601. State Department Authorization/Rule. Adoption of the rule (H Res 365) that would provide for House consideration of the bill that would authorize $20.8 billion in appropriations through fiscal 2007 for the Department of State and foreign aid programs. Adopted 228-190: R 225-0; D 3-189 (ND 3-141, SD 0-48); I 0-1. July 19, 2005.

**385.** HR 2601. State Department Authorization/U.N. Hyde, R-Ill., amendment that would withhold up to 50 percent of U.S. dues to the United Nations unless the secretary of State certifies by Oct. 1, 2007, that the organization has complied with 32 of 39 changes in its operations, such as more rigorous budget control, the creation of a U.N. independent oversight board and detailed financial disclosure for top U.N. officials. Adopted 226-195: R 217-6; D 9-188 (ND 3-147, SD 6-41); I 0-1. July 19, 2005.

**386.** HR 2601. State Department Authorization/Methamphetamine Precursors. Kennedy, R-Minn., amendment that would require the State Department to certify annually that the five biggest exporters and importers of certain methamphetamine precursors are fully cooperating with U.S. law enforcement to prevent diversion of those chemicals for illicit purposes. Countries that are not certified would be subject to foreign aid eligibility provisions under current law. Adopted 423-2: R 222-2; D 200-0 (ND 151-0, SD 49-0); I 1-0. July 19, 2005.

ND Northern Democrats, SD Southern Democrats
Southern states: Ala., Ark., Fla., Ga., Ky., La., Miss., N.C., Okla., S.C., Tenn., Texas, Va.

| | 380 | 381 | 382 | 383 | 384 | 385 | 386 |
|---|---|---|---|---|---|---|---|
| **ALABAMA** | | | | | | | |
| 1 Bonner | Y | Y | Y | Y | Y | Y | Y |
| 2 Everett | Y | Y | Y | Y | Y | Y | Y |
| 3 Rogers | Y | Y | Y | Y | Y | Y | Y |
| 4 Aderholt | Y | Y | Y | Y | Y | Y | Y |
| 5 Cramer | Y | Y | Y | N | N | ? | Y |
| 6 Bachus | Y | Y | Y | Y | Y | Y | Y |
| 7 Davis | Y | Y | Y | N | N | N | Y |
| **ALASKA** | | | | | | | |
| AL Young | Y | Y | Y | Y | Y | Y | Y |
| **ARIZONA** | | | | | | | |
| 1 Renzi | Y | Y | Y | Y | Y | Y | Y |
| 2 Franks | Y | Y | Y | Y | Y | Y | Y |
| 3 Shadegg | ? | ? | ? | Y | Y | Y | Y |
| 4 Pastor | Y | Y | Y | N | N | N | Y |
| 5 Hayworth | Y | Y | Y | Y | Y | Y | Y |
| 6 Flake | Y | N | Y | Y | Y | Y | N |
| 7 Grijalva | Y | Y | Y | N | N | N | Y |
| 8 Kolbe | Y | Y | Y | Y | Y | Y | Y |
| **ARKANSAS** | | | | | | | |
| 1 Berry | Y | Y | Y | N | N | N | Y |
| 2 Snyder | Y | Y | Y | N | N | N | Y |
| 3 Boozman | Y | Y | Y | Y | Y | Y | Y |
| 4 Ross | Y | Y | Y | N | N | N | Y |
| **CALIFORNIA** | | | | | | | |
| 1 Thompson | Y | Y | Y | N | N | N | Y |
| 2 Herger | Y | Y | Y | Y | Y | Y | Y |
| 3 Lungren | Y | Y | Y | Y | Y | Y | Y |
| 4 Doolittle | Y | Y | Y | Y | Y | Y | Y |
| 5 Matsui, D. | Y | Y | Y | N | N | N | Y |
| 6 Woolsey | Y | Y | Y | N | N | N | Y |
| 7 Miller, George | Y | Y | Y | N | N | N | Y |
| 8 Pelosi | Y | Y | Y | N | N | N | Y |
| 9 Lee | Y | Y | Y | N | N | N | Y |
| 10 Tauscher | Y | Y | Y | N | N | N | Y |
| 11 Pombo | Y | Y | Y | Y | Y | Y | Y |
| 12 Lantos | Y | Y | Y | N | N | N | Y |
| 13 Stark | ? | ? | ? | N | N | N | Y |
| 14 Eshoo | Y | Y | Y | N | ? | N | Y |
| 15 Honda | Y | Y | Y | N | N | N | Y |
| 16 Lofgren | Y | Y | Y | N | N | N | Y |
| 17 Farr | Y | Y | Y | N | N | N | Y |
| 18 Cardoza | Y | Y | Y | N | Y | N | Y |
| 19 Radanovich | Y | Y | Y | Y | Y | Y | Y |
| 20 Costa | ? | ? | ? | N | N | N | Y |
| 21 Nunes | Y | Y | Y | Y | Y | Y | Y |
| 22 Thomas | Y | Y | Y | Y | Y | Y | Y |
| 23 Capps | Y | Y | Y | N | N | N | Y |
| 24 Gallegly | Y | Y | Y | Y | Y | Y | Y |
| 25 McKeon | Y | Y | ? | Y | Y | Y | Y |
| 26 Dreier | Y | Y | Y | Y | Y | Y | Y |
| 27 Sherman | Y | Y | Y | N | N | N | Y |
| 28 Berman | Y | Y | Y | N | N | N | Y |
| 29 Schiff | Y | Y | Y | N | N | N | Y |
| 30 Waxman | Y | Y | Y | N | N | N | Y |
| 31 Becerra | Y | Y | Y | – | – | N | Y |
| 32 Solis | Y | Y | Y | N | N | N | Y |
| 33 Watson | ? | ? | ? | N | N | N | Y |
| 34 Roybal-Allard | Y | Y | Y | N | N | N | Y |
| 35 Waters | Y | Y | Y | N | ? | N | Y |
| 36 Harman | Y | Y | Y | N | N | N | Y |
| 37 Millender-McD. | Y | Y | Y | N | N | N | Y |
| 38 Napolitano | Y | Y | Y | N | N | N | Y |
| 39 Sánchez, Linda | Y | Y | Y | N | N | N | Y |
| 40 Royce | Y | Y | Y | Y | Y | Y | Y |
| 41 Lewis | Y | Y | Y | Y | Y | Y | Y |
| 42 Miller, Gary | Y | Y | Y | Y | Y | Y | Y |
| 43 Baca | Y | Y | Y | N | N | N | Y |
| 44 Calvert | Y | Y | Y | Y | Y | Y | Y |
| 45 Bono | Y | Y | Y | Y | Y | Y | Y |
| 46 Rohrabacher | Y | Y | Y | Y | Y | Y | Y |
| 47 Sanchez, Loretta | Y | Y | Y | N | N | N | Y |
| 48 Cox | Y | Y | Y | Y | Y | ? | ? |
| 49 Issa | Y | Y | Y | Y | Y | Y | Y |

| | 380 | 381 | 382 | 383 | 384 | 385 | 386 |
|---|---|---|---|---|---|---|---|
| 50 Cunningham | Y | Y | Y | Y | Y | Y | Y |
| 51 Filner | Y | Y | Y | N | N | N | Y |
| 52 Hunter | ? | ? | Y | Y | Y | Y | Y |
| 53 Davis | Y | Y | Y | N | N | N | Y |
| **COLORADO** | | | | | | | |
| 1 DeGette | Y | Y | Y | N | N | N | Y |
| 2 Udall | + | Y | Y | N | N | N | Y |
| 3 Salazar | Y | Y | Y | N | N | N | Y |
| 4 Musgrave | ? | Y | Y | Y | Y | Y | Y |
| 5 Hefley | Y | Y | Y | Y | Y | Y | Y |
| 6 Tancredo | Y | Y | Y | Y | Y | Y | ? |
| 7 Beauprez | Y | Y | Y | Y | Y | Y | Y |
| **CONNECTICUT** | | | | | | | |
| 1 Larson | Y | Y | Y | N | N | N | Y |
| 2 Simmons | Y | Y | Y | Y | Y | Y | Y |
| 3 DeLauro | Y | Y | Y | N | N | N | Y |
| 4 Shays | Y | Y | Y | Y | Y | N | Y |
| 5 Johnson | Y | Y | Y | Y | Y | Y | Y |
| **DELAWARE** | | | | | | | |
| AL Castle | Y | Y | Y | Y | Y | N | Y |
| **FLORIDA** | | | | | | | |
| 1 Miller | Y | Y | Y | Y | Y | Y | Y |
| 2 Boyd | ? | Y | Y | N | N | N | Y |
| 3 Brown | ? | ? | ? | N | N | ? | Y |
| 4 Crenshaw | Y | Y | Y | Y | Y | Y | Y |
| 5 Brown-Waite | Y | Y | Y | Y | Y | Y | Y |
| 6 Stearns | Y | Y | Y | Y | Y | Y | Y |
| 7 Mica | Y | Y | Y | Y | Y | Y | Y |
| 8 Keller | Y | Y | Y | Y | Y | Y | Y |
| 9 Bilirakis | Y | Y | Y | Y | Y | Y | Y |
| 10 Young | Y | Y | Y | Y | Y | Y | Y |
| 11 Davis | Y | Y | Y | N | N | N | Y |
| 12 Putnam | Y | Y | Y | Y | Y | Y | Y |
| 13 Harris | Y | Y | Y | Y | Y | Y | Y |
| 14 Mack | Y | Y | Y | Y | Y | Y | Y |
| 15 Weldon | Y | Y | Y | Y | Y | Y | Y |
| 16 Foley | Y | Y | Y | Y | Y | Y | Y |
| 17 Meek | Y | Y | Y | N | N | N | Y |
| 18 Ros-Lehtinen | Y | Y | Y | Y | Y | Y | Y |
| 19 Wexler | Y | Y | Y | N | N | N | Y |
| 20 Wasserman-Schultz | Y | Y | Y | N | N | N | Y |
| 21 Diaz-Balart, L. | Y | Y | Y | Y | Y | Y | Y |
| 22 Shaw | Y | Y | Y | Y | Y | Y | Y |
| 23 Hastings | Y | Y | Y | N | N | N | Y |
| 24 Feeney | Y | Y | Y | Y | Y | Y | Y |
| 25 Diaz-Balart, M. | Y | Y | Y | Y | Y | Y | Y |
| **GEORGIA** | | | | | | | |
| 1 Kingston | Y | Y | Y | Y | Y | Y | Y |
| 2 Bishop | Y | Y | Y | N | N | N | Y |
| 3 Marshall | Y | Y | Y | Y | Y | Y | Y |
| 4 McKinney | ? | ? | ? | N | N | N | Y |
| 5 Lewis | Y | Y | Y | N | N | N | Y |
| 6 Price | Y | P | Y | Y | Y | Y | Y |
| 7 Linder | Y | Y | Y | Y | Y | Y | Y |
| 8 Westmoreland | Y | N | Y | Y | Y | Y | Y |
| 9 Norwood | Y | N | Y | Y | Y | Y | Y |
| 10 Deal | Y | N | Y | Y | Y | Y | Y |
| 11 Gingrey | Y | N | Y | Y | Y | Y | Y |
| 12 Barrow | Y | Y | Y | N | N | N | Y |
| 13 Scott | Y | Y | Y | N | N | N | Y |
| **HAWAII** | | | | | | | |
| 1 Abercrombie | Y | Y | Y | N | N | N | Y |
| 2 Case | Y | Y | Y | N | N | N | Y |
| **IDAHO** | | | | | | | |
| 1 Otter | Y | Y | Y | Y | Y | Y | Y |
| 2 Simpson | Y | Y | Y | Y | Y | Y | Y |
| **ILLINOIS** | | | | | | | |
| 1 Rush | ? | ? | ? | N | N | N | Y |
| 2 Jackson | Y | Y | Y | N | N | N | Y |
| 3 Lipinski | Y | Y | Y | N | N | N | Y |
| 4 Gutierrez | ? | ? | ? | N | N | N | Y |
| 5 Emanuel | Y | Y | Y | N | N | N | Y |
| 6 Hyde | Y | Y | Y | Y | Y | Y | Y |
| 7 Davis | ? | ? | ? | N | N | N | Y |
| 8 Bean | Y | Y | Y | N | N | N | Y |
| 9 Schakowsky | ? | ? | ? | N | N | N | Y |
| 10 Kirk | Y | Y | Y | Y | Y | Y | Y |
| 11 Weller | + | + | + | Y | Y | Y | Y |
| 12 Costello | Y | Y | Y | N | N | N | Y |

**KEY** Republicans Democrats *Independents*

| | | | |
|---|---|---|---|
| Y | Voted for (yea) | X | Paired against |
| # | Paired for | – | Announced against |
| + | Announced for | P | Voted "present" |
| N | Voted against (nay) | C | Voted "present" to avoid possible conflict of interest |
| | | ? | Did not vote or otherwise make a position known |

| | 380 | 381 | 382 | 383 | 384 | 385 | 386 |
|---|---|---|---|---|---|---|---|
| 13 **Biggert** | Y | Y | Y | Y | Y | Y | Y |
| 14 **Hastert** | | | | | | | |
| 15 **Johnson** | + | + | + | Y | Y | Y | Y |
| 16 **Manzullo** | Y | Y | Y | Y | Y | Y | Y |
| 17 Evans | + | + | + | N | N | N | Y |
| 18 **LaHood** | Y | Y | Y | Y | Y | Y | Y |
| 19 **Shimkus** | Y | Y | Y | Y | Y | Y | Y |
| **INDIANA** | | | | | | | |
| 1 Visclosky | Y | Y | Y | N | N | N | Y |
| 2 **Chocola** | Y | Y | Y | Y | Y | Y | Y |
| 3 **Souder** | Y | Y | Y | Y | Y | Y | Y |
| 4 **Buyer** | ? | ? | ? | Y | Y | Y | Y |
| 5 **Burton** | Y | Y | Y | Y | Y | Y | Y |
| 6 **Pence** | Y | Y | Y | Y | Y | Y | Y |
| 7 Carson | Y | Y | Y | N | N | N | Y |
| 8 **Hostettler** | Y | Y | Y | Y | Y | Y | Y |
| 9 **Sodrel** | Y | Y | Y | Y | Y | Y | Y |
| **IOWA** | | | | | | | |
| 1 **Nussle** | ? | ? | ? | Y | Y | Y | Y |
| 2 **Leach** | ? | ? | ? | Y | Y | N | Y |
| 3 Boswell | ? | ? | ? | N | N | N | Y |
| 4 **Latham** | Y | Y | Y | Y | Y | Y | Y |
| 5 **King** | Y | N | Y | Y | Y | Y | Y |
| **KANSAS** | | | | | | | |
| 1 **Moran** | Y | Y | Y | Y | Y | Y | Y |
| 2 **Ryun** | + | + | + | Y | Y | Y | Y |
| 3 Moore | Y | Y | Y | N | N | N | Y |
| 4 **Tiahrt** | Y | Y | Y | Y | Y | Y | Y |
| **KENTUCKY** | | | | | | | |
| 1 **Whitfield** | Y | Y | Y | Y | Y | Y | Y |
| 2 **Lewis** | Y | Y | Y | Y | Y | Y | Y |
| 3 **Northup** | Y | Y | Y | Y | Y | Y | Y |
| 4 **Davis** | Y | Y | Y | Y | Y | Y | Y |
| 5 **Rogers** | Y | Y | Y | Y | Y | Y | Y |
| 6 Chandler | Y | Y | Y | N | N | N | Y |
| **LOUISIANA** | | | | | | | |
| 1 **Jindal** | ? | ? | ? | Y | Y | Y | Y |
| 2 Jefferson | Y | Y | Y | N | N | N | Y |
| 3 Melancon | Y | Y | Y | Y | N | N | Y |
| 4 **McCrery** | Y | Y | ? | Y | Y | Y | Y |
| 5 **Alexander** | Y | Y | Y | Y | Y | Y | Y |
| 6 **Baker** | Y | Y | Y | Y | Y | Y | Y |
| 7 **Boustany** | Y | Y | Y | Y | Y | Y | Y |
| **MAINE** | | | | | | | |
| 1 Allen | Y | Y | Y | N | N | N | Y |
| 2 Michaud | Y | Y | Y | N | N | N | Y |
| **MARYLAND** | | | | | | | |
| 1 **Gilchrest** | Y | Y | Y | Y | Y | Y | Y |
| 2 Ruppersberger | Y | Y | Y | N | N | N | Y |
| 3 Cardin | Y | Y | Y | N | N | N | Y |
| 4 Wynn | Y | Y | Y | N | N | N | Y |
| 5 Hoyer | Y | Y | Y | N | N | N | Y |
| 6 **Bartlett** | Y | P | Y | Y | Y | Y | Y |
| 7 Cummings | Y | Y | Y | N | N | N | Y |
| 8 Van Hollen | Y | Y | Y | N | N | N | Y |
| **MASSACHUSETTS** | | | | | | | |
| 1 Olver | Y | Y | Y | N | N | N | Y |
| 2 Neal | ? | ? | Y | N | N | N | Y |
| 3 McGovern | Y | Y | Y | N | N | N | Y |
| 4 Frank | Y | Y | Y | N | N | N | Y |
| 5 Meehan | Y | Y | Y | N | ? | N | Y |
| 6 Tierney | Y | Y | Y | N | N | N | Y |
| 7 Markey | Y | Y | Y | N | N | N | Y |
| 8 Capuano | ? | ? | ? | N | N | N | Y |
| 9 Lynch | Y | Y | Y | N | N | N | Y |
| 10 Delahunt | Y | Y | Y | N | N | N | Y |
| **MICHIGAN** | | | | | | | |
| 1 Stupak | Y | Y | Y | N | N | N | Y |
| 2 **Hoekstra** | Y | Y | Y | Y | Y | Y | Y |
| 3 **Ehlers** | Y | Y | Y | Y | Y | Y | Y |
| 4 **Camp** | Y | Y | Y | Y | Y | Y | Y |
| 5 Kildee | Y | Y | Y | N | N | N | Y |
| 6 **Upton** | Y | Y | Y | Y | Y | Y | Y |
| 7 **Schwarz** | Y | Y | Y | Y | Y | Y | Y |
| 8 **Rogers** | Y | Y | Y | Y | Y | Y | Y |
| 9 **Knollenberg** | Y | Y | Y | Y | Y | Y | Y |
| 10 **Miller** | Y | Y | Y | Y | Y | Y | Y |
| 11 **McCotter** | Y | Y | Y | Y | Y | Y | Y |
| 12 Levin | Y | Y | Y | N | N | N | Y |
| 13 Kilpatrick | Y | Y | Y | N | N | N | Y |
| 14 Conyers | Y | Y | Y | N | N | N | Y |
| 15 Dingell | Y | Y | Y | N | N | N | Y |

| | 380 | 381 | 382 | 383 | 384 | 385 | 386 |
|---|---|---|---|---|---|---|---|
| **MINNESOTA** | | | | | | | |
| 1 **Gutknecht** | Y | Y | Y | Y | Y | Y | Y |
| 2 **Kline** | Y | Y | Y | Y | Y | Y | Y |
| 3 **Ramstad** | Y | Y | Y | Y | Y | Y | Y |
| 4 McCollum | Y | Y | Y | N | N | N | Y |
| 5 Sabo | Y | Y | Y | N | N | N | Y |
| 6 **Kennedy** | Y | Y | Y | Y | Y | Y | Y |
| 7 Peterson | Y | Y | Y | N | N | N | Y |
| 8 Oberstar | Y | Y | Y | N | N | N | Y |
| **MISSISSIPPI** | | | | | | | |
| 1 **Wicker** | Y | Y | Y | Y | Y | Y | Y |
| 2 Thompson | Y | Y | Y | N | N | N | Y |
| 3 **Pickering** | Y | Y | Y | Y | Y | Y | Y |
| 4 Taylor | Y | Y | Y | N | N | Y | Y |
| **MISSOURI** | | | | | | | |
| 1 Clay | Y | Y | Y | N | N | N | Y |
| 2 **Akin** | Y | Y | Y | Y | Y | Y | Y |
| 3 Carnahan | Y | Y | Y | N | N | N | Y |
| 4 Skelton | Y | Y | Y | N | N | N | Y |
| 5 Cleaver | Y | Y | Y | N | N | N | Y |
| 6 **Graves** | Y | Y | Y | Y | Y | Y | Y |
| 7 **Blunt** | Y | Y | Y | Y | Y | Y | Y |
| 8 **Emerson** | Y | Y | Y | Y | Y | Y | Y |
| 9 **Hulshof** | Y | Y | Y | ? | Y | Y | Y |
| **MONTANA** | | | | | | | |
| AL **Rehberg** | Y | Y | Y | Y | Y | Y | Y |
| **NEBRASKA** | | | | | | | |
| 1 **Fortenberry** | Y | Y | Y | Y | Y | Y | Y |
| 2 **Terry** | Y | Y | Y | Y | Y | Y | Y |
| 3 **Osborne** | Y | Y | Y | Y | Y | Y | Y |
| **NEVADA** | | | | | | | |
| 1 Berkley | Y | Y | Y | N | N | Y | Y |
| 2 **Gibbons** | + | + | + | Y | Y | Y | Y |
| 3 **Porter** | Y | Y | Y | Y | Y | Y | Y |
| **NEW HAMPSHIRE** | | | | | | | |
| 1 **Bradley** | Y | Y | Y | Y | Y | Y | Y |
| 2 **Bass** | Y | Y | Y | Y | Y | Y | Y |
| **NEW JERSEY** | | | | | | | |
| 1 Andrews | Y | Y | Y | N | N | N | Y |
| 2 **LoBiondo** | Y | Y | Y | Y | Y | Y | Y |
| 3 **Saxton** | Y | Y | Y | Y | Y | Y | Y |
| 4 **Smith** | Y | Y | Y | Y | Y | Y | Y |
| 5 **Garrett** | Y | Y | Y | Y | Y | Y | Y |
| 6 Pallone | Y | Y | Y | N | N | N | Y |
| 7 **Ferguson** | Y | Y | Y | Y | Y | Y | Y |
| 8 Pascrell | ? | ? | ? | N | N | N | Y |
| 9 Rothman | Y | Y | Y | N | N | N | Y |
| 10 Payne | Y | Y | Y | ? | ? | ? | Y |
| 11 **Frelinghuysen** | + | + | + | + | + | + | Y |
| 12 Holt | Y | Y | Y | N | N | N | Y |
| 13 Menendez | Y | Y | Y | N | N | N | Y |
| **NEW MEXICO** | | | | | | | |
| 1 **Wilson** | Y | Y | Y | Y | Y | Y | Y |
| 2 **Pearce** | Y | Y | Y | ? | ? | Y | Y |
| 3 Udall | Y | Y | Y | N | N | N | Y |
| **NEW YORK** | | | | | | | |
| 1 Bishop | Y | Y | Y | N | N | N | Y |
| 2 Israel | Y | Y | Y | N | N | N | Y |
| 3 **King** | Y | Y | Y | Y | Y | Y | Y |
| 4 McCarthy | Y | Y | Y | N | N | N | Y |
| 5 Ackerman | Y | Y | Y | N | N | N | Y |
| 6 Meeks | Y | Y | Y | N | N | Y | Y |
| 7 Crowley | + | + | + | N | N | N | Y |
| 8 Nadler | Y | Y | Y | N | N | N | Y |
| 9 Weiner | ? | ? | ? | N | N | N | Y |
| 10 Towns | ? | ? | ? | N | N | N | Y |
| 11 Owens | Y | Y | Y | N | N | N | Y |
| 12 Velázquez | Y | Y | Y | N | N | N | Y |
| 13 **Fossella** | Y | Y | Y | Y | Y | Y | Y |
| 14 Maloney | Y | Y | Y | N | N | N | Y |
| 15 Rangel | Y | Y | Y | N | N | N | Y |
| 16 Serrano | Y | Y | Y | N | N | N | Y |
| 17 Engel | Y | Y | Y | N | N | N | Y |
| 18 Lowey | Y | Y | Y | N | N | N | Y |
| 19 **Kelly** | Y | Y | Y | Y | Y | Y | Y |
| 20 **Sweeney** | ? | ? | ? | ? | ? | ? | ? |
| 21 McNulty | Y | Y | Y | N | N | N | Y |
| 22 Hinchey | Y | Y | Y | N | N | N | Y |
| 23 **McHugh** | Y | Y | Y | Y | Y | Y | Y |
| 24 **Boehlert** | Y | Y | Y | Y | Y | N | ? |
| 25 **Walsh** | Y | Y | Y | Y | Y | Y | Y |
| 26 **Reynolds** | Y | Y | Y | Y | Y | Y | Y |
| 27 Higgins | ? | ? | ? | N | N | N | Y |
| 28 Slaughter | Y | Y | Y | N | N | N | Y |
| 29 **Kuhl** | Y | Y | ? | Y | Y | Y | Y |

| | 380 | 381 | 382 | 383 | 384 | 385 | 386 |
|---|---|---|---|---|---|---|---|
| **NORTH CAROLINA** | | | | | | | |
| 1 Butterfield | Y | Y | Y | N | N | N | Y |
| 2 Etheridge | + | + | + | N | N | N | Y |
| 3 **Jones** | Y | Y | Y | Y | Y | Y | Y |
| 4 Price | Y | Y | Y | N | N | N | Y |
| 5 **Foxx** | Y | Y | Y | Y | Y | Y | Y |
| 6 **Coble** | Y | Y | Y | Y | Y | Y | Y |
| 7 McIntyre | Y | Y | Y | N | – | Y | Y |
| 8 **Hayes** | Y | Y | Y | Y | Y | Y | Y |
| 9 **Myrick** | Y | Y | Y | Y | Y | Y | Y |
| 10 **McHenry** | Y | Y | Y | Y | Y | + | + |
| 11 **Taylor** | Y | Y | Y | Y | Y | Y | Y |
| 12 Watt | Y | Y | Y | N | N | N | Y |
| 13 Miller | Y | Y | Y | N | N | N | Y |
| **NORTH DAKOTA** | | | | | | | |
| AL Pomeroy | Y | Y | Y | N | N | N | Y |
| **OHIO** | | | | | | | |
| 1 **Chabot** | Y | Y | Y | Y | Y | Y | Y |
| 2 Vacant | | | | | | | |
| 3 **Turner** | Y | Y | Y | Y | Y | Y | Y |
| 4 **Oxley** | Y | Y | Y | Y | Y | Y | Y |
| 5 **Gillmor** | Y | Y | Y | Y | Y | Y | Y |
| 6 Strickland | ? | ? | ? | N | N | N | Y |
| 7 **Hobson** | Y | Y | Y | Y | Y | Y | Y |
| 8 **Boehner** | Y | Y | Y | Y | Y | Y | Y |
| 9 Kaptur | ? | ? | ? | N | N | N | Y |
| 10 Kucinich | Y | Y | Y | N | N | N | Y |
| 11 Jones | Y | Y | Y | ? | ? | N | Y |
| 12 **Tiberi** | Y | Y | Y | Y | Y | Y | Y |
| 13 Brown | Y | Y | Y | N | N | N | Y |
| 14 **LaTourette** | Y | Y | Y | Y | Y | Y | Y |
| 15 **Pryce** | ? | ? | ? | Y | Y | Y | Y |
| 16 **Regula** | Y | Y | Y | Y | Y | Y | Y |
| 17 Ryan | ? | Y | Y | N | N | N | Y |
| 18 **Ney** | Y | Y | Y | Y | Y | Y | Y |
| **OKLAHOMA** | | | | | | | |
| 1 **Sullivan** | Y | Y | Y | Y | Y | Y | Y |
| 2 Boren | Y | Y | Y | N | N | N | Y |
| 3 **Lucas** | Y | Y | Y | Y | Y | Y | Y |
| 4 **Cole** | Y | Y | Y | Y | Y | Y | Y |
| 5 **Istook** | Y | Y | Y | ? | ? | Y | Y |
| **OREGON** | | | | | | | |
| 1 Wu | Y | Y | Y | N | N | N | Y |
| 2 **Walden** | Y | Y | Y | Y | Y | Y | Y |
| 3 Blumenauer | Y | Y | Y | N | N | N | Y |
| 4 DeFazio | Y | Y | Y | N | N | N | Y |
| 5 Hooley | Y | Y | Y | N | N | N | Y |
| **PENNSYLVANIA** | | | | | | | |
| 1 Brady | ? | ? | ? | N | N | N | Y |
| 2 Fattah | ? | ? | ? | N | N | N | Y |
| 3 **English** | Y | Y | Y | Y | Y | Y | Y |
| 4 **Hart** | Y | Y | Y | Y | Y | Y | Y |
| 5 **Peterson** | Y | Y | Y | Y | Y | Y | Y |
| 6 **Gerlach** | Y | Y | Y | Y | Y | Y | Y |
| 7 **Weldon** | Y | Y | Y | Y | Y | Y | Y |
| 8 **Fitzpatrick** | Y | Y | Y | Y | Y | Y | Y |
| 9 **Shuster** | Y | Y | Y | Y | Y | Y | Y |
| 10 **Sherwood** | Y | Y | Y | Y | Y | Y | Y |
| 11 Kanjorski | Y | Y | Y | N | N | N | Y |
| 12 Murtha | Y | Y | Y | N | N | N | Y |
| 13 Schwartz | Y | Y | Y | N | N | N | Y |
| 14 Doyle | ? | Y | Y | N | N | N | Y |
| 15 **Dent** | Y | Y | Y | Y | Y | Y | Y |
| 16 **Pitts** | Y | Y | Y | Y | Y | Y | Y |
| 17 Holden | Y | Y | Y | N | N | N | Y |
| 18 **Murphy** | Y | Y | Y | Y | Y | Y | Y |
| 19 **Platts** | Y | Y | Y | Y | Y | Y | Y |
| **RHODE ISLAND** | | | | | | | |
| 1 Kennedy | Y | Y | Y | N | N | N | Y |
| 2 Langevin | Y | Y | Y | N | N | N | Y |
| **SOUTH CAROLINA** | | | | | | | |
| 1 **Brown** | Y | Y | Y | ? | ? | ? | ? |
| 2 **Wilson** | Y | Y | Y | Y | Y | + | Y |
| 3 **Barrett** | Y | Y | Y | Y | Y | Y | Y |
| 4 **Inglis** | Y | Y | Y | Y | Y | Y | Y |
| 5 Spratt | Y | Y | Y | N | N | N | Y |
| 6 Clyburn | Y | Y | Y | N | N | N | Y |
| **SOUTH DAKOTA** | | | | | | | |
| AL Herseth | Y | Y | Y | N | N | N | Y |
| **TENNESSEE** | | | | | | | |
| 1 **Jenkins** | ? | ? | ? | Y | Y | Y | Y |
| 2 **Duncan** | Y | Y | Y | Y | Y | Y | Y |

| | 380 | 381 | 382 | 383 | 384 | 385 | 386 |
|---|---|---|---|---|---|---|---|
| 3 **Wamp** | Y | Y | Y | Y | Y | Y | Y |
| 4 Davis | Y | Y | Y | N | N | N | Y |
| 5 Cooper | Y | Y | Y | N | N | N | Y |
| 6 Gordon | Y | Y | Y | N | N | N | Y |
| 7 **Blackburn** | Y | Y | Y | Y | Y | Y | Y |
| 8 Tanner | Y | Y | Y | N | N | N | Y |
| 9 Ford | ? | ? | ? | N | N | N | Y |
| **TEXAS** | | | | | | | |
| 1 **Gohmert** | Y | Y | Y | Y | Y | Y | Y |
| 2 **Poe** | Y | Y | Y | Y | Y | Y | Y |
| 3 **Johnson, S.** | Y | Y | Y | Y | Y | Y | Y |
| 4 **Hall** | Y | Y | Y | Y | Y | Y | Y |
| 5 **Hensarling** | Y | Y | Y | Y | Y | Y | Y |
| 6 **Barton** | Y | Y | Y | Y | Y | Y | Y |
| 7 **Culberson** | Y | Y | Y | Y | Y | Y | Y |
| 8 **Brady** | Y | Y | Y | Y | Y | Y | Y |
| 9 Green, A. | Y | Y | Y | N | N | N | Y |
| 10 **McCaul** | Y | Y | Y | Y | Y | Y | Y |
| 11 **Conaway** | Y | Y | Y | Y | Y | Y | Y |
| 12 **Granger** | Y | Y | Y | Y | Y | Y | Y |
| 13 **Thornberry** | Y | Y | Y | Y | Y | ? | Y |
| 14 **Paul** | Y | N | Y | Y | Y | N | N |
| 15 Hinojosa | ? | ? | ? | ? | ? | ? | ? |
| 16 Reyes | ? | ? | ? | ? | ? | ? | ? |
| 17 Edwards | Y | Y | Y | N | N | N | Y |
| 18 Jackson-Lee | Y | Y | Y | N | N | N | Y |
| 19 **Neugebauer** | Y | Y | Y | Y | Y | Y | Y |
| 20 Gonzalez | Y | Y | Y | N | N | N | Y |
| 21 **Smith** | Y | Y | Y | Y | Y | Y | Y |
| 22 **DeLay** | ? | ? | ? | Y | Y | Y | Y |
| 23 **Bonilla** | Y | Y | Y | Y | Y | Y | Y |
| 24 **Marchant** | Y | Y | Y | Y | Y | Y | Y |
| 25 Doggett | Y | Y | Y | N | N | N | Y |
| 26 **Burgess** | Y | Y | Y | Y | Y | Y | Y |
| 27 Ortiz | Y | Y | Y | N | N | N | Y |
| 28 Cuellar | Y | Y | Y | N | N | Y | Y |
| 29 Green, G. | Y | Y | Y | N | N | Y | Y |
| 30 Johnson, E. | Y | Y | Y | N | N | N | Y |
| 31 **Carter** | Y | Y | Y | Y | Y | Y | Y |
| 32 **Sessions** | ? | ? | ? | Y | Y | Y | Y |
| **UTAH** | | | | | | | |
| 1 **Bishop** | Y | Y | Y | Y | Y | Y | Y |
| 2 Matheson | Y | Y | Y | N | N | N | Y |
| 3 **Cannon** | Y | Y | Y | Y | Y | Y | Y |
| **VERMONT** | | | | | | | |
| AL *Sanders* | Y | Y | Y | N | N | N | Y |
| **VIRGINIA** | | | | | | | |
| 1 **Davis, J.** | Y | Y | Y | Y | Y | Y | Y |
| 2 **Drake** | Y | Y | Y | Y | Y | Y | Y |
| 3 Scott | Y | Y | Y | N | N | N | Y |
| 4 **Forbes** | Y | Y | Y | Y | Y | Y | Y |
| 5 **Goode** | Y | Y | Y | Y | Y | Y | Y |
| 6 **Goodlatte** | Y | Y | Y | Y | Y | Y | Y |
| 7 **Cantor** | Y | Y | Y | Y | Y | Y | Y |
| 8 Moran | Y | Y | Y | N | N | N | Y |
| 9 Boucher | Y | Y | Y | N | N | N | Y |
| 10 **Wolf** | Y | Y | Y | Y | Y | Y | Y |
| 11 **Davis, T.** | Y | Y | Y | Y | Y | Y | Y |
| **WASHINGTON** | | | | | | | |
| 1 Inslee | Y | Y | Y | N | N | N | Y |
| 2 Larsen | ? | ? | ? | N | N | N | Y |
| 3 Baird | Y | Y | Y | N | N | N | Y |
| 4 **Hastings** | Y | Y | Y | Y | Y | Y | Y |
| 5 **McMorris** | Y | Y | Y | Y | Y | Y | Y |
| 6 Dicks | Y | Y | Y | N | ? | N | Y |
| 7 McDermott | Y | Y | Y | N | N | N | Y |
| 8 **Reichert** | Y | Y | Y | Y | Y | N | Y |
| 9 Smith | Y | Y | Y | N | N | N | Y |
| **WEST VIRGINIA** | | | | | | | |
| 1 Mollohan | Y | Y | Y | N | N | Y | Y |
| 2 **Capito** | Y | Y | Y | Y | Y | Y | Y |
| 3 Rahall | Y | Y | Y | N | N | N | Y |
| **WISCONSIN** | | | | | | | |
| 1 **Ryan** | Y | Y | Y | Y | Y | Y | Y |
| 2 Baldwin | Y | Y | Y | N | N | N | Y |
| 3 Kind | Y | Y | Y | N | N | N | Y |
| 4 Moore | Y | Y | Y | N | N | N | Y |
| 5 **Sensenbrenner** | Y | Y | Y | Y | Y | Y | Y |
| 6 **Petri** | Y | Y | Y | Y | Y | Y | Y |
| 7 Obey | Y | Y | Y | N | Y | N | Y |
| 8 **Green** | Y | Y | Y | Y | Y | Y | Y |
| **WYOMING** | | | | | | | |
| AL **Cubin** | Y | Y | ? | Y | Y | Y | Y |

# IN THE HOUSE | By Vote Number

**387.** HR 2601. **State Department Authorization/Methamphetamines From Mexico.** Hooley, D-Ore., amendment that would direct the Bureau for International Narcotics and Law Enforcement Affairs to make a priority of stemming the influx of methamphetamine from Mexico into the United States. Adopted 424-1: R 223-1; D 200-0 (ND 151-0, SD 49-0); I 1-0. July 19, 2005.

**388.** HR 2601. **State Department Authorization/Extradition Requests for Afghans.** Souder, R-Ind., amendment that would require a State Department report on pending U.S. extradition requests for Afghans who have committed violations of narcotics laws in the United States. Adopted 426-1: R 225-1; D 200-0 (ND 151-0, SD 49-0); I 1-0. July 19, 2005.

**389.** HR 2601. **State Department Authorization/Obstetric Fistula.** Smith, R-N.J., amendment that would increase access to emergency obstetrical care for women suffering from obstetric fistula and increase the fiscal 2007 authorization for new treatment centers to $7.5 million. It would provide access to family planning services and abstinence education, and make these prevention activities discretionary. Adopted 223-205: R 202-25; D 21-179 (ND 11-140, SD 10-39); I 0-1. July 19, 2005.

**390.** HR 2601. **State Department Authorization/Palestinian Terrorist Attacks.** King, R-Iowa, amendment that would condemn attacks on U.S. citizens by Palestinian terrorists. It would also encourage Palestinian leaders to work with Israel to end all terrorist acts on innocent individuals, regardless of citizenship. Adopted 423-0: R 222-0; D 200-0 (ND 150-0, SD 50-0); I 1-0. July 20, 2005.

**391.** HR 2601. **State Department Authorization/Space-Based Weapons.** Kucinich, D-Ohio, amendment that would require the president to direct the U.S. representative to the United Nations to begin negotiations for an international treaty banning space-based weapons. Rejected 124-302: R 2-223; D 121-79 (ND 109-41, SD 12-38); I 1-0. July 20, 2005.

**392.** HR 2601. **State Department Authorization/Foreign Students.** Lantos, D-Calif., amendment to require the State Department to develop a strategy to counter perceptions among foreign students that the United States is no longer welcoming and annually consult non-governmental organizations, university officials and other interested parties on the strategy. Adopted 373-56: R 171-56; D 201-0 (ND 151-0, SD 50-0); I 1-0. July 20, 2005.

**393.** HR 2601. **State Department Authorization/Great Lakes Water.** Rogers, R-Mich., amendment that would state that Congress recognizes the efforts of the Great Lakes governors and Canadian premiers in developing a common standard for decisions related to water withdrawal from the Great Lakes and urge that the management authority remain with the governors and premiers who share stewardship over the lakes. Rejected 156-273: R 154-73; D 2-199 (ND 1-150, SD 1-49); I 0-1. July 20, 2005.

ND Northern Democrats, SD Southern Democrats
Southern states: Ala., Ark., Fla., Ga., Ky., La., Miss., N.C., Okla., S.C., Tenn., Texas, Va.

| | 387 | 388 | 389 | 390 | 391 | 392 | 393 |
|---|---|---|---|---|---|---|---|
| **ALABAMA** | | | | | | | |
| 1 Bonner | Y | Y | Y | Y | N | Y | Y |
| 2 Everett | Y | Y | Y | Y | N | Y | Y |
| 3 Rogers | Y | Y | Y | Y | N | Y | Y |
| 4 Aderholt | Y | Y | Y | Y | N | Y | Y |
| 5 Cramer | Y | Y | Y | Y | N | Y | N |
| 6 Bachus | Y | Y | Y | Y | N | Y | Y |
| 7 Davis | Y | Y | N | Y | N | Y | N |
| **ALASKA** | | | | | | | |
| AL Young | Y | Y | Y | Y | N | Y | N |
| **ARIZONA** | | | | | | | |
| 1 Renzi | Y | Y | Y | Y | N | N | N |
| 2 Franks | Y | Y | Y | Y | N | Y | Y |
| 3 Shadegg | Y | Y | Y | Y | N | Y | Y |
| 4 Pastor | Y | Y | N | Y | Y | Y | N |
| 5 Hayworth | Y | Y | Y | Y | N | N | N |
| 6 Flake | Y | Y | Y | Y | N | Y | Y |
| 7 Grijalva | Y | Y | N | Y | Y | Y | N |
| 8 Kolbe | Y | Y | N | Y | N | Y | Y |
| **ARKANSAS** | | | | | | | |
| 1 Berry | Y | Y | Y | Y | N | Y | N |
| 2 Snyder | Y | Y | N | Y | N | Y | N |
| 3 Boozman | Y | Y | Y | Y | N | Y | Y |
| 4 Ross | Y | Y | N | Y | N | Y | N |
| **CALIFORNIA** | | | | | | | |
| 1 Thompson | Y | Y | N | Y | Y | Y | N |
| 2 Herger | Y | Y | Y | Y | N | N | Y |
| 3 Lungren | Y | Y | Y | Y | N | Y | N |
| 4 Doolittle | Y | Y | Y | Y | N | N | N |
| 5 Matsui, D. | Y | Y | N | Y | Y | Y | N |
| 6 Woolsey | Y | Y | N | Y | Y | Y | N |
| 7 Miller, George | Y | Y | N | Y | Y | Y | N |
| 8 Pelosi | Y | Y | N | Y | Y | Y | N |
| 9 Lee | Y | Y | N | Y | Y | Y | N |
| 10 Tauscher | Y | Y | N | Y | Y | Y | N |
| 11 Pombo | Y | Y | Y | Y | N | N | N |
| 12 Lantos | Y | Y | N | Y | N | Y | N |
| 13 Stark | Y | Y | N | Y | Y | Y | N |
| 14 Eshoo | Y | Y | N | Y | N | Y | N |
| 15 Honda | Y | Y | N | Y | Y | Y | N |
| 16 Lofgren | Y | Y | N | Y | Y | Y | N |
| 17 Farr | Y | Y | N | Y | Y | Y | N |
| 18 Cardoza | Y | Y | N | Y | N | Y | N |
| 19 Radanovich | Y | Y | Y | Y | N | N | N |
| 20 Costa | Y | Y | N | Y | N | Y | N |
| 21 Nunes | Y | Y | Y | Y | N | Y | N |
| 22 Thomas | Y | Y | N | Y | N | Y | N |
| 23 Capps | Y | Y | N | Y | Y | Y | N |
| 24 Gallegly | Y | Y | Y | Y | N | Y | Y |
| 25 McKeon | Y | Y | Y | Y | N | Y | Y |
| 26 Dreier | Y | Y | N | Y | N | Y | Y |
| 27 Sherman | Y | Y | N | Y | Y | Y | N |
| 28 Berman | Y | Y | N | Y | N | Y | N |
| 29 Schiff | Y | Y | N | Y | N | Y | N |
| 30 Waxman | Y | Y | N | Y | Y | Y | N |
| 31 Becerra | Y | Y | N | Y | Y | Y | N |
| 32 Solis | Y | Y | N | Y | Y | Y | N |
| 33 Watson | Y | Y | N | Y | Y | Y | N |
| 34 Roybal-Allard | Y | Y | N | Y | Y | Y | N |
| 35 Waters | Y | Y | N | Y | Y | Y | N |
| 36 Harman | Y | Y | N | Y | N | Y | N |
| 37 Millender-McD. | Y | Y | N | Y | Y | Y | N |
| 38 Napolitano | Y | Y | N | Y | Y | Y | N |
| 39 Sánchez, Linda | Y | Y | N | Y | Y | Y | N |
| 40 Royce | Y | Y | Y | Y | N | N | Y |
| 41 Lewis | Y | Y | Y | Y | N | Y | Y |
| 42 Miller, Gary | Y | Y | Y | Y | N | N | Y |
| 43 Baca | Y | Y | N | Y | N | Y | N |
| 44 Calvert | Y | Y | Y | Y | N | Y | Y |
| 45 Bono | Y | Y | N | Y | N | Y | Y |
| 46 Rohrabacher | Y | Y | Y | Y | N | N | Y |
| 47 Sanchez, Loretta | Y | Y | N | Y | Y | Y | N |
| 48 Cox | ? | ? | Y | Y | N | Y | Y |
| 49 Issa | Y | Y | Y | Y | N | Y | Y |

| | 387 | 388 | 389 | 390 | 391 | 392 | 393 |
|---|---|---|---|---|---|---|---|
| 50 Cunningham | Y | Y | Y | Y | N | Y | N |
| 51 Filner | Y | Y | N | Y | Y | Y | N |
| 52 Hunter | Y | Y | Y | Y | Y | Y | N |
| 53 Davis | Y | Y | N | Y | Y | Y | N |
| **COLORADO** | | | | | | | |
| 1 DeGette | Y | Y | N | Y | N | Y | N |
| 2 Udall | Y | Y | N | Y | Y | Y | N |
| 3 Salazar | Y | Y | N | Y | N | Y | N |
| 4 Musgrave | ? | Y | Y | Y | N | Y | Y |
| 5 Hefley | Y | Y | Y | Y | N | N | Y |
| 6 Tancredo | ? | ? | ? | Y | N | N | Y |
| 7 Beauprez | Y | Y | Y | Y | N | Y | Y |
| **CONNECTICUT** | | | | | | | |
| 1 Larson | Y | Y | N | Y | Y | Y | N |
| 2 Simmons | Y | Y | N | ? | N | Y | N |
| 3 DeLauro | Y | Y | N | Y | Y | Y | N |
| 4 Shays | Y | Y | N | Y | Y | Y | N |
| 5 Johnson | Y | Y | N | Y | N | Y | N |
| **DELAWARE** | | | | | | | |
| AL Castle | Y | Y | N | Y | N | Y | N |
| **FLORIDA** | | | | | | | |
| 1 Miller | Y | Y | Y | Y | N | N | N |
| 2 Boyd | Y | Y | N | Y | N | Y | N |
| 3 Brown | Y | Y | N | Y | Y | Y | N |
| 4 Crenshaw | Y | Y | Y | Y | N | Y | N |
| 5 Brown-Waite | Y | Y | Y | Y | N | N | N |
| 6 Stearns | Y | Y | Y | Y | N | Y | N |
| 7 Mica | Y | Y | Y | Y | N | Y | N |
| 8 Keller | Y | Y | Y | Y | N | Y | N |
| 9 Bilirakis | Y | Y | Y | Y | N | Y | N |
| 10 Young | Y | Y | Y | Y | N | Y | N |
| 11 Davis | Y | Y | N | Y | N | Y | N |
| 12 Putnam | Y | Y | Y | Y | N | Y | N |
| 13 Harris | Y | Y | Y | Y | N | Y | Y |
| 14 Mack | Y | Y | Y | Y | N | Y | Y |
| 15 Weldon | Y | Y | Y | Y | N | Y | N |
| 16 Foley | Y | Y | N | Y | N | Y | Y |
| 17 Meek | Y | Y | N | Y | Y | Y | N |
| 18 Ros-Lehtinen | Y | Y | N | Y | N | Y | Y |
| 19 Wexler | Y | Y | N | Y | N | Y | N |
| 20 Wasserman-Schultz | Y | Y | N | Y | Y | Y | N |
| 21 Diaz-Balart, L. | Y | Y | N | Y | N | Y | Y |
| 22 Shaw | Y | Y | N | Y | N | N | N |
| 23 Hastings | Y | Y | N | Y | Y | Y | N |
| 24 Feeney | Y | Y | Y | ? | N | Y | Y |
| 25 Diaz-Balart, M. | Y | Y | Y | Y | N | Y | Y |
| **GEORGIA** | | | | | | | |
| 1 Kingston | Y | Y | Y | Y | N | N | Y |
| 2 Bishop | Y | Y | N | Y | N | Y | N |
| 3 Marshall | Y | Y | Y | Y | N | Y | N |
| 4 McKinney | Y | Y | N | Y | Y | Y | N |
| 5 Lewis | Y | Y | N | Y | Y | Y | N |
| 6 Price | Y | Y | Y | Y | N | N | Y |
| 7 Linder | Y | Y | Y | Y | N | N | Y |
| 8 Westmoreland | Y | Y | Y | Y | N | N | Y |
| 9 Norwood | Y | Y | Y | Y | N | N | Y |
| 10 Deal | Y | Y | Y | Y | N | N | Y |
| 11 Gingrey | Y | Y | Y | Y | N | N | Y |
| 12 Barrow | Y | Y | N | Y | N | Y | N |
| 13 Scott | Y | Y | N | Y | N | Y | N |
| **HAWAII** | | | | | | | |
| 1 Abercrombie | Y | Y | N | Y | Y | Y | N |
| 2 Case | Y | Y | N | Y | N | Y | N |
| **IDAHO** | | | | | | | |
| 1 Otter | Y | Y | Y | Y | N | N | Y |
| 2 Simpson | Y | Y | Y | Y | N | Y | Y |
| **ILLINOIS** | | | | | | | |
| 1 Rush | Y | Y | N | Y | ? | Y | N |
| 2 Jackson | Y | Y | N | Y | Y | Y | N |
| 3 Lipinski | Y | Y | Y | Y | N | Y | N |
| 4 Gutierrez | Y | Y | N | Y | N | Y | N |
| 5 Emanuel | Y | Y | N | Y | N | Y | N |
| 6 Hyde | Y | Y | Y | Y | N | Y | Y |
| 7 Davis | Y | Y | N | Y | Y | Y | N |
| 8 Bean | Y | Y | N | Y | N | Y | N |
| 9 Schakowsky | Y | Y | N | Y | Y | Y | N |
| 10 Kirk | Y | Y | N | Y | N | Y | N |
| 11 Weller | Y | Y | Y | Y | N | Y | N |
| 12 Costello | Y | Y | Y | Y | N | Y | N |

**KEY**    **Republicans**    Democrats    *Independents*

| | | | | | |
|---|---|---|---|---|---|
| Y | Voted for (yea) | X | Paired against | C | Voted "present" to avoid possible conflict of interest |
| # | Paired for | – | Announced against | | |
| + | Announced for | P | Voted "present" | ? | Did not vote or otherwise make a position known |
| N | Voted against (nay) | | | | |

| | 387 | 388 | 389 | 390 | 391 | 392 | 393 |
|---|---|---|---|---|---|---|---|
| 13 **Biggert** | Y | Y | N | Y | N | Y | Y |
| 14 **Hastert** | | | | | | | |
| 15 **Johnson** | Y | Y | Y | Y | N | Y | N |
| 16 **Manzullo** | Y | Y | Y | Y | N | N | Y |
| 17 Evans | Y | Y | N | Y | Y | Y | N |
| 18 **LaHood** | Y | Y | Y | Y | N | Y | N |
| 19 **Shimkus** | Y | Y | Y | Y | N | Y | N |
| **INDIANA** | | | | | | | |
| 1 Visclosky | Y | Y | N | Y | Y | Y | N |
| 2 **Chocola** | Y | Y | Y | Y | N | Y | Y |
| 3 **Souder** | Y | Y | Y | Y | N | Y | Y |
| 4 **Buyer** | Y | Y | Y | Y | N | Y | Y |
| 5 **Burton** | Y | Y | Y | Y | N | Y | Y |
| 6 **Pence** | Y | Y | Y | Y | N | Y | Y |
| 7 Carson | Y | Y | N | Y | Y | Y | N |
| 8 **Hostettler** | Y | Y | Y | Y | N | N | Y |
| 9 **Sodrel** | Y | Y | Y | Y | N | Y | Y |
| **IOWA** | | | | | | | |
| 1 **Nussle** | Y | Y | Y | Y | N | N | Y |
| 2 **Leach** | Y | Y | N | Y | Y | Y | N |
| 3 Boswell | Y | Y | N | Y | Y | Y | N |
| 4 **Latham** | Y | Y | Y | Y | N | Y | Y |
| 5 **King** | Y | Y | Y | Y | N | Y | Y |
| **KANSAS** | | | | | | | |
| 1 **Moran** | Y | Y | Y | Y | N | Y | Y |
| 2 **Ryun** | Y | Y | Y | Y | N | Y | Y |
| 3 Moore | Y | Y | N | Y | N | Y | N |
| 4 **Tiahrt** | Y | Y | Y | Y | N | Y | Y |
| **KENTUCKY** | | | | | | | |
| 1 **Whitfield** | Y | Y | Y | Y | N | Y | Y |
| 2 **Lewis** | Y | Y | Y | Y | N | Y | Y |
| 3 **Northup** | Y | Y | Y | Y | N | Y | Y |
| 4 **Davis** | Y | Y | Y | + | – | N | Y |
| 5 **Rogers** | Y | Y | Y | Y | N | Y | Y |
| 6 Chandler | Y | Y | N | Y | N | Y | N |
| **LOUISIANA** | | | | | | | |
| 1 **Jindal** | Y | Y | Y | ? | ? | ? | ? |
| 2 Jefferson | Y | Y | N | Y | N | Y | N |
| 3 Melancon | Y | Y | N | Y | N | Y | N |
| 4 **McCrery** | Y | Y | Y | Y | N | Y | Y |
| 5 **Alexander** | Y | Y | Y | Y | N | Y | Y |
| 6 **Baker** | Y | Y | Y | Y | N | Y | Y |
| 7 **Boustany** | Y | Y | Y | Y | N | Y | Y |
| **MAINE** | | | | | | | |
| 1 Allen | Y | Y | N | Y | Y | Y | N |
| 2 Michaud | Y | Y | N | Y | Y | Y | N |
| **MARYLAND** | | | | | | | |
| 1 **Gilchrest** | Y | Y | N | Y | N | Y | N |
| 2 Ruppersberger | Y | Y | N | Y | Y | Y | N |
| 3 Cardin | Y | Y | N | Y | N | Y | N |
| 4 Wynn | Y | Y | N | Y | Y | Y | N |
| 5 Hoyer | Y | Y | N | Y | N | Y | N |
| 6 **Bartlett** | Y | Y | Y | Y | N | N | Y |
| 7 Cummings | Y | Y | N | Y | Y | Y | N |
| 8 Van Hollen | Y | Y | N | Y | Y | Y | N |
| **MASSACHUSETTS** | | | | | | | |
| 1 Olver | Y | Y | N | Y | Y | Y | N |
| 2 Neal | Y | Y | N | Y | Y | Y | N |
| 3 McGovern | Y | Y | N | Y | Y | Y | N |
| 4 Frank | Y | Y | N | Y | Y | Y | N |
| 5 Meehan | Y | Y | N | Y | Y | Y | N |
| 6 Tierney | Y | Y | N | Y | Y | Y | N |
| 7 Markey | Y | Y | N | Y | Y | Y | N |
| 8 Capuano | Y | Y | N | Y | Y | Y | N |
| 9 Lynch | Y | Y | N | Y | N | Y | N |
| 10 Delahunt | Y | Y | N | Y | Y | Y | N |
| **MICHIGAN** | | | | | | | |
| 1 Stupak | Y | Y | Y | Y | Y | Y | N |
| 2 **Hoekstra** | Y | Y | Y | Y | N | Y | N |
| 3 **Ehlers** | Y | Y | Y | Y | N | Y | N |
| 4 **Camp** | Y | Y | Y | Y | N | Y | N |
| 5 Kildee | Y | Y | Y | Y | N | Y | N |
| 6 **Upton** | Y | Y | Y | Y | N | Y | N |
| 7 **Schwarz** | Y | Y | N | Y | N | Y | Y |
| 8 **Rogers** | Y | Y | Y | Y | N | Y | Y |
| 9 **Knollenberg** | Y | Y | Y | Y | N | Y | Y |
| 10 **Miller** | Y | Y | Y | Y | N | Y | N |
| 11 **McCotter** | Y | Y | Y | Y | N | Y | Y |
| 12 Levin | Y | Y | N | Y | N | Y | N |
| 13 Kilpatrick | Y | Y | N | Y | Y | Y | N |
| 14 Conyers | Y | Y | N | Y | Y | Y | N |
| 15 Dingell | Y | Y | N | Y | Y | Y | N |

| | 387 | 388 | 389 | 390 | 391 | 392 | 393 |
|---|---|---|---|---|---|---|---|
| **MINNESOTA** | | | | | | | |
| 1 **Gutknecht** | Y | Y | Y | Y | N | N | N |
| 2 **Kline** | Y | Y | Y | Y | N | Y | N |
| 3 **Ramstad** | Y | Y | N | Y | N | Y | N |
| 4 McCollum | Y | Y | N | Y | Y | Y | N |
| 5 Sabo | Y | Y | N | Y | Y | Y | N |
| 6 **Kennedy** | Y | Y | Y | Y | N | Y | N |
| 7 Peterson | Y | Y | Y | Y | N | Y | N |
| 8 Oberstar | Y | Y | N | Y | Y | Y | N |
| **MISSISSIPPI** | | | | | | | |
| 1 **Wicker** | Y | Y | Y | Y | N | Y | Y |
| 2 Thompson | Y | Y | N | Y | N | Y | N |
| 3 **Pickering** | Y | Y | Y | Y | N | Y | N |
| 4 Taylor | Y | Y | Y | Y | N | Y | N |
| **MISSOURI** | | | | | | | |
| 1 Clay | Y | Y | N | Y | Y | Y | N |
| 2 **Akin** | Y | Y | Y | Y | N | N | Y |
| 3 Carnahan | Y | Y | N | Y | N | Y | N |
| 4 Skelton | Y | Y | Y | Y | N | Y | N |
| 5 Cleaver | Y | Y | N | Y | Y | Y | N |
| 6 **Graves** | Y | Y | Y | Y | N | Y | Y |
| 7 **Blunt** | Y | Y | Y | Y | N | Y | Y |
| 8 **Emerson** | Y | Y | Y | Y | N | Y | Y |
| 9 **Hulshof** | Y | Y | Y | Y | N | Y | Y |
| **MONTANA** | | | | | | | |
| AL **Rehberg** | Y | Y | Y | Y | N | Y | Y |
| **NEBRASKA** | | | | | | | |
| 1 **Fortenberry** | Y | Y | Y | Y | N | Y | Y |
| 2 **Terry** | Y | Y | Y | Y | N | Y | Y |
| 3 **Osborne** | Y | Y | Y | Y | N | Y | Y |
| **NEVADA** | | | | | | | |
| 1 Berkley | Y | Y | N | Y | Y | Y | N |
| 2 **Gibbons** | Y | Y | Y | Y | N | N | Y |
| 3 **Porter** | Y | Y | Y | Y | N | Y | Y |
| **NEW HAMPSHIRE** | | | | | | | |
| 1 **Bradley** | Y | Y | N | Y | N | Y | N |
| 2 **Bass** | Y | Y | N | Y | N | Y | N |
| **NEW JERSEY** | | | | | | | |
| 1 Andrews | Y | Y | N | Y | Y | Y | N |
| 2 **LoBiondo** | Y | Y | Y | Y | N | Y | Y |
| 3 **Saxton** | Y | Y | Y | Y | N | Y | Y |
| 4 **Smith** | Y | Y | Y | Y | N | Y | N |
| 5 **Garrett** | Y | Y | Y | Y | N | N | Y |
| 6 Pallone | Y | Y | N | Y | Y | Y | N |
| 7 **Ferguson** | Y | Y | Y | Y | N | Y | N |
| 8 Pascrell | Y | Y | N | Y | Y | Y | N |
| 9 Rothman | Y | Y | N | Y | Y | Y | N |
| 10 Payne | Y | Y | N | Y | Y | Y | N |
| 11 **Frelinghuysen** | Y | Y | N | Y | N | Y | Y |
| 12 Holt | Y | Y | N | Y | Y | Y | N |
| 13 Menendez | Y | Y | N | Y | N | Y | N |
| **NEW MEXICO** | | | | | | | |
| 1 **Wilson** | Y | Y | Y | Y | N | Y | Y |
| 2 **Pearce** | Y | Y | Y | Y | N | Y | Y |
| 3 Udall | Y | Y | N | Y | Y | Y | N |
| **NEW YORK** | | | | | | | |
| 1 Bishop | Y | Y | N | Y | Y | Y | N |
| 2 Israel | Y | Y | N | Y | N | Y | N |
| 3 **King** | Y | Y | Y | Y | N | Y | Y |
| 4 McCarthy | Y | Y | N | Y | N | Y | N |
| 5 Ackerman | Y | Y | N | Y | Y | Y | N |
| 6 Meeks | Y | Y | N | Y | Y | Y | Y |
| 7 Crowley | Y | Y | N | Y | Y | Y | N |
| 8 Nadler | Y | Y | N | Y | Y | Y | N |
| 9 Weiner | Y | Y | N | Y | Y | Y | N |
| 10 Towns | Y | Y | N | Y | Y | Y | N |
| 11 Owens | Y | Y | N | Y | Y | Y | N |
| 12 Velázquez | Y | Y | N | Y | Y | Y | N |
| 13 **Fossella** | Y | Y | Y | Y | N | Y | Y |
| 14 Maloney | Y | Y | N | Y | Y | Y | N |
| 15 Rangel | Y | Y | N | Y | Y | Y | N |
| 16 Serrano | Y | Y | N | Y | Y | Y | N |
| 17 Engel | Y | Y | N | Y | Y | Y | N |
| 18 Lowey | Y | Y | N | Y | Y | Y | N |
| 19 **Kelly** | Y | Y | N | Y | N | Y | N |
| 20 **Sweeney** | ? | ? | ? | Y | N | Y | Y |
| 21 McNulty | Y | Y | N | Y | Y | Y | N |
| 22 Hinchey | Y | Y | N | Y | Y | Y | N |
| 23 **McHugh** | Y | Y | Y | Y | N | Y | Y |
| 24 **Boehlert** | Y | Y | N | Y | N | Y | Y |
| 25 **Walsh** | Y | Y | Y | Y | N | Y | Y |
| 26 **Reynolds** | Y | Y | Y | Y | N | Y | Y |
| 27 Higgins | Y | Y | N | Y | Y | Y | N |
| 28 Slaughter | Y | Y | N | + | Y | Y | N |
| 29 **Kuhl** | Y | Y | Y | Y | N | Y | Y |

| | 387 | 388 | 389 | 390 | 391 | 392 | 393 |
|---|---|---|---|---|---|---|---|
| **NORTH CAROLINA** | | | | | | | |
| 1 Butterfield | Y | Y | N | Y | N | Y | N |
| 2 Etheridge | Y | Y | N | Y | N | Y | N |
| 3 **Jones** | Y | Y | Y | Y | N | N | Y |
| 4 Price | Y | Y | N | Y | Y | Y | N |
| 5 **Foxx** | Y | Y | Y | Y | N | N | N |
| 6 **Coble** | Y | Y | Y | Y | N | N | Y |
| 7 McIntyre | Y | Y | Y | Y | N | Y | N |
| 8 **Hayes** | Y | Y | Y | Y | N | Y | Y |
| 9 **Myrick** | Y | Y | Y | Y | N | N | Y |
| 10 **McHenry** | Y | Y | Y | Y | N | N | Y |
| 11 **Taylor** | Y | Y | Y | Y | N | N | N |
| 12 Watt | Y | Y | N | Y | Y | Y | N |
| 13 Miller | Y | Y | N | Y | N | Y | N |
| **NORTH DAKOTA** | | | | | | | |
| AL Pomeroy | Y | Y | N | Y | N | Y | N |
| **OHIO** | | | | | | | |
| 1 **Chabot** | Y | Y | Y | Y | N | Y | Y |
| 2 Vacant | | | | | | | |
| 3 **Turner** | Y | Y | Y | Y | N | Y | Y |
| 4 **Oxley** | Y | Y | Y | Y | N | Y | Y |
| 5 **Gillmor** | Y | Y | Y | Y | N | Y | N |
| 6 Strickland | Y | Y | N | Y | Y | Y | N |
| 7 **Hobson** | Y | Y | Y | Y | N | Y | Y |
| 8 **Boehner** | Y | Y | Y | Y | N | Y | Y |
| 9 Kaptur | Y | Y | Y | Y | Y | Y | N |
| 10 Kucinich | Y | Y | N | Y | Y | Y | N |
| 11 Jones | Y | Y | N | Y | Y | Y | N |
| 12 **Tiberi** | Y | Y | Y | Y | N | Y | Y |
| 13 Brown | Y | Y | N | Y | Y | Y | N |
| 14 **LaTourette** | Y | Y | Y | Y | N | Y | N |
| 15 **Pryce** | Y | Y | N | Y | N | Y | N |
| 16 **Regula** | Y | Y | Y | Y | N | Y | Y |
| 17 Ryan | Y | Y | N | Y | Y | Y | N |
| 18 **Ney** | Y | Y | Y | Y | N | Y | N |
| **OKLAHOMA** | | | | | | | |
| 1 **Sullivan** | Y | Y | Y | ? | ? | Y | Y |
| 2 Boren | Y | Y | Y | Y | N | Y | N |
| 3 **Lucas** | Y | Y | Y | Y | N | Y | N |
| 4 **Cole** | Y | Y | Y | Y | N | Y | Y |
| 5 **Istook** | Y | Y | Y | Y | N | Y | N |
| **OREGON** | | | | | | | |
| 1 Wu | Y | Y | N | Y | Y | Y | N |
| 2 **Walden** | Y | Y | N | Y | N | N | Y |
| 3 Blumenauer | Y | Y | N | Y | Y | Y | N |
| 4 DeFazio | Y | Y | N | Y | Y | Y | N |
| 5 Hooley | Y | Y | N | Y | Y | Y | N |
| **PENNSYLVANIA** | | | | | | | |
| 1 Brady | Y | Y | N | Y | Y | Y | N |
| 2 Fattah | Y | Y | N | Y | Y | Y | N |
| 3 **English** | Y | Y | Y | Y | N | Y | N |
| 4 **Hart** | Y | Y | Y | Y | N | Y | N |
| 5 **Peterson** | Y | Y | Y | Y | N | Y | Y |
| 6 **Gerlach** | Y | Y | N | Y | N | Y | Y |
| 7 **Weldon** | Y | Y | Y | Y | N | Y | N |
| 8 **Fitzpatrick** | Y | Y | Y | Y | N | Y | N |
| 9 **Shuster** | Y | Y | Y | Y | N | N | N |
| 10 **Sherwood** | Y | Y | Y | Y | N | Y | Y |
| 11 Kanjorski | Y | Y | N | Y | N | Y | N |
| 12 Murtha | Y | Y | Y | Y | N | Y | N |
| 13 Schwartz | Y | Y | N | Y | Y | Y | N |
| 14 Doyle | Y | Y | N | Y | Y | Y | N |
| 15 **Dent** | Y | Y | N | Y | N | Y | Y |
| 16 **Pitts** | Y | Y | Y | Y | N | Y | Y |
| 17 Holden | Y | Y | Y | Y | N | Y | N |
| 18 **Murphy** | Y | Y | Y | Y | N | Y | Y |
| 19 **Platts** | Y | Y | Y | Y | N | Y | N |
| **RHODE ISLAND** | | | | | | | |
| 1 Kennedy | Y | Y | N | Y | N | Y | N |
| 2 Langevin | Y | Y | N | Y | N | Y | N |
| **SOUTH CAROLINA** | | | | | | | |
| 1 **Brown** | ? | ? | ? | ? | ? | ? | ? |
| 2 **Wilson** | Y | Y | Y | Y | N | Y | Y |
| 3 **Barrett** | Y | Y | Y | Y | N | N | Y |
| 4 **Inglis** | Y | Y | Y | Y | N | Y | N |
| 5 Spratt | Y | Y | N | Y | N | Y | N |
| 6 Clyburn | Y | Y | N | Y | N | Y | N |
| **SOUTH DAKOTA** | | | | | | | |
| AL Herseth | Y | Y | N | Y | N | Y | N |
| **TENNESSEE** | | | | | | | |
| 1 **Jenkins** | Y | Y | Y | Y | N | N | Y |
| 2 **Duncan** | Y | Y | Y | Y | N | N | Y |

| | 387 | 388 | 389 | 390 | 391 | 392 | 393 |
|---|---|---|---|---|---|---|---|
| 3 **Wamp** | Y | Y | Y | Y | N | Y | N |
| 4 Davis | Y | Y | Y | Y | N | Y | N |
| 5 Cooper | Y | Y | N | Y | N | Y | N |
| 6 Gordon | Y | Y | Y | Y | N | Y | N |
| 7 **Blackburn** | Y | Y | Y | Y | N | N | Y |
| 8 Tanner | Y | Y | N | Y | N | Y | N |
| 9 Ford | Y | Y | N | Y | N | Y | N |
| **TEXAS** | | | | | | | |
| 1 **Gohmert** | Y | Y | Y | Y | N | N | Y |
| 2 **Poe** | Y | Y | Y | Y | N | Y | Y |
| 3 **Johnson, S.** | Y | Y | Y | Y | N | N | Y |
| 4 **Hall** | Y | Y | Y | Y | N | Y | Y |
| 5 **Hensarling** | Y | Y | Y | Y | N | Y | Y |
| 6 **Barton** | Y | Y | Y | Y | N | Y | N |
| 7 **Culberson** | Y | Y | Y | Y | N | N | Y |
| 8 **Brady** | Y | Y | Y | ? | ? | ? | ? |
| 9 Green, A. | Y | Y | N | Y | Y | Y | N |
| 10 **McCaul** | Y | Y | Y | Y | N | Y | Y |
| 11 **Conaway** | Y | Y | Y | Y | N | Y | Y |
| 12 **Granger** | Y | Y | Y | Y | N | Y | Y |
| 13 **Thornberry** | Y | Y | Y | Y | N | Y | Y |
| 14 **Paul** | N | N | N | Y | N | N | Y |
| 15 Hinojosa | ? | ? | ? | ? | ? | ? | ? |
| 16 Reyes | ? | ? | ? | Y | N | Y | N |
| 17 Edwards | Y | Y | N | Y | N | Y | N |
| 18 Jackson-Lee | Y | Y | N | Y | Y | Y | N |
| 19 **Neugebauer** | Y | Y | Y | Y | N | Y | Y |
| 20 Gonzalez | Y | Y | N | Y | N | Y | N |
| 21 **Smith** | Y | Y | Y | Y | N | N | Y |
| 22 **DeLay** | Y | Y | Y | Y | N | Y | Y |
| 23 **Bonilla** | Y | Y | Y | Y | N | N | Y |
| 24 **Marchant** | Y | Y | Y | Y | N | N | Y |
| 25 Doggett | Y | Y | N | Y | Y | Y | N |
| 26 **Burgess** | Y | Y | Y | Y | N | N | Y |
| 27 Ortiz | Y | Y | Y | Y | N | Y | N |
| 28 Cuellar | Y | Y | Y | Y | N | Y | N |
| 29 Green, G. | Y | Y | N | Y | Y | Y | Y |
| 30 Johnson, E. | Y | Y | N | Y | Y | Y | N |
| 31 **Carter** | Y | Y | Y | Y | N | Y | Y |
| 32 **Sessions** | Y | Y | Y | Y | N | N | Y |
| **UTAH** | | | | | | | |
| 1 **Bishop** | ? | Y | Y | Y | N | Y | Y |
| 2 Matheson | Y | Y | N | Y | N | Y | N |
| 3 **Cannon** | Y | Y | Y | Y | N | Y | N |
| **VERMONT** | | | | | | | |
| AL *Sanders* | Y | Y | N | Y | Y | Y | N |
| **VIRGINIA** | | | | | | | |
| 1 **Davis, J.** | Y | Y | Y | Y | N | N | Y |
| 2 **Drake** | Y | Y | Y | Y | N | Y | Y |
| 3 Scott | Y | Y | N | Y | Y | Y | N |
| 4 **Forbes** | Y | Y | Y | Y | N | N | Y |
| 5 **Goode** | Y | Y | Y | Y | N | N | Y |
| 6 **Goodlatte** | Y | Y | Y | Y | N | Y | N |
| 7 **Cantor** | Y | Y | Y | Y | N | Y | Y |
| 8 Moran | Y | Y | N | Y | N | Y | N |
| 9 Boucher | Y | Y | N | Y | N | Y | N |
| 10 **Wolf** | Y | Y | Y | Y | N | Y | N |
| 11 **Davis, T.** | Y | Y | Y | Y | N | Y | N |
| **WASHINGTON** | | | | | | | |
| 1 Inslee | Y | Y | N | Y | Y | Y | N |
| 2 Larsen | Y | Y | N | Y | Y | Y | N |
| 3 Baird | Y | Y | N | Y | Y | Y | N |
| 4 **Hastings** | Y | Y | Y | Y | N | Y | Y |
| 5 **McMorris** | Y | Y | Y | + | N | Y | Y |
| 6 Dicks | Y | Y | N | Y | N | Y | N |
| 7 McDermott | Y | Y | N | Y | Y | Y | N |
| 8 **Reichert** | Y | Y | Y | Y | N | Y | Y |
| 9 Smith | Y | Y | N | Y | Y | Y | N |
| **WEST VIRGINIA** | | | | | | | |
| 1 Mollohan | Y | Y | Y | Y | N | Y | N |
| 2 **Capito** | Y | Y | Y | Y | N | Y | N |
| 3 Rahall | Y | Y | Y | Y | Y | Y | N |
| **WISCONSIN** | | | | | | | |
| 1 **Ryan** | Y | Y | Y | Y | N | Y | N |
| 2 Baldwin | Y | Y | N | Y | Y | Y | N |
| 3 Kind | Y | Y | N | Y | N | Y | N |
| 4 Moore | Y | Y | N | Y | Y | Y | N |
| 5 **Sensenbrenner** | Y | Y | Y | Y | N | Y | Y |
| 6 **Petri** | Y | Y | Y | Y | N | Y | N |
| 7 Obey | Y | Y | N | Y | Y | Y | N |
| 8 **Green** | Y | Y | Y | Y | N | Y | N |
| **WYOMING** | | | | | | | |
| AL **Cubin** | Y | Y | Y | Y | N | N | N |

# IN THE HOUSE | By Vote Number

**394.** HR 2601. State Department Authorization/Extradition of Charles Taylor. Watson, D-Calif., amendment that would require the United States. to seek the extradition of former Liberian President Charles Taylor to the Special Court for Sierra Leone, where he would be tried for war crimes, crimes against humanity and other violations of international humanitarian law. Adopted 422-2: R 222-2; D 199-0 (ND 150-0, SD 49-0); I 1-0. July 20, 2005.

**395.** HR 2601. State Department Authorization/Palestinian Territories. Berkley, D-Nev., amendment that would state that the United States should promote the emergence of a democratic Palestinian government that denounces and combats terrorism. It would specify that no more than 25 percent of the aid for the Palestinian Authority could be obligated and expended during any calendar quarter. Adopted 330-100: R 211-18; D 119-81 (ND 80-70, SD 39-11); I 0-1. July 20, 2005.

**396.** HR 2601. State Department Authorization/Detention of International Terrorists. Rohrabacher, R-Calif., amendment that would express the sense of Congress that the detention and lawful human interrogation of detainees at Guantánamo Bay, Cuba, is essential to U.S. defense and prosecution of the war on terrorism. Adopted 304-124: R 223-4; D 81-119 (ND 50-100, SD 31-19); I 0-1. July 20, 2005.

**397.** HR 2601. State Department Authorization/Iraqi Forces Power Transfer. Ros-Lehtinen, R-Fla., amendment that would state that it is U.S. policy not to withdraw U.S. forces prematurely from Iraq, but to do so only when it is clear that U.S. national security and foreign policy goals relating to a free and stable Iraq have been or are about to be achieved. Adopted 291-137: R 220-7; D 71-129 (ND 38-112, SD 33-17); I 0-1. July 20, 2005.

**398.** HR 2601. State Department Authorization/Recommit. Menendez, D-N.J., motion to recommit the bill to the International Relations Committee with instructions to add language asking the president to advise Congress on the benchmarks for a successful strategy in Iraq. The language would also state that it is U.S. policy to devise a plan to bring stability to Iraq so that the responsibility for Iraq's security may be transferred to the Iraqi people as soon as possible, to provide adequate equipment for U.S. troops and to provide adequate health care benefits upon their return. Motion rejected 203-227: R 2-227; D 200-0 (ND 150-0, SD 50-0); I 1-0. July 20, 2005.

**399.** HR 2601. State Department Authorization/Passage. Passage of the bill that would authorize $10.8 billion in fiscal 2006 and $10 billion in fiscal 2007 for the State Department, international broadcasting activities, international assistance programs and related agencies. Passed 351-78: R 216-13; D 135-64 (ND 95-54, SD 40-10); I 0-1. July 20, 2005.

**400.** H Res 326. Elections in Azerbaijan/Adoption. Ros-Lehtinen, R-Fla., motion to suspend the rules and adopt the resolution that would call for free and fair parliamentary elections in the Republic of Azerbaijan in November 2005. Motion agreed to 416-1: R 222-1; D 193-0 (ND 144-0, SD 49-0); I 1-0. A two-thirds majority of those present and voting (278 in this case) is required for adoption under suspension of the rules. July 20, 2005.

| | 394 | 395 | 396 | 397 | 398 | 399 | 400 |
|---|---|---|---|---|---|---|---|
| **ALABAMA** | | | | | | | |
| 1 Bonner | Y | Y | Y | Y | N | Y | Y |
| 2 Everett | Y | Y | Y | Y | N | Y | Y |
| 3 Rogers | Y | Y | Y | Y | N | Y | Y |
| 4 Aderholt | Y | Y | Y | Y | N | Y | Y |
| 5 Cramer | Y | Y | Y | Y | Y | Y | Y |
| 6 Bachus | Y | Y | Y | Y | N | Y | Y |
| 7 Davis | Y | Y | Y | Y | Y | Y | Y |
| **ALASKA** | | | | | | | |
| AL Young | Y | Y | Y | Y | N | Y | Y |
| **ARIZONA** | | | | | | | |
| 1 Renzi | Y | Y | Y | Y | N | Y | Y |
| 2 Franks | Y | Y | Y | Y | N | N | Y |
| 3 Shadegg | Y | Y | Y | Y | N | Y | Y |
| 4 Pastor | Y | N | N | N | Y | N | Y |
| 5 Hayworth | Y | Y | Y | Y | N | Y | Y |
| 6 Flake | Y | Y | Y | Y | N | N | Y |
| 7 Grijalva | Y | N | N | N | Y | N | Y |
| 8 Kolbe | Y | N | Y | Y | N | Y | Y |
| **ARKANSAS** | | | | | | | |
| 1 Berry | Y | Y | Y | Y | Y | N | Y |
| 2 Snyder | Y | N | N | N | Y | Y | Y |
| 3 Boozman | Y | Y | Y | Y | N | Y | ? |
| 4 Ross | Y | Y | Y | Y | Y | Y | Y |
| **CALIFORNIA** | | | | | | | |
| 1 Thompson | Y | Y | N | N | Y | Y | Y |
| 2 Herger | Y | Y | Y | Y | N | Y | Y |
| 3 Lungren | Y | Y | Y | Y | N | Y | Y |
| 4 Doolittle | Y | Y | Y | Y | N | Y | Y |
| 5 Matsui, D. | Y | N | N | N | Y | Y | Y |
| 6 Woolsey | Y | N | N | N | Y | N | Y |
| 7 Miller, George | Y | N | N | N | Y | N | Y |
| 8 Pelosi | Y | N | N | N | Y | N | Y |
| 9 Lee | Y | N | N | N | Y | N | Y |
| 10 Tauscher | Y | N | Y | N | Y | Y | Y |
| 11 Pombo | Y | Y | Y | Y | N | Y | Y |
| 12 Lantos | Y | Y | N | Y | Y | Y | Y |
| 13 Stark | Y | N | N | N | Y | N | Y |
| 14 Eshoo | Y | N | Y | N | Y | Y | Y |
| 15 Honda | Y | N | N | N | Y | N | Y |
| 16 Lofgren | Y | N | N | N | Y | N | Y |
| 17 Farr | Y | N | N | N | Y | N | Y |
| 18 Cardoza | Y | Y | Y | Y | Y | Y | Y |
| 19 Radanovich | Y | Y | Y | Y | N | Y | Y |
| 20 Costa | Y | Y | Y | Y | Y | Y | Y |
| 21 Nunes | Y | Y | Y | Y | N | Y | Y |
| 22 Thomas | Y | Y | Y | Y | N | Y | Y |
| 23 Capps | Y | N | N | N | Y | Y | Y |
| 24 Gallegly | Y | Y | Y | Y | N | Y | Y |
| 25 McKeon | Y | Y | Y | Y | N | Y | Y |
| 26 Dreier | N | Y | Y | Y | N | Y | Y |
| 27 Sherman | Y | Y | N | Y | Y | Y | Y |
| 28 Berman | Y | N | N | Y | Y | Y | ? |
| 29 Schiff | Y | Y | Y | Y | Y | Y | Y |
| 30 Waxman | Y | N | Y | N | Y | Y | Y |
| 31 Becerra | Y | N | N | N | Y | Y | Y |
| 32 Solis | Y | N | N | N | Y | N | Y |
| 33 Watson | Y | Y | N | N | Y | N | Y |
| 34 Roybal-Allard | Y | N | N | N | Y | Y | Y |
| 35 Waters | ? | N | N | N | Y | N | Y |
| 36 Harman | Y | Y | Y | Y | Y | Y | Y |
| 37 Millender-McD. | Y | Y | N | N | Y | Y | Y |
| 38 Napolitano | Y | N | N | N | Y | Y | Y |
| 39 Sánchez, Linda | Y | N | N | N | Y | Y | ? |
| 40 Royce | Y | Y | Y | Y | N | Y | Y |
| 41 Lewis | Y | Y | Y | Y | N | Y | Y |
| 42 Miller, Gary | Y | Y | Y | Y | N | Y | Y |
| 43 Baca | Y | Y | N | N | Y | Y | Y |
| 44 Calvert | Y | Y | Y | Y | N | Y | Y |
| 45 Bono | Y | Y | Y | Y | N | Y | Y |
| 46 Rohrabacher | Y | N | Y | Y | N | Y | Y |
| 47 Sanchez, Loretta | Y | N | Y | N | Y | Y | Y |
| 48 Cox | Y | Y | Y | Y | N | Y | Y |
| 49 Issa | Y | N | Y | Y | N | Y | Y |

| | 394 | 395 | 396 | 397 | 398 | 399 | 400 |
|---|---|---|---|---|---|---|---|
| 50 Cunningham | Y | Y | Y | Y | N | Y | Y |
| 51 Filner | Y | Y | N | N | Y | N | Y |
| 52 Hunter | Y | Y | Y | Y | N | Y | Y |
| 53 Davis | Y | Y | Y | N | Y | Y | Y |
| **COLORADO** | | | | | | | |
| 1 DeGette | Y | Y | N | N | Y | Y | Y |
| 2 Udall | Y | Y | Y | Y | Y | Y | Y |
| 3 Salazar | Y | Y | Y | Y | Y | Y | Y |
| 4 Musgrave | Y | Y | Y | Y | N | Y | Y |
| 5 Hefley | Y | Y | Y | Y | N | N | Y |
| 6 Tancredo | Y | Y | Y | Y | N | N | Y |
| 7 Beauprez | Y | Y | Y | Y | N | Y | Y |
| **CONNECTICUT** | | | | | | | |
| 1 Larson | Y | Y | N | Y | Y | Y | Y |
| 2 Simmons | ? | Y | Y | Y | N | Y | Y |
| 3 DeLauro | Y | N | N | N | Y | Y | Y |
| 4 Shays | Y | Y | N | Y | N | Y | Y |
| 5 Johnson | Y | Y | Y | Y | N | Y | Y |
| **DELAWARE** | | | | | | | |
| AL Castle | Y | Y | Y | Y | N | Y | Y |
| **FLORIDA** | | | | | | | |
| 1 Miller | Y | Y | Y | Y | N | N | Y |
| 2 Boyd | Y | Y | Y | Y | Y | Y | Y |
| 3 Brown | Y | Y | N | N | Y | Y | Y |
| 4 Crenshaw | Y | Y | Y | Y | N | Y | Y |
| 5 Brown-Waite | Y | Y | Y | Y | N | Y | Y |
| 6 Stearns | Y | Y | Y | Y | N | N | Y |
| 7 Mica | Y | Y | Y | Y | N | Y | Y |
| 8 Keller | Y | Y | Y | Y | N | Y | Y |
| 9 Bilirakis | Y | Y | Y | Y | N | Y | Y |
| 10 Young | Y | Y | N | Y | N | Y | Y |
| 11 Davis | Y | Y | Y | Y | Y | Y | ? |
| 12 Putnam | Y | Y | Y | Y | N | Y | Y |
| 13 Harris | Y | Y | Y | Y | N | Y | Y |
| 14 Mack | Y | Y | Y | Y | N | Y | Y |
| 15 Weldon | Y | Y | Y | Y | N | Y | Y |
| 16 Foley | Y | Y | Y | Y | N | Y | Y |
| 17 Meek | Y | Y | Y | Y | Y | Y | Y |
| 18 Ros-Lehtinen | Y | Y | Y | Y | N | Y | Y |
| 19 Wexler | Y | N | N | N | Y | N | Y |
| 20 Wasserman-Schultz | Y | Y | N | N | Y | Y | Y |
| 21 Diaz-Balart, L. | Y | Y | Y | Y | N | Y | Y |
| 22 Shaw | Y | Y | Y | Y | N | Y | Y |
| 23 Hastings | Y | N | N | N | Y | N | Y |
| 24 Feeney | Y | Y | Y | Y | N | Y | Y |
| 25 Diaz-Balart, M. | ? | Y | Y | Y | N | Y | Y |
| **GEORGIA** | | | | | | | |
| 1 Kingston | Y | Y | Y | Y | N | Y | Y |
| 2 Bishop | Y | Y | Y | Y | Y | Y | Y |
| 3 Marshall | Y | Y | Y | Y | Y | Y | Y |
| 4 McKinney | ? | N | N | N | Y | N | Y |
| 5 Lewis | Y | N | N | N | Y | N | Y |
| 6 Price | Y | Y | Y | Y | N | Y | Y |
| 7 Linder | Y | Y | Y | Y | N | Y | ? |
| 8 Westmoreland | Y | Y | Y | Y | N | N | Y |
| 9 Norwood | Y | Y | Y | Y | N | Y | Y |
| 10 Deal | Y | Y | Y | Y | N | Y | Y |
| 11 Gingrey | Y | Y | Y | Y | N | Y | Y |
| 12 Barrow | Y | Y | Y | Y | Y | Y | Y |
| 13 Scott | Y | Y | Y | Y | Y | Y | Y |
| **HAWAII** | | | | | | | |
| 1 Abercrombie | Y | N | N | N | Y | N | Y |
| 2 Case | Y | Y | Y | Y | Y | Y | Y |
| **IDAHO** | | | | | | | |
| 1 Otter | Y | Y | Y | Y | N | N | Y |
| 2 Simpson | Y | Y | Y | Y | N | Y | Y |
| **ILLINOIS** | | | | | | | |
| 1 Rush | Y | N | N | N | Y | Y | Y |
| 2 Jackson | Y | N | N | N | Y | N | Y |
| 3 Lipinski | Y | Y | Y | Y | Y | Y | Y |
| 4 Gutierrez | Y | N | N | N | Y | Y | Y |
| 5 Emanuel | Y | N | Y | Y | Y | Y | Y |
| 6 Hyde | Y | N | Y | Y | N | Y | Y |
| 7 Davis | Y | N | N | N | Y | N | Y |
| 8 Bean | Y | Y | Y | Y | Y | Y | Y |
| 9 Schakowsky | Y | N | N | N | Y | N | Y |
| 10 Kirk | Y | Y | Y | Y | N | Y | Y |
| 11 Weller | Y | Y | Y | Y | N | Y | Y |
| 12 Costello | Y | Y | Y | N | Y | Y | Y |

**KEY**  Republicans  Democrats  *Independents*

| | |
|---|---|
| Y Voted for (yea) | X Paired against |
| # Paired for | – Announced against |
| + Announced for | P Voted "present" |
| N Voted against (nay) | |

| |
|---|
| C Voted "present" to avoid possible conflict of interest |
| ? Did not vote or otherwise make a position known |

ND Northern Democrats, SD Southern Democrats
Southern states: Ala., Ark., Fla., Ga., Ky., La., Miss., N.C., Okla., S.C., Tenn., Texas, Va.

| | 394 | 395 | 396 | 397 | 398 | 399 | 400 |
|---|---|---|---|---|---|---|---|
| 13 **Biggert** | Y | Y | Y | Y | N | Y | Y |
| 14 **Hastert** | | | | | | | |
| 15 **Johnson** | Y | Y | Y | Y | N | Y | Y |
| 16 **Manzullo** | Y | Y | Y | Y | N | Y | Y |
| 17 Evans | Y | Y | N | N | Y | Y | Y |
| 18 **LaHood** | Y | N | Y | Y | N | Y | Y |
| 19 **Shimkus** | Y | Y | Y | Y | N | Y | Y |
| **INDIANA** | | | | | | | |
| 1 Visclosky | Y | N | N | N | Y | N | Y |
| 2 **Chocola** | Y | Y | Y | Y | N | Y | Y |
| 3 **Souder** | Y | Y | Y | Y | N | Y | Y |
| 4 **Buyer** | Y | Y | Y | Y | N | Y | Y |
| 5 **Burton** | Y | Y | Y | Y | N | Y | Y |
| 6 **Pence** | Y | Y | Y | Y | N | Y | Y |
| 7 Carson | Y | Y | Y | N | Y | Y | Y |
| 8 **Hostettler** | Y | Y | Y | N | N | Y | Y |
| 9 **Sodrel** | Y | Y | Y | Y | N | Y | Y |
| **IOWA** | | | | | | | |
| 1 **Nussle** | Y | Y | Y | Y | N | Y | Y |
| 2 **Leach** | Y | Y | N | N | N | Y | Y |
| 3 Boswell | Y | Y | Y | Y | Y | Y | Y |
| 4 **Latham** | Y | Y | Y | Y | N | Y | Y |
| 5 **King** | Y | N | Y | Y | N | Y | Y |
| **KANSAS** | | | | | | | |
| 1 **Moran** | Y | Y | Y | Y | N | Y | Y |
| 2 **Ryun** | Y | Y | Y | Y | N | Y | Y |
| 3 Moore | Y | Y | Y | Y | Y | Y | Y |
| 4 **Tiahrt** | Y | N | Y | Y | N | Y | Y |
| **KENTUCKY** | | | | | | | |
| 1 **Whitfield** | Y | Y | Y | Y | N | Y | Y |
| 2 **Lewis** | Y | Y | Y | Y | N | Y | Y |
| 3 **Northup** | Y | Y | Y | Y | N | Y | Y |
| 4 **Davis** | Y | Y | Y | Y | N | Y | Y |
| 5 **Rogers** | Y | Y | Y | Y | N | Y | Y |
| 6 Chandler | Y | Y | Y | Y | Y | Y | Y |
| **LOUISIANA** | | | | | | | |
| 1 **Jindal** | ? | Y | Y | Y | N | Y | Y |
| 2 Jefferson | Y | N | N | N | Y | Y | Y |
| 3 Melancon | Y | Y | Y | Y | Y | Y | Y |
| 4 **McCrery** | Y | N | Y | Y | N | Y | Y |
| 5 **Alexander** | Y | Y | Y | Y | N | Y | Y |
| 6 **Baker** | Y | Y | Y | Y | N | Y | Y |
| 7 **Boustany** | Y | Y | Y | Y | N | Y | Y |
| **MAINE** | | | | | | | |
| 1 Allen | Y | Y | N | N | Y | Y | Y |
| 2 Michaud | Y | Y | N | N | Y | Y | Y |
| **MARYLAND** | | | | | | | |
| 1 **Gilchrest** | Y | N | Y | Y | N | Y | Y |
| 2 Ruppersberger | Y | Y | Y | Y | Y | Y | Y |
| 3 Cardin | Y | Y | Y | Y | Y | Y | Y |
| 4 Wynn | Y | N | Y | Y | Y | Y | Y |
| 5 Hoyer | Y | Y | Y | Y | Y | Y | Y |
| 6 **Bartlett** | Y | Y | P | P | N | N | Y |
| 7 Cummings | Y | ? | ? | ? | ? | ? | ? |
| 8 Van Hollen | Y | Y | N | N | Y | Y | Y |
| **MASSACHUSETTS** | | | | | | | |
| 1 Olver | Y | N | N | N | Y | N | Y |
| 2 Neal | Y | Y | N | N | Y | N | Y |
| 3 McGovern | Y | N | N | N | Y | N | Y |
| 4 Frank | Y | N | N | N | Y | N | Y |
| 5 Meehan | Y | Y | N | N | Y | N | Y |
| 6 Tierney | Y | N | N | N | Y | N | Y |
| 7 Markey | Y | Y | N | N | Y | N | Y |
| 8 Capuano | Y | N | N | N | Y | N | Y |
| 9 Lynch | Y | N | Y | N | Y | Y | Y |
| 10 Delahunt | Y | N | N | N | Y | N | Y |
| **MICHIGAN** | | | | | | | |
| 1 Stupak | Y | Y | N | N | Y | Y | Y |
| 2 **Hoekstra** | Y | Y | Y | Y | N | Y | Y |
| 3 **Ehlers** | Y | Y | P | Y | N | Y | Y |
| 4 **Camp** | Y | Y | Y | Y | N | Y | Y |
| 5 Kildee | Y | N | Y | N | Y | Y | Y |
| 6 **Upton** | Y | Y | Y | Y | N | Y | Y |
| 7 **Schwarz** | Y | Y | Y | Y | N | Y | Y |
| 8 **Rogers** | Y | Y | Y | Y | N | Y | Y |
| 9 **Knollenberg** | Y | N | Y | Y | N | Y | ? |
| 10 **Miller** | Y | Y | Y | Y | N | Y | Y |
| 11 **McCotter** | Y | Y | Y | Y | N | Y | Y |
| 12 Levin | Y | Y | N | N | Y | N | Y |
| 13 Kilpatrick | Y | N | N | N | Y | N | Y |
| 14 Conyers | Y | N | N | N | Y | N | Y |
| 15 Dingell | Y | N | N | N | Y | Y | Y |
| **MINNESOTA** | | | | | | | |
| 1 **Gutknecht** | Y | Y | Y | Y | N | Y | Y |
| 2 **Kline** | Y | Y | Y | Y | N | Y | Y |
| 3 **Ramstad** | Y | Y | Y | Y | N | Y | Y |
| 4 McCollum | Y | N | N | N | Y | N | Y |
| 5 Sabo | Y | N | N | N | Y | N | Y |
| 6 **Kennedy** | Y | Y | Y | Y | N | Y | Y |
| 7 Peterson | Y | Y | Y | Y | Y | Y | Y |
| 8 Oberstar | Y | N | N | N | Y | N | Y |
| **MISSISSIPPI** | | | | | | | |
| 1 **Wicker** | Y | N | Y | Y | N | Y | Y |
| 2 Thompson | Y | N | N | N | Y | Y | Y |
| 3 **Pickering** | Y | Y | Y | Y | N | Y | Y |
| 4 Taylor | Y | Y | Y | Y | Y | N | Y |
| **MISSOURI** | | | | | | | |
| 1 Clay | Y | N | N | N | Y | N | Y |
| 2 **Akin** | Y | Y | Y | Y | N | Y | Y |
| 3 Carnahan | Y | Y | Y | Y | Y | Y | Y |
| 4 Skelton | Y | Y | Y | Y | Y | Y | Y |
| 5 Cleaver | Y | N | N | N | Y | Y | Y |
| 6 **Graves** | Y | Y | Y | Y | N | Y | Y |
| 7 **Blunt** | Y | Y | Y | Y | N | Y | Y |
| 8 **Emerson** | Y | Y | Y | Y | N | Y | Y |
| 9 **Hulshof** | Y | Y | Y | Y | N | Y | Y |
| **MONTANA** | | | | | | | |
| AL **Rehberg** | Y | Y | Y | Y | N | Y | Y |
| **NEBRASKA** | | | | | | | |
| 1 **Fortenberry** | Y | Y | Y | Y | N | Y | Y |
| 2 **Terry** | Y | Y | Y | Y | N | Y | Y |
| 3 **Osborne** | Y | Y | Y | Y | N | Y | Y |
| **NEVADA** | | | | | | | |
| 1 Berkley | Y | Y | Y | Y | Y | Y | Y |
| 2 **Gibbons** | Y | Y | Y | Y | N | Y | Y |
| 3 **Porter** | Y | Y | Y | Y | N | Y | Y |
| **NEW HAMPSHIRE** | | | | | | | |
| 1 **Bradley** | Y | Y | Y | Y | N | Y | Y |
| 2 **Bass** | Y | Y | Y | Y | N | Y | ? |
| **NEW JERSEY** | | | | | | | |
| 1 Andrews | Y | Y | Y | Y | Y | Y | Y |
| 2 **LoBiondo** | Y | Y | Y | Y | N | Y | Y |
| 3 **Saxton** | Y | Y | Y | Y | N | Y | Y |
| 4 **Smith** | Y | Y | Y | Y | N | Y | Y |
| 5 **Garrett** | Y | Y | Y | Y | N | Y | Y |
| 6 Pallone | Y | Y | N | N | Y | Y | Y |
| 7 **Ferguson** | Y | Y | Y | Y | N | Y | Y |
| 8 Pascrell | Y | N | N | N | Y | Y | Y |
| 9 Rothman | Y | N | N | N | Y | Y | Y |
| 10 Payne | Y | N | N | N | Y | N | Y |
| 11 **Frelinghuysen** | Y | Y | Y | Y | N | Y | Y |
| 12 Holt | Y | Y | N | N | Y | Y | Y |
| 13 Menendez | Y | Y | Y | Y | Y | Y | Y |
| **NEW MEXICO** | | | | | | | |
| 1 **Wilson** | Y | Y | Y | Y | N | Y | Y |
| 2 **Pearce** | Y | Y | Y | Y | N | Y | Y |
| 3 Udall | Y | Y | N | N | Y | Y | Y |
| **NEW YORK** | | | | | | | |
| 1 Bishop | Y | Y | Y | Y | Y | Y | Y |
| 2 Israel | Y | Y | Y | Y | Y | Y | Y |
| 3 **King** | Y | Y | Y | Y | N | Y | Y |
| 4 McCarthy | Y | Y | Y | Y | Y | Y | Y |
| 5 Ackerman | Y | N | N | N | Y | N | ? |
| 6 Meeks | Y | N | N | N | Y | Y | Y |
| 7 Crowley | Y | Y | N | N | Y | Y | Y |
| 8 Nadler | Y | Y | N | N | Y | N | Y |
| 9 Weiner | Y | Y | N | N | Y | Y | Y |
| 10 Towns | Y | Y | Y | N | Y | Y | Y |
| 11 Owens | Y | Y | N | N | Y | N | Y |
| 12 Velázquez | Y | Y | N | N | Y | N | Y |
| 13 **Fossella** | Y | Y | Y | Y | N | Y | Y |
| 14 Maloney | Y | Y | N | N | Y | N | Y |
| 15 Rangel | Y | Y | N | N | Y | Y | Y |
| 16 Serrano | Y | N | N | N | Y | N | Y |
| 17 Engel | Y | Y | Y | Y | Y | Y | Y |
| 18 Lowey | Y | N | N | N | Y | Y | Y |
| 19 **Kelly** | Y | Y | Y | Y | N | Y | Y |
| 20 **Sweeney** | Y | Y | Y | Y | N | Y | Y |
| 21 McNulty | Y | Y | N | N | Y | N | Y |
| 22 Hinchey | Y | Y | N | N | Y | N | Y |
| 23 **McHugh** | Y | Y | Y | Y | N | Y | Y |
| 24 **Boehlert** | Y | Y | Y | Y | N | Y | Y |
| 25 **Walsh** | Y | Y | Y | Y | N | Y | Y |
| 26 **Reynolds** | Y | Y | Y | Y | N | Y | Y |
| 27 Higgins | Y | Y | Y | Y | Y | Y | ? |
| 28 Slaughter | Y | N | N | N | Y | N | Y |
| 29 **Kuhl** | Y | Y | Y | Y | N | Y | Y |
| **NORTH CAROLINA** | | | | | | | |
| 1 Butterfield | Y | Y | Y | Y | Y | Y | Y |
| 2 Etheridge | Y | Y | Y | Y | Y | Y | Y |
| 3 **Jones** | Y | N | Y | P | Y | N | Y |
| 4 Price | Y | N | N | N | Y | Y | Y |
| 5 **Foxx** | Y | Y | Y | Y | N | Y | Y |
| 6 **Coble** | Y | Y | Y | Y | N | Y | ? |
| 7 McIntyre | Y | Y | Y | Y | Y | Y | Y |
| 8 **Hayes** | Y | N | Y | Y | N | Y | Y |
| 9 **Myrick** | Y | Y | Y | Y | N | Y | Y |
| 10 **McHenry** | Y | Y | Y | Y | N | Y | Y |
| 11 **Taylor** | Y | Y | Y | Y | N | Y | Y |
| 12 Watt | Y | N | N | N | Y | N | Y |
| 13 Miller | Y | Y | Y | N | Y | Y | Y |
| **NORTH DAKOTA** | | | | | | | |
| AL Pomeroy | Y | Y | Y | Y | Y | Y | Y |
| **OHIO** | | | | | | | |
| 1 **Chabot** | Y | Y | Y | Y | N | Y | Y |
| 2 Vacant | | | | | | | |
| 3 **Turner** | Y | N | Y | Y | N | Y | Y |
| 4 **Oxley** | Y | Y | Y | Y | N | Y | Y |
| 5 **Gillmor** | Y | Y | Y | Y | N | Y | Y |
| 6 Strickland | Y | Y | N | N | Y | Y | Y |
| 7 **Hobson** | Y | N | Y | Y | N | Y | Y |
| 8 **Boehner** | Y | Y | Y | Y | N | Y | Y |
| 9 Kaptur | Y | N | N | N | Y | Y | Y |
| 10 Kucinich | Y | N | N | N | Y | N | Y |
| 11 Jones | Y | Y | N | N | Y | Y | Y |
| 12 **Tiberi** | Y | Y | Y | Y | N | Y | Y |
| 13 Brown | Y | Y | N | N | Y | Y | Y |
| 14 **LaTourette** | Y | Y | Y | Y | N | Y | Y |
| 15 **Pryce** | Y | Y | Y | Y | N | Y | Y |
| 16 **Regula** | Y | Y | Y | Y | N | Y | Y |
| 17 Ryan | Y | N | Y | N | Y | Y | Y |
| 18 **Ney** | Y | Y | Y | Y | N | Y | Y |
| **OKLAHOMA** | | | | | | | |
| 1 **Sullivan** | Y | Y | Y | Y | N | Y | Y |
| 2 Boren | Y | Y | Y | Y | Y | Y | Y |
| 3 **Lucas** | Y | Y | Y | Y | N | Y | Y |
| 4 **Cole** | Y | Y | Y | Y | N | Y | Y |
| 5 **Istook** | Y | Y | Y | Y | N | Y | Y |
| **OREGON** | | | | | | | |
| 1 Wu | Y | Y | Y | N | Y | N | Y |
| 2 **Walden** | Y | Y | Y | Y | N | Y | Y |
| 3 Blumenauer | Y | N | N | N | Y | Y | Y |
| 4 DeFazio | Y | Y | Y | N | Y | N | Y |
| 5 Hooley | Y | Y | Y | N | Y | Y | Y |
| **PENNSYLVANIA** | | | | | | | |
| 1 Brady | Y | Y | N | N | Y | Y | Y |
| 2 Fattah | Y | Y | N | N | Y | Y | Y |
| 3 **English** | Y | Y | Y | Y | N | Y | Y |
| 4 **Hart** | Y | Y | Y | Y | N | Y | Y |
| 5 **Peterson** | Y | Y | Y | Y | N | Y | Y |
| 6 **Gerlach** | Y | Y | Y | Y | N | Y | Y |
| 7 **Weldon** | Y | Y | Y | Y | N | Y | Y |
| 8 **Fitzpatrick** | Y | Y | Y | Y | N | Y | Y |
| 9 **Shuster** | Y | Y | Y | Y | N | Y | Y |
| 10 **Sherwood** | Y | N | Y | Y | N | Y | Y |
| 11 Kanjorski | Y | N | N | N | Y | Y | Y |
| 12 Murtha | Y | N | N | N | Y | Y | Y |
| 13 Schwartz | Y | Y | Y | Y | Y | Y | Y |
| 14 Doyle | Y | N | N | N | Y | Y | Y |
| 15 **Dent** | Y | Y | Y | Y | N | Y | Y |
| 16 **Pitts** | Y | Y | Y | Y | N | Y | Y |
| 17 Holden | Y | Y | N | N | Y | Y | Y |
| 18 **Murphy** | Y | Y | Y | Y | N | Y | Y |
| 19 **Platts** | Y | Y | Y | Y | N | Y | Y |
| **RHODE ISLAND** | | | | | | | |
| 1 Kennedy | Y | Y | N | Y | Y | Y | Y |
| 2 Langevin | Y | Y | Y | Y | Y | Y | Y |
| **SOUTH CAROLINA** | | | | | | | |
| 1 **Brown** | ? | ? | ? | ? | ? | ? | ? |
| 2 **Wilson** | Y | Y | Y | Y | N | Y | Y |
| 3 **Barrett** | Y | N | Y | Y | N | Y | Y |
| 4 **Inglis** | Y | Y | Y | Y | N | Y | Y |
| 5 Spratt | Y | Y | Y | Y | Y | Y | Y |
| 6 Clyburn | Y | Y | Y | Y | Y | Y | Y |
| **SOUTH DAKOTA** | | | | | | | |
| AL Herseth | Y | Y | Y | Y | Y | Y | Y |
| **TENNESSEE** | | | | | | | |
| 1 **Jenkins** | Y | Y | Y | Y | N | Y | Y |
| 2 **Duncan** | Y | Y | Y | N | N | N | Y |
| 3 **Wamp** | Y | Y | Y | N | N | Y | Y |
| 4 Davis | Y | Y | Y | Y | Y | Y | Y |
| 5 Cooper | Y | Y | Y | Y | Y | Y | Y |
| 6 Gordon | Y | Y | Y | Y | Y | Y | Y |
| 7 **Blackburn** | Y | Y | Y | Y | N | Y | Y |
| 8 Tanner | Y | Y | Y | Y | Y | Y | Y |
| 9 Ford | Y | Y | Y | Y | Y | Y | Y |
| **TEXAS** | | | | | | | |
| 1 **Gohmert** | Y | Y | Y | Y | N | Y | Y |
| 2 **Poe** | Y | Y | Y | Y | N | Y | Y |
| 3 **Johnson, S.** | Y | Y | Y | Y | N | Y | Y |
| 4 **Hall** | Y | Y | Y | Y | N | Y | Y |
| 5 **Hensarling** | Y | Y | Y | Y | N | Y | Y |
| 6 **Barton** | Y | Y | Y | Y | N | Y | Y |
| 7 **Culberson** | Y | Y | Y | Y | N | Y | Y |
| 8 **Brady** | ? | Y | Y | Y | N | Y | Y |
| 9 Green, A. | Y | Y | N | N | Y | Y | Y |
| 10 **McCaul** | Y | Y | Y | Y | N | Y | Y |
| 11 **Conaway** | Y | Y | Y | Y | N | Y | Y |
| 12 **Granger** | Y | Y | Y | Y | N | Y | ? |
| 13 **Thornberry** | Y | Y | Y | Y | N | Y | Y |
| 14 **Paul** | N | N | N | N | Y | N | N |
| 15 Hinojosa | ? | ? | ? | ? | ? | ? | ? |
| 16 Reyes | Y | Y | Y | Y | Y | Y | Y |
| 17 Edwards | Y | Y | Y | Y | Y | Y | Y |
| 18 Jackson-Lee | Y | Y | N | N | Y | Y | Y |
| 19 **Neugebauer** | Y | Y | Y | Y | N | Y | Y |
| 20 Gonzalez | Y | Y | N | Y | Y | Y | Y |
| 21 **Smith** | Y | Y | Y | Y | N | Y | Y |
| 22 **DeLay** | Y | Y | Y | Y | N | Y | Y |
| 23 **Bonilla** | Y | Y | Y | Y | N | Y | Y |
| 24 **Marchant** | Y | Y | Y | Y | N | Y | Y |
| 25 Doggett | Y | N | N | N | Y | N | Y |
| 26 **Burgess** | Y | Y | Y | Y | N | Y | Y |
| 27 Ortiz | Y | Y | Y | Y | Y | Y | Y |
| 28 Cuellar | Y | Y | Y | Y | Y | Y | Y |
| 29 Green, G. | Y | Y | Y | Y | Y | Y | Y |
| 30 Johnson, E. | Y | N | N | Y | Y | Y | Y |
| 31 **Carter** | Y | Y | Y | Y | N | Y | Y |
| 32 **Sessions** | Y | Y | Y | Y | N | Y | Y |
| **UTAH** | | | | | | | |
| 1 **Bishop** | Y | Y | Y | Y | N | Y | Y |
| 2 Matheson | Y | Y | Y | Y | Y | Y | Y |
| 3 **Cannon** | Y | Y | Y | Y | N | Y | Y |
| **VERMONT** | | | | | | | |
| AL *Sanders* | Y | N | N | N | Y | N | Y |
| **VIRGINIA** | | | | | | | |
| 1 **Davis, J.** | Y | Y | Y | Y | N | Y | Y |
| 2 **Drake** | Y | Y | Y | Y | N | Y | Y |
| 3 Scott | Y | Y | N | N | Y | N | Y |
| 4 **Forbes** | Y | Y | Y | Y | N | Y | Y |
| 5 **Goode** | Y | Y | Y | Y | N | N | Y |
| 6 **Goodlatte** | Y | Y | Y | Y | N | Y | Y |
| 7 **Cantor** | ? | Y | Y | Y | N | Y | Y |
| 8 Moran | Y | N | N | N | Y | N | Y |
| 9 Boucher | Y | N | N | Y | Y | Y | Y |
| 10 **Wolf** | Y | Y | Y | Y | N | Y | Y |
| 11 **Davis, T.** | Y | Y | Y | Y | N | Y | Y |
| **WASHINGTON** | | | | | | | |
| 1 Inslee | Y | N | N | N | Y | N | Y |
| 2 Larsen | Y | Y | Y | N | Y | Y | Y |
| 3 Baird | Y | N | Y | Y | Y | Y | Y |
| 4 **Hastings** | Y | Y | Y | Y | N | Y | Y |
| 5 **McMorris** | Y | Y | Y | Y | N | Y | Y |
| 6 Dicks | Y | Y | Y | Y | Y | ? | ? |
| 7 McDermott | Y | N | N | N | Y | N | Y |
| 8 **Reichert** | Y | Y | Y | Y | N | Y | Y |
| 9 Smith | Y | N | Y | N | Y | Y | ? |
| **WEST VIRGINIA** | | | | | | | |
| 1 Mollohan | Y | N | N | N | Y | Y | Y |
| 2 **Capito** | Y | Y | Y | Y | N | Y | Y |
| 3 Rahall | Y | N | N | N | Y | N | Y |
| **WISCONSIN** | | | | | | | |
| 1 **Ryan** | Y | Y | Y | Y | N | Y | Y |
| 2 Baldwin | Y | N | N | N | Y | N | Y |
| 3 Kind | Y | Y | Y | Y | Y | N | Y |
| 4 Moore | Y | N | N | N | Y | Y | Y |
| 5 **Sensenbrenner** | Y | Y | Y | Y | N | N | Y |
| 6 **Petri** | Y | Y | N | N | N | Y | Y |
| 7 Obey | Y | N | N | N | Y | N | Y |
| 8 **Green** | Y | Y | Y | Y | N | Y | Y |
| **WYOMING** | | | | | | | |
| AL **Cubin** | Y | Y | Y | Y | N | Y | Y |

# IN THE HOUSE | By Vote Number

**401.** HR 3199. "Patriot Act" Reauthorization/Previous Question. Gingrey, R-Ga., motion to order the previous question (thus ending debate and possibility of amendment) on adoption of the rule (H Res 369) to provide for House floor consideration of the bill that would reauthorize 16 expiring provisions of the 2001 anti-terrorism law known as the Patriot Act. Motion agreed to 224-197: R 224-0; D 0-196 (ND 0-148, SD 0-48); I 0-1. July 21, 2005.

**402.** HR 3199. "Patriot Act" Reauthorization/Rule. Adoption of the rule (H Res 369) that would provide for House consideration of the bill that would reauthorize 16 expiring provisions of the 2001 anti-terrorism law known as the Patriot Act. Adopted 224-196: R 224-0; D 0-195 (ND 0-147, SD 0-48); I 0-1. July 21, 2005.

**403.** HR 3199. "Patriot Act" Reauthorization/Library or Bookstore Records. Flake, R-Ariz., amendment that would require the FBI director to personally approve a request for library or bookstore records under the business records provision of law known as the Patriot Act. Adopted 402-26: R 201-26; D 200-0 (ND 151-0, SD 49-0); I 1-0. July 21, 2005.

**404.** HR 3199. "Patriot Act" Reauthorization/Roving Wiretaps. Issa, R-Calif., amendment that would require authorities to notify the issuing judge of a venue change of a surveillance facility or place within 15 days or at the earliest reasonable time as determined by the court. It also would require authorities to specify the total number of electronic surveillances that have been or are being carried out. Adopted 406-21: R 205-21; D 200-0 (ND 151-0, SD 49-0); I 1-0. July 21, 2005.

**405.** HR 3199. "Patriot Act" Reauthorization/Violence Against Rail and Mass Transit. Capito, R-W.Va., amendment that would authorize up to 20 years in prison for individuals who commit terrorist or other violent attacks on land, water or air against railroad and mass transportation systems. It would provide a minimum sentence of 30 years if the vehicle attacked is carrying spent nuclear fuel or high-level radioactive waste, and a mandatory life sentence, with the possibility of the death penalty, if the attack results in the death of a person. Adopted 362-66: R 226-1; D 135-65 (ND 92-59, SD 43-6); I 1-0. July 21, 2005.

**406.** HR 3199. "Patriot Act" Reauthorization/National Security Letter. Flake, R-Ariz., amendment that would specify that the recipient of a national security letter may consult with an attorney and challenge the letter in court. It would authorize a judge to throw out the letter if complying with the request would be "unreasonable or oppressive." It would allow the letter recipient to challenge the non-disclosure requirements of the request in court. Adopted 394-32: R 197-28; D 196-4 (ND 148-3, SD 48-1); I 1-0. July 21, 2005.

**407.** HR 3199. "Patriot Act" Reauthorization/Forfeiture of Assets. Delahunt, D-Mass., amendment that would raise the threshold for authorities to seize assets of suspected terrorists. It would allow assets to be seized only for those specifically accused of terrorist crimes. Adopted 418-7: R 218-7; D 199-0 (ND 151-0, SD 48-0); I 1-0. July 21, 2005.

ND Northern Democrats, SD Southern Democrats
Southern states: Ala., Ark., Fla., Ga., Ky., La., Miss., N.C., Okla., S.C., Tenn., Texas, Va.

| | 401 | 402 | 403 | 404 | 405 | 406 | 407 |
|---|---|---|---|---|---|---|---|
| **ALABAMA** | | | | | | | |
| 1 Bonner | Y | Y | Y | Y | Y | N | Y |
| 2 Everett | Y | Y | Y | N | Y | N | Y |
| 3 Rogers | Y | Y | Y | Y | Y | N | Y |
| 4 Aderholt | Y | Y | Y | Y | Y | N | Y |
| 5 Cramer | N | N | Y | Y | Y | Y | Y |
| 6 Bachus | Y | Y | N | N | Y | N | Y |
| 7 Davis | N | N | Y | Y | Y | Y | Y |
| **ALASKA** | | | | | | | |
| AL Young | Y | Y | Y | Y | Y | Y | Y |
| **ARIZONA** | | | | | | | |
| 1 Renzi | Y | Y | N | Y | Y | Y | Y |
| 2 Franks | Y | Y | Y | Y | Y | N | Y |
| 3 Shadegg | Y | Y | N | Y | Y | N | Y |
| 4 Pastor | N | N | Y | Y | N | Y | Y |
| 5 Hayworth | Y | Y | Y | Y | Y | Y | Y |
| 6 Flake | Y | Y | Y | Y | Y | Y | Y |
| 7 Grijalva | N | N | Y | Y | N | Y | Y |
| 8 Kolbe | Y | Y | Y | Y | Y | Y | Y |
| **ARKANSAS** | | | | | | | |
| 1 Berry | N | N | Y | Y | Y | Y | Y |
| 2 Snyder | N | N | Y | Y | Y | Y | Y |
| 3 Boozman | Y | Y | Y | Y | Y | Y | Y |
| 4 Ross | N | N | Y | Y | Y | Y | Y |
| **CALIFORNIA** | | | | | | | |
| 1 Thompson | N | N | Y | Y | Y | Y | Y |
| 2 Herger | Y | Y | Y | Y | Y | Y | Y |
| 3 Lungren | Y | Y | Y | Y | Y | Y | Y |
| 4 Doolittle | Y | Y | Y | Y | Y | Y | Y |
| 5 Matsui, D. | N | N | Y | Y | Y | Y | Y |
| 6 Woolsey | N | N | Y | Y | N | Y | Y |
| 7 Miller, George | N | N | Y | Y | Y | Y | Y |
| 8 Pelosi | N | N | Y | Y | Y | Y | Y |
| 9 Lee | N | N | Y | Y | N | N | Y |
| 10 Tauscher | N | N | Y | Y | Y | Y | Y |
| 11 Pombo | Y | Y | Y | Y | Y | Y | Y |
| 12 Lantos | N | N | Y | Y | Y | Y | Y |
| 13 Stark | N | N | Y | Y | N | Y | Y |
| 14 Eshoo | N | N | Y | Y | Y | Y | Y |
| 15 Honda | N | N | Y | Y | N | Y | Y |
| 16 Lofgren | N | N | Y | Y | Y | Y | Y |
| 17 Farr | N | N | Y | Y | N | Y | Y |
| 18 Cardoza | N | N | Y | Y | Y | Y | Y |
| 19 Radanovich | Y | Y | Y | Y | Y | Y | Y |
| 20 Costa | N | N | Y | Y | Y | Y | Y |
| 21 Nunes | Y | Y | Y | Y | Y | Y | Y |
| 22 Thomas | Y | Y | N | Y | Y | Y | Y |
| 23 Capps | N | N | Y | Y | Y | Y | Y |
| 24 Gallegly | Y | Y | Y | Y | Y | Y | Y |
| 25 McKeon | Y | Y | Y | Y | Y | Y | Y |
| 26 Dreier | Y | Y | Y | Y | Y | Y | Y |
| 27 Sherman | N | N | Y | Y | Y | Y | Y |
| 28 Berman | N | N | Y | Y | Y | Y | Y |
| 29 Schiff | N | N | Y | Y | Y | Y | Y |
| 30 Waxman | N | N | Y | Y | N | Y | Y |
| 31 Becerra | N | N | Y | Y | N | Y | Y |
| 32 Solis | N | N | Y | Y | Y | Y | Y |
| 33 Watson | N | N | Y | Y | Y | Y | Y |
| 34 Roybal-Allard | N | N | Y | Y | Y | Y | Y |
| 35 Waters | N | N | Y | Y | N | Y | Y |
| 36 Harman | N | N | Y | Y | Y | Y | Y |
| 37 Millender-McD. | N | N | Y | Y | Y | Y | Y |
| 38 Napolitano | N | N | Y | Y | Y | Y | Y |
| 39 Sánchez, Linda | N | N | Y | Y | N | Y | Y |
| 40 Royce | Y | Y | Y | Y | Y | Y | Y |
| 41 Lewis | Y | Y | N | Y | Y | N | Y |
| 42 Miller, Gary | Y | Y | Y | Y | Y | Y | Y |
| 43 Baca | N | N | Y | Y | Y | Y | Y |
| 44 Calvert | Y | Y | N | Y | Y | Y | Y |
| 45 Bono | Y | Y | N | N | Y | N | N |
| 46 Rohrabacher | Y | P | Y | Y | Y | Y | Y |
| 47 Sanchez, Loretta | N | N | Y | Y | N | Y | Y |
| 48 Cox | Y | Y | ? | ? | ? | ? | ? |
| 49 Issa | Y | Y | Y | ? | Y | Y | Y |
| 50 Cunningham | Y | Y | Y | Y | Y | Y | Y |
| 51 Filner | N | N | Y | Y | N | Y | Y |
| 52 Hunter | Y | Y | Y | N | Y | N | N |
| 53 Davis | N | N | Y | Y | Y | Y | Y |
| **COLORADO** | | | | | | | |
| 1 DeGette | N | N | Y | Y | N | Y | Y |
| 2 Udall | N | N | Y | Y | Y | Y | Y |
| 3 Salazar | N | N | Y | Y | Y | Y | Y |
| 4 Musgrave | Y | Y | Y | Y | Y | Y | Y |
| 5 Hefley | Y | Y | Y | N | Y | Y | Y |
| 6 Tancredo | Y | Y | Y | Y | Y | Y | Y |
| 7 Beauprez | Y | Y | Y | Y | Y | Y | Y |
| **CONNECTICUT** | | | | | | | |
| 1 Larson | N | N | Y | Y | Y | Y | Y |
| 2 Simmons | Y | Y | Y | Y | Y | Y | Y |
| 3 DeLauro | N | N | Y | Y | Y | Y | Y |
| 4 Shays | Y | Y | Y | Y | Y | Y | Y |
| 5 Johnson | Y | Y | Y | Y | Y | ? | Y |
| **DELAWARE** | | | | | | | |
| AL Castle | Y | Y | Y | Y | Y | Y | Y |
| **FLORIDA** | | | | | | | |
| 1 Miller | Y | Y | + | Y | Y | Y | Y |
| 2 Boyd | N | N | Y | Y | Y | Y | Y |
| 3 Brown | N | N | Y | Y | Y | Y | ? |
| 4 Crenshaw | Y | Y | Y | Y | Y | Y | Y |
| 5 Brown-Waite | Y | Y | Y | Y | Y | Y | Y |
| 6 Stearns | Y | Y | Y | Y | Y | Y | Y |
| 7 Mica | Y | Y | Y | Y | Y | ? | Y |
| 8 Keller | Y | Y | Y | Y | Y | Y | Y |
| 9 Bilirakis | Y | Y | Y | Y | Y | Y | Y |
| 10 Young | Y | Y | Y | Y | Y | Y | Y |
| 11 Davis | N | N | Y | Y | Y | Y | Y |
| 12 Putnam | Y | Y | Y | Y | Y | Y | Y |
| 13 Harris | Y | Y | Y | Y | Y | Y | Y |
| 14 Mack | Y | Y | Y | Y | Y | Y | Y |
| 15 Weldon | Y | Y | Y | Y | Y | Y | Y |
| 16 Foley | Y | Y | Y | Y | Y | Y | Y |
| 17 Meek | N | N | Y | Y | Y | Y | Y |
| 18 Ros-Lehtinen | Y | Y | Y | ? | Y | Y | Y |
| 19 Wexler | N | N | Y | Y | Y | Y | Y |
| 20 Wasserman-Schultz | N | N | Y | Y | N | Y | Y |
| 21 Diaz-Balart, L. | Y | Y | Y | Y | Y | Y | Y |
| 22 Shaw | Y | Y | Y | Y | Y | Y | Y |
| 23 Hastings | ? | ? | ? | ? | ? | ? | ? |
| 24 Feeney | Y | Y | Y | Y | Y | Y | Y |
| 25 Diaz-Balart, M. | Y | Y | Y | Y | Y | Y | Y |
| **GEORGIA** | | | | | | | |
| 1 Kingston | Y | Y | Y | Y | Y | Y | Y |
| 2 Bishop | N | N | Y | Y | Y | Y | Y |
| 3 Marshall | N | N | Y | Y | Y | Y | Y |
| 4 McKinney | N | N | Y | Y | N | N | Y |
| 5 Lewis | N | N | Y | Y | N | Y | Y |
| 6 Price | Y | Y | N | Y | Y | Y | Y |
| 7 Linder | Y | Y | N | N | Y | N | Y |
| 8 Westmoreland | Y | Y | N | Y | N | N | Y |
| 9 Norwood | Y | Y | Y | Y | Y | Y | Y |
| 10 Deal | Y | Y | Y | Y | Y | Y | Y |
| 11 Gingrey | Y | Y | Y | Y | Y | Y | Y |
| 12 Barrow | N | N | Y | Y | Y | Y | Y |
| 13 Scott | N | N | Y | Y | Y | Y | Y |
| **HAWAII** | | | | | | | |
| 1 Abercrombie | N | N | Y | Y | N | Y | Y |
| 2 Case | N | N | Y | Y | Y | Y | Y |
| **IDAHO** | | | | | | | |
| 1 Otter | Y | P | Y | Y | Y | Y | Y |
| 2 Simpson | Y | Y | Y | Y | Y | Y | Y |
| **ILLINOIS** | | | | | | | |
| 1 Rush | N | N | Y | Y | N | Y | Y |
| 2 Jackson | N | N | Y | Y | N | Y | Y |
| 3 Lipinski | N | N | Y | Y | Y | Y | Y |
| 4 Gutierrez | N | ? | Y | Y | N | Y | Y |
| 5 Emanuel | N | N | Y | Y | Y | Y | Y |
| 6 Hyde | ? | ? | Y | Y | Y | N | Y |
| 7 Davis | N | N | Y | Y | N | Y | Y |
| 8 Bean | N | N | Y | Y | Y | Y | Y |
| 9 Schakowsky | N | N | Y | Y | N | Y | Y |
| 10 Kirk | Y | Y | Y | Y | Y | Y | Y |
| 11 Weller | Y | Y | Y | Y | Y | Y | Y |
| 12 Costello | N | N | Y | Y | N | Y | Y |

| KEY | Republicans | Democrats | *Independents* | | |
|---|---|---|---|---|---|
| Y | Voted for (yea) | X | Paired against | C | Voted "present" to avoid possible conflict of interest |
| # | Paired for | − | Announced against | | |
| + | Announced for | P | Voted "present" | ? | Did not vote or otherwise make a position known |
| N | Voted against (nay) | | | | |

| | 401 | 402 | 403 | 404 | 405 | 406 | 407 |
|---|---|---|---|---|---|---|---|
| 13 **Biggert** | Y | Y | N | N | Y | Y | Y |
| 14 **Hastert** | | | | | | | |
| 15 **Johnson** | Y | Y | Y | Y | Y | Y | Y |
| 16 **Manzullo** | Y | Y | Y | Y | Y | Y | Y |
| 17 Evans | N | N | Y | Y | Y | Y | Y |
| 18 **LaHood** | Y | Y | Y | Y | Y | N | Y |
| 19 **Shimkus** | Y | Y | Y | Y | Y | Y | Y |
| **INDIANA** | | | | | | | |
| 1 Visclosky | N | N | Y | Y | N | Y | Y |
| 2 **Chocola** | Y | Y | Y | Y | Y | Y | Y |
| 3 **Souder** | Y | Y | N | N | Y | N | Y |
| 4 **Buyer** | Y | Y | N | N | Y | Y | Y |
| 5 **Burton** | Y | Y | N | ? | Y | Y | Y |
| 6 **Pence** | Y | Y | Y | Y | Y | Y | Y |
| 7 Carson | N | N | Y | Y | N | Y | Y |
| 8 **Hostettler** | Y | Y | N | Y | Y | N | Y |
| 9 **Sodrel** | Y | Y | Y | Y | Y | Y | Y |
| **IOWA** | | | | | | | |
| 1 **Nussle** | Y | Y | Y | Y | Y | Y | Y |
| 2 **Leach** | Y | Y | Y | Y | Y | Y | Y |
| 3 Boswell | N | N | Y | Y | Y | Y | Y |
| 4 **Latham** | Y | Y | Y | Y | Y | Y | Y |
| 5 **King** | Y | Y | Y | Y | Y | Y | Y |
| **KANSAS** | | | | | | | |
| 1 **Moran** | Y | Y | Y | Y | Y | Y | Y |
| 2 **Ryun** | Y | Y | Y | Y | Y | N | Y |
| 3 Moore | N | N | Y | Y | Y | Y | Y |
| 4 **Tiahrt** | Y | Y | N | N | Y | N | Y |
| **KENTUCKY** | | | | | | | |
| 1 **Whitfield** | Y | Y | Y | Y | Y | N | Y |
| 2 **Lewis** | Y | Y | Y | Y | Y | Y | Y |
| 3 **Northup** | Y | Y | Y | Y | Y | Y | Y |
| 4 **Davis** | Y | Y | N | N | Y | Y | Y |
| 5 **Rogers** | ? | Y | Y | Y | Y | Y | Y |
| 6 Chandler | N | N | Y | Y | Y | Y | Y |
| **LOUISIANA** | | | | | | | |
| 1 **Jindal** | Y | Y | Y | Y | Y | Y | Y |
| 2 Jefferson | N | N | Y | Y | Y | Y | Y |
| 3 Melancon | N | N | Y | Y | Y | Y | Y |
| 4 **McCrery** | Y | Y | Y | Y | Y | Y | Y |
| 5 **Alexander** | Y | Y | Y | N | Y | Y | Y |
| 6 **Baker** | Y | Y | Y | Y | Y | Y | Y |
| 7 **Boustany** | Y | Y | Y | Y | Y | Y | Y |
| **MAINE** | | | | | | | |
| 1 Allen | N | N | Y | Y | N | Y | Y |
| 2 Michaud | N | N | Y | Y | N | Y | Y |
| **MARYLAND** | | | | | | | |
| 1 **Gilchrest** | Y | Y | Y | Y | Y | Y | Y |
| 2 Ruppersberger | N | N | Y | Y | Y | Y | Y |
| 3 Cardin | N | N | Y | Y | Y | Y | Y |
| 4 Wynn | N | N | Y | Y | Y | Y | Y |
| 5 Hoyer | N | N | Y | Y | Y | Y | Y |
| 6 **Bartlett** | Y | Y | Y | Y | Y | Y | Y |
| 7 Cummings | N | N | Y | Y | N | Y | Y |
| 8 Van Hollen | N | N | Y | Y | Y | Y | Y |
| **MASSACHUSETTS** | | | | | | | |
| 1 Olver | N | N | Y | Y | N | Y | Y |
| 2 Neal | N | N | Y | Y | N | Y | Y |
| 3 McGovern | N | N | Y | Y | N | Y | Y |
| 4 Frank | N | N | Y | Y | N | Y | Y |
| 5 Meehan | N | N | Y | Y | N | Y | Y |
| 6 Tierney | N | N | Y | Y | N | Y | Y |
| 7 Markey | N | N | Y | Y | N | Y | Y |
| 8 Capuano | N | N | Y | Y | N | Y | Y |
| 9 Lynch | N | N | Y | Y | Y | Y | Y |
| 10 Delahunt | N | N | Y | Y | N | Y | Y |
| **MICHIGAN** | | | | | | | |
| 1 Stupak | N | N | Y | Y | Y | Y | Y |
| 2 **Hoekstra** | Y | Y | N | Y | Y | Y | ? |
| 3 **Ehlers** | Y | Y | Y | Y | Y | Y | Y |
| 4 **Camp** | Y | Y | Y | Y | Y | Y | Y |
| 5 Kildee | N | N | Y | Y | Y | Y | Y |
| 6 **Upton** | Y | Y | Y | Y | Y | Y | Y |
| 7 **Schwarz** | Y | Y | Y | Y | Y | Y | Y |
| 8 **Rogers** | Y | Y | N | N | Y | N | N |
| 9 **Knollenberg** | Y | Y | Y | Y | Y | Y | Y |
| 10 **Miller** | Y | Y | Y | Y | Y | Y | Y |
| 11 **McCotter** | Y | Y | Y | Y | Y | Y | Y |
| 12 Levin | N | N | Y | Y | Y | Y | Y |
| 13 Kilpatrick | N | N | Y | Y | Y | N | Y |
| 14 Conyers | N | N | Y | Y | N | N | Y |
| 15 Dingell | N | N | Y | Y | Y | Y | Y |

| | 401 | 402 | 403 | 404 | 405 | 406 | 407 |
|---|---|---|---|---|---|---|---|
| **MINNESOTA** | | | | | | | |
| 1 **Gutknecht** | Y | Y | Y | Y | Y | Y | Y |
| 2 **Kline** | Y | Y | Y | Y | Y | Y | Y |
| 3 **Ramstad** | Y | Y | Y | Y | Y | Y | Y |
| 4 McCollum | N | N | Y | Y | N | Y | Y |
| 5 Sabo | N | N | Y | Y | N | Y | Y |
| 6 **Kennedy** | Y | Y | Y | Y | Y | Y | Y |
| 7 Peterson | N | N | Y | Y | Y | Y | Y |
| 8 Oberstar | N | N | Y | Y | Y | Y | Y |
| **MISSISSIPPI** | | | | | | | |
| 1 **Wicker** | Y | Y | Y | Y | Y | Y | Y |
| 2 Thompson | N | N | Y | Y | Y | Y | Y |
| 3 **Pickering** | Y | Y | Y | Y | Y | Y | Y |
| 4 Taylor | N | N | Y | Y | Y | Y | Y |
| **MISSOURI** | | | | | | | |
| 1 Clay | N | N | Y | Y | N | Y | Y |
| 2 **Akin** | Y | Y | Y | Y | Y | Y | Y |
| 3 Carnahan | N | N | Y | Y | Y | Y | Y |
| 4 Skelton | N | N | Y | Y | Y | Y | Y |
| 5 Cleaver | N | N | Y | Y | N | Y | Y |
| 6 **Graves** | Y | Y | Y | Y | Y | Y | Y |
| 7 **Blunt** | Y | Y | Y | Y | Y | Y | Y |
| 8 **Emerson** | Y | Y | Y | Y | Y | Y | Y |
| 9 **Hulshof** | Y | Y | Y | Y | Y | Y | Y |
| **MONTANA** | | | | | | | |
| AL **Rehberg** | Y | Y | Y | Y | Y | Y | Y |
| **NEBRASKA** | | | | | | | |
| 1 **Fortenberry** | Y | Y | Y | Y | Y | Y | Y |
| 2 **Terry** | Y | Y | Y | Y | Y | Y | Y |
| 3 **Osborne** | Y | Y | Y | Y | Y | Y | Y |
| **NEVADA** | | | | | | | |
| 1 Berkley | N | N | Y | Y | Y | Y | Y |
| 2 **Gibbons** | Y | Y | Y | Y | Y | Y | Y |
| 3 **Porter** | Y | Y | Y | Y | Y | Y | Y |
| **NEW HAMPSHIRE** | | | | | | | |
| 1 **Bradley** | Y | Y | Y | Y | Y | Y | Y |
| 2 **Bass** | Y | Y | Y | Y | Y | Y | Y |
| **NEW JERSEY** | | | | | | | |
| 1 Andrews | – | – | Y | Y | Y | Y | Y |
| 2 **LoBiondo** | Y | Y | Y | Y | Y | Y | Y |
| 3 **Saxton** | Y | Y | Y | Y | ? | Y | N |
| 4 **Smith** | Y | Y | Y | Y | Y | Y | Y |
| 5 **Garrett** | Y | Y | Y | Y | Y | Y | Y |
| 6 Pallone | N | N | Y | Y | Y | Y | Y |
| 7 **Ferguson** | Y | Y | Y | Y | Y | Y | Y |
| 8 Pascrell | ? | ? | Y | Y | Y | Y | Y |
| 9 Rothman | N | N | Y | Y | Y | Y | Y |
| 10 Payne | N | N | Y | Y | N | Y | Y |
| 11 **Frelinghuysen** | Y | Y | Y | Y | Y | Y | Y |
| 12 Holt | N | N | Y | Y | N | Y | Y |
| 13 Menendez | N | N | Y | Y | Y | Y | Y |
| **NEW MEXICO** | | | | | | | |
| 1 **Wilson** | Y | Y | Y | Y | Y | Y | Y |
| 2 **Pearce** | Y | Y | Y | Y | Y | Y | Y |
| 3 Udall | N | N | Y | Y | Y | Y | Y |
| **NEW YORK** | | | | | | | |
| 1 Bishop | N | N | Y | Y | Y | Y | Y |
| 2 Israel | N | N | Y | Y | Y | Y | Y |
| 3 **King** | Y | Y | Y | Y | Y | Y | Y |
| 4 McCarthy | N | N | Y | Y | Y | Y | Y |
| 5 Ackerman | N | N | Y | Y | Y | Y | Y |
| 6 Meeks | N | N | Y | Y | N | Y | Y |
| 7 Crowley | ? | ? | Y | Y | Y | Y | Y |
| 8 Nadler | N | N | Y | Y | N | Y | Y |
| 9 Weiner | N | N | Y | Y | Y | Y | Y |
| 10 Towns | N | N | Y | Y | N | Y | Y |
| 11 Owens | N | N | Y | Y | N | Y | Y |
| 12 Velázquez | N | N | Y | Y | N | Y | Y |
| 13 **Fossella** | Y | Y | Y | Y | Y | Y | Y |
| 14 Maloney | N | N | Y | Y | Y | Y | Y |
| 15 Rangel | N | N | Y | Y | N | Y | Y |
| 16 Serrano | N | N | Y | Y | N | Y | Y |
| 17 Engel | N | N | Y | Y | Y | Y | Y |
| 18 Lowey | N | N | Y | Y | Y | Y | Y |
| 19 **Kelly** | Y | Y | Y | Y | Y | Y | Y |
| 20 **Sweeney** | Y | Y | Y | Y | Y | Y | Y |
| 21 McNulty | N | N | Y | Y | N | Y | Y |
| 22 Hinchey | N | N | Y | Y | N | Y | Y |
| 23 **McHugh** | Y | Y | Y | Y | Y | Y | Y |
| 24 **Boehlert** | Y | Y | Y | Y | Y | Y | Y |
| 25 **Walsh** | Y | Y | N | Y | Y | Y | Y |
| 26 **Reynolds** | Y | Y | Y | Y | Y | Y | Y |
| 27 Higgins | N | N | Y | Y | Y | Y | Y |
| 28 Slaughter | N | N | Y | Y | N | Y | Y |
| 29 **Kuhl** | Y | Y | Y | Y | Y | Y | Y |

| | 401 | 402 | 403 | 404 | 405 | 406 | 407 |
|---|---|---|---|---|---|---|---|
| **NORTH CAROLINA** | | | | | | | |
| 1 Butterfield | N | N | Y | Y | Y | Y | Y |
| 2 Etheridge | N | N | Y | Y | Y | Y | Y |
| 3 **Jones** | Y | Y | Y | Y | Y | Y | Y |
| 4 Price | N | N | Y | Y | Y | Y | Y |
| 5 **Foxx** | Y | Y | Y | Y | Y | Y | Y |
| 6 **Coble** | Y | Y | Y | Y | Y | Y | Y |
| 7 McIntyre | N | N | Y | Y | Y | Y | Y |
| 8 **Hayes** | Y | Y | Y | Y | Y | Y | N |
| 9 **Myrick** | Y | Y | N | Y | Y | Y | Y |
| 10 **McHenry** | Y | Y | Y | Y | Y | Y | Y |
| 11 **Taylor** | Y | Y | Y | Y | Y | ? | Y |
| 12 Watt | N | N | Y | Y | N | Y | Y |
| 13 Miller | N | N | Y | Y | Y | Y | Y |
| **NORTH DAKOTA** | | | | | | | |
| AL Pomeroy | N | N | Y | Y | Y | Y | Y |
| **OHIO** | | | | | | | |
| 1 **Chabot** | Y | Y | Y | Y | Y | Y | Y |
| 2 Vacant | | | | | | | |
| 3 **Turner** | Y | Y | Y | Y | Y | Y | Y |
| 4 **Oxley** | Y | Y | N | N | Y | N | Y |
| 5 **Gillmor** | Y | Y | Y | Y | Y | Y | Y |
| 6 Strickland | N | N | Y | Y | Y | Y | Y |
| 7 **Hobson** | Y | Y | Y | Y | Y | Y | Y |
| 8 **Boehner** | Y | Y | Y | Y | Y | Y | ? |
| 9 Kaptur | N | N | Y | Y | Y | Y | Y |
| 10 Kucinich | N | N | Y | Y | N | Y | Y |
| 11 Jones | N | N | Y | Y | Y | Y | Y |
| 12 **Tiberi** | Y | Y | Y | Y | Y | Y | Y |
| 13 Brown | N | N | Y | Y | N | Y | Y |
| 14 **LaTourette** | Y | Y | Y | Y | Y | Y | Y |
| 15 **Pryce** | Y | Y | Y | Y | Y | Y | Y |
| 16 **Regula** | Y | Y | Y | Y | Y | Y | Y |
| 17 Ryan | N | N | Y | Y | Y | Y | Y |
| 18 **Ney** | Y | Y | Y | Y | Y | Y | Y |
| **OKLAHOMA** | | | | | | | |
| 1 **Sullivan** | Y | Y | Y | Y | Y | Y | Y |
| 2 Boren | N | N | Y | Y | Y | Y | Y |
| 3 **Lucas** | Y | Y | Y | Y | Y | Y | Y |
| 4 **Cole** | Y | Y | N | N | Y | Y | Y |
| 5 **Istook** | Y | Y | Y | Y | Y | Y | Y |
| **OREGON** | | | | | | | |
| 1 Wu | N | N | Y | Y | Y | Y | Y |
| 2 **Walden** | Y | Y | Y | Y | Y | Y | Y |
| 3 Blumenauer | N | N | Y | Y | N | Y | Y |
| 4 DeFazio | N | N | Y | Y | Y | Y | Y |
| 5 Hooley | N | N | Y | Y | Y | Y | Y |
| **PENNSYLVANIA** | | | | | | | |
| 1 Brady | N | N | Y | Y | Y | Y | Y |
| 2 Fattah | N | N | Y | Y | Y | Y | Y |
| 3 **English** | Y | Y | Y | Y | Y | Y | Y |
| 4 **Hart** | Y | Y | Y | Y | Y | Y | Y |
| 5 **Peterson** | Y | Y | Y | Y | Y | Y | Y |
| 6 **Gerlach** | ? | Y | Y | Y | Y | Y | Y |
| 7 **Weldon** | Y | Y | Y | Y | Y | Y | Y |
| 8 **Fitzpatrick** | Y | Y | Y | Y | Y | Y | Y |
| 9 **Shuster** | Y | Y | Y | N | Y | Y | Y |
| 10 **Sherwood** | Y | Y | Y | Y | Y | Y | Y |
| 11 Kanjorski | N | N | Y | Y | Y | Y | Y |
| 12 Murtha | N | N | Y | Y | Y | Y | Y |
| 13 Schwartz | N | N | Y | Y | Y | Y | Y |
| 14 Doyle | N | N | Y | Y | Y | Y | Y |
| 15 **Dent** | Y | Y | Y | Y | Y | Y | Y |
| 16 **Pitts** | Y | Y | Y | Y | Y | Y | Y |
| 17 Holden | N | N | Y | Y | Y | Y | Y |
| 18 **Murphy** | Y | Y | Y | Y | Y | Y | Y |
| 19 **Platts** | Y | Y | Y | Y | Y | Y | Y |
| **RHODE ISLAND** | | | | | | | |
| 1 Kennedy | N | N | Y | Y | Y | Y | Y |
| 2 Langevin | N | N | Y | Y | Y | Y | Y |
| **SOUTH CAROLINA** | | | | | | | |
| 1 **Brown** | ? | ? | ? | ? | ? | ? | ? |
| 2 **Wilson** | Y | Y | Y | Y | Y | Y | Y |
| 3 **Barrett** | Y | Y | Y | Y | Y | Y | Y |
| 4 **Inglis** | Y | Y | Y | Y | Y | Y | Y |
| 5 Spratt | N | N | Y | Y | Y | Y | Y |
| 6 Clyburn | N | N | Y | Y | Y | Y | Y |
| **SOUTH DAKOTA** | | | | | | | |
| AL Herseth | N | N | Y | Y | Y | Y | Y |
| **TENNESSEE** | | | | | | | |
| 1 **Jenkins** | Y | Y | Y | Y | Y | Y | Y |
| 2 **Duncan** | Y | Y | Y | Y | Y | Y | Y |

| | 401 | 402 | 403 | 404 | 405 | 406 | 407 |
|---|---|---|---|---|---|---|---|
| 3 **Wamp** | Y | Y | Y | Y | Y | Y | Y |
| 4 Davis | N | N | Y | Y | Y | Y | Y |
| 5 Cooper | N | N | Y | Y | Y | Y | Y |
| 6 Gordon | N | N | Y | Y | Y | Y | Y |
| 7 **Blackburn** | Y | Y | Y | Y | Y | Y | Y |
| 8 Tanner | N | N | Y | Y | Y | Y | Y |
| 9 Ford | N | N | Y | Y | Y | Y | Y |
| **TEXAS** | | | | | | | |
| 1 **Gohmert** | Y | Y | Y | Y | Y | Y | ? |
| 2 **Poe** | Y | Y | Y | Y | Y | Y | Y |
| 3 **Johnson, S.** | Y | Y | N | N | Y | N | Y |
| 4 **Hall** | Y | Y | Y | Y | Y | N | Y |
| 5 **Hensarling** | Y | Y | Y | Y | Y | Y | Y |
| 6 **Barton** | Y | Y | Y | Y | Y | N | Y |
| 7 **Culberson** | Y | Y | Y | Y | Y | Y | Y |
| 8 **Brady** | ? | Y | Y | Y | Y | Y | Y |
| 9 Green, A. | N | N | Y | Y | Y | Y | Y |
| 10 **McCaul** | Y | Y | Y | Y | Y | Y | Y |
| 11 **Conaway** | Y | Y | Y | Y | Y | Y | Y |
| 12 **Granger** | Y | Y | Y | Y | Y | Y | Y |
| 13 **Thornberry** | Y | Y | N | N | Y | N | Y |
| 14 **Paul** | Y | P | Y | Y | N | Y | Y |
| 15 Hinojosa | ? | ? | ? | ? | ? | ? | ? |
| 16 Reyes | N | N | Y | Y | Y | Y | Y |
| 17 Edwards | N | N | Y | Y | Y | Y | Y |
| 18 Jackson-Lee | N | N | Y | Y | Y | Y | Y |
| 19 **Neugebauer** | Y | Y | Y | Y | Y | Y | Y |
| 20 Gonzalez | N | N | Y | Y | Y | Y | Y |
| 21 **Smith** | Y | Y | Y | Y | Y | Y | Y |
| 22 **DeLay** | Y | Y | Y | N | Y | Y | Y |
| 23 **Bonilla** | Y | Y | N | N | Y | Y | Y |
| 24 **Marchant** | Y | Y | Y | Y | Y | Y | Y |
| 25 Doggett | N | N | Y | Y | Y | Y | Y |
| 26 **Burgess** | Y | Y | Y | Y | Y | Y | Y |
| 27 Ortiz | – | – | Y | Y | Y | Y | Y |
| 28 Cuellar | N | N | Y | Y | Y | Y | Y |
| 29 Green, G. | N | N | Y | Y | Y | Y | Y |
| 30 Johnson, E. | N | N | Y | Y | N | Y | Y |
| 31 **Carter** | Y | Y | Y | Y | Y | Y | Y |
| 32 **Sessions** | Y | Y | N | Y | Y | N | Y |
| **UTAH** | | | | | | | |
| 1 **Bishop** | Y | Y | Y | Y | Y | Y | Y |
| 2 Matheson | N | N | Y | Y | Y | Y | Y |
| 3 **Cannon** | Y | Y | Y | Y | Y | Y | Y |
| **VERMONT** | | | | | | | |
| AL *Sanders* | N | N | Y | Y | Y | Y | Y |
| **VIRGINIA** | | | | | | | |
| 1 **Davis, J.** | Y | Y | Y | Y | Y | Y | Y |
| 2 **Drake** | Y | Y | Y | Y | Y | Y | Y |
| 3 Scott | N | N | Y | Y | N | Y | Y |
| 4 **Forbes** | Y | Y | Y | Y | Y | Y | Y |
| 5 **Goode** | Y | Y | Y | Y | Y | Y | Y |
| 6 **Goodlatte** | Y | Y | Y | Y | Y | Y | Y |
| 7 **Cantor** | Y | Y | Y | N | Y | N | N |
| 8 Moran | N | N | Y | Y | Y | Y | Y |
| 9 Boucher | N | N | Y | Y | Y | Y | Y |
| 10 **Wolf** | Y | Y | Y | Y | Y | Y | Y |
| 11 **Davis, T.** | Y | Y | Y | Y | Y | Y | Y |
| **WASHINGTON** | | | | | | | |
| 1 Inslee | N | N | Y | Y | Y | Y | Y |
| 2 Larsen | N | N | Y | Y | Y | Y | Y |
| 3 Baird | N | N | Y | Y | Y | Y | Y |
| 4 **Hastings** | Y | Y | Y | Y | Y | Y | Y |
| 5 **McMorris** | Y | Y | Y | Y | Y | Y | Y |
| 6 Dicks | N | N | Y | Y | Y | Y | Y |
| 7 McDermott | N | N | Y | Y | N | Y | Y |
| 8 **Reichert** | Y | Y | Y | Y | Y | Y | Y |
| 9 Smith | N | N | Y | Y | Y | Y | Y |
| **WEST VIRGINIA** | | | | | | | |
| 1 Mollohan | N | N | Y | Y | N | Y | Y |
| 2 **Capito** | Y | Y | Y | Y | Y | Y | Y |
| 3 Rahall | N | N | Y | Y | Y | Y | Y |
| **WISCONSIN** | | | | | | | |
| 1 **Ryan** | Y | Y | Y | Y | Y | Y | Y |
| 2 Baldwin | N | N | Y | Y | N | Y | Y |
| 3 Kind | N | N | Y | Y | Y | Y | Y |
| 4 Moore | N | N | Y | Y | N | Y | Y |
| 5 **Sensenbrenner** | Y | Y | Y | Y | Y | Y | Y |
| 6 **Petri** | Y | Y | Y | Y | Y | Y | Y |
| 7 Obey | N | N | Y | Y | Y | Y | Y |
| 8 **Green** | Y | Y | Y | Y | Y | Y | Y |
| **WYOMING** | | | | | | | |
| AL **Cubin** | ? | ? | Y | Y | Y | N | N |

# IN THE HOUSE | By Vote Number

**408.** HR 3199. "Patriot Act" Reauthorization/"Sneak and Peek" Searches. Flake, R-Ariz., amendment that would require the Administrative Office of the Courts to report annually to Congress on the number of search warrants granted and eliminate unduly delaying a trial as a reason for delaying notification of "sneak and peek" searches. Adopted 407-21: R 206-21; D 200-0 (ND 151-0, SD 49-0); I 1-0. July 21, 2005.

**409.** HR 3199. "Patriot Act" Reauthorization/Data-Mining Technology. Berman, D-Calif., amendment that would require the Justice Department to report to Congress on the development and use of data-mining technology by federal departments and agencies. Adopted 261-165: R 62-165; D 198-0 (ND 151-0, SD 47-0); I 1-0. July 21, 2005.

**410.** HR 3199. "Patriot Act" Reauthorization/Maritime Security. Schiff, D-Calif., amendment that would make it a crime to use a vessel to smuggle terrorists or dangerous substances, including nuclear material, into the United States. It would impose criminal penalties for providing false information to a federal law enforcement officer at a port or on a vessel and would increase penalties for anyone who fraudulently gains access to a seaport. Adopted 381-45: R 225-2; D 155-43 (ND 114-37, SD 41-6); I 1-0. July 21, 2005.

**411.** HR 3199. "Patriot Act" Reauthorization/Terrorism Financing. Hart, R-Pa., amendment that would increase criminal penalties for anyone convicted on charges of financing terrorists to $50,000 in fines per transaction and 20 years in prison. It also would add terrorism-financing offenses to the list of crimes that constitute money laundering and would permit authorities to seize the assets of anyone who has committed terrorist acts against foreign countries or international organizations. Adopted 387-38: R 224-2; D 162-36 (ND 120-31, SD 42-5); I 1-0. July 21, 2005.

**412.** HR 3199. "Patriot Act" Reauthorization/Seizure of Assets. Jackson-Lee, D-Texas, amendment that would allow for the seizure of assets in the enforcement of a civil judgment against an individual or entity who has engaged in planning or perpetrating an act of domestic or international terrorism. Adopted 233-192: R 45-182; D 187-10 (ND 147-3, SD 40-7); I 1-0. July 21, 2005.

**413.** HR 3199. "Patriot Act" Reauthorization/Recommit. Boucher, D-Va., motion to recommit the bill to the Judiciary Committee with instructions to extend the sunsets of all 16 expiring provisions of the law known as the Patriot Act through Dec. 31, 2009. Motion rejected 209-218: R 9-218; D 199-0 (ND 151-0, SD 48-0); I 1-0. July 21, 2005.

**414.** HR 3199. "Patriot Act" Reauthorization/Passage. Passage of the bill that would make permanent 14 of the 16 provisions of the law known as the Patriot Act scheduled to expire at the end of this year and extend for 10 years the remaining two provisions on access to business and other records and "roving" wiretaps. The bill would permanently extend provisions that expand law enforcement's power to investigate suspected terrorists. Passed 257-171: R 214-14; D 43-156 (ND 19-132, SD 24-24); I 0-1. A "yea" was a vote in support of the president's position. July 21, 2005.

| | 408 | 409 | 410 | 411 | 412 | 413 | 414 |
|---|---|---|---|---|---|---|---|
| **ALABAMA** | | | | | | | |
| 1 Bonner | Y | N | Y | Y | N | N | Y |
| 2 Everett | Y | N | Y | N | N | N | Y |
| 3 Rogers | Y | N | Y | Y | N | N | Y |
| 4 Aderholt | Y | Y | Y | Y | N | N | Y |
| 5 Cramer | Y | Y | Y | Y | N | Y | Y |
| 6 Bachus | Y | N | Y | N | N | N | Y |
| 7 Davis | Y | Y | Y | Y | N | Y | Y |
| **ALASKA** | | | | | | | |
| AL Young | Y | Y | Y | Y | N | N | Y |
| **ARIZONA** | | | | | | | |
| 1 Renzi | N | N | Y | Y | N | N | Y |
| 2 Franks | Y | N | Y | Y | N | N | Y |
| 3 Shadegg | N | N | Y | Y | N | N | Y |
| 4 Pastor | Y | Y | Y | Y | Y | Y | N |
| 5 Hayworth | N | N | Y | Y | N | N | Y |
| 6 Flake | Y | Y | Y | Y | N | N | Y |
| 7 Grijalva | Y | Y | N | Y | Y | Y | N |
| 8 Kolbe | Y | N | Y | Y | N | N | Y |
| **ARKANSAS** | | | | | | | |
| 1 Berry | Y | Y | Y | Y | Y | Y | N |
| 2 Snyder | Y | Y | Y | Y | Y | Y | N |
| 3 Boozman | Y | Y | Y | Y | N | N | Y |
| 4 Ross | Y | Y | Y | Y | Y | Y | Y |
| **CALIFORNIA** | | | | | | | |
| 1 Thompson | Y | Y | Y | Y | Y | Y | N |
| 2 Herger | Y | N | Y | N | N | N | Y |
| 3 Lungren | Y | N | Y | N | N | N | Y |
| 4 Doolittle | Y | N | Y | N | N | N | Y |
| 5 Matsui, D. | Y | Y | Y | Y | Y | Y | N |
| 6 Woolsey | Y | Y | N | N | Y | Y | N |
| 7 Miller, George | Y | Y | N | N | Y | Y | N |
| 8 Pelosi | Y | Y | Y | Y | Y | Y | N |
| 9 Lee | Y | Y | N | N | Y | Y | N |
| 10 Tauscher | Y | Y | Y | Y | Y | Y | N |
| 11 Pombo | Y | N | Y | N | N | N | Y |
| 12 Lantos | Y | Y | Y | Y | Y | Y | N |
| 13 Stark | Y | Y | N | N | Y | Y | N |
| 14 Eshoo | Y | Y | Y | Y | Y | Y | N |
| 15 Honda | Y | Y | Y | Y | Y | Y | N |
| 16 Lofgren | Y | Y | Y | N | Y | Y | N |
| 17 Farr | Y | Y | Y | Y | Y | Y | N |
| 18 Cardoza | Y | Y | Y | Y | ? | Y | N |
| 19 Radanovich | Y | N | Y | Y | N | N | Y |
| 20 Costa | Y | Y | Y | Y | Y | Y | Y |
| 21 Nunes | Y | N | Y | N | N | N | Y |
| 22 Thomas | Y | ? | ? | ? | ? | ? | ? |
| 23 Capps | Y | Y | Y | Y | Y | Y | N |
| 24 Gallegly | Y | N | Y | N | N | N | Y |
| 25 McKeon | Y | N | Y | N | N | N | Y |
| 26 Dreier | Y | N | Y | N | N | N | Y |
| 27 Sherman | Y | Y | Y | Y | Y | Y | N |
| 28 Berman | Y | Y | Y | Y | Y | Y | N |
| 29 Schiff | Y | Y | Y | Y | Y | Y | N |
| 30 Waxman | Y | Y | Y | Y | Y | Y | N |
| 31 Becerra | Y | Y | Y | Y | Y | Y | N |
| 32 Solis | Y | Y | N | N | Y | Y | N |
| 33 Watson | Y | Y | Y | Y | Y | Y | N |
| 34 Roybal-Allard | Y | Y | Y | Y | Y | Y | N |
| 35 Waters | Y | Y | N | N | Y | Y | N |
| 36 Harman | Y | Y | Y | Y | Y | Y | N |
| 37 Millender-McD. | Y | Y | Y | Y | Y | Y | N |
| 38 Napolitano | Y | Y | Y | Y | Y | Y | N |
| 39 Sánchez, Linda | Y | Y | Y | N | Y | Y | N |
| 40 Royce | Y | N | Y | Y | N | N | Y |
| 41 Lewis | Y | N | Y | ? | N | N | Y |
| 42 Miller, Gary | Y | N | Y | N | N | N | Y |
| 43 Baca | Y | Y | Y | Y | Y | Y | Y |
| 44 Calvert | Y | N | Y | N | N | N | Y |
| 45 Bono | N | N | Y | N | N | N | Y |
| 46 Rohrabacher | Y | Y | Y | Y | N | Y | N |
| 47 Sanchez, Loretta | Y | Y | Y | Y | Y | Y | N |
| 48 Cox | ? | Y | Y | Y | N | N | Y |
| 49 Issa | Y | Y | Y | Y | N | N | Y |

| | 408 | 409 | 410 | 411 | 412 | 413 | 414 |
|---|---|---|---|---|---|---|---|
| 50 Cunningham | Y | Y | Y | Y | N | N | Y |
| 51 Filner | Y | Y | N | N | Y | Y | N |
| 52 Hunter | N | N | Y | Y | Y | Y | N |
| 53 Davis | Y | Y | Y | Y | Y | Y | N |
| **COLORADO** | | | | | | | |
| 1 DeGette | Y | Y | Y | Y | Y | Y | N |
| 2 Udall | Y | Y | Y | Y | Y | Y | N |
| 3 Salazar | Y | Y | Y | Y | Y | Y | N |
| 4 Musgrave | Y | N | Y | N | N | N | Y |
| 5 Hefley | Y | Y | Y | N | Y | N | Y |
| 6 Tancredo | Y | N | Y | N | N | N | Y |
| 7 Beauprez | Y | N | Y | N | N | N | Y |
| **CONNECTICUT** | | | | | | | |
| 1 Larson | Y | Y | Y | Y | Y | Y | N |
| 2 Simmons | Y | N | Y | Y | Y | N | Y |
| 3 DeLauro | Y | Y | Y | Y | Y | Y | N |
| 4 Shays | Y | N | Y | Y | Y | N | Y |
| 5 Johnson | Y | N | Y | Y | Y | N | Y |
| **DELAWARE** | | | | | | | |
| AL Castle | Y | N | Y | Y | Y | N | Y |
| **FLORIDA** | | | | | | | |
| 1 Miller | Y | N | Y | Y | N | N | Y |
| 2 Boyd | Y | Y | Y | Y | Y | Y | N |
| 3 Brown | Y | Y | Y | Y | Y | Y | N |
| 4 Crenshaw | Y | N | Y | N | N | N | Y |
| 5 Brown-Waite | Y | N | Y | N | N | N | Y |
| 6 Stearns | Y | N | Y | Y | N | N | Y |
| 7 Mica | Y | N | Y | N | N | N | Y |
| 8 Keller | Y | N | Y | N | N | N | Y |
| 9 Bilirakis | Y | N | Y | N | N | N | Y |
| 10 Young | Y | N | Y | N | N | N | Y |
| 11 Davis | Y | Y | Y | Y | Y | Y | N |
| 12 Putnam | Y | N | Y | N | N | N | Y |
| 13 Harris | Y | Y | Y | N | N | N | Y |
| 14 Mack | Y | Y | Y | Y | ? | N | Y |
| 15 Weldon | Y | N | Y | N | N | N | Y |
| 16 Foley | Y | Y | Y | Y | N | N | Y |
| 17 Meek | Y | Y | Y | Y | Y | Y | N |
| 18 Ros-Lehtinen | Y | N | Y | Y | N | N | Y |
| 19 Wexler | Y | Y | N | Y | Y | Y | N |
| 20 Wasserman-Schultz | Y | Y | N | Y | Y | Y | N |
| 21 Diaz-Balart, L. | Y | N | Y | N | N | N | Y |
| 22 Shaw | Y | N | Y | Y | N | N | Y |
| 23 Hastings | ? | ? | ? | ? | ? | ? | ? |
| 24 Feeney | Y | Y | Y | N | N | N | Y |
| 25 Diaz-Balart, M. | Y | N | Y | N | N | N | Y |
| **GEORGIA** | | | | | | | |
| 1 Kingston | Y | Y | Y | N | N | N | Y |
| 2 Bishop | Y | Y | Y | Y | Y | Y | Y |
| 3 Marshall | Y | Y | Y | Y | Y | Y | Y |
| 4 McKinney | Y | Y | N | N | Y | Y | N |
| 5 Lewis | Y | Y | N | N | Y | Y | N |
| 6 Price | Y | N | Y | Y | N | N | N |
| 7 Linder | Y | N | Y | Y | N | N | Y |
| 8 Westmoreland | N | N | Y | N | N | N | Y |
| 9 Norwood | Y | N | Y | N | N | N | Y |
| 10 Deal | Y | N | Y | N | N | N | Y |
| 11 Gingrey | Y | N | Y | N | N | N | Y |
| 12 Barrow | Y | Y | Y | Y | Y | Y | Y |
| 13 Scott | Y | Y | Y | Y | Y | Y | N |
| **HAWAII** | | | | | | | |
| 1 Abercrombie | Y | Y | Y | Y | Y | Y | N |
| 2 Case | Y | Y | Y | Y | Y | Y | Y |
| **IDAHO** | | | | | | | |
| 1 Otter | Y | Y | N | N | N | Y | N |
| 2 Simpson | Y | Y | Y | Y | N | N | Y |
| **ILLINOIS** | | | | | | | |
| 1 Rush | Y | Y | Y | Y | Y | Y | N |
| 2 Jackson | Y | Y | N | N | Y | Y | N |
| 3 Lipinski | Y | Y | Y | Y | Y | Y | Y |
| 4 Gutierrez | Y | Y | Y | N | Y | Y | Y |
| 5 Emanuel | Y | Y | Y | Y | Y | Y | Y |
| 6 Hyde | Y | N | Y | N | N | N | Y |
| 7 Davis | Y | Y | Y | Y | Y | Y | N |
| 8 Bean | Y | Y | Y | Y | Y | Y | Y |
| 9 Schakowsky | Y | Y | N | N | Y | Y | N |
| 10 Kirk | Y | N | Y | Y | ? | N | Y |
| 11 Weller | Y | N | Y | N | N | N | Y |
| 12 Costello | Y | Y | Y | Y | Y | Y | N |

**KEY**    **Republicans**    Democrats    *Independents*

| | | |
|---|---|---|
| Y   Voted for (yea) | X   Paired against | C   Voted "present" to avoid possible conflict of interest |
| #   Paired for | –   Announced against | |
| +   Announced for | P   Voted "present" | ?   Did not vote or otherwise make a position known |
| N   Voted against (nay) | | |

ND Northern Democrats, SD Southern Democrats
Southern states: Ala., Ark., Fla., Ga., Ky., La., Miss., N.C., Okla., S.C., Tenn., Texas, Va.

| | 408 | 409 | 410 | 411 | 412 | 413 | 414 |
|---|---|---|---|---|---|---|---|
| 13 **Biggert** | Y | N | Y | Y | N | N | Y |
| 14 **Hastert** | | | | | N | N | Y |
| 15 **Johnson** | Y | Y | Y | Y | Y | Y | N |
| 16 **Manzullo** | Y | N | Y | Y | N | N | N |
| 17 Evans | Y | Y | Y | Y | Y | Y | N |
| 18 **LaHood** | Y | N | Y | Y | N | N | N |
| 19 **Shimkus** | Y | N | Y | Y | N | N | Y |
| **INDIANA** | | | | | | | |
| 1 Visclosky | Y | Y | N | Y | Y | Y | N |
| 2 **Chocola** | Y | N | Y | Y | Y | N | Y |
| 3 **Souder** | N | N | Y | Y | N | N | Y |
| 4 **Buyer** | Y | N | Y | Y | N | N | Y |
| 5 **Burton** | Y | N | Y | Y | N | N | Y |
| 6 **Pence** | Y | Y | Y | Y | N | N | Y |
| 7 Carson | Y | Y | Y | N | Y | Y | N |
| 8 **Hostettler** | N | N | Y | Y | N | N | Y |
| 9 **Sodrel** | Y | N | Y | Y | N | N | Y |
| **IOWA** | | | | | | | |
| 1 **Nussle** | Y | N | Y | Y | Y | N | Y |
| 2 **Leach** | Y | Y | Y | Y | Y | Y | Y |
| 3 Boswell | Y | Y | Y | Y | Y | Y | Y |
| 4 **Latham** | Y | N | Y | Y | N | N | Y |
| 5 **King** | Y | N | Y | Y | N | N | Y |
| **KANSAS** | | | | | | | |
| 1 **Moran** | Y | N | Y | Y | N | N | Y |
| 2 **Ryun** | Y | N | Y | Y | N | N | Y |
| 3 Moore | Y | Y | Y | Y | Y | Y | N |
| 4 **Tiahrt** | N | N | Y | Y | N | N | Y |
| **KENTUCKY** | | | | | | | |
| 1 **Whitfield** | Y | N | Y | Y | Y | N | Y |
| 2 **Lewis** | Y | N | Y | Y | Y | N | Y |
| 3 **Northup** | Y | N | Y | Y | N | N | Y |
| 4 **Davis** | N | N | Y | Y | N | N | Y |
| 5 **Rogers** | Y | N | Y | Y | Y | N | Y |
| 6 Chandler | Y | Y | Y | Y | N | Y | Y |
| **LOUISIANA** | | | | | | | |
| 1 **Jindal** | Y | N | Y | Y | N | N | Y |
| 2 Jefferson | Y | ? | ? | ? | ? | Y | N |
| 3 Melancon | Y | Y | Y | Y | Y | Y | Y |
| 4 **McCrery** | Y | N | Y | Y | N | N | Y |
| 5 **Alexander** | Y | N | Y | Y | Y | N | Y |
| 6 **Baker** | Y | N | Y | Y | N | N | Y |
| 7 **Boustany** | Y | N | Y | Y | N | N | Y |
| **MAINE** | | | | | | | |
| 1 Allen | Y | Y | Y | Y | Y | Y | N |
| 2 Michaud | Y | Y | N | Y | Y | Y | N |
| **MARYLAND** | | | | | | | |
| 1 **Gilchrest** | Y | N | Y | Y | Y | N | Y |
| 2 Ruppersberger | Y | Y | Y | Y | Y | Y | Y |
| 3 Cardin | Y | Y | Y | Y | Y | Y | Y |
| 4 Wynn | Y | Y | Y | Y | Y | Y | N |
| 5 Hoyer | Y | Y | Y | Y | Y | Y | Y |
| 6 **Bartlett** | Y | Y | Y | Y | N | Y | N |
| 7 Cummings | Y | Y | Y | N | Y | Y | N |
| 8 Van Hollen | Y | Y | Y | Y | Y | Y | N |
| **MASSACHUSETTS** | | | | | | | |
| 1 Olver | Y | Y | N | Y | Y | Y | N |
| 2 Neal | Y | Y | Y | Y | Y | Y | N |
| 3 McGovern | Y | Y | N | N | Y | Y | N |
| 4 Frank | Y | Y | N | N | Y | Y | N |
| 5 Meehan | Y | Y | Y | Y | Y | Y | N |
| 6 Tierney | Y | Y | N | Y | Y | Y | N |
| 7 Markey | Y | Y | N | N | Y | Y | N |
| 8 Capuano | Y | Y | Y | N | Y | Y | N |
| 9 Lynch | Y | Y | Y | Y | Y | Y | N |
| 10 Delahunt | Y | Y | N | Y | Y | Y | N |
| **MICHIGAN** | | | | | | | |
| 1 Stupak | Y | Y | Y | Y | Y | Y | N |
| 2 **Hoekstra** | Y | N | Y | Y | N | N | Y |
| 3 **Ehlers** | Y | Y | Y | Y | N | Y | Y |
| 4 **Camp** | Y | N | Y | Y | N | N | Y |
| 5 Kildee | Y | Y | N | Y | Y | Y | N |
| 6 **Upton** | Y | Y | Y | Y | N | N | Y |
| 7 **Schwarz** | Y | Y | Y | Y | Y | N | Y |
| 8 **Rogers** | N | N | Y | Y | N | N | Y |
| 9 **Knollenberg** | N | N | Y | Y | N | N | Y |
| 10 **Miller** | Y | N | Y | Y | N | N | Y |
| 11 **McCotter** | Y | Y | Y | Y | Y | N | Y |
| 12 Levin | Y | Y | Y | Y | Y | Y | N |
| 13 Kilpatrick | Y | Y | N | Y | Y | Y | N |
| 14 Conyers | Y | Y | N | N | Y | Y | N |
| 15 Dingell | Y | Y | Y | Y | Y | Y | N |
| **MINNESOTA** | | | | | | | |
| 1 **Gutknecht** | Y | Y | Y | Y | N | N | Y |
| 2 **Kline** | Y | N | Y | Y | N | N | Y |
| 3 **Ramstad** | Y | N | Y | Y | Y | N | Y |
| 4 McCollum | Y | Y | N | Y | Y | Y | N |
| 5 Sabo | Y | Y | N | Y | Y | Y | N |
| 6 **Kennedy** | Y | Y | Y | Y | N | N | Y |
| 7 Peterson | Y | Y | Y | Y | N | Y | N |
| 8 Oberstar | Y | Y | N | Y | Y | Y | N |
| **MISSISSIPPI** | | | | | | | |
| 1 **Wicker** | Y | N | Y | Y | N | N | Y |
| 2 Thompson | Y | Y | Y | Y | Y | Y | N |
| 3 **Pickering** | Y | ? | ? | ? | ? | ? | ? |
| 4 Taylor | Y | ? | ? | ? | ? | ? | ? |
| **MISSOURI** | | | | | | | |
| 1 Clay | Y | Y | Y | N | Y | Y | N |
| 2 **Akin** | Y | N | Y | Y | N | N | Y |
| 3 Carnahan | Y | Y | Y | Y | Y | Y | Y |
| 4 Skelton | Y | Y | Y | Y | Y | Y | Y |
| 5 Cleaver | Y | Y | Y | Y | Y | Y | N |
| 6 **Graves** | Y | N | Y | Y | N | N | Y |
| 7 **Blunt** | Y | N | Y | Y | N | N | Y |
| 8 **Emerson** | Y | Y | Y | Y | N | N | Y |
| 9 **Hulshof** | Y | Y | Y | Y | N | N | Y |
| **MONTANA** | | | | | | | |
| AL **Rehberg** | Y | N | Y | Y | N | N | Y |
| **NEBRASKA** | | | | | | | |
| 1 **Fortenberry** | Y | N | Y | Y | Y | N | Y |
| 2 **Terry** | Y | N | Y | Y | Y | N | Y |
| 3 **Osborne** | Y | N | Y | Y | N | N | Y |
| **NEVADA** | | | | | | | |
| 1 Berkley | Y | Y | Y | Y | Y | Y | N |
| 2 **Gibbons** | Y | N | Y | Y | N | N | Y |
| 3 **Porter** | Y | Y | Y | Y | N | N | Y |
| **NEW HAMPSHIRE** | | | | | | | |
| 1 **Bradley** | Y | Y | Y | Y | Y | N | Y |
| 2 **Bass** | Y | N | Y | Y | Y | N | Y |
| **NEW JERSEY** | | | | | | | |
| 1 Andrews | Y | Y | Y | Y | Y | Y | Y |
| 2 **LoBiondo** | Y | N | Y | Y | Y | N | Y |
| 3 **Saxton** | Y | N | Y | Y | N | N | Y |
| 4 **Smith** | Y | Y | Y | Y | N | N | Y |
| 5 **Garrett** | Y | N | Y | Y | N | N | Y |
| 6 Pallone | Y | Y | Y | Y | Y | Y | N |
| 7 **Ferguson** | Y | N | Y | Y | N | N | Y |
| 8 Pascrell | Y | Y | Y | Y | Y | Y | N |
| 9 Rothman | Y | Y | Y | Y | Y | Y | N |
| 10 Payne | Y | Y | N | N | Y | Y | N |
| 11 **Frelinghuysen** | Y | N | Y | Y | Y | N | Y |
| 12 Holt | Y | Y | N | N | Y | Y | N |
| 13 Menendez | Y | Y | Y | Y | Y | Y | Y |
| **NEW MEXICO** | | | | | | | |
| 1 **Wilson** | Y | N | Y | Y | N | N | Y |
| 2 **Pearce** | Y | N | Y | Y | N | N | Y |
| 3 Udall | Y | Y | Y | Y | Y | Y | N |
| **NEW YORK** | | | | | | | |
| 1 Bishop | Y | Y | Y | Y | Y | Y | N |
| 2 Israel | Y | Y | Y | Y | Y | Y | N |
| 3 **King** | Y | N | Y | Y | N | N | Y |
| 4 McCarthy | Y | Y | Y | Y | Y | Y | N |
| 5 Ackerman | Y | Y | Y | Y | Y | Y | N |
| 6 Meeks | Y | Y | N | Y | Y | Y | N |
| 7 Crowley | Y | Y | Y | N | Y | Y | N |
| 8 Nadler | Y | Y | N | Y | Y | Y | N |
| 9 Weiner | Y | Y | Y | Y | Y | Y | N |
| 10 Towns | Y | Y | Y | Y | Y | Y | N |
| 11 Owens | Y | Y | N | Y | Y | Y | N |
| 12 Velázquez | Y | Y | Y | Y | Y | Y | N |
| 13 **Fossella** | Y | N | Y | Y | N | N | Y |
| 14 Maloney | Y | Y | Y | Y | Y | Y | N |
| 15 Rangel | Y | Y | Y | Y | Y | Y | N |
| 16 Serrano | Y | Y | N | N | Y | Y | N |
| 17 Engel | Y | Y | Y | Y | Y | Y | N |
| 18 Lowey | Y | Y | Y | Y | Y | Y | N |
| 19 **Kelly** | Y | N | Y | Y | N | N | Y |
| 20 **Sweeney** | Y | N | Y | Y | N | N | Y |
| 21 McNulty | Y | Y | Y | Y | Y | Y | N |
| 22 Hinchey | Y | Y | Y | Y | Y | Y | N |
| 23 **McHugh** | Y | N | Y | Y | N | N | Y |
| 24 **Boehlert** | Y | N | Y | Y | N | N | Y |
| 25 **Walsh** | Y | N | Y | Y | N | N | Y |
| 26 **Reynolds** | Y | N | Y | Y | N | N | Y |
| 27 Higgins | Y | Y | Y | Y | Y | Y | Y |
| 28 Slaughter | Y | Y | Y | Y | Y | Y | N |
| 29 **Kuhl** | Y | Y | Y | Y | N | N | Y |
| **NORTH CAROLINA** | | | | | | | |
| 1 Butterfield | Y | Y | Y | Y | Y | Y | Y |
| 2 Etheridge | Y | Y | Y | Y | Y | Y | Y |
| 3 **Jones** | Y | Y | Y | Y | Y | Y | Y |
| 4 Price | Y | Y | Y | Y | Y | Y | N |
| 5 **Foxx** | Y | N | Y | Y | N | N | Y |
| 6 **Coble** | Y | Y | Y | Y | Y | N | Y |
| 7 McIntyre | Y | Y | Y | Y | Y | Y | Y |
| 8 **Hayes** | Y | N | Y | Y | N | N | Y |
| 9 **Myrick** | Y | N | Y | Y | N | N | Y |
| 10 **McHenry** | Y | N | Y | Y | N | N | Y |
| 11 **Taylor** | Y | N | Y | Y | N | N | Y |
| 12 Watt | Y | Y | N | N | Y | Y | N |
| 13 Miller | Y | Y | Y | Y | Y | Y | Y |
| **NORTH DAKOTA** | | | | | | | |
| AL Pomeroy | Y | Y | Y | Y | Y | Y | Y |
| **OHIO** | | | | | | | |
| 1 **Chabot** | Y | N | Y | Y | N | N | Y |
| 2 Vacant | | | | | | | |
| 3 **Turner** | Y | N | Y | Y | N | N | Y |
| 4 **Oxley** | N | N | Y | Y | N | N | Y |
| 5 **Gillmor** | Y | Y | Y | Y | Y | N | Y |
| 6 Strickland | Y | Y | Y | Y | Y | Y | N |
| 7 **Hobson** | Y | N | Y | Y | Y | N | Y |
| 8 **Boehner** | Y | N | Y | Y | N | N | Y |
| 9 Kaptur | Y | Y | Y | Y | Y | Y | N |
| 10 Kucinich | Y | Y | N | N | Y | Y | N |
| 11 Jones | Y | Y | N | N | Y | Y | N |
| 12 **Tiberi** | Y | N | Y | Y | N | N | Y |
| 13 Brown | Y | Y | Y | Y | Y | Y | N |
| 14 **LaTourette** | Y | Y | Y | Y | N | N | Y |
| 15 **Pryce** | Y | N | Y | Y | N | N | Y |
| 16 **Regula** | Y | Y | Y | Y | N | N | Y |
| 17 Ryan | Y | Y | Y | Y | Y | Y | N |
| 18 **Ney** | Y | N | Y | Y | Y | N | N |
| **OKLAHOMA** | | | | | | | |
| 1 **Sullivan** | Y | N | Y | Y | N | N | Y |
| 2 Boren | Y | Y | Y | Y | Y | Y | Y |
| 3 **Lucas** | Y | N | Y | Y | N | N | N |
| 4 **Cole** | N | N | Y | Y | Y | N | Y |
| 5 **Istook** | Y | Y | Y | Y | N | N | Y |
| **OREGON** | | | | | | | |
| 1 Wu | Y | Y | Y | Y | Y | Y | N |
| 2 **Walden** | Y | Y | Y | Y | Y | N | Y |
| 3 Blumenauer | Y | Y | N | N | Y | Y | N |
| 4 DeFazio | Y | Y | Y | Y | Y | Y | N |
| 5 Hooley | Y | Y | Y | Y | Y | Y | N |
| **PENNSYLVANIA** | | | | | | | |
| 1 Brady | Y | Y | Y | Y | Y | Y | N |
| 2 Fattah | Y | Y | Y | Y | Y | Y | N |
| 3 **English** | Y | Y | Y | Y | N | N | Y |
| 4 **Hart** | Y | Y | Y | Y | N | N | Y |
| 5 **Peterson** | Y | N | Y | Y | N | N | Y |
| 6 **Gerlach** | Y | Y | Y | Y | Y | N | Y |
| 7 **Weldon** | Y | N | Y | Y | N | N | Y |
| 8 **Fitzpatrick** | Y | Y | Y | Y | Y | N | Y |
| 9 **Shuster** | N | N | Y | Y | N | N | Y |
| 10 **Sherwood** | Y | N | Y | Y | N | N | Y |
| 11 Kanjorski | Y | Y | Y | Y | N | Y | N |
| 12 Murtha | Y | Y | Y | Y | N | Y | N |
| 13 Schwartz | Y | Y | Y | Y | Y | Y | Y |
| 14 Doyle | Y | Y | Y | Y | Y | Y | N |
| 15 **Dent** | Y | N | Y | Y | Y | N | Y |
| 16 **Pitts** | Y | N | Y | Y | N | N | Y |
| 17 Holden | Y | Y | Y | Y | Y | Y | Y |
| 18 **Murphy** | Y | Y | Y | Y | N | N | Y |
| 19 **Platts** | Y | N | Y | Y | N | N | Y |
| **RHODE ISLAND** | | | | | | | |
| 1 Kennedy | Y | Y | Y | Y | Y | Y | N |
| 2 Langevin | Y | Y | Y | Y | Y | Y | N |
| **SOUTH CAROLINA** | | | | | | | |
| 1 **Brown** | ? | ? | ? | ? | ? | ? | ? |
| 2 **Wilson** | Y | N | Y | Y | N | N | Y |
| 3 **Barrett** | Y | N | Y | Y | N | N | Y |
| 4 **Inglis** | Y | Y | Y | Y | N | N | Y |
| 5 Spratt | Y | Y | Y | Y | Y | Y | Y |
| 6 Clyburn | Y | Y | Y | Y | N | Y | Y |
| **SOUTH DAKOTA** | | | | | | | |
| AL Herseth | Y | Y | Y | Y | Y | Y | Y |
| **TENNESSEE** | | | | | | | |
| 1 **Jenkins** | Y | Y | Y | Y | N | N | Y |
| 2 **Duncan** | Y | Y | Y | Y | Y | N | N |
| 3 **Wamp** | Y | Y | Y | Y | N | N | Y |
| 4 Davis | Y | Y | Y | Y | Y | Y | Y |
| 5 Cooper | Y | Y | Y | Y | N | Y | Y |
| 6 Gordon | Y | Y | Y | Y | Y | Y | Y |
| 7 **Blackburn** | Y | N | Y | Y | N | N | Y |
| 8 Tanner | Y | Y | Y | Y | Y | Y | N |
| 9 Ford | Y | Y | Y | Y | Y | Y | N |
| **TEXAS** | | | | | | | |
| 1 **Gohmert** | ? | Y | Y | Y | Y | N | Y |
| 2 **Poe** | Y | Y | Y | Y | Y | N | Y |
| 3 **Johnson, S.** | Y | N | Y | Y | N | N | Y |
| 4 **Hall** | Y | N | Y | Y | N | N | Y |
| 5 **Hensarling** | Y | Y | Y | Y | N | N | Y |
| 6 **Barton** | N | N | Y | Y | N | N | Y |
| 7 **Culberson** | Y | N | Y | Y | N | N | Y |
| 8 **Brady** | Y | N | Y | Y | Y | N | Y |
| 9 Green, A. | Y | Y | Y | Y | Y | Y | N |
| 10 **McCaul** | Y | N | Y | Y | Y | N | Y |
| 11 **Conaway** | Y | Y | Y | Y | N | N | Y |
| 12 **Granger** | Y | N | Y | Y | N | N | Y |
| 13 **Thornberry** | N | N | Y | Y | N | N | Y |
| 14 **Paul** | Y | Y | N | N | Y | Y | N |
| 15 Hinojosa | ? | ? | ? | ? | ? | ? | ? |
| 16 Reyes | Y | Y | Y | Y | Y | Y | Y |
| 17 Edwards | Y | Y | Y | Y | Y | Y | Y |
| 18 Jackson-Lee | Y | Y | N | Y | Y | Y | N |
| 19 **Neugebauer** | Y | N | Y | Y | N | N | Y |
| 20 Gonzalez | Y | Y | Y | Y | Y | Y | N |
| 21 **Smith** | Y | Y | Y | Y | N | N | Y |
| 22 **DeLay** | Y | N | Y | Y | N | N | Y |
| 23 **Bonilla** | N | N | Y | Y | N | N | Y |
| 24 **Marchant** | Y | N | Y | Y | N | N | Y |
| 25 Doggett | Y | Y | Y | Y | Y | Y | N |
| 26 **Burgess** | Y | N | Y | Y | N | N | Y |
| 27 Ortiz | Y | Y | Y | Y | Y | Y | Y |
| 28 Cuellar | Y | Y | Y | Y | Y | Y | N |
| 29 Green, G. | Y | Y | Y | Y | Y | Y | Y |
| 30 Johnson, E. | Y | Y | Y | Y | Y | Y | N |
| 31 **Carter** | Y | N | Y | Y | N | N | Y |
| 32 **Sessions** | N | N | Y | Y | N | N | Y |
| **UTAH** | | | | | | | |
| 1 **Bishop** | Y | N | Y | Y | N | N | N |
| 2 Matheson | Y | Y | Y | Y | Y | Y | N |
| 3 **Cannon** | Y | Y | Y | Y | N | N | Y |
| **VERMONT** | | | | | | | |
| AL *Sanders* | Y | Y | Y | Y | Y | Y | N |
| **VIRGINIA** | | | | | | | |
| 1 **Davis, J.** | Y | N | Y | Y | N | N | Y |
| 2 **Drake** | Y | N | Y | Y | N | N | Y |
| 3 Scott | Y | Y | N | N | N | Y | N |
| 4 **Forbes** | Y | N | Y | Y | N | N | Y |
| 5 **Goode** | Y | Y | Y | Y | N | N | Y |
| 6 **Goodlatte** | Y | Y | Y | Y | N | N | Y |
| 7 **Cantor** | N | N | Y | Y | N | N | Y |
| 8 Moran | Y | Y | Y | Y | N | Y | N |
| 9 Boucher | Y | Y | Y | Y | Y | Y | N |
| 10 **Wolf** | Y | N | Y | Y | N | N | Y |
| 11 **Davis, T.** | Y | N | Y | Y | Y | N | Y |
| **WASHINGTON** | | | | | | | |
| 1 Inslee | Y | Y | Y | Y | Y | Y | N |
| 2 Larsen | Y | Y | Y | Y | Y | Y | N |
| 3 Baird | Y | Y | Y | Y | Y | Y | N |
| 4 **Hastings** | Y | Y | Y | Y | N | N | Y |
| 5 **McMorris** | Y | N | Y | Y | N | N | Y |
| 6 Dicks | Y | Y | Y | Y | Y | Y | N |
| 7 McDermott | Y | Y | N | N | Y | Y | N |
| 8 **Reichert** | Y | N | Y | Y | N | N | Y |
| 9 Smith | Y | Y | Y | Y | Y | Y | N |
| **WEST VIRGINIA** | | | | | | | |
| 1 Mollohan | Y | Y | N | Y | Y | Y | N |
| 2 **Capito** | Y | N | Y | Y | N | N | Y |
| 3 Rahall | Y | Y | Y | Y | Y | Y | N |
| **WISCONSIN** | | | | | | | |
| 1 **Ryan** | Y | N | Y | Y | N | N | Y |
| 2 Baldwin | Y | Y | N | N | Y | Y | N |
| 3 Kind | Y | Y | Y | Y | Y | Y | N |
| 4 Moore | Y | Y | N | N | Y | Y | N |
| 5 **Sensenbrenner** | Y | Y | Y | Y | N | N | Y |
| 6 **Petri** | Y | Y | Y | N | N | N | Y |
| 7 Obey | Y | Y | Y | Y | Y | Y | N |
| 8 **Green** | Y | Y | Y | Y | N | N | Y |
| **WYOMING** | | | | | | | |
| AL **Cubin** | Y | N | Y | Y | N | N | Y |

# IN THE HOUSE | By Vote Number

**415.** **HR 3070. NASA Reauthorization/Minority-Serving Institutions.** Velázquez, D-N.Y., amendment that would create a four-year pilot program for NASA to award grants to minority-serving institutions for the development of NASA research facilities and infrastructure. Rejected 192-206: R 9-201; D 182-5 (ND 141-2, SD 41-3); I 1-0. July 22, 2005.

**416.** **HR 3070. NASA Reauthorization/Passage.** Passage of the bill that would authorize $34.7 billion for NASA — $17 billion in fiscal 2006 and $17.7 billion in fiscal 2007. It would direct NASA to manage the human space flight program with a goal of sending Americans to the moon by 2020, launch a crew exploration vehicle as close to 2010 as possible and send astronaut crews to Mars and other destinations. Passed 383-15: R 207-3; D 176-11 (ND 132-11, SD 44-0); I 0-1. July 22, 2005.

**417.** **H J Res 59. Women's Suffrage Commemoration Day/Passage.** Issa, R-Calif., motion to suspend the rules and pass the joint resolution that would express the sense of Congress that women suffragists should be revered and celebrated for working to ensure the right of women to vote in the United States. Motion agreed to 378-0: R 197-0; D 180-0 (ND 136-0, SD 44-0); I 1-0. A two-thirds majority of those present and voting (252 in this case) is required for passage under suspension of the rules. July 25, 2005.

**418.** **H Con Res 181. National Life Insurance Awareness Month/Adoption.** Issa, R-Calif., motion to suspend the rules and adopt the concurrent resolution that would support the goals and ideals of National Life Insurance Awareness Month. Motion agreed to 377-4: R 196-2; D 180-2 (ND 136-2, SD 44-0); I 1-0. A two-thirds majority of those present and voting (254 in this case) is required for adoption under suspension of the rules. July 25, 2005.

**419.** **H Res 376. Video Game Investigation/Adoption.** Upton, R-Mich., motion to suspend the rules and adopt the resolution that would urge the Federal Trade Commission to launch an investigation of the "Grand Theft Auto: San Andreas" video game and impose the strictest penalty if the game manufacturer is found guilty of deception or fraud to secure a lesser content rating. Motion agreed to 355-21: R 195-2; D 159-19 (ND 119-16, SD 40-3); I 1-0. A two-thirds majority of those present and voting (252 in this case) is required for adoption under suspension of the rules. July 25, 2005.

**420.** **HR 3200. Servicemembers' Group Life Insurance/Passage.** Buyer, R-Ind., motion to suspend the rules and pass the bill that would make permanent current law that raises the maximum federally subsidized life insurance payout to $400,000 for service members killed in the line of duty. Motion agreed to 424-0: R 224-0; D 199-0 (ND 150-0, SD 49-0); I 1-0. A two-thirds majority of those present and voting (283 in this case) is required for passage under suspension of the rules. July 26, 2005.

| | 415 | 416 | 417 | 418 | 419 | 420 |
|---|---|---|---|---|---|---|
| **ALABAMA** | | | | | | |
| 1 Bonner | N | Y | Y | Y | Y | Y |
| 2 Everett | N | Y | Y | Y | Y | Y |
| 3 Rogers | Y | Y | Y | Y | Y | Y |
| 4 Aderholt | N | Y | Y | Y | Y | Y |
| 5 Cramer | N | Y | ? | ? | ? | ? |
| 6 Bachus | N | Y | Y | ? | ? | Y |
| 7 Davis | Y | Y | Y | Y | Y | Y |
| **ALASKA** | | | | | | |
| AL Young | N | Y | Y | Y | Y | Y |
| **ARIZONA** | | | | | | |
| 1 Renzi | N | Y | Y | Y | Y | Y |
| 2 Franks | N | Y | Y | Y | Y | Y |
| 3 Shadegg | N | N | Y | Y | Y | Y |
| 4 Pastor | Y | Y | Y | Y | Y | Y |
| 5 Hayworth | N | Y | Y | Y | Y | Y |
| 6 Flake | N | N | Y | N | N | Y |
| 7 Grijalva | Y | Y | Y | Y | N | Y |
| 8 Kolbe | N | Y | Y | Y | Y | Y |
| **ARKANSAS** | | | | | | |
| 1 Berry | Y | Y | Y | Y | Y | Y |
| 2 Snyder | Y | Y | Y | Y | Y | Y |
| 3 Boozman | N | Y | Y | Y | Y | Y |
| 4 Ross | Y | Y | Y | Y | Y | Y |
| **CALIFORNIA** | | | | | | |
| 1 Thompson | Y | Y | Y | Y | Y | Y |
| 2 Herger | N | Y | Y | Y | Y | Y |
| 3 Lungren | N | Y | Y | Y | Y | Y |
| 4 Doolittle | N | Y | ? | ? | ? | Y |
| 5 Matsui, D. | Y | Y | Y | Y | Y | Y |
| 6 Woolsey | Y | Y | Y | Y | N | Y |
| 7 Miller, George | Y | Y | Y | Y | Y | Y |
| 8 Pelosi | Y | Y | ? | ? | ? | Y |
| 9 Lee | Y | Y | Y | Y | N | Y |
| 10 Tauscher | Y | Y | Y | Y | Y | Y |
| 11 Pombo | N | Y | Y | Y | Y | Y |
| 12 Lantos | Y | Y | Y | Y | Y | Y |
| 13 Stark | ? | ? | Y | N | N | Y |
| 14 Eshoo | Y | Y | Y | Y | Y | Y |
| 15 Honda | Y | Y | Y | Y | Y | Y |
| 16 Lofgren | Y | Y | Y | Y | Y | Y |
| 17 Farr | Y | Y | Y | Y | Y | Y |
| 18 Cardoza | ? | ? | Y | Y | Y | Y |
| 19 Radanovich | ? | ? | ? | ? | ? | Y |
| 20 Costa | N | Y | Y | Y | Y | Y |
| 21 Nunes | N | Y | Y | Y | Y | Y |
| 22 Thomas | ? | ? | Y | Y | Y | Y |
| 23 Capps | Y | Y | Y | Y | Y | Y |
| 24 Gallegly | N | Y | ? | ? | ? | Y |
| 25 McKeon | N | Y | Y | Y | Y | Y |
| 26 Dreier | N | Y | Y | Y | Y | Y |
| 27 Sherman | Y | Y | Y | Y | Y | Y |
| 28 Berman | Y | Y | ? | ? | ? | Y |
| 29 Schiff | Y | Y | + | Y | Y | Y |
| 30 Waxman | ? | ? | Y | Y | Y | Y |
| 31 Becerra | Y | Y | ? | ? | ? | Y |
| 32 Solis | Y | Y | Y | Y | Y | Y |
| 33 Watson | Y | Y | Y | Y | Y | Y |
| 34 Roybal-Allard | Y | Y | Y | Y | Y | Y |
| 35 Waters | Y | Y | Y | Y | Y | Y |
| 36 Harman | Y | Y | Y | Y | Y | Y |
| 37 Millender-McD. | Y | Y | Y | Y | Y | Y |
| 38 Napolitano | Y | Y | Y | Y | Y | Y |
| 39 Sánchez, Linda | Y | Y | Y | Y | Y | Y |
| 40 Royce | N | Y | Y | Y | Y | Y |
| 41 Lewis | N | Y | Y | Y | Y | Y |
| 42 Miller, Gary | N | Y | Y | Y | Y | Y |
| 43 Baca | Y | Y | Y | Y | Y | Y |
| 44 Calvert | N | Y | Y | Y | N | Y |
| 45 Bono | N | Y | Y | Y | Y | Y |
| 46 Rohrabacher | N | Y | Y | Y | Y | Y |
| 47 Sanchez, Loretta | Y | Y | Y | Y | Y | Y |
| 48 Cox | N | Y | Y | Y | Y | ? |
| 49 Issa | N | Y | Y | Y | Y | Y |
| 50 Cunningham | ? | ? | ? | ? | ? | Y |
| 51 Filner | Y | Y | Y | Y | Y | Y |
| 52 Hunter | N | Y | Y | Y | Y | Y |
| 53 Davis | Y | Y | Y | Y | Y | Y |
| **COLORADO** | | | | | | |
| 1 DeGette | ? | ? | Y | Y | Y | Y |
| 2 Udall | N | Y | Y | Y | Y | Y |
| 3 Salazar | Y | Y | Y | Y | Y | Y |
| 4 Musgrave | N | Y | Y | Y | Y | Y |
| 5 Hefley | N | Y | Y | Y | Y | Y |
| 6 Tancredo | N | Y | Y | Y | Y | Y |
| 7 Beauprez | N | Y | Y | Y | Y | Y |
| **CONNECTICUT** | | | | | | |
| 1 Larson | Y | Y | Y | Y | Y | Y |
| 2 Simmons | N | Y | Y | Y | Y | Y |
| 3 DeLauro | Y | Y | Y | Y | Y | Y |
| 4 Shays | N | Y | + | + | + | Y |
| 5 Johnson | N | Y | Y | Y | Y | Y |
| **DELAWARE** | | | | | | |
| AL Castle | N | Y | Y | Y | Y | ? |
| **FLORIDA** | | | | | | |
| 1 Miller | ? | ? | Y | Y | Y | Y |
| 2 Boyd | Y | Y | Y | Y | Y | Y |
| 3 Brown | Y | Y | ? | ? | ? | Y |
| 4 Crenshaw | ? | ? | Y | Y | Y | Y |
| 5 Brown-Waite | N | Y | + | + | + | Y |
| 6 Stearns | N | Y | Y | Y | Y | Y |
| 7 Mica | N | Y | Y | Y | Y | Y |
| 8 Keller | N | Y | Y | Y | Y | Y |
| 9 Bilirakis | N | Y | Y | Y | Y | Y |
| 10 Young | ? | ? | ? | ? | ? | Y |
| 11 Davis | Y | Y | Y | ? | ? | Y |
| 12 Putnam | N | Y | Y | Y | Y | Y |
| 13 Harris | N | Y | Y | Y | Y | Y |
| 14 Mack | N | Y | Y | Y | Y | Y |
| 15 Weldon | ? | ? | + | + | + | + |
| 16 Foley | N | Y | Y | Y | Y | Y |
| 17 Meek | Y | Y | Y | Y | Y | Y |
| 18 Ros-Lehtinen | Y | Y | Y | Y | Y | Y |
| 19 Wexler | ? | ? | Y | Y | Y | Y |
| 20 Wasserman-Schultz | Y | Y | Y | Y | Y | Y |
| 21 Diaz-Balart, L. | N | Y | Y | Y | Y | Y |
| 22 Shaw | N | Y | Y | Y | Y | Y |
| 23 Hastings | ? | ? | Y | Y | N | Y |
| 24 Feeney | N | Y | ? | ? | ? | ? |
| 25 Diaz-Balart, M. | N | Y | ? | ? | ? | Y |
| **GEORGIA** | | | | | | |
| 1 Kingston | ? | ? | Y | Y | Y | Y |
| 2 Bishop | Y | Y | Y | Y | Y | Y |
| 3 Marshall | Y | Y | Y | Y | Y | Y |
| 4 McKinney | Y | Y | Y | Y | Y | Y |
| 5 Lewis | Y | Y | Y | Y | N | Y |
| 6 Price | N | Y | Y | Y | Y | Y |
| 7 Linder | – | + | + | + | + | Y |
| 8 Westmoreland | ? | ? | Y | Y | Y | Y |
| 9 Norwood | N | Y | Y | Y | Y | Y |
| 10 Deal | N | Y | Y | Y | Y | Y |
| 11 Gingrey | N | Y | Y | Y | Y | Y |
| 12 Barrow | Y | Y | Y | Y | Y | Y |
| 13 Scott | Y | Y | Y | Y | Y | Y |
| **HAWAII** | | | | | | |
| 1 Abercrombie | Y | Y | Y | Y | N | Y |
| 2 Case | Y | Y | Y | Y | Y | Y |
| **IDAHO** | | | | | | |
| 1 Otter | N | Y | Y | Y | Y | Y |
| 2 Simpson | N | Y | Y | Y | Y | Y |
| **ILLINOIS** | | | | | | |
| 1 Rush | Y | Y | ? | ? | ? | Y |
| 2 Jackson | Y | Y | Y | Y | Y | Y |
| 3 Lipinski | Y | Y | Y | Y | Y | Y |
| 4 Gutierrez | + | + | + | + | + | Y |
| 5 Emanuel | Y | Y | Y | Y | Y | Y |
| 6 Hyde | N | Y | Y | Y | Y | Y |
| 7 Davis | Y | Y | Y | Y | Y | Y |
| 8 Bean | Y | Y | ? | ? | ? | Y |
| 9 Schakowsky | Y | Y | Y | Y | Y | Y |
| 10 Kirk | N | Y | + | Y | Y | Y |
| 11 Weller | N | Y | Y | Y | Y | Y |
| 12 Costello | Y | Y | Y | Y | ? | Y |

**KEY**    **Republicans**    Democrats    *Independents*

| | | | |
|---|---|---|---|
| Y | Voted for (yea) | X | Paired against | C | Voted "present" to avoid possible conflict of interest |
| # | Paired for | – | Announced against | |
| + | Announced for | P | Voted "present" | ? | Did not vote or otherwise make a position known |
| N | Voted against (nay) | | | |

ND Northern Democrats, SD Southern Democrats
Southern states: Ala., Ark., Fla., Ga., Ky., La., Miss., N.C., Okla., S.C., Tenn., Texas, Va.

**H-128**   2005 CQ ALMANAC | www.cq.com

| | 415 | 416 | 417 | 418 | 419 | 420 |
|---|---|---|---|---|---|---|
| 13 **Biggert** | N | Y | Y | Y | Y | Y |
| 14 **Hastert** | | | | | | |
| 15 **Johnson** | N | Y | Y | Y | Y | Y |
| 16 **Manzullo** | N | Y | Y | Y | Y | Y |
| 17 Evans | Y | Y | Y | Y | Y | Y |
| 18 **LaHood** | N | Y | Y | Y | Y | Y |
| 19 **Shimkus** | N | Y | Y | Y | Y | Y |
| **INDIANA** | | | | | | |
| 1 Visclosky | Y | Y | Y | Y | Y | Y |
| 2 **Chocola** | N | Y | Y | Y | Y | Y |
| 3 **Souder** | N | Y | ? | ? | ? | Y |
| 4 **Buyer** | N | Y | ? | ? | ? | Y |
| 5 **Burton** | N | Y | Y | Y | Y | Y |
| 6 **Pence** | N | Y | Y | Y | Y | Y |
| 7 Carson | Y | Y | Y | Y | Y | Y |
| 8 **Hostettler** | N | Y | ? | ? | ? | Y |
| 9 **Sodrel** | N | Y | ? | ? | ? | Y |
| **IOWA** | | | | | | |
| 1 **Nussle** | ? | ? | ? | ? | ? | Y |
| 2 **Leach** | N | Y | Y | Y | Y | Y |
| 3 Boswell | Y | Y | Y | Y | Y | Y |
| 4 **Latham** | N | Y | Y | Y | Y | Y |
| 5 **King** | N | Y | Y | Y | Y | Y |
| **KANSAS** | | | | | | |
| 1 **Moran** | N | Y | Y | Y | Y | Y |
| 2 **Ryun** | N | Y | Y | Y | Y | Y |
| 3 Moore | Y | Y | Y | Y | Y | Y |
| 4 **Tiahrt** | N | Y | Y | Y | Y | Y |
| **KENTUCKY** | | | | | | |
| 1 **Whitfield** | N | Y | Y | Y | Y | Y |
| 2 **Lewis** | N | Y | Y | Y | Y | Y |
| 3 **Northup** | N | Y | Y | Y | Y | Y |
| 4 **Davis** | N | Y | Y | Y | Y | Y |
| 5 **Rogers** | N | Y | Y | Y | Y | Y |
| 6 Chandler | Y | Y | Y | Y | Y | Y |
| **LOUISIANA** | | | | | | |
| 1 **Jindal** | Y | Y | Y | Y | Y | Y |
| 2 Jefferson | ? | ? | Y | Y | ? | Y |
| 3 Melancon | Y | Y | Y | Y | Y | Y |
| 4 **McCrery** | Y | Y | Y | Y | Y | Y |
| 5 **Alexander** | N | Y | Y | Y | Y | Y |
| 6 **Baker** | N | ? | Y | Y | Y | Y |
| 7 **Boustany** | Y | Y | Y | Y | Y | Y |
| **MAINE** | | | | | | |
| 1 Allen | Y | Y | Y | Y | Y | Y |
| 2 Michaud | Y | Y | Y | Y | Y | Y |
| **MARYLAND** | | | | | | |
| 1 **Gilchrest** | N | Y | Y | Y | Y | Y |
| 2 Ruppersberger | Y | Y | Y | Y | Y | Y |
| 3 Cardin | Y | Y | Y | Y | Y | Y |
| 4 Wynn | Y | Y | Y | Y | Y | Y |
| 5 Hoyer | Y | Y | Y | Y | Y | Y |
| 6 **Bartlett** | N | Y | Y | Y | Y | Y |
| 7 Cummings | Y | Y | Y | Y | Y | Y |
| 8 Van Hollen | Y | Y | Y | Y | Y | Y |
| **MASSACHUSETTS** | | | | | | |
| 1 Olver | Y | N | Y | Y | Y | Y |
| 2 Neal | Y | Y | ? | Y | Y | Y |
| 3 McGovern | Y | Y | Y | Y | Y | Y |
| 4 Frank | Y | N | Y | Y | N | Y |
| 5 Meehan | Y | N | Y | Y | Y | Y |
| 6 Tierney | Y | N | Y | Y | Y | Y |
| 7 Markey | Y | Y | Y | Y | Y | Y |
| 8 Capuano | Y | Y | Y | Y | Y | Y |
| 9 Lynch | Y | Y | Y | Y | Y | Y |
| 10 Delahunt | ? | ? | ? | ? | ? | Y |
| **MICHIGAN** | | | | | | |
| 1 Stupak | Y | Y | Y | Y | Y | Y |
| 2 **Hoekstra** | N | Y | Y | Y | Y | Y |
| 3 **Ehlers** | N | Y | Y | Y | Y | Y |
| 4 **Camp** | N | Y | Y | Y | Y | Y |
| 5 Kildee | Y | Y | Y | Y | Y | Y |
| 6 **Upton** | N | Y | Y | Y | Y | Y |
| 7 **Schwarz** | N | Y | Y | Y | Y | Y |
| 8 **Rogers** | N | Y | Y | Y | Y | Y |
| 9 **Knollenberg** | N | Y | Y | Y | Y | Y |
| 10 **Miller** | N | Y | ? | ? | ? | Y |
| 11 **McCotter** | N | Y | Y | Y | Y | Y |
| 12 Levin | Y | Y | Y | Y | Y | Y |
| 13 Kilpatrick | Y | Y | + | + | + | Y |
| 14 Conyers | Y | N | Y | Y | N | Y |
| 15 Dingell | Y | N | Y | Y | Y | Y |

| | 415 | 416 | 417 | 418 | 419 | 420 |
|---|---|---|---|---|---|---|
| **MINNESOTA** | | | | | | |
| 1 **Gutknecht** | N | Y | Y | Y | Y | Y |
| 2 **Kline** | N | Y | Y | Y | Y | Y |
| 3 **Ramstad** | N | Y | Y | Y | Y | Y |
| 4 McCollum | Y | Y | Y | Y | Y | Y |
| 5 Sabo | Y | N | Y | Y | Y | Y |
| 6 **Kennedy** | N | Y | Y | Y | Y | Y |
| 7 Peterson | Y | Y | Y | Y | Y | Y |
| 8 Oberstar | Y | N | Y | Y | Y | Y |
| **MISSISSIPPI** | | | | | | |
| 1 **Wicker** | N | Y | Y | Y | Y | Y |
| 2 Thompson | Y | Y | Y | Y | Y | Y |
| 3 **Pickering** | ? | ? | Y | Y | Y | Y |
| 4 Taylor | ? | ? | Y | Y | Y | Y |
| **MISSOURI** | | | | | | |
| 1 Clay | ? | ? | ? | ? | ? | Y |
| 2 **Akin** | N | Y | Y | Y | Y | Y |
| 3 Carnahan | Y | Y | Y | Y | Y | Y |
| 4 Skelton | Y | Y | Y | Y | Y | Y |
| 5 Cleaver | Y | Y | Y | Y | Y | Y |
| 6 **Graves** | N | Y | Y | Y | Y | Y |
| 7 **Blunt** | N | Y | Y | Y | Y | Y |
| 8 **Emerson** | N | Y | Y | Y | Y | Y |
| 9 **Hulshof** | N | Y | ? | ? | ? | Y |
| **MONTANA** | | | | | | |
| AL **Rehberg** | N | Y | Y | Y | Y | Y |
| **NEBRASKA** | | | | | | |
| 1 **Fortenberry** | N | Y | Y | Y | Y | Y |
| 2 **Terry** | N | Y | ? | ? | ? | Y |
| 3 **Osborne** | N | Y | Y | Y | Y | Y |
| **NEVADA** | | | | | | |
| 1 Berkley | Y | Y | Y | Y | N | Y |
| 2 **Gibbons** | N | Y | ? | ? | ? | ? |
| 3 **Porter** | N | Y | Y | Y | Y | Y |
| **NEW HAMPSHIRE** | | | | | | |
| 1 **Bradley** | N | Y | Y | Y | Y | Y |
| 2 **Bass** | N | Y | Y | Y | Y | Y |
| **NEW JERSEY** | | | | | | |
| 1 Andrews | Y | Y | Y | Y | Y | Y |
| 2 **LoBiondo** | N | Y | Y | Y | Y | Y |
| 3 **Saxton** | N | Y | Y | Y | Y | Y |
| 4 **Smith** | N | Y | Y | Y | Y | Y |
| 5 **Garrett** | N | Y | Y | Y | Y | Y |
| 6 Pallone | Y | Y | Y | Y | Y | Y |
| 7 **Ferguson** | N | Y | Y | Y | Y | Y |
| 8 Pascrell | Y | Y | Y | Y | Y | Y |
| 9 Rothman | Y | Y | ? | ? | ? | Y |
| 10 Payne | Y | Y | Y | Y | N | ? |
| 11 **Frelinghuysen** | N | Y | Y | Y | Y | Y |
| 12 Holt | + | Y | Y | Y | Y | Y |
| 13 Menendez | Y | Y | Y | Y | Y | Y |
| **NEW MEXICO** | | | | | | |
| 1 **Wilson** | N | Y | Y | Y | Y | Y |
| 2 **Pearce** | ? | Y | Y | Y | Y | Y |
| 3 Udall | Y | Y | Y | Y | Y | Y |
| **NEW YORK** | | | | | | |
| 1 Bishop | Y | Y | Y | Y | Y | Y |
| 2 Israel | Y | Y | Y | Y | Y | Y |
| 3 **King** | N | Y | ? | ? | ? | Y |
| 4 McCarthy | Y | Y | Y | Y | Y | Y |
| 5 Ackerman | Y | Y | Y | Y | Y | Y |
| 6 Meeks | Y | Y | Y | Y | Y | Y |
| 7 Crowley | Y | Y | Y | Y | Y | Y |
| 8 Nadler | Y | Y | Y | Y | Y | Y |
| 9 Weiner | Y | Y | Y | Y | Y | Y |
| 10 Towns | Y | Y | Y | Y | N | Y |
| 11 Owens | Y | Y | Y | Y | N | Y |
| 12 Velázquez | Y | Y | Y | Y | N | Y |
| 13 **Fossella** | N | Y | ? | ? | ? | Y |
| 14 Maloney | Y | Y | Y | Y | Y | Y |
| 15 Rangel | Y | Y | Y | Y | Y | Y |
| 16 Serrano | Y | Y | Y | Y | N | Y |
| 17 Engel | Y | Y | Y | Y | Y | Y |
| 18 Lowey | Y | Y | Y | Y | Y | Y |
| 19 **Kelly** | N | Y | Y | Y | Y | Y |
| 20 **Sweeney** | N | Y | ? | ? | ? | Y |
| 21 McNulty | Y | Y | Y | Y | Y | Y |
| 22 Hinchey | Y | Y | Y | Y | Y | Y |
| 23 **McHugh** | N | Y | Y | Y | Y | Y |
| 24 **Boehlert** | N | Y | Y | Y | Y | Y |
| 25 **Walsh** | Y | Y | Y | Y | Y | Y |
| 26 **Reynolds** | ? | Y | Y | Y | Y | Y |
| 27 Higgins | Y | Y | Y | Y | Y | Y |
| 28 Slaughter | Y | Y | Y | Y | Y | Y |
| 29 **Kuhl** | N | Y | Y | Y | Y | Y |

| | 415 | 416 | 417 | 418 | 419 | 420 |
|---|---|---|---|---|---|---|
| **NORTH CAROLINA** | | | | | | |
| 1 Butterfield | Y | Y | Y | Y | Y | Y |
| 2 Etheridge | Y | Y | Y | Y | Y | Y |
| 3 **Jones** | N | Y | Y | Y | Y | Y |
| 4 Price | Y | Y | Y | Y | Y | Y |
| 5 **Foxx** | N | Y | Y | Y | Y | Y |
| 6 **Coble** | N | Y | Y | Y | Y | Y |
| 7 McIntyre | Y | Y | Y | Y | Y | Y |
| 8 **Hayes** | N | Y | Y | Y | Y | Y |
| 9 **Myrick** | – | + | Y | Y | Y | Y |
| 10 **McHenry** | N | Y | Y | Y | Y | Y |
| 11 **Taylor** | – | + | Y | Y | Y | Y |
| 12 Watt | Y | Y | Y | Y | P | Y |
| 13 Miller | Y | Y | Y | Y | Y | Y |
| **NORTH DAKOTA** | | | | | | |
| AL Pomeroy | Y | Y | Y | Y | Y | Y |
| **OHIO** | | | | | | |
| 1 **Chabot** | N | Y | Y | Y | Y | Y |
| 2 Vacant | | | | | | |
| 3 **Turner** | N | Y | Y | Y | Y | Y |
| 4 **Oxley** | N | Y | Y | Y | Y | Y |
| 5 **Gillmor** | N | Y | Y | Y | Y | Y |
| 6 Strickland | Y | Y | ? | ? | ? | Y |
| 7 **Hobson** | N | Y | ? | ? | ? | Y |
| 8 **Boehner** | N | Y | Y | Y | Y | Y |
| 9 Kaptur | Y | Y | Y | Y | Y | Y |
| 10 Kucinich | Y | Y | Y | Y | Y | Y |
| 11 Jones | Y | Y | Y | Y | N | Y |
| 12 **Tiberi** | N | Y | + | + | + | Y |
| 13 Brown | Y | Y | Y | Y | Y | Y |
| 14 **LaTourette** | N | Y | Y | Y | Y | Y |
| 15 **Pryce** | N | Y | ? | ? | ? | Y |
| 16 **Regula** | N | Y | Y | Y | Y | Y |
| 17 Ryan | Y | Y | Y | Y | Y | Y |
| 18 **Ney** | Y | Y | Y | Y | Y | Y |
| **OKLAHOMA** | | | | | | |
| 1 **Sullivan** | N | Y | Y | Y | Y | Y |
| 2 Boren | ? | ? | Y | Y | Y | Y |
| 3 **Lucas** | N | Y | Y | Y | Y | Y |
| 4 **Cole** | N | Y | + | + | + | Y |
| 5 **Istook** | N | Y | ? | ? | ? | Y |
| **OREGON** | | | | | | |
| 1 Wu | Y | Y | Y | Y | Y | Y |
| 2 **Walden** | N | Y | Y | Y | Y | Y |
| 3 Blumenauer | Y | Y | Y | Y | N | Y |
| 4 DeFazio | Y | N | Y | Y | Y | Y |
| 5 Hooley | Y | Y | Y | Y | Y | Y |
| **PENNSYLVANIA** | | | | | | |
| 1 Brady | Y | Y | Y | Y | Y | Y |
| 2 Fattah | Y | Y | ? | ? | ? | Y |
| 3 **English** | N | Y | Y | Y | Y | Y |
| 4 **Hart** | N | Y | Y | Y | Y | Y |
| 5 **Peterson** | N | Y | Y | Y | Y | Y |
| 6 **Gerlach** | N | Y | Y | Y | Y | Y |
| 7 **Weldon** | N | Y | ? | ? | ? | Y |
| 8 **Fitzpatrick** | N | Y | Y | Y | Y | Y |
| 9 **Shuster** | N | Y | Y | Y | Y | Y |
| 10 **Sherwood** | N | Y | Y | Y | Y | Y |
| 11 Kanjorski | Y | Y | Y | Y | Y | Y |
| 12 Murtha | Y | Y | Y | Y | ? | Y |
| 13 Schwartz | Y | Y | Y | Y | Y | Y |
| 14 Doyle | Y | Y | Y | Y | Y | Y |
| 15 **Dent** | N | Y | Y | Y | Y | Y |
| 16 **Pitts** | N | Y | Y | Y | Y | Y |
| 17 Holden | Y | Y | Y | Y | Y | Y |
| 18 **Murphy** | N | Y | Y | Y | Y | Y |
| 19 **Platts** | N | Y | Y | Y | Y | Y |
| **RHODE ISLAND** | | | | | | |
| 1 Kennedy | Y | Y | Y | Y | Y | Y |
| 2 Langevin | Y | Y | Y | Y | Y | Y |
| **SOUTH CAROLINA** | | | | | | |
| 1 **Brown** | ? | ? | Y | Y | Y | Y |
| 2 **Wilson** | N | Y | Y | Y | Y | Y |
| 3 **Barrett** | N | Y | Y | Y | Y | Y |
| 4 **Inglis** | N | Y | Y | Y | Y | Y |
| 5 Spratt | Y | Y | Y | Y | Y | Y |
| 6 Clyburn | Y | Y | Y | Y | Y | Y |
| **SOUTH DAKOTA** | | | | | | |
| AL Herseth | Y | Y | Y | Y | Y | Y |
| **TENNESSEE** | | | | | | |
| 1 **Jenkins** | N | Y | ? | ? | ? | Y |
| 2 **Duncan** | N | Y | Y | Y | Y | Y |

| | 415 | 416 | 417 | 418 | 419 | 420 |
|---|---|---|---|---|---|---|
| 3 **Wamp** | N | Y | Y | Y | Y | Y |
| 4 Davis | Y | Y | Y | Y | Y | Y |
| 5 Cooper | + | + | + | + | Y | Y |
| 6 Gordon | N | Y | Y | Y | Y | Y |
| 7 **Blackburn** | N | N | Y | Y | Y | Y |
| 8 Tanner | N | Y | Y | Y | Y | Y |
| 9 Ford | Y | Y | ? | Y | Y | Y |
| **TEXAS** | | | | | | |
| 1 **Gohmert** | N | ? | Y | Y | Y | Y |
| 2 **Poe** | N | Y | Y | Y | Y | Y |
| 3 **Johnson, S.** | N | Y | Y | Y | Y | Y |
| 4 **Hall** | N | Y | Y | Y | Y | Y |
| 5 **Hensarling** | N | Y | Y | Y | Y | Y |
| 6 **Barton** | N | Y | Y | Y | Y | Y |
| 7 **Culberson** | N | Y | Y | Y | Y | Y |
| 8 **Brady** | ? | Y | Y | Y | Y | Y |
| 9 Green, A. | Y | Y | Y | Y | Y | Y |
| 10 **McCaul** | N | Y | Y | Y | Y | Y |
| 11 **Conaway** | N | Y | Y | Y | Y | Y |
| 12 **Granger** | N | Y | Y | Y | Y | Y |
| 13 **Thornberry** | N | Y | Y | Y | Y | Y |
| 14 **Paul** | N | ? | Y | N | N | Y |
| 15 Hinojosa | ? | ? | + | + | + | Y |
| 16 Reyes | Y | Y | ? | ? | ? | Y |
| 17 Edwards | Y | Y | Y | Y | Y | Y |
| 18 Jackson-Lee | Y | Y | Y | Y | Y | Y |
| 19 **Neugebauer** | N | Y | Y | Y | Y | Y |
| 20 Gonzalez | Y | Y | Y | Y | Y | Y |
| 21 **Smith** | N | Y | Y | Y | Y | Y |
| 22 **DeLay** | N | Y | Y | Y | Y | ? |
| 23 **Bonilla** | N | Y | Y | Y | Y | Y |
| 24 **Marchant** | N | Y | Y | Y | Y | Y |
| 25 Doggett | Y | Y | Y | Y | Y | Y |
| 26 **Burgess** | N | Y | Y | Y | Y | Y |
| 27 Ortiz | Y | Y | + | + | + | Y |
| 28 Cuellar | Y | Y | Y | Y | Y | Y |
| 29 Green, G. | Y | Y | Y | Y | Y | Y |
| 30 Johnson, E. | Y | Y | Y | Y | N | Y |
| 31 **Carter** | N | Y | Y | Y | Y | Y |
| 32 **Sessions** | N | Y | Y | Y | Y | Y |
| **UTAH** | | | | | | |
| 1 **Bishop** | ? | ? | ? | ? | ? | Y |
| 2 Matheson | Y | Y | Y | Y | Y | Y |
| 3 **Cannon** | N | Y | ? | ? | ? | Y |
| **VERMONT** | | | | | | |
| AL *Sanders* | Y | N | Y | Y | Y | Y |
| **VIRGINIA** | | | | | | |
| 1 **Davis, J.** | N | Y | Y | Y | Y | Y |
| 2 **Drake** | N | Y | Y | Y | Y | Y |
| 3 Scott | Y | Y | Y | Y | Y | Y |
| 4 **Forbes** | Y | Y | Y | Y | Y | Y |
| 5 **Goode** | N | Y | Y | Y | Y | Y |
| 6 **Goodlatte** | N | Y | Y | Y | Y | Y |
| 7 **Cantor** | N | Y | Y | Y | Y | Y |
| 8 Moran | Y | Y | Y | Y | Y | ? |
| 9 Boucher | Y | Y | Y | Y | Y | Y |
| 10 **Wolf** | N | Y | Y | Y | Y | Y |
| 11 **Davis, T.** | N | Y | Y | Y | Y | Y |
| **WASHINGTON** | | | | | | |
| 1 Inslee | Y | ? | Y | Y | Y | Y |
| 2 Larsen | Y | Y | Y | Y | Y | Y |
| 3 Baird | Y | Y | Y | Y | Y | Y |
| 4 **Hastings** | N | Y | Y | Y | Y | Y |
| 5 **McMorris** | N | Y | Y | Y | Y | Y |
| 6 Dicks | Y | Y | Y | Y | Y | Y |
| 7 McDermott | Y | N | Y | Y | N | Y |
| 8 **Reichert** | N | Y | Y | Y | Y | Y |
| 9 Smith | Y | Y | Y | Y | Y | Y |
| **WEST VIRGINIA** | | | | | | |
| 1 Mollohan | Y | Y | Y | Y | Y | Y |
| 2 **Capito** | N | Y | Y | Y | Y | Y |
| 3 Rahall | Y | Y | + | + | + | Y |
| **WISCONSIN** | | | | | | |
| 1 **Ryan** | N | Y | Y | Y | Y | Y |
| 2 Baldwin | Y | Y | Y | Y | Y | Y |
| 3 Kind | Y | Y | Y | Y | Y | Y |
| 4 Moore | Y | Y | Y | Y | Y | Y |
| 5 **Sensenbrenner** | N | Y | Y | Y | Y | Y |
| 6 **Petri** | N | Y | Y | Y | Y | Y |
| 7 Obey | Y | N | Y | Y | ? | Y |
| 8 **Green** | N | Y | Y | Y | Y | Y |
| **WYOMING** | | | | | | |
| AL **Cubin** | ? | ? | Y | Y | Y | Y |

# IN THE HOUSE | By Vote Number

**421.** **HR 3283. China Trade Practices/Passage.** Thomas, R-Calif., motion to suspend the rules and pass the bill that would establish mechanisms to ensure that China abides by previous trade commitments, including creating a system to monitor compliance with trade obligations on intellectual property rights, market access for U.S. goods, services and agriculture and the accounting of Chinese subsidies. Motion rejected 240-186: R 221-5; D 19-180 (ND 10-139, SD 9-41); I 0-1. A two-thirds majority of those present and voting (284 in this case) is required for passage under suspension of the rules. July 26, 2005.

**422.** **HR 2361. Fiscal 2006 Interior-Environment Appropriations/Motion to Instruct.** Obey, D-Wis., motion to instruct House conferees to accept the Senate language providing an additional $1.5 billion for veterans' medical care in fiscal 2005. Motion agreed to 426-0: R 225-0; D 200-0 (ND 150-0, SD 50-0); I 1-0. July 26, 2005.

**423.** **HR 2977. Paul Kasten Post Office/Passage.** Issa, R-Calif., motion to suspend the rules and pass the bill to designate a post office in Brockway, Mont., for Paul Kasten, a postal carrier serving eastern Montana postal routes for more than 50 years. Motion agreed to 422-0: R 224-0; D 198-0 (ND 148-0, SD 50-0); I 0-0. A two-thirds majority of those present and voting (282 in this case) is required for passage under suspension of the rules. July 26, 2005.

**424.** **HR 525. Health Plans for Small Businesses/Democratic Substitute.** Kind, D-Wis., substitute amendment that would require the Labor Department to establish a Small Employer Health Benefits Plan and make all employers with fewer than 100 employees during the previous calendar year eligible for coverage. The Labor Department would contract annually with state-licensed health insurers to offer health insurance within a state, and participating insurers would remain subject to the laws of the state in which they cover residents. Rejected 197-230: R 1-225; D 195-5 (ND 147-3, SD 48-2); I 1-0. July 26, 2005.

**425.** **HR 525. Health Plans for Small Businesses/Recommit.** Miller, D-Calif., motion to recommit the bill to the Education and Workforce Committee with instructions to maintain state health coverage for pregnancy, childbirth, child care, breast and cervical cancer screening and tests recommended by a physician, mental illness, and diabetes. Motion rejected 198-230: R 0-227; D 197-3 (ND 147-3, SD 50-0); I 1-0. July 26, 2005.

**426.** **HR 525. Health Plans for Small Businesses/Passage.** Passage of the bill that would allow for the creation of association health plans through which small companies could band together to buy insurance for their employees. Association health plans that cover employees in multiple states would be exempt from many individual state insurance regulations but would be regulated by the Labor Department. Passed 263-165: R 227-0; D 36-164 (ND 18-132, SD 18-32); I 0-1. A "yea" was a vote in support of the president's position. July 26, 2005.

| | 421 | 422 | 423 | 424 | 425 | 426 |
|---|---|---|---|---|---|---|
| **ALABAMA** | | | | | | |
| 1 Bonner | Y | Y | Y | N | N | Y |
| 2 Everett | Y | Y | Y | N | N | Y |
| 3 Rogers | Y | Y | Y | N | N | Y |
| 4 Aderholt | Y | Y | Y | N | N | Y |
| 5 Cramer | ? | ? | ? | ? | ? | ? |
| 6 Bachus | Y | Y | Y | N | N | Y |
| 7 Davis | N | Y | Y | Y | Y | Y |
| **ALASKA** | | | | | | |
| AL Young | Y | Y | Y | N | N | Y |
| **ARIZONA** | | | | | | |
| 1 Renzi | Y | Y | Y | N | N | Y |
| 2 Franks | Y | Y | Y | N | N | Y |
| 3 Shadegg | Y | Y | Y | N | N | Y |
| 4 Pastor | N | Y | Y | Y | Y | N |
| 5 Hayworth | Y | Y | Y | N | N | Y |
| 6 Flake | N | Y | Y | N | N | Y |
| 7 Grijalva | N | Y | Y | Y | Y | N |
| 8 Kolbe | N | Y | Y | N | N | Y |
| **ARKANSAS** | | | | | | |
| 1 Berry | Y | Y | Y | Y | Y | N |
| 2 Snyder | N | Y | Y | Y | Y | N |
| 3 Boozman | Y | Y | Y | N | N | Y |
| 4 Ross | N | Y | Y | Y | Y | N |
| **CALIFORNIA** | | | | | | |
| 1 Thompson | N | Y | Y | Y | Y | N |
| 2 Herger | Y | Y | Y | N | N | Y |
| 3 Lungren | Y | Y | Y | N | N | Y |
| 4 Doolittle | Y | Y | Y | N | N | Y |
| 5 Matsui, D. | N | Y | Y | Y | Y | N |
| 6 Woolsey | N | Y | Y | Y | Y | N |
| 7 Miller, George | N | Y | Y | Y | Y | N |
| 8 Pelosi | N | Y | Y | Y | Y | N |
| 9 Lee | N | Y | Y | Y | Y | N |
| 10 Tauscher | N | Y | Y | Y | Y | N |
| 11 Pombo | Y | Y | Y | N | N | Y |
| 12 Lantos | N | Y | Y | Y | Y | N |
| 13 Stark | N | Y | Y | Y | Y | N |
| 14 Eshoo | N | Y | Y | Y | Y | N |
| 15 Honda | N | Y | Y | Y | Y | N |
| 16 Lofgren | N | Y | Y | Y | Y | N |
| 17 Farr | N | Y | Y | Y | Y | N |
| 18 Cardoza | N | Y | Y | Y | Y | N |
| 19 Radanovich | Y | Y | Y | N | N | Y |
| 20 Costa | N | Y | Y | Y | Y | N |
| 21 Nunes | Y | Y | Y | N | N | Y |
| 22 Thomas | Y | Y | Y | N | N | Y |
| 23 Capps | N | Y | Y | Y | Y | N |
| 24 Gallegly | Y | Y | Y | N | N | Y |
| 25 McKeon | Y | Y | Y | N | N | Y |
| 26 Dreier | Y | Y | Y | N | N | Y |
| 27 Sherman | N | Y | Y | Y | Y | N |
| 28 Berman | N | Y | Y | Y | Y | N |
| 29 Schiff | N | Y | Y | Y | Y | N |
| 30 Waxman | N | Y | Y | Y | ? | ? |
| 31 Becerra | N | Y | Y | Y | Y | N |
| 32 Solis | N | Y | Y | Y | Y | N |
| 33 Watson | N | Y | Y | Y | Y | N |
| 34 Roybal-Allard | N | Y | Y | Y | Y | N |
| 35 Waters | N | Y | Y | Y | Y | N |
| 36 Harman | Y | Y | Y | Y | Y | N |
| 37 Millender-McD. | N | Y | Y | Y | Y | N |
| 38 Napolitano | N | Y | Y | Y | Y | N |
| 39 Sánchez, Linda | N | Y | Y | Y | Y | N |
| 40 Royce | Y | Y | Y | N | N | Y |
| 41 Lewis | Y | Y | Y | N | N | Y |
| 42 Miller, Gary | Y | Y | Y | N | N | Y |
| 43 Baca | N | Y | Y | Y | Y | N |
| 44 Calvert | Y | Y | Y | N | N | Y |
| 45 Bono | Y | Y | Y | N | N | Y |
| 46 Rohrabacher | Y | Y | Y | N | N | Y |
| 47 Sanchez, Loretta | N | Y | Y | Y | Y | N |
| 48 Cox | ? | ? | ? | N | N | Y |
| 49 Issa | Y | Y | Y | N | N | Y |

| | 421 | 422 | 423 | 424 | 425 | 426 |
|---|---|---|---|---|---|---|
| 50 Cunningham | Y | Y | Y | N | N | Y |
| 51 Filner | N | Y | Y | Y | Y | N |
| 52 Hunter | Y | Y | Y | N | N | Y |
| 53 Davis | N | Y | Y | Y | Y | N |
| **COLORADO** | | | | | | |
| 1 DeGette | N | Y | Y | Y | Y | N |
| 2 Udall | N | Y | Y | Y | Y | N |
| 3 Salazar | N | Y | Y | Y | Y | Y |
| 4 Musgrave | Y | Y | Y | N | N | Y |
| 5 Hefley | Y | Y | Y | N | N | Y |
| 6 Tancredo | Y | Y | Y | N | N | Y |
| 7 Beauprez | Y | Y | Y | N | N | Y |
| **CONNECTICUT** | | | | | | |
| 1 Larson | N | Y | Y | Y | Y | N |
| 2 Simmons | Y | Y | Y | N | N | Y |
| 3 DeLauro | N | Y | Y | Y | Y | N |
| 4 Shays | Y | Y | Y | N | N | Y |
| 5 Johnson | Y | Y | Y | N | N | Y |
| **DELAWARE** | | | | | | |
| AL Castle | Y | Y | Y | N | N | Y |
| **FLORIDA** | | | | | | |
| 1 Miller | Y | Y | Y | N | N | Y |
| 2 Boyd | N | Y | Y | Y | Y | N |
| 3 Brown | N | Y | Y | Y | Y | N |
| 4 Crenshaw | Y | Y | Y | N | N | Y |
| 5 Brown-Waite | Y | Y | Y | N | N | Y |
| 6 Stearns | Y | ? | Y | N | N | Y |
| 7 Mica | Y | Y | Y | N | N | Y |
| 8 Keller | Y | Y | Y | N | N | Y |
| 9 Bilirakis | Y | Y | Y | N | N | Y |
| 10 Young | Y | Y | Y | N | N | Y |
| 11 Davis | N | Y | Y | Y | Y | N |
| 12 Putnam | Y | Y | Y | N | N | Y |
| 13 Harris | Y | Y | Y | N | N | Y |
| 14 Mack | Y | Y | Y | N | N | Y |
| 15 Weldon | + | + | + | N | N | Y |
| 16 Foley | Y | Y | Y | N | N | Y |
| 17 Meek | N | Y | Y | Y | Y | N |
| 18 Ros-Lehtinen | Y | Y | Y | N | N | Y |
| 19 Wexler | N | Y | Y | Y | Y | N |
| 20 Wasserman-Schultz | N | Y | Y | Y | Y | N |
| 21 Diaz-Balart, L. | Y | Y | Y | N | N | Y |
| 22 Shaw | Y | Y | Y | N | N | Y |
| 23 Hastings | N | Y | Y | Y | Y | N |
| 24 Feeney | ? | ? | ? | ? | ? | ? |
| 25 Diaz-Balart, M. | Y | Y | Y | N | N | Y |
| **GEORGIA** | | | | | | |
| 1 Kingston | Y | Y | Y | N | N | Y |
| 2 Bishop | N | Y | Y | Y | Y | Y |
| 3 Marshall | N | Y | Y | Y | Y | Y |
| 4 McKinney | N | Y | Y | Y | Y | N |
| 5 Lewis | N | Y | Y | Y | Y | N |
| 6 Price | Y | Y | Y | N | N | Y |
| 7 Linder | Y | Y | Y | N | N | Y |
| 8 Westmoreland | Y | Y | Y | ? | N | Y |
| 9 Norwood | Y | Y | Y | N | N | Y |
| 10 Deal | Y | Y | Y | N | N | Y |
| 11 Gingrey | Y | Y | Y | N | N | Y |
| 12 Barrow | Y | Y | Y | Y | Y | N |
| 13 Scott | N | Y | Y | Y | Y | N |
| **HAWAII** | | | | | | |
| 1 Abercrombie | N | Y | Y | Y | Y | N |
| 2 Case | N | Y | Y | Y | Y | Y |
| **IDAHO** | | | | | | |
| 1 Otter | Y | Y | Y | N | N | Y |
| 2 Simpson | Y | Y | Y | N | N | Y |
| **ILLINOIS** | | | | | | |
| 1 Rush | N | Y | Y | Y | Y | N |
| 2 Jackson | N | Y | Y | Y | Y | N |
| 3 Lipinski | N | Y | Y | Y | Y | N |
| 4 Gutierrez | N | Y | Y | Y | Y | N |
| 5 Emanuel | N | Y | Y | Y | Y | N |
| 6 Hyde | Y | Y | Y | N | N | Y |
| 7 Davis | N | Y | Y | Y | Y | N |
| 8 Bean | N | Y | Y | Y | Y | Y |
| 9 Schakowsky | N | Y | Y | Y | Y | N |
| 10 Kirk | Y | Y | Y | N | N | Y |
| 11 Weller | Y | Y | Y | N | N | Y |
| 12 Costello | N | Y | Y | Y | Y | Y |

**KEY**    Republicans    Democrats    *Independents*

| | | |
|---|---|---|
| Y Voted for (yea) | X Paired against | C Voted "present" to avoid possible conflict of interest |
| # Paired for | – Announced against | |
| + Announced for | P Voted "present" | ? Did not vote or otherwise make a position known |
| N Voted against (nay) | | |

ND Northern Democrats, SD Southern Democrats
Southern states: Ala., Ark., Fla., Ga., Ky., La., Miss., N.C., Okla., S.C., Tenn., Texas, Va.

| | 421 | 422 | 423 | 424 | 425 | 426 |
|---|---|---|---|---|---|---|
| 13 **Biggert** | Y | Y | Y | N | N | Y |
| 14 **Hastert** | | | | | | |
| 15 **Johnson** | Y | Y | Y | N | N | Y |
| 16 **Manzullo** | Y | Y | Y | N | N | Y |
| 17 Evans | N | Y | Y | Y | N | N |
| 18 **LaHood** | Y | Y | Y | N | N | Y |
| 19 **Shimkus** | Y | Y | Y | N | N | Y |
| **INDIANA** | | | | | | |
| 1 Visclosky | N | Y | Y | Y | Y | N |
| 2 **Chocola** | Y | Y | Y | N | N | Y |
| 3 **Souder** | Y | Y | Y | N | N | Y |
| 4 **Buyer** | Y | Y | Y | N | N | Y |
| 5 **Burton** | Y | Y | Y | N | N | Y |
| 6 **Pence** | Y | Y | Y | N | N | Y |
| 7 Carson | N | Y | Y | Y | Y | N |
| 8 **Hostettler** | Y | Y | Y | N | N | Y |
| 9 **Sodrel** | Y | Y | Y | N | N | Y |
| **IOWA** | | | | | | |
| 1 **Nussle** | Y | Y | Y | N | N | Y |
| 2 **Leach** | Y | Y | Y | N | N | Y |
| 3 Boswell | Y | Y | Y | Y | Y | N |
| 4 **Latham** | Y | Y | Y | N | N | Y |
| 5 **King** | Y | Y | Y | N | N | Y |
| **KANSAS** | | | | | | |
| 1 **Moran** | Y | Y | Y | N | N | Y |
| 2 **Ryun** | Y | Y | Y | N | N | Y |
| 3 Moore | N | Y | Y | Y | Y | N |
| 4 **Tiahrt** | Y | Y | Y | N | N | Y |
| **KENTUCKY** | | | | | | |
| 1 **Whitfield** | Y | Y | Y | N | N | Y |
| 2 **Lewis** | Y | Y | Y | N | N | Y |
| 3 **Northup** | Y | Y | Y | N | N | Y |
| 4 **Davis** | Y | Y | Y | N | N | Y |
| 5 **Rogers** | Y | Y | Y | N | N | Y |
| 6 Chandler | N | Y | Y | Y | Y | N |
| **LOUISIANA** | | | | | | |
| 1 **Jindal** | Y | Y | Y | N | N | Y |
| 2 Jefferson | N | Y | Y | Y | Y | N |
| 3 Melancon | N | Y | Y | Y | Y | N |
| 4 **McCrery** | Y | Y | Y | N | N | Y |
| 5 **Alexander** | Y | Y | Y | N | N | Y |
| 6 **Baker** | Y | Y | Y | N | N | Y |
| 7 **Boustany** | Y | Y | Y | N | N | Y |
| **MAINE** | | | | | | |
| 1 Allen | N | Y | Y | Y | Y | N |
| 2 Michaud | N | Y | Y | Y | Y | N |
| **MARYLAND** | | | | | | |
| 1 **Gilchrest** | Y | Y | Y | N | N | Y |
| 2 Ruppersberger | N | Y | Y | Y | Y | N |
| 3 Cardin | N | Y | Y | Y | Y | N |
| 4 Wynn | N | Y | Y | N | N | Y |
| 5 Hoyer | N | Y | Y | Y | Y | N |
| 6 **Bartlett** | N | Y | Y | N | N | Y |
| 7 Cummings | N | Y | Y | Y | Y | N |
| 8 Van Hollen | N | Y | Y | Y | Y | N |
| **MASSACHUSETTS** | | | | | | |
| 1 Olver | N | Y | Y | Y | Y | N |
| 2 Neal | N | Y | Y | Y | Y | N |
| 3 McGovern | N | Y | Y | Y | Y | N |
| 4 Frank | N | Y | Y | Y | Y | N |
| 5 Meehan | N | Y | Y | Y | Y | N |
| 6 Tierney | N | Y | Y | Y | Y | N |
| 7 Markey | N | Y | Y | Y | Y | N |
| 8 Capuano | N | Y | Y | Y | Y | N |
| 9 Lynch | N | Y | Y | Y | Y | N |
| 10 Delahunt | N | Y | Y | Y | Y | N |
| **MICHIGAN** | | | | | | |
| 1 Stupak | N | Y | Y | Y | Y | N |
| 2 **Hoekstra** | Y | Y | Y | N | N | Y |
| 3 **Ehlers** | Y | Y | Y | N | N | Y |
| 4 **Camp** | Y | Y | Y | N | N | Y |
| 5 Kildee | N | Y | Y | Y | Y | N |
| 6 **Upton** | Y | Y | Y | N | N | Y |
| 7 **Schwarz** | Y | Y | Y | Y | N | Y |
| 8 **Rogers** | Y | Y | Y | N | N | Y |
| 9 **Knollenberg** | Y | Y | Y | N | N | Y |
| 10 **Miller** | Y | Y | Y | N | N | Y |
| 11 **McCotter** | Y | Y | Y | N | N | Y |
| 12 Levin | N | Y | Y | Y | Y | N |
| 13 Kilpatrick | N | Y | Y | Y | Y | N |
| 14 Conyers | N | Y | Y | Y | Y | N |
| 15 Dingell | N | Y | Y | Y | Y | N |

| | 421 | 422 | 423 | 424 | 425 | 426 |
|---|---|---|---|---|---|---|
| **MINNESOTA** | | | | | | |
| 1 **Gutknecht** | Y | Y | Y | N | N | Y |
| 2 **Kline** | Y | Y | Y | N | N | Y |
| 3 **Ramstad** | Y | Y | Y | N | N | Y |
| 4 McCollum | N | Y | Y | Y | Y | N |
| 5 Sabo | N | Y | Y | Y | Y | N |
| 6 **Kennedy** | Y | Y | Y | N | N | Y |
| 7 Peterson | ? | Y | Y | Y | Y | Y |
| 8 Oberstar | N | Y | ? | Y | Y | N |
| **MISSISSIPPI** | | | | | | |
| 1 **Wicker** | Y | Y | Y | N | N | Y |
| 2 Thompson | N | Y | Y | Y | Y | Y |
| 3 **Pickering** | Y | Y | Y | N | N | Y |
| 4 Taylor | Y | Y | Y | Y | Y | Y |
| **MISSOURI** | | | | | | |
| 1 Clay | N | Y | Y | Y | Y | N |
| 2 **Akin** | Y | Y | Y | N | N | Y |
| 3 Carnahan | N | Y | Y | Y | Y | N |
| 4 Skelton | Y | Y | Y | Y | Y | Y |
| 5 Cleaver | N | Y | Y | Y | Y | N |
| 6 **Graves** | Y | Y | Y | N | N | Y |
| 7 **Blunt** | Y | Y | Y | N | N | Y |
| 8 **Emerson** | Y | Y | Y | N | N | Y |
| 9 **Hulshof** | Y | Y | Y | N | N | Y |
| **MONTANA** | | | | | | |
| AL **Rehberg** | Y | Y | Y | N | N | Y |
| **NEBRASKA** | | | | | | |
| 1 **Fortenberry** | Y | Y | Y | N | N | Y |
| 2 **Terry** | Y | Y | Y | N | N | Y |
| 3 **Osborne** | Y | Y | Y | N | N | Y |
| **NEVADA** | | | | | | |
| 1 Berkley | N | Y | Y | Y | Y | N |
| 2 **Gibbons** | ? | ? | ? | ? | ? | ? |
| 3 **Porter** | Y | Y | Y | N | N | Y |
| **NEW HAMPSHIRE** | | | | | | |
| 1 **Bradley** | Y | Y | Y | N | N | Y |
| 2 **Bass** | Y | Y | Y | N | N | Y |
| **NEW JERSEY** | | | | | | |
| 1 Andrews | N | Y | Y | Y | Y | N |
| 2 **LoBiondo** | Y | Y | Y | N | N | Y |
| 3 **Saxton** | Y | Y | Y | N | N | Y |
| 4 **Smith** | Y | Y | Y | N | N | Y |
| 5 **Garrett** | Y | Y | Y | N | N | Y |
| 6 Pallone | N | Y | Y | Y | Y | N |
| 7 **Ferguson** | Y | Y | Y | N | N | Y |
| 8 Pascrell | N | Y | Y | Y | Y | N |
| 9 Rothman | N | Y | Y | Y | Y | N |
| 10 Payne | ? | ? | ? | Y | Y | N |
| 11 **Frelinghuysen** | Y | Y | Y | N | N | Y |
| 12 Holt | N | Y | Y | Y | Y | N |
| 13 Menendez | N | Y | Y | Y | Y | N |
| **NEW MEXICO** | | | | | | |
| 1 **Wilson** | Y | Y | Y | N | N | Y |
| 2 **Pearce** | Y | Y | Y | N | N | Y |
| 3 Udall | N | Y | Y | Y | Y | N |
| **NEW YORK** | | | | | | |
| 1 Bishop | N | Y | Y | Y | Y | N |
| 2 Israel | N | Y | Y | Y | Y | Y |
| 3 **King** | Y | Y | Y | N | N | Y |
| 4 McCarthy | N | Y | Y | Y | Y | N |
| 5 Ackerman | N | Y | Y | Y | Y | N |
| 6 Meeks | N | Y | Y | Y | Y | N |
| 7 Crowley | N | Y | Y | Y | Y | N |
| 8 Nadler | N | Y | Y | Y | Y | N |
| 9 Weiner | N | Y | Y | Y | Y | N |
| 10 Towns | Y | Y | Y | Y | Y | N |
| 11 Owens | N | Y | Y | ? | Y | N |
| 12 Velázquez | N | Y | Y | N | N | Y |
| 13 **Fossella** | Y | Y | Y | N | N | Y |
| 14 Maloney | N | Y | Y | Y | Y | N |
| 15 Rangel | N | Y | Y | Y | Y | N |
| 16 Serrano | N | Y | Y | Y | Y | N |
| 17 Engel | Y | Y | Y | Y | Y | N |
| 18 Lowey | N | Y | Y | Y | Y | N |
| 19 **Kelly** | Y | Y | Y | N | N | Y |
| 20 **Sweeney** | Y | Y | Y | N | N | Y |
| 21 McNulty | N | Y | Y | Y | Y | N |
| 22 Hinchey | N | Y | Y | Y | Y | N |
| 23 **McHugh** | Y | Y | Y | N | N | Y |
| 24 **Boehlert** | Y | Y | ? | N | N | Y |
| 25 **Walsh** | Y | Y | Y | N | N | Y |
| 26 **Reynolds** | Y | Y | Y | N | N | Y |
| 27 Higgins | N | Y | Y | Y | Y | N |
| 28 Slaughter | N | Y | Y | Y | Y | N |
| 29 **Kuhl** | Y | Y | Y | N | N | Y |

| | 421 | 422 | 423 | 424 | 425 | 426 |
|---|---|---|---|---|---|---|
| **NORTH CAROLINA** | | | | | | |
| 1 Butterfield | N | Y | Y | Y | Y | N |
| 2 Etheridge | Y | Y | Y | Y | Y | N |
| 3 **Jones** | Y | Y | Y | N | N | Y |
| 4 Price | N | Y | Y | Y | Y | N |
| 5 **Foxx** | Y | Y | Y | N | N | Y |
| 6 **Coble** | Y | Y | Y | N | N | Y |
| 7 McIntyre | Y | Y | Y | N | Y | Y |
| 8 **Hayes** | Y | Y | Y | N | N | Y |
| 9 **Myrick** | Y | Y | Y | N | N | Y |
| 10 **McHenry** | Y | Y | Y | N | N | Y |
| 11 **Taylor** | Y | Y | Y | N | N | Y |
| 12 Watt | N | Y | Y | Y | Y | N |
| 13 Miller | N | Y | Y | Y | Y | N |
| **NORTH DAKOTA** | | | | | | |
| AL Pomeroy | N | Y | Y | Y | Y | N |
| **OHIO** | | | | | | |
| 1 **Chabot** | Y | Y | Y | N | N | Y |
| 2 Vacant | | | | | | |
| 3 **Turner** | Y | Y | Y | N | N | Y |
| 4 **Oxley** | Y | Y | Y | ? | ? | ? |
| 5 **Gillmor** | Y | Y | ? | N | N | Y |
| 6 Strickland | N | Y | Y | Y | Y | N |
| 7 **Hobson** | Y | Y | Y | N | N | Y |
| 8 **Boehner** | Y | Y | Y | N | N | Y |
| 9 Kaptur | N | Y | Y | Y | Y | N |
| 10 Kucinich | N | Y | Y | Y | Y | N |
| 11 Jones | N | Y | Y | Y | Y | N |
| 12 **Tiberi** | Y | Y | Y | N | N | Y |
| 13 Brown | N | Y | Y | Y | Y | N |
| 14 **LaTourette** | Y | Y | Y | N | N | Y |
| 15 **Pryce** | Y | Y | Y | N | N | Y |
| 16 **Regula** | Y | Y | Y | N | N | Y |
| 17 Ryan | N | Y | Y | Y | Y | N |
| 18 **Ney** | Y | Y | Y | N | N | Y |
| **OKLAHOMA** | | | | | | |
| 1 **Sullivan** | Y | Y | Y | N | N | Y |
| 2 Boren | Y | Y | Y | N | Y | Y |
| 3 **Lucas** | Y | Y | Y | N | N | Y |
| 4 **Cole** | Y | Y | Y | N | N | Y |
| 5 **Istook** | Y | Y | Y | N | N | Y |
| **OREGON** | | | | | | |
| 1 Wu | N | Y | Y | Y | Y | N |
| 2 **Walden** | Y | Y | Y | N | N | Y |
| 3 Blumenauer | N | Y | Y | Y | Y | N |
| 4 DeFazio | N | Y | Y | Y | Y | N |
| 5 Hooley | N | Y | Y | Y | Y | N |
| **PENNSYLVANIA** | | | | | | |
| 1 Brady | N | Y | Y | Y | Y | N |
| 2 Fattah | N | Y | Y | Y | Y | N |
| 3 **English** | Y | Y | Y | N | N | Y |
| 4 **Hart** | Y | Y | Y | N | N | Y |
| 5 **Peterson** | Y | Y | Y | N | N | Y |
| 6 **Gerlach** | Y | Y | Y | N | N | Y |
| 7 **Weldon** | Y | Y | Y | N | N | Y |
| 8 **Fitzpatrick** | Y | Y | Y | N | N | Y |
| 9 **Shuster** | Y | Y | Y | N | N | Y |
| 10 **Sherwood** | Y | Y | Y | N | N | Y |
| 11 Kanjorski | N | Y | Y | Y | Y | N |
| 12 Murtha | N | Y | Y | Y | Y | N |
| 13 Schwartz | N | Y | Y | Y | Y | N |
| 14 Doyle | N | Y | Y | Y | Y | N |
| 15 **Dent** | Y | Y | Y | N | N | Y |
| 16 **Pitts** | Y | Y | Y | N | N | Y |
| 17 Holden | N | Y | Y | Y | Y | N |
| 18 **Murphy** | Y | Y | Y | N | N | Y |
| 19 **Platts** | Y | Y | Y | N | N | Y |
| **RHODE ISLAND** | | | | | | |
| 1 Kennedy | N | Y | Y | Y | Y | N |
| 2 Langevin | N | Y | Y | Y | Y | N |
| **SOUTH CAROLINA** | | | | | | |
| 1 **Brown** | Y | Y | Y | N | N | Y |
| 2 **Wilson** | Y | Y | Y | N | N | Y |
| 3 **Barrett** | Y | Y | Y | N | N | Y |
| 4 **Inglis** | Y | Y | Y | N | N | Y |
| 5 Spratt | N | Y | Y | Y | Y | N |
| 6 Clyburn | N | Y | Y | Y | Y | N |
| **SOUTH DAKOTA** | | | | | | |
| AL Herseth | Y | Y | Y | Y | Y | Y |
| **TENNESSEE** | | | | | | |
| 1 **Jenkins** | Y | Y | Y | N | N | Y |
| 2 **Duncan** | Y | Y | Y | N | N | Y |

| | 421 | 422 | 423 | 424 | 425 | 426 |
|---|---|---|---|---|---|---|
| 3 **Wamp** | Y | Y | Y | N | N | Y |
| 4 Davis | N | Y | Y | Y | Y | Y |
| 5 Cooper | N | Y | Y | Y | Y | Y |
| 6 Gordon | Y | Y | Y | Y | Y | Y |
| 7 **Blackburn** | Y | Y | Y | N | N | Y |
| 8 Tanner | Y | Y | Y | Y | Y | N |
| 9 Ford | N | Y | Y | Y | Y | Y |
| **TEXAS** | | | | | | |
| 1 **Gohmert** | Y | Y | Y | N | N | Y |
| 2 **Poe** | Y | Y | Y | N | N | Y |
| 3 **Johnson, S.** | Y | Y | Y | N | N | Y |
| 4 **Hall** | Y | Y | Y | N | N | Y |
| 5 **Hensarling** | Y | Y | Y | N | N | Y |
| 6 **Barton** | Y | Y | Y | N | N | Y |
| 7 **Culberson** | Y | Y | Y | N | N | Y |
| 8 **Brady** | Y | Y | Y | N | N | Y |
| 9 Green, A. | N | Y | Y | Y | Y | N |
| 10 **McCaul** | Y | Y | Y | N | N | Y |
| 11 **Conaway** | Y | Y | Y | N | N | Y |
| 12 **Granger** | Y | Y | Y | N | N | Y |
| 13 **Thornberry** | Y | Y | Y | N | N | Y |
| 14 **Paul** | N | Y | Y | N | N | Y |
| 15 Hinojosa | N | Y | Y | Y | Y | N |
| 16 Reyes | N | Y | Y | Y | Y | N |
| 17 Edwards | N | Y | Y | Y | Y | Y |
| 18 Jackson-Lee | N | Y | Y | Y | Y | Y |
| 19 **Neugebauer** | Y | Y | Y | N | N | Y |
| 20 Gonzalez | N | Y | Y | Y | Y | Y |
| 21 **Smith** | Y | Y | Y | N | N | Y |
| 22 **DeLay** | Y | Y | Y | N | N | Y |
| 23 **Bonilla** | Y | Y | Y | N | N | Y |
| 24 **Marchant** | Y | Y | Y | N | N | Y |
| 25 Doggett | N | Y | Y | Y | Y | N |
| 26 **Burgess** | Y | Y | Y | N | N | Y |
| 27 Ortiz | N | Y | Y | Y | Y | Y |
| 28 Cuellar | Y | Y | Y | Y | Y | Y |
| 29 Green, G. | N | Y | Y | Y | Y | N |
| 30 Johnson, E. | N | Y | Y | Y | Y | N |
| 31 **Carter** | Y | Y | Y | N | N | Y |
| 32 **Sessions** | Y | Y | Y | N | N | Y |
| **UTAH** | | | | | | |
| 1 **Bishop** | Y | Y | Y | N | N | Y |
| 2 Matheson | Y | Y | Y | Y | Y | Y |
| 3 **Cannon** | Y | Y | Y | N | N | Y |
| **VERMONT** | | | | | | |
| AL *Sanders* | N | Y | ? | Y | Y | N |
| **VIRGINIA** | | | | | | |
| 1 **Davis, J.** | Y | Y | Y | N | N | Y |
| 2 **Drake** | Y | Y | Y | N | N | Y |
| 3 Scott | N | Y | Y | Y | Y | N |
| 4 **Forbes** | Y | Y | Y | N | N | Y |
| 5 **Goode** | Y | Y | Y | N | N | Y |
| 6 **Goodlatte** | Y | Y | Y | N | N | Y |
| 7 **Cantor** | Y | Y | Y | N | N | Y |
| 8 Moran | N | Y | Y | Y | Y | Y |
| 9 Boucher | N | Y | Y | Y | Y | N |
| 10 **Wolf** | Y | Y | Y | N | N | Y |
| 11 **Davis, T.** | Y | Y | Y | N | N | Y |
| **WASHINGTON** | | | | | | |
| 1 Inslee | Y | Y | Y | Y | Y | N |
| 2 Larsen | N | Y | Y | Y | Y | N |
| 3 Baird | N | Y | Y | Y | Y | Y |
| 4 **Hastings** | Y | Y | Y | N | N | Y |
| 5 **McMorris** | Y | Y | Y | N | N | Y |
| 6 Dicks | N | Y | ? | Y | Y | N |
| 7 McDermott | N | Y | Y | Y | Y | N |
| 8 **Reichert** | Y | Y | Y | N | N | Y |
| 9 Smith | Y | Y | Y | Y | Y | N |
| **WEST VIRGINIA** | | | | | | |
| 1 Mollohan | N | Y | Y | Y | Y | Y |
| 2 **Capito** | Y | Y | Y | N | N | Y |
| 3 Rahall | N | Y | Y | Y | Y | Y |
| **WISCONSIN** | | | | | | |
| 1 **Ryan** | Y | Y | Y | N | N | Y |
| 2 Baldwin | N | Y | Y | Y | Y | N |
| 3 Kind | Y | Y | Y | Y | Y | N |
| 4 Moore | N | Y | Y | Y | Y | N |
| 5 **Sensenbrenner** | Y | Y | Y | N | N | Y |
| 6 **Petri** | Y | Y | Y | N | N | Y |
| 7 Obey | N | Y | Y | Y | Y | N |
| 8 **Green** | Y | Y | Y | N | N | Y |
| **WYOMING** | | | | | | |
| AL **Cubin** | Y | Y | Y | N | N | Y |

# IN THE HOUSE | By Vote Number

**427.** HR 2894. Abraham Lincoln Birthplace Post Office/Passage. Issa, R-Calif., motion to suspend the rules and pass the bill that would designate a post office in Hodgenville, Ky., for Abraham Lincoln, who was born Feb. 12, 1809, in Hodgenville on the Sinking Spring Farm, now a national historic site. Motion agreed to 421-0: R 221-0; D 199-0 (ND 149-0, SD 50-0); I 1-0. A two-thirds majority of those present and voting (281 in this case) is required for passage under suspension of the rules. July 26, 2005.

**428.** HR 22. Postal Service Overhaul/Postal Service Board of **Governors.** Pence, R-Ind., amendment that would strike a provision in the bill that would require the next position on the Postal Service's Board of Governors to be filled by an individual with the unanimous backing of labor unions. Rejected 82-345: R 82-146; D 0-198 (ND 0-149, SD 0-49); I 0-1. July 26, 2005.

**429.** HR 22. Postal Service Overhaul/Alternative Delivery Services. Flake, R-Ariz., amendment that would create pilot programs for up to 20 communities to determine the feasibility of alternative mail delivery services. Rejected 51-379: R 51-177; D 0-201 (ND 0-150, SD 0-51); I 0-1. July 26, 2005.

**430.** HR 22. Postal Service Overhaul/Passage. Passage of the bill that would overhaul the operations of the U.S. Postal Service. The bill would replace the existing Postal Rate Commission with a Postal Regulatory Commission that has expanded regulatory powers. It would require separate rate regulation systems for market-dominant products and competitive products, including Express and Priority Mail. It would require the Treasury Department to pay postal worker retirement costs related to military service and would establish the Postal Service Retiree Health Benefits Fund. Passed 410-20: R 208-20; D 201-0 (ND 150-0, SD 51-0); I 1-0. A "nay" was a vote in support of the president's position. July 26, 2005.

**431.** HR 3339. James T. Molloy Post Office/Passage. Issa, R-Calif., motion to suspend the rules and pass the bill that would designate a post office in Buffalo, N.Y., for James T. Molloy, a former doorkeeper of the House. Motion agreed to 423-0: R 225-0; D 197-0 (ND 149-0, SD 48-0); I 1-0. A two-thirds majority of those present and voting (282 in this case) is required for passage under suspension of the rules. July 26, 2005.

**432.** HR 3283. China Trade Practices/Previous Question. Putnam, R-Fla., motion to order the previous question (thus ending debate and possibility of amendment) on adoption of the rule (H Res 387) to provide for House floor consideration of the bill that would establish mechanisms to ensure that China abides by previous trade agreement commitments. Motion agreed to 226-202: R 226-0; D 0-201 (ND 0-150, SD 0-51); I 0-1. July 27, 2005.

**433.** HR 3283. China Trade Practices/Rule. Adoption of the rule (H Res 387) to provide for House floor consideration of the bill that would establish mechanisms to ensure that China abides by previous trade agreement commitments. Adopted 228-200: R 228-0; D 0-199 (ND 0-150, SD 0-49); I 0-1. July 27, 2005.

| | 427 | 428 | 429 | 430 | 431 | 432 | 433 |
|---|---|---|---|---|---|---|---|
| **ALABAMA** | | | | | | | |
| 1 Bonner | Y | N | N | Y | Y | Y | Y |
| 2 Everett | Y | N | N | Y | Y | Y | Y |
| 3 Rogers | Y | N | N | Y | Y | Y | Y |
| 4 Aderholt | Y | Y | N | Y | Y | Y | Y |
| 5 Cramer | ? | N | N | Y | Y | N | N |
| 6 Bachus | Y | N | N | Y | Y | Y | Y |
| 7 Davis | Y | N | N | Y | Y | N | N |
| **ALASKA** | | | | | | | |
| AL Young | Y | N | N | Y | Y | Y | Y |
| **ARIZONA** | | | | | | | |
| 1 Renzi | Y | N | N | Y | Y | Y | Y |
| 2 Franks | Y | Y | Y | N | Y | Y | Y |
| 3 Shadegg | Y | Y | Y | N | Y | Y | Y |
| 4 Pastor | Y | N | N | Y | Y | N | N |
| 5 Hayworth | Y | Y | Y | N | Y | Y | Y |
| 6 Flake | Y | Y | Y | N | Y | Y | Y |
| 7 Grijalva | Y | N | N | Y | N | N | N |
| 8 Kolbe | Y | N | Y | Y | Y | Y | Y |
| **ARKANSAS** | | | | | | | |
| 1 Berry | Y | N | N | Y | Y | N | N |
| 2 Snyder | Y | N | N | Y | Y | N | N |
| 3 Boozman | Y | N | N | Y | Y | Y | Y |
| 4 Ross | Y | N | N | Y | Y | N | N |
| **CALIFORNIA** | | | | | | | |
| 1 Thompson | Y | N | N | Y | Y | N | N |
| 2 Herger | Y | Y | N | Y | Y | Y | Y |
| 3 Lungren | Y | N | Y | Y | Y | Y | Y |
| 4 Doolittle | Y | N | N | Y | Y | Y | Y |
| 5 Matsui, D. | Y | N | N | Y | Y | N | N |
| 6 Woolsey | Y | N | N | Y | Y | N | N |
| 7 Miller, George | Y | ? | ? | ? | ? | N | N |
| 8 Pelosi | Y | N | N | Y | Y | N | N |
| 9 Lee | Y | N | N | Y | Y | N | N |
| 10 Tauscher | Y | N | N | Y | Y | N | N |
| 11 Pombo | Y | N | N | Y | Y | Y | Y |
| 12 Lantos | Y | N | N | Y | Y | N | N |
| 13 Stark | Y | N | N | Y | Y | N | N |
| 14 Eshoo | Y | N | N | Y | Y | N | N |
| 15 Honda | Y | N | N | Y | Y | N | N |
| 16 Lofgren | Y | N | N | Y | Y | N | N |
| 17 Farr | Y | N | N | Y | Y | N | N |
| 18 Cardoza | Y | N | N | Y | Y | N | N |
| 19 Radanovich | Y | N | N | Y | ? | Y | Y |
| 20 Costa | Y | N | N | Y | Y | N | N |
| 21 Nunes | Y | N | N | Y | Y | Y | Y |
| 22 Thomas | Y | N | N | Y | Y | Y | Y |
| 23 Capps | Y | N | N | Y | Y | N | N |
| 24 Gallegly | Y | N | N | Y | Y | Y | Y |
| 25 McKeon | Y | N | N | Y | Y | Y | Y |
| 26 Dreier | Y | N | N | Y | Y | Y | Y |
| 27 Sherman | Y | N | N | Y | Y | N | N |
| 28 Berman | ? | N | N | Y | Y | N | N |
| 29 Schiff | Y | N | N | Y | Y | N | N |
| 30 Waxman | ? | N | N | Y | Y | N | N |
| 31 Becerra | Y | N | N | Y | Y | N | N |
| 32 Solis | Y | N | N | Y | Y | N | N |
| 33 Watson | Y | N | N | Y | Y | N | N |
| 34 Roybal-Allard | Y | N | N | Y | Y | N | N |
| 35 Waters | Y | N | N | Y | Y | N | N |
| 36 Harman | Y | N | N | Y | Y | N | N |
| 37 Millender-McD. | Y | N | N | Y | Y | N | N |
| 38 Napolitano | Y | N | N | Y | Y | N | N |
| 39 Sánchez, Linda | Y | N | N | Y | Y | N | N |
| 40 Royce | Y | Y | Y | N | Y | Y | Y |
| 41 Lewis | Y | N | N | Y | ? | Y | Y |
| 42 Miller, Gary | Y | Y | N | Y | Y | Y | Y |
| 43 Baca | Y | N | N | Y | Y | N | N |
| 44 Calvert | Y | N | N | Y | Y | Y | Y |
| 45 Bono | Y | N | N | Y | Y | Y | Y |
| 46 Rohrabacher | Y | Y | Y | N | Y | Y | Y |
| 47 Sanchez, Loretta | Y | N | N | Y | Y | N | N |
| 48 Cox | Y | Y | Y | Y | Y | Y | Y |
| 49 Issa | Y | Y | N | Y | Y | ? | ? |
| 50 Cunningham | Y | N | Y | Y | Y | Y | Y |
| 51 Filner | Y | N | N | Y | Y | N | N |
| 52 Hunter | Y | N | Y | Y | Y | Y | Y |
| 53 Davis | Y | N | N | Y | Y | N | N |
| **COLORADO** | | | | | | | |
| 1 DeGette | Y | N | N | Y | Y | N | N |
| 2 Udall | Y | N | N | Y | Y | N | N |
| 3 Salazar | Y | N | N | Y | Y | N | N |
| 4 Musgrave | Y | Y | N | Y | Y | Y | Y |
| 5 Hefley | Y | Y | N | Y | ? | Y | Y |
| 6 Tancredo | Y | Y | Y | Y | Y | Y | Y |
| 7 Beauprez | Y | Y | N | Y | Y | Y | Y |
| **CONNECTICUT** | | | | | | | |
| 1 Larson | Y | N | N | Y | Y | N | N |
| 2 Simmons | Y | N | N | Y | Y | Y | Y |
| 3 DeLauro | Y | N | N | Y | Y | N | N |
| 4 Shays | Y | N | N | Y | Y | Y | Y |
| 5 Johnson | Y | N | N | Y | Y | Y | Y |
| **DELAWARE** | | | | | | | |
| AL Castle | Y | N | N | Y | Y | Y | Y |
| **FLORIDA** | | | | | | | |
| 1 Miller | Y | Y | Y | Y | Y | Y | Y |
| 2 Boyd | Y | N | N | Y | Y | N | N |
| 3 Brown | Y | N | N | Y | Y | N | N |
| 4 Crenshaw | Y | N | N | Y | Y | Y | Y |
| 5 Brown-Waite | ? | N | N | Y | Y | Y | Y |
| 6 Stearns | Y | Y | Y | Y | Y | Y | Y |
| 7 Mica | Y | N | Y | Y | Y | Y | Y |
| 8 Keller | Y | N | N | Y | Y | Y | Y |
| 9 Bilirakis | Y | N | N | Y | Y | Y | Y |
| 10 Young | Y | N | N | Y | Y | Y | Y |
| 11 Davis | Y | N | N | Y | ? | N | N |
| 12 Putnam | Y | N | N | Y | Y | Y | Y |
| 13 Harris | Y | N | Y | Y | Y | Y | Y |
| 14 Mack | Y | Y | Y | Y | Y | Y | Y |
| 15 Weldon | Y | Y | Y | N | Y | Y | Y |
| 16 Foley | Y | N | N | Y | Y | Y | Y |
| 17 Meek | Y | N | N | Y | Y | N | N |
| 18 Ros-Lehtinen | Y | N | N | Y | Y | N | N |
| 19 Wexler | Y | N | N | Y | ? | N | N |
| 20 Wasserman-Schultz | Y | N | N | Y | Y | N | N |
| 21 Diaz-Balart, L. | Y | N | N | Y | Y | Y | Y |
| 22 Shaw | Y | N | N | Y | Y | Y | Y |
| 23 Hastings | Y | N | N | Y | Y | N | N |
| 24 Feeney | ? | Y | Y | N | Y | Y | Y |
| 25 Diaz-Balart, M. | Y | N | N | Y | Y | Y | Y |
| **GEORGIA** | | | | | | | |
| 1 Kingston | Y | Y | Y | Y | Y | Y | Y |
| 2 Bishop | Y | N | N | Y | Y | N | N |
| 3 Marshall | Y | N | N | Y | ? | N | N |
| 4 McKinney | Y | N | N | Y | Y | N | ? |
| 5 Lewis | Y | N | N | Y | Y | N | N |
| 6 Price | Y | Y | Y | N | Y | Y | Y |
| 7 Linder | Y | N | Y | Y | Y | Y | Y |
| 8 Westmoreland | Y | Y | Y | N | Y | Y | Y |
| 9 Norwood | Y | Y | Y | Y | Y | Y | Y |
| 10 Deal | Y | N | N | Y | Y | Y | Y |
| 11 Gingrey | Y | Y | Y | Y | Y | Y | Y |
| 12 Barrow | Y | N | N | Y | Y | N | N |
| 13 Scott | Y | N | N | Y | Y | N | N |
| **HAWAII** | | | | | | | |
| 1 Abercrombie | Y | N | N | Y | Y | N | N |
| 2 Case | Y | N | N | Y | Y | N | N |
| **IDAHO** | | | | | | | |
| 1 Otter | ? | Y | Y | N | Y | Y | Y |
| 2 Simpson | Y | N | N | Y | Y | Y | Y |
| **ILLINOIS** | | | | | | | |
| 1 Rush | Y | N | N | Y | Y | N | N |
| 2 Jackson | Y | N | N | Y | Y | N | N |
| 3 Lipinski | Y | N | N | Y | Y | N | N |
| 4 Gutierrez | Y | N | N | Y | Y | N | N |
| 5 Emanuel | Y | N | N | Y | Y | N | N |
| 6 Hyde | Y | Y | N | Y | Y | Y | Y |
| 7 Davis | Y | N | N | Y | Y | N | N |
| 8 Bean | Y | N | N | Y | Y | N | N |
| 9 Schakowsky | Y | N | N | Y | Y | N | N |
| 10 Kirk | Y | N | N | Y | Y | Y | Y |
| 11 Weller | Y | N | N | Y | Y | Y | Y |
| 12 Costello | Y | N | N | Y | Y | N | N |

**KEY**  Republicans  Democrats  *Independents*

| | | | |
|---|---|---|---|
| **Y** | Voted for (yea) | **X** Paired against | **C** Voted "present" to avoid possible conflict of interest |
| **#** | Paired for | **–** Announced against | **?** Did not vote or otherwise make a position known |
| **+** | Announced for | **P** Voted "present" | |
| **N** | Voted against (nay) | | |

ND Northern Democrats, SD Southern Democrats
Southern states: Ala., Ark., Fla., Ga., Ky., La., Miss., N.C., Okla., S.C., Tenn., Texas, Va.

| | 427 | 428 | 429 | 430 | 431 | 432 | 433 |
|---|---|---|---|---|---|---|---|
| 13 **Biggert** | Y | N | N | Y | Y | Y | Y |
| 14 **Hastert** | | | | | | | |
| 15 **Johnson** | Y | N | N | Y | Y | ? | Y |
| 16 **Manzullo** | Y | N | N | Y | Y | Y | Y |
| 17 Evans | Y | N | N | Y | Y | N | N |
| 18 **LaHood** | Y | N | N | Y | Y | Y | Y |
| 19 **Shimkus** | Y | N | N | Y | Y | Y | Y |
| **INDIANA** | | | | | | | |
| 1 Visclosky | Y | N | N | Y | Y | N | N |
| 2 **Chocola** | Y | Y | Y | N | Y | Y | Y |
| 3 **Souder** | Y | N | N | Y | Y | Y | Y |
| 4 **Buyer** | Y | Y | Y | Y | Y | Y | Y |
| 5 **Burton** | Y | N | N | Y | Y | Y | Y |
| 6 **Pence** | Y | Y | Y | N | Y | Y | Y |
| 7 Carson | Y | N | N | Y | Y | N | N |
| 8 **Hostettler** | Y | Y | N | Y | Y | Y | Y |
| 9 **Sodrel** | Y | N | N | Y | Y | Y | Y |
| **IOWA** | | | | | | | |
| 1 **Nussle** | Y | N | N | N | Y | Y | Y |
| 2 **Leach** | Y | N | N | Y | Y | Y | Y |
| 3 Boswell | Y | N | N | Y | Y | N | N |
| 4 **Latham** | Y | N | N | Y | Y | Y | Y |
| 5 **King** | Y | Y | Y | Y | Y | Y | Y |
| **KANSAS** | | | | | | | |
| 1 **Moran** | Y | N | N | Y | Y | Y | Y |
| 2 **Ryun** | Y | Y | N | Y | Y | Y | Y |
| 3 Moore | Y | N | N | Y | Y | N | N |
| 4 **Tiahrt** | Y | Y | N | Y | Y | Y | Y |
| **KENTUCKY** | | | | | | | |
| 1 **Whitfield** | Y | Y | N | Y | Y | Y | Y |
| 2 **Lewis** | Y | N | N | Y | Y | Y | Y |
| 3 **Northup** | Y | N | N | Y | Y | Y | Y |
| 4 **Davis** | Y | N | N | Y | Y | Y | Y |
| 5 **Rogers** | Y | N | N | Y | Y | Y | Y |
| 6 Chandler | Y | N | N | Y | Y | N | N |
| **LOUISIANA** | | | | | | | |
| 1 **Jindal** | Y | Y | Y | Y | Y | Y | Y |
| 2 Jefferson | Y | N | N | Y | Y | N | ? |
| 3 Melancon | Y | N | N | Y | Y | N | N |
| 4 **McCrery** | Y | Y | N | Y | Y | Y | Y |
| 5 **Alexander** | Y | N | N | Y | Y | Y | Y |
| 6 **Baker** | Y | N | N | Y | Y | Y | Y |
| 7 **Boustany** | Y | Y | N | Y | Y | Y | Y |
| **MAINE** | | | | | | | |
| 1 Allen | Y | N | N | Y | Y | N | N |
| 2 Michaud | Y | N | N | Y | Y | N | N |
| **MARYLAND** | | | | | | | |
| 1 **Gilchrest** | Y | N | N | Y | Y | Y | Y |
| 2 Ruppersberger | Y | N | N | Y | Y | N | N |
| 3 Cardin | Y | N | N | Y | Y | N | N |
| 4 Wynn | Y | N | N | Y | Y | N | N |
| 5 Hoyer | Y | N | N | Y | Y | N | N |
| 6 **Bartlett** | Y | Y | Y | Y | Y | Y | Y |
| 7 Cummings | Y | N | N | Y | Y | N | N |
| 8 Van Hollen | Y | N | N | Y | Y | N | N |
| **MASSACHUSETTS** | | | | | | | |
| 1 Olver | Y | N | N | Y | Y | N | N |
| 2 Neal | Y | N | N | Y | Y | N | N |
| 3 McGovern | Y | N | N | Y | Y | N | N |
| 4 Frank | Y | N | N | Y | Y | N | N |
| 5 Meehan | Y | N | N | Y | Y | N | N |
| 6 Tierney | Y | N | N | Y | Y | N | N |
| 7 Markey | Y | N | N | Y | Y | N | N |
| 8 Capuano | Y | N | N | Y | Y | N | N |
| 9 Lynch | Y | N | N | Y | Y | N | N |
| 10 Delahunt | Y | N | N | Y | Y | N | N |
| **MICHIGAN** | | | | | | | |
| 1 Stupak | Y | N | N | Y | Y | N | N |
| 2 **Hoekstra** | Y | N | N | Y | Y | Y | Y |
| 3 **Ehlers** | Y | N | N | Y | Y | Y | Y |
| 4 **Camp** | Y | N | N | Y | Y | Y | Y |
| 5 Kildee | Y | N | N | Y | Y | N | N |
| 6 **Upton** | Y | N | N | Y | Y | Y | Y |
| 7 **Schwarz** | Y | N | N | Y | Y | Y | Y |
| 8 **Rogers** | Y | N | N | Y | Y | Y | Y |
| 9 **Knollenberg** | Y | N | N | Y | Y | Y | Y |
| 10 **Miller** | Y | N | N | Y | Y | Y | Y |
| 11 **McCotter** | Y | N | N | Y | Y | Y | Y |
| 12 Levin | Y | N | N | Y | Y | N | N |
| 13 Kilpatrick | Y | N | N | Y | Y | N | N |
| 14 Conyers | Y | N | N | Y | Y | N | N |
| 15 Dingell | Y | N | N | Y | Y | N | N |

| | 427 | 428 | 429 | 430 | 431 | 432 | 433 |
|---|---|---|---|---|---|---|---|
| **MINNESOTA** | | | | | | | |
| 1 **Gutknecht** | Y | N | N | Y | Y | Y | Y |
| 2 **Kline** | Y | N | N | Y | Y | Y | Y |
| 3 **Ramstad** | Y | N | N | Y | Y | Y | Y |
| 4 McCollum | Y | N | N | Y | Y | N | N |
| 5 Sabo | Y | N | N | Y | Y | N | N |
| 6 **Kennedy** | Y | N | N | Y | Y | Y | Y |
| 7 Peterson | Y | N | N | Y | Y | N | N |
| 8 Oberstar | Y | N | N | Y | Y | N | N |
| **MISSISSIPPI** | | | | | | | |
| 1 **Wicker** | Y | N | N | Y | Y | Y | Y |
| 2 Thompson | Y | N | N | Y | Y | N | N |
| 3 **Pickering** | Y | N | N | Y | Y | Y | Y |
| 4 Taylor | Y | N | N | Y | Y | N | N |
| **MISSOURI** | | | | | | | |
| 1 Clay | Y | N | N | Y | Y | N | N |
| 2 **Akin** | Y | Y | Y | N | Y | Y | Y |
| 3 Carnahan | Y | N | N | Y | Y | N | N |
| 4 Skelton | Y | N | N | Y | Y | N | N |
| 5 Cleaver | Y | N | N | Y | Y | N | N |
| 6 **Graves** | Y | N | N | Y | Y | Y | Y |
| 7 **Blunt** | Y | Y | N | Y | Y | Y | Y |
| 8 **Emerson** | Y | N | N | Y | Y | Y | Y |
| 9 **Hulshof** | Y | N | N | Y | Y | Y | Y |
| **MONTANA** | | | | | | | |
| AL **Rehberg** | Y | N | N | Y | Y | Y | Y |
| **NEBRASKA** | | | | | | | |
| 1 **Fortenberry** | Y | N | N | Y | Y | Y | Y |
| 2 **Terry** | Y | N | N | Y | Y | Y | Y |
| 3 **Osborne** | Y | N | N | Y | Y | Y | Y |
| **NEVADA** | | | | | | | |
| 1 Berkley | Y | N | N | Y | Y | N | N |
| 2 **Gibbons** | ? | ? | ? | ? | ? | Y | Y |
| 3 **Porter** | Y | N | N | Y | Y | Y | Y |
| **NEW HAMPSHIRE** | | | | | | | |
| 1 **Bradley** | Y | N | N | Y | Y | Y | Y |
| 2 **Bass** | Y | Y | N | Y | Y | Y | Y |
| **NEW JERSEY** | | | | | | | |
| 1 Andrews | Y | N | N | Y | Y | N | N |
| 2 **LoBiondo** | Y | N | N | Y | Y | Y | Y |
| 3 **Saxton** | Y | N | N | Y | Y | Y | Y |
| 4 **Smith** | Y | N | N | Y | Y | Y | Y |
| 5 **Garrett** | Y | Y | Y | Y | Y | Y | Y |
| 6 Pallone | Y | N | N | Y | Y | N | N |
| 7 **Ferguson** | Y | N | N | Y | Y | Y | Y |
| 8 Pascrell | Y | N | N | Y | Y | N | N |
| 9 Rothman | Y | N | N | Y | Y | N | N |
| 10 Payne | Y | N | N | Y | Y | N | N |
| 11 **Frelinghuysen** | Y | N | N | Y | Y | Y | Y |
| 12 Holt | Y | N | N | Y | Y | N | N |
| 13 Menendez | Y | N | N | Y | Y | N | N |
| **NEW MEXICO** | | | | | | | |
| 1 **Wilson** | Y | N | N | Y | Y | Y | Y |
| 2 **Pearce** | Y | N | N | Y | Y | Y | Y |
| 3 Udall | Y | N | N | Y | Y | N | N |
| **NEW YORK** | | | | | | | |
| 1 Bishop | Y | N | N | Y | Y | N | N |
| 2 Israel | Y | N | N | Y | Y | N | N |
| 3 **King** | Y | N | N | Y | Y | Y | Y |
| 4 McCarthy | Y | N | N | Y | Y | N | N |
| 5 Ackerman | Y | N | N | Y | Y | N | N |
| 6 Meeks | Y | N | N | Y | Y | N | N |
| 7 Crowley | Y | N | N | Y | Y | N | N |
| 8 Nadler | Y | N | N | Y | Y | N | N |
| 9 Weiner | Y | N | N | Y | Y | N | N |
| 10 Towns | Y | N | N | Y | Y | N | N |
| 11 Owens | Y | N | N | Y | Y | N | N |
| 12 Velázquez | Y | N | N | Y | Y | N | N |
| 13 **Fossella** | Y | N | N | Y | Y | Y | Y |
| 14 Maloney | Y | N | N | Y | Y | N | N |
| 15 Rangel | Y | N | N | Y | Y | N | N |
| 16 Serrano | Y | N | N | Y | Y | N | N |
| 17 Engel | Y | N | N | Y | Y | N | N |
| 18 Lowey | Y | N | N | Y | Y | N | N |
| 19 **Kelly** | Y | N | N | Y | Y | Y | Y |
| 20 **Sweeney** | Y | N | N | Y | Y | Y | Y |
| 21 McNulty | Y | N | N | Y | Y | N | N |
| 22 Hinchey | Y | N | N | Y | Y | N | N |
| 23 **McHugh** | Y | N | N | Y | Y | Y | Y |
| 24 **Boehlert** | Y | N | N | Y | Y | Y | Y |
| 25 **Walsh** | Y | N | N | Y | Y | Y | Y |
| 26 **Reynolds** | Y | N | N | Y | Y | Y | Y |
| 27 Higgins | Y | N | N | Y | Y | N | N |
| 28 Slaughter | Y | N | N | Y | Y | N | N |
| 29 **Kuhl** | Y | N | N | Y | Y | Y | Y |

| | 427 | 428 | 429 | 430 | 431 | 432 | 433 |
|---|---|---|---|---|---|---|---|
| **NORTH CAROLINA** | | | | | | | |
| 1 Butterfield | Y | N | N | Y | Y | N | N |
| 2 Etheridge | Y | N | N | Y | Y | N | N |
| 3 **Jones** | Y | Y | N | Y | Y | Y | Y |
| 4 Price | Y | N | N | Y | Y | N | N |
| 5 **Foxx** | Y | Y | Y | Y | Y | Y | Y |
| 6 **Coble** | Y | N | N | Y | Y | Y | Y |
| 7 McIntyre | Y | N | N | Y | Y | N | N |
| 8 **Hayes** | Y | Y | N | Y | Y | Y | Y |
| 9 **Myrick** | Y | Y | Y | Y | Y | Y | Y |
| 10 **McHenry** | ? | Y | Y | Y | Y | Y | Y |
| 11 **Taylor** | Y | N | N | Y | Y | Y | Y |
| 12 Watt | Y | N | N | Y | Y | N | N |
| 13 Miller | Y | N | N | Y | Y | N | N |
| **NORTH DAKOTA** | | | | | | | |
| AL Pomeroy | Y | N | N | Y | Y | N | N |
| **OHIO** | | | | | | | |
| 1 **Chabot** | Y | Y | N | Y | Y | Y | Y |
| 2 Vacant | | | | | | | |
| 3 **Turner** | Y | N | N | Y | Y | Y | Y |
| 4 **Oxley** | ? | ? | ? | ? | ? | Y | Y |
| 5 **Gillmor** | Y | N | N | Y | Y | Y | Y |
| 6 Strickland | Y | N | N | Y | Y | N | N |
| 7 **Hobson** | Y | N | N | Y | Y | Y | Y |
| 8 **Boehner** | Y | N | N | Y | Y | Y | Y |
| 9 Kaptur | Y | N | N | Y | Y | N | N |
| 10 Kucinich | Y | N | N | Y | Y | N | N |
| 11 Jones | Y | N | N | Y | Y | N | N |
| 12 **Tiberi** | Y | N | N | Y | Y | Y | Y |
| 13 Brown | Y | N | N | Y | Y | N | N |
| 14 **LaTourette** | ? | N | N | Y | Y | Y | Y |
| 15 **Pryce** | Y | N | N | Y | Y | Y | Y |
| 16 **Regula** | Y | N | N | Y | Y | Y | Y |
| 17 Ryan | Y | N | N | Y | Y | N | N |
| 18 **Ney** | Y | N | N | Y | Y | Y | Y |
| **OKLAHOMA** | | | | | | | |
| 1 **Sullivan** | Y | Y | Y | Y | Y | Y | Y |
| 2 Boren | Y | N | N | Y | Y | N | N |
| 3 **Lucas** | Y | N | N | Y | Y | Y | Y |
| 4 **Cole** | Y | Y | N | Y | Y | Y | Y |
| 5 **Istook** | Y | Y | N | N | Y | Y | Y |
| **OREGON** | | | | | | | |
| 1 Wu | Y | N | N | Y | Y | N | N |
| 2 **Walden** | Y | N | N | Y | Y | Y | Y |
| 3 Blumenauer | Y | N | N | Y | Y | N | N |
| 4 DeFazio | Y | N | N | Y | Y | N | N |
| 5 Hooley | Y | N | N | Y | Y | N | N |
| **PENNSYLVANIA** | | | | | | | |
| 1 Brady | Y | N | N | Y | Y | ? | ? |
| 2 Fattah | Y | N | N | Y | Y | N | N |
| 3 **English** | Y | N | N | Y | Y | Y | Y |
| 4 **Hart** | Y | N | N | Y | Y | Y | Y |
| 5 **Peterson** | ? | N | N | Y | Y | Y | Y |
| 6 **Gerlach** | Y | N | N | Y | Y | Y | Y |
| 7 **Weldon** | Y | N | N | Y | Y | Y | Y |
| 8 **Fitzpatrick** | Y | N | N | Y | Y | Y | Y |
| 9 **Shuster** | Y | N | N | Y | Y | Y | Y |
| 10 **Sherwood** | Y | N | N | Y | Y | Y | Y |
| 11 Kanjorski | Y | N | N | Y | Y | N | N |
| 12 Murtha | Y | N | N | Y | ? | N | N |
| 13 Schwartz | Y | N | N | Y | Y | N | N |
| 14 Doyle | Y | N | N | Y | Y | N | N |
| 15 **Dent** | Y | N | N | Y | Y | Y | Y |
| 16 **Pitts** | Y | Y | N | Y | Y | Y | Y |
| 17 Holden | Y | N | N | Y | Y | N | N |
| 18 **Murphy** | Y | N | N | Y | Y | ? | ? |
| 19 **Platts** | Y | N | N | Y | Y | ? | Y |
| **RHODE ISLAND** | | | | | | | |
| 1 Kennedy | Y | N | N | Y | Y | N | N |
| 2 Langevin | Y | N | N | Y | Y | N | N |
| **SOUTH CAROLINA** | | | | | | | |
| 1 **Brown** | Y | N | N | Y | Y | Y | Y |
| 2 **Wilson** | Y | Y | Y | Y | Y | Y | Y |
| 3 **Barrett** | Y | Y | Y | N | Y | Y | Y |
| 4 **Inglis** | Y | Y | Y | Y | Y | Y | Y |
| 5 Spratt | Y | N | N | Y | Y | N | N |
| 6 Clyburn | Y | N | N | Y | Y | N | N |
| **SOUTH DAKOTA** | | | | | | | |
| AL Herseth | Y | N | N | Y | Y | N | N |
| **TENNESSEE** | | | | | | | |
| 1 **Jenkins** | Y | N | N | Y | Y | Y | Y |
| 2 **Duncan** | Y | N | Y | Y | Y | Y | Y |

| | 427 | 428 | 429 | 430 | 431 | 432 | 433 |
|---|---|---|---|---|---|---|---|
| 3 **Wamp** | Y | N | N | Y | Y | Y | Y |
| 4 Davis | Y | N | N | Y | Y | N | N |
| 5 Cooper | Y | ? | N | Y | Y | N | N |
| 6 Gordon | Y | N | N | Y | Y | N | N |
| 7 **Blackburn** | Y | Y | Y | Y | Y | Y | Y |
| 8 Tanner | Y | N | N | Y | Y | N | N |
| 9 Ford | Y | N | N | Y | Y | N | N |
| **TEXAS** | | | | | | | |
| 1 **Gohmert** | Y | Y | N | N | Y | Y | Y |
| 2 **Poe** | Y | Y | Y | Y | Y | Y | Y |
| 3 **Johnson, S.** | Y | Y | Y | N | Y | Y | Y |
| 4 **Hall** | Y | Y | N | Y | Y | Y | Y |
| 5 **Hensarling** | Y | Y | Y | N | Y | Y | Y |
| 6 **Barton** | Y | N | N | Y | Y | Y | Y |
| 7 **Culberson** | Y | Y | Y | N | Y | Y | Y |
| 8 **Brady** | Y | Y | Y | Y | Y | Y | Y |
| 9 Green, A. | Y | N | N | Y | Y | N | N |
| 10 **McCaul** | Y | Y | Y | Y | Y | Y | Y |
| 11 **Conaway** | Y | Y | Y | Y | Y | Y | Y |
| 12 **Granger** | Y | Y | N | Y | Y | Y | Y |
| 13 **Thornberry** | Y | Y | N | Y | Y | Y | Y |
| 14 **Paul** | ? | Y | Y | N | Y | Y | Y |
| 15 Hinojosa | Y | – | N | Y | Y | N | N |
| 16 Reyes | Y | N | N | Y | Y | N | N |
| 17 Edwards | Y | N | N | Y | Y | N | N |
| 18 Jackson-Lee | Y | N | N | Y | Y | N | N |
| 19 **Neugebauer** | Y | Y | Y | Y | Y | Y | Y |
| 20 Gonzalez | Y | N | N | Y | Y | N | N |
| 21 **Smith** | Y | N | N | Y | Y | Y | Y |
| 22 **DeLay** | Y | Y | N | Y | Y | Y | Y |
| 23 **Bonilla** | Y | Y | N | Y | Y | Y | Y |
| 24 **Marchant** | Y | Y | N | Y | Y | Y | Y |
| 25 Doggett | Y | N | N | Y | Y | N | N |
| 26 **Burgess** | Y | Y | N | Y | Y | Y | Y |
| 27 Ortiz | Y | N | N | Y | Y | N | N |
| 28 Cuellar | Y | N | N | Y | Y | N | N |
| 29 Green, G. | Y | N | N | Y | Y | N | N |
| 30 Johnson, E. | Y | N | N | Y | Y | N | N |
| 31 **Carter** | Y | Y | Y | Y | Y | Y | Y |
| 32 **Sessions** | Y | Y | Y | Y | Y | Y | Y |
| **UTAH** | | | | | | | |
| 1 **Bishop** | Y | N | N | Y | Y | Y | Y |
| 2 Matheson | Y | N | N | Y | Y | N | N |
| 3 **Cannon** | Y | N | N | Y | Y | Y | Y |
| **VERMONT** | | | | | | | |
| AL *Sanders* | Y | N | N | Y | Y | N | N |
| **VIRGINIA** | | | | | | | |
| 1 **Davis, J.** | Y | N | N | N | Y | Y | Y |
| 2 **Drake** | Y | N | N | Y | Y | Y | Y |
| 3 Scott | Y | N | N | Y | Y | N | N |
| 4 **Forbes** | Y | N | N | Y | Y | Y | Y |
| 5 **Goode** | Y | N | N | Y | Y | Y | Y |
| 6 **Goodlatte** | Y | Y | N | Y | Y | Y | Y |
| 7 **Cantor** | Y | Y | N | Y | Y | Y | Y |
| 8 Moran | Y | N | N | Y | Y | N | N |
| 9 Boucher | Y | N | N | Y | Y | N | N |
| 10 **Wolf** | Y | N | N | Y | Y | Y | Y |
| 11 **Davis, T.** | Y | N | N | Y | Y | Y | Y |
| **WASHINGTON** | | | | | | | |
| 1 Inslee | Y | N | N | Y | Y | N | N |
| 2 Larsen | Y | N | N | Y | Y | N | N |
| 3 Baird | Y | N | N | Y | Y | N | N |
| 4 **Hastings** | Y | N | N | Y | Y | Y | Y |
| 5 **McMorris** | Y | Y | Y | Y | Y | Y | Y |
| 6 Dicks | Y | N | N | Y | Y | N | N |
| 7 McDermott | Y | N | N | Y | Y | N | N |
| 8 **Reichert** | Y | N | N | Y | Y | Y | Y |
| 9 Smith | Y | N | N | Y | Y | N | N |
| **WEST VIRGINIA** | | | | | | | |
| 1 Mollohan | Y | N | N | Y | Y | N | N |
| 2 **Capito** | Y | N | N | Y | Y | Y | Y |
| 3 Rahall | Y | N | N | Y | Y | N | N |
| **WISCONSIN** | | | | | | | |
| 1 **Ryan** | Y | N | N | Y | Y | Y | Y |
| 2 Baldwin | Y | N | N | Y | Y | N | N |
| 3 Kind | Y | N | N | Y | Y | N | N |
| 4 Moore | Y | N | N | Y | Y | N | N |
| 5 **Sensenbrenner** | Y | N | N | Y | Y | Y | Y |
| 6 **Petri** | Y | N | N | Y | Y | Y | Y |
| 7 Obey | Y | ? | N | Y | Y | N | N |
| 8 **Green** | Y | N | N | Y | Y | Y | Y |
| **WYOMING** | | | | | | | |
| AL **Cubin** | Y | N | N | Y | Y | Y | Y |

# IN THE HOUSE | By Vote Number

**434.** **S 544. Medical Error Reporting/Passage.** Deal, R-Ga., motion to suspend the rules and pass the bill that would establish a set of procedures for the voluntary and confidential reporting of medical errors to patient safety organizations that would analyze the data and develop ways to improve patient safety and reduce medical errors. Motion agreed to 428-3: R 226-3; D 201-0 (ND 150-0, SD 51-0); I 1-0. A two-thirds majority of those present and voting (288 in this case) is required for passage under suspension of the rules. July 27, 2005.

**435.** **S 45. Drug Addiction Treatment/Passage.** Deal, R-Ga., motion to suspend the rules and pass the bill that would lift the 30-patient limit on group practices for treating drug addicts with narcotic drugs in a maintenance or detoxification-treatment program. Motion agreed to 429-0: R 228-0; D 200-0 (ND 149-0, SD 51-0); I 1-0. A two-thirds majority of those present and voting (286 in this case) is required for passage under suspension of the rules. July 27, 2005.

**436.** **HR 3283. China Trade Practices/Recommit.** Cardin, D-Md., motion to recommit the bill to the Ways and Means Committee with instructions to add language that would require the U.S. trade representative to conduct an investigation, make applicable determinations and implement any necessary action on China's currency practices. Motion rejected 195-232: R 0-227; D 194-5 (ND 144-4, SD 50-1); I 1-0. July 27, 2005.

**437.** **HR 3283. China Trade Practices/Passage.** Passage of the bill that would establish mechanisms to ensure that China abides by previous trade agreement commitments, including creating a system to monitor compliance with trade obligations on intellectual property rights, market access for U.S. goods, services and agriculture and the accounting of Chinese subsidies. Passed 255-168: R 221-5; D 34-162 (ND 14-133, SD 20-29); I 0-1. July 27, 2005.

**438.** **H Res 383. Rights of Iraqi Women/Adoption.** Ros-Lehtinen, R-Fla., motion to suspend the rules and adopt the resolution that would strongly encourage Iraq to adopt a constitution that grants women equal rights. Motion agreed to 426-0: R 226-0; D 199-0 (ND 148-0, SD 51-0); I 1-0. A two-thirds majority of those present and voting (284 in this case) is required for adoption under suspension of the rules. July 27, 2005.

**439.** **H Res 384. Terrorist Attacks in Egypt/Adoption.** Ros-Lehtinen, R-Fla., motion to suspend the rules and adopt the resolution that would strongly condemn the terrorist attacks in Sharm el-Sheikh, Egypt, and other terrorist attacks against Egypt, and express condolences to the families and friends of those injured and killed in the attacks. Motion agreed to 428-0: R 229-0; D 198-0 (ND 148-0, SD 50-0); I 1-0. A two-thirds majority of those present and voting (286 in this case) is required for adoption under suspension of the rules. July 27, 2005.

ND Northern Democrats, SD Southern Democrats
Southern states: Ala., Ark., Fla., Ga., Ky., La., Miss., N.C., Okla., S.C., Tenn., Texas, Va.

| | 434 | 435 | 436 | 437 | 438 | 439 |
|---|---|---|---|---|---|---|
| **ALABAMA** | | | | | | |
| 1 **Bonner** | Y | Y | N | Y | Y | Y |
| 2 **Everett** | Y | Y | N | Y | Y | Y |
| 3 **Rogers** | Y | Y | N | Y | Y | Y |
| 4 **Aderholt** | Y | Y | N | Y | Y | Y |
| 5 **Cramer** | Y | Y | Y | Y | Y | Y |
| 6 **Bachus** | Y | Y | N | Y | Y | Y |
| 7 Davis | Y | Y | Y | Y | Y | Y |
| **ALASKA** | | | | | | |
| AL **Young** | Y | Y | N | Y | Y | Y |
| **ARIZONA** | | | | | | |
| 1 **Renzi** | Y | Y | N | Y | Y | Y |
| 2 **Franks** | Y | Y | N | Y | Y | Y |
| 3 **Shadegg** | Y | Y | N | Y | Y | Y |
| 4 Pastor | Y | Y | Y | N | Y | Y |
| 5 **Hayworth** | Y | Y | N | Y | Y | Y |
| 6 **Flake** | N | N | N | Y | Y | Y |
| 7 Grijalva | Y | Y | Y | N | Y | Y |
| 8 **Kolbe** | Y | Y | N | N | Y | Y |
| **ARKANSAS** | | | | | | |
| 1 Berry | Y | Y | Y | Y | Y | Y |
| 2 Snyder | Y | Y | Y | N | Y | Y |
| 3 **Boozman** | Y | Y | N | Y | Y | Y |
| 4 Ross | Y | Y | Y | N | Y | Y |
| **CALIFORNIA** | | | | | | |
| 1 Thompson | Y | Y | Y | Y | Y | Y |
| 2 **Herger** | Y | Y | N | Y | Y | Y |
| 3 **Lungren** | Y | Y | N | Y | Y | Y |
| 4 **Doolittle** | Y | Y | N | Y | Y | Y |
| 5 Matsui, D. | Y | Y | Y | N | Y | Y |
| 6 Woolsey | Y | Y | Y | N | Y | Y |
| 7 Miller, George | Y | Y | Y | N | Y | Y |
| 8 Pelosi | Y | Y | Y | N | Y | Y |
| 9 Lee | Y | Y | Y | N | Y | Y |
| 10 Tauscher | Y | Y | Y | N | Y | Y |
| 11 **Pombo** | Y | Y | N | Y | Y | Y |
| 12 Lantos | Y | Y | Y | N | Y | Y |
| 13 Stark | Y | Y | Y | N | Y | Y |
| 14 Eshoo | Y | Y | Y | N | Y | Y |
| 15 Honda | Y | Y | Y | N | Y | Y |
| 16 Lofgren | Y | Y | N | N | Y | Y |
| 17 Farr | Y | Y | Y | N | Y | Y |
| 18 Cardoza | Y | Y | Y | N | Y | Y |
| 19 **Radanovich** | Y | Y | N | Y | Y | Y |
| 20 Costa | Y | Y | Y | N | Y | Y |
| 21 **Nunes** | Y | Y | N | Y | Y | Y |
| 22 **Thomas** | Y | Y | N | Y | Y | Y |
| 23 Capps | Y | Y | Y | N | Y | Y |
| 24 **Gallegly** | Y | Y | N | Y | Y | Y |
| 25 **McKeon** | Y | Y | N | Y | Y | Y |
| 26 **Dreier** | Y | Y | N | Y | Y | Y |
| 27 Sherman | Y | Y | Y | N | Y | Y |
| 28 Berman | Y | Y | Y | N | Y | Y |
| 29 Schiff | Y | Y | Y | N | Y | Y |
| 30 Waxman | Y | Y | Y | N | Y | Y |
| 31 Becerra | Y | Y | Y | N | Y | Y |
| 32 Solis | Y | Y | Y | N | Y | Y |
| 33 Watson | Y | Y | Y | N | Y | Y |
| 34 Roybal-Allard | Y | Y | Y | N | Y | Y |
| 35 Waters | Y | Y | Y | N | Y | Y |
| 36 Harman | Y | Y | Y | N | Y | Y |
| 37 Millender-McD. | Y | Y | Y | N | Y | Y |
| 38 Napolitano | Y | Y | Y | N | Y | Y |
| 39 Sánchez, Linda | Y | Y | Y | N | Y | Y |
| 40 **Royce** | Y | Y | N | Y | Y | Y |
| 41 **Lewis** | Y | Y | N | Y | Y | Y |
| 42 Miller, Gary | Y | Y | N | Y | Y | Y |
| 43 Baca | Y | Y | Y | N | Y | Y |
| 44 **Calvert** | Y | Y | N | Y | Y | Y |
| 45 **Bono** | Y | Y | N | Y | Y | Y |
| 46 **Rohrabacher** | Y | Y | N | Y | Y | Y |
| 47 Sanchez, Loretta | Y | Y | Y | N | Y | Y |
| 48 **Cox** | Y | Y | ? | ? | ? | Y |
| 49 **Issa** | Y | Y | N | Y | Y | Y |
| 50 **Cunningham** | Y | Y | N | Y | Y | Y |
| 51 Filner | Y | Y | Y | N | Y | Y |
| 52 **Hunter** | Y | Y | N | Y | Y | Y |
| 53 Davis | Y | Y | Y | N | Y | Y |
| **COLORADO** | | | | | | |
| 1 DeGette | Y | Y | Y | N | Y | Y |
| 2 Udall | Y | Y | Y | N | Y | Y |
| 3 Salazar | Y | Y | Y | N | Y | Y |
| 4 **Musgrave** | Y | Y | N | Y | Y | Y |
| 5 **Hefley** | Y | Y | N | Y | Y | Y |
| 6 **Tancredo** | Y | Y | N | Y | Y | Y |
| 7 **Beauprez** | Y | Y | N | Y | Y | Y |
| **CONNECTICUT** | | | | | | |
| 1 Larson | Y | Y | Y | N | Y | Y |
| 2 **Simmons** | Y | Y | N | Y | Y | Y |
| 3 DeLauro | Y | Y | Y | N | Y | Y |
| 4 **Shays** | Y | Y | N | Y | Y | Y |
| 5 **Johnson** | Y | Y | N | Y | Y | Y |
| **DELAWARE** | | | | | | |
| AL **Castle** | Y | Y | N | Y | Y | Y |
| **FLORIDA** | | | | | | |
| 1 **Miller** | Y | Y | N | Y | Y | Y |
| 2 Boyd | Y | Y | Y | N | Y | Y |
| 3 Brown | Y | Y | Y | N | Y | Y |
| 4 **Crenshaw** | Y | Y | N | Y | Y | Y |
| 5 **Brown-Waite** | Y | Y | N | Y | Y | Y |
| 6 **Stearns** | Y | Y | N | Y | Y | Y |
| 7 **Mica** | Y | Y | N | Y | Y | Y |
| 8 **Keller** | Y | Y | N | Y | Y | Y |
| 9 **Bilirakis** | Y | Y | N | Y | Y | Y |
| 10 **Young** | Y | Y | N | Y | Y | Y |
| 11 Davis | Y | Y | Y | N | Y | Y |
| 12 **Putnam** | Y | Y | N | Y | Y | Y |
| 13 **Harris** | Y | Y | N | Y | Y | Y |
| 14 **Mack** | Y | Y | N | Y | Y | Y |
| 15 **Weldon** | Y | Y | N | Y | Y | Y |
| 16 **Foley** | Y | Y | N | Y | Y | Y |
| 17 Meek | Y | Y | Y | N | Y | Y |
| 18 **Ros-Lehtinen** | Y | Y | N | Y | Y | Y |
| 19 Wexler | Y | Y | Y | N | Y | Y |
| 20 Wasserman-Schultz | Y | Y | Y | N | Y | Y |
| 21 **Diaz-Balart, L.** | Y | Y | N | ? | Y | Y |
| 22 **Shaw** | Y | Y | N | Y | Y | Y |
| 23 Hastings | Y | Y | Y | ? | Y | Y |
| 24 **Feeney** | Y | Y | N | Y | Y | Y |
| 25 **Diaz-Balart, M.** | Y | Y | N | Y | Y | Y |
| **GEORGIA** | | | | | | |
| 1 **Kingston** | Y | Y | N | Y | Y | Y |
| 2 Bishop | Y | Y | Y | N | Y | Y |
| 3 Marshall | Y | Y | Y | Y | Y | Y |
| 4 McKinney | Y | Y | Y | N | Y | Y |
| 5 Lewis | Y | Y | Y | N | Y | Y |
| 6 **Price** | Y | Y | N | Y | Y | Y |
| 7 **Linder** | Y | Y | N | Y | Y | Y |
| 8 **Westmoreland** | Y | Y | N | Y | Y | Y |
| 9 **Norwood** | Y | Y | N | Y | Y | Y |
| 10 **Deal** | Y | Y | N | Y | Y | Y |
| 11 **Gingrey** | Y | Y | N | Y | Y | Y |
| 12 **Barrow** | Y | Y | Y | Y | Y | Y |
| 13 Scott | Y | Y | Y | N | Y | Y |
| **HAWAII** | | | | | | |
| 1 Abercrombie | Y | Y | Y | N | Y | Y |
| 2 Case | Y | Y | Y | N | Y | Y |
| **IDAHO** | | | | | | |
| 1 **Otter** | Y | Y | N | Y | Y | Y |
| 2 **Simpson** | Y | Y | N | Y | Y | Y |
| **ILLINOIS** | | | | | | |
| 1 Rush | Y | Y | Y | N | Y | Y |
| 2 Jackson | Y | Y | Y | N | Y | Y |
| 3 Lipinski | Y | Y | Y | N | Y | Y |
| 4 Gutierrez | Y | Y | Y | N | Y | Y |
| 5 Emanuel | Y | Y | Y | N | Y | Y |
| 6 **Hyde** | Y | Y | N | Y | Y | Y |
| 7 Davis | Y | Y | Y | N | Y | Y |
| 8 Bean | Y | Y | Y | N | Y | Y |
| 9 Schakowsky | Y | Y | Y | N | Y | Y |
| 10 **Kirk** | Y | Y | N | Y | Y | Y |
| 11 **Weller** | Y | Y | N | Y | Y | Y |
| 12 Costello | Y | Y | Y | N | Y | Y |

**KEY**    Republicans    Democrats    *Independents*

| | | |
|---|---|---|
| **Y** Voted for (yea) | **X** Paired against | **C** Voted "present" to avoid possible conflict of interest |
| **#** Paired for | **−** Announced against | |
| **+** Announced for | **P** Voted "present" | **?** Did not vote or otherwise make a position known |
| **N** Voted against (nay) | | |

| | 434 | 435 | 436 | 437 | 438 | 439 |
|---|---|---|---|---|---|---|
| 13 **Biggert** | Y | Y | N | Y | Y | Y |
| 14 **Hastert** | | | | | | |
| 15 **Johnson** | Y | Y | N | Y | Y | Y |
| 16 **Manzullo** | Y | Y | N | Y | Y | Y |
| 17 Evans | Y | Y | Y | N | Y | Y |
| 18 **LaHood** | Y | Y | N | Y | Y | Y |
| 19 **Shimkus** | Y | Y | N | Y | Y | Y |
| **INDIANA** | | | | | | |
| 1 Visclosky | Y | Y | Y | N | Y | Y |
| 2 **Chocola** | Y | Y | N | Y | Y | Y |
| 3 **Souder** | Y | Y | N | Y | Y | Y |
| 4 **Buyer** | Y | Y | N | Y | Y | Y |
| 5 **Burton** | Y | Y | N | Y | Y | Y |
| 6 **Pence** | Y | Y | N | Y | Y | Y |
| 7 Carson | Y | Y | Y | N | Y | Y |
| 8 **Hostettler** | Y | Y | N | Y | Y | Y |
| 9 **Sodrel** | Y | Y | N | Y | Y | Y |
| **IOWA** | | | | | | |
| 1 **Nussle** | Y | Y | N | Y | Y | Y |
| 2 **Leach** | Y | Y | N | Y | Y | Y |
| 3 Boswell | Y | Y | Y | Y | Y | Y |
| 4 **Latham** | Y | Y | N | Y | Y | Y |
| 5 **King** | Y | Y | N | Y | Y | Y |
| **KANSAS** | | | | | | |
| 1 **Moran** | Y | Y | N | Y | Y | Y |
| 2 **Ryun** | Y | Y | N | Y | Y | Y |
| 3 Moore | Y | Y | Y | N | Y | Y |
| 4 **Tiahrt** | Y | Y | N | Y | ? | Y |
| **KENTUCKY** | | | | | | |
| 1 **Whitfield** | Y | Y | N | Y | Y | Y |
| 2 **Lewis** | Y | Y | N | Y | Y | Y |
| 3 **Northup** | Y | Y | N | Y | Y | Y |
| 4 **Davis** | Y | Y | N | Y | Y | Y |
| 5 **Rogers** | Y | Y | N | Y | Y | Y |
| 6 Chandler | Y | Y | Y | N | Y | Y |
| **LOUISIANA** | | | | | | |
| 1 **Jindal** | Y | Y | N | Y | Y | Y |
| 2 Jefferson | Y | Y | Y | N | Y | ? |
| 3 Melancon | Y | Y | Y | Y | Y | Y |
| 4 **McCrery** | Y | Y | N | Y | Y | Y |
| 5 **Alexander** | Y | Y | N | Y | Y | Y |
| 6 **Baker** | Y | Y | N | Y | Y | Y |
| 7 **Boustany** | Y | Y | N | Y | Y | Y |
| **MAINE** | | | | | | |
| 1 Allen | Y | Y | Y | N | Y | Y |
| 2 Michaud | Y | Y | Y | N | Y | Y |
| **MARYLAND** | | | | | | |
| 1 **Gilchrest** | Y | Y | N | Y | Y | Y |
| 2 Ruppersberger | Y | Y | Y | N | Y | Y |
| 3 Cardin | Y | Y | Y | N | Y | Y |
| 4 Wynn | Y | Y | Y | Y | Y | Y |
| 5 Hoyer | Y | Y | Y | N | Y | Y |
| 6 **Bartlett** | Y | Y | N | N | Y | Y |
| 7 Cummings | Y | Y | ? | ? | ? | ? |
| 8 Van Hollen | Y | Y | Y | N | Y | Y |
| **MASSACHUSETTS** | | | | | | |
| 1 Olver | Y | Y | Y | N | Y | Y |
| 2 Neal | Y | Y | Y | N | Y | Y |
| 3 McGovern | Y | Y | Y | N | Y | Y |
| 4 Frank | Y | Y | Y | N | Y | Y |
| 5 Meehan | Y | Y | Y | N | Y | Y |
| 6 Tierney | Y | Y | Y | N | Y | Y |
| 7 Markey | Y | Y | Y | N | Y | Y |
| 8 Capuano | Y | Y | Y | N | Y | Y |
| 9 Lynch | Y | Y | Y | N | Y | Y |
| 10 Delahunt | Y | Y | Y | N | Y | Y |
| **MICHIGAN** | | | | | | |
| 1 Stupak | Y | Y | Y | N | Y | Y |
| 2 **Hoekstra** | Y | Y | N | Y | Y | Y |
| 3 **Ehlers** | Y | Y | N | Y | Y | Y |
| 4 **Camp** | Y | Y | N | Y | Y | Y |
| 5 Kildee | Y | Y | Y | N | Y | Y |
| 6 **Upton** | Y | Y | N | Y | Y | Y |
| 7 **Schwarz** | Y | Y | N | Y | Y | Y |
| 8 **Rogers** | Y | Y | N | Y | Y | Y |
| 9 **Knollenberg** | Y | Y | N | Y | Y | Y |
| 10 **Miller** | Y | Y | N | Y | Y | Y |
| 11 **McCotter** | Y | Y | N | Y | Y | Y |
| 12 Levin | Y | Y | Y | N | Y | Y |
| 13 Kilpatrick | Y | Y | Y | N | Y | Y |
| 14 Conyers | Y | Y | Y | N | Y | Y |
| 15 Dingell | Y | Y | Y | N | Y | Y |
| **MINNESOTA** | | | | | | |
| 1 **Gutknecht** | Y | Y | N | Y | Y | Y |
| 2 **Kline** | Y | Y | N | Y | Y | Y |
| 3 **Ramstad** | Y | Y | N | Y | Y | Y |
| 4 McCollum | Y | Y | Y | N | Y | Y |
| 5 Sabo | Y | Y | Y | N | Y | Y |
| 6 **Kennedy** | Y | Y | N | Y | Y | Y |
| 7 Peterson | Y | Y | Y | N | Y | Y |
| 8 Oberstar | Y | Y | Y | N | Y | Y |
| **MISSISSIPPI** | | | | | | |
| 1 **Wicker** | Y | Y | N | Y | Y | Y |
| 2 Thompson | Y | Y | Y | N | Y | Y |
| 3 **Pickering** | Y | Y | N | Y | Y | Y |
| 4 Taylor | Y | Y | Y | Y | Y | Y |
| **MISSOURI** | | | | | | |
| 1 Clay | Y | Y | Y | ? | Y | Y |
| 2 **Akin** | Y | Y | N | Y | Y | Y |
| 3 Carnahan | Y | Y | Y | N | Y | Y |
| 4 Skelton | Y | Y | Y | Y | Y | Y |
| 5 Cleaver | Y | Y | Y | N | Y | Y |
| 6 **Graves** | Y | Y | N | Y | Y | Y |
| 7 **Blunt** | Y | Y | N | Y | Y | Y |
| 8 **Emerson** | Y | Y | N | Y | Y | Y |
| 9 **Hulshof** | Y | Y | N | Y | Y | Y |
| **MONTANA** | | | | | | |
| AL **Rehberg** | Y | Y | N | Y | Y | Y |
| **NEBRASKA** | | | | | | |
| 1 **Fortenberry** | Y | Y | N | Y | Y | Y |
| 2 **Terry** | Y | Y | N | Y | Y | Y |
| 3 **Osborne** | Y | Y | N | Y | Y | Y |
| **NEVADA** | | | | | | |
| 1 Berkley | Y | Y | Y | N | Y | Y |
| 2 **Gibbons** | Y | Y | N | Y | Y | Y |
| 3 **Porter** | Y | Y | N | Y | Y | Y |
| **NEW HAMPSHIRE** | | | | | | |
| 1 **Bradley** | Y | Y | N | Y | Y | Y |
| 2 **Bass** | Y | Y | N | Y | Y | Y |
| **NEW JERSEY** | | | | | | |
| 1 Andrews | Y | Y | Y | N | Y | Y |
| 2 **LoBiondo** | Y | Y | N | Y | Y | Y |
| 3 **Saxton** | Y | Y | N | Y | Y | Y |
| 4 **Smith** | Y | Y | N | Y | Y | Y |
| 5 **Garrett** | Y | Y | N | Y | Y | Y |
| 6 Pallone | Y | Y | Y | N | Y | Y |
| 7 **Ferguson** | Y | Y | N | Y | Y | Y |
| 8 Pascrell | Y | Y | Y | N | Y | Y |
| 9 Rothman | Y | Y | Y | N | Y | Y |
| 10 Payne | Y | Y | Y | N | Y | Y |
| 11 **Frelinghuysen** | Y | Y | N | Y | Y | Y |
| 12 Holt | Y | Y | Y | N | Y | Y |
| 13 Menendez | Y | Y | Y | N | Y | Y |
| **NEW MEXICO** | | | | | | |
| 1 **Wilson** | Y | Y | N | Y | Y | Y |
| 2 **Pearce** | Y | Y | N | Y | Y | Y |
| 3 Udall | Y | Y | Y | N | Y | Y |
| **NEW YORK** | | | | | | |
| 1 Bishop | Y | Y | Y | N | Y | Y |
| 2 Israel | Y | Y | Y | N | Y | Y |
| 3 **King** | Y | Y | N | Y | Y | Y |
| 4 McCarthy | Y | Y | Y | N | Y | Y |
| 5 Ackerman | Y | Y | Y | Y | Y | Y |
| 6 Meeks | Y | Y | Y | N | Y | Y |
| 7 Crowley | Y | Y | Y | N | Y | Y |
| 8 Nadler | Y | Y | Y | N | Y | Y |
| 9 Weiner | Y | Y | Y | N | Y | Y |
| 10 Towns | Y | Y | Y | N | Y | Y |
| 11 Owens | Y | Y | Y | N | Y | Y |
| 12 Velázquez | Y | Y | Y | N | Y | Y |
| 13 **Fossella** | Y | Y | N | Y | Y | Y |
| 14 Maloney | Y | Y | Y | N | Y | Y |
| 15 Rangel | Y | Y | Y | N | Y | Y |
| 16 Serrano | Y | Y | Y | N | Y | Y |
| 17 Engel | Y | Y | Y | Y | Y | Y |
| 18 Lowey | Y | Y | Y | N | Y | Y |
| 19 **Kelly** | Y | Y | N | Y | Y | Y |
| 20 **Sweeney** | Y | Y | N | Y | Y | Y |
| 21 McNulty | Y | Y | Y | N | Y | Y |
| 22 Hinchey | Y | Y | Y | N | Y | Y |
| 23 **McHugh** | Y | Y | N | Y | Y | Y |
| 24 **Boehlert** | Y | Y | N | Y | Y | Y |
| 25 **Walsh** | Y | Y | N | Y | Y | Y |
| 26 **Reynolds** | Y | Y | N | Y | Y | Y |
| 27 Higgins | Y | Y | Y | Y | Y | Y |
| 28 Slaughter | Y | Y | Y | N | Y | Y |
| 29 **Kuhl** | Y | Y | N | Y | Y | Y |
| **NORTH CAROLINA** | | | | | | |
| 1 Butterfield | Y | Y | Y | Y | Y | Y |
| 2 Etheridge | Y | Y | Y | Y | Y | Y |
| 3 **Jones** | Y | Y | N | Y | Y | Y |
| 4 Price | Y | Y | Y | Y | Y | Y |
| 5 **Foxx** | N | Y | N | Y | Y | Y |
| 6 **Coble** | Y | Y | N | Y | Y | Y |
| 7 McIntyre | Y | Y | Y | Y | Y | Y |
| 8 **Hayes** | Y | Y | N | Y | Y | Y |
| 9 **Myrick** | Y | Y | N | Y | Y | Y |
| 10 **McHenry** | Y | Y | N | Y | Y | Y |
| 11 **Taylor** | Y | Y | N | Y | Y | Y |
| 12 Watt | Y | Y | Y | N | Y | Y |
| 13 Miller | Y | Y | Y | N | Y | Y |
| **NORTH DAKOTA** | | | | | | |
| AL Pomeroy | Y | Y | Y | N | Y | Y |
| **OHIO** | | | | | | |
| 1 **Chabot** | Y | Y | N | Y | Y | Y |
| 2 Vacant | | | | | | |
| 3 **Turner** | Y | Y | N | Y | Y | Y |
| 4 **Oxley** | Y | Y | N | Y | Y | Y |
| 5 **Gillmor** | Y | Y | N | Y | Y | Y |
| 6 Strickland | Y | Y | Y | N | Y | Y |
| 7 **Hobson** | Y | Y | N | Y | Y | Y |
| 8 **Boehner** | Y | Y | N | Y | Y | Y |
| 9 Kaptur | Y | Y | Y | N | Y | Y |
| 10 Kucinich | Y | Y | Y | N | Y | Y |
| 11 Jones | Y | Y | Y | N | Y | Y |
| 12 **Tiberi** | Y | Y | N | Y | Y | Y |
| 13 Brown | Y | Y | Y | N | Y | Y |
| 14 **LaTourette** | Y | Y | N | Y | Y | Y |
| 15 **Pryce** | Y | Y | N | Y | Y | Y |
| 16 **Regula** | Y | Y | N | Y | Y | Y |
| 17 Ryan | Y | Y | Y | N | Y | Y |
| 18 **Ney** | Y | Y | N | Y | Y | Y |
| **OKLAHOMA** | | | | | | |
| 1 **Sullivan** | Y | Y | N | Y | Y | Y |
| 2 Boren | Y | Y | Y | Y | Y | Y |
| 3 **Lucas** | Y | Y | N | Y | Y | Y |
| 4 **Cole** | Y | Y | N | Y | Y | Y |
| 5 **Istook** | Y | Y | N | Y | Y | Y |
| **OREGON** | | | | | | |
| 1 Wu | Y | Y | Y | Y | Y | Y |
| 2 **Walden** | Y | Y | N | Y | Y | Y |
| 3 Blumenauer | Y | ? | Y | N | Y | Y |
| 4 DeFazio | Y | Y | Y | N | Y | Y |
| 5 Hooley | Y | Y | Y | N | Y | Y |
| **PENNSYLVANIA** | | | | | | |
| 1 Brady | ? | ? | ? | ? | ? | ? |
| 2 Fattah | Y | Y | Y | N | Y | Y |
| 3 **English** | Y | Y | N | Y | Y | Y |
| 4 **Hart** | Y | Y | N | Y | Y | Y |
| 5 **Peterson** | Y | Y | N | Y | Y | Y |
| 6 **Gerlach** | Y | Y | N | Y | Y | Y |
| 7 **Weldon** | Y | Y | N | Y | Y | Y |
| 8 **Fitzpatrick** | Y | Y | N | Y | Y | Y |
| 9 **Shuster** | Y | Y | N | Y | Y | Y |
| 10 **Sherwood** | Y | Y | N | Y | Y | Y |
| 11 Kanjorski | Y | Y | Y | N | Y | Y |
| 12 Murtha | Y | Y | ? | ? | ? | ? |
| 13 Schwartz | Y | Y | Y | N | Y | Y |
| 14 Doyle | Y | Y | Y | N | Y | Y |
| 15 **Dent** | Y | Y | N | Y | Y | Y |
| 16 **Pitts** | Y | Y | N | Y | Y | Y |
| 17 Holden | Y | Y | Y | N | Y | Y |
| 18 **Murphy** | ? | ? | ? | ? | ? | ? |
| 19 **Platts** | Y | Y | N | Y | Y | Y |
| **RHODE ISLAND** | | | | | | |
| 1 Kennedy | Y | Y | Y | N | Y | Y |
| 2 Langevin | Y | Y | Y | N | Y | Y |
| **SOUTH CAROLINA** | | | | | | |
| 1 **Brown** | Y | Y | N | Y | Y | Y |
| 2 **Wilson** | Y | Y | N | Y | Y | Y |
| 3 **Barrett** | Y | Y | N | Y | Y | Y |
| 4 **Inglis** | Y | Y | N | Y | Y | Y |
| 5 Spratt | Y | Y | Y | N | Y | Y |
| 6 Clyburn | Y | Y | Y | N | Y | Y |
| **SOUTH DAKOTA** | | | | | | |
| AL Herseth | Y | Y | Y | Y | Y | Y |
| **TENNESSEE** | | | | | | |
| 1 **Jenkins** | Y | Y | ? | ? | ? | Y |
| 2 **Duncan** | Y | Y | N | Y | Y | Y |
| 3 **Wamp** | Y | Y | N | Y | Y | Y |
| 4 Davis | Y | Y | Y | N | Y | Y |
| 5 Cooper | Y | Y | Y | Y | Y | Y |
| 6 Gordon | Y | Y | Y | Y | Y | Y |
| 7 **Blackburn** | Y | Y | N | Y | Y | Y |
| 8 Tanner | Y | Y | Y | Y | Y | Y |
| 9 Ford | Y | Y | Y | Y | Y | Y |
| **TEXAS** | | | | | | |
| 1 **Gohmert** | Y | Y | N | Y | Y | Y |
| 2 **Poe** | Y | Y | N | Y | Y | Y |
| 3 **Johnson, S.** | Y | Y | N | Y | Y | Y |
| 4 **Hall** | Y | Y | N | Y | Y | Y |
| 5 **Hensarling** | Y | Y | N | Y | Y | Y |
| 6 **Barton** | Y | Y | N | Y | Y | Y |
| 7 **Culberson** | Y | Y | N | Y | Y | Y |
| 8 **Brady** | Y | Y | N | Y | Y | Y |
| 9 Green, A. | Y | Y | Y | N | Y | Y |
| 10 **McCaul** | Y | Y | N | Y | Y | Y |
| 11 **Conaway** | Y | Y | N | Y | Y | Y |
| 12 **Granger** | Y | Y | N | Y | Y | Y |
| 13 **Thornberry** | Y | Y | N | Y | Y | Y |
| 14 **Paul** | N | Y | N | N | Y | Y |
| 15 Hinojosa | Y | Y | Y | N | Y | Y |
| 16 Reyes | Y | Y | Y | ? | Y | Y |
| 17 Edwards | Y | Y | Y | N | Y | Y |
| 18 Jackson-Lee | Y | Y | Y | N | Y | Y |
| 19 **Neugebauer** | Y | Y | N | Y | Y | Y |
| 20 Gonzalez | Y | Y | Y | N | Y | Y |
| 21 **Smith** | Y | Y | N | Y | Y | Y |
| 22 **DeLay** | Y | Y | N | Y | Y | Y |
| 23 **Bonilla** | Y | Y | N | Y | Y | Y |
| 24 **Marchant** | Y | Y | N | Y | Y | Y |
| 25 Doggett | Y | Y | Y | N | Y | Y |
| 26 **Burgess** | Y | Y | N | Y | Y | Y |
| 27 Ortiz | Y | Y | Y | Y | Y | Y |
| 28 Cuellar | Y | Y | Y | Y | Y | Y |
| 29 Green, G. | Y | Y | Y | N | Y | Y |
| 30 Johnson, E. | Y | Y | Y | N | Y | Y |
| 31 **Carter** | Y | ? | N | Y | Y | Y |
| 32 **Sessions** | Y | Y | N | Y | Y | Y |
| **UTAH** | | | | | | |
| 1 **Bishop** | Y | Y | N | Y | Y | Y |
| 2 Matheson | Y | Y | Y | Y | Y | Y |
| 3 **Cannon** | Y | Y | N | Y | Y | Y |
| **VERMONT** | | | | | | |
| AL *Sanders* | Y | Y | Y | N | Y | Y |
| **VIRGINIA** | | | | | | |
| 1 **Davis, J.** | Y | Y | N | Y | Y | Y |
| 2 **Drake** | Y | Y | N | Y | Y | Y |
| 3 Scott | Y | Y | Y | N | Y | Y |
| 4 **Forbes** | Y | Y | N | Y | Y | Y |
| 5 **Goode** | Y | Y | N | Y | Y | Y |
| 6 **Goodlatte** | Y | Y | N | Y | Y | Y |
| 7 **Cantor** | Y | Y | N | Y | Y | Y |
| 8 Moran | Y | Y | N | N | Y | Y |
| 9 Boucher | Y | Y | Y | Y | Y | Y |
| 10 **Wolf** | Y | Y | N | Y | Y | Y |
| 11 **Davis, T.** | Y | Y | N | Y | Y | Y |
| **WASHINGTON** | | | | | | |
| 1 Inslee | Y | Y | Y | Y | Y | Y |
| 2 Larsen | Y | Y | N | N | Y | Y |
| 3 Baird | Y | Y | Y | N | Y | Y |
| 4 **Hastings** | Y | Y | N | Y | Y | Y |
| 5 **McMorris** | Y | Y | N | Y | Y | Y |
| 6 Dicks | Y | Y | N | Y | Y | Y |
| 7 McDermott | Y | Y | Y | N | Y | Y |
| 8 **Reichert** | Y | Y | N | Y | Y | Y |
| 9 Smith | Y | Y | N | Y | Y | Y |
| **WEST VIRGINIA** | | | | | | |
| 1 Mollohan | Y | Y | Y | N | Y | Y |
| 2 **Capito** | Y | Y | N | Y | Y | Y |
| 3 Rahall | Y | Y | Y | N | Y | Y |
| **WISCONSIN** | | | | | | |
| 1 **Ryan** | Y | Y | N | Y | Y | Y |
| 2 Baldwin | Y | Y | Y | N | Y | Y |
| 3 Kind | Y | Y | Y | Y | Y | Y |
| 4 Moore | Y | Y | Y | N | Y | Y |
| 5 **Sensenbrenner** | Y | Y | N | Y | Y | Y |
| 6 **Petri** | Y | Y | N | Y | Y | Y |
| 7 Obey | Y | Y | Y | N | Y | Y |
| 8 **Green** | Y | Y | N | Y | Y | Y |
| **WYOMING** | | | | | | |
| AL **Cubin** | Y | Y | N | Y | Y | Y |

# IN THE HOUSE | By Vote Number

**440.** **HR 5. Medical Malpractice/Previous Question.** Gingrey, R-Ga., motion to order the previous question (thus ending debate and the possibility of amendment) on adoption of the rule (H Res 385) to provide for House floor consideration of the bill that would cap the awards plaintiffs and their attorneys could receive in medical malpractice cases. Motion agreed to 226-200: R 226-0; D 0-199 (ND 0-148, SD 0-51); I 0-1. July 27, 2005.

**441.** **HR 5. Medical Malpractice/Rule.** Adoption of the rule (H Res 385) to provide for House consideration of the bill that would cap the awards plaintiffs and their attorneys could receive in medical malpractice cases. Adopted 226-200: R 225-1; D 1-198 (ND 1-147, SD 0-51); I 0-1. July 27, 2005.

**442.** **HR 3045. Central American Free Trade Agreement/Rule.** Adoption of the rule (H Res 386) to provide for House consideration of the bill that would implement a free trade agreement between the United States and Costa Rica, El Salvador, Guatemala, Honduras and Nicaragua and a separate pact with the Dominican Republic. Adopted 227-201: R 227-0; D 0-200 (ND 0-149, SD 0-51); I 0-1. July 27, 2005.

**443.** **HR 3045. Central American Free Trade Agreement/Passage.** Passage of the bill that would implement a free trade agreement between the United States and Costa Rica, El Salvador, Guatemala, Honduras and Nicaragua and a separate pact with the Dominican Republic. Passed 217-215: R 202-27; D 15-187 (ND 7-144, SD 8-43); I 0-1. A "yea" was a vote in support of the president's position. July 28, 2005 (in the session that began and the Congressional Record dated July 27, 2005).

**444.** **H Res 308. National Marina Day/Adoption.** Coble, R-N.C., motion to suspend the rules and adopt the resolution that would support the goals of National Marina Day and urge U.S. marinas to continue to provide environmentally friendly gateways to boating for Americans. Motion agreed to 385-0: R 203-0; D 181-0 (ND 137-0, SD 44-0); I 1-0. A two-thirds majority of those present and voting (257 in this case) is required for adoption under suspension of the rules. July 28, 2005 (in the session that began and the Congressional Record dated July 27, 2005).

**445.** **HR 6. Energy Policy/Conference Report.** Adoption of the conference report on the bill that would overhaul the nation's energy policy and provide for $14.6 billion in energy-related tax incentives. It would allow lawsuits involving the gasoline additive methyl tertiary butyl ether to be moved to a federal district court and require refiners to use 7.5 billion gallons of renewable fuels annually by 2012. It would grant the Federal Energy Regulatory Commission jurisdiction over reliability standards for electricity transmission networks and extend daylight-saving time by one month. Adopted (thus sent to the Senate) 275-156: R 200-31; D 75-124 (ND 41-107, SD 34-17); I 0-1. A "yea" was a vote in support of the president's position. July 28, 2005.

**446.** **HR 2361. Fiscal 2006 Interior-Environment Appropriations/Rule.** Adoption of the rule (H Res 392) to provide for House floor consideration of the conference report on the bill that would appropriate $26.2 billion in fiscal 2006 for the Department of Interior, the EPA and related agencies. Adopted 402-4: R 207-0; D 194-4 (ND 145-3, SD 49-1); I 1-0. July 28, 2005.

ND Northern Democrats, SD Southern Democrats
Southern states: Ala., Ark., Fla., Ga., Ky., La., Miss., N.C., Okla., S.C., Tenn., Texas, Va.

| | 440 | 441 | 442 | 443 | 444 | 445 | 446 |
|---|---|---|---|---|---|---|---|
| **ALABAMA** | | | | | | | |
| 1 Bonner | Y | Y | Y | Y | Y | N | Y |
| 2 Everett | Y | Y | Y | Y | Y | Y | Y |
| 3 Rogers | Y | Y | Y | Y | Y | Y | Y |
| 4 Aderholt | Y | Y | Y | Y | Y | Y | Y |
| 5 Cramer | N | N | N | N | ? | Y | Y |
| 6 Bachus | Y | Y | Y | Y | Y | Y | Y |
| 7 Davis | N | N | N | N | Y | Y | Y |
| **ALASKA** | | | | | | | |
| AL Young | Y | Y | Y | Y | Y | Y | Y |
| **ARIZONA** | | | | | | | |
| 1 Renzi | Y | Y | Y | Y | Y | Y | Y |
| 2 Franks | Y | Y | Y | Y | Y | Y | P |
| 3 Shadegg | Y | Y | Y | Y | Y | Y | Y |
| 4 Pastor | N | N | N | N | Y | N | Y |
| 5 Hayworth | Y | Y | Y | Y | Y | Y | Y |
| 6 Flake | Y | Y | Y | Y | Y | N | P |
| 7 Grijalva | N | N | N | N | ? | N | Y |
| 8 Kolbe | Y | Y | Y | Y | Y | Y | Y |
| **ARKANSAS** | | | | | | | |
| 1 Berry | N | N | N | N | Y | Y | Y |
| 2 Snyder | N | N | N | N | Y | N | Y |
| 3 Boozman | Y | Y | Y | Y | Y | Y | Y |
| 4 Ross | N | N | N | N | Y | Y | Y |
| **CALIFORNIA** | | | | | | | |
| 1 Thompson | N | N | N | N | N | Y | Y |
| 2 Herger | Y | Y | Y | Y | Y | Y | Y |
| 3 Lungren | Y | Y | Y | Y | Y | Y | P |
| 4 Doolittle | Y | Y | Y | Y | Y | Y | Y |
| 5 Matsui, D. | N | N | N | N | Y | N | Y |
| 6 Woolsey | N | N | N | N | Y | N | Y |
| 7 Miller, George | N | N | N | N | Y | N | Y |
| 8 Pelosi | N | N | N | N | Y | N | Y |
| 9 Lee | N | N | N | N | Y | N | Y |
| 10 Tauscher | N | N | N | N | Y | Y | Y |
| 11 Pombo | Y | Y | Y | Y | Y | Y | Y |
| 12 Lantos | N | N | N | N | Y | N | Y |
| 13 Stark | N | N | N | N | ? | N | Y |
| 14 Eshoo | N | N | N | N | Y | N | Y |
| 15 Honda | N | N | N | N | Y | N | Y |
| 16 Lofgren | N | N | N | N | Y | N | Y |
| 17 Farr | N | N | N | N | Y | N | Y |
| 18 Cardoza | N | N | N | N | Y | Y | Y |
| 19 Radanovich | Y | Y | Y | Y | Y | Y | Y |
| 20 Costa | N | N | N | N | Y | Y | Y |
| 21 Nunes | Y | Y | Y | Y | Y | Y | Y |
| 22 Thomas | Y | Y | Y | Y | Y | Y | Y |
| 23 Capps | N | N | N | N | Y | N | Y |
| 24 Gallegly | Y | Y | Y | Y | Y | Y | Y |
| 25 McKeon | Y | Y | Y | Y | Y | Y | Y |
| 26 Dreier | Y | Y | Y | Y | Y | Y | Y |
| 27 Sherman | N | N | N | N | Y | N | Y |
| 28 Berman | N | N | N | N | Y | N | Y |
| 29 Schiff | N | N | N | N | Y | N | Y |
| 30 Waxman | N | N | N | N | Y | N | Y |
| 31 Becerra | N | N | N | N | Y | N | Y |
| 32 Solis | N | N | N | N | Y | N | Y |
| 33 Watson | N | N | N | N | Y | N | Y |
| 34 Roybal-Allard | N | N | N | N | Y | N | Y |
| 35 Waters | N | N | N | N | Y | N | Y |
| 36 Harman | N | N | N | N | Y | N | Y |
| 37 Millender-McD. | N | N | N | N | Y | N | Y |
| 38 Napolitano | N | N | N | N | Y | N | Y |
| 39 Sánchez, Linda | ? | N | N | N | Y | N | Y |
| 40 Royce | Y | Y | Y | Y | Y | N | Y |
| 41 Lewis | Y | Y | Y | Y | Y | Y | Y |
| 42 Miller, Gary | Y | Y | Y | Y | ? | Y | Y |
| 43 Baca | N | N | N | N | Y | Y | Y |
| 44 Calvert | Y | Y | Y | Y | Y | Y | Y |
| 45 Bono | Y | Y | Y | Y | Y | Y | Y |
| 46 Rohrabacher | Y | Y | Y | Y | Y | N | Y |
| 47 Sanchez, Loretta | N | N | N | N | Y | N | Y |
| 48 Cox | Y | Y | Y | Y | Y | Y | Y |
| 49 Issa | Y | Y | Y | Y | Y | Y | Y |

| | 440 | 441 | 442 | 443 | 444 | 445 | 446 |
|---|---|---|---|---|---|---|---|
| 50 Cunningham | Y | Y | Y | Y | ? | Y | Y |
| 51 Filner | N | N | N | N | Y | N | Y |
| 52 Hunter | Y | Y | Y | Y | Y | Y | Y |
| 53 Davis | N | N | N | N | Y | N | Y |
| **COLORADO** | | | | | | | |
| 1 DeGette | N | N | N | N | Y | N | Y |
| 2 Udall | N | N | N | N | Y | N | Y |
| 3 Salazar | N | N | N | N | ? | Y | Y |
| 4 Musgrave | Y | Y | Y | Y | Y | Y | P |
| 5 Hefley | Y | N | Y | Y | ? | Y | P |
| 6 Tancredo | Y | Y | Y | N | ? | Y | P |
| 7 Beauprez | Y | Y | Y | Y | Y | Y | Y |
| **CONNECTICUT** | | | | | | | |
| 1 Larson | N | N | N | N | Y | N | Y |
| 2 Simmons | Y | Y | Y | N | Y | N | Y |
| 3 DeLauro | N | N | N | N | Y | N | Y |
| 4 Shays | Y | Y | Y | Y | Y | N | Y |
| 5 Johnson | Y | Y | Y | Y | Y | Y | Y |
| **DELAWARE** | | | | | | | |
| AL Castle | Y | Y | Y | Y | Y | N | Y |
| **FLORIDA** | | | | | | | |
| 1 Miller | Y | Y | Y | Y | Y | N | P |
| 2 Boyd | N | N | N | N | Y | N | Y |
| 3 Brown | N | N | N | N | Y | N | Y |
| 4 Crenshaw | Y | Y | Y | Y | Y | N | Y |
| 5 Brown-Waite | Y | Y | Y | Y | Y | N | Y |
| 6 Stearns | Y | Y | Y | Y | ? | Y | Y |
| 7 Mica | Y | Y | Y | Y | Y | Y | Y |
| 8 Keller | Y | Y | Y | Y | Y | N | Y |
| 9 Bilirakis | Y | Y | Y | Y | Y | Y | Y |
| 10 Young | Y | Y | Y | Y | ? | N | Y |
| 11 Davis | N | N | N | N | Y | N | Y |
| 12 Putnam | Y | Y | Y | Y | Y | Y | Y |
| 13 Harris | Y | Y | Y | Y | Y | Y | Y |
| 14 Mack | Y | Y | Y | Y | N | Y | Y |
| 15 Weldon | Y | Y | Y | Y | Y | N | Y |
| 16 Foley | Y | Y | Y | Y | Y | Y | Y |
| 17 Meek | N | N | N | N | Y | N | Y |
| 18 Ros-Lehtinen | Y | Y | Y | Y | Y | N | Y |
| 19 Wexler | N | N | N | N | Y | N | Y |
| 20 Wasserman-Schultz | N | N | N | N | Y | N | Y |
| 21 Diaz-Balart, L. | Y | Y | Y | Y | Y | N | Y |
| 22 Shaw | Y | Y | Y | Y | Y | N | Y |
| 23 Hastings | N | N | N | N | Y | N | Y |
| 24 Feeney | Y | Y | Y | Y | Y | N | Y |
| 25 Diaz-Balart, M. | Y | Y | Y | Y | Y | N | Y |
| **GEORGIA** | | | | | | | |
| 1 Kingston | Y | Y | Y | Y | Y | Y | Y |
| 2 Bishop | N | N | N | N | Y | Y | Y |
| 3 Marshall | N | N | N | N | Y | Y | Y |
| 4 McKinney | N | N | N | N | Y | N | Y |
| 5 Lewis | N | N | N | N | Y | N | Y |
| 6 Price | Y | Y | Y | Y | Y | Y | P |
| 7 Linder | Y | Y | Y | Y | Y | Y | Y |
| 8 Westmoreland | Y | Y | Y | Y | Y | Y | P |
| 9 Norwood | Y | Y | Y | N | ? | Y | Y |
| 10 Deal | Y | Y | Y | Y | Y | Y | Y |
| 11 Gingrey | Y | Y | Y | Y | Y | Y | Y |
| 12 Barrow | N | N | N | N | Y | Y | Y |
| 13 Scott | N | N | N | N | Y | Y | Y |
| **HAWAII** | | | | | | | |
| 1 Abercrombie | N | ? | N | N | Y | Y | Y |
| 2 Case | N | N | N | N | Y | N | Y |
| **IDAHO** | | | | | | | |
| 1 Otter | Y | Y | Y | N | ? | Y | P |
| 2 Simpson | Y | Y | Y | N | ? | Y | Y |
| **ILLINOIS** | | | | | | | |
| 1 Rush | N | N | N | N | Y | Y | Y |
| 2 Jackson | N | N | N | N | Y | N | Y |
| 3 Lipinski | N | N | N | N | Y | N | Y |
| 4 Gutierrez | N | N | N | N | Y | N | Y |
| 5 Emanuel | N | N | N | N | Y | N | Y |
| 6 Hyde | Y | Y | Y | Y | Y | Y | Y |
| 7 Davis | N | N | N | N | Y | N | Y |
| 8 Bean | N | N | N | Y | Y | Y | Y |
| 9 Schakowsky | N | N | N | N | Y | ? | ? |
| 10 Kirk | Y | Y | Y | Y | Y | Y | Y |
| 11 Weller | Y | Y | Y | Y | Y | Y | Y |
| 12 Costello | N | N | N | N | Y | N | Y |

**KEY**  **Republicans**    Democrats    *Independents*

| | | | |
|---|---|---|---|
| Y | Voted for (yea) | X | Paired against |
| # | Paired for | – | Announced against |
| + | Announced for | P | Voted "present" |
| N | Voted against (nay) | | |
| C | Voted "present" to avoid possible conflict of interest | | |
| ? | Did not vote or otherwise make a position known | | |

| | 440 | 441 | 442 | 443 | 444 | 445 | 446 |
|---|---|---|---|---|---|---|---|
| 13 **Biggert** | Y | Y | Y | Y | Y | Y | Y |
| 14 **Hastert** | | | | Y | | Y | |
| 15 **Johnson** | Y | Y | Y | Y | Y | Y | Y |
| 16 **Manzullo** | Y | Y | Y | Y | Y | Y | Y |
| 17 Evans | N | N | N | N | Y | Y | Y |
| 18 **LaHood** | Y | Y | Y | Y | Y | Y | Y |
| 19 **Shimkus** | Y | Y | Y | Y | Y | Y | Y |
| **INDIANA** | | | | | | | |
| 1 Visclosky | N | N | N | N | Y | Y | Y |
| 2 **Chocola** | Y | Y | Y | Y | Y | Y | Y |
| 3 **Souder** | Y | Y | Y | Y | Y | Y | Y |
| 4 **Buyer** | Y | Y | Y | Y | ? | Y | Y |
| 5 **Burton** | Y | Y | Y | Y | Y | Y | Y |
| 6 **Pence** | Y | Y | Y | Y | Y | Y | P |
| 7 Carson | ? | ? | ? | N | ? | Y | Y |
| 8 **Hostettler** | Y | Y | Y | N | Y | Y | Y |
| 9 **Sodrel** | Y | Y | Y | Y | Y | Y | P |
| **IOWA** | | | | | | | |
| 1 **Nussle** | Y | Y | Y | Y | Y | Y | Y |
| 2 **Leach** | ? | ? | ? | Y | Y | Y | Y |
| 3 Boswell | N | N | N | N | Y | Y | Y |
| 4 **Latham** | Y | Y | Y | Y | Y | Y | Y |
| 5 **King** | Y | Y | Y | Y | Y | Y | P |
| **KANSAS** | | | | | | | |
| 1 **Moran** | Y | Y | Y | Y | Y | Y | Y |
| 2 **Ryun** | Y | Y | Y | Y | Y | Y | Y |
| 3 Moore | N | N | N | Y | Y | Y | Y |
| 4 **Tiahrt** | Y | Y | Y | Y | Y | Y | Y |
| **KENTUCKY** | | | | | | | |
| 1 **Whitfield** | Y | Y | Y | Y | ? | Y | Y |
| 2 **Lewis** | Y | Y | Y | Y | Y | Y | Y |
| 3 **Northup** | Y | Y | Y | Y | Y | Y | Y |
| 4 **Davis** | Y | Y | Y | Y | Y | Y | Y |
| 5 **Rogers** | Y | Y | Y | Y | Y | Y | Y |
| 6 Chandler | N | N | N | N | Y | N | Y |
| **LOUISIANA** | | | | | | | |
| 1 **Jindal** | Y | Y | Y | N | Y | Y | Y |
| 2 Jefferson | N | N | N | Y | ? | Y | Y |
| 3 Melancon | N | N | N | N | Y | Y | Y |
| 4 **McCrery** | Y | Y | Y | Y | Y | Y | Y |
| 5 **Alexander** | Y | Y | Y | Y | Y | Y | Y |
| 6 **Baker** | Y | Y | Y | Y | ? | Y | Y |
| 7 **Boustany** | Y | Y | Y | N | Y | Y | Y |
| **MAINE** | | | | | | | |
| 1 Allen | N | N | N | N | Y | N | Y |
| 2 Michaud | N | N | N | N | Y | N | Y |
| **MARYLAND** | | | | | | | |
| 1 **Gilchrest** | Y | Y | Y | Y | Y | Y | Y |
| 2 Ruppersberger | N | N | N | N | Y | Y | Y |
| 3 Cardin | N | N | N | N | Y | N | Y |
| 4 Wynn | N | N | N | N | Y | Y | Y |
| 5 Hoyer | N | N | N | N | Y | Y | Y |
| 6 **Bartlett** | Y | Y | Y | Y | Y | N | P |
| 7 Cummings | N | N | N | N | Y | N | Y |
| 8 Van Hollen | N | N | N | N | Y | N | Y |
| **MASSACHUSETTS** | | | | | | | |
| 1 Olver | N | N | N | N | Y | N | Y |
| 2 Neal | N | N | N | N | Y | N | Y |
| 3 McGovern | N | N | N | N | Y | N | Y |
| 4 Frank | N | N | N | N | Y | N | Y |
| 5 Meehan | N | N | N | N | Y | N | Y |
| 6 Tierney | N | N | N | N | Y | N | Y |
| 7 Markey | N | N | N | N | ? | N | Y |
| 8 Capuano | N | N | N | N | Y | N | N |
| 9 Lynch | N | N | N | N | Y | N | Y |
| 10 Delahunt | N | N | N | N | Y | N | Y |
| **MICHIGAN** | | | | | | | |
| 1 Stupak | N | N | N | N | Y | Y | N |
| 2 **Hoekstra** | Y | Y | Y | Y | Y | Y | Y |
| 3 **Ehlers** | Y | Y | Y | Y | Y | Y | Y |
| 4 **Camp** | Y | Y | Y | Y | Y | Y | Y |
| 5 Kildee | N | N | N | N | Y | N | Y |
| 6 **Upton** | Y | Y | Y | Y | Y | Y | Y |
| 7 **Schwarz** | Y | Y | Y | Y | Y | Y | Y |
| 8 **Rogers** | Y | Y | Y | Y | Y | Y | Y |
| 9 **Knollenberg** | Y | Y | Y | Y | Y | Y | Y |
| 10 **Miller** | Y | Y | Y | N | Y | Y | Y |
| 11 **McCotter** | Y | Y | Y | N | Y | Y | Y |
| 12 Levin | N | N | N | N | Y | Y | Y |
| 13 Kilpatrick | N | N | N | N | Y | N | Y |
| 14 Conyers | N | N | N | N | Y | N | Y |
| 15 Dingell | N | N | N | N | ? | Y | N |

| | 440 | 441 | 442 | 443 | 444 | 445 | 446 |
|---|---|---|---|---|---|---|---|
| **MINNESOTA** | | | | | | | |
| 1 **Gutknecht** | Y | Y | Y | N | ? | Y | P |
| 2 **Kline** | Y | Y | Y | Y | Y | Y | Y |
| 3 **Ramstad** | Y | Y | Y | Y | Y | Y | Y |
| 4 McCollum | N | N | N | N | Y | N | Y |
| 5 Sabo | N | N | N | N | Y | N | Y |
| 6 **Kennedy** | Y | Y | Y | Y | Y | Y | Y |
| 7 Peterson | N | Y | N | N | Y | Y | Y |
| 8 Oberstar | N | N | N | N | Y | Y | Y |
| **MISSISSIPPI** | | | | | | | |
| 1 **Wicker** | Y | Y | Y | Y | Y | Y | Y |
| 2 Thompson | N | N | N | N | Y | Y | Y |
| 3 **Pickering** | Y | Y | Y | Y | Y | Y | Y |
| 4 Taylor | N | N | N | N | Y | N | Y |
| **MISSOURI** | | | | | | | |
| 1 Clay | N | N | N | N | ? | N | Y |
| 2 **Akin** | Y | Y | Y | Y | Y | Y | P |
| 3 Carnahan | N | N | N | N | Y | N | Y |
| 4 Skelton | N | N | N | Y | ? | Y | Y |
| 5 Cleaver | N | N | N | N | Y | N | Y |
| 6 **Graves** | Y | Y | Y | Y | Y | Y | Y |
| 7 **Blunt** | Y | Y | Y | Y | ? | Y | Y |
| 8 **Emerson** | Y | Y | Y | Y | Y | Y | Y |
| 9 **Hulshof** | Y | Y | Y | Y | Y | Y | Y |
| **MONTANA** | | | | | | | |
| AL **Rehberg** | Y | Y | Y | N | Y | Y | Y |
| **NEBRASKA** | | | | | | | |
| 1 **Fortenberry** | Y | Y | Y | Y | Y | Y | Y |
| 2 **Terry** | Y | Y | Y | Y | Y | Y | Y |
| 3 **Osborne** | Y | Y | Y | Y | Y | Y | Y |
| **NEVADA** | | | | | | | |
| 1 Berkley | N | N | N | N | Y | N | Y |
| 2 **Gibbons** | Y | Y | Y | Y | Y | Y | Y |
| 3 **Porter** | Y | Y | Y | Y | Y | Y | Y |
| **NEW HAMPSHIRE** | | | | | | | |
| 1 **Bradley** | Y | Y | Y | Y | Y | N | Y |
| 2 **Bass** | Y | Y | Y | Y | ? | Y | Y |
| **NEW JERSEY** | | | | | | | |
| 1 Andrews | N | N | N | N | Y | N | Y |
| 2 **LoBiondo** | Y | Y | Y | N | Y | N | Y |
| 3 **Saxton** | Y | Y | Y | Y | Y | N | Y |
| 4 **Smith** | Y | Y | Y | N | Y | N | Y |
| 5 **Garrett** | Y | Y | Y | N | ? | Y | Y |
| 6 Pallone | N | N | N | N | Y | N | Y |
| 7 **Ferguson** | Y | Y | Y | Y | Y | Y | Y |
| 8 Pascrell | N | N | N | N | Y | N | Y |
| 9 Rothman | N | N | N | N | Y | N | Y |
| 10 Payne | N | N | N | N | Y | ? | ? |
| 11 **Frelinghuysen** | Y | Y | Y | Y | Y | Y | Y |
| 12 Holt | N | N | N | N | Y | N | Y |
| 13 Menendez | N | N | N | N | Y | N | Y |
| **NEW MEXICO** | | | | | | | |
| 1 **Wilson** | Y | Y | Y | Y | Y | Y | Y |
| 2 **Pearce** | Y | Y | Y | Y | Y | Y | Y |
| 3 Udall | N | N | N | N | Y | Y | Y |
| **NEW YORK** | | | | | | | |
| 1 Bishop | N | N | N | N | Y | N | Y |
| 2 Israel | N | N | N | N | Y | N | Y |
| 3 **King** | Y | Y | Y | Y | Y | Y | Y |
| 4 McCarthy | N | N | N | N | Y | N | Y |
| 5 Ackerman | N | N | N | N | Y | N | Y |
| 6 Meeks | N | N | N | Y | ? | Y | Y |
| 7 Crowley | N | N | N | N | Y | N | Y |
| 8 Nadler | N | N | N | N | Y | N | Y |
| 9 Weiner | N | N | N | N | Y | N | Y |
| 10 Towns | N | N | N | Y | ? | Y | Y |
| 11 Owens | N | N | N | N | Y | N | Y |
| 12 Velázquez | N | N | N | N | ? | N | Y |
| 13 **Fossella** | Y | Y | Y | Y | Y | Y | Y |
| 14 Maloney | N | N | N | N | Y | N | Y |
| 15 Rangel | N | N | N | N | Y | N | Y |
| 16 Serrano | N | N | N | N | Y | N | Y |
| 17 Engel | N | N | N | N | Y | N | Y |
| 18 Lowey | N | N | N | N | Y | N | Y |
| 19 **Kelly** | Y | Y | Y | Y | Y | N | Y |
| 20 **Sweeney** | Y | Y | Y | Y | Y | Y | Y |
| 21 McNulty | N | N | N | N | Y | N | Y |
| 22 Hinchey | N | N | N | N | Y | N | Y |
| 23 **McHugh** | Y | Y | Y | N | ? | Y | Y |
| 24 **Boehlert** | Y | Y | Y | Y | Y | N | Y |
| 25 **Walsh** | Y | Y | Y | Y | Y | Y | Y |
| 26 **Reynolds** | Y | Y | Y | Y | Y | Y | Y |
| 27 Higgins | N | N | N | N | Y | N | Y |
| 28 Slaughter | N | N | N | N | Y | Y | Y |
| 29 **Kuhl** | Y | Y | Y | Y | Y | Y | Y |

| | 440 | 441 | 442 | 443 | 444 | 445 | 446 |
|---|---|---|---|---|---|---|---|
| **NORTH CAROLINA** | | | | | | | |
| 1 Butterfield | N | N | N | N | Y | Y | Y |
| 2 Etheridge | N | N | N | N | Y | Y | Y |
| 3 **Jones** | Y | Y | Y | N | Y | N | P |
| 4 Price | N | N | N | N | Y | N | Y |
| 5 **Foxx** | Y | Y | Y | N | Y | Y | P |
| 6 **Coble** | Y | Y | Y | N | Y | Y | Y |
| 7 McIntyre | N | N | N | N | Y | Y | Y |
| 8 **Hayes** | Y | Y | Y | Y | Y | Y | Y |
| 9 **Myrick** | Y | Y | Y | Y | Y | Y | Y |
| 10 **McHenry** | Y | Y | Y | N | Y | Y | Y |
| 11 **Taylor** | Y | Y | Y | ? | ? | Y | Y |
| 12 Watt | N | N | N | N | Y | N | Y |
| 13 Miller | N | N | N | N | Y | N | Y |
| **NORTH DAKOTA** | | | | | | | |
| AL Pomeroy | N | N | N | N | Y | Y | Y |
| **OHIO** | | | | | | | |
| 1 **Chabot** | Y | Y | Y | Y | Y | Y | Y |
| 2 Vacant | | | | | | | |
| 3 **Turner** | Y | Y | Y | Y | Y | Y | Y |
| 4 **Oxley** | Y | Y | Y | Y | ? | Y | Y |
| 5 **Gillmor** | Y | Y | Y | Y | Y | Y | Y |
| 6 Strickland | N | N | N | N | Y | Y | Y |
| 7 **Hobson** | Y | Y | Y | Y | Y | Y | Y |
| 8 **Boehner** | Y | Y | Y | Y | Y | Y | Y |
| 9 Kaptur | N | N | N | N | Y | N | Y |
| 10 Kucinich | N | N | N | N | Y | N | Y |
| 11 Jones | N | N | N | N | Y | N | Y |
| 12 **Tiberi** | Y | Y | Y | Y | Y | Y | Y |
| 13 Brown | N | N | N | N | Y | N | Y |
| 14 **LaTourette** | Y | Y | Y | Y | Y | Y | Y |
| 15 **Pryce** | Y | Y | Y | Y | Y | Y | Y |
| 16 **Regula** | Y | Y | Y | Y | Y | Y | Y |
| 17 Ryan | N | N | N | N | Y | Y | Y |
| 18 **Ney** | Y | Y | Y | N | Y | Y | Y |
| **OKLAHOMA** | | | | | | | |
| 1 **Sullivan** | Y | Y | Y | Y | Y | Y | Y |
| 2 Boren | N | N | N | N | Y | Y | Y |
| 3 **Lucas** | Y | Y | Y | Y | Y | Y | Y |
| 4 **Cole** | Y | Y | Y | Y | Y | Y | Y |
| 5 **Istook** | Y | Y | Y | Y | ? | Y | Y |
| **OREGON** | | | | | | | |
| 1 Wu | N | N | N | N | Y | N | Y |
| 2 **Walden** | Y | Y | Y | Y | Y | Y | Y |
| 3 Blumenauer | N | N | N | N | Y | N | Y |
| 4 DeFazio | N | N | N | N | Y | N | Y |
| 5 Hooley | N | N | N | N | Y | N | Y |
| **PENNSYLVANIA** | | | | | | | |
| 1 Brady | ? | ? | ? | N | Y | ? | ? |
| 2 Fattah | N | N | N | N | Y | N | Y |
| 3 **English** | Y | Y | Y | Y | Y | Y | Y |
| 4 **Hart** | Y | Y | Y | Y | Y | Y | Y |
| 5 **Peterson** | Y | Y | Y | Y | Y | Y | Y |
| 6 **Gerlach** | Y | Y | Y | Y | Y | Y | Y |
| 7 **Weldon** | Y | Y | Y | Y | Y | Y | Y |
| 8 **Fitzpatrick** | Y | Y | Y | Y | Y | N | Y |
| 9 **Shuster** | Y | Y | Y | Y | Y | Y | Y |
| 10 **Sherwood** | Y | Y | Y | Y | Y | Y | Y |
| 11 Kanjorski | N | N | N | N | Y | N | Y |
| 12 Murtha | N | N | N | N | ? | Y | Y |
| 13 Schwartz | N | N | N | N | Y | N | Y |
| 14 Doyle | N | N | N | N | Y | N | Y |
| 15 **Dent** | Y | Y | Y | Y | Y | Y | Y |
| 16 **Pitts** | Y | Y | Y | Y | Y | Y | Y |
| 17 Holden | N | N | N | N | ? | Y | Y |
| 18 **Murphy** | ? | ? | ? | Y | Y | Y | Y |
| 19 **Platts** | Y | Y | Y | Y | Y | Y | Y |
| **RHODE ISLAND** | | | | | | | |
| 1 Kennedy | N | N | N | N | Y | N | Y |
| 2 Langevin | N | N | N | N | Y | N | Y |
| **SOUTH CAROLINA** | | | | | | | |
| 1 **Brown** | Y | Y | Y | Y | Y | Y | Y |
| 2 **Wilson** | Y | Y | Y | Y | ? | Y | Y |
| 3 **Barrett** | Y | Y | Y | Y | Y | Y | P |
| 4 **Inglis** | Y | Y | Y | Y | Y | Y | Y |
| 5 Spratt | N | N | N | N | Y | Y | Y |
| 6 Clyburn | N | N | N | N | Y | Y | Y |
| **SOUTH DAKOTA** | | | | | | | |
| AL Herseth | N | N | N | N | Y | Y | Y |
| **TENNESSEE** | | | | | | | |
| 1 **Jenkins** | Y | Y | Y | Y | ? | Y | Y |
| 2 **Duncan** | Y | Y | Y | Y | Y | Y | Y |

| | 440 | 441 | 442 | 443 | 444 | 445 | 446 |
|---|---|---|---|---|---|---|---|
| 3 **Wamp** | Y | Y | Y | Y | Y | Y | Y |
| 4 Davis | N | N | N | N | Y | Y | Y |
| 5 Cooper | N | N | N | Y | Y | N | N |
| 6 Gordon | N | N | N | N | ? | Y | Y |
| 7 **Blackburn** | Y | Y | Y | Y | Y | Y | Y |
| 8 Tanner | N | N | N | Y | Y | Y | P |
| 9 Ford | N | N | N | N | Y | Y | Y |
| **TEXAS** | | | | | | | |
| 1 **Gohmert** | Y | Y | Y | Y | Y | Y | P |
| 2 **Poe** | Y | Y | Y | Y | Y | Y | Y |
| 3 **Johnson, S.** | Y | Y | Y | Y | Y | Y | Y |
| 4 **Hall** | Y | Y | Y | Y | Y | Y | Y |
| 5 **Hensarling** | Y | Y | Y | Y | Y | Y | P |
| 6 **Barton** | Y | Y | Y | Y | Y | Y | Y |
| 7 **Culberson** | Y | Y | Y | Y | Y | Y | Y |
| 8 **Brady** | Y | Y | Y | Y | ? | Y | Y |
| 9 Green, A. | N | N | N | N | Y | Y | Y |
| 10 **McCaul** | Y | Y | Y | Y | Y | Y | Y |
| 11 **Conaway** | Y | Y | Y | Y | Y | Y | Y |
| 12 **Granger** | Y | Y | Y | Y | Y | Y | Y |
| 13 **Thornberry** | Y | Y | Y | Y | ? | Y | Y |
| 14 **Paul** | Y | Y | Y | N | Y | N | ? |
| 15 Hinojosa | N | N | N | Y | ? | Y | Y |
| 16 Reyes | N | N | N | N | ? | Y | Y |
| 17 Edwards | N | N | N | N | ? | Y | Y |
| 18 Jackson-Lee | N | N | N | N | Y | Y | Y |
| 19 **Neugebauer** | Y | Y | Y | Y | Y | Y | Y |
| 20 Gonzalez | N | N | N | N | Y | Y | Y |
| 21 **Smith** | Y | Y | Y | Y | Y | Y | Y |
| 22 **DeLay** | Y | Y | Y | Y | Y | Y | Y |
| 23 **Bonilla** | Y | Y | Y | Y | Y | Y | Y |
| 24 **Marchant** | Y | Y | Y | Y | Y | Y | Y |
| 25 Doggett | N | N | N | N | Y | N | Y |
| 26 **Burgess** | Y | Y | Y | Y | Y | Y | Y |
| 27 Ortiz | N | N | N | Y | Y | Y | Y |
| 28 Cuellar | N | N | N | Y | Y | Y | Y |
| 29 Green, G. | N | N | N | N | Y | Y | Y |
| 30 Johnson, E. | N | N | N | N | Y | Y | Y |
| 31 **Carter** | Y | Y | Y | Y | Y | Y | Y |
| 32 **Sessions** | Y | Y | Y | Y | Y | Y | Y |
| **UTAH** | | | | | | | |
| 1 **Bishop** | Y | Y | Y | Y | Y | Y | Y |
| 2 Matheson | N | N | N | Y | Y | Y | Y |
| 3 **Cannon** | Y | Y | Y | Y | Y | Y | Y |
| **VERMONT** | | | | | | | |
| AL *Sanders* | N | N | N | N | Y | N | Y |
| **VIRGINIA** | | | | | | | |
| 1 **Davis, J.** | ? | ? | ? | ? | ? | Y | Y |
| 2 **Drake** | Y | Y | Y | Y | Y | Y | Y |
| 3 Scott | N | N | N | N | Y | Y | Y |
| 4 **Forbes** | Y | Y | Y | Y | Y | Y | Y |
| 5 **Goode** | Y | Y | Y | N | ? | Y | Y |
| 6 **Goodlatte** | Y | Y | Y | Y | Y | Y | Y |
| 7 **Cantor** | Y | Y | Y | Y | Y | Y | Y |
| 8 Moran | N | N | N | Y | Y | N | Y |
| 9 Boucher | N | N | N | N | ? | Y | Y |
| 10 **Wolf** | Y | Y | Y | Y | Y | Y | Y |
| 11 **Davis, T.** | Y | Y | Y | Y | Y | Y | Y |
| **WASHINGTON** | | | | | | | |
| 1 Inslee | N | N | N | N | Y | N | Y |
| 2 Larsen | N | N | N | N | Y | Y | Y |
| 3 Baird | N | N | N | N | Y | N | Y |
| 4 **Hastings** | Y | Y | Y | Y | Y | Y | Y |
| 5 **McMorris** | Y | Y | Y | Y | Y | Y | Y |
| 6 Dicks | N | N | N | Y | ? | Y | Y |
| 7 McDermott | N | N | N | N | Y | N | Y |
| 8 **Reichert** | Y | Y | Y | Y | Y | Y | Y |
| 9 Smith | N | N | N | N | Y | N | Y |
| **WEST VIRGINIA** | | | | | | | |
| 1 Mollohan | N | N | N | N | Y | Y | Y |
| 2 **Capito** | Y | Y | Y | N | Y | Y | Y |
| 3 Rahall | N | N | N | N | Y | Y | Y |
| **WISCONSIN** | | | | | | | |
| 1 **Ryan** | Y | Y | Y | Y | Y | Y | P |
| 2 Baldwin | N | N | N | N | Y | N | Y |
| 3 Kind | N | N | N | N | Y | N | Y |
| 4 Moore | N | N | N | N | Y | N | Y |
| 5 **Sensenbrenner** | P | P | Y | Y | Y | Y | Y |
| 6 **Petri** | Y | Y | Y | Y | Y | Y | Y |
| 7 Obey | N | N | N | N | Y | N | Y |
| 8 **Green** | Y | Y | Y | Y | Y | Y | Y |
| **WYOMING** | | | | | | | |
| AL **Cubin** | Y | Y | Y | N | ? | Y | Y |

# IN THE HOUSE | By Vote Number

## 447. HR 2985. Fiscal 2006 Legislative Branch Appropriations/Rule.
Adoption of the rule (H Res 396) to provide for House floor consideration of the conference report on the bill that would appropriate $3.8 billion in fiscal 2006 for legislative branch operations. Adopted 375-27: R 204-0; D 170-27 (ND 126-22, SD 44-5); I 1-0. July 28, 2005.

## 448. HR 5. Medical Malpractice/Recommit.
Conyers, D-Mich., motion to recommit the bill to the House Judiciary and Energy and Commerce committees with instructions to include language that would establish an independent advisory commission on medical malpractice insurance and require plaintiff attorneys in medical malpractice cases to file a certificate of merit. Motion rejected 193-234: R 0-227; D 192-7 (ND 144-4, SD 48-3); I 1-0. July 28, 2005.

## 449. HR 5. Medical Malpractice/Passage.
Passage of the bill that would cap the awards that plaintiffs and their attorneys could receive in medical malpractice cases. The bill would limit non-economic damages to $250,000 and cap punitive damages at $250,000 or double economic damages, whichever is greater. Punitive damages could only be awarded if economic damages were found. The bill would not pre-empt state damage caps but would impose federal caps on any states that do not have their own. Passed 230-194: R 216-9; D 14-184 (ND 6-141, SD 8-43); I 0-1. A "yea" was a vote in support of the president's position. July 28, 2005.

## 450. HR 2361. Fiscal 2006 Interior-Environment Appropriations/ Conference Report.
Adoption of the conference report on the bill that would appropriate $26.2 billion in fiscal 2006 for the Interior Department, the EPA and related agencies. It would provide $9.9 billion for the Interior Department, $7.7 billion for the EPA, $4.3 billion for the Forest Service, and $3.1 billion for the Indian Health Service. It also would provide $1.5 billion in fiscal 2005 funding for veterans' medical care, which would remain available through fiscal 2006. Adopted (thus sent to the Senate) 410-10: R 218-9; D 191-1 (ND 144-1, SD 47-0); I 1-0. July 28, 2005.

| | 447 | 448 | 449 | 450 |
|---|---|---|---|---|
| **ALABAMA** | | | | |
| 1 **Bonner** | Y | N | Y | Y |
| 2 **Everett** | Y | N | Y | Y |
| 3 **Rogers** | Y | N | Y | Y |
| 4 **Aderholt** | Y | N | Y | Y |
| 5 **Cramer** | Y | N | Y | ? |
| 6 **Bachus** | Y | N | Y | Y |
| 7 Davis | Y | Y | N | Y |
| **ALASKA** | | | | |
| AL **Young** | Y | N | Y | Y |
| **ARIZONA** | | | | |
| 1 **Renzi** | Y | N | Y | + |
| 2 **Franks** | P | N | Y | N |
| 3 **Shadegg** | Y | N | Y | Y |
| 4 Pastor | Y | Y | N | Y |
| 5 **Hayworth** | Y | N | Y | Y |
| 6 **Flake** | P | N | N | N |
| 7 Grijalva | Y | Y | N | Y |
| 8 **Kolbe** | Y | N | Y | Y |
| **ARKANSAS** | | | | |
| 1 Berry | Y | Y | N | Y |
| 2 Snyder | Y | Y | N | Y |
| 3 **Boozman** | Y | N | Y | Y |
| 4 Ross | Y | Y | N | Y |
| **CALIFORNIA** | | | | |
| 1 Thompson | Y | Y | N | Y |
| 2 **Herger** | Y | N | Y | Y |
| 3 **Lungren** | P | N | Y | Y |
| 4 **Doolittle** | Y | N | Y | Y |
| 5 Matsui, D. | Y | Y | N | Y |
| 6 Woolsey | Y | Y | N | Y |
| 7 Miller, George | N | Y | N | Y |
| 8 Pelosi | Y | Y | N | Y |
| 9 Lee | Y | Y | N | Y |
| 10 Tauscher | Y | Y | N | Y |
| 11 **Pombo** | Y | N | Y | Y |
| 12 Lantos | Y | Y | N | Y |
| 13 Stark | N | Y | N | Y |
| 14 Eshoo | Y | Y | N | Y |
| 15 Honda | Y | Y | N | Y |
| 16 Lofgren | N | Y | N | Y |
| 17 Farr | Y | Y | N | Y |
| 18 Cardoza | Y | Y | Y | Y |
| 19 **Radanovich** | Y | N | Y | Y |
| 20 Costa | Y | Y | N | Y |
| 21 **Nunes** | Y | N | Y | Y |
| 22 **Thomas** | Y | N | Y | Y |
| 23 Capps | Y | Y | N | Y |
| 24 **Gallegly** | Y | N | Y | Y |
| 25 **McKeon** | Y | N | Y | Y |
| 26 **Dreier** | Y | N | Y | Y |
| 27 Sherman | Y | Y | N | Y |
| 28 Berman | Y | Y | N | Y |
| 29 Schiff | Y | Y | N | Y |
| 30 Waxman | Y | Y | N | ? |
| 31 Becerra | Y | Y | N | Y |
| 32 Solis | Y | Y | N | Y |
| 33 Watson | Y | Y | N | Y |
| 34 Roybal-Allard | Y | Y | N | Y |
| 35 Waters | Y | Y | N | Y |
| 36 Harman | Y | Y | N | Y |
| 37 Millender-McD. | Y | Y | N | Y |
| 38 Napolitano | Y | Y | N | Y |
| 39 Sánchez, Linda | Y | Y | N | + |
| 40 **Royce** | Y | N | Y | Y |
| 41 **Lewis** | Y | N | Y | Y |
| 42 **Miller, Gary** | Y | N | Y | Y |
| 43 Baca | Y | Y | N | Y |
| 44 **Calvert** | Y | N | Y | Y |
| 45 **Bono** | Y | N | Y | Y |
| 46 **Rohrabacher** | Y | N | Y | Y |
| 47 Sanchez, Loretta | Y | Y | N | Y |
| 48 **Cox** | Y | N | Y | ? |
| 49 **Issa** | Y | N | Y | Y |

| | 447 | 448 | 449 | 450 |
|---|---|---|---|---|
| 50 **Cunningham** | Y | N | Y | Y |
| 51 Filner | Y | Y | N | Y |
| 52 **Hunter** | Y | N | Y | Y |
| 53 Davis | Y | Y | N | Y |
| **COLORADO** | | | | |
| 1 DeGette | Y | Y | N | Y |
| 2 Udall | Y | Y | N | Y |
| 3 Salazar | Y | Y | N | Y |
| 4 **Musgrave** | Y | N | Y | Y |
| 5 **Hefley** | P | N | Y | N |
| 6 **Tancredo** | P | N | Y | Y |
| 7 **Beauprez** | Y | N | Y | Y |
| **CONNECTICUT** | | | | |
| 1 Larson | Y | Y | N | Y |
| 2 **Simmons** | Y | N | Y | Y |
| 3 DeLauro | Y | Y | N | Y |
| 4 **Shays** | Y | N | Y | Y |
| 5 **Johnson** | Y | N | Y | Y |
| **DELAWARE** | | | | |
| AL **Castle** | Y | N | Y | Y |
| **FLORIDA** | | | | |
| 1 **Miller** | P | N | Y | Y |
| 2 Boyd | Y | Y | Y | Y |
| 3 Brown | Y | Y | N | Y |
| 4 **Crenshaw** | Y | N | Y | Y |
| 5 **Brown-Waite** | Y | N | Y | Y |
| 6 **Stearns** | Y | N | Y | Y |
| 7 **Mica** | Y | N | Y | Y |
| 8 **Keller** | Y | N | Y | Y |
| 9 **Bilirakis** | Y | N | Y | Y |
| 10 **Young** | Y | N | Y | Y |
| 11 Davis | Y | Y | N | ? |
| 12 **Putnam** | Y | N | Y | Y |
| 13 **Harris** | Y | N | Y | Y |
| 14 **Mack** | Y | N | Y | Y |
| 15 **Weldon** | Y | N | Y | Y |
| 16 **Foley** | Y | N | Y | Y |
| 17 Meek | Y | Y | N | Y |
| 18 **Ros-Lehtinen** | Y | N | Y | Y |
| 19 Wexler | Y | Y | N | Y |
| 20 Wasserman-Schultz | Y | Y | N | Y |
| 21 **Diaz-Balart, L.** | Y | N | N | Y |
| 22 **Shaw** | Y | N | Y | Y |
| 23 Hastings | Y | Y | N | Y |
| 24 **Feeney** | ? | N | Y | Y |
| 25 **Diaz-Balart, M.** | Y | N | Y | Y |
| **GEORGIA** | | | | |
| 1 **Kingston** | Y | N | Y | Y |
| 2 Bishop | Y | Y | N | Y |
| 3 Marshall | Y | Y | N | Y |
| 4 McKinney | Y | Y | N | Y |
| 5 Lewis | Y | Y | N | Y |
| 6 **Price** | P | N | Y | Y |
| 7 **Linder** | Y | N | Y | Y |
| 8 **Westmoreland** | P | N | Y | Y |
| 9 **Norwood** | Y | N | Y | Y |
| 10 **Deal** | Y | N | Y | Y |
| 11 **Gingrey** | Y | N | Y | Y |
| 12 Barrow | N | Y | N | Y |
| 13 Scott | Y | Y | Y | ? |
| **HAWAII** | | | | |
| 1 Abercrombie | Y | Y | N | Y |
| 2 Case | Y | Y | N | Y |
| **IDAHO** | | | | |
| 1 **Otter** | P | N | Y | Y |
| 2 **Simpson** | Y | N | Y | Y |
| **ILLINOIS** | | | | |
| 1 Rush | Y | Y | N | Y |
| 2 Jackson | Y | Y | N | Y |
| 3 Lipinski | Y | Y | N | Y |
| 4 Gutierrez | Y | Y | N | Y |
| 5 Emanuel | Y | Y | N | Y |
| 6 **Hyde** | Y | N | Y | Y |
| 7 Davis | Y | Y | N | Y |
| 8 Bean | Y | Y | N | Y |
| 9 Schakowsky | ? | ? | ? | ? |
| 10 **Kirk** | Y | N | Y | Y |
| 11 **Weller** | Y | N | Y | Y |
| 12 Costello | Y | Y | N | Y |

**KEY**    **Republicans**    Democrats    *Independents*

| | | | |
|---|---|---|---|
| **Y** Voted for (yea) | **X** Paired against | **C** Voted "present" to avoid possible conflict of interest |
| **#** Paired for | **–** Announced against | |
| **+** Announced for | **P** Voted "present" | **?** Did not vote or otherwise make a position known |
| **N** Voted against (nay) | | |

ND Northern Democrats, SD Southern Democrats
Southern states: Ala., Ark., Fla., Ga., Ky., La., Miss., N.C., Okla., S.C., Tenn., Texas, Va.

| | 447 | 448 | 449 | 450 |
|---|---|---|---|---|
| 13 Biggert | Y | N | Y | Y |
| 14 Hastert | | | | Y |
| 15 Johnson | Y | N | N | Y |
| 16 Manzullo | Y | N | Y | Y |
| 17 Evans | Y | Y | N | Y |
| 18 LaHood | Y | N | Y | Y |
| 19 Shimkus | Y | N | Y | Y |
| **INDIANA** | | | | |
| 1 Visclosky | Y | Y | N | Y |
| 2 Chocola | Y | N | Y | Y |
| 3 Souder | Y | N | Y | Y |
| 4 Buyer | Y | N | Y | Y |
| 5 Burton | Y | N | P | Y |
| 6 Pence | P | N | Y | N |
| 7 Carson | Y | ? | ? | ? |
| 8 Hostettler | Y | N | Y | Y |
| 9 Sodrel | P | N | Y | Y |
| **IOWA** | | | | |
| 1 Nussle | Y | N | Y | Y |
| 2 Leach | Y | N | Y | Y |
| 3 Boswell | Y | Y | N | Y |
| 4 Latham | Y | N | Y | Y |
| 5 King | P | N | Y | Y |
| **KANSAS** | | | | |
| 1 Moran | Y | N | Y | Y |
| 2 Ryun | Y | N | Y | Y |
| 3 Moore | Y | Y | N | Y |
| 4 Tiahrt | Y | N | Y | Y |
| **KENTUCKY** | | | | |
| 1 Whitfield | Y | N | Y | Y |
| 2 Lewis | Y | N | Y | Y |
| 3 Northup | Y | N | Y | Y |
| 4 Davis | Y | N | Y | Y |
| 5 Rogers | Y | N | Y | Y |
| 6 Chandler | Y | Y | N | Y |
| **LOUISIANA** | | | | |
| 1 Jindal | Y | N | Y | Y |
| 2 Jefferson | Y | Y | N | Y |
| 3 Melancon | Y | Y | N | Y |
| 4 McCrery | Y | N | Y | Y |
| 5 Alexander | Y | N | Y | Y |
| 6 Baker | Y | N | Y | Y |
| 7 Boustany | Y | N | Y | Y |
| **MAINE** | | | | |
| 1 Allen | Y | Y | N | Y |
| 2 Michaud | Y | Y | N | Y |
| **MARYLAND** | | | | |
| 1 Gilchrest | Y | N | Y | Y |
| 2 Ruppersberger | Y | Y | N | Y |
| 3 Cardin | Y | Y | N | Y |
| 4 Wynn | Y | Y | N | Y |
| 5 Hoyer | Y | Y | N | Y |
| 6 Bartlett | P | N | Y | Y |
| 7 Cummings | Y | Y | N | Y |
| 8 Van Hollen | Y | Y | N | Y |
| **MASSACHUSETTS** | | | | |
| 1 Olver | N | Y | N | ? |
| 2 Neal | Y | Y | N | Y |
| 3 McGovern | Y | Y | N | Y |
| 4 Frank | N | Y | N | Y |
| 5 Meehan | N | Y | N | Y |
| 6 Tierney | N | Y | N | Y |
| 7 Markey | N | Y | N | Y |
| 8 Capuano | N | Y | N | Y |
| 9 Lynch | Y | Y | N | ? |
| 10 Delahunt | Y | Y | N | Y |
| **MICHIGAN** | | | | |
| 1 Stupak | Y | Y | N | Y |
| 2 Hoekstra | Y | N | Y | Y |
| 3 Ehlers | Y | N | Y | Y |
| 4 Camp | Y | N | Y | Y |
| 5 Kildee | N | Y | N | Y |
| 6 Upton | Y | N | Y | Y |
| 7 Schwarz | Y | N | Y | Y |
| 8 Rogers | Y | N | Y | Y |
| 9 Knollenberg | Y | N | Y | Y |
| 10 Miller | Y | N | Y | Y |
| 11 McCotter | Y | N | Y | Y |
| 12 Levin | Y | Y | N | Y |
| 13 Kilpatrick | Y | Y | N | Y |
| 14 Conyers | N | Y | N | Y |
| 15 Dingell | Y | Y | N | N |

| | 447 | 448 | 449 | 450 |
|---|---|---|---|---|
| **MINNESOTA** | | | | |
| 1 Gutknecht | P | N | Y | Y |
| 2 Kline | Y | N | Y | Y |
| 3 Ramstad | Y | N | Y | Y |
| 4 McCollum | Y | Y | N | Y |
| 5 Sabo | Y | Y | N | Y |
| 6 Kennedy | Y | N | Y | Y |
| 7 Peterson | Y | Y | Y | Y |
| 8 Oberstar | Y | Y | N | Y |
| **MISSISSIPPI** | | | | |
| 1 Wicker | Y | N | Y | Y |
| 2 Thompson | ? | N | Y | Y |
| 3 Pickering | Y | N | Y | Y |
| 4 Taylor | N | N | Y | Y |
| **MISSOURI** | | | | |
| 1 Clay | Y | Y | N | Y |
| 2 Akin | P | N | Y | Y |
| 3 Carnahan | Y | Y | N | Y |
| 4 Skelton | Y | Y | N | Y |
| 5 Cleaver | Y | Y | N | Y |
| 6 Graves | Y | N | Y | N |
| 7 Blunt | Y | N | Y | Y |
| 8 Emerson | Y | N | Y | Y |
| 9 Hulshof | Y | N | Y | Y |
| **MONTANA** | | | | |
| AL Rehberg | Y | N | Y | Y |
| **NEBRASKA** | | | | |
| 1 Fortenberry | Y | N | Y | Y |
| 2 Terry | Y | N | N | Y |
| 3 Osborne | Y | N | Y | Y |
| **NEVADA** | | | | |
| 1 Berkley | Y | Y | N | Y |
| 2 Gibbons | Y | N | Y | Y |
| 3 Porter | Y | N | Y | Y |
| **NEW HAMPSHIRE** | | | | |
| 1 Bradley | Y | N | Y | Y |
| 2 Bass | Y | N | Y | Y |
| **NEW JERSEY** | | | | |
| 1 Andrews | Y | + | - | + |
| 2 LoBiondo | Y | N | Y | Y |
| 3 Saxton | Y | N | Y | Y |
| 4 Smith | Y | N | Y | Y |
| 5 Garrett | P | N | Y | Y |
| 6 Pallone | Y | Y | N | Y |
| 7 Ferguson | Y | Y | N | Y |
| 8 Pascrell | Y | Y | N | Y |
| 9 Rothman | Y | Y | N | Y |
| 10 Payne | ? | Y | N | Y |
| 11 Frelinghuysen | Y | N | Y | Y |
| 12 Holt | Y | Y | N | Y |
| 13 Menendez | Y | Y | N | Y |
| **NEW MEXICO** | | | | |
| 1 Wilson | Y | N | Y | Y |
| 2 Pearce | Y | N | Y | Y |
| 3 Udall | N | Y | N | Y |
| **NEW YORK** | | | | |
| 1 Bishop | Y | Y | N | Y |
| 2 Israel | N | Y | N | Y |
| 3 King | Y | N | N | Y |
| 4 McCarthy | Y | Y | N | Y |
| 5 Ackerman | Y | Y | N | Y |
| 6 Meeks | Y | Y | N | Y |
| 7 Crowley | Y | Y | N | Y |
| 8 Nadler | Y | Y | N | Y |
| 9 Weiner | Y | Y | N | Y |
| 10 Towns | Y | Y | N | Y |
| 11 Owens | Y | Y | N | Y |
| 12 Velázquez | N | Y | N | Y |
| 13 Fossella | Y | N | Y | Y |
| 14 Maloney | Y | Y | N | Y |
| 15 Rangel | Y | Y | N | Y |
| 16 Serrano | Y | Y | N | Y |
| 17 Engel | Y | Y | N | Y |
| 18 Lowey | Y | Y | N | Y |
| 19 Kelly | Y | ? | Y | Y |
| 20 Sweeney | Y | N | Y | Y |
| 21 McNulty | Y | Y | N | Y |
| 22 Hinchey | Y | Y | N | Y |
| 23 McHugh | Y | N | Y | Y |
| 24 Boehlert | Y | N | Y | Y |
| 25 Walsh | Y | N | Y | Y |
| 26 Reynolds | ? | N | Y | Y |
| 27 Higgins | Y | Y | N | Y |
| 28 Slaughter | Y | Y | N | Y |
| 29 Kuhl | Y | N | Y | Y |

| | 447 | 448 | 449 | 450 |
|---|---|---|---|---|
| **NORTH CAROLINA** | | | | |
| 1 Butterfield | Y | Y | N | Y |
| 2 Etheridge | Y | Y | N | Y |
| 3 Jones | P | N | Y | N |
| 4 Price | Y | Y | N | Y |
| 5 Foxx | P | N | Y | Y |
| 6 Coble | Y | N | Y | Y |
| 7 McIntyre | Y | Y | N | Y |
| 8 Hayes | Y | N | Y | Y |
| 9 Myrick | Y | N | Y | Y |
| 10 McHenry | Y | N | Y | Y |
| 11 Taylor | Y | N | Y | Y |
| 12 Watt | Y | Y | N | Y |
| 13 Miller | Y | Y | N | Y |
| **NORTH DAKOTA** | | | | |
| AL Pomeroy | Y | Y | Y | Y |
| **OHIO** | | | | |
| 1 Chabot | Y | N | Y | Y |
| 2 Vacant | | | | |
| 3 Turner | Y | N | Y | Y |
| 4 Oxley | Y | N | Y | Y |
| 5 Gillmor | Y | N | Y | ? |
| 6 Strickland | Y | Y | N | Y |
| 7 Hobson | Y | N | Y | Y |
| 8 Boehner | Y | N | Y | Y |
| 9 Kaptur | Y | Y | N | Y |
| 10 Kucinich | N | Y | N | Y |
| 11 Jones | Y | Y | N | Y |
| 12 Tiberi | Y | N | Y | Y |
| 13 Brown | N | Y | N | Y |
| 14 LaTourette | Y | N | Y | Y |
| 15 Pryce | Y | N | Y | Y |
| 16 Regula | Y | N | Y | Y |
| 17 Ryan | N | Y | N | Y |
| 18 Ney | Y | N | Y | Y |
| **OKLAHOMA** | | | | |
| 1 Sullivan | Y | N | Y | Y |
| 2 Boren | Y | Y | Y | Y |
| 3 Lucas | Y | N | Y | Y |
| 4 Cole | Y | N | Y | Y |
| 5 Istook | Y | N | N | Y |
| **OREGON** | | | | |
| 1 Wu | N | Y | ? | Y |
| 2 Walden | Y | N | Y | Y |
| 3 Blumenauer | Y | Y | N | Y |
| 4 DeFazio | Y | Y | N | Y |
| 5 Hooley | Y | Y | N | Y |
| **PENNSYLVANIA** | | | | |
| 1 Brady | ? | Y | N | Y |
| 2 Fattah | Y | Y | N | Y |
| 3 English | Y | N | Y | Y |
| 4 Hart | Y | N | Y | Y |
| 5 Peterson | Y | N | Y | Y |
| 6 Gerlach | Y | N | Y | Y |
| 7 Weldon | Y | N | Y | Y |
| 8 Fitzpatrick | Y | N | Y | Y |
| 9 Shuster | Y | N | Y | Y |
| 10 Sherwood | Y | N | Y | Y |
| 11 Kanjorski | Y | Y | N | Y |
| 12 Murtha | Y | Y | N | Y |
| 13 Schwartz | Y | Y | N | Y |
| 14 Doyle | Y | Y | N | Y |
| 15 Dent | Y | N | Y | Y |
| 16 Pitts | Y | N | Y | Y |
| 17 Holden | Y | N | Y | Y |
| 18 Murphy | Y | N | Y | Y |
| 19 Platts | Y | N | Y | Y |
| **RHODE ISLAND** | | | | |
| 1 Kennedy | N | Y | N | Y |
| 2 Langevin | Y | Y | N | Y |
| **SOUTH CAROLINA** | | | | |
| 1 Brown | Y | N | Y | Y |
| 2 Wilson | Y | N | Y | Y |
| 3 Barrett | P | N | Y | Y |
| 4 Inglis | Y | N | Y | Y |
| 5 Spratt | Y | Y | N | Y |
| 6 Clyburn | Y | Y | N | Y |
| **SOUTH DAKOTA** | | | | |
| AL Herseth | Y | Y | N | Y |
| **TENNESSEE** | | | | |
| 1 Jenkins | Y | N | N | Y |
| 2 Duncan | Y | N | N | N |

| | 447 | 448 | 449 | 450 |
|---|---|---|---|---|
| 3 Wamp | Y | N | Y | Y |
| 4 Davis | Y | Y | Y | Y |
| 5 Cooper | N | Y | N | Y |
| 6 Gordon | Y | N | Y | Y |
| 7 Blackburn | Y | N | Y | Y |
| 8 Tanner | P | Y | N | Y |
| 9 Ford | Y | Y | N | Y |
| **TEXAS** | | | | |
| 1 Gohmert | P | N | Y | Y |
| 2 Poe | Y | N | Y | Y |
| 3 Johnson, S. | Y | N | ? | Y |
| 4 Hall | Y | N | Y | Y |
| 5 Hensarling | P | N | Y | N |
| 6 Barton | Y | N | Y | Y |
| 7 Culberson | Y | N | Y | Y |
| 8 Brady | Y | N | Y | Y |
| 9 Green, A. | Y | Y | N | Y |
| 10 McCaul | Y | N | Y | Y |
| 11 Conaway | Y | N | Y | Y |
| 12 Granger | Y | N | Y | Y |
| 13 Thornberry | Y | N | Y | Y |
| 14 Paul | ? | ? | ? | ? |
| 15 Hinojosa | Y | Y | N | Y |
| 16 Reyes | Y | Y | N | Y |
| 17 Edwards | Y | Y | N | Y |
| 18 Jackson-Lee | N | Y | N | Y |
| 19 Neugebauer | Y | N | Y | Y |
| 20 Gonzalez | Y | Y | N | Y |
| 21 Smith | Y | N | Y | Y |
| 22 DeLay | Y | N | Y | Y |
| 23 Bonilla | Y | N | Y | Y |
| 24 Marchant | P | N | Y | Y |
| 25 Doggett | N | Y | N | Y |
| 26 Burgess | Y | N | + | Y |
| 27 Ortiz | Y | Y | N | Y |
| 28 Cuellar | Y | Y | Y | + |
| 29 Green, G. | Y | Y | N | Y |
| 30 Johnson, E. | Y | Y | N | Y |
| 31 Carter | Y | N | Y | Y |
| 32 Sessions | Y | N | Y | Y |
| **UTAH** | | | | |
| 1 Bishop | Y | N | Y | Y |
| 2 Matheson | Y | N | Y | Y |
| 3 Cannon | Y | N | Y | Y |
| **VERMONT** | | | | |
| AL Sanders | Y | Y | N | Y |
| **VIRGINIA** | | | | |
| 1 Davis, J. | Y | N | Y | Y |
| 2 Drake | Y | N | Y | Y |
| 3 Scott | Y | Y | N | Y |
| 4 Forbes | Y | N | Y | Y |
| 5 Goode | Y | N | Y | Y |
| 6 Goodlatte | Y | N | Y | Y |
| 7 Cantor | Y | N | Y | Y |
| 8 Moran | Y | Y | N | Y |
| 9 Boucher | Y | Y | N | Y |
| 10 Wolf | Y | N | Y | Y |
| 11 Davis, T. | Y | N | Y | Y |
| **WASHINGTON** | | | | |
| 1 Inslee | Y | Y | N | Y |
| 2 Larsen | Y | Y | N | Y |
| 3 Baird | N | Y | N | Y |
| 4 Hastings | Y | N | Y | Y |
| 5 McMorris | Y | N | Y | Y |
| 6 Dicks | Y | Y | N | Y |
| 7 McDermott | Y | Y | N | Y |
| 8 Reichert | Y | N | Y | Y |
| 9 Smith | Y | Y | N | Y |
| **WEST VIRGINIA** | | | | |
| 1 Mollohan | Y | N | Y | Y |
| 2 Capito | Y | N | Y | Y |
| 3 Rahall | Y | Y | N | Y |
| **WISCONSIN** | | | | |
| 1 Ryan | P | N | Y | Y |
| 2 Baldwin | N | Y | N | Y |
| 3 Kind | Y | Y | N | Y |
| 4 Moore | Y | Y | N | Y |
| 5 Sensenbrenner | Y | P | P | Y |
| 6 Petri | Y | N | Y | N |
| 7 Obey | Y | N | Y | Y |
| 8 Green | Y | N | Y | Y |
| **WYOMING** | | | | |
| AL Cubin | Y | N | Y | Y |

# IN THE HOUSE | By Vote Number

## 451. HR 2985. Fiscal 2006 Legislative Branch Appropriations/
**Conference Report.** Adoption of the conference report on the bill that would appropriate $3.8 billion in fiscal 2006 for legislative branch operations, including $1.1 billion for operations of the House of Representatives and $786 million for Senate operations. It also would require special elections if needed to replace members after a catastrophe. Adopted (thus sent to the Senate) 305-122: R 195-34; D 110-87 (ND 78-68, SD 32-19); I 0-1. July 28, 2005.

## 452. H Con Res 225. Adjournment/Adoption. Adoption of the concurrent
resolution that would provide for adjournment of the House until 2 p.m., Tuesday, Sept. 6 and adjournment of the Senate until 12 p.m. on Tuesday, Sept. 6. Adopted 404-16: R 227-0; D 177-16 (ND 134-9, SD 43-7); I 0-0. July 28, 2005.

## 453. HR 3. Surface Transportation Reauthorization/Conference Report.
Adoption of the conference report on the bill that would bring total authorization for federal highway, mass transit, safety and research programs, including fiscal 2004 funding, to $286.5 billion through 2009. The bill would increase the rate of return to states on their Highway Trust Fund contributions to 92 percent by fiscal 2008. It would make the Transportation Department the lead agency in the environmental review process for transportation projects. Adopted (thus sent to the Senate) 412-8: R 217-8; D 194-0 (ND 144-0, SD 50-0); I 1-0. July 29, 2005.

| | 451 | 452 | 453 |
|---|---|---|---|
| **ALABAMA** | | | |
| 1 Bonner | Y | Y | Y |
| 2 Everett | Y | Y | Y |
| 3 Rogers | Y | Y | Y |
| 4 Aderholt | Y | Y | Y |
| 5 Cramer | Y | Y | Y |
| 6 Bachus | Y | Y | Y |
| 7 Davis | Y | Y | Y |
| **ALASKA** | | | |
| AL Young | Y | Y | Y |
| **ARIZONA** | | | |
| 1 Renzi | + | + | Y |
| 2 Franks | N | Y | Y |
| 3 Shadegg | Y | Y | N |
| 4 Pastor | Y | Y | Y |
| 5 Hayworth | N | Y | Y |
| 6 Flake | N | Y | N |
| 7 Grijalva | N | Y | Y |
| 8 Kolbe | Y | Y | Y |
| **ARKANSAS** | | | |
| 1 Berry | N | Y | Y |
| 2 Snyder | N | Y | Y |
| 3 Boozman | Y | Y | Y |
| 4 Ross | N | Y | Y |
| **CALIFORNIA** | | | |
| 1 Thompson | Y | Y | Y |
| 2 Herger | Y | Y | Y |
| 3 Lungren | Y | Y | Y |
| 4 Doolittle | Y | Y | Y |
| 5 Matsui, D. | Y | Y | Y |
| 6 Woolsey | N | Y | Y |
| 7 Miller, George | N | Y | ? |
| 8 Pelosi | N | Y | Y |
| 9 Lee | N | Y | Y |
| 10 Tauscher | N | Y | Y |
| 11 Pombo | Y | Y | + |
| 12 Lantos | Y | Y | Y |
| 13 Stark | N | Y | ? |
| 14 Eshoo | Y | ? | Y |
| 15 Honda | N | Y | Y |
| 16 Lofgren | N | N | Y |
| 17 Farr | Y | Y | Y |
| 18 Cardoza | N | Y | Y |
| 19 Radanovich | Y | Y | Y |
| 20 Costa | Y | Y | Y |
| 21 Nunes | Y | Y | Y |
| 22 Thomas | Y | Y | Y |
| 23 Capps | Y | Y | + |
| 24 Gallegly | Y | Y | Y |
| 25 McKeon | Y | Y | Y |
| 26 Dreier | Y | Y | Y |
| 27 Sherman | N | N | Y |
| 28 Berman | N | Y | Y |
| 29 Schiff | Y | Y | Y |
| 30 Waxman | Y | Y | Y |
| 31 Becerra | N | Y | Y |
| 32 Solis | N | Y | Y |
| 33 Watson | Y | Y | Y |
| 34 Roybal-Allard | N | Y | Y |
| 35 Waters | Y | Y | Y |
| 36 Harman | Y | Y | Y |
| 37 Millender-McD. | Y | Y | Y |
| 38 Napolitano | Y | Y | Y |
| 39 Sánchez, Linda | Y | Y | Y |
| 40 Royce | Y | Y | N |
| 41 Lewis | Y | Y | Y |
| 42 Miller, Gary | Y | Y | Y |
| 43 Baca | Y | Y | Y |
| 44 Calvert | Y | Y | Y |
| 45 Bono | Y | Y | Y |
| 46 Rohrabacher | N | Y | Y |
| 47 Sanchez, Loretta | N | N | Y |
| 48 Cox | Y | Y | Y |
| 49 Issa | Y | Y | Y |

| | 451 | 452 | 453 |
|---|---|---|---|
| 50 Cunningham | Y | Y | Y |
| 51 Filner | Y | Y | Y |
| 52 Hunter | Y | Y | Y |
| 53 Davis | N | Y | Y |
| **COLORADO** | | | |
| 1 DeGette | N | Y | Y |
| 2 Udall | N | N | Y |
| 3 Salazar | N | Y | Y |
| 4 Musgrave | N | Y | Y |
| 5 Hefley | N | Y | Y |
| 6 Tancredo | N | Y | Y |
| 7 Beauprez | Y | Y | Y |
| **CONNECTICUT** | | | |
| 1 Larson | Y | ? | Y |
| 2 Simmons | Y | Y | Y |
| 3 DeLauro | Y | Y | Y |
| 4 Shays | N | Y | Y |
| 5 Johnson | Y | Y | Y |
| **DELAWARE** | | | |
| AL Castle | Y | Y | Y |
| **FLORIDA** | | | |
| 1 Miller | N | Y | Y |
| 2 Boyd | Y | Y | Y |
| 3 Brown | Y | Y | Y |
| 4 Crenshaw | Y | Y | Y |
| 5 Brown-Waite | N | Y | Y |
| 6 Stearns | N | Y | Y |
| 7 Mica | Y | Y | ? |
| 8 Keller | Y | Y | Y |
| 9 Bilirakis | Y | Y | Y |
| 10 Young | Y | Y | Y |
| 11 Davis | Y | Y | Y |
| 12 Putnam | Y | Y | Y |
| 13 Harris | N | Y | Y |
| 14 Mack | Y | Y | Y |
| 15 Weldon | Y | Y | Y |
| 16 Foley | Y | Y | Y |
| 17 Meek | N | Y | Y |
| 18 Ros-Lehtinen | Y | Y | Y |
| 19 Wexler | Y | Y | ? |
| 20 Wasserman-Schultz | Y | Y | Y |
| 21 Diaz-Balart, L. | Y | Y | Y |
| 22 Shaw | Y | Y | Y |
| 23 Hastings | Y | Y | Y |
| 24 Feeney | N | Y | Y |
| 25 Diaz-Balart, M. | Y | Y | Y |
| **GEORGIA** | | | |
| 1 Kingston | Y | Y | Y |
| 2 Bishop | Y | Y | Y |
| 3 Marshall | N | N | Y |
| 4 McKinney | N | Y | Y |
| 5 Lewis | N | N | Y |
| 6 Price | N | Y | Y |
| 7 Linder | Y | Y | Y |
| 8 Westmoreland | N | Y | Y |
| 9 Norwood | Y | Y | Y |
| 10 Deal | Y | Y | Y |
| 11 Gingrey | Y | Y | Y |
| 12 Barrow | N | Y | Y |
| 13 Scott | Y | Y | Y |
| **HAWAII** | | | |
| 1 Abercrombie | Y | Y | Y |
| 2 Case | Y | Y | Y |
| **IDAHO** | | | |
| 1 Otter | Y | Y | Y |
| 2 Simpson | Y | Y | Y |
| **ILLINOIS** | | | |
| 1 Rush | Y | Y | Y |
| 2 Jackson | Y | Y | Y |
| 3 Lipinski | N | Y | Y |
| 4 Gutierrez | N | Y | Y |
| 5 Emanuel | Y | Y | Y |
| 6 Hyde | Y | Y | Y |
| 7 Davis | Y | Y | Y |
| 8 Bean | N | Y | Y |
| 9 Schakowsky | ? | ? | ? |
| 10 Kirk | Y | Y | Y |
| 11 Weller | Y | Y | Y |
| 12 Costello | N | Y | Y |

**KEY**   Republicans   Democrats   *Independents*

| | | |
|---|---|---|
| **Y** Voted for (yea) | **X** Paired against | **C** Voted "present" to avoid possible conflict of interest |
| **#** Paired for | **–** Announced against | |
| **+** Announced for | **P** Voted "present" | **?** Did not vote or otherwise make a position known |
| **N** Voted against (nay) | | |

ND Northern Democrats, SD Southern Democrats
Southern states: Ala., Ark., Fla., Ga., Ky., La., Miss., N.C., Okla., S.C., Tenn., Texas, Va.

| | 451 | 452 | 453 |
|---|---|---|---|
| 13 Biggert | Y | Y | Y |
| 14 Hastert | Y | | Y |
| 15 Johnson | Y | Y | Y |
| 16 Manzullo | Y | Y | Y |
| 17 Evans | Y | Y | Y |
| 18 LaHood | Y | Y | Y |
| 19 Shimkus | N | Y | Y |
| **INDIANA** | | | |
| 1 Visclosky | Y | Y | Y |
| 2 Chocola | N | Y | Y |
| 3 Souder | Y | Y | Y |
| 4 Buyer | Y | Y | Y |
| 5 Burton | Y | Y | Y |
| 6 Pence | N | Y | Y |
| 7 Carson | ? | ? | Y |
| 8 Hostettler | Y | Y | Y |
| 9 Sodrel | Y | Y | Y |
| **IOWA** | | | |
| 1 Nussle | Y | Y | Y |
| 2 Leach | Y | Y | Y |
| 3 Boswell | N | N | Y |
| 4 Latham | Y | Y | Y |
| 5 King | Y | Y | Y |
| **KANSAS** | | | |
| 1 Moran | Y | Y | Y |
| 2 Ryun | Y | Y | Y |
| 3 Moore | N | ? | Y |
| 4 Tiahrt | Y | Y | Y |
| **KENTUCKY** | | | |
| 1 Whitfield | Y | Y | Y |
| 2 Lewis | Y | Y | Y |
| 3 Northup | Y | Y | Y |
| 4 Davis | Y | Y | Y |
| 5 Rogers | Y | Y | Y |
| 6 Chandler | N | N | Y |
| **LOUISIANA** | | | |
| 1 Jindal | Y | Y | Y |
| 2 Jefferson | Y | Y | Y |
| 3 Melancon | N | Y | Y |
| 4 McCrery | Y | Y | Y |
| 5 Alexander | Y | Y | Y |
| 6 Baker | Y | Y | Y |
| 7 Boustany | Y | Y | Y |
| **MAINE** | | | |
| 1 Allen | Y | Y | Y |
| 2 Michaud | Y | Y | Y |
| **MARYLAND** | | | |
| 1 Gilchrest | Y | Y | Y |
| 2 Ruppersberger | Y | Y | Y |
| 3 Cardin | Y | Y | Y |
| 4 Wynn | Y | Y | Y |
| 5 Hoyer | Y | Y | Y |
| 6 Bartlett | Y | Y | Y |
| 7 Cummings | Y | Y | Y |
| 8 Van Hollen | N | Y | Y |
| **MASSACHUSETTS** | | | |
| 1 Olver | N | N | Y |
| 2 Neal | Y | Y | Y |
| 3 McGovern | N | Y | Y |
| 4 Frank | N | Y | Y |
| 5 Meehan | N | Y | Y |
| 6 Tierney | N | Y | Y |
| 7 Markey | N | Y | Y |
| 8 Capuano | Y | Y | Y |
| 9 Lynch | ? | ? | Y |
| 10 Delahunt | Y | Y | ? |
| **MICHIGAN** | | | |
| 1 Stupak | Y | Y | Y |
| 2 Hoekstra | Y | Y | Y |
| 3 Ehlers | Y | Y | Y |
| 4 Camp | Y | Y | Y |
| 5 Kildee | N | Y | Y |
| 6 Upton | Y | Y | Y |
| 7 Schwarz | Y | Y | ? |
| 8 Rogers | Y | Y | Y |
| 9 Knollenberg | Y | Y | Y |
| 10 Miller | Y | Y | Y |
| 11 McCotter | Y | Y | Y |
| 12 Levin | Y | Y | Y |
| 13 Kilpatrick | N | Y | Y |
| 14 Conyers | N | Y | Y |
| 15 Dingell | Y | Y | Y |

| | 451 | 452 | 453 |
|---|---|---|---|
| **MINNESOTA** | | | |
| 1 Gutknecht | N | Y | Y |
| 2 Kline | Y | Y | Y |
| 3 Ramstad | Y | Y | Y |
| 4 McCollum | N | Y | Y |
| 5 Sabo | Y | Y | Y |
| 6 Kennedy | N | Y | Y |
| 7 Peterson | N | Y | Y |
| 8 Oberstar | N | Y | Y |
| **MISSISSIPPI** | | | |
| 1 Wicker | Y | Y | Y |
| 2 Thompson | Y | Y | Y |
| 3 Pickering | Y | Y | Y |
| 4 Taylor | N | N | Y |
| **MISSOURI** | | | |
| 1 Clay | ? | Y | Y |
| 2 Akin | Y | Y | Y |
| 3 Carnahan | Y | Y | Y |
| 4 Skelton | Y | Y | Y |
| 5 Cleaver | Y | Y | Y |
| 6 Graves | N | Y | Y |
| 7 Blunt | Y | Y | Y |
| 8 Emerson | Y | Y | Y |
| 9 Hulshof | N | Y | Y |
| **MONTANA** | | | |
| AL Rehberg | Y | Y | Y |
| **NEBRASKA** | | | |
| 1 Fortenberry | Y | Y | Y |
| 2 Terry | Y | Y | Y |
| 3 Osborne | Y | Y | Y |
| **NEVADA** | | | |
| 1 Berkley | Y | Y | Y |
| 2 Gibbons | Y | Y | Y |
| 3 Porter | Y | Y | Y |
| **NEW HAMPSHIRE** | | | |
| 1 Bradley | Y | Y | Y |
| 2 Bass | Y | Y | Y |
| **NEW JERSEY** | | | |
| 1 Andrews | – | + | Y |
| 2 LoBiondo | Y | Y | Y |
| 3 Saxton | Y | Y | Y |
| 4 Smith | Y | Y | Y |
| 5 Garrett | N | Y | Y |
| 6 Pallone | N | Y | Y |
| 7 Ferguson | Y | Y | Y |
| 8 Pascrell | Y | Y | Y |
| 9 Rothman | Y | Y | Y |
| 10 Payne | Y | Y | Y |
| 11 Frelinghuysen | Y | Y | Y |
| 12 Holt | Y | Y | Y |
| 13 Menendez | N | Y | Y |
| **NEW MEXICO** | | | |
| 1 Wilson | Y | Y | Y |
| 2 Pearce | Y | Y | Y |
| 3 Udall | N | N | Y |
| **NEW YORK** | | | |
| 1 Bishop | N | Y | Y |
| 2 Israel | N | Y | Y |
| 3 King | Y | Y | Y |
| 4 McCarthy | Y | Y | Y |
| 5 Ackerman | Y | Y | Y |
| 6 Meeks | Y | Y | Y |
| 7 Crowley | Y | Y | Y |
| 8 Nadler | N | Y | Y |
| 9 Weiner | Y | Y | Y |
| 10 Towns | Y | Y | Y |
| 11 Owens | Y | Y | Y |
| 12 Velázquez | N | ? | Y |
| 13 Fossella | N | Y | Y |
| 14 Maloney | N | Y | Y |
| 15 Rangel | Y | Y | Y |
| 16 Serrano | Y | Y | Y |
| 17 Engel | Y | Y | Y |
| 18 Lowey | N | Y | Y |
| 19 Kelly | Y | Y | Y |
| 20 Sweeney | Y | Y | Y |
| 21 McNulty | Y | Y | Y |
| 22 Hinchey | N | Y | Y |
| 23 McHugh | Y | Y | Y |
| 24 Boehlert | Y | Y | Y |
| 25 Walsh | Y | Y | Y |
| 26 Reynolds | Y | Y | Y |
| 27 Higgins | Y | Y | Y |
| 28 Slaughter | N | Y | Y |
| 29 Kuhl | Y | Y | Y |

| | 451 | 452 | 453 |
|---|---|---|---|
| **NORTH CAROLINA** | | | |
| 1 Butterfield | Y | ? | Y |
| 2 Etheridge | N | Y | Y |
| 3 Jones | N | Y | N |
| 4 Price | Y | Y | Y |
| 5 Foxx | Y | Y | Y |
| 6 Coble | N | Y | Y |
| 7 McIntyre | Y | Y | Y |
| 8 Hayes | Y | Y | Y |
| 9 Myrick | Y | Y | Y |
| 10 McHenry | Y | Y | Y |
| 11 Taylor | Y | Y | Y |
| 12 Watt | Y | Y | Y |
| 13 Miller | Y | Y | Y |
| **NORTH DAKOTA** | | | |
| AL Pomeroy | N | Y | Y |
| **OHIO** | | | |
| 1 Chabot | N | Y | Y |
| 2 Vacant | | | |
| 3 Turner | Y | Y | Y |
| 4 Oxley | Y | Y | Y |
| 5 Gillmor | Y | Y | Y |
| 6 Strickland | Y | Y | Y |
| 7 Hobson | Y | Y | Y |
| 8 Boehner | Y | Y | N |
| 9 Kaptur | N | Y | Y |
| 10 Kucinich | N | Y | Y |
| 11 Jones | N | Y | Y |
| 12 Tiberi | Y | Y | Y |
| 13 Brown | N | Y | Y |
| 14 LaTourette | Y | Y | Y |
| 15 Pryce | Y | Y | Y |
| 16 Regula | Y | Y | Y |
| 17 Ryan | Y | Y | Y |
| 18 Ney | Y | Y | Y |
| **OKLAHOMA** | | | |
| 1 Sullivan | Y | Y | Y |
| 2 Boren | Y | Y | Y |
| 3 Lucas | Y | Y | Y |
| 4 Cole | Y | Y | Y |
| 5 Istook | Y | Y | Y |
| **OREGON** | | | |
| 1 Wu | N | N | Y |
| 2 Walden | Y | Y | Y |
| 3 Blumenauer | N | Y | Y |
| 4 DeFazio | N | Y | Y |
| 5 Hooley | N | Y | Y |
| **PENNSYLVANIA** | | | |
| 1 Brady | Y | Y | ? |
| 2 Fattah | Y | Y | ? |
| 3 English | Y | Y | Y |
| 4 Hart | Y | Y | Y |
| 5 Peterson | Y | Y | Y |
| 6 Gerlach | Y | Y | Y |
| 7 Weldon | Y | Y | Y |
| 8 Fitzpatrick | Y | Y | Y |
| 9 Shuster | Y | Y | Y |
| 10 Sherwood | Y | Y | Y |
| 11 Kanjorski | Y | Y | Y |
| 12 Murtha | Y | Y | Y |
| 13 Schwartz | Y | Y | Y |
| 14 Doyle | Y | Y | Y |
| 15 Dent | Y | Y | Y |
| 16 Pitts | Y | Y | ? |
| 17 Holden | Y | Y | Y |
| 18 Murphy | Y | Y | Y |
| 19 Platts | Y | Y | Y |
| **RHODE ISLAND** | | | |
| 1 Kennedy | Y | Y | Y |
| 2 Langevin | Y | Y | Y |
| **SOUTH CAROLINA** | | | |
| 1 Brown | Y | Y | Y |
| 2 Wilson | Y | Y | Y |
| 3 Barrett | Y | ? | Y |
| 4 Inglis | Y | Y | Y |
| 5 Spratt | N | Y | Y |
| 6 Clyburn | Y | Y | Y |
| **SOUTH DAKOTA** | | | |
| AL Herseth | N | Y | Y |
| **TENNESSEE** | | | |
| 1 Jenkins | Y | Y | Y |
| 2 Duncan | N | Y | Y |

| | 451 | 452 | 453 |
|---|---|---|---|
| 3 Wamp | Y | Y | Y |
| 4 Davis | Y | Y | Y |
| 5 Cooper | N | N | Y |
| 6 Gordon | N | Y | Y |
| 7 Blackburn | Y | Y | Y |
| 8 Tanner | N | Y | Y |
| 9 Ford | N | N | Y |
| **TEXAS** | | | |
| 1 Gohmert | Y | Y | Y |
| 2 Poe | Y | Y | Y |
| 3 Johnson, S. | Y | Y | ? |
| 4 Hall | Y | Y | Y |
| 5 Hensarling | N | Y | N |
| 6 Barton | Y | Y | Y |
| 7 Culberson | Y | Y | Y |
| 8 Brady | Y | Y | Y |
| 9 Green, A. | Y | Y | Y |
| 10 McCaul | Y | Y | Y |
| 11 Conaway | Y | Y | Y |
| 12 Granger | Y | Y | Y |
| 13 Thornberry | Y | Y | N |
| 14 Paul | ? | ? | ? |
| 15 Hinojosa | Y | Y | Y |
| 16 Reyes | Y | Y | Y |
| 17 Edwards | Y | Y | Y |
| 18 Jackson-Lee | Y | Y | Y |
| 19 Neugebauer | Y | Y | Y |
| 20 Gonzalez | Y | Y | Y |
| 21 Smith | Y | Y | Y |
| 22 DeLay | Y | Y | Y |
| 23 Bonilla | Y | Y | Y |
| 24 Marchant | Y | Y | Y |
| 25 Doggett | N | N | Y |
| 26 Burgess | Y | Y | Y |
| 27 Ortiz | Y | Y | Y |
| 28 Cuellar | Y | Y | Y |
| 29 Green, G. | N | Y | Y |
| 30 Johnson, E. | Y | Y | Y |
| 31 Carter | Y | Y | Y |
| 32 Sessions | Y | Y | Y |
| **UTAH** | | | |
| 1 Bishop | Y | Y | Y |
| 2 Matheson | N | N | Y |
| 3 Cannon | Y | Y | Y |
| **VERMONT** | | | |
| AL *Sanders* | N | ? | Y |
| **VIRGINIA** | | | |
| 1 Davis, J. | N | Y | Y |
| 2 Drake | Y | Y | Y |
| 3 Scott | Y | Y | Y |
| 4 Forbes | N | Y | Y |
| 5 Goode | N | Y | Y |
| 6 Goodlatte | Y | Y | Y |
| 7 Cantor | Y | Y | Y |
| 8 Moran | Y | Y | Y |
| 9 Boucher | Y | Y | Y |
| 10 Wolf | Y | Y | Y |
| 11 Davis, T. | Y | Y | Y |
| **WASHINGTON** | | | |
| 1 Inslee | N | Y | Y |
| 2 Larsen | Y | Y | Y |
| 3 Baird | N | Y | Y |
| 4 Hastings | Y | Y | Y |
| 5 McMorris | Y | Y | Y |
| 6 Dicks | N | Y | Y |
| 7 McDermott | N | Y | Y |
| 8 Reichert | Y | Y | Y |
| 9 Smith | Y | Y | Y |
| **WEST VIRGINIA** | | | |
| 1 Mollohan | Y | Y | Y |
| 2 Capito | Y | Y | Y |
| 3 Rahall | Y | Y | Y |
| **WISCONSIN** | | | |
| 1 Ryan | Y | Y | Y |
| 2 Baldwin | N | Y | Y |
| 3 Kind | N | Y | Y |
| 4 Moore | N | Y | Y |
| 5 Sensenbrenner | Y | Y | N |
| 6 Petri | N | Y | Y |
| 7 Obey | N | Y | Y |
| 8 Green | N | Y | Y |
| **WYOMING** | | | |
| AL Cubin | Y | Y | Y |

# IN THE HOUSE | By Vote Number

**454.** **H Res 360. V-J Day 60th Anniversary/Adoption.** Smith, R-N.J., motion to suspend the rules and adopt the resolution that would commemorate the 60th anniversary of Victory over Japan Day (V-J Day) and the end of World War II and express appreciation for the members of the armed services who served in the Pacific during the war. Motion agreed to 394-0: R 216-0; D 177-0 (ND 129-0, SD 48-0); I 1-0. A two-thirds majority of those present and voting (263 in this case) is required for adoption under suspension of the rules. Sept. 6, 2005.

**455.** **S J Res 19. Helsinki Final Act 30th Anniversary/Passage.** Smith, R-N.J., motion to suspend the rules and pass the joint resolution that would call on the president to issue a proclamation recognizing the 30th anniversary of the Helsinki Final Act signing and reassert U.S. commitment to its full implementation. Motion agreed to 393-1: R 215-1; D 177-0 (ND 130-0, SD 47-0); I 1-0. A two-thirds majority of those present and voting (263 in this case) is required for passage under suspension of the rules. Sept. 6, 2005.

**456.** **HR 3650. Federal Judiciary Emergency Special Sessions/Passage.** Sensenbrenner, R-Wis., motion to suspend the rules and pass the bill that would allow circuit courts, district courts and bankruptcy courts to hold special sessions outside their normal geographic region if no area within their jurisdiction is reasonably available because of emergency conditions. Motion agreed to 409-0: R 218-0; D 190-0 (ND 143-0, SD 47-0); I 1-0. A two-thirds majority of those present and voting (273 in this case) is required for passage under suspension of the rules. Sept. 7, 2005.

**457.** **HR 3169. Pell Grant Disaster Relief/Passage.** Keller, R-Fla., motion to suspend the rules and pass the bill that would allow the Education Department to waive the repayment requirement for Pell Grant recipients whose school attendance is interrupted because of the impact of a disaster if students were living, working or attending school in an area designated by the president to warrant major disaster assistance. Motion agreed to 412-0: R 220-0; D 191-0 (ND 144-0, SD 47-0); I 1-0. A two-thirds majority of those present and voting (275 in this case) is required for passage under suspension of the rules. Sept. 7, 2005.

**458.** **H Res 426. Suspension Motions/Previous Question.** L. Diaz-Balart, R-Fla., motion to order the previous question (thus ending debate and possibility of amendment) on adoption of the resolution (H Res 426) to provide for House floor consideration of bills under suspension of the rules on Thursday, Sept. 8, 2005. Motion agreed to 221-193: R 221-0; D 0-192 (ND 0-145, SD 0-47); I 0-1. Sept. 8, 2005.

**459.** **H Res 426. Suspension Motions/Rule.** Adoption of the resolution (H Res 426) to provide for House floor consideration of bills under suspension of the rules on Thursday, Sept. 8, 2005. Adopted 235-179: R 219-2; D 16-176 (ND 11-133, SD 5-43); I 0-1. Sept. 8, 2005.

[1] Rep. Christopher Cox, R-Calif., resigned effective Aug. 2. The last vote for which he was eligible was vote 453.

[2] Rep. Jean Schmidt, R-Ohio, was sworn in Sept. 6. The first vote for which she was eligible was vote 454.

ND Northern Democrats, SD Southern Democrats
Southern states: Ala., Ark., Fla., Ga., Ky., La., Miss., N.C., Okla., S.C., Tenn., Texas, Va.

| | 454 | 455 | 456 | 457 | 458 | 459 |
|---|---|---|---|---|---|---|
| **ALABAMA** | | | | | | |
| 1 Bonner | Y | Y | Y | Y | Y | Y |
| 2 Everett | Y | Y | Y | Y | Y | Y |
| 3 Rogers | Y | Y | Y | Y | Y | Y |
| 4 Aderholt | Y | Y | Y | Y | Y | Y |
| 5 Cramer | Y | Y | Y | Y | N | N |
| 6 Bachus | Y | Y | Y | Y | Y | Y |
| 7 Davis | Y | Y | Y | Y | N | N |
| **ALASKA** | | | | | | |
| AL Young | ? | ? | ? | ? | ? | ? |
| **ARIZONA** | | | | | | |
| 1 Renzi | Y | Y | Y | Y | Y | Y |
| 2 Franks | Y | Y | Y | Y | Y | Y |
| 3 Shadegg | Y | Y | Y | Y | Y | Y |
| 4 Pastor | Y | Y | Y | Y | N | N |
| 5 Hayworth | Y | Y | Y | Y | Y | Y |
| 6 Flake | Y | Y | Y | Y | Y | N |
| 7 Grijalva | Y | Y | Y | Y | N | N |
| 8 Kolbe | Y | Y | Y | Y | Y | Y |
| **ARKANSAS** | | | | | | |
| 1 Berry | Y | Y | Y | Y | N | N |
| 2 Snyder | Y | Y | Y | Y | N | N |
| 3 Boozman | Y | Y | Y | Y | Y | Y |
| 4 Ross | Y | Y | Y | Y | N | N |
| **CALIFORNIA** | | | | | | |
| 1 Thompson | Y | Y | Y | Y | N | N |
| 2 Herger | Y | Y | Y | Y | Y | Y |
| 3 Lungren | Y | Y | Y | Y | Y | Y |
| 4 Doolittle | Y | Y | Y | Y | Y | Y |
| 5 Matsui, D. | Y | Y | Y | Y | N | N |
| 6 Woolsey | Y | Y | Y | Y | N | N |
| 7 Miller, George | Y | Y | Y | Y | N | N |
| 8 Pelosi | Y | Y | Y | Y | N | N |
| 9 Lee | Y | Y | Y | Y | N | N |
| 10 Tauscher | Y | Y | Y | Y | N | N |
| 11 Pombo | Y | Y | Y | Y | Y | Y |
| 12 Lantos | Y | Y | Y | Y | N | N |
| 13 Stark | ? | ? | Y | Y | N | N |
| 14 Eshoo | Y | Y | Y | Y | N | Y |
| 15 Honda | Y | Y | Y | Y | N | N |
| 16 Lofgren | Y | Y | Y | Y | N | N |
| 17 Farr | Y | Y | Y | Y | N | N |
| 18 Cardoza | Y | Y | Y | Y | N | Y |
| 19 Radanovich | Y | Y | Y | Y | Y | Y |
| 20 Costa | Y | Y | Y | Y | N | N |
| 21 Nunes | Y | Y | Y | Y | Y | Y |
| 22 Thomas | Y | Y | Y | Y | Y | Y |
| 23 Capps | Y | Y | Y | Y | N | N |
| 24 Gallegly | + | + | Y | Y | Y | Y |
| 25 McKeon | Y | Y | Y | Y | Y | Y |
| 26 Dreier | Y | Y | + | + | Y | Y |
| 27 Sherman | Y | Y | Y | Y | N | N |
| 28 Berman | Y | Y | Y | Y | N | N |
| 29 Schiff | Y | Y | Y | Y | N | N |
| 30 Waxman | Y | Y | Y | Y | N | N |
| 31 Becerra | Y | Y | Y | Y | N | N |
| 32 Solis | Y | Y | Y | Y | N | N |
| 33 Watson | Y | Y | Y | Y | N | N |
| 34 Roybal-Allard | Y | Y | Y | Y | N | N |
| 35 Waters | ? | ? | Y | Y | N | N |
| 36 Harman | Y | Y | Y | Y | N | N |
| 37 Millender-McD. | Y | Y | Y | Y | N | N |
| 38 Napolitano | Y | Y | Y | Y | N | ? |
| 39 Sánchez, Linda | Y | Y | Y | Y | N | N |
| 40 Royce | Y | Y | Y | Y | Y | Y |
| 41 Lewis | Y | Y | Y | Y | Y | Y |
| 42 Miller, Gary | Y | Y | Y | Y | Y | Y |
| 43 Baca | Y | Y | Y | Y | N | N |
| 44 Calvert | Y | Y | Y | Y | Y | Y |
| 45 Bono | Y | Y | Y | Y | Y | Y |
| 46 Rohrabacher | Y | Y | Y | Y | Y | Y |
| 47 Sanchez, Loretta | + | + | + | + | – | – |
| 48 Vacant[1] | | | | | | |
| 49 Issa | Y | Y | Y | Y | Y | Y |
| 50 Cunningham | Y | Y | Y | Y | Y | Y |
| 51 Filner | Y | Y | Y | Y | N | N |
| 52 Hunter | ? | ? | Y | Y | Y | Y |
| 53 Davis | Y | Y | Y | Y | N | N |
| **COLORADO** | | | | | | |
| 1 DeGette | Y | Y | Y | Y | N | N |
| 2 Udall | Y | Y | Y | Y | N | N |
| 3 Salazar | Y | Y | Y | Y | N | N |
| 4 Musgrave | Y | Y | Y | Y | Y | Y |
| 5 Hefley | ? | ? | Y | Y | Y | Y |
| 6 Tancredo | ? | ? | Y | Y | Y | Y |
| 7 Beauprez | Y | Y | Y | Y | Y | Y |
| **CONNECTICUT** | | | | | | |
| 1 Larson | Y | Y | Y | Y | N | N |
| 2 Simmons | Y | Y | Y | Y | N | N |
| 3 DeLauro | Y | Y | Y | Y | N | N |
| 4 Shays | Y | Y | Y | Y | Y | Y |
| 5 Johnson | Y | Y | Y | Y | Y | Y |
| **DELAWARE** | | | | | | |
| AL Castle | Y | Y | Y | Y | Y | Y |
| **FLORIDA** | | | | | | |
| 1 Miller | Y | Y | Y | Y | Y | Y |
| 2 Boyd | Y | Y | Y | Y | N | N |
| 3 Brown | Y | Y | Y | Y | N | N |
| 4 Crenshaw | Y | Y | Y | Y | Y | Y |
| 5 Brown-Waite | Y | Y | Y | Y | Y | Y |
| 6 Stearns | Y | Y | Y | Y | Y | Y |
| 7 Mica | Y | Y | Y | Y | Y | Y |
| 8 Keller | Y | Y | Y | Y | Y | Y |
| 9 Bilirakis | + | + | Y | Y | Y | Y |
| 10 Young | Y | Y | Y | Y | Y | Y |
| 11 Davis | Y | Y | Y | Y | N | N |
| 12 Putnam | Y | Y | Y | Y | Y | Y |
| 13 Harris | Y | Y | Y | Y | Y | Y |
| 14 Mack | Y | Y | Y | Y | Y | Y |
| 15 Weldon | Y | Y | Y | Y | Y | Y |
| 16 Foley | Y | Y | Y | Y | Y | Y |
| 17 Meek | Y | Y | Y | Y | N | N |
| 18 Ros-Lehtinen | Y | Y | Y | Y | Y | Y |
| 19 Wexler | Y | Y | Y | Y | ? | N |
| 20 Wasserman-Schultz | Y | Y | Y | Y | N | N |
| 21 Diaz-Balart, L. | Y | Y | Y | Y | Y | Y |
| 22 Shaw | Y | Y | Y | Y | Y | Y |
| 23 Hastings | Y | Y | Y | Y | N | N |
| 24 Feeney | Y | Y | Y | Y | Y | Y |
| 25 Diaz-Balart, M. | Y | Y | Y | Y | Y | Y |
| **GEORGIA** | | | | | | |
| 1 Kingston | Y | Y | Y | Y | Y | Y |
| 2 Bishop | Y | Y | Y | Y | N | N |
| 3 Marshall | Y | Y | Y | Y | N | N |
| 4 McKinney | Y | Y | Y | Y | N | N |
| 5 Lewis | Y | Y | Y | Y | N | N |
| 6 Price | Y | Y | Y | Y | Y | Y |
| 7 Linder | Y | Y | Y | Y | Y | Y |
| 8 Westmoreland | Y | Y | Y | Y | Y | Y |
| 9 Norwood | Y | Y | Y | Y | Y | Y |
| 10 Deal | Y | Y | Y | Y | Y | Y |
| 11 Gingrey | Y | Y | Y | Y | Y | Y |
| 12 Barrow | Y | Y | Y | Y | N | N |
| 13 Scott | Y | Y | Y | Y | N | N |
| **HAWAII** | | | | | | |
| 1 Abercrombie | Y | Y | Y | Y | N | N |
| 2 Case | ? | Y | Y | Y | N | N |
| **IDAHO** | | | | | | |
| 1 Otter | Y | Y | Y | Y | Y | Y |
| 2 Simpson | Y | Y | Y | Y | Y | Y |
| **ILLINOIS** | | | | | | |
| 1 Rush | ? | ? | Y | Y | N | N |
| 2 Jackson | Y | Y | Y | Y | N | N |
| 3 Lipinski | Y | Y | Y | Y | N | N |
| 4 Gutierrez | Y | Y | Y | Y | N | N |
| 5 Emanuel | Y | Y | Y | Y | N | N |
| 6 Hyde | Y | Y | Y | Y | ? | ? |
| 7 Davis | Y | Y | Y | Y | N | N |
| 8 Bean | Y | Y | Y | Y | N | N |
| 9 Schakowsky | Y | Y | Y | Y | N | N |
| 10 Kirk | Y | Y | Y | Y | Y | Y |
| 11 Weller | Y | Y | Y | Y | Y | Y |
| 12 Costello | ? | ? | ? | ? | N | N |

| KEY | Republicans | Democrats | Independents | | |
|---|---|---|---|---|---|
| Y | Voted for (yea) | X | Paired against | C | Voted "present" to avoid possible conflict of interest |
| # | Paired for | – | Announced against | | |
| + | Announced for | P | Voted "present" | ? | Did not vote or otherwise make a position known |
| N | Voted against (nay) | | | | |

| | 454 | 455 | 456 | 457 | 458 | 459 |
|---|---|---|---|---|---|---|
| 13 **Biggert** | Y | Y | Y | Y | Y | Y |
| 14 **Hastert** | | | | | | |
| 15 **Johnson** | Y | Y | Y | Y | Y | Y |
| 16 **Manzullo** | Y | Y | Y | Y | Y | Y |
| 17 Evans | Y | Y | Y | Y | N | N |
| 18 **LaHood** | Y | Y | Y | Y | Y | Y |
| 19 **Shimkus** | Y | Y | Y | Y | Y | Y |
| **INDIANA** | | | | | | |
| 1 Visclosky | Y | Y | Y | Y | N | N |
| 2 **Chocola** | Y | Y | Y | Y | Y | Y |
| 3 **Souder** | Y | Y | Y | Y | Y | Y |
| 4 **Buyer** | ? | ? | ? | ? | ? | ? |
| 5 **Burton** | Y | Y | Y | Y | Y | Y |
| 6 **Pence** | Y | Y | Y | Y | Y | Y |
| 7 Carson | Y | Y | Y | Y | N | N |
| 8 **Hostettler** | Y | Y | Y | Y | Y | Y |
| 9 **Sodrel** | Y | Y | Y | Y | Y | Y |
| **IOWA** | | | | | | |
| 1 **Nussle** | Y | Y | Y | Y | Y | Y |
| 2 **Leach** | Y | Y | Y | Y | Y | Y |
| 3 Boswell | Y | Y | Y | Y | N | Y |
| 4 **Latham** | ? | ? | Y | Y | Y | Y |
| 5 **King** | Y | Y | Y | Y | Y | Y |
| **KANSAS** | | | | | | |
| 1 **Moran** | Y | Y | Y | Y | Y | Y |
| 2 **Ryun** | Y | Y | Y | Y | Y | Y |
| 3 Moore | ? | ? | Y | Y | N | Y |
| 4 **Tiahrt** | Y | Y | Y | Y | Y | Y |
| **KENTUCKY** | | | | | | |
| 1 **Whitfield** | Y | Y | Y | Y | Y | Y |
| 2 **Lewis** | Y | Y | Y | Y | Y | Y |
| 3 **Northup** | Y | Y | Y | Y | Y | Y |
| 4 **Davis** | Y | Y | Y | Y | Y | Y |
| 5 **Rogers** | Y | Y | Y | Y | Y | Y |
| 6 Chandler | Y | Y | Y | Y | N | Y |
| **LOUISIANA** | | | | | | |
| 1 **Jindal** | Y | Y | Y | Y | Y | Y |
| 2 Jefferson | Y | ? | Y | Y | N | N |
| 3 Melancon | ? | ? | ? | ? | ? | ? |
| 4 **McCrery** | ? | ? | Y | Y | ? | ? |
| 5 **Alexander** | Y | Y | Y | Y | Y | Y |
| 6 **Baker** | Y | Y | ? | ? | ? | ? |
| 7 **Boustany** | Y | Y | Y | Y | Y | Y |
| **MAINE** | | | | | | |
| 1 Allen | Y | Y | Y | Y | N | N |
| 2 Michaud | Y | Y | Y | Y | N | N |
| **MARYLAND** | | | | | | |
| 1 **Gilchrest** | Y | Y | Y | Y | Y | Y |
| 2 Ruppersberger | Y | Y | Y | Y | N | Y |
| 3 Cardin | ? | ? | Y | Y | N | Y |
| 4 Wynn | Y | Y | Y | Y | N | Y |
| 5 Hoyer | Y | Y | Y | Y | N | N |
| 6 **Bartlett** | Y | Y | Y | Y | Y | Y |
| 7 Cummings | Y | Y | Y | Y | N | N |
| 8 Van Hollen | Y | Y | Y | Y | N | N |
| **MASSACHUSETTS** | | | | | | |
| 1 Olver | ? | ? | ? | ? | ? | ? |
| 2 Neal | Y | Y | Y | Y | N | N |
| 3 McGovern | Y | Y | Y | Y | N | N |
| 4 Frank | Y | Y | Y | Y | N | N |
| 5 Meehan | Y | Y | Y | Y | N | N |
| 6 Tierney | Y | Y | Y | Y | N | N |
| 7 Markey | Y | Y | Y | Y | N | N |
| 8 Capuano | Y | Y | Y | Y | N | N |
| 9 Lynch | Y | Y | Y | Y | N | Y |
| 10 Delahunt | ? | ? | Y | Y | N | N |
| **MICHIGAN** | | | | | | |
| 1 Stupak | Y | Y | Y | Y | N | N |
| 2 **Hoekstra** | Y | Y | ? | ? | Y | Y |
| 3 **Ehlers** | Y | Y | Y | Y | Y | Y |
| 4 **Camp** | Y | Y | Y | Y | Y | Y |
| 5 Kildee | Y | Y | Y | Y | N | N |
| 6 **Upton** | Y | Y | Y | Y | Y | Y |
| 7 **Schwarz** | Y | Y | Y | Y | Y | Y |
| 8 **Rogers** | Y | Y | Y | Y | Y | Y |
| 9 **Knollenberg** | Y | Y | Y | Y | Y | Y |
| 10 **Miller** | Y | Y | Y | Y | Y | Y |
| 11 **McCotter** | Y | Y | Y | Y | Y | Y |
| 12 Levin | Y | Y | ? | Y | N | N |
| 13 Kilpatrick | Y | Y | Y | Y | N | N |
| 14 Conyers | Y | Y | Y | Y | N | N |
| 15 Dingell | Y | Y | Y | Y | N | N |

| | 454 | 455 | 456 | 457 | 458 | 459 |
|---|---|---|---|---|---|---|
| **MINNESOTA** | | | | | | |
| 1 **Gutknecht** | Y | Y | Y | Y | Y | Y |
| 2 **Kline** | Y | Y | Y | Y | Y | Y |
| 3 **Ramstad** | Y | Y | Y | Y | Y | Y |
| 4 McCollum | Y | Y | Y | Y | N | N |
| 5 Sabo | Y | Y | Y | Y | N | N |
| 6 **Kennedy** | Y | Y | Y | Y | Y | Y |
| 7 Peterson | Y | Y | Y | Y | N | N |
| 8 Oberstar | Y | Y | Y | Y | ? | ? |
| **MISSISSIPPI** | | | | | | |
| 1 **Wicker** | Y | Y | Y | Y | Y | Y |
| 2 Thompson | Y | Y | Y | Y | N | N |
| 3 **Pickering** | + | + | ? | ? | Y | Y |
| 4 Taylor | ? | ? | ? | ? | ? | ? |
| **MISSOURI** | | | | | | |
| 1 Clay | Y | Y | Y | Y | N | N |
| 2 **Akin** | Y | Y | Y | Y | Y | Y |
| 3 Carnahan | Y | Y | Y | Y | N | N |
| 4 Skelton | Y | Y | Y | Y | N | N |
| 5 Cleaver | Y | Y | Y | Y | N | N |
| 6 **Graves** | Y | Y | Y | Y | Y | Y |
| 7 **Blunt** | Y | Y | Y | Y | Y | Y |
| 8 **Emerson** | + | + | + | + | + | + |
| 9 **Hulshof** | Y | Y | Y | Y | Y | Y |
| **MONTANA** | | | | | | |
| AL **Rehberg** | Y | Y | Y | Y | Y | Y |
| **NEBRASKA** | | | | | | |
| 1 **Fortenberry** | Y | Y | Y | Y | Y | Y |
| 2 **Terry** | Y | Y | Y | Y | Y | Y |
| 3 **Osborne** | Y | Y | Y | Y | Y | Y |
| **NEVADA** | | | | | | |
| 1 Berkley | ? | ? | ? | ? | ? | ? |
| 2 **Gibbons** | Y | Y | Y | Y | Y | Y |
| 3 **Porter** | Y | Y | Y | Y | Y | Y |
| **NEW HAMPSHIRE** | | | | | | |
| 1 **Bradley** | Y | Y | Y | Y | Y | Y |
| 2 **Bass** | Y | Y | Y | Y | Y | Y |
| **NEW JERSEY** | | | | | | |
| 1 Andrews | Y | Y | Y | Y | N | N |
| 2 **LoBiondo** | Y | Y | Y | Y | Y | Y |
| 3 **Saxton** | Y | Y | Y | Y | Y | Y |
| 4 **Smith** | Y | Y | Y | Y | Y | Y |
| 5 **Garrett** | Y | Y | Y | Y | Y | Y |
| 6 Pallone | Y | Y | Y | Y | N | N |
| 7 **Ferguson** | Y | Y | Y | Y | Y | Y |
| 8 Pascrell | Y | Y | Y | Y | N | N |
| 9 Rothman | Y | Y | Y | Y | N | N |
| 10 Payne | Y | Y | Y | Y | N | N |
| 11 **Frelinghuysen** | Y | Y | Y | Y | Y | Y |
| 12 Holt | Y | Y | Y | Y | N | N |
| 13 Menendez | Y | Y | Y | Y | N | Y |
| **NEW MEXICO** | | | | | | |
| 1 **Wilson** | Y | Y | Y | Y | Y | Y |
| 2 **Pearce** | Y | Y | Y | Y | Y | Y |
| 3 Udall | Y | Y | Y | Y | N | N |
| **NEW YORK** | | | | | | |
| 1 Bishop | Y | Y | Y | Y | N | N |
| 2 Israel | Y | Y | Y | Y | N | N |
| 3 **King** | Y | Y | Y | Y | Y | Y |
| 4 McCarthy | Y | Y | Y | Y | N | N |
| 5 Ackerman | Y | Y | Y | Y | N | N |
| 6 Meeks | Y | Y | Y | Y | N | N |
| 7 Crowley | Y | Y | Y | Y | N | N |
| 8 Nadler | Y | Y | Y | Y | N | N |
| 9 Weiner | ? | ? | ? | ? | ? | ? |
| 10 Towns | Y | Y | Y | Y | N | N |
| 11 Owens | Y | Y | Y | Y | N | N |
| 12 Velázquez | Y | Y | Y | Y | N | N |
| 13 **Fossella** | Y | Y | Y | Y | Y | Y |
| 14 Maloney | + | + | + | + | ? | ? |
| 15 Rangel | Y | Y | Y | Y | N | N |
| 16 Serrano | Y | Y | Y | Y | N | N |
| 17 Engel | ? | ? | Y | Y | N | N |
| 18 Lowey | Y | Y | Y | Y | N | N |
| 19 **Kelly** | Y | Y | Y | Y | Y | Y |
| 20 **Sweeney** | Y | Y | Y | Y | Y | Y |
| 21 McNulty | Y | Y | ? | ? | N | N |
| 22 Hinchey | Y | Y | Y | Y | N | N |
| 23 **McHugh** | Y | Y | Y | Y | Y | Y |
| 24 **Boehlert** | Y | Y | Y | Y | Y | Y |
| 25 **Walsh** | Y | Y | Y | Y | Y | Y |
| 26 **Reynolds** | Y | Y | ? | Y | Y | Y |
| 27 Higgins | Y | Y | Y | Y | N | N |
| 28 Slaughter | Y | Y | Y | Y | N | N |
| 29 **Kuhl** | Y | Y | Y | Y | Y | Y |

| | 454 | 455 | 456 | 457 | 458 | 459 |
|---|---|---|---|---|---|---|
| **NORTH CAROLINA** | | | | | | |
| 1 Butterfield | Y | Y | ? | ? | ? | ? |
| 2 Etheridge | Y | Y | Y | Y | N | N |
| 3 **Jones** | Y | Y | Y | Y | Y | Y |
| 4 Price | Y | Y | Y | Y | N | N |
| 5 **Foxx** | Y | Y | Y | Y | Y | Y |
| 6 **Coble** | Y | Y | Y | Y | Y | Y |
| 7 McIntyre | Y | Y | Y | Y | N | Y |
| 8 **Hayes** | Y | Y | Y | Y | Y | Y |
| 9 **Myrick** | Y | Y | Y | Y | Y | Y |
| 10 **McHenry** | Y | Y | Y | Y | Y | Y |
| 11 **Taylor** | Y | Y | Y | Y | Y | Y |
| 12 Watt | Y | Y | Y | Y | N | N |
| 13 Miller | Y | Y | Y | Y | N | N |
| **NORTH DAKOTA** | | | | | | |
| AL Pomeroy | Y | Y | Y | Y | N | N |
| **OHIO** | | | | | | |
| 1 **Chabot** | Y | Y | Y | Y | Y | Y |
| 2 **Schmidt**[2] | Y | Y | Y | Y | Y | Y |
| 3 **Turner** | Y | Y | Y | Y | Y | Y |
| 4 **Oxley** | Y | Y | Y | Y | Y | Y |
| 5 **Gillmor** | Y | Y | Y | Y | Y | Y |
| 6 Strickland | ? | ? | Y | Y | N | N |
| 7 **Hobson** | Y | Y | Y | Y | Y | Y |
| 8 **Boehner** | Y | Y | Y | Y | Y | Y |
| 9 Kaptur | Y | Y | Y | Y | N | N |
| 10 Kucinich | Y | Y | Y | Y | N | N |
| 11 Jones | Y | Y | Y | Y | N | N |
| 12 **Tiberi** | Y | Y | Y | Y | Y | Y |
| 13 Brown | Y | Y | Y | Y | N | N |
| 14 **LaTourette** | Y | Y | Y | Y | Y | Y |
| 15 **Pryce** | Y | Y | Y | Y | Y | Y |
| 16 **Regula** | Y | Y | Y | Y | Y | Y |
| 17 Ryan | Y | Y | Y | Y | N | N |
| 18 **Ney** | Y | Y | Y | Y | Y | Y |
| **OKLAHOMA** | | | | | | |
| 1 **Sullivan** | Y | Y | Y | Y | Y | Y |
| 2 Boren | Y | Y | Y | Y | N | N |
| 3 **Lucas** | Y | Y | Y | Y | Y | Y |
| 4 **Cole** | Y | Y | Y | Y | Y | Y |
| 5 **Istook** | Y | Y | Y | Y | Y | Y |
| **OREGON** | | | | | | |
| 1 Wu | Y | Y | Y | Y | N | N |
| 2 **Walden** | Y | Y | Y | Y | Y | Y |
| 3 Blumenauer | Y | Y | Y | Y | N | N |
| 4 DeFazio | Y | Y | Y | Y | N | N |
| 5 Hooley | Y | Y | Y | Y | N | N |
| **PENNSYLVANIA** | | | | | | |
| 1 Brady | ? | ? | Y | Y | N | N |
| 2 Fattah | ? | ? | Y | Y | N | N |
| 3 **English** | Y | Y | Y | Y | Y | Y |
| 4 **Hart** | Y | Y | Y | Y | Y | Y |
| 5 **Peterson** | Y | Y | Y | Y | Y | Y |
| 6 **Gerlach** | Y | Y | Y | Y | Y | Y |
| 7 **Weldon** | Y | Y | ? | Y | Y | Y |
| 8 **Fitzpatrick** | Y | Y | Y | Y | Y | Y |
| 9 **Shuster** | Y | Y | Y | Y | Y | Y |
| 10 **Sherwood** | Y | Y | Y | Y | Y | Y |
| 11 Kanjorski | Y | Y | Y | Y | N | N |
| 12 Murtha | ? | ? | Y | Y | N | N |
| 13 Schwartz | Y | Y | Y | Y | N | N |
| 14 Doyle | Y | Y | Y | Y | N | N |
| 15 **Dent** | Y | Y | Y | Y | Y | Y |
| 16 **Pitts** | Y | Y | Y | Y | Y | Y |
| 17 Holden | Y | Y | Y | Y | N | N |
| 18 **Murphy** | Y | Y | Y | Y | Y | Y |
| 19 **Platts** | Y | Y | Y | Y | Y | Y |
| **RHODE ISLAND** | | | | | | |
| 1 Kennedy | Y | Y | Y | Y | N | N |
| 2 Langevin | Y | Y | Y | Y | N | Y |
| **SOUTH CAROLINA** | | | | | | |
| 1 **Brown** | Y | Y | Y | Y | Y | Y |
| 2 **Wilson** | Y | Y | Y | Y | Y | Y |
| 3 **Barrett** | Y | Y | Y | Y | Y | Y |
| 4 **Inglis** | Y | Y | Y | Y | Y | Y |
| 5 Spratt | Y | Y | Y | Y | N | N |
| 6 Clyburn | Y | Y | Y | Y | N | N |
| **SOUTH DAKOTA** | | | | | | |
| AL Herseth | Y | Y | Y | Y | N | N |
| **TENNESSEE** | | | | | | |
| 1 **Jenkins** | Y | Y | Y | Y | Y | Y |
| 2 **Duncan** | Y | Y | Y | Y | Y | Y |

| | 454 | 455 | 456 | 457 | 458 | 459 |
|---|---|---|---|---|---|---|
| 3 **Wamp** | Y | Y | Y | Y | Y | Y |
| 4 Davis | Y | Y | Y | Y | N | N |
| 5 Cooper | Y | Y | Y | Y | N | N |
| 6 Gordon | Y | Y | Y | Y | N | N |
| 7 **Blackburn** | Y | Y | Y | Y | Y | Y |
| 8 Tanner | Y | Y | Y | Y | N | N |
| 9 Ford | Y | Y | ? | ? | N | N |
| **TEXAS** | | | | | | |
| 1 **Gohmert** | Y | Y | Y | Y | Y | Y |
| 2 **Poe** | Y | Y | Y | Y | Y | Y |
| 3 **Johnson, S.** | Y | Y | Y | Y | Y | Y |
| 4 **Hall** | Y | Y | Y | Y | Y | Y |
| 5 **Hensarling** | Y | Y | Y | Y | Y | Y |
| 6 **Barton** | Y | Y | Y | Y | Y | Y |
| 7 **Culberson** | Y | Y | Y | Y | Y | Y |
| 8 **Brady** | ? | ? | ? | ? | ? | ? |
| 9 Green, A. | Y | Y | Y | Y | N | N |
| 10 **McCaul** | Y | Y | Y | Y | Y | Y |
| 11 **Conaway** | ? | ? | ? | ? | ? | ? |
| 12 **Granger** | Y | Y | Y | Y | Y | Y |
| 13 **Thornberry** | Y | Y | Y | Y | Y | Y |
| 14 **Paul** | Y | N | Y | Y | Y | Y |
| 15 Hinojosa | Y | Y | Y | Y | N | N |
| 16 Reyes | Y | Y | Y | Y | N | N |
| 17 Edwards | Y | Y | Y | Y | N | Y |
| 18 Jackson-Lee | Y | Y | Y | Y | N | N |
| 19 **Neugebauer** | Y | Y | Y | Y | Y | Y |
| 20 Gonzalez | Y | Y | Y | Y | N | Y |
| 21 **Smith** | Y | Y | Y | Y | Y | Y |
| 22 **DeLay** | Y | Y | Y | Y | Y | Y |
| 23 **Bonilla** | Y | Y | Y | Y | Y | Y |
| 24 **Marchant** | Y | Y | ? | ? | Y | Y |
| 25 Doggett | Y | Y | Y | Y | N | N |
| 26 **Burgess** | Y | Y | Y | Y | Y | Y |
| 27 Ortiz | Y | Y | Y | Y | N | N |
| 28 Cuellar | Y | Y | Y | Y | N | N |
| 29 Green, G. | Y | Y | Y | Y | N | N |
| 30 Johnson, E. | Y | Y | Y | Y | N | N |
| 31 **Carter** | Y | Y | Y | Y | Y | Y |
| 32 **Sessions** | ? | ? | Y | Y | Y | Y |
| **UTAH** | | | | | | |
| 1 **Bishop** | Y | Y | Y | Y | Y | Y |
| 2 Matheson | Y | Y | Y | Y | N | N |
| 3 **Cannon** | Y | Y | Y | Y | Y | Y |
| **VERMONT** | | | | | | |
| AL *Sanders* | Y | Y | Y | Y | N | N |
| **VIRGINIA** | | | | | | |
| 1 **Davis, J.** | Y | Y | Y | Y | Y | Y |
| 2 **Drake** | Y | Y | Y | Y | Y | Y |
| 3 Scott | Y | Y | Y | Y | N | N |
| 4 **Forbes** | Y | Y | Y | Y | Y | Y |
| 5 **Goode** | Y | Y | Y | Y | Y | Y |
| 6 **Goodlatte** | Y | Y | Y | Y | Y | Y |
| 7 **Cantor** | Y | Y | Y | Y | Y | Y |
| 8 Moran | Y | Y | Y | Y | N | N |
| 9 Boucher | ? | ? | Y | Y | N | N |
| 10 **Wolf** | Y | Y | Y | Y | Y | Y |
| 11 **Davis, T.** | Y | Y | Y | Y | Y | Y |
| **WASHINGTON** | | | | | | |
| 1 Inslee | + | + | Y | Y | N | N |
| 2 Larsen | Y | Y | Y | Y | N | N |
| 3 Baird | Y | Y | Y | Y | N | N |
| 4 **Hastings** | Y | Y | Y | Y | Y | Y |
| 5 **McMorris** | Y | Y | Y | Y | Y | Y |
| 6 Dicks | ? | ? | Y | Y | N | Y |
| 7 McDermott | + | + | Y | Y | N | N |
| 8 **Reichert** | Y | Y | Y | Y | Y | Y |
| 9 Smith | Y | Y | Y | Y | N | N |
| **WEST VIRGINIA** | | | | | | |
| 1 Mollohan | ? | ? | Y | Y | N | N |
| 2 **Capito** | Y | Y | Y | Y | Y | Y |
| 3 Rahall | Y | Y | Y | Y | N | N |
| **WISCONSIN** | | | | | | |
| 1 **Ryan** | Y | Y | Y | Y | Y | Y |
| 2 Baldwin | Y | Y | Y | Y | N | N |
| 3 Kind | Y | Y | Y | Y | N | N |
| 4 Moore | Y | Y | Y | Y | N | N |
| 5 **Sensenbrenner** | Y | Y | Y | Y | Y | Y |
| 6 **Petri** | Y | Y | Y | Y | Y | Y |
| 7 Obey | Y | Y | Y | Y | N | N |
| 8 **Green** | Y | Y | Y | Y | Y | Y |
| **WYOMING** | | | | | | |
| AL **Cubin** | Y | Y | Y | Y | ? | ? |

# IN THE HOUSE | By Vote Number

**460.** **HR 3673. Fiscal 2005 Emergency Supplemental Appropriations/Passage.** Lewis, R-Calif., motion to suspend the rules and pass the bill that would appropriate $51.8 billion in fiscal 2005 supplemental spending for disaster relief to areas affected by Hurricane Katrina. The bill would provide $50 billion for the Federal Emergency Management Agency, $1.4 billion for the Defense Department and $400 million for the Army Corps of Engineers. Motion agreed to 410-11: R 213-11; D 196-0 (ND 147-0, SD 49-0); I 1-0. A two-thirds majority of those present and voting (281 in this case) is required for passage under suspension of the rules. Sept. 8, 2005.

**461.** **HR 3669. National Flood Insurance Program/Passage.** Ney, R-Ohio, motion to suspend the rules and pass the bill that would temporarily increase to $3.5 billion, from $1.5 billion, the amount that the Federal Emergency Management Agency may borrow to pay claims under the National Flood Insurance Program that exceed collected premiums in the National Flood Insurance Fund. Motion agreed to 416-0: R 223-0; D 192-0 (ND 144-0, SD 48-0); I 1-0. A two-thirds majority of those present and voting (278 in this case) is required for passage under suspension of the rules. Sept. 8, 2005.

**462.** **HR 3668. Federal Student Grant Assistance/Passage.** Boustany, R-La., motion to suspend the rules and pass the bill that would allow the Education Department to waive the repayment requirement for any federal student grant assistance provided to students under Title IV of the Higher Education Act if their school attendance is interrupted because of the impact of a major disaster. To qualify for the waiver, students must have lived, worked, or attended schools in an area designated by the president as a major disaster. Motion agreed to 414-0: R 222-0; D 191-0 (ND 142-0, SD 49-0); I 1-0. A two-thirds majority of those present and voting (276 in this case) is required for passage under suspension of the rules. Sept. 8, 2005.

**463.** **H Res 428. Gratitude to Foreign Individuals and Governments/Adoption.** Leach, R-Iowa, motion to suspend the rules and adopt the resolution that would express the sincere gratitude of the House to foreign individuals, organizations and governments that have offered material assistance and other forms of support to people affected by Hurricane Katrina. Motion agreed to 410-0: R 220-0; D 189-0 (ND 141-0, SD 48-0); I 1-0. A two-thirds majority of those present and voting (274 in this case) is required for adoption under suspension of the rules. Sept. 8, 2005.

**464.** **H Res 427. September 11 Remembrance/Adoption.** Leach, R-Iowa, motion to suspend the rules and adopt the resolution that would express the sense of the House on the anniversary of the Sept. 11 terrorist attacks. The resolution would extend the deepest sympathies of the House to the victims of the attacks and thank foreign leaders and citizens of all nations who assisted the United States in its fight against terrorism. Motion agreed to 402-6: R 219-0; D 182-6 (ND 135-5, SD 47-1); I 1-0. A two-thirds majority of those present and voting (272 in this case) is required for adoption under suspension of the rules. Sept. 8, 2005.

ND Northern Democrats, SD Southern Democrats
Southern states: Ala., Ark., Fla., Ga., Ky., La., Miss., N.C., Okla., S.C., Tenn., Texas, Va.

| | 460 | 461 | 462 | 463 | 464 |
|---|---|---|---|---|---|
| **ALABAMA** | | | | | |
| 1 Bonner | Y | Y | Y | Y | Y |
| 2 Everett | ? | ? | ? | ? | ? |
| 3 Rogers | Y | Y | Y | Y | Y |
| 4 Aderholt | Y | Y | Y | Y | Y |
| 5 Cramer | Y | Y | Y | Y | Y |
| 6 Bachus | Y | Y | Y | Y | Y |
| 7 Davis | Y | Y | Y | Y | Y |
| **ALASKA** | | | | | |
| AL Young | ? | ? | ? | ? | ? |
| **ARIZONA** | | | | | |
| 1 Renzi | Y | Y | Y | Y | Y |
| 2 Franks | Y | Y | Y | Y | Y |
| 3 Shadegg | Y | Y | Y | Y | Y |
| 4 Pastor | Y | Y | Y | Y | Y |
| 5 Hayworth | Y | Y | Y | Y | Y |
| 6 Flake | N | Y | Y | Y | Y |
| 7 Grijalva | Y | Y | Y | Y | Y |
| 8 Kolbe | Y | Y | Y | Y | Y |
| **ARKANSAS** | | | | | |
| 1 Berry | Y | Y | Y | Y | Y |
| 2 Snyder | Y | Y | Y | Y | Y |
| 3 Boozman | Y | Y | Y | Y | Y |
| 4 Ross | Y | Y | Y | Y | Y |
| **CALIFORNIA** | | | | | |
| 1 Thompson | Y | Y | Y | Y | Y |
| 2 Herger | Y | Y | Y | Y | Y |
| 3 Lungren | Y | Y | Y | Y | Y |
| 4 Doolittle | Y | Y | Y | Y | Y |
| 5 Matsui, D. | Y | Y | Y | Y | Y |
| 6 Woolsey | Y | Y | Y | Y | N |
| 7 Miller, George | Y | Y | Y | Y | Y |
| 8 Pelosi | Y | Y | Y | Y | Y |
| 9 Lee | Y | Y | Y | Y | N |
| 10 Tauscher | Y | Y | Y | Y | Y |
| 11 Pombo | Y | Y | Y | Y | Y |
| 12 Lantos | Y | Y | Y | Y | Y |
| 13 Stark | Y | Y | Y | Y | N |
| 14 Eshoo | Y | Y | Y | Y | Y |
| 15 Honda | Y | Y | Y | Y | Y |
| 16 Lofgren | Y | Y | Y | Y | Y |
| 17 Farr | Y | Y | Y | Y | Y |
| 18 Cardoza | Y | Y | Y | Y | Y |
| 19 Radanovich | Y | Y | Y | Y | Y |
| 20 Costa | Y | Y | Y | Y | Y |
| 21 Nunes | Y | Y | Y | Y | Y |
| 22 Thomas | Y | Y | Y | Y | Y |
| 23 Capps | Y | Y | Y | Y | Y |
| 24 Gallegly | Y | Y | Y | Y | Y |
| 25 McKeon | Y | Y | Y | ? | ? |
| 26 Dreier | Y | Y | Y | Y | Y |
| 27 Sherman | Y | Y | Y | Y | Y |
| 28 Berman | Y | Y | Y | ? | ? |
| 29 Schiff | Y | Y | Y | Y | Y |
| 30 Waxman | Y | Y | Y | Y | Y |
| 31 Becerra | Y | Y | Y | Y | Y |
| 32 Solis | Y | Y | Y | Y | Y |
| 33 Watson | Y | Y | Y | Y | Y |
| 34 Roybal-Allard | Y | Y | Y | Y | Y |
| 35 Waters | Y | Y | Y | Y | Y |
| 36 Harman | Y | Y | Y | Y | Y |
| 37 Millender-McD. | Y | Y | Y | Y | Y |
| 38 Napolitano | Y | Y | Y | Y | Y |
| 39 Sánchez, Linda | Y | Y | Y | Y | Y |
| 40 Royce | Y | Y | Y | Y | Y |
| 41 Lewis | Y | Y | Y | Y | Y |
| 42 Miller, Gary | Y | Y | Y | ? | ? |
| 43 Baca | Y | Y | Y | Y | Y |
| 44 Calvert | Y | Y | Y | Y | Y |
| 45 Bono | Y | Y | Y | Y | Y |
| 46 Rohrabacher | Y | Y | Y | Y | Y |
| 47 Sanchez, Loretta | + | + | + | + | + |
| 48 Vacant | | | | | |
| 49 Issa | Y | ? | ? | ? | ? |
| 50 Cunningham | Y | Y | Y | Y | Y |
| 51 Filner | Y | + | + | + | + |
| 52 Hunter | Y | Y | Y | Y | Y |
| 53 Davis | Y | Y | Y | Y | Y |
| **COLORADO** | | | | | |
| 1 DeGette | Y | Y | Y | Y | ? |
| 2 Udall | Y | Y | Y | Y | Y |
| 3 Salazar | Y | Y | Y | Y | Y |
| 4 Musgrave | Y | Y | Y | Y | Y |
| 5 Hefley | Y | Y | Y | Y | Y |
| 6 Tancredo | N | Y | Y | Y | Y |
| 7 Beauprez | Y | Y | Y | Y | Y |
| **CONNECTICUT** | | | | | |
| 1 Larson | Y | Y | Y | Y | Y |
| 2 Simmons | Y | Y | Y | Y | Y |
| 3 DeLauro | Y | Y | Y | Y | Y |
| 4 Shays | Y | Y | Y | Y | Y |
| 5 Johnson | Y | Y | Y | Y | Y |
| **DELAWARE** | | | | | |
| AL Castle | Y | Y | Y | Y | |
| **FLORIDA** | | | | | |
| 1 Miller | Y | Y | Y | Y | Y |
| 2 Boyd | Y | Y | Y | Y | Y |
| 3 Brown | Y | Y | Y | Y | Y |
| 4 Crenshaw | Y | Y | Y | Y | Y |
| 5 Brown-Waite | Y | Y | Y | Y | Y |
| 6 Stearns | Y | Y | Y | Y | Y |
| 7 Mica | Y | Y | Y | Y | Y |
| 8 Keller | Y | Y | Y | Y | Y |
| 9 Bilirakis | Y | Y | Y | Y | Y |
| 10 Young | Y | Y | Y | Y | Y |
| 11 Davis | Y | Y | Y | Y | Y |
| 12 Putnam | Y | Y | Y | Y | Y |
| 13 Harris | Y | Y | Y | Y | Y |
| 14 Mack | Y | Y | Y | Y | Y |
| 15 Weldon | Y | Y | Y | Y | Y |
| 16 Foley | Y | Y | Y | Y | Y |
| 17 Meek | Y | Y | Y | Y | Y |
| 18 Ros-Lehtinen | Y | Y | Y | Y | Y |
| 19 Wexler | Y | Y | Y | Y | Y |
| 20 Wasserman-Schultz | Y | Y | Y | Y | Y |
| 21 Diaz-Balart, L. | Y | Y | Y | Y | Y |
| 22 Shaw | Y | Y | Y | Y | Y |
| 23 Hastings | Y | Y | Y | Y | Y |
| 24 Feeney | Y | Y | Y | Y | Y |
| 25 Diaz-Balart, M. | Y | Y | Y | Y | Y |
| **GEORGIA** | | | | | |
| 1 Kingston | Y | Y | Y | Y | Y |
| 2 Bishop | Y | ? | Y | Y | Y |
| 3 Marshall | Y | Y | Y | Y | Y |
| 4 McKinney | Y | Y | Y | Y | N |
| 5 Lewis | Y | Y | Y | Y | Y |
| 6 Price | Y | Y | Y | Y | Y |
| 7 Linder | Y | Y | Y | Y | Y |
| 8 Westmoreland | N | Y | Y | Y | Y |
| 9 Norwood | Y | Y | Y | Y | Y |
| 10 Deal | Y | Y | Y | Y | Y |
| 11 Gingrey | Y | Y | Y | Y | Y |
| 12 Barrow | Y | Y | Y | Y | Y |
| 13 Scott | Y | Y | Y | Y | Y |
| **HAWAII** | | | | | |
| 1 Abercrombie | Y | Y | Y | Y | Y |
| 2 Case | Y | Y | Y | Y | Y |
| **IDAHO** | | | | | |
| 1 Otter | N | Y | Y | Y | Y |
| 2 Simpson | Y | Y | Y | Y | Y |
| **ILLINOIS** | | | | | |
| 1 Rush | Y | Y | Y | Y | Y |
| 2 Jackson | Y | Y | Y | Y | Y |
| 3 Lipinski | Y | Y | Y | Y | Y |
| 4 Gutierrez | Y | Y | Y | Y | Y |
| 5 Emanuel | Y | Y | Y | Y | Y |
| 6 Hyde | Y | Y | Y | Y | Y |
| 7 Davis | Y | Y | Y | Y | Y |
| 8 Bean | Y | Y | Y | Y | Y |
| 9 Schakowsky | Y | Y | Y | Y | Y |
| 10 Kirk | Y | Y | Y | Y | Y |
| 11 Weller | Y | Y | Y | Y | Y |
| 12 Costello | Y | Y | Y | Y | Y |

**KEY**   Republicans   Democrats   *Independents*

| | | |
|---|---|---|
| **Y** Voted for (yea) | **X** Paired against | **C** Voted "present" to avoid possible conflict of interest |
| **#** Paired for | **–** Announced against | |
| **+** Announced for | **P** Voted "present" | **?** Did not vote or otherwise make a position known |
| **N** Voted against (nay) | | |

| | 460 | 461 | 462 | 463 | 464 |
|---|---|---|---|---|---|
| 13 **Biggert** | Y | Y | Y | Y | Y |
| 14 **Hastert** | | | | | Y |
| 15 **Johnson** | Y | Y | Y | Y | Y |
| 16 **Manzullo** | Y | Y | Y | Y | Y |
| 17 Evans | Y | Y | Y | Y | Y |
| 18 **LaHood** | Y | Y | Y | Y | Y |
| 19 **Shimkus** | Y | Y | Y | Y | Y |
| **INDIANA** | | | | | |
| 1 Visclosky | Y | Y | Y | Y | Y |
| 2 **Chocola** | Y | Y | Y | Y | Y |
| 3 **Souder** | Y | Y | Y | Y | Y |
| 4 **Buyer** | Y | Y | Y | Y | Y |
| 5 **Burton** | Y | Y | Y | Y | Y |
| 6 **Pence** | Y | Y | Y | Y | Y |
| 7 Carson | Y | Y | Y | Y | Y |
| 8 **Hostettler** | N | Y | Y | Y | Y |
| 9 **Sodrel** | Y | Y | Y | Y | Y |
| **IOWA** | | | | | |
| 1 **Nussle** | Y | Y | Y | Y | Y |
| 2 **Leach** | Y | Y | Y | Y | Y |
| 3 Boswell | Y | Y | Y | Y | Y |
| 4 **Latham** | Y | Y | Y | Y | Y |
| 5 **King** | N | Y | Y | Y | Y |
| **KANSAS** | | | | | |
| 1 **Moran** | Y | Y | Y | Y | Y |
| 2 **Ryun** | Y | Y | Y | Y | Y |
| 3 Moore | Y | Y | Y | Y | Y |
| 4 **Tiahrt** | Y | Y | Y | Y | Y |
| **KENTUCKY** | | | | | |
| 1 **Whitfield** | Y | Y | Y | Y | Y |
| 2 **Lewis** | Y | Y | Y | Y | Y |
| 3 **Northup** | Y | Y | Y | Y | Y |
| 4 **Davis** | Y | Y | Y | Y | Y |
| 5 **Rogers** | Y | Y | Y | Y | Y |
| 6 Chandler | Y | Y | Y | Y | Y |
| **LOUISIANA** | | | | | |
| 1 **Jindal** | Y | Y | Y | Y | Y |
| 2 Jefferson | Y | Y | Y | Y | Y |
| 3 Melancon | Y | Y | Y | Y | Y |
| 4 **McCrery** | ? | ? | ? | ? | ? |
| 5 **Alexander** | Y | Y | Y | Y | Y |
| 6 **Baker** | ? | ? | ? | ? | ? |
| 7 **Boustany** | Y | Y | Y | Y | Y |
| **MAINE** | | | | | |
| 1 Allen | Y | Y | Y | Y | Y |
| 2 Michaud | Y | Y | Y | Y | Y |
| **MARYLAND** | | | | | |
| 1 **Gilchrest** | Y | Y | Y | Y | Y |
| 2 Ruppersberger | Y | Y | Y | Y | Y |
| 3 Cardin | Y | Y | Y | Y | Y |
| 4 Wynn | Y | Y | Y | Y | Y |
| 5 Hoyer | Y | Y | Y | Y | Y |
| 6 **Bartlett** | Y | Y | Y | Y | Y |
| 7 Cummings | Y | Y | Y | Y | Y |
| 8 Van Hollen | Y | Y | Y | Y | Y |
| **MASSACHUSETTS** | | | | | |
| 1 Olver | ? | ? | ? | ? | ? |
| 2 Neal | Y | Y | Y | Y | Y |
| 3 McGovern | Y | Y | Y | Y | Y |
| 4 Frank | Y | Y | Y | Y | Y |
| 5 Meehan | Y | ? | ? | ? | ? |
| 6 Tierney | Y | Y | Y | Y | Y |
| 7 Markey | Y | Y | Y | Y | Y |
| 8 Capuano | Y | Y | Y | Y | Y |
| 9 Lynch | Y | Y | Y | ? | ? |
| 10 Delahunt | Y | Y | Y | Y | Y |
| **MICHIGAN** | | | | | |
| 1 Stupak | Y | Y | Y | Y | Y |
| 2 **Hoekstra** | Y | Y | Y | Y | Y |
| 3 **Ehlers** | Y | Y | Y | Y | Y |
| 4 **Camp** | Y | Y | Y | Y | Y |
| 5 Kildee | Y | Y | Y | Y | Y |
| 6 **Upton** | Y | Y | Y | Y | Y |
| 7 **Schwarz** | Y | Y | Y | Y | Y |
| 8 **Rogers** | Y | Y | Y | Y | Y |
| 9 **Knollenberg** | Y | Y | Y | Y | Y |
| 10 **Miller** | Y | Y | Y | Y | Y |
| 11 **McCotter** | Y | Y | Y | Y | Y |
| 12 Levin | Y | Y | Y | Y | Y |
| 13 Kilpatrick | Y | Y | Y | Y | Y |
| 14 Conyers | Y | Y | Y | Y | N |
| 15 Dingell | Y | Y | Y | Y | Y |

| | 460 | 461 | 462 | 463 | 464 |
|---|---|---|---|---|---|
| **MINNESOTA** | | | | | |
| 1 **Gutknecht** | Y | Y | Y | Y | Y |
| 2 **Kline** | Y | Y | Y | Y | Y |
| 3 **Ramstad** | Y | Y | Y | Y | Y |
| 4 McCollum | Y | Y | Y | Y | Y |
| 5 Sabo | Y | Y | Y | Y | Y |
| 6 **Kennedy** | Y | Y | Y | Y | Y |
| 7 Peterson | Y | Y | Y | Y | Y |
| 8 Oberstar | Y | Y | Y | Y | Y |
| **MISSISSIPPI** | | | | | |
| 1 **Wicker** | Y | Y | Y | Y | Y |
| 2 Thompson | Y | Y | Y | Y | Y |
| 3 **Pickering** | Y | Y | ? | Y | Y |
| 4 Taylor | ? | ? | ? | ? | ? |
| **MISSOURI** | | | | | |
| 1 Clay | Y | Y | Y | Y | Y |
| 2 **Akin** | Y | Y | Y | Y | Y |
| 3 Carnahan | Y | Y | Y | Y | Y |
| 4 Skelton | Y | Y | Y | Y | Y |
| 5 Cleaver | Y | Y | Y | Y | Y |
| 6 **Graves** | Y | Y | Y | Y | Y |
| 7 **Blunt** | Y | Y | Y | Y | Y |
| 8 **Emerson** | Y | Y | Y | Y | Y |
| 9 **Hulshof** | Y | Y | Y | Y | Y |
| **MONTANA** | | | | | |
| AL **Rehberg** | Y | Y | Y | Y | Y |
| **NEBRASKA** | | | | | |
| 1 **Fortenberry** | Y | Y | Y | Y | Y |
| 2 **Terry** | Y | Y | Y | Y | Y |
| 3 **Osborne** | Y | Y | Y | Y | Y |
| **NEVADA** | | | | | |
| 1 Berkley | ? | ? | ? | ? | ? |
| 2 **Gibbons** | Y | Y | Y | Y | Y |
| 3 **Porter** | Y | Y | Y | Y | Y |
| **NEW HAMPSHIRE** | | | | | |
| 1 **Bradley** | Y | Y | Y | Y | Y |
| 2 **Bass** | Y | Y | Y | Y | + |
| **NEW JERSEY** | | | | | |
| 1 Andrews | Y | Y | Y | Y | Y |
| 2 **LoBiondo** | Y | Y | Y | Y | Y |
| 3 **Saxton** | Y | Y | Y | Y | Y |
| 4 **Smith** | Y | Y | Y | Y | Y |
| 5 **Garrett** | N | Y | Y | Y | Y |
| 6 Pallone | Y | Y | Y | Y | Y |
| 7 **Ferguson** | Y | Y | Y | Y | Y |
| 8 Pascrell | Y | Y | Y | Y | Y |
| 9 Rothman | Y | Y | Y | Y | Y |
| 10 Payne | Y | Y | Y | Y | Y |
| 11 **Frelinghuysen** | Y | Y | Y | Y | Y |
| 12 Holt | Y | Y | Y | Y | Y |
| 13 Menendez | Y | Y | Y | Y | Y |
| **NEW MEXICO** | | | | | |
| 1 **Wilson** | Y | Y | Y | Y | Y |
| 2 **Pearce** | Y | Y | Y | Y | Y |
| 3 Udall | Y | Y | Y | Y | Y |
| **NEW YORK** | | | | | |
| 1 Bishop | Y | Y | Y | Y | Y |
| 2 Israel | Y | Y | Y | Y | Y |
| 3 **King** | Y | Y | Y | Y | Y |
| 4 McCarthy | Y | Y | Y | Y | Y |
| 5 Ackerman | Y | Y | Y | Y | Y |
| 6 Meeks | Y | Y | Y | Y | Y |
| 7 Crowley | Y | Y | Y | Y | Y |
| 8 Nadler | Y | Y | Y | Y | Y |
| 9 Weiner | Y | Y | Y | Y | Y |
| 10 Towns | Y | Y | ? | ? | ? |
| 11 Owens | Y | Y | Y | Y | Y |
| 12 Velázquez | Y | Y | Y | Y | Y |
| 13 **Fossella** | Y | Y | Y | Y | Y |
| 14 Maloney | ? | ? | ? | ? | ? |
| 15 Rangel | Y | Y | Y | Y | Y |
| 16 Serrano | Y | Y | Y | Y | Y |
| 17 Engel | Y | Y | Y | Y | Y |
| 18 Lowey | Y | Y | Y | Y | Y |
| 19 **Kelly** | Y | Y | Y | Y | Y |
| 20 **Sweeney** | Y | Y | Y | Y | Y |
| 21 McNulty | Y | Y | Y | Y | Y |
| 22 Hinchey | Y | Y | Y | Y | Y |
| 23 **McHugh** | Y | Y | Y | Y | Y |
| 24 **Boehlert** | Y | Y | Y | Y | Y |
| 25 **Walsh** | Y | Y | Y | Y | Y |
| 26 **Reynolds** | Y | Y | Y | Y | Y |
| 27 Higgins | Y | Y | Y | Y | Y |
| 28 Slaughter | Y | Y | Y | Y | Y |
| 29 **Kuhl** | Y | Y | Y | Y | Y |

| | 460 | 461 | 462 | 463 | 464 |
|---|---|---|---|---|---|
| **NORTH CAROLINA** | | | | | |
| 1 Butterfield | ? | ? | ? | ? | ? |
| 2 Etheridge | Y | Y | Y | Y | Y |
| 3 **Jones** | Y | Y | Y | Y | Y |
| 4 Price | Y | Y | Y | Y | Y |
| 5 **Foxx** | N | Y | Y | Y | Y |
| 6 **Coble** | Y | Y | Y | Y | Y |
| 7 McIntyre | Y | Y | Y | Y | Y |
| 8 **Hayes** | Y | Y | Y | Y | Y |
| 9 **Myrick** | Y | Y | Y | Y | Y |
| 10 **McHenry** | Y | Y | Y | Y | Y |
| 11 **Taylor** | Y | Y | Y | Y | Y |
| 12 Watt | Y | Y | Y | Y | Y |
| 13 Miller | Y | Y | Y | Y | Y |
| **NORTH DAKOTA** | | | | | |
| AL Pomeroy | Y | Y | Y | Y | Y |
| **OHIO** | | | | | |
| 1 **Chabot** | Y | Y | Y | Y | Y |
| 2 **Schmidt** | Y | Y | Y | Y | Y |
| 3 **Turner** | Y | Y | Y | Y | Y |
| 4 **Oxley** | Y | Y | Y | Y | Y |
| 5 **Gillmor** | Y | Y | Y | Y | Y |
| 6 Strickland | Y | Y | Y | Y | Y |
| 7 **Hobson** | Y | Y | Y | Y | Y |
| 8 **Boehner** | Y | Y | Y | Y | Y |
| 9 Kaptur | Y | ? | ? | Y | Y |
| 10 Kucinich | Y | Y | Y | Y | Y |
| 11 Jones | Y | Y | Y | Y | Y |
| 12 **Tiberi** | Y | Y | Y | Y | Y |
| 13 Brown | Y | Y | Y | Y | Y |
| 14 **LaTourette** | Y | Y | Y | Y | Y |
| 15 **Pryce** | Y | Y | Y | Y | Y |
| 16 **Regula** | Y | Y | Y | Y | Y |
| 17 Ryan | Y | Y | Y | Y | Y |
| 18 **Ney** | Y | Y | Y | Y | ? |
| **OKLAHOMA** | | | | | |
| 1 **Sullivan** | Y | Y | Y | Y | Y |
| 2 Boren | Y | Y | Y | Y | Y |
| 3 **Lucas** | Y | Y | Y | Y | Y |
| 4 **Cole** | Y | Y | Y | Y | Y |
| 5 **Istook** | Y | Y | Y | Y | Y |
| **OREGON** | | | | | |
| 1 Wu | Y | Y | Y | Y | Y |
| 2 **Walden** | Y | Y | Y | Y | Y |
| 3 Blumenauer | Y | Y | ? | ? | ? |
| 4 DeFazio | Y | Y | Y | Y | Y |
| 5 Hooley | Y | Y | Y | Y | Y |
| **PENNSYLVANIA** | | | | | |
| 1 Brady | Y | Y | Y | Y | Y |
| 2 Fattah | Y | Y | Y | Y | Y |
| 3 **English** | Y | Y | Y | Y | Y |
| 4 **Hart** | Y | Y | Y | Y | Y |
| 5 **Peterson** | Y | Y | Y | Y | Y |
| 6 **Gerlach** | Y | Y | Y | Y | Y |
| 7 **Weldon** | Y | Y | Y | Y | Y |
| 8 **Fitzpatrick** | Y | Y | Y | Y | Y |
| 9 **Shuster** | Y | Y | Y | Y | Y |
| 10 **Sherwood** | Y | Y | Y | Y | Y |
| 11 Kanjorski | Y | Y | Y | Y | Y |
| 12 Murtha | Y | Y | Y | Y | Y |
| 13 Schwartz | Y | Y | Y | Y | Y |
| 14 Doyle | Y | Y | Y | Y | Y |
| 15 **Dent** | Y | Y | Y | Y | Y |
| 16 **Pitts** | Y | Y | Y | Y | Y |
| 17 Holden | Y | Y | Y | Y | Y |
| 18 **Murphy** | Y | Y | Y | Y | Y |
| 19 **Platts** | Y | Y | Y | Y | Y |
| **RHODE ISLAND** | | | | | |
| 1 Kennedy | Y | Y | Y | Y | Y |
| 2 Langevin | Y | Y | Y | Y | Y |
| **SOUTH CAROLINA** | | | | | |
| 1 **Brown** | Y | Y | Y | Y | Y |
| 2 **Wilson** | Y | Y | Y | Y | Y |
| 3 **Barrett** | Y | Y | Y | Y | Y |
| 4 **Inglis** | Y | Y | Y | Y | Y |
| 5 Spratt | Y | Y | Y | Y | Y |
| 6 Clyburn | Y | Y | Y | Y | Y |
| **SOUTH DAKOTA** | | | | | |
| AL Herseth | Y | Y | Y | Y | Y |
| **TENNESSEE** | | | | | |
| 1 **Jenkins** | Y | Y | Y | Y | Y |
| 2 **Duncan** | Y | Y | Y | Y | Y |

| | 460 | 461 | 462 | 463 | 464 |
|---|---|---|---|---|---|
| 3 **Wamp** | Y | Y | Y | Y | Y |
| 4 Davis | Y | Y | Y | Y | Y |
| 5 Cooper | Y | Y | Y | Y | Y |
| 6 Gordon | Y | Y | Y | Y | ? |
| 7 **Blackburn** | Y | Y | Y | Y | Y |
| 8 Tanner | Y | Y | Y | Y | Y |
| 9 Ford | Y | Y | Y | Y | Y |
| **TEXAS** | | | | | |
| 1 **Gohmert** | Y | Y | Y | Y | Y |
| 2 **Poe** | Y | Y | Y | Y | Y |
| 3 **Johnson, S.** | Y | Y | Y | Y | Y |
| 4 **Hall** | Y | Y | Y | Y | Y |
| 5 **Hensarling** | Y | Y | Y | Y | Y |
| 6 **Barton** | N | Y | Y | ? | ? |
| 7 **Culberson** | Y | Y | Y | Y | Y |
| 8 **Brady** | ? | ? | ? | ? | ? |
| 9 Green, A. | Y | Y | Y | Y | Y |
| 10 **McCaul** | Y | Y | Y | Y | Y |
| 11 **Conaway** | ? | ? | ? | ? | ? |
| 12 **Granger** | Y | Y | Y | Y | Y |
| 13 **Thornberry** | Y | Y | Y | Y | Y |
| 14 **Paul** | N | Y | Y | Y | Y |
| 15 Hinojosa | Y | Y | Y | Y | Y |
| 16 Reyes | Y | Y | Y | Y | Y |
| 17 Edwards | Y | Y | Y | Y | Y |
| 18 Jackson-Lee | Y | Y | Y | Y | Y |
| 19 **Neugebauer** | Y | Y | Y | Y | Y |
| 20 Gonzalez | Y | Y | Y | Y | Y |
| 21 **Smith** | Y | Y | Y | Y | Y |
| 22 **DeLay** | Y | Y | Y | Y | Y |
| 23 **Bonilla** | Y | Y | Y | Y | Y |
| 24 **Marchant** | Y | Y | Y | Y | Y |
| 25 Doggett | Y | Y | Y | Y | Y |
| 26 **Burgess** | Y | Y | Y | Y | Y |
| 27 Ortiz | Y | Y | Y | Y | Y |
| 28 Cuellar | Y | Y | Y | Y | Y |
| 29 Green, G. | Y | Y | Y | Y | Y |
| 30 Johnson, E. | Y | Y | Y | + | Y |
| 31 **Carter** | Y | Y | Y | Y | Y |
| 32 **Sessions** | Y | Y | Y | Y | Y |
| **UTAH** | | | | | |
| 1 **Bishop** | Y | Y | Y | Y | Y |
| 2 Matheson | Y | Y | Y | Y | Y |
| 3 **Cannon** | Y | Y | Y | Y | Y |
| **VERMONT** | | | | | |
| AL *Sanders* | Y | Y | Y | Y | Y |
| **VIRGINIA** | | | | | |
| 1 **Davis, J.** | Y | Y | Y | Y | Y |
| 2 **Drake** | Y | Y | Y | Y | Y |
| 3 Scott | Y | Y | Y | Y | Y |
| 4 **Forbes** | Y | Y | Y | Y | Y |
| 5 **Goode** | Y | Y | Y | Y | Y |
| 6 **Goodlatte** | Y | Y | Y | Y | Y |
| 7 **Cantor** | Y | Y | Y | Y | Y |
| 8 Moran | Y | Y | Y | Y | Y |
| 9 Boucher | Y | Y | Y | Y | Y |
| 10 **Wolf** | Y | Y | Y | Y | Y |
| 11 **Davis, T.** | Y | Y | Y | Y | Y |
| **WASHINGTON** | | | | | |
| 1 Inslee | Y | Y | Y | Y | Y |
| 2 Larsen | Y | Y | Y | Y | Y |
| 3 Baird | Y | Y | Y | Y | Y |
| 4 **Hastings** | Y | Y | Y | Y | Y |
| 5 **McMorris** | Y | Y | Y | Y | Y |
| 6 Dicks | Y | Y | Y | Y | Y |
| 7 McDermott | Y | Y | Y | Y | N |
| 8 **Reichert** | Y | Y | Y | Y | Y |
| 9 Smith | Y | Y | Y | Y | Y |
| **WEST VIRGINIA** | | | | | |
| 1 Mollohan | Y | Y | Y | Y | Y |
| 2 **Capito** | Y | Y | Y | Y | Y |
| 3 Rahall | Y | Y | Y | Y | Y |
| **WISCONSIN** | | | | | |
| 1 **Ryan** | Y | Y | Y | Y | Y |
| 2 Baldwin | Y | Y | Y | Y | Y |
| 3 Kind | Y | Y | Y | Y | Y |
| 4 Moore | Y | Y | Y | Y | Y |
| 5 **Sensenbrenner** | N | Y | Y | Y | Y |
| 6 **Petri** | Y | Y | Y | Y | Y |
| 7 Obey | Y | Y | Y | Y | Y |
| 8 **Green** | Y | Y | Y | Y | Y |
| **WYOMING** | | | | | |
| AL **Cubin** | Y | Y | Y | Y | Y |

# IN THE HOUSE | By Vote Number

**465.** **S Con Res 26. United Airlines Flight 93 Memorial/Adoption.**
Shuster, R-Pa., motion to suspend the rules and adopt the concurrent resolution that would establish a panel of congressional leaders to select a Capitol memorial honoring the passengers and crew of Flight 93, which crashed in Pennsylvania on Sept. 11, 2001. Motion agreed to 403-0: R 219-0; D 183-0 (ND 135-0, SD 48-0); I 1-0. A two-thirds majority of those present and voting (269 in this case) is required for adoption under suspension of the rules. Sept. 13, 2005.

**466.** **HR 3649. Sportfishing and Recreational Boating Safety/Passage.**
Shuster, R-Pa., motion to suspend the rules and pass the bill that would continue funding through fiscal 2005 for various sportfishing and recreational boating programs. Motion agreed to 401-1: R 217-1; D 183-0 (ND 135-0, SD 48-0); I 1-0. A two-thirds majority of those present and voting (268 in this case) is required for passage under suspension of the rules. Sept. 13, 2005.

**467.** **S 276. Wind Cave National Park Boundary Revision/Passage.**
Fortuño, R-P.R., motion to suspend the rules and pass the bill that would authorize the Interior Department to acquire 5,675 acres of land to expand the Wind Cave National Park in South Dakota. Motion agreed to 295-106: R 111-106; D 183-0 (ND 135-0, SD 48-0); I 1-0. A two-thirds majority of those present and voting (268 in this case) is required for passage under suspension of the rules. Sept. 13, 2005.

**468.** **HR 3132. Sex Offender Registration/Mandatory Minimum Sentences.** Inglis, R-S.C., amendment that would eliminate the mandatory minimum sentences of five years in prison for failing to register as a sex offender or for making false statements during registration. Rejected 106-316: R 7-217; D 98-99 (ND 81-67, SD 17-32); I 1-0. Sept. 14, 2005.

**469.** **HR 3132. Sex Offender Registration/Hate Crimes.** Conyers, D-Mich., amendment that would broaden the categories covered by hate crimes to include crimes motivated by the victim's gender, sexual orientation or disability. The amendment would require the Justice Department to certify that bias was a motivating factor in the crime and that the state does not object to the federal government assuming jurisdiction. It also would authorize $5 million per year for fiscal 2006 and 2007 for the Justice Department to assist states and local authorities in investigating and prosecuting hate crimes. Adopted 223-199: R 30-194; D 192-5 (ND 148-0, SD 44-5); I 1-0. Sept. 14, 2005.

**470.** **HR 3132. Sex Offender Registration/Passage.** Passage of the bill that would create a national sex offender registry database and require individuals convicted of a sex crime to register before completing a prison term or within five days of being sentenced if they are not sentenced to prison. Convicted sex offenders who fail to register would face fines and five to 20 years in prison. The penalty for sexual exploitation of children would increase to 25 years to life in prison. State foster care programs would be required to check child abuse and neglect registries in all areas where prospective foster care families have lived within the past five years. Passed 371-52: R 195-29; D 175-23 (ND 130-19, SD 45-4); I 1-0. Sept. 14, 2005.

ND Northern Democrats, SD Southern Democrats
Southern states: Ala., Ark., Fla., Ga., Ky., La., Miss., N.C., Okla., S.C., Tenn., Texas, Va.

| | 465 | 466 | 467 | 468 | 469 | 470 |
|---|---|---|---|---|---|---|
| **ALABAMA** | | | | | | |
| 1 Bonner | Y | Y | N | N | N | Y |
| 2 Everett | Y | Y | N | N | N | Y |
| 3 Rogers | Y | Y | Y | N | N | Y |
| 4 Aderholt | Y | Y | Y | N | N | Y |
| 5 Cramer | Y | Y | Y | N | Y | Y |
| 6 Bachus | Y | Y | N | N | N | Y |
| 7 Davis | Y | Y | Y | N | Y | Y |
| **ALASKA** | | | | | | |
| AL Young | Y | Y | Y | N | N | Y |
| **ARIZONA** | | | | | | |
| 1 Renzi | Y | Y | Y | N | N | Y |
| 2 Franks | Y | Y | N | N | N | Y |
| 3 Shadegg | Y | Y | N | N | N | N |
| 4 Pastor | Y | Y | Y | Y | Y | Y |
| 5 Hayworth | Y | Y | N | N | N | Y |
| 6 Flake | Y | N | N | N | N | N |
| 7 Grijalva | Y | Y | Y | Y | Y | Y |
| 8 Kolbe | Y | Y | Y | N | Y | Y |
| **ARKANSAS** | | | | | | |
| 1 Berry | Y | Y | Y | N | N | Y |
| 2 Snyder | Y | Y | Y | Y | Y | Y |
| 3 Boozman | Y | Y | N | N | N | Y |
| 4 Ross | Y | Y | Y | N | Y | Y |
| **CALIFORNIA** | | | | | | |
| 1 Thompson | Y | Y | Y | N | Y | Y |
| 2 Herger | Y | Y | N | N | N | Y |
| 3 Lungren | Y | Y | Y | N | Y | Y |
| 4 Doolittle | Y | Y | N | N | N | Y |
| 5 Matsui, D. | Y | Y | Y | Y | Y | Y |
| 6 Woolsey | Y | Y | Y | Y | Y | N |
| 7 Miller, George | Y | Y | Y | Y | Y | Y |
| 8 Pelosi | Y | Y | Y | Y | Y | Y |
| 9 Lee | Y | Y | Y | Y | Y | N |
| 10 Tauscher | Y | Y | Y | Y | Y | Y |
| 11 Pombo | Y | Y | Y | N | N | Y |
| 12 Lantos | Y | Y | Y | Y | Y | Y |
| 13 Stark | Y | Y | Y | Y | N | N |
| 14 Eshoo | Y | Y | N | N | Y | Y |
| 15 Honda | Y | Y | Y | Y | N | N |
| 16 Lofgren | Y | Y | N | N | Y | Y |
| 17 Farr | Y | Y | Y | Y | Y | Y |
| 18 Cardoza | Y | Y | Y | N | Y | Y |
| 19 Radanovich | Y | Y | ? | N | N | Y |
| 20 Costa | Y | Y | Y | N | Y | Y |
| 21 Nunes | Y | Y | N | N | N | Y |
| 22 Thomas | Y | Y | N | N | N | Y |
| 23 Capps | Y | Y | Y | N | N | Y |
| 24 Gallegly | + | + | + | N | N | Y |
| 25 McKeon | Y | Y | N | N | N | Y |
| 26 Dreier | Y | Y | N | N | N | Y |
| 27 Sherman | Y | Y | Y | Y | Y | Y |
| 28 Berman | Y | Y | Y | Y | Y | Y |
| 29 Schiff | Y | Y | Y | N | Y | Y |
| 30 Waxman | Y | Y | Y | Y | Y | N |
| 31 Becerra | Y | Y | Y | Y | Y | Y |
| 32 Solis | Y | Y | Y | Y | Y | Y |
| 33 Watson | Y | Y | Y | Y | Y | N |
| 34 Roybal-Allard | Y | Y | Y | Y | Y | Y |
| 35 Waters | Y | Y | Y | Y | N | N |
| 36 Harman | Y | Y | Y | ? | ? | Y |
| 37 Millender-McD. | Y | Y | Y | Y | Y | Y |
| 38 Napolitano | Y | Y | Y | Y | Y | Y |
| 39 Sánchez, Linda | Y | Y | Y | Y | Y | Y |
| 40 Royce | Y | Y | N | ? | ? | ? |
| 41 Lewis | Y | Y | Y | N | N | Y |
| 42 Miller, Gary | Y | Y | N | N | N | Y |
| 43 Baca | Y | Y | Y | N | Y | Y |
| 44 Calvert | Y | Y | N | N | N | Y |
| 45 Bono | Y | Y | Y | N | Y | Y |
| 46 Rohrabacher | Y | Y | N | N | N | Y |
| 47 Sanchez, Loretta | Y | Y | Y | N | Y | Y |
| 48 Vacant | | | | | | |
| 49 Issa | Y | Y | N | N | N | Y |

| | 465 | 466 | 467 | 468 | 469 | 470 |
|---|---|---|---|---|---|---|
| 50 Cunningham | Y | Y | Y | N | N | Y |
| 51 Filner | Y | Y | Y | Y | Y | Y |
| 52 Hunter | Y | Y | Y | N | N | N |
| 53 Davis | Y | Y | N | Y | Y | Y |
| **COLORADO** | | | | | | |
| 1 DeGette | Y | Y | Y | Y | Y | Y |
| 2 Udall | Y | Y | Y | N | Y | Y |
| 3 Salazar | Y | Y | Y | N | Y | Y |
| 4 Musgrave | Y | Y | N | N | N | Y |
| 5 Hefley | Y | Y | N | N | N | N |
| 6 Tancredo | Y | Y | N | N | N | N |
| 7 Beauprez | ? | ? | ? | ? | ? | ? |
| **CONNECTICUT** | | | | | | |
| 1 Larson | Y | Y | Y | N | Y | Y |
| 2 Simmons | Y | Y | Y | N | Y | Y |
| 3 DeLauro | Y | Y | Y | N | Y | Y |
| 4 Shays | Y | Y | Y | N | Y | Y |
| 5 Johnson | Y | Y | Y | N | Y | Y |
| **DELAWARE** | | | | | | |
| AL Castle | Y | Y | Y | N | Y | Y |
| **FLORIDA** | | | | | | |
| 1 Miller | Y | Y | N | N | N | Y |
| 2 Boyd | Y | Y | Y | N | Y | Y |
| 3 Brown | Y | Y | Y | Y | Y | Y |
| 4 Crenshaw | Y | Y | Y | N | N | Y |
| 5 Brown-Waite | Y | Y | N | N | N | Y |
| 6 Stearns | Y | Y | N | N | N | Y |
| 7 Mica | Y | Y | N | N | N | Y |
| 8 Keller | Y | Y | N | N | N | Y |
| 9 Bilirakis | Y | Y | N | N | N | Y |
| 10 Young | Y | Y | N | N | N | Y |
| 11 Davis | Y | Y | Y | N | Y | Y |
| 12 Putnam | Y | Y | N | N | N | Y |
| 13 Harris | Y | Y | N | N | N | Y |
| 14 Mack | Y | Y | N | N | N | Y |
| 15 Weldon | Y | Y | N | N | N | Y |
| 16 Foley | Y | Y | Y | N | Y | Y |
| 17 Meek | Y | Y | Y | Y | Y | Y |
| 18 Ros-Lehtinen | Y | Y | Y | N | Y | Y |
| 19 Wexler | Y | Y | Y | N | Y | Y |
| 20 Wasserman-Schultz | Y | Y | Y | Y | Y | Y |
| 21 Diaz-Balart, L. | Y | Y | Y | N | Y | Y |
| 22 Shaw | Y | Y | Y | N | N | Y |
| 23 Hastings | Y | Y | Y | Y | Y | Y |
| 24 Feeney | Y | Y | N | N | N | Y |
| 25 Diaz-Balart, M. | Y | Y | N | N | Y | Y |
| **GEORGIA** | | | | | | |
| 1 Kingston | Y | Y | N | N | N | N |
| 2 Bishop | Y | Y | Y | Y | Y | Y |
| 3 Marshall | Y | Y | Y | Y | Y | Y |
| 4 McKinney | Y | Y | Y | Y | Y | N |
| 5 Lewis | Y | Y | Y | Y | Y | N |
| 6 Price | Y | Y | N | N | N | N |
| 7 Linder | Y | Y | N | N | Y | Y |
| 8 Westmoreland | Y | Y | N | N | N | N |
| 9 Norwood | Y | Y | N | N | N | N |
| 10 Deal | Y | Y | N | Y | N | N |
| 11 Gingrey | Y | Y | N | N | N | Y |
| 12 Barrow | Y | Y | Y | N | Y | Y |
| 13 Scott | Y | Y | Y | N | Y | Y |
| **HAWAII** | | | | | | |
| 1 Abercrombie | Y | Y | Y | Y | Y | Y |
| 2 Case | Y | Y | Y | Y | Y | Y |
| **IDAHO** | | | | | | |
| 1 Otter | Y | Y | N | N | N | Y |
| 2 Simpson | Y | Y | N | N | N | Y |
| **ILLINOIS** | | | | | | |
| 1 Rush | Y | Y | Y | Y | Y | Y |
| 2 Jackson | Y | Y | Y | Y | Y | Y |
| 3 Lipinski | Y | Y | Y | Y | Y | Y |
| 4 Gutierrez | Y | Y | Y | Y | Y | Y |
| 5 Emanuel | Y | Y | N | Y | Y | Y |
| 6 Hyde | Y | Y | N | N | Y | Y |
| 7 Davis | Y | Y | Y | Y | Y | N |
| 8 Bean | Y | Y | N | Y | Y | Y |
| 9 Schakowsky | Y | Y | Y | Y | Y | N |
| 10 Kirk | Y | ? | Y | N | Y | Y |
| 11 Weller | Y | Y | N | N | Y | Y |
| 12 Costello | Y | Y | N | Y | Y | Y |

**KEY**    Republicans    Democrats    *Independents*

| | | | | |
|---|---|---|---|---|
| Y | Voted for (yea) | X | Paired against | C Voted "present" to avoid possible conflict of interest |
| # | Paired for | – | Announced against | |
| + | Announced for | P | Voted "present" | ? Did not vote or otherwise make a position known |
| N | Voted against (nay) | | | |

| | 465 | 466 | 467 | 468 | 469 | 470 |
|---|---|---|---|---|---|---|
| 13 **Biggert** | Y | Y | Y | N | Y | Y |
| 14 **Hastert** | | | | | | |
| 15 **Johnson** | Y | Y | Y | N | N | Y |
| 16 **Manzullo** | Y | Y | Y | N | N | Y |
| 17 Evans | Y | Y | Y | Y | Y | Y |
| 18 **LaHood** | Y | Y | N | N | Y | Y |
| 19 **Shimkus** | Y | Y | Y | N | Y | Y |
| **INDIANA** | | | | | | |
| 1 Visclosky | Y | Y | Y | N | Y | Y |
| 2 **Chocola** | Y | Y | N | N | N | Y |
| 3 **Souder** | Y | Y | Y | N | N | N |
| 4 **Buyer** | Y | Y | Y | N | N | N |
| 5 **Burton** | Y | Y | N | N | N | Y |
| 6 **Pence** | Y | Y | N | N | N | Y |
| 7 Carson | Y | Y | Y | Y | Y | Y |
| 8 **Hostettler** | Y | Y | N | N | N | Y |
| 9 **Sodrel** | Y | Y | N | N | N | Y |
| **IOWA** | | | | | | |
| 1 **Nussle** | ? | ? | ? | N | N | Y |
| 2 **Leach** | Y | Y | Y | N | Y | Y |
| 3 Boswell | Y | Y | Y | N | Y | Y |
| 4 **Latham** | Y | Y | Y | N | N | Y |
| 5 **King** | Y | Y | N | N | N | Y |
| **KANSAS** | | | | | | |
| 1 **Moran** | Y | Y | N | N | N | N |
| 2 **Ryun** | Y | Y | N | N | N | N |
| 3 Moore | Y | Y | Y | N | Y | Y |
| 4 **Tiahrt** | Y | Y | N | N | N | Y |
| **KENTUCKY** | | | | | | |
| 1 **Whitfield** | Y | Y | Y | N | N | Y |
| 2 **Lewis** | Y | Y | N | N | N | Y |
| 3 **Northup** | Y | Y | Y | N | N | Y |
| 4 **Davis** | Y | Y | Y | N | N | Y |
| 5 **Rogers** | Y | Y | Y | N | N | Y |
| 6 Chandler | Y | Y | Y | N | Y | Y |
| **LOUISIANA** | | | | | | |
| 1 **Jindal** | ? | ? | ? | N | N | Y |
| 2 Jefferson | Y | Y | Y | Y | Y | Y |
| 3 Melancon | ? | ? | ? | ? | ? | ? |
| 4 **McCrery** | Y | Y | Y | N | N | Y |
| 5 **Alexander** | Y | Y | Y | N | N | Y |
| 6 **Baker** | Y | Y | N | N | N | Y |
| 7 **Boustany** | Y | Y | Y | N | N | Y |
| **MAINE** | | | | | | |
| 1 Allen | Y | Y | Y | N | Y | Y |
| 2 Michaud | Y | Y | Y | N | Y | Y |
| **MARYLAND** | | | | | | |
| 1 **Gilchrest** | ? | ? | ? | ? | ? | + |
| 2 Ruppersberger | Y | Y | Y | N | Y | Y |
| 3 Cardin | Y | Y | Y | N | Y | Y |
| 4 Wynn | Y | Y | Y | Y | Y | Y |
| 5 Hoyer | Y | Y | Y | Y | Y | Y |
| 6 **Bartlett** | Y | Y | N | N | N | Y |
| 7 Cummings | Y | Y | Y | Y | Y | Y |
| 8 Van Hollen | Y | Y | Y | N | Y | Y |
| **MASSACHUSETTS** | | | | | | |
| 1 Olver | Y | Y | Y | Y | Y | Y |
| 2 Neal | Y | Y | Y | Y | Y | Y |
| 3 McGovern | Y | Y | Y | Y | Y | Y |
| 4 Frank | Y | Y | Y | Y | Y | Y |
| 5 Meehan | Y | Y | Y | Y | Y | Y |
| 6 Tierney | Y | Y | Y | Y | Y | Y |
| 7 Markey | Y | Y | Y | Y | Y | Y |
| 8 Capuano | Y | Y | Y | Y | Y | Y |
| 9 Lynch | Y | Y | Y | N | Y | Y |
| 10 Delahunt | Y | Y | Y | Y | Y | Y |
| **MICHIGAN** | | | | | | |
| 1 Stupak | Y | Y | Y | Y | Y | Y |
| 2 **Hoekstra** | ? | ? | ? | ? | ? | Y |
| 3 **Ehlers** | Y | Y | Y | Y | N | Y |
| 4 **Camp** | Y | ? | ? | N | N | ? |
| 5 Kildee | Y | Y | Y | Y | Y | Y |
| 6 **Upton** | Y | Y | Y | N | N | Y |
| 7 **Schwarz** | Y | Y | Y | Y | Y | Y |
| 8 **Rogers** | Y | Y | Y | N | N | Y |
| 9 **Knollenberg** | Y | Y | Y | N | N | Y |
| 10 **Miller** | Y | Y | N | N | N | Y |
| 11 **McCotter** | Y | Y | N | N | Y | Y |
| 12 Levin | Y | Y | Y | Y | Y | Y |
| 13 Kilpatrick | Y | Y | Y | Y | Y | Y |
| 14 Conyers | Y | Y | Y | Y | Y | Y |
| 15 Dingell | ? | ? | ? | Y | Y | Y |
| **MINNESOTA** | | | | | | |
| 1 **Gutknecht** | Y | Y | N | N | N | Y |
| 2 **Kline** | Y | Y | N | N | N | Y |
| 3 **Ramstad** | Y | Y | Y | N | N | Y |
| 4 McCollum | Y | Y | Y | N | Y | Y |
| 5 Sabo | Y | Y | Y | Y | Y | N |
| 6 **Kennedy** | Y | Y | Y | N | N | Y |
| 7 Peterson | Y | Y | Y | N | Y | Y |
| 8 Oberstar | Y | Y | Y | Y | Y | N |
| **MISSISSIPPI** | | | | | | |
| 1 **Wicker** | Y | Y | N | N | N | Y |
| 2 Thompson | Y | Y | Y | N | Y | Y |
| 3 **Pickering** | Y | Y | Y | N | N | Y |
| 4 Taylor | Y | Y | Y | N | N | Y |
| **MISSOURI** | | | | | | |
| 1 Clay | Y | Y | Y | Y | Y | Y |
| 2 **Akin** | Y | Y | N | N | N | N |
| 3 Carnahan | Y | Y | Y | N | Y | Y |
| 4 Skelton | Y | Y | Y | N | Y | Y |
| 5 Cleaver | Y | Y | Y | Y | Y | Y |
| 6 **Graves** | Y | Y | Y | N | N | Y |
| 7 **Blunt** | Y | Y | N | N | N | N |
| 8 **Emerson** | Y | Y | Y | N | N | Y |
| 9 **Hulshof** | Y | Y | Y | N | N | Y |
| **MONTANA** | | | | | | |
| AL **Rehberg** | Y | Y | N | N | N | Y |
| **NEBRASKA** | | | | | | |
| 1 **Fortenberry** | + | + | + | N | N | Y |
| 2 **Terry** | Y | Y | N | N | N | Y |
| 3 **Osborne** | Y | Y | Y | N | N | Y |
| **NEVADA** | | | | | | |
| 1 Berkley | Y | Y | Y | N | Y | Y |
| 2 **Gibbons** | Y | Y | N | N | N | Y |
| 3 **Porter** | Y | Y | Y | N | N | Y |
| **NEW HAMPSHIRE** | | | | | | |
| 1 **Bradley** | Y | Y | Y | N | N | Y |
| 2 **Bass** | Y | Y | Y | N | Y | Y |
| **NEW JERSEY** | | | | | | |
| 1 Andrews | Y | Y | Y | N | Y | Y |
| 2 **LoBiondo** | Y | Y | Y | N | Y | Y |
| 3 **Saxton** | Y | Y | Y | N | Y | Y |
| 4 **Smith** | Y | Y | Y | N | N | Y |
| 5 **Garrett** | Y | Y | N | N | N | Y |
| 6 Pallone | Y | Y | Y | N | Y | Y |
| 7 **Ferguson** | Y | Y | Y | N | N | Y |
| 8 Pascrell | Y | Y | Y | N | Y | Y |
| 9 Rothman | Y | Y | Y | N | Y | Y |
| 10 Payne | Y | Y | Y | ? | ? | ? |
| 11 **Frelinghuysen** | Y | Y | Y | N | N | Y |
| 12 Holt | Y | Y | Y | Y | Y | N |
| 13 Menendez | Y | Y | Y | N | Y | Y |
| **NEW MEXICO** | | | | | | |
| 1 **Wilson** | Y | Y | Y | N | N | Y |
| 2 **Pearce** | Y | Y | N | N | N | Y |
| 3 Udall | Y | Y | Y | Y | Y | Y |
| **NEW YORK** | | | | | | |
| 1 Bishop | Y | Y | Y | N | Y | Y |
| 2 Israel | Y | Y | Y | N | Y | Y |
| 3 **King** | Y | Y | Y | N | N | Y |
| 4 McCarthy | Y | Y | Y | N | Y | Y |
| 5 Ackerman | Y | Y | Y | Y | Y | Y |
| 6 Meeks | ? | ? | ? | Y | Y | Y |
| 7 Crowley | Y | Y | Y | Y | Y | Y |
| 8 Nadler | ? | ? | ? | Y | Y | Y |
| 9 Weiner | ? | ? | ? | ? | ? | ? |
| 10 Towns | ? | ? | ? | Y | Y | Y |
| 11 Owens | + | + | + | Y | Y | Y |
| 12 Velázquez | ? | ? | ? | Y | Y | N |
| 13 **Fossella** | ? | ? | ? | N | N | Y |
| 14 Maloney | + | + | + | Y | Y | Y |
| 15 Rangel | Y | Y | Y | Y | Y | Y |
| 16 Serrano | ? | ? | ? | Y | Y | Y |
| 17 Engel | ? | ? | ? | Y | Y | Y |
| 18 Lowey | Y | Y | Y | N | Y | Y |
| 19 **Kelly** | Y | Y | Y | N | Y | Y |
| 20 **Sweeney** | Y | Y | N | N | N | Y |
| 21 McNulty | ? | ? | ? | N | Y | Y |
| 22 Hinchey | Y | Y | Y | Y | Y | N |
| 23 **McHugh** | ? | ? | ? | N | N | Y |
| 24 **Boehlert** | Y | Y | Y | N | Y | Y |
| 25 **Walsh** | ? | ? | ? | ? | ? | ? |
| 26 **Reynolds** | Y | Y | N | N | N | Y |
| 27 Higgins | Y | Y | Y | N | Y | Y |
| 28 Slaughter | Y | Y | Y | N | Y | Y |
| 29 **Kuhl** | Y | Y | Y | N | N | Y |
| **NORTH CAROLINA** | | | | | | |
| 1 Butterfield | Y | Y | Y | Y | Y | Y |
| 2 Etheridge | Y | Y | Y | N | Y | Y |
| 3 **Jones** | Y | Y | N | N | N | N |
| 4 Price | Y | Y | Y | Y | Y | Y |
| 5 **Foxx** | Y | Y | N | N | N | Y |
| 6 **Coble** | Y | Y | N | N | N | Y |
| 7 McIntyre | Y | Y | Y | N | Y | Y |
| 8 **Hayes** | Y | Y | Y | N | N | Y |
| 9 **Myrick** | Y | Y | N | N | N | Y |
| 10 **McHenry** | Y | Y | N | N | N | Y |
| 11 **Taylor** | Y | Y | N | N | N | Y |
| 12 Watt | Y | Y | Y | Y | Y | N |
| 13 Miller | Y | Y | Y | N | Y | Y |
| **NORTH DAKOTA** | | | | | | |
| AL Pomeroy | Y | Y | Y | N | Y | Y |
| **OHIO** | | | | | | |
| 1 **Chabot** | Y | Y | N | N | N | Y |
| 2 **Schmidt** | Y | Y | N | N | N | Y |
| 3 **Turner** | Y | Y | Y | N | N | Y |
| 4 **Oxley** | Y | Y | N | N | N | Y |
| 5 **Gillmor** | Y | Y | Y | N | N | Y |
| 6 Strickland | ? | ? | ? | N | Y | Y |
| 7 **Hobson** | Y | Y | Y | N | N | Y |
| 8 **Boehner** | Y | Y | Y | N | N | Y |
| 9 Kaptur | Y | Y | Y | Y | Y | Y |
| 10 Kucinich | Y | Y | Y | Y | Y | N |
| 11 Jones | ? | ? | ? | Y | Y | N |
| 12 **Tiberi** | Y | Y | Y | N | N | Y |
| 13 Brown | Y | Y | Y | Y | Y | Y |
| 14 **LaTourette** | Y | Y | N | Y | N | Y |
| 15 **Pryce** | Y | Y | Y | N | N | Y |
| 16 **Regula** | Y | Y | Y | N | N | Y |
| 17 Ryan | Y | Y | Y | N | Y | Y |
| 18 **Ney** | Y | Y | N | N | N | Y |
| **OKLAHOMA** | | | | | | |
| 1 **Sullivan** | Y | Y | N | N | N | Y |
| 2 Boren | Y | Y | Y | N | N | Y |
| 3 **Lucas** | Y | Y | Y | N | N | Y |
| 4 **Cole** | Y | Y | Y | N | N | Y |
| 5 **Istook** | Y | Y | N | N | N | Y |
| **OREGON** | | | | | | |
| 1 Wu | Y | Y | Y | N | Y | Y |
| 2 **Walden** | Y | Y | Y | N | Y | Y |
| 3 Blumenauer | Y | Y | Y | N | Y | Y |
| 4 DeFazio | ? | ? | ? | N | Y | Y |
| 5 Hooley | ? | ? | ? | N | Y | Y |
| **PENNSYLVANIA** | | | | | | |
| 1 Brady | Y | Y | Y | N | Y | Y |
| 2 Fattah | ? | ? | ? | N | Y | Y |
| 3 **English** | Y | Y | Y | N | N | Y |
| 4 **Hart** | Y | Y | ? | N | N | Y |
| 5 **Peterson** | Y | Y | N | N | N | Y |
| 6 **Gerlach** | Y | Y | Y | N | Y | Y |
| 7 **Weldon** | Y | Y | Y | N | Y | Y |
| 8 **Fitzpatrick** | Y | Y | Y | N | Y | Y |
| 9 **Shuster** | Y | Y | Y | N | N | Y |
| 10 **Sherwood** | Y | Y | N | N | N | Y |
| 11 Kanjorski | Y | Y | Y | N | Y | Y |
| 12 Murtha | Y | Y | Y | N | Y | Y |
| 13 Schwartz | Y | Y | Y | N | Y | Y |
| 14 Doyle | Y | Y | Y | N | Y | Y |
| 15 **Dent** | Y | Y | Y | N | Y | Y |
| 16 **Pitts** | Y | Y | Y | N | N | Y |
| 17 Holden | Y | Y | Y | N | Y | Y |
| 18 **Murphy** | Y | Y | Y | N | N | Y |
| 19 **Platts** | Y | Y | Y | N | Y | Y |
| **RHODE ISLAND** | | | | | | |
| 1 Kennedy | Y | Y | Y | N | Y | Y |
| 2 Langevin | Y | Y | Y | N | Y | Y |
| **SOUTH CAROLINA** | | | | | | |
| 1 **Brown** | Y | Y | Y | N | N | Y |
| 2 **Wilson** | Y | Y | N | N | N | Y |
| 3 **Barrett** | Y | Y | N | N | N | N |
| 4 **Inglis** | Y | Y | N | Y | N | Y |
| 5 Spratt | Y | Y | Y | N | Y | Y |
| 6 Clyburn | Y | Y | Y | ? | ? | ? |
| **SOUTH DAKOTA** | | | | | | |
| AL Herseth | Y | Y | Y | N | Y | Y |
| **TENNESSEE** | | | | | | |
| 1 **Jenkins** | Y | Y | Y | N | N | Y |
| 2 **Duncan** | Y | Y | N | N | N | N |
| 3 **Wamp** | Y | Y | N | N | N | N |
| 4 Davis | Y | Y | Y | N | N | Y |
| 5 Cooper | Y | Y | Y | N | Y | Y |
| 6 Gordon | Y | Y | Y | N | Y | Y |
| 7 **Blackburn** | Y | Y | N | N | N | Y |
| 8 Tanner | Y | Y | Y | N | N | Y |
| 9 Ford | Y | Y | Y | N | Y | Y |
| **TEXAS** | | | | | | |
| 1 **Gohmert** | Y | Y | N | N | N | N |
| 2 **Poe** | Y | Y | N | N | N | Y |
| 3 **Johnson, S.** | Y | Y | N | N | N | N |
| 4 **Hall** | Y | Y | N | N | N | Y |
| 5 **Hensarling** | Y | Y | N | N | N | Y |
| 6 **Barton** | Y | Y | N | ? | ? | ? |
| 7 **Culberson** | Y | Y | Y | N | N | Y |
| 8 **Brady** | Y | Y | Y | N | N | Y |
| 9 Green, A. | Y | Y | Y | Y | Y | Y |
| 10 **McCaul** | Y | Y | N | N | N | Y |
| 11 **Conaway** | Y | Y | N | N | N | N |
| 12 **Granger** | Y | Y | Y | N | N | Y |
| 13 **Thornberry** | Y | Y | N | N | N | N |
| 14 **Paul** | Y | Y | N | Y | N | N |
| 15 Hinojosa | + | + | + | N | Y | Y |
| 16 Reyes | Y | Y | Y | N | Y | Y |
| 17 Edwards | Y | Y | Y | N | Y | Y |
| 18 Jackson-Lee | Y | Y | Y | Y | Y | Y |
| 19 **Neugebauer** | Y | Y | N | N | N | Y |
| 20 Gonzalez | Y | Y | Y | N | Y | Y |
| 21 **Smith** | Y | Y | Y | N | N | Y |
| 22 **DeLay** | Y | Y | Y | N | N | Y |
| 23 **Bonilla** | Y | Y | Y | N | N | N |
| 24 **Marchant** | Y | Y | N | N | N | Y |
| 25 Doggett | Y | Y | Y | N | Y | Y |
| 26 **Burgess** | Y | Y | N | N | N | Y |
| 27 Ortiz | Y | Y | Y | N | Y | Y |
| 28 Cuellar | Y | Y | Y | N | Y | Y |
| 29 Green, G. | Y | Y | Y | N | Y | Y |
| 30 Johnson, E. | Y | Y | Y | Y | Y | Y |
| 31 **Carter** | Y | Y | N | N | N | Y |
| 32 **Sessions** | Y | Y | N | N | N | Y |
| **UTAH** | | | | | | |
| 1 **Bishop** | ? | Y | N | N | N | Y |
| 2 Matheson | Y | Y | Y | N | Y | Y |
| 3 **Cannon** | Y | Y | N | N | N | Y |
| **VERMONT** | | | | | | |
| AL *Sanders* | Y | Y | Y | Y | Y | Y |
| **VIRGINIA** | | | | | | |
| 1 **Davis, J.** | Y | Y | N | N | N | Y |
| 2 **Drake** | Y | Y | N | N | N | Y |
| 3 Scott | Y | Y | Y | Y | Y | N |
| 4 **Forbes** | Y | Y | N | N | N | Y |
| 5 **Goode** | Y | Y | N | N | N | Y |
| 6 **Goodlatte** | Y | Y | Y | N | N | Y |
| 7 **Cantor** | Y | Y | Y | N | N | Y |
| 8 Moran | ? | ? | ? | Y | Y | Y |
| 9 Boucher | Y | Y | Y | Y | Y | Y |
| 10 **Wolf** | Y | Y | Y | N | N | Y |
| 11 **Davis, T.** | Y | Y | Y | N | N | Y |
| **WASHINGTON** | | | | | | |
| 1 Inslee | Y | Y | Y | N | Y | Y |
| 2 Larsen | Y | Y | Y | Y | Y | Y |
| 3 Baird | Y | Y | Y | Y | Y | Y |
| 4 **Hastings** | Y | Y | Y | N | N | Y |
| 5 **McMorris** | Y | Y | N | N | N | Y |
| 6 Dicks | Y | Y | Y | N | Y | Y |
| 7 McDermott | Y | Y | Y | Y | Y | N |
| 8 **Reichert** | Y | Y | Y | N | Y | Y |
| 9 Smith | Y | Y | Y | Y | Y | Y |
| **WEST VIRGINIA** | | | | | | |
| 1 Mollohan | Y | Y | Y | Y | Y | N |
| 2 **Capito** | Y | Y | Y | N | N | Y |
| 3 Rahall | Y | Y | Y | Y | Y | N |
| **WISCONSIN** | | | | | | |
| 1 **Ryan** | Y | Y | N | N | N | Y |
| 2 Baldwin | Y | Y | Y | Y | Y | Y |
| 3 Kind | Y | Y | Y | N | Y | Y |
| 4 Moore | Y | Y | Y | Y | Y | Y |
| 5 **Sensenbrenner** | Y | Y | N | N | N | Y |
| 6 **Petri** | Y | Y | N | N | N | Y |
| 7 Obey | Y | Y | Y | N | Y | Y |
| 8 **Green** | Y | Y | N | N | N | Y |
| **WYOMING** | | | | | | |
| AL **Cubin** | Y | Y | N | N | N | Y |

# IN THE HOUSE | By Vote Number

**471.** H Res 437. Hurricane Katrina Investigatory Committee/Previous Question. Dreier, R-Calif., motion to order the previous question (thus ending debate and the possibility of amendment) on adoption of the rule (H Res 439) to provide for House floor consideration of the resolution that would create a bipartisan select committee to investigate the actions of federal, state and local governments before and after Hurricane Katrina. Motion agreed to 222-193: R 222-0; D 0-192 (ND 0-144, SD 0-48); I 0-1. Sept. 15, 2005.

**472.** H Res 437. Hurricane Katrina Investigatory Committee/Rule. Adoption of the rule (H Res 439) to provide for House floor consideration of the resolution that would create a bipartisan select committee to investigate the actions of federal, state and local governments before and after Hurricane Katrina. Adopted 221-193: R 221-0; D 0-192 (ND 0-144, SD 0-48); I 0-1. Sept. 15, 2005.

**473.** HR 889. Coast Guard Reauthorization/Liquefied Natural Gas. Markey, D-Mass., amendment that would require the Coast Guard to conduct a comprehensive security and safety review of the proposed construction, expansion or operation of a waterfront facility for transferring liquefied natural gas between ships and land. Rejected 163-254: R 7-213; D 155-41 (ND 121-27, SD 34-14); I 1-0. Sept. 15, 2005.

**474.** HR 889. Coast Guard Reauthorization/Passage. Passage of the bill that would authorize $8.7 billion in fiscal 2006 for the Coast Guard, including $5.6 billion for operation and maintenance, $1 billion in mandatory spending for retired pay and $1.6 billion for the Deepwater program to replace aging ships and aircraft. It would require a new implementation plan for the program. Passed 415-0: R 220-0; D 194-0 (ND 147-0, SD 47-0); I 1-0. Sept. 15, 2005.

**475.** H Res 437. Hurricane Katrina Investigatory Committee/Adoption. Adoption of the resolution that would establish a bipartisan select committee to investigate the government preparation and response to Hurricane Katrina. The Speaker would select 20 members to the committee, including nine Democrats appointed after consultation with the minority leader. The resolution would earmark $500,000 out of existing House accounts for the committee. Adopted 224-188: R 217-1; D 7-186 (ND 2-144, SD 5-42); I 0-1. Sept. 15, 2005.

| | 471 | 472 | 473 | 474 | 475 |
|---|---|---|---|---|---|
| **ALABAMA** | | | | | |
| 1 Bonner | Y | Y | Y | Y | Y |
| 2 Everett | Y | Y | N | Y | Y |
| 3 Rogers | Y | Y | N | Y | Y |
| 4 Aderholt | Y | Y | N | Y | Y |
| 5 Cramer | N | N | Y | Y | N |
| 6 Bachus | Y | Y | N | Y | Y |
| 7 Davis | N | N | Y | Y | N |
| **ALASKA** | | | | | |
| AL Young | Y | Y | N | Y | Y |
| **ARIZONA** | | | | | |
| 1 Renzi | Y | Y | N | Y | Y |
| 2 Franks | Y | Y | N | Y | Y |
| 3 Shadegg | Y | Y | N | Y | Y |
| 4 Pastor | N | N | Y | Y | N |
| 5 Hayworth | Y | Y | N | Y | Y |
| 6 Flake | Y | Y | N | Y | Y |
| 7 Grijalva | N | N | Y | Y | N |
| 8 Kolbe | Y | Y | N | Y | Y |
| **ARKANSAS** | | | | | |
| 1 Berry | N | N | N | Y | N |
| 2 Snyder | N | N | Y | Y | N |
| 3 Boozman | Y | Y | N | Y | Y |
| 4 Ross | N | N | N | Y | N |
| **CALIFORNIA** | | | | | |
| 1 Thompson | N | N | Y | Y | N |
| 2 Herger | Y | Y | N | Y | Y |
| 3 Lungren | Y | Y | N | Y | Y |
| 4 Doolittle | ? | Y | N | Y | Y |
| 5 Matsui, D. | N | N | Y | Y | N |
| 6 Woolsey | ? | ? | Y | Y | N |
| 7 Miller, George | N | N | Y | Y | N |
| 8 Pelosi | N | N | Y | Y | N |
| 9 Lee | N | N | Y | Y | N |
| 10 Tauscher | N | N | Y | Y | N |
| 11 Pombo | Y | Y | N | Y | Y |
| 12 Lantos | N | N | Y | Y | N |
| 13 Stark | N | N | Y | Y | N |
| 14 Eshoo | N | N | Y | Y | N |
| 15 Honda | N | N | Y | Y | N |
| 16 Lofgren | N | N | Y | Y | N |
| 17 Farr | N | N | Y | Y | N |
| 18 Cardoza | N | N | Y | Y | N |
| 19 Radanovich | Y | Y | N | Y | Y |
| 20 Costa | N | N | N | Y | N |
| 21 Nunes | Y | Y | N | Y | Y |
| 22 Thomas | Y | Y | N | Y | Y |
| 23 Capps | N | N | Y | Y | N |
| 24 Gallegly | Y | Y | N | Y | ? |
| 25 McKeon | Y | Y | N | Y | Y |
| 26 Dreier | Y | Y | N | Y | Y |
| 27 Sherman | N | N | Y | Y | N |
| 28 Berman | N | N | Y | ? | ? |
| 29 Schiff | N | N | Y | Y | N |
| 30 Waxman | N | N | Y | Y | N |
| 31 Becerra | N | N | Y | Y | N |
| 32 Solis | ? | N | Y | Y | N |
| 33 Watson | N | N | Y | Y | N |
| 34 Roybal-Allard | N | N | Y | Y | N |
| 35 Waters | N | N | Y | Y | N |
| 36 Harman | N | N | Y | Y | N |
| 37 Millender-McD. | N | N | Y | Y | N |
| 38 Napolitano | N | N | Y | Y | N |
| 39 Sánchez, Linda | N | N | Y | Y | N |
| 40 Royce | Y | Y | Y | Y | Y |
| 41 Lewis | Y | Y | N | Y | Y |
| 42 Miller, Gary | Y | Y | ? | ? | ? |
| 43 Baca | N | N | Y | Y | ? |
| 44 Calvert | Y | Y | ? | ? | ? |
| 45 Bono | Y | Y | N | Y | Y |
| 46 Rohrabacher | Y | Y | N | Y | Y |
| 47 Sanchez, Loretta | N | N | Y | Y | N |
| 48 Vacant | | | | | |
| 49 Issa | Y | Y | N | Y | Y |
| 50 Cunningham | Y | Y | ? | ? | ? |
| 51 Filner | N | N | Y | Y | N |
| 52 Hunter | Y | Y | N | Y | Y |
| 53 Davis | N | N | Y | Y | N |
| **COLORADO** | | | | | |
| 1 DeGette | N | N | Y | Y | N |
| 2 Udall | N | N | Y | Y | N |
| 3 Salazar | N | N | Y | Y | N |
| 4 Musgrave | Y | Y | N | Y | ? |
| 5 Hefley | Y | Y | N | Y | Y |
| 6 Tancredo | Y | ? | N | Y | Y |
| 7 Beauprez | ? | ? | ? | ? | ? |
| **CONNECTICUT** | | | | | |
| 1 Larson | N | N | Y | Y | N |
| 2 Simmons | Y | Y | Y | Y | Y |
| 3 DeLauro | N | N | Y | Y | N |
| 4 Shays | Y | + | Y | Y | Y |
| 5 Johnson | Y | Y | Y | Y | Y |
| **DELAWARE** | | | | | |
| AL Castle | Y | Y | N | Y | Y |
| **FLORIDA** | | | | | |
| 1 Miller | Y | + | N | Y | Y |
| 2 Boyd | N | N | Y | Y | N |
| 3 Brown | N | N | Y | Y | N |
| 4 Crenshaw | Y | Y | N | Y | Y |
| 5 Brown-Waite | Y | Y | N | Y | Y |
| 6 Stearns | Y | Y | N | Y | Y |
| 7 Mica | Y | Y | N | Y | Y |
| 8 Keller | Y | Y | N | Y | Y |
| 9 Bilirakis | Y | Y | N | Y | Y |
| 10 Young | Y | Y | N | Y | Y |
| 11 Davis | N | N | Y | Y | N |
| 12 Putnam | Y | Y | N | Y | Y |
| 13 Harris | Y | Y | N | Y | Y |
| 14 Mack | Y | Y | N | Y | Y |
| 15 Weldon | Y | Y | N | Y | Y |
| 16 Foley | Y | Y | N | Y | Y |
| 17 Meek | N | N | Y | Y | N |
| 18 Ros-Lehtinen | Y | Y | N | Y | Y |
| 19 Wexler | N | N | Y | Y | N |
| 20 Wasserman-Schultz | N | N | Y | Y | N |
| 21 Diaz-Balart, L. | Y | Y | N | Y | Y |
| 22 Shaw | Y | Y | N | Y | Y |
| 23 Hastings | N | N | Y | Y | N |
| 24 Feeney | Y | Y | N | Y | Y |
| 25 Diaz-Balart, M. | Y | Y | N | Y | Y |
| **GEORGIA** | | | | | |
| 1 Kingston | Y | Y | N | Y | Y |
| 2 Bishop | N | N | N | Y | N |
| 3 Marshall | N | N | Y | Y | Y |
| 4 McKinney | N | N | Y | Y | N |
| 5 Lewis | N | ? | Y | Y | N |
| 6 Price | Y | Y | N | Y | Y |
| 7 Linder | Y | Y | N | Y | Y |
| 8 Westmoreland | Y | Y | N | Y | Y |
| 9 Norwood | Y | Y | N | Y | Y |
| 10 Deal | Y | Y | N | Y | Y |
| 11 Gingrey | Y | Y | N | Y | Y |
| 12 Barrow | N | N | Y | Y | Y |
| 13 Scott | N | N | Y | Y | N |
| **HAWAII** | | | | | |
| 1 Abercrombie | N | N | Y | Y | N |
| 2 Case | N | N | Y | Y | N |
| **IDAHO** | | | | | |
| 1 Otter | Y | Y | N | Y | Y |
| 2 Simpson | Y | Y | N | Y | Y |
| **ILLINOIS** | | | | | |
| 1 Rush | N | N | N | Y | N |
| 2 Jackson | N | N | Y | Y | N |
| 3 Lipinski | N | N | N | Y | N |
| 4 Gutierrez | N | N | Y | Y | N |
| 5 Emanuel | N | N | Y | Y | N |
| 6 Hyde | Y | Y | N | Y | Y |
| 7 Davis | N | N | Y | Y | N |
| 8 Bean | N | N | N | Y | N |
| 9 Schakowsky | N | N | Y | Y | N |
| 10 Kirk | Y | Y | N | Y | Y |
| 11 Weller | Y | Y | N | Y | Y |
| 12 Costello | N | N | N | Y | N |

| KEY | Republicans | Democrats | *Independents* |
|---|---|---|---|

| | | |
|---|---|---|
| Y Voted for (yea) | X Paired against | C Voted "present" to avoid possible conflict of interest |
| # Paired for | − Announced against | |
| + Announced for | P Voted "present" | ? Did not vote or otherwise make a position known |
| N Voted against (nay) | | |

ND Northern Democrats, SD Southern Democrats
Southern states: Ala., Ark., Fla., Ga., Ky., La., Miss., N.C., Okla., S.C., Tenn., Texas, Va.

| | | 471 | 472 | 473 | 474 | 475 |
|---|---|---|---|---|---|---|
| 13 | Biggert | Y | Y | N | Y | Y |
| 14 | Hastert | | | | | |
| 15 | Johnson | Y | Y | N | Y | Y |
| 16 | Manzullo | Y | Y | N | Y | Y |
| 17 | Evans | N | N | Y | Y | N |
| 18 | LaHood | Y | Y | N | Y | Y |
| 19 | Shimkus | Y | Y | N | Y | Y |
| **INDIANA** | | | | | | |
| 1 | Visclosky | N | N | Y | Y | N |
| 2 | Chocola | Y | Y | N | Y | Y |
| 3 | Souder | Y | Y | N | Y | Y |
| 4 | Buyer | Y | Y | N | Y | Y |
| 5 | Burton | Y | Y | N | Y | Y |
| 6 | Pence | Y | Y | N | Y | Y |
| 7 | Carson | N | N | Y | Y | N |
| 8 | Hostettler | Y | Y | N | Y | Y |
| 9 | Sodrel | Y | Y | N | Y | Y |
| **IOWA** | | | | | | |
| 1 | Nussle | Y | Y | N | Y | Y |
| 2 | Leach | Y | Y | N | Y | Y |
| 3 | Boswell | N | N | N | Y | N |
| 4 | Latham | Y | Y | N | Y | Y |
| 5 | King | Y | Y | N | Y | Y |
| **KANSAS** | | | | | | |
| 1 | Moran | Y | Y | N | Y | Y |
| 2 | Ryun | Y | Y | N | Y | Y |
| 3 | Moore | N | N | Y | Y | N |
| 4 | Tiahrt | Y | Y | N | Y | Y |
| **KENTUCKY** | | | | | | |
| 1 | Whitfield | Y | Y | N | Y | N |
| 2 | Lewis | Y | Y | N | Y | Y |
| 3 | Northup | Y | Y | N | Y | Y |
| 4 | Davis | Y | Y | N | Y | Y |
| 5 | Rogers | Y | Y | N | Y | Y |
| 6 | Chandler | N | N | Y | Y | N |
| **LOUISIANA** | | | | | | |
| 1 | Jindal | ? | ? | N | Y | Y |
| 2 | Jefferson | N | N | Y | Y | N |
| 3 | Melancon | ? | ? | ? | ? | ? |
| 4 | McCrery | Y | Y | N | Y | Y |
| 5 | Alexander | Y | Y | N | Y | Y |
| 6 | Baker | Y | Y | N | Y | Y |
| 7 | Boustany | Y | Y | N | Y | Y |
| **MAINE** | | | | | | |
| 1 | Allen | N | N | Y | Y | N |
| 2 | Michaud | N | N | N | Y | N |
| **MARYLAND** | | | | | | |
| 1 | Gilchrest | Y | Y | N | Y | Y |
| 2 | Ruppersberger | N | N | N | Y | N |
| 3 | Cardin | N | N | Y | Y | N |
| 4 | Wynn | N | N | N | Y | N |
| 5 | Hoyer | N | N | Y | Y | N |
| 6 | Bartlett | Y | Y | N | Y | Y |
| 7 | Cummings | N | N | Y | Y | N |
| 8 | Van Hollen | N | N | Y | Y | N |
| **MASSACHUSETTS** | | | | | | |
| 1 | Olver | N | N | ? | ? | ? |
| 2 | Neal | N | N | Y | Y | N |
| 3 | McGovern | N | N | Y | Y | N |
| 4 | Frank | N | N | Y | Y | N |
| 5 | Meehan | N | N | Y | Y | N |
| 6 | Tierney | N | N | Y | Y | N |
| 7 | Markey | N | N | Y | Y | N |
| 8 | Capuano | N | N | Y | Y | N |
| 9 | Lynch | N | N | Y | Y | N |
| 10 | Delahunt | N | N | Y | Y | N |
| **MICHIGAN** | | | | | | |
| 1 | Stupak | N | N | Y | Y | N |
| 2 | Hoekstra | Y | Y | N | Y | Y |
| 3 | Ehlers | Y | Y | N | Y | Y |
| 4 | Camp | Y | Y | N | Y | Y |
| 5 | Kildee | N | N | Y | Y | N |
| 6 | Upton | Y | Y | N | Y | Y |
| 7 | Schwarz | ? | Y | N | Y | Y |
| 8 | Rogers | ? | ? | ? | ? | ? |
| 9 | Knollenberg | Y | Y | N | Y | Y |
| 10 | Miller | Y | Y | N | Y | Y |
| 11 | McCotter | Y | Y | N | Y | Y |
| 12 | Levin | N | N | Y | Y | N |
| 13 | Kilpatrick | N | N | Y | Y | N |
| 14 | Conyers | N | N | Y | Y | N |
| 15 | Dingell | N | N | Y | Y | N |

| | | 471 | 472 | 473 | 474 | 475 |
|---|---|---|---|---|---|---|
| **MINNESOTA** | | | | | | |
| 1 | Gutknecht | Y | Y | N | Y | Y |
| 2 | Kline | Y | Y | N | Y | Y |
| 3 | Ramstad | Y | Y | N | Y | Y |
| 4 | McCollum | N | N | Y | Y | N |
| 5 | Sabo | N | N | Y | Y | N |
| 6 | Kennedy | Y | Y | N | Y | Y |
| 7 | Peterson | N | N | N | Y | N |
| 8 | Oberstar | N | N | N | Y | N |
| **MISSISSIPPI** | | | | | | |
| 1 | Wicker | Y | Y | N | Y | Y |
| 2 | Thompson | N | N | N | Y | N |
| 3 | Pickering | Y | Y | ? | ? | ? |
| 4 | Taylor | N | N | Y | Y | Y |
| **MISSOURI** | | | | | | |
| 1 | Clay | N | N | Y | Y | N |
| 2 | Akin | Y | Y | N | Y | Y |
| 3 | Carnahan | N | N | Y | Y | N |
| 4 | Skelton | N | N | Y | Y | N |
| 5 | Cleaver | N | N | Y | Y | N |
| 6 | Graves | Y | Y | N | Y | Y |
| 7 | Blunt | Y | Y | N | Y | Y |
| 8 | Emerson | Y | Y | N | Y | Y |
| 9 | Hulshof | Y | Y | N | Y | Y |
| **MONTANA** | | | | | | |
| AL | Rehberg | Y | Y | N | Y | Y |
| **NEBRASKA** | | | | | | |
| 1 | Fortenberry | Y | Y | N | Y | Y |
| 2 | Terry | Y | Y | N | Y | Y |
| 3 | Osborne | Y | Y | N | Y | Y |
| **NEVADA** | | | | | | |
| 1 | Berkley | N | N | Y | Y | N |
| 2 | Gibbons | Y | Y | N | Y | Y |
| 3 | Porter | Y | Y | N | Y | Y |
| **NEW HAMPSHIRE** | | | | | | |
| 1 | Bradley | Y | Y | N | Y | Y |
| 2 | Bass | Y | Y | N | Y | Y |
| **NEW JERSEY** | | | | | | |
| 1 | Andrews | N | N | Y | Y | N |
| 2 | LoBiondo | Y | Y | N | Y | Y |
| 3 | Saxton | Y | Y | N | Y | Y |
| 4 | Smith | Y | Y | N | Y | Y |
| 5 | Garrett | Y | Y | N | Y | Y |
| 6 | Pallone | N | N | Y | Y | N |
| 7 | Ferguson | Y | Y | N | Y | Y |
| 8 | Pascrell | N | N | Y | Y | N |
| 9 | Rothman | ? | ? | ? | ? | ? |
| 10 | Payne | N | N | Y | Y | N |
| 11 | Frelinghuysen | Y | Y | N | Y | Y |
| 12 | Holt | N | N | Y | Y | N |
| 13 | Menendez | N | N | Y | Y | N |
| **NEW MEXICO** | | | | | | |
| 1 | Wilson | Y | Y | N | Y | Y |
| 2 | Pearce | Y | Y | N | Y | Y |
| 3 | Udall | N | N | Y | Y | N |
| **NEW YORK** | | | | | | |
| 1 | Bishop | N | N | Y | Y | N |
| 2 | Israel | N | N | Y | Y | N |
| 3 | King | Y | Y | N | Y | N |
| 4 | McCarthy | N | N | Y | Y | N |
| 5 | Ackerman | N | N | Y | Y | N |
| 6 | Meeks | N | N | Y | Y | N |
| 7 | Crowley | N | N | Y | Y | N |
| 8 | Nadler | ? | ? | ? | ? | ? |
| 9 | Weiner | ? | ? | Y | Y | N |
| 10 | Towns | N | N | Y | Y | N |
| 11 | Owens | N | N | Y | Y | N |
| 12 | Velázquez | N | N | Y | Y | N |
| 13 | Fossella | Y | Y | N | Y | Y |
| 14 | Maloney | N | N | Y | Y | N |
| 15 | Rangel | N | N | Y | Y | N |
| 16 | Serrano | N | N | Y | Y | N |
| 17 | Engel | N | N | Y | Y | N |
| 18 | Lowey | N | N | Y | Y | N |
| 19 | Kelly | Y | Y | N | Y | Y |
| 20 | Sweeney | Y | Y | N | Y | Y |
| 21 | McNulty | N | N | Y | Y | N |
| 22 | Hinchey | ? | ? | Y | Y | N |
| 23 | McHugh | Y | Y | N | Y | Y |
| 24 | Boehlert | Y | Y | N | Y | Y |
| 25 | Walsh | Y | Y | N | Y | Y |
| 26 | Reynolds | Y | Y | N | Y | Y |
| 27 | Higgins | N | N | Y | Y | N |
| 28 | Slaughter | N | N | Y | Y | N |
| 29 | Kuhl | Y | Y | N | Y | Y |

| | | 471 | 472 | 473 | 474 | 475 |
|---|---|---|---|---|---|---|
| **NORTH CAROLINA** | | | | | | |
| 1 | Butterfield | N | N | Y | Y | N |
| 2 | Etheridge | N | N | Y | Y | N |
| 3 | Jones | Y | Y | Y | Y | Y |
| 4 | Price | N | N | Y | Y | N |
| 5 | Foxx | Y | Y | N | Y | Y |
| 6 | Coble | Y | Y | N | Y | Y |
| 7 | McIntyre | N | N | Y | Y | N |
| 8 | Hayes | Y | Y | N | Y | Y |
| 9 | Myrick | Y | Y | N | Y | Y |
| 10 | McHenry | Y | Y | N | Y | Y |
| 11 | Taylor | Y | Y | ? | ? | ? |
| 12 | Watt | N | N | Y | Y | N |
| 13 | Miller | N | N | Y | Y | N |
| **NORTH DAKOTA** | | | | | | |
| AL | Pomeroy | N | N | N | Y | N |
| **OHIO** | | | | | | |
| 1 | Chabot | Y | Y | N | Y | Y |
| 2 | Schmidt | Y | Y | N | Y | Y |
| 3 | Turner | Y | Y | N | Y | Y |
| 4 | Oxley | Y | Y | N | Y | Y |
| 5 | Gillmor | Y | Y | N | Y | Y |
| 6 | Strickland | N | N | Y | Y | N |
| 7 | Hobson | Y | Y | N | Y | Y |
| 8 | Boehner | Y | Y | N | Y | Y |
| 9 | Kaptur | N | N | Y | Y | N |
| 10 | Kucinich | N | N | Y | Y | N |
| 11 | Jones | ? | ? | Y | Y | N |
| 12 | Tiberi | Y | Y | N | Y | Y |
| 13 | Brown | N | N | Y | Y | N |
| 14 | LaTourette | Y | Y | N | Y | Y |
| 15 | Pryce | Y | Y | N | Y | Y |
| 16 | Regula | Y | Y | N | Y | Y |
| 17 | Ryan | N | N | Y | Y | N |
| 18 | Ney | Y | Y | N | Y | Y |
| **OKLAHOMA** | | | | | | |
| 1 | Sullivan | Y | Y | N | Y | Y |
| 2 | Boren | N | N | N | Y | N |
| 3 | Lucas | Y | Y | N | Y | Y |
| 4 | Cole | Y | Y | N | Y | Y |
| 5 | Istook | ? | ? | ? | ? | ? |
| **OREGON** | | | | | | |
| 1 | Wu | N | N | Y | Y | N |
| 2 | Walden | Y | Y | N | Y | Y |
| 3 | Blumenauer | N | N | Y | Y | N |
| 4 | DeFazio | N | N | Y | Y | N |
| 5 | Hooley | N | N | Y | Y | N |
| **PENNSYLVANIA** | | | | | | |
| 1 | Brady | N | N | Y | Y | N |
| 2 | Fattah | N | N | Y | Y | N |
| 3 | English | Y | Y | N | Y | Y |
| 4 | Hart | Y | Y | N | Y | Y |
| 5 | Peterson | Y | Y | N | Y | Y |
| 6 | Gerlach | Y | Y | N | Y | Y |
| 7 | Weldon | Y | Y | N | Y | Y |
| 8 | Fitzpatrick | Y | Y | N | Y | Y |
| 9 | Shuster | Y | Y | N | Y | Y |
| 10 | Sherwood | Y | Y | N | Y | Y |
| 11 | Kanjorski | N | N | Y | Y | N |
| 12 | Murtha | N | ? | N | Y | N |
| 13 | Schwartz | N | N | Y | Y | N |
| 14 | Doyle | N | N | Y | Y | N |
| 15 | Dent | Y | Y | N | Y | Y |
| 16 | Pitts | Y | Y | N | Y | Y |
| 17 | Holden | N | N | N | Y | N |
| 18 | Murphy | Y | Y | N | Y | Y |
| 19 | Platts | Y | Y | N | Y | Y |
| **RHODE ISLAND** | | | | | | |
| 1 | Kennedy | N | N | Y | Y | N |
| 2 | Langevin | N | N | Y | Y | N |
| **SOUTH CAROLINA** | | | | | | |
| 1 | Brown | Y | Y | N | Y | Y |
| 2 | Wilson | Y | Y | N | Y | Y |
| 3 | Barrett | Y | Y | N | Y | Y |
| 4 | Inglis | Y | Y | N | Y | Y |
| 5 | Spratt | N | N | Y | Y | N |
| 6 | Clyburn | N | N | N | Y | N |
| **SOUTH DAKOTA** | | | | | | |
| AL | Herseth | N | N | N | Y | N |
| **TENNESSEE** | | | | | | |
| 1 | Jenkins | Y | Y | N | Y | Y |
| 2 | Duncan | Y | Y | N | Y | Y |

| | | 471 | 472 | 473 | 474 | 475 |
|---|---|---|---|---|---|---|
| 3 | Wamp | Y | Y | N | Y | Y |
| 4 | Davis | N | N | Y | Y | Y |
| 5 | Cooper | N | N | ? | ? | ? |
| 6 | Gordon | N | N | Y | Y | N |
| 7 | Blackburn | Y | Y | N | Y | Y |
| 8 | Tanner | ? | ? | ? | ? | ? |
| 9 | Ford | N | N | Y | ? | ? |
| **TEXAS** | | | | | | |
| 1 | Gohmert | Y | Y | N | Y | Y |
| 2 | Poe | Y | Y | N | Y | Y |
| 3 | Johnson, S. | Y | Y | N | Y | Y |
| 4 | Hall | Y | Y | N | Y | Y |
| 5 | Hensarling | Y | Y | N | Y | Y |
| 6 | Barton | ? | ? | ? | ? | ? |
| 7 | Culberson | Y | Y | N | Y | Y |
| 8 | Brady | Y | Y | N | Y | Y |
| 9 | Green, A. | N | N | N | Y | N |
| 10 | McCaul | Y | Y | N | Y | Y |
| 11 | Conaway | Y | Y | N | Y | Y |
| 12 | Granger | Y | Y | N | Y | Y |
| 13 | Thornberry | Y | Y | N | Y | Y |
| 14 | Paul | Y | Y | N | Y | Y |
| 15 | Hinojosa | N | N | N | Y | N |
| 16 | Reyes | N | N | N | Y | N |
| 17 | Edwards | N | N | Y | Y | N |
| 18 | Jackson-Lee | N | N | Y | Y | N |
| 19 | Neugebauer | Y | Y | N | Y | Y |
| 20 | Gonzalez | N | N | N | Y | N |
| 21 | Smith | Y | Y | N | Y | Y |
| 22 | DeLay | Y | Y | N | Y | Y |
| 23 | Bonilla | Y | Y | N | Y | Y |
| 24 | Marchant | Y | Y | N | Y | Y |
| 25 | Doggett | ? | N | Y | Y | N |
| 26 | Burgess | Y | Y | N | Y | Y |
| 27 | Ortiz | N | N | N | Y | N |
| 28 | Cuellar | N | N | N | Y | N |
| 29 | Green, G. | N | N | N | Y | N |
| 30 | Johnson, E. | N | N | N | Y | N |
| 31 | Carter | Y | Y | N | Y | Y |
| 32 | Sessions | Y | Y | N | Y | Y |
| **UTAH** | | | | | | |
| 1 | Bishop | ? | ? | ? | ? | ? |
| 2 | Matheson | N | N | N | Y | Y |
| 3 | Cannon | Y | Y | N | Y | Y |
| **VERMONT** | | | | | | |
| AL | Sanders | N | N | Y | Y | N |
| **VIRGINIA** | | | | | | |
| 1 | Davis, J. | Y | Y | N | Y | Y |
| 2 | Drake | Y | Y | N | Y | Y |
| 3 | Scott | N | N | Y | Y | N |
| 4 | Forbes | Y | Y | N | Y | Y |
| 5 | Goode | Y | Y | N | Y | Y |
| 6 | Goodlatte | Y | Y | N | Y | Y |
| 7 | Cantor | Y | Y | N | Y | Y |
| 8 | Moran | N | N | Y | Y | N |
| 9 | Boucher | N | N | Y | Y | N |
| 10 | Wolf | Y | Y | N | Y | Y |
| 11 | Davis, T. | Y | Y | N | Y | Y |
| **WASHINGTON** | | | | | | |
| 1 | Inslee | N | N | Y | Y | N |
| 2 | Larsen | N | N | Y | Y | N |
| 3 | Baird | N | N | Y | Y | N |
| 4 | Hastings | Y | Y | N | Y | Y |
| 5 | McMorris | Y | Y | N | Y | Y |
| 6 | Dicks | N | N | Y | Y | N |
| 7 | McDermott | N | N | Y | Y | N |
| 8 | Reichert | Y | Y | N | Y | Y |
| 9 | Smith | N | N | N | Y | N |
| **WEST VIRGINIA** | | | | | | |
| 1 | Mollohan | N | N | Y | Y | N |
| 2 | Capito | Y | Y | N | Y | Y |
| 3 | Rahall | N | N | N | Y | N |
| **WISCONSIN** | | | | | | |
| 1 | Ryan | Y | Y | N | Y | Y |
| 2 | Baldwin | N | N | Y | Y | N |
| 3 | Kind | N | N | Y | Y | N |
| 4 | Moore | N | N | Y | Y | N |
| 5 | Sensenbrenner | Y | Y | N | Y | Y |
| 6 | Petri | Y | Y | N | Y | Y |
| 7 | Obey | N | N | Y | Y | N |
| 8 | Green | Y | Y | N | Y | Y |
| **WYOMING** | | | | | | |
| AL | Cubin | Y | Y | N | Y | Y |

# IN THE HOUSE | By Vote Number

**476.** HR 3761. **Flexibility for Displaced Workers/Passage.** Boustany, R-La., motion to suspend the rules and pass the bill that would give more flexibility for a Labor Department program that provides temporary disaster relief and training to individuals who take part in projects that assist victims of a disaster. Motion agreed to 400-0: R 215-0; D 185-0 (ND 139-0, SD 46-0); I 0-0. A two-thirds majority of those present and voting (267 in this case) is required for passage under suspension of the rules. Sept. 20, 2005.

**477.** H Res 441. **Congratulate NASA and Space Shuttle Discovery Crew/Adoption.** Calvert, R-Calif., motion to suspend the rules and adopt the resolution that would commend the NASA team and community for the recent Space Shuttle Discovery flight and recognize the achievements of the Discovery crew, including Commander Eileen Collins, the first female space shuttle commander. Motion agreed to 401-0: R 216-0; D 185-0 (ND 139-0, SD 46-0); I 0-0. A two-thirds majority of those present and voting (268 in this case) is required for adoption under suspension of the rules. Sept. 20, 2005.

**478.** HR 250. **Manufacturing Technology/Rule.** Adoption of the rule (H Res 451) that would provide for House floor consideration of the bill that would authorize $2.1 billion in fiscal 2006 through 2008 for activities designed to improve the competitiveness of the U.S. manufacturing sector, including grant programs, scientific research and education. Adopted 222-198: R 222-0; D 0-197 (ND 0-148, SD 0-49); I 0-1. Sept. 21, 2005.

**479.** H J Res 61. **Gold Star Mothers Day/Passage.** Gutknecht, R-Minn., motion to suspend the rules and pass the joint resolution that would express the support of the House of Representatives for the goals and ideals of Gold Star Mothers Day. Motion agreed to 419-0: R 222-0; D 197-0 (ND 147-0, SD 50-0); I 0-0. A two-thirds majority of those present and voting (280 in this case) is required for passage under suspension of the rules. Sept. 21, 2005.

**480.** HR 3768. **Hurricane Katrina Tax Relief/Adoption.** McCrery, R-La., motion to suspend the rules and adopt the resolution (H Res 454) that would agree to the Senate amendment, with an amendment. The bill, as modified, would provide tax breaks to Hurricane Katrina victims, including provisions to waive penalties for early withdrawal from retirement funds, increase deductions for charitable donations by individuals and businesses and allow low-income workers to maintain benefits such as the earned income tax credit. Motion agreed to 422-0: R 223-0; D 198-0 (ND 148-0, SD 50-0); I 1-0. A two-thirds majority of those present and voting (282 in this case) is required for adoption under suspension of the rules. Sept. 21, 2005.

**481.** HR 250. **Manufacturing Technology/Minority-Serving Institutions.** Jackson-Lee, D-Texas, amendment that would make funds authorized in the bill for scientific, technical research and general services available, to the maximum extent practical, to historically black colleges and universities and other minority-serving institutions. Adopted 416-8: R 216-8; D 199-0 (ND 149-0, SD 50-0); I 1-0. Sept. 21, 2005.

| | 476 | 477 | 478 | 479 | 480 | 481 |
|---|---|---|---|---|---|---|
| **ALABAMA** | | | | | | |
| 1 Bonner | Y | Y | Y | Y | Y | Y |
| 2 Everett | Y | Y | Y | Y | Y | Y |
| 3 Rogers | Y | Y | Y | Y | Y | Y |
| 4 Aderholt | Y | Y | Y | Y | Y | Y |
| 5 Cramer | Y | Y | N | Y | Y | Y |
| 6 Bachus | Y | Y | Y | Y | Y | Y |
| 7 Davis | Y | Y | N | Y | Y | Y |
| **ALASKA** | | | | | | |
| AL Young | Y | Y | Y | Y | Y | N |
| **ARIZONA** | | | | | | |
| 1 Renzi | Y | Y | Y | Y | Y | Y |
| 2 Franks | Y | Y | Y | Y | Y | Y |
| 3 Shadegg | Y | Y | Y | Y | Y | Y |
| 4 Pastor | Y | Y | N | Y | Y | Y |
| 5 Hayworth | Y | Y | Y | Y | Y | Y |
| 6 Flake | Y | Y | Y | Y | Y | Y |
| 7 Grijalva | Y | Y | N | Y | Y | Y |
| 8 Kolbe | Y | + | Y | Y | Y | Y |
| **ARKANSAS** | | | | | | |
| 1 Berry | Y | Y | N | Y | Y | Y |
| 2 Snyder | Y | Y | N | Y | Y | Y |
| 3 Boozman | Y | Y | Y | Y | Y | Y |
| 4 Ross | Y | Y | N | Y | Y | Y |
| **CALIFORNIA** | | | | | | |
| 1 Thompson | Y | Y | N | Y | Y | Y |
| 2 Herger | Y | Y | Y | Y | Y | Y |
| 3 Lungren | Y | Y | Y | Y | Y | Y |
| 4 Doolittle | ? | ? | ? | ? | ? | ? |
| 5 Matsui, D. | Y | Y | N | Y | Y | Y |
| 6 Woolsey | Y | Y | N | Y | Y | Y |
| 7 Miller, George | Y | Y | N | Y | Y | Y |
| 8 Pelosi | Y | Y | N | Y | Y | Y |
| 9 Lee | Y | Y | N | Y | Y | Y |
| 10 Tauscher | Y | Y | N | Y | Y | Y |
| 11 Pombo | Y | Y | Y | Y | Y | Y |
| 12 Lantos | Y | Y | N | Y | Y | Y |
| 13 Stark | Y | Y | N | Y | Y | Y |
| 14 Eshoo | Y | Y | N | Y | Y | Y |
| 15 Honda | Y | Y | N | Y | Y | Y |
| 16 Lofgren | Y | Y | N | Y | Y | Y |
| 17 Farr | Y | Y | N | Y | Y | Y |
| 18 Cardoza | Y | Y | N | Y | Y | Y |
| 19 Radanovich | ? | ? | Y | Y | Y | Y |
| 20 Costa | Y | Y | N | Y | Y | Y |
| 21 Nunes | Y | Y | Y | Y | Y | Y |
| 22 Thomas | Y | Y | Y | Y | Y | Y |
| 23 Capps | Y | Y | N | Y | Y | Y |
| 24 Gallegly | Y | Y | Y | Y | Y | Y |
| 25 McKeon | Y | Y | Y | Y | Y | Y |
| 26 Dreier | Y | Y | Y | Y | Y | Y |
| 27 Sherman | Y | Y | N | Y | Y | Y |
| 28 Berman | Y | Y | N | Y | Y | Y |
| 29 Schiff | Y | Y | N | Y | Y | Y |
| 30 Waxman | Y | Y | N | Y | Y | Y |
| 31 Becerra | Y | Y | N | + | Y | Y |
| 32 Solis | Y | Y | N | Y | Y | Y |
| 33 Watson | Y | Y | N | Y | Y | Y |
| 34 Roybal-Allard | Y | Y | N | Y | Y | Y |
| 35 Waters | Y | Y | N | Y | Y | Y |
| 36 Harman | Y | Y | N | Y | Y | Y |
| 37 Millender-McD. | Y | Y | N | Y | Y | Y |
| 38 Napolitano | Y | Y | N | Y | Y | Y |
| 39 Sánchez, Linda | Y | Y | N | Y | Y | Y |
| 40 Royce | Y | Y | Y | Y | Y | Y |
| 41 Lewis | Y | Y | Y | Y | Y | Y |
| 42 Miller, Gary | Y | Y | Y | Y | Y | Y |
| 43 Baca | Y | Y | N | Y | Y | Y |
| 44 Calvert | Y | Y | Y | Y | Y | Y |
| 45 Bono | Y | Y | Y | Y | Y | Y |
| 46 Rohrabacher | Y | Y | Y | Y | Y | Y |
| 47 Sanchez, Loretta | Y | Y | N | Y | Y | Y |
| 48 Vacant | | | | | | |
| 49 Issa | Y | Y | Y | Y | Y | Y |

| | 476 | 477 | 478 | 479 | 480 | 481 |
|---|---|---|---|---|---|---|
| 50 Cunningham | Y | Y | Y | Y | Y | Y |
| 51 Filner | Y | Y | N | Y | Y | Y |
| 52 Hunter | Y | Y | Y | Y | Y | Y |
| 53 Davis | Y | Y | N | Y | Y | Y |
| **COLORADO** | | | | | | |
| 1 DeGette | Y | Y | N | Y | Y | Y |
| 2 Udall | Y | Y | N | Y | Y | Y |
| 3 Salazar | Y | Y | N | Y | Y | Y |
| 4 Musgrave | Y | Y | Y | Y | Y | Y |
| 5 Hefley | Y | Y | ? | ? | ? | ? |
| 6 Tancredo | Y | Y | Y | Y | Y | Y |
| 7 Beauprez | Y | Y | Y | Y | Y | Y |
| **CONNECTICUT** | | | | | | |
| 1 Larson | Y | Y | N | Y | Y | Y |
| 2 Simmons | Y | Y | Y | Y | Y | Y |
| 3 DeLauro | Y | Y | N | Y | Y | Y |
| 4 Shays | Y | Y | Y | Y | Y | Y |
| 5 Johnson | Y | Y | Y | Y | Y | Y |
| **DELAWARE** | | | | | | |
| AL Castle | Y | Y | Y | Y | Y | Y |
| **FLORIDA** | | | | | | |
| 1 Miller | Y | Y | Y | Y | Y | Y |
| 2 Boyd | Y | Y | N | Y | Y | Y |
| 3 Brown | ? | ? | N | Y | Y | Y |
| 4 Crenshaw | Y | Y | Y | Y | Y | Y |
| 5 Brown-Waite | Y | Y | Y | Y | Y | N |
| 6 Stearns | Y | Y | Y | Y | Y | Y |
| 7 Mica | Y | Y | Y | Y | Y | Y |
| 8 Keller | Y | Y | Y | Y | Y | Y |
| 9 Bilirakis | Y | Y | Y | Y | Y | Y |
| 10 Young | Y | Y | Y | Y | Y | Y |
| 11 Davis | ? | ? | N | Y | Y | Y |
| 12 Putnam | Y | Y | Y | Y | Y | Y |
| 13 Harris | Y | Y | Y | Y | Y | Y |
| 14 Mack | Y | Y | Y | Y | Y | Y |
| 15 Weldon | Y | Y | Y | Y | Y | Y |
| 16 Foley | Y | Y | Y | Y | Y | Y |
| 17 Meek | Y | Y | N | Y | Y | Y |
| 18 Ros-Lehtinen | ? | ? | Y | Y | Y | Y |
| 19 Wexler | Y | Y | N | Y | Y | Y |
| 20 Wasserman-Schultz | Y | Y | N | Y | Y | Y |
| 21 Diaz-Balart, L. | ? | ? | Y | Y | Y | Y |
| 22 Shaw | Y | Y | Y | Y | Y | Y |
| 23 Hastings | Y | Y | N | Y | Y | Y |
| 24 Feeney | Y | Y | Y | Y | Y | Y |
| 25 Diaz-Balart, M. | ? | ? | Y | Y | Y | Y |
| **GEORGIA** | | | | | | |
| 1 Kingston | Y | Y | Y | Y | Y | Y |
| 2 Bishop | Y | Y | N | Y | Y | Y |
| 3 Marshall | Y | ? | N | Y | Y | Y |
| 4 McKinney | ? | ? | Y | Y | Y | Y |
| 5 Lewis | Y | Y | N | Y | Y | Y |
| 6 Price | Y | Y | Y | Y | Y | Y |
| 7 Linder | Y | Y | + | + | + | Y |
| 8 Westmoreland | Y | Y | Y | Y | Y | Y |
| 9 Norwood | Y | Y | Y | Y | Y | Y |
| 10 Deal | Y | Y | Y | Y | Y | Y |
| 11 Gingrey | Y | Y | Y | Y | Y | Y |
| 12 Barrow | Y | Y | N | Y | Y | Y |
| 13 Scott | Y | Y | N | Y | Y | Y |
| **HAWAII** | | | | | | |
| 1 Abercrombie | Y | Y | N | Y | Y | Y |
| 2 Case | Y | Y | N | Y | Y | Y |
| **IDAHO** | | | | | | |
| 1 Otter | Y | Y | Y | Y | Y | Y |
| 2 Simpson | Y | Y | Y | Y | Y | Y |
| **ILLINOIS** | | | | | | |
| 1 Rush | ? | ? | N | Y | Y | Y |
| 2 Jackson | Y | Y | N | Y | Y | Y |
| 3 Lipinski | Y | Y | N | Y | Y | Y |
| 4 Gutierrez | Y | Y | N | Y | Y | Y |
| 5 Emanuel | Y | Y | N | Y | Y | Y |
| 6 Hyde | Y | Y | Y | Y | Y | Y |
| 7 Davis | Y | Y | N | Y | Y | Y |
| 8 Bean | Y | Y | N | Y | Y | Y |
| 9 Schakowsky | Y | Y | N | Y | Y | Y |
| 10 Kirk | Y | Y | Y | Y | Y | Y |
| 11 Weller | Y | Y | ? | ? | ? | ? |
| 12 Costello | Y | Y | N | Y | Y | Y |

**KEY** | **Republicans** | Democrats | *Independents*

| | | |
|---|---|---|
| Y Voted for (yea) | X Paired against | C Voted "present" to avoid possible conflict of interest |
| # Paired for | – Announced against | |
| + Announced for | P Voted "present" | ? Did not vote or otherwise make a position known |
| N Voted against (nay) | | |

ND Northern Democrats, SD Southern Democrats
Southern states: Ala., Ark., Fla., Ga., Ky., La., Miss., N.C., Okla., S.C., Tenn., Texas, Va.

| | 476 | 477 | 478 | 479 | 480 | 481 |
|---|---|---|---|---|---|---|
| 13 **Biggert** | Y | Y | Y | Y | Y | Y |
| 14 **Hastert** | | | | | | |
| 15 **Johnson** | Y | Y | Y | Y | Y | Y |
| 16 **Manzullo** | ? | ? | Y | Y | Y | Y |
| 17 Evans | Y | Y | N | Y | Y | Y |
| 18 **LaHood** | Y | Y | Y | Y | Y | Y |
| 19 **Shimkus** | Y | Y | Y | Y | Y | Y |
| **INDIANA** | | | | | | |
| 1 Visclosky | Y | Y | N | Y | Y | Y |
| 2 **Chocola** | Y | Y | Y | Y | Y | Y |
| 3 **Souder** | Y | Y | Y | Y | Y | Y |
| 4 **Buyer** | Y | Y | ? | Y | Y | Y |
| 5 **Burton** | + | + | Y | Y | Y | Y |
| 6 **Pence** | Y | Y | Y | Y | Y | Y |
| 7 Carson | Y | Y | N | Y | Y | Y |
| 8 **Hostettler** | Y | Y | Y | Y | Y | Y |
| 9 **Sodrel** | Y | Y | Y | Y | Y | Y |
| **IOWA** | | | | | | |
| 1 **Nussle** | Y | Y | Y | Y | Y | Y |
| 2 **Leach** | Y | Y | Y | Y | Y | Y |
| 3 Boswell | ? | ? | ? | ? | ? | ? |
| 4 **Latham** | Y | Y | Y | Y | Y | Y |
| 5 **King** | Y | Y | Y | Y | Y | N |
| **KANSAS** | | | | | | |
| 1 **Moran** | Y | Y | Y | Y | Y | Y |
| 2 **Ryun** | Y | Y | Y | Y | Y | Y |
| 3 Moore | Y | Y | N | Y | Y | Y |
| 4 **Tiahrt** | Y | Y | Y | Y | Y | Y |
| **KENTUCKY** | | | | | | |
| 1 **Whitfield** | Y | Y | Y | Y | Y | Y |
| 2 **Lewis** | Y | Y | Y | Y | Y | Y |
| 3 **Northup** | Y | Y | Y | Y | Y | Y |
| 4 **Davis** | Y | Y | Y | Y | Y | Y |
| 5 **Rogers** | Y | Y | Y | Y | Y | Y |
| 6 Chandler | Y | Y | N | Y | Y | Y |
| **LOUISIANA** | | | | | | |
| 1 **Jindal** | Y | Y | Y | Y | Y | Y |
| 2 Jefferson | Y | Y | N | Y | Y | Y |
| 3 Melancon | Y | Y | N | Y | Y | Y |
| 4 **McCrery** | Y | Y | Y | Y | Y | Y |
| 5 **Alexander** | Y | Y | Y | Y | Y | Y |
| 6 **Baker** | ? | Y | Y | Y | Y | Y |
| 7 **Boustany** | Y | Y | Y | Y | Y | Y |
| **MAINE** | | | | | | |
| 1 Allen | Y | Y | N | Y | Y | Y |
| 2 Michaud | Y | Y | N | Y | Y | Y |
| **MARYLAND** | | | | | | |
| 1 **Gilchrest** | Y | Y | Y | Y | Y | Y |
| 2 Ruppersberger | Y | Y | N | Y | Y | Y |
| 3 Cardin | Y | Y | N | Y | Y | Y |
| 4 Wynn | Y | Y | N | Y | Y | Y |
| 5 Hoyer | Y | Y | N | Y | Y | Y |
| 6 **Bartlett** | Y | Y | Y | Y | Y | Y |
| 7 Cummings | ? | Y | N | Y | Y | Y |
| 8 Van Hollen | Y | Y | N | Y | Y | Y |
| **MASSACHUSETTS** | | | | | | |
| 1 Olver | Y | Y | N | Y | Y | Y |
| 2 Neal | Y | Y | N | Y | Y | Y |
| 3 McGovern | Y | Y | N | Y | Y | Y |
| 4 Frank | Y | Y | N | Y | Y | Y |
| 5 Meehan | Y | Y | N | Y | Y | Y |
| 6 Tierney | Y | Y | N | Y | Y | Y |
| 7 Markey | Y | Y | N | Y | Y | Y |
| 8 Capuano | Y | Y | N | Y | Y | Y |
| 9 Lynch | ? | ? | N | Y | Y | Y |
| 10 Delahunt | Y | Y | N | Y | Y | Y |
| **MICHIGAN** | | | | | | |
| 1 Stupak | Y | Y | N | Y | Y | Y |
| 2 **Hoekstra** | ? | ? | Y | Y | Y | Y |
| 3 **Ehlers** | Y | Y | Y | Y | Y | Y |
| 4 **Camp** | ? | ? | ? | ? | ? | ? |
| 5 Kildee | Y | Y | N | Y | Y | Y |
| 6 **Upton** | Y | Y | Y | Y | Y | Y |
| 7 **Schwarz** | Y | Y | Y | Y | Y | Y |
| 8 **Rogers** | Y | Y | Y | Y | Y | Y |
| 9 **Knollenberg** | Y | Y | Y | Y | Y | Y |
| 10 **Miller** | Y | Y | Y | Y | Y | Y |
| 11 **McCotter** | Y | Y | Y | Y | Y | Y |
| 12 Levin | Y | Y | N | Y | Y | Y |
| 13 Kilpatrick | Y | Y | N | Y | Y | Y |
| 14 Conyers | Y | Y | N | Y | Y | Y |
| 15 Dingell | Y | Y | N | Y | Y | Y |

| | 476 | 477 | 478 | 479 | 480 | 481 |
|---|---|---|---|---|---|---|
| **MINNESOTA** | | | | | | |
| 1 **Gutknecht** | Y | Y | Y | Y | Y | Y |
| 2 **Kline** | Y | Y | Y | Y | Y | Y |
| 3 **Ramstad** | Y | Y | Y | Y | Y | Y |
| 4 McCollum | Y | Y | N | Y | Y | Y |
| 5 Sabo | Y | Y | N | Y | Y | Y |
| 6 **Kennedy** | Y | Y | Y | Y | Y | Y |
| 7 Peterson | Y | Y | N | Y | Y | Y |
| 8 Oberstar | Y | Y | N | Y | Y | Y |
| **MISSISSIPPI** | | | | | | |
| 1 **Wicker** | Y | Y | Y | Y | Y | Y |
| 2 Thompson | Y | Y | N | Y | Y | Y |
| 3 **Pickering** | Y | Y | Y | Y | Y | Y |
| 4 Taylor | ? | ? | N | Y | Y | Y |
| **MISSOURI** | | | | | | |
| 1 Clay | Y | Y | N | Y | Y | Y |
| 2 **Akin** | Y | Y | Y | Y | Y | Y |
| 3 Carnahan | Y | Y | N | Y | Y | Y |
| 4 Skelton | ? | Y | N | Y | Y | Y |
| 5 Cleaver | Y | Y | N | Y | Y | Y |
| 6 **Graves** | Y | Y | Y | Y | Y | Y |
| 7 **Blunt** | Y | Y | Y | Y | Y | Y |
| 8 **Emerson** | Y | Y | Y | Y | Y | Y |
| 9 **Hulshof** | Y | Y | Y | Y | Y | Y |
| **MONTANA** | | | | | | |
| AL **Rehberg** | Y | Y | Y | Y | Y | Y |
| **NEBRASKA** | | | | | | |
| 1 **Fortenberry** | Y | Y | Y | Y | Y | Y |
| 2 **Terry** | Y | Y | Y | Y | Y | Y |
| 3 **Osborne** | Y | Y | Y | Y | Y | Y |
| **NEVADA** | | | | | | |
| 1 Berkley | Y | Y | N | Y | Y | Y |
| 2 **Gibbons** | + | + | Y | Y | Y | Y |
| 3 **Porter** | Y | Y | Y | Y | Y | Y |
| **NEW HAMPSHIRE** | | | | | | |
| 1 **Bradley** | Y | Y | Y | Y | Y | Y |
| 2 **Bass** | Y | Y | Y | Y | Y | Y |
| **NEW JERSEY** | | | | | | |
| 1 Andrews | + | + | N | Y | Y | Y |
| 2 **LoBiondo** | Y | Y | Y | Y | Y | Y |
| 3 **Saxton** | Y | Y | Y | Y | Y | Y |
| 4 **Smith** | Y | Y | Y | Y | Y | Y |
| 5 **Garrett** | Y | Y | Y | Y | Y | Y |
| 6 Pallone | ? | ? | N | Y | Y | Y |
| 7 **Ferguson** | Y | Y | Y | Y | Y | Y |
| 8 Pascrell | Y | Y | N | Y | Y | Y |
| 9 Rothman | Y | Y | N | Y | Y | Y |
| 10 Payne | Y | Y | N | Y | Y | Y |
| 11 **Frelinghuysen** | Y | Y | Y | Y | Y | Y |
| 12 Holt | Y | Y | N | Y | Y | Y |
| 13 Menendez | + | + | N | Y | Y | Y |
| **NEW MEXICO** | | | | | | |
| 1 **Wilson** | Y | Y | Y | Y | Y | Y |
| 2 **Pearce** | Y | Y | Y | Y | Y | Y |
| 3 Udall | Y | Y | N | Y | Y | Y |
| **NEW YORK** | | | | | | |
| 1 Bishop | Y | Y | N | Y | Y | Y |
| 2 Israel | Y | Y | N | Y | Y | Y |
| 3 **King** | Y | Y | Y | Y | Y | Y |
| 4 McCarthy | Y | Y | N | Y | Y | Y |
| 5 Ackerman | Y | Y | N | Y | Y | Y |
| 6 Meeks | Y | Y | N | Y | Y | Y |
| 7 Crowley | Y | Y | N | Y | Y | Y |
| 8 Nadler | Y | Y | N | Y | Y | Y |
| 9 Weiner | Y | Y | N | Y | Y | Y |
| 10 Towns | ? | ? | ? | ? | ? | Y |
| 11 Owens | Y | Y | N | Y | Y | Y |
| 12 Velázquez | Y | Y | N | Y | Y | Y |
| 13 **Fossella** | Y | Y | Y | + | Y | Y |
| 14 Maloney | Y | Y | N | Y | Y | Y |
| 15 Rangel | Y | Y | N | Y | Y | Y |
| 16 Serrano | Y | Y | N | Y | Y | Y |
| 17 Engel | Y | Y | N | Y | Y | Y |
| 18 Lowey | Y | Y | N | Y | Y | Y |
| 19 **Kelly** | Y | Y | Y | Y | Y | Y |
| 20 **Sweeney** | Y | Y | Y | Y | Y | Y |
| 21 McNulty | Y | Y | N | Y | Y | Y |
| 22 Hinchey | Y | Y | N | Y | Y | Y |
| 23 **McHugh** | Y | Y | Y | Y | Y | Y |
| 24 **Boehlert** | Y | Y | Y | Y | Y | Y |
| 25 **Walsh** | Y | Y | Y | Y | Y | Y |
| 26 **Reynolds** | Y | Y | Y | Y | Y | Y |
| 27 Higgins | Y | Y | N | Y | Y | Y |
| 28 Slaughter | Y | Y | N | Y | Y | Y |
| 29 **Kuhl** | Y | Y | Y | Y | Y | Y |

| | 476 | 477 | 478 | 479 | 480 | 481 |
|---|---|---|---|---|---|---|
| **NORTH CAROLINA** | | | | | | |
| 1 Butterfield | Y | Y | N | Y | Y | Y |
| 2 Etheridge | Y | Y | N | Y | Y | Y |
| 3 **Jones** | Y | Y | Y | Y | Y | Y |
| 4 Price | Y | Y | N | Y | Y | Y |
| 5 **Foxx** | Y | Y | Y | Y | Y | Y |
| 6 **Coble** | Y | Y | Y | Y | Y | Y |
| 7 McIntyre | Y | Y | N | Y | Y | Y |
| 8 **Hayes** | Y | Y | Y | Y | Y | Y |
| 9 **Myrick** | + | + | Y | Y | Y | Y |
| 10 **McHenry** | ? | ? | Y | Y | Y | N |
| 11 **Taylor** | Y | Y | Y | Y | Y | N |
| 12 Watt | Y | Y | N | Y | Y | Y |
| 13 Miller | Y | Y | N | Y | Y | Y |
| **NORTH DAKOTA** | | | | | | |
| AL Pomeroy | Y | ? | N | Y | Y | Y |
| **OHIO** | | | | | | |
| 1 **Chabot** | Y | Y | Y | Y | Y | Y |
| 2 **Schmidt** | Y | Y | Y | Y | Y | Y |
| 3 **Turner** | Y | Y | Y | Y | Y | Y |
| 4 **Oxley** | Y | Y | Y | Y | Y | Y |
| 5 **Gillmor** | Y | Y | Y | Y | Y | Y |
| 6 Strickland | ? | ? | N | Y | Y | Y |
| 7 **Hobson** | Y | Y | Y | Y | Y | Y |
| 8 **Boehner** | Y | Y | Y | Y | Y | Y |
| 9 Kaptur | Y | Y | N | Y | Y | Y |
| 10 Kucinich | Y | Y | N | Y | Y | Y |
| 11 Jones | Y | Y | N | Y | Y | Y |
| 12 **Tiberi** | Y | Y | Y | Y | Y | Y |
| 13 Brown | Y | Y | N | Y | Y | Y |
| 14 **LaTourette** | Y | Y | Y | Y | Y | Y |
| 15 **Pryce** | Y | Y | Y | Y | Y | Y |
| 16 **Regula** | Y | Y | Y | Y | Y | Y |
| 17 Ryan | Y | Y | N | Y | Y | Y |
| 18 **Ney** | Y | Y | Y | Y | Y | Y |
| **OKLAHOMA** | | | | | | |
| 1 **Sullivan** | Y | Y | Y | Y | Y | Y |
| 2 Boren | Y | Y | N | Y | Y | Y |
| 3 **Lucas** | Y | Y | Y | Y | Y | Y |
| 4 **Cole** | Y | Y | Y | Y | Y | Y |
| 5 **Istook** | Y | Y | Y | Y | Y | Y |
| **OREGON** | | | | | | |
| 1 Wu | Y | Y | N | Y | Y | Y |
| 2 **Walden** | Y | Y | Y | Y | Y | Y |
| 3 Blumenauer | Y | Y | N | Y | Y | Y |
| 4 DeFazio | Y | Y | N | Y | Y | Y |
| 5 Hooley | Y | Y | N | Y | Y | Y |
| **PENNSYLVANIA** | | | | | | |
| 1 Brady | Y | Y | N | Y | Y | Y |
| 2 Fattah | Y | Y | N | Y | Y | Y |
| 3 **English** | Y | Y | Y | Y | Y | Y |
| 4 **Hart** | Y | Y | Y | Y | Y | Y |
| 5 **Peterson** | Y | Y | Y | Y | Y | Y |
| 6 **Gerlach** | Y | Y | Y | Y | Y | Y |
| 7 **Weldon** | Y | Y | Y | Y | Y | Y |
| 8 **Fitzpatrick** | Y | Y | Y | Y | Y | Y |
| 9 **Shuster** | Y | Y | Y | Y | Y | Y |
| 10 **Sherwood** | Y | Y | Y | Y | Y | Y |
| 11 Kanjorski | Y | Y | N | Y | Y | Y |
| 12 Murtha | ? | ? | N | Y | Y | Y |
| 13 Schwartz | Y | Y | N | Y | Y | Y |
| 14 Doyle | Y | Y | N | Y | Y | Y |
| 15 **Dent** | Y | Y | Y | Y | Y | Y |
| 16 **Pitts** | Y | Y | Y | Y | Y | Y |
| 17 Holden | Y | Y | N | Y | Y | Y |
| 18 **Murphy** | Y | Y | Y | Y | Y | Y |
| 19 **Platts** | ? | Y | Y | Y | Y | Y |
| **RHODE ISLAND** | | | | | | |
| 1 Kennedy | Y | Y | N | Y | Y | Y |
| 2 Langevin | Y | Y | N | Y | Y | Y |
| **SOUTH CAROLINA** | | | | | | |
| 1 **Brown** | Y | Y | Y | Y | Y | Y |
| 2 **Wilson** | Y | Y | Y | Y | Y | Y |
| 3 **Barrett** | Y | Y | Y | Y | Y | Y |
| 4 **Inglis** | Y | Y | Y | Y | Y | Y |
| 5 Spratt | Y | Y | N | Y | Y | Y |
| 6 Clyburn | Y | Y | N | Y | Y | Y |
| **SOUTH DAKOTA** | | | | | | |
| AL Herseth | Y | Y | N | Y | Y | Y |
| **TENNESSEE** | | | | | | |
| 1 **Jenkins** | Y | Y | Y | Y | Y | Y |
| 2 **Duncan** | Y | Y | Y | Y | Y | Y |

| | 76 | 477 | 478 | 479 | 480 | 481 |
|---|---|---|---|---|---|---|
| 3 **Wamp** | Y | Y | Y | Y | Y | Y |
| 4 Davis | Y | Y | N | Y | Y | Y |
| 5 Cooper | Y | Y | N | Y | Y | Y |
| 6 Gordon | Y | Y | N | Y | Y | Y |
| 7 **Blackburn** | Y | Y | Y | Y | Y | Y |
| 8 Tanner | Y | Y | N | Y | Y | Y |
| 9 Ford | ? | ? | N | Y | Y | Y |
| **TEXAS** | | | | | | |
| 1 **Gohmert** | Y | Y | Y | Y | Y | Y |
| 2 **Poe** | Y | Y | Y | Y | Y | Y |
| 3 **Johnson, S.** | Y | Y | Y | Y | Y | N |
| 4 **Hall** | Y | Y | Y | Y | Y | Y |
| 5 **Hensarling** | Y | Y | Y | Y | Y | Y |
| 6 **Barton** | Y | Y | ? | ? | ? | ? |
| 7 **Culberson** | Y | Y | Y | Y | Y | N |
| 8 **Brady** | Y | Y | Y | Y | Y | Y |
| 9 Green, A. | Y | Y | N | Y | Y | Y |
| 10 **McCaul** | Y | Y | Y | Y | Y | Y |
| 11 **Conaway** | Y | Y | Y | Y | Y | Y |
| 12 **Granger** | Y | Y | Y | Y | Y | Y |
| 13 **Thornberry** | Y | Y | Y | Y | Y | Y |
| 14 **Paul** | Y | Y | Y | Y | Y | Y |
| 15 Hinojosa | Y | Y | N | Y | Y | Y |
| 16 Reyes | Y | Y | N | Y | Y | Y |
| 17 Edwards | Y | Y | N | Y | Y | Y |
| 18 Jackson-Lee | Y | Y | N | Y | Y | Y |
| 19 **Neugebauer** | Y | Y | Y | Y | Y | Y |
| 20 Gonzalez | Y | Y | N | Y | Y | Y |
| 21 **Smith** | Y | Y | Y | Y | Y | Y |
| 22 **DeLay** | Y | Y | ? | ? | ? | ? |
| 23 **Bonilla** | Y | Y | Y | Y | Y | Y |
| 24 **Marchant** | Y | Y | Y | Y | Y | Y |
| 25 Doggett | Y | Y | N | Y | Y | Y |
| 26 **Burgess** | Y | Y | Y | Y | Y | Y |
| 27 Ortiz | Y | Y | – | + | + | + |
| 28 Cuellar | Y | Y | N | Y | Y | Y |
| 29 Green, G. | Y | Y | N | Y | Y | Y |
| 30 Johnson, E. | Y | Y | N | Y | Y | Y |
| 31 **Carter** | Y | Y | Y | Y | Y | Y |
| 32 **Sessions** | ? | ? | Y | Y | Y | N |
| **UTAH** | | | | | | |
| 1 **Bishop** | Y | Y | Y | Y | Y | Y |
| 2 Matheson | Y | Y | N | Y | Y | Y |
| 3 **Cannon** | Y | Y | Y | Y | Y | Y |
| **VERMONT** | | | | | | |
| AL *Sanders* | ? | ? | N | ? | Y | Y |
| **VIRGINIA** | | | | | | |
| 1 **Davis, J.** | Y | Y | Y | Y | Y | Y |
| 2 **Drake** | Y | Y | Y | Y | Y | Y |
| 3 Scott | Y | Y | N | Y | Y | Y |
| 4 **Forbes** | Y | Y | Y | Y | Y | Y |
| 5 **Goode** | Y | Y | Y | Y | Y | Y |
| 6 **Goodlatte** | Y | Y | Y | Y | Y | Y |
| 7 **Cantor** | Y | Y | Y | Y | Y | Y |
| 8 Moran | Y | Y | N | Y | Y | Y |
| 9 Boucher | Y | Y | N | Y | Y | Y |
| 10 **Wolf** | Y | Y | Y | Y | Y | Y |
| 11 **Davis, T.** | Y | Y | Y | Y | Y | Y |
| **WASHINGTON** | | | | | | |
| 1 Inslee | Y | Y | N | Y | Y | Y |
| 2 Larsen | Y | Y | N | Y | Y | Y |
| 3 Baird | Y | Y | N | Y | Y | Y |
| 4 **Hastings** | Y | Y | Y | Y | Y | Y |
| 5 **McMorris** | Y | Y | Y | Y | Y | Y |
| 6 Dicks | Y | Y | N | Y | Y | Y |
| 7 McDermott | Y | Y | N | Y | Y | Y |
| 8 **Reichert** | Y | Y | Y | Y | Y | Y |
| 9 Smith | Y | ? | N | Y | Y | Y |
| **WEST VIRGINIA** | | | | | | |
| 1 Mollohan | Y | Y | N | Y | Y | Y |
| 2 **Capito** | Y | Y | Y | Y | Y | Y |
| 3 Rahall | Y | Y | N | Y | Y | Y |
| **WISCONSIN** | | | | | | |
| 1 **Ryan** | Y | Y | Y | Y | Y | Y |
| 2 Baldwin | Y | Y | N | Y | Y | Y |
| 3 Kind | ? | ? | ? | ? | ? | ? |
| 4 Moore | Y | Y | N | Y | Y | Y |
| 5 **Sensenbrenner** | Y | Y | Y | Y | Y | Y |
| 6 **Petri** | Y | Y | Y | Y | Y | Y |
| 7 Obey | Y | Y | N | Y | Y | Y |
| 8 **Green** | Y | Y | Y | Y | Y | Y |
| **WYOMING** | | | | | | |
| AL **Cubin** | Y | Y | Y | Y | Y | Y |

# IN THE HOUSE | By Vote Number

**482.** **HR 250. Manufacturing Technology/Manufacturing and Technology Administration.** Larson, D-Conn., amendment that would establish a Manufacturing and Technology Administration within the Commerce Department. It would direct the president to appoint an undersecretary to supervise the new office. Rejected 210-213: R 10-213; D 199-0 (ND 149-0, SD 50-0); I 1-0. Sept. 21, 2005.

**483.** **HR 250. Manufacturing Technology/Advanced Technological Education Program.** Udall, D-Colo., amendment that would increase to $220.5 million the authorization for fiscal 2006 through 2008 for the National Science Foundation's Advanced Technological Education Program. Rejected 210-212: R 12-212; D 197-0 (ND 147-0, SD 50-0); I 1-0. Sept. 21, 2005.

**484.** **HR 250. Manufacturing Technology/Recommit.** Honda, D-Calif., motion to recommit the bill to the Science Committee with instructions to add language that would authorize $140 million in fiscal 2006 for the Advanced Technology Program. Motion rejected 196-226: R 0-224; D 196-1 (ND 147-1, SD 49-0); I 0-1. Sept. 21, 2005.

**485.** **HR 250. Manufacturing Technology/Passage.** Passage of the bill that would authorize $2.1 billion in fiscal 2006 through 2008 for activities designed to improve the competitiveness of the U.S. manufacturing sector, including grant programs, scientific research and education. The bill includes $1.3 billion in fiscal 2006 through 2008 for laboratory activities and technical research run by the National Institute of Standards and Technology. Passed 394-24: R 196-24; D 197-0 (ND 148-0, SD 49-0); I 1-0. Sept. 21, 2005.

**486.** **HR 2123. Head Start Reauthorization/Rule.** Adoption of the rule (H Res 455) that would provide for House floor consideration of the bill that would reauthorize the Head Start program through fiscal 2011. Adopted 221-189: R 221-0; D 0-188 (ND 0-142, SD 0-46); I 0-1. Sept. 22, 2005.

**487.** **Procedural Motion/Journal.** Approval of the House Journal of Wednesday Sept. 21, 2005. Approved 346-59: R 200-17; D 145-42 (ND 111-31, SD 34-11); I 1-0. Sept. 22, 2005.

ND Northern Democrats, SD Southern Democrats
Southern states: Ala., Ark., Fla., Ga., Ky., La., Miss., N.C., Okla., S.C., Tenn., Texas, Va.

| | 482 | 483 | 484 | 485 | 486 | 487 |
|---|---|---|---|---|---|---|
| **ALABAMA** | | | | | | |
| 1 Bonner | N | N | N | Y | Y | Y |
| 2 Everett | N | N | N | Y | Y | Y |
| 3 Rogers | N | N | N | Y | Y | Y |
| 4 Aderholt | N | N | N | Y | Y | Y |
| 5 Cramer | Y | Y | Y | Y | N | Y |
| 6 Bachus | N | N | N | Y | Y | Y |
| 7 Davis | Y | Y | Y | Y | N | Y |
| **ALASKA** | | | | | | |
| AL Young | N | N | N | Y | Y | Y |
| **ARIZONA** | | | | | | |
| 1 Renzi | N | Y | N | Y | Y | Y |
| 2 Franks | N | N | N | N | Y | Y |
| 3 Shadegg | N | N | N | N | Y | Y |
| 4 Pastor | Y | Y | Y | Y | N | Y |
| 5 Hayworth | N | N | N | N | Y | Y |
| 6 Flake | N | N | N | N | Y | Y |
| 7 Grijalva | Y | Y | Y | Y | N | Y |
| 8 Kolbe | N | N | N | Y | Y | Y |
| **ARKANSAS** | | | | | | |
| 1 Berry | Y | Y | Y | Y | N | N |
| 2 Snyder | Y | Y | Y | Y | N | Y |
| 3 Boozman | N | N | N | Y | Y | Y |
| 4 Ross | Y | Y | Y | Y | N | Y |
| **CALIFORNIA** | | | | | | |
| 1 Thompson | Y | Y | Y | Y | N | N |
| 2 Herger | N | N | N | Y | Y | Y |
| 3 Lungren | N | N | N | Y | Y | Y |
| 4 Doolittle | ? | ? | ? | ? | ? | ? |
| 5 Matsui, D. | Y | Y | Y | Y | N | Y |
| 6 Woolsey | Y | Y | Y | Y | N | Y |
| 7 Miller, George | Y | Y | Y | Y | N | N |
| 8 Pelosi | Y | Y | Y | Y | N | Y |
| 9 Lee | Y | Y | Y | Y | N | Y |
| 10 Tauscher | Y | Y | Y | Y | N | Y |
| 11 Pombo | N | N | N | Y | Y | Y |
| 12 Lantos | Y | Y | Y | Y | N | Y |
| 13 Stark | Y | Y | Y | Y | N | Y |
| 14 Eshoo | Y | Y | Y | Y | N | Y |
| 15 Honda | Y | Y | Y | Y | N | Y |
| 16 Lofgren | Y | Y | Y | Y | N | Y |
| 17 Farr | Y | Y | Y | Y | N | Y |
| 18 Cardoza | Y | Y | Y | Y | N | Y |
| 19 Radanovich | N | N | N | Y | Y | Y |
| 20 Costa | Y | Y | Y | Y | N | Y |
| 21 Nunes | N | N | N | Y | Y | Y |
| 22 Thomas | N | N | N | Y | Y | Y |
| 23 Capps | Y | Y | Y | Y | N | Y |
| 24 Gallegly | N | N | N | Y | Y | Y |
| 25 McKeon | N | N | N | Y | Y | Y |
| 26 Dreier | N | N | N | Y | Y | Y |
| 27 Sherman | Y | Y | Y | Y | N | Y |
| 28 Berman | Y | Y | Y | Y | N | ? |
| 29 Schiff | Y | Y | Y | Y | N | Y |
| 30 Waxman | Y | Y | ? | Y | N | Y |
| 31 Becerra | Y | Y | Y | Y | N | N |
| 32 Solis | Y | Y | Y | Y | N | Y |
| 33 Watson | Y | Y | Y | Y | N | Y |
| 34 Roybal-Allard | Y | Y | Y | Y | N | Y |
| 35 Waters | Y | Y | Y | Y | N | N |
| 36 Harman | Y | Y | Y | Y | N | Y |
| 37 Millender-McD. | Y | Y | Y | Y | ? | ? |
| 38 Napolitano | Y | Y | Y | Y | N | Y |
| 39 Sánchez, Linda | Y | Y | Y | Y | N | Y |
| 40 Royce | N | N | N | N | Y | Y |
| 41 Lewis | N | N | N | Y | Y | Y |
| 42 Miller, Gary | N | N | N | N | Y | Y |
| 43 Baca | Y | Y | Y | Y | N | Y |
| 44 Calvert | N | N | N | Y | Y | Y |
| 45 Bono | N | N | N | Y | Y | Y |
| 46 Rohrabacher | N | N | N | Y | Y | Y |
| 47 Sanchez, Loretta | Y | Y | Y | Y | N | N |
| 48 Vacant | | | | | | |
| 49 Issa | N | N | N | Y | Y | Y |

| | 482 | 483 | 484 | 485 | 486 | 487 |
|---|---|---|---|---|---|---|
| 50 Cunningham | N | N | N | Y | Y | Y |
| 51 Filner | Y | Y | Y | Y | N | N |
| 52 Hunter | N | N | N | Y | Y | Y |
| 53 Davis | Y | Y | Y | Y | N | Y |
| **COLORADO** | | | | | | |
| 1 DeGette | Y | Y | Y | Y | N | Y |
| 2 Udall | Y | Y | Y | Y | N | N |
| 3 Salazar | Y | Y | Y | Y | N | Y |
| 4 Musgrave | N | N | N | N | Y | Y |
| 5 Hefley | ? | ? | ? | ? | ? | ? |
| 6 Tancredo | N | N | N | N | Y | P |
| 7 Beauprez | N | N | N | Y | Y | Y |
| **CONNECTICUT** | | | | | | |
| 1 Larson | Y | Y | Y | Y | N | Y |
| 2 Simmons | Y | N | N | Y | Y | Y |
| 3 DeLauro | Y | Y | Y | Y | N | Y |
| 4 Shays | Y | Y | N | Y | Y | Y |
| 5 Johnson | Y | N | N | Y | Y | Y |
| **DELAWARE** | | | | | | |
| AL Castle | N | N | N | Y | Y | Y |
| **FLORIDA** | | | | | | |
| 1 Miller | N | N | N | N | Y | Y |
| 2 Boyd | Y | Y | Y | Y | N | Y |
| 3 Brown | Y | Y | Y | Y | ? | ? |
| 4 Crenshaw | N | N | N | Y | Y | Y |
| 5 Brown-Waite | N | N | N | Y | Y | Y |
| 6 Stearns | N | N | N | N | Y | Y |
| 7 Mica | N | N | N | Y | Y | Y |
| 8 Keller | N | N | N | Y | Y | Y |
| 9 Bilirakis | N | N | N | Y | Y | Y |
| 10 Young | N | N | N | Y | Y | Y |
| 11 Davis | Y | Y | Y | Y | N | Y |
| 12 Putnam | N | N | N | Y | Y | Y |
| 13 Harris | N | N | N | + | Y | Y |
| 14 Mack | N | N | N | Y | Y | Y |
| 15 Weldon | N | N | N | Y | Y | Y |
| 16 Foley | N | N | N | Y | Y | Y |
| 17 Meek | Y | Y | Y | Y | N | N |
| 18 Ros-Lehtinen | N | N | N | Y | Y | Y |
| 19 Wexler | Y | Y | Y | Y | N | Y |
| 20 Wasserman-Schultz | Y | Y | Y | Y | N | Y |
| 21 Diaz-Balart, L. | N | N | N | Y | Y | Y |
| 22 Shaw | N | N | N | Y | Y | Y |
| 23 Hastings | Y | Y | Y | Y | N | N |
| 24 Feeney | N | N | N | Y | Y | Y |
| 25 Diaz-Balart, M. | N | N | N | Y | Y | Y |
| **GEORGIA** | | | | | | |
| 1 Kingston | N | N | N | Y | Y | Y |
| 2 Bishop | Y | Y | Y | Y | N | Y |
| 3 Marshall | Y | Y | Y | Y | N | N |
| 4 McKinney | Y | Y | ? | Y | N | Y |
| 5 Lewis | Y | Y | Y | Y | N | Y |
| 6 Price | N | N | N | Y | Y | Y |
| 7 Linder | N | N | N | Y | Y | Y |
| 8 Westmoreland | N | N | N | N | Y | Y |
| 9 Norwood | N | N | N | Y | Y | Y |
| 10 Deal | N | N | N | Y | Y | Y |
| 11 Gingrey | N | N | N | Y | Y | Y |
| 12 Barrow | Y | Y | Y | Y | N | Y |
| 13 Scott | Y | Y | Y | Y | N | Y |
| **HAWAII** | | | | | | |
| 1 Abercrombie | Y | Y | Y | Y | N | Y |
| 2 Case | Y | Y | Y | Y | N | Y |
| **IDAHO** | | | | | | |
| 1 Otter | N | N | N | Y | Y | Y |
| 2 Simpson | N | N | N | Y | Y | Y |
| **ILLINOIS** | | | | | | |
| 1 Rush | Y | Y | Y | Y | ? | ? |
| 2 Jackson | Y | Y | Y | Y | N | Y |
| 3 Lipinski | Y | Y | Y | Y | N | Y |
| 4 Gutierrez | Y | Y | Y | Y | N | Y |
| 5 Emanuel | Y | Y | Y | Y | N | Y |
| 6 Hyde | N | N | N | Y | Y | Y |
| 7 Davis | Y | Y | Y | Y | ? | ? |
| 8 Bean | Y | Y | Y | + | N | Y |
| 9 Schakowsky | Y | Y | Y | Y | N | N |
| 10 Kirk | N | N | N | Y | Y | Y |
| 11 Weller | ? | ? | ? | ? | ? | ? |
| 12 Costello | Y | Y | Y | Y | N | N |

## KEY

**Republicans**    Democrats    *Independents*

| | | |
|---|---|---|
| Y Voted for (yea) | X Paired against | C Voted "present" to avoid possible conflict of interest |
| # Paired for | – Announced against | |
| + Announced for | P Voted "present" | ? Did not vote or otherwise make a position known |
| N Voted against (nay) | | |

| | 482 | 483 | 484 | 485 | 486 | 487 |
|---|---|---|---|---|---|---|
| 13 **Biggert** | N | N | N | Y | Y | Y |
| 14 **Hastert** | | | | | | |
| 15 **Johnson** | N | N | N | Y | Y | Y |
| 16 **Manzullo** | N | N | N | Y | Y | Y |
| 17 Evans | Y | Y | Y | Y | N | N |
| 18 **LaHood** | N | N | N | Y | Y | Y |
| 19 **Shimkus** | N | N | N | Y | Y | Y |
| **INDIANA** | | | | | | |
| 1 Visclosky | Y | Y | Y | Y | N | N |
| 2 **Chocola** | N | N | N | Y | Y | Y |
| 3 **Souder** | N | N | N | Y | Y | Y |
| 4 **Buyer** | N | N | N | Y | Y | Y |
| 5 **Burton** | N | N | N | Y | Y | Y |
| 6 **Pence** | N | N | N | N | Y | Y |
| 7 Carson | Y | Y | Y | Y | N | Y |
| 8 **Hostettler** | N | N | N | N | Y | ? |
| 9 **Sodrel** | N | N | N | Y | Y | Y |
| **IOWA** | | | | | | |
| 1 **Nussle** | N | N | N | Y | Y | Y |
| 2 **Leach** | N | N | N | Y | Y | Y |
| 3 Boswell | ? | ? | ? | ? | ? | ? |
| 4 **Latham** | N | N | N | Y | Y | N |
| 5 **King** | N | N | N | N | Y | Y |
| **KANSAS** | | | | | | |
| 1 **Moran** | N | N | N | Y | Y | N |
| 2 **Ryun** | N | N | N | Y | Y | Y |
| 3 Moore | Y | Y | Y | Y | N | Y |
| 4 **Tiahrt** | N | N | N | Y | Y | N |
| **KENTUCKY** | | | | | | |
| 1 **Whitfield** | N | N | N | Y | Y | Y |
| 2 **Lewis** | N | N | N | Y | Y | Y |
| 3 **Northup** | N | N | N | Y | Y | Y |
| 4 **Davis** | N | N | N | + | Y | Y |
| 5 **Rogers** | N | N | N | Y | Y | Y |
| 6 Chandler | Y | Y | Y | Y | N | N |
| **LOUISIANA** | | | | | | |
| 1 **Jindal** | N | N | N | Y | Y | Y |
| 2 Jefferson | Y | Y | Y | Y | N | Y |
| 3 Melancon | Y | Y | Y | Y | N | Y |
| 4 **McCrery** | N | N | N | Y | Y | Y |
| 5 **Alexander** | N | N | N | Y | Y | Y |
| 6 **Baker** | N | N | N | Y | Y | Y |
| 7 **Boustany** | N | N | N | Y | ? | ? |
| **MAINE** | | | | | | |
| 1 Allen | Y | Y | Y | Y | N | Y |
| 2 Michaud | Y | Y | Y | Y | N | Y |
| **MARYLAND** | | | | | | |
| 1 **Gilchrest** | N | N | N | Y | Y | Y |
| 2 Ruppersberger | Y | Y | Y | Y | N | Y |
| 3 Cardin | Y | Y | Y | Y | N | Y |
| 4 Wynn | Y | Y | Y | Y | N | Y |
| 5 Hoyer | Y | Y | Y | Y | N | Y |
| 6 **Bartlett** | N | N | N | Y | Y | Y |
| 7 Cummings | Y | Y | Y | Y | N | Y |
| 8 Van Hollen | Y | Y | Y | Y | N | Y |
| **MASSACHUSETTS** | | | | | | |
| 1 Olver | Y | Y | Y | Y | N | N |
| 2 Neal | Y | Y | Y | Y | N | Y |
| 3 McGovern | Y | Y | Y | Y | N | N |
| 4 Frank | Y | Y | Y | Y | N | Y |
| 5 Meehan | Y | Y | Y | Y | N | Y |
| 6 Tierney | Y | Y | Y | Y | N | Y |
| 7 Markey | Y | Y | Y | Y | N | Y |
| 8 Capuano | Y | Y | Y | Y | N | N |
| 9 Lynch | Y | Y | Y | Y | N | Y |
| 10 Delahunt | Y | Y | Y | Y | N | Y |
| **MICHIGAN** | | | | | | |
| 1 Stupak | Y | Y | Y | Y | N | N |
| 2 **Hoekstra** | N | N | N | Y | Y | Y |
| 3 **Ehlers** | N | N | N | Y | Y | Y |
| 4 **Camp** | ? | ? | ? | ? | ? | ? |
| 5 Kildee | Y | Y | Y | Y | N | Y |
| 6 **Upton** | N | N | N | Y | Y | Y |
| 7 **Schwarz** | N | N | N | Y | Y | Y |
| 8 **Rogers** | N | N | N | Y | Y | Y |
| 9 **Knollenberg** | N | N | N | Y | Y | Y |
| 10 **Miller** | N | N | N | Y | Y | Y |
| 11 **McCotter** | N | N | N | Y | Y | N |
| 12 Levin | Y | Y | Y | Y | N | Y |
| 13 Kilpatrick | Y | Y | Y | Y | N | Y |
| 14 Conyers | Y | ? | Y | Y | ? | ? |
| 15 Dingell | Y | Y | Y | Y | N | Y |

| | 482 | 483 | 484 | 485 | 486 | 487 |
|---|---|---|---|---|---|---|
| **MINNESOTA** | | | | | | |
| 1 **Gutknecht** | N | N | N | N | Y | N |
| 2 **Kline** | N | N | N | Y | Y | Y |
| 3 **Ramstad** | N | N | N | Y | Y | N |
| 4 McCollum | Y | Y | Y | Y | N | Y |
| 5 Sabo | Y | Y | Y | Y | ? | ? |
| 6 **Kennedy** | N | Y | N | Y | Y | Y |
| 7 Peterson | Y | Y | Y | Y | ? | N |
| 8 Oberstar | Y | Y | Y | Y | N | N |
| **MISSISSIPPI** | | | | | | |
| 1 **Wicker** | N | N | N | Y | Y | Y |
| 2 Thompson | Y | Y | Y | Y | N | N |
| 3 **Pickering** | N | N | N | Y | Y | Y |
| 4 Taylor | Y | Y | Y | Y | N | N |
| **MISSOURI** | | | | | | |
| 1 Clay | Y | Y | Y | Y | N | Y |
| 2 **Akin** | N | N | N | Y | Y | Y |
| 3 Carnahan | Y | Y | Y | Y | N | Y |
| 4 Skelton | Y | Y | Y | Y | N | Y |
| 5 Cleaver | Y | Y | Y | Y | N | Y |
| 6 **Graves** | N | N | N | Y | Y | N |
| 7 **Blunt** | N | N | N | Y | Y | ? |
| 8 **Emerson** | N | N | N | Y | Y | Y |
| 9 **Hulshof** | N | N | N | Y | Y | N |
| **MONTANA** | | | | | | |
| AL **Rehberg** | N | N | N | Y | Y | Y |
| **NEBRASKA** | | | | | | |
| 1 **Fortenberry** | N | N | N | Y | Y | Y |
| 2 **Terry** | N | N | N | Y | Y | Y |
| 3 **Osborne** | N | N | N | Y | Y | Y |
| **NEVADA** | | | | | | |
| 1 Berkley | Y | Y | Y | Y | N | Y |
| 2 **Gibbons** | N | Y | N | Y | Y | Y |
| 3 **Porter** | N | Y | N | Y | Y | Y |
| **NEW HAMPSHIRE** | | | | | | |
| 1 **Bradley** | N | N | N | Y | Y | Y |
| 2 **Bass** | N | N | N | Y | Y | Y |
| **NEW JERSEY** | | | | | | |
| 1 Andrews | Y | Y | Y | Y | N | Y |
| 2 **LoBiondo** | N | N | N | Y | Y | N |
| 3 **Saxton** | N | N | N | Y | Y | Y |
| 4 **Smith** | Y | N | N | Y | Y | Y |
| 5 **Garrett** | N | N | N | N | Y | Y |
| 6 Pallone | Y | Y | Y | Y | N | Y |
| 7 **Ferguson** | N | N | N | Y | Y | Y |
| 8 Pascrell | Y | Y | Y | Y | N | Y |
| 9 Rothman | Y | Y | Y | Y | N | Y |
| 10 Payne | Y | Y | Y | Y | N | Y |
| 11 **Frelinghuysen** | N | N | N | Y | Y | Y |
| 12 Holt | Y | Y | Y | Y | N | N |
| 13 Menendez | Y | Y | Y | Y | N | Y |
| **NEW MEXICO** | | | | | | |
| 1 **Wilson** | N | Y | N | Y | Y | Y |
| 2 **Pearce** | N | N | N | Y | Y | Y |
| 3 Udall | Y | Y | Y | Y | N | N |
| **NEW YORK** | | | | | | |
| 1 Bishop | Y | Y | Y | Y | N | Y |
| 2 Israel | Y | Y | Y | Y | N | Y |
| 3 **King** | N | N | N | Y | Y | Y |
| 4 McCarthy | Y | Y | Y | Y | N | Y |
| 5 Ackerman | Y | Y | Y | Y | N | Y |
| 6 Meeks | Y | ? | Y | Y | N | Y |
| 7 Crowley | Y | Y | Y | Y | N | Y |
| 8 Nadler | Y | Y | Y | Y | N | Y |
| 9 Weiner | Y | Y | Y | Y | N | Y |
| 10 Towns | Y | Y | Y | Y | N | Y |
| 11 Owens | Y | Y | Y | Y | N | Y |
| 12 Velázquez | Y | Y | Y | Y | N | N |
| 13 **Fossella** | N | N | N | Y | Y | N |
| 14 Maloney | Y | Y | Y | Y | N | Y |
| 15 Rangel | Y | Y | Y | Y | N | Y |
| 16 Serrano | Y | Y | Y | Y | N | Y |
| 17 Engel | Y | Y | Y | Y | N | Y |
| 18 Lowey | Y | Y | Y | Y | N | Y |
| 19 **Kelly** | N | N | N | Y | Y | Y |
| 20 **Sweeney** | N | N | N | Y | Y | N |
| 21 McNulty | Y | Y | Y | Y | N | N |
| 22 Hinchey | Y | Y | Y | Y | N | Y |
| 23 **McHugh** | N | N | N | Y | Y | Y |
| 24 **Boehlert** | N | N | N | Y | Y | Y |
| 25 **Walsh** | N | N | N | Y | Y | Y |
| 26 **Reynolds** | N | N | N | Y | Y | Y |
| 27 Higgins | Y | Y | Y | Y | N | Y |
| 28 Slaughter | Y | Y | Y | Y | N | N |
| 29 **Kuhl** | N | N | N | Y | Y | Y |

| | 482 | 483 | 484 | 485 | 486 | 487 |
|---|---|---|---|---|---|---|
| **NORTH CAROLINA** | | | | | | |
| 1 Butterfield | Y | Y | Y | Y | N | Y |
| 2 Etheridge | Y | Y | Y | Y | N | Y |
| 3 **Jones** | Y | N | N | N | Y | Y |
| 4 Price | Y | Y | Y | Y | N | Y |
| 5 **Foxx** | N | N | N | N | Y | Y |
| 6 **Coble** | N | Y | N | Y | Y | Y |
| 7 McIntyre | Y | Y | Y | Y | N | Y |
| 8 **Hayes** | N | N | N | Y | Y | Y |
| 9 **Myrick** | N | N | N | N | Y | Y |
| 10 **McHenry** | N | N | N | N | Y | Y |
| 11 **Taylor** | N | N | N | Y | Y | Y |
| 12 Watt | Y | Y | Y | Y | N | Y |
| 13 Miller | Y | Y | Y | Y | N | Y |
| **NORTH DAKOTA** | | | | | | |
| AL Pomeroy | Y | Y | Y | Y | N | Y |
| **OHIO** | | | | | | |
| 1 **Chabot** | N | N | N | Y | Y | Y |
| 2 **Schmidt** | N | N | N | Y | Y | Y |
| 3 **Turner** | N | N | N | Y | Y | Y |
| 4 **Oxley** | N | N | N | Y | Y | Y |
| 5 **Gillmor** | N | N | N | Y | Y | Y |
| 6 Strickland | Y | Y | Y | Y | N | Y |
| 7 **Hobson** | N | N | N | Y | Y | Y |
| 8 **Boehner** | N | N | N | Y | Y | Y |
| 9 Kaptur | Y | Y | Y | Y | N | Y |
| 10 Kucinich | Y | Y | Y | Y | N | N |
| 11 Jones | Y | Y | Y | Y | N | Y |
| 12 **Tiberi** | N | N | N | Y | Y | N |
| 13 Brown | Y | Y | Y | Y | N | Y |
| 14 **LaTourette** | N | N | N | Y | Y | Y |
| 15 **Pryce** | N | N | N | Y | Y | Y |
| 16 **Regula** | N | N | N | Y | Y | Y |
| 17 Ryan | Y | Y | Y | Y | N | Y |
| 18 **Ney** | N | N | N | Y | Y | Y |
| **OKLAHOMA** | | | | | | |
| 1 **Sullivan** | N | N | N | Y | Y | Y |
| 2 Boren | Y | Y | Y | Y | N | Y |
| 3 **Lucas** | N | N | N | Y | Y | Y |
| 4 **Cole** | N | N | N | Y | Y | Y |
| 5 **Istook** | N | N | N | Y | Y | Y |
| **OREGON** | | | | | | |
| 1 Wu | Y | Y | Y | Y | N | N |
| 2 **Walden** | N | N | N | Y | Y | Y |
| 3 Blumenauer | Y | Y | Y | Y | N | Y |
| 4 DeFazio | Y | Y | N | Y | N | N |
| 5 Hooley | Y | Y | Y | Y | N | Y |
| **PENNSYLVANIA** | | | | | | |
| 1 Brady | Y | Y | Y | Y | N | N |
| 2 Fattah | Y | Y | Y | Y | ? | ? |
| 3 **English** | N | N | N | Y | Y | N |
| 4 **Hart** | N | N | N | Y | Y | N |
| 5 **Peterson** | Y | Y | N | Y | Y | Y |
| 6 **Gerlach** | N | N | N | Y | Y | Y |
| 7 **Weldon** | Y | N | N | Y | Y | Y |
| 8 **Fitzpatrick** | Y | N | N | Y | Y | N |
| 9 **Shuster** | N | N | N | Y | Y | Y |
| 10 **Sherwood** | N | N | N | Y | Y | N |
| 11 Kanjorski | Y | Y | Y | Y | N | Y |
| 12 Murtha | Y | Y | Y | Y | ? | ? |
| 13 Schwartz | Y | Y | Y | Y | N | Y |
| 14 Doyle | Y | Y | Y | Y | N | Y |
| 15 **Dent** | N | N | N | Y | Y | Y |
| 16 **Pitts** | N | N | N | Y | Y | Y |
| 17 Holden | Y | Y | Y | Y | N | Y |
| 18 **Murphy** | N | N | N | Y | Y | Y |
| 19 **Platts** | Y | N | N | Y | Y | Y |
| **RHODE ISLAND** | | | | | | |
| 1 Kennedy | Y | Y | Y | Y | N | Y |
| 2 Langevin | Y | Y | Y | Y | N | Y |
| **SOUTH CAROLINA** | | | | | | |
| 1 **Brown** | N | N | N | Y | Y | Y |
| 2 **Wilson** | N | N | N | Y | Y | Y |
| 3 **Barrett** | N | N | N | N | Y | Y |
| 4 **Inglis** | N | N | N | Y | Y | Y |
| 5 Spratt | Y | Y | Y | Y | N | Y |
| 6 Clyburn | Y | Y | Y | Y | N | Y |
| **SOUTH DAKOTA** | | | | | | |
| AL Herseth | Y | Y | Y | Y | N | Y |
| **TENNESSEE** | | | | | | |
| 1 **Jenkins** | N | N | N | Y | Y | Y |
| 2 **Duncan** | N | N | N | N | Y | Y |

| | 482 | 483 | 484 | 485 | 486 | 487 |
|---|---|---|---|---|---|---|
| 3 **Wamp** | N | N | N | Y | Y | Y |
| 4 Davis | Y | Y | Y | Y | N | Y |
| 5 Cooper | Y | Y | Y | Y | N | Y |
| 6 Gordon | Y | Y | Y | Y | N | Y |
| 7 **Blackburn** | N | N | N | Y | Y | Y |
| 8 Tanner | Y | Y | Y | Y | N | N |
| 9 Ford | Y | Y | Y | Y | N | N |
| **TEXAS** | | | | | | |
| 1 **Gohmert** | N | N | N | Y | Y | Y |
| 2 **Poe** | N | N | N | Y | ? | ? |
| 3 **Johnson, S.** | N | N | N | N | Y | Y |
| 4 **Hall** | N | N | N | Y | Y | Y |
| 5 **Hensarling** | N | N | N | N | Y | Y |
| 6 **Barton** | ? | ? | ? | ? | Y | Y |
| 7 **Culberson** | N | N | N | Y | Y | Y |
| 8 **Brady** | N | N | N | Y | ? | ? |
| 9 Green, A. | Y | Y | Y | Y | N | Y |
| 10 **McCaul** | N | N | N | Y | Y | Y |
| 11 **Conaway** | N | N | N | Y | Y | Y |
| 12 **Granger** | N | N | N | Y | Y | Y |
| 13 **Thornberry** | N | N | N | Y | Y | Y |
| 14 **Paul** | N | N | N | ? | Y | ? |
| 15 Hinojosa | Y | Y | Y | Y | ? | ? |
| 16 Reyes | Y | Y | Y | Y | N | Y |
| 17 Edwards | Y | Y | Y | Y | N | ? |
| 18 Jackson-Lee | Y | Y | Y | Y | ? | ? |
| 19 **Neugebauer** | N | N | N | Y | Y | Y |
| 20 Gonzalez | Y | Y | Y | Y | N | Y |
| 21 **Smith** | N | N | N | Y | Y | Y |
| 22 **DeLay** | ? | ? | ? | ? | ? | ? |
| 23 **Bonilla** | N | N | N | Y | Y | Y |
| 24 **Marchant** | N | N | N | N | Y | Y |
| 25 Doggett | Y | Y | Y | Y | N | Y |
| 26 **Burgess** | N | N | N | Y | Y | Y |
| 27 Ortiz | + | + | + | + | − | + |
| 28 Cuellar | Y | Y | Y | Y | N | Y |
| 29 Green, G. | Y | Y | Y | Y | + | + |
| 30 Johnson, E. | Y | Y | Y | Y | N | N |
| 31 **Carter** | ? | N | N | Y | Y | Y |
| 32 **Sessions** | N | N | N | Y | Y | Y |
| **UTAH** | | | | | | |
| 1 **Bishop** | N | N | N | Y | Y | Y |
| 2 Matheson | Y | Y | Y | Y | N | N |
| 3 **Cannon** | N | N | N | Y | Y | Y |
| **VERMONT** | | | | | | |
| AL *Sanders* | Y | Y | N | Y | N | Y |
| **VIRGINIA** | | | | | | |
| 1 **Davis, J.** | N | N | N | Y | Y | Y |
| 2 **Drake** | N | N | N | Y | Y | Y |
| 3 Scott | Y | Y | Y | Y | N | Y |
| 4 **Forbes** | N | N | N | Y | Y | Y |
| 5 **Goode** | Y | N | N | Y | Y | Y |
| 6 **Goodlatte** | N | N | N | Y | Y | Y |
| 7 **Cantor** | N | N | N | Y | Y | ? |
| 8 Moran | Y | Y | Y | Y | N | Y |
| 9 Boucher | Y | Y | Y | ? | N | Y |
| 10 **Wolf** | N | N | N | Y | Y | Y |
| 11 **Davis, T.** | N | Y | N | Y | Y | Y |
| **WASHINGTON** | | | | | | |
| 1 Inslee | Y | Y | Y | Y | N | Y |
| 2 Larsen | Y | Y | Y | Y | N | N |
| 3 Baird | Y | Y | Y | Y | N | N |
| 4 **Hastings** | N | N | N | Y | Y | Y |
| 5 **McMorris** | N | N | N | Y | + | Y |
| 6 Dicks | Y | Y | Y | Y | N | Y |
| 7 McDermott | Y | Y | Y | Y | N | N |
| 8 **Reichert** | N | N | N | Y | Y | Y |
| 9 Smith | Y | Y | Y | Y | N | Y |
| **WEST VIRGINIA** | | | | | | |
| 1 Mollohan | Y | Y | Y | Y | N | Y |
| 2 **Capito** | N | N | N | Y | Y | N |
| 3 Rahall | Y | Y | Y | Y | N | Y |
| **WISCONSIN** | | | | | | |
| 1 **Ryan** | N | N | N | Y | Y | Y |
| 2 Baldwin | Y | Y | Y | Y | N | N |
| 3 Kind | ? | ? | ? | ? | N | Y |
| 4 Moore | Y | Y | Y | Y | N | Y |
| 5 **Sensenbrenner** | N | N | N | Y | Y | Y |
| 6 **Petri** | N | N | N | Y | Y | Y |
| 7 Obey | Y | Y | Y | Y | N | Y |
| 8 **Green** | N | Y | N | Y | Y | Y |
| **WYOMING** | | | | | | |
| AL **Cubin** | N | N | N | Y | Y | Y |

# IN THE HOUSE | By Vote Number

**488.** **HR 2123. Head Start Reauthorization/Policy Councils.** Souder, R-Ind., amendment that would allow the policy councils of the Head Start program to approve or disapprove most program planning and operation activities along with the board of directors. Rejected 153-266: R 69-152; D 83-114 (ND 64-85, SD 19-29); I 1-0. Sept. 22, 2005.

**489.** **HR 2123. Head Start Reauthorization/Children with Disabilities.** Stearns, R-Fla., amendment that would provide staff and teacher training concerning children with disabilities. Adopted 411-0: R 217-0; D 193-0 (ND 148-0, SD 45-0); I 1-0. Sept. 22, 2005.

**490.** **HR 2123. Head Start Reauthorization/Outreach Program.** Davis, D-Ill., amendment that would direct the Health and Human Services Department to conduct an outreach program to train and recruit African-American and Latino-American men to become Head Start teachers. Adopted 401-14: R 204-14; D 196-0 (ND 148-0, SD 48-0); I 1-0. Sept. 22, 2005.

**491.** **HR 2123. Head Start Reauthorization/For-Profit Head Start Programs.** Musgrave, R-Colo., amendment that would allow for-profit Head Start programs that spend less than 15 percent of their grant money on administration to take as profit the difference between the 15 percent and the amount they actually spend. Rejected 175-241: R 175-44; D 0-196 (ND 0-148, SD 0-48); I 0-1. Sept. 22, 2005.

**492.** **HR 2123. Head Start Reauthorization/Religious Organizations.** Boehner, R-Ohio, amendment that would allow faith-based charities that operate Head Start programs to consider religion as a factor in hiring decisions. Adopted 220-196: R 210-9; D 10-186 (ND 3-145, SD 7-41); I 0-1. A "yea" was a vote in support of the president's position. Sept. 22, 2005.

**493.** **HR 2123. Head Start Reauthorization/Passage.** Passage of the bill that would reauthorize the Head Start program through fiscal 2011. It would authorize $6.8 billion for the program in fiscal 2006. Half of all Head Start teachers would be required to have at least a bachelor's degree by 2011. The bill would authorize the Health and Human Services Department (HHS) to conduct unscheduled reviews of Head Start programs and allow HHS to contract out monitoring activities to third parties. As amended, it would allow faith-based charities that operate Head Start programs to consider religion as a factor in hiring decisions. Passed 231-184: R 208-10; D 23-173 (ND 11-137, SD 12-36); I 0-1. A "yea" was a vote in support of the president's position. Sept. 22, 2005.

ND Northern Democrats, SD Southern Democrats
Southern states: Ala., Ark., Fla., Ga., Ky., La., Miss., N.C., Okla., S.C., Tenn., Texas, Va.

| | 488 | 489 | 490 | 491 | 492 | 493 |
|---|---|---|---|---|---|---|
| **ALABAMA** | | | | | | |
| 1 Bonner | N | Y | Y | Y | Y | Y |
| 2 Everett | N | Y | Y | Y | Y | Y |
| 3 Rogers | N | Y | Y | Y | Y | Y |
| 4 Aderholt | N | Y | Y | Y | Y | Y |
| 5 Cramer | Y | Y | Y | N | N | Y |
| 6 Bachus | N | Y | Y | Y | Y | Y |
| 7 Davis | N | Y | Y | N | N | N |
| **ALASKA** | | | | | | |
| AL Young | N | Y | Y | Y | Y | Y |
| **ARIZONA** | | | | | | |
| 1 Renzi | N | Y | Y | N | Y | Y |
| 2 Franks | Y | Y | N | Y | Y | Y |
| 3 Shadegg | Y | Y | N | Y | Y | Y |
| 4 Pastor | N | Y | Y | N | N | N |
| 5 Hayworth | Y | Y | Y | Y | Y | Y |
| 6 Flake | Y | Y | N | Y | Y | Y |
| 7 Grijalva | N | Y | Y | N | N | N |
| 8 Kolbe | N | Y | Y | Y | Y | Y |
| **ARKANSAS** | | | | | | |
| 1 Berry | N | Y | Y | N | N | N |
| 2 Snyder | N | Y | Y | N | N | N |
| 3 Boozman | Y | Y | Y | Y | Y | Y |
| 4 Ross | N | Y | Y | N | N | N |
| **CALIFORNIA** | | | | | | |
| 1 Thompson | N | Y | Y | N | N | N |
| 2 Herger | Y | Y | N | N | Y | Y |
| 3 Lungren | Y | Y | Y | Y | Y | Y |
| 4 Doolittle | Y | Y | Y | Y | Y | Y |
| 5 Matsui, D. | Y | Y | Y | N | N | N |
| 6 Woolsey | N | Y | Y | N | N | N |
| 7 Miller, George | N | Y | Y | N | N | N |
| 8 Pelosi | N | Y | Y | N | N | N |
| 9 Lee | Y | Y | Y | N | N | N |
| 10 Tauscher | N | Y | Y | N | N | N |
| 11 Pombo | N | Y | Y | Y | Y | Y |
| 12 Lantos | N | Y | Y | N | N | N |
| 13 Stark | N | Y | Y | N | N | N |
| 14 Eshoo | N | Y | Y | N | N | N |
| 15 Honda | N | Y | Y | N | N | N |
| 16 Lofgren | Y | Y | Y | N | N | N |
| 17 Farr | Y | Y | Y | N | N | N |
| 18 Cardoza | N | Y | Y | N | N | N |
| 19 Radanovich | Y | Y | Y | Y | Y | Y |
| 20 Costa | N | Y | Y | N | N | N |
| 21 Nunes | Y | Y | Y | Y | Y | Y |
| 22 Thomas | N | Y | Y | Y | Y | Y |
| 23 Capps | N | Y | Y | N | N | N |
| 24 Gallegly | N | Y | Y | Y | Y | Y |
| 25 McKeon | N | Y | Y | Y | Y | Y |
| 26 Dreier | N | Y | Y | Y | Y | Y |
| 27 Sherman | N | Y | Y | N | N | N |
| 28 Berman | N | Y | Y | N | N | N |
| 29 Schiff | Y | Y | Y | N | N | N |
| 30 Waxman | N | Y | Y | N | N | N |
| 31 Becerra | Y | Y | Y | N | N | N |
| 32 Solis | N | Y | Y | N | N | N |
| 33 Watson | N | Y | Y | N | N | N |
| 34 Roybal-Allard | Y | Y | Y | N | N | N |
| 35 Waters | Y | Y | Y | N | N | N |
| 36 Harman | N | Y | Y | N | N | N |
| 37 Millender-McD. | Y | Y | Y | N | N | N |
| 38 Napolitano | Y | Y | Y | N | N | N |
| 39 Sánchez, Linda | Y | Y | Y | N | N | N |
| 40 Royce | Y | Y | Y | Y | Y | Y |
| 41 Lewis | N | Y | Y | Y | Y | Y |
| 42 Miller, Gary | Y | Y | Y | Y | Y | Y |
| 43 Baca | Y | Y | Y | N | N | N |
| 44 Calvert | N | Y | Y | Y | Y | Y |
| 45 Bono | N | Y | Y | Y | Y | Y |
| 46 Rohrabacher | Y | Y | Y | Y | Y | Y |
| 47 Sanchez, Loretta | Y | Y | Y | N | N | N |
| 48 Vacant | | | | | | |
| 49 Issa | N | Y | Y | Y | Y | Y |

| | 488 | 489 | 490 | 491 | 492 | 493 |
|---|---|---|---|---|---|---|
| 50 Cunningham | N | Y | Y | Y | Y | Y |
| 51 Filner | Y | Y | Y | N | N | N |
| 52 Hunter | N | Y | Y | Y | Y | Y |
| 53 Davis | N | Y | Y | N | N | N |
| **COLORADO** | | | | | | |
| 1 DeGette | N | Y | Y | N | N | N |
| 2 Udall | Y | Y | Y | N | N | Y |
| 3 Salazar | N | Y | Y | N | N | N |
| 4 Musgrave | Y | Y | Y | Y | Y | Y |
| 5 Hefley | ? | ? | ? | ? | ? | ? |
| 6 Tancredo | Y | Y | Y | Y | Y | N |
| 7 Beauprez | N | Y | Y | Y | Y | Y |
| **CONNECTICUT** | | | | | | |
| 1 Larson | Y | Y | Y | N | N | N |
| 2 Simmons | Y | Y | Y | N | N | Y |
| 3 DeLauro | Y | Y | Y | N | N | N |
| 4 Shays | N | Y | Y | N | N | Y |
| 5 Johnson | Y | ? | Y | N | N | Y |
| **DELAWARE** | | | | | | |
| AL Castle | N | Y | Y | N | Y | Y |
| **FLORIDA** | | | | | | |
| 1 Miller | Y | Y | Y | Y | Y | Y |
| 2 Boyd | N | Y | Y | N | N | N |
| 3 Brown | Y | Y | Y | N | N | N |
| 4 Crenshaw | N | Y | Y | Y | Y | Y |
| 5 Brown-Waite | N | Y | Y | Y | Y | Y |
| 6 Stearns | Y | Y | Y | Y | Y | Y |
| 7 Mica | N | Y | Y | N | Y | Y |
| 8 Keller | Y | Y | Y | N | Y | Y |
| 9 Bilirakis | Y | Y | Y | N | Y | Y |
| 10 Young | N | ? | Y | Y | Y | Y |
| 11 Davis | N | Y | Y | N | N | N |
| 12 Putnam | N | Y | Y | Y | Y | Y |
| 13 Harris | N | Y | Y | Y | Y | Y |
| 14 Mack | N | Y | Y | Y | Y | Y |
| 15 Weldon | Y | Y | Y | Y | Y | Y |
| 16 Foley | N | Y | Y | Y | Y | Y |
| 17 Meek | N | Y | Y | N | N | N |
| 18 Ros-Lehtinen | N | Y | Y | Y | Y | Y |
| 19 Wexler | N | Y | Y | N | N | N |
| 20 Wasserman-Schultz | N | Y | Y | N | N | N |
| 21 Diaz-Balart, L. | N | Y | ? | Y | Y | Y |
| 22 Shaw | Y | Y | Y | Y | Y | Y |
| 23 Hastings | N | Y | Y | N | N | N |
| 24 Feeney | Y | Y | Y | Y | Y | Y |
| 25 Diaz-Balart, M. | N | Y | Y | Y | Y | Y |
| **GEORGIA** | | | | | | |
| 1 Kingston | N | Y | Y | Y | Y | Y |
| 2 Bishop | Y | Y | Y | N | N | N |
| 3 Marshall | Y | Y | Y | N | Y | N |
| 4 McKinney | Y | Y | Y | N | N | N |
| 5 Lewis | Y | Y | Y | N | N | N |
| 6 Price | N | Y | N | Y | Y | Y |
| 7 Linder | N | Y | Y | Y | Y | Y |
| 8 Westmoreland | N | Y | Y | Y | Y | Y |
| 9 Norwood | N | Y | Y | Y | Y | Y |
| 10 Deal | N | Y | Y | Y | Y | Y |
| 11 Gingrey | N | Y | Y | Y | Y | Y |
| 12 Barrow | Y | Y | Y | N | Y | Y |
| 13 Scott | Y | Y | Y | N | N | N |
| **HAWAII** | | | | | | |
| 1 Abercrombie | N | Y | Y | N | N | N |
| 2 Case | Y | Y | Y | N | Y | Y |
| **IDAHO** | | | | | | |
| 1 Otter | Y | Y | Y | Y | Y | Y |
| 2 Simpson | N | Y | Y | Y | Y | Y |
| **ILLINOIS** | | | | | | |
| 1 Rush | N | Y | Y | N | N | N |
| 2 Jackson | N | Y | Y | N | N | N |
| 3 Lipinski | Y | Y | Y | N | N | N |
| 4 Gutierrez | Y | Y | Y | N | N | N |
| 5 Emanuel | Y | Y | Y | N | N | N |
| 6 Hyde | N | Y | Y | Y | Y | Y |
| 7 Davis | Y | Y | Y | N | N | N |
| 8 Bean | N | Y | Y | N | Y | Y |
| 9 Schakowsky | Y | ? | Y | N | N | N |
| 10 Kirk | N | Y | Y | N | Y | Y |
| 11 Weller | ? | ? | ? | ? | ? | ? |
| 12 Costello | Y | Y | Y | N | N | N |

**KEY**   Republicans   Democrats   *Independents*

| | | |
|---|---|---|
| Y Voted for (yea) | X Paired against | C Voted "present" to avoid possible conflict of interest |
| # Paired for | – Announced against | |
| + Announced for | P Voted "present" | ? Did not vote or otherwise make a position known |
| N Voted against (nay) | | |

| | 488 | 489 | 490 | 491 | 492 | 493 |
|---|---|---|---|---|---|---|
| 13 **Biggert** | Y | Y | Y | N | Y | Y |
| 14 **Hastert** | | | | | | |
| 15 **Johnson** | Y | Y | Y | Y | Y | Y |
| 16 **Manzullo** | Y | Y | Y | Y | Y | N |
| 17 Evans | Y | Y | Y | N | N | N |
| 18 **LaHood** | N | Y | Y | N | Y | N |
| 19 **Shimkus** | N | Y | Y | N | Y | Y |
| **INDIANA** | | | | | | |
| 1 Visclosky | Y | Y | Y | N | N | N |
| 2 **Chocola** | N | Y | Y | Y | Y | Y |
| 3 **Souder** | Y | Y | Y | Y | Y | Y |
| 4 **Buyer** | ? | ? | ? | ? | ? | ? |
| 5 **Burton** | Y | Y | Y | Y | Y | Y |
| 6 **Pence** | Y | Y | Y | Y | Y | Y |
| 7 Carson | N | Y | Y | N | N | N |
| 8 **Hostettler** | Y | Y | Y | Y | Y | Y |
| 9 **Sodrel** | Y | Y | Y | Y | Y | Y |
| **IOWA** | | | | | | |
| 1 **Nussle** | N | Y | Y | Y | Y | Y |
| 2 **Leach** | N | Y | Y | N | N | N |
| 3 Boswell | ? | ? | ? | ? | ? | ? |
| 4 **Latham** | N | Y | Y | Y | Y | Y |
| 5 **King** | N | Y | N | Y | Y | Y |
| **KANSAS** | | | | | | |
| 1 **Moran** | Y | Y | Y | Y | Y | Y |
| 2 **Ryun** | Y | Y | Y | Y | Y | Y |
| 3 Moore | Y | Y | Y | N | N | N |
| 4 **Tiahrt** | Y | Y | Y | Y | Y | Y |
| **KENTUCKY** | | | | | | |
| 1 **Whitfield** | Y | Y | Y | Y | Y | Y |
| 2 **Lewis** | Y | Y | Y | Y | Y | Y |
| 3 **Northup** | N | Y | Y | Y | Y | Y |
| 4 **Davis** | N | Y | Y | Y | Y | Y |
| 5 **Rogers** | Y | Y | Y | Y | Y | Y |
| 6 Chandler | Y | Y | Y | N | Y | Y |
| **LOUISIANA** | | | | | | |
| 1 **Jindal** | N | Y | Y | Y | Y | Y |
| 2 Jefferson | Y | Y | Y | N | N | N |
| 3 Melancon | Y | ? | Y | N | N | N |
| 4 **McCrery** | N | Y | Y | Y | Y | Y |
| 5 **Alexander** | N | Y | Y | Y | Y | Y |
| 6 **Baker** | N | Y | ? | ? | ? | ? |
| 7 **Boustany** | – | + | + | + | + | + |
| **MAINE** | | | | | | |
| 1 Allen | N | Y | Y | N | N | N |
| 2 Michaud | N | Y | Y | N | N | N |
| **MARYLAND** | | | | | | |
| 1 **Gilchrest** | N | Y | Y | Y | Y | Y |
| 2 Ruppersberger | N | Y | Y | N | N | N |
| 3 Cardin | Y | Y | Y | N | N | N |
| 4 Wynn | Y | Y | Y | N | N | N |
| 5 Hoyer | N | Y | Y | N | N | N |
| 6 **Bartlett** | Y | Y | Y | Y | Y | N |
| 7 Cummings | Y | Y | Y | N | N | N |
| 8 Van Hollen | Y | Y | Y | N | N | N |
| **MASSACHUSETTS** | | | | | | |
| 1 Olver | N | Y | Y | N | N | N |
| 2 Neal | N | Y | Y | N | N | N |
| 3 McGovern | N | Y | Y | N | N | N |
| 4 Frank | N | Y | Y | N | N | N |
| 5 Meehan | N | Y | Y | N | N | N |
| 6 Tierney | N | Y | Y | N | N | N |
| 7 Markey | N | Y | Y | N | N | N |
| 8 Capuano | Y | Y | Y | N | N | N |
| 9 Lynch | Y | Y | ? | ? | ? | ? |
| 10 Delahunt | N | Y | Y | N | N | N |
| **MICHIGAN** | | | | | | |
| 1 Stupak | N | Y | Y | N | N | N |
| 2 **Hoekstra** | Y | Y | Y | Y | Y | Y |
| 3 **Ehlers** | N | Y | Y | Y | Y | Y |
| 4 **Camp** | ? | ? | ? | ? | ? | ? |
| 5 Kildee | N | Y | Y | N | N | N |
| 6 **Upton** | N | Y | Y | N | Y | Y |
| 7 **Schwarz** | N | Y | Y | N | N | Y |
| 8 **Rogers** | N | Y | Y | N | Y | Y |
| 9 **Knollenberg** | N | Y | Y | Y | Y | Y |
| 10 **Miller** | N | Y | Y | Y | Y | Y |
| 11 **McCotter** | N | Y | Y | N | Y | Y |
| 12 Levin | N | Y | Y | N | N | N |
| 13 Kilpatrick | N | Y | Y | N | N | N |
| 14 Conyers | N | Y | Y | N | N | N |
| 15 Dingell | N | Y | Y | N | N | N |

| | 488 | 489 | 490 | 491 | 492 | 493 |
|---|---|---|---|---|---|---|
| **MINNESOTA** | | | | | | |
| 1 **Gutknecht** | Y | Y | Y | Y | Y | Y |
| 2 **Kline** | N | Y | Y | Y | Y | Y |
| 3 **Ramstad** | Y | Y | Y | N | Y | Y |
| 4 McCollum | N | Y | Y | N | N | N |
| 5 Sabo | Y | Y | Y | N | N | N |
| 6 **Kennedy** | Y | Y | Y | Y | Y | Y |
| 7 Peterson | Y | Y | Y | N | Y | N |
| 8 Oberstar | Y | Y | Y | N | N | N |
| **MISSISSIPPI** | | | | | | |
| 1 **Wicker** | N | Y | Y | Y | Y | Y |
| 2 Thompson | N | Y | Y | N | N | N |
| 3 **Pickering** | N | Y | Y | Y | Y | Y |
| 4 Taylor | N | Y | Y | N | Y | Y |
| **MISSOURI** | | | | | | |
| 1 Clay | N | Y | Y | N | N | N |
| 2 **Akin** | Y | Y | Y | Y | Y | Y |
| 3 Carnahan | N | Y | Y | N | N | N |
| 4 Skelton | N | Y | Y | N | N | Y |
| 5 Cleaver | N | Y | Y | N | N | N |
| 6 **Graves** | N | Y | Y | Y | Y | Y |
| 7 **Blunt** | N | Y | N | Y | Y | Y |
| 8 **Emerson** | N | Y | Y | N | Y | Y |
| 9 **Hulshof** | Y | Y | Y | N | Y | Y |
| **MONTANA** | | | | | | |
| AL **Rehberg** | N | Y | Y | Y | Y | Y |
| **NEBRASKA** | | | | | | |
| 1 **Fortenberry** | N | Y | Y | Y | Y | Y |
| 2 **Terry** | N | Y | Y | N | Y | Y |
| 3 **Osborne** | N | Y | Y | N | Y | Y |
| **NEVADA** | | | | | | |
| 1 Berkley | N | Y | Y | N | N | N |
| 2 **Gibbons** | Y | Y | Y | Y | Y | Y |
| 3 **Porter** | N | Y | Y | N | Y | Y |
| **NEW HAMPSHIRE** | | | | | | |
| 1 **Bradley** | N | Y | Y | N | N | Y |
| 2 **Bass** | N | Y | Y | N | Y | Y |
| **NEW JERSEY** | | | | | | |
| 1 Andrews | N | Y | Y | N | N | N |
| 2 **LoBiondo** | N | Y | Y | N | Y | Y |
| 3 **Saxton** | N | Y | Y | N | Y | Y |
| 4 **Smith** | Y | Y | Y | Y | Y | ? |
| 5 **Garrett** | Y | Y | Y | Y | Y | Y |
| 6 Pallone | Y | Y | Y | N | N | N |
| 7 **Ferguson** | N | Y | Y | Y | Y | Y |
| 8 Pascrell | N | Y | Y | N | N | N |
| 9 Rothman | Y | Y | Y | N | N | N |
| 10 Payne | Y | Y | Y | N | N | N |
| 11 **Frelinghuysen** | Y | Y | Y | N | Y | Y |
| 12 Holt | Y | Y | Y | N | N | N |
| 13 Menendez | Y | Y | Y | N | N | N |
| **NEW MEXICO** | | | | | | |
| 1 **Wilson** | N | Y | Y | Y | Y | Y |
| 2 **Pearce** | N | Y | Y | Y | Y | Y |
| 3 Udall | Y | Y | Y | N | N | N |
| **NEW YORK** | | | | | | |
| 1 Bishop | N | Y | Y | N | N | N |
| 2 Israel | Y | Y | Y | N | N | N |
| 3 **King** | N | Y | Y | Y | Y | Y |
| 4 McCarthy | N | Y | Y | N | N | N |
| 5 Ackerman | N | Y | Y | N | N | N |
| 6 Meeks | Y | Y | Y | N | N | N |
| 7 Crowley | Y | Y | Y | N | N | N |
| 8 Nadler | Y | Y | Y | N | N | N |
| 9 Weiner | Y | Y | Y | N | N | N |
| 10 Towns | Y | Y | Y | N | N | N |
| 11 Owens | N | Y | Y | N | N | N |
| 12 Velázquez | Y | Y | Y | N | N | N |
| 13 **Fossella** | N | Y | Y | Y | Y | Y |
| 14 Maloney | Y | Y | Y | N | N | N |
| 15 Rangel | N | Y | Y | N | N | N |
| 16 Serrano | Y | Y | Y | N | N | N |
| 17 Engel | N | Y | Y | N | N | N |
| 18 Lowey | Y | Y | Y | N | N | N |
| 19 **Kelly** | N | Y | Y | N | N | Y |
| 20 **Sweeney** | N | Y | Y | N | Y | Y |
| 21 McNulty | Y | Y | Y | N | N | N |
| 22 Hinchey | N | Y | Y | N | N | N |
| 23 **McHugh** | N | Y | Y | N | N | Y |
| 24 **Boehlert** | N | Y | Y | N | Y | Y |
| 25 **Walsh** | N | ? | Y | N | Y | Y |
| 26 **Reynolds** | N | Y | Y | Y | Y | Y |
| 27 Higgins | N | Y | Y | N | N | N |
| 28 Slaughter | N | Y | Y | N | N | N |
| 29 **Kuhl** | N | Y | Y | N | Y | Y |

| | 488 | 489 | 490 | 491 | 492 | 493 |
|---|---|---|---|---|---|---|
| **NORTH CAROLINA** | | | | | | |
| 1 Butterfield | N | Y | Y | N | N | N |
| 2 Etheridge | Y | Y | Y | N | N | N |
| 3 **Jones** | Y | Y | Y | Y | Y | N |
| 4 Price | N | Y | Y | N | N | N |
| 5 **Foxx** | Y | Y | Y | Y | Y | Y |
| 6 **Coble** | N | Y | Y | Y | Y | Y |
| 7 McIntyre | N | Y | Y | N | Y | Y |
| 8 **Hayes** | N | Y | Y | Y | Y | Y |
| 9 **Myrick** | N | ? | N | Y | Y | Y |
| 10 **McHenry** | Y | Y | N | Y | Y | Y |
| 11 **Taylor** | Y | Y | Y | Y | Y | Y |
| 12 Watt | Y | ? | Y | N | N | N |
| 13 Miller | N | Y | Y | N | N | N |
| **NORTH DAKOTA** | | | | | | |
| AL Pomeroy | N | Y | Y | N | N | N |
| **OHIO** | | | | | | |
| 1 **Chabot** | Y | Y | Y | Y | Y | Y |
| 2 **Schmidt** | N | Y | Y | Y | Y | Y |
| 3 **Turner** | N | Y | Y | Y | Y | Y |
| 4 **Oxley** | N | Y | Y | Y | Y | Y |
| 5 **Gillmor** | N | Y | Y | Y | Y | Y |
| 6 Strickland | Y | Y | Y | N | N | N |
| 7 **Hobson** | N | Y | Y | Y | Y | Y |
| 8 **Boehner** | N | Y | Y | Y | Y | Y |
| 9 Kaptur | N | Y | Y | N | N | N |
| 10 Kucinich | N | Y | Y | N | N | N |
| 11 Jones | Y | Y | Y | N | N | N |
| 12 **Tiberi** | N | Y | Y | Y | Y | Y |
| 13 Brown | N | Y | Y | N | N | N |
| 14 **LaTourette** | N | Y | Y | N | Y | Y |
| 15 **Pryce** | N | Y | Y | Y | Y | Y |
| 16 **Regula** | N | Y | Y | N | Y | Y |
| 17 Ryan | N | Y | Y | N | N | N |
| 18 **Ney** | N | Y | Y | N | Y | Y |
| **OKLAHOMA** | | | | | | |
| 1 **Sullivan** | N | Y | Y | Y | Y | Y |
| 2 Boren | N | Y | Y | N | Y | Y |
| 3 **Lucas** | N | Y | Y | Y | Y | Y |
| 4 **Cole** | N | Y | Y | Y | Y | Y |
| 5 **Istook** | N | Y | Y | Y | Y | Y |
| **OREGON** | | | | | | |
| 1 Wu | Y | Y | Y | N | N | Y |
| 2 **Walden** | N | Y | Y | N | Y | Y |
| 3 Blumenauer | Y | Y | Y | N | N | N |
| 4 DeFazio | Y | Y | Y | N | N | N |
| 5 Hooley | N | Y | Y | N | N | N |
| **PENNSYLVANIA** | | | | | | |
| 1 Brady | N | Y | Y | N | N | N |
| 2 Fattah | N | Y | Y | N | N | N |
| 3 **English** | Y | Y | Y | Y | Y | Y |
| 4 **Hart** | N | Y | Y | N | Y | Y |
| 5 **Peterson** | N | Y | Y | ? | Y | Y |
| 6 **Gerlach** | N | Y | Y | N | Y | Y |
| 7 **Weldon** | N | Y | Y | N | Y | Y |
| 8 **Fitzpatrick** | Y | Y | Y | N | Y | Y |
| 9 **Shuster** | N | Y | Y | Y | Y | Y |
| 10 **Sherwood** | N | Y | Y | N | Y | Y |
| 11 Kanjorski | N | Y | Y | N | N | N |
| 12 Murtha | N | Y | Y | N | N | N |
| 13 Schwartz | N | Y | Y | N | N | N |
| 14 Doyle | N | Y | Y | N | N | N |
| 15 **Dent** | Y | Y | Y | N | Y | Y |
| 16 **Pitts** | N | Y | Y | Y | Y | Y |
| 17 Holden | Y | Y | Y | N | N | Y |
| 18 **Murphy** | N | Y | Y | N | Y | Y |
| 19 **Platts** | Y | Y | Y | N | Y | Y |
| **RHODE ISLAND** | | | | | | |
| 1 Kennedy | Y | Y | Y | N | N | N |
| 2 Langevin | Y | Y | Y | N | N | N |
| **SOUTH CAROLINA** | | | | | | |
| 1 **Brown** | N | Y | Y | Y | Y | Y |
| 2 **Wilson** | N | Y | Y | Y | Y | Y |
| 3 **Barrett** | N | Y | Y | Y | Y | Y |
| 4 **Inglis** | N | Y | Y | Y | Y | Y |
| 5 Spratt | N | Y | Y | N | N | N |
| 6 Clyburn | N | Y | Y | N | N | N |
| **SOUTH DAKOTA** | | | | | | |
| AL Herseth | N | Y | Y | N | N | Y |
| **TENNESSEE** | | | | | | |
| 1 **Jenkins** | N | Y | Y | Y | Y | Y |
| 2 **Duncan** | Y | Y | Y | Y | Y | N |

| | 488 | 489 | 490 | 491 | 492 | 493 |
|---|---|---|---|---|---|---|
| 3 **Wamp** | Y | Y | Y | Y | Y | Y |
| 4 Davis | N | Y | Y | N | Y | Y |
| 5 Cooper | N | Y | Y | N | N | N |
| 6 Gordon | N | Y | Y | N | N | Y |
| 7 **Blackburn** | N | Y | Y | Y | Y | Y |
| 8 Tanner | Y | Y | Y | N | N | N |
| 9 Ford | N | Y | Y | N | N | Y |
| **TEXAS** | | | | | | |
| 1 **Gohmert** | N | Y | Y | Y | ? | ? |
| 2 **Poe** | ? | ? | ? | ? | ? | ? |
| 3 **Johnson, S.** | N | Y | N | Y | Y | Y |
| 4 **Hall** | N | Y | N | Y | Y | Y |
| 5 **Hensarling** | Y | Y | Y | Y | Y | Y |
| 6 **Barton** | N | Y | Y | Y | Y | Y |
| 7 **Culberson** | Y | Y | Y | Y | Y | N |
| 8 **Brady** | ? | ? | ? | ? | ? | ? |
| 9 Green, A. | Y | Y | Y | N | N | N |
| 10 **McCaul** | N | Y | Y | Y | Y | Y |
| 11 **Conaway** | N | Y | Y | Y | Y | Y |
| 12 **Granger** | N | Y | Y | Y | Y | Y |
| 13 **Thornberry** | N | Y | Y | Y | Y | Y |
| 14 **Paul** | Y | Y | Y | Y | Y | N |
| 15 Hinojosa | ? | ? | ? | ? | ? | ? |
| 16 Reyes | N | Y | Y | N | N | N |
| 17 Edwards | N | ? | Y | N | N | Y |
| 18 Jackson-Lee | Y | Y | Y | N | N | N |
| 19 **Neugebauer** | N | Y | Y | Y | Y | Y |
| 20 Gonzalez | Y | Y | Y | N | N | N |
| 21 **Smith** | N | Y | Y | Y | Y | Y |
| 22 **DeLay** | ? | ? | ? | ? | ? | ? |
| 23 **Bonilla** | N | Y | Y | Y | Y | Y |
| 24 **Marchant** | N | Y | N | Y | Y | Y |
| 25 Doggett | N | Y | Y | N | N | N |
| 26 **Burgess** | N | Y | Y | Y | Y | Y |
| 27 Ortiz | + | + | + | – | – | – |
| 28 Cuellar | Y | Y | Y | N | N | Y |
| 29 Green, G. | + | + | + | – | – | + |
| 30 Johnson, E. | Y | Y | Y | N | N | N |
| 31 **Carter** | N | Y | N | Y | Y | Y |
| 32 **Sessions** | N | Y | N | Y | Y | Y |
| **UTAH** | | | | | | |
| 1 **Bishop** | Y | Y | Y | Y | Y | Y |
| 2 Matheson | Y | Y | Y | N | N | N |
| 3 **Cannon** | Y | Y | Y | Y | Y | Y |
| **VERMONT** | | | | | | |
| AL *Sanders* | Y | Y | Y | N | N | N |
| **VIRGINIA** | | | | | | |
| 1 **Davis, J.** | Y | Y | Y | Y | Y | Y |
| 2 **Drake** | N | Y | Y | Y | Y | Y |
| 3 Scott | Y | Y | Y | N | N | N |
| 4 **Forbes** | Y | Y | Y | Y | Y | Y |
| 5 **Goode** | Y | Y | ? | Y | Y | Y |
| 6 **Goodlatte** | N | Y | Y | Y | Y | Y |
| 7 **Cantor** | N | Y | Y | Y | Y | Y |
| 8 Moran | N | Y | Y | N | N | N |
| 9 Boucher | N | Y | Y | N | N | N |
| 10 **Wolf** | N | Y | Y | Y | Y | Y |
| 11 **Davis, T.** | N | Y | Y | Y | Y | Y |
| **WASHINGTON** | | | | | | |
| 1 Inslee | Y | Y | Y | N | N | N |
| 2 Larsen | N | Y | Y | N | N | N |
| 3 Baird | Y | Y | Y | N | N | N |
| 4 **Hastings** | ? | ? | ? | ? | ? | ? |
| 5 **McMorris** | N | Y | Y | Y | Y | Y |
| 6 Dicks | N | Y | Y | N | N | N |
| 7 McDermott | N | Y | Y | N | N | N |
| 8 **Reichert** | N | Y | Y | Y | Y | Y |
| 9 Smith | N | Y | Y | N | N | N |
| **WEST VIRGINIA** | | | | | | |
| 1 Mollohan | N | Y | Y | N | Y | Y |
| 2 **Capito** | Y | Y | Y | N | Y | Y |
| 3 Rahall | N | Y | Y | N | N | N |
| **WISCONSIN** | | | | | | |
| 1 **Ryan** | N | Y | Y | Y | Y | Y |
| 2 Baldwin | N | Y | Y | N | N | N |
| 3 Kind | ? | ? | ? | ? | ? | ? |
| 4 Moore | Y | Y | Y | N | N | N |
| 5 **Sensenbrenner** | N | Y | Y | Y | Y | Y |
| 6 **Petri** | N | Y | Y | Y | Y | Y |
| 7 Obey | N | Y | Y | N | N | N |
| 8 **Green** | N | Y | Y | Y | Y | Y |
| **WYOMING** | | | | | | |
| AL **Cubin** | Y | Y | Y | Y | Y | Y |

## IN THE HOUSE | By Vote Number

**494.** H J Res 66. After-School Programs/Passage. Ehlers, R-Mich., motion to suspend the rules and pass the joint resolution that would support the goals and ideals of "Lights on Afterschool!"and call on the president to issue a proclamation requesting that communities nationwide institute after-school programs. Motion agreed to 403-0: R 222-0; D 180-0 (ND 135-0, SD 45-0); I 1-0. A two-thirds majority of those present and voting (269 in this case) is required for passage under suspension of the rules. Sept. 27, 2005.

**495.** HR 438. Maudelle Shirek Post Office/Passage. Brown-Waite, R-Fla., motion to suspend the rules and pass the bill that would designate a post office in Berkeley, Calif., for Maudelle Shirek, who was active in the movements for civil rights and the rights of unions and their workers. Motion rejected 190-215: R 9-212; D 180-3 (ND 138-0, SD 42-3); I 1-0. A two-thirds majority of those present and voting (270 in this case) is required for passage under suspension of the rules. Sept. 27, 2005.

**496.** H Con Res 209. Domestic Violence Awareness Month/Adoption. Brown-Waite, R-Fla., motion to suspend the rules and adopt the concurrent resolution that would support the goals and ideals of National Domestic Violence Awareness Month. Motion agreed to 404-0: R 221-0; D 182-0 (ND 138-0, SD 44-0); I 1-0. A two-thirds majority of those present and voting (270 in this case) is required for adoption under suspension of the rules. Sept. 27, 2005.

**497.** HR 2360. Fiscal 2006 Homeland Security Appropriations/Motion to Instruct. Sabo, D-Minn., motion to instruct House conferees to include language that would insist that the Homeland Security secretary delay a proposal to reorganize the department's existing preparedness functions under a new preparedness directorate while making the Federal Emergency Management Agency a separate office focused on recovery and response. Motion rejected 196-227: R 0-226; D 195-1 (ND 147-0, SD 48-1); I 1-0. Sept. 28, 2005.

**498.** HR 3402. Justice Department Authorization/Rule. Adoption of the rule (H Res 462) to provide for House floor consideration of the bill that would reauthorize funds for the Justice Department for fiscal 2006 through 2009. Adopted 330-89: R 224-0; D 105-89 (ND 70-75, SD 35-14); I 1-0. Sept. 28, 2005.

**499.** HR 3402. Justice Department Reauthorization/Manager's Amendment. Sensenbrenner, R-Wis., amendment that would authorize $7.5 million per year in fiscal 2006 through 2010 for grants to assist state and local law enforcement agencies in prosecuting child abuse cases. It also would encourage the chief justice of each U.S. District Court to respond to requests by state and local courts to make federal facilities available for the proceedings of courts whose operations have been "significantly disrupted" by hurricanes Katrina or Rita. Adopted 225-191: R 220-5; D 5-185 (ND 1-140, SD 4-45); I 0-1. Sept. 28, 2005.

ND Northern Democrats, SD Southern Democrats
Southern states: Ala., Ark., Fla., Ga., Ky., La., Miss., N.C., Okla., S.C., Tenn., Texas, Va.

| | 494 | 495 | 496 | 497 | 498 | 499 |
|---|---|---|---|---|---|---|
| **ALABAMA** | | | | | | |
| 1 Bonner | Y | N | Y | N | Y | Y |
| 2 Everett | Y | N | Y | N | Y | Y |
| 3 Rogers | Y | N | Y | N | Y | Y |
| 4 Aderholt | Y | N | Y | N | Y | Y |
| 5 Cramer | Y | N | Y | Y | N | Y |
| 6 Bachus | Y | N | Y | N | Y | Y |
| 7 Davis | Y | Y | Y | Y | Y | N |
| **ALASKA** | | | | | | |
| AL Young | Y | N | Y | N | Y | Y |
| **ARIZONA** | | | | | | |
| 1 Renzi | Y | N | Y | N | ? | Y |
| 2 Franks | Y | N | Y | N | Y | Y |
| 3 Shadegg | ? | ? | ? | N | Y | Y |
| 4 Pastor | Y | Y | Y | Y | N | N |
| 5 Hayworth | Y | N | Y | N | Y | Y |
| 6 Flake | Y | N | Y | N | Y | Y |
| 7 Grijalva | + | + | + | Y | N | N |
| 8 Kolbe | Y | N | Y | N | Y | Y |
| **ARKANSAS** | | | | | | |
| 1 Berry | Y | Y | Y | Y | N | N |
| 2 Snyder | Y | Y | Y | Y | Y | N |
| 3 Boozman | Y | N | Y | N | Y | Y |
| 4 Ross | Y | Y | Y | Y | Y | N |
| **CALIFORNIA** | | | | | | |
| 1 Thompson | Y | Y | Y | Y | N | N |
| 2 Herger | Y | N | Y | N | Y | Y |
| 3 Lungren | Y | N | Y | N | Y | Y |
| 4 Doolittle | Y | N | Y | N | Y | Y |
| 5 Matsui, D. | Y | Y | Y | Y | N | N |
| 6 Woolsey | Y | Y | Y | Y | N | N |
| 7 Miller, George | Y | Y | Y | Y | N | N |
| 8 Pelosi | Y | Y | Y | Y | ? | N |
| 9 Lee | Y | Y | Y | Y | N | N |
| 10 Tauscher | Y | Y | Y | Y | N | ? |
| 11 Pombo | Y | ? | Y | N | Y | Y |
| 12 Lantos | Y | Y | Y | Y | N | N |
| 13 Stark | Y | Y | Y | Y | N | N |
| 14 Eshoo | Y | Y | Y | Y | N | N |
| 15 Honda | Y | Y | Y | Y | N | N |
| 16 Lofgren | Y | Y | Y | Y | N | N |
| 17 Farr | Y | Y | Y | Y | N | N |
| 18 Cardoza | Y | Y | Y | Y | Y | N |
| 19 Radanovich | Y | N | Y | N | Y | Y |
| 20 Costa | Y | Y | Y | Y | Y | ? |
| 21 Nunes | Y | N | Y | N | Y | Y |
| 22 Thomas | Y | N | Y | N | Y | Y |
| 23 Capps | ? | Y | Y | Y | N | N |
| 24 Gallegly | Y | N | Y | N | Y | Y |
| 25 McKeon | Y | N | Y | N | Y | Y |
| 26 Dreier | Y | N | Y | N | Y | Y |
| 27 Sherman | Y | Y | Y | Y | N | N |
| 28 Berman | Y | Y | Y | Y | Y | N |
| 29 Schiff | Y | Y | Y | Y | N | N |
| 30 Waxman | Y | Y | Y | Y | N | N |
| 31 Becerra | Y | Y | Y | Y | N | N |
| 32 Solis | Y | Y | Y | Y | N | N |
| 33 Watson | Y | Y | Y | Y | N | N |
| 34 Roybal-Allard | Y | Y | Y | Y | N | N |
| 35 Waters | Y | Y | Y | Y | N | N |
| 36 Harman | ? | ? | ? | ? | ? | ? |
| 37 Millender-McD. | Y | Y | ? | Y | Y | N |
| 38 Napolitano | Y | Y | Y | Y | N | N |
| 39 Sánchez, Linda | Y | Y | Y | Y | N | N |
| 40 Royce | Y | N | Y | N | Y | Y |
| 41 Lewis | Y | N | Y | N | Y | Y |
| 42 Miller, Gary | Y | N | Y | N | Y | Y |
| 43 Baca | Y | Y | Y | Y | Y | N |
| 44 Calvert | Y | N | Y | N | Y | Y |
| 45 Bono | Y | Y | Y | N | Y | Y |
| 46 Rohrabacher | Y | N | Y | N | Y | Y |
| 47 Sanchez, Loretta | Y | Y | Y | Y | N | N |
| 48 Vacant | | | | | | |
| 49 Issa | Y | N | Y | N | Y | Y |

| | 494 | 495 | 496 | 497 | 498 | 499 |
|---|---|---|---|---|---|---|
| 50 Cunningham | Y | N | Y | N | Y | Y |
| 51 Filner | Y | Y | Y | Y | N | N |
| 52 Hunter | ? | ? | ? | ? | ? | ? |
| 53 Davis | Y | Y | Y | Y | Y | N |
| **COLORADO** | | | | | | |
| 1 DeGette | Y | Y | Y | Y | Y | N |
| 2 Udall | Y | Y | Y | Y | Y | N |
| 3 Salazar | Y | Y | Y | Y | Y | N |
| 4 Musgrave | Y | N | Y | N | Y | Y |
| 5 Hefley | Y | N | Y | N | Y | Y |
| 6 Tancredo | Y | N | Y | N | Y | ? |
| 7 Beauprez | Y | N | Y | N | Y | Y |
| **CONNECTICUT** | | | | | | |
| 1 Larson | Y | Y | Y | Y | Y | N |
| 2 Simmons | Y | N | Y | N | Y | Y |
| 3 DeLauro | Y | Y | Y | Y | Y | N |
| 4 Shays | Y | N | Y | ? | ? | Y |
| 5 Johnson | Y | Y | Y | N | Y | Y |
| **DELAWARE** | | | | | | |
| AL Castle | Y | N | Y | N | Y | Y |
| **FLORIDA** | | | | | | |
| 1 Miller | Y | N | Y | N | Y | Y |
| 2 Boyd | Y | Y | Y | Y | N | N |
| 3 Brown | Y | Y | Y | Y | N | N |
| 4 Crenshaw | Y | N | Y | N | Y | Y |
| 5 Brown-Waite | Y | N | Y | N | Y | Y |
| 6 Stearns | Y | N | Y | N | Y | Y |
| 7 Mica | Y | N | Y | N | Y | Y |
| 8 Keller | Y | N | Y | N | Y | Y |
| 9 Bilirakis | Y | N | Y | N | Y | Y |
| 10 Young | Y | N | Y | N | Y | Y |
| 11 Davis | ? | ? | ? | ? | ? | ? |
| 12 Putnam | Y | N | Y | N | Y | Y |
| 13 Harris | Y | N | Y | N | Y | Y |
| 14 Mack | Y | N | Y | N | Y | Y |
| 15 Weldon | Y | N | Y | N | Y | Y |
| 16 Foley | Y | N | Y | N | Y | Y |
| 17 Meek | ? | ? | ? | Y | N | N |
| 18 Ros-Lehtinen | ? | ? | ? | N | Y | Y |
| 19 Wexler | Y | Y | Y | Y | N | N |
| 20 Wasserman-Schultz | Y | Y | Y | Y | N | N |
| 21 Diaz-Balart, L. | Y | N | Y | N | Y | Y |
| 22 Shaw | Y | N | Y | N | Y | Y |
| 23 Hastings | Y | Y | Y | Y | N | N |
| 24 Feeney | Y | N | Y | N | Y | Y |
| 25 Diaz-Balart, M. | Y | N | Y | N | Y | Y |
| **GEORGIA** | | | | | | |
| 1 Kingston | Y | N | Y | N | Y | Y |
| 2 Bishop | Y | Y | Y | Y | Y | N |
| 3 Marshall | Y | Y | ? | Y | Y | N |
| 4 McKinney | ? | ? | ? | Y | N | N |
| 5 Lewis | Y | Y | Y | Y | N | N |
| 6 Price | Y | N | Y | N | Y | Y |
| 7 Linder | Y | N | Y | N | Y | Y |
| 8 Westmoreland | Y | N | Y | N | Y | Y |
| 9 Norwood | Y | N | Y | N | Y | Y |
| 10 Deal | Y | N | Y | N | Y | Y |
| 11 Gingrey | Y | N | Y | N | Y | Y |
| 12 Barrow | Y | Y | Y | Y | N | N |
| 13 Scott | Y | Y | Y | Y | Y | N |
| **HAWAII** | | | | | | |
| 1 Abercrombie | Y | Y | Y | Y | N | N |
| 2 Case | Y | Y | Y | Y | N | N |
| **IDAHO** | | | | | | |
| 1 Otter | Y | N | Y | N | Y | Y |
| 2 Simpson | Y | N | Y | N | Y | Y |
| **ILLINOIS** | | | | | | |
| 1 Rush | ? | ? | ? | Y | N | N |
| 2 Jackson | Y | Y | Y | Y | N | N |
| 3 Lipinski | Y | Y | Y | Y | Y | N |
| 4 Gutierrez | + | + | + | + | + | – |
| 5 Emanuel | Y | Y | Y | Y | Y | N |
| 6 Hyde | Y | N | Y | N | Y | Y |
| 7 Davis | Y | Y | Y | Y | N | N |
| 8 Bean | Y | Y | Y | Y | N | N |
| 9 Schakowsky | Y | Y | Y | Y | N | N |
| 10 Kirk | Y | N | Y | N | Y | Y |
| 11 Weller | + | – | + | N | Y | Y |
| 12 Costello | Y | Y | Y | Y | Y | N |

**KEY**

| Republicans | Democrats | *Independents* |
|---|---|---|

| | | | | | |
|---|---|---|---|---|---|
| Y | Voted for (yea) | X | Paired against | C | Voted "present" to avoid possible conflict of interest |
| # | Paired for | – | Announced against | | |
| + | Announced for | P | Voted "present" | ? | Did not vote or otherwise make a position known |
| N | Voted against (nay) | | | | |

| | 494 | 495 | 496 | 497 | 498 | 499 |
|---|---|---|---|---|---|---|
| 13 **Biggert** | Y | N | Y | N | Y | Y |
| 14 **Hastert** | | | | | | |
| 15 **Johnson** | Y | N | Y | N | Y | N |
| 16 **Manzullo** | Y | N | Y | N | Y | Y |
| 17 Evans | Y | Y | Y | Y | N | N |
| 18 **LaHood** | Y | N | Y | N | Y | Y |
| 19 **Shimkus** | Y | N | Y | N | Y | Y |
| **INDIANA** | | | | | | |
| 1 Visclosky | Y | Y | Y | Y | Y | N |
| 2 **Chocola** | Y | N | Y | N | Y | Y |
| 3 **Souder** | Y | N | Y | N | Y | Y |
| 4 **Buyer** | Y | N | Y | N | Y | Y |
| 5 **Burton** | Y | N | Y | N | Y | Y |
| 6 **Pence** | Y | N | Y | N | Y | Y |
| 7 Carson | Y | Y | Y | Y | N | N |
| 8 **Hostettler** | Y | N | Y | N | Y | Y |
| 9 **Sodrel** | Y | N | Y | N | Y | Y |
| **IOWA** | | | | | | |
| 1 **Nussle** | Y | N | Y | N | Y | Y |
| 2 **Leach** | Y | Y | Y | N | Y | N |
| 3 Boswell | ? | ? | ? | ? | ? | ? |
| 4 **Latham** | Y | N | Y | N | Y | Y |
| 5 **King** | Y | N | Y | N | Y | Y |
| **KANSAS** | | | | | | |
| 1 **Moran** | Y | N | Y | N | Y | Y |
| 2 **Ryun** | Y | N | Y | N | Y | Y |
| 3 Moore | Y | Y | Y | Y | Y | N |
| 4 **Tiahrt** | Y | N | Y | N | Y | Y |
| **KENTUCKY** | | | | | | |
| 1 **Whitfield** | Y | N | Y | N | Y | Y |
| 2 **Lewis** | Y | N | Y | N | Y | Y |
| 3 **Northup** | ? | ? | ? | N | Y | Y |
| 4 **Davis** | Y | N | Y | N | Y | Y |
| 5 **Rogers** | Y | N | Y | N | Y | Y |
| 6 Chandler | Y | Y | Y | Y | Y | N |
| **LOUISIANA** | | | | | | |
| 1 **Jindal** | Y | N | Y | N | Y | Y |
| 2 Jefferson | Y | Y | Y | Y | N | N |
| 3 Melancon | ? | ? | ? | ? | ? | ? |
| 4 **McCrery** | Y | Y | Y | N | Y | Y |
| 5 **Alexander** | Y | N | Y | N | Y | ? |
| 6 **Baker** | Y | N | Y | N | Y | Y |
| 7 **Boustany** | ? | ? | ? | N | Y | Y |
| **MAINE** | | | | | | |
| 1 Allen | Y | Y | Y | Y | Y | N |
| 2 Michaud | Y | Y | Y | Y | Y | N |
| **MARYLAND** | | | | | | |
| 1 **Gilchrest** | Y | Y | Y | N | Y | Y |
| 2 Ruppersberger | Y | Y | Y | Y | Y | – |
| 3 Cardin | ? | ? | ? | Y | Y | N |
| 4 Wynn | Y | Y | Y | Y | Y | N |
| 5 Hoyer | Y | Y | Y | Y | N | N |
| 6 **Bartlett** | Y | N | Y | N | Y | Y |
| 7 Cummings | Y | Y | Y | Y | N | N |
| 8 Van Hollen | Y | Y | Y | Y | N | N |
| **MASSACHUSETTS** | | | | | | |
| 1 Olver | ? | Y | Y | Y | N | N |
| 2 Neal | Y | Y | Y | Y | N | N |
| 3 McGovern | Y | Y | Y | Y | N | N |
| 4 Frank | Y | Y | Y | Y | N | N |
| 5 Meehan | Y | Y | Y | Y | N | N |
| 6 Tierney | Y | Y | Y | Y | N | N |
| 7 Markey | Y | Y | Y | Y | N | N |
| 8 Capuano | Y | Y | Y | Y | Y | N |
| 9 Lynch | Y | Y | Y | Y | Y | N |
| 10 Delahunt | Y | Y | Y | Y | Y | N |
| **MICHIGAN** | | | | | | |
| 1 Stupak | Y | Y | Y | Y | N | N |
| 2 **Hoekstra** | Y | N | Y | N | Y | Y |
| 3 **Ehlers** | Y | N | Y | N | Y | Y |
| 4 **Camp** | Y | N | Y | N | Y | Y |
| 5 Kildee | Y | Y | Y | Y | Y | N |
| 6 **Upton** | Y | N | Y | N | Y | Y |
| 7 **Schwarz** | Y | N | Y | N | Y | Y |
| 8 **Rogers** | Y | N | Y | N | Y | Y |
| 9 **Knollenberg** | Y | N | Y | N | Y | Y |
| 10 **Miller** | Y | N | Y | N | Y | Y |
| 11 **McCotter** | Y | N | Y | N | Y | Y |
| 12 Levin | Y | Y | Y | Y | Y | N |
| 13 Kilpatrick | Y | Y | Y | Y | Y | N |
| 14 Conyers | Y | Y | Y | Y | N | N |
| 15 Dingell | Y | Y | Y | Y | Y | N |

| | 494 | 495 | 496 | 497 | 498 | 499 |
|---|---|---|---|---|---|---|
| **MINNESOTA** | | | | | | |
| 1 **Gutknecht** | Y | N | Y | N | Y | Y |
| 2 **Kline** | Y | N | Y | N | Y | Y |
| 3 **Ramstad** | Y | N | Y | N | Y | Y |
| 4 McCollum | Y | Y | Y | Y | ? | N |
| 5 Sabo | Y | Y | Y | Y | Y | N |
| 6 **Kennedy** | Y | N | Y | N | Y | Y |
| 7 Peterson | Y | Y | Y | Y | Y | N |
| 8 Oberstar | Y | Y | Y | Y | Y | N |
| **MISSISSIPPI** | | | | | | |
| 1 **Wicker** | Y | N | Y | N | Y | Y |
| 2 Thompson | Y | Y | Y | Y | N | N |
| 3 **Pickering** | Y | N | Y | N | Y | ? |
| 4 Taylor | Y | Y | Y | N | Y | Y |
| **MISSOURI** | | | | | | |
| 1 Clay | Y | Y | Y | Y | Y | N |
| 2 **Akin** | Y | N | Y | N | Y | Y |
| 3 Carnahan | Y | Y | Y | Y | Y | N |
| 4 Skelton | Y | Y | Y | Y | Y | – |
| 5 Cleaver | Y | Y | Y | Y | Y | ? |
| 6 **Graves** | Y | N | Y | N | Y | Y |
| 7 **Blunt** | Y | N | Y | N | Y | Y |
| 8 **Emerson** | Y | N | Y | N | Y | Y |
| 9 **Hulshof** | Y | N | Y | N | Y | Y |
| **MONTANA** | | | | | | |
| AL **Rehberg** | Y | N | Y | N | Y | Y |
| **NEBRASKA** | | | | | | |
| 1 **Fortenberry** | Y | N | Y | N | Y | Y |
| 2 **Terry** | Y | N | Y | N | Y | Y |
| 3 **Osborne** | Y | N | Y | N | Y | Y |
| **NEVADA** | | | | | | |
| 1 Berkley | Y | Y | Y | Y | N | ? |
| 2 **Gibbons** | Y | N | Y | N | Y | Y |
| 3 **Porter** | Y | N | Y | N | Y | Y |
| **NEW HAMPSHIRE** | | | | | | |
| 1 **Bradley** | Y | N | Y | N | Y | N |
| 2 **Bass** | Y | N | Y | N | Y | Y |
| **NEW JERSEY** | | | | | | |
| 1 Andrews | Y | Y | Y | Y | Y | N |
| 2 **LoBiondo** | Y | N | Y | N | Y | Y |
| 3 **Saxton** | Y | N | Y | N | Y | Y |
| 4 **Smith** | Y | N | Y | N | Y | Y |
| 5 **Garrett** | Y | N | Y | N | Y | Y |
| 6 Pallone | Y | Y | Y | Y | N | N |
| 7 **Ferguson** | Y | N | Y | N | Y | Y |
| 8 Pascrell | Y | Y | Y | Y | Y | N |
| 9 Rothman | Y | Y | Y | Y | Y | N |
| 10 Payne | Y | Y | Y | Y | N | N |
| 11 **Frelinghuysen** | Y | N | Y | N | Y | Y |
| 12 Holt | Y | Y | Y | Y | N | N |
| 13 Menendez | + | ? | + | Y | N | N |
| **NEW MEXICO** | | | | | | |
| 1 **Wilson** | Y | N | Y | N | Y | Y |
| 2 **Pearce** | Y | N | Y | N | Y | Y |
| 3 Udall | Y | Y | Y | Y | N | N |
| **NEW YORK** | | | | | | |
| 1 Bishop | Y | Y | Y | Y | N | N |
| 2 Israel | Y | Y | Y | Y | N | N |
| 3 **King** | Y | N | Y | N | Y | Y |
| 4 McCarthy | Y | Y | Y | Y | N | N |
| 5 Ackerman | Y | Y | Y | Y | N | N |
| 6 Meeks | Y | Y | Y | Y | N | N |
| 7 Crowley | Y | Y | Y | Y | N | N |
| 8 Nadler | Y | Y | Y | Y | N | N |
| 9 Weiner | Y | Y | Y | Y | N | N |
| 10 Towns | Y | Y | Y | Y | N | N |
| 11 Owens | Y | Y | Y | Y | N | N |
| 12 Velázquez | Y | Y | Y | Y | N | N |
| 13 **Fossella** | Y | Y | Y | N | Y | Y |
| 14 Maloney | Y | Y | Y | Y | N | N |
| 15 Rangel | Y | Y | Y | Y | N | N |
| 16 Serrano | Y | Y | Y | Y | N | N |
| 17 Engel | Y | Y | Y | Y | N | N |
| 18 Lowey | Y | Y | Y | Y | N | N |
| 19 **Kelly** | Y | N | Y | N | Y | Y |
| 20 **Sweeney** | Y | N | Y | N | Y | Y |
| 21 McNulty | Y | Y | Y | Y | Y | N |
| 22 Hinchey | Y | Y | Y | Y | N | N |
| 23 **McHugh** | Y | N | Y | N | Y | Y |
| 24 **Boehlert** | Y | Y | Y | N | Y | Y |
| 25 **Walsh** | Y | N | Y | N | Y | Y |
| 26 **Reynolds** | Y | N | Y | N | Y | Y |
| 27 Higgins | Y | Y | Y | Y | N | N |
| 28 Slaughter | Y | Y | Y | Y | N | N |
| 29 **Kuhl** | Y | N | Y | N | Y | Y |

| | 494 | 495 | 496 | 497 | 498 | 499 |
|---|---|---|---|---|---|---|
| **NORTH CAROLINA** | | | | | | |
| 1 Butterfield | Y | Y | Y | Y | Y | N |
| 2 Etheridge | Y | Y | Y | Y | Y | N |
| 3 **Jones** | Y | N | Y | N | Y | Y |
| 4 Price | Y | Y | Y | Y | Y | N |
| 5 **Foxx** | Y | N | Y | N | Y | Y |
| 6 **Coble** | Y | N | Y | N | Y | Y |
| 7 McIntyre | Y | ? | Y | Y | N | N |
| 8 **Hayes** | Y | N | Y | N | Y | Y |
| 9 **Myrick** | Y | N | Y | N | Y | Y |
| 10 **McHenry** | Y | N | Y | N | Y | Y |
| 11 **Taylor** | Y | N | Y | N | Y | Y |
| 12 Watt | ? | ? | ? | Y | N | N |
| 13 Miller | Y | Y | Y | Y | Y | N |
| **NORTH DAKOTA** | | | | | | |
| AL Pomeroy | Y | Y | Y | Y | Y | N |
| **OHIO** | | | | | | |
| 1 **Chabot** | Y | N | Y | N | Y | Y |
| 2 **Schmidt** | Y | N | Y | N | Y | Y |
| 3 **Turner** | Y | N | Y | N | Y | Y |
| 4 **Oxley** | Y | N | Y | N | Y | Y |
| 5 **Gillmor** | Y | N | Y | N | Y | Y |
| 6 Strickland | ? | ? | ? | Y | N | N |
| 7 **Hobson** | Y | N | Y | N | Y | Y |
| 8 **Boehner** | Y | N | ? | N | Y | Y |
| 9 Kaptur | ? | Y | Y | Y | N | N |
| 10 Kucinich | Y | Y | Y | Y | N | N |
| 11 Jones | Y | Y | Y | Y | N | N |
| 12 **Tiberi** | Y | N | Y | N | Y | Y |
| 13 Brown | Y | Y | Y | Y | Y | N |
| 14 **LaTourette** | Y | N | Y | N | Y | Y |
| 15 **Pryce** | Y | N | Y | N | Y | Y |
| 16 **Regula** | Y | N | Y | N | Y | Y |
| 17 Ryan | ? | ? | Y | Y | Y | N |
| 18 **Ney** | Y | N | Y | N | Y | Y |
| **OKLAHOMA** | | | | | | |
| 1 **Sullivan** | Y | N | Y | N | Y | Y |
| 2 Boren | Y | N | Y | Y | Y | Y |
| 3 **Lucas** | Y | N | Y | N | ? | Y |
| 4 **Cole** | Y | N | Y | N | Y | Y |
| 5 **Istook** | Y | N | Y | N | Y | Y |
| **OREGON** | | | | | | |
| 1 Wu | Y | Y | Y | Y | Y | N |
| 2 **Walden** | Y | N | Y | N | Y | Y |
| 3 Blumenauer | ? | ? | ? | ? | ? | ? |
| 4 DeFazio | Y | Y | Y | Y | N | N |
| 5 Hooley | Y | Y | Y | Y | Y | N |
| **PENNSYLVANIA** | | | | | | |
| 1 Brady | Y | Y | Y | Y | Y | N |
| 2 Fattah | ? | ? | ? | Y | N | N |
| 3 **English** | Y | N | Y | N | Y | Y |
| 4 **Hart** | Y | N | Y | N | Y | Y |
| 5 **Peterson** | Y | N | Y | N | Y | Y |
| 6 **Gerlach** | Y | N | Y | N | Y | Y |
| 7 **Weldon** | Y | N | Y | N | Y | Y |
| 8 **Fitzpatrick** | Y | N | Y | N | Y | Y |
| 9 **Shuster** | Y | N | Y | N | Y | Y |
| 10 **Sherwood** | Y | N | Y | N | Y | Y |
| 11 Kanjorski | Y | Y | Y | Y | Y | N |
| 12 Murtha | ? | ? | ? | Y | Y | N |
| 13 Schwartz | Y | Y | Y | Y | N | N |
| 14 Doyle | Y | Y | Y | Y | Y | N |
| 15 **Dent** | Y | N | Y | N | Y | Y |
| 16 **Pitts** | Y | N | Y | N | Y | Y |
| 17 Holden | Y | Y | Y | Y | Y | N |
| 18 **Murphy** | Y | N | Y | N | Y | Y |
| 19 **Platts** | Y | N | Y | N | Y | Y |
| **RHODE ISLAND** | | | | | | |
| 1 Kennedy | Y | Y | Y | Y | Y | N |
| 2 Langevin | Y | Y | Y | Y | N | N |
| **SOUTH CAROLINA** | | | | | | |
| 1 **Brown** | Y | N | Y | N | Y | Y |
| 2 **Wilson** | Y | N | Y | N | Y | Y |
| 3 **Barrett** | Y | N | Y | N | Y | Y |
| 4 **Inglis** | Y | N | Y | N | Y | Y |
| 5 Spratt | Y | Y | Y | Y | Y | N |
| 6 Clyburn | Y | Y | Y | Y | N | N |
| **SOUTH DAKOTA** | | | | | | |
| AL Herseth | Y | Y | Y | Y | Y | N |
| **TENNESSEE** | | | | | | |
| 1 **Jenkins** | Y | N | Y | N | Y | Y |
| 2 **Duncan** | Y | N | Y | N | Y | Y |

| | 494 | 495 | 496 | 497 | 498 | 499 |
|---|---|---|---|---|---|---|
| 3 **Wamp** | Y | N | Y | N | Y | Y |
| 4 Davis | Y | Y | Y | Y | Y | Y |
| 5 Cooper | Y | Y | Y | Y | Y | N |
| 6 Gordon | Y | Y | ? | Y | Y | N |
| 7 **Blackburn** | Y | N | Y | N | Y | Y |
| 8 Tanner | Y | Y | Y | Y | Y | N |
| 9 Ford | Y | Y | Y | Y | Y | N |
| **TEXAS** | | | | | | |
| 1 **Gohmert** | Y | N | Y | N | Y | Y |
| 2 **Poe** | Y | N | Y | N | Y | Y |
| 3 **Johnson, S.** | Y | N | Y | N | Y | Y |
| 4 **Hall** | Y | N | Y | N | Y | Y |
| 5 **Hensarling** | Y | N | Y | N | Y | Y |
| 6 **Barton** | Y | N | Y | N | Y | Y |
| 7 **Culberson** | ? | ? | ? | ? | ? | ? |
| 8 **Brady** | ? | ? | ? | N | Y | Y |
| 9 Green, A. | Y | Y | Y | Y | Y | N |
| 10 **McCaul** | Y | N | Y | N | Y | Y |
| 11 **Conaway** | Y | N | Y | N | Y | Y |
| 12 **Granger** | Y | N | Y | N | Y | Y |
| 13 **Thornberry** | Y | N | Y | N | Y | Y |
| 14 **Paul** | Y | N | Y | N | Y | N |
| 15 Hinojosa | + | Y | Y | Y | Y | N |
| 16 Reyes | Y | Y | Y | Y | Y | N |
| 17 Edwards | Y | Y | Y | Y | Y | N |
| 18 Jackson-Lee | Y | Y | Y | Y | Y | N |
| 19 **Neugebauer** | Y | N | Y | N | Y | Y |
| 20 Gonzalez | Y | Y | Y | Y | N | N |
| 21 **Smith** | Y | N | Y | N | Y | Y |
| 22 **DeLay** | Y | N | Y | N | Y | Y |
| 23 **Bonilla** | Y | N | Y | N | Y | Y |
| 24 **Marchant** | Y | N | Y | N | Y | Y |
| 25 Doggett | Y | Y | Y | Y | N | N |
| 26 **Burgess** | Y | N | Y | N | Y | Y |
| 27 Ortiz | Y | Y | Y | Y | Y | N |
| 28 Cuellar | Y | Y | Y | Y | Y | N |
| 29 Green, G. | Y | Y | Y | Y | Y | N |
| 30 Johnson, E. | Y | Y | Y | Y | N | N |
| 31 **Carter** | Y | N | Y | N | Y | Y |
| 32 **Sessions** | Y | N | Y | N | Y | Y |
| **UTAH** | | | | | | |
| 1 **Bishop** | Y | N | Y | N | Y | Y |
| 2 Matheson | Y | Y | Y | Y | Y | N |
| 3 **Cannon** | Y | N | Y | N | Y | Y |
| **VERMONT** | | | | | | |
| AL *Sanders* | Y | Y | Y | Y | Y | N |
| **VIRGINIA** | | | | | | |
| 1 **Davis, J.** | Y | N | Y | ? | ? | Y |
| 2 **Drake** | Y | N | Y | N | Y | Y |
| 3 Scott | Y | Y | Y | Y | Y | N |
| 4 **Forbes** | Y | N | Y | N | Y | Y |
| 5 **Goode** | Y | N | Y | N | Y | Y |
| 6 **Goodlatte** | Y | N | Y | N | Y | Y |
| 7 **Cantor** | Y | N | Y | N | Y | Y |
| 8 Moran | Y | Y | Y | Y | Y | N |
| 9 Boucher | Y | Y | Y | Y | Y | N |
| 10 **Wolf** | Y | N | Y | N | Y | Y |
| 11 **Davis, T.** | Y | Y | Y | N | Y | Y |
| **WASHINGTON** | | | | | | |
| 1 Inslee | Y | Y | Y | Y | N | N |
| 2 Larsen | Y | Y | Y | Y | Y | N |
| 3 Baird | Y | Y | Y | Y | N | N |
| 4 **Hastings** | Y | N | Y | N | Y | Y |
| 5 **McMorris** | Y | N | Y | N | Y | Y |
| 6 Dicks | Y | Y | Y | Y | Y | N |
| 7 McDermott | + | + | + | Y | N | N |
| 8 **Reichert** | Y | N | Y | N | Y | Y |
| 9 Smith | Y | Y | Y | Y | Y | N |
| **WEST VIRGINIA** | | | | | | |
| 1 Mollohan | Y | Y | Y | Y | Y | N |
| 2 **Capito** | Y | N | Y | N | Y | Y |
| 3 Rahall | Y | Y | Y | Y | Y | N |
| **WISCONSIN** | | | | | | |
| 1 **Ryan** | Y | N | Y | N | Y | Y |
| 2 Baldwin | Y | Y | Y | Y | N | N |
| 3 Kind | Y | Y | Y | Y | Y | N |
| 4 Moore | Y | Y | Y | Y | Y | N |
| 5 **Sensenbrenner** | Y | N | Y | N | Y | Y |
| 6 **Petri** | Y | N | Y | N | Y | Y |
| 7 Obey | Y | Y | Y | Y | Y | N |
| 8 **Green** | Y | N | Y | N | Y | Y |
| **WYOMING** | | | | | | |
| AL **Cubin** | Y | Y | Y | N | Y | Y |

# IN THE HOUSE | By Vote Number

**500.** **HR 3402. Justice Department Reauthorization/Recommit.**
Stupak, D-Mich., motion to recommit the bill to the Judiciary Committee with instructions to add language that would give the Justice Department authority to prosecute oil companies that engage in gas price gouging and impose fines of up to $100 million on corporations, as well as up to $1 million in fines or 10 years in prison or both for individuals. Motion rejected 195-226: R 0-226; D 194-0 (ND 145-0, SD 49-0); I 1-0. Sept. 28, 2005.

**501.** **HR 3402. Justice Department Reauthorization/Passage.** Passage of the bill that would authorize nearly $85 billion for the Justice Department, related programs and agencies for fiscal 2006 through 2009, including $24.4 billion for the FBI, $21.5 billion for the Federal Prison System and $7.3 billion for the Drug Enforcement Administration. The measure also would reauthorize provisions of the Violence Against Women Act, require the attorney general to report to Congress annually on the number of U.S. citizens or legal residents detained on suspicion of terrorism and create a privacy officer for the department. Passed 415-4: R 225-2; D 189-2 (ND 140-2, SD 49-0); I 1-0. Sept. 28, 2005.

**502.** **HR 3824. Endangered Species Act Overhaul/Rule.** Adoption of the rule (H Res 470) that would provide for House floor consideration of the bill that would overhaul the Endangered Species Act. Adopted 252-171: R 228-0; D 24-170 (ND 11-133, SD 13-37); I 0-1. Sept. 29, 2005.

**503.** **H Res 388. Cuban Human Rights/Adoption.** Boozman, R-Ark., motion to suspend the rules and adopt the resolution that would condemn human rights violations by the Cuban government and urge an international solidarity campaign to demand the immediate release of all Cuban political prisoners. Motion agreed to 393-31: R 228-1; D 164-30 (ND 119-25, SD 45-5); I 1-0. A two-thirds majority of those present and voting (283 in this case) is required for adoption under suspension of the rules. Sept. 29, 2005.

**504.** **H Con Res 245. Pledge of Allegiance/Adoption.** Sensenbrenner, R-Wis., motion to suspend the rules and adopt the concurrent resolution that would express the sense of Congress that the Supreme Court should speedily recognize the constitutional right of children to recite the pledge in school. Motion agreed to 383-31: R 226-0; D 156-31 (ND 114-26, SD 42-5); I 1-0. A two-thirds majority of those present and voting (276 in this case) is required for adoption under suspension of the rules. Sept. 29, 2005.

ND Northern Democrats, SD Southern Democrats
Southern states: Ala., Ark., Fla., Ga., Ky., La., Miss., N.C., Okla., S.C., Tenn., Texas, Va.

| | 500 | 501 | 502 | 503 | 504 |
|---|---|---|---|---|---|
| **ALABAMA** | | | | | |
| 1 Bonner | N | Y | Y | Y | Y |
| 2 Everett | N | Y | Y | Y | Y |
| 3 Rogers | N | Y | Y | Y | Y |
| 4 Aderholt | N | Y | Y | Y | Y |
| 5 Cramer | Y | Y | Y | Y | Y |
| 6 Bachus | N | Y | Y | Y | Y |
| 7 Davis | Y | Y | Y | Y | Y |
| **ALASKA** | | | | | |
| AL Young | ? | Y | Y | Y | Y |
| **ARIZONA** | | | | | |
| 1 Renzi | N | Y | Y | Y | Y |
| 2 Franks | N | Y | Y | Y | Y |
| 3 Shadegg | N | Y | Y | Y | Y |
| 4 Pastor | Y | Y | N | N | N |
| 5 Hayworth | N | Y | Y | Y | Y |
| 6 Flake | N | Y | Y | Y | Y |
| 7 Grijalva | Y | Y | N | N | N |
| 8 Kolbe | N | Y | Y | Y | Y |
| **ARKANSAS** | | | | | |
| 1 Berry | Y | Y | Y | Y | Y |
| 2 Snyder | Y | Y | N | Y | Y |
| 3 Boozman | N | Y | Y | Y | Y |
| 4 Ross | Y | Y | Y | Y | Y |
| **CALIFORNIA** | | | | | |
| 1 Thompson | Y | Y | N | Y | Y |
| 2 Herger | N | Y | Y | Y | Y |
| 3 Lungren | N | Y | Y | Y | Y |
| 4 Doolittle | N | Y | Y | Y | Y |
| 5 Matsui, D. | Y | Y | N | Y | Y |
| 6 Woolsey | Y | Y | N | N | N |
| 7 Miller, George | Y | Y | N | N | Y |
| 8 Pelosi | Y | Y | N | Y | Y |
| 9 Lee | Y | Y | ? | ? | ? |
| 10 Tauscher | Y | Y | N | Y | Y |
| 11 Pombo | N | Y | Y | Y | Y |
| 12 Lantos | Y | Y | N | Y | Y |
| 13 Stark | Y | Y | N | N | N |
| 14 Eshoo | Y | Y | N | Y | Y |
| 15 Honda | Y | Y | N | N | N |
| 16 Lofgren | Y | Y | N | Y | Y |
| 17 Farr | Y | Y | N | N | N |
| 18 Cardoza | Y | Y | Y | Y | Y |
| 19 Radanovich | N | Y | Y | Y | Y |
| 20 Costa | ? | ? | Y | Y | Y |
| 21 Nunes | N | Y | Y | Y | Y |
| 22 Thomas | N | Y | Y | Y | Y |
| 23 Capps | Y | Y | N | Y | Y |
| 24 Gallegly | N | Y | Y | Y | Y |
| 25 McKeon | N | Y | Y | Y | Y |
| 26 Dreier | N | Y | Y | Y | Y |
| 27 Sherman | Y | Y | N | Y | Y |
| 28 Berman | Y | Y | N | Y | Y |
| 29 Schiff | Y | Y | N | Y | Y |
| 30 Waxman | Y | Y | N | Y | N |
| 31 Becerra | Y | Y | N | Y | Y |
| 32 Solis | Y | Y | N | Y | Y |
| 33 Watson | Y | N | N | N | N |
| 34 Roybal-Allard | Y | Y | N | Y | Y |
| 35 Waters | Y | ? | N | N | N |
| 36 Harman | ? | ? | ? | ? | ? |
| 37 Millender-McD. | Y | Y | N | Y | Y |
| 38 Napolitano | Y | Y | N | Y | Y |
| 39 Sánchez, Linda | Y | Y | N | Y | P |
| 40 Royce | N | Y | Y | Y | Y |
| 41 Lewis | N | Y | Y | Y | Y |
| 42 Miller, Gary | N | Y | Y | Y | Y |
| 43 Baca | Y | Y | Y | Y | Y |
| 44 Calvert | N | Y | Y | Y | Y |
| 45 Bono | N | Y | Y | Y | Y |
| 46 Rohrabacher | N | Y | Y | Y | Y |
| 47 Sanchez, Loretta | Y | Y | N | Y | Y |
| 48 Vacant | | | | | |
| 49 Issa | N | Y | Y | Y | + |

| | 500 | 501 | 502 | 503 | 504 |
|---|---|---|---|---|---|
| 50 Cunningham | N | Y | Y | Y | Y |
| 51 Filner | Y | Y | N | Y | Y |
| 52 Hunter | ? | ? | Y | Y | Y |
| 53 Davis | Y | Y | N | Y | Y |
| **COLORADO** | | | | | |
| 1 DeGette | Y | Y | N | Y | N |
| 2 Udall | Y | Y | N | Y | Y |
| 3 Salazar | Y | Y | Y | Y | Y |
| 4 Musgrave | N | Y | Y | Y | Y |
| 5 Hefley | N | Y | Y | Y | Y |
| 6 Tancredo | N | Y | Y | Y | Y |
| 7 Beauprez | N | Y | Y | Y | Y |
| **CONNECTICUT** | | | | | |
| 1 Larson | Y | Y | N | Y | Y |
| 2 Simmons | N | Y | Y | Y | Y |
| 3 DeLauro | Y | Y | N | Y | Y |
| 4 Shays | N | Y | Y | Y | Y |
| 5 Johnson | N | Y | Y | Y | Y |
| **DELAWARE** | | | | | |
| AL Castle | N | Y | Y | Y | Y |
| **FLORIDA** | | | | | |
| 1 Miller | N | Y | Y | Y | Y |
| 2 Boyd | Y | Y | Y | Y | Y |
| 3 Brown | Y | Y | N | Y | Y |
| 4 Crenshaw | N | Y | Y | Y | Y |
| 5 Brown-Waite | N | Y | Y | Y | Y |
| 6 Stearns | N | Y | Y | Y | Y |
| 7 Mica | N | Y | Y | Y | Y |
| 8 Keller | N | Y | Y | Y | Y |
| 9 Bilirakis | N | Y | Y | Y | Y |
| 10 Young | N | Y | Y | Y | Y |
| 11 Davis | ? | ? | ? | ? | ? |
| 12 Putnam | N | Y | Y | Y | Y |
| 13 Harris | N | Y | Y | Y | Y |
| 14 Mack | N | Y | Y | Y | Y |
| 15 Weldon | N | Y | Y | Y | Y |
| 16 Foley | N | Y | Y | Y | Y |
| 17 Meek | Y | Y | N | Y | Y |
| 18 Ros-Lehtinen | N | Y | Y | Y | Y |
| 19 Wexler | Y | Y | N | Y | Y |
| 20 Wasserman-Schultz | Y | Y | N | Y | N |
| 21 Diaz-Balart, L. | N | Y | Y | Y | Y |
| 22 Shaw | N | Y | Y | Y | Y |
| 23 Hastings | Y | Y | N | Y | N |
| 24 Feeney | N | Y | Y | Y | Y |
| 25 Diaz-Balart, M. | N | Y | Y | Y | Y |
| **GEORGIA** | | | | | |
| 1 Kingston | N | Y | Y | Y | Y |
| 2 Bishop | Y | Y | Y | Y | Y |
| 3 Marshall | Y | Y | N | Y | Y |
| 4 McKinney | Y | Y | N | N | ? |
| 5 Lewis | Y | Y | N | N | N |
| 6 Price | N | Y | Y | Y | Y |
| 7 Linder | N | Y | Y | Y | Y |
| 8 Westmoreland | N | Y | Y | Y | Y |
| 9 Norwood | N | Y | Y | Y | Y |
| 10 Deal | N | Y | Y | Y | Y |
| 11 Gingrey | N | Y | Y | Y | Y |
| 12 Barrow | Y | Y | N | Y | Y |
| 13 Scott | Y | Y | Y | Y | Y |
| **HAWAII** | | | | | |
| 1 Abercrombie | Y | Y | Y | Y | Y |
| 2 Case | Y | Y | N | Y | Y |
| **IDAHO** | | | | | |
| 1 Otter | N | Y | Y | Y | Y |
| 2 Simpson | N | Y | Y | Y | Y |
| **ILLINOIS** | | | | | |
| 1 Rush | Y | Y | N | N | P |
| 2 Jackson | Y | Y | N | Y | Y |
| 3 Lipinski | Y | Y | N | Y | Y |
| 4 Gutierrez | + | + | – | + | ? |
| 5 Emanuel | Y | Y | N | Y | Y |
| 6 Hyde | – | + | Y | Y | Y |
| 7 Davis | Y | Y | N | N | Y |
| 8 Bean | Y | Y | N | Y | Y |
| 9 Schakowsky | Y | Y | N | N | N |
| 10 Kirk | N | Y | Y | Y | Y |
| 11 Weller | N | Y | Y | Y | Y |
| 12 Costello | Y | Y | N | Y | Y |

| | 500 | 501 | 502 | 503 | 504 |
|---|---|---|---|---|---|
| 13 Biggert | N | Y | Y | Y | Y |
| 14 Hastert | N | Y | Y | Y | Y |
| 15 Johnson | N | Y | Y | Y | Y |
| 16 Manzullo | N | Y | Y | Y | Y |
| 17 Evans | Y | Y | N | Y | Y |
| 18 LaHood | N | Y | Y | Y | Y |
| 19 Shimkus | N | Y | Y | Y | Y |
| **INDIANA** | | | | | |
| 1 Visclosky | Y | ? | N | Y | Y |
| 2 Chocola | N | Y | Y | Y | Y |
| 3 Souder | N | Y | Y | Y | Y |
| 4 Buyer | N | Y | Y | Y | Y |
| 5 Burton | N | Y | Y | Y | Y |
| 6 Pence | N | Y | Y | Y | Y |
| 7 Carson | Y | Y | N | N | N |
| 8 Hostettler | N | Y | Y | Y | Y |
| 9 Sodrel | N | Y | Y | Y | Y |
| **IOWA** | | | | | |
| 1 Nussle | N | Y | Y | Y | Y |
| 2 Leach | N | Y | Y | Y | Y |
| 3 Boswell | ? | ? | ? | ? | ? |
| 4 Latham | N | Y | Y | Y | Y |
| 5 King | N | Y | Y | Y | Y |
| **KANSAS** | | | | | |
| 1 Moran | N | Y | Y | Y | Y |
| 2 Ryun | N | Y | Y | Y | Y |
| 3 Moore | Y | Y | N | Y | Y |
| 4 Tiahrt | N | Y | Y | Y | Y |
| **KENTUCKY** | | | | | |
| 1 Whitfield | N | Y | Y | Y | Y |
| 2 Lewis | N | Y | Y | Y | Y |
| 3 Northup | N | Y | Y | Y | Y |
| 4 Davis | N | Y | Y | Y | Y |
| 5 Rogers | N | Y | Y | Y | Y |
| 6 Chandler | Y | Y | N | Y | Y |
| **LOUISIANA** | | | | | |
| 1 Jindal | N | Y | Y | Y | Y |
| 2 Jefferson | Y | Y | N | Y | Y |
| 3 Melancon | ? | ? | Y | Y | Y |
| 4 McCrery | N | Y | Y | Y | Y |
| 5 Alexander | N | Y | Y | Y | Y |
| 6 Baker | N | Y | Y | Y | Y |
| 7 Boustany | N | Y | Y | Y | Y |
| **MAINE** | | | | | |
| 1 Allen | Y | Y | N | Y | Y |
| 2 Michaud | Y | Y | N | Y | Y |
| **MARYLAND** | | | | | |
| 1 Gilchrest | N | Y | Y | Y | Y |
| 2 Ruppersberger | + | + | N | Y | Y |
| 3 Cardin | Y | Y | N | Y | Y |
| 4 Wynn | Y | Y | N | N | Y |
| 5 Hoyer | Y | Y | N | Y | Y |
| 6 Bartlett | N | Y | Y | Y | Y |
| 7 Cummings | Y | Y | N | Y | Y |
| 8 Van Hollen | Y | Y | N | Y | Y |
| **MASSACHUSETTS** | | | | | |
| 1 Olver | Y | Y | N | Y | Y |
| 2 Neal | Y | Y | N | Y | Y |
| 3 McGovern | Y | Y | N | Y | Y |
| 4 Frank | Y | Y | N | Y | N |
| 5 Meehan | Y | N | Y | N | Y |
| 6 Tierney | Y | Y | N | Y | P |
| 7 Markey | Y | Y | N | Y | N |
| 8 Capuano | Y | Y | N | Y | P |
| 9 Lynch | Y | Y | N | Y | Y |
| 10 Delahunt | Y | Y | N | Y | Y |
| **MICHIGAN** | | | | | |
| 1 Stupak | Y | Y | N | Y | Y |
| 2 Hoekstra | N | Y | Y | Y | Y |
| 3 Ehlers | N | Y | Y | Y | Y |
| 4 Camp | N | Y | Y | Y | Y |
| 5 Kildee | Y | Y | N | Y | Y |
| 6 Upton | N | Y | Y | Y | Y |
| 7 Schwarz | N | Y | Y | Y | Y |
| 8 Rogers | N | Y | Y | Y | Y |
| 9 Knollenberg | N | Y | Y | Y | Y |
| 10 Miller | N | Y | Y | Y | Y |
| 11 McCotter | N | Y | Y | Y | Y |
| 12 Levin | Y | Y | N | Y | Y |
| 13 Kilpatrick | Y | Y | N | Y | Y |
| 14 Conyers | Y | Y | N | N | N |
| 15 Dingell | Y | Y | N | Y | Y |

| | 500 | 501 | 502 | 503 | 504 |
|---|---|---|---|---|---|
| **MINNESOTA** | | | | | |
| 1 Gutknecht | N | Y | Y | Y | Y |
| 2 Kline | N | Y | Y | Y | Y |
| 3 Ramstad | N | Y | Y | Y | Y |
| 4 McCollum | Y | Y | N | Y | Y |
| 5 Sabo | Y | Y | N | Y | Y |
| 6 Kennedy | N | Y | Y | Y | Y |
| 7 Peterson | Y | Y | N | Y | Y |
| 8 Oberstar | Y | Y | N | Y | Y |
| **MISSISSIPPI** | | | | | |
| 1 Wicker | N | Y | Y | Y | Y |
| 2 Thompson | Y | Y | Y | N | Y |
| 3 Pickering | N | Y | Y | Y | Y |
| 4 Taylor | Y | Y | N | Y | Y |
| **MISSOURI** | | | | | |
| 1 Clay | Y | Y | N | N | Y |
| 2 Akin | N | Y | Y | Y | Y |
| 3 Carnahan | Y | Y | N | Y | Y |
| 4 Skelton | Y | Y | N | Y | Y |
| 5 Cleaver | Y | Y | N | Y | N |
| 6 Graves | N | Y | Y | Y | Y |
| 7 Blunt | N | Y | Y | Y | Y |
| 8 Emerson | N | Y | Y | Y | Y |
| 9 Hulshof | N | Y | Y | Y | Y |
| **MONTANA** | | | | | |
| AL Rehberg | N | Y | Y | Y | Y |
| **NEBRASKA** | | | | | |
| 1 Fortenberry | N | Y | Y | Y | Y |
| 2 Terry | N | Y | Y | Y | Y |
| 3 Osborne | N | Y | Y | Y | Y |
| **NEVADA** | | | | | |
| 1 Berkley | Y | Y | N | Y | Y |
| 2 Gibbons | N | Y | Y | Y | + |
| 3 Porter | N | Y | Y | Y | Y |
| **NEW HAMPSHIRE** | | | | | |
| 1 Bradley | N | Y | Y | Y | Y |
| 2 Bass | N | Y | Y | Y | Y |
| **NEW JERSEY** | | | | | |
| 1 Andrews | Y | Y | – | Y | Y |
| 2 LoBiondo | N | Y | Y | Y | Y |
| 3 Saxton | N | Y | Y | Y | Y |
| 4 Smith | N | Y | Y | Y | Y |
| 5 Garrett | N | Y | Y | Y | Y |
| 6 Pallone | Y | Y | N | Y | Y |
| 7 Ferguson | N | Y | Y | Y | Y |
| 8 Pascrell | Y | Y | N | Y | Y |
| 9 Rothman | Y | Y | N | Y | Y |
| 10 Payne | Y | Y | N | N | N |
| 11 Frelinghuysen | N | Y | Y | Y | Y |
| 12 Holt | Y | Y | N | Y | Y |
| 13 Menendez | Y | Y | N | Y | Y |
| **NEW MEXICO** | | | | | |
| 1 Wilson | N | Y | Y | Y | Y |
| 2 Pearce | N | Y | Y | Y | Y |
| 3 Udall | Y | Y | N | Y | Y |
| **NEW YORK** | | | | | |
| 1 Bishop | Y | Y | N | Y | Y |
| 2 Israel | Y | Y | N | Y | Y |
| 3 King | N | Y | Y | Y | Y |
| 4 McCarthy | Y | Y | N | Y | Y |
| 5 Ackerman | Y | Y | N | Y | N |
| 6 Meeks | Y | Y | N | N | Y |
| 7 Crowley | Y | Y | N | Y | Y |
| 8 Nadler | Y | Y | N | Y | N |
| 9 Weiner | Y | Y | N | Y | Y |
| 10 Towns | Y | Y | N | Y | N |
| 11 Owens | Y | Y | N | Y | P |
| 12 Velázquez | Y | Y | N | N | N |
| 13 Fossella | N | Y | Y | Y | Y |
| 14 Maloney | Y | Y | N | Y | Y |
| 15 Rangel | Y | Y | N | Y | Y |
| 16 Serrano | Y | Y | N | N | Y |
| 17 Engel | Y | Y | N | Y | Y |
| 18 Lowey | Y | Y | N | Y | Y |
| 19 Kelly | N | Y | Y | Y | Y |
| 20 Sweeney | N | Y | Y | Y | Y |
| 21 McNulty | Y | Y | N | Y | Y |
| 22 Hinchey | Y | Y | N | N | N |
| 23 McHugh | N | Y | Y | Y | Y |
| 24 Boehlert | N | Y | Y | Y | Y |
| 25 Walsh | N | Y | Y | Y | Y |
| 26 Reynolds | N | Y | Y | Y | Y |
| 27 Higgins | Y | Y | N | Y | Y |
| 28 Slaughter | Y | Y | ? | ? | ? |
| 29 Kuhl | N | Y | Y | Y | Y |

| | 500 | 501 | 502 | 503 | 504 |
|---|---|---|---|---|---|
| **NORTH CAROLINA** | | | | | |
| 1 Butterfield | Y | Y | N | Y | Y |
| 2 Etheridge | Y | Y | N | Y | Y |
| 3 Jones | N | Y | Y | Y | Y |
| 4 Price | Y | Y | N | Y | Y |
| 5 Foxx | N | Y | Y | Y | Y |
| 6 Coble | N | Y | Y | Y | Y |
| 7 McIntyre | Y | Y | N | Y | Y |
| 8 Hayes | N | Y | Y | Y | Y |
| 9 Myrick | N | Y | Y | Y | Y |
| 10 McHenry | N | Y | Y | Y | Y |
| 11 Taylor | N | Y | Y | Y | Y |
| 12 Watt | Y | Y | N | Y | P |
| 13 Miller | Y | Y | N | Y | Y |
| **NORTH DAKOTA** | | | | | |
| AL Pomeroy | Y | Y | Y | Y | Y |
| **OHIO** | | | | | |
| 1 Chabot | N | Y | Y | Y | Y |
| 2 Schmidt | N | Y | Y | Y | Y |
| 3 Turner | N | Y | Y | Y | Y |
| 4 Oxley | N | Y | Y | Y | Y |
| 5 Gillmor | N | Y | Y | Y | Y |
| 6 Strickland | Y | Y | N | Y | Y |
| 7 Hobson | N | Y | Y | Y | Y |
| 8 Boehner | N | Y | Y | Y | Y |
| 9 Kaptur | Y | Y | N | ? | Y |
| 10 Kucinich | Y | Y | N | N | Y |
| 11 Jones | Y | Y | N | N | N |
| 12 Tiberi | N | Y | Y | Y | Y |
| 13 Brown | Y | Y | N | Y | Y |
| 14 LaTourette | N | Y | Y | Y | Y |
| 15 Pryce | N | Y | Y | Y | Y |
| 16 Regula | N | Y | Y | Y | Y |
| 17 Ryan | Y | Y | N | Y | Y |
| 18 Ney | N | Y | Y | Y | Y |
| **OKLAHOMA** | | | | | |
| 1 Sullivan | N | Y | Y | Y | Y |
| 2 Boren | Y | Y | Y | Y | Y |
| 3 Lucas | N | Y | Y | Y | Y |
| 4 Cole | N | Y | Y | Y | Y |
| 5 Istook | N | Y | Y | Y | Y |
| **OREGON** | | | | | |
| 1 Wu | Y | Y | N | Y | Y |
| 2 Walden | N | Y | Y | Y | Y |
| 3 Blumenauer | ? | ? | N | Y | N |
| 4 DeFazio | Y | Y | N | Y | Y |
| 5 Hooley | Y | Y | N | Y | Y |
| **PENNSYLVANIA** | | | | | |
| 1 Brady | Y | Y | N | Y | Y |
| 2 Fattah | Y | Y | N | Y | Y |
| 3 English | N | Y | Y | Y | Y |
| 4 Hart | N | Y | Y | Y | Y |
| 5 Peterson | N | Y | Y | Y | Y |
| 6 Gerlach | N | Y | ? | Y | Y |
| 7 Weldon | N | Y | Y | Y | Y |
| 8 Fitzpatrick | N | Y | Y | Y | Y |
| 9 Shuster | N | Y | Y | Y | Y |
| 10 Sherwood | N | Y | Y | Y | Y |
| 11 Kanjorski | Y | Y | N | Y | Y |
| 12 Murtha | Y | Y | N | Y | Y |
| 13 Schwartz | Y | Y | N | Y | Y |
| 14 Doyle | Y | Y | N | Y | Y |
| 15 Dent | N | Y | Y | Y | Y |
| 16 Pitts | N | Y | Y | Y | Y |
| 17 Holden | Y | Y | N | Y | Y |
| 18 Murphy | N | Y | Y | Y | Y |
| 19 Platts | N | Y | Y | Y | Y |
| **RHODE ISLAND** | | | | | |
| 1 Kennedy | Y | Y | N | Y | Y |
| 2 Langevin | Y | Y | N | Y | Y |
| **SOUTH CAROLINA** | | | | | |
| 1 Brown | N | Y | Y | Y | Y |
| 2 Wilson | N | Y | Y | Y | Y |
| 3 Barrett | N | Y | Y | Y | Y |
| 4 Inglis | N | Y | Y | Y | Y |
| 5 Spratt | Y | Y | N | Y | Y |
| 6 Clyburn | Y | Y | N | Y | Y |
| **SOUTH DAKOTA** | | | | | |
| AL Herseth | Y | Y | Y | Y | Y |
| **TENNESSEE** | | | | | |
| 1 Jenkins | N | Y | Y | Y | Y |
| 2 Duncan | N | Y | Y | Y | Y |

| | 500 | 501 | 502 | 503 | 504 |
|---|---|---|---|---|---|
| 3 Wamp | N | Y | Y | Y | Y |
| 4 Davis | Y | Y | N | Y | Y |
| 5 Cooper | Y | Y | N | Y | Y |
| 6 Gordon | Y | Y | N | Y | Y |
| 7 Blackburn | N | Y | Y | Y | Y |
| 8 Tanner | Y | Y | N | Y | Y |
| 9 Ford | Y | Y | N | Y | Y |
| **TEXAS** | | | | | |
| 1 Gohmert | N | Y | Y | Y | Y |
| 2 Poe | N | Y | Y | Y | Y |
| 3 Johnson, S. | N | Y | Y | Y | Y |
| 4 Hall | N | Y | Y | Y | Y |
| 5 Hensarling | N | Y | Y | Y | Y |
| 6 Barton | N | Y | Y | Y | Y |
| 7 Culberson | ? | ? | ? | ? | ? |
| 8 Brady | N | Y | Y | Y | Y |
| 9 Green, A. | Y | Y | N | Y | P |
| 10 McCaul | N | Y | Y | Y | Y |
| 11 Conaway | N | Y | Y | Y | Y |
| 12 Granger | N | Y | Y | Y | Y |
| 13 Thornberry | N | Y | Y | Y | Y |
| 14 Paul | N | N | Y | N | Y |
| 15 Hinojosa | Y | Y | N | Y | Y |
| 16 Reyes | Y | Y | N | Y | Y |
| 17 Edwards | Y | Y | N | Y | Y |
| 18 Jackson-Lee | Y | Y | N | N | Y |
| 19 Neugebauer | N | Y | Y | Y | Y |
| 20 Gonzalez | Y | Y | N | Y | Y |
| 21 Smith | N | Y | Y | Y | Y |
| 22 DeLay | N | Y | Y | Y | Y |
| 23 Bonilla | N | Y | Y | Y | Y |
| 24 Marchant | N | Y | Y | Y | ? |
| 25 Doggett | Y | Y | N | Y | Y |
| 26 Burgess | N | Y | Y | Y | Y |
| 27 Ortiz | Y | Y | N | Y | Y |
| 28 Cuellar | Y | Y | N | Y | Y |
| 29 Green, G. | Y | Y | N | Y | Y |
| 30 Johnson, E. | Y | Y | N | N | N |
| 31 Carter | N | Y | Y | Y | Y |
| 32 Sessions | N | Y | Y | Y | Y |
| **UTAH** | | | | | |
| 1 Bishop | N | Y | Y | Y | Y |
| 2 Matheson | Y | Y | N | Y | Y |
| 3 Cannon | N | Y | Y | Y | Y |
| **VERMONT** | | | | | |
| AL *Sanders* | Y | Y | N | Y | Y |
| **VIRGINIA** | | | | | |
| 1 Davis, J. | N | Y | Y | Y | Y |
| 2 Drake | N | Y | Y | Y | Y |
| 3 Scott | Y | Y | N | Y | N |
| 4 Forbes | N | Y | Y | Y | Y |
| 5 Goode | N | Y | Y | Y | Y |
| 6 Goodlatte | N | Y | Y | Y | Y |
| 7 Cantor | N | Y | Y | Y | Y |
| 8 Moran | Y | Y | N | Y | Y |
| 9 Boucher | Y | Y | N | Y | Y |
| 10 Wolf | N | Y | Y | Y | Y |
| 11 Davis, T. | N | Y | Y | Y | Y |
| **WASHINGTON** | | | | | |
| 1 Inslee | Y | Y | N | Y | Y |
| 2 Larsen | Y | Y | N | Y | Y |
| 3 Baird | Y | Y | N | Y | Y |
| 4 Hastings | N | Y | Y | Y | Y |
| 5 McMorris | N | Y | Y | Y | Y |
| 6 Dicks | Y | ? | N | Y | Y |
| 7 McDermott | Y | Y | N | N | N |
| 8 Reichert | N | Y | Y | Y | Y |
| 9 Smith | Y | Y | N | Y | Y |
| **WEST VIRGINIA** | | | | | |
| 1 Mollohan | Y | Y | N | Y | Y |
| 2 Capito | N | Y | Y | Y | Y |
| 3 Rahall | Y | Y | N | Y | Y |
| **WISCONSIN** | | | | | |
| 1 Ryan | N | Y | Y | Y | Y |
| 2 Baldwin | Y | Y | N | Y | Y |
| 3 Kind | Y | Y | N | Y | P |
| 4 Moore | Y | Y | ? | Y | P |
| 5 Sensenbrenner | N | Y | Y | Y | Y |
| 6 Petri | N | Y | Y | Y | Y |
| 7 Obey | Y | Y | N | ? | Y |
| 8 Green | N | Y | Y | Y | Y |
| **WYOMING** | | | | | |
| AL Cubin | N | Y | Y | Y | Y |

# IN THE HOUSE | By Vote Number

**505.** **HR 3824. Endangered Species Act Overhaul/Substitute.** Miller, D-Calif., substitute amendment that would reauthorize the Endangered Species Act through 2010 and make changes to the species recovery plan process. It would require recovery plans to identify publicly owned land necessary to achieve species recovery. It would establish a program to promote voluntary habitat conservation for endangered species on privately owned land. The definition of putting a species in jeopardy would be changed to any action that directly or indirectly "makes it less likely" that a threatened or endangered species would recover, or significantly delays or increases the cost of species recovery. Rejected 206-216: R 29-198; D 176-18 (ND 138-6, SD 38-12); I 1-0. Sept. 29, 2005.

**506.** **HR 3824. Endangered Species Act Overhaul/Passage.** Passage of the bill that would overhaul and reauthorize the Endangered Species Act through 2010. It would replace the critical habitat designation with expanded authority to develop recovery plans for species that take into account areas of "special value" in conserving an endangered or threatened species. The Interior Department would be required to reimburse landowners who are not allowed to develop their land because of protections for endangered species. It also would authorize grants for private landowners to protect endangered species. Passed 229-193: R 193-34; D 36-158 (ND 15-129, SD 21-29); I 0-1. Sept. 29, 2005.

**507.** **H J Res 68. Fiscal 2006 Continuing Resolution/Passage.** Passage of the joint resolution that would provide continuing appropriations through Nov. 18 for all federal departments and agencies whose fiscal 2006 appropriations bills have not been enacted. Passed 348-65: R 219-2; D 129-62 (ND 87-54, SD 42-8); I 0-1. Sept. 29, 2005.

**508.** **H Con Res 178. Idiopathic Pulmonary Fibrosis/Adoption.** Deal, R-Ga., motion to suspend the rules and adopt the concurrent resolution that would recognize the need to increase awareness of idiopathic pulmonary fibrosis and to work to find a cure. Motion agreed to 401-0: R 218-0; D 182-0 (ND 133-0, SD 49-0); I 1-0. A two-thirds majority of those present and voting (268 in this case) is required for adoption under suspension of the rules. Sept. 29, 2005.

| | 505 | 506 | 507 | 508 |
|---|---|---|---|---|
| **ALABAMA** | | | | |
| 1 Bonner | N | Y | Y | Y |
| 2 Everett | N | Y | Y | Y |
| 3 Rogers | N | Y | Y | Y |
| 4 Aderholt | N | Y | Y | Y |
| 5 Cramer | N | Y | Y | Y |
| 6 Bachus | N | Y | Y | Y |
| 7 Davis | N | Y | Y | Y |
| **ALASKA** | | | | |
| AL Young | N | Y | Y | Y |
| **ARIZONA** | | | | |
| 1 Renzi | N | Y | Y | Y |
| 2 Franks | N | Y | Y | Y |
| 3 Shadegg | N | Y | Y | ? |
| 4 Pastor | Y | N | N | Y |
| 5 Hayworth | N | Y | Y | Y |
| 6 Flake | N | Y | Y | Y |
| 7 Grijalva | Y | N | N | Y |
| 8 Kolbe | N | Y | Y | Y |
| **ARKANSAS** | | | | |
| 1 Berry | N | Y | Y | Y |
| 2 Snyder | Y | N | Y | Y |
| 3 Boozman | N | Y | Y | Y |
| 4 Ross | N | Y | Y | Y |
| **CALIFORNIA** | | | | |
| 1 Thompson | Y | N | Y | Y |
| 2 Herger | N | Y | Y | Y |
| 3 Lungren | N | Y | Y | Y |
| 4 Doolittle | N | Y | Y | ? |
| 5 Matsui, D. | Y | N | Y | Y |
| 6 Woolsey | Y | N | N | Y |
| 7 Miller, George | Y | N | N | ? |
| 8 Pelosi | Y | N | Y | Y |
| 9 Lee | ? | ? | ? | ? |
| 10 Tauscher | Y | N | Y | Y |
| 11 Pombo | N | Y | Y | Y |
| 12 Lantos | Y | N | Y | Y |
| 13 Stark | Y | N | N | ? |
| 14 Eshoo | Y | N | Y | Y |
| 15 Honda | Y | N | N | Y |
| 16 Lofgren | Y | N | Y | ? |
| 17 Farr | Y | N | N | Y |
| 18 Cardoza | N | Y | Y | ? |
| 19 Radanovich | N | Y | Y | Y |
| 20 Costa | N | Y | Y | Y |
| 21 Nunes | N | Y | Y | Y |
| 22 Thomas | N | Y | Y | Y |
| 23 Capps | Y | N | N | Y |
| 24 Gallegly | N | Y | ? | ? |
| 25 McKeon | N | Y | Y | Y |
| 26 Dreier | N | Y | Y | Y |
| 27 Sherman | Y | N | Y | Y |
| 28 Berman | Y | N | ? | ? |
| 29 Schiff | Y | N | Y | Y |
| 30 Waxman | Y | N | Y | Y |
| 31 Becerra | Y | N | Y | Y |
| 32 Solis | Y | N | Y | Y |
| 33 Watson | Y | N | Y | Y |
| 34 Roybal-Allard | Y | N | Y | Y |
| 35 Waters | Y | N | N | Y |
| 36 Harman | ? | ? | ? | ? |
| 37 Millender-McD. | Y | N | Y | Y |
| 38 Napolitano | Y | N | Y | Y |
| 39 Sánchez, Linda | Y | N | Y | Y |
| 40 Royce | N | Y | Y | Y |
| 41 Lewis | N | Y | Y | Y |
| 42 Miller, Gary | N | Y | ? | ? |
| 43 Baca | N | Y | Y | Y |
| 44 Calvert | N | Y | Y | Y |
| 45 Bono | N | Y | Y | Y |
| 46 Rohrabacher | N | Y | Y | Y |
| 47 Sanchez, Loretta | Y | N | Y | Y |
| 48 Vacant | | | | |
| 49 Issa | N | Y | Y | Y |

| | 505 | 506 | 507 | 508 |
|---|---|---|---|---|
| 50 Cunningham | N | Y | Y | Y |
| 51 Filner | Y | N | N | Y |
| 52 Hunter | N | Y | Y | Y |
| 53 Davis | Y | N | Y | Y |
| **COLORADO** | | | | |
| 1 DeGette | Y | N | N | Y |
| 2 Udall | Y | N | Y | Y |
| 3 Salazar | N | Y | Y | Y |
| 4 Musgrave | N | Y | Y | Y |
| 5 Hefley | N | Y | Y | Y |
| 6 Tancredo | N | Y | Y | Y |
| 7 Beauprez | N | Y | Y | Y |
| **CONNECTICUT** | | | | |
| 1 Larson | Y | N | N | Y |
| 2 Simmons | N | N | Y | Y |
| 3 DeLauro | Y | N | N | Y |
| 4 Shays | Y | N | Y | Y |
| 5 Johnson | Y | N | Y | Y |
| **DELAWARE** | | | | |
| AL Castle | Y | N | Y | Y |
| **FLORIDA** | | | | |
| 1 Miller | N | Y | Y | ? |
| 2 Boyd | Y | Y | Y | Y |
| 3 Brown | Y | N | Y | Y |
| 4 Crenshaw | N | Y | Y | Y |
| 5 Brown-Waite | N | Y | Y | Y |
| 6 Stearns | N | Y | Y | Y |
| 7 Mica | N | Y | Y | Y |
| 8 Keller | N | Y | Y | Y |
| 9 Bilirakis | N | Y | Y | Y |
| 10 Young | N | Y | Y | Y |
| 11 Davis | ? | ? | ? | ? |
| 12 Putnam | N | Y | Y | Y |
| 13 Harris | N | Y | Y | Y |
| 14 Mack | N | Y | Y | Y |
| 15 Weldon | N | Y | Y | Y |
| 16 Foley | N | Y | Y | Y |
| 17 Meek | Y | N | Y | Y |
| 18 Ros-Lehtinen | N | Y | Y | ? |
| 19 Wexler | Y | N | Y | Y |
| 20 Wasserman-Schultz | Y | N | Y | Y |
| 21 Diaz-Balart, L. | N | Y | Y | Y |
| 22 Shaw | N | N | Y | Y |
| 23 Hastings | Y | N | Y | Y |
| 24 Feeney | N | Y | Y | Y |
| 25 Diaz-Balart, M. | N | Y | Y | Y |
| **GEORGIA** | | | | |
| 1 Kingston | N | Y | Y | Y |
| 2 Bishop | N | Y | Y | Y |
| 3 Marshall | Y | Y | Y | Y |
| 4 McKinney | Y | N | N | Y |
| 5 Lewis | Y | N | N | Y |
| 6 Price | N | Y | Y | Y |
| 7 Linder | N | Y | Y | Y |
| 8 Westmoreland | N | Y | Y | Y |
| 9 Norwood | N | Y | Y | Y |
| 10 Deal | N | Y | Y | Y |
| 11 Gingrey | N | Y | Y | Y |
| 12 Barrow | Y | Y | Y | Y |
| 13 Scott | N | Y | Y | ? |
| **HAWAII** | | | | |
| 1 Abercrombie | Y | Y | Y | Y |
| 2 Case | Y | N | Y | Y |
| **IDAHO** | | | | |
| 1 Otter | N | Y | Y | Y |
| 2 Simpson | N | Y | Y | Y |
| **ILLINOIS** | | | | |
| 1 Rush | Y | N | Y | Y |
| 2 Jackson | Y | N | Y | Y |
| 3 Lipinski | Y | N | Y | Y |
| 4 Gutierrez | + | – | + | + |
| 5 Emanuel | Y | N | N | Y |
| 6 Hyde | N | Y | Y | Y |
| 7 Davis | Y | N | Y | Y |
| 8 Bean | Y | N | Y | Y |
| 9 Schakowsky | Y | N | N | Y |
| 10 Kirk | Y | N | Y | Y |
| 11 Weller | N | Y | Y | Y |
| 12 Costello | Y | Y | N | Y |

| KEY | Republicans | Democrats | Independents |
|---|---|---|---|

| | | | | |
|---|---|---|---|---|
| Y | Voted for (yea) | X | Paired against | C Voted "present" to avoid possible conflict of interest |
| # | Paired for | – | Announced against | |
| + | Announced for | P | Voted "present" | ? Did not vote or otherwise make a position known |
| N | Voted against (nay) | | | |

ND Northern Democrats, SD Southern Democrats
Southern states: Ala., Ark., Fla., Ga., Ky., La., Miss., N.C., Okla., S.C., Tenn., Texas, Va.

H-160    2005 CQ ALMANAC | www.cq.com

| | 505 | 506 | 507 | 508 |
|---|---|---|---|---|
| 13 Biggert | Y | N | Y | Y |
| 14 Hastert | | | | |
| 15 Johnson | Y | N | Y | Y |
| 16 Manzullo | N | Y | Y | Y |
| 17 Evans | Y | N | Y | Y |
| 18 LaHood | N | N | Y | Y |
| 19 Shimkus | N | Y | Y | Y |
| **INDIANA** | | | | |
| 1 Visclosky | Y | N | Y | Y |
| 2 Chocola | N | Y | Y | Y |
| 3 Souder | N | Y | Y | Y |
| 4 Buyer | N | Y | ? | Y |
| 5 Burton | N | Y | Y | Y |
| 6 Pence | N | Y | Y | Y |
| 7 Carson | Y | N | N | Y |
| 8 Hostettler | N | Y | Y | Y |
| 9 Sodrel | N | Y | Y | Y |
| **IOWA** | | | | |
| 1 Nussle | N | Y | Y | Y |
| 2 Leach | Y | N | Y | Y |
| 3 Boswell | ? | ? | ? | ? |
| 4 Latham | N | Y | Y | Y |
| 5 King | N | Y | Y | Y |
| **KANSAS** | | | | |
| 1 Moran | N | Y | Y | Y |
| 2 Ryun | N | Y | Y | Y |
| 3 Moore | Y | N | Y | Y |
| 4 Tiahrt | N | Y | Y | Y |
| **KENTUCKY** | | | | |
| 1 Whitfield | N | Y | Y | Y |
| 2 Lewis | N | Y | Y | Y |
| 3 Northup | N | Y | Y | Y |
| 4 Davis | N | Y | Y | Y |
| 5 Rogers | N | Y | Y | Y |
| 6 Chandler | Y | N | Y | Y |
| **LOUISIANA** | | | | |
| 1 Jindal | N | Y | Y | Y |
| 2 Jefferson | Y | N | Y | Y |
| 3 Melancon | N | Y | Y | Y |
| 4 McCrery | N | Y | Y | Y |
| 5 Alexander | N | Y | Y | Y |
| 6 Baker | N | Y | Y | Y |
| 7 Boustany | N | Y | Y | Y |
| **MAINE** | | | | |
| 1 Allen | Y | N | Y | Y |
| 2 Michaud | Y | N | Y | Y |
| **MARYLAND** | | | | |
| 1 Gilchrest | Y | N | Y | Y |
| 2 Ruppersberger | Y | N | Y | Y |
| 3 Cardin | Y | N | Y | Y |
| 4 Wynn | Y | Y | Y | Y |
| 5 Hoyer | Y | N | Y | Y |
| 6 Bartlett | N | Y | Y | Y |
| 7 Cummings | Y | N | ? | ? |
| 8 Van Hollen | Y | N | Y | Y |
| **MASSACHUSETTS** | | | | |
| 1 Olver | Y | N | N | Y |
| 2 Neal | Y | N | N | Y |
| 3 McGovern | Y | N | N | Y |
| 4 Frank | Y | N | N | Y |
| 5 Meehan | Y | N | N | Y |
| 6 Tierney | Y | N | N | Y |
| 7 Markey | Y | N | N | Y |
| 8 Capuano | Y | N | N | Y |
| 9 Lynch | Y | N | Y | ? |
| 10 Delahunt | Y | N | ? | ? |
| **MICHIGAN** | | | | |
| 1 Stupak | Y | N | Y | Y |
| 2 Hoekstra | N | Y | Y | Y |
| 3 Ehlers | Y | N | Y | Y |
| 4 Camp | N | Y | Y | Y |
| 5 Kildee | Y | N | N | Y |
| 6 Upton | N | Y | Y | Y |
| 7 Schwarz | Y | N | Y | Y |
| 8 Rogers | N | Y | Y | Y |
| 9 Knollenberg | N | Y | Y | Y |
| 10 Miller | N | Y | Y | Y |
| 11 McCotter | N | Y | Y | Y |
| 12 Levin | Y | N | Y | Y |
| 13 Kilpatrick | Y | N | Y | + |
| 14 Conyers | Y | N | N | Y |
| 15 Dingell | Y | N | Y | Y |

| | 505 | 506 | 507 | 508 |
|---|---|---|---|---|
| **MINNESOTA** | | | | |
| 1 Gutknecht | N | Y | Y | Y |
| 2 Kline | N | Y | Y | Y |
| 3 Ramstad | Y | N | Y | Y |
| 4 McCollum | Y | N | N | Y |
| 5 Sabo | Y | N | Y | Y |
| 6 Kennedy | N | Y | Y | Y |
| 7 Peterson | N | Y | Y | Y |
| 8 Oberstar | Y | N | N | Y |
| **MISSISSIPPI** | | | | |
| 1 Wicker | N | Y | Y | Y |
| 2 Thompson | Y | Y | Y | Y |
| 3 Pickering | N | Y | Y | Y |
| 4 Taylor | Y | Y | Y | Y |
| **MISSOURI** | | | | |
| 1 Clay | Y | N | N | Y |
| 2 Akin | N | Y | Y | Y |
| 3 Carnahan | Y | N | Y | Y |
| 4 Skelton | Y | Y | Y | Y |
| 5 Cleaver | Y | N | Y | Y |
| 6 Graves | N | Y | Y | Y |
| 7 Blunt | N | Y | Y | Y |
| 8 Emerson | N | Y | Y | ? |
| 9 Hulshof | N | Y | Y | Y |
| **MONTANA** | | | | |
| AL Rehberg | N | Y | Y | Y |
| **NEBRASKA** | | | | |
| 1 Fortenberry | N | Y | Y | Y |
| 2 Terry | N | Y | Y | Y |
| 3 Osborne | N | Y | Y | Y |
| **NEVADA** | | | | |
| 1 Berkley | Y | N | Y | Y |
| 2 Gibbons | N | Y | Y | Y |
| 3 Porter | N | Y | Y | Y |
| **NEW HAMPSHIRE** | | | | |
| 1 Bradley | Y | N | Y | Y |
| 2 Bass | Y | N | Y | Y |
| **NEW JERSEY** | | | | |
| 1 Andrews | Y | N | Y | Y |
| 2 LoBiondo | Y | N | Y | Y |
| 3 Saxton | Y | N | Y | Y |
| 4 Smith | Y | N | Y | Y |
| 5 Garrett | N | Y | Y | Y |
| 6 Pallone | Y | N | Y | Y |
| 7 Ferguson | Y | N | Y | Y |
| 8 Pascrell | Y | N | Y | Y |
| 9 Rothman | Y | N | Y | Y |
| 10 Payne | ? | ? | ? | ? |
| 11 Frelinghuysen | Y | N | Y | Y |
| 12 Holt | Y | N | N | Y |
| 13 Menendez | Y | N | Y | Y |
| **NEW MEXICO** | | | | |
| 1 Wilson | N | Y | Y | Y |
| 2 Pearce | N | Y | Y | Y |
| 3 Udall | Y | N | N | Y |
| **NEW YORK** | | | | |
| 1 Bishop | Y | N | Y | Y |
| 2 Israel | Y | N | Y | Y |
| 3 King | N | Y | Y | Y |
| 4 McCarthy | Y | N | Y | Y |
| 5 Ackerman | Y | N | Y | ? |
| 6 Meeks | Y | N | Y | Y |
| 7 Crowley | Y | N | N | Y |
| 8 Nadler | Y | N | N | Y |
| 9 Weiner | Y | N | N | Y |
| 10 Towns | ? | ? | ? | ? |
| 11 Owens | Y | N | Y | Y |
| 12 Velázquez | Y | N | Y | Y |
| 13 Fossella | N | Y | Y | Y |
| 14 Maloney | Y | N | Y | Y |
| 15 Rangel | Y | N | Y | Y |
| 16 Serrano | Y | N | Y | Y |
| 17 Engel | Y | N | Y | Y |
| 18 Lowey | Y | N | Y | Y |
| 19 Kelly | Y | N | Y | Y |
| 20 Sweeney | N | Y | Y | Y |
| 21 McNulty | Y | N | Y | ? |
| 22 Hinchey | Y | N | N | Y |
| 23 McHugh | N | Y | Y | Y |
| 24 Boehlert | Y | N | Y | Y |
| 25 Walsh | Y | N | Y | Y |
| 26 Reynolds | N | Y | Y | Y |
| 27 Higgins | Y | N | Y | Y |
| 28 Slaughter | Y | N | Y | Y |
| 29 Kuhl | N | Y | Y | Y |

| | 505 | 506 | 507 | 508 |
|---|---|---|---|---|
| **NORTH CAROLINA** | | | | |
| 1 Butterfield | Y | N | Y | Y |
| 2 Etheridge | Y | N | Y | Y |
| 3 Jones | N | Y | Y | Y |
| 4 Price | Y | N | Y | Y |
| 5 Foxx | N | Y | Y | Y |
| 6 Coble | N | Y | Y | Y |
| 7 McIntyre | N | Y | N | Y |
| 8 Hayes | N | Y | Y | Y |
| 9 Myrick | N | Y | Y | Y |
| 10 McHenry | N | Y | Y | Y |
| 11 Taylor | N | Y | Y | Y |
| 12 Watt | Y | N | N | Y |
| 13 Miller | Y | N | Y | Y |
| **NORTH DAKOTA** | | | | |
| AL Pomeroy | Y | Y | Y | Y |
| **OHIO** | | | | |
| 1 Chabot | N | Y | Y | Y |
| 2 Schmidt | N | Y | Y | Y |
| 3 Turner | N | Y | Y | Y |
| 4 Oxley | N | Y | Y | Y |
| 5 Gillmor | N | Y | Y | Y |
| 6 Strickland | Y | N | Y | Y |
| 7 Hobson | ? | ? | ? | ? |
| 8 Boehner | N | Y | Y | Y |
| 9 Kaptur | Y | N | N | Y |
| 10 Kucinich | Y | N | N | Y |
| 11 Jones | Y | N | N | Y |
| 12 Tiberi | N | Y | Y | Y |
| 13 Brown | Y | N | Y | Y |
| 14 LaTourette | N | N | Y | Y |
| 15 Pryce | N | Y | Y | Y |
| 16 Regula | N | Y | Y | Y |
| 17 Ryan | Y | N | Y | Y |
| 18 Ney | N | Y | Y | Y |
| **OKLAHOMA** | | | | |
| 1 Sullivan | N | Y | Y | Y |
| 2 Boren | N | Y | Y | Y |
| 3 Lucas | N | Y | Y | Y |
| 4 Cole | N | Y | Y | Y |
| 5 Istook | N | Y | Y | Y |
| **OREGON** | | | | |
| 1 Wu | Y | N | N | Y |
| 2 Walden | N | Y | Y | Y |
| 3 Blumenauer | Y | N | N | Y |
| 4 DeFazio | Y | N | N | Y |
| 5 Hooley | Y | N | Y | Y |
| **PENNSYLVANIA** | | | | |
| 1 Brady | Y | N | N | Y |
| 2 Fattah | + | - | ? | ? |
| 3 English | N | Y | ? | Y |
| 4 Hart | N | Y | Y | Y |
| 5 Peterson | N | Y | Y | Y |
| 6 Gerlach | Y | N | Y | Y |
| 7 Weldon | Y | N | Y | Y |
| 8 Fitzpatrick | Y | N | Y | Y |
| 9 Shuster | N | Y | Y | Y |
| 10 Sherwood | N | Y | Y | Y |
| 11 Kanjorski | Y | N | Y | Y |
| 12 Murtha | Y | N | Y | Y |
| 13 Schwartz | Y | N | Y | Y |
| 14 Doyle | Y | N | Y | Y |
| 15 Dent | Y | N | Y | Y |
| 16 Pitts | N | Y | Y | Y |
| 17 Holden | Y | Y | Y | Y |
| 18 Murphy | N | Y | Y | Y |
| 19 Platts | Y | N | Y | Y |
| **RHODE ISLAND** | | | | |
| 1 Kennedy | Y | N | N | Y |
| 2 Langevin | Y | N | N | Y |
| **SOUTH CAROLINA** | | | | |
| 1 Brown | N | Y | Y | Y |
| 2 Wilson | N | Y | Y | Y |
| 3 Barrett | N | Y | Y | Y |
| 4 Inglis | Y | Y | Y | Y |
| 5 Spratt | Y | N | Y | Y |
| 6 Clyburn | Y | N | Y | Y |
| **SOUTH DAKOTA** | | | | |
| AL Herseth | N | Y | Y | Y |
| **TENNESSEE** | | | | |
| 1 Jenkins | N | Y | Y | Y |
| 2 Duncan | N | Y | Y | Y |

| | 505 | 506 | 507 | 508 |
|---|---|---|---|---|
| 3 Wamp | N | Y | Y | Y |
| 4 Davis | Y | Y | Y | Y |
| 5 Cooper | Y | N | Y | Y |
| 6 Gordon | Y | N | Y | Y |
| 7 Blackburn | N | Y | Y | Y |
| 8 Tanner | Y | Y | Y | Y |
| 9 Ford | Y | Y | N | Y |
| **TEXAS** | | | | |
| 1 Gohmert | N | Y | Y | Y |
| 2 Poe | N | Y | Y | Y |
| 3 Johnson, S. | N | Y | Y | Y |
| 4 Hall | N | Y | Y | Y |
| 5 Hensarling | N | Y | Y | Y |
| 6 Barton | N | Y | Y | Y |
| 7 Culberson | ? | ? | ? | ? |
| 8 Brady | N | Y | ? | Y |
| 9 Green, A. | Y | N | Y | Y |
| 10 McCaul | N | Y | Y | Y |
| 11 Conaway | N | Y | Y | Y |
| 12 Granger | N | Y | Y | Y |
| 13 Thornberry | N | Y | Y | Y |
| 14 Paul | ? | ? | ? | ? |
| 15 Hinojosa | Y | Y | Y | Y |
| 16 Reyes | Y | N | Y | Y |
| 17 Edwards | N | Y | Y | Y |
| 18 Jackson-Lee | Y | N | Y | Y |
| 19 Neugebauer | N | Y | Y | Y |
| 20 Gonzalez | Y | N | Y | Y |
| 21 Smith | N | Y | Y | Y |
| 22 DeLay | N | Y | Y | ? |
| 23 Bonilla | N | Y | Y | Y |
| 24 Marchant | N | Y | Y | Y |
| 25 Doggett | Y | N | Y | Y |
| 26 Burgess | N | Y | Y | Y |
| 27 Ortiz | Y | N | Y | Y |
| 28 Cuellar | Y | N | Y | Y |
| 29 Green, G. | Y | N | Y | Y |
| 30 Johnson, E. | Y | N | Y | Y |
| 31 Carter | N | Y | Y | Y |
| 32 Sessions | N | Y | Y | Y |
| **UTAH** | | | | |
| 1 Bishop | N | Y | Y | Y |
| 2 Matheson | Y | Y | Y | Y |
| 3 Cannon | N | Y | Y | Y |
| **VERMONT** | | | | |
| AL Sanders | Y | N | N | Y |
| **VIRGINIA** | | | | |
| 1 Davis, J. | N | Y | Y | Y |
| 2 Drake | N | Y | Y | Y |
| 3 Scott | Y | N | N | Y |
| 4 Forbes | N | Y | Y | Y |
| 5 Goode | N | Y | Y | Y |
| 6 Goodlatte | N | Y | Y | Y |
| 7 Cantor | N | Y | Y | Y |
| 8 Moran | Y | N | Y | Y |
| 9 Boucher | Y | N | N | Y |
| 10 Wolf | Y | N | Y | Y |
| 11 Davis, T. | Y | N | Y | Y |
| **WASHINGTON** | | | | |
| 1 Inslee | Y | N | Y | Y |
| 2 Larsen | Y | N | Y | Y |
| 3 Baird | Y | N | Y | Y |
| 4 Hastings | N | Y | Y | Y |
| 5 McMorris | N | Y | Y | Y |
| 6 Dicks | Y | N | Y | Y |
| 7 McDermott | Y | N | N | Y |
| 8 Reichert | N | Y | Y | Y |
| 9 Smith | Y | N | Y | Y |
| **WEST VIRGINIA** | | | | |
| 1 Mollohan | Y | Y | Y | Y |
| 2 Capito | N | Y | Y | Y |
| 3 Rahall | Y | N | Y | Y |
| **WISCONSIN** | | | | |
| 1 Ryan | N | Y | N | Y |
| 2 Baldwin | Y | N | N | Y |
| 3 Kind | Y | N | N | Y |
| 4 Moore | Y | N | N | Y |
| 5 Sensenbrenner | N | Y | Y | Y |
| 6 Petri | Y | Y | ? | ? |
| 7 Obey | Y | N | N | Y |
| 8 Green | Y | N | N | Y |
| **WYOMING** | | | | |
| AL Cubin | N | Y | Y | Y |

# IN THE HOUSE | By Vote Number

**509.** **S 1786. Airport Emergency Grants/Passage.** Mica, R-Fla., motion to suspend the rules and pass the bill that would authorize the Transportation Department to provide emergency grants to certain airports in Louisiana, Mississippi, Alabama and Texas that were damaged by hurricanes Katrina and Rita. Motion agreed to 420-0: R 225-0; D 194-0 (ND 144-0, SD 50-0); I 1-0. A two-thirds majority of those present and voting (280 in this case) is required for passage under suspension of the rules. Oct. 6, 2005.

**510.** **H Res 276. Pancreatic Cancer Awareness Month/Adoption.** Duncan, R-Tenn., motion to suspend the rules and adopt the resolution that would support the goals and ideals of Pancreatic Cancer Awareness Month, to be designated for November. Motion agreed to 415-0: R 220-0; D 194-0 (ND 144-0, SD 50-0); I 1-0. A two-thirds majority of those present and voting (277 in this case) is required for adoption under suspension of the rules. Oct. 6, 2005.

**511.** **HR 3894. Hurricane Katrina Section 8 Housing Relief/Passage.** Baker, R-La., motion to suspend the rules and pass the bill that would direct the Housing and Urban Development Department to waive eligibility requirements for the Section 8 housing voucher program for anyone who resided in a federal disaster area and whose residence became uninhabitable as a result of Hurricane Katrina. Motion agreed to 418-0: R 223-0; D 194-0 (ND 144-0, SD 50-0); I 1-0. A two-thirds majority of those present and voting (279 in this case) is required for passage under suspension of the rules. Oct. 6, 2005.

**512.** **HR 2360. Fiscal 2006 Homeland Security Appropriations/ Conference Report.** Adoption of the conference report on the bill that would appropriate $31.9 billion in fiscal 2006 for the Homeland Security Department and related agencies. The bill includes $6 billion for customs and border protection; $5.9 billion for the Transportation Security Administration, including fees; $7.8 billion for the Coast Guard; $1.2 billion for the Secret Service and $2.6 billion for response and recovery efforts conducted by the Federal Emergency Management Agency. Adopted (thus sent to the Senate) 347-70: R 223-2; D 124-67 (ND 83-58, SD 41-9); I 0-1. Oct. 6, 2005.

**513.** **HR 3895. Rural Housing Hurricane Katrina Relief/Passage.** Baker, R-La., motion to suspend the rules and pass the bill that would allow the Agricultural Department, in the event of a presidentially declared natural disaster, to convert rural rental assistance into urban and rural housing vouchers. Motion agreed to 335-81: R 149-76; D 185-5 (ND 136-4, SD 49-1); I 1-0. A two-thirds majority of those present and voting (278 in this case) is required for passage under suspension of the rules. Oct. 6, 2005.

**514.** **HR 3896. CDBG Hurricane Katrina Relief/Passage.** Baker, R-La., motion to suspend the rules and pass the bill that would direct the Housing and Urban Development Department to suspend Community Development Block Grant caps for fiscal 2005 through 2008 for communities directly affected by hurricanes Katrina and Rita. Motion agreed to 415-0: R 224-0; D 190-0 (ND 140-0, SD 50-0); I 1-0. A two-thirds majority of those present and voting (277 in this case) is required for passage under suspension of the rules. Oct. 6, 2005.

ND Northern Democrats, SD Southern Democrats
Southern states: Ala., Ark., Fla., Ga., Ky., La., Miss., N.C., Okla., S.C., Tenn., Texas, Va.

| | 509 | 510 | 511 | 512 | 513 | 514 |
|---|---|---|---|---|---|---|
| **ALABAMA** | | | | | | |
| 1 Bonner | Y | Y | Y | Y | Y | Y |
| 2 Everett | Y | Y | Y | Y | Y | Y |
| 3 Rogers | Y | Y | Y | Y | Y | Y |
| 4 Aderholt | Y | Y | Y | Y | Y | Y |
| 5 Cramer | Y | Y | Y | Y | Y | Y |
| 6 Bachus | Y | Y | Y | Y | Y | Y |
| 7 Davis | Y | Y | Y | Y | Y | |
| **ALASKA** | | | | | | |
| AL Young | Y | Y | Y | ? | ? | ? |
| **ARIZONA** | | | | | | |
| 1 Renzi | Y | Y | Y | Y | Y | Y |
| 2 Franks | Y | Y | Y | Y | N | Y |
| 3 Shadegg | Y | Y | Y | Y | Y | Y |
| 4 Pastor | Y | Y | Y | N | Y | Y |
| 5 Hayworth | Y | Y | Y | Y | Y | Y |
| 6 Flake | Y | Y | Y | N | Y | N |
| 7 Grijalva | Y | Y | Y | N | N | Y |
| 8 Kolbe | Y | Y | Y | Y | N | Y |
| **ARKANSAS** | | | | | | |
| 1 Berry | Y | Y | Y | N | Y | Y |
| 2 Snyder | Y | Y | Y | Y | Y | Y |
| 3 Boozman | Y | Y | Y | Y | N | Y |
| 4 Ross | Y | Y | Y | Y | Y | Y |
| **CALIFORNIA** | | | | | | |
| 1 Thompson | Y | Y | Y | Y | Y | Y |
| 2 Herger | Y | Y | Y | Y | N | Y |
| 3 Lungren | Y | Y | Y | Y | Y | Y |
| 4 Doolittle | Y | Y | Y | Y | N | Y |
| 5 Matsui, D. | Y | Y | Y | Y | Y | Y |
| 6 Woolsey | Y | Y | Y | N | Y | Y |
| 7 Miller, George | Y | Y | Y | N | Y | Y |
| 8 Pelosi | Y | Y | Y | Y | Y | Y |
| 9 Lee | Y | Y | Y | N | Y | Y |
| 10 Tauscher | Y | Y | Y | Y | Y | Y |
| 11 Pombo | Y | Y | Y | Y | Y | Y |
| 12 Lantos | Y | Y | Y | Y | Y | Y |
| 13 Stark | Y | Y | Y | ? | ? | ? |
| 14 Eshoo | Y | Y | Y | Y | Y | Y |
| 15 Honda | Y | Y | Y | N | Y | Y |
| 16 Lofgren | Y | Y | Y | Y | Y | Y |
| 17 Farr | Y | Y | Y | Y | Y | Y |
| 18 Cardoza | Y | Y | Y | Y | Y | Y |
| 19 Radanovich | Y | Y | Y | Y | Y | Y |
| 20 Costa | Y | Y | Y | Y | Y | Y |
| 21 Nunes | Y | ? | Y | Y | Y | Y |
| 22 Thomas | Y | Y | Y | Y | Y | Y |
| 23 Capps | Y | Y | Y | N | Y | Y |
| 24 Gallegly | Y | Y | Y | Y | Y | Y |
| 25 McKeon | Y | Y | Y | Y | Y | Y |
| 26 Dreier | Y | Y | Y | Y | Y | Y |
| 27 Sherman | Y | Y | Y | Y | Y | Y |
| 28 Berman | Y | Y | Y | Y | Y | Y |
| 29 Schiff | Y | Y | Y | Y | Y | Y |
| 30 Waxman | Y | Y | Y | N | Y | Y |
| 31 Becerra | Y | Y | Y | Y | Y | Y |
| 32 Solis | Y | Y | Y | Y | Y | Y |
| 33 Watson | ? | ? | ? | ? | ? | ? |
| 34 Roybal-Allard | Y | Y | Y | Y | Y | Y |
| 35 Waters | Y | Y | Y | N | Y | Y |
| 36 Harman | Y | Y | Y | Y | Y | Y |
| 37 Millender-McD. | Y | Y | Y | Y | Y | Y |
| 38 Napolitano | Y | Y | Y | N | Y | Y |
| 39 Sánchez, Linda | Y | Y | Y | Y | Y | Y |
| 40 Royce | ? | ? | ? | ? | ? | ? |
| 41 Lewis | Y | ? | Y | N | Y | Y |
| 42 Miller, Gary | Y | Y | Y | N | Y | Y |
| 43 Baca | Y | Y | Y | N | Y | Y |
| 44 Calvert | Y | Y | Y | N | Y | Y |
| 45 Bono | Y | Y | Y | Y | Y | Y |
| 46 Rohrabacher | Y | Y | Y | N | Y | Y |
| 47 Sanchez, Loretta | Y | Y | Y | Y | Y | Y |
| 48 Vacant | | | | | | |
| 49 Issa | Y | Y | Y | Y | Y | Y |
| 50 Cunningham | Y | Y | Y | N | Y | Y |
| 51 Filner | Y | Y | Y | N | Y | Y |
| 52 Hunter | Y | Y | Y | Y | N | Y |
| 53 Davis | Y | Y | Y | Y | Y | Y |
| **COLORADO** | | | | | | |
| 1 DeGette | Y | Y | Y | N | Y | Y |
| 2 Udall | Y | Y | Y | Y | Y | Y |
| 3 Salazar | Y | Y | Y | Y | Y | Y |
| 4 Musgrave | Y | Y | Y | Y | Y | Y |
| 5 Hefley | Y | Y | Y | Y | Y | Y |
| 6 Tancredo | Y | Y | Y | Y | Y | Y |
| 7 Beauprez | Y | Y | Y | Y | Y | Y |
| **CONNECTICUT** | | | | | | |
| 1 Larson | Y | Y | Y | N | Y | Y |
| 2 Simmons | Y | Y | Y | N | Y | Y |
| 3 DeLauro | Y | Y | Y | N | Y | Y |
| 4 Shays | Y | Y | Y | Y | Y | Y |
| 5 Johnson | Y | Y | Y | Y | Y | Y |
| **DELAWARE** | | | | | | |
| AL Castle | Y | Y | Y | Y | Y | Y |
| **FLORIDA** | | | | | | |
| 1 Miller | Y | Y | Y | Y | Y | Y |
| 2 Boyd | Y | Y | Y | Y | Y | Y |
| 3 Brown | Y | Y | Y | N | Y | Y |
| 4 Crenshaw | Y | Y | Y | Y | N | Y |
| 5 Brown-Waite | Y | Y | Y | Y | N | Y |
| 6 Stearns | Y | Y | Y | Y | N | Y |
| 7 Mica | Y | Y | Y | Y | Y | Y |
| 8 Keller | Y | Y | Y | Y | Y | Y |
| 9 Bilirakis | Y | Y | Y | Y | N | Y |
| 10 Young | Y | Y | Y | Y | N | Y |
| 11 Davis | Y | Y | Y | Y | Y | Y |
| 12 Putnam | Y | Y | Y | Y | N | Y |
| 13 Harris | Y | Y | Y | Y | Y | Y |
| 14 Mack | Y | Y | Y | Y | Y | Y |
| 15 Weldon | Y | Y | Y | Y | Y | Y |
| 16 Foley | Y | Y | Y | Y | Y | Y |
| 17 Meek | Y | Y | Y | Y | Y | Y |
| 18 Ros-Lehtinen | Y | Y | Y | Y | Y | Y |
| 19 Wexler | Y | Y | Y | N | Y | Y |
| 20 Wasserman-Schultz | Y | Y | Y | N | Y | Y |
| 21 Diaz-Balart, L. | Y | Y | Y | Y | Y | Y |
| 22 Shaw | Y | Y | Y | Y | Y | Y |
| 23 Hastings | ? | ? | ? | ? | ? | ? |
| 24 Feeney | Y | Y | Y | Y | Y | Y |
| 25 Diaz-Balart, M. | Y | Y | Y | Y | Y | Y |
| **GEORGIA** | | | | | | |
| 1 Kingston | Y | Y | Y | N | N | Y |
| 2 Bishop | Y | Y | Y | Y | Y | Y |
| 3 Marshall | Y | Y | Y | Y | Y | Y |
| 4 McKinney | Y | Y | Y | N | Y | Y |
| 5 Lewis | Y | Y | Y | N | Y | Y |
| 6 Price | Y | Y | Y | Y | Y | Y |
| 7 Linder | ? | ? | ? | Y | Y | Y |
| 8 Westmoreland | Y | Y | Y | Y | Y | Y |
| 9 Norwood | Y | Y | Y | Y | Y | Y |
| 10 Deal | Y | Y | Y | Y | Y | Y |
| 11 Gingrey | Y | Y | Y | Y | Y | Y |
| 12 Barrow | Y | Y | Y | Y | Y | Y |
| 13 Scott | Y | Y | Y | Y | Y | Y |
| **HAWAII** | | | | | | |
| 1 Abercrombie | Y | Y | Y | N | Y | Y |
| 2 Case | Y | Y | Y | Y | Y | Y |
| **IDAHO** | | | | | | |
| 1 Otter | Y | Y | Y | Y | N | Y |
| 2 Simpson | Y | Y | Y | Y | Y | Y |
| **ILLINOIS** | | | | | | |
| 1 Rush | Y | Y | Y | N | Y | Y |
| 2 Jackson | Y | Y | Y | N | Y | Y |
| 3 Lipinski | Y | Y | Y | Y | Y | Y |
| 4 Gutierrez | Y | Y | Y | N | Y | Y |
| 5 Emanuel | Y | Y | Y | Y | Y | Y |
| 6 Hyde | Y | Y | Y | Y | Y | Y |
| 7 Davis | Y | Y | Y | N | Y | Y |
| 8 Bean | Y | Y | Y | Y | Y | Y |
| 9 Schakowsky | Y | Y | Y | N | Y | Y |
| 10 Kirk | Y | Y | Y | ? | Y | Y |
| 11 Weller | Y | Y | Y | Y | Y | Y |
| 12 Costello | Y | Y | Y | N | Y | Y |

**KEY**   Republicans   Democrats   Independents

| | | |
|---|---|---|
| Y Voted for (yea) | X Paired against | C Voted "present" to avoid possible conflict of interest |
| # Paired for | – Announced against | |
| + Announced for | P Voted "present" | ? Did not vote or otherwise make a position known |
| N Voted against (nay) | | |

| | 509 | 510 | 511 | 512 | 513 | 514 |
|---|---|---|---|---|---|---|
| 13 **Biggert** | Y | Y | Y | Y | Y | Y |
| 14 **Hastert** | | | | | | |
| 15 **Johnson** | Y | Y | Y | Y | Y | Y |
| 16 **Manzullo** | Y | Y | Y | Y | Y | Y |
| 17 Evans | Y | Y | Y | ? | ? | ? |
| 18 **LaHood** | Y | Y | Y | Y | N | Y |
| 19 **Shimkus** | Y | Y | Y | Y | Y | Y |
| **INDIANA** | | | | | | |
| 1 Visclosky | Y | Y | Y | Y | Y | Y |
| 2 **Chocola** | Y | Y | Y | Y | Y | Y |
| 3 **Souder** | Y | Y | Y | Y | Y | Y |
| 4 **Buyer** | Y | Y | Y | Y | Y | Y |
| 5 **Burton** | Y | Y | Y | Y | Y | Y |
| 6 **Pence** | Y | Y | Y | Y | Y | Y |
| 7 Carson | Y | Y | Y | Y | Y | Y |
| 8 **Hostettler** | Y | Y | Y | Y | Y | Y |
| 9 **Sodrel** | Y | Y | Y | Y | Y | Y |
| **IOWA** | | | | | | |
| 1 **Nussle** | Y | Y | Y | Y | Y | Y |
| 2 **Leach** | Y | Y | Y | Y | Y | Y |
| 3 Boswell | ? | ? | ? | ? | ? | ? |
| 4 **Latham** | Y | Y | Y | Y | N | Y |
| 5 **King** | Y | Y | Y | Y | Y | Y |
| **KANSAS** | | | | | | |
| 1 **Moran** | Y | Y | Y | Y | N | Y |
| 2 **Ryun** | Y | Y | Y | Y | Y | Y |
| 3 Moore | Y | Y | Y | Y | Y | Y |
| 4 **Tiahrt** | Y | Y | Y | Y | N | Y |
| **KENTUCKY** | | | | | | |
| 1 **Whitfield** | ? | ? | ? | Y | N | Y |
| 2 **Lewis** | Y | Y | Y | Y | N | Y |
| 3 **Northup** | Y | Y | Y | Y | N | Y |
| 4 **Davis** | Y | Y | Y | Y | Y | Y |
| 5 **Rogers** | Y | Y | Y | Y | N | Y |
| 6 Chandler | Y | Y | Y | Y | Y | Y |
| **LOUISIANA** | | | | | | |
| 1 **Jindal** | Y | Y | Y | Y | Y | Y |
| 2 Jefferson | Y | Y | Y | Y | Y | Y |
| 3 Melancon | Y | Y | Y | Y | Y | Y |
| 4 **McCrery** | Y | Y | Y | Y | Y | Y |
| 5 **Alexander** | Y | Y | Y | Y | Y | Y |
| 6 **Baker** | Y | Y | Y | Y | Y | Y |
| 7 **Boustany** | Y | Y | Y | Y | Y | Y |
| **MAINE** | | | | | | |
| 1 Allen | Y | Y | Y | N | Y | Y |
| 2 Michaud | Y | Y | Y | N | Y | Y |
| **MARYLAND** | | | | | | |
| 1 **Gilchrest** | Y | Y | Y | Y | Y | Y |
| 2 Ruppersberger | Y | Y | Y | Y | Y | Y |
| 3 Cardin | Y | Y | Y | Y | Y | Y |
| 4 Wynn | Y | Y | Y | Y | Y | Y |
| 5 Hoyer | Y | Y | Y | Y | Y | Y |
| 6 **Bartlett** | Y | Y | Y | Y | N | Y |
| 7 Cummings | Y | Y | Y | Y | Y | Y |
| 8 Van Hollen | Y | Y | Y | Y | Y | Y |
| **MASSACHUSETTS** | | | | | | |
| 1 Olver | ? | ? | ? | ? | ? | ? |
| 2 Neal | Y | Y | Y | N | ? | ? |
| 3 McGovern | Y | Y | Y | N | Y | Y |
| 4 Frank | Y | Y | Y | N | Y | Y |
| 5 Meehan | Y | Y | Y | N | Y | Y |
| 6 Tierney | Y | Y | Y | N | Y | Y |
| 7 Markey | Y | Y | Y | N | Y | Y |
| 8 Capuano | Y | Y | Y | N | Y | Y |
| 9 Lynch | Y | Y | Y | N | Y | Y |
| 10 Delahunt | ? | ? | ? | ? | ? | ? |
| **MICHIGAN** | | | | | | |
| 1 Stupak | Y | Y | Y | Y | Y | Y |
| 2 **Hoekstra** | Y | Y | Y | Y | N | Y |
| 3 **Ehlers** | Y | Y | Y | Y | N | Y |
| 4 **Camp** | Y | Y | Y | Y | Y | Y |
| 5 Kildee | Y | Y | Y | Y | Y | Y |
| 6 **Upton** | Y | Y | Y | Y | N | Y |
| 7 **Schwarz** | ? | ? | ? | ? | ? | ? |
| 8 **Rogers** | Y | Y | Y | Y | Y | Y |
| 9 **Knollenberg** | Y | Y | Y | Y | N | Y |
| 10 **Miller** | Y | Y | Y | Y | N | Y |
| 11 **McCotter** | Y | Y | Y | Y | Y | Y |
| 12 Levin | Y | Y | Y | Y | Y | Y |
| 13 Kilpatrick | Y | Y | Y | Y | Y | Y |
| 14 Conyers | Y | Y | Y | N | Y | Y |
| 15 Dingell | Y | Y | Y | Y | Y | Y |

| | 509 | 510 | 511 | 512 | 513 | 514 |
|---|---|---|---|---|---|---|
| **MINNESOTA** | | | | | | |
| 1 **Gutknecht** | Y | Y | Y | Y | N | Y |
| 2 **Kline** | Y | Y | Y | Y | N | Y |
| 3 **Ramstad** | Y | Y | Y | Y | Y | Y |
| 4 McCollum | Y | Y | Y | N | Y | Y |
| 5 Sabo | Y | Y | Y | Y | Y | Y |
| 6 **Kennedy** | Y | Y | Y | Y | Y | Y |
| 7 Peterson | Y | Y | Y | Y | N | Y |
| 8 Oberstar | Y | Y | Y | N | Y | Y |
| **MISSISSIPPI** | | | | | | |
| 1 **Wicker** | Y | Y | Y | Y | Y | Y |
| 2 Thompson | Y | Y | Y | Y | Y | Y |
| 3 **Pickering** | Y | Y | Y | Y | Y | Y |
| 4 Taylor | Y | Y | Y | Y | Y | Y |
| **MISSOURI** | | | | | | |
| 1 Clay | Y | Y | Y | N | Y | Y |
| 2 **Akin** | Y | Y | Y | Y | Y | Y |
| 3 Carnahan | Y | Y | Y | Y | Y | Y |
| 4 Skelton | Y | Y | Y | Y | Y | Y |
| 5 Cleaver | Y | Y | Y | Y | Y | Y |
| 6 **Graves** | Y | Y | Y | Y | Y | Y |
| 7 **Blunt** | Y | Y | Y | Y | Y | Y |
| 8 **Emerson** | Y | Y | Y | Y | N | Y |
| 9 **Hulshof** | Y | Y | Y | Y | Y | Y |
| **MONTANA** | | | | | | |
| AL **Rehberg** | Y | Y | Y | Y | N | Y |
| **NEBRASKA** | | | | | | |
| 1 **Fortenberry** | Y | Y | Y | Y | Y | Y |
| 2 **Terry** | Y | Y | Y | Y | Y | Y |
| 3 **Osborne** | Y | Y | Y | Y | Y | Y |
| **NEVADA** | | | | | | |
| 1 Berkley | Y | Y | Y | Y | Y | Y |
| 2 **Gibbons** | Y | Y | Y | Y | Y | Y |
| 3 **Porter** | Y | Y | Y | Y | Y | Y |
| **NEW HAMPSHIRE** | | | | | | |
| 1 **Bradley** | Y | Y | Y | Y | Y | Y |
| 2 **Bass** | Y | Y | Y | Y | Y | Y |
| **NEW JERSEY** | | | | | | |
| 1 Andrews | Y | Y | Y | N | Y | Y |
| 2 **LoBiondo** | Y | + | Y | Y | Y | Y |
| 3 **Saxton** | Y | Y | Y | Y | N | Y |
| 4 **Smith** | Y | Y | Y | Y | Y | Y |
| 5 **Garrett** | Y | Y | Y | Y | Y | Y |
| 6 Pallone | Y | Y | Y | N | Y | Y |
| 7 **Ferguson** | Y | Y | Y | Y | Y | Y |
| 8 Pascrell | Y | Y | Y | Y | Y | Y |
| 9 Rothman | ? | ? | ? | ? | ? | ? |
| 10 Payne | ? | ? | ? | ? | ? | ? |
| 11 **Frelinghuysen** | Y | Y | Y | Y | N | Y |
| 12 Holt | Y | Y | Y | N | Y | Y |
| 13 Menendez | Y | Y | Y | N | Y | Y |
| **NEW MEXICO** | | | | | | |
| 1 **Wilson** | Y | Y | Y | Y | Y | Y |
| 2 **Pearce** | Y | Y | Y | Y | Y | Y |
| 3 Udall | Y | Y | Y | Y | Y | Y |
| **NEW YORK** | | | | | | |
| 1 Bishop | Y | Y | Y | Y | Y | Y |
| 2 Israel | Y | Y | Y | Y | Y | Y |
| 3 **King** | Y | Y | Y | Y | Y | Y |
| 4 McCarthy | Y | Y | Y | Y | Y | Y |
| 5 Ackerman | Y | Y | Y | Y | Y | Y |
| 6 Meeks | Y | Y | Y | Y | Y | Y |
| 7 Crowley | ? | ? | ? | ? | ? | ? |
| 8 Nadler | Y | Y | Y | N | Y | Y |
| 9 Weiner | Y | Y | Y | Y | Y | Y |
| 10 Towns | Y | Y | Y | Y | Y | Y |
| 11 Owens | Y | Y | Y | N | Y | Y |
| 12 Velázquez | Y | Y | Y | N | Y | Y |
| 13 **Fossella** | Y | Y | Y | Y | Y | Y |
| 14 Maloney | Y | Y | Y | N | Y | Y |
| 15 Rangel | Y | Y | Y | Y | Y | Y |
| 16 Serrano | Y | Y | Y | Y | Y | Y |
| 17 Engel | Y | Y | Y | Y | Y | Y |
| 18 Lowey | Y | Y | Y | Y | Y | Y |
| 19 **Kelly** | Y | Y | Y | Y | Y | Y |
| 20 **Sweeney** | Y | Y | Y | Y | N | Y |
| 21 McNulty | Y | Y | Y | Y | Y | Y |
| 22 Hinchey | Y | Y | Y | N | Y | Y |
| 23 **McHugh** | Y | Y | Y | Y | N | Y |
| 24 **Boehlert** | Y | Y | Y | Y | Y | Y |
| 25 **Walsh** | Y | Y | Y | Y | Y | Y |
| 26 **Reynolds** | Y | Y | Y | Y | Y | Y |
| 27 Higgins | Y | Y | Y | Y | Y | Y |
| 28 Slaughter | Y | Y | Y | N | Y | Y |
| 29 **Kuhl** | Y | Y | Y | Y | N | Y |

| | 509 | 510 | 511 | 512 | 513 | 514 |
|---|---|---|---|---|---|---|
| **NORTH CAROLINA** | | | | | | |
| 1 Butterfield | Y | Y | Y | Y | Y | Y |
| 2 Etheridge | Y | Y | Y | Y | Y | Y |
| 3 **Jones** | Y | Y | Y | Y | N | Y |
| 4 Price | Y | Y | Y | Y | Y | Y |
| 5 **Foxx** | Y | Y | Y | Y | Y | Y |
| 6 **Coble** | Y | Y | Y | Y | N | Y |
| 7 McIntyre | Y | Y | Y | Y | Y | Y |
| 8 **Hayes** | Y | Y | Y | Y | Y | Y |
| 9 **Myrick** | Y | Y | Y | Y | N | Y |
| 10 **McHenry** | Y | Y | Y | Y | N | Y |
| 11 **Taylor** | Y | Y | Y | Y | N | Y |
| 12 Watt | Y | Y | Y | N | Y | Y |
| 13 Miller | Y | Y | Y | Y | Y | Y |
| **NORTH DAKOTA** | | | | | | |
| AL Pomeroy | Y | Y | Y | Y | Y | Y |
| **OHIO** | | | | | | |
| 1 **Chabot** | Y | Y | Y | Y | N | Y |
| 2 **Schmidt** | Y | Y | Y | Y | N | Y |
| 3 **Turner** | Y | Y | Y | Y | Y | Y |
| 4 **Oxley** | Y | Y | Y | Y | Y | Y |
| 5 **Gillmor** | Y | Y | ? | Y | Y | Y |
| 6 Strickland | Y | Y | Y | ? | ? | ? |
| 7 **Hobson** | Y | Y | Y | Y | N | Y |
| 8 **Boehner** | Y | Y | Y | Y | Y | Y |
| 9 Kaptur | Y | Y | Y | Y | Y | Y |
| 10 Kucinich | Y | Y | Y | N | Y | Y |
| 11 Jones | Y | Y | Y | N | Y | Y |
| 12 **Tiberi** | Y | Y | Y | Y | Y | Y |
| 13 Brown | Y | Y | Y | Y | Y | Y |
| 14 **LaTourette** | Y | Y | Y | Y | Y | Y |
| 15 **Pryce** | Y | Y | Y | Y | Y | Y |
| 16 **Regula** | Y | Y | Y | Y | N | Y |
| 17 Ryan | Y | Y | Y | Y | Y | Y |
| 18 **Ney** | Y | Y | Y | Y | Y | Y |
| **OKLAHOMA** | | | | | | |
| 1 **Sullivan** | Y | ? | Y | Y | Y | Y |
| 2 Boren | Y | Y | Y | Y | Y | Y |
| 3 **Lucas** | Y | Y | Y | Y | Y | Y |
| 4 **Cole** | Y | Y | Y | Y | Y | Y |
| 5 **Istook** | Y | Y | Y | Y | Y | Y |
| **OREGON** | | | | | | |
| 1 Wu | Y | Y | Y | N | Y | Y |
| 2 **Walden** | Y | Y | Y | Y | Y | Y |
| 3 Blumenauer | Y | Y | Y | N | Y | Y |
| 4 DeFazio | Y | Y | Y | Y | Y | Y |
| 5 Hooley | Y | Y | Y | Y | Y | Y |
| **PENNSYLVANIA** | | | | | | |
| 1 Brady | Y | Y | Y | N | Y | Y |
| 2 Fattah | Y | Y | Y | N | Y | Y |
| 3 **English** | Y | Y | Y | Y | N | Y |
| 4 **Hart** | Y | Y | Y | Y | Y | Y |
| 5 **Peterson** | Y | Y | Y | Y | N | Y |
| 6 **Gerlach** | Y | Y | Y | Y | Y | Y |
| 7 **Weldon** | Y | Y | Y | Y | Y | Y |
| 8 **Fitzpatrick** | Y | Y | Y | Y | Y | Y |
| 9 **Shuster** | Y | Y | Y | Y | Y | Y |
| 10 **Sherwood** | Y | Y | Y | Y | N | Y |
| 11 Kanjorski | Y | Y | Y | Y | Y | Y |
| 12 Murtha | Y | Y | Y | Y | N | Y |
| 13 Schwartz | Y | Y | Y | Y | Y | Y |
| 14 Doyle | Y | Y | Y | N | Y | Y |
| 15 **Dent** | Y | Y | Y | Y | Y | Y |
| 16 **Pitts** | Y | Y | Y | Y | Y | Y |
| 17 Holden | Y | Y | Y | Y | Y | Y |
| 18 **Murphy** | Y | Y | Y | Y | Y | Y |
| 19 **Platts** | Y | Y | Y | Y | Y | Y |
| **RHODE ISLAND** | | | | | | |
| 1 Kennedy | Y | Y | Y | Y | Y | Y |
| 2 Langevin | Y | Y | Y | Y | Y | Y |
| **SOUTH CAROLINA** | | | | | | |
| 1 **Brown** | Y | Y | Y | Y | N | Y |
| 2 **Wilson** | Y | Y | Y | Y | Y | ? |
| 3 **Barrett** | Y | Y | Y | Y | Y | Y |
| 4 **Inglis** | Y | Y | Y | ? | ? | ? |
| 5 Spratt | Y | Y | Y | Y | Y | Y |
| 6 Clyburn | Y | Y | Y | Y | Y | Y |
| **SOUTH DAKOTA** | | | | | | |
| AL Herseth | Y | Y | Y | Y | Y | Y |
| **TENNESSEE** | | | | | | |
| 1 **Jenkins** | Y | Y | Y | Y | N | Y |
| 2 **Duncan** | Y | Y | Y | Y | Y | Y |

| | 509 | 510 | 511 | 512 | 513 | 514 |
|---|---|---|---|---|---|---|
| 3 **Wamp** | Y | Y | Y | Y | N | Y |
| 4 Davis | Y | Y | Y | Y | Y | Y |
| 5 Cooper | Y | Y | Y | N | Y | Y |
| 6 Gordon | Y | Y | Y | Y | Y | Y |
| 7 **Blackburn** | Y | Y | Y | Y | N | Y |
| 8 Tanner | Y | Y | Y | Y | Y | Y |
| 9 Ford | Y | Y | Y | N | Y | Y |
| **TEXAS** | | | | | | |
| 1 **Gohmert** | Y | Y | Y | Y | N | Y |
| 2 **Poe** | ? | ? | ? | ? | ? | ? |
| 3 **Johnson, S.** | Y | ? | Y | Y | N | Y |
| 4 **Hall** | Y | Y | Y | Y | Y | Y |
| 5 **Hensarling** | Y | Y | Y | Y | Y | Y |
| 6 **Barton** | Y | Y | Y | Y | Y | Y |
| 7 **Culberson** | Y | Y | Y | Y | Y | Y |
| 8 **Brady** | Y | Y | Y | Y | Y | Y |
| 9 Green, A. | Y | Y | Y | Y | Y | Y |
| 10 **McCaul** | Y | Y | Y | Y | Y | Y |
| 11 **Conaway** | Y | Y | Y | Y | Y | Y |
| 12 **Granger** | Y | Y | Y | Y | N | Y |
| 13 **Thornberry** | Y | Y | Y | Y | N | Y |
| 14 **Paul** | Y | Y | Y | N | Y | Y |
| 15 Hinojosa | Y | Y | Y | Y | Y | Y |
| 16 Reyes | Y | Y | Y | Y | Y | Y |
| 17 Edwards | Y | Y | Y | Y | Y | Y |
| 18 Jackson-Lee | Y | Y | Y | Y | Y | Y |
| 19 **Neugebauer** | Y | Y | Y | Y | N | Y |
| 20 Gonzalez | Y | Y | Y | Y | Y | Y |
| 21 **Smith** | Y | Y | Y | Y | Y | Y |
| 22 **DeLay** | Y | Y | Y | Y | Y | Y |
| 23 **Bonilla** | Y | Y | Y | Y | N | Y |
| 24 **Marchant** | Y | Y | Y | Y | N | Y |
| 25 Doggett | Y | Y | Y | Y | Y | Y |
| 26 **Burgess** | Y | Y | Y | Y | Y | Y |
| 27 Ortiz | Y | Y | Y | Y | Y | Y |
| 28 Cuellar | Y | Y | Y | Y | Y | Y |
| 29 Green, G. | Y | Y | Y | Y | Y | Y |
| 30 Johnson, E. | Y | Y | Y | Y | Y | Y |
| 31 **Carter** | Y | Y | Y | Y | N | Y |
| 32 **Sessions** | Y | Y | Y | Y | Y | Y |
| **UTAH** | | | | | | |
| 1 **Bishop** | Y | Y | Y | Y | Y | Y |
| 2 Matheson | Y | Y | Y | Y | Y | Y |
| 3 **Cannon** | Y | Y | Y | Y | N | Y |
| **VERMONT** | | | | | | |
| AL *Sanders* | Y | Y | Y | N | Y | Y |
| **VIRGINIA** | | | | | | |
| 1 **Davis, J.** | Y | Y | Y | Y | N | Y |
| 2 **Drake** | Y | Y | Y | Y | Y | Y |
| 3 Scott | Y | Y | Y | Y | Y | Y |
| 4 **Forbes** | Y | Y | Y | Y | N | Y |
| 5 **Goode** | Y | Y | Y | Y | N | Y |
| 6 **Goodlatte** | Y | Y | Y | Y | N | Y |
| 7 **Cantor** | Y | Y | Y | Y | N | Y |
| 8 Moran | Y | Y | Y | Y | N | Y |
| 9 Boucher | Y | Y | Y | Y | Y | Y |
| 10 **Wolf** | Y | Y | Y | Y | Y | Y |
| 11 **Davis, T.** | Y | Y | Y | Y | Y | Y |
| **WASHINGTON** | | | | | | |
| 1 Inslee | Y | Y | Y | Y | Y | Y |
| 2 Larsen | Y | Y | Y | Y | Y | Y |
| 3 Baird | Y | Y | Y | Y | Y | Y |
| 4 **Hastings** | Y | Y | Y | Y | Y | Y |
| 5 **McMorris** | Y | Y | Y | Y | Y | Y |
| 6 Dicks | Y | Y | Y | Y | Y | Y |
| 7 McDermott | Y | Y | Y | N | Y | Y |
| 8 **Reichert** | Y | Y | Y | Y | Y | Y |
| 9 Smith | Y | Y | Y | Y | Y | Y |
| **WEST VIRGINIA** | | | | | | |
| 1 Mollohan | Y | Y | Y | Y | Y | Y |
| 2 **Capito** | Y | Y | Y | Y | Y | Y |
| 3 Rahall | Y | Y | Y | Y | Y | Y |
| **WISCONSIN** | | | | | | |
| 1 **Ryan** | Y | Y | Y | Y | N | Y |
| 2 Baldwin | Y | Y | Y | N | Y | Y |
| 3 Kind | Y | Y | Y | N | Y | Y |
| 4 Moore | Y | Y | Y | Y | Y | Y |
| 5 **Sensenbrenner** | Y | Y | Y | Y | N | Y |
| 6 **Petri** | Y | Y | Y | Y | N | Y |
| 7 Obey | Y | Y | Y | N | N | Y |
| 8 **Green** | Y | Y | Y | Y | Y | Y |
| **WYOMING** | | | | | | |
| AL **Cubin** | Y | Y | Y | Y | N | Y |

# IN THE HOUSE | By Vote Number

**515.** **HR 3893. Oil Refinery Construction/Rule.** Adoption of the rule (H Res 481) that would provide for House floor consideration of the bill that would allow state governors to opt into a streamlined regulatory process for refinery expansion and construction projects. Adopted 216-201: R 216-5; D 0-195 (ND 0-145, SD 0-50); I 0-1. Oct. 7, 2005.

**516.** **Procedural Motion/Journal.** Approval of the House Journal of Thursday, Oct. 6, 2005. Approved 348-63: R 203-16; D 144-47 (ND 103-41, SD 41-6); I 1-0. Oct. 7, 2005.

**517.** **HR 3893. Oil Refinery Construction/Democratic Substitute.** Stupak, D-Mich., substitute amendment that would outlaw gasoline price gouging in a time of a presidentially declared energy emergency, authorize the Federal Trade Commission to impose fines for price gouging, and authorize the Energy Department to construct new refineries or open closed refineries to create a strategic refinery reserve that would have a capacity equaling 5 percent of the daily U.S. demand for gasoline, home heating oil and other refined petroleum products. Rejected 199-222: R 2-222; D 196-0 (ND 146-0, SD 50-0); I 1-0. Oct. 7, 2005.

**518.** **HR 3893. Oil Refinery Construction/Recommit.** Bishop, D-N.Y., motion to recommit the bill to the Energy and Commerce Committee with instructions to add language that would provide for stricter penalties dealing with gasoline price gouging, outlaw market manipulation and empower state attorneys general to enforce the law. Motion rejected 200-222: R 3-222; D 196-0 (ND 146-0, SD 50-0); I 1-0. Oct. 7, 2005.

**519.** **HR 3893. Oil Refinery Construction/Passage.** Passage of the bill that would allow state governors to opt into a streamlined regulatory process for refinery expansion and construction projects. It would require the president to designate federal sites for new oil refineries and allow the federal government to pay new refineries for the costs of significant delays due to lawsuits and government regulations. Price gouging on gasoline would be banned in times of emergencies. The bill also would direct the Federal Trade Commission to investigate price gouging after Hurricane Katrina. It would specify that the federal government could provide loan guarantees for the Alaska natural gas pipeline up to two years after enactment, unless the state of Alaska has a contractual agreement to complete construction of the pipeline. Passed 212-210: R 212-13; D 0-196 (ND 0-146, SD 0-50); I 0-1. Oct. 7, 2005.

**520.** **H Con Res 248. Simon Wiesenthal Tribute/Adoption.** Smith, R-N.J., motion to suspend the rules and adopt the resolution that would honor the life and work of Simon Wiesenthal to memorialize the victims of the Holocaust and to bring the perpetrators of crimes against humanity to justice. Motion agreed to 354-0: R 187-0; D 166-0 (ND 120-0, SD 46-0); I 1-0. A two-thirds majority of those present and voting (236 in this case) is required for adoption under suspension of the rules. Oct. 7, 2005.

| | 515 | 516 | 517 | 518 | 519 | 520 |
|---|---|---|---|---|---|---|
| **ALABAMA** | | | | | | |
| 1 Bonner | Y | Y | N | N | Y | Y |
| 2 Everett | Y | Y | N | N | Y | ? |
| 3 Rogers | Y | Y | N | N | Y | Y |
| 4 Aderholt | Y | Y | N | N | Y | Y |
| 5 Cramer | N | Y | Y | Y | N | Y |
| 6 Bachus | Y | Y | N | N | Y | ? |
| 7 Davis | N | Y | Y | Y | N | Y |
| **ALASKA** | | | | | | |
| AL Young | ? | ? | N | N | Y | Y |
| **ARIZONA** | | | | | | |
| 1 Renzi | Y | Y | N | N | Y | Y |
| 2 Franks | Y | Y | N | N | Y | Y |
| 3 Shadegg | Y | Y | N | N | Y | Y |
| 4 Pastor | N | Y | Y | Y | N | Y |
| 5 Hayworth | Y | Y | N | N | Y | Y |
| 6 Flake | Y | Y | N | N | Y | Y |
| 7 Grijalva | N | Y | Y | Y | N | Y |
| 8 Kolbe | Y | Y | N | N | Y | Y |
| **ARKANSAS** | | | | | | |
| 1 Berry | N | N | Y | Y | N | Y |
| 2 Snyder | N | Y | Y | Y | N | Y |
| 3 Boozman | Y | Y | N | N | Y | Y |
| 4 Ross | N | Y | Y | Y | N | Y |
| **CALIFORNIA** | | | | | | |
| 1 Thompson | N | N | Y | Y | N | Y |
| 2 Herger | Y | Y | N | N | Y | Y |
| 3 Lungren | Y | Y | N | N | Y | Y |
| 4 Doolittle | Y | Y | N | N | Y | Y |
| 5 Matsui, D. | N | Y | Y | Y | N | Y |
| 6 Woolsey | N | Y | Y | Y | N | Y |
| 7 Miller, George | N | N | Y | Y | N | Y |
| 8 Pelosi | N | Y | Y | Y | N | Y |
| 9 Lee | N | Y | Y | Y | N | Y |
| 10 Tauscher | N | Y | Y | Y | N | Y |
| 11 Pombo | Y | Y | N | N | Y | ? |
| 12 Lantos | N | Y | Y | Y | N | Y |
| 13 Stark | N | N | Y | Y | N | ? |
| 14 Eshoo | N | Y | Y | Y | N | ? |
| 15 Honda | N | Y | Y | Y | N | Y |
| 16 Lofgren | N | Y | Y | Y | N | Y |
| 17 Farr | N | Y | Y | Y | N | Y |
| 18 Cardoza | N | Y | Y | Y | N | Y |
| 19 Radanovich | Y | Y | N | N | Y | Y |
| 20 Costa | N | Y | Y | Y | N | Y |
| 21 Nunes | Y | Y | N | N | Y | Y |
| 22 Thomas | Y | Y | N | N | Y | Y |
| 23 Capps | N | Y | Y | Y | N | + |
| 24 Gallegly | Y | Y | N | N | Y | Y |
| 25 McKeon | Y | Y | N | N | Y | Y |
| 26 Dreier | Y | Y | N | N | Y | Y |
| 27 Sherman | N | Y | Y | Y | N | Y |
| 28 Berman | N | Y | Y | Y | N | Y |
| 29 Schiff | N | Y | Y | Y | N | Y |
| 30 Waxman | N | Y | Y | Y | N | Y |
| 31 Becerra | N | Y | Y | Y | N | Y |
| 32 Solis | N | Y | Y | Y | N | Y |
| 33 Watson | N | N | Y | Y | N | ? |
| 34 Roybal-Allard | N | Y | Y | Y | N | Y |
| 35 Waters | N | N | Y | Y | N | ? |
| 36 Harman | N | Y | Y | Y | N | Y |
| 37 Millender-McD. | N | Y | Y | Y | N | Y |
| 38 Napolitano | N | Y | Y | Y | N | Y |
| 39 Sánchez, Linda | N | Y | Y | Y | N | Y |
| 40 Royce | ? | ? | ? | ? | ? | ? |
| 41 Lewis | Y | ? | N | N | Y | Y |
| 42 Miller, Gary | Y | Y | N | N | Y | Y |
| 43 Baca | N | Y | Y | Y | N | Y |
| 44 Calvert | Y | Y | N | N | Y | Y |
| 45 Bono | Y | Y | N | N | Y | Y |
| 46 Rohrabacher | Y | Y | N | N | Y | Y |
| 47 Sanchez, Loretta | N | N | Y | Y | N | Y |
| 48 Vacant | | | | | | |
| 49 Issa | Y | Y | N | N | Y | Y |

| | 515 | 516 | 517 | 518 | 519 | 520 |
|---|---|---|---|---|---|---|
| 50 Cunningham | Y | Y | N | N | Y | Y |
| 51 Filner | N | N | Y | Y | N | + |
| 52 Hunter | Y | Y | N | N | Y | Y |
| 53 Davis | N | Y | Y | Y | N | Y |
| **COLORADO** | | | | | | |
| 1 DeGette | N | Y | Y | Y | N | Y |
| 2 Udall | N | N | Y | Y | N | Y |
| 3 Salazar | N | Y | Y | Y | N | Y |
| 4 Musgrave | Y | Y | N | N | Y | ? |
| 5 Hefley | Y | N | N | N | Y | Y |
| 6 Tancredo | Y | Y | N | N | Y | Y |
| 7 Beauprez | ? | ? | ? | ? | ? | ? |
| **CONNECTICUT** | | | | | | |
| 1 Larson | N | N | Y | Y | N | + |
| 2 Simmons | + | + | N | N | Y | Y |
| 3 DeLauro | N | Y | Y | Y | N | ? |
| 4 Shays | N | Y | Y | Y | N | Y |
| 5 Johnson | Y | Y | N | N | Y | Y |
| **DELAWARE** | | | | | | |
| AL Castle | N | Y | N | N | N | Y |
| **FLORIDA** | | | | | | |
| 1 Miller | Y | Y | N | N | Y | Y |
| 2 Boyd | N | Y | Y | Y | N | Y |
| 3 Brown | N | Y | Y | Y | N | Y |
| 4 Crenshaw | Y | Y | N | N | Y | Y |
| 5 Brown-Waite | Y | Y | N | N | Y | ? |
| 6 Stearns | Y | Y | N | N | Y | Y |
| 7 Mica | Y | Y | N | N | Y | + |
| 8 Keller | Y | Y | N | N | Y | Y |
| 9 Bilirakis | Y | Y | N | N | Y | Y |
| 10 Young | Y | Y | N | N | Y | Y |
| 11 Davis | N | Y | Y | Y | N | ? |
| 12 Putnam | Y | Y | N | N | Y | Y |
| 13 Harris | Y | Y | N | N | Y | ? |
| 14 Mack | Y | Y | N | N | Y | Y |
| 15 Weldon | Y | Y | N | N | Y | Y |
| 16 Foley | Y | Y | N | N | Y | Y |
| 17 Meek | N | Y | Y | Y | N | Y |
| 18 Ros-Lehtinen | Y | Y | N | N | Y | Y |
| 19 Wexler | N | ? | Y | Y | N | Y |
| 20 Wasserman-Schultz | N | Y | Y | Y | N | Y |
| 21 Diaz-Balart, L. | Y | Y | N | N | Y | Y |
| 22 Shaw | Y | Y | N | N | Y | Y |
| 23 Hastings | ? | ? | ? | ? | ? | ? |
| 24 Feeney | Y | Y | N | N | Y | ? |
| 25 Diaz-Balart, M. | Y | Y | N | N | Y | Y |
| **GEORGIA** | | | | | | |
| 1 Kingston | Y | Y | N | N | Y | Y |
| 2 Bishop | N | Y | Y | Y | N | Y |
| 3 Marshall | N | N | Y | Y | N | Y |
| 4 McKinney | N | Y | Y | Y | N | Y |
| 5 Lewis | N | Y | Y | Y | N | Y |
| 6 Price | Y | Y | N | N | Y | Y |
| 7 Linder | Y | ? | N | N | Y | Y |
| 8 Westmoreland | Y | Y | N | N | Y | ? |
| 9 Norwood | ? | ? | ? | ? | ? | ? |
| 10 Deal | ? | ? | ? | ? | ? | ? |
| 11 Gingrey | Y | Y | N | N | Y | Y |
| 12 Barrow | N | N | Y | Y | N | Y |
| 13 Scott | N | Y | Y | Y | N | Y |
| **HAWAII** | | | | | | |
| 1 Abercrombie | N | Y | Y | Y | N | Y |
| 2 Case | N | Y | Y | Y | N | Y |
| **IDAHO** | | | | | | |
| 1 Otter | Y | Y | N | N | Y | Y |
| 2 Simpson | Y | Y | N | N | Y | Y |
| **ILLINOIS** | | | | | | |
| 1 Rush | N | Y | Y | Y | N | Y |
| 2 Jackson | N | Y | Y | Y | N | Y |
| 3 Lipinski | N | Y | Y | Y | N | Y |
| 4 Gutierrez | N | Y | Y | Y | N | + |
| 5 Emanuel | N | Y | Y | Y | N | Y |
| 6 Hyde | Y | Y | N | N | Y | Y |
| 7 Davis | N | Y | Y | Y | N | Y |
| 8 Bean | N | Y | Y | Y | N | Y |
| 9 Schakowsky | N | N | Y | Y | N | Y |
| 10 Kirk | Y | Y | N | N | Y | Y |
| 11 Weller | Y | N | N | N | Y | Y |
| 12 Costello | N | N | Y | Y | N | Y |

ND Northern Democrats, SD Southern Democrats
Southern states: Ala., Ark., Fla., Ga., Ky., La., Miss., N.C., Okla., S.C., Tenn., Texas, Va.

| | 515 | 516 | 517 | 518 | 519 | 520 |
|---|---|---|---|---|---|---|
| 13 **Biggert** | Y | Y | N | N | Y | Y |
| 14 **Hastert** | | | | N | Y | |
| 15 **Johnson** | N | Y | N | N | N | + |
| 16 **Manzullo** | Y | Y | N | N | Y | Y |
| 17 Evans | N | N | Y | Y | N | Y |
| 18 **LaHood** | Y | Y | N | N | N | ? |
| 19 **Shimkus** | Y | Y | N | N | Y | Y |
| **INDIANA** | | | | | | |
| 1 Visclosky | N | N | Y | Y | N | Y |
| 2 **Chocola** | Y | Y | N | N | Y | Y |
| 3 **Souder** | Y | Y | N | N | Y | Y |
| 4 **Buyer** | Y | Y | N | N | Y | Y |
| 5 **Burton** | Y | Y | N | N | Y | Y |
| 6 **Pence** | Y | Y | N | N | Y | + |
| 7 Carson | N | Y | Y | Y | N | ? |
| 8 **Hostettler** | Y | Y | N | N | Y | Y |
| 9 **Sodrel** | Y | Y | N | N | Y | Y |
| **IOWA** | | | | | | |
| 1 **Nussle** | Y | Y | N | N | Y | ? |
| 2 **Leach** | N | Y | N | N | N | Y |
| 3 Boswell | ? | ? | ? | ? | ? | ? |
| 4 **Latham** | Y | N | N | N | Y | Y |
| 5 **King** | Y | Y | N | N | Y | Y |
| **KANSAS** | | | | | | |
| 1 **Moran** | Y | N | N | N | Y | ? |
| 2 **Ryun** | Y | Y | N | N | Y | Y |
| 3 Moore | N | Y | Y | Y | N | Y |
| 4 **Tiahrt** | Y | Y | N | N | Y | Y |
| **KENTUCKY** | | | | | | |
| 1 **Whitfield** | Y | N | N | N | Y | Y |
| 2 **Lewis** | Y | Y | N | N | Y | Y |
| 3 **Northup** | Y | Y | N | N | Y | Y |
| 4 **Davis** | Y | N | N | N | Y | Y |
| 5 **Rogers** | Y | Y | N | N | Y | Y |
| 6 Chandler | N | N | Y | Y | N | Y |
| **LOUISIANA** | | | | | | |
| 1 **Jindal** | Y | Y | N | N | Y | Y |
| 2 Jefferson | N | Y | Y | Y | N | Y |
| 3 Melancon | N | ? | Y | Y | N | Y |
| 4 **McCrery** | Y | Y | N | N | Y | Y |
| 5 **Alexander** | Y | Y | N | N | Y | Y |
| 6 **Baker** | Y | Y | N | N | Y | Y |
| 7 **Boustany** | Y | Y | N | N | Y | Y |
| **MAINE** | | | | | | |
| 1 Allen | N | Y | Y | Y | N | Y |
| 2 Michaud | N | Y | Y | Y | N | Y |
| **MARYLAND** | | | | | | |
| 1 **Gilchrest** | Y | Y | N | N | Y | Y |
| 2 Ruppersberger | N | Y | Y | Y | N | Y |
| 3 Cardin | N | Y | Y | Y | N | Y |
| 4 Wynn | N | Y | Y | Y | N | Y |
| 5 Hoyer | N | Y | Y | Y | N | Y |
| 6 **Bartlett** | Y | Y | N | N | Y | Y |
| 7 Cummings | N | Y | Y | Y | N | Y |
| 8 Van Hollen | N | Y | Y | Y | N | Y |
| **MASSACHUSETTS** | | | | | | |
| 1 Olver | ? | ? | ? | ? | ? | ? |
| 2 Neal | ? | ? | ? | ? | ? | ? |
| 3 McGovern | N | Y | Y | Y | N | Y |
| 4 Frank | N | Y | Y | Y | N | Y |
| 5 Meehan | N | Y | Y | Y | N | ? |
| 6 Tierney | N | Y | Y | Y | N | Y |
| 7 Markey | N | N | Y | Y | N | Y |
| 8 Capuano | N | N | Y | Y | N | Y |
| 9 Lynch | N | N | Y | Y | N | ? |
| 10 Delahunt | ? | ? | ? | ? | ? | ? |
| **MICHIGAN** | | | | | | |
| 1 Stupak | N | N | Y | Y | N | ? |
| 2 **Hoekstra** | Y | Y | N | N | Y | Y |
| 3 **Ehlers** | Y | Y | N | N | Y | Y |
| 4 **Camp** | Y | Y | N | N | Y | Y |
| 5 Kildee | N | Y | Y | Y | N | Y |
| 6 **Upton** | Y | Y | N | N | Y | Y |
| 7 **Schwarz** | ? | ? | ? | ? | ? | ? |
| 8 **Rogers** | Y | Y | N | N | Y | Y |
| 9 **Knollenberg** | Y | Y | N | N | Y | Y |
| 10 **Miller** | Y | Y | N | N | Y | Y |
| 11 **McCotter** | Y | N | N | N | Y | Y |
| 12 Levin | N | Y | Y | Y | N | Y |
| 13 Kilpatrick | N | Y | Y | Y | N | Y |
| 14 Conyers | N | Y | Y | Y | N | Y |
| 15 Dingell | N | Y | Y | Y | N | Y |
| **MINNESOTA** | | | | | | |
| 1 **Gutknecht** | Y | N | N | N | Y | Y |
| 2 **Kline** | Y | Y | N | N | Y | Y |
| 3 **Ramstad** | Y | N | N | N | Y | Y |
| 4 McCollum | N | Y | Y | Y | N | Y |
| 5 Sabo | N | N | Y | Y | N | ? |
| 6 **Kennedy** | Y | N | N | N | Y | Y |
| 7 Peterson | N | Y | Y | Y | N | ? |
| 8 Oberstar | N | N | Y | Y | N | Y |
| **MISSISSIPPI** | | | | | | |
| 1 **Wicker** | Y | Y | N | N | Y | ? |
| 2 Thompson | N | N | Y | Y | N | Y |
| 3 **Pickering** | Y | Y | N | N | Y | Y |
| 4 Taylor | N | N | Y | Y | N | Y |
| **MISSOURI** | | | | | | |
| 1 Clay | ? | ? | Y | Y | N | Y |
| 2 **Akin** | Y | Y | N | N | Y | Y |
| 3 Carnahan | N | Y | Y | Y | N | Y |
| 4 Skelton | N | Y | Y | Y | N | Y |
| 5 Cleaver | N | Y | Y | Y | N | + |
| 6 **Graves** | Y | N | N | N | Y | ? |
| 7 **Blunt** | Y | Y | N | N | Y | Y |
| 8 **Emerson** | Y | Y | Y | N | Y | Y |
| 9 **Hulshof** | Y | Y | N | N | Y | Y |
| **MONTANA** | | | | | | |
| AL **Rehberg** | Y | Y | N | N | Y | Y |
| **NEBRASKA** | | | | | | |
| 1 **Fortenberry** | Y | Y | N | N | Y | Y |
| 2 **Terry** | Y | Y | N | N | Y | ? |
| 3 **Osborne** | Y | Y | N | N | Y | ? |
| **NEVADA** | | | | | | |
| 1 Berkley | N | Y | Y | Y | N | Y |
| 2 **Gibbons** | Y | Y | N | N | Y | Y |
| 3 **Porter** | Y | Y | N | N | Y | Y |
| **NEW HAMPSHIRE** | | | | | | |
| 1 **Bradley** | Y | Y | N | N | N | Y |
| 2 **Bass** | Y | Y | N | N | Y | Y |
| **NEW JERSEY** | | | | | | |
| 1 Andrews | N | ? | Y | Y | N | Y |
| 2 **LoBiondo** | Y | N | N | Y | N | Y |
| 3 **Saxton** | Y | Y | N | N | N | Y |
| 4 **Smith** | Y | Y | N | N | N | Y |
| 5 **Garrett** | Y | Y | N | N | Y | Y |
| 6 Pallone | N | Y | Y | Y | N | Y |
| 7 **Ferguson** | Y | Y | N | N | Y | Y |
| 8 Pascrell | N | Y | Y | Y | N | ? |
| 9 Rothman | N | Y | Y | Y | N | Y |
| 10 Payne | ? | ? | ? | ? | ? | ? |
| 11 **Frelinghuysen** | Y | Y | N | N | Y | ? |
| 12 Holt | N | N | Y | Y | N | Y |
| 13 Menendez | N | Y | Y | Y | N | Y |
| **NEW MEXICO** | | | | | | |
| 1 **Wilson** | Y | Y | N | N | Y | Y |
| 2 **Pearce** | Y | Y | N | N | Y | Y |
| 3 Udall | N | N | Y | Y | N | Y |
| **NEW YORK** | | | | | | |
| 1 Bishop | N | Y | Y | Y | N | Y |
| 2 Israel | N | N | Y | Y | N | ? |
| 3 **King** | Y | Y | N | N | Y | ? |
| 4 McCarthy | N | N | Y | Y | N | ? |
| 5 Ackerman | N | N | Y | Y | N | ? |
| 6 Meeks | N | Y | Y | Y | N | Y |
| 7 Crowley | N | Y | Y | Y | N | Y |
| 8 Nadler | N | Y | Y | Y | N | Y |
| 9 Weiner | N | Y | Y | Y | N | Y |
| 10 Towns | N | N | Y | Y | N | Y |
| 11 Owens | N | Y | Y | Y | N | Y |
| 12 Velázquez | N | N | Y | Y | N | Y |
| 13 **Fossella** | Y | N | N | N | Y | Y |
| 14 Maloney | N | N | Y | Y | N | Y |
| 15 Rangel | N | Y | Y | Y | N | Y |
| 16 Serrano | N | Y | Y | Y | N | Y |
| 17 Engel | N | Y | Y | Y | N | Y |
| 18 Lowey | N | Y | Y | Y | N | Y |
| 19 **Kelly** | Y | Y | N | N | Y | Y |
| 20 **Sweeney** | Y | N | N | Y | Y | Y |
| 21 McNulty | N | N | Y | Y | N | Y |
| 22 Hinchey | N | N | Y | Y | N | ? |
| 23 **McHugh** | Y | Y | N | N | Y | Y |
| 24 **Boehlert** | N | Y | N | N | N | Y |
| 25 **Walsh** | Y | Y | N | N | Y | ? |
| 26 **Reynolds** | Y | Y | N | N | Y | Y |
| 27 Higgins | N | Y | Y | Y | N | Y |
| 28 Slaughter | N | N | Y | Y | N | Y |
| 29 **Kuhl** | Y | Y | N | N | Y | Y |
| **NORTH CAROLINA** | | | | | | |
| 1 Butterfield | N | Y | Y | Y | N | Y |
| 2 Etheridge | N | Y | Y | Y | N | Y |
| 3 **Jones** | Y | Y | N | N | N | Y |
| 4 Price | N | Y | Y | Y | N | Y |
| 5 **Foxx** | Y | Y | N | N | Y | ? |
| 6 **Coble** | Y | Y | N | N | Y | ? |
| 7 McIntyre | N | Y | Y | Y | N | Y |
| 8 **Hayes** | Y | Y | N | N | Y | Y |
| 9 **Myrick** | Y | Y | N | N | Y | Y |
| 10 **McHenry** | Y | Y | N | N | Y | Y |
| 11 **Taylor** | Y | Y | N | N | Y | ? |
| 12 Watt | N | Y | Y | Y | N | Y |
| 13 Miller | N | Y | Y | Y | N | Y |
| **NORTH DAKOTA** | | | | | | |
| AL Pomeroy | N | Y | Y | Y | N | Y |
| **OHIO** | | | | | | |
| 1 **Chabot** | Y | Y | N | N | Y | Y |
| 2 **Schmidt** | Y | Y | N | N | Y | Y |
| 3 **Turner** | Y | Y | N | N | Y | Y |
| 4 **Oxley** | Y | Y | N | N | Y | ? |
| 5 **Gillmor** | Y | Y | N | N | Y | ? |
| 6 Strickland | N | N | Y | Y | N | Y |
| 7 **Hobson** | Y | Y | N | N | Y | Y |
| 8 **Boehner** | Y | Y | N | N | Y | Y |
| 9 Kaptur | N | Y | Y | Y | N | Y |
| 10 Kucinich | N | N | Y | Y | N | Y |
| 11 Jones | N | Y | Y | Y | N | Y |
| 12 **Tiberi** | Y | Y | N | N | Y | ? |
| 13 Brown | N | Y | Y | Y | N | Y |
| 14 **LaTourette** | Y | Y | N | N | Y | Y |
| 15 **Pryce** | Y | Y | N | N | Y | Y |
| 16 **Regula** | Y | Y | N | N | Y | Y |
| 17 Ryan | N | Y | Y | Y | N | Y |
| 18 **Ney** | Y | Y | N | N | Y | ? |
| **OKLAHOMA** | | | | | | |
| 1 **Sullivan** | Y | Y | N | N | Y | Y |
| 2 Boren | N | Y | Y | Y | N | Y |
| 3 **Lucas** | Y | Y | N | N | Y | Y |
| 4 **Cole** | Y | Y | N | N | Y | Y |
| 5 **Istook** | Y | Y | N | N | Y | Y |
| **OREGON** | | | | | | |
| 1 Wu | N | N | Y | Y | N | Y |
| 2 **Walden** | Y | Y | N | N | Y | Y |
| 3 Blumenauer | N | Y | Y | Y | N | Y |
| 4 DeFazio | N | N | Y | Y | N | ? |
| 5 Hooley | N | Y | Y | Y | N | ? |
| **PENNSYLVANIA** | | | | | | |
| 1 Brady | N | N | Y | Y | N | Y |
| 2 Fattah | N | Y | Y | Y | N | Y |
| 3 **English** | Y | N | N | N | Y | Y |
| 4 **Hart** | Y | Y | N | N | Y | Y |
| 5 **Peterson** | Y | Y | N | N | Y | ? |
| 6 **Gerlach** | Y | Y | N | N | Y | Y |
| 7 **Weldon** | Y | Y | N | ? | N | Y |
| 8 **Fitzpatrick** | ? | ? | N | N | N | Y |
| 9 **Shuster** | Y | N | N | N | Y | Y |
| 10 **Sherwood** | Y | Y | N | N | Y | Y |
| 11 Kanjorski | N | Y | Y | Y | N | Y |
| 12 Murtha | N | Y | Y | Y | N | ? |
| 13 Schwartz | N | Y | Y | Y | N | Y |
| 14 Doyle | N | Y | Y | Y | N | Y |
| 15 **Dent** | Y | Y | N | N | Y | Y |
| 16 **Pitts** | Y | Y | N | N | Y | Y |
| 17 Holden | N | Y | Y | Y | N | Y |
| 18 **Murphy** | Y | Y | N | N | Y | Y |
| 19 **Platts** | Y | Y | N | N | Y | Y |
| **RHODE ISLAND** | | | | | | |
| 1 Kennedy | N | Y | Y | Y | N | Y |
| 2 Langevin | N | Y | Y | Y | N | Y |
| **SOUTH CAROLINA** | | | | | | |
| 1 **Brown** | Y | Y | N | N | Y | Y |
| 2 **Wilson** | Y | Y | N | N | Y | Y |
| 3 **Barrett** | Y | Y | N | N | Y | Y |
| 4 **Inglis** | Y | Y | N | N | Y | Y |
| 5 Spratt | N | Y | Y | Y | N | Y |
| 6 Clyburn | N | Y | Y | Y | N | ? |
| **SOUTH DAKOTA** | | | | | | |
| AL Herseth | N | Y | Y | Y | N | Y |
| **TENNESSEE** | | | | | | |
| 1 **Jenkins** | Y | Y | N | N | Y | ? |
| 2 **Duncan** | Y | Y | N | N | Y | Y |
| 3 **Wamp** | Y | Y | N | N | Y | ? |
| 4 Davis | N | Y | Y | Y | N | ? |
| 5 Cooper | N | Y | Y | Y | N | Y |
| 6 Gordon | N | Y | Y | Y | N | Y |
| 7 **Blackburn** | Y | Y | N | N | Y | ? |
| 8 Tanner | N | Y | Y | Y | N | Y |
| 9 Ford | N | Y | Y | Y | N | Y |
| **TEXAS** | | | | | | |
| 1 **Gohmert** | Y | Y | N | N | Y | Y |
| 2 **Poe** | + | + | – | N | Y | Y |
| 3 **Johnson, S.** | Y | Y | N | N | Y | Y |
| 4 **Hall** | Y | Y | N | N | Y | Y |
| 5 **Hensarling** | Y | Y | N | N | Y | Y |
| 6 **Barton** | Y | Y | N | N | Y | Y |
| 7 **Culberson** | Y | Y | N | N | Y | Y |
| 8 **Brady** | Y | Y | N | N | Y | ? |
| 9 Green, A. | N | Y | Y | Y | N | Y |
| 10 **McCaul** | Y | Y | N | N | Y | Y |
| 11 **Conaway** | Y | Y | N | N | Y | Y |
| 12 **Granger** | Y | Y | N | N | Y | ? |
| 13 **Thornberry** | Y | Y | N | N | Y | Y |
| 14 **Paul** | Y | Y | N | N | ? | Y |
| 15 Hinojosa | N | Y | Y | Y | N | Y |
| 16 Reyes | N | Y | Y | Y | N | Y |
| 17 Edwards | N | ? | Y | Y | N | Y |
| 18 Jackson-Lee | N | Y | Y | Y | N | Y |
| 19 **Neugebauer** | Y | Y | N | N | Y | Y |
| 20 Gonzalez | N | Y | Y | Y | N | Y |
| 21 **Smith** | Y | Y | N | N | Y | Y |
| 22 **DeLay** | Y | Y | N | N | Y | Y |
| 23 **Bonilla** | Y | Y | N | N | Y | Y |
| 24 **Marchant** | Y | Y | N | N | Y | ? |
| 25 Doggett | N | Y | Y | Y | N | Y |
| 26 **Burgess** | Y | Y | N | N | Y | Y |
| 27 Ortiz | N | Y | Y | Y | N | Y |
| 28 Cuellar | N | Y | Y | Y | N | Y |
| 29 Green, G. | N | Y | Y | Y | N | Y |
| 30 Johnson, E. | N | Y | Y | Y | N | Y |
| 31 **Carter** | Y | Y | N | N | Y | Y |
| 32 **Sessions** | Y | Y | N | N | Y | Y |
| **UTAH** | | | | | | |
| 1 **Bishop** | Y | Y | N | N | Y | Y |
| 2 Matheson | N | N | Y | Y | N | Y |
| 3 **Cannon** | Y | Y | N | N | Y | Y |
| **VERMONT** | | | | | | |
| AL *Sanders* | N | Y | Y | Y | N | Y |
| **VIRGINIA** | | | | | | |
| 1 **Davis, J.** | Y | Y | N | N | Y | ? |
| 2 **Drake** | Y | Y | N | N | Y | Y |
| 3 Scott | N | Y | Y | Y | N | Y |
| 4 **Forbes** | Y | Y | N | N | Y | Y |
| 5 **Goode** | Y | Y | N | N | Y | ? |
| 6 **Goodlatte** | Y | Y | N | N | Y | Y |
| 7 **Cantor** | Y | Y | N | N | Y | Y |
| 8 Moran | N | Y | Y | Y | N | Y |
| 9 Boucher | N | Y | Y | Y | N | ? |
| 10 **Wolf** | Y | Y | N | N | Y | Y |
| 11 **Davis, T.** | Y | Y | N | N | Y | Y |
| **WASHINGTON** | | | | | | |
| 1 Inslee | N | Y | Y | Y | N | Y |
| 2 Larsen | N | N | Y | Y | N | Y |
| 3 Baird | N | N | Y | Y | N | Y |
| 4 **Hastings** | Y | Y | N | N | Y | Y |
| 5 **McMorris** | Y | Y | N | N | Y | Y |
| 6 Dicks | N | Y | Y | Y | N | ? |
| 7 McDermott | N | N | Y | Y | N | ? |
| 8 **Reichert** | Y | Y | N | N | Y | Y |
| 9 Smith | N | Y | Y | Y | N | Y |
| **WEST VIRGINIA** | | | | | | |
| 1 Mollohan | N | Y | Y | Y | N | Y |
| 2 **Capito** | Y | Y | N | N | Y | Y |
| 3 Rahall | N | Y | Y | Y | N | Y |
| **WISCONSIN** | | | | | | |
| 1 **Ryan** | Y | Y | N | N | Y | Y |
| 2 Baldwin | N | N | Y | Y | N | Y |
| 3 Kind | N | Y | Y | Y | N | Y |
| 4 Moore | N | Y | Y | Y | N | Y |
| 5 **Sensenbrenner** | Y | Y | N | N | Y | Y |
| 6 **Petri** | Y | Y | N | N | Y | Y |
| 7 Obey | N | Y | Y | Y | N | Y |
| 8 **Green** | Y | Y | N | N | Y | + |
| **WYOMING** | | | | | | |
| AL **Cubin** | Y | Y | N | N | Y | Y |

# IN THE HOUSE | By Vote Number

**521.** **Procedural Motion/Journal.** Approval of the House Journal of Friday, October 7, 2005. Approved 317-52: R 188-17; D 129-35 (ND 96-28, SD 33-7); I 0-0. Oct. 17, 2005.

**522.** **H Res 457. National Chemistry Week/Adoption.** Smith, R-Texas, motion to suspend the rules and adopt the resolution that would support the goals of National Chemistry Week. Motion agreed to 366-2: R 202-2; D 164-0 (ND 124-0, SD 40-0); I 0-0. A two-thirds majority of those present and voting (246 in this case) is required for adoption under suspension of the rules. Oct. 17, 2005.

**523.** **H Res 491. Cyber Security Awareness Month/Adoption.** Smith, R-Texas, motion to suspend the rules and adopt the resolution that would express support for the goals and ideals of National Cyber Security Awareness Month. Motion agreed to 354-13: R 192-13; D 162-0 (ND 123-0, SD 39-0); I 0-0. A two-thirds majority of those present and voting (245 in this case) is required for adoption under suspension of the rules. Oct. 17, 2005.

**524.** **HR 554. Food Industry Lawsuits/Rule.** Adoption of the rule (H Res 494) that would provide for House floor consideration of the bill that would prohibit lawsuits in federal or state courts against restaurants, food manufacturers and distributors based on claims that the food contributed to the plaintiff's obesity or weight gain. Adopted 310-114: R 228-0; D 81-114 (ND 50-96, SD 31-18); I 1-0. Oct. 18, 2005.

**525.** **HR 1409. Orphan Assistance in Developing Countries/Passage.** Hyde, R-Ill., motion to suspend the rules and pass the bill that would establish a special adviser within the U.S. Agency for International Development who would be responsible for reviewing and approving all assistance provided by the agency to orphans and vulnerable children in developing countries. Motion agreed to 415-9: R 219-9; D 195-0 (ND 146-0, SD 49-0); I 1-0. A two-thirds majority of those present and voting (283 in this case) is required for passage under suspension of the rules. Oct. 18, 2005.

**526.** **H Res 492. Earthquake Victims Condolence/Adoption.** Hyde, R-Ill., motion to suspend the rules and adopt the resolution that would mourn the loss of life and suffering caused by the earthquake that occurred in Pakistan and India on Oct. 8, 2005. Motion agreed to 423-0: R 227-0; D 195-0 (ND 146-0, SD 49-0); I 1-0. A two-thirds majority of those present and voting (282 in this case) is required for adoption under suspension of the rules. Oct. 18, 2005.

**527.** **HR 3549. William F. Clinger Post Office/Passage.** Porter, R-Nev., motion to suspend the rules and pass the bill that would designate a post office in Warren, Pa., for William F. Clinger, R-Pa. (1979-97), who represented Pennsylvania in the House for nine successive terms and was chairman of the Government Reform and Oversight Committee in the 104th Congress. Motion agreed to 422-1: R 228-0; D 193-1 (ND 144-1, SD 49-0); I 1-0. A two-thirds majority of those present and voting (282 in this case) is required for passage under suspension of the rules. Oct. 18, 2005.

**528.** **HR 3853. Willie Vaughn Post Office/Passage.** Porter, R-Nev., motion to suspend the rules and pass the bill that would designate a post office in Parkdale, Ark., for Willie Vaughn, a church, civic and community leader in Parkdale. Motion agreed to 421-0: R 227-0; D 193-0 (ND 144-0, SD 49-0); I 1-0. A two-thirds majority of those present and voting (281 in this case) is required for passage under suspension of the rules. Oct. 18, 2005.

ND Northern Democrats, SD Southern Democrats
Southern states: Ala., Ark., Fla., Ga., Ky., La., Miss., N.C., Okla., S.C., Tenn., Va.

| | 521 | 522 | 523 | 524 | 525 | 526 | 527 | 528 |
|---|---|---|---|---|---|---|---|---|
| **ALABAMA** | | | | | | | | |
| 1 Bonner | Y | Y | Y | Y | Y | Y | Y | Y |
| 2 Everett | Y | Y | Y | Y | Y | Y | Y | Y |
| 3 Rogers | Y | Y | Y | Y | Y | Y | Y | Y |
| 4 Aderholt | Y | Y | Y | Y | Y | Y | Y | Y |
| 5 Cramer | Y | Y | Y | Y | Y | Y | Y | Y |
| 6 Bachus | Y | Y | Y | Y | Y | Y | Y | Y |
| 7 Davis | Y | Y | Y | Y | Y | Y | Y | Y |
| **ALASKA** | | | | | | | | |
| AL Young | Y | Y | Y | Y | Y | Y | Y | Y |
| **ARIZONA** | | | | | | | | |
| 1 Renzi | Y | Y | Y | Y | Y | Y | Y | Y |
| 2 Franks | Y | Y | Y | Y | Y | Y | Y | Y |
| 3 Shadegg | Y | N | N | Y | N | Y | Y | Y |
| 4 Pastor | N | Y | Y | N | Y | Y | Y | Y |
| 5 Hayworth | Y | Y | Y | Y | Y | Y | Y | Y |
| 6 Flake | Y | N | N | Y | N | Y | Y | Y |
| 7 Grijalva | – | + | + | – | + | + | + | + |
| 8 Kolbe | Y | Y | Y | Y | Y | Y | Y | Y |
| **ARKANSAS** | | | | | | | | |
| 1 Berry | Y | Y | Y | Y | Y | Y | Y | Y |
| 2 Snyder | Y | Y | Y | Y | Y | Y | Y | Y |
| 3 Boozman | Y | Y | Y | Y | Y | Y | Y | Y |
| 4 Ross | Y | Y | Y | Y | Y | Y | Y | Y |
| **CALIFORNIA** | | | | | | | | |
| 1 Thompson | N | Y | Y | Y | Y | Y | Y | Y |
| 2 Herger | Y | Y | Y | Y | Y | Y | Y | Y |
| 3 Lungren | Y | Y | Y | Y | Y | Y | Y | Y |
| 4 Doolittle | Y | Y | Y | Y | ? | Y | Y | Y |
| 5 Matsui, D. | Y | Y | Y | N | Y | Y | Y | Y |
| 6 Woolsey | Y | Y | Y | N | Y | Y | Y | Y |
| 7 Miller, George | Y | Y | Y | N | Y | Y | Y | Y |
| 8 Pelosi | Y | Y | Y | Y | Y | Y | Y | Y |
| 9 Lee | Y | Y | Y | N | Y | Y | Y | Y |
| 10 Tauscher | Y | Y | Y | N | Y | Y | Y | Y |
| 11 Pombo | Y | ? | Y | Y | Y | Y | Y | Y |
| 12 Lantos | Y | Y | Y | N | Y | Y | Y | Y |
| 13 Stark | ? | ? | ? | N | Y | Y | ? | Y |
| 14 Eshoo | Y | Y | Y | N | Y | Y | Y | Y |
| 15 Honda | Y | Y | Y | N | Y | Y | Y | Y |
| 16 Lofgren | Y | Y | Y | N | Y | Y | Y | Y |
| 17 Farr | Y | Y | Y | N | Y | Y | Y | Y |
| 18 Cardoza | Y | Y | Y | N | Y | Y | Y | Y |
| 19 Radanovich | Y | Y | Y | Y | Y | Y | Y | Y |
| 20 Costa | Y | Y | Y | Y | Y | Y | Y | Y |
| 21 Nunes | Y | Y | Y | Y | Y | Y | Y | Y |
| 22 Thomas | Y | Y | Y | Y | Y | Y | Y | Y |
| 23 Capps | Y | Y | Y | N | Y | Y | Y | Y |
| 24 Gallegly | + | + | + | Y | Y | Y | Y | Y |
| 25 McKeon | ? | ? | ? | Y | Y | Y | Y | Y |
| 26 Dreier | Y | Y | Y | Y | Y | Y | Y | Y |
| 27 Sherman | Y | Y | Y | N | Y | Y | Y | Y |
| 28 Berman | Y | Y | Y | N | Y | Y | Y | Y |
| 29 Schiff | ? | ? | ? | ? | ? | ? | ? | ? |
| 30 Waxman | Y | Y | Y | N | Y | Y | Y | Y |
| 31 Becerra | + | + | + | N | Y | Y | Y | Y |
| 32 Solis | Y | Y | Y | N | Y | Y | Y | Y |
| 33 Watson | Y | Y | Y | N | Y | Y | Y | Y |
| 34 Roybal-Allard | ? | ? | ? | ? | ? | ? | ? | ? |
| 35 Waters | N | Y | Y | N | Y | Y | Y | Y |
| 36 Harman | ? | ? | ? | Y | Y | Y | Y | Y |
| 37 Millender-McD. | Y | Y | Y | N | Y | Y | Y | Y |
| 38 Napolitano | Y | Y | Y | N | Y | Y | Y | Y |
| 39 Sánchez, Linda | Y | Y | Y | Y | Y | Y | Y | Y |
| 40 Royce | Y | Y | Y | Y | Y | Y | Y | Y |
| 41 Lewis | Y | Y | Y | Y | Y | Y | Y | Y |
| 42 Miller, Gary | Y | Y | Y | Y | Y | Y | Y | Y |
| 43 Baca | Y | Y | Y | Y | Y | Y | Y | Y |
| 44 Calvert | ? | ? | ? | Y | Y | Y | Y | Y |
| 45 Bono | Y | Y | Y | Y | Y | Y | Y | Y |
| 46 Rohrabacher | Y | Y | Y | Y | Y | Y | Y | Y |
| 47 Sanchez, Loretta | N | Y | Y | Y | Y | Y | Y | Y |
| 48 Vacant | | | | | | | | |
| 49 Issa | Y | Y | Y | Y | Y | Y | Y | Y |
| **COLORADO** | | | | | | | | |
| 1 DeGette | Y | Y | Y | Y | Y | Y | Y | Y |
| 2 Udall | N | Y | Y | N | Y | Y | Y | Y |
| 3 Salazar | Y | Y | Y | Y | Y | Y | Y | Y |
| 4 Musgrave | Y | Y | Y | Y | Y | Y | Y | Y |
| 5 Hefley | N | Y | Y | Y | Y | Y | Y | Y |
| 6 Tancredo | P | Y | Y | Y | Y | Y | Y | Y |
| 7 Beauprez | Y | Y | Y | Y | Y | Y | Y | Y |
| **CONNECTICUT** | | | | | | | | |
| 1 Larson | Y | Y | Y | N | Y | Y | Y | Y |
| 2 Simmons | Y | Y | Y | Y | Y | Y | Y | Y |
| 3 DeLauro | Y | Y | Y | N | Y | Y | Y | Y |
| 4 Shays | Y | Y | Y | Y | Y | Y | Y | Y |
| 5 Johnson | Y | Y | Y | Y | Y | Y | Y | Y |
| **DELAWARE** | | | | | | | | |
| AL Castle | Y | Y | Y | Y | Y | Y | Y | Y |
| **FLORIDA** | | | | | | | | |
| 1 Miller | Y | Y | Y | Y | Y | Y | Y | Y |
| 2 Boyd | Y | Y | Y | Y | Y | Y | Y | Y |
| 3 Brown | ? | ? | ? | N | Y | Y | Y | Y |
| 4 Crenshaw | Y | Y | Y | Y | Y | Y | Y | Y |
| 5 Brown-Waite | Y | Y | Y | N | Y | Y | Y | Y |
| 6 Stearns | Y | Y | Y | N | Y | Y | Y | Y |
| 7 Mica | Y | Y | Y | Y | Y | Y | Y | Y |
| 8 Keller | ? | ? | ? | ? | ? | ? | ? | ? |
| 9 Bilirakis | Y | Y | Y | Y | Y | Y | Y | Y |
| 10 Young | Y | Y | Y | Y | Y | Y | Y | Y |
| 11 Davis | ? | ? | ? | ? | ? | ? | ? | ? |
| 12 Putnam | Y | Y | Y | Y | Y | Y | Y | Y |
| 13 Harris | ? | ? | ? | Y | Y | Y | Y | Y |
| 14 Mack | Y | Y | Y | Y | Y | Y | Y | Y |
| 15 Weldon | Y | Y | Y | Y | Y | Y | Y | Y |
| 16 Foley | Y | Y | Y | Y | Y | Y | Y | Y |
| 17 Meek | Y | Y | Y | N | Y | Y | Y | Y |
| 18 Ros-Lehtinen | ? | ? | ? | Y | Y | Y | Y | Y |
| 19 Wexler | Y | Y | Y | N | Y | Y | Y | Y |
| 20 Wasserman-Schultz | ? | ? | ? | Y | Y | Y | Y | Y |
| 21 Diaz-Balart, L. | ? | ? | ? | Y | Y | Y | Y | Y |
| 22 Shaw | Y | Y | Y | Y | Y | Y | Y | Y |
| 23 Hastings | N | Y | Y | N | Y | Y | Y | Y |
| 24 Feeney | ? | ? | ? | Y | Y | Y | Y | Y |
| 25 Diaz-Balart, M. | Y | Y | Y | Y | Y | Y | Y | Y |
| **GEORGIA** | | | | | | | | |
| 1 Kingston | Y | Y | Y | ? | ? | ? | ? | ? |
| 2 Bishop | Y | Y | Y | Y | Y | Y | Y | Y |
| 3 Marshall | N | Y | Y | Y | Y | Y | Y | Y |
| 4 McKinney | Y | Y | Y | N | Y | Y | Y | Y |
| 5 Lewis | N | Y | Y | ? | ? | ? | ? | ? |
| 6 Price | Y | Y | Y | Y | Y | Y | Y | Y |
| 7 Linder | Y | Y | Y | Y | Y | Y | Y | Y |
| 8 Westmoreland | Y | Y | N | Y | N | Y | Y | Y |
| 9 Norwood | Y | Y | N | Y | Y | Y | Y | Y |
| 10 Deal | Y | Y | Y | Y | Y | Y | Y | Y |
| 11 Gingrey | Y | Y | Y | Y | Y | Y | Y | Y |
| 12 Barrow | ? | ? | ? | Y | Y | Y | Y | Y |
| 13 Scott | Y | Y | Y | Y | Y | Y | Y | Y |
| **HAWAII** | | | | | | | | |
| 1 Abercrombie | N | Y | Y | N | Y | Y | N | Y |
| 2 Case | ? | ? | ? | Y | Y | Y | Y | Y |
| **IDAHO** | | | | | | | | |
| 1 Otter | Y | Y | Y | Y | Y | Y | Y | Y |
| 2 Simpson | Y | Y | Y | Y | Y | Y | Y | Y |
| **ILLINOIS** | | | | | | | | |
| 1 Rush | ? | ? | ? | N | Y | Y | Y | Y |
| 2 Jackson | Y | Y | Y | N | Y | Y | Y | Y |
| 3 Lipinski | Y | Y | Y | N | Y | Y | Y | Y |
| 4 Gutierrez | + | + | ? | Y | Y | Y | Y | Y |
| 5 Emanuel | Y | Y | Y | N | Y | Y | Y | Y |
| 6 Hyde | Y | Y | Y | Y | Y | Y | Y | Y |
| 7 Davis | Y | Y | Y | N | Y | Y | Y | Y |
| 8 Bean | Y | Y | Y | Y | Y | Y | Y | Y |
| 9 Schakowsky | Y | Y | Y | N | Y | Y | Y | Y |
| 10 Kirk | + | Y | Y | Y | Y | Y | Y | Y |
| 11 Weller | N | Y | Y | N | Y | Y | Y | Y |
| 12 Costello | N | Y | N | N | Y | Y | Y | Y |
| **50 Cunningham** | Y | Y | Y | Y | Y | Y | Y | Y |
| **51 Filner** | N | Y | Y | N | Y | Y | Y | Y |
| **52 Hunter** | Y | Y | Y | Y | Y | Y | Y | Y |
| **53 Davis** | Y | Y | Y | Y | Y | Y | Y | Y |

**KEY** Republicans | Democrats | *Independents*

| | | | | | |
|---|---|---|---|---|---|
| Y | Voted for (yea) | X | Paired against | C | Voted "present" to avoid possible conflict of interest |
| # | Paired for | – | Announced against | | |
| + | Announced for | P | Voted "present" | ? | Did not vote or otherwise make a position known |
| N | Voted against (nay) | | | | |

| | 521 | 522 | 523 | 524 | 525 | 526 | 527 | 528 |
|---|---|---|---|---|---|---|---|---|
| 13 **Biggert** | ? | ? | ? | Y | Y | Y | Y | Y |
| 14 **Hastert** | | | | | | | | |
| 15 **Johnson** | Y | Y | Y | Y | Y | Y | Y | Y |
| 16 **Manzullo** | Y | Y | Y | Y | Y | Y | Y | Y |
| 17 Evans | Y | Y | Y | N | Y | Y | Y | Y |
| 18 **LaHood** | ? | ? | ? | Y | Y | Y | Y | Y |
| 19 **Shimkus** | Y | Y | N | Y | Y | Y | Y | Y |
| **INDIANA** | | | | | | | | |
| 1 Visclosky | ? | ? | ? | N | Y | Y | Y | Y |
| 2 **Chocola** | Y | Y | Y | Y | Y | Y | Y | Y |
| 3 **Souder** | Y | Y | Y | Y | Y | Y | Y | Y |
| 4 **Buyer** | Y | Y | Y | Y | Y | Y | Y | Y |
| 5 **Burton** | Y | Y | Y | Y | Y | Y | Y | Y |
| 6 **Pence** | Y | Y | Y | Y | Y | Y | Y | Y |
| 7 Carson | Y | Y | Y | Y | Y | Y | Y | Y |
| 8 **Hostettler** | Y | Y | Y | Y | Y | Y | Y | Y |
| 9 **Sodrel** | Y | Y | Y | Y | Y | Y | Y | Y |
| **IOWA** | | | | | | | | |
| 1 **Nussle** | N | Y | Y | Y | Y | Y | Y | Y |
| 2 **Leach** | Y | Y | Y | Y | Y | Y | Y | Y |
| 3 Boswell | ? | ? | ? | ? | ? | ? | ? | ? |
| 4 **Latham** | N | Y | Y | Y | Y | Y | Y | Y |
| 5 **King** | + | + | ? | Y | Y | Y | Y | Y |
| **KANSAS** | | | | | | | | |
| 1 **Moran** | N | Y | Y | Y | Y | Y | Y | Y |
| 2 **Ryun** | + | + | + | Y | Y | Y | Y | Y |
| 3 Moore | Y | Y | Y | Y | Y | Y | Y | Y |
| 4 **Tiahrt** | Y | Y | ? | Y | Y | Y | Y | Y |
| **KENTUCKY** | | | | | | | | |
| 1 **Whitfield** | Y | Y | Y | Y | Y | Y | Y | Y |
| 2 **Lewis** | Y | Y | Y | Y | Y | Y | Y | Y |
| 3 **Northup** | Y | Y | Y | Y | Y | Y | Y | Y |
| 4 **Davis** | N | Y | Y | Y | Y | Y | Y | Y |
| 5 **Rogers** | + | + | + | Y | Y | Y | Y | Y |
| 6 Chandler | N | Y | Y | Y | Y | Y | Y | Y |
| **LOUISIANA** | | | | | | | | |
| 1 **Jindal** | Y | Y | Y | Y | Y | Y | Y | Y |
| 2 Jefferson | Y | Y | Y | N | Y | Y | Y | Y |
| 3 Melancon | Y | Y | Y | Y | Y | Y | Y | Y |
| 4 **McCrery** | Y | Y | Y | Y | Y | Y | Y | Y |
| 5 **Alexander** | ? | ? | ? | Y | Y | Y | Y | Y |
| 6 **Baker** | Y | Y | Y | Y | Y | Y | Y | Y |
| 7 **Boustany** | Y | Y | Y | Y | Y | Y | Y | Y |
| **MAINE** | | | | | | | | |
| 1 Allen | Y | Y | Y | N | Y | Y | Y | Y |
| 2 Michaud | Y | Y | Y | Y | Y | Y | Y | Y |
| **MARYLAND** | | | | | | | | |
| 1 **Gilchrest** | Y | Y | Y | Y | Y | Y | Y | Y |
| 2 Ruppersberger | Y | Y | Y | Y | Y | Y | Y | Y |
| 3 Cardin | ? | ? | ? | N | Y | Y | Y | Y |
| 4 Wynn | Y | Y | Y | Y | Y | Y | Y | Y |
| 5 Hoyer | Y | Y | Y | Y | Y | Y | Y | Y |
| 6 **Bartlett** | Y | Y | Y | Y | Y | Y | Y | Y |
| 7 Cummings | Y | Y | Y | N | Y | Y | Y | Y |
| 8 Van Hollen | Y | Y | Y | Y | Y | Y | Y | Y |
| **MASSACHUSETTS** | | | | | | | | |
| 1 Olver | N | Y | ? | N | Y | Y | Y | Y |
| 2 Neal | ? | ? | ? | Y | Y | Y | Y | Y |
| 3 McGovern | ? | ? | ? | N | Y | Y | Y | Y |
| 4 Frank | Y | Y | Y | Y | Y | Y | Y | Y |
| 5 Meehan | Y | Y | Y | N | Y | Y | Y | Y |
| 6 Tierney | Y | Y | Y | N | Y | Y | Y | Y |
| 7 Markey | N | Y | Y | N | Y | Y | Y | Y |
| 8 Capuano | N | Y | Y | N | Y | Y | Y | Y |
| 9 Lynch | Y | Y | Y | Y | Y | Y | Y | Y |
| 10 Delahunt | Y | Y | Y | N | Y | Y | Y | Y |
| **MICHIGAN** | | | | | | | | |
| 1 Stupak | N | Y | Y | N | Y | Y | Y | Y |
| 2 **Hoekstra** | Y | Y | Y | Y | Y | Y | Y | Y |
| 3 **Ehlers** | Y | Y | Y | Y | Y | Y | Y | Y |
| 4 **Camp** | Y | Y | Y | Y | Y | Y | Y | Y |
| 5 Kildee | Y | Y | Y | Y | Y | Y | Y | Y |
| 6 **Upton** | Y | Y | N | Y | Y | Y | Y | Y |
| 7 **Schwarz** | Y | Y | Y | Y | Y | Y | Y | Y |
| 8 **Rogers** | Y | Y | Y | Y | Y | Y | Y | Y |
| 9 **Knollenberg** | Y | Y | Y | Y | Y | Y | Y | Y |
| 10 **Miller** | Y | Y | Y | Y | Y | Y | Y | Y |
| 11 **McCotter** | ? | ? | ? | Y | Y | Y | Y | Y |
| 12 Levin | Y | Y | Y | N | Y | Y | Y | Y |
| 13 Kilpatrick | + | + | + | N | Y | Y | Y | Y |
| 14 Conyers | Y | Y | Y | Y | Y | Y | Y | Y |
| 15 Dingell | Y | Y | Y | Y | Y | Y | Y | Y |
| **MINNESOTA** | | | | | | | | |
| 1 **Gutknecht** | Y | Y | Y | Y | Y | Y | Y | Y |
| 2 **Kline** | Y | Y | Y | Y | Y | Y | Y | Y |
| 3 **Ramstad** | N | Y | Y | Y | Y | Y | Y | Y |
| 4 McCollum | N | Y | Y | N | Y | Y | Y | Y |
| 5 Sabo | N | Y | Y | N | Y | Y | Y | Y |
| 6 **Kennedy** | N | Y | Y | Y | Y | Y | Y | Y |
| 7 Peterson | N | Y | Y | Y | Y | Y | Y | Y |
| 8 Oberstar | N | Y | Y | N | Y | Y | Y | Y |
| **MISSISSIPPI** | | | | | | | | |
| 1 **Wicker** | Y | Y | Y | Y | Y | Y | Y | Y |
| 2 Thompson | Y | Y | Y | N | Y | Y | Y | Y |
| 3 **Pickering** | ? | ? | ? | Y | Y | Y | Y | Y |
| 4 Taylor | N | Y | Y | Y | Y | Y | Y | Y |
| **MISSOURI** | | | | | | | | |
| 1 Clay | Y | Y | Y | N | Y | Y | Y | Y |
| 2 **Akin** | Y | Y | Y | Y | Y | Y | Y | Y |
| 3 Carnahan | Y | Y | Y | N | Y | Y | Y | Y |
| 4 Skelton | Y | Y | Y | Y | Y | Y | Y | Y |
| 5 Cleaver | Y | Y | Y | N | Y | Y | Y | Y |
| 6 **Graves** | Y | Y | Y | Y | Y | Y | Y | Y |
| 7 **Blunt** | Y | Y | Y | Y | Y | Y | Y | ? |
| 8 **Emerson** | Y | Y | Y | Y | Y | Y | Y | Y |
| 9 **Hulshof** | Y | Y | Y | Y | Y | Y | Y | Y |
| **MONTANA** | | | | | | | | |
| AL **Rehberg** | Y | Y | Y | Y | Y | Y | Y | Y |
| **NEBRASKA** | | | | | | | | |
| 1 **Fortenberry** | Y | Y | Y | Y | Y | Y | Y | Y |
| 2 **Terry** | ? | ? | ? | Y | Y | Y | Y | Y |
| 3 **Osborne** | Y | Y | Y | Y | Y | Y | Y | Y |
| **NEVADA** | | | | | | | | |
| 1 Berkley | Y | Y | Y | Y | Y | Y | Y | Y |
| 2 **Gibbons** | + | + | + | Y | Y | Y | Y | Y |
| 3 **Porter** | Y | Y | Y | Y | Y | Y | Y | Y |
| **NEW HAMPSHIRE** | | | | | | | | |
| 1 **Bradley** | Y | Y | Y | Y | Y | Y | Y | Y |
| 2 **Bass** | Y | Y | Y | Y | Y | Y | Y | Y |
| **NEW JERSEY** | | | | | | | | |
| 1 Andrews | Y | Y | Y | - | + | + | + | + |
| 2 **LoBiondo** | N | Y | Y | Y | Y | Y | Y | Y |
| 3 **Saxton** | Y | ? | Y | Y | Y | Y | Y | Y |
| 4 **Smith** | Y | Y | Y | Y | Y | Y | Y | Y |
| 5 **Garrett** | Y | Y | Y | Y | Y | Y | Y | Y |
| 6 Pallone | Y | Y | Y | N | Y | Y | Y | Y |
| 7 **Ferguson** | Y | Y | N | Y | Y | Y | Y | Y |
| 8 Pascrell | + | + | + | N | Y | Y | Y | Y |
| 9 Rothman | Y | Y | Y | N | Y | Y | Y | Y |
| 10 Payne | Y | Y | Y | N | Y | Y | Y | Y |
| 11 **Frelinghuysen** | Y | Y | Y | Y | Y | Y | Y | Y |
| 12 Holt | Y | Y | Y | N | Y | Y | Y | Y |
| 13 Menendez | + | + | Y | Y | Y | Y | Y | Y |
| **NEW MEXICO** | | | | | | | | |
| 1 **Wilson** | Y | Y | Y | Y | Y | Y | Y | Y |
| 2 **Pearce** | Y | Y | Y | Y | Y | Y | Y | Y |
| 3 Udall | N | Y | Y | N | Y | Y | Y | Y |
| **NEW YORK** | | | | | | | | |
| 1 Bishop | Y | Y | Y | Y | Y | Y | Y | Y |
| 2 Israel | Y | Y | Y | Y | Y | Y | Y | Y |
| 3 **King** | Y | Y | Y | Y | Y | Y | Y | Y |
| 4 McCarthy | N | Y | Y | N | Y | Y | Y | Y |
| 5 Ackerman | Y | Y | Y | N | Y | Y | Y | Y |
| 6 Meeks | ? | ? | ? | N | Y | Y | Y | Y |
| 7 Crowley | Y | Y | Y | N | Y | Y | Y | Y |
| 8 Nadler | Y | Y | Y | N | Y | Y | Y | Y |
| 9 Weiner | Y | Y | Y | N | Y | Y | Y | Y |
| 10 Towns | ? | ? | ? | N | Y | Y | Y | Y |
| 11 Owens | Y | Y | Y | N | Y | Y | Y | Y |
| 12 Velázquez | N | Y | Y | N | Y | Y | Y | Y |
| 13 **Fossella** | N | Y | Y | Y | Y | Y | Y | Y |
| 14 Maloney | Y | Y | Y | N | Y | Y | Y | Y |
| 15 Rangel | ? | ? | ? | Y | Y | Y | Y | Y |
| 16 Serrano | Y | Y | Y | N | Y | Y | Y | Y |
| 17 Engel | ? | ? | ? | N | Y | Y | Y | Y |
| 18 Lowey | Y | Y | Y | N | Y | Y | Y | Y |
| 19 **Kelly** | Y | Y | Y | Y | Y | Y | Y | Y |
| 20 **Sweeney** | N | Y | Y | Y | Y | Y | Y | Y |
| 21 McNulty | Y | Y | Y | N | Y | Y | Y | Y |
| 22 Hinchey | Y | Y | Y | N | Y | Y | Y | Y |
| 23 **McHugh** | Y | Y | Y | Y | Y | Y | Y | Y |
| 24 **Boehlert** | Y | Y | Y | Y | Y | Y | Y | Y |
| 25 **Walsh** | Y | Y | Y | Y | Y | Y | Y | Y |
| 26 **Reynolds** | Y | ? | Y | Y | Y | Y | Y | Y |
| 27 Higgins | Y | Y | Y | Y | Y | Y | Y | Y |
| 28 Slaughter | Y | Y | Y | N | Y | Y | Y | Y |
| 29 **Kuhl** | Y | Y | Y | Y | Y | Y | Y | Y |
| **NORTH CAROLINA** | | | | | | | | |
| 1 Butterfield | ? | ? | ? | N | Y | Y | Y | Y |
| 2 Etheridge | N | Y | Y | N | Y | Y | Y | Y |
| 3 **Jones** | Y | Y | N | Y | Y | Y | Y | Y |
| 4 Price | Y | Y | ? | N | Y | Y | Y | Y |
| 5 **Foxx** | Y | Y | Y | Y | Y | Y | Y | Y |
| 6 **Coble** | Y | Y | Y | Y | Y | Y | Y | Y |
| 7 McIntyre | Y | Y | Y | Y | Y | Y | Y | Y |
| 8 **Hayes** | Y | Y | Y | Y | Y | Y | Y | Y |
| 9 **Myrick** | Y | Y | Y | Y | Y | Y | Y | Y |
| 10 **McHenry** | Y | Y | Y | Y | Y | Y | Y | Y |
| 11 **Taylor** | Y | Y | Y | Y | Y | Y | Y | Y |
| 12 Watt | ? | ? | ? | N | Y | Y | Y | Y |
| 13 Miller | Y | Y | Y | N | Y | Y | Y | Y |
| **NORTH DAKOTA** | | | | | | | | |
| AL Pomeroy | Y | Y | Y | Y | Y | Y | Y | Y |
| **OHIO** | | | | | | | | |
| 1 **Chabot** | Y | Y | Y | Y | Y | Y | Y | Y |
| 2 **Schmidt** | Y | Y | Y | Y | Y | Y | Y | Y |
| 3 **Turner** | Y | Y | Y | Y | Y | Y | Y | Y |
| 4 **Oxley** | + | + | + | Y | Y | Y | Y | Y |
| 5 **Gillmor** | Y | Y | Y | Y | Y | Y | Y | Y |
| 6 Strickland | ? | ? | ? | N | Y | Y | Y | Y |
| 7 **Hobson** | Y | Y | Y | Y | Y | Y | Y | Y |
| 8 **Boehner** | Y | Y | Y | Y | Y | Y | Y | Y |
| 9 Kaptur | Y | Y | Y | N | Y | Y | Y | Y |
| 10 Kucinich | N | Y | Y | N | Y | Y | Y | Y |
| 11 Jones | ? | ? | ? | N | Y | Y | Y | Y |
| 12 **Tiberi** | N | Y | Y | Y | Y | Y | Y | Y |
| 13 Brown | Y | Y | Y | N | Y | Y | Y | Y |
| 14 **LaTourette** | Y | Y | Y | Y | Y | Y | Y | Y |
| 15 **Pryce** | Y | Y | Y | Y | Y | Y | Y | Y |
| 16 **Regula** | Y | Y | Y | Y | Y | Y | Y | Y |
| 17 Ryan | Y | Y | Y | N | Y | Y | Y | Y |
| 18 **Ney** | Y | Y | Y | Y | Y | Y | Y | Y |
| **OKLAHOMA** | | | | | | | | |
| 1 **Sullivan** | ? | ? | ? | Y | Y | Y | Y | Y |
| 2 Boren | Y | Y | Y | Y | Y | Y | Y | Y |
| 3 **Lucas** | Y | Y | Y | Y | Y | Y | Y | Y |
| 4 **Cole** | Y | Y | Y | Y | Y | Y | Y | Y |
| 5 **Istook** | ? | ? | ? | Y | Y | Y | Y | Y |
| **OREGON** | | | | | | | | |
| 1 Wu | N | Y | Y | Y | Y | Y | Y | Y |
| 2 **Walden** | Y | Y | N | Y | Y | Y | Y | Y |
| 3 Blumenauer | + | + | + | N | Y | Y | Y | Y |
| 4 DeFazio | ? | ? | ? | Y | Y | Y | Y | Y |
| 5 Hooley | Y | Y | Y | Y | Y | Y | Y | Y |
| **PENNSYLVANIA** | | | | | | | | |
| 1 Brady | ? | ? | ? | N | Y | Y | Y | Y |
| 2 Fattah | N | Y | Y | N | Y | Y | Y | ? |
| 3 **English** | N | Y | Y | Y | Y | Y | Y | Y |
| 4 **Hart** | N | Y | Y | Y | Y | Y | Y | Y |
| 5 **Peterson** | Y | Y | Y | Y | Y | Y | Y | Y |
| 6 **Gerlach** | + | + | + | Y | Y | Y | Y | Y |
| 7 **Weldon** | Y | Y | Y | Y | Y | Y | Y | Y |
| 8 **Fitzpatrick** | N | Y | Y | Y | Y | Y | Y | Y |
| 9 **Shuster** | N | Y | Y | Y | N | Y | Y | Y |
| 10 **Sherwood** | Y | Y | Y | Y | Y | Y | Y | Y |
| 11 Kanjorski | N | Y | Y | N | Y | Y | Y | Y |
| 12 Murtha | Y | Y | ? | N | Y | Y | Y | ? |
| 13 Schwartz | Y | Y | Y | Y | Y | Y | Y | Y |
| 14 Doyle | Y | Y | Y | Y | Y | Y | Y | Y |
| 15 **Dent** | Y | Y | Y | Y | Y | Y | Y | Y |
| 16 **Pitts** | Y | Y | Y | Y | Y | Y | Y | Y |
| 17 Holden | N | Y | Y | N | Y | Y | Y | Y |
| 18 **Murphy** | Y | Y | Y | Y | Y | Y | Y | Y |
| 19 **Platts** | Y | Y | Y | Y | Y | Y | Y | Y |
| **RHODE ISLAND** | | | | | | | | |
| 1 Kennedy | + | + | + | Y | Y | Y | Y | Y |
| 2 Langevin | Y | Y | Y | Y | Y | Y | Y | Y |
| **SOUTH CAROLINA** | | | | | | | | |
| 1 **Brown** | Y | Y | Y | Y | Y | Y | Y | Y |
| 2 **Wilson** | Y | Y | Y | Y | Y | Y | Y | Y |
| 3 **Barrett** | Y | Y | Y | Y | Y | Y | Y | Y |
| 4 **Inglis** | Y | Y | Y | Y | Y | Y | Y | Y |
| 5 Spratt | Y | Y | Y | N | Y | Y | Y | Y |
| 6 Clyburn | Y | Y | Y | N | Y | Y | Y | Y |
| **SOUTH DAKOTA** | | | | | | | | |
| AL Herseth | Y | Y | Y | Y | Y | Y | Y | Y |
| **TENNESSEE** | | | | | | | | |
| 1 **Jenkins** | Y | Y | Y | Y | Y | Y | Y | Y |
| 2 **Duncan** | Y | Y | Y | Y | Y | Y | Y | Y |
| 3 **Wamp** | Y | Y | Y | Y | Y | Y | Y | Y |
| 4 Davis | Y | Y | Y | Y | Y | Y | Y | Y |
| 5 Cooper | Y | Y | Y | Y | Y | Y | Y | Y |
| 6 Gordon | Y | Y | Y | Y | Y | Y | Y | Y |
| 7 **Blackburn** | Y | Y | Y | Y | Y | Y | Y | Y |
| 8 Tanner | Y | Y | Y | Y | Y | Y | Y | Y |
| 9 Ford | ? | ? | ? | N | Y | Y | Y | Y |
| **TEXAS** | | | | | | | | |
| 1 **Gohmert** | Y | Y | Y | Y | N | Y | Y | Y |
| 2 **Poe** | Y | Y | Y | Y | Y | Y | Y | Y |
| 3 **Johnson, S.** | Y | Y | Y | Y | N | Y | Y | Y |
| 4 **Hall** | Y | Y | Y | Y | Y | Y | Y | Y |
| 5 **Hensarling** | Y | Y | N | Y | Y | Y | Y | Y |
| 6 **Barton** | Y | Y | N | Y | Y | Y | Y | Y |
| 7 **Culberson** | Y | Y | Y | Y | Y | Y | Y | Y |
| 8 **Brady** | Y | Y | Y | Y | Y | Y | Y | Y |
| 9 Green, A. | Y | Y | Y | N | Y | Y | Y | Y |
| 10 **McCaul** | Y | Y | Y | Y | Y | Y | Y | Y |
| 11 **Conaway** | Y | Y | Y | Y | Y | Y | Y | Y |
| 12 **Granger** | Y | Y | Y | Y | Y | Y | Y | Y |
| 13 **Thornberry** | Y | Y | Y | Y | Y | Y | Y | Y |
| 14 **Paul** | Y | Y | N | Y | N | Y | Y | Y |
| 15 Hinojosa | Y | Y | Y | Y | Y | Y | Y | Y |
| 16 Reyes | ? | ? | ? | Y | Y | Y | Y | Y |
| 17 Edwards | Y | Y | Y | Y | Y | Y | Y | Y |
| 18 Jackson-Lee | + | + | + | Y | Y | Y | Y | Y |
| 19 **Neugebauer** | Y | Y | Y | Y | Y | Y | Y | Y |
| 20 Gonzalez | Y | Y | Y | Y | Y | Y | Y | Y |
| 21 **Smith** | Y | Y | ? | Y | Y | Y | Y | Y |
| 22 **DeLay** | Y | Y | Y | Y | Y | Y | Y | Y |
| 23 **Bonilla** | Y | Y | Y | Y | Y | Y | Y | Y |
| 24 **Marchant** | Y | Y | Y | Y | Y | Y | Y | Y |
| 25 Doggett | Y | Y | Y | N | Y | Y | Y | Y |
| 26 **Burgess** | Y | Y | Y | Y | Y | Y | Y | Y |
| 27 Ortiz | Y | Y | Y | Y | Y | Y | Y | Y |
| 28 Cuellar | Y | Y | Y | Y | Y | Y | Y | Y |
| 29 Green, G. | N | Y | Y | Y | Y | Y | Y | Y |
| 30 Johnson, E. | Y | Y | Y | N | Y | Y | Y | Y |
| 31 **Carter** | Y | Y | Y | Y | Y | Y | Y | Y |
| 32 **Sessions** | Y | Y | N | Y | Y | Y | Y | Y |
| **UTAH** | | | | | | | | |
| 1 **Bishop** | Y | Y | Y | Y | Y | Y | Y | Y |
| 2 Matheson | N | Y | Y | Y | Y | Y | Y | Y |
| 3 **Cannon** | Y | Y | Y | Y | Y | Y | Y | Y |
| **VERMONT** | | | | | | | | |
| AL *Sanders* | ? | ? | ? | Y | Y | Y | Y | Y |
| **VIRGINIA** | | | | | | | | |
| 1 **Davis, J.** | Y | Y | Y | Y | Y | Y | Y | Y |
| 2 **Drake** | Y | Y | Y | Y | Y | Y | Y | Y |
| 3 Scott | Y | Y | Y | Y | Y | Y | Y | Y |
| 4 **Forbes** | Y | Y | Y | Y | Y | Y | Y | Y |
| 5 **Goode** | ? | ? | ? | Y | Y | Y | Y | Y |
| 6 **Goodlatte** | Y | Y | Y | Y | Y | Y | Y | Y |
| 7 **Cantor** | Y | Y | Y | Y | Y | Y | Y | Y |
| 8 Moran | ? | ? | ? | Y | Y | Y | Y | Y |
| 9 Boucher | ? | ? | ? | Y | Y | Y | Y | Y |
| 10 **Wolf** | Y | Y | Y | Y | Y | Y | Y | Y |
| 11 **Davis, T.** | Y | Y | Y | Y | Y | Y | Y | Y |
| **WASHINGTON** | | | | | | | | |
| 1 Inslee | Y | Y | Y | N | Y | Y | Y | Y |
| 2 Larsen | Y | Y | Y | Y | Y | Y | Y | Y |
| 3 Baird | N | Y | Y | N | Y | Y | Y | Y |
| 4 **Hastings** | Y | Y | Y | Y | Y | Y | Y | Y |
| 5 **McMorris** | Y | Y | Y | Y | Y | Y | Y | Y |
| 6 Dicks | Y | Y | Y | Y | Y | Y | Y | Y |
| 7 McDermott | N | Y | Y | N | Y | Y | Y | Y |
| 8 **Reichert** | Y | Y | Y | Y | Y | Y | Y | Y |
| 9 Smith | Y | Y | Y | Y | Y | Y | Y | Y |
| **WEST VIRGINIA** | | | | | | | | |
| 1 Mollohan | Y | Y | Y | N | Y | Y | Y | Y |
| 2 **Capito** | N | Y | Y | Y | Y | Y | Y | Y |
| 3 Rahall | Y | Y | Y | N | Y | Y | Y | Y |
| **WISCONSIN** | | | | | | | | |
| 1 **Ryan** | Y | Y | Y | Y | Y | Y | Y | Y |
| 2 Baldwin | N | Y | Y | N | Y | Y | Y | Y |
| 3 Kind | Y | Y | Y | Y | Y | Y | Y | Y |
| 4 Moore | Y | Y | Y | N | Y | Y | Y | Y |
| 5 **Sensenbrenner** | Y | Y | Y | Y | Y | Y | Y | Y |
| 6 **Petri** | Y | Y | Y | Y | Y | Y | Y | Y |
| 7 Obey | Y | Y | Y | N | Y | Y | Y | Y |
| 8 **Green** | Y | Y | Y | Y | Y | Y | Y | Y |
| **WYOMING** | | | | | | | | |
| AL **Cubin** | Y | Y | Y | Y | Y | Y | Y | Y |

# IN THE HOUSE | By Vote Number

**529.** HR 554. Food Industry Lawsuits/Lawsuits by Food Manufacturers. Jackson-Lee, D-Texas, amendment that would prohibit food manufacturers, vendors or trade associations from filing lawsuits against any individual due to that person's consumption of food that has led to weight gain, obesity or related health problems. Rejected 67-357: R 0-227; D 66-130 (ND 53-95, SD 13-35); I 1-0. Oct. 19, 2005.

**530.** HR 554. Food Industry Lawsuits/Lawsuits for Children. Filner, D-Calif., amendment that would allow lawsuits for obesity-related injuries of children age 8 and under against chain outlets with at least 20 stores that have marketed food to children under age 8. Rejected 129-298: R 1-227; D 127-71 (ND 105-44, SD 22-27); I 1-0. Oct. 19, 2005.

**531.** HR 554. Food Industry Lawsuits/State Consumer Protection Laws. Scott, D-Va., amendment that would exempt from the bill an action brought by a state agency to enforce state consumer protection laws concerning mislabeling or other unfair and deceptive trade practices. Rejected 192-234: R 6-221; D 185-13 (ND 145-4, SD 40-9); I 1-0. Oct. 19, 2005.

**532.** HR 554. Food Industry Lawsuits/Dietary Supplement Makers. Waxman, D-Calif., amendment that would allow lawsuits against dietary supplement makers for damages because of obesity, weight gain or related health problems. Rejected 177-247: R 5-221; D 171-26 (ND 137-11, SD 34-15); I 1-0. Oct. 19, 2005.

**533.** HR 554. Food Industry Lawsuits/Passage. Passage of the bill that would prohibit lawsuits in federal or state courts against restaurants, food manufacturers or distributors based on claims that the food contributed to the plaintiff's obesity or weight gain. Suits would be allowed if the defendant knowingly violated federal or state laws governing the labeling, advertising or selling of food products. Passed 306-120: R 226-1; D 80-118 (ND 49-100, SD 31-18); I 0-1. A "yea" was a vote in support of the president's position. Oct. 19, 2005.

**534.** S 397. Gun Liability/Passage. Passage of the bill that would bar certain civil lawsuits against manufacturers, distributors, dealers and importers of firearms and ammunition, principally those lawsuits aimed at making them liable for gun violence. Trade groups also would be protected, and all pending legal action against gunmakers would be dismissed. The bill would also, with certain exceptions, make it unlawful for licensed gun importers, manufacturers or dealers to sell, deliver or transfer handguns without a secure gun storage or safety device. Passed (thus cleared for the president) 283-144: R 223-4; D 59-140 (ND 31-118, SD 28-22); I 1-0. A "yea" was a vote in support of the president's position. Oct. 20, 2005.

**535.** HR 2744. Fiscal 2006 Agriculture Appropriations/Motion to Instruct. DeLauro, D-Conn., motion to instruct House conferees to include language that would agree to a Senate provision that would block use of funds in the bill from being used to close or relocate state Farm Service Agency offices unless the Agriculture Department reports that such closures are necessary and cost effective. It also would instruct conferees to agree to a new provision that would prohibit a state agency from using federal funds for administrative costs related to Food Stamp Program operations that are contracted to a private entity. Motion rejected 209-216: R 12-215; D 196-1 (ND 147-1, SD 49-0); I 1-0. Oct. 20, 2005.

ND Northern Democrats, SD Southern Democrats
Southern states: Ala., Ark., Fla., Ga., Ky., La., Miss., N.C., Okla., S.C., Tenn., Texas, Va.

| | 529 | 530 | 531 | 532 | 533 | 534 | 535 |
|---|---|---|---|---|---|---|---|
| **ALABAMA** | | | | | | | |
| 1 Bonner | N | N | N | N | Y | Y | N |
| 2 Everett | N | N | N | N | Y | Y | N |
| 3 Rogers | N | N | N | N | Y | Y | N |
| 4 Aderholt | N | N | N | N | Y | Y | N |
| 5 Cramer | N | N | N | N | Y | Y | Y |
| 6 Bachus | N | N | N | N | Y | Y | N |
| 7 Davis | N | N | Y | N | Y | Y | Y |
| **ALASKA** | | | | | | | |
| AL Young | N | N | N | N | Y | Y | N |
| **ARIZONA** | | | | | | | |
| 1 Renzi | N | N | N | N | Y | Y | N |
| 2 Franks | N | N | N | N | Y | Y | N |
| 3 Shadegg | N | N | N | N | Y | Y | N |
| 4 Pastor | Y | Y | Y | Y | N | N | Y |
| 5 Hayworth | N | N | N | N | Y | Y | N |
| 6 Flake | N | N | N | N | Y | Y | N |
| 7 Grijalva | Y | Y | Y | Y | N | N | Y |
| 8 Kolbe | N | N | N | N | Y | Y | N |
| **ARKANSAS** | | | | | | | |
| 1 Berry | N | N | Y | Y | Y | Y | Y |
| 2 Snyder | N | N | Y | Y | N | Y | N |
| 3 Boozman | N | N | N | N | Y | Y | N |
| 4 Ross | N | N | Y | Y | Y | Y | Y |
| **CALIFORNIA** | | | | | | | |
| 1 Thompson | N | N | N | N | Y | Y | Y |
| 2 Herger | N | N | N | N | Y | Y | N |
| 3 Lungren | N | N | N | N | Y | Y | N |
| 4 Doolittle | N | N | N | N | Y | Y | N |
| 5 Matsui, D. | N | Y | Y | Y | N | N | Y |
| 6 Woolsey | Y | Y | Y | Y | N | N | Y |
| 7 Miller, George | N | Y | Y | Y | N | N | Y |
| 8 Pelosi | Y | Y | Y | Y | N | N | Y |
| 9 Lee | Y | Y | Y | Y | N | N | Y |
| 10 Tauscher | N | Y | Y | Y | N | N | Y |
| 11 Pombo | N | N | N | N | Y | Y | N |
| 12 Lantos | N | Y | Y | Y | N | N | Y |
| 13 Stark | Y | Y | Y | Y | N | N | ? |
| 14 Eshoo | N | N | Y | Y | N | N | Y |
| 15 Honda | Y | Y | Y | Y | N | N | Y |
| 16 Lofgren | N | Y | Y | Y | N | N | Y |
| 17 Farr | Y | Y | Y | Y | N | N | Y |
| 18 Cardoza | N | Y | N | N | Y | Y | Y |
| 19 Radanovich | N | N | N | N | Y | Y | N |
| 20 Costa | N | N | Y | Y | Y | Y | Y |
| 21 Nunes | N | N | N | N | Y | Y | N |
| 22 Thomas | N | N | N | N | Y | Y | N |
| 23 Capps | N | Y | Y | Y | N | N | Y |
| 24 Gallegly | N | N | N | N | Y | Y | N |
| 25 McKeon | N | N | N | N | Y | Y | N |
| 26 Dreier | N | N | N | N | Y | Y | N |
| 27 Sherman | N | Y | Y | Y | N | N | Y |
| 28 Berman | N | Y | Y | Y | N | N | Y |
| 29 Schiff | N | Y | Y | Y | N | N | Y |
| 30 Waxman | N | Y | Y | Y | N | N | Y |
| 31 Becerra | N | Y | Y | Y | N | N | Y |
| 32 Solis | N | Y | Y | Y | N | N | Y |
| 33 Watson | Y | Y | Y | Y | N | N | Y |
| 34 Roybal-Allard | ? | ? | ? | ? | ? | ? | ? |
| 35 Waters | Y | Y | Y | Y | N | N | Y |
| 36 Harman | N | N | Y | Y | N | N | Y |
| 37 Millender-McD. | Y | N | Y | Y | Y | N | Y |
| 38 Napolitano | Y | Y | Y | Y | N | N | Y |
| 39 Sánchez, Linda | Y | Y | Y | Y | N | N | Y |
| 40 Royce | N | N | N | N | Y | Y | N |
| 41 Lewis | N | N | N | N | Y | Y | N |
| 42 Miller, Gary | N | N | N | N | Y | Y | N |
| 43 Baca | N | N | Y | Y | Y | Y | Y |
| 44 Calvert | N | N | N | N | Y | Y | N |
| 45 Bono | N | N | N | N | Y | Y | N |
| 46 Rohrabacher | N | N | Y | N | Y | Y | N |
| 47 Sanchez, Loretta | N | N | Y | Y | Y | Y | Y |
| 48 Vacant | | | | | | | |
| 49 Issa | N | N | N | N | Y | Y | N |

| | 529 | 530 | 531 | 532 | 533 | 534 | 535 |
|---|---|---|---|---|---|---|---|
| 50 Cunningham | N | N | Y | N | Y | Y | N |
| 51 Filner | N | Y | Y | Y | N | N | Y |
| 52 Hunter | N | N | N | N | Y | Y | N |
| 53 Davis | N | Y | Y | Y | N | N | Y |
| **COLORADO** | | | | | | | |
| 1 DeGette | N | N | Y | Y | N | N | Y |
| 2 Udall | N | N | Y | Y | Y | N | Y |
| 3 Salazar | N | N | Y | Y | Y | Y | Y |
| 4 Musgrave | N | N | N | N | Y | + | N |
| 5 Hefley | N | N | N | N | Y | Y | N |
| 6 Tancredo | N | N | N | N | Y | Y | N |
| 7 Beauprez | N | N | N | N | Y | Y | N |
| **CONNECTICUT** | | | | | | | |
| 1 Larson | Y | Y | Y | Y | N | N | Y |
| 2 Simmons | N | N | N | Y | Y | Y | Y |
| 3 DeLauro | N | Y | Y | Y | N | N | Y |
| 4 Shays | N | N | N | N | Y | Y | Y |
| 5 Johnson | N | N | N | N | Y | Y | Y |
| **DELAWARE** | | | | | | | |
| AL Castle | N | N | N | N | Y | N | N |
| **FLORIDA** | | | | | | | |
| 1 Miller | N | N | N | N | Y | Y | N |
| 2 Boyd | N | N | N | Y | Y | Y | Y |
| 3 Brown | N | Y | Y | Y | Y | N | Y |
| 4 Crenshaw | N | N | N | N | Y | Y | N |
| 5 Brown-Waite | N | N | N | N | Y | Y | N |
| 6 Stearns | N | N | N | N | Y | Y | N |
| 7 Mica | N | N | N | N | Y | Y | N |
| 8 Keller | ? | ? | ? | ? | ? | ? | ? |
| 9 Bilirakis | N | N | N | N | Y | Y | N |
| 10 Young | N | N | N | N | Y | Y | N |
| 11 Davis | ? | ? | ? | ? | ? | ? | ? |
| 12 Putnam | N | N | N | N | Y | Y | N |
| 13 Harris | N | N | N | N | Y | Y | N |
| 14 Mack | N | N | N | N | Y | Y | N |
| 15 Weldon | N | N | N | N | Y | Y | N |
| 16 Foley | N | N | N | N | Y | Y | N |
| 17 Meek | N | Y | Y | Y | N | N | Y |
| 18 Ros-Lehtinen | N | N | N | N | Y | Y | N |
| 19 Wexler | Y | Y | Y | Y | N | N | Y |
| 20 Wasserman-Schultz | Y | N | Y | Y | N | N | Y |
| 21 Diaz-Balart, L. | N | N | N | N | Y | Y | N |
| 22 Shaw | N | N | N | N | Y | Y | N |
| 23 Hastings | N | Y | Y | Y | N | N | Y |
| 24 Feeney | ? | N | N | N | Y | Y | N |
| 25 Diaz-Balart, M. | N | N | N | N | Y | Y | N |
| **GEORGIA** | | | | | | | |
| 1 Kingston | N | N | N | N | Y | Y | Y |
| 2 Bishop | N | N | Y | Y | Y | Y | Y |
| 3 Marshall | N | N | Y | Y | Y | Y | Y |
| 4 McKinney | Y | Y | Y | Y | N | N | Y |
| 5 Lewis | ? | ? | ? | ? | ? | N | Y |
| 6 Price | N | N | N | N | Y | Y | N |
| 7 Linder | N | N | N | N | Y | Y | N |
| 8 Westmoreland | N | N | N | N | Y | Y | N |
| 9 Norwood | N | N | N | N | Y | Y | N |
| 10 Deal | N | N | N | N | Y | Y | N |
| 11 Gingrey | N | N | N | N | Y | Y | N |
| 12 Barrow | N | N | N | N | Y | Y | Y |
| 13 Scott | N | N | Y | N | Y | Y | Y |
| **HAWAII** | | | | | | | |
| 1 Abercrombie | N | Y | Y | Y | N | N | Y |
| 2 Case | N | N | Y | N | N | N | Y |
| **IDAHO** | | | | | | | |
| 1 Otter | N | N | N | N | Y | Y | N |
| 2 Simpson | N | N | ? | ? | Y | Y | N |
| **ILLINOIS** | | | | | | | |
| 1 Rush | Y | Y | Y | Y | N | N | Y |
| 2 Jackson | Y | Y | Y | Y | N | N | Y |
| 3 Lipinski | N | Y | Y | Y | N | N | Y |
| 4 Gutierrez | Y | Y | Y | Y | N | N | Y |
| 5 Emanuel | N | Y | Y | Y | N | N | Y |
| 6 Hyde | N | N | N | N | Y | Y | N |
| 7 Davis | N | N | Y | Y | N | N | Y |
| 8 Bean | N | N | Y | Y | Y | Y | Y |
| 9 Schakowsky | Y | Y | Y | Y | N | N | Y |
| 10 Kirk | N | N | N | N | Y | N | N |
| 11 Weller | N | N | N | N | Y | Y | N |
| 12 Costello | N | Y | Y | Y | N | Y | Y |

| KEY | Republicans | Democrats | Independents |
|---|---|---|---|
| Y | Voted for (yea) | X | Paired against | C | Voted "present" to avoid possible conflict of interest |
| # | Paired for | – | Announced against | |
| + | Announced for | P | Voted "present" | ? | Did not vote or otherwise make a position known |
| N | Voted against (nay) | | |

| | 529 | 530 | 531 | 532 | 533 | 534 | 535 |
|---|---|---|---|---|---|---|---|
| 13 **Biggert** | N | N | N | N | Y | Y | N |
| 14 **Hastert** | | | | | | | |
| 15 **Johnson** | N | N | N | N | Y | Y | Y |
| 16 **Manzullo** | N | N | N | N | Y | Y | N |
| 17 Evans | N | Y | Y | Y | N | N | Y |
| 18 **LaHood** | N | N | N | N | Y | Y | N |
| 19 **Shimkus** | N | N | N | N | Y | Y | N |
| **INDIANA** | | | | | | | |
| 1 Visclosky | Y | N | Y | Y | N | N | Y |
| 2 **Chocola** | N | N | N | N | Y | Y | N |
| 3 **Souder** | N | N | N | N | Y | Y | N |
| 4 **Buyer** | N | N | N | N | Y | Y | N |
| 5 **Burton** | N | N | N | N | Y | Y | N |
| 6 **Pence** | N | N | N | N | Y | Y | N |
| 7 Carson | Y | Y | Y | Y | N | N | Y |
| 8 **Hostettler** | N | N | N | N | Y | Y | N |
| 9 **Sodrel** | N | N | N | N | Y | Y | N |
| **IOWA** | | | | | | | |
| 1 **Nussle** | N | N | N | N | Y | Y | N |
| 2 **Leach** | N | N | N | N | Y | Y | Y |
| 3 Boswell | ? | ? | ? | ? | ? | ? | ? |
| 4 **Latham** | N | N | N | N | Y | Y | N |
| 5 **King** | N | N | N | N | Y | Y | N |
| **KANSAS** | | | | | | | |
| 1 **Moran** | N | N | N | N | Y | Y | N |
| 2 **Ryun** | N | N | N | N | Y | Y | N |
| 3 Moore | N | N | Y | Y | Y | N | Y |
| 4 **Tiahrt** | N | N | N | N | Y | Y | N |
| **KENTUCKY** | | | | | | | |
| 1 **Whitfield** | N | N | N | N | Y | Y | Y |
| 2 **Lewis** | N | N | N | N | Y | Y | Y |
| 3 **Northup** | N | N | N | N | Y | Y | N |
| 4 **Davis** | N | N | N | N | Y | Y | N |
| 5 **Rogers** | N | N | N | N | Y | Y | N |
| 6 Chandler | N | Y | Y | Y | N | Y | Y |
| **LOUISIANA** | | | | | | | |
| 1 **Jindal** | N | N | N | N | Y | Y | N |
| 2 Jefferson | N | Y | Y | Y | N | N | Y |
| 3 Melancon | N | N | N | Y | Y | Y | Y |
| 4 **McCrery** | N | N | N | N | Y | Y | N |
| 5 **Alexander** | N | N | N | N | Y | Y | N |
| 6 **Baker** | N | N | N | N | Y | Y | N |
| 7 **Boustany** | N | N | N | N | Y | Y | N |
| **MAINE** | | | | | | | |
| 1 Allen | N | N | Y | Y | N | N | Y |
| 2 Michaud | N | N | Y | Y | Y | Y | Y |
| **MARYLAND** | | | | | | | |
| 1 **Gilchrest** | N | N | N | N | Y | Y | N |
| 2 Ruppersberger | N | N | Y | Y | Y | N | Y |
| 3 Cardin | N | Y | Y | Y | N | N | Y |
| 4 Wynn | Y | N | Y | Y | Y | N | Y |
| 5 Hoyer | N | Y | Y | Y | N | N | Y |
| 6 **Bartlett** | N | N | N | N | Y | Y | N |
| 7 Cummings | Y | Y | Y | Y | N | N | Y |
| 8 Van Hollen | N | Y | Y | Y | N | N | Y |
| **MASSACHUSETTS** | | | | | | | |
| 1 Olver | N | Y | Y | Y | N | N | Y |
| 2 Neal | N | N | Y | Y | N | N | Y |
| 3 McGovern | N | Y | Y | Y | N | N | Y |
| 4 Frank | N | N | Y | Y | N | N | Y |
| 5 Meehan | Y | Y | Y | Y | N | N | Y |
| 6 Tierney | N | Y | Y | Y | N | N | Y |
| 7 Markey | Y | Y | Y | Y | N | N | Y |
| 8 Capuano | Y | Y | Y | Y | N | N | Y |
| 9 Lynch | N | N | Y | Y | Y | N | Y |
| 10 Delahunt | Y | Y | Y | Y | N | N | Y |
| **MICHIGAN** | | | | | | | |
| 1 Stupak | N | Y | Y | Y | Y | Y | Y |
| 2 **Hoekstra** | N | N | N | N | Y | Y | N |
| 3 **Ehlers** | N | N | N | N | Y | Y | N |
| 4 **Camp** | N | N | N | N | Y | Y | Y |
| 5 Kildee | N | Y | Y | Y | N | N | Y |
| 6 **Upton** | N | N | N | N | Y | Y | N |
| 7 **Schwarz** | N | N | N | N | Y | Y | N |
| 8 **Rogers** | N | N | N | N | Y | Y | N |
| 9 **Knollenberg** | N | N | N | N | Y | Y | N |
| 10 **Miller** | N | N | N | N | Y | Y | N |
| 11 **McCotter** | N | N | N | N | Y | Y | N |
| 12 Levin | N | Y | Y | Y | N | N | Y |
| 13 Kilpatrick | Y | Y | Y | Y | N | N | Y |
| 14 Conyers | N | Y | Y | Y | N | N | Y |
| 15 Dingell | ? | Y | Y | Y | Y | Y | Y |
| **MINNESOTA** | | | | | | | |
| 1 **Gutknecht** | N | N | N | N | Y | Y | N |
| 2 **Kline** | N | N | N | N | Y | Y | N |
| 3 **Ramstad** | N | N | N | N | Y | Y | N |
| 4 McCollum | N | N | Y | Y | N | N | Y |
| 5 Sabo | N | Y | Y | Y | N | N | Y |
| 6 **Kennedy** | N | N | N | N | Y | Y | N |
| 7 Peterson | N | N | N | N | Y | Y | Y |
| 8 Oberstar | N | Y | Y | Y | N | N | Y |
| **MISSISSIPPI** | | | | | | | |
| 1 **Wicker** | N | N | N | N | Y | Y | N |
| 2 Thompson | Y | Y | Y | Y | N | N | Y |
| 3 **Pickering** | N | N | N | N | Y | Y | N |
| 4 Taylor | N | N | Y | N | Y | Y | Y |
| **MISSOURI** | | | | | | | |
| 1 Clay | Y | Y | Y | Y | Y | N | Y |
| 2 **Akin** | N | N | N | N | Y | Y | N |
| 3 Carnahan | Y | Y | Y | Y | N | N | Y |
| 4 Skelton | N | N | Y | Y | Y | Y | Y |
| 5 Cleaver | Y | Y | Y | Y | N | N | Y |
| 6 **Graves** | N | N | N | N | Y | Y | N |
| 7 **Blunt** | N | N | N | N | Y | Y | N |
| 8 **Emerson** | N | N | N | N | Y | Y | N |
| 9 **Hulshof** | N | N | N | N | Y | Y | N |
| **MONTANA** | | | | | | | |
| AL **Rehberg** | N | N | N | N | Y | Y | N |
| **NEBRASKA** | | | | | | | |
| 1 **Fortenberry** | N | N | N | N | Y | Y | N |
| 2 **Terry** | N | N | N | N | Y | Y | N |
| 3 **Osborne** | N | N | N | N | Y | Y | N |
| **NEVADA** | | | | | | | |
| 1 Berkley | Y | N | Y | Y | Y | Y | Y |
| 2 **Gibbons** | N | N | N | N | Y | Y | N |
| 3 **Porter** | N | N | N | N | Y | Y | N |
| **NEW HAMPSHIRE** | | | | | | | |
| 1 **Bradley** | N | N | N | N | Y | Y | N |
| 2 **Bass** | N | N | N | N | Y | Y | N |
| **NEW JERSEY** | | | | | | | |
| 1 Andrews | N | Y | Y | Y | N | N | Y |
| 2 **LoBiondo** | N | N | N | N | Y | Y | N |
| 3 **Saxton** | N | N | N | N | Y | Y | N |
| 4 **Smith** | N | N | N | N | Y | Y | N |
| 5 **Garrett** | N | N | N | N | Y | Y | N |
| 6 Pallone | Y | Y | Y | Y | N | N | Y |
| 7 **Ferguson** | N | N | N | N | Y | Y | N |
| 8 Pascrell | Y | N | Y | Y | N | N | Y |
| 9 Rothman | N | N | Y | Y | N | N | Y |
| 10 Payne | Y | Y | Y | Y | N | N | Y |
| 11 **Frelinghuysen** | N | N | N | N | Y | Y | N |
| 12 Holt | N | Y | Y | Y | N | N | Y |
| 13 Menendez | N | Y | Y | Y | Y | N | Y |
| **NEW MEXICO** | | | | | | | |
| 1 **Wilson** | N | N | N | N | Y | Y | N |
| 2 **Pearce** | N | N | N | N | Y | Y | N |
| 3 Udall | N | Y | Y | Y | N | N | Y |
| **NEW YORK** | | | | | | | |
| 1 Bishop | N | Y | Y | Y | N | N | Y |
| 2 Israel | N | Y | Y | Y | N | N | Y |
| 3 **King** | N | N | N | N | Y | Y | N |
| 4 McCarthy | N | Y | Y | Y | N | N | Y |
| 5 Ackerman | N | Y | Y | Y | N | N | Y |
| 6 Meeks | N | Y | Y | Y | Y | N | Y |
| 7 Crowley | Y | Y | Y | Y | N | N | Y |
| 8 Nadler | Y | Y | Y | Y | N | N | Y |
| 9 Weiner | N | Y | Y | Y | N | N | Y |
| 10 Towns | N | N | Y | Y | Y | N | Y |
| 11 Owens | Y | Y | Y | Y | N | N | Y |
| 12 Velázquez | N | Y | Y | Y | Y | N | Y |
| 13 **Fossella** | N | N | N | N | Y | Y | N |
| 14 Maloney | N | Y | Y | ? | N | N | Y |
| 15 Rangel | N | Y | Y | Y | N | N | Y |
| 16 Serrano | Y | Y | Y | Y | N | N | Y |
| 17 Engel | N | Y | Y | Y | N | N | Y |
| 18 Lowey | N | Y | Y | Y | N | N | Y |
| 19 **Kelly** | N | N | N | N | Y | Y | N |
| 20 **Sweeney** | N | N | N | Y | Y | Y | N |
| 21 McNulty | Y | Y | Y | Y | Y | N | Y |
| 22 Hinchey | Y | Y | Y | Y | N | N | Y |
| 23 **McHugh** | N | N | N | N | Y | Y | N |
| 24 **Boehlert** | N | N | N | N | Y | Y | N |
| 25 **Walsh** | N | N | N | N | Y | Y | N |
| 26 **Reynolds** | N | N | N | N | Y | Y | N |
| 27 Higgins | Y | Y | Y | Y | Y | Y | Y |
| 28 Slaughter | Y | Y | Y | Y | Y | N | Y |
| 29 **Kuhl** | N | N | N | N | Y | Y | N |
| **NORTH CAROLINA** | | | | | | | |
| 1 Butterfield | Y | Y | Y | Y | N | Y | Y |
| 2 Etheridge | N | Y | Y | Y | N | N | Y |
| 3 **Jones** | N | N | N | N | Y | Y | Y |
| 4 Price | N | Y | Y | Y | N | N | Y |
| 5 **Foxx** | N | N | N | N | Y | Y | N |
| 6 **Coble** | N | N | N | N | Y | Y | N |
| 7 McIntyre | N | N | Y | Y | Y | Y | Y |
| 8 **Hayes** | N | N | N | N | Y | Y | N |
| 9 **Myrick** | - | - | - | - | + | Y | ? |
| 10 **McHenry** | N | N | N | N | Y | Y | N |
| 11 **Taylor** | N | N | N | N | Y | Y | N |
| 12 Watt | Y | Y | Y | Y | N | N | Y |
| 13 Miller | N | Y | Y | Y | N | N | Y |
| **NORTH DAKOTA** | | | | | | | |
| AL Pomeroy | N | N | Y | Y | Y | Y | Y |
| **OHIO** | | | | | | | |
| 1 **Chabot** | N | N | N | N | Y | Y | N |
| 2 **Schmidt** | N | N | N | N | Y | Y | N |
| 3 **Turner** | N | N | N | N | Y | Y | N |
| 4 **Oxley** | N | N | N | N | Y | Y | N |
| 5 **Gillmor** | N | N | N | N | Y | Y | N |
| 6 Strickland | N | N | Y | Y | N | Y | Y |
| 7 **Hobson** | N | N | N | N | Y | Y | N |
| 8 **Boehner** | N | N | N | N | Y | Y | N |
| 9 Kaptur | N | Y | Y | Y | N | Y | Y |
| 10 Kucinich | Y | Y | Y | Y | N | N | Y |
| 11 Jones | Y | Y | Y | Y | N | N | Y |
| 12 **Tiberi** | N | N | N | N | Y | Y | N |
| 13 Brown | Y | Y | Y | Y | N | N | Y |
| 14 **LaTourette** | N | N | N | N | Y | Y | N |
| 15 **Pryce** | N | N | N | N | ? | Y | Y |
| 16 **Regula** | N | N | N | N | Y | Y | N |
| 17 Ryan | N | Y | Y | Y | Y | Y | Y |
| 18 **Ney** | N | N | N | N | Y | Y | N |
| **OKLAHOMA** | | | | | | | |
| 1 **Sullivan** | N | N | N | N | Y | Y | Y |
| 2 Boren | N | N | N | N | Y | Y | Y |
| 3 **Lucas** | N | N | N | N | Y | Y | N |
| 4 **Cole** | N | N | N | N | Y | Y | N |
| 5 **Istook** | N | N | N | N | Y | Y | N |
| **OREGON** | | | | | | | |
| 1 Wu | N | Y | Y | Y | Y | N | Y |
| 2 **Walden** | N | N | N | N | Y | Y | N |
| 3 Blumenauer | N | Y | Y | Y | N | N | Y |
| 4 DeFazio | Y | N | Y | N | Y | Y | Y |
| 5 Hooley | N | N | Y | Y | Y | N | Y |
| **PENNSYLVANIA** | | | | | | | |
| 1 Brady | Y | Y | Y | Y | N | N | Y |
| 2 Fattah | Y | Y | Y | Y | N | N | Y |
| 3 **English** | N | N | N | N | Y | Y | N |
| 4 **Hart** | N | N | N | N | Y | Y | N |
| 5 **Peterson** | N | N | N | N | Y | Y | N |
| 6 **Gerlach** | N | N | Y | N | Y | Y | N |
| 7 **Weldon** | N | N | N | N | Y | Y | N |
| 8 **Fitzpatrick** | N | N | Y | Y | Y | Y | N |
| 9 **Shuster** | N | N | N | N | Y | Y | N |
| 10 **Sherwood** | N | N | N | N | Y | Y | N |
| 11 Kanjorski | N | Y | Y | N | N | Y | Y |
| 12 Murtha | N | N | Y | N | N | Y | Y |
| 13 Schwartz | N | Y | Y | Y | N | N | Y |
| 14 Doyle | N | Y | Y | Y | Y | N | Y |
| 15 **Dent** | N | N | N | N | Y | Y | N |
| 16 **Pitts** | N | N | N | N | Y | Y | N |
| 17 Holden | N | N | Y | N | Y | Y | Y |
| 18 **Murphy** | N | N | N | N | Y | Y | N |
| 19 **Platts** | N | N | N | N | Y | Y | N |
| **RHODE ISLAND** | | | | | | | |
| 1 Kennedy | N | Y | Y | Y | N | N | Y |
| 2 Langevin | Y | N | Y | Y | Y | N | Y |
| **SOUTH CAROLINA** | | | | | | | |
| 1 **Brown** | N | N | N | N | Y | Y | N |
| 2 **Wilson** | N | N | N | N | Y | Y | N |
| 3 **Barrett** | N | N | N | N | Y | Y | N |
| 4 **Inglis** | N | N | N | N | Y | Y | N |
| 5 Spratt | N | N | Y | N | Y | Y | Y |
| 6 Clyburn | N | N | Y | Y | Y | N | Y |
| **SOUTH DAKOTA** | | | | | | | |
| AL Herseth | N | N | Y | N | Y | Y | Y |
| **TENNESSEE** | | | | | | | |
| 1 **Jenkins** | N | N | N | N | Y | Y | N |
| 2 **Duncan** | N | N | Y | N | Y | Y | N |
| 3 **Wamp** | N | N | N | N | Y | Y | N |
| 4 Davis | N | N | N | N | Y | Y | Y |
| 5 Cooper | N | N | Y | N | Y | Y | Y |
| 6 Gordon | N | N | N | N | Y | Y | Y |
| 7 **Blackburn** | N | N | N | N | Y | Y | N |
| 8 Tanner | N | N | N | N | Y | Y | Y |
| 9 Ford | N | N | Y | Y | Y | Y | Y |
| **TEXAS** | | | | | | | |
| 1 **Gohmert** | N | N | N | N | Y | Y | N |
| 2 **Poe** | N | N | N | N | Y | Y | N |
| 3 **Johnson, S.** | N | N | N | N | Y | Y | N |
| 4 **Hall** | N | N | N | N | Y | Y | N |
| 5 **Hensarling** | N | N | N | N | Y | Y | N |
| 6 **Barton** | N | N | N | N | Y | Y | N |
| 7 **Culberson** | N | N | N | N | Y | Y | N |
| 8 **Brady** | N | N | N | N | Y | Y | N |
| 9 Green, A. | Y | Y | Y | Y | N | N | Y |
| 10 **McCaul** | N | N | N | N | Y | Y | N |
| 11 **Conaway** | N | N | N | N | Y | Y | N |
| 12 **Granger** | N | N | N | N | Y | Y | N |
| 13 **Thornberry** | N | N | N | N | Y | Y | N |
| 14 **Paul** | N | N | Y | N | N | N | N |
| 15 Hinojosa | Y | N | Y | Y | Y | Y | Y |
| 16 Reyes | N | N | Y | Y | Y | Y | Y |
| 17 Edwards | ? | N | N | N | Y | Y | Y |
| 18 Jackson-Lee | Y | Y | Y | N | N | N | Y |
| 19 **Neugebauer** | N | N | N | N | Y | Y | N |
| 20 Gonzalez | N | Y | Y | Y | N | N | Y |
| 21 **Smith** | N | N | N | N | Y | Y | N |
| 22 **DeLay** | N | N | N | N | Y | ? | ? |
| 23 **Bonilla** | N | N | N | N | Y | Y | N |
| 24 **Marchant** | N | N | N | ? | Y | Y | N |
| 25 Doggett | Y | Y | Y | Y | N | N | Y |
| 26 **Burgess** | N | N | N | N | Y | Y | N |
| 27 Ortiz | N | N | Y | Y | Y | Y | Y |
| 28 Cuellar | N | Y | Y | N | Y | Y | Y |
| 29 Green, G. | Y | Y | Y | Y | Y | Y | Y |
| 30 Johnson, E. | Y | Y | Y | Y | N | N | Y |
| 31 **Carter** | N | N | N | N | Y | Y | N |
| 32 **Sessions** | N | N | N | N | Y | Y | N |
| **UTAH** | | | | | | | |
| 1 **Bishop** | N | N | N | N | Y | Y | N |
| 2 Matheson | N | N | N | N | Y | Y | Y |
| 3 **Cannon** | N | N | N | N | Y | Y | N |
| **VERMONT** | | | | | | | |
| AL *Sanders* | Y | Y | Y | Y | N | Y | Y |
| **VIRGINIA** | | | | | | | |
| 1 **Davis, J.** | N | N | N | N | Y | Y | N |
| 2 **Drake** | N | N | N | N | Y | Y | N |
| 3 Scott | Y | Y | Y | Y | N | N | Y |
| 4 **Forbes** | N | N | N | N | Y | Y | N |
| 5 **Goode** | N | N | N | N | Y | Y | N |
| 6 **Goodlatte** | N | N | N | N | Y | Y | N |
| 7 **Cantor** | N | N | N | N | Y | Y | N |
| 8 Moran | N | Y | Y | Y | Y | N | ? |
| 9 Boucher | N | N | Y | Y | Y | Y | Y |
| 10 **Wolf** | N | N | N | Y | Y | Y | N |
| 11 **Davis, T.** | N | N | N | Y | Y | Y | N |
| **WASHINGTON** | | | | | | | |
| 1 Inslee | N | N | Y | Y | N | N | Y |
| 2 Larsen | N | N | Y | Y | Y | Y | Y |
| 3 Baird | N | N | Y | N | Y | Y | Y |
| 4 **Hastings** | N | N | N | N | Y | Y | N |
| 5 **McMorris** | N | N | N | N | Y | Y | N |
| 6 Dicks | N | Y | Y | Y | Y | N | Y |
| 7 McDermott | Y | Y | Y | Y | N | N | Y |
| 8 **Reichert** | N | N | N | N | Y | Y | N |
| 9 Smith | N | N | Y | Y | Y | N | N |
| **WEST VIRGINIA** | | | | | | | |
| 1 Mollohan | N | Y | Y | Y | N | Y | Y |
| 2 **Capito** | N | N | N | N | Y | Y | N |
| 3 Rahall | N | Y | Y | Y | N | Y | Y |
| **WISCONSIN** | | | | | | | |
| 1 **Ryan** | N | N | N | N | Y | Y | N |
| 2 Baldwin | N | Y | Y | Y | N | N | Y |
| 3 Kind | N | N | Y | Y | Y | Y | Y |
| 4 Moore | Y | Y | Y | Y | N | N | Y |
| 5 **Sensenbrenner** | N | N | N | N | Y | Y | N |
| 6 **Petri** | N | N | N | N | Y | Y | N |
| 7 Obey | Y | Y | Y | Y | Y | Y | Y |
| 8 **Green** | N | N | N | N | Y | Y | N |
| **WYOMING** | | | | | | | |
| AL **Cubin** | N | N | N | N | Y | Y | N |

# IN THE HOUSE | By Vote Number

**536.** **HR 3675. Fraud in Emergencies/Passage.** Stearns, R-Fla., motion to suspend the rules and pass the bill that would increase civil penalties to $22,000 per violation for individuals or companies that commit unfair or deceptive acts that exploit the popular reaction to disasters and national emergencies. Motion agreed to 399-3: R 216-3; D 182-0 (ND 139-0, SD 43-0); I 1-0. A two-thirds majority of those present and voting (268 in this case) is required for passage under suspension of the rules. Oct. 25, 2005.

**537.** **H Con Res 269. White House Fellows Program/Adoption.** Schmidt, R-Ohio, motion to suspend the rules and adopt the concurrent resolution that would recognize the 40th anniversary of the White House Fellows Program and the contributions of the fellows to their communities, the United States and the world. Motion agreed to 401-0: R 218-0; D 182-0 (ND 139-0, SD 43-0); I 1-0. A two-thirds majority of those present and voting (268 in this case) is required for adoption under suspension of the rules. Oct. 25, 2005.

**538.** **HR 3256. James Grove Fulton Post Office/Passage.** Schmidt, R-Ohio, motion to suspend the rules and pass the bill that would designate a post office in Pittsburgh, Pa., for James Grove Fulton, R-Pa. (1945-71), who served in the House for 13 full terms, including more than two terms as the ranking member of the then-Science and Astronautics Committee. Motion agreed to 396-1: R 215-0; D 180-1 (ND 137-1, SD 43-0); I 1-0. A two-thirds majority of those present and voting (265 in this case) is required for passage under suspension of the rules. Oct. 25, 2005.

**539.** **HR 1461. Government-Sponsored Enterprises/Rule.** Adoption of the rule (H Res 509) that would provide for House floor consideration of the bill that would overhaul the regulation of government-sponsored enterprises, including Fannie Mae, Freddie Mac and the 12 Federal Home Loan Banks. Adopted 220-196: R 220-1; D 0-194 (ND 0-148, SD 0-46); I 0-1. Oct. 26, 2005.

**540.** **Procedural Motion/Journal.** Approval of the House Journal of Tuesday, October 25, 2005. Approved 349-62: R 199-19; D 149-43 (ND 113-35, SD 36-8); I 1-0. Oct. 26, 2005.

**541.** **HR 1461. Government-Sponsored Enterprises/Manager's Amendment.** Oxley, R-Ohio, amendment that would sunset the affordable housing fund in the bill after five years and require Fannie Mae and Freddie Mac to allocate 3.5 percent of their profits for the fund in the first two years and 5 percent in the final three years. Priority for funds in the first two years would go to areas affected by hurricanes Katrina and Rita. It also would prohibit the use of funds in the bill for purposes such as political activities, lobbying, travel expenses or providing advice on tax returns. Adopted 210-205: R 208-13; D 2-191 (ND 1-146, SD 1-45); I 0-1. Oct. 26, 2005.

**542.** **HR 1461. Government-Sponsored Enterprises/Minimum Capital Levels.** Leach, R-Iowa, amendment that would allow the new regulator that would be created under the bill — the Federal Housing Finance Agency — to establish a minimum capital level for Fannie Mae, Freddie Mac or any Federal Home Loan Bank if it is needed for the long-term viability of any of the institutions. Rejected 36-378: R 31-190; D 5-187 (ND 3-143, SD 2-44); I 0-1. Oct. 26, 2005.

| Member | 536 | 537 | 538 | 539 | 540 | 541 | 542 |
|---|---|---|---|---|---|---|---|
| **ALABAMA** | | | | | | | |
| 1 Bonner | Y | Y | Y | Y | Y | Y | N |
| 2 Everett | Y | Y | Y | Y | Y | Y | N |
| 3 Rogers | Y | Y | Y | Y | Y | Y | N |
| 4 Aderholt | Y | Y | Y | Y | Y | Y | N |
| 5 Cramer | Y | Y | Y | N | Y | N | N |
| 6 Bachus | Y | Y | Y | Y | Y | Y | N |
| 7 Davis | Y | Y | Y | N | Y | N | N |
| **ALASKA** | | | | | | | |
| AL Young | Y | Y | Y | Y | Y | Y | N |
| **ARIZONA** | | | | | | | |
| 1 Renzi | Y | Y | Y | Y | Y | Y | N |
| 2 Franks | Y | Y | Y | Y | Y | Y | Y |
| 3 Shadegg | Y | Y | Y | Y | Y | Y | Y |
| 4 Pastor | Y | Y | Y | N | N | N | N |
| 5 Hayworth | Y | Y | Y | Y | Y | N | N |
| 6 Flake | N | Y | Y | Y | Y | Y | Y |
| 7 Grijalva | Y | Y | Y | N | N | N | N |
| 8 Kolbe | Y | Y | Y | Y | Y | Y | N |
| **ARKANSAS** | | | | | | | |
| 1 Berry | Y | Y | Y | N | N | N | N |
| 2 Snyder | Y | Y | Y | N | N | N | N |
| 3 Boozman | Y | Y | Y | Y | Y | N | N |
| 4 Ross | Y | Y | Y | N | Y | N | N |
| **CALIFORNIA** | | | | | | | |
| 1 Thompson | Y | Y | Y | N | N | N | N |
| 2 Herger | Y | Y | Y | Y | Y | Y | N |
| 3 Lungren | Y | Y | Y | Y | Y | Y | Y |
| 4 Doolittle | Y | Y | Y | Y | Y | Y | N |
| 5 Matsui, D. | Y | Y | Y | N | N | N | N |
| 6 Woolsey | Y | Y | Y | N | N | N | N |
| 7 Miller, George | Y | Y | Y | N | N | N | N |
| 8 Pelosi | Y | Y | Y | N | N | N | N |
| 9 Lee | Y | Y | Y | N | N | N | N |
| 10 Tauscher | Y | Y | Y | N | N | N | N |
| 11 Pombo | Y | Y | ? | Y | Y | Y | N |
| 12 Lantos | Y | Y | Y | N | N | N | N |
| 13 Stark | Y | Y | Y | N | N | N | N |
| 14 Eshoo | Y | Y | Y | N | N | N | N |
| 15 Honda | ? | ? | Y | N | Y | N | N |
| 16 Lofgren | Y | Y | Y | N | N | N | N |
| 17 Farr | Y | Y | Y | N | N | Y | N |
| 18 Cardoza | Y | Y | Y | N | N | N | N |
| 19 Radanovich | Y | Y | Y | Y | Y | N | N |
| 20 Costa | Y | Y | Y | N | N | N | N |
| 21 Nunes | Y | Y | Y | N | Y | N | N |
| 22 Thomas | Y | Y | Y | N | N | N | N |
| 23 Capps | Y | Y | Y | N | N | N | N |
| 24 Gallegly | Y | Y | Y | Y | Y | N | N |
| 25 McKeon | Y | Y | Y | Y | Y | Y | N |
| 26 Dreier | Y | Y | Y | Y | Y | Y | N |
| 27 Sherman | Y | Y | Y | N | N | N | ? |
| 28 Berman | Y | Y | Y | N | N | N | N |
| 29 Schiff | Y | Y | Y | N | Y | N | N |
| 30 Waxman | Y | Y | Y | N | N | N | N |
| 31 Becerra | Y | Y | Y | N | N | N | N |
| 32 Solis | Y | Y | Y | N | N | N | N |
| 33 Watson | Y | Y | Y | N | N | N | N |
| 34 Roybal-Allard | ? | ? | ? | ? | ? | ? | ? |
| 35 Waters | Y | Y | ? | N | Y | N | N |
| 36 Harman | Y | Y | Y | N | N | N | N |
| 37 Millender-McD. | Y | Y | Y | N | N | N | N |
| 38 Napolitano | Y | Y | Y | N | N | N | N |
| 39 Sánchez, Linda | Y | Y | Y | N | N | N | N |
| 40 Royce | Y | Y | Y | Y | Y | Y | Y |
| 41 Lewis | Y | Y | Y | Y | Y | Y | N |
| 42 Miller, Gary | Y | Y | Y | Y | Y | Y | Y |
| 43 Baca | Y | Y | Y | N | Y | N | N |
| 44 Calvert | Y | Y | Y | Y | Y | Y | N |
| 45 Bono | Y | Y | Y | Y | Y | Y | N |
| 46 Rohrabacher | Y | Y | Y | Y | Y | Y | N |
| 47 Sanchez, Loretta | Y | Y | Y | N | N | N | N |
| 48 Vacant | | | | | | | |
| 49 Issa | Y | Y | Y | Y | Y | Y | N |
| 50 Cunningham | Y | Y | Y | Y | Y | Y | N |
| 51 Filner | Y | Y | Y | N | N | N | N |
| 52 Hunter | Y | Y | Y | N | Y | N | N |
| 53 Davis | Y | Y | Y | N | Y | N | N |
| **COLORADO** | | | | | | | |
| 1 DeGette | Y | Y | Y | N | Y | N | N |
| 2 Udall | Y | Y | Y | N | N | N | N |
| 3 Salazar | Y | Y | Y | N | Y | N | N |
| 4 Musgrave | Y | Y | Y | Y | Y | Y | Y |
| 5 Hefley | Y | Y | Y | N | Y | N | N |
| 6 Tancredo | Y | Y | Y | Y | P | Y | N |
| 7 Beauprez | Y | Y | Y | Y | Y | Y | Y |
| **CONNECTICUT** | | | | | | | |
| 1 Larson | Y | Y | Y | N | N | N | N |
| 2 Simmons | Y | Y | Y | Y | N | N | N |
| 3 DeLauro | Y | Y | Y | N | Y | N | N |
| 4 Shays | Y | Y | Y | Y | Y | Y | N |
| 5 Johnson | Y | Y | Y | Y | Y | Y | Y |
| **DELAWARE** | | | | | | | |
| AL Castle | Y | Y | Y | Y | Y | Y | N |
| **FLORIDA** | | | | | | | |
| 1 Miller | Y | Y | ? | Y | Y | Y | N |
| 2 Boyd | Y | Y | Y | N | Y | N | N |
| 3 Brown | ? | ? | ? | N | Y | N | N |
| 4 Crenshaw | Y | Y | Y | Y | Y | Y | N |
| 5 Brown-Waite | ? | ? | ? | ? | ? | ? | ? |
| 6 Stearns | Y | Y | Y | Y | Y | Y | N |
| 7 Mica | Y | Y | ? | Y | Y | Y | N |
| 8 Keller | Y | Y | ? | Y | Y | Y | N |
| 9 Bilirakis | Y | Y | Y | Y | Y | Y | N |
| 10 Young | ? | ? | ? | ? | ? | ? | Y |
| 11 Davis | Y | Y | Y | N | N | N | N |
| 12 Putnam | Y | Y | Y | Y | Y | Y | N |
| 13 Harris | Y | Y | Y | Y | Y | Y | N |
| 14 Mack | Y | Y | Y | Y | Y | Y | N |
| 15 Weldon | Y | Y | Y | Y | Y | Y | N |
| 16 Foley | ? | ? | ? | ? | ? | ? | ? |
| 17 Meek | ? | ? | ? | ? | ? | ? | ? |
| 18 Ros-Lehtinen | ? | ? | ? | ? | ? | ? | ? |
| 19 Wexler | ? | ? | ? | ? | ? | ? | ? |
| 20 Wasserman-Schultz | ? | ? | ? | ? | ? | N | N |
| 21 Diaz-Balart, L. | ? | ? | ? | ? | ? | ? | ? |
| 22 Shaw | ? | ? | ? | ? | ? | ? | ? |
| 23 Hastings | Y | Y | Y | N | N | N | N |
| 24 Feeney | Y | Y | Y | ? | Y | Y | N |
| 25 Diaz-Balart, M. | ? | ? | ? | ? | ? | ? | ? |
| **GEORGIA** | | | | | | | |
| 1 Kingston | Y | Y | Y | Y | Y | Y | Y |
| 2 Bishop | Y | Y | Y | ? | ? | ? | ? |
| 3 Marshall | Y | Y | Y | N | Y | N | N |
| 4 McKinney | Y | Y | Y | N | N | N | N |
| 5 Lewis | Y | Y | Y | N | N | N | N |
| 6 Price | Y | Y | Y | Y | Y | Y | N |
| 7 Linder | Y | Y | Y | Y | Y | Y | N |
| 8 Westmoreland | Y | Y | Y | Y | Y | Y | Y |
| 9 Norwood | Y | Y | Y | Y | Y | Y | N |
| 10 Deal | Y | Y | Y | Y | Y | Y | N |
| 11 Gingrey | ? | ? | ? | Y | Y | Y | N |
| 12 Barrow | Y | Y | Y | N | N | N | N |
| 13 Scott | Y | Y | Y | N | Y | N | N |
| **HAWAII** | | | | | | | |
| 1 Abercrombie | Y | Y | N | N | Y | N | N |
| 2 Case | Y | Y | Y | N | Y | N | N |
| **IDAHO** | | | | | | | |
| 1 Otter | Y | Y | Y | Y | N | N | N |
| 2 Simpson | Y | Y | Y | Y | Y | Y | N |
| **ILLINOIS** | | | | | | | |
| 1 Rush | Y | Y | Y | N | N | N | N |
| 2 Jackson | Y | Y | Y | N | Y | N | N |
| 3 Lipinski | Y | Y | Y | N | N | N | N |
| 4 Gutierrez | + | + | + | N | Y | N | N |
| 5 Emanuel | Y | Y | Y | ? | Y | ? | ? |
| 6 Hyde | Y | Y | Y | Y | Y | Y | N |
| 7 Davis | Y | Y | Y | N | N | N | N |
| 8 Bean | Y | Y | Y | N | N | N | N |
| 9 Schakowsky | Y | Y | Y | N | N | N | N |
| 10 Kirk | Y | Y | Y | Y | Y | Y | N |
| 11 Weller | Y | Y | Y | Y | N | Y | N |
| 12 Costello | Y | Y | Y | N | N | N | N |

**KEY**    Republicans    Democrats    *Independents*

| | | |
|---|---|---|
| Y Voted for (yea) | X Paired against | C Voted "present" to avoid possible conflict of interest |
| # Paired for | − Announced against | |
| + Announced for | P Voted "present" | ? Did not vote or otherwise make a position known |
| N Voted against (nay) | | |

ND Northern Democrats, SD Southern Democrats
Southern states: Ala., Ark., Fla., Ga., Ky., La., Miss., N.C., Okla., S.C., Tenn., Texas, Va.

| | 536 | 537 | 538 | 539 | 540 | 541 | 542 |
|---|---|---|---|---|---|---|---|
| 13 **Biggert** | Y | Y | Y | Y | Y | Y | N |
| 14 **Hastert** | | | | | | Y | |
| 15 **Johnson** | Y | Y | Y | Y | Y | N | N |
| 16 **Manzullo** | Y | ? | ? | Y | Y | Y | N |
| 17 Evans | ? | Y | Y | N | Y | N | N |
| 18 **LaHood** | Y | Y | Y | Y | Y | Y | N |
| 19 **Shimkus** | Y | Y | Y | Y | Y | Y | N |
| **INDIANA** | | | | | | | |
| 1 Visclosky | ? | ? | ? | N | N | N | N |
| 2 **Chocola** | Y | Y | Y | Y | Y | Y | Y |
| 3 **Souder** | Y | Y | Y | Y | Y | Y | N |
| 4 **Buyer** | Y | Y | Y | Y | Y | Y | N |
| 5 **Burton** | Y | Y | Y | Y | Y | Y | N |
| 6 **Pence** | Y | Y | Y | Y | Y | Y | Y |
| 7 Carson | + | + | + | N | P | N | N |
| 8 **Hostettler** | Y | Y | Y | Y | Y | Y | Y |
| 9 **Sodrel** | Y | Y | Y | Y | Y | Y | N |
| **IOWA** | | | | | | | |
| 1 **Nussle** | Y | Y | Y | Y | Y | Y | Y |
| 2 **Leach** | Y | Y | Y | Y | ? | N | Y |
| 3 Boswell | ? | ? | ? | ? | ? | ? | ? |
| 4 **Latham** | Y | Y | Y | Y | N | Y | Y |
| 5 **King** | Y | Y | Y | Y | Y | Y | Y |
| **KANSAS** | | | | | | | |
| 1 **Moran** | Y | Y | Y | Y | N | Y | N |
| 2 **Ryun** | Y | Y | Y | Y | Y | Y | N |
| 3 Moore | Y | Y | Y | N | N | N | N |
| 4 **Tiahrt** | Y | Y | Y | Y | Y | Y | N |
| **KENTUCKY** | | | | | | | |
| 1 **Whitfield** | Y | Y | Y | Y | Y | ? | ? |
| 2 **Lewis** | Y | Y | Y | Y | Y | Y | N |
| 3 **Northup** | Y | Y | Y | Y | Y | Y | N |
| 4 **Davis** | Y | Y | Y | Y | N | Y | N |
| 5 **Rogers** | Y | Y | Y | Y | Y | Y | N |
| 6 Chandler | Y | Y | Y | N | N | N | N |
| **LOUISIANA** | | | | | | | |
| 1 **Jindal** | Y | Y | Y | Y | Y | Y | N |
| 2 Jefferson | Y | Y | Y | N | Y | N | N |
| 3 Melancon | Y | Y | Y | N | Y | N | N |
| 4 **McCrery** | Y | Y | Y | Y | Y | Y | N |
| 5 **Alexander** | Y | Y | Y | Y | Y | Y | N |
| 6 **Baker** | Y | Y | Y | Y | Y | Y | N |
| 7 **Boustany** | Y | Y | Y | Y | Y | Y | N |
| **MAINE** | | | | | | | |
| 1 Allen | Y | Y | Y | N | Y | N | N |
| 2 Michaud | Y | Y | Y | N | Y | N | N |
| **MARYLAND** | | | | | | | |
| 1 **Gilchrest** | Y | Y | Y | Y | Y | N | Y |
| 2 Ruppersberger | Y | Y | Y | N | Y | N | N |
| 3 Cardin | Y | Y | Y | N | Y | N | N |
| 4 Wynn | Y | Y | Y | N | Y | N | Y |
| 5 Hoyer | Y | Y | Y | N | Y | N | N |
| 6 **Bartlett** | Y | Y | Y | Y | Y | Y | N |
| 7 Cummings | Y | Y | Y | N | Y | N | N |
| 8 Van Hollen | Y | Y | Y | N | Y | N | N |
| **MASSACHUSETTS** | | | | | | | |
| 1 Olver | Y | Y | Y | N | N | N | N |
| 2 Neal | Y | Y | Y | N | Y | N | N |
| 3 McGovern | Y | Y | Y | N | Y | N | N |
| 4 Frank | Y | Y | Y | N | Y | N | N |
| 5 Meehan | Y | Y | Y | N | Y | N | N |
| 6 Tierney | Y | Y | Y | N | Y | N | N |
| 7 Markey | Y | Y | Y | N | Y | N | ? |
| 8 Capuano | Y | Y | Y | N | N | N | N |
| 9 Lynch | Y | Y | Y | N | Y | N | N |
| 10 Delahunt | Y | Y | Y | N | Y | N | N |
| **MICHIGAN** | | | | | | | |
| 1 Stupak | Y | Y | Y | N | N | N | N |
| 2 **Hoekstra** | Y | Y | Y | Y | Y | Y | N |
| 3 **Ehlers** | Y | Y | Y | Y | Y | N | Y |
| 4 **Camp** | Y | Y | Y | Y | Y | Y | N |
| 5 Kildee | Y | Y | Y | N | Y | N | N |
| 6 **Upton** | Y | Y | Y | Y | Y | Y | N |
| 7 **Schwarz** | Y | Y | Y | Y | Y | Y | N |
| 8 **Rogers** | Y | Y | Y | Y | Y | Y | N |
| 9 **Knollenberg** | Y | Y | Y | Y | Y | Y | N |
| 10 **Miller** | Y | Y | Y | Y | Y | Y | N |
| 11 **McCotter** | Y | Y | Y | Y | N | Y | N |
| 12 Levin | Y | Y | Y | N | Y | N | N |
| 13 Kilpatrick | Y | Y | Y | N | Y | N | N |
| 14 Conyers | Y | Y | Y | N | Y | N | N |
| 15 Dingell | Y | Y | Y | N | Y | N | Y |

| | 536 | 537 | 538 | 539 | 540 | 541 | 542 |
|---|---|---|---|---|---|---|---|
| **MINNESOTA** | | | | | | | |
| 1 **Gutknecht** | Y | Y | Y | Y | N | Y | Y |
| 2 **Kline** | Y | Y | Y | Y | Y | Y | N |
| 3 **Ramstad** | Y | Y | Y | Y | N | N | N |
| 4 McCollum | Y | Y | Y | N | Y | N | N |
| 5 Sabo | Y | Y | Y | N | N | N | N |
| 6 **Kennedy** | Y | Y | Y | N | N | N | N |
| 7 Peterson | Y | ? | Y | N | N | N | N |
| 8 Oberstar | Y | Y | Y | N | N | N | N |
| **MISSISSIPPI** | | | | | | | |
| 1 **Wicker** | Y | Y | Y | Y | Y | Y | N |
| 2 Thompson | Y | Y | Y | N | N | N | N |
| 3 **Pickering** | Y | Y | Y | Y | Y | Y | N |
| 4 Taylor | Y | Y | Y | N | N | Y | Y |
| **MISSOURI** | | | | | | | |
| 1 Clay | Y | Y | Y | N | Y | N | N |
| 2 **Akin** | Y | Y | Y | Y | Y | Y | N |
| 3 Carnahan | Y | Y | Y | N | Y | N | N |
| 4 Skelton | Y | Y | Y | N | Y | N | N |
| 5 Cleaver | Y | Y | Y | N | Y | N | N |
| 6 **Graves** | Y | Y | Y | Y | N | Y | N |
| 7 **Blunt** | Y | Y | Y | Y | Y | Y | N |
| 8 **Emerson** | Y | Y | Y | Y | Y | Y | N |
| 9 **Hulshof** | ? | ? | ? | Y | Y | Y | N |
| **MONTANA** | | | | | | | |
| AL **Rehberg** | Y | Y | Y | Y | Y | Y | N |
| **NEBRASKA** | | | | | | | |
| 1 **Fortenberry** | Y | Y | Y | Y | Y | Y | N |
| 2 **Terry** | Y | Y | Y | Y | Y | Y | N |
| 3 **Osborne** | Y | Y | Y | Y | Y | Y | N |
| **NEVADA** | | | | | | | |
| 1 Berkley | Y | Y | Y | N | Y | N | N |
| 2 **Gibbons** | Y | Y | Y | Y | Y | Y | N |
| 3 **Porter** | Y | Y | Y | Y | Y | Y | N |
| **NEW HAMPSHIRE** | | | | | | | |
| 1 **Bradley** | Y | Y | Y | Y | Y | N | N |
| 2 **Bass** | Y | Y | Y | Y | Y | Y | N |
| **NEW JERSEY** | | | | | | | |
| 1 Andrews | + | + | + | N | Y | N | N |
| 2 **LoBiondo** | Y | Y | Y | Y | N | Y | N |
| 3 **Saxton** | Y | Y | Y | Y | Y | Y | N |
| 4 **Smith** | Y | Y | Y | Y | Y | N | N |
| 5 **Garrett** | Y | Y | Y | Y | Y | Y | Y |
| 6 Pallone | Y | Y | Y | N | Y | N | N |
| 7 **Ferguson** | Y | Y | Y | Y | Y | Y | N |
| 8 Pascrell | Y | Y | Y | N | Y | N | N |
| 9 Rothman | Y | Y | Y | N | Y | N | N |
| 10 Payne | ? | ? | ? | N | Y | N | N |
| 11 **Frelinghuysen** | Y | Y | Y | Y | Y | Y | N |
| 12 Holt | Y | Y | Y | N | N | N | N |
| 13 Menendez | Y | Y | Y | N | Y | N | N |
| **NEW MEXICO** | | | | | | | |
| 1 **Wilson** | Y | Y | Y | Y | Y | Y | N |
| 2 **Pearce** | Y | Y | Y | Y | Y | Y | N |
| 3 Udall | Y | Y | Y | N | N | N | N |
| **NEW YORK** | | | | | | | |
| 1 Bishop | Y | Y | Y | N | Y | N | N |
| 2 Israel | Y | Y | Y | N | Y | N | N |
| 3 **King** | Y | Y | Y | Y | Y | Y | N |
| 4 McCarthy | Y | Y | Y | N | Y | N | N |
| 5 Ackerman | Y | Y | Y | N | Y | N | N |
| 6 Meeks | Y | Y | Y | N | Y | N | N |
| 7 Crowley | Y | Y | Y | N | Y | N | N |
| 8 Nadler | Y | Y | Y | N | Y | N | N |
| 9 Weiner | Y | Y | Y | N | Y | N | N |
| 10 Towns | Y | Y | Y | N | Y | ? | N |
| 11 Owens | Y | Y | Y | N | Y | N | N |
| 12 Velázquez | Y | Y | Y | N | N | N | N |
| 13 **Fossella** | Y | Y | Y | Y | N | Y | N |
| 14 Maloney | Y | Y | ? | N | Y | N | N |
| 15 Rangel | Y | Y | Y | N | Y | N | N |
| 16 Serrano | Y | Y | Y | N | Y | N | N |
| 17 Engel | Y | Y | Y | N | Y | N | N |
| 18 Lowey | Y | Y | Y | N | Y | N | N |
| 19 **Kelly** | Y | Y | Y | Y | Y | Y | N |
| 20 **Sweeney** | Y | Y | Y | Y | N | N | N |
| 21 McNulty | Y | Y | Y | N | N | N | N |
| 22 Hinchey | Y | Y | Y | N | Y | N | N |
| 23 **McHugh** | Y | Y | Y | Y | Y | N | N |
| 24 **Boehlert** | Y | Y | Y | Y | Y | Y | N |
| 25 **Walsh** | Y | Y | Y | Y | Y | Y | N |
| 26 **Reynolds** | ? | ? | ? | ? | ? | ? | ? |
| 27 Higgins | ? | ? | ? | N | Y | N | N |
| 28 Slaughter | Y | Y | Y | N | N | N | N |
| 29 **Kuhl** | Y | Y | Y | Y | Y | Y | N |

| | 536 | 537 | 538 | 539 | 540 | 541 | 542 |
|---|---|---|---|---|---|---|---|
| **NORTH CAROLINA** | | | | | | | |
| 1 Butterfield | Y | Y | Y | N | Y | N | N |
| 2 Etheridge | Y | Y | Y | N | Y | N | N |
| 3 **Jones** | Y | Y | Y | Y | Y | Y | N |
| 4 Price | Y | Y | Y | N | Y | N | N |
| 5 **Foxx** | Y | Y | Y | Y | Y | Y | N |
| 6 **Coble** | Y | Y | Y | Y | Y | Y | N |
| 7 McIntyre | Y | Y | Y | N | Y | N | N |
| 8 **Hayes** | Y | Y | Y | Y | Y | Y | N |
| 9 **Myrick** | Y | Y | Y | Y | Y | Y | N |
| 10 **McHenry** | Y | Y | Y | Y | Y | Y | N |
| 11 **Taylor** | Y | Y | Y | Y | Y | Y | Y |
| 12 Watt | Y | Y | Y | N | Y | N | N |
| 13 Miller | Y | Y | Y | N | Y | N | N |
| **NORTH DAKOTA** | | | | | | | |
| AL Pomeroy | Y | Y | Y | N | Y | N | N |
| **OHIO** | | | | | | | |
| 1 **Chabot** | Y | Y | Y | Y | Y | Y | N |
| 2 **Schmidt** | Y | Y | Y | Y | Y | Y | N |
| 3 **Turner** | Y | Y | Y | Y | Y | Y | N |
| 4 **Oxley** | Y | Y | Y | Y | Y | Y | N |
| 5 **Gillmor** | Y | Y | Y | Y | Y | Y | Y |
| 6 Strickland | ? | ? | ? | N | N | N | N |
| 7 **Hobson** | Y | Y | Y | Y | Y | Y | N |
| 8 **Boehner** | Y | Y | Y | Y | Y | Y | N |
| 9 Kaptur | Y | Y | Y | N | Y | N | N |
| 10 Kucinich | Y | Y | Y | N | N | N | N |
| 11 Jones | Y | Y | Y | N | N | N | N |
| 12 **Tiberi** | Y | Y | Y | Y | N | Y | N |
| 13 Brown | Y | Y | Y | N | Y | N | N |
| 14 **LaTourette** | Y | Y | Y | Y | Y | Y | N |
| 15 **Pryce** | Y | Y | Y | Y | Y | Y | N |
| 16 **Regula** | Y | Y | Y | Y | Y | Y | N |
| 17 Ryan | Y | Y | Y | N | Y | N | N |
| 18 **Ney** | Y | Y | Y | Y | Y | Y | N |
| **OKLAHOMA** | | | | | | | |
| 1 **Sullivan** | Y | Y | Y | Y | Y | Y | N |
| 2 Boren | Y | Y | Y | N | Y | N | N |
| 3 **Lucas** | Y | Y | Y | Y | Y | Y | N |
| 4 **Cole** | Y | Y | Y | Y | Y | Y | N |
| 5 **Istook** | Y | Y | Y | Y | Y | Y | N |
| **OREGON** | | | | | | | |
| 1 Wu | Y | Y | Y | N | N | N | N |
| 2 **Walden** | Y | Y | Y | Y | Y | Y | N |
| 3 Blumenauer | Y | Y | Y | N | Y | N | N |
| 4 DeFazio | Y | Y | Y | N | N | N | N |
| 5 Hooley | Y | Y | Y | N | Y | N | N |
| **PENNSYLVANIA** | | | | | | | |
| 1 Brady | Y | Y | Y | N | N | N | N |
| 2 Fattah | ? | ? | ? | N | Y | N | N |
| 3 **English** | Y | Y | Y | Y | N | Y | N |
| 4 **Hart** | Y | Y | Y | Y | N | Y | N |
| 5 **Peterson** | Y | Y | Y | Y | Y | Y | N |
| 6 **Gerlach** | Y | Y | Y | Y | Y | Y | N |
| 7 **Weldon** | Y | Y | Y | Y | Y | Y | N |
| 8 **Fitzpatrick** | Y | Y | Y | Y | N | Y | N |
| 9 **Shuster** | Y | Y | Y | Y | N | Y | N |
| 10 **Sherwood** | Y | Y | Y | Y | Y | Y | N |
| 11 Kanjorski | Y | Y | Y | N | Y | N | N |
| 12 Murtha | Y | Y | ? | N | Y | N | N |
| 13 Schwartz | Y | Y | Y | N | Y | N | N |
| 14 Doyle | Y | Y | Y | N | Y | N | N |
| 15 **Dent** | Y | Y | Y | Y | Y | Y | N |
| 16 **Pitts** | Y | Y | Y | Y | Y | Y | N |
| 17 Holden | Y | Y | Y | N | Y | N | N |
| 18 **Murphy** | Y | Y | Y | Y | Y | Y | N |
| 19 **Platts** | Y | Y | Y | ? | ? | ? | ? |
| **RHODE ISLAND** | | | | | | | |
| 1 Kennedy | Y | Y | Y | N | Y | N | N |
| 2 Langevin | Y | Y | Y | N | Y | N | N |
| **SOUTH CAROLINA** | | | | | | | |
| 1 **Brown** | Y | Y | Y | Y | Y | Y | N |
| 2 **Wilson** | Y | Y | Y | Y | Y | Y | N |
| 3 **Barrett** | Y | Y | Y | Y | Y | Y | N |
| 4 **Inglis** | Y | Y | Y | Y | Y | Y | N |
| 5 Spratt | Y | Y | Y | N | Y | N | N |
| 6 Clyburn | Y | Y | Y | N | Y | N | N |
| **SOUTH DAKOTA** | | | | | | | |
| AL Herseth | Y | Y | Y | N | Y | N | N |
| **TENNESSEE** | | | | | | | |
| 1 **Jenkins** | Y | Y | Y | Y | Y | Y | N |
| 2 **Duncan** | Y | Y | Y | Y | Y | Y | Y |

| | 536 | 537 | 538 | 539 | 540 | 541 | 542 |
|---|---|---|---|---|---|---|---|
| 3 **Wamp** | Y | Y | Y | Y | Y | Y | Y |
| 4 Davis | Y | Y | Y | N | Y | N | N |
| 5 Cooper | Y | Y | Y | N | Y | N | Y |
| 6 Gordon | Y | Y | Y | N | Y | N | N |
| 7 **Blackburn** | Y | Y | Y | Y | Y | Y | Y |
| 8 Tanner | Y | Y | Y | N | N | N | N |
| 9 Ford | ? | ? | ? | N | Y | N | N |
| **TEXAS** | | | | | | | |
| 1 **Gohmert** | Y | Y | Y | Y | Y | Y | N |
| 2 **Poe** | Y | Y | Y | Y | Y | Y | N |
| 3 **Johnson, S.** | Y | Y | Y | Y | Y | Y | N |
| 4 **Hall** | Y | Y | Y | Y | Y | Y | N |
| 5 **Hensarling** | Y | Y | Y | Y | Y | Y | Y |
| 6 **Barton** | Y | Y | Y | Y | Y | Y | N |
| 7 **Culberson** | Y | Y | Y | Y | Y | Y | N |
| 8 **Brady** | ? | ? | ? | Y | Y | Y | N |
| 9 Green, A. | Y | Y | Y | N | Y | N | N |
| 10 **McCaul** | Y | Y | Y | Y | Y | Y | N |
| 11 **Conaway** | N | Y | Y | Y | Y | Y | N |
| 12 **Granger** | Y | Y | Y | Y | Y | Y | N |
| 13 **Thornberry** | Y | Y | Y | Y | Y | Y | N |
| 14 **Paul** | N | Y | Y | Y | Y | Y | Y |
| 15 Hinojosa | Y | Y | Y | N | Y | N | N |
| 16 Reyes | ? | ? | ? | ? | ? | ? | ? |
| 17 Edwards | ? | ? | ? | N | Y | N | N |
| 18 Jackson-Lee | ? | ? | ? | N | Y | N | N |
| 19 **Neugebauer** | Y | Y | Y | Y | Y | Y | N |
| 20 Gonzalez | Y | Y | Y | N | Y | N | N |
| 21 **Smith** | Y | Y | Y | Y | Y | Y | N |
| 22 **DeLay** | Y | Y | Y | Y | Y | Y | N |
| 23 **Bonilla** | Y | Y | Y | Y | Y | Y | N |
| 24 **Marchant** | Y | Y | Y | Y | Y | Y | N |
| 25 Doggett | Y | Y | Y | N | Y | N | N |
| 26 **Burgess** | Y | Y | Y | Y | Y | Y | N |
| 27 Ortiz | Y | Y | Y | N | Y | N | N |
| 28 Cuellar | Y | Y | Y | N | Y | N | N |
| 29 Green, G. | Y | Y | Y | N | ? | N | N |
| 30 Johnson, E. | Y | Y | Y | N | Y | N | N |
| 31 **Carter** | Y | Y | Y | Y | Y | Y | N |
| 32 **Sessions** | Y | Y | Y | Y | Y | Y | N |
| **UTAH** | | | | | | | |
| 1 **Bishop** | Y | Y | Y | Y | Y | Y | N |
| 2 Matheson | Y | Y | Y | N | N | N | N |
| 3 **Cannon** | Y | Y | Y | Y | Y | ? | N |
| **VERMONT** | | | | | | | |
| AL *Sanders* | Y | Y | Y | N | Y | N | N |
| **VIRGINIA** | | | | | | | |
| 1 **Davis, J.** | Y | Y | Y | Y | Y | Y | N |
| 2 **Drake** | Y | Y | Y | Y | Y | Y | N |
| 3 Scott | Y | Y | Y | N | Y | N | N |
| 4 **Forbes** | Y | Y | Y | Y | Y | Y | N |
| 5 **Goode** | Y | Y | Y | Y | Y | Y | N |
| 6 **Goodlatte** | Y | Y | Y | Y | Y | Y | N |
| 7 **Cantor** | Y | Y | Y | Y | Y | Y | N |
| 8 Moran | Y | Y | Y | N | ? | ? | ? |
| 9 Boucher | Y | Y | Y | N | Y | N | N |
| 10 **Wolf** | Y | Y | Y | Y | Y | Y | N |
| 11 **Davis, T.** | Y | Y | Y | Y | Y | Y | N |
| **WASHINGTON** | | | | | | | |
| 1 Inslee | Y | Y | Y | N | Y | N | N |
| 2 Larsen | Y | Y | Y | N | N | N | N |
| 3 Baird | Y | Y | Y | N | N | N | N |
| 4 **Hastings** | Y | Y | Y | Y | Y | Y | N |
| 5 **McMorris** | Y | Y | Y | Y | Y | Y | N |
| 6 Dicks | Y | Y | Y | N | Y | N | Y |
| 7 McDermott | Y | Y | Y | N | N | N | N |
| 8 **Reichert** | Y | Y | Y | Y | Y | Y | N |
| 9 Smith | Y | Y | Y | N | Y | N | N |
| **WEST VIRGINIA** | | | | | | | |
| 1 Mollohan | Y | Y | Y | N | Y | N | N |
| 2 **Capito** | Y | Y | Y | Y | Y | Y | N |
| 3 Rahall | Y | Y | Y | N | Y | N | N |
| **WISCONSIN** | | | | | | | |
| 1 **Ryan** | Y | Y | Y | Y | Y | Y | Y |
| 2 Baldwin | Y | Y | Y | N | N | N | N |
| 3 Kind | Y | Y | Y | N | Y | N | N |
| 4 Moore | Y | Y | Y | N | Y | N | N |
| 5 **Sensenbrenner** | Y | Y | Y | Y | Y | Y | N |
| 6 **Petri** | Y | Y | Y | Y | Y | N | Y |
| 7 Obey | Y | Y | Y | N | Y | N | N |
| 8 **Green** | Y | Y | Y | Y | Y | Y | N |
| **WYOMING** | | | | | | | |
| AL **Cubin** | Y | Y | Y | Y | Y | Y | N |

# IN THE HOUSE | By Vote Number

**543.** **HR 1461. Government-Sponsored Enterprises/Systemic Risk.** Royce, R-Calif., amendment that would authorize the new regulator to require Fannie Mae or Freddie Mac to sell or acquire assets or liabilities, if an asset or liability is deemed to be a potential systemic risk to the housing market, the capital markets or the financial system. Rejected 73-346: R 70-153; D 3-192 (ND 1-147, SD 2-45); I 0-1. Oct. 26, 2005.

**544.** **HR 1461. Government-Sponsored Enterprises/U.S. Treasury Borrowing.** Paul, R-Texas, amendment that would eliminate the ability of Fannie Mae, Freddie Mac and the Federal Home Loan Bank Board to borrow from the U.S. Treasury. Rejected 47-371: R 47-176; D 0-194 (ND 0-147, SD 0-47); I 0-1. Oct. 26, 2005.

**545.** **HR 1461. Government-Sponsored Enterprises/Loan Limit.** Garrett, R-N.J., amendment that would strike language in the bill that would increase by 50 percent the maximum mortgages Fannie Mae and Freddie Mac can buy in areas with high home prices. Rejected 57-358: R 53-168; D 4-189 (ND 2-145, SD 2-44); I 0-1. Oct. 26, 2005.

**546.** **HR 1461. Government-Sponsored Enterprises/Recommit.** Frank, D-Mass., motion to recommit the bill to the Financial Services Committee with instructions to add language clarifying that housing must be among a nonprofit organization's primary purposes and that recipients of money from the affordable housing fund may participate in any voter registration or get-out-the-vote-activity conducted on a nonpartisan basis. Motion rejected 200-220: R 3-220; D 196-0 (ND 148-0, SD 48-0); I 1-0. Oct. 26, 2005.

**547.** **HR 1461. Government-Sponsored Enterprises/Passage.** Passage of the bill that would overhaul the regulation of government-sponsored enterprises, including Fannie Mae, Freddie Mac and the 12 Federal Home Loan Banks. The bill would create a new independent agency, the Federal Housing Finance Agency, to regulate Fannie Mae, Freddie Mac and the Federal Home Loan Bank System. It also would establish an affordable housing fund. Passed 331-90: R 209-15; D 122-74 (ND 90-58, SD 32-16); I 0-1. A "nay" was a vote in support of the president's position. Oct. 26, 2005.

**548.** **H J Res 65. Base Closure and Realignment Commission/Passage.** Passage of the joint resolution that would disapprove the recommendations of the Base Realignment and Closure Commission for the fifth round of base closures and realignments. Rejected 85-324: R 34-183; D 51-140 (ND 35-109, SD 16-31); I 0-1. A "nay" was a vote in support of the president's position. Oct. 27, 2005.

| | 543 | 544 | 545 | 546 | 547 | 548 |
|---|---|---|---|---|---|---|
| **ALABAMA** | | | | | | |
| 1 Bonner | N | N | N | N | Y | N |
| 2 Everett | N | N | N | N | Y | N |
| 3 Rogers | N | N | N | N | Y | N |
| 4 Aderholt | N | N | N | N | Y | N |
| 5 Cramer | N | N | N | Y | Y | N |
| 6 Bachus | N | N | N | N | Y | N |
| 7 Davis | N | N | N | Y | Y | N |
| **ALASKA** | | | | | | |
| AL Young | N | Y | N | N | N | N |
| **ARIZONA** | | | | | | |
| 1 Renzi | N | N | N | N | Y | N |
| 2 Franks | Y | Y | Y | N | Y | N |
| 3 Shadegg | Y | Y | Y | N | N | N |
| 4 Pastor | N | N | N | Y | N | N |
| 5 Hayworth | Y | N | N | N | Y | N |
| 6 Flake | Y | Y | Y | N | N | N |
| 7 Grijalva | N | N | N | Y | N | N |
| 8 Kolbe | Y | N | Y | N | Y | N |
| **ARKANSAS** | | | | | | |
| 1 Berry | N | N | N | Y | Y | N |
| 2 Snyder | N | N | N | Y | Y | N |
| 3 Boozman | N | N | N | N | Y | N |
| 4 Ross | N | N | N | Y | Y | N |
| **CALIFORNIA** | | | | | | |
| 1 Thompson | N | N | N | Y | Y | - |
| 2 Herger | N | N | N | N | Y | N |
| 3 Lungren | Y | N | N | N | Y | N |
| 4 Doolittle | N | N | N | N | Y | Y |
| 5 Matsui, D. | N | N | N | Y | Y | N |
| 6 Woolsey | N | N | N | Y | N | N |
| 7 Miller, George | N | N | N | Y | N | N |
| 8 Pelosi | N | N | ? | Y | N | N |
| 9 Lee | N | N | N | Y | N | N |
| 10 Tauscher | N | N | N | Y | Y | ? |
| 11 Pombo | N | N | N | N | Y | N |
| 12 Lantos | N | N | N | Y | Y | N |
| 13 Stark | N | N | N | Y | N | N |
| 14 Eshoo | N | N | N | Y | N | N |
| 15 Honda | N | N | N | Y | N | N |
| 16 Lofgren | N | N | N | Y | N | N |
| 17 Farr | N | N | N | Y | N | N |
| 18 Cardoza | Y | N | N | Y | Y | N |
| 19 Radanovich | Y | N | Y | N | Y | N |
| 20 Costa | N | N | N | Y | Y | N |
| 21 Nunes | N | N | N | N | Y | N |
| 22 Thomas | N | N | N | N | Y | N |
| 23 Capps | N | N | N | Y | Y | Y |
| 24 Gallegly | N | N | N | N | Y | Y |
| 25 McKeon | N | N | N | N | Y | N |
| 26 Dreier | Y | N | N | N | Y | N |
| 27 Sherman | N | ? | N | Y | Y | N |
| 28 Berman | N | N | N | Y | Y | N |
| 29 Schiff | N | N | N | Y | Y | N |
| 30 Waxman | N | N | N | Y | N | N |
| 31 Becerra | N | N | N | Y | Y | N |
| 32 Solis | N | N | N | Y | Y | N |
| 33 Watson | N | N | N | Y | N | Y |
| 34 Roybal-Allard | ? | ? | ? | ? | ? | ? |
| 35 Waters | N | N | N | Y | N | N |
| 36 Harman | N | N | N | Y | Y | N |
| 37 Millender-McD. | N | N | N | Y | N | N |
| 38 Napolitano | N | N | N | Y | Y | N |
| 39 Sánchez, Linda | N | N | N | Y | N | N |
| 40 Royce | Y | Y | Y | N | N | N |
| 41 Lewis | N | N | N | N | Y | N |
| 42 Miller, Gary | N | N | N | N | Y | N |
| 43 Baca | N | N | N | Y | Y | N |
| 44 Calvert | N | N | N | Y | Y | N |
| 45 Bono | N | N | N | N | Y | N |
| 46 Rohrabacher | Y | Y | Y | N | N | N |
| 47 Sanchez, Loretta | N | N | N | Y | Y | N |
| 48 Vacant | | | | | | |
| 49 Issa | N | N | N | N | Y | N |
| **50 Cunningham** | N | N | N | N | Y | ? |
| **51 Filner** | N | N | N | Y | Y | N |
| **52 Hunter** | Y | N | N | N | Y | N |
| **53 Davis** | N | N | N | Y | Y | N |
| **COLORADO** | | | | | | |
| 1 DeGette | N | N | N | Y | N | Y |
| 2 Udall | N | N | N | Y | Y | N |
| 3 Salazar | N | N | N | Y | Y | N |
| 4 Musgrave | Y | N | Y | N | N | N |
| 5 Hefley | N | N | N | N | Y | N |
| 6 Tancredo | Y | N | Y | N | N | N |
| 7 Beauprez | Y | N | N | N | Y | N |
| **CONNECTICUT** | | | | | | |
| 1 Larson | N | N | N | Y | Y | Y |
| 2 Simmons | N | N | N | Y | Y | ? |
| 3 DeLauro | N | N | N | Y | Y | Y |
| 4 Shays | Y | Y | N | Y | N | N |
| 5 Johnson | N | N | N | N | Y | N |
| **DELAWARE** | | | | | | |
| AL Castle | N | N | Y | N | Y | N |
| **FLORIDA** | | | | | | |
| 1 Miller | N | Y | N | N | N | Y |
| 2 Boyd | N | N | N | Y | Y | N |
| 3 Brown | N | N | N | Y | Y | Y |
| 4 Crenshaw | N | N | N | N | Y | N |
| 5 Brown-Waite | ? | ? | ? | ? | ? | ? |
| 6 Stearns | Y | N | N | N | N | N |
| 7 Mica | N | N | N | N | Y | N |
| 8 Keller | N | N | N | N | Y | N |
| 9 Bilirakis | N | N | N | N | Y | N |
| 10 Young | N | N | N | N | Y | N |
| 11 Davis | N | N | ? | Y | Y | N |
| 12 Putnam | N | N | N | N | Y | N |
| 13 Harris | N | N | Y | N | Y | ? |
| 14 Mack | N | Y | N | N | N | ? |
| 15 Weldon | Y | N | N | N | Y | N |
| 16 Foley | ? | ? | ? | ? | ? | ? |
| 17 Meek | ? | ? | N | Y | N | N |
| 18 Ros-Lehtinen | ? | ? | ? | Y | ? | ? |
| 19 Wexler | ? | ? | ? | ? | ? | ? |
| 20 Wasserman-Schultz | N | N | N | Y | N | N |
| 21 Diaz-Balart, L. | ? | ? | ? | ? | ? | ? |
| 22 Shaw | ? | ? | ? | Y | ? | ? |
| 23 Hastings | N | N | N | Y | N | ? |
| 24 Feeney | Y | Y | N | N | Y | N |
| 25 Diaz-Balart, M. | ? | ? | ? | ? | ? | ? |
| **GEORGIA** | | | | | | |
| 1 Kingston | Y | Y | N | N | Y | N |
| 2 Bishop | ? | ? | ? | ? | ? | N |
| 3 Marshall | N | N | ? | Y | Y | N |
| 4 McKinney | N | N | N | Y | N | N |
| 5 Lewis | N | N | N | Y | N | Y |
| 6 Price | Y | N | N | N | Y | N |
| 7 Linder | N | Y | N | N | Y | N |
| 8 Westmoreland | Y | Y | Y | N | N | N |
| 9 Norwood | Y | Y | Y | N | Y | N |
| 10 Deal | Y | Y | Y | N | Y | N |
| 11 Gingrey | N | N | N | N | Y | N |
| 12 Barrow | N | N | N | Y | Y | Y |
| 13 Scott | N | N | N | Y | N | Y |
| **HAWAII** | | | | | | |
| 1 Abercrombie | N | N | N | Y | N | Y |
| 2 Case | N | N | N | Y | Y | N |
| **IDAHO** | | | | | | |
| 1 Otter | Y | Y | Y | N | N | N |
| 2 Simpson | N | N | N | N | N | N |
| **ILLINOIS** | | | | | | |
| 1 Rush | N | N | Y | Y | Y | Y |
| 2 Jackson | N | N | N | Y | Y | Y |
| 3 Lipinski | N | N | N | Y | Y | N |
| 4 Gutierrez | N | N | N | Y | N | N |
| 5 Emanuel | ? | ? | ? | ? | ? | Y |
| 6 Hyde | N | N | N | N | Y | N |
| 7 Davis | N | N | N | Y | Y | Y |
| 8 Bean | N | N | N | Y | Y | N |
| 9 Schakowsky | N | N | N | Y | N | N |
| 10 Kirk | Y | N | N | N | Y | N |
| 11 Weller | N | N | N | N | Y | Y |
| 12 Costello | N | N | N | Y | Y | N |

**KEY**    **Republicans**    Democrats    *Independents*

| | | | |
|---|---|---|---|
| Y | Voted for (yea) | X Paired against | C Voted "present" to avoid possible conflict of interest |
| # | Paired for | − Announced against | |
| + | Announced for | P Voted "present" | ? Did not vote or otherwise make a position known |
| N | Voted against (nay) | | |

ND Northern Democrats, SD Southern Democrats
Southern states: Ala., Ark., Fla., Ga., Ky., La., Miss., N.C., Okla., S.C., Tenn., Texas, Va.

| | 543 | 544 | 545 | 546 | 547 | 548 |
|---|---|---|---|---|---|---|
| 13 **Biggert** | N | N | N | N | Y | N |
| 14 **Hastert** | | | | | | |
| 15 **Johnson** | N | N | N | N | Y | Y |
| 16 **Manzullo** | Y | Y | N | N | Y | Y |
| 17 Evans | N | N | N | Y | Y | Y |
| 18 **LaHood** | N | N | N | N | Y | Y |
| 19 **Shimkus** | N | N | N | N | Y | N |
| **INDIANA** | | | | | | |
| 1 Visclosky | N | N | N | Y | N | N |
| 2 **Chocola** | Y | Y | Y | N | N | N |
| 3 **Souder** | N | N | N | N | Y | N |
| 4 **Buyer** | N | N | N | N | Y | N |
| 5 **Burton** | N | Y | N | N | Y | N |
| 6 **Pence** | Y | Y | Y | N | Y | N |
| 7 Carson | N | N | N | Y | N | N |
| 8 **Hostettler** | Y | Y | Y | N | Y | Y |
| 9 **Sodrel** | N | N | Y | N | Y | N |
| **IOWA** | | | | | | |
| 1 **Nussle** | Y | Y | Y | N | Y | Y |
| 2 **Leach** | Y | Y | Y | Y | N | Y |
| 3 Boswell | ? | ? | ? | ? | ? | ? |
| 4 **Latham** | N | N | N | N | Y | N |
| 5 **King** | Y | N | Y | N | Y | N |
| **KANSAS** | | | | | | |
| 1 **Moran** | N | N | N | N | Y | N |
| 2 **Ryun** | N | N | N | N | Y | N |
| 3 Moore | N | N | N | Y | Y | N |
| 4 **Tiahrt** | Y | N | Y | N | Y | N |
| **KENTUCKY** | | | | | | |
| 1 **Whitfield** | ? | ? | ? | ? | ? | N |
| 2 **Lewis** | N | N | N | N | Y | N |
| 3 **Northup** | N | N | N | N | Y | N |
| 4 **Davis** | N | N | N | N | Y | N |
| 5 **Rogers** | N | N | N | N | Y | N |
| 6 Chandler | N | N | N | Y | Y | N |
| **LOUISIANA** | | | | | | |
| 1 **Jindal** | N | N | Y | N | Y | Y |
| 2 Jefferson | N | N | N | Y | Y | N |
| 3 Melancon | N | N | N | Y | Y | N |
| 4 **McCrery** | N | N | Y | N | Y | N |
| 5 **Alexander** | N | N | Y | N | Y | N |
| 6 **Baker** | N | N | Y | N | Y | N |
| 7 **Boustany** | N | N | Y | N | Y | N |
| **MAINE** | | | | | | |
| 1 Allen | N | N | N | Y | Y | Y |
| 2 Michaud | N | N | N | Y | Y | N |
| **MARYLAND** | | | | | | |
| 1 **Gilchrest** | N | N | N | N | Y | N |
| 2 Ruppersberger | N | N | N | Y | Y | N |
| 3 Cardin | N | N | N | Y | Y | N |
| 4 Wynn | N | N | N | Y | Y | N |
| 5 Hoyer | N | N | N | Y | Y | N |
| 6 **Bartlett** | Y | Y | Y | N | Y | N |
| 7 Cummings | N | N | N | Y | Y | N |
| 8 Van Hollen | N | N | N | Y | Y | N |
| **MASSACHUSETTS** | | | | | | |
| 1 Olver | N | N | N | Y | N | N |
| 2 Neal | N | N | N | Y | Y | N |
| 3 McGovern | N | N | N | Y | N | N |
| 4 Frank | N | N | N | Y | N | N |
| 5 Meehan | N | N | N | Y | Y | N |
| 6 Tierney | N | N | N | Y | Y | N |
| 7 Markey | N | N | N | Y | N | N |
| 8 Capuano | N | N | N | Y | N | N |
| 9 Lynch | N | N | N | Y | Y | Y |
| 10 Delahunt | N | N | Y | Y | Y | Y |
| **MICHIGAN** | | | | | | |
| 1 Stupak | N | N | N | Y | Y | Y |
| 2 **Hoekstra** | Y | Y | N | N | Y | N |
| 3 **Ehlers** | Y | N | N | N | Y | N |
| 4 **Camp** | N | N | N | N | Y | N |
| 5 Kildee | N | N | N | Y | Y | N |
| 6 **Upton** | Y | N | N | N | Y | N |
| 7 **Schwarz** | N | N | N | N | Y | N |
| 8 **Rogers** | N | N | N | N | Y | N |
| 9 **Knollenberg** | N | N | N | N | Y | N |
| 10 **Miller** | N | N | N | N | Y | N |
| 11 **McCotter** | N | N | N | N | Y | N |
| 12 Levin | N | N | N | Y | Y | N |
| 13 Kilpatrick | N | N | N | Y | N | N |
| 14 Conyers | N | N | N | Y | N | N |
| 15 Dingell | N | N | N | Y | N | N |

| | 543 | 544 | 545 | 546 | 547 | 548 |
|---|---|---|---|---|---|---|
| **MINNESOTA** | | | | | | |
| 1 **Gutknecht** | Y | N | Y | N | Y | N |
| 2 **Kline** | Y | N | N | N | Y | N |
| 3 **Ramstad** | Y | N | N | Y | N | N |
| 4 McCollum | N | N | N | Y | N | N |
| 5 Sabo | N | N | N | Y | N | N |
| 6 **Kennedy** | Y | N | N | N | Y | N |
| 7 Peterson | N | N | N | Y | Y | N |
| 8 Oberstar | N | N | N | Y | N | N |
| **MISSISSIPPI** | | | | | | |
| 1 **Wicker** | N | N | N | N | Y | Y |
| 2 Thompson | N | N | N | Y | Y | N |
| 3 **Pickering** | N | N | N | N | Y | Y |
| 4 Taylor | Y | N | Y | Y | Y | Y |
| **MISSOURI** | | | | | | |
| 1 Clay | N | N | N | Y | N | Y |
| 2 **Akin** | Y | Y | Y | N | Y | Y |
| 3 Carnahan | N | N | N | Y | Y | Y |
| 4 Skelton | N | N | N | Y | Y | N |
| 5 Cleaver | N | N | N | Y | N | N |
| 6 **Graves** | N | N | N | N | Y | N |
| 7 **Blunt** | Y | N | N | N | Y | N |
| 8 **Emerson** | N | N | N | N | Y | Y |
| 9 **Hulshof** | N | N | N | N | Y | Y |
| **MONTANA** | | | | | | |
| AL **Rehberg** | N | N | N | N | Y | N |
| **NEBRASKA** | | | | | | |
| 1 **Fortenberry** | Y | N | N | N | Y | N |
| 2 **Terry** | N | N | N | N | Y | N |
| 3 **Osborne** | N | N | N | N | Y | N |
| **NEVADA** | | | | | | |
| 1 Berkley | N | N | N | Y | Y | N |
| 2 **Gibbons** | N | N | N | N | Y | N |
| 3 **Porter** | N | N | N | N | Y | N |
| **NEW HAMPSHIRE** | | | | | | |
| 1 **Bradley** | N | N | N | N | Y | N |
| 2 **Bass** | N | N | N | N | Y | N |
| **NEW JERSEY** | | | | | | |
| 1 Andrews | N | N | N | Y | Y | Y |
| 2 **LoBiondo** | N | N | N | N | Y | N |
| 3 **Saxton** | Y | N | N | N | Y | N |
| 4 **Smith** | Y | N | N | N | Y | Y |
| 5 **Garrett** | Y | Y | Y | N | N | N |
| 6 Pallone | N | N | N | Y | Y | Y |
| 7 **Ferguson** | Y | N | N | N | Y | N |
| 8 Pascrell | N | N | N | Y | Y | Y |
| 9 Rothman | N | N | N | Y | Y | Y |
| 10 Payne | N | N | N | Y | N | ? |
| 11 **Frelinghuysen** | N | N | N | N | Y | N |
| 12 Holt | N | N | N | Y | Y | Y |
| 13 Menendez | N | N | N | Y | Y | Y |
| **NEW MEXICO** | | | | | | |
| 1 **Wilson** | N | N | N | N | Y | Y |
| 2 **Pearce** | N | N | N | N | Y | N |
| 3 Udall | N | N | N | Y | Y | Y |
| **NEW YORK** | | | | | | |
| 1 Bishop | N | N | N | Y | Y | N |
| 2 Israel | N | N | N | Y | N | N |
| 3 **King** | N | N | N | N | Y | N |
| 4 McCarthy | N | N | N | Y | Y | N |
| 5 Ackerman | N | N | N | Y | N | N |
| 6 Meeks | N | N | N | Y | N | N |
| 7 Crowley | N | N | N | Y | N | Y |
| 8 Nadler | N | N | N | Y | N | N |
| 9 Weiner | N | N | N | Y | N | N |
| 10 Towns | N | N | N | Y | N | N |
| 11 Owens | N | N | N | Y | N | N |
| 12 Velázquez | N | N | N | Y | N | N |
| 13 **Fossella** | N | N | N | N | Y | N |
| 14 Maloney | N | N | N | Y | N | N |
| 15 Rangel | N | N | N | Y | N | ? |
| 16 Serrano | N | N | N | Y | N | N |
| 17 Engel | N | N | N | Y | Y | N |
| 18 Lowey | N | N | N | Y | Y | N |
| 19 **Kelly** | N | N | N | N | Y | N |
| 20 **Sweeney** | N | N | N | N | Y | N |
| 21 McNulty | N | N | N | Y | N | N |
| 22 Hinchey | N | N | N | Y | N | N |
| 23 **McHugh** | N | N | N | N | Y | N |
| 24 **Boehlert** | N | N | N | N | Y | N |
| 25 **Walsh** | N | N | N | N | Y | N |
| 26 **Reynolds** | N | N | N | N | Y | N |
| 27 Higgins | N | N | N | Y | Y | N |
| 28 Slaughter | N | N | N | Y | Y | N |
| 29 **Kuhl** | N | N | N | N | Y | N |

| | 543 | 544 | 545 | 546 | 547 | 548 |
|---|---|---|---|---|---|---|
| **NORTH CAROLINA** | | | | | | |
| 1 Butterfield | N | N | N | Y | Y | N |
| 2 Etheridge | N | N | N | Y | Y | N |
| 3 **Jones** | Y | Y | Y | N | Y | N |
| 4 Price | N | N | N | Y | N | N |
| 5 **Foxx** | Y | Y | N | N | Y | N |
| 6 **Coble** | N | N | N | N | Y | N |
| 7 McIntyre | N | N | N | Y | Y | N |
| 8 **Hayes** | N | N | N | N | Y | N |
| 9 **Myrick** | N | Y | N | N | Y | N |
| 10 **McHenry** | Y | Y | N | N | Y | N |
| 11 **Taylor** | Y | N | N | N | Y | N |
| 12 Watt | N | N | N | Y | N | N |
| 13 Miller | N | N | N | Y | N | N |
| **NORTH DAKOTA** | | | | | | |
| AL Pomeroy | N | N | N | Y | Y | N |
| **OHIO** | | | | | | |
| 1 **Chabot** | Y | N | N | N | Y | N |
| 2 **Schmidt** | N | N | N | N | Y | N |
| 3 **Turner** | N | N | N | N | Y | N |
| 4 **Oxley** | N | N | N | N | Y | Y |
| 5 **Gillmor** | Y | N | N | N | Y | N |
| 6 Strickland | N | N | N | Y | Y | N |
| 7 **Hobson** | N | N | N | N | Y | Y |
| 8 **Boehner** | N | Y | N | N | Y | N |
| 9 Kaptur | N | N | N | Y | N | N |
| 10 Kucinich | N | N | N | Y | N | N |
| 11 Jones | N | N | N | Y | N | N |
| 12 **Tiberi** | N | N | N | N | Y | N |
| 13 Brown | N | N | N | Y | Y | Y |
| 14 **LaTourette** | N | N | N | N | Y | N |
| 15 **Pryce** | N | N | N | N | Y | N |
| 16 **Regula** | Y | N | N | N | Y | N |
| 17 Ryan | N | N | N | Y | Y | N |
| 18 **Ney** | N | N | N | N | Y | N |
| **OKLAHOMA** | | | | | | |
| 1 **Sullivan** | N | N | N | N | Y | N |
| 2 Boren | N | N | N | Y | Y | N |
| 3 **Lucas** | N | N | N | N | Y | N |
| 4 **Cole** | N | N | N | N | Y | N |
| 5 **Istook** | N | Y | Y | N | Y | N |
| **OREGON** | | | | | | |
| 1 Wu | N | N | N | Y | Y | N |
| 2 **Walden** | N | N | N | N | Y | N |
| 3 Blumenauer | N | N | N | Y | Y | N |
| 4 DeFazio | N | N | N | Y | Y | N |
| 5 Hooley | N | N | N | Y | Y | N |
| **PENNSYLVANIA** | | | | | | |
| 1 Brady | N | N | N | Y | N | Y |
| 2 Fattah | N | N | N | Y | N | Y |
| 3 **English** | N | N | Y | N | Y | N |
| 4 **Hart** | N | N | N | N | Y | N |
| 5 **Peterson** | N | N | N | N | Y | N |
| 6 **Gerlach** | N | N | N | N | Y | Y |
| 7 **Weldon** | N | N | N | N | Y | N |
| 8 **Fitzpatrick** | N | N | N | N | Y | Y |
| 9 **Shuster** | N | N | N | N | Y | N |
| 10 **Sherwood** | Y | N | N | N | Y | N |
| 11 Kanjorski | N | N | N | Y | N | N |
| 12 Murtha | N | N | N | Y | Y | Y |
| 13 Schwartz | N | N | N | Y | Y | Y |
| 14 Doyle | N | N | N | Y | N | N |
| 15 **Dent** | N | N | N | N | Y | Y |
| 16 **Pitts** | Y | Y | Y | N | Y | N |
| 17 Holden | N | N | N | Y | Y | N |
| 18 **Murphy** | N | N | N | N | Y | N |
| 19 **Platts** | Y | Y | Y | N | N | N |
| **RHODE ISLAND** | | | | | | |
| 1 Kennedy | N | N | N | Y | N | N |
| 2 Langevin | N | N | N | Y | Y | N |
| **SOUTH CAROLINA** | | | | | | |
| 1 **Brown** | N | N | N | N | Y | Y |
| 2 **Wilson** | N | N | N | N | Y | N |
| 3 **Barrett** | N | N | Y | N | Y | N |
| 4 **Inglis** | Y | Y | N | N | Y | N |
| 5 Spratt | N | N | N | Y | Y | N |
| 6 Clyburn | N | N | N | Y | N | N |
| **SOUTH DAKOTA** | | | | | | |
| AL Herseth | N | N | N | Y | Y | N |
| **TENNESSEE** | | | | | | |
| 1 **Jenkins** | N | N | N | N | Y | Y |
| 2 **Duncan** | Y | Y | Y | N | Y | N |

| | 543 | 544 | 545 | 546 | 547 | 548 |
|---|---|---|---|---|---|---|
| 3 **Wamp** | N | N | N | N | Y | N |
| 4 Davis | N | N | N | Y | Y | N |
| 5 Cooper | Y | N | Y | Y | N | Y |
| 6 Gordon | N | N | N | Y | Y | Y |
| 7 **Blackburn** | Y | Y | Y | N | N | N |
| 8 Tanner | N | N | N | Y | Y | N |
| 9 Ford | N | N | N | Y | Y | Y |
| **TEXAS** | | | | | | |
| 1 **Gohmert** | Y | Y | Y | N | Y | ? |
| 2 **Poe** | N | N | N | N | Y | Y |
| 3 **Johnson, S.** | N | N | ? | N | Y | N |
| 4 **Hall** | Y | N | N | N | Y | ? |
| 5 **Hensarling** | Y | Y | Y | N | Y | N |
| 6 **Barton** | N | Y | Y | N | Y | N |
| 7 **Culberson** | Y | N | Y | N | Y | N |
| 8 **Brady** | N | N | N | N | Y | N |
| 9 Green, A. | N | N | N | Y | N | Y |
| 10 **McCaul** | N | N | N | N | Y | Y |
| 11 **Conaway** | N | N | N | N | Y | N |
| 12 **Granger** | N | N | N | N | Y | N |
| 13 **Thornberry** | N | N | N | N | Y | N |
| 14 **Paul** | Y | Y | Y | N | N | Y |
| 15 Hinojosa | N | N | N | Y | Y | Y |
| 16 Reyes | ? | ? | ? | ? | ? | ? |
| 17 Edwards | N | N | N | Y | Y | Y |
| 18 Jackson-Lee | N | N | N | Y | N | N |
| 19 **Neugebauer** | N | N | N | N | Y | N |
| 20 Gonzalez | N | N | N | Y | Y | N |
| 21 **Smith** | N | N | N | N | Y | N |
| 22 **DeLay** | Y | N | N | N | Y | Y |
| 23 **Bonilla** | N | N | N | N | Y | N |
| 24 **Marchant** | N | N | N | N | Y | N |
| 25 Doggett | N | N | N | Y | Y | N |
| 26 **Burgess** | N | N | Y | N | Y | N |
| 27 Ortiz | N | N | N | Y | Y | Y |
| 28 Cuellar | N | N | N | Y | Y | P |
| 29 Green, G. | N | N | N | Y | N | Y |
| 30 Johnson, E. | N | N | N | Y | N | Y |
| 31 **Carter** | N | N | Y | N | Y | N |
| 32 **Sessions** | N | N | N | N | Y | N |
| **UTAH** | | | | | | |
| 1 **Bishop** | N | N | ? | N | Y | N |
| 2 Matheson | N | N | N | Y | Y | N |
| 3 **Cannon** | N | N | N | N | Y | N |
| **VERMONT** | | | | | | |
| AL *Sanders* | N | N | N | Y | N | N |
| **VIRGINIA** | | | | | | |
| 1 **Davis, J.** | N | N | Y | N | Y | Y |
| 2 **Drake** | N | N | N | N | Y | Y |
| 3 Scott | N | N | N | Y | N | Y |
| 4 **Forbes** | N | N | N | N | Y | Y |
| 5 **Goode** | Y | Y | N | N | Y | N |
| 6 **Goodlatte** | N | N | N | N | Y | N |
| 7 **Cantor** | N | N | N | N | Y | N |
| 8 Moran | N | N | N | Y | Y | Y |
| 9 Boucher | N | N | N | Y | Y | N |
| 10 **Wolf** | N | N | N | N | Y | N |
| 11 **Davis, T.** | N | N | N | N | Y | Y |
| **WASHINGTON** | | | | | | |
| 1 Inslee | N | N | N | Y | N | N |
| 2 Larsen | N | N | N | Y | Y | N |
| 3 Baird | N | N | N | Y | Y | N |
| 4 **Hastings** | N | N | N | N | Y | N |
| 5 **McMorris** | N | N | N | N | Y | N |
| 6 Dicks | N | N | N | Y | Y | N |
| 7 McDermott | N | N | N | Y | N | N |
| 8 **Reichert** | N | N | N | N | Y | N |
| 9 Smith | N | N | N | Y | Y | N |
| **WEST VIRGINIA** | | | | | | |
| 1 Mollohan | N | N | N | Y | Y | Y |
| 2 **Capito** | N | N | N | N | Y | N |
| 3 Rahall | N | N | N | Y | Y | N |
| **WISCONSIN** | | | | | | |
| 1 **Ryan** | Y | Y | Y | N | Y | N |
| 2 Baldwin | N | N | N | Y | Y | N |
| 3 Kind | N | N | N | Y | Y | N |
| 4 Moore | N | N | N | Y | Y | Y |
| 5 **Sensenbrenner** | Y | Y | Y | N | Y | ? |
| 6 **Petri** | Y | N | Y | N | Y | N |
| 7 Obey | N | N | N | Y | Y | ? |
| 8 **Green** | N | N | Y | N | Y | N |
| **WYOMING** | | | | | | |
| AL **Cubin** | N | N | N | N | Y | N |

# IN THE HOUSE | By Vote Number

**549.** **HR 3945. Hurricane Katrina Financial Services Relief/Passage.** Baker, R-La., motion to suspend the rules and pass the bill that would require Federal Reserve banks to waive or rebate any transaction fees for wire transfer services to insured depository institutions or credit unions that are head-quartered in an area declared a disaster after Hurricane Katrina. Motion agreed to 411-0: R 216-0; D 194-0 (ND 146-0, SD 48-0); I 1-0. A two-thirds majority of those present and voting (274 in this case) is required for passage under suspension of the rules. Oct. 27, 2005.

**550.** **H Res 368. Vice President of the U.N. General Assembly/ Adoption.** Chabot, R-Ohio, motion to suspend the rules and adopt the resolution that would congratulate Ambassador Dan Gillerman, Israel's permanent representative to the United Nations, and the Israeli government and people on Gillerman's election as vice president of the 60th U.N. General Assembly. Motion agreed to 407-0: R 215-0; D 191-0 (ND 144-0, SD 47-0); I 1-0. A two-thirds majority of those present and voting (272 in this case) is required for adoption under suspension of the rules. Oct. 27, 2005.

**551.** **HR 420. "Meritless" Lawsuits/Democratic Substitute.** Schiff, D-Calif., substitute amendment that would require mandatory sanctions against attorneys who file frivolous civil lawsuits, including payment of costs and attorney fees. Attorneys would be allowed to appeal. It would prevent a court from sealing or otherwise restricting access to a court record unless the court finds that such a restriction is justified. Rejected 184-226: R 1-215; D 182-11 (ND 137-9, SD 45-2); I 1-0. Oct. 27, 2005.

**552.** **HR 420. "Meritless" Lawsuits/Recommit.** Barrow, D-Ga., motion to recommit the bill to the Judiciary Committee with instructions to add language that would exempt from the bill claims against "disaster profiteering businesses." Motion rejected 196-217: R 1-217; D 194-0 (ND 147-0, SD 47-0); I 1-0. Oct. 27, 2005.

**553.** **HR 420. "Meritless" Lawsuits/Passage.** Passage of the bill that would increase federal sanctions on attorneys who file "meritless" civil lawsuits. It would restore mandatory sanctions against such attorneys instead of giving judges the discretion to implement sanctions. The bill would strike a "safe harbor" provision in existing law that allows attorneys to avoid sanctions by withdrawing or correcting questionable claims. Passed 228-184: R 212-5; D 16-178 (ND 5-142, SD 11-36); I 0-1. A "yea" was a vote in support of the president's position. Oct. 27, 2005.

**554.** **HR 3057. Fiscal 2006 Foreign Operations Appropriations/Motion to Instruct.** Lowey, D-N.Y., motion to instruct House conferees to include language that would agree to a Senate provision allowing for $3 billion to combat HIV/AIDS, tuberculosis and malaria, including $500 million for a U.S. contribution to the Global Fund to Fight AIDS, Tuberculosis and Malaria. Motion agreed to 259-147: R 69-145; D 189-2 (ND 145-0, SD 44-2); I 1-0. Oct. 27, 2005.

| | 549 | 550 | 551 | 552 | 553 | 554 |
|---|---|---|---|---|---|---|
| **ALABAMA** | | | | | | |
| 1 Bonner | Y | Y | N | N | Y | N |
| 2 Everett | Y | Y | N | N | Y | N |
| 3 Rogers | Y | Y | N | N | Y | Y |
| 4 Aderholt | Y | Y | N | N | Y | Y |
| 5 Cramer | Y | Y | Y | Y | Y | Y |
| 6 Bachus | Y | Y | N | N | Y | N |
| 7 Davis | Y | Y | Y | Y | N | Y |
| **ALASKA** | | | | | | |
| AL Young | Y | Y | N | N | Y | N |
| **ARIZONA** | | | | | | |
| 1 Renzi | Y | Y | N | N | Y | N |
| 2 Franks | Y | Y | N | N | Y | N |
| 3 Shadegg | Y | Y | N | N | Y | N |
| 4 Pastor | Y | Y | Y | Y | N | Y |
| 5 Hayworth | Y | Y | N | N | Y | N |
| 6 Flake | Y | Y | N | N | Y | N |
| 7 Grijalva | Y | Y | Y | Y | N | Y |
| 8 Kolbe | Y | Y | N | N | Y | Y |
| **ARKANSAS** | | | | | | |
| 1 Berry | Y | Y | Y | Y | N | N |
| 2 Snyder | Y | Y | N | Y | N | Y |
| 3 Boozman | Y | Y | N | N | Y | N |
| 4 Ross | Y | Y | Y | Y | N | Y |
| **CALIFORNIA** | | | | | | |
| 1 Thompson | Y | Y | Y | Y | N | Y |
| 2 Herger | Y | Y | N | N | Y | N |
| 3 Lungren | Y | Y | N | N | Y | N |
| 4 Doolittle | Y | Y | N | N | N | N |
| 5 Matsui, D. | Y | Y | Y | Y | N | Y |
| 6 Woolsey | Y | Y | Y | Y | N | Y |
| 7 Miller, George | Y | Y | Y | Y | N | Y |
| 8 Pelosi | Y | Y | Y | Y | N | Y |
| 9 Lee | Y | Y | Y | Y | N | Y |
| 10 Tauscher | ? | ? | ? | ? | ? | ? |
| 11 Pombo | Y | Y | N | N | Y | N |
| 12 Lantos | Y | Y | Y | Y | N | Y |
| 13 Stark | Y | Y | Y | Y | N | Y |
| 14 Eshoo | Y | Y | Y | Y | N | Y |
| 15 Honda | Y | Y | Y | Y | N | Y |
| 16 Lofgren | Y | Y | N | Y | N | Y |
| 17 Farr | Y | Y | Y | Y | N | Y |
| 18 Cardoza | Y | Y | Y | Y | N | Y |
| 19 Radanovich | Y | Y | N | N | Y | Y |
| 20 Costa | Y | Y | Y | Y | N | Y |
| 21 Nunes | Y | Y | N | N | Y | N |
| 22 Thomas | Y | Y | N | N | Y | N |
| 23 Capps | Y | Y | Y | Y | N | Y |
| 24 Gallegly | Y | Y | N | N | Y | ? |
| 25 McKeon | Y | Y | N | N | Y | Y |
| 26 Dreier | Y | Y | N | N | Y | N |
| 27 Sherman | Y | Y | Y | Y | N | Y |
| 28 Berman | Y | Y | Y | Y | N | Y |
| 29 Schiff | Y | Y | Y | Y | N | Y |
| 30 Waxman | Y | Y | Y | Y | N | Y |
| 31 Becerra | Y | Y | Y | Y | N | Y |
| 32 Solis | Y | Y | Y | Y | N | Y |
| 33 Watson | Y | Y | Y | Y | N | Y |
| 34 Roybal-Allard | ? | ? | ? | ? | ? | ? |
| 35 Waters | Y | Y | Y | Y | N | Y |
| 36 Harman | Y | Y | Y | Y | N | Y |
| 37 Millender-McD. | Y | Y | Y | Y | N | Y |
| 38 Napolitano | Y | Y | Y | Y | N | Y |
| 39 Sánchez, Linda | Y | Y | Y | Y | N | Y |
| 40 Royce | Y | Y | N | N | Y | N |
| 41 Lewis | Y | Y | N | N | Y | N |
| 42 Miller, Gary | Y | Y | N | N | Y | N |
| 43 Baca | Y | Y | Y | Y | N | Y |
| 44 Calvert | Y | Y | N | N | Y | N |
| 45 Bono | Y | Y | N | N | Y | N |
| 46 Rohrabacher | Y | Y | N | N | Y | N |
| 47 Sanchez, Loretta | Y | Y | Y | Y | N | Y |
| 48 Vacant | | | | | | |
| 49 Issa | Y | Y | N | N | Y | N |

| | 549 | 550 | 551 | 552 | 553 | 554 |
|---|---|---|---|---|---|---|
| 50 Cunningham | ? | ? | N | N | Y | N |
| 51 Filner | Y | Y | Y | Y | N | Y |
| 52 Hunter | Y | Y | N | N | Y | N |
| 53 Davis | Y | Y | Y | Y | N | Y |
| **COLORADO** | | | | | | |
| 1 DeGette | Y | Y | Y | Y | N | Y |
| 2 Udall | Y | Y | Y | Y | N | Y |
| 3 Salazar | Y | Y | Y | Y | N | Y |
| 4 Musgrave | Y | Y | N | N | Y | N |
| 5 Hefley | Y | Y | N | N | Y | N |
| 6 Tancredo | Y | Y | N | N | Y | N |
| 7 Beauprez | Y | Y | N | N | Y | Y |
| **CONNECTICUT** | | | | | | |
| 1 Larson | Y | Y | Y | Y | N | Y |
| 2 Simmons | ? | ? | ? | ? | ? | ? |
| 3 DeLauro | Y | Y | Y | Y | N | Y |
| 4 Shays | Y | Y | N | N | Y | Y |
| 5 Johnson | Y | Y | N | N | Y | Y |
| **DELAWARE** | | | | | | |
| AL Castle | Y | Y | N | N | Y | ? |
| **FLORIDA** | | | | | | |
| 1 Miller | Y | Y | N | N | Y | N |
| 2 Boyd | Y | Y | Y | Y | Y | Y |
| 3 Brown | Y | Y | Y | Y | N | Y |
| 4 Crenshaw | Y | Y | N | N | Y | N |
| 5 Brown-Waite | ? | ? | ? | ? | ? | ? |
| 6 Stearns | Y | Y | N | N | Y | N |
| 7 Mica | Y | Y | N | N | Y | N |
| 8 Keller | Y | Y | N | N | Y | N |
| 9 Bilirakis | Y | Y | N | N | Y | N |
| 10 Young | Y | Y | Y | Y | N | Y |
| 11 Davis | Y | Y | Y | Y | N | Y |
| 12 Putnam | Y | Y | N | N | Y | N |
| 13 Harris | ? | ? | ? | ? | ? | ? |
| 14 Mack | ? | ? | ? | ? | ? | ? |
| 15 Weldon | Y | Y | N | N | Y | N |
| 16 Foley | ? | ? | ? | ? | ? | ? |
| 17 Meek | Y | Y | Y | Y | N | Y |
| 18 Ros-Lehtinen | ? | ? | ? | ? | ? | ? |
| 19 Wexler | ? | ? | ? | ? | ? | ? |
| 20 Wasserman-Schultz | Y | ? | Y | Y | N | Y |
| 21 Diaz-Balart, L. | ? | ? | ? | ? | ? | ? |
| 22 Shaw | ? | ? | ? | ? | ? | ? |
| 23 Hastings | ? | ? | ? | ? | ? | ? |
| 24 Feeney | Y | Y | N | N | Y | N |
| 25 Diaz-Balart, M. | ? | ? | ? | ? | ? | ? |
| **GEORGIA** | | | | | | |
| 1 Kingston | Y | Y | N | N | Y | N |
| 2 Bishop | Y | Y | Y | Y | N | Y |
| 3 Marshall | Y | Y | Y | Y | Y | Y |
| 4 McKinney | Y | Y | Y | Y | N | Y |
| 5 Lewis | Y | Y | Y | Y | N | Y |
| 6 Price | Y | Y | N | N | Y | N |
| 7 Linder | Y | Y | N | N | Y | N |
| 8 Westmoreland | Y | Y | N | N | Y | N |
| 9 Norwood | Y | Y | N | N | Y | N |
| 10 Deal | Y | Y | N | N | Y | N |
| 11 Gingrey | Y | Y | ? | N | Y | N |
| 12 Barrow | Y | Y | Y | Y | N | Y |
| 13 Scott | Y | Y | Y | Y | N | Y |
| **HAWAII** | | | | | | |
| 1 Abercrombie | Y | Y | Y | Y | N | Y |
| 2 Case | Y | Y | Y | Y | Y | Y |
| **IDAHO** | | | | | | |
| 1 Otter | Y | Y | N | N | Y | N |
| 2 Simpson | Y | Y | N | N | Y | N |
| **ILLINOIS** | | | | | | |
| 1 Rush | Y | Y | Y | Y | N | Y |
| 2 Jackson | Y | Y | Y | Y | N | Y |
| 3 Lipinski | Y | Y | Y | Y | N | Y |
| 4 Gutierrez | Y | Y | Y | Y | N | Y |
| 5 Emanuel | Y | Y | Y | Y | N | Y |
| 6 Hyde | Y | Y | N | N | Y | Y |
| 7 Davis | Y | Y | Y | Y | N | Y |
| 8 Bean | Y | Y | Y | Y | N | Y |
| 9 Schakowsky | Y | Y | Y | Y | N | Y |
| 10 Kirk | Y | Y | N | N | Y | Y |
| 11 Weller | Y | Y | N | N | Y | Y |
| 12 Costello | Y | Y | N | N | Y | Y |

ND Northern Democrats, SD Southern Democrats
Southern states: Ala., Ark., Fla., Ga., Ky., La., Miss., N.C., Okla., S.C., Tenn., Texas, Va.

| | 549 | 550 | 551 | 552 | 553 | 554 |
|---|---|---|---|---|---|---|
| 13 **Biggert** | Y | Y | N | N | Y | Y |
| 14 **Hastert** | | | | | | |
| 15 **Johnson** | Y | Y | Y | Y | Y | Y |
| 16 **Manzullo** | Y | Y | N | N | N | Y |
| 17 Evans | Y | Y | Y | Y | N | Y |
| 18 **LaHood** | Y | Y | N | N | Y | Y |
| 19 **Shimkus** | Y | Y | N | N | Y | Y |
| **INDIANA** | | | | | | |
| 1 Visclosky | Y | Y | Y | Y | N | Y |
| 2 **Chocola** | Y | Y | N | N | Y | Y |
| 3 **Souder** | Y | Y | N | N | Y | N |
| 4 **Buyer** | Y | Y | N | N | Y | N |
| 5 **Burton** | Y | Y | N | N | Y | N |
| 6 **Pence** | Y | Y | N | N | Y | N |
| 7 Carson | Y | Y | Y | Y | N | Y |
| 8 **Hostettler** | Y | Y | N | N | Y | N |
| 9 **Sodrel** | Y | Y | N | N | Y | N |
| **IOWA** | | | | | | |
| 1 **Nussle** | Y | Y | N | N | Y | Y |
| 2 **Leach** | Y | Y | N | N | Y | Y |
| 3 Boswell | ? | ? | ? | ? | ? | ? |
| 4 **Latham** | Y | Y | N | N | Y | Y |
| 5 **King** | Y | Y | N | N | Y | N |
| **KANSAS** | | | | | | |
| 1 **Moran** | Y | Y | N | N | Y | N |
| 2 **Ryun** | Y | Y | N | N | Y | N |
| 3 Moore | Y | Y | Y | Y | N | Y |
| 4 **Tiahrt** | Y | Y | N | N | Y | N |
| **KENTUCKY** | | | | | | |
| 1 **Whitfield** | ? | Y | N | N | Y | Y |
| 2 **Lewis** | Y | Y | N | N | Y | N |
| 3 **Northup** | Y | Y | N | N | Y | Y |
| 4 **Davis** | Y | Y | N | N | Y | N |
| 5 **Rogers** | Y | Y | N | N | Y | N |
| 6 Chandler | Y | Y | Y | Y | N | Y |
| **LOUISIANA** | | | | | | |
| 1 **Jindal** | Y | Y | N | N | Y | N |
| 2 Jefferson | Y | Y | Y | Y | N | Y |
| 3 Melancon | Y | Y | Y | Y | N | Y |
| 4 **McCrery** | Y | Y | N | N | Y | N |
| 5 **Alexander** | Y | Y | N | N | Y | N |
| 6 **Baker** | Y | Y | N | N | Y | N |
| 7 **Boustany** | Y | Y | N | N | Y | N |
| **MAINE** | | | | | | |
| 1 Allen | Y | Y | N | Y | N | Y |
| 2 Michaud | Y | Y | Y | Y | N | Y |
| **MARYLAND** | | | | | | |
| 1 **Gilchrest** | Y | Y | N | N | Y | Y |
| 2 Ruppersberger | Y | Y | Y | Y | N | Y |
| 3 Cardin | Y | Y | Y | Y | N | Y |
| 4 Wynn | Y | Y | Y | Y | N | Y |
| 5 Hoyer | Y | Y | Y | Y | N | Y |
| 6 **Bartlett** | Y | Y | N | N | Y | N |
| 7 Cummings | Y | Y | Y | Y | N | Y |
| 8 Van Hollen | Y | Y | Y | Y | N | Y |
| **MASSACHUSETTS** | | | | | | |
| 1 Olver | Y | Y | Y | Y | N | Y |
| 2 Neal | Y | ? | Y | Y | N | Y |
| 3 McGovern | Y | Y | Y | Y | N | Y |
| 4 Frank | Y | Y | Y | Y | N | Y |
| 5 Meehan | Y | Y | Y | Y | N | Y |
| 6 Tierney | Y | Y | Y | Y | N | Y |
| 7 Markey | Y | Y | Y | Y | N | Y |
| 8 Capuano | Y | Y | Y | Y | N | Y |
| 9 Lynch | Y | Y | Y | Y | N | ? |
| 10 Delahunt | Y | Y | Y | Y | N | Y |
| **MICHIGAN** | | | | | | |
| 1 Stupak | Y | Y | Y | Y | N | Y |
| 2 **Hoekstra** | Y | Y | N | N | Y | N |
| 3 **Ehlers** | Y | Y | N | N | Y | Y |
| 4 **Camp** | Y | Y | N | N | Y | N |
| 5 Kildee | Y | Y | Y | Y | N | Y |
| 6 **Upton** | Y | Y | N | N | Y | Y |
| 7 **Schwarz** | Y | Y | N | N | Y | Y |
| 8 **Rogers** | Y | Y | N | N | Y | N |
| 9 **Knollenberg** | Y | Y | N | N | Y | Y |
| 10 **Miller** | Y | Y | N | N | Y | N |
| 11 **McCotter** | Y | Y | N | N | Y | Y |
| 12 Levin | Y | Y | Y | Y | N | Y |
| 13 Kilpatrick | Y | Y | Y | Y | N | Y |
| 14 Conyers | Y | Y | Y | Y | N | Y |
| 15 Dingell | Y | Y | Y | Y | N | Y |
| **MINNESOTA** | | | | | | |
| 1 **Gutknecht** | Y | Y | N | N | Y | N |
| 2 **Kline** | Y | Y | N | N | Y | N |
| 3 **Ramstad** | Y | Y | N | N | Y | Y |
| 4 McCollum | Y | Y | Y | Y | N | Y |
| 5 Sabo | Y | Y | Y | Y | N | Y |
| 6 **Kennedy** | Y | Y | N | N | Y | N |
| 7 Peterson | Y | Y | N | Y | Y | Y |
| 8 Oberstar | Y | Y | Y | Y | N | Y |
| **MISSISSIPPI** | | | | | | |
| 1 **Wicker** | Y | Y | N | N | Y | Y |
| 2 Thompson | Y | Y | Y | Y | N | Y |
| 3 **Pickering** | Y | Y | N | N | Y | N |
| 4 Taylor | Y | Y | Y | Y | Y | N |
| **MISSOURI** | | | | | | |
| 1 Clay | Y | Y | Y | Y | N | Y |
| 2 **Akin** | Y | Y | N | N | Y | N |
| 3 Carnahan | Y | Y | Y | Y | N | Y |
| 4 Skelton | Y | Y | Y | Y | N | Y |
| 5 Cleaver | Y | Y | Y | Y | N | Y |
| 6 **Graves** | Y | Y | N | N | ? | N |
| 7 **Blunt** | Y | Y | ? | ? | ? | ? |
| 8 **Emerson** | Y | Y | N | N | Y | Y |
| 9 **Hulshof** | Y | Y | N | N | Y | Y |
| **MONTANA** | | | | | | |
| AL **Rehberg** | Y | Y | N | N | Y | N |
| **NEBRASKA** | | | | | | |
| 1 **Fortenberry** | Y | Y | N | N | Y | N |
| 2 **Terry** | Y | Y | N | N | N | N |
| 3 **Osborne** | Y | Y | N | N | Y | Y |
| **NEVADA** | | | | | | |
| 1 Berkley | Y | Y | Y | Y | N | Y |
| 2 **Gibbons** | Y | Y | N | N | Y | N |
| 3 **Porter** | Y | Y | N | N | Y | N |
| **NEW HAMPSHIRE** | | | | | | |
| 1 **Bradley** | Y | Y | N | N | Y | N |
| 2 **Bass** | Y | Y | N | N | Y | N |
| **NEW JERSEY** | | | | | | |
| 1 Andrews | Y | Y | N | Y | N | Y |
| 2 **LoBiondo** | Y | Y | N | N | Y | Y |
| 3 **Saxton** | Y | Y | N | N | Y | Y |
| 4 **Smith** | Y | Y | N | N | Y | ? |
| 5 **Garrett** | Y | ? | N | N | Y | N |
| 6 Pallone | Y | Y | Y | Y | N | Y |
| 7 **Ferguson** | Y | Y | N | N | Y | Y |
| 8 Pascrell | Y | Y | Y | Y | N | Y |
| 9 Rothman | Y | Y | Y | Y | N | Y |
| 10 Payne | ? | ? | Y | Y | N | Y |
| 11 **Frelinghuysen** | Y | Y | N | N | Y | N |
| 12 Holt | Y | Y | Y | Y | N | Y |
| 13 Menendez | Y | Y | Y | Y | N | Y |
| **NEW MEXICO** | | | | | | |
| 1 **Wilson** | Y | Y | N | N | Y | Y |
| 2 **Pearce** | Y | Y | N | N | Y | N |
| 3 Udall | Y | Y | Y | Y | N | Y |
| **NEW YORK** | | | | | | |
| 1 Bishop | Y | Y | Y | Y | N | Y |
| 2 Israel | Y | Y | Y | Y | N | Y |
| 3 **King** | Y | Y | N | N | N | Y |
| 4 McCarthy | Y | Y | Y | Y | N | Y |
| 5 Ackerman | Y | Y | Y | Y | N | Y |
| 6 Meeks | Y | Y | ? | Y | N | Y |
| 7 Crowley | Y | Y | Y | Y | N | Y |
| 8 Nadler | Y | Y | N | Y | N | Y |
| 9 Weiner | Y | Y | Y | Y | N | Y |
| 10 Towns | Y | Y | Y | Y | N | Y |
| 11 Owens | Y | Y | Y | Y | N | Y |
| 12 Velázquez | Y | Y | Y | Y | N | ? |
| 13 **Fossella** | Y | Y | N | N | Y | Y |
| 14 Maloney | Y | Y | Y | Y | N | Y |
| 15 Rangel | Y | Y | Y | Y | N | Y |
| 16 Serrano | Y | Y | Y | Y | N | Y |
| 17 Engel | Y | Y | Y | Y | N | Y |
| 18 Lowey | Y | Y | Y | Y | N | Y |
| 19 **Kelly** | Y | Y | N | N | Y | N |
| 20 **Sweeney** | Y | Y | N | N | Y | Y |
| 21 McNulty | Y | Y | Y | Y | N | Y |
| 22 Hinchey | Y | Y | Y | Y | N | Y |
| 23 **McHugh** | Y | Y | N | N | Y | Y |
| 24 **Boehlert** | Y | Y | N | N | Y | Y |
| 25 **Walsh** | Y | Y | N | N | Y | N |
| 26 **Reynolds** | Y | Y | N | N | Y | Y |
| 27 Higgins | Y | Y | Y | Y | N | Y |
| 28 Slaughter | Y | Y | Y | Y | N | Y |
| 29 **Kuhl** | Y | Y | N | N | Y | Y |
| **NORTH CAROLINA** | | | | | | |
| 1 Butterfield | Y | Y | Y | Y | N | Y |
| 2 Etheridge | Y | Y | Y | Y | N | Y |
| 3 **Jones** | Y | Y | N | N | Y | N |
| 4 Price | Y | Y | Y | Y | N | Y |
| 5 **Foxx** | Y | Y | N | N | Y | N |
| 6 **Coble** | Y | Y | N | N | Y | N |
| 7 McIntyre | Y | Y | Y | Y | N | Y |
| 8 **Hayes** | Y | Y | N | N | Y | N |
| 9 **Myrick** | Y | Y | N | N | Y | N |
| 10 **McHenry** | Y | Y | N | N | Y | N |
| 11 **Taylor** | Y | Y | N | N | Y | N |
| 12 Watt | Y | Y | Y | Y | N | Y |
| 13 Miller | Y | Y | Y | Y | N | Y |
| **NORTH DAKOTA** | | | | | | |
| AL Pomeroy | Y | Y | Y | Y | N | Y |
| **OHIO** | | | | | | |
| 1 **Chabot** | Y | Y | N | N | Y | N |
| 2 **Schmidt** | Y | Y | N | N | Y | N |
| 3 **Turner** | Y | Y | N | N | Y | Y |
| 4 **Oxley** | Y | Y | N | N | Y | N |
| 5 **Gillmor** | Y | Y | N | N | Y | Y |
| 6 Strickland | Y | Y | Y | Y | N | Y |
| 7 **Hobson** | Y | Y | N | N | Y | Y |
| 8 **Boehner** | Y | Y | N | N | Y | N |
| 9 Kaptur | Y | Y | Y | Y | N | Y |
| 10 Kucinich | Y | Y | N | Y | N | Y |
| 11 Jones | Y | Y | N | Y | N | Y |
| 12 **Tiberi** | Y | Y | N | N | Y | N |
| 13 Brown | Y | Y | Y | Y | N | Y |
| 14 **LaTourette** | Y | Y | N | N | Y | Y |
| 15 **Pryce** | Y | Y | N | N | Y | Y |
| 16 **Regula** | Y | Y | N | N | Y | Y |
| 17 Ryan | Y | Y | Y | Y | N | Y |
| 18 **Ney** | Y | Y | N | N | Y | Y |
| **OKLAHOMA** | | | | | | |
| 1 **Sullivan** | Y | Y | N | N | Y | N |
| 2 Boren | Y | Y | Y | Y | Y | Y |
| 3 **Lucas** | Y | Y | N | N | Y | N |
| 4 **Cole** | Y | Y | N | N | Y | N |
| 5 **Istook** | Y | Y | N | N | Y | N |
| **OREGON** | | | | | | |
| 1 Wu | Y | Y | Y | Y | N | Y |
| 2 **Walden** | Y | Y | N | N | Y | N |
| 3 Blumenauer | Y | Y | Y | Y | N | Y |
| 4 DeFazio | Y | Y | Y | Y | N | Y |
| 5 Hooley | Y | Y | Y | Y | N | Y |
| **PENNSYLVANIA** | | | | | | |
| 1 Brady | Y | Y | Y | Y | N | Y |
| 2 Fattah | Y | Y | Y | Y | N | Y |
| 3 **English** | Y | Y | N | N | Y | Y |
| 4 **Hart** | Y | Y | N | N | Y | N |
| 5 **Peterson** | Y | Y | N | N | Y | N |
| 6 **Gerlach** | Y | Y | N | N | Y | Y |
| 7 **Weldon** | Y | Y | N | N | Y | Y |
| 8 **Fitzpatrick** | Y | Y | N | N | N | Y |
| 9 **Shuster** | Y | Y | N | N | Y | N |
| 10 **Sherwood** | Y | Y | N | N | Y | Y |
| 11 Kanjorski | Y | Y | Y | Y | N | Y |
| 12 Murtha | Y | Y | Y | Y | N | Y |
| 13 Schwartz | Y | Y | Y | Y | N | Y |
| 14 Doyle | Y | Y | Y | Y | N | Y |
| 15 **Dent** | Y | Y | N | N | Y | Y |
| 16 **Pitts** | Y | Y | N | N | Y | N |
| 17 Holden | Y | Y | Y | Y | Y | Y |
| 18 **Murphy** | Y | Y | N | N | Y | N |
| 19 **Platts** | Y | Y | N | N | Y | Y |
| **RHODE ISLAND** | | | | | | |
| 1 Kennedy | Y | Y | Y | Y | N | Y |
| 2 Langevin | Y | Y | Y | Y | N | Y |
| **SOUTH CAROLINA** | | | | | | |
| 1 **Brown** | Y | Y | N | N | Y | N |
| 2 **Wilson** | Y | Y | N | N | Y | N |
| 3 **Barrett** | Y | Y | N | N | Y | N |
| 4 **Inglis** | Y | Y | N | N | Y | N |
| 5 Spratt | Y | Y | Y | Y | N | Y |
| 6 Clyburn | Y | Y | ? | ? | ? | ? |
| **SOUTH DAKOTA** | | | | | | |
| AL Herseth | Y | Y | Y | Y | N | Y |
| **TENNESSEE** | | | | | | |
| 1 **Jenkins** | Y | Y | N | N | Y | N |
| 2 **Duncan** | Y | Y | N | N | Y | N |
| 3 **Wamp** | Y | Y | N | N | Y | N |
| 4 Davis | Y | Y | Y | Y | Y | Y |
| 5 Cooper | Y | Y | Y | Y | N | Y |
| 6 Gordon | Y | Y | Y | Y | Y | Y |
| 7 **Blackburn** | Y | Y | N | N | Y | N |
| 8 Tanner | Y | Y | Y | Y | Y | Y |
| 9 Ford | Y | Y | Y | Y | N | ? |
| **TEXAS** | | | | | | |
| 1 **Gohmert** | ? | ? | N | N | Y | N |
| 2 **Poe** | Y | Y | N | N | Y | N |
| 3 **Johnson, S.** | Y | Y | N | N | Y | N |
| 4 **Hall** | ? | ? | ? | ? | ? | ? |
| 5 **Hensarling** | Y | Y | N | N | Y | N |
| 6 **Barton** | Y | Y | N | N | Y | N |
| 7 **Culberson** | Y | ? | N | N | Y | N |
| 8 **Brady** | Y | Y | N | N | Y | N |
| 9 Green, A. | Y | Y | Y | Y | N | Y |
| 10 **McCaul** | Y | Y | N | N | Y | N |
| 11 **Conaway** | Y | Y | N | N | Y | Y |
| 12 **Granger** | Y | Y | N | N | Y | ? |
| 13 **Thornberry** | Y | Y | N | N | Y | N |
| 14 **Paul** | Y | Y | N | N | Y | N |
| 15 Hinojosa | Y | Y | Y | Y | N | Y |
| 16 Reyes | ? | ? | ? | ? | ? | ? |
| 17 Edwards | Y | Y | Y | Y | Y | Y |
| 18 Jackson-Lee | Y | Y | Y | Y | N | Y |
| 19 **Neugebauer** | Y | Y | N | N | Y | N |
| 20 Gonzalez | Y | Y | Y | Y | N | Y |
| 21 **Smith** | Y | Y | N | N | Y | N |
| 22 **DeLay** | Y | Y | N | N | Y | N |
| 23 **Bonilla** | Y | Y | N | N | Y | N |
| 24 **Marchant** | Y | Y | ? | N | Y | N |
| 25 Doggett | Y | Y | N | Y | N | Y |
| 26 **Burgess** | Y | Y | N | N | Y | N |
| 27 Ortiz | Y | Y | Y | Y | N | Y |
| 28 Cuellar | Y | Y | Y | Y | Y | Y |
| 29 Green, G. | Y | Y | Y | Y | N | Y |
| 30 Johnson, E. | Y | Y | Y | Y | N | Y |
| 31 **Carter** | Y | Y | N | N | Y | N |
| 32 **Sessions** | Y | Y | N | N | Y | N |
| **UTAH** | | | | | | |
| 1 **Bishop** | Y | Y | N | N | Y | N |
| 2 Matheson | Y | Y | Y | Y | Y | Y |
| 3 **Cannon** | Y | Y | N | N | Y | N |
| **VERMONT** | | | | | | |
| AL *Sanders* | Y | Y | Y | Y | N | Y |
| **VIRGINIA** | | | | | | |
| 1 **Davis, J.** | Y | Y | N | N | Y | N |
| 2 **Drake** | Y | Y | N | N | Y | N |
| 3 Scott | Y | Y | Y | Y | N | Y |
| 4 **Forbes** | Y | Y | N | N | Y | N |
| 5 **Goode** | Y | Y | N | N | Y | N |
| 6 **Goodlatte** | Y | Y | N | N | Y | N |
| 7 **Cantor** | Y | Y | N | N | Y | N |
| 8 Moran | Y | Y | Y | Y | N | Y |
| 9 Boucher | Y | Y | Y | Y | N | Y |
| 10 **Wolf** | Y | Y | N | N | Y | Y |
| 11 **Davis, T.** | Y | Y | N | N | Y | Y |
| **WASHINGTON** | | | | | | |
| 1 Inslee | Y | Y | Y | Y | N | Y |
| 2 Larsen | Y | Y | Y | Y | N | Y |
| 3 Baird | Y | Y | Y | Y | N | Y |
| 4 **Hastings** | Y | Y | N | N | Y | N |
| 5 **McMorris** | Y | Y | N | N | Y | N |
| 6 Dicks | Y | ? | Y | Y | N | Y |
| 7 McDermott | Y | Y | Y | Y | N | Y |
| 8 **Reichert** | Y | Y | N | N | Y | Y |
| 9 Smith | Y | Y | Y | Y | N | Y |
| **WEST VIRGINIA** | | | | | | |
| 1 Mollohan | Y | Y | Y | Y | N | Y |
| 2 **Capito** | Y | Y | N | N | Y | Y |
| 3 Rahall | Y | Y | Y | Y | N | Y |
| **WISCONSIN** | | | | | | |
| 1 **Ryan** | Y | Y | N | N | Y | Y |
| 2 Baldwin | Y | Y | Y | Y | N | Y |
| 3 Kind | Y | Y | Y | Y | N | Y |
| 4 Moore | Y | Y | Y | Y | N | Y |
| 5 **Sensenbrenner** | ? | ? | ? | ? | ? | ? |
| 6 **Petri** | Y | Y | N | N | Y | N |
| 7 Obey | ? | ? | ? | ? | ? | ? |
| 8 **Green** | Y | Y | N | N | Y | N |
| **WYOMING** | | | | | | |
| AL **Cubin** | Y | Y | N | N | Y | N |

# IN THE HOUSE | By Vote Number

**555.** **HR 2744. Fiscal 2006 Agriculture Appropriations/Conference Report.** Adoption of the conference report on the bill that would appropriate $101 billion in fiscal 2006 for the Department of Agriculture, the Food and Drug Administration (FDA) and related agencies. The bill would provide $40.7 billion for the food stamp program, $12.7 billion for child nutrition, $25.7 billion for the Commodity Credit Corporation, $5.3 billion for the Women, Infants and Children program and $1.5 billion for the FDA. Adopted (thus sent to the Senate) 318-63: R 163-41; D 154-22 (ND 114-18, SD 40-4); I 1-0. Oct. 28, 2005.

**556.** **H Res 523. Condemnation Against Iran President/Adoption.** Adoption of the resolution that would condemn Iranian President Mahmoud Ahmadinejad's threats against Israel and nations that support Israel. Adopted 383-0: R 204-0; D 178-0 (ND 135-0, SD 43-0); I 1-0. Oct. 28, 2005.

**557.** **HR 3548. Heinz Ahlmeyer Jr. Post Office/Passage.** Gutknecht, R-Minn, motion to suspend the rules and pass the bill that would designate a post office in Pearl River, N.Y., for Heinz Ahlmeyer Jr., who was killed in action in Vietnam. Motion agreed to 390-0: R 214-0; D 175-0 (ND 131-0, SD 44-0); I 1-0. A two-thirds majority of those present and voting (260 in this case) is required for passage under suspension of the rules. Nov. 1, 2005.

**558.** **HR 3989. Albert Harold Quie Post Office/Passage.** Gutknecht, R-Minn, motion to suspend the rules and pass the bill that would designate a post office in Dennison, Minn., for Albert Harold Quie, R-Minn. (1958-79), who served 10 full terms in the House and one term as governor. Motion agreed to 391-1: R 213-0; D 177-1 (ND 132-1, SD 45-0); I 1-0. A two-thirds majority of those present and voting (262 in this case) is required for passage under suspension of the rules. Nov. 1, 2005.

**559.** **HR 1606. Online Freedom of Speech/Passage.** Miller, R-Mich., motion to suspend the rules and pass the bill that would exempt the Internet, including blogs and e-mail, from being considered a form of public communication subject to Federal Election Commission regulation and disclosure requirements. Motion rejected 225-182: R 179-38; D 46-143 (ND 34-108, SD 12-35); I 0-1. A two-thirds majority of those present and voting (272 in this case) is required for passage under suspension of the rules. Nov. 2, 2005.

**560.** **HR 4061. Veterans' Affairs Information Technology/Passage.** Buyer, R-Ind., motion to suspend the rules and pass the bill that would reorganize the information technology (IT) division of the Department of Veterans Affairs (VA) and give the VA chief information officer authority over all IT resources, budget and personnel. Motion agreed to 408-0: R 218-0; D 189-0 (ND 142-0, SD 47-0); I 1-0. A two-thirds majority of those present and voting (272 in this case) is required for passage under suspension of the rules. Nov. 2, 2005.

**561.** **HR 1691. John H. Bradley Outpatient Clinic/Passage.** Buyer, R-Ind., motion to suspend the rules and pass the bill that would designate a Veterans Affairs Department outpatient clinic in Appleton, Wis., for John H. Bradley, one of six Marines who raised a U.S. flag on the top of Mt. Suribachi at Iwo Jima. Motion agreed to 407-0: R 218-0; D 188-0 (ND 141-0, SD 47-0); I 1-0. A two-thirds majority of those present and voting (272 in this case) is required for passage under suspension of the rules. Nov. 2, 2005.

| | 555 | 556 | 557 | 558 | 559 | 560 | 561 |
|---|---|---|---|---|---|---|---|
| **ALABAMA** | | | | | | | |
| 1 Bonner | Y | Y | Y | Y | Y | Y | Y |
| 2 Everett | Y | Y | Y | Y | Y | Y | Y |
| 3 Rogers | Y | Y | Y | Y | Y | Y | Y |
| 4 Aderholt | Y | Y | Y | Y | Y | Y | Y |
| 5 Cramer | Y | Y | Y | Y | Y | Y | Y |
| 6 Bachus | Y | Y | Y | Y | Y | Y | Y |
| 7 Davis | Y | Y | Y | Y | N | Y | Y |
| **ALASKA** | | | | | | | |
| AL Young | Y | Y | Y | Y | ? | ? | ? |
| **ARIZONA** | | | | | | | |
| 1 Renzi | Y | Y | Y | Y | Y | Y | Y |
| 2 Franks | N | Y | Y | Y | Y | Y | Y |
| 3 Shadegg | ? | ? | Y | Y | Y | Y | Y |
| 4 Pastor | Y | Y | Y | Y | N | Y | Y |
| 5 Hayworth | N | Y | Y | Y | Y | Y | Y |
| 6 Flake | N | Y | Y | Y | Y | Y | Y |
| 7 Grijalva | Y | Y | Y | Y | N | Y | Y |
| 8 Kolbe | Y | Y | Y | Y | Y | Y | Y |
| **ARKANSAS** | | | | | | | |
| 1 Berry | Y | Y | Y | Y | N | Y | Y |
| 2 Snyder | Y | Y | Y | Y | N | Y | Y |
| 3 Boozman | Y | Y | Y | Y | Y | Y | Y |
| 4 Ross | Y | Y | Y | Y | Y | Y | Y |
| **CALIFORNIA** | | | | | | | |
| 1 Thompson | Y | Y | Y | Y | Y | Y | Y |
| 2 Herger | Y | Y | Y | Y | Y | Y | Y |
| 3 Lungren | Y | Y | Y | Y | Y | Y | Y |
| 4 Doolittle | Y | Y | Y | Y | Y | Y | Y |
| 5 Matsui, D. | Y | Y | Y | Y | N | Y | Y |
| 6 Woolsey | Y | Y | Y | Y | Y | Y | Y |
| 7 Miller, George | Y | Y | Y | Y | N | Y | Y |
| 8 Pelosi | ? | ? | Y | Y | N | Y | Y |
| 9 Lee | N | Y | Y | Y | Y | Y | Y |
| 10 Tauscher | ? | ? | Y | Y | N | Y | Y |
| 11 Pombo | Y | Y | + | + | + | + | + |
| 12 Lantos | Y | Y | Y | Y | Y | Y | Y |
| 13 Stark | ? | Y | Y | Y | ? | ? | ? |
| 14 Eshoo | + | + | Y | Y | Y | Y | Y |
| 15 Honda | N | Y | Y | Y | Y | Y | Y |
| 16 Lofgren | Y | Y | Y | Y | Y | Y | Y |
| 17 Farr | Y | Y | Y | Y | N | Y | Y |
| 18 Cardoza | Y | Y | Y | Y | Y | Y | Y |
| 19 Radanovich | Y | Y | Y | Y | ? | ? | ? |
| 20 Costa | Y | Y | Y | Y | Y | Y | Y |
| 21 Nunes | + | + | Y | Y | Y | Y | Y |
| 22 Thomas | Y | Y | Y | Y | Y | Y | Y |
| 23 Capps | Y | Y | Y | Y | N | Y | Y |
| 24 Gallegly | + | + | + | + | N | Y | Y |
| 25 McKeon | ? | ? | Y | Y | Y | Y | Y |
| 26 Dreier | Y | Y | Y | Y | Y | Y | Y |
| 27 Sherman | Y | Y | Y | Y | N | Y | Y |
| 28 Berman | ? | Y | ? | Y | Y | Y | Y |
| 29 Schiff | Y | Y | Y | Y | N | Y | Y |
| 30 Waxman | Y | Y | Y | Y | N | Y | Y |
| 31 Becerra | + | + | Y | Y | N | Y | Y |
| 32 Solis | Y | Y | Y | Y | N | Y | Y |
| 33 Watson | Y | Y | Y | Y | N | Y | Y |
| 34 Roybal-Allard | ? | ? | ? | ? | ? | ? | ? |
| 35 Waters | Y | Y | Y | Y | Y | Y | Y |
| 36 Harman | Y | Y | Y | Y | ? | ? | ? |
| 37 Millender-McD. | Y | Y | Y | Y | N | Y | Y |
| 38 Napolitano | ? | ? | Y | Y | N | Y | Y |
| 39 Sánchez, Linda | Y | Y | Y | Y | N | Y | Y |
| 40 Royce | N | Y | Y | Y | Y | Y | Y |
| 41 Lewis | Y | Y | Y | Y | Y | Y | Y |
| 42 Miller, Gary | ? | ? | ? | ? | Y | Y | Y |
| 43 Baca | Y | Y | Y | Y | Y | Y | Y |
| 44 Calvert | ? | ? | Y | Y | Y | Y | Y |
| 45 Bono | N | Y | Y | Y | Y | Y | Y |
| 46 Rohrabacher | N | Y | ? | ? | Y | Y | Y |
| 47 Sanchez, Loretta | Y | Y | Y | Y | Y | Y | Y |
| 48 Vacant | | | | | | | |
| 49 Issa | Y | Y | Y | Y | Y | Y | Y |

| | 555 | 556 | 557 | 558 | 559 | 560 | 561 |
|---|---|---|---|---|---|---|---|
| 50 Cunningham | Y | Y | Y | Y | Y | Y | Y |
| 51 Filner | Y | Y | Y | Y | N | Y | Y |
| 52 Hunter | Y | Y | Y | Y | Y | Y | Y |
| 53 Davis | Y | Y | Y | Y | N | Y | Y |
| **COLORADO** | | | | | | | |
| 1 DeGette | Y | Y | Y | Y | N | Y | Y |
| 2 Udall | Y | Y | + | + | Y | Y | Y |
| 3 Salazar | Y | Y | Y | Y | Y | Y | Y |
| 4 Musgrave | Y | Y | Y | Y | Y | Y | Y |
| 5 Hefley | N | Y | Y | Y | N | Y | Y |
| 6 Tancredo | N | Y | Y | Y | Y | Y | Y |
| 7 Beauprez | Y | Y | Y | Y | Y | Y | Y |
| **CONNECTICUT** | | | | | | | |
| 1 Larson | Y | Y | Y | Y | N | Y | Y |
| 2 Simmons | N | Y | Y | Y | N | Y | Y |
| 3 DeLauro | Y | Y | Y | Y | N | Y | Y |
| 4 Shays | N | Y | ? | ? | N | Y | Y |
| 5 Johnson | Y | Y | Y | Y | N | Y | Y |
| **DELAWARE** | | | | | | | |
| AL Castle | Y | Y | Y | Y | N | Y | Y |
| **FLORIDA** | | | | | | | |
| 1 Miller | Y | Y | Y | Y | + | – | + |
| 2 Boyd | Y | Y | Y | Y | N | Y | Y |
| 3 Brown | Y | Y | ? | ? | N | Y | Y |
| 4 Crenshaw | Y | Y | Y | Y | Y | Y | Y |
| 5 Brown-Waite | ? | ? | ? | ? | Y | ? | ? |
| 6 Stearns | N | Y | Y | Y | Y | Y | Y |
| 7 Mica | Y | Y | Y | Y | Y | Y | Y |
| 8 Keller | Y | Y | Y | Y | Y | Y | Y |
| 9 Bilirakis | N | Y | Y | Y | Y | Y | Y |
| 10 Young | Y | Y | Y | Y | Y | Y | Y |
| 11 Davis | ? | ? | ? | ? | N | Y | Y |
| 12 Putnam | Y | Y | Y | Y | Y | Y | Y |
| 13 Harris | ? | Y | ? | ? | Y | Y | Y |
| 14 Mack | Y | Y | Y | Y | Y | Y | Y |
| 15 Weldon | Y | Y | Y | Y | Y | Y | Y |
| 16 Foley | ? | ? | Y | Y | Y | Y | Y |
| 17 Meek | ? | Y | Y | Y | N | Y | Y |
| 18 Ros-Lehtinen | Y | Y | Y | Y | Y | Y | Y |
| 19 Wexler | N | Y | Y | Y | N | Y | Y |
| 20 Wasserman-Schultz | Y | Y | Y | Y | N | Y | Y |
| 21 Diaz-Balart, L. | ? | ? | Y | Y | Y | Y | Y |
| 22 Shaw | ? | ? | Y | Y | Y | Y | Y |
| 23 Hastings | Y | Y | ? | ? | ? | ? | ? |
| 24 Feeney | N | Y | Y | Y | Y | Y | Y |
| 25 Diaz-Balart, M. | ? | ? | Y | Y | Y | Y | Y |
| **GEORGIA** | | | | | | | |
| 1 Kingston | ? | ? | Y | Y | Y | Y | Y |
| 2 Bishop | Y | Y | Y | Y | Y | Y | Y |
| 3 Marshall | Y | Y | Y | Y | ? | ? | ? |
| 4 McKinney | Y | ? | Y | Y | Y | Y | Y |
| 5 Lewis | N | Y | Y | Y | N | Y | Y |
| 6 Price | N | Y | Y | Y | Y | Y | Y |
| 7 Linder | + | + | Y | Y | Y | Y | Y |
| 8 Westmoreland | ? | ? | Y | Y | Y | Y | Y |
| 9 Norwood | Y | Y | ? | ? | ? | ? | ? |
| 10 Deal | Y | Y | Y | Y | Y | Y | Y |
| 11 Gingrey | Y | Y | Y | Y | Y | Y | Y |
| 12 Barrow | Y | Y | Y | Y | Y | Y | Y |
| 13 Scott | Y | Y | Y | Y | Y | Y | Y |
| **HAWAII** | | | | | | | |
| 1 Abercrombie | Y | Y | Y | N | N | Y | Y |
| 2 Case | Y | Y | Y | N | N | Y | Y |
| **IDAHO** | | | | | | | |
| 1 Otter | N | Y | Y | Y | Y | Y | Y |
| 2 Simpson | Y | Y | Y | Y | Y | Y | Y |
| **ILLINOIS** | | | | | | | |
| 1 Rush | Y | Y | ? | ? | N | Y | Y |
| 2 Jackson | Y | Y | ? | Y | N | Y | Y |
| 3 Lipinski | Y | Y | Y | Y | N | Y | Y |
| 4 Gutierrez | + | + | + | + | N | Y | Y |
| 5 Emanuel | Y | Y | Y | Y | N | Y | Y |
| 6 Hyde | Y | Y | + | + | – | + | + |
| 7 Davis | Y | Y | Y | Y | N | Y | Y |
| 8 Bean | N | Y | Y | Y | N | Y | Y |
| 9 Schakowsky | N | Y | Y | Y | N | Y | Y |
| 10 Kirk | N | Y | Y | Y | N | Y | Y |
| 11 Weller | Y | Y | Y | Y | Y | Y | Y |
| 12 Costello | Y | Y | ? | ? | N | Y | Y |

**KEY**    Republicans    Democrats    *Independents*

| | | | |
|---|---|---|---|
| **Y** Voted for (yea) | **X** Paired against | **C** Voted "present" to avoid possible conflict of interest |
| **#** Paired for | **–** Announced against | |
| **+** Announced for | **P** Voted "present" | **?** Did not vote or otherwise make a position known |
| **N** Voted against (nay) | | |

ND Northern Democrats, SD Southern Democrats
Southern states: Ala., Ark., Fla., Ga., Ky., La., Miss., N.C., Okla., S.C., Tenn., Texas, Va.

| | 555 | 556 | 557 | 558 | 559 | 560 | 561 |
|---|---|---|---|---|---|---|---|
| 13 **Biggert** | N | Y | Y | Y | Y | Y | Y |
| 14 **Hastert** | | | | | | | |
| 15 **Johnson** | Y | Y | Y | Y | N | Y | Y |
| 16 **Manzullo** | Y | Y | Y | Y | Y | Y | Y |
| 17 Evans | Y | Y | Y | Y | N | Y | Y |
| 18 **LaHood** | Y | Y | Y | Y | N | Y | Y |
| 19 **Shimkus** | Y | Y | Y | Y | Y | Y | Y |
| **INDIANA** | | | | | | | |
| 1 Visclosky | Y | Y | Y | Y | N | Y | Y |
| 2 **Chocola** | N | Y | Y | Y | Y | Y | Y |
| 3 **Souder** | Y | Y | Y | Y | Y | Y | Y |
| 4 **Buyer** | Y | Y | Y | Y | Y | Y | Y |
| 5 **Burton** | Y | Y | Y | Y | Y | Y | Y |
| 6 **Pence** | N | Y | Y | Y | Y | Y | Y |
| 7 Carson | Y | Y | Y | Y | N | Y | Y |
| 8 **Hostettler** | N | Y | Y | Y | Y | Y | Y |
| 9 **Sodrel** | Y | Y | Y | Y | Y | Y | Y |
| **IOWA** | | | | | | | |
| 1 **Nussle** | Y | Y | Y | Y | Y | Y | Y |
| 2 **Leach** | Y | Y | Y | Y | N | Y | Y |
| 3 Boswell | ? | ? | ? | ? | ? | ? | ? |
| 4 **Latham** | Y | Y | Y | Y | Y | Y | Y |
| 5 **King** | Y | Y | Y | Y | Y | Y | Y |
| **KANSAS** | | | | | | | |
| 1 **Moran** | Y | Y | Y | Y | Y | Y | Y |
| 2 **Ryun** | Y | Y | Y | Y | Y | Y | Y |
| 3 Moore | Y | Y | Y | Y | N | Y | Y |
| 4 **Tiahrt** | + | + | Y | Y | Y | Y | Y |
| **KENTUCKY** | | | | | | | |
| 1 **Whitfield** | N | Y | Y | Y | Y | Y | Y |
| 2 **Lewis** | Y | Y | Y | Y | Y | Y | Y |
| 3 **Northup** | Y | Y | Y | Y | Y | Y | Y |
| 4 **Davis** | Y | Y | Y | Y | Y | Y | Y |
| 5 **Rogers** | Y | Y | Y | Y | Y | Y | Y |
| 6 Chandler | Y | Y | Y | Y | Y | Y | Y |
| **LOUISIANA** | | | | | | | |
| 1 **Jindal** | Y | Y | Y | Y | Y | Y | Y |
| 2 Jefferson | ? | ? | Y | Y | N | Y | Y |
| 3 Melancon | Y | Y | Y | Y | Y | Y | Y |
| 4 **McCrery** | Y | Y | Y | Y | Y | Y | Y |
| 5 **Alexander** | Y | Y | Y | Y | Y | Y | Y |
| 6 **Baker** | ? | ? | Y | Y | Y | Y | Y |
| 7 **Boustany** | Y | Y | Y | Y | Y | Y | Y |
| **MAINE** | | | | | | | |
| 1 Allen | Y | Y | Y | Y | N | Y | Y |
| 2 Michaud | Y | Y | Y | Y | N | Y | Y |
| **MARYLAND** | | | | | | | |
| 1 **Gilchrest** | Y | Y | Y | Y | N | Y | Y |
| 2 Ruppersberger | Y | Y | Y | Y | N | Y | Y |
| 3 Cardin | Y | Y | Y | Y | N | Y | Y |
| 4 Wynn | Y | Y | ? | ? | Y | Y | Y |
| 5 Hoyer | Y | Y | ? | ? | Y | Y | Y |
| 6 **Bartlett** | Y | Y | Y | Y | Y | Y | Y |
| 7 Cummings | Y | Y | ? | ? | N | Y | Y |
| 8 Van Hollen | Y | Y | Y | Y | N | Y | Y |
| **MASSACHUSETTS** | | | | | | | |
| 1 Olver | Y | Y | Y | Y | N | Y | Y |
| 2 Neal | Y | Y | Y | Y | N | Y | Y |
| 3 McGovern | Y | Y | Y | Y | N | Y | Y |
| 4 Frank | Y | Y | Y | Y | N | Y | Y |
| 5 Meehan | Y | Y | Y | Y | N | Y | Y |
| 6 Tierney | Y | Y | Y | Y | N | Y | Y |
| 7 Markey | Y | Y | Y | Y | N | Y | Y |
| 8 Capuano | N | Y | ? | ? | Y | Y | Y |
| 9 Lynch | ? | Y | Y | Y | N | Y | Y |
| 10 Delahunt | Y | Y | Y | Y | N | Y | Y |
| **MICHIGAN** | | | | | | | |
| 1 Stupak | Y | Y | Y | Y | N | Y | Y |
| 2 **Hoekstra** | Y | Y | Y | Y | Y | Y | Y |
| 3 **Ehlers** | Y | Y | Y | Y | Y | Y | Y |
| 4 **Camp** | Y | Y | Y | Y | Y | Y | Y |
| 5 Kildee | Y | Y | Y | Y | N | Y | Y |
| 6 **Upton** | Y | Y | Y | Y | N | Y | Y |
| 7 **Schwarz** | Y | Y | Y | Y | N | Y | Y |
| 8 **Rogers** | Y | Y | Y | Y | Y | Y | Y |
| 9 **Knollenberg** | Y | Y | Y | Y | Y | Y | Y |
| 10 **Miller** | Y | Y | Y | Y | Y | Y | Y |
| 11 **McCotter** | Y | Y | Y | Y | Y | Y | Y |
| 12 Levin | Y | Y | Y | Y | N | Y | Y |
| 13 Kilpatrick | Y | Y | Y | Y | N | Y | Y |
| 14 Conyers | N | Y | Y | Y | Y | Y | Y |
| 15 Dingell | Y | Y | ? | ? | N | Y | Y |

| | 555 | 556 | 557 | 558 | 559 | 560 | 561 |
|---|---|---|---|---|---|---|---|
| **MINNESOTA** | | | | | | | |
| 1 **Gutknecht** | Y | Y | Y | Y | Y | Y | Y |
| 2 **Kline** | Y | Y | Y | Y | Y | Y | Y |
| 3 **Ramstad** | N | Y | Y | Y | N | Y | Y |
| 4 McCollum | N | Y | ? | ? | ? | ? | ? |
| 5 Sabo | Y | Y | Y | Y | ? | ? | ? |
| 6 **Kennedy** | Y | Y | Y | Y | Y | Y | Y |
| 7 Peterson | Y | Y | Y | Y | Y | Y | Y |
| 8 Oberstar | Y | Y | Y | Y | N | Y | Y |
| **MISSISSIPPI** | | | | | | | |
| 1 **Wicker** | Y | ? | Y | Y | Y | Y | Y |
| 2 Thompson | Y | Y | ? | ? | N | Y | Y |
| 3 **Pickering** | Y | Y | Y | Y | Y | Y | Y |
| 4 Taylor | Y | Y | Y | Y | N | Y | Y |
| **MISSOURI** | | | | | | | |
| 1 Clay | Y | Y | Y | Y | Y | Y | Y |
| 2 **Akin** | Y | Y | Y | Y | Y | Y | Y |
| 3 Carnahan | Y | Y | Y | Y | N | Y | Y |
| 4 Skelton | Y | Y | Y | Y | N | Y | Y |
| 5 Cleaver | Y | Y | Y | Y | N | Y | Y |
| 6 **Graves** | Y | Y | Y | Y | Y | Y | Y |
| 7 **Blunt** | ? | ? | Y | Y | Y | Y | Y |
| 8 **Emerson** | Y | Y | Y | Y | N | Y | Y |
| 9 **Hulshof** | Y | Y | Y | Y | Y | Y | Y |
| **MONTANA** | | | | | | | |
| AL **Rehberg** | N | Y | Y | Y | Y | Y | Y |
| **NEBRASKA** | | | | | | | |
| 1 **Fortenberry** | Y | Y | Y | Y | Y | Y | Y |
| 2 **Terry** | Y | Y | ? | ? | Y | Y | Y |
| 3 **Osborne** | Y | Y | Y | Y | N | Y | Y |
| **NEVADA** | | | | | | | |
| 1 Berkley | Y | Y | Y | Y | N | Y | Y |
| 2 **Gibbons** | N | Y | Y | Y | Y | Y | Y |
| 3 **Porter** | Y | Y | Y | Y | Y | Y | Y |
| **NEW HAMPSHIRE** | | | | | | | |
| 1 **Bradley** | N | Y | Y | Y | N | Y | Y |
| 2 **Bass** | N | Y | Y | Y | N | Y | Y |
| **NEW JERSEY** | | | | | | | |
| 1 Andrews | N | Y | + | + | N | Y | Y |
| 2 **LoBiondo** | Y | Y | Y | Y | N | Y | Y |
| 3 **Saxton** | Y | Y | Y | Y | N | Y | Y |
| 4 **Smith** | Y | Y | Y | Y | N | Y | Y |
| 5 **Garrett** | N | Y | Y | Y | Y | Y | Y |
| 6 Pallone | Y | Y | Y | Y | N | Y | Y |
| 7 **Ferguson** | N | Y | Y | Y | Y | Y | Y |
| 8 Pascrell | Y | Y | Y | Y | N | Y | Y |
| 9 Rothman | Y | Y | Y | Y | N | Y | Y |
| 10 Payne | N | Y | Y | Y | N | Y | Y |
| 11 **Frelinghuysen** | Y | Y | Y | Y | N | Y | Y |
| 12 Holt | Y | Y | Y | Y | N | Y | Y |
| 13 Menendez | Y | Y | Y | Y | – | + | + |
| **NEW MEXICO** | | | | | | | |
| 1 **Wilson** | Y | Y | Y | Y | N | Y | Y |
| 2 **Pearce** | Y | Y | ? | ? | ? | ? | ? |
| 3 Udall | Y | Y | Y | Y | N | Y | Y |
| **NEW YORK** | | | | | | | |
| 1 Bishop | Y | Y | Y | Y | N | Y | Y |
| 2 Israel | N | Y | Y | Y | N | Y | Y |
| 3 **King** | Y | Y | Y | Y | ? | ? | ? |
| 4 McCarthy | Y | Y | Y | Y | N | Y | Y |
| 5 Ackerman | Y | Y | Y | Y | ? | ? | ? |
| 6 Meeks | Y | Y | Y | Y | N | Y | Y |
| 7 Crowley | Y | Y | Y | Y | N | Y | Y |
| 8 Nadler | N | Y | Y | Y | N | Y | Y |
| 9 Weiner | Y | Y | Y | Y | N | Y | Y |
| 10 Towns | ? | ? | Y | Y | N | Y | ? |
| 11 Owens | N | Y | Y | Y | N | Y | Y |
| 12 Velázquez | ? | ? | Y | Y | N | Y | Y |
| 13 **Fossella** | N | Y | Y | Y | Y | Y | Y |
| 14 Maloney | Y | Y | + | + | N | Y | Y |
| 15 Rangel | Y | Y | Y | Y | N | Y | Y |
| 16 Serrano | Y | Y | Y | Y | Y | Y | Y |
| 17 Engel | N | Y | Y | Y | N | Y | Y |
| 18 Lowey | Y | Y | Y | Y | N | Y | Y |
| 19 **Kelly** | Y | Y | Y | Y | Y | Y | Y |
| 20 **Sweeney** | N | Y | Y | Y | Y | Y | Y |
| 21 McNulty | Y | Y | Y | Y | N | Y | Y |
| 22 Hinchey | Y | Y | ? | Y | N | Y | Y |
| 23 **McHugh** | Y | Y | Y | Y | Y | Y | Y |
| 24 **Boehlert** | ? | ? | Y | Y | N | Y | Y |
| 25 **Walsh** | Y | Y | Y | Y | N | Y | Y |
| 26 **Reynolds** | Y | Y | Y | Y | Y | Y | Y |
| 27 Higgins | Y | Y | Y | Y | N | Y | Y |
| 28 Slaughter | ? | ? | Y | Y | N | Y | Y |
| 29 **Kuhl** | Y | Y | Y | Y | Y | Y | Y |

| | 555 | 556 | 557 | 558 | 559 | 560 | 561 |
|---|---|---|---|---|---|---|---|
| **NORTH CAROLINA** | | | | | | | |
| 1 Butterfield | Y | Y | Y | Y | N | Y | Y |
| 2 Etheridge | Y | Y | Y | Y | – | + | + |
| 3 **Jones** | – | + | Y | Y | Y | Y | Y |
| 4 Price | Y | Y | Y | Y | N | Y | Y |
| 5 **Foxx** | Y | Y | Y | Y | Y | Y | Y |
| 6 **Coble** | Y | Y | Y | Y | N | Y | Y |
| 7 McIntyre | Y | Y | Y | Y | N | Y | Y |
| 8 **Hayes** | Y | Y | Y | Y | Y | Y | Y |
| 9 **Myrick** | Y | Y | Y | Y | Y | Y | Y |
| 10 **McHenry** | Y | Y | Y | Y | Y | Y | Y |
| 11 **Taylor** | Y | Y | Y | Y | Y | Y | Y |
| 12 Watt | Y | Y | Y | Y | N | Y | Y |
| 13 Miller | Y | Y | Y | Y | N | Y | Y |
| **NORTH DAKOTA** | | | | | | | |
| AL Pomeroy | Y | Y | Y | Y | N | Y | Y |
| **OHIO** | | | | | | | |
| 1 **Chabot** | Y | Y | Y | Y | Y | Y | Y |
| 2 **Schmidt** | Y | Y | Y | Y | N | Y | Y |
| 3 **Turner** | Y | Y | Y | Y | N | Y | Y |
| 4 **Oxley** | Y | Y | + | + | ? | ? | ? |
| 5 **Gillmor** | Y | Y | Y | Y | N | Y | Y |
| 6 Strickland | Y | Y | Y | ? | Y | Y | Y |
| 7 **Hobson** | Y | Y | Y | Y | N | Y | Y |
| 8 **Boehner** | Y | Y | Y | Y | Y | Y | Y |
| 9 Kaptur | Y | Y | Y | Y | N | Y | Y |
| 10 Kucinich | N | Y | Y | Y | N | Y | Y |
| 11 Jones | Y | Y | Y | Y | N | Y | Y |
| 12 **Tiberi** | Y | Y | Y | Y | Y | Y | Y |
| 13 Brown | Y | Y | Y | Y | Y | Y | Y |
| 14 **LaTourette** | ? | Y | Y | Y | N | Y | Y |
| 15 **Pryce** | Y | Y | Y | Y | ? | Y | Y |
| 16 **Regula** | Y | Y | Y | Y | N | Y | Y |
| 17 Ryan | Y | Y | Y | Y | Y | Y | Y |
| 18 **Ney** | + | + | Y | Y | Y | Y | Y |
| **OKLAHOMA** | | | | | | | |
| 1 **Sullivan** | Y | Y | Y | Y | Y | Y | Y |
| 2 Boren | Y | Y | Y | Y | Y | Y | Y |
| 3 **Lucas** | Y | Y | Y | Y | Y | Y | Y |
| 4 **Cole** | Y | Y | Y | Y | Y | Y | Y |
| 5 **Istook** | Y | Y | ? | ? | Y | Y | Y |
| **OREGON** | | | | | | | |
| 1 Wu | ? | Y | Y | Y | N | Y | Y |
| 2 **Walden** | Y | Y | Y | Y | N | Y | Y |
| 3 Blumenauer | N | Y | Y | Y | Y | Y | Y |
| 4 DeFazio | N | Y | Y | Y | N | Y | Y |
| 5 Hooley | Y | Y | Y | Y | N | Y | Y |
| **PENNSYLVANIA** | | | | | | | |
| 1 Brady | Y | Y | Y | Y | ? | ? | ? |
| 2 Fattah | Y | Y | Y | Y | Y | Y | Y |
| 3 **English** | Y | Y | Y | Y | Y | Y | Y |
| 4 **Hart** | Y | Y | Y | Y | Y | Y | Y |
| 5 **Peterson** | Y | Y | Y | Y | Y | Y | Y |
| 6 **Gerlach** | Y | Y | Y | Y | Y | Y | Y |
| 7 **Weldon** | Y | Y | Y | Y | N | Y | Y |
| 8 **Fitzpatrick** | Y | Y | Y | Y | Y | Y | Y |
| 9 **Shuster** | Y | Y | Y | Y | Y | Y | Y |
| 10 **Sherwood** | Y | Y | Y | Y | Y | Y | Y |
| 11 Kanjorski | Y | Y | Y | Y | N | Y | Y |
| 12 Murtha | Y | Y | ? | ? | Y | Y | Y |
| 13 Schwartz | Y | Y | Y | Y | N | Y | Y |
| 14 Doyle | Y | Y | ? | ? | N | Y | Y |
| 15 **Dent** | Y | Y | Y | Y | Y | Y | Y |
| 16 **Pitts** | N | Y | Y | Y | Y | Y | Y |
| 17 Holden | Y | Y | Y | Y | N | Y | Y |
| 18 **Murphy** | Y | Y | Y | Y | Y | Y | Y |
| 19 **Platts** | Y | Y | Y | Y | N | Y | Y |
| **RHODE ISLAND** | | | | | | | |
| 1 Kennedy | Y | Y | Y | Y | Y | Y | Y |
| 2 Langevin | Y | Y | Y | Y | N | Y | Y |
| **SOUTH CAROLINA** | | | | | | | |
| 1 **Brown** | Y | Y | Y | Y | Y | Y | Y |
| 2 **Wilson** | Y | Y | Y | Y | Y | Y | Y |
| 3 **Barrett** | N | Y | Y | Y | Y | Y | Y |
| 4 **Inglis** | Y | Y | Y | Y | Y | Y | Y |
| 5 Spratt | Y | Y | ? | ? | N | Y | Y |
| 6 Clyburn | ? | ? | Y | Y | N | Y | Y |
| **SOUTH DAKOTA** | | | | | | | |
| AL Herseth | N | Y | ? | ? | Y | Y | Y |
| **TENNESSEE** | | | | | | | |
| 1 **Jenkins** | Y | Y | ? | ? | Y | Y | Y |
| 2 **Duncan** | N | Y | Y | Y | Y | Y | Y |

| | 555 | 556 | 557 | 558 | 559 | 560 | 561 |
|---|---|---|---|---|---|---|---|
| 3 **Wamp** | Y | Y | Y | Y | N | Y | Y |
| 4 Davis | Y | Y | ? | Y | Y | Y | Y |
| 5 Cooper | N | Y | Y | Y | N | Y | Y |
| 6 Gordon | Y | Y | Y | Y | N | Y | Y |
| 7 **Blackburn** | N | Y | Y | Y | Y | Y | Y |
| 8 Tanner | Y | Y | Y | Y | N | Y | Y |
| 9 Ford | ? | ? | ? | ? | N | Y | Y |
| **TEXAS** | | | | | | | |
| 1 **Gohmert** | Y | Y | Y | Y | Y | Y | Y |
| 2 **Poe** | Y | Y | Y | Y | Y | Y | Y |
| 3 **Johnson, S.** | Y | Y | Y | Y | Y | Y | Y |
| 4 **Hall** | Y | Y | ? | ? | ? | ? | ? |
| 5 **Hensarling** | N | Y | Y | Y | Y | Y | Y |
| 6 **Barton** | Y | Y | Y | Y | Y | Y | Y |
| 7 **Culberson** | Y | Y | Y | Y | Y | Y | Y |
| 8 **Brady** | Y | Y | Y | Y | Y | Y | Y |
| 9 Green, A. | Y | Y | Y | Y | N | Y | Y |
| 10 **McCaul** | Y | Y | Y | Y | Y | Y | Y |
| 11 **Conaway** | Y | Y | Y | Y | Y | Y | Y |
| 12 **Granger** | Y | Y | Y | Y | Y | Y | Y |
| 13 **Thornberry** | Y | Y | Y | Y | Y | Y | Y |
| 14 **Paul** | N | P | Y | Y | Y | Y | Y |
| 15 Hinojosa | Y | Y | Y | Y | N | Y | Y |
| 16 Reyes | ? | ? | Y | Y | ? | ? | ? |
| 17 Edwards | Y | Y | Y | Y | N | Y | Y |
| 18 Jackson-Lee | N | Y | Y | Y | N | Y | Y |
| 19 **Neugebauer** | Y | Y | Y | Y | Y | Y | Y |
| 20 Gonzalez | Y | Y | Y | Y | N | Y | Y |
| 21 **Smith** | ? | ? | Y | Y | Y | Y | Y |
| 22 **DeLay** | Y | Y | ? | ? | Y | Y | Y |
| 23 **Bonilla** | Y | Y | Y | Y | Y | Y | Y |
| 24 **Marchant** | N | Y | Y | Y | Y | Y | Y |
| 25 Doggett | Y | Y | Y | Y | N | Y | Y |
| 26 **Burgess** | Y | Y | Y | Y | Y | Y | Y |
| 27 Ortiz | + | + | Y | Y | N | Y | Y |
| 28 Cuellar | Y | Y | Y | Y | Y | Y | Y |
| 29 Green, G. | Y | Y | Y | Y | N | Y | Y |
| 30 Johnson, E. | Y | Y | Y | Y | N | Y | Y |
| 31 **Carter** | Y | Y | Y | Y | Y | Y | Y |
| 32 **Sessions** | Y | Y | Y | Y | Y | Y | Y |
| **UTAH** | | | | | | | |
| 1 **Bishop** | Y | Y | Y | Y | Y | Y | Y |
| 2 Matheson | Y | Y | Y | Y | Y | Y | Y |
| 3 **Cannon** | Y | Y | Y | Y | Y | Y | Y |
| **VERMONT** | | | | | | | |
| AL *Sanders* | Y | Y | Y | Y | N | Y | Y |
| **VIRGINIA** | | | | | | | |
| 1 **Davis, J.** | + | + | Y | Y | Y | Y | Y |
| 2 **Drake** | ? | ? | Y | Y | Y | Y | Y |
| 3 Scott | Y | Y | Y | Y | N | Y | Y |
| 4 **Forbes** | Y | Y | Y | Y | Y | Y | Y |
| 5 **Goode** | Y | Y | Y | Y | Y | Y | Y |
| 6 **Goodlatte** | Y | Y | Y | Y | Y | Y | Y |
| 7 **Cantor** | Y | Y | Y | Y | Y | Y | Y |
| 8 Moran | Y | Y | Y | Y | N | Y | Y |
| 9 Boucher | Y | Y | Y | Y | Y | Y | Y |
| 10 **Wolf** | Y | Y | Y | Y | N | Y | Y |
| 11 **Davis, T.** | N | Y | Y | Y | Y | Y | Y |
| **WASHINGTON** | | | | | | | |
| 1 Inslee | N | Y | Y | Y | N | Y | Y |
| 2 Larsen | Y | Y | Y | Y | N | Y | Y |
| 3 Baird | Y | Y | Y | Y | N | Y | Y |
| 4 **Hastings** | Y | Y | Y | Y | Y | Y | Y |
| 5 **McMorris** | Y | Y | Y | Y | Y | Y | Y |
| 6 Dicks | Y | Y | Y | Y | N | Y | Y |
| 7 McDermott | – | + | Y | Y | N | Y | Y |
| 8 **Reichert** | Y | Y | Y | Y | Y | Y | Y |
| 9 Smith | Y | Y | Y | Y | Y | Y | Y |
| **WEST VIRGINIA** | | | | | | | |
| 1 Mollohan | Y | Y | Y | Y | N | Y | Y |
| 2 **Capito** | Y | Y | Y | Y | Y | Y | Y |
| 3 Rahall | Y | Y | Y | Y | Y | Y | Y |
| **WISCONSIN** | | | | | | | |
| 1 **Ryan** | N | Y | Y | Y | Y | Y | Y |
| 2 Baldwin | Y | Y | Y | Y | N | Y | Y |
| 3 Kind | ? | ? | Y | Y | Y | Y | Y |
| 4 Moore | Y | Y | Y | Y | N | Y | Y |
| 5 **Sensenbrenner** | ? | ? | Y | Y | Y | Y | Y |
| 6 **Petri** | N | Y | Y | Y | N | Y | Y |
| 7 Obey | ? | ? | Y | Y | N | Y | Y |
| 8 **Green** | N | Y | Y | Y | Y | Y | Y |
| **WYOMING** | | | | | | | |
| AL **Cubin** | Y | Y | ? | ? | ? | ? | ? |

# IN THE HOUSE | By Vote Number

**562.** **Iraq War Investigation/Appeal Ruling of the Chair.** Walsh, R-N.Y., motion to table (kill) the Pelosi, D-Calif., appeal of the ruling of the chair that the Pelosi resolution did not qualify as a question of privilege as it relates to the safety and efficiency of the House. The Pelosi resolution would ask the Republican leadership and the chairmen of the committees of jurisdiction to conduct an investigation into possible abuses in the Iraq War. Motion agreed to 220-191: R 219-0; D 1-190 (ND 0-144, SD 1-46); I 0-1. Nov. 3, 2005.

**563.** **HR 4128. Eminent Domain/Rule.** Adoption of the rule (H Res 527) that would provide for House floor consideration of the bill that would prohibit state and local governments that receive federal economic development funds from using eminent domain to seize land for economic development purposes. Adopted 401-11: R 219-0; D 181-11 (ND 135-10, SD 46-1); I 1-0. Nov. 3, 2005.

**564.** **HR 4128. Eminent Domain/Court Action.** Nadler, D-N.Y., amendment that would permit a property owner to go to court before any property is taken to challenge a government's use of eminent domain to seize their property. It would strike provisions that would prohibit state and local governments that violate the restrictions in the bill from receiving federal economic development funds for two fiscal years. Rejected 63-355: R 1-222; D 62-132 (ND 56-92, SD 6-40); I 0-1. Nov. 3, 2005.

**565.** **HR 4128. Eminent Domain/Economic Development Definition.** Moran, D-Va., amendment that would define economic development as the use of property for commercial for-profit enterprises, or where the primary purpose is to increase tax revenue or the tax base. Rejected 49-368: R 1-221; D 48-146 (ND 42-106, SD 6-40); I 0-1. Nov. 3, 2005.

**566.** **HR 4128. Eminent Domain/Harmful Uses of Land.** Turner, R-Ohio, amendment that would specify harmful uses of land that would constitute a threat to public health and safety. It would permit the use of eminent domain in such cases. Rejected 56-357: R 28-192; D 28-164 (ND 24-123, SD 4-41); I 0-1. Nov. 3, 2005.

**567.** **HR 4128. Eminent Domain/Sense of Congress.** Watt, D-N.C., amendment that would strike all sections of the bill and retain only a provision expressing the sense of Congress that recognizes the importance of property rights and states that the Supreme Court's decision in *Kelo v. City of New London* may lead to abuses of eminent domain power. Rejected 44-371: R 0-221; D 44-149 (ND 40-107, SD 4-42); I 0-1. Nov. 3, 2005.

**568.** **HR 4128. Eminent Domain/Passage.** Passage of the bill that would prohibit state and local governments that receive federal economic development funds from using eminent domain to seize land for economic development purposes. Any private property owner who suffers injury as a result of such actions by a state or local government would be able to bring a lawsuit against the government or seek a temporary restraining order or a preliminary injunction. State and local governments that violate the restrictions in the bill could be barred from receiving federal economic development funds for two years. Passed 376-38: R 218-2; D 157-36 (ND 116-32, SD 41-4); I 1-0. Nov. 3, 2005.

| | 562 | 563 | 564 | 565 | 566 | 567 | 568 |
|---|---|---|---|---|---|---|---|
| **ALABAMA** | | | | | | | |
| 1 Bonner | Y | Y | N | N | N | N | Y |
| 2 Everett | Y | Y | N | N | N | N | Y |
| 3 Rogers | Y | Y | N | N | N | N | Y |
| 4 Aderholt | Y | Y | Y | N | N | N | Y |
| 5 Cramer | N | N | N | N | N | N | Y |
| 6 Bachus | Y | Y | N | N | N | N | + |
| 7 Davis | N | Y | N | N | N | N | Y |
| **ALASKA** | | | | | | | |
| AL Young | Y | Y | N | N | N | N | Y |
| **ARIZONA** | | | | | | | |
| 1 Renzi | Y | Y | N | N | N | N | Y |
| 2 Franks | Y | Y | N | N | N | N | Y |
| 3 Shadegg | Y | Y | N | N | N | N | Y |
| 4 Pastor | N | N | Y | N | N | Y | N |
| 5 Hayworth | Y | Y | N | N | N | N | Y |
| 6 Flake | Y | Y | N | N | N | N | Y |
| 7 Grijalva | N | N | N | N | N | N | Y |
| 8 Kolbe | Y | Y | N | N | N | N | Y |
| **ARKANSAS** | | | | | | | |
| 1 Berry | N | Y | N | N | N | N | Y |
| 2 Snyder | N | Y | N | N | N | N | Y |
| 3 Boozman | Y | Y | N | N | N | N | Y |
| 4 Ross | N | Y | N | N | N | N | Y |
| **CALIFORNIA** | | | | | | | |
| 1 Thompson | N | Y | Y | N | N | N | Y |
| 2 Herger | Y | Y | N | N | N | N | Y |
| 3 Lungren | Y | Y | N | N | N | N | Y |
| 4 Doolittle | Y | Y | N | N | N | N | Y |
| 5 Matsui, D. | N | Y | Y | N | Y | Y | Y |
| 6 Woolsey | N | Y | Y | Y | Y | N | N |
| 7 Miller, George | N | Y | Y | Y | Y | Y | N |
| 8 Pelosi | N | Y | Y | Y | N | Y | N |
| 9 Lee | N | Y | N | N | N | N | Y |
| 10 Tauscher | N | Y | N | N | N | N | Y |
| 11 Pombo | ? | ? | ? | ? | ? | ? | + |
| 12 Lantos | N | Y | N | N | N | N | Y |
| 13 Stark | N | Y | N | N | N | Y | N |
| 14 Eshoo | N | Y | N | N | Y | N | Y |
| 15 Honda | N | Y | N | N | N | N | Y |
| 16 Lofgren | N | Y | N | N | N | Y | Y |
| 17 Farr | N | Y | Y | N | Y | N | Y |
| 18 Cardoza | N | Y | N | N | N | N | Y |
| 19 Radanovich | Y | Y | N | N | N | N | Y |
| 20 Costa | N | Y | N | N | N | N | Y |
| 21 Nunes | Y | Y | N | N | N | N | Y |
| 22 Thomas | Y | Y | N | N | N | N | Y |
| 23 Capps | N | Y | N | N | N | N | Y |
| 24 Gallegly | Y | Y | N | N | N | N | Y |
| 25 McKeon | Y | Y | N | N | N | N | Y |
| 26 Dreier | Y | Y | N | N | N | N | Y |
| 27 Sherman | N | Y | N | Y | N | N | Y |
| 28 Berman | N | Y | N | N | N | N | Y |
| 29 Schiff | ? | ? | ? | ? | ? | ? | ? |
| 30 Waxman | N | Y | N | Y | N | Y | N |
| 31 Becerra | N | Y | N | N | N | Y | N |
| 32 Solis | N | Y | N | Y | N | N | Y |
| 33 Watson | N | Y | N | N | Y | N | Y |
| 34 Roybal-Allard | ? | ? | ? | ? | ? | ? | ? |
| 35 Waters | N | Y | N | N | N | N | Y |
| 36 Harman | N | Y | N | N | N | N | Y |
| 37 Millender-McD. | N | Y | N | N | N | N | Y |
| 38 Napolitano | N | Y | N | N | N | N | Y |
| 39 Sánchez, Linda | N | Y | N | N | N | N | Y |
| 40 Royce | Y | Y | N | N | N | N | Y |
| 41 Lewis | Y | Y | N | N | N | N | Y |
| 42 Miller, Gary | Y | Y | N | N | N | N | Y |
| 43 Baca | N | Y | N | N | N | N | Y |
| 44 Calvert | Y | Y | N | N | N | N | Y |
| 45 Bono | Y | Y | N | N | N | N | Y |
| 46 Rohrabacher | Y | Y | N | N | N | N | Y |
| 47 Sanchez, Loretta | N | Y | N | N | Y | ? | Y |
| 48 Vacant | | | | | | | |
| 49 Issa | Y | Y | N | N | N | N | Y |

| | 562 | 563 | 564 | 565 | 566 | 567 | 568 |
|---|---|---|---|---|---|---|---|
| 50 Cunningham | Y | Y | N | N | N | N | Y |
| 51 Filner | N | Y | N | N | N | N | Y |
| 52 Hunter | Y | Y | N | N | ? | N | Y |
| 53 Davis | N | Y | N | N | N | N | Y |
| **COLORADO** | | | | | | | |
| 1 DeGette | N | Y | Y | Y | Y | Y | N |
| 2 Udall | N | Y | N | N | Y | N | Y |
| 3 Salazar | N | Y | N | N | N | N | Y |
| 4 Musgrave | Y | Y | N | N | N | N | Y |
| 5 Hefley | Y | Y | N | N | N | N | Y |
| 6 Tancredo | Y | Y | N | N | N | N | Y |
| 7 Beauprez | Y | Y | N | N | Y | N | Y |
| **CONNECTICUT** | | | | | | | |
| 1 Larson | N | Y | Y | Y | Y | Y | N |
| 2 Simmons | Y | Y | N | N | N | N | Y |
| 3 DeLauro | N | Y | N | N | N | N | Y |
| 4 Shays | Y | Y | N | Y | N | N | Y |
| 5 Johnson | Y | Y | N | N | N | N | Y |
| **DELAWARE** | | | | | | | |
| AL Castle | Y | Y | N | N | N | N | Y |
| **FLORIDA** | | | | | | | |
| 1 Miller | Y | Y | N | N | N | N | Y |
| 2 Boyd | ? | ? | ? | ? | ? | ? | ? |
| 3 Brown | N | Y | Y | N | N | N | Y |
| 4 Crenshaw | Y | Y | N | N | N | N | Y |
| 5 Brown-Waite | ? | ? | ? | ? | ? | ? | ? |
| 6 Stearns | Y | Y | N | N | N | N | Y |
| 7 Mica | Y | Y | N | N | N | N | Y |
| 8 Keller | Y | Y | N | N | N | N | Y |
| 9 Bilirakis | Y | Y | N | N | N | N | Y |
| 10 Young | Y | Y | N | N | N | N | Y |
| 11 Davis | ? | ? | ? | ? | ? | ? | ? |
| 12 Putnam | Y | Y | N | N | N | N | Y |
| 13 Harris | Y | Y | N | N | N | ? | Y |
| 14 Mack | Y | Y | N | N | N | N | Y |
| 15 Weldon | Y | Y | N | N | N | N | Y |
| 16 Foley | Y | Y | N | N | N | N | Y |
| 17 Meek | N | Y | N | N | N | N | Y |
| 18 Ros-Lehtinen | Y | Y | N | N | N | N | Y |
| 19 Wexler | N | Y | N | N | N | N | Y |
| 20 Wasserman-Schultz | N | Y | N | N | N | N | Y |
| 21 Diaz-Balart, L. | Y | Y | N | N | N | N | Y |
| 22 Shaw | Y | Y | N | N | N | N | Y |
| 23 Hastings | ? | ? | ? | ? | ? | ? | ? |
| 24 Feeney | Y | Y | N | ? | N | N | Y |
| 25 Diaz-Balart, M. | Y | Y | N | N | N | N | Y |
| **GEORGIA** | | | | | | | |
| 1 Kingston | Y | Y | N | N | N | N | Y |
| 2 Bishop | N | Y | N | N | Y | N | Y |
| 3 Marshall | Y | Y | N | N | N | N | Y |
| 4 McKinney | N | Y | N | N | N | N | Y |
| 5 Lewis | N | Y | ? | ? | ? | ? | ? |
| 6 Price | Y | Y | N | N | N | N | Y |
| 7 Linder | Y | Y | N | N | N | N | Y |
| 8 Westmoreland | Y | Y | N | N | N | N | Y |
| 9 Norwood | ? | ? | ? | ? | ? | ? | ? |
| 10 Deal | Y | Y | N | N | N | N | Y |
| 11 Gingrey | Y | Y | N | N | N | N | Y |
| 12 Barrow | N | Y | N | N | N | N | Y |
| 13 Scott | N | Y | N | N | N | N | Y |
| **HAWAII** | | | | | | | |
| 1 Abercrombie | N | Y | Y | N | N | N | Y |
| 2 Case | N | Y | Y | Y | Y | Y | N |
| **IDAHO** | | | | | | | |
| 1 Otter | Y | Y | N | N | N | N | Y |
| 2 Simpson | Y | Y | N | N | N | N | Y |
| **ILLINOIS** | | | | | | | |
| 1 Rush | N | Y | N | N | N | N | Y |
| 2 Jackson | N | Y | N | Y | Y | Y | N |
| 3 Lipinski | N | Y | N | N | N | N | Y |
| 4 Gutierrez | N | Y | N | N | N | N | Y |
| 5 Emanuel | N | Y | Y | Y | N | Y | N |
| 6 Hyde | Y | Y | N | N | N | N | Y |
| 7 Davis | N | Y | N | N | N | N | Y |
| 8 Bean | N | Y | N | N | N | N | Y |
| 9 Schakowsky | N | Y | N | Y | N | Y | N |
| 10 Kirk | Y | Y | N | N | N | N | Y |
| 11 Weller | Y | Y | N | N | N | N | Y |
| 12 Costello | N | Y | N | N | N | N | Y |

**KEY**   Republicans   Democrats   *Independents*

| | | | | |
|---|---|---|---|---|
| Y | Voted for (yea) | X | Paired against | C Voted "present" to avoid possible conflict of interest |
| # | Paired for | – | Announced against | |
| + | Announced for | P | Voted "present" | ? Did not vote or otherwise make a position known |
| N | Voted against (nay) | | | |

ND Northern Democrats, SD Southern Democrats
Southern states: Ala., Ark., Fla., Ga., Ky., La., Miss., N.C., Okla., S.C., Tenn., Texas, Va.

| | 562 | 563 | 564 | 565 | 566 | 567 | 568 |
|---|---|---|---|---|---|---|---|
| 13 **Biggert** | Y | Y | N | N | N | N | Y |
| 14 **Hastert** | | | | | | | |
| 15 **Johnson** | Y | Y | N | N | N | N | Y |
| 16 **Manzullo** | Y | Y | N | N | N | N | Y |
| 17 Evans | N | Y | N | N | N | N | Y |
| 18 **LaHood** | Y | Y | N | N | N | N | Y |
| 19 **Shimkus** | Y | Y | N | N | N | N | Y |
| **INDIANA** | | | | | | | |
| 1 Visclosky | N | Y | N | N | N | Y | N |
| 2 **Chocola** | Y | Y | N | N | Y | N | Y |
| 3 **Souder** | Y | Y | N | N | Y | N | Y |
| 4 **Buyer** | Y | Y | ? | ? | ? | ? | ? |
| 5 **Burton** | Y | Y | N | N | N | N | Y |
| 6 **Pence** | Y | Y | N | N | N | N | Y |
| 7 Carson | N | Y | N | Y | N | Y | Y |
| 8 **Hostettler** | Y | Y | N | N | N | N | Y |
| 9 **Sodrel** | Y | Y | N | N | N | N | Y |
| **IOWA** | | | | | | | |
| 1 **Nussle** | Y | Y | N | N | N | N | Y |
| 2 **Leach** | Y | Y | N | N | N | N | Y |
| 3 Boswell | ? | ? | ? | ? | ? | ? | ? |
| 4 **Latham** | Y | Y | N | N | N | N | Y |
| 5 **King** | Y | Y | N | N | N | N | Y |
| **KANSAS** | | | | | | | |
| 1 **Moran** | Y | Y | N | N | N | N | Y |
| 2 **Ryun** | Y | Y | N | N | N | N | Y |
| 3 Moore | N | Y | N | N | N | N | Y |
| 4 **Tiahrt** | + | + | – | – | – | – | + |
| **KENTUCKY** | | | | | | | |
| 1 **Whitfield** | Y | Y | N | N | N | N | Y |
| 2 **Lewis** | Y | Y | N | N | N | N | Y |
| 3 **Northup** | Y | Y | N | N | N | N | Y |
| 4 **Davis** | Y | Y | N | N | N | N | Y |
| 5 **Rogers** | Y | Y | N | N | N | N | Y |
| 6 Chandler | N | Y | N | N | N | N | Y |
| **LOUISIANA** | | | | | | | |
| 1 **Jindal** | Y | Y | N | N | N | N | Y |
| 2 Jefferson | N | Y | N | Y | N | N | Y |
| 3 Melancon | N | Y | N | N | N | N | Y |
| 4 **McCrery** | Y | Y | N | N | N | N | Y |
| 5 **Alexander** | Y | Y | N | N | N | N | Y |
| 6 **Baker** | Y | Y | N | N | Y | N | Y |
| 7 **Boustany** | Y | Y | N | N | N | N | Y |
| **MAINE** | | | | | | | |
| 1 Allen | N | Y | N | N | N | N | Y |
| 2 Michaud | N | Y | N | N | N | N | Y |
| **MARYLAND** | | | | | | | |
| 1 **Gilchrest** | Y | Y | N | N | N | N | Y |
| 2 Ruppersberger | N | Y | N | N | N | N | Y |
| 3 Cardin | N | Y | N | N | N | N | Y |
| 4 Wynn | N | Y | N | Y | Y | Y | N |
| 5 Hoyer | N | Y | Y | N | N | N | Y |
| 6 **Bartlett** | Y | Y | N | N | N | N | Y |
| 7 Cummings | ? | Y | N | N | N | N | Y |
| 8 Van Hollen | N | Y | N | N | N | N | Y |
| **MASSACHUSETTS** | | | | | | | |
| 1 Olver | N | N | Y | Y | N | Y | N |
| 2 Neal | N | Y | Y | Y | Y | Y | N |
| 3 McGovern | N | Y | N | Y | Y | N | Y |
| 4 Frank | N | Y | N | N | N | N | Y |
| 5 Meehan | N | Y | N | N | N | N | Y |
| 6 Tierney | N | Y | N | N | Y | N | Y |
| 7 Markey | N | Y | Y | Y | N | Y | Y |
| 8 Capuano | N | Y | Y | Y | Y | Y | N |
| 9 Lynch | N | Y | N | N | N | N | Y |
| 10 Delahunt | N | Y | Y | Y | Y | Y | Y |
| **MICHIGAN** | | | | | | | |
| 1 Stupak | N | Y | N | N | N | N | Y |
| 2 **Hoekstra** | Y | Y | N | N | N | N | Y |
| 3 **Ehlers** | Y | Y | N | N | Y | N | ? |
| 4 **Camp** | Y | Y | N | N | N | N | Y |
| 5 Kildee | N | Y | Y | N | N | N | Y |
| 6 **Upton** | Y | Y | N | N | N | N | Y |
| 7 **Schwarz** | Y | Y | N | N | N | N | Y |
| 8 **Rogers** | Y | Y | N | N | N | N | Y |
| 9 **Knollenberg** | Y | Y | N | N | N | N | Y |
| 10 **Miller** | Y | Y | N | N | Y | N | Y |
| 11 **McCotter** | Y | Y | N | N | N | N | Y |
| 12 Levin | N | Y | Y | Y | N | Y | N |
| 13 Kilpatrick | N | Y | N | N | N | N | Y |
| 14 Conyers | N | Y | N | N | N | N | Y |
| 15 Dingell | N | Y | Y | Y | ? | Y | N |
| **MINNESOTA** | | | | | | | |
| 1 **Gutknecht** | Y | Y | N | N | N | N | Y |
| 2 **Kline** | Y | Y | N | N | N | N | Y |
| 3 **Ramstad** | Y | Y | N | N | N | N | Y |
| 4 McCollum | N | Y | Y | N | N | N | Y |
| 5 Sabo | N | N | Y | Y | N | Y | N |
| 6 **Kennedy** | Y | Y | N | N | N | N | Y |
| 7 Peterson | N | Y | N | N | N | N | Y |
| 8 Oberstar | N | Y | Y | N | N | N | Y |
| **MISSISSIPPI** | | | | | | | |
| 1 **Wicker** | Y | Y | N | N | Y | N | Y |
| 2 Thompson | N | Y | N | N | N | N | Y |
| 3 **Pickering** | Y | Y | N | N | Y | N | Y |
| 4 Taylor | N | N | N | N | N | N | Y |
| **MISSOURI** | | | | | | | |
| 1 Clay | N | Y | N | N | N | Y | Y |
| 2 **Akin** | Y | Y | N | N | N | N | Y |
| 3 Carnahan | N | Y | N | N | N | N | Y |
| 4 Skelton | N | Y | N | N | N | N | Y |
| 5 Cleaver | N | Y | Y | Y | N | Y | N |
| 6 **Graves** | Y | Y | N | N | N | N | Y |
| 7 **Blunt** | Y | Y | N | N | Y | N | Y |
| 8 **Emerson** | Y | Y | N | N | N | N | Y |
| 9 **Hulshof** | Y | Y | N | N | N | N | Y |
| **MONTANA** | | | | | | | |
| AL **Rehberg** | Y | Y | N | N | N | N | Y |
| **NEBRASKA** | | | | | | | |
| 1 **Fortenberry** | Y | Y | N | N | Y | N | Y |
| 2 **Terry** | Y | Y | N | N | N | N | Y |
| 3 **Osborne** | Y | Y | N | N | N | N | Y |
| **NEVADA** | | | | | | | |
| 1 Berkley | N | Y | N | N | N | N | Y |
| 2 **Gibbons** | Y | Y | N | N | N | N | Y |
| 3 **Porter** | Y | Y | N | N | N | N | Y |
| **NEW HAMPSHIRE** | | | | | | | |
| 1 **Bradley** | Y | Y | N | N | N | N | Y |
| 2 **Bass** | Y | Y | N | N | N | N | Y |
| **NEW JERSEY** | | | | | | | |
| 1 Andrews | N | Y | N | N | N | N | Y |
| 2 **LoBiondo** | Y | Y | N | N | N | N | Y |
| 3 **Saxton** | Y | Y | N | N | N | ? | Y |
| 4 **Smith** | Y | Y | N | N | N | N | Y |
| 5 **Garrett** | Y | Y | N | N | N | N | Y |
| 6 Pallone | N | Y | N | N | N | N | Y |
| 7 **Ferguson** | Y | Y | N | N | N | N | Y |
| 8 Pascrell | N | Y | N | N | Y | N | Y |
| 9 Rothman | N | N | Y | Y | Y | Y | N |
| 10 Payne | N | Y | Y | Y | N | Y | Y |
| 11 **Frelinghuysen** | Y | Y | N | N | N | N | Y |
| 12 Holt | N | N | Y | Y | N | N | Y |
| 13 Menendez | N | Y | N | N | N | N | Y |
| **NEW MEXICO** | | | | | | | |
| 1 **Wilson** | Y | Y | N | N | N | N | Y |
| 2 **Pearce** | Y | Y | N | N | N | N | Y |
| 3 Udall | N | Y | N | N | N | N | Y |
| **NEW YORK** | | | | | | | |
| 1 Bishop | N | Y | Y | N | N | N | Y |
| 2 Israel | N | Y | N | N | N | N | Y |
| 3 **King** | ? | ? | N | N | N | N | Y |
| 4 McCarthy | N | ? | N | N | N | N | Y |
| 5 Ackerman | N | Y | Y | N | N | Y | N |
| 6 Meeks | N | Y | Y | N | N | N | N |
| 7 Crowley | N | Y | N | N | N | N | Y |
| 8 Nadler | N | N | Y | Y | N | Y | N |
| 9 Weiner | N | Y | Y | Y | N | N | Y |
| 10 Towns | ? | ? | Y | N | N | N | Y |
| 11 Owens | N | Y | Y | N | N | N | Y |
| 12 Velázquez | N | Y | N | N | N | N | Y |
| 13 **Fossella** | Y | Y | N | N | N | N | Y |
| 14 Maloney | N | Y | Y | N | N | N | Y |
| 15 Rangel | N | Y | Y | Y | N | Y | Y |
| 16 Serrano | ? | Y | Y | N | N | N | Y |
| 17 Engel | N | Y | Y | Y | N | N | Y |
| 18 Lowey | N | Y | Y | Y | N | Y | N |
| 19 **Kelly** | Y | Y | N | N | Y | N | Y |
| 20 **Sweeney** | Y | Y | N | N | Y | N | Y |
| 21 McNulty | N | Y | N | N | N | N | Y |
| 22 Hinchey | N | Y | Y | Y | N | Y | N |
| 23 **McHugh** | Y | Y | N | N | N | N | Y |
| 24 **Boehlert** | Y | Y | N | N | Y | N | N |
| 25 **Walsh** | Y | Y | N | N | N | N | Y |
| 26 **Reynolds** | Y | Y | N | N | N | N | Y |
| 27 Higgins | N | Y | N | N | N | N | Y |
| 28 Slaughter | N | Y | Y | Y | N | Y | Y |
| 29 **Kuhl** | Y | Y | N | N | N | N | Y |
| **NORTH CAROLINA** | | | | | | | |
| 1 Butterfield | – | + | N | N | N | N | Y |
| 2 Etheridge | N | Y | N | N | N | N | Y |
| 3 **Jones** | Y | Y | N | N | N | N | Y |
| 4 Price | N | Y | N | Y | N | N | Y |
| 5 **Foxx** | Y | Y | N | N | N | N | Y |
| 6 **Coble** | Y | Y | N | N | N | N | Y |
| 7 McIntyre | N | Y | N | N | N | N | Y |
| 8 **Hayes** | Y | Y | N | N | N | N | Y |
| 9 **Myrick** | Y | Y | N | N | N | N | Y |
| 10 **McHenry** | Y | Y | N | N | N | N | Y |
| 11 **Taylor** | Y | Y | N | N | N | N | Y |
| 12 Watt | N | Y | Y | Y | N | Y | N |
| 13 Miller | N | Y | Y | Y | Y | Y | N |
| **NORTH DAKOTA** | | | | | | | |
| AL Pomeroy | N | Y | N | N | N | N | Y |
| **OHIO** | | | | | | | |
| 1 **Chabot** | ? | ? | N | N | Y | N | Y |
| 2 **Schmidt** | Y | Y | N | N | Y | N | Y |
| 3 **Turner** | Y | Y | N | N | Y | N | N |
| 4 **Oxley** | Y | Y | N | N | Y | N | Y |
| 5 **Gillmor** | Y | Y | N | N | N | N | Y |
| 6 Strickland | N | Y | N | N | N | N | Y |
| 7 **Hobson** | Y | Y | N | N | Y | N | Y |
| 8 **Boehner** | Y | Y | N | N | N | N | Y |
| 9 Kaptur | N | Y | Y | N | N | N | Y |
| 10 Kucinich | N | Y | N | N | N | N | Y |
| 11 Jones | N | N | N | N | N | N | Y |
| 12 **Tiberi** | Y | Y | N | N | Y | N | Y |
| 13 Brown | N | Y | Y | N | N | N | Y |
| 14 **LaTourette** | Y | Y | N | N | Y | N | Y |
| 15 **Pryce** | Y | Y | N | N | Y | N | Y |
| 16 **Regula** | Y | Y | N | N | Y | N | Y |
| 17 Ryan | N | Y | Y | N | N | N | Y |
| 18 **Ney** | Y | Y | N | N | N | N | Y |
| **OKLAHOMA** | | | | | | | |
| 1 **Sullivan** | Y | Y | ? | ? | ? | ? | ? |
| 2 Boren | N | Y | N | N | N | N | Y |
| 3 **Lucas** | Y | Y | N | N | N | N | Y |
| 4 **Cole** | Y | Y | N | N | N | N | Y |
| 5 **Istook** | ? | ? | N | N | N | N | Y |
| **OREGON** | | | | | | | |
| 1 Wu | N | N | N | N | N | N | Y |
| 2 **Walden** | Y | Y | N | N | N | N | Y |
| 3 Blumenauer | N | Y | Y | Y | Y | Y | N |
| 4 DeFazio | N | Y | N | N | N | N | Y |
| 5 Hooley | N | Y | Y | Y | N | N | Y |
| **PENNSYLVANIA** | | | | | | | |
| 1 Brady | ? | ? | N | Y | N | Y | N |
| 2 Fattah | N | Y | Y | Y | N | Y | N |
| 3 **English** | Y | Y | N | N | N | N | Y |
| 4 **Hart** | Y | Y | N | N | N | N | Y |
| 5 **Peterson** | Y | Y | N | N | N | N | Y |
| 6 **Gerlach** | Y | Y | N | N | Y | N | Y |
| 7 **Weldon** | ? | Y | N | N | N | N | Y |
| 8 **Fitzpatrick** | Y | Y | N | N | N | N | Y |
| 9 **Shuster** | Y | Y | N | N | N | N | Y |
| 10 **Sherwood** | Y | Y | N | N | N | N | Y |
| 11 Kanjorski | N | Y | Y | Y | Y | Y | Y |
| 12 Murtha | N | Y | N | Y | N | N | Y |
| 13 Schwartz | N | Y | Y | Y | N | Y | N |
| 14 Doyle | N | Y | N | N | N | N | Y |
| 15 **Dent** | Y | Y | N | N | N | N | Y |
| 16 **Pitts** | Y | Y | N | N | N | N | Y |
| 17 Holden | N | Y | N | N | N | N | Y |
| 18 **Murphy** | Y | Y | N | N | N | N | Y |
| 19 **Platts** | Y | Y | N | N | N | N | Y |
| **RHODE ISLAND** | | | | | | | |
| 1 Kennedy | N | Y | Y | Y | Y | N | Y |
| 2 Langevin | N | Y | N | N | Y | N | Y |
| **SOUTH CAROLINA** | | | | | | | |
| 1 **Brown** | Y | Y | N | N | N | N | Y |
| 2 **Wilson** | Y | Y | N | N | N | N | Y |
| 3 **Barrett** | Y | Y | N | N | N | N | Y |
| 4 **Inglis** | Y | Y | N | N | N | N | Y |
| 5 Spratt | N | Y | N | N | N | N | Y |
| 6 Clyburn | N | Y | N | N | N | N | Y |
| **SOUTH DAKOTA** | | | | | | | |
| AL Herseth | N | Y | N | N | N | N | Y |
| **TENNESSEE** | | | | | | | |
| 1 **Jenkins** | Y | Y | N | N | N | N | Y |
| 2 **Duncan** | Y | Y | N | N | N | N | Y |
| 3 **Wamp** | Y | Y | N | N | N | N | Y |
| 4 Davis | N | Y | N | N | N | N | Y |
| 5 Cooper | N | Y | N | N | N | N | Y |
| 6 Gordon | N | Y | N | N | N | N | Y |
| 7 **Blackburn** | Y | Y | N | N | N | N | Y |
| 8 Tanner | N | Y | N | N | N | N | Y |
| 9 Ford | N | Y | N | N | N | N | Y |
| **TEXAS** | | | | | | | |
| 1 **Gohmert** | Y | Y | N | N | N | N | Y |
| 2 **Poe** | Y | Y | N | N | N | N | Y |
| 3 **Johnson, S.** | Y | Y | N | N | N | N | Y |
| 4 **Hall** | ? | ? | N | N | N | N | Y |
| 5 **Hensarling** | Y | Y | N | N | N | N | Y |
| 6 **Barton** | Y | Y | N | N | N | N | Y |
| 7 **Culberson** | Y | Y | N | N | N | N | Y |
| 8 **Brady** | Y | Y | N | N | ? | N | Y |
| 9 Green, A. | N | Y | N | N | – | N | Y |
| 10 **McCaul** | Y | ? | N | N | N | N | Y |
| 11 **Conaway** | Y | Y | N | N | N | N | Y |
| 12 **Granger** | Y | Y | N | N | Y | N | Y |
| 13 **Thornberry** | Y | Y | N | N | N | N | Y |
| 14 **Paul** | Y | Y | N | N | N | N | Y |
| 15 Hinojosa | N | Y | N | N | N | N | Y |
| 16 Reyes | N | Y | N | N | N | N | Y |
| 17 Edwards | N | Y | N | N | N | N | Y |
| 18 Jackson-Lee | N | Y | N | N | N | N | Y |
| 19 **Neugebauer** | Y | Y | N | N | N | N | Y |
| 20 Gonzalez | N | Y | N | N | N | N | Y |
| 21 **Smith** | Y | Y | N | N | N | N | Y |
| 22 **DeLay** | Y | Y | N | N | N | N | Y |
| 23 **Bonilla** | Y | Y | N | N | N | N | Y |
| 24 **Marchant** | Y | Y | N | N | N | N | Y |
| 25 Doggett | N | Y | N | N | N | N | Y |
| 26 **Burgess** | Y | Y | N | N | N | N | Y |
| 27 Ortiz | N | Y | – | – | – | – | + |
| 28 Cuellar | N | Y | N | N | N | N | Y |
| 29 Green, G. | N | Y | N | N | Y | N | Y |
| 30 Johnson, E. | N | Y | N | N | N | N | Y |
| 31 **Carter** | Y | Y | N | N | N | N | Y |
| 32 **Sessions** | Y | Y | N | N | N | N | Y |
| **UTAH** | | | | | | | |
| 1 **Bishop** | ? | ? | N | N | ? | N | Y |
| 2 Matheson | N | Y | N | N | N | N | Y |
| 3 **Cannon** | Y | Y | N | N | N | N | Y |
| **VERMONT** | | | | | | | |
| AL *Sanders* | N | Y | N | N | N | N | Y |
| **VIRGINIA** | | | | | | | |
| 1 **Davis, J.** | Y | Y | N | N | Y | N | Y |
| 2 **Drake** | Y | Y | N | N | N | N | Y |
| 3 Scott | N | Y | Y | Y | N | Y | N |
| 4 **Forbes** | Y | Y | N | N | N | N | Y |
| 5 **Goode** | Y | Y | N | N | N | N | Y |
| 6 **Goodlatte** | Y | Y | N | N | N | N | Y |
| 7 **Cantor** | Y | Y | N | N | N | N | Y |
| 8 Moran | N | Y | Y | Y | Y | Y | N |
| 9 Boucher | N | Y | N | N | N | N | ? |
| 10 **Wolf** | Y | Y | N | N | N | N | ? |
| 11 **Davis, T.** | Y | Y | N | N | Y | N | Y |
| **WASHINGTON** | | | | | | | |
| 1 Inslee | N | Y | N | N | N | N | Y |
| 2 Larsen | N | Y | N | N | N | N | Y |
| 3 Baird | N | Y | N | Y | N | N | Y |
| 4 **Hastings** | Y | Y | N | N | N | N | Y |
| 5 **McMorris** | ? | ? | ? | ? | ? | ? | ? |
| 6 Dicks | N | Y | Y | N | N | N | Y |
| 7 McDermott | N | N | Y | N | Y | Y | N |
| 8 **Reichert** | Y | Y | N | N | N | N | Y |
| 9 Smith | N | Y | N | Y | N | N | Y |
| **WEST VIRGINIA** | | | | | | | |
| 1 Mollohan | N | Y | N | N | N | N | Y |
| 2 **Capito** | Y | Y | N | N | N | N | Y |
| 3 Rahall | N | Y | N | N | N | N | Y |
| **WISCONSIN** | | | | | | | |
| 1 **Ryan** | Y | Y | N | N | N | N | Y |
| 2 Baldwin | N | Y | N | N | N | N | Y |
| 3 Kind | N | Y | N | N | N | N | Y |
| 4 Moore | N | Y | N | N | N | N | Y |
| 5 **Sensenbrenner** | Y | Y | N | N | N | N | Y |
| 6 **Petri** | Y | Y | N | N | N | N | Y |
| 7 Obey | N | Y | N | N | N | N | Y |
| 8 **Green** | Y | Y | N | N | N | N | Y |
| **WYOMING** | | | | | | | |
| AL **Cubin** | Y | Y | N | N | N | N | Y |

# IN THE HOUSE | By Vote Number

**569.** **HR 3057. Fiscal 2006 Foreign Operations Appropriations/ Conference Report.** Adoption of the conference report on the bill that would provide $21 billion in fiscal 2006 for foreign operations and related programs, including $2.8 billion to fight HIV/AIDS, tuberculosis and malaria; $1.8 billion for the Millennium Challenge Corporation; and $1.6 billion for the Child Survival and Health Programs Fund. Adopted (thus sent to the Senate) 358-39: R 179-32; D 178-7 (ND 137-3, SD 41-4); I 1-0. Nov. 4, 2005.

**570.** **H Con Res 260. Nostra Aetate Tribute/Adoption.** Poe, R-Texas, motion to suspend the rules and adopt the concurrent resolution that would recognize the 40th anniversary of Nostra Aetate, the Second Vatican Council's Declaration on the Relation of the Church to Non-Christian Religions, and also recognize the religious diversity of the United States and the world. Motion agreed to 349-0: R 202-0; D 146-0 (ND 104-0, SD 42-0); I 1-0. A two-thirds majority of those present and voting (233 in this case) is required for adoption under suspension of the rules. Nov. 7, 2005.

**571.** **HR 1973. Water for the Poor/Passage.** Poe, R-Texas, motion to suspend the rules and pass the bill that would authorize unspecified sums to provide safe water and sanitation to people in developing countries. Motion agreed to 319-34: R 170-34; D 148-0 (ND 106-0, SD 42-0); I 1-0. A two-thirds majority of those present and voting (236 in this case) is required for passage under suspension of the rules. Nov. 7, 2005.

**572.** **H Res 444. Ovarian Cancer Awareness Month/Adoption.** Upton, R-Mich., motion to suspend the rules and adopt the resolution that would support the goals and ideals of National Ovarian Cancer Awareness Month in September. Motion agreed to 348-0: R 201-0; D 146-0 (ND 105-0, SD 41-0); I 1-0. A two-thirds majority of those present and voting (232 in this case) is required for adoption under suspension of the rules. Nov. 7, 2005.

**573.** **HR 3010. Fiscal 2006 Labor-HHS-Education Appropriations/ Appeal Ruling of the Chair.** Regula, R-Ohio., motion to table (kill) the Obey, D-Wis., appeal of the ruling of the chair against the Regula point of order against the Obey motion. The Obey motion would instruct House conferees to agree to various Senate provisions including $8.1 billion for avian flu preparation and $5.1 billion for the Low Income Home Energy Assistance Program, offset by reducing tax cuts for the wealthy. Motion agreed to 218-173: R 218-0; D 0-172 (ND 0-125, SD 0-47); I 0-1. Nov. 8, 2005.

**574.** **H Res 38. Israel and the OECD/Adoption.** Ros-Lehtinen, R-Fla., motion to suspend the rules and adopt the resolution that would express the sense of the House that the U.S. government should support the accession of Israel to the Organization for Economic Co-Operation and Development. Motion agreed to 391-0: R 219-0; D 171-0 (ND 123-0, SD 48-0); I 1-0. A two-thirds majority of those present and voting (261 in this case) is required for adoption under suspension of the rules. Nov. 8, 2005.

| | 569 | 570 | 571 | 572 | 573 | 574 |
|---|---|---|---|---|---|---|
| **ALABAMA** | | | | | | |
| 1 Bonner | Y | Y | Y | Y | Y | Y |
| 2 Everett | Y | Y | Y | Y | Y | Y |
| 3 Rogers | Y | Y | Y | Y | Y | Y |
| 4 Aderholt | Y | Y | Y | Y | Y | Y |
| 5 Cramer | Y | Y | Y | Y | N | Y |
| 6 Bachus | Y | Y | Y | Y | Y | Y |
| 7 Davis | Y | Y | Y | Y | N | Y |
| **ALASKA** | | | | | | |
| AL Young | Y | Y | Y | Y | Y | Y |
| **ARIZONA** | | | | | | |
| 1 Renzi | Y | Y | Y | Y | Y | Y |
| 2 Franks | N | Y | N | ? | Y | Y |
| 3 Shadegg | Y | Y | N | Y | Y | Y |
| 4 Pastor | Y | Y | Y | Y | N | Y |
| 5 Hayworth | Y | Y | Y | Y | Y | Y |
| 6 Flake | N | Y | N | Y | Y | Y |
| 7 Grijalva | Y | Y | Y | Y | N | Y |
| 8 Kolbe | Y | Y | Y | Y | Y | Y |
| **ARKANSAS** | | | | | | |
| 1 Berry | N | Y | Y | Y | N | Y |
| 2 Snyder | Y | Y | Y | Y | N | Y |
| 3 Boozman | Y | Y | Y | Y | Y | Y |
| 4 Ross | Y | Y | Y | Y | N | Y |
| **CALIFORNIA** | | | | | | |
| 1 Thompson | Y | Y | Y | Y | N | Y |
| 2 Herger | Y | Y | N | Y | Y | Y |
| 3 Lungren | Y | Y | Y | Y | Y | Y |
| 4 Doolittle | Y | Y | Y | Y | Y | Y |
| 5 Matsui, D. | Y | Y | Y | Y | N | Y |
| 6 Woolsey | Y | Y | Y | Y | N | Y |
| 7 Miller, George | Y | Y | Y | Y | N | Y |
| 8 Pelosi | Y | Y | Y | Y | N | Y |
| 9 Lee | Y | + | + | + | ? | ? |
| 10 Tauscher | Y | Y | Y | Y | N | Y |
| 11 Pombo | - | Y | Y | Y | Y | Y |
| 12 Lantos | Y | ? | Y | Y | N | Y |
| 13 Stark | N | ? | ? | ? | N | Y |
| 14 Eshoo | Y | Y | Y | Y | N | Y |
| 15 Honda | Y | Y | Y | Y | N | Y |
| 16 Lofgren | Y | Y | Y | Y | N | Y |
| 17 Farr | Y | Y | Y | Y | N | Y |
| 18 Cardoza | Y | Y | Y | Y | N | Y |
| 19 Radanovich | Y | Y | Y | Y | Y | Y |
| 20 Costa | Y | Y | Y | Y | N | Y |
| 21 Nunes | + | Y | Y | Y | Y | Y |
| 22 Thomas | Y | Y | Y | Y | Y | Y |
| 23 Capps | Y | Y | Y | Y | N | Y |
| 24 Gallegly | + | Y | Y | Y | Y | Y |
| 25 McKeon | Y | Y | Y | Y | Y | Y |
| 26 Dreier | Y | Y | Y | Y | Y | Y |
| 27 Sherman | Y | ? | ? | ? | ? | ? |
| 28 Berman | Y | ? | ? | ? | ? | ? |
| 29 Schiff | + | Y | Y | Y | N | Y |
| 30 Waxman | Y | Y | Y | Y | N | Y |
| 31 Becerra | + | + | + | + | N | Y |
| 32 Solis | Y | + | + | + | - | + |
| 33 Watson | Y | Y | Y | Y | N | Y |
| 34 Roybal-Allard | + | Y | Y | Y | N | Y |
| 35 Waters | Y | ? | ? | ? | ? | ? |
| 36 Harman | Y | Y | Y | Y | N | Y |
| 37 Millender-McD. | Y | ? | ? | ? | ? | ? |
| 38 Napolitano | Y | Y | Y | Y | N | Y |
| 39 Sánchez, Linda | Y | ? | ? | ? | N | Y |
| 40 Royce | Y | Y | Y | Y | Y | Y |
| 41 Lewis | Y | Y | Y | Y | Y | Y |
| 42 Miller, Gary | ? | Y | N | Y | Y | Y |
| 43 Baca | Y | ? | ? | ? | N | Y |
| 44 Calvert | ? | Y | Y | Y | Y | Y |
| 45 Bono | Y | Y | Y | Y | Y | Y |
| 46 Rohrabacher | N | Y | Y | Y | Y | Y |
| 47 Sanchez, Loretta | Y | Y | Y | Y | N | Y |
| 48 Vacant | | | | | | |
| 49 Issa | ? | Y | Y | Y | Y | Y |
| 50 Cunningham | Y | Y | Y | Y | Y | Y |
| 51 Filner | + | Y | Y | Y | N | Y |
| 52 Hunter | Y | Y | Y | Y | Y | Y |
| 53 Davis | Y | Y | Y | Y | N | Y |
| **COLORADO** | | | | | | |
| 1 DeGette | Y | Y | Y | Y | N | ? |
| 2 Udall | Y | Y | Y | Y | N | Y |
| 3 Salazar | Y | Y | Y | Y | N | Y |
| 4 Musgrave | Y | Y | N | Y | Y | Y |
| 5 Hefley | N | Y | Y | Y | Y | Y |
| 6 Tancredo | N | Y | Y | Y | Y | Y |
| 7 Beauprez | Y | Y | Y | Y | Y | Y |
| **CONNECTICUT** | | | | | | |
| 1 Larson | Y | Y | Y | ? | N | Y |
| 2 Simmons | Y | Y | Y | Y | Y | Y |
| 3 DeLauro | Y | Y | Y | Y | N | Y |
| 4 Shays | Y | Y | Y | Y | Y | Y |
| 5 Johnson | Y | ? | ? | ? | Y | ? |
| **DELAWARE** | | | | | | |
| AL Castle | Y | Y | Y | Y | Y | Y |
| **FLORIDA** | | | | | | |
| 1 Miller | N | Y | N | Y | Y | Y |
| 2 Boyd | ? | Y | Y | Y | N | Y |
| 3 Brown | Y | ? | ? | ? | ? | ? |
| 4 Crenshaw | Y | ? | ? | ? | ? | ? |
| 5 Brown-Waite | ? | ? | ? | ? | ? | ? |
| 6 Stearns | N | Y | N | Y | Y | Y |
| 7 Mica | Y | Y | Y | Y | Y | Y |
| 8 Keller | N | Y | Y | Y | Y | Y |
| 9 Bilirakis | Y | Y | Y | Y | Y | Y |
| 10 Young | Y | ? | ? | ? | ? | ? |
| 11 Davis | ? | Y | Y | Y | N | Y |
| 12 Putnam | Y | Y | Y | Y | Y | Y |
| 13 Harris | Y | ? | ? | ? | ? | ? |
| 14 Mack | Y | Y | Y | Y | Y | Y |
| 15 Weldon | Y | ? | ? | ? | ? | ? |
| 16 Foley | Y | Y | Y | Y | Y | Y |
| 17 Meek | Y | Y | Y | Y | N | Y |
| 18 Ros-Lehtinen | Y | Y | Y | Y | Y | Y |
| 19 Wexler | Y | Y | Y | Y | N | Y |
| 20 Wasserman-Schultz | Y | Y | Y | Y | N | Y |
| 21 Diaz-Balart, L. | Y | Y | Y | Y | Y | Y |
| 22 Shaw | Y | Y | Y | Y | Y | Y |
| 23 Hastings | ? | ? | ? | ? | ? | ? |
| 24 Feeney | Y | Y | N | Y | Y | Y |
| 25 Diaz-Balart, M. | Y | Y | Y | Y | Y | Y |
| **GEORGIA** | | | | | | |
| 1 Kingston | Y | Y | Y | Y | Y | Y |
| 2 Bishop | Y | Y | Y | Y | N | Y |
| 3 Marshall | Y | Y | Y | ? | N | Y |
| 4 McKinney | Y | ? | ? | ? | N | Y |
| 5 Lewis | Y | Y | Y | Y | N | Y |
| 6 Price | Y | Y | N | Y | Y | Y |
| 7 Linder | Y | Y | Y | Y | Y | Y |
| 8 Westmoreland | N | Y | N | Y | ? | ? |
| 9 Norwood | - | + | - | + | + | + |
| 10 Deal | Y | Y | N | Y | Y | Y |
| 11 Gingrey | Y | Y | N | Y | Y | Y |
| 12 Barrow | Y | Y | Y | Y | N | Y |
| 13 Scott | Y | Y | Y | Y | N | Y |
| **HAWAII** | | | | | | |
| 1 Abercrombie | Y | Y | Y | Y | N | Y |
| 2 Case | Y | ? | ? | ? | N | Y |
| **IDAHO** | | | | | | |
| 1 Otter | N | Y | Y | Y | Y | Y |
| 2 Simpson | Y | Y | Y | Y | Y | Y |
| **ILLINOIS** | | | | | | |
| 1 Rush | Y | ? | ? | ? | N | Y |
| 2 Jackson | Y | Y | Y | Y | N | Y |
| 3 Lipinski | Y | ? | ? | ? | N | Y |
| 4 Gutierrez | + | ? | ? | ? | N | Y |
| 5 Emanuel | Y | Y | Y | Y | N | Y |
| 6 Hyde | Y | Y | Y | Y | Y | Y |
| 7 Davis | Y | Y | Y | Y | N | Y |
| 8 Bean | Y | Y | Y | Y | N | Y |
| 9 Schakowsky | Y | Y | Y | Y | N | Y |
| 10 Kirk | Y | + | + | + | Y | Y |
| 11 Weller | Y | Y | Y | Y | Y | Y |
| 12 Costello | Y | Y | Y | Y | N | Y |

ND Northern Democrats, SD Southern Democrats
Southern states: Ala., Ark., Fla., Ga., Ky., La., Miss., N.C., Okla., S.C., Tenn., Texas, Va.

| | 569 | 570 | 571 | 572 | 573 | 574 |
|---|---|---|---|---|---|---|
| 13 **Biggert** | Y | Y | Y | Y | Y | Y |
| 14 **Hastert** | | | | | | |
| 15 **Johnson** | Y | Y | Y | Y | Y | Y |
| 16 **Manzullo** | Y | Y | Y | Y | Y | Y |
| 17 Evans | Y | Y | Y | Y | N | Y |
| 18 **LaHood** | Y | ? | ? | ? | Y | Y |
| 19 **Shimkus** | Y | ? | ? | ? | Y | Y |
| **INDIANA** | | | | | | |
| 1 Visclosky | Y | Y | Y | Y | N | Y |
| 2 **Chocola** | Y | ? | Y | Y | Y | Y |
| 3 **Souder** | Y | ? | ? | ? | ? | Y |
| 4 **Buyer** | ? | Y | Y | Y | Y | Y |
| 5 **Burton** | Y | Y | Y | Y | Y | Y |
| 6 **Pence** | Y | Y | N | Y | Y | Y |
| 7 Carson | Y | Y | Y | Y | N | Y |
| 8 **Hostettler** | N | Y | N | Y | Y | Y |
| 9 **Sodrel** | Y | Y | N | Y | Y | Y |
| **IOWA** | | | | | | |
| 1 **Nussle** | Y | Y | Y | Y | Y | Y |
| 2 **Leach** | Y | ? | ? | ? | Y | Y |
| 3 Boswell | ? | ? | ? | ? | ? | ? |
| 4 **Latham** | Y | Y | Y | Y | Y | Y |
| 5 **King** | Y | Y | N | Y | Y | Y |
| **KANSAS** | | | | | | |
| 1 **Moran** | N | Y | Y | Y | Y | Y |
| 2 **Ryun** | N | Y | Y | Y | Y | Y |
| 3 Moore | Y | Y | Y | Y | N | Y |
| 4 **Tiahrt** | + | Y | Y | Y | Y | Y |
| **KENTUCKY** | | | | | | |
| 1 **Whitfield** | Y | ? | ? | ? | ? | ? |
| 2 **Lewis** | Y | + | + | + | Y | Y |
| 3 **Northup** | Y | Y | Y | Y | Y | Y |
| 4 **Davis** | Y | Y | N | Y | Y | Y |
| 5 **Rogers** | Y | Y | Y | Y | Y | Y |
| 6 Chandler | Y | Y | Y | Y | N | Y |
| **LOUISIANA** | | | | | | |
| 1 **Jindal** | Y | Y | Y | Y | Y | Y |
| 2 Jefferson | Y | Y | Y | Y | N | Y |
| 3 Melancon | N | Y | Y | Y | N | Y |
| 4 **McCrery** | Y | Y | Y | Y | Y | Y |
| 5 **Alexander** | Y | Y | Y | Y | Y | Y |
| 6 **Baker** | ? | Y | Y | Y | Y | Y |
| 7 **Boustany** | Y | ? | ? | ? | Y | Y |
| **MAINE** | | | | | | |
| 1 Allen | Y | Y | Y | Y | N | Y |
| 2 Michaud | Y | Y | Y | Y | N | Y |
| **MARYLAND** | | | | | | |
| 1 **Gilchrest** | Y | Y | Y | Y | Y | Y |
| 2 Ruppersberger | Y | Y | Y | Y | N | Y |
| 3 Cardin | Y | ? | ? | ? | N | Y |
| 4 Wynn | Y | Y | Y | Y | N | Y |
| 5 Hoyer | ? | Y | Y | Y | N | Y |
| 6 **Bartlett** | N | Y | N | Y | Y | Y |
| 7 Cummings | Y | ? | Y | Y | ? | ? |
| 8 Van Hollen | Y | Y | Y | Y | N | Y |
| **MASSACHUSETTS** | | | | | | |
| 1 Olver | Y | Y | Y | Y | N | Y |
| 2 Neal | Y | ? | ? | ? | N | Y |
| 3 McGovern | Y | Y | Y | Y | N | Y |
| 4 Frank | Y | Y | Y | Y | N | Y |
| 5 Meehan | Y | Y | Y | Y | N | Y |
| 6 Tierney | Y | Y | Y | Y | N | Y |
| 7 Markey | Y | Y | Y | Y | N | Y |
| 8 Capuano | Y | ? | ? | ? | N | Y |
| 9 Lynch | Y | Y | Y | Y | N | Y |
| 10 Delahunt | Y | Y | Y | Y | N | Y |
| **MICHIGAN** | | | | | | |
| 1 Stupak | Y | ? | ? | ? | N | Y |
| 2 **Hoekstra** | Y | ? | ? | ? | Y | Y |
| 3 **Ehlers** | Y | Y | Y | Y | Y | Y |
| 4 **Camp** | Y | Y | Y | Y | Y | Y |
| 5 Kildee | Y | Y | Y | Y | N | Y |
| 6 **Upton** | Y | Y | Y | Y | Y | Y |
| 7 **Schwarz** | Y | ? | ? | ? | Y | Y |
| 8 **Rogers** | Y | Y | Y | Y | Y | Y |
| 9 **Knollenberg** | Y | Y | Y | Y | Y | Y |
| 10 **Miller** | Y | Y | N | Y | Y | Y |
| 11 **McCotter** | Y | Y | Y | Y | Y | Y |
| 12 Levin | Y | Y | Y | Y | N | Y |
| 13 Kilpatrick | Y | + | + | + | – | + |
| 14 Conyers | Y | ? | ? | ? | ? | ? |
| 15 Dingell | Y | Y | Y | Y | ? | ? |
| **MINNESOTA** | | | | | | |
| 1 **Gutknecht** | N | + | + | + | + | + |
| 2 **Kline** | Y | Y | Y | Y | Y | Y |
| 3 **Ramstad** | Y | Y | Y | Y | Y | Y |
| 4 McCollum | Y | Y | Y | Y | N | Y |
| 5 Sabo | Y | Y | Y | Y | N | Y |
| 6 **Kennedy** | Y | Y | Y | Y | Y | Y |
| 7 Peterson | Y | Y | Y | Y | N | Y |
| 8 Oberstar | Y | Y | Y | Y | N | Y |
| **MISSISSIPPI** | | | | | | |
| 1 **Wicker** | Y | Y | Y | Y | Y | Y |
| 2 Thompson | ? | Y | Y | Y | N | Y |
| 3 **Pickering** | Y | Y | Y | Y | Y | Y |
| 4 Taylor | N | Y | Y | Y | N | Y |
| **MISSOURI** | | | | | | |
| 1 Clay | Y | Y | Y | Y | N | Y |
| 2 **Akin** | Y | Y | Y | Y | Y | Y |
| 3 Carnahan | Y | Y | Y | Y | N | Y |
| 4 Skelton | Y | Y | Y | Y | N | + |
| 5 Cleaver | Y | Y | Y | Y | N | Y |
| 6 **Graves** | N | Y | Y | Y | Y | Y |
| 7 **Blunt** | Y | Y | Y | Y | Y | Y |
| 8 **Emerson** | + | Y | Y | Y | Y | Y |
| 9 **Hulshof** | N | ? | ? | ? | Y | Y |
| **MONTANA** | | | | | | |
| AL **Rehberg** | Y | Y | Y | Y | Y | Y |
| **NEBRASKA** | | | | | | |
| 1 **Fortenberry** | Y | Y | Y | Y | Y | Y |
| 2 **Terry** | Y | ? | ? | ? | Y | Y |
| 3 **Osborne** | + | Y | Y | Y | Y | Y |
| **NEVADA** | | | | | | |
| 1 Berkley | Y | Y | Y | Y | N | Y |
| 2 **Gibbons** | N | + | + | + | Y | Y |
| 3 **Porter** | Y | Y | Y | Y | Y | Y |
| **NEW HAMPSHIRE** | | | | | | |
| 1 **Bradley** | Y | Y | Y | Y | Y | Y |
| 2 **Bass** | Y | Y | Y | Y | Y | Y |
| **NEW JERSEY** | | | | | | |
| 1 Andrews | Y | + | + | + | – | + |
| 2 **LoBiondo** | Y | Y | Y | Y | Y | Y |
| 3 **Saxton** | Y | Y | Y | Y | Y | Y |
| 4 **Smith** | Y | Y | Y | Y | Y | Y |
| 5 **Garrett** | Y | Y | N | Y | Y | Y |
| 6 Pallone | Y | ? | ? | ? | ? | ? |
| 7 **Ferguson** | Y | Y | Y | Y | Y | Y |
| 8 Pascrell | Y | + | + | + | – | + |
| 9 Rothman | Y | Y | Y | Y | N | Y |
| 10 Payne | Y | ? | ? | ? | ? | ? |
| 11 **Frelinghuysen** | Y | Y | Y | Y | Y | Y |
| 12 Holt | Y | Y | Y | Y | N | Y |
| 13 Menendez | Y | Y | Y | Y | N | Y |
| **NEW MEXICO** | | | | | | |
| 1 **Wilson** | Y | Y | Y | Y | Y | Y |
| 2 **Pearce** | Y | Y | Y | Y | Y | Y |
| 3 Udall | Y | Y | Y | Y | N | Y |
| **NEW YORK** | | | | | | |
| 1 Bishop | Y | ? | ? | ? | N | Y |
| 2 Israel | Y | ? | ? | ? | N | Y |
| 3 **King** | Y | Y | Y | Y | Y | Y |
| 4 McCarthy | Y | ? | ? | ? | N | Y |
| 5 Ackerman | Y | ? | ? | ? | ? | ? |
| 6 Meeks | Y | ? | ? | ? | ? | ? |
| 7 Crowley | Y | ? | ? | ? | ? | ? |
| 8 Nadler | Y | Y | Y | Y | N | Y |
| 9 Weiner | Y | Y | Y | Y | N | Y |
| 10 Towns | Y | ? | ? | ? | ? | ? |
| 11 Owens | Y | + | + | + | – | + |
| 12 Velázquez | Y | ? | ? | ? | ? | ? |
| 13 **Fossella** | Y | Y | Y | Y | Y | Y |
| 14 Maloney | Y | Y | Y | Y | N | Y |
| 15 Rangel | Y | ? | ? | ? | N | Y |
| 16 Serrano | Y | ? | ? | ? | ? | ? |
| 17 Engel | Y | Y | Y | Y | N | Y |
| 18 Lowey | Y | Y | Y | Y | N | Y |
| 19 **Kelly** | Y | Y | Y | Y | Y | Y |
| 20 **Sweeney** | Y | Y | Y | Y | Y | Y |
| 21 McNulty | Y | Y | Y | Y | N | Y |
| 22 Hinchey | ? | ? | ? | ? | ? | ? |
| 23 **McHugh** | Y | Y | Y | Y | Y | Y |
| 24 **Boehlert** | ? | Y | Y | Y | Y | Y |
| 25 **Walsh** | Y | Y | Y | Y | Y | Y |
| 26 **Reynolds** | Y | Y | Y | Y | Y | Y |
| 27 Higgins | Y | Y | Y | Y | N | Y |
| 28 Slaughter | Y | + | + | + | N | Y |
| 29 **Kuhl** | Y | Y | Y | Y | Y | Y |
| **NORTH CAROLINA** | | | | | | |
| 1 Butterfield | Y | Y | Y | Y | N | Y |
| 2 Etheridge | Y | Y | Y | Y | N | Y |
| 3 **Jones** | N | Y | N | Y | ? | Y |
| 4 Price | Y | ? | ? | ? | N | Y |
| 5 **Foxx** | Y | Y | N | Y | Y | Y |
| 6 **Coble** | Y | Y | N | Y | Y | Y |
| 7 McIntyre | Y | Y | Y | Y | N | Y |
| 8 **Hayes** | N | Y | N | Y | Y | Y |
| 9 **Myrick** | Y | Y | Y | Y | Y | Y |
| 10 **McHenry** | Y | Y | N | Y | Y | Y |
| 11 **Taylor** | Y | ? | ? | ? | Y | Y |
| 12 Watt | Y | Y | Y | Y | N | Y |
| 13 Miller | Y | Y | Y | Y | N | Y |
| **NORTH DAKOTA** | | | | | | |
| AL Pomeroy | Y | ? | ? | ? | N | Y |
| **OHIO** | | | | | | |
| 1 **Chabot** | Y | Y | Y | Y | Y | Y |
| 2 **Schmidt** | Y | Y | Y | Y | Y | Y |
| 3 **Turner** | Y | Y | Y | Y | Y | Y |
| 4 **Oxley** | Y | Y | Y | Y | Y | Y |
| 5 **Gillmor** | Y | Y | Y | Y | Y | Y |
| 6 Strickland | Y | ? | ? | ? | N | Y |
| 7 **Hobson** | Y | Y | Y | Y | Y | Y |
| 8 **Boehner** | Y | Y | Y | Y | Y | Y |
| 9 Kaptur | Y | Y | Y | Y | N | Y |
| 10 Kucinich | Y | Y | Y | Y | N | Y |
| 11 Jones | Y | ? | ? | ? | ? | ? |
| 12 **Tiberi** | Y | Y | Y | Y | Y | Y |
| 13 Brown | Y | + | + | + | N | Y |
| 14 **LaTourette** | Y | Y | Y | Y | Y | Y |
| 15 **Pryce** | Y | Y | Y | Y | Y | Y |
| 16 **Regula** | Y | Y | Y | Y | Y | Y |
| 17 Ryan | Y | Y | Y | Y | N | Y |
| 18 **Ney** | Y | Y | Y | Y | Y | Y |
| **OKLAHOMA** | | | | | | |
| 1 **Sullivan** | ? | Y | Y | Y | Y | Y |
| 2 Boren | Y | Y | Y | Y | N | Y |
| 3 **Lucas** | N | Y | Y | Y | Y | Y |
| 4 **Cole** | Y | Y | Y | Y | Y | Y |
| 5 **Istook** | Y | ? | ? | ? | Y | Y |
| **OREGON** | | | | | | |
| 1 Wu | Y | Y | Y | Y | N | Y |
| 2 **Walden** | Y | Y | Y | Y | Y | Y |
| 3 Blumenauer | Y | Y | Y | Y | N | Y |
| 4 DeFazio | N | Y | Y | Y | N | Y |
| 5 Hooley | Y | Y | Y | Y | N | Y |
| **PENNSYLVANIA** | | | | | | |
| 1 Brady | ? | Y | Y | Y | ? | ? |
| 2 Fattah | Y | Y | Y | Y | N | Y |
| 3 **English** | Y | Y | Y | Y | Y | Y |
| 4 **Hart** | Y | Y | Y | Y | Y | Y |
| 5 **Peterson** | Y | Y | Y | Y | Y | Y |
| 6 **Gerlach** | Y | Y | Y | Y | Y | Y |
| 7 **Weldon** | Y | ? | Y | Y | Y | Y |
| 8 **Fitzpatrick** | Y | Y | Y | Y | Y | Y |
| 9 **Shuster** | Y | Y | Y | Y | Y | Y |
| 10 **Sherwood** | Y | Y | Y | Y | Y | Y |
| 11 Kanjorski | Y | Y | Y | Y | N | Y |
| 12 Murtha | Y | ? | ? | ? | N | Y |
| 13 Schwartz | Y | Y | Y | Y | N | Y |
| 14 Doyle | Y | ? | ? | ? | ? | ? |
| 15 **Dent** | Y | Y | Y | Y | Y | Y |
| 16 **Pitts** | Y | Y | Y | Y | Y | Y |
| 17 Holden | Y | ? | ? | ? | N | Y |
| 18 **Murphy** | Y | Y | Y | Y | Y | Y |
| 19 **Platts** | Y | Y | Y | Y | Y | Y |
| **RHODE ISLAND** | | | | | | |
| 1 Kennedy | Y | Y | Y | Y | N | Y |
| 2 Langevin | Y | Y | Y | Y | N | Y |
| **SOUTH CAROLINA** | | | | | | |
| 1 **Brown** | Y | Y | Y | Y | ? | ? |
| 2 **Wilson** | Y | Y | Y | ? | Y | Y |
| 3 **Barrett** | Y | Y | Y | Y | Y | Y |
| 4 **Inglis** | Y | Y | Y | Y | Y | Y |
| 5 Spratt | Y | Y | Y | Y | N | Y |
| 6 Clyburn | Y | Y | Y | Y | N | Y |
| **SOUTH DAKOTA** | | | | | | |
| AL Herseth | Y | Y | Y | Y | N | Y |
| **TENNESSEE** | | | | | | |
| 1 **Jenkins** | N | ? | ? | ? | Y | Y |
| 2 **Duncan** | N | Y | N | Y | Y | Y |
| 3 **Wamp** | Y | Y | Y | Y | Y | Y |
| 4 Davis | Y | ? | ? | ? | ? | ? |
| 5 Cooper | Y | Y | Y | Y | N | Y |
| 6 Gordon | Y | ? | ? | ? | N | Y |
| 7 **Blackburn** | Y | Y | Y | Y | Y | Y |
| 8 Tanner | N | Y | Y | Y | N | Y |
| 9 Ford | ? | ? | ? | ? | N | Y |
| **TEXAS** | | | | | | |
| 1 **Gohmert** | Y | Y | Y | Y | Y | Y |
| 2 **Poe** | ? | Y | Y | Y | + | Y |
| 3 **Johnson, S.** | Y | Y | N | ? | Y | Y |
| 4 **Hall** | Y | Y | Y | Y | Y | Y |
| 5 **Hensarling** | N | Y | N | Y | Y | Y |
| 6 **Barton** | Y | Y | Y | Y | Y | Y |
| 7 **Culberson** | Y | Y | Y | Y | Y | Y |
| 8 **Brady** | ? | Y | Y | Y | Y | Y |
| 9 Green, A. | Y | Y | Y | Y | N | Y |
| 10 **McCaul** | Y | Y | Y | Y | Y | Y |
| 11 **Conaway** | Y | Y | N | Y | Y | Y |
| 12 **Granger** | Y | Y | Y | Y | Y | Y |
| 13 **Thornberry** | Y | Y | Y | Y | Y | Y |
| 14 **Paul** | N | Y | N | Y | Y | ? |
| 15 Hinojosa | Y | Y | Y | Y | N | Y |
| 16 Reyes | Y | ? | ? | ? | N | Y |
| 17 Edwards | Y | Y | Y | Y | N | Y |
| 18 Jackson-Lee | Y | Y | Y | Y | N | Y |
| 19 **Neugebauer** | Y | Y | N | Y | Y | Y |
| 20 Gonzalez | Y | Y | Y | Y | N | Y |
| 21 **Smith** | Y | Y | Y | Y | Y | Y |
| 22 **DeLay** | Y | Y | Y | Y | Y | Y |
| 23 **Bonilla** | Y | Y | Y | Y | Y | Y |
| 24 **Marchant** | Y | ? | ? | ? | ? | ? |
| 25 Doggett | Y | Y | Y | Y | N | Y |
| 26 **Burgess** | Y | Y | Y | Y | Y | Y |
| 27 Ortiz | + | Y | Y | Y | N | Y |
| 28 Cuellar | Y | Y | Y | Y | N | Y |
| 29 Green, G. | Y | Y | Y | Y | N | Y |
| 30 Johnson, E. | Y | Y | Y | Y | N | Y |
| 31 **Carter** | Y | Y | Y | Y | Y | Y |
| 32 **Sessions** | Y | Y | Y | Y | Y | Y |
| **UTAH** | | | | | | |
| 1 **Bishop** | Y | Y | Y | Y | Y | Y |
| 2 Matheson | Y | Y | Y | Y | N | Y |
| 3 **Cannon** | Y | Y | Y | Y | Y | Y |
| **VERMONT** | | | | | | |
| AL *Sanders* | Y | Y | Y | Y | N | Y |
| **VIRGINIA** | | | | | | |
| 1 **Davis, J.** | N | Y | Y | Y | Y | Y |
| 2 **Drake** | Y | Y | Y | Y | Y | Y |
| 3 Scott | Y | ? | ? | ? | N | Y |
| 4 **Forbes** | Y | Y | Y | Y | Y | Y |
| 5 **Goode** | N | Y | N | Y | Y | Y |
| 6 **Goodlatte** | N | Y | Y | Y | Y | Y |
| 7 **Cantor** | Y | ? | ? | ? | Y | Y |
| 8 Moran | Y | Y | Y | Y | – | Y |
| 9 Boucher | Y | Y | Y | Y | N | Y |
| 10 **Wolf** | Y | Y | Y | Y | Y | Y |
| 11 **Davis, T.** | Y | Y | Y | Y | Y | Y |
| **WASHINGTON** | | | | | | |
| 1 Inslee | Y | Y | Y | Y | N | Y |
| 2 Larsen | Y | Y | Y | Y | N | Y |
| 3 Baird | Y | Y | Y | Y | N | Y |
| 4 **Hastings** | Y | Y | Y | Y | Y | Y |
| 5 **McMorris** | ? | Y | Y | Y | Y | Y |
| 6 Dicks | ? | Y | Y | Y | N | Y |
| 7 McDermott | Y | Y | Y | Y | N | Y |
| 8 **Reichert** | Y | Y | Y | Y | Y | Y |
| 9 Smith | Y | Y | Y | Y | N | Y |
| **WEST VIRGINIA** | | | | | | |
| 1 Mollohan | Y | Y | Y | Y | N | Y |
| 2 **Capito** | Y | Y | Y | Y | Y | Y |
| 3 Rahall | N | Y | Y | Y | N | Y |
| **WISCONSIN** | | | | | | |
| 1 **Ryan** | + | + | + | + | Y | Y |
| 2 Baldwin | Y | Y | Y | Y | N | Y |
| 3 Kind | ? | Y | Y | Y | N | Y |
| 4 Moore | Y | Y | Y | Y | N | Y |
| 5 **Sensenbrenner** | N | Y | N | Y | Y | Y |
| 6 **Petri** | N | Y | N | Y | Y | Y |
| 7 Obey | Y | Y | Y | Y | N | Y |
| 8 **Green** | N | Y | Y | Y | Y | Y |
| **WYOMING** | | | | | | |
| AL **Cubin** | N | Y | Y | Y | Y | Y |

# IN THE HOUSE | By Vote Number

**575.** **H Res 302. Employers of National Guard and Reserve Forces/ Adoption.** Johnson, R-Texas., motion to suspend the rules and adopt the resolution that would recognize and support employers of National Guard and other reserve forces for their strong support of U.S. goals and struggles in the war on terrorism. Motion agreed to 395-0: R 221-0; D 173-0 (ND 125-0, SD 48-0); I 1-0. A two-thirds majority of those present and voting (264 in this case) is required for adoption under suspension of the rules. Nov. 8, 2005.

**576.** **HR 3770. Grant W. Green Post Office/Passage.** Westmoreland, R-Ga., motion to suspend the rules and pass the bill that would designate a post office in Knox, Ind., for Grant W. Green, who was a postal worker for 50 years, serving from 1920 to 1970. Motion agreed to 393-1: R 221-0; D 171-1 (ND 123-1, SD 48-0); I 1-0. A two-thirds majority of those present and voting (263 in this case) is required for passage under suspension of the rules. Nov. 8, 2005.

**577.** **HR 2419. Fiscal 2006 Energy-Water Appropriations/Rule.** Adoption of the rule (H Res 539) that would provide for House floor consideration of the conference report on the bill that would appropriate $30.5 billion in fiscal 2006 for energy and water development projects. Adopted 412-2: R 220-1; D 191-1 (ND 142-1, SD 49-0); I 1-0. Nov. 9, 2005.

**578.** **HR 2862. Fiscal 2006 Commerce-Justice-Science Appropriations/ Rule.** Adoption of the rule (H Res 538) that would provide for House floor consideration of the conference report on the bill that would appropriate $61.8 billion in fiscal 2006 for the departments of Commerce, Justice and State, and various science and other related agencies. Adopted 410-0: R 220-0; D 189-0 (ND 142-0, SD 47-0); I 1-0. Nov. 9, 2005.

**579.** **HR 1751. Court Security/Rule.** Adoption of the rule (H Res 540) that would provide for House floor consideration of the bill that would increase federal penalties for the assault, murder or kidnapping of judges or their immediate family members. Adopted 412-0: R 221-0; D 190-0 (ND 142-0, SD 48-0); I 1-0. Nov. 9, 2005.

**580.** **HR 2419. Fiscal 2006 Energy-Water Appropriations/Conference Report.** Adoption of the conference report on the bill that would provide $30.5 billion in fiscal 2006 for energy and water development projects, including $24.3 billion for the Energy Department, $5.4 billion for the Army Corps of Engineers and $1.1 billion for Interior Department water projects. Adopted (thus sent to the Senate) 399-17: R 209-12; D 189-5 (ND 140-5, SD 49-0); I 1-0. Nov. 9, 2005.

| | 575 | 576 | 577 | 578 | 579 | 580 |
|---|---|---|---|---|---|---|
| **ALABAMA** | | | | | | |
| 1 Bonner | Y | Y | Y | Y | Y | Y |
| 2 Everett | Y | Y | Y | Y | Y | Y |
| 3 Rogers | Y | Y | Y | Y | Y | Y |
| 4 Aderholt | Y | Y | Y | Y | Y | Y |
| 5 Cramer | Y | Y | Y | Y | Y | Y |
| 6 Bachus | Y | Y | Y | Y | Y | Y |
| 7 Davis | Y | Y | Y | Y | Y | Y |
| **ALASKA** | | | | | | |
| AL Young | Y | Y | Y | Y | Y | Y |
| **ARIZONA** | | | | | | |
| 1 Renzi | Y | Y | Y | Y | Y | Y |
| 2 Franks | Y | Y | Y | Y | Y | Y |
| 3 Shadegg | Y | Y | Y | Y | Y | Y |
| 4 Pastor | Y | Y | Y | Y | Y | Y |
| 5 Hayworth | Y | Y | Y | Y | Y | Y |
| 6 Flake | Y | Y | Y | Y | Y | N |
| 7 Grijalva | Y | Y | Y | Y | Y | Y |
| 8 Kolbe | Y | Y | Y | Y | Y | Y |
| **ARKANSAS** | | | | | | |
| 1 Berry | Y | Y | Y | Y | Y | Y |
| 2 Snyder | Y | Y | Y | Y | Y | Y |
| 3 Boozman | Y | Y | Y | Y | Y | Y |
| 4 Ross | Y | Y | Y | Y | Y | Y |
| **CALIFORNIA** | | | | | | |
| 1 Thompson | Y | Y | Y | Y | Y | Y |
| 2 Herger | Y | Y | Y | Y | Y | Y |
| 3 Lungren | Y | Y | Y | Y | Y | Y |
| 4 Doolittle | Y | Y | Y | Y | Y | Y |
| 5 Matsui, D. | Y | Y | Y | Y | Y | Y |
| 6 Woolsey | Y | Y | Y | Y | Y | Y |
| 7 Miller, George | Y | Y | Y | Y | Y | Y |
| 8 Pelosi | Y | Y | Y | Y | Y | Y |
| 9 Lee | ? | ? | Y | Y | Y | Y |
| 10 Tauscher | Y | Y | Y | Y | Y | Y |
| 11 Pombo | Y | Y | Y | Y | Y | Y |
| 12 Lantos | Y | Y | Y | Y | Y | Y |
| 13 Stark | Y | Y | Y | ? | Y | Y |
| 14 Eshoo | Y | Y | Y | Y | Y | Y |
| 15 Honda | Y | Y | Y | Y | Y | Y |
| 16 Lofgren | Y | Y | Y | Y | Y | Y |
| 17 Farr | ? | Y | Y | Y | Y | Y |
| 18 Cardoza | Y | Y | Y | Y | Y | Y |
| 19 Radanovich | Y | Y | Y | Y | Y | Y |
| 20 Costa | Y | Y | Y | Y | Y | Y |
| 21 Nunes | Y | Y | Y | Y | Y | Y |
| 22 Thomas | Y | Y | Y | Y | Y | Y |
| 23 Capps | Y | Y | Y | Y | Y | Y |
| 24 Gallegly | Y | Y | Y | Y | Y | Y |
| 25 McKeon | Y | Y | Y | Y | Y | Y |
| 26 Dreier | Y | Y | Y | Y | Y | Y |
| 27 Sherman | ? | ? | Y | Y | Y | Y |
| 28 Berman | ? | ? | ? | ? | ? | Y |
| 29 Schiff | Y | Y | Y | Y | Y | Y |
| 30 Waxman | Y | Y | Y | Y | Y | Y |
| 31 Becerra | Y | Y | Y | Y | Y | Y |
| 32 Solis | + | + | + | + | + | + |
| 33 Watson | Y | Y | Y | Y | Y | Y |
| 34 Roybal-Allard | Y | Y | Y | Y | Y | Y |
| 35 Waters | ? | ? | Y | Y | Y | Y |
| 36 Harman | Y | Y | Y | Y | Y | Y |
| 37 Millender-McD. | ? | ? | ? | ? | ? | ? |
| 38 Napolitano | Y | ? | Y | Y | Y | Y |
| 39 Sánchez, Linda | Y | Y | Y | Y | Y | Y |
| 40 Royce | Y | Y | Y | Y | Y | Y |
| 41 Lewis | Y | Y | Y | Y | Y | Y |
| 42 Miller, Gary | Y | Y | Y | Y | Y | Y |
| 43 Baca | Y | Y | Y | Y | Y | Y |
| 44 Calvert | Y | Y | Y | Y | Y | Y |
| 45 Bono | Y | Y | Y | Y | Y | Y |
| 46 Rohrabacher | Y | Y | Y | Y | Y | Y |
| 47 Sanchez, Loretta | Y | Y | Y | Y | Y | Y |
| 48 Vacant | | | | | | |
| 49 Issa | Y | Y | Y | Y | Y | Y |

| | 575 | 576 | 577 | 578 | 579 | 580 |
|---|---|---|---|---|---|---|
| 50 Cunningham | Y | Y | Y | Y | Y | Y |
| 51 Filner | Y | Y | Y | Y | Y | Y |
| 52 Hunter | Y | Y | Y | Y | Y | Y |
| 53 Davis | Y | Y | Y | Y | Y | Y |
| **COLORADO** | | | | | | |
| 1 DeGette | Y | Y | Y | Y | Y | Y |
| 2 Udall | Y | Y | Y | Y | Y | Y |
| 3 Salazar | Y | Y | Y | Y | Y | Y |
| 4 Musgrave | Y | Y | Y | Y | Y | Y |
| 5 Hefley | Y | Y | Y | Y | Y | N |
| 6 Tancredo | Y | Y | Y | Y | Y | N |
| 7 Beauprez | Y | Y | Y | Y | Y | Y |
| **CONNECTICUT** | | | | | | |
| 1 Larson | Y | Y | Y | Y | Y | Y |
| 2 Simmons | Y | Y | Y | Y | Y | Y |
| 3 DeLauro | Y | Y | Y | Y | Y | Y |
| 4 Shays | Y | Y | Y | Y | Y | Y |
| 5 Johnson | Y | Y | Y | Y | Y | Y |
| **DELAWARE** | | | | | | |
| AL Castle | Y | Y | Y | Y | Y | Y |
| **FLORIDA** | | | | | | |
| 1 Miller | Y | Y | Y | Y | Y | N |
| 2 Boyd | Y | Y | Y | Y | Y | Y |
| 3 Brown | ? | ? | Y | Y | Y | Y |
| 4 Crenshaw | Y | Y | Y | Y | Y | Y |
| 5 Brown-Waite | ? | ? | ? | ? | ? | ? |
| 6 Stearns | Y | Y | Y | Y | Y | N |
| 7 Mica | Y | Y | Y | Y | Y | Y |
| 8 Keller | Y | Y | Y | Y | Y | Y |
| 9 Bilirakis | Y | Y | Y | Y | Y | Y |
| 10 Young | ? | ? | ? | ? | ? | ? |
| 11 Davis | Y | Y | ? | Y | ? | ? |
| 12 Putnam | Y | Y | Y | Y | Y | Y |
| 13 Harris | ? | ? | Y | Y | Y | Y |
| 14 Mack | Y | Y | Y | Y | Y | Y |
| 15 Weldon | Y | Y | Y | Y | Y | Y |
| 16 Foley | Y | Y | Y | Y | Y | Y |
| 17 Meek | Y | Y | Y | Y | Y | Y |
| 18 Ros-Lehtinen | Y | Y | Y | Y | Y | Y |
| 19 Wexler | Y | Y | Y | Y | Y | Y |
| 20 Wasserman-Schultz | Y | Y | Y | Y | Y | Y |
| 21 Diaz-Balart, L. | Y | Y | ? | ? | Y | Y |
| 22 Shaw | Y | Y | Y | Y | Y | Y |
| 23 Hastings | ? | ? | ? | ? | ? | ? |
| 24 Feeney | Y | Y | Y | Y | Y | Y |
| 25 Diaz-Balart, M. | Y | Y | Y | Y | Y | Y |
| **GEORGIA** | | | | | | |
| 1 Kingston | Y | Y | Y | Y | Y | Y |
| 2 Bishop | Y | Y | Y | Y | Y | Y |
| 3 Marshall | Y | Y | Y | Y | Y | Y |
| 4 McKinney | Y | Y | Y | Y | Y | Y |
| 5 Lewis | Y | Y | Y | Y | Y | Y |
| 6 Price | Y | Y | Y | Y | Y | Y |
| 7 Linder | Y | Y | Y | Y | Y | Y |
| 8 Westmoreland | ? | ? | Y | Y | Y | Y |
| 9 Norwood | + | + | + | + | + | – |
| 10 Deal | Y | Y | Y | Y | Y | N |
| 11 Gingrey | Y | Y | Y | Y | Y | Y |
| 12 Barrow | Y | Y | Y | Y | Y | Y |
| 13 Scott | Y | Y | Y | Y | Y | Y |
| **HAWAII** | | | | | | |
| 1 Abercrombie | Y | N | Y | Y | Y | Y |
| 2 Case | Y | Y | Y | Y | Y | Y |
| **IDAHO** | | | | | | |
| 1 Otter | Y | Y | Y | Y | Y | Y |
| 2 Simpson | Y | Y | Y | Y | Y | Y |
| **ILLINOIS** | | | | | | |
| 1 Rush | Y | Y | Y | Y | Y | Y |
| 2 Jackson | Y | Y | Y | Y | Y | Y |
| 3 Lipinski | Y | Y | Y | Y | Y | Y |
| 4 Gutierrez | Y | Y | Y | Y | Y | Y |
| 5 Emanuel | Y | Y | Y | ? | ? | Y |
| 6 Hyde | Y | Y | Y | Y | Y | Y |
| 7 Davis | Y | Y | Y | Y | Y | Y |
| 8 Bean | Y | Y | Y | Y | Y | Y |
| 9 Schakowsky | Y | Y | Y | Y | Y | Y |
| 10 Kirk | Y | Y | Y | Y | Y | Y |
| 11 Weller | Y | Y | Y | Y | Y | Y |
| 12 Costello | Y | Y | Y | Y | Y | Y |

| KEY | Republicans | Democrats | *Independents* | | |
|---|---|---|---|---|---|
| Y | Voted for (yea) | X | Paired against | C | Voted "present" to avoid possible conflict of interest |
| # | Paired for | – | Announced against | | |
| + | Announced for | P | Voted "present" | ? | Did not vote or otherwise make a position known |
| N | Voted against (nay) | | | | |

ND Northern Democrats, SD Southern Democrats
Southern states: Ala., Ark., Fla., Ga., Ky., La., Miss., N.C., Okla., S.C., Tenn., Texas, Va.

| | 575 | 576 | 577 | 578 | 579 | 580 |
|---|---|---|---|---|---|---|
| 13 **Biggert** | Y | Y | Y | Y | Y | Y |
| 14 **Hastert** | | | | | | |
| 15 **Johnson** | Y | Y | Y | Y | Y | Y |
| 16 **Manzullo** | Y | Y | Y | Y | Y | Y |
| 17 Evans | Y | Y | Y | Y | Y | Y |
| 18 **LaHood** | Y | Y | Y | Y | Y | Y |
| 19 **Shimkus** | Y | Y | Y | Y | Y | Y |
| **INDIANA** | | | | | | |
| 1 Visclosky | Y | Y | Y | Y | Y | Y |
| 2 **Chocola** | Y | Y | Y | Y | Y | Y |
| 3 **Souder** | Y | Y | Y | Y | Y | Y |
| 4 **Buyer** | Y | Y | Y | Y | Y | Y |
| 5 **Burton** | Y | Y | Y | Y | Y | Y |
| 6 **Pence** | Y | Y | Y | Y | Y | Y |
| 7 Carson | Y | Y | Y | Y | Y | Y |
| 8 **Hostettler** | Y | Y | Y | Y | Y | N |
| 9 **Sodrel** | Y | Y | Y | Y | Y | Y |
| **IOWA** | | | | | | |
| 1 **Nussle** | Y | Y | Y | Y | Y | Y |
| 2 **Leach** | Y | Y | Y | Y | Y | Y |
| 3 Boswell | ? | ? | ? | ? | ? | ? |
| 4 **Latham** | Y | Y | Y | Y | Y | Y |
| 5 **King** | Y | Y | Y | Y | Y | Y |
| **KANSAS** | | | | | | |
| 1 **Moran** | Y | Y | Y | Y | Y | Y |
| 2 **Ryun** | Y | Y | Y | Y | Y | Y |
| 3 Moore | Y | Y | Y | Y | Y | Y |
| 4 **Tiahrt** | Y | Y | Y | Y | Y | Y |
| **KENTUCKY** | | | | | | |
| 1 **Whitfield** | ? | ? | Y | Y | Y | Y |
| 2 **Lewis** | Y | Y | Y | Y | Y | Y |
| 3 **Northup** | Y | Y | Y | Y | Y | Y |
| 4 **Davis** | Y | Y | Y | Y | Y | Y |
| 5 **Rogers** | Y | Y | Y | Y | Y | Y |
| 6 Chandler | Y | Y | Y | Y | Y | Y |
| **LOUISIANA** | | | | | | |
| 1 **Jindal** | Y | Y | Y | Y | Y | Y |
| 2 Jefferson | Y | Y | Y | ? | Y | Y |
| 3 Melancon | Y | Y | Y | Y | Y | Y |
| 4 **McCrery** | Y | Y | Y | Y | Y | Y |
| 5 **Alexander** | Y | Y | Y | Y | Y | Y |
| 6 **Baker** | Y | Y | Y | Y | Y | Y |
| 7 **Boustany** | Y | Y | Y | Y | Y | Y |
| **MAINE** | | | | | | |
| 1 Allen | Y | Y | Y | Y | Y | Y |
| 2 Michaud | Y | Y | Y | Y | Y | Y |
| **MARYLAND** | | | | | | |
| 1 **Gilchrest** | Y | Y | Y | Y | Y | Y |
| 2 Ruppersberger | Y | Y | Y | Y | Y | Y |
| 3 Cardin | Y | Y | Y | Y | Y | Y |
| 4 Wynn | Y | Y | Y | Y | Y | Y |
| 5 Hoyer | Y | Y | Y | Y | Y | Y |
| 6 **Bartlett** | Y | Y | Y | Y | Y | Y |
| 7 Cummings | ? | ? | Y | Y | Y | Y |
| 8 Van Hollen | Y | Y | Y | Y | Y | Y |
| **MASSACHUSETTS** | | | | | | |
| 1 Olver | Y | Y | Y | Y | Y | Y |
| 2 Neal | Y | Y | Y | Y | Y | Y |
| 3 McGovern | Y | Y | Y | Y | Y | Y |
| 4 Frank | Y | Y | Y | Y | Y | Y |
| 5 Meehan | Y | Y | Y | Y | Y | Y |
| 6 Tierney | Y | Y | Y | Y | Y | Y |
| 7 Markey | Y | Y | Y | Y | Y | Y |
| 8 Capuano | Y | Y | Y | Y | Y | Y |
| 9 Lynch | Y | Y | Y | Y | Y | Y |
| 10 Delahunt | Y | Y | Y | Y | Y | Y |
| **MICHIGAN** | | | | | | |
| 1 Stupak | Y | Y | Y | Y | Y | Y |
| 2 **Hoekstra** | Y | Y | Y | Y | Y | Y |
| 3 **Ehlers** | Y | Y | Y | Y | Y | Y |
| 4 **Camp** | Y | Y | Y | Y | Y | Y |
| 5 Kildee | Y | Y | Y | Y | Y | Y |
| 6 **Upton** | Y | Y | Y | Y | Y | Y |
| 7 **Schwarz** | Y | Y | Y | Y | Y | Y |
| 8 **Rogers** | Y | Y | Y | Y | Y | Y |
| 9 **Knollenberg** | Y | Y | Y | Y | Y | Y |
| 10 **Miller** | Y | Y | Y | Y | Y | Y |
| 11 **McCotter** | Y | Y | Y | Y | Y | Y |
| 12 Levin | Y | Y | Y | Y | Y | Y |
| 13 Kilpatrick | + | + | ? | ? | ? | Y |
| 14 Conyers | ? | ? | Y | Y | Y | Y |
| 15 Dingell | ? | ? | Y | Y | Y | Y |

| | 575 | 576 | 577 | 578 | 579 | 580 |
|---|---|---|---|---|---|---|
| **MINNESOTA** | | | | | | |
| 1 **Gutknecht** | + | + | Y | Y | Y | Y |
| 2 **Kline** | Y | Y | Y | Y | Y | Y |
| 3 **Ramstad** | Y | Y | Y | Y | Y | Y |
| 4 McCollum | Y | Y | Y | Y | Y | Y |
| 5 Sabo | Y | Y | Y | Y | Y | Y |
| 6 **Kennedy** | Y | Y | Y | Y | Y | Y |
| 7 Peterson | Y | Y | Y | Y | Y | Y |
| 8 Oberstar | Y | Y | Y | Y | Y | Y |
| **MISSISSIPPI** | | | | | | |
| 1 **Wicker** | Y | Y | Y | Y | Y | Y |
| 2 Thompson | Y | Y | Y | Y | Y | Y |
| 3 **Pickering** | Y | Y | Y | Y | Y | Y |
| 4 Taylor | Y | Y | Y | Y | Y | Y |
| **MISSOURI** | | | | | | |
| 1 Clay | Y | Y | Y | Y | Y | Y |
| 2 **Akin** | Y | Y | Y | Y | Y | Y |
| 3 Carnahan | Y | Y | Y | Y | Y | Y |
| 4 Skelton | Y | + | Y | Y | Y | Y |
| 5 Cleaver | Y | Y | Y | Y | Y | Y |
| 6 **Graves** | Y | Y | Y | Y | Y | Y |
| 7 **Blunt** | Y | Y | Y | Y | Y | Y |
| 8 **Emerson** | Y | Y | Y | Y | Y | Y |
| 9 **Hulshof** | Y | Y | Y | Y | Y | Y |
| **MONTANA** | | | | | | |
| AL **Rehberg** | Y | Y | Y | Y | Y | Y |
| **NEBRASKA** | | | | | | |
| 1 **Fortenberry** | Y | Y | Y | Y | Y | Y |
| 2 **Terry** | Y | Y | Y | Y | Y | Y |
| 3 **Osborne** | Y | Y | Y | Y | Y | Y |
| **NEVADA** | | | | | | |
| 1 Berkley | Y | Y | N | Y | Y | N |
| 2 **Gibbons** | Y | Y | Y | Y | Y | N |
| 3 **Porter** | Y | Y | N | Y | Y | N |
| **NEW HAMPSHIRE** | | | | | | |
| 1 **Bradley** | Y | Y | Y | Y | Y | Y |
| 2 **Bass** | Y | Y | Y | Y | Y | Y |
| **NEW JERSEY** | | | | | | |
| 1 Andrews | + | + | Y | Y | Y | N |
| 2 **LoBiondo** | Y | Y | Y | Y | Y | Y |
| 3 **Saxton** | Y | Y | Y | Y | Y | Y |
| 4 **Smith** | Y | Y | Y | Y | Y | Y |
| 5 **Garrett** | Y | Y | Y | Y | Y | Y |
| 6 Pallone | ? | ? | Y | Y | Y | Y |
| 7 **Ferguson** | Y | Y | Y | Y | Y | Y |
| 8 Pascrell | + | + | Y | Y | Y | Y |
| 9 Rothman | Y | Y | Y | Y | Y | Y |
| 10 Payne | ? | ? | Y | Y | Y | Y |
| 11 **Frelinghuysen** | Y | Y | Y | Y | Y | Y |
| 12 Holt | Y | Y | Y | Y | Y | Y |
| 13 Menendez | Y | Y | Y | Y | Y | Y |
| **NEW MEXICO** | | | | | | |
| 1 **Wilson** | Y | Y | Y | Y | Y | Y |
| 2 **Pearce** | Y | Y | Y | Y | Y | Y |
| 3 Udall | Y | Y | Y | Y | Y | Y |
| **NEW YORK** | | | | | | |
| 1 Bishop | Y | Y | Y | Y | Y | N |
| 2 Israel | Y | Y | Y | Y | Y | Y |
| 3 **King** | Y | Y | Y | Y | Y | Y |
| 4 McCarthy | Y | Y | Y | Y | Y | Y |
| 5 Ackerman | ? | ? | Y | Y | ? | Y |
| 6 Meeks | ? | ? | Y | Y | Y | ? |
| 7 Crowley | ? | ? | Y | Y | Y | Y |
| 8 Nadler | Y | Y | Y | Y | Y | Y |
| 9 Weiner | Y | Y | Y | Y | Y | Y |
| 10 Towns | ? | ? | Y | Y | Y | Y |
| 11 Owens | + | + | Y | Y | Y | Y |
| 12 Velázquez | ? | ? | Y | Y | Y | Y |
| 13 **Fossella** | Y | Y | ? | ? | ? | Y |
| 14 Maloney | Y | Y | Y | Y | Y | Y |
| 15 Rangel | Y | Y | Y | Y | Y | Y |
| 16 Serrano | ? | ? | Y | Y | Y | Y |
| 17 Engel | Y | Y | Y | Y | Y | Y |
| 18 Lowey | Y | Y | Y | Y | Y | Y |
| 19 **Kelly** | Y | Y | Y | Y | Y | Y |
| 20 **Sweeney** | Y | Y | ? | ? | ? | ? |
| 21 McNulty | Y | Y | Y | Y | Y | Y |
| 22 Hinchey | ? | ? | Y | Y | Y | Y |
| 23 **McHugh** | Y | Y | Y | Y | Y | Y |
| 24 **Boehlert** | Y | Y | Y | Y | Y | Y |
| 25 **Walsh** | Y | Y | ? | ? | ? | Y |
| 26 **Reynolds** | Y | Y | Y | Y | Y | Y |
| 27 Higgins | Y | Y | Y | Y | Y | Y |
| 28 Slaughter | Y | Y | Y | Y | Y | ? |
| 29 **Kuhl** | Y | Y | Y | Y | Y | Y |

| | 575 | 576 | 577 | 578 | 579 | 580 |
|---|---|---|---|---|---|---|
| **NORTH CAROLINA** | | | | | | |
| 1 Butterfield | Y | Y | Y | Y | Y | Y |
| 2 Etheridge | Y | Y | Y | Y | Y | Y |
| 3 **Jones** | Y | Y | Y | Y | Y | Y |
| 4 Price | Y | Y | Y | Y | Y | Y |
| 5 **Foxx** | Y | Y | Y | Y | Y | Y |
| 6 **Coble** | Y | Y | Y | Y | Y | Y |
| 7 McIntyre | Y | Y | Y | Y | Y | Y |
| 8 **Hayes** | + | + | Y | Y | Y | Y |
| 9 **Myrick** | Y | Y | Y | Y | Y | Y |
| 10 **McHenry** | Y | Y | Y | Y | Y | Y |
| 11 **Taylor** | Y | Y | Y | Y | Y | Y |
| 12 Watt | Y | Y | Y | Y | Y | Y |
| 13 Miller | Y | Y | Y | Y | Y | Y |
| **NORTH DAKOTA** | | | | | | |
| AL Pomeroy | Y | Y | Y | Y | Y | Y |
| **OHIO** | | | | | | |
| 1 **Chabot** | Y | Y | Y | Y | Y | Y |
| 2 **Schmidt** | Y | Y | Y | Y | Y | Y |
| 3 **Turner** | Y | Y | ? | ? | ? | ? |
| 4 **Oxley** | Y | Y | Y | Y | Y | + |
| 5 **Gillmor** | Y | Y | Y | Y | Y | Y |
| 6 Strickland | Y | Y | ? | ? | ? | ? |
| 7 **Hobson** | Y | Y | Y | Y | Y | Y |
| 8 **Boehner** | Y | Y | Y | Y | Y | Y |
| 9 Kaptur | Y | Y | Y | Y | Y | Y |
| 10 Kucinich | Y | Y | Y | Y | Y | N |
| 11 Jones | ? | ? | ? | ? | ? | Y |
| 12 **Tiberi** | Y | Y | Y | Y | Y | Y |
| 13 Brown | Y | Y | Y | Y | Y | Y |
| 14 **LaTourette** | Y | Y | Y | Y | Y | Y |
| 15 **Pryce** | Y | Y | Y | Y | Y | Y |
| 16 **Regula** | Y | Y | Y | Y | Y | Y |
| 17 Ryan | Y | Y | Y | Y | Y | Y |
| 18 **Ney** | Y | Y | Y | Y | Y | Y |
| **OKLAHOMA** | | | | | | |
| 1 **Sullivan** | Y | Y | Y | Y | Y | Y |
| 2 Boren | Y | Y | Y | Y | Y | Y |
| 3 **Lucas** | Y | Y | Y | Y | Y | Y |
| 4 **Cole** | Y | Y | Y | Y | Y | Y |
| 5 **Istook** | Y | Y | Y | Y | Y | Y |
| **OREGON** | | | | | | |
| 1 Wu | Y | Y | Y | Y | Y | Y |
| 2 **Walden** | Y | Y | Y | Y | Y | Y |
| 3 Blumenauer | Y | Y | ? | Y | Y | Y |
| 4 DeFazio | Y | Y | Y | Y | Y | Y |
| 5 Hooley | Y | Y | Y | Y | Y | Y |
| **PENNSYLVANIA** | | | | | | |
| 1 Brady | ? | ? | Y | Y | Y | Y |
| 2 Fattah | Y | Y | Y | Y | Y | Y |
| 3 **English** | Y | Y | Y | Y | Y | Y |
| 4 **Hart** | Y | Y | Y | Y | Y | Y |
| 5 **Peterson** | Y | Y | Y | Y | Y | Y |
| 6 **Gerlach** | Y | Y | Y | Y | Y | Y |
| 7 **Weldon** | Y | Y | Y | Y | Y | Y |
| 8 **Fitzpatrick** | Y | Y | Y | Y | Y | Y |
| 9 **Shuster** | Y | Y | Y | Y | Y | Y |
| 10 **Sherwood** | Y | Y | Y | Y | Y | Y |
| 11 Kanjorski | Y | Y | Y | Y | Y | Y |
| 12 Murtha | Y | Y | Y | Y | Y | Y |
| 13 Schwartz | Y | Y | Y | Y | Y | Y |
| 14 Doyle | Y | Y | Y | Y | Y | Y |
| 15 **Dent** | Y | Y | Y | Y | Y | Y |
| 16 **Pitts** | Y | Y | Y | Y | Y | Y |
| 17 Holden | Y | Y | Y | Y | Y | Y |
| 18 **Murphy** | Y | Y | Y | Y | Y | Y |
| 19 **Platts** | Y | Y | Y | Y | Y | Y |
| **RHODE ISLAND** | | | | | | |
| 1 Kennedy | Y | Y | Y | Y | Y | Y |
| 2 Langevin | Y | Y | Y | Y | Y | Y |
| **SOUTH CAROLINA** | | | | | | |
| 1 **Brown** | Y | Y | Y | Y | Y | Y |
| 2 **Wilson** | Y | Y | Y | Y | Y | Y |
| 3 **Barrett** | Y | Y | Y | Y | Y | Y |
| 4 **Inglis** | Y | Y | Y | Y | Y | Y |
| 5 Spratt | Y | Y | Y | Y | Y | Y |
| 6 Clyburn | Y | Y | Y | Y | Y | Y |
| **SOUTH DAKOTA** | | | | | | |
| AL Herseth | Y | Y | Y | Y | Y | Y |
| **TENNESSEE** | | | | | | |
| 1 **Jenkins** | Y | Y | Y | ? | Y | Y |
| 2 **Duncan** | Y | Y | Y | Y | Y | N |

| | 575 | 576 | 577 | 578 | 579 | 580 |
|---|---|---|---|---|---|---|
| 3 **Wamp** | Y | Y | Y | Y | Y | Y |
| 4 Davis | ? | ? | Y | Y | Y | Y |
| 5 Cooper | Y | Y | Y | Y | Y | Y |
| 6 Gordon | Y | Y | Y | Y | Y | Y |
| 7 **Blackburn** | Y | Y | Y | Y | Y | Y |
| 8 Tanner | Y | Y | Y | Y | Y | Y |
| 9 Ford | Y | Y | Y | Y | Y | Y |
| **TEXAS** | | | | | | |
| 1 **Gohmert** | Y | Y | Y | Y | Y | Y |
| 2 **Poe** | Y | Y | Y | Y | Y | Y |
| 3 **Johnson, S.** | Y | Y | Y | Y | Y | Y |
| 4 **Hall** | Y | Y | Y | Y | Y | Y |
| 5 **Hensarling** | Y | Y | Y | Y | Y | Y |
| 6 **Barton** | Y | Y | Y | Y | Y | Y |
| 7 **Culberson** | Y | Y | Y | Y | Y | Y |
| 8 **Brady** | Y | Y | Y | Y | Y | Y |
| 9 Green, A. | Y | Y | Y | Y | Y | Y |
| 10 **McCaul** | Y | Y | Y | Y | Y | Y |
| 11 **Conaway** | Y | Y | ? | ? | ? | ? |
| 12 **Granger** | Y | Y | Y | Y | Y | Y |
| 13 **Thornberry** | Y | Y | Y | Y | Y | Y |
| 14 **Paul** | Y | Y | Y | Y | Y | ? |
| 15 Hinojosa | Y | Y | Y | Y | Y | Y |
| 16 Reyes | Y | Y | Y | Y | Y | Y |
| 17 Edwards | Y | Y | Y | Y | Y | Y |
| 18 Jackson-Lee | Y | Y | Y | Y | Y | Y |
| 19 **Neugebauer** | Y | Y | Y | Y | Y | Y |
| 20 Gonzalez | Y | Y | Y | ? | ? | Y |
| 21 **Smith** | Y | Y | Y | Y | Y | Y |
| 22 **DeLay** | Y | Y | Y | Y | Y | Y |
| 23 **Bonilla** | Y | Y | Y | Y | Y | Y |
| 24 **Marchant** | ? | ? | Y | Y | Y | Y |
| 25 Doggett | Y | Y | Y | Y | Y | Y |
| 26 **Burgess** | Y | Y | Y | Y | Y | Y |
| 27 Ortiz | Y | Y | Y | Y | Y | Y |
| 28 Cuellar | Y | Y | Y | Y | Y | Y |
| 29 Green, G. | Y | Y | Y | Y | Y | Y |
| 30 Johnson, E. | Y | Y | Y | Y | Y | Y |
| 31 **Carter** | Y | Y | Y | Y | Y | Y |
| 32 **Sessions** | Y | Y | Y | Y | Y | ? |
| **UTAH** | | | | | | |
| 1 **Bishop** | Y | Y | Y | Y | Y | Y |
| 2 Matheson | Y | Y | Y | Y | Y | N |
| 3 **Cannon** | Y | Y | Y | Y | Y | Y |
| **VERMONT** | | | | | | |
| AL *Sanders* | Y | Y | Y | Y | Y | Y |
| **VIRGINIA** | | | | | | |
| 1 **Davis, J.** | Y | Y | Y | Y | ? | Y |
| 2 **Drake** | Y | Y | Y | Y | Y | Y |
| 3 Scott | Y | Y | Y | Y | Y | Y |
| 4 **Forbes** | Y | Y | Y | Y | Y | Y |
| 5 **Goode** | Y | Y | Y | Y | Y | Y |
| 6 **Goodlatte** | Y | Y | Y | Y | Y | Y |
| 7 **Cantor** | Y | Y | Y | Y | Y | Y |
| 8 Moran | Y | Y | Y | Y | Y | Y |
| 9 Boucher | Y | Y | Y | Y | Y | Y |
| 10 **Wolf** | Y | Y | Y | Y | Y | Y |
| 11 **Davis, T.** | Y | Y | Y | Y | Y | Y |
| **WASHINGTON** | | | | | | |
| 1 Inslee | Y | Y | Y | Y | Y | Y |
| 2 Larsen | Y | Y | Y | Y | Y | Y |
| 3 Baird | Y | Y | Y | Y | Y | Y |
| 4 **Hastings** | Y | Y | Y | Y | Y | Y |
| 5 **McMorris** | Y | Y | Y | Y | Y | Y |
| 6 Dicks | Y | Y | Y | Y | Y | Y |
| 7 McDermott | Y | Y | Y | Y | Y | Y |
| 8 **Reichert** | Y | Y | Y | Y | Y | Y |
| 9 Smith | Y | Y | Y | Y | Y | Y |
| **WEST VIRGINIA** | | | | | | |
| 1 Mollohan | Y | Y | Y | Y | Y | Y |
| 2 **Capito** | Y | Y | Y | Y | Y | Y |
| 3 Rahall | Y | Y | Y | Y | Y | Y |
| **WISCONSIN** | | | | | | |
| 1 **Ryan** | Y | Y | Y | Y | Y | Y |
| 2 Baldwin | Y | Y | Y | Y | Y | Y |
| 3 Kind | Y | Y | Y | Y | Y | Y |
| 4 Moore | Y | Y | Y | Y | Y | Y |
| 5 **Sensenbrenner** | Y | Y | Y | Y | Y | N |
| 6 **Petri** | Y | Y | Y | Y | Y | Y |
| 7 Obey | Y | Y | Y | Y | Y | Y |
| 8 **Green** | Y | Y | Y | Y | Y | N |
| **WYOMING** | | | | | | |
| AL **Cubin** | Y | Y | Y | Y | Y | Y |

# IN THE HOUSE | By Vote Number

**581.** **HR 2862. Fiscal 2006 Commerce-Justice-Science Appropriations/ Conference Report.** Adoption of the conference report on the bill that would provide $61.8 billion, including $57.9 billion in discretionary spending, in fiscal 2006 for the departments of Commerce, Justice and State, as well as various science and other related agencies. It would provide $21.7 billion for Justice, $6.6 billion for Commerce, $9.7 billion for the State Department and international broadcasting agencies, $16.5 billion for NASA and $5.6 billion for the National Science Foundation. Adopted (thus sent to the Senate) 397-19: R 211-9; D 185-10 (ND 138-8, SD 47-2); I 1-0. Nov. 9, 2005.

**582.** **S 1894. Access to Foster Care/Passage.** Herger, R-Calif., motion to suspend the rules and pass the bill that would clarify that federal foster care payments could be made to private, for-profit — as well as nonprofit — therapeutic foster care agencies. Motion agreed to 408-1: R 218-0; D 189-1 (ND 142-1, SD 47-0); I 1-0. A two-thirds majority of those present and voting (273 in this case) is required for passage under suspension of the rules. Nov. 9, 2005.

**583.** **HR 1751. Court Security/Penalty for Killing Federal Officers.** Scott, D-Va., amendment to eliminate the death penalty authorized in the bill for individuals convicted of killing federal public safety officers, and instead allow a sentence of up to life in prison for the same crime. Rejected 97-325: R 5-218; D 91-107 (ND 82-67, SD 9-40); I 1-0. Nov. 9, 2005.

**584.** **HR 1751. Court Security/Recommit.** Higgins, D-N.Y., motion to recommit the bill to the Judiciary Committee with instructions to add language to impose stricter criminal and civil penalties on corporations that intentionally overcharge the federal government for the provision of goods and services in response to a presidentially declared major disaster, emergency or military action, including in Iraq and Afghanistan. Motion rejected 201-221: R 2-221; D 198-0 (ND 149-0, SD 49-0); I 1-0. Nov. 9, 2005.

**585.** **HR 1751. Court Security/Passage.** Passage of the bill that would increase federal penalties for the assault, murder or kidnapping of judges or their immediate family members. It would make it a federal crime to kill or assault public safety officers or other court personnel. The bill would bar the possession of dangerous weapons, in addition to guns, in federal courts. It would give presiding judges in federal appellate or circuit courts the authority to allow news media to photograph, broadcast, televise or electronically record court proceedings. Passed 375-45: R 221-1; D 153-44 (ND 108-40, SD 45-4); I 1-0. Nov. 9, 2005.

| | 581 | 582 | 583 | 584 | 585 |
|---|---|---|---|---|---|
| **ALABAMA** | | | | | |
| 1 Bonner | Y | Y | N | N | Y |
| 2 Everett | Y | Y | N | N | Y |
| 3 Rogers | Y | Y | N | N | Y |
| 4 Aderholt | Y | Y | N | N | Y |
| 5 Cramer | Y | Y | N | Y | Y |
| 6 Bachus | Y | Y | N | N | Y |
| 7 Davis | Y | Y | N | Y | Y |
| **ALASKA** | | | | | |
| AL Young | Y | Y | N | N | Y |
| **ARIZONA** | | | | | |
| 1 Renzi | Y | Y | N | N | Y |
| 2 Franks | Y | Y | N | N | Y |
| 3 Shadegg | Y | Y | N | N | Y |
| 4 Pastor | Y | Y | Y | Y | Y |
| 5 Hayworth | Y | Y | N | N | Y |
| 6 Flake | N | Y | N | N | Y |
| 7 Grijalva | Y | Y | N | Y | N |
| 8 Kolbe | Y | Y | N | N | Y |
| **ARKANSAS** | | | | | |
| 1 Berry | Y | Y | N | Y | Y |
| 2 Snyder | Y | Y | N | Y | Y |
| 3 Boozman | Y | Y | N | N | Y |
| 4 Ross | Y | Y | N | Y | Y |
| **CALIFORNIA** | | | | | |
| 1 Thompson | Y | Y | N | Y | Y |
| 2 Herger | Y | Y | N | N | Y |
| 3 Lungren | Y | Y | N | N | Y |
| 4 Doolittle | Y | Y | N | N | Y |
| 5 Matsui, D. | Y | Y | N | Y | Y |
| 6 Woolsey | Y | Y | Y | Y | Y |
| 7 Miller, George | Y | Y | Y | Y | N |
| 8 Pelosi | Y | Y | Y | Y | Y |
| 9 Lee | Y | Y | Y | Y | N |
| 10 Tauscher | Y | Y | N | Y | Y |
| 11 Pombo | Y | Y | N | N | Y |
| 12 Lantos | Y | Y | N | Y | Y |
| 13 Stark | Y | Y | Y | Y | N |
| 14 Eshoo | Y | Y | Y | Y | Y |
| 15 Honda | Y | ? | Y | Y | Y |
| 16 Lofgren | Y | Y | N | Y | Y |
| 17 Farr | Y | Y | Y | Y | Y |
| 18 Cardoza | Y | Y | N | Y | Y |
| 19 Radanovich | Y | Y | N | N | Y |
| 20 Costa | Y | Y | N | Y | Y |
| 21 Nunes | Y | Y | N | N | Y |
| 22 Thomas | Y | Y | N | N | Y |
| 23 Capps | Y | Y | N | Y | Y |
| 24 Gallegly | Y | Y | N | N | Y |
| 25 McKeon | Y | Y | N | N | Y |
| 26 Dreier | Y | Y | N | N | Y |
| 27 Sherman | Y | Y | N | Y | Y |
| 28 Berman | Y | Y | Y | Y | Y |
| 29 Schiff | Y | Y | N | Y | Y |
| 30 Waxman | Y | Y | Y | Y | N |
| 31 Becerra | Y | Y | N | Y | Y |
| 32 Solis | + | + | Y | Y | N |
| 33 Watson | Y | Y | Y | Y | Y |
| 34 Roybal-Allard | Y | Y | Y | Y | N |
| 35 Waters | Y | ? | Y | Y | N |
| 36 Harman | Y | Y | N | Y | Y |
| 37 Millender-McD. | ? | ? | Y | Y | Y |
| 38 Napolitano | Y | Y | N | Y | Y |
| 39 Sánchez, Linda | Y | Y | N | Y | Y |
| 40 Royce | Y | Y | N | N | Y |
| 41 Lewis | Y | Y | N | N | Y |
| 42 Miller, Gary | Y | Y | N | N | Y |
| 43 Baca | Y | Y | N | Y | Y |
| 44 Calvert | Y | Y | N | N | Y |
| 45 Bono | Y | Y | N | N | Y |
| 46 Rohrabacher | Y | Y | N | N | Y |
| 47 Sanchez, Loretta | Y | Y | Y | Y | Y |
| 48 Vacant | | | | | |
| 49 Issa | Y | Y | N | N | Y |
| 50 Cunningham | Y | Y | N | N | Y |
| 51 Filner | Y | Y | N | N | N |
| 52 Hunter | Y | Y | N | N | Y |
| 53 Davis | Y | Y | N | Y | Y |
| **COLORADO** | | | | | |
| 1 DeGette | Y | Y | Y | Y | Y |
| 2 Udall | Y | Y | Y | Y | Y |
| 3 Salazar | Y | Y | N | Y | Y |
| 4 Musgrave | Y | Y | N | N | Y |
| 5 Hefley | N | Y | N | N | Y |
| 6 Tancredo | N | ? | N | N | Y |
| 7 Beauprez | Y | Y | N | N | Y |
| **CONNECTICUT** | | | | | |
| 1 Larson | Y | Y | N | Y | Y |
| 2 Simmons | Y | Y | N | Y | Y |
| 3 DeLauro | Y | Y | N | Y | Y |
| 4 Shays | Y | Y | N | Y | Y |
| 5 Johnson | Y | Y | N | N | Y |
| **DELAWARE** | | | | | |
| AL Castle | ? | Y | N | N | Y |
| **FLORIDA** | | | | | |
| 1 Miller | Y | Y | N | N | Y |
| 2 Boyd | Y | Y | N | Y | Y |
| 3 Brown | Y | Y | N | Y | Y |
| 4 Crenshaw | Y | Y | N | N | Y |
| 5 Brown-Waite | ? | ? | ? | ? | ? |
| 6 Stearns | Y | Y | N | N | Y |
| 7 Mica | Y | Y | N | N | Y |
| 8 Keller | Y | Y | N | N | Y |
| 9 Bilirakis | Y | Y | N | N | Y |
| 10 Young | ? | ? | ? | ? | ? |
| 11 Davis | ? | ? | ? | ? | ? |
| 12 Putnam | Y | Y | N | N | Y |
| 13 Harris | Y | Y | N | N | Y |
| 14 Mack | Y | Y | N | N | Y |
| 15 Weldon | Y | Y | N | N | Y |
| 16 Foley | Y | Y | N | N | Y |
| 17 Meek | Y | Y | N | Y | Y |
| 18 Ros-Lehtinen | Y | Y | N | N | Y |
| 19 Wexler | Y | Y | N | Y | Y |
| 20 Wasserman-Schultz | Y | Y | Y | Y | Y |
| 21 Diaz-Balart, L. | Y | Y | N | N | Y |
| 22 Shaw | Y | Y | N | N | Y |
| 23 Hastings | ? | ? | ? | ? | ? |
| 24 Feeney | Y | Y | N | N | Y |
| 25 Diaz-Balart, M. | Y | Y | N | N | Y |
| **GEORGIA** | | | | | |
| 1 Kingston | Y | Y | N | N | Y |
| 2 Bishop | Y | Y | N | Y | Y |
| 3 Marshall | Y | Y | N | Y | Y |
| 4 McKinney | Y | Y | Y | Y | N |
| 5 Lewis | Y | Y | Y | Y | N |
| 6 Price | Y | Y | N | N | + |
| 7 Linder | Y | Y | N | N | Y |
| 8 Westmoreland | Y | Y | N | N | Y |
| 9 Norwood | + | + | – | – | + |
| 10 Deal | Y | Y | N | N | Y |
| 11 Gingrey | Y | Y | N | N | Y |
| 12 Barrow | Y | Y | N | Y | Y |
| 13 Scott | Y | Y | N | Y | Y |
| **HAWAII** | | | | | |
| 1 Abercrombie | Y | Y | Y | Y | Y |
| 2 Case | Y | Y | N | Y | Y |
| **IDAHO** | | | | | |
| 1 Otter | N | Y | N | N | Y |
| 2 Simpson | Y | Y | N | N | Y |
| **ILLINOIS** | | | | | |
| 1 Rush | Y | Y | Y | Y | N |
| 2 Jackson | Y | Y | Y | Y | N |
| 3 Lipinski | Y | Y | N | Y | Y |
| 4 Gutierrez | Y | Y | N | Y | Y |
| 5 Emanuel | Y | Y | N | Y | Y |
| 6 Hyde | Y | Y | N | N | Y |
| 7 Davis | Y | Y | Y | Y | Y |
| 8 Bean | Y | Y | N | Y | Y |
| 9 Schakowsky | Y | Y | Y | Y | N |
| 10 Kirk | Y | Y | N | N | Y |
| 11 Weller | Y | Y | N | N | Y |
| 12 Costello | Y | Y | N | Y | Y |

**KEY**   Republicans   Democrats   *Independents*

| | | | |
|---|---|---|---|
| Y | Voted for (yea) | X  Paired against | C  Voted "present" to avoid possible conflict of interest |
| # | Paired for | –  Announced against | |
| + | Announced for | P  Voted "present" | ?  Did not vote or otherwise make a position known |
| N | Voted against (nay) | | |

ND Northern Democrats, SD Southern Democrats
Southern states: Ala., Ark., Fla., Ga., Ky., La., Miss., N.C., Okla., S.C., Tenn., Texas, Va.

| | 581 | 582 | 583 | 584 | 585 |
|---|---|---|---|---|---|
| 13 Biggert | Y | Y | N | N | Y |
| 14 Hastert | | | | | |
| 15 Johnson | Y | Y | N | N | Y |
| 16 Manzullo | Y | Y | N | N | Y |
| 17 Evans | Y | Y | Y | Y | Y |
| 18 LaHood | Y | Y | N | N | Y |
| 19 Shimkus | Y | Y | N | N | Y |
| **INDIANA** | | | | | |
| 1 Visclosky | Y | Y | N | Y | Y |
| 2 Chocola | Y | Y | N | N | Y |
| 3 Souder | Y | Y | N | N | Y |
| 4 Buyer | Y | Y | N | N | Y |
| 5 Burton | Y | Y | N | N | Y |
| 6 Pence | + | + | - | - | + |
| 7 Carson | Y | Y | Y | Y | N |
| 8 Hostettler | N | Y | N | N | Y |
| 9 Sodrel | Y | Y | N | N | Y |
| **IOWA** | | | | | |
| 1 Nussle | Y | Y | N | N | Y |
| 2 Leach | Y | Y | N | Y | Y |
| 3 Boswell | ? | ? | ? | ? | ? |
| 4 Latham | Y | Y | N | N | Y |
| 5 King | Y | Y | N | N | Y |
| **KANSAS** | | | | | |
| 1 Moran | Y | Y | N | N | Y |
| 2 Ryun | Y | Y | N | N | Y |
| 3 Moore | Y | Y | N | Y | Y |
| 4 Tiahrt | Y | Y | N | N | Y |
| **KENTUCKY** | | | | | |
| 1 Whitfield | Y | Y | N | N | Y |
| 2 Lewis | Y | Y | N | N | Y |
| 3 Northup | Y | Y | N | N | Y |
| 4 Davis | Y | Y | N | N | Y |
| 5 Rogers | Y | Y | N | N | Y |
| 6 Chandler | Y | Y | N | Y | Y |
| **LOUISIANA** | | | | | |
| 1 Jindal | Y | Y | N | N | Y |
| 2 Jefferson | Y | Y | N | Y | Y |
| 3 Melancon | Y | ? | N | Y | Y |
| 4 McCrery | Y | Y | N | N | Y |
| 5 Alexander | Y | Y | N | N | Y |
| 6 Baker | Y | Y | N | N | Y |
| 7 Boustany | Y | Y | N | N | Y |
| **MAINE** | | | | | |
| 1 Allen | Y | Y | Y | Y | Y |
| 2 Michaud | Y | Y | Y | Y | N |
| **MARYLAND** | | | | | |
| 1 Gilchrest | Y | Y | N | N | Y |
| 2 Ruppersberger | Y | Y | N | Y | Y |
| 3 Cardin | Y | Y | N | Y | Y |
| 4 Wynn | Y | Y | N | Y | Y |
| 5 Hoyer | Y | Y | N | Y | Y |
| 6 Bartlett | Y | Y | Y | N | Y |
| 7 Cummings | Y | Y | Y | Y | N |
| 8 Van Hollen | Y | Y | Y | Y | Y |
| **MASSACHUSETTS** | | | | | |
| 1 Olver | Y | Y | Y | Y | N |
| 2 Neal | Y | Y | Y | Y | Y |
| 3 McGovern | Y | Y | Y | Y | N |
| 4 Frank | Y | Y | Y | Y | Y |
| 5 Meehan | Y | Y | Y | Y | Y |
| 6 Tierney | N | Y | Y | Y | Y |
| 7 Markey | Y | Y | Y | Y | N |
| 8 Capuano | N | Y | Y | Y | Y |
| 9 Lynch | Y | Y | Y | Y | Y |
| 10 Delahunt | Y | Y | Y | Y | N |
| **MICHIGAN** | | | | | |
| 1 Stupak | Y | Y | N | Y | Y |
| 2 Hoekstra | Y | Y | Y | N | Y |
| 3 Ehlers | Y | Y | Y | N | Y |
| 4 Camp | Y | Y | N | N | Y |
| 5 Kildee | Y | Y | Y | Y | N |
| 6 Upton | Y | Y | Y | N | Y |
| 7 Schwarz | Y | Y | N | N | Y |
| 8 Rogers | Y | Y | N | N | Y |
| 9 Knollenberg | Y | Y | N | N | Y |
| 10 Miller | Y | Y | N | N | Y |
| 11 McCotter | Y | Y | N | N | Y |
| 12 Levin | Y | Y | Y | Y | Y |
| 13 Kilpatrick | Y | Y | Y | Y | N |
| 14 Conyers | N | Y | Y | Y | N |
| 15 Dingell | Y | Y | Y | Y | Y |

| | 581 | 582 | 583 | 584 | 585 |
|---|---|---|---|---|---|
| **MINNESOTA** | | | | | |
| 1 Gutknecht | Y | Y | N | N | Y |
| 2 Kline | Y | Y | N | N | Y |
| 3 Ramstad | Y | Y | N | N | Y |
| 4 McCollum | Y | Y | Y | Y | ? |
| 5 Sabo | Y | Y | Y | Y | N |
| 6 Kennedy | Y | Y | N | N | Y |
| 7 Peterson | Y | Y | N | Y | Y |
| 8 Oberstar | Y | Y | Y | Y | Y |
| **MISSISSIPPI** | | | | | |
| 1 Wicker | Y | Y | N | N | Y |
| 2 Thompson | Y | Y | N | Y | Y |
| 3 Pickering | Y | Y | N | N | Y |
| 4 Taylor | N | Y | N | Y | Y |
| **MISSOURI** | | | | | |
| 1 Clay | Y | Y | Y | Y | N |
| 2 Akin | Y | Y | N | N | Y |
| 3 Carnahan | Y | Y | N | Y | Y |
| 4 Skelton | Y | Y | N | Y | Y |
| 5 Cleaver | Y | Y | Y | Y | Y |
| 6 Graves | Y | Y | N | N | Y |
| 7 Blunt | Y | Y | N | N | Y |
| 8 Emerson | Y | ? | N | N | Y |
| 9 Hulshof | Y | Y | N | N | Y |
| **MONTANA** | | | | | |
| AL Rehberg | Y | Y | N | N | Y |
| **NEBRASKA** | | | | | |
| 1 Fortenberry | Y | Y | N | N | Y |
| 2 Terry | Y | Y | N | N | Y |
| 3 Osborne | Y | Y | N | N | Y |
| **NEVADA** | | | | | |
| 1 Berkley | Y | Y | N | Y | Y |
| 2 Gibbons | Y | Y | N | N | Y |
| 3 Porter | Y | Y | N | N | Y |
| **NEW HAMPSHIRE** | | | | | |
| 1 Bradley | Y | Y | N | N | Y |
| 2 Bass | Y | Y | N | N | Y |
| **NEW JERSEY** | | | | | |
| 1 Andrews | Y | Y | N | Y | Y |
| 2 LoBiondo | Y | Y | N | N | Y |
| 3 Saxton | Y | Y | N | N | Y |
| 4 Smith | Y | Y | Y | Y | Y |
| 5 Garrett | Y | Y | N | N | Y |
| 6 Pallone | Y | Y | N | Y | Y |
| 7 Ferguson | Y | Y | N | N | Y |
| 8 Pascrell | Y | Y | N | Y | Y |
| 9 Rothman | Y | Y | N | Y | Y |
| 10 Payne | Y | Y | Y | Y | N |
| 11 Frelinghuysen | Y | Y | N | N | Y |
| 12 Holt | Y | Y | Y | Y | N |
| 13 Menendez | Y | Y | N | Y | Y |
| **NEW MEXICO** | | | | | |
| 1 Wilson | Y | Y | N | N | Y |
| 2 Pearce | Y | Y | N | N | Y |
| 3 Udall | Y | Y | N | Y | Y |
| **NEW YORK** | | | | | |
| 1 Bishop | Y | Y | N | Y | Y |
| 2 Israel | Y | Y | N | Y | Y |
| 3 King | Y | Y | N | N | Y |
| 4 McCarthy | Y | Y | Y | Y | Y |
| 5 Ackerman | Y | Y | N | Y | Y |
| 6 Meeks | ? | ? | Y | Y | Y |
| 7 Crowley | Y | Y | N | Y | Y |
| 8 Nadler | Y | Y | Y | Y | N |
| 9 Weiner | Y | Y | N | Y | Y |
| 10 Towns | Y | Y | Y | Y | Y |
| 11 Owens | Y | Y | Y | Y | N |
| 12 Velázquez | N | Y | N | Y | Y |
| 13 Fossella | Y | Y | N | N | Y |
| 14 Maloney | Y | Y | N | Y | Y |
| 15 Rangel | Y | Y | Y | Y | Y |
| 16 Serrano | Y | Y | Y | Y | Y |
| 17 Engel | Y | Y | Y | Y | Y |
| 18 Lowey | Y | Y | N | Y | Y |
| 19 Kelly | Y | Y | N | N | Y |
| 20 Sweeney | ? | ? | ? | ? | ? |
| 21 McNulty | Y | Y | Y | Y | Y |
| 22 Hinchey | Y | Y | Y | Y | N |
| 23 McHugh | Y | Y | N | N | Y |
| 24 Boehlert | Y | Y | N | N | Y |
| 25 Walsh | Y | Y | N | N | Y |
| 26 Reynolds | Y | Y | N | N | Y |
| 27 Higgins | Y | ? | N | Y | Y |
| 28 Slaughter | Y | Y | Y | Y | Y |
| 29 Kuhl | Y | Y | N | N | Y |

| | 581 | 582 | 583 | 584 | 585 |
|---|---|---|---|---|---|
| **NORTH CAROLINA** | | | | | |
| 1 Butterfield | Y | Y | N | Y | Y |
| 2 Etheridge | Y | Y | N | Y | Y |
| 3 Jones | N | Y | N | N | Y |
| 4 Price | Y | Y | N | Y | Y |
| 5 Foxx | Y | Y | N | N | Y |
| 6 Coble | Y | Y | N | N | Y |
| 7 McIntyre | Y | Y | N | Y | Y |
| 8 Hayes | Y | Y | N | N | Y |
| 9 Myrick | Y | Y | N | N | Y |
| 10 McHenry | Y | Y | N | N | Y |
| 11 Taylor | Y | Y | N | N | Y |
| 12 Watt | Y | Y | N | Y | N |
| 13 Miller | Y | Y | N | Y | Y |
| **NORTH DAKOTA** | | | | | |
| AL Pomeroy | Y | Y | N | Y | Y |
| **OHIO** | | | | | |
| 1 Chabot | Y | Y | N | N | Y |
| 2 Schmidt | Y | Y | N | N | Y |
| 3 Turner | ? | ? | N | N | Y |
| 4 Oxley | + | + | N | N | Y |
| 5 Gillmor | Y | Y | N | N | Y |
| 6 Strickland | ? | ? | ? | ? | ? |
| 7 Hobson | Y | Y | N | N | Y |
| 8 Boehner | Y | Y | N | N | Y |
| 9 Kaptur | Y | Y | N | Y | Y |
| 10 Kucinich | Y | Y | Y | Y | N |
| 11 Jones | Y | Y | N | Y | Y |
| 12 Tiberi | Y | Y | N | N | Y |
| 13 Brown | Y | Y | Y | Y | Y |
| 14 LaTourette | Y | Y | N | N | Y |
| 15 Pryce | Y | Y | N | N | Y |
| 16 Regula | Y | Y | N | N | Y |
| 17 Ryan | Y | Y | Y | Y | Y |
| 18 Ney | Y | Y | N | N | Y |
| **OKLAHOMA** | | | | | |
| 1 Sullivan | Y | Y | N | N | Y |
| 2 Boren | Y | Y | N | Y | Y |
| 3 Lucas | Y | Y | N | N | Y |
| 4 Cole | Y | Y | N | N | Y |
| 5 Istook | Y | Y | N | N | Y |
| **OREGON** | | | | | |
| 1 Wu | Y | Y | N | Y | Y |
| 2 Walden | Y | Y | N | N | Y |
| 3 Blumenauer | Y | Y | Y | Y | Y |
| 4 DeFazio | Y | Y | N | Y | Y |
| 5 Hooley | Y | Y | N | Y | Y |
| **PENNSYLVANIA** | | | | | |
| 1 Brady | Y | Y | N | Y | Y |
| 2 Fattah | Y | Y | Y | Y | Y |
| 3 English | Y | Y | N | N | Y |
| 4 Hart | Y | Y | N | N | Y |
| 5 Peterson | Y | Y | N | N | Y |
| 6 Gerlach | Y | Y | N | N | Y |
| 7 Weldon | Y | Y | N | N | Y |
| 8 Fitzpatrick | Y | Y | N | N | Y |
| 9 Shuster | Y | Y | N | N | Y |
| 10 Sherwood | Y | Y | N | N | Y |
| 11 Kanjorski | Y | Y | N | Y | Y |
| 12 Murtha | Y | Y | N | Y | Y |
| 13 Schwartz | Y | Y | N | Y | Y |
| 14 Doyle | Y | Y | N | Y | Y |
| 15 Dent | Y | Y | N | N | Y |
| 16 Pitts | Y | Y | N | N | Y |
| 17 Holden | Y | Y | N | Y | Y |
| 18 Murphy | Y | Y | N | N | Y |
| 19 Platts | Y | Y | N | N | Y |
| **RHODE ISLAND** | | | | | |
| 1 Kennedy | Y | Y | N | Y | Y |
| 2 Langevin | Y | Y | N | Y | Y |
| **SOUTH CAROLINA** | | | | | |
| 1 Brown | Y | Y | N | N | Y |
| 2 Wilson | Y | Y | N | N | Y |
| 3 Barrett | Y | Y | N | N | Y |
| 4 Inglis | Y | Y | N | N | Y |
| 5 Spratt | Y | Y | N | Y | Y |
| 6 Clyburn | Y | Y | Y | Y | Y |
| **SOUTH DAKOTA** | | | | | |
| AL Herseth | Y | Y | N | Y | Y |
| **TENNESSEE** | | | | | |
| 1 Jenkins | Y | Y | N | N | Y |
| 2 Duncan | N | Y | N | N | Y |

| | 581 | 582 | 583 | 584 | 585 |
|---|---|---|---|---|---|
| 3 Wamp | Y | Y | N | N | Y |
| 4 Davis | Y | Y | N | Y | Y |
| 5 Cooper | Y | Y | N | Y | Y |
| 6 Gordon | Y | Y | N | Y | Y |
| 7 Blackburn | Y | Y | N | N | Y |
| 8 Tanner | Y | Y | N | Y | Y |
| 9 Ford | Y | Y | N | Y | Y |
| **TEXAS** | | | | | |
| 1 Gohmert | Y | ? | N | N | Y |
| 2 Poe | Y | Y | N | N | Y |
| 3 Johnson, S. | Y | Y | N | N | Y |
| 4 Hall | Y | Y | N | N | Y |
| 5 Hensarling | Y | Y | N | N | Y |
| 6 Barton | Y | Y | N | N | Y |
| 7 Culberson | Y | Y | N | N | Y |
| 8 Brady | Y | Y | N | N | Y |
| 9 Green, A. | Y | Y | Y | Y | Y |
| 10 McCaul | Y | Y | N | N | Y |
| 11 Conaway | ? | ? | ? | ? | ? |
| 12 Granger | Y | Y | N | N | Y |
| 13 Thornberry | Y | Y | N | N | Y |
| 14 Paul | N | Y | N | N | N |
| 15 Hinojosa | Y | Y | N | Y | Y |
| 16 Reyes | Y | Y | N | Y | Y |
| 17 Edwards | Y | Y | N | Y | Y |
| 18 Jackson-Lee | Y | Y | Y | Y | Y |
| 19 Neugebauer | Y | Y | N | N | Y |
| 20 Gonzalez | Y | Y | N | Y | Y |
| 21 Smith | Y | Y | N | N | Y |
| 22 DeLay | Y | Y | N | N | Y |
| 23 Bonilla | Y | Y | N | N | Y |
| 24 Marchant | Y | Y | N | N | Y |
| 25 Doggett | N | Y | N | Y | Y |
| 26 Burgess | Y | Y | N | N | Y |
| 27 Ortiz | Y | ? | N | Y | Y |
| 28 Cuellar | Y | Y | N | Y | Y |
| 29 Green, G. | Y | Y | N | Y | Y |
| 30 Johnson, E. | Y | Y | Y | Y | Y |
| 31 Carter | Y | Y | N | N | Y |
| 32 Sessions | ? | ? | ? | ? | ? |
| **UTAH** | | | | | |
| 1 Bishop | Y | Y | N | N | Y |
| 2 Matheson | N | Y | N | Y | Y |
| 3 Cannon | Y | Y | N | N | Y |
| **VERMONT** | | | | | |
| AL *Sanders* | Y | Y | Y | Y | Y |
| **VIRGINIA** | | | | | |
| 1 Davis, J. | Y | Y | N | N | Y |
| 2 Drake | Y | Y | N | N | Y |
| 3 Scott | Y | Y | Y | Y | N |
| 4 Forbes | Y | Y | N | N | Y |
| 5 Goode | Y | Y | N | N | Y |
| 6 Goodlatte | Y | Y | N | N | Y |
| 7 Cantor | Y | Y | N | N | Y |
| 8 Moran | Y | Y | N | Y | Y |
| 9 Boucher | Y | Y | N | Y | Y |
| 10 Wolf | Y | Y | N | N | Y |
| 11 Davis, T. | Y | Y | N | N | Y |
| **WASHINGTON** | | | | | |
| 1 Inslee | Y | Y | N | Y | Y |
| 2 Larsen | Y | Y | N | Y | Y |
| 3 Baird | Y | Y | N | Y | Y |
| 4 Hastings | Y | Y | N | N | Y |
| 5 McMorris | Y | Y | N | N | Y |
| 6 Dicks | Y | Y | N | Y | Y |
| 7 McDermott | N | Y | Y | Y | N |
| 8 Reichert | Y | Y | N | N | Y |
| 9 Smith | Y | Y | Y | Y | Y |
| **WEST VIRGINIA** | | | | | |
| 1 Mollohan | Y | Y | Y | Y | N |
| 2 Capito | Y | Y | N | N | Y |
| 3 Rahall | Y | Y | Y | Y | N |
| **WISCONSIN** | | | | | |
| 1 Ryan | Y | Y | N | N | Y |
| 2 Baldwin | N | Y | Y | Y | Y |
| 3 Kind | Y | Y | N | Y | Y |
| 4 Moore | Y | N | Y | Y | Y |
| 5 Sensenbrenner | Y | Y | N | N | Y |
| 6 Petri | Y | Y | N | N | Y |
| 7 Obey | N | Y | Y | Y | Y |
| 8 Green | N | Y | N | N | Y |
| **WYOMING** | | | | | |
| AL Cubin | Y | Y | N | N | Y |

# IN THE HOUSE | By Vote Number

**586.** **HR 1564. Yakima-Tieton Irrigation District/Passage.** Musgrave, R-Colo., motion to suspend the rules and pass the bill that would transfer nine acres of federal land and several buildings to the Yakima-Tieton Irrigation District in Washington. Motion agreed to 420-0: R 226-0; D 193-0 (ND 144-0, SD 49-0); I 1-0. A two-thirds majority of those present and voting (280 in this case) is required for passage under suspension of the rules. Nov. 15, 2005.

**587.** **HR 323. Bob Hope Memorial Library/Passage.** Musgrave, R-Colo., motion to suspend the rules and pass the bill that would redesignate the Ellis Island Library, which is part of the Ellis Island Immigration Museum, as the Bob Hope Memorial Library. Motion agreed to 419-0: R 226-0; D 192-0 (ND 143-0, SD 49-0); I 1-0. A two-thirds majority of those present and voting (280 in this case) is required for passage under suspension of the rules. Nov. 15, 2005.

**588.** **HR 856. Federal Youth Coordination/Passage.** Osborne, R-Neb., motion to suspend the rules and pass the bill that would establish a Federal Youth Development Council to allow for better communication among federal agencies serving youth, assess the needs of disadvantaged youth and report on youth programs. Motion agreed to 353-62: R 163-62; D 189-0 (ND 140-0, SD 49-0); I 1-0. A two-thirds majority of those present and voting (277 in this case) is required for passage under suspension of the rules. Nov. 15, 2005.

**589.** **HR 1065. U.S. Boxing Commission/Rule.** Adoption of the rule (H Res 553) that would provide for House floor consideration of the bill that would create a federal boxing commission within the Commerce Department to regulate professional boxing. Adopted 366-56: R 224-1; D 141-55 (ND 107-40, SD 34-15); I 1-0. Nov. 16, 2005.

**590.** **HR 1790. Child Medication in Schools/Passage.** Kline, R-Minn., motion to suspend the rules and pass the bill that would require states, as a condition of receiving federal education funds, to prohibit schools from requiring a child to be medicated as a condition of attending school or receiving services. Motion agreed to 407-12: R 221-1; D 185-11 (ND 137-10, SD 48-1); I 1-0. A two-thirds majority of those present and voting (280 in this case) is required for passage under suspension of the rules. Nov. 16, 2005.

**591.** **H Res 547. Disapprove 9th Circuit Court Ruling/Adoption.** Sensenbrenner, R-Wis., motion to suspend the rules and adopt the resolution that would express the sense of the House that parents have a "fundamental right" to direct their children's education and that the 9th Circuit Court of Appeals' ruling in *Fields v. Palmdale School District* would undermine that right. Motion agreed to 320-91: R 225-0; D 94-91 (ND 61-78, SD 33-13); I 1-0. A two-thirds majority of those present and voting (274 in this case) is required for adoption under suspension of the rules. Nov. 16, 2005.

| | 586 | 587 | 588 | 589 | 590 | 591 |
|---|---|---|---|---|---|---|
| **ALABAMA** | | | | | | |
| 1 Bonner | Y | Y | Y | Y | Y | Y |
| 2 Everett | Y | Y | Y | Y | Y | Y |
| 3 Rogers | Y | Y | Y | Y | Y | Y |
| 4 Aderholt | Y | Y | Y | Y | Y | Y |
| 5 Cramer | Y | Y | Y | Y | Y | Y |
| 6 Bachus | Y | Y | Y | Y | Y | Y |
| 7 Davis | Y | Y | Y | Y | Y | Y |
| **ALASKA** | | | | | | |
| AL Young | Y | Y | Y | Y | Y | Y |
| **ARIZONA** | | | | | | |
| 1 Renzi | Y | Y | Y | Y | Y | Y |
| 2 Franks | Y | Y | N | Y | Y | Y |
| 3 Shadegg | Y | Y | N | Y | Y | Y |
| 4 Pastor | Y | Y | Y | N | Y | N |
| 5 Hayworth | Y | Y | N | Y | Y | Y |
| 6 Flake | Y | Y | N | Y | Y | Y |
| 7 Grijalva | Y | Y | Y | Y | Y | N |
| 8 Kolbe | Y | Y | Y | Y | Y | Y |
| **ARKANSAS** | | | | | | |
| 1 Berry | Y | Y | Y | N | Y | Y |
| 2 Snyder | Y | Y | Y | Y | Y | P |
| 3 Boozman | Y | Y | Y | Y | Y | Y |
| 4 Ross | Y | Y | Y | Y | Y | Y |
| **CALIFORNIA** | | | | | | |
| 1 Thompson | Y | Y | Y | Y | Y | N |
| 2 Herger | Y | Y | N | Y | Y | Y |
| 3 Lungren | Y | Y | Y | Y | Y | Y |
| 4 Doolittle | Y | Y | Y | Y | Y | Y |
| 5 Matsui, D. | Y | Y | Y | Y | Y | N |
| 6 Woolsey | Y | Y | Y | N | Y | N |
| 7 Miller, George | Y | Y | ? | Y | N | N |
| 8 Pelosi | Y | Y | Y | Y | Y | P |
| 9 Lee | Y | Y | Y | N | Y | N |
| 10 Tauscher | Y | Y | Y | Y | Y | N |
| 11 Pombo | Y | Y | Y | Y | Y | Y |
| 12 Lantos | Y | Y | Y | ? | ? | ? |
| 13 Stark | ? | ? | ? | ? | ? | ? |
| 14 Eshoo | Y | Y | Y | Y | Y | P |
| 15 Honda | Y | Y | Y | N | Y | N |
| 16 Lofgren | Y | P | Y | Y | Y | P |
| 17 Farr | Y | Y | Y | Y | Y | N |
| 18 Cardoza | Y | Y | Y | Y | Y | Y |
| 19 Radanovich | Y | Y | Y | Y | Y | Y |
| 20 Costa | Y | Y | Y | Y | Y | Y |
| 21 Nunes | Y | Y | Y | Y | Y | Y |
| 22 Thomas | Y | Y | Y | Y | Y | Y |
| 23 Capps | Y | Y | Y | Y | Y | N |
| 24 Gallegly | Y | Y | Y | Y | Y | Y |
| 25 McKeon | Y | Y | Y | Y | Y | Y |
| 26 Dreier | Y | Y | Y | Y | Y | Y |
| 27 Sherman | Y | Y | Y | Y | Y | N |
| 28 Berman | Y | Y | Y | N | Y | N |
| 29 Schiff | Y | Y | Y | Y | Y | Y |
| 30 Waxman | Y | Y | Y | N | Y | N |
| 31 Becerra | Y | Y | Y | Y | Y | N |
| 32 Solis | Y | Y | Y | N | Y | N |
| 33 Watson | Y | Y | Y | N | Y | N |
| 34 Roybal-Allard | Y | Y | Y | Y | Y | N |
| 35 Waters | Y | Y | Y | N | Y | N |
| 36 Harman | Y | Y | Y | Y | Y | N |
| 37 Millender-McD. | Y | Y | Y | Y | Y | N |
| 38 Napolitano | Y | Y | Y | Y | Y | N |
| 39 Sánchez, Linda | Y | Y | Y | Y | Y | N |
| 40 Royce | Y | Y | N | Y | Y | Y |
| 41 Lewis | Y | Y | Y | Y | Y | Y |
| 42 Miller, Gary | Y | Y | N | Y | Y | Y |
| 43 Baca | Y | Y | Y | Y | Y | Y |
| 44 Calvert | Y | Y | Y | Y | Y | Y |
| 45 Bono | Y | Y | Y | Y | Y | Y |
| 46 Rohrabacher | Y | Y | N | Y | Y | Y |
| 47 Sanchez, Loretta | Y | Y | Y | Y | Y | Y |
| 48 Vacant | | | | | | |
| 49 Issa | Y | Y | Y | Y | Y | Y |
| 50 Cunningham | ? | ? | ? | ? | ? | ? |
| 51 Filner | Y | Y | Y | Y | Y | Y |
| 52 Hunter | Y | Y | Y | ? | Y | Y |
| 53 Davis | Y | Y | Y | N | N | N |
| **COLORADO** | | | | | | |
| 1 DeGette | Y | Y | Y | Y | Y | N |
| 2 Udall | Y | Y | Y | Y | Y | Y |
| 3 Salazar | Y | Y | Y | Y | Y | Y |
| 4 Musgrave | Y | Y | N | Y | Y | Y |
| 5 Hefley | Y | Y | N | Y | Y | Y |
| 6 Tancredo | Y | Y | N | Y | Y | Y |
| 7 Beauprez | Y | Y | N | Y | Y | Y |
| **CONNECTICUT** | | | | | | |
| 1 Larson | Y | Y | Y | Y | Y | Y |
| 2 Simmons | Y | Y | Y | Y | ? | Y |
| 3 DeLauro | Y | Y | Y | Y | Y | Y |
| 4 Shays | Y | Y | Y | Y | Y | Y |
| 5 Johnson | Y | Y | Y | Y | Y | Y |
| **DELAWARE** | | | | | | |
| AL Castle | Y | Y | Y | Y | Y | Y |
| **FLORIDA** | | | | | | |
| 1 Miller | Y | Y | N | Y | Y | Y |
| 2 Boyd | Y | Y | Y | Y | Y | Y |
| 3 Brown | Y | Y | Y | N | Y | Y |
| 4 Crenshaw | Y | Y | N | Y | Y | Y |
| 5 Brown-Waite | Y | Y | N | Y | Y | Y |
| 6 Stearns | Y | Y | N | Y | Y | Y |
| 7 Mica | Y | Y | Y | Y | Y | Y |
| 8 Keller | Y | Y | Y | Y | Y | Y |
| 9 Bilirakis | Y | Y | Y | Y | Y | Y |
| 10 Young | Y | Y | N | Y | Y | Y |
| 11 Davis | Y | Y | Y | ? | ? | ? |
| 12 Putnam | Y | Y | Y | Y | Y | Y |
| 13 Harris | Y | Y | Y | ? | ? | Y |
| 14 Mack | Y | Y | N | Y | Y | Y |
| 15 Weldon | Y | Y | Y | Y | Y | Y |
| 16 Foley | Y | Y | Y | Y | Y | Y |
| 17 Meek | Y | Y | Y | N | Y | Y |
| 18 Ros-Lehtinen | Y | Y | Y | Y | Y | Y |
| 19 Wexler | ? | ? | ? | Y | Y | N |
| 20 Wasserman-Schultz | Y | Y | Y | Y | Y | N |
| 21 Diaz-Balart, L. | Y | Y | Y | Y | Y | Y |
| 22 Shaw | Y | Y | Y | Y | Y | Y |
| 23 Hastings | Y | Y | Y | N | Y | N |
| 24 Feeney | Y | Y | N | Y | Y | Y |
| 25 Diaz-Balart, M. | Y | Y | N | Y | Y | Y |
| **GEORGIA** | | | | | | |
| 1 Kingston | Y | Y | N | Y | Y | Y |
| 2 Bishop | Y | Y | Y | Y | Y | Y |
| 3 Marshall | Y | Y | Y | Y | Y | Y |
| 4 McKinney | Y | Y | N | N | Y | N |
| 5 Lewis | Y | Y | N | Y | Y | N |
| 6 Price | Y | Y | N | Y | Y | Y |
| 7 Linder | Y | Y | N | Y | Y | Y |
| 8 Westmoreland | Y | Y | N | Y | Y | Y |
| 9 Norwood | Y | Y | Y | Y | Y | Y |
| 10 Deal | Y | Y | Y | Y | Y | Y |
| 11 Gingrey | Y | Y | N | Y | P | Y |
| 12 Barrow | Y | Y | Y | Y | Y | Y |
| 13 Scott | Y | Y | N | Y | Y | Y |
| **HAWAII** | | | | | | |
| 1 Abercrombie | Y | Y | Y | Y | Y | N |
| 2 Case | Y | Y | Y | Y | Y | N |
| **IDAHO** | | | | | | |
| 1 Otter | Y | Y | Y | Y | Y | Y |
| 2 Simpson | Y | Y | Y | Y | Y | Y |
| **ILLINOIS** | | | | | | |
| 1 Rush | Y | Y | Y | Y | Y | N |
| 2 Jackson | Y | Y | ? | Y | N | Y |
| 3 Lipinski | Y | Y | Y | Y | Y | Y |
| 4 Gutierrez | + | + | + | N | Y | N |
| 5 Emanuel | Y | Y | Y | Y | Y | N |
| 6 Hyde | Y | Y | Y | Y | Y | Y |
| 7 Davis | Y | Y | Y | N | Y | N |
| 8 Bean | Y | Y | Y | Y | Y | Y |
| 9 Schakowsky | Y | Y | ? | Y | Y | N |
| 10 Kirk | Y | Y | Y | Y | Y | Y |
| 11 Weller | Y | Y | Y | Y | Y | Y |
| 12 Costello | Y | Y | N | Y | Y | Y |

**KEY**    Republicans    Democrats    *Independents*

| | | |
|---|---|---|
| **Y** Voted for (yea) | **X** Paired against | **C** Voted "present" to avoid possible conflict of interest |
| **#** Paired for | **–** Announced against | |
| **+** Announced for | **P** Voted "present" | **?** Did not vote or otherwise make a position known |
| **N** Voted against (nay) | | |

ND Northern Democrats, SD Southern Democrats
Southern states: Ala., Ark., Fla., Ga., Ky., La., Miss., N.C., Okla., S.C., Tenn., Texas, Va.

| | 586 | 587 | 588 | 589 | 590 | 591 |
|---|---|---|---|---|---|---|
| 13 **Biggert** | Y | Y | Y | Y | Y | P |
| 14 **Hastert** | | | | | | |
| 15 **Johnson** | Y | Y | Y | Y | Y | Y |
| 16 **Manzullo** | Y | Y | N | Y | Y | Y |
| 17 Evans | Y | Y | Y | Y | Y | Y |
| 18 **LaHood** | Y | Y | Y | Y | Y | Y |
| 19 **Shimkus** | Y | Y | Y | Y | Y | Y |
| **INDIANA** | | | | | | |
| 1 Visclosky | Y | Y | Y | Y | Y | Y |
| 2 **Chocola** | Y | Y | N | Y | Y | Y |
| 3 **Souder** | Y | Y | Y | Y | Y | Y |
| 4 **Buyer** | Y | Y | Y | Y | Y | Y |
| 5 **Burton** | Y | Y | N | Y | Y | Y |
| 6 **Pence** | Y | Y | N | Y | Y | Y |
| 7 Carson | Y | Y | Y | N | Y | N |
| 8 **Hostettler** | Y | Y | N | Y | Y | Y |
| 9 **Sodrel** | Y | Y | N | Y | Y | Y |
| **IOWA** | | | | | | |
| 1 **Nussle** | Y | Y | Y | Y | Y | Y |
| 2 **Leach** | Y | Y | Y | Y | Y | Y |
| 3 Boswell | ? | ? | ? | ? | ? | ? |
| 4 **Latham** | Y | Y | Y | Y | Y | Y |
| 5 **King** | Y | Y | Y | Y | Y | Y |
| **KANSAS** | | | | | | |
| 1 **Moran** | Y | Y | Y | Y | Y | Y |
| 2 **Ryun** | Y | Y | N | Y | Y | Y |
| 3 Moore | Y | Y | Y | Y | Y | Y |
| 4 **Tiahrt** | Y | Y | N | Y | Y | Y |
| **KENTUCKY** | | | | | | |
| 1 **Whitfield** | Y | Y | Y | Y | Y | Y |
| 2 **Lewis** | Y | Y | Y | Y | Y | Y |
| 3 **Northup** | Y | Y | Y | Y | Y | Y |
| 4 **Davis** | Y | Y | N | Y | Y | Y |
| 5 **Rogers** | Y | Y | Y | Y | Y | Y |
| 6 Chandler | Y | Y | Y | Y | Y | Y |
| **LOUISIANA** | | | | | | |
| 1 **Jindal** | Y | Y | N | Y | Y | Y |
| 2 Jefferson | Y | Y | Y | N | Y | Y |
| 3 Melancon | Y | Y | Y | N | Y | Y |
| 4 **McCrery** | Y | Y | Y | Y | Y | Y |
| 5 **Alexander** | Y | Y | Y | Y | Y | Y |
| 6 **Baker** | Y | Y | Y | Y | Y | Y |
| 7 **Boustany** | Y | Y | Y | Y | Y | Y |
| **MAINE** | | | | | | |
| 1 Allen | Y | Y | Y | Y | Y | P |
| 2 Michaud | Y | Y | Y | Y | Y | Y |
| **MARYLAND** | | | | | | |
| 1 **Gilchrest** | Y | Y | Y | Y | Y | Y |
| 2 Ruppersberger | Y | Y | Y | Y | Y | Y |
| 3 Cardin | Y | Y | Y | Y | Y | Y |
| 4 Wynn | Y | Y | Y | Y | Y | Y |
| 5 Hoyer | Y | Y | Y | Y | Y | N |
| 6 **Bartlett** | Y | Y | N | Y | Y | Y |
| 7 Cummings | Y | Y | Y | Y | Y | Y |
| 8 Van Hollen | Y | Y | Y | Y | Y | N |
| **MASSACHUSETTS** | | | | | | |
| 1 Olver | Y | Y | Y | N | N | N |
| 2 Neal | Y | Y | Y | N | Y | Y |
| 3 McGovern | Y | Y | Y | Y | Y | N |
| 4 Frank | Y | Y | Y | Y | N | N |
| 5 Meehan | Y | Y | Y | Y | Y | N |
| 6 Tierney | Y | Y | Y | N | Y | N |
| 7 Markey | Y | Y | Y | Y | Y | N |
| 8 Capuano | Y | Y | Y | N | Y | P |
| 9 Lynch | Y | Y | Y | Y | Y | Y |
| 10 Delahunt | Y | Y | Y | N | Y | N |
| **MICHIGAN** | | | | | | |
| 1 Stupak | Y | Y | Y | Y | Y | Y |
| 2 **Hoekstra** | Y | Y | Y | Y | Y | Y |
| 3 **Ehlers** | Y | Y | Y | Y | Y | Y |
| 4 **Camp** | Y | Y | Y | Y | Y | Y |
| 5 Kildee | Y | Y | Y | Y | Y | Y |
| 6 **Upton** | Y | Y | Y | Y | Y | Y |
| 7 **Schwarz** | Y | Y | Y | Y | Y | Y |
| 8 **Rogers** | Y | Y | Y | Y | Y | Y |
| 9 **Knollenberg** | Y | Y | Y | Y | Y | Y |
| 10 **Miller** | Y | Y | Y | Y | Y | Y |
| 11 **McCotter** | Y | Y | Y | Y | Y | Y |
| 12 Levin | Y | Y | Y | Y | Y | N |
| 13 Kilpatrick | Y | Y | Y | Y | Y | Y |
| 14 Conyers | Y | Y | ? | N | Y | N |
| 15 Dingell | Y | Y | Y | Y | N | N |

| | 586 | 587 | 588 | 589 | 590 | 591 |
|---|---|---|---|---|---|---|
| **MINNESOTA** | | | | | | |
| 1 **Gutknecht** | Y | Y | Y | Y | Y | Y |
| 2 **Kline** | Y | Y | Y | Y | Y | Y |
| 3 **Ramstad** | Y | Y | Y | Y | Y | Y |
| 4 McCollum | Y | Y | Y | Y | Y | P |
| 5 Sabo | Y | Y | Y | N | Y | P |
| 6 **Kennedy** | Y | Y | Y | Y | Y | Y |
| 7 Peterson | Y | Y | Y | Y | Y | Y |
| 8 Oberstar | Y | Y | Y | Y | Y | N |
| **MISSISSIPPI** | | | | | | |
| 1 **Wicker** | Y | Y | Y | Y | Y | Y |
| 2 Thompson | Y | Y | Y | N | Y | Y |
| 3 **Pickering** | Y | Y | Y | Y | Y | Y |
| 4 Taylor | ? | ? | ? | ? | ? | ? |
| **MISSOURI** | | | | | | |
| 1 Clay | Y | Y | Y | N | Y | N |
| 2 **Akin** | Y | Y | N | Y | Y | Y |
| 3 Carnahan | Y | Y | Y | Y | Y | Y |
| 4 Skelton | Y | Y | Y | Y | Y | Y |
| 5 Cleaver | Y | Y | Y | N | Y | N |
| 6 **Graves** | Y | Y | Y | Y | Y | Y |
| 7 **Blunt** | Y | Y | Y | Y | Y | Y |
| 8 **Emerson** | Y | Y | Y | Y | Y | Y |
| 9 **Hulshof** | Y | Y | Y | Y | Y | Y |
| **MONTANA** | | | | | | |
| AL **Rehberg** | Y | Y | Y | Y | Y | Y |
| **NEBRASKA** | | | | | | |
| 1 **Fortenberry** | Y | Y | Y | Y | Y | Y |
| 2 **Terry** | Y | Y | Y | Y | Y | Y |
| 3 **Osborne** | Y | Y | Y | Y | Y | Y |
| **NEVADA** | | | | | | |
| 1 Berkley | Y | Y | Y | Y | N | Y |
| 2 **Gibbons** | Y | Y | Y | Y | Y | Y |
| 3 **Porter** | Y | Y | Y | Y | Y | Y |
| **NEW HAMPSHIRE** | | | | | | |
| 1 **Bradley** | Y | Y | Y | Y | Y | Y |
| 2 **Bass** | Y | Y | Y | Y | Y | Y |
| **NEW JERSEY** | | | | | | |
| 1 Andrews | + | + | + | N | Y | N |
| 2 **LoBiondo** | Y | Y | Y | Y | Y | Y |
| 3 **Saxton** | Y | Y | Y | Y | Y | Y |
| 4 **Smith** | Y | Y | Y | Y | Y | Y |
| 5 **Garrett** | Y | Y | N | Y | N | Y |
| 6 Pallone | Y | Y | Y | N | Y | N |
| 7 **Ferguson** | Y | Y | Y | + | + | + |
| 8 Pascrell | Y | Y | Y | Y | Y | Y |
| 9 Rothman | Y | Y | Y | N | Y | Y |
| 10 Payne | Y | Y | Y | N | Y | N |
| 11 **Frelinghuysen** | Y | Y | Y | Y | Y | Y |
| 12 Holt | Y | Y | Y | Y | Y | N |
| 13 Menendez | Y | Y | Y | N | Y | Y |
| **NEW MEXICO** | | | | | | |
| 1 **Wilson** | Y | Y | Y | Y | Y | Y |
| 2 **Pearce** | Y | Y | Y | Y | Y | Y |
| 3 Udall | Y | Y | Y | N | Y | N |
| **NEW YORK** | | | | | | |
| 1 Bishop | Y | Y | Y | Y | Y | Y |
| 2 Israel | Y | Y | Y | Y | Y | N |
| 3 **King** | Y | Y | Y | Y | Y | Y |
| 4 McCarthy | Y | Y | Y | Y | Y | Y |
| 5 Ackerman | Y | Y | Y | N | Y | N |
| 6 Meeks | Y | Y | Y | Y | Y | N |
| 7 Crowley | Y | Y | Y | Y | Y | Y |
| 8 Nadler | Y | Y | Y | N | Y | N |
| 9 Weiner | Y | Y | Y | Y | Y | Y |
| 10 Towns | Y | Y | Y | N | Y | Y |
| 11 Owens | Y | Y | Y | Y | Y | N |
| 12 Velázquez | Y | Y | Y | N | Y | N |
| 13 **Fossella** | Y | Y | Y | Y | Y | Y |
| 14 Maloney | Y | Y | Y | Y | Y | N |
| 15 Rangel | Y | Y | Y | N | Y | N |
| 16 Serrano | Y | Y | Y | N | Y | N |
| 17 Engel | Y | Y | Y | Y | Y | P |
| 18 Lowey | Y | Y | Y | Y | Y | N |
| 19 **Kelly** | Y | Y | Y | Y | Y | Y |
| 20 **Sweeney** | Y | Y | Y | Y | Y | Y |
| 21 McNulty | ? | ? | ? | ? | ? | ? |
| 22 Hinchey | Y | Y | Y | N | Y | N |
| 23 **McHugh** | Y | Y | Y | Y | Y | Y |
| 24 **Boehlert** | Y | Y | Y | Y | Y | Y |
| 25 **Walsh** | Y | Y | Y | Y | Y | Y |
| 26 **Reynolds** | Y | Y | Y | Y | Y | Y |
| 27 Higgins | Y | Y | Y | Y | Y | Y |
| 28 Slaughter | Y | Y | ? | N | Y | N |
| 29 **Kuhl** | Y | Y | Y | Y | Y | Y |

| | 586 | 587 | 588 | 589 | 590 | 591 |
|---|---|---|---|---|---|---|
| **NORTH CAROLINA** | | | | | | |
| 1 Butterfield | Y | Y | Y | Y | Y | Y |
| 2 Etheridge | Y | Y | Y | Y | Y | Y |
| 3 **Jones** | Y | Y | N | Y | Y | Y |
| 4 Price | Y | Y | Y | Y | Y | N |
| 5 **Foxx** | Y | Y | N | Y | Y | Y |
| 6 **Coble** | Y | Y | N | Y | Y | Y |
| 7 McIntyre | Y | Y | Y | Y | Y | Y |
| 8 **Hayes** | Y | Y | Y | Y | Y | Y |
| 9 **Myrick** | Y | Y | N | Y | Y | Y |
| 10 **McHenry** | Y | Y | N | Y | Y | Y |
| 11 **Taylor** | Y | Y | Y | Y | Y | Y |
| 12 Watt | Y | Y | Y | N | Y | P |
| 13 Miller | Y | Y | Y | Y | Y | N |
| **NORTH DAKOTA** | | | | | | |
| AL Pomeroy | Y | Y | Y | Y | Y | Y |
| **OHIO** | | | | | | |
| 1 **Chabot** | Y | Y | Y | Y | Y | Y |
| 2 **Schmidt** | Y | Y | Y | Y | Y | Y |
| 3 **Turner** | Y | Y | Y | Y | Y | Y |
| 4 **Oxley** | Y | Y | Y | Y | Y | Y |
| 5 **Gillmor** | Y | Y | Y | Y | Y | Y |
| 6 Strickland | Y | Y | Y | Y | Y | Y |
| 7 **Hobson** | Y | Y | Y | Y | Y | Y |
| 8 **Boehner** | Y | Y | Y | Y | Y | Y |
| 9 Kaptur | Y | Y | Y | Y | Y | Y |
| 10 Kucinich | Y | Y | Y | N | Y | Y |
| 11 Jones | Y | Y | Y | Y | N | N |
| 12 **Tiberi** | Y | Y | Y | Y | Y | Y |
| 13 Brown | Y | Y | Y | Y | Y | Y |
| 14 **LaTourette** | Y | Y | Y | Y | Y | Y |
| 15 **Pryce** | Y | Y | Y | Y | Y | Y |
| 16 **Regula** | Y | Y | Y | Y | Y | Y |
| 17 Ryan | Y | Y | Y | Y | Y | Y |
| 18 **Ney** | Y | Y | Y | Y | Y | Y |
| **OKLAHOMA** | | | | | | |
| 1 **Sullivan** | Y | Y | Y | Y | Y | Y |
| 2 Boren | Y | Y | Y | Y | Y | Y |
| 3 **Lucas** | Y | Y | Y | Y | Y | Y |
| 4 **Cole** | Y | Y | Y | Y | Y | Y |
| 5 **Istook** | Y | Y | N | Y | Y | Y |
| **OREGON** | | | | | | |
| 1 Wu | Y | Y | Y | N | Y | Y |
| 2 **Walden** | Y | Y | Y | Y | Y | Y |
| 3 Blumenauer | Y | Y | Y | Y | Y | N |
| 4 DeFazio | Y | Y | Y | Y | Y | Y |
| 5 Hooley | Y | Y | Y | Y | Y | Y |
| **PENNSYLVANIA** | | | | | | |
| 1 Brady | Y | Y | Y | Y | Y | N |
| 2 Fattah | Y | Y | Y | Y | Y | Y |
| 3 **English** | Y | Y | Y | Y | Y | Y |
| 4 **Hart** | Y | Y | Y | Y | Y | Y |
| 5 **Peterson** | Y | Y | Y | Y | Y | Y |
| 6 **Gerlach** | Y | Y | Y | Y | Y | Y |
| 7 **Weldon** | Y | Y | Y | Y | Y | Y |
| 8 **Fitzpatrick** | Y | Y | Y | Y | Y | Y |
| 9 **Shuster** | Y | Y | Y | Y | Y | Y |
| 10 **Sherwood** | Y | Y | Y | Y | Y | Y |
| 11 Kanjorski | Y | Y | Y | Y | Y | N |
| 12 Murtha | ? | ? | ? | Y | Y | N |
| 13 Schwartz | Y | Y | Y | Y | Y | Y |
| 14 Doyle | Y | Y | Y | Y | Y | N |
| 15 **Dent** | Y | Y | Y | Y | Y | Y |
| 16 **Pitts** | Y | Y | N | Y | Y | Y |
| 17 Holden | Y | Y | Y | Y | Y | Y |
| 18 **Murphy** | Y | Y | Y | Y | Y | Y |
| 19 **Platts** | Y | Y | Y | Y | Y | Y |
| **RHODE ISLAND** | | | | | | |
| 1 Kennedy | Y | Y | Y | N | Y | N |
| 2 Langevin | Y | Y | Y | Y | Y | N |
| **SOUTH CAROLINA** | | | | | | |
| 1 **Brown** | Y | Y | Y | Y | Y | Y |
| 2 **Wilson** | Y | Y | N | Y | Y | Y |
| 3 **Barrett** | Y | Y | N | Y | Y | Y |
| 4 **Inglis** | Y | Y | N | Y | Y | Y |
| 5 Spratt | Y | Y | Y | Y | Y | Y |
| 6 Clyburn | Y | Y | Y | Y | Y | Y |
| **SOUTH DAKOTA** | | | | | | |
| AL Herseth | Y | Y | Y | Y | Y | Y |
| **TENNESSEE** | | | | | | |
| 1 **Jenkins** | ? | ? | ? | ? | ? | ? |
| 2 **Duncan** | Y | Y | Y | Y | Y | Y |

| | 586 | 587 | 588 | 589 | 590 | 591 |
|---|---|---|---|---|---|---|
| 3 **Wamp** | Y | Y | Y | Y | Y | Y |
| 4 Davis | Y | Y | Y | N | Y | Y |
| 5 Cooper | Y | Y | Y | N | Y | Y |
| 6 Gordon | Y | Y | Y | Y | Y | Y |
| 7 **Blackburn** | Y | Y | N | Y | Y | Y |
| 8 Tanner | Y | Y | Y | Y | Y | Y |
| 9 Ford | Y | Y | Y | Y | Y | Y |
| **TEXAS** | | | | | | |
| 1 **Gohmert** | Y | Y | Y | Y | Y | Y |
| 2 **Poe** | Y | Y | N | Y | Y | Y |
| 3 **Johnson, S.** | Y | Y | N | Y | Y | Y |
| 4 **Hall** | Y | Y | Y | Y | Y | Y |
| 5 **Hensarling** | Y | Y | N | Y | Y | Y |
| 6 **Barton** | Y | Y | Y | Y | Y | Y |
| 7 **Culberson** | Y | Y | N | Y | Y | Y |
| 8 **Brady** | Y | Y | Y | Y | Y | Y |
| 9 Green, A. | Y | Y | Y | Y | Y | P |
| 10 **McCaul** | Y | Y | Y | Y | Y | Y |
| 11 **Conaway** | Y | Y | N | Y | Y | Y |
| 12 **Granger** | ? | ? | ? | Y | Y | Y |
| 13 **Thornberry** | Y | Y | Y | Y | Y | Y |
| 14 **Paul** | Y | Y | N | Y | Y | Y |
| 15 Hinojosa | Y | Y | Y | Y | Y | Y |
| 16 Reyes | Y | Y | Y | Y | Y | Y |
| 17 Edwards | Y | Y | Y | Y | Y | Y |
| 18 Jackson-Lee | Y | Y | Y | N | Y | Y |
| 19 **Neugebauer** | Y | Y | N | Y | Y | Y |
| 20 Gonzalez | Y | Y | Y | Y | Y | N |
| 21 **Smith** | Y | Y | Y | Y | Y | Y |
| 22 **DeLay** | Y | Y | N | Y | Y | Y |
| 23 **Bonilla** | Y | Y | Y | Y | Y | Y |
| 24 **Marchant** | Y | Y | N | Y | Y | Y |
| 25 Doggett | Y | Y | Y | Y | Y | N |
| 26 **Burgess** | Y | Y | Y | Y | Y | Y |
| 27 Ortiz | Y | Y | Y | Y | Y | Y |
| 28 Cuellar | Y | Y | Y | Y | Y | Y |
| 29 Green, G. | Y | Y | Y | Y | Y | Y |
| 30 Johnson, E. | Y | Y | Y | Y | Y | N |
| 31 **Carter** | Y | Y | ? | Y | Y | Y |
| 32 **Sessions** | Y | Y | N | Y | Y | Y |
| **UTAH** | | | | | | |
| 1 **Bishop** | Y | Y | N | Y | ? | Y |
| 2 Matheson | Y | Y | Y | Y | Y | Y |
| 3 **Cannon** | Y | Y | Y | Y | Y | Y |
| **VERMONT** | | | | | | |
| AL *Sanders* | Y | Y | Y | Y | Y | Y |
| **VIRGINIA** | | | | | | |
| 1 **Davis, J.** | Y | Y | N | Y | Y | Y |
| 2 **Drake** | Y | Y | N | Y | Y | Y |
| 3 Scott | Y | Y | Y | N | N | N |
| 4 **Forbes** | Y | Y | Y | Y | Y | Y |
| 5 **Goode** | Y | Y | N | Y | Y | Y |
| 6 **Goodlatte** | Y | Y | Y | Y | Y | Y |
| 7 **Cantor** | Y | Y | Y | Y | Y | Y |
| 8 Moran | Y | Y | Y | Y | Y | N |
| 9 Boucher | Y | Y | Y | Y | Y | N |
| 10 **Wolf** | Y | Y | Y | Y | Y | Y |
| 11 **Davis, T.** | Y | Y | Y | Y | Y | Y |
| **WASHINGTON** | | | | | | |
| 1 Inslee | Y | Y | Y | Y | Y | N |
| 2 Larsen | Y | Y | Y | Y | Y | N |
| 3 Baird | Y | Y | Y | Y | N | N |
| 4 **Hastings** | Y | Y | Y | Y | Y | Y |
| 5 **McMorris** | Y | Y | Y | Y | Y | Y |
| 6 Dicks | Y | Y | Y | Y | Y | Y |
| 7 McDermott | Y | Y | Y | N | N | N |
| 8 **Reichert** | ? | ? | ? | ? | ? | ? |
| 9 Smith | Y | Y | Y | Y | Y | Y |
| **WEST VIRGINIA** | | | | | | |
| 1 Mollohan | ? | ? | ? | Y | Y | Y |
| 2 **Capito** | Y | Y | Y | Y | Y | Y |
| 3 Rahall | Y | Y | Y | Y | Y | Y |
| **WISCONSIN** | | | | | | |
| 1 **Ryan** | Y | Y | N | Y | Y | Y |
| 2 Baldwin | Y | Y | Y | N | Y | Y |
| 3 Kind | Y | Y | Y | Y | Y | Y |
| 4 Moore | Y | Y | Y | Y | Y | N |
| 5 **Sensenbrenner** | Y | Y | N | Y | Y | Y |
| 6 **Petri** | Y | Y | Y | Y | Y | Y |
| 7 Obey | Y | Y | Y | N | Y | Y |
| 8 **Green** | Y | Y | N | Y | Y | Y |
| **WYOMING** | | | | | | |
| AL **Cubin** | Y | Y | Y | Y | Y | Y |

# IN THE HOUSE | By Vote Number

**592.** **HR 1065. United States Boxing Commission/Passage.** Passage of the bill that would create a federal boxing commission within the Commerce Department to regulate professional boxing. Rejected 190-233: R 43-183; D 146-50 (ND 116-32, SD 30-18); I 1-0. Nov. 16, 2005.

**593.** **H Con Res 230. Enforcing Intellectual Property Rights/Adoption.** Shaw, R-Fla., motion to suspend the rules and adopt the concurrent resolution that would express the sense of Congress that Russia should provide adequate and effective protection of intellectual property rights, or risk losing its eligibility to participate in the Generalized System of Preferences. Motion agreed to 421-2: R 224-2; D 196-0 (ND 148-0, SD 48-0); I 1-0. A two-thirds majority of those present and voting (282 in this case) is required for adoption under suspension of the rules. Nov. 16, 2005.

**594.** **H Con Res 268. Internet Corporation for Assigned Names and Numbers/Adoption.** Upton, R-Mich., motion to suspend the rules and adopt the concurrent resolution that would express the sense of Congress that the authoritative root zone server should remain physically located in the United States, with the Commerce Department maintaining oversight of the Internet Corporation for Assigned Names and Numbers. Motion agreed to 423-0: R 225-0; D 197-0 (ND 148-0, SD 49-0); I 1-0. A two-thirds majority of those present and voting (282 in this case) is required for adoption under suspension of the rules. Nov. 16, 2005.

**595.** **H Res 558, H J Res 72. Fiscal 2006 Continuing Resolution/Rule.** Adoption of the rule (H Res 558) that would provide for House floor consideration of the joint resolution that would provide continuing appropriations through Dec. 17 for all federal departments and agencies whose fiscal 2006 appropriations bills have not been enacted. Adopted 407-21: R 229-0; D 177-21 (ND 132-17, SD 45-4); I 1-0. Nov. 17, 2005.

**596.** **H Res 559, HR 3010. Fiscal 2006 Labor-HHS-Education Appropriations/Rule.** Adoption of the rule (H Res 559) that would provide for House floor consideration of the conference report on the bill that would appropriate $601.7 billion, including $142.5 billion in discretionary spending, in fiscal 2006 for the departments of Labor, Health and Human Services and Education, and for other various agencies and programs. Adopted 244-185: R 227-2; D 17-182 (ND 9-140, SD 8-42); I 0-1. Nov. 17, 2005.

**597.** **H Res 500. 60th Anniversary of Flight 19 Rescue/Adoption.** J. Davis, R-Va., motion to suspend the rules and adopt the resolution which would recognize the 60th anniversary of the disappearance of the five naval Avenger torpedo bombers of Flight 19 and the naval Mariner rescue aircraft sent to search for Flight 19. Motion agreed to 420-2: R 222-2; D 197-0 (ND 148-0, SD 49-0); I 1-0. A two-thirds majority of those present and voting (282 in this case) is required for adoption under suspension of the rules. Nov. 17, 2005.

ND Northern Democrats, SD Southern Democrats
Southern states: Ala., Ark., Fla., Ga., Ky., La., Miss., N.C., Okla., S.C., Tenn., Texas, Va.

| | 592 | 593 | 594 | 595 | 596 | 597 |
|---|---|---|---|---|---|---|
| **ALABAMA** | | | | | | |
| 1 Bonner | N | Y | Y | Y | Y | Y |
| 2 Everett | N | Y | Y | Y | Y | Y |
| 3 Rogers | N | Y | Y | Y | N | Y |
| 4 Aderholt | N | Y | Y | Y | Y | Y |
| 5 Cramer | Y | Y | Y | Y | Y | Y |
| 6 Bachus | N | Y | Y | Y | Y | Y |
| 7 Davis | Y | Y | Y | Y | N | Y |
| **ALASKA** | | | | | | |
| AL Young | N | Y | Y | Y | N | Y |
| **ARIZONA** | | | | | | |
| 1 Renzi | N | Y | Y | Y | Y | Y |
| 2 Franks | N | Y | Y | Y | Y | Y |
| 3 Shadegg | N | Y | Y | Y | Y | Y |
| 4 Pastor | N | Y | Y | N | N | Y |
| 5 Hayworth | N | Y | Y | Y | Y | Y |
| 6 Flake | N | Y | Y | Y | Y | Y |
| 7 Grijalva | Y | Y | Y | N | N | Y |
| 8 Kolbe | N | Y | ? | Y | Y | + |
| **ARKANSAS** | | | | | | |
| 1 Berry | N | Y | Y | Y | N | Y |
| 2 Snyder | N | Y | Y | Y | N | Y |
| 3 Boozman | N | Y | Y | Y | Y | Y |
| 4 Ross | N | Y | Y | Y | N | Y |
| **CALIFORNIA** | | | | | | |
| 1 Thompson | Y | Y | Y | Y | N | Y |
| 2 Herger | N | Y | Y | Y | Y | Y |
| 3 Lungren | Y | Y | Y | Y | Y | Y |
| 4 Doolittle | N | Y | Y | Y | Y | Y |
| 5 Matsui, D. | Y | Y | Y | Y | N | Y |
| 6 Woolsey | Y | Y | Y | Y | N | Y |
| 7 Miller, George | Y | Y | Y | N | N | Y |
| 8 Pelosi | Y | Y | Y | Y | N | Y |
| 9 Lee | Y | Y | Y | N | N | Y |
| 10 Tauscher | Y | Y | Y | Y | N | Y |
| 11 Pombo | N | Y | Y | ? | Y | Y |
| 12 Lantos | ? | ? | ? | Y | N | Y |
| 13 Stark | ? | ? | ? | ? | ? | Y |
| 14 Eshoo | Y | Y | Y | Y | N | Y |
| 15 Honda | Y | Y | Y | N | N | Y |
| 16 Lofgren | Y | Y | Y | Y | N | Y |
| 17 Farr | Y | Y | Y | Y | N | Y |
| 18 Cardoza | N | Y | Y | Y | N | Y |
| 19 Radanovich | N | Y | Y | Y | Y | Y |
| 20 Costa | N | Y | Y | Y | N | Y |
| 21 Nunes | N | Y | Y | Y | Y | Y |
| 22 Thomas | Y | Y | Y | Y | Y | Y |
| 23 Capps | Y | Y | Y | Y | N | Y |
| 24 Gallegly | N | Y | Y | Y | Y | Y |
| 25 McKeon | N | Y | Y | Y | Y | Y |
| 26 Dreier | N | Y | Y | Y | Y | Y |
| 27 Sherman | Y | Y | Y | Y | N | Y |
| 28 Berman | Y | Y | Y | Y | N | Y |
| 29 Schiff | Y | Y | Y | Y | N | Y |
| 30 Waxman | Y | Y | Y | Y | N | Y |
| 31 Becerra | Y | Y | Y | N | N | Y |
| 32 Solis | Y | Y | Y | Y | N | Y |
| 33 Watson | Y | Y | Y | Y | N | Y |
| 34 Roybal-Allard | Y | Y | Y | Y | N | Y |
| 35 Waters | Y | Y | Y | Y | N | Y |
| 36 Harman | Y | Y | Y | Y | N | Y |
| 37 Millender-McD. | Y | Y | Y | Y | N | Y |
| 38 Napolitano | Y | Y | Y | Y | N | Y |
| 39 Sánchez, Linda | Y | Y | Y | Y | N | Y |
| 40 Royce | N | Y | Y | Y | Y | Y |
| 41 Lewis | N | Y | Y | Y | Y | Y |
| 42 Miller, Gary | N | Y | Y | Y | Y | Y |
| 43 Baca | Y | Y | Y | Y | N | Y |
| 44 Calvert | N | Y | Y | Y | Y | Y |
| 45 Bono | N | Y | Y | Y | Y | Y |
| 46 Rohrabacher | N | Y | Y | Y | Y | Y |
| 47 Sanchez, Loretta | Y | Y | Y | Y | N | Y |
| 48 Vacant | | | | | | |
| 49 Issa | Y | Y | Y | Y | Y | Y |

| | 592 | 593 | 594 | 595 | 596 | 597 |
|---|---|---|---|---|---|---|
| 50 Cunningham | ? | ? | ? | Y | Y | Y |
| 51 Filner | Y | Y | Y | Y | N | Y |
| 52 Hunter | N | Y | Y | Y | Y | Y |
| 53 Davis | Y | Y | Y | Y | N | Y |
| **COLORADO** | | | | | | |
| 1 DeGette | Y | Y | Y | Y | Y | ? |
| 2 Udall | Y | Y | Y | N | N | Y |
| 3 Salazar | N | Y | Y | Y | N | Y |
| 4 Musgrave | N | Y | Y | Y | Y | Y |
| 5 Hefley | N | Y | Y | Y | Y | Y |
| 6 Tancredo | N | Y | Y | Y | Y | Y |
| 7 Beauprez | N | Y | Y | Y | Y | Y |
| **CONNECTICUT** | | | | | | |
| 1 Larson | Y | Y | Y | Y | N | Y |
| 2 Simmons | Y | Y | Y | Y | Y | Y |
| 3 DeLauro | Y | Y | Y | Y | N | Y |
| 4 Shays | Y | Y | Y | Y | Y | Y |
| 5 Johnson | Y | Y | Y | Y | Y | Y |
| **DELAWARE** | | | | | | |
| AL Castle | Y | Y | Y | Y | Y | Y |
| **FLORIDA** | | | | | | |
| 1 Miller | N | Y | Y | Y | Y | Y |
| 2 Boyd | Y | Y | Y | Y | N | Y |
| 3 Brown | Y | Y | Y | Y | N | Y |
| 4 Crenshaw | N | Y | Y | Y | Y | Y |
| 5 Brown-Waite | N | Y | Y | Y | Y | Y |
| 6 Stearns | Y | Y | Y | Y | Y | Y |
| 7 Mica | N | Y | Y | Y | Y | Y |
| 8 Keller | N | Y | Y | Y | Y | Y |
| 9 Bilirakis | N | Y | Y | Y | Y | Y |
| 10 Young | Y | Y | Y | Y | Y | Y |
| 11 Davis | ? | ? | ? | Y | N | Y |
| 12 Putnam | N | Y | Y | Y | Y | Y |
| 13 Harris | N | Y | Y | Y | Y | Y |
| 14 Mack | N | Y | Y | Y | Y | Y |
| 15 Weldon | Y | Y | Y | Y | Y | Y |
| 16 Foley | N | Y | Y | Y | Y | Y |
| 17 Meek | N | Y | Y | Y | N | Y |
| 18 Ros-Lehtinen | ? | Y | Y | Y | Y | Y |
| 19 Wexler | Y | Y | Y | ? | N | Y |
| 20 Wasserman-Schultz | N | Y | Y | Y | Y | Y |
| 21 Diaz-Balart, L. | Y | Y | Y | Y | Y | Y |
| 22 Shaw | N | Y | ? | Y | Y | Y |
| 23 Hastings | N | Y | Y | N | N | Y |
| 24 Feeney | N | Y | Y | Y | Y | Y |
| 25 Diaz-Balart, M. | N | Y | Y | Y | Y | Y |
| **GEORGIA** | | | | | | |
| 1 Kingston | N | Y | Y | Y | Y | Y |
| 2 Bishop | Y | Y | Y | Y | Y | Y |
| 3 Marshall | N | Y | Y | Y | N | Y |
| 4 McKinney | Y | Y | Y | Y | N | Y |
| 5 Lewis | Y | Y | Y | Y | N | Y |
| 6 Price | N | Y | Y | Y | Y | Y |
| 7 Linder | N | Y | Y | Y | Y | Y |
| 8 Westmoreland | N | Y | Y | Y | Y | Y |
| 9 Norwood | N | Y | Y | Y | Y | Y |
| 10 Deal | N | Y | Y | Y | Y | Y |
| 11 Gingrey | N | Y | Y | Y | Y | Y |
| 12 Barrow | Y | Y | Y | Y | N | Y |
| 13 Scott | Y | Y | Y | Y | N | Y |
| **HAWAII** | | | | | | |
| 1 Abercrombie | Y | Y | Y | Y | N | Y |
| 2 Case | N | Y | Y | Y | N | Y |
| **IDAHO** | | | | | | |
| 1 Otter | N | Y | Y | Y | Y | Y |
| 2 Simpson | N | Y | Y | Y | Y | Y |
| **ILLINOIS** | | | | | | |
| 1 Rush | Y | Y | Y | N | N | Y |
| 2 Jackson | Y | Y | Y | N | N | Y |
| 3 Lipinski | Y | Y | Y | Y | N | Y |
| 4 Gutierrez | Y | Y | Y | Y | N | Y |
| 5 Emanuel | Y | Y | Y | Y | N | Y |
| 6 Hyde | Y | Y | Y | Y | Y | Y |
| 7 Davis | Y | Y | Y | N | N | Y |
| 8 Bean | N | Y | Y | Y | N | Y |
| 9 Schakowsky | Y | Y | Y | Y | N | Y |
| 10 Kirk | Y | Y | Y | Y | Y | N |
| 11 Weller | N | Y | Y | Y | Y | Y |
| 12 Costello | N | Y | Y | Y | N | Y |

| | 592 | 593 | 594 | 595 | 596 | 597 |
|---|---|---|---|---|---|---|
| 13 **Biggert** | N | Y | Y | Y | Y | Y |
| 14 **Hastert** | | | | | | |
| 15 **Johnson** | N | Y | Y | Y | Y | ? |
| 16 **Manzullo** | N | Y | Y | Y | Y | Y |
| 17 Evans | Y | Y | Y | Y | N | Y |
| 18 **LaHood** | N | Y | Y | Y | Y | Y |
| 19 **Shimkus** | Y | Y | Y | Y | Y | Y |
| **INDIANA** | | | | | | |
| 1 Visclosky | Y | Y | Y | Y | N | Y |
| 2 **Chocola** | N | Y | Y | Y | Y | Y |
| 3 **Souder** | N | Y | Y | Y | Y | Y |
| 4 **Buyer** | Y | Y | Y | Y | Y | Y |
| 5 **Burton** | N | Y | Y | Y | Y | Y |
| 6 **Pence** | N | Y | Y | Y | Y | Y |
| 7 Carson | N | Y | Y | Y | N | Y |
| 8 **Hostettler** | N | Y | Y | Y | Y | Y |
| 9 **Sodrel** | N | Y | Y | Y | Y | Y |
| **IOWA** | | | | | | |
| 1 **Nussle** | N | Y | Y | Y | Y | Y |
| 2 **Leach** | N | Y | Y | Y | Y | Y |
| 3 Boswell | ? | ? | ? | ? | ? | ? |
| 4 **Latham** | N | Y | Y | Y | Y | Y |
| 5 **King** | N | Y | Y | Y | Y | Y |
| **KANSAS** | | | | | | |
| 1 **Moran** | Y | Y | Y | Y | Y | Y |
| 2 **Ryun** | N | Y | Y | Y | Y | Y |
| 3 Moore | Y | Y | Y | Y | N | Y |
| 4 **Tiahrt** | N | Y | Y | Y | Y | Y |
| **KENTUCKY** | | | | | | |
| 1 **Whitfield** | Y | Y | Y | Y | Y | Y |
| 2 **Lewis** | N | Y | Y | Y | Y | Y |
| 3 **Northup** | N | Y | Y | Y | Y | Y |
| 4 **Davis** | N | Y | Y | Y | Y | Y |
| 5 **Rogers** | Y | Y | Y | Y | Y | Y |
| 6 Chandler | Y | Y | Y | Y | N | Y |
| **LOUISIANA** | | | | | | |
| 1 **Jindal** | N | Y | Y | Y | Y | Y |
| 2 Jefferson | Y | Y | Y | Y | N | Y |
| 3 Melancon | N | Y | Y | Y | N | Y |
| 4 **McCrery** | N | Y | Y | Y | Y | ? |
| 5 **Alexander** | N | Y | Y | Y | Y | Y |
| 6 **Baker** | N | Y | Y | Y | Y | Y |
| 7 **Boustany** | N | Y | Y | Y | Y | Y |
| **MAINE** | | | | | | |
| 1 Allen | Y | Y | Y | Y | N | Y |
| 2 Michaud | Y | Y | Y | Y | N | Y |
| **MARYLAND** | | | | | | |
| 1 **Gilchrest** | Y | Y | Y | Y | Y | Y |
| 2 Ruppersberger | Y | Y | Y | Y | N | Y |
| 3 Cardin | Y | Y | Y | Y | N | Y |
| 4 Wynn | Y | Y | Y | Y | N | Y |
| 5 Hoyer | Y | Y | Y | Y | N | Y |
| 6 **Bartlett** | N | Y | Y | Y | Y | Y |
| 7 Cummings | Y | Y | Y | Y | N | Y |
| 8 Van Hollen | Y | Y | Y | Y | N | Y |
| **MASSACHUSETTS** | | | | | | |
| 1 Olver | Y | Y | Y | Y | N | Y |
| 2 Neal | Y | Y | Y | Y | N | Y |
| 3 McGovern | Y | Y | Y | Y | N | Y |
| 4 Frank | N | Y | Y | N | N | Y |
| 5 Meehan | Y | Y | Y | Y | N | Y |
| 6 Tierney | N | Y | Y | Y | N | Y |
| 7 Markey | Y | Y | Y | N | N | Y |
| 8 Capuano | N | Y | Y | Y | N | Y |
| 9 Lynch | Y | Y | Y | Y | N | Y |
| 10 Delahunt | Y | Y | Y | Y | N | Y |
| **MICHIGAN** | | | | | | |
| 1 Stupak | Y | Y | Y | N | N | Y |
| 2 **Hoekstra** | N | Y | Y | Y | Y | Y |
| 3 **Ehlers** | Y | Y | Y | Y | Y | Y |
| 4 **Camp** | N | Y | Y | Y | Y | Y |
| 5 Kildee | Y | Y | Y | Y | N | Y |
| 6 **Upton** | Y | Y | Y | Y | Y | Y |
| 7 **Schwarz** | Y | Y | Y | Y | Y | Y |
| 8 **Rogers** | N | Y | Y | Y | Y | Y |
| 9 **Knollenberg** | N | Y | Y | Y | Y | Y |
| 10 **Miller** | N | Y | Y | Y | Y | Y |
| 11 **McCotter** | N | Y | Y | Y | Y | Y |
| 12 Levin | Y | Y | Y | Y | N | Y |
| 13 Kilpatrick | Y | Y | Y | Y | N | Y |
| 14 Conyers | Y | Y | Y | N | N | Y |
| 15 Dingell | Y | Y | Y | Y | N | Y |

| | 592 | 593 | 594 | 595 | 596 | 597 |
|---|---|---|---|---|---|---|
| **MINNESOTA** | | | | | | |
| 1 **Gutknecht** | Y | Y | Y | Y | Y | Y |
| 2 **Kline** | N | Y | Y | Y | Y | Y |
| 3 **Ramstad** | N | Y | Y | Y | Y | Y |
| 4 McCollum | Y | Y | Y | Y | N | Y |
| 5 Sabo | Y | Y | Y | Y | N | Y |
| 6 **Kennedy** | N | Y | Y | Y | Y | Y |
| 7 Peterson | N | Y | Y | Y | N | Y |
| 8 Oberstar | Y | Y | Y | Y | Y | Y |
| **MISSISSIPPI** | | | | | | |
| 1 **Wicker** | N | Y | Y | Y | Y | Y |
| 2 Thompson | Y | Y | Y | Y | N | Y |
| 3 **Pickering** | Y | Y | Y | Y | Y | Y |
| 4 Taylor | ? | ? | ? | Y | N | Y |
| **MISSOURI** | | | | | | |
| 1 Clay | Y | Y | Y | Y | N | Y |
| 2 **Akin** | N | Y | Y | Y | Y | Y |
| 3 Carnahan | Y | Y | Y | Y | N | Y |
| 4 Skelton | Y | Y | Y | Y | N | Y |
| 5 Cleaver | N | Y | Y | Y | N | Y |
| 6 **Graves** | N | Y | Y | Y | Y | Y |
| 7 **Blunt** | Y | Y | Y | Y | Y | Y |
| 8 **Emerson** | N | Y | Y | Y | Y | Y |
| 9 **Hulshof** | N | Y | Y | Y | Y | Y |
| **MONTANA** | | | | | | |
| AL **Rehberg** | N | Y | Y | Y | Y | Y |
| **NEBRASKA** | | | | | | |
| 1 **Fortenberry** | Y | Y | Y | Y | Y | Y |
| 2 **Terry** | N | Y | Y | Y | Y | Y |
| 3 **Osborne** | Y | Y | Y | Y | Y | Y |
| **NEVADA** | | | | | | |
| 1 Berkley | Y | Y | Y | Y | N | Y |
| 2 **Gibbons** | Y | Y | Y | Y | Y | Y |
| 3 **Porter** | Y | Y | Y | Y | Y | Y |
| **NEW HAMPSHIRE** | | | | | | |
| 1 **Bradley** | N | Y | Y | Y | Y | Y |
| 2 **Bass** | Y | Y | Y | Y | Y | Y |
| **NEW JERSEY** | | | | | | |
| 1 Andrews | N | Y | Y | N | N | Y |
| 2 **LoBiondo** | N | Y | Y | Y | Y | Y |
| 3 **Saxton** | N | Y | Y | Y | Y | Y |
| 4 **Smith** | Y | Y | Y | Y | Y | Y |
| 5 **Garrett** | N | Y | Y | Y | Y | Y |
| 6 Pallone | N | Y | Y | Y | N | Y |
| 7 **Ferguson** | N | Y | Y | Y | Y | Y |
| 8 Pascrell | Y | Y | Y | Y | N | Y |
| 9 Rothman | N | Y | Y | Y | N | Y |
| 10 Payne | N | Y | Y | Y | N | Y |
| 11 **Frelinghuysen** | N | Y | Y | Y | Y | Y |
| 12 Holt | N | Y | Y | Y | N | Y |
| 13 Menendez | N | Y | Y | Y | N | Y |
| **NEW MEXICO** | | | | | | |
| 1 **Wilson** | N | Y | Y | Y | Y | Y |
| 2 **Pearce** | N | Y | Y | Y | Y | Y |
| 3 Udall | N | Y | Y | N | N | Y |
| **NEW YORK** | | | | | | |
| 1 Bishop | Y | Y | Y | Y | N | Y |
| 2 Israel | Y | Y | Y | Y | N | Y |
| 3 **King** | Y | Y | Y | Y | Y | Y |
| 4 McCarthy | Y | Y | Y | Y | N | Y |
| 5 Ackerman | Y | Y | Y | Y | N | Y |
| 6 Meeks | Y | Y | Y | Y | N | Y |
| 7 Crowley | Y | Y | Y | N | N | Y |
| 8 Nadler | N | Y | Y | Y | N | ? |
| 9 Weiner | Y | Y | Y | Y | N | Y |
| 10 Towns | Y | Y | Y | Y | N | Y |
| 11 Owens | Y | Y | Y | Y | N | Y |
| 12 Velázquez | Y | Y | Y | Y | N | Y |
| 13 **Fossella** | N | Y | Y | Y | Y | Y |
| 14 Maloney | Y | Y | Y | Y | N | Y |
| 15 Rangel | Y | Y | Y | Y | N | Y |
| 16 Serrano | Y | Y | Y | Y | Y | Y |
| 17 Engel | Y | Y | Y | Y | N | Y |
| 18 Lowey | Y | Y | Y | Y | N | Y |
| 19 **Kelly** | N | Y | Y | Y | Y | Y |
| 20 **Sweeney** | N | Y | Y | Y | Y | Y |
| 21 McNulty | Y | Y | Y | Y | N | Y |
| 22 Hinchey | Y | Y | Y | Y | N | Y |
| 23 **McHugh** | N | Y | Y | Y | Y | Y |
| 24 **Boehlert** | N | Y | Y | Y | Y | Y |
| 25 **Walsh** | N | Y | Y | Y | Y | Y |
| 26 **Reynolds** | N | Y | Y | Y | Y | Y |
| 27 Higgins | Y | Y | Y | Y | N | Y |
| 28 Slaughter | Y | Y | Y | Y | N | Y |
| 29 **Kuhl** | N | Y | Y | Y | Y | Y |

| | 592 | 593 | 594 | 595 | 596 | 597 |
|---|---|---|---|---|---|---|
| **NORTH CAROLINA** | | | | | | |
| 1 Butterfield | Y | Y | Y | Y | N | Y |
| 2 Etheridge | N | Y | Y | Y | N | Y |
| 3 **Jones** | N | N | Y | Y | Y | Y |
| 4 Price | Y | Y | Y | Y | N | Y |
| 5 **Foxx** | N | Y | Y | Y | Y | ? |
| 6 **Coble** | N | Y | Y | Y | Y | Y |
| 7 McIntyre | Y | Y | Y | Y | N | Y |
| 8 **Hayes** | N | Y | Y | Y | Y | Y |
| 9 **Myrick** | N | Y | Y | Y | Y | Y |
| 10 **McHenry** | N | Y | Y | Y | Y | Y |
| 11 **Taylor** | N | Y | Y | Y | Y | Y |
| 12 Watt | N | Y | Y | Y | N | Y |
| 13 Miller | Y | Y | Y | Y | Y | Y |
| **NORTH DAKOTA** | | | | | | |
| AL Pomeroy | Y | Y | Y | Y | N | Y |
| **OHIO** | | | | | | |
| 1 **Chabot** | N | Y | Y | Y | Y | ? |
| 2 **Schmidt** | N | Y | Y | Y | Y | Y |
| 3 **Turner** | N | Y | Y | Y | Y | Y |
| 4 **Oxley** | N | Y | Y | Y | Y | Y |
| 5 **Gillmor** | Y | Y | Y | Y | Y | Y |
| 6 Strickland | Y | Y | Y | Y | N | Y |
| 7 **Hobson** | N | Y | Y | Y | Y | Y |
| 8 **Boehner** | N | Y | Y | Y | Y | Y |
| 9 Kaptur | N | Y | Y | Y | N | Y |
| 10 Kucinich | Y | Y | Y | N | N | Y |
| 11 Jones | N | Y | Y | Y | N | Y |
| 12 **Tiberi** | N | Y | Y | Y | Y | Y |
| 13 Brown | Y | Y | Y | Y | N | Y |
| 14 **LaTourette** | N | Y | Y | Y | Y | Y |
| 15 **Pryce** | Y | Y | Y | Y | Y | Y |
| 16 **Regula** | N | Y | Y | Y | Y | Y |
| 17 Ryan | Y | Y | Y | Y | N | Y |
| 18 **Ney** | N | Y | Y | Y | Y | Y |
| **OKLAHOMA** | | | | | | |
| 1 **Sullivan** | N | Y | Y | Y | Y | Y |
| 2 Boren | Y | Y | Y | Y | N | Y |
| 3 **Lucas** | N | Y | Y | Y | Y | Y |
| 4 **Cole** | N | Y | Y | Y | Y | Y |
| 5 **Istook** | N | Y | Y | Y | Y | Y |
| **OREGON** | | | | | | |
| 1 Wu | N | Y | Y | N | Y | Y |
| 2 **Walden** | Y | Y | Y | Y | Y | Y |
| 3 Blumenauer | N | Y | Y | Y | N | Y |
| 4 DeFazio | N | Y | Y | N | N | Y |
| 5 Hooley | Y | Y | Y | Y | N | Y |
| **PENNSYLVANIA** | | | | | | |
| 1 Brady | Y | Y | Y | Y | N | Y |
| 2 Fattah | Y | Y | Y | Y | N | Y |
| 3 **English** | N | Y | Y | Y | Y | Y |
| 4 **Hart** | N | Y | Y | Y | Y | Y |
| 5 **Peterson** | N | Y | Y | Y | Y | Y |
| 6 **Gerlach** | Y | Y | Y | Y | Y | Y |
| 7 **Weldon** | N | Y | Y | Y | Y | Y |
| 8 **Fitzpatrick** | Y | Y | Y | Y | Y | Y |
| 9 **Shuster** | N | Y | Y | Y | Y | Y |
| 10 **Sherwood** | N | Y | Y | Y | Y | Y |
| 11 Kanjorski | N | Y | Y | Y | Y | Y |
| 12 Murtha | N | Y | Y | Y | Y | Y |
| 13 Schwartz | Y | Y | Y | Y | N | Y |
| 14 Doyle | Y | Y | Y | Y | N | Y |
| 15 **Dent** | N | Y | Y | Y | Y | Y |
| 16 **Pitts** | Y | Y | Y | Y | Y | Y |
| 17 Holden | Y | Y | Y | Y | N | Y |
| 18 **Murphy** | N | Y | Y | Y | Y | Y |
| 19 **Platts** | N | Y | Y | Y | Y | Y |
| **RHODE ISLAND** | | | | | | |
| 1 Kennedy | Y | Y | Y | Y | N | Y |
| 2 Langevin | Y | Y | Y | Y | N | Y |
| **SOUTH CAROLINA** | | | | | | |
| 1 **Brown** | N | Y | Y | Y | Y | Y |
| 2 **Wilson** | N | Y | Y | Y | Y | Y |
| 3 **Barrett** | N | Y | Y | Y | Y | Y |
| 4 **Inglis** | N | Y | Y | Y | Y | Y |
| 5 Spratt | Y | Y | Y | Y | N | Y |
| 6 Clyburn | Y | Y | Y | Y | N | Y |
| **SOUTH DAKOTA** | | | | | | |
| AL Herseth | Y | Y | Y | Y | N | Y |
| **TENNESSEE** | | | | | | |
| 1 **Jenkins** | ? | ? | ? | Y | Y | Y |
| 2 **Duncan** | N | Y | Y | Y | Y | Y |

| | 592 | 593 | 594 | 595 | 596 | 597 |
|---|---|---|---|---|---|---|
| 3 **Wamp** | N | Y | Y | Y | Y | Y |
| 4 Davis | N | Y | Y | Y | N | Y |
| 5 Cooper | N | Y | Y | N | N | Y |
| 6 Gordon | N | Y | Y | Y | Y | Y |
| 7 **Blackburn** | N | Y | Y | Y | Y | Y |
| 8 Tanner | N | Y | Y | Y | N | Y |
| 9 Ford | N | Y | Y | N | N | ? |
| **TEXAS** | | | | | | |
| 1 **Gohmert** | N | Y | Y | Y | Y | N |
| 2 **Poe** | N | Y | Y | Y | Y | Y |
| 3 **Johnson, S.** | N | Y | Y | Y | Y | Y |
| 4 **Hall** | Y | Y | Y | Y | Y | Y |
| 5 **Hensarling** | N | Y | Y | Y | Y | Y |
| 6 **Barton** | Y | Y | Y | Y | ? | Y |
| 7 **Culberson** | N | ? | Y | Y | Y | Y |
| 8 **Brady** | N | Y | Y | Y | Y | Y |
| 9 Green, A. | N | Y | Y | Y | N | Y |
| 10 **McCaul** | N | Y | Y | Y | Y | Y |
| 11 **Conaway** | N | Y | Y | Y | Y | Y |
| 12 **Granger** | N | Y | Y | Y | Y | Y |
| 13 **Thornberry** | N | Y | Y | Y | Y | Y |
| 14 **Paul** | N | N | Y | Y | Y | Y |
| 15 Hinojosa | Y | Y | Y | Y | Y | Y |
| 16 Reyes | Y | Y | Y | Y | N | Y |
| 17 Edwards | ? | ? | Y | Y | N | Y |
| 18 Jackson-Lee | Y | Y | Y | N | N | Y |
| 19 **Neugebauer** | N | Y | Y | Y | Y | Y |
| 20 Gonzalez | Y | Y | Y | Y | N | Y |
| 21 **Smith** | N | Y | Y | Y | Y | ? |
| 22 **DeLay** | N | Y | Y | Y | Y | Y |
| 23 **Bonilla** | N | Y | Y | Y | Y | Y |
| 24 **Marchant** | N | Y | Y | Y | Y | Y |
| 25 Doggett | Y | Y | Y | Y | N | Y |
| 26 **Burgess** | Y | Y | Y | Y | Y | Y |
| 27 Ortiz | Y | Y | Y | Y | N | Y |
| 28 Cuellar | N | Y | Y | Y | Y | Y |
| 29 Green, G. | Y | Y | Y | Y | N | Y |
| 30 Johnson, E. | N | Y | Y | Y | N | Y |
| 31 **Carter** | N | Y | Y | Y | Y | Y |
| 32 **Sessions** | N | Y | Y | Y | Y | Y |
| **UTAH** | | | | | | |
| 1 **Bishop** | N | Y | Y | Y | Y | Y |
| 2 Matheson | Y | Y | Y | Y | N | Y |
| 3 **Cannon** | N | Y | Y | Y | Y | Y |
| **VERMONT** | | | | | | |
| AL *Sanders* | Y | Y | Y | Y | N | Y |
| **VIRGINIA** | | | | | | |
| 1 **Davis, J.** | N | Y | Y | Y | Y | Y |
| 2 **Drake** | N | Y | Y | Y | Y | Y |
| 3 Scott | Y | Y | Y | Y | N | Y |
| 4 **Forbes** | N | Y | Y | Y | Y | Y |
| 5 **Goode** | N | Y | Y | Y | Y | Y |
| 6 **Goodlatte** | N | Y | Y | Y | Y | Y |
| 7 **Cantor** | N | Y | Y | Y | Y | Y |
| 8 Moran | Y | Y | Y | ? | ? | ? |
| 9 Boucher | Y | Y | Y | Y | N | Y |
| 10 **Wolf** | N | Y | Y | Y | Y | Y |
| 11 **Davis, T.** | Y | Y | Y | Y | Y | Y |
| **WASHINGTON** | | | | | | |
| 1 Inslee | Y | Y | Y | Y | N | Y |
| 2 Larsen | N | Y | Y | Y | N | Y |
| 3 Baird | Y | Y | Y | Y | N | Y |
| 4 **Hastings** | N | Y | Y | Y | Y | Y |
| 5 **McMorris** | N | Y | Y | Y | Y | Y |
| 6 Dicks | Y | Y | Y | Y | N | Y |
| 7 McDermott | N | Y | Y | Y | N | Y |
| 8 **Reichert** | ? | ? | ? | Y | Y | Y |
| 9 Smith | Y | Y | Y | Y | Y | Y |
| **WEST VIRGINIA** | | | | | | |
| 1 Mollohan | N | Y | Y | Y | Y | Y |
| 2 **Capito** | N | Y | Y | Y | Y | Y |
| 3 Rahall | N | Y | Y | Y | N | Y |
| **WISCONSIN** | | | | | | |
| 1 **Ryan** | N | Y | Y | Y | Y | Y |
| 2 Baldwin | Y | Y | Y | Y | N | Y |
| 3 Kind | Y | Y | Y | Y | Y | Y |
| 4 Moore | Y | Y | Y | Y | N | Y |
| 5 **Sensenbrenner** | N | Y | Y | Y | Y | Y |
| 6 **Petri** | N | Y | Y | Y | Y | Y |
| 7 Obey | Y | Y | Y | Y | N | Y |
| 8 **Green** | N | Y | Y | Y | Y | Y |
| **WYOMING** | | | | | | |
| AL **Cubin** | Y | Y | Y | Y | Y | Y |

# IN THE HOUSE | By Vote Number

**598.** **HR 3010. Fiscal 2006 Labor-HHS-Education Appropriations/Conference Report.** Adoption of the conference report on the bill that would appropriate $601.7 billion, including $142.5 billion in discretionary spending, for the Labor, Health and Human Services (HHS) and Education departments and related agencies in fiscal 2006. It would provide $63.5 billion for the Education Department, $14.8 billion for the Labor Department and $474.1 billion for Health and Human Services. Rejected 209-224: R 209-22; D 0-201 (ND 0-150, SD 0-51); I 0-1. Nov. 17, 2005.

**599.** **H J Res 72. Fiscal 2006 Continuing Resolution/Passage.** Passage of the joint resolution that would provide continuing appropriations through Dec. 17 for all federal departments and agencies whose fiscal 2006 appropriations bills have not been enacted. Passed 413-16: R 230-0; D 182-16 (ND 135-13, SD 47-3); I 1-0. Nov. 17, 2005.

**600.** **HR 4241. Budget Reconciliation/Question of Consideration.** Question of whether the House should consider the rule (H Res 560) to provide for House floor consideration of the bill that would make changes to programs for a net savings of approximately $49.9 billion over five years. Agreed to consider 224-198: R 224-1; D 0-196 (ND 0-145, SD 0-51); I 0-1. Nov. 17, 2005.

**601.** **HR 4241. Budget Reconciliation/Passage.** Passage of the bill that would make changes to programs for a net savings of $49.9 billion over five years. It would reduce subsidies to lenders of student loans, reduce aid to states to enforce child support payments, reduce federal spending on Medicaid and repeal a law that sends anti-dumping trade penalties to aggrieved corporations instead of to the U.S. Treasury. It would provide $2.5 billion in Medicaid and other assistance to Hurricane Katrina victims. Passed 217-215: R 217-14; D 0-200 (ND 0-149, SD 0-51); I 0-1. A "yea" was a vote in support of the president's position. Nov. 18, 2005 (in the session that began and the Congressional Record dated Nov. 17, 2005).

**602.** **H Res 546. Condemn Terrorist Attacks in Jordan/Adoption.** Ros-Lehtinen, R-Fla., motion to suspend the rules and adopt the resolution that would condemn the Nov. 9 terrorist attacks in Amman, Jordan, and express the condolences of the House of Representatives to the families and friends of those killed in the attacks. Motion agreed to 409-0: R 217-0; D 191-0 (ND 143-0, SD 48-0); I 1-0. A two-thirds majority of those present and voting (273 in this case) is required for adoption under suspension of the rules. Nov. 18, 2005 (in the session that began and the Congressional Record dated Nov. 17, 2005).

| | 598 | 599 | 600 | 601 | 602 |
|---|---|---|---|---|---|
| **ALABAMA** | | | | | |
| 1 Bonner | Y | Y | Y | Y | Y |
| 2 Everett | Y | Y | Y | Y | Y |
| 3 Rogers | N | Y | Y | Y | Y |
| 4 Aderholt | Y | Y | Y | Y | Y |
| 5 Cramer | N | Y | N | N | Y |
| 6 Bachus | Y | Y | Y | Y | Y |
| 7 Davis | N | Y | N | N | Y |
| **ALASKA** | | | | | |
| AL Young | Y | Y | Y | Y | Y |
| **ARIZONA** | | | | | |
| 1 Renzi | N | Y | Y | Y | Y |
| 2 Franks | Y | Y | Y | Y | Y |
| 3 Shadegg | Y | Y | Y | Y | Y |
| 4 Pastor | N | Y | N | N | Y |
| 5 Hayworth | Y | Y | Y | Y | Y |
| 6 Flake | Y | Y | Y | Y | Y |
| 7 Grijalva | N | N | N | N | Y |
| 8 Kolbe | Y | Y | Y | Y | Y |
| **ARKANSAS** | | | | | |
| 1 Berry | N | Y | N | N | Y |
| 2 Snyder | N | Y | N | N | Y |
| 3 Boozman | Y | Y | Y | Y | Y |
| 4 Ross | N | Y | N | N | Y |
| **CALIFORNIA** | | | | | |
| 1 Thompson | N | Y | N | N | Y |
| 2 Herger | Y | Y | Y | Y | Y |
| 3 Lungren | Y | Y | Y | Y | Y |
| 4 Doolittle | Y | Y | Y | Y | Y |
| 5 Matsui, D. | N | Y | N | N | Y |
| 6 Woolsey | N | Y | N | N | Y |
| 7 Miller, George | N | Y | N | N | Y |
| 8 Pelosi | N | Y | N | N | Y |
| 9 Lee | N | Y | N | N | Y |
| 10 Tauscher | N | Y | N | N | Y |
| 11 Pombo | Y | Y | Y | Y | Y |
| 12 Lantos | N | Y | N | N | Y |
| 13 Stark | N | Y | N | N | ? |
| 14 Eshoo | N | Y | N | N | Y |
| 15 Honda | N | Y | N | N | Y |
| 16 Lofgren | N | N | N | N | Y |
| 17 Farr | N | Y | N | N | Y |
| 18 Cardoza | N | Y | N | N | Y |
| 19 Radanovich | Y | Y | ? | Y | ? |
| 20 Costa | N | Y | N | N | Y |
| 21 Nunes | N | Y | Y | Y | Y |
| 22 Thomas | N | Y | Y | Y | Y |
| 23 Capps | N | Y | N | N | Y |
| 24 Gallegly | Y | Y | Y | Y | Y |
| 25 McKeon | Y | Y | Y | Y | Y |
| 26 Dreier | Y | Y | Y | Y | Y |
| 27 Sherman | N | Y | N | N | Y |
| 28 Berman | N | Y | N | N | Y |
| 29 Schiff | N | Y | N | N | Y |
| 30 Waxman | N | Y | N | N | Y |
| 31 Becerra | N | N | N | N | Y |
| 32 Solis | N | Y | N | N | Y |
| 33 Watson | N | Y | N | N | Y |
| 34 Roybal-Allard | N | Y | N | N | Y |
| 35 Waters | N | Y | N | N | Y |
| 36 Harman | N | Y | N | N | Y |
| 37 Millender-McD. | N | Y | N | N | Y |
| 38 Napolitano | N | Y | N | N | Y |
| 39 Sánchez, Linda | N | Y | N | N | Y |
| 40 Royce | Y | Y | Y | Y | Y |
| 41 Lewis | Y | Y | Y | Y | Y |
| 42 Miller, Gary | Y | Y | Y | Y | Y |
| 43 Baca | N | Y | N | N | Y |
| 44 Calvert | Y | Y | Y | Y | Y |
| 45 Bono | Y | Y | Y | Y | Y |
| 46 Rohrabacher | Y | Y | Y | Y | Y |
| 47 Sanchez, Loretta | N | Y | N | N | Y |
| 48 Vacant | | | | | |
| 49 Issa | Y | Y | Y | Y | Y |

| | 598 | 599 | 600 | 601 | 602 |
|---|---|---|---|---|---|
| 50 Cunningham | Y | Y | N | N | Y |
| 51 Filner | N | Y | N | N | Y |
| 52 Hunter | Y | Y | Y | Y | Y |
| 53 Davis | N | Y | N | N | Y |
| **COLORADO** | | | | | |
| 1 DeGette | N | Y | N | N | Y |
| 2 Udall | N | Y | N | N | Y |
| 3 Salazar | N | Y | N | N | Y |
| 4 Musgrave | Y | Y | Y | Y | Y |
| 5 Hefley | Y | Y | Y | Y | ? |
| 6 Tancredo | Y | Y | Y | Y | ? |
| 7 Beauprez | Y | Y | Y | Y | Y |
| **CONNECTICUT** | | | | | |
| 1 Larson | N | Y | N | N | Y |
| 2 Simmons | Y | Y | N | N | Y |
| 3 DeLauro | N | Y | N | N | Y |
| 4 Shays | Y | Y | Y | N | Y |
| 5 Johnson | N | Y | Y | N | Y |
| **DELAWARE** | | | | | |
| AL Castle | N | Y | Y | Y | Y |
| **FLORIDA** | | | | | |
| 1 Miller | Y | Y | Y | Y | Y |
| 2 Boyd | N | Y | N | N | Y |
| 3 Brown | N | Y | N | N | Y |
| 4 Crenshaw | Y | Y | Y | Y | Y |
| 5 Brown-Waite | Y | Y | Y | Y | Y |
| 6 Stearns | N | Y | Y | Y | Y |
| 7 Mica | Y | Y | Y | Y | Y |
| 8 Keller | Y | Y | Y | Y | Y |
| 9 Bilirakis | Y | Y | Y | Y | Y |
| 10 Young | Y | Y | ? | Y | Y |
| 11 Davis | N | Y | N | N | Y |
| 12 Putnam | Y | Y | Y | Y | Y |
| 13 Harris | Y | Y | Y | Y | Y |
| 14 Mack | Y | Y | Y | Y | Y |
| 15 Weldon | Y | Y | Y | Y | Y |
| 16 Foley | Y | Y | Y | Y | Y |
| 17 Meek | N | Y | N | N | Y |
| 18 Ros-Lehtinen | Y | Y | Y | Y | Y |
| 19 Wexler | N | Y | N | N | Y |
| 20 Wasserman-Schultz | N | Y | N | N | Y |
| 21 Diaz-Balart, L. | Y | Y | Y | Y | Y |
| 22 Shaw | Y | Y | Y | Y | Y |
| 23 Hastings | N | N | N | N | Y |
| 24 Feeney | Y | Y | Y | Y | Y |
| 25 Diaz-Balart, M. | Y | Y | Y | Y | Y |
| **GEORGIA** | | | | | |
| 1 Kingston | Y | Y | Y | Y | Y |
| 2 Bishop | N | Y | N | N | Y |
| 3 Marshall | N | Y | N | N | ? |
| 4 McKinney | N | Y | N | N | Y |
| 5 Lewis | N | Y | N | N | Y |
| 6 Price | Y | Y | Y | Y | Y |
| 7 Linder | Y | Y | Y | Y | Y |
| 8 Westmoreland | Y | Y | Y | Y | Y |
| 9 Norwood | Y | Y | Y | Y | Y |
| 10 Deal | Y | Y | Y | Y | Y |
| 11 Gingrey | Y | Y | Y | Y | Y |
| 12 Barrow | N | Y | N | N | Y |
| 13 Scott | N | Y | N | N | Y |
| **HAWAII** | | | | | |
| 1 Abercrombie | N | Y | N | N | Y |
| 2 Case | N | Y | N | N | Y |
| **IDAHO** | | | | | |
| 1 Otter | N | Y | Y | Y | Y |
| 2 Simpson | Y | Y | Y | Y | Y |
| **ILLINOIS** | | | | | |
| 1 Rush | N | Y | N | N | Y |
| 2 Jackson | N | N | N | N | Y |
| 3 Lipinski | N | Y | N | N | Y |
| 4 Gutierrez | N | Y | N | N | Y |
| 5 Emanuel | N | Y | N | N | Y |
| 6 Hyde | Y | Y | ? | Y | Y |
| 7 Davis | N | Y | N | N | Y |
| 8 Bean | N | Y | N | N | ? |
| 9 Schakowsky | N | Y | N | N | Y |
| 10 Kirk | N | Y | N | N | Y |
| 11 Weller | Y | Y | Y | Y | Y |
| 12 Costello | N | Y | N | N | Y |

**KEY**   Republicans   Democrats   *Independents*

| | | | | | |
|---|---|---|---|---|---|
| Y | Voted for (yea) | X | Paired against | C | Voted "present" to avoid possible conflict of interest |
| # | Paired for | – | Announced against | | |
| + | Announced for | P | Voted "present" | ? | Did not vote or otherwise make a position known |
| N | Voted against (nay) | | | | |

ND Northern Democrats, SD Southern Democrats
Southern states: Ala., Ark., Fla., Ga., Ky., La., Miss., N.C., Okla., S.C., Tenn., Texas, Va.

H-190   2005 CQ ALMANAC | www.cq.com

| | 598 | 599 | 600 | 601 | 602 |
|---|---|---|---|---|---|
| 13 Biggert | Y | Y | Y | Y | Y |
| 14 Hastert | Y | | Y | Y | |
| 15 Johnson | Y | Y | Y | N | Y |
| 16 Manzullo | Y | Y | Y | Y | Y |
| 17 Evans | N | Y | N | N | Y |
| 18 LaHood | Y | Y | Y | Y | Y |
| 19 Shimkus | Y | Y | Y | Y | Y |
| **INDIANA** | | | | | |
| 1 Visclosky | N | Y | N | N | Y |
| 2 Chocola | Y | Y | Y | Y | Y |
| 3 Souder | Y | Y | Y | Y | Y |
| 4 Buyer | Y | Y | Y | Y | Y |
| 5 Burton | Y | Y | Y | Y | Y |
| 6 Pence | Y | Y | Y | Y | Y |
| 7 Carson | N | Y | N | N | Y |
| 8 Hostettler | Y | Y | Y | Y | Y |
| 9 Sodrel | Y | Y | Y | Y | Y |
| **IOWA** | | | | | |
| 1 Nussle | Y | Y | Y | Y | Y |
| 2 Leach | N | Y | Y | N | Y |
| 3 Boswell | ? | ? | ? | ? | ? |
| 4 Latham | Y | Y | Y | Y | ? |
| 5 King | Y | Y | Y | Y | Y |
| **KANSAS** | | | | | |
| 1 Moran | N | Y | Y | Y | Y |
| 2 Ryun | Y | Y | Y | Y | Y |
| 3 Moore | N | Y | N | N | Y |
| 4 Tiahrt | Y | Y | Y | Y | Y |
| **KENTUCKY** | | | | | |
| 1 Whitfield | Y | Y | Y | Y | Y |
| 2 Lewis | Y | Y | Y | Y | Y |
| 3 Northup | Y | Y | Y | Y | Y |
| 4 Davis | Y | Y | Y | Y | Y |
| 5 Rogers | Y | Y | Y | Y | Y |
| 6 Chandler | N | Y | N | N | Y |
| **LOUISIANA** | | | | | |
| 1 Jindal | Y | Y | Y | Y | Y |
| 2 Jefferson | N | Y | N | N | Y |
| 3 Melancon | N | Y | N | N | Y |
| 4 McCrery | Y | Y | Y | Y | Y |
| 5 Alexander | Y | Y | Y | Y | Y |
| 6 Baker | Y | Y | Y | Y | ? |
| 7 Boustany | Y | Y | Y | Y | Y |
| **MAINE** | | | | | |
| 1 Allen | N | Y | N | N | Y |
| 2 Michaud | N | Y | N | N | Y |
| **MARYLAND** | | | | | |
| 1 Gilchrest | Y | Y | Y | Y | Y |
| 2 Ruppersberger | N | Y | N | N | Y |
| 3 Cardin | N | Y | ? | N | Y |
| 4 Wynn | N | Y | N | N | Y |
| 5 Hoyer | N | Y | N | N | Y |
| 6 Bartlett | Y | Y | Y | Y | Y |
| 7 Cummings | N | Y | N | N | Y |
| 8 Van Hollen | N | Y | N | N | Y |
| **MASSACHUSETTS** | | | | | |
| 1 Olver | N | Y | N | N | Y |
| 2 Neal | N | Y | N | N | Y |
| 3 McGovern | N | Y | N | N | Y |
| 4 Frank | N | N | N | N | Y |
| 5 Meehan | N | Y | N | N | Y |
| 6 Tierney | N | N | N | N | Y |
| 7 Markey | N | Y | N | N | Y |
| 8 Capuano | N | Y | N | N | Y |
| 9 Lynch | N | Y | N | N | Y |
| 10 Delahunt | N | Y | N | N | Y |
| **MICHIGAN** | | | | | |
| 1 Stupak | N | N | N | N | Y |
| 2 Hoekstra | Y | Y | ? | Y | Y |
| 3 Ehlers | Y | Y | Y | Y | Y |
| 4 Camp | Y | Y | Y | Y | Y |
| 5 Kildee | N | Y | N | N | Y |
| 6 Upton | Y | Y | Y | Y | Y |
| 7 Schwarz | Y | Y | Y | Y | Y |
| 8 Rogers | Y | Y | Y | Y | Y |
| 9 Knollenberg | Y | Y | Y | Y | Y |
| 10 Miller | Y | Y | Y | Y | Y |
| 11 McCotter | Y | Y | Y | Y | Y |
| 12 Levin | N | Y | N | N | Y |
| 13 Kilpatrick | N | Y | N | N | Y |
| 14 Conyers | N | N | N | N | Y |
| 15 Dingell | N | N | N | N | Y |

| | 598 | 599 | 600 | 601 | 602 |
|---|---|---|---|---|---|
| **MINNESOTA** | | | | | |
| 1 Gutknecht | Y | Y | Y | Y | Y |
| 2 Kline | Y | Y | Y | Y | Y |
| 3 Ramstad | N | Y | Y | N | ? |
| 4 McCollum | N | Y | N | N | Y |
| 5 Sabo | N | Y | N | N | Y |
| 6 Kennedy | Y | Y | Y | Y | Y |
| 7 Peterson | N | Y | N | N | Y |
| 8 Oberstar | N | Y | N | N | Y |
| **MISSISSIPPI** | | | | | |
| 1 Wicker | Y | Y | Y | Y | Y |
| 2 Thompson | N | Y | N | N | Y |
| 3 Pickering | N | Y | Y | Y | Y |
| 4 Taylor | N | Y | N | N | Y |
| **MISSOURI** | | | | | |
| 1 Clay | N | Y | N | N | ? |
| 2 Akin | Y | Y | Y | Y | Y |
| 3 Carnahan | N | ? | N | N | Y |
| 4 Skelton | N | Y | N | N | Y |
| 5 Cleaver | N | Y | N | N | Y |
| 6 Graves | Y | Y | Y | Y | Y |
| 7 Blunt | Y | Y | Y | Y | Y |
| 8 Emerson | N | Y | Y | Y | Y |
| 9 Hulshof | Y | Y | Y | Y | Y |
| **MONTANA** | | | | | |
| AL Rehberg | Y | Y | Y | Y | Y |
| **NEBRASKA** | | | | | |
| 1 Fortenberry | Y | Y | ? | Y | Y |
| 2 Terry | Y | Y | Y | Y | Y |
| 3 Osborne | Y | Y | Y | Y | Y |
| **NEVADA** | | | | | |
| 1 Berkley | N | Y | N | N | Y |
| 2 Gibbons | N | Y | Y | Y | Y |
| 3 Porter | Y | Y | Y | Y | Y |
| **NEW HAMPSHIRE** | | | | | |
| 1 Bradley | Y | Y | Y | Y | Y |
| 2 Bass | Y | Y | Y | Y | Y |
| **NEW JERSEY** | | | | | |
| 1 Andrews | N | Y | N | N | Y |
| 2 LoBiondo | Y | Y | Y | Y | Y |
| 3 Saxton | Y | Y | Y | Y | Y |
| 4 Smith | Y | Y | Y | N | Y |
| 5 Garrett | Y | Y | Y | Y | Y |
| 6 Pallone | N | Y | N | N | Y |
| 7 Ferguson | Y | Y | Y | Y | Y |
| 8 Pascrell | N | Y | N | N | Y |
| 9 Rothman | N | Y | N | N | Y |
| 10 Payne | N | Y | N | N | Y |
| 11 Frelinghuysen | Y | Y | Y | Y | Y |
| 12 Holt | N | Y | N | N | Y |
| 13 Menendez | N | Y | N | N | Y |
| **NEW MEXICO** | | | | | |
| 1 Wilson | N | Y | Y | N | Y |
| 2 Pearce | Y | Y | Y | Y | Y |
| 3 Udall | N | Y | N | N | Y |
| **NEW YORK** | | | | | |
| 1 Bishop | N | Y | N | N | Y |
| 2 Israel | N | Y | N | N | Y |
| 3 King | Y | Y | Y | Y | Y |
| 4 McCarthy | N | Y | N | N | Y |
| 5 Ackerman | N | Y | N | N | Y |
| 6 Meeks | N | Y | N | N | Y |
| 7 Crowley | N | Y | N | N | Y |
| 8 Nadler | N | Y | N | N | Y |
| 9 Weiner | N | Y | N | N | Y |
| 10 Towns | N | ? | ? | ? | ? |
| 11 Owens | N | Y | N | N | Y |
| 12 Velázquez | N | Y | N | N | Y |
| 13 Fossella | Y | Y | Y | Y | Y |
| 14 Maloney | N | Y | N | N | Y |
| 15 Rangel | N | Y | N | N | ? |
| 16 Serrano | N | Y | N | N | Y |
| 17 Engel | N | Y | ? | N | Y |
| 18 Lowey | N | Y | N | N | Y |
| 19 Kelly | Y | Y | Y | Y | Y |
| 20 Sweeney | Y | Y | Y | Y | Y |
| 21 McNulty | N | Y | N | N | Y |
| 22 Hinchey | N | Y | N | N | Y |
| 23 McHugh | Y | Y | Y | Y | ? |
| 24 Boehlert | Y | Y | Y | Y | Y |
| 25 Walsh | Y | Y | Y | Y | Y |
| 26 Reynolds | Y | Y | Y | Y | Y |
| 27 Higgins | N | Y | N | N | Y |
| 28 Slaughter | N | Y | N | N | Y |
| 29 Kuhl | Y | Y | Y | Y | Y |

| | 598 | 599 | 600 | 601 | 602 |
|---|---|---|---|---|---|
| **NORTH CAROLINA** | | | | | |
| 1 Butterfield | N | Y | N | N | Y |
| 2 Etheridge | N | Y | N | N | Y |
| 3 Jones | Y | Y | Y | N | ? |
| 4 Price | N | Y | N | N | Y |
| 5 Foxx | Y | Y | Y | Y | Y |
| 6 Coble | Y | Y | Y | Y | Y |
| 7 McIntyre | N | Y | N | N | Y |
| 8 Hayes | Y | Y | Y | Y | Y |
| 9 Myrick | Y | Y | Y | Y | Y |
| 10 McHenry | Y | Y | Y | Y | Y |
| 11 Taylor | Y | Y | Y | Y | Y |
| 12 Watt | N | Y | N | N | Y |
| 13 Miller | N | Y | N | N | Y |
| **NORTH DAKOTA** | | | | | |
| AL Pomeroy | N | Y | N | N | Y |
| **OHIO** | | | | | |
| 1 Chabot | Y | Y | Y | Y | Y |
| 2 Schmidt | Y | Y | Y | Y | Y |
| 3 Turner | Y | Y | Y | Y | Y |
| 4 Oxley | Y | Y | Y | Y | ? |
| 5 Gillmor | Y | Y | Y | Y | Y |
| 6 Strickland | N | Y | N | N | Y |
| 7 Hobson | Y | Y | Y | Y | Y |
| 8 Boehner | Y | Y | Y | Y | ? |
| 9 Kaptur | N | Y | N | N | Y |
| 10 Kucinich | N | N | N | N | Y |
| 11 Jones | N | Y | N | N | Y |
| 12 Tiberi | Y | Y | Y | Y | Y |
| 13 Brown | N | Y | N | N | Y |
| 14 LaTourette | Y | Y | Y | Y | Y |
| 15 Pryce | Y | Y | Y | Y | Y |
| 16 Regula | Y | Y | Y | Y | Y |
| 17 Ryan | N | ? | Y | N | Y |
| 18 Ney | Y | Y | Y | N | Y |
| **OKLAHOMA** | | | | | |
| 1 Sullivan | Y | Y | Y | Y | Y |
| 2 Boren | N | Y | N | N | Y |
| 3 Lucas | Y | Y | Y | Y | Y |
| 4 Cole | Y | Y | Y | Y | Y |
| 5 Istook | Y | Y | Y | Y | Y |
| **OREGON** | | | | | |
| 1 Wu | N | N | N | N | Y |
| 2 Walden | Y | Y | ? | Y | Y |
| 3 Blumenauer | N | Y | N | N | Y |
| 4 DeFazio | N | N | N | N | Y |
| 5 Hooley | N | Y | N | N | Y |
| **PENNSYLVANIA** | | | | | |
| 1 Brady | N | Y | N | N | Y |
| 2 Fattah | N | Y | N | N | Y |
| 3 English | Y | Y | Y | Y | Y |
| 4 Hart | Y | Y | Y | Y | Y |
| 5 Peterson | Y | Y | Y | Y | Y |
| 6 Gerlach | Y | Y | Y | Y | Y |
| 7 Weldon | Y | Y | Y | Y | Y |
| 8 Fitzpatrick | N | Y | Y | Y | Y |
| 9 Shuster | Y | Y | Y | Y | Y |
| 10 Sherwood | Y | Y | Y | Y | Y |
| 11 Kanjorski | N | Y | N | N | Y |
| 12 Murtha | N | Y | N | N | ? |
| 13 Schwartz | N | Y | N | N | Y |
| 14 Doyle | N | Y | N | N | Y |
| 15 Dent | Y | Y | Y | Y | Y |
| 16 Pitts | Y | Y | Y | Y | Y |
| 17 Holden | N | Y | N | N | Y |
| 18 Murphy | N | Y | Y | Y | Y |
| 19 Platts | N | Y | Y | Y | Y |
| **RHODE ISLAND** | | | | | |
| 1 Kennedy | N | Y | N | N | Y |
| 2 Langevin | N | Y | N | N | Y |
| **SOUTH CAROLINA** | | | | | |
| 1 Brown | Y | Y | Y | Y | Y |
| 2 Wilson | Y | Y | Y | Y | Y |
| 3 Barrett | Y | Y | Y | Y | Y |
| 4 Inglis | Y | Y | Y | Y | Y |
| 5 Spratt | N | Y | N | N | Y |
| 6 Clyburn | N | Y | N | N | Y |
| **SOUTH DAKOTA** | | | | | |
| AL Herseth | N | Y | N | N | Y |
| **TENNESSEE** | | | | | |
| 1 Jenkins | Y | Y | Y | Y | Y |
| 2 Duncan | Y | Y | Y | Y | Y |

| | 598 | 599 | 600 | 601 | 602 |
|---|---|---|---|---|---|
| 3 Wamp | Y | Y | Y | Y | Y |
| 4 Davis | N | Y | N | N | Y |
| 5 Cooper | N | N | N | N | Y |
| 6 Gordon | N | Y | N | N | Y |
| 7 Blackburn | Y | Y | Y | Y | Y |
| 8 Tanner | N | Y | N | N | Y |
| 9 Ford | N | N | N | N | Y |
| **TEXAS** | | | | | |
| 1 Gohmert | Y | Y | Y | Y | Y |
| 2 Poe | Y | Y | Y | Y | Y |
| 3 Johnson, S. | Y | Y | Y | Y | Y |
| 4 Hall | Y | Y | Y | Y | ? |
| 5 Hensarling | Y | Y | Y | Y | Y |
| 6 Barton | Y | Y | Y | Y | Y |
| 7 Culberson | Y | Y | Y | Y | Y |
| 8 Brady | Y | Y | Y | Y | Y |
| 9 Green, A. | N | Y | N | N | Y |
| 10 McCaul | Y | Y | Y | Y | Y |
| 11 Conaway | Y | Y | Y | Y | Y |
| 12 Granger | Y | Y | Y | Y | Y |
| 13 Thornberry | Y | Y | Y | Y | Y |
| 14 Paul | N | Y | N | N | ? |
| 15 Hinojosa | N | Y | N | N | Y |
| 16 Reyes | N | Y | N | N | Y |
| 17 Edwards | N | ? | N | N | Y |
| 18 Jackson-Lee | N | Y | N | N | Y |
| 19 Neugebauer | Y | Y | Y | Y | Y |
| 20 Gonzalez | N | Y | N | N | Y |
| 21 Smith | Y | Y | Y | Y | Y |
| 22 DeLay | Y | Y | Y | Y | Y |
| 23 Bonilla | Y | Y | Y | Y | Y |
| 24 Marchant | Y | Y | Y | Y | Y |
| 25 Doggett | N | Y | N | N | ? |
| 26 Burgess | Y | Y | Y | Y | Y |
| 27 Ortiz | N | Y | N | N | Y |
| 28 Cuellar | N | Y | N | N | Y |
| 29 Green, G. | N | Y | N | N | Y |
| 30 Johnson, E. | N | Y | N | N | ? |
| 31 Carter | Y | Y | Y | Y | Y |
| 32 Sessions | Y | Y | Y | Y | Y |
| **UTAH** | | | | | |
| 1 Bishop | Y | Y | Y | Y | Y |
| 2 Matheson | N | Y | N | N | Y |
| 3 Cannon | Y | Y | Y | Y | Y |
| **VERMONT** | | | | | |
| AL *Sanders* | N | Y | N | N | Y |
| **VIRGINIA** | | | | | |
| 1 Davis, J. | Y | Y | Y | Y | ? |
| 2 Drake | Y | Y | Y | Y | Y |
| 3 Scott | N | Y | N | N | Y |
| 4 Forbes | Y | Y | Y | Y | Y |
| 5 Goode | Y | Y | Y | Y | Y |
| 6 Goodlatte | Y | Y | Y | Y | Y |
| 7 Cantor | Y | Y | Y | Y | Y |
| 8 Moran | N | Y | N | N | Y |
| 9 Boucher | N | Y | N | N | Y |
| 10 Wolf | Y | Y | Y | Y | Y |
| 11 Davis, T. | Y | Y | Y | Y | Y |
| **WASHINGTON** | | | | | |
| 1 Inslee | N | Y | N | N | Y |
| 2 Larsen | N | Y | N | N | Y |
| 3 Baird | N | Y | N | N | Y |
| 4 Hastings | Y | Y | Y | Y | Y |
| 5 McMorris | Y | Y | Y | Y | Y |
| 6 Dicks | N | Y | N | N | ? |
| 7 McDermott | N | N | N | N | Y |
| 8 Reichert | Y | Y | N | Y | Y |
| 9 Smith | N | Y | N | N | Y |
| **WEST VIRGINIA** | | | | | |
| 1 Mollohan | N | Y | ? | N | Y |
| 2 Capito | Y | Y | Y | Y | Y |
| 3 Rahall | N | Y | N | N | Y |
| **WISCONSIN** | | | | | |
| 1 Ryan | Y | Y | Y | Y | Y |
| 2 Baldwin | N | Y | N | N | Y |
| 3 Kind | N | Y | N | N | Y |
| 4 Moore | N | Y | N | N | Y |
| 5 Sensenbrenner | Y | Y | Y | Y | Y |
| 6 Petri | Y | Y | Y | Y | Y |
| 7 Obey | N | Y | N | N | Y |
| 8 Green | Y | Y | Y | Y | Y |
| **WYOMING** | | | | | |
| AL Cubin | Y | Y | Y | Y | Y |

# IN THE HOUSE | By Vote Number

**603.** **Quorum Call.*** 417 members responded. Nov. 18, 2005.

**604.** **HR 2528. Fiscal 2006 Military Construction-VA Appropriations/ Conference Report.** Adoption of the conference report on the bill that would provide $82.6 billion in fiscal 2006 for the Department of Veterans Affairs, military construction and military housing. The bill would provide $22.5 billion for veterans' medical services, $6.2 billion for military construction, $4 billion for military family housing and $1.5 billion for the latest round of base closures. Adopted (thus sent to the Senate) 427-0: R 227-0; D 199-0 (ND 148-0, SD 51-0); I 1-0. Nov. 18, 2005.

**605.** **HR 3058. Fiscal 2006 Transportation-Treasury-Housing Appropriations/Conference Report.** Adoption of the conference report on the bill that would appropriate $137.6 billion in fiscal 2006, including $65.9 billion in discretionary spending, for the departments of Housing and Urban Development (HUD), Treasury, and Transportation, and related agencies. It would provide $34 billion for HUD, $34.7 billion for the Federal Highway Administration, $13.8 billion for the Federal Aviation Administration, $11.7 billion for the Treasury Department and $5.8 billion for the judiciary. It also includes $603 million for the District of Columbia. Adopted (thus sent to the Senate) 392-31: R 204-21; D 187-10 (ND 137-9, SD 50-1); I 1-0. Nov. 18, 2005.

**606.** **H Res 563. Immediate Iraq Withdrawal/Consideration of Rule.** Adoption of the resolution (H Res 563) that would waive the two-thirds vote requirement for same-day consideration of any rule to provide for House floor consideration of a resolution relating to U.S. forces in Iraq, or any outstanding conference reports on fiscal 2006 appropriations bills, a conference report on the bill (HR 3199) that would reauthorize the law known as the Patriot Act, a bill or joint resolution relating to flood insurance, or a fiscal 2006 tax reconciliation measure. Adopted 211-204: R 211-6; D 0-197 (ND 0-147, SD 0-50); I 0-1. Nov. 18, 2005.

**607.** **H Res 571. Immediate Iraq Withdrawal/Rule.** Adoption of the rule (H Res 572) that would provide for House floor consideration of the resolution that would express the sense of the House of Representatives that deployment of U.S. forces in Iraq should be terminated immediately. Adopted 210-202: R 210-5; D 0-196 (ND 0-147, SD 0-49); I 0-1. Nov. 18, 2005.

**608.** **H Res 571. Immediate Iraq Withdrawal/Adoption.** Adoption of the resolution that would express the sense of the House of Representatives that deployment of U.S. forces in Iraq should be terminated immediately. Rejected 3-403: R 0-215; D 3-187 (ND 1-140, SD 2-47); I 0-1. Nov. 18, 2005.

*CQ does not include quorum calls in its vote charts.

ND Northern Democrats, SD Southern Democrats
Southern states: Ala., Ark., Fla., Ga., Ky., La., Miss., N.C., Okla., S.C., Tenn., Texas, Va.

| | 604 | 605 | 606 | 607 | 608 |
|---|---|---|---|---|---|
| **ALABAMA** | | | | | |
| 1 Bonner | Y | Y | Y | Y | N |
| 2 Everett | Y | Y | Y | Y | N |
| 3 Rogers | Y | Y | Y | Y | N |
| 4 Aderholt | Y | Y | Y | Y | N |
| 5 Cramer | Y | Y | N | N | N |
| 6 Bachus | Y | Y | Y | Y | N |
| 7 Davis | Y | Y | N | ? | ? |
| **ALASKA** | | | | | |
| AL Young | Y | N | Y | ? | ? |
| **ARIZONA** | | | | | |
| 1 Renzi | Y | Y | Y | Y | N |
| 2 Franks | Y | N | Y | Y | N |
| 3 Shadegg | Y | N | ? | ? | ? |
| 4 Pastor | Y | Y | N | N | N |
| 5 Hayworth | Y | Y | Y | Y | N |
| 6 Flake | Y | N | ? | ? | ? |
| 7 Grijalva | Y | Y | N | N | N |
| 8 Kolbe | Y | Y | Y | Y | N |
| **ARKANSAS** | | | | | |
| 1 Berry | Y | Y | N | N | N |
| 2 Snyder | Y | Y | N | N | N |
| 3 Boozman | Y | Y | Y | Y | N |
| 4 Ross | Y | Y | N | N | N |
| **CALIFORNIA** | | | | | |
| 1 Thompson | Y | Y | N | N | N |
| 2 Herger | Y | Y | Y | Y | N |
| 3 Lungren | Y | Y | Y | Y | N |
| 4 Doolittle | Y | Y | Y | Y | N |
| 5 Matsui, D. | Y | Y | N | N | N |
| 6 Woolsey | Y | Y | N | N | N |
| 7 Miller, George | Y | Y | N | N | N |
| 8 Pelosi | Y | Y | N | N | N |
| 9 Lee | Y | Y | N | N | N |
| 10 Tauscher | Y | Y | N | N | N |
| 11 Pombo | Y | Y | Y | Y | N |
| 12 Lantos | Y | Y | N | N | N |
| 13 Stark | Y | N | N | N | N |
| 14 Eshoo | Y | Y | N | N | N |
| 15 Honda | Y | Y | N | N | N |
| 16 Lofgren | Y | Y | N | N | N |
| 17 Farr | Y | Y | N | N | N |
| 18 Cardoza | Y | Y | N | N | N |
| 19 Radanovich | Y | Y | Y | Y | N |
| 20 Costa | Y | Y | N | N | N |
| 21 Nunes | Y | Y | Y | Y | N |
| 22 Thomas | Y | Y | N | N | N |
| 23 Capps | Y | Y | N | N | N |
| 24 Gallegly | Y | Y | ? | ? | ? |
| 25 McKeon | Y | Y | Y | Y | N |
| 26 Dreier | Y | Y | Y | Y | N |
| 27 Sherman | Y | Y | N | N | N |
| 28 Berman | + | + | − | − | − |
| 29 Schiff | Y | Y | N | N | N |
| 30 Waxman | Y | Y | N | N | N |
| 31 Becerra | Y | Y | N | N | N |
| 32 Solis | Y | Y | N | N | N |
| 33 Watson | Y | Y | N | N | N |
| 34 Roybal-Allard | Y | Y | N | N | N |
| 35 Waters | Y | N | N | N | N |
| 36 Harman | Y | Y | N | N | N |
| 37 Millender-McD. | Y | Y | N | N | N |
| 38 Napolitano | Y | Y | N | N | N |
| 39 Sánchez, Linda | Y | Y | N | N | N |
| 40 Royce | Y | Y | Y | Y | N |
| 41 Lewis | Y | Y | Y | Y | N |
| 42 Miller, Gary | Y | Y | ? | ? | ? |
| 43 Baca | Y | Y | N | N | N |
| 44 Calvert | Y | Y | Y | Y | N |
| 45 Bono | Y | Y | Y | Y | N |
| 46 Rohrabacher | Y | Y | Y | Y | N |
| 47 Sanchez, Loretta | Y | Y | N | N | N |
| 48 Vacant | | | | | |
| 49 Issa | Y | Y | Y | Y | N |

| | 604 | 605 | 606 | 607 | 608 |
|---|---|---|---|---|---|
| 50 Cunningham | Y | Y | ? | ? | ? |
| 51 Filner | Y | Y | N | N | N |
| 52 Hunter | Y | Y | Y | Y | N |
| 53 Davis | Y | N | N | N | N |
| **COLORADO** | | | | | |
| 1 DeGette | Y | Y | N | N | N |
| 2 Udall | Y | Y | N | N | N |
| 3 Salazar | Y | N | N | N | N |
| 4 Musgrave | Y | Y | Y | Y | N |
| 5 Hefley | Y | N | Y | Y | N |
| 6 Tancredo | Y | N | Y | Y | N |
| 7 Beauprez | Y | Y | ? | ? | ? |
| **CONNECTICUT** | | | | | |
| 1 Larson | Y | Y | N | N | N |
| 2 Simmons | Y | Y | Y | Y | N |
| 3 DeLauro | Y | Y | N | N | N |
| 4 Shays | Y | Y | Y | Y | N |
| 5 Johnson | Y | Y | Y | Y | N |
| **DELAWARE** | | | | | |
| AL Castle | Y | N | Y | Y | N |
| **FLORIDA** | | | | | |
| 1 Miller | Y | N | Y | Y | N |
| 2 Boyd | Y | Y | ? | ? | ? |
| 3 Brown | Y | Y | N | N | N |
| 4 Crenshaw | Y | Y | Y | Y | N |
| 5 Brown-Waite | Y | Y | Y | Y | N |
| 6 Stearns | Y | Y | Y | Y | N |
| 7 Mica | Y | Y | Y | Y | N |
| 8 Keller | Y | Y | Y | Y | N |
| 9 Bilirakis | Y | Y | Y | Y | N |
| 10 Young | Y | Y | Y | Y | N |
| 11 Davis | Y | Y | N | N | N |
| 12 Putnam | Y | Y | Y | Y | N |
| 13 Harris | Y | ? | Y | Y | N |
| 14 Mack | Y | Y | Y | Y | N |
| 15 Weldon | Y | Y | Y | Y | N |
| 16 Foley | Y | Y | Y | Y | N |
| 17 Meek | Y | Y | N | N | N |
| 18 Ros-Lehtinen | Y | Y | Y | Y | N |
| 19 Wexler | Y | Y | N | N | Y |
| 20 Wasserman-Schultz | Y | Y | N | N | N |
| 21 Diaz-Balart, L. | Y | Y | Y | Y | N |
| 22 Shaw | Y | Y | Y | Y | N |
| 23 Hastings | Y | Y | N | N | N |
| 24 Feeney | Y | ? | Y | Y | N |
| 25 Diaz-Balart, M. | Y | Y | Y | Y | N |
| **GEORGIA** | | | | | |
| 1 Kingston | Y | Y | Y | Y | N |
| 2 Bishop | Y | Y | N | N | N |
| 3 Marshall | Y | Y | N | N | N |
| 4 McKinney | Y | Y | N | N | Y |
| 5 Lewis | Y | Y | N | N | N |
| 6 Price | Y | N | Y | Y | N |
| 7 Linder | Y | Y | Y | Y | N |
| 8 Westmoreland | Y | Y | Y | Y | N |
| 9 Norwood | Y | Y | Y | Y | N |
| 10 Deal | Y | Y | Y | Y | N |
| 11 Gingrey | Y | Y | Y | Y | N |
| 12 Barrow | Y | Y | N | N | N |
| 13 Scott | Y | Y | N | N | N |
| **HAWAII** | | | | | |
| 1 Abercrombie | Y | Y | N | N | N |
| 2 Case | Y | Y | N | N | N |
| **IDAHO** | | | | | |
| 1 Otter | Y | Y | Y | Y | N |
| 2 Simpson | Y | Y | N | N | N |
| **ILLINOIS** | | | | | |
| 1 Rush | Y | Y | N | N | N |
| 2 Jackson | Y | Y | N | N | N |
| 3 Lipinski | Y | Y | N | N | N |
| 4 Gutierrez | Y | Y | N | N | N |
| 5 Emanuel | Y | Y | N | N | N |
| 6 Hyde | Y | Y | Y | Y | N |
| 7 Davis | Y | Y | N | N | N |
| 8 Bean | Y | Y | N | N | N |
| 9 Schakowsky | Y | Y | N | N | N |
| 10 Kirk | Y | Y | Y | Y | N |
| 11 Weller | Y | Y | Y | Y | N |
| 12 Costello | Y | N | N | N | N |

**KEY**

| | Republicans | | Democrats | | *Independents* | |
|---|---|---|---|---|---|---|
| Y | Voted for (yea) | X | Paired against | C | Voted "present" to avoid possible conflict of interest |
| # | Paired for | − | Announced against | | |
| + | Announced for | P | Voted "present" | ? | Did not vote or otherwise make a position known |
| N | Voted against (nay) | | | | |

| | | 604 | 605 | 606 | 607 | 608 |
|---|---|---|---|---|---|---|
| 13 | Biggert | Y | Y | Y | Y | N |
| 14 | Hastert | | | | Y | N |
| 15 | Johnson | Y | Y | Y | Y | N |
| 16 | Manzullo | Y | Y | Y | Y | N |
| 17 | Evans | Y | Y | N | N | N |
| 18 | LaHood | Y | Y | ? | ? | ? |
| 19 | Shimkus | Y | Y | Y | Y | N |
| **INDIANA** | | | | | | |
| 1 | Visclosky | Y | Y | N | N | N |
| 2 | Chocola | Y | Y | Y | Y | N |
| 3 | Souder | Y | Y | Y | Y | N |
| 4 | Buyer | Y | Y | Y | Y | N |
| 5 | Burton | Y | Y | Y | Y | N |
| 6 | Pence | Y | Y | Y | Y | N |
| 7 | Carson | Y | Y | N | N | N |
| 8 | Hostettler | Y | Y | N | N | N |
| 9 | Sodrel | Y | Y | Y | Y | N |
| **IOWA** | | | | | | |
| 1 | Nussle | Y | Y | Y | Y | N |
| 2 | Leach | Y | Y | N | N | N |
| 3 | Boswell | ? | ? | ? | ? | ? |
| 4 | Latham | Y | Y | Y | Y | N |
| 5 | King | Y | Y | Y | Y | N |
| **KANSAS** | | | | | | |
| 1 | Moran | Y | Y | ? | ? | ? |
| 2 | Ryun | Y | Y | Y | Y | N |
| 3 | Moore | Y | Y | N | N | N |
| 4 | Tiahrt | Y | Y | Y | Y | N |
| **KENTUCKY** | | | | | | |
| 1 | Whitfield | Y | Y | Y | Y | N |
| 2 | Lewis | Y | Y | Y | Y | N |
| 3 | Northup | Y | Y | Y | ? | – |
| 4 | Davis | Y | Y | Y | Y | N |
| 5 | Rogers | Y | Y | Y | Y | N |
| 6 | Chandler | Y | Y | N | N | N |
| **LOUISIANA** | | | | | | |
| 1 | Jindal | Y | Y | ? | ? | ? |
| 2 | Jefferson | Y | Y | N | N | N |
| 3 | Melancon | Y | Y | Y | Y | N |
| 4 | McCrery | Y | Y | Y | Y | N |
| 5 | Alexander | Y | Y | Y | Y | N |
| 6 | Baker | Y | Y | Y | Y | N |
| 7 | Boustany | Y | N | Y | Y | N |
| **MAINE** | | | | | | |
| 1 | Allen | Y | Y | N | N | N |
| 2 | Michaud | Y | Y | N | N | N |
| **MARYLAND** | | | | | | |
| 1 | Gilchrest | Y | Y | N | N | N |
| 2 | Ruppersberger | Y | Y | N | N | N |
| 3 | Cardin | Y | ? | N | N | N |
| 4 | Wynn | Y | Y | N | N | N |
| 5 | Hoyer | Y | Y | N | N | N |
| 6 | Bartlett | Y | Y | N | Y | N |
| 7 | Cummings | Y | Y | N | N | N |
| 8 | Van Hollen | Y | Y | N | N | N |
| **MASSACHUSETTS** | | | | | | |
| 1 | Olver | Y | Y | N | N | N |
| 2 | Neal | Y | Y | N | N | N |
| 3 | McGovern | Y | Y | N | N | N |
| 4 | Frank | Y | Y | N | N | N |
| 5 | Meehan | Y | Y | N | N | N |
| 6 | Tierney | Y | Y | N | N | N |
| 7 | Markey | Y | Y | N | N | N |
| 8 | Capuano | Y | Y | N | N | P |
| 9 | Lynch | Y | Y | N | N | N |
| 10 | Delahunt | Y | Y | N | N | N |
| **MICHIGAN** | | | | | | |
| 1 | Stupak | Y | Y | N | N | N |
| 2 | Hoekstra | Y | Y | Y | Y | N |
| 3 | Ehlers | Y | Y | Y | Y | N |
| 4 | Camp | Y | Y | Y | ? | ? |
| 5 | Kildee | Y | Y | N | N | N |
| 6 | Upton | Y | Y | Y | Y | N |
| 7 | Schwarz | Y | Y | Y | Y | N |
| 8 | Rogers | Y | Y | Y | Y | N |
| 9 | Knollenberg | Y | Y | Y | Y | N |
| 10 | Miller | Y | Y | Y | Y | N |
| 11 | McCotter | Y | Y | Y | Y | N |
| 12 | Levin | Y | Y | N | N | N |
| 13 | Kilpatrick | Y | Y | N | N | N |
| 14 | Conyers | Y | Y | N | N | N |
| 15 | Dingell | Y | Y | N | N | N |

| | | 604 | 605 | 606 | 607 | 608 |
|---|---|---|---|---|---|---|
| **MINNESOTA** | | | | | | |
| 1 | Gutknecht | Y | Y | Y | Y | N |
| 2 | Kline | Y | Y | Y | Y | N |
| 3 | Ramstad | Y | Y | Y | Y | N |
| 4 | McCollum | Y | Y | N | N | N |
| 5 | Sabo | Y | Y | N | N | N |
| 6 | Kennedy | Y | Y | Y | Y | N |
| 7 | Peterson | Y | Y | N | N | N |
| 8 | Oberstar | Y | N | N | N | N |
| **MISSISSIPPI** | | | | | | |
| 1 | Wicker | Y | Y | Y | Y | N |
| 2 | Thompson | Y | Y | N | N | N |
| 3 | Pickering | Y | Y | Y | Y | N |
| 4 | Taylor | Y | Y | N | N | N |
| **MISSOURI** | | | | | | |
| 1 | Clay | Y | Y | N | N | P |
| 2 | Akin | Y | Y | Y | Y | N |
| 3 | Carnahan | Y | Y | N | N | N |
| 4 | Skelton | Y | Y | N | N | N |
| 5 | Cleaver | Y | Y | N | N | N |
| 6 | Graves | Y | Y | Y | Y | N |
| 7 | Blunt | Y | Y | Y | Y | N |
| 8 | Emerson | Y | Y | Y | Y | N |
| 9 | Hulshof | Y | Y | Y | Y | N |
| **MONTANA** | | | | | | |
| AL | Rehberg | Y | Y | Y | Y | N |
| **NEBRASKA** | | | | | | |
| 1 | Fortenberry | + | + | Y | Y | N |
| 2 | Terry | Y | Y | Y | Y | N |
| 3 | Osborne | Y | Y | Y | Y | N |
| **NEVADA** | | | | | | |
| 1 | Berkley | Y | Y | N | N | N |
| 2 | Gibbons | Y | Y | Y | Y | N |
| 3 | Porter | Y | Y | Y | Y | N |
| **NEW HAMPSHIRE** | | | | | | |
| 1 | Bradley | Y | Y | Y | Y | N |
| 2 | Bass | Y | Y | Y | Y | N |
| **NEW JERSEY** | | | | | | |
| 1 | Andrews | Y | Y | N | N | N |
| 2 | LoBiondo | Y | Y | Y | Y | N |
| 3 | Saxton | Y | Y | Y | Y | N |
| 4 | Smith | Y | Y | Y | Y | N |
| 5 | Garrett | Y | Y | Y | Y | N |
| 6 | Pallone | Y | Y | N | N | N |
| 7 | Ferguson | Y | Y | Y | Y | N |
| 8 | Pascrell | Y | Y | N | N | N |
| 9 | Rothman | Y | Y | N | N | N |
| 10 | Payne | Y | Y | N | N | N |
| 11 | Frelinghuysen | Y | Y | Y | Y | N |
| 12 | Holt | Y | + | N | N | N |
| 13 | Menendez | Y | Y | N | N | N |
| **NEW MEXICO** | | | | | | |
| 1 | Wilson | Y | Y | Y | Y | N |
| 2 | Pearce | Y | Y | Y | Y | N |
| 3 | Udall | Y | Y | N | N | N |
| **NEW YORK** | | | | | | |
| 1 | Bishop | Y | Y | N | N | N |
| 2 | Israel | Y | Y | N | N | N |
| 3 | King | Y | Y | Y | Y | N |
| 4 | McCarthy | Y | Y | N | N | N |
| 5 | Ackerman | Y | Y | N | N | N |
| 6 | Meeks | Y | Y | N | N | N |
| 7 | Crowley | Y | Y | N | N | N |
| 8 | Nadler | Y | Y | N | N | P |
| 9 | Weiner | Y | Y | N | N | N |
| 10 | Towns | ? | ? | ? | ? | ? |
| 11 | Owens | Y | Y | N | N | P |
| 12 | Velázquez | Y | N | N | N | N |
| 13 | Fossella | Y | Y | ? | ? | ? |
| 14 | Maloney | Y | Y | N | N | N |
| 15 | Rangel | Y | Y | N | N | N |
| 16 | Serrano | Y | Y | N | N | Y |
| 17 | Engel | Y | Y | N | N | N |
| 18 | Lowey | Y | Y | N | N | N |
| 19 | Kelly | Y | Y | Y | Y | N |
| 20 | Sweeney | Y | Y | Y | Y | N |
| 21 | McNulty | Y | Y | N | N | N |
| 22 | Hinchey | Y | Y | N | N | P |
| 23 | McHugh | Y | Y | Y | Y | N |
| 24 | Boehlert | Y | Y | Y | Y | N |
| 25 | Walsh | Y | Y | Y | Y | N |
| 26 | Reynolds | Y | Y | Y | Y | N |
| 27 | Higgins | Y | Y | N | N | N |
| 28 | Slaughter | Y | Y | N | N | N |
| 29 | Kuhl | Y | Y | Y | Y | N |

| | | 604 | 605 | 606 | 607 | 608 |
|---|---|---|---|---|---|---|
| **NORTH CAROLINA** | | | | | | |
| 1 | Butterfield | Y | Y | N | N | N |
| 2 | Etheridge | Y | Y | N | N | N |
| 3 | Jones | Y | N | N | N | N |
| 4 | Price | Y | Y | N | N | N |
| 5 | Foxx | Y | Y | Y | Y | N |
| 6 | Coble | Y | Y | Y | Y | N |
| 7 | McIntyre | Y | Y | N | N | N |
| 8 | Hayes | Y | Y | Y | Y | N |
| 9 | Myrick | Y | Y | Y | Y | N |
| 10 | McHenry | Y | Y | Y | Y | N |
| 11 | Taylor | Y | Y | Y | Y | N |
| 12 | Watt | Y | Y | N | N | N |
| 13 | Miller | Y | Y | N | N | N |
| **NORTH DAKOTA** | | | | | | |
| AL | Pomeroy | Y | Y | N | N | N |
| **OHIO** | | | | | | |
| 1 | Chabot | Y | Y | Y | Y | N |
| 2 | Schmidt | Y | Y | Y | Y | N |
| 3 | Turner | Y | Y | Y | Y | N |
| 4 | Oxley | Y | Y | Y | Y | N |
| 5 | Gillmor | Y | Y | Y | Y | N |
| 6 | Strickland | Y | Y | N | N | N |
| 7 | Hobson | Y | Y | Y | Y | N |
| 8 | Boehner | Y | Y | Y | Y | N |
| 9 | Kaptur | Y | Y | N | N | N |
| 10 | Kucinich | Y | N | N | N | N |
| 11 | Jones | Y | Y | N | N | N |
| 12 | Tiberi | Y | Y | Y | Y | N |
| 13 | Brown | Y | Y | N | N | N |
| 14 | LaTourette | Y | N | Y | Y | N |
| 15 | Pryce | Y | Y | Y | Y | N |
| 16 | Regula | Y | Y | Y | Y | N |
| 17 | Ryan | Y | Y | N | N | N |
| 18 | Ney | Y | Y | Y | Y | N |
| **OKLAHOMA** | | | | | | |
| 1 | Sullivan | Y | Y | Y | Y | N |
| 2 | Boren | Y | Y | N | N | N |
| 3 | Lucas | Y | Y | Y | Y | N |
| 4 | Cole | Y | Y | Y | Y | N |
| 5 | Istook | Y | Y | Y | Y | N |
| **OREGON** | | | | | | |
| 1 | Wu | Y | Y | N | N | N |
| 2 | Walden | Y | Y | Y | Y | N |
| 3 | Blumenauer | Y | Y | N | N | N |
| 4 | DeFazio | Y | N | N | N | N |
| 5 | Hooley | Y | Y | N | N | N |
| **PENNSYLVANIA** | | | | | | |
| 1 | Brady | Y | Y | N | N | N |
| 2 | Fattah | Y | Y | N | N | N |
| 3 | English | Y | Y | Y | Y | N |
| 4 | Hart | Y | Y | Y | Y | N |
| 5 | Peterson | Y | Y | ? | ? | ? |
| 6 | Gerlach | Y | Y | Y | Y | N |
| 7 | Weldon | Y | Y | Y | Y | N |
| 8 | Fitzpatrick | Y | Y | Y | Y | N |
| 9 | Shuster | Y | N | Y | Y | N |
| 10 | Sherwood | Y | Y | Y | Y | N |
| 11 | Kanjorski | Y | Y | N | N | N |
| 12 | Murtha | Y | Y | N | N | N |
| 13 | Schwartz | Y | Y | N | N | N |
| 14 | Doyle | Y | Y | N | N | N |
| 15 | Dent | Y | Y | Y | Y | N |
| 16 | Pitts | Y | Y | Y | Y | N |
| 17 | Holden | Y | Y | N | N | N |
| 18 | Murphy | Y | Y | Y | Y | N |
| 19 | Platts | Y | Y | Y | Y | N |
| **RHODE ISLAND** | | | | | | |
| 1 | Kennedy | Y | Y | N | N | N |
| 2 | Langevin | Y | Y | N | N | N |
| **SOUTH CAROLINA** | | | | | | |
| 1 | Brown | Y | Y | Y | Y | N |
| 2 | Wilson | Y | Y | Y | Y | N |
| 3 | Barrett | Y | Y | Y | Y | N |
| 4 | Inglis | Y | Y | Y | Y | N |
| 5 | Spratt | Y | Y | N | N | N |
| 6 | Clyburn | Y | Y | N | N | N |
| **SOUTH DAKOTA** | | | | | | |
| AL | Herseth | Y | Y | N | N | N |
| **TENNESSEE** | | | | | | |
| 1 | Jenkins | Y | Y | Y | Y | N |
| 2 | Duncan | Y | N | Y | Y | N |

| | | 604 | 605 | 606 | 607 | 608 |
|---|---|---|---|---|---|---|
| 3 | Wamp | Y | Y | Y | Y | N |
| 4 | Davis | Y | Y | N | N | N |
| 5 | Cooper | Y | Y | N | N | N |
| 6 | Gordon | Y | Y | N | N | N |
| 7 | Blackburn | Y | Y | Y | Y | N |
| 8 | Tanner | Y | Y | N | N | N |
| 9 | Ford | Y | Y | N | N | N |
| **TEXAS** | | | | | | |
| 1 | Gohmert | Y | Y | Y | Y | N |
| 2 | Poe | Y | N | Y | Y | N |
| 3 | Johnson, S. | Y | Y | Y | Y | N |
| 4 | Hall | ? | ? | ? | ? | ? |
| 5 | Hensarling | Y | Y | Y | Y | N |
| 6 | Barton | Y | N | Y | Y | N |
| 7 | Culberson | Y | Y | Y | Y | N |
| 8 | Brady | Y | Y | Y | Y | N |
| 9 | Green, A. | Y | Y | N | N | N |
| 10 | McCaul | Y | Y | Y | Y | N |
| 11 | Conaway | Y | Y | Y | Y | N |
| 12 | Granger | Y | Y | Y | Y | N |
| 13 | Thornberry | Y | Y | Y | Y | N |
| 14 | Paul | ? | ? | ? | ? | ? |
| 15 | Hinojosa | Y | Y | N | N | N |
| 16 | Reyes | Y | Y | N | N | N |
| 17 | Edwards | Y | Y | N | N | N |
| 18 | Jackson-Lee | Y | Y | Y | Y | N |
| 19 | Neugebauer | Y | Y | Y | Y | N |
| 20 | Gonzalez | Y | Y | N | N | N |
| 21 | Smith | Y | Y | Y | Y | N |
| 22 | DeLay | Y | Y | Y | Y | N |
| 23 | Bonilla | Y | Y | Y | Y | N |
| 24 | Marchant | Y | N | Y | Y | N |
| 25 | Doggett | Y | Y | N | N | N |
| 26 | Burgess | Y | Y | Y | Y | N |
| 27 | Ortiz | Y | Y | N | N | N |
| 28 | Cuellar | Y | Y | N | N | N |
| 29 | Green, G. | Y | Y | N | N | N |
| 30 | Johnson, E. | Y | Y | N | N | N |
| 31 | Carter | Y | Y | Y | Y | N |
| 32 | Sessions | Y | Y | Y | Y | N |
| **UTAH** | | | | | | |
| 1 | Bishop | Y | Y | Y | Y | N |
| 2 | Matheson | Y | N | N | N | N |
| 3 | Cannon | Y | Y | Y | Y | N |
| **VERMONT** | | | | | | |
| AL | *Sanders* | Y | Y | N | N | N |
| **VIRGINIA** | | | | | | |
| 1 | Davis, J. | Y | Y | Y | Y | N |
| 2 | Drake | Y | Y | Y | Y | N |
| 3 | Scott | Y | Y | N | N | N |
| 4 | Forbes | Y | Y | Y | Y | N |
| 5 | Goode | Y | Y | Y | Y | N |
| 6 | Goodlatte | Y | Y | Y | Y | N |
| 7 | Cantor | Y | Y | Y | Y | N |
| 8 | Moran | Y | Y | N | N | N |
| 9 | Boucher | Y | Y | N | N | N |
| 10 | Wolf | Y | Y | Y | Y | N |
| 11 | Davis, T. | Y | Y | Y | Y | N |
| **WASHINGTON** | | | | | | |
| 1 | Inslee | Y | Y | N | N | N |
| 2 | Larsen | Y | Y | N | N | N |
| 3 | Baird | Y | Y | N | N | N |
| 4 | Hastings | Y | Y | Y | Y | N |
| 5 | McMorris | Y | Y | Y | Y | N |
| 6 | Dicks | Y | Y | N | N | N |
| 7 | McDermott | Y | N | N | N | P |
| 8 | Reichert | Y | Y | Y | Y | N |
| 9 | Smith | Y | Y | N | N | N |
| **WEST VIRGINIA** | | | | | | |
| 1 | Mollohan | Y | Y | N | N | N |
| 2 | Capito | Y | Y | Y | Y | N |
| 3 | Rahall | Y | Y | N | N | N |
| **WISCONSIN** | | | | | | |
| 1 | Ryan | Y | N | Y | Y | N |
| 2 | Baldwin | Y | Y | N | N | N |
| 3 | Kind | Y | Y | ? | ? | ? |
| 4 | Moore | Y | Y | N | N | N |
| 5 | Sensenbrenner | Y | N | Y | Y | N |
| 6 | Petri | Y | N | Y | Y | N |
| 7 | Obey | Y | Y | N | N | N |
| 8 | Green | Y | N | Y | Y | N |
| **WYOMING** | | | | | | |
| AL | Cubin | Y | Y | Y | Y | N |

# IN THE HOUSE | By Vote Number

**609.** **H Res 438. Anti-Israel Resolutions/Adoption.** Ros-Lehtinen, R-Fla., motion to suspend the rules and adopt the resolution that would state that the House of Representatives urges U.N. member states to stop supporting resolutions that unfairly castigate Israel. Motion agreed to 400-1: R 219-1; D 180-0 (ND 137-0, SD 43-0); I 1-0. A two-thirds majority of those present and voting (268 in this case) is required for adoption under suspension of the rules. Dec. 6, 2005.

**610.** **H Res 535. Yitzhak Rabin Commemoration/Adoption.** Ros-Lehtinen, R-Fla., motion to suspend the rules and adopt the resolution that would honor the late Yitzhak Rabin, former Israeli prime minister, for his contributions to the country and express condolences on the 10th anniversary of his death. Motion agreed to 399-0: R 219-0; D 179-0 (ND 136-0, SD 43-0); I 1-0. A two-thirds majority of those present and voting (266 in this case) is required for adoption under suspension of the rules. Dec. 6, 2005.

**611.** **H Res 479. 50th Anniversary of Hungarian Revolution/Adoption.** Gallegly, R-Calif., motion to suspend the rules and adopt the resolution that would commend the people of Hungary as they mark the 50th anniversary of the 1956 Hungarian Revolution, which set the stage for the ultimate collapse of communism in 1989 throughout central and eastern Europe. Motion agreed to 395-0: R 217-0; D 177-0 (ND 136-0, SD 41-0); I 1-0. A two-thirds majority of those present and voting (264 in this case) is required for adoption under suspension of the rules. Dec. 6, 2005.

**612.** **S 467. Terrorism Risk Insurance Extension/Passage.** Oxley, R-Ohio, motion to suspend the rules and pass the bill, as amended, that would reauthorize the federal terrorism insurance program through Dec. 31, 2007. It would increase the "trigger" level from the current $5 million aggregate industry insured losses to $50 million in 2006 and $100 million in 2007. The bill also would extend the $100 billion annual cap on covered losses. Motion agreed to 371-49: R 178-46; D 192-3 (ND 146-2, SD 46-1); I 1-0. A two-thirds majority of those present and voting (280 in this case) is required for passage under suspension of the rules. A "nay" was a vote in support of the president's position. Dec. 7, 2005.

**613.** **HR 4096. Alternative Minimum Tax Relief/Passage.** Reynolds, R-N.Y., motion to suspend the rules and pass the bill that would extend for one year, through 2006, the higher exemption levels for the alternative minimum tax, adjusted for inflation. Motion agreed to 414-4: R 225-0; D 188-4 (ND 143-3, SD 45-1); I 1-0. A two-thirds majority of those present and voting (279 in this case) is required for passage under suspension of the rules. Dec. 7, 2005.

\*Rep. Randy "Duke" Cunningham, R-Calif., resigned effective Dec. 1, 2005. The last vote for which he was eligible was vote 608.

ND Northern Democrats, SD Southern Democrats
Southern states: Ala., Ark., Fla., Ga., Ky., La., Miss., N.C., Okla., S.C., Tenn., Va.

| | 609 | 610 | 611 | 612 | 613 |
|---|---|---|---|---|---|
| **ALABAMA** | | | | | |
| 1 Bonner | Y | Y | Y | Y | Y |
| 2 Everett | Y | Y | Y | Y | Y |
| 3 Rogers | Y | Y | Y | Y | Y |
| 4 Aderholt | Y | Y | Y | N | Y |
| 5 Cramer | ? | ? | ? | Y | Y |
| 6 Bachus | Y | Y | Y | Y | Y |
| 7 Davis | Y | Y | Y | Y | Y |
| **ALASKA** | | | | | |
| AL Young | Y | Y | Y | Y | Y |
| **ARIZONA** | | | | | |
| 1 Renzi | Y | Y | Y | Y | Y |
| 2 Franks | Y | Y | Y | N | Y |
| 3 Shadegg | Y | Y | Y | N | Y |
| 4 Pastor | Y | Y | Y | Y | Y |
| 5 Hayworth | Y | Y | Y | Y | Y |
| 6 Flake | Y | Y | Y | N | Y |
| 7 Grijalva | Y | Y | Y | Y | Y |
| 8 Kolbe | Y | Y | Y | N | Y |
| **ARKANSAS** | | | | | |
| 1 Berry | Y | Y | Y | Y | Y |
| 2 Snyder | Y | Y | Y | Y | Y |
| 3 Boozman | Y | Y | Y | Y | Y |
| 4 Ross | Y | Y | Y | Y | Y |
| **CALIFORNIA** | | | | | |
| 1 Thompson | Y | Y | Y | Y | Y |
| 2 Herger | Y | Y | Y | Y | Y |
| 3 Lungren | Y | Y | Y | Y | Y |
| 4 Doolittle | ? | ? | ? | N | Y |
| 5 Matsui, D. | Y | Y | Y | Y | Y |
| 6 Woolsey | Y | Y | Y | Y | Y |
| 7 Miller, George | Y | Y | Y | Y | Y |
| 8 Pelosi | Y | Y | Y | Y | ? |
| 9 Lee | Y | Y | Y | Y | Y |
| 10 Tauscher | Y | Y | Y | Y | Y |
| 11 Pombo | Y | Y | Y | Y | Y |
| 12 Lantos | Y | Y | Y | Y | Y |
| 13 Stark | Y | Y | Y | Y | Y |
| 14 Eshoo | Y | Y | Y | Y | Y |
| 15 Honda | Y | Y | Y | Y | ? |
| 16 Lofgren | Y | Y | Y | Y | Y |
| 17 Farr | Y | Y | Y | Y | Y |
| 18 Cardoza | Y | Y | Y | Y | Y |
| 19 Radanovich | Y | Y | Y | Y | Y |
| 20 Costa | Y | Y | Y | Y | Y |
| 21 Nunes | Y | Y | Y | Y | Y |
| 22 Thomas | Y | Y | Y | Y | Y |
| 23 Capps | + | + | + | Y | Y |
| 24 Gallegly | Y | Y | Y | Y | Y |
| 25 McKeon | Y | Y | Y | Y | Y |
| 26 Dreier | Y | Y | Y | Y | Y |
| 27 Sherman | Y | Y | Y | Y | Y |
| 28 Berman | Y | Y | Y | Y | Y |
| 29 Schiff | Y | Y | Y | Y | Y |
| 30 Waxman | Y | Y | Y | Y | Y |
| 31 Becerra | Y | Y | Y | Y | Y |
| 32 Solis | Y | Y | Y | Y | Y |
| 33 Watson | Y | Y | Y | Y | Y |
| 34 Roybal-Allard | Y | Y | Y | Y | Y |
| 35 Waters | Y | Y | Y | Y | ? |
| 36 Harman | Y | Y | Y | Y | Y |
| 37 Millender-McD. | Y | Y | Y | Y | Y |
| 38 Napolitano | Y | Y | Y | Y | Y |
| 39 Sánchez, Linda | Y | Y | Y | Y | Y |
| 40 Royce | Y | Y | Y | N | Y |
| 41 Lewis | Y | Y | Y | Y | Y |
| 42 Miller, Gary | Y | Y | Y | Y | Y |
| 43 Baca | Y | Y | Y | Y | Y |
| 44 Calvert | Y | Y | Y | Y | Y |
| 45 Bono | Y | Y | Y | Y | Y |
| 46 Rohrabacher | Y | Y | Y | N | Y |
| 47 Sanchez, Loretta | Y | Y | Y | Y | Y |
| 48 Vacant | | | | | |
| 49 Issa | Y | Y | Y | Y | Y |

| | 609 | 610 | 611 | 612 | 613 |
|---|---|---|---|---|---|
| 50 Vacant\* | | | | | |
| 51 Filner | Y | Y | Y | Y | Y |
| 52 Hunter | Y | Y | Y | Y | Y |
| 53 Davis | Y | Y | Y | Y | Y |
| **COLORADO** | | | | | |
| 1 DeGette | Y | Y | Y | Y | Y |
| 2 Udall | Y | Y | Y | Y | Y |
| 3 Salazar | Y | Y | Y | Y | Y |
| 4 Musgrave | Y | Y | Y | Y | Y |
| 5 Hefley | Y | Y | Y | Y | Y |
| 6 Tancredo | Y | Y | Y | N | Y |
| 7 Beauprez | Y | Y | Y | Y | Y |
| **CONNECTICUT** | | | | | |
| 1 Larson | Y | Y | Y | Y | Y |
| 2 Simmons | ? | ? | ? | Y | Y |
| 3 DeLauro | Y | Y | Y | Y | Y |
| 4 Shays | Y | Y | Y | Y | Y |
| 5 Johnson | Y | Y | Y | Y | Y |
| **DELAWARE** | | | | | |
| AL Castle | Y | Y | Y | Y | Y |
| **FLORIDA** | | | | | |
| 1 Miller | Y | Y | Y | N | Y |
| 2 Boyd | Y | Y | ? | Y | Y |
| 3 Brown | ? | ? | ? | Y | Y |
| 4 Crenshaw | Y | Y | Y | Y | Y |
| 5 Brown-Waite | ? | ? | ? | ? | ? |
| 6 Stearns | Y | Y | Y | Y | Y |
| 7 Mica | Y | Y | Y | Y | Y |
| 8 Keller | Y | Y | Y | Y | Y |
| 9 Bilirakis | Y | Y | Y | Y | Y |
| 10 Young | Y | Y | Y | Y | Y |
| 11 Davis | ? | ? | ? | ? | ? |
| 12 Putnam | Y | Y | Y | N | Y |
| 13 Harris | Y | Y | Y | Y | Y |
| 14 Mack | Y | Y | Y | N | Y |
| 15 Weldon | Y | Y | Y | N | Y |
| 16 Foley | Y | Y | Y | Y | Y |
| 17 Meek | Y | Y | ? | Y | Y |
| 18 Ros-Lehtinen | Y | Y | Y | Y | Y |
| 19 Wexler | ? | ? | ? | ? | ? |
| 20 Wasserman-Schultz | Y | ? | ? | Y | Y |
| 21 Diaz-Balart, L. | Y | Y | Y | Y | Y |
| 22 Shaw | Y | Y | Y | Y | Y |
| 23 Hastings | Y | Y | Y | Y | Y |
| 24 Feeney | Y | Y | Y | N | Y |
| 25 Diaz-Balart, M. | ? | ? | ? | ? | Y |
| **GEORGIA** | | | | | |
| 1 Kingston | Y | Y | Y | Y | Y |
| 2 Bishop | Y | Y | Y | Y | Y |
| 3 Marshall | Y | Y | Y | Y | Y |
| 4 McKinney | ? | Y | Y | Y | Y |
| 5 Lewis | Y | Y | Y | Y | Y |
| 6 Price | Y | Y | Y | Y | Y |
| 7 Linder | Y | Y | Y | Y | Y |
| 8 Westmoreland | Y | Y | Y | N | Y |
| 9 Norwood | Y | Y | Y | Y | Y |
| 10 Deal | Y | Y | Y | Y | Y |
| 11 Gingrey | Y | Y | Y | Y | Y |
| 12 Barrow | Y | Y | Y | Y | Y |
| 13 Scott | Y | Y | Y | Y | ? |
| **HAWAII** | | | | | |
| 1 Abercrombie | Y | Y | Y | Y | Y |
| 2 Case | Y | Y | Y | Y | Y |
| **IDAHO** | | | | | |
| 1 Otter | Y | Y | Y | N | Y |
| 2 Simpson | Y | Y | Y | Y | Y |
| **ILLINOIS** | | | | | |
| 1 Rush | Y | Y | Y | Y | Y |
| 2 Jackson | Y | Y | Y | Y | Y |
| 3 Lipinski | Y | Y | Y | Y | Y |
| 4 Gutierrez | + | + | + | Y | Y |
| 5 Emanuel | Y | Y | Y | Y | Y |
| 6 Hyde | Y | Y | Y | Y | Y |
| 7 Davis | Y | Y | Y | Y | Y |
| 8 Bean | Y | Y | Y | Y | Y |
| 9 Schakowsky | Y | Y | Y | Y | Y |
| 10 Kirk | Y | Y | Y | Y | Y |
| 11 Weller | Y | Y | Y | Y | Y |
| 12 Costello | Y | Y | Y | N | N |

| | | 609 | 610 | 611 | 612 | 613 |
|---|---|---|---|---|---|---|
| 13 | Biggert | Y | Y | Y | Y | Y |
| 14 | Hastert | | | | | |
| 15 | Johnson | Y | Y | Y | Y | Y |
| 16 | Manzullo | Y | Y | Y | Y | Y |
| 17 | Evans | Y | Y | Y | Y | Y |
| 18 | LaHood | Y | Y | Y | Y | Y |
| 19 | Shimkus | Y | Y | Y | Y | Y |
| **INDIANA** | | | | | | |
| 1 | Visclosky | Y | Y | Y | Y | Y |
| 2 | Chocola | Y | Y | Y | Y | Y |
| 3 | Souder | Y | Y | Y | Y | Y |
| 4 | Buyer | Y | Y | Y | Y | Y |
| 5 | Burton | Y | Y | Y | Y | Y |
| 6 | Pence | Y | Y | Y | ? | ? |
| 7 | Carson | + | + | + | Y | Y |
| 8 | Hostettler | Y | Y | Y | Y | Y |
| 9 | Sodrel | Y | Y | Y | Y | Y |
| **IOWA** | | | | | | |
| 1 | Nussle | Y | Y | Y | Y | Y |
| 2 | Leach | Y | Y | Y | Y | Y |
| 3 | Boswell | Y | Y | Y | Y | Y |
| 4 | Latham | Y | Y | Y | Y | Y |
| 5 | King | Y | Y | Y | Y | Y |
| **KANSAS** | | | | | | |
| 1 | Moran | Y | Y | Y | Y | Y |
| 2 | Ryun | Y | Y | Y | Y | Y |
| 3 | Moore | Y | Y | Y | Y | Y |
| 4 | Tiahrt | Y | Y | Y | Y | Y |
| **KENTUCKY** | | | | | | |
| 1 | Whitfield | Y | Y | Y | Y | Y |
| 2 | Lewis | Y | Y | Y | Y | Y |
| 3 | Northup | Y | Y | Y | Y | Y |
| 4 | Davis | Y | Y | Y | Y | Y |
| 5 | Rogers | Y | Y | Y | Y | Y |
| 6 | Chandler | Y | Y | Y | Y | |
| **LOUISIANA** | | | | | | |
| 1 | Jindal | Y | Y | Y | Y | Y |
| 2 | Jefferson | Y | Y | Y | Y | Y |
| 3 | Melancon | Y | Y | Y | Y | Y |
| 4 | McCrery | Y | Y | Y | Y | Y |
| 5 | Alexander | Y | Y | Y | Y | Y |
| 6 | Baker | Y | Y | Y | Y | Y |
| 7 | Boustany | Y | Y | Y | Y | Y |
| **MAINE** | | | | | | |
| 1 | Allen | Y | Y | Y | Y | Y |
| 2 | Michaud | Y | Y | Y | Y | Y |
| **MARYLAND** | | | | | | |
| 1 | Gilchrest | Y | Y | ? | Y | Y |
| 2 | Ruppersberger | Y | Y | Y | Y | Y |
| 3 | Cardin | Y | Y | Y | Y | Y |
| 4 | Wynn | Y | Y | Y | Y | Y |
| 5 | Hoyer | Y | Y | Y | Y | Y |
| 6 | Bartlett | Y | Y | Y | N | Y |
| 7 | Cummings | Y | Y | Y | Y | Y |
| 8 | Van Hollen | Y | Y | Y | Y | Y |
| **MASSACHUSETTS** | | | | | | |
| 1 | Olver | ? | ? | ? | Y | Y |
| 2 | Neal | Y | Y | Y | Y | Y |
| 3 | McGovern | Y | Y | Y | Y | Y |
| 4 | Frank | ? | ? | ? | Y | Y |
| 5 | Meehan | Y | Y | Y | Y | Y |
| 6 | Tierney | ? | ? | ? | Y | Y |
| 7 | Markey | Y | Y | Y | Y | Y |
| 8 | Capuano | Y | Y | Y | Y | Y |
| 9 | Lynch | Y | Y | Y | Y | Y |
| 10 | Delahunt | Y | Y | Y | Y | Y |
| **MICHIGAN** | | | | | | |
| 1 | Stupak | Y | Y | Y | Y | Y |
| 2 | Hoekstra | Y | Y | Y | Y | Y |
| 3 | Ehlers | Y | Y | Y | Y | Y |
| 4 | Camp | Y | Y | Y | Y | Y |
| 5 | Kildee | Y | Y | Y | Y | Y |
| 6 | Upton | Y | Y | Y | Y | Y |
| 7 | Schwarz | Y | Y | Y | Y | Y |
| 8 | Rogers | Y | Y | Y | Y | Y |
| 9 | Knollenberg | Y | Y | Y | Y | Y |
| 10 | Miller | Y | Y | Y | Y | Y |
| 11 | McCotter | Y | Y | Y | Y | Y |
| 12 | Levin | Y | Y | Y | Y | Y |
| 13 | Kilpatrick | Y | Y | Y | Y | Y |
| 14 | Conyers | Y | Y | Y | Y | Y |
| 15 | Dingell | Y | Y | Y | Y | Y |

| | | 609 | 610 | 611 | 612 | 613 |
|---|---|---|---|---|---|---|
| **MINNESOTA** | | | | | | |
| 1 | Gutknecht | Y | Y | Y | N | Y |
| 2 | Kline | Y | Y | Y | Y | Y |
| 3 | Ramstad | Y | Y | Y | Y | Y |
| 4 | McCollum | Y | Y | Y | Y | Y |
| 5 | Sabo | Y | Y | Y | Y | N |
| 6 | Kennedy | Y | Y | Y | Y | Y |
| 7 | Peterson | Y | Y | Y | N | N |
| 8 | Oberstar | Y | Y | Y | Y | |
| **MISSISSIPPI** | | | | | | |
| 1 | Wicker | Y | Y | Y | Y | Y |
| 2 | Thompson | Y | Y | Y | Y | Y |
| 3 | Pickering | Y | Y | Y | Y | Y |
| 4 | Taylor | Y | Y | Y | N | Y |
| **MISSOURI** | | | | | | |
| 1 | Clay | ? | ? | ? | ? | ? |
| 2 | Akin | Y | Y | Y | N | Y |
| 3 | Carnahan | Y | Y | Y | Y | Y |
| 4 | Skelton | Y | Y | Y | Y | Y |
| 5 | Cleaver | Y | Y | Y | Y | Y |
| 6 | Graves | Y | Y | Y | Y | Y |
| 7 | Blunt | Y | Y | Y | Y | Y |
| 8 | Emerson | Y | Y | Y | Y | Y |
| 9 | Hulshof | Y | Y | Y | Y | Y |
| **MONTANA** | | | | | | |
| AL | Rehberg | Y | Y | Y | Y | Y |
| **NEBRASKA** | | | | | | |
| 1 | Fortenberry | Y | Y | Y | Y | Y |
| 2 | Terry | Y | Y | Y | Y | Y |
| 3 | Osborne | Y | Y | Y | Y | Y |
| **NEVADA** | | | | | | |
| 1 | Berkley | Y | Y | Y | Y | Y |
| 2 | Gibbons | Y | Y | Y | Y | Y |
| 3 | Porter | Y | Y | Y | Y | Y |
| **NEW HAMPSHIRE** | | | | | | |
| 1 | Bradley | Y | Y | Y | Y | Y |
| 2 | Bass | Y | Y | Y | Y | Y |
| **NEW JERSEY** | | | | | | |
| 1 | Andrews | Y | Y | Y | + | + |
| 2 | LoBiondo | Y | Y | Y | Y | Y |
| 3 | Saxton | Y | Y | Y | Y | Y |
| 4 | Smith | Y | Y | Y | Y | Y |
| 5 | Garrett | Y | Y | Y | Y | Y |
| 6 | Pallone | Y | Y | Y | Y | Y |
| 7 | Ferguson | Y | Y | Y | Y | Y |
| 8 | Pascrell | Y | Y | Y | Y | Y |
| 9 | Rothman | Y | Y | Y | Y | Y |
| 10 | Payne | Y | Y | Y | Y | Y |
| 11 | Frelinghuysen | Y | Y | Y | Y | Y |
| 12 | Holt | Y | Y | Y | Y | Y |
| 13 | Menendez | Y | Y | Y | Y | Y |
| **NEW MEXICO** | | | | | | |
| 1 | Wilson | Y | Y | Y | Y | Y |
| 2 | Pearce | Y | Y | Y | Y | Y |
| 3 | Udall | Y | Y | Y | Y | Y |
| **NEW YORK** | | | | | | |
| 1 | Bishop | Y | Y | Y | Y | Y |
| 2 | Israel | Y | Y | Y | Y | Y |
| 3 | King | Y | Y | Y | Y | Y |
| 4 | McCarthy | Y | Y | Y | Y | Y |
| 5 | Ackerman | Y | Y | Y | Y | Y |
| 6 | Meeks | Y | Y | Y | Y | Y |
| 7 | Crowley | Y | Y | Y | Y | Y |
| 8 | Nadler | Y | Y | Y | Y | Y |
| 9 | Weiner | ? | ? | ? | Y | Y |
| 10 | Towns | Y | Y | Y | Y | Y |
| 11 | Owens | Y | Y | Y | Y | Y |
| 12 | Velázquez | Y | Y | Y | Y | Y |
| 13 | Fossella | Y | Y | Y | Y | Y |
| 14 | Maloney | Y | Y | Y | Y | Y |
| 15 | Rangel | Y | Y | Y | Y | Y |
| 16 | Serrano | Y | Y | Y | Y | Y |
| 17 | Engel | Y | Y | Y | Y | Y |
| 18 | Lowey | Y | Y | Y | Y | Y |
| 19 | Kelly | Y | Y | Y | Y | Y |
| 20 | Sweeney | ? | ? | ? | ? | ? |
| 21 | McNulty | Y | Y | Y | Y | Y |
| 22 | Hinchey | ? | ? | ? | Y | Y |
| 23 | McHugh | Y | Y | Y | Y | Y |
| 24 | Boehlert | Y | Y | Y | Y | Y |
| 25 | Walsh | Y | Y | Y | Y | Y |
| 26 | Reynolds | Y | Y | Y | Y | Y |
| 27 | Higgins | Y | Y | Y | Y | Y |
| 28 | Slaughter | Y | Y | Y | Y | Y |
| 29 | Kuhl | Y | Y | Y | Y | Y |

| | | 609 | 610 | 611 | 612 | 613 |
|---|---|---|---|---|---|---|
| **NORTH CAROLINA** | | | | | | |
| 1 | Butterfield | Y | Y | Y | Y | Y |
| 2 | Etheridge | Y | Y | Y | Y | Y |
| 3 | Jones | Y | Y | Y | N | Y |
| 4 | Price | Y | Y | Y | Y | Y |
| 5 | Foxx | Y | Y | Y | N | Y |
| 6 | Coble | Y | Y | Y | Y | Y |
| 7 | McIntyre | Y | Y | Y | Y | Y |
| 8 | Hayes | Y | Y | Y | Y | Y |
| 9 | Myrick | Y | Y | Y | N | Y |
| 10 | McHenry | Y | Y | Y | Y | Y |
| 11 | Taylor | ? | ? | ? | Y | Y |
| 12 | Watt | Y | Y | Y | ? | ? |
| 13 | Miller | Y | Y | Y | Y | Y |
| **NORTH DAKOTA** | | | | | | |
| AL | Pomeroy | Y | Y | Y | Y | Y |
| **OHIO** | | | | | | |
| 1 | Chabot | Y | Y | Y | N | Y |
| 2 | Schmidt | Y | Y | Y | Y | Y |
| 3 | Turner | Y | Y | Y | Y | Y |
| 4 | Oxley | Y | ? | ? | Y | Y |
| 5 | Gillmor | Y | Y | Y | Y | Y |
| 6 | Strickland | Y | Y | Y | Y | Y |
| 7 | Hobson | Y | Y | Y | Y | Y |
| 8 | Boehner | Y | Y | ? | ? | Y |
| 9 | Kaptur | ? | ? | ? | Y | Y |
| 10 | Kucinich | Y | Y | Y | Y | Y |
| 11 | Jones | + | + | + | Y | Y |
| 12 | Tiberi | Y | Y | Y | Y | Y |
| 13 | Brown | Y | + | + | Y | Y |
| 14 | LaTourette | Y | Y | Y | Y | Y |
| 15 | Pryce | Y | Y | Y | Y | Y |
| 16 | Regula | Y | Y | Y | Y | Y |
| 17 | Ryan | Y | Y | Y | Y | Y |
| 18 | Ney | Y | Y | Y | Y | Y |
| **OKLAHOMA** | | | | | | |
| 1 | Sullivan | Y | Y | Y | Y | Y |
| 2 | Boren | Y | Y | Y | Y | Y |
| 3 | Lucas | Y | Y | Y | Y | Y |
| 4 | Cole | Y | Y | Y | Y | Y |
| 5 | Istook | Y | Y | Y | Y | Y |
| **OREGON** | | | | | | |
| 1 | Wu | Y | Y | Y | Y | Y |
| 2 | Walden | Y | Y | Y | Y | Y |
| 3 | Blumenauer | Y | Y | Y | Y | Y |
| 4 | DeFazio | Y | Y | Y | Y | Y |
| 5 | Hooley | Y | Y | Y | Y | Y |
| **PENNSYLVANIA** | | | | | | |
| 1 | Brady | Y | Y | Y | Y | Y |
| 2 | Fattah | Y | Y | Y | Y | Y |
| 3 | English | Y | Y | Y | Y | Y |
| 4 | Hart | Y | Y | Y | Y | Y |
| 5 | Peterson | Y | Y | Y | Y | Y |
| 6 | Gerlach | Y | Y | Y | + | + |
| 7 | Weldon | Y | Y | Y | Y | Y |
| 8 | Fitzpatrick | Y | Y | Y | Y | Y |
| 9 | Shuster | Y | Y | Y | Y | Y |
| 10 | Sherwood | Y | Y | Y | Y | Y |
| 11 | Kanjorski | Y | Y | Y | Y | Y |
| 12 | Murtha | ? | ? | ? | ? | ? |
| 13 | Schwartz | + | + | + | Y | Y |
| 14 | Doyle | Y | Y | Y | Y | Y |
| 15 | Dent | Y | Y | Y | Y | Y |
| 16 | Pitts | Y | Y | Y | N | Y |
| 17 | Holden | Y | Y | Y | Y | Y |
| 18 | Murphy | Y | Y | Y | Y | Y |
| 19 | Platts | Y | Y | Y | Y | Y |
| **RHODE ISLAND** | | | | | | |
| 1 | Kennedy | Y | Y | Y | Y | Y |
| 2 | Langevin | Y | Y | Y | Y | Y |
| **SOUTH CAROLINA** | | | | | | |
| 1 | Brown | Y | Y | Y | Y | Y |
| 2 | Wilson | Y | Y | Y | Y | Y |
| 3 | Barrett | Y | Y | Y | N | Y |
| 4 | Inglis | Y | Y | Y | Y | Y |
| 5 | Spratt | Y | Y | Y | Y | Y |
| 6 | Clyburn | Y | Y | Y | Y | Y |
| **SOUTH DAKOTA** | | | | | | |
| AL | Herseth | Y | Y | Y | Y | Y |
| **TENNESSEE** | | | | | | |
| 1 | Jenkins | Y | Y | Y | Y | Y |
| 2 | Duncan | Y | Y | Y | N | Y |

| | | 609 | 610 | 611 | 612 | 613 |
|---|---|---|---|---|---|---|
| 3 | Wamp | Y | Y | Y | Y | Y |
| 4 | Davis | Y | Y | Y | Y | Y |
| 5 | Cooper | Y | Y | Y | Y | Y |
| 6 | Gordon | Y | Y | Y | Y | Y |
| 7 | Blackburn | + | Y | Y | N | Y |
| 8 | Tanner | Y | Y | Y | Y | Y |
| 9 | Ford | ? | ? | ? | Y | Y |
| **TEXAS** | | | | | | |
| 1 | Gohmert | Y | Y | Y | N | Y |
| 2 | Poe | Y | Y | Y | N | Y |
| 3 | Johnson, S. | Y | Y | Y | N | Y |
| 4 | Hall | Y | Y | Y | Y | Y |
| 5 | Hensarling | Y | Y | Y | N | Y |
| 6 | Barton | Y | Y | Y | N | Y |
| 7 | Culberson | Y | Y | Y | N | Y |
| 8 | Brady | Y | Y | Y | N | Y |
| 9 | Green, A. | Y | Y | Y | Y | Y |
| 10 | McCaul | Y | Y | Y | Y | Y |
| 11 | Conaway | Y | Y | Y | Y | Y |
| 12 | Granger | Y | Y | Y | N | Y |
| 13 | Thornberry | Y | Y | Y | N | Y |
| 14 | Paul | N | Y | N | N | Y |
| 15 | Hinojosa | Y | Y | Y | Y | Y |
| 16 | Reyes | ? | ? | ? | ? | ? |
| 17 | Edwards | Y | Y | Y | Y | Y |
| 18 | Jackson-Lee | Y | Y | Y | Y | Y |
| 19 | Neugebauer | Y | Y | Y | Y | Y |
| 20 | Gonzalez | Y | Y | Y | Y | Y |
| 21 | Smith | Y | Y | Y | Y | Y |
| 22 | DeLay | Y | Y | Y | N | Y |
| 23 | Bonilla | Y | Y | Y | N | Y |
| 24 | Marchant | Y | Y | Y | Y | Y |
| 25 | Doggett | Y | Y | Y | Y | Y |
| 26 | Burgess | Y | Y | Y | N | Y |
| 27 | Ortiz | Y | Y | Y | Y | Y |
| 28 | Cuellar | Y | Y | Y | Y | Y |
| 29 | Green, G. | Y | Y | Y | Y | Y |
| 30 | Johnson, E. | Y | Y | Y | Y | Y |
| 31 | Carter | Y | Y | Y | N | Y |
| 32 | Sessions | Y | Y | Y | Y | Y |
| **UTAH** | | | | | | |
| 1 | Bishop | Y | Y | Y | Y | Y |
| 2 | Matheson | Y | Y | Y | Y | Y |
| 3 | Cannon | Y | Y | Y | Y | Y |
| **VERMONT** | | | | | | |
| AL | Sanders | Y | Y | Y | Y | Y |
| **VIRGINIA** | | | | | | |
| 1 | Davis, J. | Y | Y | Y | N | Y |
| 2 | Drake | Y | Y | Y | Y | Y |
| 3 | Scott | Y | Y | Y | Y | N |
| 4 | Forbes | Y | Y | Y | N | Y |
| 5 | Goode | Y | Y | Y | Y | Y |
| 6 | Goodlatte | Y | Y | Y | Y | Y |
| 7 | Cantor | Y | ? | ? | Y | Y |
| 8 | Moran | ? | ? | ? | Y | Y |
| 9 | Boucher | Y | Y | Y | Y | Y |
| 10 | Wolf | Y | Y | Y | Y | Y |
| 11 | Davis, T. | Y | Y | Y | Y | Y |
| **WASHINGTON** | | | | | | |
| 1 | Inslee | Y | Y | Y | Y | Y |
| 2 | Larsen | ? | ? | ? | Y | Y |
| 3 | Baird | Y | Y | Y | Y | Y |
| 4 | Hastings | Y | Y | Y | Y | Y |
| 5 | McMorris | Y | Y | Y | Y | Y |
| 6 | Dicks | Y | Y | Y | Y | Y |
| 7 | McDermott | Y | Y | Y | Y | Y |
| 8 | Reichert | Y | Y | Y | Y | Y |
| 9 | Smith | Y | Y | Y | Y | Y |
| **WEST VIRGINIA** | | | | | | |
| 1 | Mollohan | Y | Y | Y | Y | Y |
| 2 | Capito | Y | Y | Y | Y | Y |
| 3 | Rahall | Y | Y | Y | Y | Y |
| **WISCONSIN** | | | | | | |
| 1 | Ryan | Y | Y | Y | N | Y |
| 2 | Baldwin | Y | Y | Y | Y | Y |
| 3 | Kind | Y | Y | Y | Y | Y |
| 4 | Moore | Y | Y | Y | Y | Y |
| 5 | Sensenbrenner | Y | Y | Y | N | Y |
| 6 | Petri | Y | Y | Y | Y | Y |
| 7 | Obey | Y | Y | Y | Y | Y |
| 8 | Green | + | + | + | Y | Y |
| **WYOMING** | | | | | | |
| AL | Cubin | ? | ? | ? | Y | Y |

# IN THE HOUSE | By Vote Number

**614.** **H Con Res 196. Federal Flight Deck Officer Program/Adoption.** Pearce, R-N.M., motion to suspend the rules and adopt the concurrent resolution that would recognize volunteer pilots in the Federal Flight Deck Officer Program and applaud them for taking a stand against terrorism. Motion agreed to 413-2: R 221-0; D 191-2 (ND 145-2, SD 46-0); I 1-0. A two-thirds majority of those present and voting (277 in this case) is required for adoption under suspension of the rules. Dec. 7, 2005.

**615.** **HR 3010. Fiscal 2006 Labor-HHS-Education Appropriations/ Appeal Ruling of the Chair.** Regula, R-Ohio., motion to table (kill) the Obey, D-Wis., appeal of the ruling of the chair against the Regula point of order against the Obey motion to instruct House conferees on the grounds that the provisions in the motion exceed the scope of the conference. The Obey motion would instruct House conferees to include language that would appropriate $4.2 billion for the Low Income Home Energy Assistance Program, with $2 billion of the total designated as emergency funding. Motion agreed to 226-196: R 226-0; D 0-195 (ND 0-146, SD 0-49); I 0-1. Dec. 7, 2005.

**616.** **HR 4340. United States-Bahrain Free Trade Agreement/Passage.** Passage of the bill that would implement a trade agreement between the United States and Bahrain. It would provide immediate duty-free access for 98 percent of U.S. agricultural exports and phase out tariffs on the remaining products within 10 years. It also would provide immediate duty-free access on all of Bahrain's agricultural exports to the United States. Passed 327-95: R 212-13; D 115-81 (ND 82-65, SD 33-16); I 0-1. A "yea" was a vote in support of the president's position. Dec. 7, 2005.

**617.** **HR 4388. Tax Breaks Extensions/Passage.** McCrery, R-La., motion to suspend the rules and pass the bill that would extend for one year various expiring tax provisions including one that would allow military combat pay to continue to be counted for purposes of calculating the earned income tax credit. Motion agreed to 423-0: R 226-0; D 196-0 (ND 147-0, SD 49-0); I 1-0. A two-thirds majority of those present and voting (282 in this case) is required for passage under suspension of the rules. Dec. 7, 2005.

**618.** **HR 4440. Gulf Zone Tax Relief/Passage.** McCrery, R-La., motion to suspend the rules and pass the bill that would provide tax benefits for areas of Alabama, Louisiana and Mississippi affected by Hurricane Katrina. It would provide authority for tax-exempt bonds to help rebuild infrastructure, authorize additional credits for low-income housing and authorize federal guarantees for up to $3 billion in bonds to aid local governments that cannot meet certain financing requirements. Motion agreed to 415-4: R 223-3; D 191-1 (ND 144-1, SD 47-0); I 1-0. A two-thirds majority of those present and voting (280 in this case) is required for passage under suspension of the rules. Dec. 7, 2005.

| | 614 | 615 | 616 | 617 | 618 |
|---|---|---|---|---|---|
| **ALABAMA** | | | | | |
| 1 Bonner | Y | Y | Y | Y | Y |
| 2 Everett | Y | Y | N | Y | Y |
| 3 Rogers | Y | Y | N | Y | Y |
| 4 Aderholt | Y | Y | Y | Y | Y |
| 5 Cramer | Y | N | Y | Y | Y |
| 6 Bachus | Y | Y | Y | Y | Y |
| 7 Davis | Y | N | Y | Y | Y |
| **ALASKA** | | | | | |
| AL Young | Y | Y | Y | Y | Y |
| **ARIZONA** | | | | | |
| 1 Renzi | Y | Y | Y | Y | Y |
| 2 Franks | Y | Y | Y | Y | Y |
| 3 Shadegg | Y | Y | Y | Y | Y |
| 4 Pastor | Y | N | N | Y | Y |
| 5 Hayworth | Y | Y | Y | Y | Y |
| 6 Flake | Y | Y | Y | Y | Y |
| 7 Grijalva | Y | N | N | Y | Y |
| 8 Kolbe | Y | Y | Y | Y | Y |
| **ARKANSAS** | | | | | |
| 1 Berry | Y | N | N | Y | Y |
| 2 Snyder | Y | N | Y | Y | Y |
| 3 Boozman | Y | Y | Y | Y | Y |
| 4 Ross | Y | N | Y | Y | Y |
| **CALIFORNIA** | | | | | |
| 1 Thompson | Y | N | Y | Y | Y |
| 2 Herger | Y | Y | Y | Y | Y |
| 3 Lungren | Y | Y | Y | Y | Y |
| 4 Doolittle | Y | Y | Y | Y | Y |
| 5 Matsui, D. | Y | N | Y | Y | Y |
| 6 Woolsey | Y | N | N | Y | Y |
| 7 Miller, George | Y | N | Y | Y | Y |
| 8 Pelosi | ? | ? | ? | ? | ? |
| 9 Lee | Y | N | N | Y | Y |
| 10 Tauscher | Y | N | Y | Y | Y |
| 11 Pombo | Y | Y | Y | Y | Y |
| 12 Lantos | Y | N | N | Y | Y |
| 13 Stark | N | N | N | Y | Y |
| 14 Eshoo | Y | N | Y | Y | Y |
| 15 Honda | Y | N | Y | Y | Y |
| 16 Lofgren | Y | N | Y | Y | Y |
| 17 Farr | Y | N | Y | Y | Y |
| 18 Cardoza | Y | N | Y | Y | Y |
| 19 Radanovich | Y | Y | Y | Y | Y |
| 20 Costa | Y | N | Y | Y | Y |
| 21 Nunes | Y | Y | Y | Y | Y |
| 22 Thomas | Y | Y | Y | Y | Y |
| 23 Capps | Y | N | Y | Y | Y |
| 24 Gallegly | Y | Y | Y | Y | Y |
| 25 McKeon | Y | Y | Y | Y | Y |
| 26 Dreier | Y | Y | Y | Y | Y |
| 27 Sherman | Y | N | Y | Y | Y |
| 28 Berman | Y | N | Y | Y | Y |
| 29 Schiff | Y | N | Y | Y | Y |
| 30 Waxman | Y | N | Y | Y | Y |
| 31 Becerra | Y | N | Y | Y | Y |
| 32 Solis | Y | N | N | Y | Y |
| 33 Watson | Y | N | Y | Y | Y |
| 34 Roybal-Allard | Y | N | Y | Y | Y |
| 35 Waters | Y | N | N | Y | Y |
| 36 Harman | Y | N | Y | Y | Y |
| 37 Millender-McD. | Y | N | N | Y | Y |
| 38 Napolitano | Y | – | N | Y | Y |
| 39 Sánchez, Linda | Y | N | N | Y | Y |
| 40 Royce | Y | Y | ? | Y | Y |
| 41 Lewis | Y | Y | Y | Y | Y |
| 42 Miller, Gary | Y | Y | Y | Y | Y |
| 43 Baca | Y | N | N | Y | Y |
| 44 Calvert | Y | Y | Y | Y | Y |
| 45 Bono | Y | Y | Y | Y | Y |
| 46 Rohrabacher | Y | Y | Y | Y | Y |
| 47 Sanchez, Loretta | Y | N | Y | Y | Y |
| 48 Vacant | | | | | |
| 49 Issa | Y | Y | Y | Y | Y |
| 50 Vacant | | | | | |
| 51 Filner | Y | N | N | Y | Y |
| 52 Hunter | Y | Y | Y | Y | Y |
| 53 Davis | Y | N | Y | Y | Y |
| **COLORADO** | | | | | |
| 1 DeGette | Y | N | Y | Y | Y |
| 2 Udall | Y | N | Y | Y | Y |
| 3 Salazar | Y | N | Y | Y | Y |
| 4 Musgrave | Y | Y | Y | Y | Y |
| 5 Hefley | Y | Y | Y | Y | Y |
| 6 Tancredo | Y | Y | Y | Y | Y |
| 7 Beauprez | Y | Y | Y | Y | Y |
| **CONNECTICUT** | | | | | |
| 1 Larson | Y | N | Y | Y | Y |
| 2 Simmons | Y | Y | Y | Y | Y |
| 3 DeLauro | Y | N | N | Y | Y |
| 4 Shays | Y | Y | Y | Y | Y |
| 5 Johnson | Y | Y | Y | Y | Y |
| **DELAWARE** | | | | | |
| AL Castle | Y | Y | Y | Y | Y |
| **FLORIDA** | | | | | |
| 1 Miller | Y | Y | Y | Y | Y |
| 2 Boyd | Y | N | Y | Y | Y |
| 3 Brown | Y | N | N | Y | Y |
| 4 Crenshaw | Y | Y | Y | Y | Y |
| 5 Brown-Waite | ? | ? | ? | ? | ? |
| 6 Stearns | Y | Y | Y | Y | Y |
| 7 Mica | Y | Y | Y | Y | Y |
| 8 Keller | Y | Y | Y | Y | Y |
| 9 Bilirakis | Y | Y | Y | Y | Y |
| 10 Young | Y | Y | Y | Y | Y |
| 11 Davis | ? | ? | ? | ? | ? |
| 12 Putnam | Y | Y | Y | Y | Y |
| 13 Harris | Y | Y | Y | Y | Y |
| 14 Mack | Y | Y | Y | Y | Y |
| 15 Weldon | Y | Y | Y | Y | Y |
| 16 Foley | Y | Y | Y | Y | Y |
| 17 Meek | Y | N | Y | Y | Y |
| 18 Ros-Lehtinen | Y | Y | Y | Y | Y |
| 19 Wexler | ? | ? | ? | ? | ? |
| 20 Wasserman-Schultz | Y | N | Y | Y | Y |
| 21 Diaz-Balart, L. | Y | Y | Y | Y | Y |
| 22 Shaw | Y | Y | Y | Y | Y |
| 23 Hastings | Y | N | N | Y | Y |
| 24 Feeney | Y | Y | Y | Y | Y |
| 25 Diaz-Balart, M. | Y | Y | Y | Y | Y |
| **GEORGIA** | | | | | |
| 1 Kingston | Y | Y | Y | Y | Y |
| 2 Bishop | Y | N | Y | Y | Y |
| 3 Marshall | Y | N | Y | Y | Y |
| 4 McKinney | Y | N | N | Y | Y |
| 5 Lewis | Y | N | Y | Y | Y |
| 6 Price | Y | Y | Y | Y | Y |
| 7 Linder | Y | Y | Y | Y | Y |
| 8 Westmoreland | Y | Y | Y | Y | Y |
| 9 Norwood | Y | Y | Y | Y | Y |
| 10 Deal | Y | Y | Y | Y | Y |
| 11 Gingrey | Y | Y | Y | Y | Y |
| 12 Barrow | Y | N | Y | Y | Y |
| 13 Scott | Y | N | Y | Y | Y |
| **HAWAII** | | | | | |
| 1 Abercrombie | Y | N | N | Y | Y |
| 2 Case | Y | N | Y | Y | Y |
| **IDAHO** | | | | | |
| 1 Otter | Y | Y | Y | Y | Y |
| 2 Simpson | Y | Y | Y | Y | Y |
| **ILLINOIS** | | | | | |
| 1 Rush | Y | N | Y | Y | Y |
| 2 Jackson | Y | N | N | Y | Y |
| 3 Lipinski | Y | N | N | Y | Y |
| 4 Gutierrez | Y | N | N | Y | + |
| 5 Emanuel | Y | N | Y | Y | Y |
| 6 Hyde | Y | Y | Y | Y | Y |
| 7 Davis | Y | N | N | Y | Y |
| 8 Bean | Y | N | Y | Y | Y |
| 9 Schakowsky | Y | N | N | Y | Y |
| 10 Kirk | Y | Y | Y | Y | Y |
| 11 Weller | Y | Y | Y | Y | Y |
| 12 Costello | Y | N | N | Y | Y |

**KEY**    **Republicans**    Democrats    *Independents*

| | | | | | |
|---|---|---|---|---|---|
| Y | Voted for (yea) | X | Paired against | C | Voted "present" to avoid possible conflict of interest |
| # | Paired for | – | Announced against | | |
| + | Announced for | P | Voted "present" | ? | Did not vote or otherwise make a position known |
| N | Voted against (nay) | | | | |

ND Northern Democrats, SD Southern Democrats
Southern states: Ala., Ark., Fla., Ga., Ky., La., Miss., N.C., Okla., S.C., Tenn., Texas, Va.

| | | 614 | 615 | 616 | 617 | 618 |
|---|---|---|---|---|---|---|
| 13 | Biggert | Y | Y | Y | Y | Y |
| 14 | Hastert | | | | | |
| 15 | Johnson | Y | Y | Y | Y | Y |
| 16 | Manzullo | Y | Y | Y | Y | Y |
| 17 | Evans | Y | N | N | Y | Y |
| 18 | LaHood | Y | Y | Y | Y | Y |
| 19 | Shimkus | Y | Y | Y | Y | Y |
| **INDIANA** | | | | | | |
| 1 | Visclosky | Y | N | N | Y | Y |
| 2 | Chocola | Y | Y | Y | Y | Y |
| 3 | Souder | Y | Y | Y | Y | Y |
| 4 | Buyer | Y | Y | Y | Y | Y |
| 5 | Burton | Y | Y | Y | Y | Y |
| 6 | Pence | ? | ? | ? | ? | ? |
| 7 | Carson | Y | N | N | Y | Y |
| 8 | Hostettler | Y | Y | N | Y | Y |
| 9 | Sodrel | Y | Y | Y | Y | Y |
| **IOWA** | | | | | | |
| 1 | Nussle | Y | Y | Y | Y | Y |
| 2 | Leach | Y | Y | Y | Y | Y |
| 3 | Boswell | Y | N | Y | Y | Y |
| 4 | Latham | Y | Y | Y | Y | Y |
| 5 | King | Y | Y | Y | Y | Y |
| **KANSAS** | | | | | | |
| 1 | Moran | Y | Y | Y | Y | Y |
| 2 | Ryun | Y | Y | Y | Y | Y |
| 3 | Moore | Y | N | Y | Y | Y |
| 4 | Tiahrt | Y | Y | Y | Y | Y |
| **KENTUCKY** | | | | | | |
| 1 | Whitfield | Y | Y | Y | Y | Y |
| 2 | Lewis | Y | Y | Y | Y | Y |
| 3 | Northup | Y | Y | Y | Y | Y |
| 4 | Davis | Y | Y | Y | Y | Y |
| 5 | Rogers | Y | Y | Y | Y | Y |
| 6 | Chandler | Y | N | Y | Y | Y |
| **LOUISIANA** | | | | | | |
| 1 | Jindal | Y | Y | Y | Y | Y |
| 2 | Jefferson | Y | N | Y | Y | Y |
| 3 | Melancon | Y | Y | Y | Y | Y |
| 4 | McCrery | Y | Y | Y | Y | Y |
| 5 | Alexander | Y | Y | Y | Y | Y |
| 6 | Baker | Y | Y | Y | Y | Y |
| 7 | Boustany | Y | Y | Y | Y | Y |
| **MAINE** | | | | | | |
| 1 | Allen | Y | N | Y | Y | Y |
| 2 | Michaud | Y | N | N | Y | Y |
| **MARYLAND** | | | | | | |
| 1 | Gilchrest | Y | Y | Y | Y | Y |
| 2 | Ruppersberger | Y | N | Y | Y | Y |
| 3 | Cardin | Y | N | Y | Y | Y |
| 4 | Wynn | Y | N | Y | Y | Y |
| 5 | Hoyer | Y | N | Y | Y | Y |
| 6 | Bartlett | Y | Y | Y | Y | Y |
| 7 | Cummings | Y | N | Y | Y | Y |
| 8 | Van Hollen | Y | N | Y | Y | Y |
| **MASSACHUSETTS** | | | | | | |
| 1 | Olver | Y | N | N | Y | Y |
| 2 | Neal | Y | N | Y | Y | Y |
| 3 | McGovern | Y | N | N | Y | Y |
| 4 | Frank | Y | N | Y | Y | Y |
| 5 | Meehan | Y | N | N | Y | Y |
| 6 | Tierney | Y | N | N | Y | Y |
| 7 | Markey | Y | N | N | Y | Y |
| 8 | Capuano | Y | N | N | Y | Y |
| 9 | Lynch | Y | N | N | Y | Y |
| 10 | Delahunt | Y | N | Y | Y | Y |
| **MICHIGAN** | | | | | | |
| 1 | Stupak | Y | N | N | Y | Y |
| 2 | Hoekstra | Y | Y | Y | Y | Y |
| 3 | Ehlers | Y | Y | Y | Y | Y |
| 4 | Camp | Y | Y | Y | Y | Y |
| 5 | Kildee | Y | N | N | Y | Y |
| 6 | Upton | Y | Y | Y | Y | Y |
| 7 | Schwarz | Y | Y | Y | Y | Y |
| 8 | Rogers | Y | Y | Y | Y | Y |
| 9 | Knollenberg | Y | Y | Y | Y | Y |
| 10 | Miller | Y | Y | Y | Y | Y |
| 11 | McCotter | Y | Y | Y | Y | Y |
| 12 | Levin | Y | N | Y | Y | Y |
| 13 | Kilpatrick | Y | N | N | Y | Y |
| 14 | Conyers | Y | N | N | Y | Y |
| 15 | Dingell | Y | N | Y | Y | Y |

| | | 614 | 615 | 616 | 617 | 618 |
|---|---|---|---|---|---|---|
| **MINNESOTA** | | | | | | |
| 1 | Gutknecht | Y | Y | Y | Y | Y |
| 2 | Kline | Y | Y | Y | Y | Y |
| 3 | Ramstad | Y | Y | Y | Y | Y |
| 4 | McCollum | Y | N | N | Y | Y |
| 5 | Sabo | Y | N | N | Y | Y |
| 6 | Kennedy | Y | Y | Y | Y | Y |
| 7 | Peterson | Y | N | Y | Y | Y |
| 8 | Oberstar | Y | N | N | Y | Y |
| **MISSISSIPPI** | | | | | | |
| 1 | Wicker | Y | Y | Y | Y | Y |
| 2 | Thompson | Y | N | N | Y | Y |
| 3 | Pickering | Y | Y | Y | Y | Y |
| 4 | Taylor | ? | N | N | Y | Y |
| **MISSOURI** | | | | | | |
| 1 | Clay | ? | ? | ? | ? | ? |
| 2 | Akin | Y | Y | Y | Y | Y |
| 3 | Carnahan | Y | N | N | Y | Y |
| 4 | Skelton | Y | N | Y | Y | Y |
| 5 | Cleaver | Y | N | Y | Y | Y |
| 6 | Graves | Y | Y | Y | Y | Y |
| 7 | Blunt | Y | Y | Y | Y | Y |
| 8 | Emerson | Y | Y | Y | Y | Y |
| 9 | Hulshof | Y | Y | Y | Y | Y |
| **MONTANA** | | | | | | |
| AL | Rehberg | Y | Y | Y | Y | Y |
| **NEBRASKA** | | | | | | |
| 1 | Fortenberry | Y | Y | Y | Y | Y |
| 2 | Terry | Y | Y | Y | Y | Y |
| 3 | Osborne | Y | Y | Y | Y | Y |
| **NEVADA** | | | | | | |
| 1 | Berkley | Y | N | Y | Y | N |
| 2 | Gibbons | Y | Y | Y | Y | N |
| 3 | Porter | Y | Y | Y | Y | N |
| **NEW HAMPSHIRE** | | | | | | |
| 1 | Bradley | Y | Y | Y | Y | Y |
| 2 | Bass | Y | Y | Y | Y | Y |
| **NEW JERSEY** | | | | | | |
| 1 | Andrews | + | – | – | + | + |
| 2 | LoBiondo | Y | Y | Y | Y | N |
| 3 | Saxton | Y | Y | Y | Y | Y |
| 4 | Smith | Y | Y | Y | Y | Y |
| 5 | Garrett | Y | Y | Y | Y | Y |
| 6 | Pallone | Y | N | N | Y | Y |
| 7 | Ferguson | Y | Y | Y | Y | Y |
| 8 | Pascrell | Y | N | Y | Y | Y |
| 9 | Rothman | Y | N | Y | Y | Y |
| 10 | Payne | Y | N | Y | Y | Y |
| 11 | Frelinghuysen | Y | Y | Y | Y | Y |
| 12 | Holt | Y | N | Y | Y | Y |
| 13 | Menendez | Y | N | N | Y | Y |
| **NEW MEXICO** | | | | | | |
| 1 | Wilson | Y | Y | Y | Y | Y |
| 2 | Pearce | Y | Y | Y | Y | Y |
| 3 | Udall | Y | N | Y | Y | Y |
| **NEW YORK** | | | | | | |
| 1 | Bishop | Y | N | Y | Y | Y |
| 2 | Israel | Y | N | Y | Y | Y |
| 3 | King | Y | Y | Y | Y | Y |
| 4 | McCarthy | + | N | Y | Y | Y |
| 5 | Ackerman | Y | N | Y | Y | Y |
| 6 | Meeks | Y | N | Y | Y | Y |
| 7 | Crowley | Y | N | Y | Y | Y |
| 8 | Nadler | Y | – | – | + | + |
| 9 | Weiner | Y | N | Y | Y | Y |
| 10 | Towns | Y | N | Y | Y | Y |
| 11 | Owens | Y | N | N | Y | Y |
| 12 | Velázquez | Y | N | Y | Y | Y |
| 13 | Fossella | Y | Y | Y | Y | Y |
| 14 | Maloney | Y | N | Y | Y | Y |
| 15 | Rangel | Y | N | Y | Y | Y |
| 16 | Serrano | Y | N | N | Y | Y |
| 17 | Engel | Y | N | Y | Y | Y |
| 18 | Lowey | Y | N | Y | Y | Y |
| 19 | Kelly | Y | Y | Y | Y | Y |
| 20 | Sweeney | ? | Y | Y | Y | Y |
| 21 | McNulty | Y | N | Y | Y | Y |
| 22 | Hinchey | Y | N | N | Y | Y |
| 23 | McHugh | Y | Y | Y | Y | Y |
| 24 | Boehlert | Y | Y | Y | Y | Y |
| 25 | Walsh | ? | Y | Y | Y | Y |
| 26 | Reynolds | Y | Y | Y | Y | Y |
| 27 | Higgins | Y | N | Y | Y | Y |
| 28 | Slaughter | Y | N | N | Y | ? |
| 29 | Kuhl | Y | Y | Y | Y | Y |

| | | 614 | 615 | 616 | 617 | 618 |
|---|---|---|---|---|---|---|
| **NORTH CAROLINA** | | | | | | |
| 1 | Butterfield | Y | N | Y | Y | Y |
| 2 | Etheridge | Y | N | Y | Y | Y |
| 3 | Jones | Y | Y | N | Y | Y |
| 4 | Price | Y | N | Y | Y | Y |
| 5 | Foxx | Y | Y | Y | Y | Y |
| 6 | Coble | Y | Y | N | Y | Y |
| 7 | McIntyre | Y | N | N | Y | Y |
| 8 | Hayes | Y | Y | Y | Y | Y |
| 9 | Myrick | Y | Y | Y | Y | Y |
| 10 | McHenry | Y | Y | Y | Y | Y |
| 11 | Taylor | Y | Y | Y | Y | Y |
| 12 | Watt | ? | N | N | Y | Y |
| 13 | Miller | Y | N | N | Y | Y |
| **NORTH DAKOTA** | | | | | | |
| AL | Pomeroy | Y | N | Y | Y | Y |
| **OHIO** | | | | | | |
| 1 | Chabot | Y | Y | Y | Y | Y |
| 2 | Schmidt | Y | Y | Y | Y | Y |
| 3 | Turner | Y | Y | Y | Y | Y |
| 4 | Oxley | Y | Y | Y | Y | Y |
| 5 | Gillmor | Y | Y | Y | Y | Y |
| 6 | Strickland | Y | N | N | Y | Y |
| 7 | Hobson | Y | Y | Y | Y | Y |
| 8 | Boehner | Y | Y | Y | Y | Y |
| 9 | Kaptur | Y | N | N | Y | Y |
| 10 | Kucinich | Y | N | N | Y | Y |
| 11 | Jones | Y | N | N | Y | Y |
| 12 | Tiberi | Y | Y | Y | Y | Y |
| 13 | Brown | Y | N | N | Y | Y |
| 14 | LaTourette | Y | Y | Y | Y | Y |
| 15 | Pryce | Y | Y | Y | Y | Y |
| 16 | Regula | Y | Y | Y | Y | Y |
| 17 | Ryan | Y | N | N | Y | Y |
| 18 | Ney | Y | Y | Y | Y | Y |
| **OKLAHOMA** | | | | | | |
| 1 | Sullivan | Y | Y | Y | Y | Y |
| 2 | Boren | Y | N | Y | Y | Y |
| 3 | Lucas | Y | Y | Y | Y | Y |
| 4 | Cole | + | Y | Y | Y | Y |
| 5 | Istook | Y | Y | Y | Y | Y |
| **OREGON** | | | | | | |
| 1 | Wu | N | N | Y | Y | Y |
| 2 | Walden | Y | Y | Y | Y | Y |
| 3 | Blumenauer | Y | N | Y | Y | Y |
| 4 | DeFazio | Y | N | N | Y | Y |
| 5 | Hooley | Y | N | Y | Y | Y |
| **PENNSYLVANIA** | | | | | | |
| 1 | Brady | Y | N | N | Y | Y |
| 2 | Fattah | Y | N | N | Y | Y |
| 3 | English | Y | Y | Y | Y | Y |
| 4 | Hart | Y | Y | Y | Y | Y |
| 5 | Peterson | Y | Y | Y | Y | Y |
| 6 | Gerlach | + | Y | Y | Y | Y |
| 7 | Weldon | Y | Y | Y | Y | Y |
| 8 | Fitzpatrick | Y | Y | Y | Y | Y |
| 9 | Shuster | Y | Y | Y | Y | Y |
| 10 | Sherwood | Y | Y | Y | Y | Y |
| 11 | Kanjorski | Y | N | N | Y | Y |
| 12 | Murtha | Y | N | N | Y | Y |
| 13 | Schwartz | Y | N | N | Y | Y |
| 14 | Doyle | Y | N | N | Y | Y |
| 15 | Dent | Y | Y | Y | Y | Y |
| 16 | Pitts | Y | Y | Y | Y | Y |
| 17 | Holden | Y | N | Y | Y | Y |
| 18 | Murphy | Y | Y | Y | Y | Y |
| 19 | Platts | Y | Y | Y | Y | Y |
| **RHODE ISLAND** | | | | | | |
| 1 | Kennedy | Y | N | Y | Y | Y |
| 2 | Langevin | Y | N | Y | Y | Y |
| **SOUTH CAROLINA** | | | | | | |
| 1 | Brown | Y | Y | Y | Y | Y |
| 2 | Wilson | Y | Y | Y | Y | Y |
| 3 | Barrett | Y | Y | N | Y | Y |
| 4 | Inglis | Y | Y | N | Y | Y |
| 5 | Spratt | Y | N | N | Y | Y |
| 6 | Clyburn | Y | N | N | Y | Y |
| **SOUTH DAKOTA** | | | | | | |
| AL | Herseth | Y | N | Y | Y | Y |
| **TENNESSEE** | | | | | | |
| 1 | Jenkins | Y | Y | Y | Y | Y |
| 2 | Duncan | Y | Y | Y | Y | Y |

| | | 614 | 615 | 616 | 617 | 618 |
|---|---|---|---|---|---|---|
| 3 | Wamp | Y | Y | Y | Y | Y |
| 4 | Davis | Y | N | Y | Y | Y |
| 5 | Cooper | Y | N | Y | Y | Y |
| 6 | Gordon | Y | N | Y | Y | Y |
| 7 | Blackburn | Y | Y | Y | Y | Y |
| 8 | Tanner | Y | N | Y | Y | Y |
| 9 | Ford | Y | N | Y | Y | Y |
| **TEXAS** | | | | | | |
| 1 | Gohmert | Y | Y | Y | Y | Y |
| 2 | Poe | Y | Y | Y | Y | Y |
| 3 | Johnson, S. | ? | Y | Y | Y | Y |
| 4 | Hall | Y | Y | Y | Y | Y |
| 5 | Hensarling | Y | Y | Y | Y | Y |
| 6 | Barton | Y | Y | Y | Y | Y |
| 7 | Culberson | Y | Y | Y | Y | Y |
| 8 | Brady | Y | Y | Y | Y | Y |
| 9 | Green, A. | Y | N | N | Y | Y |
| 10 | McCaul | Y | Y | Y | Y | Y |
| 11 | Conaway | Y | Y | Y | Y | Y |
| 12 | Granger | Y | Y | Y | Y | Y |
| 13 | Thornberry | Y | Y | Y | Y | Y |
| 14 | Paul | Y | N | Y | Y | Y |
| 15 | Hinojosa | Y | N | Y | Y | Y |
| 16 | Reyes | ? | N | Y | Y | Y |
| 17 | Edwards | Y | N | Y | Y | Y |
| 18 | Jackson-Lee | Y | N | N | Y | Y |
| 19 | Neugebauer | Y | Y | Y | Y | Y |
| 20 | Gonzalez | Y | N | Y | Y | Y |
| 21 | Smith | Y | Y | Y | Y | Y |
| 22 | DeLay | Y | Y | Y | Y | Y |
| 23 | Bonilla | Y | Y | Y | Y | Y |
| 24 | Marchant | Y | Y | Y | Y | Y |
| 25 | Doggett | Y | N | Y | Y | Y |
| 26 | Burgess | Y | Y | Y | Y | Y |
| 27 | Ortiz | Y | N | Y | Y | Y |
| 28 | Cuellar | Y | N | Y | Y | Y |
| 29 | Green, G. | Y | N | N | Y | Y |
| 30 | Johnson, E. | Y | N | Y | Y | ? |
| 31 | Carter | Y | Y | Y | Y | Y |
| 32 | Sessions | Y | Y | Y | Y | Y |
| **UTAH** | | | | | | |
| 1 | Bishop | Y | Y | N | Y | Y |
| 2 | Matheson | Y | N | Y | Y | Y |
| 3 | Cannon | Y | Y | Y | Y | Y |
| **VERMONT** | | | | | | |
| AL | *Sanders* | Y | N | N | Y | Y |
| **VIRGINIA** | | | | | | |
| 1 | Davis, J. | Y | Y | N | Y | Y |
| 2 | Drake | Y | Y | Y | Y | Y |
| 3 | Scott | Y | N | N | Y | ? |
| 4 | Forbes | Y | Y | Y | Y | Y |
| 5 | Goode | Y | Y | Y | Y | Y |
| 6 | Goodlatte | Y | Y | Y | Y | Y |
| 7 | Cantor | Y | Y | Y | Y | Y |
| 8 | Moran | Y | N | N | Y | Y |
| 9 | Boucher | Y | N | Y | Y | Y |
| 10 | Wolf | Y | Y | Y | Y | Y |
| 11 | Davis, T. | Y | Y | Y | Y | Y |
| **WASHINGTON** | | | | | | |
| 1 | Inslee | Y | N | Y | Y | Y |
| 2 | Larsen | Y | N | Y | Y | Y |
| 3 | Baird | Y | N | Y | Y | Y |
| 4 | Hastings | Y | ? | ? | ? | ? |
| 5 | McMorris | Y | Y | Y | Y | Y |
| 6 | Dicks | Y | N | Y | Y | Y |
| 7 | McDermott | Y | N | Y | Y | Y |
| 8 | Reichert | Y | Y | Y | Y | Y |
| 9 | Smith | Y | N | Y | Y | Y |
| **WEST VIRGINIA** | | | | | | |
| 1 | Mollohan | Y | N | N | Y | Y |
| 2 | Capito | ? | Y | Y | Y | Y |
| 3 | Rahall | Y | N | N | Y | Y |
| **WISCONSIN** | | | | | | |
| 1 | Ryan | Y | Y | Y | Y | Y |
| 2 | Baldwin | Y | N | N | Y | Y |
| 3 | Kind | Y | N | Y | Y | Y |
| 4 | Moore | Y | N | Y | Y | Y |
| 5 | Sensenbrenner | Y | Y | Y | Y | Y |
| 6 | Petri | Y | Y | Y | Y | Y |
| 7 | Obey | Y | N | Y | Y | Y |
| 8 | Green | Y | Y | Y | Y | Y |
| **WYOMING** | | | | | | |
| AL | Cubin | Y | Y | Y | Y | Y |

# IN THE HOUSE | By Vote Number

**619.** **HR 4297. Fiscal 2006 Tax Reconciliation/Democratic Substitute.** Rangel, D-N.Y., substitute amendment that would extend for one year many expiring provisions such as the deduction for state and local retail sales taxes, the deduction for college tuition expenses, tax incentives for the District of Columbia and Indian reservations, the 15-year depreciation period for leasehold and restaurant improvements, qualified zone academy bonds and the Brownfields cleanup tax incentive. The amendment would also eliminate all individual minimum tax liability for incomes below $200,000 in the case of joint returns and below $100,000 in all other cases for taxable year 2006. Rejected 192-239: R 2-226; D 189-13 (ND 141-10, SD 48-3); I 1-0. Dec. 8, 2005.

**620.** **HR 4297. Fiscal 2006 Tax Reconciliation/Recommit.** Rangel, D-N.Y., motion to recommit the bill to the Ways and Means Committee with instructions to strike language related to the capital gains and dividend tax breaks as well as add a new section to the bill dealing with tax relief for the alternative minimum tax. Motion rejected 193-235: R 0-226; D 192-9 (ND 145-5, SD 47-4); I 1-0. Dec. 8, 2005.

**621.** **HR 4297. Fiscal 2006 Tax Reconciliation/Passage.** Passage of bill that would provide $56.1 billion to extend a series of tax cuts set to expire between 2005 and 2010. It would extend for two years, through 2010, reduced tax rates on capital gains and dividends. It would extend, for two years, a tax provision that allows small businesses to write off more than $100,000 in capital investments in the year they are made. It would allow for a one-year extension of the college tuition deduction, the research and experimentation tax credit, and the state and local sales tax deduction in states without income taxes. Passed 234-197: R 225-3; D 9-193 (ND 1-150, SD 8-43); I 0-1. A "yea" is a vote in support of the president's position. Dec. 8, 2005.

**622.** **H Res 591. Ethics and the Medicare Drug Benefit Vote/Motion to Table.** Putnam, R-Fla., motion to table (kill) the Pelosi, D-Calif., privileged resolution that would denounce a "culture of corruption" by Republican leaders who have held open votes — particularly on the 2003 Medicare drug benefit bill — beyond a reasonable time "for the sole purpose of circumventing the will of the House." Motion agreed to 219-188: R 218-0; D 1-187 (ND 1-139, SD 0-48); I 0-1. Dec. 8, 2005.

\* Rep. John Campbell, R-Calif., was sworn in Dec. 7, 2005. The first vote for which he was eligible was vote 619.

ND Northern Democrats, SD Southern Democrats
Southern states: Ala., Ark., Fla., Ga., Ky., La., Miss., N.C., Okla., S.C., Tenn., Texas, Va.

| | 619 | 620 | 621 | 622 |
|---|---|---|---|---|
| **ALABAMA** | | | | |
| 1 Bonner | N | N | Y | Y |
| 2 Everett | N | N | Y | ? |
| 3 Rogers | N | N | Y | Y |
| 4 Aderholt | N | N | Y | Y |
| 5 Cramer | Y | N | Y | N |
| 6 Bachus | N | N | Y | Y |
| 7 Davis | Y | Y | N | N |
| **ALASKA** | | | | |
| AL Young | N | N | Y | Y |
| **ARIZONA** | | | | |
| 1 Renzi | N | N | Y | Y |
| 2 Franks | N | N | + | Y |
| 3 Shadegg | N | N | Y | Y |
| 4 Pastor | Y | Y | N | N |
| 5 Hayworth | N | N | Y | Y |
| 6 Flake | N | N | Y | Y |
| 7 Grijalva | Y | Y | N | N |
| 8 Kolbe | N | N | Y | Y |
| **ARKANSAS** | | | | |
| 1 Berry | Y | Y | N | N |
| 2 Snyder | Y | Y | N | N |
| 3 Boozman | N | ? | Y | Y |
| 4 Ross | Y | Y | N | N |
| **CALIFORNIA** | | | | |
| 1 Thompson | Y | Y | N | N |
| 2 Herger | N | N | Y | Y |
| 3 Lungren | N | N | Y | Y |
| 4 Doolittle | N | N | Y | Y |
| 5 Matsui, D. | Y | Y | N | N |
| 6 Woolsey | Y | Y | N | ? |
| 7 Miller, George | Y | Y | N | N |
| 8 Pelosi | Y | Y | N | N |
| 9 Lee | Y | Y | N | N |
| 10 Tauscher | Y | Y | N | N |
| 11 Pombo | N | N | Y | Y |
| 12 Lantos | Y | Y | N | N |
| 13 Stark | Y | Y | N | N |
| 14 Eshoo | Y | Y | N | N |
| 15 Honda | Y | Y | N | N |
| 16 Lofgren | Y | Y | N | N |
| 17 Farr | Y | Y | N | N |
| 18 Cardoza | Y | Y | N | N |
| 19 Radanovich | N | N | Y | Y |
| 20 Costa | Y | Y | N | N |
| 21 Nunes | N | N | Y | Y |
| 22 Thomas | N | N | Y | Y |
| 23 Capps | Y | Y | N | N |
| 24 Gallegly | N | N | Y | Y |
| 25 McKeon | N | N | Y | Y |
| 26 Dreier | N | N | Y | Y |
| 27 Sherman | Y | Y | N | N |
| 28 Berman | Y | Y | N | N |
| 29 Schiff | Y | Y | N | N |
| 30 Waxman | Y | Y | N | N |
| 31 Becerra | Y | Y | N | N |
| 32 Solis | Y | Y | N | N |
| 33 Watson | Y | Y | N | N |
| 34 Roybal-Allard | Y | Y | N | N |
| 35 Waters | Y | Y | N | ? |
| 36 Harman | Y | Y | N | N |
| 37 Millender-McD. | Y | Y | N | N |
| 38 Napolitano | Y | Y | N | N |
| 39 Sánchez, Linda | Y | Y | N | N |
| 40 Royce | N | N | Y | Y |
| 41 Lewis | N | N | Y | Y |
| 42 Miller, Gary | N | N | Y | Y |
| 43 Baca | Y | Y | N | N |
| 44 Calvert | N | N | Y | Y |
| 45 Bono | N | N | Y | Y |
| 46 Rohrabacher | N | N | Y | Y |
| 47 Sanchez, Loretta | Y | Y | N | N |
| 48 Campbell* | N | N | Y | Y |
| 49 Issa | N | N | Y | Y |

| | 619 | 620 | 621 | 622 |
|---|---|---|---|---|
| 50 Vacant | | | | |
| 51 Filner | Y | Y | N | N |
| 52 Hunter | N | N | Y | Y |
| 53 Davis | Y | Y | N | N |
| **COLORADO** | | | | |
| 1 DeGette | Y | Y | N | N |
| 2 Udall | Y | Y | N | N |
| 3 Salazar | Y | Y | N | N |
| 4 Musgrave | N | N | Y | Y |
| 5 Hefley | N | N | Y | Y |
| 6 Tancredo | N | N | Y | Y |
| 7 Beauprez | N | N | Y | Y |
| **CONNECTICUT** | | | | |
| 1 Larson | Y | Y | N | N |
| 2 Simmons | N | N | Y | Y |
| 3 DeLauro | Y | Y | N | N |
| 4 Shays | N | N | Y | Y |
| 5 Johnson | N | N | Y | Y |
| **DELAWARE** | | | | |
| AL Castle | N | N | Y | Y |
| **FLORIDA** | | | | |
| 1 Miller | N | N | Y | Y |
| 2 Boyd | Y | Y | N | ? |
| 3 Brown | Y | Y | N | N |
| 4 Crenshaw | N | N | Y | Y |
| 5 Brown-Waite | ? | ? | ? | ? |
| 6 Stearns | N | N | Y | Y |
| 7 Mica | N | N | Y | Y |
| 8 Keller | N | N | Y | Y |
| 9 Bilirakis | N | N | Y | Y |
| 10 Young | N | N | Y | Y |
| 11 Davis | Y | Y | N | N |
| 12 Putnam | N | N | Y | Y |
| 13 Harris | N | N | Y | Y |
| 14 Mack | N | N | Y | Y |
| 15 Weldon | N | N | Y | Y |
| 16 Foley | N | N | Y | Y |
| 17 Meek | Y | Y | N | N |
| 18 Ros-Lehtinen | N | N | Y | Y |
| 19 Wexler | Y | Y | N | N |
| 20 Wasserman-Schultz | Y | Y | N | N |
| 21 Diaz-Balart, L. | N | N | Y | Y |
| 22 Shaw | N | N | Y | Y |
| 23 Hastings | Y | Y | N | N |
| 24 Feeney | N | N | Y | Y |
| 25 Diaz-Balart, M. | N | N | Y | Y |
| **GEORGIA** | | | | |
| 1 Kingston | N | N | Y | Y |
| 2 Bishop | Y | Y | N | N |
| 3 Marshall | N | Y | Y | N |
| 4 McKinney | Y | Y | N | N |
| 5 Lewis | Y | Y | N | N |
| 6 Price | N | N | Y | Y |
| 7 Linder | N | N | Y | Y |
| 8 Westmoreland | N | N | Y | Y |
| 9 Norwood | N | N | Y | Y |
| 10 Deal | N | N | Y | Y |
| 11 Gingrey | N | N | Y | Y |
| 12 Barrow | N | Y | Y | N |
| 13 Scott | Y | Y | N | N |
| **HAWAII** | | | | |
| 1 Abercrombie | Y | Y | N | Y |
| 2 Case | Y | Y | N | N |
| **IDAHO** | | | | |
| 1 Otter | N | N | Y | Y |
| 2 Simpson | N | N | Y | Y |
| **ILLINOIS** | | | | |
| 1 Rush | Y | Y | N | N |
| 2 Jackson | Y | Y | N | N |
| 3 Lipinski | Y | Y | N | N |
| 4 Gutierrez | Y | Y | N | N |
| 5 Emanuel | Y | Y | N | N |
| 6 Hyde | N | N | Y | ? |
| 7 Davis | Y | Y | N | N |
| 8 Bean | N | N | Y | N |
| 9 Schakowsky | Y | Y | N | N |
| 10 Kirk | N | N | Y | Y |
| 11 Weller | N | N | Y | Y |
| 12 Costello | N | Y | N | N |

## KEY

| Republicans | Democrats | *Independents* |
|---|---|---|

| | | |
|---|---|---|
| **Y** Voted for (yea) | **X** Paired against | **C** Voted "present" to avoid possible conflict of interest |
| **#** Paired for | **−** Announced against | |
| **+** Announced for | **P** Voted "present" | **?** Did not vote or otherwise make a position known |
| **N** Voted against (nay) | | |

| | | 619 | 620 | 621 | 622 |
|---|---|---|---|---|---|
| 13 | Biggert | N | N | Y | Y |
| 14 | Hastert | | | Y | Y |
| 15 | Johnson | N | N | Y | Y |
| 16 | Manzullo | N | N | Y | Y |
| 17 | Evans | Y | Y | N | N |
| 18 | LaHood | N | N | Y | Y |
| 19 | Shimkus | N | N | Y | Y |
| **INDIANA** | | | | | |
| 1 | Visclosky | N | Y | N | N |
| 2 | Chocola | N | N | Y | ? |
| 3 | Souder | N | N | Y | Y |
| 4 | Buyer | N | N | Y | ? |
| 5 | Burton | N | N | Y | Y |
| 6 | Pence | N | N | Y | Y |
| 7 | Carson | Y | Y | N | N |
| 8 | Hostettler | N | N | Y | Y |
| 9 | Sodrel | N | N | Y | Y |
| **IOWA** | | | | | |
| 1 | Nussle | N | N | Y | Y |
| 2 | Leach | Y | N | N | Y |
| 3 | Boswell | Y | Y | N | N |
| 4 | Latham | N | N | Y | Y |
| 5 | King | N | N | Y | Y |
| **KANSAS** | | | | | |
| 1 | Moran | N | N | Y | Y |
| 2 | Ryun | N | N | Y | Y |
| 3 | Moore | Y | Y | N | N |
| 4 | Tiahrt | N | N | Y | Y |
| **KENTUCKY** | | | | | |
| 1 | Whitfield | N | N | Y | Y |
| 2 | Lewis | N | N | Y | Y |
| 3 | Northup | N | N | Y | Y |
| 4 | Davis | N | N | Y | Y |
| 5 | Rogers | N | N | Y | Y |
| 6 | Chandler | Y | Y | N | N |
| **LOUISIANA** | | | | | |
| 1 | Jindal | N | N | Y | Y |
| 2 | Jefferson | Y | Y | N | N |
| 3 | Melancon | Y | Y | N | N |
| 4 | McCrery | N | N | Y | Y |
| 5 | Alexander | N | N | Y | Y |
| 6 | Baker | N | N | Y | Y |
| 7 | Boustany | N | N | Y | Y |
| **MAINE** | | | | | |
| 1 | Allen | Y | Y | N | N |
| 2 | Michaud | Y | Y | N | N |
| **MARYLAND** | | | | | |
| 1 | Gilchrest | N | N | Y | Y |
| 2 | Ruppersberger | Y | Y | N | N |
| 3 | Cardin | Y | Y | N | N |
| 4 | Wynn | Y | Y | N | N |
| 5 | Hoyer | Y | Y | N | N |
| 6 | Bartlett | N | N | Y | Y |
| 7 | Cummings | Y | Y | N | N |
| 8 | Van Hollen | Y | Y | N | N |
| **MASSACHUSETTS** | | | | | |
| 1 | Olver | Y | Y | N | N |
| 2 | Neal | Y | Y | N | N |
| 3 | McGovern | Y | Y | N | N |
| 4 | Frank | Y | Y | N | N |
| 5 | Meehan | Y | Y | N | N |
| 6 | Tierney | Y | Y | N | N |
| 7 | Markey | Y | ? | N | N |
| 8 | Capuano | Y | Y | N | N |
| 9 | Lynch | Y | Y | N | N |
| 10 | Delahunt | Y | Y | N | N |
| **MICHIGAN** | | | | | |
| 1 | Stupak | Y | Y | N | N |
| 2 | Hoekstra | N | N | Y | Y |
| 3 | Ehlers | N | N | Y | Y |
| 4 | Camp | N | N | Y | Y |
| 5 | Kildee | Y | Y | N | N |
| 6 | Upton | N | N | N | Y |
| 7 | Schwarz | N | N | Y | Y |
| 8 | Rogers | N | N | Y | Y |
| 9 | Knollenberg | N | N | Y | Y |
| 10 | Miller | N | N | Y | Y |
| 11 | McCotter | N | N | Y | Y |
| 12 | Levin | Y | Y | N | N |
| 13 | Kilpatrick | Y | Y | N | N |
| 14 | Conyers | Y | Y | N | N |
| 15 | Dingell | Y | Y | N | N |

| | | 619 | 620 | 621 | 622 |
|---|---|---|---|---|---|
| **MINNESOTA** | | | | | |
| 1 | Gutknecht | N | N | Y | Y |
| 2 | Kline | N | N | Y | Y |
| 3 | Ramstad | N | N | Y | Y |
| 4 | McCollum | N | Y | N | N |
| 5 | Sabo | N | Y | N | N |
| 6 | Kennedy | N | N | Y | Y |
| 7 | Peterson | N | N | N | N |
| 8 | Oberstar | N | Y | N | N |
| **MISSISSIPPI** | | | | | |
| 1 | Wicker | N | N | Y | Y |
| 2 | Thompson | Y | Y | N | N |
| 3 | Pickering | N | N | Y | Y |
| 4 | Taylor | Y | N | N | N |
| **MISSOURI** | | | | | |
| 1 | Clay | Y | Y | N | N |
| 2 | Akin | N | N | Y | Y |
| 3 | Carnahan | Y | Y | N | N |
| 4 | Skelton | Y | Y | N | N |
| 5 | Cleaver | Y | Y | N | N |
| 6 | Graves | N | N | Y | Y |
| 7 | Blunt | N | N | Y | Y |
| 8 | Emerson | N | N | Y | Y |
| 9 | Hulshof | N | N | Y | Y |
| **MONTANA** | | | | | |
| AL | Rehberg | N | N | Y | Y |
| **NEBRASKA** | | | | | |
| 1 | Fortenberry | N | N | Y | Y |
| 2 | Terry | N | N | Y | Y |
| 3 | Osborne | N | N | Y | Y |
| **NEVADA** | | | | | |
| 1 | Berkley | Y | Y | N | N |
| 2 | Gibbons | N | N | Y | Y |
| 3 | Porter | N | N | Y | Y |
| **NEW HAMPSHIRE** | | | | | |
| 1 | Bradley | N | N | Y | Y |
| 2 | Bass | N | N | Y | Y |
| **NEW JERSEY** | | | | | |
| 1 | Andrews | Y | Y | N | N |
| 2 | LoBiondo | N | N | Y | Y |
| 3 | Saxton | N | N | Y | Y |
| 4 | Smith | N | ? | Y | Y |
| 5 | Garrett | N | N | Y | Y |
| 6 | Pallone | Y | Y | N | N |
| 7 | Ferguson | N | N | Y | Y |
| 8 | Pascrell | Y | Y | N | ? |
| 9 | Rothman | Y | Y | N | N |
| 10 | Payne | Y | Y | N | N |
| 11 | Frelinghuysen | N | N | Y | Y |
| 12 | Holt | Y | Y | N | N |
| 13 | Menendez | Y | Y | N | ? |
| **NEW MEXICO** | | | | | |
| 1 | Wilson | Y | N | Y | Y |
| 2 | Pearce | N | N | Y | Y |
| 3 | Udall | Y | Y | N | N |
| **NEW YORK** | | | | | |
| 1 | Bishop | Y | Y | N | N |
| 2 | Israel | Y | Y | N | N |
| 3 | King | N | N | Y | Y |
| 4 | McCarthy | Y | Y | N | N |
| 5 | Ackerman | Y | Y | N | N |
| 6 | Meeks | Y | Y | N | N |
| 7 | Crowley | Y | Y | N | N |
| 8 | Nadler | Y | Y | N | N |
| 9 | Weiner | Y | Y | N | N |
| 10 | Towns | Y | Y | N | N |
| 11 | Owens | Y | Y | N | N |
| 12 | Velázquez | Y | Y | N | N |
| 13 | Fossella | N | N | Y | Y |
| 14 | Maloney | Y | Y | N | N |
| 15 | Rangel | Y | Y | N | N |
| 16 | Serrano | Y | Y | N | N |
| 17 | Engel | Y | Y | N | N |
| 18 | Lowey | Y | Y | N | N |
| 19 | Kelly | N | N | Y | Y |
| 20 | Sweeney | N | N | Y | Y |
| 21 | McNulty | Y | Y | N | ? |
| 22 | Hinchey | Y | Y | N | N |
| 23 | McHugh | N | N | Y | Y |
| 24 | Boehlert | N | N | Y | Y |
| 25 | Walsh | N | N | Y | Y |
| 26 | Reynolds | N | N | Y | Y |
| 27 | Higgins | Y | Y | N | N |
| 28 | Slaughter | Y | Y | N | N |
| 29 | Kuhl | N | N | Y | Y |

| | | 619 | 620 | 621 | 622 |
|---|---|---|---|---|---|
| **NORTH CAROLINA** | | | | | |
| 1 | Butterfield | Y | Y | N | N |
| 2 | Etheridge | Y | Y | N | ? |
| 3 | Jones | N | N | Y | ? |
| 4 | Price | Y | Y | N | N |
| 5 | Foxx | N | N | Y | Y |
| 6 | Coble | N | N | Y | ? |
| 7 | McIntyre | Y | Y | N | N |
| 8 | Hayes | N | N | Y | ? |
| 9 | Myrick | N | N | Y | Y |
| 10 | McHenry | N | N | Y | Y |
| 11 | Taylor | N | N | Y | Y |
| 12 | Watt | Y | Y | N | N |
| 13 | Miller | Y | Y | N | N |
| **NORTH DAKOTA** | | | | | |
| AL | Pomeroy | Y | Y | N | N |
| **OHIO** | | | | | |
| 1 | Chabot | N | N | Y | Y |
| 2 | Schmidt | N | N | Y | Y |
| 3 | Turner | N | N | Y | Y |
| 4 | Oxley | N | N | Y | Y |
| 5 | Gillmor | N | N | Y | Y |
| 6 | Strickland | Y | Y | N | N |
| 7 | Hobson | N | N | Y | Y |
| 8 | Boehner | N | N | Y | Y |
| 9 | Kaptur | Y | Y | N | N |
| 10 | Kucinich | Y | Y | N | N |
| 11 | Jones | Y | Y | N | N |
| 12 | Tiberi | N | N | Y | Y |
| 13 | Brown | Y | Y | N | N |
| 14 | LaTourette | N | N | Y | Y |
| 15 | Pryce | N | N | Y | Y |
| 16 | Regula | N | N | Y | Y |
| 17 | Ryan | Y | Y | N | N |
| 18 | Ney | N | N | Y | Y |
| **OKLAHOMA** | | | | | |
| 1 | Sullivan | N | N | Y | ? |
| 2 | Boren | N | N | Y | N |
| 3 | Lucas | N | N | Y | Y |
| 4 | Cole | N | N | Y | Y |
| 5 | Istook | N | N | Y | Y |
| **OREGON** | | | | | |
| 1 | Wu | Y | Y | N | N |
| 2 | Walden | N | N | Y | ? |
| 3 | Blumenauer | Y | Y | N | ? |
| 4 | DeFazio | Y | Y | N | ? |
| 5 | Hooley | Y | Y | N | N |
| **PENNSYLVANIA** | | | | | |
| 1 | Brady | Y | Y | N | N |
| 2 | Fattah | Y | Y | N | N |
| 3 | English | N | N | Y | Y |
| 4 | Hart | N | N | Y | Y |
| 5 | Peterson | N | N | Y | ? |
| 6 | Gerlach | N | N | Y | Y |
| 7 | Weldon | N | N | Y | Y |
| 8 | Fitzpatrick | N | N | Y | Y |
| 9 | Shuster | N | N | Y | Y |
| 10 | Sherwood | N | N | Y | Y |
| 11 | Kanjorski | N | N | N | N |
| 12 | Murtha | Y | Y | N | N |
| 13 | Schwartz | Y | Y | N | N |
| 14 | Doyle | Y | Y | N | ? |
| 15 | Dent | N | N | Y | Y |
| 16 | Pitts | N | N | Y | Y |
| 17 | Holden | Y | Y | N | ? |
| 18 | Murphy | N | N | Y | Y |
| 19 | Platts | N | N | Y | Y |
| **RHODE ISLAND** | | | | | |
| 1 | Kennedy | Y | Y | N | N |
| 2 | Langevin | Y | Y | N | N |
| **SOUTH CAROLINA** | | | | | |
| 1 | Brown | N | N | Y | Y |
| 2 | Wilson | N | N | Y | Y |
| 3 | Barrett | N | N | Y | Y |
| 4 | Inglis | N | N | Y | Y |
| 5 | Spratt | Y | Y | N | N |
| 6 | Clyburn | Y | Y | N | N |
| **SOUTH DAKOTA** | | | | | |
| AL | Herseth | Y | Y | N | N |
| **TENNESSEE** | | | | | |
| 1 | Jenkins | N | N | Y | Y |
| 2 | Duncan | N | N | Y | Y |

| | | 619 | 620 | 621 | 622 |
|---|---|---|---|---|---|
| 3 | Wamp | N | N | Y | Y |
| 4 | Davis | Y | Y | Y | N |
| 5 | Cooper | Y | Y | N | N |
| 6 | Gordon | Y | Y | Y | N |
| 7 | Blackburn | N | N | Y | Y |
| 8 | Tanner | Y | Y | N | N |
| 9 | Ford | Y | Y | N | N |
| **TEXAS** | | | | | |
| 1 | Gohmert | N | N | Y | Y |
| 2 | Poe | N | N | Y | Y |
| 3 | Johnson, S. | N | N | Y | Y |
| 4 | Hall | N | N | Y | Y |
| 5 | Hensarling | N | N | Y | Y |
| 6 | Barton | N | N | Y | Y |
| 7 | Culberson | N | N | Y | Y |
| 8 | Brady | N | N | Y | Y |
| 9 | Green, A. | Y | Y | N | N |
| 10 | McCaul | N | N | Y | Y |
| 11 | Conaway | N | N | Y | Y |
| 12 | Granger | N | N | Y | Y |
| 13 | Thornberry | N | N | Y | Y |
| 14 | Paul | N | N | Y | ? |
| 15 | Hinojosa | Y | Y | N | N |
| 16 | Reyes | Y | Y | N | N |
| 17 | Edwards | Y | Y | N | N |
| 18 | Jackson-Lee | Y | Y | N | N |
| 19 | Neugebauer | N | N | Y | Y |
| 20 | Gonzalez | Y | Y | N | N |
| 21 | Smith | N | N | Y | Y |
| 22 | DeLay | N | N | Y | Y |
| 23 | Bonilla | N | N | Y | Y |
| 24 | Marchant | N | N | Y | Y |
| 25 | Doggett | Y | Y | N | N |
| 26 | Burgess | N | N | Y | Y |
| 27 | Ortiz | Y | Y | N | N |
| 28 | Cuellar | Y | Y | N | N |
| 29 | Green, G. | Y | Y | N | ? |
| 30 | Johnson, E. | Y | Y | N | N |
| 31 | Carter | N | N | Y | Y |
| 32 | Sessions | N | N | Y | Y |
| **UTAH** | | | | | |
| 1 | Bishop | N | N | Y | Y |
| 2 | Matheson | N | N | N | N |
| 3 | Cannon | N | N | Y | Y |
| **VERMONT** | | | | | |
| AL | *Sanders* | Y | Y | N | N |
| **VIRGINIA** | | | | | |
| 1 | Davis, J. | N | N | Y | Y |
| 2 | Drake | N | N | Y | Y |
| 3 | Scott | Y | Y | N | N |
| 4 | Forbes | N | N | Y | Y |
| 5 | Goode | N | N | Y | Y |
| 6 | Goodlatte | N | N | Y | Y |
| 7 | Cantor | N | N | Y | Y |
| 8 | Moran | Y | Y | N | N |
| 9 | Boucher | Y | Y | N | N |
| 10 | Wolf | N | N | Y | Y |
| 11 | Davis, T. | N | N | Y | Y |
| **WASHINGTON** | | | | | |
| 1 | Inslee | Y | Y | N | N |
| 2 | Larsen | Y | Y | N | N |
| 3 | Baird | Y | Y | N | N |
| 4 | Hastings | ? | ? | ? | ? |
| 5 | McMorris | N | N | Y | Y |
| 6 | Dicks | Y | Y | N | N |
| 7 | McDermott | Y | Y | N | ? |
| 8 | Reichert | N | N | Y | Y |
| 9 | Smith | Y | Y | N | N |
| **WEST VIRGINIA** | | | | | |
| 1 | Mollohan | Y | Y | N | N |
| 2 | Capito | N | N | Y | Y |
| 3 | Rahall | Y | Y | N | N |
| **WISCONSIN** | | | | | |
| 1 | Ryan | N | N | Y | Y |
| 2 | Baldwin | Y | Y | N | N |
| 3 | Kind | Y | Y | N | ? |
| 4 | Moore | Y | Y | N | N |
| 5 | Sensenbrenner | N | N | Y | Y |
| 6 | Petri | N | N | Y | Y |
| 7 | Obey | Y | Y | N | N |
| 8 | Green | N | N | Y | Y |
| **WYOMING** | | | | | |
| AL | Cubin | N | N | Y | Y |

# IN THE HOUSE | By Vote Number

**623.** **H Res 487. Korean-American Day/Adoption.** Cannon, R-Utah, motion to suspend the rules and adopt the resolution that would support the goals and ideals of Korean-American Day and urge all Americans to observe the day in appreciation of the contributions that Korean-Americans have made to the United States. Motion agreed to 405-0: R 215-0; D 189-0 (ND 142-0, SD 47-0); I 1-0. A two-thirds majority of those present and voting (270 in this case) is required for adoption under suspension of the rules. Dec. 13, 2005.

**624.** **S 1047. Presidential Coin/Passage.** Oxley, R-Ohio, motion to suspend the rules and pass the bill that would authorize the U.S. Mint to issue a redesigned $1 coin to commemorate U.S. presidents, a series of $10 gold bullion coins to honor first ladies and a new $50 gold bullion coin. It also would authorize the redesign of the penny in 2009 to commemorate the 200th anniversary of President Abraham Lincoln's birth. Motion agreed to 291-113: R 103-111; D 187-2 (ND 141-1, SD 46-1); I 1-0. A two-thirds majority of those present and voting (270 in this case) is required for passage under suspension of the rules. Dec. 13, 2005.

**625.** **HR 3422. Small Public Housing Authority/Passage.** Oxley, R-Ohio, motion to suspend the rules and pass the bill that would exempt qualified small public housing authorities from the requirement of preparing an annual housing agency plan. Motion agreed to 387-2: R 203-2; D 183-0 (ND 137-0, SD 46-0); I 1-0. A two-thirds majority of those present and voting (260 in this case) is required for passage under suspension of the rules. Dec. 13, 2005.

**626.** **HR 3199. "Patriot Act" Reauthorization/Recommit.** Conyers, D-Mich., motion to recommit the bill to the Judiciary Committee with instructions to replace the text of the conference report on the bill with the Senate-passed version of the bill. Motion rejected 202-224: R 5-221; D 196-3 (ND 146-2, SD 50-1); I 1-0. Dec. 14, 2005.

**627.** **HR 3199. "Patriot Act" Reauthorization/Conference Report.** Adoption of the conference report on the bill that would make permanent 14 of the 16 provisions of the anti-terrorism law known as the Patriot Act set to expire at the end of the year, and extend for four years two provisions on access to business and other records and "roving" wiretaps. The measure would allow recipients of "national security letters" demanding information to consult with lawyers and to challenge the letters in court. Adopted (thus sent to the Senate) 251-174: R 207-18; D 44-155 (ND 22-127, SD 22-28); I 0-1. A "yea" is a vote in support of the president's position. Dec. 14, 2005.

**628.** **HR 3010. Fiscal 2006 Labor-HHS-Education Appropriations/Conference Report.** Adoption of the conference report on the bill that would appropriate $601.6 billion, including $142.5 billion in discretionary spending, for the Labor, Health and Human Services, and Education departments and related agencies in fiscal 2006. It would provide $63.5 billion for the Education Department, $14.8 billion for the Labor Department and $474.1 billion for Health and Human Services, including $28.6 billion for the National Institutes of Health. Adopted (thus sent to the Senate) 215-213: R 215-12; D 0-200 (ND 0-149, SD 0-51); I 0-1. Dec. 14, 2005.

**629.** **HR 2863. Fiscal 2006 Defense Appropriations/Motion to Close Conference.** Young, R-Fla., motion to close portions of the conference on the bill that would appropriate funding for Defense programs for fiscal 2006. Motion agreed to 415-9: R 225-0; D 189-9 (ND 141-8, SD 48-1); I 1-0. Dec. 14, 2005.

| | 623 | 624 | 625 | 626 | 627 | 628 | 629 |
|---|---|---|---|---|---|---|---|
| **ALABAMA** | | | | | | | |
| 1 Bonner | ? | ? | ? | N | Y | Y | Y |
| 2 Everett | ? | ? | ? | N | Y | Y | Y |
| 3 Rogers | Y | Y | N | Y | Y | Y | Y |
| 4 Aderholt | Y | Y | Y | N | Y | Y | Y |
| 5 Cramer | Y | Y | Y | Y | N | Y | Y |
| 6 Bachus | ? | ? | ? | N | Y | Y | Y |
| 7 Davis | Y | Y | Y | Y | Y | N | Y |
| **ALASKA** | | | | | | | |
| AL Young | Y | N | Y | N | N | Y | Y |
| **ARIZONA** | | | | | | | |
| 1 Renzi | Y | Y | Y | N | Y | N | Y |
| 2 Franks | Y | N | Y | N | Y | Y | Y |
| 3 Shadegg | Y | N | Y | N | Y | Y | Y |
| 4 Pastor | Y | Y | Y | Y | N | N | Y |
| 5 Hayworth | ? | ? | ? | N | Y | Y | Y |
| 6 Flake | Y | N | Y | N | Y | Y | Y |
| 7 Grijalva | Y | Y | Y | Y | N | N | Y |
| 8 Kolbe | Y | N | Y | N | Y | Y | Y |
| **ARKANSAS** | | | | | | | |
| 1 Berry | Y | Y | Y | Y | N | N | Y |
| 2 Snyder | Y | Y | Y | Y | N | N | Y |
| 3 Boozman | Y | N | Y | N | Y | Y | Y |
| 4 Ross | Y | Y | Y | Y | Y | N | Y |
| **CALIFORNIA** | | | | | | | |
| 1 Thompson | Y | Y | Y | Y | N | N | Y |
| 2 Herger | Y | N | Y | N | Y | Y | Y |
| 3 Lungren | Y | N | Y | N | Y | Y | Y |
| 4 Doolittle | Y | N | Y | N | Y | Y | Y |
| 5 Matsui, D. | Y | Y | Y | Y | N | N | Y |
| 6 Woolsey | Y | Y | Y | Y | N | N | N |
| 7 Miller, George | Y | Y | Y | Y | N | N | Y |
| 8 Pelosi | Y | Y | Y | Y | N | N | Y |
| 9 Lee | Y | Y | Y | Y | N | N | Y |
| 10 Tauscher | Y | Y | Y | Y | N | N | Y |
| 11 Pombo | Y | Y | Y | N | Y | Y | Y |
| 12 Lantos | Y | Y | Y | Y | N | N | Y |
| 13 Stark | Y | Y | Y | Y | N | N | N |
| 14 Eshoo | Y | Y | Y | Y | N | N | Y |
| 15 Honda | Y | Y | Y | Y | N | N | Y |
| 16 Lofgren | Y | Y | Y | Y | N | N | Y |
| 17 Farr | Y | Y | Y | Y | N | N | Y |
| 18 Cardoza | Y | Y | Y | Y | N | N | Y |
| 19 Radanovich | Y | Y | Y | N | ? | Y | Y |
| 20 Costa | Y | Y | Y | Y | Y | N | + |
| 21 Nunes | Y | Y | Y | N | Y | Y | Y |
| 22 Thomas | Y | Y | N | Y | Y | Y | Y |
| 23 Capps | Y | Y | Y | Y | N | N | Y |
| 24 Gallegly | + | + | + | N | Y | Y | Y |
| 25 McKeon | Y | Y | Y | N | Y | Y | Y |
| 26 Dreier | Y | Y | N | Y | Y | Y | Y |
| 27 Sherman | Y | Y | Y | Y | N | N | Y |
| 28 Berman | Y | Y | Y | Y | N | N | Y |
| 29 Schiff | Y | Y | Y | Y | Y | N | Y |
| 30 Waxman | Y | Y | Y | Y | N | N | Y |
| 31 Becerra | Y | Y | Y | Y | N | N | Y |
| 32 Solis | Y | Y | ? | Y | N | N | Y |
| 33 Watson | Y | Y | Y | Y | N | N | Y |
| 34 Roybal-Allard | Y | Y | Y | Y | N | N | Y |
| 35 Waters | Y | Y | ? | Y | N | N | Y |
| 36 Harman | Y | Y | Y | Y | N | N | Y |
| 37 Millender-McD. | Y | Y | Y | Y | N | N | Y |
| 38 Napolitano | Y | Y | Y | Y | N | N | Y |
| 39 Sánchez, Linda | Y | Y | ? | Y | N | N | Y |
| 40 Royce | Y | N | Y | N | Y | Y | Y |
| 41 Lewis | Y | Y | ? | N | Y | Y | Y |
| 42 Miller, Gary | Y | N | Y | N | Y | Y | Y |
| 43 Baca | Y | Y | Y | Y | N | N | Y |
| 44 Calvert | ? | ? | ? | N | Y | Y | Y |
| 45 Bono | Y | N | Y | N | Y | Y | Y |
| 46 Rohrabacher | Y | Y | Y | N | Y | Y | Y |
| 47 Sanchez, Loretta | Y | Y | Y | Y | N | N | Y |
| 48 Campbell | Y | N | Y | N | Y | Y | Y |
| 49 Issa | Y | Y | Y | N | Y | Y | Y |

| | 623 | 624 | 625 | 626 | 627 | 628 | 629 |
|---|---|---|---|---|---|---|---|
| 50 Vacant | | | | | | | |
| 51 Filner | Y | Y | Y | Y | N | N | Y |
| 52 Hunter | Y | N | Y | N | Y | Y | Y |
| 53 Davis | Y | Y | Y | Y | N | N | Y |
| **COLORADO** | | | | | | | |
| 1 DeGette | ? | ? | ? | ? | ? | ? | Y |
| 2 Udall | + | + | + | Y | N | N | Y |
| 3 Salazar | Y | Y | Y | Y | N | N | Y |
| 4 Musgrave | Y | N | Y | N | Y | Y | Y |
| 5 Hefley | Y | N | Y | N | Y | Y | Y |
| 6 Tancredo | Y | Y | Y | N | Y | Y | Y |
| 7 Beauprez | Y | N | Y | N | Y | Y | Y |
| **CONNECTICUT** | | | | | | | |
| 1 Larson | Y | Y | Y | Y | N | N | Y |
| 2 Simmons | Y | Y | Y | N | Y | N | Y |
| 3 DeLauro | Y | Y | Y | Y | N | N | Y |
| 4 Shays | Y | Y | Y | Y | Y | N | Y |
| 5 Johnson | Y | Y | ? | N | Y | N | Y |
| **DELAWARE** | | | | | | | |
| AL Castle | Y | Y | Y | N | Y | N | Y |
| **FLORIDA** | | | | | | | |
| 1 Miller | Y | N | N | N | Y | Y | Y |
| 2 Boyd | Y | Y | Y | Y | N | N | Y |
| 3 Brown | ? | ? | ? | Y | N | N | Y |
| 4 Crenshaw | Y | Y | Y | N | Y | Y | Y |
| 5 Brown-Waite | Y | N | Y | N | Y | Y | Y |
| 6 Stearns | Y | N | Y | N | Y | Y | Y |
| 7 Mica | Y | Y | Y | N | Y | Y | Y |
| 8 Keller | Y | Y | Y | N | Y | Y | Y |
| 9 Bilirakis | Y | N | Y | N | Y | Y | Y |
| 10 Young | Y | N | Y | N | Y | Y | Y |
| 11 Davis | ? | ? | ? | Y | Y | N | Y |
| 12 Putnam | Y | Y | N | N | Y | Y | Y |
| 13 Harris | ? | ? | ? | N | Y | Y | Y |
| 14 Mack | Y | N | Y | N | Y | Y | Y |
| 15 Weldon | Y | N | Y | N | Y | Y | Y |
| 16 Foley | Y | Y | Y | N | Y | Y | Y |
| 17 Meek | Y | Y | Y | Y | N | N | Y |
| 18 Ros-Lehtinen | ? | ? | ? | ? | ? | ? | ? |
| 19 Wexler | Y | Y | Y | Y | N | N | Y |
| 20 Wasserman-Schultz | Y | Y | Y | Y | N | N | Y |
| 21 Diaz-Balart, L. | Y | Y | N | Y | Y | Y | Y |
| 22 Shaw | Y | Y | ? | N | Y | Y | Y |
| 23 Hastings | Y | Y | Y | Y | N | N | Y |
| 24 Feeney | Y | N | Y | N | Y | ? | Y |
| 25 Diaz-Balart, M. | + | – | + | – | + | + | + |
| **GEORGIA** | | | | | | | |
| 1 Kingston | Y | N | Y | N | Y | Y | Y |
| 2 Bishop | Y | Y | Y | Y | Y | N | Y |
| 3 Marshall | Y | Y | Y | Y | N | N | Y |
| 4 McKinney | Y | Y | Y | N | N | N | N |
| 5 Lewis | Y | Y | Y | Y | N | N | Y |
| 6 Price | Y | N | ? | N | Y | Y | Y |
| 7 Linder | Y | Y | Y | N | Y | Y | Y |
| 8 Westmoreland | Y | N | Y | N | Y | Y | ? |
| 9 Norwood | Y | N | Y | N | Y | Y | Y |
| 10 Deal | Y | Y | ? | N | Y | Y | Y |
| 11 Gingrey | Y | N | Y | N | Y | Y | Y |
| 12 Barrow | Y | Y | Y | Y | N | N | Y |
| 13 Scott | Y | Y | Y | Y | Y | N | Y |
| **HAWAII** | | | | | | | |
| 1 Abercrombie | Y | Y | Y | Y | N | N | ? |
| 2 Case | Y | Y | Y | Y | N | N | Y |
| **IDAHO** | | | | | | | |
| 1 Otter | Y | N | Y | Y | N | Y | Y |
| 2 Simpson | Y | Y | Y | N | Y | Y | ? |
| **ILLINOIS** | | | | | | | |
| 1 Rush | Y | Y | Y | Y | N | N | Y |
| 2 Jackson | Y | Y | Y | Y | N | N | Y |
| 3 Lipinski | Y | Y | Y | Y | Y | N | Y |
| 4 Gutierrez | Y | Y | Y | Y | N | N | Y |
| 5 Emanuel | Y | Y | Y | Y | N | N | Y |
| 6 Hyde | + | – | + | – | + | + | + |
| 7 Davis | Y | Y | Y | Y | N | N | Y |
| 8 Bean | Y | Y | Y | Y | N | N | Y |
| 9 Schakowsky | Y | Y | Y | Y | N | N | Y |
| 10 Kirk | Y | Y | Y | N | Y | Y | Y |
| 11 Weller | Y | Y | Y | N | Y | Y | Y |
| 12 Costello | ? | ? | ? | Y | N | N | Y |

**KEY**    Republicans    Democrats    *Independents*

| | | | |
|---|---|---|---|
| **Y** Voted for (yea) | **X** Paired against | **C** Voted "present" to avoid possible conflict of interest |
| **#** Paired for | **–** Announced against | |
| **+** Announced for | **P** Voted "present" | **?** Did not vote or otherwise make a position known |
| **N** Voted against (nay) | | |

ND Northern Democrats, SD Southern Democrats
Southern states: Ala., Ark., Fla., Ga., Ky., La., Miss., N.C., Okla., S.C., Tenn., Texas, Va.

| | 623 | 624 | 625 | 626 | 627 | 628 | 629 |
|---|---|---|---|---|---|---|---|
| 13 **Biggert** | Y | Y | Y | N | Y | Y | Y |
| 14 **Hastert** | | | | | Y | Y | |
| 15 **Johnson** | Y | N | Y | Y | N | Y | Y |
| 16 **Manzullo** | Y | Y | Y | N | N | Y | Y |
| 17 Evans | Y | Y | Y | Y | N | N | Y |
| 18 **LaHood** | Y | Y | Y | N | Y | Y | Y |
| 19 **Shimkus** | Y | Y | Y | N | Y | Y | Y |
| **INDIANA** | | | | | | | |
| 1 Visclosky | Y | Y | Y | Y | N | N | Y |
| 2 **Chocola** | Y | N | Y | N | Y | Y | Y |
| 3 **Souder** | Y | N | Y | N | Y | Y | Y |
| 4 **Buyer** | Y | N | Y | N | Y | Y | Y |
| 5 **Burton** | Y | N | Y | N | Y | Y | Y |
| 6 **Pence** | Y | N | Y | N | Y | Y | Y |
| 7 Carson | Y | Y | Y | Y | N | N | Y |
| 8 **Hostettler** | Y | Y | Y | N | Y | Y | Y |
| 9 **Sodrel** | Y | N | Y | N | Y | Y | Y |
| **IOWA** | | | | | | | |
| 1 **Nussle** | Y | Y | Y | N | Y | Y | Y |
| 2 **Leach** | Y | Y | Y | Y | Y | Y | Y |
| 3 Boswell | Y | Y | Y | Y | Y | N | Y |
| 4 **Latham** | Y | Y | Y | N | Y | Y | Y |
| 5 **King** | Y | N | Y | N | Y | Y | Y |
| **KANSAS** | | | | | | | |
| 1 **Moran** | Y | Y | Y | N | Y | Y | Y |
| 2 **Ryun** | Y | N | Y | N | Y | Y | Y |
| 3 Moore | Y | Y | Y | Y | Y | N | Y |
| 4 **Tiahrt** | Y | N | Y | N | Y | Y | Y |
| **KENTUCKY** | | | | | | | |
| 1 **Whitfield** | Y | N | Y | N | Y | Y | Y |
| 2 **Lewis** | Y | N | Y | N | Y | Y | Y |
| 3 **Northup** | Y | Y | Y | N | Y | Y | Y |
| 4 **Davis** | Y | N | Y | N | Y | Y | Y |
| 5 **Rogers** | Y | Y | Y | N | Y | Y | Y |
| 6 Chandler | Y | Y | Y | Y | Y | N | Y |
| **LOUISIANA** | | | | | | | |
| 1 **Jindal** | Y | N | Y | N | Y | Y | Y |
| 2 Jefferson | Y | Y | ? | Y | N | N | Y |
| 3 Melancon | Y | Y | Y | Y | Y | N | Y |
| 4 **McCrery** | Y | N | Y | N | Y | Y | Y |
| 5 **Alexander** | Y | N | Y | N | Y | Y | Y |
| 6 **Baker** | Y | Y | Y | N | Y | Y | Y |
| 7 **Boustany** | Y | Y | Y | N | Y | Y | Y |
| **MAINE** | | | | | | | |
| 1 Allen | Y | Y | Y | Y | N | N | Y |
| 2 Michaud | Y | Y | Y | Y | N | N | Y |
| **MARYLAND** | | | | | | | |
| 1 **Gilchrest** | Y | Y | Y | N | Y | Y | Y |
| 2 Ruppersberger | Y | Y | Y | Y | Y | N | Y |
| 3 Cardin | Y | Y | Y | Y | Y | N | Y |
| 4 Wynn | ? | ? | ? | Y | N | N | Y |
| 5 Hoyer | Y | Y | Y | Y | Y | N | Y |
| 6 **Bartlett** | Y | N | Y | N | N | Y | Y |
| 7 Cummings | Y | Y | Y | Y | N | N | Y |
| 8 Van Hollen | Y | Y | Y | Y | N | N | Y |
| **MASSACHUSETTS** | | | | | | | |
| 1 Olver | Y | Y | Y | Y | N | N | N |
| 2 Neal | Y | Y | Y | Y | N | N | Y |
| 3 McGovern | Y | Y | Y | Y | N | N | Y |
| 4 Frank | Y | Y | Y | Y | N | N | Y |
| 5 Meehan | Y | Y | Y | Y | N | N | Y |
| 6 Tierney | Y | Y | Y | Y | N | N | Y |
| 7 Markey | Y | Y | Y | Y | N | N | Y |
| 8 Capuano | Y | Y | Y | Y | N | N | Y |
| 9 Lynch | Y | Y | Y | Y | N | N | Y |
| 10 Delahunt | Y | Y | Y | Y | N | N | Y |
| **MICHIGAN** | | | | | | | |
| 1 Stupak | Y | Y | Y | Y | N | N | Y |
| 2 **Hoekstra** | Y | Y | Y | N | Y | Y | Y |
| 3 **Ehlers** | Y | Y | Y | N | N | Y | Y |
| 4 **Camp** | Y | N | Y | N | Y | Y | Y |
| 5 Kildee | Y | Y | Y | Y | N | N | Y |
| 6 **Upton** | Y | N | Y | N | Y | Y | Y |
| 7 **Schwarz** | Y | Y | Y | N | Y | Y | Y |
| 8 **Rogers** | Y | Y | Y | N | Y | Y | Y |
| 9 **Knollenberg** | Y | Y | ? | N | Y | Y | Y |
| 10 **Miller** | Y | N | Y | N | Y | Y | Y |
| 11 **McCotter** | Y | N | Y | N | Y | Y | Y |
| 12 Levin | Y | Y | Y | Y | N | N | Y |
| 13 Kilpatrick | Y | Y | Y | Y | N | N | Y |
| 14 Conyers | Y | Y | Y | Y | N | N | Y |
| 15 Dingell | Y | Y | Y | Y | N | N | Y |
| **MINNESOTA** | | | | | | | |
| 1 **Gutknecht** | Y | Y | Y | N | Y | Y | Y |
| 2 **Kline** | Y | N | Y | N | Y | Y | Y |
| 3 **Ramstad** | Y | Y | Y | N | Y | N | Y |
| 4 McCollum | Y | Y | Y | Y | N | N | Y |
| 5 Sabo | ? | ? | ? | Y | N | N | Y |
| 6 **Kennedy** | Y | N | Y | N | Y | Y | Y |
| 7 Peterson | Y | Y | Y | Y | N | N | Y |
| 8 Oberstar | Y | Y | Y | Y | N | N | Y |
| **MISSISSIPPI** | | | | | | | |
| 1 **Wicker** | Y | N | Y | N | Y | Y | Y |
| 2 Thompson | Y | Y | Y | Y | N | N | Y |
| 3 **Pickering** | Y | Y | Y | N | Y | Y | Y |
| 4 Taylor | Y | Y | Y | Y | Y | N | Y |
| **MISSOURI** | | | | | | | |
| 1 Clay | Y | Y | Y | Y | N | N | Y |
| 2 **Akin** | Y | N | Y | N | Y | Y | Y |
| 3 Carnahan | Y | Y | Y | Y | Y | N | Y |
| 4 Skelton | Y | Y | Y | Y | Y | N | Y |
| 5 Cleaver | Y | Y | Y | Y | N | N | Y |
| 6 **Graves** | Y | Y | Y | N | Y | Y | Y |
| 7 **Blunt** | Y | N | Y | N | Y | Y | Y |
| 8 **Emerson** | Y | Y | Y | N | Y | Y | Y |
| 9 **Hulshof** | Y | Y | Y | N | Y | Y | Y |
| **MONTANA** | | | | | | | |
| AL **Rehberg** | ? | Y | Y | N | Y | Y | Y |
| **NEBRASKA** | | | | | | | |
| 1 **Fortenberry** | + | + | Y | N | Y | Y | Y |
| 2 **Terry** | Y | N | Y | N | Y | Y | Y |
| 3 **Osborne** | Y | Y | Y | N | Y | Y | Y |
| **NEVADA** | | | | | | | |
| 1 Berkley | Y | Y | Y | Y | N | N | Y |
| 2 **Gibbons** | Y | Y | Y | N | Y | N | Y |
| 3 **Porter** | Y | Y | Y | N | Y | Y | Y |
| **NEW HAMPSHIRE** | | | | | | | |
| 1 **Bradley** | Y | Y | Y | N | Y | Y | Y |
| 2 **Bass** | Y | Y | Y | N | Y | Y | Y |
| **NEW JERSEY** | | | | | | | |
| 1 Andrews | Y | Y | Y | Y | Y | N | Y |
| 2 **LoBiondo** | Y | N | Y | N | Y | Y | Y |
| 3 **Saxton** | Y | N | Y | N | Y | Y | Y |
| 4 **Smith** | Y | Y | Y | N | Y | Y | Y |
| 5 **Garrett** | Y | N | Y | N | Y | Y | Y |
| 6 Pallone | Y | Y | Y | Y | N | N | Y |
| 7 **Ferguson** | Y | Y | Y | N | Y | Y | Y |
| 8 Pascrell | Y | Y | Y | Y | N | N | Y |
| 9 Rothman | Y | Y | Y | Y | Y | N | Y |
| 10 Payne | Y | Y | Y | ? | N | N | Y |
| 11 **Frelinghuysen** | Y | Y | Y | N | Y | Y | Y |
| 12 Holt | Y | Y | Y | Y | N | N | Y |
| 13 Menendez | Y | Y | Y | Y | N | N | Y |
| **NEW MEXICO** | | | | | | | |
| 1 **Wilson** | Y | Y | Y | N | Y | N | Y |
| 2 **Pearce** | Y | Y | Y | N | Y | Y | Y |
| 3 Udall | Y | Y | Y | Y | N | N | Y |
| **NEW YORK** | | | | | | | |
| 1 Bishop | Y | Y | Y | Y | N | N | Y |
| 2 Israel | Y | Y | Y | Y | N | N | Y |
| 3 **King** | Y | Y | Y | N | Y | Y | Y |
| 4 McCarthy | Y | Y | ? | Y | Y | N | Y |
| 5 Ackerman | Y | Y | Y | Y | N | N | Y |
| 6 Meeks | Y | Y | Y | Y | N | N | Y |
| 7 Crowley | Y | Y | Y | Y | N | N | Y |
| 8 Nadler | Y | Y | Y | Y | N | N | Y |
| 9 Weiner | ? | ? | ? | Y | N | N | Y |
| 10 Towns | Y | Y | Y | Y | N | N | Y |
| 11 Owens | Y | Y | Y | Y | N | N | Y |
| 12 Velázquez | Y | Y | Y | Y | N | N | Y |
| 13 **Fossella** | Y | Y | Y | N | Y | Y | Y |
| 14 Maloney | Y | Y | Y | Y | N | N | Y |
| 15 Rangel | Y | Y | ? | Y | N | N | Y |
| 16 Serrano | Y | Y | Y | N | N | N | Y |
| 17 Engel | Y | Y | Y | Y | N | N | Y |
| 18 Lowey | Y | Y | Y | Y | N | N | Y |
| 19 **Kelly** | Y | Y | Y | N | Y | Y | Y |
| 20 **Sweeney** | Y | N | Y | N | N | Y | Y |
| 21 McNulty | Y | Y | Y | Y | N | N | Y |
| 22 Hinchey | ? | ? | Y | Y | N | N | N |
| 23 **McHugh** | Y | Y | Y | N | Y | Y | Y |
| 24 **Boehlert** | Y | Y | Y | N | Y | Y | Y |
| 25 **Walsh** | Y | Y | Y | N | Y | Y | Y |
| 26 **Reynolds** | ? | ? | ? | N | Y | Y | Y |
| 27 Higgins | Y | Y | Y | Y | Y | N | Y |
| 28 Slaughter | Y | Y | Y | Y | N | N | Y |
| 29 **Kuhl** | Y | N | Y | N | Y | Y | Y |
| **NORTH CAROLINA** | | | | | | | |
| 1 Butterfield | Y | Y | Y | Y | N | N | Y |
| 2 Etheridge | Y | Y | Y | Y | Y | N | Y |
| 3 **Jones** | Y | N | Y | N | N | N | Y |
| 4 Price | Y | Y | Y | Y | N | N | Y |
| 5 **Foxx** | Y | N | N | N | Y | Y | Y |
| 6 **Coble** | Y | N | ? | N | Y | Y | Y |
| 7 McIntyre | Y | Y | Y | Y | Y | N | Y |
| 8 **Hayes** | Y | N | Y | N | Y | Y | Y |
| 9 **Myrick** | Y | N | Y | N | Y | Y | Y |
| 10 **McHenry** | Y | N | Y | N | Y | Y | Y |
| 11 **Taylor** | Y | N | Y | N | N | Y | Y |
| 12 Watt | Y | Y | Y | Y | N | N | ? |
| 13 Miller | Y | Y | Y | Y | Y | N | Y |
| **NORTH DAKOTA** | | | | | | | |
| AL Pomeroy | Y | Y | Y | Y | Y | N | Y |
| **OHIO** | | | | | | | |
| 1 **Chabot** | Y | N | Y | N | Y | Y | Y |
| 2 **Schmidt** | Y | N | Y | N | Y | Y | Y |
| 3 **Turner** | Y | N | Y | N | Y | Y | Y |
| 4 **Oxley** | Y | Y | ? | N | Y | Y | Y |
| 5 **Gillmor** | Y | Y | Y | N | Y | Y | Y |
| 6 Strickland | Y | N | Y | Y | N | N | Y |
| 7 **Hobson** | Y | Y | Y | N | Y | Y | Y |
| 8 **Boehner** | Y | Y | Y | N | Y | Y | Y |
| 9 Kaptur | Y | Y | Y | Y | N | N | Y |
| 10 Kucinich | Y | Y | Y | Y | N | N | N |
| 11 Jones | Y | Y | Y | Y | N | N | Y |
| 12 **Tiberi** | Y | N | Y | N | Y | Y | Y |
| 13 Brown | Y | Y | Y | Y | N | N | Y |
| 14 **LaTourette** | Y | Y | Y | N | Y | Y | Y |
| 15 **Pryce** | Y | Y | Y | N | Y | Y | Y |
| 16 **Regula** | Y | Y | Y | N | Y | Y | Y |
| 17 Ryan | Y | Y | Y | Y | N | N | Y |
| 18 **Ney** | Y | Y | Y | N | N | Y | Y |
| **OKLAHOMA** | | | | | | | |
| 1 **Sullivan** | Y | N | Y | N | Y | Y | Y |
| 2 Boren | Y | Y | Y | Y | Y | N | Y |
| 3 **Lucas** | Y | Y | Y | N | N | Y | Y |
| 4 **Cole** | Y | ? | Y | N | Y | Y | Y |
| 5 **Istook** | Y | N | Y | N | Y | Y | Y |
| **OREGON** | | | | | | | |
| 1 Wu | Y | Y | Y | Y | N | N | Y |
| 2 **Walden** | Y | Y | Y | N | Y | Y | Y |
| 3 Blumenauer | Y | Y | Y | Y | N | N | N |
| 4 DeFazio | Y | Y | Y | Y | N | N | N |
| 5 Hooley | Y | Y | Y | Y | N | N | Y |
| **PENNSYLVANIA** | | | | | | | |
| 1 Brady | Y | Y | Y | Y | N | N | Y |
| 2 Fattah | Y | Y | Y | Y | N | N | Y |
| 3 **English** | Y | Y | Y | N | Y | Y | Y |
| 4 **Hart** | Y | N | Y | N | Y | Y | Y |
| 5 **Peterson** | Y | N | Y | N | + | Y | Y |
| 6 **Gerlach** | Y | Y | Y | N | Y | N | Y |
| 7 **Weldon** | Y | Y | Y | N | Y | Y | Y |
| 8 **Fitzpatrick** | Y | Y | Y | N | N | N | Y |
| 9 **Shuster** | Y | N | Y | N | Y | Y | Y |
| 10 **Sherwood** | Y | Y | Y | N | Y | Y | Y |
| 11 Kanjorski | Y | Y | Y | Y | N | N | Y |
| 12 Murtha | Y | Y | ? | Y | Y | N | Y |
| 13 Schwartz | Y | Y | Y | Y | Y | N | Y |
| 14 Doyle | Y | Y | Y | Y | N | N | Y |
| 15 **Dent** | Y | Y | Y | N | Y | Y | Y |
| 16 **Pitts** | Y | N | Y | N | Y | Y | Y |
| 17 Holden | Y | Y | Y | Y | Y | N | Y |
| 18 **Murphy** | Y | N | Y | N | Y | Y | Y |
| 19 **Platts** | Y | ? | ? | N | Y | N | Y |
| **RHODE ISLAND** | | | | | | | |
| 1 Kennedy | Y | Y | Y | Y | N | N | Y |
| 2 Langevin | Y | Y | Y | Y | N | N | Y |
| **SOUTH CAROLINA** | | | | | | | |
| 1 **Brown** | Y | Y | Y | N | Y | Y | Y |
| 2 **Wilson** | Y | Y | Y | N | Y | Y | Y |
| 3 **Barrett** | Y | N | Y | N | Y | Y | Y |
| 4 **Inglis** | Y | Y | Y | N | Y | Y | Y |
| 5 Spratt | Y | Y | Y | Y | Y | N | Y |
| 6 Clyburn | ? | ? | ? | Y | N | N | Y |
| **SOUTH DAKOTA** | | | | | | | |
| AL Herseth | Y | Y | Y | Y | Y | N | Y |
| **TENNESSEE** | | | | | | | |
| 1 **Jenkins** | Y | Y | ? | N | Y | Y | Y |
| 2 **Duncan** | Y | N | Y | N | N | Y | Y |
| 3 **Wamp** | Y | N | Y | N | Y | Y | Y |
| 4 Davis | Y | Y | Y | Y | Y | N | Y |
| 5 Cooper | Y | Y | Y | Y | Y | N | Y |
| 6 Gordon | Y | Y | Y | Y | N | N | Y |
| 7 **Blackburn** | Y | N | Y | N | Y | Y | Y |
| 8 Tanner | Y | Y | Y | Y | N | N | ? |
| 9 Ford | ? | ? | ? | Y | N | N | Y |
| **TEXAS** | | | | | | | |
| 1 **Gohmert** | Y | N | Y | N | Y | Y | Y |
| 2 **Poe** | Y | N | Y | ? | ? | Y | Y |
| 3 **Johnson, S.** | Y | Y | Y | N | Y | Y | Y |
| 4 **Hall** | Y | N | Y | N | Y | Y | Y |
| 5 **Hensarling** | Y | N | Y | N | Y | Y | Y |
| 6 **Barton** | Y | Y | Y | N | Y | Y | Y |
| 7 **Culberson** | Y | N | Y | N | Y | Y | Y |
| 8 **Brady** | Y | Y | Y | N | Y | Y | Y |
| 9 Green, A. | Y | Y | Y | Y | N | N | Y |
| 10 **McCaul** | Y | Y | Y | N | Y | Y | Y |
| 11 **Conaway** | Y | N | Y | N | Y | Y | Y |
| 12 **Granger** | Y | N | Y | N | Y | Y | Y |
| 13 **Thornberry** | Y | N | Y | N | Y | Y | Y |
| 14 **Paul** | Y | N | Y | Y | N | N | Y |
| 15 Hinojosa | Y | Y | Y | Y | N | N | Y |
| 16 Reyes | Y | Y | Y | Y | Y | N | Y |
| 17 Edwards | Y | Y | Y | N | Y | N | Y |
| 18 Jackson-Lee | Y | Y | Y | Y | N | N | Y |
| 19 **Neugebauer** | Y | N | Y | N | Y | Y | Y |
| 20 Gonzalez | Y | Y | Y | Y | N | N | Y |
| 21 **Smith** | Y | Y | Y | N | Y | Y | Y |
| 22 **DeLay** | Y | N | Y | N | Y | Y | Y |
| 23 **Bonilla** | Y | N | Y | N | Y | Y | Y |
| 24 **Marchant** | Y | Y | Y | N | Y | Y | Y |
| 25 Doggett | Y | Y | Y | Y | N | N | Y |
| 26 **Burgess** | Y | N | Y | N | Y | Y | Y |
| 27 Ortiz | Y | Y | Y | Y | + | N | Y |
| 28 Cuellar | Y | Y | Y | Y | Y | N | Y |
| 29 Green, G. | Y | Y | Y | Y | N | N | Y |
| 30 Johnson, E. | Y | N | Y | Y | N | N | Y |
| 31 **Carter** | Y | N | Y | N | Y | Y | Y |
| 32 **Sessions** | Y | N | Y | N | Y | Y | Y |
| **UTAH** | | | | | | | |
| 1 **Bishop** | Y | N | Y | N | N | Y | ? |
| 2 Matheson | Y | Y | Y | Y | N | N | Y |
| 3 **Cannon** | Y | N | Y | N | Y | Y | Y |
| **VERMONT** | | | | | | | |
| AL *Sanders* | Y | Y | Y | Y | N | N | Y |
| **VIRGINIA** | | | | | | | |
| 1 **Davis, J.** | Y | N | Y | N | Y | Y | Y |
| 2 **Drake** | Y | N | Y | N | Y | Y | Y |
| 3 Scott | Y | Y | Y | Y | N | N | Y |
| 4 **Forbes** | Y | N | Y | N | Y | Y | Y |
| 5 **Goode** | ? | ? | ? | N | Y | Y | Y |
| 6 **Goodlatte** | Y | N | Y | N | Y | Y | Y |
| 7 **Cantor** | Y | Y | ? | N | Y | Y | Y |
| 8 Moran | Y | Y | Y | Y | N | N | Y |
| 9 Boucher | Y | Y | Y | Y | N | N | Y |
| 10 **Wolf** | Y | Y | Y | N | Y | Y | Y |
| 11 **Davis, T.** | Y | N | ? | N | Y | Y | Y |
| **WASHINGTON** | | | | | | | |
| 1 Inslee | Y | Y | Y | Y | N | N | Y |
| 2 Larsen | Y | Y | Y | Y | N | N | Y |
| 3 Baird | Y | Y | Y | Y | N | N | Y |
| 4 **Hastings** | Y | Y | Y | N | Y | Y | Y |
| 5 **McMorris** | Y | N | Y | N | Y | Y | Y |
| 6 Dicks | Y | Y | Y | Y | N | N | Y |
| 7 McDermott | + | + | ? | + | - | - | Y |
| 8 **Reichert** | Y | Y | Y | N | Y | Y | Y |
| 9 Smith | Y | Y | Y | Y | N | N | Y |
| **WEST VIRGINIA** | | | | | | | |
| 1 Mollohan | Y | Y | Y | Y | N | N | Y |
| 2 **Capito** | Y | Y | Y | N | Y | Y | Y |
| 3 Rahall | Y | Y | Y | Y | N | N | Y |
| **WISCONSIN** | | | | | | | |
| 1 **Ryan** | Y | N | Y | N | Y | Y | Y |
| 2 Baldwin | Y | Y | Y | Y | N | N | Y |
| 3 Kind | ? | ? | ? | Y | N | N | Y |
| 4 Moore | Y | Y | Y | Y | N | N | Y |
| 5 **Sensenbrenner** | Y | N | Y | N | Y | Y | Y |
| 6 **Petri** | Y | Y | Y | N | Y | Y | Y |
| 7 Obey | Y | Y | Y | Y | N | N | Y |
| 8 **Green** | Y | N | Y | N | Y | Y | Y |
| **WYOMING** | | | | | | | |
| AL **Cubin** | ? | ? | ? | N | Y | Y | Y |

# IN THE HOUSE | By Vote Number

**630.** **HR 2863. Fiscal 2006 Defense Appropriations/Motion to Instruct.** Murtha, D-Pa., motion to instruct House conferees to include Senate-passed language that would establish the U.S. Army Field Manual on Intelligence Interrogation as the uniform standard for interrogating persons detained by the Department of Defense, and prohibit cruel, inhuman or degrading treatment of any prisoner detained by the U.S. government. Motion agreed to 308-122: R 107-121; D 200-1 (ND 150-0, SD 50-1); I 1-0. A "nay" was a vote was a vote in support of the president's position. Dec. 14, 2005.

**631.** **H Res 599. Ocean Policy Task Force/Adoption.** Hastings, R-Wash., motion to suspend the rules and adopt the resolution that would establish a House Task Force on Ocean Policy to make recommendations on the final report of the U.S. Commission on Ocean Policy and report these recommendations to the House. Motion rejected 103-327: R 93-134; D 10-192 (ND 9-142, SD 1-50); I 0-1. A two-thirds majority of those present and voting (287 in this case) is required for adoption under suspension of the rules. Dec. 14, 2005.

**632.** **HR 972. Trafficking Victims Protection Reauthorization/Passage.** Smith, R-N.J., motion to suspend the rules and pass the bill that would reauthorize the Trafficking Victims Protection Act of 2000. It would authorize $15 million in fiscal 2006 to remain available until spent for the FBI to investigate severe forms of trafficking and $18 million per year in fiscal 2006-07 for investigations by Immigration and Customs Enforcement in the Homeland Security Department. Motion agreed to 426-0: R 225-0; D 201-0 (ND 151-0, SD 50-0); I 0-0. A two-thirds majority of those present and voting (284 in this case) is required for passage under suspension of the rules. Dec. 14, 2005.

**633.** **HR 2830. Pension Overhaul/Rule.** Adoption of the rule (H Res 602) to provide for House floor consideration of the bill that would overhaul federal pension laws. Adopted 226-199: R 224-1; D 2-197 (ND 1-149, SD 1-48); I 0-1. Dec. 15, 2005.

**634.** **HR 2830. Pension Overhaul/Recommit.** Miller, D-Calif., motion to recommit the bill to the Education and the Workforce and Ways and Means committees with instructions to substitute the text of a Democratic bill that would make it harder for companies to declare bankruptcy or eliminate workers' pensions, and include relief for struggling airlines and multi-employer plans. Motion rejected 200-227: R 0-226; D 199-1 (ND 149-1, SD 50-0); I 1-0. Dec. 15, 2005.

**635.** **HR 2830. Pension Overhaul/Passage.** Passage of the bill that would overhaul federal pension law and increase the premiums companies pay to the Pension Benefit Guaranty Corporation to $30 per participant from $19. It would establish a premium for employers who terminate their pension plans on an involuntary basis. It also would require employers to make sufficient contributions to meet a 100 percent funding target. Passed 294-132: R 224-1; D 70-130 (ND 49-101, SD 21-29); I 0-1. Dec. 15, 2005.

**636.** **HR 4437. Border Security/Rule.** Adoption of the rule (H Res 610) that would provide for House floor consideration of the bill to increase security at the international border and at ports of entry into the United States. Adopted 220-206: R 219-7; D 1-198 (ND 1-148, SD 0-50); I 0-1. Dec. 15, 2005.

| Member | 630 | 631 | 632 | 633 | 634 | 635 | 636 |
|---|---|---|---|---|---|---|---|
| **ALABAMA** | | | | | | | |
| 1 Bonner | N | N | Y | Y | N | Y | Y |
| 2 Everett | N | N | Y | Y | N | Y | Y |
| 3 Rogers | N | Y | Y | Y | N | Y | Y |
| 4 Aderholt | N | N | Y | Y | N | Y | N |
| 5 Cramer | Y | N | Y | N | Y | Y | N |
| 6 Bachus | Y | N | Y | N | Y | N | Y |
| 7 Davis | Y | N | Y | N | Y | N | N |
| **ALASKA** | | | | | | | |
| AL Young | N | Y | Y | Y | N | Y | Y |
| **ARIZONA** | | | | | | | |
| 1 Renzi | N | N | Y | Y | N | Y | Y |
| 2 Franks | N | N | Y | Y | N | Y | Y |
| 3 Shadegg | N | N | Y | Y | N | Y | Y |
| 4 Pastor | Y | N | Y | N | Y | Y | N |
| 5 Hayworth | N | N | Y | Y | N | Y | Y |
| 6 Flake | Y | N | Y | Y | Y | Y | Y |
| 7 Grijalva | Y | N | Y | N | Y | N | N |
| 8 Kolbe | Y | Y | Y | Y | N | Y | N |
| **ARKANSAS** | | | | | | | |
| 1 Berry | Y | N | Y | N | Y | Y | N |
| 2 Snyder | Y | N | Y | N | Y | Y | N |
| 3 Boozman | Y | N | Y | Y | N | Y | Y |
| 4 Ross | Y | N | Y | N | Y | Y | N |
| **CALIFORNIA** | | | | | | | |
| 1 Thompson | Y | N | Y | N | Y | N | N |
| 2 Herger | N | N | Y | Y | N | Y | Y |
| 3 Lungren | N | N | Y | Y | N | Y | Y |
| 4 Doolittle | N | N | Y | Y | N | Y | Y |
| 5 Matsui, D. | Y | N | Y | N | Y | N | N |
| 6 Woolsey | Y | N | Y | N | Y | N | N |
| 7 Miller, George | Y | N | Y | N | Y | N | N |
| 8 Pelosi | Y | N | Y | N | Y | N | N |
| 9 Lee | Y | N | Y | N | Y | N | N |
| 10 Tauscher | Y | N | Y | N | Y | N | N |
| 11 Pombo | Y | N | Y | Y | N | Y | Y |
| 12 Lantos | Y | N | Y | N | Y | N | N |
| 13 Stark | Y | N | Y | N | Y | N | N |
| 14 Eshoo | Y | N | Y | N | Y | N | N |
| 15 Honda | Y | N | Y | N | Y | N | N |
| 16 Lofgren | Y | N | Y | N | Y | N | N |
| 17 Farr | Y | N | Y | N | Y | N | N |
| 18 Cardoza | Y | Y | Y | N | Y | N | N |
| 19 Radanovich | N | N | Y | Y | N | Y | Y |
| 20 Costa | + | N | Y | N | Y | N | N |
| 21 Nunes | N | N | Y | Y | N | Y | Y |
| 22 Thomas | Y | N | Y | Y | N | Y | Y |
| 23 Capps | Y | N | Y | N | Y | N | N |
| 24 Gallegly | N | N | Y | Y | N | Y | Y |
| 25 McKeon | N | N | Y | Y | N | Y | Y |
| 26 Dreier | N | Y | Y | Y | N | Y | Y |
| 27 Sherman | Y | N | Y | N | Y | N | N |
| 28 Berman | Y | N | Y | N | Y | N | N |
| 29 Schiff | Y | N | Y | N | Y | N | N |
| 30 Waxman | Y | N | Y | N | Y | N | N |
| 31 Becerra | Y | N | Y | N | Y | N | N |
| 32 Solis | Y | N | Y | N | Y | N | N |
| 33 Watson | Y | N | Y | N | Y | N | N |
| 34 Roybal-Allard | Y | N | Y | N | Y | N | N |
| 35 Waters | Y | N | Y | N | ? | ? | ? |
| 36 Harman | Y | N | Y | N | Y | Y | N |
| 37 Millender-McD. | Y | N | Y | N | Y | N | N |
| 38 Napolitano | Y | N | Y | N | Y | N | N |
| 39 Sánchez, Linda | Y | N | Y | N | Y | N | N |
| 40 Royce | N | N | Y | Y | N | Y | Y |
| 41 Lewis | N | N | Y | Y | N | Y | Y |
| 42 Miller, Gary | N | N | Y | Y | N | Y | Y |
| 43 Baca | Y | N | Y | N | Y | N | N |
| 44 Calvert | N | N | Y | Y | N | Y | Y |
| 45 Bono | N | N | Y | Y | N | Y | Y |
| 46 Rohrabacher | N | N | Y | Y | N | Y | Y |
| 47 Sanchez, Loretta | Y | N | Y | N | Y | N | N |
| 48 Campbell | N | N | Y | Y | N | Y | Y |
| 49 Issa | Y | N | Y | Y | N | Y | Y |
| 50 Vacant | | | | | | | |
| 51 Filner | Y | N | Y | N | Y | N | N |
| 52 Hunter | N | Y | Y | Y | N | Y | ? |
| 53 Davis | Y | N | Y | N | Y | N | N |
| **COLORADO** | | | | | | | |
| 1 DeGette | Y | N | Y | N | Y | N | N |
| 2 Udall | Y | N | Y | N | Y | N | N |
| 3 Salazar | Y | N | Y | N | Y | N | N |
| 4 Musgrave | N | N | Y | Y | N | Y | Y |
| 5 Hefley | N | N | Y | Y | N | Y | Y |
| 6 Tancredo | Y | N | Y | N | Y | N | Y |
| 7 Beauprez | Y | N | Y | N | Y | N | Y |
| **CONNECTICUT** | | | | | | | |
| 1 Larson | Y | N | Y | N | Y | N | N |
| 2 Simmons | Y | Y | Y | N | Y | Y | Y |
| 3 DeLauro | Y | N | Y | N | Y | N | N |
| 4 Shays | Y | Y | Y | Y | N | Y | Y |
| 5 Johnson | Y | Y | Y | Y | N | Y | Y |
| **DELAWARE** | | | | | | | |
| AL Castle | Y | Y | Y | Y | N | Y | Y |
| **FLORIDA** | | | | | | | |
| 1 Miller | N | N | Y | Y | N | Y | Y |
| 2 Boyd | Y | N | Y | N | Y | N | N |
| 3 Brown | Y | N | Y | N | Y | N | N |
| 4 Crenshaw | N | N | Y | Y | N | Y | Y |
| 5 Brown-Waite | N | N | Y | Y | N | Y | Y |
| 6 Stearns | N | N | Y | Y | N | Y | Y |
| 7 Mica | N | Y | Y | Y | N | Y | Y |
| 8 Keller | Y | N | Y | Y | N | Y | Y |
| 9 Bilirakis | N | Y | Y | Y | N | Y | Y |
| 10 Young | N | Y | Y | N | Y | Y | Y |
| 11 Davis | Y | N | ? | ? | ? | ? | ? |
| 12 Putnam | N | Y | Y | Y | N | Y | Y |
| 13 Harris | Y | Y | Y | Y | N | Y | Y |
| 14 Mack | N | Y | Y | Y | N | Y | Y |
| 15 Weldon | N | Y | Y | Y | N | Y | Y |
| 16 Foley | Y | N | Y | N | Y | Y | Y |
| 17 Meek | Y | N | Y | N | Y | Y | N |
| 18 Ros-Lehtinen | Y | Y | Y | Y | N | Y | Y |
| 19 Wexler | Y | N | Y | N | Y | N | N |
| 20 Wasserman-Schultz | Y | N | Y | N | Y | N | N |
| 21 Diaz-Balart, L. | Y | Y | Y | N | ? | Y | Y |
| 22 Shaw | Y | Y | Y | Y | N | Y | Y |
| 23 Hastings | Y | N | Y | N | Y | Y | N |
| 24 Feeney | N | N | Y | N | Y | Y | Y |
| 25 Diaz-Balart, M. | + | + | + | + | − | + | + |
| **GEORGIA** | | | | | | | |
| 1 Kingston | N | Y | Y | Y | N | Y | Y |
| 2 Bishop | Y | N | Y | N | Y | Y | N |
| 3 Marshall | N | N | Y | N | Y | Y | N |
| 4 McKinney | Y | N | Y | N | Y | N | N |
| 5 Lewis | Y | N | Y | N | Y | N | N |
| 6 Price | N | Y | Y | Y | N | Y | Y |
| 7 Linder | N | N | Y | Y | N | Y | Y |
| 8 Westmoreland | N | N | Y | Y | N | Y | Y |
| 9 Norwood | N | N | Y | Y | N | Y | Y |
| 10 Deal | N | N | Y | Y | N | Y | Y |
| 11 Gingrey | N | N | Y | Y | N | Y | Y |
| 12 Barrow | Y | N | Y | N | Y | N | N |
| 13 Scott | Y | N | Y | N | Y | N | N |
| **HAWAII** | | | | | | | |
| 1 Abercrombie | Y | Y | Y | N | Y | N | N |
| 2 Case | Y | Y | Y | N | Y | Y | N |
| **IDAHO** | | | | | | | |
| 1 Otter | Y | N | Y | Y | N | Y | Y |
| 2 Simpson | N | Y | Y | Y | N | Y | Y |
| **ILLINOIS** | | | | | | | |
| 1 Rush | Y | N | Y | N | Y | N | N |
| 2 Jackson | Y | N | Y | N | Y | N | N |
| 3 Lipinski | Y | N | Y | N | Y | Y | N |
| 4 Gutierrez | Y | N | Y | N | Y | N | N |
| 5 Emanuel | Y | N | Y | N | Y | N | − |
| 6 Hyde | + | − | + | + | − | + | + |
| 7 Davis | Y | N | Y | N | Y | N | N |
| 8 Bean | Y | N | Y | N | Y | Y | N |
| 9 Schakowsky | Y | N | Y | N | Y | N | N |
| 10 Kirk | Y | Y | Y | Y | N | Y | Y |
| 11 Weller | Y | Y | Y | N | Y | Y | Y |
| 12 Costello | Y | N | Y | N | Y | Y | N |

ND Northern Democrats, SD Southern Democrats
Southern states: Ala., Ark., Fla., Ga., Ky., La., Miss., N.C., Okla., S.C., Tenn., Texas, Va.

| | 630 | 631 | 632 | 633 | 634 | 635 | 636 |
|---|---|---|---|---|---|---|---|
| 13 **Biggert** | Y | Y | Y | Y | N | Y | Y |
| 14 **Hastert** | | | | | | | |
| 15 **Johnson** | Y | Y | Y | Y | N | Y | Y |
| 16 **Manzullo** | Y | N | Y | Y | N | Y | Y |
| 17 Evans | Y | N | Y | N | Y | N | N |
| 18 **LaHood** | N | N | Y | Y | N | Y | Y |
| 19 **Shimkus** | Y | N | Y | Y | N | Y | Y |
| **INDIANA** | | | | | | | |
| 1 Visclosky | Y | N | Y | N | Y | N | N |
| 2 **Chocola** | Y | N | Y | Y | N | Y | Y |
| 3 **Souder** | N | Y | Y | Y | N | Y | ? |
| 4 **Buyer** | N | N | ? | Y | N | Y | Y |
| 5 **Burton** | N | N | Y | Y | N | Y | Y |
| 6 **Pence** | N | N | Y | Y | N | Y | Y |
| 7 Carson | Y | N | Y | N | Y | N | N |
| 8 **Hostettler** | N | N | Y | Y | N | N | N |
| 9 **Sodrel** | Y | N | Y | Y | N | Y | Y |
| **IOWA** | | | | | | | |
| 1 **Nussle** | Y | N | Y | Y | N | Y | Y |
| 2 **Leach** | Y | Y | Y | Y | N | Y | N |
| 3 Boswell | Y | N | Y | N | Y | Y | N |
| 4 **Latham** | Y | Y | Y | Y | N | Y | Y |
| 5 **King** | N | N | Y | Y | N | Y | Y |
| **KANSAS** | | | | | | | |
| 1 **Moran** | Y | N | Y | Y | N | Y | Y |
| 2 **Ryun** | N | N | Y | Y | N | Y | Y |
| 3 Moore | Y | N | Y | N | Y | Y | N |
| 4 **Tiahrt** | N | N | Y | Y | N | Y | Y |
| **KENTUCKY** | | | | | | | |
| 1 **Whitfield** | Y | Y | Y | Y | N | Y | Y |
| 2 **Lewis** | N | Y | Y | Y | N | Y | Y |
| 3 **Northup** | Y | N | Y | Y | N | Y | Y |
| 4 **Davis** | Y | N | Y | Y | N | Y | Y |
| 5 **Rogers** | N | Y | Y | Y | N | Y | Y |
| 6 Chandler | Y | N | Y | N | Y | Y | N |
| **LOUISIANA** | | | | | | | |
| 1 **Jindal** | N | N | Y | Y | N | Y | Y |
| 2 Jefferson | Y | N | Y | N | Y | N | N |
| 3 Melancon | Y | Y | Y | N | Y | Y | N |
| 4 **McCrery** | Y | Y | Y | Y | N | Y | Y |
| 5 **Alexander** | Y | N | Y | Y | N | Y | Y |
| 6 **Baker** | N | N | Y | Y | N | Y | Y |
| 7 **Boustany** | Y | N | Y | Y | N | Y | Y |
| **MAINE** | | | | | | | |
| 1 Allen | Y | Y | Y | N | Y | N | N |
| 2 Michaud | Y | Y | Y | N | Y | N | N |
| **MARYLAND** | | | | | | | |
| 1 **Gilchrest** | Y | Y | Y | Y | N | ? | Y |
| 2 Ruppersberger | Y | Y | Y | N | Y | N | N |
| 3 Cardin | Y | Y | Y | N | Y | N | N |
| 4 Wynn | Y | N | Y | N | Y | Y | N |
| 5 Hoyer | Y | N | Y | N | Y | N | N |
| 6 **Bartlett** | Y | Y | Y | Y | N | Y | Y |
| 7 Cummings | Y | N | Y | N | Y | N | N |
| 8 Van Hollen | Y | Y | Y | N | Y | N | N |
| **MASSACHUSETTS** | | | | | | | |
| 1 Olver | Y | N | Y | N | Y | N | N |
| 2 Neal | Y | N | Y | N | Y | N | N |
| 3 McGovern | Y | N | Y | N | Y | N | N |
| 4 Frank | Y | N | Y | N | Y | N | N |
| 5 Meehan | Y | N | Y | N | Y | N | N |
| 6 Tierney | Y | N | Y | N | Y | N | N |
| 7 Markey | Y | N | Y | N | Y | N | N |
| 8 Capuano | Y | N | Y | N | Y | Y | N |
| 9 Lynch | Y | N | Y | N | Y | Y | N |
| 10 Delahunt | Y | N | Y | N | Y | N | N |
| **MICHIGAN** | | | | | | | |
| 1 Stupak | Y | N | Y | N | Y | Y | N |
| 2 **Hoekstra** | N | Y | Y | Y | N | Y | Y |
| 3 **Ehlers** | Y | Y | Y | Y | N | Y | Y |
| 4 **Camp** | Y | N | Y | Y | N | Y | Y |
| 5 Kildee | Y | N | Y | N | Y | Y | N |
| 6 **Upton** | Y | Y | Y | Y | N | Y | N |
| 7 **Schwarz** | Y | Y | Y | Y | N | Y | Y |
| 8 **Rogers** | N | Y | Y | Y | N | Y | Y |
| 9 **Knollenberg** | Y | N | Y | Y | N | Y | Y |
| 10 **Miller** | Y | Y | Y | Y | N | Y | Y |
| 11 **McCotter** | Y | N | Y | Y | N | Y | Y |
| 12 Levin | Y | N | Y | N | Y | N | N |
| 13 Kilpatrick | Y | N | Y | N | Y | Y | N |
| 14 Conyers | Y | N | Y | N | Y | Y | N |
| 15 Dingell | Y | N | Y | N | Y | Y | N |

| | 630 | 631 | 632 | 633 | 634 | 635 | 636 |
|---|---|---|---|---|---|---|---|
| **MINNESOTA** | | | | | | | |
| 1 **Gutknecht** | Y | N | Y | Y | N | Y | Y |
| 2 **Kline** | Y | N | Y | Y | N | Y | Y |
| 3 **Ramstad** | Y | Y | Y | Y | N | Y | Y |
| 4 McCollum | Y | N | Y | N | Y | N | N |
| 5 Sabo | Y | N | Y | N | Y | N | N |
| 6 **Kennedy** | Y | N | Y | Y | N | Y | Y |
| 7 Peterson | Y | N | Y | N | Y | Y | N |
| 8 Oberstar | Y | N | Y | Y | Y | Y | N |
| **MISSISSIPPI** | | | | | | | |
| 1 **Wicker** | N | N | Y | Y | N | Y | Y |
| 2 Thompson | Y | N | Y | N | Y | N | N |
| 3 **Pickering** | Y | N | Y | Y | - | + | Y |
| 4 Taylor | Y | N | Y | N | Y | N | N |
| **MISSOURI** | | | | | | | |
| 1 Clay | Y | N | Y | N | Y | Y | N |
| 2 **Akin** | N | Y | Y | Y | N | Y | Y |
| 3 Carnahan | Y | N | Y | N | Y | N | N |
| 4 Skelton | Y | N | Y | N | Y | N | N |
| 5 Cleaver | Y | N | Y | N | Y | Y | N |
| 6 **Graves** | N | N | Y | Y | N | Y | Y |
| 7 **Blunt** | N | Y | Y | Y | N | Y | Y |
| 8 **Emerson** | Y | N | Y | Y | N | Y | Y |
| 9 **Hulshof** | Y | N | Y | Y | N | Y | Y |
| **MONTANA** | | | | | | | |
| AL **Rehberg** | N | Y | Y | Y | N | Y | Y |
| **NEBRASKA** | | | | | | | |
| 1 **Fortenberry** | Y | Y | Y | Y | N | Y | Y |
| 2 **Terry** | N | N | Y | Y | N | Y | Y |
| 3 **Osborne** | Y | Y | Y | Y | N | Y | Y |
| **NEVADA** | | | | | | | |
| 1 Berkley | Y | N | Y | - | Y | N | N |
| 2 **Gibbons** | Y | N | Y | Y | N | Y | Y |
| 3 **Porter** | Y | N | Y | Y | N | Y | Y |
| **NEW HAMPSHIRE** | | | | | | | |
| 1 **Bradley** | Y | Y | Y | Y | N | Y | Y |
| 2 **Bass** | Y | Y | Y | Y | N | Y | Y |
| **NEW JERSEY** | | | | | | | |
| 1 Andrews | Y | N | Y | N | Y | Y | N |
| 2 **LoBiondo** | Y | N | Y | Y | N | Y | Y |
| 3 **Saxton** | Y | Y | Y | Y | N | Y | Y |
| 4 **Smith** | Y | Y | Y | Y | N | Y | Y |
| 5 **Garrett** | N | N | Y | Y | N | Y | Y |
| 6 Pallone | Y | N | Y | N | Y | N | N |
| 7 **Ferguson** | Y | ? | ? | Y | N | Y | Y |
| 8 Pascrell | Y | N | Y | N | Y | Y | N |
| 9 Rothman | Y | N | Y | N | Y | Y | N |
| 10 Payne | Y | N | Y | N | Y | N | N |
| 11 **Frelinghuysen** | N | Y | Y | Y | N | Y | Y |
| 12 Holt | Y | N | Y | N | Y | N | N |
| 13 Menendez | Y | N | Y | N | Y | Y | N |
| **NEW MEXICO** | | | | | | | |
| 1 **Wilson** | Y | Y | Y | Y | N | Y | N |
| 2 **Pearce** | N | N | Y | Y | ? | Y | Y |
| 3 Udall | Y | N | Y | N | Y | N | N |
| **NEW YORK** | | | | | | | |
| 1 Bishop | Y | N | Y | N | Y | N | N |
| 2 Israel | Y | N | Y | N | Y | Y | N |
| 3 **King** | N | Y | Y | Y | N | Y | Y |
| 4 McCarthy | Y | N | Y | N | Y | Y | N |
| 5 Ackerman | Y | N | Y | N | Y | N | N |
| 6 Meeks | Y | N | Y | N | Y | Y | N |
| 7 Crowley | Y | N | Y | N | Y | N | N |
| 8 Nadler | Y | N | Y | N | Y | N | N |
| 9 Weiner | Y | N | Y | N | Y | N | N |
| 10 Towns | Y | N | Y | N | Y | N | N |
| 11 Owens | Y | N | Y | N | Y | Y | N |
| 12 Velázquez | Y | N | Y | N | Y | N | N |
| 13 **Fossella** | N | Y | Y | ? | N | Y | Y |
| 14 Maloney | Y | N | Y | N | Y | N | N |
| 15 Rangel | Y | N | Y | N | Y | N | N |
| 16 Serrano | Y | N | Y | N | Y | N | N |
| 17 Engel | Y | N | Y | N | Y | Y | N |
| 18 Lowey | Y | N | Y | N | Y | N | N |
| 19 **Kelly** | Y | Y | Y | Y | N | Y | Y |
| 20 **Sweeney** | Y | Y | Y | Y | N | Y | Y |
| 21 McNulty | Y | N | Y | N | Y | Y | N |
| 22 Hinchey | Y | N | Y | N | Y | N | N |
| 23 **McHugh** | Y | Y | Y | ? | N | Y | Y |
| 24 **Boehlert** | Y | Y | Y | Y | N | Y | Y |
| 25 **Walsh** | Y | Y | Y | Y | N | Y | Y |
| 26 **Reynolds** | Y | Y | Y | Y | N | Y | Y |
| 27 Higgins | Y | N | Y | N | Y | N | N |
| 28 Slaughter | Y | N | Y | N | Y | N | N |
| 29 **Kuhl** | Y | N | Y | Y | N | Y | Y |

| | 630 | 631 | 632 | 633 | 634 | 635 | 636 |
|---|---|---|---|---|---|---|---|
| **NORTH CAROLINA** | | | | | | | |
| 1 Butterfield | Y | N | Y | N | Y | N | N |
| 2 Etheridge | Y | N | Y | N | Y | N | N |
| 3 **Jones** | Y | Y | Y | Y | N | Y | Y |
| 4 Price | Y | N | Y | N | Y | N | N |
| 5 **Foxx** | N | N | Y | Y | N | Y | Y |
| 6 **Coble** | N | N | Y | Y | N | Y | Y |
| 7 McIntyre | Y | N | Y | N | Y | Y | N |
| 8 **Hayes** | N | N | Y | Y | N | Y | Y |
| 9 **Myrick** | N | Y | Y | Y | N | Y | Y |
| 10 **McHenry** | N | N | Y | Y | N | Y | Y |
| 11 **Taylor** | N | N | Y | Y | N | Y | Y |
| 12 Watt | Y | N | Y | N | Y | N | N |
| 13 Miller | Y | N | Y | N | Y | N | N |
| **NORTH DAKOTA** | | | | | | | |
| AL Pomeroy | Y | N | Y | N | Y | N | N |
| **OHIO** | | | | | | | |
| 1 **Chabot** | N | N | Y | Y | N | Y | Y |
| 2 **Schmidt** | N | N | Y | Y | N | Y | Y |
| 3 **Turner** | N | N | Y | Y | N | Y | Y |
| 4 **Oxley** | N | N | Y | Y | N | Y | Y |
| 5 **Gillmor** | N | Y | Y | Y | N | Y | Y |
| 6 Strickland | Y | N | Y | N | Y | Y | N |
| 7 **Hobson** | N | Y | Y | Y | N | Y | Y |
| 8 **Boehner** | N | Y | Y | Y | N | Y | Y |
| 9 Kaptur | Y | N | Y | N | Y | N | N |
| 10 Kucinich | Y | N | Y | N | Y | Y | N |
| 11 Jones | Y | N | Y | N | Y | N | N |
| 12 **Tiberi** | Y | N | Y | Y | N | Y | Y |
| 13 Brown | Y | N | Y | N | Y | Y | N |
| 14 **LaTourette** | Y | N | Y | Y | N | Y | Y |
| 15 **Pryce** | Y | Y | Y | Y | N | Y | Y |
| 16 **Regula** | Y | Y | Y | Y | N | Y | Y |
| 17 Ryan | Y | N | Y | N | Y | Y | N |
| 18 **Ney** | N | N | Y | Y | N | Y | Y |
| **OKLAHOMA** | | | | | | | |
| 1 **Sullivan** | N | N | Y | Y | N | Y | Y |
| 2 Boren | Y | N | Y | N | Y | Y | N |
| 3 **Lucas** | N | N | Y | Y | N | Y | Y |
| 4 **Cole** | N | N | Y | Y | N | Y | Y |
| 5 **Istook** | N | N | ? | Y | N | Y | Y |
| **OREGON** | | | | | | | |
| 1 Wu | Y | N | Y | N | Y | Y | N |
| 2 **Walden** | Y | Y | Y | Y | N | Y | Y |
| 3 Blumenauer | Y | N | Y | N | Y | N | N |
| 4 DeFazio | Y | N | Y | N | Y | N | N |
| 5 Hooley | Y | N | Y | N | Y | Y | N |
| **PENNSYLVANIA** | | | | | | | |
| 1 Brady | Y | N | Y | N | Y | Y | N |
| 2 Fattah | Y | N | Y | N | Y | Y | N |
| 3 **English** | Y | Y | Y | Y | N | Y | Y |
| 4 **Hart** | N | N | Y | Y | N | Y | Y |
| 5 **Peterson** | N | N | Y | Y | N | Y | Y |
| 6 **Gerlach** | Y | Y | Y | Y | N | Y | Y |
| 7 **Weldon** | Y | Y | Y | Y | N | Y | Y |
| 8 **Fitzpatrick** | Y | N | Y | ? | N | Y | Y |
| 9 **Shuster** | N | Y | Y | Y | N | Y | Y |
| 10 **Sherwood** | Y | Y | Y | Y | N | Y | Y |
| 11 Kanjorski | Y | N | Y | N | Y | N | N |
| 12 Murtha | Y | N | Y | N | Y | N | N |
| 13 Schwartz | Y | N | Y | N | Y | N | N |
| 14 Doyle | Y | N | Y | N | Y | N | N |
| 15 **Dent** | Y | Y | Y | Y | N | Y | Y |
| 16 **Pitts** | Y | N | Y | Y | N | Y | Y |
| 17 Holden | Y | N | Y | N | Y | Y | N |
| 18 **Murphy** | Y | N | Y | Y | N | Y | Y |
| 19 **Platts** | Y | Y | Y | Y | N | Y | Y |
| **RHODE ISLAND** | | | | | | | |
| 1 Kennedy | Y | N | Y | N | Y | N | N |
| 2 Langevin | Y | N | Y | N | Y | N | N |
| **SOUTH CAROLINA** | | | | | | | |
| 1 **Brown** | N | N | Y | Y | N | Y | Y |
| 2 **Wilson** | N | N | Y | Y | N | Y | Y |
| 3 **Barrett** | N | N | Y | Y | N | Y | Y |
| 4 **Inglis** | Y | N | Y | Y | N | Y | Y |
| 5 Spratt | Y | N | Y | N | Y | N | N |
| 6 Clyburn | Y | N | Y | N | Y | N | N |
| **SOUTH DAKOTA** | | | | | | | |
| AL Herseth | Y | N | Y | N | Y | Y | N |
| **TENNESSEE** | | | | | | | |
| 1 **Jenkins** | Y | Y | Y | Y | N | Y | Y |
| 2 **Duncan** | Y | Y | Y | Y | N | Y | Y |

| | 630 | 631 | 632 | 633 | 634 | 635 | 636 |
|---|---|---|---|---|---|---|---|
| 3 **Wamp** | Y | Y | Y | Y | N | Y | Y |
| 4 Davis | Y | N | Y | N | Y | Y | N |
| 5 Cooper | Y | N | Y | N | Y | Y | N |
| 6 Gordon | Y | N | Y | N | Y | Y | N |
| 7 **Blackburn** | N | N | Y | Y | N | Y | Y |
| 8 Tanner | Y | N | Y | N | Y | Y | N |
| 9 Ford | Y | N | Y | N | Y | Y | N |
| **TEXAS** | | | | | | | |
| 1 **Gohmert** | N | N | Y | Y | N | Y | Y |
| 2 **Poe** | N | N | Y | Y | N | Y | Y |
| 3 **Johnson, S.** | N | N | Y | Y | N | Y | Y |
| 4 **Hall** | N | N | Y | Y | N | Y | Y |
| 5 **Hensarling** | N | N | Y | Y | N | Y | Y |
| 6 **Barton** | N | Y | Y | Y | N | Y | Y |
| 7 **Culberson** | N | N | Y | Y | N | Y | Y |
| 8 **Brady** | N | N | Y | Y | N | Y | Y |
| 9 Green, A. | Y | N | Y | N | Y | N | N |
| 10 **McCaul** | Y | Y | Y | Y | N | Y | Y |
| 11 **Conaway** | N | N | Y | Y | N | Y | Y |
| 12 **Granger** | N | N | Y | Y | N | Y | Y |
| 13 **Thornberry** | N | N | Y | Y | N | Y | Y |
| 14 **Paul** | Y | N | Y | N | N | Y | Y |
| 15 Hinojosa | Y | N | Y | N | Y | N | N |
| 16 Reyes | Y | N | Y | N | Y | N | N |
| 17 Edwards | Y | N | Y | N | Y | Y | N |
| 18 Jackson-Lee | Y | N | Y | N | Y | N | N |
| 19 **Neugebauer** | N | N | Y | Y | N | Y | Y |
| 20 Gonzalez | Y | N | Y | N | Y | N | N |
| 21 **Smith** | N | Y | Y | Y | N | Y | Y |
| 22 **DeLay** | N | Y | Y | Y | N | Y | Y |
| 23 **Bonilla** | N | N | Y | Y | N | Y | Y |
| 24 **Marchant** | N | N | Y | Y | N | Y | Y |
| 25 Doggett | Y | N | Y | N | Y | N | N |
| 26 **Burgess** | N | Y | Y | Y | N | Y | Y |
| 27 Ortiz | Y | N | Y | N | Y | N | N |
| 28 Cuellar | Y | N | Y | Y | Y | Y | N |
| 29 Green, G. | Y | N | Y | N | Y | Y | N |
| 30 Johnson, E. | Y | N | Y | N | Y | N | N |
| 31 **Carter** | N | N | Y | Y | N | Y | Y |
| 32 **Sessions** | N | N | Y | Y | N | Y | Y |
| **UTAH** | | | | | | | |
| 1 **Bishop** | N | Y | Y | Y | N | Y | Y |
| 2 Matheson | Y | N | Y | N | N | Y | N |
| 3 **Cannon** | N | Y | Y | Y | N | Y | Y |
| **VERMONT** | | | | | | | |
| AL *Sanders* | Y | N | ? | N | Y | N | N |
| **VIRGINIA** | | | | | | | |
| 1 **Davis, J.** | Y | N | Y | Y | N | Y | Y |
| 2 **Drake** | N | N | Y | Y | N | Y | Y |
| 3 Scott | Y | N | Y | N | Y | N | N |
| 4 **Forbes** | Y | N | Y | Y | N | Y | Y |
| 5 **Goode** | N | N | Y | Y | N | Y | Y |
| 6 **Goodlatte** | Y | N | Y | Y | N | Y | Y |
| 7 **Cantor** | N | N | Y | Y | N | Y | Y |
| 8 Moran | Y | N | Y | N | Y | N | N |
| 9 Boucher | Y | N | Y | ? | Y | N | N |
| 10 **Wolf** | Y | Y | Y | Y | N | Y | Y |
| 11 **Davis, T.** | Y | Y | Y | Y | N | Y | Y |
| **WASHINGTON** | | | | | | | |
| 1 Inslee | Y | Y | Y | N | Y | Y | N |
| 2 Larsen | Y | N | Y | N | Y | Y | N |
| 3 Baird | Y | N | Y | N | Y | N | N |
| 4 **Hastings** | N | Y | Y | Y | N | Y | Y |
| 5 **McMorris** | Y | N | Y | Y | N | Y | Y |
| 6 Dicks | Y | N | Y | N | Y | N | N |
| 7 McDermott | Y | N | Y | N | Y | N | N |
| 8 **Reichert** | Y | N | Y | Y | N | Y | Y |
| 9 Smith | Y | N | Y | N | Y | Y | N |
| **WEST VIRGINIA** | | | | | | | |
| 1 Mollohan | Y | N | Y | N | Y | N | N |
| 2 **Capito** | Y | Y | Y | Y | N | Y | Y |
| 3 Rahall | Y | N | Y | N | Y | Y | N |
| **WISCONSIN** | | | | | | | |
| 1 **Ryan** | Y | N | Y | Y | N | Y | Y |
| 2 Baldwin | Y | N | Y | N | Y | N | N |
| 3 Kind | Y | N | Y | N | Y | Y | N |
| 4 Moore | Y | N | Y | N | Y | N | N |
| 5 **Sensenbrenner** | Y | Y | Y | Y | N | Y | Y |
| 6 **Petri** | Y | Y | Y | Y | N | Y | Y |
| 7 Obey | Y | N | Y | N | Y | N | N |
| 8 **Green** | Y | N | Y | Y | N | Y | Y |
| **WYOMING** | | | | | | | |
| AL **Cubin** | N | Y | Y | Y | N | Y | Y |

# IN THE HOUSE | By Vote Number

**637.** **H Res 579. Christmas Symbols and Traditions/Adoption.** Porter, R-Nev., motion to suspend the rules and adopt the resolution that would recognize the importance of the symbols and traditions of Christmas and strongly disapprove of attempts to ban references to Christmas. Motion agreed to 401-22: R 228-0; D 172-22 (ND 128-16, SD 44-6); I 1-0. A two-thirds majority of those present and voting (282 in this case) is required for adoption under suspension of the rules. Dec. 15, 2005.

**638.** **H Con Res 315. American Jewish History Month/Adoption.** Porter, R-Nev., motion to suspend the rules and adopt the concurrent resolution that would urge the president to issue an annual proclamation calling for the observance of an American Jewish History Month in January. Motion agreed to 423-0: R 225-0; D 197-0 (ND 148-0, SD 49-0); I 1-0. A two-thirds majority of those present and voting (282 in this case) is required for adoption under suspension of the rules. Dec. 15, 2005.

**639.** **HR 4437. Border Security/Removal Process.** Jackson-Lee, D-Texas, amendment that would direct the Homeland Security Department to create a program under which certain illegal immigrants undergoing expedited removal could be released to the custody of an individual or group who would monitor them and ensure that they make required court appearances. Rejected 162-252: R 0-218; D 161-34 (ND 128-17, SD 33-17); I 1-0. Dec. 15, 2005.

**640.** **HR 4437. Border Security/Security Fencing.** Hunter, R-Calif., amendment that would require the construction of security fencing, including lights and cameras, along certain ports of entry along the U.S.-Mexico border. Adopted 260-159: R 211-12; D 49-146 (ND 28-117, SD 21-29); I 0-1. Dec. 15, 2005.

**641.** **H Con Res 312. Russia and NGOs/Adoption.** Smith, R-N.J., motion to suspend the rules and adopt the concurrent resolution that would state that Congress urges the Russian government to withdraw draft legislation that would have the effect of severely restricting the activities of non-governmental organizations in Russia. Motion agreed to 405-15: R 211-12; D 193-3 (ND 145-2, SD 48-1); I 1-0. A two-thirds majority of those present and voting (280 in this case) is required for adoption under suspension of the rules. Dec. 15, 2005.

**642.** **HR 1815. Fiscal 2006 Defense Authorization/Motion to Close Conference.** Drake, R-Va., motion to close portions of the conference on the bill that would authorize funding for defense programs for fiscal 2006. Motion agreed to 409-12: R 221-0; D 187-12 (ND 138-10, SD 49-2); I 1-0. Dec. 16, 2005.

**643.** **HR 1815. Fiscal 2006 Defense Authorization/Motion to Instruct.** Skelton, D-Mo., motion to instruct House conferees to include Senate-passed language that would require the Defense secretary and the director of National Intelligence to submit a report within 60 days of the bill's enactment on clandestine U.S. detention facilities abroad. Motion agreed to 228-187: R 31-186; D 196-1 (ND 147-0, SD 49-1); I 1-0. Dec. 16, 2005.

**644.** **H Res 612. Commitment to Iraq Victory/Previous Question.** Dreier, R-Calif., motion to order the previous question (thus ending debate and the possibility of amendment) on adoption of the rule (H Res 619) for House floor consideration of the resolution that would express the commitment of the House of Representatives to achieving victory in Iraq. Motion agreed to 221-200: R 221-0; D 0-199 (ND 0-148, SD 0-51); I 0-1. Dec. 16, 2005.

| | 637 | 638 | 639 | 640 | 641 | 642 | 643 | 644 |
|---|---|---|---|---|---|---|---|---|
| **ALABAMA** | | | | | | | | |
| 1 Bonner | Y | Y | N | Y | Y | Y | N | Y |
| 2 Everett | Y | Y | N | Y | Y | Y | N | Y |
| 3 Rogers | Y | Y | N | Y | Y | Y | N | Y |
| 4 Aderholt | Y | Y | N | Y | Y | Y | N | Y |
| 5 Cramer | Y | Y | N | Y | Y | Y | Y | N |
| 6 Bachus | Y | Y | N | Y | Y | Y | N | Y |
| 7 Davis | Y | Y | N | N | Y | Y | Y | N |
| **ALASKA** | | | | | | | | |
| AL Young | Y | Y | ? | ? | ? | Y | N | Y |
| **ARIZONA** | | | | | | | | |
| 1 Renzi | Y | Y | N | Y | Y | Y | N | Y |
| 2 Franks | Y | Y | N | Y | Y | Y | N | Y |
| 3 Shadegg | Y | Y | N | Y | Y | Y | N | Y |
| 4 Pastor | Y | Y | Y | N | Y | Y | Y | N |
| 5 Hayworth | Y | Y | N | Y | Y | Y | N | Y |
| 6 Flake | Y | Y | N | Y | Y | Y | N | Y |
| 7 Grijalva | Y | Y | Y | N | Y | Y | Y | N |
| 8 Kolbe | Y | Y | N | Y | Y | Y | N | Y |
| **ARKANSAS** | | | | | | | | |
| 1 Berry | Y | Y | N | Y | Y | Y | Y | N |
| 2 Snyder | Y | Y | N | Y | Y | Y | Y | N |
| 3 Boozman | Y | Y | N | Y | Y | Y | N | Y |
| 4 Ross | Y | Y | N | Y | Y | Y | Y | N |
| **CALIFORNIA** | | | | | | | | |
| 1 Thompson | Y | Y | N | N | Y | Y | Y | N |
| 2 Herger | Y | ? | N | Y | Y | Y | N | Y |
| 3 Lungren | Y | Y | N | Y | Y | Y | N | Y |
| 4 Doolittle | Y | Y | N | Y | Y | Y | N | Y |
| 5 Matsui, D. | Y | Y | Y | N | Y | Y | Y | N |
| 6 Woolsey | N | Y | Y | N | Y | N | Y | N |
| 7 Miller, George | N | Y | Y | N | Y | Y | Y | N |
| 8 Pelosi | Y | Y | Y | N | Y | Y | Y | N |
| 9 Lee | N | Y | Y | N | Y | N | Y | N |
| 10 Tauscher | Y | Y | Y | N | Y | Y | Y | N |
| 11 Pombo | Y | Y | N | Y | Y | Y | N | Y |
| 12 Lantos | Y | Y | Y | N | Y | Y | Y | N |
| 13 Stark | N | Y | N | N | Y | N | Y | N |
| 14 Eshoo | Y | Y | Y | N | Y | Y | Y | N |
| 15 Honda | N | Y | Y | N | Y | Y | Y | N |
| 16 Lofgren | Y | Y | Y | N | Y | Y | Y | N |
| 17 Farr | Y | Y | Y | N | Y | Y | Y | N |
| 18 Cardoza | Y | Y | N | Y | Y | Y | Y | N |
| 19 Radanovich | Y | Y | N | N | Y | Y | N | Y |
| 20 Costa | Y | Y | Y | Y | Y | Y | Y | N |
| 21 Nunes | Y | Y | N | Y | Y | Y | N | Y |
| 22 Thomas | Y | Y | ? | Y | Y | Y | N | Y |
| 23 Capps | N | Y | Y | N | Y | Y | Y | N |
| 24 Gallegly | Y | Y | N | Y | Y | Y | N | Y |
| 25 McKeon | Y | Y | N | Y | Y | Y | N | Y |
| 26 Dreier | Y | Y | N | Y | Y | Y | N | Y |
| 27 Sherman | Y | Y | Y | N | Y | Y | Y | N |
| 28 Berman | Y | Y | Y | N | Y | Y | Y | N |
| 29 Schiff | Y | Y | Y | N | Y | Y | + | N |
| 30 Waxman | Y | Y | Y | N | Y | Y | Y | N |
| 31 Becerra | Y | Y | Y | N | Y | Y | Y | N |
| 32 Solis | Y | Y | Y | N | Y | Y | Y | N |
| 33 Watson | Y | Y | Y | N | Y | Y | Y | N |
| 34 Roybal-Allard | Y | Y | Y | N | Y | Y | Y | N |
| 35 Waters | ? | ? | ? | ? | ? | N | Y | N |
| 36 Harman | N | Y | N | N | Y | Y | Y | N |
| 37 Millender-McD. | Y | Y | Y | N | Y | Y | Y | N |
| 38 Napolitano | Y | Y | Y | N | Y | ? | ? | ? |
| 39 Sánchez, Linda | Y | Y | Y | N | Y | Y | Y | N |
| 40 Royce | Y | Y | N | Y | Y | Y | N | Y |
| 41 Lewis | Y | Y | N | Y | Y | Y | N | Y |
| 42 Miller, Gary | Y | Y | N | Y | Y | Y | N | Y |
| 43 Baca | Y | Y | Y | N | Y | Y | Y | N |
| 44 Calvert | Y | Y | N | Y | Y | Y | N | Y |
| 45 Bono | Y | Y | N | Y | Y | Y | N | Y |
| 46 Rohrabacher | Y | Y | N | Y | Y | Y | N | Y |
| 47 Sanchez, Loretta | Y | Y | Y | N | Y | Y | Y | N |
| 48 Campbell | Y | Y | N | Y | Y | Y | N | Y |
| 49 Issa | Y | Y | N | Y | Y | Y | N | Y |

| | 637 | 638 | 639 | 640 | 641 | 642 | 643 | 644 |
|---|---|---|---|---|---|---|---|---|
| 50 Vacant | | | | | | | | |
| 51 Filner | Y | Y | N | Y | Y | Y | Y | N |
| 52 Hunter | Y | ? | N | Y | Y | Y | N | Y |
| 53 Davis | Y | Y | N | Y | Y | Y | Y | N |
| **COLORADO** | | | | | | | | |
| 1 DeGette | N | Y | Y | N | Y | Y | Y | N |
| 2 Udall | Y | Y | N | Y | Y | Y | Y | N |
| 3 Salazar | Y | Y | Y | N | Y | Y | Y | N |
| 4 Musgrave | Y | Y | N | Y | Y | Y | N | Y |
| 5 Hefley | Y | Y | N | Y | Y | Y | N | Y |
| 6 Tancredo | Y | Y | N | Y | Y | Y | N | Y |
| 7 Beauprez | Y | Y | N | Y | Y | Y | N | Y |
| **CONNECTICUT** | | | | | | | | |
| 1 Larson | Y | Y | N | Y | Y | Y | Y | N |
| 2 Simmons | Y | Y | N | Y | Y | Y | Y | Y |
| 3 DeLauro | Y | Y | N | Y | Y | Y | Y | N |
| 4 Shays | Y | Y | N | Y | Y | Y | Y | N |
| 5 Johnson | Y | Y | N | Y | Y | Y | N | Y |
| **DELAWARE** | | | | | | | | |
| AL Castle | Y | Y | N | Y | Y | Y | Y | Y |
| **FLORIDA** | | | | | | | | |
| 1 Miller | Y | Y | N | Y | Y | Y | N | Y |
| 2 Boyd | Y | Y | N | Y | Y | Y | Y | N |
| 3 Brown | Y | Y | Y | N | ? | Y | Y | N |
| 4 Crenshaw | Y | Y | N | Y | Y | Y | N | Y |
| 5 Brown-Waite | Y | Y | N | Y | Y | Y | N | Y |
| 6 Stearns | Y | Y | N | Y | Y | Y | N | Y |
| 7 Mica | Y | Y | N | Y | Y | Y | N | Y |
| 8 Keller | Y | Y | N | Y | Y | Y | N | Y |
| 9 Bilirakis | Y | Y | N | Y | Y | Y | N | Y |
| 10 Young | Y | Y | N | Y | Y | Y | N | Y |
| 11 Davis | ? | ? | ? | ? | ? | Y | Y | N |
| 12 Putnam | Y | Y | N | Y | Y | Y | - | Y |
| 13 Harris | Y | Y | N | Y | Y | Y | N | Y |
| 14 Mack | Y | Y | N | Y | Y | Y | N | Y |
| 15 Weldon | Y | Y | N | Y | Y | Y | N | Y |
| 16 Foley | Y | Y | N | Y | Y | Y | N | Y |
| 17 Meek | Y | Y | Y | N | Y | Y | Y | N |
| 18 Ros-Lehtinen | Y | Y | N | N | Y | Y | N | Y |
| 19 Wexler | N | Y | Y | N | Y | Y | Y | N |
| 20 Wasserman-Schultz | N | Y | Y | N | Y | Y | Y | N |
| 21 Diaz-Balart, L. | Y | Y | N | Y | Y | Y | N | Y |
| 22 Shaw | Y | Y | N | Y | Y | Y | N | Y |
| 23 Hastings | N | Y | Y | N | N | Y | Y | N |
| 24 Feeney | Y | Y | ? | Y | Y | Y | ? | Y |
| 25 Diaz-Balart, M. | + | + | - | - | + | + | - | + |
| **GEORGIA** | | | | | | | | |
| 1 Kingston | Y | Y | N | Y | Y | Y | N | Y |
| 2 Bishop | Y | Y | Y | Y | Y | Y | Y | N |
| 3 Marshall | Y | Y | N | Y | Y | Y | N | N |
| 4 McKinney | Y | Y | Y | N | Y | N | Y | N |
| 5 Lewis | N | Y | Y | N | Y | N | Y | N |
| 6 Price | Y | Y | N | Y | Y | Y | N | Y |
| 7 Linder | Y | Y | N | Y | Y | Y | N | Y |
| 8 Westmoreland | Y | Y | N | Y | Y | Y | N | Y |
| 9 Norwood | Y | Y | N | Y | Y | Y | N | Y |
| 10 Deal | Y | ? | N | Y | Y | Y | N | Y |
| 11 Gingrey | Y | Y | N | Y | Y | Y | N | Y |
| 12 Barrow | Y | Y | N | Y | Y | Y | Y | N |
| 13 Scott | Y | Y | Y | Y | Y | Y | Y | N |
| **HAWAII** | | | | | | | | |
| 1 Abercrombie | Y | Y | N | Y | N | Y | Y | N |
| 2 Case | Y | Y | N | Y | Y | Y | Y | N |
| **IDAHO** | | | | | | | | |
| 1 Otter | Y | Y | N | Y | N | Y | N | Y |
| 2 Simpson | Y | Y | N | Y | Y | Y | N | Y |
| **ILLINOIS** | | | | | | | | |
| 1 Rush | N | Y | Y | N | Y | Y | Y | N |
| 2 Jackson | Y | Y | N | Y | N | Y | Y | N |
| 3 Lipinski | Y | Y | Y | Y | Y | Y | Y | N |
| 4 Gutierrez | Y | Y | N | Y | Y | Y | Y | N |
| 5 Emanuel | + | + | + | - | + | Y | Y | N |
| 6 Hyde | + | + | - | + | + | + | - | + |
| 7 Davis | Y | Y | Y | N | Y | Y | Y | N |
| 8 Bean | Y | Y | N | Y | Y | Y | Y | N |
| 9 Schakowsky | N | Y | N | Y | Y | Y | Y | N |
| 10 Kirk | Y | Y | N | Y | ? | Y | - | Y |
| 11 Weller | Y | Y | N | Y | Y | Y | N | Y |
| 12 Costello | Y | Y | N | Y | Y | Y | Y | N |

**KEY**  Republicans    Democrats    *Independents*

| | | | |
|---|---|---|---|
| Y Voted for (yea) | X Paired against | C Voted "present" to avoid possible conflict of interest |
| # Paired for | – Announced against | |
| + Announced for | P Voted "present" | ? Did not vote or otherwise make a position known |
| N Voted against (nay) | | |

ND Northern Democrats, SD Southern Democrats
Southern states: Ala., Ark., Fla., Ga., Ky., La., Miss., N.C., Okla., S.C., Tenn., Va.

| | 637 | 638 | 639 | 640 | 641 | 642 | 643 | 644 |
|---|---|---|---|---|---|---|---|---|
| 13 **Biggert** | Y | Y | N | Y | Y | Y | N | Y |
| 14 **Hastert** | | | | | | | | |
| 15 **Johnson** | Y | Y | N | Y | Y | Y | N | Y |
| 16 **Manzullo** | Y | Y | N | Y | Y | Y | N | Y |
| 17 Evans | Y | Y | Y | N | Y | Y | Y | N |
| 18 **LaHood** | Y | Y | ? | ? | ? | ? | ? | ? |
| 19 **Shimkus** | Y | Y | N | Y | Y | Y | N | Y |
| INDIANA | | | | | | | | |
| 1 Visclosky | Y | Y | N | N | Y | Y | Y | N |
| 2 **Chocola** | Y | Y | N | Y | Y | Y | N | Y |
| 3 **Souder** | Y | Y | N | Y | Y | Y | N | Y |
| 4 **Buyer** | Y | Y | N | Y | Y | Y | N | Y |
| 5 **Burton** | Y | Y | N | Y | Y | Y | N | Y |
| 6 **Pence** | Y | Y | N | Y | Y | Y | N | Y |
| 7 Carson | Y | Y | Y | N | Y | Y | Y | N |
| 8 **Hostettler** | Y | Y | N | Y | Y | Y | N | Y |
| 9 **Sodrel** | Y | Y | N | Y | Y | Y | N | Y |
| IOWA | | | | | | | | |
| 1 **Nussle** | Y | Y | N | Y | Y | Y | N | Y |
| 2 **Leach** | Y | Y | N | Y | Y | Y | Y | Y |
| 3 Boswell | Y | Y | Y | Y | Y | Y | Y | N |
| 4 **Latham** | Y | Y | N | Y | Y | Y | N | Y |
| 5 **King** | Y | Y | N | Y | Y | Y | N | Y |
| KANSAS | | | | | | | | |
| 1 **Moran** | Y | Y | N | Y | Y | Y | Y | Y |
| 2 **Ryun** | Y | Y | N | Y | Y | Y | N | Y |
| 3 Moore | Y | Y | Y | Y | Y | Y | Y | N |
| 4 **Tiahrt** | Y | Y | N | Y | Y | Y | N | Y |
| KENTUCKY | | | | | | | | |
| 1 **Whitfield** | Y | Y | N | Y | Y | Y | Y | Y |
| 2 **Lewis** | Y | Y | N | Y | Y | Y | N | Y |
| 3 **Northup** | Y | Y | N | Y | Y | Y | N | Y |
| 4 **Davis** | Y | Y | N | Y | Y | Y | Y | Y |
| 5 **Rogers** | Y | Y | N | Y | Y | Y | N | Y |
| 6 Chandler | Y | Y | N | Y | Y | Y | Y | N |
| LOUISIANA | | | | | | | | |
| 1 **Jindal** | Y | Y | N | Y | Y | Y | N | Y |
| 2 Jefferson | Y | Y | Y | N | Y | Y | Y | N |
| 3 Melancon | Y | Y | N | Y | Y | Y | Y | N |
| 4 **McCrery** | Y | Y | N | Y | Y | Y | N | Y |
| 5 **Alexander** | Y | Y | N | Y | Y | Y | N | Y |
| 6 **Baker** | Y | Y | N | Y | Y | Y | N | Y |
| 7 **Boustany** | Y | Y | N | Y | Y | Y | N | Y |
| MAINE | | | | | | | | |
| 1 Allen | Y | Y | Y | N | Y | Y | Y | N |
| 2 Michaud | Y | Y | Y | N | Y | Y | Y | N |
| MARYLAND | | | | | | | | |
| 1 **Gilchrest** | Y | Y | N | Y | Y | Y | Y | Y |
| 2 Ruppersberger | Y | Y | Y | Y | Y | Y | Y | N |
| 3 Cardin | Y | Y | Y | N | Y | Y | Y | N |
| 4 Wynn | Y | Y | Y | N | Y | Y | Y | N |
| 5 Hoyer | Y | Y | Y | N | Y | Y | Y | N |
| 6 **Bartlett** | Y | Y | N | Y | Y | Y | Y | Y |
| 7 Cummings | Y | Y | Y | N | Y | Y | Y | N |
| 8 Van Hollen | Y | Y | Y | N | Y | Y | Y | N |
| MASSACHUSETTS | | | | | | | | |
| 1 Olver | Y | Y | Y | N | Y | N | Y | N |
| 2 Neal | Y | Y | Y | N | Y | Y | Y | N |
| 3 McGovern | Y | Y | Y | N | Y | Y | Y | N |
| 4 Frank | Y | Y | Y | N | Y | Y | Y | N |
| 5 Meehan | Y | Y | Y | N | Y | Y | Y | N |
| 6 Tierney | Y | ? | Y | N | Y | Y | Y | N |
| 7 Markey | Y | Y | Y | N | Y | Y | Y | N |
| 8 Capuano | Y | Y | Y | N | Y | Y | Y | N |
| 9 Lynch | Y | Y | ? | ? | Y | Y | Y | N |
| 10 Delahunt | Y | Y | Y | N | Y | Y | Y | N |
| MICHIGAN | | | | | | | | |
| 1 Stupak | Y | Y | N | Y | Y | Y | Y | N |
| 2 **Hoekstra** | Y | Y | N | Y | Y | Y | N | Y |
| 3 **Ehlers** | Y | Y | N | N | Y | Y | Y | Y |
| 4 **Camp** | Y | Y | N | Y | Y | Y | N | Y |
| 5 Kildee | Y | Y | Y | N | Y | Y | Y | N |
| 6 **Upton** | Y | Y | N | Y | Y | Y | Y | Y |
| 7 **Schwarz** | Y | Y | N | Y | Y | Y | N | Y |
| 8 **Rogers** | Y | Y | ? | Y | Y | Y | N | Y |
| 9 **Knollenberg** | Y | Y | N | Y | Y | Y | N | Y |
| 10 **Miller** | Y | Y | N | Y | Y | Y | N | Y |
| 11 **McCotter** | Y | Y | N | Y | Y | Y | Y | Y |
| 12 Levin | Y | Y | Y | N | Y | Y | Y | N |
| 13 Kilpatrick | Y | Y | Y | N | Y | Y | Y | N |
| 14 Conyers | Y | Y | Y | N | Y | Y | Y | N |
| 15 Dingell | Y | Y | Y | N | Y | Y | Y | N |
| MINNESOTA | | | | | | | | |
| 1 **Gutknecht** | Y | Y | N | Y | N | Y | N | Y |
| 2 **Kline** | Y | Y | N | Y | Y | Y | N | Y |
| 3 **Ramstad** | Y | Y | N | Y | Y | Y | N | Y |
| 4 McCollum | Y | Y | Y | N | Y | Y | Y | N |
| 5 Sabo | Y | Y | Y | N | Y | Y | Y | N |
| 6 **Kennedy** | Y | Y | N | Y | Y | Y | N | Y |
| 7 Peterson | Y | Y | N | Y | Y | Y | Y | N |
| 8 Oberstar | Y | Y | Y | N | Y | Y | Y | N |
| MISSISSIPPI | | | | | | | | |
| 1 **Wicker** | Y | Y | N | Y | Y | Y | N | Y |
| 2 Thompson | Y | Y | Y | N | Y | Y | Y | N |
| 3 **Pickering** | Y | Y | N | Y | Y | Y | N | Y |
| 4 Taylor | Y | Y | N | Y | Y | Y | Y | N |
| MISSOURI | | | | | | | | |
| 1 Clay | Y | Y | ? | ? | Y | Y | Y | N |
| 2 **Akin** | Y | Y | N | Y | Y | Y | ? | Y |
| 3 Carnahan | Y | Y | Y | N | Y | Y | Y | N |
| 4 Skelton | Y | Y | N | Y | Y | Y | Y | N |
| 5 Cleaver | N | Y | Y | N | Y | Y | Y | N |
| 6 **Graves** | Y | Y | N | Y | Y | Y | N | Y |
| 7 **Blunt** | Y | Y | N | Y | Y | Y | N | Y |
| 8 **Emerson** | Y | Y | N | Y | Y | Y | Y | Y |
| 9 **Hulshof** | Y | Y | N | Y | Y | Y | Y | Y |
| MONTANA | | | | | | | | |
| AL **Rehberg** | Y | Y | N | Y | Y | Y | N | Y |
| NEBRASKA | | | | | | | | |
| 1 **Fortenberry** | Y | Y | N | Y | Y | Y | N | Y |
| 2 **Terry** | Y | Y | N | Y | Y | Y | N | Y |
| 3 **Osborne** | Y | Y | N | Y | Y | Y | N | Y |
| NEVADA | | | | | | | | |
| 1 Berkley | Y | Y | Y | Y | Y | Y | Y | N |
| 2 **Gibbons** | Y | Y | N | Y | Y | Y | Y | Y |
| 3 **Porter** | Y | Y | N | Y | Y | Y | Y | Y |
| NEW HAMPSHIRE | | | | | | | | |
| 1 **Bradley** | Y | Y | N | Y | Y | Y | N | Y |
| 2 **Bass** | Y | Y | N | Y | Y | Y | N | Y |
| NEW JERSEY | | | | | | | | |
| 1 Andrews | Y | Y | Y | N | Y | Y | Y | N |
| 2 **LoBiondo** | Y | Y | N | Y | Y | Y | N | Y |
| 3 **Saxton** | Y | Y | ? | Y | N | Y | N | Y |
| 4 **Smith** | Y | Y | N | Y | Y | Y | Y | Y |
| 5 **Garrett** | Y | Y | N | Y | Y | Y | N | Y |
| 6 Pallone | Y | Y | Y | N | Y | Y | Y | N |
| 7 **Ferguson** | Y | Y | N | Y | Y | Y | N | Y |
| 8 Pascrell | Y | Y | Y | N | Y | Y | Y | N |
| 9 Rothman | Y | Y | Y | N | Y | Y | Y | N |
| 10 Payne | N | Y | Y | N | Y | ? | ? | ? |
| 11 **Frelinghuysen** | Y | Y | N | Y | Y | Y | N | Y |
| 12 Holt | P | Y | Y | N | Y | Y | Y | N |
| 13 Menendez | Y | Y | Y | N | Y | Y | Y | N |
| NEW MEXICO | | | | | | | | |
| 1 **Wilson** | Y | Y | N | N | Y | Y | N | Y |
| 2 **Pearce** | Y | Y | N | N | Y | ? | ? | ? |
| 3 Udall | Y | Y | Y | N | Y | Y | Y | N |
| NEW YORK | | | | | | | | |
| 1 Bishop | Y | Y | Y | Y | Y | Y | Y | N |
| 2 Israel | P | Y | Y | Y | Y | Y | Y | N |
| 3 **King** | Y | Y | N | Y | Y | Y | N | Y |
| 4 McCarthy | Y | Y | + | + | + | + | + | – |
| 5 Ackerman | N | Y | Y | N | Y | Y | Y | N |
| 6 Meeks | Y | Y | ? | ? | Y | Y | Y | N |
| 7 Crowley | Y | Y | Y | N | Y | Y | Y | N |
| 8 Nadler | Y | Y | Y | N | Y | Y | Y | N |
| 9 Weiner | Y | Y | Y | N | Y | Y | Y | N |
| 10 Towns | Y | Y | Y | N | Y | Y | Y | N |
| 11 Owens | P | Y | Y | N | Y | Y | Y | N |
| 12 Velázquez | Y | Y | Y | N | Y | Y | Y | N |
| 13 **Fossella** | Y | Y | N | Y | Y | Y | N | Y |
| 14 Maloney | Y | Y | Y | Y | Y | Y | Y | N |
| 15 Rangel | Y | Y | Y | N | Y | Y | Y | N |
| 16 Serrano | Y | Y | Y | N | Y | Y | Y | N |
| 17 Engel | Y | Y | Y | N | Y | Y | Y | N |
| 18 Lowey | P | Y | Y | N | Y | Y | Y | N |
| 19 **Kelly** | Y | Y | N | Y | Y | Y | Y | Y |
| 20 **Sweeney** | Y | Y | ? | ? | ? | ? | ? | ? |
| 21 McNulty | Y | Y | Y | N | Y | Y | Y | N |
| 22 Hinchey | Y | Y | Y | Y | Y | N | Y | N |
| 23 **McHugh** | Y | Y | N | Y | Y | Y | N | Y |
| 24 **Boehlert** | Y | Y | N | N | Y | Y | Y | Y |
| 25 **Walsh** | Y | Y | N | Y | Y | Y | N | Y |
| 26 **Reynolds** | Y | Y | N | N | Y | Y | N | Y |
| 27 Higgins | Y | Y | Y | Y | Y | Y | Y | N |
| 28 Slaughter | Y | Y | Y | N | Y | Y | Y | N |
| 29 **Kuhl** | Y | Y | N | Y | Y | Y | N | Y |
| NORTH CAROLINA | | | | | | | | |
| 1 Butterfield | Y | Y | Y | N | Y | Y | Y | N |
| 2 Etheridge | Y | Y | Y | Y | Y | Y | Y | N |
| 3 **Jones** | Y | Y | N | Y | N | Y | Y | Y |
| 4 Price | Y | Y | Y | N | Y | Y | Y | N |
| 5 **Foxx** | Y | Y | N | Y | Y | Y | N | Y |
| 6 **Coble** | Y | Y | N | Y | N | Y | N | Y |
| 7 McIntyre | Y | Y | N | Y | Y | Y | Y | N |
| 8 **Hayes** | Y | Y | N | Y | Y | Y | N | Y |
| 9 **Myrick** | Y | Y | N | Y | Y | Y | N | Y |
| 10 **McHenry** | Y | Y | N | Y | Y | Y | N | Y |
| 11 **Taylor** | Y | Y | N | Y | N | Y | N | Y |
| 12 Watt | Y | Y | Y | N | Y | Y | Y | N |
| 13 Miller | Y | Y | Y | Y | Y | Y | Y | N |
| NORTH DAKOTA | | | | | | | | |
| AL Pomeroy | Y | Y | N | Y | Y | Y | Y | N |
| OHIO | | | | | | | | |
| 1 **Chabot** | Y | Y | N | Y | Y | Y | Y | Y |
| 2 **Schmidt** | Y | Y | N | Y | Y | Y | N | Y |
| 3 **Turner** | Y | Y | N | Y | Y | Y | N | Y |
| 4 **Oxley** | Y | Y | N | Y | Y | Y | N | Y |
| 5 **Gillmor** | Y | Y | N | Y | Y | Y | N | Y |
| 6 Strickland | Y | Y | Y | N | Y | Y | Y | N |
| 7 **Hobson** | Y | Y | N | Y | Y | Y | N | Y |
| 8 **Boehner** | Y | Y | N | Y | Y | Y | N | Y |
| 9 Kaptur | Y | Y | Y | N | Y | Y | Y | N |
| 10 Kucinich | Y | Y | Y | N | N | N | Y | N |
| 11 Jones | Y | Y | Y | N | Y | Y | Y | N |
| 12 **Tiberi** | Y | Y | N | Y | Y | Y | N | Y |
| 13 Brown | Y | Y | Y | N | Y | Y | Y | N |
| 14 **LaTourette** | Y | Y | N | Y | Y | Y | N | Y |
| 15 **Pryce** | Y | Y | N | Y | Y | Y | N | Y |
| 16 **Regula** | Y | Y | N | Y | Y | Y | N | Y |
| 17 Ryan | Y | Y | Y | Y | Y | Y | Y | N |
| 18 **Ney** | Y | Y | N | Y | Y | Y | N | Y |
| OKLAHOMA | | | | | | | | |
| 1 **Sullivan** | Y | Y | N | Y | Y | Y | N | Y |
| 2 Boren | Y | Y | N | Y | Y | Y | Y | N |
| 3 **Lucas** | Y | Y | N | Y | Y | Y | N | Y |
| 4 **Cole** | Y | Y | N | Y | Y | Y | N | Y |
| 5 **Istook** | Y | Y | N | Y | Y | ? | ? | ? |
| OREGON | | | | | | | | |
| 1 Wu | Y | Y | Y | N | Y | Y | Y | N |
| 2 **Walden** | Y | Y | N | Y | Y | Y | Y | Y |
| 3 Blumenauer | N | Y | Y | N | Y | N | Y | N |
| 4 DeFazio | Y | Y | Y | N | Y | N | Y | N |
| 5 Hooley | Y | Y | Y | Y | Y | Y | Y | N |
| PENNSYLVANIA | | | | | | | | |
| 1 Brady | Y | Y | Y | N | Y | Y | Y | N |
| 2 Fattah | Y | Y | Y | N | Y | Y | Y | N |
| 3 **English** | Y | Y | N | Y | Y | Y | N | Y |
| 4 **Hart** | Y | Y | N | Y | Y | Y | N | Y |
| 5 **Peterson** | Y | Y | N | Y | Y | Y | N | Y |
| 6 **Gerlach** | Y | Y | N | Y | Y | Y | Y | Y |
| 7 **Weldon** | Y | Y | N | Y | N | Y | N | Y |
| 8 **Fitzpatrick** | Y | Y | N | Y | Y | Y | Y | Y |
| 9 **Shuster** | Y | Y | N | Y | Y | Y | N | Y |
| 10 **Sherwood** | Y | Y | N | Y | Y | Y | N | Y |
| 11 Kanjorski | Y | Y | N | Y | Y | Y | Y | N |
| 12 Murtha | Y | Y | Y | Y | ? | Y | Y | N |
| 13 Schwartz | P | Y | Y | N | Y | Y | Y | N |
| 14 Doyle | Y | Y | Y | N | Y | Y | Y | N |
| 15 **Dent** | Y | Y | N | Y | Y | Y | N | Y |
| 16 **Pitts** | Y | Y | N | Y | Y | Y | N | Y |
| 17 Holden | Y | Y | N | Y | Y | Y | Y | N |
| 18 **Murphy** | Y | Y | N | Y | Y | Y | N | Y |
| 19 **Platts** | Y | Y | N | Y | Y | Y | Y | Y |
| RHODE ISLAND | | | | | | | | |
| 1 Kennedy | Y | Y | Y | N | Y | Y | Y | N |
| 2 Langevin | Y | Y | Y | N | Y | Y | Y | N |
| SOUTH CAROLINA | | | | | | | | |
| 1 **Brown** | Y | Y | N | Y | Y | Y | N | Y |
| 2 **Wilson** | Y | Y | N | Y | Y | Y | N | Y |
| 3 **Barrett** | Y | Y | N | Y | Y | + | – | + |
| 4 **Inglis** | Y | Y | N | Y | Y | Y | Y | Y |
| 5 Spratt | Y | Y | Y | Y | Y | Y | Y | N |
| 6 Clyburn | Y | Y | Y | N | Y | Y | Y | N |
| SOUTH DAKOTA | | | | | | | | |
| AL Herseth | Y | Y | N | Y | Y | Y | Y | N |
| TENNESSEE | | | | | | | | |
| 1 **Jenkins** | Y | Y | N | Y | N | Y | N | Y |
| 2 **Duncan** | Y | Y | N | Y | N | Y | N | Y |
| 3 **Wamp** | Y | Y | N | Y | N | Y | N | Y |
| 4 Davis | Y | Y | N | Y | Y | Y | Y | N |
| 5 Cooper | Y | Y | Y | N | Y | Y | Y | N |
| 6 Gordon | Y | Y | N | Y | Y | Y | Y | N |
| 7 **Blackburn** | Y | Y | N | Y | Y | Y | N | Y |
| 8 Tanner | Y | Y | N | Y | Y | Y | Y | N |
| 9 Ford | Y | Y | Y | N | Y | Y | Y | N |
| TEXAS | | | | | | | | |
| 1 **Gohmert** | Y | Y | N | Y | Y | Y | N | Y |
| 2 **Poe** | Y | Y | N | Y | Y | Y | N | Y |
| 3 **Johnson, S.** | Y | Y | N | Y | Y | Y | N | Y |
| 4 **Hall** | Y | Y | N | Y | Y | Y | N | Y |
| 5 **Hensarling** | Y | Y | N | Y | Y | Y | N | Y |
| 6 **Barton** | Y | Y | – | + | + | + | – | + |
| 7 **Culberson** | Y | Y | N | Y | Y | Y | N | Y |
| 8 **Brady** | Y | Y | N | Y | Y | Y | N | Y |
| 9 Green, A. | Y | Y | Y | N | Y | Y | Y | N |
| 10 **McCaul** | Y | Y | N | Y | Y | Y | N | Y |
| 11 **Conaway** | Y | Y | N | N | Y | Y | N | Y |
| 12 **Granger** | Y | Y | N | N | Y | Y | N | Y |
| 13 **Thornberry** | Y | Y | N | Y | Y | Y | N | Y |
| 14 **Paul** | Y | Y | N | N | N | Y | Y | Y |
| 15 Hinojosa | Y | Y | Y | N | Y | Y | Y | N |
| 16 Reyes | Y | Y | Y | N | Y | Y | Y | N |
| 17 Edwards | Y | Y | N | Y | Y | Y | ? | N |
| 18 Jackson-Lee | Y | Y | Y | N | Y | Y | Y | N |
| 19 **Neugebauer** | Y | Y | N | Y | Y | Y | N | Y |
| 20 Gonzalez | Y | + | Y | N | Y | Y | Y | N |
| 21 **Smith** | Y | Y | N | Y | Y | Y | N | Y |
| 22 **DeLay** | Y | Y | ? | Y | Y | Y | N | Y |
| 23 **Bonilla** | Y | Y | N | N | Y | Y | N | Y |
| 24 **Marchant** | Y | Y | N | Y | Y | Y | N | Y |
| 25 Doggett | Y | Y | Y | N | Y | Y | Y | N |
| 26 **Burgess** | Y | Y | N | Y | Y | Y | N | Y |
| 27 Ortiz | Y | Y | Y | N | Y | Y | Y | N |
| 28 Cuellar | Y | Y | Y | N | Y | Y | Y | N |
| 29 Green, G. | Y | Y | Y | N | Y | Y | Y | N |
| 30 Johnson, E. | Y | Y | Y | N | Y | Y | Y | N |
| 31 **Carter** | Y | Y | N | Y | Y | Y | N | Y |
| 32 **Sessions** | Y | Y | N | Y | Y | Y | N | Y |
| UTAH | | | | | | | | |
| 1 **Bishop** | Y | Y | N | Y | Y | Y | N | Y |
| 2 Matheson | Y | Y | N | Y | Y | Y | Y | N |
| 3 **Cannon** | Y | Y | N | ? | Y | Y | N | Y |
| VERMONT | | | | | | | | |
| AL *Sanders* | Y | Y | Y | N | Y | Y | Y | N |
| VIRGINIA | | | | | | | | |
| 1 **Davis, J.** | Y | Y | N | Y | Y | + | + | + |
| 2 **Drake** | Y | Y | N | Y | Y | Y | N | Y |
| 3 Scott | N | Y | Y | N | Y | Y | Y | N |
| 4 **Forbes** | Y | Y | N | Y | Y | Y | N | Y |
| 5 **Goode** | Y | Y | N | Y | Y | Y | N | Y |
| 6 **Goodlatte** | Y | Y | N | Y | Y | Y | N | Y |
| 7 **Cantor** | Y | Y | ? | Y | Y | Y | N | Y |
| 8 Moran | N | Y | Y | N | Y | Y | Y | N |
| 9 Boucher | Y | Y | Y | Y | Y | Y | Y | N |
| 10 **Wolf** | Y | Y | N | Y | Y | Y | Y | Y |
| 11 **Davis, T.** | Y | Y | N | Y | Y | Y | N | Y |
| WASHINGTON | | | | | | | | |
| 1 Inslee | Y | Y | Y | N | Y | Y | Y | N |
| 2 Larsen | Y | Y | Y | N | Y | Y | Y | N |
| 3 Baird | Y | Y | Y | N | Y | Y | Y | N |
| 4 **Hastings** | Y | Y | N | Y | Y | Y | N | Y |
| 5 **McMorris** | Y | Y | N | Y | Y | Y | N | Y |
| 6 Dicks | Y | Y | Y | N | Y | Y | Y | N |
| 7 McDermott | N | Y | Y | N | Y | N | Y | N |
| 8 **Reichert** | Y | Y | N | Y | Y | Y | N | Y |
| 9 Smith | Y | Y | N | Y | Y | Y | Y | N |
| WEST VIRGINIA | | | | | | | | |
| 1 Mollohan | Y | Y | Y | N | Y | Y | Y | N |
| 2 **Capito** | Y | Y | N | Y | Y | Y | N | Y |
| 3 Rahall | Y | Y | Y | N | Y | Y | Y | N |
| WISCONSIN | | | | | | | | |
| 1 **Ryan** | Y | Y | N | Y | Y | Y | N | Y |
| 2 Baldwin | Y | Y | Y | N | Y | Y | Y | N |
| 3 Kind | Y | Y | Y | Y | Y | Y | Y | N |
| 4 Moore | N | Y | Y | N | Y | Y | Y | N |
| 5 **Sensenbrenner** | Y | Y | N | Y | N | Y | N | Y |
| 6 **Petri** | Y | Y | N | Y | Y | Y | Y | Y |
| 7 Obey | Y | Y | Y | N | Y | Y | Y | N |
| 8 **Green** | Y | Y | N | Y | Y | Y | N | Y |
| WYOMING | | | | | | | | |
| AL **Cubin** | Y | Y | N | Y | Y | Y | N | Y |

# IN THE HOUSE | By Vote Number

**645.** **H Res 612. Commitment to Iraq Victory/Rule.** Adoption of the rule (H Res 619) that would provide for House floor consideration of the resolution that would express the commitment of the House of Representatives to achieving victory in Iraq. Adopted 217-202: R 217-3; D 0-198 (ND 0-147, SD 0-51); I 0-1. Dec. 16, 2005.

**646.** **HR 4437. Border Security/Rule.** Adoption of the rule (H Res 621) that would provide for House floor consideration of the bill that would increase security at international borders and at ports of entry into the United States. Adopted 216-203: R 213-8; D 3-194 (ND 3-143, SD 0-51); I 0-1. Dec. 16, 2005.

**647.** **H Con Res 294. Condemn Prison Camps in China/Adoption.** Smith, R-N.J., motion to suspend the rules and adopt the concurrent resolution that would call on the international community to condemn the Laogai, the system of forced labor prison camps in China, as a tool for suppression maintained by the Chinese government. Motion agreed to 413-1: R 216-1; D 196-0 (ND 146-0, SD 50-0); I 1-0. A two-thirds majority of those present and voting (276 in this case) is required for adoption under suspension of the rules. Dec. 16, 2005.

**648.** **H Res 612. Commitment to Iraq Victory/Adoption.** Adoption of the resolution that would state the commitment of the House of Representatives to achieving victory in Iraq. Adopted 279-109: R 220-0; D 59-108 (ND 28-92, SD 31-16); I 0-1. Dec. 16, 2005.

**649.** **H Res 409. Operation Murambatsvina Condemnation/Adoption.** Smith, R-N.J., motion to suspend the rules and adopt the resolution that would condemn Operation Murambatsvina as a major humanitarian catastrophe caused by the Zimbabwean government's callousness toward its own people, disregard for the rule of law, and lack of planning to move families and businesses to more desirable locations. Motion agreed to 421-1: R 221-1; D 199-0 (ND 148-0, SD 51-0); I 1-0. A two-thirds majority of those present and voting (282 in this case) is required for adoption under suspension of the rules. Dec. 16, 2005.

**650.** **H Res 575. Palestinian Elections/Adoption.** Ros-Lehtinen, R-Fla., motion to suspend the rules and adopt the resolution that would assert that organizations that carry out terrorist acts, such as Hamas, should not be allowed to participate in Palestinian elections until they recognize Israel, disarm and cease terrorist activities. Motion agreed to 397-17: R 217-1; D 179-16 (ND 132-12, SD 47-4); I 1-0. A two-thirds majority of those present and voting (276 in this case) is required for adoption under suspension of the rules. Dec. 16, 2005.

**651.** **H Res 534. Iraqi Judiciary/Adoption.** Ros-Lehtinen, R-Fla., motion to suspend the rules and adopt the resolution that would recognize the importance of the Iraqi judiciary. Motion agreed to 408-1: R 213-1; D 194-0 (ND 143-0, SD 51-0); I 1-0. A two-thirds majority of those present and voting (273 in this case) is required for adoption under suspension of the rules. Dec. 16, 2005.

**652.** **S 1932. Budget Reconciliation/Motion to Instruct.** Spratt, D-S.C., motion to instruct House conferees to eliminate House provisions that would reduce eligibility for food stamps and funding for child support enforcement, repeal the Byrd amendment in the House-passed bill and accept the Senate-passed language eliminating the stabilization fund for Medicare Advantage payments. Motion agreed to 246-175: R 46-175; D 199-0 (ND 148-0, SD 51-0); I 1-0. Dec. 16, 2005.

ND Northern Democrats, SD Southern Democrats
Southern states: Ala., Ark., Fla., Ga., Ky., La., Miss., N.C., Okla., S.C., Tenn., Texas, Va.

| | 645 | 646 | 647 | 648 | 649 | 650 | 651 | 652 |
|---|---|---|---|---|---|---|---|---|
| **ALABAMA** | | | | | | | | |
| 1 Bonner | Y | Y | Y | Y | Y | Y | Y | N |
| 2 Everett | Y | Y | Y | Y | Y | Y | Y | N |
| 3 Rogers | Y | Y | Y | Y | Y | Y | Y | N |
| 4 Aderholt | Y | Y | Y | Y | Y | Y | Y | N |
| 5 Cramer | N | N | Y | Y | Y | Y | Y | Y |
| 6 Bachus | Y | Y | Y | Y | Y | Y | ? | N |
| 7 Davis | N | N | Y | Y | Y | Y | Y | Y |
| **ALASKA** | | | | | | | | |
| AL Young | Y | Y | Y | Y | Y | Y | Y | N |
| **ARIZONA** | | | | | | | | |
| 1 Renzi | Y | Y | Y | Y | Y | Y | Y | N |
| 2 Franks | Y | Y | Y | Y | Y | Y | Y | N |
| 3 Shadegg | Y | Y | Y | Y | Y | Y | Y | N |
| 4 Pastor | N | N | Y | N | Y | Y | Y | Y |
| 5 Hayworth | Y | N | Y | Y | Y | Y | Y | N |
| 6 Flake | Y | Y | Y | Y | Y | Y | Y | N |
| 7 Grijalva | N | N | Y | N | Y | Y | Y | Y |
| 8 Kolbe | Y | N | Y | Y | Y | P | Y | ? |
| **ARKANSAS** | | | | | | | | |
| 1 Berry | N | N | Y | Y | Y | Y | Y | Y |
| 2 Snyder | N | N | Y | Y | Y | Y | Y | Y |
| 3 Boozman | Y | Y | Y | Y | Y | Y | Y | N |
| 4 Ross | N | N | Y | Y | Y | Y | Y | Y |
| **CALIFORNIA** | | | | | | | | |
| 1 Thompson | N | N | Y | P | Y | Y | Y | Y |
| 2 Herger | Y | Y | Y | Y | Y | Y | Y | N |
| 3 Lungren | Y | Y | Y | Y | Y | Y | Y | N |
| 4 Doolittle | Y | Y | Y | Y | ? | Y | Y | N |
| 5 Matsui, D. | N | N | P | Y | Y | Y | Y | Y |
| 6 Woolsey | N | N | Y | N | Y | Y | Y | Y |
| 7 Miller, George | N | N | Y | N | Y | Y | ? | Y |
| 8 Pelosi | N | N | Y | N | Y | Y | Y | Y |
| 9 Lee | N | N | Y | N | Y | N | Y | Y |
| 10 Tauscher | N | N | Y | P | Y | Y | Y | Y |
| 11 Pombo | Y | Y | Y | Y | Y | Y | Y | N |
| 12 Lantos | N | N | Y | P | Y | Y | ? | Y |
| 13 Stark | N | N | ? | N | Y | N | Y | Y |
| 14 Eshoo | N | N | P | Y | Y | Y | Y | Y |
| 15 Honda | N | N | Y | N | Y | Y | Y | Y |
| 16 Lofgren | N | N | Y | P | Y | Y | Y | Y |
| 17 Farr | N | N | Y | N | Y | Y | Y | Y |
| 18 Cardoza | N | N | Y | N | Y | Y | Y | Y |
| 19 Radanovich | Y | Y | Y | Y | Y | Y | ? | N |
| 20 Costa | N | N | Y | Y | Y | Y | Y | Y |
| 21 Nunes | Y | Y | Y | Y | Y | Y | Y | N |
| 22 Thomas | Y | Y | Y | Y | Y | Y | N | N |
| 23 Capps | N | N | Y | N | Y | Y | Y | Y |
| 24 Gallegly | Y | Y | Y | Y | Y | Y | Y | N |
| 25 McKeon | Y | Y | Y | Y | Y | Y | Y | N |
| 26 Dreier | Y | Y | Y | Y | Y | Y | Y | N |
| 27 Sherman | N | N | Y | P | Y | Y | Y | Y |
| 28 Berman | N | N | Y | Y | Y | Y | Y | Y |
| 29 Schiff | N | N | Y | P | Y | Y | Y | Y |
| 30 Waxman | N | N | Y | N | Y | Y | Y | Y |
| 31 Becerra | N | N | Y | N | Y | P | Y | Y |
| 32 Solis | N | N | Y | N | Y | Y | Y | Y |
| 33 Watson | N | N | Y | N | Y | N | Y | Y |
| 34 Roybal-Allard | N | N | Y | N | Y | Y | Y | Y |
| 35 Waters | N | N | Y | N | Y | N | Y | Y |
| 36 Harman | N | N | Y | P | Y | Y | Y | Y |
| 37 Millender-McD. | N | N | Y | N | Y | Y | Y | Y |
| 38 Napolitano | ? | ? | ? | ? | ? | ? | ? | ? |
| 39 Sánchez, Linda | N | N | Y | N | Y | Y | Y | Y |
| 40 Royce | Y | Y | Y | Y | Y | Y | Y | N |
| 41 Lewis | Y | Y | ? | Y | Y | Y | Y | N |
| 42 Miller, Gary | Y | Y | Y | Y | Y | Y | Y | N |
| 43 Baca | N | N | Y | N | Y | Y | Y | Y |
| 44 Calvert | Y | Y | Y | Y | Y | Y | Y | N |
| 45 Bono | Y | Y | Y | Y | Y | Y | Y | Y |
| 46 Rohrabacher | Y | Y | Y | Y | Y | Y | Y | N |
| 47 Sanchez, Loretta | N | N | Y | P | Y | Y | Y | Y |
| 48 Campbell | Y | Y | Y | Y | Y | Y | Y | N |
| 49 Issa | Y | Y | Y | Y | Y | Y | Y | N |

| | 645 | 646 | 647 | 648 | 649 | 650 | 651 | 652 |
|---|---|---|---|---|---|---|---|---|
| 50 Vacant | | | | | | | | |
| 51 Filner | N | N | Y | N | Y | Y | Y | Y |
| 52 Hunter | Y | Y | Y | Y | Y | Y | Y | N |
| 53 Davis | N | N | Y | Y | Y | Y | Y | Y |
| **COLORADO** | | | | | | | | |
| 1 DeGette | N | N | Y | N | Y | Y | Y | Y |
| 2 Udall | N | N | Y | Y | Y | Y | Y | Y |
| 3 Salazar | N | N | Y | Y | Y | Y | Y | Y |
| 4 Musgrave | Y | Y | Y | Y | Y | Y | Y | N |
| 5 Hefley | Y | N | Y | Y | Y | Y | Y | N |
| 6 Tancredo | Y | Y | Y | Y | Y | Y | Y | N |
| 7 Beauprez | Y | Y | Y | Y | Y | Y | Y | N |
| **CONNECTICUT** | | | | | | | | |
| 1 Larson | N | N | Y | N | Y | Y | Y | Y |
| 2 Simmons | Y | Y | Y | Y | Y | Y | Y | Y |
| 3 DeLauro | N | N | Y | N | Y | Y | Y | Y |
| 4 Shays | Y | N | Y | Y | Y | Y | Y | Y |
| 5 Johnson | Y | Y | Y | Y | Y | Y | Y | N |
| **DELAWARE** | | | | | | | | |
| AL Castle | Y | Y | Y | Y | Y | Y | Y | Y |
| **FLORIDA** | | | | | | | | |
| 1 Miller | Y | Y | Y | Y | Y | Y | ? | N |
| 2 Boyd | N | N | Y | P | Y | Y | Y | Y |
| 3 Brown | N | N | Y | N | Y | Y | Y | Y |
| 4 Crenshaw | Y | Y | Y | Y | Y | Y | Y | N |
| 5 Brown-Waite | Y | Y | Y | Y | Y | Y | Y | N |
| 6 Stearns | Y | Y | Y | Y | Y | Y | Y | N |
| 7 Mica | Y | Y | Y | Y | Y | Y | ? | N |
| 8 Keller | Y | Y | Y | Y | Y | Y | Y | N |
| 9 Bilirakis | Y | Y | Y | Y | Y | Y | Y | N |
| 10 Young | Y | Y | Y | Y | Y | Y | Y | ? |
| 11 Davis | N | N | Y | Y | Y | Y | Y | Y |
| 12 Putnam | Y | Y | Y | Y | Y | Y | Y | N |
| 13 Harris | Y | Y | Y | Y | Y | Y | Y | N |
| 14 Mack | Y | Y | Y | Y | Y | Y | Y | N |
| 15 Weldon | Y | Y | Y | Y | Y | Y | Y | N |
| 16 Foley | Y | Y | Y | Y | Y | Y | Y | N |
| 17 Meek | N | N | Y | P | Y | Y | Y | Y |
| 18 Ros-Lehtinen | Y | Y | Y | Y | Y | Y | Y | Y |
| 19 Wexler | N | N | Y | N | Y | Y | Y | Y |
| 20 Wasserman-Schultz | N | N | Y | N | Y | Y | Y | Y |
| 21 Diaz-Balart, L. | Y | Y | Y | Y | Y | Y | Y | Y |
| 22 Shaw | Y | Y | Y | Y | Y | Y | Y | N |
| 23 Hastings | N | N | Y | N | Y | Y | Y | Y |
| 24 Feeney | Y | Y | Y | Y | Y | Y | Y | N |
| 25 Diaz-Balart, M. | + | + | + | + | + | + | + | - |
| **GEORGIA** | | | | | | | | |
| 1 Kingston | Y | Y | Y | Y | Y | Y | Y | N |
| 2 Bishop | N | N | Y | Y | Y | Y | Y | Y |
| 3 Marshall | N | N | Y | Y | Y | Y | Y | Y |
| 4 McKinney | N | N | Y | N | Y | N | Y | Y |
| 5 Lewis | N | N | Y | N | Y | Y | Y | Y |
| 6 Price | Y | Y | Y | Y | Y | Y | Y | N |
| 7 Linder | Y | Y | Y | Y | Y | Y | Y | N |
| 8 Westmoreland | Y | Y | Y | Y | Y | Y | Y | N |
| 9 Norwood | Y | Y | Y | Y | Y | Y | Y | N |
| 10 Deal | Y | Y | Y | Y | Y | Y | Y | N |
| 11 Gingrey | Y | Y | Y | Y | Y | Y | Y | N |
| 12 Barrow | N | N | Y | Y | Y | Y | Y | Y |
| 13 Scott | N | N | Y | Y | Y | Y | Y | Y |
| **HAWAII** | | | | | | | | |
| 1 Abercrombie | N | N | Y | N | Y | N | Y | Y |
| 2 Case | N | Y | Y | Y | Y | Y | Y | Y |
| **IDAHO** | | | | | | | | |
| 1 Otter | Y | Y | Y | Y | Y | Y | Y | Y |
| 2 Simpson | Y | Y | Y | Y | Y | Y | Y | Y |
| **ILLINOIS** | | | | | | | | |
| 1 Rush | N | N | Y | N | Y | Y | Y | Y |
| 2 Jackson | N | N | Y | N | Y | Y | Y | Y |
| 3 Lipinski | N | N | Y | Y | Y | Y | Y | Y |
| 4 Gutierrez | N | N | Y | N | P | Y | Y | Y |
| 5 Emanuel | N | N | Y | P | Y | Y | Y | Y |
| 6 Hyde | + | + | + | ? | ? | ? | ? | ? |
| 7 Davis | N | N | Y | N | Y | Y | Y | Y |
| 8 Bean | N | N | Y | Y | Y | Y | Y | Y |
| 9 Schakowsky | N | N | Y | N | Y | Y | Y | Y |
| 10 Kirk | Y | Y | Y | Y | Y | Y | Y | N |
| 11 Weller | Y | Y | Y | Y | Y | Y | Y | N |
| 12 Costello | N | N | Y | Y | Y | Y | Y | Y |

**KEY**    Republicans    Democrats    *Independents*

| | | | |
|---|---|---|---|
| **Y** Voted for (yea) | **X** Paired against | **C** Voted "present" to avoid possible conflict of interest |
| **#** Paired for | **–** Announced against | |
| **+** Announced for | **P** Voted "present" | **?** Did not vote or otherwise make a position known |
| **N** Voted against (nay) | | |

| | 645 | 646 | 647 | 648 | 649 | 650 | 651 | 652 |
|---|---|---|---|---|---|---|---|---|
| 13 **Biggert** | Y | Y | Y | Y | Y | Y | Y | N |
| 14 **Hastert** | | Y | | | | | | |
| 15 **Johnson** | Y | Y | Y | Y | Y | Y | Y | Y |
| 16 **Manzullo** | Y | Y | Y | Y | Y | Y | Y | N |
| 17 Evans | N | N | Y | N | Y | Y | Y | Y |
| 18 **LaHood** | ? | ? | ? | ? | ? | ? | ? | ? |
| 19 **Shimkus** | Y | Y | Y | Y | Y | Y | Y | Y |
| **INDIANA** | | | | | | | | |
| 1 Visclosky | N | N | Y | N | Y | Y | Y | Y |
| 2 **Chocola** | Y | Y | Y | Y | Y | Y | ? | N |
| 3 **Souder** | Y | Y | Y | Y | Y | Y | Y | N |
| 4 **Buyer** | Y | Y | Y | Y | Y | Y | Y | N |
| 5 **Burton** | Y | Y | Y | Y | Y | Y | Y | N |
| 6 **Pence** | Y | Y | Y | Y | Y | Y | Y | N |
| 7 Carson | N | N | Y | P | Y | Y | Y | Y |
| 8 **Hostettler** | Y | Y | Y | Y | Y | Y | Y | N |
| 9 **Sodrel** | Y | Y | Y | Y | Y | Y | Y | N |
| **IOWA** | | | | | | | | |
| 1 **Nussle** | Y | Y | Y | Y | Y | Y | Y | N |
| 2 **Leach** | N | N | Y | P | Y | P | Y | Y |
| 3 Boswell | N | N | Y | Y | Y | Y | Y | Y |
| 4 **Latham** | Y | Y | Y | Y | Y | Y | Y | N |
| 5 **King** | Y | Y | Y | Y | Y | Y | Y | N |
| **KANSAS** | | | | | | | | |
| 1 **Moran** | Y | Y | Y | Y | Y | Y | Y | N |
| 2 **Ryun** | Y | Y | Y | Y | Y | Y | Y | N |
| 3 Moore | N | N | Y | Y | Y | Y | Y | Y |
| 4 **Tiahrt** | Y | Y | Y | Y | Y | Y | Y | N |
| **KENTUCKY** | | | | | | | | |
| 1 **Whitfield** | Y | Y | Y | Y | Y | Y | Y | N |
| 2 **Lewis** | Y | Y | Y | Y | Y | Y | Y | N |
| 3 **Northup** | Y | Y | Y | Y | Y | Y | Y | N |
| 4 **Davis** | Y | Y | Y | Y | Y | Y | Y | N |
| 5 **Rogers** | Y | Y | Y | Y | Y | Y | Y | N |
| 6 Chandler | N | N | Y | Y | Y | Y | Y | Y |
| **LOUISIANA** | | | | | | | | |
| 1 **Jindal** | Y | Y | Y | Y | Y | Y | Y | N |
| 2 Jefferson | N | N | Y | Y | Y | Y | Y | Y |
| 3 Melancon | N | N | Y | Y | Y | Y | Y | Y |
| 4 **McCrery** | Y | Y | Y | Y | Y | Y | Y | N |
| 5 **Alexander** | Y | Y | Y | Y | Y | Y | Y | N |
| 6 **Baker** | Y | Y | Y | Y | Y | Y | Y | N |
| 7 **Boustany** | Y | Y | Y | Y | Y | Y | Y | N |
| **MAINE** | | | | | | | | |
| 1 Allen | N | N | Y | N | Y | Y | Y | Y |
| 2 Michaud | N | N | Y | P | Y | Y | Y | Y |
| **MARYLAND** | | | | | | | | |
| 1 **Gilchrest** | Y | Y | ? | Y | Y | Y | Y | Y |
| 2 Ruppersberger | N | N | Y | Y | Y | Y | Y | Y |
| 3 Cardin | N | N | Y | N | Y | Y | Y | Y |
| 4 Wynn | N | N | Y | N | Y | Y | Y | Y |
| 5 Hoyer | N | N | Y | P | Y | Y | Y | Y |
| 6 **Bartlett** | Y | Y | Y | Y | Y | Y | Y | N |
| 7 Cummings | N | N | Y | N | Y | Y | Y | Y |
| 8 Van Hollen | N | N | Y | P | Y | Y | Y | Y |
| **MASSACHUSETTS** | | | | | | | | |
| 1 Olver | N | N | Y | N | Y | Y | Y | Y |
| 2 Neal | N | N | ? | N | Y | Y | Y | Y |
| 3 McGovern | N | N | Y | N | Y | Y | Y | Y |
| 4 Frank | N | N | Y | N | Y | Y | Y | Y |
| 5 Meehan | N | N | Y | N | Y | Y | Y | Y |
| 6 Tierney | N | N | Y | N | Y | Y | Y | Y |
| 7 Markey | N | N | Y | N | Y | Y | Y | Y |
| 8 Capuano | N | N | Y | N | Y | P | Y | Y |
| 9 Lynch | N | N | Y | N | Y | Y | Y | Y |
| 10 Delahunt | N | N | Y | N | Y | Y | ? | Y |
| **MICHIGAN** | | | | | | | | |
| 1 Stupak | N | N | Y | N | Y | Y | Y | Y |
| 2 **Hoekstra** | Y | Y | ? | Y | Y | Y | Y | N |
| 3 **Ehlers** | Y | Y | Y | Y | Y | Y | Y | Y |
| 4 **Camp** | Y | Y | Y | Y | Y | Y | Y | N |
| 5 Kildee | N | N | Y | N | Y | Y | Y | Y |
| 6 **Upton** | Y | N | Y | Y | Y | Y | Y | Y |
| 7 **Schwarz** | Y | Y | Y | Y | Y | Y | Y | Y |
| 8 **Rogers** | Y | Y | Y | Y | Y | Y | Y | N |
| 9 **Knollenberg** | Y | Y | Y | Y | Y | Y | Y | N |
| 10 **Miller** | Y | Y | Y | Y | Y | Y | Y | Y |
| 11 **McCotter** | Y | Y | Y | Y | Y | Y | Y | Y |
| 12 Levin | N | N | Y | N | Y | Y | Y | Y |
| 13 Kilpatrick | N | N | Y | N | Y | N | Y | Y |
| 14 Conyers | N | N | Y | N | Y | Y | Y | Y |
| 15 Dingell | N | N | Y | N | Y | N | Y | Y |

| | 645 | 646 | 647 | 648 | 649 | 650 | 651 | 652 |
|---|---|---|---|---|---|---|---|---|
| **MINNESOTA** | | | | | | | | |
| 1 **Gutknecht** | Y | Y | Y | Y | Y | P | Y | N |
| 2 **Kline** | Y | Y | Y | Y | Y | Y | Y | N |
| 3 **Ramstad** | Y | Y | Y | Y | Y | Y | Y | Y |
| 4 McCollum | N | N | Y | N | Y | Y | Y | Y |
| 5 Sabo | N | N | Y | N | Y | Y | Y | Y |
| 6 **Kennedy** | Y | Y | Y | Y | Y | Y | Y | N |
| 7 Peterson | N | Y | Y | Y | Y | Y | Y | Y |
| 8 Oberstar | N | N | Y | N | Y | Y | Y | Y |
| **MISSISSIPPI** | | | | | | | | |
| 1 **Wicker** | Y | Y | Y | Y | Y | Y | Y | N |
| 2 Thompson | N | N | Y | N | Y | Y | Y | Y |
| 3 **Pickering** | Y | Y | Y | Y | Y | Y | Y | N |
| 4 Taylor | N | N | Y | Y | Y | Y | Y | Y |
| **MISSOURI** | | | | | | | | |
| 1 Clay | N | N | Y | N | Y | Y | Y | Y |
| 2 **Akin** | Y | Y | Y | Y | Y | Y | Y | N |
| 3 Carnahan | N | N | Y | Y | Y | Y | Y | Y |
| 4 Skelton | N | N | Y | Y | Y | Y | Y | Y |
| 5 Cleaver | N | N | Y | N | Y | Y | Y | Y |
| 6 **Graves** | Y | Y | Y | Y | Y | Y | Y | N |
| 7 **Blunt** | Y | Y | Y | Y | Y | Y | Y | N |
| 8 **Emerson** | Y | Y | Y | Y | Y | Y | Y | Y |
| 9 **Hulshof** | Y | Y | Y | Y | Y | Y | Y | N |
| **MONTANA** | | | | | | | | |
| AL **Rehberg** | Y | Y | Y | Y | Y | Y | Y | Y |
| **NEBRASKA** | | | | | | | | |
| 1 **Fortenberry** | Y | Y | Y | Y | Y | Y | Y | N |
| 2 **Terry** | Y | Y | Y | Y | Y | Y | Y | N |
| 3 **Osborne** | Y | Y | Y | Y | Y | Y | Y | N |
| **NEVADA** | | | | | | | | |
| 1 Berkley | N | N | Y | Y | Y | Y | Y | Y |
| 2 **Gibbons** | Y | Y | Y | Y | Y | Y | Y | N |
| 3 **Porter** | Y | Y | Y | Y | Y | Y | Y | N |
| **NEW HAMPSHIRE** | | | | | | | | |
| 1 **Bradley** | Y | Y | Y | Y | Y | Y | Y | N |
| 2 **Bass** | Y | Y | Y | Y | Y | Y | Y | N |
| **NEW JERSEY** | | | | | | | | |
| 1 Andrews | N | N | Y | P | Y | Y | Y | Y |
| 2 **LoBiondo** | Y | Y | Y | Y | Y | Y | Y | Y |
| 3 **Saxton** | Y | Y | Y | Y | Y | Y | Y | Y |
| 4 **Smith** | Y | Y | Y | Y | Y | Y | Y | Y |
| 5 **Garrett** | Y | Y | Y | Y | Y | Y | Y | N |
| 6 Pallone | N | N | Y | N | Y | Y | Y | Y |
| 7 **Ferguson** | Y | Y | Y | Y | Y | Y | Y | N |
| 8 Pascrell | N | N | Y | N | Y | Y | Y | Y |
| 9 Rothman | N | N | Y | N | Y | Y | Y | Y |
| 10 Payne | ? | ? | ? | ? | ? | ? | ? | ? |
| 11 **Frelinghuysen** | Y | Y | Y | Y | Y | Y | Y | N |
| 12 Holt | N | N | Y | N | Y | Y | Y | Y |
| 13 Menendez | N | N | Y | N | Y | Y | Y | Y |
| **NEW MEXICO** | | | | | | | | |
| 1 **Wilson** | Y | Y | Y | Y | Y | Y | Y | Y |
| 2 **Pearce** | ? | ? | ? | Y | Y | Y | Y | N |
| 3 Udall | N | N | Y | N | Y | Y | Y | Y |
| **NEW YORK** | | | | | | | | |
| 1 Bishop | N | N | Y | P | Y | Y | Y | Y |
| 2 Israel | N | N | Y | Y | Y | Y | Y | Y |
| 3 **King** | Y | Y | Y | Y | Y | Y | Y | N |
| 4 McCarthy | - | - | + | + | + | + | + | + |
| 5 Ackerman | N | N | Y | N | Y | Y | Y | Y |
| 6 Meeks | N | N | Y | N | Y | Y | Y | Y |
| 7 Crowley | N | N | Y | N | Y | Y | Y | Y |
| 8 Nadler | N | N | Y | N | Y | Y | Y | Y |
| 9 Weiner | N | N | Y | N | Y | Y | Y | Y |
| 10 Towns | N | N | Y | N | Y | Y | Y | Y |
| 11 Owens | N | N | Y | P | Y | Y | Y | Y |
| 12 Velázquez | N | N | Y | N | Y | Y | Y | Y |
| 13 **Fossella** | Y | Y | Y | Y | Y | Y | Y | N |
| 14 Maloney | N | N | Y | P | Y | Y | Y | Y |
| 15 Rangel | N | N | Y | N | Y | Y | ? | Y |
| 16 Serrano | N | N | Y | N | Y | Y | Y | Y |
| 17 Engel | N | N | Y | P | Y | Y | Y | Y |
| 18 Lowey | N | N | Y | P | Y | Y | Y | Y |
| 19 **Kelly** | Y | Y | Y | Y | Y | Y | Y | Y |
| 20 **Sweeney** | ? | ? | ? | ? | ? | ? | ? | Y |
| 21 McNulty | N | Y | Y | P | Y | Y | Y | Y |
| 22 Hinchey | N | N | Y | N | Y | Y | Y | Y |
| 23 **McHugh** | Y | Y | Y | Y | Y | Y | Y | Y |
| 24 **Boehlert** | Y | Y | Y | Y | Y | Y | Y | Y |
| 25 **Walsh** | Y | Y | ? | Y | Y | Y | Y | N |
| 26 **Reynolds** | Y | Y | Y | Y | Y | Y | Y | N |
| 27 Higgins | N | N | Y | Y | Y | Y | Y | Y |
| 28 Slaughter | N | N | Y | P | Y | Y | Y | Y |
| 29 **Kuhl** | Y | Y | Y | Y | Y | Y | Y | Y |

| | 645 | 646 | 647 | 648 | 649 | 650 | 651 | 652 |
|---|---|---|---|---|---|---|---|---|
| **NORTH CAROLINA** | | | | | | | | |
| 1 Butterfield | N | N | Y | P | Y | Y | Y | Y |
| 2 Etheridge | N | N | Y | Y | Y | Y | Y | Y |
| 3 **Jones** | N | Y | Y | Y | Y | Y | Y | Y |
| 4 Price | N | N | Y | N | Y | Y | Y | Y |
| 5 **Foxx** | Y | Y | Y | Y | Y | Y | Y | N |
| 6 **Coble** | Y | Y | Y | Y | Y | Y | Y | Y |
| 7 McIntyre | N | N | Y | Y | Y | Y | Y | Y |
| 8 **Hayes** | Y | Y | Y | Y | Y | Y | Y | Y |
| 9 **Myrick** | Y | Y | Y | Y | Y | Y | Y | N |
| 10 **McHenry** | Y | Y | Y | Y | Y | Y | Y | N |
| 11 **Taylor** | Y | Y | Y | Y | Y | Y | Y | N |
| 12 Watt | N | N | ? | N | Y | N | Y | Y |
| 13 Miller | N | N | Y | N | Y | Y | Y | Y |
| **NORTH DAKOTA** | | | | | | | | |
| AL Pomeroy | N | N | Y | Y | Y | Y | Y | Y |
| **OHIO** | | | | | | | | |
| 1 **Chabot** | Y | N | Y | Y | Y | Y | Y | N |
| 2 **Schmidt** | Y | Y | Y | Y | Y | Y | Y | N |
| 3 **Turner** | Y | Y | Y | Y | Y | Y | Y | N |
| 4 **Oxley** | Y | Y | Y | Y | Y | Y | Y | N |
| 5 **Gillmor** | Y | Y | Y | Y | Y | Y | Y | N |
| 6 Strickland | N | N | Y | N | Y | Y | Y | Y |
| 7 **Hobson** | Y | Y | Y | Y | Y | Y | Y | N |
| 8 **Boehner** | Y | Y | Y | Y | Y | Y | Y | N |
| 9 Kaptur | N | N | Y | P | Y | Y | Y | Y |
| 10 Kucinich | N | N | Y | N | Y | N | Y | Y |
| 11 Jones | N | - | Y | N | Y | Y | Y | Y |
| 12 **Tiberi** | Y | Y | Y | Y | Y | Y | Y | N |
| 13 Brown | N | N | Y | N | Y | Y | Y | Y |
| 14 **LaTourette** | Y | Y | Y | Y | Y | Y | Y | N |
| 15 **Pryce** | Y | Y | Y | Y | Y | Y | Y | N |
| 16 **Regula** | Y | Y | Y | Y | Y | Y | Y | Y |
| 17 Ryan | N | N | Y | N | Y | Y | Y | Y |
| 18 **Ney** | Y | Y | Y | Y | Y | Y | Y | Y |
| **OKLAHOMA** | | | | | | | | |
| 1 **Sullivan** | Y | Y | Y | Y | Y | Y | Y | N |
| 2 Boren | N | N | Y | Y | Y | Y | Y | Y |
| 3 **Lucas** | Y | Y | Y | Y | Y | Y | Y | N |
| 4 **Cole** | Y | Y | Y | Y | Y | Y | + | N |
| 5 **Istook** | ? | ? | ? | ? | ? | ? | ? | ? |
| **OREGON** | | | | | | | | |
| 1 Wu | N | N | Y | N | Y | Y | Y | Y |
| 2 **Walden** | Y | Y | Y | Y | Y | Y | Y | N |
| 3 Blumenauer | N | N | Y | N | Y | N | Y | Y |
| 4 DeFazio | N | N | Y | P | Y | Y | Y | Y |
| 5 Hooley | N | N | Y | P | Y | Y | Y | Y |
| **PENNSYLVANIA** | | | | | | | | |
| 1 Brady | N | N | Y | N | Y | Y | Y | Y |
| 2 Fattah | N | N | Y | N | Y | Y | Y | Y |
| 3 **English** | Y | Y | Y | Y | Y | Y | Y | N |
| 4 **Hart** | ? | Y | Y | Y | Y | Y | Y | N |
| 5 **Peterson** | Y | Y | Y | Y | Y | Y | Y | N |
| 6 **Gerlach** | Y | Y | Y | Y | Y | Y | Y | Y |
| 7 **Weldon** | Y | Y | Y | Y | Y | Y | Y | Y |
| 8 **Fitzpatrick** | Y | Y | Y | Y | Y | Y | Y | Y |
| 9 **Shuster** | Y | Y | Y | Y | Y | Y | Y | N |
| 10 **Sherwood** | Y | Y | Y | Y | Y | Y | Y | N |
| 11 Kanjorski | N | N | Y | N | Y | Y | Y | Y |
| 12 Murtha | N | N | Y | N | Y | Y | Y | Y |
| 13 Schwartz | ? | N | Y | N | Y | Y | Y | Y |
| 14 Doyle | N | N | Y | N | Y | Y | Y | Y |
| 15 **Dent** | Y | Y | Y | Y | Y | Y | Y | Y |
| 16 **Pitts** | Y | Y | Y | Y | Y | Y | Y | N |
| 17 Holden | N | N | Y | Y | Y | Y | Y | Y |
| 18 **Murphy** | Y | Y | Y | Y | Y | Y | Y | N |
| 19 **Platts** | Y | Y | Y | Y | Y | Y | Y | Y |
| **RHODE ISLAND** | | | | | | | | |
| 1 Kennedy | N | N | Y | Y | Y | Y | Y | Y |
| 2 Langevin | N | N | Y | Y | Y | Y | Y | Y |
| **SOUTH CAROLINA** | | | | | | | | |
| 1 **Brown** | Y | Y | Y | Y | Y | Y | Y | N |
| 2 **Wilson** | Y | Y | Y | Y | Y | Y | Y | N |
| 3 **Barrett** | + | + | + | + | + | + | + | - |
| 4 **Inglis** | Y | Y | Y | Y | Y | Y | Y | N |
| 5 Spratt | N | N | Y | Y | Y | Y | Y | Y |
| 6 Clyburn | N | N | Y | N | Y | Y | Y | Y |
| **SOUTH DAKOTA** | | | | | | | | |
| AL Herseth | N | N | Y | Y | Y | Y | Y | Y |
| **TENNESSEE** | | | | | | | | |
| 1 **Jenkins** | Y | Y | Y | Y | Y | Y | Y | N |
| 2 **Duncan** | Y | Y | Y | Y | Y | Y | Y | N |

| | 645 | 646 | 647 | 648 | 649 | 650 | 651 | 652 |
|---|---|---|---|---|---|---|---|---|
| 3 **Wamp** | Y | Y | Y | Y | Y | Y | Y | N |
| 4 Davis | N | N | Y | Y | Y | Y | Y | Y |
| 5 Cooper | N | N | Y | Y | Y | Y | Y | Y |
| 6 Gordon | N | N | Y | Y | Y | Y | Y | Y |
| 7 **Blackburn** | Y | ? | Y | Y | Y | Y | Y | N |
| 8 Tanner | N | N | Y | Y | Y | Y | Y | Y |
| 9 Ford | N | N | Y | Y | Y | Y | Y | Y |
| **TEXAS** | | | | | | | | |
| 1 **Gohmert** | Y | Y | Y | Y | Y | Y | Y | N |
| 2 **Poe** | Y | Y | Y | Y | Y | Y | Y | N |
| 3 **Johnson, S.** | Y | Y | Y | Y | Y | Y | ? | N |
| 4 **Hall** | Y | Y | Y | Y | Y | Y | Y | N |
| 5 **Hensarling** | Y | Y | Y | Y | Y | Y | Y | N |
| 6 **Barton** | + | + | + | + | + | + | + | - |
| 7 **Culberson** | Y | Y | Y | Y | Y | Y | Y | N |
| 8 **Brady** | Y | Y | Y | Y | Y | Y | ? | N |
| 9 Green, A. | N | N | Y | N | Y | Y | Y | Y |
| 10 **McCaul** | Y | Y | Y | Y | Y | Y | Y | N |
| 11 **Conaway** | Y | Y | Y | Y | Y | Y | Y | N |
| 12 **Granger** | Y | Y | Y | Y | Y | Y | Y | N |
| 13 **Thornberry** | Y | Y | Y | Y | Y | Y | Y | N |
| 14 **Paul** | N | N | N | P | N | N | N | N |
| 15 Hinojosa | N | N | Y | Y | Y | Y | Y | Y |
| 16 Reyes | N | N | Y | Y | Y | Y | Y | Y |
| 17 Edwards | N | N | Y | Y | Y | Y | Y | Y |
| 18 Jackson-Lee | N | N | Y | N | Y | Y | Y | Y |
| 19 **Neugebauer** | Y | Y | Y | Y | Y | Y | Y | N |
| 20 Gonzalez | N | N | Y | Y | Y | Y | Y | Y |
| 21 **Smith** | Y | Y | Y | Y | Y | Y | Y | N |
| 22 **DeLay** | Y | Y | Y | Y | Y | Y | Y | N |
| 23 **Bonilla** | Y | Y | Y | Y | Y | Y | Y | N |
| 24 **Marchant** | Y | Y | Y | Y | Y | Y | Y | N |
| 25 Doggett | N | N | Y | N | Y | Y | Y | Y |
| 26 **Burgess** | Y | Y | Y | Y | Y | Y | Y | N |
| 27 Ortiz | N | N | Y | Y | Y | Y | Y | Y |
| 28 Cuellar | N | N | Y | Y | Y | Y | Y | Y |
| 29 Green, G. | N | N | Y | Y | Y | Y | Y | Y |
| 30 Johnson, E. | N | N | Y | P | Y | N | Y | Y |
| 31 **Carter** | Y | Y | Y | Y | Y | Y | Y | N |
| 32 **Sessions** | Y | Y | Y | Y | Y | Y | Y | N |
| **UTAH** | | | | | | | | |
| 1 **Bishop** | Y | Y | Y | Y | Y | Y | Y | N |
| 2 Matheson | N | N | Y | Y | Y | Y | Y | Y |
| 3 **Cannon** | Y | Y | Y | Y | Y | Y | Y | N |
| **VERMONT** | | | | | | | | |
| AL *Sanders* | N | N | Y | N | Y | Y | Y | Y |
| **VIRGINIA** | | | | | | | | |
| 1 **Davis, J.** | + | + | + | + | + | + | + | - |
| 2 **Drake** | Y | Y | Y | Y | Y | Y | Y | N |
| 3 Scott | N | N | Y | N | Y | Y | Y | Y |
| 4 **Forbes** | Y | Y | Y | Y | Y | Y | Y | N |
| 5 **Goode** | Y | Y | Y | Y | Y | Y | Y | N |
| 6 **Goodlatte** | Y | Y | Y | Y | Y | Y | Y | N |
| 7 **Cantor** | Y | Y | Y | Y | Y | Y | Y | N |
| 8 Moran | N | N | Y | N | Y | N | Y | Y |
| 9 Boucher | N | N | Y | Y | Y | Y | Y | Y |
| 10 **Wolf** | Y | Y | Y | Y | Y | Y | Y | N |
| 11 **Davis, T.** | Y | Y | Y | Y | Y | Y | Y | Y |
| **WASHINGTON** | | | | | | | | |
| 1 Inslee | N | N | Y | N | Y | Y | Y | Y |
| 2 Larsen | N | N | Y | P | Y | Y | Y | Y |
| 3 Baird | N | N | Y | P | Y | Y | Y | Y |
| 4 **Hastings** | Y | Y | Y | Y | Y | Y | Y | N |
| 5 **McMorris** | Y | Y | Y | Y | Y | Y | Y | N |
| 6 Dicks | N | N | Y | Y | Y | Y | Y | Y |
| 7 McDermott | N | N | Y | N | Y | N | + | Y |
| 8 **Reichert** | Y | Y | Y | Y | Y | Y | Y | Y |
| 9 Smith | N | N | Y | Y | Y | Y | Y | Y |
| **WEST VIRGINIA** | | | | | | | | |
| 1 Mollohan | N | N | Y | N | Y | Y | Y | Y |
| 2 **Capito** | Y | Y | Y | Y | Y | Y | Y | Y |
| 3 Rahall | N | N | Y | N | Y | N | Y | Y |
| **WISCONSIN** | | | | | | | | |
| 1 **Ryan** | Y | Y | Y | Y | Y | Y | Y | N |
| 2 Baldwin | N | N | Y | N | Y | Y | Y | Y |
| 3 Kind | N | N | Y | Y | Y | Y | Y | Y |
| 4 Moore | N | ? | Y | N | Y | P | Y | Y |
| 5 **Sensenbrenner** | Y | Y | Y | Y | Y | Y | Y | N |
| 6 **Petri** | Y | Y | Y | Y | Y | Y | Y | N |
| 7 Obey | N | N | Y | N | Y | N | Y | Y |
| 8 **Green** | Y | Y | Y | Y | Y | Y | Y | N |
| **WYOMING** | | | | | | | | |
| AL **Cubin** | Y | Y | Y | Y | Y | Y | Y | N |

# IN THE HOUSE | By Vote Number

**653.** **HR 4437. Border Security/Diversity Visa Program.** Goodlatte, R-Va., amendment that would eliminate the diversity visa program, which makes available 50,000 permanent resident visas annually, drawn from a random selection of entries from people who meet eligibility requirements from countries with low rates of immigration into the United States. Adopted 273-148: R 215-6; D 57-142 (ND 32-116, SD 25-26); I 1-0. Dec. 16, 2005.

**654.** **HR 4437. Border Security/Legal Immigration Status.** Stearns, R-Fla., amendment that would prohibit the Homeland Security and Justice departments and courts from granting any kind of legal immigration status to an alien until all the relevant criminal records databases and terrorist watch lists are checked. Adopted 420-0: R 220-0; D 199-0 (ND 148-0, SD 51-0); I 1-0. Dec. 16, 2005.

**655.** **HR 4437. Border Security/Illegal Entry.** Sensenbrenner, R-Wis., amendment that would strike language in the bill that would increase the maximum sentence for illegal presence or illegal entry into the United States to one year and a day. Rejected 164-257: R 156-65; D 8-191 (ND 3-145, SD 5-46); I 0-1 . Dec. 16, 2005.

**656.** **HR 4437. Border Security/Illegal Immigrants.** Norwood, R-Ga., amendment that would require the Homeland Security Department to provide training at no cost to local and state law enforcement, authorize $1 billion each year for the State Criminal Alien Assistance Program and require the department to submit for entry into the National Crime Information Database the names of certain categories of aliens. Adopted 237-180: R 207-11; D 30-168 (ND 13-134, SD 17-34); I 0-1. Dec. 16, 2005.

**657.** **HR 4437. Border Security/Penalties for Unauthorized Aliens.** Westmoreland, R-Ga., amendment that would cap the monetary penalties for hiring or employing unauthorized aliens at $7,500 for first time offenses, $15,000 for second offenses, and $40,000 for all subsequent offenses. It would provide an exemption for initial good faith violations and a safe harbor for contractors if their subcontractor hires an unauthorized alien. Adopted 247-170: R 217-2; D 30-167 (ND 10-137, SD 20-30); I 0-1. Dec. 16, 2005.

**658.** **HR 4437. Border Security/Increase Fines on Businesses.** Gonzalez, D-Texas, amendment that would increase the fines on businesses for knowingly hiring unauthorized aliens to $50,000, and provide that proceeds be shared with state and local governments to help cover the costs associated with providing services to undocumented immigrants. Rejected 87-332: R 0-219; D 86-113 (ND 69-79, SD 17-34); I 1-0. Dec. 16, 2005.

**659.** **HR 4437. Border Security/Deportation of Illegal Immigrants.** Sullivan, R-Okla., amendment that would expand deportation for illegal immigrants who cannot prove that they have been in the United States for longer than one year to be applicable nationwide. It also would require federal authorities to detain all illegal immigrants reported to the Homeland Security Department by state and local authorities and require all non-citizens to be processed through the UH-VISIT system. Rejected 163-251: R 139-77; D 24-173 (ND 7-139, SD 17-34); I 0-1. Dec. 16, 2005.

| | 653 | 654 | 655 | 656 | 657 | 658 | 659 |
|---|---|---|---|---|---|---|---|
| **ALABAMA** | | | | | | | |
| 1 Bonner | Y | Y | Y | Y | Y | N | Y |
| 2 Everett | Y | Y | Y | Y | Y | N | Y |
| 3 Rogers | Y | Y | N | Y | Y | N | Y |
| 4 Aderholt | Y | Y | Y | Y | Y | N | Y |
| 5 Cramer | Y | Y | N | Y | Y | N | Y |
| 6 Bachus | Y | Y | Y | Y | Y | N | Y |
| 7 Davis | N | Y | N | N | Y | N | N |
| **ALASKA** | | | | | | | |
| AL Young | Y | Y | Y | N | ? | ? | ? |
| **ARIZONA** | | | | | | | |
| 1 Renzi | Y | Y | N | Y | Y | N | Y |
| 2 Franks | Y | Y | N | Y | Y | N | Y |
| 3 Shadegg | Y | Y | Y | Y | Y | N | N |
| 4 Pastor | N | Y | N | N | N | N | N |
| 5 Hayworth | Y | Y | N | Y | Y | N | Y |
| 6 Flake | Y | Y | N | Y | N | N | N |
| 7 Grijalva | N | Y | N | N | N | N | N |
| 8 Kolbe | ? | ? | ? | ? | ? | ? | ? |
| **ARKANSAS** | | | | | | | |
| 1 Berry | Y | Y | Y | Y | Y | N | Y |
| 2 Snyder | Y | Y | N | N | N | N | N |
| 3 Boozman | Y | Y | N | Y | Y | N | Y |
| 4 Ross | Y | Y | N | Y | N | N | Y |
| **CALIFORNIA** | | | | | | | |
| 1 Thompson | Y | Y | N | N | N | Y | N |
| 2 Herger | Y | Y | N | Y | Y | N | Y |
| 3 Lungren | Y | Y | Y | Y | Y | N | Y |
| 4 Doolittle | Y | Y | Y | Y | Y | N | Y |
| 5 Matsui, D. | N | Y | N | N | N | Y | N |
| 6 Woolsey | N | Y | N | ? | N | N | N |
| 7 Miller, George | N | Y | N | N | N | N | N |
| 8 Pelosi | N | Y | N | N | N | N | N |
| 9 Lee | N | Y | N | N | N | N | N |
| 10 Tauscher | N | Y | N | N | N | N | N |
| 11 Pombo | Y | Y | Y | Y | Y | N | Y |
| 12 Lantos | N | Y | N | N | N | N | N |
| 13 Stark | N | Y | N | N | N | Y | N |
| 14 Eshoo | N | Y | N | N | N | Y | N |
| 15 Honda | N | Y | N | N | N | N | N |
| 16 Lofgren | N | Y | N | N | N | Y | N |
| 17 Farr | N | Y | N | N | N | N | N |
| 18 Cardoza | Y | Y | N | N | N | N | N |
| 19 Radanovich | Y | Y | Y | Y | Y | N | N |
| 20 Costa | Y | Y | N | N | N | N | N |
| 21 Nunes | Y | Y | Y | Y | Y | N | N |
| 22 Thomas | Y | Y | Y | Y | Y | N | N |
| 23 Capps | N | Y | N | N | N | Y | N |
| 24 Gallegly | Y | Y | N | Y | Y | N | Y |
| 25 McKeon | Y | Y | Y | Y | Y | N | Y |
| 26 Dreier | Y | Y | Y | Y | Y | N | N |
| 27 Sherman | Y | Y | N | N | N | N | N |
| 28 Berman | Y | Y | N | N | N | Y | N |
| 29 Schiff | N | Y | N | N | N | Y | N |
| 30 Waxman | Y | Y | N | N | N | Y | N |
| 31 Becerra | N | Y | N | N | N | Y | N |
| 32 Solis | N | Y | N | N | N | N | N |
| 33 Watson | N | Y | N | N | N | N | N |
| 34 Roybal-Allard | N | Y | N | N | N | Y | N |
| 35 Waters | N | Y | N | N | N | Y | N |
| 36 Harman | N | Y | N | N | Y | N | N |
| 37 Millender-McD. | N | Y | N | N | N | N | N |
| 38 Napolitano | ? | ? | ? | ? | ? | ? | ? |
| 39 Sánchez, Linda | N | Y | N | N | N | Y | N |
| 40 Royce | Y | Y | Y | Y | Y | N | Y |
| 41 Lewis | Y | Y | Y | Y | Y | N | ? |
| 42 Miller, Gary | Y | Y | Y | Y | Y | N | Y |
| 43 Baca | N | Y | N | N | N | N | N |
| 44 Calvert | Y | Y | Y | Y | Y | N | Y |
| 45 Bono | Y | Y | Y | Y | Y | N | Y |
| 46 Rohrabacher | Y | Y | Y | Y | Y | N | Y |
| 47 Sanchez, Loretta | N | Y | N | N | N | N | N |
| 48 Campbell | Y | Y | Y | Y | Y | N | Y |
| 49 Issa | Y | Y | Y | Y | Y | N | Y |

| | 653 | 654 | 655 | 656 | 657 | 658 | 659 |
|---|---|---|---|---|---|---|---|
| 50 Vacant | | | | | | | |
| 51 Filner | N | Y | N | N | N | N | Y |
| 52 Hunter | Y | Y | N | Y | Y | N | Y |
| 53 Davis | N | Y | N | N | N | Y | N |
| **COLORADO** | | | | | | | |
| 1 DeGette | N | Y | N | N | N | Y | N |
| 2 Udall | Y | Y | N | Y | N | N | N |
| 3 Salazar | N | Y | N | N | Y | N | N |
| 4 Musgrave | Y | Y | Y | Y | Y | N | Y |
| 5 Hefley | Y | Y | Y | Y | Y | N | Y |
| 6 Tancredo | Y | Y | Y | Y | Y | N | Y |
| 7 Beauprez | Y | Y | Y | Y | Y | N | Y |
| **CONNECTICUT** | | | | | | | |
| 1 Larson | N | Y | N | N | N | Y | N |
| 2 Simmons | Y | Y | Y | Y | Y | N | N |
| 3 DeLauro | N | Y | N | N | N | Y | N |
| 4 Shays | Y | Y | Y | Y | Y | N | N |
| 5 Johnson | Y | Y | Y | Y | Y | N | N |
| **DELAWARE** | | | | | | | |
| AL Castle | Y | Y | Y | N | Y | N | N |
| **FLORIDA** | | | | | | | |
| 1 Miller | Y | Y | N | Y | Y | N | Y |
| 2 Boyd | Y | Y | N | Y | Y | N | Y |
| 3 Brown | N | Y | N | N | N | N | N |
| 4 Crenshaw | Y | Y | Y | Y | Y | N | Y |
| 5 Brown-Waite | Y | Y | N | Y | Y | N | Y |
| 6 Stearns | Y | Y | N | Y | Y | N | Y |
| 7 Mica | Y | Y | N | Y | Y | N | Y |
| 8 Keller | Y | Y | Y | Y | Y | N | Y |
| 9 Bilirakis | Y | Y | Y | Y | Y | N | Y |
| 10 Young | ? | ? | ? | ? | ? | ? | ? |
| 11 Davis | Y | Y | N | N | N | N | N |
| 12 Putnam | Y | Y | Y | Y | Y | N | Y |
| 13 Harris | N | Y | Y | Y | Y | N | Y |
| 14 Mack | Y | Y | Y | Y | Y | N | Y |
| 15 Weldon | Y | Y | Y | Y | Y | N | Y |
| 16 Foley | Y | Y | Y | Y | Y | N | N |
| 17 Meek | N | Y | N | N | N | N | N |
| 18 Ros-Lehtinen | N | Y | N | Y | N | N | N |
| 19 Wexler | N | Y | N | N | N | Y | N |
| 20 Wasserman-Schultz | N | Y | N | N | N | N | N |
| 21 Diaz-Balart, L. | N | Y | N | Y | N | N | N |
| 22 Shaw | Y | Y | Y | Y | Y | N | N |
| 23 Hastings | N | Y | N | N | N | N | N |
| 24 Feeney | Y | Y | Y | Y | Y | N | N |
| 25 Diaz-Balart, M. | – | + | + | – | + | – | – |
| **GEORGIA** | | | | | | | |
| 1 Kingston | Y | Y | Y | Y | Y | N | Y |
| 2 Bishop | N | Y | N | N | Y | N | N |
| 3 Marshall | Y | Y | N | Y | Y | Y | Y |
| 4 McKinney | N | Y | N | N | N | N | N |
| 5 Lewis | N | Y | N | N | N | N | N |
| 6 Price | Y | Y | Y | Y | N | N | Y |
| 7 Linder | Y | Y | Y | Y | Y | N | Y |
| 8 Westmoreland | Y | Y | Y | Y | Y | N | Y |
| 9 Norwood | Y | Y | Y | Y | Y | N | Y |
| 10 Deal | Y | Y | Y | Y | Y | N | Y |
| 11 Gingrey | Y | Y | Y | Y | Y | N | Y |
| 12 Barrow | Y | Y | Y | Y | N | N | Y |
| 13 Scott | Y | Y | N | Y | N | N | N |
| **HAWAII** | | | | | | | |
| 1 Abercrombie | N | Y | N | N | N | N | N |
| 2 Case | Y | Y | N | Y | N | Y | Y |
| **IDAHO** | | | | | | | |
| 1 Otter | Y | Y | N | Y | Y | N | Y |
| 2 Simpson | Y | Y | Y | Y | Y | N | Y |
| **ILLINOIS** | | | | | | | |
| 1 Rush | N | Y | N | N | N | Y | N |
| 2 Jackson | N | Y | N | N | N | Y | N |
| 3 Lipinski | Y | Y | N | N | N | Y | N |
| 4 Gutierrez | N | Y | N | N | N | Y | N |
| 5 Emanuel | Y | Y | N | N | N | Y | N |
| 6 Hyde | ? | ? | ? | ? | ? | ? | ? |
| 7 Davis | N | Y | N | N | N | N | N |
| 8 Bean | Y | Y | N | N | N | N | N |
| 9 Schakowsky | N | Y | N | N | N | N | N |
| 10 Kirk | Y | Y | Y | Y | Y | N | N |
| 11 Weller | Y | ? | Y | Y | Y | N | N |
| 12 Costello | Y | Y | N | Y | N | Y | N |

**KEY**  Republicans  Democrats  *Independents*

| | | |
|---|---|---|
| **Y** Voted for (yea) | **X** Paired against | **C** Voted "present" to avoid possible conflict of interest |
| **#** Paired for | **–** Announced against | |
| **+** Announced for | **P** Voted "present" | **?** Did not vote or otherwise make a position known |
| **N** Voted against (nay) | | |

ND Northern Democrats, SD Southern Democrats
Southern states: Ala., Ark., Fla., Ga., Ky., La., Miss., N.C., Okla., S.C., Tenn., Texas, Va.

| | 653 | 654 | 655 | 656 | 657 | 658 | 659 |
|---|---|---|---|---|---|---|---|
| 13 **Biggert** | Y | Y | Y | Y | Y | N | N |
| 14 **Hastert** | | | | | | | |
| 15 **Johnson** | Y | Y | Y | Y | Y | N | N |
| 16 **Manzullo** | Y | Y | Y | Y | Y | N | Y |
| 17 Evans | N | Y | N | N | N | Y | N |
| 18 **LaHood** | ? | ? | ? | ? | ? | ? | ? |
| 19 **Shimkus** | Y | Y | Y | Y | Y | N | Y |
| **INDIANA** | | | | | | | |
| 1 Visclosky | Y | Y | N | N | N | N | N |
| 2 **Chocola** | Y | Y | Y | Y | Y | N | Y |
| 3 **Souder** | Y | Y | Y | Y | P | N | N |
| 4 **Buyer** | Y | Y | Y | Y | Y | N | Y |
| 5 **Burton** | Y | Y | Y | Y | Y | N | N |
| 6 **Pence** | Y | Y | Y | Y | Y | N | N |
| 7 Carson | N | Y | N | N | N | N | N |
| 8 **Hostettler** | Y | Y | Y | Y | Y | N | Y |
| 9 **Sodrel** | Y | Y | N | Y | Y | N | N |
| **IOWA** | | | | | | | |
| 1 **Nussle** | Y | Y | Y | Y | Y | N | Y |
| 2 **Leach** | N | Y | Y | Y | Y | N | N |
| 3 Boswell | N | Y | N | Y | Y | N | Y |
| 4 **Latham** | Y | Y | Y | Y | Y | N | Y |
| 5 **King** | Y | Y | N | Y | Y | N | Y |
| **KANSAS** | | | | | | | |
| 1 **Moran** | Y | Y | Y | Y | Y | N | Y |
| 2 **Ryun** | Y | Y | Y | Y | Y | N | Y |
| 3 Moore | Y | Y | Y | N | N | N | N |
| 4 **Tiahrt** | Y | Y | Y | Y | Y | N | N |
| **KENTUCKY** | | | | | | | |
| 1 **Whitfield** | Y | Y | N | Y | Y | N | Y |
| 2 **Lewis** | Y | Y | N | Y | Y | N | Y |
| 3 **Northup** | Y | Y | Y | Y | Y | N | N |
| 4 **Davis** | Y | Y | Y | Y | Y | N | Y |
| 5 **Rogers** | N | Y | N | Y | Y | N | N |
| 6 Chandler | Y | Y | N | Y | Y | N | Y |
| **LOUISIANA** | | | | | | | |
| 1 **Jindal** | Y | Y | Y | Y | Y | N | Y |
| 2 Jefferson | N | Y | N | N | N | N | N |
| 3 Melancon | Y | Y | N | N | N | Y | Y |
| 4 **McCrery** | Y | Y | Y | Y | Y | N | Y |
| 5 **Alexander** | Y | Y | Y | Y | Y | N | Y |
| 6 **Baker** | Y | Y | Y | Y | Y | N | Y |
| 7 **Boustany** | Y | Y | Y | Y | Y | N | N |
| **MAINE** | | | | | | | |
| 1 Allen | N | Y | N | N | N | N | N |
| 2 Michaud | Y | Y | N | N | N | N | N |
| **MARYLAND** | | | | | | | |
| 1 **Gilchrest** | Y | Y | Y | Y | Y | N | N |
| 2 Ruppersberger | Y | Y | N | N | N | N | N |
| 3 Cardin | N | Y | N | N | N | N | N |
| 4 Wynn | N | Y | N | N | Y | N | N |
| 5 Hoyer | N | Y | N | N | N | N | N |
| 6 **Bartlett** | Y | Y | Y | Y | Y | N | Y |
| 7 Cummings | N | Y | N | N | N | Y | N |
| 8 Van Hollen | N | Y | N | N | N | Y | N |
| **MASSACHUSETTS** | | | | | | | |
| 1 Olver | N | Y | N | N | N | N | N |
| 2 Neal | N | Y | N | N | N | N | N |
| 3 McGovern | N | Y | N | N | N | Y | N |
| 4 Frank | N | Y | N | N | N | N | N |
| 5 Meehan | N | Y | N | N | N | N | N |
| 6 Tierney | N | Y | N | N | N | Y | N |
| 7 Markey | N | Y | N | N | N | Y | N |
| 8 Capuano | N | Y | N | N | N | Y | N |
| 9 Lynch | N | Y | N | N | N | N | N |
| 10 Delahunt | N | Y | N | N | N | N | N |
| **MICHIGAN** | | | | | | | |
| 1 Stupak | N | Y | N | N | N | N | N |
| 2 **Hoekstra** | Y | Y | Y | Y | Y | N | N |
| 3 **Ehlers** | Y | Y | Y | N | Y | N | N |
| 4 **Camp** | Y | Y | Y | Y | Y | N | N |
| 5 Kildee | N | Y | N | N | N | N | N |
| 6 **Upton** | Y | Y | Y | Y | Y | N | N |
| 7 **Schwarz** | Y | Y | Y | Y | Y | N | N |
| 8 **Rogers** | Y | Y | N | Y | Y | N | Y |
| 9 **Knollenberg** | Y | Y | Y | Y | Y | N | N |
| 10 **Miller** | Y | Y | N | Y | Y | N | N |
| 11 **McCotter** | Y | Y | N | Y | Y | N | P |
| 12 Levin | N | Y | N | N | N | N | N |
| 13 Kilpatrick | N | Y | N | N | N | Y | N |
| 14 Conyers | N | Y | N | N | N | Y | N |
| 15 Dingell | N | Y | N | N | N | N | N |
| **MINNESOTA** | | | | | | | |
| 1 **Gutknecht** | Y | Y | Y | Y | Y | N | Y |
| 2 **Kline** | Y | Y | Y | Y | Y | N | Y |
| 3 **Ramstad** | Y | Y | N | Y | Y | N | Y |
| 4 McCollum | N | Y | N | N | N | Y | N |
| 5 Sabo | Y | Y | N | N | N | N | N |
| 6 **Kennedy** | Y | Y | Y | Y | Y | N | Y |
| 7 Peterson | Y | Y | N | Y | Y | N | Y |
| 8 Oberstar | N | Y | N | N | N | N | N |
| **MISSISSIPPI** | | | | | | | |
| 1 **Wicker** | Y | Y | Y | Y | Y | N | Y |
| 2 Thompson | N | Y | N | N | N | Y | N |
| 3 **Pickering** | Y | Y | Y | Y | Y | N | Y |
| 4 Taylor | Y | Y | N | Y | Y | N | Y |
| **MISSOURI** | | | | | | | |
| 1 Clay | N | Y | N | N | N | Y | N |
| 2 **Akin** | Y | Y | Y | Y | Y | N | N |
| 3 Carnahan | N | Y | N | N | N | Y | N |
| 4 Skelton | Y | Y | N | N | N | N | Y |
| 5 Cleaver | N | Y | N | N | N | Y | N |
| 6 **Graves** | Y | Y | N | Y | Y | N | Y |
| 7 **Blunt** | Y | Y | Y | Y | Y | N | Y |
| 8 **Emerson** | Y | Y | Y | Y | Y | N | Y |
| 9 **Hulshof** | Y | Y | Y | Y | Y | N | Y |
| **MONTANA** | | | | | | | |
| AL **Rehberg** | Y | Y | N | Y | Y | N | N |
| **NEBRASKA** | | | | | | | |
| 1 **Fortenberry** | Y | Y | Y | Y | Y | N | Y |
| 2 **Terry** | Y | Y | Y | N | Y | N | N |
| 3 **Osborne** | Y | Y | Y | Y | Y | N | Y |
| **NEVADA** | | | | | | | |
| 1 Berkley | N | Y | N | N | Y | N | N |
| 2 **Gibbons** | Y | Y | N | Y | Y | N | Y |
| 3 **Porter** | Y | Y | N | Y | Y | N | Y |
| **NEW HAMPSHIRE** | | | | | | | |
| 1 **Bradley** | Y | Y | Y | Y | Y | N | Y |
| 2 **Bass** | Y | Y | Y | Y | Y | N | N |
| **NEW JERSEY** | | | | | | | |
| 1 Andrews | N | Y | N | N | N | Y | N |
| 2 **LoBiondo** | Y | Y | N | Y | Y | N | Y |
| 3 **Saxton** | Y | Y | N | Y | Y | N | Y |
| 4 **Smith** | Y | Y | N | Y | Y | N | N |
| 5 **Garrett** | Y | Y | Y | Y | Y | N | Y |
| 6 Pallone | N | Y | N | N | N | Y | N |
| 7 **Ferguson** | Y | Y | N | Y | Y | N | N |
| 8 Pascrell | N | Y | N | N | N | Y | N |
| 9 Rothman | N | Y | N | N | N | N | ? |
| 10 Payne | ? | ? | ? | ? | ? | ? | ? |
| 11 **Frelinghuysen** | Y | Y | Y | N | Y | N | N |
| 12 Holt | N | Y | N | N | N | N | N |
| 13 Menendez | N | Y | N | N | N | Y | N |
| **NEW MEXICO** | | | | | | | |
| 1 **Wilson** | Y | Y | Y | N | Y | N | N |
| 2 **Pearce** | Y | Y | Y | Y | Y | N | N |
| 3 Udall | Y | Y | N | N | N | Y | N |
| **NEW YORK** | | | | | | | |
| 1 Bishop | N | Y | N | Y | N | Y | N |
| 2 Israel | N | Y | N | Y | N | Y | N |
| 3 **King** | Y | Y | Y | Y | Y | N | N |
| 4 McCarthy | – | + | + | – | – | – | – |
| 5 Ackerman | N | Y | N | N | N | Y | N |
| 6 Meeks | N | Y | N | N | N | N | N |
| 7 Crowley | N | Y | N | N | N | Y | N |
| 8 Nadler | N | Y | N | N | N | N | N |
| 9 Weiner | N | Y | N | N | N | N | N |
| 10 Towns | N | Y | N | N | N | Y | N |
| 11 Owens | N | Y | N | N | N | Y | N |
| 12 Velázquez | N | Y | N | N | N | Y | N |
| 13 **Fossella** | Y | Y | Y | Y | Y | N | N |
| 14 Maloney | N | Y | N | N | N | Y | N |
| 15 Rangel | N | Y | N | N | N | N | N |
| 16 Serrano | N | Y | N | N | N | N | N |
| 17 Engel | N | Y | N | N | N | Y | N |
| 18 Lowey | N | Y | N | N | N | N | N |
| 19 **Kelly** | Y | Y | Y | Y | Y | N | Y |
| 20 **Sweeney** | Y | Y | N | Y | Y | N | Y |
| 21 McNulty | N | Y | Y | N | N | N | N |
| 22 Hinchey | N | Y | N | N | N | N | N |
| 23 **McHugh** | Y | Y | N | Y | Y | N | ? |
| 24 **Boehlert** | Y | Y | Y | Y | Y | N | N |
| 25 **Walsh** | Y | Y | Y | Y | Y | N | N |
| 26 **Reynolds** | Y | Y | Y | Y | Y | – | Y |
| 27 Higgins | N | Y | N | Y | Y | N | N |
| 28 Slaughter | N | Y | N | N | N | N | N |
| 29 **Kuhl** | Y | Y | N | Y | Y | N | N |
| **NORTH CAROLINA** | | | | | | | |
| 1 Butterfield | N | Y | N | N | N | N | N |
| 2 Etheridge | N | Y | N | N | Y | N | N |
| 3 **Jones** | Y | Y | N | ? | Y | N | Y |
| 4 Price | N | Y | N | N | N | N | N |
| 5 **Foxx** | Y | Y | N | Y | Y | N | N |
| 6 **Coble** | Y | Y | Y | Y | Y | N | Y |
| 7 McIntyre | Y | Y | N | Y | Y | N | Y |
| 8 **Hayes** | Y | Y | Y | Y | Y | N | Y |
| 9 **Myrick** | Y | Y | Y | Y | Y | N | Y |
| 10 **McHenry** | Y | Y | N | Y | Y | N | Y |
| 11 **Taylor** | Y | Y | N | Y | Y | N | Y |
| 12 Watt | N | Y | N | N | N | N | N |
| 13 Miller | N | Y | N | N | N | Y | N |
| **NORTH DAKOTA** | | | | | | | |
| AL Pomeroy | N | Y | N | N | ? | Y | N |
| **OHIO** | | | | | | | |
| 1 **Chabot** | Y | Y | Y | Y | Y | N | Y |
| 2 **Schmidt** | Y | Y | N | Y | Y | N | Y |
| 3 **Turner** | Y | Y | Y | Y | Y | N | N |
| 4 **Oxley** | Y | Y | Y | ? | Y | N | N |
| 5 **Gillmor** | Y | Y | Y | Y | Y | N | N |
| 6 Strickland | Y | Y | N | N | N | N | N |
| 7 **Hobson** | Y | Y | Y | Y | Y | N | N |
| 8 **Boehner** | Y | Y | N | Y | Y | N | Y |
| 9 Kaptur | N | Y | N | N | N | N | N |
| 10 Kucinich | N | Y | N | N | N | Y | N |
| 11 Jones | N | Y | N | N | N | N | N |
| 12 **Tiberi** | Y | Y | Y | Y | Y | N | Y |
| 13 Brown | Y | Y | N | N | N | Y | N |
| 14 **LaTourette** | Y | Y | N | Y | Y | N | N |
| 15 **Pryce** | Y | Y | Y | ? | Y | N | Y |
| 16 **Regula** | Y | Y | Y | Y | Y | N | N |
| 17 Ryan | N | Y | N | N | N | Y | N |
| 18 **Ney** | Y | Y | N | Y | Y | N | Y |
| **OKLAHOMA** | | | | | | | |
| 1 **Sullivan** | Y | Y | N | Y | Y | N | Y |
| 2 Boren | Y | Y | N | Y | Y | N | Y |
| 3 **Lucas** | Y | Y | Y | Y | Y | N | Y |
| 4 **Cole** | Y | Y | Y | Y | Y | N | + |
| 5 **Istook** | ? | ? | ? | ? | ? | ? | ? |
| **OREGON** | | | | | | | |
| 1 Wu | N | Y | N | N | N | Y | N |
| 2 **Walden** | Y | Y | Y | Y | Y | N | Y |
| 3 Blumenauer | N | Y | N | N | N | N | N |
| 4 DeFazio | Y | Y | N | Y | N | Y | N |
| 5 Hooley | Y | Y | N | Y | N | Y | N |
| **PENNSYLVANIA** | | | | | | | |
| 1 Brady | N | Y | N | N | N | Y | N |
| 2 Fattah | N | Y | N | N | N | Y | N |
| 3 **English** | Y | Y | Y | Y | Y | N | Y |
| 4 **Hart** | Y | Y | N | Y | Y | N | Y |
| 5 **Peterson** | Y | Y | Y | Y | Y | N | Y |
| 6 **Gerlach** | Y | Y | N | Y | Y | N | N |
| 7 **Weldon** | Y | Y | N | Y | Y | N | N |
| 8 **Fitzpatrick** | Y | Y | N | Y | Y | N | N |
| 9 **Shuster** | Y | Y | N | Y | Y | N | Y |
| 10 **Sherwood** | Y | Y | Y | Y | Y | N | Y |
| 11 Kanjorski | N | Y | N | Y | N | N | N |
| 12 Murtha | N | Y | N | N | N | N | N |
| 13 Schwartz | Y | Y | N | N | N | Y | N |
| 14 Doyle | N | Y | N | N | N | N | N |
| 15 **Dent** | Y | Y | N | Y | Y | N | Y |
| 16 **Pitts** | Y | Y | Y | Y | Y | N | Y |
| 17 Holden | Y | Y | N | Y | N | N | Y |
| 18 **Murphy** | Y | Y | Y | Y | Y | N | Y |
| 19 **Platts** | Y | Y | N | Y | Y | N | Y |
| **RHODE ISLAND** | | | | | | | |
| 1 Kennedy | N | Y | N | N | N | N | ? |
| 2 Langevin | N | Y | N | N | N | N | N |
| **SOUTH CAROLINA** | | | | | | | |
| 1 **Brown** | Y | Y | Y | Y | Y | N | Y |
| 2 **Wilson** | Y | Y | N | Y | Y | N | Y |
| 3 **Barrett** | + | + | – | + | + | – | + |
| 4 **Inglis** | Y | Y | Y | Y | Y | N | Y |
| 5 Spratt | Y | Y | Y | Y | Y | N | N |
| 6 Clyburn | N | Y | N | N | N | Y | N |
| **SOUTH DAKOTA** | | | | | | | |
| AL Herseth | Y | Y | N | Y | N | Y | Y |
| **TENNESSEE** | | | | | | | |
| 1 **Jenkins** | Y | Y | Y | Y | Y | N | Y |
| 2 **Duncan** | Y | Y | N | Y | Y | N | Y |
| 3 **Wamp** | Y | Y | Y | Y | Y | N | Y |
| 4 Davis | Y | Y | N | Y | Y | N | Y |
| 5 Cooper | Y | Y | N | Y | Y | Y | Y |
| 6 Gordon | Y | Y | N | N | Y | N | Y |
| 7 **Blackburn** | Y | Y | Y | Y | Y | N | Y |
| 8 Tanner | Y | Y | Y | Y | Y | Y | Y |
| 9 Ford | Y | Y | N | Y | Y | N | Y |
| **TEXAS** | | | | | | | |
| 1 **Gohmert** | Y | Y | N | Y | Y | N | Y |
| 2 **Poe** | Y | Y | N | Y | Y | N | Y |
| 3 **Johnson, S.** | Y | Y | Y | Y | Y | N | Y |
| 4 **Hall** | Y | Y | Y | Y | Y | N | Y |
| 5 **Hensarling** | Y | Y | Y | Y | Y | N | N |
| 6 **Barton** | + | + | + | + | + | – | + |
| 7 **Culberson** | Y | Y | N | Y | Y | N | Y |
| 8 **Brady** | Y | Y | Y | Y | Y | N | Y |
| 9 Green, A. | N | Y | N | N | N | Y | N |
| 10 **McCaul** | Y | Y | Y | Y | Y | N | Y |
| 11 **Conaway** | Y | Y | N | Y | Y | N | Y |
| 12 **Granger** | Y | Y | Y | Y | Y | N | N |
| 13 **Thornberry** | Y | Y | Y | Y | Y | N | N |
| 14 **Paul** | Y | Y | Y | Y | Y | N | Y |
| 15 Hinojosa | N | Y | N | N | N | N | N |
| 16 Reyes | N | Y | N | N | N | Y | N |
| 17 Edwards | Y | Y | Y | Y | Y | N | Y |
| 18 Jackson-Lee | N | Y | N | N | N | Y | N |
| 19 **Neugebauer** | Y | Y | N | Y | Y | N | Y |
| 20 Gonzalez | N | Y | N | N | N | Y | N |
| 21 **Smith** | Y | Y | Y | Y | Y | N | Y |
| 22 **DeLay** | Y | Y | Y | Y | Y | N | N |
| 23 **Bonilla** | Y | Y | Y | Y | Y | N | N |
| 24 **Marchant** | Y | Y | N | Y | Y | N | Y |
| 25 Doggett | N | Y | N | N | N | N | N |
| 26 **Burgess** | Y | Y | Y | Y | Y | N | N |
| 27 Ortiz | N | Y | N | N | N | Y | N |
| 28 Cuellar | Y | Y | N | N | Y | N | N |
| 29 Green, G. | Y | Y | N | N | N | Y | N |
| 30 Johnson, E. | N | Y | N | N | N | Y | N |
| 31 **Carter** | Y | Y | N | Y | Y | N | N |
| 32 **Sessions** | Y | Y | Y | Y | Y | N | Y |
| **UTAH** | | | | | | | |
| 1 **Bishop** | Y | Y | Y | Y | Y | N | Y |
| 2 Matheson | Y | Y | Y | Y | Y | N | Y |
| 3 **Cannon** | N | Y | Y | N | Y | N | N |
| **VERMONT** | | | | | | | |
| AL *Sanders* | Y | Y | N | N | N | Y | N |
| **VIRGINIA** | | | | | | | |
| 1 **Davis, J.** | + | + | + | + | + | – | + |
| 2 **Drake** | Y | Y | N | Y | Y | N | Y |
| 3 Scott | N | Y | N | N | N | N | N |
| 4 **Forbes** | Y | Y | N | Y | Y | N | Y |
| 5 **Goode** | Y | Y | N | Y | Y | N | Y |
| 6 **Goodlatte** | Y | Y | N | Y | Y | N | Y |
| 7 **Cantor** | Y | Y | Y | Y | Y | N | Y |
| 8 Moran | Y | Y | N | N | – | N | N |
| 9 Boucher | Y | Y | N | Y | N | Y | N |
| 10 **Wolf** | Y | Y | N | Y | Y | N | N |
| 11 **Davis, T.** | Y | Y | N | Y | Y | N | N |
| **WASHINGTON** | | | | | | | |
| 1 Inslee | N | Y | N | N | N | N | N |
| 2 Larsen | N | Y | N | N | N | N | N |
| 3 Baird | Y | Y | N | N | N | N | N |
| 4 **Hastings** | Y | Y | Y | Y | Y | N | N |
| 5 **McMorris** | Y | Y | Y | Y | Y | N | N |
| 6 Dicks | Y | Y | N | N | N | N | N |
| 7 McDermott | N | Y | N | N | N | Y | N |
| 8 **Reichert** | Y | Y | Y | Y | Y | N | N |
| 9 Smith | N | Y | N | N | N | Y | N |
| **WEST VIRGINIA** | | | | | | | |
| 1 Mollohan | N | Y | N | N | N | N | N |
| 2 **Capito** | Y | Y | Y | Y | Y | N | Y |
| 3 Rahall | N | Y | N | N | N | Y | N |
| **WISCONSIN** | | | | | | | |
| 1 **Ryan** | Y | Y | Y | N | Y | N | N |
| 2 Baldwin | N | Y | N | N | N | N | N |
| 3 Kind | Y | Y | N | N | Y | N | N |
| 4 Moore | N | Y | N | N | N | N | N |
| 5 **Sensenbrenner** | Y | Y | Y | Y | Y | N | N |
| 6 **Petri** | Y | Y | Y | Y | Y | N | N |
| 7 Obey | Y | Y | N | N | N | Y | N |
| 8 **Green** | Y | Y | Y | Y | Y | N | N |
| **WYOMING** | | | | | | | |
| AL **Cubin** | Y | Y | Y | Y | Y | N | Y |

# IN THE HOUSE | By Vote Number

**660.** **HR 4437. Border Security/Recommit.** Reyes, D-Texas, motion to recommit the bill to the Homeland Security and Judiciary committees with instructions to substitute language that would require the Department of Homeland Security to develop a comprehensive security strategy for all U.S. borders and ports, provide increased personnel including 12,000 additional Border Patrol agents, and provide 100,000 additional detention beds. Motion rejected 198-221: R 0-219; D 197-2 (ND 148-1, SD 49-1); I 1-0. Dec. 16, 2005.

**661.** **HR 4437. Border Security/Passage.** Passage of the bill that would tighten border security and increase enforcement of immigration laws. It would designate unlawful presence, in addition to illegal migration, as a criminal, rather than a civil, offense. It also would increase penalties for a variety of immigration-related crimes. It would create a mandatory program under which all employers would have to verify employees' work eligibility with the federal government. As amended, it would require the construction of security fencing, including lights and cameras, along certain ports of entry along the U.S.-Mexico border. Passed 239-182: R 203-17; D 36-164 (ND 20-129, SD 16-35); I 0-1. A "yea" was a vote in support of the president's position. Dec. 16, 2005.

**662.** **H Res 598. Lebanese Prime Minister Assassination/Adoption.** Ros-Lehtinen, R-Fla., motion to suspend the rules and adopt the resolution that would condemn the Syrian government for hindering and failing to fully cooperate in a timely manner with the U.N. investigation of the assassination of former Lebanese Prime Minister Rafik Hariri. Motion agreed to 404-5: R 214-1; D 189-4 (ND 140-3, SD 49-1); I 1-0. A two-thirds majority of those present and voting (273 in this case) is required for adoption under suspension of the rules. Dec. 16, 2005.

**663.** **H Res 623. Suspension Motions/Rule.** Adoption of the rule (H Res 623) to provide for House floor consideration of bills under suspension of the rules on Saturday, Nov. 17, 2005. Adopted 213-190: R 212-0; D 1-189 (ND 1-140, SD 0-49); I 0-1. Dec. 17, 2005.

**664.** **HR 2520. Cord Blood Stem Cell Research/Passage.** Deal, R-Ga., motion to suspend the rules and agree to the Senate amendment to the bill that would create a new federal program to collect and store umbilical cord blood stem cells. The bill also would reauthorize and expand the current bone marrow registry program. Motion agreed to 413-0: R 216-0; D 196-0 (ND 145-0, SD 51-0); I 1-0. A two-thirds majority of those present and voting (276 in this case) is required for passage under suspension of the rules. Dec. 17, 2005.

**665.** **HR 1815. Fiscal 2006 Defense Authorization/Conference Report.** Adoption of the conference report on the bill that would authorize $441.5 billion for defense programs and $50 billion for military operations in Iraq and Afghanistan. The bill includes $77 billion for weapons procurement, $108.9 billion for personnel and $12.2 billion for military construction and family housing. It would also authorize $6.6 billion for Hurricane Katrina relief, $130 million for flu preparedness and $40 million for Pakistan earthquake relief. It would prohibit cruel, inhuman or degrading treatment of any prisoner detained by the U.S. government. Adopted (thus sent to the Senate) 374-41: R 218-1; D 155-40 (ND 109-36, SD 46-4); I 1-0. Dec. 19, 2005 (in the session that began and the Congressional Record dated Dec. 18, 2005).

| | 660 | 661 | 662 | 663 | 664 | 665 |
|---|---|---|---|---|---|---|
| **ALABAMA** | | | | | | |
| 1 Bonner | N | Y | Y | Y | Y | Y |
| 2 Everett | N | Y | Y | Y | Y | Y |
| 3 Rogers | N | Y | Y | Y | Y | Y |
| 4 Aderholt | N | Y | Y | Y | Y | Y |
| 5 Cramer | Y | Y | Y | N | Y | Y |
| 6 Bachus | N | Y | Y | Y | Y | Y |
| 7 Davis | Y | N | Y | N | Y | Y |
| **ALASKA** | | | | | | |
| AL Young | ? | ? | ? | Y | Y | Y |
| **ARIZONA** | | | | | | |
| 1 Renzi | N | Y | Y | Y | Y | Y |
| 2 Franks | N | Y | Y | Y | Y | Y |
| 3 Shadegg | N | Y | Y | Y | Y | Y |
| 4 Pastor | Y | N | Y | ? | Y | Y |
| 5 Hayworth | N | N | Y | Y | Y | Y |
| 6 Flake | N | Y | Y | Y | Y | Y |
| 7 Grijalva | Y | N | Y | N | Y | N |
| 8 Kolbe | ? | ? | ? | ? | ? | ? |
| **ARKANSAS** | | | | | | |
| 1 Berry | Y | Y | Y | N | Y | Y |
| 2 Snyder | Y | N | Y | N | Y | Y |
| 3 Boozman | N | Y | Y | Y | Y | Y |
| 4 Ross | Y | Y | Y | N | Y | Y |
| **CALIFORNIA** | | | | | | |
| 1 Thompson | Y | N | Y | N | Y | Y |
| 2 Herger | N | Y | Y | Y | Y | Y |
| 3 Lungren | N | Y | Y | Y | Y | Y |
| 4 Doolittle | N | Y | Y | Y | Y | Y |
| 5 Matsui, D. | Y | N | Y | N | Y | Y |
| 6 Woolsey | Y | N | N | N | Y | N |
| 7 Miller, George | Y | N | Y | N | Y | N |
| 8 Pelosi | Y | N | Y | N | Y | N |
| 9 Lee | Y | N | Y | N | Y | N |
| 10 Tauscher | Y | N | Y | N | Y | Y |
| 11 Pombo | N | Y | Y | Y | Y | Y |
| 12 Lantos | Y | N | N | N | Y | Y |
| 13 Stark | Y | N | Y | N | Y | N |
| 14 Eshoo | Y | N | Y | N | Y | Y |
| 15 Honda | Y | N | Y | N | Y | Y |
| 16 Lofgren | Y | N | Y | N | Y | Y |
| 17 Farr | Y | N | ? | N | Y | Y |
| 18 Cardoza | Y | N | Y | ? | Y | Y |
| 19 Radanovich | N | N | ? | Y | ? | ? |
| 20 Costa | Y | N | Y | N | Y | Y |
| 21 Nunes | N | N | Y | Y | Y | Y |
| 22 Thomas | N | N | Y | Y | Y | Y |
| 23 Capps | Y | N | Y | N | Y | Y |
| 24 Gallegly | N | Y | Y | Y | Y | Y |
| 25 McKeon | N | Y | Y | Y | Y | Y |
| 26 Dreier | N | Y | Y | Y | Y | Y |
| 27 Sherman | Y | N | Y | N | Y | Y |
| 28 Berman | Y | N | ? | N | Y | Y |
| 29 Schiff | Y | N | Y | N | Y | Y |
| 30 Waxman | Y | N | Y | N | Y | Y |
| 31 Becerra | Y | N | Y | - | + | Y |
| 32 Solis | Y | N | Y | N | Y | N |
| 33 Watson | Y | N | Y | ? | ? | N |
| 34 Roybal-Allard | Y | N | Y | N | Y | ? |
| 35 Waters | Y | N | Y | ? | Y | N |
| 36 Harman | Y | N | Y | N | Y | ? |
| 37 Millender-McD. | Y | N | Y | N | Y | Y |
| 38 Napolitano | ? | ? | ? | N | Y | Y |
| 39 Sánchez, Linda | Y | N | Y | N | Y | Y |
| 40 Royce | N | Y | Y | Y | Y | Y |
| 41 Lewis | N | Y | Y | Y | Y | Y |
| 42 Miller, Gary | N | Y | Y | Y | Y | Y |
| 43 Baca | Y | N | Y | ? | ? | ? |
| 44 Calvert | N | Y | Y | Y | Y | Y |
| 45 Bono | N | Y | Y | Y | Y | Y |
| 46 Rohrabacher | N | Y | Y | Y | Y | Y |
| 47 Sanchez, Loretta | Y | N | Y | N | Y | Y |
| 48 Campbell | N | Y | Y | Y | Y | Y |
| 49 Issa | N | Y | Y | Y | Y | Y |
| 50 Vacant | | | | | | |
| 51 Filner | Y | N | Y | N | Y | N |
| 52 Hunter | N | Y | Y | Y | Y | Y |
| 53 Davis | Y | N | Y | N | Y | Y |
| **COLORADO** | | | | | | |
| 1 DeGette | Y | N | Y | N | Y | Y |
| 2 Udall | Y | Y | Y | N | Y | Y |
| 3 Salazar | Y | Y | Y | N | Y | Y |
| 4 Musgrave | N | Y | Y | Y | Y | Y |
| 5 Hefley | N | Y | Y | Y | Y | ? |
| 6 Tancredo | N | Y | Y | Y | Y | Y |
| 7 Beauprez | N | Y | Y | Y | Y | Y |
| **CONNECTICUT** | | | | | | |
| 1 Larson | Y | N | Y | N | Y | Y |
| 2 Simmons | N | Y | Y | Y | Y | Y |
| 3 DeLauro | Y | N | Y | N | Y | Y |
| 4 Shays | N | Y | Y | Y | Y | Y |
| 5 Johnson | N | Y | Y | Y | Y | Y |
| **DELAWARE** | | | | | | |
| AL Castle | N | Y | Y | Y | Y | Y |
| **FLORIDA** | | | | | | |
| 1 Miller | N | Y | Y | Y | Y | Y |
| 2 Boyd | Y | N | Y | N | Y | Y |
| 3 Brown | Y | N | Y | N | Y | Y |
| 4 Crenshaw | N | Y | Y | Y | Y | Y |
| 5 Brown-Waite | N | Y | Y | Y | Y | Y |
| 6 Stearns | N | Y | Y | + | Y | Y |
| 7 Mica | N | Y | Y | Y | Y | Y |
| 8 Keller | N | Y | Y | Y | Y | Y |
| 9 Bilirakis | N | Y | Y | Y | Y | Y |
| 10 Young | ? | ? | ? | ? | Y | Y |
| 11 Davis | Y | N | Y | N | Y | Y |
| 12 Putnam | N | Y | Y | Y | Y | Y |
| 13 Harris | N | Y | Y | Y | Y | Y |
| 14 Mack | N | Y | Y | Y | Y | Y |
| 15 Weldon | N | Y | Y | Y | Y | Y |
| 16 Foley | N | Y | Y | Y | Y | Y |
| 17 Meek | Y | N | Y | N | Y | Y |
| 18 Ros-Lehtinen | N | Y | Y | Y | Y | Y |
| 19 Wexler | Y | N | Y | ? | Y | Y |
| 20 Wasserman-Schultz | Y | N | Y | N | Y | Y |
| 21 Diaz-Balart, L. | N | Y | Y | Y | Y | Y |
| 22 Shaw | N | Y | Y | Y | Y | Y |
| 23 Hastings | Y | N | Y | N | Y | N |
| 24 Feeney | N | Y | Y | Y | Y | Y |
| 25 Diaz-Balart, M. | - | - | ? | ? | ? | Y |
| **GEORGIA** | | | | | | |
| 1 Kingston | N | Y | Y | Y | Y | Y |
| 2 Bishop | Y | N | Y | N | Y | Y |
| 3 Marshall | Y | Y | Y | N | Y | Y |
| 4 McKinney | Y | N | N | N | Y | Y |
| 5 Lewis | Y | N | Y | N | Y | N |
| 6 Price | N | Y | Y | Y | Y | + |
| 7 Linder | N | Y | Y | Y | Y | Y |
| 8 Westmoreland | N | Y | Y | ? | Y | Y |
| 9 Norwood | N | Y | Y | Y | Y | Y |
| 10 Deal | N | Y | Y | Y | Y | Y |
| 11 Gingrey | N | Y | Y | Y | Y | Y |
| 12 Barrow | N | Y | Y | N | Y | Y |
| 13 Scott | Y | N | Y | N | Y | Y |
| **HAWAII** | | | | | | |
| 1 Abercrombie | Y | N | P | N | Y | Y |
| 2 Case | N | Y | Y | N | Y | Y |
| **IDAHO** | | | | | | |
| 1 Otter | N | Y | Y | Y | Y | Y |
| 2 Simpson | N | Y | Y | Y | Y | Y |
| **ILLINOIS** | | | | | | |
| 1 Rush | Y | N | Y | N | Y | N |
| 2 Jackson | Y | N | Y | N | Y | N |
| 3 Lipinski | Y | Y | Y | N | Y | Y |
| 4 Gutierrez | Y | N | Y | N | Y | ? |
| 5 Emanuel | Y | N | Y | N | Y | ? |
| 6 Hyde | ? | ? | ? | ? | ? | ? |
| 7 Davis | Y | N | Y | N | Y | N |
| 8 Bean | Y | Y | Y | N | Y | N |
| 9 Schakowsky | Y | N | Y | N | Y | N |
| 10 Kirk | N | Y | Y | Y | Y | Y |
| 11 Weller | N | Y | Y | Y | Y | Y |
| 12 Costello | Y | Y | Y | N | Y | Y |

| KEY | Republicans | Democrats | *Independents* |
|---|---|---|---|

| | | |
|---|---|---|
| Y Voted for (yea) | X Paired against | C Voted "present" to avoid possible conflict of interest |
| # Paired for | - Announced against | |
| + Announced for | P Voted "present" | ? Did not vote or otherwise make a position known |
| N Voted against (nay) | | |

ND Northern Democrats, SD Southern Democrats
Southern states: Ala., Ark., Fla., Ga., Ky., La., Miss., N.C., Okla., S.C., Tenn., Texas, Va.

| | 660 | 661 | 662 | 663 | 664 | 665 |
|---|---|---|---|---|---|---|
| 13 **Biggert** | N | Y | Y | Y | Y | Y |
| 14 **Hastert** | | Y | | | | Y |
| 15 **Johnson** | N | Y | Y | Y | Y | Y |
| 16 **Manzullo** | N | Y | Y | Y | ? | Y |
| 17 Evans | Y | N | Y | N | Y | Y |
| 18 **LaHood** | ? | ? | ? | Y | Y | Y |
| 19 **Shimkus** | N | Y | Y | Y | Y | Y |
| **INDIANA** | | | | | | |
| 1 Visclosky | Y | Y | Y | N | Y | Y |
| 2 **Chocola** | N | Y | Y | Y | Y | Y |
| 3 **Souder** | N | N | Y | Y | Y | Y |
| 4 **Buyer** | N | Y | Y | Y | Y | Y |
| 5 **Burton** | N | Y | Y | Y | Y | Y |
| 6 **Pence** | N | Y | Y | Y | Y | Y |
| 7 Carson | Y | N | Y | N | Y | Y |
| 8 **Hostettler** | N | Y | Y | Y | ? | ? |
| 9 **Sodrel** | N | Y | Y | Y | Y | Y |
| **IOWA** | | | | | | |
| 1 **Nussle** | ? | Y | ? | Y | Y | Y |
| 2 **Leach** | N | N | Y | Y | Y | Y |
| 3 Boswell | Y | Y | Y | N | Y | Y |
| 4 **Latham** | N | Y | Y | Y | Y | Y |
| 5 **King** | N | Y | Y | Y | Y | Y |
| **KANSAS** | | | | | | |
| 1 **Moran** | N | Y | Y | Y | Y | Y |
| 2 **Ryun** | N | Y | Y | Y | Y | Y |
| 3 Moore | Y | Y | Y | N | Y | Y |
| 4 **Tiahrt** | N | Y | Y | Y | Y | Y |
| **KENTUCKY** | | | | | | |
| 1 **Whitfield** | N | Y | Y | Y | Y | Y |
| 2 **Lewis** | N | Y | Y | Y | Y | Y |
| 3 **Northup** | N | Y | Y | Y | Y | Y |
| 4 **Davis** | N | Y | Y | Y | Y | Y |
| 5 **Rogers** | N | Y | Y | Y | Y | Y |
| 6 Chandler | Y | Y | Y | N | Y | Y |
| **LOUISIANA** | | | | | | |
| 1 **Jindal** | N | Y | Y | Y | Y | Y |
| 2 Jefferson | ? | N | Y | N | Y | Y |
| 3 Melancon | Y | Y | Y | N | Y | Y |
| 4 **McCrery** | N | Y | Y | ? | Y | Y |
| 5 **Alexander** | N | Y | Y | Y | Y | Y |
| 6 **Baker** | N | Y | ? | Y | Y | Y |
| 7 **Boustany** | N | Y | Y | Y | Y | Y |
| **MAINE** | | | | | | |
| 1 Allen | Y | N | Y | N | Y | Y |
| 2 Michaud | Y | N | Y | N | Y | Y |
| **MARYLAND** | | | | | | |
| 1 **Gilchrest** | N | Y | Y | ? | Y | Y |
| 2 Ruppersberger | Y | N | Y | N | Y | Y |
| 3 Cardin | Y | N | Y | N | Y | Y |
| 4 Wynn | Y | N | Y | N | Y | Y |
| 5 Hoyer | Y | N | Y | ? | Y | Y |
| 6 **Bartlett** | N | N | Y | Y | Y | Y |
| 7 Cummings | Y | N | Y | ? | Y | Y |
| 8 Van Hollen | Y | N | Y | N | Y | Y |
| **MASSACHUSETTS** | | | | | | |
| 1 Olver | Y | N | Y | N | Y | N |
| 2 Neal | Y | N | Y | N | Y | Y |
| 3 McGovern | Y | N | Y | N | Y | N |
| 4 Frank | Y | N | Y | N | Y | N |
| 5 Meehan | Y | N | Y | N | Y | Y |
| 6 Tierney | Y | N | Y | N | Y | N |
| 7 Markey | Y | N | ? | N | Y | N |
| 8 Capuano | Y | N | Y | N | Y | Y |
| 9 Lynch | Y | N | Y | N | Y | Y |
| 10 Delahunt | Y | N | Y | N | Y | Y |
| **MICHIGAN** | | | | | | |
| 1 Stupak | Y | N | Y | N | Y | Y |
| 2 **Hoekstra** | N | Y | Y | Y | Y | Y |
| 3 **Ehlers** | N | Y | Y | ? | ? | Y |
| 4 **Camp** | N | Y | Y | Y | Y | Y |
| 5 Kildee | Y | N | Y | N | Y | Y |
| 6 **Upton** | N | Y | Y | Y | Y | Y |
| 7 **Schwarz** | N | Y | Y | Y | Y | Y |
| 8 **Rogers** | N | Y | Y | Y | Y | Y |
| 9 **Knollenberg** | N | Y | Y | Y | Y | Y |
| 10 **Miller** | N | Y | Y | Y | Y | Y |
| 11 **McCotter** | N | Y | Y | Y | Y | Y |
| 12 Levin | Y | N | Y | N | Y | Y |
| 13 Kilpatrick | Y | N | ? | N | Y | N |
| 14 Conyers | Y | N | Y | N | Y | N |
| 15 Dingell | Y | N | Y | N | Y | Y |
| **MINNESOTA** | | | | | | |
| 1 **Gutknecht** | N | Y | Y | Y | Y | Y |
| 2 **Kline** | N | Y | Y | Y | Y | Y |
| 3 **Ramstad** | N | Y | Y | Y | Y | Y |
| 4 McCollum | Y | N | Y | N | Y | Y |
| 5 Sabo | Y | N | Y | N | Y | Y |
| 6 **Kennedy** | N | Y | Y | Y | Y | Y |
| 7 Peterson | Y | Y | Y | N | Y | Y |
| 8 Oberstar | Y | N | Y | N | Y | N |
| **MISSISSIPPI** | | | | | | |
| 1 **Wicker** | N | Y | Y | Y | Y | Y |
| 2 Thompson | Y | N | Y | N | Y | Y |
| 3 **Pickering** | N | Y | Y | Y | Y | Y |
| 4 Taylor | Y | Y | Y | N | Y | Y |
| **MISSOURI** | | | | | | |
| 1 Clay | Y | N | Y | ? | Y | ? |
| 2 **Akin** | N | Y | Y | ? | ? | Y |
| 3 Carnahan | Y | N | Y | N | Y | Y |
| 4 Skelton | Y | Y | Y | N | Y | Y |
| 5 Cleaver | Y | N | Y | N | Y | Y |
| 6 **Graves** | N | Y | Y | Y | Y | Y |
| 7 **Blunt** | N | Y | Y | Y | Y | Y |
| 8 **Emerson** | N | Y | Y | Y | Y | Y |
| 9 **Hulshof** | N | Y | Y | Y | Y | Y |
| **MONTANA** | | | | | | |
| AL **Rehberg** | N | Y | Y | Y | Y | Y |
| **NEBRASKA** | | | | | | |
| 1 **Fortenberry** | N | Y | Y | Y | Y | Y |
| 2 **Terry** | N | Y | Y | Y | Y | Y |
| 3 **Osborne** | N | Y | Y | Y | Y | Y |
| **NEVADA** | | | | | | |
| 1 Berkley | Y | N | Y | N | Y | Y |
| 2 **Gibbons** | N | Y | Y | Y | Y | Y |
| 3 **Porter** | N | Y | Y | Y | Y | Y |
| **NEW HAMPSHIRE** | | | | | | |
| 1 **Bradley** | N | Y | Y | Y | Y | Y |
| 2 **Bass** | N | Y | Y | Y | Y | Y |
| **NEW JERSEY** | | | | | | |
| 1 Andrews | Y | N | Y | N | Y | Y |
| 2 **LoBiondo** | N | Y | Y | Y | Y | Y |
| 3 **Saxton** | N | Y | Y | Y | Y | Y |
| 4 **Smith** | N | N | Y | Y | Y | Y |
| 5 **Garrett** | N | Y | Y | Y | Y | Y |
| 6 Pallone | Y | N | Y | N | Y | Y |
| 7 **Ferguson** | N | Y | Y | Y | Y | Y |
| 8 Pascrell | Y | N | Y | N | Y | Y |
| 9 Rothman | Y | N | Y | Y | Y | Y |
| 10 Payne | Y | N | Y | N | Y | N |
| 11 **Frelinghuysen** | N | Y | Y | Y | Y | Y |
| 12 Holt | Y | N | Y | N | Y | Y |
| 13 Menendez | Y | N | Y | N | Y | Y |
| **NEW MEXICO** | | | | | | |
| 1 **Wilson** | N | N | Y | Y | Y | Y |
| 2 **Pearce** | N | N | Y | Y | Y | Y |
| 3 Udall | Y | N | Y | N | Y | Y |
| **NEW YORK** | | | | | | |
| 1 Bishop | Y | N | Y | N | Y | Y |
| 2 Israel | Y | N | Y | N | Y | Y |
| 3 **King** | N | Y | Y | Y | Y | Y |
| 4 McCarthy | + | – | + | – | + | Y |
| 5 Ackerman | Y | N | Y | N | Y | Y |
| 6 Meeks | Y | N | Y | N | Y | Y |
| 7 Crowley | Y | N | Y | N | Y | Y |
| 8 Nadler | Y | N | Y | N | Y | N |
| 9 Weiner | Y | N | Y | N | Y | Y |
| 10 Towns | Y | N | Y | N | Y | N |
| 11 Owens | Y | N | Y | N | Y | N |
| 12 Velázquez | Y | N | Y | N | Y | N |
| 13 **Fossella** | N | Y | Y | Y | ? | Y |
| 14 Maloney | Y | N | Y | N | Y | Y |
| 15 Rangel | Y | N | Y | N | Y | N |
| 16 Serrano | Y | N | Y | N | Y | N |
| 17 Engel | Y | N | Y | N | Y | Y |
| 18 Lowey | Y | N | Y | N | Y | Y |
| 19 **Kelly** | N | Y | Y | Y | Y | Y |
| 20 **Sweeney** | N | Y | Y | Y | Y | Y |
| 21 McNulty | Y | N | Y | N | Y | N |
| 22 Hinchey | Y | N | Y | N | Y | N |
| 23 **McHugh** | N | Y | Y | Y | Y | Y |
| 24 **Boehlert** | N | Y | Y | Y | Y | Y |
| 25 **Walsh** | N | Y | Y | Y | Y | Y |
| 26 **Reynolds** | N | Y | Y | Y | Y | Y |
| 27 Higgins | Y | Y | Y | N | Y | Y |
| 28 Slaughter | Y | N | Y | N | ? | Y |
| 29 **Kuhl** | N | Y | Y | Y | Y | Y |
| **NORTH CAROLINA** | | | | | | |
| 1 Butterfield | Y | N | Y | N | Y | Y |
| 2 Etheridge | Y | N | Y | N | Y | Y |
| 3 **Jones** | N | Y | Y | Y | Y | ? |
| 4 Price | Y | N | Y | N | Y | Y |
| 5 **Foxx** | N | Y | Y | Y | Y | Y |
| 6 **Coble** | N | Y | Y | Y | Y | Y |
| 7 McIntyre | Y | Y | Y | N | Y | Y |
| 8 **Hayes** | N | Y | Y | Y | Y | Y |
| 9 **Myrick** | N | Y | Y | ? | ? | ? |
| 10 **McHenry** | N | Y | Y | Y | Y | Y |
| 11 **Taylor** | N | Y | Y | Y | Y | Y |
| 12 Watt | Y | N | Y | N | Y | N |
| 13 Miller | Y | N | Y | N | Y | Y |
| **NORTH DAKOTA** | | | | | | |
| AL Pomeroy | Y | Y | Y | N | Y | Y |
| **OHIO** | | | | | | |
| 1 **Chabot** | N | Y | Y | Y | Y | Y |
| 2 **Schmidt** | N | Y | Y | Y | Y | Y |
| 3 **Turner** | N | N | Y | Y | Y | Y |
| 4 **Oxley** | N | Y | ? | Y | Y | Y |
| 5 **Gillmor** | N | Y | Y | Y | Y | Y |
| 6 Strickland | Y | Y | Y | N | Y | Y |
| 7 **Hobson** | N | N | Y | Y | Y | Y |
| 8 **Boehner** | N | N | Y | Y | Y | Y |
| 9 Kaptur | Y | N | N | N | Y | Y |
| 10 Kucinich | Y | N | Y | N | Y | N |
| 11 Jones | Y | N | Y | N | Y | N |
| 12 **Tiberi** | N | N | Y | Y | Y | Y |
| 13 Brown | Y | N | Y | N | Y | Y |
| 14 **LaTourette** | N | Y | Y | Y | Y | Y |
| 15 **Pryce** | N | Y | Y | Y | Y | Y |
| 16 **Regula** | N | Y | Y | Y | Y | Y |
| 17 Ryan | Y | N | Y | N | Y | Y |
| 18 **Ney** | N | Y | Y | Y | Y | Y |
| **OKLAHOMA** | | | | | | |
| 1 **Sullivan** | N | Y | Y | Y | Y | Y |
| 2 Boren | Y | Y | Y | N | Y | Y |
| 3 **Lucas** | N | Y | Y | Y | Y | Y |
| 4 **Cole** | N | + | Y | Y | Y | Y |
| 5 **Istook** | ? | ? | ? | ? | ? | ? |
| **OREGON** | | | | | | |
| 1 Wu | Y | N | Y | N | Y | Y |
| 2 **Walden** | N | Y | ? | Y | Y | Y |
| 3 Blumenauer | Y | N | Y | N | Y | N |
| 4 DeFazio | Y | Y | Y | N | Y | Y |
| 5 Hooley | Y | N | Y | N | Y | Y |
| **PENNSYLVANIA** | | | | | | |
| 1 Brady | Y | N | Y | N | Y | Y |
| 2 Fattah | Y | N | Y | N | Y | Y |
| 3 **English** | N | Y | Y | Y | Y | Y |
| 4 **Hart** | N | Y | Y | Y | Y | Y |
| 5 **Peterson** | N | Y | Y | Y | Y | Y |
| 6 **Gerlach** | N | Y | Y | Y | Y | Y |
| 7 **Weldon** | N | Y | Y | ? | Y | Y |
| 8 **Fitzpatrick** | N | Y | Y | Y | Y | Y |
| 9 **Shuster** | N | Y | Y | Y | Y | Y |
| 10 **Sherwood** | N | Y | Y | Y | Y | Y |
| 11 Kanjorski | Y | Y | Y | N | Y | Y |
| 12 Murtha | Y | N | ? | N | ? | Y |
| 13 Schwartz | Y | N | Y | N | Y | Y |
| 14 Doyle | Y | N | Y | N | Y | Y |
| 15 **Dent** | N | Y | Y | Y | Y | Y |
| 16 **Pitts** | N | Y | Y | Y | Y | Y |
| 17 Holden | Y | Y | Y | N | Y | Y |
| 18 **Murphy** | N | Y | Y | Y | Y | Y |
| 19 **Platts** | N | Y | Y | ? | Y | Y |
| **RHODE ISLAND** | | | | | | |
| 1 Kennedy | Y | N | Y | N | Y | Y |
| 2 Langevin | Y | N | Y | N | Y | Y |
| **SOUTH CAROLINA** | | | | | | |
| 1 **Brown** | N | Y | Y | Y | Y | Y |
| 2 **Wilson** | N | Y | Y | Y | Y | Y |
| 3 **Barrett** | – | + | + | Y | Y | Y |
| 4 **Inglis** | N | Y | Y | Y | Y | Y |
| 5 Spratt | Y | N | Y | ? | Y | Y |
| 6 Clyburn | Y | N | Y | N | Y | Y |
| **SOUTH DAKOTA** | | | | | | |
| AL Herseth | Y | Y | Y | N | Y | Y |
| **TENNESSEE** | | | | | | |
| 1 **Jenkins** | N | Y | Y | Y | Y | Y |
| 2 **Duncan** | N | Y | Y | Y | Y | Y |
| 3 **Wamp** | N | Y | Y | Y | Y | Y |
| 4 Davis | Y | Y | Y | N | Y | Y |
| 5 Cooper | Y | N | Y | N | Y | Y |
| 6 Gordon | Y | Y | Y | N | Y | Y |
| 7 **Blackburn** | N | Y | Y | Y | Y | Y |
| 8 Tanner | Y | Y | Y | N | Y | Y |
| 9 Ford | Y | Y | ? | N | Y | Y |
| **TEXAS** | | | | | | |
| 1 **Gohmert** | N | Y | Y | Y | Y | Y |
| 2 **Poe** | N | Y | Y | Y | Y | Y |
| 3 **Johnson, S.** | N | Y | Y | Y | Y | ? |
| 4 **Hall** | N | Y | Y | Y | Y | Y |
| 5 **Hensarling** | N | Y | Y | Y | Y | Y |
| 6 **Barton** | – | + | + | + | + | Y |
| 7 **Culberson** | N | Y | Y | Y | Y | Y |
| 8 **Brady** | N | Y | Y | Y | Y | Y |
| 9 Green, A. | Y | N | Y | N | Y | Y |
| 10 **McCaul** | N | Y | Y | Y | Y | Y |
| 11 **Conaway** | N | Y | Y | Y | Y | Y |
| 12 **Granger** | N | Y | Y | Y | Y | Y |
| 13 **Thornberry** | N | Y | Y | Y | Y | Y |
| 14 **Paul** | N | Y | N | Y | ? | N |
| 15 Hinojosa | Y | N | Y | N | Y | Y |
| 16 Reyes | Y | N | Y | N | Y | ? |
| 17 Edwards | Y | Y | Y | N | Y | Y |
| 18 Jackson-Lee | Y | N | Y | N | Y | Y |
| 19 **Neugebauer** | N | Y | Y | Y | Y | Y |
| 20 Gonzalez | Y | N | Y | N | Y | Y |
| 21 **Smith** | N | Y | Y | Y | Y | Y |
| 22 **DeLay** | N | Y | Y | Y | Y | Y |
| 23 **Bonilla** | N | Y | Y | Y | Y | Y |
| 24 **Marchant** | N | Y | Y | Y | Y | Y |
| 25 Doggett | Y | N | Y | N | Y | Y |
| 26 **Burgess** | N | Y | Y | Y | Y | Y |
| 27 Ortiz | Y | N | Y | N | Y | Y |
| 28 Cuellar | Y | N | Y | N | Y | Y |
| 29 Green, G. | Y | N | Y | N | Y | Y |
| 30 Johnson, E. | Y | N | Y | N | Y | Y |
| 31 **Carter** | N | Y | Y | Y | Y | Y |
| 32 **Sessions** | N | Y | Y | Y | Y | Y |
| **UTAH** | | | | | | |
| 1 **Bishop** | N | Y | Y | Y | Y | Y |
| 2 Matheson | Y | Y | Y | N | Y | Y |
| 3 **Cannon** | N | Y | Y | Y | Y | Y |
| **VERMONT** | | | | | | |
| AL *Sanders* | Y | N | Y | N | Y | Y |
| **VIRGINIA** | | | | | | |
| 1 **Davis, J.** | – | + | + | + | + | ? |
| 2 **Drake** | N | Y | Y | Y | Y | Y |
| 3 Scott | Y | N | Y | N | Y | Y |
| 4 **Forbes** | N | Y | Y | Y | Y | Y |
| 5 **Goode** | N | Y | Y | Y | Y | Y |
| 6 **Goodlatte** | N | Y | Y | Y | Y | Y |
| 7 **Cantor** | N | Y | Y | Y | Y | Y |
| 8 Moran | Y | N | Y | N | Y | Y |
| 9 Boucher | Y | Y | Y | N | Y | Y |
| 10 **Wolf** | N | Y | Y | Y | Y | Y |
| 11 **Davis, T.** | N | Y | Y | ? | Y | Y |
| **WASHINGTON** | | | | | | |
| 1 Inslee | Y | N | Y | N | Y | Y |
| 2 Larsen | Y | Y | Y | N | Y | Y |
| 3 Baird | Y | N | Y | N | Y | N |
| 4 **Hastings** | N | N | Y | Y | Y | Y |
| 5 **McMorris** | N | Y | Y | Y | Y | Y |
| 6 Dicks | Y | N | Y | N | Y | Y |
| 7 McDermott | Y | N | N | N | Y | N |
| 8 **Reichert** | N | Y | Y | Y | Y | Y |
| 9 Smith | Y | N | Y | N | Y | Y |
| **WEST VIRGINIA** | | | | | | |
| 1 Mollohan | Y | N | Y | N | Y | Y |
| 2 **Capito** | N | Y | Y | Y | Y | Y |
| 3 Rahall | Y | N | Y | N | Y | Y |
| **WISCONSIN** | | | | | | |
| 1 **Ryan** | N | Y | Y | Y | Y | Y |
| 2 Baldwin | Y | N | Y | N | Y | N |
| 3 Kind | Y | N | Y | N | Y | Y |
| 4 Moore | Y | N | Y | N | Y | Y |
| 5 **Sensenbrenner** | N | Y | Y | Y | Y | Y |
| 6 **Petri** | N | Y | Y | Y | Y | Y |
| 7 Obey | Y | N | Y | N | Y | Y |
| 8 **Green** | N | Y | Y | Y | Y | Y |
| **WYOMING** | | | | | | |
| AL **Cubin** | N | Y | Y | ? | Y | Y |

# IN THE HOUSE | By Vote Number

**666.** **HR 2863. Fiscal 2006 Defense Appropriations/Rule.** Adoption of the rule (H Res 639) to provide for House floor consideration of the conference report on the bill that would appropriate $453.5 billion in fiscal 2006 for Defense, including $50 billion for operations in Iraq and Afghanistan. Adopted 214-201: R 198-21; D 16-179 (ND 7-138, SD 9-41); I 0-1. Dec. 19, 2005 (in the session that began and the Congressional Record dated Dec. 18, 2005).

**667.** **H Con Res 284. Egyptian Elections/Adoption.** Ros-Lehtinen, R-Fla., motion to suspend the rules and adopt the concurrent resolution to express the sense of Congress recognizing the importance of the Egyptian presidential election held Sept. 7, 2005, as a first step toward greater openness and political changes in that country. Motion agreed to 388-22: R 214-3; D 173-19 (ND 128-16, SD 45-3); I 1-0. A two-thirds majority of those present and voting (274 in this case) is required for adoption under suspension of the rules. Dec. 19, 2005 (in the session that began and the Congressional Record dated Dec. 18, 2005).

**668.** **HR 2863. Fiscal 2006 Defense Appropriations/Recommit.** Obey, D-Wis., motion to recommit the conference report on the bill to the Appropriations Committee with instructions to eliminate the legislation's across-the-board spending cuts. Motion rejected 183-231: R 1-218; D 181-13 (ND 135-9, SD 46-4); I 1-0. Dec. 19, 2005 (in the session that began and the Congressional Record dated Dec. 18, 2005).

**669.** **HR 2863. Fiscal 2006 Defense Appropriations/Conference Report.** Adoption of the conference report on the bill that would appropriate $453.5 billion for Defense spending, including $50 billion for operations in Iraq and Afghanistan. The total includes $123.6 billion for operations and maintenance, $76.5 billion for procurement and $72.1 billion for research and development. It would require a 1 percent across-the-board cut to all fiscal 2006 discretionary spending except Veterans Administration funding that was added to the legislation. It would provide $29 billion for disaster assistance to hurricane-damaged areas and $3.8 billion for flu preparedness. It would allow oil and gas leasing in the Arctic National Wildlife Refuge. Adopted (thus sent to the Senate) 308-106: R 202-16; D 106-89 (ND 65-80, SD 41-9); I 0-1. Dec. 19, 2005 (in the session that began and the Congressional Record dated Dec. 18, 2005).

**670.** **S 1932. Budget Reconciliation/Conference Report.** Adoption of the conference report on the bill that would make changes to programs for a net savings of $38.8 billion over five years. The total includes savings of roughly $12.7 billion from the student loan program, $1.5 billion from aid to states to enforce child support payments and $4.8 billion from Medicaid. The bill would provide $2.1 billion in hurricane assistance, authorize an additional $1 billion for low-income energy assistance and provide $7.3 billion to avoid a scheduled Medicare reimbursement cut to physicians. Adopted (thus sent to the Senate) 212-206: R 212-9; D 0-196 (ND 0-146, SD 0-50); I 0-1. A "yea" was a vote in support of the president's position. Dec. 19, 2005 (in the session that began and the Congressional Record dated Dec. 18, 2005).

**671.** **H Con Res 275. Education Curriculum in Saudi Arabia/Adoption.** Ros-Lehtinen, R-Fla., motion to suspend the rules and adopt the concurrent resolution that would urge the Saudi Arabian government to revise its textbooks and education curriculum to promote tolerance and peaceful coexistence with others, develop civil society and encourage functionality in the global economy. Motion agreed to 351-1: R 175-1; D 175-0 (ND 128-0, SD 47-0); I 1-0. A two-thirds majority of those present and voting (235 in this case) is required for adoption under suspension of the rules. Dec. 19, 2005 (in the session that began and the Congressional Record dated Dec. 18, 2005).

ND Northern Democrats, SD Southern Democrats
Southern states: Ala., Ark., Fla., Ga., Ky., La., Miss., N.C., Okla., S.C., Tenn., Texas, Va.

| | 666 | 667 | 668 | 669 | 670 | 671 |
|---|---|---|---|---|---|---|
| **ALABAMA** | | | | | | |
| 1 Bonner | Y | Y | N | Y | Y | Y |
| 2 Everett | Y | Y | N | Y | Y | ? |
| 3 Rogers | Y | Y | N | Y | Y | Y |
| 4 Aderholt | Y | Y | N | Y | Y | Y |
| 5 Cramer | Y | Y | Y | Y | N | Y |
| 6 Bachus | Y | Y | N | Y | Y | Y |
| 7 Davis | N | Y | Y | Y | N | Y |
| **ALASKA** | | | | | | |
| AL Young | Y | Y | N | Y | Y | Y |
| **ARIZONA** | | | | | | |
| 1 Renzi | Y | Y | N | Y | Y | Y |
| 2 Franks | Y | Y | N | Y | Y | Y |
| 3 Shadegg | Y | Y | N | Y | Y | Y |
| 4 Pastor | N | N | Y | N | N | Y |
| 5 Hayworth | Y | Y | N | Y | Y | Y |
| 6 Flake | Y | Y | N | Y | Y | ? |
| 7 Grijalva | N | Y | Y | N | N | Y |
| 8 Kolbe | ? | ? | ? | ? | ? | ? |
| **ARKANSAS** | | | | | | |
| 1 Berry | N | Y | Y | Y | N | Y |
| 2 Snyder | N | Y | Y | Y | N | Y |
| 3 Boozman | Y | Y | N | Y | Y | Y |
| 4 Ross | N | Y | Y | Y | N | Y |
| **CALIFORNIA** | | | | | | |
| 1 Thompson | N | Y | Y | N | N | Y |
| 2 Herger | Y | Y | N | Y | Y | Y |
| 3 Lungren | Y | Y | N | Y | Y | Y |
| 4 Doolittle | Y | Y | N | Y | Y | Y |
| 5 Matsui, D. | N | Y | Y | Y | N | Y |
| 6 Woolsey | N | Y | Y | N | N | Y |
| 7 Miller, George | N | N | Y | N | N | Y |
| 8 Pelosi | N | Y | Y | Y | N | Y |
| 9 Lee | N | N | Y | N | N | Y |
| 10 Tauscher | N | Y | Y | N | N | Y |
| 11 Pombo | Y | Y | N | Y | Y | Y |
| 12 Lantos | N | Y | Y | Y | N | Y |
| 13 Stark | N | Y | ? | N | N | Y |
| 14 Eshoo | N | Y | Y | N | N | Y |
| 15 Honda | N | Y | Y | N | N | Y |
| 16 Lofgren | N | Y | Y | N | N | Y |
| 17 Farr | N | Y | Y | N | N | Y |
| 18 Cardoza | N | Y | N | Y | N | ? |
| 19 Radanovich | ? | ? | ? | ? | ? | ? |
| 20 Costa | N | Y | Y | Y | N | Y |
| 21 Nunes | Y | Y | N | Y | Y | Y |
| 22 Thomas | Y | Y | N | Y | Y | Y |
| 23 Capps | N | Y | Y | N | N | Y |
| 24 Gallegly | Y | Y | N | Y | Y | Y |
| 25 McKeon | Y | Y | N | Y | Y | ? |
| 26 Dreier | Y | Y | N | Y | Y | Y |
| 27 Sherman | N | Y | Y | N | N | Y |
| 28 Berman | N | Y | Y | Y | N | Y |
| 29 Schiff | N | Y | Y | Y | N | Y |
| 30 Waxman | N | Y | Y | N | N | Y |
| 31 Becerra | N | Y | Y | N | N | Y |
| 32 Solis | N | Y | Y | N | N | Y |
| 33 Watson | N | Y | Y | N | N | Y |
| 34 Roybal-Allard | ? | ? | ? | ? | ? | ? |
| 35 Waters | N | N | Y | N | N | ? |
| 36 Harman | ? | ? | ? | ? | ? | ? |
| 37 Millender-McD. | N | Y | Y | N | N | Y |
| 38 Napolitano | N | Y | Y | N | N | Y |
| 39 Sánchez, Linda | N | Y | Y | N | N | Y |
| 40 Royce | Y | Y | N | Y | Y | Y |
| 41 Lewis | Y | Y | N | Y | Y | ? |
| 42 Miller, Gary | ? | ? | ? | ? | ? | ? |
| 43 Baca | ? | ? | ? | ? | ? | ? |
| 44 Calvert | Y | Y | N | Y | Y | ? |
| 45 Bono | Y | Y | N | Y | Y | Y |
| 46 Rohrabacher | Y | Y | N | Y | Y | ? |
| 47 Sanchez, Loretta | N | Y | Y | N | N | Y |
| 48 Campbell | Y | Y | N | Y | Y | Y |
| 49 Issa | Y | Y | N | Y | Y | Y |

| | 666 | 667 | 668 | 669 | 670 | 671 |
|---|---|---|---|---|---|---|
| 50 Vacant | | | | | | |
| 51 Filner | N | Y | Y | N | N | Y |
| 52 Hunter | Y | Y | N | Y | Y | ? |
| 53 Davis | N | Y | Y | Y | N | Y |
| **COLORADO** | | | | | | |
| 1 DeGette | N | Y | Y | N | N | Y |
| 2 Udall | N | Y | Y | N | N | Y |
| 3 Salazar | N | Y | Y | Y | N | Y |
| 4 Musgrave | Y | Y | N | Y | Y | Y |
| 5 Hefley | ? | ? | ? | ? | Y | Y |
| 6 Tancredo | Y | Y | N | Y | Y | Y |
| 7 Beauprez | Y | Y | N | Y | Y | Y |
| **CONNECTICUT** | | | | | | |
| 1 Larson | N | Y | Y | Y | N | ? |
| 2 Simmons | N | Y | N | Y | Y | Y |
| 3 DeLauro | N | Y | Y | N | N | Y |
| 4 Shays | N | Y | N | N | Y | Y |
| 5 Johnson | N | Y | N | Y | N | ? |
| **DELAWARE** | | | | | | |
| AL Castle | N | Y | N | N | Y | Y |
| **FLORIDA** | | | | | | |
| 1 Miller | Y | Y | N | Y | Y | ? |
| 2 Boyd | N | Y | Y | Y | N | ? |
| 3 Brown | N | Y | Y | Y | N | Y |
| 4 Crenshaw | Y | Y | N | Y | Y | Y |
| 5 Brown-Waite | Y | Y | N | Y | Y | Y |
| 6 Stearns | Y | Y | N | Y | Y | Y |
| 7 Mica | Y | Y | N | Y | Y | Y |
| 8 Keller | Y | Y | N | Y | Y | Y |
| 9 Bilirakis | Y | Y | N | Y | Y | Y |
| 10 Young | Y | Y | N | Y | Y | Y |
| 11 Davis | N | Y | Y | Y | N | Y |
| 12 Putnam | Y | Y | N | Y | Y | Y |
| 13 Harris | Y | Y | N | Y | Y | Y |
| 14 Mack | Y | Y | N | Y | Y | Y |
| 15 Weldon | Y | Y | N | Y | Y | Y |
| 16 Foley | Y | Y | N | Y | Y | Y |
| 17 Meek | N | Y | Y | N | N | Y |
| 18 Ros-Lehtinen | Y | Y | N | Y | Y | Y |
| 19 Wexler | N | Y | Y | N | N | Y |
| 20 Wasserman-Schultz | N | Y | Y | Y | N | Y |
| 21 Diaz-Balart, L. | Y | ? | N | Y | Y | ? |
| 22 Shaw | Y | Y | N | Y | Y | Y |
| 23 Hastings | N | ? | Y | N | N | Y |
| 24 Feeney | Y | Y | ? | Y | Y | Y |
| 25 Diaz-Balart, M. | Y | ? | N | Y | Y | ? |
| **GEORGIA** | | | | | | |
| 1 Kingston | Y | Y | N | Y | Y | Y |
| 2 Bishop | Y | Y | N | Y | N | Y |
| 3 Marshall | N | ? | Y | Y | N | Y |
| 4 McKinney | N | N | Y | N | N | ? |
| 5 Lewis | N | Y | Y | N | N | Y |
| 6 Price | + | Y | N | Y | Y | Y |
| 7 Linder | Y | Y | N | Y | Y | Y |
| 8 Westmoreland | Y | Y | N | Y | Y | Y |
| 9 Norwood | Y | Y | N | Y | Y | Y |
| 10 Deal | Y | Y | N | Y | Y | Y |
| 11 Gingrey | Y | Y | N | Y | Y | Y |
| 12 Barrow | N | Y | Y | Y | N | Y |
| 13 Scott | N | Y | Y | N | N | Y |
| **HAWAII** | | | | | | |
| 1 Abercrombie | N | Y | Y | Y | N | P |
| 2 Case | N | Y | Y | N | N | Y |
| **IDAHO** | | | | | | |
| 1 Otter | Y | Y | N | Y | Y | Y |
| 2 Simpson | Y | Y | N | Y | Y | Y |
| **ILLINOIS** | | | | | | |
| 1 Rush | N | Y | Y | N | N | Y |
| 2 Jackson | N | N | Y | N | N | Y |
| 3 Lipinski | N | Y | Y | Y | N | Y |
| 4 Gutierrez | ? | ? | ? | ? | ? | ? |
| 5 Emanuel | ? | ? | ? | ? | ? | ? |
| 6 Hyde | ? | ? | ? | ? | ? | ? |
| 7 Davis | N | Y | Y | N | N | Y |
| 8 Bean | N | Y | N | Y | N | Y |
| 9 Schakowsky | N | Y | Y | N | N | Y |
| 10 Kirk | Y | Y | N | N | Y | Y |
| 11 Weller | Y | Y | N | Y | Y | Y |
| 12 Costello | N | Y | Y | Y | N | Y |

**KEY** Republicans Democrats *Independents*

| | | | |
|---|---|---|---|
| **Y** Voted for (yea) | **X** Paired against | **C** Voted "present" to avoid possible conflict of interest |
| **#** Paired for | **–** Announced against | |
| **+** Announced for | **P** Voted "present" | **?** Did not vote or otherwise make a position known |
| **N** Voted against (nay) | | |

| | 666 | 667 | 668 | 669 | 670 | 671 |
|---|---|---|---|---|---|---|
| 13 **Biggert** | N | Y | N | Y | Y | Y |
| 14 **Hastert** | Y | Y | N | Y | Y | |
| 15 **Johnson** | N | Y | N | N | N | Y |
| 16 **Manzullo** | Y | Y | N | Y | Y | Y |
| 17 Evans | N | Y | Y | Y | N | Y |
| 18 **LaHood** | Y | Y | N | Y | Y | Y |
| 19 **Shimkus** | Y | Y | N | Y | Y | Y |
| **INDIANA** | | | | | | |
| 1 Visclosky | N | Y | Y | Y | N | Y |
| 2 **Chocola** | Y | Y | N | Y | Y | ? |
| 3 **Souder** | Y | Y | N | Y | Y | Y |
| 4 **Buyer** | Y | Y | N | Y | N | ? |
| 5 **Burton** | Y | Y | N | P | Y | ? |
| 6 **Pence** | Y | Y | N | Y | Y | Y |
| 7 Carson | N | Y | Y | Y | N | Y |
| 8 **Hostettler** | ? | ? | ? | ? | ? | ? |
| 9 **Sodrel** | Y | Y | N | Y | Y | Y |
| **IOWA** | | | | | | |
| 1 **Nussle** | Y | Y | N | Y | Y | Y |
| 2 **Leach** | N | Y | Y | N | N | ? |
| 3 Boswell | N | Y | Y | N | N | Y |
| 4 **Latham** | Y | Y | N | Y | Y | Y |
| 5 **King** | Y | Y | N | Y | Y | Y |
| **KANSAS** | | | | | | |
| 1 **Moran** | Y | Y | N | Y | Y | ? |
| 2 **Ryun** | Y | Y | N | Y | Y | Y |
| 3 Moore | N | Y | Y | Y | N | Y |
| 4 **Tiahrt** | Y | Y | N | Y | Y | Y |
| **KENTUCKY** | | | | | | |
| 1 **Whitfield** | Y | Y | N | Y | Y | Y |
| 2 **Lewis** | Y | Y | N | Y | Y | Y |
| 3 **Northup** | Y | Y | N | Y | Y | Y |
| 4 **Davis** | Y | Y | N | Y | Y | Y |
| 5 **Rogers** | Y | Y | N | Y | Y | Y |
| 6 Chandler | N | Y | Y | Y | N | Y |
| **LOUISIANA** | | | | | | |
| 1 **Jindal** | Y | Y | N | Y | Y | Y |
| 2 Jefferson | N | Y | N | Y | N | Y |
| 3 Melancon | Y | Y | N | Y | N | Y |
| 4 **McCrery** | Y | Y | N | Y | Y | ? |
| 5 **Alexander** | Y | Y | N | Y | Y | Y |
| 6 **Baker** | Y | Y | N | Y | Y | ? |
| 7 **Boustany** | Y | Y | N | Y | Y | Y |
| **MAINE** | | | | | | |
| 1 Allen | N | Y | Y | Y | N | Y |
| 2 Michaud | N | Y | Y | N | N | Y |
| **MARYLAND** | | | | | | |
| 1 **Gilchrest** | N | Y | N | Y | Y | Y |
| 2 Ruppersberger | N | Y | Y | Y | N | Y |
| 3 Cardin | N | Y | Y | N | N | ? |
| 4 Wynn | N | N | Y | Y | N | Y |
| 5 Hoyer | N | Y | Y | Y | N | Y |
| 6 **Bartlett** | N | Y | N | Y | Y | Y |
| 7 Cummings | N | Y | Y | N | N | Y |
| 8 Van Hollen | N | Y | Y | N | N | Y |
| **MASSACHUSETTS** | | | | | | |
| 1 Olver | N | Y | Y | N | N | Y |
| 2 Neal | N | Y | Y | Y | N | ? |
| 3 McGovern | N | Y | + | – | N | Y |
| 4 Frank | N | Y | Y | N | N | Y |
| 5 Meehan | N | Y | Y | Y | N | Y |
| 6 Tierney | N | Y | Y | N | N | Y |
| 7 Markey | N | Y | Y | N | N | Y |
| 8 Capuano | N | Y | Y | Y | N | Y |
| 9 Lynch | N | Y | Y | Y | N | ? |
| 10 Delahunt | N | Y | Y | N | N | ? |
| **MICHIGAN** | | | | | | |
| 1 Stupak | N | Y | Y | N | N | Y |
| 2 **Hoekstra** | Y | Y | N | N | Y | ? |
| 3 **Ehlers** | N | Y | N | N | Y | Y |
| 4 **Camp** | Y | Y | N | Y | Y | Y |
| 5 Kildee | N | Y | Y | N | N | Y |
| 6 **Upton** | Y | Y | N | Y | Y | Y |
| 7 **Schwarz** | N | Y | N | Y | Y | Y |
| 8 **Rogers** | Y | Y | N | Y | Y | Y |
| 9 **Knollenberg** | Y | Y | N | Y | Y | Y |
| 10 **Miller** | Y | Y | N | Y | Y | Y |
| 11 **McCotter** | Y | Y | N | Y | Y | Y |
| 12 Levin | N | Y | Y | Y | N | Y |
| 13 Kilpatrick | N | N | Y | N | N | Y |
| 14 Conyers | N | N | Y | N | N | Y |
| 15 Dingell | N | Y | Y | N | N | Y |
| **MINNESOTA** | | | | | | |
| 1 **Gutknecht** | Y | Y | N | Y | Y | Y |
| 2 **Kline** | Y | Y | N | Y | Y | Y |
| 3 **Ramstad** | N | Y | N | N | Y | Y |
| 4 McCollum | N | Y | Y | N | N | Y |
| 5 Sabo | N | Y | Y | N | N | Y |
| 6 **Kennedy** | Y | Y | N | Y | Y | Y |
| 7 Peterson | N | Y | N | Y | N | Y |
| 8 Oberstar | N | Y | Y | N | N | Y |
| **MISSISSIPPI** | | | | | | |
| 1 **Wicker** | Y | Y | N | Y | Y | Y |
| 2 Thompson | N | Y | Y | Y | N | Y |
| 3 **Pickering** | Y | Y | N | Y | Y | Y |
| 4 Taylor | Y | Y | N | Y | N | Y |
| **MISSOURI** | | | | | | |
| 1 Clay | ? | ? | Y | Y | N | Y |
| 2 **Akin** | Y | Y | N | Y | Y | Y |
| 3 Carnahan | N | Y | Y | Y | N | Y |
| 4 Skelton | N | Y | Y | Y | N | Y |
| 5 Cleaver | N | ? | Y | Y | N | Y |
| 6 **Graves** | Y | Y | N | Y | Y | ? |
| 7 **Blunt** | Y | Y | N | Y | Y | ? |
| 8 **Emerson** | Y | Y | N | Y | Y | Y |
| 9 **Hulshof** | Y | Y | N | Y | Y | ? |
| **MONTANA** | | | | | | |
| AL **Rehberg** | Y | Y | N | Y | Y | Y |
| **NEBRASKA** | | | | | | |
| 1 **Fortenberry** | Y | N | N | Y | Y | Y |
| 2 **Terry** | Y | Y | N | Y | Y | Y |
| 3 **Osborne** | N | Y | N | Y | Y | Y |
| **NEVADA** | | | | | | |
| 1 Berkley | N | Y | Y | Y | N | Y |
| 2 **Gibbons** | Y | Y | N | Y | Y | Y |
| 3 **Porter** | Y | Y | N | Y | Y | Y |
| **NEW HAMPSHIRE** | | | | | | |
| 1 **Bradley** | Y | Y | N | Y | Y | Y |
| 2 **Bass** | N | Y | N | N | Y | Y |
| **NEW JERSEY** | | | | | | |
| 1 Andrews | N | Y | Y | N | N | Y |
| 2 **LoBiondo** | N | Y | N | N | Y | Y |
| 3 **Saxton** | Y | Y | N | P | Y | Y |
| 4 **Smith** | N | Y | N | N | N | Y |
| 5 **Garrett** | Y | Y | N | Y | Y | Y |
| 6 Pallone | N | Y | Y | N | N | Y |
| 7 **Ferguson** | Y | Y | N | Y | Y | Y |
| 8 Pascrell | Y | Y | Y | Y | N | Y |
| 9 Rothman | N | Y | Y | N | N | Y |
| 10 Payne | N | N | Y | N | N | Y |
| 11 **Frelinghuysen** | Y | Y | N | Y | Y | Y |
| 12 Holt | N | Y | Y | N | N | Y |
| 13 Menendez | N | Y | Y | N | N | Y |
| **NEW MEXICO** | | | | | | |
| 1 **Wilson** | Y | Y | N | Y | N | Y |
| 2 **Pearce** | Y | Y | N | Y | Y | ? |
| 3 Udall | N | Y | Y | N | N | Y |
| **NEW YORK** | | | | | | |
| 1 Bishop | N | Y | Y | Y | N | Y |
| 2 Israel | N | Y | Y | Y | N | Y |
| 3 **King** | Y | Y | N | Y | Y | Y |
| 4 McCarthy | N | Y | Y | Y | N | Y |
| 5 Ackerman | N | Y | Y | N | N | ? |
| 6 Meeks | N | Y | Y | N | N | Y |
| 7 Crowley | N | Y | Y | Y | N | ? |
| 8 Nadler | N | Y | Y | N | N | Y |
| 9 Weiner | N | Y | Y | N | N | Y |
| 10 Towns | N | Y | Y | N | N | Y |
| 11 Owens | N | Y | Y | N | N | Y |
| 12 Velázquez | N | Y | Y | N | N | ? |
| 13 **Fossella** | Y | Y | N | Y | Y | ? |
| 14 Maloney | N | Y | Y | N | N | Y |
| 15 Rangel | N | Y | Y | N | N | ? |
| 16 Serrano | N | Y | Y | N | N | Y |
| 17 Engel | N | Y | Y | N | N | Y |
| 18 Lowey | N | Y | Y | Y | N | Y |
| 19 **Kelly** | Y | Y | N | N | Y | Y |
| 20 **Sweeney** | Y | Y | N | Y | Y | Y |
| 21 McNulty | N | Y | Y | N | N | ? |
| 22 Hinchey | N | N | Y | N | N | Y |
| 23 **McHugh** | Y | Y | N | Y | N | ? |
| 24 **Boehlert** | N | Y | N | Y | Y | Y |
| 25 **Walsh** | Y | Y | N | Y | Y | Y |
| 26 **Reynolds** | Y | Y | N | Y | Y | Y |
| 27 Higgins | N | Y | Y | Y | N | Y |
| 28 Slaughter | N | Y | Y | N | N | ? |
| 29 **Kuhl** | Y | Y | N | Y | Y | Y |
| **NORTH CAROLINA** | | | | | | |
| 1 Butterfield | N | Y | Y | Y | N | Y |
| 2 Etheridge | N | Y | Y | Y | N | Y |
| 3 **Jones** | ? | ? | ? | ? | ? | ? |
| 4 Price | N | Y | Y | Y | N | Y |
| 5 **Foxx** | Y | Y | N | Y | Y | Y |
| 6 **Coble** | Y | Y | N | Y | Y | ? |
| 7 McIntyre | N | Y | Y | Y | N | Y |
| 8 **Hayes** | Y | Y | N | Y | Y | ? |
| 9 **Myrick** | ? | ? | ? | ? | ? | ? |
| 10 **McHenry** | Y | Y | N | Y | Y | Y |
| 11 **Taylor** | Y | N | N | Y | Y | P |
| 12 Watt | N | Y | Y | N | N | Y |
| 13 Miller | N | Y | Y | Y | N | Y |
| **NORTH DAKOTA** | | | | | | |
| AL Pomeroy | N | Y | Y | Y | N | Y |
| **OHIO** | | | | | | |
| 1 **Chabot** | Y | Y | N | Y | Y | Y |
| 2 **Schmidt** | Y | Y | N | Y | Y | Y |
| 3 **Turner** | Y | Y | N | Y | Y | Y |
| 4 **Oxley** | Y | Y | N | Y | Y | Y |
| 5 **Gillmor** | Y | Y | N | Y | Y | Y |
| 6 Strickland | N | Y | Y | Y | N | Y |
| 7 **Hobson** | Y | Y | N | Y | Y | Y |
| 8 **Boehner** | Y | Y | N | Y | Y | Y |
| 9 Kaptur | N | Y | Y | Y | N | Y |
| 10 Kucinich | N | N | Y | N | N | Y |
| 11 Jones | N | Y | Y | N | N | Y |
| 12 **Tiberi** | Y | Y | N | Y | Y | Y |
| 13 Brown | N | Y | Y | Y | N | ? |
| 14 **LaTourette** | Y | Y | N | Y | N | ? |
| 15 **Pryce** | Y | Y | N | Y | Y | ? |
| 16 **Regula** | Y | Y | N | Y | Y | Y |
| 17 Ryan | N | Y | Y | Y | N | Y |
| 18 **Ney** | Y | Y | N | Y | N | Y |
| **OKLAHOMA** | | | | | | |
| 1 **Sullivan** | Y | Y | N | Y | Y | Y |
| 2 Boren | Y | Y | Y | Y | N | Y |
| 3 **Lucas** | Y | Y | N | Y | Y | Y |
| 4 **Cole** | Y | Y | N | Y | Y | Y |
| 5 **Istook** | ? | ? | ? | ? | ? | ? |
| **OREGON** | | | | | | |
| 1 Wu | N | Y | Y | N | N | Y |
| 2 **Walden** | Y | Y | N | Y | Y | Y |
| 3 Blumenauer | N | N | Y | N | N | Y |
| 4 DeFazio | N | N | Y | Y | N | Y |
| 5 Hooley | N | Y | Y | Y | N | Y |
| **PENNSYLVANIA** | | | | | | |
| 1 Brady | Y | Y | N | Y | N | Y |
| 2 Fattah | N | Y | Y | Y | N | Y |
| 3 **English** | Y | Y | N | Y | Y | Y |
| 4 **Hart** | Y | Y | N | Y | Y | Y |
| 5 **Peterson** | Y | Y | N | Y | Y | ? |
| 6 **Gerlach** | N | Y | N | Y | Y | Y |
| 7 **Weldon** | Y | Y | N | Y | Y | Y |
| 8 **Fitzpatrick** | N | Y | N | N | Y | Y |
| 9 **Shuster** | Y | Y | N | Y | Y | Y |
| 10 **Sherwood** | Y | Y | N | Y | Y | ? |
| 11 Kanjorski | Y | Y | N | Y | N | Y |
| 12 Murtha | Y | Y | N | Y | N | ? |
| 13 Schwartz | N | Y | Y | Y | N | Y |
| 14 Doyle | Y | Y | Y | Y | N | ? |
| 15 **Dent** | Y | Y | N | Y | Y | Y |
| 16 **Pitts** | Y | Y | N | Y | Y | ? |
| 17 Holden | Y | Y | N | Y | N | Y |
| 18 **Murphy** | Y | Y | N | Y | Y | Y |
| 19 **Platts** | N | Y | N | Y | Y | Y |
| **RHODE ISLAND** | | | | | | |
| 1 Kennedy | N | Y | Y | Y | N | Y |
| 2 Langevin | N | Y | Y | Y | N | Y |
| **SOUTH CAROLINA** | | | | | | |
| 1 **Brown** | Y | Y | N | Y | Y | Y |
| 2 **Wilson** | Y | Y | N | Y | Y | Y |
| 3 **Barrett** | Y | Y | N | Y | Y | Y |
| 4 **Inglis** | Y | Y | N | Y | Y | Y |
| 5 Spratt | N | Y | Y | Y | N | Y |
| 6 Clyburn | N | Y | Y | Y | N | Y |
| **SOUTH DAKOTA** | | | | | | |
| AL Herseth | N | Y | Y | Y | N | Y |
| **TENNESSEE** | | | | | | |
| 1 **Jenkins** | Y | Y | N | Y | Y | ? |
| 2 **Duncan** | Y | Y | N | Y | Y | Y |
| 3 **Wamp** | Y | Y | N | Y | Y | Y |
| 4 Davis | Y | Y | Y | Y | N | Y |
| 5 Cooper | N | Y | Y | N | N | Y |
| 6 Gordon | N | Y | Y | Y | N | Y |
| 7 **Blackburn** | Y | Y | N | Y | Y | Y |
| 8 Tanner | N | Y | Y | Y | N | Y |
| 9 Ford | N | Y | Y | Y | N | Y |
| **TEXAS** | | | | | | |
| 1 **Gohmert** | Y | Y | N | Y | Y | Y |
| 2 **Poe** | Y | Y | N | Y | Y | Y |
| 3 **Johnson, S.** | ? | ? | ? | ? | ? | ? |
| 4 **Hall** | Y | Y | N | Y | Y | ? |
| 5 **Hensarling** | Y | Y | N | Y | Y | Y |
| 6 **Barton** | Y | Y | N | Y | Y | ? |
| 7 **Culberson** | Y | Y | N | Y | Y | Y |
| 8 **Brady** | Y | Y | N | Y | Y | ? |
| 9 Green, A. | N | Y | Y | Y | N | Y |
| 10 **McCaul** | Y | Y | N | Y | Y | Y |
| 11 **Conaway** | Y | Y | N | Y | Y | Y |
| 12 **Granger** | Y | Y | N | Y | Y | ? |
| 13 **Thornberry** | Y | Y | N | Y | Y | ? |
| 14 **Paul** | Y | N | N | N | N | N |
| 15 Hinojosa | N | Y | Y | Y | N | ? |
| 16 Reyes | ? | ? | ? | ? | ? | ? |
| 17 Edwards | N | Y | Y | Y | N | Y |
| 18 Jackson-Lee | N | N | Y | Y | N | Y |
| 19 **Neugebauer** | Y | Y | N | Y | Y | Y |
| 20 Gonzalez | N | Y | Y | Y | N | Y |
| 21 **Smith** | Y | Y | N | Y | Y | Y |
| 22 **DeLay** | Y | Y | N | Y | Y | Y |
| 23 **Bonilla** | Y | ? | N | Y | Y | ? |
| 24 **Marchant** | Y | Y | N | Y | Y | Y |
| 25 Doggett | N | Y | Y | N | N | Y |
| 26 **Burgess** | Y | Y | N | Y | Y | Y |
| 27 Ortiz | Y | Y | Y | Y | N | ? |
| 28 Cuellar | Y | Y | Y | Y | N | Y |
| 29 Green, G. | Y | Y | Y | Y | N | Y |
| 30 Johnson, E. | N | N | Y | N | N | Y |
| 31 **Carter** | Y | Y | N | Y | Y | ? |
| 32 **Sessions** | Y | Y | N | Y | Y | Y |
| **UTAH** | | | | | | |
| 1 **Bishop** | Y | Y | N | Y | Y | Y |
| 2 Matheson | N | Y | Y | Y | N | Y |
| 3 **Cannon** | Y | Y | N | Y | Y | Y |
| **VERMONT** | | | | | | |
| AL *Sanders* | N | Y | Y | N | N | Y |
| **VIRGINIA** | | | | | | |
| 1 **Davis, J.** | ? | ? | ? | ? | ? | ? |
| 2 **Drake** | Y | Y | N | Y | Y | Y |
| 3 Scott | N | Y | Y | N | N | Y |
| 4 **Forbes** | Y | Y | N | Y | Y | ? |
| 5 **Goode** | Y | Y | N | Y | Y | Y |
| 6 **Goodlatte** | Y | Y | N | Y | Y | Y |
| 7 **Cantor** | Y | Y | N | Y | Y | Y |
| 8 Moran | N | Y | Y | Y | N | Y |
| 9 Boucher | N | Y | Y | Y | N | Y |
| 10 **Wolf** | Y | Y | N | Y | Y | Y |
| 11 **Davis, T.** | Y | Y | N | Y | Y | Y |
| **WASHINGTON** | | | | | | |
| 1 Inslee | N | Y | Y | N | N | Y |
| 2 Larsen | N | Y | Y | Y | N | Y |
| 3 Baird | N | N | Y | N | N | Y |
| 4 **Hastings** | Y | Y | N | Y | Y | Y |
| 5 **McMorris** | Y | Y | N | Y | Y | Y |
| 6 Dicks | N | Y | N | Y | N | Y |
| 7 McDermott | N | Y | Y | N | N | Y |
| 8 **Reichert** | N | Y | N | Y | Y | Y |
| 9 Smith | N | Y | Y | N | N | Y |
| **WEST VIRGINIA** | | | | | | |
| 1 Mollohan | Y | Y | N | Y | N | Y |
| 2 **Capito** | Y | Y | N | Y | Y | Y |
| 3 Rahall | N | N | Y | Y | N | Y |
| **WISCONSIN** | | | | | | |
| 1 **Ryan** | Y | Y | N | Y | Y | ? |
| 2 Baldwin | N | Y | Y | N | N | Y |
| 3 Kind | N | Y | Y | Y | N | Y |
| 4 Moore | N | Y | Y | N | N | Y |
| 5 **Sensenbrenner** | Y | Y | N | Y | Y | Y |
| 6 **Petri** | Y | Y | N | N | Y | ? |
| 7 Obey | N | N | Y | N | N | ? |
| 8 **Green** | Y | Y | N | Y | Y | Y |
| **WYOMING** | | | | | | |
| AL **Cubin** | Y | Y | N | Y | Y | Y |

# House Roll Call Index by Subject

**Appendix S**

# SENATE
# ROLL CALL
# VOTES

# Senate Roll Call Index By Bill Number

# IN THE SENATE | By Vote Number

**1. Electoral Vote Count.** Rep. Stephanie Tubbs Jones, D-Ohio, and Sen. Barbara Boxer, D-Calif., objection to the certification of the Ohio electoral votes to protest voting irregularities in that state. Rejected 1-74: R 0-38; D 1-35 (ND 1-32, SD 0-3); I 0-1. Jan. 6, 2005.

**2. Rice Nomination/Confirmation.** Confirmation of President Bush's nomination of Condoleezza Rice to be secretary of State. Confirmed 85-13: R 53-0; D 32-12 (ND 28-12, SD 4-0); I 0-1. A "yea" was a vote in support of the president's position. Jan. 25, 2005.

**3. Gonzales Nomination/Confirmation.** Confirmation of President Bush's nomination of Alberto R. Gonzales of Texas to be attorney general. Confirmed 60-36: R 54-0; D 6-35 (ND 3-34, SD 3-1); I 0-1. A "yea" was a vote in support of the president's position. Feb. 3, 2005.

| | 1 | 2 | 3 | | | 1 | 2 | 3 |
|---|---|---|---|---|---|---|---|---|
| **ALABAMA** | | | | | **MONTANA** | | | |
| Shelby | ? | Y | Y | | Baucus | N | Y | ? |
| Sessions | N | Y | Y | | Burns | ? | + | + |
| **ALASKA** | | | | | **NEBRASKA** | | | |
| Stevens | N | Y | Y | | Hagel | N | Y | Y |
| Murkowski | ? | Y | Y | | Nelson | N | Y | Y |
| **ARIZONA** | | | | | **NEVADA** | | | |
| McCain | - | Y | Y | | Reid | N | Y | N |
| Kyl | - | Y | Y | | Ensign | ? | Y | Y |
| **ARKANSAS** | | | | | **NEW HAMPSHIRE** | | | |
| Lincoln | N | Y | N | | Gregg | N | ? | Y |
| Pryor | N | Y | Y | | Sununu | N | Y | Y |
| **CALIFORNIA** | | | | | **NEW JERSEY** | | | |
| Feinstein | ? | Y | N | | Corzine | ? | Y | N |
| Boxer | Y | N | N | | Lautenberg | N | N | N |
| **COLORADO** | | | | | **NEW MEXICO** | | | |
| Allard | N | Y | Y | | Domenici | N | Y | Y |
| Salazar | N | Y | Y | | Bingaman | ? | Y | N |
| **CONNECTICUT** | | | | | **NEW YORK** | | | |
| Dodd | N | Y | N | | Schumer | N | Y | N |
| Lieberman | N | Y | Y | | Clinton | N | Y | N |
| **DELAWARE** | | | | | **NORTH CAROLINA** | | | |
| Biden | N | Y | N | | Dole | N | Y | Y |
| Carper | N | Y | N | | Burr | N | Y | Y |
| **FLORIDA** | | | | | **NORTH DAKOTA** | | | |
| Nelson | N | Y | Y | | Conrad | N | Y | ? |
| Martinez | ? | Y | Y | | Dorgan | N | Y | N |
| **GEORGIA** | | | | | **OHIO** | | | |
| Chambliss | N | Y | Y | | DeWine | N | Y | Y |
| Isakson | N | Y | Y | | Voinovich | N | Y | Y |
| **HAWAII** | | | | | **OKLAHOMA** | | | |
| Inouye | N | Y | - | | Inhofe | - | Y | Y |
| Akaka | ? | N | N | | Coburn | N | Y | Y |
| **IDAHO** | | | | | **OREGON** | | | |
| Craig | ? | Y | Y | | Wyden | N | Y | N |
| Crapo | N | Y | Y | | Smith | N | Y | Y |
| **ILLINOIS** | | | | | **PENNSYLVANIA** | | | |
| Durbin | N | N | N | | Specter | N | Y | Y |
| Obama | N | Y | N | | Santorum | N | Y | Y |
| **INDIANA** | | | | | **RHODE ISLAND** | | | |
| Lugar | ? | Y | Y | | Reed | N | N | N |
| Bayh | ? | N | N | | Chafee | ? | Y | Y |
| **IOWA** | | | | | **SOUTH CAROLINA** | | | |
| Grassley | N | Y | Y | | Graham | N | Y | Y |
| Harkin | N | N | N | | DeMint | N | Y | Y |
| **KANSAS** | | | | | **SOUTH DAKOTA** | | | |
| Brownback | N | Y | Y | | Johnson | N | Y | N |
| Roberts | N | Y | Y | | Thune | N | Y | Y |
| **KENTUCKY** | | | | | **TENNESSEE** | | | |
| McConnell | N | Y | Y | | Frist | ? | Y | Y |
| Bunning | - | Y | Y | | Alexander | N | Y | Y |
| **LOUISIANA** | | | | | **TEXAS** | | | |
| Landrieu | ? | Y | Y | | Hutchison | ? | Y | Y |
| Vitter | - | Y | Y | | Cornyn | N | Y | Y |
| **MAINE** | | | | | **UTAH** | | | |
| Snowe | N | Y | Y | | Hatch | N | Y | Y |
| Collins | N | Y | Y | | Bennett | N | Y | Y |
| **MARYLAND** | | | | | **VERMONT** | | | |
| Sarbanes | N | Y | N | | Leahy | N | Y | N |
| Mikulski | N | Y | N | | *Jeffords* | N | N | N |
| **MASSACHUSETTS** | | | | | **VIRGINIA** | | | |
| Kennedy | N | N | N | | Warner | N | Y | Y |
| Kerry | ? | N | N | | Allen | ? | Y | Y |
| **MICHIGAN** | | | | | **WASHINGTON** | | | |
| Levin | N | N | N | | Murray | ? | Y | N |
| Stabenow | N | Y | N | | Cantwell | N | Y | N |
| **MINNESOTA** | | | | | **WEST VIRGINIA** | | | |
| Dayton | N | N | N | | Byrd | N | N | N |
| Coleman | N | Y | Y | | Rockefeller | N | Y | N |
| **MISSISSIPPI** | | | | | **WISCONSIN** | | | |
| Cochran | N | Y | Y | | Kohl | N | Y | N |
| Lott | N | Y | Y | | Feingold | N | Y | N |
| **MISSOURI** | | | | | **WYOMING** | | | |
| Bond | N | Y | Y | | Thomas | ? | Y | Y |
| Talent | N | Y | Y | | Enzi | N | Y | Y |

**KEY**    **Republicans**    Democrats    *Independents*

| | | | | | | |
|---|---|---|---|---|---|---|
| Y | Voted for (yea) | | X | Paired against | C | Voted "present" to avoid possible conflict of interest |
| # | Paired for | | - | Announced against | | |
| + | Announced for | | P | Voted "present" | ? | Did not vote or otherwise make a position known |
| N | Voted against (nay) | | | | | |

ND Northern Democrats, SD Southern Democrats

Southern states: Ala., Ark., Fla., Ga., Ky., La., Miss., N.C., Okla., S.C., Tenn., Texas, Va.

# IN THE SENATE | By Vote Number

**4.** **S Res 38. Iraqi Elections/Adoption.** Adoption of the resolution that would commend the people of Iraq on the Jan. 30, 2005, elections, express support for the establishment of a fully democratic Iraqi government, and condemn "all acts of violence and intimidation" committed by insurgents. Adopted 93-0: R 49-0; D 43-0 (ND 39-0, SD 4-0); I 1-0. Feb. 7, 2005.

**5.** **S 5. Class Action Overhaul/State Attorneys General.** Specter, R-Pa., motion to table (kill) the Pryor, D-Ark., amendment that would exempt class action suits brought by state attorneys general from the provisions of the bill. Motion agreed to 60-39: R 54-0; D 6-38 (ND 5-35, SD 1-3); I 0-1. Feb. 9, 2005.

**6.** **S 5. Class Action Overhaul/Civil Rights and Labor Cases.** Kennedy, D-Mass., amendment that would exclude civil rights class action suits and class action claims for lost wages and overtime from the bill's provisions. Rejected 40-59: R 0-54; D 39-5 (ND 35-5, SD 4-0); I 1-0. Feb. 9, 2005.

**7.** **S 5. Class Action Overhaul/Judicial Discretion.** Feinstein, D-Calif., amendment that would give federal judges additional discretion in deciding which state consumer protection laws to apply in class action suits where plaintiffs are from multiple states. Rejected 38-61: R 1-53; D 37-7 (ND 34-6, SD 3-1); I 0-1. Feb. 9, 2005.

**8.** **S 5. Class Action Overhaul/Time Limit.** Feingold, D-Wis., amendment that would place a 60-day limit on the amount of time federal judges have to consider whether to send class action cases back to state courts. Rejected 37-61: R 0-53; D 36-8 (ND 33-7, SD 3-1); I 1-0. Feb. 10, 2005.

**9.** **S 5. Class Action Overhaul/Passage.** Passage of the bill that would give federal courts jurisdiction over class action cases involving at least 100 plaintiffs if at least $5 million was at stake and two-thirds of the plaintiffs lived in different states. It would require judges to review all non-cash settlements, such as coupons for goods and services, and limit attorney's fees paid in such settlements. It also would prohibit federal judges from approving a net loss settlement without finding that the loss was outweighed by non-monetary benefits. Passed 72-26: R 53-0; D 18-26 (ND 16-24, SD 2-2); I 1-0. A "yea" was a vote in support of the president's position. Feb. 10, 2005.

| State / Senator | 4 | 5 | 6 | 7 | 8 | 9 |
|---|---|---|---|---|---|---|
| **ALABAMA** | | | | | | |
| Shelby | Y | Y | N | N | N | Y |
| Sessions | Y | Y | N | N | N | Y |
| **ALASKA** | | | | | | |
| Stevens | Y | Y | N | N | N | Y |
| Murkowski | ? | Y | N | N | N | Y |
| **ARIZONA** | | | | | | |
| McCain | Y | Y | N | N | N | Y |
| Kyl | Y | Y | N | N | N | Y |
| **ARKANSAS** | | | | | | |
| Lincoln | Y | Y | Y | N | Y | Y |
| Pryor | Y | N | Y | Y | Y | N |
| **CALIFORNIA** | | | | | | |
| Feinstein | Y | N | N | Y | Y | Y |
| Boxer | Y | N | Y | Y | Y | N |
| **COLORADO** | | | | | | |
| Allard | Y | Y | N | N | N | Y |
| Salazar | Y | N | Y | Y | Y | Y |
| **CONNECTICUT** | | | | | | |
| Dodd | Y | Y | N | N | N | Y |
| Lieberman | Y | N | Y | N | N | Y |
| **DELAWARE** | | | | | | |
| Biden | Y | N | Y | Y | Y | N |
| Carper | Y | Y | N | N | Y | Y |
| **FLORIDA** | | | | | | |
| Nelson | Y | N | Y | Y | Y | N |
| Martinez | Y | Y | N | N | N | Y |
| **GEORGIA** | | | | | | |
| Chambliss | Y | Y | N | N | N | Y |
| Isakson | Y | Y | N | N | N | Y |
| **HAWAII** | | | | | | |
| Inouye | Y | N | Y | Y | Y | N |
| Akaka | ? | N | Y | Y | Y | N |
| **IDAHO** | | | | | | |
| Craig | Y | Y | N | N | N | Y |
| Crapo | Y | Y | N | N | N | Y |
| **ILLINOIS** | | | | | | |
| Durbin | Y | N | Y | Y | Y | N |
| Obama | Y | N | Y | Y | Y | Y |
| **INDIANA** | | | | | | |
| Lugar | Y | Y | N | N | ? | Y |
| Bayh | Y | N | Y | N | N | Y |
| **IOWA** | | | | | | |
| Grassley | Y | Y | N | N | N | Y |
| Harkin | Y | N | Y | Y | Y | N |
| **KANSAS** | | | | | | |
| Brownback | Y | Y | N | N | N | Y |
| Roberts | Y | Y | N | N | N | Y |
| **KENTUCKY** | | | | | | |
| McConnell | Y | Y | N | N | N | Y |
| Bunning | Y | Y | N | N | N | Y |
| **LOUISIANA** | | | | | | |
| Landrieu | Y | N | Y | Y | N | Y |
| Vitter | + | Y | N | N | N | Y |
| **MAINE** | | | | | | |
| Snowe | Y | Y | N | N | N | Y |
| Collins | Y | Y | N | N | N | Y |
| **MARYLAND** | | | | | | |
| Sarbanes | Y | N | Y | Y | Y | N |
| Mikulski | Y | N | Y | Y | Y | N |
| **MASSACHUSETTS** | | | | | | |
| Kennedy | Y | N | Y | Y | Y | N |
| Kerry | Y | N | Y | Y | Y | N |
| **MICHIGAN** | | | | | | |
| Levin | Y | N | Y | Y | Y | N |
| Stabenow | Y | N | Y | Y | Y | N |
| **MINNESOTA** | | | | | | |
| Dayton | Y | N | Y | Y | Y | N |
| Coleman | Y | Y | N | N | N | Y |
| **MISSISSIPPI** | | | | | | |
| Cochran | Y | Y | N | N | N | Y |
| Lott | Y | Y | N | N | N | Y |
| **MISSOURI** | | | | | | |
| Bond | Y | Y | N | N | N | Y |
| Talent | Y | Y | N | N | N | Y |
| **MONTANA** | | | | | | |
| Baucus | Y | N | Y | Y | Y | N |
| Burns | + | Y | N | N | N | Y |
| **NEBRASKA** | | | | | | |
| Hagel | Y | Y | N | N | N | Y |
| Nelson | Y | Y | N | N | N | Y |
| **NEVADA** | | | | | | |
| Reid | Y | N | Y | Y | Y | N |
| Ensign | ? | Y | N | N | N | Y |
| **NEW HAMPSHIRE** | | | | | | |
| Gregg | Y | Y | N | N | N | Y |
| Sununu | Y | ? | ? | ? | ? | ? |
| **NEW JERSEY** | | | | | | |
| Corzine | Y | N | Y | Y | Y | N |
| Lautenberg | Y | N | Y | Y | Y | N |
| **NEW MEXICO** | | | | | | |
| Domenici | Y | Y | N | N | N | Y |
| Bingaman | Y | N | Y | Y | Y | Y |
| **NEW YORK** | | | | | | |
| Schumer | Y | Y | Y | Y | N | Y |
| Clinton | Y | N | Y | Y | Y | N |
| **NORTH CAROLINA** | | | | | | |
| Dole | Y | Y | N | N | N | Y |
| Burr | Y | Y | N | N | N | Y |
| **NORTH DAKOTA** | | | | | | |
| Conrad | Y | N | Y | Y | Y | Y |
| Dorgan | Y | N | Y | Y | Y | N |
| **OHIO** | | | | | | |
| DeWine | ? | Y | N | N | N | Y |
| Voinovich | Y | Y | N | N | N | Y |
| **OKLAHOMA** | | | | | | |
| Inhofe | Y | Y | N | N | N | Y |
| Coburn | Y | Y | N | N | N | Y |
| **OREGON** | | | | | | |
| Wyden | Y | N | Y | Y | Y | N |
| Smith | Y | Y | N | N | N | Y |
| **PENNSYLVANIA** | | | | | | |
| Specter | Y | Y | N | Y | N | Y |
| Santorum | Y | Y | N | N | N | ? |
| **RHODE ISLAND** | | | | | | |
| Reed | Y | N | Y | Y | Y | Y |
| Chafee | Y | Y | N | N | N | Y |
| **SOUTH CAROLINA** | | | | | | |
| Graham | Y | Y | N | N | N | Y |
| DeMint | Y | Y | N | N | N | Y |
| **SOUTH DAKOTA** | | | | | | |
| Johnson | Y | N | Y | Y | Y | Y |
| Thune | Y | Y | N | N | N | Y |
| **TENNESSEE** | | | | | | |
| Frist | Y | Y | N | N | N | Y |
| Alexander | Y | Y | N | N | N | Y |
| **TEXAS** | | | | | | |
| Hutchison | ? | Y | N | N | N | Y |
| Cornyn | Y | Y | N | N | N | Y |
| **UTAH** | | | | | | |
| Hatch | Y | Y | N | N | N | Y |
| Bennett | Y | Y | N | N | N | Y |
| **VERMONT** | | | | | | |
| Leahy | Y | N | Y | Y | Y | N |
| *Jeffords* | Y | N | Y | N | Y | Y |
| **VIRGINIA** | | | | | | |
| Warner | Y | Y | N | N | N | Y |
| Allen | Y | Y | N | N | N | Y |
| **WASHINGTON** | | | | | | |
| Murray | Y | N | Y | Y | Y | N |
| Cantwell | Y | N | Y | Y | Y | Y |
| **WEST VIRGINIA** | | | | | | |
| Byrd | Y | N | Y | Y | Y | N |
| Rockefeller | Y | N | Y | Y | Y | Y |
| **WISCONSIN** | | | | | | |
| Kohl | Y | Y | N | N | N | Y |
| Feingold | Y | N | Y | Y | Y | N |
| **WYOMING** | | | | | | |
| Thomas | Y | Y | N | N | N | Y |
| Enzi | Y | Y | N | N | N | Y |

**KEY** Republicans  Democrats  *Independents*

| | | | |
|---|---|---|---|
| Y Voted for (yea) | X Paired against | C Voted "present" to avoid possible conflict of interest |
| # Paired for | – Announced against | |
| + Announced for | P Voted "present" | ? Did not vote or otherwise make a position known |
| N Voted against (nay) | | |

ND Northern Democrats, SD Southern Democrats
Southern states: Ala., Ark., Fla., Ga., Ky., La., Miss., N.C., Okla., S.C., Tenn., Texas, Va.

## IN THE SENATE | By Vote Number

**10. Chertoff Nomination/Confirmation.** Confirmation of President Bush's nomination of Michael Chertoff to be secretary of Homeland Security. Confirmed 98-0: R 54-0; D 43-0 (ND 39-0, SD 4-0); I 1-0. A "yea" was a vote in support of the president's position. Feb. 15, 2005.

**11. S 306. Genetic Non-Discrimination/Passage.** Passage of a bill that would ban employers and health insurers from discriminating based on an individual's genetic profile. Employers would be barred from using genetic information in employment decisions, and insurers would be prohibited from using genetic information to deny coverage or set or adjust premiums. Passed 98-0: R 54-0; D 43-0 (ND 39-0, SD 4-0); I 1-0. Feb. 17, 2005.

| | 10 | 11 | | | 10 | 11 |
|---|---|---|---|---|---|---|
| **ALABAMA** | | | | **MONTANA** | | |
| Shelby | Y | Y | | Baucus | ? | Y |
| Sessions | Y | Y | | Burns | Y | Y |
| **ALASKA** | | | | **NEBRASKA** | | |
| Stevens | Y | Y | | Hagel | Y | Y |
| Murkowski | Y | Y | | Nelson | Y | Y |
| **ARIZONA** | | | | **NEVADA** | | |
| McCain | Y | Y | | Reid | Y | Y |
| Kyl | Y | Y | | Ensign | Y | Y |
| **ARKANSAS** | | | | **NEW HAMPSHIRE** | | |
| Lincoln | Y | Y | | Gregg | Y | Y |
| Pryor | Y | Y | | Sununu | Y | Y |
| **CALIFORNIA** | | | | **NEW JERSEY** | | |
| Feinstein | Y | Y | | Corzine | Y | Y |
| Boxer | Y | Y | | Lautenberg | Y | Y |
| **COLORADO** | | | | **NEW MEXICO** | | |
| Allard | Y | Y | | Domenici | Y | Y |
| Salazar | Y | Y | | Bingaman | Y | Y |
| **CONNECTICUT** | | | | **NEW YORK** | | |
| Dodd | Y | Y | | Schumer | Y | Y |
| Lieberman | Y | Y | | Clinton | Y | Y |
| **DELAWARE** | | | | **NORTH CAROLINA** | | |
| Biden | Y | + | | Dole | Y | Y |
| Carper | Y | Y | | Burr | Y | Y |
| **FLORIDA** | | | | **NORTH DAKOTA** | | |
| Nelson | Y | Y | | Conrad | Y | Y |
| Martinez | Y | Y | | Dorgan | Y | Y |
| **GEORGIA** | | | | **OHIO** | | |
| Chambliss | Y | Y | | DeWine | Y | Y |
| Isakson | Y | Y | | Voinovich | Y | Y |
| **HAWAII** | | | | **OKLAHOMA** | | |
| Inouye | Y | Y | | Inhofe | Y | Y |
| Akaka | Y | Y | | Coburn | Y | Y |
| **IDAHO** | | | | **OREGON** | | |
| Craig | Y | Y | | Wyden | Y | Y |
| Crapo | Y | Y | | Smith | Y | Y |
| **ILLINOIS** | | | | **PENNSYLVANIA** | | |
| Durbin | Y | Y | | Specter | ? | ? |
| Obama | Y | Y | | Santorum | Y | Y |
| **INDIANA** | | | | **RHODE ISLAND** | | |
| Lugar | Y | Y | | Reed | Y | Y |
| Bayh | Y | Y | | Chafee | Y | Y |
| **IOWA** | | | | **SOUTH CAROLINA** | | |
| Grassley | Y | Y | | Graham | Y | Y |
| Harkin | Y | Y | | DeMint | Y | Y |
| **KANSAS** | | | | **SOUTH DAKOTA** | | |
| Brownback | Y | Y | | Johnson | Y | Y |
| Roberts | Y | Y | | Thune | Y | Y |
| **KENTUCKY** | | | | **TENNESSEE** | | |
| McConnell | Y | Y | | Frist | Y | Y |
| Bunning | Y | Y | | Alexander | Y | Y |
| **LOUISIANA** | | | | **TEXAS** | | |
| Landrieu | Y | Y | | Hutchison | Y | Y |
| Vitter | Y | Y | | Cornyn | Y | Y |
| **MAINE** | | | | **UTAH** | | |
| Snowe | Y | Y | | Hatch | Y | Y |
| Collins | Y | Y | | Bennett | Y | Y |
| **MARYLAND** | | | | **VERMONT** | | |
| Sarbanes | Y | Y | | Leahy | Y | Y |
| Mikulski | Y | Y | | Jeffords | Y | Y |
| **MASSACHUSETTS** | | | | **VIRGINIA** | | |
| Kennedy | Y | Y | | Warner | Y | Y |
| Kerry | Y | Y | | Allen | Y | Y |
| **MICHIGAN** | | | | **WASHINGTON** | | |
| Levin | Y | Y | | Murray | Y | Y |
| Stabenow | Y | Y | | Cantwell | Y | Y |
| **MINNESOTA** | | | | **WEST VIRGINIA** | | |
| Dayton | Y | Y | | Byrd | Y | Y |
| Coleman | Y | Y | | Rockefeller | Y | Y |
| **MISSISSIPPI** | | | | **WISCONSIN** | | |
| Cochran | Y | Y | | Kohl | Y | Y |
| Lott | Y | Y | | Feingold | Y | Y |
| **MISSOURI** | | | | **WYOMING** | | |
| Bond | Y | Y | | Thomas | Y | Y |
| Talent | Y | Y | | Enzi | Y | Y |

**KEY**  Republicans  Democrats  *Independents*

| | | | | | |
|---|---|---|---|---|---|
| Y | Voted for (yea) | X | Paired against | C | Voted "present" to avoid possible conflict of interest |
| # | Paired for | – | Announced against | | |
| + | Announced for | P | Voted "present" | ? | Did not vote or otherwise make a position known |
| N | Voted against (nay) | | | | |

ND Northern Democrats, SD Southern Democrats
Southern states: Ala., Ark., Fla., Ga., Ky., La., Miss., N.C., Okla., S.C., Tenn., Texas, Va.

# IN THE SENATE | By Vote Number

**12.** **S 256. Bankruptcy Overhaul/Safe Harbor.** Sessions, R-Ala., amendment that would clarify that the bill's "safe harbor" provision would apply to low-income veterans, debtors who have medical conditions, or those called or ordered to active duty. It would require such individuals to satisfy all the procedural requirements of a means test used by bankruptcy judges to determine whether debtors have the ability to repay some or all of their debts. Adopted 63-32: R 52-0; D 11-31 (ND 9-29, SD 2-2); I 0-1. March 1, 2005.

**13.** **S 256. Bankruptcy Overhaul/Means Test Exemptions.** Durbin, D-Ill., amendment that would exempt members of the armed forces, veterans and spouses of service members who die in military service from application of the bill's means test provisions. It also would allow such individuals to claim a minimum homestead exemption of $75,000 or choose the exemption in the state in which they file, whichever is higher. Rejected 38-58: R 1-52; D 36-6 (ND 32-6, SD 4-0); I 1-0. March 1, 2005.

**14.** **S 256. Bankruptcy Overhaul/Elderly Homestead Exemption.** Feingold, D-Wis., amendment that would create a federal homestead exemption of $75,000 for debtors over the age of 62. Rejected 40-59: R 0-55; D 40-3 (ND 36-3, SD 4-0); I 0-1. March 2, 2005.

**15.** **S 256. Bankruptcy Overhaul/Credit Cards.** Akaka, D-Hawaii, amendment that would require credit card companies to issue a warning notification on monthly statements stating that a minimum payment will increase the amount of interest paid and the time it will take to repay the outstanding balance. It would require companies to disclose the amount required for the consumer to pay off the outstanding balance in three years, if no further advances are made. It also would require credit card companies to provide a toll-free number for consumers to receive information about credit counseling and debt management assistance. Rejected 40-59: R 1-54; D 38-5 (ND 34-5, SD 4-0); I 1-0. March 2, 2005.

**16.** **S 256. Bankruptcy Overhaul/Medical Expenses.** Kennedy, D-Mass., amendment that would exempt debtors from the means test if their financial troubles were caused by medical expenses. Rejected 39-58: R 0-54; D 38-4 (ND 34-4, SD 4-0); I 1-0. March 2, 2005.

**17.** **S 256. Bankruptcy Overhaul/Medical Homestead Exemption.** Kennedy, D-Mass., amendment that would provide a homestead exemption of at least $150,000 of the equity in the property the debtor uses as a primary residence if the bankruptcy stems from medical expenses. Rejected 39-58: R 0-54; D 38-4 (ND 34-4, SD 4-0); I 1-0. March 2, 2005.

**18.** **S 256. Bankruptcy Overhaul/Caregivers Exemption.** Corzine, D-N.J., amendment that would exempt from the means test individuals who have incurred substantial medical debt on behalf of dependent or non-dependent family members, such as a parent or grandparent, or who have experienced a reduction in employment status while caring for such a family member. Rejected 37-60: R 0-54; D 37-5 (ND 33-5, SD 4-0); I 0-1. March 2, 2005.

ND Northern Democrats, SD Southern Democrats
Southern states: Ala., Ark., Fla., Ga., Ky., La., Miss., N.C., Okla., S.C., Tenn., Texas, Va.

| | 12 | 13 | 14 | 15 | 16 | 17 | 18 |
|---|---|---|---|---|---|---|---|
| **ALABAMA** | | | | | | | |
| Shelby | Y | N | N | N | N | N | N |
| Sessions | Y | N | N | N | N | N | N |
| **ALASKA** | | | | | | | |
| Stevens | Y | N | N | N | N | N | N |
| Murkowski | Y | N | N | N | N | N | N |
| **ARIZONA** | | | | | | | |
| McCain | Y | N | N | N | N | N | N |
| Kyl | Y | N | N | N | N | N | N |
| **ARKANSAS** | | | | | | | |
| Lincoln | Y | Y | Y | Y | Y | Y | Y |
| Pryor | N | Y | Y | Y | Y | Y | Y |
| **CALIFORNIA** | | | | | | | |
| Feinstein | Y | Y | Y | Y | Y | Y | Y |
| Boxer | N | Y | Y | Y | Y | Y | Y |
| **COLORADO** | | | | | | | |
| Allard | Y | N | N | N | N | N | N |
| Salazar | N | Y | Y | Y | Y | Y | Y |
| **CONNECTICUT** | | | | | | | |
| Dodd | N | Y | Y | Y | ? | Y | Y |
| Lieberman | N | Y | Y | Y | Y | Y | Y |
| **DELAWARE** | | | | | | | |
| Biden | Y | N | N | N | N | ? | ? |
| Carper | Y | N | N | N | N | N | N |
| **FLORIDA** | | | | | | | |
| Nelson | Y | Y | Y | Y | Y | Y | Y |
| Martinez | Y | N | N | N | N | N | N |
| **GEORGIA** | | | | | | | |
| Chambliss | Y | N | N | N | N | N | N |
| Isakson | Y | N | N | N | N | N | N |
| **HAWAII** | | | | | | | |
| Inouye | ? | ? | ? | ? | ? | ? | ? |
| Akaka | N | Y | Y | Y | Y | Y | Y |
| **IDAHO** | | | | | | | |
| Craig | Y | N | N | N | N | N | N |
| Crapo | Y | N | N | N | N | N | N |
| **ILLINOIS** | | | | | | | |
| Durbin | N | Y | Y | Y | Y | Y | Y |
| Obama | N | Y | Y | Y | Y | Y | Y |
| **INDIANA** | | | | | | | |
| Lugar | Y | N | N | N | N | N | N |
| Bayh | N | Y | Y | Y | Y | Y | Y |
| **IOWA** | | | | | | | |
| Grassley | Y | N | N | N | N | N | N |
| Harkin | N | Y | Y | Y | Y | Y | Y |
| **KANSAS** | | | | | | | |
| Brownback | Y | N | N | N | N | N | N |
| Roberts | Y | N | N | N | N | N | N |
| **KENTUCKY** | | | | | | | |
| McConnell | Y | N | N | N | N | N | N |
| Bunning | Y | N | N | N | N | N | N |
| **LOUISIANA** | | | | | | | |
| Landrieu | N | Y | Y | Y | Y | Y | Y |
| Vitter | Y | N | N | N | N | N | N |
| **MAINE** | | | | | | | |
| Snowe | Y | N | N | N | N | N | N |
| Collins | Y | N | N | N | N | N | N |
| **MARYLAND** | | | | | | | |
| Sarbanes | N | Y | Y | Y | Y | Y | Y |
| Mikulski | N | Y | Y | Y | Y | Y | Y |
| **MASSACHUSETTS** | | | | | | | |
| Kennedy | N | Y | Y | Y | Y | Y | Y |
| Kerry | N | Y | Y | Y | Y | Y | Y |
| **MICHIGAN** | | | | | | | |
| Levin | N | Y | Y | Y | Y | Y | Y |
| Stabenow | N | Y | Y | Y | Y | Y | Y |
| **MINNESOTA** | | | | | | | |
| Dayton | ? | ? | Y | Y | Y | Y | Y |
| Coleman | ? | ? | N | N | N | N | N |
| **MISSISSIPPI** | | | | | | | |
| Cochran | Y | N | N | N | N | N | N |
| Lott | Y | N | N | N | N | N | N |
| **MISSOURI** | | | | | | | |
| Bond | Y | N | N | N | N | N | N |
| Talent | Y | N | N | N | N | N | N |
| **MONTANA** | | | | | | | |
| Baucus | Y | N | Y | N | Y | Y | N |
| Burns | Y | N | N | N | N | N | N |
| **NEBRASKA** | | | | | | | |
| Hagel | Y | N | N | N | N | N | N |
| Nelson | Y | N | N | N | N | N | N |
| **NEVADA** | | | | | | | |
| Reid | N | Y | Y | Y | Y | Y | Y |
| Ensign | Y | N | N | N | N | N | N |
| **NEW HAMPSHIRE** | | | | | | | |
| Gregg | Y | N | N | N | N | N | N |
| Sununu | Y | N | N | N | N | N | N |
| **NEW JERSEY** | | | | | | | |
| Corzine | N | Y | Y | Y | Y | Y | Y |
| Lautenberg | N | Y | Y | Y | Y | Y | Y |
| **NEW MEXICO** | | | | | | | |
| Domenici | Y | N | N | N | N | N | N |
| Bingaman | N | Y | Y | Y | Y | N | N |
| **NEW YORK** | | | | | | | |
| Schumer | N | Y | Y | Y | Y | Y | Y |
| Clinton | N | Y | Y | Y | Y | Y | Y |
| **NORTH CAROLINA** | | | | | | | |
| Dole | Y | N | N | N | N | N | N |
| Burr | Y | N | N | N | N | N | N |
| **NORTH DAKOTA** | | | | | | | |
| Conrad | Y | Y | Y | Y | Y | Y | Y |
| Dorgan | N | Y | Y | Y | Y | Y | Y |
| **OHIO** | | | | | | | |
| DeWine | Y | N | N | Y | N | N | N |
| Voinovich | Y | N | N | N | N | N | N |
| **OKLAHOMA** | | | | | | | |
| Inhofe | Y | N | N | N | N | N | N |
| Coburn | Y | N | N | N | N | N | N |
| **OREGON** | | | | | | | |
| Wyden | N | Y | Y | Y | Y | Y | Y |
| Smith | Y | N | N | N | N | N | N |
| **PENNSYLVANIA** | | | | | | | |
| Specter | Y | Y | N | N | N | N | N |
| Santorum | Y | N | N | N | ? | ? | ? |
| **RHODE ISLAND** | | | | | | | |
| Reed | N | Y | Y | Y | Y | Y | Y |
| Chafee | Y | N | N | N | N | N | N |
| **SOUTH CAROLINA** | | | | | | | |
| Graham | Y | N | N | N | N | N | N |
| DeMint | Y | N | N | N | N | N | N |
| **SOUTH DAKOTA** | | | | | | | |
| Johnson | Y | N | Y | N | N | N | N |
| Thune | Y | N | N | N | N | N | N |
| **TENNESSEE** | | | | | | | |
| Frist | Y | N | N | N | N | N | N |
| Alexander | Y | N | N | N | N | N | N |
| **TEXAS** | | | | | | | |
| Hutchison | Y | N | N | N | N | N | N |
| Cornyn | ? | ? | N | N | N | N | N |
| **UTAH** | | | | | | | |
| Hatch | Y | N | N | N | N | N | N |
| Bennett | Y | N | N | N | N | N | N |
| **VERMONT** | | | | | | | |
| Leahy | N | Y | Y | Y | Y | Y | Y |
| *Jeffords* | N | Y | N | Y | Y | Y | N |
| **VIRGINIA** | | | | | | | |
| Warner | ? | N | N | N | N | N | N |
| Allen | Y | N | N | N | N | N | N |
| **WASHINGTON** | | | | | | | |
| Murray | N | Y | Y | Y | Y | Y | Y |
| Cantwell | N | Y | Y | Y | Y | Y | Y |
| **WEST VIRGINIA** | | | | | | | |
| Byrd | Y | N | Y | Y | Y | Y | Y |
| Rockefeller | N | Y | Y | Y | Y | Y | Y |
| **WISCONSIN** | | | | | | | |
| Kohl | Y | Y | Y | Y | Y | Y | Y |
| Feingold | N | Y | Y | Y | Y | Y | Y |
| **WYOMING** | | | | | | | |
| Thomas | Y | N | N | N | N | N | N |
| Enzi | Y | N | N | N | N | N | N |

**KEY**   Republicans   Democrats   *Independents*

| | | | | | |
|---|---|---|---|---|---|
| Y | Voted for (yea) | X | Paired against | C | Voted "present" to avoid possible conflict of interest |
| # | Paired for | – | Announced against | | |
| + | Announced for | P | Voted "present" | ? | Did not vote or otherwise make a position known |
| N | Voted against (nay) | | | | |

## IN THE SENATE | By Vote Number

**19.** **S J Res 4. Agriculture Department Rule Disapproval/Passage.**
Passage of the joint resolution that would block a proposed Agriculture Department regulation that would ease restrictions on Canadian beef. Passed 52-46: R 13-42; D 38-4 (ND 37-1, SD 1-3); I 1-0. A "nay" was a vote in support of the president's position. March 3, 2005.

**20.** **S 256. Bankruptcy Overhaul/Interest Rates.** Dayton, D-Minn., amendment that would set a 30 percent ceiling on interest rates for loans or credit cards. Rejected 24-74: R 0-55; D 23-19 (ND 22-16, SD 1-3); I 1-0. March 3, 2005.

**21.** **S 256. Bankruptcy Overhaul/Identity Theft Exemption.** Nelson, D-Fla., amendment that would exempt identity theft victims from the bill's means test provisions and amend the bankruptcy code to include definitions of identity theft and identity theft victims. Rejected 37-61: R 0-55; D 36-6 (ND 32-6, SD 4-0); I 1-0. March 3, 2005.

**22.** **S 256. Bankruptcy Overhaul/Predatory Lending.** Durbin, D-Ill., amendment that would prohibit high cost mortgage lenders from collecting on their claims in bankruptcy court if they extend credit in violation of the Truth in Lending Act. Rejected 40-58: R 1-54; D 38-4 (ND 34-4, SD 4-0); I 1-0. March 3, 2005.

**23.** **S 256. Bankruptcy Overhaul/Asset Protection Trusts.** Schumer, D-N.Y., amendment that would prohibit debtors from transferring more than $125,000 in assets into an asset protection trust within the 10-year period prior to filing bankruptcy. Rejected 39-56: R 1-53; D 37-3 (ND 33-3, SD 4-0); I 1-0. March 3, 2005.

**24.** **S 256. Bankruptcy Overhaul/Wage and Benefit Payments.** Rockefeller, D-W.Va., amendment that would allow employees to recover up to $15,000 in back pay or other compensation owed to them and entitle retirees to payment equal to the cost of buying health insurance for a period of 18 months if an employer reduces retiree health care benefits as part of a bankruptcy plan. Rejected 40-54: R 2-51; D 37-3 (ND 33-3, SD 4-0); I 1-0. March 3, 2005.

**25.** **S 256. Bankruptcy Overhaul/Corporate Fraud.** Durbin, D-Ill., amendment that would increase from one to four years the period of time during which a bankruptcy court can recapture assets of corporate executives who make fraudulent transfers. It also would give employees and retirees a priority unsecured claim in bankruptcy for the value of company stock held for their benefit in an employee pension plan, unless the beneficiary had the option to invest the assets in another way. Rejected 40-54: R 0-53; D 39-1 (ND 35-1, SD 4-0); I 1-0. March 3, 2005.

| | 19 | 20 | 21 | 22 | 23 | 24 | 25 |
|---|---|---|---|---|---|---|---|
| **ALABAMA** | | | | | | | |
| Shelby | Y | N | N | N | N | N | N |
| Sessions | Y | N | N | N | N | N | N |
| **ALASKA** | | | | | | | |
| Stevens | N | N | N | N | N | N | N |
| Murkowski | N | N | N | N | N | N | N |
| **ARIZONA** | | | | | | | |
| McCain | N | N | N | N | N | N | N |
| Kyl | N | N | N | N | N | N | N |
| **ARKANSAS** | | | | | | | |
| Lincoln | N | N | Y | Y | Y | Y | Y |
| Pryor | N | Y | Y | Y | Y | Y | Y |
| **CALIFORNIA** | | | | | | | |
| Feinstein | Y | Y | Y | Y | Y | Y | Y |
| Boxer | Y | Y | Y | Y | ? | ? | ? |
| **COLORADO** | | | | | | | |
| Allard | N | N | N | N | N | N | N |
| Salazar | Y | Y | Y | Y | Y | Y | Y |
| **CONNECTICUT** | | | | | | | |
| Dodd | Y | Y | Y | Y | Y | Y | Y |
| Lieberman | Y | Y | Y | Y | Y | Y | Y |
| **DELAWARE** | | | | | | | |
| Biden | Y | N | N | N | Y | N | Y |
| Carper | Y | N | N | N | N | N | Y |
| **FLORIDA** | | | | | | | |
| Nelson | N | N | Y | Y | Y | Y | Y |
| Martinez | N | N | N | N | N | N | N |
| **GEORGIA** | | | | | | | |
| Chambliss | N | N | N | N | N | N | N |
| Isakson | N | N | N | N | N | N | N |
| **HAWAII** | | | | | | | |
| Inouye | ? | ? | ? | ? | ? | ? | ? |
| Akaka | Y | Y | Y | Y | Y | Y | Y |
| **IDAHO** | | | | | | | |
| Craig | Y | N | N | N | N | N | N |
| Crapo | Y | N | N | N | N | N | N |
| **ILLINOIS** | | | | | | | |
| Durbin | Y | N | Y | Y | Y | Y | Y |
| Obama | Y | N | Y | Y | Y | Y | Y |
| **INDIANA** | | | | | | | |
| Lugar | N | N | N | N | N | N | N |
| Bayh | Y | Y | Y | Y | Y | Y | Y |
| **IOWA** | | | | | | | |
| Grassley | N | N | N | N | N | N | N |
| Harkin | Y | Y | Y | Y | Y | Y | Y |
| **KANSAS** | | | | | | | |
| Brownback | N | N | N | N | N | N | N |
| Roberts | N | N | N | N | N | N | N |
| **KENTUCKY** | | | | | | | |
| McConnell | N | N | N | N | N | N | N |
| Bunning | N | N | N | N | N | N | N |
| **LOUISIANA** | | | | | | | |
| Landrieu | Y | N | Y | Y | Y | Y | Y |
| Vitter | N | N | N | N | N | N | N |
| **MAINE** | | | | | | | |
| Snowe | N | N | N | N | N | Y | N |
| Collins | N | N | N | Y | N | N | N |
| **MARYLAND** | | | | | | | |
| Sarbanes | Y | N | Y | Y | Y | Y | Y |
| Mikulski | Y | Y | Y | Y | Y | Y | Y |
| **MASSACHUSETTS** | | | | | | | |
| Kennedy | Y | Y | Y | Y | Y | Y | Y |
| Kerry | Y | N | Y | Y | Y | Y | Y |
| **MICHIGAN** | | | | | | | |
| Levin | Y | Y | Y | Y | Y | Y | Y |
| Stabenow | Y | Y | Y | Y | Y | Y | Y |
| **MINNESOTA** | | | | | | | |
| Dayton | Y | Y | Y | Y | Y | Y | Y |
| Coleman | N | N | N | N | N | N | N |
| **MISSISSIPPI** | | | | | | | |
| Cochran | N | N | N | N | N | N | N |
| Lott | N | N | N | N | N | N | N |
| **MISSOURI** | | | | | | | |
| Bond | N | N | N | N | N | N | N |
| Talent | N | N | N | N | N | N | N |
| **MONTANA** | | | | | | | |
| Baucus | Y | N | Y | Y | Y | Y | Y |
| Burns | Y | N | N | N | N | N | N |
| **NEBRASKA** | | | | | | | |
| Hagel | N | N | N | N | N | N | N |
| Nelson | Y | N | N | N | N | N | N |
| **NEVADA** | | | | | | | |
| Reid | Y | N | Y | Y | Y | Y | Y |
| Ensign | Y | N | N | N | N | N | N |
| **NEW HAMPSHIRE** | | | | | | | |
| Gregg | N | N | N | N | N | N | N |
| Sununu | N | N | N | N | N | N | N |
| **NEW JERSEY** | | | | | | | |
| Corzine | Y | Y | Y | Y | ? | ? | ? |
| Lautenberg | Y | Y | Y | Y | Y | Y | Y |
| **NEW MEXICO** | | | | | | | |
| Domenici | Y | N | N | N | N | N | N |
| Bingaman | Y | N | N | Y | Y | Y | Y |
| **NEW YORK** | | | | | | | |
| Schumer | Y | Y | Y | Y | Y | Y | Y |
| Clinton | Y | Y | Y | Y | Y | Y | Y |
| **NORTH CAROLINA** | | | | | | | |
| Dole | N | N | N | N | N | N | N |
| Burr | N | N | N | N | N | N | N |
| **NORTH DAKOTA** | | | | | | | |
| Conrad | Y | Y | Y | Y | Y | Y | Y |
| Dorgan | Y | Y | Y | Y | Y | Y | Y |
| **OHIO** | | | | | | | |
| DeWine | N | N | N | N | N | N | N |
| Voinovich | N | N | N | N | N | N | N |
| **OKLAHOMA** | | | | | | | |
| Inhofe | Y | N | N | N | – | ? | ? |
| Coburn | Y | N | N | N | N | N | N |
| **OREGON** | | | | | | | |
| Wyden | Y | N | Y | Y | Y | Y | Y |
| Smith | Y | N | N | N | N | N | N |
| **PENNSYLVANIA** | | | | | | | |
| Specter | N | N | N | N | N | ? | ? |
| Santorum | N | N | N | N | N | N | N |
| **RHODE ISLAND** | | | | | | | |
| Reed | Y | N | Y | Y | Y | Y | Y |
| Chafee | N | N | N | N | Y | N | N |
| **SOUTH CAROLINA** | | | | | | | |
| Graham | N | N | N | N | N | N | N |
| DeMint | N | N | N | N | N | N | N |
| **SOUTH DAKOTA** | | | | | | | |
| Johnson | N | N | N | N | N | Y | Y |
| Thune | Y | N | N | N | N | N | N |
| **TENNESSEE** | | | | | | | |
| Frist | N | N | N | N | N | N | N |
| Alexander | N | N | N | N | N | N | N |
| **TEXAS** | | | | | | | |
| Hutchison | N | N | N | N | N | N | N |
| Cornyn | N | N | N | N | N | N | N |
| **UTAH** | | | | | | | |
| Hatch | N | N | N | N | N | N | N |
| Bennett | N | N | N | N | N | N | N |
| **VERMONT** | | | | | | | |
| Leahy | Y | N | Y | Y | Y | Y | Y |
| Jeffords | Y | Y | Y | Y | Y | Y | Y |
| **VIRGINIA** | | | | | | | |
| Warner | N | N | N | N | N | N | N |
| Allen | N | N | N | N | N | N | N |
| **WASHINGTON** | | | | | | | |
| Murray | Y | Y | Y | Y | Y | Y | Y |
| Cantwell | Y | N | Y | Y | Y | Y | Y |
| **WEST VIRGINIA** | | | | | | | |
| Byrd | Y | Y | Y | Y | Y | Y | Y |
| Rockefeller | N | Y | Y | Y | Y | Y | Y |
| **WISCONSIN** | | | | | | | |
| Kohl | Y | N | Y | Y | Y | Y | Y |
| Feingold | ? | ? | ? | ? | ? | ? | ? |
| **WYOMING** | | | | | | | |
| Thomas | Y | N | N | N | N | N | N |
| Enzi | Y | N | N | N | N | N | N |

**KEY**   Republicans   Democrats   *Independents*

| | | |
|---|---|---|
| **Y** Voted for (yea) | **X** Paired against | **C** Voted "present" to avoid possible conflict of interest |
| **#** Paired for | **–** Announced against | |
| **+** Announced for | **P** Voted "present" | **?** Did not vote or otherwise make a position known |
| **N** Voted against (nay) | | |

ND Northern Democrats, SD Southern Democrats
Southern states: Ala., Ark., Fla., Ga., Ky., La., Miss., N.C., Okla., S.C., Tenn., Texas, Va.

# IN THE SENATE | By Vote Number

**26.** **S 256. Bankruptcy Overhaul/Minimum Wage.** Kennedy, D-Mass., amendment that would raise the minimum wage from $5.15 an hour to $7.25 an hour over 26 months. Rejected 46-49: R 4-49; D 41-0 (ND 37-0, SD 4-0); I 1-0. March 7, 2005.

**27.** **S 256. Bankruptcy Overhaul/Minimum Wage.** Santorum, R-Pa., amendment that would raise the minimum wage from $5.15 to $6.25 over 18 months in two increments of 55 cents. It also would provide several tax cuts for small businesses. Rejected 38-61: R 38-17; D 0-43 (ND 0-39, SD 0-4); I 0-1. March 7, 2005.

**28.** **S 256. Bankruptcy Overhaul/Violent Protesters.** Schumer, D-N.Y., amendment that would prohibit violent protesters, such as anti-abortion activists, from escaping court-ordered fines or judgments by filing for bankruptcy protection. It would bar such debtors from discharging debts, such as damages, court fines, penalties, citations or attorney fees, incurred from acts of violence or potential acts of violence. Rejected 46-53: R 4-51; D 41-2 (ND 37-2, SD 4-0); I 1-0. March 8, 2005.

**29.** **S 256. Bankruptcy Overhaul/Cloture.** Motion to invoke cloture (thus limiting debate) on the bill that would revise bankruptcy laws to make it easier for courts to move debtors from Chapter 7 of the bankruptcy code, which allows most debts to be discharged, to Chapter 13, which requires a reorganization of debts under a repayment. Motion agreed to 69-31: R 55-0; D 14-30 (ND 10-30, SD 4-0); I 0-1. Three-fifths of the total Senate (60) is required to invoke cloture. March 8, 2005.

**30.** **S 256. Bankruptcy Overhaul/Small Business Provisions.** Feingold, D-Wis., amendment that would strike certain small business-related bankruptcy provisions in the bill, including the 300-day deadline for small businesses seeking to reorganize under Chapter 11. Rejected 41-59: R 0-55; D 40-4 (ND 36-4, SD 4-0); I 1-0. March 8, 2005.

**31.** **S 256. Bankruptcy Overhaul/Median Income.** Durbin, D-Ill., amendment that would clarify that the means test would not apply to debtors whose incomes fell below the median. Rejected 42-58: R 0-55; D 41-3 (ND 37-3, SD 4-0); I 1-0. March 9, 2005.

**32.** **S 256. Bankruptcy Overhaul/Employee Wage Priority.** Harkin, D-Iowa, amendment that would strike the 180-day limit on the accrual period for the employee wage priority to protect the back pay and severance for workers whose employers are in bankruptcy. Rejected 48-52: R 3-52; D 44-0 (ND 40-0, SD 4-0); I 1-0. March 9, 2005.

| | 26 | 27 | 28 | 29 | 30 | 31 | 32 |
|---|---|---|---|---|---|---|---|
| **ALABAMA** | | | | | | | |
| Shelby | N | Y | N | Y | N | N | N |
| Sessions | N | Y | N | Y | N | N | N |
| **ALASKA** | | | | | | | |
| Stevens | N | Y | N | Y | N | N | N |
| Murkowski | N | Y | N | Y | N | N | N |
| **ARIZONA** | | | | | | | |
| McCain | N | Y | N | Y | N | N | N |
| Kyl | N | Y | N | Y | N | N | N |
| **ARKANSAS** | | | | | | | |
| Lincoln | Y | N | Y | Y | Y | Y | Y |
| Pryor | Y | N | Y | Y | Y | Y | Y |
| **CALIFORNIA** | | | | | | | |
| Feinstein | Y | N | Y | N | Y | Y | Y |
| Boxer | Y | N | Y | N | Y | Y | Y |
| **COLORADO** | | | | | | | |
| Allard | N | N | N | Y | N | N | N |
| Salazar | Y | N | Y | Y | Y | Y | Y |
| **CONNECTICUT** | | | | | | | |
| Dodd | Y | N | Y | N | Y | Y | Y |
| Lieberman | Y | N | Y | Y | Y | Y | Y |
| **DELAWARE** | | | | | | | |
| Biden | Y | N | Y | Y | N | Y | Y |
| Carper | Y | N | Y | Y | N | N | Y |
| **FLORIDA** | | | | | | | |
| Nelson | Y | N | Y | Y | Y | Y | Y |
| Martinez | N | Y | N | Y | N | N | N |
| **GEORGIA** | | | | | | | |
| Chambliss | N | N | N | Y | N | N | N |
| Isakson | N | N | N | Y | N | N | N |
| **HAWAII** | | | | | | | |
| Inouye | Y | N | Y | N | Y | Y | Y |
| Akaka | Y | N | Y | N | Y | Y | Y |
| **IDAHO** | | | | | | | |
| Craig | N | Y | N | Y | N | N | N |
| Crapo | N | Y | N | Y | N | N | N |
| **ILLINOIS** | | | | | | | |
| Durbin | Y | N | Y | N | Y | Y | Y |
| Obama | Y | N | Y | N | Y | Y | Y |
| **INDIANA** | | | | | | | |
| Lugar | N | Y | N | Y | N | N | N |
| Bayh | Y | N | Y | N | Y | Y | Y |
| **IOWA** | | | | | | | |
| Grassley | N | Y | N | Y | N | N | N |
| Harkin | Y | N | Y | N | Y | Y | Y |
| **KANSAS** | | | | | | | |
| Brownback | N | Y | N | Y | N | N | N |
| Roberts | N | Y | N | Y | N | N | N |
| **KENTUCKY** | | | | | | | |
| McConnell | N | Y | N | Y | N | N | N |
| Bunning | N | Y | N | Y | N | N | N |
| **LOUISIANA** | | | | | | | |
| Landrieu | Y | N | Y | Y | Y | Y | Y |
| Vitter | N | N | N | Y | N | N | N |
| **MAINE** | | | | | | | |
| Snowe | N | Y | Y | Y | N | N | Y |
| Collins | N | N | Y | Y | N | N | Y |
| **MARYLAND** | | | | | | | |
| Sarbanes | Y | N | Y | N | Y | Y | Y |
| Mikulski | ? | ? | Y | N | Y | Y | Y |
| **MASSACHUSETTS** | | | | | | | |
| Kennedy | Y | N | Y | N | Y | Y | Y |
| Kerry | Y | N | Y | N | Y | Y | Y |
| **MICHIGAN** | | | | | | | |
| Levin | Y | N | Y | N | Y | Y | Y |
| Stabenow | Y | N | Y | Y | Y | Y | Y |
| **MINNESOTA** | | | | | | | |
| Dayton | Y | N | Y | N | Y | Y | Y |
| Coleman | Y | Y | N | Y | N | N | N |
| **MISSISSIPPI** | | | | | | | |
| Cochran | N | N | N | Y | N | N | N |
| Lott | N | N | N | Y | N | N | N |
| **MISSOURI** | | | | | | | |
| Bond | N | N | N | Y | N | N | N |
| Talent | N | Y | N | Y | N | N | N |
| **MONTANA** | | | | | | | |
| Baucus | ? | N | Y | N | Y | Y | Y |
| Burns | N | Y | N | Y | N | N | N |
| **NEBRASKA** | | | | | | | |
| Hagel | N | Y | N | Y | N | N | N |
| Nelson | Y | N | N | Y | N | N | Y |
| **NEVADA** | | | | | | | |
| Reid | Y | N | Y | N | Y | Y | Y |
| Ensign | ? | Y | N | Y | N | N | N |
| **NEW HAMPSHIRE** | | | | | | | |
| Gregg | N | N | N | Y | N | N | N |
| Sununu | N | N | N | Y | N | N | N |
| **NEW JERSEY** | | | | | | | |
| Corzine | Y | N | ? | N | Y | Y | Y |
| Lautenberg | Y | N | Y | N | Y | Y | Y |
| **NEW MEXICO** | | | | | | | |
| Domenici | Y | Y | N | Y | N | N | N |
| Bingaman | Y | N | Y | N | Y | Y | Y |
| **NEW YORK** | | | | | | | |
| Schumer | Y | N | Y | N | Y | Y | Y |
| Clinton | Y | N | Y | N | Y | Y | Y |
| **NORTH CAROLINA** | | | | | | | |
| Dole | N | Y | N | Y | N | N | N |
| Burr | N | N | N | Y | N | N | N |
| **NORTH DAKOTA** | | | | | | | |
| Conrad | ? | N | Y | Y | Y | Y | Y |
| Dorgan | Y | N | Y | N | Y | Y | Y |
| **OHIO** | | | | | | | |
| DeWine | Y | Y | N | Y | N | N | N |
| Voinovich | N | Y | N | Y | N | N | N |
| **OKLAHOMA** | | | | | | | |
| Inhofe | N | N | N | Y | N | N | N |
| Coburn | N | N | N | Y | N | N | N |
| **OREGON** | | | | | | | |
| Wyden | Y | N | Y | N | Y | Y | Y |
| Smith | N | Y | N | Y | N | N | N |
| **PENNSYLVANIA** | | | | | | | |
| Specter | ? | Y | Y | Y | N | N | Y |
| Santorum | N | Y | N | Y | N | N | N |
| **RHODE ISLAND** | | | | | | | |
| Reed | Y | N | Y | N | Y | Y | Y |
| Chafee | Y | N | Y | Y | N | N | N |
| **SOUTH CAROLINA** | | | | | | | |
| Graham | N | Y | N | Y | N | N | N |
| DeMint | N | N | N | Y | N | N | N |
| **SOUTH DAKOTA** | | | | | | | |
| Johnson | Y | N | Y | N | Y | Y | Y |
| Thune | N | Y | N | Y | N | N | N |
| **TENNESSEE** | | | | | | | |
| Frist | N | Y | N | Y | N | N | N |
| Alexander | N | N | N | Y | N | N | N |
| **TEXAS** | | | | | | | |
| Hutchison | N | Y | N | Y | N | N | N |
| Cornyn | N | N | N | Y | N | N | N |
| **UTAH** | | | | | | | |
| Hatch | N | Y | N | Y | N | N | N |
| Bennett | N | Y | N | Y | N | N | N |
| **VERMONT** | | | | | | | |
| Leahy | Y | N | Y | N | Y | Y | Y |
| *Jeffords* | Y | N | Y | N | Y | Y | Y |
| **VIRGINIA** | | | | | | | |
| Warner | N | Y | N | Y | N | N | N |
| Allen | N | Y | N | Y | N | N | N |
| **WASHINGTON** | | | | | | | |
| Murray | Y | N | Y | N | Y | Y | Y |
| Cantwell | Y | N | Y | N | Y | Y | Y |
| **WEST VIRGINIA** | | | | | | | |
| Byrd | Y | N | N | Y | Y | Y | Y |
| Rockefeller | Y | N | Y | N | Y | Y | Y |
| **WISCONSIN** | | | | | | | |
| Kohl | Y | N | Y | Y | Y | Y | Y |
| Feingold | Y | N | Y | N | Y | Y | Y |
| **WYOMING** | | | | | | | |
| Thomas | N | Y | N | Y | N | N | N |
| Enzi | N | Y | N | Y | N | N | N |

**KEY** — Republicans — Democrats — *Independents*

| | | | |
|---|---|---|---|
| Y | Voted for (yea) | X | Paired against |
| # | Paired for | – | Announced against |
| + | Announced for | P | Voted "present" |
| N | Voted against (nay) | C | Voted "present" to avoid possible conflict of interest |
| | | ? | Did not vote or otherwise make a position known |

ND Northern Democrats, SD Southern Democrats
Southern states: Ala., Ark., Fla., Ga., Ky., La., Miss., N.C., Okla., S.C., Tenn., Texas, Va.

# IN THE SENATE | By Vote Number

**33.** **S 256. Bankruptcy Overhaul/Disallowance of Claims.** Boxer, D-Calif., amendment that would not allow creditors to file a bankruptcy claim if the claim was based on the extension of credit to an individual age 21 or younger who, at the time the credit was extended, did not have a parental or spousal co-signer, had an income level below the poverty line, and already had six or more unsecured credit cards. Rejected 40-60: R 1-54; D 38-6 (ND 35-5, SD 3-1); I 1-0. March 9, 2005.

**34.** **S 256. Bankruptcy Overhaul/Family-Related Provisions.** Dodd, D-Conn., amendment that would alter the means test to provide greater flexibility when calculating a debtor's ability to pay, and broaden allowable monthly expenses to ensure that parents had the resources to support their children throughout bankruptcy. It also would allow debtors to keep personal property found in or around the home, excluding cars, and ensure that support payments and tax refunds do not become the property of the bankruptcy estate. Rejected 42-58: R 0-55; D 41-3 (ND 37-3, SD 4-0); I 1-0. March 9, 2005.

**35.** **S 256. Bankruptcy Overhaul/Homestead Exemption Cap.** Kennedy, D-Mass., amendment that would place a $300,000 cap on the bill's homestead exemption. Rejected 47-53: R 5-50; D 41-3 (ND 38-2, SD 3-1); I 1-0. March 9, 2005.

**36.** **S 256. Bankruptcy Overhaul/Means Test Exemption.** Kennedy, D-Mass., amendment that would exempt debtors from the means test if they failed to receive alimony or child support in any consecutive 12-month period in the two years before filing a bankruptcy petition and the amount exceeded 35 percent of the debtor's household income. Rejected 41-58: R 1-54; D 39-4 (ND 35-4, SD 4-0); I 1-0. March 10, 2005.

**37.** **S 256. Bankruptcy Overhaul/Current Monthly Income.** Kennedy, D-Mass., amendment that would change the bill's definition of current monthly income to specifically exclude income from a debtor's former job and income from any activity the debtor can no longer engage in due to disability. Rejected 41-58: R 0-55; D 40-3 (ND 36-3, SD 4-0); I 1-0. March 10, 2005.

**38.** **S 256. Bankruptcy Overhaul/Unsecured Creditors.** Akaka, D-Hawaii, amendment that would disallow an unsecured creditor's claim in bankruptcy if the creditor did not have a policy of waiving additional interest for all debtors who participate in a debt management plan administered by a nonprofit budget and credit counseling agency. Rejected 38-61: R 0-55; D 37-6 (ND 33-6, SD 4-0); I 1-0. March 10, 2005.

ND Northern Democrats, SD Southern Democrats
Southern states: Ala., Ark., Fla., Ga., Ky., La., Miss., N.C., Okla., S.C., Tenn., Texas, Va.

| | 33 | 34 | 35 | 36 | 37 | 38 |
|---|---|---|---|---|---|---|
| **ALABAMA** | | | | | | |
| Shelby | N | N | N | N | N | N |
| Sessions | N | N | N | N | N | N |
| **ALASKA** | | | | | | |
| Stevens | N | N | N | N | N | N |
| Murkowski | N | N | N | N | N | N |
| **ARIZONA** | | | | | | |
| McCain | N | N | N | N | N | N |
| Kyl | N | N | N | N | N | N |
| **ARKANSAS** | | | | | | |
| Lincoln | Y | Y | Y | Y | Y | Y |
| Pryor | Y | Y | Y | Y | Y | Y |
| **CALIFORNIA** | | | | | | |
| Feinstein | Y | Y | Y | Y | Y | Y |
| Boxer | Y | Y | Y | Y | Y | Y |
| **COLORADO** | | | | | | |
| Allard | N | N | N | N | N | N |
| Salazar | Y | Y | Y | Y | Y | Y |
| **CONNECTICUT** | | | | | | |
| Dodd | Y | Y | Y | Y | Y | Y |
| Lieberman | Y | Y | Y | Y | Y | Y |
| **DELAWARE** | | | | | | |
| Biden | Y | N | Y | N | Y | N |
| Carper | N | N | Y | N | N | N |
| **FLORIDA** | | | | | | |
| Nelson | N | Y | N | Y | Y | Y |
| Martinez | N | N | N | N | N | N |
| **GEORGIA** | | | | | | |
| Chambliss | N | N | N | N | N | N |
| Isakson | N | N | N | N | N | N |
| **HAWAII** | | | | | | |
| Inouye | Y | Y | Y | Y | Y | Y |
| Akaka | Y | Y | Y | Y | Y | Y |
| **IDAHO** | | | | | | |
| Craig | N | N | N | N | N | N |
| Crapo | N | N | N | N | N | N |
| **ILLINOIS** | | | | | | |
| Durbin | Y | Y | Y | Y | Y | Y |
| Obama | Y | Y | Y | Y | Y | Y |
| **INDIANA** | | | | | | |
| Lugar | N | N | N | N | N | N |
| Bayh | N | Y | Y | Y | Y | Y |
| **IOWA** | | | | | | |
| Grassley | N | N | N | N | N | N |
| Harkin | Y | Y | Y | Y | Y | Y |
| **KANSAS** | | | | | | |
| Brownback | N | N | N | N | N | N |
| Roberts | N | N | N | N | N | N |
| **KENTUCKY** | | | | | | |
| McConnell | N | N | N | N | N | N |
| Bunning | N | N | N | N | N | N |
| **LOUISIANA** | | | | | | |
| Landrieu | Y | Y | Y | Y | Y | Y |
| Vitter | N | N | N | N | N | N |
| **MAINE** | | | | | | |
| Snowe | N | N | Y | N | Y | N |
| Collins | N | N | Y | N | N | N |
| **MARYLAND** | | | | | | |
| Sarbanes | Y | Y | Y | Y | Y | Y |
| Mikulski | Y | Y | Y | Y | Y | Y |
| **MASSACHUSETTS** | | | | | | |
| Kennedy | Y | Y | Y | Y | Y | Y |
| Kerry | Y | Y | Y | Y | Y | Y |
| **MICHIGAN** | | | | | | |
| Levin | Y | Y | Y | Y | Y | Y |
| Stabenow | Y | Y | Y | Y | Y | Y |
| **MINNESOTA** | | | | | | |
| Dayton | Y | Y | Y | Y | Y | Y |
| Coleman | N | N | N | N | N | N |
| **MISSISSIPPI** | | | | | | |
| Cochran | N | N | N | N | N | N |
| Lott | N | N | N | N | N | N |
| **MISSOURI** | | | | | | |
| Bond | N | N | N | N | N | N |
| Talent | N | N | N | N | N | N |
| **MONTANA** | | | | | | |
| Baucus | N | Y | N | Y | Y | Y |
| Burns | N | N | N | N | N | N |
| **NEBRASKA** | | | | | | |
| Hagel | N | N | N | N | N | N |
| Nelson | N | N | N | N | N | N |
| **NEVADA** | | | | | | |
| Reid | Y | Y | Y | Y | Y | Y |
| Ensign | N | N | N | N | N | N |
| **NEW HAMPSHIRE** | | | | | | |
| Gregg | N | N | N | N | N | N |
| Sununu | N | N | N | N | N | N |
| **NEW JERSEY** | | | | | | |
| Corzine | Y | Y | Y | Y | Y | Y |
| Lautenberg | Y | Y | Y | Y | Y | Y |
| **NEW MEXICO** | | | | | | |
| Domenici | N | N | N | N | N | N |
| Bingaman | Y | Y | Y | Y | N | N |
| **NEW YORK** | | | | | | |
| Schumer | Y | Y | Y | Y | Y | Y |
| Clinton | Y | Y | Y | ? | ? | ? |
| **NORTH CAROLINA** | | | | | | |
| Dole | N | N | N | N | N | N |
| Burr | N | N | N | N | N | N |
| **NORTH DAKOTA** | | | | | | |
| Conrad | Y | Y | Y | Y | Y | Y |
| Dorgan | Y | Y | Y | Y | Y | Y |
| **OHIO** | | | | | | |
| DeWine | N | N | N | N | N | N |
| Voinovich | N | N | N | N | N | N |
| **OKLAHOMA** | | | | | | |
| Inhofe | N | N | N | N | N | N |
| Coburn | N | N | N | N | N | N |
| **OREGON** | | | | | | |
| Wyden | Y | Y | Y | Y | Y | Y |
| Smith | N | N | N | N | N | N |
| **PENNSYLVANIA** | | | | | | |
| Specter | N | N | Y | N | N | N |
| Santorum | N | N | N | N | N | N |
| **RHODE ISLAND** | | | | | | |
| Reed | Y | Y | Y | Y | Y | Y |
| Chafee | Y | N | Y | Y | Y | Y |
| **SOUTH CAROLINA** | | | | | | |
| Graham | N | N | N | N | N | N |
| DeMint | N | N | N | N | N | N |
| **SOUTH DAKOTA** | | | | | | |
| Johnson | N | Y | N | Y | Y | Y |
| Thune | N | N | N | N | N | N |
| **TENNESSEE** | | | | | | |
| Frist | N | N | N | N | N | N |
| Alexander | N | N | N | N | N | N |
| **TEXAS** | | | | | | |
| Hutchison | N | N | N | N | N | N |
| Cornyn | N | N | N | N | N | N |
| **UTAH** | | | | | | |
| Hatch | N | N | N | N | N | N |
| Bennett | N | N | N | N | N | N |
| **VERMONT** | | | | | | |
| Leahy | Y | Y | Y | Y | Y | Y |
| Jeffords | Y | Y | Y | Y | Y | Y |
| **VIRGINIA** | | | | | | |
| Warner | N | N | N | N | N | N |
| Allen | N | N | N | N | N | N |
| **WASHINGTON** | | | | | | |
| Murray | Y | Y | Y | Y | Y | Y |
| Cantwell | Y | Y | Y | Y | Y | Y |
| **WEST VIRGINIA** | | | | | | |
| Byrd | Y | Y | Y | Y | Y | Y |
| Rockefeller | Y | Y | Y | Y | Y | Y |
| **WISCONSIN** | | | | | | |
| Kohl | Y | Y | Y | Y | Y | Y |
| Feingold | Y | Y | Y | Y | Y | Y |
| **WYOMING** | | | | | | |
| Thomas | N | N | N | N | N | N |
| Enzi | N | N | N | N | N | N |

**KEY**    Republicans    Democrats    *Independents*

| Y | Voted for (yea) | X | Paired against | C | Voted "present" to avoid possible conflict of interest |
|---|---|---|---|---|---|
| # | Paired for | – | Announced against | | |
| + | Announced for | P | Voted "present" | ? | Did not vote or otherwise make a position known |
| N | Voted against (nay) | | | | |

# IN THE SENATE | By Vote Number

**39.** **S 256. Bankruptcy Overhaul/Conflict of Interest.** Leahy, D-Vt., amendment that would prohibit investment bankers from acting as financial advisers to debtor companies filing for bankruptcy if they have advised those same companies within five years of the company's bankruptcy. Rejected 44-55: R 5-50; D 38-5 (ND 35-4, SD 2-2); I 1-0. March 10, 2005.

**40.** **S 256. Bankruptcy Overhaul/Disabled Veterans.** Durbin, D-Ill., amendment that would exempt disabled veterans from the means test if their debts were incurred primarily when they were on active duty or performing homeland defense duties. Adopted 99-0: R 55-0; D 43-0 (ND 39-0, SD 4-0); I 1-0. March 10, 2005.

**41.** **S 256. Bankruptcy Overhaul/Asset Protection Trusts.** Schumer, D-N.Y., amendment to the Talent, R-Mo., amendment. The Schumer amendment would strike language in the underlying amendment that would require bankruptcy courts to show that the owner of an asset protection trust had the intent of defrauding creditors and employees. The Talent amendment would allow bankruptcy courts to access assets in such trusts up to 10 years before the owner filed a bankruptcy petition. Rejected 43-56: R 1-54; D 41-2 (ND 37-2, SD 4-0); I 1-0. March 10, 2005.

**42.** **S 256. Bankruptcy Overhaul/Asset Protection Trusts.** Talent, R-Mo., amendment that would allow bankruptcy courts to access assets in asset protection trusts up to 10 years before the owner filed a bankruptcy petition. It also would require courts to show that the owner of such a trust had the intent of defrauding creditors and employees. Adopted 73-26: R 55-0; D 18-25 (ND 15-24, SD 3-1); I 0-1. March 10, 2005.

**43.** **S 250. Vocational-Technical Education/Passage.** Passage of the bill that would reauthorize the Carl D. Perkins Vocational and Technical Education Act, which provides federal grants to states to develop and support vocational training programs. It would set the within-state allotment at a minimum of 85 percent and remove spending caps on non-traditional programs such as prisoner retraining. It would eliminate the Tech-Prep demonstration program. Passed 99-0: R 55-0; D 43-0 (ND 39-0, SD 4-0); I 1-0. March 10, 2005.

**44.** **S 256. Bankruptcy Overhaul/Passage.** Passage of the bill that would create a means test tied to the median incomes of individual states to determine whether personal bankruptcy filers were able to repay some or all of their debts. Those deemed able to pay would be pushed into Chapter 13 bankruptcy, which results in a court-ordered repayment plan; those with insufficient assets would be allowed to file under Chapter 7, which erases debts after the forfeiture of certain assets. The bill would exempt disabled veterans from the means test if their debts were incurred primarily when they were on active duty or performing homeland defense duties. It also would make a number of debts non-dischargeable, including student loans, child support, alimony and luxury payments over $500 made within three months of a bankruptcy filing. Passed 74-25: R 55-0; D 18-25 (ND 14-25, SD 4-0); I 1-0. March 10, 2005.

ND Northern Democrats, SD Southern Democrats
Southern states: Ala., Ark., Fla., Ga., Ky., La., Miss., N.C., Okla., S.C., Tenn., Texas, Va.

| | 39 | 40 | 41 | 42 | 43 | 44 |
|---|---|---|---|---|---|---|
| **ALABAMA** | | | | | | |
| Shelby | N | Y | N | Y | Y | Y |
| Sessions | N | Y | N | Y | Y | Y |
| **ALASKA** | | | | | | |
| Stevens | N | Y | N | Y | Y | Y |
| Murkowski | N | Y | N | Y | Y | Y |
| **ARIZONA** | | | | | | |
| McCain | N | Y | N | Y | Y | Y |
| Kyl | N | Y | N | Y | Y | Y |
| **ARKANSAS** | | | | | | |
| Lincoln | N | Y | Y | Y | Y | Y |
| Pryor | N | Y | Y | Y | Y | Y |
| **CALIFORNIA** | | | | | | |
| Feinstein | Y | Y | Y | N | Y | N |
| Boxer | Y | Y | Y | N | Y | N |
| **COLORADO** | | | | | | |
| Allard | N | Y | N | Y | Y | Y |
| Salazar | Y | Y | Y | Y | Y | Y |
| **CONNECTICUT** | | | | | | |
| Dodd | Y | Y | Y | Y | N | N |
| Lieberman | Y | Y | Y | N | Y | N |
| **DELAWARE** | | | | | | |
| Biden | Y | Y | Y | Y | Y | Y |
| Carper | Y | Y | N | N | Y | Y |
| **FLORIDA** | | | | | | |
| Nelson | Y | Y | Y | Y | Y | Y |
| Martinez | N | Y | N | Y | Y | Y |
| **GEORGIA** | | | | | | |
| Chambliss | N | Y | N | Y | Y | Y |
| Isakson | N | Y | N | Y | Y | Y |
| **HAWAII** | | | | | | |
| Inouye | Y | Y | Y | N | Y | Y |
| Akaka | Y | Y | Y | N | Y | N |
| **IDAHO** | | | | | | |
| Craig | N | Y | N | Y | Y | Y |
| Crapo | N | Y | N | Y | Y | Y |
| **ILLINOIS** | | | | | | |
| Durbin | Y | Y | Y | N | Y | N |
| Obama | Y | Y | Y | N | Y | N |
| **INDIANA** | | | | | | |
| Lugar | N | Y | N | Y | Y | Y |
| Bayh | N | Y | Y | N | Y | Y |
| **IOWA** | | | | | | |
| Grassley | N | Y | N | Y | Y | Y |
| Harkin | Y | Y | Y | Y | Y | N |
| **KANSAS** | | | | | | |
| Brownback | N | Y | N | Y | Y | Y |
| Roberts | N | Y | N | Y | Y | Y |
| **KENTUCKY** | | | | | | |
| McConnell | N | Y | N | Y | Y | Y |
| Bunning | N | Y | N | Y | Y | Y |
| **LOUISIANA** | | | | | | |
| Landrieu | Y | Y | Y | N | Y | Y |
| Vitter | N | Y | Y | Y | Y | Y |
| **MAINE** | | | | | | |
| Snowe | Y | Y | Y | Y | Y | Y |
| Collins | Y | Y | N | Y | Y | Y |
| **MARYLAND** | | | | | | |
| Sarbanes | Y | Y | Y | N | Y | N |
| Mikulski | Y | Y | Y | N | Y | N |
| **MASSACHUSETTS** | | | | | | |
| Kennedy | Y | Y | Y | N | Y | N |
| Kerry | Y | Y | Y | N | Y | N |
| **MICHIGAN** | | | | | | |
| Levin | Y | Y | Y | N | Y | N |
| Stabenow | N | Y | Y | N | Y | Y |
| **MINNESOTA** | | | | | | |
| Dayton | Y | Y | Y | Y | N | Y |
| Coleman | N | Y | N | Y | Y | Y |
| **MISSISSIPPI** | | | | | | |
| Cochran | N | Y | N | Y | Y | Y |
| Lott | N | Y | N | Y | Y | Y |
| **MISSOURI** | | | | | | |
| Bond | N | Y | N | Y | Y | Y |
| Talent | N | Y | N | Y | Y | Y |

| | 39 | 40 | 41 | 42 | 43 | 44 |
|---|---|---|---|---|---|---|
| **MONTANA** | | | | | | |
| Baucus | N | Y | Y | Y | Y | Y |
| Burns | N | Y | N | Y | Y | Y |
| **NEBRASKA** | | | | | | |
| Hagel | N | Y | N | Y | Y | Y |
| Nelson | Y | Y | N | Y | Y | Y |
| **NEVADA** | | | | | | |
| Reid | Y | Y | Y | N | Y | Y |
| Ensign | N | Y | N | Y | Y | Y |
| **NEW HAMPSHIRE** | | | | | | |
| Gregg | N | Y | N | Y | Y | Y |
| Sununu | N | Y | N | Y | Y | Y |
| **NEW JERSEY** | | | | | | |
| Corzine | Y | Y | Y | Y | Y | N |
| Lautenberg | Y | Y | Y | N | Y | N |
| **NEW MEXICO** | | | | | | |
| Domenici | N | Y | N | Y | Y | Y |
| Bingaman | Y | Y | Y | Y | Y | Y |
| **NEW YORK** | | | | | | |
| Schumer | Y | Y | Y | N | Y | N |
| Clinton | ? | ? | ? | ? | ? | ? |
| **NORTH CAROLINA** | | | | | | |
| Dole | N | Y | N | Y | Y | Y |
| Burr | N | Y | N | Y | Y | Y |
| **NORTH DAKOTA** | | | | | | |
| Conrad | Y | Y | Y | Y | Y | Y |
| Dorgan | Y | Y | Y | Y | Y | N |
| **OHIO** | | | | | | |
| DeWine | N | Y | N | Y | Y | Y |
| Voinovich | Y | Y | N | Y | Y | Y |
| **OKLAHOMA** | | | | | | |
| Inhofe | N | Y | N | Y | Y | Y |
| Coburn | N | Y | N | Y | Y | Y |
| **OREGON** | | | | | | |
| Wyden | Y | Y | Y | N | Y | N |
| Smith | N | Y | N | Y | Y | Y |
| **PENNSYLVANIA** | | | | | | |
| Specter | Y | Y | N | Y | Y | Y |
| Santorum | N | Y | N | Y | Y | Y |
| **RHODE ISLAND** | | | | | | |
| Reed | Y | Y | Y | N | Y | N |
| Chafee | N | Y | Y | Y | Y | Y |
| **SOUTH CAROLINA** | | | | | | |
| Graham | N | Y | N | Y | Y | Y |
| DeMint | N | Y | N | Y | Y | Y |
| **SOUTH DAKOTA** | | | | | | |
| Johnson | Y | Y | N | Y | Y | Y |
| Thune | N | Y | N | Y | Y | Y |
| **TENNESSEE** | | | | | | |
| Frist | N | Y | N | Y | Y | Y |
| Alexander | N | Y | N | Y | Y | Y |
| **TEXAS** | | | | | | |
| Hutchison | N | Y | N | Y | Y | Y |
| Cornyn | N | Y | N | Y | Y | Y |
| **UTAH** | | | | | | |
| Hatch | N | Y | N | Y | Y | Y |
| Bennett | N | Y | N | Y | Y | Y |
| **VERMONT** | | | | | | |
| Leahy | Y | Y | Y | N | Y | N |
| *Jeffords* | Y | Y | Y | N | Y | Y |
| **VIRGINIA** | | | | | | |
| Warner | Y | Y | N | Y | Y | Y |
| Allen | N | Y | N | Y | Y | Y |
| **WASHINGTON** | | | | | | |
| Murray | Y | Y | Y | N | Y | N |
| Cantwell | Y | Y | Y | Y | Y | N |
| **WEST VIRGINIA** | | | | | | |
| Byrd | Y | Y | Y | Y | Y | Y |
| Rockefeller | Y | Y | Y | N | Y | N |
| **WISCONSIN** | | | | | | |
| Kohl | Y | Y | Y | Y | Y | Y |
| Feingold | Y | Y | Y | N | Y | N |
| **WYOMING** | | | | | | |
| Thomas | N | Y | N | Y | Y | Y |
| Enzi | N | Y | N | Y | Y | Y |

**KEY**   Republicans   Democrats   *Independents*

| | | |
|---|---|---|
| Y Voted for (yea) | X Paired against | C Voted "present" to avoid possible conflict of interest |
| # Paired for | − Announced against | |
| + Announced for | P Voted "present" | ? Did not vote or otherwise make a position known |
| N Voted against (nay) | | |

# IN THE SENATE | By Vote Number

**45.** **S Con Res 18. Fiscal 2006 Budget Resolution/Education Funding.**
Bingaman, D-N.M., amendment that would increase education funding for fiscal 2006 by $4.75 billion, restoring it to fiscal 2005 levels, and reduce the federal deficit by $4.75 billion. It would be offset by a $9.5 billion reduction in tax cuts. Rejected 44-49: R 3-49; D 40-0 (ND 36-0, SD 4-0); I 1-0. March 14, 2005.

**46.** **S Con Res 18. Fiscal 2006 Budget Resolution/Social Security Solvency.** Graham, R-S.C., amendment that would express the sense of the Senate that the president, Congress and the American people should work together to enact legislation that would achieve a solvent and permanently sustainable Social Security system. Adopted 100-0: R 55-0; D 44-0 (ND 40-0, SD 4-0); I 1-0. March 15, 2005.

**47.** **S Con Res 18. Fiscal 2006 Budget Resolution/Social Security Solvency.** Conrad, D-N.D., amendment that would make the consideration of new tax cuts or net mandatory spending that would increase the deficit subject to a 60-vote point of order unless Congress had restored the solvency of Social Security for 75 years. Rejected 45-55: R 0-55; D 44-0 (ND 40-0, SD 4-0); I 1-0. March 15, 2005.

**48.** **S Con Res 18. Fiscal 2006 Budget Resolution/Social Security Benefit Cuts.** DeMint, R-S.C., amendment that would express the sense of the Senate that Congress should reject any Social Security plan that requires deep benefit cuts or a massive increase in debt, and that a failure to act on Social Security would result in massive debt, deep benefit cuts and tax increases. Adopted 56-43: R 53-2; D 3-40 (ND 2-38, SD 1-2); I 0-1. March 15, 2005.

**49.** **S Con Res 18. Fiscal 2006 Budget Resolution/Social Security.**
Nelson, D-Fla., amendment that would express the sense of the Senate that Congress should reject any Social Security plan that requires deep benefit cuts or a massive increase in debt. It also would urge Congress to take action to address Social Security solvency. Rejected 50-50: R 5-50; D 44-0 (ND 40-0, SD 4-0); I 1-0. March 15, 2005.

**50.** **S Con Res 18. Fiscal 2006 Budget Resolution/First-Responder Funding.** Stabenow, D-Mich., amendment that would increase funding for first-responder programs by $1.6 billion in fiscal 2006 and reduce the federal deficit by $1.6 billion. It would be offset by a $3.2 billion reduction in tax reconciliation provisions. Rejected 46-54: R 1-54; D 44-0 (ND 40-0, SD 4-0); I 1-0. March 15, 2005.

**51.** **S Con Res 18. Fiscal 2006 Budget Resolution/Amtrak Funding.** Byrd, D-W.Va., amendment that would allow $1.04 billion in additional fiscal 2006 funding for Amtrak and increase the fiscal 2006 discretionary spending limit by $1.04 billion. The spending would be offset by revenue increases. Rejected 46-52: R 4-51; D 41-1 (ND 38-1, SD 3-0); I 1-0. March 16, 2005.

**52.** **S Con Res 18. Fiscal 2006 Budget Resolution/ANWR Oil Drilling.**
Cantwell, D-Wash., amendment that would strike language in the resolution that would give procedural protection to legislation authorizing oil drilling in part of the Arctic National Wildlife Refuge (ANWR) in Alaska. Rejected 49-51: R 7-48; D 41-3 (ND 38-2, SD 3-1); I 1-0. A "nay" was a vote in support of the president's position. March 16, 2005.

| | 45 | 46 | 47 | 48 | 49 | 50 | 51 | 52 |
|---|---|---|---|---|---|---|---|---|
| **ALABAMA** | | | | | | | | |
| Shelby | N | Y | N | Y | N | N | N | N |
| Sessions | N | Y | N | Y | N | N | N | N |
| **ALASKA** | | | | | | | | |
| Stevens | N | Y | N | Y | N | N | N | N |
| Murkowski | N | Y | N | Y | N | N | N | N |
| **ARIZONA** | | | | | | | | |
| McCain | ? | Y | N | Y | N | N | N | Y |
| Kyl | N | Y | N | Y | N | N | N | N |
| **ARKANSAS** | | | | | | | | |
| Lincoln | Y | Y | Y | N | Y | Y | Y | Y |
| Pryor | Y | Y | Y | N | Y | Y | ? | Y |
| **CALIFORNIA** | | | | | | | | |
| Feinstein | Y | Y | Y | N | Y | Y | Y | Y |
| Boxer | Y | Y | Y | N | Y | Y | Y | Y |
| **COLORADO** | | | | | | | | |
| Allard | N | Y | N | Y | N | N | N | N |
| Salazar | Y | Y | Y | N | Y | Y | Y | Y |
| **CONNECTICUT** | | | | | | | | |
| Dodd | Y | Y | Y | N | Y | Y | Y | Y |
| Lieberman | Y | Y | Y | N | Y | Y | Y | Y |
| **DELAWARE** | | | | | | | | |
| Biden | Y | Y | Y | N | Y | Y | Y | Y |
| Carper | Y | Y | Y | N | Y | Y | Y | Y |
| **FLORIDA** | | | | | | | | |
| Nelson | Y | Y | Y | Y | Y | Y | N | Y |
| Martinez | N | Y | N | Y | N | N | N | N |
| **GEORGIA** | | | | | | | | |
| Chambliss | N | Y | N | Y | N | N | N | N |
| Isakson | N | Y | N | Y | N | N | N | N |
| **HAWAII** | | | | | | | | |
| Inouye | Y | Y | Y | N | Y | Y | Y | N |
| Akaka | Y | Y | Y | N | Y | Y | Y | N |
| **IDAHO** | | | | | | | | |
| Craig | N | Y | N | Y | N | N | N | N |
| Crapo | N | Y | N | Y | N | N | N | N |
| **ILLINOIS** | | | | | | | | |
| Durbin | Y | Y | Y | N | Y | Y | Y | Y |
| Obama | Y | Y | Y | N | Y | Y | Y | Y |
| **INDIANA** | | | | | | | | |
| Lugar | N | Y | N | Y | N | N | N | N |
| Bayh | Y | Y | Y | N | Y | Y | Y | Y |
| **IOWA** | | | | | | | | |
| Grassley | N | Y | N | Y | N | N | N | N |
| Harkin | ? | Y | Y | N | Y | Y | Y | Y |
| **KANSAS** | | | | | | | | |
| Brownback | N | Y | N | Y | N | N | N | N |
| Roberts | ? | Y | N | Y | N | N | N | N |
| **KENTUCKY** | | | | | | | | |
| McConnell | N | Y | N | Y | N | N | N | N |
| Bunning | N | Y | N | Y | N | N | N | N |
| **LOUISIANA** | | | | | | | | |
| Landrieu | Y | Y | Y | ? | Y | Y | Y | N |
| Vitter | N | Y | N | Y | N | N | N | N |
| **MAINE** | | | | | | | | |
| Snowe | N | Y | N | N | Y | N | Y | Y |
| Collins | N | Y | N | Y | Y | N | Y | Y |
| **MARYLAND** | | | | | | | | |
| Sarbanes | Y | Y | Y | N | Y | Y | Y | Y |
| Mikulski | Y | Y | Y | N | Y | Y | Y | Y |
| **MASSACHUSETTS** | | | | | | | | |
| Kennedy | Y | Y | Y | N | Y | Y | Y | Y |
| Kerry | Y | Y | Y | N | Y | Y | Y | Y |
| **MICHIGAN** | | | | | | | | |
| Levin | Y | Y | Y | N | Y | Y | Y | Y |
| Stabenow | Y | Y | Y | N | Y | Y | Y | Y |
| **MINNESOTA** | | | | | | | | |
| Dayton | Y | Y | Y | N | Y | Y | Y | Y |
| Coleman | Y | Y | N | Y | N | N | N | Y |
| **MISSISSIPPI** | | | | | | | | |
| Cochran | N | Y | N | Y | N | N | N | N |
| Lott | N | Y | N | Y | N | N | N | N |
| **MISSOURI** | | | | | | | | |
| Bond | N | Y | N | Y | N | N | N | N |
| Talent | N | Y | N | Y | N | N | N | N |
| **MONTANA** | | | | | | | | |
| Baucus | Y | Y | Y | N | Y | Y | Y | Y |
| Burns | N | Y | N | Y | N | N | N | N |
| **NEBRASKA** | | | | | | | | |
| Hagel | N | Y | N | Y | N | N | N | N |
| Nelson | Y | Y | Y | Y | Y | Y | Y | Y |
| **NEVADA** | | | | | | | | |
| Reid | Y | Y | Y | N | Y | Y | Y | Y |
| Ensign | N | Y | N | Y | N | N | N | N |
| **NEW HAMPSHIRE** | | | | | | | | |
| Gregg | N | Y | N | Y | N | N | N | N |
| Sununu | N | Y | N | Y | N | N | N | N |
| **NEW JERSEY** | | | | | | | | |
| Corzine | ? | Y | Y | N | Y | Y | Y | Y |
| Lautenberg | Y | Y | Y | N | Y | Y | Y | Y |
| **NEW MEXICO** | | | | | | | | |
| Domenici | N | Y | N | Y | N | N | N | N |
| Bingaman | Y | Y | Y | N | Y | Y | Y | Y |
| **NEW YORK** | | | | | | | | |
| Schumer | Y | Y | Y | N | Y | Y | Y | Y |
| Clinton | ? | Y | Y | N | Y | Y | Y | Y |
| **NORTH CAROLINA** | | | | | | | | |
| Dole | N | Y | N | Y | N | N | N | N |
| Burr | N | Y | N | Y | N | N | N | N |
| **NORTH DAKOTA** | | | | | | | | |
| Conrad | Y | Y | Y | N | Y | Y | Y | Y |
| Dorgan | Y | Y | Y | N | Y | Y | Y | Y |
| **OHIO** | | | | | | | | |
| DeWine | Y | Y | N | Y | Y | Y | Y | Y |
| Voinovich | N | Y | N | N | N | N | N | N |
| **OKLAHOMA** | | | | | | | | |
| Inhofe | N | Y | N | Y | N | N | N | N |
| Coburn | N | Y | N | Y | N | N | N | N |
| **OREGON** | | | | | | | | |
| Wyden | Y | Y | Y | N | Y | Y | Y | Y |
| Smith | N | Y | N | Y | N | N | N | Y |
| **PENNSYLVANIA** | | | | | | | | |
| Specter | N | Y | N | Y | Y | N | Y | N |
| Santorum | N | Y | N | Y | N | N | N | N |
| **RHODE ISLAND** | | | | | | | | |
| Reed | Y | Y | Y | N | Y | Y | ? | Y |
| Chafee | Y | Y | Y | N | Y | Y | Y | Y |
| **SOUTH CAROLINA** | | | | | | | | |
| Graham | ? | Y | N | Y | N | N | N | N |
| DeMint | N | Y | N | Y | N | N | N | N |
| **SOUTH DAKOTA** | | | | | | | | |
| Johnson | Y | Y | Y | N | Y | Y | Y | Y |
| Thune | N | Y | N | Y | N | N | N | N |
| **TENNESSEE** | | | | | | | | |
| Frist | N | Y | N | Y | N | N | N | N |
| Alexander | N | Y | N | Y | N | N | N | N |
| **TEXAS** | | | | | | | | |
| Hutchison | N | Y | N | Y | N | N | N | N |
| Cornyn | N | Y | N | Y | N | N | N | N |
| **UTAH** | | | | | | | | |
| Hatch | N | Y | N | Y | N | N | N | N |
| Bennett | N | Y | N | Y | N | N | N | N |
| **VERMONT** | | | | | | | | |
| Leahy | ? | Y | Y | N | Y | Y | Y | Y |
| Jeffords | Y | Y | Y | N | Y | Y | Y | Y |
| **VIRGINIA** | | | | | | | | |
| Warner | N | Y | N | Y | N | N | N | N |
| Allen | N | Y | N | Y | N | N | N | N |
| **WASHINGTON** | | | | | | | | |
| Murray | Y | Y | Y | N | Y | Y | Y | Y |
| Cantwell | Y | Y | Y | N | Y | Y | Y | Y |
| **WEST VIRGINIA** | | | | | | | | |
| Byrd | Y | Y | Y | Y | Y | Y | Y | Y |
| Rockefeller | Y | Y | Y | N | Y | Y | Y | Y |
| **WISCONSIN** | | | | | | | | |
| Kohl | Y | Y | Y | N | Y | Y | Y | Y |
| Feingold | Y | Y | Y | N | Y | Y | Y | Y |
| **WYOMING** | | | | | | | | |
| Thomas | N | Y | N | Y | N | N | N | N |
| Enzi | N | Y | N | Y | N | N | N | N |

**KEY**    Republicans    Democrats    *Independents*

| | | |
|---|---|---|
| **Y** Voted for (yea) | **X** Paired against | **C** Voted "present" to avoid possible conflict of interest |
| **#** Paired for | **–** Announced against | |
| **+** Announced for | **P** Voted "present" | **?** Did not vote or otherwise make a position known |
| **N** Voted against (nay) | | |

ND Northern Democrats, SD Southern Democrats
Southern states: Ala., Ark., Fla., Ga., Ky., La., Miss., N.C., Okla., S.C., Tenn., Texas, Va.

# IN THE SENATE | By Vote Number

## 53. S Con Res 18. Fiscal 2006 Budget Resolution/PAYGO Rules.
Feingold, D-Wis., amendment that would restore pay-as-you-go (PAYGO) rules, which would create a 60-vote point of order against any direct spending or revenue legislation that would increase the on-budget deficit or cause an on-budget deficit. Tax cuts and new entitlement spending would have to be offset with revenue increases or spending cuts. Rejected 50-50: R 5-50 D 44-0 (ND 40-0, SD 4-0); I 1-0. March 16, 2005.

## 54. S Con Res 18. Fiscal 2006 Budget Resolution/Veterans' Health Care Funding.
Ensign, R-Nev., amendment that would increase fiscal 2006 health care funding for veterans by $410 million. It would be offset by a reduction in foreign aid funding. Adopted 96-4: R 51-4; D 44-0 (ND 40-0, SD 4-0); I 1-0. March 16, 2005.

## 55. S Con Res 18. Fiscal 2006 Budget Resolution/Veterans' Health Care and Deficit Reduction.
Akaka, D-Hawaii, amendment that would increase funding for veterans health care by $2.8 billion for fiscal 2006 and reduce the deficit by $2.8 billion. Rejected 47-53: R 2-53; D 44-0 (ND 40-0, SD 4-0); I 1-0. March 16, 2005.

## 56. S Con Res 18. Fiscal 2006 Budget Resolution/Health and Education Funding.
Specter, R-Pa., amendment that would increase fiscal 2006 funding for the National Institutes of Health by $1.5 billion and education funding by $500 million. It would be offset by a $2 billion cut in the allowances account. Adopted 63-37: R 18-37; D 44-0 (ND 40-0, SD 4-0); I 1-0. March 16, 2005.

## 57. S Con Res 18. Fiscal 2006 Budget Resolution/Medicaid.
Gregg, R-N.H., amendment that would express the sense of the Senate that the Health and Human Services secretary, working with a bipartisan group of governors and stakeholders, should make recommendations for changes to Medicaid. It also would express the sense of the Senate that the Finance Committee should report a reconciliation bill that allows Medicaid savings to be shared by federal and state governments, emphasizes state flexibility through voluntary options for states and would not cause Medicaid recipients to lose coverage. Rejected 49-51: R 49-6; D 0-44 (ND 0-40, SD 0-4); I 0-1. March 17, 2005.

## 58. S Con Res 18. Fiscal 2006 Budget Resolution/Medicaid Cuts.
Smith, R-Ore., amendment that would strip out reconciliation instructions to the Finance Committee to reduce its outlays by $15 billion over five years that would likely result in a cut of $14 billion to Medicaid. It also would set up a reserve fund for the creation of a 23-member Bipartisan Medicaid Commission to study Medicaid before any cuts are made. Adopted 52-48: R 7-48; D 44-0 (ND 40-0, SD 4-0); I 1-0. March 17, 2005.

## 59. S Con Res 18. Fiscal 2006 Budget Resolution/Tax Cuts.
Carper, D-Del., amendment that would strike language in the resolution that would give reconciliation protection to tax cuts. Rejected 49-51: R 5-50; D 43-1 (ND 39-1, SD 4-0); I 1-0. March 17, 2005.

## 60. S Con Res 18. Fiscal 2006 Budget Resolution/Prescription Drug Prices.
Snowe, R-Maine, amendment that would insert language that would allow the secretary of Health and Human Services to negotiate with drug manufacturers for lower drug prices under Medicare. Rejected 49-50: R 6-48; D 42-2 (ND 39-1, SD 3-1); I 1-0. March 17, 2005.

ND Northern Democrats, SD Southern Democrats
Southern states: Ala., Ark., Fla., Ga., Ky., La., Miss., N.C., Okla., S.C., Tenn., Texas, Va.

| | 53 | 54 | 55 | 56 | 57 | 58 | 59 | 60 |
|---|---|---|---|---|---|---|---|---|
| **ALABAMA** | | | | | | | | |
| Shelby | N | Y | N | Y | Y | N | N | N |
| **Sessions** | N | Y | N | N | Y | N | N | N |
| **ALASKA** | | | | | | | | |
| Stevens | N | Y | N | N | Y | N | N | N |
| **Murkowski** | N | Y | N | N | Y | N | N | N |
| **ARIZONA** | | | | | | | | |
| McCain | Y | Y | N | N | Y | N | Y | Y |
| **Kyl** | N | Y | N | N | Y | N | N | N |
| **ARKANSAS** | | | | | | | | |
| Lincoln | Y | Y | Y | Y | N | Y | Y | Y |
| Pryor | Y | Y | Y | Y | N | Y | Y | Y |
| **CALIFORNIA** | | | | | | | | |
| Feinstein | Y | Y | Y | Y | N | Y | Y | Y |
| Boxer | Y | Y | Y | Y | N | Y | Y | Y |
| **COLORADO** | | | | | | | | |
| Allard | N | Y | N | N | Y | N | N | N |
| Salazar | Y | Y | Y | Y | N | Y | Y | Y |
| **CONNECTICUT** | | | | | | | | |
| Dodd | Y | Y | Y | Y | N | Y | Y | Y |
| Lieberman | Y | Y | Y | Y | N | Y | Y | Y |
| **DELAWARE** | | | | | | | | |
| Biden | Y | Y | Y | Y | N | Y | Y | Y |
| Carper | Y | Y | Y | Y | N | Y | Y | Y |
| **FLORIDA** | | | | | | | | |
| Nelson | Y | Y | Y | Y | N | Y | Y | Y |
| **Martinez** | N | Y | N | N | Y | N | N | N |
| **GEORGIA** | | | | | | | | |
| **Chambliss** | N | Y | N | N | Y | N | N | N |
| **Isakson** | N | Y | N | N | Y | N | N | N |
| **HAWAII** | | | | | | | | |
| Inouye | Y | Y | Y | Y | N | Y | Y | Y |
| **Akaka** | Y | Y | Y | Y | N | Y | Y | Y |
| **IDAHO** | | | | | | | | |
| **Craig** | N | Y | N | Y | Y | N | N | N |
| **Crapo** | N | Y | N | Y | Y | N | N | N |
| **ILLINOIS** | | | | | | | | |
| Durbin | Y | Y | Y | Y | N | Y | Y | Y |
| **Obama** | Y | Y | Y | Y | N | Y | Y | Y |
| **INDIANA** | | | | | | | | |
| **Lugar** | N | N | Y | Y | Y | N | N | N |
| Bayh | Y | Y | Y | Y | N | Y | Y | Y |
| **IOWA** | | | | | | | | |
| **Grassley** | N | Y | N | Y | Y | N | N | N |
| Harkin | Y | Y | Y | Y | N | Y | Y | Y |
| **KANSAS** | | | | | | | | |
| **Brownback** | N | Y | N | Y | Y | N | N | N |
| **Roberts** | N | Y | N | N | Y | N | N | N |
| **KENTUCKY** | | | | | | | | |
| **McConnell** | N | Y | N | N | Y | N | N | N |
| **Bunning** | N | Y | N | N | Y | N | N | N |
| **LOUISIANA** | | | | | | | | |
| Landrieu | Y | Y | Y | Y | N | Y | Y | Y |
| **Vitter** | N | Y | N | N | Y | N | N | N |
| **MAINE** | | | | | | | | |
| **Snowe** | Y | Y | N | Y | N | Y | Y | Y |
| **Collins** | Y | Y | N | Y | N | Y | Y | Y |
| **MARYLAND** | | | | | | | | |
| Sarbanes | Y | Y | Y | Y | N | Y | Y | Y |
| Mikulski | Y | Y | Y | Y | N | Y | Y | Y |
| **MASSACHUSETTS** | | | | | | | | |
| Kennedy | Y | Y | Y | Y | N | Y | Y | Y |
| Kerry | Y | Y | Y | Y | N | Y | Y | Y |
| **MICHIGAN** | | | | | | | | |
| Levin | Y | Y | Y | Y | N | Y | Y | Y |
| Stabenow | Y | Y | Y | Y | N | Y | Y | Y |
| **MINNESOTA** | | | | | | | | |
| Dayton | Y | Y | Y | Y | N | Y | Y | Y |
| **Coleman** | N | N | Y | Y | N | Y | N | N |
| **MISSISSIPPI** | | | | | | | | |
| **Cochran** | N | Y | N | N | Y | N | N | N |
| **Lott** | N | Y | N | N | Y | N | N | N |
| **MISSOURI** | | | | | | | | |
| **Bond** | N | Y | N | N | Y | N | N | N |
| **Talent** | N | Y | N | Y | Y | N | N | N |

| | 53 | 54 | 55 | 56 | 57 | 58 | 59 | 60 |
|---|---|---|---|---|---|---|---|---|
| **MONTANA** | | | | | | | | |
| Baucus | Y | Y | Y | Y | N | Y | Y | Y |
| **Burns** | N | Y | N | N | Y | N | N | N |
| **NEBRASKA** | | | | | | | | |
| **Hagel** | N | Y | N | N | Y | N | N | N |
| Nelson | Y | Y | Y | Y | N | Y | N | N |
| **NEVADA** | | | | | | | | |
| Reid | Y | Y | Y | Y | N | Y | Y | Y |
| **Ensign** | N | Y | N | N | Y | N | N | N |
| **NEW HAMPSHIRE** | | | | | | | | |
| **Gregg** | N | Y | N | N | Y | N | N | N |
| **Sununu** | N | Y | N | N | Y | N | N | N |
| **NEW JERSEY** | | | | | | | | |
| Corzine | Y | Y | Y | Y | N | Y | Y | Y |
| Lautenberg | Y | Y | Y | Y | N | Y | Y | Y |
| **NEW MEXICO** | | | | | | | | |
| **Domenici** | N | Y | N | N | Y | N | N | N |
| Bingaman | Y | Y | Y | Y | N | Y | Y | Y |
| **NEW YORK** | | | | | | | | |
| Schumer | Y | Y | Y | Y | N | Y | Y | Y |
| Clinton | Y | Y | Y | Y | N | Y | Y | Y |
| **NORTH CAROLINA** | | | | | | | | |
| **Dole** | N | Y | N | Y | Y | N | N | N |
| **Burr** | N | Y | N | N | Y | N | N | N |
| **NORTH DAKOTA** | | | | | | | | |
| Conrad | Y | Y | Y | Y | N | Y | Y | Y |
| Dorgan | Y | Y | Y | Y | N | Y | Y | Y |
| **OHIO** | | | | | | | | |
| **DeWine** | N | Y | N | Y | Y | N | N | N |
| **Voinovich** | Y | N | N | N | Y | N | Y | ? |
| **OKLAHOMA** | | | | | | | | |
| **Inhofe** | N | Y | N | N | Y | N | N | N |
| **Coburn** | N | Y | N | N | Y | N | N | N |
| **OREGON** | | | | | | | | |
| Wyden | Y | Y | Y | Y | N | Y | Y | Y |
| **Smith** | N | Y | N | N | Y | N | N | N |
| **PENNSYLVANIA** | | | | | | | | |
| **Specter** | N | Y | N | Y | Y | N | N | N |
| **Santorum** | N | Y | N | Y | Y | N | N | N |
| **RHODE ISLAND** | | | | | | | | |
| Reed | Y | Y | Y | Y | N | Y | Y | Y |
| **Chafee** | Y | N | Y | Y | N | Y | Y | Y |
| **SOUTH CAROLINA** | | | | | | | | |
| **Graham** | N | Y | N | N | Y | N | N | Y |
| **DeMint** | N | Y | N | N | Y | N | N | N |
| **SOUTH DAKOTA** | | | | | | | | |
| Johnson | Y | Y | Y | Y | N | Y | Y | Y |
| **Thune** | N | Y | N | Y | Y | N | N | N |
| **TENNESSEE** | | | | | | | | |
| **Frist** | N | Y | N | N | Y | N | N | N |
| **Alexander** | N | Y | N | N | Y | N | N | N |
| **TEXAS** | | | | | | | | |
| **Hutchison** | N | Y | N | N | Y | N | N | N |
| **Cornyn** | N | Y | N | N | Y | N | N | N |
| **UTAH** | | | | | | | | |
| **Hatch** | N | Y | N | Y | Y | N | N | N |
| **Bennett** | N | Y | N | Y | Y | N | N | N |
| **VERMONT** | | | | | | | | |
| Leahy | Y | Y | Y | Y | N | Y | Y | Y |
| *Jeffords* | Y | Y | Y | Y | N | Y | Y | Y |
| **VIRGINIA** | | | | | | | | |
| **Warner** | N | Y | N | N | Y | N | N | N |
| **Allen** | N | Y | N | Y | Y | N | N | N |
| **WASHINGTON** | | | | | | | | |
| Murray | Y | Y | Y | Y | N | Y | Y | Y |
| Cantwell | Y | Y | Y | Y | N | Y | Y | Y |
| **WEST VIRGINIA** | | | | | | | | |
| Byrd | Y | Y | Y | Y | N | Y | Y | Y |
| Rockefeller | Y | Y | Y | Y | N | Y | Y | Y |
| **WISCONSIN** | | | | | | | | |
| Kohl | Y | Y | Y | Y | N | Y | Y | Y |
| Feingold | Y | Y | Y | Y | N | Y | Y | Y |
| **WYOMING** | | | | | | | | |
| **Thomas** | N | Y | N | N | Y | N | N | N |
| **Enzi** | N | Y | N | N | Y | N | N | N |

**KEY**   Republicans   Democrats   *Independents*

| | | |
|---|---|---|
| **Y** Voted for (yea) | **X** Paired against | **C** Voted "present" to avoid possible conflict of interest |
| **#** Paired for | **–** Announced against | |
| **+** Announced for | **P** Voted "present" | **?** Did not vote or otherwise make a position known |
| **N** Voted against (nay) | | |

# IN THE SENATE | By Vote Number

**61.** S Con Res 18. Fiscal 2006 Budget Resolution/Perkins Loans. Harkin, D-Iowa, amendment that would reinstate two provisions of the tax code and use $7.46 billion to increase funding under the Perkins Vocational and Technical Education Act and the remainder to reduce the deficit. Rejected 44-56: R 1-54; D 42-2 (ND 38-2, SD 4-0); I 1-0. March 17, 2005.

**62.** S Con Res 18. Fiscal 2006 Budget Resolution/Reserve Fund. Landrieu, D-La., amendment that would add language to create a deficit-neutral reserve fund if legislation is passed that would provide a 50 percent tax credit for employers who continue to pay the salaries of National Guard and Reserve members called to active duty. Adopted 100-0: R 55-0; D 44-0 (ND 40-0, SD 4-0); I 1-0. March 17, 2005.

**63.** S Con Res 18. Fiscal 2006 Budget Resolution/Offshore Companies. Dorgan, D-N.D., amendment that would repeal tax incentives for domestic companies that move their manufacturing plants to offshore locations; it would use the resulting revenue to reduce the federal deficit by $3.2 billion from 2006 to 2010. Rejected 40-59: R 0-54; D 40-4 (ND 37-3, SD 3-1); I 0-1. March 17, 2005.

**64.** S Con Res 18. Fiscal 2006 Budget Resolution/Homeland Security Grants. Lieberman, D-Conn., amendment that would increase fiscal 2006 funding for the Community and Regional Development account by $715 million and for the Administration of Justice account by $140 million. It would stipulate that the funding be used for first-responder programs, port security grants and border patrol agents. It would be offset by a cut in the Allowances account. Adopted 63-37: R 18-37; D 44-0 (ND 39-1, SD 4-0); I 1-0. March 17, 2005.

**65.** S Con Res 18. Fiscal 2006 Budget Resolution/Community Development Block Grants. Sarbanes, D-Md., amendment that would restore $1.9 billion in cuts to the block grant program and other programs proposed for elimination, restoring funding to fiscal 2005 levels. It would be offset by striking $1.8 billion from the reconciliation instruction's tax cut figure. Rejected 49-51: R 4-51; D 44-0 (ND 40-0, SD 4-0); I 1-0. March 17, 2005.

**66.** S Con Res 18. Fiscal 2006 Budget Resolution/Community Development Block Grant Program. Coleman, R-Minn., amendment that would restore funding for the block grants and other programs to fiscal 2005 levels. It would be offset by cuts to the Allowances account. Adopted 68-31: R 24-31; D 43-0 (ND 39-0, SD 4-0); I 1-0. March 17, 2005.

**67.** S Con Res 18. Fiscal 2006 Budget Resolution/Emergency Spending. Cochran, R-Miss., amendment that would strike language giving the president the authority to designate funding as emergency spending. Adopted 73-26: R 32-22; D 40-4 (ND 36-4, SD 4-0); I 1-0. March 17, 2005.

**68.** S Con Res 18. Fiscal 2006 Budget Resolution/Education Funding. Kennedy, D-Mass., amendment that would increase the discretionary spending limit in the budget by $5.4 billion to $848.8 billion to restore education program cuts and increase the maximum Pell Grant award to $4,500. It would decrease the five-year tax cut reconciliation instruction figure by $5.4 billion. Adopted 51-49: R 6-49; D 44-0 (ND 40-0, SD 4-0); I 1-0. March 17, 2005.

ND Northern Democrats, SD Southern Democrats
Southern states: Ala., Ark., Fla., Ga., Ky., La., Miss., N.C., Okla., S.C., Tenn., Texas, Va.

| | 61 | 62 | 63 | 64 | 65 | 66 | 67 | 68 |
|---|---|---|---|---|---|---|---|---|
| **ALABAMA** | | | | | | | | |
| Shelby | N | Y | N | N | N | N | Y | N |
| Sessions | N | Y | N | N | N | N | N | N |
| **ALASKA** | | | | | | | | |
| Stevens | N | Y | N | N | N | N | Y | N |
| Murkowski | N | Y | N | Y | N | Y | Y | N |
| **ARIZONA** | | | | | | | | |
| McCain | N | Y | N | N | N | N | N | N |
| Kyl | N | Y | ? | N | N | N | N | N |
| **ARKANSAS** | | | | | | | | |
| Lincoln | Y | Y | Y | Y | Y | Y | Y | Y |
| Pryor | Y | Y | N | Y | Y | Y | Y | Y |
| **CALIFORNIA** | | | | | | | | |
| Feinstein | Y | Y | Y | Y | Y | Y | Y | Y |
| Boxer | Y | Y | Y | Y | Y | Y | Y | Y |
| **COLORADO** | | | | | | | | |
| Allard | N | Y | N | N | N | N | Y | N |
| Salazar | Y | Y | Y | Y | Y | Y | Y | Y |
| **CONNECTICUT** | | | | | | | | |
| Dodd | Y | Y | Y | Y | Y | Y | N | Y |
| Lieberman | Y | Y | Y | Y | Y | ? | N | Y |
| **DELAWARE** | | | | | | | | |
| Biden | Y | Y | Y | Y | Y | Y | Y | Y |
| Carper | Y | Y | Y | Y | Y | Y | Y | Y |
| **FLORIDA** | | | | | | | | |
| Nelson | Y | Y | Y | Y | Y | Y | Y | Y |
| Martinez | N | Y | N | Y | N | Y | Y | N |
| **GEORGIA** | | | | | | | | |
| Chambliss | N | Y | N | N | N | Y | Y | N |
| Isakson | N | Y | N | Y | N | Y | Y | N |
| **HAWAII** | | | | | | | | |
| Inouye | Y | Y | Y | Y | Y | Y | Y | Y |
| Akaka | Y | Y | Y | Y | Y | Y | Y | Y |
| **IDAHO** | | | | | | | | |
| Craig | N | Y | N | N | N | N | Y | N |
| Crapo | N | Y | N | N | N | N | N | N |
| **ILLINOIS** | | | | | | | | |
| Durbin | Y | Y | Y | Y | Y | Y | Y | Y |
| Obama | Y | Y | Y | Y | Y | Y | Y | Y |
| **INDIANA** | | | | | | | | |
| Lugar | N | Y | N | Y | N | Y | N | N |
| Bayh | Y | Y | Y | Y | Y | Y | N | Y |
| **IOWA** | | | | | | | | |
| Grassley | N | Y | N | N | N | N | N | N |
| Harkin | Y | Y | Y | Y | Y | Y | Y | Y |
| **KANSAS** | | | | | | | | |
| Brownback | N | Y | N | N | N | N | Y | N |
| Roberts | N | Y | N | Y | N | N | Y | N |
| **KENTUCKY** | | | | | | | | |
| McConnell | N | Y | N | N | N | N | Y | N |
| Bunning | N | Y | N | N | N | N | Y | N |
| **LOUISIANA** | | | | | | | | |
| Landrieu | Y | Y | Y | Y | Y | Y | Y | Y |
| Vitter | N | Y | N | Y | N | Y | N | N |
| **MAINE** | | | | | | | | |
| Snowe | N | Y | N | Y | N | Y | Y | Y |
| Collins | N | Y | N | Y | N | Y | Y | Y |
| **MARYLAND** | | | | | | | | |
| Sarbanes | Y | Y | Y | Y | Y | Y | Y | Y |
| Mikulski | Y | Y | Y | Y | Y | Y | Y | Y |
| **MASSACHUSETTS** | | | | | | | | |
| Kennedy | Y | Y | Y | Y | Y | Y | Y | Y |
| Kerry | Y | Y | Y | Y | Y | Y | Y | Y |
| **MICHIGAN** | | | | | | | | |
| Levin | Y | Y | Y | Y | Y | Y | Y | Y |
| Stabenow | Y | Y | Y | Y | Y | Y | Y | Y |
| **MINNESOTA** | | | | | | | | |
| Dayton | Y | Y | Y | Y | Y | Y | Y | Y |
| Coleman | N | Y | N | Y | Y | Y | Y | Y |
| **MISSISSIPPI** | | | | | | | | |
| Cochran | N | Y | N | N | N | N | Y | N |
| Lott | N | Y | N | N | N | N | Y | N |
| **MISSOURI** | | | | | | | | |
| Bond | N | Y | N | N | N | Y | Y | N |
| Talent | N | Y | N | Y | N | Y | Y | N |

| | 61 | 62 | 63 | 64 | 65 | 66 | 67 | 68 |
|---|---|---|---|---|---|---|---|---|
| **MONTANA** | | | | | | | | |
| Baucus | N | Y | N | Y | Y | Y | Y | Y |
| Burns | N | Y | N | N | N | Y | Y | N |
| **NEBRASKA** | | | | | | | | |
| Hagel | N | Y | N | N | N | N | N | N |
| Nelson | N | Y | N | Y | Y | Y | Y | Y |
| **NEVADA** | | | | | | | | |
| Reid | Y | Y | Y | Y | Y | Y | Y | Y |
| Ensign | N | Y | N | N | N | N | N | N |
| **NEW HAMPSHIRE** | | | | | | | | |
| Gregg | N | Y | N | N | N | N | N | N |
| Sununu | N | Y | N | N | N | N | N | N |
| **NEW JERSEY** | | | | | | | | |
| Corzine | Y | Y | Y | Y | Y | Y | Y | Y |
| Lautenberg | Y | Y | Y | Y | Y | Y | Y | Y |
| **NEW MEXICO** | | | | | | | | |
| Domenici | N | Y | N | N | N | Y | N | N |
| Bingaman | Y | Y | Y | Y | Y | Y | Y | Y |
| **NEW YORK** | | | | | | | | |
| Schumer | Y | Y | Y | Y | Y | Y | N | Y |
| Clinton | Y | Y | Y | Y | Y | Y | Y | Y |
| **NORTH CAROLINA** | | | | | | | | |
| Dole | N | Y | N | Y | N | Y | Y | N |
| Burr | N | Y | N | N | N | N | Y | N |
| **NORTH DAKOTA** | | | | | | | | |
| Conrad | Y | Y | Y | Y | Y | Y | Y | Y |
| Dorgan | Y | Y | Y | Y | Y | Y | Y | Y |
| **OHIO** | | | | | | | | |
| DeWine | N | Y | N | N | Y | Y | Y | Y |
| Voinovich | N | Y | N | N | Y | Y | N | N |
| **OKLAHOMA** | | | | | | | | |
| Inhofe | N | Y | N | N | N | N | N | N |
| Coburn | N | Y | N | N | N | N | N | N |
| **OREGON** | | | | | | | | |
| Wyden | Y | Y | Y | Y | Y | Y | Y | Y |
| Smith | N | Y | N | N | N | Y | Y | N |
| **PENNSYLVANIA** | | | | | | | | |
| Specter | N | Y | N | Y | N | Y | Y | Y |
| Santorum | N | Y | N | N | N | Y | ? | N |
| **RHODE ISLAND** | | | | | | | | |
| Reed | Y | Y | Y | Y | Y | Y | Y | Y |
| Chafee | Y | Y | Y | Y | Y | Y | N | Y |
| **SOUTH CAROLINA** | | | | | | | | |
| Graham | N | Y | N | N | N | N | N | N |
| DeMint | N | Y | N | N | N | N | N | N |
| **SOUTH DAKOTA** | | | | | | | | |
| Johnson | Y | Y | Y | Y | Y | Y | Y | Y |
| Thune | N | Y | N | Y | N | Y | Y | N |
| **TENNESSEE** | | | | | | | | |
| Frist | N | Y | N | N | N | N | N | N |
| Alexander | N | Y | N | N | N | N | N | N |
| **TEXAS** | | | | | | | | |
| Hutchison | N | Y | N | Y | N | Y | Y | N |
| Cornyn | N | Y | N | N | N | N | Y | N |
| **UTAH** | | | | | | | | |
| Hatch | N | Y | N | N | N | N | Y | N |
| Bennett | N | Y | N | N | N | N | Y | N |
| **VERMONT** | | | | | | | | |
| Leahy | Y | Y | Y | Y | Y | Y | Y | Y |
| Jeffords | Y | Y | N | Y | Y | Y | Y | Y |
| **VIRGINIA** | | | | | | | | |
| Warner | N | Y | N | N | N | Y | Y | N |
| Allen | N | Y | N | Y | N | Y | Y | N |
| **WASHINGTON** | | | | | | | | |
| Murray | Y | Y | Y | Y | Y | Y | Y | Y |
| Cantwell | Y | Y | N | Y | Y | Y | Y | Y |
| **WEST VIRGINIA** | | | | | | | | |
| Byrd | Y | Y | Y | Y | Y | Y | Y | Y |
| Rockefeller | Y | Y | Y | Y | Y | Y | Y | Y |
| **WISCONSIN** | | | | | | | | |
| Kohl | Y | Y | Y | Y | Y | Y | Y | Y |
| Feingold | Y | Y | Y | Y | Y | Y | Y | Y |
| **WYOMING** | | | | | | | | |
| Thomas | N | Y | N | N | N | N | N | N |
| Enzi | N | Y | N | Y | N | Y | N | N |

**KEY**  Republicans  Democrats  *Independents*

| | | |
|---|---|---|
| Y Voted for (yea) | X Paired against | C Voted "present" to avoid possible conflict of interest |
| # Paired for | – Announced against | |
| + Announced for | P Voted "present" | ? Did not vote or otherwise make a position known |
| N Voted against (nay) | | |

# IN THE SENATE | By Vote Number

**69.** **S Con Res 18. Fiscal 2006 Budget Resolution/Agriculture Cuts.**
Baucus, D-Mont., amendment that would strike language in the resolution
that would instruct the Agriculture Committee to cut mandatory spending for
agriculture programs by $2.8 billion between 2006 and 2010. Rejected 46-54:
R 1-54; D 44-0 (ND 40-0, SD 4-0); I 1-0. March 17, 2005.

**70.** **S Con Res 18. Fiscal 2006 Budget Resolution/Community Oriented
Policing Services.** Biden, D-Del., amendment that would increase the
discretionary spending limit by $1 billion and decrease the five-year tax cut rec-
onciliation instruction figure by $2 billion. It would increase funding for the
Office of Community Oriented Policing Services by $1 billion and use
$1 billion to reduce the deficit. Rejected 45-55: R 0-55; D 44-0 (ND 40-0, SD 4-
0); I 1-0. March 17, 2005.

**71.** **S Con Res 18. Fiscal 2006 Budget Resolution/Surface
Transportation Funding.** Byrd, D-W.Va., amendment that would increase
revenue by $13.8 billion and use it to increase spending for surface
transportation projects. It also would add a section designating $34.7 billion in
outlays for highways in fiscal 2006 and $7.1 billion for public transit. Rejected
45-54: R 0-54; D 44-0 (ND 40-0, SD 4-0); I 1-0. March 17, 2005.

**72.** **S Con Res 18. Fiscal 2006 Budget Resolution/Surface
Transportation Adjustments.** Talent, R-Mo., amendment that would alter language in the section on adjustment for surface transportation to make it possible to consider all available transportation funding options. Adopted 81-19:
R 36-19; D 44-0 (ND 40-0, SD 4-0); I 1-0. March 17, 2005.

**73.** **S Con Res 18. Fiscal 2006 Budget Resolution/Social Security
Benefits Tax.** Conrad, D-N.D., amendment that would express the sense of the
Senate that the tax cuts assumed in the resolution include the repeal of the
1993 income tax increase on Social Security benefits. Adopted 94-6: R 49-6;
D 44-0 (ND 40-0, SD 4-0); I 1-0. March 17, 2005.

**74.** **S Con Res 18. Fiscal 2006 Budget Resolution/Social Security
Benefit Tax.** Bunning, R-Ky., amendment that would repeal the 1993 tax
increase on Social Security benefits and increase the five-year tax cut reconciliation instruction figure by $63.9 billion. Adopted 55-45: R 50-5; D 5-39 (ND 3-
37, SD 2-2); I 0-1. March 17, 2005.

**75.** **S Con Res 18. Fiscal 2006 Budget Resolution/Family Planning
Programs.** Clinton, D-N.Y., amendment that would reduce the five-year tax cut
reconciliation instructions by $198 million and increase the discretionary
spending limit in the budget by $36 million. It also would express the sense of
the Senate that $1 billion should be used for family planning programs, such as
teen pregnancy prevention. Rejected 47-53: R 3-52; D 43-1 (ND 39-1, SD 4-0);
I 1-0. March 17, 2005.

ND Northern Democrats, SD Southern Democrats
Southern states: Ala., Ark., Fla., Ga., Ky., La., Miss., N.C., Okla., S.C., Tenn., Texas, Va.

| | 69 | 70 | 71 | 72 | 73 | 74 | 75 | | | 69 | 70 | 71 | 72 | 73 | 74 | 75 |
|---|---|---|---|---|---|---|---|---|---|---|---|---|---|---|---|---|
| **ALABAMA** | | | | | | | | | **MONTANA** | | | | | | | |
| Shelby | N | N | N | Y | Y | Y | N | | Baucus | Y | Y | Y | Y | Y | N | Y |
| Sessions | N | N | N | N | Y | Y | N | | Burns | N | N | N | Y | Y | Y | N |
| **ALASKA** | | | | | | | | | **NEBRASKA** | | | | | | | |
| Stevens | N | N | N | Y | N | Y | N | | Hagel | N | N | N | N | N | Y | N |
| Murkowski | N | N | N | Y | Y | Y | N | | Nelson | Y | Y | Y | Y | Y | Y | N |
| **ARIZONA** | | | | | | | | | **NEVADA** | | | | | | | |
| McCain | N | N | N | N | Y | Y | N | | Reid | Y | Y | Y | Y | Y | N | Y |
| Kyl | N | N | N | N | N | Y | N | | Ensign | N | N | N | N | Y | Y | N |
| **ARKANSAS** | | | | | | | | | **NEW HAMPSHIRE** | | | | | | | |
| Lincoln | Y | Y | Y | Y | Y | N | Y | | Gregg | N | N | N | Y | Y | Y | N |
| Pryor | Y | Y | Y | Y | Y | N | Y | | Sununu | N | N | N | Y | Y | Y | N |
| **CALIFORNIA** | | | | | | | | | **NEW JERSEY** | | | | | | | |
| Feinstein | Y | Y | Y | Y | Y | N | Y | | Corzine | Y | Y | Y | Y | Y | N | Y |
| Boxer | Y | Y | Y | Y | Y | N | Y | | Lautenberg | Y | Y | Y | Y | Y | N | Y |
| **COLORADO** | | | | | | | | | **NEW MEXICO** | | | | | | | |
| Allard | N | N | N | N | N | Y | N | | Domenici | N | N | N | N | N | N | N |
| Salazar | Y | Y | Y | Y | Y | Y | Y | | Bingaman | Y | Y | Y | Y | Y | N | Y |
| **CONNECTICUT** | | | | | | | | | **NEW YORK** | | | | | | | |
| Dodd | Y | Y | Y | Y | Y | N | Y | | Schumer | Y | Y | Y | Y | Y | N | Y |
| Lieberman | Y | Y | Y | Y | Y | N | Y | | Clinton | Y | Y | Y | Y | Y | N | Y |
| **DELAWARE** | | | | | | | | | **NORTH CAROLINA** | | | | | | | |
| Biden | Y | Y | Y | Y | Y | N | Y | | Dole | N | N | N | Y | Y | Y | N |
| Carper | Y | Y | Y | Y | Y | N | Y | | Burr | N | N | N | Y | Y | Y | N |
| **FLORIDA** | | | | | | | | | **NORTH DAKOTA** | | | | | | | |
| Nelson | Y | Y | Y | Y | Y | Y | Y | | Conrad | Y | Y | Y | Y | Y | N | Y |
| Martinez | N | N | N | Y | Y | Y | N | | Dorgan | Y | Y | Y | Y | Y | N | Y |
| **GEORGIA** | | | | | | | | | **OHIO** | | | | | | | |
| Chambliss | N | N | N | Y | Y | Y | N | | DeWine | N | N | N | Y | Y | Y | N |
| Isakson | N | N | N | Y | Y | Y | N | | Voinovich | N | N | N | Y | N | N | N |
| **HAWAII** | | | | | | | | | **OKLAHOMA** | | | | | | | |
| Inouye | Y | Y | Y | Y | Y | N | Y | | Inhofe | N | N | N | N | Y | Y | N |
| Akaka | Y | Y | Y | Y | Y | N | Y | | Coburn | N | N | N | N | Y | Y | N |
| **IDAHO** | | | | | | | | | **OREGON** | | | | | | | |
| Craig | N | N | N | Y | Y | Y | N | | Wyden | Y | Y | Y | Y | Y | N | Y |
| Crapo | N | N | N | Y | Y | Y | N | | Smith | N | N | N | Y | Y | Y | N |
| **ILLINOIS** | | | | | | | | | **PENNSYLVANIA** | | | | | | | |
| Durbin | Y | Y | Y | Y | Y | N | Y | | Specter | N | N | N | Y | Y | Y | N |
| Obama | Y | Y | Y | Y | Y | N | Y | | Santorum | N | N | N | Y | Y | Y | N |
| **INDIANA** | | | | | | | | | **RHODE ISLAND** | | | | | | | |
| Lugar | N | N | N | N | N | Y | N | | Reed | Y | Y | Y | Y | Y | N | Y |
| Bayh | Y | Y | Y | Y | Y | N | Y | | Chafee | N | N | N | Y | Y | N | Y |
| **IOWA** | | | | | | | | | **SOUTH CAROLINA** | | | | | | | |
| Grassley | N | N | N | Y | Y | Y | N | | Graham | N | N | N | N | Y | Y | N |
| Harkin | Y | Y | Y | Y | Y | N | Y | | DeMint | N | N | N | Y | Y | Y | N |
| **KANSAS** | | | | | | | | | **SOUTH DAKOTA** | | | | | | | |
| Brownback | N | N | N | Y | Y | Y | N | | Johnson | Y | Y | Y | Y | Y | N | Y |
| Roberts | N | N | N | Y | Y | Y | N | | Thune | N | N | N | Y | Y | Y | N |
| **KENTUCKY** | | | | | | | | | **TENNESSEE** | | | | | | | |
| McConnell | N | N | N | Y | Y | Y | N | | Frist | N | N | N | N | Y | Y | N |
| Bunning | N | N | N | Y | N | Y | N | | Alexander | N | N | N | N | Y | Y | N |
| **LOUISIANA** | | | | | | | | | **TEXAS** | | | | | | | |
| Landrieu | Y | Y | Y | Y | Y | Y | Y | | Hutchison | N | N | N | Y | Y | Y | N |
| Vitter | N | N | N | Y | Y | Y | N | | Cornyn | N | N | ? | Y | Y | Y | N |
| **MAINE** | | | | | | | | | **UTAH** | | | | | | | |
| Snowe | N | N | N | Y | Y | N | Y | | Hatch | N | N | N | Y | Y | Y | N |
| Collins | N | N | N | Y | Y | Y | N | | Bennett | N | N | N | Y | Y | Y | N |
| **MARYLAND** | | | | | | | | | **VERMONT** | | | | | | | |
| Sarbanes | Y | Y | Y | Y | Y | N | Y | | Leahy | Y | Y | Y | Y | Y | N | Y |
| Mikulski | Y | Y | Y | Y | Y | N | Y | | *Jeffords* | Y | Y | Y | Y | Y | N | Y |
| **MASSACHUSETTS** | | | | | | | | | **VIRGINIA** | | | | | | | |
| Kennedy | Y | Y | Y | Y | Y | N | Y | | Warner | N | N | N | Y | Y | Y | N |
| Kerry | Y | Y | Y | Y | Y | N | Y | | Allen | N | N | N | Y | Y | Y | N |
| **MICHIGAN** | | | | | | | | | **WASHINGTON** | | | | | | | |
| Levin | Y | Y | Y | Y | Y | N | Y | | Murray | Y | Y | Y | Y | Y | N | Y |
| Stabenow | Y | Y | Y | Y | Y | N | Y | | Cantwell | Y | Y | Y | Y | Y | N | Y |
| **MINNESOTA** | | | | | | | | | **WEST VIRGINIA** | | | | | | | |
| Dayton | Y | Y | Y | Y | Y | N | Y | | Byrd | Y | Y | Y | Y | Y | N | Y |
| Coleman | N | N | N | Y | Y | Y | N | | Rockefeller | Y | Y | Y | Y | Y | N | Y |
| **MISSISSIPPI** | | | | | | | | | **WISCONSIN** | | | | | | | |
| Cochran | N | N | N | Y | Y | Y | N | | Kohl | Y | Y | Y | Y | Y | N | Y |
| Lott | N | N | N | Y | Y | Y | N | | Feingold | Y | Y | Y | Y | Y | N | Y |
| **MISSOURI** | | | | | | | | | **WYOMING** | | | | | | | |
| Bond | N | N | N | Y | Y | Y | N | | Thomas | N | N | N | Y | Y | Y | N |
| Talent | N | N | N | Y | Y | Y | N | | Enzi | N | N | N | N | Y | Y | N |

**KEY**  Republicans  Democrats  *Independents*

| | | | |
|---|---|---|---|
| Y | Voted for (yea) | X | Paired against | C | Voted "present" to avoid possible conflict of interest |
| # | Paired for | – | Announced against | | |
| + | Announced for | P | Voted "present" | ? | Did not vote or otherwise make a position known |
| N | Voted against (nay) | | | | |

# IN THE SENATE | By Vote Number

**76.** **S Con Res 18. Fiscal 2006 Budget Resolution/Debt Limit.**
Lautenberg, D-N.J., amendment that would strike reconciliation instructions in the budget related to the debt limit. Rejected 45-54: R 1-53; D 43-1 (ND 39-1, SD 4-0); I 1-0. March 17, 2005.

**77.** **S Con Res 18. Fiscal 2006 Budget Resolution/News Packages.** Boxer, D-Calif., amendment that would establish a point of order in the Senate against any appropriations bill if it allows funds to be provided for "prepackaged news stories" that do not have a disclaimer stating "Paid for by the United States Government" running throughout the presentation. Rejected 44-54: R 0-54; D 43-0 (ND 39-0, SD 4-0); I 1-0. March 17, 2005.

**78.** **S Con Res 18. Fiscal 2006 Budget Resolution/Tribal Program Funding.** Dorgan, D-N.D., amendment that would decrease the five-year tax cut reconciliation instruction figure by $3.2 billion and increase the discretionary spending limit in the budget by $1 billion. The funds would be used to increase spending for tribal programs and reduce the deficit. Rejected 45-55: R 0-55; D 44-0 (ND 40-0, SD 4-0); I 1-0. March 17, 2005.

**79.** **S Con Res 18. Fiscal 2006 Budget Resolution/Special Education Funding.** Dayton, D-Minn., amendment that would create a reserve fund that would provide $71.3 billion for special education programs under the Individuals with Disabilities Education Act. It would be offset by a $73.8 billion cut in the five-year tax cut reconciliation instruction figure. It also would reduce the deficit by $2.5 billion. Rejected 37-63: R 1-54; D 35-9 (ND 32-8, SD 3-1); I 1-0. March 17, 2005.

**80.** **S Con Res 18. Fiscal 2006 Budget Resolution/Technology Funding.** Levin, D-Mich., amendment that would express the sense of the Senate that the Appropriations Committee should make every effort to provide funding for the Advanced Technology Program in fiscal 2006. Adopted 53-46: R 9-45; D 43-1 (ND 39-1, SD 4-0); I 1-0. March 17, 2005.

**81.** **S Con Res 18. Fiscal 2006 Budget Resolution/Adoption.** Adoption of the concurrent resolution that would set broad spending and revenue targets over the next five years. The resolution would allow up to $848.8 billion in discretionary spending for fiscal 2006 and call for $17 billion in cuts in mandatory spending over five years. It also would give procedural protection to legislation authorizing oil drilling in part of the Arctic National Wildlife Refuge (ANWR) in Alaska. Adopted 51-49: R 51-4; D 0-44 (ND 0-40, SD 0-4); I 0-1. March 17, 2005.

| State / Senator | 76 | 77 | 78 | 79 | 80 | 81 |
|---|---|---|---|---|---|---|
| **ALABAMA** | | | | | | |
| Shelby | N | N | N | N | Y | Y |
| Sessions | N | N | N | N | N | Y |
| **ALASKA** | | | | | | |
| Stevens | N | N | N | N | N | Y |
| Murkowski | N | N | N | N | N | Y |
| **ARIZONA** | | | | | | |
| McCain | Y | N | N | N | N | Y |
| Kyl | N | N | N | N | N | Y |
| **ARKANSAS** | | | | | | |
| Lincoln | Y | Y | Y | Y | Y | N |
| Pryor | Y | Y | Y | Y | Y | N |
| **CALIFORNIA** | | | | | | |
| Feinstein | Y | Y | Y | Y | Y | N |
| Boxer | Y | Y | Y | Y | Y | N |
| **COLORADO** | | | | | | |
| Allard | N | N | N | N | N | Y |
| Salazar | Y | Y | Y | N | Y | N |
| **CONNECTICUT** | | | | | | |
| Dodd | Y | Y | Y | Y | Y | N |
| Lieberman | Y | Y | Y | Y | Y | N |
| **DELAWARE** | | | | | | |
| Biden | Y | Y | Y | Y | Y | N |
| Carper | Y | Y | Y | N | Y | N |
| **FLORIDA** | | | | | | |
| Nelson | Y | Y | Y | N | Y | N |
| Martinez | N | N | N | N | N | Y |
| **GEORGIA** | | | | | | |
| Chambliss | ? | N | N | N | N | Y |
| Isakson | N | N | N | N | N | Y |
| **HAWAII** | | | | | | |
| Inouye | Y | Y | Y | Y | Y | N |
| Akaka | Y | Y | Y | Y | Y | N |
| **IDAHO** | | | | | | |
| Craig | N | N | N | N | N | Y |
| Crapo | N | N | N | N | N | Y |
| **ILLINOIS** | | | | | | |
| Durbin | Y | Y | Y | Y | Y | N |
| Obama | Y | Y | Y | Y | Y | N |
| **INDIANA** | | | | | | |
| Lugar | N | N | N | N | N | Y |
| Bayh | Y | Y | Y | Y | Y | N |
| **IOWA** | | | | | | |
| Grassley | N | N | N | N | N | Y |
| Harkin | Y | Y | Y | Y | Y | N |
| **KANSAS** | | | | | | |
| Brownback | N | N | N | N | N | Y |
| Roberts | N | N | N | N | N | Y |
| **KENTUCKY** | | | | | | |
| McConnell | N | N | N | N | N | Y |
| Bunning | N | N | N | N | N | Y |
| **LOUISIANA** | | | | | | |
| Landrieu | Y | Y | Y | Y | Y | N |
| Vitter | N | N | N | N | N | Y |
| **MAINE** | | | | | | |
| Snowe | N | N | N | N | Y | N |
| Collins | N | N | N | N | N | N |
| **MARYLAND** | | | | | | |
| Sarbanes | Y | Y | Y | Y | Y | N |
| Mikulski | Y | Y | Y | Y | Y | N |
| **MASSACHUSETTS** | | | | | | |
| Kennedy | Y | Y | Y | Y | Y | N |
| Kerry | Y | Y | Y | Y | Y | N |
| **MICHIGAN** | | | | | | |
| Levin | Y | Y | Y | Y | Y | N |
| Stabenow | Y | Y | Y | Y | Y | N |
| **MINNESOTA** | | | | | | |
| Dayton | Y | Y | Y | Y | Y | N |
| Coleman | N | N | N | N | Y | Y |
| **MISSISSIPPI** | | | | | | |
| Cochran | N | N | N | N | N | Y |
| Lott | N | N | N | N | N | Y |
| **MISSOURI** | | | | | | |
| Bond | N | N | N | N | N | Y |
| Talent | N | N | N | N | N | Y |
| **MONTANA** | | | | | | |
| Baucus | Y | Y | Y | Y | Y | N |
| Burns | N | ? | N | N | N | Y |
| **NEBRASKA** | | | | | | |
| Hagel | N | N | N | N | N | Y |
| Nelson | N | Y | Y | Y | Y | N |
| **NEVADA** | | | | | | |
| Reid | Y | Y | Y | Y | Y | N |
| Ensign | N | N | N | N | N | Y |
| **NEW HAMPSHIRE** | | | | | | |
| Gregg | N | N | N | N | N | Y |
| Sununu | N | N | N | N | N | Y |
| **NEW JERSEY** | | | | | | |
| Corzine | Y | Y | Y | Y | Y | N |
| Lautenberg | Y | Y | Y | Y | Y | N |
| **NEW MEXICO** | | | | | | |
| Domenici | N | N | N | N | N | Y |
| Bingaman | Y | Y | Y | N | Y | N |
| **NEW YORK** | | | | | | |
| Schumer | Y | Y | Y | Y | Y | N |
| Clinton | Y | ? | Y | Y | Y | N |
| **NORTH CAROLINA** | | | | | | |
| Dole | N | N | N | N | N | Y |
| Burr | N | N | N | N | N | Y |
| **NORTH DAKOTA** | | | | | | |
| Conrad | Y | Y | Y | N | Y | N |
| Dorgan | Y | Y | Y | N | Y | N |
| **OHIO** | | | | | | |
| DeWine | N | N | N | N | N | Y |
| Voinovich | N | N | N | N | Y | N |
| **OKLAHOMA** | | | | | | |
| Inhofe | N | N | N | N | N | Y |
| Coburn | N | N | N | N | N | Y |
| **OREGON** | | | | | | |
| Wyden | Y | Y | Y | Y | Y | N |
| Smith | N | N | N | N | N | Y |
| **PENNSYLVANIA** | | | | | | |
| Specter | N | N | N | N | Y | Y |
| Santorum | N | N | N | N | ? | Y |
| **RHODE ISLAND** | | | | | | |
| Reed | Y | Y | Y | Y | Y | N |
| Chafee | N | N | N | Y | N | N |
| **SOUTH CAROLINA** | | | | | | |
| Graham | N | N | N | N | N | Y |
| DeMint | N | N | N | N | N | Y |
| **SOUTH DAKOTA** | | | | | | |
| Johnson | Y | Y | Y | N | Y | N |
| Thune | N | N | N | N | N | Y |
| **TENNESSEE** | | | | | | |
| Frist | N | N | N | N | N | Y |
| Alexander | N | N | N | N | N | Y |
| **TEXAS** | | | | | | |
| Hutchison | N | N | N | N | Y | Y |
| Cornyn | N | N | N | N | N | Y |
| **UTAH** | | | | | | |
| Hatch | N | N | N | N | N | Y |
| Bennett | N | N | N | N | N | Y |
| **VERMONT** | | | | | | |
| Leahy | Y | Y | Y | Y | Y | N |
| Jeffords | Y | Y | Y | Y | Y | N |
| **VIRGINIA** | | | | | | |
| Warner | N | N | N | N | Y | Y |
| Allen | N | N | N | N | Y | Y |
| **WASHINGTON** | | | | | | |
| Murray | Y | Y | Y | Y | Y | N |
| Cantwell | Y | Y | Y | Y | Y | N |
| **WEST VIRGINIA** | | | | | | |
| Byrd | Y | Y | Y | Y | Y | N |
| Rockefeller | Y | Y | Y | Y | Y | N |
| **WISCONSIN** | | | | | | |
| Kohl | Y | Y | Y | N | Y | N |
| Feingold | Y | Y | Y | N | N | N |
| **WYOMING** | | | | | | |
| Thomas | N | N | N | N | N | Y |
| Enzi | N | N | N | N | N | Y |

**KEY**   Republicans   Democrats   *Independents*

| | | |
|---|---|---|
| **Y** Voted for (yea) | **X** Paired against | **C** Voted "present" to avoid possible conflict of interest |
| **#** Paired for | **–** Announced against | |
| **+** Announced for | **P** Voted "present" | **?** Did not vote or otherwise make a position known |
| **N** Voted against (nay) | | |

ND Northern Democrats, SD Southern Democrats
Southern states: Ala., Ark., Fla., Ga., Ky., La., Miss., N.C., Okla., S.C., Tenn., Texas, Va.

# IN THE SENATE | By Vote Number

**82.** **S Res 95. Pope John Paul II Tribute/Adoption.** Adoption of the resolution that would pay tribute to Pope John Paul II, who died April 2, 2005, and state that the Congress joins the world in mourning his death. Adopted 98-0: R 54-0; D 43-0 (ND 39-0, SD 4-0); I 1-0. April 5, 2005.

**83.** **S 600. Fiscal 2006 State Department Authorization/"Mexico City" Policy.** Boxer, D-Calif., amendment that would repeal the "Mexico City" policy, which bars U.S. aid to international family planning organizations that perform or promote abortions, even if they use their own funds to do so. Under the amendment, organizations could receive U.S. aid if they used their own funds to provide health or medical services that do not violate federal law or the laws of the country in which they are being provided. Adopted 52-46: R 8-46; D 43-0 (ND 39-0, SD 4-0); I 1-0. A "nay" was a vote in support of the president's position. April 5, 2005.

**84.** **S 600. Fiscal 2006 State Department Authorization/U.N. Peacekeepers.** Biden, D-Del., amendment to the Lugar, R-Ind., amendment. The Biden amendment would cap U.S. contributions for U.N. peacekeeping at 27.1 percent for calendar year 2005 through 2007. The Lugar amendment would delete a permanent 27.1 percent cap provided in the bill. Rejected 40-57: R 0-54; D 39-3 (ND 35-3, SD 4-0); I 1-0. (Subsequently, the Lugar amendment was adopted by voice vote.) A "nay" was a vote in support of the president's position. April 6, 2005.

**85.** **S 600. Fiscal 2006 State Department Authorization/Television Broadcasting to Cuba.** Lugar, R-Ind., motion to table (kill) the Dorgan, D-N.D., amendment that would reduce funding for international broadcasting operations from $641 million to $620 million in fiscal 2006 and prohibit the use of funds for television broadcasts to Cuba. It also would bar broadcasting capital improvement funds for this purpose. Motion agreed to 65-35: R 53-2; D 12-32 (ND 11-29, SD 1-3); I 0-1. April 6, 2005.

**86.** **S 600. Fiscal 2006 State Department Authorization/Tariffs on Chinese Imports.** Lugar, R-Ind., motion to table (kill) the Schumer, D-N.Y., amendment that would impose a 27.5 percent duty on Chinese imports 180 days after enactment of the bill if China does not allow its currency to appreciate relative to the value of the U.S dollar. It would allow the president to delay implementation of the tariffs and permit their removal if he certified that China had agreed to revalue its currency upward to at, or near, fair market value. Motion rejected 33-67: R 26-29; D 7-37 (ND 7-33, SD 0-4); I 0-1. April 6, 2005.

ND Northern Democrats, SD Southern Democrats
Southern states: Ala., Ark., Fla., Ga., Ky., La., Miss., N.C., Okla., S.C., Tenn., Texas, Va.

| | 82 | 83 | 84 | 85 | 86 |
|---|---|---|---|---|---|
| **ALABAMA** | | | | | |
| Shelby | Y | N | N | Y | N |
| Sessions | Y | N | N | Y | N |
| **ALASKA** | | | | | |
| Stevens | Y | Y | N | Y | Y |
| Murkowski | Y | Y | N | Y | Y |
| **ARIZONA** | | | | | |
| McCain | Y | N | N | Y | Y |
| Kyl | Y | N | N | Y | Y |
| **ARKANSAS** | | | | | |
| Lincoln | Y | Y | Y | N | N |
| Pryor | Y | Y | Y | N | N |
| **CALIFORNIA** | | | | | |
| Feinstein | Y | Y | Y | N | Y |
| Boxer | Y | Y | Y | N | N |
| **COLORADO** | | | | | |
| Allard | ? | ? | N | Y | Y |
| Salazar | Y | Y | Y | Y | N |
| **CONNECTICUT** | | | | | |
| Dodd | Y | Y | Y | N | N |
| Lieberman | Y | Y | Y | N | N |
| **DELAWARE** | | | | | |
| Biden | Y | Y | Y | N | N |
| Carper | Y | Y | Y | N | Y |
| **FLORIDA** | | | | | |
| Nelson | Y | Y | Y | Y | N |
| Martinez | Y | N | N | Y | N |
| **GEORGIA** | | | | | |
| Chambliss | Y | N | N | Y | N |
| Isakson | Y | N | N | Y | N |
| **HAWAII** | | | | | |
| Inouye | Y | Y | Y | N | N |
| Akaka | Y | Y | Y | N | N |
| **IDAHO** | | | | | |
| Craig | Y | N | N | Y | N |
| Crapo | Y | N | ? | Y | N |
| **ILLINOIS** | | | | | |
| Durbin | Y | Y | Y | N | N |
| Obama | Y | Y | Y | N | N |
| **INDIANA** | | | | | |
| Lugar | Y | N | N | Y | Y |
| Bayh | Y | Y | Y | Y | N |
| **IOWA** | | | | | |
| Grassley | Y | N | N | Y | Y |
| Harkin | Y | Y | Y | N | N |
| **KANSAS** | | | | | |
| Brownback | Y | N | N | Y | Y |
| Roberts | Y | N | N | Y | Y |
| **KENTUCKY** | | | | | |
| McConnell | Y | N | N | Y | Y |
| Bunning | Y | N | N | Y | N |
| **LOUISIANA** | | | | | |
| Landrieu | Y | Y | Y | N | N |
| Vitter | Y | N | N | Y | N |
| **MAINE** | | | | | |
| Snowe | Y | Y | N | Y | N |
| Collins | Y | Y | N | Y | Y |
| **MARYLAND** | | | | | |
| Sarbanes | Y | Y | Y | Y | N |
| Mikulski | Y | Y | Y | N | N |
| **MASSACHUSETTS** | | | | | |
| Kennedy | ? | ? | Y | N | N |
| Kerry | Y | Y | Y | Y | N |
| **MICHIGAN** | | | | | |
| Levin | Y | Y | Y | N | N |
| Stabenow | Y | Y | Y | N | N |
| **MINNESOTA** | | | | | |
| Dayton | Y | Y | ? | N | N |
| Coleman | Y | N | N | Y | Y |
| **MISSISSIPPI** | | | | | |
| Cochran | Y | N | N | Y | Y |
| Lott | Y | N | N | Y | Y |
| **MISSOURI** | | | | | |
| Bond | Y | N | N | Y | Y |
| Talent | Y | N | N | Y | N |

| | 82 | 83 | 84 | 85 | 86 |
|---|---|---|---|---|---|
| **NTANA** | | | | | |
| Baucus | Y | Y | N | N | Y |
| Burns | Y | N | N | Y | Y |
| **NEBRASKA** | | | | | |
| Hagel | Y | N | N | Y | Y |
| Nelson | Y | Y | N | Y | Y |
| **NEVADA** | | | | | |
| Reid | Y | Y | Y | Y | N |
| Ensign | Y | N | N | Y | Y |
| **NEW HAMPSHIRE** | | | | | |
| Gregg | Y | N | N | Y | Y |
| Sununu | Y | N | N | N | Y |
| **NEW JERSEY** | | | | | |
| Corzine | Y | Y | Y | N | N |
| Lautenberg | Y | Y | Y | Y | N |
| **NEW MEXICO** | | | | | |
| Domenici | Y | N | N | Y | N |
| Bingaman | Y | Y | Y | N | N |
| **NEW YORK** | | | | | |
| Schumer | Y | Y | Y | Y | N |
| Clinton | Y | Y | Y | Y | N |
| **NORTH CAROLINA** | | | | | |
| Dole | Y | N | N | Y | N |
| Burr | Y | N | N | Y | N |
| **NORTH DAKOTA** | | | | | |
| Conrad | Y | Y | Y | N | N |
| Dorgan | Y | Y | Y | N | N |
| **OHIO** | | | | | |
| DeWine | Y | N | N | Y | N |
| Voinovich | Y | N | N | Y | N |
| **OKLAHOMA** | | | | | |
| Inhofe | Y | N | N | Y | N |
| Coburn | Y | N | N | Y | N |
| **OREGON** | | | | | |
| Wyden | Y | Y | Y | N | Y |
| Smith | Y | Y | Y | Y | Y |
| **PENNSYLVANIA** | | | | | |
| Specter | Y | Y | N | Y | N |
| Santorum | Y | N | N | Y | N |
| **RHODE ISLAND** | | | | | |
| Reed | Y | Y | Y | N | N |
| Chafee | Y | Y | N | Y | Y |
| **SOUTH CAROLINA** | | | | | |
| Graham | Y | N | N | Y | Y |
| DeMint | Y | N | N | Y | Y |
| **SOUTH DAKOTA** | | | | | |
| Johnson | Y | Y | Y | N | N |
| Thune | Y | N | N | Y | N |
| **TENNESSEE** | | | | | |
| Frist | Y | N | N | Y | Y |
| Alexander | Y | N | N | Y | Y |
| **TEXAS** | | | | | |
| Hutchison | Y | N | N | Y | N |
| Cornyn | Y | N | N | Y | N |
| **UTAH** | | | | | |
| Hatch | Y | N | N | Y | N |
| Bennett | Y | N | N | Y | N |
| **VERMONT** | | | | | |
| Leahy | Y | Y | Y | N | N |
| *Jeffords* | Y | Y | Y | N | N |
| **VIRGINIA** | | | | | |
| Warner | Y | Y | N | Y | N |
| Allen | Y | N | N | Y | N |
| **WASHINGTON** | | | | | |
| Murray | Y | Y | Y | N | Y |
| Cantwell | Y | Y | Y | N | Y |
| **WEST VIRGINIA** | | | | | |
| Byrd | Y | Y | N | N | N |
| Rockefeller | Y | Y | ? | N | N |
| **WISCONSIN** | | | | | |
| Kohl | Y | Y | Y | N | N |
| Feingold | Y | Y | Y | N | N |
| **WYOMING** | | | | | |
| Thomas | Y | N | N | Y | N |
| Enzi | Y | N | N | Y | N |

**KEY**  Republicans  Democrats  *Independents*

| Y | Voted for (yea) | X | Paired against | C | Voted "present" to avoid possible conflict of interest |
|---|---|---|---|---|---|
| # | Paired for | – | Announced against | | |
| + | Announced for | P | Voted "present" | ? | Did not vote or otherwise make a position known |
| N | Voted against (nay) | | | | |

# IN THE SENATE | By Vote Number

**87. Crotty Nomination/Confirmation.** Confirmation of President Bush's nomination of Paul A. Crotty of New York to be U.S. district judge for the Southern District of New York. Confirmed 95-0: R 53-0; D 41-0 (ND 37-0, SD 4-0); I 1-0. A "yea" was a vote in support of the president's position. April 11, 2005.

**88. S Con Res 25. Airbus Subsidies/Adoption.** Adoption of the concurrent resolution that would express the sense of the Congress that European governments should reject a pending launch aid application by the airplane manufacturer Airbus for the A350 aircraft and any future models. It also would urge the U.S. Trade Representative to request a World Trade Organization dispute resolution panel if no immediate agreement is reached and if there is no progress toward a comprehensive bilateral agreement covering all government subsidies of the large aircraft sector. Adopted 96-0: R 53-0; D 42-0 (ND 38-0, SD 4-0); I 1-0. April 11, 2005.

**89. HR 1268. Fiscal 2005 Supplemental Appropriations/Veterans' Health Care Funding.** Murray, D-Wash., motion to waive the Budget Act with respect to the Cochran, R-Miss., point of order against the Murray amendment. The Murray amendment would increase funding for the Veterans Affairs Department by $1.98 billion and designate it as emergency spending. It would stipulate that $840 million be used for veterans' regional health networks; $610 million be used to address the needs of service members deployed in Iraq and Afghanistan; and $525 million be used to provide mental health care and treatment. Motion rejected 46-54: R 1-54; D 44-0 (ND 40-0, SD 4-0); I 1-0. A three-fifths majority vote (60) of the total Senate is required to waive the Budget Act. (Subsequently, the chair upheld the point of order, and the emergency designation was stricken.) April 12, 2005.

**90. HR 1268. Fiscal 2005 Supplemental Appropriations/Veterans' Health Care Funding.** Murray, D-Wash., motion to waive the Budget Act with respect to the Cochran, R-Miss., point of order against the Murray amendment, modified to remove the emergency designation. Motion rejected 46-54: R 1-54; D 44-0 (ND 40-0, SD 4-0); I 1-0. A three-fifths majority (60) of the total Senate is required to waive the Budget Act. (Subsequently, the chair upheld the point of order, and the amendment fell.) April 12, 2005.

**91. HR 1268. Fiscal 2005 Supplemental Appropriations/Salary Reimbursement for Federal Employees.** Stevens, R-Alaska, motion to table (kill) the Durbin, D-Ill., amendment that would require that federal employees who take a leave without pay to perform certain services as a member of the uniformed service or the National Guard, be reimbursed for the difference between their salary and the pay and allowances they receive while on duty. Motion rejected 39-61: R 39-16; D 0-44 (ND 0-40, SD 0-4); I 0-1. (Subsequently, the amendment was adopted by voice vote.) April 13, 2005.

| | 87 | 88 | 89 | 90 | 91 |
|---|---|---|---|---|---|
| **ALABAMA** | | | | | |
| Shelby | Y | Y | N | N | Y |
| Sessions | Y | Y | N | N | Y |
| **ALASKA** | | | | | |
| Stevens | Y | Y | N | N | Y |
| Murkowski | ? | ? | N | N | Y |
| **ARIZONA** | | | | | |
| McCain | Y | Y | N | N | Y |
| Kyl | Y | Y | N | N | Y |
| **ARKANSAS** | | | | | |
| Lincoln | Y | Y | Y | Y | N |
| Pryor | Y | Y | Y | Y | N |
| **CALIFORNIA** | | | | | |
| Feinstein | Y | Y | Y | Y | N |
| Boxer | Y | Y | Y | Y | N |
| **COLORADO** | | | | | |
| Allard | Y | Y | N | N | Y |
| Salazar | Y | Y | Y | Y | N |
| **CONNECTICUT** | | | | | |
| Dodd | Y | Y | Y | Y | N |
| Lieberman | Y | Y | Y | Y | N |
| **DELAWARE** | | | | | |
| Biden | Y | Y | Y | Y | N |
| Carper | Y | Y | Y | Y | N |
| **FLORIDA** | | | | | |
| Nelson | Y | Y | Y | Y | N |
| Martinez | Y | Y | N | N | Y |
| **GEORGIA** | | | | | |
| Chambliss | Y | Y | N | N | Y |
| Isakson | Y | Y | N | N | Y |
| **HAWAII** | | | | | |
| Inouye | Y | Y | Y | Y | N |
| Akaka | Y | Y | Y | Y | N |
| **IDAHO** | | | | | |
| Craig | Y | Y | N | N | Y |
| Crapo | Y | Y | N | N | Y |
| **ILLINOIS** | | | | | |
| Durbin | Y | Y | Y | Y | N |
| Obama | Y | Y | Y | Y | N |
| **INDIANA** | | | | | |
| Lugar | Y | Y | N | N | Y |
| Bayh | Y | Y | Y | Y | N |
| **IOWA** | | | | | |
| Grassley | Y | Y | N | N | Y |
| Harkin | ? | ? | Y | Y | N |
| **KANSAS** | | | | | |
| Brownback | Y | Y | N | N | Y |
| Roberts | Y | Y | N | N | N |
| **KENTUCKY** | | | | | |
| McConnell | Y | Y | N | N | Y |
| Bunning | Y | Y | N | N | Y |
| **LOUISIANA** | | | | | |
| Landrieu | Y | Y | Y | Y | N |
| Vitter | Y | Y | N | N | Y |
| **MAINE** | | | | | |
| Snowe | Y | Y | N | N | N |
| Collins | Y | Y | N | N | N |
| **MARYLAND** | | | | | |
| Sarbanes | Y | Y | Y | Y | N |
| Mikulski | Y | Y | Y | Y | N |
| **MASSACHUSETTS** | | | | | |
| Kennedy | Y | Y | Y | Y | N |
| Kerry | Y | Y | Y | Y | N |
| **MICHIGAN** | | | | | |
| Levin | Y | Y | Y | Y | N |
| Stabenow | Y | Y | Y | Y | N |
| **MINNESOTA** | | | | | |
| Dayton | Y | Y | Y | Y | N |
| Coleman | Y | Y | N | N | N |
| **MISSISSIPPI** | | | | | |
| Cochran | Y | Y | N | N | Y |
| Lott | Y | Y | N | N | Y |
| **MISSOURI** | | | | | |
| Bond | Y | Y | N | N | Y |
| Talent | Y | Y | N | N | Y |
| **MONTANA** | | | | | |
| Baucus | Y | Y | Y | Y | N |
| Burns | Y | Y | N | N | Y |
| **NEBRASKA** | | | | | |
| Hagel | Y | Y | N | N | Y |
| Nelson | Y | Y | Y | Y | N |
| **NEVADA** | | | | | |
| Reid | Y | Y | Y | Y | N |
| Ensign | Y | Y | N | N | Y |
| **NEW HAMPSHIRE** | | | | | |
| Gregg | Y | Y | N | N | Y |
| Sununu | Y | Y | N | N | Y |
| **NEW JERSEY** | | | | | |
| Corzine | Y | Y | Y | Y | N |
| Lautenberg | ? | ? | Y | Y | N |
| **NEW MEXICO** | | | | | |
| Domenici | Y | Y | N | N | N |
| Bingaman | Y | Y | Y | Y | N |
| **NEW YORK** | | | | | |
| Schumer | Y | Y | Y | Y | N |
| Clinton | Y | Y | Y | Y | N |
| **NORTH CAROLINA** | | | | | |
| Dole | Y | Y | N | N | N |
| Burr | Y | Y | N | N | Y |
| **NORTH DAKOTA** | | | | | |
| Conrad | Y | Y | Y | Y | N |
| Dorgan | + | Y | Y | Y | N |
| **OHIO** | | | | | |
| DeWine | Y | Y | N | N | N |
| Voinovich | Y | Y | N | N | Y |
| **OKLAHOMA** | | | | | |
| Inhofe | Y | Y | N | N | Y |
| Coburn | Y | Y | N | N | Y |
| **OREGON** | | | | | |
| Wyden | Y | Y | Y | Y | N |
| Smith | Y | Y | N | N | Y |
| **PENNSYLVANIA** | | | | | |
| Specter | Y | Y | Y | Y | N |
| Santorum | Y | Y | N | N | Y |
| **RHODE ISLAND** | | | | | |
| Reed | Y | Y | Y | Y | N |
| Chafee | Y | Y | N | N | N |
| **SOUTH CAROLINA** | | | | | |
| Graham | Y | Y | N | N | Y |
| DeMint | Y | Y | N | N | Y |
| **SOUTH DAKOTA** | | | | | |
| Johnson | Y | Y | Y | Y | N |
| Thune | Y | Y | N | N | Y |
| **TENNESSEE** | | | | | |
| Frist | Y | Y | N | N | Y |
| Alexander | Y | Y | N | N | N |
| **TEXAS** | | | | | |
| Hutchison | Y | Y | N | N | N |
| Cornyn | Y | Y | N | N | N |
| **UTAH** | | | | | |
| Hatch | Y | Y | N | N | Y |
| Bennett | Y | Y | N | N | Y |
| **VERMONT** | | | | | |
| Leahy | Y | Y | Y | Y | N |
| Jeffords | Y | Y | Y | Y | N |
| **VIRGINIA** | | | | | |
| Warner | Y | Y | N | N | N |
| Allen | Y | Y | N | N | N |
| **WASHINGTON** | | | | | |
| Murray | Y | Y | Y | Y | N |
| Cantwell | Y | Y | Y | Y | N |
| **WEST VIRGINIA** | | | | | |
| Byrd | Y | Y | Y | Y | N |
| Rockefeller | Y | Y | Y | Y | N |
| **WISCONSIN** | | | | | |
| Kohl | Y | Y | Y | Y | N |
| Feingold | Y | Y | Y | Y | N |
| **WYOMING** | | | | | |
| Thomas | Y | Y | N | N | N |
| Enzi | ? | ? | N | N | N |

**KEY** — Republicans — Democrats — *Independents*

| | | |
|---|---|---|
| Y Voted for (yea) | X Paired against | C Voted "present" to avoid possible conflict of interest |
| # Paired for | − Announced against | |
| + Announced for | P Voted "present" | ? Did not vote or otherwise make a position known |
| N Voted against (nay) | | |

ND Northern Democrats, SD Southern Democrats
Southern states: Ala., Ark., Fla., Ga., Ky., La., Miss., N.C., Okla., S.C., Tenn., Texas, Va.

# IN THE SENATE | By Vote Number

**92.** **HR 1268. Fiscal 2005 Supplemental Appropriations/Military Death Benefits.** Stevens, R-Alaska, motion to table (kill) the Kerry, D-Mass., amendment that would increase the military death benefit from $12,420 to $100,000 for all military members who died on active duty on or after Oct. 7, 2001, not just those serving in combat. Motion rejected 25-75: R 25-30; D 0-44 (ND 0-40, SD 0-4); I 0-1. (Subsequently, the amendment was adopted by voice vote.) April 13, 2005.

**93.** **HR 1268. Fiscal 2005 Supplemental Appropriations/Prison Construction.** Byrd, D-W.Va., amendment that would delete $36 million from the bill's appropriation for military construction earmarked to pay for a new maximum security prison at Guantánamo, Cuba. Rejected 27-71: R 1-54; D 25-17 (ND 23-15, SD 2-2); I 1-0. April 13, 2005.

**94.** **HR 1268. Fiscal 2005 Supplemental Appropriations/Immigration Debate.** Cornyn, R-Texas, amendment that would express the sense of the Senate that Congress should not delay enactment of the supplemental appropriations bill by conducting a debate about immigration overhaul while the measure is pending on the Senate floor. Adopted 61-38: R 48-7; D 13-30 (ND 10-29, SD 3-1); I 0-1. April 13, 2005.

**95.** **HR 1268. Fiscal 2005 Supplemental Appropriations/News Packages.** Byrd, D-W.Va., amendment that would prohibit a federal agency, unless otherwise authorized by existing law, to use funds in the bill or any other act to produce a "prepackaged news" story, unless it includes a clear notification within the text or audio that it was prepared or funded by that agency. Adopted 98-0: R 54-0; D 43-0 (ND 39-0, SD 4-0); I 1-0. April 14, 2005.

| | 92 | 93 | 94 | 95 | | 92 | 93 | 94 | 95 |
|---|---|---|---|---|---|---|---|---|---|
| **ALABAMA** | | | | | **MONTANA** | | | | |
| **Shelby** | Y | N | Y | Y | Baucus | N | Y | N | Y |
| **Sessions** | Y | N | Y | Y | **Burns** | Y | N | Y | Y |
| **ALASKA** | | | | | **NEBRASKA** | | | | |
| **Stevens** | Y | N | Y | Y | **Hagel** | N | N | Y | Y |
| **Murkowski** | N | N | Y | Y | Nelson | N | N | Y | Y |
| **ARIZONA** | | | | | **NEVADA** | | | | |
| McCain | N | N | Y | Y | Reid | N | Y | Y | Y |
| Kyl | N | N | Y | Y | **Ensign** | N | N | Y | Y |
| **ARKANSAS** | | | | | **NEW HAMPSHIRE** | | | | |
| Lincoln | N | Y | Y | Y | **Gregg** | N | N | Y | Y |
| Pryor | N | Y | Y | Y | **Sununu** | N | N | Y | Y |
| **CALIFORNIA** | | | | | **NEW JERSEY** | | | | |
| Feinstein | N | Y | Y | Y | Corzine | N | N | N | Y |
| Boxer | N | Y | N | Y | Lautenberg | N | Y | N | Y |
| **COLORADO** | | | | | **NEW MEXICO** | | | | |
| **Allard** | Y | N | Y | Y | **Domenici** | Y | N | Y | Y |
| Salazar | N | N | Y | Y | Bingaman | N | N | N | Y |
| **CONNECTICUT** | | | | | **NEW YORK** | | | | |
| Dodd | N | N | N | Y | Schumer | N | N | Y | Y |
| Lieberman | N | N | N | Y | Clinton | N | N | Y | Y |
| **DELAWARE** | | | | | **NORTH CAROLINA** | | | | |
| Biden | N | Y | N | Y | **Dole** | Y | N | Y | Y |
| Carper | N | Y | N | Y | **Burr** | Y | N | Y | Y |
| **FLORIDA** | | | | | **NORTH DAKOTA** | | | | |
| Nelson | N | N | N | Y | Conrad | N | N | N | Y |
| **Martinez** | N | N | Y | Y | Dorgan | N | Y | N | Y |
| **GEORGIA** | | | | | **OHIO** | | | | |
| **Chambliss** | N | N | Y | Y | **DeWine** | N | N | N | Y |
| **Isakson** | N | N | N | Y | **Voinovich** | Y | N | N | Y |
| **HAWAII** | | | | | **OKLAHOMA** | | | | |
| Inouye | N | Y | N | Y | **Inhofe** | Y | N | Y | ? |
| Akaka | N | Y | N | Y | **Coburn** | N | N | Y | Y |
| **IDAHO** | | | | | **OREGON** | | | | |
| **Craig** | N | N | N | Y | Wyden | N | Y | Y | Y |
| **Crapo** | N | N | N | Y | **Smith** | N | N | Y | Y |
| **ILLINOIS** | | | | | **PENNSYLVANIA** | | | | |
| Durbin | N | N | N | Y | **Specter** | N | Y | Y | Y |
| Obama | N | N | N | Y | **Santorum** | Y | N | Y | Y |
| **INDIANA** | | | | | **RHODE ISLAND** | | | | |
| **Lugar** | N | N | Y | Y | Reed | N | Y | N | Y |
| Bayh | N | N | N | Y | **Chafee** | N | N | Y | Y |
| **IOWA** | | | | | **SOUTH CAROLINA** | | | | |
| **Grassley** | Y | N | Y | Y | **Graham** | N | N | Y | Y |
| Harkin | N | Y | N | Y | **DeMint** | Y | N | Y | Y |
| **KANSAS** | | | | | **SOUTH DAKOTA** | | | | |
| **Brownback** | N | N | Y | Y | Johnson | N | Y | N | Y |
| **Roberts** | N | N | Y | Y | **Thune** | N | N | Y | Y |
| **KENTUCKY** | | | | | **TENNESSEE** | | | | |
| **McConnell** | Y | N | Y | Y | **Frist** | Y | N | Y | Y |
| **Bunning** | Y | N | Y | Y | **Alexander** | N | N | Y | Y |
| **LOUISIANA** | | | | | **TEXAS** | | | | |
| Landrieu | N | N | Y | Y | **Hutchison** | N | N | Y | Y |
| **Vitter** | N | N | Y | Y | **Cornyn** | Y | N | Y | Y |
| **MAINE** | | | | | **UTAH** | | | | |
| **Snowe** | N | N | N | Y | **Hatch** | Y | N | Y | Y |
| **Collins** | N | N | Y | Y | **Bennett** | Y | N | Y | Y |
| **MARYLAND** | | | | | **VERMONT** | | | | |
| Sarbanes | N | Y | N | ? | Leahy | N | Y | N | Y |
| Mikulski | N | Y | N | Y | *Jeffords* | N | Y | N | Y |
| **MASSACHUSETTS** | | | | | **VIRGINIA** | | | | |
| Kennedy | N | ? | N | Y | **Warner** | Y | N | N | Y |
| Kerry | N | N | N | Y | **Allen** | N | N | Y | Y |
| **MICHIGAN** | | | | | **WASHINGTON** | | | | |
| Levin | N | Y | N | Y | Murray | N | N | Y | Y |
| Stabenow | N | Y | N | Y | Cantwell | N | N | Y | Y |
| **MINNESOTA** | | | | | **WEST VIRGINIA** | | | | |
| Dayton | N | ? | ? | Y | Byrd | N | Y | Y | Y |
| **Coleman** | N | N | Y | Y | Rockefeller | N | Y | N | Y |
| **MISSISSIPPI** | | | | | **WISCONSIN** | | | | |
| **Cochran** | Y | N | Y | Y | Kohl | N | Y | N | Y |
| **Lott** | Y | N | Y | Y | Feingold | N | Y | N | Y |
| **MISSOURI** | | | | | **WYOMING** | | | | |
| **Bond** | Y | N | Y | Y | **Thomas** | Y | N | Y | Y |
| **Talent** | N | N | Y | Y | **Enzi** | Y | N | Y | Y |

**KEY**      Republicans      Democrats      *Independents*

| | | |
|---|---|---|
| Y    Voted for (yea) | X    Paired against | C    Voted "present" to avoid |
| #    Paired for | –    Announced against | possible conflict of interest |
| +    Announced for | P    Voted "present" | ?    Did not vote or otherwise |
| N    Voted against (nay) | | make a position known |

ND Northern Democrats, SD Southern Democrats
Southern states: Ala., Ark., Fla., Ga., Ky., La., Miss., N.C., Okla., S.C., Tenn., Texas, Va.

# IN THE SENATE | By Vote Number

**96.** HR 1268. Fiscal 2005 Supplemental Appropriations/Overseas **Military Funding.** Byrd, D-W.Va., amendment that would express the sense of the Senate that any funds for ongoing military operations overseas, including those in Afghanistan and Iraq, should be included in the president's annual budget request and urge the president to detail cost estimates for ongoing overseas military operations by Sept. 1, 2005. Adopted 61-31: R 21-31; D 39-0 (ND 36-0, SD 3-0); I 1-0. April 18, 2005.

**97.** HR 1268. Fiscal 2005 Supplemental Appropriations/Cloture. Motion to invoke cloture (thus limiting debate) on the Chambliss, R-Ga., amendment that would create a "blue card" program that would grant foreign workers temporary legal status if an employer could show they unsuccessfully tried to recruit and hire U.S. workers. Motion rejected 21-77: R 19-36; D 2-40 (ND 1-37, SD 1-3); I 0-1. Three-fifths of the total Senate (60) is required to invoke cloture. April 19, 2005.

**98.** HR 1268. Fiscal 2005 Supplemental Appropriations/Cloture. Motion to invoke cloture (thus limiting debate) on the Craig, R-Idaho, amendment that would grant certain agricultural workers who are in the country illegally temporary resident status and put them on the path toward permanent resident status if they meet specified employment and residency requirements. Motion rejected 53-45: R 15-40; D 37-5 (ND 33-5, SD 4-0); I 1-0. Three-fifths of the total Senate (60) is required to invoke cloture. April 19, 2005.

**99.** Procedural Motion/Require Attendance. Frist, R-Tenn., motion to instruct the sergeant at arms to request the attendance of absent senators. Motion agreed to 91-7: R 54-1; D 36-6 (ND 32-6, SD 4-0); I 1-0. April 19, 2005.

**100.** Procedural Motion/Recess. Frist, R-Tenn., motion to recess until 5 p.m. on Tuesday, April 19, 2005. Motion agreed to 56-42: R 55-0; D 1-41 (ND 1-37, SD 0-4); I 0-1. April 19, 2005.

**101.** HR 1268. Fiscal 2005 Supplemental Appropriation/Cloture. Motion to invoke cloture (thus limiting debate) on the Mikulski, D-Md., amendment that would exempt returning seasonal workers from the national H-2B visa cap of 66,000 if they have already successfully participated in the program. Motion agreed to 83-17: R 39-16; D 43-1 (ND 39-1, SD 4-0); I 1-0. Three-fifths of the total Senate (60) is required to invoke cloture. April 19, 2005.

**102.** HR 1268. Fiscal 2005 Supplemental Appropriations/Seasonal **Workers.** Mikulski, D-Md., amendment that would exempt returning seasonal workers from the national H-2B visa cap of 66,000 if they have already successfully participated in the program. It also would require employers to pay an anti-fraud fee of $150 on each H-2B petition and require the Department of Homeland Security to certify that the foreign employee is a returning worker. Adopted 94-6: R 51-4; D 42-2 (ND 39-1, SD 3-1); I 1-0. April 19, 2005.

**103.** HR 1268. Fiscal 2005 Supplemental Appropriations/Cloture. Motion to invoke cloture (thus limiting debate) on the bill that would appropriate $80.7 billion in fiscal 2005 supplemental spending for military operations and reconstruction in Iraq and Afghanistan and for disaster assistance to victims of the December 2004 tsunami in South Asia. Motion agreed to 100-0: R 55-0; D 44-0 (ND 40-0, SD 4-0); I 1-0. April 19, 2005.

ND Northern Democrats, SD Southern Democrats
Southern states: Ala., Ark., Fla., Ga., Ky., La., Miss., N.C., Okla., S.C., Tenn., Texas, Va.

| | 96 | 97 | 98 | 99 | 100 | 101 | 102 | 103 |
|---|---|---|---|---|---|---|---|---|
| **ALABAMA** | | | | | | | | |
| Shelby | N | N | N | Y | Y | N | N | Y |
| Sessions | N | N | N | Y | Y | N | N | Y |
| **ALASKA** | | | | | | | | |
| Stevens | Y | Y | N | Y | Y | Y | Y | Y |
| Murkowski | N | N | N | Y | Y | Y | Y | Y |
| **ARIZONA** | | | | | | | | |
| McCain | Y | N | Y | Y | Y | Y | Y | Y |
| Kyl | N | Y | N | Y | Y | Y | Y | Y |
| **ARKANSAS** | | | | | | | | |
| Lincoln | Y | N | Y | N | Y | N | Y | Y |
| Pryor | Y | N | Y | N | Y | N | Y | Y |
| **CALIFORNIA** | | | | | | | | |
| Feinstein | Y | N | N | Y | Y | Y | Y | Y |
| Boxer | Y | N | Y | N | N | Y | Y | Y |
| **COLORADO** | | | | | | | | |
| Allard | N | Y | N | Y | Y | Y | Y | Y |
| Salazar | Y | Y | Y | N | Y | N | Y | Y |
| **CONNECTICUT** | | | | | | | | |
| Dodd | Y | N | N | N | Y | Y | Y | Y |
| Lieberman | Y | N | Y | N | Y | N | Y | Y |
| **DELAWARE** | | | | | | | | |
| Biden | ? | N | Y | Y | N | Y | Y | Y |
| Carper | Y | N | Y | N | Y | N | Y | Y |
| **FLORIDA** | | | | | | | | |
| Nelson | Y | N | Y | N | Y | N | Y | N |
| Martinez | N | N | Y | Y | Y | Y | Y | Y |
| **GEORGIA** | | | | | | | | |
| Chambliss | N | Y | N | Y | Y | Y | Y | Y |
| Isakson | N | N | N | Y | Y | Y | Y | Y |
| **HAWAII** | | | | | | | | |
| Inouye | Y | N | Y | N | Y | Y | Y | Y |
| Akaka | Y | N | Y | N | Y | N | Y | Y |
| **IDAHO** | | | | | | | | |
| Craig | Y | N | Y | Y | Y | Y | Y | Y |
| Crapo | Y | N | N | Y | Y | Y | Y | Y |
| **ILLINOIS** | | | | | | | | |
| Durbin | ? | ? | ? | ? | ? | Y | Y | Y |
| Obama | ? | ? | ? | ? | ? | Y | Y | Y |
| **INDIANA** | | | | | | | | |
| Lugar | N | N | Y | Y | Y | Y | Y | Y |
| Bayh | Y | N | Y | N | Y | N | Y | Y |
| **IOWA** | | | | | | | | |
| Grassley | N | Y | N | Y | Y | N | Y | Y |
| Harkin | Y | N | Y | N | Y | N | Y | Y |
| **KANSAS** | | | | | | | | |
| Brownback | N | N | N | Y | Y | N | Y | Y |
| Roberts | N | N | N | Y | Y | N | Y | Y |
| **KENTUCKY** | | | | | | | | |
| McConnell | ? | N | N | Y | Y | N | Y | Y |
| Bunning | N | N | N | Y | Y | N | Y | Y |
| **LOUISIANA** | | | | | | | | |
| Landrieu | ? | Y | Y | N | Y | N | Y | Y |
| Vitter | N | N | N | Y | Y | N | N | Y |
| **MAINE** | | | | | | | | |
| Snowe | Y | N | Y | Y | Y | Y | Y | Y |
| Collins | Y | Y | N | Y | Y | Y | Y | Y |
| **MARYLAND** | | | | | | | | |
| Sarbanes | Y | N | Y | N | Y | N | Y | Y |
| Mikulski | Y | N | Y | N | N | Y | Y | Y |
| **MASSACHUSETTS** | | | | | | | | |
| Kennedy | Y | N | Y | N | Y | N | Y | Y |
| Kerry | ? | N | Y | N | Y | N | Y | Y |
| **MICHIGAN** | | | | | | | | |
| Levin | Y | N | Y | N | Y | N | Y | Y |
| Stabenow | Y | N | Y | N | Y | N | Y | Y |
| **MINNESOTA** | | | | | | | | |
| Dayton | Y | N | Y | N | Y | N | Y | Y |
| Coleman | Y | N | Y | N | Y | Y | Y | Y |
| **MISSISSIPPI** | | | | | | | | |
| Cochran | N | Y | N | Y | Y | N | Y | Y |
| Lott | N | Y | N | Y | Y | N | Y | Y |
| **MISSOURI** | | | | | | | | |
| Bond | ? | Y | N | Y | Y | Y | Y | Y |
| Talent | Y | N | N | Y | Y | Y | Y | Y |
| **MONTANA** | | | | | | | | |
| Baucus | Y | N | Y | N | N | Y | Y | Y |
| Burns | ? | Y | Y | Y | Y | Y | Y | Y |
| **NEBRASKA** | | | | | | | | |
| Hagel | Y | N | Y | N | Y | Y | Y | Y |
| Nelson | Y | N | Y | N | N | Y | Y | Y |
| **NEVADA** | | | | | | | | |
| Reid | Y | N | Y | N | N | Y | Y | Y |
| Ensign | N | N | N | Y | N | Y | N | Y |
| **NEW HAMPSHIRE** | | | | | | | | |
| Gregg | N | Y | N | Y | Y | Y | Y | Y |
| Sununu | Y | Y | N | Y | Y | Y | Y | Y |
| **NEW JERSEY** | | | | | | | | |
| Corzine | Y | N | Y | N | Y | Y | Y | Y |
| Lautenberg | Y | N | Y | N | Y | N | Y | Y |
| **NEW MEXICO** | | | | | | | | |
| Domenici | N | N | Y | Y | Y | Y | Y | Y |
| Bingaman | Y | N | Y | N | Y | N | Y | Y |
| **NEW YORK** | | | | | | | | |
| Schumer | Y | N | Y | N | Y | Y | Y | Y |
| Clinton | Y | N | Y | N | Y | N | Y | Y |
| **NORTH CAROLINA** | | | | | | | | |
| Dole | N | Y | N | Y | Y | Y | Y | Y |
| Burr | N | Y | N | Y | Y | Y | Y | Y |
| **NORTH DAKOTA** | | | | | | | | |
| Conrad | Y | N | N | Y | N | Y | Y | Y |
| Dorgan | Y | N | N | Y | N | Y | Y | Y |
| **OHIO** | | | | | | | | |
| DeWine | N | N | Y | Y | Y | Y | Y | Y |
| Voinovich | Y | N | Y | Y | Y | Y | Y | Y |
| **OKLAHOMA** | | | | | | | | |
| Inhofe | N | N | N | Y | Y | N | N | Y |
| Coburn | Y | N | N | Y | Y | Y | Y | Y |
| **OREGON** | | | | | | | | |
| Wyden | Y | N | Y | N | Y | Y | Y | Y |
| Smith | Y | N | Y | Y | Y | Y | Y | Y |
| **PENNSYLVANIA** | | | | | | | | |
| Specter | Y | N | Y | Y | Y | Y | Y | Y |
| Santorum | N | Y | N | Y | Y | Y | Y | Y |
| **RHODE ISLAND** | | | | | | | | |
| Reed | Y | N | Y | N | Y | Y | Y | Y |
| Chafee | Y | N | Y | Y | Y | Y | Y | Y |
| **SOUTH CAROLINA** | | | | | | | | |
| Graham | N | Y | N | Y | Y | Y | Y | Y |
| DeMint | N | Y | N | Y | Y | Y | Y | Y |
| **SOUTH DAKOTA** | | | | | | | | |
| Johnson | Y | N | Y | N | Y | Y | Y | Y |
| Thune | Y | N | N | Y | Y | Y | Y | Y |
| **TENNESSEE** | | | | | | | | |
| Frist | N | N | N | Y | Y | N | Y | Y |
| Alexander | N | N | N | Y | Y | N | Y | Y |
| **TEXAS** | | | | | | | | |
| Hutchison | Y | N | N | Y | Y | N | Y | Y |
| Cornyn | N | N | N | Y | Y | N | N | Y |
| **UTAH** | | | | | | | | |
| Hatch | Y | N | Y | Y | Y | Y | Y | Y |
| Bennett | Y | N | Y | Y | Y | Y | Y | Y |
| **VERMONT** | | | | | | | | |
| Leahy | Y | N | Y | N | Y | Y | Y | Y |
| Jeffords | Y | N | Y | N | Y | N | Y | Y |
| **VIRGINIA** | | | | | | | | |
| Warner | Y | Y | Y | Y | Y | Y | Y | Y |
| Allen | Y | N | N | N | Y | Y | Y | Y |
| **WASHINGTON** | | | | | | | | |
| Murray | Y | N | Y | N | Y | Y | Y | Y |
| Cantwell | Y | N | Y | N | Y | N | Y | Y |
| **WEST VIRGINIA** | | | | | | | | |
| Byrd | Y | N | N | N | N | N | N | Y |
| Rockefeller | Y | N | N | Y | N | Y | Y | Y |
| **WISCONSIN** | | | | | | | | |
| Kohl | Y | N | Y | N | Y | Y | Y | Y |
| Feingold | Y | N | Y | N | N | Y | Y | Y |
| **WYOMING** | | | | | | | | |
| Thomas | N | Y | N | Y | Y | Y | Y | Y |
| Enzi | N | N | N | Y | Y | Y | Y | Y |

**KEY**  Republicans  Democrats  *Independents*

| | | |
|---|---|---|
| Y  Voted for (yea) | X  Paired against | C  Voted "present" to avoid possible conflict of interest |
| #  Paired for | –  Announced against | |
| +  Announced for | P  Voted "present" | ?  Did not vote or otherwise make a position known |
| N  Voted against (nay) | | |

# IN THE SENATE | By Vote Number

**104.** HR 1268. Fiscal 2005 Supplemental Appropriations/Iraq Embassy **Funding.** Cochran, R-Miss., motion to table (kill) the Coburn, R-Okla., amendment that would reduce appropriations for the security, construction and maintenance of U.S. embassies from $592 million to $106 million, effectively cutting funding for the construction of a new U.S. embassy in Iraq. Motion agreed to 54-45: R 29-26; D 25-19 (ND 23-17, SD 2-2); I 0-0. A "yea" was a vote in support of the president's position. April 20, 2005.

**105.** HR 1268. Fiscal 2005 Supplemental Appropriations/Border **Security Funding.** Byrd, D-W.Va., amendment that would increase funding for immigration and customs enforcement at the Homeland Security Department by $389.6 million and reduce funding for diplomatic and consular programs at the State Department by $400 million. It would provide for the hiring of additional border patrol agents and fund the operation of unmanned aerial vehicles along the southwest U.S.-Mexico border. Adopted 65-34: R 21-34; D 44-0 (ND 40-0, SD 4-0); I 0-0. April 20, 2005.

**106.** HR 1268. Fiscal 2005 Supplemental Appropriations/Navy Aircraft **Carriers.** Warner, R-Va., amendment that would bar funds appropriated or made available in the bill from being obligated or spent to reduce the number of active Navy aircraft carriers to less than 12 until certain conditions are met. It also would require funding to be made available to the Navy for the repair and maintenance of the *USS John F. Kennedy.* Adopted 58-38: R 24-31; D 34-7 (ND 30-7, SD 4-0); I 0-0. April 20, 2005.

**107.** Negroponte Nomination/Confirmation. Confirmation of President Bush's nomination of John D. Negroponte of New York to be director of national intelligence. Confirmed 98-2: R 55-0; D 42-2 (ND 38-2, SD 4-0); I 1-0. A "yea" was a vote in support of the president's position. April 21, 2005.

**108.** HR 1268. Fiscal 2005 Supplemental Appropriations/Humvees **Funding.** Bayh, D-Ind., amendment that would appropriate an additional $213 million to the army for the procurement of up-armored high mobility multipurpose-wheeled vehicles, known as Humvees. Adopted 61-39: R 17-38; D 43-1 (ND 39-1, SD 4-0); I 1-0. April 21, 2005.

**109.** HR 1268. Fiscal 2005 Supplemental Appropriations/Passage. Passage of the bill that would appropriate $81.3 billion in fiscal 2005 supplemental spending for military operations and reconstruction in Iraq and Afghanistan, and for disaster assistance to victims of the December 2004 tsunami in South Asia. The bill would provide $17.5 billion for military personnel, $37.4 billion for operations and maintenance, and $16.1 billion for procurement. It also would provide $907.3 million for tsunami relief and recovery, and $592 million for the security, construction and maintenance of U.S. embassies, such as one in Iraq. Passed 99-0: R 55-0; D 43-0 (ND 39-0, SD 4-0); I 1-0. April 21, 2005.

| | 104 | 105 | 106 | 107 | 108 | 109 | | | 104 | 105 | 106 | 107 | 108 | 109 |
|---|---|---|---|---|---|---|---|---|---|---|---|---|---|---|
| **ALABAMA** | | | | | | | | **MONTANA** | | | | | | |
| Shelby | Y | N | N | Y | N | Y | | Baucus | Y | Y | Y | Y | Y | Y |
| Sessions | N | Y | N | Y | N | Y | | Burns | Y | N | N | Y | Y | Y |
| **ALASKA** | | | | | | | | **NEBRASKA** | | | | | | |
| Stevens | Y | N | N | Y | N | Y | | Hagel | Y | N | Y | Y | N | Y |
| Murkowski | Y | N | N | Y | N | Y | | Nelson | N | Y | Y | Y | Y | Y |
| **ARIZONA** | | | | | | | | **NEVADA** | | | | | | |
| McCain | Y | N | N | Y | Y | Y | | Reid | Y | Y | Y | Y | Y | Y |
| Kyl | N | Y | N | Y | N | Y | | Ensign | N | Y | Y | Y | N | Y |
| **ARKANSAS** | | | | | | | | **NEW HAMPSHIRE** | | | | | | |
| Lincoln | N | Y | Y | Y | Y | Y | | Gregg | N | Y | N | Y | N | Y |
| Pryor | N | Y | Y | Y | Y | Y | | Sununu | N | Y | N | Y | N | Y |
| **CALIFORNIA** | | | | | | | | **NEW JERSEY** | | | | | | |
| Feinstein | Y | Y | Y | Y | Y | Y | | Corzine | Y | Y | Y | Y | Y | Y |
| Boxer | N | Y | Y | Y | Y | Y | | Lautenberg | Y | Y | Y | Y | Y | Y |
| **COLORADO** | | | | | | | | **NEW MEXICO** | | | | | | |
| Allard | Y | N | N | Y | N | Y | | Domenici | Y | Y | Y | Y | N | Y |
| Salazar | Y | Y | Y | Y | Y | Y | | Bingaman | Y | Y | Y | Y | Y | Y |
| **CONNECTICUT** | | | | | | | | **NEW YORK** | | | | | | |
| Dodd | N | Y | Y | Y | Y | Y | | Schumer | N | Y | N | Y | Y | Y |
| Lieberman | Y | Y | Y | Y | Y | Y | | Clinton | N | Y | Y | Y | Y | Y |
| **DELAWARE** | | | | | | | | **NORTH CAROLINA** | | | | | | |
| Biden | Y | Y | Y | Y | Y | Y | | Dole | Y | N | Y | Y | N | Y |
| Carper | N | Y | Y | Y | Y | Y | | Burr | N | N | Y | Y | N | Y |
| **FLORIDA** | | | | | | | | **NORTH DAKOTA** | | | | | | |
| Nelson | Y | Y | Y | Y | Y | Y | | Conrad | N | Y | ? | Y | Y | Y |
| Martinez | Y | N | Y | Y | Y | Y | | Dorgan | N | Y | N | Y | Y | Y |
| **GEORGIA** | | | | | | | | **OHIO** | | | | | | |
| Chambliss | N | Y | Y | N | N | Y | | DeWine | Y | N | Y | Y | N | Y |
| Isakson | N | Y | Y | N | N | Y | | Voinovich | Y | N | N | Y | N | Y |
| **HAWAII** | | | | | | | | **OKLAHOMA** | | | | | | |
| Inouye | Y | Y | Y | Y | Y | ? | | Inhofe | N | Y | Y | Y | N | Y |
| Akaka | Y | Y | Y | Y | Y | Y | | Coburn | N | Y | Y | Y | N | Y |
| **IDAHO** | | | | | | | | **OREGON** | | | | | | |
| Craig | N | Y | N | Y | N | Y | | Wyden | N | Y | N | Y | Y | Y |
| Crapo | N | Y | N | Y | N | Y | | Smith | Y | N | N | Y | N | Y |
| **ILLINOIS** | | | | | | | | **PENNSYLVANIA** | | | | | | |
| Durbin | Y | Y | Y | Y | Y | Y | | Specter | Y | N | N | Y | Y | Y |
| Obama | N | Y | Y | Y | Y | Y | | Santorum | Y | Y | N | Y | Y | Y |
| **INDIANA** | | | | | | | | **RHODE ISLAND** | | | | | | |
| Lugar | Y | N | N | Y | Y | Y | | Reed | Y | Y | Y | Y | Y | Y |
| Bayh | N | Y | Y | Y | Y | Y | | Chafee | N | N | N | Y | Y | Y |
| **IOWA** | | | | | | | | **SOUTH CAROLINA** | | | | | | |
| Grassley | N | N | N | Y | N | Y | | Graham | N | N | Y | Y | N | Y |
| Harkin | N | Y | Y | N | Y | Y | | DeMint | N | N | N | Y | N | Y |
| **KANSAS** | | | | | | | | **SOUTH DAKOTA** | | | | | | |
| Brownback | N | N | Y | Y | N | Y | | Johnson | Y | Y | Y | Y | Y | Y |
| Roberts | Y | Y | N | Y | N | Y | | Thune | N | Y | Y | Y | Y | Y |
| **KENTUCKY** | | | | | | | | **TENNESSEE** | | | | | | |
| McConnell | Y | N | N | Y | N | Y | | Frist | Y | N | N | Y | N | Y |
| Bunning | N | Y | N | Y | N | Y | | Alexander | Y | N | N | Y | Y | Y |
| **LOUISIANA** | | | | | | | | **TEXAS** | | | | | | |
| Landrieu | Y | Y | Y | Y | Y | Y | | Hutchison | Y | Y | N | Y | Y | Y |
| Vitter | N | Y | Y | Y | N | Y | | Cornyn | N | Y | Y | Y | Y | Y |
| **MAINE** | | | | | | | | **UTAH** | | | | | | |
| Snowe | Y | Y | Y | Y | Y | Y | | Hatch | N | N | Y | Y | N | Y |
| Collins | N | N | Y | Y | Y | Y | | Bennett | Y | N | N | Y | N | Y |
| **MARYLAND** | | | | | | | | **VERMONT** | | | | | | |
| Sarbanes | N | Y | Y | Y | Y | Y | | Leahy | Y | Y | Y | Y | Y | Y |
| Mikulski | Y | Y | Y | Y | Y | Y | | *Jeffords* | ? | ? | ? | Y | Y | Y |
| **MASSACHUSETTS** | | | | | | | | **VIRGINIA** | | | | | | |
| Kennedy | N | Y | ? | Y | Y | Y | | Warner | Y | N | Y | Y | N | Y |
| Kerry | Y | Y | Y | Y | Y | Y | | Allen | Y | N | Y | Y | Y | Y |
| **MICHIGAN** | | | | | | | | **WASHINGTON** | | | | | | |
| Levin | Y | Y | Y | Y | Y | Y | | Murray | Y | Y | Y | Y | Y | Y |
| Stabenow | Y | Y | Y | Y | Y | Y | | Cantwell | Y | Y | Y | Y | Y | Y |
| **MINNESOTA** | | | | | | | | **WEST VIRGINIA** | | | | | | |
| Dayton | Y | Y | Y | Y | Y | Y | | Byrd | N | Y | ? | Y | Y | Y |
| Coleman | Y | N | Y | Y | Y | Y | | Rockefeller | Y | Y | N | Y | Y | Y |
| **MISSISSIPPI** | | | | | | | | **WISCONSIN** | | | | | | |
| Cochran | Y | N | N | Y | N | Y | | Kohl | N | Y | N | Y | Y | Y |
| Lott | N | N | Y | Y | Y | Y | | Feingold | N | Y | N | Y | Y | Y |
| **MISSOURI** | | | | | | | | **WYOMING** | | | | | | |
| Bond | Y | N | N | Y | N | Y | | Thomas | N | N | N | Y | N | Y |
| Talent | Y | Y | Y | Y | Y | Y | | Enzi | N | N | N | Y | N | Y |

**KEY**   Republicans   Democrats   *Independents*

| | | | |
|---|---|---|---|
| Y  Voted for (yea) | X  Paired against | C  Voted "present" to avoid possible conflict of interest |
| #  Paired for | –  Announced against | |
| +  Announced for | P  Voted "present" | ?  Did not vote or otherwise make a position known |
| N  Voted against (nay) | | |

ND Northern Democrats, SD Southern Democrats
Southern states: Ala., Ark., Fla., Ga., Ky., La., Miss., N.C., Okla., S.C., Tenn., Texas, Va.

# IN THE SENATE | By Vote Number

**110.** **HR 3. Surface Transportation Reauthorization/Cloture.** Motion to invoke cloture (thus limiting debate) on the motion to proceed to the bill that would authorize $283.9 billion for federal-aid highway, mass transit, safety and research programs through fiscal 2009. Motion agreed to 94-6: R 49-6; D 44-0 (ND 40-0, SD 4-0); I 1-0. Three-fifths of the total Senate (60) is required to invoke cloture. April 26, 2005.

**111.** **Seabright Nomination/Confirmation.** Confirmation of President Bush's nomination of J. Michael Seabright of Hawaii to be U.S. district judge for the District of Hawaii. Confirmed 98-0: R 55-0; D 42-0 (ND 38-0, SD 4-0); I 1-0. A "yea" was a vote in support of the president's position. April 27, 2005.

**112.** **Procedural Motion/Recess.** Frist, R-Tenn., motion to recess until 2 p.m. on Thursday, April 28, 2005. Motion agreed to 98-1: R 55-0; D 42-1 (ND 38-1, SD 4-0); I 1-0. April, 28, 2005.

**113.** **HR 3. Surface Transportation Reauthorization/Stormwater Mitigation.** Warner, R-Va., motion to table (kill) the Bond, R-Mo., amendment to the Inhofe, R-Okla., substitute amendment. The Bond amendment would strike a section that would require every state to set aside 2 percent of its surface transportation funds and associated equity bonus funding to be used for stormwater mitigation activities. The substitute amendment would authorize $283.9 billion for federal-aid highway, mass transit, safety and research programs through fiscal 2009 and guarantee that every state receives at least 92 cents in funding for every dollar in gas taxes it pays into the Highway Trust Fund. Motion agreed to 51-49: R 9-46; D 41-3 (ND 38-2, SD 3-1); I 1-0. April 28, 2005.

**114.** **H Con Res 95. Fiscal 2006 Budget Resolution/Conference Report.** Adoption of the conference report on the concurrent resolution that would set broad spending and revenue targets for five years, limit discretionary spending to $843 billion in fiscal 2006, and provide instructions for reconciliation bills that would achieve $70 billion in tax cuts and $34.7 billion in savings to mandatory programs, including $10 billion in Medicaid savings. Adopted 52-47: R 52-3; D 0-43 (ND 0-39, SD 0-4); I 0-1. April 28, 2005.

**115.** **Johnson Nomination/Cloture.** Motion to invoke cloture (thus limiting debate) on the nomination of Stephen L. Johnson of Maryland to be the EPA administrator. Motion agreed to 61-37: R 54-0; D 7-36 (ND 6-33, SD 1-3); I 0-1. Three-fifths of the total Senate (60) is required to invoke cloture. (Subsequently, the nomination was confirmed by voice vote.) April 29, 2005 (in the session that began and the Congressional Record dated April 28, 2005).

| | 110 | 111 | 112 | 113 | 114 | 115 |
|---|---|---|---|---|---|---|
| **ALABAMA** | | | | | | |
| Shelby | Y | Y | Y | N | Y | Y |
| Sessions | Y | Y | Y | N | Y | Y |
| **ALASKA** | | | | | | |
| Stevens | Y | Y | Y | N | Y | Y |
| Murkowski | Y | Y | Y | N | Y | Y |
| **ARIZONA** | | | | | | |
| McCain | N | Y | Y | Y | Y | Y |
| Kyl | N | Y | Y | N | Y | Y |
| **ARKANSAS** | | | | | | |
| Lincoln | Y | Y | Y | Y | N | N |
| Pryor | Y | Y | Y | Y | N | N |
| **CALIFORNIA** | | | | | | |
| Feinstein | Y | Y | Y | Y | N | N |
| Boxer | Y | Y | Y | Y | N | N |
| **COLORADO** | | | | | | |
| Allard | Y | Y | Y | N | Y | Y |
| Salazar | Y | Y | Y | Y | N | N |
| **CONNECTICUT** | | | | | | |
| Dodd | Y | Y | Y | Y | N | N |
| Lieberman | Y | Y | Y | Y | ? | ? |
| **DELAWARE** | | | | | | |
| Biden | Y | ? | Y | Y | N | N |
| Carper | Y | Y | Y | Y | N | N |
| **FLORIDA** | | | | | | |
| Nelson | Y | Y | Y | Y | N | Y |
| Martinez | Y | Y | Y | N | Y | Y |
| **GEORGIA** | | | | | | |
| Chambliss | Y | Y | Y | N | Y | Y |
| Isakson | Y | Y | Y | N | Y | Y |
| **HAWAII** | | | | | | |
| Inouye | Y | Y | Y | Y | N | N |
| Akaka | Y | Y | Y | Y | N | N |
| **IDAHO** | | | | | | |
| Craig | Y | Y | Y | N | Y | Y |
| Crapo | Y | Y | Y | N | Y | Y |
| **ILLINOIS** | | | | | | |
| Durbin | Y | Y | Y | Y | N | N |
| Obama | Y | Y | Y | Y | N | N |
| **INDIANA** | | | | | | |
| Lugar | Y | Y | Y | N | Y | Y |
| Bayh | Y | Y | Y | Y | N | N |
| **IOWA** | | | | | | |
| Grassley | Y | Y | Y | N | Y | Y |
| Harkin | Y | Y | Y | Y | N | N |
| **KANSAS** | | | | | | |
| Brownback | Y | Y | Y | N | Y | Y |
| Roberts | Y | Y | Y | N | Y | Y |
| **KENTUCKY** | | | | | | |
| McConnell | Y | Y | Y | N | Y | Y |
| Bunning | Y | Y | Y | N | Y | Y |
| **LOUISIANA** | | | | | | |
| Landrieu | Y | Y | Y | N | N | N |
| Vitter | Y | Y | Y | N | Y | Y |
| **MAINE** | | | | | | |
| Snowe | Y | Y | Y | N | Y | Y |
| Collins | Y | Y | Y | N | Y | Y |
| **MARYLAND** | | | | | | |
| Sarbanes | Y | Y | Y | Y | N | N |
| Mikulski | Y | Y | Y | Y | N | N |
| **MASSACHUSETTS** | | | | | | |
| Kennedy | Y | Y | Y | Y | N | N |
| Kerry | Y | Y | Y | Y | N | N |
| **MICHIGAN** | | | | | | |
| Levin | Y | Y | Y | Y | N | N |
| Stabenow | Y | Y | Y | Y | N | N |
| **MINNESOTA** | | | | | | |
| Dayton | Y | Y | Y | Y | N | N |
| Coleman | Y | Y | Y | Y | Y | Y |
| **MISSISSIPPI** | | | | | | |
| Cochran | Y | Y | Y | N | Y | Y |
| Lott | Y | Y | Y | N | Y | ? |
| **MISSOURI** | | | | | | |
| Bond | Y | Y | Y | N | Y | Y |
| Talent | Y | Y | Y | N | Y | Y |

| | 110 | 111 | 112 | 113 | 114 | 115 |
|---|---|---|---|---|---|---|
| **MONTANA** | | | | | | |
| Baucus | Y | ? | ? | Y | N | Y |
| Burns | Y | Y | Y | N | Y | Y |
| **NEBRASKA** | | | | | | |
| Hagel | Y | Y | Y | N | Y | Y |
| Nelson | Y | Y | Y | Y | N | Y |
| **NEVADA** | | | | | | |
| Reid | Y | Y | Y | Y | N | N |
| Ensign | Y | Y | Y | Y | Y | Y |
| **NEW HAMPSHIRE** | | | | | | |
| Gregg | N | Y | Y | N | Y | Y |
| Sununu | N | Y | Y | N | Y | Y |
| **NEW JERSEY** | | | | | | |
| Corzine | Y | Y | Y | Y | N | N |
| Lautenberg | Y | Y | Y | Y | N | N |
| **NEW MEXICO** | | | | | | |
| Domenici | Y | Y | Y | N | Y | Y |
| Bingaman | Y | Y | Y | Y | N | N |
| **NEW YORK** | | | | | | |
| Schumer | Y | Y | Y | Y | N | N |
| Clinton | Y | Y | Y | N | N | N |
| **NORTH CAROLINA** | | | | | | |
| Dole | Y | Y | Y | N | Y | Y |
| Burr | Y | Y | Y | N | Y | Y |
| **NORTH DAKOTA** | | | | | | |
| Conrad | Y | Y | Y | N | N | N |
| Dorgan | Y | Y | Y | N | N | N |
| **OHIO** | | | | | | |
| DeWine | Y | Y | Y | N | N | Y |
| Voinovich | Y | Y | Y | N | N | Y |
| **OKLAHOMA** | | | | | | |
| Inhofe | Y | Y | Y | N | Y | Y |
| Coburn | Y | Y | Y | N | Y | Y |
| **OREGON** | | | | | | |
| Wyden | Y | Y | Y | Y | N | N |
| Smith | Y | Y | Y | Y | Y | Y |
| **PENNSYLVANIA** | | | | | | |
| Specter | Y | Y | Y | N | N | Y |
| Santorum | Y | Y | Y | N | Y | Y |
| **RHODE ISLAND** | | | | | | |
| Reed | Y | Y | Y | Y | N | N |
| Chafee | Y | Y | Y | N | N | Y |
| **SOUTH CAROLINA** | | | | | | |
| Graham | Y | Y | Y | N | Y | Y |
| DeMint | Y | Y | Y | N | Y | Y |
| **SOUTH DAKOTA** | | | | | | |
| Johnson | Y | Y | Y | N | N | N |
| Thune | Y | Y | Y | N | Y | Y |
| **TENNESSEE** | | | | | | |
| Frist | Y | Y | Y | N | Y | Y |
| Alexander | Y | Y | Y | Y | Y | Y |
| **TEXAS** | | | | | | |
| Hutchison | N | Y | Y | N | Y | Y |
| Cornyn | N | Y | Y | N | Y | Y |
| **UTAH** | | | | | | |
| Hatch | Y | Y | Y | Y | Y | Y |
| Bennett | Y | Y | Y | Y | Y | Y |
| **VERMONT** | | | | | | |
| Leahy | Y | Y | Y | Y | N | N |
| *Jeffords* | Y | Y | Y | Y | N | N |
| **VIRGINIA** | | | | | | |
| Warner | Y | Y | Y | Y | Y | Y |
| Allen | Y | Y | Y | N | Y | Y |
| **WASHINGTON** | | | | | | |
| Murray | Y | Y | Y | Y | N | N |
| Cantwell | Y | Y | Y | Y | N | N |
| **WEST VIRGINIA** | | | | | | |
| Byrd | Y | Y | Y | N | N | Y |
| Rockefeller | Y | Y | Y | N | N | Y |
| **WISCONSIN** | | | | | | |
| Kohl | Y | Y | Y | Y | N | N |
| Feingold | Y | Y | Y | N | N | N |
| **WYOMING** | | | | | | |
| Thomas | Y | Y | Y | N | Y | Y |
| Enzi | Y | Y | Y | N | Y | Y |

**KEY**   Republicans   Democrats   *Independents*

| | | |
|---|---|---|
| **Y** Voted for (yea) | **X** Paired against | **C** Voted "present" to avoid possible conflict of interest |
| **#** Paired for | **–** Announced against | |
| **+** Announced for | **P** Voted "present" | **?** Did not vote or otherwise make a position known |
| **N** Voted against (nay) | | |

ND Northern Democrats, SD Southern Democrats
Southern states: Ala., Ark., Fla., Ga., Ky., La., Miss., N.C., Okla., S.C., Tenn., Texas, Va.

# IN THE SENATE | By Vote Number

**116.** **HR 3. Surface Transportation Reauthorization/Minority Contractors.** Talent, R-Mo., amendment to the Inhofe, R-Okla., substitute amendment. The Talent amendment would direct the Transportation secretary to notify state and local governments that receive federal funds of a new law providing that once certain minority-owned small businesses are certified at the federal level they do not have be re-certified at the state and local level to compete for federal contracts such as federal highway projects. The substitute would authorize $283.9 billion for federal-aid highway, mass transit, safety and research programs in fiscal 2004 through 2009 and guarantee that every state receives at least 92 cents in funding for every dollar in gas taxes it pays into the Highway Trust Fund. Adopted 89-0: R 49-0; D 39-0 (ND 35-0, SD 4-0); I 1-0. May 9, 2005.

**117.** **HR 1268. Fiscal 2005 Supplemental Appropriations/Adoption.** Adoption of the conference report on the bill that would appropriate $82 billion in fiscal 2005 supplemental spending for military operations and reconstruction in Iraq and Afghanistan and for disaster assistance to victims of the December 2004 tsunami in South Asia. It also would establish national driver's license standards, stiffen asylum requirements and speed completion of a fence on the U.S.-Mexico border. Adopted (thus cleared for the president) 100-0: R 55-0; D 44-0 (ND 40-0, SD 4-0); I 1-0. May 10, 2005.

**118.** **HR 3. Surface Transportation Reauthorization/Substitute.** Inhofe, R-Okla., motion to waive the Budget Act with respect to the Gregg, R-N.H., point of order against the Inhofe substitute amendment. The substitute would authorize $295 billion for federal-aid highway, mass transit, safety and research programs from fiscal 2004 through 2009. The funding total includes $234 billion for highway programs and $54 billion for public transportation programs. Motion agreed to 76-22: R 33-21; D 42-1 (ND 38-1, SD 4-0); I 1-0. A three-fifths majority (60) of the total Senate is required to waive the Budget Act. May 11, 2005.

**119.** **HR 3. Surface Transportation Reauthorization/Contractor Campaign Contributions.** Inhofe, R-Okla., motion to table (kill) the Corzine, D-N.J., amendment to the Inhofe substitute amendment. The Corzine amendment would allow states to enact laws limiting political campaign contributions by contractors for transportation contracts awarded by the state, without losing federal transportation funding. Motion agreed to 57-40: R 48-5; D 8-35 (ND 7-32, SD 1-3); I 1-0. May 11, 2005.

| | 116 | 117 | 118 | 119 | | | 116 | 117 | 118 | 119 |
|---|---|---|---|---|---|---|---|---|---|---|
| **ALABAMA** | | | | | | **MONTANA** | | | | |
| Shelby | Y | Y | Y | Y | | Baucus | Y | Y | Y | Y |
| Sessions | Y | Y | N | Y | | Burns | Y | Y | Y | Y |
| **ALASKA** | | | | | | **NEBRASKA** | | | | |
| Stevens | Y | Y | Y | Y | | Hagel | Y | Y | N | Y |
| Murkowski | ? | Y | Y | Y | | Nelson | Y | Y | Y | Y |
| **ARIZONA** | | | | | | **NEVADA** | | | | |
| McCain | ? | Y | N | N | | Reid | Y | Y | Y | Y |
| Kyl | ? | Y | N | Y | | Ensign | Y | Y | N | Y |
| **ARKANSAS** | | | | | | **NEW HAMPSHIRE** | | | | |
| Lincoln | Y | Y | Y | N | | Gregg | Y | Y | N | N |
| Pryor | Y | Y | Y | N | | Sununu | Y | Y | N | Y |
| **CALIFORNIA** | | | | | | **NEW JERSEY** | | | | |
| Feinstein | Y | Y | Y | N | | Corzine | Y | Y | Y | N |
| Boxer | Y | Y | Y | N | | Lautenberg | Y | Y | Y | N |
| **COLORADO** | | | | | | **NEW MEXICO** | | | | |
| Allard | Y | Y | N | Y | | Domenici | Y | Y | Y | ? |
| Salazar | Y | Y | Y | N | | Bingaman | Y | Y | Y | N |
| **CONNECTICUT** | | | | | | **NEW YORK** | | | | |
| Dodd | Y | Y | Y | N | | Schumer | Y | Y | Y | N |
| Lieberman | Y | Y | Y | N | | Clinton | Y | Y | Y | N |
| **DELAWARE** | | | | | | **NORTH CAROLINA** | | | | |
| Biden | ? | Y | Y | N | | Dole | Y | Y | Y | Y |
| Carper | Y | Y | Y | N | | Burr | Y | Y | Y | Y |
| **FLORIDA** | | | | | | **NORTH DAKOTA** | | | | |
| Nelson | Y | Y | Y | N | | Conrad | Y | Y | Y | Y |
| Martinez | Y | Y | Y | Y | | Dorgan | ? | Y | Y | Y |
| **GEORGIA** | | | | | | **OHIO** | | | | |
| Chambliss | Y | Y | N | Y | | DeWine | Y | Y | Y | Y |
| Isakson | Y | Y | N | Y | | Voinovich | Y | Y | Y | Y |
| **HAWAII** | | | | | | **OKLAHOMA** | | | | |
| Inouye | Y | Y | Y | N | | Inhofe | Y | Y | Y | Y |
| Akaka | Y | Y | Y | N | | Coburn | Y | Y | N | Y |
| **IDAHO** | | | | | | **OREGON** | | | | |
| Craig | Y | Y | N | Y | | Wyden | Y | Y | Y | N |
| Crapo | Y | Y | Y | Y | | Smith | Y | Y | Y | Y |
| **ILLINOIS** | | | | | | **PENNSYLVANIA** | | | | |
| Durbin | Y | Y | Y | N | | Specter | Y | Y | Y | Y |
| Obama | Y | Y | Y | N | | Santorum | Y | Y | Y | Y |
| **INDIANA** | | | | | | **RHODE ISLAND** | | | | |
| Lugar | Y | Y | Y | Y | | Reed | Y | Y | Y | N |
| Bayh | Y | Y | Y | N | | Chafee | Y | Y | N | N |
| **IOWA** | | | | | | **SOUTH CAROLINA** | | | | |
| Grassley | Y | Y | Y | Y | | Graham | Y | Y | N | Y |
| Harkin | ? | Y | Y | N | | DeMint | Y | Y | N | Y |
| **KANSAS** | | | | | | **SOUTH DAKOTA** | | | | |
| Brownback | Y | Y | N | Y | | Johnson | Y | Y | Y | N |
| Roberts | Y | Y | Y | Y | | Thune | Y | Y | Y | Y |
| **KENTUCKY** | | | | | | **TENNESSEE** | | | | |
| McConnell | Y | Y | N | Y | | Frist | Y | Y | N | Y |
| Bunning | Y | Y | Y | Y | | Alexander | ? | Y | Y | Y |
| **LOUISIANA** | | | | | | **TEXAS** | | | | |
| Landrieu | Y | Y | Y | Y | | Hutchison | Y | Y | N | Y |
| Vitter | Y | Y | Y | Y | | Cornyn | Y | Y | N | Y |
| **MAINE** | | | | | | **UTAH** | | | | |
| Snowe | Y | Y | Y | N | | Hatch | Y | Y | Y | Y |
| Collins | Y | Y | Y | N | | Bennett | Y | Y | Y | Y |
| **MARYLAND** | | | | | | **VERMONT** | | | | |
| Sarbanes | ? | Y | Y | N | | Leahy | Y | Y | Y | N |
| Mikulski | Y | Y | Y | N | | *Jeffords* | Y | Y | Y | Y |
| **MASSACHUSETTS** | | | | | | **VIRGINIA** | | | | |
| Kennedy | Y | Y | Y | N | | Warner | Y | Y | Y | Y |
| Kerry | Y | Y | Y | N | | Allen | Y | Y | Y | Y |
| **MICHIGAN** | | | | | | **WASHINGTON** | | | | |
| Levin | Y | Y | Y | N | | Murray | Y | Y | Y | Y |
| Stabenow | Y | Y | Y | N | | Cantwell | Y | Y | Y | N |
| **MINNESOTA** | | | | | | **WEST VIRGINIA** | | | | |
| Dayton | ? | Y | ? | ? | | Byrd | Y | Y | Y | Y |
| Coleman | Y | Y | ? | ? | | Rockefeller | Y | Y | Y | N |
| **MISSISSIPPI** | | | | | | **WISCONSIN** | | | | |
| Cochran | ? | Y | Y | Y | | Kohl | Y | Y | Y | N |
| Lott | Y | Y | Y | Y | | Feingold | Y | Y | N | N |
| **MISSOURI** | | | | | | **WYOMING** | | | | |
| Bond | Y | Y | Y | Y | | Thomas | Y | Y | N | Y |
| Talent | Y | Y | Y | Y | | Enzi | ? | Y | N | Y |

**KEY**    Republicans    Democrats    *Independents*

| | | | |
|---|---|---|---|
| Y | Voted for (yea) | X Paired against | C Voted "present" to avoid possible conflict of interest |
| # | Paired for | – Announced against | |
| + | Announced for | P Voted "present" | ? Did not vote or otherwise make a position known |
| N | Voted against (nay) | | |

ND Northern Democrats, SD Southern Democrats
Southern states: Ala., Ark., Fla., Ga., Ky., La., Miss., N.C., Okla., S.C., Tenn., Texas, Va.

# IN THE SENATE | By Vote Number

**120.** HR 3. Surface Transportation Reauthorization/Motorcycle Safety
**Programs.** Lautenberg, D-N.J., amendment to the Inhofe, R-Okla., substitute
amendment. The Lautenberg amendment would stipulate that, beginning in
fiscal 2008, funding for motorcycle safety training programs in states without
helmet laws would come from the state's share of federal highway funds. Rejected 28-69: R 6-47; D 22-21 (ND 21-18, SD 1-3); I 0-1. May 11, 2005.

**121.** HR 3. Surface Transportation Reauthorization/Pedestrian and
**Bicycle Safety.** Harkin, D-Iowa, amendment to the Inhofe, R-Okla., substitute
amendment. The Harkin amendment would direct the Transportation
secretary to promote a goal of increasing the percentage of pedestrian and bicycle trips relative to motorized trips, while reducing accidents involving bicyclists
and pedestrians by 10 percent. It would encourage local action on bicycle and
pedestrian safety. Rejected 44-53: R 4-49; D 40-3 (ND 36-3, SD 4-0); I 0-1.
May 11, 2005.

**122.** HR 3. Surface Transportation Reauthorization/Cloture. Motion to
invoke cloture (thus limiting debate) on the Inhofe, R-Okla., substitute amendment that would authorize $295 billion for federal aid highway, mass transit,
safety and research programs from fiscal 2004 through 2009. The funding total
includes $234 billion for highway programs and $54 billion for public
transportation programs. Motion agreed to 92-7: R 47-7; D 44-0 (ND 40-0,
SD 4-0); I 1-0. Three-fifths of the total Senate (60) is required to invoke cloture.
May 12, 2005.

| | 120 | 121 | 122 | | 120 | 121 | 122 |
|---|---|---|---|---|---|---|---|
| **ALABAMA** | | | | **MONTANA** | | | |
| Shelby | N | N | Y | Baucus | N | N | Y |
| Sessions | N | N | Y | Burns | N | N | Y |
| **ALASKA** | | | | **NEBRASKA** | | | |
| Stevens | N | N | Y | Hagel | N | N | Y |
| Murkowski | N | N | Y | Nelson | N | N | Y |
| **ARIZONA** | | | | **NEVADA** | | | |
| McCain | N | N | N | Reid | Y | Y | Y |
| Kyl | N | N | N | Ensign | N | Y | Y |
| **ARKANSAS** | | | | **NEW HAMPSHIRE** | | | |
| Lincoln | N | Y | Y | Gregg | N | N | N |
| Pryor | N | Y | Y | Sununu | N | N | N |
| **CALIFORNIA** | | | | **NEW JERSEY** | | | |
| Feinstein | Y | Y | Y | Corzine | Y | Y | Y |
| Boxer | Y | Y | Y | Lautenberg | Y | Y | Y |
| **COLORADO** | | | | **NEW MEXICO** | | | |
| Allard | N | N | Y | Domenici | ? | ? | Y |
| Salazar | N | Y | Y | Bingaman | N | Y | Y |
| **CONNECTICUT** | | | | **NEW YORK** | | | |
| Dodd | Y | Y | Y | Schumer | N | Y | Y |
| Lieberman | Y | Y | Y | Clinton | N | Y | Y |
| **DELAWARE** | | | | **NORTH CAROLINA** | | | |
| Biden | Y | Y | Y | Dole | Y | N | Y |
| Carper | N | Y | Y | Burr | N | N | Y |
| **FLORIDA** | | | | **NORTH DAKOTA** | | | |
| Nelson | N | Y | Y | Conrad | N | N | Y |
| Martinez | Y | N | N | Dorgan | N | Y | Y |
| **GEORGIA** | | | | **OHIO** | | | |
| Chambliss | N | N | Y | DeWine | Y | N | Y |
| Isakson | N | N | Y | Voinovich | N | N | Y |
| **HAWAII** | | | | **OKLAHOMA** | | | |
| Inouye | Y | Y | Y | Inhofe | N | N | Y |
| Akaka | Y | Y | Y | Coburn | N | N | Y |
| **IDAHO** | | | | **OREGON** | | | |
| Craig | N | N | Y | Wyden | Y | Y | Y |
| Crapo | N | N | Y | Smith | N | N | Y |
| **ILLINOIS** | | | | **PENNSYLVANIA** | | | |
| Durbin | Y | Y | Y | Specter | N | N | Y |
| Obama | N | Y | Y | Santorum | N | N | ? |
| **INDIANA** | | | | **RHODE ISLAND** | | | |
| Lugar | N | N | Y | Reed | N | Y | Y |
| Bayh | N | Y | Y | Chafee | Y | N | Y |
| **IOWA** | | | | **SOUTH CAROLINA** | | | |
| Grassley | N | N | Y | Graham | N | N | Y |
| Harkin | Y | Y | Y | DeMint | N | N | Y |
| **KANSAS** | | | | **SOUTH DAKOTA** | | | |
| Brownback | N | N | Y | Johnson | N | Y | Y |
| Roberts | N | N | Y | Thune | N | N | Y |
| **KENTUCKY** | | | | **TENNESSEE** | | | |
| McConnell | N | N | Y | Frist | Y | N | Y |
| Bunning | N | N | Y | Alexander | N | N | Y |
| **LOUISIANA** | | | | **TEXAS** | | | |
| Landrieu | Y | Y | Y | Hutchison | N | N | N |
| Vitter | N | N | Y | Cornyn | N | N | N |
| **MAINE** | | | | **UTAH** | | | |
| Snowe | N | Y | Y | Hatch | N | N | Y |
| Collins | N | Y | Y | Bennett | N | N | Y |
| **MARYLAND** | | | | **VERMONT** | | | |
| Sarbanes | Y | Y | Y | Leahy | N | Y | Y |
| Mikulski | Y | Y | Y | *Jeffords* | N | N | Y |
| **MASSACHUSETTS** | | | | **VIRGINIA** | | | |
| Kennedy | Y | Y | Y | Warner | Y | Y | Y |
| Kerry | N | Y | Y | Allen | N | N | Y |
| **MICHIGAN** | | | | **WASHINGTON** | | | |
| Levin | Y | Y | Y | Murray | Y | Y | Y |
| Stabenow | N | Y | Y | Cantwell | Y | Y | Y |
| **MINNESOTA** | | | | **WEST VIRGINIA** | | | |
| Dayton | ? | ? | Y | Byrd | Y | Y | Y |
| Coleman | ? | ? | Y | Rockefeller | Y | Y | Y |
| **MISSISSIPPI** | | | | **WISCONSIN** | | | |
| Cochran | N | N | Y | Kohl | N | Y | Y |
| Lott | N | N | Y | Feingold | N | Y | Y |
| **MISSOURI** | | | | **WYOMING** | | | |
| Bond | N | N | Y | Thomas | N | N | Y |
| Talent | N | N | Y | Enzi | N | N | Y |

**KEY**   Republicans   Democrats   *Independents*

| Y | Voted for (yea) | X | Paired against | C | Voted "present" to avoid possible conflict of interest |
|---|---|---|---|---|---|
| # | Paired for | – | Announced against | | |
| + | Announced for | P | Voted "present" | ? | Did not vote or otherwise make a position known |
| N | Voted against (nay) | | | | |

ND Northern Democrats, SD Southern Democrats
Southern states: Ala., Ark., Fla., Ga., Ky., La., Miss., N.C., Okla., S.C., Tenn., Texas, Va.

# IN THE SENATE | By Vote Number

**123.** **HR 3. Surface Transportation Reauthorization/Seat Belts.** Allen, R-Va., amendment to the Inhofe, R-Okla., substitute amendment. The Allen amendment would revise the Occupant Protection Incentive Grant program to base grant awards on an 85 percent safety belt use rate in the preceding calendar year. It would strike the requirement that to receive funds under the program, states must either have a primary safety belt law in effect, or have a safety belt use rate of 90 percent. The substitute amendment would bring the total authorization for federal-aid highway, mass transit, safety and research programs, including fiscal 2004 funds, to $295 billion through 2009. The funding total includes $234 billion for highway programs and $54 billion for public transportation programs. Rejected 14-86: R 11-44; D 3-41 (ND 2-38, SD 1-3); I 0-1. May 17, 2005.

**124.** **HR 3. Surface Transportation Reauthorization/Funding Reduction.** Sessions, R-Ala., amendment to the Inhofe, R-Okla., substitute amendment. The Sessions amendment would reduce funding for certain programs by $10.7 billion, including a $5 billion cut for mass transit, a $4 billion cut for the congestion mitigation and air quality improvement program, and a $1.1 billion cut for surface transportation enhancement projects. Rejected 16-84: R 16-39; D 0-44 (ND 0-40, SD 0-4); I 0-1. May 17, 2005.

**125.** **HR 3. Surface Transportation Reauthorization/Passage.** Passage of the bill that would bring the total authorization for federal-aid highway, mass transit, safety and research programs, including fiscal 2004 funds, to $295 billion through 2009. The bill includes $234 billion for highway programs and $54 billion for public transportation programs. It would increase the rate of return to states on their Highway Trust Fund contributions to 92 percent by 2009. Passed 89-11: R 46-9; D 42-2 (ND 38-2, SD 4-0); I 1-0. A "nay" was a vote in support of the president's position. (Before passage, the Senate adopted the Inhofe substitute by voice vote.) May 17, 2005.

| | 123 | 124 | 125 | | 123 | 124 | 125 |
|---|---|---|---|---|---|---|---|
| **ALABAMA** | | | | **MONTANA** | | | |
| Shelby | N | N | Y | Baucus | Y | N | Y |
| Sessions | N | Y | Y | Burns | N | N | Y |
| **ALASKA** | | | | **NEBRASKA** | | | |
| Stevens | N | N | Y | Hagel | N | Y | Y |
| Murkowski | N | N | Y | Nelson | N | N | Y |
| **ARIZONA** | | | | **NEVADA** | | | |
| McCain | N | Y | N | Reid | N | N | Y |
| Kyl | Y | Y | N | Ensign | Y | N | Y |
| **ARKANSAS** | | | | **NEW HAMPSHIRE** | | | |
| Lincoln | N | N | Y | Gregg | Y | Y | N |
| Pryor | N | N | Y | Sununu | Y | Y | N |
| **CALIFORNIA** | | | | **NEW JERSEY** | | | |
| Feinstein | N | N | Y | Corzine | N | N | Y |
| Boxer | N | N | Y | Lautenberg | N | N | Y |
| **COLORADO** | | | | **NEW MEXICO** | | | |
| Allard | N | N | Y | Domenici | N | N | Y |
| Salazar | N | N | Y | Bingaman | N | N | Y |
| **CONNECTICUT** | | | | **NEW YORK** | | | |
| Dodd | N | N | Y | Schumer | N | N | Y |
| Lieberman | N | N | Y | Clinton | N | N | Y |
| **DELAWARE** | | | | **NORTH CAROLINA** | | | |
| Biden | N | N | Y | Dole | N | N | Y |
| Carper | N | N | Y | Burr | N | Y | Y |
| **FLORIDA** | | | | **NORTH DAKOTA** | | | |
| Nelson | Y | N | Y | Conrad | N | N | Y |
| Martinez | N | N | Y | Dorgan | N | N | Y |
| **GEORGIA** | | | | **OHIO** | | | |
| Chambliss | N | N | Y | DeWine | N | N | Y |
| Isakson | N | N | Y | Voinovich | N | N | Y |
| **HAWAII** | | | | **OKLAHOMA** | | | |
| Inouye | N | N | Y | Inhofe | N | N | Y |
| Akaka | N | N | Y | Coburn | N | Y | Y |
| **IDAHO** | | | | **OREGON** | | | |
| Craig | N | N | Y | Wyden | N | N | Y |
| Crapo | N | N | Y | Smith | N | N | Y |
| **ILLINOIS** | | | | **PENNSYLVANIA** | | | |
| Durbin | N | N | Y | Specter | N | N | Y |
| Obama | N | N | Y | Santorum | N | N | Y |
| **INDIANA** | | | | **RHODE ISLAND** | | | |
| Lugar | Y | N | Y | Reed | N | N | Y |
| Bayh | N | N | Y | Chafee | N | N | Y |
| **IOWA** | | | | **SOUTH CAROLINA** | | | |
| Grassley | N | N | Y | Graham | N | Y | N |
| Harkin | N | N | Y | DeMint | N | Y | N |
| **KANSAS** | | | | **SOUTH DAKOTA** | | | |
| Brownback | N | Y | N | Johnson | N | N | Y |
| Roberts | N | N | Y | Thune | N | N | Y |
| **KENTUCKY** | | | | **TENNESSEE** | | | |
| McConnell | N | N | Y | Frist | Y | Y | Y |
| Bunning | N | N | Y | Alexander | Y | N | Y |
| **LOUISIANA** | | | | **TEXAS** | | | |
| Landrieu | N | N | Y | Hutchison | N | Y | N |
| Vitter | Y | N | Y | Cornyn | N | Y | N |
| **MAINE** | | | | **UTAH** | | | |
| Snowe | Y | N | Y | Hatch | N | N | Y |
| Collins | Y | N | Y | Bennett | N | N | Y |
| **MARYLAND** | | | | **VERMONT** | | | |
| Sarbanes | N | N | Y | Leahy | N | N | Y |
| Mikulski | N | N | Y | Jeffords | N | N | Y |
| **MASSACHUSETTS** | | | | **VIRGINIA** | | | |
| Kennedy | N | N | Y | Warner | N | N | Y |
| Kerry | N | N | Y | Allen | Y | N | Y |
| **MICHIGAN** | | | | **WASHINGTON** | | | |
| Levin | N | N | Y | Murray | N | N | Y |
| Stabenow | N | N | Y | Cantwell | N | N | Y |
| **MINNESOTA** | | | | **WEST VIRGINIA** | | | |
| Dayton | N | N | Y | Byrd | N | N | Y |
| Coleman | N | N | Y | Rockefeller | N | N | Y |
| **MISSISSIPPI** | | | | **WISCONSIN** | | | |
| Cochran | N | N | Y | Kohl | N | N | N |
| Lott | N | N | Y | Feingold | Y | N | N |
| **MISSOURI** | | | | **WYOMING** | | | |
| Bond | Y | N | Y | Thomas | N | Y | Y |
| Talent | N | N | Y | Enzi | N | Y | Y |

**KEY**   Republicans   Democrats   *Independents*

| | | | |
|---|---|---|---|
| Y | Voted for (yea) | X | Paired against |
| # | Paired for | – | Announced against |
| + | Announced for | P | Voted "present" |
| N | Voted against (nay) | | |

| | |
|---|---|
| C | Voted "present" to avoid possible conflict of interest |
| ? | Did not vote or otherwise make a position known |

ND Northern Democrats, SD Southern Democrats
Southern states: Ala., Ark., Fla., Ga., Ky., La., Miss., N.C., Okla., S.C., Tenn., Texas, Va.

# IN THE SENATE | By Vote Number

**126. Procedural Motion/Require Attendance.** Frist, R-Tenn., motion to instruct the sergeant at arms to request the attendance of absent senators. Motion agreed to 90-1: R 49-1; D 40-0 (ND 37-0, SD 3-0); I 1-0. May 23, 2005.

**127. Owen Nomination/Cloture.** Motion to invoke cloture (thus limiting debate) on President Bush's nomination of Priscilla R. Owen of Texas to be a judge for the U.S. Court of Appeals for the 5th Circuit. Motion agreed to 81-18: R 55-0; D 26-17 (ND 23-16, SD 3-1); I 0-1. Three-fifths of the total Senate (60) is required to invoke cloture. May 24, 2005.

**128. Owen Nomination/Confirmation.** Confirmation of President Bush's nomination of Priscilla R. Owen of Texas to be a judge for the U.S. Court of Appeals for the 5th Circuit. Confirmed 55-43: R 53-1; D 2-41 (ND 1-38, SD 1-3); I 0-1. A "yea" was a vote in support of the president's position. May 25, 2005.

**129. Bolton Nomination/Cloture.** Motion to invoke cloture (thus limiting debate) on President Bush's nomination of John R. Bolton of Maryland to be the permanent U.S. representative to the United Nations. Motion rejected 56-42: R 53-1; D 3-40 (ND 1-38, SD 2-2); I 0-1. Three-fifths of the total Senate (60) is required to invoke cloture. A "yea" was a vote in support of the president's position. May 26, 2005.

| | 126 | 127 | 128 | 129 | | | 126 | 127 | 128 | 129 |
|---|---|---|---|---|---|---|---|---|---|---|
| **ALABAMA** | | | | | | **MONTANA** | | | | |
| Shelby | Y | Y | Y | Y | | Baucus | Y | Y | N | N |
| Sessions | Y | Y | Y | Y | | Burns | Y | Y | Y | Y |
| **ALASKA** | | | | | | **NEBRASKA** | | | | |
| Stevens | Y | Y | P | Y | | Hagel | Y | Y | Y | Y |
| Murkowski | ? | Y | Y | Y | | Nelson | Y | Y | N | Y |
| **ARIZONA** | | | | | | **NEVADA** | | | | |
| McCain | Y | Y | Y | Y | | Reid | Y | Y | N | N |
| Kyl | Y | Y | Y | Y | | Ensign | Y | Y | Y | Y |
| **ARKANSAS** | | | | | | **NEW HAMPSHIRE** | | | | |
| Lincoln | ? | N | N | N | | Gregg | ? | Y | Y | Y |
| Pryor | Y | Y | N | Y | | Sununu | Y | Y | Y | Y |
| **CALIFORNIA** | | | | | | **NEW JERSEY** | | | | |
| Feinstein | Y | Y | N | N | | Corzine | Y | N | N | N |
| Boxer | Y | N | N | N | | Lautenberg | Y | N | N | N |
| **COLORADO** | | | | | | **NEW MEXICO** | | | | |
| Allard | Y | Y | Y | Y | | Domenici | Y | Y | Y | Y |
| Salazar | Y | Y | N | N | | Bingaman | Y | Y | N | N |
| **CONNECTICUT** | | | | | | **NEW YORK** | | | | |
| Dodd | Y | N | N | N | | Schumer | Y | Y | N | N |
| Lieberman | Y | Y | N | N | | Clinton | Y | Y | N | N |
| **DELAWARE** | | | | | | **NORTH CAROLINA** | | | | |
| Biden | Y | N | N | N | | Dole | Y | Y | Y | Y |
| Carper | Y | Y | N | N | | Burr | Y | Y | Y | Y |
| **FLORIDA** | | | | | | **NORTH DAKOTA** | | | | |
| Nelson | Y | Y | N | N | | Conrad | Y | Y | N | N |
| Martinez | Y | Y | Y | Y | | Dorgan | Y | N | N | N |
| **GEORGIA** | | | | | | **OHIO** | | | | |
| Chambliss | Y | Y | Y | Y | | DeWine | Y | Y | Y | Y |
| Isakson | Y | Y | Y | Y | | Voinovich | Y | Y | Y | Y |
| **HAWAII** | | | | | | **OKLAHOMA** | | | | |
| Inouye | ? | ? | – | ? | | Inhofe | Y | Y | Y | Y |
| Akaka | Y | Y | N | N | | Coburn | Y | Y | Y | Y |
| **IDAHO** | | | | | | **OREGON** | | | | |
| Craig | Y | Y | Y | Y | | Wyden | Y | Y | N | N |
| Crapo | Y | Y | Y | Y | | Smith | Y | Y | Y | Y |
| **ILLINOIS** | | | | | | **PENNSYLVANIA** | | | | |
| Durbin | Y | Y | N | N | | Specter | Y | Y | Y | ? |
| Obama | Y | Y | N | N | | Santorum | Y | Y | Y | Y |
| **INDIANA** | | | | | | **RHODE ISLAND** | | | | |
| Lugar | Y | Y | Y | Y | | Reed | Y | N | N | N |
| Bayh | Y | Y | N | N | | Chafee | Y | Y | N | Y |
| **IOWA** | | | | | | **SOUTH CAROLINA** | | | | |
| Grassley | Y | Y | Y | Y | | Graham | Y | Y | Y | Y |
| Harkin | Y | Y | N | N | | DeMint | Y | Y | Y | Y |
| **KANSAS** | | | | | | **SOUTH DAKOTA** | | | | |
| Brownback | Y | Y | Y | Y | | Johnson | Y | Y | N | N |
| Roberts | Y | Y | Y | Y | | Thune | Y | Y | Y | Y |
| **KENTUCKY** | | | | | | **TENNESSEE** | | | | |
| McConnell | Y | Y | Y | Y | | Frist | Y | Y | Y | N |
| Bunning | Y | Y | Y | Y | | Alexander | Y | Y | Y | Y |
| **LOUISIANA** | | | | | | **TEXAS** | | | | |
| Landrieu | Y | Y | Y | Y | | Hutchison | Y | Y | Y | Y |
| Vitter | Y | Y | Y | Y | | Cornyn | + | Y | Y | Y |
| **MAINE** | | | | | | **UTAH** | | | | |
| Snowe | Y | Y | Y | Y | | Hatch | Y | Y | Y | Y |
| Collins | Y | Y | Y | Y | | Bennett | Y | Y | Y | Y |
| **MARYLAND** | | | | | | **VERMONT** | | | | |
| Sarbanes | Y | N | N | N | | Leahy | Y | Y | N | N |
| Mikulski | Y | Y | N | N | | Jeffords | Y | N | N | N |
| **MASSACHUSETTS** | | | | | | **VIRGINIA** | | | | |
| Kennedy | ? | N | N | N | | Warner | Y | Y | Y | Y |
| Kerry | Y | N | N | N | | Allen | N | Y | Y | Y |
| **MICHIGAN** | | | | | | **WASHINGTON** | | | | |
| Levin | Y | N | N | N | | Murray | Y | N | N | N |
| Stabenow | Y | N | N | N | | Cantwell | Y | N | N | N |
| **MINNESOTA** | | | | | | **WEST VIRGINIA** | | | | |
| Dayton | ? | N | N | N | | Byrd | Y | Y | Y | N |
| Coleman | Y | Y | Y | Y | | Rockefeller | Y | Y | N | N |
| **MISSISSIPPI** | | | | | | **WISCONSIN** | | | | |
| Cochran | ? | Y | Y | Y | | Kohl | Y | N | N | N |
| Lott | ? | Y | Y | Y | | Feingold | Y | N | N | N |
| **MISSOURI** | | | | | | **WYOMING** | | | | |
| Bond | Y | Y | Y | Y | | Thomas | Y | Y | Y | Y |
| Talent | Y | Y | Y | Y | | Enzi | Y | Y | Y | Y |

| **KEY** | **Republicans** | Democrats | *Independents* | | |
|---|---|---|---|---|---|
| Y | Voted for (yea) | X | Paired against | C | Voted "present" to avoid possible conflict of interest |
| # | Paired for | – | Announced against | | |
| + | Announced for | P | Voted "present" | ? | Did not vote or otherwise make a position known |
| N | Voted against (nay) | | | | |

ND Northern Democrats, SD Southern Democrats
Southern states: Ala., Ark., Fla., Ga., Ky., La., Miss., N.C., Okla., S.C., Tenn., Texas, Va.

# IN THE SENATE | By Vote Number

**130. Brown Nomination/Cloture.** Motion to invoke cloture (thus limiting debate) on President Bush's nomination of Janice R. Brown of California to be a judge for the U.S. Court of Appeals for the District of Columbia Circuit. Motion agreed to 65-32: R 55-0; D 10-32 (ND 7-31, SD 3-1); I 0-0. Three-fifths of the total Senate (60) is required to invoke cloture. June 7, 2005.

**131. Brown Nomination/Confirmation.** Confirmation of President Bush's nomination of Janice R. Brown of California to be a judge for the U.S. Court of Appeals for the District of Columbia Circuit. Confirmed 56-43: R 55-0; D 1-43 (ND 1-39, SD 0-4); I 0-0. A "yea" was a vote in support of the president's position. June 8, 2005.

**132. Pryor Nomination/Cloture.** Motion to invoke cloture (thus limiting debate) on President Bush's nomination of William H. Pryor Jr. of Alabama to be a judge for the U.S. Court of Appeals for the 11th Circuit. Motion agreed to 67-32: R 55-0; D 12-32 (ND 9-31, SD 3-1); I 0-0. Three-fifths of the total Senate (60) is required to invoke cloture. June 8, 2005.

**133. Pryor Nomination/Confirmation.** Confirmation of President Bush's nomination of William H. Pryor Jr. of Alabama to be a judge for the U.S. Court of Appeals for the 11th Circuit. Confirmed 53-45: R 51-3; D 2-42 (ND 2-38, SD 0-4); I 0-0. A "yea" was a vote in support of the president's position. June 9, 2005.

**134. Griffin Nomination/Confirmation.** Confirmation of President Bush's nomination of Richard A. Griffin of Michigan to be a judge for the U.S. Court of Appeals for the 6th Circuit. Confirmed 95-0: R 53-0; D 42-0 (ND 38-0, SD 4-0); I 0-0. A "yea" was a vote in support of the president's position. June 9, 2005.

**135. McKeague Nomination/Confirmation.** Confirmation of President Bush's nomination of David W. McKeague of Michigan to be a judge for the U.S. Court of Appeals for the 6th Circuit. Confirmed 96-0: R 53-0; D 43-0 (ND 39-0, SD 4-0); I 0-0. A "yea" was a vote in support of the president's position. June 9, 2005.

| | 130 | 131 | 132 | 133 | 134 | 135 |
|---|---|---|---|---|---|---|
| **ALABAMA** | | | | | | |
| Shelby | Y | Y | Y | Y | Y | Y |
| Sessions | Y | Y | Y | Y | Y | Y |
| **ALASKA** | | | | | | |
| Stevens | Y | Y | Y | Y | Y | Y |
| Murkowski | Y | Y | Y | ? | ? | ? |
| **ARIZONA** | | | | | | |
| McCain | Y | Y | Y | Y | Y | Y |
| Kyl | Y | Y | Y | Y | Y | Y |
| **ARKANSAS** | | | | | | |
| Lincoln | N | N | N | N | Y | Y |
| Pryor | Y | N | Y | N | Y | Y |
| **CALIFORNIA** | | | | | | |
| Feinstein | N | N | N | N | Y | Y |
| Boxer | N | N | N | N | Y | Y |
| **COLORADO** | | | | | | |
| Allard | Y | Y | Y | Y | Y | Y |
| Salazar | Y | N | Y | Y | Y | Y |
| **CONNECTICUT** | | | | | | |
| Dodd | N | N | N | N | Y | Y |
| Lieberman | Y | N | Y | N | Y | Y |
| **DELAWARE** | | | | | | |
| Biden | N | N | N | N | + | + |
| Carper | Y | N | N | N | Y | Y |
| **FLORIDA** | | | | | | |
| Nelson | Y | N | Y | N | Y | Y |
| Martinez | Y | Y | Y | Y | Y | Y |
| **GEORGIA** | | | | | | |
| Chambliss | Y | Y | Y | Y | Y | Y |
| Isakson | Y | Y | Y | Y | Y | Y |
| **HAWAII** | | | | | | |
| Inouye | Y | N | Y | N | Y | Y |
| Akaka | N | N | N | N | Y | Y |
| **IDAHO** | | | | | | |
| Craig | Y | Y | Y | Y | Y | Y |
| Crapo | Y | Y | Y | Y | Y | Y |
| **ILLINOIS** | | | | | | |
| Durbin | N | N | N | N | Y | Y |
| Obama | N | N | N | N | ? | Y |
| **INDIANA** | | | | | | |
| Lugar | Y | Y | Y | Y | Y | Y |
| Bayh | N | N | N | N | Y | Y |
| **IOWA** | | | | | | |
| Grassley | Y | Y | Y | Y | Y | Y |
| Harkin | N | N | N | N | Y | Y |
| **KANSAS** | | | | | | |
| Brownback | Y | Y | Y | Y | Y | Y |
| Roberts | Y | Y | Y | Y | Y | Y |
| **KENTUCKY** | | | | | | |
| McConnell | Y | Y | Y | Y | Y | Y |
| Bunning | Y | Y | Y | Y | Y | Y |
| **LOUISIANA** | | | | | | |
| Landrieu | Y | N | Y | N | Y | Y |
| Vitter | Y | Y | Y | Y | Y | Y |
| **MAINE** | | | | | | |
| Snowe | Y | Y | Y | N | Y | Y |
| Collins | Y | Y | Y | N | Y | Y |
| **MARYLAND** | | | | | | |
| Sarbanes | N | N | N | N | Y | Y |
| Mikulski | N | N | N | N | Y | Y |
| **MASSACHUSETTS** | | | | | | |
| Kennedy | N | N | N | N | Y | Y |
| Kerry | N | N | N | N | Y | Y |
| **MICHIGAN** | | | | | | |
| Levin | N | N | N | N | Y | Y |
| Stabenow | N | N | N | N | Y | Y |
| **MINNESOTA** | | | | | | |
| Dayton | N | N | N | N | Y | Y |
| Coleman | Y | Y | Y | Y | Y | Y |
| **MISSISSIPPI** | | | | | | |
| Cochran | Y | Y | Y | Y | Y | Y |
| Lott | Y | Y | Y | Y | Y | Y |
| **MISSOURI** | | | | | | |
| Bond | Y | Y | Y | Y | Y | Y |
| Talent | Y | Y | Y | Y | Y | Y |
| **MONTANA** | | | | | | |
| Baucus | N | N | N | N | Y | Y |
| Burns | Y | Y | Y | Y | Y | Y |
| **NEBRASKA** | | | | | | |
| Hagel | Y | Y | Y | Y | Y | Y |
| Nelson | Y | Y | Y | Y | Y | Y |
| **NEVADA** | | | | | | |
| Reid | N | N | N | N | Y | Y |
| Ensign | Y | Y | Y | Y | Y | Y |
| **NEW HAMPSHIRE** | | | | | | |
| Gregg | Y | Y | Y | Y | Y | Y |
| Sununu | Y | Y | Y | Y | Y | Y |
| **NEW JERSEY** | | | | | | |
| Corzine | N | N | N | N | Y | Y |
| Lautenberg | ? | N | N | N | Y | Y |
| **NEW MEXICO** | | | | | | |
| Domenici | Y | Y | Y | Y | Y | Y |
| Bingaman | N | N | Y | N | Y | Y |
| **NEW YORK** | | | | | | |
| Schumer | N | N | N | N | Y | Y |
| Clinton | N | N | N | N | Y | Y |
| **NORTH CAROLINA** | | | | | | |
| Dole | Y | Y | Y | Y | Y | Y |
| Burr | Y | Y | Y | Y | Y | Y |
| **NORTH DAKOTA** | | | | | | |
| Conrad | Y | N | Y | N | Y | Y |
| Dorgan | N | N | N | N | Y | Y |
| **OHIO** | | | | | | |
| DeWine | Y | Y | Y | Y | Y | Y |
| Voinovich | Y | Y | Y | Y | Y | Y |
| **OKLAHOMA** | | | | | | |
| Inhofe | Y | Y | Y | Y | Y | Y |
| Coburn | Y | Y | Y | Y | Y | Y |
| **OREGON** | | | | | | |
| Wyden | N | N | N | N | Y | Y |
| Smith | Y | Y | Y | Y | Y | Y |
| **PENNSYLVANIA** | | | | | | |
| Specter | Y | Y | Y | Y | Y | Y |
| Santorum | Y | Y | Y | Y | Y | Y |
| **RHODE ISLAND** | | | | | | |
| Reed | N | N | N | N | Y | Y |
| Chafee | Y | Y | Y | N | Y | Y |
| **SOUTH CAROLINA** | | | | | | |
| Graham | Y | Y | Y | Y | Y | Y |
| DeMint | Y | Y | Y | Y | Y | Y |
| **SOUTH DAKOTA** | | | | | | |
| Johnson | N | N | Y | N | Y | Y |
| Thune | Y | Y | Y | Y | Y | Y |
| **TENNESSEE** | | | | | | |
| Frist | Y | Y | Y | Y | Y | Y |
| Alexander | Y | Y | Y | Y | ? | ? |
| **TEXAS** | | | | | | |
| Hutchison | Y | Y | Y | Y | Y | Y |
| Cornyn | Y | Y | Y | Y | Y | Y |
| **UTAH** | | | | | | |
| Hatch | Y | Y | Y | Y | Y | Y |
| Bennett | Y | Y | Y | Y | Y | Y |
| **VERMONT** | | | | | | |
| Leahy | N | N | N | N | Y | Y |
| *Jeffords* | ? | ? | ? | ? | ? | ? |
| **VIRGINIA** | | | | | | |
| Warner | Y | Y | Y | Y | Y | Y |
| Allen | Y | Y | Y | Y | Y | Y |
| **WASHINGTON** | | | | | | |
| Murray | N | N | N | N | Y | Y |
| Cantwell | N | N | N | N | Y | Y |
| **WEST VIRGINIA** | | | | | | |
| Byrd | Y | N | Y | N | Y | Y |
| Rockefeller | N | N | N | N | Y | Y |
| **WISCONSIN** | | | | | | |
| Kohl | ? | N | N | N | Y | Y |
| Feingold | N | N | N | N | Y | Y |
| **WYOMING** | | | | | | |
| Thomas | Y | Y | Y | Y | Y | Y |
| Enzi | Y | Y | Y | Y | Y | Y |

**KEY**  Republicans  Democrats  *Independents*

| | | | |
|---|---|---|---|
| Y | Voted for (yea) | X Paired against | C Voted "present" to avoid possible conflict of interest |
| # | Paired for | – Announced against | ? Did not vote or otherwise make a position known |
| + | Announced for | P Voted "present" | |
| N | Voted against (nay) | | |

ND Northern Democrats, SD Southern Democrats
Southern states: Ala., Ark., Fla., Ga., Ky., La., Miss., N.C., Okla., S.C., Tenn., Texas, Va.

# IN THE SENATE | By Vote Number

**136.** **Griffith Nomination/Confirmation.** Confirmation of President Bush's nomination of Thomas B. Griffith of Utah to be a judge for the U.S. Court of Appeals for the District of Columbia Circuit. Confirmed 73-24: R 53-0; D 20-24 (ND 17-23, SD 3-1); I 0-0. A "yea" was a vote in support of the president's position. June 14, 2005.

**137.** **HR 6. Energy Policy/Ethanol Liability.** Domenici, R-N.M., motion to table (kill) the Boxer, D-Calif., amendment to the Domenici amendment. The Boxer amendment would strike a provision in the underlying amendment that would provide liability protection for ethanol manufacturers. The Domenici amendment would require refiners to annually use 8 billion gallons of renewable fuels by 2012, grant liability protection for ethanol manufacturers, phase out the use of gasoline additive methyl tertiary butyl ether and eliminate the oxygen content requirement for reformulated gasoline. Motion agreed to 59-38: R 45-9; D 14-28 (ND 11-27, SD 3-1); I 0-1. June 14, 2005.

**138.** **HR 6. Energy Policy/Ethanol Mandate.** Domenici, R-N.M., motion to table (kill) the Schumer, D-N.Y., amendment to the Domenici amendment. The Schumer amendment would strike a section in the underlying amendment that would require refiners to annually use 8 billion gallons of renewable fuels, most likely ethanol, by 2012. Motion agreed to 69-28: R 39-14; D 30-14 (ND 26-14, SD 4-0); I 0-0. June 15, 2005.

**139.** **HR 6. Energy Policy/Renewable Fuel Mandate.** Domenici, R-N.M., amendment that would require refiners to annually use 8 billion gallons of renewable fuels by 2012, grant liability protection for ethanol manufacturers, phase out the use of the gasoline additive methyl tertiary butyl ether and elimi-nate the oxygen content requirement for reformulated gasoline. Adopted 70-26: R 38-14; D 32-12 (ND 28-12, SD 4-0); I 0-0. June 15, 2005.

**140.** **HR 6. Energy Policy/Foreign Oil Dependence.** Cantwell, D-Wash., amendment that would call on the president to develop and implement measures to reduce 40 percent foreign petroleum imports projected for 2025. It also would require the president to submit an annual report to Congress that would assess the progress made toward achieving that goal. Rejected 47-53: R 3-52; D 43-1 (ND 39-1, SD 4-0); I 1-0. June 16, 2005.

**141.** **HR 6. Energy Policy/Electric Utilities.** Bingaman, D-N.M., amendment that would mandate that at least 10 percent of the electricity sold by electric utilities by 2020 must be produced from renewable energy sources, beginning with a minimum annual standard of 2.5 percent for calendar years 2008 through 2011. Adopted 52-48: R 9-46; D 42-2 (ND 38-2, SD 4-0); I 1-0. June 16, 2005.

ND Northern Democrats, SD Southern Democrats
Southern states: Ala., Ark., Fla., Ga., Ky., La., Miss., N.C., Okla., S.C., Tenn., Texas, Va.

| | 136 | 137 | 138 | 139 | 140 | 141 |
|---|---|---|---|---|---|---|
| **ALABAMA** | | | | | | |
| Shelby | Y | Y | Y | N | N | N |
| Sessions | Y | Y | Y | Y | N | N |
| **ALASKA** | | | | | | |
| Stevens | Y | Y | ? | ? | N | N |
| Murkowski | Y | Y | ? | ? | N | N |
| **ARIZONA** | | | | | | |
| McCain | Y | N | N | N | N | N |
| Kyl | Y | Y | N | N | N | N |
| **ARKANSAS** | | | | | | |
| Lincoln | Y | Y | Y | Y | Y | Y |
| Pryor | Y | Y | Y | Y | Y | Y |
| **CALIFORNIA** | | | | | | |
| Feinstein | Y | – | N | N | Y | Y |
| Boxer | N | N | N | N | Y | Y |
| **COLORADO** | | | | | | |
| Allard | Y | Y | N | N | N | N |
| Salazar | N | Y | Y | Y | Y | Y |
| **CONNECTICUT** | | | | | | |
| Dodd | Y | N | N | N | Y | Y |
| Lieberman | Y | N | N | N | Y | Y |
| **DELAWARE** | | | | | | |
| Biden | Y | N | Y | Y | Y | Y |
| Carper | Y | N | Y | Y | Y | Y |
| **FLORIDA** | | | | | | |
| Nelson | Y | N | Y | Y | Y | Y |
| Martinez | Y | Y | Y | Y | N | N |
| **GEORGIA** | | | | | | |
| Chambliss | Y | Y | Y | N | N | N |
| Isakson | Y | Y | Y | N | N | N |
| **HAWAII** | | | | | | |
| Inouye | Y | N | Y | Y | Y | Y |
| Akaka | N | N | Y | Y | Y | Y |
| **IDAHO** | | | | | | |
| Craig | Y | Y | Y | Y | N | N |
| Crapo | Y | Y | Y | ? | N | N |
| **ILLINOIS** | | | | | | |
| Durbin | Y | N | Y | Y | Y | Y |
| Obama | Y | N | Y | Y | Y | Y |
| **INDIANA** | | | | | | |
| Lugar | Y | Y | Y | Y | N | N |
| Bayh | N | Y | Y | Y | Y | Y |
| **IOWA** | | | | | | |
| Grassley | Y | Y | Y | Y | N | N |
| Harkin | N | Y | Y | Y | Y | Y |
| **KANSAS** | | | | | | |
| Brownback | Y | Y | Y | Y | N | N |
| Roberts | Y | Y | Y | Y | N | N |
| **KENTUCKY** | | | | | | |
| McConnell | Y | Y | Y | Y | N | N |
| Bunning | Y | Y | Y | Y | N | N |
| **LOUISIANA** | | | | | | |
| Landrieu | N | Y | Y | Y | Y | Y |
| Vitter | Y | Y | Y | Y | N | N |
| **MAINE** | | | | | | |
| Snowe | Y | N | N | Y | Y | Y |
| Collins | Y | N | N | Y | Y | Y |
| **MARYLAND** | | | | | | |
| Sarbanes | N | N | Y | Y | Y | Y |
| Mikulski | N | N | N | Y | Y | Y |
| **MASSACHUSETTS** | | | | | | |
| Kennedy | N | N | N | N | Y | Y |
| Kerry | N | N | Y | Y | Y | Y |
| **MICHIGAN** | | | | | | |
| Levin | Y | N | Y | Y | Y | Y |
| Stabenow | N | Y | Y | Y | N | Y |
| **MINNESOTA** | | | | | | |
| Dayton | N | N | Y | Y | Y | Y |
| Coleman | Y | Y | Y | Y | N | Y |
| **MISSISSIPPI** | | | | | | |
| Cochran | Y | Y | Y | Y | N | N |
| Lott | Y | Y | N | N | N | N |
| **MISSOURI** | | | | | | |
| Bond | Y | Y | Y | Y | N | N |
| Talent | Y | Y | Y | Y | N | N |

| | 136 | 137 | 138 | 139 | 140 | 141 |
|---|---|---|---|---|---|---|
| **MONTANA** | | | | | | |
| Baucus | Y | Y | Y | Y | Y | Y |
| Burns | Y | Y | Y | N | N | N |
| **NEBRASKA** | | | | | | |
| Hagel | Y | Y | Y | Y | N | N |
| Nelson | Y | Y | Y | Y | N | N |
| **NEVADA** | | | | | | |
| Reid | Y | N | Y | Y | Y | Y |
| Ensign | Y | N | N | N | N | Y |
| **NEW HAMPSHIRE** | | | | | | |
| Gregg | Y | N | N | N | N | N |
| Sununu | Y | N | N | N | N | N |
| **NEW JERSEY** | | | | | | |
| Corzine | N | ? | N | N | Y | Y |
| Lautenberg | N | N | N | N | Y | Y |
| **NEW MEXICO** | | | | | | |
| Domenici | Y | Y | Y | Y | N | N |
| Bingaman | Y | N | Y | Y | Y | Y |
| **NEW YORK** | | | | | | |
| Schumer | Y | N | N | N | Y | Y |
| Clinton | N | N | N | N | Y | Y |
| **NORTH CAROLINA** | | | | | | |
| Dole | Y | Y | Y | N | N | N |
| Burr | Y | Y | Y | N | N | N |
| **NORTH DAKOTA** | | | | | | |
| Conrad | Y | Y | Y | Y | Y | Y |
| Dorgan | Y | Y | Y | Y | Y | Y |
| **OHIO** | | | | | | |
| DeWine | Y | ? | Y | N | N | N |
| Voinovich | Y | Y | Y | N | N | N |
| **OKLAHOMA** | | | | | | |
| Inhofe | Y | Y | Y | N | N | N |
| Coburn | Y | N | N | N | N | N |
| **OREGON** | | | | | | |
| Wyden | N | N | N | N | Y | Y |
| Smith | Y | Y | Y | Y | N | Y |
| **PENNSYLVANIA** | | | | | | |
| Specter | ? | N | N | N | Y | Y |
| Santorum | ? | Y | N | N | N | N |
| **RHODE ISLAND** | | | | | | |
| Reed | N | N | N | N | Y | Y |
| Chafee | Y | N | N | N | Y | Y |
| **SOUTH CAROLINA** | | | | | | |
| Graham | Y | Y | Y | N | N | N |
| DeMint | Y | Y | N | N | N | N |
| **SOUTH DAKOTA** | | | | | | |
| Johnson | N | Y | Y | Y | Y | Y |
| Thune | Y | Y | Y | N | N | N |
| **TENNESSEE** | | | | | | |
| Frist | Y | Y | Y | N | N | N |
| Alexander | Y | Y | Y | N | N | N |
| **TEXAS** | | | | | | |
| Hutchison | Y | Y | Y | Y | N | N |
| Cornyn | Y | Y | Y | N | N | N |
| **UTAH** | | | | | | |
| Hatch | Y | Y | Y | Y | N | N |
| Bennett | Y | Y | Y | Y | N | N |
| **VERMONT** | | | | | | |
| Leahy | N | N | N | N | Y | Y |
| *Jeffords* | ? | N | ? | ? | Y | Y |
| **VIRGINIA** | | | | | | |
| Warner | Y | N | N | N | N | N |
| Allen | Y | Y | Y | N | N | N |
| **WASHINGTON** | | | | | | |
| Murray | N | N | Y | Y | Y | Y |
| Cantwell | N | N | Y | Y | Y | Y |
| **WEST VIRGINIA** | | | | | | |
| Byrd | N | N | Y | Y | Y | N |
| Rockefeller | N | Y | N | N | Y | Y |
| **WISCONSIN** | | | | | | |
| Kohl | Y | Y | Y | Y | Y | Y |
| Feingold | N | N | Y | Y | Y | Y |
| **WYOMING** | | | | | | |
| Thomas | Y | Y | Y | Y | N | N |
| Enzi | Y | Y | Y | Y | N | N |

**KEY**  Republicans  Democrats  *Independents*

| | | | |
|---|---|---|---|
| **Y** | Voted for (yea) | **X** Paired against | **C** Voted "present" to avoid possible conflict of interest |
| **#** | Paired for | **–** Announced against | |
| **+** | Announced for | **P** Voted "present" | **?** Did not vote or otherwise make a position known |
| **N** | Voted against (nay) | | |

# IN THE SENATE | By Vote Number

**142. Bolton Nomination/Cloture.** Motion to invoke cloture (thus limiting debate) on President Bush's nomination of John R. Bolton to be the permanent U.S. representative to the United Nations. Motion rejected 54-38: R 51-1; D 3-36 (ND 1-34, SD 2-2); I 0-1. Three-fifths of the total Senate (60) is required to invoke cloture. June 20, 2005.

**143. HR 6. Energy Policy/Outer Continental Shelf Inventory.** Martinez, R-Fla., amendment that would strike a section in the bill directing the Interior Department to make an assessment of oil and natural gas resources in the Outer Continental Shelf. Rejected 44-52: R 12-42; D 31-10 (ND 30-7, SD 1-3); I 1-0. June 21, 2005.

**144. HR 6. Energy Policy/Climate Change.** Hagel, R-Neb., amendment that would direct the Energy secretary to lead an interagency process to implement a national climate change strategy and authorize such sums as necessary for projects using technologies that reduce greenhouse gases. It would establish an interagency working group to promote exports of greenhouse gas-reducing technology to developing countries. Adopted 66-29: R 47-7; D 19-22 (ND 16-21, SD 3-1); I 0-0. June 21, 2005.

**145. HR 6. Energy Policy/Diesel Emissions.** Voinovich, R-Ohio, amendment that would authorize $1 billion over five years to establish voluntary national and state-level grant and loan programs to promote the reduction of diesel emissions. Adopted 92-1: R 53-1; D 39-0 (ND 35-0, SD 4-0); I 0-0. June 21, 2005.

**146. HR 6. Energy Policy/Liquefied Natural Gas Terminals.** Domenici, R-N.M., motion to table (kill) the Feinstein, D-Calif., amendment that would prohibit the Federal Energy Regulatory Commission from approving an application for a liquefied natural gas terminal located on shore or in state waters without the approval of the state's governor. Motion agreed to 52-45: R 44-10; D 8-34 (ND 6-32, SD 2-2); I 0-1. June 22, 2005.

**147. HR 6. Energy Policy/Gas Prices.** Domenici, R-N.M., motion to table (kill) the Schumer, D-N.Y., amendment that would express the sense of the Senate that the president should challenge the Organization of Petroleum Exporting Countries to immediately increase oil production, and require that 1 million barrels of oil a day be released from the Strategic Petroleum Reserve for 30 days after the bill's enactment. Motion agreed to 57-39: R 51-3; D 6-35 (ND 5-32, SD 1-3); I 0-1. June 22, 2005.

| | 142 | 143 | 144 | 145 | 146 | 147 |
|---|---|---|---|---|---|---|
| **ALABAMA** | | | | | | |
| Shelby | Y | N | Y | Y | Y | Y |
| Sessions | Y | N | Y | Y | N | Y |
| **ALASKA** | | | | | | |
| Stevens | Y | N | Y | Y | Y | Y |
| Murkowski | Y | N | Y | Y | Y | Y |
| **ARIZONA** | | | | | | |
| McCain | Y | Y | N | Y | Y | Y |
| Kyl | Y | N | Y | Y | Y | Y |
| **ARKANSAS** | | | | | | |
| Lincoln | N | N | Y | Y | Y | N |
| Pryor | Y | N | Y | Y | Y | N |
| **CALIFORNIA** | | | | | | |
| Feinstein | N | Y | N | Y | N | N |
| Boxer | N | Y | N | Y | N | N |
| **COLORADO** | | | | | | |
| Allard | Y | N | Y | Y | Y | Y |
| Salazar | N | N | Y | Y | Y | N |
| **CONNECTICUT** | | | | | | |
| Dodd | N | Y | N | Y | N | N |
| Lieberman | N | Y | N | Y | N | N |
| **DELAWARE** | | | | | | |
| Biden | N | Y | N | Y | N | N |
| Carper | N | N | N | Y | N | N |
| **FLORIDA** | | | | | | |
| Nelson | N | Y | Y | Y | Y | N |
| Martinez | Y | Y | Y | Y | N | Y |
| **GEORGIA** | | | | | | |
| Chambliss | Y | N | Y | Y | Y | Y |
| Isakson | Y | N | Y | Y | Y | Y |
| **HAWAII** | | | | | | |
| Inouye | N | Y | N | Y | N | ? |
| Akaka | N | Y | N | Y | N | N |
| **IDAHO** | | | | | | |
| Craig | Y | N | Y | Y | Y | Y |
| Crapo | Y | N | Y | Y | Y | Y |
| **ILLINOIS** | | | | | | |
| Durbin | N | Y | N | Y | N | N |
| Obama | N | Y | N | Y | N | N |
| **INDIANA** | | | | | | |
| Lugar | Y | N | Y | Y | Y | Y |
| Bayh | N | Y | Y | Y | N | Y |
| **IOWA** | | | | | | |
| Grassley | Y | N | Y | Y | Y | Y |
| Harkin | N | Y | N | Y | N | N |
| **KANSAS** | | | | | | |
| Brownback | Y | N | Y | Y | Y | Y |
| Roberts | Y | N | Y | Y | Y | Y |
| **KENTUCKY** | | | | | | |
| McConnell | Y | N | Y | Y | Y | Y |
| Bunning | Y | N | N | Y | Y | Y |
| **LOUISIANA** | | | | | | |
| Landrieu | Y | N | Y | Y | N | Y |
| Vitter | Y | N | Y | Y | N | Y |
| **MAINE** | | | | | | |
| Snowe | Y | Y | N | Y | N | N |
| Collins | Y | Y | N | Y | N | N |
| **MARYLAND** | | | | | | |
| Sarbanes | N | Y | N | Y | N | N |
| Mikulski | N | Y | Y | Y | N | N |
| **MASSACHUSETTS** | | | | | | |
| Kennedy | N | Y | N | Y | N | N |
| Kerry | ? | ? | ? | ? | N | N |
| **MICHIGAN** | | | | | | |
| Levin | ? | Y | Y | Y | N | N |
| Stabenow | N | Y | Y | Y | N | N |
| **MINNESOTA** | | | | | | |
| Dayton | N | Y | Y | Y | N | N |
| Coleman | + | Y | Y | Y | Y | Y |
| **MISSISSIPPI** | | | | | | |
| Cochran | Y | N | Y | Y | Y | Y |
| Lott | Y | N | Y | Y | Y | Y |
| **MISSOURI** | | | | | | |
| Bond | Y | N | Y | Y | Y | Y |
| Talent | Y | N | Y | Y | Y | Y |

| | 142 | 143 | 144 | 145 | 146 | 147 |
|---|---|---|---|---|---|---|
| **MONTANA** | | | | | | |
| Baucus | N | N | Y | Y | Y | Y |
| Burns | ? | N | Y | Y | Y | Y |
| **NEBRASKA** | | | | | | |
| Hagel | Y | N | Y | Y | Y | Y |
| Nelson | Y | N | Y | Y | Y | N |
| **NEVADA** | | | | | | |
| Reid | N | Y | Y | Y | N | N |
| Ensign | Y | N | Y | Y | Y | Y |
| **NEW HAMPSHIRE** | | | | | | |
| Gregg | Y | N | N | Y | Y | Y |
| Sununu | Y | Y | N | Y | N | Y |
| **NEW JERSEY** | | | | | | |
| Corzine | N | Y | N | Y | N | N |
| Lautenberg | N | Y | N | ? | N | N |
| **NEW MEXICO** | | | | | | |
| Domenici | Y | N | Y | Y | Y | Y |
| Bingaman | N | N | Y | Y | Y | N |
| **NEW YORK** | | | | | | |
| Schumer | N | Y | Y | Y | N | N |
| Clinton | N | Y | Y | Y | N | N |
| **NORTH CAROLINA** | | | | | | |
| Dole | Y | Y | Y | Y | Y | Y |
| Burr | Y | Y | Y | Y | Y | Y |
| **NORTH DAKOTA** | | | | | | |
| Conrad | N | N | Y | ? | ? | ? |
| Dorgan | N | ? | ? | ? | Y | N |
| **OHIO** | | | | | | |
| DeWine | Y | N | Y | Y | Y | Y |
| Voinovich | N | N | Y | Y | Y | Y |
| **OKLAHOMA** | | | | | | |
| Inhofe | Y | N | Y | Y | Y | Y |
| Coburn | Y | N | Y | Y | Y | Y |
| **OREGON** | | | | | | |
| Wyden | N | Y | N | Y | N | N |
| Smith | Y | Y | Y | Y | N | Y |
| **PENNSYLVANIA** | | | | | | |
| Specter | Y | N | Y | Y | Y | N |
| Santorum | Y | N | Y | Y | Y | Y |
| **RHODE ISLAND** | | | | | | |
| Reed | N | Y | N | Y | N | N |
| Chafee | Y | Y | N | Y | N | N |
| **SOUTH CAROLINA** | | | | | | |
| Graham | Y | Y | Y | Y | Y | Y |
| DeMint | Y | Y | Y | Y | Y | Y |
| **SOUTH DAKOTA** | | | | | | |
| Johnson | ? | ? | ? | ? | ? | ? |
| Thune | ? | ? | ? | ? | ? | ? |
| **TENNESSEE** | | | | | | |
| Frist | Y | N | Y | Y | Y | Y |
| Alexander | Y | N | Y | Y | Y | Y |
| **TEXAS** | | | | | | |
| Hutchison | Y | N | Y | Y | Y | Y |
| Cornyn | Y | N | Y | Y | Y | Y |
| **UTAH** | | | | | | |
| Hatch | Y | N | Y | Y | Y | Y |
| Bennett | Y | N | Y | Y | Y | Y |
| **VERMONT** | | | | | | |
| Leahy | N | Y | N | Y | N | N |
| *Jeffords* | N | Y | ? | ? | N | N |
| **VIRGINIA** | | | | | | |
| Warner | Y | N | Y | Y | Y | Y |
| Allen | Y | N | Y | Y | N | Y |
| **WASHINGTON** | | | | | | |
| Murray | N | Y | Y | Y | N | Y |
| Cantwell | N | Y | N | Y | N | Y |
| **WEST VIRGINIA** | | | | | | |
| Byrd | N | N | N | Y | N | N |
| Rockefeller | N | Y | Y | Y | N | N |
| **WISCONSIN** | | | | | | |
| Kohl | ? | Y | N | Y | N | N |
| Feingold | ? | Y | N | Y | N | N |
| **WYOMING** | | | | | | |
| Thomas | Y | N | Y | Y | Y | Y |
| Enzi | Y | N | Y | N | Y | Y |

**KEY**    Republicans    Democrats    *Independents*

| | | | |
|---|---|---|---|
| Y | Voted for (yea) | X | Paired against |
| # | Paired for | – | Announced against |
| + | Announced for | P | Voted "present" |
| N | Voted against (nay) | | |

| | |
|---|---|
| C | Voted "present" to avoid possible conflict of interest |
| ? | Did not vote or otherwise make a position known |

ND Northern Democrats, SD Southern Democrats
Southern states: Ala., Ark., Fla., Ga., Ky., La., Miss., N.C., Okla., S.C., Tenn., Texas, Va.

# IN THE SENATE | By Vote Number

**148.** **HR 6. Energy Policy/Climate Change.** McCain, R-Ariz., amendment that would cap greenhouse gas emissions at 2000 levels by 2010. It would provide for the trading of emission allowances and reductions through a government-provided greenhouse gas database that would contain an inventory of emissions and a registry of reductions. Rejected 38-60: R 6-49; D 31-11 (ND 30-8, SD 1-3); I 1-0. A "nay" was a vote in support of the president's position. June 22, 2005.

**149.** **HR 6. Energy Policy/Climate Change.** Inhofe, R-Okla., motion to table (kill) the Bingaman, D-N.M., amendment that would express the sense of the Senate that Congress should enact a national program of mandatory, market-based limits and incentives on greenhouse gas emissions that slow, stop and reverse their growth at a rate that would not harm the economy significantly, and would encourage comparable action by other nations. Motion rejected 44-53: R 42-12; D 2-40 (ND 2-36, SD 0-4); I 0-1. (Subsequently, the amendment was adopted by voice vote.) A "yea" was a vote in support of the president's position. June 22, 2005.

**150.** **HR 6. Energy Policy/Wind Power Projects.** Alexander, R-Tenn., amendment that would bar subsidies for all wind power projects within 20 miles of highly scenic areas and federal land, including national parks, lakeshores and wildlife refuges. Environmental impact statements for all projects within 20 miles of such areas would be required and communities would be given six months notice before a project is permitted. Rejected 32-63: R 31-23; D 1-40 (ND 0-37, SD 1-3); I 0-0. June 22, 2005.

**151.** **HR 6. Energy Policy/Climate Change.** Kerry, D-Mass., amendment that would express the sense of the Senate that the United States should act to reduce the health, environmental and economic risks posed by global climate change and foster sustained economic growth through new technologies by engaging in international negotiations under the United Nations Framework Convention of Climate Change. Rejected 46-49: R 7-47; D 39-2 (ND 37-0, SD 2-2); I 0-0. June 22, 2005.

**152.** **HR 6. Energy Policy/Cloture.** Domenici, R-N.M., motion to invoke cloture on the bill that would overhaul the nation's energy policy and provide for approximately $18 billion in energy-related tax incentives. It would require refiners to annually use 8 billion gallons of renewable fuels by 2012, grant liability protection for ethanol manufacturers and phase out the use of the gasoline additive methyl tertiary butyl ether. Motion agreed to 92-4: R 53-1; D 38-3 (ND 34-3, SD 4-0); I 1-0. Three-fifths of the total Senate (60) is required to invoke cloture. June 23, 2005.

| | 148 | 149 | 150 | 151 | 152 | | | 148 | 149 | 150 | 151 | 152 |
|---|---|---|---|---|---|---|---|---|---|---|---|---|
| **ALABAMA** | | | | | | | **MONTANA** | | | | | |
| Shelby | N | Y | N | N | Y | | Baucus | N | Y | N | Y | Y |
| Sessions | N | Y | Y | N | Y | | Burns | N | Y | Y | N | Y |
| **ALASKA** | | | | | | | **NEBRASKA** | | | | | |
| Stevens | N | Y | Y | N | Y | | Hagel | N | Y | N | N | Y |
| Murkowski | N | Y | Y | N | Y | | Nelson | N | Y | N | Y | Y |
| **ARIZONA** | | | | | | | **NEVADA** | | | | | |
| McCain | Y | N | Y | Y | N | | Reid | Y | N | N | Y | Y |
| Kyl | N | Y | Y | N | Y | | Ensign | N | Y | Y | N | Y |
| **ARKANSAS** | | | | | | | **NEW HAMPSHIRE** | | | | | |
| Lincoln | N | N | N | Y | Y | | Gregg | Y | N | Y | Y | Y |
| Pryor | N | N | N | N | Y | | Sununu | N | Y | Y | N | Y |
| **CALIFORNIA** | | | | | | | **NEW JERSEY** | | | | | |
| Feinstein | Y | N | N | Y | Y | | Corzine | Y | N | N | Y | N |
| Boxer | N | N | N | Y | Y | | Lautenberg | Y | N | N | Y | N |
| **COLORADO** | | | | | | | **NEW MEXICO** | | | | | |
| Allard | N | Y | N | N | Y | | Domenici | N | N | Y | N | Y |
| Salazar | Y | N | N | Y | Y | | Bingaman | Y | N | N | Y | Y |
| **CONNECTICUT** | | | | | | | **NEW YORK** | | | | | |
| Dodd | Y | N | N | Y | Y | | Schumer | Y | N | N | Y | Y |
| Lieberman | Y | N | N | Y | Y | | Clinton | Y | N | N | Y | Y |
| **DELAWARE** | | | | | | | **NORTH CAROLINA** | | | | | |
| Biden | Y | N | N | Y | Y | | Dole | N | Y | N | N | Y |
| Carper | Y | N | N | Y | Y | | Burr | N | Y | Y | N | Y |
| **FLORIDA** | | | | | | | **NORTH DAKOTA** | | | | | |
| Nelson | Y | N | N | Y | Y | | Conrad | ? | ? | ? | ? | ? |
| Martinez | N | Y | Y | N | Y | | Dorgan | ? | ? | ? | ? | ? |
| **GEORGIA** | | | | | | | **OHIO** | | | | | |
| Chambliss | N | Y | N | N | Y | | DeWine | N | N | Y | N | Y |
| Isakson | N | Y | N | N | Y | | Voinovich | N | Y | Y | N | Y |
| **HAWAII** | | | | | | | **OKLAHOMA** | | | | | |
| Inouye | Y | N | N | Y | Y | | Inhofe | N | Y | N | N | Y |
| Akaka | Y | N | N | Y | Y | | Coburn | N | Y | N | N | Y |
| **IDAHO** | | | | | | | **OREGON** | | | | | |
| Craig | N | Y | N | N | Y | | Wyden | Y | N | N | Y | Y |
| Crapo | N | Y | N | N | Y | | Smith | N | Y | N | Y | Y |
| **ILLINOIS** | | | | | | | **PENNSYLVANIA** | | | | | |
| Durbin | Y | N | N | Y | N | | Specter | N | N | Y | N | Y |
| Obama | Y | N | N | Y | Y | | Santorum | N | Y | Y | N | Y |
| **INDIANA** | | | | | | | **RHODE ISLAND** | | | | | |
| Lugar | Y | N | Y | Y | Y | | Reed | Y | N | N | Y | Y |
| Bayh | Y | N | N | Y | Y | | Chafee | Y | N | N | Y | Y |
| **IOWA** | | | | | | | **SOUTH CAROLINA** | | | | | |
| Grassley | N | Y | N | Y | Y | | Graham | N | Y | N | N | Y |
| Harkin | N | N | N | Y | Y | | DeMint | N | Y | N | N | Y |
| **KANSAS** | | | | | | | **SOUTH DAKOTA** | | | | | |
| Brownback | N | Y | Y | N | Y | | Johnson | Y | N | N | Y | Y |
| Roberts | N | Y | N | N | Y | | Thune | N | Y | N | N | Y |
| **KENTUCKY** | | | | | | | **TENNESSEE** | | | | | |
| McConnell | N | Y | Y | N | Y | | Frist | N | Y | Y | N | Y |
| Bunning | N | Y | Y | N | Y | | Alexander | N | N | Y | N | Y |
| **LOUISIANA** | | | | | | | **TEXAS** | | | | | |
| Landrieu | N | N | N | N | Y | | Hutchison | N | Y | N | N | Y |
| Vitter | N | Y | Y | N | Y | | Cornyn | N | Y | Y | N | Y |
| **MAINE** | | | | | | | **UTAH** | | | | | |
| Snowe | Y | N | N | Y | Y | | Hatch | N | Y | N | N | Y |
| Collins | Y | N | N | Y | Y | | Bennett | N | Y | N | N | Y |
| **MARYLAND** | | | | | | | **VERMONT** | | | | | |
| Sarbanes | Y | N | N | Y | Y | | Leahy | Y | N | N | Y | Y |
| Mikulski | Y | N | N | Y | Y | | Jeffords | Y | N | ? | ? | Y |
| **MASSACHUSETTS** | | | | | | | **VIRGINIA** | | | | | |
| Kennedy | Y | N | N | Y | Y | | Warner | N | N | Y | N | Y |
| Kerry | Y | N | N | Y | Y | | Allen | N | Y | Y | N | Y |
| **MICHIGAN** | | | | | | | **WASHINGTON** | | | | | |
| Levin | N | N | N | Y | Y | | Murray | Y | N | N | Y | Y |
| Stabenow | Y | N | N | Y | Y | | Cantwell | Y | N | N | Y | Y |
| **MINNESOTA** | | | | | | | **WEST VIRGINIA** | | | | | |
| Dayton | N | N | ? | ? | ? | | Byrd | N | N | N | Y | Y |
| Coleman | N | – | – | – | + | | Rockefeller | Y | N | N | Y | Y |
| **MISSISSIPPI** | | | | | | | **WISCONSIN** | | | | | |
| Cochran | N | Y | Y | N | Y | | Kohl | Y | N | N | Y | Y |
| Lott | N | Y | Y | N | Y | | Feingold | N | N | N | Y | Y |
| **MISSOURI** | | | | | | | **WYOMING** | | | | | |
| Bond | N | Y | N | N | Y | | Thomas | N | Y | N | N | Y |
| Talent | N | Y | Y | N | Y | | Enzi | N | Y | N | N | Y |

**KEY**   Republicans   Democrats   *Independents*

| | | | |
|---|---|---|---|
| Y | Voted for (yea) | X | Paired against |
| # | Paired for | – | Announced against |
| + | Announced for | P | Voted "present" |
| N | Voted against (nay) | | |

| | |
|---|---|
| C | Voted "present" to avoid possible conflict of interest |
| ? | Did not vote or otherwise make a position known |

ND Northern Democrats, SD Southern Democrats
Southern states: Ala., Ark., Fla., Ga., Ky., La., Miss., N.C., Okla., S.C., Tenn., Texas, Va.

# IN THE SENATE | By Vote Number

**153.** **HR 6. Energy Policy/Coastal Impact Assistance Program.** Vitter, R-La., motion to waive the Budget Act with respect to the Gregg, R-N.H., point of order against the Domenici, R-N.M., amendment.The Domenici amendment would provide $250 million per year for fiscal 2007 through 2010 from existing royalties to six coastal states that have offshore oil and gas facilities. Motion agreed to 69-26: R 32-21; D 36-5 (ND 32-5, SD 4-0); I 1-0. A three-fifths majority (60) of the total Senate is required to waive the Budget Act. (Subsequently, the amendment was adopted by voice vote.) June 23, 2005.

**154.** **HR 6. Energy Policy/Medical Isotope Production.** Schumer, D-N.Y., amendment that would strike a provision related to the production of medical isotopes. Adopted 52-46: R 15-39; D 37-6 (ND 36-3, SD 1-3); I 0-1. June 23, 2005.

**155.** **HR 6. Energy Policy/Federal Loan Guarantees.** Sununu, R-N.H., amendment that would strike a provision that would provide incentives in the form of loan guarantees for the development of innovative technology such as those used in nuclear power plants. Rejected 21-76: R 9-44; D 12-31 (ND 12-27, SD 0-4); I 0-1. June 23, 2005.

**156.** **HR 6. Energy Policy/Fuel Economy Standards.** Bond, R-Mo., amendment that would require the Transportation secretary to consider several factors, including technological feasibility and economic practicability, when determining the Corporate Average Fuel (CAFE) Economy standards. It would direct the secretary to issue an environmental assessment of the effects of increased fuel efficiency standards on the environment and would authorize $5 million annually from fiscal 2006 through 2010 for it. Adopted 64-31: R 46-7; D 18-23 (ND 15-22, SD 3-1); I 0-1. June 23, 2005.

**157.** **HR 6. Energy Policy/Fuel Economy Standards.** Durbin, D-Ill., amendment that would mandate phased increases in the CAFE standards. Passenger vehicles made before 2008 would have to average 25 miles per gallon. The standard would gradually increase to 40 mpg by model year 2016. Non-passenger vehicles made before 2008 would have to average 17 mpg. By model year 2016, the standard would rise to an average of 27.5 mpg. Rejected 28-67: R 5-48; D 22-19 (ND 21-16, SD 1-3); I 1-0. A "nay" was a vote in support of the president's position. June 23, 2005.

| | 153 | 154 | 155 | 156 | 157 |
|---|---|---|---|---|---|
| **ALABAMA** | | | | | |
| Shelby | Y | N | N | Y | N |
| Sessions | Y | N | N | Y | N |
| **ALASKA** | | | | | |
| Stevens | ? | N | N | Y | N |
| Murkowski | Y | N | N | Y | N |
| **ARIZONA** | | | | | |
| McCain | N | Y | Y | N | N |
| Kyl | N | Y | Y | Y | N |
| **ARKANSAS** | | | | | |
| Lincoln | Y | N | N | Y | N |
| Pryor | Y | N | N | Y | N |
| **CALIFORNIA** | | | | | |
| Feinstein | Y | Y | N | N | Y |
| Boxer | Y | Y | Y | N | + |
| **COLORADO** | | | | | |
| Allard | N | N | Y | Y | N |
| Salazar | Y | Y | N | Y | N |
| **CONNECTICUT** | | | | | |
| Dodd | Y | Y | N | ? | Y |
| Lieberman | Y | Y | N | N | Y |
| **DELAWARE** | | | | | |
| Biden | Y | Y | N | N | N |
| Carper | Y | N | N | Y | Y |
| **FLORIDA** | | | | | |
| Nelson | Y | Y | N | N | Y |
| Martinez | Y | Y | N | Y | N |
| **GEORGIA** | | | | | |
| Chambliss | N | N | N | Y | N |
| Isakson | N | N | N | Y | N |
| **HAWAII** | | | | | |
| Inouye | Y | Y | N | ? | ? |
| Akaka | Y | Y | N | N | Y |
| **IDAHO** | | | | | |
| Craig | Y | N | N | Y | N |
| Crapo | N | N | N | Y | N |
| **ILLINOIS** | | | | | |
| Durbin | Y | Y | Y | N | Y |
| Obama | Y | Y | N | N | Y |
| **INDIANA** | | | | | |
| Lugar | N | Y | N | Y | Y |
| Bayh | Y | Y | N | Y | N |
| **IOWA** | | | | | |
| Grassley | Y | N | N | Y | N |
| Harkin | N | Y | Y | N | Y |
| **KANSAS** | | | | | |
| Brownback | Y | N | N | Y | N |
| Roberts | Y | N | N | Y | N |
| **KENTUCKY** | | | | | |
| McConnell | N | N | N | Y | N |
| Bunning | N | N | N | Y | N |
| **LOUISIANA** | | | | | |
| Landrieu | Y | N | N | Y | N |
| Vitter | Y | Y | N | Y | N |
| **MAINE** | | | | | |
| Snowe | Y | Y | N | N | Y |
| Collins | N | Y | Y | N | Y |
| **MARYLAND** | | | | | |
| Sarbanes | Y | Y | N | N | Y |
| Mikulski | Y | Y | Y | Y | N |
| **MASSACHUSETTS** | | | | | |
| Kennedy | Y | Y | Y | N | Y |
| Kerry | Y | Y | N | Y | N |
| **MICHIGAN** | | | | | |
| Levin | Y | Y | N | Y | N |
| Stabenow | Y | Y | N | Y | N |
| **MINNESOTA** | | | | | |
| Dayton | ? | Y | N | Y | Y |
| Coleman | + | N | N | Y | N |
| **MISSISSIPPI** | | | | | |
| Cochran | Y | N | N | Y | N |
| Lott | Y | Y | N | ? | ? |
| **MISSOURI** | | | | | |
| Bond | Y | N | N | Y | N |
| Talent | Y | N | N | Y | N |

| | 153 | 154 | 155 | 156 | 157 |
|---|---|---|---|---|---|
| **MONTANA** | | | | | |
| Baucus | Y | N | N | Y | N |
| Burns | N | N | N | Y | N |
| **NEBRASKA** | | | | | |
| Hagel | Y | N | N | Y | N |
| Nelson | Y | Y | N | Y | N |
| **NEVADA** | | | | | |
| Reid | Y | Y | N | N | Y |
| Ensign | Y | Y | ? | Y | N |
| **NEW HAMPSHIRE** | | | | | |
| Gregg | N | Y | Y | N | Y |
| Sununu | N | Y | Y | N | N |
| **NEW JERSEY** | | | | | |
| Corzine | Y | Y | Y | N | Y |
| Lautenberg | Y | Y | Y | N | Y |
| **NEW MEXICO** | | | | | |
| Domenici | Y | ? | ? | ? | ? |
| Bingaman | Y | ? | ? | ? | ? |
| **NEW YORK** | | | | | |
| Schumer | Y | Y | Y | N | Y |
| Clinton | Y | Y | N | N | Y |
| **NORTH CAROLINA** | | | | | |
| Dole | Y | N | N | Y | N |
| Burr | Y | N | N | Y | N |
| **NORTH DAKOTA** | | | | | |
| Conrad | ? | Y | N | Y | N |
| Dorgan | ? | Y | N | Y | N |
| **OHIO** | | | | | |
| DeWine | Y | N | N | Y | N |
| Voinovich | Y | N | N | Y | N |
| **OKLAHOMA** | | | | | |
| Inhofe | N | N | N | Y | N |
| Coburn | N | N | Y | Y | N |
| **OREGON** | | | | | |
| Wyden | N | Y | Y | N | Y |
| Smith | Y | N | N | Y | N |
| **PENNSYLVANIA** | | | | | |
| Specter | N | Y | N | Y | N |
| Santorum | N | Y | N | Y | N |
| **RHODE ISLAND** | | | | | |
| Reed | Y | Y | Y | N | Y |
| Chafee | N | N | N | N | Y |
| **SOUTH CAROLINA** | | | | | |
| Graham | Y | N | N | Y | N |
| DeMint | N | N | Y | Y | N |
| **SOUTH DAKOTA** | | | | | |
| Johnson | Y | N | N | Y | N |
| Thune | Y | N | N | Y | N |
| **TENNESSEE** | | | | | |
| Frist | Y | N | N | Y | N |
| Alexander | Y | Y | N | Y | N |
| **TEXAS** | | | | | |
| Hutchison | Y | N | N | Y | N |
| Cornyn | Y | Y | N | Y | N |
| **UTAH** | | | | | |
| Hatch | Y | N | N | Y | N |
| Bennett | Y | N | N | Y | N |
| **VERMONT** | | | | | |
| Leahy | N | Y | N | N | Y |
| Jeffords | Y | N | N | N | Y |
| **VIRGINIA** | | | | | |
| Warner | Y | N | N | Y | N |
| Allen | Y | N | N | Y | N |
| **WASHINGTON** | | | | | |
| Murray | Y | Y | N | N | Y |
| Cantwell | Y | Y | N | N | Y |
| **WEST VIRGINIA** | | | | | |
| Byrd | N | Y | N | Y | N |
| Rockefeller | Y | Y | N | N | Y |
| **WISCONSIN** | | | | | |
| Kohl | Y | Y | N | Y | N |
| Feingold | N | Y | Y | Y | N |
| **WYOMING** | | | | | |
| Thomas | N | N | N | N | N |
| Enzi | N | N | N | Y | N |

**KEY**  Republicans   Democrats   *Independents*

| | | | |
|---|---|---|---|
| Y | Voted for (yea) | X | Paired against |
| # | Paired for | – | Announced against |
| + | Announced for | P | Voted "present" |
| N | Voted against (nay) | | |

C  Voted "present" to avoid possible conflict of interest
?  Did not vote or otherwise make a position known

ND Northern Democrats, SD Southern Democrats
Southern states: Ala., Ark., Fla., Ga., Ky., La., Miss., N.C., Okla., S.C., Tenn., Texas, Va.

# IN THE SENATE | By Vote Number

**158.** **HR 6. Energy Policy/Passage.** Passage of the bill that would overhaul the nation's energy policy and provide for about $18 billion in energy-related tax incentives. It would require refiners to use 8 billion gallons of renewable fuels per year by 2012, grant liability protection for ethanol manufacturers and phase out the use of the gasoline additive methyl tertiary butyl ether. It also would direct the Energy secretary to lead an interagency process to implement a national climate change strategy and authorize funding for projects using technologies that reduce greenhouse gases. Passed 85-12: R 49-5; D 35-7 (ND 32-6, SD 3-1); I 1-0. A "yea" was a vote in support of the president's position. June 28, 2005.

**159.** **HR 2361. Fiscal 2006 Interior-Environment Appropriations/ Indian Health Funding.** Coburn, R-Okla., motion to waive the Budget Act with respect to the Burns, R-Mont., point of order against the Coburn amendment. The Coburn amendment would reduce funding for land acquisition by $121 million, to $33 million, and transfer the money to the Indian Health Service. Motion rejected 17-75: R 10-41; D 7-33 (ND 7-29, SD 0-4); I 0-1. A three-fifths majority (60) of the total Senate is required to waive the Budget Act. (Subsequently, the chair upheld the point of order, and the amendment fell.) June 28, 2005.

**160.** **HR 2361. Fiscal 2006 Interior-Environment Appropriations/ Conference Report Language.** Coburn, R-Okla., amendment that would require that any limitation, directive or earmark be included in the bill's conference report to give both chambers the opportunity to vote on all provisions. Rejected 33-59: R 13-38; D 20-20 (ND 18-18, SD 2-2); I 0-1. June 28, 2005.

**161.** **HR 2361 Fiscal 2006 Interior-Environment Appropriations/ Pesticide Testing.** Burns, R-Mont., amendment that would direct the EPA administrator to conduct a review of all third-party intentional human dosing studies. It also would direct the administrator to issue a final rule within 180 days of enactment that addresses the application of ethical standards to third-party studies involving intentional human dosing to identify or quantify toxic effects. Adopted 57-40: R 49-4; D 8-35 (ND 5-34, SD 3-1); I 0-1. June 29, 2005.

**162.** **HR 2361. Fiscal 2006 Interior-Environment Appropriations/ Pesticide Testing.** Boxer, D-Calif., amendment that would prohibit the EPA administrator from using fiscal 2006 funds to accept, consider or rely on third-party intentional human studies on the effects of pesticides or to conduct intentional human dosing studies of pesticides. Adopted 60-37: R 16-37; D 43-0 (ND 39-0, SD 4-0); I 1-0. June 29, 2005.

ND Northern Democrats, SD Southern Democrats
Southern states: Ala., Ark., Fla., Ga., Ky., La., Miss., N.C., Okla., S.C., Tenn., Texas, Va.

| | 158 | 159 | 160 | 161 | 162 | | 158 | 159 | 160 | 161 | 162 |
|---|---|---|---|---|---|---|---|---|---|---|---|
| **ALABAMA** | | | | | | **MONTANA** | | | | | |
| Shelby | Y | N | N | Y | N | Baucus | Y | N | N | Y | Y |
| Sessions | + | N | Y | Y | N | Burns | Y | N | N | Y | N |
| **ALASKA** | | | | | | **NEBRASKA** | | | | | |
| Stevens | Y | Y | N | Y | N | Hagel | Y | N | N | Y | N |
| Murkowski | Y | Y | N | Y | Y | Nelson | Y | Y | Y | Y | Y |
| **ARIZONA** | | | | | | **NEVADA** | | | | | |
| McCain | N | Y | Y | Y | Y | Reid | Y | Y | N | N | Y |
| Kyl | N | Y | Y | Y | N | Ensign | Y | N | Y | Y | Y |
| **ARKANSAS** | | | | | | **NEW HAMPSHIRE** | | | | | |
| Lincoln | Y | N | N | Y | Y | Gregg | N | N | N | Y | N |
| Pryor | Y | N | N | Y | Y | Sununu | N | N | Y | Y | N |
| **CALIFORNIA** | | | | | | **NEW JERSEY** | | | | | |
| Feinstein | Y | N | Y | N | Y | Corzine | N | N | Y | N | Y |
| Boxer | Y | N | Y | N | Y | Lautenberg | N | N | N | N | Y |
| **COLORADO** | | | | | | **NEW MEXICO** | | | | | |
| Allard | Y | N | N | Y | N | Domenici | Y | N | N | Y | N |
| Salazar | Y | N | N | N | Y | Bingaman | Y | N | Y | N | Y |
| **CONNECTICUT** | | | | | | **NEW YORK** | | | | | |
| Dodd | ? | ? | ? | N | Y | Schumer | N | N | N | Y | Y |
| Lieberman | ? | ? | ? | ? | ? | Clinton | Y | N | N | Y | Y |
| **DELAWARE** | | | | | | **NORTH CAROLINA** | | | | | |
| Biden | Y | N | Y | N | Y | Dole | Y | ? | ? | Y | N |
| Carper | Y | N | N | N | Y | Burr | Y | ? | ? | Y | N |
| **FLORIDA** | | | | | | **NORTH DAKOTA** | | | | | |
| Nelson | N | N | N | Y | Y | Conrad | Y | Y | N | Y | Y |
| Martinez | N | N | N | Y | N | Dorgan | Y | Y | N | Y | Y |
| **GEORGIA** | | | | | | **OHIO** | | | | | |
| Chambliss | Y | N | N | Y | N | DeWine | Y | N | N | Y | Y |
| Isakson | Y | N | Y | Y | N | Voinovich | Y | N | N | Y | Y |
| **HAWAII** | | | | | | **OKLAHOMA** | | | | | |
| Inouye | Y | N | N | N | Y | Inhofe | Y | Y | Y | Y | N |
| Akaka | Y | Y | Y | N | Y | Coburn | Y | Y | Y | Y | Y |
| **IDAHO** | | | | | | **OREGON** | | | | | |
| Craig | Y | N | N | Y | N | Wyden | N | N | N | N | Y |
| Crapo | Y | N | N | Y | N | Smith | Y | N | N | Y | Y |
| **ILLINOIS** | | | | | | **PENNSYLVANIA** | | | | | |
| Durbin | Y | N | N | N | Y | Specter | Y | Y | Y | Y | Y |
| Obama | Y | N | N | N | Y | Santorum | Y | N | N | Y | N |
| **INDIANA** | | | | | | **RHODE ISLAND** | | | | | |
| Lugar | Y | N | ? | ? | ? | Reed | N | N | N | N | Y |
| Bayh | Y | N | Y | N | Y | Chafee | Y | N | N | N | Y |
| **IOWA** | | | | | | **SOUTH CAROLINA** | | | | | |
| Grassley | Y | N | N | Y | N | Graham | Y | ? | ? | Y | Y |
| Harkin | Y | N | N | N | Y | DeMint | Y | ? | ? | Y | N |
| **KANSAS** | | | | | | **SOUTH DAKOTA** | | | | | |
| Brownback | Y | Y | N | Y | N | Johnson | Y | N | N | N | Y |
| Roberts | Y | N | N | Y | N | Thune | Y | Y | N | Y | Y |
| **KENTUCKY** | | | | | | **TENNESSEE** | | | | | |
| McConnell | Y | N | N | Y | N | Frist | Y | N | N | Y | N |
| Bunning | Y | N | N | Y | N | Alexander | Y | N | Y | Y | N |
| **LOUISIANA** | | | | | | **TEXAS** | | | | | |
| Landrieu | Y | N | Y | Y | Y | Hutchison | Y | N | N | Y | N |
| Vitter | Y | N | N | Y | N | Cornyn | Y | N | Y | Y | N |
| **MAINE** | | | | | | **UTAH** | | | | | |
| Snowe | Y | N | N | N | Y | Hatch | Y | N | Y | N | N |
| Collins | Y | N | N | N | Y | Bennett | Y | N | N | ? | ? |
| **MARYLAND** | | | | | | **VERMONT** | | | | | |
| Sarbanes | Y | N | N | N | Y | Leahy | Y | N | N | N | Y |
| Mikulski | Y | N | N | N | Y | Jeffords | Y | N | N | N | Y |
| **MASSACHUSETTS** | | | | | | **VIRGINIA** | | | | | |
| Kennedy | Y | Y | N | N | Y | Warner | Y | N | N | Y | Y |
| Kerry | Y | N | Y | N | Y | Allen | Y | N | N | Y | N |
| **MICHIGAN** | | | | | | **WASHINGTON** | | | | | |
| Levin | Y | N | Y | N | Y | Murray | Y | N | N | N | Y |
| Stabenow | Y | N | Y | N | Y | Cantwell | Y | N | Y | N | Y |
| **MINNESOTA** | | | | | | **WEST VIRGINIA** | | | | | |
| Dayton | Y | N | Y | N | Y | Byrd | Y | ? | ? | Y | Y |
| Coleman | Y | N | N | Y | N | Rockefeller | Y | ? | ? | N | Y |
| **MISSISSIPPI** | | | | | | **WISCONSIN** | | | | | |
| Cochran | Y | N | N | Y | N | Kohl | Y | N | N | N | Y |
| Lott | Y | N | N | Y | N | Feingold | N | N | Y | N | Y |
| **MISSOURI** | | | | | | **WYOMING** | | | | | |
| Bond | Y | N | N | Y | N | Thomas | Y | N | N | Y | N |
| Talent | Y | N | N | Y | Y | Enzi | Y | Y | N | Y | N |

| KEY | Republicans | Democrats | *Independents* | | |
|---|---|---|---|---|---|
| Y | Voted for (yea) | X | Paired against | C | Voted "present" to avoid possible conflict of interest |
| # | Paired for | – | Announced against | | |
| + | Announced for | P | Voted "present" | ? | Did not vote or otherwise make a position known |
| N | Voted against (nay) | | | | |

# IN THE SENATE | By Vote Number

**163.** **HR 2361. Fiscal 2006 Interior-Environment Appropriations/ Indian Health Care.** Dorgan, D-N.D., motion to waive the Budget Act with respect to the Burns, R-Mont., point of order against the Dorgan amendment. The Dorgan amendment would require the Federal Reserve banks to transfer $1 billion in fiscal 2006 from surplus funds to the general fund of the Treasury for Indian health care services. A three-fifths majority (60) of the total Senate is required to waive the Budget Act. (Subsequently, the chair upheld the point of order, and the amendment fell.) Motion rejected 47-51: R 3-51; D 43-0 (ND 39-0, SD 4-0); I 1-0. June 29, 2005.

**164.** **HR 2361. Fiscal 2006 Interior-Environment Appropriations/ Tongass National Forest.** Sununu, R-N.H., amendment that would prohibit the use of funds to plan, design, study or construct new roads in the Tongass National Forest in Alaska for the purpose of harvesting timber by private companies or individuals. Rejected 39-59: R 3-51; D 35-8 (ND 34-5, SD 1-3); I 1-0. June 29, 2005.

**165.** **HR 2361. Fiscal 2006 Interior-Environment Appropriations/ Veterans' Heath Care Funding.** Santorum, R-Pa., amendment to the Murray, D-Wash., amendment. The Santorum amendment would appropriate $1.5 billion in supplemental fiscal 2005 funding to the Department of Veterans Affairs for medical services provided by the Veterans Health Administration (VHA). The Murray amendment would appropriate $1.42 billion in supplemental fiscal 2005 funding for the same purpose. Adopted 96-0: R 52-0; D 43-0 (ND 39-0, SD 4-0); I 1-0. June 29, 2005.

**166.** **HR 2361. Fiscal 2006 Interior-Environment Appropriations/ Veterans' Health Care Funding.** Murray, D-Wash., amendment, as amended, that would provide $1.5 billion in fiscal 2005 supplemental appropriations to the Department of Veterans Affairs for medical services provided by the VHA. Adopted 96-0: R 52-0; D 43-0 (ND 39-0, SD 4-0); I 1-0. June 29, 2005.

**167.** **HR 2361 . Fiscal 2006 Interior-Environment Appropriations/ Family Travel to Cuba.** Dorgan, D-N.D., motion to suspend the rule against legislating on an appropriations bill with respect to the Dorgan amendment. The Dorgan amendment would require the Treasury secretary to issue a general license to individuals subject to U.S. jurisdiction and their immediate families to travel to Cuba to visit immediate family for humanitarian reasons. Motion rejected 60-35: R 20-31; D 39-4 (ND 36-3, SD 3-1); I 1-0. A two-thirds majority of those present and voting (64 in this case) is required to suspend the rule. (Subsequently, a point of order was made and the amendment fell.) A "yea" was a vote in support of the president's position. June 29, 2005.

| | 163 | 164 | 165 | 166 | 167 | | | 163 | 164 | 165 | 166 | 167 |
|---|---|---|---|---|---|---|---|---|---|---|---|---|
| **ALABAMA** | | | | | | | **MONTANA** | | | | | |
| Shelby | N | N | Y | Y | N | | Baucus | Y | N | Y | Y | Y |
| Sessions | N | N | Y | Y | N | | Burns | N | N | Y | Y | N |
| **ALASKA** | | | | | | | **NEBRASKA** | | | | | |
| Stevens | N | N | Y | Y | N | | Hagel | N | N | Y | Y | Y |
| Murkowski | N | N | Y | Y | N | | Nelson | Y | N | Y | Y | Y |
| **ARIZONA** | | | | | | | **NEVADA** | | | | | |
| McCain | N | Y | ? | ? | ? | | Reid | Y | Y | Y | Y | N |
| Kyl | N | N | Y | Y | Y | | Ensign | N | N | Y | Y | N |
| **ARKANSAS** | | | | | | | **NEW HAMPSHIRE** | | | | | |
| Lincoln | Y | N | Y | Y | Y | | Gregg | N | N | Y | Y | Y |
| Pryor | Y | N | Y | Y | Y | | Sununu | N | Y | Y | Y | Y |
| **CALIFORNIA** | | | | | | | **NEW JERSEY** | | | | | |
| Feinstein | Y | Y | Y | Y | Y | | Corzine | Y | Y | Y | Y | N |
| Boxer | Y | Y | Y | Y | Y | | Lautenberg | Y | Y | Y | Y | Y |
| **COLORADO** | | | | | | | **NEW MEXICO** | | | | | |
| Allard | N | N | Y | Y | N | | Domenici | N | N | Y | Y | N |
| Salazar | Y | Y | Y | Y | Y | | Bingaman | Y | Y | Y | Y | Y |
| **CONNECTICUT** | | | | | | | **NEW YORK** | | | | | |
| Dodd | Y | Y | Y | Y | Y | | Schumer | Y | Y | Y | Y | Y |
| Lieberman | ? | ? | ? | ? | ? | | Clinton | Y | Y | Y | Y | Y |
| **DELAWARE** | | | | | | | **NORTH CAROLINA** | | | | | |
| Biden | Y | Y | Y | Y | Y | | Dole | N | N | Y | Y | N |
| Carper | Y | Y | Y | Y | Y | | Burr | N | N | Y | Y | Y |
| **FLORIDA** | | | | | | | **NORTH DAKOTA** | | | | | |
| Nelson | Y | Y | Y | Y | N | | Conrad | Y | Y | Y | Y | Y |
| Martinez | N | N | ? | ? | X | | Dorgan | Y | Y | Y | Y | Y |
| **GEORGIA** | | | | | | | **OHIO** | | | | | |
| Chambliss | N | N | Y | Y | N | | DeWine | N | N | Y | Y | Y |
| Isakson | N | N | Y | Y | N | | Voinovich | N | N | Y | Y | Y |
| **HAWAII** | | | | | | | **OKLAHOMA** | | | | | |
| Inouye | Y | N | Y | Y | Y | | Inhofe | N | N | Y | Y | N |
| Akaka | Y | N | Y | Y | Y | | Coburn | N | N | Y | Y | # |
| **IDAHO** | | | | | | | **OREGON** | | | | | |
| Craig | N | N | Y | Y | Y | | Wyden | Y | Y | Y | Y | Y |
| Crapo | N | N | Y | Y | Y | | Smith | Y | N | Y | Y | N |
| **ILLINOIS** | | | | | | | **PENNSYLVANIA** | | | | | |
| Durbin | Y | Y | Y | Y | Y | | Specter | N | N | Y | Y | N |
| Obama | Y | Y | Y | Y | Y | | Santorum | N | N | Y | Y | N |
| **INDIANA** | | | | | | | **RHODE ISLAND** | | | | | |
| Lugar | N | N | Y | Y | Y | | Reed | Y | Y | Y | Y | Y |
| Bayh | Y | Y | Y | Y | Y | | Chafee | N | Y | Y | Y | Y |
| **IOWA** | | | | | | | **SOUTH CAROLINA** | | | | | |
| Grassley | N | N | Y | Y | N | | Graham | N | N | Y | Y | N |
| Harkin | Y | Y | Y | Y | Y | | DeMint | N | N | Y | Y | Y |
| **KANSAS** | | | | | | | **SOUTH DAKOTA** | | | | | |
| Brownback | N | N | Y | Y | N | | Johnson | Y | Y | Y | Y | Y |
| Roberts | N | N | Y | Y | Y | | Thune | Y | N | Y | Y | Y |
| **KENTUCKY** | | | | | | | **TENNESSEE** | | | | | |
| McConnell | N | N | Y | Y | N | | Frist | N | N | Y | Y | N |
| Bunning | N | N | Y | Y | N | | Alexander | N | N | Y | Y | N |
| **LOUISIANA** | | | | | | | **TEXAS** | | | | | |
| Landrieu | Y | N | Y | Y | Y | | Hutchison | N | N | Y | Y | N |
| Vitter | N | N | Y | Y | N | | Cornyn | N | N | Y | Y | N |
| **MAINE** | | | | | | | **UTAH** | | | | | |
| Snowe | N | N | Y | Y | Y | | Hatch | N | N | Y | Y | N |
| Collins | N | N | Y | Y | Y | | Bennett | ? | ? | ? | ? | ? |
| **MARYLAND** | | | | | | | **VERMONT** | | | | | |
| Sarbanes | Y | Y | Y | Y | Y | | Leahy | Y | Y | Y | Y | Y |
| Mikulski | Y | Y | Y | Y | Y | | Jeffords | Y | Y | Y | Y | Y |
| **MASSACHUSETTS** | | | | | | | **VIRGINIA** | | | | | |
| Kennedy | Y | Y | Y | Y | Y | | Warner | N | N | Y | Y | Y |
| Kerry | Y | Y | Y | Y | Y | | Allen | N | N | Y | Y | N |
| **MICHIGAN** | | | | | | | **WASHINGTON** | | | | | |
| Levin | Y | Y | Y | Y | Y | | Murray | Y | Y | Y | Y | Y |
| Stabenow | Y | Y | Y | Y | Y | | Cantwell | Y | Y | Y | Y | Y |
| **MINNESOTA** | | | | | | | **WEST VIRGINIA** | | | | | |
| Dayton | Y | Y | Y | Y | Y | | Byrd | Y | N | Y | Y | Y |
| Coleman | Y | N | Y | Y | N | | Rockefeller | Y | Y | Y | Y | Y |
| **MISSISSIPPI** | | | | | | | **WISCONSIN** | | | | | |
| Cochran | N | N | Y | Y | N | | Kohl | Y | Y | Y | Y | Y |
| Lott | N | N | Y | Y | N | | Feingold | Y | Y | Y | Y | Y |
| **MISSOURI** | | | | | | | **WYOMING** | | | | | |
| Bond | N | N | Y | Y | Y | | Thomas | N | N | Y | Y | Y |
| Talent | N | N | Y | Y | Y | | Enzi | N | N | Y | Y | Y |

**KEY**   Republicans   Democrats   *Independents*

| | | | |
|---|---|---|---|
| Y | Voted for (yea) | X | Paired against |
| # | Paired for | – | Announced against |
| + | Announced for | P | Voted "present" |
| N | Voted against (nay) | | |

C   Voted "present" to avoid possible conflict of interest
?   Did not vote or otherwise make a position known

ND Northern Democrats, SD Southern Democrats
Southern states: Ala., Ark., Fla., Ga., Ky., La., Miss., N.C., Okla., S.C., Tenn., Texas, Va.

# IN THE SENATE | By Vote Number

**168.** HR 2361. Fiscal 2006 Interior-Environment Appropriations/ **Passage.** Passage of the bill that would provide $26.3 billion in fiscal 2006 for the Department of Interior and related agencies, including $9.9 billion for the Interior Department, $7.8 billion for the EPA and $4.1 billion for the Forest Service. It also would provide $1.5 billion in emergency fiscal 2005 funding for medical services provided by the Veterans Health Administration. Passed 94-0: R 50-0; D 43-0 (ND 39-0, SD 4-0); I 1-0. June 29, 2005.

**169.** S 1307. Central American Free Trade Agreement/Motion to **Proceed.** Frist, R-Tenn., motion to proceed to consideration of a bill that would implement a free trade agreement between the United States and Costa Rica, El Salvador, Guatemala, Honduras, Nicaragua and the Dominican Republic. Motion agreed to 61-34: R 46-5; D 14-29 (ND 12-27, SD 2-2); I 1-0. June 29, 2005.

**170.** S 1307. Central American Free Trade Agreement/Passage. Passage of the bill that would implement a free trade agreement between the United States and Costa Rica, El Salvador, Guatemala, Honduras, Nicaragua and a separate pact with the Dominican Republic. It also would eliminate customs duties on all originating goods traded among the participating nations within 10 days. Passed 54-45: R 43-12; D 10-33 (ND 7-32, SD 3-1); I 1-0. A "yea" was a vote in support of the president's position. June 30, 2005.

**171.** HR 2419. Fiscal 2006 Energy and Water Appropriations/Nuclear **Weapons Funding.** Feinstein, D-Calif., amendment that would prohibit the use of funds in the bill for any purpose related to the Robust Nuclear Earth Penetrator. It would stipulate that the funds appropriated for this purpose be used to reduce the national debt. Rejected 43-53: R 3-50; D 39-3 (ND 36-2, SD 3-1); I 1-0. A "nay" was a vote in support of the president's position. July 1, 2005 (in the session that began and the Congressional Record dated June 30, 2005).

**172.** HR 2419. Fiscal 2006 Energy and Water Appropriations/Passage. Passage of the bill that would provide $31.2 billion in fiscal 2006 for energy and water development projects, including $5.3 billion for the Army Corps of Engineers and $25 billion for the Energy Department. It also would provide $577 million for the Yucca Mountain nuclear waste repository. Passed 92-3: R 50-3; D 41-0 (ND 37-0, SD 4-0); I 1-0. July 1, 2005 (in the session that began and the Congressional Record dated June 30, 2005).

| | 168 | 169 | 170 | 171 | 172 |
|---|---|---|---|---|---|
| **ALABAMA** | | | | | |
| Shelby | Y | Y | N | N | Y |
| Sessions | Y | Y | Y | N | Y |
| **ALASKA** | | | | | |
| Stevens | Y | Y | Y | N | Y |
| Murkowski | Y | Y | Y | N | Y |
| **ARIZONA** | | | | | |
| McCain | ? | Y | Y | N | N |
| Kyl | Y | Y | Y | N | Y |
| **ARKANSAS** | | | | | |
| Lincoln | Y | Y | Y | Y | Y |
| Pryor | Y | Y | Y | Y | Y |
| **CALIFORNIA** | | | | | |
| Feinstein | Y | Y | Y | Y | Y |
| Boxer | Y | N | N | Y | Y |
| **COLORADO** | | | | | |
| Allard | Y | Y | Y | N | Y |
| Salazar | Y | N | N | Y | Y |
| **CONNECTICUT** | | | | | |
| Dodd | Y | Y | N | Y | Y |
| Lieberman | ? | ? | ? | ? | ? |
| **DELAWARE** | | | | | |
| Biden | Y | N | N | Y | Y |
| Carper | Y | Y | Y | Y | Y |
| **FLORIDA** | | | | | |
| Nelson | Y | N | N | N | Y |
| Martinez | ? | ? | Y | N | Y |
| **GEORGIA** | | | | | |
| Chambliss | Y | Y | Y | N | Y |
| Isakson | Y | Y | Y | N | Y |
| **HAWAII** | | | | | |
| Inouye | Y | N | N | Y | Y |
| Akaka | Y | N | N | Y | Y |
| **IDAHO** | | | | | |
| Craig | Y | Y | N | N | Y |
| Crapo | Y | Y | N | N | Y |
| **ILLINOIS** | | | | | |
| Durbin | Y | N | N | Y | Y |
| Obama | Y | N | N | Y | Y |
| **INDIANA** | | | | | |
| Lugar | Y | Y | Y | N | Y |
| Bayh | Y | N | N | N | ? |
| **IOWA** | | | | | |
| Grassley | Y | Y | Y | N | Y |
| Harkin | Y | Y | N | Y | Y |
| **KANSAS** | | | | | |
| Brownback | Y | Y | Y | N | Y |
| Roberts | Y | Y | Y | N | Y |
| **KENTUCKY** | | | | | |
| McConnell | Y | Y | Y | N | Y |
| Bunning | Y | Y | Y | ? | ? |
| **LOUISIANA** | | | | | |
| Landrieu | Y | N | N | Y | Y |
| Vitter | Y | N | N | N | Y |
| **MAINE** | | | | | |
| Snowe | Y | N | N | N | Y |
| Collins | Y | Y | N | Y | Y |
| **MARYLAND** | | | | | |
| Sarbanes | Y | N | N | Y | Y |
| Mikulski | Y | N | N | ? | ? |
| **MASSACHUSETTS** | | | | | |
| Kennedy | Y | N | N | Y | Y |
| Kerry | Y | N | N | Y | Y |
| **MICHIGAN** | | | | | |
| Levin | Y | N | N | Y | Y |
| Stabenow | Y | N | N | Y | Y |
| **MINNESOTA** | | | | | |
| Dayton | Y | N | N | Y | Y |
| Coleman | Y | Y | Y | N | Y |
| **MISSISSIPPI** | | | | | |
| Cochran | Y | Y | Y | N | Y |
| Lott | Y | Y | Y | N | Y |
| **MISSOURI** | | | | | |
| Bond | Y | Y | Y | N | Y |
| Talent | Y | Y | Y | N | Y |

| | 168 | 169 | 170 | 171 | 172 |
|---|---|---|---|---|---|
| **MONTANA** | | | | | |
| Baucus | Y | Y | N | Y | Y |
| Burns | Y | Y | N | N | Y |
| **NEBRASKA** | | | | | |
| Hagel | Y | Y | Y | N | Y |
| Nelson | Y | Y | Y | N | Y |
| **NEVADA** | | | | | |
| Reid | Y | N | N | Y | Y |
| Ensign | Y | Y | Y | N | Y |
| **NEW HAMPSHIRE** | | | | | |
| Gregg | ? | ? | Y | N | Y |
| Sununu | Y | Y | Y | N | N |
| **NEW JERSEY** | | | | | |
| Corzine | Y | N | N | Y | Y |
| Lautenberg | Y | N | N | Y | Y |
| **NEW MEXICO** | | | | | |
| Domenici | Y | Y | Y | N | Y |
| Bingaman | Y | Y | Y | Y | Y |
| **NEW YORK** | | | | | |
| Schumer | Y | N | N | Y | Y |
| Clinton | Y | N | N | Y | Y |
| **NORTH CAROLINA** | | | | | |
| Dole | Y | Y | Y | N | Y |
| Burr | Y | Y | Y | N | Y |
| **NORTH DAKOTA** | | | | | |
| Conrad | Y | N | N | Y | Y |
| Dorgan | Y | N | N | Y | Y |
| **OHIO** | | | | | |
| DeWine | Y | Y | Y | N | Y |
| Voinovich | Y | Y | Y | Y | Y |
| **OKLAHOMA** | | | | | |
| Inhofe | Y | Y | Y | N | Y |
| Coburn | ? | ? | Y | N | N |
| **OREGON** | | | | | |
| Wyden | Y | Y | Y | Y | Y |
| Smith | Y | Y | Y | N | Y |
| **PENNSYLVANIA** | | | | | |
| Specter | Y | Y | N | ? | ? |
| Santorum | Y | Y | Y | N | Y |
| **RHODE ISLAND** | | | | | |
| Reed | Y | N | N | Y | Y |
| Chafee | Y | Y | Y | Y | Y |
| **SOUTH CAROLINA** | | | | | |
| Graham | Y | Y | N | N | Y |
| DeMint | Y | Y | Y | N | Y |
| **SOUTH DAKOTA** | | | | | |
| Johnson | Y | N | N | Y | Y |
| Thune | Y | N | N | N | Y |
| **TENNESSEE** | | | | | |
| Frist | Y | Y | Y | N | Y |
| Alexander | Y | Y | Y | N | Y |
| **TEXAS** | | | | | |
| Hutchison | Y | Y | Y | N | Y |
| Cornyn | Y | Y | Y | N | Y |
| **UTAH** | | | | | |
| Hatch | Y | Y | Y | N | Y |
| Bennett | ? | ? | Y | N | Y |
| **VERMONT** | | | | | |
| Leahy | Y | Y | N | Y | Y |
| Jeffords | Y | Y | Y | Y | Y |
| **VIRGINIA** | | | | | |
| Warner | Y | Y | Y | N | Y |
| Allen | Y | Y | Y | N | Y |
| **WASHINGTON** | | | | | |
| Murray | Y | Y | Y | Y | Y |
| Cantwell | Y | Y | Y | Y | Y |
| **WEST VIRGINIA** | | | | | |
| Byrd | Y | N | N | Y | Y |
| Rockefeller | Y | N | N | Y | Y |
| **WISCONSIN** | | | | | |
| Kohl | Y | N | N | Y | Y |
| Feingold | Y | N | N | Y | Y |
| **WYOMING** | | | | | |
| Thomas | Y | N | N | N | Y |
| Enzi | Y | N | N | N | Y |

**KEY**    Republicans    Democrats    *Independents*

| | | |
|---|---|---|
| **Y** Voted for (yea) | **X** Paired against | **C** Voted "present" to avoid possible conflict of interest |
| **#** Paired for | **–** Announced against | |
| **+** Announced for | **P** Voted "present" | **?** Did not vote or otherwise make a position known |
| **N** Voted against (nay) | | |

ND Northern Democrats, SD Southern Democrats
Southern states: Ala., Ark., Fla., Ga., Ky., La., Miss., N.C., Okla., S.C., Tenn., Texas, Va.

# IN THE SENATE | By Vote Number

**173.** **S Res 193. London Bombings/Adoption.** Adoption of the resolution that would express the deepest sympathies and condolences to the people of the United Kingdom in the aftermath of the July 7, 2005, terrorist attacks in London. Adopted 76-0: R 41-0; D 34-0 (ND 34-0, SD 0-0); I 1-0. July 11, 2005.

**174.** **HR 2360. Fiscal 2006 Homeland Security Appropriations/ Veterans' Health Care.** Murray, D-Wash., amendment that would provide $1.5 billion in fiscal 2005 supplemental appropriations to the Department of Veterans Affairs for medical services provided by the Veterans Health Administration. Adopted 95-0: R 51-0; D 43-0 (ND 39-0, SD 4-0); I 1-0. July 12, 2005.

**175.** **HR 2360. Fiscal 2006 Homeland Security Appropriations/First-Responders.** Collins, R-Maine, amendment that would change the distribution of certain first-responder grants and guarantee that each state receive a minimum of 0.55 percent of total funding for such grants. States with larger populations and higher population densities would receive a higher guaranteed amount on a sliding scale; the remaining funds would be distributed based on the relative threat of terrorist attack faced by an area. Adopted 71-26: R 42-11; D 28-15 (ND 26-13, SD 2-2); I 1-0. A "nay" was a vote in support of the president's position. July 12, 2005.

**176.** **HR 2360. Fiscal 2006 Homeland Security Appropriations/First-Responders.** Feinstein, D-Calif., amendment that would change the distribution of certain first-responder grants and guarantee that each state receive 0.25 percent of the total available funding. It would direct the Homeland Security secretary to allocate the remainder of the funds based on a risk assessment carried out by the department. Rejected 32-65: R 13-40; D 19-24 (ND 17-22, SD 2-2); I 0-1. July 12, 2005.

**177.** **HR 2360. Fiscal 2006 Homeland Security Appropriations/First-Responders.** Dodd, D-Conn., motion to waive the Budget Act with respect to the Gregg, R-N.H., point of order against the Dodd amendment. The Dodd amendment would increase funding for emergency first-responders and transit, rail, truck and port security programs by approximately $16 billion. Motion rejected 36-60: R 0-53; D 35-7 (ND 33-6, SD 2-1); I 1-0. A three-fifths majority (60) of the total Senate is required to waive the Budget Act. (Subsequently, the chair upheld the point of order, and the amendment fell.) July 13, 2005.

**178.** **HR 2360. Fiscal 2006 Homeland Security Appropriations/First-Responders.** Akaka, D-Hawaii, motion to waive the Budget Act with respect to the Gregg, R-N.H., point of order against the Akaka amendment. The Akaka amendment would add $487 million for state and local first-responder grant programs. Motion rejected 42-55: R 0-54; D 41-1 (ND 38-1, SD 3-0); I 1-0. A three-fifths majority (60) of the total Senate is required to waive the Budget Act. (Subsequently, the chair upheld the point of order, and the amendment fell.) July 13, 2005.

| | 173 | 174 | 175 | 176 | 177 | 178 | | 173 | 174 | 175 | 176 | 177 | 178 |
|---|---|---|---|---|---|---|---|---|---|---|---|---|---|
| **ALABAMA** | | | | | | | **MONTANA** | | | | | | |
| Shelby | Y | Y | Y | N | N | N | Baucus | ? | Y | Y | N | N | Y |
| Sessions | + | + | Y | N | N | N | Burns | Y | Y | Y | N | N | N |
| **ALASKA** | | | | | | | **NEBRASKA** | | | | | | |
| Stevens | Y | Y | Y | N | N | N | Hagel | Y | Y | Y | N | N | N |
| Murkowski | ? | Y | Y | N | N | N | Nelson | Y | Y | Y | N | N | Y |
| **ARIZONA** | | | | | | | **NEVADA** | | | | | | |
| McCain | ? | Y | Y | Y | N | N | Reid | Y | Y | Y | N | Y | Y |
| Kyl | Y | Y | N | Y | N | N | Ensign | Y | Y | Y | Y | N | N |
| **ARKANSAS** | | | | | | | **NEW HAMPSHIRE** | | | | | | |
| Lincoln | + | Y | Y | N | Y | Y | Gregg | Y | Y | N | N | N | N |
| Pryor | + | Y | Y | N | Y | Y | Sununu | Y | Y | Y | N | N | N |
| **CALIFORNIA** | | | | | | | **NEW JERSEY** | | | | | | |
| Feinstein | Y | Y | N | Y | Y | Y | Corzine | Y | Y | N | Y | Y | Y |
| Boxer | + | Y | N | Y | Y | Y | Lautenberg | Y | Y | N | Y | Y | Y |
| **COLORADO** | | | | | | | **NEW MEXICO** | | | | | | |
| Allard | Y | Y | N | Y | N | N | Domenici | Y | Y | Y | N | N | N |
| Salazar | Y | Y | Y | N | Y | Y | Bingaman | Y | Y | Y | N | N | Y |
| **CONNECTICUT** | | | | | | | **NEW YORK** | | | | | | |
| Dodd | Y | Y | Y | N | Y | Y | Schumer | Y | Y | Y | N | Y | Y |
| Lieberman | Y | Y | Y | N | Y | Y | Clinton | Y | Y | N | Y | Y | Y |
| **DELAWARE** | | | | | | | **NORTH CAROLINA** | | | | | | |
| Biden | Y | Y | Y | N | Y | Y | Dole | Y | Y | Y | N | N | N |
| Carper | Y | Y | Y | N | N | Y | Burr | Y | Y | Y | N | N | N |
| **FLORIDA** | | | | | | | **NORTH DAKOTA** | | | | | | |
| Nelson | ? | Y | N | Y | N | Y | Conrad | Y | Y | Y | N | N | N |
| Martinez | ? | Y | N | Y | N | N | Dorgan | Y | Y | Y | N | N | Y |
| **GEORGIA** | | | | | | | **OHIO** | | | | | | |
| Chambliss | ? | Y | Y | N | N | N | DeWine | Y | Y | Y | N | N | N |
| Isakson | Y | Y | Y | N | N | N | Voinovich | Y | Y | Y | N | N | N |
| **HAWAII** | | | | | | | **OKLAHOMA** | | | | | | |
| Inouye | Y | Y | Y | Y | Y | Y | Inhofe | ? | Y | Y | N | N | N |
| Akaka | Y | Y | Y | N | Y | Y | Coburn | Y | Y | Y | N | N | N |
| **IDAHO** | | | | | | | **OREGON** | | | | | | |
| Craig | Y | Y | Y | N | N | N | Wyden | Y | Y | Y | Y | Y | Y |
| Crapo | Y | Y | Y | N | N | N | Smith | ? | Y | Y | N | N | N |
| **ILLINOIS** | | | | | | | **PENNSYLVANIA** | | | | | | |
| Durbin | Y | Y | N | Y | Y | Y | Specter | Y | Y | Y | Y | N | N |
| Obama | ? | Y | N | Y | Y | Y | Santorum | Y | Y | N | Y | N | N |
| **INDIANA** | | | | | | | **RHODE ISLAND** | | | | | | |
| Lugar | Y | Y | Y | N | N | N | Reed | Y | Y | Y | N | Y | Y |
| Bayh | ? | Y | Y | N | Y | Y | Chafee | Y | Y | Y | N | N | N |
| **IOWA** | | | | | | | **SOUTH CAROLINA** | | | | | | |
| Grassley | Y | Y | Y | N | N | N | Graham | Y | Y | Y | N | N | N |
| Harkin | Y | Y | Y | N | Y | Y | DeMint | Y | Y | Y | N | N | N |
| **KANSAS** | | | | | | | **SOUTH DAKOTA** | | | | | | |
| Brownback | Y | Y | Y | N | N | N | Johnson | Y | Y | Y | N | Y | Y |
| Roberts | Y | Y | Y | N | N | N | Thune | ? | ? | ? | ? | ? | N |
| **KENTUCKY** | | | | | | | **TENNESSEE** | | | | | | |
| McConnell | Y | Y | Y | N | N | N | Frist | Y | Y | Y | N | N | N |
| Bunning | Y | Y | Y | N | N | N | Alexander | + | + | Y | N | N | N |
| **LOUISIANA** | | | | | | | **TEXAS** | | | | | | |
| Landrieu | ? | Y | N | Y | ? | ? | Hutchison | ? | Y | N | Y | N | N |
| Vitter | Y | Y | N | Y | N | N | Cornyn | ? | Y | N | Y | N | N |
| **MAINE** | | | | | | | **UTAH** | | | | | | |
| Snowe | Y | Y | Y | N | N | N | Hatch | Y | Y | N | N | N | N |
| Collins | Y | Y | Y | N | N | N | Bennett | Y | Y | Y | N | N | N |
| **MARYLAND** | | | | | | | **VERMONT** | | | | | | |
| Sarbanes | Y | Y | N | Y | Y | Y | Leahy | Y | Y | N | Y | N | Y |
| Mikulski | ? | ? | ? | ? | ? | ? | Jeffords | Y | Y | Y | N | Y | Y |
| **MASSACHUSETTS** | | | | | | | **VIRGINIA** | | | | | | |
| Kennedy | Y | Y | N | Y | Y | Y | Warner | Y | Y | N | Y | N | N |
| Kerry | Y | Y | N | Y | Y | Y | Allen | Y | Y | N | Y | N | N |
| **MICHIGAN** | | | | | | | **WASHINGTON** | | | | | | |
| Levin | Y | Y | Y | Y | Y | Y | Murray | Y | Y | Y | Y | Y | Y |
| Stabenow | Y | Y | Y | Y | Y | Y | Cantwell | Y | Y | Y | Y | Y | Y |
| **MINNESOTA** | | | | | | | **WEST VIRGINIA** | | | | | | |
| Dayton | ? | Y | Y | N | Y | Y | Byrd | Y | Y | N | Y | Y | Y |
| Coleman | Y | Y | Y | N | N | N | Rockefeller | Y | Y | Y | N | Y | Y |
| **MISSISSIPPI** | | | | | | | **WISCONSIN** | | | | | | |
| Cochran | ? | Y | Y | N | N | N | Kohl | Y | Y | Y | N | Y | Y |
| Lott | ? | ? | ? | ? | ? | ? | Feingold | Y | Y | Y | N | Y | Y |
| **MISSOURI** | | | | | | | **WYOMING** | | | | | | |
| Bond | Y | Y | Y | N | N | N | Thomas | ? | Y | Y | N | N | N |
| Talent | Y | Y | Y | N | N | N | Enzi | Y | Y | Y | N | N | N |

**KEY**    **Republicans**    Democrats    *Independents*

| | | | | | |
|---|---|---|---|---|---|
| Y | Voted for (yea) | X | Paired against | C | Voted "present" to avoid possible conflict of interest |
| # | Paired for | – | Announced against | | |
| + | Announced for | P | Voted "present" | ? | Did not vote or otherwise make a position known |
| N | Voted against (nay) | | | | |

ND Northern Democrats, SD Southern Democrats
Southern states: Ala., Ark., Fla., Ga., Ky., La., Miss., N.C., Okla., S.C., Tenn., Texas, Va.

# IN THE SENATE | By Vote Number

**179.** **HR 2360. Fiscal 2006 Homeland Security Appropriations/Border Security.** Ensign, R-Nev., amendment to the Ensign amendment. The second-degree amendment would allow the transfer of $367.6 million to Customs and Border Protection to hire an additional 1,000 border agents. The underlying amendment would require the transfer of such funds for this purpose. Rejected 38-60: R 36-18; D 2-41 (ND 2-37, SD 0-4); I 0-1. (Subsequently, the underlying Ensign amendment was rejected by voice vote.) July 14, 2005.

**180.** **HR 2360. Fiscal 2006 Homeland Security Appropriations/Air Cargo Security.** Schumer, D-N.Y., motion to waive the Budget Act with respect to the Gregg, R-N.H., point of order against the Schumer amendment. The Schumer amendment would appropriate approximately $302 million for aviation security programs. Motion rejected 45-53: R 2-52; D 42-1 (ND 38-1, SD 4-0); I 1-0. A three-fifths majority (60) of the total Senate is required to waive the Budget Act. (Subsequently, the chair upheld the point of order, and the amendment fell.) July 14, 2005.

**181.** **HR 2360. Fiscal 2006 Homeland Security Appropriations/Truck Security.** Schumer, D-N.Y., motion to waive the Budget Act with respect to the Gregg, R-N.H., point of order against the Schumer amendment. The Schumer amendment would appropriate $70 million to the Transportation Security Administration to identify and track shipments by truck of hazardous materials using global positioning system (GPS) technology. Motion rejected 36-62: R 0-54; D 35-8 (ND 33-6, SD 2-2); I 1-0. A three-fifths majority (60) of the total Senate is required to waive the Budget Act. (Subsequently, the chair upheld the point of order, and the amendment fell.) July 14, 2005.

**182.** **HR 2360. Fiscal 2006 Homeland Security Appropriations/ Immigration and Customs Enforcement.** McCain, R-Ariz., amendment that would increase funding for immigration and customs enforcement by about $200 million to add 5,760 detention beds and hire more personnel. It would be offset by a reduction for state and local programs. Rejected 42-56: R 35-19; D 6-37 (ND 6-33, SD 0-4); I 1-0. July 14, 2005.

**183.** **HR 2360. Fiscal 2006 Homeland Security Appropriations/ Interoperable Communications Equipment.** Stabenow, D-Mich., motion to waive the Budget Act with respect to the Gregg, R-N.H., point of order against the Stabenow amendment. The Stabenow amendment would appropriate $5 billion for interoperable communications equipment grants and designate it as emergency spending. Motion rejected 35-63: R 0-54; D 34-9 (ND 31-8, SD 3-1); I 1-0. A three-fifths majority (60) of the total Senate is required to waive the Budget Act. (Subsequently, the chair upheld the point of order, and the emergency designation was stricken. The amendment was then rejected by voice vote.) July 14, 2005.

**184.** **HR 2360. Fiscal 2006 Homeland Security Appropriations/Rail and Transit Security.** Byrd, D-W.Va., motion to waive the Budget Act with respect to the Gregg, R-N.H., point of order against the Byrd amendment. The Byrd amendment would appropriate $1.2 billion for transit security grants and $265 million for intercity rail transportation. Motion rejected 43-55: R 0-54; D 42-1 (ND 38-1, SD 4-0); I 1-0. A three-fifths majority (60) of the total Senate is required to waive the Budget Act. (Subsequently, the chair upheld the point of order, and the amendment fell.) July 14, 2005.

ND Northern Democrats, SD Southern Democrats
Southern states: Ala., Ark., Fla., Ga., Ky., La., Miss., N.C., Okla., S.C., Tenn., Texas, Va.

| | 179 | 180 | 181 | 182 | 183 | 184 |
|---|---|---|---|---|---|---|
| **ALABAMA** | | | | | | |
| Shelby | Y | N | N | N | N | N |
| Sessions | Y | N | N | Y | N | N |
| **ALASKA** | | | | | | |
| Stevens | N | N | N | N | N | N |
| Murkowski | Y | N | N | N | N | N |
| **ARIZONA** | | | | | | |
| McCain | Y | N | N | Y | N | N |
| Kyl | Y | N | N | Y | N | N |
| **ARKANSAS** | | | | | | |
| Lincoln | N | Y | N | N | Y | Y |
| Pryor | N | Y | N | N | Y | Y |
| **CALIFORNIA** | | | | | | |
| Feinstein | N | Y | N | Y | Y | Y |
| Boxer | N | Y | Y | Y | Y | Y |
| **COLORADO** | | | | | | |
| Allard | Y | N | N | Y | N | N |
| Salazar | Y | Y | Y | Y | Y | N |
| **CONNECTICUT** | | | | | | |
| Dodd | N | Y | Y | Y | Y | Y |
| Lieberman | N | Y | Y | N | Y | Y |
| **DELAWARE** | | | | | | |
| Biden | N | Y | Y | N | Y | Y |
| Carper | N | Y | Y | N | N | Y |
| **FLORIDA** | | | | | | |
| Nelson | N | Y | N | N | N | Y |
| Martinez | Y | N | N | Y | N | N |
| **GEORGIA** | | | | | | |
| Chambliss | Y | N | N | Y | N | N |
| Isakson | Y | N | N | Y | N | N |
| **HAWAII** | | | | | | |
| Inouye | N | Y | N | N | N | Y |
| Akaka | N | Y | Y | N | Y | Y |
| **IDAHO** | | | | | | |
| Craig | Y | N | N | Y | N | N |
| Crapo | Y | N | N | Y | N | N |
| **ILLINOIS** | | | | | | |
| Durbin | N | Y | Y | N | Y | Y |
| Obama | N | Y | Y | N | Y | Y |
| **INDIANA** | | | | | | |
| Lugar | N | N | N | Y | N | N |
| Bayh | N | Y | Y | Y | Y | Y |
| **IOWA** | | | | | | |
| Grassley | Y | N | N | Y | N | N |
| Harkin | N | Y | Y | N | Y | N |
| **KANSAS** | | | | | | |
| Brownback | Y | N | N | Y | N | N |
| Roberts | Y | N | N | N | N | N |
| **KENTUCKY** | | | | | | |
| McConnell | Y | N | N | Y | N | N |
| Bunning | Y | N | N | Y | N | N |
| **LOUISIANA** | | | | | | |
| Landrieu | N | Y | Y | N | Y | Y |
| Vitter | N | N | N | Y | N | N |
| **MAINE** | | | | | | |
| Snowe | N | Y | N | N | N | Y |
| Collins | N | N | N | N | N | N |
| **MARYLAND** | | | | | | |
| Sarbanes | N | Y | Y | N | Y | Y |
| Mikulski | ? | ? | ? | ? | ? | ? |
| **MASSACHUSETTS** | | | | | | |
| Kennedy | N | Y | Y | N | Y | Y |
| Kerry | N | Y | Y | N | Y | Y |
| **MICHIGAN** | | | | | | |
| Levin | N | Y | Y | N | Y | Y |
| Stabenow | N | Y | Y | N | Y | Y |
| **MINNESOTA** | | | | | | |
| Dayton | N | Y | Y | N | Y | Y |
| Coleman | N | N | N | N | N | N |
| **MISSISSIPPI** | | | | | | |
| Cochran | N | N | N | N | N | N |
| Lott | ? | ? | ? | ? | ? | ? |
| **MISSOURI** | | | | | | |
| Bond | N | N | N | N | N | N |
| Talent | N | N | N | N | N | N |

| | 179 | 180 | 181 | 182 | 183 | 184 |
|---|---|---|---|---|---|---|
| **MONTANA** | | | | | | |
| Baucus | N | Y | N | N | Y | Y |
| Burns | Y | N | N | Y | N | N |
| **NEBRASKA** | | | | | | |
| Hagel | Y | N | N | Y | N | N |
| Nelson | N | Y | N | N | N | Y |
| **NEVADA** | | | | | | |
| Reid | N | Y | N | N | Y | Y |
| Ensign | Y | N | N | Y | N | N |
| **NEW HAMPSHIRE** | | | | | | |
| Gregg | Y | N | N | N | N | N |
| Sununu | Y | N | N | N | N | N |
| **NEW JERSEY** | | | | | | |
| Corzine | N | Y | Y | N | Y | Y |
| Lautenberg | N | Y | Y | N | Y | Y |
| **NEW MEXICO** | | | | | | |
| Domenici | Y | N | N | Y | N | N |
| Bingaman | Y | Y | Y | Y | Y | N |
| **NEW YORK** | | | | | | |
| Schumer | N | Y | N | N | Y | Y |
| Clinton | N | Y | Y | N | Y | Y |
| **NORTH CAROLINA** | | | | | | |
| Dole | Y | N | N | Y | N | N |
| Burr | Y | N | N | Y | N | N |
| **NORTH DAKOTA** | | | | | | |
| Conrad | N | Y | Y | N | N | Y |
| Dorgan | N | Y | Y | N | N | Y |
| **OHIO** | | | | | | |
| DeWine | N | N | N | N | N | N |
| Voinovich | N | N | N | N | N | N |
| **OKLAHOMA** | | | | | | |
| Inhofe | N | N | N | Y | N | N |
| Coburn | Y | N | N | Y | N | N |
| **OREGON** | | | | | | |
| Wyden | N | Y | Y | N | N | Y |
| Smith | N | N | N | N | N | N |
| **PENNSYLVANIA** | | | | | | |
| Specter | N | N | N | N | N | N |
| Santorum | N | N | N | Y | N | N |
| **RHODE ISLAND** | | | | | | |
| Reed | N | Y | Y | N | Y | Y |
| Chafee | N | N | N | N | N | N |
| **SOUTH CAROLINA** | | | | | | |
| Graham | N | N | N | Y | N | N |
| DeMint | Y | N | N | Y | N | N |
| **SOUTH DAKOTA** | | | | | | |
| Johnson | N | Y | Y | N | Y | Y |
| Thune | Y | N | N | Y | N | N |
| **TENNESSEE** | | | | | | |
| Frist | Y | N | N | Y | N | N |
| Alexander | N | N | N | N | N | N |
| **TEXAS** | | | | | | |
| Hutchison | Y | N | N | Y | N | N |
| Cornyn | Y | N | N | Y | N | N |
| **UTAH** | | | | | | |
| Hatch | Y | N | N | Y | N | N |
| Bennett | Y | N | N | Y | N | N |
| **VERMONT** | | | | | | |
| Leahy | N | Y | Y | N | Y | Y |
| Jeffords | N | Y | Y | Y | Y | Y |
| **VIRGINIA** | | | | | | |
| Warner | Y | N | N | Y | N | N |
| Allen | Y | N | N | Y | N | N |
| **WASHINGTON** | | | | | | |
| Murray | N | Y | Y | N | Y | Y |
| Cantwell | N | Y | Y | N | Y | Y |
| **WEST VIRGINIA** | | | | | | |
| Byrd | N | Y | Y | N | Y | Y |
| Rockefeller | N | Y | Y | N | Y | Y |
| **WISCONSIN** | | | | | | |
| Kohl | N | Y | Y | N | Y | Y |
| Feingold | N | Y | Y | N | N | Y |
| **WYOMING** | | | | | | |
| Thomas | Y | N | N | N | N | N |
| Enzi | Y | N | N | N | N | N |

**KEY**    Republicans    Democrats    *Independents*

| | | |
|---|---|---|
| **Y** Voted for (yea) | **X** Paired against | **C** Voted "present" to avoid possible conflict of interest |
| **#** Paired for | **–** Announced against | |
| **+** Announced for | **P** Voted "present" | **?** Did not vote or otherwise make a position known |
| **N** Voted against (nay) | | |

# IN THE SENATE | By Vote Number

**185.** HR 2360. Fiscal 2006 Homeland Security Appropriations/Rail and Transit Security. Gregg, R-N.H., amendment that would provide an additional $100 million for transportation and infrastructure grants, and increase intercity bus security grants to $15 million. It would be offset by cuts to state and local aid accounts. Rejected 46-52: R 45-9; D 1-42 (ND 1-38, SD 0-4); I 0-1. July 14, 2005.

**186.** HR 2360. Fiscal 2006 Homeland Security Appropriations/Transit Security. Shelby, R-Ala., motion to waive the Budget Act with respect to the Gregg, R-N.H., point of order against the Shelby amendment. The Shelby amendment would appropriate $1.5 billion for discretionary transportation and infrastructure grants, of which $1.2 billion would be for transit security grants. Motion rejected 53-45: R 9-45; D 43-0 (ND 39-0, SD 4-0); I 1-0. A three-fifths majority (60) of the total Senate is required to waive the Budget Act. (Subsequently, the chair upheld the point of order, and the amendment fell.) July 14, 2005.

**187.** HR 2360. Fiscal 2006 Homeland Security Appropriations/ Disclosure of Classified Information. Frist, R-Tenn., amendment that would bar any federal officeholder who refers to a classified FBI report on the Senate floor or makes a statement based on FBI agent comments that is then used as terrorist propaganda from having access to such information. Rejected 32-65: R 32-21; D 0-43 (ND 0-39, SD 0-4); I 0-1. July 14, 2005.

**188.** HR 2360. Fiscal 2006 Homeland Security Appropriations/ Disclosure of Classified Information. Reid, D-Nev., amendment that would bar federal employees from holding security clearances for access to classified information if they disclose, or have disclosed, classified information, including the identity of a covert CIA agent to an unauthorized person. Rejected 44-53: R 0-53; D 43-0 (ND 39-0, SD 4-0); I 1-0. July 14, 2005.

**189.** HR 2360. Fiscal 2006 Homeland Security Appropriations/Passage. Passage of the bill that would provide $31.9 billion in fiscal 2006 for the Homeland Security Department, including $7.9 billion for the Coast Guard, $6 billion for border security, $5.1 billion for the Transportation Security Administration, not including assumed fees, and $3.8 billion for investigating and enforcing immigration and customs laws. Each state would receive a minimum of 0.55 percent of total funding for first-responder grants. Passed 96-1: R 52-1; D 43-0 (ND 39-0, SD 4-0); I 1-0. July 14, 2005.

| | 185 | 186 | 187 | 188 | 189 | | 185 | 186 | 187 | 188 | 189 |
|---|---|---|---|---|---|---|---|---|---|---|---|
| **ALABAMA** | | | | | | **MONTANA** | | | | | |
| Shelby* | N | Y | N | N | Y | Baucus | N | Y | N | Y | Y |
| Sessions | Y | N | N | N | Y | Burns | Y | N | Y | N | Y |
| **ALASKA** | | | | | | **NEBRASKA** | | | | | |
| Stevens | Y | N | Y | N | Y | Hagel | Y | N | N | N | Y |
| Murkowski | Y | N | N | N | Y | Nelson | N | Y | N | Y | Y |
| **ARIZONA** | | | | | | **NEVADA** | | | | | |
| McCain | Y | N | N | N | Y | Reid | N | Y | N | Y | Y |
| Kyl | Y | N | Y | N | Y | Ensign | Y | N | Y | N | Y |
| **ARKANSAS** | | | | | | **NEW HAMPSHIRE** | | | | | |
| Lincoln | N | Y | N | Y | Y | Gregg | Y | N | Y | N | Y |
| Pryor | N | Y | N | Y | Y | Sununu | Y | N | N | N | Y |
| **CALIFORNIA** | | | | | | **NEW JERSEY** | | | | | |
| Feinstein | N | Y | N | Y | Y | Corzine | N | Y | N | Y | Y |
| Boxer | N | Y | N | Y | Y | Lautenberg | N | Y | N | Y | Y |
| **COLORADO** | | | | | | **NEW MEXICO** | | | | | |
| Allard | Y | N | Y | N | Y | Domenici | Y | N | Y | N | Y |
| Salazar | N | Y | N | Y | Y | Bingaman | N | Y | N | Y | Y |
| **CONNECTICUT** | | | | | | **NEW YORK** | | | | | |
| Dodd | N | Y | N | Y | Y | Schumer | N | Y | N | Y | Y |
| Lieberman | N | Y | N | Y | Y | Clinton | N | Y | N | Y | Y |
| **DELAWARE** | | | | | | **NORTH CAROLINA** | | | | | |
| Biden | N | Y | N | Y | Y | Dole | N | Y | Y | N | Y |
| Carper | N | Y | N | Y | Y | Burr | Y | N | Y | N | Y |
| **FLORIDA** | | | | | | **NORTH DAKOTA** | | | | | |
| Nelson | N | Y | N | Y | Y | Conrad | Y | Y | N | Y | Y |
| Martinez | Y | N | Y | N | Y | Dorgan | N | Y | N | Y | Y |
| **GEORGIA** | | | | | | **OHIO** | | | | | |
| Chambliss | Y | N | N | N | Y | DeWine | Y | Y | N | N | Y |
| Isakson | Y | N | Y | N | Y | Voinovich | Y | N | Y | N | Y |
| **HAWAII** | | | | | | **OKLAHOMA** | | | | | |
| Inouye | N | Y | N | Y | Y | Inhofe | N | N | Y | N | Y |
| Akaka | N | Y | N | Y | Y | Coburn | Y | N | Y | N | N |
| **IDAHO** | | | | | | **OREGON** | | | | | |
| Craig | Y | N | Y | N | Y | Wyden | N | Y | N | Y | Y |
| Crapo | Y | N | Y | N | Y | Smith | Y | N | Y | N | Y |
| **ILLINOIS** | | | | | | **PENNSYLVANIA** | | | | | |
| Durbin | N | Y | N | Y | Y | Specter | Y | Y | Y | N | Y |
| Obama | N | Y | N | Y | Y | Santorum | Y | N | Y | N | Y |
| **INDIANA** | | | | | | **RHODE ISLAND** | | | | | |
| Lugar | Y | N | N | N | Y | Reed | N | Y | N | Y | Y |
| Bayh | N | Y | N | Y | Y | Chafee | N | Y | N | N | Y |
| **IOWA** | | | | | | **SOUTH CAROLINA** | | | | | |
| Grassley | Y | N | N | N | Y | Graham | Y | N | N | N | Y |
| Harkin | N | Y | N | Y | Y | DeMint | N | N | + | − | + |
| **KANSAS** | | | | | | **SOUTH DAKOTA** | | | | | |
| Brownback | Y | N | N | N | Y | Johnson | N | Y | N | Y | Y |
| Roberts | Y | N | N | N | Y | Thune | N | N | N | N | Y |
| **KENTUCKY** | | | | | | **TENNESSEE** | | | | | |
| McConnell | Y | N | Y | N | Y | Frist | Y | N | Y | N | Y |
| Bunning | Y | N | Y | N | Y | Alexander | Y | N | Y | N | Y |
| **LOUISIANA** | | | | | | **TEXAS** | | | | | |
| Landrieu | N | Y | N | Y | Y | Hutchison | Y | N | Y | N | Y |
| Vitter | Y | N | Y | N | Y | Cornyn | Y | N | Y | N | Y |
| **MAINE** | | | | | | **UTAH** | | | | | |
| Snowe | Y | N | N | N | Y | Hatch | Y | Y | Y | N | Y |
| Collins | N | N | N | N | Y | Bennett | Y | Y | Y | N | Y |
| **MARYLAND** | | | | | | **VERMONT** | | | | | |
| Sarbanes | N | Y | N | Y | Y | Leahy | N | Y | N | Y | Y |
| Mikulski | ? | ? | ? | ? | ? | *Jeffords* | N | Y | N | Y | Y |
| **MASSACHUSETTS** | | | | | | **VIRGINIA** | | | | | |
| Kennedy | N | Y | N | Y | Y | Warner | Y | N | N | N | Y |
| Kerry | N | Y | N | Y | Y | Allen | Y | N | N | N | Y |
| **MICHIGAN** | | | | | | **WASHINGTON** | | | | | |
| Levin | N | Y | N | Y | Y | Murray | N | Y | N | Y | Y |
| Stabenow | N | Y | N | Y | Y | Cantwell | N | Y | N | Y | Y |
| **MINNESOTA** | | | | | | **WEST VIRGINIA** | | | | | |
| Dayton | N | Y | N | Y | Y | Byrd | N | Y | N | Y | Y |
| Coleman | N | Y | Y | N | Y | Rockefeller | N | Y | N | Y | Y |
| **MISSISSIPPI** | | | | | | **WISCONSIN** | | | | | |
| Cochran | Y | N | Y | N | Y | Kohl | N | Y | N | Y | Y |
| Lott | ? | ? | ? | ? | ? | Feingold | N | Y | N | Y | Y |
| **MISSOURI** | | | | | | **WYOMING** | | | | | |
| Bond | Y | N | Y | N | Y | Thomas | Y | N | N | N | Y |
| Talent | N | Y | N | N | Y | Enzi | Y | N | Y | N | Y |

| **KEY** | **Republicans** | Democrats | *Independents* | |
|---|---|---|---|---|
| **Y** Voted for (yea) | | **X** Paired against | | **C** Voted "present" to avoid possible conflict of interest |
| **#** Paired for | | **−** Announced against | | |
| **+** Announced for | | **P** Voted "present" | | **?** Did not vote or otherwise make a position known |
| **N** Voted against (nay) | | | | |

*Sen. Richard C. Shelby, R-Ala., received unanimous consent July 18 to switch from "yea" to "nay" on vote 187, taken on July 14. The switch did not affect the outcome. The corrected tally is given above.

ND Northern Democrats, SD Southern Democrats
Southern states: Ala., Ark., Fla., Ga., Ky., La., Miss., N.C., Okla., S.C., Tenn., Texas, Va.

# IN THE SENATE | By Vote Number

**190. Crawford Nomination/Confirmation.** Confirmation of President Bush's nomination of Lester M. Crawford of Maryland to be commissioner of the Food and Drug Administration. Confirmed 78-16: R 49-3; D 28-13 (ND 25-13, SD 3-0); I 1-0. A "yea" was a vote in support of the president's position. July 18, 2005.

**191. H J Res 52. Myanmar Sanctions/Passage.** Passage of the joint resolution that would extend for one year import restrictions on products from Myanmar, formerly known as Burma, until the president certifies that the Myanmar government has made significant progress toward practicing democracy and ending human rights violations. Passed (thus cleared for the president) 97-1: R 54-1; D 42-0 (ND 39-0, SD 3-0); I 1-0. July 19, 2005.

**192. HR 3057. Fiscal 2006 Foreign Operations Appropriation/Nuclear Power Plants in China.** Coburn, R-Okla., amendment that would prohibit the Export-Import Bank from approving federal loans or loan guarantees for the construction of nuclear power plants in China. Rejected 37-62: R 14-41; D 23-20 (ND 23-17, SD 0-3); I 0-1. July 19, 2005.

**193. HR 3057. Fiscal 2006 Foreign Operations Appropriations/USAID Funding.** Coburn, R-Okla., amendment that would prohibit the use of funds in the bill for entertainment expenses of the U.S. Agency for International Development. Adopted 59-40: R 51-4; D 8-35 (ND 8-32, SD 0-3); I 0-1. July 19, 2005.

**194. HR 3057. Fiscal 2006 Foreign Operations Appropriations/Television Broadcasting to Cuba.** Dorgan, D-N.D., amendment that would reduce funding for international broadcasting operations by $20 million for broadcasting to Cuba and increase Peace Corps funding by that amount. It would prohibit the use of funds for television broadcasts to Cuba and bar the use of capital improvement funds for this purpose. Rejected 33-66: R 2-53; D 30-13 (ND 28-12, SD 2-1); I 1-0. July 19, 2005.

**195. HR 3057. Fiscal 2006 Foreign Operations Appropriations/International Adoption.** Landrieu, D-La., amendment that would reaffirm congressional funding commitment to the founding principle of the Hague Convention related to intercountry adoption and affirm the benefits of international adoption. Adopted 98-0: R 55-0; D 42-0 (ND 38-0, SD 4-0); I 1-0. July 20, 2005.

| | 190 | 191 | 192 | 193 | 194 | 195 |
|---|---|---|---|---|---|---|
| **ALABAMA** | | | | | | |
| Shelby | Y | Y | N | Y | N | Y |
| Sessions | Y | Y | Y | Y | N | Y |
| **ALASKA** | | | | | | |
| Stevens | Y | Y | N | Y | N | Y |
| Murkowski | ? | Y | N | Y | N | Y |
| **ARIZONA** | | | | | | |
| McCain | ? | Y | N | Y | N | Y |
| Kyl | Y | Y | N | Y | N | Y |
| **ARKANSAS** | | | | | | |
| Lincoln | ? | Y | N | N | Y | Y |
| Pryor | Y | Y | N | N | N | Y |
| **CALIFORNIA** | | | | | | |
| Feinstein | Y | Y | N | N | Y | Y |
| Boxer | N | Y | Y | Y | Y | Y |
| **COLORADO** | | | | | | |
| Allard | Y | Y | Y | Y | N | Y |
| Salazar | Y | Y | Y | Y | N | Y |
| **CONNECTICUT** | | | | | | |
| Dodd | ? | Y | N | N | Y | Y |
| Lieberman | Y | Y | N | N | N | Y |
| **DELAWARE** | | | | | | |
| Biden | Y | Y | N | N | Y | Y |
| Carper | Y | Y | N | N | Y | Y |
| **FLORIDA** | | | | | | |
| Nelson | Y | Y | N | N | N | Y |
| Martinez | Y | Y | Y | N | N | Y |
| **GEORGIA** | | | | | | |
| Chambliss | Y | Y | N | Y | N | Y |
| Isakson | Y | Y | N | Y | N | Y |
| **HAWAII** | | | | | | |
| Inouye | Y | Y | N | N | Y | Y |
| Akaka | Y | Y | N | N | Y | Y |
| **IDAHO** | | | | | | |
| Craig | Y | Y | N | Y | N | Y |
| Crapo | Y | Y | N | Y | N | Y |
| **ILLINOIS** | | | | | | |
| Durbin | N | Y | Y | N | Y | Y |
| Obama | N | Y | Y | N | Y | Y |
| **INDIANA** | | | | | | |
| Lugar | Y | Y | N | N | N | Y |
| Bayh | Y | Y | N | Y | N | Y |
| **IOWA** | | | | | | |
| Grassley | N | Y | N | Y | N | Y |
| Harkin | Y | Y | Y | N | Y | Y |
| **KANSAS** | | | | | | |
| Brownback | Y | Y | Y | Y | N | Y |
| Roberts | Y | Y | N | Y | N | Y |
| **KENTUCKY** | | | | | | |
| McConnell | Y | Y | N | Y | N | Y |
| Bunning | Y | Y | N | Y | N | Y |
| **LOUISIANA** | | | | | | |
| Landrieu | Y | ? | ? | ? | ? | Y |
| Vitter | N | Y | N | Y | N | Y |
| **MAINE** | | | | | | |
| Snowe | N | Y | Y | Y | N | Y |
| Collins | Y | Y | Y | Y | N | Y |
| **MARYLAND** | | | | | | |
| Sarbanes | Y | Y | Y | N | N | Y |
| Mikulski | N | Y | Y | N | Y | Y |
| **MASSACHUSETTS** | | | | | | |
| Kennedy | Y | Y | Y | N | Y | Y |
| Kerry | Y | Y | N | N | N | Y |
| **MICHIGAN** | | | | | | |
| Levin | Y | Y | Y | N | Y | Y |
| Stabenow | N | Y | Y | Y | Y | Y |
| **MINNESOTA** | | | | | | |
| Dayton | N | Y | Y | Y | Y | Y |
| Coleman | Y | Y | N | Y | N | Y |
| **MISSISSIPPI** | | | | | | |
| Cochran | Y | Y | N | Y | N | Y |
| Lott | Y | Y | N | Y | N | Y |
| **MISSOURI** | | | | | | |
| Bond | Y | Y | N | Y | N | Y |
| Talent | Y | Y | N | Y | N | Y |
| **MONTANA** | | | | | | |
| Baucus | N | Y | N | N | Y | Y |
| Burns | Y | Y | N | Y | N | Y |
| **NEBRASKA** | | | | | | |
| Hagel | Y | Y | N | N | N | Y |
| Nelson | Y | Y | N | N | N | Y |
| **NEVADA** | | | | | | |
| Reid | Y | Y | N | N | N | Y |
| Ensign | Y | Y | Y | Y | N | Y |
| **NEW HAMPSHIRE** | | | | | | |
| Gregg | Y | Y | Y | Y | N | Y |
| Sununu | Y | Y | Y | Y | Y | Y |
| **NEW JERSEY** | | | | | | |
| Corzine | ? | Y | N | N | N | Y |
| Lautenberg | N | Y | N | N | N | Y |
| **NEW MEXICO** | | | | | | |
| Domenici | Y | Y | N | N | N | Y |
| Bingaman | Y | Y | N | N | Y | Y |
| **NEW YORK** | | | | | | |
| Schumer | N | Y | Y | N | N | Y |
| Clinton | N | Y | Y | N | N | Y |
| **NORTH CAROLINA** | | | | | | |
| Dole | Y | Y | N | Y | N | Y |
| Burr | Y | Y | N | Y | N | Y |
| **NORTH DAKOTA** | | | | | | |
| Conrad | Y | Y | Y | Y | Y | Y |
| Dorgan | N | Y | Y | Y | Y | Y |
| **OHIO** | | | | | | |
| DeWine | Y | Y | N | Y | N | Y |
| Voinovich | Y | Y | N | N | N | Y |
| **OKLAHOMA** | | | | | | |
| Inhofe | Y | Y | Y | Y | N | Y |
| Coburn | ? | Y | Y | Y | N | Y |
| **OREGON** | | | | | | |
| Wyden | Y | Y | Y | Y | N | Y |
| Smith | Y | Y | Y | Y | N | Y |
| **PENNSYLVANIA** | | | | | | |
| Specter | Y | Y | N | Y | N | Y |
| Santorum | Y | Y | N | Y | N | Y |
| **RHODE ISLAND** | | | | | | |
| Reed | Y | Y | N | Y | Y | Y |
| Chafee | Y | Y | N | N | N | Y |
| **SOUTH CAROLINA** | | | | | | |
| Graham | Y | Y | N | Y | N | Y |
| DeMint | Y | Y | N | Y | N | Y |
| **SOUTH DAKOTA** | | | | | | |
| Johnson | Y | Y | Y | Y | N | Y |
| Thune | Y | Y | N | Y | N | Y |
| **TENNESSEE** | | | | | | |
| Frist | Y | Y | N | Y | N | Y |
| Alexander | Y | Y | N | Y | N | Y |
| **TEXAS** | | | | | | |
| Hutchison | Y | Y | N | Y | N | Y |
| Cornyn | Y | Y | N | Y | N | Y |
| **UTAH** | | | | | | |
| Hatch | Y | Y | N | Y | N | Y |
| Bennett | Y | Y | N | Y | N | Y |
| **VERMONT** | | | | | | |
| Leahy | Y | Y | Y | N | Y | Y |
| Jeffords | Y | Y | N | N | Y | Y |
| **VIRGINIA** | | | | | | |
| Warner | Y | Y | N | Y | N | Y |
| Allen | Y | Y | N | Y | N | Y |
| **WASHINGTON** | | | | | | |
| Murray | N | Y | N | N | Y | Y |
| Cantwell | N | Y | N | N | Y | Y |
| **WEST VIRGINIA** | | | | | | |
| Byrd | Y | Y | Y | Y | Y | ? |
| Rockefeller | Y | ? | N | N | Y | ? |
| **WISCONSIN** | | | | | | |
| Kohl | Y | Y | N | N | Y | Y |
| Feingold | Y | Y | Y | N | Y | Y |
| **WYOMING** | | | | | | |
| Thomas | Y | Y | N | Y | N | Y |
| Enzi | Y | N | Y | Y | Y | Y |

**KEY**  Republicans  Democrats  *Independents*

| | | | |
|---|---|---|---|
| Y | Voted for (yea) | X | Paired against |
| # | Paired for | – | Announced against |
| + | Announced for | P | Voted "present" |
| N | Voted against (nay) | | |

| | |
|---|---|
| C | Voted "present" to avoid possible conflict of interest |
| ? | Did not vote or otherwise make a position known |

ND Northern Democrats, SD Southern Democrats
Southern states: Ala., Ark., Fla., Ga., Ky., La., Miss., N.C., Okla., S.C., Tenn., Texas, Va.

# IN THE SENATE | By Vote Number

**196. HR 3057. Fiscal 2006 Foreign Operations Appropriations/ Extradition Refusal.** Chambliss, R-Ga., amendment that would prohibit the State Department from providing assistance to any country that has refused to extradite individuals charged with committing certain crimes in the United States, regardless of their citizenship. Adopted 86-12: R 52-3; D 34-9 (ND 30-9, SD 4-0); I 0-1. July 20, 2005.

**197. HR 3057. Fiscal 2006 Foreign Operations Appropriations/Passage.** Passage of the bill that would appropriate $31.8 billion in fiscal 2006 for foreign operations and the State Department. It would appropriate $9.7 billion for the State Department and related agencies, and $22.1 billion for foreign aid programs, including $2.9 billion for programs to combat HIV/AIDS and related diseases, and $1.8 billion for the Millennium Challenge Corporation. Passed 98-1: R 54-0; D 43-1 (ND 39-1, SD 4-0); I 1-0. July 20, 2005.

**198. Dorr Nomination/Confirmation.** Confirmation of President Bush's nomination of Thomas C. Dorr as undersecretary of Agriculture for rural development. Confirmed 62-38: R 55-0; D 7-37 (ND 5-35, SD 2-2); I 0-1. A "yea" was a vote in support of the president's position. (Subsequently, Dorr was confirmed by voice vote as a member of the board of directors of the Commodity Credit Corporation.) July 21, 2005.

**199. S 1042. Fiscal 2006 Defense Authorization/Vehicle Armor.** Warner, R-Va., amendment that would authorize an additional $105 million to the Army and $340.4 million to the Marine Corps for the procurement of various high-mobility vehicles and add-on armor protection. It would be offset by a reduction of $445.4 million for the Iraq Freedom Fund. Adopted 100-0: R 55-0; D 44-0 (ND 40-0, SD 4-0); I 1-0. July 21, 2005.

**200. S 1042. Fiscal 2006 Defense Authorization/Non-Proliferation Programs.** Lugar, R-Ind., amendment that would remove certain restrictions on provisions of the Cooperative Threat Reduction Assistance program, including the removal of certifications the president must make for countries receiving assistance under it. Adopted 78-19: R 34-19; D 43-0 (ND 39-0, SD 4-0); I 1-0. July 21, 2005.

| | 196 | 197 | 198 | 199 | 200 |
|---|---|---|---|---|---|
| **ALABAMA** | | | | | |
| Shelby | Y | Y | Y | Y | N |
| Sessions | Y | Y | Y | Y | N |
| **ALASKA** | | | | | |
| Stevens | Y | Y | Y | Y | Y |
| Murkowski | Y | Y | Y | Y | Y |
| **ARIZONA** | | | | | |
| McCain | Y | Y | Y | Y | Y |
| Kyl | Y | Y | Y | Y | N |
| **ARKANSAS** | | | | | |
| Lincoln | Y | Y | Y | Y | Y |
| Pryor | Y | Y | Y | Y | Y |
| **CALIFORNIA** | | | | | |
| Feinstein | Y | Y | N | Y | Y |
| Boxer | Y | Y | N | Y | + |
| **COLORADO** | | | | | |
| Allard | Y | Y | Y | Y | N |
| Salazar | Y | Y | Y | Y | Y |
| **CONNECTICUT** | | | | | |
| Dodd | Y | Y | N | Y | Y |
| Lieberman | Y | Y | Y | Y | Y |
| **DELAWARE** | | | | | |
| Biden | Y | Y | N | Y | Y |
| Carper | Y | Y | N | Y | Y |
| **FLORIDA** | | | | | |
| Nelson | Y | Y | N | Y | Y |
| Martinez | Y | Y | Y | Y | Y |
| **GEORGIA** | | | | | |
| Chambliss | Y | Y | Y | Y | N |
| Isakson | Y | Y | Y | Y | N |
| **HAWAII** | | | | | |
| Inouye | Y | Y | Y | Y | Y |
| Akaka | N | Y | Y | Y | Y |
| **IDAHO** | | | | | |
| Craig | Y | Y | Y | Y | Y |
| Crapo | Y | Y | Y | Y | Y |
| **ILLINOIS** | | | | | |
| Durbin | Y | Y | N | Y | Y |
| Obama | Y | Y | N | Y | Y |
| **INDIANA** | | | | | |
| Lugar | N | Y | Y | Y | Y |
| Bayh | Y | Y | N | Y | Y |
| **IOWA** | | | | | |
| Grassley | Y | Y | Y | Y | N |
| Harkin | Y | Y | N | Y | Y |
| **KANSAS** | | | | | |
| Brownback | Y | Y | Y | Y | Y |
| Roberts | Y | Y | Y | Y | N |
| **KENTUCKY** | | | | | |
| McConnell | Y | Y | Y | Y | Y |
| Bunning | Y | Y | Y | Y | N |
| **LOUISIANA** | | | | | |
| Landrieu | Y | Y | N | Y | Y |
| Vitter | Y | Y | Y | Y | N |
| **MAINE** | | | | | |
| Snowe | Y | Y | Y | Y | Y |
| Collins | Y | Y | Y | Y | Y |
| **MARYLAND** | | | | | |
| Sarbanes | N | Y | N | Y | Y |
| Mikulski | N | Y | N | Y | Y |
| **MASSACHUSETTS** | | | | | |
| Kennedy | N | Y | N | Y | Y |
| Kerry | Y | Y | N | Y | Y |
| **MICHIGAN** | | | | | |
| Levin | Y | Y | N | Y | Y |
| Stabenow | Y | Y | N | Y | Y |
| **MINNESOTA** | | | | | |
| Dayton | N | Y | N | Y | Y |
| Coleman | Y | Y | Y | Y | Y |
| **MISSISSIPPI** | | | | | |
| Cochran | Y | Y | Y | Y | ? |
| Lott | Y | Y | Y | Y | Y |
| **MISSOURI** | | | | | |
| Bond | Y | Y | Y | Y | Y |
| Talent | Y | Y | Y | Y | N |
| **MONTANA** | | | | | |
| Baucus | Y | Y | N | Y | Y |
| Burns | Y | Y | Y | Y | Y |
| **NEBRASKA** | | | | | |
| Hagel | N | Y | Y | Y | Y |
| Nelson | Y | Y | Y | Y | Y |
| **NEVADA** | | | | | |
| Reid | Y | Y | N | Y | Y |
| Ensign | Y | Y | Y | Y | N |
| **NEW HAMPSHIRE** | | | | | |
| Gregg | Y | Y | Y | Y | Y |
| Sununu | Y | Y | Y | Y | Y |
| **NEW JERSEY** | | | | | |
| Corzine | Y | Y | N | Y | Y |
| Lautenberg | Y | Y | N | Y | Y |
| **NEW MEXICO** | | | | | |
| Domenici | Y | Y | Y | Y | Y |
| Bingaman | Y | Y | N | Y | Y |
| **NEW YORK** | | | | | |
| Schumer | Y | Y | N | Y | Y |
| Clinton | Y | Y | N | Y | Y |
| **NORTH CAROLINA** | | | | | |
| Dole | Y | Y | Y | Y | N |
| Burr | Y | Y | Y | Y | N |
| **NORTH DAKOTA** | | | | | |
| Conrad | Y | Y | N | Y | Y |
| Dorgan | Y | Y | N | Y | Y |
| **OHIO** | | | | | |
| DeWine | Y | Y | Y | Y | Y |
| Voinovich | N | Y | Y | Y | Y |
| **OKLAHOMA** | | | | | |
| Inhofe | Y | N | Y | Y | N |
| Coburn | Y | Y | Y | Y | Y |
| **OREGON** | | | | | |
| Wyden | Y | Y | N | Y | Y |
| Smith | Y | Y | Y | Y | Y |
| **PENNSYLVANIA** | | | | | |
| Specter | Y | Y | Y | Y | Y |
| Santorum | Y | Y | Y | Y | N |
| **RHODE ISLAND** | | | | | |
| Reed | N | Y | N | Y | Y |
| Chafee | Y | Y | Y | Y | Y |
| **SOUTH CAROLINA** | | | | | |
| Graham | Y | Y | Y | Y | Y |
| DeMint | Y | Y | Y | Y | N |
| **SOUTH DAKOTA** | | | | | |
| Johnson | Y | Y | N | Y | Y |
| Thune | Y | Y | Y | Y | Y |
| **TENNESSEE** | | | | | |
| Frist | Y | Y | Y | Y | ? |
| Alexander | Y | Y | Y | Y | Y |
| **TEXAS** | | | | | |
| Hutchison | Y | Y | Y | Y | Y |
| Cornyn | Y | Y | Y | Y | N |
| **UTAH** | | | | | |
| Hatch | Y | Y | Y | Y | Y |
| Bennett | Y | Y | Y | Y | Y |
| **VERMONT** | | | | | |
| Leahy | N | Y | N | Y | Y |
| Jeffords | N | Y | N | Y | Y |
| **VIRGINIA** | | | | | |
| Warner | Y | Y | Y | Y | N |
| Allen | Y | Y | Y | Y | Y |
| **WASHINGTON** | | | | | |
| Murray | Y | Y | N | Y | Y |
| Cantwell | Y | Y | N | Y | Y |
| **WEST VIRGINIA** | | | | | |
| Byrd | ? | Y | N | Y | Y |
| Rockefeller | ? | ? | N | Y | Y |
| **WISCONSIN** | | | | | |
| Kohl | Y | Y | N | Y | Y |
| Feingold | N | Y | N | Y | Y |
| **WYOMING** | | | | | |
| Thomas | Y | Y | Y | Y | Y |
| Enzi | Y | Y | Y | Y | Y |

**KEY**  Republicans  Democrats  *Independents*

| | | | |
|---|---|---|---|
| Y | Voted for (yea) | X | Paired against |
| # | Paired for | – | Announced against |
| + | Announced for | P | Voted "present" |
| N | Voted against (nay) | C | Voted "present" to avoid possible conflict of interest |
| | | ? | Did not vote or otherwise make a position known |

ND Northern Democrats, SD Southern Democrats
Southern states: Ala., Ark., Fla., Ga., Ky., La., Miss., N.C., Okla., S.C., Tenn., Texas, Va.

# IN THE SENATE | By Vote Number

**201.** **S Res 207. Americans with Disabilities Act Anniversary/Adoption.**
Adoption of the resolution that would commemorate the 15th anniversary of the enactment of the Americans with Disabilities Act of 1990 and salute those who contributed to it. Adopted 87-0: R 47-0; D 39-0 (ND 35-0, SD 4-0); I 1-0. July 25, 2005.

**202.** **S 1042. Fiscal 2006 Defense Authorization/Terrorist Financing.**
Collins, R-Maine, amendment that would strengthen penalties for U.S. parent companies and their employees that do business with terrorist nations. It would increase the statutory limit in civil penalties under the International Emergency Economic Powers Act from $10,000 to $250,000 and from $50,000 to $500,000 for willful violations. It also would grant the Treasury Department subpoena power. Adopted 98-0: R 54-0; D 43-0 (ND 39-0, SD 4-0); I 1-0. July 26, 2005.

**203.** **S 1042. Fiscal 2006 Defense Authorization/Terrorist Financing.**
Lautenberg, D-N.J., amendment that would make certain foreign subsidiaries controlled by U.S. parent companies subject to sanctions under the International Emergency Economic Powers Act if they engage in business with terrorist nations. It also would require all firms subject to U.S. law to annually disclose an ownership stake of more than 10 percent in companies that are engaged in transactions that violate the terrorist financing law. Rejected 47-51: R 3-51; D 43-0 (ND 39-0, SD 4-0); I 1-0. July 26, 2005.

**204.** **S 1042. Fiscal 2006 Defense Authorization/Support of Youth Organizations.** Frist, R-Tenn., amendment that would stipulate that a federal agency cannot provide less support to youth organizations than the agency has in the past, except under certain special circumstances. It also would stipulate that the Defense secretary should provide at least the same level of support for a national or world Boy Scouts Jamboree as the department has provided in the past. Adopted 98-0: R 54-0; D 43-0 (ND 39-0, SD 4-0); I 1-0. July 26, 2005.

**205.** **S 1042. Fiscal 2006 Defense Authorization/Cloture.** McConnell, R-Ky., motion to invoke cloture on the bill that would authorize $441.6 billion for defense programs and another $50 billion for military action in Iraq and Afghanistan for fiscal 2006. Motion rejected 50-48: R 47-7; D 3-40 (ND 2-37, SD 1-3); I 0-1. Three-fifths of the total Senate (60) is required to invoke cloture. July 26, 2005.

ND Northern Democrats, SD Southern Democrats
Southern states: Ala., Ark., Fla., Ga., Ky., La., Miss., N.C., Okla., S.C., Tenn., Texas, Va.

| | 201 | 202 | 203 | 204 | 205 | | 201 | 202 | 203 | 204 | 205 |
|---|---|---|---|---|---|---|---|---|---|---|---|
| **ALABAMA** | | | | | | **MONTANA** | | | | | |
| Shelby | Y | Y | N | Y | Y | Baucus | Y | Y | Y | Y | N |
| Sessions | Y | Y | N | Y | Y | Burns | Y | Y | N | Y | Y |
| **ALASKA** | | | | | | **NEBRASKA** | | | | | |
| Stevens | Y | Y | N | Y | Y | Hagel | Y | Y | N | Y | Y |
| Murkowski | Y | Y | N | Y | Y | Nelson | Y | Y | Y | Y | Y |
| **ARIZONA** | | | | | | **NEVADA** | | | | | |
| McCain | Y | Y | N | Y | N | Reid | Y | Y | Y | Y | N |
| Kyl | ? | Y | Y | Y | Y | Ensign | Y | Y | Y | Y | Y |
| **ARKANSAS** | | | | | | **NEW HAMPSHIRE** | | | | | |
| Lincoln | Y | Y | Y | Y | N | Gregg | Y | Y | N | Y | Y |
| Pryor | Y | Y | Y | Y | N | Sununu | Y | Y | N | Y | Y |
| **CALIFORNIA** | | | | | | **NEW JERSEY** | | | | | |
| Feinstein | Y | Y | Y | Y | N | Corzine | ? | Y | Y | Y | N |
| Boxer | Y | Y | Y | Y | N | Lautenberg | Y | Y | Y | Y | N |
| **COLORADO** | | | | | | **NEW MEXICO** | | | | | |
| Allard | Y | Y | N | Y | Y | Domenici | Y | Y | N | Y | Y |
| Salazar | Y | Y | Y | Y | N | Bingaman | Y | Y | Y | Y | N |
| **CONNECTICUT** | | | | | | **NEW YORK** | | | | | |
| Dodd | Y | Y | Y | Y | N | Schumer | Y | Y | Y | Y | N |
| Lieberman | Y | Y | Y | Y | N | Clinton | Y | Y | Y | Y | N |
| **DELAWARE** | | | | | | **NORTH CAROLINA** | | | | | |
| Biden | ? | Y | Y | Y | N | Dole | Y | Y | N | Y | Y |
| Carper | Y | Y | Y | Y | N | Burr | Y | Y | N | Y | Y |
| **FLORIDA** | | | | | | **NORTH DAKOTA** | | | | | |
| Nelson | Y | Y | Y | Y | Y | Conrad | Y | Y | Y | Y | Y |
| Martinez | ? | Y | N | Y | Y | Dorgan | Y | Y | Y | Y | N |
| **GEORGIA** | | | | | | **OHIO** | | | | | |
| Chambliss | ? | Y | N | Y | Y | DeWine | Y | Y | N | Y | Y |
| Isakson | Y | Y | N | Y | Y | Voinovich | Y | Y | N | Y | Y |
| **HAWAII** | | | | | | **OKLAHOMA** | | | | | |
| Inouye | Y | Y | Y | Y | N | Inhofe | Y | Y | N | Y | Y |
| Akaka | Y | Y | Y | Y | N | Coburn | Y | Y | N | Y | Y |
| **IDAHO** | | | | | | **OREGON** | | | | | |
| Craig | ? | ? | ? | ? | ? | Wyden | Y | Y | Y | Y | N |
| Crapo | Y | Y | N | Y | Y | Smith | Y | Y | N | Y | Y |
| **ILLINOIS** | | | | | | **PENNSYLVANIA** | | | | | |
| Durbin | Y | Y | Y | Y | N | Specter | Y | Y | N | Y | Y |
| Obama | Y | Y | Y | Y | N | Santorum | ? | Y | N | Y | Y |
| **INDIANA** | | | | | | **RHODE ISLAND** | | | | | |
| Lugar | Y | Y | N | Y | Y | Reed | Y | Y | Y | Y | N |
| Bayh | ? | Y | Y | Y | N | Chafee | Y | Y | N | Y | Y |
| **IOWA** | | | | | | **SOUTH CAROLINA** | | | | | |
| Grassley | Y | Y | N | Y | Y | Graham | Y | Y | N | Y | N |
| Harkin | Y | Y | Y | Y | N | DeMint | Y | Y | N | Y | Y |
| **KANSAS** | | | | | | **SOUTH DAKOTA** | | | | | |
| Brownback | Y | Y | N | Y | Y | Johnson | Y | Y | Y | Y | N |
| Roberts | Y | Y | N | Y | Y | Thune | Y | Y | N | Y | N |
| **KENTUCKY** | | | | | | **TENNESSEE** | | | | | |
| McConnell | Y | Y | N | Y | Y | Frist | ? | Y | N | Y | Y |
| Bunning | Y | Y | N | Y | Y | Alexander | Y | Y | N | Y | Y |
| **LOUISIANA** | | | | | | **TEXAS** | | | | | |
| Landrieu | Y | Y | Y | Y | N | Hutchison | Y | Y | N | Y | Y |
| Vitter | Y | Y | N | Y | Y | Cornyn | Y | Y | N | Y | Y |
| **MAINE** | | | | | | **UTAH** | | | | | |
| Snowe | Y | Y | N | Y | N | Hatch | Y | Y | N | Y | Y |
| Collins | Y | Y | N | Y | N | Bennett | ? | Y | N | Y | Y |
| **MARYLAND** | | | | | | **VERMONT** | | | | | |
| Sarbanes | Y | Y | Y | Y | N | Leahy | Y | Y | Y | Y | N |
| Mikulski | Y | Y | Y | Y | N | Jeffords | Y | Y | Y | Y | N |
| **MASSACHUSETTS** | | | | | | **VIRGINIA** | | | | | |
| Kennedy | ? | Y | Y | Y | N | Warner | Y | Y | N | Y | Y |
| Kerry | Y | Y | Y | Y | N | Allen | Y | Y | N | Y | Y |
| **MICHIGAN** | | | | | | **WASHINGTON** | | | | | |
| Levin | Y | Y | Y | Y | N | Murray | Y | Y | Y | Y | N |
| Stabenow | Y | Y | Y | Y | N | Cantwell | Y | Y | Y | Y | N |
| **MINNESOTA** | | | | | | **WEST VIRGINIA** | | | | | |
| Dayton | Y | Y | Y | Y | N | Byrd | Y | Y | Y | Y | N |
| Coleman | Y | Y | N | Y | Y | Rockefeller | ? | ? | ? | ? | ? |
| **MISSISSIPPI** | | | | | | **WISCONSIN** | | | | | |
| Cochran | ? | Y | N | Y | Y | Kohl | Y | Y | Y | Y | N |
| Lott | Y | Y | N | Y | N | Feingold | Y | Y | Y | Y | N |
| **MISSOURI** | | | | | | **WYOMING** | | | | | |
| Bond | Y | Y | N | Y | Y | Thomas | Y | Y | N | Y | Y |
| Talent | Y | Y | N | Y | Y | Enzi | Y | Y | N | Y | Y |

**KEY**    Republicans    Democrats    *Independents*

| | | | | | |
|---|---|---|---|---|---|
| Y | Voted for (yea) | X | Paired against | C | Voted "present" to avoid possible conflict of interest |
| # | Paired for | – | Announced against | | |
| + | Announced for | P | Voted "present" | ? | Did not vote or otherwise make a position known |
| N | Voted against (nay) | | | | |

# IN THE SENATE | By Vote Number

**206.** **S 397. Gun Liability/Cloture.** McConnell, R-Ky., motion to invoke cloture (thus limiting debate) on the motion to proceed to the bill that would prohibit civil liability actions from being brought in any state or federal court against manufacturers, distributors, dealers and importers of firearms and ammunition resulting from the misuse of their products by others. Motion agreed to 66-32: R 53-1; D 13-30 (ND 9-30, SD 4-0); I 0-1. Three-fifths of the total Senate (60) is required to invoke cloture. July 26, 2005.

**207.** **S 397. Gun Liability/Safety Locks.** Kohl, D-Wis., amendment that would add a section to the bill that would, with certain exceptions, make it unlawful for licensed gun importers, manufacturers or dealers to sell, deliver or transfer handguns without a secure gun storage or safety device. It also would establish penalties for non-compliance, including a six-month suspension of a license, the revocation of a license or a $2,500 fine. Adopted 70-30: R 25-30; D 44-0 (ND 40-0, SD 4-0); I 1-0. July 28, 2005.

**208.** **S 397. Gun Liability/Civil Liability.** Craig, R-Idaho, motion to table (kill) the Levin, D-Mich., amendment that would add a section to the bill allowing civil liability action against all gun dealers and manufacturers who commit reckless or grossly negligent practices that contribute to a death or injury. Motion agreed to 62-37: R 50-4; D 12-32 (ND 9-31, SD 3-1); I 0-1. July 28, 2005.

**209.** **HR 3045. Central American Free Trade Agreement/Passage.** Passage of the bill that would implement a free trade agreement between the United States and Costa Rica, El Salvador, Guatemala, Honduras, Nicaragua and a separate pact with the Dominican Republic. Passed (thus cleared for the president) 55-45: R 43-12; D 11-33 (ND 8-32, SD 3-1); I 1-0. July 28, 2005.

| | 206 | 207 | 208 | 209 |
|---|---|---|---|---|
| **ALABAMA** | | | | |
| Shelby | Y | N | Y | N |
| Sessions | Y | N | Y | Y |
| **ALASKA** | | | | |
| Stevens | Y | Y | Y | Y |
| Murkowski | Y | Y | Y | Y |
| **ARIZONA** | | | | |
| McCain | Y | Y | Y | Y |
| Kyl | Y | N | Y | Y |
| **ARKANSAS** | | | | |
| Lincoln | Y | Y | Y | Y |
| Pryor | Y | Y | Y | Y |
| **CALIFORNIA** | | | | |
| Feinstein | N | Y | N | Y |
| Boxer | N | Y | N | N |
| **COLORADO** | | | | |
| Allard | Y | N | Y | Y |
| Salazar | Y | Y | Y | N |
| **CONNECTICUT** | | | | |
| Dodd | N | Y | N | N |
| Lieberman | N | Y | N | Y |
| **DELAWARE** | | | | |
| Biden | N | Y | N | N |
| Carper | N | Y | N | Y |
| **FLORIDA** | | | | |
| Nelson | Y | Y | N | Y |
| Martinez | Y | N | Y | Y |
| **GEORGIA** | | | | |
| Chambliss | Y | N | Y | Y |
| Isakson | Y | N | Y | Y |
| **HAWAII** | | | | |
| Inouye | N | Y | N | N |
| Akaka | N | Y | N | N |
| **IDAHO** | | | | |
| Craig | ? | N | Y | N |
| Crapo | Y | N | Y | N |
| **ILLINOIS** | | | | |
| Durbin | N | Y | N | N |
| Obama | N | Y | N | N |
| **INDIANA** | | | | |
| Lugar | Y | Y | N | Y |
| Bayh | N | Y | N | N |
| **IOWA** | | | | |
| Grassley | Y | Y | Y | Y |
| Harkin | N | Y | N | N |
| **KANSAS** | | | | |
| Brownback | Y | Y | Y | Y |
| Roberts | Y | Y | Y | Y |
| **KENTUCKY** | | | | |
| McConnell | Y | Y | Y | Y |
| Bunning | Y | N | Y | Y |
| **LOUISIANA** | | | | |
| Landrieu | Y | Y | Y | N |
| Vitter | Y | N | Y | N |
| **MAINE** | | | | |
| Snowe | Y | Y | N | N |
| Collins | Y | Y | N | N |
| **MARYLAND** | | | | |
| Sarbanes | N | Y | N | N |
| Mikulski | N | Y | N | N |
| **MASSACHUSETTS** | | | | |
| Kennedy | N | Y | N | N |
| Kerry | N | Y | N | N |
| **MICHIGAN** | | | | |
| Levin | N | Y | N | N |
| Stabenow | N | Y | N | N |
| **MINNESOTA** | | | | |
| Dayton | N | Y | N | N |
| Coleman | Y | Y | Y | Y |
| **MISSISSIPPI** | | | | |
| Cochran | Y | N | Y | Y |
| Lott | Y | N | Y | Y |
| **MISSOURI** | | | | |
| Bond | Y | N | Y | Y |
| Talent | Y | N | Y | Y |

| | 206 | 207 | 208 | 209 |
|---|---|---|---|---|
| **MONTANA** | | | | |
| Baucus | Y | Y | Y | N |
| Burns | Y | N | Y | N |
| **NEBRASKA** | | | | |
| Hagel | Y | Y | Y | Y |
| Nelson | Y | Y | Y | Y |
| **NEVADA** | | | | |
| Reid | Y | Y | Y | N |
| Ensign | Y | N | Y | Y |
| **NEW HAMPSHIRE** | | | | |
| Gregg | Y | Y | Y | Y |
| Sununu | Y | Y | Y | Y |
| **NEW JERSEY** | | | | |
| Corzine | N | Y | N | N |
| Lautenberg | N | Y | N | N |
| **NEW MEXICO** | | | | |
| Domenici | Y | Y | ? | Y |
| Bingaman | N | Y | N | Y |
| **NEW YORK** | | | | |
| Schumer | N | Y | N | N |
| Clinton | N | Y | N | N |
| **NORTH CAROLINA** | | | | |
| Dole | Y | N | Y | Y |
| Burr | Y | N | Y | Y |
| **NORTH DAKOTA** | | | | |
| Conrad | Y | Y | Y | N |
| Dorgan | Y | Y | Y | N |
| **OHIO** | | | | |
| DeWine | N | Y | N | Y |
| Voinovich | Y | Y | Y | Y |
| **OKLAHOMA** | | | | |
| Inhofe | Y | N | Y | Y |
| Coburn | Y | N | Y | Y |
| **OREGON** | | | | |
| Wyden | N | Y | N | Y |
| Smith | Y | Y | Y | Y |
| **PENNSYLVANIA** | | | | |
| Specter | Y | Y | Y | N |
| Santorum | Y | Y | Y | Y |
| **RHODE ISLAND** | | | | |
| Reed | N | Y | N | N |
| Chafee | Y | Y | N | Y |
| **SOUTH CAROLINA** | | | | |
| Graham | Y | Y | Y | N |
| DeMint | Y | N | Y | Y |
| **SOUTH DAKOTA** | | | | |
| Johnson | Y | Y | Y | N |
| Thune | Y | N | Y | N |
| **TENNESSEE** | | | | |
| Frist | Y | Y | Y | Y |
| Alexander | Y | N | Y | Y |
| **TEXAS** | | | | |
| Hutchison | Y | Y | Y | Y |
| Cornyn | Y | N | Y | Y |
| **UTAH** | | | | |
| Hatch | Y | N | Y | Y |
| Bennett | Y | N | Y | Y |
| **VERMONT** | | | | |
| Leahy | N | Y | N | N |
| Jeffords | N | Y | N | N |
| **VIRGINIA** | | | | |
| Warner | Y | Y | N | Y |
| Allen | Y | N | Y | Y |
| **WASHINGTON** | | | | |
| Murray | N | Y | N | Y |
| Cantwell | N | Y | N | Y |
| **WEST VIRGINIA** | | | | |
| Byrd | Y | Y | Y | N |
| Rockefeller | ? | Y | Y | N |
| **WISCONSIN** | | | | |
| Kohl | Y | Y | N | N |
| Feingold | N | Y | N | N |
| **WYOMING** | | | | |
| Thomas | Y | N | Y | N |
| Enzi | Y | N | Y | N |

**KEY** — Republicans — Democrats — *Independents*

| | | | |
|---|---|---|---|
| Y | Voted for (yea) | X | Paired against |
| # | Paired for | − | Announced against |
| + | Announced for | P | Voted "present" |
| N | Voted against (nay) | | |

| | |
|---|---|
| C | Voted "present" to avoid possible conflict of interest |
| ? | Did not vote or otherwise make a position known |

ND Northern Democrats, SD Southern Democrats
Southern states: Ala., Ark., Fla., Ga., Ky., La., Miss., N.C., Okla., S.C., Tenn., Texas, Va.

# IN THE SENATE | By Vote Number

**210.** **HR 2361. Fiscal 2006 Interior-Environment Appropriations/ Conference Report.** Adoption of the conference report on the bill that would appropriate $26.2 billion in fiscal 2006 for the Interior Department, the EPA and related agencies. It would provide $9.9 billion for the Interior Department, $7.7 billion for the EPA, $4.3 billion for the Forest Service and $3.1 billion for the Indian Health Service. It also would provide $1.5 billion in fiscal 2005 funding for veterans' medical care. Adopted (thus cleared for the president) 99-1: R 54-1; D 44-0 (ND 40-0, SD 4-0); I 1-0. July 29, 2005.

**211.** **HR 2985. Fiscal 2006 Legislative Branch Appropriations/ Conference Report.** Adoption of the conference report on the bill that would appropriate $3.8 billion in fiscal 2006 for legislative branch operations, including $1.1 billion for operations of the House of Representatives and $786 million for Senate operations. It also would require states to hold special elections within 49 days in the event that more than 100 lawmakers are killed or incapacitated. Adopted (thus cleared for the president) 96-4: R 52-3; D 43-1 (ND 39-1, SD 4-0); I 1-0. July 29, 2005.

**212.** **HR 6. Energy Policy/Conference Report.** Domenici, R-N.M., motion to waive the Budget Act with respect to the Feingold, D-Wis., point of order against the conference report on the bill that would overhaul the nation's energy policy and provide for $14.6 billion in energy-related tax incentives. Motion agreed to 71-29: R 46-9; D 25-19 (ND 22-18, SD 3-1); I 0-1. A three-fifths majority (60) of the total Senate is required to waive the Budget Act. July 29, 2005.

**213.** **HR 6. Energy Policy/Conference Report.** Adoption of the conference report on the bill that would overhaul the nation's energy policy and provide for $14.6 billion in energy-related tax incentives. It would allow lawsuits involving the gasoline additive methyl tertiary butyl ether (MTBE) to be moved to federal district court and require refiners to use 7.5 billion gallons of renewable fuels annually by 2012. It would grant the Federal Energy Regulatory Commission jurisdiction over reliability standards for electricity transmission networks and extend daylight-saving time by one month. Adopted (thus cleared for the president) 74-26: R 49-6; D 25-19 (ND 22-18, SD 3-1); I 0-1. A "yea" was a vote in support of the president's position. July 29, 2005.

**214.** **S 397. Gun Liability/Child Victims.** Craig, R-Idaho, amendment that would insert language to clarify that nothing in the bill would limit the right of individuals under the age of 17 to recover damages authorized under federal or state law in a civil action suit that meets the existing exceptions in the bill. Adopted 72-26: R 52-2; D 20-23 (ND 16-23, SD 4-0); I 0-1. July 29, 2005.

| | 210 | 211 | 212 | 213 | 214 |
|---|---|---|---|---|---|
| **ALABAMA** | | | | | |
| Shelby | Y | Y | Y | Y | Y |
| Sessions | Y | Y | Y | Y | Y |
| **ALASKA** | | | | | |
| Stevens | Y | Y | Y | Y | Y |
| Murkowski | Y | Y | Y | Y | Y |
| **ARIZONA** | | | | | |
| McCain | Y | Y | N | N | Y |
| Kyl | Y | Y | N | N | Y |
| **ARKANSAS** | | | | | |
| Lincoln | Y | Y | Y | Y | Y |
| Pryor | Y | Y | Y | Y | Y |
| **CALIFORNIA** | | | | | |
| Feinstein | Y | Y | Y | N | N |
| Boxer | Y | Y | N | N | N |
| **COLORADO** | | | | | |
| Allard | Y | Y | Y | Y | Y |
| Salazar | Y | Y | Y | Y | Y |
| **CONNECTICUT** | | | | | |
| Dodd | Y | Y | Y | N | N |
| Lieberman | Y | Y | Y | Y | Y |
| **DELAWARE** | | | | | |
| Biden | Y | Y | N | N | – |
| Carper | Y | Y | N | N | N |
| **FLORIDA** | | | | | |
| Nelson | Y | Y | N | N | Y |
| Martinez | Y | Y | N | N | Y |
| **GEORGIA** | | | | | |
| Chambliss | Y | Y | N | Y | Y |
| Isakson | Y | Y | N | Y | Y |
| **HAWAII** | | | | | |
| Inouye | Y | Y | Y | Y | N |
| Akaka | Y | Y | Y | Y | N |
| **IDAHO** | | | | | |
| Craig | Y | Y | Y | Y | Y |
| Crapo | Y | Y | Y | Y | Y |
| **ILLINOIS** | | | | | |
| Durbin | Y | Y | Y | Y | N |
| Obama | Y | Y | Y | Y | N |
| **INDIANA** | | | | | |
| Lugar | Y | Y | Y | Y | Y |
| Bayh | Y | Y | N | Y | Y |
| **IOWA** | | | | | |
| Grassley | Y | Y | Y | Y | Y |
| Harkin | Y | Y | Y | Y | N |
| **KANSAS** | | | | | |
| Brownback | Y | Y | Y | Y | Y |
| Roberts | Y | Y | Y | Y | Y |
| **KENTUCKY** | | | | | |
| McConnell | Y | Y | Y | Y | Y |
| Bunning | Y | Y | Y | Y | Y |
| **LOUISIANA** | | | | | |
| Landrieu | Y | Y | Y | Y | Y |
| Vitter | Y | Y | Y | Y | Y |
| **MAINE** | | | | | |
| Snowe | Y | Y | Y | Y | Y |
| Collins | Y | Y | Y | Y | Y |
| **MARYLAND** | | | | | |
| Sarbanes | Y | Y | N | N | N |
| Mikulski | Y | Y | Y | Y | N |
| **MASSACHUSETTS** | | | | | |
| Kennedy | Y | Y | N | N | N |
| Kerry | Y | Y | N | N | N |
| **MICHIGAN** | | | | | |
| Levin | Y | Y | Y | Y | N |
| Stabenow | Y | Y | Y | Y | Y |
| **MINNESOTA** | | | | | |
| Dayton | Y | Y | Y | Y | N |
| Coleman | Y | Y | Y | Y | Y |
| **MISSISSIPPI** | | | | | |
| Cochran | Y | Y | Y | Y | Y |
| Lott | Y | Y | Y | Y | Y |
| **MISSOURI** | | | | | |
| Bond | Y | Y | Y | Y | Y |
| Talent | Y | Y | Y | Y | Y |

| | 210 | 211 | 212 | 213 | 214 |
|---|---|---|---|---|---|
| **MONTANA** | | | | | |
| Baucus | Y | Y | Y | Y | Y |
| Burns | Y | Y | Y | Y | Y |
| **NEBRASKA** | | | | | |
| Hagel | Y | Y | Y | Y | Y |
| Nelson | Y | Y | Y | Y | Y |
| **NEVADA** | | | | | |
| Reid | Y | Y | N | N | Y |
| Ensign | Y | N | Y | Y | Y |
| **NEW HAMPSHIRE** | | | | | |
| Gregg | Y | Y | N | N | Y |
| Sununu | Y | Y | N | N | ? |
| **NEW JERSEY** | | | | | |
| Corzine | Y | Y | N | N | N |
| Lautenberg | Y | Y | N | N | N |
| **NEW MEXICO** | | | | | |
| Domenici | Y | Y | Y | Y | Y |
| Bingaman | Y | Y | Y | Y | Y |
| **NEW YORK** | | | | | |
| Schumer | Y | Y | N | N | N |
| Clinton | Y | Y | N | N | N |
| **NORTH CAROLINA** | | | | | |
| Dole | Y | Y | Y | Y | Y |
| Burr | Y | Y | Y | Y | Y |
| **NORTH DAKOTA** | | | | | |
| Conrad | Y | N | Y | Y | Y |
| Dorgan | Y | Y | Y | Y | Y |
| **OHIO** | | | | | |
| DeWine | Y | Y | Y | N | N |
| Voinovich | Y | Y | Y | Y | Y |
| **OKLAHOMA** | | | | | |
| Inhofe | Y | N | Y | Y | Y |
| Coburn | N | N | Y | Y | Y |
| **OREGON** | | | | | |
| Wyden | Y | Y | N | N | N |
| Smith | Y | Y | Y | Y | Y |
| **PENNSYLVANIA** | | | | | |
| Specter | Y | Y | Y | Y | Y |
| Santorum | Y | Y | Y | Y | Y |
| **RHODE ISLAND** | | | | | |
| Reed | Y | Y | N | N | N |
| Chafee | Y | Y | N | N | N |
| **SOUTH CAROLINA** | | | | | |
| Graham | Y | Y | Y | Y | Y |
| DeMint | Y | Y | Y | Y | Y |
| **SOUTH DAKOTA** | | | | | |
| Johnson | Y | Y | Y | Y | Y |
| Thune | Y | Y | Y | Y | Y |
| **TENNESSEE** | | | | | |
| Frist | Y | Y | Y | Y | Y |
| Alexander | Y | Y | Y | Y | Y |
| **TEXAS** | | | | | |
| Hutchison | Y | Y | Y | Y | Y |
| Cornyn | Y | Y | N | Y | Y |
| **UTAH** | | | | | |
| Hatch | Y | Y | Y | Y | Y |
| Bennett | Y | Y | Y | Y | Y |
| **VERMONT** | | | | | |
| Leahy | Y | Y | N | N | N |
| Jeffords | Y | Y | N | N | N |
| **VIRGINIA** | | | | | |
| Warner | Y | Y | Y | Y | Y |
| Allen | Y | Y | Y | Y | Y |
| **WASHINGTON** | | | | | |
| Murray | Y | Y | N | N | Y |
| Cantwell | Y | Y | Y | Y | Y |
| **WEST VIRGINIA** | | | | | |
| Byrd | Y | Y | Y | Y | Y |
| Rockefeller | Y | Y | Y | Y | Y |
| **WISCONSIN** | | | | | |
| Kohl | Y | Y | N | Y | Y |
| Feingold | Y | Y | N | N | N |
| **WYOMING** | | | | | |
| Thomas | Y | Y | Y | Y | Y |
| Enzi | Y | Y | Y | Y | Y |

**KEY**    Republicans    Democrats    *Independents*

| | | | |
|---|---|---|---|
| Y | Voted for (yea) | X | Paired against |
| # | Paired for | – | Announced against |
| + | Announced for | P | Voted "present" |
| N | Voted against (nay) | C | Voted "present" to avoid possible conflict of interest |
| | | ? | Did not vote or otherwise make a position known |

ND Northern Democrats, SD Southern Democrats
Southern states: Ala., Ark., Fla., Ga., Ky., La., Miss., N.C., Okla., S.C., Tenn., Texas, Va.

# IN THE SENATE | By Vote Number

**215.** **S 397. Gun Liability/Child Victims.** Lautenberg, D-N.J., amendment that would exempt lawsuits involving injuries to individuals age 17 and under from the bill's definition of qualified civil liability action. Rejected 35-64: R 2-52; D 32-12 (ND 31-9, SD 1-3); I 1-0. July 29, 2005.

**216.** **S 397. Gun Liability/Armor-Piercing Ammunition.** Craig, R-Idaho, amendment that would require the attorney general to commission a study to determine whether a uniform standard for the testing of projectiles against body armor is feasible. It also would increase the penalties for violent or drug trafficking crimes in which the perpetrator uses or possesses armor-piercing ammunition to a minimum of 15 years imprisonment. Adopted 87-11: R 53-0; D 33-11 (ND 29-11, SD 4-0); I 1-0. July 29, 2005.

**217.** **S 397. Gun Liability/Armor-Piercing Ammunition.** Kennedy, D-Mass., amendment that would expand the current ban on armor-piercing handgun ammunition by adding a performance standard to the current content-based standard and by prohibiting certain ammunition for sniper rifles and assault weapons. Rejected 31-64: R 1-50; D 30-13 (ND 29-10, SD 1-3); I 0-1. July 29, 2005.

**218.** **S 397. Gun Liability/Substitute.** Reed, D-R.I., substitute amendment that would bar certain civil lawsuits against manufacturers, distributors, dealers and importers of firearms and ammunition, principally those lawsuits aimed at making them liable for gun violence. The substitute would block municipalities from suing for damages caused by firearms but would allow individuals to sue. Rejected 33-63: R 2-50; D 30-13 (ND 29-10, SD 1-3); I 1-0. July 29, 2005.

**219.** **S 397. Gun Liability/Passage.** Passage of the bill that would bar certain civil lawsuits against manufacturers, distributors, dealers and importers of firearms and ammunition, principally those lawsuits aimed at making them liable for gun violence. Trade groups also would be protected, and all pending legal action against gunmakers would be dismissed. It also would, with certain exceptions, make it unlawful for licensed gun importers, manufacturers or dealers to sell, deliver or transfer handguns without a secure gun storage or safety device. Passed 65-31: R 50-2; D 14-29 (ND 10-29, SD 4-0); I 1-0. A "yea" was a vote in support of the president's position. July 29, 2005.

**220.** **HR 3. Surface Transportation Reauthorization/Conference Report.** Adoption of the conference report on the bill that would bring total authorization for federal aid highway, mass transit, safety and research programs, including fiscal 2004 funding, to $286.5 billion through 2009. The bill would increase the rate of return to states on their Highway Trust Fund contributions to 92 percent by fiscal 2008. It would make the Transportation Department the lead agency in the environmental review process for transportation projects. Adopted (thus cleared for the president) 91-4: R 48-4; D 42-0 (ND 38-0, SD 4-0); I 1-0. July 29, 2005.

ND Northern Democrats, SD Southern Democrats
Southern states: Ala., Ark., Fla., Ga., Ky., La., Miss., N.C., Okla., S.C., Tenn., Texas, Va.

| | 215 | 216 | 217 | 218 | 219 | 220 | | 215 | 216 | 217 | 218 | 219 | 220 |
|---|---|---|---|---|---|---|---|---|---|---|---|---|---|
| **ALABAMA** | | | | | | | **MONTANA** | | | | | | |
| Shelby | N | Y | N | N | Y | Y | Baucus | N | Y | N | N | Y | Y |
| Sessions | N | Y | N | N | Y | Y | Burns | N | Y | N | N | Y | Y |
| **ALASKA** | | | | | | | **NEBRASKA** | | | | | | |
| Stevens | N | Y | N | N | Y | Y | Hagel | N | Y | N | N | Y | Y |
| Murkowski | N | Y | N | N | Y | Y | Nelson | N | Y | N | N | Y | Y |
| **ARIZONA** | | | | | | | **NEVADA** | | | | | | |
| McCain | N | Y | N | N | Y | N | Reid | N | Y | N | N | Y | Y |
| Kyl | N | Y | N | N | Y | N | Ensign | N | Y | N | N | Y | Y |
| **ARKANSAS** | | | | | | | **NEW HAMPSHIRE** | | | | | | |
| Lincoln | N | Y | N | N | Y | Y | Gregg | N | Y | N | N | Y | N |
| Pryor | N | Y | N | N | Y | Y | Sununu | ? | ? | ? | ? | ? | ? |
| **CALIFORNIA** | | | | | | | **NEW JERSEY** | | | | | | |
| Feinstein | Y | Y | + | + | – | + | Corzine | Y | N | Y | Y | N | Y |
| Boxer | Y | N | Y | Y | N | + | Lautenberg | Y | N | Y | Y | N | Y |
| **COLORADO** | | | | | | | **NEW MEXICO** | | | | | | |
| Allard | N | Y | N | N | Y | Y | Domenici | N | Y | N | N | Y | Y |
| Salazar | N | Y | N | N | Y | Y | Bingaman | Y | Y | N | Y | N | Y |
| **CONNECTICUT** | | | | | | | **NEW YORK** | | | | | | |
| Dodd | Y | Y | Y | Y | N | Y | Schumer | Y | Y | Y | Y | N | Y |
| Lieberman | Y | N | Y | N | N | Y | Clinton | Y | Y | Y | Y | N | Y |
| **DELAWARE** | | | | | | | **NORTH CAROLINA** | | | | | | |
| Biden | Y | Y | Y | Y | N | Y | Dole | N | Y | N | N | Y | Y |
| Carper | Y | Y | Y | Y | N | Y | Burr | N | Y | N | N | Y | Y |
| **FLORIDA** | | | | | | | **NORTH DAKOTA** | | | | | | |
| Nelson | Y | Y | Y | Y | Y | Y | Conrad | N | Y | N | N | Y | Y |
| Martinez | N | Y | N | N | Y | Y | Dorgan | N | Y | N | N | Y | Y |
| **GEORGIA** | | | | | | | **OHIO** | | | | | | |
| Chambliss | N | Y | N | N | Y | Y | DeWine | Y | Y | N | Y | N | Y |
| Isakson | N | Y | N | N | Y | Y | Voinovich | N | Y | N | N | Y | Y |
| **HAWAII** | | | | | | | **OKLAHOMA** | | | | | | |
| Inouye | Y | Y | Y | Y | N | Y | Inhofe | N | Y | N | N | Y | Y |
| Akaka | Y | N | Y | Y | N | Y | Coburn | N | Y | N | N | Y | Y |
| **IDAHO** | | | | | | | **OREGON** | | | | | | |
| Craig | N | Y | N | N | Y | Y | Wyden | Y | N | Y | Y | N | Y |
| Crapo | N | Y | N | N | Y | Y | Smith | N | Y | ? | – | + | + |
| **ILLINOIS** | | | | | | | **PENNSYLVANIA** | | | | | | |
| Durbin | Y | Y | Y | Y | N | Y | Specter | N | Y | N | N | Y | Y |
| Obama | Y | Y | Y | Y | N | Y | Santorum | N | Y | N | N | Y | Y |
| **INDIANA** | | | | | | | **RHODE ISLAND** | | | | | | |
| Lugar | N | Y | N | N | Y | Y | Reed | Y | N | Y | Y | N | Y |
| Bayh | Y | Y | Y | Y | N | Y | Chafee | Y | Y | Y | Y | N | Y |
| **IOWA** | | | | | | | **SOUTH CAROLINA** | | | | | | |
| Grassley | N | Y | N | N | Y | Y | Graham | N | Y | N | N | Y | Y |
| Harkin | Y | Y | Y | Y | N | Y | DeMint | N | Y | N | N | Y | Y |
| **KANSAS** | | | | | | | **SOUTH DAKOTA** | | | | | | |
| Brownback | N | Y | N | N | Y | Y | Johnson | N | Y | N | N | Y | Y |
| Roberts | N | + | – | – | + | + | Thune | N | Y | N | N | Y | Y |
| **KENTUCKY** | | | | | | | **TENNESSEE** | | | | | | |
| McConnell | N | Y | N | N | Y | Y | Frist | N | Y | N | N | Y | Y |
| Bunning | N | Y | N | N | Y | Y | Alexander | N | Y | N | N | Y | Y |
| **LOUISIANA** | | | | | | | **TEXAS** | | | | | | |
| Landrieu | N | Y | N | N | Y | Y | Hutchison | N | Y | N | N | Y | Y |
| Vitter | N | Y | N | N | Y | Y | Cornyn | N | Y | ? | N | Y | N |
| **MAINE** | | | | | | | **UTAH** | | | | | | |
| Snowe | N | Y | N | N | Y | Y | Hatch | N | Y | N | N | Y | Y |
| Collins | N | Y | N | N | Y | Y | Bennett | N | Y | N | N | Y | Y |
| **MARYLAND** | | | | | | | **VERMONT** | | | | | | |
| Sarbanes | Y | N | Y | Y | N | Y | Leahy | Y | Y | N | Y | N | Y |
| Mikulski | Y | Y | Y | Y | N | Y | Jeffords | Y | Y | N | Y | Y | Y |
| **MASSACHUSETTS** | | | | | | | **VIRGINIA** | | | | | | |
| Kennedy | Y | N | Y | Y | N | Y | Warner | N | Y | N | N | Y | Y |
| Kerry | Y | Y | Y | Y | N | Y | Allen | N | Y | N | N | Y | Y |
| **MICHIGAN** | | | | | | | **WASHINGTON** | | | | | | |
| Levin | Y | N | Y | Y | N | Y | Murray | Y | Y | Y | Y | N | Y |
| Stabenow | Y | Y | Y | Y | N | Y | Cantwell | Y | Y | Y | Y | N | Y |
| **MINNESOTA** | | | | | | | **WEST VIRGINIA** | | | | | | |
| Dayton | Y | Y | Y | Y | N | Y | Byrd | N | Y | N | N | Y | Y |
| Coleman | N | Y | N | N | Y | Y | Rockefeller | N | Y | Y | N | Y | Y |
| **MISSISSIPPI** | | | | | | | **WISCONSIN** | | | | | | |
| Cochran | N | Y | N | N | Y | Y | Kohl | Y | Y | Y | Y | Y | Y |
| Lott | N | Y | N | N | Y | Y | Feingold | Y | N | Y | Y | N | Y |
| **MISSOURI** | | | | | | | **WYOMING** | | | | | | |
| Bond | N | Y | N | N | Y | Y | Thomas | N | Y | N | N | Y | Y |
| Talent | N | Y | N | N | Y | Y | Enzi | N | Y | N | N | Y | Y |

**KEY**    **Republicans**    Democrats    *Independents*

| | | |
|---|---|---|
| Y   Voted for (yea) | X   Paired against | C   Voted "present" to avoid possible conflict of interest |
| #   Paired for | –   Announced against | |
| +   Announced for | P   Voted "present" | ?   Did not vote or otherwise make a position known |
| N   Voted against (nay) | | |

# IN THE SENATE | By Vote Number

**221.** **S Res 233. Condolences for Hurricane Victims/Adoption.** Adoption of the resolution that would express the nation's condolences to the victims of Hurricane Katrina and commit to providing the necessary resources to the affected states for relief, recovery and rebuilding efforts. Adopted 94-0: R 52-0; D 41-0 (ND 38-0, SD 3-0); I 1-0. Sept. 6, 2005.

**222.** **S Res 234. Rehnquist Tribute/Adoption.** Adoption of the resolution that would pay tribute to the late William H. Rehnquist, chief justice of the Supreme Court, who died Sept. 3. Adopted 95-0: R 54-0; D 40-0 (ND 37-0, SD 3-0); I 1-0. Sept. 7, 2005.

**223.** **HR 3673. Fiscal 2005 Emergency Supplemental Appropriations/ Passage.** Passage of the bill that would appropriate $51.8 billion in fiscal 2005 supplemental spending for disaster relief to areas affected by Hurricane Katrina. The bill would provide $50 billion for the Federal Emergency Management Agency, $1.4 billion for the Defense Department and $400 million for the Army Corps of Engineers. Passed (thus cleared for the president) 97-0: R 52-0; D 44-0 (ND 40-0, SD 4-0); I 1-0. Sept. 8, 2005.

| | 221 | 222 | 223 | | | | 221 | 222 | 223 |
|---|---|---|---|---|---|---|---|---|---|
| **ALABAMA** | | | | | **MONTANA** | | | |
| Shelby | Y | Y | Y | | Baucus | Y | Y | Y |
| Sessions | Y | Y | Y | | Burns | Y | Y | Y |
| **ALASKA** | | | | | **NEBRASKA** | | | |
| Stevens | Y | Y | ? | | Hagel | Y | Y | Y |
| Murkowski | Y | Y | Y | | Nelson | Y | Y | Y |
| **ARIZONA** | | | | | **NEVADA** | | | |
| McCain | Y | Y | Y | | Reid | Y | Y | Y |
| Kyl | Y | Y | Y | | Ensign | Y | Y | Y |
| **ARKANSAS** | | | | | **NEW HAMPSHIRE** | | | |
| Lincoln | Y | Y | Y | | Gregg | Y | Y | Y |
| Pryor | Y | Y | Y | | Sununu | Y | Y | Y |
| **CALIFORNIA** | | | | | **NEW JERSEY** | | | |
| Feinstein | Y | Y | Y | | Corzine | Y | ? | Y |
| Boxer | Y | Y | Y | | Lautenberg | Y | Y | Y |
| **COLORADO** | | | | | **NEW MEXICO** | | | |
| Allard | ? | Y | Y | | Domenici | Y | Y | Y |
| Salazar | Y | Y | Y | | Bingaman | Y | Y | Y |
| **CONNECTICUT** | | | | | **NEW YORK** | | | |
| Dodd | Y | Y | Y | | Schumer | Y | Y | Y |
| Lieberman | Y | Y | Y | | Clinton | Y | Y | Y |
| **DELAWARE** | | | | | **NORTH CAROLINA** | | | |
| Biden | Y | ? | Y | | Dole | Y | Y | Y |
| Carper | Y | Y | Y | | Burr | Y | Y | Y |
| **FLORIDA** | | | | | **NORTH DAKOTA** | | | |
| Nelson | Y | Y | Y | | Conrad | Y | Y | Y |
| Martinez | Y | Y | Y | | Dorgan | Y | Y | Y |
| **GEORGIA** | | | | | **OHIO** | | | |
| Chambliss | Y | Y | Y | | DeWine | Y | Y | Y |
| Isakson | Y | Y | Y | | Voinovich | Y | Y | Y |
| **HAWAII** | | | | | **OKLAHOMA** | | | |
| Inouye | + | Y | ? | | Inhofe | Y | Y | Y |
| Akaka | Y | Y | Y | | Coburn | Y | Y | Y |
| **IDAHO** | | | | | **OREGON** | | | |
| Craig | Y | Y | Y | | Wyden | Y | Y | Y |
| Crapo | Y | Y | Y | | Smith | Y | Y | Y |
| **ILLINOIS** | | | | | **PENNSYLVANIA** | | | |
| Durbin | Y | Y | Y | | Specter | ? | Y | Y |
| Obama | Y | Y | Y | | Santorum | Y | Y | Y |
| **INDIANA** | | | | | **RHODE ISLAND** | | | |
| Lugar | Y | Y | Y | | Reed | Y | Y | Y |
| Bayh | Y | Y | Y | | Chafee | Y | Y | Y |
| **IOWA** | | | | | **SOUTH CAROLINA** | | | |
| Grassley | Y | Y | Y | | Graham | Y | Y | Y |
| Harkin | Y | Y | Y | | DeMint | Y | Y | Y |
| **KANSAS** | | | | | **SOUTH DAKOTA** | | | |
| Brownback | Y | Y | Y | | Johnson | Y | Y | Y |
| Roberts | Y | Y | Y | | Thune | Y | Y | Y |
| **KENTUCKY** | | | | | **TENNESSEE** | | | |
| McConnell | Y | Y | Y | | Frist | Y | Y | Y |
| Bunning | Y | Y | Y | | Alexander | Y | Y | Y |
| **LOUISIANA** | | | | | **TEXAS** | | | |
| Landrieu | ? | ? | Y | | Hutchison | Y | Y | Y |
| Vitter | + | ? | ? | | Cornyn | Y | Y | Y |
| **MAINE** | | | | | **UTAH** | | | |
| Snowe | Y | Y | Y | | Hatch | Y | Y | Y |
| Collins | Y | Y | Y | | Bennett | Y | Y | Y |
| **MARYLAND** | | | | | **VERMONT** | | | |
| Sarbanes | Y | Y | Y | | Leahy | Y | Y | Y |
| Mikulski | Y | Y | Y | | *Jeffords* | Y | Y | Y |
| **MASSACHUSETTS** | | | | | **VIRGINIA** | | | |
| Kennedy | Y | Y | Y | | Warner | Y | Y | Y |
| Kerry | Y | Y | Y | | Allen | Y | Y | Y |
| **MICHIGAN** | | | | | **WASHINGTON** | | | |
| Levin | Y | Y | Y | | Murray | Y | Y | Y |
| Stabenow | Y | Y | Y | | Cantwell | Y | Y | Y |
| **MINNESOTA** | | | | | **WEST VIRGINIA** | | | |
| Dayton | Y | Y | Y | | Byrd | Y | Y | Y |
| Coleman | Y | Y | Y | | Rockefeller | ? | ? | Y |
| **MISSISSIPPI** | | | | | **WISCONSIN** | | | |
| Cochran | Y | Y | Y | | Kohl | Y | Y | Y |
| Lott | Y | Y | Y | | Feingold | Y | Y | Y |
| **MISSOURI** | | | | | **WYOMING** | | | |
| Bond | Y | Y | Y | | Thomas | Y | Y | Y |
| Talent | Y | Y | Y | | Enzi | Y | Y | Y |

**KEY**    **Republicans**    Democrats    *Independents*

| | | | | | | |
|---|---|---|---|---|---|---|
| Y | Voted for (yea) | X | Paired against | C | Voted "present" to avoid possible conflict of interest |
| # | Paired for | – | Announced against | | |
| + | Announced for | P | Voted "present" | ? | Did not vote or otherwise make a position known |
| N | Voted against (nay) | | | | |

ND Northern Democrats, SD Southern Democrats
Southern states: Ala., Ark., Fla., Ga., Ky., La., Miss., N.C., Okla., S.C., Tenn., Texas, Va.

# IN THE SENATE | By Vote Number

**224.** **S J Res 20. EPA Rule Disapproval/Motion to Proceed.** Inhofe, R-Okla., motion to proceed to consideration of a joint resolution that would provide for congressional disapproval of an EPA rule that removes coal and oil-fired electric generating units from the list of major sources of hazardous air pollutants as defined by the Clean Air Act. Motion agreed to 92-0: R 50-0; D 41-0 (ND 37-0, SD 4-0); I 1-0. Sept. 12, 2005.

**225.** **S J Res 20. EPA Rule Disapproval/Passage.** Passage of a joint resolution that would provide for congressional disapproval of an EPA rule that removes coal and oil-fired electric generating units from the list of major sources of hazardous air pollutants as defined by the Clean Air Act. Rejected 47-51: R 9-45; D 37-6 (ND 34-5, SD 3-1); I 1-0. A "nay" was a vote in support of the president's position. Sept. 13, 2005.

**226.** **HR 2862. Fiscal 2006 Commerce-Justice-Science Appropriations/ Law Enforcement Programs.** Biden, D-Del., motion to waive the Budget Act with respect to the Gregg, R-N.H., point of order against the emergency designation of the Biden amendment. The Biden amendment would increase funding for the Community Oriented Policing Services program by $1 billion; the National Center for Missing and Exploited Children by $10 million; and the Office of Violence Against Women by $9 million, and designate the increases as emergency spending. Motion rejected 41-56: R 1-53; D 39-3 (ND 35-3, SD 4-0); I 1-0. A three-fifths majority (60) of the total Senate is required to waive the Budget Act. (Subsequently, the chair upheld the point of order, and the emergency designation was stricken. The amendment fell after a second budgetary point of order was upheld.) Sept. 13, 2005.

**227.** **HR 2862. Fiscal 2006 Commerce-Justice-Science Appropriations/ Interoperable Communications Funding.** Stabenow, D-Mich., motion to waive the Budget Act with respect to the Gregg, R-N.H., point of order against the Stabenow amendment. The Stabenow amendment would increase funding for interoperable communications equipment grants by $5 billion. Motion rejected 40-58: R 0-54; D 39-4 (ND 35-4, SD 4-0); I 1-0. A three-fifths majority vote (60) of the total Senate is required to waive the Budget Act. (Subsequently, the chair upheld the point of order and the amendment fell.) Sept. 14, 2005.

**228.** **HR 2862. Fiscal 2006 Commerce-Justice-Science Appropriations/ Special Committee.** Dorgan, D-N.D., motion to suspend the rule against legislating on an appropriations bill with respect to the Dorgan amendment, which would establish a special Senate committee to investigate the awarding and carrying out of contracts in Afghanistan and Iraq. Motion rejected 44-53: R 0-53; D 43-0 (ND 39-0, SD 4-0); I 1-0. A two-thirds majority of those present and voting (65 in this case) is required to suspend the rule. (Subsequently, the amendment fell on a previous point of order.) Sept. 14, 2005.

**229.** **HR 2862. Fiscal 2006 Commerce-Justice-Science Appropriations/ Hurricane Katrina Commission.** Dorgan, D-N.D., motion to suspend the rule against legislating on an appropriations bill with respect to the Clinton, D-N.Y., amendment. The Clinton amendment would establish an independent commission to examine the federal, state and local response to Hurricane Katrina and make immediate corrective measures to improve future responses. Motion rejected 44-54: R 0-54; D 43-0 (ND 39-0, SD 4-0); I 1-0. A two-thirds majority of those present and voting (66 in this case) is required to suspend the rule. (Subsequently, the amendment fell on a previous point of order.) Sept. 14, 2005.

ND Northern Democrats, SD Southern Democrats
Southern states: Ala., Ark., Fla., Ga., Ky., La., Miss., N.C., Okla., S.C., Tenn., Texas, Va.

| | 224 | 225 | 226 | 227 | 228 | 229 | | 224 | 225 | 226 | 227 | 228 | 229 |
|---|---|---|---|---|---|---|---|---|---|---|---|---|---|
| **ALABAMA** | | | | | | | **MONTANA** | | | | | | |
| Shelby | Y | N | N | N | N | N | Baucus | Y | N | Y | Y | Y | Y |
| Sessions | Y | N | N | N | N | N | Burns | ? | N | N | N | N | N |
| **ALASKA** | | | | | | | **NEBRASKA** | | | | | | |
| Stevens | Y | N | N | N | N | N | Hagel | Y | N | N | N | N | N |
| Murkowski | Y | N | N | N | N | N | Nelson | Y | N | N | N | Y | Y |
| **ARIZONA** | | | | | | | **NEVADA** | | | | | | |
| McCain | Y | Y | N | N | N | N | Reid | Y | Y | Y | Y | Y | Y |
| Kyl | Y | N | N | N | N | N | Ensign | Y | N | N | N | N | N |
| **ARKANSAS** | | | | | | | **NEW HAMPSHIRE** | | | | | | |
| Lincoln | Y | Y | Y | Y | Y | Y | Gregg | Y | Y | N | N | N | N |
| Pryor | Y | N | Y | Y | Y | Y | Sununu | Y | Y | N | N | N | N |
| **CALIFORNIA** | | | | | | | **NEW JERSEY** | | | | | | |
| Feinstein | Y | Y | Y | Y | Y | Y | Corzine | Y | Y | ? | ? | ? | ? |
| Boxer | Y | Y | Y | Y | Y | Y | Lautenberg | Y | Y | Y | Y | Y | Y |
| **COLORADO** | | | | | | | **NEW MEXICO** | | | | | | |
| Allard | Y | N | N | N | N | N | Domenici | Y | N | N | N | N | N |
| Salazar | Y | Y | Y | Y | Y | Y | Bingaman | Y | Y | Y | Y | Y | Y |
| **CONNECTICUT** | | | | | | | **NEW YORK** | | | | | | |
| Dodd | Y | Y | Y | Y | Y | Y | Schumer | Y | Y | Y | Y | Y | Y |
| Lieberman | Y | Y | Y | Y | Y | Y | Clinton | Y | Y | Y | Y | Y | Y |
| **DELAWARE** | | | | | | | **NORTH CAROLINA** | | | | | | |
| Biden | Y | Y | Y | Y | Y | Y | Dole | Y | N | N | N | N | N |
| Carper | Y | Y | Y | N | Y | Y | Burr | Y | N | N | N | N | N |
| **FLORIDA** | | | | | | | **NORTH DAKOTA** | | | | | | |
| Nelson | Y | Y | Y | Y | Y | Y | Conrad | Y | N | N | N | N | N |
| Martinez | ? | N | N | N | N | N | Dorgan | Y | N | Y | Y | Y | Y |
| **GEORGIA** | | | | | | | **OHIO** | | | | | | |
| Chambliss | ? | N | N | N | N | N | DeWine | Y | N | N | N | N | N |
| Isakson | Y | N | N | N | N | N | Voinovich | Y | N | N | N | N | N |
| **HAWAII** | | | | | | | **OKLAHOMA** | | | | | | |
| Inouye | ? | Y | Y | Y | Y | Y | Inhofe | Y | N | N | N | N | N |
| Akaka | Y | Y | Y | Y | Y | Y | Coburn | Y | N | N | N | N | N |
| **IDAHO** | | | | | | | **OREGON** | | | | | | |
| Craig | Y | N | N | N | N | N | Wyden | Y | Y | Y | Y | Y | Y |
| Crapo | Y | N | N | N | N | N | Smith | Y | Y | Y | N | N | N |
| **ILLINOIS** | | | | | | | **PENNSYLVANIA** | | | | | | |
| Durbin | Y | Y | Y | Y | Y | Y | Specter | Y | N | N | N | N | N |
| Obama | Y | Y | Y | Y | Y | Y | Santorum | Y | N | N | N | N | N |
| **INDIANA** | | | | | | | **RHODE ISLAND** | | | | | | |
| Lugar | Y | N | N | N | N | N | Reed | Y | Y | Y | Y | Y | Y |
| Bayh | Y | Y | Y | Y | Y | Y | Chafee | Y | Y | N | N | N | N |
| **IOWA** | | | | | | | **SOUTH CAROLINA** | | | | | | |
| Grassley | Y | N | N | N | N | N | Graham | + | N | N | N | N | N |
| Harkin | Y | Y | Y | Y | Y | Y | DeMint | Y | N | N | N | N | N |
| **KANSAS** | | | | | | | **SOUTH DAKOTA** | | | | | | |
| Brownback | Y | N | N | N | N | N | Johnson | Y | Y | N | Y | Y | Y |
| Roberts | ? | N | N | N | N | N | Thune | Y | N | N | N | N | N |
| **KENTUCKY** | | | | | | | **TENNESSEE** | | | | | | |
| McConnell | Y | N | N | N | N | N | Frist | Y | N | N | N | N | N |
| Bunning | Y | N | N | N | N | N | Alexander | Y | N | N | N | N | N |
| **LOUISIANA** | | | | | | | **TEXAS** | | | | | | |
| Landrieu | Y | Y | Y | Y | Y | Y | Hutchison | Y | N | N | N | N | N |
| Vitter | Y | N | ? | ? | ? | ? | Cornyn | Y | N | N | N | N | N |
| **MAINE** | | | | | | | **UTAH** | | | | | | |
| Snowe | Y | Y | N | N | N | N | Hatch | Y | ? | N | N | N | N |
| Collins | Y | Y | N | N | N | N | Bennett | Y | N | N | N | N | N |
| **MARYLAND** | | | | | | | **VERMONT** | | | | | | |
| Sarbanes | Y | Y | Y | Y | Y | Y | Leahy | Y | Y | Y | Y | Y | Y |
| Mikulski | Y | Y | Y | Y | Y | Y | Jeffords | Y | Y | Y | Y | Y | Y |
| **MASSACHUSETTS** | | | | | | | **VIRGINIA** | | | | | | |
| Kennedy | Y | Y | Y | Y | Y | Y | Warner | Y | N | N | N | ? | N |
| Kerry | ? | Y | Y | Y | Y | Y | Allen | Y | N | N | N | N | N |
| **MICHIGAN** | | | | | | | **WASHINGTON** | | | | | | |
| Levin | Y | Y | Y | Y | Y | Y | Murray | Y | Y | Y | Y | Y | Y |
| Stabenow | Y | Y | Y | Y | Y | Y | Cantwell | Y | Y | Y | Y | Y | Y |
| **MINNESOTA** | | | | | | | **WEST VIRGINIA** | | | | | | |
| Dayton | Y | Y | Y | Y | Y | Y | Byrd | Y | N | N | Y | Y | Y |
| Coleman | Y | Y | N | N | N | N | Rockefeller | ? | ? | ? | Y | Y | Y |
| **MISSISSIPPI** | | | | | | | **WISCONSIN** | | | | | | |
| Cochran | Y | N | N | N | N | N | Kohl | Y | Y | Y | Y | Y | Y |
| Lott | Y | N | N | N | N | N | Feingold | Y | Y | Y | N | Y | Y |
| **MISSOURI** | | | | | | | **WYOMING** | | | | | | |
| Bond | Y | N | N | N | N | N | Thomas | Y | N | N | N | N | N |
| Talent | Y | N | Y | N | N | N | Enzi | Y | N | N | N | N | N |

**KEY**  Republicans   Democrats   *Independents*

| | | | |
|---|---|---|---|
| Y | Voted for (yea) | X Paired against | C Voted "present" to avoid possible conflict of interest |
| # | Paired for | − Announced against | |
| + | Announced for | P Voted "present" | ? Did not vote or otherwise make a position known |
| N | Voted against (nay) | | |

# IN THE SENATE | By Vote Number

**230.** HR 2862. Fiscal 2006 Commerce-Justice-Science Appropriations/ **Advanced Technology Program.** Shelby, R-Ala., motion to table (kill) the Coburn, R-Okla., amendment that would eliminate funding for the Advanced Technology Program and increase funding for the National Oceanic and Atmospheric Administration by $4.9 million, Community Oriented Policing Services by $72 million and state and local law enforcement assistance by $48 million. Motion agreed to 68-29: R 28-25; D 39-4 (ND 35-4, SD 4-0); I 1-0. Sept. 14, 2005.

**231.** HR 2862. Fiscal 2006 Commerce-Justice-Science Appropriations/ **Trade Promotion Authority Enforcement.** Grassley, R-Iowa, amendment that would require that funds appropriated in the bill be used in a manner consistent with the Bipartisan Trade Promotion Authority Act of 2002. Adopted 99-0: R 55-0; D 43-0 (ND 39-0, SD 4-0); I 1-0. Sept. 15, 2005.

**232.** HR 2862. Fiscal 2006 Commerce-Justice-Science Appropriations/ **Trade Negotiating Restrictions.** Dorgan, D-N.D., amendment that would prohibit the U.S. trade representative from using funds appropriated in the bill to change or establish any trade agreement that would alter U.S. law relating to national security import restrictions or remedies to domestic firms harmed by the trade practices of foreign competitors. Rejected 39-60: R 8-47; D 31-12 (ND 28-11, SD 3-1); I 0-1. Sept. 15, 2005.

**233.** HR 2862. Fiscal 2006 Commerce-Justice-Science Appropriations/ **Small Business Emergency Relief.** Snowe, R-Maine, amendment that would provide $595 million in disaster aid to victims of Hurricane Katrina through modified Small Business Administration programs for small-business owners, homeowners and renters. The funds would be designated as emergency spending. Adopted 96-0: R 52-0; D 43-0 (ND 39-0, SD 4-0); I 1-0. Sept. 15, 2005.

**234.** HR 2862. Fiscal 2006 Commerce-Justice-Science Appropriations/ **Financial Relief for Hurricane Katrina Victims.** Lieberman, D-Conn., motion to suspend the rule against legislating on an appropriations bill with respect to the Lieberman amendment. The Lieberman amendment would allow for up to 52 weeks of unemployment benefits for an individual as a result of a major disaster and provide other relief. Motion rejected 43-52: R 1-51; D 41-1 (ND 38-1, SD 3-0); I 1-0. A two-thirds majority of those present and voting (64 in this case) is required to suspend the rule. (Subsequently the amendment fell on a point of order.) Sept. 15, 2005.

**235.** HR 2862. Fiscal 2006 Commerce-Justice-Science Appropriations/ **Passage.** Passage of the bill that would provide $52.4 billion in fiscal 2006, including $48.6 billion in discretionary funds, for the Commerce and Justice departments, as well as agencies such as NASA. It would provide $21.2 billion for the Justice Department, $7.2 billion for the Commerce Department and related agencies and $16.4 billion for NASA. Passed 91-4: R 48-4; D 42-0 (ND 39-0, SD 3-0); I 1-0. Sept. 15, 2005.

| | 230 | 231 | 232 | 233 | 234 | 235 | | | 230 | 231 | 232 | 233 | 234 | 235 |
|---|---|---|---|---|---|---|---|---|---|---|---|---|---|---|
| **ALABAMA** | | | | | | | | **MONTANA** | | | | | | |
| Shelby | Y | Y | Y | Y | N | Y | | Baucus | Y | Y | N | Y | Y | Y |
| Sessions | Y | Y | N | Y | N | Y | | Burns | Y | Y | N | Y | N | Y |
| **ALASKA** | | | | | | | | **NEBRASKA** | | | | | | |
| Stevens | N | Y | N | Y | N | Y | | Hagel | Y | Y | N | Y | N | Y |
| Murkowski | ? | Y | N | Y | N | Y | | Nelson | Y | Y | N | Y | N | Y |
| **ARIZONA** | | | | | | | | **NEVADA** | | | | | | |
| McCain | N | Y | N | Y | N | Y | | Reid | Y | Y | Y | Y | Y | Y |
| Kyl | N | Y | N | Y | N | Y | | Ensign | N | Y | N | Y | N | Y |
| **ARKANSAS** | | | | | | | | **NEW HAMPSHIRE** | | | | | | |
| Lincoln | Y | Y | N | Y | Y | Y | | Gregg | Y | Y | N | Y | N | Y |
| Pryor | Y | Y | Y | Y | Y | Y | | Sununu | N | Y | N | Y | N | Y |
| **CALIFORNIA** | | | | | | | | **NEW JERSEY** | | | | | | |
| Feinstein | Y | Y | N | Y | Y | Y | | Corzine | ? | ? | ? | ? | ? | ? |
| Boxer | Y | Y | Y | Y | Y | Y | | Lautenberg | Y | Y | Y | Y | Y | Y |
| **COLORADO** | | | | | | | | **NEW MEXICO** | | | | | | |
| Allard | Y | Y | N | Y | N | Y | | Domenici | Y | Y | N | Y | N | Y |
| Salazar | Y | Y | Y | Y | Y | Y | | Bingaman | Y | Y | Y | Y | Y | Y |
| **CONNECTICUT** | | | | | | | | **NEW YORK** | | | | | | |
| Dodd | Y | Y | Y | Y | Y | Y | | Schumer | Y | Y | Y | Y | Y | Y |
| Lieberman | Y | Y | N | Y | Y | Y | | Clinton | Y | Y | Y | Y | Y | Y |
| **DELAWARE** | | | | | | | | **NORTH CAROLINA** | | | | | | |
| Biden | Y | Y | Y | Y | Y | Y | | Dole | Y | Y | N | Y | N | Y |
| Carper | Y | Y | N | Y | Y | Y | | Burr | N | Y | N | Y | N | Y |
| **FLORIDA** | | | | | | | | **NORTH DAKOTA** | | | | | | |
| Nelson | Y | Y | Y | Y | Y | Y | | Conrad | N | Y | Y | Y | Y | Y |
| Martinez | N | Y | N | Y | N | Y | | Dorgan | N | Y | Y | Y | Y | Y |
| **GEORGIA** | | | | | | | | **OHIO** | | | | | | |
| Chambliss | N | Y | Y | Y | N | Y | | DeWine | Y | Y | N | Y | N | Y |
| Isakson | N | Y | N | Y | N | Y | | Voinovich | Y | Y | N | Y | N | Y |
| **HAWAII** | | | | | | | | **OKLAHOMA** | | | | | | |
| Inouye | Y | Y | Y | Y | Y | Y | | Inhofe | N | Y | N | Y | N | N |
| Akaka | Y | Y | Y | Y | Y | Y | | Coburn | N | Y | Y | Y | N | N |
| **IDAHO** | | | | | | | | **OREGON** | | | | | | |
| Craig | N | Y | N | Y | N | Y | | Wyden | Y | Y | N | Y | Y | Y |
| Crapo | Y | Y | N | Y | N | Y | | Smith | Y | Y | N | Y | N | Y |
| **ILLINOIS** | | | | | | | | **PENNSYLVANIA** | | | | | | |
| Durbin | Y | Y | Y | Y | Y | Y | | Specter | Y | Y | Y | Y | Y | Y |
| Obama | Y | Y | N | Y | Y | Y | | Santorum | N | Y | N | Y | N | Y |
| **INDIANA** | | | | | | | | **RHODE ISLAND** | | | | | | |
| Lugar | Y | Y | N | Y | N | Y | | Reed | Y | Y | N | Y | Y | Y |
| Bayh | Y | Y | Y | Y | Y | Y | | Chafee | Y | Y | N | Y | Y | Y |
| **IOWA** | | | | | | | | **SOUTH CAROLINA** | | | | | | |
| Grassley | N | Y | N | Y | N | Y | | Graham | N | Y | Y | Y | N | Y |
| Harkin | N | Y | Y | Y | Y | Y | | DeMint | N | Y | N | Y | N | Y |
| **KANSAS** | | | | | | | | **SOUTH DAKOTA** | | | | | | |
| Brownback | N | Y | N | Y | N | Y | | Johnson | Y | Y | Y | Y | Y | Y |
| Roberts | Y | Y | N | Y | N | Y | | Thune | N | Y | N | + | - | + |
| **KENTUCKY** | | | | | | | | **TENNESSEE** | | | | | | |
| McConnell | N | Y | N | Y | N | Y | | Frist | Y | Y | N | Y | N | Y |
| Bunning | Y | Y | N | Y | N | Y | | Alexander | Y | Y | N | Y | N | Y |
| **LOUISIANA** | | | | | | | | **TEXAS** | | | | | | |
| Landrieu | Y | Y | Y | Y | ? | ? | | Hutchison | Y | Y | N | Y | N | Y |
| Vitter | ? | Y | N | ? | ? | ? | | Cornyn | Y | Y | N | Y | N | Y |
| **MAINE** | | | | | | | | **UTAH** | | | | | | |
| Snowe | N | Y | Y | Y | N | Y | | Hatch | Y | Y | N | Y | N | Y |
| Collins | N | Y | N | Y | N | Y | | Bennett | Y | Y | N | Y | N | Y |
| **MARYLAND** | | | | | | | | **VERMONT** | | | | | | |
| Sarbanes | Y | Y | Y | Y | Y | Y | | Leahy | Y | Y | Y | Y | Y | Y |
| Mikulski | Y | Y | Y | Y | Y | Y | | Jeffords | Y | Y | Y | Y | Y | Y |
| **MASSACHUSETTS** | | | | | | | | **VIRGINIA** | | | | | | |
| Kennedy | Y | Y | Y | Y | Y | Y | | Warner | Y | Y | N | Y | N | Y |
| Kerry | Y | Y | Y | Y | Y | Y | | Allen | Y | Y | N | Y | N | Y |
| **MICHIGAN** | | | | | | | | **WASHINGTON** | | | | | | |
| Levin | Y | Y | Y | Y | Y | Y | | Murray | Y | Y | N | Y | Y | Y |
| Stabenow | Y | Y | Y | Y | Y | Y | | Cantwell | Y | Y | N | Y | Y | Y |
| **MINNESOTA** | | | | | | | | **WEST VIRGINIA** | | | | | | |
| Dayton | Y | Y | Y | Y | Y | Y | | Byrd | Y | Y | Y | Y | Y | Y |
| Coleman | N | Y | N | Y | N | Y | | Rockefeller | Y | Y | Y | Y | Y | Y |
| **MISSISSIPPI** | | | | | | | | **WISCONSIN** | | | | | | |
| Cochran | Y | Y | N | Y | N | Y | | Kohl | Y | Y | Y | Y | Y | Y |
| Lott | N | Y | N | ? | ? | ? | | Feingold | N | Y | Y | Y | Y | Y |
| **MISSOURI** | | | | | | | | **WYOMING** | | | | | | |
| Bond | Y | Y | N | Y | N | Y | | Thomas | N | Y | N | Y | N | N |
| Talent | N | Y | N | Y | N | Y | | Enzi | Y | Y | N | Y | N | N |

**KEY**   Republicans   Democrats   *Independents*

| | | | | | | |
|---|---|---|---|---|---|---|
| Y | Voted for (yea) | X | Paired against | C | Voted "present" to avoid possible conflict of interest |
| # | Paired for | - | Announced against | | |
| + | Announced for | P | Voted "present" | ? | Did not vote or otherwise make a position known |
| N | Voted against (nay) | | | | |

ND Northern Democrats, SD Southern Democrats
Southern states: Ala., Ark., Fla., Ga., Ky., La., Miss., N.C., Okla., S.C., Tenn., Texas, Va.

# IN THE SENATE | By Vote Number

**236.** HR 2744. Fiscal 2006 Agriculture Appropriations/Japanese Beef **Importation.** Nelson, D-Neb., amendment that would prohibit the Agriculture Department from using funds in the bill to develop a final rule to allow the importation of beef from Japan unless the president certifies to Congress that Japan has granted open access for U.S. beef and beef products. Adopted 72-26: R 31-24; D 40-2 (ND 36-2, SD 4-0); I 1-0. Sept. 20, 2005.

**237.** HR 2744. Fiscal 2006 Agriculture Appropriations/Horse **Slaughtering Ban.** Ensign, R-Nev., amendment that would prohibit the use of funds in the bill to pay the salaries or expenses of personnel to inspect horses being sent to slaughter for human consumption. Adopted 69-28: R 35-20; D 33-8 (ND 32-6, SD 1-2); I 1-0. Sept. 20, 2005.

**238.** HR 2744. Fiscal 2006 Agriculture Appropriations/Sunshine **Report Language.** Coburn, R-Okla., amendment that would require any limitation, directive or earmark contained in the House or Senate report accompanying the bill to be included in the conference report to be considered as approved by both chambers. Adopted 55-39: R 32-21; D 23-17 (ND 21-15, SD 2-2); I 0-1. Sept. 21, 2005.

**239.** HR 2744. Fiscal 2006 Agriculture Appropriations/Nutrition **Education.** Bingaman, D-N.M., amendment that would increase funding for Team Nutrition programs by $10 million with an offset of $10 million from the Common Computer Environment program. Adopted 66-29: R 25-29; D 40-0 (ND 36-0, SD 4-0); I 1-0. Sept. 21, 2005.

**240.** HR 2744. Fiscal 2006 Agriculture Appropriations/Prevented **Planting Payments.** Dayton, D-Minn., amendment that would modify the timetable for the Prevented Planting Payment program for one year to help farmers in areas that have been declared agriculture disasters in calendar 2005 by the president or Agriculture secretary, with an increase in funding by $1 million offset by a reduction in departmental travel expenses. Rejected 47-52: R 3-52; D 43-0 (ND 39-0, SD 4-0); I 1-0. Sept. 22, 2005.

**241.** HR 2744. Fiscal 2006 Agriculture Appropriations/Passage. Passage of the bill that would provide $100.7 billion in fiscal 2006 for the Agriculture Department, the Food and Drug Administration and related agencies, including $17.3 billion in discretionary spending. The bill includes $40.7 billion for the food stamp program, $25.7 billion for the Commodity Credit Corporation and $12.4 billion for school meal programs. Passed 97-2: R 53-2; D 43-0 (ND 39-0, SD 4-0); I 1-0. Sept. 22, 2005.

**242.** HR 2528. Fiscal 2006 Military Construction-VA Appropriations/ **Counseling Service Funding.** Akaka, D-Hawaii, amendment that would shift $10 million from a Veterans Affairs Department (VA) information technology program to a readjustment counseling program for veterans. Rejected 48-50: R 4-50; D 43-0 (ND 39-0, SD 4-0); I 1-0. Sept. 22, 2005.

**243.** HR 2528. Fiscal 2006 Military Construction-VA Appropriations/ **Passage.** Passage of the bill that would provide $83 billion in fiscal 2006 for the VA and military construction, including $46.4 billion for discretionary spending. It would provide $70.7 billion for the VA, $12 billion for military construction and $2 billion in emergency spending to address a shortfall in veterans' health care funding. Passed 98-0: R 54-0; D 43-0 (ND 39-0, SD 4-0); I 1-0. Sept. 22, 2005.

ND Northern Democrats, SD Southern Democrats
Southern states: Ala., Ark., Fla., Ga., Ky., La., Miss., N.C., Okla., S.C., Tenn., Texas, Va.

| | 236 | 237 | 238 | 239 | 240 | 241 | 242 | 243 |
|---|---|---|---|---|---|---|---|---|
| **ALABAMA** | | | | | | | | |
| Shelby | Y | N | N | Y | N | Y | N | Y |
| Sessions | Y | N | Y | Y | N | Y | N | Y |
| **ALASKA** | | | | | | | | |
| Stevens | N | Y | N | N | N | Y | N | Y |
| Murkowski | N | Y | Y | Y | N | Y | N | Y |
| **ARIZONA** | | | | | | | | |
| McCain | N | Y | Y | N | N | Y | N | Y |
| Kyl | N | Y | Y | N | N | Y | N | Y |
| **ARKANSAS** | | | | | | | | |
| Lincoln | Y | N | N | Y | Y | Y | Y | Y |
| Pryor | Y | N | N | Y | Y | Y | Y | Y |
| **CALIFORNIA** | | | | | | | | |
| Feinstein | Y | Y | Y | Y | Y | Y | Y | Y |
| Boxer | Y | Y | Y | Y | Y | Y | Y | Y |
| **COLORADO** | | | | | | | | |
| Allard | N | N | N | N | N | Y | N | Y |
| Salazar | N | N | Y | Y | Y | Y | Y | Y |
| **CONNECTICUT** | | | | | | | | |
| Dodd | Y | Y | Y | Y | Y | Y | Y | Y |
| Lieberman | Y | Y | Y | Y | Y | Y | Y | Y |
| **DELAWARE** | | | | | | | | |
| Biden | Y | Y | Y | Y | Y | Y | Y | Y |
| Carper | Y | Y | N | Y | Y | Y | Y | Y |
| **FLORIDA** | | | | | | | | |
| Nelson | Y | Y | Y | Y | Y | Y | Y | Y |
| Martinez | N | Y | Y | N | N | Y | ? | + |
| **GEORGIA** | | | | | | | | |
| Chambliss | Y | Y | N | N | N | Y | N | Y |
| Isakson | N | Y | Y | N | N | Y | N | Y |
| **HAWAII** | | | | | | | | |
| Inouye | N | Y | ? | ? | Y | Y | Y | Y |
| Akaka | Y | Y | Y | Y | Y | Y | Y | Y |
| **IDAHO** | | | | | | | | |
| Craig | Y | N | Y | N | N | Y | N | Y |
| Crapo | Y | N | N | N | N | Y | N | Y |
| **ILLINOIS** | | | | | | | | |
| Durbin | Y | Y | N | Y | Y | Y | Y | Y |
| Obama | Y | Y | Y | Y | Y | Y | Y | Y |
| **INDIANA** | | | | | | | | |
| Lugar | N | Y | Y | N | Y | Y | N | Y |
| Bayh | Y | Y | Y | Y | Y | Y | Y | Y |
| **IOWA** | | | | | | | | |
| Grassley | N | N | N | Y | Y | Y | N | Y |
| Harkin | Y | Y | Y | N | Y | Y | Y | Y |
| **KANSAS** | | | | | | | | |
| Brownback | Y | N | Y | N | N | Y | N | Y |
| Roberts | Y | N | Y | N | N | Y | N | Y |
| **KENTUCKY** | | | | | | | | |
| McConnell | N | Y | Y | Y | N | Y | N | Y |
| Bunning | N | Y | N | N | N | Y | N | Y |
| **LOUISIANA** | | | | | | | | |
| Landrieu | Y | ? | Y | Y | Y | Y | Y | Y |
| Vitter | Y | Y | N | N | N | Y | N | Y |
| **MAINE** | | | | | | | | |
| Snowe | Y | Y | Y | Y | N | Y | Y | Y |
| Collins | Y | Y | Y | Y | N | Y | Y | Y |
| **MARYLAND** | | | | | | | | |
| Sarbanes | Y | Y | N | Y | Y | Y | Y | Y |
| Mikulski | Y | Y | ? | ? | Y | Y | Y | Y |
| **MASSACHUSETTS** | | | | | | | | |
| Kennedy | Y | Y | N | N | Y | Y | Y | Y |
| Kerry | Y | Y | Y | Y | Y | Y | Y | Y |
| **MICHIGAN** | | | | | | | | |
| Levin | Y | Y | Y | Y | Y | Y | Y | Y |
| Stabenow | Y | Y | Y | Y | Y | Y | Y | Y |
| **MINNESOTA** | | | | | | | | |
| Dayton | Y | Y | Y | Y | Y | Y | Y | Y |
| Coleman | Y | Y | N | Y | Y | Y | N | Y |
| **MISSISSIPPI** | | | | | | | | |
| Cochran | N | N | N | N | N | Y | N | Y |
| Lott | N | Y | N | N | N | Y | N | Y |
| **MISSOURI** | | | | | | | | |
| Bond | Y | N | N | N | N | Y | N | Y |
| Talent | Y | N | Y | N | N | Y | N | Y |
| **MONTANA** | | | | | | | | |
| Baucus | Y | N | N | Y | Y | Y | Y | Y |
| Burns | Y | N | N | N | N | Y | N | Y |
| **NEBRASKA** | | | | | | | | |
| Hagel | N | Y | N | N | N | Y | N | Y |
| Nelson | Y | Y | Y | Y | Y | Y | Y | Y |
| **NEVADA** | | | | | | | | |
| Reid | Y | Y | Y | Y | Y | Y | Y | Y |
| Ensign | Y | Y | Y | Y | N | N | N | Y |
| **NEW HAMPSHIRE** | | | | | | | | |
| Gregg | N | Y | N | N | N | Y | N | Y |
| Sununu | N | Y | Y | N | N | N | N | Y |
| **NEW JERSEY** | | | | | | | | |
| Corzine | ? | ? | ? | ? | ? | ? | ? | ? |
| Lautenberg | Y | N | Y | Y | Y | Y | Y | Y |
| **NEW MEXICO** | | | | | | | | |
| Domenici | Y | N | ? | ? | N | Y | N | Y |
| Bingaman | Y | N | Y | Y | Y | Y | Y | Y |
| **NEW YORK** | | | | | | | | |
| Schumer | Y | Y | Y | Y | Y | Y | Y | Y |
| Clinton | Y | Y | Y | Y | Y | Y | Y | Y |
| **NORTH CAROLINA** | | | | | | | | |
| Dole | N | Y | N | Y | N | Y | N | Y |
| Burr | N | Y | Y | N | N | Y | N | Y |
| **NORTH DAKOTA** | | | | | | | | |
| Conrad | Y | N | N | Y | Y | Y | Y | Y |
| Dorgan | Y | N | N | Y | Y | Y | Y | Y |
| **OHIO** | | | | | | | | |
| DeWine | Y | Y | N | N | N | Y | N | Y |
| Voinovich | Y | N | Y | N | N | N | N | Y |
| **OKLAHOMA** | | | | | | | | |
| Inhofe | Y | N | Y | N | N | Y | N | Y |
| Coburn | Y | N | Y | N | Y | N | N | Y |
| **OREGON** | | | | | | | | |
| Wyden | Y | Y | Y | Y | Y | Y | Y | Y |
| Smith | Y | Y | N | Y | N | Y | N | Y |
| **PENNSYLVANIA** | | | | | | | | |
| Specter | Y | Y | Y | Y | N | Y | N | Y |
| Santorum | Y | Y | Y | N | N | Y | N | Y |
| **RHODE ISLAND** | | | | | | | | |
| Reed | Y | Y | Y | Y | Y | Y | Y | Y |
| Chafee | N | Y | Y | N | Y | Y | Y | Y |
| **SOUTH CAROLINA** | | | | | | | | |
| Graham | Y | Y | Y | N | N | Y | N | Y |
| DeMint | N | Y | Y | N | N | Y | N | Y |
| **SOUTH DAKOTA** | | | | | | | | |
| Johnson | Y | N | N | Y | Y | Y | Y | Y |
| Thune | Y | N | N | Y | Y | Y | N | Y |
| **TENNESSEE** | | | | | | | | |
| Frist | N | Y | N | N | N | Y | N | Y |
| Alexander | N | Y | Y | N | N | Y | N | Y |
| **TEXAS** | | | | | | | | |
| Hutchison | Y | Y | N | N | N | Y | N | Y |
| Cornyn | Y | N | Y | N | N | Y | N | Y |
| **UTAH** | | | | | | | | |
| Hatch | N | Y | N | N | N | Y | N | Y |
| Bennett | N | Y | N | N | N | Y | N | Y |
| **VERMONT** | | | | | | | | |
| Leahy | Y | Y | Y | Y | Y | Y | Y | Y |
| Jeffords | Y | N | Y | N | Y | Y | Y | Y |
| **VIRGINIA** | | | | | | | | |
| Warner | Y | Y | Y | Y | N | Y | N | Y |
| Allen | Y | Y | Y | N | N | Y | N | Y |
| **WASHINGTON** | | | | | | | | |
| Murray | Y | N | N | Y | Y | Y | Y | Y |
| Cantwell | Y | Y | N | Y | Y | Y | Y | Y |
| **WEST VIRGINIA** | | | | | | | | |
| Byrd | Y | N | N | Y | Y | Y | Y | Y |
| Rockefeller | ? | ? | ? | ? | ? | Y | Y | Y |
| **WISCONSIN** | | | | | | | | |
| Kohl | Y | Y | N | Y | Y | Y | Y | Y |
| Feingold | Y | Y | Y | Y | Y | Y | Y | Y |
| **WYOMING** | | | | | | | | |
| Thomas | Y | N | Y | N | N | Y | N | Y |
| Enzi | Y | N | ? | N | N | Y | N | Y |

**KEY**    Republicans    Democrats    *Independents*

| | | | |
|---|---|---|---|
| Y | Voted for (yea) | X Paired against | C Voted "present" to avoid possible conflict of interest |
| # | Paired for | – Announced against | |
| + | Announced for | P Voted "present" | ? Did not vote or otherwise make a position known |
| N | Voted against (nay) | | |

# IN THE SENATE | By Vote Number

## 244. Treaty Doc 108-6. Customs Simplification Treaty/Adoption.

Adoption of the resolution of ratification of the Protocol of Amendment to the International Convention on Simplification and Harmonization of Customs Procedures that would require participants to implement standardized customs procedures, continuously modernize customs procedures and provide transparency in administrative and judicial reviews of customs decisions. Adopted (thus consenting to ratification) 87-0: R 48-0; D 38-0 (ND 36-0, SD 2-0); I 1-0. A two-thirds majority of those present and voting (58 in this case) is required for adoption of resolutions of ratification. Sept. 26, 2005.

## 245. Roberts Nomination/Confirmation.

Confirmation of President Bush's nomination of John G. Roberts Jr. of Maryland to be chief justice of the United States. Confirmed 78-22: R 55-0; D 22-22 (ND 18-22, SD 4-0); I 1-0. A "yea" was a vote in support of the president's position. Sept. 29, 2005.

| | 244 | 245 | | | 244 | 245 |
|---|---|---|---|---|---|---|
| **ALABAMA** | | | **MONTANA** | | |
| Shelby | Y | Y | Baucus | Y | Y |
| Sessions | Y | Y | Burns | Y | Y |
| **ALASKA** | | | **NEBRASKA** | | |
| Stevens | Y | Y | Hagel | ? | Y |
| Murkowski | Y | Y | Nelson | Y | Y |
| **ARIZONA** | | | **NEVADA** | | |
| McCain | Y | Y | Reid | Y | N |
| Kyl | Y | Y | Ensign | Y | Y |
| **ARKANSAS** | | | **NEW HAMPSHIRE** | | |
| Lincoln | Y | Y | Gregg | Y | Y |
| Pryor | Y | Y | Sununu | Y | Y |
| **CALIFORNIA** | | | **NEW JERSEY** | | |
| Feinstein | Y | N | Corzine | ? | N |
| Boxer | Y | N | Lautenberg | Y | N |
| **COLORADO** | | | **NEW MEXICO** | | |
| Allard | Y | Y | Domenici | Y | Y |
| Salazar | Y | Y | Bingaman | Y | Y |
| **CONNECTICUT** | | | **NEW YORK** | | |
| Dodd | Y | Y | Schumer | Y | N |
| Lieberman | Y | Y | Clinton | Y | N |
| **DELAWARE** | | | **NORTH CAROLINA** | | |
| Biden | ? | N | Dole | Y | Y |
| Carper | Y | Y | Burr | ? | Y |
| **FLORIDA** | | | **NORTH DAKOTA** | | |
| Nelson | + | Y | Conrad | Y | Y |
| Martinez | + | Y | Dorgan | Y | Y |
| **GEORGIA** | | | **OHIO** | | |
| Chambliss | Y | Y | DeWine | Y | Y |
| Isakson | Y | Y | Voinovich | Y | Y |
| **HAWAII** | | | **OKLAHOMA** | | |
| Inouye | Y | N | Inhofe | Y | Y |
| Akaka | Y | N | Coburn | Y | Y |
| **IDAHO** | | | **OREGON** | | |
| Craig | Y | Y | Wyden | Y | Y |
| Crapo | Y | Y | Smith | Y | Y |
| **ILLINOIS** | | | **PENNSYLVANIA** | | |
| Durbin | Y | N | Specter | Y | Y |
| Obama | Y | N | Santorum | Y | Y |
| **INDIANA** | | | **RHODE ISLAND** | | |
| Lugar | Y | Y | Reed | Y | N |
| Bayh | Y | N | Chafee | Y | Y |
| **IOWA** | | | **SOUTH CAROLINA** | | |
| Grassley | Y | Y | Graham | Y | Y |
| Harkin | ? | N | DeMint | Y | Y |
| **KANSAS** | | | **SOUTH DAKOTA** | | |
| Brownback | ? | Y | Johnson | Y | Y |
| Roberts | Y | Y | Thune | Y | Y |
| **KENTUCKY** | | | **TENNESSEE** | | |
| McConnell | Y | Y | Frist | Y | Y |
| Bunning | Y | Y | Alexander | Y | Y |
| **LOUISIANA** | | | **TEXAS** | | |
| Landrieu | ? | Y | Hutchison | ? | Y |
| Vitter | + | Y | Cornyn | + | Y |
| **MAINE** | | | **UTAH** | | |
| Snowe | Y | Y | Hatch | Y | Y |
| Collins | Y | Y | Bennett | Y | Y |
| **MARYLAND** | | | **VERMONT** | | |
| Sarbanes | Y | N | Leahy | Y | Y |
| Mikulski | Y | N | Jeffords | Y | Y |
| **MASSACHUSETTS** | | | **VIRGINIA** | | |
| Kennedy | Y | N | Warner | Y | Y |
| Kerry | Y | N | Allen | Y | Y |
| **MICHIGAN** | | | **WASHINGTON** | | |
| Levin | Y | Y | Murray | Y | Y |
| Stabenow | ? | N | Cantwell | Y | N |
| **MINNESOTA** | | | **WEST VIRGINIA** | | |
| Dayton | Y | N | Byrd | Y | Y |
| Coleman | Y | Y | Rockefeller | Y | Y |
| **MISSISSIPPI** | | | **WISCONSIN** | | |
| Cochran | Y | Y | Kohl | Y | Y |
| Lott | Y | Y | Feingold | Y | Y |
| **MISSOURI** | | | **WYOMING** | | |
| Bond | Y | Y | Thomas | Y | Y |
| Talent | Y | Y | Enzi | Y | Y |

**KEY**   Republicans   Democrats   *Independents*

| | | | | | | |
|---|---|---|---|---|---|---|
| Y | Voted for (yea) | X | Paired against | C | Voted "present" to avoid possible conflict of interest |
| # | Paired for | – | Announced against | | |
| + | Announced for | P | Voted "present" | ? | Did not vote or otherwise make a position known |
| N | Voted against (nay) | | | | |

ND Northern Democrats, SD Southern Democrats
Southern states: Ala., Ark., Fla., Ga., Ky., La., Miss., N.C., Okla., S.C., Tenn., Texas, Va.

# IN THE SENATE | By Vote Number

**246.** H J Res 68. Fiscal 2006 Continuing Resolution/Community Services Block Grant Funding. Harkin, D-Iowa, amendment that would continue funding for the Community Services Block Grant at no less than the fiscal 2005 level. Rejected 39-53: R 0-53; D 38-0 (ND 34-0, SD 4-0); I 1-0. Sept. 30, 2005.

**247.** HR 2863. Fiscal 2006 Defense Appropriations/Defense Authorization. Judgment of the Senate on the germaneness of the Warner, R-Va., amendment that would authorize funding for defense programs in fiscal 2006, plus another $50 billion for military operations in Iraq and Afghanistan. Ruled not germane 49-50: R 17-38; D 31-12 (ND 28-11, SD 3-1); I 1-0. Oct. 5, 2005.

**248.** HR 2863. Fiscal 2006 Defense Appropriations/Armored Vehicle Funding. Bayh, D-Ind., motion to waive the Budget Act with respect to the Stevens, R-Alaska, point of order against the Bayh amendment. The Bayh amendment would increase funding by $360.8 million for the procurement of armored Tactical Wheeled Vehicles for use in Iraq and Afghanistan, or to reconstitute certain facilities at Fort Polk, La. Motion rejected 56-43: R 13-42; D 42-1 (ND 38-1, SD 4-0); I 1-0. A three-fifths majority vote (60) of the total Senate is required to waive the Budget Act. (Subsequently, the chair upheld the point of order, and the amendment fell.) Oct. 5, 2005.

**249.** HR 2863. Fiscal 2006 Defense Appropriations/Detainee Standards. McCain, R-Ariz., amendment that would establish the U.S. Army Field Manual on Intelligence Interrogation as the uniform standard for interrogating persons detained by the Department of Defense, and prohibit cruel, inhuman or degrading treatment of any prisoner detained by the U.S. government. Adopted 90-9: R 46-9; D 43-0 (ND 39-0, SD 4-0); I 1-0. A "nay" was a vote in support of the president's position. Oct. 5, 2005.

**250.** HR 2863. Fiscal 2006 Defense Appropriations/Low Income Heating Funding. Kerry, D-Mass., motion to waive the Budget Act with respect to the Stevens, R-Alaska, point of order against the emergency designation of the Kerry amendment. The Kerry amendment would appropriate $3.1 billion for the Low Income Home Energy Assistance Program and designate it as emergency spending. Motion rejected 50-49: R 9-46; D 40-3 (ND 36-3, SD 4-0); I 1-0. A three-fifths majority vote (60) of the total Senate is required to waive the Budget Act. (Subsequently, the chair upheld the point of order, and the emergency designation was stricken. The amendment later fell on a second budget point of order.) Oct. 5, 2005.

| | 246 | 247 | 248 | 249 | 250 | | | 246 | 247 | 248 | 249 | 250 |
|---|---|---|---|---|---|---|---|---|---|---|---|---|
| **ALABAMA** | | | | | | | **MONTANA** | | | | | |
| Shelby | N | N | N | Y | N | | Baucus | Y | Y | Y | Y | Y |
| Sessions | N | Y | N | N | N | | Burns | N | N | N | Y | N |
| **ALASKA** | | | | | | | **NEBRASKA** | | | | | |
| Stevens | N | N | N | N | N | | Hagel | N | Y | N | Y | N |
| Murkowski | N | N | N | Y | N | | Nelson | Y | Y | Y | Y | N |
| **ARIZONA** | | | | | | | **NEVADA** | | | | | |
| McCain | N | Y | N | Y | N | | Reid | Y | Y | Y | Y | Y |
| Kyl | N | N | N | Y | N | | Ensign | N | Y | N | Y | N |
| **ARKANSAS** | | | | | | | **NEW HAMPSHIRE** | | | | | |
| Lincoln | Y | Y | Y | Y | Y | | Gregg | ? | N | N | Y | N |
| Pryor | Y | Y | Y | Y | Y | | Sununu | N | N | N | Y | N |
| **CALIFORNIA** | | | | | | | **NEW JERSEY** | | | | | |
| Feinstein | Y | N | Y | Y | Y | | Corzine | ? | ? | ? | ? | ? |
| Boxer | Y | Y | Y | Y | Y | | Lautenberg | Y | Y | Y | Y | Y |
| **COLORADO** | | | | | | | **NEW MEXICO** | | | | | |
| Allard | N | N | N | N | N | | Domenici | N | N | N | Y | N |
| Salazar | Y | Y | Y | Y | Y | | Bingaman | Y | Y | Y | Y | Y |
| **CONNECTICUT** | | | | | | | **NEW YORK** | | | | | |
| Dodd | Y | Y | Y | Y | Y | | Schumer | Y | Y | Y | Y | Y |
| Lieberman | Y | Y | Y | Y | Y | | Clinton | Y | Y | Y | Y | Y |
| **DELAWARE** | | | | | | | **NORTH CAROLINA** | | | | | |
| Biden | ? | Y | Y | Y | Y | | Dole | N | N | N | Y | N |
| Carper | Y | Y | Y | Y | N | | Burr | N | N | N | Y | N |
| **FLORIDA** | | | | | | | **NORTH DAKOTA** | | | | | |
| Nelson | Y | Y | Y | Y | Y | | Conrad | Y | N | Y | Y | Y |
| Martinez | N | N | N | Y | N | | Dorgan | Y | N | Y | Y | Y |
| **GEORGIA** | | | | | | | **OHIO** | | | | | |
| Chambliss | N | Y | N | Y | N | | DeWine | N | N | Y | Y | Y |
| Isakson | N | N | N | Y | N | | Voinovich | N | N | Y | Y | Y |
| **HAWAII** | | | | | | | **OKLAHOMA** | | | | | |
| Inouye | Y | N | N | Y | N | | Inhofe | N | Y | N | N | N |
| Akaka | Y | Y | Y | Y | Y | | Coburn | N | N | N | N | N |
| **IDAHO** | | | | | | | **OREGON** | | | | | |
| Craig | N | N | N | Y | N | | Wyden | Y | N | Y | Y | Y |
| Crapo | N | N | N | Y | N | | Smith | N | N | N | Y | N |
| **ILLINOIS** | | | | | | | **PENNSYLVANIA** | | | | | |
| Durbin | Y | Y | Y | Y | Y | | Specter | N | N | N | Y | Y |
| Obama | Y | Y | Y | Y | Y | | Santorum | N | N | N | Y | Y |
| **INDIANA** | | | | | | | **RHODE ISLAND** | | | | | |
| Lugar | N | Y | Y | Y | Y | | Reed | Y | Y | Y | Y | Y |
| Bayh | Y | Y | Y | Y | Y | | Chafee | N | Y | Y | Y | Y |
| **IOWA** | | | | | | | **SOUTH CAROLINA** | | | | | |
| Grassley | N | N | N | Y | N | | Graham | N | Y | N | Y | N |
| Harkin | Y | N | Y | Y | Y | | DeMint | N | N | N | Y | N |
| **KANSAS** | | | | | | | **SOUTH DAKOTA** | | | | | |
| Brownback | N | N | N | Y | N | | Johnson | Y | Y | Y | Y | Y |
| Roberts | N | N | N | N | N | | Thune | N | Y | Y | Y | N |
| **KENTUCKY** | | | | | | | **TENNESSEE** | | | | | |
| McConnell | N | N | N | Y | N | | Frist | N | N | N | Y | N |
| Bunning | N | N | N | N | N | | Alexander | N | N | Y | Y | N |
| **LOUISIANA** | | | | | | | **TEXAS** | | | | | |
| Landrieu | Y | N | Y | Y | Y | | Hutchison | N | N | N | Y | N |
| Vitter | ? | N | N | Y | N | | Cornyn | N | Y | N | N | N |
| **MAINE** | | | | | | | **UTAH** | | | | | |
| Snowe | N | Y | Y | Y | Y | | Hatch | N | N | N | Y | N |
| Collins | N | Y | Y | Y | Y | | Bennett | N | N | N | Y | N |
| **MARYLAND** | | | | | | | **VERMONT** | | | | | |
| Sarbanes | Y | Y | Y | Y | Y | | Leahy | Y | Y | Y | Y | Y |
| Mikulski | ? | N | Y | Y | Y | | Jeffords | Y | Y | Y | Y | Y |
| **MASSACHUSETTS** | | | | | | | **VIRGINIA** | | | | | |
| Kennedy | Y | Y | Y | Y | Y | | Warner | N | Y | Y | Y | N |
| Kerry | Y | Y | Y | Y | Y | | Allen | N | Y | Y | Y | N |
| **MICHIGAN** | | | | | | | **WASHINGTON** | | | | | |
| Levin | Y | Y | Y | Y | Y | | Murray | ? | N | Y | Y | Y |
| Stabenow | Y | Y | Y | Y | Y | | Cantwell | Y | Y | Y | Y | Y |
| **MINNESOTA** | | | | | | | **WEST VIRGINIA** | | | | | |
| Dayton | Y | Y | Y | Y | Y | | Byrd | ? | N | Y | Y | Y |
| Coleman | N | N | Y | Y | Y | | Rockefeller | ? | Y | Y | Y | Y |
| **MISSISSIPPI** | | | | | | | **WISCONSIN** | | | | | |
| Cochran | N | N | N | N | N | | Kohl | Y | N | Y | Y | Y |
| Lott | N | N | N | Y | N | | Feingold | Y | Y | Y | Y | Y |
| **MISSOURI** | | | | | | | **WYOMING** | | | | | |
| Bond | N | N | N | N | N | | Thomas | N | N | N | Y | N |
| Talent | N | Y | Y | Y | Y | | Enzi | N | N | N | Y | N |

**KEY**   Republicans   Democrats   *Independents*

| | | |
|---|---|---|
| Y  Voted for (yea) | X  Paired against | C  Voted "present" to avoid possible conflict of interest |
| #  Paired for | −  Announced against | |
| +  Announced for | P  Voted "present" | ?  Did not vote or otherwise make a position known |
| N  Voted against (nay) | | |

ND Northern Democrats, SD Southern Democrats
Southern states: Ala., Ark., Fla., Ga., Ky., La., Miss., N.C., Okla., S.C., Tenn., Texas, Va.

# IN THE SENATE | By Vote Number

**251.** **HR 2863. Fiscal 2006 Defense Appropriations/Veterans' Health Care Funding.** Stabenow, D-Mich., motion to waive the Budget Act with respect to the Stevens, R-Alaska, point of order against the Stabenow amendment. The Stabenow amendment would establish a formula that would adjust health care funding for veterans to account for changes in population and inflation. Motion rejected 48-51: R 5-50; D 42-1 (ND 38-1, SD 4-0); I 1-0. A three-fifths majority vote (60) of the total Senate is required to waive the Budget Act. (Subsequently, the chair upheld the point of order, and the amendment fell.) Oct. 5, 2005.

**252.** **HR 2863. Fiscal 2006 Defense Appropriations/Cloture.** Frist, R-Tenn., motion to invoke cloture (thus limiting debate) on the bill that would provide $445.4 billion in defense spending, including $50 billion in bridge funding for continued military operations in Iraq and Afghanistan. Motion agreed to 95-4: R 55-0; D 39-4 (ND 35-4, SD 4-0); I 1-0. Three-fifths of the total Senate (60) is required to invoke cloture. Oct. 5, 2005.

**253.** **HR 2863. Fiscal 2006 Defense Appropriations/Web-Based Travel Program.** Stevens, R-Alaska, motion to table (kill) the Coburn, R-Okla., amendment that would prohibit use of funds in the bill for a Web-based travel system being developed by the Pentagon. Motion agreed to 65-32: R 37-16; D 27-16 (ND 25-14, SD 2-2); I 1-0. Oct. 6, 2005.

**254.** **HR 2863. Fiscal 2006 Defense Appropriations/Passage.** Passage of the bill that would provide $445.4 billion for fiscal 2006 military operations, including $390 billion in discretionary spending. The total also includes $50 billion in bridge funding for continued military operations in Iraq and Afghanistan. The bill would provide $95.7 billion for personnel, $75.8 billion for procurement and $125 billion for operations and maintenance. Passed 97-0: R 53-0; D 43-0 (ND 39-0, SD 4-0); I 1-0. Oct. 7, 2005.

| | 251 | 252 | 253 | 254 | | | 251 | 252 | 253 | 254 |
|---|---|---|---|---|---|---|---|---|---|---|
| **ALABAMA** | | | | | | **MONTANA** | | | | |
| Shelby | N | Y | Y | Y | | Baucus | Y | Y | Y | Y |
| Sessions | N | Y | N | Y | | Burns | N | Y | Y | Y |
| **ALASKA** | | | | | | **NEBRASKA** | | | | |
| Stevens | N | Y | Y | Y | | Hagel | N | Y | Y | Y |
| Murkowski | N | Y | Y | Y | | Nelson | Y | Y | Y | Y |
| **ARIZONA** | | | | | | **NEVADA** | | | | |
| McCain | N | Y | N | Y | | Reid | Y | N | Y | Y |
| Kyl | N | Y | N | Y | | Ensign | N | Y | Y | Y |
| **ARKANSAS** | | | | | | **NEW HAMPSHIRE** | | | | |
| Lincoln | Y | Y | N | Y | | Gregg | N | Y | N | ? |
| Pryor | Y | Y | Y | Y | | Sununu | N | Y | N | Y |
| **CALIFORNIA** | | | | | | **NEW JERSEY** | | | | |
| Feinstein | Y | Y | Y | Y | | Corzine | ? | ? | ? | Y |
| Boxer | Y | N | N | Y | | Lautenberg | Y | Y | Y | Y |
| **COLORADO** | | | | | | **NEW MEXICO** | | | | |
| Allard | N | Y | ? | Y | | Domenici | N | Y | Y | Y |
| Salazar | Y | Y | Y | Y | | Bingaman | Y | N | N | Y |
| **CONNECTICUT** | | | | | | **NEW YORK** | | | | |
| Dodd | Y | Y | N | Y | | Schumer | Y | Y | Y | Y |
| Lieberman | Y | Y | Y | Y | | Clinton | Y | Y | Y | Y |
| **DELAWARE** | | | | | | **NORTH CAROLINA** | | | | |
| Biden | Y | Y | Y | Y | | Dole | N | Y | N | Y |
| Carper | Y | Y | Y | Y | | Burr | N | Y | N | Y |
| **FLORIDA** | | | | | | **NORTH DAKOTA** | | | | |
| Nelson | Y | Y | N | Y | | Conrad | Y | Y | Y | Y |
| Martinez | N | Y | Y | Y | | Dorgan | Y | Y | Y | Y |
| **GEORGIA** | | | | | | **OHIO** | | | | |
| Chambliss | N | Y | Y | Y | | DeWine | N | Y | Y | Y |
| Isakson | N | Y | Y | Y | | Voinovich | N | Y | Y | Y |
| **HAWAII** | | | | | | **OKLAHOMA** | | | | |
| Inouye | N | Y | Y | Y | | Inhofe | N | Y | N | Y |
| Akaka | Y | Y | Y | Y | | Coburn | N | Y | N | Y |
| **IDAHO** | | | | | | **OREGON** | | | | |
| Craig | N | Y | Y | Y | | Wyden | Y | Y | N | Y |
| Crapo | N | Y | Y | Y | | Smith | N | Y | Y | Y |
| **ILLINOIS** | | | | | | **PENNSYLVANIA** | | | | |
| Durbin | Y | Y | N | Y | | Specter | Y | Y | Y | Y |
| Obama | Y | Y | N | Y | | Santorum | N | Y | Y | Y |
| **INDIANA** | | | | | | **RHODE ISLAND** | | | | |
| Lugar | N | Y | Y | Y | | Reed | Y | Y | Y | Y |
| Bayh | Y | Y | N | Y | | Chafee | Y | Y | Y | Y |
| **IOWA** | | | | | | **SOUTH CAROLINA** | | | | |
| Grassley | N | Y | N | Y | | Graham | N | Y | N | Y |
| Harkin | Y | Y | Y | Y | | DeMint | N | Y | N | Y |
| **KANSAS** | | | | | | **SOUTH DAKOTA** | | | | |
| Brownback | N | Y | N | Y | | Johnson | Y | Y | Y | Y |
| Roberts | N | Y | Y | Y | | Thune | Y | Y | N | Y |
| **KENTUCKY** | | | | | | **TENNESSEE** | | | | |
| McConnell | N | Y | Y | Y | | Frist | N | Y | Y | Y |
| Bunning | N | Y | Y | + | | Alexander | N | Y | Y | Y |
| **LOUISIANA** | | | | | | **TEXAS** | | | | |
| Landrieu | Y | Y | Y | Y | | Hutchison | N | Y | Y | Y |
| Vitter | N | Y | Y | Y | | Cornyn | N | Y | Y | Y |
| **MAINE** | | | | | | **UTAH** | | | | |
| Snowe | Y | Y | N | Y | | Hatch | N | Y | + | Y |
| Collins | Y | Y | Y | Y | | Bennett | N | Y | Y | Y |
| **MARYLAND** | | | | | | **VERMONT** | | | | |
| Sarbanes | Y | Y | Y | Y | | Leahy | Y | Y | Y | ? |
| Mikulski | Y | Y | Y | Y | | Jeffords | Y | Y | Y | Y |
| **MASSACHUSETTS** | | | | | | **VIRGINIA** | | | | |
| Kennedy | Y | Y | Y | Y | | Warner | N | Y | Y | Y |
| Kerry | Y | Y | N | Y | | Allen | N | Y | Y | Y |
| **MICHIGAN** | | | | | | **WASHINGTON** | | | | |
| Levin | Y | N | Y | Y | | Murray | Y | Y | Y | Y |
| Stabenow | Y | Y | N | Y | | Cantwell | Y | Y | N | Y |
| **MINNESOTA** | | | | | | **WEST VIRGINIA** | | | | |
| Dayton | Y | Y | N | Y | | Byrd | Y | Y | N | Y |
| Coleman | N | Y | Y | Y | | Rockefeller | Y | Y | Y | Y |
| **MISSISSIPPI** | | | | | | **WISCONSIN** | | | | |
| Cochran | N | Y | Y | Y | | Kohl | Y | Y | N | Y |
| Lott | N | Y | Y | Y | | Feingold | Y | Y | N | Y |
| **MISSOURI** | | | | | | **WYOMING** | | | | |
| Bond | N | Y | Y | Y | | Thomas | N | Y | N | Y |
| Talent | N | Y | Y | Y | | Enzi | N | Y | Y | Y |

| **KEY** | **Republicans** | Democrats | *Independents* | | |
|---|---|---|---|---|---|
| Y | Voted for (yea) | X | Paired against | C | Voted "present" to avoid possible conflict of interest |
| # | Paired for | – | Announced against | | |
| + | Announced for | P | Voted "present" | ? | Did not vote or otherwise make a position known |
| N | Voted against (nay) | | | | |

ND Northern Democrats, SD Southern Democrats
Southern states: Ala., Ark., Fla., Ga., Ky., La., Miss., N.C., Okla., S.C., Tenn., Texas, Va.

# IN THE SENATE | By Vote Number

**255.** HR 3058. Fiscal 2006 Transportation-Treasury-Housing Appropriations/HUD Authority. Bond, R-Mo., amendment that would clarify the authority of the Housing and Urban Development (HUD) Department to recover losses from owners of multifamily houses who are intentionally withholding assets from rent receipts on Federal Housing Administration loans. It would allow the agency to recover double damages from individuals, groups or heirs who have violated HUD project agreements. Adopted 93-0: R 52-0; D 40-0 (ND 36-0, SD 4-0); I 1-0. Oct. 17, 2005.

**256.** HR 3058. Fiscal 2006 Transportation-Treasury-Housing Appropriations/Congressional Pay Raise. Kyl, R-Ariz., amendment that would prevent members of Congress from receiving their automatic yearly pay increase in fiscal 2006. Adopted 92-6: R 52-2; D 40-3 (ND 36-3, SD 4-0); I 0-1. Oct. 18, 2005.

**257.** HR 3058. Fiscal 2006 Transportation-Treasury-Housing Appropriations/Minimum Wage Increase. Kennedy, D-Mass., motion to waive the Budget Act with respect to the Bond, R-Mo., point of order against the Kennedy amendment. The Kennedy amendment would increase the minimum hourly wage to $5.70 six months after the bill's enactment and to $6.25 one year after enactment. Motion rejected 47-51: R 4-51; D 42-0 (ND 38-0, SD 4-0); I 1-0. A three-fifths majority vote (60) of the total Senate is required to waive the Budget Act. (Subsequently, the chair upheld the point of order, and the amendment fell.) Oct. 19, 2005.

**258.** HR 3058. Fiscal 2006 Transportation-Treasury-Housing Appropriations/Minimum Wage Increase. Enzi, R-Wyo., motion to waive the Budget Act with respect to the Kennedy, D-Mass., point of order against an Enzi amendment. The Enzi amendment would increase the minimum hourly wage to $5.70 six months after enactment and to $6.25 eighteen months after enactment. It also would exempt businesses with gross annual sales of under $1 million; permit private-sector workers to participate in biweekly flex-hour programs; exclude tips from the minimum wage rates paid to restaurant workers; and provide tax benefits for small-business owners. Motion rejected 42-57: R 42-13; D 0-43 (ND 0-39, SD 0-4); I 0-1. A three-fifths majority vote (60) of the total Senate is required to waive the Budget Act. (Subsequently, the chair upheld the point of order, and the amendment fell.) Oct. 19, 2005.

**259.** HR 3058. Fiscal 2006 Transportation-Treasury-Housing Appropriations/Independent Investigation. Dorgan, D-N.D., motion to suspend the rule against legislating on an appropriations bill with respect to the Dorgan amendment. The Dorgan amendment would establish a special committee to investigate waste, fraud and abuse in the awarding and perform- ing of contracts in Iraq and Afghanistan, and for the reconstruction of damage done by hurricanes Katrina and Rita. Motion rejected 44-54: R 0-54; D 43-0 (ND 39-0, SD 4-0); I 1-0. A two-thirds majority of those present and voting (66 in this case) is required to suspend the rule. Oct. 19, 2005.

| | 255 | 256 | 257 | 258 | 259 |
|---|---|---|---|---|---|
| **ALABAMA** | | | | | |
| Shelby | Y | Y | N | Y | N |
| Sessions | Y | Y | N | Y | N |
| **ALASKA** | | | | | |
| Stevens | Y | Y | N | Y | N |
| Murkowski | Y | Y | N | Y | N |
| **ARIZONA** | | | | | |
| McCain | ? | Y | N | Y | N |
| Kyl | Y | Y | N | Y | N |
| **ARKANSAS** | | | | | |
| Lincoln | Y | Y | Y | N | Y |
| Pryor | Y | Y | Y | N | Y |
| **CALIFORNIA** | | | | | |
| Feinstein | Y | Y | Y | N | Y |
| Boxer | Y | Y | Y | N | Y |
| **COLORADO** | | | | | |
| Allard | Y | Y | N | N | N |
| Salazar | Y | Y | Y | N | Y |
| **CONNECTICUT** | | | | | |
| Dodd | Y | Y | Y | N | Y |
| Lieberman | Y | Y | Y | N | Y |
| **DELAWARE** | | | | | |
| Biden | ? | Y | Y | N | Y |
| Carper | Y | Y | Y | N | Y |
| **FLORIDA** | | | | | |
| Nelson | Y | Y | Y | N | Y |
| Martinez | Y | Y | N | Y | N |
| **GEORGIA** | | | | | |
| Chambliss | Y | ? | N | N | N |
| Isakson | Y | Y | N | N | N |
| **HAWAII** | | | | | |
| Inouye | Y | N | ? | ? | ? |
| Akaka | Y | Y | Y | N | Y |
| **IDAHO** | | | | | |
| Craig | Y | Y | N | Y | N |
| Crapo | Y | Y | N | Y | N |
| **ILLINOIS** | | | | | |
| Durbin | Y | Y | Y | N | Y |
| Obama | Y | Y | Y | N | Y |
| **INDIANA** | | | | | |
| Lugar | Y | N | N | Y | N |
| Bayh | Y | Y | Y | N | Y |
| **IOWA** | | | | | |
| Grassley | Y | Y | N | Y | N |
| Harkin | ? | Y | Y | N | Y |
| **KANSAS** | | | | | |
| Brownback | Y | Y | N | Y | N |
| Roberts | Y | Y | N | Y | N |
| **KENTUCKY** | | | | | |
| McConnell | Y | Y | N | Y | N |
| Bunning | Y | Y | N | Y | N |
| **LOUISIANA** | | | | | |
| Landrieu | Y | Y | Y | N | Y |
| Vitter | ? | Y | N | N | N |
| **MAINE** | | | | | |
| Snowe | Y | Y | N | Y | N |
| Collins | Y | Y | N | Y | N |
| **MARYLAND** | | | | | |
| Sarbanes | Y | N | Y | N | Y |
| Mikulski | Y | Y | Y | N | Y |
| **MASSACHUSETTS** | | | | | |
| Kennedy | Y | Y | Y | N | Y |
| Kerry | Y | Y | Y | N | Y |
| **MICHIGAN** | | | | | |
| Levin | Y | Y | Y | N | Y |
| Stabenow | Y | Y | Y | N | Y |
| **MINNESOTA** | | | | | |
| Dayton | Y | Y | Y | N | Y |
| Coleman | Y | Y | N | Y | N |
| **MISSISSIPPI** | | | | | |
| Cochran | Y | Y | N | Y | N |
| Lott | Y | Y | N | N | N |
| **MISSOURI** | | | | | |
| Bond | Y | N | N | Y | N |
| Talent | Y | Y | N | Y | N |
| **MONTANA** | | | | | |
| Baucus | Y | Y | Y | N | Y |
| Burns | Y | Y | N | Y | ? |
| **NEBRASKA** | | | | | |
| Hagel | Y | Y | N | Y | N |
| Nelson | Y | Y | Y | N | Y |
| **NEVADA** | | | | | |
| Reid | Y | Y | Y | N | Y |
| Ensign | Y | Y | N | Y | N |
| **NEW HAMPSHIRE** | | | | | |
| Gregg | Y | Y | N | Y | N |
| Sununu | Y | Y | N | N | N |
| **NEW JERSEY** | | | | | |
| Corzine | ? | ? | + | N | Y |
| Lautenberg | ? | Y | Y | N | Y |
| **NEW MEXICO** | | | | | |
| Domenici | Y | Y | N | Y | N |
| Bingaman | Y | N | Y | N | Y |
| **NEW YORK** | | | | | |
| Schumer | Y | Y | Y | N | Y |
| Clinton | Y | Y | Y | N | Y |
| **NORTH CAROLINA** | | | | | |
| Dole | Y | Y | N | Y | N |
| Burr | Y | Y | N | N | N |
| **NORTH DAKOTA** | | | | | |
| Conrad | Y | Y | Y | N | Y |
| Dorgan | Y | Y | Y | N | Y |
| **OHIO** | | | | | |
| DeWine | Y | Y | Y | Y | N |
| Voinovich | Y | Y | N | Y | N |
| **OKLAHOMA** | | | | | |
| Inhofe | Y | Y | N | N | N |
| Coburn | Y | Y | N | N | N |
| **OREGON** | | | | | |
| Wyden | Y | Y | Y | N | Y |
| Smith | Y | Y | N | Y | N |
| **PENNSYLVANIA** | | | | | |
| Specter | Y | Y | Y | Y | N |
| Santorum | Y | Y | Y | Y | N |
| **RHODE ISLAND** | | | | | |
| Reed | Y | Y | Y | N | Y |
| Chafee | Y | Y | Y | N | N |
| **SOUTH CAROLINA** | | | | | |
| Graham | Y | Y | N | N | N |
| DeMint | + | Y | N | N | N |
| **SOUTH DAKOTA** | | | | | |
| Johnson | Y | Y | Y | N | Y |
| Thune | Y | Y | N | Y | N |
| **TENNESSEE** | | | | | |
| Frist | Y | Y | N | Y | N |
| Alexander | Y | Y | N | Y | N |
| **TEXAS** | | | | | |
| Hutchison | Y | Y | N | Y | N |
| Cornyn | Y | Y | N | N | N |
| **UTAH** | | | | | |
| Hatch | Y | Y | N | Y | N |
| Bennett | Y | Y | N | Y | N |
| **VERMONT** | | | | | |
| Leahy | Y | Y | Y | N | Y |
| Jeffords | Y | N | Y | N | Y |
| **VIRGINIA** | | | | | |
| Warner | Y | Y | Y | Y | N |
| Allen | Y | Y | N | Y | N |
| **WASHINGTON** | | | | | |
| Murray | Y | Y | Y | N | Y |
| Cantwell | Y | Y | Y | N | Y |
| **WEST VIRGINIA** | | | | | |
| Byrd | Y | Y | Y | N | Y |
| Rockefeller | Y | Y | Y | N | Y |
| **WISCONSIN** | | | | | |
| Kohl | Y | Y | Y | N | Y |
| Feingold | Y | Y | Y | N | Y |
| **WYOMING** | | | | | |
| Thomas | Y | Y | N | Y | N |
| Enzi | Y | Y | N | Y | N |

**KEY**    Republicans    Democrats    *Independents*

| | | |
|---|---|---|
| Y Voted for (yea) | X Paired against | C Voted "present" to avoid possible conflict of interest |
| # Paired for | – Announced against | |
| + Announced for | P Voted "present" | ? Did not vote or otherwise make a position known |
| N Voted against (nay) | | |

ND Northern Democrats, SD Southern Democrats
Southern states: Ala., Ark., Fla., Ga., Ky., La., Miss., N.C., Okla., S.C., Tenn., Texas, Va.

# IN THE SENATE | By Vote Number

**260.** HR 3058. Fiscal 2006 Transportation-Treasury-Housing Appropriations/Bar Funds for Earmark Projects. Bond, R-Mo., motion to table (kill) Coburn, R-Okla., amendment that would prohibit use of funds in the bill from for several earmarked projects, including the Joslyn Art Museum in Omaha, Neb.; the Stand Up for Animals shelter in Westerly, R.I.; and the Seattle Art Museum's sculpture park in Seattle, Wash. Motion agreed to 86-13: R 43-12; D 42-1 (ND 38-1, SD 4-0); I 1-0. Oct. 20, 2005.

**261.** HR 3058. Fiscal 2006 Transportation-Treasury-Housing Appropriations/LIHEAP. Reed, D-R.I., motion to waive the Budget Act with respect to the Bond, R-Mo., point of order against the Reed amendment. The Reed amendment would provide an additional $3.1 billion in emergency funding for the Low-Income Home Energy Assistance Program (LIHEAP). Motion rejected 53-46: R 11-44; D 41-2 (ND 37-2, SD 4-0); I 1-0. A three-fifths majority vote (60) of the total Senate is required to waive the Budget Act. (Subsequently, the chair upheld the point of order, and the amendment fell.) Oct. 20, 2005.

**262.** HR 3058. Fiscal 2006 Transportation-Treasury-Housing Appropriations/Bridge Funding. Coburn, R-Okla., amendment that would transfer $125 million in funding from the Ketchikan-Gravina and Knik Arm bridge projects in Alaska to the reconstruction of the Twin Spans Bridge connecting New Orleans and Slidell, La. It would place remaining Alaska bridge funds into a general highway fund for Alaska. Rejected 15-82: R 11-43; D 4-38 (ND 3-35, SD 1-3); I 0-1. (By unanimous consent, the Senate agreed to raise the majority requirement for adoption of the Coburn amendment to 60 votes.) Oct. 20, 2005.

**263.** HR 3058. Fiscal 2006 Transportation-Treasury-Housing Appropriations/Bridge Funding. Stevens, R-Alaska, amendment that would prevent any new bridge projects funded by the surface transportation law from going forward until the reconstruction of the Twin Spans Bridge connecting New Orleans and Slidell, La., is fully funded through non-emergency accounts. Rejected 33-61: R 30-22; D 3-38 (ND 2-35, SD 1-3); I 0-1. (By unanimous consent, the Senate agreed to raise the majority requirement for adoption of the Stevens amendment to 60 votes.) Oct. 20, 2005.

**264.** HR 3058. Fiscal 2006 Transportation-Treasury-Housing Appropriations/Passage. Passage of the bill that would provide $141.6 billion in fiscal 2006, including $65.8 billion in discretionary spending for the departments of Housing and Urban Development, Treasury, and Transportation and for related agencies. It would provide $40.2 billion in highway spending, $34.8 billion for the Department of Housing and Urban Development and $14.3 billion for the Federal Aviation Administration. It also would provide $1.5 billion for Amtrak and $593 million in federal funds for the District of Columbia. Passed 93-1: R 53-0; D 39-1 (ND 35-1, SD 4-0); I 1-0. Oct. 20, 2005.

| | 260 | 261 | 262 | 263 | 264 | | 260 | 261 | 262 | 263 | 264 |
|---|---|---|---|---|---|---|---|---|---|---|---|
| **ALABAMA** | | | | | | **MONTANA** | | | | | |
| Shelby | Y | N | N | Y | Y | Baucus | Y | Y | N | ? | ? |
| Sessions | N | N | Y | Y | Y | Burns | Y | N | N | N | Y |
| **ALASKA** | | | | | | **NEBRASKA** | | | | | |
| Stevens | Y | N | N | Y | Y | Hagel | N | N | N | N | Y |
| Murkowski | Y | N | N | Y | Y | Nelson | Y | N | N | N | Y |
| **ARIZONA** | | | | | | **NEVADA** | | | | | |
| McCain | N | N | ? | ? | ? | Reid | Y | Y | N | N | Y |
| Kyl | N | N | Y | Y | Y | Ensign | N | N | N | N | Y |
| **ARKANSAS** | | | | | | **NEW HAMPSHIRE** | | | | | |
| Lincoln | Y | Y | N | N | Y | Gregg | Y | N | N | N | Y |
| Pryor | Y | Y | N | N | Y | Sununu | N | Y | Y | Y | ? |
| **CALIFORNIA** | | | | | | **NEW JERSEY** | | | | | |
| Feinstein | Y | Y | N | N | Y | Corzine | ? | ? | ? | ? | ? |
| Boxer | Y | Y | N | N | Y | Lautenberg | Y | Y | N | N | Y |
| **COLORADO** | | | | | | **NEW MEXICO** | | | | | |
| Allard | Y | N | Y | Y | Y | Domenici | Y | N | N | N | Y |
| Salazar | Y | Y | N | Y | Y | Bingaman | Y | Y | N | N | Y |
| **CONNECTICUT** | | | | | | **NEW YORK** | | | | | |
| Dodd | Y | Y | N | N | Y | Schumer | Y | Y | ? | ? | ? |
| Lieberman | Y | Y | N | N | Y | Clinton | Y | Y | N | N | Y |
| **DELAWARE** | | | | | | **NORTH CAROLINA** | | | | | |
| Biden | Y | Y | N | N | Y | Dole | Y | N | N | Y | Y |
| Carper | Y | N | N | N | Y | Burr | N | N | Y | Y | Y |
| **FLORIDA** | | | | | | **NORTH DAKOTA** | | | | | |
| Nelson | Y | Y | N | N | Y | Conrad | Y | Y | N | N | Y |
| Martinez | Y | N | N | Y | Y | Dorgan | Y | Y | N | N | Y |
| **GEORGIA** | | | | | | **OHIO** | | | | | |
| Chambliss | Y | N | N | Y | Y | DeWine | Y | Y | N | N | Y |
| Isakson | Y | N | N | Y | Y | Voinovich | Y | N | N | N | Y |
| **HAWAII** | | | | | | **OKLAHOMA** | | | | | |
| Inouye | Y | Y | N | N | ? | Inhofe | Y | N | N | Y | Y |
| Akaka | Y | Y | N | N | Y | Coburn | N | N | Y | Y | Y |
| **IDAHO** | | | | | | **OREGON** | | | | | |
| Craig | Y | N | N | N | Y | Wyden | Y | Y | N | N | Y |
| Crapo | Y | N | N | N | Y | Smith | Y | Y | N | N | Y |
| **ILLINOIS** | | | | | | **PENNSYLVANIA** | | | | | |
| Durbin | Y | Y | N | N | Y | Specter | Y | Y | N | Y | Y |
| Obama | Y | Y | N | N | Y | Santorum | Y | Y | N | Y | Y |
| **INDIANA** | | | | | | **RHODE ISLAND** | | | | | |
| Lugar | Y | Y | N | N | Y | Reed | Y | Y | N | Y | Y |
| Bayh | Y | Y | Y | Y | N | Chafee | Y | Y | N | Y | Y |
| **IOWA** | | | | | | **SOUTH CAROLINA** | | | | | |
| Grassley | Y | N | N | N | Y | Graham | N | N | Y | Y | Y |
| Harkin | Y | Y | N | N | Y | DeMint | N | N | Y | Y | Y |
| **KANSAS** | | | | | | **SOUTH DAKOTA** | | | | | |
| Brownback | Y | N | N | Y | Y | Johnson | Y | Y | N | N | Y |
| Roberts | Y | N | N | N | Y | Thune | Y | N | N | N | Y |
| **KENTUCKY** | | | | | | **TENNESSEE** | | | | | |
| McConnell | Y | N | N | Y | Y | Frist | Y | N | N | Y | Y |
| Bunning | Y | N | N | Y | Y | Alexander | Y | N | N | N | Y |
| **LOUISIANA** | | | | | | **TEXAS** | | | | | |
| Landrieu | Y | Y | Y | Y | Y | Hutchison | Y | N | N | N | Y |
| Vitter | Y | N | Y | Y | Y | Cornyn | Y | N | N | Y | Y |
| **MAINE** | | | | | | **UTAH** | | | | | |
| Snowe | Y | Y | N | N | Y | Hatch | Y | N | N | N | Y |
| Collins | Y | Y | N | N | Y | Bennett | Y | N | N | Y | Y |
| **MARYLAND** | | | | | | **VERMONT** | | | | | |
| Sarbanes | Y | Y | N | N | Y | Leahy | Y | Y | N | N | Y |
| Mikulski | Y | Y | N | N | Y | Jeffords | Y | Y | N | N | Y |
| **MASSACHUSETTS** | | | | | | **VIRGINIA** | | | | | |
| Kennedy | Y | Y | N | N | Y | Warner | Y | N | N | Y | Y |
| Kerry | Y | Y | N | N | Y | Allen | N | N | Y | Y | Y |
| **MICHIGAN** | | | | | | **WASHINGTON** | | | | | |
| Levin | Y | Y | N | N | Y | Murray | Y | Y | N | N | Y |
| Stabenow | Y | Y | N | N | Y | Cantwell | Y | Y | N | N | Y |
| **MINNESOTA** | | | | | | **WEST VIRGINIA** | | | | | |
| Dayton | Y | Y | N | N | Y | Byrd | Y | Y | N | N | Y |
| Coleman | Y | Y | N | Y | Y | Rockefeller | Y | Y | N | N | Y |
| **MISSISSIPPI** | | | | | | **WISCONSIN** | | | | | |
| Cochran | Y | N | N | N | Y | Kohl | Y | Y | N | N | Y |
| Lott | Y | N | N | N | Y | Feingold | N | Y | Y | Y | Y |
| **MISSOURI** | | | | | | **WYOMING** | | | | | |
| Bond | Y | N | N | N | Y | Thomas | Y | N | N | ? | ? |
| Talent | N | Y | N | N | Y | Enzi | Y | N | N | ? | Y |

**KEY**    Republicans    Democrats    *Independents*

| | | |
|---|---|---|
| Y Voted for (yea) | X Paired against | C Voted "present" to avoid possible conflict of interest |
| # Paired for | – Announced against | |
| + Announced for | P Voted "present" | ? Did not vote or otherwise make a position known |
| N Voted against (nay) | | |

ND Northern Democrats, SD Southern Democrats
Southern states: Ala., Ark., Fla., Ga., Ky., La., Miss., N.C., Okla., S.C., Tenn., Texas, Va.

# IN THE SENATE | By Vote Number

**265.** **Sandoval Nomination/Confirmation.** Confirmation of President Bush's nomination of Brian Sandoval of Nevada to be a judge for the U.S. District Court for the District of Nevada. Confirmed 89-0: R 52-0; D 36-0 (ND 33-0, SD 3-0); I 1-0. A "yea" was a vote in support of the president's position. Oct. 24, 2005.

**266.** **Mattice Nomination/Confirmation.** Confirmation of President Bush's nomination of Harry Sandlin Mattice Jr. of Tennessee to be a judge for the U.S. District Court for the Eastern District of Tennessee. Confirmed 91-0: R 52-0; D 38-0 (ND 35-0, SD 3-0); I 1-0. A "yea" was a vote in support of the president's position. Oct. 24, 2005.

**267.** **HR 3010. Fiscal 2006 Labor-HHS-Education Appropriations/ Patient Identifiers.** Durbin, D-Ill., amendment that would require the secretary of Health and Human Services (HHS) to submit a report to Congress by June 30, 2006, outlining a plan for discontinuing the use of Social Security numbers as numerical patient identifiers for Medicare and Medicaid recipients and the costs of implementing the plan. Adopted 98-0: R 54-0; D 43-0 (ND 39-0, SD 4-0); I 1-0. Oct. 25, 2005.

**268.** **HR 3010. Fiscal 2006 Labor-HHS-Education Appropriations/ Pell Grant Increase.** Kennedy, D-Mass., motion to waive the Budget Act with respect to the Specter, R-Pa., point of order against the Kennedy amendment. The Kennedy amendment would add $836 million for Pell Grants, increasing the maximum Pell Grant for the 2006-07 award year to $4,250. Motion rejected 48-51: R 6-49; D 41-2 (ND 38-1, SD 3-1); I 1-0. A three-fifths majority vote (60) of the total Senate is required to waive the Budget Act. (Subsequently, the chair upheld the point of order, and the amendment fell.) Oct. 25, 2005.

**269.** **HR 3010. Fiscal 2006 Labor-HHS-Education Appropriations/ Title I Funding.** Byrd, D-W.Va., motion to waive the Budget Act with respect to the Specter, R-Pa., point of order against the Byrd amendment. The Byrd amendment would add $5 billion for Title I of the Elementary and Secondary Education Act, split evenly between targeted grants and finance incentives. Motion rejected 44-51: R 3-50; D 40-1 (ND 37-1, SD 3-0); I 1-0. A three-fifths majority vote (60) of the total Senate is required to waive the Budget Act. (Subsequently, the chair upheld the point of order, and the amendment fell.) Oct. 26, 2005.

**270.** **HR 3010. Fiscal 2006 Labor-HHS-Education Appropriations/ LIHEAP.** Reed, D-R.I., motion to waive the Budget Act with respect to the Crapo, R-Idaho, point of order against the Reed amendment. The Reed amendment would provide an additional $2.9 billion in emergency funding for the Low-Income Home Energy Assistance Program (LIHEAP). Motion rejected 54-43: R 12-41; D 41-2 (ND 37-2, SD 4-0); I 1-0. A three-fifths majority vote (60) of the total Senate is required to waive the Budget Act. (Subsequently, the chair upheld the point of order, and the amendment fell.) Oct. 26, 2005.

**271.** **HR 3010. Fiscal 2006 Labor-HHS-Education Appropriations/ LIHEAP.** Gregg, R-N.H., amendment that would provide an additional $1.3 billion for LIHEAP, offset with a 0.92 percent across-the-board cut in budget authority in the bill. Rejected 46-53: R 46-9; D 0-43 (ND 0-39, SD 0-4); I 0-1. Oct. 26, 2005.

| | 265 | 266 | 267 | 268 | 269 | 270 | 271 | | 265 | 266 | 267 | 268 | 269 | 270 | 271 |
|---|---|---|---|---|---|---|---|---|---|---|---|---|---|---|---|
| **ALABAMA** | | | | | | | | **MONTANA** | | | | | | | |
| Shelby | Y | Y | ? | N | N | N | Y | Baucus | Y | Y | Y | Y | Y | Y | N |
| Sessions | ? | ? | Y | N | N | ? | Y | Burns | Y | Y | Y | N | N | N | Y |
| **ALASKA** | | | | | | | | **NEBRASKA** | | | | | | | |
| Stevens | Y | Y | Y | N | N | N | Y | Hagel | Y | Y | Y | N | N | N | Y |
| Murkowski | Y | Y | Y | N | N | ? | Y | Nelson | Y | Y | Y | Y | Y | N | N |
| **ARIZONA** | | | | | | | | **NEVADA** | | | | | | | |
| McCain | ? | ? | N | N | N | N | Y | Reid | Y | Y | Y | Y | Y | Y | N |
| Kyl | Y | Y | Y | N | N | N | Y | Ensign | Y | Y | Y | N | N | N | Y |
| **ARKANSAS** | | | | | | | | **NEW HAMPSHIRE** | | | | | | | |
| Lincoln | Y | Y | Y | Y | Y | Y | N | Gregg | Y | Y | Y | N | N | N | Y |
| Pryor | Y | Y | Y | Y | Y | Y | N | Sununu | Y | Y | Y | N | N | Y | Y |
| **CALIFORNIA** | | | | | | | | **NEW JERSEY** | | | | | | | |
| Feinstein | ? | Y | Y | Y | Y | Y | N | Corzine | ? | ? | ? | ? | ? | ? | ? |
| Boxer | Y | Y | Y | Y | Y | Y | N | Lautenberg | Y | Y | Y | Y | Y | Y | N |
| **COLORADO** | | | | | | | | **NEW MEXICO** | | | | | | | |
| Allard | Y | Y | Y | N | N | N | Y | Domenici | Y | Y | Y | N | N | N | Y |
| Salazar | Y | Y | Y | Y | Y | Y | N | Bingaman | Y | Y | Y | Y | Y | Y | N |
| **CONNECTICUT** | | | | | | | | **NEW YORK** | | | | | | | |
| Dodd | Y | Y | Y | Y | Y | Y | N | Schumer | Y | Y | Y | Y | Y | Y | N |
| Lieberman | Y | Y | Y | Y | Y | Y | N | Clinton | Y | Y | Y | Y | Y | Y | N |
| **DELAWARE** | | | | | | | | **NORTH CAROLINA** | | | | | | | |
| Biden | ? | ? | Y | Y | Y | Y | N | Dole | Y | Y | Y | N | N | N | Y |
| Carper | Y | Y | Y | Y | Y | N | N | Burr | Y | Y | Y | N | N | N | Y |
| **FLORIDA** | | | | | | | | **NORTH DAKOTA** | | | | | | | |
| Nelson | ? | ? | N | N | ? | Y | N | Conrad | Y | Y | Y | Y | Y | Y | N |
| Martinez | Y | Y | N | N | ? | N | Y | Dorgan | Y | Y | Y | Y | Y | Y | N |
| **GEORGIA** | | | | | | | | **OHIO** | | | | | | | |
| Chambliss | Y | Y | N | N | N | N | Y | DeWine | Y | Y | Y | Y | N | Y | Y |
| Isakson | Y | Y | N | N | N | N | Y | Voinovich | Y | Y | Y | N | N | Y | Y |
| **HAWAII** | | | | | | | | **OKLAHOMA** | | | | | | | |
| Inouye | ? | ? | Y | Y | Y | Y | N | Inhofe | Y | Y | Y | N | N | N | N |
| Akaka | Y | Y | Y | Y | Y | Y | N | Coburn | Y | Y | Y | N | N | N | N |
| **IDAHO** | | | | | | | | **OREGON** | | | | | | | |
| Craig | Y | Y | Y | N | N | N | Y | Wyden | ? | ? | Y | Y | Y | Y | N |
| Crapo | Y | Y | Y | N | N | N | Y | Smith | ? | ? | Y | N | N | Y | N |
| **ILLINOIS** | | | | | | | | **PENNSYLVANIA** | | | | | | | |
| Durbin | Y | Y | Y | Y | Y | Y | N | Specter | Y | Y | Y | N | N | Y | N |
| Obama | ? | Y | Y | Y | Y | Y | N | Santorum | Y | Y | Y | N | N | Y | Y |
| **INDIANA** | | | | | | | | **RHODE ISLAND** | | | | | | | |
| Lugar | Y | Y | Y | N | Y | Y | Y | Reed | Y | Y | Y | Y | Y | Y | N |
| Bayh | Y | Y | Y | Y | Y | Y | N | Chafee | Y | Y | Y | Y | N | Y | N |
| **IOWA** | | | | | | | | **SOUTH CAROLINA** | | | | | | | |
| Grassley | Y | Y | Y | N | N | N | Y | Graham | Y | Y | Y | N | N | N | Y |
| Harkin | Y | Y | Y | Y | Y | Y | N | DeMint | Y | Y | Y | N | N | N | Y |
| **KANSAS** | | | | | | | | **SOUTH DAKOTA** | | | | | | | |
| Brownback | Y | Y | Y | N | N | N | Y | Johnson | Y | Y | Y | Y | Y | Y | N |
| Roberts | Y | Y | Y | N | N | N | Y | Thune | Y | Y | Y | N | N | N | Y |
| **KENTUCKY** | | | | | | | | **TENNESSEE** | | | | | | | |
| McConnell | Y | Y | Y | N | N | N | Y | Frist | Y | Y | Y | N | N | N | Y |
| Bunning | Y | Y | Y | N | N | N | Y | Alexander | Y | Y | Y | N | N | N | Y |
| **LOUISIANA** | | | | | | | | **TEXAS** | | | | | | | |
| Landrieu | Y | Y | Y | Y | Y | Y | N | Hutchison | Y | Y | Y | N | N | N | Y |
| Vitter | Y | Y | Y | N | N | N | N | Cornyn | Y | Y | Y | N | N | N | Y |
| **MAINE** | | | | | | | | **UTAH** | | | | | | | |
| Snowe | Y | Y | Y | Y | Y | Y | N | Hatch | Y | Y | Y | N | N | N | Y |
| Collins | Y | Y | Y | Y | Y | Y | N | Bennett | Y | Y | Y | N | N | N | Y |
| **MARYLAND** | | | | | | | | **VERMONT** | | | | | | | |
| Sarbanes | Y | Y | Y | Y | Y | Y | N | Leahy | Y | Y | Y | Y | Y | Y | N |
| Mikulski | Y | Y | Y | Y | Y | Y | N | Jeffords | Y | Y | Y | Y | Y | Y | N |
| **MASSACHUSETTS** | | | | | | | | **VIRGINIA** | | | | | | | |
| Kennedy | ? | ? | Y | Y | Y | Y | N | Warner | Y | Y | Y | N | ? | N | Y |
| Kerry | Y | Y | Y | Y | Y | Y | N | Allen | Y | Y | Y | N | N | N | Y |
| **MICHIGAN** | | | | | | | | **WASHINGTON** | | | | | | | |
| Levin | Y | Y | Y | Y | Y | Y | N | Murray | Y | Y | Y | Y | Y | Y | N |
| Stabenow | Y | Y | Y | Y | Y | Y | N | Cantwell | Y | Y | Y | Y | Y | Y | N |
| **MINNESOTA** | | | | | | | | **WEST VIRGINIA** | | | | | | | |
| Dayton | Y | Y | Y | Y | ? | Y | N | Byrd | Y | Y | Y | Y | Y | Y | N |
| Coleman | Y | Y | Y | Y | N | Y | N | Rockefeller | Y | Y | Y | Y | Y | Y | N |
| **MISSISSIPPI** | | | | | | | | **WISCONSIN** | | | | | | | |
| Cochran | Y | Y | Y | N | N | N | Y | Kohl | Y | Y | Y | Y | Y | Y | N |
| Lott | Y | Y | Y | N | N | N | N | Feingold | Y | Y | Y | Y | Y | Y | N |
| **MISSOURI** | | | | | | | | **WYOMING** | | | | | | | |
| Bond | Y | Y | Y | N | N | N | Y | Thomas | Y | Y | Y | N | N | N | Y |
| Talent | Y | Y | Y | Y | N | Y | N | Enzi | Y | Y | Y | N | N | N | Y |

| KEY | Republicans | Democrats | *Independents* |
|---|---|---|---|

| Y | Voted for (yea) | X | Paired against | C | Voted "present" to avoid possible conflict of interest |
|---|---|---|---|---|---|
| # | Paired for | – | Announced against | | |
| + | Announced for | P | Voted "present" | ? | Did not vote or otherwise make a position known |
| N | Voted against (nay) | | | | |

ND Northern Democrats, SD Southern Democrats
Southern states: Ala., Ark., Fla., Ga., Ky., La., Miss., N.C., Okla., S.C., Tenn., Texas, Va.

# IN THE SENATE | By Vote Number

**272.** **HR 3010. Fiscal 2006 Labor-HHS-Education Appropriations/ Head Start.** Dodd, D-Conn., motion to waive the Budget Act with respect to the Specter, R-Pa., point of order against Dodd amendment. The Dodd amendment would add $153 million for Head Start programs. Motion rejected 47-52: R 5-50; D 41-2 (ND 37-2, SD 4-0); I 1-0. A three-fifths majority vote (60) of the total Senate is required to waive the Budget Act. (Subsequently, the chair upheld the point of order, and the amendment fell.) Oct. 26, 2005.

**273.** **HR 3010. Fiscal 2006 Labor-HHS-Education Appropriations/ Special Education Funding.** Clinton, D-N.Y., motion to waive the Budget Act with respect to the Specter, R-Pa., point of order against Clinton amendment. The Clinton amendment would provide $4 billion in additional funding for state-administered federal grants for disabled and special education students. Motion rejected 46-53: R 4-51; D 41-2 (ND 37-2, SD 4-0); I 1-0. A three-fifths majority vote (60) of the total Senate is required to waive the Budget Act. (Subsequently, the chair upheld the point of order, and the amendment fell.) Oct. 26, 2005.

**274.** **HR 3010. Fiscal 2006 Labor-HHS-Education Appropriations/ AIDS Drug Assistance.** Coburn, R-Okla., amendment that would transfer $60 million in funding from construction and renovation of the Centers for Disease Control and Prevention complex to the AIDS Drug Assistance Program. Rejected 14-85: R 10-45; D 4-39 (ND 4-35, SD 0-4); I 0-1. Oct. 26, 2005.

**275.** **HR 3010. Fiscal 2006 Labor-HHS-Education Appropriations/ Cloture.** Motion to invoke cloture (thus limiting debate) on bill, that would provide $604.4 billion in 2006 for the Labor, Health and Human Services, and Education departments and related agencies, including $141.7 billion in discretionary funding. Motion agreed to 97-0: R 54-0; D 42-0 (ND 38-0, SD 4-0); I 1-0. Three-fifths of the total Senate (60) is required to invoke cloture. Oct. 27, 2005.

**276.** **Smoak Nomination/Confirmation.** Confirmation of President Bush's nomination of John R. Smoak of Florida to be a judge for the U.S. District Court for the Northern District of Florida. Confirmed 97-0: R 55-0; D 41-0 (ND 37-0, SD 4-0); I 1-0. A "yea" was a vote in support of the president's position. Oct. 27, 2005.

**277.** **Neilson Nomination/Confirmation.** Confirmation of President Bush's nomination of Susan Neilson of Michigan to be a judge for the U.S. Court of Appeals for the 6th Circuit. Confirmed 97-0: R 55-0; D 41-0 (ND 37-0, SD 4-0); I 1-0. A "yea" was a vote in support of the president's position. Oct. 27, 2005.

**278.** **HR 3010. Fiscal 2006 Labor-HHS-Education Appropriations/AIDS Drug Assistance.** Harkin, D-Iowa, motion to waive the Budget Act with respect to the Specter, R-Pa., point of order against Bingaman, D-N.M., amendment. The Bingaman amendment would provide an additional $74 million for the AIDS Drug Assistance Program. Motion rejected 46-50: R 6-48; D 39-2 (ND 36-1, SD 3-1); I 1-0. A three-fifths majority vote (60) of the total Senate is required to waive the Budget Act. (Subsequently, the chair upheld the point of order, and the amendment fell.) Oct. 27, 2005.

| | 272 | 273 | 274 | 275 | 276 | 277 | 278 | | | 272 | 273 | 274 | 275 | 276 | 277 | 278 |
|---|---|---|---|---|---|---|---|---|---|---|---|---|---|---|---|---|
| **ALABAMA** | | | | | | | | | **MONTANA** | | | | | | | |
| Shelby | N | N | N | Y | Y | Y | N | | Baucus | Y | Y | N | Y | Y | Y | Y |
| Sessions | N | N | N | Y | Y | Y | N | | Burns | N | N | N | Y | Y | Y | N |
| **ALASKA** | | | | | | | | | **NEBRASKA** | | | | | | | |
| Stevens | N | N | N | Y | Y | Y | N | | Hagel | N | N | N | Y | Y | Y | N |
| Murkowski | N | N | N | Y | Y | Y | N | | Nelson | N | Y | N | Y | Y | Y | N |
| **ARIZONA** | | | | | | | | | **NEVADA** | | | | | | | |
| McCain | N | N | Y | Y | Y | Y | N | | Reid | Y | Y | N | Y | Y | Y | Y |
| Kyl | N | N | N | Y | Y | Y | N | | Ensign | N | N | N | Y | Y | Y | N |
| **ARKANSAS** | | | | | | | | | **NEW HAMPSHIRE** | | | | | | | |
| Lincoln | Y | Y | N | Y | Y | Y | Y | | Gregg | N | N | N | Y | Y | Y | N |
| Pryor | Y | Y | N | Y | Y | Y | Y | | Sununu | N | N | N | Y | Y | Y | N |
| **CALIFORNIA** | | | | | | | | | **NEW JERSEY** | | | | | | | |
| Feinstein | Y | Y | N | Y | Y | Y | Y | | Corzine | ? | ? | ? | ? | ? | ? | ? |
| Boxer | Y | Y | N | Y | Y | Y | Y | | Lautenberg | Y | Y | N | Y | Y | Y | Y |
| **COLORADO** | | | | | | | | | **NEW MEXICO** | | | | | | | |
| Allard | N | N | N | Y | Y | Y | N | | Domenici | N | N | N | Y | Y | Y | N |
| Salazar | Y | Y | N | Y | Y | Y | Y | | Bingaman | Y | Y | N | Y | Y | Y | Y |
| **CONNECTICUT** | | | | | | | | | **NEW YORK** | | | | | | | |
| Dodd | Y | Y | N | Y | Y | Y | Y | | Schumer | Y | Y | N | Y | Y | Y | Y |
| Lieberman | Y | Y | N | Y | Y | Y | Y | | Clinton | Y | Y | N | Y | Y | Y | Y |
| **DELAWARE** | | | | | | | | | **NORTH CAROLINA** | | | | | | | |
| Biden | Y | Y | N | Y | Y | Y | Y | | Dole | N | N | N | Y | Y | Y | N |
| Carper | Y | Y | N | Y | Y | Y | N | | Burr | N | N | N | Y | Y | Y | ? |
| **FLORIDA** | | | | | | | | | **NORTH DAKOTA** | | | | | | | |
| Nelson | Y | Y | N | Y | Y | Y | Y | | Conrad | N | N | N | Y | Y | Y | Y |
| Martinez | N | N | N | Y | Y | Y | N | | Dorgan | Y | Y | N | Y | Y | Y | Y |
| **GEORGIA** | | | | | | | | | **OHIO** | | | | | | | |
| Chambliss | N | N | N | Y | Y | N | N | | DeWine | Y | N | Y | Y | Y | Y | Y |
| Isakson | N | N | N | Y | Y | Y | N | | Voinovich | N | N | N | Y | Y | Y | N |
| **HAWAII** | | | | | | | | | **OKLAHOMA** | | | | | | | |
| Inouye | Y | Y | N | Y | ? | ? | ? | | Inhofe | N | N | N | Y | Y | Y | N |
| Akaka | Y | Y | N | Y | Y | Y | Y | | Coburn | N | N | Y | Y | Y | N | N |
| **IDAHO** | | | | | | | | | **OREGON** | | | | | | | |
| Craig | N | N | N | Y | Y | Y | N | | Wyden | Y | Y | Y | Y | Y | Y | Y |
| Crapo | N | N | N | Y | Y | Y | N | | Smith | N | N | Y | Y | Y | Y | Y |
| **ILLINOIS** | | | | | | | | | **PENNSYLVANIA** | | | | | | | |
| Durbin | Y | Y | N | Y | Y | Y | Y | | Specter | N | N | N | Y | Y | Y | N |
| Obama | Y | Y | N | Y | Y | Y | Y | | Santorum | N | N | N | Y | Y | Y | N |
| **INDIANA** | | | | | | | | | **RHODE ISLAND** | | | | | | | |
| Lugar | Y | Y | Y | Y | Y | Y | N | | Reed | Y | Y | N | Y | Y | Y | Y |
| Bayh | Y | Y | N | Y | Y | Y | Y | | Chafee | Y | Y | Y | Y | Y | Y | Y |
| **IOWA** | | | | | | | | | **SOUTH CAROLINA** | | | | | | | |
| Grassley | N | N | Y | Y | Y | Y | N | | Graham | N | N | N | Y | Y | Y | N |
| Harkin | Y | Y | Y | Y | Y | Y | Y | | DeMint | N | N | N | Y | Y | Y | N |
| **KANSAS** | | | | | | | | | **SOUTH DAKOTA** | | | | | | | |
| Brownback | N | N | N | Y | Y | Y | N | | Johnson | Y | Y | N | Y | Y | Y | Y |
| Roberts | N | N | N | Y | Y | Y | N | | Thune | N | N | N | Y | Y | Y | N |
| **KENTUCKY** | | | | | | | | | **TENNESSEE** | | | | | | | |
| McConnell | N | N | N | Y | Y | Y | N | | Frist | N | N | N | Y | Y | Y | N |
| Bunning | N | N | N | Y | Y | Y | N | | Alexander | N | N | N | Y | Y | Y | N |
| **LOUISIANA** | | | | | | | | | **TEXAS** | | | | | | | |
| Landrieu | Y | Y | N | Y | Y | Y | Y | | Hutchison | N | N | N | Y | Y | Y | N |
| Vitter | N | N | N | Y | Y | Y | N | | Cornyn | N | N | N | Y | Y | Y | N |
| **MAINE** | | | | | | | | | **UTAH** | | | | | | | |
| Snowe | Y | Y | N | Y | Y | Y | N | | Hatch | N | N | N | Y | Y | Y | N |
| Collins | Y | Y | N | Y | Y | Y | N | | Bennett | N | N | N | Y | Y | Y | N |
| **MARYLAND** | | | | | | | | | **VERMONT** | | | | | | | |
| Sarbanes | Y | Y | N | Y | Y | Y | Y | | Leahy | Y | Y | N | Y | Y | Y | Y |
| Mikulski | Y | Y | N | Y | Y | Y | Y | | Jeffords | Y | Y | N | Y | Y | Y | Y |
| **MASSACHUSETTS** | | | | | | | | | **VIRGINIA** | | | | | | | |
| Kennedy | Y | Y | N | Y | Y | Y | Y | | Warner | N | N | N | Y | Y | Y | N |
| Kerry | Y | Y | N | Y | Y | Y | Y | | Allen | N | N | N | Y | Y | Y | N |
| **MICHIGAN** | | | | | | | | | **WASHINGTON** | | | | | | | |
| Levin | Y | Y | N | Y | Y | Y | Y | | Murray | Y | Y | N | Y | Y | Y | Y |
| Stabenow | Y | Y | Y | Y | Y | Y | Y | | Cantwell | Y | Y | N | Y | Y | Y | Y |
| **MINNESOTA** | | | | | | | | | **WEST VIRGINIA** | | | | | | | |
| Dayton | Y | Y | Y | Y | Y | Y | Y | | Byrd | Y | Y | N | Y | Y | Y | Y |
| Coleman | N | N | N | Y | Y | Y | Y | | Rockefeller | Y | Y | N | ? | ? | ? | ? |
| **MISSISSIPPI** | | | | | | | | | **WISCONSIN** | | | | | | | |
| Cochran | N | N | N | Y | Y | Y | N | | Kohl | Y | Y | N | Y | Y | Y | Y |
| Lott | N | N | N | ? | Y | Y | N | | Feingold | Y | Y | Y | Y | Y | Y | Y |
| **MISSOURI** | | | | | | | | | **WYOMING** | | | | | | | |
| Bond | N | N | N | Y | Y | Y | N | | Thomas | N | N | N | Y | Y | Y | N |
| Talent | N | N | N | Y | Y | Y | N | | Enzi | N | N | N | Y | Y | Y | N |

**KEY**    Republicans    Democrats    *Independents*

| | | | | | |
|---|---|---|---|---|---|
| **Y** | Voted for (yea) | **X** | Paired against | **C** | Voted "present" to avoid possible conflict of interest |
| **#** | Paired for | **–** | Announced against | | |
| **+** | Announced for | **P** | Voted "present" | **?** | Did not vote or otherwise make a position known |
| **N** | Voted against (nay) | | | | |

ND Northern Democrats, SD Southern Democrats
Southern states: Ala., Ark., Fla., Ga., Ky., La., Miss., N.C., Okla., S.C., Tenn., Texas, Va.

# IN THE SENATE | By Vote Number

**279.** **HR 3010. Fiscal 2006 Labor-HHS-Education Appropriations/ Learning Centers.** Boxer, D-Calif., motion to waive the Budget Act with respect to the Specter, R-Pa., point of order against Boxer amendment. The Boxer amendment would provide an additional $51.9 million for after-school programs under the 21st Century Community Learning Centers, part of the 2001 education overhaul law. Motion rejected 41-56: R 0-55; D 40-1 (ND 36-1, SD 4-0); I 1-0. A three-fifths majority vote (60) of the total Senate is required to waive the Budget Act. (Subsequently, the chair upheld the point of order, and the amendment fell.) Oct. 27, 2005.

**280.** **HR 3010. Fiscal 2006 Labor-HHS-Education Appropriations/ e-Language System Distribution.** Ensign, R-Nev., amendment that would prohibit funds in the bill from being used to develop or distribute the Education Department's e-Language Learning System. Rejected 41-56: R 35-20; D 6-35 (ND 6-31, SD 0-4); I 0-1. Oct. 27, 2005.

**281.** **HR 3010. Fiscal 2006 Labor-HHS-Education Appropriations/ Passage.** Passage of the bill that would provide $604.4 billion in fiscal 2006 for the Labor, Health and Human Services (HHS), and Education departments and related agencies, including $141.7 billion in discretionary spending. The bill includes $15 billion for the Labor Department; $476.2 billion for HHS, and $63.7 billion for the Education Department. It would shift $3.3 billion in mandatory Supplemental Security Income payments from fiscal 2006 to fiscal 2007. Passed 94-3: R 53-2; D 40-1 (ND 36-1, SD 4-0); I 1-0. Oct. 27, 2005.

| | 279 | 280 | 281 | | | 279 | 280 | 281 |
|---|---|---|---|---|---|---|---|---|
| **ALABAMA** | | | | | **MONTANA** | | | |
| Shelby | N | Y | Y | | Baucus | Y | N | Y |
| Sessions | N | Y | Y | | Burns | N | N | Y |
| **ALASKA** | | | | | **NEBRASKA** | | | |
| Stevens | N | N | Y | | Hagel | N | N | Y |
| Murkowski | N | N | Y | | Nelson | N | Y | Y |
| **ARIZONA** | | | | | **NEVADA** | | | |
| McCain | N | N | Y | | Reid | Y | N | Y |
| Kyl | N | Y | Y | | Ensign | N | Y | N |
| **ARKANSAS** | | | | | **NEW HAMPSHIRE** | | | |
| Lincoln | Y | N | Y | | Gregg | N | Y | Y |
| Pryor | Y | N | Y | | Sununu | N | Y | Y |
| **CALIFORNIA** | | | | | **NEW JERSEY** | | | |
| Feinstein | Y | N | Y | | Corzine | ? | ? | ? |
| Boxer | Y | N | Y | | Lautenberg | Y | N | Y |
| **COLORADO** | | | | | **NEW MEXICO** | | | |
| Allard | N | Y | Y | | Domenici | N | N | Y |
| Salazar | Y | N | Y | | Bingaman | Y | N | Y |
| **CONNECTICUT** | | | | | **NEW YORK** | | | |
| Dodd | Y | N | Y | | Schumer | Y | Y | Y |
| Lieberman | Y | N | Y | | Clinton | Y | N | Y |
| **DELAWARE** | | | | | **NORTH CAROLINA** | | | |
| Biden | Y | N | Y | | Dole | N | Y | Y |
| Carper | Y | N | Y | | Burr | N | Y | Y |
| **FLORIDA** | | | | | **NORTH DAKOTA** | | | |
| Nelson | Y | N | Y | | Conrad | Y | N | N |
| Martinez | N | Y | Y | | Dorgan | Y | Y | Y |
| **GEORGIA** | | | | | **OHIO** | | | |
| Chambliss | N | Y | Y | | DeWine | N | N | Y |
| Isakson | N | Y | Y | | Voinovich | N | N | Y |
| **HAWAII** | | | | | **OKLAHOMA** | | | |
| Inouye | ? | ? | ? | | Inhofe | N | Y | N |
| Akaka | Y | N | Y | | Coburn | N | Y | Y |
| **IDAHO** | | | | | **OREGON** | | | |
| Craig | N | Y | Y | | Wyden | Y | Y | Y |
| Crapo | N | Y | Y | | Smith | N | Y | Y |
| **ILLINOIS** | | | | | **PENNSYLVANIA** | | | |
| Durbin | Y | N | Y | | Specter | N | N | Y |
| Obama | Y | N | Y | | Santorum | N | Y | Y |
| **INDIANA** | | | | | **RHODE ISLAND** | | | |
| Lugar | N | N | Y | | Reed | Y | N | Y |
| Bayh | Y | Y | Y | | Chafee | N | N | Y |
| **IOWA** | | | | | **SOUTH CAROLINA** | | | |
| Grassley | N | Y | Y | | Graham | N | Y | Y |
| Harkin | Y | N | Y | | DeMint | N | Y | Y |
| **KANSAS** | | | | | **SOUTH DAKOTA** | | | |
| Brownback | N | Y | Y | | Johnson | Y | N | Y |
| Roberts | N | Y | Y | | Thune | N | Y | Y |
| **KENTUCKY** | | | | | **TENNESSEE** | | | |
| McConnell | N | N | Y | | Frist | N | N | Y |
| Bunning | N | N | Y | | Alexander | N | N | Y |
| **LOUISIANA** | | | | | **TEXAS** | | | |
| Landrieu | Y | N | Y | | Hutchison | N | Y | Y |
| Vitter | N | Y | Y | | Cornyn | N | Y | Y |
| **MAINE** | | | | | **UTAH** | | | |
| Snowe | N | Y | Y | | Hatch | N | Y | Y |
| Collins | N | N | Y | | Bennett | N | Y | Y |
| **MARYLAND** | | | | | **VERMONT** | | | |
| Sarbanes | Y | N | Y | | Leahy | Y | N | Y |
| Mikulski | Y | N | Y | | *Jeffords* | Y | N | Y |
| **MASSACHUSETTS** | | | | | **VIRGINIA** | | | |
| Kennedy | Y | N | Y | | Warner | N | Y | Y |
| Kerry | Y | N | Y | | Allen | N | Y | Y |
| **MICHIGAN** | | | | | **WASHINGTON** | | | |
| Levin | Y | N | Y | | Murray | Y | N | Y |
| Stabenow | Y | N | Y | | Cantwell | Y | N | Y |
| **MINNESOTA** | | | | | **WEST VIRGINIA** | | | |
| Dayton | Y | N | Y | | Byrd | Y | N | Y |
| Coleman | N | N | Y | | Rockefeller | ? | ? | ? |
| **MISSISSIPPI** | | | | | **WISCONSIN** | | | |
| Cochran | N | N | Y | | Kohl | Y | Y | Y |
| Lott | N | Y | Y | | Feingold | Y | N | Y |
| **MISSOURI** | | | | | **WYOMING** | | | |
| Bond | N | N | Y | | Thomas | N | N | Y |
| Talent | N | Y | Y | | Enzi | N | Y | Y |

**KEY** **Republicans** Democrats *Independents*

| | | | |
|---|---|---|---|
| Y | Voted for (yea) | X Paired against | C Voted "present" to avoid possible conflict of interest |
| # | Paired for | − Announced against | |
| + | Announced for | P Voted "present" | ? Did not vote or otherwise make a position known |
| N | Voted against (nay) | | |

ND Northern Democrats, SD Southern Democrats
Southern states: Ala., Ark., Fla., Ga., Ky., La., Miss., N.C., Okla., S.C., Tenn., Texas, Va.

# IN THE SENATE | By Vote Number

**282.** **HR 2744. Fiscal 2006 Agriculture Appropriations/Conference Report.** Adoption of the conference report on the bill that would appropriate $101 billion in fiscal 2006 for the Department of Agriculture, the Food and Drug Administration (FDA) and related agencies. The bill would provide $40.7 billion for the food stamp program, $12.7 billion for child nutrition, $25.7 billion for the Commodity Credit Corporation, $5.3 billion for the Women, Infants and Children program, and $1.5 billion for the FDA. Adopted (thus cleared for the president) 81-18: R 45-10; D 35-8 (ND 31-8, SD 4-0); I 1-0. Nov. 3, 2005.

**283.** **S 1932. Budget Reconciliation/PAYGO Rules.** Conrad, D-N.D., motion to waive the Budget Act with respect to the Gregg, R-N.H., point of order against the Conrad amendment. The Conrad amendment would restore pay-as-you-go (PAYGO) rules, which would create a 60-vote point of order against any direct spending or revenue legislation that would increase the on-budget deficit or cause an on-budget deficit, until Sept. 30, 2010. Tax cuts and new entitlement spending would have to be offset with revenue increases or spending cuts. Motion rejected 50-49: R 6-49; D 43-0 (ND 39-0, SD 4-0); I 1-0. A three-fifths majority vote (60) of the total Senate is required to waive the Budget Act. (Subsequently, the chair upheld the point of order, and the amendment fell.) Nov. 3, 2005.

**284.** **S 1932. Budget Reconciliation/Private School Aid.** Ensign, R-Nev., motion to waive the Budget Act with respect to the Enzi, R-Wyo., point of order against the Ensign amendment to the Enzi amendment. The Ensign amendment would allow federal funds to go to states, which would have to send checks to schools that receive Katrina evacuees. Non-public schools would be required to obtain permission from parents of displaced children before they could use the government money. The Enzi amendment would provide $1.2 billion in financial assistance for displaced students attending public, private or religious schools, $450 million in grants to schools in the Gulf Coast region, and $900 million to reduce loan origination fees for college students to 2 percent. Motion rejected 31-68: R 31-24; D 0-43 (ND 0-39, SD 0-4); I 0-1. A three-fifths majority vote (60) of the total Senate is required to waive the Budget Act. (Subsequently, the chair upheld the point of order, and the Ensign amendment fell. The Enzi amendment was adopted by voice vote.) Nov. 3, 2005.

**285.** **S 1932. Budget Reconciliation/Emergency Health Care for Katrina Victims.** Lincoln, D-Ark., motion to waive the Budget Act with respect to the Gregg, R-N.H., point of order against the Lincoln amendment. The Lincoln amendment would grant access to Medicaid to Hurricane Katrina victims for five months; provide full federal funding for Medicaid in Louisiana, Mississippi and Alabama for one year and provide other health assistance for the hurricane victims. It would be paid for with unspent Federal Emergency Management Agency funds. Motion rejected 48-51: R 4-51; D 43-0 (ND 39-0, SD 4-0); I 1-0. A three-fifths majority vote (60) of the total Senate is required to waive the Budget Act. (Subsequently, the chair upheld the point of order, and the amendment fell.) Nov. 3, 2005.

**286.** **S 1932. Budget Reconciliation/Discretionary Spending Cap.** Inhofe, R-Okla., motion to waive the Budget Act with respect to the Cochran, R-Miss., point of order against the Inhofe amendment. The Inhofe amendment would cap non-defense, non-trust fund spending at fiscal 2006 levels beginning in fiscal 2007. The Senate could waive the cap and increase spending with a two-thirds majority vote. Motion rejected 32-67: R 32-23; D 0-43 (ND 0-39, SD 0-4); I 0-1. A three-fifths majority vote (60) of the total Senate is required to waive the Budget Act. (Subsequently, the chair upheld the point of order, and the amendment fell.) Nov. 3, 2005.

ND Northern Democrats, SD Southern Democrats
Southern states: Ala., Ark., Fla., Ga., Ky., La., Miss., N.C., Okla., S.C., Tenn., Texas, Va.

| | 282 | 283 | 284 | 285 | 286 |
|---|---|---|---|---|---|
| **ALABAMA** | | | | | |
| Shelby | Y | N | Y | N | Y |
| Sessions | Y | N | Y | N | Y |
| **ALASKA** | | | | | |
| Stevens | Y | N | N | N | Y |
| Murkowski | Y | N | N | N | N |
| **ARIZONA** | | | | | |
| McCain | N | Y | Y | N | Y |
| Kyl | N | N | Y | N | Y |
| **ARKANSAS** | | | | | |
| Lincoln | Y | Y | N | Y | N |
| Pryor | Y | Y | N | Y | N |
| **CALIFORNIA** | | | | | |
| Feinstein | Y | Y | N | Y | N |
| Boxer | Y | Y | N | Y | N |
| **COLORADO** | | | | | |
| Allard | Y | N | N | N | Y |
| Salazar | Y | Y | N | Y | N |
| **CONNECTICUT** | | | | | |
| Dodd | N | Y | N | Y | N |
| Lieberman | Y | Y | N | Y | N |
| **DELAWARE** | | | | | |
| Biden | Y | Y | N | Y | N |
| Carper | Y | Y | N | Y | N |
| **FLORIDA** | | | | | |
| Nelson | Y | Y | N | Y | N |
| Martinez | Y | N | Y | N | Y |
| **GEORGIA** | | | | | |
| Chambliss | Y | N | N | N | Y |
| Isakson | Y | N | N | N | Y |
| **HAWAII** | | | | | |
| Inouye | Y | Y | N | Y | N |
| Akaka | Y | Y | N | Y | N |
| **IDAHO** | | | | | |
| Craig | Y | N | Y | N | Y |
| Crapo | Y | N | Y | N | Y |
| **ILLINOIS** | | | | | |
| Durbin | Y | Y | N | Y | N |
| Obama | Y | Y | N | Y | N |
| **INDIANA** | | | | | |
| Lugar | Y | N | N | N | N |
| Bayh | N | Y | N | Y | N |
| **IOWA** | | | | | |
| Grassley | N | N | Y | N | Y |
| Harkin | N | Y | N | Y | N |
| **KANSAS** | | | | | |
| Brownback | Y | N | Y | N | Y |
| Roberts | Y | N | N | N | N |
| **KENTUCKY** | | | | | |
| McConnell | Y | N | Y | N | Y |
| Bunning | Y | N | Y | N | Y |
| **LOUISIANA** | | | | | |
| Landrieu | Y | Y | N | Y | N |
| Vitter | Y | N | Y | Y | Y |
| **MAINE** | | | | | |
| Snowe | Y | Y | N | Y | N |
| Collins | Y | Y | N | N | N |
| **MARYLAND** | | | | | |
| Sarbanes | Y | Y | N | Y | N |
| Mikulski | Y | Y | N | Y | N |
| **MASSACHUSETTS** | | | | | |
| Kennedy | Y | Y | N | Y | N |
| Kerry | N | Y | N | Y | N |
| **MICHIGAN** | | | | | |
| Levin | Y | Y | N | Y | N |
| Stabenow | Y | Y | N | Y | N |
| **MINNESOTA** | | | | | |
| Dayton | Y | Y | N | Y | N |
| Coleman | Y | N | Y | N | N |
| **MISSISSIPPI** | | | | | |
| Cochran | Y | N | N | N | N |
| Lott | Y | N | N | N | N |
| **MISSOURI** | | | | | |
| Bond | Y | N | N | N | N |
| Talent | Y | N | N | N | N |
| **MONTANA** | | | | | |
| Baucus | N | Y | N | Y | N |
| Burns | N | N | N | N | Y |
| **NEBRASKA** | | | | | |
| Hagel | Y | N | Y | N | Y |
| Nelson | Y | Y | N | Y | N |
| **NEVADA** | | | | | |
| Reid | Y | Y | N | Y | N |
| Ensign | N | N | Y | N | Y |
| **NEW HAMPSHIRE** | | | | | |
| Gregg | Y | N | Y | N | N |
| Sununu | N | N | Y | N | Y |
| **NEW JERSEY** | | | | | |
| Corzine | ? | ? | ? | ? | ? |
| Lautenberg | Y | Y | N | Y | N |
| **NEW MEXICO** | | | | | |
| Domenici | Y | N | N | N | N |
| Bingaman | Y | Y | N | Y | N |
| **NEW YORK** | | | | | |
| Schumer | Y | Y | N | Y | N |
| Clinton | Y | Y | N | Y | N |
| **NORTH CAROLINA** | | | | | |
| Dole | Y | N | Y | N | Y |
| Burr | Y | N | N | N | Y |
| **NORTH DAKOTA** | | | | | |
| Conrad | Y | Y | N | Y | N |
| Dorgan | N | Y | N | Y | N |
| **OHIO** | | | | | |
| DeWine | Y | N | Y | N | Y |
| Voinovich | Y | Y | Y | N | N |
| **OKLAHOMA** | | | | | |
| Inhofe | Y | N | Y | N | Y |
| Coburn | N | Y | Y | N | Y |
| **OREGON** | | | | | |
| Wyden | Y | Y | N | Y | N |
| Smith | Y | N | N | N | N |
| **PENNSYLVANIA** | | | | | |
| Specter | Y | N | N | N | N |
| Santorum | Y | N | Y | N | N |
| **RHODE ISLAND** | | | | | |
| Reed | Y | Y | N | Y | N |
| Chafee | Y | Y | N | N | N |
| **SOUTH CAROLINA** | | | | | |
| Graham | Y | N | Y | N | Y |
| DeMint | Y | N | Y | N | Y |
| **SOUTH DAKOTA** | | | | | |
| Johnson | N | Y | N | Y | N |
| Thune | N | N | Y | N | Y |
| **TENNESSEE** | | | | | |
| Frist | Y | N | Y | N | Y |
| Alexander | Y | N | N | N | N |
| **TEXAS** | | | | | |
| Hutchison | Y | N | N | N | Y |
| Cornyn | Y | N | N | Y | Y |
| **UTAH** | | | | | |
| Hatch | Y | N | Y | N | N |
| Bennett | Y | N | Y | N | N |
| **VERMONT** | | | | | |
| Leahy | Y | Y | N | Y | N |
| Jeffords | Y | Y | N | Y | N |
| **VIRGINIA** | | | | | |
| Warner | Y | N | N | N | N |
| Allen | Y | N | Y | N | Y |
| **WASHINGTON** | | | | | |
| Murray | Y | Y | N | Y | N |
| Cantwell | Y | Y | N | Y | N |
| **WEST VIRGINIA** | | | | | |
| Byrd | Y | Y | N | Y | N |
| Rockefeller | Y | Y | N | Y | N |
| **WISCONSIN** | | | | | |
| Kohl | Y | Y | N | Y | N |
| Feingold | N | Y | N | Y | N |
| **WYOMING** | | | | | |
| Thomas | N | N | N | N | Y |
| Enzi | N | N | N | N | Y |

**KEY**   Republicans   Democrats   *Independents*

| | | |
|---|---|---|
| Y  Voted for (yea) | X  Paired against | C  Voted "present" to avoid possible conflict of interest |
| #  Paired for | −  Announced against | |
| +  Announced for | P  Voted "present" | ?  Did not vote or otherwise make a position known |
| N  Voted against (nay) | | |

# IN THE SENATE | By Vote Number

**287.** **S 1932. Budget Reconciliation/Medicare Part B Premiums.** Nelson, D-Fla., amendment that would prevent an increase in monthly Part B premiums for Medicare recipients that might result from a boost in payments to doctors. It would be offset with rebate payments by drug companies for Medicaid programs administered by health maintenance organizations (HMOs). Rejected 49-50: R 5-50; D 43-0 (ND 39-0, SD 4-0); I 1-0. Nov. 3, 2005.

**288.** **S 1932. Budget Reconciliation/ANWR Oil and Gas Leasing.** Cantwell, D-Wash., amendment that would strike language from the underlying bill permitting oil and gas leasing in Alaska's Arctic National Wildlife Refuge (ANWR). Rejected 48-51: R 7-48; D 40-3 (ND 37-2, SD 3-1); I 1-0. A "nay" was a vote in support of the president's position. Nov. 3, 2005.

**289.** **S 1932. Budget Reconciliation/ANWR Exports.** Wyden, D-Ore., amendment that would prohibit any oil or gas produced from leases in ANWR from being sold outside the United States. Adopted 83-16: R 40-15; D 42-1 (ND 39-0, SD 3-1); I 1-0. Nov. 3, 2005.

**290.** **S 1932. Budget Reconciliation/Farm Programs.** Grassley, R-Iowa, motion to waive the Budget Act with respect to the Chambliss, R-Ga., point of order against the Grassley amendment. The Grassley amendment would cap farm commodity program payments at $250,000 a year for married couples and $125,000 for individuals and delay the onset of the 2.5 percent across-the-board reduction in farm program payments by one year until 2007. Motion rejected 46-53: R 19-36; D 27-16 (ND 27-12, SD 0-4); I 0-1. A three-fifths majority vote (60) of the total Senate is required to waive the Budget Act. (Subsequently, the chair upheld the point of order, and the amendment fell.) Nov. 3, 2005.

**291.** **S 1932. Budget Reconciliation/Medicaid FMAP.** Bingaman, D-N.M., amendment that would prevent the Medicaid federal medical assistance percentage (FMAP) from falling below 0.1 in for Delaware and Michigan, 0.3 for Kentucky and 0.5 for any other state in fiscal 2006. The amendment also would extend prescription drug rebates to Medicaid recipients enrolled in HMOs or preferred provider organizations. Adopted 54-45: R 10-45; D 43-0 (ND 39-0, SD 4-0); I 1-0. Nov. 3, 2005.

**292.** **S 1932. Budget Reconciliation/Amtrak Funding.** Lott, R-Miss., amendment that would partially restructure Amtrak and authorize more than $12 billion over six years through fiscal 2011 for operations, capital improvements and rail security. Adopted 93-6: R 49-6; D 43-0 (ND 39-0, SD 4-0); I 1-0. Nov. 3, 2005.

| | 287 | 288 | 289 | 290 | 291 | 292 | | 287 | 288 | 289 | 290 | 291 | 292 |
|---|---|---|---|---|---|---|---|---|---|---|---|---|---|
| **ALABAMA** | | | | | | | **MONTANA** | | | | | | |
| Shelby | N | N | Y | N | N | Y | Baucus | Y | Y | Y | N | Y | Y |
| Sessions | N | N | N | N | N | N | Burns | Y | N | Y | N | N | Y |
| **ALASKA** | | | | | | | **NEBRASKA** | | | | | | |
| Stevens | N | N | Y | N | N | Y | Hagel | N | N | Y | Y | N | Y |
| Murkowski | N | N | Y | N | Y | Y | Nelson | Y | Y | Y | Y | Y | Y |
| **ARIZONA** | | | | | | | **NEVADA** | | | | | | |
| McCain | N | Y | N | N | N | Y | Reid | Y | Y | Y | Y | Y | Y |
| Kyl | N | N | N | N | N | Y | Ensign | N | N | Y | Y | N | N |
| **ARKANSAS** | | | | | | | **NEW HAMPSHIRE** | | | | | | |
| Lincoln | Y | Y | Y | N | Y | Y | Gregg | N | N | N | N | N | N |
| Pryor | Y | Y | Y | N | Y | Y | Sununu | N | N | N | Y | N | N |
| **CALIFORNIA** | | | | | | | **NEW JERSEY** | | | | | | |
| Feinstein | Y | Y | Y | N | Y | Y | Corzine | ? | ? | ? | ? | ? | ? |
| Boxer | Y | Y | Y | N | Y | Y | Lautenberg | Y | Y | Y | Y | Y | Y |
| **COLORADO** | | | | | | | **NEW MEXICO** | | | | | | |
| Allard | N | N | N | Y | N | Y | Domenici | N | N | Y | N | Y | Y |
| Salazar | Y | Y | Y | Y | Y | Y | Bingaman | Y | Y | Y | Y | Y | Y |
| **CONNECTICUT** | | | | | | | **NEW YORK** | | | | | | |
| Dodd | Y | Y | Y | N | Y | Y | Schumer | Y | Y | Y | Y | Y | Y |
| Lieberman | Y | Y | Y | N | Y | Y | Clinton | Y | Y | Y | Y | Y | Y |
| **DELAWARE** | | | | | | | **NORTH CAROLINA** | | | | | | |
| Biden | Y | Y | Y | N | Y | Y | Dole | N | N | Y | N | N | Y |
| Carper | Y | Y | Y | N | Y | Y | Burr | N | N | N | N | N | Y |
| **FLORIDA** | | | | | | | **NORTH DAKOTA** | | | | | | |
| Nelson | Y | Y | Y | N | Y | Y | Conrad | Y | Y | Y | Y | Y | Y |
| Martinez | N | N | Y | N | N | Y | Dorgan | Y | Y | Y | Y | Y | Y |
| **GEORGIA** | | | | | | | **OHIO** | | | | | | |
| Chambliss | N | N | Y | N | N | Y | DeWine | Y | Y | Y | Y | N | Y |
| Isakson | N | N | Y | N | N | Y | Voinovich | N | N | Y | N | Y | N |
| **HAWAII** | | | | | | | **OKLAHOMA** | | | | | | |
| Inouye | Y | N | Y | N | Y | Y | Inhofe | N | N | N | N | Y | Y |
| Akaka | Y | N | Y | N | Y | Y | Coburn | N | N | Y | N | Y | Y |
| **IDAHO** | | | | | | | **OREGON** | | | | | | |
| Craig | N | N | N | N | N | Y | Wyden | Y | Y | Y | N | Y | Y |
| Crapo | N | N | Y | N | N | Y | Smith | N | Y | Y | N | Y | Y |
| **ILLINOIS** | | | | | | | **PENNSYLVANIA** | | | | | | |
| Durbin | Y | Y | Y | Y | Y | Y | Specter | N | N | Y | N | Y | Y |
| Obama | Y | Y | Y | Y | Y | Y | Santorum | N | N | Y | N | N | Y |
| **INDIANA** | | | | | | | **RHODE ISLAND** | | | | | | |
| Lugar | N | N | Y | N | N | Y | Reed | Y | Y | Y | Y | Y | Y |
| Bayh | Y | Y | Y | Y | Y | Y | Chafee | N | Y | Y | Y | Y | Y |
| **IOWA** | | | | | | | **SOUTH CAROLINA** | | | | | | |
| Grassley | N | N | Y | Y | N | Y | Graham | N | N | Y | N | N | Y |
| Harkin | Y | Y | Y | Y | Y | Y | DeMint | N | N | Y | N | N | N |
| **KANSAS** | | | | | | | **SOUTH DAKOTA** | | | | | | |
| Brownback | N | N | N | Y | N | Y | Johnson | Y | Y | Y | Y | Y | Y |
| Roberts | N | N | Y | N | N | Y | Thune | N | N | Y | N | N | Y |
| **KENTUCKY** | | | | | | | **TENNESSEE** | | | | | | |
| McConnell | N | N | Y | N | N | Y | Frist | N | N | Y | N | N | Y |
| Bunning | N | N | N | N | N | Y | Alexander | N | N | N | N | N | Y |
| **LOUISIANA** | | | | | | | **TEXAS** | | | | | | |
| Landrieu | Y | N | N | N | Y | Y | Hutchison | N | N | Y | N | Y | Y |
| Vitter | N | N | Y | N | N | Y | Cornyn | N | N | N | N | Y | Y |
| **MAINE** | | | | | | | **UTAH** | | | | | | |
| Snowe | Y | Y | Y | Y | Y | Y | Hatch | N | N | Y | N | N | Y |
| Collins | Y | Y | Y | Y | Y | Y | Bennett | N | N | N | N | N | Y |
| **MARYLAND** | | | | | | | **VERMONT** | | | | | | |
| Sarbanes | Y | Y | Y | Y | Y | Y | Leahy | Y | Y | Y | N | Y | Y |
| Mikulski | Y | Y | Y | Y | Y | Y | Jeffords | Y | Y | Y | Y | Y | Y |
| **MASSACHUSETTS** | | | | | | | **VIRGINIA** | | | | | | |
| Kennedy | Y | Y | Y | Y | Y | Y | Warner | N | N | Y | N | N | Y |
| Kerry | Y | Y | Y | Y | Y | Y | Allen | N | N | N | N | N | Y |
| **MICHIGAN** | | | | | | | **WASHINGTON** | | | | | | |
| Levin | Y | Y | Y | Y | Y | Y | Murray | Y | Y | Y | Y | Y | Y |
| Stabenow | Y | Y | Y | Y | Y | Y | Cantwell | Y | Y | Y | Y | Y | Y |
| **MINNESOTA** | | | | | | | **WEST VIRGINIA** | | | | | | |
| Dayton | Y | Y | Y | Y | Y | Y | Byrd | Y | Y | Y | N | Y | Y |
| Coleman | N | Y | Y | N | N | Y | Rockefeller | Y | Y | Y | N | Y | Y |
| **MISSISSIPPI** | | | | | | | **WISCONSIN** | | | | | | |
| Cochran | N | N | Y | N | N | Y | Kohl | Y | Y | Y | N | Y | Y |
| Lott | N | N | Y | N | N | Y | Feingold | Y | Y | Y | Y | Y | Y |
| **MISSOURI** | | | | | | | **WYOMING** | | | | | | |
| Bond | N | N | Y | N | N | Y | Thomas | N | N | Y | Y | N | Y |
| Talent | Y | N | Y | N | N | Y | Enzi | N | N | Y | Y | N | Y |

**KEY**   Republicans   Democrats   *Independents*

| | | | |
|---|---|---|---|
| Y | Voted for (yea) | X Paired against | C Voted "present" to avoid possible conflict of interest |
| # | Paired for | – Announced against | |
| + | Announced for | P Voted "present" | ? Did not vote or otherwise make a position known |
| N | Voted against (nay) | | |

ND Northern Democrats, SD Southern Democrats
Southern states: Ala., Ark., Fla., Ga., Ky., La., Miss., N.C., Okla., S.C., Tenn., Texas, Va.

## IN THE SENATE | By Vote Number

**293.** **S 1932. Budget Reconciliation/Broadcast Spectrum.** McCain, R-Ariz., amendment that would move the date when broadcasters must relinquish certain segments of the broadcast spectrum forward by one year to April 7, 2008. Rejected 30-69: R 9-46; D 20-23 (ND 19-20, SD 1-3); I 1-0. Nov. 3, 2005.

**294.** **S 1932. Budget Reconciliation/Medicare Dual Eligibility.** Murray, D-Wash., motion to waive the Budget Act with respect to the Gregg, R-N.H., point of order against the Murray amendment. The Murray amendment would provide an extra six months for Medicaid patients who are also seniors to enroll in the new Medicare prescription drug program. Motion rejected 43-56: R 0-55; D 42-1 (ND 38-1, SD 4-0); I 1-0. A three-fifths majority vote (60) of the total Senate is required to waive the Budget Act. (Subsequently, the chair upheld the point of order, and the amendment fell.) Nov. 3, 2005.

**295.** **S 1932. Budget Reconciliation/Non-Immigrant Visa Fee.** Byrd, D-W.Va., amendment that would strike the section of the bill related to immigrant visas and insert language that would impose a fee of $1,500 on employers filing L1 visa request for a non-immigrant employer. Rejected 14-85: R 3-52; D 10-33 (ND 9-30, SD 1-3); I 1-0. Nov. 3, 2005.

**296.** **S 1932. Budget Reconciliation/Reconciliation Consideration.** Byrd, D-W.Va., motion to waive the Budget Act with respect to the Gregg, R-N.H., point of order against the Byrd amendment. The Byrd amendment would suspend the 20-hour time limit on debate for any reconciliation bill that would increase the deficit. Motion rejected 44-55: R 0-55; D 43-0 (ND 39-0, SD 4-0); I 1-0. A three-fifths majority vote (60) of the total Senate is required to waive the Budget Act. (Subsequently, the chair upheld the point of order, and the amendment fell.) Nov. 3, 2005.

**297.** **S 1932. Budget Reconciliation/Prescription Drug Enrollment.** Lautenberg, D-N.J., motion to waive the Budget Act with respect to the Gregg, R-N.H., point of order against the Lautenberg amendment. The Lautenberg amendment would require applicants for Medicare Advantage prescription drug plans to sign a certification prior to enrollment stating that they understand that the plan may contain a potential coverage gap. Motion rejected 43-56: R 0-55; D 43-0 (ND 39-0, SD 4-0); I 0-1. A three-fifths majority vote (60) of the total Senate is required to waive the Budget Act. (Subsequently, the chair upheld the point of order, and the amendment fell.) Nov. 3, 2005.

**298.** **S 1932. Budget Reconciliation/ANWR Revenue Split.** Cantwell, D-Wash., amendment that would ensure that 50 percent of revenues from oil and natural gas leasing and production in ANWR be paid to the state of Alaska and 50 percent to the U.S. Treasury. If the state of Alaska brings a civil suit against the federal government to secure more than 50 percent, oil and gas production would cease until a non-appealable decision is handed down. Rejected 48-51: R 6-49; D 41-2 (ND 37-2, SD 4-0); I 1-0. Nov. 3, 2005.

ND Northern Democrats, SD Southern Democrats
Southern states: Ala., Ark., Fla., Ga., Ky., La., Miss., N.C., Okla., S.C., Tenn., Texas, Va.

| | 293 | 294 | 295 | 296 | 297 | 298 | | 293 | 294 | 295 | 296 | 297 | 298 |
|---|---|---|---|---|---|---|---|---|---|---|---|---|---|
| **ALABAMA** | | | | | | | **MONTANA** | | | | | | |
| Shelby | N | N | N | N | N | N | Baucus | N | Y | N | Y | Y | Y |
| Sessions | N | N | Y | N | N | N | Burns | N | N | N | N | N | N |
| **ALASKA** | | | | | | | **NEBRASKA** | | | | | | |
| Stevens | N | N | N | N | N | N | Hagel | N | N | N | N | N | N |
| Murkowski | N | N | N | N | N | N | Nelson | N | N | N | Y | Y | N |
| **ARIZONA** | | | | | | | **NEVADA** | | | | | | |
| McCain | Y | N | N | N | N | Y | Reid | N | Y | N | Y | Y | Y |
| Kyl | Y | N | N | N | N | N | Ensign | Y | N | N | N | N | N |
| **ARKANSAS** | | | | | | | **NEW HAMPSHIRE** | | | | | | |
| Lincoln | N | Y | N | Y | Y | Y | Gregg | N | N | N | N | N | N |
| Pryor | N | Y | N | Y | Y | Y | Sununu | Y | N | N | N | N | N |
| **CALIFORNIA** | | | | | | | **NEW JERSEY** | | | | | | |
| Feinstein | Y | Y | N | Y | Y | Y | Corzine | ? | ? | ? | ? | ? | ? |
| Boxer | Y | Y | N | Y | Y | Y | Lautenberg | Y | Y | N | Y | Y | Y |
| **COLORADO** | | | | | | | **NEW MEXICO** | | | | | | |
| Allard | N | N | N | N | N | N | Domenici | N | N | N | N | N | N |
| Salazar | Y | Y | N | Y | Y | Y | Bingaman | N | Y | N | Y | Y | Y |
| **CONNECTICUT** | | | | | | | **NEW YORK** | | | | | | |
| Dodd | Y | Y | Y | Y | Y | Y | Schumer | Y | Y | N | Y | Y | Y |
| Lieberman | Y | Y | N | Y | Y | Y | Clinton | Y | Y | N | Y | Y | Y |
| **DELAWARE** | | | | | | | **NORTH CAROLINA** | | | | | | |
| Biden | Y | Y | N | Y | Y | Y | Dole | N | N | N | N | N | N |
| Carper | Y | Y | N | Y | Y | Y | Burr | N | N | N | N | N | N |
| **FLORIDA** | | | | | | | **NORTH DAKOTA** | | | | | | |
| Nelson | Y | Y | N | Y | Y | Y | Conrad | N | Y | N | Y | Y | Y |
| Martinez | N | N | N | N | N | N | Dorgan | N | Y | Y | Y | Y | Y |
| **GEORGIA** | | | | | | | **OHIO** | | | | | | |
| Chambliss | N | N | N | N | N | N | DeWine | N | N | N | N | N | N |
| Isakson | N | N | N | N | N | N | Voinovich | N | N | N | N | N | N |
| **HAWAII** | | | | | | | **OKLAHOMA** | | | | | | |
| Inouye | N | Y | Y | Y | Y | N | Inhofe | N | N | N | N | N | N |
| Akaka | N | Y | Y | Y | Y | N | Coburn | Y | N | N | N | N | N |
| **IDAHO** | | | | | | | **OREGON** | | | | | | |
| Craig | N | N | N | N | N | N | Wyden | N | Y | N | Y | Y | Y |
| Crapo | N | N | N | N | N | N | Smith | N | N | N | N | N | N |
| **ILLINOIS** | | | | | | | **PENNSYLVANIA** | | | | | | |
| Durbin | N | Y | Y | Y | Y | Y | Specter | N | N | N | N | N | N |
| Obama | N | Y | N | Y | Y | Y | Santorum | N | N | N | N | N | N |
| **INDIANA** | | | | | | | **RHODE ISLAND** | | | | | | |
| Lugar | N | N | N | N | N | N | Reed | N | Y | N | Y | Y | Y |
| Bayh | Y | Y | N | Y | Y | Y | Chafee | N | N | N | N | N | Y |
| **IOWA** | | | | | | | **SOUTH CAROLINA** | | | | | | |
| Grassley | N | N | N | N | N | N | Graham | Y | N | N | N | N | N |
| Harkin | Y | Y | N | Y | Y | Y | DeMint | Y | N | N | N | N | N |
| **KANSAS** | | | | | | | **SOUTH DAKOTA** | | | | | | |
| Brownback | N | N | N | N | N | N | Johnson | N | Y | N | Y | Y | Y |
| Roberts | N | N | N | N | N | N | Thune | N | N | N | N | N | N |
| **KENTUCKY** | | | | | | | **TENNESSEE** | | | | | | |
| McConnell | N | N | N | N | N | N | Frist | N | N | N | N | N | N |
| Bunning | N | N | N | N | N | N | Alexander | N | N | N | N | N | N |
| **LOUISIANA** | | | | | | | **TEXAS** | | | | | | |
| Landrieu | N | Y | Y | Y | Y | Y | Hutchison | N | N | N | N | N | N |
| Vitter | N | N | Y | N | N | N | Cornyn | N | N | N | N | N | N |
| **MAINE** | | | | | | | **UTAH** | | | | | | |
| Snowe | N | N | N | N | N | Y | Hatch | N | N | N | N | N | N |
| Collins | Y | N | N | N | N | N | Bennett | N | N | N | N | N | N |
| **MARYLAND** | | | | | | | **VERMONT** | | | | | | |
| Sarbanes | N | Y | N | Y | Y | Y | Leahy | N | Y | N | Y | Y | Y |
| Mikulski | Y | Y | N | Y | Y | Y | Jeffords | Y | Y | Y | Y | N | Y |
| **MASSACHUSETTS** | | | | | | | **VIRGINIA** | | | | | | |
| Kennedy | Y | Y | N | Y | Y | Y | Warner | Y | N | N | N | N | N |
| Kerry | Y | Y | N | Y | Y | Y | Allen | N | N | N | N | N | N |
| **MICHIGAN** | | | | | | | **WASHINGTON** | | | | | | |
| Levin | Y | Y | N | Y | Y | Y | Murray | N | Y | N | Y | Y | Y |
| Stabenow | Y | Y | Y | Y | Y | Y | Cantwell | N | Y | N | Y | Y | Y |
| **MINNESOTA** | | | | | | | **WEST VIRGINIA** | | | | | | |
| Dayton | N | Y | Y | Y | Y | Y | Byrd | N | Y | Y | Y | Y | Y |
| Coleman | N | N | N | N | N | Y | Rockefeller | Y | Y | Y | Y | Y | Y |
| **MISSISSIPPI** | | | | | | | **WISCONSIN** | | | | | | |
| Cochran | N | N | N | N | N | N | Kohl | N | Y | N | Y | Y | Y |
| Lott | N | N | N | N | N | N | Feingold | Y | Y | Y | Y | Y | Y |
| **MISSOURI** | | | | | | | **WYOMING** | | | | | | |
| Bond | N | N | N | N | N | N | Thomas | N | N | N | N | N | N |
| Talent | N | N | N | N | N | N | Enzi | N | N | N | N | N | N |

**KEY**  Republicans  Democrats  *Independents*

| | | | | | | |
|---|---|---|---|---|---|---|
| Y | Voted for (yea) | X | Paired against | C | Voted "present" to avoid possible conflict of interest |
| # | Paired for | – | Announced against | | |
| + | Announced for | P | Voted "present" | ? | Did not vote or otherwise make a position known |
| N | Voted against (nay) | | | | |

# IN THE SENATE | By Vote Number

**299.** S 1932. Budget Reconciliation/Drug Rebates. Schumer, D-N.Y., amendment to strike provisions in the bill that would increase the manufacturer's rebate on generic drugs from 11 percent to 17 percent. Rejected 49-50: R 5-50; D 43-0 (ND 39-0, SD 4-0); I 1-0. Nov. 3, 2005.

**300.** S 1932. Budget Reconciliation/Targeted Case Management. Reed, D-R.I., amendment that would strike the section of the bill that would prohibit Medicaid reimbursements for "targeted case management" services, including assessment activities for foster care services, in cases when a third party could provide coverage. Rejected 46-52: R 2-52; D 43-0 (ND 39-0, SD 4-0); I 1-0. Nov. 3, 2005.

**301.** S 1932. Budget Reconciliation/FHA Assets. Reed, D-R.I., amendment that would strike language in the bill that would change the process of a Federal Housing Administration program that issues grants to rehabilitate multifamily properties or sells those properties at below-market prices, subject the program to appropriations and authorize $100 million in fiscal 2006 for asset disposition. Rejected 48-51: R 4-51; D 43-0 (ND 39-0, SD 4-0); I 1-0. Nov. 3, 2005.

**302.** S 1932. Budget Reconciliation/Drug Price Negotiations. Snowe, R-Maine, motion to waive the Budget Act with respect to the Grassley R-Iowa, point of order against the Snowe amendment. The Snowe amendment would authorize the secretary of Health and Human Services to negotiate prices for prescription drugs under Medicare. It also would specify that such authority may not be used to set prices. Motion rejected 51-48: R 9-46; D 41-2 (ND 37-2, SD 4-0); I 1-0. A three-fifths majority vote (60) of the total Senate is required to waive the Budget Act. (Subsequently, the chair upheld the point of order, and the amendment fell.) Nov. 3, 2005.

**303.** S 1932. Budget Reconciliation/Passage. Passage of a bill that would make changes to mandatory programs for a net savings of approximately $35 billion over five years, including cuts in the growth of Medicare and Medicaid. It would provide $2.6 billion in education aid, including $1.7 billion for Hurricane Katrina victims; prohibit export of any oil or gas produced from leases in Alaska's Arctic National Wildlife Refuge; and authorize more than $12 billion over six years for Amtrak. Passed 52-47: R 50-5; D 2-41 (ND 1-38, SD 1-3); I 0-1. A " yea" was a vote in support of the president's position. Nov. 3, 2005.

ND Northern Democrats, SD Southern Democrats
Southern states: Ala., Ark., Fla., Ga., Ky., La., Miss., N.C., Okla., S.C., Tenn., Texas, Va.

| | 299 | 300 | 301 | 302 | 303 | | | 299 | 300 | 301 | 302 | 303 |
|---|---|---|---|---|---|---|---|---|---|---|---|---|
| **ALABAMA** | | | | | | | **MONTANA** | | | | | |
| Shelby | N | N | N | N | Y | | Baucus | Y | Y | Y | N | N |
| Sessions | N | N | N | N | Y | | Burns | N | N | N | N | Y |
| **ALASKA** | | | | | | | **NEBRASKA** | | | | | |
| Stevens | N | N | N | N | Y | | Hagel | N | N | N | N | Y |
| Murkowski | N | N | N | N | Y | | Nelson | Y | Y | Y | N | Y |
| **ARIZONA** | | | | | | | **NEVADA** | | | | | |
| McCain | Y | N | N | Y | Y | | Reid | Y | Y | Y | Y | N |
| Kyl | N | N | N | N | Y | | Ensign | N | N | N | N | Y |
| **ARKANSAS** | | | | | | | **NEW HAMPSHIRE** | | | | | |
| Lincoln | Y | Y | Y | Y | N | | Gregg | N | N | N | N | Y |
| Pryor | Y | Y | Y | Y | N | | Sununu | N | N | N | N | Y |
| **CALIFORNIA** | | | | | | | **NEW JERSEY** | | | | | |
| Feinstein | Y | Y | Y | Y | N | | Corzine | ? | ? | ? | ? | ? |
| Boxer | Y | Y | Y | Y | N | | Lautenberg | Y | Y | Y | Y | N |
| **COLORADO** | | | | | | | **NEW MEXICO** | | | | | |
| Allard | N | N | N | N | Y | | Domenici | N | N | N | N | Y |
| Salazar | Y | Y | Y | Y | N | | Bingaman | Y | Y | Y | Y | N |
| **CONNECTICUT** | | | | | | | **NEW YORK** | | | | | |
| Dodd | Y | Y | Y | Y | N | | Schumer | Y | Y | Y | Y | N |
| Lieberman | Y | Y | Y | Y | N | | Clinton | Y | Y | Y | Y | N |
| **DELAWARE** | | | | | | | **NORTH CAROLINA** | | | | | |
| Biden | Y | Y | Y | Y | N | | Dole | N | N | N | N | Y |
| Carper | Y | Y | Y | Y | N | | Burr | N | N | N | N | Y |
| **FLORIDA** | | | | | | | **NORTH DAKOTA** | | | | | |
| Nelson | Y | Y | Y | Y | N | | Conrad | Y | Y | Y | Y | N |
| Martinez | N | N | N | N | Y | | Dorgan | Y | Y | Y | Y | N |
| **GEORGIA** | | | | | | | **OHIO** | | | | | |
| Chambliss | N | N | N | N | Y | | DeWine | N | Y | Y | Y | N |
| Isakson | N | N | N | N | Y | | Voinovich | N | N | N | N | Y |
| **HAWAII** | | | | | | | **OKLAHOMA** | | | | | |
| Inouye | Y | Y | Y | Y | N | | Inhofe | N | N | N | N | Y |
| Akaka | Y | Y | Y | Y | N | | Coburn | N | ? | N | Y | Y |
| **IDAHO** | | | | | | | **OREGON** | | | | | |
| Craig | N | N | N | N | Y | | Wyden | Y | Y | Y | Y | N |
| Crapo | N | N | N | N | Y | | Smith | N | N | N | N | Y |
| **ILLINOIS** | | | | | | | **PENNSYLVANIA** | | | | | |
| Durbin | Y | Y | Y | Y | N | | Specter | Y | N | Y | Y | Y |
| Obama | Y | Y | Y | Y | N | | Santorum | N | N | N | N | Y |
| **INDIANA** | | | | | | | **RHODE ISLAND** | | | | | |
| Lugar | N | N | N | N | Y | | Reed | Y | Y | Y | Y | N |
| Bayh | Y | Y | Y | Y | N | | Chafee | N | Y | Y | Y | N |
| **IOWA** | | | | | | | **SOUTH CAROLINA** | | | | | |
| Grassley | N | N | N | N | Y | | Graham | N | N | N | Y | Y |
| Harkin | Y | Y | Y | Y | N | | DeMint | N | N | N | N | Y |
| **KANSAS** | | | | | | | **SOUTH DAKOTA** | | | | | |
| Brownback | N | N | N | Y | Y | | Johnson | Y | Y | Y | Y | N |
| Roberts | N | N | N | N | Y | | Thune | N | N | N | N | Y |
| **KENTUCKY** | | | | | | | **TENNESSEE** | | | | | |
| McConnell | N | N | N | N | Y | | Frist | N | N | N | N | Y |
| Bunning | N | N | N | N | Y | | Alexander | N | N | N | N | Y |
| **LOUISIANA** | | | | | | | **TEXAS** | | | | | |
| Landrieu | Y | Y | Y | Y | Y | | Hutchison | N | N | N | N | Y |
| Vitter | N | N | N | N | Y | | Cornyn | N | N | N | N | Y |
| **MAINE** | | | | | | | **UTAH** | | | | | |
| Snowe | Y | N | N | Y | N | | Hatch | N | N | N | N | Y |
| Collins | Y | N | N | Y | N | | Bennett | N | N | N | N | Y |
| **MARYLAND** | | | | | | | **VERMONT** | | | | | |
| Sarbanes | Y | Y | Y | Y | N | | Leahy | Y | Y | Y | Y | N |
| Mikulski | Y | Y | Y | Y | N | | Jeffords | Y | Y | Y | Y | N |
| **MASSACHUSETTS** | | | | | | | **VIRGINIA** | | | | | |
| Kennedy | Y | Y | Y | Y | N | | Warner | N | N | N | N | Y |
| Kerry | Y | Y | Y | Y | N | | Allen | N | N | N | N | Y |
| **MICHIGAN** | | | | | | | **WASHINGTON** | | | | | |
| Levin | Y | Y | Y | Y | N | | Murray | Y | Y | Y | Y | N |
| Stabenow | Y | Y | Y | Y | N | | Cantwell | Y | Y | Y | Y | N |
| **MINNESOTA** | | | | | | | **WEST VIRGINIA** | | | | | |
| Dayton | Y | Y | Y | Y | N | | Byrd | Y | Y | Y | Y | N |
| Coleman | N | N | N | N | N | | Rockefeller | Y | Y | Y | Y | N |
| **MISSISSIPPI** | | | | | | | **WISCONSIN** | | | | | |
| Cochran | N | N | N | N | Y | | Kohl | Y | Y | Y | Y | N |
| Lott | N | N | N | N | Y | | Feingold | Y | Y | Y | Y | N |
| **MISSOURI** | | | | | | | **WYOMING** | | | | | |
| Bond | N | N | Y | N | Y | | Thomas | N | N | N | N | Y |
| Talent | N | N | N | N | Y | | Enzi | N | N | N | N | Y |

| KEY | Republicans | Democrats | *Independents* | | |
|---|---|---|---|---|---|
| Y | Voted for (yea) | X | Paired against | C | Voted "present" to avoid possible conflict of interest |
| # | Paired for | – | Announced against | | |
| + | Announced for | P | Voted "present" | ? | Did not vote or otherwise make a position known |
| N | Voted against (nay) | | | | |

# IN THE SENATE | By Vote Number

**304.** **S 1042. Fiscal 2006 Defense Authorization/Retirement Benefits for Rocky Flats Employees.** Allard, R-Colo., amendment that would authorize $15 million to provide health, medical and life insurance benefits for employees of the Energy Department's Rocky Flats, Colo., Environmental Technology Site even if their retirement goes into effect before Dec. 15, 2006. Rejected 38-53: R 13-40; D 24-13 (ND 22-11, SD 2-2); I 1-0. Nov. 7, 2005.

**305.** **S 1042. Fiscal 2006 Defense Authorization/Armed Forces Network.** Inhofe, R-Okla., amendment that would express the sense of the Senate commending the Armed Forces Network and state that censorship on the network is unacceptable. It also would allow the Defense secretary to create an ombudsman's office for the radio network. Adopted 55-43: R 52-0; D 3-42 (ND 2-39, SD 1-3); I 0-1. Nov. 8, 2005.

**306.** **S 1042. Fiscal 2006 Defense Authorization/Armed Forces Network.** Harkin, D-Iowa, amendment that would require the Defense secretary to establish an ombudsman's office to conduct programming reviews of the Armed Forces Network, and field questions and concerns from listeners. It also would call for political balance in Armed Forces Network programming. Rejected 44-54: R 0-54; D 43-0 (ND 39-0, SD 4-0); I 1-0. Nov. 8, 2005.

**307.** **S 1042. Fiscal 2006 Defense Authorization/Survivor Benefits.** Nelson, D-Fla., amendment that would eliminate the requirement that widows and orphans of deceased or fully disabled military personnel who receive pensions under the Defense Department's Survivor Benefits Plan have those benefits reduced dollar for dollar by the amount received from the Department of Veterans Affairs Dependency and Indemnity Compensation program. Adopted 92-6: R 48-6; D 43-0 (ND 39-0, SD 4-0); I 1-0. Nov. 8, 2005.

**308.** **S 1042. Fiscal 2006 Defense Authorization/BRAC Sites.** Snowe, R-Maine, amendment that would require the Defense Department to grant a free transfer of lands to local communities when bases are closed under the Base Realignment and Closure (BRAC) process, rather than requiring communities to pay the Defense Department fair market value for the land. Rejected 36-62: R 14-40; D 21-22 (ND 18-21, SD 3-1); I 1-0. Nov. 8, 2005.

**309.** **S 1042. Fiscal 2006 Defense Authorization/Detainee Abuse.** Levin, D-Mich., amendment that would create an independent bipartisan commission to examine detainee abuse at U.S. military prisons around the world. Rejected 43-55: R 0-54; D 42-1 (ND 39-0, SD 3-1); I 1-0. A "nay" was a vote in support of the president's position. Nov. 8, 2005.

| | 304 | 305 | 306 | 307 | 308 | 309 |
|---|---|---|---|---|---|---|
| **ALABAMA** | | | | | | |
| Shelby | N | Y | N | Y | N | N |
| Sessions | N | Y | N | N | N | N |
| **ALASKA** | | | | | | |
| Stevens | N | Y | N | Y | N | N |
| Murkowski | Y | Y | N | Y | N | N |
| **ARIZONA** | | | | | | |
| McCain | ? | ? | ? | ? | ? | ? |
| Kyl | N | Y | N | Y | N | N |
| **ARKANSAS** | | | | | | |
| Lincoln | N | N | Y | Y | Y | Y |
| Pryor | Y | N | Y | Y | Y | Y |
| **CALIFORNIA** | | | | | | |
| Feinstein | Y | N | Y | Y | N | Y |
| Boxer | Y | N | Y | Y | Y | Y |
| **COLORADO** | | | | | | |
| Allard | Y | Y | N | N | N | N |
| Salazar | Y | N | Y | Y | N | Y |
| **CONNECTICUT** | | | | | | |
| Dodd | N | N | Y | Y | Y | Y |
| Lieberman | Y | N | Y | Y | N | Y |
| **DELAWARE** | | | | | | |
| Biden | ? | N | Y | Y | N | Y |
| Carper | N | N | Y | Y | N | Y |
| **FLORIDA** | | | | | | |
| Nelson | N | N | Y | Y | N | Y |
| Martinez | N | Y | N | Y | N | N |
| **GEORGIA** | | | | | | |
| Chambliss | N | Y | N | Y | N | N |
| Isakson | N | Y | N | Y | N | N |
| **HAWAII** | | | | | | |
| Inouye | ? | N | Y | Y | Y | Y |
| Akaka | N | N | Y | Y | N | Y |
| **IDAHO** | | | | | | |
| Craig | Y | Y | N | Y | N | N |
| Crapo | Y | Y | N | Y | N | N |
| **ILLINOIS** | | | | | | |
| Durbin | Y | N | Y | Y | Y | Y |
| Obama | Y | N | Y | Y | Y | Y |
| **INDIANA** | | | | | | |
| Lugar | N | Y | N | Y | N | N |
| Bayh | ? | N | Y | Y | Y | Y |
| **IOWA** | | | | | | |
| Grassley | N | Y | N | Y | N | N |
| Harkin | Y | N | Y | Y | Y | Y |
| **KANSAS** | | | | | | |
| Brownback | N | Y | N | Y | N | N |
| Roberts | N | Y | N | Y | Y | N |
| **KENTUCKY** | | | | | | |
| McConnell | N | Y | N | Y | N | N |
| Bunning | N | Y | N | Y | N | N |
| **LOUISIANA** | | | | | | |
| Landrieu | Y | N | Y | Y | Y | Y |
| Vitter | N | Y | N | Y | Y | N |
| **MAINE** | | | | | | |
| Snowe | N | Y | N | Y | N | N |
| Collins | N | Y | N | Y | N | N |
| **MARYLAND** | | | | | | |
| Sarbanes | Y | N | Y | Y | N | Y |
| Mikulski | Y | N | Y | Y | N | Y |
| **MASSACHUSETTS** | | | | | | |
| Kennedy | ? | N | Y | Y | N | Y |
| Kerry | Y | N | Y | Y | Y | Y |
| **MICHIGAN** | | | | | | |
| Levin | N | N | Y | Y | N | Y |
| Stabenow | ? | N | Y | Y | Y | Y |
| **MINNESOTA** | | | | | | |
| Dayton | Y | N | Y | Y | N | Y |
| Coleman | N | Y | N | Y | Y | N |
| **MISSISSIPPI** | | | | | | |
| Cochran | N | Y | N | Y | N | N |
| Lott | N | Y | N | Y | N | N |
| **MISSOURI** | | | | | | |
| Bond | Y | Y | N | Y | N | N |
| Talent | Y | Y | N | Y | N | N |

| | 304 | 305 | 306 | 307 | 308 | 309 |
|---|---|---|---|---|---|---|
| **MONTANA** | | | | | | |
| Baucus | Y | N | Y | Y | N | Y |
| Burns | Y | Y | N | Y | N | N |
| **NEBRASKA** | | | | | | |
| Hagel | N | Y | N | Y | Y | N |
| Nelson | N | Y | Y | Y | N | N |
| **NEVADA** | | | | | | |
| Reid | N | N | Y | Y | N | Y |
| Ensign | N | Y | N | Y | N | N |
| **NEW HAMPSHIRE** | | | | | | |
| Gregg | N | Y | N | Y | Y | N |
| Sununu | N | Y | N | Y | Y | N |
| **NEW JERSEY** | | | | | | |
| Corzine | ? | ? | ? | ? | ? | ? |
| Lautenberg | Y | N | Y | Y | Y | Y |
| **NEW MEXICO** | | | | | | |
| Domenici | Y | Y | N | Y | N | N |
| Bingaman | Y | N | Y | Y | N | Y |
| **NEW YORK** | | | | | | |
| Schumer | N | N | Y | Y | Y | Y |
| Clinton | N | N | Y | Y | Y | Y |
| **NORTH CAROLINA** | | | | | | |
| Dole | N | Y | N | Y | N | N |
| Burr | N | Y | N | Y | N | N |
| **NORTH DAKOTA** | | | | | | |
| Conrad | Y | N | Y | Y | Y | Y |
| Dorgan | ? | N | Y | Y | Y | Y |
| **OHIO** | | | | | | |
| DeWine | Y | Y | N | Y | N | N |
| Voinovich | N | Y | N | N | N | N |
| **OKLAHOMA** | | | | | | |
| Inhofe | N | Y | N | N | N | N |
| Coburn | N | Y | N | N | N | N |
| **OREGON** | | | | | | |
| Wyden | Y | N | Y | Y | N | Y |
| Smith | N | Y | N | Y | Y | N |
| **PENNSYLVANIA** | | | | | | |
| Specter | Y | Y | N | Y | N | N |
| Santorum | N | Y | N | Y | N | N |
| **RHODE ISLAND** | | | | | | |
| Reed | N | N | Y | Y | N | Y |
| Chafee | N | Y | N | Y | N | Y |
| **SOUTH CAROLINA** | | | | | | |
| Graham | Y | Y | N | Y | N | N |
| DeMint | Y | Y | N | N | N | N |
| **SOUTH DAKOTA** | | | | | | |
| Johnson | Y | N | Y | Y | N | Y |
| Thune | N | Y | N | Y | Y | N |
| **TENNESSEE** | | | | | | |
| Frist | N | Y | N | Y | N | N |
| Alexander | Y | Y | N | Y | N | N |
| **TEXAS** | | | | | | |
| Hutchison | N | Y | N | Y | N | N |
| Cornyn | N | Y | N | Y | N | N |
| **UTAH** | | | | | | |
| Hatch | – | Y | N | Y | N | N |
| Bennett | N | Y | N | Y | N | N |
| **VERMONT** | | | | | | |
| Leahy | Y | N | Y | Y | N | Y |
| Jeffords | Y | N | Y | Y | Y | Y |
| **VIRGINIA** | | | | | | |
| Warner | N | Y | N | Y | N | N |
| Allen | N | Y | N | Y | N | N |
| **WASHINGTON** | | | | | | |
| Murray | Y | N | Y | Y | Y | Y |
| Cantwell | Y | N | Y | Y | Y | Y |
| **WEST VIRGINIA** | | | | | | |
| Byrd | N | N | Y | Y | N | Y |
| Rockefeller | N | N | Y | Y | N | Y |
| **WISCONSIN** | | | | | | |
| Kohl | Y | N | Y | Y | Y | Y |
| Feingold | Y | N | Y | Y | N | Y |
| **WYOMING** | | | | | | |
| Thomas | N | Y | N | Y | N | N |
| Enzi | N | Y | N | Y | N | N |

**KEY**    **Republicans**    Democrats    *Independents*

| | | | | | |
|---|---|---|---|---|---|
| **Y** | Voted for (yea) | **X** | Paired against | **C** | Voted "present" to avoid possible conflict of interest |
| **#** | Paired for | **–** | Announced against | | |
| **+** | Announced for | **P** | Voted "present" | **?** | Did not vote or otherwise make a position known |
| **N** | Voted against (nay) | | | | |

ND Northern Democrats, SD Southern Democrats
Southern states: Ala., Ark., Fla., Ga., Ky., La., Miss., N.C., Okla., S.C., Tenn., Texas, Va.

# IN THE SENATE | By Vote Number

**310.** **S 1042. Fiscal 2006 Defense Authorization/Management Study.**
Byrd, D-W.Va., amendment that would authorize a feasibility study on creating a deputy secretary of Defense for management to oversee the spending and financial management at the Defense Department. Adopted 97-0: R 54-0; D 42-0 (ND 38-0, SD 4-0); I 1-0. Nov. 8, 2005.

**311.** **S 1042. Fiscal 2006 Defense Authorization/Cooperative Threat Reduction Funding.** Reed, D-R.I., amendment that would move $50 million from missile defense accounts to the Cooperative Threat Reduction program. Rejected 37-60: R 2-52; D 34-8 (ND 30-8, SD 4-0); I 1-0. Nov. 8, 2005.

**312.** **S 1042. Fiscal 2006 Defense Authorization/Prayer at Service Academies.** Inhofe, R-Okla., amendment that would grant the superintendent of each institution the authority for setting rules for offering non-denominational, voluntary prayer at the U.S. military service academies. Adopted 99-0: R 55-0; D 43-0 (ND 39-0, SD 4-0); I 1-0. Nov. 9, 2005.

**313.** **S 1042. Fiscal 2006 Defense Authorization/Tear Gas.** Ensign, R-Nev., amendment that would state that it is U.S. policy that tear gas and other non-lethal riot-control agents are not chemical weapons and that they should be permitted for use by the military in combat situations. Adopted 98-1: R 55-0; D 42-1 (ND 38-1, SD 4-0); I 1-0. Nov. 9, 2005.

**314.** **S 1042. Fiscal 2006 Defense Authorization/Reserve Retirement.**
Chambliss, R-Ga., amendment that would create a formula for reducing the eligibility age for reservists to receive retiree benefits based on the amount of time served in an active-duty capacity. Reservists would be able to receive retirement pay no earlier than age 50. Adopted 99-0: R 55-0; D 43-0 (ND 39-0, SD 4-0); I 1-0. Nov. 9, 2005.

**315.** **S 1042. Fiscal 2006 Defense Authorization/Reserve Retirement.**
Durbin, D-Ill., amendment that would create a formula for reducing the eligibility age for reservists to receive retiree benefits based on the amount of time served in an active-duty capacity. Rejected 40-59: R 0-55; D 39-4 (ND 35-4, SD 4-0); I 1-0. Nov. 9, 2005.

| | 310 | 311 | 312 | 313 | 314 | 315 |
|---|---|---|---|---|---|---|
| **ALABAMA** | | | | | | |
| Shelby | Y | N | Y | Y | Y | N |
| Sessions | Y | N | Y | Y | Y | N |
| **ALASKA** | | | | | | |
| Stevens | Y | N | Y | Y | Y | N |
| Murkowski | Y | N | Y | Y | Y | N |
| **ARIZONA** | | | | | | |
| McCain | ? | ? | Y | Y | Y | N |
| Kyl | Y | N | Y | Y | Y | N |
| **ARKANSAS** | | | | | | |
| Lincoln | Y | Y | Y | Y | Y | Y |
| Pryor | Y | Y | Y | Y | Y | Y |
| **CALIFORNIA** | | | | | | |
| Feinstein | Y | Y | Y | Y | Y | Y |
| Boxer | Y | Y | Y | Y | Y | Y |
| **COLORADO** | | | | | | |
| Allard | Y | N | Y | Y | Y | N |
| Salazar | Y | N | Y | Y | Y | Y |
| **CONNECTICUT** | | | | | | |
| Dodd | Y | Y | Y | Y | Y | Y |
| Lieberman | Y | N | Y | Y | Y | Y |
| **DELAWARE** | | | | | | |
| Biden | Y | Y | Y | Y | Y | Y |
| Carper | Y | Y | Y | Y | Y | N |
| **FLORIDA** | | | | | | |
| Nelson | Y | Y | Y | Y | Y | Y |
| Martinez | Y | N | Y | Y | Y | N |
| **GEORGIA** | | | | | | |
| Chambliss | Y | N | Y | Y | Y | N |
| Isakson | Y | N | Y | Y | Y | N |
| **HAWAII** | | | | | | |
| Inouye | Y | N | Y | Y | Y | Y |
| Akaka | Y | N | Y | Y | Y | Y |
| **IDAHO** | | | | | | |
| Craig | Y | N | Y | Y | Y | N |
| Crapo | Y | N | Y | Y | Y | N |
| **ILLINOIS** | | | | | | |
| Durbin | Y | Y | Y | Y | Y | Y |
| Obama | Y | Y | Y | Y | Y | Y |
| **INDIANA** | | | | | | |
| Lugar | Y | Y | Y | Y | Y | N |
| Bayh | Y | N | Y | Y | Y | Y |
| **IOWA** | | | | | | |
| Grassley | Y | N | Y | Y | Y | N |
| Harkin | Y | Y | Y | N | Y | Y |
| **KANSAS** | | | | | | |
| Brownback | Y | N | Y | Y | Y | N |
| Roberts | Y | N | Y | Y | Y | N |
| **KENTUCKY** | | | | | | |
| McConnell | Y | N | Y | Y | Y | N |
| Bunning | Y | N | Y | Y | Y | N |
| **LOUISIANA** | | | | | | |
| Landrieu | Y | Y | Y | Y | Y | Y |
| Vitter | Y | N | Y | Y | Y | N |
| **MAINE** | | | | | | |
| Snowe | Y | N | Y | Y | Y | N |
| Collins | Y | N | Y | Y | Y | N |
| **MARYLAND** | | | | | | |
| Sarbanes | Y | Y | Y | Y | Y | Y |
| Mikulski | Y | Y | Y | Y | Y | Y |
| **MASSACHUSETTS** | | | | | | |
| Kennedy | Y | Y | Y | Y | Y | Y |
| Kerry | Y | Y | Y | Y | Y | Y |
| **MICHIGAN** | | | | | | |
| Levin | Y | Y | Y | Y | Y | Y |
| Stabenow | Y | Y | Y | Y | Y | Y |
| **MINNESOTA** | | | | | | |
| Dayton | Y | N | Y | Y | Y | Y |
| Coleman | Y | N | Y | Y | Y | N |
| **MISSISSIPPI** | | | | | | |
| Cochran | Y | N | Y | Y | Y | N |
| Lott | Y | N | Y | Y | Y | N |
| **MISSOURI** | | | | | | |
| Bond | Y | N | Y | Y | Y | N |
| Talent | Y | N | Y | Y | Y | N |
| **MONTANA** | | | | | | |
| Baucus | Y | N | Y | Y | Y | N |
| Burns | Y | N | Y | Y | Y | N |
| **NEBRASKA** | | | | | | |
| Hagel | Y | N | Y | Y | Y | N |
| Nelson | Y | N | Y | Y | Y | N |
| **NEVADA** | | | | | | |
| Reid | Y | Y | Y | Y | Y | Y |
| Ensign | Y | N | Y | Y | Y | N |
| **NEW HAMPSHIRE** | | | | | | |
| Gregg | Y | N | Y | Y | Y | N |
| Sununu | Y | N | Y | Y | Y | N |
| **NEW JERSEY** | | | | | | |
| Corzine | ? | ? | ? | ? | ? | ? |
| Lautenberg | ? | ? | Y | Y | Y | Y |
| **NEW MEXICO** | | | | | | |
| Domenici | Y | N | Y | Y | Y | N |
| Bingaman | Y | Y | Y | Y | Y | Y |
| **NEW YORK** | | | | | | |
| Schumer | Y | Y | Y | Y | Y | Y |
| Clinton | Y | Y | Y | Y | Y | Y |
| **NORTH CAROLINA** | | | | | | |
| Dole | Y | N | Y | Y | Y | N |
| Burr | Y | N | Y | Y | Y | N |
| **NORTH DAKOTA** | | | | | | |
| Conrad | Y | Y | Y | Y | Y | N |
| Dorgan | Y | Y | Y | Y | Y | Y |
| **OHIO** | | | | | | |
| DeWine | Y | N | Y | Y | Y | N |
| Voinovich | Y | N | Y | Y | Y | N |
| **OKLAHOMA** | | | | | | |
| Inhofe | Y | N | Y | Y | Y | N |
| Coburn | Y | N | Y | Y | Y | N |
| **OREGON** | | | | | | |
| Wyden | Y | Y | Y | Y | Y | Y |
| Smith | Y | N | Y | Y | Y | N |
| **PENNSYLVANIA** | | | | | | |
| Specter | Y | N | Y | Y | Y | N |
| Santorum | Y | N | Y | Y | Y | N |
| **RHODE ISLAND** | | | | | | |
| Reed | Y | Y | Y | Y | Y | Y |
| Chafee | Y | Y | Y | Y | Y | N |
| **SOUTH CAROLINA** | | | | | | |
| Graham | Y | N | Y | Y | Y | N |
| DeMint | Y | N | Y | Y | Y | N |
| **SOUTH DAKOTA** | | | | | | |
| Johnson | Y | Y | Y | Y | Y | Y |
| Thune | Y | N | Y | Y | Y | N |
| **TENNESSEE** | | | | | | |
| Frist | Y | N | Y | Y | Y | N |
| Alexander | Y | N | Y | Y | Y | N |
| **TEXAS** | | | | | | |
| Hutchison | Y | N | Y | Y | Y | N |
| Cornyn | Y | N | Y | Y | Y | N |
| **UTAH** | | | | | | |
| Hatch | Y | N | Y | Y | Y | N |
| Bennett | Y | N | Y | Y | Y | N |
| **VERMONT** | | | | | | |
| Leahy | Y | Y | Y | Y | Y | Y |
| Jeffords | Y | Y | Y | Y | Y | Y |
| **VIRGINIA** | | | | | | |
| Warner | Y | N | Y | Y | Y | N |
| Allen | Y | N | Y | Y | Y | N |
| **WASHINGTON** | | | | | | |
| Murray | Y | Y | Y | Y | Y | Y |
| Cantwell | Y | Y | Y | Y | Y | Y |
| **WEST VIRGINIA** | | | | | | |
| Byrd | Y | Y | Y | Y | Y | Y |
| Rockefeller | Y | Y | Y | Y | Y | Y |
| **WISCONSIN** | | | | | | |
| Kohl | Y | Y | Y | Y | Y | Y |
| Feingold | Y | Y | Y | Y | Y | Y |
| **WYOMING** | | | | | | |
| Thomas | Y | N | Y | Y | Y | N |
| Enzi | Y | N | Y | Y | Y | N |

**KEY**    Republicans    Democrats    *Independents*

| | | | |
|---|---|---|---|
| Y | Voted for (yea) | X | Paired against |
| # | Paired for | – | Announced against |
| + | Announced for | P | Voted "present" |
| N | Voted against (nay) | | |

C   Voted "present" to avoid possible conflict of interest
?   Did not vote or otherwise make a position known

ND Northern Democrats, SD Southern Democrats
Southern states: Ala., Ark., Fla., Ga., Ky., La., Miss., N.C., Okla., S.C., Tenn., Texas, Va.

# IN THE SENATE | By Vote Number

**316.** **S 1042. Fiscal 2006 Defense Authorization/Contracting Investigation.** Dorgan, D-N.D., amendment that would establish a special Senate committee to investigate the awarding and carrying out of contracts in Afghanistan and Iraq. Rejected 44-53: R 1-53; D 42-0 (ND 38-0, SD 4-0); I 1-0. Nov. 10, 2005.

**317.** **S 1042. Fiscal 2006 Defense Authorization/C-17 Cargo Planes.** Talent, R-Mo., amendment that would permit the Air Force to enter into contracts for advanced procurement for up to 42 C-17 Globemaster III cargo planes. Adopted 89-8: R 48-6; D 40-2 (ND 36-2, SD 4-0); I 1-0. Nov. 10, 2005.

**318.** **S 1042. Fiscal 2006 Defense Authorization/Reports on Detainee Camps.** Kerry, D-Mass., amendment that would require the Defense secretary and the director of National Intelligence to submit reports within 60 days of the bill's enactment on clandestine U.S. detention facilities abroad. Adopted 82-9: R 39-9; D 42-0 (ND 38-0, SD 4-0); I 1-0. Nov. 10, 2005.

**319.** **S 1042. Fiscal 2006 Defense Authorization/Habeas Corpus and Guantánamo Bay.** Graham, R-S.C., substitute amendment to the Graham amendment. The substitute amendment would make the underlying amendment effective one day after the bill's enactment. The underlying amendment would deny non-citizens held at Guantánamo Bay, Cuba, habeas corpus access to U.S. civilian courts to contest their detention or conviction. It would allow one appellate court review of any military tribunal decision to detain prisoners under Defense Department procedure. It also would require the Defense Secretary to submit a report to Congress detailing review procedures at Guantánamo Bay. Adopted 49-42: R 44-4; D 5-37 (ND 4-34, SD 1-3); I 0-1. Nov. 10, 2005.

**320.** **HR 3057. Fiscal 2006 Foreign Operations Appropriations/ Conference Report.** Adoption of the conference report on the bill that would provide $21 billion in fiscal 2006 for foreign operations and related programs, including $2.8 billion to fight HIV/AIDS, tuberculosis and malaria; $1.8 billion for the Millennium Challenge Corporation; and $1.6 billion for the Child Survival and Health Programs Fund. Adopted (thus cleared for the president) 91-0: R 48-0; D 42-0 (ND 38-0, SD 4-0); I 1-0. Nov. 10, 2005.

| | 316 | 317 | 318 | 319 | 320 |
|---|---|---|---|---|---|
| **ALABAMA** | | | | | |
| Shelby | N | Y | Y | Y | Y |
| Sessions | N | N | N | Y | Y |
| **ALASKA** | | | | | |
| Stevens | N | Y | N | Y | Y |
| Murkowski | N | Y | Y | Y | Y |
| **ARIZONA** | | | | | |
| McCain | N | N | Y | Y | Y |
| Kyl | N | N | N | Y | Y |
| **ARKANSAS** | | | | | |
| Lincoln | Y | Y | Y | N | Y |
| Pryor | Y | Y | Y | N | Y |
| **CALIFORNIA** | | | | | |
| Feinstein | Y | Y | Y | N | Y |
| Boxer | Y | Y | Y | N | Y |
| **COLORADO** | | | | | |
| Allard | N | N | Y | Y | Y |
| Salazar | Y | Y | Y | N | Y |
| **CONNECTICUT** | | | | | |
| Dodd | Y | Y | Y | N | Y |
| Lieberman | Y | Y | Y | Y | Y |
| **DELAWARE** | | | | | |
| Biden | Y | Y | Y | N | Y |
| Carper | Y | Y | Y | N | Y |
| **FLORIDA** | | | | | |
| Nelson | Y | Y | Y | N | Y |
| Martinez | N | Y | N | Y | Y |
| **GEORGIA** | | | | | |
| Chambliss | N | Y | N | Y | Y |
| Isakson | N | Y | N | Y | Y |
| **HAWAII** | | | | | |
| Inouye | ? | ? | ? | ? | ? |
| Akaka | Y | Y | Y | N | Y |
| **IDAHO** | | | | | |
| Craig | N | Y | Y | Y | Y |
| Crapo | N | Y | Y | Y | Y |
| **ILLINOIS** | | | | | |
| Durbin | Y | Y | Y | N | Y |
| Obama | Y | Y | Y | N | Y |
| **INDIANA** | | | | | |
| Lugar | N | Y | ? | ? | ? |
| Bayh | Y | Y | Y | N | Y |
| **IOWA** | | | | | |
| Grassley | N | Y | Y | Y | Y |
| Harkin | Y | Y | Y | N | Y |
| **KANSAS** | | | | | |
| Brownback | N | Y | Y | Y | Y |
| Roberts | N | Y | Y | Y | Y |
| **KENTUCKY** | | | | | |
| McConnell | N | Y | Y | Y | Y |
| Bunning | N | Y | Y | Y | Y |
| **LOUISIANA** | | | | | |
| Landrieu | Y | Y | Y | Y | Y |
| Vitter | N | Y | N | Y | Y |
| **MAINE** | | | | | |
| Snowe | N | Y | Y | Y | Y |
| Collins | N | Y | Y | Y | Y |
| **MARYLAND** | | | | | |
| Sarbanes | Y | Y | Y | N | Y |
| Mikulski | Y | Y | Y | N | Y |
| **MASSACHUSETTS** | | | | | |
| Kennedy | Y | Y | Y | N | Y |
| Kerry | Y | Y | Y | N | Y |
| **MICHIGAN** | | | | | |
| Levin | Y | Y | Y | N | Y |
| Stabenow | Y | Y | Y | N | Y |
| **MINNESOTA** | | | | | |
| Dayton | Y | Y | Y | N | Y |
| Coleman | N | Y | Y | Y | Y |
| **MISSISSIPPI** | | | | | |
| Cochran | N | Y | Y | Y | Y |
| Lott | N | Y | Y | Y | Y |
| **MISSOURI** | | | | | |
| Bond | N | Y | Y | Y | Y |
| Talent | N | Y | Y | Y | Y |
| **MONTANA** | | | | | |
| Baucus | Y | Y | Y | N | Y |
| Burns | N | Y | Y | Y | Y |
| **NEBRASKA** | | | | | |
| Hagel | N | Y | ? | ? | ? |
| Nelson | Y | Y | Y | Y | Y |
| **NEVADA** | | | | | |
| Reid | Y | Y | Y | N | Y |
| Ensign | N | Y | Y | Y | Y |
| **NEW HAMPSHIRE** | | | | | |
| Gregg | N | Y | Y | Y | Y |
| Sununu | N | N | N | Y | Y |
| **NEW JERSEY** | | | | | |
| Corzine | ? | ? | ? | ? | ? |
| Lautenberg | Y | Y | Y | N | Y |
| **NEW MEXICO** | | | | | |
| Domenici | N | Y | ? | ? | ? |
| Bingaman | Y | Y | Y | N | Y |
| **NEW YORK** | | | | | |
| Schumer | Y | Y | Y | N | Y |
| Clinton | Y | Y | Y | N | Y |
| **NORTH CAROLINA** | | | | | |
| Dole | N | Y | Y | Y | Y |
| Burr | N | Y | N | Y | Y |
| **NORTH DAKOTA** | | | | | |
| Conrad | Y | Y | Y | Y | Y |
| Dorgan | Y | Y | Y | N | Y |
| **OHIO** | | | | | |
| DeWine | N | Y | Y | Y | Y |
| Voinovich | N | Y | Y | Y | Y |
| **OKLAHOMA** | | | | | |
| Inhofe | N | Y | Y | Y | Y |
| Coburn | N | Y | Y | Y | Y |
| **OREGON** | | | | | |
| Wyden | Y | Y | Y | N | Y |
| Smith | N | Y | Y | N | Y |
| **PENNSYLVANIA** | | | | | |
| Specter | N | Y | Y | N | Y |
| Santorum | N | Y | ? | ? | ? |
| **RHODE ISLAND** | | | | | |
| Reed | Y | Y | Y | N | Y |
| Chafee | Y | Y | Y | N | Y |
| **SOUTH CAROLINA** | | | | | |
| Graham | N | Y | Y | Y | Y |
| DeMint | N | Y | N | Y | Y |
| **SOUTH DAKOTA** | | | | | |
| Johnson | Y | Y | Y | N | Y |
| Thune | N | Y | Y | Y | Y |
| **TENNESSEE** | | | | | |
| Frist | N | Y | Y | Y | Y |
| Alexander | ? | ? | ? | ? | ? |
| **TEXAS** | | | | | |
| Hutchison | N | Y | Y | Y | Y |
| Cornyn | N | Y | Y | Y | Y |
| **UTAH** | | | | | |
| Hatch | N | Y | Y | Y | Y |
| Bennett | N | Y | Y | Y | Y |
| **VERMONT** | | | | | |
| Leahy | Y | Y | Y | N | Y |
| Jeffords | Y | Y | Y | N | Y |
| **VIRGINIA** | | | | | |
| Warner | N | Y | Y | Y | Y |
| Allen | N | Y | Y | Y | Y |
| **WASHINGTON** | | | | | |
| Murray | Y | Y | Y | N | Y |
| Cantwell | Y | Y | Y | N | Y |
| **WEST VIRGINIA** | | | | | |
| Byrd | Y | Y | Y | N | Y |
| Rockefeller | Y | Y | Y | N | Y |
| **WISCONSIN** | | | | | |
| Kohl | Y | N | Y | N | Y |
| Feingold | Y | N | Y | N | Y |
| **WYOMING** | | | | | |
| Thomas | N | N | ? | ? | ? |
| Enzi | N | Y | ? | ? | ? |

**KEY**   Republicans   Democrats   *Independents*

| | | | |
|---|---|---|---|
| **Y** | Voted for (yea) | **X** | Paired against |
| **#** | Paired for | **–** | Announced against |
| **+** | Announced for | **P** | Voted "present" |
| **N** | Voted against (nay) | | |

| | |
|---|---|
| **C** | Voted "present" to avoid possible conflict of interest |
| **?** | Did not vote or otherwise make a position known |

ND Northern Democrats, SD Southern Democrats
Southern states: Ala., Ark., Fla., Ga., Ky., La., Miss., N.C., Okla., S.C., Tenn., Texas, Va.

# IN THE SENATE | By Vote Number

**321.** **HR 2419. Fiscal 2006 Energy-Water Appropriations/Conference Report.** Adoption of the conference report on the bill that would provide $30.5 billion in fiscal 2006 for energy and water development projects, including $24.3 billion for the Energy Department, $5.4 billion for the Army Corps of Engineers and $1.1 billion for Interior Department water projects. Adopted (thus cleared for the president) 84-4: R 48-2; D 35-2 (ND 31-2, SD 4-0); I 1-0. Nov. 14, 2005.

**322.** **S 1042. Fiscal 2006 Defense Authorization/Iraq Withdrawal.** Levin, D-Mich., amendment that would state that U.S. military forces should not stay in Iraq indefinitely and require the president to report to Congress within 30 days of the bill's enactment with a timetable for withdrawal and a campaign plan, including dates, outlining phased redeployment of U.S. troops from Iraq. Rejected 40-58: R 1-53; D 38-5 (ND 36-3, SD 2-2); I 1-0. Nov. 15, 2005.

**323.** **S 1042. Fiscal 2006 Defense Authorization/Iraq Withdrawal.** Warner, R-Va., amendment that would require the president to submit an unclassified report to Congress on U.S. policy and operations in Iraq 90 days after enactment and every three months thereafter. It would also state that 2006 should be a period of significant transition to Iraqi sovereignty, that U.S. forces should not remain in Iraq any longer than necessary, and that the Bush administration needs to explain to Congress and the American public the strategy for completing the Iraq mission. Adopted 79-19: R 41-13; D 37-6 (ND 33-6, SD 4-0); I 1-0. Nov. 15, 2005.

**324.** **S 1042. Fiscal 2006 Defense Authorization/Habeas Corpus.** Bingaman, D-N.M., amendment to the Graham, R-S.C., amendment. The Bingaman amendment would grant detainees and enemy combatants the right to petition for habeas corpus in the U.S. Circuit Court of Appeals for the District of Columbia, provided a review tribunal has been conducted. The Graham amendment would deny non-citizens held at Guantánamo Bay, Cuba, habeas corpus access to U.S. civilian courts to contest their detention or conviction. It would allow one appellate court review of any military tribunal decision to detain prisoners under Defense Department procedure. It also would require the Defense secretary to submit a report to Congress detailing procedures at Guantánamo Bay. Rejected 44-54: R 4-50; D 39-4 (ND 35-4, SD 4-0); I 1-0. Nov. 15, 2005.

**325.** **S 1042. Fiscal 2006 Defense Authorization/Habeas Corpus.** Graham, R-S.C., amendment to the Graham amendment. The second-degree amendment would prevent Combatant Status Review Tribunals from considering statements obtained under undue coercion. It also would establish a "designated civilian official," appointed by the president with the advice and consent of the Senate, to oversee the release of detainees. Adopted 84-14: R 53-1; D 30-13 (ND 26-13, SD 4-0); I 1-0. (Subsequently, the underlying Graham amendment, as modified, was adopted by voice vote.) Nov. 15, 2005.

| | 321 | 322 | 323 | 324 | 325 |
|---|---|---|---|---|---|
| **ALABAMA** | | | | | |
| Shelby | Y | N | Y | N | Y |
| Sessions | Y | N | N | N | Y |
| **ALASKA** | | | | | |
| Stevens | Y | N | Y | N | Y |
| Murkowski | ? | N | Y | N | Y |
| **ARIZONA** | | | | | |
| McCain | ? | N | N | N | Y |
| Kyl | Y | N | N | N | Y |
| **ARKANSAS** | | | | | |
| Lincoln | Y | Y | Y | Y | Y |
| Pryor | Y | N | Y | Y | Y |
| **CALIFORNIA** | | | | | |
| Feinstein | Y | Y | Y | Y | Y |
| Boxer | ? | Y | Y | Y | Y |
| **COLORADO** | | | | | |
| Allard | Y | N | Y | N | Y |
| Salazar | Y | Y | Y | Y | Y |
| **CONNECTICUT** | | | | | |
| Dodd | Y | Y | Y | Y | Y |
| Lieberman | Y | N | Y | N | Y |
| **DELAWARE** | | | | | |
| Biden | ? | Y | Y | Y | N |
| Carper | Y | Y | Y | Y | Y |
| **FLORIDA** | | | | | |
| Nelson | Y | N | Y | Y | Y |
| Martinez | Y | N | Y | N | Y |
| **GEORGIA** | | | | | |
| Chambliss | Y | N | N | N | Y |
| Isakson | Y | N | N | N | Y |
| **HAWAII** | | | | | |
| Inouye | Y | Y | Y | Y | Y |
| Akaka | Y | Y | Y | Y | Y |
| **IDAHO** | | | | | |
| Craig | Y | N | Y | N | Y |
| Crapo | Y | N | Y | N | Y |
| **ILLINOIS** | | | | | |
| Durbin | Y | Y | Y | Y | N |
| Obama | Y | Y | Y | Y | Y |
| **INDIANA** | | | | | |
| Lugar | Y | N | Y | N | Y |
| Bayh | ? | Y | Y | N | Y |
| **IOWA** | | | | | |
| Grassley | Y | N | Y | N | Y |
| Harkin | Y | Y | N | Y | N |
| **KANSAS** | | | | | |
| Brownback | Y | N | Y | N | Y |
| Roberts | Y | N | Y | N | Y |
| **KENTUCKY** | | | | | |
| McConnell | Y | N | Y | N | Y |
| Bunning | Y | N | N | N | Y |
| **LOUISIANA** | | | | | |
| Landrieu | Y | Y | Y | Y | Y |
| Vitter | Y | N | N | N | Y |
| **MAINE** | | | | | |
| Snowe | Y | N | Y | N | Y |
| Collins | Y | N | Y | N | Y |
| **MARYLAND** | | | | | |
| Sarbanes | Y | Y | Y | Y | N |
| Mikulski | Y | Y | Y | Y | Y |
| **MASSACHUSETTS** | | | | | |
| Kennedy | ? | Y | N | Y | N |
| Kerry | Y | Y | N | Y | Y |
| **MICHIGAN** | | | | | |
| Levin | Y | Y | Y | Y | Y |
| Stabenow | Y | Y | Y | Y | Y |
| **MINNESOTA** | | | | | |
| Dayton | Y | Y | Y | Y | N |
| Coleman | Y | N | Y | N | Y |
| **MISSISSIPPI** | | | | | |
| Cochran | Y | N | Y | N | Y |
| Lott | Y | N | Y | N | Y |
| **MISSOURI** | | | | | |
| Bond | Y | N | Y | N | Y |
| Talent | Y | N | Y | N | Y |

| | 321 | 322 | 323 | 324 | 325 |
|---|---|---|---|---|---|
| **MONTANA** | | | | | |
| Baucus | Y | Y | Y | Y | N |
| Burns | + | N | Y | N | Y |
| **NEBRASKA** | | | | | |
| Hagel | Y | N | Y | N | Y |
| Nelson | Y | N | Y | N | Y |
| **NEVADA** | | | | | |
| Reid | Y | Y | Y | Y | Y |
| Ensign | Y | N | Y | N | Y |
| **NEW HAMPSHIRE** | | | | | |
| Gregg | Y | N | Y | N | Y |
| Sununu | N | N | Y | Y | Y |
| **NEW JERSEY** | | | | | |
| Corzine | ? | ? | ? | ? | ? |
| Lautenberg | Y | Y | Y | Y | N |
| **NEW MEXICO** | | | | | |
| Domenici | Y | N | Y | N | Y |
| Bingaman | Y | Y | Y | Y | N |
| **NEW YORK** | | | | | |
| Schumer | N | Y | Y | Y | Y |
| Clinton | ? | Y | Y | Y | Y |
| **NORTH CAROLINA** | | | | | |
| Dole | Y | N | N | N | Y |
| Burr | ? | N | N | N | Y |
| **NORTH DAKOTA** | | | | | |
| Conrad | Y | N | N | N | Y |
| Dorgan | Y | Y | Y | Y | Y |
| **OHIO** | | | | | |
| DeWine | Y | N | Y | N | Y |
| Voinovich | Y | N | Y | N | Y |
| **OKLAHOMA** | | | | | |
| Inhofe | Y | N | N | N | Y |
| Coburn | N | N | N | N | Y |
| **OREGON** | | | | | |
| Wyden | Y | Y | Y | Y | Y |
| Smith | Y | N | Y | Y | Y |
| **PENNSYLVANIA** | | | | | |
| Specter | Y | N | Y | N | N |
| Santorum | Y | N | Y | N | Y |
| **RHODE ISLAND** | | | | | |
| Reed | Y | Y | Y | Y | Y |
| Chafee | Y | Y | Y | Y | Y |
| **SOUTH CAROLINA** | | | | | |
| Graham | Y | N | N | N | Y |
| DeMint | Y | N | N | N | Y |
| **SOUTH DAKOTA** | | | | | |
| Johnson | Y | Y | Y | Y | Y |
| Thune | Y | N | N | N | Y |
| **TENNESSEE** | | | | | |
| Frist | Y | N | Y | N | Y |
| Alexander | Y | - | + | - | + |
| **TEXAS** | | | | | |
| Hutchison | Y | N | Y | N | Y |
| Cornyn | + | N | Y | N | Y |
| **UTAH** | | | | | |
| Hatch | Y | N | Y | N | Y |
| Bennett | Y | N | Y | N | Y |
| **VERMONT** | | | | | |
| Leahy | Y | Y | N | Y | N |
| Jeffords | Y | Y | Y | Y | Y |
| **VIRGINIA** | | | | | |
| Warner | Y | N | Y | N | Y |
| Allen | Y | N | Y | N | Y |
| **WASHINGTON** | | | | | |
| Murray | Y | Y | Y | Y | Y |
| Cantwell | Y | Y | Y | Y | Y |
| **WEST VIRGINIA** | | | | | |
| Byrd | ? | Y | N | Y | N |
| Rockefeller | Y | Y | Y | Y | N |
| **WISCONSIN** | | | | | |
| Kohl | Y | Y | Y | Y | Y |
| Feingold | N | Y | Y | Y | N |
| **WYOMING** | | | | | |
| Thomas | Y | N | Y | N | Y |
| Enzi | Y | N | Y | N | Y |

**KEY**    Republicans    Democrats    *Independents*

| | | |
|---|---|---|
| Y Voted for (yea) | X Paired against | C Voted "present" to avoid possible conflict of interest |
| # Paired for | − Announced against | |
| + Announced for | P Voted "present" | ? Did not vote or otherwise make a position known |
| N Voted against (nay) | | |

ND Northern Democrats, SD Southern Democrats
Southern states: Ala., Ark., Fla., Ga., Ky., La., Miss., N.C., Okla., S.C., Tenn., Texas, Va.

# IN THE SENATE | By Vote Number

**326.** S 1042. Fiscal 2006 Defense Authorization/Passage. Passage of the bill that would authorize $491.6 billion for fiscal 2006 defense spending, including a $50 billion bridge supplemental for war costs in Iraq and Afghanistan; $109.2 billion for military personnel; $78.2 billion for procurement; $69.8 billion for research, development, testing and evaluation; and $1.6 billion for Energy department non-proliferation programs. Passed 98-0: R 54-0; D 43-0 (ND 39-0, SD 4-0); I 1-0. Nov. 15, 2005.

**327.** S 1783. Pension Overhaul/Airline Pilot Annuity Benefits. Akaka, D-Hawaii, amendment that would calculate the actuarial value of monthly life annuity benefits beginning at age 60 for airline pilots. Adopted 58-41: R 16-39; D 41-2 (ND 37-2, SD 4-0); I 1-0. Nov. 16, 2005.

**328.** S 1783. Pension Overhaul/Passage. Passage of the bill that would overhaul pension funding rules by requiring companies to use a modified yield curve to determine their plan's funding status and to fund 100 percent of their pension obligations. Companies with underfunded plans would have seven years to make up any underfunding. Annual per-employee premiums would increase to $30 from $19 starting in 2006. Passed 97-2: R 55-0; D 41-2 (ND 37-2, SD 4-0); I 1-0. Nov. 16, 2005.

**329.** HR 2862. Fiscal 2006 Commerce-Justice-Science Appropriations/Conference Report. Adoption of the conference report on the bill that would provide $61.8 billion, including $57.9 billion in discretionary funding, in fiscal 2006 for the departments of Commerce, Justice and State, as well as various science and other related agencies. It would provide $21.7 billion for Justice, $6.6 billion for Commerce and $9.7 billion for the State Department and international broadcasting agencies. It also would appropriate $16.5 billion for NASA and $5.6 billion for the National Science Foundation. Adopted (thus cleared for the president) 94-5: R 53-2; D 40-3 (ND 36-3, SD 4-0); I 1-0. Nov. 16, 2005.

**330.** S 2020. Fiscal 2006 Tax Reconciliation/2005 Tax Cut Extension. Conrad, D-N.D., motion to waive the Budget Act with respect to the Grassley, R-Iowa, point of order against the Conrad amendment. The Conrad amendment would extend only the tax cuts that expire in 2005, offsetting the cost by altering other tax provisions. Motion rejected 44-55: R 2-53; D 41-2 (ND 38-1, SD 3-1); I 1-0. A three-fifths majority vote (60) of the total Senate is required to waive the Budget Act. (Subsequently, the chair upheld the point of order, and the amendment fell.) Nov. 17, 2005.

**331.** S 2020. Fiscal 2006 Tax Reconciliation/Windfall Profits. Dorgan, D-N.D., motion to waive the Budget Act with respect to the Grassley, R-Iowa, point of order against the Dorgan amendment. The Dorgan amendment would impose a temporary 50 percent tax on oil company profits from the sale of crude oil. Funds from the tax would be used to provide a consumer tax credit for petroleum products. Motion rejected 35-64: R 0-55; D 34-9 (ND 33-6, SD 1-3); I 1-0. A three-fifths majority vote (60) of the total Senate is required to waive the Budget Act. (Subsequently, the chair upheld the point of order, and the amendment fell.) Nov. 17, 2005.

| State / Senator | 326 | 327 | 328 | 329 | 330 | 331 |
|---|---|---|---|---|---|---|
| **ALABAMA** Shelby | Y | N | Y | Y | N | N |
| Sessions | Y | N | Y | Y | N | N |
| **ALASKA** Stevens | Y | N | Y | Y | N | N |
| Murkowski | Y | N | Y | Y | N | N |
| **ARIZONA** McCain | Y | N | Y | Y | N | N |
| Kyl | Y | N | Y | Y | N | N |
| **ARKANSAS** Lincoln | Y | Y | Y | Y | Y | N |
| Pryor | Y | Y | Y | Y | Y | N |
| **CALIFORNIA** Feinstein | Y | Y | Y | Y | Y | Y |
| Boxer | Y | Y | Y | Y | Y | Y |
| **COLORADO** Allard | Y | N | Y | Y | N | N |
| Salazar | Y | Y | Y | Y | Y | N |
| **CONNECTICUT** Dodd | Y | Y | Y | Y | Y | Y |
| Lieberman | Y | Y | Y | Y | Y | Y |
| **DELAWARE** Biden | Y | Y | Y | Y | Y | Y |
| Carper | Y | Y | Y | Y | N | Y |
| **FLORIDA** Nelson | Y | Y | Y | Y | Y | Y |
| Martinez | Y | N | Y | Y | N | N |
| **GEORGIA** Chambliss | Y | Y | Y | Y | N | N |
| Isakson | Y | Y | Y | Y | N | N |
| **HAWAII** Inouye | Y | Y | Y | Y | Y | Y |
| Akaka | Y | Y | Y | Y | Y | Y |
| **IDAHO** Craig | Y | N | Y | Y | N | N |
| Crapo | Y | N | Y | Y | N | N |
| **ILLINOIS** Durbin | Y | Y | Y | Y | Y | Y |
| Obama | Y | Y | Y | Y | Y | Y |
| **INDIANA** Lugar | Y | Y | Y | Y | N | N |
| Bayh | Y | Y | Y | Y | Y | Y |
| **IOWA** Grassley | Y | N | Y | Y | N | N |
| Harkin | Y | Y | Y | Y | Y | Y |
| **KANSAS** Brownback | Y | N | Y | Y | N | N |
| Roberts | Y | N | Y | Y | N | N |
| **KENTUCKY** McConnell | Y | N | Y | Y | N | N |
| Bunning | Y | N | Y | Y | N | N |
| **LOUISIANA** Landrieu | Y | Y | Y | Y | N | Y |
| Vitter | Y | N | Y | Y | N | N |
| **MAINE** Snowe | Y | N | Y | Y | N | N |
| Collins | Y | N | Y | Y | N | N |
| **MARYLAND** Sarbanes | Y | Y | Y | Y | Y | Y |
| Mikulski | Y | Y | Y | Y | Y | Y |
| **MASSACHUSETTS** Kennedy | Y | Y | Y | Y | Y | Y |
| Kerry | Y | Y | Y | Y | Y | Y |
| **MICHIGAN** Levin | Y | Y | N | Y | Y | Y |
| Stabenow | Y | Y | N | Y | Y | Y |
| **MINNESOTA** Dayton | Y | Y | Y | N | Y | Y |
| Coleman | Y | Y | Y | Y | N | N |
| **MISSISSIPPI** Cochran | Y | N | Y | Y | N | N |
| Lott | Y | N | Y | Y | N | N |
| **MISSOURI** Bond | Y | Y | Y | Y | N | N |
| Talent | Y | Y | Y | Y | N | N |

| State / Senator | 326 | 327 | 328 | 329 | 330 | 331 |
|---|---|---|---|---|---|---|
| **MONTANA** Baucus | Y | N | Y | N | Y | N |
| Burns | Y | N | Y | Y | N | N |
| **NEBRASKA** Hagel | Y | N | Y | Y | N | N |
| Nelson | Y | Y | Y | Y | Y | N |
| **NEVADA** Reid | Y | Y | Y | Y | Y | Y |
| Ensign | Y | N | Y | Y | N | N |
| **NEW HAMPSHIRE** Gregg | Y | N | Y | Y | N | N |
| Sununu | Y | N | Y | Y | N | N |
| **NEW JERSEY** Corzine | ? | ? | ? | ? | ? | ? |
| Lautenberg | Y | Y | Y | Y | Y | Y |
| **NEW MEXICO** Domenici | Y | N | Y | Y | N | N |
| Bingaman | Y | Y | Y | Y | Y | N |
| **NEW YORK** Schumer | Y | Y | Y | Y | Y | Y |
| Clinton | Y | Y | Y | Y | Y | Y |
| **NORTH CAROLINA** Dole | Y | Y | Y | Y | N | N |
| Burr | Y | Y | Y | Y | N | N |
| **NORTH DAKOTA** Conrad | Y | Y | Y | N | Y | Y |
| Dorgan | Y | Y | Y | Y | Y | Y |
| **OHIO** DeWine | Y | Y | Y | Y | N | N |
| Voinovich | Y | N | Y | Y | N | N |
| **OKLAHOMA** Inhofe | Y | N | Y | N | N | N |
| Coburn | Y | N | Y | N | N | N |
| **OREGON** Wyden | Y | Y | Y | Y | N | Y |
| Smith | Y | N | Y | Y | N | N |
| **PENNSYLVANIA** Specter | Y | Y | Y | Y | N | N |
| Santorum | Y | Y | Y | Y | N | N |
| **RHODE ISLAND** Reed | Y | Y | Y | Y | Y | Y |
| Chafee | Y | Y | Y | Y | Y | N |
| **SOUTH CAROLINA** Graham | Y | N | Y | Y | N | N |
| DeMint | Y | N | Y | Y | N | N |
| **SOUTH DAKOTA** Johnson | Y | Y | Y | Y | Y | Y |
| Thune | Y | N | Y | Y | N | N |
| **TENNESSEE** Frist | Y | N | Y | Y | N | N |
| Alexander | + | N | Y | Y | N | N |
| **TEXAS** Hutchison | Y | N | Y | Y | N | N |
| Cornyn | Y | N | Y | Y | N | N |
| **UTAH** Hatch | Y | Y | Y | Y | N | N |
| Bennett | Y | Y | Y | Y | N | N |
| **VERMONT** Leahy | Y | Y | Y | Y | Y | Y |
| Jeffords | Y | Y | Y | Y | Y | Y |
| **VIRGINIA** Warner | Y | Y | Y | Y | N | N |
| Allen | Y | N | Y | Y | N | N |
| **WASHINGTON** Murray | Y | Y | Y | Y | Y | Y |
| Cantwell | Y | Y | Y | Y | Y | N |
| **WEST VIRGINIA** Byrd | Y | Y | Y | Y | Y | Y |
| Rockefeller | Y | N | Y | Y | Y | Y |
| **WISCONSIN** Kohl | Y | Y | Y | Y | Y | Y |
| Feingold | Y | Y | Y | Y | Y | Y |
| **WYOMING** Thomas | Y | N | Y | N | N | N |
| Enzi | Y | N | Y | N | N | N |

**KEY** Republicans  Democrats  *Independents*

| | | |
|---|---|---|
| Y Voted for (yea) | X Paired against | C Voted "present" to avoid possible conflict of interest |
| # Paired for | − Announced against | |
| + Announced for | P Voted "present" | ? Did not vote or otherwise make a position known |
| N Voted against (nay) | | |

ND Northern Democrats, SD Southern Democrats
Southern states: Ala., Ark., Fla., Ga., Ky., La., Miss., N.C., Okla., S.C., Tenn., Texas, Va.

# IN THE SENATE | By Vote Number

**332.** **S 2020. Fiscal 2006 Tax Reconciliation/Oil Company Tax Credits.** Feinstein, D-Calif., motion to waive the Budget Act with respect to the Grassley, R-Iowa, point of order against the Feinstein amendment. The Feinstein amendment would repeal tax deductions granted to major integrated oil companies for intangible drilling and exploration costs. Motion rejected 48-51: R 12-43; D 35-8 (ND 32-7, SD 3-1); I 1-0. A three-fifths majority vote (60) of the total Senate is required to waive the Budget Act. (Subsequently, the chair upheld the point of order, and the amendment fell.) Nov. 17, 2005.

**333.** **S 2020. Fiscal 2006 Tax Reconciliation/Top Tax Rate.** Feinstein, D-Calif., motion to waive the Budget Act with respect to the Grassley, R-Iowa, point of order against the Feinstein amendment. The Feinstein amendment would reinstate a 39.6 percent tax rate for individuals with annual incomes of more than $1 million. It also would repeal lower dividend and capital gains tax rates for those individuals until the federal budget is balanced. Motion rejected 40-59: R 1-54; D 38-5 (ND 35-4, SD 3-1); I 1-0. A three-fifths majority vote (60) of the total Senate is required to waive the Budget Act. (Subsequently, the chair upheld the point of order, and the amendment fell.) Nov. 17, 2005.

**334.** **S 2020. Fiscal 2006 Tax Reconciliation/Price Gouging.** Cantwell, D-Wash., motion to waive the Budget Act with respect to the Stevens, R-Alaska, point of order against the Cantwell amendment. The Cantwell amendment would make price gouging on energy products, services or markets a federal crime. Motion rejected 57-42: R 13-42; D 43-0 (ND 39-0, SD 4-0); I 1-0. A three-fifths majority vote (60) of the total Senate is required to waive the Budget Act. (Subsequently, the chair upheld the point of order, and the amendment fell.) Nov. 17, 2005.

**335.** **S 2020. Fiscal 2006 Tax Reconciliation/Physician Senators.** Lott, R-Miss., motion to waive the Budget Act with respect to the Voinovich, R-Ohio, point of order against the Lott amendment. The Lott amendment would allow senators who are physicians to continue their medical practice while serving in the Senate, provided they do not charge more than the amount necessary to cover practice expenses. Motion rejected 51-47: R 47-8; D 4-38 (ND 3-35, SD 1-3); I 0-1. A three-fifths majority vote (60) of the total Senate is required to waive the Budget Act. (Subsequently, the chair upheld the point of order, and the amendment fell.) Nov. 17, 2005.

**336.** **S 2020. Fiscal 2006 Tax Reconciliation/Insurance for Children.** Grassley, R-Iowa, motion to waive the Budget Act with respect to the Durbin, D-Ill., point of order against the Grassley amendment. The Grassley amendment would express the sense of the Senate that current tax policy should be continued to help insure children. Motion rejected 53-45: R 52-2; D 1-42 (ND 1-38, SD 0-4); I 0-1. A three-fifths majority vote (60) of the total Senate is required to waive the Budget Act. (Subsequently, the chair upheld the point of order, and the amendment fell.) Nov. 17, 2005.

**337.** **S 2020. Fiscal 2006 Tax Reconciliation/State Children's Health Insurance Program.** Durbin, D-Ill., motion to waive the Budget Act with respect to the Grassley, R-Iowa, point of order against the Durbin amendment. The Durbin amendment would express the sense of the Senate that the Senate should not extend the 15 percent dividend and capital-gains tax rates for high-income taxpayers until the federal government provides funding to state and local entities to enroll children in the State Children's Health Insurance Program. Motion rejected 43-55: R 0-54; D 42-1 (ND 39-0, SD 3-1); I 1-0. A three-fifths majority vote (60) of the total Senate is required to waive the Budget Act. (Subsequently, the chair upheld the point of order, and the amendment fell.) Nov. 17, 2005.

ND Northern Democrats, SD Southern Democrats
Southern states: Ala., Ark., Fla., Ga., Ky., La., Miss., N.C., Okla., S.C., Tenn., Texas, Va.

| | 332 | 333 | 334 | 335 | 336 | 337 |
|---|---|---|---|---|---|---|
| **ALABAMA** | | | | | | |
| Shelby | N | N | N | N | Y | N |
| Sessions | N | N | N | Y | Y | N |
| **ALASKA** | | | | | | |
| Stevens | N | N | N | Y | Y | N |
| Murkowski | N | N | N | N | Y | N |
| **ARIZONA** | | | | | | |
| McCain | Y | N | N | Y | Y | N |
| Kyl | N | N | N | Y | Y | N |
| **ARKANSAS** | | | | | | |
| Lincoln | Y | Y | Y | N | N | Y |
| Pryor | Y | Y | Y | N | N | Y |
| **CALIFORNIA** | | | | | | |
| Feinstein | Y | Y | Y | N | N | Y |
| Boxer | Y | Y | Y | N | N | Y |
| **COLORADO** | | | | | | |
| Allard | N | N | N | Y | Y | N |
| Salazar | N | Y | Y | N | N | Y |
| **CONNECTICUT** | | | | | | |
| Dodd | Y | Y | Y | N | N | Y |
| Lieberman | Y | Y | Y | N | N | Y |
| **DELAWARE** | | | | | | |
| Biden | Y | Y | Y | N | N | Y |
| Carper | Y | Y | Y | Y | N | Y |
| **FLORIDA** | | | | | | |
| Nelson | Y | Y | Y | N | N | Y |
| Martinez | N | N | N | Y | Y | N |
| **GEORGIA** | | | | | | |
| Chambliss | N | N | N | Y | Y | N |
| Isakson | N | N | N | Y | Y | N |
| **HAWAII** | | | | | | |
| Inouye | Y | Y | Y | ? | N | Y |
| Akaka | Y | Y | Y | N | N | Y |
| **IDAHO** | | | | | | |
| Craig | N | N | N | Y | Y | N |
| Crapo | N | N | N | Y | Y | N |
| **ILLINOIS** | | | | | | |
| Durbin | Y | Y | Y | N | N | Y |
| Obama | Y | Y | Y | Y | N | Y |
| **INDIANA** | | | | | | |
| Lugar | N | N | N | Y | Y | N |
| Bayh | Y | Y | Y | N | N | Y |
| **IOWA** | | | | | | |
| Grassley | N | N | N | Y | Y | N |
| Harkin | Y | Y | Y | N | N | Y |
| **KANSAS** | | | | | | |
| Brownback | N | N | N | Y | Y | N |
| Roberts | N | N | N | N | Y | N |
| **KENTUCKY** | | | | | | |
| McConnell | N | N | N | Y | Y | N |
| Bunning | N | N | N | N | Y | N |
| **LOUISIANA** | | | | | | |
| Landrieu | N | N | Y | Y | N | Y |
| Vitter | N | N | N | Y | Y | N |
| **MAINE** | | | | | | |
| Snowe | Y | N | Y | Y | N | N |
| Collins | Y | N | Y | Y | N | N |
| **MARYLAND** | | | | | | |
| Sarbanes | Y | Y | Y | N | N | Y |
| Mikulski | Y | Y | Y | N | N | Y |
| **MASSACHUSETTS** | | | | | | |
| Kennedy | Y | Y | Y | N | N | Y |
| Kerry | Y | Y | Y | N | N | Y |
| **MICHIGAN** | | | | | | |
| Levin | N | Y | Y | N | N | Y |
| Stabenow | Y | Y | Y | N | N | Y |
| **MINNESOTA** | | | | | | |
| Dayton | Y | Y | Y | Y | N | Y |
| Coleman | Y | N | Y | Y | Y | N |
| **MISSISSIPPI** | | | | | | |
| Cochran | N | N | N | Y | Y | N |
| Lott | N | N | N | Y | ? | ? |
| **MISSOURI** | | | | | | |
| Bond | N | N | N | Y | Y | N |
| Talent | Y | N | Y | Y | Y | N |
| **MONTANA** | | | | | | |
| Baucus | N | N | Y | N | N | Y |
| Burns | N | N | N | Y | Y | N |
| **NEBRASKA** | | | | | | |
| Hagel | N | N | Y | Y | Y | N |
| Nelson | N | N | Y | N | Y | N |
| **NEVADA** | | | | | | |
| Reid | Y | Y | Y | N | N | Y |
| Ensign | N | N | N | Y | Y | N |
| **NEW HAMPSHIRE** | | | | | | |
| Gregg | Y | N | N | Y | Y | N |
| Sununu | Y | N | N | Y | Y | N |
| **NEW JERSEY** | | | | | | |
| Corzine | ? | ? | ? | ? | ? | ? |
| Lautenberg | Y | Y | Y | N | N | Y |
| **NEW MEXICO** | | | | | | |
| Domenici | N | N | N | Y | Y | N |
| Bingaman | N | N | Y | N | N | Y |
| **NEW YORK** | | | | | | |
| Schumer | Y | Y | Y | N | N | Y |
| Clinton | Y | Y | Y | N | N | Y |
| **NORTH CAROLINA** | | | | | | |
| Dole | N | N | N | Y | Y | N |
| Burr | Y | N | N | Y | Y | N |
| **NORTH DAKOTA** | | | | | | |
| Conrad | N | Y | Y | N | N | Y |
| Dorgan | N | Y | Y | N | N | Y |
| **OHIO** | | | | | | |
| DeWine | Y | N | Y | Y | Y | N |
| Voinovich | N | N | N | N | Y | N |
| **OKLAHOMA** | | | | | | |
| Inhofe | N | N | N | Y | Y | N |
| Coburn | N | N | N | Y | Y | N |
| **OREGON** | | | | | | |
| Wyden | Y | Y | Y | Y | N | Y |
| Smith | N | N | Y | Y | Y | N |
| **PENNSYLVANIA** | | | | | | |
| Specter | Y | N | Y | Y | Y | N |
| Santorum | N | N | Y | Y | Y | N |
| **RHODE ISLAND** | | | | | | |
| Reed | Y | Y | Y | N | N | Y |
| Chafee | Y | Y | Y | Y | N | Y |
| **SOUTH CAROLINA** | | | | | | |
| Graham | N | N | Y | Y | Y | N |
| DeMint | Y | N | N | Y | Y | N |
| **SOUTH DAKOTA** | | | | | | |
| Johnson | Y | Y | Y | N | N | Y |
| Thune | N | N | Y | Y | Y | N |
| **TENNESSEE** | | | | | | |
| Frist | N | N | N | N | Y | N |
| Alexander | N | N | N | Y | Y | N |
| **TEXAS** | | | | | | |
| Hutchison | N | N | Y | Y | Y | N |
| Cornyn | N | N | Y | Y | Y | N |
| **UTAH** | | | | | | |
| Hatch | N | N | N | Y | Y | N |
| Bennett | N | N | N | Y | Y | N |
| **VERMONT** | | | | | | |
| Leahy | Y | Y | Y | N | N | Y |
| Jeffords | Y | Y | Y | N | N | Y |
| **VIRGINIA** | | | | | | |
| Warner | N | N | N | N | Y | N |
| Allen | N | N | N | Y | Y | N |
| **WASHINGTON** | | | | | | |
| Murray | Y | Y | Y | N | N | Y |
| Cantwell | Y | N | Y | N | N | Y |
| **WEST VIRGINIA** | | | | | | |
| Byrd | Y | Y | Y | N | N | Y |
| Rockefeller | Y | Y | Y | N | N | Y |
| **WISCONSIN** | | | | | | |
| Kohl | Y | Y | Y | N | N | Y |
| Feingold | Y | Y | Y | N | N | Y |
| **WYOMING** | | | | | | |
| Thomas | N | N | N | Y | Y | N |
| Enzi | N | N | N | Y | Y | N |

**KEY**   Republicans   Democrats   *Independents*

| | | |
|---|---|---|
| Y Voted for (yea) | X Paired against | C Voted "present" to avoid possible conflict of interest |
| # Paired for | – Announced against | |
| + Announced for | P Voted "present" | ? Did not vote or otherwise make a position known |
| N Voted against (nay) | | |

# IN THE SENATE | By Vote Number

**338.** S 2020. Fiscal 2006 Tax Reconciliation/Child Poverty Elimination Fund. Kennedy, D-Mass., motion to waive the Budget Act with respect to the Grassley, R-Iowa, point of order against the Kennedy amendment. The Kennedy amendment would create a child poverty elimination trust fund with the goal of reducing child poverty within a decade. The new program would be funded by an additional 1 percent tax on people with incomes above $500,000, or $1 million for married couples. Motion rejected 36-62: R 0-54; D 35-8 (ND 33-6, SD 2-2); I 1-0. A three-fifths majority vote (60) of the total Senate is required to waive the Budget Act. (Subsequently, the chair upheld the point of order, and the amendment fell.) Nov. 17, 2005.

**339.** S 2020. Fiscal 2006 Tax Reconciliation/LIHEAP. Reed, D-R.I., motion to waive the Budget Act with respect to the Grassley, R-Iowa, point of order against the Reed amendment. The Reed amendment would fund the Low-Income Home Energy Assistance Program (LIHEAP) by imposing a one-year temporary tax on oil company profits from the sale of crude oil. Motion rejected 50-48: R 9-45; D 40-3 (ND 37-2, SD 3-1); I 1-0. A three-fifths majority vote (60) of the total Senate is required to waive the Budget Act. (Subsequently, the chair upheld the point of order, and the amendment fell.) Nov. 17, 2005.

**340.** S 2020. Fiscal 2006 Tax Reconciliation/PAYGO. Feingold, D-Wis., motion to waive the Budget Act with respect to the Grassley, R-Iowa, point of order against the Feingold amendment. The Feingold amendment would restore pay-as-you-go (PAYGO) rules, which would create a 60-vote point of order against any direct spending or revenue legislation that would increase the on-budget deficit or cause an on-budget deficit. Tax cuts and new entitlement spending would have to be offset with revenue increases or spending cuts. The amendment would sunset Sept. 30, 2010. Motion rejected 50-48: R 6-48; D 43-0 (ND 39-0, SD 4-0); I 1-0. A three-fifths majority vote (60) of the total Senate is required to waive the Budget Act. (Subsequently, the chair upheld the point of order, and the amendment fell.) Nov. 17, 2005.

**341.** S 2020. Fiscal 2006 Tax Reconciliation/Windfall Oil Profits. Schumer, D-N.Y., motion to waive the Budget Act with respect to the Grassley, R-Iowa, point of order against the Schumer amendment. The Schumer amendment would impose a temporary tax on oil company profits from the sale of crude oil. The funds would be used to provide every taxpayer with a $100 non-refundable tax credit for 2005 for each person in their household. Motion rejected 33-65: R 0-54; D 32-11 (ND 31-8, SD 1-3); I 1-0. A three-fifths majority vote (60) of the total Senate is required to waive the Budget Act. (Subsequently, the chair upheld the point of order, and the amendment fell.) Nov. 17, 2005.

**342.** S 2020. Fiscal 2006 Tax Reconciliation/Medicare Enrollment. Nelson, D-Fla., motion to waive the Budget Act with respect to the Grassley, R-Iowa, point of order against the Nelson, D-Fla., amendment. The Nelson amendment would extend the initial enrollment period for the Medicare prescription drug benefit by six months, through the end of 2006. Motion rejected 51-47: R 7-47; D 43-0 (ND 39-0, SD 4-0); I 1-0. A three-fifths majority vote (60) of the total Senate is required to waive the Budget Act. (Subsequently, the chair upheld the point of order, and the amendment fell.) Nov. 17, 2005.

| | 338 | 339 | 340 | 341 | 342 | | | 338 | 339 | 340 | 341 | 342 |
|---|---|---|---|---|---|---|---|---|---|---|---|---|
| **ALABAMA** | | | | | | | **MONTANA** | | | | | |
| Shelby | N | N | N | N | N | | Baucus | N | Y | Y | N | Y |
| Sessions | N | N | N | N | N | | Burns | N | N | N | N | N |
| **ALASKA** | | | | | | | **NEBRASKA** | | | | | |
| Stevens | N | N | N | N | N | | Hagel | N | N | N | N | N |
| Murkowski | N | N | N | N | N | | Nelson | N | N | Y | N | Y |
| **ARIZONA** | | | | | | | **NEVADA** | | | | | |
| McCain | N | N | Y | N | N | | Reid | Y | Y | Y | Y | Y |
| Kyl | N | N | N | N | N | | Ensign | N | N | N | N | N |
| **ARKANSAS** | | | | | | | **NEW HAMPSHIRE** | | | | | |
| Lincoln | N | Y | Y | N | Y | | Gregg | N | Y | N | N | N |
| Pryor | N | Y | Y | N | Y | | Sununu | N | Y | N | N | N |
| **CALIFORNIA** | | | | | | | **NEW JERSEY** | | | | | |
| Feinstein | Y | Y | Y | Y | Y | | Corzine | ? | ? | ? | ? | ? |
| Boxer | Y | Y | Y | Y | Y | | Lautenberg | Y | Y | Y | Y | Y |
| **COLORADO** | | | | | | | **NEW MEXICO** | | | | | |
| Allard | N | N | N | N | N | | Domenici | N | N | N | N | N |
| Salazar | N | Y | Y | N | Y | | Bingaman | Y | N | Y | N | Y |
| **CONNECTICUT** | | | | | | | **NEW YORK** | | | | | |
| Dodd | Y | Y | Y | Y | Y | | Schumer | Y | Y | Y | Y | Y |
| Lieberman | Y | Y | Y | Y | Y | | Clinton | Y | Y | Y | Y | Y |
| **DELAWARE** | | | | | | | **NORTH CAROLINA** | | | | | |
| Biden | N | Y | Y | N | Y | | Dole | N | N | N | N | N |
| Carper | N | Y | Y | N | Y | | Burr | N | N | N | N | N |
| **FLORIDA** | | | | | | | **NORTH DAKOTA** | | | | | |
| Nelson | Y | Y | Y | Y | Y | | Conrad | Y | Y | Y | N | Y |
| Martinez | N | N | N | N | N | | Dorgan | Y | Y | Y | Y | Y |
| **GEORGIA** | | | | | | | **OHIO** | | | | | |
| Chambliss | N | N | N | N | N | | DeWine | N | N | N | N | Y |
| Isakson | N | N | N | N | N | | Voinovich | N | Y | Y | N | Y |
| **HAWAII** | | | | | | | **OKLAHOMA** | | | | | |
| Inouye | Y | Y | Y | Y | Y | | Inhofe | N | N | N | N | N |
| Akaka | Y | Y | Y | Y | Y | | Coburn | N | N | Y | N | N |
| **IDAHO** | | | | | | | **OREGON** | | | | | |
| Craig | N | N | N | N | N | | Wyden | Y | Y | Y | Y | Y |
| Crapo | N | N | N | N | N | | Smith | N | N | N | N | N |
| **ILLINOIS** | | | | | | | **PENNSYLVANIA** | | | | | |
| Durbin | Y | Y | Y | Y | Y | | Specter | N | N | N | N | Y |
| Obama | Y | Y | Y | Y | Y | | Santorum | N | N | N | N | N |
| **INDIANA** | | | | | | | **RHODE ISLAND** | | | | | |
| Lugar | N | N | N | N | N | | Reed | Y | Y | Y | Y | Y |
| Bayh | Y | Y | Y | Y | Y | | Chafee | N | Y | Y | N | Y |
| **IOWA** | | | | | | | **SOUTH CAROLINA** | | | | | |
| Grassley | N | N | N | N | N | | Graham | N | N | N | N | N |
| Harkin | Y | Y | Y | Y | Y | | DeMint | N | N | N | N | N |
| **KANSAS** | | | | | | | **SOUTH DAKOTA** | | | | | |
| Brownback | N | N | N | N | N | | Johnson | Y | Y | Y | Y | Y |
| Roberts | N | N | N | N | N | | Thune | N | Y | N | N | N |
| **KENTUCKY** | | | | | | | **TENNESSEE** | | | | | |
| McConnell | N | N | N | N | N | | Frist | N | N | N | N | N |
| Bunning | N | N | N | N | N | | Alexander | N | N | N | N | N |
| **LOUISIANA** | | | | | | | **TEXAS** | | | | | |
| Landrieu | Y | N | Y | N | Y | | Hutchison | N | N | N | N | N |
| Vitter | N | N | N | N | N | | Cornyn | N | N | N | N | N |
| **MAINE** | | | | | | | **UTAH** | | | | | |
| Snowe | N | Y | Y | N | Y | | Hatch | N | N | N | N | N |
| Collins | N | Y | Y | N | Y | | Bennett | N | N | N | N | N |
| **MARYLAND** | | | | | | | **VERMONT** | | | | | |
| Sarbanes | Y | Y | Y | Y | Y | | Leahy | Y | Y | Y | Y | Y |
| Mikulski | Y | Y | Y | Y | Y | | *Jeffords* | Y | Y | Y | Y | Y |
| **MASSACHUSETTS** | | | | | | | **VIRGINIA** | | | | | |
| Kennedy | Y | Y | Y | Y | Y | | Warner | N | N | N | N | Y |
| Kerry | Y | Y | Y | Y | Y | | Allen | N | N | N | N | N |
| **MICHIGAN** | | | | | | | **WASHINGTON** | | | | | |
| Levin | Y | Y | Y | Y | Y | | Murray | Y | Y | Y | Y | Y |
| Stabenow | Y | Y | Y | Y | Y | | Cantwell | N | Y | N | N | Y |
| **MINNESOTA** | | | | | | | **WEST VIRGINIA** | | | | | |
| Dayton | Y | Y | Y | Y | Y | | Byrd | Y | Y | Y | Y | Y |
| Coleman | N | Y | N | N | N | | Rockefeller | Y | Y | Y | Y | Y |
| **MISSISSIPPI** | | | | | | | **WISCONSIN** | | | | | |
| Cochran | N | N | N | N | N | | Kohl | Y | Y | Y | Y | Y |
| Lott | ? | ? | ? | ? | ? | | Feingold | Y | Y | Y | Y | Y |
| **MISSOURI** | | | | | | | **WYOMING** | | | | | |
| Bond | N | N | N | N | N | | Thomas | N | N | N | N | N |
| Talent | N | N | N | N | N | | Enzi | N | N | N | N | N |

**KEY**   Republicans   Democrats   *Independents*

| Y | Voted for (yea) | X | Paired against | C | Voted "present" to avoid possible conflict of interest |
|---|---|---|---|---|---|
| # | Paired for | – | Announced against | | |
| + | Announced for | P | Voted "present" | ? | Did not vote or otherwise make a position known |
| N | Voted against (nay) | | | | |

ND Northern Democrats, SD Southern Democrats
Southern states: Ala., Ark., Fla., Ga., Ky., La., Miss., N.C., Okla., S.C., Tenn., Texas, Va.

# IN THE SENATE | By Vote Number

**343.** **S 2020. Fiscal 2006 Tax Reconciliation/Veterans.** Boxer, D-Calif., motion to waive the Budget Act with respect to the Grassley, R-Iowa, point of order against the Boxer amendment. The Boxer amendment would provide an additional $500 million per year for the next five years for mental health services for veterans. It would be offset by deferring tax cuts for those making $1 million per year. Motion rejected 43-55: R 1-53; D 41-2 (ND 37-2, SD 4-0); I 1-0. A three-fifths majority vote (60) of the total Senate is required to waive the Budget Act. (Subsequently, the chair upheld the point of order, and the amendment fell.) Nov. 17, 2005.

**344.** **S 2020. Fiscal 2006 Tax Reconciliation/Combat Pay.** Kerry, D-Mass., motion to waive the Budget Act with respect to the Grassley, R-Iowa, point of order against the Kerry amendment. The Kerry amendment would extend through 2007 the inclusion of combat pay in earned income. It also would accelerate so-called marriage penalty tax relief for the earned-income tax credit and extend the effective dates of leasing provisions of the American Jobs Creation Act. Motion rejected 55-43: R 11-43; D 43-0 (ND 39-0, SD 4-0); I 1-0. A three-fifths majority vote (60) of the total Senate is required to waive the Budget Act. (Subsequently, the chair upheld the point of order, and the amendment fell.) Nov. 17, 2005.

**345.** **S 2020. Fiscal 2006 Tax Reconciliation/Farmers Tax Credit.** Dayton, D-Minn., motion to waive the Budget Act with respect to the Grassley, R-Iowa, point of order against the Dayton amendment. The Dayton amendment would provide a refundable tax credit for farmers equal to the lesser of 30 percent of their energy costs for 2005, or $3,000. It would increase taxes on foreign oil and gas income for U.S. energy companies through modifications to foreign-tax credit rules. Motion rejected 47-51: R 3-51; D 43-0 (ND 39-0, SD 4-0); I 1-0. A three-fifths majority vote (60) of the total Senate is required to waive the Budget Act. (Subsequently, the chair upheld the point of order, and the amendment fell.) Nov. 17, 2005.

**346.** **S 2020. Fiscal 2006 Tax Reconciliation/Child Tax Credit.** Harkin, D-Iowa, motion to waive the Budget Act with respect to the Grassley, R-Iowa, point of order against the Harkin amendment. The Harkin amendment would reinstate the personal exemption phase-out and phase-out of itemized deductions provisions of the tax code, and would use those revenues to lower the income threshold for calculating the child tax credit from $10,000 to $9,000. Motion rejected 42-56: R 0-54; D 41-2 (ND 37-2, SD 4-0); I 1-0. A three-fifths majority vote (60) of the total Senate is required to waive the Budget Act. (Subsequently, the chair upheld the point of order, and the amendment fell.) Nov. 17, 2005.

**347.** **S 2020. Fiscal 2006 Tax Reconciliation/Passage.** Passage of bill that would extend a series of tax cuts set to expire between 2005 and 2010, including the college tuition deduction and the state and local sales tax deduction in states without income taxes. It would extend through 2006 protections for middle-class taxpayers from alternative-minimum tax liability, and include $7 billion in tax incentives to encourage reconstruction along the hurricane-damaged Gulf Coast, along with a new tax deduction for charitable giving by taxpayers who do not itemize. Passed 64-33: R 49-4; D 15-28 (ND 11-28, SD 4-0); I 0-1. Nov. 18, 2005 (in the session that began and the Congressional Record dated Nov. 17, 2005).

| | 343 | 344 | 345 | 346 | 347 | | 343 | 344 | 345 | 346 | 347 |
|---|---|---|---|---|---|---|---|---|---|---|---|
| **ALABAMA** | | | | | | **MONTANA** | | | | | |
| Shelby | N | N | N | N | ? | Baucus | N | Y | Y | N | Y |
| Sessions | N | N | N | N | Y | Burns | N | Y | Y | N | Y |
| **ALASKA** | | | | | | **NEBRASKA** | | | | | |
| Stevens | N | N | N | N | Y | Hagel | N | N | N | N | Y |
| Murkowski | N | N | N | N | Y | Nelson | N | Y | Y | N | Y |
| **ARIZONA** | | | | | | **NEVADA** | | | | | |
| McCain | N | Y | N | N | Y | Reid | Y | Y | Y | Y | N |
| Kyl | N | N | N | N | Y | Ensign | N | N | N | N | Y |
| **ARKANSAS** | | | | | | **NEW HAMPSHIRE** | | | | | |
| Lincoln | Y | Y | Y | Y | Y | Gregg | N | N | N | N | Y |
| Pryor | Y | Y | Y | Y | Y | Sununu | N | N | N | N | Y |
| **CALIFORNIA** | | | | | | **NEW JERSEY** | | | | | |
| Feinstein | Y | Y | Y | Y | Y | Corzine | ? | ? | ? | ? | ? |
| Boxer | Y | Y | Y | Y | N | Lautenberg | Y | Y | Y | Y | N |
| **COLORADO** | | | | | | **NEW MEXICO** | | | | | |
| Allard | N | N | N | N | Y | Domenici | N | N | N | N | Y |
| Salazar | Y | Y | Y | Y | Y | Bingaman | Y | Y | Y | Y | N |
| **CONNECTICUT** | | | | | | **NEW YORK** | | | | | |
| Dodd | Y | Y | Y | Y | N | Schumer | Y | Y | Y | Y | Y |
| Lieberman | Y | Y | Y | Y | N | Clinton | Y | Y | Y | Y | Y |
| **DELAWARE** | | | | | | **NORTH CAROLINA** | | | | | |
| Biden | Y | Y | Y | Y | N | Dole | N | Y | N | N | Y |
| Carper | Y | Y | Y | Y | Y | Burr | N | N | N | N | N |
| **FLORIDA** | | | | | | **NORTH DAKOTA** | | | | | |
| Nelson | Y | Y | Y | Y | Y | Conrad | Y | Y | Y | Y | N |
| Martinez | N | N | N | N | Y | Dorgan | Y | Y | Y | Y | N |
| **GEORGIA** | | | | | | **OHIO** | | | | | |
| Chambliss | N | N | N | N | Y | DeWine | N | Y | N | N | Y |
| Isakson | N | N | N | N | Y | Voinovich | N | N | N | N | N |
| **HAWAII** | | | | | | **OKLAHOMA** | | | | | |
| Inouye | Y | Y | Y | Y | N | Inhofe | N | N | N | N | Y |
| Akaka | Y | Y | Y | Y | N | Coburn | N | N | N | N | Y |
| **IDAHO** | | | | | | **OREGON** | | | | | |
| Craig | N | N | N | N | N | Wyden | Y | Y | Y | Y | N |
| Crapo | N | N | N | N | Y | Smith | Y | N | N | N | Y |
| **ILLINOIS** | | | | | | **PENNSYLVANIA** | | | | | |
| Durbin | Y | Y | Y | Y | N | Specter | N | Y | N | N | Y |
| Obama | Y | Y | Y | Y | N | Santorum | N | Y | N | N | Y |
| **INDIANA** | | | | | | **RHODE ISLAND** | | | | | |
| Lugar | N | N | N | N | Y | Reed | Y | Y | Y | Y | N |
| Bayh | Y | Y | Y | Y | N | Chafee | N | Y | N | N | N |
| **IOWA** | | | | | | **SOUTH CAROLINA** | | | | | |
| Grassley | N | N | N | N | Y | Graham | N | N | N | N | Y |
| Harkin | Y | Y | Y | Y | N | DeMint | N | N | N | N | Y |
| **KANSAS** | | | | | | **SOUTH DAKOTA** | | | | | |
| Brownback | N | N | N | N | Y | Johnson | Y | Y | Y | Y | Y |
| Roberts | N | N | N | N | Y | Thune | N | N | N | N | Y |
| **KENTUCKY** | | | | | | **TENNESSEE** | | | | | |
| McConnell | N | N | N | N | Y | Frist | N | N | N | N | Y |
| Bunning | N | N | N | N | Y | Alexander | N | N | N | N | Y |
| **LOUISIANA** | | | | | | **TEXAS** | | | | | |
| Landrieu | Y | Y | Y | Y | Y | Hutchison | N | N | N | N | Y |
| Vitter | N | N | N | N | Y | Cornyn | N | N | N | N | Y |
| **MAINE** | | | | | | **UTAH** | | | | | |
| Snowe | N | N | N | N | Y | Hatch | N | N | N | N | Y |
| Collins | N | Y | N | N | Y | Bennett | N | N | N | N | Y |
| **MARYLAND** | | | | | | **VERMONT** | | | | | |
| Sarbanes | Y | Y | Y | Y | N | Leahy | Y | Y | Y | Y | N |
| Mikulski | Y | Y | Y | Y | N | Jeffords | Y | Y | Y | Y | N |
| **MASSACHUSETTS** | | | | | | **VIRGINIA** | | | | | |
| Kennedy | Y | Y | Y | Y | N | Warner | N | N | N | N | Y |
| Kerry | Y | Y | Y | Y | N | Allen | N | N | N | N | Y |
| **MICHIGAN** | | | | | | **WASHINGTON** | | | | | |
| Levin | Y | Y | Y | Y | N | Murray | Y | Y | Y | Y | N |
| Stabenow | Y | Y | Y | Y | Y | Cantwell | Y | Y | Y | Y | Y |
| **MINNESOTA** | | | | | | **WEST VIRGINIA** | | | | | |
| Dayton | Y | Y | Y | Y | Y | Byrd | Y | Y | Y | Y | N |
| Coleman | N | Y | Y | N | Y | Rockefeller | Y | Y | Y | Y | N |
| **MISSISSIPPI** | | | | | | **WISCONSIN** | | | | | |
| Cochran | N | N | N | N | Y | Kohl | Y | Y | Y | Y | N |
| Lott | ? | ? | ? | ? | ? | Feingold | Y | Y | Y | Y | N |
| **MISSOURI** | | | | | | **WYOMING** | | | | | |
| Bond | N | N | N | N | Y | Thomas | N | N | N | N | Y |
| Talent | N | Y | Y | N | Y | Enzi | N | N | N | N | Y |

**KEY**    **Republicans**    Democrats    *Independents*

| | | | |
|---|---|---|---|
| Y | Voted for (yea) | X | Paired against |
| # | Paired for | – | Announced against |
| + | Announced for | P | Voted "present" |
| N | Voted against (nay) | | |

| |
|---|
| C  Voted "present" to avoid possible conflict of interest |
| ?  Did not vote or otherwise make a position known |

ND Northern Democrats, SD Southern Democrats
Southern states: Ala., Ark., Fla., Ga., Ky., La., Miss., N.C., Okla., S.C., Tenn., Texas, Va.

# IN THE SENATE | By Vote Number

**348.** **H J Res 72. Fiscal 2006 Continuing Resolution/Community Services Block Grant Funding.** Harkin, D-Iowa, amendment that would increase the amount appropriated for the Community Services Block Grant, ensuring that its funding for Oct. 1, 2005, through Dec. 17, 2005, would continue at no less than the fiscal 2005 level. Rejected 46-50: R 4-50; D 41-0 (ND 37-0, SD 4-0); I 1-0. (Subsequently, the joint resolution was passed by voice vote.) Nov. 18, 2005.

**349.** **HR 3010. Fiscal 2006 Labor-HHS-Education Appropriations/ LIHEAP.** Specter, R-Pa., motion to instruct conferees to insist that $2.2 billion be available for the Low Income Home Energy Heating Assistance Program (LIHEAP), with the funding designated as emergency spending. Motion agreed to 66-28: R 30-24; D 35-4 (ND 33-2, SD 2-2); I 1-0. Nov. 18, 2005.

**350.** **HR 3010. Fiscal 2006 Labor-HHS-Education Appropriations/ NIH Funding.** Durbin, D-Ill., motion to instruct conferees to insist that the conference report retain the $1 billion increase for the National Institutes of Health (NIH) called for in the Senate-passed bill. Motion agreed to 58-36: R 18-36; D 39-0 (ND 35-0, SD 4-0); I 1-0. Nov. 18, 2005.

| | 348 | 349 | 350 | | | 348 | 349 | 350 |
|---|---|---|---|---|---|---|---|---|
| **ALABAMA** | | | | | **MONTANA** | | | |
| Shelby | N | Y | N | | Baucus | Y | Y | Y |
| Sessions | N | N | N | | Burns | N | Y | N |
| **ALASKA** | | | | | **NEBRASKA** | | | |
| Stevens | N | Y | N | | Hagel | N | Y | N |
| Murkowski | N | Y | N | | Nelson | Y | + | + |
| **ARIZONA** | | | | | **NEVADA** | | | |
| McCain | N | N | N | | Reid | Y | Y | Y |
| Kyl | N | N | N | | Ensign | N | ? | ? |
| **ARKANSAS** | | | | | **NEW HAMPSHIRE** | | | |
| Lincoln | Y | N | Y | | Gregg | N | N | N |
| Pryor | Y | N | Y | | Sununu | N | Y | N |
| **CALIFORNIA** | | | | | **NEW JERSEY** | | | |
| Feinstein | Y | Y | Y | | Corzine | ? | ? | ? |
| Boxer | Y | Y | Y | | Lautenberg | Y | Y | Y |
| **COLORADO** | | | | | **NEW MEXICO** | | | |
| Allard | N | N | N | | Domenici | N | Y | N |
| Salazar | Y | Y | Y | | Bingaman | Y | Y | Y |
| **CONNECTICUT** | | | | | **NEW YORK** | | | |
| Dodd | Y | Y | Y | | Schumer | Y | Y | Y |
| Lieberman | Y | Y | Y | | Clinton | Y | Y | Y |
| **DELAWARE** | | | | | **NORTH CAROLINA** | | | |
| Biden | Y | ? | ? | | Dole | N | Y | N |
| Carper | Y | N | Y | | Burr | N | Y | Y |
| **FLORIDA** | | | | | **NORTH DAKOTA** | | | |
| Nelson | Y | Y | Y | | Conrad | Y | Y | Y |
| Martinez | N | Y | N | | Dorgan | Y | Y | Y |
| **GEORGIA** | | | | | **OHIO** | | | |
| Chambliss | N | N | Y | | DeWine | N | Y | Y |
| Isakson | N | N | Y | | Voinovich | N | Y | N |
| **HAWAII** | | | | | **OKLAHOMA** | | | |
| Inouye | ? | ? | ? | | Inhofe | N | N | N |
| Akaka | Y | Y | Y | | Coburn | N | Y | N |
| **IDAHO** | | | | | **OREGON** | | | |
| Craig | N | N | N | | Wyden | Y | Y | Y |
| Crapo | N | N | N | | Smith | ? | Y | Y |
| **ILLINOIS** | | | | | **PENNSYLVANIA** | | | |
| Durbin | Y | Y | Y | | Specter | Y | Y | Y |
| Obama | Y | Y | Y | | Santorum | N | Y | N |
| **INDIANA** | | | | | **RHODE ISLAND** | | | |
| Lugar | N | Y | Y | | Reed | Y | N | Y |
| Bayh | Y | Y | Y | | Chafee | Y | N | Y |
| **IOWA** | | | | | **SOUTH CAROLINA** | | | |
| Grassley | N | Y | N | | Graham | N | N | N |
| Harkin | Y | Y | Y | | DeMint | N | N | N |
| **KANSAS** | | | | | **SOUTH DAKOTA** | | | |
| Brownback | N | N | N | | Johnson | Y | Y | Y |
| Roberts | N | N | Y | | Thune | N | Y | N |
| **KENTUCKY** | | | | | **TENNESSEE** | | | |
| McConnell | N | N | N | | Frist | N | Y | N |
| Bunning | N | N | N | | Alexander | N | N | Y |
| **LOUISIANA** | | | | | **TEXAS** | | | |
| Landrieu | Y | Y | Y | | Hutchison | N | Y | N |
| Vitter | N | N | N | | Cornyn | N | N | Y |
| **MAINE** | | | | | **UTAH** | | | |
| Snowe | Y | Y | Y | | Hatch | N | Y | N |
| Collins | Y | Y | Y | | Bennett | N | Y | N |
| **MARYLAND** | | | | | **VERMONT** | | | |
| Sarbanes | Y | Y | Y | | Leahy | Y | Y | Y |
| Mikulski | Y | Y | Y | | Jeffords | Y | Y | Y |
| **MASSACHUSETTS** | | | | | **VIRGINIA** | | | |
| Kennedy | Y | Y | Y | | Warner | N | Y | Y |
| Kerry | Y | Y | Y | | Allen | N | N | Y |
| **MICHIGAN** | | | | | **WASHINGTON** | | | |
| Levin | Y | Y | Y | | Murray | Y | Y | Y |
| Stabenow | + | + | + | | Cantwell | Y | Y | Y |
| **MINNESOTA** | | | | | **WEST VIRGINIA** | | | |
| Dayton | Y | Y | Y | | Byrd | Y | Y | Y |
| Coleman | N | Y | Y | | Rockefeller | Y | Y | Y |
| **MISSISSIPPI** | | | | | **WISCONSIN** | | | |
| Cochran | N | Y | N | | Kohl | Y | Y | Y |
| Lott | N | N | N | | Feingold | Y | Y | Y |
| **MISSOURI** | | | | | **WYOMING** | | | |
| Bond | N | Y | N | | Thomas | N | N | N |
| Talent | N | Y | N | | Enzi | N | N | N |

**KEY**   Republicans   Democrats   *Independents*

| | | | | | |
|---|---|---|---|---|---|
| Y | Voted for (yea) | X | Paired against | C | Voted "present" to avoid possible conflict of interest |
| # | Paired for | – | Announced against | | |
| + | Announced for | P | Voted "present" | ? | Did not vote or otherwise make a position known |
| N | Voted against (nay) | | | | |

ND Northern Democrats, SD Southern Democrats
Southern states: Ala., Ark., Fla., Ga., Ky., La., Miss., N.C., Okla., S.C., Tenn., Texas, Va.

# IN THE SENATE | By Vote Number

**351.** S 1932. **Budget Reconciliation/Motion to Instruct.** Carper, D-Del., motion to instruct conferees to insist that the conference report not include any provisions related to the Temporary Assistance for Needy Families (TANF) program, particularly those that would increase work hours for single mothers or cut child care funding. Motion agreed to 64-27: R 24-27; D 39-0 (ND 35-0, SD 4-0); I 1-0. Dec. 14, 2005.

**352.** S 1932. **Budget Reconciliation/Motion to Instruct.** Baucus, D-Mont., motion to instruct conferees to insist that the conference report not contain any provisions that would increase Medicaid beneficiary cost-sharing or otherwise increase costs for Medicaid recipients. Motion agreed to 75-16: R 35-16; D 39-0 (ND 35-0, SD 4-0); I 1-0. Dec. 14, 2005.

**353.** S 1932. **Budget Reconciliation/Motion to Instruct.** Harkin, D-Iowa, motion to instruct conferees to insist that the conference report not contain cuts to any federal food assistance programs, including the federal food stamp program. Motion agreed to 66-26: R 26-26; D 39-0 (ND 35-0, SD 4-0); I 1-0. Dec. 14, 2005.

**354.** S 1932. **Budget Reconciliation/Motion to Instruct.** DeWine, R-Ohio, motion to instruct conferees to insist that the conference report not include any provisions to repeal the Continued Dumping and Subsidies Offset Act. Motion agreed to 71-20: R 30-20; D 40-0 (ND 36-0, SD 4-0); I 1-0. Dec. 15, 2005.

**355.** S 1932. **Budget Reconciliation/Motion to Instruct.** Kohl, D-Wis., motion to instruct conferees not to include in the conference report any provision that would reduce states' access to funding for the child support programs under existing Social Security law. Motion agreed to 75-16: R 34-16; D 40-0 (ND 36-0, SD 4-0); I 1-0. Dec. 15, 2005.

**356.** S 1932. **Budget Reconciliation/Motion to Instruct.** Kennedy, D-Mass., motion to instruct conferees to insist that the conference report include provisions to increase need-based financial aid for college tuition. Motion agreed to 83-8: R 42-8; D 40-0 (ND 36-0, SD 4-0); I 1-0. Dec. 15, 2005.

**357.** S 1932. **Budget Reconciliation/Motion to Instruct.** Reed, D-R.I., motion to instruct conferees to insist that the conference report include $2.9 billion for the Low-Income Home Energy Assistance Program. Motion agreed to 63-28: R 23-27; D 39-1 (ND 35-1, SD 4-0); I 1-0. Dec. 15, 2005.

**358.** HR 3199. **"Patriot Act" Reauthorization/Cloture.** Motion to invoke cloture (thus limiting debate) on the conference report accompanying the bill that would make permanent 14 of the 16 provisions of the law known as the Patriot Act (PL 107-56) set to expire at the end of the year, and extend for four years the provisions on access to business and other records and "roving" wiretaps. Motion rejected 52-47: R 50-5; D 2-41 (ND 2-37, SD 0-4); I 0-1. Three-fifths of the total Senate (60) is required to invoke cloture. A "yea" was a vote in support of the president's position. Dec. 16, 2005.

| | 351 | 352 | 353 | 354 | 355 | 356 | 357 | 358 |
|---|---|---|---|---|---|---|---|---|
| **ALABAMA** | | | | | | | | |
| Shelby | N | N | N | Y | Y | Y | N | Y |
| Sessions | N | N | N | Y | Y | Y | N | Y |
| **ALASKA** | | | | | | | | |
| Stevens | Y | Y | Y | Y | Y | Y | Y | Y |
| Murkowski | Y | Y | Y | N | Y | Y | Y | N |
| **ARIZONA** | | | | | | | | |
| McCain | ? | ? | ? | N | Y | Y | Y | Y |
| Kyl | Y | Y | N | N | Y | Y | N | Y |
| **ARKANSAS** | | | | | | | | |
| Lincoln | Y | Y | Y | Y | Y | Y | Y | N |
| Pryor | Y | Y | Y | Y | Y | Y | Y | N |
| **CALIFORNIA** | | | | | | | | |
| Feinstein | Y | Y | Y | Y | Y | Y | Y | N |
| Boxer | + | + | + | + | + | + | + | N |
| **COLORADO** | | | | | | | | |
| Allard | N | N | N | N | N | Y | N | Y |
| Salazar | Y | Y | Y | Y | Y | Y | Y | N |
| **CONNECTICUT** | | | | | | | | |
| Dodd | ? | ? | ? | ? | ? | ? | ? | ? |
| Lieberman | + | + | + | Y | Y | Y | Y | N |
| **DELAWARE** | | | | | | | | |
| Biden | ? | ? | ? | ? | ? | ? | ? | N |
| Carper | Y | Y | Y | Y | Y | Y | Y | N |
| **FLORIDA** | | | | | | | | |
| Nelson | Y | Y | Y | Y | Y | Y | Y | N |
| Martinez | N | Y | Y | Y | N | Y | Y | Y |
| **GEORGIA** | | | | | | | | |
| Chambliss | ? | ? | ? | ? | ? | ? | ? | Y |
| Isakson | N | N | N | ? | ? | ? | ? | Y |
| **HAWAII** | | | | | | | | |
| Inouye | Y | Y | Y | Y | Y | Y | Y | N |
| Akaka | Y | Y | Y | Y | Y | Y | Y | N |
| **IDAHO** | | | | | | | | |
| Craig | N | Y | N | Y | Y | Y | N | N |
| Crapo | N | Y | N | Y | Y | Y | Y | Y |
| **ILLINOIS** | | | | | | | | |
| Durbin | Y | Y | Y | Y | Y | Y | Y | N |
| Obama | Y | Y | Y | Y | Y | Y | Y | N |
| **INDIANA** | | | | | | | | |
| Lugar | Y | Y | Y | N | Y | Y | Y | Y |
| Bayh | Y | Y | Y | Y | Y | Y | Y | N |
| **IOWA** | | | | | | | | |
| Grassley | Y | Y | Y | N | Y | Y | Y | Y |
| Harkin | Y | Y | Y | Y | Y | Y | Y | N |
| **KANSAS** | | | | | | | | |
| Brownback | N | Y | Y | N | N | Y | N | Y |
| Roberts | Y | Y | Y | N | Y | Y | N | Y |
| **KENTUCKY** | | | | | | | | |
| McConnell | N | Y | N | N | N | Y | N | Y |
| Bunning | N | N | N | Y | N | Y | N | Y |
| **LOUISIANA** | | | | | | | | |
| Landrieu | Y | Y | Y | Y | Y | Y | Y | N |
| Vitter | N | Y | N | + | ? | ? | ? | Y |
| **MAINE** | | | | | | | | |
| Snowe | Y | Y | Y | Y | Y | Y | Y | Y |
| Collins | Y | Y | Y | Y | Y | Y | Y | Y |
| **MARYLAND** | | | | | | | | |
| Sarbanes | Y | Y | Y | Y | Y | Y | Y | N |
| Mikulski | Y | Y | Y | Y | Y | Y | Y | N |
| **MASSACHUSETTS** | | | | | | | | |
| Kennedy | Y | Y | Y | Y | Y | Y | Y | N |
| Kerry | Y | Y | Y | Y | Y | Y | Y | N |
| **MICHIGAN** | | | | | | | | |
| Levin | Y | Y | Y | Y | Y | Y | Y | N |
| Stabenow | Y | Y | Y | Y | Y | Y | Y | N |
| **MINNESOTA** | | | | | | | | |
| Dayton | Y | Y | Y | Y | Y | Y | Y | N |
| Coleman | Y | Y | Y | Y | Y | Y | Y | Y |
| **MISSISSIPPI** | | | | | | | | |
| Cochran | N | Y | N | Y | N | Y | N | Y |
| Lott | N | N | N | Y | N | Y | N | Y |
| **MISSOURI** | | | | | | | | |
| Bond | N | Y | N | N | N | N | N | Y |
| Talent | N | Y | Y | Y | Y | Y | Y | Y |

| | 351 | 352 | 353 | 354 | 355 | 356 | 357 | 358 |
|---|---|---|---|---|---|---|---|---|
| **MONTANA** | | | | | | | | |
| Baucus | Y | Y | Y | Y | Y | Y | Y | N |
| Burns | Y | Y | Y | Y | Y | Y | Y | Y |
| **NEBRASKA** | | | | | | | | |
| Hagel | N | N | Y | N | N | N | N | N |
| Nelson | Y | Y | Y | Y | Y | Y | N | Y |
| **NEVADA** | | | | | | | | |
| Reid | Y | Y | Y | Y | Y | Y | Y | N |
| Ensign | N | N | N | N | N | Y | N | Y |
| **NEW HAMPSHIRE** | | | | | | | | |
| Gregg | N | Y | N | N | N | N | N | Y |
| Sununu | N | N | N | N | N | N | N | Y |
| **NEW JERSEY** | | | | | | | | |
| Corzine | Y | Y | Y | Y | Y | Y | Y | N |
| Lautenberg | Y | Y | Y | Y | Y | Y | Y | N |
| **NEW MEXICO** | | | | | | | | |
| Domenici | ? | ? | N | Y | Y | Y | Y | Y |
| Bingaman | Y | Y | Y | Y | Y | Y | Y | N |
| **NEW YORK** | | | | | | | | |
| Schumer | Y | Y | Y | Y | Y | Y | Y | N |
| Clinton | Y | Y | Y | Y | Y | Y | Y | N |
| **NORTH CAROLINA** | | | | | | | | |
| Dole | Y | Y | Y | Y | Y | Y | Y | Y |
| Burr | N | N | Y | Y | N | N | Y | Y |
| **NORTH DAKOTA** | | | | | | | | |
| Conrad | Y | Y | Y | Y | Y | Y | Y | N |
| Dorgan | Y | Y | Y | Y | Y | Y | Y | N |
| **OHIO** | | | | | | | | |
| DeWine | Y | Y | Y | Y | Y | Y | Y | Y |
| Voinovich | Y | N | Y | Y | Y | Y | Y | Y |
| **OKLAHOMA** | | | | | | | | |
| Inhofe | N | N | N | N | N | N | N | Y |
| Coburn | N | N | N | Y | N | N | N | Y |
| **OREGON** | | | | | | | | |
| Wyden | Y | Y | Y | Y | Y | Y | Y | N |
| Smith | Y | Y | Y | Y | Y | Y | Y | Y |
| **PENNSYLVANIA** | | | | | | | | |
| Specter | Y | Y | Y | Y | Y | Y | Y | Y |
| Santorum | Y | Y | Y | + | ? | ? | + | Y |
| **RHODE ISLAND** | | | | | | | | |
| Reed | Y | Y | Y | Y | Y | Y | Y | N |
| Chafee | Y | Y | Y | N | Y | Y | Y | N |
| **SOUTH CAROLINA** | | | | | | | | |
| Graham | ? | ? | ? | ? | ? | ? | ? | Y |
| DeMint | N | N | N | N | N | N | N | Y |
| **SOUTH DAKOTA** | | | | | | | | |
| Johnson | Y | Y | Y | Y | Y | Y | Y | Y |
| Thune | Y | Y | Y | Y | Y | Y | Y | Y |
| **TENNESSEE** | | | | | | | | |
| Frist | Y | Y | N | Y | Y | N | N | Y |
| Alexander | Y | Y | N | N | Y | Y | N | Y |
| **TEXAS** | | | | | | | | |
| Hutchison | Y | Y | N | Y | Y | Y | N | Y |
| Cornyn | N | N | N | Y | Y | Y | N | Y |
| **UTAH** | | | | | | | | |
| Hatch | Y | Y | Y | Y | Y | Y | N | Y |
| Bennett | Y | Y | Y | Y | Y | Y | N | Y |
| **VERMONT** | | | | | | | | |
| Leahy | Y | Y | Y | Y | Y | Y | Y | N |
| Jeffords | Y | Y | Y | Y | Y | Y | Y | N |
| **VIRGINIA** | | | | | | | | |
| Warner | Y | Y | Y | Y | Y | Y | Y | Y |
| Allen | N | N | N | Y | N | Y | N | Y |
| **WASHINGTON** | | | | | | | | |
| Murray | Y | Y | Y | Y | Y | Y | Y | N |
| Cantwell | ? | ? | ? | ? | ? | ? | ? | N |
| **WEST VIRGINIA** | | | | | | | | |
| Byrd | Y | Y | Y | Y | Y | Y | Y | N |
| Rockefeller | Y | Y | Y | Y | Y | Y | Y | N |
| **WISCONSIN** | | | | | | | | |
| Kohl | Y | Y | Y | Y | Y | Y | Y | N |
| Feingold | Y | Y | Y | Y | Y | Y | Y | N |
| **WYOMING** | | | | | | | | |
| Thomas | N | Y | N | N | Y | Y | N | Y |
| Enzi | N | Y | N | Y | Y | Y | N | Y |

**KEY**   Republicans   Democrats   *Independents*

| | | | |
|---|---|---|---|
| Y | Voted for (yea) | X | Paired against | C | Voted "present" to avoid possible conflict of interest |
| # | Paired for | – | Announced against | |
| + | Announced for | P | Voted "present" | ? | Did not vote or otherwise make a position known |
| N | Voted against (nay) | | | |

ND Northern Democrats, SD Southern Democrats
Southern states: Ala., Ark., Fla., Ga., Ky., La., Miss., N.C., Okla., S.C., Tenn., Texas, Va.

# IN THE SENATE | By Vote Number

**359.** **HR 2863. Fiscal 2006 Defense Appropriations/Motion to Proceed.** Frist, R-Tenn., motion to proceed to consideration of the conference report on the bill that would appropriate $453.5 billion for Defense spending in fiscal 2006, including $50 billion for operations in Iraq and Afghanistan. It also would require a 1 percent across-the-board cut to all fiscal 2006 discretionary spending except Veterans Administration funding that was added to the legislation. It would provide $29 billion for disaster assistance to hurricane-damaged areas and $3.8 billion for flu preparedness. It would allow oil and gas leasing in the Arctic National Wildlife Refuge. Motion agreed to 94-1: R 53-0; D 41-0 (ND 37-0, SD 4-0); I 0-1. Dec. 19, 2005.

**360.** **HR 1815. Fiscal 2006 Defense Authorization/Motion to Proceed.** Frist, R-Tenn., motion to proceed to consideration of the conference report on the bill that would authorize $441.5 billion for defense programs and $50 billion for military operations in Iraq and Afghanistan. Motion agreed to 95-0: R 53-0; D 41-0 (ND 37-0, SD 4-0); I 1-0. Dec. 19, 2005.

**361.** **S 1932. Budget Reconciliation/Motion to Proceed.** Frist, R-Tenn., motion to proceed to consideration of the conference report on the bill that would make changes to programs for a net savings in the federal budget of $38.8 billion over five years. Motion agreed to 86-9: R 52-1; D 34-7 (ND 30-7, SD 4-0); I 0-1. Dec. 19, 2005.

**362.** **S 1932. Budget Reconciliation/Budget Act Waiver.** Gregg, R-N.H., motion to waive the Budget Act with respect to the Conrad, D-N.D., points of order against two reporting provisions and Medicaid liability provisions in the conference report on the bill that would make changes to programs for a net savings in the federal budget of $38.8 billion over five years. Motion rejected 52-48: R 52-3; D 0-44 (ND 0-40, SD 0-4); I 0-1. A three-fifths majority vote (60) of the total Senate is required to waive the Budget Act. (Subsequently, the chair upheld the points of order, and the provisions were struck.) Dec. 21, 2005.

**363.** **S 1932. Budget Reconciliation/Concur With House Amendment.** Gregg, R-N.H., motion to concur in the House amendment with a Senate amendment on the bill that would make changes to programs for a net savings of $38.8 billion over five years. The Senate amendment would strike two reporting provisions and language that would allow for a Medicaid liability provision regarding hospitals that deny treatment to low-income individuals unable to pay. Motion agreed to, with Vice President Cheney casting a "yea" vote to break the tie, 50-50: R 50-5; D 0-44 (ND 0-40, SD 0-4); I 0-1. A "yea" was a vote in support of the president's position. Dec. 21, 2005.

| | 359 | 360 | 361 | 362 | 363 |
|---|---|---|---|---|---|
| **ALABAMA** | | | | | |
| Shelby | Y | Y | Y | Y | Y |
| Sessions | Y | Y | Y | Y | Y |
| **ALASKA** | | | | | |
| Stevens | Y | Y | Y | Y | Y |
| Murkowski | Y | Y | Y | Y | Y |
| **ARIZONA** | | | | | |
| McCain | ? | ? | ? | Y | Y |
| Kyl | Y | Y | Y | Y | Y |
| **ARKANSAS** | | | | | |
| Lincoln | Y | Y | Y | N | N |
| Pryor | Y | Y | Y | N | N |
| **CALIFORNIA** | | | | | |
| Feinstein | Y | Y | Y | N | N |
| Boxer | Y | Y | Y | N | N |
| **COLORADO** | | | | | |
| Allard | Y | Y | Y | Y | Y |
| Salazar | Y | Y | Y | N | N |
| **CONNECTICUT** | | | | | |
| Dodd | ? | ? | ? | N | N |
| Lieberman | Y | Y | Y | N | N |
| **DELAWARE** | | | | | |
| Biden | ? | ? | ? | N | N |
| Carper | Y | Y | Y | N | N |
| **FLORIDA** | | | | | |
| Nelson | Y | Y | Y | N | N |
| Martinez | Y | Y | Y | Y | Y |
| **GEORGIA** | | | | | |
| Chambliss | Y | Y | Y | Y | Y |
| Isakson | Y | Y | Y | Y | Y |
| **HAWAII** | | | | | |
| Inouye | Y | Y | Y | N | N |
| Akaka | Y | Y | Y | N | N |
| **IDAHO** | | | | | |
| Craig | Y | Y | Y | Y | Y |
| Crapo | Y | Y | Y | Y | Y |
| **ILLINOIS** | | | | | |
| Durbin | Y | Y | N | N | N |
| Obama | Y | Y | N | N | N |
| **INDIANA** | | | | | |
| Lugar | Y | Y | Y | Y | Y |
| Bayh | Y | Y | Y | N | N |
| **IOWA** | | | | | |
| Grassley | Y | Y | Y | Y | Y |
| Harkin | Y | Y | N | N | N |
| **KANSAS** | | | | | |
| Brownback | Y | Y | Y | Y | Y |
| Roberts | Y | Y | Y | Y | Y |
| **KENTUCKY** | | | | | |
| McConnell | Y | Y | Y | Y | Y |
| Bunning | Y | Y | Y | Y | Y |
| **LOUISIANA** | | | | | |
| Landrieu | Y | Y | Y | N | N |
| Vitter | Y | Y | Y | Y | Y |
| **MAINE** | | | | | |
| Snowe | Y | Y | N | N | N |
| Collins | Y | Y | Y | Y | N |
| **MARYLAND** | | | | | |
| Sarbanes | Y | Y | Y | N | N |
| Mikulski | Y | Y | Y | N | N |
| **MASSACHUSETTS** | | | | | |
| Kennedy | Y | Y | Y | N | N |
| Kerry | Y | Y | Y | N | N |
| **MICHIGAN** | | | | | |
| Levin | Y | Y | Y | N | N |
| Stabenow | Y | Y | Y | N | N |
| **MINNESOTA** | | | | | |
| Dayton | Y | Y | Y | N | N |
| Coleman | Y | Y | Y | Y | Y |
| **MISSISSIPPI** | | | | | |
| Cochran | Y | Y | Y | Y | Y |
| Lott | Y | Y | Y | Y | Y |
| **MISSOURI** | | | | | |
| Bond | Y | Y | Y | Y | Y |
| Talent | Y | Y | Y | Y | Y |
| **MONTANA** | | | | | |
| Baucus | Y | Y | Y | N | N |
| Burns | Y | Y | Y | Y | Y |
| **NEBRASKA** | | | | | |
| Hagel | Y | Y | Y | Y | Y |
| Nelson | Y | Y | N | N | N |
| **NEVADA** | | | | | |
| Reid | Y | Y | Y | N | N |
| Ensign | Y | Y | Y | Y | Y |
| **NEW HAMPSHIRE** | | | | | |
| Gregg | Y | Y | Y | Y | Y |
| Sununu | Y | Y | Y | Y | Y |
| **NEW JERSEY** | | | | | |
| Corzine | ? | ? | ? | N | N |
| Lautenberg | Y | Y | Y | N | N |
| **NEW MEXICO** | | | | | |
| Domenici | Y | Y | Y | Y | Y |
| Bingaman | Y | Y | Y | N | N |
| **NEW YORK** | | | | | |
| Schumer | Y | Y | Y | N | N |
| Clinton | Y | Y | N | N | N |
| **NORTH CAROLINA** | | | | | |
| Dole | Y | Y | Y | Y | Y |
| Burr | ? | ? | ? | Y | Y |
| **NORTH DAKOTA** | | | | | |
| Conrad | Y | Y | Y | N | N |
| Dorgan | Y | Y | Y | N | N |
| **OHIO** | | | | | |
| DeWine | Y | Y | Y | Y | N |
| Voinovich | Y | Y | Y | Y | Y |
| **OKLAHOMA** | | | | | |
| Inhofe | Y | Y | Y | Y | Y |
| Coburn | Y | Y | Y | Y | Y |
| **OREGON** | | | | | |
| Wyden | Y | Y | Y | N | N |
| Smith | Y | Y | Y | N | N |
| **PENNSYLVANIA** | | | | | |
| Specter | Y | Y | Y | Y | Y |
| Santorum | Y | Y | Y | Y | Y |
| **RHODE ISLAND** | | | | | |
| Reed | Y | Y | Y | N | N |
| Chafee | Y | Y | Y | N | N |
| **SOUTH CAROLINA** | | | | | |
| Graham | Y | Y | Y | Y | Y |
| DeMint | Y | Y | Y | Y | Y |
| **SOUTH DAKOTA** | | | | | |
| Johnson | Y | Y | Y | N | N |
| Thune | Y | Y | Y | Y | Y |
| **TENNESSEE** | | | | | |
| Frist | Y | Y | Y | Y | Y |
| Alexander | Y | Y | Y | Y | Y |
| **TEXAS** | | | | | |
| Hutchison | Y | Y | Y | Y | Y |
| Cornyn | Y | Y | Y | Y | Y |
| **UTAH** | | | | | |
| Hatch | Y | Y | Y | Y | Y |
| Bennett | Y | Y | Y | Y | Y |
| **VERMONT** | | | | | |
| Leahy | Y | Y | Y | N | N |
| Jeffords | N | Y | N | N | N |
| **VIRGINIA** | | | | | |
| Warner | Y | Y | Y | Y | Y |
| Allen | Y | Y | Y | Y | Y |
| **WASHINGTON** | | | | | |
| Murray | Y | Y | N | N | N |
| Cantwell | Y | Y | N | N | N |
| **WEST VIRGINIA** | | | | | |
| Byrd | Y | Y | Y | N | N |
| Rockefeller | Y | Y | Y | N | N |
| **WISCONSIN** | | | | | |
| Kohl | Y | Y | Y | N | N |
| Feingold | Y | N | N | N | N |
| **WYOMING** | | | | | |
| Thomas | Y | Y | Y | Y | Y |
| Enzi | Y | Y | Y | Y | Y |

**KEY**   Republicans   Democrats   *Independents*

| | | |
|---|---|---|
| **Y** Voted for (yea) | **X** Paired against | **C** Voted "present" to avoid possible conflict of interest |
| **#** Paired for | **−** Announced against | |
| **+** Announced for | **P** Voted "present" | **?** Did not vote or otherwise make a position known |
| **N** Voted against (nay) | | |

ND Northern Democrats, SD Southern Democrats
Southern states: Ala., Ark., Fla., Ga., Ky., La., Miss., N.C., Okla., S.C., Tenn., Texas, Va.

# IN THE SENATE | By Vote Number

**364.** HR 2863. Fiscal 2006 Defense Appropriations/Cloture. Motion to invoke cloture (thus limiting debate) on the conference report on the bill that would appropriate $453.5 billion for Defense spending, including $50 billion for operations in Iraq and Afghanistan. Motion rejected 56-44: R 52-3; D 4-40 (ND 3-37, SD 1-3); I 0-1. Three-fifths of the total Senate (60) is required to invoke cloture. A "yea" was a vote in support of the president's position. Dec. 21, 2005.

**365.** HR 2863. Fiscal 2006 Defense Appropriations/Enrolling Resolution. Adoption of the concurrent resolution (S Con Res 74) that would instruct the Clerk of the House to strike certain provisions from the conference report accompanying the bill. Those provisions would allow oil drilling in the Arctic National Wildlife Refuge and provide additional funding for hurricane recovery and other purposes. Adopted 48-45: R 7-44; D 40-1 (ND 37-0, SD 3-1); I 1-0. Dec. 21, 2005.

**366.** HR 2863. Fiscal 2006 Defense Appropriations/Conference Report. Adoption of the conference report on the bill that would appropriate $453.5 billion for Defense spending, including $50 billion for operations in Iraq and Afghanistan. The total includes $123.6 billion for operations and maintenance, $76.5 billion for procurement and $72.1 billion for research and development. It would require a 1 percent across-the-board cut to all fiscal 2006 discretionary spending except Veterans Administration funding that was added to the legislation. It would provide $29 billion for disaster assistance to hurricane-damaged areas and $3.8 billion for flu preparedness. Adopted (thus cleared for the president, pending House adoption of S Con Res 74) 93-0: R 51-0; D 41-0 (ND 37-0, SD 4-0); I 1-0. (Subsequently, the House adopted S Con Res 74 by voice vote Dec. 22.) Dec. 21, 2005.

| | 364 | 365 | 366 | | | 364 | 365 | 366 |
|---|---|---|---|---|---|---|---|---|
| **ALABAMA** | | | | | **MONTANA** | | | |
| Shelby | Y | N | Y | | Baucus | N | Y | Y |
| Sessions | Y | N | Y | | Burns | Y | N | Y |
| **ALASKA** | | | | | **NEBRASKA** | | | |
| Stevens | Y | N | Y | | Hagel | Y | N | Y |
| Murkowski | Y | N | Y | | Nelson | Y | Y | Y |
| **ARIZONA** | | | | | **NEVADA** | | | |
| McCain | Y | ? | ? | | Reid | N | Y | Y |
| Kyl | Y | N | Y | | Ensign | Y | N | Y |
| **ARKANSAS** | | | | | **NEW HAMPSHIRE** | | | |
| Lincoln | N | Y | Y | | Gregg | Y | ? | ? |
| Pryor | N | Y | Y | | Sununu | Y | N | Y |
| **CALIFORNIA** | | | | | **NEW JERSEY** | | | |
| Feinstein | N | Y | Y | | Corzine | N | ? | ? |
| Boxer | N | Y | Y | | Lautenberg | N | Y | Y |
| **COLORADO** | | | | | **NEW MEXICO** | | | |
| Allard | Y | N | Y | | Domenici | Y | N | Y |
| Salazar | N | Y | Y | | Bingaman | N | Y | Y |
| **CONNECTICUT** | | | | | **NEW YORK** | | | |
| Dodd | N | ? | ? | | Schumer | N | Y | Y |
| Lieberman | N | Y | Y | | Clinton | N | Y | Y |
| **DELAWARE** | | | | | **NORTH CAROLINA** | | | |
| Biden | N | Y | Y | | Dole | Y | N | Y |
| Carper | N | Y | Y | | Burr | Y | N | Y |
| **FLORIDA** | | | | | **NORTH DAKOTA** | | | |
| Nelson | N | Y | Y | | Conrad | N | Y | Y |
| Martinez | Y | N | Y | | Dorgan | N | Y | Y |
| **GEORGIA** | | | | | **OHIO** | | | |
| Chambliss | Y | N | Y | | DeWine | N | Y | Y |
| Isakson | Y | N | Y | | Voinovich | Y | N | Y |
| **HAWAII** | | | | | **OKLAHOMA** | | | |
| Inouye | Y | Y | Y | | Inhofe | Y | N | Y |
| Akaka | Y | Y | Y | | Coburn | Y | N | Y |
| **IDAHO** | | | | | **OREGON** | | | |
| Craig | Y | N | Y | | Wyden | N | Y | Y |
| Crapo | Y | N | Y | | Smith | Y | Y | Y |
| **ILLINOIS** | | | | | **PENNSYLVANIA** | | | |
| Durbin | N | Y | Y | | Specter | Y | Y | Y |
| Obama | N | Y | Y | | Santorum | Y | N | Y |
| **INDIANA** | | | | | **RHODE ISLAND** | | | |
| Lugar | Y | Y | Y | | Reed | N | Y | Y |
| Bayh | N | Y | Y | | Chafee | N | ? | ? |
| **IOWA** | | | | | **SOUTH CAROLINA** | | | |
| Grassley | Y | N | Y | | Graham | Y | N | Y |
| Harkin | N | ? | ? | | DeMint | Y | – | ? |
| **KANSAS** | | | | | **SOUTH DAKOTA** | | | |
| Brownback | Y | N | Y | | Johnson | N | Y | Y |
| Roberts | Y | N | Y | | Thune | Y | N | Y |
| **KENTUCKY** | | | | | **TENNESSEE** | | | |
| McConnell | Y | N | Y | | Frist | N | N | Y |
| Bunning | Y | N | Y | | Alexander | Y | N | Y |
| **LOUISIANA** | | | | | **TEXAS** | | | |
| Landrieu | Y | N | Y | | Hutchison | Y | N | Y |
| Vitter | Y | N | Y | | Cornyn | Y | N | Y |
| **MAINE** | | | | | **UTAH** | | | |
| Snowe | Y | Y | Y | | Hatch | Y | N | Y |
| Collins | Y | Y | Y | | Bennett | Y | N | Y |
| **MARYLAND** | | | | | **VERMONT** | | | |
| Sarbanes | N | Y | Y | | Leahy | N | Y | Y |
| Mikulski | N | Y | Y | | Jeffords | N | Y | Y |
| **MASSACHUSETTS** | | | | | **VIRGINIA** | | | |
| Kennedy | N | Y | Y | | Warner | Y | N | Y |
| Kerry | N | Y | Y | | Allen | Y | N | Y |
| **MICHIGAN** | | | | | **WASHINGTON** | | | |
| Levin | N | Y | Y | | Murray | N | Y | Y |
| Stabenow | N | Y | Y | | Cantwell | N | Y | Y |
| **MINNESOTA** | | | | | **WEST VIRGINIA** | | | |
| Dayton | N | Y | Y | | Byrd | N | Y | Y |
| Coleman | Y | Y | Y | | Rockefeller | N | Y | Y |
| **MISSISSIPPI** | | | | | **WISCONSIN** | | | |
| Cochran | Y | N | Y | | Kohl | N | Y | Y |
| Lott | Y | N | Y | | Feingold | N | Y | Y |
| **MISSOURI** | | | | | **WYOMING** | | | |
| Bond | Y | N | Y | | Thomas | Y | N | Y |
| Talent | Y | N | Y | | Enzi | Y | N | Y |

**KEY**    Republicans    Democrats    *Independents*

| | | | | | | |
|---|---|---|---|---|---|---|
| Y | Voted for (yea) | | X | Paired against | | C | Voted "present" to avoid possible conflict of interest |
| # | Paired for | | – | Announced against | | |
| + | Announced for | | P | Voted "present" | | ? | Did not vote or otherwise make a position known |
| N | Voted against (nay) | | | | | |

ND Northern Democrats, SD Southern Democrats
Southern states: Ala., Ark., Fla., Ga., Ky., La., Miss., N.C., Okla., S.C., Tenn., Texas, Va.

# Senate Roll Call Index by Subject

**Appendix I**

# GENERAL INDEX

# General Index

## A

**Foreign Intelligence Surveillance Act**
Library and bookseller records, 2-11
"Patriot Act" highlights, 12-3, 12-4
**Foreign Relations Committee (Senate)**
Bolton nomination as U.N. ambassador, 10-4
Foreign operations authorization, 9-3
**Forrester, Doug**
New Jersey gubernatorial election, 5-10
**Fortuño, Luis, R-P.R.**
Higher education authorization, 7-5
**Fossella, Vito J., R-N.Y. (13)**
Coast Guard reauthorization, 12-7
**Foster care**
Cost reductions, 4-16
**Fox, Michael J.**
Stem cell research, 11-7
**Foxx, Virginia, R-N.C. (5)**
Higher education authorization, 7-5
**Frank, Barney, D-Mass. (4)**
Fannie Mae and Freddie Mac regulation, 3-11–3-12
**Freddie Mac**
Regulation, 3-11–3-12
**Frist, Bill, R-Tenn.**
Asbestos compensation, 14-9
Budget reconciliation, 4-15, 4-17
Budget resolution, 4-11, 4-14
Campaign finance, 2-50
Defense authorization, 2-17, 6-6, 6-8
Estate tax, 15-7
Ethics issues, 5-7
Gun manufacturer liability, 14-13–14-14
Highway program reauthorization, 18-5
Home heating assistance, 2-40
Hurricane Katrina inquiry, 12-7
Immigration, 13-3, 13-4
Judicial nominations, 14-8–14-9
Parental consent for abortion, 14-15
"Patriot Act," 12-3, 12-6
Schiavo case, 14-16–14-17
Stem cell research, 11-7–11-8
Tax cuts, 15-4
Vaccine liability, 2-17, 2-19
**Fruits and vegetables**
Labeling, 2-5
**Future Combat System**
Defense appropriations, 2-14–2-16, 2-19
Defense authorization, 6-3–6-4, 6-6, 6-9

## G

**Gainer, Terrance W.**
Capitol Police appropriations, 2-41, 2-42
**Gambling**
Casinos operated by Native American tribes, 5-3, 5-5
Hurricane-related tax relief, 15-6
**Gangs**
Illegal immigrants, 13-8
**Garrett, Scott, R-N.J. (5)**
Eminent domain, 2-49
**Gasoline**
Fuel surcharges, 18-7
Prices, 2-23, 8-3, 8-6, 8-17–8-18
Refinery construction, 8-17–8-18
Taxes, 18-3, 18-4, 18-6, 18-7
**Geneva Conventions**
Detainee treatment
Defense appropriations, 2-14, 2-16, 2-17

Defense authorization, 6-3, 6-6
Key votes, C-9
**Georgia**
Redistricting, 5-11
**Gephardt, Richard A., D-Mo. (3)**
Debt limit, 4-11
**Gilchrist, Jim**
California special election, 5-10
**Gingrey, Phil, R-Ga. (11)**
Redistricting, 5-11
**Global Environment Facility**
Funding, 2-25, 2-26, 2-27
**Global Fund to Fight AIDS, Tuberculosis and Malaria**
Appropriations, 2-25–2-27
**Global War on Terror Partners Fund**
Appropriations, 2-56
**Global warming**
Greenhouse gas emissions, 8-3–8-4, 8-7–8-8, 8-14
Key votes, C-3, C-6
**Goldwater, former Sen. Barry, R-Ariz.**
O'Connor profile, 14-7
**Gonzales, Attorney General Alberto R.**
Judicial nominations, 14-7
Nomination as attorney general, 10-3
**Goode, Virgil H. Jr., R-Va. (5)**
Agriculture appropriations, 2-6
Defense authorization, 6-5
**Goodlatte, Robert W., R-Va. (6)**
Border security legislation, 13-8
Spyware, 16-4
**Gordon, Bart, D-Tenn. (6)**
NASA reauthorization, 11-9
**Gore, Al**
2000 election results, 14-4
**Government Accountability Office**
Appropriations, 2-41, 2-42
Capitol Visitor Center costs, 2-41
Digital television transition, 16-5
Eminent domain, 2-12
Head Start program, 7-4
Iraq reconstruction funding investigation, 2-54
Postal Service overhaul, 10-6
Sensitive security information, 2-30
**Government Printing Office**
Appropriations, 2-41
**Government Reform Committee (House)**
Energy bill, 8-4
Postal Service overhaul, 10-6–10-7
Schiavo case, 14-17
**Governors**
Congressional continuity following catastrophe, 5-8
**Graham, Lindsey, R-S.C.**
Asbestos compensation, 14-10
Defense authorization, 6-7
**Grassley, Charles E., R-Iowa**
Budget reconciliation, 4-16–4-17, 11-4
Cisneros investigation, 2-50
Energy bill, 8-6
Estate tax, 15-7
Highway program reauthorization, 18-6
Pension system overhaul, 3-14
Tax cuts, 15-4
Unfair trade practices, 2-12
**Gray, William H. III**
Blacks as congressional leaders, 5-10
**Great Britain**
London bombings, 2-28, 2-31
**Greenspan, Alan**
Fannie Mae and Freddie Mac regulation, 3-11

**Greer, Judge George**
Schiavo case, 14-17
**Gregg, Judd, R-N.H.**
Budget reconciliation, 4-15, 4-17
Budget resolution, 4-10–4-12, 4-14, 11-4
Bush budget proposal, 4-3
Highway program reauthorization, 18-6
Homeland Security appropriations, 2-28, 2-30–2-31
Labor-HHS-Education appropriations, 2-40
Offshore drilling, 8-7
**Griffin, Richard A.**
Judicial nomination, 14-9
**Grijalva, Raúl M., D-Ariz. (7)**
Energy bill, 8-4
**Gross domestic product**
Economic forecasting, 4-8
**Guantánamo Bay, Cuba**
Detainee legal rights, 6-3, 6-7, 6-8
Detainee treatment, 2-17
Detentions and war on terror, 9-4
**Guatemala**
Trade agreement, 17-3
Key votes, C-6–C-7, C-16
**Gubernatorial elections**
Members of Congress running for governor, 5-10 (chart)
New Jersey, 5-10
Virginia, 5-10
**Gulf Opportunity Zones**
Background, 15-6
**Gun control**
Armor-piercing bullets, 14-14
District of Columbia, 2-20–2-21
Rehnquist obituary, 14-5
**Gunn, David L.**
Amtrak funding, 2-48, 2-49
**Guns**
Manufacturer liability, 14-13–14-14
Key votes, C-7–C-8
Manufacturer tax exemption, 18-6
Safety, 14-13–14-14
Sales records, 12-4, 12-5
**Gutierrez, Secretary of Commerce Carlos**
Central American trade, 17-4, 17-5
Nomination as secretary of Commerce, 10-4

## H

**Hackett, Paul**
Ohio special election, 5-10
**Hadley, Stephen**
Central American trade, 17-4
**Hagel, Chuck, R-Neb.**
Climate change, 8-7
"Patriot Act," 12-6
**Hager, Worth**
Water projects, 2-24
**Haiti**
U.S. aid, 2-52, 9-3
**Hallmark Cards Inc.**
Postal Service overhaul, 10-6
**Hariri, Rafiq**
Assassination, 11-9
**Harkin, Tom, D-Iowa**
Agriculture appropriations, 2-7
Defense appropriations, 2-17
Labor-HHS-Education appropriations, 2-17, 2-39
Stem cell research, 11-7

**Harlan, John Marshall**
Rehnquist obituary, 14-5
**Harman, Jane, D-Calif. (36)**
Border fence, 13-4
Intelligence authorization, 9-5
**Hart, Judge Joseph H.**
DeLay Texas court ruling, 5-4
**Hart, Melissa A., R-Pa. (4)**
"Patriot Act," 12-5
**Hastert, J. Dennis, R-Ill. (14)**
Budget reconciliation, 4-17
Budget resolution, 4-12, 4-14, 4-16
Congressional continuity following catastrophe, 2-41, 5-7–5-8
Debt limit, 4-11
Energy legislation, 8-17
Ethics committee staff changes, 5-7
Highway program reauthorization, 18-3
House leadership issues, 5-3–5-6
Portman confirmation as U.S. Trade Representative, 10-5
Schiavo case, 14-16, 14-17
**Hastings, Alcee L., D-Fla (23)**
Schiavo case, 14-16
**Hastings, Doc, R-Wash. (4)**
Ethics committee chairmanship, 5-3, 5-7
**Hatch, Orrin G., R-Utah**
Bankruptcy overhaul, 3-4, 3-5
Class action lawsuits, 14-11
Judicial nominations, 14-3
Stem cell research, 11-8
Tax cuts, 15-4
**Hayden, Michael V.**
Nomination as deputy director of national intelligence, 10-5
**Hayes, Robin, R-N.C. (8)**
Central American trade, 17-5
**Hayworth, J.D., R-Ariz. (5)**
House rules changes, 5-3
**Hazardous materials**
Highway bill, 18-7
Highway program reauthorization, 18-16–18-17
Shipment tracking, 2-31
**Hazardous waste**
EPA funding, 2-33, 2-35
**HCA Corp.**
Frist ethics issues, 5-7
**Head Start**
Appropriations, 2-37
Reauthorization, 7-3–7-4
**Health and Human Services, Department of**
Appropriations, 2-37–2-40
Flu emergency spending, 2-17
Head Start reauthorization, 7-3, 7-4
Hurricane Katrina supplemental appropriations, 2-58
Leavitt nomination as secretary, 10-5, 11-3
Medicaid overhaul, 11-3–11-5
Medical errors reporting, 11-6
Prescription drug reimbursements, 4-17
Stem cell research, 11-7, 11-8
**Health care**
Bankruptcy and health costs, 3-4–3-5
Budget resolution, 4-10, 4-12
Children, 9-3, 11-3–11-5
Head Start program, 7-3
Home health care, 4-14, 11-4
Illegal immigrants, 2-39, 13-7
Immigration legislation, 13-4, 13-6, 13-7